GENERAL STATUTES
OF NORTH CAROLINA

ANNOTATED

Volume 9

Chapters 55B Through 58

Prepared Under the Supervision of
THE DEPARTMENT OF JUSTICE
OF THE STATE OF NORTH CAROLINA
by
The Editorial Staff of the Publisher

LexisNexis™

QUESTIONS ABOUT THIS PUBLICATION?

For EDITORIAL QUESTIONS concerning this publication, or REPRINT PERMISSION, please call:

800-833-9844

For CUSTOMER SERVICE ASSISTANCE concerning replacement pages, shipments, billing or other matters, please call:

Customer Service Department at	800-833-9844
Outside the United States and Canada	518-487-3000
FAX	518-487-3584

For INFORMATION ON OTHER MATTHEW BENDER PUBLICATIONS, please call:

Your account manager or	800-223-1940
Outside the United States and Canada	518-487-3000

4537511 (hardbound volume)
4535011 (hardbound set)
4640513 (softbound set)

ISBN 0-8205-9810-0 (hardbound volume)
ISBN 0-8205-9801-1 (hardbound set)
ISBN 0-8205-9800-3 (softbound set)

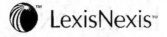

Matthew Bender & Company, Inc.

P.O. Box 7587, Charlottesville, VA 22906-7587

www.lexisnexis.com

(Pub.45350) (HB)
(Pub.46405) (SB)

Preface

This volume contains the general laws of a permanent nature enacted by the General Assembly through the 2003 Regular Session that are within Chapters 55B through 58, and brings to date the annotations included therein.

A majority of the Session Laws are made effective upon becoming law, but a few provide for stated effective dates. If the Session Law makes no provision for an effective date, the law becomes effective under G.S. 120-20 "from and after 60 days after the adjournment of the session" in which passed.

A ready reference index is included at the back of this volume. This index is intended to give the user a quick reference to larger bodies of statutes within this volume only. For detailed research on any subject, both within this volume and the General Statutes as a whole, see the General Index to the General Statutes.

Beginning with formal opinions issued by the North Carolina Attorney General on July 1, 1969, selected opinions which construe a specific statute are cited in the annotations to that statute. For a copy of an opinion or of its headnotes, write the Attorney General, P.O. Box 629, Raleigh, N.C. 27602.

This recompiled volume has been prepared and published under the supervision of the Department of Justice of the State of North Carolina. The members of the North Carolina Bar are requested to communicate any suggestions they may have for improving the General Statutes to the Department, or to LexisNexis, Charlottesville, Virginia.

Roy Cooper
Attorney General

Scope of Volume

Statutes:

Permanent portions of the General Laws enacted by the General Assembly through the 2003 Regular Session affecting Chapters 55B through 58 of the General Statutes.

Annotations:

This publication contains annotations taken from decisions of the North Carolina Supreme Court posted on LEXIS through June 13, 2003, decisions of the North Carolina Court of Appeals posted on LEXIS through June 17, 2003, and decisions of the appropriate federal courts posted through June 20, 2003. These cases will be printed in the following reporters:

South Eastern Reporter 2nd Series.
Federal Reporter 3rd Series.
Federal Supplement 2nd Series.
Federal Rules Decisions.
Bankruptcy Reports.
Supreme Court Reporter.

Additionally, annotations have been taken from the following sources:

North Carolina Law Review through Volume 81, no. 2, p. 900.
Wake Forest Law Review through Volume 37, Pamphlet No. 4, p. 1174.
Campbell Law Review through Volume 24, no. 2, p. 346.
Duke Law Journal through Volume 52, no. 1, p. 273.
North Carolina Central Law Journal through Volume 24, no. 1, p. 180.
Opinions of the Attorney General.

User's Guide

In order to assist both the legal profession and the layperson in obtaining the maximum benefit from the North Carolina General Statutes, a User's Guide has been included in Volume 1. This guide contains comments and information on the many features found within the General Statutes intended to increase the usefulness of this set of laws to the user. See Volume 1 for the complete User's Guide.

Abbreviations

(The abbreviations below are those found in the General Statutes that refer to prior codes.)

P.R. .... Potter's Revisal (1821, 1827)
R.S. .... Revised Statutes (1837)
R.C. .... Revised Code (1854)
C.C.P. .... Code of Civil Procedure (1868)
Code .... Code (1883)
Rev. .... Revisal of 1905
C.S. .... Consolidated Statutes (1919, 1924)

STATE OF NORTH CAROLINA

DEPARTMENT OF JUSTICE

Raleigh, North Carolina

November 2003

I, Roy Cooper, Attorney General of North Carolina, do hereby certify that the foregoing 2003 Replacement Code to the General Statutes of North Carolina was prepared and published by LexisNexis under the supervision of the Department of Justice of the State of North Carolina.

ROY COOPER

Attorney General of North Carolina

Table of Contents

For complete listing of chapters set out in the North Carolina General Statutes, see the Table of Contents included in Volume 1.

VOLUME 9

Chapter 55B.

Professional Corporation Act.

§ 55B-1. Title.

This Chapter may be cited as "The Professional Corporation Act." (1969, c. 718, s. 1.)

Cross References. — As to limited liability companies and their powers, see G.S. 57C-2-01 et seq.

Legal Periodicals. — For note discussing the liability of members of a professional corporation, in light of Nelson v. Patrick, 73 N.C. App. 1, 326 S.E.2d 45 (1985), see 64 N.C.L. Rev. 1216 (1986).

For comment, "North Carolina's Limited Liability Company Act: A Legislative Mandate for Professional Limited Liability," see 29 Wake Forest L. Rev. 857 (1994).

CASE NOTES

Cited in Harris v. Maready, 64 N.C. App. 1, 306 S.E.2d 799 (1983).

§ 55B-2. Definitions.

As used in this Chapter, the following words shall, unless the context requires otherwise, have the following meanings:

(1) "Disqualified person" means a licensed person who for any reason becomes legally disqualified to render the same professional services which are or were being rendered by the professional corporation of which such person is an officer, director, shareholder or employee.

(2) "Licensee" means any natural person who is duly licensed by the appropriate licensing board to render the same professional services which will be rendered by the professional corporation of which he is, or intends to become, an officer, director, shareholder or employee.

(3) "Licensing board" means a board which is charged with the licensing and regulating of the profession or practice in this State in which the professional corporation is organized to engage.

(4) The term "licensing board," as the same applies to attorneys at law, shall mean the Council of the North Carolina State Bar, and it shall include the North Carolina State Board of Law Examiners only to the extent that the North Carolina Board of Law Examiners is authorized to issue licenses for the practice of law under the supervision of the Council of the North Carolina State Bar.

(5) "Professional corporation" means a corporation which is engaged in rendering the professional services as herein specified and defined, pursuant to a certificate of registration issued by the Licensing Board

1

regulating the profession or practice, and which has as its shareholders only those individuals permitted by G.S. 55B-6 of this Chapter to be shareholders and which designates itself as may be required by this statute, and which is organized under the provisions of this Chapter and of Chapter 55, the North Carolina Business Corporation Act.

(6) The term "professional service" means any type of personal or professional service of the public which requires as a condition precedent to the rendering of such service the obtaining of a license from a licensing board as herein defined, and pursuant to the following provisions of the General Statutes: Chapter 83A, "Architects"; Chapter 84, "Attorneys-at-Law"; Chapter 93, "Public Accountants"; and the following Articles in Chapter 90: Article 1, "Practice of Medicine," Article 2, "Dentistry," Article 6, "Optometry," Article 7, "Osteopathy," Article 8, "Chiropractic," Article 9A, "Nursing Practice Act," with regard to registered nurses, Article 11, "Veterinarians," Article 12A, "Podiatrists," Article 18A, "Practicing Psychologists," Article 18C, "Marriage and Family Therapy Licensure," Article 18D, "Occupational Therapy," and Article 24, "Licensed Professional Counselors"; Chapter 89C, "Engineering and Land Surveying"; Chapter 89A, "Landscape Architects"; Chapter 90B, "Social Worker Certification and Licensure Act" with regard to Certified [Licensed] Clinical Social Workers as defined by G.S. 90B-3; Chapter 89E, "Geologists"; Chapter 89B, "Foresters"; and Chapter 89F, "North Carolina Soil Scientist Licensing Act." (1969, c. 718, s. 2; 1971, c. 196, s. 1; 1977, c. 53; c. 855, s. 1; 1979, c. 460; 1989 (Reg. Sess., 1990), c. 1024, s. 3; 1991, c. 205, s. 1; 1995, c. 382, s. 2; 1997-421, s. 2; 2000-115, s. 4; 2001-487, s. 40(d); 2003-117, s. 3.)

Editor's Note. — Session Laws 1999-313, s. 1, changed the term "Certified Clinical Social Worker" to "Licensed Clinical Social Worker." The term was changed without engrossing by Session Laws 2001-487, s. 40(d) in subdivision (6).

Effect of Amendments. — Session Laws 2003-117, s. 3, effective June 1, 2003, in subdivision (6), inserted "the following Articles in Chapter 90" and "Article 18C, 'Marriage and Family Therapy Licensure,'" substituted "Counselors" for "Counselors, of Chapter 90," and made minor punctuation changes.

OPINIONS OF ATTORNEY GENERAL

North Carolina Licensing Board Must License Foreign Professional. — See opinion of Attorney General to Mr. Joseph G. Maddrey, Corporation Attorney, Office of Secretary of State, 40 N.C.A.G. 46 (1970).

§ 55B-3. North Carolina Business Corporation Act applicable; other applicable law.

(a) Chapter 55 of the General Statutes, the North Carolina Business Corporation Act, applies to professional corporations, including their organization, and professional corporations shall enjoy the powers and privileges and shall be subject to the duties, restrictions and liabilities of other corporations, except insofar as the same may be limited or enlarged by this Chapter. If any provision of this Chapter conflicts with the provisions of Chapter 55 of the General Statutes, the North Carolina Business Corporation Act, the provisions of this Chapter shall prevail.

(b) A document required or permitted by this Chapter to be filed by the Secretary of State shall be filed under Chapter 55D of the General Statutes, Filings, Names, and Registered Agents for Corporations, Nonprofit Corporations, Limited Liability Companies, Limited Partnerships, and Limited Partnerships. (1969, c. 718, s. 3; 1989 (Reg. Sess., 1990), c. 1024, s. 3; 2001-358, s. 11; 2001-387, ss. 173, 175(a); 2001-413, s. 6.)

Editor's Note. — Session Laws 2001-358, s. 53, provided that the act, which amended this section, was effective October 1, 2001, and applicable to documents submitted for filing on or after that date. Section 173 of Session Laws 2001-387 changed the effective date of Session Laws 2001-358 from October 1, 2001, to January 1, 2002. Section 6 of Session Laws 2001-413, effective September 14, 2001, added a sentence to s. 175(a) of Session Laws 2001-387, making s. 173 of that act effective when it became law (August 26, 2001). As a result of these changes, the amendment by Session Laws 2001-358 is effective January 1, 2002, and applicable to documents submitted for filing on or after that date.

Effect of Amendments. — Session Laws 2001-358, s. 11, effective January 1, 2002, and applicable to documents submitted for filing on or after that date, added "other applicable law" in the section catchline; inserted the subsection (a) designation, and in subsection (a) inserted "Chapter 55 of the General Statutes" in the first and second sentences, and substituted "applies to" for "shall be applicable to such" in the first sentence; and added subsection (b).

Legal Periodicals. — For note discussing the liability of members of a professional corporation, in light of Nelson v. Patrick, 73 N.C. App. 1, 326 S.E.2d 45 (1985), see 64 N.C.L. Rev. 1216 (1986).

CASE NOTES

Cited in Buchele v. Pinehurst Surgical Clinic, 80 N.C. App. 256, 341 S.E.2d 772 (1986).

§ 55B-4. Formation of corporation.

A professional corporation under this Chapter may be formed pursuant to the provisions of Chapter 55, the North Carolina Business Corporation Act, with the following limitations:

(1) At least one incorporator shall be a "licensee" as hereinabove defined in G.S. 55B-2(2).

(2) All of the shares of stock of the corporation shall be owned and held by a licensee, or licensees, as hereinabove defined in G.S. 55B-2(2), except as otherwise permitted in G.S. 55B-6.

(3) At least one director and one officer shall be a "licensee" as hereinabove defined in G.S. 55B-2(2).

(4) The articles of incorporation, in addition to the requirements of Chapter 55, shall designate the personal services to be rendered by the professional corporation and shall be accompanied by a certification by the appropriate licensing board that the ownership of the shares of stock is in compliance with the requirements of G.S. 55B-4(2) and G.S. 55B-6. (1969, c. 718, s. 4; 1977, c. 855, s. 1; 1989 (Reg. Sess., 1990), c. 1024, s. 3; 1991, c. 205, s. 2; 1995, c. 351, s. 15.)

Legal Periodicals. — For comment on tax and corporate aspects of professional incorporation in North Carolina, see 48 N.C.L. Rev. 573 (1970).

CASE NOTES

Cited in Harris v. Maready, 64 N.C. App. 1, 306 S.E.2d 799 (1983); In re Wake Kidney Clinic, 85 N.C. App. 639, 355 S.E.2d 788 (1987).

OPINIONS OF ATTORNEY GENERAL

North Carolina Licensing Board Must License Foreign Professional. — See opinion of Attorney General to Mr. Joseph G. Maddrey, Corporation Attorney, Office of Secretary of State, 40 N.C.A.G. 46 (1970).

§ 55B-5. Corporate name.

The corporate name used by professional corporations under this Chapter, except as limited by the licensing acts of the respective professions, shall be governed by the provisions of Chapter 55D, provided that professional corporations may use the words "Professional Association, P.A.," "Professional Corporation," or "P.C." in lieu of the corporate designations specified in Chapter 55D, and provided further that licensing boards by regulations may make further corporate name requirements or limitations for the respective professions, but such regulations may not prohibit the continued use of any corporate name duly adopted in conformity with the General Statutes and with the pertinent licensing board regulations in effect at the date of such adoption. (1969, c. 718, s. 5; 1983, c. 22; 1989 (Reg. Sess., 1990), c. 1024, s. 3; 2001-358, s. 25; 2001-387, ss. 173, 175(a); 2001-413, s. 6.)

Editor's Note. — Session Laws 2001-358, s. 53, provided that the act, which amended this section, was effective October 1, 2001, and applicable to documents submitted for filing on or after that date. Section 173 of Session Laws 2001-387 changed the effective date of Session Laws 2001-358 from October 1, 2001, to January 1, 2002. Section 6 of Session Laws 2001-413, effective September 14, 2001, added a sentence to s. 175(a) of Session Laws 2001-387, making s. 173 of that act effective when it became law (August 26, 2001). As a result of these changes, the amendment by Session Laws 2001-358 is effective January 1, 2002, and applicable to documents submitted for filing on or after that date.

Effect of Amendments. — Session Laws 2001-358, s. 25, effective January 1, 2002, and applicable to documents submitted for filing on or after that date, substituted "provisions of Chapter 55D" for "provisions of Chapter 55, the North Carolina Business Corporation Act", and substituted "specified in Chapter 55D" for "specified in Chapter 55."

CASE NOTES

Cited in Harris v. Maready, 64 N.C. App. 1, 306 S.E.2d 799 (1983).

§ 55B-6. Capital stock.

(a) Except as provided in subsections (a1) and (b) of this section, a professional corporation may issue shares of its capital stock only to a licensee as defined in G.S. 55B-2, and a shareholder may voluntarily transfer shares of stock issued to the shareholder only to another licensee. No share or shares of any stock of a professional corporation shall be transferred upon the books of the corporation unless the corporation has received a certification of the appropriate licensing board that the transferee is a licensee. Provided, it shall be lawful in the case of professional corporations rendering services as defined in Chapters 83A, 89A, 89C, 89E, and 89F, for non-licensed employees of the corporation to own not more than one-third of the total issued and outstanding shares of the corporation; and provided further, with respect to a professional corporation rendering such services as defined in Chapters 83A, 89A, 89C, and 89E of the General Statutes, an employee retirement plan qualified under section 401 of the Internal Revenue Code of 1986, as amended (or any successor section), is deemed for purposes of this section to be a licensee if the trustee or trustees of the plan are licensees. Provided further, subject to any additional conditions that the appropriate licensing board may by rule or order impose in the public interest, it shall be lawful for individuals who are not licensees but who perform professional services on behalf of a professional corporation in another jurisdiction in which the corporation maintains an office, and who are duly licensed to perform professional services under the laws of the other jurisdiction, to be shareholders of the corporation so long as there is at least one shareholder who is a licensee as defined in G.S. 55B-2, and the corporation renders its professional services in the State only through those shareholders that are licensed in North Carolina. Upon the transfer of any shares of such corporation to a non-licensed employee of such corporation, the corporation shall inform the appropriate licensing board of the name and address of the transferee and the number of shares issued to such nonprofessional transferee. Any share of stock of such corporation issued or transferred in violation of this section shall be null and void. No shareholder of a professional corporation shall enter into a voting trust agreement or any other type of agreement vesting in another person the authority to exercise the voting power of any or all of his stock.

(a1) Any person may own up to forty-nine percent of the stock of a professional corporation rendering services under Chapter 93 of the General Statutes as long as:

(1) Licensees continue to own and control voting stock that represents at least fifty-one percent (51%) the votes entitled to be cast in the election of directors of the professional corporation; and

(2) All licensees who perform professional services on behalf of the corporation comply with Chapter 93 of the General Statutes and the rules adopted thereunder.

(b) A professional corporation formed pursuant to this Chapter may issue one hundred percent (100%) of its capital stock to another professional corporation in order for that corporation (the distributing corporation) to distribute in accordance with section 355 of the Internal Revenue Code of 1986, as amended (or any succeeding section), the stock of the controlled corporation to one or more shareholders of the distributing corporation authorized under this section to hold the shares. The distributing corporation shall distribute the stock of the controlled corporation within 30 days after the stock is issued to the distributing corporation. A share of stock of the controlled corporation that is not transferred in accordance with this subsection within 30 days after the share was issued to the distributing corporation is void. (1969, c. 718, s. 6; 1977, c. 855, s. 1; 1989, c. 258; 1991, c. 179, s. 1; c. 205, s. 3; 1995, c. 351, s. 16; 1999-440, s. 1; 2000-115, s. 5.)

OPINIONS OF ATTORNEY GENERAL

An architectural professional corporation may establish an employee stock ownership plan (ESOP) wherein up to one third of the outstanding shares of the professional corporation are held in trust, by a trustee who is a licensed employee of the corporation, for the benefit of nonlicensed employees of the corporation. See opinion of Attorney General to Mr. Julian Mann, III, Attorney for the North Carolina Board of Architecture, 56 N.C.A.G. 43 (1986).

§ 55B-7. Death or disqualification of a stockholder or employee.

(a) If any officer, shareholder, agent or employee of a corporation organized under this Chapter who is a licensee becomes legally disqualified to render professional services within this State, he shall sever all employment with, and financial interest in, such corporation forthwith. A corporation's failure to comply with this provision shall constitute grounds for the forfeiture of its certificate of incorporation and its dissolution. When a corporation's failure to comply with this provision is brought to the attention of the Secretary of State, the Secretary of State shall forthwith certify that fact to the Attorney General for appropriate action to dissolve the corporation.

(b) A professional corporation shall report to the appropriate licensing board the death of any of its shareholders within 30 days thereafter. Within one year of the date of such death, all of the shares owned by such deceased shareholder shall be transferred to and acquired by the professional corporation or persons qualified to own such shares. In the absence of an agreement which determines the equitable value of the shares, then the price for such shares shall be the fair market value of the stock, but not less than the book value as of the end of the month immediately preceding the death or disqualification. Notwithstanding any other provisions of this Chapter, the shares of stock owned by such deceased shareholder may be owned and held by the person or persons who may be legally entitled to receive such shares for a period of one year after the death of such deceased shareholder, or in the case of the death of the owner of all the shares of such corporation, for such period of time as may be necessary to liquidate the corporation. (1969, c. 718, s. 7.)

§ 55B-8. Rendition of professional services.

A professional service corporation may render professional services only through its officers, employees and agents who are duly licensed to render such professional services; provided, however, this provision shall not be interpreted to include in the term "employee," as used herein, clerks, secretaries, bookkeepers, technicians and other assistants who are not considered by law to be rendering professional services to the public. (1969, c. 718, s. 8.)

§ 55B-9. Professional relationship and liability.

(a) Relationship. — Nothing in this Chapter shall be interpreted to abolish, modify, restrict, limit or alter the law in this State applicable to the professional relationship and liabilities between the licensee furnishing the professional services and the person receiving such professional service, or the standards of professional conduct applicable to the rendering therein of such services.

(b) Liability. — A shareholder, a director, or an officer of a professional corporation is not individually liable, directly or indirectly, including by indemnification, contribution, assessment, or otherwise, for the debts, obligations, and liabilities of, or chargeable to, the professional corporation that arise from errors, omissions, negligence, malpractice, incompetence, or malfeasance committed by another shareholder, director, or officer or by a representative of the professional corporation; provided, however, nothing in this Chapter shall affect the liability of a shareholder, director, or officer of a professional corporation for his or her own errors, omissions, negligence, malpractice, incompetence, or malfeasance committed in the rendering of professional services. (1969, c. 718, s. 9; 1993, c. 354, s. 2; 1999-362, s. 2; 2000-140, s. 101(f).)

Legal Periodicals. — For note discussing the liability of members of a professional corporation, in light of Nelson v. Patrick, 73 N.C. App. 1, 326 S.E.2d 45 (1985), see 64 N.C.L. Rev. 1216 (1986).

CASE NOTES

Liability of Professional Corporations. — A professional corporation is liable to the same extent as if it were a partnership. Zimmerman v. Hogg, 22 N.C. App. 544, 207

S.E.2d 267, rev'd on other grounds, 286 N.C. 24,
209 S.E.2d 795 (1974).

§ 55B-10. Registration with licensing board.

No professional corporation shall open, operate, or maintain an establishment for any of the purposes set forth in this Chapter without first having obtained a certificate of registration from the licensing board or boards. Applications for such registration shall be made to the licensing board or boards in writing and shall contain the name and address of the corporation and such other information as may be required by the licensing board or boards. If the board finds that no disciplinary action is pending before the board against any of the licensed incorporators, officers, directors, shareholders or employees of such corporation, and if it appears that such corporation will be conducted in compliance with the law and the regulations of the board, the board shall issue, upon the payment of a registration fee, not to exceed fifty dollars ($50.00), a certificate of registration which shall remain effective until January 1 following the date of such registration or until such other expiration or renewal date as may be established by law or by the regulations of the licensing board. (1969, c. 718, s. 10.)

§ 55B-11. Renewal of certificate of registration.

Upon written application of the holder, accompanied by a fee not to exceed the sum of twenty-five dollars ($25.00), the licensing board shall renew the certificate of registration of a professional corporation as required by law or the regulations of the licensing board if the board finds that the corporation has complied with its regulations and the provisions of this section. If the corporation does not apply for renewal of its certificate of registration within 30 days after the date of the expiration of such certificate, the certificate of registration shall be automatically suspended and may be reinstated within the calendar year upon the payment of the required renewal fee plus a penalty of ten dollars ($10.00), if such corporation is then otherwise qualified and entitled to a renewal of its certificate of registration. (1969, c. 718, s. 11.)

§ 55B-12. Application of regulations of licensing boards.

A professional corporation shall be subject to the applicable rules and regulations adopted by, and all the disciplinary powers of, the licensing board as herein defined. Nothing in this Chapter shall impair the disciplinary powers of any licensing board applicable to a licensee as herein defined. No professional corporation may do any act which its shareholders as licensees are prohibited from doing. (1969, c. 718, s. 12.)

§ 55B-13. Suspension or revocation of certificate of registration.

A licensing board may suspend or revoke a certificate of registration issued by it to a domestic or foreign professional corporation for any of the following reasons:

    (1) Upon the failure of such corporation to promptly remove or discharge an officer, director, shareholder or employee who becomes disqualified by reason of the revocation or suspension of his license to practice; or

    (2) Upon a finding by the licensing board that the professional corporation has failed to comply with the provisions of this Chapter or the regulations of the licensing board.

Upon the suspension or revocation of a certificate of registration issued to a professional corporation, such corporation shall cease forthwith to render professional services, and the Secretary of State shall be notified to the end that the corporation may be removed from active status and remain as such until reinstatement. (1969, c. 718, s. 13; 1995, c. 351, s. 17.)

§ 55B-14. Types of professional services.

(a) A professional corporation shall render only one specific type professional service, and such services as may be ancillary thereto, and shall not engage in any other business or profession; provided, however, such corporation may own real and personal property necessary or appropriate for rendering the type of professional services it was organized to render and it may invest in real estate, mortgages, stocks, bonds, and any other type of investments.

(b) Notwithstanding subsection (a) of this section, in the case of architectural, landscape architectural, engineering or land surveying, geological, and soil science services, as defined in Chapters 83A, 89A, 89C, 89E, and 89F respectively, one corporation may be authorized to provide such of these services where such corporation, and at least one corporate officer who is a stockholder thereof, is duly licensed by the licensing board of each such profession.

(c) A professional corporation may also be formed by and between or among:

(1) A licensed psychologist and a physician practicing psychiatry to render psychotherapeutic and related services.

(2) Any combination of a registered nurse, nurse practitioner, certified clinical specialist in psychiatric and mental health nursing, certified nurse midwife, and certified nurse anesthetist, to render nursing and related services that the respective stockholders are licensed, certified, or otherwise approved to provide.

(3) A physician and a physician assistant who is licensed, registered, or otherwise certified under Chapter 90 of the General Statutes to render medical and related services.

(4) A physician, or a licensed psychologist, or both, and a certified clinical specialist in psychiatric and mental health nursing, a licensed clinical social worker, a licensed marriage and family therapist, a licensed professional counselor, or each of them, to render psychotherapeutic and related services that the respective stockholders are licensed, certified, or otherwise approved to provide.

(5) A physician and any combination of a nurse practitioner, certified clinical specialist in psychiatric and mental health nursing, or certified nurse midwife, registered or otherwise certified under Chapter 90 of the General Statutes, to render medical and related services that the respective stockholders are licensed, certified, or otherwise approved to provide.

(6) A physician practicing anesthesiology and a certified nurse anesthetist to render anesthesia and related medical services that the respective stockholders are licensed, certified, or otherwise approved to provide.

(7) A physician and an audiologist who is licensed under Article 22 of Chapter 90 of the General Statutes to render audiological and related medical services that the respective stockholders are licensed, certified, or otherwise approved to provide.

(8) A physician practicing ophthalmology and an optometrist who is licensed under Article 6 of Chapter 90 of the General Statutes to render either or both of ophthalmic services and optometric and related services that the respective stockholders are licensed, certi-

fied, or otherwise approved to provide. (1969, c. 718, s. 14; 1971, c. 196, s. 2; 1973, c. 1446, s. 9; 1985, c. 251; 1991, c. 205, s. 4; 1995, c. 382, s. 1; 1997-421, s. 1; 1997-500, s. 1; 1999-136, s. 1; 2000-115, s. 6; 2001-487, s. 40(e); 2003-117, s. 4.)

Effect of Amendments. — Session Laws 2003-117, s. 4, effective June 1, 2003, inserted "a licensed marriage and family therapist" in subdivision (c)(4).

§ 55B-15. Applicability of Chapter.

(a) This Chapter shall not apply to the following:
   (1) A corporation which prior to June 5, 1969, was permitted by law to render professional services or the corporate successor of that corporation by merger or otherwise by operation of law, provided there is no substantial change in the direct or indirect beneficial ownership of the shares of that corporation as the result of the merger or other transaction. For purposes of this subdivision, a change of twenty percent (20%) or less shall not be considered substantial.
   (2) A corporation authorized in this State to render primary services governed by Articles 1, 2, 4, or 5 of Chapter 87 of the General Statutes, if the corporation renders services as defined in Chapter 89C of the General Statutes, that are reasonably necessary and connected with the primary services performed by individuals regularly employed in the ordinary course of business by the corporation. The professional services may not be offered, performed, or rendered independently from the primary services rendered by the corporation. This subdivision does not restrict, limit, or modify the requirement that professional services must be provided by individuals regularly employed in the ordinary course of business by the corporation and duly licensed to render these professional services in this State. Nothing in this subdivision shall be interpreted to abolish, modify, restrict, limit, or alter the law in this State applicable to the professional relationship and liabilities between licensees furnishing the professional service and the person receiving the professional service, or the standards of professional conduct applicable to the rendering of the professional service.
(b) A corporation or its successor exempt under subsection (a) of this section may be brought within the provisions of this Chapter by the filing of an amendment to its articles of incorporation declaring that its shareholders have elected to bring the corporation within the provisions of this Chapter and to make the same conform to all of the provisions of this Chapter. (1969, c. 718, s. 15; 1991, c. 645, s. 20; 1997-244, s. 1.)

§ 55B-16. Foreign professional corporations.

(a) A foreign professional corporation may apply for a certificate of authority to transact business in this State pursuant to the provisions of this Chapter and Chapter 55 of the General Statutes provided that:
   (1) The corporation obtains a certificate of registration from the appropriate licensing board or boards in this State;
   (2) With respect to each professional service practiced through the corporation in this State, at least one director and one officer shall be a licensee of the licensing board which regulates the profession in this State;
   (3) Each officer, employee, and agent of the corporation who will provide professional services to persons in this State shall be a licensee of the appropriate licensing board in this State;

(4) The corporation shall be subject to the applicable rules and regulations adopted by, and all the disciplinary powers of, the appropriate licensing board or boards in this State;

(5) The corporation's activities in this State shall be limited as provided by G.S. 55B-14; and

(6) The application for certificate of authority, in addition to the requirements of G.S. 55-15-03, shall set forth the personal services to be rendered by the foreign professional corporation and the individual or individuals who will satisfy the requirements of G.S. 55B-16(a)(2) and shall be accompanied by a certification by the appropriate licensing board that each individual is a "licensee" as defined in G.S. 55B-2(2) and by additional certifications as may be required to establish that the corporation is a "foreign professional corporation" as defined in G.S. 55B-16(b).

(b) For purposes of this section, "foreign professional corporation" means a corporation for profit that:

(1) Is incorporated under a law other than the law of this State;

(2) Is incorporated for the purpose of rendering professional services of the type that if rendered in this State would require the obtaining of a license from a licensing board pursuant to the statutory provisions referred to in G.S. 55B-2(6); and

(3) Has as its shareholders only individuals who:

  a. Qualify to hold shares of a corporation organized under this Chapter;

  b. Are licensed to provide professional services as defined in G.S. 55B-2(6) in a state in which the corporation is incorporated or is authorized to transact business, provided that such professional services are the same as the professional service rendered by the corporation;

  c. Are nonlicensed employees of a corporation rendering services of the type defined in Chapters 83A, 89A, 89C, and 89E of the General Statutes, provided that all such nonlicensed employees own no more than one-third of the total issued and outstanding shares of such corporation in the aggregate; or

  d. With respect to a professional corporation rendering services under Chapter 93 of the General Statutes, are persons who own not more than forty-nine percent (49%) of the stock in the professional corporation as long as:

    1. Individuals who meet the requirements of sub-subdivision a. or b. of this subdivision own and control voting stock that represents at least fifty-one percent (51%) of the votes entitled to be cast in the election of directors of the professional corporation; and

    2. All licensees who perform professional services on behalf of the corporation in this State comply with Chapter 93 of the General Statutes and the rules adopted thereunder.

(b1) With respect to a professional corporation rendering services as defined in Chapters 83A, 89A, 89C, and 89E of the General Statutes, an employee retirement plan qualified under section 401 of the Internal Revenue Code of 1986, as amended (or any successor section), is deemed for purposes of this section to be an individual licensee if at least one trustee of the plan is a licensee and all other trustees are licensees or are individuals who are licensed under the laws of a state in which the corporation maintains an office to perform at least one of the professional services, as defined in Chapter 83A, 89A, 89C, or 89E of the General Statutes, rendered by the corporation.

(c) A foreign professional corporation with a valid certificate of authority has the same but no greater rights and privileges as, and is subject to the same duties, restrictions, penalties, and liabilities now or later imposed on, a domestic professional corporation of like character, except that the provisions of G.S. 55B-6 and G.S. 55B-7 do not apply. (1995, c. 351, s. 18; 1997-485, s. 23; 1999-440, s. 2.)

Legal Periodicals. — For 1997 legislative survey, see 20 Campbell L. Rev. 389.

Chapter 55C.

Foreign Trade Zones.

§ 55C-1. Public corporations authorized to apply for privilege of establishing a foreign trade zone.

Any public corporation of the State of North Carolina, as that term is hereinafter defined is hereby authorized to make application for the privilege of establishing, operating and maintaining a foreign trade zone in accordance with an act of Congress approved June 18, 1934, entitled, "An Act to Provide for the Establishment, Operation and Maintenance of Foreign Trade Zones in Ports of Entry of the United States," to expedite and encourage foreign commerce, and for other purposes. (1975, 2nd Sess., c. 983, s. 132.)

Legal Periodicals. — For survey of 1977 law on taxation, see 56 N.C.L. Rev. 1128 (1978).

§ 55C-2. "Public corporation" defined.

The term "public corporation" for the purposes of this Chapter, means the State of North Carolina or any political subdivision thereof, or any public agency of this State or any political subdivision thereof, or any public board, bureau, commission or authority created by the General Assembly. (1975, 2nd Sess., c. 983, s. 132.)

§ 55C-3. Private corporations authorized to apply for privilege of establishing a foreign trade zone.

Any private corporation hereafter organized under the laws of this State for the specific purpose of establishing, operating and maintaining a foreign trade zone in accordance with the act of Congress referred to in G.S. 55C-1 is likewise authorized to make application for the privilege of establishing, operating and maintaining a foreign trade zone in accordance with the said act of Congress. (1975, 2nd Sess., c. 983, s. 132.)

§ 55C-4. Public or private corporation establishing foreign trade zone to be governed by federal law.

Any public or private corporation authorized by this Chapter to make application for the privilege of establishing, operating, and maintaining said foreign trade zone, whose application is granted pursuant to the terms of the aforementioned act of Congress is hereby authorized to establish such foreign trade zone and to operate and maintain the same subject to the conditions and restrictions of the said act of Congress and any amendments thereto, and under such rules and regulations and for the period of time that may be prescribed by the board established by said act of Congress to carry out the provisions of such act. (1975, 2nd Sess., c. 983, s. 132; 1977, c. 782, s. 1.)

Chapter 55D.

Filings, Names, and Registered Agents for Corporations, Nonprofit Corporations, and Partnerships.

Editor's Note. — Session Laws 2001-358, s. 52, effective January 1, 2002, and applicable to documents submitted for filing on or after that date, authorizes the Revisor of Statutes to transfer, as historical annotations, the Official Comments and the North Carolina Comments to those portions of Chapter 55 of the General Statutes that are recodified by this act to the corresponding locations in Chapter 55D of the General Statutes, as the Revisor deems appropriate.

ARTICLE 1.

General Provisions.

§ 55D-1. Applicable definitions.

The following definitions apply in this Chapter:
(1) "Corporation" or "domestic corporation" is defined in G.S. 55-1-40(4).
(2) "Deliver" is defined in G.S. 55-1-40(5).
(3) "Entity" is defined in G.S. 55-1-40(9).
(4) "Foreign corporation" is defined in G.S. 55-1-40(10).
(5) "Foreign limited liability company" is defined in G.S. 57C-1-03(8).
(5a) "Foreign limited liability limited partnership" is defined in G.S. 59-102(4c).
(6) "Foreign limited liability partnership" is defined in G.S. 59-32(4g).
(7) "Foreign limited partnership" is defined in G.S. 59-102(5).
(8) "Foreign nonprofit corporation" means a foreign corporation as defined in G.S. 55A-1-40(11).
(9) "Individual" is defined in G.S. 55-1-40(13).

(10) "Limited liability company" or "domestic limited liability company" is defined in G.S. 57C-1-03(11).

(11) "Limited liability limited partnership" is defined in G.S. 59-102(6a).

(12) "Limited liability partnership" or "registered limited liability partnership" means a registered limited liability partnership as defined in G.S. 59-32(7).

(13) "Limited partnership" or "domestic limited partnership" is defined in G.S. 59-102(8).

(14) "Nonprofit corporation" or "domestic nonprofit corporation" means a corporation as defined in G.S. 55A-1-40(5).

(15) "Person" is defined in G.S. 55-1-40(16). (2001-358, s. 1; 2001-387, ss. 161, 173, 175(a); 2001-413, s. 6.)

Editor's Note. — Session Laws 2001-358, s. 53, provided that the act, which enacted this article, was effective October 1, 2001, and applicable to documents submitted for filing on or after that date. Section 173 of Session Laws 2001-387 changed the effective date of Session Laws 2001-358 from October 1, 2001, to January 1, 2002. Section 6 of Session Laws 2001-413, effective September 14, 2001, added a sentence to s. 175(a) of Session Laws 2001-387, making s. 173 of that act effective when it became law (August 26, 2001). As a result of these changes, the enactment of this article by Session Laws 2001-358 is effective January 1, 2002, and applicable to documents submitted for filing on or after that date.

Session Laws 2001-387, s. 154(b), provides that nothing in this act shall supersede the provisions of Article 10 or 65 of Chapter 58 of the General Statutes, and this act does not create an alternate means for an entity governed by Article 65 of Chapter 58 of the General Statutes to convert to a different business form.

Effect of Amendments. — Session Laws 2001-358, s. 12, inserted "and Names" in the chapter heading and Session Laws 2001-358, s. 42, as amended by s. 12, substituted "Filings, Names, and Registered Agents" for "Filings and Names." See editor's note for effective date and applicability.

Session Laws 2001-387, effective January 1, 2002, deleted "Limited Liability Companies, Limited partnerships, and Limited Liability" following "Nonprofit Corporations" in the chapter heading; inserted subdivision (5a); substituted "G.S. 59-32(4g)" for "G.S. 59-32(4a)" in subdivision (6); and inserted present subdivision (11) and redesignated former subdivisions (11) through (14) as present subdivisions (12) through (15).

§§ 55D-2 through 55D-4: Reserved for future codification purposes.

§ 55D-5. Rule-making authority.

The Secretary of State may adopt rules to implement the Secretary of State's responsibilities under this Chapter. (2001-358, s. 1; 2001-387, s. 173; 2001-413, s. 6.)

§§ 55D-6 through 55D-9: Reserved for future codification purposes.

ARTICLE 2.

Submission of Documents to the Secretary of State for Filing.

§ 55D-10. Filing requirements.

(a) To be entitled to filing by the Secretary of State under Chapter 55, 55A, 55B, 57C, or 59 of the General Statutes, a document must satisfy the requirements of this section, and of any other section of the General Statutes that adds to or varies these requirements.

(b) The document must meet all of the following requirements:

(1) The document must be one that is required or permitted by Chapter 55, 55A, 55B, 57C, or 59 of the General Statutes to be filed in the office of the Secretary of State.

(2) The document must contain the information required by Chapter 55, 55A, 55B, 57C, or 59 of the General Statutes for that document. It may contain other information as well.

(3) The document must be typewritten, printed, or in an electronic form acceptable to the Secretary of State.

(4) The document must be in the English language. A name need not be in English if written in English letters or Arabic or Roman numerals, and the certificate of existence required of foreign corporations, foreign nonprofit corporations, foreign limited liability companies, and foreign limited liability partnerships need not be in English if accompanied by a reasonably authenticated English translation.

(5) A document submitted by an entity must be executed by a person authorized to execute documents (i) under G.S. 55-1-20 if the entity is a domestic or foreign corporation, (ii) under G.S. 55A-1-20 if the entity is a domestic or foreign nonprofit corporation, (iii) under G.S. 57C-1-20 if the entity is a domestic or foreign limited liability company, (iv) under G.S. 59-204 if the entity is a domestic or foreign limited partnership, or (v) under G.S. 59-35.1 if the entity is any other partnership as defined in G.S. 59-36 whether or not formed under the laws of the State.

(6) The person executing the document must sign it and state beneath or opposite the person's signature, the person's name, and the capacity in which the person signs. Any signature on the document may be a facsimile or an electronic signature in a form acceptable to the Secretary of State. The document may but need not contain a seal, attestation, acknowledgment, verification, or proof.

(7) If the Secretary of State has prescribed a mandatory form for the document, the document must be in or on the prescribed form.

(8) The document must be delivered to the office of the Secretary of State for filing and must be accompanied by the applicable fees. (1955, c. 1371, s. 1; 1967, c. 13, s. 1; c. 823, s. 16; 1989, c. 265, s. 1; 1989 (Reg. Sess., 1990), c. 1024, s. 12.1(a); 1991, c. 645, s. 15; 1999-369, s. 1.1; 2001-358, ss. 3(a), 4; 2001-387, ss. 173, 175(a); 2001-413, s. 6.)

FORMER OFFICIAL COMMENT TO § 55-1-20

Editor's Note. — The Official Comments below were formerly located under G.S. 55-1-20 prior to its amendment in 2001. At the request of the Revisor of Statutes, the Official Comments have been transferred to this section as historical annotations pursuant to Session Laws 2001-358, s. 52.

Section 1.20 standardizes the filing requirements for all documents required or permitted by the Model Act to be filed with the secretary of state. In a few instances, other sections of the Act impose additional requirements which must also be complied with if the document in question is to be filed. Section 1.20 relates only to documents which the Model Act expressly requires or permits to be filed with the secretary of state; it does not authorize or direct the secretary of state to accept or reject for filing other documents relating to corporations and does not treat documents required or permitted to be filed under other statutes.

The purposes of the filing requirements of chapter 1 are: (1) to simplify the filing requirements by the elimination of formal or technical requirements that serve little purpose, (2) to minimize the number of pieces of paper to be processed by the secretary of state, and (3) to eliminate all possible disputes between persons seeking to file documents and the secretary of state as to the legal efficacy of documents.

The requirements of section 1.20 may be summarized as follows:

1. FORM

To be eligible for filing, a document must be typed or printed and in the English language (except to the limited extent permitted by section 1.20(e)). The secretary of state is not authorized to prescribe forms (except to the extent permitted by section 1.21) and as a result may not reject documents on the basis of form (see section 1.25) if they contain the information called for by the specific statutory requirement and meet the minimal formal requirements of this section.

2. EXECUTION

To be filed a document must simply be executed by a corporate officer. Section 1.21(f). No specific corporate officer is designated as the appropriate officer to sign though the signing officer must designate his office or the capacity in which he signs the document. Among the officers who are expressly authorized to sign a document is the chairman of the board of directors, a choice that may be appropriate if the corporation has a board of directors but has not appointed officers. If a corporation has not been formed or has neither officers nor a board of directors, an incorporator may execute the document.

The requirement in earlier versions of the Model Act and in many state statutes that documents must be acknowledge or verified as a condition for filing has been eliminated. These requirements serve little purpose in connection with documents filed under corporation statutes. (See in this connection section 1.29, which makes it a criminal offense for any person to sign a document for filing with knowledge that it contains false information.) On the other hand, many organizations, like lenders or title companies, may desire that specific documents include acknowledgments, verifications, or seals; section 1.21(g) therefore provides that the addition of these forms of execution does not affect the eligibility of the document for filing.

3. CONTENTS

A document must be filed by the secretary of state if it contains the information required by the Model Act. The document may contain additional information or statements and their presence is not ground for the secretary of state to reject the document for filing. These documents must be accepted for filing even though the secretary of state believes that the language is illegal or unenforceable. In view of this very limited discretion granted to secretaries of state under this section, section 1.25(d) defines the secretary of state's role as "ministerial" and provides that no inference or presumption arises from the fact that the secretary of state accepted a document for filing. See the Official Comments to sections 1.25 and 1.30.

4. NUMBER OF COPIES

Section 1.20(i) requires that a document filed with the secretary of state must be accompanied by "one exact or conformed copy." The requirement in early versions of the Model Act and in many state statutes that "duplicate originals" (each being executed as an original document) be submitted has been eliminated. Under section 1.20(i) an "exact" copy is a reproduction of the executed original document by photographic or xerographic process; a "conformed" copy is a copy on which the existence of signatures is entered or noted on the copy. The substitution of exact or conformed copies for duplicate originals reflects advances in the art of office copying machines that permit the routine reproduction of exact copies of executed documents. However, a person submitting "duplicate originals" meets the requirement of this section since the secretary of state may treat the duplicate original as a "conformed copy." The reasons for requiring an exact or conformed copy of a filed document to accompany the signed original, and the processing of these documents by the secretary of state, are discussed in the Official Comment to section 1.25.

FORMER NORTH CAROLINA COMMENTARY TO § 55-1-20

Editor's Note. — The North Carolina Commentary below was formerly located under G.S. 55-1-20 prior to its amendment in 2001. At the request of the Revisor of Statutes, the North Carolina Commentary has been transferred to this section as historical annotations pursuant to Session Laws 2001-358, s. 52.

This section differs from prior law in three minor substantive respects. First, former G.S. 55-4(a) (2) required the signatures of two specified officers, whereas this section requires only one and permits incorporators or fiduciaries to sign in appropriate circumstances. Second, former G.S. 55-4(a) (3) required verification except where acknowledgment was otherwise required, whereas the present section permits either verification or acknowledgment but does not require either. Third, former G.S. 55-4(a) (6) required delivery of a copy of the document to the register of deeds of the county in which the corporation's registered office was located; the new statute does not.

Because subsection (g) does not require verification or acknowledgment, G.S. 55-1-29 makes it a criminal offense for any person to sign a document for filing with knowledge that it contains false information. Other leading states, such as Delaware, do not require the acknowledgment or verification of corporate documents for filing, apparently without any problems. Finally, it does not appear that third parties can be injured by the elimination of the requirement of acknowledgment or verification. Third parties are entitled to rely on what is on file in the Secretary of State's office and are only charged with notice of any limitations on corporate powers expressly stated in the corporation's articles of incorporation.

This section differs from the corresponding section of the Model Act in three minor respects. First, the addition of the language "under this Act" in subsection (a) makes it clear that the subsection is referring to documents filed under this Act and not other filings such as UCC filings and securities law filings. Second, subsection (b) was rewritten for stylistic consistency. Third, subsection (i) limits the Model Act's requirement that a document presented for filing be accompanied by any franchise tax, license fee, or penalty required by this Act or other law *whether or not* related to the filing. The North Carolina version limits the necessary payments to those required by the Act and thus continues the former North Carolina practice.

Editor's Note. — Session Laws 2001-358, s. 2, effective January 1, 2002, and applicable to documents submitted for filing on or after that date, added the Article 2 head and its catchline.

Session Laws 2001-358, s. 3(b), effective January 1, 2002, and applicable to documents submitted for filing on or after that date, recodified 55-1-22.1, 55-1-22.2, 55-1-23, 55-1-24, 55-1-25, 55-1-26, 55-1-27, 55-1-29 as 55D-11, 55D-12, 55D-13, 55D-14, 55D-15, 55D-16, 55D-17, and 55D-18, respectively, in Article 2 of Chapter 55D of the General Statutes.

Session Laws 2001-358, s. 53, provided that the act, which amended this section, was effective October 1, 2001, and applicable to documents submitted for filing on or after that date. Section 173 of Session Laws 2001-387 changed the effective date of Session Laws 2001-358 from October 1, 2001, to January 1, 2002. Section 6 of Session Laws 2001-413, effective September 14, 2001, added a sentence to s. 175(a) of Session Laws 2001-387, making s. 173 of that act effective when it became law (August 26, 2001). As a result of these changes, the amendment by Session Laws 2001-358 is effective January 1, 2002, and applicable to documents submitted for filing on or after that date.

Effect of Amendments. — Session Laws 2001-358, ss. 3(a) and 4, effective January 1, 2002, and applicable to documents submitted for filing on or after that date, recodified G.S. 55-1-20(a) through (e) and (g) through (i) as this section; added the section head; and rewrote the section.

Legal Periodicals. — For article, "Revolving Funds: In the Vanguard of the Preservation Movement," see 11 N.C. Cent. L.J. 256 (1980).

For "Legislative Survey: Business & Banking," see 22 Campbell L. Rev. 253 (2000).

§ 55D-11. Expedited filings.

A person submitting a document for filing may request an expedited filing only at the time the document is submitted. The Secretary of State shall guarantee the expedited filing of the document if the document is in proper form and accompanied by all applicable fees, including the following fee:

(1) Two hundred dollars ($200.00) for the filing by the end of the same business day of a document received by 12:00 noon; or

(2) One hundred dollars ($100.00) for the filing of a document within 24 hours after receipt, excluding weekends and holidays.

The Secretary of State shall not collect the fees allowed in this section unless the person submitting the document for filing is informed by the Secretary of State of the fees prior to the filing of the document. (1995, c. 539, s. 1; 2001-358, ss. 3(b), 4; 2001-387, ss. 173, 175(a); 2001-413, s. 6.)

Editor's Note. — Session Laws 2001-358, s. 53, provided that the act, which amended this section, was effective October 1, 2001, and applicable to documents submitted for filing on or after that date. Section 173 of Session Laws 2001-387 changed the effective date of Session Laws 2001-358 from October 1, 2001, to January 1, 2002. Section 6 of Session Laws 2001-413, effective September 14, 2001, added a sentence to s. 175(a) of Session Laws 2001-387, making s. 173 of that act effective when it became law (August 26, 2001). As a result of these changes, the amendment by Session Laws 2001-358 is effective January 1, 2002, and applicable to documents submitted for filing on or after that date.

Effect of Amendments. — Session Laws 2001-358, ss. 3(b) and 4, effective January 1, 2002, and applicable to documents submitted for filing on or after that date, recodified G.S. 55-1-22.1 as this section; rewrote the first paragraph; substituted "noon; or" for "noon Eastern Standard Time; and" at the end of subdivision (1); and deleted "requests an expedited filing and" preceding "is informed" in the last paragraph.

§ 55D-12. Advisory review of documents.

Upon request, the Secretary of State shall review a document prior to its submission for filing to determine whether it satisfies applicable filing requirements. Submission of a document for review shall be accompanied by a fee of two hundred dollars ($200.00) and shall be in accordance with procedures adopted by rule by the Secretary of State. The advisory review shall be completed within 24 hours after submission, excluding weekends and holidays, unless the person submitting the document is otherwise notified in accordance with procedures adopted by rule by the Secretary of State fixing priority between submissions under this section and filings under G.S. 55D-11. Upon completion of the advisory review, the Secretary of State shall notify the person submitting the document of any deficiencies in the document that would prevent its filing. (1997-485, s. 6; 2001-358, ss. 3(b), 4; 2001-387, ss. 173, 175(a); 2001-413, s. 6.)

Editor's Note. — Session Laws 2001-358, s. 53, provided that the act, which amended this section, was effective October 1, 2001, and applicable to documents submitted for filing on or after that date. Section 173 of Session Laws 2001-387 changed the effective date of Session Laws 2001-358 from October 1, 2001, to January 1, 2002. Section 6 of Session Laws 2001-413, effective September 14, 2001, added a sentence to s. 175(a) of Session Laws 2001-387, making s. 173 of that act effective when it became law (August 26, 2001). As a result of these changes, the amendment by Session Laws 2001-358 is effective January 1, 2002, and applicable to documents submitted for filing on or after that date.

Effect of Amendments. — Session Laws 2001-358, ss. 3(b) and 4, effective January 1, 2002, and applicable to documents submitted for filing on or after that date, recodified G.S. 55-1-22.2 as this section; in the first sentence, substituted "review" for "provide for the review of" and substituted "applicable filing requirements" for "the requirements of this Chapter"; substituted "a fee of two hundred dollars ($200.00)" for "the proper fee" in the second sentence; and substituted "G.S. 55D-11" for "G.S. 55-1-22.1" in the next to last sentence.

Legal Periodicals. — For 1997 legislative survey, see 20 Campbell L. Rev. 389.

§ 55D-13. Effective time and date of document.

(a) Except as provided in subsection (b) of this section and in G.S. 55D-14, a document accepted for filing is effective:
(1) At the time of filing on the date it is filed, as evidenced by the Secretary of State's date and time endorsement on the filed document; or
(2) At the time specified in the document as its effective time on the date it is filed.
(b) A document may specify a delayed effective time and date, and if it does so the document becomes effective at the time and date specified. If a delayed effective date but no time is specified, the document is effective at 11:59:59 P.M. on that date. A delayed effective date for a document may not be later than the 90th day after the date it is filed.
(c) Except as provided in G.S. 55-2-03(b), 55A-2-03(b), and 57C-2-20(b), the fact that a document has become effective under this section does not determine its validity or invalidity or the correctness or incorrectness of the information contained in the document. (1955, c. 1371, s. 1; 1967, c. 13, s. 1; c. 823, s. 16; 1989, c. 265, s. 1; 1993, c. 552, s. 1; 2001-358, ss. 3(b), 4; 2001-387, ss. 173, 175(a); 2001-413, s. 6.)

OFFICIAL COMMENT TO FORMER § 55-1-23

Editor's Note. — The Official Comments below were formerly located under G.S. 55-1-23 prior to its transfer in 2001. At the request of the Revisor of Statutes, the Official Comments have been transferred to this section as historical annotations pursuant to Session Laws 2001-358, s. 52.

Section 1.23(a) provides that documents accepted for filing become effective at the time and date of filing, or at another specified time on that date, unless a delayed effective date is selected under section 1.23(b). This section gives express statutory authority to the common practice of most secretaries of state of ignoring processing time and treating a document as effective as of the date it is submitted for filing even though it may not be reviewed and accepted for filing until several days later.

Section 1.23(a) requires secretaries of state to maintain a date and time stamp for recording the receipt of documents and provides that documents become effective at the stamped time on the date of filing. This provision should eliminate any doubt about situations involving same-day transactions in which documents, for example articles of merger, are filed on the morning of the date the merger is to become effective. Section 1.23(a) contemplates that the time of filing, as well as the date, will be routinely recorded.

Section 1.23(b) provides an alternative method of establishing the effective date of a document. The document itself may fix as its effective date any date within 90 days after the date it is filed; it may also fix the time it becomes effective on that date. If no time is specified, the document becomes effective as of the close of business on the specified date. The Model Act also allows the effective date fixed in a document to be corrected to a limited extent. See the Official Comment to section 1.24.

Section 1.23(b) does not authorize or contemplate the retroactive establishment of an effective date before the date of filing.

NORTH CAROLINA COMMENTARY TO FORMER § 55-1-23

Editor's Note. — The North Carolina Commentary below was formerly located under G.S. 55-1-23 prior to its transfer in 2001. At the request of the Revisor of Statutes, the North Carolina Commentary has been transferred to this section as historical annotations pursuant to Session Laws 2001-358, s. 52.

This section differs from prior law in three respects. First, it increases from 20 to 90 days the maximum time by which the effective date of a filed document may be delayed. Second, it specifies a time of day (11:59:59 P.M.) for the effectiveness of documents that specify a delayed effective date but no time. Third, it deletes reference to a penalty for a failure to deliver documents to the register of deeds, since that requirement no longer exists.

This section differs in two respects from the Model Act. First, it specifies 11:59:59 P.M. (rather than the close of business) as the time of effectiveness of documents that specify a delayed effective date but no time. Second, it makes explicit in subsection (c) the limited effect of the Secretary of State's acceptance of documents for filing. This is probably implicit under the Model Act. *See* North Carolina Comment to G.S. 55-1-25(d), *infra*.

Editor's Note. — Session Laws 2001-358, s. 53, provided that the act, which amended this section, was effective October 1, 2001, and applicable to documents submitted for filing on or after that date. Section 173 of Session Laws 2001-387 changed the effective date of Session Laws 2001-358 from October 1, 2001, to January 1, 2002. Section 6 of Session Laws 2001-413, effective September 14, 2001, added a sentence to s. 175(a) of Session Laws 2001-387, making s. 173 of that act effective when it became law (August 26, 2001). As a result of these changes, the amendment by Session Laws 2001-358 is effective January 1, 2002, and applicable to documents submitted for filing on or after that date.

Effect of Amendments. — Session Laws 2001-358, ss. 3(b) and 4, s. 173, effective January 1, 2002, and applicable to documents submitted for filing on or after that date, recodified G.S. 55-1-23 as this section; substituted "of this section" and in G.S. 55D-14" for "and G.S. 55-1-24(c)" in the introductory language of subsection (a); substituted "filed document" for "original document" in subdivision (a)(1); and inserted "55A-2-03(b), and 57C-2-20(b)" in subsection (c).

§ 55D-14. Correcting filed document.

(a) A person on whose behalf a document was filed in the Office of the Secretary of State may correct that document if it (i) contains a statement that is incorrect and was incorrect when filed or (ii) was defectively executed, attested, sealed, verified, or acknowledged.

(b) A document is corrected by delivering to the Secretary of State for filing articles of correction that do all of the following:

(1) Describe the document (including its filing date) or have attached to them a copy of the document.

(2) Specify the incorrect statement and the reason it is incorrect or the nature of the defect.

(3) Correct the incorrect statement or defect.

(c) Articles of correction are effective as of the effective time and date of the document they correct except as to persons relying on the uncorrected document and adversely affected by the correction. As to those persons, articles of correction are effective when filed. (1989, c. 265, s. 1; 1997-485, s. 14; 2001-358, ss. 3(b), 4; 2001-387, ss. 173, 175(a); 2001-413, s. 6.)

OFFICIAL COMMENT TO FORMER § 55-1-24

Editor's Note. — The Official Comments below were formerly located under G.S. 55-1-24 prior to its transfer in 2001. At the request of the Revisor of Statutes, the Official Comments have been transferred to this section as historical annotations pursuant to Session Laws 2001-358, s. 52.

Section 1.24 permits making corrections in filed documents without refiling the entire document or submitting formal articles of amendment. This correction procedure has two advantages: (1) filing articles of correction may be less expensive than refiling the document or filing articles of amendment, and (2) articles of correction do not alter the effective date of the underlying document being corrected. Indeed, under section 1.24(c), even the correction relates back to the original effective date of the document except as to persons relying on the original document and adversely affected by the correction. As to these persons, the effective date of articles of correction is the date the articles are filed.

A document may be corrected either because it contains an "incorrect statement" or because it was defectively executed (including defects in optional forms of execution that do not affect the eligibility of the original document for filing).

A provision in a document setting an effective date (section 1.23) may be corrected under this section, but the corrected effective date must comply with section 1.23 measured from the date of the original filing of the document being corrected, i.e. it cannot be before the date of filing of the document or more than 90 days thereafter.

NORTH CAROLINA COMMENTARY TO FORMER § 55-1-24

Editor's Note. — The North Carolina Commentary below was formerly located under G.S. 55-1-24 prior to its transfer in 2001. At the request of the Revisor of Statutes, the North Carolina Commentary has been transferred to this section as historical annotations pursuant to Session Laws 2001-358, s. 52.

This section has no counterpart in prior law.

Editor's Note. — Session Laws 2001-358, s. 53, provided that the act, which amended this section, was effective October 1, 2001, and applicable to documents submitted for filing on or after that date. Section 173 of Session Laws 2001-387 changed the effective date of Session Laws 2001-358 from October 1, 2001, to January 1, 2002. Section 6 of Session Laws 2001-413, effective September 14, 2001, added a sentence to s. 175(a) of Session Laws 2001-387, making s. 173 of that act effective when it became law (August 26, 2001). As a result of these changes, the amendment by Session Laws 2001-358 is effective January 1, 2002, and applicable to documents submitted for filing on or after that date.

Effect of Amendments. — Session Laws 2001-358, ss. 3(b) and (4), effective January 1,

2002, and applicable to documents submitted for filing on or after that date, recodified G.S. 55-1-24 as this section; rewrote subsections (a) and (b); and substituted "as of the effective time and date" for "on the effective date" in subsection (c).

§ 55D-15. Filing duty of Secretary of State.

(a) If a document delivered to the office of the Secretary of State for filing satisfies the requirements of this Chapter and of Chapter 55, 55A, 55B, 57C, or 59 of the General Statutes, the Secretary of State shall file it. Documents filed with the Secretary of State under this Chapter may be maintained by the Secretary either in their original form or in photographic, microfilm, optical disk media, or other reproduced form. The Secretary may make reproductions of documents filed under this Chapter, or under any predecessor law, by photographic, microfilm, optical disk media, or other means of reproduction, and may destroy the originals of those documents reproduced.

(b) The Secretary of State files a document by endorsing "Filed", together with the Secretary's name and official title and the date and time of filing, on the document. After filing a document, the Secretary of State shall deliver a document copy to the person submitting the document for filing and as provided in G.S. 55D-32.

(c) If the Secretary of State refuses to file a document, the Secretary shall return it to the person submitting the document for filing within five days after the document was received, together with a written statement of the date of the refusal and a brief explanation of the reason for refusal. The Secretary of State may correct apparent errors and omissions on a document submitted for filing if authorized to make the corrections by the person submitting the document for filing.

(d) The Secretary of State's duty is to review and file documents that satisfy the requirements of this Chapter and of Chapter 55, 55A, 55B, 57C, or 59 of the General Statutes. The Secretary of State's filing or refusing to file a document does not do any of the following:

　(1) Except as provided in G.S. 55-2-03(b), 55A-2-03(b), or 57C-2-20(b), affect the validity or invalidity of the document in whole or part.

　(2) Relate to the correctness or incorrectness of information contained in the document.

　(3) Create a presumption that the document is valid or invalid or that information contained in the document is correct or incorrect. (1955, c. 1371, s. 1; 1967, c. 13, s. 1; c. 823, s. 16; 1989, c. 265, s. 1; 1989 (Reg. Sess., 1990), c. 1024, s. 12.2; 1993, c. 552, s. 2; 1995, c. 539, s. 2; 2001-358, ss. 3(b), 4, 46; 2001-387, ss. 173, 175(a); 2001-413, s. 6.)

OFFICIAL COMMENT TO FORMER § 55-1-25

Editor's Note. — *The Official Comments below were formerly located under G.S. 55-1-25 prior to its transfer in 2001. At the request of the Revisor of Statutes, the Official Comments have been transferred to this section as historical annotations pursuant to Session Laws 2001-358, s. 52.*

1. FILING DUTY IN GENERAL

Under section 1.25 the secretary of state is required to file a document if it "satisfies the requirements of section 1.20." This language should be contrasted with earlier versions of the Model Act (and many state statutes) that required the secretary of state to ascertain whether the document "conformed with law" before filing it. The purpose of this change is to limit the discretion of the secretary of state to a ministerial role in reviewing the contents of documents. If the document submitted is in the form prescribed and contains the information required by section 1.20 and the applicable provision of the Model Act, the secretary of state under section 1.25 must file it even though it contains additional provisions the secretary of state may feel are irrelevant or not authorized by the Model Act or by general legal principles. Consistently with this approach, section 1.25(d) states that the filing duty of the secretary of state is ministerial and provides that filing a document with the secretary of state does not affect the validity or invalidity of any provision contained in the document and does not create any presumption with respect to any provision. Persons adversely affected by provisions in a document may test their validity in a proceeding appropriate for that purpose. Similarly, the attorney general of the state may also question the validity of provisions of documents filed with the secretary of state in an independent suit brought for that purpose; in neither case should any presumption or inference be drawn about the validity of the provision from the fact that the secretary of state accepted the document for filing.

2. MECHANICS OF FILING

Section 1.25(b) provides that when the secretary of state files a document, he stamps or endorses it as filed, retains the signed original document for his records, and returns the exact or conformed copy (which must accompany the document under section 1.20(i)) to the corporation or its representative with the secretary of state's fee receipt or acknowledgement of receipt if no fee is required. This will establish that a document has been filed in the form of the copy. Consideration was given to dispensing with the document copy entirely and providing only for the return of a fee receipt or equivalent document. Several states currently follow this practice with respect to articles of incorporation and other documents. It was felt to be important, however, to continue a practice by which each corporation receives back from the secretary of state for its records a document that on its face shows that it is an exact conformed copy of the document that was filed with the secre-

tary of state. This copy is usually placed in the minute book and is available for informal inspection without requiring a person to examine the records of the secretary of state. Of course, a person desiring a certified copy of any filed document may obtain it from the office of the secretary of state by paying the fee prescribed in section 1.22(c).

3. ELIMINATION OF CERTIFICATES OF INCORPORATION AND SIMILAR DOCUMENTS

Section 1.25(b) provides that acceptance of articles of incorporation or other documents is evidenced merely by the issuance of a fee receipt or acknowledgement of receipt if no fee is required. Earlier versions of the Model Act and the statutes of many states provided that acceptance by the secretary of state is evidenced by a "certificate" (e.g., of incorporation, of merger, or of amendment). This older practice was not retained in the revised Model Act because it was felt desirable to reduce the number of pieces of paper issued by the secretary of state. Under the older practice most state offices routinely issued both fee receipts and certificates. A single document—the fee receipt or acknowledgment—should sufficiently indicate that the document has been accepted for filing, and in fact many states in recent years have dispensed with the formal certificate.

4. REJECTION OF DOCUMENT BY SECRETARY OF STATE

Because of the simplification of formal filing requirements and the limited discretion granted to the secretary of state by the Model Act, it is probable that rejection of documents for filing will occur only rarely. Section 1.25(c) provides that if the secretary of state does reject a document for filing he must return it to the corporation or its representative within five days together with a brief written explanation of his reason for rejection. This rejection may be the basis of judicial review under section 1.26.

NORTH CAROLINA COMMENTARY TO FORMER § 55-1-25

Editor's Note. — *The North Carolina Commentary below was formerly located under G.S. 55-1-25 prior to its transfer in 2001. At the request of the Revisor of Statutes, the North Carolina Commentary has been transferred to this section as historical annotations pursuant to Session Laws 2001-358, s. 52.*

Former G.S. 55-4(a) (5) required the Secretary of State to file a document unless it did not "conform to law." Although this section omits the filing standard of former G.S. 55-4(a) (5) — that a document shall be filed only if it "conforms to law" — the drafters rejected the Official Comment's suggestion that there is a conflict between the Secretary of State's

ministerial filing duty under section 1.25 of the Model Act and his review of a document to determine whether it conforms to law. The drafters intend that the Secretary of State's office continue the practice under former G.S. 55-4(a) (5) of calling attention to mistakes apparent on the face of a document presented for filing and to inconsistencies between a document presented for filing and other documents previously filed by the same corporation. For example, if a document presented for filing contains a reference (e.g., par value of authorized shares; number of outstanding shares) that, on its face, is inconsistent with the corporation's articles of incorporation, then the Secretary of State may refuse to file it. Similarly, a document may be refused if, on its face, it shows that the action referred to therein has not been authorized in the manner prescribed by the statute (e.g. no shareholders' vote on a matter requiring shareholder action). The drafters concluded that continuation of the practice under former G.S. 55-4(a) (5) was necessary to preserve the integrity and reliability of documents on file in the office of the Secretary of State. Accordingly, to clarify their intention, the drafters modified the Model Act in subsection (a) to provide that in order to be filed, a document must satisfy the requirements of "this Chapter."

The Model Act was modified in subsection (b) to omit the requirement that the Secretary of State provide a filing fee receipt in all cases. However, it is intended that a filing fee receipt will be provided upon request.

The Model Act was also modified in subsec-

tion (c) by substituting "received" for "delivered." "Deliver" is defined in G.S. 55-1-40(5) as including "mail," which creates an ambiguity as to when the five-day period for returning a document presented for filing begins to run. The modification was made to clarify this point.

Former G.S. 55-169 provided that a certificate issued by the Secretary of State with respect to a document on file in his office constituted prima facie evidence of the facts therein stated. Subsection (d) eliminates that presumption with respect to extrinsic facts in a document on file (e.g. the number of shares issued and outstanding; the number of shares voted on a particular matter). In that respect G.S. 55-1-23(c) was added to make a clear distinction between the word "validity," as used in subsection (d), and the word "effective" as used elsewhere in the statute. "Validity" refers to the substance and legal sufficiency of a filed document, and "effective" refers only to whether the document has been accepted and become operative under the formal filing procedures of the Act. Subsection (d) was also modified from the Model Act to describe the Secretary of State's duty under this section instead of merely characterizing it as ministerial.

Editor's Note. — Session Laws 2001-358, s. 53, provided that the act, which amended this section, was effective October 1, 2001, and applicable to documents submitted for filing on or after that date. Section 173 of Session Laws 2001-387 changed the effective date of Session Laws 2001-358 from October 1, 2001, to January 1, 2002. Section 6 of Session Laws 2001-413, effective September 14, 2001, added a sentence to s. 175(a) of Session Laws 2001-387, making s. 173 of that act effective when it

became law (August 26, 2001). As a result of these changes, the amendment by Session Laws 2001-358 is effective January 1, 2002, and applicable to documents submitted for filing on or after that date.

Effect of Amendments. — Session Laws 2001-358, ss. 3(b), (4), and (46), effective January 1, 2002, and applicable to documents submitted for filing on or after that date, recodified G.S. 55-1-25 as this section, and rewrote the section.

§ 55D-16. Appeal from Secretary of State's refusal to file document.

(a) If the Secretary of State refuses to file a document delivered to the Secretary of State's office for filing, the person on whose behalf the document was submitted for filing may, within 30 days after the date of the refusal, appeal the refusal to the Superior Court of Wake County. The appeal is commenced by filing a petition with the court and with the Secretary of State requesting the court to compel the Secretary of State to file the document. The petition must have attached to it the document to be filed and the Secretary of State's explanation for the refusal to file. No service of process on the Secretary of State is required except for the filing of the petition as set forth in this subsection. The appeal to the superior court is not governed by Chapter 150B of the General Statutes, the Administrative Procedure Act, and shall be determined by a judge of the superior court upon such further notice and opportunity to be heard, if any, as the court may deem appropriate under the circumstances.

(b) Upon consideration of the petition and any response made by the Secretary of State, the court may, prior to entering final judgment, order the Secretary of State to file the document or take other action the court considers appropriate.

(c) The court's final decision may be appealed as in other civil proceedings. (1989, c. 265, s. 1; 1989 (Reg. Sess., 1990), c. 1024, s. 12.3; 2001-358, ss. 3(b), 4; 2001-387, ss. 173, 175(a); 2001-413, s. 6.)

OFFICIAL COMMENT TO FORMER § 55-1-26

Editor's Note. — *The Official Comments below were formerly located under G.S. 55-1-26 prior to its transfer in 2001. At the request of the Revisor of Statutes, the Official Comments have been transferred to this section as historical annotations pursuant to Session Laws 2001-358, s. 52.*

1. THE COURT WITH JURISDICTION TO HEAR APPEALS FROM THE SECRETARY OF STATE

The identity of the specific court with jurisdiction to hear appeals from the secretary of state under section 1.26 must be supplied by each state when enacting this section. It is intended that this should be a court of general civil jurisdiction. It may either be the court located in the capital of the state or the court in the county where the corporation's principal business office is located in the state or, if the corporation does not have a principal office in the state, the court located in the county in which its registered office is located. The annual report of the corporation must state where the principal office of the corporation (which need not be within the state) is located. See section 16.22. Other sections of the Model Act also contemplate that the court with jurisdiction over substantive corporate matters will be designated in the statute. See, for example, section 7.03, relating to the ordering of a shareholders' meeting after the corporation fails to hold such a meeting. It is expected that jurisdiction over litigation with respect to substantive matters will normally be vested in the court in the county of the corporation's princi-pal or registered office. See the Official Comment to section 7.03.

2. "SUMMARY" ORDERS

In view of the limited discretion of the secretary of state under the Act, a "summary" order appears to be appropriate in section 1.26. Throughout the Model Act the term "summarily order" or similar language is used where courts are authorized to order action taken and the person charged with taking the original action has little or no discretion. The word "summary" is not used in a technical sense but to refer to a class of cases where the court might appropriately order that action be taken on the face of the pleadings or after an oral hearing but without any need to resolve disputed factual issues.

3. BURDEN OF PROOF AND REVIEW STANDARD

The revised Model Act, unlike earlier versions, does not address either the burden of proof or the standard for review in judicial proceedings challenging action of the secretary of state. It is contemplated that these matters will be governed by general principles of judicial review of agency action in each adopting state.

AMENDED NORTH CAROLINA COMMENTARY TO FORMER § 55-1-26

Editor's Note. — *The North Carolina Commentary below was formerly located under G.S. 55-1-26 prior to its transfer in 2001. At the request of the Revisor of Statutes, the North Carolina Commentary has been transferred to this section as historical annotations pursuant to Session Laws 2001-358, s. 52.*

The prior law contained no explicit procedure for appeal from the Secretary of State's refusal to file a document.

This section varies from the Model Act in that it avoids use of the word "summarily" and instead sets out a specific procedure, in the nature of a petition for a writ of mandamus, which (1) requires the appellant to file a copy of its petition with the Secretary of State, (2) makes it clear that the Administrative Procedure Act does not govern such appeal, and (3) provides that the court may give the Secretary of State further notice and an opportunity to be heard if it chooses to do so. In addition, to clarify that a refusal to file initial articles of incorporation or reservations of corporate names may be appealed pursuant to this section, this section uses the words "person tendering the document for filing" to describe the appellant where the Model Act uses the words "domestic or foreign corporation."

Editor's Note. — The Administrative Procedure Act, referred to in this section, is codified at Chapter 150B, G.S. 150B-1 et seq.

Session Laws 2001-358, s. 53, provided that the act, which amended this section, was effective October 1, 2001, and applicable to documents submitted for filing on or after that date. Section 173 of Session Laws 2001-387 changed the effective date of Session Laws 2001-358 from October 1, 2001, to January 1, 2002. Section 6 of Session Laws 2001-413, effective September 14, 2001, added a sentence to s. 175(a) of Session Laws 2001-387, making s. 173 of that act effective when it became law (August 26, 2001). As a result of these changes, the amendment by Session Laws 2001-358 is effective January 1, 2002, and applicable to docu-

ments submitted for filing on or after that date.

Effect of Amendments. — Session Laws 2001-358, ss. 3(b) and (4), effective January 1, 2002, and applicable to documents submitted for filing on or after that date, recodified G.S. 55-1-26 as this section; and in subsection (a), in the first sentence, substituted "the Secretary of State's office" for "his office," substituted "on whose behalf the document was submitted" for "tendering the document," and substituted "the date of the refusal" for "such refusal," in the third sentence, substituted "must" for "shall" and substituted "the refusal" for "his refusal," inserted the present fourth sentence, and in the final sentence, inserted "Chapter 150B of the General Statutes" and inserted "by a judge of the superior court."

§ 55D-17. Evidentiary effect of copy of filed document.

A certificate attached to a copy of a document filed by the Secretary of State, bearing the Secretary of State's signature and the seal of office (both of which may be in facsimile or in any electronic form approved by the Secretary of State) and certifying that the copy is a true copy of the document, is conclusive evidence that the original document is on file with the Secretary of State. A photographic, microfilm, optical disk media, or other reproduced copy of a document filed under this Chapter, Chapter 55, 55A, 55B, 57C, or 59 of the General Statutes, or any predecessor law, when certified by the Secretary, shall be considered an original for all purposes and is admissible in evidence in like manner as an original. (1955, c. 1371, s. 1; 1989, c. 265, s. 1; 1995, c. 539, s. 3; 2001-358, ss. 3(b), 4; 2001-387, ss. 173, 175(a); 2001-413, s. 6.)

OFFICIAL COMMENT TO FORMER § 55-1-27

Editor's Note. — The Official Comments below were formerly located under G.S. 55-1-27 prior to its transfer in 2001. At the request of the Revisor of Statutes, the Official Comments have been transferred to this section as historical annotations pursuant to Session Laws 2001-358, s. 52.

The secretary of state may be requested to certify that a specific document has been filed with him upon payment of the fees specified in section 1.22(c). Section 1.27 provides that the certificate is conclusive evidence only that the

original document is on file. The limited effect of the certificate is consistent with the ministerial filing obligation imposed on the secretary of state under the Model Act.

NORTH CAROLINA COMMENTARY TO FORMER § 55-1-27

Editor's Note. — The North Carolina Commentary below was formerly located under G.S. 55-1-27 prior to its transfer in 2001. At the request of the Revisor of Statutes, the North Carolina Commentary has been transferred to this section as historical annotations pursuant to Session Laws 2001-358, s. 52.

This section makes the Secretary of State's certificate of a document conclusive that the

original is on file in his office. It differs from former G.S. 55-169, which made such certificate "prima facie" evidence of the facts stated in the certificate and in the certified document.

The section differs from the Model Act by inserting the requirement that the Secretary of State certify that the attached copy of the document is a true copy and by providing for the use of the Secretary of State's seal rather than the State seal.

Editor's Note. — Session Laws 2001-358, s. 53, provided that the act, which amended this section, was effective October 1, 2001, and applicable to documents submitted for filing on or after that date. Section 173 of Session Laws 2001-387 changed the effective date of Session Laws 2001-358 from October 1, 2001, to January 1, 2002. Section 6 of Session Laws 2001-413, effective September 14, 2001, added a sentence to s. 175(a) of Session Laws 2001-387, making s. 173 of that act effective when it became law (August 26, 2001). As a result of these changes, the amendment by Session Laws 2001-358 is effective January 1, 2002, and applicable to documents submitted for fil-ing on or after that date.

Effect of Amendments. — Session Laws 2001-358, ss. 3(b) and (4), effective January 1, 2002, and applicable to documents submitted for filing on or after that date, recodified G.S. 55-1-27 as this section; substituted "and the seal of office (both of which may be in facsimile or in any electronic form approved by the Secretary of State)" for "(which may be in facsimile) and the seal of office" in the first sentence, and substituted "under this Chapter, Chapter 55, 55A, 55B, 57C, or 59 of the General Statutes, or any predecessor law" for "pursuant to this Chapter or any predecessor act" in the final sentence.

§ 55D-18. Penalty for signing false document.

(a) A person commits an offense if the person signs a document the person knows is false in any material respect with intent that the document be delivered to the Secretary of State for filing.

(b) An offense under this section is a Class 1 misdemeanor. (1989, c. 265, s. 1; 1993, c. 539, s. 439; 1994, Ex. Sess., c. 24, s. 14(c); 2001-358, ss. 3(b), 4; 2001-387, ss. 173, 175(a); 2001-413, s. 6.)

OFFICIAL COMMENT TO FORMER § 55-1-29

Editor's Note. — The Official Comments below were formerly located under G.S. 55-1-29 prior to its transfer in 2001. At the request of the Revisor of Statutes, the Official Comments have been transferred to this section as historical annotations pursuant to Session Laws 2001-358, s. 52.

Section 1.29 makes it a criminal offense for any person to sign a document that he knows is false in any material respect with intent that the document be submitted for filing to the secretary of state.

Section 1.29(b) is keyed to the classification of offenses provided by the Model Penal Code. If a state has not adopted this classification, the dollar amount of the fine should be substituted for the misdemeanor classification.

Editor's Note. — Session Laws 2001-358, s. 53, provided that the act, which amended this section, was effective October 1, 2001, and applicable to documents submitted for filing on or after that date. Section 173 of Session Laws 2001-387 changed the effective date of Session Laws 2001-358 from October 1, 2001, to January 1, 2002. Section 6 of Session Laws 2001-413, effective September 14, 2001, added a sentence to s. 175(a) of Session Laws 2001-387, making s. 173 of that act effective when it became law (August 26, 2001). As a result of these changes, the amendment by Session Laws 2001-358 is effective January 1, 2002, and applicable to documents submitted for filing on or after that date.

Effect of Amendments. — Session Laws 2001-358, ss. 3(b) and (4), effective January 1, 2002, and applicable to documents submitted for filing on or after that date, recodified G.S. 55-1-29 as this section; and substituted "the person" for "he" in two places in subsection (a).

§ **55D-19:** Reserved for future codification purposes.

ARTICLE 3.

Names.

§ 55D-20. Name requirements.

(a) In addition to the requirements of any other applicable section of the General Statutes:

(1) The name of a corporation must contain the word "corporation", "incorporated", "company", or "limited", or the abbreviation "corp.", "inc.", "co.", or "ltd.".

(2) The name of a limited liability company must contain the words "limited liability company" or the abbreviation "L.L.C." or "LLC", or the combination "ltd. liability co.", "limited liability co.", or "ltd. liability company".

(3) The name of a limited partnership that is not a limited liability limited partnership must contain the words "limited partnership", the abbreviation "L.P." or "LP", or the combination "ltd. partnership".

(4) The name of a limited liability limited partnership must contain the words "registered limited liability limited partnership" or "limited liability limited partnership" or the abbreviation "L.L.L.P.", "R.L.L.L.P.", "LLLP", or "RLLLP".

(5) A registered limited liability partnership's name must contain the words "registered limited liability partnership" or "limited liability partnership" or the abbreviation "L.L.P.", "R.L.L.P.", "LLP" or "RLLP".

(b) In addition to the requirements of subsection (a) of this section, the name of a limited partnership shall not contain the name of a limited partner unless (i) it is also the name of a general partner or the corporate name of a corporate general partner, or (ii) the business of the limited partnership has been carried on under that name before the admission of that limited partner.

(c) The name of a corporation, nonprofit corporation, or limited liability company shall not contain language stating or implying that the entity is organized for a purpose other than that permitted by G.S. 55-3-01, 55A-3-01, or 57C-2-01 and by its articles of incorporation or organization.

(d) The use of assumed names or fictitious names, as provided for in Chapter 66, is not affected by this Chapter or by Chapter 55, 55A, 57C, or 59 of the General Statutes.

(e) The filing of any document, the reservation or registration of any name under this Chapter or under Chapter 55, 55A, 55B, 57C, or 59 of the General Statutes, or the issuance of a certificate of authority to transact business or conduct affairs or a statement of foreign registration does not authorize the use in this State of a name in violation of the rights of any third party under the federal trademark act, the trademark act of this State, or other statutory or common law, and is not a defense to an action for violation of any of those rights. (1901, c. 2, s. 8; 1903, c. 453; Rev., s. 1137; 1913, c. 5, s. 1; C.S., s. 1114; 1935, cc. 166, 320; 1939, c. 222; G.S., s. 55-2; 1955, c. 1371, s. 1; 1959, c. 1316, s. 28; 1969, c. 751, ss. 4-6; 1973, c. 469, s. 45.3; 1989, c. 265, s. 1; 1989 (Reg. Sess., 1990), c. 1024, s. 12.5; 1995, c. 539, ss. 4, 5; 2001-358, ss. 14(a), 15; 2001-387, ss. 162, 173, 175(a); 2001-413, s. 6.)

OFFICIAL COMMENT TO FORMER § 55-4-01

Editor's Note. — The Official Comments below were formerly located under G.S. 55-4-01 prior to its transfer in 2001. At the request of the Revisor of Statutes, the Official Comments have been transferred to this section as historical annotations pursuant to Session Laws 2001-358, s. 52.

All of chapter 4, relating to corporate names, has been reviewed and revised in light of the responsibilities that should reasonably be placed on secretaries of state considering their available resources.

Section 4.01 deals with two basic name requirements: (1) the name must indicate "corporateness," and (2) the name must be distinguishable upon the records of the secretary of state.

1. INDICATION OF CORPORATENESS

Section 4.01(a) permits the words indicating corporateness to include "corporation," "incorporated," "limited," or "company" or an abbreviation of them. While the words "company" and "limited" are commonly used by partnerships or limited partnerships, and therefore do not uniquely indicate corporateness, their use is widespread and is continued since it creates no discernible harm. The Act also permits the use of words or abbreviations in another language that import corporateness.

2. NAMES THAT ARE "DISTINGUISHABLE UPON THE RECORDS OF THE SECRETARY OF STATE"

The revision of the Model Act is based on the fundamental premise that its name provisions should only ensure that each corporation has a sufficiently distinctive name so that it may be distinguished from other corporations upon the records of the secretary of state. The general business corporation statute should not be a partial substitute for a general assumed name, unfair competition, or antifraud statute. As a result, the Model Act does not restrict the power of a corporation to adopt or use an assumed or fictitious name with the same freedom as an individual or impose a requirement that an "official" name not be "deceptively similar" to another corporate name (a requirement of earlier versions of the Model Act). Principles of unfair competition, not the business corporation act, provide the limits on the competitive use of similar names.

The phrase "distinguishable upon the records of the secretary of state" is drawn from section 102(a)(1) of the Delaware General Corporation Law. The principal justifications for requiring a distinguishable official name are (1) to prevent confusion within the secretary of state's office and the tax office and (2) to permit accuracy in naming and serving corporate defendants in litigation. Thus, confusion in an absolute or linguistic sense is the appropriate test under the Model Act, not the competitive relationship between the corporations, which is the test for fraud or unfair competition. The precise scope of "distinguishable upon the records of the secretary of state" is an appropriate subject of regulation by the office of secretary of state in order to ensure uniformity of administration.

Corporate names that differ only in the words used to indicate corporateness are generally not distinguishable. Thus, if ABC Corporation is in existence, the names "ABC Inc.," "ABC Co.," or "ABC Corp." should not be viewed as distinguishable. Similarly, minor variations between names that are unlikely to be noticed, such as the substitution of a "." for a ",," or the substitution of an arabic numeral for a word, such as "2" for "Two", or the substitution of a lower case letter for a capital, such as "d" for "D," generally should not be viewed as being distinguishable.

The elimination of the "deceptively similar" requirement that appeared in earlier versions of the Model Act and the specific recognition appearing in section 4.01(e), that corporations may use artificial or fictitious names to the same extent an individual can, are based on the fact that the secretary of state does not generally police the unfair competitive use of names and, indeed, usually has no resources to do so. For example, assume that "ABC Corporation" operates a retail furniture store in Albany, New York, and another group wants to use the same name to engage in a business involving imports of textiles in New York City. An attempt to incorporate a second "ABC Corporation" (or a very close variant such as "ABC Corp." or "ABC Inc.") should be rejected because the names are not distinguishable upon the records of the secretary of state. If the second group uses a distinguishable official name, like "ABD Corporation," it probably may lawfully assume the fictitious name "ABC Corporation" to import goods in New York City if it files the assumed name certificate required by New York law. In these situations, the secretary of state will usually not know in what business or in what geographical area "ABC Corporation" is active or what name ABD Corporation is actually using in its business; he simply maintains an alphabetical list of "official" corporate names as they appear from corporate records and makes his decision about whether a proposed name is distinguishable from other "official names" by comparing the proposed name with those on the list. This assumes that there is either no assumed name statute or that if there is such a statute it requires only local filing in counties or, as in New York, a central filing which does not become part of the corporate records maintained by the secretary of state's office. These assumptions are generally if not universally correct.

3. CLASSES OF UNAVAILABLE NAMES

Section 4.01(b)(3) lists classes of "official names" that are not available. Names in use and thus unavailable from the standpoint of the secretary of state's uniqueness test for "official names" come from the following sources: (1) official names of profit or not-for-profit domestic corporations, (2) official names of foreign profit or not-for-profit corporations qualified to transact business, (3) reserved names, and (4) registered names. The secretary of state becomes involved with fictitious or assumed names only in the situation where a foreign corporation, planning to transact business in a state, discovers that its name is not available in that state. To qualify it must adopt an assumed or fictitious name as its "official name" in the state, see section 15.06. Such a fictitious or assumed name is thereafter an "official" name and is unavailable to the same extent as any other "official name" in use is unavailable.

4. CONSENT TO USE

Section 4.01(c)(1) authorizes the secretary of state to accept a name that is indistinguishable from the name of another corporation if that corporation files an undertaking in a form satisfactory to the secretary of state that it will thereafter change its name to a name that is distinguishable upon the records of the secretary of state. This privilege may be important in acquisition transactions where a new corporation is to take over the business of an existing corporation without a change in corporate name. The secretary of state may require the undertaking to specify the new name which the corporation will adopt and the time period within which the change will be made. The requirements imposed on the undertaking should be consistent with the limited role of the secretary of state in the administration of section 4.01.

FORMER AMENDED NORTH CAROLINA COMMENTARY TO § 55-4-01

Editor's Note. — *The North Carolina Commentary below was formerly located under G.S. 55-1-23 prior to its transfer in 2001. At the request of the Revisor of Statutes, the North Carolina Commentary has been transferred to this section as historical annotations pursuant to Session Laws 2001-358, s. 52.*

Unlike the Model Act, former G.S. 55-12(a) did not permit a corporate name to contain "words or abbreviations of like import in another language." The drafters concluded that a corporate name should not contain foreign words or abbreviations to indicate corporateness and that it would be confusing to the Secretary of State's office to determine what foreign words or abbreviations are "of like import." Therefore, consistent with the provisions of the prior law, they omitted the Model Act language "or words or abbreviations of like import in another language" from subdivision (a)(1).

The Model Act was modified in subsection (c) to clarify that any person (not just a corporation) may apply for authorization under this subsection.

Subsection 4.01(d) of the Model Act is a restatement of the trade name law and therefore was deemed unnecessary.

Subsection (e) was rewritten for clarification.

Subsection (f) was added to bring forward the provisions of former G.S. 55-12(k).

Subsection (g), which is not in the Model Act, is an entirely new section that addresses the use of a dissolved corporation's name.

Former G.S. 55-12(b), which provided that a corporate name could not contain "any word or phrase which is likely to mislead the public or which indicates or implies that it is organized for any purpose other than one or more of the purposes contained in its charter," was not brought forward. The provision was aimed at preventing fraudulent business practices, and the drafters decided that this should be policed by the Attorney General rather than by the Secretary of State through the corporation laws.

Editor's Note. — Session Laws 2001-358, s. 14(a), effective January 1, 2002, and applicable to documents submitted for filing on or after that date, provides that: "G.S. 55-4-01(a), (e), and (f) are recodified as G.S. 55D-20(a), (c), and (d), respectively, in Article 3 of Chapter 55D of the General Statutes. The catch line of G.S. 55D-20, as enacted by this section, is 'Name requirements.' G.S. 55-4-01(b), (c), and (g) are recodified as G.S. 55D-21(b), (c), and (d), respectively, in Article 3 of Chapter 55D of the General Statutes. The catch line of G.S.55D-21, as enacted by this section, is 'Entity names on the records of the Secretary of State; availability.'"

Session Laws 2001-358, s. 14(b), as amended by Session Laws 2001-387, s. 173, effective January 1, 2002, and applicable to documents submitted for filing on or after that date, recodified G.S. 55-4-02, 55-4-03, 55-4-04, 55-4-05 as G.S. 55D-23, 55D-24, 55D-25, 55D-26, respectively, in Article 3 of Chapter 55D of the General Statutes.

Session Laws 2001-358, s. 53, provided that the act, which amended this section, was effective October 1, 2001, and applicable to documents submitted for filing on or after that date. Section 173 of Session Laws 2001-387 changed the effective date of Session Laws 2001-358 from October 1, 2001, to January 1, 2002. Section 6 of Session Laws 2001-413, effective September 14, 2001, added a sentence to s. 175(a) of Session Laws 2001-387, making s. 173 of that act effective when it became law (August 26, 2001). As a result of these changes, the amendment by Session Laws 2001-358 is effective January 1, 2002, and applicable to documents submitted for filing on or after that date.

Session Laws 2001-387, s. 154(b), provides that: "Nothing in this act shall supersede the provisions of Article 10 or 65 of Chapter 58 of the General Statutes, and this act does not create an alternate means for an entity governed by Article 65 of Chapter 58 of the General Statutes to convert to a different business form."

Effect of Amendments. — Session Laws 2001-358, ss. 14(a) and 15, effective January 1, 2002, and applicable to documents submitted for filing on or after that date, recodified G.S. 55-4-01(a), (e), and (f) as subsections (a), (c), and (d) of this section; added the section catchline; and rewrote the section.

Session Laws 2001-387, s. 162, effective January 1, 2002, rewrote subdivision (a)(3); inserted present subdivision (a)(4) and redesignated former subdivision (a)(4) as subdivision (a)(5); deleted "as the last words or letters of its name" from the end of subdivision (a)(5); inserted present subsection (b) and redesignated former subsections (b) through (d) as subsections (c) through (e); and made minor stylistic changes throughout the section.

Legal Periodicals. — For article, "The Creation of North Carolina's Limited Liability Corporation Act," see 32 Wake Forest L. Rev. 179 (1997).

§ 55D-21. Entity names on the records of the Secretary of State; availability.

(a) The following entities are subject to this section:
    (1) Domestic corporations, nonprofit corporations, limited liability companies, limited partnerships, and registered limited liability partnerships.
    (2) Foreign corporations, foreign nonprofit corporations, foreign limited liability companies, and foreign limited partnerships applying for or maintaining a certificate of authority to transact business or conduct affairs in this State.
    (3) Foreign limited liability partnerships applying for or maintaining a statement of foreign registration.

(b) Except as authorized by subsection (c) of this section, the name of an entity subject to this section, including a fictitious name for a foreign entity, must be distinguishable upon the records of the Secretary of State from:
    (1) The name of a domestic corporation, nonprofit corporation, limited liability company, limited partnership, or registered limited liability partnership, or of a foreign corporation, foreign nonprofit corporation, foreign limited liability company, or foreign limited partnership authorized to transact business or conduct affairs in this State, or a foreign limited liability partnership maintaining a statement of foreign registration in this State;
    (2) A name reserved or registered under G.S. 55D-23 or registered under G.S. 55D-24; and
    (3) The fictitious name adopted by a foreign corporation, foreign nonprofit corporation, foreign limited liability company, or foreign limited partnership authorized to transact business or conduct affairs, or a foreign limited liability partnership maintaining a statement of foreign registration in this State because its real name is unavailable.

(c) A person may apply to the Secretary of State for authorization to use a name that is not distinguishable upon the Secretary of State's records from one or more of the names described in subsection (b) of this section. The Secretary of State shall authorize use of the name applied for if:

    (1) The other person who has or uses the name or who has reserved or registered the name consents in writing to the use and submits an undertaking in form satisfactory to the Secretary of State to change its name to a name that is distinguishable upon the records of the Secretary of State from the name of the applicant; or

    (2) The applicant delivers to the Secretary of State a certified copy of the final judgment of a court of competent jurisdiction establishing the applicant's right to use the name applied for in this State.

(d) Except as otherwise provided in this subsection, the name of a corporation dissolved under Article 14 of Chapter 55 of the General Statutes, of a nonprofit corporation dissolved under Article 14 of Chapter 55A of the General Statutes, of a limited liability company dissolved under Article 6 of Chapter 57C of the General Statutes, of a limited partnership dissolved under Part 8 of Article 5 of Chapter 59 of the General Statutes, or of a limited liability partnership whose registration as a limited liability partnership has been cancelled under G.S. 59-84.2 or revoked under G.S. 59-84.4, may not be used by another entity until one of the following occurs:

    (1) In the case of a nonjudicial dissolution other than an administrative dissolution or cancellation of registration as a limited liability partnership, 120 days after the effective date of the dissolution or cancellation.

    (2) In the case of an administrative dissolution or revocation of registration as a limited liability partnership, the expiration of five years after the effective date of the administrative dissolution or revocation.

    (3) In the case of a judicial dissolution, 120 days after the later of the date the judgment has become final or the effective date of the dissolution. The person applying for the name must certify to the Secretary of State that no appeal or other judicial review of the judgment directing dissolution is pending.

    (4) The dissolved entity changes its name to a name that is distinguishable upon the records of the Secretary of State from the names of other domestic corporations, nonprofit corporations, limited liability companies, limited partnerships, or registered limited liability partnerships or foreign corporations, foreign nonprofit corporations, foreign limited liability companies, or foreign limited partnerships authorized to transact business or conduct affairs in this State, or foreign limited liability partnerships maintaining a statement of foreign registration in this State. (1901, c. 2, s. 8; 1903, c. 453; Rev., s. 1137; 1913, c. 5, s. 1; C.S., s. 1114; 1935, cc. 166, 320; 1939, c. 222; G.S., s. 55-2; 1955, c. 1371, s. 1; 1959, c. 1316, s. 28; 1969, c. 751, ss. 4-6; 1973, c. 469, s. 45.3; 1989, c. 265, s. 1; 1989 (Reg. Sess., 1990), c. 1024, s. 12.5; 1995, c. 539, ss. 4, 5; 2001-358, ss. 14(a), 15; 2001-387, ss. 163, 173, 175(a); 2001-390, s. 15; 2001-413, s. 6; 2001-487, s. 62(h); 2002-159, s. 23.)

FORMER OFFICIAL COMMENT TO § 55-4-01

Editor's Note. — *The Official Comments located under G.S. 55D-20 were formerly located under G.S. 55-4-01, parts of which were recodified as G.S. 55D-20 and G.S. 55D-21 in 2001. At the request of the Revisor of Statutes, the Official Comments have been transferred to G.S. 55D-20 as historical annotations pursuant to Session Laws 2001-358, s. 52. The Official Comments under that section apply to this section as well.*

FORMER AMENDED NORTH CAROLINA COMMENTARY TO § 55-4-01

Editor's Note. — *The North Carolina Commentary located under G.S. 55D-20 was formerly located under G.S. 55-4-01, parts of which were recodified as G.S. 55D-20 and G.S. 55D-21 in 2001. At the request of the Revisor of Statutes, the North Carolina Commentary has been transferred to*

G.S. 55D-20 as historical annotations pursuant to Session Laws 2001-358, s. 52. The North Carolina Commentary under that section applies to this section as well.

Editor's Note. — Session Laws 2001-358, s. 53, provided that the act, which amended this section, was effective October 1, 2001, and applicable to documents submitted for filing on or after that date. Section 173 of Session Laws 2001-387 changed the effective date of Session Laws 2001-358 from October 1, 2001, to January 1, 2002. Section 6 of Session Laws 2001-413, effective September 14, 2001, added a sentence to s. 175(a) of Session Laws 2001-387, making s. 173 of that act effective when it became law (August 26, 2001). As a result of these changes, the amendment by Session Laws 2001-358 is effective January 1, 2002, and applicable to documents submitted for filing on or after that date.

Session Laws 2001-387, s. 154(b), provides that "Nothing in the act shall supersede the provisions of Article 10 or 65 of Chapter 58 of the General Statutes, and this act does not create an alternate means for an entity governed by Article 65 of Chapter 58 of the General Statutes to convert to a different business form."

Session Laws 2001-390, s. 14, provides: "The Secretary of State shall report to the General Assembly by June 30, 2003, on whether a time limit should be placed upon the period of time within which an entity may be permitted to apply for reinstatement from administrative dissolution or revocation."

Session Laws 2001-390, s. 8, effective August 26, 2001, and applicable retroactively to applications for reinstatement made on or after December 1, 1999, amending former G.S. 55-4-01(g) before the recodification to subsection (d) of this section, added "until one of the following occurs" at the end of the introductory language of subsection (g); deleted "or" at the end of subdivision (g)(1); substituted "five years after the effective date of the administrative dissolution" for "the period within which the corporation may be reinstated pursuant to G.S. 55-14-

21" at the end of subdivision (g)(2); inserted the subdivision (g)(3) designation, and deleted "unless" at the beginning of that subdivision. Session Laws 2002-159, s. 23, repealed Session Law 2001-390, s. 8, effective January 1, 2002.

Effect of Amendments. — Session Laws 2001-358, ss. 14(a) and 15, effective January 1, 2002, and applicable to documents submitted for filing on or after that date, recodified G.S. 55-4-01(b), (c) and (g) as subsections (b), (c) and (d) of this section; added the section catchline; and rewrote the section.

Session Laws 2001-387, s. 163, effective January 1, 2002, inserted "cancelled under G.S. 59-84.2 or" near the end of the introductory language of subsection (d); rewrote subdivision (d)(1) and (d)(2); and made a minor stylistic change.

Session Laws 2001-390, s. 15, effective January 1, 2002, in this section as enacted by Session Laws 2001-358 and amended by Session Laws 387, added "one of the following occurs" to the end of the introductory language of subsection (d); substituted "five years after the effective date of the administrative dissolution or revocation" for "the period within which the entity or its registration may be reinstated" in subdivision (d)(2); redesignated the former last paragraph of subsection (d) as present subdivision (d)(4); and substituted "The dissolved entity" for "The name of a dissolved entity may be used at any time if the entity" at the beginning of subdivision (d)(4).

Session Laws 2001-487, s. 62(h), effective January 1, 2002, as enacted by Session Laws 2001-358 and amended by s. 163 of Session Laws 2001-387, deleted a comma preceding "in this State" at the end of the last sentence of subsection (d) (now subdivision (d)(4)).

Legal Periodicals. — For article, "The Creation of North Carolina's Limited Liability Corporation Act," see 32 Wake Forest L. Rev. 179 (1997).

CASE NOTES

Editor's Note. — The cases below were decided under the Business Corporation Act adopted in 1955.

Generally Descriptive Phrases Not Covered by Subsection (c). — The proscription in former G.S. 55-12(c) against deceptively similar corporate names remained circumscribed by the salutary common law principle that generally descriptive phrases may not be exclusively appropriated in a trade name. Two Way Radio Serv., Inc. v. Two Way Radio of Carolina, Inc.,

322 N.C. 809, 370 S.E.2d 408 (1988).

Use of a Generally Descriptive Term Did Not Exclude Others. — Plaintiff did not, by its prior incorporation under a name that included the generally descriptive phrase "two way radio," acquire a right to the use of that phrase in its corporate name to the exclusion of that right in defendant and others subsequently incorporated. Two Way Radio Serv., Inc. v. Two Way Radio of Carolina, Inc., 322 N.C. 809, 370 S.E.2d 408 (1988).

"Homestead Builders" Insufficient. — Where a contract or sale entered into by a purported corporation used only the name "Homestead Builders," and, similarly, the bank account of the purported corporation was opened in the name of "Homestead Builders," the corporate name did not comply with former G.S. 55-12(a). Keels v. Turner, 45 N.C. App. 213, 262 S.E.2d 845, cert. denied, 300 N.C. 197, 269 S.E.2d 624, reh'g denied, 270 S.E.2d 109 (N.C. 1980).

Applied in State v. Woody, 132 N.C. App. 788, 513 S.E.2d 801 (1999).

§ 55D-22. Names of foreign entities.

(a) If the name of a foreign corporation, foreign nonprofit corporation, foreign limited liability company, foreign limited partnership, or foreign limited liability partnership does not satisfy the requirements of G.S. 55D-20 and G.S. 55D-21, then to obtain or maintain a certificate of authority to transact business or conduct affairs in this State or a statement of foreign registration in this State, the entity may:

(1) If a foreign corporation or foreign nonprofit corporation, add the word "corporation", "incorporated", "company", or "limited", or the abbreviation "corp.", "inc.", "co.", or "ltd." to its corporate name for use in this State;

(2) If a foreign limited liability company, add the words "limited liability company", or the abbreviation "L.L.C.", or "LLC", or the combination "ltd. liability co.", "limited liability co.", or "ltd. liability company" to its name for use in this State if the addition will cause the name to satisfy the requirements of G.S. 55D-20 and G.S. 55D-21;

(3) If a foreign limited partnership that is not a foreign limited liability limited partnership, add the words "limited partnership" or the abbreviation "L.P." or "LP", or the combination "ltd. partnership";

(4) If a foreign limited partnership that is a foreign limited liability limited partnership, add the words "registered limited liability limited partnership" or "limited liability limited partnership" or the abbreviation "L.L.L.P.", "R.L.L.L.P.", "LLLP", or "RLLLP";

(5) If a foreign limited liability partnership, add the words "registered limited liability partnership", or "limited liability partnership" or the abbreviation "L.L.P.", "R.L.L.P.", "LLP", or "RLLP"; or

(6) Use a fictitious name, which includes one or more of the words, abbreviations, or combinations in subdivisions (1) through (5) of this subsection if applicable, to transact business or conduct affairs in this State if its real name is unavailable and it delivers to the Secretary of State for filing a copy of the resolution adopting the fictitious name.

(b) If a foreign corporation, foreign nonprofit corporation, foreign limited liability company, or foreign limited partnership authorized to transact business or conduct affairs in this State, or a foreign limited liability partnership maintaining a statement of foreign registration, changes its name to one that does not satisfy the requirements of this Article, it may not transact business or conduct affairs in this State under the changed name until it adopts a name satisfying the requirements of this Article and obtains an amended certificate of authority or statement of foreign registration under G.S. 55-15-04, 55A-15-04, 57C-7-05, 59-91, or 59-905, as applicable. (2001-358, s. 15; 2001-387, ss. 164, 173, 175(a); 2001-413, s. 6.)

Editor's Note. — Session Laws 2001-358, s. 53, provided that the act, which amended this section, was effective October 1, 2001, and applicable to documents submitted for filing on or after that date. Section 173 of Session Laws 2001-387 changed the effective date of Session Laws 2001-358 from October 1, 2001, to January 1, 2002. Section 6 of Session Laws 2001-413, effective September 14, 2001, added a sentence to s. 175(a) of Session Laws 2001-387, making s. 173 of that act effective when it became law (August 26, 2001). As a result of these changes, the amendment by Session Laws 2001-358 is effective January 1, 2002, and applicable to documents submitted for filing on or after that date.

Session Laws 2001-387, s. 154(b), provides that "Nothing in the act shall supersede the provisions of Article 10 or 65 of Chapter 58 of the General Statutes, and this act does not create an alternate means for an entity governed by Article 65 of Chapter 58 of the General Statutes to convert to a different business form."

Effect of Amendments. — Session Laws 2001-387, s. 164, effective January 1, 2002, inserted "that is not a foreign limited liability limited partnership" in subdivision (a)(3); inserted subdivision (a)(4) and redesignated former subdivisions (a)(4) and (5) as present subdivisions (a)(5) and (6); deleted "as the last words or letters of its name" following "RLLP" in subdivision (a)(5); and substituted "subdivisions (1) through (5)" for "subdivisions (1) through (4)" in subdivision (a)(6).

§ 55D-23. Reserved name.

(a) A person may reserve the exclusive use of a name for an entity, including a fictitious name for a foreign corporation, foreign nonprofit corporation, foreign limited liability company, foreign limited partnership, or foreign limited liability partnership whose name is not available, by filing an application with the Secretary of State. The application must set forth the name and address of the applicant and the name proposed to be reserved. If the Secretary of State finds that the name applied for is available, the Secretary of State shall reserve the name for the applicant's exclusive use for a nonrenewable 120-day period.

(b) The owner of a reserved name may transfer the reservation to another person by filing with the Secretary of State a signed notice of the transfer that states the name and address of the transferee.

(c) Any person acquiring the goodwill of a domestic corporation, nonprofit corporation, limited liability company, limited partnership, or registered limited liability partnership, or of a foreign corporation, foreign nonprofit corporation, foreign limited liability company, or foreign limited partnership authorized to transact business or conduct affairs in this State, or of a foreign limited liability partnership maintaining a statement of foreign registration in this State may, on furnishing the Secretary of State satisfactory evidence of such acquisition, reserve for 10 years the exclusive right to any name that became available as a result of the acquisition. (1901, c. 2, s. 8; 1903, c. 453; Rev., s. 1137; 1913, c. 5, s. 1; C.S., s. 1114; 1935, cc. 166, 320; 1939, c. 222; G.S., s. 55-2; 1955, c. 1371, s. 1; 1959, c. 1316, s. 28; 1969, c. 751, ss. 4-6; 1973, c. 469, s. 45.3; 1989, c. 265, s. 1; 2001-358, ss. 14(b), 15; 2001-387, ss. 173, 175(a); 2001-413, s. 6.)

OFFICIAL COMMENT TO FORMER § 55-4-02

Editor's Note. — *The Official Comments below were formerly located under G.S. 55-4-02 prior to its transfer in 2001. At the request of the Revisor of Statutes, the Official Comments have been transferred to this section as historical annotations pursuant to Session Laws 2001-358, s. 52.*

The "reservation" of a corporate name is basically a device to simplify the formation of a new corporation or the qualification of a foreign corporation. By reserving a name, the persons considering the formation or qualification of the corporation can order stationery, prepare documents, etc. on the assumption that the reserved name will be available. Reference to a specific intent to form a new corporation is not required by the statute, however, since a secretary of state is not equipped and should not be asked to determine whether the requisite intent actually exists. For the same reason, "any person" is permitted to reserve a corporate name without reference to specific classes of persons who might wish to reserve a corporate name for various purposes.

Under section 4.02 of the Model Act, an available corporate name may be reserved:
(1) by persons considering the formation of a new domestic corporation;
(2) by persons considering the formation of a corporation in another state and the immediate qualification of that new corporation in this state; and
(3) by a foreign corporation planning or consid-

ering qualification in this state. The name reserved may be the foreign corporation's "official name" (if that name is available) or another name. The foreign corporation may thereafter use the reserved name as the name of a domestic subsidiary or, if its real name is unavailable, as a fictitious "official name" for its qualification under section 15.06.

These illustrations are designed to suggest the scope and flexibility of section 4.02, and not to exhaust the possible uses to which a reserved name may be put.

Consideration was also given to whether reservation of a corporate name should be made renewable. The modern requirements for incorporation of a domestic corporation or the qual-

ification of a foreign corporation are so simple that it is unlikely that more than 120 days could ever be realistically required to form or qualify a corporation. Also, it was believed to be undesirable to allow the reservation procedure to be used for other purposes, such as permanently setting aside a name by successive renewals. Therefore, only a single, one-time reservation is provided for, although after the 120-day period expires the name becomes available again and anyone, including the original reserver, may reserve the name. And nothing prevents the formation of an inactive corporation specifically to hold the desired name if a longer period of reservation is desired than the 120-day period specified by section 4.02.

NORTH CAROLINA COMMENTARY TO FORMER § 55-4-02

Editor's Note. — The North Carolina Commentary below was formerly located under G.S. 55-4-02 prior to its transfer in 2001. At the request of the Revisor of Statutes, the North Carolina Commentary has been transferred to this section as historical annotations pursuant to Session Laws 2001-358, s. 52.

Subsection (c) was added to the Model Act's provisions to bring forward the provisions of former G.S. 55-12(e). Other minor changes to

the Model Act in this section were made for clarification.

Editor's Note. — Session Laws 2001-358, s. 53, provided that the act, which amended this section, was effective October 1, 2001, and applicable to documents submitted for filing on or after that date. Section 173 of Session Laws 2001-387 changed the effective date of Session Laws 2001-358 from October 1, 2001, to January 1, 2002. Section 6 of Session Laws 2001-413, effective September 14, 2001, added a sentence to s. 175(a) of Session Laws 2001-387, making s. 173 of that act effective when it became law (August 26, 2001). As a result of these changes, the amendment by Session Laws 2001-358 is effective January 1, 2002, and applicable to documents submitted for filing on or after that date.

Effect of Amendments. — Session Laws 2001-358, ss. 14(b) and 15, effective January 1, 2002, and applicable to documents submitted for filing on or after that date, recodified G.S. 55-4-02 as this section; in subsection (a), in the first sentence, substituted "exclusive use of a name for an entity" for "exclusive use of a corporate name" and inserted "foreign nonprofit corporation, foreign limited liability company, foreign limited partnership, or foreign limited liability partnership," and in the last sentence, deleted "corporate" preceding "name applied," and substituted "the Secretary of State" for "he"; deleted "corporate" preceding "name may" in subsection (b); and rewrote subsection (c).

§ 55D-24. Registered name.

(a) A foreign corporation, foreign nonprofit corporation, foreign limited liability company, foreign limited partnership, or foreign limited liability partnership may register its name, or its name with any addition required by G.S. 55D-22, if the name to be registered is distinguishable upon the records of the Secretary of State from the names that are not available under G.S. 55D-21(b).

(b) An entity described in subsection (a) of this section registers its name, or its name with any addition required by G.S. 55D-22, by filing with the Secretary of State an application:

(1) Setting forth its name, or its name with any addition required by G.S. 55D-22, the state or country and date of its incorporation or formation, and a brief description of the nature of the business or activities in which it is engaged; and

(2) Accompanied by a certificate of existence (or a document of a similar import) from the state or country of incorporation or formation.

(c) The name is registered for the applicant's exclusive use upon the effective date of the application and until the end of the calendar year in which it became effective.

(d) An entity whose registration is effective may renew it for successive years by filing with the Secretary of State a renewal application, which complies with the requirements of subsection (b) of this section, between October 1 and December 31 of the preceding year. The renewal application renews the registration for the following calendar year. Any renewal application filed after the expiration of the registration shall be treated as a new application for registration.

(e) An entity whose registration is effective may thereafter become authorized to transact business or conduct affairs under that name or consent in writing to the use of that name by:

(1) A domestic corporation, nonprofit corporation, limited liability company, limited partnership, or registered limited liability partnership thereafter incorporated, formed, or registered in this State under that name;

(2) A domestic corporation, nonprofit corporation, limited liability company, limited partnership, or registered limited liability partnership that changes its name to that name; or

(3) Another foreign corporation, foreign nonprofit corporation, foreign limited liability company, foreign limited partnership, or foreign limited liability partnership that becomes authorized to transact business or conduct affairs in this State under that name.

The registration terminates when the domestic corporation, nonprofit corporation, limited liability company, limited partnership, or registered limited liability partnership is incorporated, formed, registered, or changes its name or the foreign corporation, foreign nonprofit corporation, foreign limited liability company, foreign limited partnership, or foreign limited liability partnership qualifies or registers or consents to the qualification or registration of another entity under the registered name. (1901, c. 2, s. 8; 1903, c. 453; Rev., s. 1137; 1913, c. 5, s. 1; C.S., s. 1114; 1935, cc. 166, 320; 1939, c. 222; G.S., s. 55-2; 1955, c. 1371, s. 1; 1959, c. 1316, s. 28; 1969, c. 751, ss. 4-6; 1973, c. 469, s. 45.3; 1989, c. 265, s. 1; 2001-358, ss. 14(b), 15; 2001-387, ss. 165(a), 165(b), 173, 175(a); 2001-413, s. 6.)

OFFICIAL COMMENT TO FORMER § 55-4-03

Editor's Note. — The Official Comments below were formerly located under G.S. 55-4-03 prior to its transfer in 2001. At the request of the Revisor of Statutes, the Official Comments have been transferred to this section as historical annotations pursuant to Session Laws 2001-358, s. 52.

The "registration" of a corporate name is basically a device by which a foreign corporation, not qualified to transact business in the state, can preserve the right to use its unique "real" name if it decides later to qualify in the state. In effect, registration ensures "real" name availability in areas of potential future expansion.

It is believed desirable to limit section 4.03 to this purpose and not allow it to become an indirect device for the preservation of trademarks, trade names, or possible assumed names. For this reason, generally only "real" names of foreign corporations may be registered (with exceptions described below). A broader approach would create issues better resolved under a trademark or similar statute, or by litigation under unfair competition principles, and might impose duties on secretaries of state that they are generally not equipped to handle, or could handle only at increased cost.

Registration of a name other than the "real" name is permitted in only one situation: if the "real" name of a foreign corporation is not available solely because it does not comply with section 15.06, requiring the words "incorporated," "corporation," "company," or "limited," or an abbreviation of one of these words, the corporation may add one of these words or abbreviations and register its "real" name as so modified under section 4.03(a).

Confusion sometimes exists between "reservation" of names under section 4.02 and registration of names under section 4.03. A foreign corporation that is planning to qualify as a foreign corporation and finds that its name is available in the state may either register or reserve the name. Often a foreign corporation will have to decide whether to qualify or to create a domestic subsidiary; this well may be decided after the exclusive right to use the corporate name in the state is obtained either by reservation or by registration. If the corporation registers its name, it will be kept indefinitely; if it reserves, it will be kept for 120 days and then become available again. That is the foreign corporation's choice. If a foreign corpo-

ration registers its name and then elects to form a domestic or foreign subsidiary, the written consent procedure of section 4.03(e) allows the secretary of state to ascertain that the domestic subsidiary is related to the foreign corporation and that use of the registered name by that subsidiary is acceptable to the foreign parent.

If a foreign corporation's "real" name is unavailable, a foreign corporation may *reserve* any name — including one that is assumed or fictitious when compared with the corporation's "real" name — for 120 days. But it may not *register* this type of name in light of the policy against allowing the name provisions of the Model Act to be used for purposes broader than the "unique name" issue. Nevertheless, a foreign corporation that wishes to be certain that a particular fictitious or assumed name will be available in the future may create an inactive domestic subsidiary with the desired name to preserve its future availability. See also the Official Comment to section 15.06.

Section 4.03(e) provides that the protection of the name provided by this section terminates when the name is used pursuant to this section by the foreign corporation or its domestic or foreign subsidiary.

NORTH CAROLINA COMMENTARY TO FORMER § 55-4-03

Editor's Note. — *The North Carolina Commentary below was formerly located under G.S. 55-4-03 prior to its transfer in 2001. At the request of the Revisor of Statutes, the North Carolina Commentary has been transferred to this section as historical annotations pursuant to Session Laws 2001-358, s. 52.*

Subsection (c) differs from the Model Act in providing that registration of a corporate name remains effective "until the end of the calendar year in which it became effective."

The last sentence of subsection (d) was added from former G.S. 55-12(h). Former G.S. 55-

12(h) permitted renewals on a year-to-year basis for ten years, whereas this Act does not contain this limitation.

Other minor changes to the Model Act in this section were made for clarification.

Editor's Note. — Session Laws 2001-358, s. 53, provided that the act, which amended this section, was effective October 1, 2001, and applicable to documents submitted for filing on or after that date. Section 173 of Session Laws 2001-387 changed the effective date of Session Laws 2001-358 from October 1, 2001, to January 1, 2002. Section 6 of Session Laws 2001-413, effective September 14, 2001, added a sentence to s. 175(a) of Session Laws 2001-387, making s. 173 of that act effective when it became law (August 26, 2001). As a result of these changes, the amendment by Session Laws 2001-358 is effective January 1, 2002, and applicable to documents submitted for filing on or after that date.

Session Laws 2001-387, s. 154(b), provides that "Nothing in the act shall supersede the provisions of Article 10 or 65 of Chapter 58 of the General Statutes, and this act does not create an alternate means for an entity governed by Article 65 of Chapter 58 of the General Statutes to convert to a different business form."

Effect of Amendments. — Session Laws 2001-358, ss. 14(b) and 15, effective January 1, 2002, and applicable to documents submitted for filing on or after that date, recodified G.S. 55-4-03 as this section; rewrote subsections (a) and (e); in the introductory language of subsection (b), substituted "An entity registers its name, or its name with" for "A foreign corporation registers its corporate name, or its corporate name with" and substituted "G.S. 55D-22" for "G.S. 55-15-06"; in subdivision (b)(1), substituted "its name, or its name with any addition required by G.S. 55D-22" for "its corporate name, or its corporate name with any addition required by G.S. 55-15-06," and inserted "organization, or formation" and "or activities"; added "organization, or formation" to the end of subdivision (b)(2); and in the first sentence of subsection (d), substituted "An entity" for "A foreign corporation" and inserted "of this section."

Session Laws 2001-387, ss. 165(a) and

165(b), effective January 1, 2002, inserted "described in subsection (a) of this section" in the introductory language of subsection (b); deleted "organization" following "incorporation" in subdivisions (b)(1) and (2), and made minor punctuation changes; and, substituted "incorporated, formed, or registered" for "incorporated, organized, or formed" in subdivision (e)(1); and in the last paragraph of subsection (e), substituted "incorporated, formed, registered, or changes" for "incorporated, organized, formed, or changes," and inserted "or registers" and "or registration."

§ 55D-25. Reserved and registered names; powers of the Secretary of State.

The Secretary of State may revoke any reservation or registration of a name if the Secretary of State:

(1) Gives written notice by registered or certified mail, return receipt requested, to the person who made the reservation or registration of the date and time of a hearing;

(2) Conducts a hearing not less that 15 days after receipt of the notice as shown by the return receipt; and

(3) Finds that the application therefor or any transfer thereof was not made in good faith or that any statement contained in the application for reservation or registration was false when such application was filed or has thereafter become false. (1901, c. 2, s. 8; 1903, c. 453; Rev., s. 1137; 1913, c. 5, s. 1; C.S., s. 1114; 1935, cc. 166, 320; 1939, c. 222; G.S., s. 55-2; 1955, c. 1371, s. 1; 1959, c. 1316, s. 28; 1969, c. 751, ss. 4-6; 1973, c. 469, s. 45.3; 1989, c. 265, s. 1; 1993, c. 552, s. 7; 2001-358, ss. 14(b), 15; 2001-387, ss. 173, 175(a); 2001-413, s. 6.)

NORTH CAROLINA COMMENTARY TO FORMER § 55-4-04

Editor's Note. — *The North Carolina Commentary below was formerly located under G.S. 55-4-04 prior to its transfer in 2001. At the request of the Revisor of Statutes, the North Carolina Commentary has been transferred to this section as historical annotations pursuant to Session Laws 2001-358, s. 52.*

This section, which is not part of the Model Act, was added to bring forward the provisions of former G.S. 55-12(i), relating to the power of the Secretary of State to revoke any reservation or registration of a corporate name, and the provisions of former G.S. 55-12(j), relating to enjoining the use by a corporation of a name in violation of Article 4. The drafters concluded that such powers should be explicit.

Editor's Note. — Session Laws 2001-358, s. 53, provided that the act, which amended this section, was effective October 1, 2001, and applicable to documents submitted for filing on or after that date. Section 173 of Session Laws 2001-387 changed the effective date of Session Laws 2001-358 from October 1, 2001, to January 1, 2002. Section 6 of Session Laws 2001-413, effective September 14, 2001, added a sentence to s. 175(a) of Session Laws 2001-387, making s. 173 of that act effective when it became law (August 26, 2001). As a result of these changes, the amendment by Session Laws 2001-358 is effective January 1, 2002, and applicable to documents submitted for filing on or after that date.

Effect of Amendments. — Session Laws 2001-358, ss. 14(b) and 15, effective January 1,

2002, and applicable to documents submitted for filing on or after that date, recodified G.S. 55-4-04 as this section; and rewrote the section.

§ 55D-26. Real property records.

(a) A certificate issued by the Secretary of State as described in subsection (b) of this section must be recorded when:

(1) The name of any domestic corporation, nonprofit corporation, limited liability company, limited partnership, or registered limited liability partnership or foreign corporation, foreign nonprofit corporation, foreign limited liability company, foreign limited partnership, or foreign limited liability partnership that holds title to real property in this State is changed upon amendment to its articles of incorporation or organization, its certificate of limited partnership, or its registration as a limited liability partnership or foreign limited liability partnership; or

(2) Title to real property in this State held by any entity listed in subdivision (1) of this subsection is vested by operation of law in another entity upon merger, consolidation, or conversion of the entity.

The certificate must recite the name change, merger, consolidation, or conversion and must be recorded in the office of the register of deeds of the county where the property lies or, if the property is located in more than one county in each county where any portion of the property lies.

(b) The Secretary of State shall issue uniform certificates for recordation in accordance with this section. In the case of a foreign corporation, foreign nonprofit corporation, foreign limited liability company, foreign limited partnership, or foreign limited liability partnership, a similar certificate by any competent authority of the jurisdiction of incorporation may be recorded in accordance with this section.

(c) The certificate required by this section must be recorded by the register of deeds in the same manner as deeds, and for the same fees, but no formalities as to acknowledgement, probate, or approval by any other officer shall be required. The former name of the entity holding title to the real property before the name change, merger, consolidation, or conversion shall appear in the "Grantor" index, and the new name of the corporation or the name of the other entity holding title to the real property by virtue of the merger, consolidation, or conversion shall appear in the "Grantee" index. (1989, c. 265, s. 1; 1991, c. 645, s. 2(a); 1999-369, s. 1.4; 2001-358, ss. 14(b), 15; 2001-387, ss. 166, 173, 175(a); 2001-413, s. 6.)

NORTH CAROLINA COMMENTARY TO FORMER § 55-4-05

Editor's Note. — The North Carolina Commentary below was formerly located under G.S. 55-4-05 prior to its transfer in 2001. At the request of the Revisor of Statutes, the North Carolina Commentary has been transferred to this section as historical annotations pursuant to Session Laws 2001-358, s. 52.

This section, which is not part of the Model Act, relates to updating real property records when the name of a corporation is changed or when title to real property is transferred by operation of law in a merger. It is a blend of section 13.1-633 of the Virginia act and G.S. 47-18.1.

Editor's Note. — Session Laws 2001-358, s. 53, provided that the act, which amended this section, was effective October 1, 2001, and applicable to documents submitted for filing on or after that date. Section 173 of Session Laws 2001-387 changed the effective date of Session Laws 2001-358 from October 1, 2001, to January 1, 2002. Section 6 of Session Laws 2001-413, effective September 14, 2001, added a sentence to s. 175(a) of Session Laws 2001-387, making s. 173 of that act effective when it became law (August 26, 2001). As a result of these changes, the amendment by Session Laws 2001-358 is effective January 1, 2002, and applicable to documents submitted for filing on or after that date.

Session Laws 2001-387, s. 154(b), provides that "Nothing in the act shall supersede the provisions of Article 10 or 65 of Chapter 58 of the General Statutes, and this act does not create an alternate means for an entity governed by Article 65 of Chapter 58 of the General Statutes to convert to a different business form."

Effect of Amendments. — Session Laws 2001-358, ss. 14(b) and 15, effective January 1, 2002, and applicable to documents submitted for filing on or after that date, recodified G.S. 55-4-05 as this section; rewrote subsections (a) and (b); and in subsection (c), substituted "must be recorded" for "shall be recorded" in the first sentence, and substituted "entity holding" for "corporation holding" in the second sentence.

Session Laws 2001-387, s. 166, effective January 1, 2002, in subdivision (a)(1), inserted the first occurrence of "limited partnership" and substituted "or its registration as a limited liability partnership or foreign limited liability partnership" for "or its application for registration as a limited liability partnership" at the end.

§§ 55D-27 through 55D-29: Reserved for future codification purposes.

ARTICLE 4.

Registered Office and Registered Agent.

§ 55D-30. Registered office and registered agent required.

(a) Each domestic corporation, nonprofit corporation, limited liability company, limited partnership, and limited liability partnership, each foreign limited liability partnership maintaining a statement of foreign registration, and each foreign corporation, nonprofit corporation, limited liability company, and limited partnership authorized to transact business or conduct affairs in this State must continuously maintain in this State:

(1) A registered office that may be the same as any of its places of business or any place where it conducts affairs; and

(2) A registered agent, who must be:

    a. An individual who resides in this State and whose business office is identical with the registered office;

    b. A domestic corporation, nonprofit corporation, or limited liability company whose business office is identical with the registered office; or

    c. A foreign corporation, foreign nonprofit corporation, or foreign limited liability company authorized to transact business or conduct affairs in this State whose business office is identical with the registered office.

(b) The sole duty of the registered agent to the entity is to forward to the entity at its last known address any notice, process, or demand that is served on the registered agent. (1901, c. 5; Rev., s. 1243; C.S., s. 1137; 1937, c. 133, ss. 1-3; G.S., ss. 55-38, 55-39; 1955, c. 1371, s. 1; 1957, c. 979, s. 17; 1989, c. 265, s. 1; 2000-140, s. 101(a); 2001-358, ss. 44, 45; 2001-387, ss. 173, 175(a); 2001-413, s. 6.)

FORMER OFFICIAL COMMENT TO § 55-5-01

Editor's Note. — *The Official Comments below were formerly located under G.S. 55-5-01 prior to its amendment in 2001. At the request of the Revisor of Statutes, the Official Comments have been transferred to this section as historical annotations pursuant to Session Laws 2001-358, s. 52.*

The requirements that a corporation continuously maintain a registered office and a registered agent at that office are based on the premises that at all times a corporation should have an office where it may be found and a person at that office on whom any notice or process required or permitted by law may be served. This covers not only service of process in connection with litigation but also tax notices and communications from the secretary of state and other governmental offices. The street address of the registered office must appear in the public records maintained by the secretary of state. A mailing address, such as a post office box, is not sufficient since the registered office is the designated location for service of process.

The Model Act assumes that formal communications to the corporation will normally be addressed to the registered agent at the registered office. If the communication itself deals with the registered office or registered agent, however, copies must be sent to the principal office of the corporation. Moreover, the Act authorizes corporations to retain records at, or to provide information to shareholders through, offices other than the registered office. The

Model Act consistently recognizes that the registered office may be a "legal" rather than a "business" office.

Many corporations designate their registered office to be a business office of the corporation and a corporate officer at that office to be the registered agent. Since most of the communication to the registered agent at the registered office deals with legal matters, however, corporations often designate their regular legal counsel or his nominee as their registered agent and the counsel's office as the registered office of the corporation. This practice may also encourage regular communication between the corporation and its legal counsel.

The registered agent need not be an individual. Corporation service companies often provide, as a commercial service, registered offices and registered agents at the office of the corporation service company.

The voluntary dissolution of the corporation does not of itself terminate the authority of the registered agent to accept service of process or other communications on behalf of the dissolved corporation. See section 14.05.

FORMER NORTH CAROLINA COMMENTARY TO § 55-5-01

Editor's Note. — The North Carolina Commentary below was formerly located under G.S. 55-5-01 prior to its amendment in 2001. At the request of the Revisor of Statutes, the North Carolina Commentary has been transferred to this section as historical annotations pursuant to Session Laws 2001-358, s. 52.

Subsection (a) is the same as section 5.01 of the Model Act, except that "nonprofit" has been substituted for "not-for-profit" and "shall" has been substituted for "may" in subdivision (2).

Subsection (b) was added to define precisely and exclusively what a registered agent is obligated to do.

Editor's Note. — Session Laws 2001-358, s. 44, effective January 1, 2002, and applicable to documents submitted for filing on or after that date, recodified G.S. 55-5-01(b) as G.S. 55D-30(b) and G.S. 55-5-02, 55-5-03, and 55-5-04 as G.S. 55D-31, 55D-32, and 55D-33, respectively, in Article 4 of Chapter 55D of the General Statutes.

Session Laws 2001-358, s. 53, provided that the act, which amended this section, was effective October 1, 2001, and applicable to documents submitted for filing on or after that date. Section 173 of Session Laws 2001-387 changed the effective date of Session Laws 2001-358 from October 1, 2001, to January 1, 2002. Section 6 of Session Laws 2001-413, effective September 14, 2001, added a sentence to s. 175(a) of Session Laws 2001-387, making s. 173 of that act effective when it became law (August 26, 2001). As a result of these changes, the amendment by Session Laws 2001-358 is effec-

tive January 1, 2002, and applicable to documents submitted for filing on or after that date.

Effect of Amendments. — Session Laws 2000-140, s. 101(a), effective July 21, 2000, in subdivision (a)(2), substituted "corporation, nonprofit corporation, or limited liability company" for "corporation or nonprofit domestic corporation" in (ii) and substituted "corporation, nonprofit corporation, or limited liability company authorized to transact business or conduct affairs" for "corporation or nonprofit foreign corporation authorized to transact business" in (iii).

Session Laws 2001-358, ss. 44 and 45, effective January 1, 2002, and applicable to documents submitted for filing on or after that date, recodified G.S. 55-5-01(b) as subsection (b) of this section; added subsection (a) of this section; and substituted "entity" for "corporation" in two places in subsection (b).

Legal Periodicals. — For article, "The Cre-

ation of North Carolina's Limited Liability Corporation Act," see 32 Wake Forest L. Rev. 179
(1997).

CASE NOTES

Editor's Note. — *The case below was decided under the Business Corporation Act
adopted in 1955.*
**The listing of an agent for corporate
service of process is not a voluntary action,** subject to the discretion of the corporation. This listing is legislatively mandated.
South Carolina Ins. Co. v. Hallmark Enters.,
Inc., 88 N.C. App. 642, 364 S.E.2d 678, cert.
denied, 322 N.C. 482, 370 S.E.2d 228 (1988).
Failure to Notify Insurer of Suit Where

**Corporation Without Agent Received No
Notice Thereof.** — Corporation could not rely
on its violation of former G.S. 55-13 to justify its
failure to receive notice of suit. Consequently, it
did not give notice of suit to its insurer at the
time it was reasonably expected to receive
actual notice thereof, thus failing to notify
insurer as soon as practicable. South Carolina
Ins. Co. v. Hallmark Enters., Inc., 88 N.C. App.
642, 364 S.E.2d 678, cert. denied, 322 N.C. 482,
370 S.E.2d 228 (1988).

§ 55D-31. Change of registered office or registered agent.

(a) An entity required to maintain a registered office and registered agent
under G.S. 55D-30 may change its registered office or registered agent by
delivering to the Secretary of State for filing a statement of change that sets
forth all of the following:

   (1) The name of the entity.

   (2) The street address, and the mailing address if different from the street
       address, of its current registered office, and the county in which it is
       located.

   (3) If the address of the entity's registered office is to be changed, the
       street address, and the mailing address if different from the street
       address, of the new registered office, and the county in which it is
       located.

   (4) The name of its current registered agent.

   (5) If the current registered agent is to be changed, the name of the new
       registered agent and the new agent's written consent (either on the
       statement or attached to it) to the appointment.

   (6) That after the change or changes are made, the addresses of its
       registered office and the business office of its registered agent will be
       identical.

(b) If a registered agent changes the address of the agent's business office,
the agent may change the address of the registered office of any entity for
which the agent is the registered agent in this State by notifying the entity in
writing of the change and signing and delivering to the Secretary of State for
filing a statement that complies with the requirements of subsection (a) of this
section and recites that the entity has been notified of the change.

(c) A domestic corporation, limited liability company, limited liability limited partnership, registered limited liability partnership, foreign corporation,
foreign limited liability company, or foreign limited liability partnership may
change its registered office or registered agent by including in its annual report
required by G.S. 55-16-22, 57C-2-23, 59-84.4, or 59-210 the information and
any written consent required by subsection (a) of this section. (1901, c. 2, s. 31;
Rev., s. 1176; C.S., s. 1133; G.S., s. 55-34; 1955, c. 1371, s. 1; 1957, c. 979, ss. 6,
7; 1965, c. 298, s. 1; 1967, c. 823, s. 17; 1973, c. 262; c. 469, s. 3; 1989, c. 265,
s. 1; 1991, c. 645, s. 3; 2001-358, ss. 44, 45; 2001-387, ss. 167, 173, 175(a);
2001-413, s. 6.)

OFFICIAL COMMENT TO FORMER § 55-5-02

Editor's Note. — The Official Comments below were formerly located under G.S. 55-5-02 prior to its transfer in 2001. At the request of the Revisor of Statutes, the Official Comments have been transferred to this section as historical annotations pursuant to Session Laws 2001-358, s. 52.

Changes of registered office or registered agent are usually routine matters which do not affect the rights of shareholders. The purpose of this section is to permit these changes without a formal amendment of the articles of incorporation, without approval of the shareholders, and, indeed, even without formal approval of the board of directors.

Changes of registered office or registered agent are often of particular concern to corporation service companies which routinely serve as registered agent and routinely provide a registered office for literally thousands of corporations within many states.

Experience with the change of registered agent and registered office provisions in earlier versions of the Model Act and the statutes of many states revealed several minor problems with these largely formal provisions that are addressed in the revised Model Act.

(1) Changes of registered office or registered agent need not be authorized by the board of directors. Many changes (such as the name of a specific registered agent at a registered office) are so routine that they should not require action by the board of directors, particularly in publicly held corporations.

(2) In the case of a change of registered agent, the written consent of the new registered agent is required. This is designed to prevent naming persons as registered agents without their knowledge.

(3) The procedure by which a registered agent may change the street address of the registered office applies to any location within the state and the agent is expressly required to notify the corporation of the change. But a facsimile signature of the agent is acceptable since a corporation service company changing its street address may be required to file a form for each of the thousands of corporations for which it serves as registered agent and to notify each corporation of the change. Resignation of the registered agent is separately treated in section 5.03.

NORTH CAROLINA COMMENTARY TO FORMER § 55-5-02

Editor's Note. — The North Carolina Commentary below was formerly located under G.S. 55-5-02 prior to its transfer in 2001. At the request of the Revisor of Statutes, the North Carolina Commentary has been transferred to this section as historical annotations pursuant to Session Laws 2001-358, s. 52.

The provisions requiring a mailing address (if different from the street address) and the name of the county were added to the Model Act's provisions.

Editor's Note. — Session Laws 2001-358, s. 53, provided that the act, which amended this section, was effective October 1, 2001, and applicable to documents submitted for filing on or after that date. Section 173 of Session Laws 2001-387 changed the effective date of Session Laws 2001-358 from October 1, 2001, to January 1, 2002. Section 6 of Session Laws 2001-413, effective September 14, 2001, added a sentence to s. 175(a) of Session Laws 2001-387, making s. 173 of that act effective when it became law (August 26, 2001). As a result of these changes, the amendment by Session Laws 2001-358 is effective January 1, 2002, and applicable to documents submitted for filing on or after that date.

Session Laws 2001-387, s. 154(b), provides that nothing in this act shall supersede the provisions of Article 10 or 65 of Chapter 58 of the General Statutes, and this act does not create an alternate means for an entity governed by Article 65 of Chapter 58 of the General Statutes to convert to a different business form.

Effect of Amendments. — Session Laws 2001-358, ss. 44 and 45, effective January 1, 2002, and applicable to documents submitted for filing on or after that date, recodified G.S. 55-5-02 as this section; in the introductory language of subsection (a), substituted "An entity required to maintain a registered office and registered agent under G.S. 55D-30" for "A corporation" and added "all of the following" to the end; substituted "entity" for "corporation" in subdivision (a)(1); substituted "its" for "the corporation's" in subdivision (a)(2); substituted "entity's" for "corporation's" in subdivision (a)(3); deleted "and" at the end of subdivision (a)(5); in subsection (b), substituted "the agent's" for "his," substituted "the agent" for "he" in two places, substituted "entity" for "corporation" in three places, inserted "in this State," deleted "(either manually or in facsimile)" following "and signing," and inserted "of this section"; and rewrote subsection (c).

Session Laws 2001-387, s. 167, effective January 1, 2002, in subsection (c), inserted "limited liability limited partnership" and substituted "59-84.4, or 59-210" for "or 59-84.4."

§ 55D-32. Resignation of registered agent.

(a) The registered agent of an entity may resign by signing and filing with the Secretary of State a statement of resignation which may include a statement that the registered office is also discontinued. The statement must include or be accompanied by a certification from the registered agent that the agent has mailed or delivered to the entity at its last known address written notice of this resignation. This certification shall include the name and title of the individual notified, if any, and the address to which the notice was mailed or delivered.

(b) After filing the statement the Secretary of State shall mail a copy to the registered office (if not discontinued) and a copy to the entity at its principal office address on file with the Secretary of State or, if none is on file, at the address contained in the certification included in or accompanying the statement of resignation.

(c) The agency appointment is terminated, and, if applicable, the registered office discontinued on the 31st day after the date on which the statement was filed. (1901, c. 2, s. 31; Rev., s. 1176; C.S., s. 1133; G.S., s. 55-34; 1955, c. 1371, s. 1; 1957, c. 979, ss. 6, 7; 1965, c. 298, s. 1; 1967, c. 823, s. 17; 1973, c. 262; c. 469, s. 3; 1989, c. 265, s. 1; 1989 (Reg. Sess., 1990), c. 1024, s. 12.6; 2001-358, ss. 44, 45; 2001-387, ss. 168, 173, 175(a); 2001-413, s. 6.)

OFFICIAL COMMENT TO FORMER § 55-5-03

Editor's Note. — *The Official Comments below were formerly located under G.S. 55-5-03 prior to its transfer in 2001. At the request of the Revisor of Statutes, the Official Comments have been transferred to this section as historical annotations pursuant to Session Laws 2001-358, s. 52.*

The resignation of registered agents in states with statutes similar to earlier versions of the Model Act created special problems. Most of these problems arose in connection with corporation service companies who serve as registered agent for an annual fee. If the fee was not paid, the corporation service company obviously desired to terminate the representation promptly. Often the agent did not have a current business address for the corporation and was uncertain whether the corporation was still actively engaged in business. The earlier Model Act provision required the agent to submit his statement of resignation in duplicate and the secretary of state was directed to mail one copy "forthwith ... to the corporation at its registered office." This resulted in a circularity in notice: the duplicate was mailed back to the resigned agent who originally filed the copy. The probability that the corporation would re-

ceive a copy of the resignation under these circumstances was obviously low.

Section 5.03 resolves the circularity problem by requiring the resigning agent to submit two copies of its statement of resignation, one to be sent to the corporation at its registered office and the other to the corporation "at its principal office." Mailing to this second address appears to be the only option regularly available to "break the circle" of the corporation "receiving" the notice through an agent whose resignation is being communicated.

This section also permits the discontinuance of the registered office as well as the resignation of the agent. Corporation service companies desiring to resign their agency for nonpayment of fees will normally wish to discontinue the registered office as well as the registered agent.

AMENDED NORTH CAROLINA COMMENTARY TO FORMER § 55-5-03

Editor's Note. — *The North Carolina Commentary below was formerly located under G.S. 55-5-03 prior to its transfer in 2001. At the request of the Revisor of Statutes, the North Carolina Commentary has been transferred to this section as historical annotations pursuant to Session Laws 2001-358, s. 52.*

The Model Act was modified in subsection (a) to require that the statement of resignation include or be accompanied by a certification that written notice of the resignation was mailed or delivered to the corporation. The certification must include the name and title of the officer notified (if any) and the address to which the notice of resignation was mailed or delivered.

Editor's Note. — Session Laws 2001-358, s. 53, provided that the act, which amended this section, was effective October 1, 2001, and applicable to documents submitted for filing on or after that date. Section 173 of Session Laws 2001-387 changed the effective date of Session Laws 2001-358 from October 1, 2001, to January 1, 2002. Section 6 of Session Laws 2001-413, effective September 14, 2001, added a sentence to s. 175(a) of Session Laws 2001-387, making s. 173 of that act effective when it became law (August 26, 2001). As a result of these changes, the amendment by Session Laws 2001-358 is effective January 1, 2002, and applicable to documents submitted for filing on or after that date.

Session Laws 2001-387, s. 154(b), provides that "Nothing in the act shall supersede the provisions of Article 10 or 65 of Chapter 58 of the General Statutes, and this act does not create an alternate means for an entity governed by Article 65 of Chapter 58 of the General Statutes to convert to a different business form."

Effect of Amendments. — Session Laws 2001-358, ss. 44 and 45, effective January 1, 2002, and applicable to documents submitted for filing on or after that date, recodified G.S. 55-5-03 as this section; in subsection (a), in the first sentence, substituted "The registered agent of an entity may resign" for "A registered agent may resign his agency appointment" and deleted "the signed original and two exact or conformed copies of" preceding "a statement of resignation," in the second sentence, substituted "the agent" for "he" and substituted "entity" for "corporation," and, in the last sentence, substituted "This" for "Such" and substituted "individual" for "officer"; rewrote subsection (b); and in subsection (c), inserted "if applicable" and deleted "if so provided" following "discontinued."

Session Laws 2001-387, s. 168, effective January 1, 2002, insubsection (b), inserted "at its principal office address on file with the Secretary of State or, if none is on file" and deleted "or, if different, at the address indicated in the latest document filed by the Secretary of State stating the entity's current mailing address" from the end.

§ 55D-33. Service on entities.

(a) Service of process, notice or demand required or permitted by law to be served on an entity may be served on the registered agent required by G.S. 55D-30.

(b) When an entity required to maintain a registered office and registered agent under G.S. 55D-30 fails to appoint or maintain a registered agent in this State, or when its registered agent cannot with due diligence be found at the registered office, or when the Secretary of State revokes a certificate of authority or a statement of foreign registration of a foreign entity authorized to transact business or conduct affairs in this State, the Secretary of State becomes an agent of the entity upon whom any such process, notice or demand may be served. Service on the Secretary of State of any such process, notice or demand is made by delivering to and leaving with the Secretary of State or any clerk authorized by the Secretary of State to accept service of process, duplicate copies of the process, notice or demand and the applicable fee. In the event any such process, notice or demand is served on the Secretary of State in the manner provided by this subsection, the Secretary of State shall immediately mail one of the copies thereof, by registered or certified mail, return receipt requested, to the entity at its principal office or, if there is no mailing address for the principal office on file, to the entity at its registered office. Service on an entity under this subsection is effective for all purposes from and after the date of the service on the Secretary of State.

(c) The Secretary of State shall keep a record of all processes, notices and demands served upon the Secretary of State under this section and shall record therein the date of service and the Secretary of State's action with reference thereto.

(d) Nothing in this section affects the right to serve any process, notice or demand required or permitted by law to be served upon an entity in any other manner now or hereafter permitted by law. (1937, c. 133, ss. 1-3; G.S., s. 55-39; 1955, c. 1371, s. 1; 1977, 2nd Sess., c. 1219, s. 33; 1989, c. 265, s. 1; 2000-140, s. 43; 2001-358, ss. 44, 45; 2001-387, ss. 173, 175(a); 2001-413, s. 6.)

OFFICIAL COMMENT TO FORMER § 55-5-04

Editor's Note. — *The Official Comments below were formerly located under G.S. 55-5-04 prior to its transfer in 2001. At the request of the Revisor of Statutes, the Official Comments have been transferred to this section as historical annotations pursuant to Session Laws 2001-358, s. 52.*

Somewhat the same circularity problem that arose in connection with the resignation of registered agents (see the Official Comment to section 5.03) also sometimes arose in connection with service of process under statutes based on the former Model Act provision. Under that provision, if service could not be made on the registered agent at its registered office, a duplicate of the process was forwarded to the secretary of state who served it at the registered office (where the agent previously could not be found). It is unlikely that this arrangement resulted in the copy being forwarded routinely to the corporation. Instead of providing for service on the secretary of state if service cannot be perfected on the registered agent, therefore, section 5.04 provides for service by registered or certified mail addressed to the secretary of the corporation at its principal office shown in its most recent annual report.

If service is not perfected on the corporation at its registered office, section 5.04(b) provides that service is deemed perfected at the earliest of:

(1) the date the corporation receives the mail;
(2) the date shown on the return receipt if the receipt is signed on behalf of the corporation;
(3) five days after the certified or registered mail is delivered to the post office or deposited in the mail by the person seeking to serve the corporation, if the return receipt was not returned or not signed on behalf of the corporation.

Section 5.04 also simplifies the recordkeeping requirements of the secretary of state, who is no longer required to keep records of service of process on domestic corporations.

Section 5.04(c) provides that this section does not prescribe the only, or necessarily the required, means of serving a corporation. Service may also be perfected under civil practice statutes, under rules of civil procedure, or under statutes that provide special service requirements applicable to certain types of corporations.

NORTH CAROLINA COMMENTARY TO FORMER § 55-5-04

Editor's Note. — *The North Carolina Commentary below was formerly located under G.S. 55-5-04 prior to its transfer in 2001. At the request of the Revisor of Statutes, the North Carolina Commentary has been transferred to this section as historical annotations pursuant to Session Laws 2001-358, s. 52.*

Subsection (a) follows the Model Act except for specifying that the registered agent is "an" agent rather than "the" agent for service on the corporation. Subsections (b), (c) and (d) bring forward former G.S. 55-15(b), (c) and (d), with minor conforming changes in subsection (b). Service on the Secretary of State under the circumstances permitted by former G.S. 55-15(b) has been retained as an alternative.

Editor's Note. — Session Laws 2001-358, s. 53, provided that the act, which amended this section, was effective October 1, 2001, and applicable to documents submitted for filing on or after that date. Section 173 of Session Laws 2001-387 changed the effective date of Session Laws 2001-358 from October 1, 2001, to January 1, 2002. Section 6 of Session Laws 2001-413, effective September 14, 2001, added a sentence to s. 175(a) of Session Laws 2001-387, making s. 173 of that act effective when it became law (August 26, 2001). As a result of these changes, the amendment by Session Laws 2001-358 is effective January 1, 2002, and applicable to documents submitted for filing on or after that date.

Effect of Amendments. — Session Laws 2001-358, ss. 44 and 45, effective January 1, 2002, and applicable to documents submitted for filing on or after that date, recodified G.S. 55-5-04 as this section; and rewrote the section.

CASE NOTES

Editor's Note. — *Most of the cases below were decided under the Business Corporation Act adopted in 1955 or under prior law.*

Purpose of Service on Secretary of State. — The provision for service of process on the Secretary of State is not in the nature of a penalty upon the corporation for not having an agent upon whom service could be had, and not keeping the name of such agent on file with the Secretary of State, which might be condoned because of the alleged inability of the corporation to comply with the statute. It is a device for public convenience and is sustained upon the theory that it is reasonably adequate notice, either to be employed alternatively or where other forms of notice are unavailable. Sisk v. Old Hickory Motor Freight, 222 N.C. 631, 24 S.E.2d 488 (1943).

Service upon a corporation by substituted service upon the Secretary of State does not violate due process of law. Royal Bus. Funds Corp. v. South E. Dev. Corp., 32 N.C. App. 362, 232 S.E.2d 215, cert. denied, 292 N.C. 728, 235 S.E.2d 784 (1977).

Violation of Due Process Where Attorney Had Actual Knowledge of Defendant's Address. — Where plaintiff's attorney had actual knowledge of an address where defendant could be served and did not attempt to serve defendant at the known address, substitute service of process on the Secretary of State was ineffective and violated defendant's due process rights. Interior Distribs., Inc. v. Hartland Constr. Co., 116 N.C. App. 627, 449 S.E.2d 193 (1994).

To obtain proper service upon a domestic corporation, (i) service must first be made upon the Secretary of State, and (ii) the Secretary of State must forward a copy of the summons and complaint to the corporation. Huggins v. Hallmark Enters., Inc., 84 N.C. App. 15, 351 S.E.2d 779 (1987).

Test of Sufficiency of Notice. — The test is not whether defendants received actual notice, but whether the notice was of a nature reasonably calculated to give them actual notice and the opportunity to defend. Royal Bus. Funds Corp. v. South E. Dev. Corp., 32 N.C. App. 362, 232 S.E.2d 215, cert. denied, 292 N.C. 728, 235 S.E.2d 784 (1977).

Actual Receipt of Notice Not Required. — Former G.S. 55-15(b), which directed the Secretary of State to forward process by registered mail, did not require that the defendant corporation receive actual notice. Royal Bus. Funds Corp. v. South E. Dev. Corp., 32 N.C. App. 362, 232 S.E.2d 215, cert. denied, 292 N.C. 728, 235 S.E.2d 784 (1977).

Effect of Failure to Comply with Statutory Registration Requirements. — Where defendants were required by former G.S. 55-13 to maintain a registered office and registered agent, and their failure to do so caused process to be twice returned without personal service, while had they conformed to the statutory requirements, both methods of service would have resulted in their receiving actual notice of the lawsuit, the notice given (attempted personal service on the Secretary of State) was in fact reasonably calculated, under all the circumstances, to apprise interested parties of the pendency of the action and afford them an opportunity to present their objections. Accordingly, the service upon the Secretary of State was constitutionally valid and the trial court acquired in personam jurisdiction over the North Carolina corporations. Royal Bus. Funds Corp. v. South E. Dev. Corp., 32 N.C. App. 362, 232 S.E.2d 215, cert. denied, 292 N.C. 728, 235 S.E.2d 784 (1977).

Failure of Secretary of State to Mail Copy of Process to Registered Office. — Where the Secretary of State's office, contrary to the mandate in former G.S. 55-15(b), failed to mail a copy of process to the registered office of defendant corporation, plaintiff did not obtain proper service upon defendant, and the fact that even if the Secretary of State had forwarded the summons and complaint to defendant's then recorded address, such would not have been received, would not change this result. Huggins v. Hallmark Enters., Inc., 84 N.C. App. 15, 351 S.E.2d 779 (1987).

Service After Forfeiture of Charter. — The continuance of corporate existence by former G.S. 55-132 made service of process on a corporation after it had been adjudged a bankrupt and its charter forfeited reasonable notice and a valid service. Sisk v. Old Hickory Motor Freight, 222 N.C. 631, 24 S.E.2d 488 (1943).

Continuously Doing Business as Presence. — Where the seller has continuously done business in this State since plaintiff's claims accrued, the seller has been sufficiently "present" in the state to warrant the protection of the statutes of limitations. Bobbitt v. Tannewitz, 538 F. Supp. 654 (M.D.N.C. 1982).

Presence Through Agents in State. — A corporation can actually be present in the State by continuously doing business in this State through its agents, even though its place of incorporation and principal place of business are in foreign states. Bobbitt v. Tannewitz, 538 F. Supp. 654 (M.D.N.C. 1982).

Corporation Bound upon Service of Agent. — Service of process upon a corporation's registered agent binds that corporation when the agent is served, not when the service actually comes to the attention of an officer or agent charged with defending actions against the corporation. Anderson Trucking Serv., Inc. v. Key Way Transp., Inc., 94 N.C. App. 36, 379 S.E.2d 665 (1989), decided under the former Business Corporation Act.

Cited in Patridge v. Associated Cleaning Consultants & Servs., Inc., 108 N.C. App. 625, 424 S.E.2d 664 (1993).

Chapter 56.
Electric, Telegraph and Power Companies.

§§ 56-1 through 56-11: Repealed by Session Laws 1963, c. 1165, s. 1.

Chapter 57.

Hospital, Medical and Dental Service Corporations.

§§ 57-1 through 57-38: Recodified as Articles 65 and 66 of Chapter 58.

Editor's Note. — This Chapter has been recodified as Articles 65 and 66 of Chapter 58, under the authority of Session Laws 1987, c. 752, s. 9 and Session Laws 1987 (Reg. Sess., 1988), c. 975, s. 34.

Former G.S. 57-14 was repealed by Session Laws 1987, c. 814, s. 5, effective July 1, 1988. Former G.S. 57-21 to 57-29 had been reserved.

For old to new section correlations, see the table of disposition provided at the end of Chapter 58.

Chapter 57A.

Health Maintenance Organization Act.

§§ 57A-1 through 57A-29: Recodified.

Editor's Note. — This Chapter was rewritten by Session Laws 1979, c. 876, s. 1, effective July 1, 1979, and was recodified as Chapter 57B, which in turn has been recodified as Article 67 of Chapter 58.

Chapter 57B.

Health Maintenance Organization Act.

§§ 57B-1 through 57B-25: Recodified as Article 67 of Chapter 58.

Editor's Note. — This Chapter has been recodified as Article 67 of Chapter 58, under the authority of Session Laws 1987, c. 752, s. 9 and Session Laws 1987 (Reg. Sess., 1988), c. 975, s. 34.

For old to new section correlations, see the table of disposition provided at the end of Chapter 58.

Chapter 57C.

North Carolina Limited Liability Company Act.

Article 1.

General Provisions.

Part 1. Short Title; Reservation of Power; Definitions.

§ 57C-1-01. Short title.

This Chapter is the "North Carolina Limited Liability Company Act" and may be cited by that name. (1993, c. 354, s. 1.)

Legal Periodicals. — For note, "Corporate Law — Limited Liability Company Act, N.C. Gen. Stat. G.S. 57C-1-01 to 57C-10-07 (1993)," see 72 N.C.L. Rev. 1654 (1994).

For comment, "How the Uniform Partnership Act Determines Ultimate Liability for a Claim Against a General Partnership and Provides for the Settling of Accounts Between Partners," see 17 Campbell L. Rev. 333 (1995).

For article, "The Creation of North Carolina's Limited Liability Corporation Act," see 32 Wake Forest L. Rev. 179 (1997).

§ 57C-1-02. Reservation of power to amend or repeal.

The General Assembly has power to amend or repeal all or part of this Chapter at any time and all domestic limited liability companies and foreign limited liability companies subject to this Chapter are governed by the amendment or repeal. (1993, c. 354, s. 1.)

§ 57C-1-03. Definitions.

The following definitions apply in this Chapter, unless otherwise specifically provided:

(1) Articles of organization. — The document filed under G.S. 57C-2-20 of this Chapter for the purpose of forming a limited liability company, as amended or restated.

(2) Bankrupt. — Bankrupt under the United States Bankruptcy Code, as amended, or insolvent under State insolvency laws.

(3) Business. — Any lawful trade, investment, or other purpose or activity, whether or not such trade, investment, purpose, or activity is carried on for profit.

(3a) Business entity. — A corporation (including a professional corporation as defined in G.S. 55B-2), a foreign corporation (including a foreign professional corporation defined in G.S. 55B-16), a domestic or foreign nonprofit corporation, a domestic or foreign limited liability company, a domestic or foreign limited partnership, a registered limited liability partnership or foreign limited liability partnership as defined in G.S. 59-32, or any other partnership as defined in G.S. 59-36 whether or not formed under the laws of this State.

(4) Corporation or domestic corporation. — Has the same meaning as in G.S. 55-1-40(4).

(5) Court. — Includes every court and judge having jurisdiction in the case.

(5a) Director. — For any limited liability company the management of whose affairs is vested in whole or in part in persons other than its managers pursuant to G.S. 57C-3-20(b), any person who is so vested with, or is one of a group of persons so vested with, the authority to direct the management of the limited liability company's affairs.

(6) Distribution. — A direct or indirect transfer of money or other property or incurrence of indebtedness by a limited liability company to or for the benefit of its members in respect of their membership interests.

(6a) Domestic nonprofit corporation. — A corporation as defined in G.S. 55A-1-40(5).

(6b) Executive. — For any limited liability company the management of whose affairs is vested in whole or in part in persons other than its managers pursuant to G.S. 57C-3-20(b), any person who is so vested with authority to participate in the management of the limited liability company's affairs under the direction of the limited liability company's managers or directors.

(7) Foreign corporation. — Has the same meaning as in G.S. 55-1-40(10).

(8) Foreign limited liability company. — An unincorporated organization formed under laws other than the laws of this State, that affords to each of its members, pursuant to the laws under which it is formed, limited liability with respect to the liabilities of the organization.

(9) Foreign limited partnership. — Has the same meaning as in G.S. 59-102(5).

(9a) Foreign nonprofit corporation. — A foreign corporation as defined in G.S. 55A-1-40(11).

(10) Individual. — A human being.

(10a) Liabilities, debts, and obligations. — Have one and the same meaning and are used interchangeably throughout this Chapter. Reference to "liabilities," "debts," or "obligations" whether individually or in any combination, is deemed to reference "all liabilities, debts, and obligations, whether arising in contract, tort, or otherwise."

(11) Limited liability company or domestic limited liability company. — An entity formed and existing under this Chapter.

(12) Limited partnership or domestic limited partnership. — Has the same meaning as in G.S. 59-102(8).

(12a) Management of the affairs. — In respect of an entity, unless the context indicates otherwise, the authority to direct and participate in the management of the entity.

(13) Manager. — Has the following meanings: (i) with respect to a domestic limited liability company, any person designated in, or in accordance with, G.S. 57C-3-20(a), and (ii) with respect to a foreign limited liability company, any person authorized to act for and bind the foreign limited liability company.

(14) Member. — A person who has been admitted to membership in the limited liability company as provided in G.S. 57C-3-01 until the person's membership ceases as provided in G.S. 57C-3-02 or G.S. 57C-5-02.

(15) Membership interest or interest. — In the context of a member of a limited liability company, the terms mean all of a member's rights in the limited liability company, including any share of the profits and losses of the limited liability company, any right to receive distributions of the limited liability company assets, any right to vote on matters relating to the limited liability company, and any right to participate in the management of the limited liability company's affairs.

(16) Operating agreement. — Any agreement, written or oral, of the members with respect to the affairs of a limited liability company and the conduct of its business that is binding on all the members. An operating agreement shall include, in the case of a limited liability company with only one member, any writing signed by the member, without regard to whether the writing constitutes an agreement, that relates to the affairs of the limited liability company and the conduct of its business.

(16a) Organizer. — A person who executes the articles of organization of a limited liability company in the capacity of an organizer.

(17) Person. — An individual, a trust, an estate, or a domestic or foreign corporation, a domestic or foreign professional corporation, a domestic or foreign partnership, a domestic or foreign limited partnership, a domestic or foreign limited liability company, an unincorporated association, or another entity.

(17a) Principal office. — The office, in or out of this State, where the principal executive offices of a domestic or foreign limited liability company are located, as designated in its most recent annual report filed with the Secretary of State or, in the case of a domestic or foreign limited liability company that has not yet filed an annual report, in its articles of organization or application for a certificate of authority, respectively.

(18) State. — A state, territory, or possession of the United States, the District of Columbia, or the Commonwealth of Puerto Rico. (1993, c. 354, s. 1; 1995, c. 351, ss. 1, 2; 1999-189, s. 1; 1999-369, ss. 3.2, 3.3; 1999-456, s. 52(a); 2000-140, s. 101(t); 2001-387, ss. 48-52.)

Editor's Note. — Session Laws 2001-387, s. 154(b) provides that: "Nothing in this act shall supersede the provisions of Article 10 or 65 of Chapter 58 of the General Statutes, and this act does not create an alternate means for an entity governed by Article 65 of Chapter 58 of the General Statutes to convert to a different business form."

Effect of Amendments. — Session Laws 2001-387, ss. 48 through 52, effective January 1, 2002, added subdivisions (5a), (6a), (6b), (9a), (12a) and (17a); in subdivision (3a), substituted "corporation, a domestic or foreign limited liability company, a domestic or foreign limited partnership, a registered limited liability part-nership or foreign limited liability partnership as defined in G.S. 59-32" for "corporation as defined in G.S. 55A-1-40, a domestic or foreign limited liability company, a domestic or foreign limited partnership as defined in G.S. 59-102" and deleted "(including a registered limited liability partnership as defined in G.S. 59-32 and any other limited liability partnership formed under a law other than the laws of this State)" from the end; added "or domestic corporation" to the subheading in subdivision (4); and rewrote subdivisions (13) and (15).

Legal Periodicals. — For "Legislative Survey: Business & Banking," see 22 Campbell L. Rev. 253 (2000).

§§ 57C-1-04 through 57C-1-19: Reserved for future codification purposes.

Part 2. Filing Documents.

§ 57C-1-20. Filing requirements.

(a) A document required or permitted by this Chapter to be filed by the Secretary of State must be filed under Chapter 55D of the General Statutes.

(b) A document submitted on behalf of a domestic or foreign limited liability company must be executed:

(1) By a manager of the limited liability company;

(2) If the limited liability company has not been formed or if no initial members of the limited liability company have been identified in the manner provided in this Chapter, by an organizer; or

(3) If the limited liability company is in the hands of a receiver, trustee, or other court-appointed fiduciary, by that fiduciary. (1993, c. 354, s. 1; 1999-189, s. 2.1; 1999-369, s. 3.1; 2000-140, s. 101(t); 2001-358, s. 8(a); 2001-387, ss. 53, 155, 173, 175(a); 2001-413, s. 6.)

Editor's Note. — Session Laws 2001-358, s. 53, provided that the act, which amended this section, was effective October 1, 2001, and applicable to documents submitted for filing on or after that date. Section 173 of Session Laws 2001-387 changed the effective date of Session Laws 2001-358 from October 1, 2001, to January 1, 2002. Section 6 of Session Laws 2001-

413, effective September 14, 2001, added a sentence to s. 175(a) of Session Laws 2001-387, making s. 173 of that act effective when it became law (August 26, 2001). As a result of these changes, the amendment by Session Laws 2001-358 is effective January 1, 2002, and applicable to documents submitted for filing on or after that date.

Session Laws 2001-387, s. 53, had amended this section. However, s. 155 of c. 387 repealed s. 53, contingent upon the enactment of Session Laws 2001-358. Session Laws 2001-358 was enacted on August 10, 2001.

Effect of Amendments. — Session Laws 2001-358, s. 8(a), effective January 1, 2002, and applicable to documents submitted for filing on or after that date, rewrote the section.

Legal Periodicals. — For comment, "Creating the Legal Monster: The Expansion and Effect of Legal Malpractice Liability in North Carolina", see 18 Campbell L. Rev. 121 (1996).

§ 57C-1-21. Forms.

(a) The Secretary of State may promulgate and furnish on request forms for:
 (1) An application for a certificate of existence;
 (2) A foreign limited liability company's application for a certificate of authority to transact business in this State; and
 (3) A foreign limited liability company's application for a certificate of withdrawal.
If the Secretary of State so requires, use of these forms is mandatory.

(b) The Secretary of State may promulgate and furnish on request forms for other documents required or permitted to be filed by this Chapter but their use is not mandatory. (1993, c. 354, s. 1.)

§ 57C-1-22. Filing, service, and copying fees.

(a) The Secretary of State shall collect the following fees when the documents described in this subsection are delivered to the Secretary of State for filing:

Document		Fee
(1)	Articles of organization	$125.00
(2)	Application for reserved name	10.00
(3)	Notice of transfer of reserved name	10.00
(4)	Application for registered name	10.00
(5)	Application for renewal of registered name	10.00
(6)	Limited liability company's statement of change of registered agent or registered office or both	5.00
(7)	Agent's statement of change of registered office for each affected limited liability company	5.00
(8)	Agent's statement of resignation	No fee
(9)	Designation of registered agent or registered office or both	5.00
(10)	Amendment of articles of organization	50.00
(11)	Restated articles of organization without amendment of articles	10.00
(12)	Restated articles of organization with amendment of articles	50.00
(12a)	Articles of conversion (other than articles of conversion included as part of another document)	50.00
(13)	Articles of merger	50.00
(14)	Articles of dissolution	30.00

Document	Fee
(15) Cancellation of articles of dissolution	10.00
(16) Certificate of administrative dissolution	No fee
(16a) Application for reinstatement following administrative dissolution	100.00
(17) Certificate of reinstatement	No fee
(18) Certificate of judicial dissolution	No fee
(19) Application for certificate of authority	250.00
(20) Application for amended certificate of authority	50.00
(21) Application for certificate of withdrawal	10.00
(22) Certificate of revocation of authority to transact business	No fee
(23) Articles of correction	10.00
(24) Application for certificate of existence or authorization (paper)	15.00
(24a) Application for certificate of existence or authorization (electronic)	10.00
(25) Annual report	200.00
(26) Any other document required or permitted to be filed by this Chapter	10.00
(27) Repealed by Session Laws 2001-358, s. 8(c), effective January 1, 2002.	

(b) The Secretary of State shall collect a fee of ten dollars ($10.00) each time process is served on the Secretary of State under this Chapter. The party to a proceeding causing service of process is entitled to recover this fee as costs if the party prevails in the proceeding.

(c) The Secretary of State shall collect the following fees for copying, comparing, and certifying a copy of any filed document relating to a domestic or foreign limited liability company:

    (1) One dollar ($1.00) a page for copying or comparing a copy to the original; and

    (2) Fifteen dollars ($15.00) for a paper certificate.

    (3) Ten dollars ($10.00) for an electronic certificate. (1993, c. 354, s. 1; 1997-456, s. 55.3; 1997-475, s. 5.3; 1997-485, ss. 12, 20; 2001-358, s. 8(c); 2001-387, ss. 54, 173, 175(a); 2001-413, s. 6; 2002-126, ss. 29A.29, 29A.30.)

Editor's Note. — Session Laws 2001-358, s. 53, provided that the act, which amended this section, was effective October 1, 2001, and applicable to documents submitted for filing on or after that date. Section 173 of Session Laws 2001-387 changed the effective date of Session Laws 2001-358 from October 1, 2001, to January 1, 2002. Section 6 of Session Laws 2001-413, effective September 14, 2001, added a sentence to s. 175(a) of Session Laws 2001-387, making s. 173 of that act effective when it became law (August 26, 2001). As a result of these changes, the amendment by Session Laws 2001-358 is effective January 1, 2002, and applicable to documents submitted for filing on or after that date.

Session Laws 2001-387, s. 154(b) provides that: "Nothing in this act shall supersede the provisions of Article 10 or 65 of Chapter 58 of the General Statutes, and this act does not create an alternate means for an entity governed by Article 65 of Chapter 58 of the General Statutes to convert to a different business form."

Session Laws 2002-126, s. 1.2, provides: "This act shall be known as 'The Current Operations, Capitol Improvements, and Finance Act of 2002'."

Session Laws 2002-126, s. 31.6 is a severability clause.

Effect of Amendments. — Session Laws 2001-358, s. 8(c), effective January 1, 2002, and applicable to documents submitted for filing on or after that date, repealed subdivision (a)(27), which related to the fee for advisory review of a document.

Session Laws 2001-387, s. 54, effective January 1, 2002, added subdivision (a)(12a).

Session Laws 2002-126, ss. 29A.29 and 29A.30, effective November 1, 2002, substituted "(paper) 15.00" for "5.00" in subdivision (a)(24); added subdivision (a)(24a); rewrote

subdivision (c)(2), which formerly read: "Five dollars ($5.00) for the certificate"; and added subdivision (c)(3).

Legal Periodicals. — For 1997 legislative survey, see 20 Campbell L. Rev. 389.

§§ 57C-1-22.1, 57C-1-22.2: Repealed by Session Laws 2001-358, s. 8(b), effective January 1, 2002.

Editor's Note. — Session Laws 2001-358, s. 53, provided that the act, which amended this section, was effective October 1, 2001, and applicable to documents submitted for filing on or after that date. Section 173 of Session Laws 2001-387 changed the effective date of Session Laws 2001-358 from October 1, 2001, to January 1, 2002. Section 6 of Session Laws 2001-

413, effective September 14, 2001, added a sentence to s. 175(a) of Session Laws 2001-387, making s. 173 of that act effective when it became law (August 26, 2001). As a result of these changes, the amendment by Session Laws 2001-358 is effective January 1, 2002, and applicable to documents submitted for filing on or after that date.

§§ 57C-1-23 through 57C-1-27: Repealed by Session Laws 2001-358, s. 8(b), effective January 1, 2002.

Editor's Note. — Session Laws 2001-358, s. 53, provided that the act, which amended this section, was effective October 1, 2001, and applicable to documents submitted for filing on or after that date. Section 173 of Session Laws 2001-387 changed the effective date of Session Laws 2001-358 from October 1, 2001, to January 1, 2002. Section 6 of Session Laws 2001-

413, effective September 14, 2001, added a sentence to s. 175(a) of Session Laws 2001-387, making s. 173 of that act effective when it became law (August 26, 2001). As a result of these changes, the amendment by Session Laws 2001-358 is effective January 1, 2002, and applicable to documents submitted for filing on or after that date.

§ 57C-1-28. Certificate of existence.

(a) Anyone may apply to the Secretary of State to furnish a certificate of existence for a domestic limited liability company or a certificate of authorization for a foreign limited liability company.

(b) A certificate of existence or authorization sets forth:

(1) The domestic limited liability company's name or the foreign limited liability company's name used in this State;

(2) That (i) the domestic limited liability company is duly formed under the law of this State, the date of its formation, and the period of its duration, or (ii) that the foreign limited liability company is authorized to transact business in this State;

(3) That the articles of organization of a domestic limited liability company or the certificate of authority of a foreign limited liability company has not been suspended under G.S. 105-230 for failure to pay a tax or fee or file a report or return, and that the limited liability company has not been administratively dissolved for failure to comply with the provisions of this Chapter;

(4) That articles of dissolution have not been filed; and

(5) Other facts of record in the Office of the Secretary of State that may be requested by the applicant.

(c) Subject to any qualification stated in the certificate, a certificate of existence or authorization issued by the Secretary of State may be relied upon as conclusive evidence that the domestic or foreign limited liability company is in existence or is authorized to transact business in this State. (1993, c. 354, s. 1.)

§ 57C-1-29: Repealed by Session Laws 2001-358, s. 8(b), effective January 1, 2002.

Editor's Note. — Session Laws 2001-358, s. 53, provided that the act, which amended this section, was effective October 1, 2001, and applicable to documents submitted for filing on or after that date. Section 173 of Session Laws 2001-387 changed the effective date of Session Laws 2001-358 from October 1, 2001, to January 1, 2002. Section 6 of Session Laws 2001- 413, effective September 14, 2001, added a sentence to s. 175(a) of Session Laws 2001-387, making s. 173 of that act effective when it became law (August 26, 2001). As a result of these changes, the amendment by Session Laws 2001-358 is effective January 1, 2002, and applicable to documents submitted for filing on or after that date.

Part 3. Secretary of State.

§ 57C-1-30. Powers of the Secretary of State.

The Secretary of State has the power reasonably necessary to perform the duties required by this Chapter. (1993, c. 354, s. 1.)

§ 57C-1-31. Interrogatories by Secretary of State.

The Secretary of State may propound to any foreign or domestic limited liability company that the Secretary of State has reason to believe is subject to the provisions of this Chapter, and to any manager thereof, such written interrogatories as may be reasonably necessary and proper to enable the Secretary of State to ascertain whether the limited liability company is subject to the provisions of this Chapter or has complied with all of the provisions of this Chapter applicable to it. Subject to applicable jurisdictional requirements, the interrogatories shall be answered within 30 days after the mailing thereof, or within such additional time as shall be fixed by the Secretary of State, and the answers thereto shall be full and complete and shall be made in writing and under oath. If the interrogatories are directed to an individual, they shall be answered by the individual, and if directed to a foreign or domestic limited liability company, they shall be answered by any manager thereof. The Secretary of State shall certify to the Attorney General for such action as the Attorney General may deem appropriate, all interrogatories and answers thereto which disclose a violation of any of the provisions of this Chapter requiring or permitting action by the Attorney General. (1993, c. 354, s. 1.)

§ 57C-1-32. Penalties imposed upon domestic and foreign limited liability companies for failure to answer interrogatories.

(a) If a foreign or domestic limited liability company fails or refuses to answer truthfully and fully within the time prescribed in this Chapter interrogatories propounded by the Secretary of State in accordance with the provisions of this Chapter, the Secretary of State may suspend its articles of organization or its certificate of authority to do business in this State.

(b) Each manager of a foreign or domestic limited liability company who fails or refuses within the time prescribed by this Chapter to answer truthfully and fully interrogatories propounded to the manager by the Secretary of State in accordance with the provisions of this Chapter shall be guilty of a Class 1 misdemeanor. (1993, c. 354, s. 1; 1994, Ex. Sess., c. 14, s. 39.)

§ 57C-1-33. Information disclosed by interrogatories.

Interrogatories propounded by the Secretary of State and the answers thereto shall not be open to public inspection nor shall the Secretary of State disclose any facts or information obtained therefrom except insofar as the Secretary of State's official duty may require the same to be made public or in the event the interrogatories or the answers thereto are required for evidence in any criminal proceedings or in any other action or proceedings by this State. (1993, c. 354, s. 1.)

ARTICLE 2.

Purposes, Powers, Formation, Annual Report, Name, Registered Office, and Agent.

Part 1. Purposes and Powers.

§ 57C-2-01. Purposes.

(a) Every limited liability company formed under this Chapter has the purpose of engaging in any lawful business unless a more limited lawful purpose is set forth in its articles of organization.

(b) A domestic or foreign limited liability company engaging in a business that is subject to regulation under another statute of this State may be formed or authorized to transact business under this Chapter only if permitted by and subject to all limitations of the other statute giving effect to subsection (c) of this section.

(c) Subsections (a) and (b) of this section to the contrary notwithstanding and except as set forth in this subsection, a domestic or foreign limited liability company shall engage in rendering professional services only to the extent that a professional corporation acting pursuant to Chapter 55B of the General Statutes or a corporation acting pursuant to Chapter 55 of the General Statutes may engage in rendering professional services under the conditions and limitations imposed by an applicable licensing statute. Chapter 55B of the General Statutes and each applicable licensing statute are deemed amended to provide that professionals licensed under the applicable licensing statute may render professional services through a domestic or foreign limited liability company. For purposes of applying the provisions, conditions, and limitations of Chapter 55B of the General Statutes and the applicable licensing statute to domestic and foreign limited liability companies that engage in rendering professional services, (i) unless the context clearly requires otherwise, references to Chapter 55 of the General Statutes (the North Carolina Business Corporation Act) shall be treated as references to this Chapter, and references to a "corporation" or "foreign corporation" shall be treated as references to a limited liability company or foreign limited liability company, respectively, (ii) members shall be treated in the same manner as shareholders of a professional corporation, (iii) managers and directors shall be treated in the same manner as directors of a professional corporation, (iv) the persons signing the articles of organization of a limited liability company shall be treated in the same manner as the incorporators of a professional corporation, and (v) the name of a domestic or foreign limited liability company so engaged shall comply with Article 3 of Chapter 55D of the General Statutes and, in addition, shall contain the word "Professional" or the abbreviation "P.L.L.C." or "PLLC". For purposes of this subsection, "applicable licensing statute" shall mean those provisions of the General Statutes referred to in G.S. 55B-2(6).

Nothing in this Chapter shall be interpreted to abolish, modify, restrict, limit, or alter the law in this State applicable to the professional relationship and liabilities between the individual furnishing the professional services and the person receiving the professional services, the standards of professional conduct applicable to the rendering of the services, or any responsibilities, obligations, or sanctions imposed under applicable licensing statutes. A member, manager, director, or executive of a professional limited liability company is not individually liable, directly or indirectly, including by indemnification, contribution, assessment, or otherwise, for debts, obligations, and liabilities of, or chargeable to, the professional limited liability company that arise from errors, omissions, negligence, malpractice, incompetence, or malfeasance committed by another member, manager, director, executive, employee, agent, or other representative of the professional limited liability company; provided, however, nothing in this Chapter shall affect the liability of a member, manager, director, or executive of a professional limited liability company for his or her own errors, omissions, negligence, malpractice, incompetence, or malfeasance committed in the rendering of professional services. (1993, c. 354, s. 1; 1995, c. 351, s. 21; 1999-362, s. 3; 2001-358, s. 26; 2001-387, ss. 55, 173, 175(a); 2001-413, s. 6.)

Editor's Note. — Session Laws 2001-358, s. 53, provided that the act, which amended this section, was effective October 1, 2001, and applicable to documents submitted for filing on or after that date. Section 173 of Session Laws 2001-387 changed the effective date of Session Laws 2001-358 from October 1, 2001, to January 1, 2002. Section 6 of Session Laws 2001-413, effective September 14, 2001, added a sentence to s. 175(a) of Session Laws 2001-387, making s. 173 of that act effective when it became law (August 26, 2001). As a result of these changes, the amendment by Session Laws 2001-358 is effective January 1, 2002, and applicable to documents submitted for filing on or after that date.

Session Laws 2001-387, s. 154(b) provides that nothing in this act shall supersede the provisions of Article 10 or 65 of Chapter 58 of the General Statutes, and this act does not create an alternate means for an entity governed by Article 65 of Chapter 58 of the General Statutes to convert to a different business form.

Effect of Amendments. — Session Laws 2001-358, s. 26, effective January 1, 2002, and applicable to documents submitted for filing on or after that date, substituted "Article 3 of Chapter 55D of the General Statutes" for "G.S. 57C-2-30 or G.S. 57C-7-06" near the end of the first paragraph of subsection (c).

Session Laws 2001-387, s. 55, effective January 1, 2002, in subsection (a) substituted "formed" for "organized"; in subsection (c) inserted "and directors" following "(iii) managers"; and in the undesignated paragraph, twice substituted "member, manager, director, or executive" for "member or," and also inserted "director, executive" preceding "employee, agent".

Legal Periodicals. — For note, "Corporate Law — Limited Liability Company Act, N.C. Gen. Stat. G.S. 57C-1-01 to 57C-10-07 (1993)," see 72 N.C.L. Rev. 1654 (1994).

For comment, "Creating the legal monster: the expansion and effect of legal malpractice liability in North Carolina", see 18 Campbell L. Rev. 121 (1996).

For article, "The Creation of North Carolina's Limited Liability Corporation Act," see 32 Wake Forest L. Rev. 179 (1997).

§ 57C-2-02. Powers of the limited liability company.

Unless its articles of organization or this Chapter provide otherwise, each limited liability company has the same powers as an individual to do all things necessary or convenient to carry out its business and affairs, including, without limitation, power:

(1) To sue and be sued, complain, and defend in its own name;

(2) To make and amend operating agreements, not inconsistent with its articles of organization or with the laws of this State, for managing the business and regulating the affairs of the limited liability company;

(3) To purchase, receive, lease, or otherwise acquire, and own, hold, improve, use, and otherwise deal with, real or personal property, or any legal or equitable interest in property, wherever located;

(4) To sell, convey, mortgage, pledge, lease, exchange, and otherwise dispose of all or any part of its property;

(5) To purchase, receive, subscribe for, or otherwise acquire; own, hold, vote, use, sell, mortgage, lend, pledge, or otherwise dispose of; and deal in and with shares or other interests in, or obligations of, any other entity;

(6) To make contracts and guarantees, incur liabilities, borrow money, issue its notes, bonds, and other obligations (which may be convertible into or include the option to purchase other interests in the limited liability company), and secure any of its obligations by mortgage or pledge of any of its property, franchises, or income;

(7) To lend money, invest and reinvest its funds, and receive and hold real and personal property as security for repayment;

(8) To be a promoter, partner, member, associate, or manager of any partnership, joint venture, trust, or other entity;

(9) To conduct its business, locate offices, and exercise the powers granted by this Chapter within or without this State;

(10) To elect or appoint managers, directors, executives, officers, employees, and agents of the limited liability company, define their duties, fix their compensation, and lend them money and credit;

(11) To pay pensions and establish pension plans, pension trusts, profit-sharing plans, and other benefit or incentive plans for any or all of its current or former managers, directors, executives, officers, employees, and agents;

(12) To make donations for the public welfare or for charitable, religious, cultural, scientific, or educational purposes;

(13) To transact any lawful business that will aid governmental policy;

(14) To make payments or donations, or do any other act, not inconsistent with law, that furthers the business and affairs of the limited liability company;

(15) To provide insurance for its benefit on the life or physical or mental ability of any of its managers, directors, executives, officers, or employees or on the life or physical or mental ability of any owner of any interest in the limited liability company for the purpose of acquiring the interest owned by him at the time of his death or disability, and for these purposes the limited liability company is deemed to have an insurable interest in its managers, directors, executives, officers, employees, or members and other interest owners; and to provide insurance for its benefit on the life or physical or mental ability of any other person in whom it has an insurable interest; and

(16) To render professional services, subject to G.S. 57C-2-01(c). (1993, c. 354, s. 1; 2001-387, s. 56.)

Editor's Note. — Session Laws 2001-387, s. 154(b) provides that nothing in this act shall supersede the provisions of Article 10 or 65 of Chapter 58 of the General Statutes, and this act does not create an alternate means for an entity governed by Article 65 of Chapter 58 of the General Statutes to convert to a different business form.

Effect of Amendments. — Session Laws 2001-387, s. 56, effective January 1, 2002, in subdivision (10) inserted "directors, executives," preceding "officers, employees"; in subdivision (11) inserted "directors, executives," preceding "officers, employees"; and in subdivision (15) inserted "directors, executives," preceding "officers, or employees" and preceding "officers, employees."

§§ 57C-2-03 through 57C-2-19: Reserved for future codification purposes.

Part 2. Formation; Articles of Organization; Amendment of Articles; Annual Report.

§ 57C-2-20. Formation.

(a) One or more persons may form a limited liability company by delivering executed articles of organization to the Secretary of State for filing. A limited liability company may also be formed through the conversion of another business entity pursuant to Part 1 of Article 9A of this Chapter.

(b)(1) When the filing by the Secretary of State of the articles of organization becomes effective, the proposed organization becomes a limited liability company subject to this Chapter and to the purposes, conditions, and provisions stated in the articles of organization.

(2) Filing of the articles of organization by the Secretary of State is conclusive evidence of the formation of the limited liability company, except in a proceeding by the State to cancel or revoke the articles of organization or involuntarily dissolve the limited liability company.

(c) Organization of a limited liability company requires one or more initial members and any further action as may be determined by the initial member or members. If initial members are not identified in the articles of organization of a limited liability company in the manner provided in G.S. 57C-3-01(a), the organizers shall hold one or more meetings at the call of a majority of the organizers to identify the initial members of the limited liability company. Unless otherwise provided in this Chapter or in the articles of organization of the limited liability company, all decisions to be made by the organizers at such meetings shall require the approval, consent, agreement, or ratification of a majority of the organizers. Unless otherwise provided in the articles of organization, the organizers may, in lieu of a meeting, take action as described in this subsection by written consent signed by all of the organizers. The written consent may be incorporated in, or otherwise made part of, the initial written operating agreement of the limited liability company. (1993, c. 354, s. 1; 1997-485, s. 28; 1999-189, s. 2.2; 1999-369, s. 3.4; 1999-456, s. 50; 2000-140, ss. 10(a), 10(b); 2001-387, s. 57.)

Editor's Note. — The section above was amended by Session Laws 1999-189, s. 2.2, and Session Laws 1999-456, s. 50, in the coded bill drafting format provided by G.S. 120-20.1. The amendment by 1999-456 rewrote the section, as amended by Session Laws 1999-189, s. 2, and failed to incorporate changes made by Session Laws 1999-189, including the addition of subsection (d), regarding formation of a limited liability company through the conversion of another business entity. As added by Session Laws 1999-189, s. 2, subsection (d) read as follows: "(d) A limited liability company may also be formed through the conversion of another business entity in accordance with Part 1 of Article 9 of this Chapter." Subsequently, Session Laws 2000-140, s. 10(a), repealed s. 2.2 of Session Laws 1999-189 and s. 50 of Session Laws 1999-456, effective July 21, 2000.

Session Laws 2001-387, s. 154(b) provides that nothing in this act shall supersede the provisions of Article 10 or 65 of Chapter 58 of the General Statutes, and this act does not create an alternate means for an entity governed by Article 65 of Chapter 58 of the General Statutes to convert to a different business form.

Effect of Amendments. — Session Laws 2001-387, s. 57, effective January 1, 2002, added the first sentence in subsection (c).

Legal Periodicals. — For 1997 legislative survey, see 20 Campbell L. Rev. 389.

§ 57C-2-21. Articles of organization.

(a) The articles of organization must set forth:
  (1) A name for the limited liability company that satisfies the provisions of G.S. 55D-20 and G.S. 55D-21;
  (2) If the limited liability company is to dissolve by a specific date, the latest date on which the limited liability company is to dissolve. If no date for dissolution is specified, there shall be no limit on the duration of the limited liability company;
  (3) The name and address of each person executing the articles of organization and whether the person is executing the articles of organization in the capacity of a member or an organizer;
  (4) The street address, and the mailing address if different from the street address, of the limited liability company's initial registered office, the county in which the initial registered office is located, and the name of the limited liability company's initial registered agent at that address;
  (4a) The street address, and the mailing address if different from the street address, of the limited liability company's principal office, if any, and the county in which the principal office, if any, is located; and
  (5) Unless all of the members by virtue of their status as members shall be managers of the limited liability company, a statement that, except as provided in G.S. 57C-3-20(a), the members shall not be managers by virtue of their status as members.

(b) The articles of organization may set forth any other provision, not inconsistent with law, including any other matter that under this Chapter is permitted to be set forth in an operating agreement.

(c) The articles of organization need not set forth any of the powers enumerated in this Chapter. (1993, c. 354, s. 1; 1999-189, s. 2.3; 2000-140, s. 101(t); 2001-358, s. 27; 2001-387, ss. 58, 173, 175(a); 2001-413, s. 6.)

Editor's Note. — Session Laws 2001-358, s. 53, provided that the act, which amended this section, was effective October 1, 2001, and applicable to documents submitted for filing on or after that date. Section 173 of Session Laws 2001-387 changed the effective date of Session Laws 2001-358 from October 1, 2001, to January 1, 2002. Section 6 of Session Laws 2001-413, effective September 14, 2001, added a sentence to s. 175(a) of Session Laws 2001-387, making s. 173 of that act effective when it became law (August 26, 2001). As a result of these changes, the amendment by Session Laws 2001-358 is effective January 1, 2002, and applicable to documents submitted for filing on or after that date.

Session Laws 2001-387, s. 154(b) provides that nothing in this act shall supersede the provisions of Article 10 or 65 of Chapter 58 of the General Statutes, and this act does not create an alternate means for an entity governed by Article 65 of Chapter 58 of the General Statutes to convert to a different business form.

Effect of Amendments. — Session Laws 2001-358, s. 27, effective January 1, 2002, and applicable to documents submitted for filing on or after that date, substituted "G.S. 55D-20 and G.S. 55D-21" for "G.S. 57C-2-30" in subdivision (a)(1).

Session Laws 2001-387, s. 58, effective January 1, 2002, added subdivision (4a).

§ 57C-2-22. Amendment of articles of organization.

(a) The articles of organization shall be amended when:
  (1) There is a change in the name of the limited liability company;
  (2) There is a false or erroneous statement in the articles of organization;
  (3) There is a change in the time as stated in the articles of organization for the dissolution of the limited liability company; or
  (4) The members desire to make a change in the articles of organization.

(b) Unless otherwise provided in the articles of organization or a written operating agreement, any amendment to the articles of organization shall require the unanimous vote of the members or, if no initial members of the limited liability company have been identified in the manner provided in this Chapter, by the unanimous vote of the organizers. (1993, c. 354, s. 1; 1999-189, s. 2.4; 2000-140, s. 101(t).)

§ 57C-2-22.1. Restated articles of organization.

(a) A limited liability company may restate its articles of organization at any time with or without member action.

(b) The restated articles of organization may include one or more amendments to the articles of organization. Unless otherwise provided in the articles of organization or a written operating agreement, any amendment requires the unanimous vote of the members or, if no initial members of the limited liability company have been identified in the manner provided in this Chapter, by the unanimous vote of the organizers. The restated articles of organization may include a statement of the address of the current registered office and the name of the current registered agent of the limited liability company.

(c) A limited liability company restating its articles of organization shall deliver to the Secretary of State for filing articles of restatement that:

(1) Set forth the name of the limited liability company.

(2) Attach as an exhibit thereto the text of the restated articles of organization.

(3) State that the restated articles of organization do not contain an amendment or, if the articles do contain an amendment, that there is an amendment that was approved as required by this Chapter.

(d) Duly adopted restated articles of organization supersede the original articles of organization and all amendments to them.

(e) The Secretary of State may certify restated articles of organization as the articles of organization currently in effect, without including the other information required by subsection (c) of this section. (1997-485, s. 18; 1999-189, s. 2.5; 2000-140, s. 101(t).)

Legal Periodicals. — For 1997 legislative survey, see 20 Campbell L. Rev. 389.

§ 57C-2-23. Annual report for Secretary of State.

(a) Each domestic limited liability company other than a professional limited liability company governed by G.S. 57C-2-01(c) and each foreign limited liability company authorized to transact business in this State, shall deliver to the Secretary of State for filing an annual report, in a form prescribed by the Secretary of State, that sets forth all of the following:

(1) The name of the limited liability or foreign limited liability company and the state or country under whose law it is formed.

(2) The street address, and the mailing address if different from the street address, of the registered office, the county in which the registered office is located, and the name of its registered agent at that office in this State, and a statement of any change of the registered office or registered agent, or both.

(3) The address and telephone number of its principal office.

(4) The names and business addresses of its managers or, if the limited liability company has never had members, its organizers.

(5) A brief description of the nature of its business.

If the information contained in the most recently filed annual report has not changed, a certification to that effect may be made instead of setting forth the information required by subdivisions (2) through (5) of this subsection. The Secretary of State shall make available the form required to file an annual report.

(b) Information in the annual report must be current as of the date the annual report is executed on behalf of the limited liability company or the foreign limited liability company.

(c) The Secretary of State must notify limited liability companies of the annual report filing requirement. The annual report shall be delivered to the Secretary of State by April 15th of each year.

(d) If an annual report does not contain the information required by this section, the Secretary of State shall promptly notify the reporting domestic or foreign limited liability company in writing and return the report to it for correction. If the report is corrected to contain the information required by this section and delivered to the Secretary of State within 30 days after the effective date of notice, it is deemed to be timely filed.

(e) Amendments to any previously filed annual report may be filed with the Secretary of State at any time for the purpose of correcting, updating, or augmenting the information contained in the annual report. (1993, c. 354, s. 1; 1997-475, s. 6.7; 2001-387, ss. 59, 59A.)

Editor's Note. — Session Laws 2001-387, s. 154(b) provides that nothing in this act shall supersede the provisions of Article 10 or 65 of Chapter 58 of the General Statutes, and this act does not create an alternate means for an entity governed by Article 65 of Chapter 58 of the General Statutes to convert to a different business form.

Legal Periodicals. — For 1997 legislative survey, see 20 Campbell L. Rev. 389.

§§ 57C-2-24 through 57C-2-29: Reserved for future codification purposes.

Part 3. Name.

§§ 57C-2-30 through 57C-2-34: Repealed by Session Laws 2001-358, s. 30, effective January 1, 2002.

Editor's Note. — Prior to the repeal of this Part, G.S. 57C-2-35 through 57C-2-39 had been set out as reserved for future codification purposes.

Session Laws 2001-358, s. 53, provided that the act, which amended this section, was effective October 1, 2001, and applicable to documents submitted for filing on or after that date. Section 173 of Session Laws 2001-387 changed the effective date of Session Laws 2001-358 from October 1, 2001, to January 1, 2002. Section 6 of Session Laws 2001-413, effective September 14, 2001, added a sentence to s. 175(a) of Session Laws 2001-387, making s. 173 of that act effective when it became law (August 26, 2001). As a result of these changes, the amendment by Session Laws 2001-358 is effective January 1, 2002, and applicable to documents submitted for filing on or after that date.

Session Laws 2001-387, ss. 60 through 63, amended these sections. However, s. 155 of c. 387 repealed ss. 60 through 63, contingent upon the enactment of Session Laws 2001-358. Session Laws 2001-358 was enacted on August 10, 2001.

Session Laws 2001-390, s. 12, rewrote G.S. 57C-2-30(f), effective August 26, 2001, and applicable retroactively to applications for reinstatement made on or after December 1, 1999.

§§ 57C-2-35 through 57C-2-39: Reserved for future codification purposes.

Part 4. Registered Office and Registered Agent.

§ 57C-2-40. Registered office and registered agent.

Each limited liability company must maintain a registered office and registered agent as required by Article 4 of Chapter 55D of the General Statutes and is subject to service on the Secretary of State under that Article. (1993, c. 354, s. 1; 2000-140, s. 101(g); 2001-358, s. 49(a); 2001-387, ss. 173, 175(a); 2001-413, s. 6.)

Editor's Note. — Session Laws 2001-358, s. 53, provided that the act, which amended this section, was effective October 1, 2001, and applicable to documents submitted for filing on or after that date. Section 173 of Session Laws 2001-387 changed the effective date of Session Laws 2001-358 from October 1, 2001, to January 1, 2002. Section 6 of Session Laws 2001-413, effective September 14, 2001, added a sentence to s. 175(a) of Session Laws 2001-387, making s. 173 of that act effective when it became law (August 26, 2001). As a result of these changes, the amendment by Session Laws 2001-358 is effective January 1, 2002, and applicable to documents submitted for filing on or after that date.

Effect of Amendments. — Session Laws 2001-358, s. 49(a), effective January 1, 2002, and applicable to documents submitted for filing on or after that date, rewrote the section.

§§ 57C-2-41, 57C-2-42: Repealed by Session Laws 2001-358, s. 49(c), effective January 1, 2002.

Editor's Note. — Session Laws 2001-358, s. 53, provided that the act, which amended this section, was effective October 1, 2001, and applicable to documents submitted for filing on or after that date. Section 173 of Session Laws 2001-387 changed the effective date of Session Laws 2001-358 from October 1, 2001, to January 1, 2002. Section 6 of Session Laws 2001-413, effective September 14, 2001, added a sentence to s. 175(a) of Session Laws 2001-387, making s. 173 of that act effective when it became law (August 26, 2001). As a result of these changes, the amendment by Session Laws 2001-358 is effective January 1, 2002, and applicable to documents submitted for filing on or after that date.

§ 57C-2-43. Service on limited liability company.

(a) A limited liability company's registered agent is an agent of the limited liability company for service of process, notice, or demand required or permitted by law to be served on the limited liability company.

(b) Whenever a limited liability company shall fail to appoint or maintain a registered agent in this State, or whenever its registered agent cannot with due diligence be found at the registered office, then the Secretary of State shall be an agent of the limited liability company upon whom any process, notice, or demand may be served. Service on the Secretary of State of any such process, notice, or demand shall be made by delivering to and leaving with the Secretary of State or with any clerk authorized by the Secretary of State to accept service of process, duplicate copies of the process, notice, or demand and the fee required by G.S. 57C-1-22(b). In the event any such process, notice, or demand is served on the Secretary of State in the manner provided for in this section, the Secretary of State shall immediately mail one of the copies thereof, by registered or certified mail, return receipt requested, to the limited liability company at its principal office or, if there is no mailing address for the principal office on file, to the limited liability company at its registered office. Service on a limited liability company under this subsection shall be effective for all purposes from and after the date of the service on the Secretary of State.

(c) The Secretary of State shall keep a record of all processes, notices, and demands served upon the Secretary of State under this section and shall record therein the time of the service and his action with reference thereto.

(d) Nothing herein contained shall limit or affect the right to serve any process, notice, or demand required or permitted by law to be served upon a limited liability company in any other manner now or hereafter permitted by law. (1993, c. 354, s. 1; 2000-140, s. 49.)

ARTICLE 3.

Membership and Management.

Part 1. Membership.

§ 57C-3-01. Admission of members.

(a) Unless the articles of organization of a limited liability company provide otherwise, each person executing the articles of organization of a limited liability company in the capacity of a member, and each person who is otherwise named in the articles of organization as a member of the limited liability company, becomes a member at the time that the filing by the Secretary of State of the articles of organization of the limited liability company becomes effective.

(b) A person may be admitted as a member of a limited liability company:

(1) In the case of a person acquiring a membership interest directly from the limited liability company, (i) upon being so identified by the organizers of the limited liability company in accordance with G.S. 57C-2-20(c) or (ii) upon compliance with the articles of organization or operating agreement or, if the articles of organization or operating agreement do not so provide, upon the unanimous consent of the members; and

(2) In the case of an assignee of an interest of a member, upon compliance with the provisions of G.S. 57C-5-04(a).

(c) Nothing in this Chapter precludes a person from being a member of a limited liability company because that person has not made, and has no obligation to make, any contributions to the limited liability company and has no right to receive any distributions from the limited liability company or share in any profits or losses of the limited liability company. (1993, c. 354, s. 1; 1999-189, s. 4.1; 2000-140, s. 101(t); 2001-387, s. 64.)

Editor's Note. — Session Laws 2001-387, s. 154(b) provides that nothing in this act shall supersede the provisions of Article 10 or 65 of Chapter 58 of the General Statutes, and this act does not create an alternate means for an entity governed by Article 65 of Chapter 58 of the General Statutes to convert to a different business form.

Effect of Amendments. — Session laws 2001-387, s. 64, effective January 1, 2002, added subsection (c).

Legal Periodicals. — For note, "Corporate Law — Limited Liability Company Act, N.C. Gen. Stat. G.S. 57C-1-01 to 57C-10-07 (1993)," see 72 N.C.L. Rev. 1654 (1994).

For article, "The Creation of North Carolina's Limited Liability Corporation Act," see 32 Wake Forest L. Rev. 179 (1997).

§ 57C-3-02. Cessation of membership.

Unless otherwise provided in this Chapter, the articles of organization, or a written operating agreement, a person who has ceased to be a member shall have only the rights of an assignee as provided in G.S. 57C-5-02, but shall not be released from his liability to the limited liability company under G.S. 57C-4-02 (liability for contribution) and G.S. 57C-4-07 (liability upon wrongful distribution). A person ceases to be a member of a limited liability company upon the happening of any of the following events of withdrawal:

(1) The person's voluntary withdrawal from the limited liability company as provided in G.S. 57C-5-06;

(2) The person's removal as a member in accordance with the articles of organization or an operating agreement;

(3) Unless otherwise provided in the articles of organization or a written operating agreement or with the consent of all other members, the person's:
   a. Making an assignment for the benefit of creditors;
   b. Filing a voluntary petition in bankruptcy;
   c. Being adjudged bankrupt or insolvent or having entered against him an order for relief in any bankruptcy or insolvency proceeding;
   d. Filing a petition or answer seeking for him any reorganization, arrangement, composition, readjustment, liquidation, dissolution, or similar relief under any statute, law, or regulation;
   e. Seeking, consenting to, or acquiescing in, the appointment of a trustee or receiver for, or liquidation of the person or of all or any substantial part of that person's properties; or
   f. Filing an answer or other pleading admitting or failing to contest the material allegations of a petition filed against the person in any proceeding described in this subdivision;

(4) Unless otherwise provided in the articles of organization or a written operating agreement or with the consent of all other members, the continuation of any proceeding against the person seeking reorganization, arrangement, composition, readjustment, liquidation, dissolution, or similar relief under any statute, law, or regulation, for 120 days after the commencement thereof or the appointment of a trustee, receiver, or liquidator for the person or all or any substantial part of the person's properties without the person's agreement or acquiescence, which appointment is not vacated or stayed for 120 days or, if the appointment is stayed, for 120 days after the expiration of the stay during which period the appointment is not vacated;

(5) Unless otherwise provided in the articles of organization or a written operating agreement or with the consent of all other members, in the case of a member who is an individual, the individual's:
   a. Death; or
   b. Adjudication by a court of competent jurisdiction as incompetent to manage his person or property;

(6) Unless otherwise provided in the articles of organization or a written operating agreement or with the consent of all other members, in the case of a member who is acting as a member by virtue of being a trustee of a trust, the termination of the trust (but not merely the substitution of a new trustee);

(7) Unless otherwise provided in the articles of organization or a written operating agreement or with the consent of all other members, in the case of a member that is a domestic or foreign partnership, a domestic or foreign limited partnership, or another domestic or foreign limited liability company, the dissolution and commencement of winding up of the partnership, limited partnership, or limited liability company;

(8) Unless otherwise provided in the articles of organization or a written operating agreement or with the consent of all other members, in the case of a member that is a domestic or foreign corporation, the dissolution of the corporation or the revocation of its charter; or

(9) Unless otherwise provided in the articles of organization or a written operating agreement or with the consent of all other members, in the case of a member that is an estate, the distribution by the fiduciary of

the estate's entire interest in the limited liability company. (1993, c. 354, s. 1; 1995, c. 351, ss. 5, 6; 2001-387, s. 65.)

Editor's Note. — Session Laws 2001-387, s. 154(b) provides that nothing in this act shall supersede the provisions of Article 10 or 65 of Chapter 58 of the General Statutes, and this act does not create an alternate means for an entity governed by Article 65 of Chapter 58 of the General Statutes to convert to a different business form.

Effect of Amendments. — Session Laws 2001-387, s. 65, effective January 1, 2002, in subdivision (3)e, substituted "the person" for "the member" and substituted "part of that person's" for "part of his."

§ 57C-3-03. Voting of members.

Except as provided in the articles of organization or a written operating agreement, the affirmative vote, approval, agreement, or consent of all members shall be required to:

(1) Adopt or amend an operating agreement;
(2) Admit any person as a member;
(3) Sell, transfer, or otherwise dispose of all or substantially all of the assets of the limited liability company prior to the dissolution of the limited liability company.
(4) Repealed by Session Laws 1999-456, s. 51, effective August 13, 1999. (1993, c. 354, s. 1; 1999-456, s. 51.)

CASE NOTES

Applied in Herring v. Keasler, 150 N.C. App. 598, 563 S.E.2d 614, 2002 N.C. App. LEXIS 585 (2002), review denied, 356 N.C. 435, 572 S.E.2d 431 (2002).

§ 57C-3-04. Members' access to information; records.

(a) Each member has the right, subject to such reasonable standards (including standards governing what information and documents are to be furnished, at what time and location and at whose expense) as may be set forth in the articles of organization or a written operating agreement, to obtain from the limited liability company from time to time upon reasonable demand for any purpose reasonably related to the member's interest as a member:

(1) Information regarding the status of the business and the financial condition of the limited liability company;
(2) Promptly after becoming available, a copy of the limited liability company's federal, State, and local income tax returns for each year;
(3) A current list of the name and last known business, residence, or mailing address of each member;
(4) A copy of the articles of organization and any written operating agreement and all amendments thereto, together with copies of any written powers of attorney pursuant to which the articles of organization, operating agreement, and all amendments thereto have been executed;
(5) Information regarding the amount of cash and a description and statement of the agreed value of any other property or services contributed by each member, and the property and services that each member has agreed to contribute in the future, and the date on which each became a member; and
(6) Such other information regarding the affairs of the limited liability company as is just and reasonable.

(b) A limited liability company may maintain its records in other than written form if the form is capable of conversion into written form within a reasonable time.

(c) Any demand under this section shall (i) be in writing, (ii) be made in good faith and for a proper purpose, and (iii) describe with reasonable particularity the purpose and the records or information desired.

(d) Failure of the limited liability company to keep or maintain any of the records or information required pursuant to this section shall not be grounds for imposing liability on any person for the debts and obligations of the limited liability company.

(e) The managers shall have the right to keep confidential from members who are not managers, for such period of time as the managers deem reasonable, any information which the managers reasonably believe to be in the nature of trade secrets or other information the disclosure of which the managers in good faith believe is not in the best interest of the limited liability company. The authority authorized in this subsection may be vested in directors instead of managers to the extent provided in the articles of organization or a written operating agreement. (1993, c. 354, s. 1; 2001-387, s. 66; 2001-487, s. 62(i).)

Editor's Note. — Session Laws 2001-387, s. 154(b) provides that nothing in this act shall supersede the provisions of Article 10 or 65 of Chapter 58 of the General Statutes, and this act does not create an alternate means for an entity governed by Article 65 of Chapter 58 of the General Statutes to convert to a different business form.

Effect of Amendments. — Session Laws 2001-387, s. 66, effective January 1, 2002, inserted "or directors" following "managers" throughout subsection (e).

Session Laws 2001-487, s. 62(i), effective January 1, 2002, in subsection (e), as amended by Session Laws 2001-387, s. 66, substituted "managers" for "managers or directors" throughout, and added the second sentence.

§ 57C-3-05. Members bound by operating agreements.

A member shall be bound by any operating agreement, including any amendment thereto, otherwise valid under this Chapter and other applicable law, (i) to which the member has expressly assented, or (ii) which was in effect at the time the member became a member and either was in writing or the terms of which were actually known to the member, or (iii) with respect to any amendment, if the member was bound by the operating agreement as in effect immediately prior to such amendment and such amendment was adopted in accordance with the terms of such operating agreement. The articles of organization or written operating agreement may require that all agreements of the members constituting the operating agreement be in writing, in which case the term "operating agreement" shall not include oral agreements of the members. Except to the extent otherwise provided in a written operating agreement, a limited liability company shall be deemed for all purposes to be a party to the operating agreement of its member or members. (1993, c. 354, s. 1; 1999-189, s. 4.2; 2000-140, s. 101(t).)

§§ 57C-3-06 through 57C-3-19: Reserved for future codification purposes.

Part 2. Managers.

§ 57C-3-20. Determination of managers; management.

(a) Unless the articles of organization provide otherwise, all members by virtue of their status as members shall be managers of the limited liability company, together with any other persons that may be designated as managers in, or in accordance with, the articles of organization or a written operating agreement. If the articles of organization provide that all members are not necessarily managers by virtue of their status as members, then those persons designated as managers in, or in accordance with, the articles of organization or a written operating agreement shall be managers, but for any period during which no such designation has been made or is in effect, all members shall be managers.

(b) Except to the extent otherwise provided in the articles of organization or a written operating agreement, management of the affairs of the limited liability company shall be vested in the managers. Subject to any provisions in the articles of organization or a written operating agreement or this Chapter restricting, enlarging, or modifying the management rights and duties of any manager or managers, or management procedures, each manager shall have equal rights and authority to participate in the management of the limited liability company, and management decisions shall require the approval, consent, agreement, or ratification of a majority of the managers. (1993, c. 354, s. 1; 1999-189, s. 4.3; 2000-140, s. 101(t); 2001-387, s. 67.)

Editor's Note. — Session Laws 2001-387, s. 154(b) provides that nothing in this act shall supersede the provisions of Article 10 or 65 of Chapter 58 of the General Statutes, and this act does not create an alternate means for an entity governed by Article 65 of Chapter 58 of the General Statutes to convert to a different business form.

Effect of Amendments. — Session Laws 2001-387, s. 67, effective January 1, 2002, in subsection (a), substituted "managers in, or in accordance with the articles of organization or a written" for "managers in a written" three times.

§ 57C-3-21. Qualification, designation, and removal of managers.

Subject to G.S. 57C-3-20(a), the articles of organization or a written operating agreement may set forth the number and qualification of managers and the manner in which they are to be designated, removed, and replaced. Unless otherwise provided in the articles of organization, a written operating agreement, or this Chapter:

(1) Managers need not be members and, unless otherwise required by G.S. 57C-3-20(a), members need not be managers;

(2) Designation of managers (other than those managers who are such by virtue of their status as members) shall be evidenced in a written operating agreement, as amended from time to time;

(3) Upon designation as manager and the person's consent to such designation, the designated person shall serve as manager until the earliest to occur of (i) the person's resignation, (ii) any event described in G.S. 57C-3-02 with respect to the manager, (iii) any event specified in the articles of organization or written operating agreement that results in a manager ceasing to be a manager, or (iv) in the case of a person designated as a manager in a written operating agreement, the amendment of the written operating agreement removing the person's designation as a manager. (1993, c. 354, s. 1; 1995, c. 351, s. 7; 2001-487, s. 62(j).)

Effect of Amendments. — Session Laws 2001-487, s. 62(j), effective January 1, 2002, in subdivision (3), deleted "in a written operating agreement" following "Upon designation as manager" and inserted "in the case of a person designated as a manager in a written operating agreement" at the beginning of clause (iv).

§ 57C-3-22. Duties of managers.

(a) The provisions of this section are all subject to G.S. 57C-3-30.

(b) A manager shall discharge his duties as manager in good faith, with the care an ordinary prudent person in a like position would exercise under similar circumstances, and in the manner the manager reasonably believes to be in the best interests of the limited liability company. In discharging his duties, a manager is entitled to rely on information, opinions, reports, or statements, including, but not limited to, financial statements or other financial data, if prepared or presented by:

    (1) One or more employees of the limited liability company whom the manager reasonably believes to be reliable and competent in the matters presented;

    (2) Legal counsel, certified public accountants, or other persons on matters the manager reasonably believes are within the person's professional or expert competence; or

    (3) A committee of managers of which the manager is not a member if the manager reasonably believes the committee merits confidence.

(c) A manager is not acting in good faith if the manager has actual knowledge concerning the matter in question that makes reliance otherwise permitted by subsection (b) of this section unwarranted.

(d) A manager is not liable for any action taken as a manager, or any failure to take any action, if the manager performs the duties of his office in compliance with this section.

(e) Except as otherwise provided in the articles of organization or a written operating agreement, every manager must account to the limited liability company and hold as trustee for it any profit or benefit derived without the informed consent of the members by the manager from any transaction connected with the formation, conduct, or liquidation of the limited liability company or from any personal use by the manager of its property.

(f) Except to the extent otherwise provided in the articles of organization or a written operating agreement, each director and executive shall be subject to the same requirements and afforded the same rights as are provided in this section for a manager when the director or executive exercises authority in the management of a limited liability company's affairs that would otherwise be vested in the managers pursuant to G.S. 57C-3-20(b). (1993, c. 354, s. 1; 2001-387, s. 68.)

Editor's Note. — Session Laws 2001-387, s. 154(b) provides that nothing in this act shall supersede the provisions of Article 10 or 65 of Chapter 58 of the General Statutes, and this act does not create an alternate means for an entity governed by Article 65 of Chapter 58 of the General Statutes to convert to a different business form.

Effect of Amendments. — Session Laws 2001-387, s. 68, effective January 1, 2002, added subsection (f).

§ 57C-3-23. Agency power of managers.

Every manager is an agent of the limited liability company for the purpose of its business, and the act of every manager, including execution in the name of the limited liability company of any instrument, for apparently carrying on in the usual way the business of the limited liability company of which he is a manager, binds the limited liability company, unless the manager so acting has in fact no authority to act for the limited liability company in the particular matter and the person with whom the manager is dealing has knowledge of the fact that the manager has no authority. An act of a manager that is not apparently for carrying on the usual course of the business of the limited liability company does not bind the limited liability company unless authorized in fact or ratified by the limited liability company. (1993, c. 354, s. 1; 2001-487, s. 62(l).)

Effect of Amendments. — Session Laws 2001-487, s. 62(l), effective January 1, 2002, deleted "the managers of" preceding "the limited liability company" at the end of the section.

§ 57C-3-24. Delegation of authority of managers.

(a) The authority of a manager or the managers to act on behalf of the limited liability company may be delegated by such manager or the managers to persons other than managers if and to the extent a written operating agreement so provides. The delegation of authority may be general or limited to specific matters. The act of any such person within the scope of the authority so delegated shall be as effective to bind the limited liability company as would the act of such manager or the managers, unless the delegation has been revoked and the person with whom such person is dealing has actual knowledge of the fact that the delegation has been revoked.

(b) The creation of, delegation of authority to, or action by a manager's delegate does not alone constitute compliance by a manager with the standards of conduct described in G.S. 57C-3-22.

(c) Each person acting on behalf of the limited liability company within the scope of authority delegated by a manager or the managers pursuant to subsection (a) of this section, or reasonably and in good faith believing himself to be so acting, shall be entitled, with respect to such acts, to the same limitation on personal liability as is afforded to a manager pursuant to G.S. 57C-3-30. A limited liability company may, but is not required to, provide persons acting on behalf of the limited liability company within the scope of the authority delegated by a manager or the managers pursuant to subsection (a) of this section with the same limitation on personal liability and rights to indemnification as are, or may be, afforded to managers pursuant to G.S. 57C-3-31 and G.S. 57C-3-32. (1993, c. 354, s. 1.)

§ 57C-3-25. Identity of managers, authentication of records, and execution of documents.

(a) Any person dealing with a limited liability company or a foreign limited liability company may rely conclusively upon its most recent annual report and any amendments to it on file with the Secretary of State as to the identity of its managers, except to the extent the person has actual knowledge that a person identified therein as a manager is not a manager.

(b) The documents, if any, constituting the operating agreement of a limited liability company or a foreign limited liability company authorized to transact business in this State, and records of the actions of its members, managers, directors, or executives may be authenticated by any manager of the domestic or foreign limited liability company. Any person dealing with the domestic or foreign limited liability company may rely conclusively upon the certificate or written statement of a manager authenticating the documents and records except to the extent the person has actual knowledge that the certificate or written statement is false.

(c) Any document or instrument required or permitted by law to be filed, registered, or recorded with any public authority and to be executed by a limited liability company or a foreign limited liability company authorized to transact business in this State shall be sufficiently executed for such purpose if signed on its behalf by one of its managers. (1993, c. 354, s. 1; 1997-475, s. 6.8; 2001-487, s. 62(m).)

Editor's Note. — Session Laws 1997-475, s. 6.12, effective September 4, 1997, provides, in part, that the 1997 amendment to this section "becomes effective January 1, 1998, and applies to tax years ending on or after December 31, 1997, in the case of corporations required to file annual reports with the Secretary of Revenue and to fiscal years ending on or after December 31, 1997, in the case of corporations and limited liability companies required to file annual reports with the Secretary of State."

Effect of Amendments. — Session Laws 2001-487, s. 62(m), effective January 1, 2002, substituted "members, managers, directors, or executives" for "members or managers" in the first sentence in subsection (b).

§§ 57C-3-26 through 57C-3-29: Reserved for future codification purposes.

Part 3. Liability.

§ 57C-3-30. Liability to third parties of members, managers, directors, and executives; parties to actions; governing law.

(a) A person who is a member, manager, director, executive, or any combination thereof of a limited liability company is not liable for the obligations of a limited liability company solely by reason of being a member, manager, director, or executive and does not become so by participating, in whatever capacity, in the management or control of the business. A member, manager, director, or executive may, however, become personally liable by reason of that person's own acts or conduct.

(b) A member of a limited liability company is not a proper party to proceedings by or against a limited liability company, except where the object of the proceeding is to enforce a member's right against or liability to the limited liability company.

(c) The liability of members, managers, directors, and executives of a limited liability company formed and existing under this Chapter shall at all times be determined solely and exclusively by this Chapter and the laws of this State.

(d) If a conflict arises between the laws of this State and the laws of any other jurisdiction with regard to the liability of members, managers, directors, or executives of a limited liability company formed and existing under this Chapter for the debts, obligations, and liabilities of the limited liability company, this Chapter and the laws of this State shall govern in determining the liability. (1993, c. 354, s. 1; 2001-387, s. 69.)

Editor's Note. — Session Laws 2001-387, s. 154(b) provides that nothing in this act shall supersede the provisions of Article 10 or 65 of Chapter 58 of the General Statutes, and this act does not create an alternate means for an entity governed by Article 65 of Chapter 58 of the General Statutes to convert to a different business form.

Effect of Amendments. — Session Laws 2001-387, s. 69, effective January 1, 2002, sub-stituted "members, managers, directors, and executives" for "members and managers" in the section heading; rewrote subsection (a); substituted "members, managers, directors, and executives" for "members and managers" and substituted "formed" for "organized" in subsections (c) and (d); and substituted "members, managers, directors, or executives" for "member or manager" in subsection (d).

CASE NOTES

Violation to Name Individual Member as Party Defendant. — Under this section, it was improper to name an individual member of a limited liability company as a party defendant without any evidence to support it; thus, the naming of member as an individual defen-

dant was not well-grounded in law and therefore a violation of G.S. 1A-1-11. Page v. Roscoe,
128 N.C. App. 678, 497 S.E.2d 422 (1998).

§ 57C-3-31. Mandatory indemnification of managers, directors, executives, and members.

(a) Unless otherwise provided in the articles of organization or a written
operating agreement, a limited liability company must indemnify every
manager, director, and executive in respect of payments made and personal
liabilities reasonably incurred by the manager, director, and executive in the
authorized conduct of its business or for the preservation of its business or
property.

(b) Unless otherwise provided in the articles of organization or a written
operating agreement, a limited liability company shall indemnify a member,
manager, director, or executive who is wholly successful, on the merits or
otherwise, in the defense of any proceeding to which the person was a party
because the person is or was a member, manager, director, or executive of the
limited liability company against reasonable expenses incurred by the person
in connection with the proceeding. (1993, c. 354, s. 1; 2001-387, s. 70.)

Editor's Note. — Session Laws 2001-387, s.
154(b) provides that nothing in this act shall
supersede the provisions of Article 10 or 65 of
Chapter 58 of the General Statutes, and this
act does not create an alternate means for an
entity governed by Article 65 of Chapter 58 of
the General Statutes to convert to a different
business form.

Effect of Amendments. — Session Laws
2001-387, s. 70, effective January 1, 2002, rewrote the section.

§ 57C-3-32. Limitation of liability of managers, directors, executives, and members and permissive indemnification of managers, directors, executives, and members; insurance.

(a) Subject to subsection (b) of this section, the articles of organization or a
written operating agreement may:

(1) Eliminate or limit the personal liability of a manager, director, or
executive for monetary damages for breach of any duty provided for in
G.S. 57C-3-22 (other than liability under G.S. 57C-4-07); and

(2) Provide for indemnification of a manager, member, director, or executive for judgments, settlements, penalties, fines, or expenses incurred
in a proceeding to which the member, manager, director, or executive
is a party because the person is or was a manager, member, director,
or executive. For purposes of this subdivision, the words "expenses",
"proceeding", and "party" shall have the meanings set forth in G.S.
55-8-50(b).

(b) No provision permitted under subsection (a) of this section shall limit,
eliminate, or indemnify against the liability of a manager, director, or executive for (i) acts or omissions that the manager, director, or executive knew at
the time of the acts or omissions were clearly in conflict with the interests of
the limited liability company, (ii) any transaction from which the manager,
director, or executive derived an improper personal benefit, or (iii) acts or
omissions occurring prior to the date the provision became effective, except
that indemnification pursuant to subdivision (2) of subsection (a) of this section
may be provided if approved by all the members. As used in this subsection,
"improper personal benefit" does not include reasonable compensation or other
reasonable incidental benefit for or on account of service as a manager,

director, executive, officer, employee, independent contractor, attorney, or consultant of the limited liability company.

(c) A limited liability company may purchase and maintain insurance on behalf of an individual who is or was a manager, director, executive, officer, employee, or agent of the limited liability company, or who, while a manager, director, executive, officer, employee, or agent of the limited liability company is or was serving at the request of the limited liability company as a director, executive, officer, partner, member, manager, trustee, employee, or agent of a person, against liability asserted against or incurred by the person in that capacity or arising from the person's status as a manager, director, executive, officer, employee, or agent, whether or not the limited liability company would have the power to indemnify the person against the same liability under any provision of this Chapter. (1993, c. 354, s. 1; 1995, c. 351, ss. 8, 9; 1999-189, s. 4.4; 2000-140, s. 101(t); 2001-387, s. 71.)

Editor's Note. — Session Laws 2001-387, s. 154(b) provides that nothing in this act shall supersede the provisions of Article 10 or 65 of Chapter 58 of the General Statutes, and this act does not create an alternate means for an entity governed by Article 65 of Chapter 58 of the General Statutes to convert to a different business form.

Effect of Amendments. — Session Laws 2001-387, s. 71, effective January 1, 2002, inserted "directors, executives" twice in the catchline; inserted "director, or executive" in subdivision (a)(1) and throughout subsection (b); rewrote subdivision (a)(2); in subsection (b), inserted "director, executive" in the second sentence; in subsection (c), inserted "director, executive, officer" throughout, inserted "executive" following "as a director" and inserted "member" following "officer, partner"; and made minor stylistic changes throughout the section.

ARTICLE 4.

Finance.

§ 57C-4-01. Contributions to capital.

The contribution of a member may be in the form of any tangible or intangible property or benefit to the limited liability company that a person contributes in cash, property, services rendered, promissory notes, or other binding obligation to contribute cash or property or to render services. Except as provided in an operating agreement, in the case of noncash contributions, the value of the contribution to the limited liability company shall be the fair market value of the contribution on the date it is made, as agreed to by the limited liability company and the contributor. (1993, c. 354, s. 1.)

Legal Periodicals. — For note, "Corporate Law — Limited Liability Company Act, N.C. Gen. Stat. G.S. 57C-1-01 to 57C-10-07 (1993)," see 72 N.C.L. Rev. 1654 (1994).

For article, "The Creation of North Carolina's Limited Liability Corporation Act," see 32 Wake Forest L. Rev. 179 (1997).

§ 57C-4-02. Liability for contribution.

(a) A promise by a member to contribute to the limited liability company is not enforceable unless set out in a writing signed by the member.

(b) Except as provided in an operating agreement, a member is obligated to the limited liability company to perform any enforceable promises to contribute cash or property or to render services, even if the member is unable to perform because of death, disability, or any other reason. If a member does not make the required contribution of property or services, the member (or the member's estate or personal representative) is obligated, at the option of the limited liability company, to contribute cash equal to that portion of the value of the stated contribution that has not been made.

(c) Unless otherwise provided in the operating agreement, the obligation of a member to make a contribution or to return money or other property paid or distributed in violation of this Chapter may be compromised only with the unanimous consent of the members. Any such compromise, however, shall not affect the rights of a creditor of a limited liability company to enforce a claim that arose prior to the date of the compromise. (1993, c. 354, s. 1.)

§ 57C-4-03. Allocation of income, gain, loss, deduction, or credit.

Income, gain, loss, deduction, or credit of a limited liability company shall be allocated among the members, and among classes of members, in the manner agreed to in an operating agreement. To the extent an operating agreement does not so provide for the allocation of such items, income, gain, loss, deduction, or credit shall be allocated among the members in proportion to the agreed value, as stated in the limited liability company records required to be kept pursuant to G.S. 57C-3-04(a)(5), of the contributions made by each member, taking into account variations in the capital contributions of each member during the period for which the allocations are made using any reasonable method selected by the managers. (1993, c. 354, s. 1.)

§ 57C-4-04. Interim distributions.

Except as provided in this Chapter, a member is entitled to receive distributions from a limited liability company before the withdrawal of the member from the limited liability company and before the dissolution and winding up of the limited liability company as provided in an operating agreement. In the absence of any provision for interim distributions in an operating agreement, such distributions may be made at such times and in such amounts as determined by the managers, in proportion to the agreed value, as stated in the limited liability company records required to be kept pursuant to G.S. 57C-3-04(a)(5), of the contributions made by each member as of the date of such distribution, or as of such date within 90 days prior to the distribution that may be determined by the managers. (1993, c. 354, s. 1.)

§ 57C-4-05. Distribution in kind.

Except as provided in an operating agreement:
  (1) A member, regardless of the nature of the member's contribution, has no right to demand or receive any distribution from a limited liability company in any form other than cash; and
  (2) No member may be compelled to accept from a limited liability company a distribution of any asset in kind unless all persons with interests in the limited liability company receive at the same time as a distribution an interest in the property distributed that is proportionate to their interests in the limited liability company. (1993, c. 354, s. 1.)

§ 57C-4-06. Restrictions on making distributions.

(a) No distribution may be made if, after giving effect to the distribution:
  (1) The limited liability company would not be able to pay its debts as they become due in the usual course of business; or

(2) The limited liability company's total assets would be less than the sum of its total liabilities plus, unless the operating agreement provides otherwise, the amount that would be needed, if the limited liability company were to be dissolved at the time of the distribution, to satisfy the preferential rights upon dissolution of members whose preferential rights are superior to the rights of the member receiving the distribution.

(b) The limited liability company may base a determination that a distribution is not prohibited under subsection (a) of this section on financial statements prepared on the basis of accounting practices and principles that are reasonable under the circumstances; and for this purpose may determine asset values based on book values or on a fair market valuation or other method that is reasonable under the circumstances.

(c) Except as provided in subsection (e) of this section, the effect of a distribution under subsection (a) of this section is measured as of (i) the date the distribution is authorized if the payment occurs within 120 days after the date of authorization; or (ii) the date payment is made if it occurs more than 120 days after the date of authorization.

(d) A limited liability company's indebtedness issued as a distribution made in accordance with this section is at parity with the limited liability company's indebtedness to its general, unsecured creditors except to the extent otherwise provided by agreement.

(e) Indebtedness of a limited liability company, including indebtedness issued as a distribution, is not considered a liability for purposes of determinations under subsection (a) of this section if its terms provide that payment of principal and interest are made only if, and to the extent that, payment of a distribution to members could then be made under this section. If indebtedness with such terms is issued as a distribution, each payment of principal or interest, and not the issuance of the indebtedness, is treated as a distribution, the effect of which is measured on the date the payment is actually made. (1993, c. 354, s. 1.)

§ 57C-4-07. Liability upon wrongful distribution.

(a) A manager or director who votes for or assents to a distribution in violation of G.S. 57C-4-06 or a written operating agreement is personally liable to the limited liability company for the amount of the distribution that exceeds what could have been distributed without violating G.S. 57C-4-06 or the operating agreement if it is established that the manager or director did not act in compliance with G.S. 57C-3-22.

(b) Each manager or director held liable under subsection (a) of this section for a wrongful distribution is entitled to:
(1) Contribution from each other manager or director who could be held liable under subsection (a) of this section for the wrongful distribution; and
(2) Reimbursement from each member for the amount the member received knowing that the distribution was made in violation of G.S. 57C-4-06 or the operating agreement.

(c) A proceeding under this section is barred unless it is commenced within three years after the date on which the effect of the distribution is measured under G.S. 57C-4-06(c). (1993, c. 354, s. 1; 2001-387, s. 72.)

Editor's Note. — Session Laws 2001-387, s. 154(b) provides that nothing in this act shall supersede the provisions of Article 10 or 65 of Chapter 58 of the General Statutes, and this act does not create an alternate means for an entity governed by Article 65 of Chapter 58 of the General Statutes to convert to a different business form.

Effect of Amendments. — Session Laws 2001-387, s. 72, effective January 1, 2002, inserted "or director" following "manager" throughout the section.

§ 57C-4-08. Right to distribution.

Subject to the provisions of this Article, at the time a member becomes entitled to receive a distribution, the member has the status of, and is entitled to all remedies available to, a creditor of the limited liability company with respect to the distribution. (1993, c. 354, s. 1.)

ARTICLE 5.

Assignment of Membership Interests; Withdrawal.

§ 57C-5-01. Nature of membership interest.

A membership interest is personal property. A member has no interest in specific limited liability company property. (1993, c. 354, s. 1.)

Legal Periodicals. — For note, "Corporate Law — Limited Liability Company Act, N.C. Gen. Stat. G.S. 57C-1-01 to 57C-10-07 (1993)," see 72 N.C.L. Rev. 1654 (1994).

For article, "The Creation of North Carolina's Limited Liability Corporation Act," see 32 Wake Forest L. Rev. 179 (1997).

§ 57C-5-02. Assignment of membership interest.

Except as provided in the articles of organization or a written operating agreement, a membership interest is assignable in whole or in part. An assignment of a membership interest does not dissolve the limited liability company or entitle the assignee to become or exercise any rights of a member. An assignment entitles the assignee to receive, to the extent assigned, only the distributions and allocations to which the assignor would be entitled but for the assignment. Except as provided in the articles of organization or a written operating agreement, a member ceases to be a member upon assignment of all of his membership interest. Except as provided in the articles of organization or a written operating agreement, the pledge of, or granting of a security interest, lien, or other encumbrance in or against, all or any part of the membership interest of a member shall not cause the member to cease to be a member or the secured party to have the power to exercise any rights or powers of a member. (1993, c. 354, s. 1.)

CASE NOTES

Applied in Herring v. Keasler, 150 N.C. App. 598, 563 S.E.2d 614, 2002 N.C. App. LEXIS 585 (2002), review denied, 356 N.C. 435, 572 S.E.2d 431 (2002).

§ 57C-5-03. Rights of judgment creditor.

On application to a court of competent jurisdiction by any judgment creditor of a member, the court may charge the membership interest of the member with payment of the unsatisfied amount of the judgment with interest. To the extent so charged, the judgment creditor has only the rights of an assignee of the membership interest. This Chapter does not deprive any member of the benefit of any exemption laws applicable to his membership interest. (1993, c. 354, s. 1.)

CASE NOTES

Forced Sale of Judgment Debtor's Membership Interests Properly Refused. — Trial court properly ordered defendant debtor's distributions and allocations from certain limited liability companies in which the debtor had membership interests to be applied to satisfy a judgment, and properly denied plaintiff assignee's motion to order the membership interests to be seized and sold, because pursuant to G.S. 57C-5-03, the trial court was allowed to charge the membership interests with payment of the judgment. Nevertheless, such charging did not entitle the assignee to become a member or exercise a member's rights, and therefore, because forcing the sale of the membership interests to satisfy the debt would have entailed the assignee becoming a member of the limited liability companies, a forced sale like that otherwise allowed by G.S. 1-362 was prohibited. Herring v. Keasler, 150 N.C. App. 598, 563 S.E.2d 614, 2002 N.C. App. LEXIS 585 (2002), review denied, 356 N.C. 435, 572 S.E.2d 431 (2002).

§ 57C-5-04. Right of assignee to become a member.

(a) An assignee of an interest in a limited liability company may become a member only with the assignee's consent and, except as otherwise provided in the articles of organization or operating agreement, only if the other members unanimously agree. The consent of a member may be evidenced in any manner specified in the operating agreement, but in the absence of such specification, consent shall be evidenced by a written instrument, dated and signed by the member, or evidenced by a vote taken at a meeting of members.

(b) An assignee who becomes a member has, to the extent assigned, the rights and powers, and is subject to the restrictions and liabilities, of a member under the articles of organization, any operating agreements, and this Chapter. Notwithstanding the preceding sentence, unless otherwise provided in a written operating agreement, an assignee who becomes a member is liable for any obligations of his assignor to make contributions under G.S. 57C-4-02 (liability for contribution) but shall not be liable for obligations of his assignor under G.S. 57C-4-07 (liability upon wrongful distribution). However, the assignee is not obligated for liabilities unknown to the assignee at the time the assignee became a member and which could not be ascertained from the articles of organization or a written operating agreement.

(c) Whether or not an assignee of a membership interest becomes a member, the assignor is not released from his liability to the limited liability company under G.S. 57C-4-02 (liability for contribution) and G.S. 57C-4-07 (liability upon wrongful distribution). (1993, c. 354, s. 1.)

§ 57C-5-05. Powers of legal representative of a deceased, incompetent, or dissolved member.

Unless otherwise provided in the articles of organization or a written operating agreement, if a member who is an individual dies or a court of competent jurisdiction adjudges the member to be incompetent to manage his person or his property, the member's executor, administrator, guardian, conservator, or other legal representative may exercise all of the member's rights for the purpose of settling his estate or administering his property, including any power the member had under the articles of organization or a written operating agreement to give an assignee the right to become a member. If a member is a corporation, trust, or other entity and is dissolved or terminated, the powers of that member may be exercised by its legal representative or successor for the purpose of liquidating, winding up, and making final distributions of the entity's assets to its owners, beneficiaries, or creditors. (1993, c. 354, s. 1.)

§ 57C-5-06. Voluntary withdrawal of member.

A member may withdraw only at the time or upon the happening of the events specified in the articles of organization or a written operating agreement. (1993, c. 354, s. 1; 1999-189, s. 4.5; 2000-140, s. 101(t).)

§ 57C-5-07. Distribution upon withdrawal.

Except as provided in and to the extent provided under this Chapter, upon withdrawal, any withdrawing member is entitled to receive any distribution to which he is otherwise entitled under the articles of organization or a written operating agreement, or, if not otherwise provided in the articles of organization or a written operating agreement, upon a reasonable time after withdrawal, the fair value of the member's interest in the limited liability company as of the date of withdrawal based upon the member's right to share in distributions from the limited liability company. (1995, c. 351, s. 10; 1999-189, s. 4.6; 2000-140, s. 101(t).)

ARTICLE 6.

Dissolution.

§ 57C-6-01. Dissolution.

A limited liability company is dissolved and its affairs shall be wound up at or upon the first to occur of the following:
  (1) The time specified in the articles of organization or a written operating agreement;
  (2) The happening of an event specified in the articles of organization or a written operating agreement;
  (3) The written consent of all members;
  (4) Unless otherwise provided in the articles of organization or a written operating agreement, at such time that the limited liability company no longer has any members. The foregoing to the contrary notwithstanding, unless otherwise provided in the articles of organization or a written operating agreement, a limited liability company shall not be dissolved and is not required to be wound up by reason of any event of withdrawal of the last remaining member if, within 90 days after the event of withdrawal, the assignee or the fiduciary of the estate of the last remaining member agrees in writing that the business of the limited liability company may be continued until the admission of the assignee or the fiduciary of the estate of the member or its designee to the limited liability company as a member, effective as of the occurrence of the event that causes the withdrawal of the last remaining member; or
  (5) Entry of a decree of judicial dissolution under G.S. 57C-6-02, or the filing by the Secretary of State of a certificate of dissolution under G.S. 57C-6-03. (1993, c. 354, s. 1; 1995, c. 351, s. 12; 1999-189, s. 5.1; 2000-140, s. 101(t).)

Legal Periodicals. — For note, "Corporate Law — Limited Liability Company Act, N.C. Gen. Stat. G.S. 57C-1-01 to 57C-10-07 (1993)," see 72 N.C.L. Rev. 1654 (1994). For article, "The Creation of North Carolina's Limited Liability Corporation Act," see 32 Wake Forest L. Rev. 179 (1997).

§ 57C-6-02. Grounds for judicial dissolution.

The superior court may dissolve a limited liability company in a proceeding by the following:

(1) The Attorney General if it is established that (i) the limited liability company obtained its articles of organization through fraud; or (ii) the limited liability company has, after written notice by the Attorney General given at least 120 days prior thereto, continued to exceed or abuse the authority conferred upon it by law;

(2) A member if it is established that (i) the managers, directors, or any other persons in control of the limited liability company are deadlocked in the management of the affairs of the limited liability company, the members are unable to break the deadlock, and irreparable injury to the limited liability company is threatened or being suffered, or the business and affairs of the limited liability company can no longer be conducted to the advantage of the members generally, because of the deadlock; (ii) liquidation is reasonably necessary for the protection of the rights or interests of the complaining member, (iii) the assets of the limited liability company are being misapplied or wasted; or (iv) the articles of organization or a written operating agreement entitles the complaining member to dissolution of the limited liability company; or

(3) The limited liability company to have its voluntary dissolution continued under court supervision. (1993, c. 354, s. 1; 1995, c. 351, s. 11; 1999-189, s. 5.2; 2000-140, s. 101(t); 2001-387, s. 73.)

Editor's Note. — Session Laws 2001-387, s. 154(b) provides that nothing in this act shall supersede the provisions of Article 10 or 65 of Chapter 58 of the General Statutes, and this act does not create an alternate means for an entity governed by Article 65 of Chapter 58 of the General Statutes to convert to a different business form.

Effect of Amendments. — Session Laws 2001-387, s. 73, effective January 1, 2002, substituted "managers, directors, or any other persons in control" for "managers or those in control" near the beginning of subdivision (2).

§ 57C-6-02.1. Procedure for judicial dissolution.

(a) Venue for a proceeding to dissolve a limited liability company lies in the county where the limited liability company's principal office (or, if none in this State, its registered office) is or was last located.

(b) It is not necessary to join members as parties to a proceeding to dissolve a limited liability company unless relief is sought against them individually, however the court shall order that appropriate notice of the dissolution proceeding be given to all members by the party initiating the proceeding.

(c) A court in a proceeding brought to dissolve a limited liability company may issue injunctions, appoint a receiver with all powers and duties the court directs, take other action required to preserve the assets of the limited liability company, wherever located, and carry on the business of the limited liability company.

(d) In any proceeding brought by a member under G.S. 57C-6-02(2)(ii) in which the court determines that dissolution would be appropriate, the court shall not order dissolution if, after the court's determination, the limited liability company elects to purchase the membership interest of the complaining member at its fair value, as determined in accordance with any procedures the court may provide. (1999-189, s. 5.3; 2000-140, s. 101(t).)

§ 57C-6-02.2. Receivership.

(a) A court in a judicial proceeding brought to dissolve a limited liability company may appoint one or more receivers to wind up or to manage the business and affairs of the limited liability company. Before appointing a receiver, the court shall hold a hearing after notifying all parties to the proceeding and any interested persons designated by the court. The court appointing a receiver has exclusive jurisdiction over the limited liability company and all of its property, wherever located.

(b) The court may appoint an individual or other person as a receiver. The court may require the receiver to post bond, with or without sureties, in an amount the court directs.

(c) The court shall describe the powers and duties of the receiver in its appointing order, which may be amended from time to time. The powers may include the authority to:

    (1) Dispose of all or any part of the assets of the limited liability company wherever located, at a public or private sale, if authorized by the court;

    (2) Sue and defend in the receiver's own name as receiver of the limited liability company in all courts of this State; and

    (3) Exercise all of the powers of the limited liability company, through or in place of its managers, to the extent necessary to manage the affairs of the limited liability company in the best interests of its members and creditors.

(d) From time to time during the receivership, the court may order compensation paid and expense disbursements or reimbursements made to the receiver and the receiver's counsel from the assets of the limited liability company or proceeds from the sale of the assets. (1999-189, s. 5.4; 2000-140, s. 101(t).)

§ 57C-6-02.3. Decree of dissolution.

(a) If, after a hearing, the court determines that one or more grounds for judicial dissolution described in G.S. 57C-6-02 exist, it may enter a decree dissolving the limited liability company and specifying the effective date of the dissolution, and the clerk of the court shall deliver a certified copy of the decree to the Secretary of State, who shall file it.

(b) After entering the decree of dissolution, the court shall direct the winding up of the limited liability company's business and affairs in accordance with G.S. 57C-6-04 and G.S. 57C-6-05 and the notification of claimants in accordance with G.S. 57C-6-07 and G.S. 57C-6-08. The limited liability company's name becomes available for use by another entity as provided in G.S. 55D-21. (1999-189, s. 5.5; 2000-140, s. 101(t); 2001-358, s. 31; 2001-387, ss. 173, 175(a); 2001-413, s. 6.)

Editor's Note. — Session Laws 2001-358, s. 53, provided that the act, which amended this section, was effective October 1, 2001, and applicable to documents submitted for filing on or after that date. Section 173 of Session Laws 2001-387 changed the effective date of Session Laws 2001-358 from October 1, 2001, to January 1, 2002. Section 6 of Session Laws 2001-413, effective September 14, 2001, added a sentence to s. 175(a) of Session Laws 2001-387, making s. 173 of that act effective when it became law (August 26, 2001). As a result of these changes, the amendment by Session Laws 2001-358 is effective January 1, 2002, and applicable to documents submitted for filing on ar after that date.

Effect of Amendments. — Session Laws 2001-358, s. 31, effective January 1, 2002, and applicable to documents submitted for filing on or after that date, added the last sentence to subsection (b).

§ 57C-6-03. Administrative dissolution.

(a) The Secretary of State may administratively dissolve a limited liability company if the Secretary of State determines that:

    (1) The limited liability company has not paid within 60 days after they are due any penalties, fees, or other payments due under this Chapter;

    (2) The limited liability company does not deliver its annual report to the Secretary of State on or before the date it is due;

    (3) The limited liability company has been without a registered agent or registered office in this State for 60 days or more;

    (4) The limited liability company has not notified the Secretary of State within 60 days that its registered agent or registered office has been changed, that its registered agent has resigned, or that its registered office has been discontinued; or

    (5) The limited liability company's period of duration stated in its articles of organization has expired.

(b) If the Secretary of State determines that one or more grounds exist under subsection (a) of this section for dissolving a limited liability company, the Secretary of State shall mail the limited liability company written notice of that determination. If, within 60 days after the notice is mailed, the limited liability company does not correct each ground for dissolution or demonstrate to the reasonable satisfaction of the Secretary of State that each ground does not exist, the Secretary of State shall administratively dissolve a limited liability company by signing a certificate of dissolution that recites the ground or grounds for dissolution and its effective date. The Secretary of State shall file the original certificate of dissolution and mail a copy to the limited liability company.

(c) A limited liability company administratively dissolved under this section may apply to the Secretary of State for reinstatement. The procedures for reinstatement and for the appeal of any denial of the limited liability company's application for reinstatement shall be the same procedures applicable to corporations under G.S. 55-14-22, 55-14-23, and 55-14-24. If, at the time the limited liability company applies for reinstatement, the name of the limited liability company is not distinguishable from the name of another entity authorized to be used under G.S. 55D-21, then the limited liability company must change its name to a name that is distinguishable upon the records of the Secretary of State from the name of the other entity before the Secretary of State may prepare a certificate of reinstatement. The effect of reinstatement of a limited liability company shall be the same as for a corporation under G.S. 55-14-22. (1993, c. 354, s. 1; 1996, 2nd Ex. Sess., c. 17, s. 15.1(e); 1997-485, s. 3; 2001-387, s. 74; 2001-390, s. 11; 2001-413, s. 7.4; 2001-487, s. 62(ee).)

Editor's Note. — Session Laws 2001-387, s. 154(b), provides that nothing in this act shall supersede the provisions of Article 10 or 65 of Chapter 58 of the General Statutes, and this act does not create an alternate means for an entity governed by Article 65 of Chapter 58 of the General Statutes to convert to a different business form.

Session Laws 2001-390, s. 14, provides: "The Secretary of State shall report to the General Assembly by June 30, 2003, on whether a time limit should be placed upon the period of time within which an entity may be permitted to apply for reinstatement from administrative dissolution or revocation."

Session Laws 2001-390, s. 16, provided in part that 2001-390, s. 11, which amended subsection (c) of this section, was effective August 26, 2001 and applicable retroactively to reinstatements made on or after December 1, 1999.

Session Laws 2001-487, s. 62(ee), effective January 1, 2002, repealed Session Laws 2001-387, s. 74, which, effective January 1, 2002, would have amended subsection (c) of this section.

Effect of Amendments. — Session Laws 2001-413, s. 7.4, effective January 1, 2002, in this section as amended by Session Laws 2001-

390, substituted "G.S. 55D-21" for "G.S. 57C-2-30" in subsection (c).

Legal Periodicals. — For 1997 legislative survey, see 20 Campbell L. Rev. 389.

§ 57C-6-03.1: Repealed by Session Laws 1998-228, s. 17, effective December 1, 1999.

§ 57C-6-04. Winding up.

(a) Except as otherwise provided in this Chapter, the articles of organization, or a written operating agreement, the managers shall wind up the limited liability company's affairs following its dissolution. If the dissolved limited liability company has no managers, and provision is not otherwise made in the articles of organization or a written operating agreement, the legal representative of or successor to the last remaining member may wind up the limited liability company's affairs. The court may wind up the limited liability company's affairs, or appoint a person to wind up its affairs, on application of any member, his legal representative, or assignee.

(b) As promptly as reasonably possible following dissolution as is consistent with obtaining the fair market value for the limited liability company's assets, the persons charged with winding up the limited liability company shall collect its assets, dispose of its properties that will not be distributed in kind to its members, discharge or make provision for discharging its liabilities, and distribute its remaining assets as provided in G.S. 57C-6-05. The limited liability company shall continue in existence following its dissolution and during its winding up, but shall carry on only that business appropriate to wind up and liquidate its business and affairs.

(c) The dissolution of the limited liability company does not transfer title to its assets, prevent assignment of its member interests, subject its managers to standards of conduct different from those prescribed in Article 3 of this Chapter, change any provisions of its operating agreement except as provided in subsection (b) of this section, prevent commencement of a proceeding by or against the limited liability company in its own name, abate or suspend a proceeding by or against the limited liability company, or terminate the authority of the registered agent of the limited liability company. (1993, c. 354, s. 1; 2001-387, s. 75.)

Editor's Note. — Session Laws 2001-387, s. 154(b) provides that nothing in this act shall supersede the provisions of Article 10 or 65 of Chapter 58 of the General Statutes, and this act does not create an alternate means for an entity governed by Article 65 of Chapter 58 of the General Statutes to convert to a different business form.

Effect of Amendments. — Session Laws 2001-387, s. 75, effective January 1, 2002, rewrote the second sentence in subsection (a).

§ 57C-6-05. Distribution of assets.

Upon the winding up of a limited liability company, its assets shall be applied as follows:

(1) To creditors, including members who are creditors, to the extent permitted by law, in satisfaction of liabilities of the limited liability company other than liabilities for distributions to members under G.S. 57C-4-04;

(2) Except as provided in the articles of organization or a written operating agreement, to members or former members in satisfaction of liabilities for distributions under G.S. 57C-4-04; and

(3) Except as provided in the articles of organization or a written operating agreement, by distribution to the members and to any

former member whose event of withdrawal resulted in the dissolution in proportion to the agreed value, as stated in the limited liability company records required to be kept pursuant to G.S. 57C-3-04(a)(5), of the contributions made by each such member and former member, after such agreed values are adjusted by: (i) adding thereto the person's share of the profits of the limited liability company, and (ii) deducting therefrom the person's share of the losses of the limited liability company and all distributions previously received by the person. (1993, c. 354, s. 1.)

§ 57C-6-06. Articles of dissolution.

Upon the dissolution and the commencement of winding up of the limited liability company, articles of dissolution shall be filed in the Office of the Secretary of State and shall set forth:
(1) The name of the limited liability company;
(2) The dates of filing of its articles of organization and all amendments thereto;
(3) The reason for filing the articles of dissolution;
(4) The effective date (which shall be a date certain) of the dissolution, as determined in accordance with G.S. 57C-6-01; and
(5) Any other information the managers filing the articles of dissolution determine. (1993, c. 354, s. 1; 2001-387, s. 76.)

Editor's Note. — Session Laws 2001-387, s. 154(b) provides that nothing in this act shall supersede the provisions of Article 10 or 65 of Chapter 58 of the General Statutes, and this act does not create an alternate means for an entity governed by Article 65 of Chapter 58 of the General Statutes to convert to a different business form.

Effect of Amendments. — Session Laws 2001-387, s. 76, effective January 1, 2002, deleted "members or" preceding "managers" in subdivision (5).

§ 57C-6-06.1. Cancellation of articles of dissolution.

After the filing of articles of dissolution by a limited liability company dissolved pursuant to G.S. 57C-6-01(4) because of the happening of an event of withdrawal, the articles of dissolution may be cancelled if, within 90 days after the event of withdrawal, all remaining members agree in writing that the business of the limited liability company should be continued and the limited liability company files articles of cancellation with the Secretary of State. The articles of cancellation shall set forth:
(1) The name of the limited liability company;
(2) The date of the event of withdrawal described in the articles of dissolution;
(3) The date of filing of the company's articles of dissolution;
(4) A statement that within 90 days after the event of withdrawal all remaining members have agreed in writing that the business of the limited liability company may be continued; and
(5) Any other information the managers filing the articles of cancellation determine. (1997-485, s. 19; 2001-387, s. 77.)

Editor's Note. — Session Laws 2001-387, s. 154(b) provides that nothing in this act shall supersede the provisions of Article 10 or 65 of Chapter 58 of the General Statutes, and this act does not create an alternate means for an entity governed by Article 65 of Chapter 58 of the General Statutes to convert to a different business form.

Effect of Amendments. — Session Laws 2001-387, s. 77, effective January 1, 2002, deleted "members or" preceding "managers" in subdivision (5).

Legal Periodicals. — For 1997 legislative survey, see 20 Campbell L. Rev. 389.

§ 57C-6-07. Known claims against dissolved limited liability company.

(a) A dissolved limited liability company may dispose of the known claims against it by following the procedure described in this section.

(b) The dissolved limited liability company shall notify its known claimants in writing of the dissolution at any time after it has filed its articles of dissolution. The written notice must:

    (1) Describe information that must be included in a claim;

    (2) Provide a mailing address where claims may be sent;

    (3) State the deadline, which may not be fewer than 120 days from the date of the written notice, by which the dissolved limited liability company must receive the claim; and

    (4) State that the claim will be barred if not received by the deadline.

(c) A claim against the dissolved limited liability company is barred:

    (1) If the limited liability company does not receive the claim by the deadline from a claimant who received written notice under subsection (b) of this section; or

    (2) If a claimant whose claim was rejected by written notice from the dissolved limited liability company does not commence a proceeding to enforce the claim within 90 days from the date of receipt of the rejection notice.

(d) For purposes of this section, "claim" does not include a contingent liability or a claim based on an event occurring after the filing of the articles of dissolution. (1993, c. 354, s. 1.)

§ 57C-6-08. Unknown and certain other claims against dissolved limited liability company.

(a) A dissolved limited liability company that has filed articles of dissolution may also publish notice of its dissolution and request that persons with claims against the limited liability company present them in accordance with the notice.

(b) The notice must:

    (1) Be published one time in a newspaper of general circulation in the county where the dissolved limited liability company's principal office (or, if none in this State, its registered office) is or was last located;

    (2) Describe the information that must be included in a claim and provide a mailing address where the claim may be sent; and

    (3) State that a claim against the limited liability company will be barred unless a proceeding to enforce the claim is commenced within five years after the publication of the notice.

(c) If the dissolved limited liability company publishes a newspaper notice in accordance with subsections (a) and (b) of this section, the claim of each of the following claimants is barred unless the claimant commences a proceeding to enforce the claim against the dissolved limited liability company within five years after the publication date of the newspaper notice:

    (1) A claimant who was known but did not receive written notice under G.S. 57C-6-07;

    (2) A claimant whose claim was timely sent to the dissolved limited liability company but not acted on; or

    (3) A claimant whose claim is contingent or based on an event occurring after the filing of the articles of dissolution. (1993, c. 354, s. 1.)

§ 57C-6-09. Enforcement of claims.

(a) A claim under G.S. 57C-6-07 or G.S. 57C-6-08 may be enforced:

(1) Against the dissolved limited liability company, to the extent of its undistributed assets, including coverage under any applicable insurance policy; or

(2) If the assets have been distributed in winding up, against a member of the dissolved limited liability company to the extent of his pro rata share of the claim or the limited liability company assets distributed to him in winding up, whichever is less, but a member's total liability for all claims under this section may not exceed the total amount of assets distributed to him.

(b) Nothing in G.S. 57C-6-07 or G.S. 57C-6-08 shall extend any applicable period of limitation. (1993, c. 354, s. 1.)

ARTICLE 7.

Foreign Limited Liability Companies.

§ 57C-7-01. Law governing.

The laws of the state or other jurisdiction under which a foreign limited liability company is formed shall govern its formation, organization, and internal affairs and the liability of its managers and members, regardless of whether the foreign limited liability company procured or should have procured a certificate of authority under this Chapter, and a foreign limited liability company shall not be denied a certificate of authority by reason of any difference between the laws under which it is formed and the laws of this State. A foreign limited liability company with a valid certificate of authority has the same but no greater rights and has the same but no greater privileges as, and is subject to the same duties, restrictions, penalties, and liabilities now or later imposed on, a domestic limited liability company of like character. (1993, c. 354, s. 1; 2001-387, s. 78.)

Editor's Note. — Session Laws 2001-387, s. 154(b) provides that nothing in this act shall supersede the provisions of Article 10 or 65 of Chapter 58 of the General Statutes, and this act does not create an alternate means for an entity governed by Article 65 of Chapter 58 of the General Statutes to convert to a different business form.

Effect of Amendments. — Session Laws 2001-387, s. 78, effective January 1, 2002, substituted "formed" for "organized" in two places; substituted "its formation, organization" for "its organization"; and substituted "shall" for "may" following "foreign limited liability company."

Legal Periodicals. — For note, "Corporate Law — Limited Liability Company Act, N.C. Gen. Stat. G.S. 57C-1-01 to 57C-10-07 (1993)," see 72 N.C.L. Rev. 1654 (1994).

For article, "The Creation of North Carolina's Limited Liability Corporation Act," see 32 Wake Forest L. Rev. 179 (1997).

§ 57C-7-02. Authority to transact business required.

(a) A foreign limited liability company may not transact business in this State until it obtains a certificate of authority from the Secretary of State.

(b) Without excluding other activities that may not constitute transacting business in this State, a foreign limited liability company shall not be considered to be transacting business in this State for the purposes of this Chapter by reason of carrying on in this State any one or more of the following activities:

(1) Maintaining or defending any action or suit or any administrative or arbitration proceeding, or effecting the settlement thereof or the settlement of claims or disputes;

(2) Holding meetings of its managers or members or carrying on other activities concerning its internal affairs;

(3) Maintaining bank accounts or borrowing money in this State, with or without security, even if such borrowings are repeated and continuous transactions;

(4) Maintaining offices or agencies for the transfer, exchange, and registration of its membership interests, or appointing and maintaining trustees or depositories with relation to its membership interests;

(5) Soliciting or procuring orders, whether by mail or through employees or agents or otherwise, where the orders require acceptance without this State before becoming binding contracts;

(6) Making or investing in loans with or without security including servicing of mortgages or deeds of trust through independent agencies within the State, the conducting of foreclosure proceedings and sales, the acquiring of property at foreclosure sale, and the management and rental of such property for a reasonable time while liquidating its investment, provided no office or agency therefor is maintained in this State;

(7) Taking security for or collecting debts due to it or enforcing any rights in property securing the same;

(8) Transacting business in interstate commerce;

(9) Conducting an isolated transaction completed within a period of six months and not in the course of a number of repeated transactions of like nature;

(10) Selling through independent contractors; and

(11) Owning, without more, real or personal property.

(c) This section does not apply in determining the contacts or activities that may subject a foreign limited liability company to service of process or taxation in this State or to regulation under any other law of this State. (1993, c. 354, s. 1.)

§ 57C-7-03. Consequences of transacting business without authority.

(a) No foreign limited liability company transacting business in this State without permission obtained through a certificate of authority under this Chapter shall be permitted to maintain any action or proceeding in any court of this State unless the foreign limited liability company shall have obtained a certificate of authority prior to trial. An issue arising under this subsection must be raised by motion and determined by the trial judge prior to trial.

(b) A foreign limited liability company failing to obtain a certificate of authority as required by this Chapter shall be liable to the State for the years or parts thereof during which it transacted business in this State without a certificate of authority in an amount equal to all fees and taxes which would have been imposed by law upon the foreign limited liability company had it duly applied for and received such permission, plus interest and all penalties imposed by law for failure to pay such fees and taxes. In addition, the foreign limited liability company shall be liable for a civil penalty of ten dollars ($10.00) for each day, but not to exceed a total of one thousand dollars ($1,000) for each year or part thereof, it transacts business in this State without a certificate of authority. The Attorney General may bring actions to recover all amounts due the State under the provisions of this subsection. The clear proceeds of civil penalties provided for in this subsection shall be remitted to the Civil Penalty and Forfeiture Fund in accordance with G.S. 115C-457.2.

(c) Notwithstanding subsection (a) of this section, the failure of a foreign limited liability company to obtain a certificate of authority does not impair the validity of its acts or prevent it from defending any proceeding in this State.

(d) The Secretary of State is directed to require that every foreign limited liability company transacting business in this State comply with the provisions of this Chapter. The Secretary of State may employ such assistants as shall be deemed necessary in the Secretary of State's office for the purpose of enforcing the provisions of this Article and for making such investigations as shall be necessary to ascertain foreign limited liability companies transacting business in this State that may have failed to comply with the provisions of this Chapter. (1993, c. 354, s. 1; 1998-215, s. 119.)

§ 57C-7-04. Application for certificate of authority.

(a) A foreign limited liability company may apply for a certificate of authority to transact business in this State by delivering an application to the Secretary of State for filing. The application must set forth:

(1) The name of the foreign limited liability company or a name that satisfies the requirements of Article 3 of Chapter 55D of the General Statutes;

(2) The name of the state or country under whose law it is formed;

(3) Its date of formation and period of duration;

(4) The street address, and the mailing address if different from the street address, of its principal office, if any, and the county in which the principal office, if any, is located;

(5) The street address, and the mailing address if different from the street address, of its registered office in this State and the name of its registered agent at that office; and

(6) The names and usual business addresses of its current managers.

(b) The foreign limited liability company shall deliver with the completed application a certificate of existence (or a document of similar import) duly authenticated by the Secretary of State or other official having custody of limited liability company records in the state or country under whose law it is formed.

(c) If the Secretary of State finds that the application conforms to law, the Secretary of State shall, when all taxes and fees have been tendered as prescribed in this Chapter:

(1) Endorse on the application and an exact or conformed copy thereof the word "filed" and the hour, day, month, and year of the filing thereof;

(2) File in his office the application and the certificate of existence (or document of similar import as described in subsection (b) of this section);

(3) Issue a certificate of authority to transact business in this State to which the Secretary of State shall affix the exact or conformed copy of the application; and

(4) Send to the foreign limited liability company or its representative the certificate of authority, together with the exact or conformed copy of the application affixed thereto. (1993, c. 354, s. 1; 2000-140, s. 50; 2001-358, s. 28; 2001-387, ss. 79, 80, 173, 175(a); 2001-413, s. 6.)

Editor's Note. — Session Laws 2001-358, s. 53, provided that the act, which amended this section, was effective October 1, 2001, and applicable to documents submitted for filing on or after that date. Section 173 of Session Laws 2001-387 changed the effective date of Session Laws 2001-358 from October 1, 2001, to January 1, 2002. Section 6 of Session Laws 2001-413, effective September 14, 2001, added a sentence to s. 175(a) of Session Laws 2001-387, making s. 173 of that act effective when it became law (August 26, 2001). As a result of these changes, the amendment by Session Laws 2001-358 is effective January 1, 2002, and applicable to documents submitted for filing on or after that date.

Session Laws 2001-387, s. 154(b) provides that nothing in this act shall supersede the provisions of Article 10 or 65 of Chapter 58 of the General Statutes, and this act does not create an alternate means for an entity governed by Article 65 of Chapter 58 of the General Statutes to convert to a different business form.

Effect of Amendments. — Session Laws 2001-358, s. 28, effective January 1, 2002, and applicable to documents submitted for filing on or after that date, substituted "or a name that satisfies the requirements of Article 3 of Chapter 55D of the General Statutes" for "or, if its name is unavailable for use in this State, a name that satisfies the requirements of G.S. 57C-7-06" in subdivision (a)(1).

Session Laws 2001-387, ss. 79 and 80, effective January 1, 2002, and applicable to documents submitted for filing on or after that date, in subsection (a), substituted "formed" for "organized" in subdivision (a)(2), substituted "formation" for "organization" in subdivision (a)(3), and rewrote subdivision (a)(4); and substituted "formed" for "organized" at the end of subsection (b).

§ 57C-7-05. Amended certificate of authority.

(a) A foreign limited liability company authorized to transact business in this State must obtain an amended certificate of authority from the Secretary of State if it changes:

(1) Its name;

(2) The period of its duration; or

(3) The state or country of its formation.

(b) A foreign limited liability company may apply for an amended certificate of authority by delivering an application to the Secretary of State for filing that sets forth:

(1) The name of the limited liability company and the name in which the limited liability company is authorized to transact business in North Carolina if different;

(2) The name of the state or country under whose law it is formed;

(3) The date it was originally authorized to transact business in this State; and

(4) A statement of the change or changes being made.

Except for the content of the application, the requirements of G.S. 57C-7-03 for obtaining an original certificate of authority apply to obtaining an amended certificate under this section. (1993, c. 354, s. 1; 2001-387, ss. 81, 82.)

Editor's Note. — Session Laws 2001-387, s. 154(b) provides that nothing in this act shall supersede the provisions of Article 10 or 65 of Chapter 58 of the General Statutes, and this act does not create an alternate means for an entity governed by Article 65 of Chapter 58 of the General Statutes to convert to a different business form.

Effect of Amendments. — Session Laws 2001-387, ss. 81 and 82, effective January 1, 2002, substituted "formation" for "organization" in subdivision (a)(3) and substituted "formed" for "organized" in subdivision (b)(2).

§ 57C-7-06: Repealed by Session Laws 2001-358, s. 29, effective January 1, 2002.

Editor's Note. — Session Laws 2001-358, s. 53, provided that the act, which repealed this section, was effective October 1, 2001, and applicable to documents submitted for filing on or after that date. Section 173 of Session Laws 2001-387 changed the effective date of Session Laws 2001-358 from October 1, 2001, to January 1, 2002. Section 6 of Session Laws 2001-413, effective September 14, 2001, added a sentence to s. 175(a) of Session Laws 2001-387, making s. 173 of that act effective when it became law (August 26, 2001). As a result of these changes, the amendment by Session Laws 2001-358 is effective January 1, 2002, and applicable to documents submitted for filing on or after that date.

Session Laws 2001-387, ss. 83 and 84 had amended this section. However, s. 155 of Session Laws 2001-387 repealed ss. 83 and 84, contingent upon the enactment of Session Laws

2001-358. Session Laws 2001-358 was enacted on August 10, 2001.

§ 57C-7-07. Registered office and registered agent of foreign limited liability company.

Each foreign limited liability company authorized to transact business or conduct affairs in this State must maintain a registered office and registered agent as required by Article 4 of Chapter 55D of the General Statutes and is subject to service on the Secretary of State under that Article. (1993, c. 354, s. 1; 2000-140, s. 101(h); 2001-358, s. 49(b); 2001-387, ss. 173, 175(a); 2001-413, s. 6.)

Editor's Note. — Session Laws 2001-358, s. 53, provided that the act, which amended this section, was effective October 1, 2001, and applicable to documents submitted for filing on or after that date. Section 173 of Session Laws 2001-387 changed the effective date of Session Laws 2001-358 from October 1, 2001, to January 1, 2002. Section 6 of Session Laws 2001-413, effective September 14, 2001, added a sentence to s. 175(a) of Session Laws 2001-387, making s. 173 of that act effective when it became law (August 26, 2001). As a result of these changes, the amendment by Session Laws 2001-358 is effective January 1, 2002, and applicable to documents submitted for filing on ar after that date.

Effect of Amendments. — Session Laws 2001-358, s. 49(b), effective January 1, 2002, and applicable to documents submitted for filing on or after that date, rewrote the section.

CASE NOTES

Cited in Bruggeman v. Meditrust Acquisition Co., 138 N.C. App. 612, 532 S.E.2d 215, 2000 N.C. App. LEXIS 774 (2000).

§§ 57C-7-08 through 57C-7-10: Repealed by Session Laws 2001-358, s. 49(c), effective January 1, 2002.

Editor's Note. — Session Laws 2001-358, s. 53, provided that the act, which repealed this section, was effective October 1, 2001, and applicable to documents submitted for filing on or after that date. Section 173 of Session Laws 2001-387 changed the effective date of Session Laws 2001-358 from October 1, 2001, to January 1, 2002. Section 6 of Session Laws 2001-413, effective September 14, 2001, added a sentence to s. 175(a) of Session Laws 2001-387, making s. 173 of that act effective when it became law (August 26, 2001). As a result of these changes, the amendment by Session Laws 2001-358 is effective January 1, 2002, and applicable to documents submitted for filing on ar after that date.

Session Laws 2001-387, s. 85, amended G.S. 57C-7-10(b).

§ 57C-7-11. Withdrawal of foreign limited liability company.

(a) A foreign limited liability company authorized to transact business in this State may not withdraw from this State until it obtains a certificate of withdrawal from the Secretary of State.

(b) A foreign limited liability company authorized to transact business in this State may apply for a certificate of withdrawal by delivering an application to the Secretary of State for filing. The application must set forth:

(1) The name of the foreign limited liability company and the name of the state or country under whose law it is formed;

(2) That it is not transacting business in this State and that it surrenders its authority to transact business in this State;

(3) That the foreign limited liability company revokes the authority of its registered agent to accept service of process and consents that service of process in any action or proceeding based upon any cause of action arising in this State, or arising out of business transacted in this State, during the time the foreign limited liability company was authorized to transact business in this State, may thereafter be made on such foreign limited liability company by service thereof on the Secretary of State;

(4) A mailing address to which the Secretary of State may mail a copy of any process served on the Secretary of State under subdivision (3) of this subsection; and

(5) A commitment to file with the Secretary of State a statement of any subsequent change in its mailing address.

(c) If the Secretary of State finds that the application conforms to law, the Secretary of State shall:

(1) Endorse on the application and an exact or conformed copy thereof the word "filed" and the hour, day, month, and year of the filing thereof;

(2) File the application in the Secretary of State's office;

(3) Issue a certificate of withdrawal to which the Secretary of State shall affix the exact or conformed copy of the application; and

(4) Send to the foreign limited liability company or its representative the certificate of withdrawal together with the exact or conformed copy of the application affixed thereto.

(d) After the withdrawal of the foreign limited liability company is effective, service of process on the Secretary of State in accordance with subsection (b) of this section shall be made by delivering to and leaving with the Secretary of State, or with any clerk authorized by the Secretary of State to accept service of process, duplicate copies of that process and the fee required by G.S. 57C-1-22(b). Upon receipt of process in the manner provided in this subsection, the Secretary of State shall mail a copy of the process by registered or certified mail, return receipt requested, to the foreign limited liability company at the mailing address designated pursuant to subsection (b) of this section. (1993, c. 354, s. 1; 2001-387, ss. 86, 87.)

Editor's Note. — Session Laws 2001-387, s. 154(b) provides that nothing in this act shall supersede the provisions of Article 10 or 65 of Chapter 58 of the General Statutes, and this act does not create an alternate means for an entity governed by Article 65 of Chapter 58 of the General Statutes to convert to a different business form.

Effect of Amendments. — Session Laws 2001-387, ss. 86 and 87, effective January 1, 2002, in subsection (b), substituted "formed" for "organized" at the end of subdivision (1), substituted "the Secretary of State" for "him" in subdivision (4), and substituted "file with the Secretary of State a statement of any subsequent change" for "notify the Secretary of State in the future of any change" in subdivision (5) and rewrote subsection (d).

§ 57C-7-12. Withdrawal of limited liability company by reason of a merger, consolidation, or conversion.

(a) Whenever a foreign limited liability company authorized to transact business in this State ceases its separate existence as a result of a statutory merger, consolidation, or conversion permitted by the laws of the state or country under which it was formed, or converts into another type of entity as permitted by those laws, the surviving or resulting entity shall apply for a certificate of withdrawal for the foreign limited liability company by delivering to the Secretary of State for filing a copy of the articles of merger, consolidation, or conversion or a certificate reciting the facts of the merger, consolidation, or conversion, duly authenticated by the Secretary of State or other official having custody of limited liability company records in the state or country under the laws of which the foreign limited liability company was formed. If the surviving or resulting entity is not authorized to transact business or conduct affairs in this State, the articles or certificate must be accompanied by an application which must set forth:

 (1) The name of the foreign limited liability company authorized to transact business in this State, the type of entity and name of the surviving or resulting entity, and a statement that the surviving or resulting entity is not authorized to transact business or conduct affairs in this State;

 (2) A statement that the surviving or resulting entity consents that service of process based upon any cause of action arising in this State, or arising out of business transacted in this State, during the time the foreign limited liability company was authorized to transact business in this State, may thereafter be made by service thereof on the Secretary of State;

 (3) A mailing address to which the Secretary of State may mail a copy of any process served on the Secretary of State under subdivision (a)(2) of this section; and

 (4) A commitment to file with the Secretary of State a statement of any subsequent change in its mailing address.

(b) If the Secretary of State finds that the articles or certificate and the application for withdrawal, if required, conform to law, the Secretary of State shall:

 (1) Endorse on the articles or certificate and the application for withdrawal, if required, the word "filed" and the hour, day, month, and year of filing thereof;

 (2) File the articles or certificate and the application, if required;

 (3) Issue a certificate of withdrawal; and

 (4) Send to the surviving or resulting entity or its representative the certificate of withdrawal, together with the exact or conformed copy of the application, if required, affixed thereto.

(c) After the withdrawal of the foreign limited liability company is effective, service of process on the Secretary of State in accordance with subsection (a) of this section shall be made by delivering to and leaving with the Secretary of State, or with any clerk authorized by the Secretary of State to accept service of process, duplicate copies of process and the fee required by G.S. 57C-1-22(b). Upon receipt of process in the manner provided in this subsection, the Secretary of State shall immediately mail a copy of the process by registered or certified mail, return receipt requested, to the surviving or resulting entity at the mailing address designated pursuant to subsection (a) of this section. (1993, c. 354, s. 1; 1999-369, s. 3.6; 2000-140, s. 101(i); 2001-387, ss. 88, 89; 2001-487, s. 62(k).)

Editor's Note. — Session Laws 2001-387, s. 154(b) provides that nothing in this act shall supersede the provisions of Article 10 or 65 of Chapter 58 of the General Statutes, and this act does not create an alternate means for an entity governed by Article 65 of Chapter 58 of the General Statutes to convert to a different business form.

Effect of Amendments. — Session Laws 2001-387, ss. 88 and 89, effective January 1, 2002, in subsection (a), substituted "formed" for "organized" in two places in the first sentence of the introductory language, substituted "the Secretary of State" for "him" in subdivision (a)(3), and in subdivision (a)(4), inserted "subsequent" following "any" and deleted "subsequent" preceding "mailing"; and added subsection (c).

Session Laws 2001-487, s. 62(k), effective January 1, 2002, in subsection (a) as amended by Session Laws 2001-387, s. 88, inserted "or conduct affairs" following "to transact a business" near the end of the introductory language and in subdivision (a)(1).

§ 57C-7-13. Action by Attorney General.

The Attorney General may maintain an action to restrain a foreign limited liability company from transacting business in this State in violation of this Article. (1993, c. 354, s. 1.)

§ 57C-7-14. Revocation of certificate of authority.

(a) The Secretary of State may administratively revoke the certificate of authority of a foreign limited liability company authorized to transact business in this State if the Secretary of State determines that:

(1) The foreign limited liability company has not paid, within 60 days after they are due, any penalties, fees, or other payments due under this Chapter;

(2) The foreign limited liability company has not delivered its annual report to the Secretary of State on or before the date it is due;

(3) The foreign limited liability company has been without a registered agent or a registered office in this State for 60 days or more;

(4) The foreign limited liability company does not inform the Secretary of State as required by this Chapter that its registered agent or registered office has been changed, that its registered agent has resigned, or that its registered office has been discontinued within 60 days of the change, resignation, or discontinuance;

(5) An organizer, member, manager, or agent of the foreign limited liability company has signed a document that he knew was false in any material respect with the intent the document be delivered to the Secretary of State for filing;

(6) The Secretary of State receives a duly authenticated certificate from the secretary of state or other official having custody of limited liability company records in the state or country under whose law the foreign limited liability company is organized stating that it has been dissolved or has ceased to exist as the result of a merger or otherwise; or

(7) The limited liability company is exceeding the authority conferred upon it by this Chapter.

(b) If the Secretary of State determines that one or more grounds exist under this section for revocation of the certificate of authority, the Secretary of State shall mail the foreign limited liability company written notice of his determination. If, within 60 days after notice is mailed, a foreign limited liability company does not correct each ground for revocation, or demonstrate to the reasonable satisfaction of the Secretary of State that each ground does not exist, the Secretary of State shall revoke the foreign limited liability company's certificate of authority by signing a certificate of revocation that recites the ground or grounds for the revocation, shall file the certificate of revocation, and shall mail a copy to the foreign limited liability company. The authority of the foreign limited liability company to transact business in this State shall cease on the date the certificate of authority is revoked by the filing of the certificate of revocation by the Secretary of State.

(c) Upon the revocation of a foreign limited liability company's certificate of authority, the Secretary of State shall become the foreign limited liability company's agent for service of process in any proceeding based on a cause of action arising in this State or arising out of business transacted in this State during the time the foreign limited liability company was authorized to transact business in this State. The Secretary of State shall then proceed in accordance with G.S. 55D-33.

(d) A foreign limited liability company may appeal the Secretary of State's revocation of its certificate of authority under the same procedures that a foreign corporation may appeal the revocation of its certificate of authority pursuant to G.S. 55-15-32 and G.S. 55-15-33. (1993, c. 354, s. 1; 2001-358, s. 49(d); 2001-387, ss. 173, 175(a); 2001-413, s. 6.)

Effect of Amendments. — Session Laws 2001-358, s. 49(d), effective January 1, 2002, and applicable to documents submitted for fil- ing on or after that date, substituted "G.S. 55D-33" for "G.S. 57C-7" in subsection (c).

ARTICLE 8.

Derivative Actions.

§ 57C-8-01. Members' derivative actions.

(a) A member may bring an action in the superior court of this State in the right of any domestic or foreign limited liability company to recover a judgment in its favor if the following conditions are met:

  (1) The plaintiff does not have the authority to cause the limited liability company to sue in its own right; and

  (2) The plaintiff (i) is a member of the limited liability company at the time of bringing the action, and (ii) was a member of the limited liability company at the time of the transaction of which the plaintiff complains, or the plaintiff's status as a member of the limited liability company thereafter devolved upon the plaintiff pursuant to the terms of the operating agreement from a person who was a member at such time.

(b) The complaint shall allege with particularity the efforts, if any, made by the plaintiff to obtain the action the plaintiff desires from the managers, directors, or other applicable authority and the reasons for the plaintiff's failure to obtain the action, or for not making the effort. Whether or not a demand for action was made, if the limited liability company commences an investigation of the charges made in the demand or complaint, the court may stay any proceeding until the investigation is completed.

(c) Upon motion of the limited liability company, the court may appoint a committee composed of two or more disinterested managers, directors, or other disinterested persons, acceptable to the limited liability company, to determine whether it is in the best interest of the limited liability company to pursue a particular legal right or remedy. The committee shall report its findings to the court. After considering the report and any other relevant evidence, the court shall determine whether the proceeding should be continued or not.

(d) No action on behalf of a limited liability company shall be discontinued, dismissed, compromised, or settled without the approval of the court. If the court shall determine that the interest of the members or any class or classes thereof or of the creditors of the limited liability company will be substantially affected by such discontinuance, dismissal, compromise, or settlement, the court, in its discretion, may direct that notice, by publication or otherwise, shall be given to such members or creditors whose interests it determines will be so affected. If notice is so directed to be given, the court may determine which one or more of the parties to the action shall bear the expense of giving the same, in such amount as the court shall determine and find to be reasonable in the circumstances, and the amount of such expense shall be awarded as costs of the action.

(e) If the action on behalf of the limited liability company is successful, in whole or in part, whether by means of a compromise and settlement or by a judgment, the court may award the plaintiff the reasonable expenses of maintaining the action, including reasonable attorneys' fees, and shall direct the plaintiff to account to the limited liability company for the remainder of any proceeds of the action.

(f) In any such action the court, upon final judgment and a finding that the action was brought without reasonable cause, may require the plaintiff or plaintiffs to pay to the defendant or defendants the reasonable expenses, including attorneys' fees, incurred by them in the defense of the action.

(g) In proceedings hereunder, no member shall be entitled to obtain or have access to any communication within the scope of the limited liability company's attorney-client privilege which could not be obtained by or would not be accessible to a party in an action other than on behalf of the limited liability company. (1993, c. 354, s. 1; 2001-387, ss. 90, 91.)

Editor's Note. — Session Laws 2001-387, s. 154(b) provides that nothing in this act shall supersede the provisions of Article 10 or 65 of Chapter 58 of the General Statutes, and this act does not create an alternate means for an entity governed by Article 65 of Chapter 58 of the General Statutes to convert to a different business form.

Effect of Amendments. — Session Laws 2001-387, ss. 90 and 91, effective January 1, 2002, substituted "managers, directors, or other applicable" for "managers or comparable" in subsection (b) and in subsection (c), inserted "directors" and made a minor punctuation change in the first sentence.

Legal Periodicals. — For note, "Corporate Law — Limited Liability Company Act, N.C. Gen. Stat. G.S. 57C-1-01 to 57C-10-07 (1993)," see 72 N.C.L. Rev. 1654 (1994).

For article, "The Creation of North Carolina's Limited Liability Corporation Act," see 32 Wake Forest L. Rev. 179 (1997).

ARTICLES 9.

§§ 57C-9-01 through 57C-9-06: Repealed by Session Laws 1999-369, s. 3.7, effective December 15, 1999.

Cross References. — For present provisions as to conversion and merger amongst limited liability companies, see Article 9A of Chapter 57C.

ARTICLE 9A.

Conversion and Merger.

Part 1. Conversion to Limited Liability Company.

Editor's Note. — Session Laws 2001-387, s. 154(b) provides that nothing in this act shall supersede the provisions of Article 10 or 65 of Chapter 58 of the General Statutes, and this act does not create an alternate means for an entity governed by Article 65 of Chapter 58 of the General Statutes to convert to a different business form.

Effect of Amendments. — Session Laws 2001-387, s. 92, effective January 1, 2002, rewrote the Part 1 heading.

§ 57C-9A-01. Conversion.

A business entity other than a domestic limited liability company may convert to a domestic limited liability company if:

(1) The conversion is permitted by the laws of the state or country governing the organization and internal affairs of the converting business entity; and

(2) The converting business entity complies with the requirements of this Part and, to the extent applicable, the laws referred to in subdivision (1) of this section. (1999-369, s. 3.7; 2001-387, s. 93.)

Editor's Note. — Session Laws 2001-387, s. 154(b) provides that nothing in this act shall supersede the provisions of Article 10 or 65 of Chapter 58 of the General Statutes, and this act does not create an alternate means for an entity governed by Article 65 of Chapter 58 of the General Statutes to convert to a different business form.

Effect of Amendments. — Session Laws 2001-387, s. 93, effective January 1, 2002, rewrote the section.

Legal Periodicals. — For note, "Corporate Law — Limited Liability Company Act, N.C. Gen. Stat. G.S. 57C-1-01 to 57C-10-07 (1993)," see 72 N.C.L. Rev. 1654 (1994).

For article, "The Creation of North Carolina's Limited Liability Corporation Act," see 32 Wake Forest L. Rev. 179 (1997).

For "Legislative Survey: Business & Banking," see 22 Campbell L. Rev. 253 (2000).

§ 57C-9A-02. Plan of conversion.

(a) The converting business entity shall approve a written plan of conversion containing:

    (1) The name of the resulting domestic limited liability company into which the converting business entity shall convert;

    (1a) The name of the converting business entity, its type of business entity, and the state or country whose laws govern its organization and internal affairs;

    (2) The terms and conditions of the conversion; and

    (3) The manner and basis for converting the interests in the converting business entity into interests, obligations, or securities of the resulting domestic limited liability company or into cash or other property in whole or in part.

The plan of conversion may contain other provisions relating to the conversion.

(b) The plan of conversion must be approved in accordance with the laws of the state or country governing the organization and internal affairs of the converting business entity.

(c) After a plan of conversion has been approved as provided in subsection (b) of this section, but before articles of organization for the resulting domestic limited liability company become effective, the plan of conversion may be amended or abandoned to the extent permitted by the laws that govern the organization and internal affairs of the converting business entity. (1999-369, s. 3.7; 2001-387, s. 94.)

Editor's Note. — Session Laws 2001-387, s. 154(b) provides that nothing in this act shall supersede the provisions of Article 10 or 65 of Chapter 58 of the General Statutes, and this act does not create an alternate means for an entity governed by Article 65 of Chapter 58 of the General Statutes to convert to a different business form.

Effect of Amendments. — Session Laws

2001-387, s. 94, effective January 1, 2002, deleted "holders of the interests in the" following "The" at the beginning of the introductory language of subsection (a) and inserted subdivision (a)(1a); rewrote subsection (b); and substituted "permited by the ... coverting business entity" for "provided in the plan of conversion" at the end of subsection (c).

§ 57C-9A-03. Filing of articles of organization by converting business entity.

(a) After a plan of conversion has been approved by the converting business entity as provided in G.S. 57C-9A-02, the converting business entity shall deliver articles of organization to the Secretary of State for filing. In addition to the matters required or permitted by G.S. 57C-2-21, the articles of organization shall contain articles of conversion stating:

    (1) That the domestic limited liability company is being formed pursuant to a conversion of another business entity;

(2) The name of the converting business entity, its type of business entity, and the state or country whose laws govern its organization and internal affairs; and

(3) That a plan of conversion has been approved by the converting business entity as required by law.

If the plan of conversion is abandoned after the articles of organization have been filed with the Secretary of State but before the articles of organization become effective, the converting business entity shall deliver to the Secretary of State for filing prior to the time the articles of organization become effective an amendment to the articles of organization withdrawing the articles of organization.

(b) The conversion takes effect when the articles of organization become effective.

(c) Repealed by Session Laws 2001-387, s. 95, effective January 1, 2002.

(d) Certificates of conversion shall also be registered as provided in G.S. 47-18.1. (1999-369, s. 3.7; 2001-387, s. 95.)

Editor's Note. — Session Laws 2001-387, s. 154(b) provides that nothing in this act shall supersede the provisions of Article 10 or 65 of Chapter 58 of the General Statutes, and this act does not create an alternate means for an entity governed by Article 65 of Chapter 58 of the General Statutes to convert to a different business form.

Effect of Amendments. — Session Laws 2001-387, s. 95, effective January 1, 2002, in subsection (a), substituted "shall contain articles of conversion stating" for "shall state" at the end of the introductory language, and rewrote the last paragraph; and deleted subsection (c).

§ 57C-9A-04. Effects of conversion.

When the conversion takes effect:
(1) The converting business entity ceases its prior form of organization and continues in existence as the resulting domestic limited liability company;

(2) The title to all real estate and other property owned by the converting business entity continues vested in the resulting domestic limited liability company without reversion or impairment;

(3) All liabilities of the converting business entity continue as liabilities of the resulting domestic limited liability company;

(4) A proceeding pending by or against the converting business entity may be continued as if the conversion did not occur; and

(5) The interests in the converting business entity that are to be converted into interests, obligations, or securities of the resulting domestic limited liability company or into the right to receive cash or other property are thereupon so converted, and the former holders of interests in the converting business entity are entitled only to the rights provided in the plan of conversion.

The conversion shall not affect the liability or absence of liability of any holder of an interest in the converting business entity for any acts, omissions, or obligations of the converting business entity made or incurred prior to the effectiveness of the conversion. The cessation of the existence of the converting business entity in its prior form of organization in the conversion shall not constitute a dissolution or termination of the converting business entity. (1999-369, s. 3.7.)

Legal Periodicals. — For "Legislative Survey: Business & Banking," see 22 Campbell L. Rev. 253 (2000)

§§ 57C-9A-05 through 57C-9A-09: Reserved for future codification purposes.

Part 1A. Conversion of Limited Liability Company.

§ 57C-9A-10. Conversion.

A domestic limited liability company may convert to a different business entity if:

    (1) The conversion is permitted by the laws of the state or country governing the organization and internal affairs of such other business entity; and

    (2) The converting domestic limited liability company complies with the requirements of this Part and, to the extent applicable, the laws referred to in subdivision (1) of this section. (2001-387, s. 96.)

Editor's Note. — Session Laws 2001-387, s. 175(a), made this Part effective January 1, 2002.

Session Laws 2001-387, s. 154(b) provides that nothing in this act shall supersede the provisions of Article 10 or 65 of Chapter 58 of the General Statutes, and this act does not create an alternate means for an entity governed by Article 65 of Chapter 58 of the General Statutes to convert to a different business form.

§ 57C-9A-11. Plan of conversion.

(a) The converting domestic limited liability company shall approve a written plan of conversion containing:

    (1) The name of the converting domestic limited liability company;

    (2) The name of the resulting business entity into which the domestic limited liability company shall convert, its type of business entity, and the state or country whose laws govern its organization and internal affairs;

    (3) The terms and conditions of the conversion; and

    (4) The manner and basis for converting the interests in the domestic limited liability company into interests, obligations, or securities of the resulting business entity or into cash or other property in whole or in part.

The plan of conversion may contain other provisions relating to the conversion.

(b) The plan of conversion shall be approved by the domestic limited liability company in the manner provided for the approval of such conversion in its articles of organization or a written operating agreement or, if there is no such provision, by the unanimous consent of its members. If any member of the converting domestic limited liability company has or will have personal liability for any existing or future obligation of the resulting business entity solely as a result of holding an interest in the resulting business entity, then in addition to the requirements of the preceding sentence, approval of the plan of conversion by the domestic limited liability company shall require the consent of that member. The converting domestic limited liability company shall provide a copy of the plan of conversion to each member of the converting domestic limited liability company at the time provided in its articles of organization or a written operating agreement or, if there is no such provision, prior to its approval of the plan of conversion.

(c) After a plan of conversion has been approved by a domestic limited liability company but before the articles of conversion become effective, the plan of conversion (i) may be amended as provided in the plan of conversion, or (ii) may be abandoned, subject to any contractual rights, as provided in the plan of conversion, articles of organization, or written operating agreement or, if not so provided, as determined by the managers or directors of the domestic limited liability company in accordance with G.S. 57C-3-20(b). (2001-387, s. 96; 2001-487, s. 62(n).)

Effect of Amendments. — Session Laws 2001-487, s. 62(n), effective January 1, 2002, in subsection (c) as enacted by Session Laws 2001-387, s. 96, inserted a comma following "conversion" at the end of item (i).

§ 57C-9A-12. Articles of conversion.

(a) After a plan of conversion has been approved by the converting domestic limited liability company as provided in G.S. 57C-9A-11, the converting domestic limited liability company shall deliver articles of conversion to the Secretary of State for filing. The articles of conversion shall state:

(1) The name of the converting domestic limited liability company;

(2) The name of the resulting business entity, its type of business entity, the state or country whose laws govern its organization and internal affairs, and, if the resulting business entity is not authorized to transact business or conduct affairs in this State, a designation of its mailing address and a commitment to file with the Secretary of State a statement of any subsequent change in its mailing address; and

(3) That a plan of conversion has been approved by the domestic limited liability company as required by law.

(b) If the domestic limited liability company is converting to a business entity whose formation, or whose status as a registered limited liability partnership as defined in G.S. 59-32, requires the filing of a document with the Secretary of State, then notwithstanding subsection (a) of this section the articles of conversion shall be included as part of that document and shall contain the information required by the laws governing the organization and internal affairs of the resulting business entity.

(c) If the plan of conversion is abandoned after the articles of conversion have been filed with the Secretary of State but before the articles of conversion become effective, the converting domestic limited liability company shall deliver to the Secretary of State for filing prior to the time the articles of conversion become effective an amendment of the articles of conversion withdrawing the articles of conversion.

(d) The conversion takes effect when the articles of conversion become effective.

(e) Certificates of conversion shall also be registered as provided in G.S. 47-18.1. (2001-387, s. 96; 2001-487, s. 62(o).)

Effect of Amendments. — Session Laws 2001-487, s. 62(o), effective January 1, 2002, in this section as enacted by Session Laws 2001-387, s. 96, designated the last two paragraphs of subsection (a) as subsections (b) and (c), and redesignated former subsections (b) and (c) as subsections (d) and (e); and rewrote present subsection (b).

§ 57C-9A-13. Effects of conversion.

(a) When the conversion takes effect:

(1) The converting domestic limited liability company ceases its prior form of organization and continues in existence as the resulting business entity;

(2) The title to all real estate and other property owned by the converting domestic limited liability company continues vested in the resulting business entity without reversion or impairment;

(3) All liabilities of the converting domestic limited liability company continue as liabilities of the resulting business entity;

(4) A proceeding pending by or against the converting domestic limited liability company may be continued as if the conversion did not occur; and

(5) The interests in the converting domestic limited liability company that are to be converted into interests, obligations, or securities of the resulting business entity or into the right to receive cash or other property are thereupon so converted, and the former holders of interests in the converting domestic limited liability company are entitled only to the rights provided in the plan of conversion.

The conversion shall not affect the liability or absence of liability of any holder of an interest in the converting domestic limited liability company for any acts, omissions, or obligations of the converting domestic limited liability company made or incurred prior to the effectiveness of the conversion. The cessation of the existence of the converting domestic limited liability company in its form of organization as a domestic limited liability company in the conversion shall not constitute a dissolution or termination of the converting domestic limited liability company.

(b) If the resulting business entity is not a domestic corporation or a domestic limited partnership, when the conversion takes effect the resulting business entity is deemed:

(1) To agree that it may be served with process in this State for enforcement of (i) any obligation of the converting domestic limited liability company and (ii) any obligation of the resulting business entity arising from the conversion; and

(2) To have appointed the Secretary of State as its agent for service of process in any such proceeding. Service on the Secretary of State of any such process shall be made by delivering to and leaving with the Secretary of State, or with any clerk authorized by the Secretary of State to accept service of process, duplicate copies of the process and the fee required by G.S. 57C-1-22(b). Upon receipt of service of process on behalf of a resulting business entity in the manner provided for in this section, the Secretary of State shall immediately mail a copy of the process by registered or certified mail, return receipt requested, to the resulting business entity. If the resulting business entity is authorized to transact business or conduct affairs in this State, the address for mailing shall be its principal office designated in the latest document filed with the Secretary of State that is authorized by law to designate the principal office or, if there is no principal office on file, its registered office. If the resulting business entity is not authorized to transact business or conduct affairs in this State, the address for mailing shall be the mailing address designated pursuant to G.S. 57C-9A-12(a)(2). (2001-387, s. 96.)

§§ 57C-9A-14 through 57C-9A-19: Reserved for future codification purposes.

Part 2. Merger.

§ 57C-9A-20. Merger.

A domestic limited liability company may merge with one or more other domestic limited liability companies or other business entities if:

(1) The merger is permitted by the laws of the state or country governing the organization and internal affairs of each other merging business entity; and

(2) Each merging domestic limited liability company and each other merging business entity comply with the requirements of this Part and, to the extent applicable, the laws referred to in subdivision (1) of this section. (1999-369, s. 3.7.)

Editor's Note. — Sections 57C-9A-20 to 57C-9A-23 were designated as such by the Revisor of Statutes, having been designated as G.S. 57C-9A-05 to 57C-9A-08 by Session Laws 1999-369, s. 3.7.

§ 57C-9A-21. Plan of merger.

(a) Each merging domestic limited liability company and each other merging business entity shall approve a written plan of merger containing:

(1) For each merging business entity, its name, type of business entity, and the state or country whose laws govern its organization and internal affairs;

(2) The name of the merging business entity that shall survive the merger;

(3) The terms and conditions of the merger;

(4) The manner and basis for converting the interests in each merging business entity into interests, obligations, or securities of the surviving business entity or into cash or other property in whole or in part; and

(5) If the surviving business entity is a domestic limited liability company, any amendments to its articles of organization that are to be made in connection with the merger.

The plan of merger may contain other provisions relating to the merger.

(b) In the case of a merging domestic limited liability company, the plan of merger must be approved in the manner provided in its articles of organization or a written operating agreement for approval of a merger with the type of business entity contemplated in the plan of merger, or, if there is no provision, by the unanimous consent of its members. If any member of a merging domestic limited liability company has or will have personal liability for any existing or future obligation of the surviving business entity solely as a result of holding an interest in the surviving business entity, then in addition to the requirements of the preceding sentence, approval of the plan of merger by the domestic limited liability company shall require the consent of each such member. In the case of each other merging business entity, the plan of merger must be approved in accordance with the laws of the state or country governing the organization and internal affairs of the merging business entity.

(c) After a plan of merger has been approved by a domestic limited liability company but before the articles of merger become effective, the plan of merger (i) may be amended as provided in the plan of merger, or (ii) may be abandoned (subject to any contractual rights) as provided in the plan of merger, articles of organization, or written operating agreement or, if not so provided, as determined by the managers of the domestic limited liability company in accordance with G.S. 57C-3-20(b). (1999-369, s. 3.7; 2001-387, s. 97; 2001-487, s. 62(p).)

Editor's Note. — Session Laws 2001-387, s. 154(b) provides that nothing in this act shall supersede the provisions of Article 10 or 65 of Chapter 58 of the General Statutes, and this act does not create an alternate means for an entity governed by Article 65 of Chapter 58 of the General Statutes to convert to a different business form.

Effect of Amendments. — Session Laws 2001-387, s. 97, effective January 1, 2002, inserted the second sentence in subsection (b).

Session Laws 2001-487, s. 62(p), effective January 1, 2002, inserted "has or" near the

beginning of the second sentence in subsection (b) as amended by Session Laws 2001-387, s. 97.

§ 57C-9A-22. Articles of merger.

(a) After a plan of merger has been approved by each merging domestic limited liability company and each other merging business entity as provided in G.S. 57C-9A-21, the surviving business entity shall deliver articles of merger to the Secretary of State for filing. The articles of merger shall set forth:

(1) The plan of merger;

(2) For each merging business entity, its name, type of business entity, and the state or country whose laws govern its organization and internal affairs;

(3) The name of the surviving business entity and, if the surviving business entity is not authorized to transact business or conduct affairs in this State, a designation of its mailing address and a commitment to file with the Secretary of State a statement of any subsequent change in its mailing address;

(4) A statement that the plan of merger has been approved by each merging business entity in the manner required by law; and

(5) The effective date and time of the merger if it is not to be effective at the time of filing of the articles of merger.

If the plan of merger is amended or abandoned after the articles of merger have been filed but before the articles of merger become effective, the surviving business entity shall deliver to the Secretary of State for filing prior to the time the articles of merger become effective an amendment to the articles of merger reflecting the amendment or abandonment of the plan of merger.

(b) A merger takes effect when the articles of merger become effective.

(c) Certificates of merger shall also be registered as provided in G.S. 47-18.1. (1999-369, s. 3.7; 2001-387, s. 98.)

Editor's Note. — Session Laws 2001-387, s. 154(b), provides that nothing in this act shall supersede the provisions of Article 10 or 65 of Chapter 58 of the General Statutes, and this act does not create an alternate means for an entity governed by Article 65 of Chapter 58 of the General Statutes to convert to a different business form.

Effect of Amendments. — Session Laws 2001-387, s. 98, effective January 1, 2002, rewrote subdivision (a)(3), and in the last paragraph of subsection (a), inserted "after the articles of merger have been filed but," deleted "promptly" preceding "shall deliver," and inserted "prior to the time the articles of merger become effective."

§ 57C-9A-23. Effects of merger.

(a) When the merger takes effect:

(1) Each other merging business entity merges into the surviving business entity, and the separate existence of each merging business entity except the surviving business entity ceases;

(2) The title to all real estate and other property owned by each merging business entity is vested in the surviving business entity without reversion or impairment;

(3) The surviving business entity has all liabilities of each merging business entity;

(4) A proceeding pending by or against any merging business entity may be continued as if the merger did not occur, or the surviving business entity may be substituted in the proceeding for a merging business entity whose separate existence ceases in the merger;

(5) If a domestic limited liability company is the surviving business entity, its articles of organization shall be amended to the extent provided in the plan of merger;

(6) The interests in each merging business entity that are to be converted into interests, obligations, or securities of the surviving business entity or into the right to receive cash or other property are thereupon so converted, and the former holders of the interests are entitled only to the rights provided to them in the articles of merger or, in the case of former holders of shares in a domestic corporation, any rights they may have under Article 13 of Chapter 55 of the General Statutes; and

(7) If the surviving business entity is not a domestic corporation, the surviving business entity is deemed to agree that it will promptly pay to the dissenting shareholders of any merging domestic corporation the amount, if any, to which they are entitled under Article 13 of Chapter 55 of the General Statutes and otherwise to comply with the requirements of Article 13 as if it were a surviving domestic corporation in the merger.

The merger shall not affect the liability or absence of liability of any holder of an interest in a merging business entity for any acts, omissions, or obligations of any merging business entity made or incurred prior to the effectiveness of the merger. The cessation of separate existence of a merging business entity in the merger shall not constitute a dissolution or termination of that merging business entity.

(b) If the surviving business entity is not a domestic limited liability company, a domestic corporation, a domestic nonprofit corporation, or a domestic limited partnership, when the merger takes effect the surviving business entity is deemed:

(1) To agree that it may be served with process in this State in any proceeding for enforcement of (i) any obligation of any merging domestic limited liability company, domestic corporation, domestic nonprofit corporation, domestic limited partnership, or other partnership as defined in G.S. 59-36 that is formed under the laws of this State, (ii) the rights of dissenting shareholders of any merging domestic corporation under Article 13 of Chapter 55 of the General Statutes, and (iii) any obligation of the surviving business entity arising from the merger; and

(2) To have appointed the Secretary of State as its registered agent for service of process in any such proceeding. Service on the Secretary of State of any such process shall be made by delivering to and leaving with the Secretary of State, or with any clerk authorized by the Secretary of State to accept service of process, duplicate copies of such process and the fee required by G.S. 57C-1-22(b). Upon receipt of service of process on behalf of a surviving business entity in the manner provided for in this section, the Secretary of State shall immediately mail a copy of the process by registered or certified mail, return receipt requested, to the surviving business entity. If the surviving business entity is authorized to transact business or conduct affairs in this State, the address for mailing shall be its principal office designated in the latest document filed with the Secretary of State that is authorized by law to designate the principal office or, if there is no principal office on file, its registered office. If the surviving business entity is not authorized to transact business or conduct affairs in this State, the address for mailing shall be the mailing address designated pursuant to G.S. 57C-9A-22(a)(3). (1999-369, s. 3.7; 1999-456, s. 52(b); 2000-140, s. 51; 2001-387, s. 99.)

Editor's Note. — The subsection (b) designation was added at the direction of the Revisor of Statutes.

Session Laws 2001-387, s. 154(b) provides that nothing in this act shall supersede the provisions of Article 10 or 65 of Chapter 58 of the General Statutes, and this act does not create an alternate means for an entity governed by Article 65 of Chapter 58 of the General Statutes to convert to a different business form.

Effect of Amendments. — Session Laws 2001-387, s. 99, effective January 1, 2002, made minor punctuation changes throughout subsection (b); and in subdivision (b)(2), inserted "entity" and substituted "G.S. 57C-9A-22(a)(3)" for "subdivision (3) of subsection (d) of this section" in the last sentence.

§§ 57C-9A-24 through 57C-9A-29: Reserved for future codification purposes.

ARTICLE 10.

Miscellaneous.

§ 57C-10-01. Execution by judicial act.

Any person who is adversely affected by the failure or refusal of any person to execute and file any articles or other document to be filed under this Chapter may petition the superior court in the county where the limited liability company's principal office (or, if none in this State, its registered office) is or was last located or, if there is no such office, in the County of Wake, to direct the execution and filing of the articles or other document. If the court finds that it is proper for the articles or the document to be executed and filed and that there has been failure or refusal to execute and file the document, it shall order the Secretary of State to file the appropriate articles or other document. (1993, c. 354, s. 1.)

Legal Periodicals. — For note, "Corporate Law — Limited Liability Company Act, N.C. Gen. Stat. G.S. 57C-1-01 to 57C-10-07 (1993)," see 72 N.C.L. Rev. 1654 (1994).

For article, "The Creation of North Carolina's Limited Liability Corporation Act," see 32 Wake Forest L. Rev. 179 (1997).

§ 57C-10-02. Applicability of provisions to foreign and interstate commerce.

The provisions of this Chapter shall apply to determine the rights and obligations of a limited liability company formed hereunder in commerce with foreign nations and among the several states, except as prohibited by law. (1993, c. 354, s. 1; 2001-387, s. 100.)

Editor's Note. — Session Laws 2001-387, s. 154(b) provides that nothing in this act shall supersede the provisions of Article 10 or 65 of Chapter 58 of the General Statutes, and this act does not create an alternate means for an entity governed by Article 65 of Chapter 58 of the General Statutes to convert to a different business form.

Effect of Amendments. — Session Laws 2001-387, effective January 1, 2002, substituted "formed" for "organized."

§ 57C-10-03. Rules of construction.

(a) The rules that statutes in derogation of the common law are to be strictly construed shall have no application to this Chapter.

(b) The law of estoppel shall apply to this Chapter.

(c) The law of agency shall apply under this Chapter.

(d) This Chapter shall not be construed so as to impair the obligations of any contract existing when this Chapter goes into effect, nor to affect any action or proceedings begun or right accrued before this Chapter takes effect. (1993, c. 354, s. 1.)

§ 57C-10-04. Jurisdiction of the superior courts.

The superior courts shall have jurisdiction to enforce the provisions of this Chapter. (1993, c. 354, s. 1.)

§ 57C-10-05. Rules for cases not provided for in this Chapter.

In any case not provided for in this Chapter, the rules of law and equity shall govern. (1993, c. 354, s. 1.)

§ 57C-10-06. Income taxation.

A limited liability company, a foreign limited liability company authorized to transact business in this State, and a member of one of these companies are subject to taxation under Article 4 of Chapter 105 of the General Statutes in accordance with their classification for federal income tax purposes. Accordingly, if a limited liability company or a foreign limited liability company authorized to transact business in this State is classified for federal income tax purposes as a C corporation as defined in G.S. 105-131(b)(2) or an S corporation as defined in G.S. 105-131(b)(8), the company and its members are subject to tax under Article 4 of Chapter 105 of the General Statutes to the same extent as a C corporation or an S corporation, as the case may be, and its shareholders. If a limited liability company or a foreign limited liability company authorized to transact business in this State is classified for federal income tax purposes as a partnership, the company and its members are subject to tax under Article 4 of Chapter 105 of the General Statutes to the same extent as a partnership and its members. If a limited liability company or a foreign limited liability company authorized to transact business in this State is classified for federal income tax purposes as other than a corporation or a partnership, the company and its members are subject to tax under Article 4 of Chapter 105 of the General Statutes in a manner consistent with that classification. This section does not require a limited liability company or a foreign limited liability company to obtain an administrative ruling from the Internal Revenue Service on its classification under the Internal Revenue Code. (1993, c. 354, s. 1; 2001-387, s. 101.)

Editor's Note. — Session Laws 2001-387, s. 154(b) provides that nothing in this act shall supersede the provisions of Article 10 or 65 of Chapter 58 of the General Statutes, and this act does not create an alternate means for an entity governed by Article 65 of Chapter 58 of the General Statutes to convert to a different business form.

Effect of Amendments. — Session Laws 2001-387, s. 101, effective January 1, 2002, rewrote the second sentence, inserted "of the General Statutes" in the third sentence, and inserted "of Chapter 105 of the General Statutes" in the fourth sentence.

§ 57C-10-07. Intent.

It is the intent of the General Assembly that the legal existence of limited liability companies formed under this Chapter be recognized outside the boundaries of this State and that, subject to any reasonable requirement of registration, a domestic limited liability company transacting business outside this State be granted full faith and credit under Section 1 of Article IV of the Constitution of the United States. (1993, c. 354, s. 1; 2001-387, s. 102.)

Editor's Note. — Session Laws 2001-387, s. 154(b) provides that nothing in this act shall supersede the provisions of Article 10 or 65 of Chapter 58 of the General Statutes, and this act does not create an alternate means for an entity governed by Article 65 of Chapter 58 of the General Statutes to convert to a different business form.

Effect of Amendments. — Session Laws 2001-387, s. 102, effective January 1, 2002, substituted "formed" for "organized."

Chapter 58.

Insurance.

Article 3.

General Regulations for Insurance.

Article 66.

Hospital, Medical and Dental Service Corporation Readable Insurance Certificates Act.

Article 67.

Health Maintenance Organization Act.

ARTICLE 1.

Title and Definitions.

§ 58-1-1. Title of the Chapter.

Articles 1 through 64 of this Chapter may be cited and shall be known as the Insurance Law. (1899, c. 54; Rev., s. 4677; C.S., s. 6260.)

Cross References. — As to hospital, medical, and dental service corporations, see Articles 65 and 66 of this Chapter. For the Health Maintenance Organization Act of 1979, see Article 67 of this Chapter. For provisions applicable to corporations governed by Articles 1 through 64 of this Chapter which relate to the elimination of discrimination in treatment of handicapped and disabled persons, see G.S. 168-10.

Editor's Note. — Pursuant to Session Laws 1987, c. 752, s. 9, as amended by Session Laws 1987 (1988 Reg. Sess.), c. 975, s. 34, the insurance and related laws of North Carolina in former Chapters 57, 57B, 58, 58A, 85C, 109, and 118, Articles 9B and 9C of Chapter 66, and Articles 1, 3, 4, 5, and 6 of Chapter 69 have been renumbered, rearranged and consolidated into a new Chapter 58. This recodification was performed by the Attorney General, through the Revisor of Statutes, and the Commissioner of Insurance, through the Legal Division of the Department of Insurance. Historical citations and case annotations to the sections in the former Chapters have been added to the corresponding sections in new Chapter 58 as recodified. The new Chapter uses a three-part numbering scheme, with the Chapter number as the first part of the code section number, the Article number as the second part, and the sections of the Chapter numbered in increments of five as the final part. At the end of new Chapter 58 are tables showing comparable sections and their disposition between the various former chapters and new Chapter 58.

Session Laws 1999-294, s. 13 provides that the Codifier of Rules may amend the text of the administrative rules in Title 11 of the North Carolina Administrative Code to reflect the recodification of Chapter 58 of the General Statutes. An amendment pursuant to this section is exempt from Chapter 150B of the General Statutes and review by the Rules Review Commission to the extent that it does not change the substance of the rule.

Legal Periodicals. — For article on the 1945 revision of the Insurance Law, see 23 N.C.L. Rev. 283 (1945).

For discussion of changes made by the Session Laws of 1947, see 25 N.C.L. Rev. 429 (1947).

For case law survey as to insurance, see 44 N.C.L. Rev. 1022 (1966); 45 N.C.L. Rev. 955 (1967).

For legislative survey on insurance, see 22 Campbell L. Rev. 253 (2000).

CASE NOTES

Purpose of Chapter. — The statute law makes elaborate and minute provisions for the protection of the people from imposition under the guise of insurance, and the Department of Insurance is charged with the special duty of seeing that these provisions are complied with. State v. Arlington, 157 N.C. 640, 73 S.E. 122 (1911).

Chapter 58 does not provide the exclusive remedy for those damaged by unfair trade practices in the insurance industry. Phillips v. Integon Corp., 70 N.C. App. 440, 319 S.E.2d 673 (1984).

There is no authority which expressly declares that Chapter 58 is the exclusive vehicle of obtaining relief from those who engage in unfair trade practices in the insurance industry. Phillips v. Integon Corp., 70 N.C. App. 440, 319 S.E.2d 673 (1984).

Chapter 75 is applicable to the sale of insurance. Phillips v. Integon Corp., 70 N.C. App. 440, 319 S.E.2d 673 (1984).

Therefore, if a cause of action relating to insurance practices can arise under the first chapter, then surely it also can arise under the second. Phillips v. Integon Corp., 70 N.C. App. 440, 319 S.E.2d 673 (1984).

Section 75-1.1 provides a remedy for unfair trade practices in the insurance industry. Allegations of unfair fixing of insurance rates should be permitted to be raised under G.S. 75-5 as well and reject defendant's claim that any expansion of Chapter 75 should not be limited only to G.S. 75-1.1. Although G.S. 75-1.1 contains a general prohibition of unfair methods of competition and unfair or deceptive practices affecting commerce, G.S. 75-5 (now repealed) lists particular acts that constitute unfair or deceptive acts. Phillips v. Integon Corp., 70 N.C. App. 440, 319 S.E.2d 673 (1984).

Insurance Policy as Thing of Value. — Former section 75-5(b)(3), (4) and (5) address fixing the price of "goods." Goods are defined in the statute to include "other things of value." An insurance policy is a thing of value. Phillips v. Integon Corp., 70 N.C. App. 440, 319 S.E.2d 673 (1984).

Cited in In re North Carolina Auto. Rate Admin. Office, 278 N.C. 302, 180 S.E.2d 155 (1971); State ex rel. Comm'r of Ins. v. North Carolina Rate Bureau, 61 N.C. App. 262, 300 S.E.2d 586 (1983); United Va. Bank v. Air-Lift Assocs., 79 N.C. App. 315, 339 S.E.2d 90 (1986).

§ 58-1-5. Definitions.

In this Chapter, unless the context clearly requires otherwise:

(1) "Alien company" means a company incorporated or organized under the laws of any jurisdiction outside of the United States.

(1a) "Commercial aircraft" means aircraft used in domestic, flag, supplemental, commuter, or on-demand operations, as defined in Federal Aviation Administration Regulations, 14 C.F.R. § 119.3, as amended.

(2) "Commissioner" means the Commissioner of Insurance of North Carolina or an authorized designee of the Commissioner.

(3) "Company" or "insurance company" or "insurer" includes any corporation, association, partnership, society, order, individual or aggregation of individuals engaging or proposing or attempting to engage as principals in any kind of insurance business, including the exchanging of reciprocal or interinsurance contracts between individuals, partnerships and corporations. "Company" or "insurance company" or "insurer" does not mean the State of North Carolina or any county, city, or other political subdivision of the State of North Carolina.

(4) "Department" means the Department of Insurance of North Carolina.

(5) "Domestic company" means a company incorporated or organized under the laws of this State.

(6) "Foreign company" means a company incorporated or organized under the laws of the United States or of any jurisdiction within the United States other than this State.

(7) "NAIC" means the National Association of Insurance Commissioners.

(8) Repealed by Session Laws 1999-219, s. 5.5, effective October 1, 1999.

(9) "Person" means an individual, partnership, firm, association, corporation, joint-stock company, trust, any similar entity, or any combination of the foregoing acting in concert.

(10) The singular form includes the plural, and the masculine form includes the feminine wherever appropriate. (1899, c. 54, s. 1; Rev., s. 4678; C.S., s. 6261; 1945, c. 383; 1971, c. 510, s. 1; 1987, c. 864, s. 34; 1995, c. 193, s. 1; 1999-219, s. 5.5; 2001-334, s. 18.2.)

CASE NOTES

The Insurance Law clearly contemplates both incorporated and unincorporated companies. State v. Arlington, 157 N.C. 640, 73 S.E. 122 (1911).

Cited in Wake County Hosp. Sys. v. National Cas. Co., 804 F. Supp. 768 (E.D.N.C. 1992); North Carolina Steel, Inc. v. National Council on Comp. Ins., 123 N.C. App. 163, 472 S.E.2d 578 (1996), aff'd in part and rev'd in part, 347 N.C. 627, 496 S.E.2d 369 (1998).

§ 58-1-10. Contract of insurance.

A contract of insurance is an agreement by which the insurer is bound to pay money or its equivalent or to do some act of value to the insured upon, and as an indemnity or reimbursement for the destruction, loss, or injury of something in which the other party has an interest. (1899, c. 54, s. 2; Rev., s. 4679; C.S., s. 6262; 1945, c. 383.)

Legal Periodicals. — For comment, "Insurance Contract and Policy in General as it Relates to North Carolina," see 3 N.C. Cent. L.J. 259 (1972).

For note, "Searching for Limits on a Municipality's Retention of Governmental Immunity," see 76 N.C.L. Rev. 269 (1997).

CASE NOTES

Contract to Indemnify Assured for Loss Is Insurance Contract. — That portion of a contract under which a company agrees to indemnify the assured for loss or damage from perils therein defined, with provision for subrogation of the company to the right of the assured against third persons, constitutes a contract of insurance. American Nat'l Fire Ins. Co. v. Gibbs, 260 N.C. 681, 133 S.E.2d 669 (1963).

But Contract to Pay Claims for Which Assured Is Liable Is Surety Contract. — A contract under which a company obligates itself to pay, to any shipper or consignee, claims for which the assured would be liable by provision of G.S. 62-111, with stipulation that the assured should reimburse the company for any such payment, is a surety contract and not a contract of insurance. American Nat'l Fire Ins.

Co. v. Gibbs, 260 N.C. 681, 133 S.E.2d 669 (1963).

Requirement That Risk Shift. — One characteristic of an insurance contract is the shifting of a risk from the insured to the insurer. If no risk is shifted there is not an insurance contract. Blackwelder v. City of Winston-Salem, 332 N.C. 319, 420 S.E.2d 432 (1992).

Applied in Miller Brewing Co. v. Morgan Mechanical Contractors, 90 N.C. App. 310, 368 S.E.2d 438 (1988).

Cited in Charleston & W. Carolina Ry. v. Robert G. Lassiter & Co., 207 N.C. 408, 177 S.E. 9 (1934); Kraemer v. Moore, 67 N.C. App. 505, 313 S.E.2d 610 (1984); Wake County Hosp. Sys. v. National Cas. Co., 804 F. Supp. 768 (E.D.N.C. 1992).

§ 58-1-15. Warranties by manufacturers, distributors, or sellers of goods or services.

(a) As used in this section:

(1) "Goods" means all things that are moveable at the time of sale or at the time the buyer takes possession. "Goods" includes things not in existence at the time the transaction is entered into; and includes

things that are furnished or used at the time of sale or subsequently in modernization, rehabilitation, repair, alteration, improvement, or construction on real property so as to become a part of real property whether or not they are severable from real property.

(2) "Services" means work, labor, and other personal services.

(b) Any warranty made solely by a manufacturer, distributor, or seller of goods or services without charge, or an extended warranty offered as an option and made solely by a manufacturer, distributor, or seller of goods or services for charge, that guarantees indemnity for defective parts, mechanical or electrical breakdown, labor, or any other remedial measure, including replacement of goods or repetition of services, shall not be a contract of insurance under Articles 1 through 64 of this Chapter; however, service agreements on motor vehicles are governed by G.S. 58-1-25, 58-1-35, and 58-1-36. Service agreements on home appliances are governed by G.S. 58-1-30, 58-1-35, and 58-1-36.

(c) Nothing in this section affects the provisions of Article 28 of this Chapter. Any warranty or extended warranty made by any person other than the manufacturer, distributor, or seller of the warranted goods or services is a contract of insurance.

(d) Repealed by Session Laws 1989 (Regular Session, 1990), c. 1021, s. 3. (1959, c. 866; 1975, cc. 643, 788; 1977, c. 185; 1987, c. 369; 1989, c. 789, s. 2; 1989 (Reg. Sess., 1990), c. 1021, s. 3; 1991 (Reg. Sess., 1992), c. 1014, s. 2; 1995, c. 193, s. 2.)

§ 58-1-20. Real property warranties.

(a) Any warranty relating to fixtures to real property issued by a person is a contract of insurance, except the following:

(1) A warranty made by a builder or seller of the real property;

(2) A warranty providing for the repair or replacement of the items covered by the warranty for defective parts and mechanical failure or resulting from ordinary wear and tear, and excluding from its coverage damage from recognizable perils, such as fire, flood, and wind, that neither relate to any defect in the items covered nor result from ordinary wear and tear.

(b) It is unlawful for any person to issue a warranty specified in subdivision (a)(2) of this section unless that person has posted a surety bond with the Secretary of State in the principal sum of not less than one hundred thousand dollars ($100,000). The bond must be issued by a surety company licensed to do business in this State and is subject to the approval of the Secretary of State. Any person to whom the warranty is issued may institute an action to recover against the warrantor and the surety bond for any breach of warranty.

(c) Persons issuing real property warranties shall comply with the requirements of G.S. 58-1-36. (1979, c. 773, s. 1; 1987, c. 864, s. 9; 1991, c. 644, s. 43; 2003-290, s. 1(a).)

Effect of Amendments. — Session Laws 2003-290, s. 1.(a), effective October 1, 2003, added subsection (c).

§ 58-1-25. Motor vehicle service agreement companies.

(a) This section applies to all motor vehicle service agreement companies soliciting business in this State, but it does not apply to performance guarantees, warranties, or motor vehicle service agreements made by

(1) A manufacturer,

(2) A distributor, or

    (3) A subsidiary or affiliate of a manufacturer or a distributor, where fifty-one percent (51%) or more of the subsidiary or affiliate is owned directly or indirectly by

        a. The manufacturer,

        b. The distributor, or

        c. The common owner of fifty-one percent (51%) or more of the manufacturer or distributor

in connection with the sale of motor vehicles. This section does not apply to any motor vehicle dealer licensed to do business in this State (i) whose primary business is the retail sale and service of motor vehicles; (ii) who makes and administers its own service agreements with or without association with a third-party administrator or who makes its own service agreements in association with a manufacturer, distributor, or their subsidiaries or affiliates; and (iii) whose service agreements cover only vehicles sold by the dealer to its retail customer; provided that the dealer complies with G.S. 58-1-35 and G.S. 58-1-36. A motor vehicle dealer who sells a motor vehicle service agreement to a consumer, as defined in 15 U.S.C. § 2301(3), is not deemed to have made a written warranty to the consumer with respect to the motor vehicle sold or to have entered into a service contract with the consumer that applies to the motor vehicle, as provided in 15 U.S.C. § 2308(a), if: (i) the motor vehicle dealer acts as a mere agent of a third party in selling the motor vehicle service agreement; and (ii) the motor vehicle dealer would, after the sale of the motor vehicle service agreement, have no further obligation under the motor vehicle service agreement to the consumer to service or repair the vehicle sold to the consumer at or within 90 days before the dealer sold the motor vehicle service agreement to the consumer.

    (b) The following definitions apply in this section and in G.S. 58-1-30, 58-1-35, and 58-1-36:

    (1) Authorized insurer. — An insurance company authorized to write liability insurance under Articles 7, 16, 21, or 22 of this Chapter.

    (2) Distributor. — Defined in G.S. 20-286(3).

    (3) Licensed insurer. — An insurance company licensed to write liability insurance under Article 7 or 16 of this Chapter.

    (4) Motor vehicle. — Defined in G.S. 20-4.01(23), but also including mopeds as defined in G.S. 20-4.01(27)d1.

    (5) Motor vehicle service agreement. — Any contract or agreement indemnifying the motor vehicle service agreement holder against loss caused by failure, arising out of the ownership, operation, or use of a motor vehicle, of a mechanical or other component part of the motor vehicle that is listed in the agreement. The term does not mean a contract or agreement guaranteeing the performance of parts or lubricants manufactured by the guarantor and sold for use in connection with a motor vehicle where no additional consideration is paid or given to the guarantor for the contract or agreement beyond the price of the parts or lubricants.

    (6) Motor vehicle service agreement company. — Any person that issues motor vehicle service agreements and that is not a licensed insurer.

    (c) through (g) Repealed by Session Laws 1993 (Reg. Sess., 1994), c. 730, s. 3. (1991 (Reg. Sess., 1992), c. 1014, s. 1; 1993, c. 504, ss. 47, 48, 52; c. 539, s. 442; 1994, Ex. Sess., c. 24, s. 14(c); 1993 (Reg. Sess., 1994), c. 730, ss. 3, 4; 1995, c. 193, s. 3.)

§ 58-1-30. Home appliance service agreement companies.

    (a) This section applies to all home appliance service agreement companies soliciting business in this State, but it does not apply to performance guarantees or warranties made by manufacturers in connection with the sale of new home appliances. This section does not apply to any home appliance dealer licensed to do business in this State (i) whose primary business is the retail sale and service of home appliances; (ii) who makes and administers its own service agreements without association with any other entity; and (iii) whose service agreements cover primarily appliances sold by the dealer to its retail customers, provided that the dealer complies with G.S. 58-1-35 and G.S. 58-1-36. This section does not apply to any warranty made by a builder or seller of real property relating to home appliances that are sold along with real property. This section does not apply to any issuer of credit cards or charge cards that markets home appliance service agreements as an ancillary part of its business; provided, however, that such issuer maintains insurance in accordance with G.S. 58-1-36.

(b) The following definitions apply in this section:

(1) "Home appliance" means a clothes washing machine or dryer; kitchen appliance; vacuum cleaner; sewing machine; home audio or video electronic equipment; home electronic data processing equipment; home exercise and fitness equipment; home health care equipment; power tools; heater or air conditioner, other than a permanently installed unit using internal ductwork; or other personal consumer goods.

(2) "Home appliance service agreement" means any contract or agreement indemnifying the home appliance service agreement holder against loss caused by failure, arising out of the ownership, operation, or use of a home appliance, of a mechanical or other component part of the home appliance that is listed in the agreement.

(3) "Home appliance service agreement company" means any person that issues home appliance service agreements and that is not a licensed insurer.

(c) through (g) Repealed by Session Laws 1993 (Reg. Sess., 1994), c. 730, s. 3. (1991 (Reg. Sess., 1992), c. 1014, s. 1; 1993, c. 504, ss. 49, 52; c. 539, s. 443; 1994, Ex. Sess., c. 24, s. 14(c); 1993 (Reg. Sess., 1994), c. 730, ss. 3, 4, 6; 2003-290, s. 1(b).)

Effect of Amendments. — Session Laws 2003-290, s. 1.(b), effective October 1, 2003, in subsection (a), substituted "primarily appliances" for "only appliances" in the second sentence, and deleted the former third sentence, which read "Provided, however, that G.S. 58-1-36 does not apply to a service agreement contract offered by a person primarily engaged in the retail sale of goods and services who incidentally offers service agreement contracts and has a net worth of one hundred million dollars ($100,000,000), has offered service agreement contracts for at least the preceding 10 years, and is required to file an SEC Form 10K"; made stylistic changes in subdivisions (b)(1), (2), and (3); and in subdivision (b)(1), inserted "home exercise and fitness equipment; home health care equipment; power tools;" and added "or other personal consumer goods" at the end of the subdivision.

§ 58-1-35. Miscellaneous requirements for motor vehicle and home appliance service agreement companies.

(a) The provisions of this section and G.S. 58-1-36 apply to companies specified in G.S. 58-1-25 and G.S. 58-1-30.

(b) The following definitions apply in this section and in G.S. 58-1-36:

(1) Service agreement. — Includes motor vehicle service agreements and home appliance service agreements.

(2) Service agreement company. — Includes motor vehicle service agreement companies and home appliance service agreement companies.

(c) Before the sale of any service agreement, the service agreement company shall give written notice to the customer clearly disclosing that the purchase of the agreement is not required either to purchase or to obtain financing for a motor vehicle or home appliance, as the case may be.

(d) No service agreement may be used in this State by any service agreement company if the agreement:

    (1) In any respect violates, or does not comply with, the laws of this State;

    (2) Contains, or incorporates by reference when incorporation is otherwise permissible, any inconsistent, ambiguous, or misleading clauses or any exceptions and conditions that deceptively affect the risk purported to be assumed in the general coverage of the agreement;

    (3) Has any title, heading, or other indication of its provisions that is misleading; or

    (4) Is printed or otherwise reproduced in a manner that renders any material provision of the agreement substantially illegible.

(e) All service agreements used in this State by a service agreement company shall:

    (1) Not contain provisions that allow the company to cancel the agreement in its discretion other than for nonpayment of premiums or for a direct violation of the agreement by the consumer where the service agreement states that violation of the agreement would subject the agreement to cancellation;

    (2) With respect to a motor vehicle service agreement as defined in G.S. 58-1-25(b)(1), provide for a right of assignability by the consumer to a subsequent purchaser before expiration of coverage if the subsequent purchaser meets the same criteria for motor vehicle service agreement acceptability as the original purchaser; and

    (3) Contain a cancellation provision allowing the consumer to cancel at any time after purchase and receive a pro rata refund less any claims paid on the agreement and a reasonable administrative fee, not to exceed ten percent (10%) of the amount of the pro rata refund.

(f) Each service agreement company, as a minimum requirement for permanent office records, shall maintain:

    (1) A complete set of accounting records, including a general ledger, cash receipts and disbursements journals, accounts receivable registers, and accounts payable registers.

    (2) Memorandum journals showing the service agreement forms issued to the company salespersons and recording the delivery of the forms to dealers.

    (3) Memorandum journals showing the service agreement forms received by dealers and indicating the disposition of the forms by the dealers.

    (4) A detailed service agreement register, in numerical order by agreement number, of agreements in force. The register shall include the following: agreement number, date of issue, issuing dealer, name of agreement holder, description of item covered, service agreement period (and, if applicable, mileage), gross premium, total commission paid, and net premium.

    (5) A detailed claims register, in numerical order by service agreement number. The register shall include the following information: agreement number, date of issue, date claim paid, and, if applicable, disposition other than payment and reason for the disposition.

(g) Repealed by Session Laws 1993 (Reg. Sess., 1994), c. 730, s. 3.

(h) No insurer or service agreement company shall act as a fronting company for any unauthorized insurer or service agreement company that is not in compliance with this section. As used in this subsection, "fronting company" means a licensed insurer or service agreement company that, by reinsurance or otherwise, generally transfers to one or more unauthorized insurers or service agreement companies that are not in compliance with this section a substantial portion of the risk of loss under agreements it writes in this State.

(i) All funds belonging to insurers, companies, or others received by a salesperson of a service agreement are trust funds received by the salesperson in a fiduciary capacity; and the salesperson, in the applicable regular course of business, shall account for and pay the funds to the person entitled to the funds. Any salesperson who, not being entitled to the funds, diverts or appropriates the funds or any portion of the funds, other than funds representing the salesperson's commission if authorized by the salesperson agreement, to his or her own use, upon conviction is guilty of embezzlement under G.S. 14-90.

(j) Any person who knowingly offers for sale or sells a service agreement for a company that has failed to comply with the provisions of this section is guilty of a Class 1 misdemeanor. All service agreement companies and individuals selling service agreements are subject to G.S. 75-1 through G.S. 75-19.

(k) Repealed by Session Laws 1993 (Reg. Sess., 1994), c. 730, s. 2.

(l) No service agreement company shall use in its name, contracts, literature, advertising in any medium, or any other printed matter the words "insurance", "casualty", "surety", "mutual", or any other words descriptive of the insurance business or deceptively similar to the name or description of any insurer doing business in this State, except to indicate that the obligations of the contract are insured by an insurance company.

(m) If not submitted electronically, all contracts, literature, advertising materials, letters, and other documents submitted to the Department to comply with the filing requirements of this Chapter or an administrative rule adopted pursuant to this Chapter shall be submitted on paper eight and one-half inches by eleven inches. Brochures and pamphlets shall not be stapled or bound. (1991 (Reg. Sess., 1992), c. 1014, s. 1; 1993, c. 504, ss. 50, 51, 52; c. 539, s. 444; 1994, Ex. Sess., c. 24, s. 14(c); 1993 (Reg. Sess., 1994), c. 730, ss. 2, 3, 5; 1995, c. 193, ss. 4, 5; 2003-290, s. 2.)

Editor's Note. — This section was amended by Session Laws 1993 (Reg. Sess., 1994), c. 730, s. 5, in the coded bill drafting format provided by G.S. 120-20.1. In part, the amendment added the duplicate language "a substantial portion of the risk of loss under agreements it writes in this State" at the end of subsection (h). This section has been set out in the form above at the direction of the Revisor of Statutes.

Effect of Amendments. — Session Laws 2003-290, s. 2, effective October 1, 2003, added subsection (m).

§ 58-1-36. Insurance policy requirements.

(a) Each company or person subject to this section shall maintain contractual liability insurance or service agreement reimbursement insurance with an authorized insurer for one hundred percent (100%) of claims exposure, including reported and incurred but not reported claims and claims expenses, on business written in this State unless the company or person:

(1) Maintains an audited net worth of one hundred million dollars ($100,000,000);

(2) Has offered service agreement contracts or warranties, as applicable to the respective company, its parent company, or person, for at least the preceding 10 years; and

(3) Either is required to file and has filed an SEC Form 10K or Form 20-F with the Securities and Exchange Commission (SEC) within the last calendar year or, if the company does not file with the SEC, can produce, upon request, a copy of the company's audited financial statements, which show a net worth of the company or person of at

least one hundred million dollars ($100,000,000). A company or person may utilize its parent company's Form 10-K, Form 20-F, or audited financial statements to satisfy this requirement if the parent company agrees to guarantee the obligations of the company or person relating to service agreement contracts or warranties, as applicable to the respective company or person, sold by the company or person in this State.

(b) All forms relating to insurance policies written by authorized insurers under this section shall be filed with and approved by the Commissioner before they may be used for any purpose in this State, irrespective of whether the insurers are licensed insurers.

(c) Each policy shall contain the following provisions:

(1) If the company or person does not fulfill its obligations under service agreements or warranties issued in this State for any reason, including federal bankruptcy or state receivership proceedings, the insurer will pay losses and unearned premium refunds directly to any person making the claim under the service agreement.

(2) The insurer shall assume full responsibility for the administration of claims if the company or person is unable to do so.

(3) The policy is subject to the cancellation, nonrenewal, and renewal provisions of G.S. 58-41-15, 58-41-20, 58-41-25, and 58-41-40.

(4) The policy shall insure all service agreements and warranties that were issued while the policy was in effect, regardless of whether the premium was remitted to the insurer.

(5) If the insurer is fulfilling any service agreement covered by the policy and if the service agreement holder cancels the service agreement, the insurer shall make a full refund of the unearned premium to the consumer pursuant to G.S. 58-1-35(e)(3). This subdivision applies only to service agreement companies.

(d) The Commissioner may adopt rules, in addition to the requirements of this section, governing the terms and conditions of policy forms for the insurance required by this section.

(e) Persons and companies subject to G.S. 58-1-15, 58-1-20, 58-1-25, 58-1-30, and 58-1-42 are subject to and shall comply with this section. The Commissioner may enforce compliance with this section using the provisions of Article 2 of this Chapter. (1993 (Reg. Sess., 1994), c. 730, s. 1; 2003-290, s. 1(c).)

Effect of Amendments. — Session Laws 2003-290, s. 1.(c), effective October 1, 2003, in subsection (a), substituted "Each company or person subject to this section shall maintain" for "Each service agreement company shall maintain," and added "unless the company or person:" in the introductory paragraph, and added subdivisions (1), (2), and (3); in subdivisions (c)(1) and (c)(2), substituted "company or person" for "service agreement company"; in subdivision (c)(1), inserted "or warranties"; in subdivision (c)(4), inserted "and warranties"; in subdivision (c)(5), added the last sentence; and added subsection (e).

§ **58-1-40:** Repealed by Session Laws 1993 (Reg. Sess., 1994), c. 730, s. 3.

§ 58-1-42. Mechanical breakdown service agreements.

(a) Except as provided in subsection (c) of this section, all mechanical breakdown service agreement companies soliciting business in this State shall comply with G.S. 58-1-35 and G.S. 58-1-36.

(b) As used in this section, "mechanical breakdown service agreement companies" include any person that issues mechanical breakdown service agreements and is not a licensed insurer, and "mechanical breakdown service agreements" are applicable to mechanized equipment, including automobiles, riding mowers, scooters, generators, farm implements, logging equipment, road graders, bulldozers, and power equipment not licensed for road use, whether mobile or not.

(c) This section does not apply to performance guarantees, warranties, mechanical breakdown service agreements, or motor vehicle service agreements made by:

    (1) A manufacturer.

    (2) A distributor.

    (3) A subsidiary of a manufacturer or distributor. (2003-290, s. 4.)

Editor's Note. — Session Laws 2003-290, s. 6, made this section effective October 1, 2003. This section was enacted as G.S. 58-1-40. It has been recodified as G.S. 58-1-42 at the direction of the Revisor of Statutes.

§§ 58-1-45, 58-1-50: Repealed by Session Laws 1993 (Reg. Sess., 1994), c. 730, s. 3.

ARTICLE 2.

Commissioner of Insurance.

§ 58-2-1. Department established.

The Department is hereby established as a separate and distinct department, which is charged with the execution of laws relating to insurance and other subjects placed under the Department. (1899, c. 54, s. 3; 1901, c. 391, s. 1; Rev., s. 4680; C.S., s. 6263; 1991, c. 720, s. 5.)

Legal Periodicals. — For note discussing changes in automobile rate regulation and the role of the Insurance Commissioner in North Carolina, see 17 Wake Forest L. Rev. 822 (1981).

CASE NOTES

Cited in O'Neal v. Wake County, 196 N.C. 184, 145 S.E. 28 (1928); In re North Carolina Auto. Rate Admin. Office, 278 N.C. 302, 180 S.E.2d 155 (1971); North Carolina Steel, Inc. v. National Council on Comp. Ins., 123 N.C. App. 163, 472 S.E.2d 578 (1996), aff'd in part and rev'd in part, 347 N.C. 627, 496 S.E.2d 369 (1998); State ex rel. Commissioner of Ins. v. North Carolina Rate Bureau, 350 N.C. 539, 516 S.E.2d 150 (1999).

§ 58-2-5. Commissioner's election and term of office.

The chief officer of the Insurance Department shall be called the Commissioner of Insurance; whenever in the statutes of this State the words "Insurance Commissioner" appear, they shall be deemed to refer to and to be synonymous with the term "Commissioner of Insurance." He shall be elected by the people in the manner prescribed for the election of members of the General Assembly and State officers, and the result of the election shall be declared in the same manner and at the same time as the election of State officers is now declared. His term of office begins on the first day of January next after his election, and is for four years or until his successor is elected and qualified. If a vacancy occurs during the term, it shall be filled by the Governor for the unexpired term. (Rev., ss. 4680, 4681; 1907, c. 868; C.S., s. 6264; 1943, c. 170.)

Cross References. — As to penalty for failure to take oath, see G.S. 128-5. As to Commissioner's taking of oath and induction into office, see G.S. 147-4.

Cited in Allstate Ins. Co. v. Lanier, 242 F. Supp. 73 (E.D.N.C. 1965); In re North Carolina Auto. Rate Admin. Office, 278 N.C. 302, 180 S.E.2d 155 (1971).

§ 58-2-10. Salary of Commissioner.

The salary of the Commissioner shall be set by the General Assembly in the Current Operations Appropriations Act. In addition to the salary set by the General Assembly in the Current Operations Appropriations Act, longevity pay shall be paid on the same basis as is provided to employees of the State who are subject to the State Personnel Act. (1899, c. 54, ss. 3, 8; 1901, c. 710; 1903, c. 42; c. 771, s. 3; Rev., s. 2756; 1907, c. 830, s. 10; c. 994; 1909, c. 839; 1913, c. 194; 1915, cc. 158, 171; 1917, c. 70; 1919, c. 247, s. 4; C.S., s. 3874; 1921, c. 25, s. 1; 1933, c. 282, s. 5; 1935, c. 293; 1937, c. 342; 1945, c. 383; 1947, c. 1041; 1949, c. 1278; 1953, c. 1, s. 2; 1957, c. 1; 1963, c. 1178, s. 6; 1967, c. 1130; c. 1237, s. 6; 1969, c. 1214, s. 6; 1971, c. 912, s. 6; 1973, c. 778, s. 6; 1975, 2nd Sess., c. 983, s. 21; 1977, c. 802, s. 42.12; 1983, c. 761, s. 206; 1983 (Reg. Sess., 1984), c. 1034, s. 164; 1987, c. 738, s. 32(b); 1991, c. 720, s. 4.)

§ 58-2-15. Chief deputy commissioner.

The Commissioner shall appoint and may remove at his discretion a chief deputy commissioner, who, in the event of the absence, death, resignation, disability or disqualification of the Commissioner, or in case the office of Commissioner shall for any reason become vacant, shall have and exercise all the powers and duties vested by law in the Commissioner. He shall receive such compensation as fixed and provided by the Department of Administration. (1945, c. 383; 1987, c. 864, s. 19(a).)

For discussion of respective powers and duties of the Commissioner and his designated hearing officer in the review of filed rates and entry of a final agency decision in a contested insurance rate case, see State ex rel. Comm'r of Ins. v. North Carolina Rate Bureau, 61 N.C. App. 506, 300 S.E.2d 845 (1983).

Cited in In re North Carolina Auto. Rate Admin. Office, 278 N.C. 302, 180 S.E.2d 155 (1971); State ex rel. Comm'r of Ins. v. North Carolina Rate Bureau, 61 N.C. App. 262, 300 S.E.2d 586 (1983).

Attendance at Meetings Through Delegates or Designated Subordinates. — Those members of the Council of State who have statutory authority to delegate duties may, in conformity with such statutes, attend and vote at meetings of Boards of which they are ex officio members through delegates or designated subordinates. The remaining members of the Council of State may make similar delegations or designations where, in the member's judgment, other duties necessitate his absence and the statute creating his ex officio membership does not express or clearly imply an intent of the General Assembly that the powers of such membership be exercised personally. See opinion of Attorney General to the Honorable James E. Long, Commissioner of Insurance, 55 N.C.A.G. 116 (1986).

§ 58-2-20. Chief actuary.

The Commissioner shall appoint and may remove at his discretion a chief actuary, who shall receive such compensation as fixed and provided by the Department of Administration. (1945, c. 383; 1987, c. 864, s. 19(b).)

CASE NOTES

Cited in In re North Carolina Auto. Rate Admin. Office, 278 N.C. 302, 180 S.E.2d 155 (1971).

§ 58-2-25. Other deputies, actuaries, examiners and employees.

(a) The Commissioner shall appoint or employ such other deputies, actuaries, economists, financial analysts, financial examiners, licensed attorneys, rate and policy analysts, accountants, fire and rescue training instructors, market conduct analysts, insurance complaint analysts, investigators, engineers, building inspectors, risk managers, clerks and other employees that the Commissioner considers to be necessary for the proper execution of the work of the Department, at the compensation that is fixed and provided by the Department of Administration. If the Commissioner considers it to be necessary for the proper execution of the work of the Department to contract with persons, except to fill authorized employee positions, all of those contracts, except those provided for in Articles 36 and 37 of this Chapter, shall be made pursuant to the provisions of Article 3C of Chapter 143 of the General Statutes.

Whenever the Commissioner or any deputy or employee of the Department is requested or subpoenaed to testify as an expert witness in any civil or administrative action, the party making the request or filing the subpoena and on whose behalf the testimony is given shall, upon receiving a statement of the cost from the Commissioner, reimburse the Department for the actual time and expenses incurred by the Department in connection with the testimony.

(b) The minimum education requirements for financial analysts and examiners referred to in subsection (a) of this section are a bachelors degree, with the appropriate courses in accounting as defined in 21 NCAC 8A.0309, and other courses that are required to qualify the applicant as a candidate for the uniform certified public accountant examination, based on the examination requirements in effect at the time of graduation by the analyst or examiner from an accredited college or university. (1945, c. 383; 1981, c. 859, s. 94; 1987, c. 864, s. 20; 1989 (Reg. Sess., 1990), c. 1069, s. 20; 1991, c. 681, s. 1; 2000-122, s. 4.)

Cross References. — As to assistant attorney general assigned to Commissioner and Insurance Department, see G.S. 114-4.2A.

CASE NOTES

Cited in In re North Carolina Auto. Rate Admin. Office, 278 N.C. 302, 180 S.E.2d 155 (1971).

§ 58-2-30. Appointments of committees or councils.

(a) As used in this section, the term "committee" means a collective body that consults with and advises the Commissioner or his designee in detailed technical areas; and the term "council" means a collective body that consults with and advises the Commissioner or his designee as representative of citizen advice in specific areas of interest.

(b) The Commissioner may create and appoint committees and councils, each of which shall consist of no more than 13 members unless otherwise provided by law. The members of any committee or council shall serve at the pleasure of the Commissioner and may be paid per diem and necessary travel and subsistence expenses within the limits of appropriations and in accordance with G.S. 138-5. Per diem, travel, and subsistence payments to members of committees or councils that are created in connection with federal programs shall be paid from federal funds unless otherwise provided by law. (1985, c. 666, s. 44.)

§ 58-2-35. Seal of Department.

The Commissioner, with the approval of the Governor, shall devise a seal, with suitable inscription, for his office, a description of which, with the certificate of approval by the Governor, shall be filed in the office of the Secretary of State, with an impression thereof, which seal shall thereupon become the seal of office of the Commissioner of the Department. The seal may be renewed whenever necessary. (1899, c. 54, s. 11; Rev., s. 4682; C.S., s. 6266; 1991, c. 720, ss. 4, 5.)

§ 58-2-40. Powers and duties of Commissioner.

The Commissioner shall:

    (1) See that all laws of this State that the Commissioner is responsible for administering and the provisions of this Chapter are faithfully executed; and to that end the Commissioner is authorized to adopt rules in accordance with Chapter 150B of the General Statutes, in order to enforce, carry out and make effective the provisions of those laws. The Commissioner is also authorized to adopt such further rules not contrary to those laws that will prevent persons subject to the Commissioner's regulatory authority from engaging in practices injurious to the public.

    (2) Have the power and authority to adopt rules pertaining to and governing the solicitation of proxies, including financial reporting in connection therewith, with respect to the capital stock or other equity securities of any domestic stock insurance company.

    (3) Prescribe to the companies, associations, orders, or bureaus required by Articles 1 through 64 of this Chapter to report to the Commissioner, the necessary forms for the statements required. The Commissioner may change those forms from time to time when necessary to secure full information as to the standing, condition, and such other information desired of companies, associations, orders, or bureaus under the jurisdiction of the Department.

    (4) Receive and thoroughly examine each financial statement required by Articles 1 through 64 of this Chapter.

    (5) Report in detail to the Attorney General any violations of the laws relative to insurance companies, associations, orders and bureaus or the business of insurance; and the Commissioner may institute civil actions or criminal prosecutions either by the Attorney General or

another attorney whom the Attorney General may select, for any violation of the provisions of Articles 1 through 64 of this Chapter.

(6) Upon a proper application by any citizen of this State, give a statement or synopsis of the provisions of any insurance contract offered or issued to the citizen.

(7) Administer, or the Commissioner's deputy may administer, all oaths required in the discharge of the Commissioner's official duty.

(8) Compile and make available to the public such lists of rates charged, including deviations, and such explanations of coverages that are provided by insurers for and in connection with contracts or policies of (i) insurance against loss to residential real property with not more than four housing units located in this State and any contents thereof or valuable interest therein and other insurance coverages written in connection with the sale of such property insurance and (ii) private passenger (nonfleet) motor vehicle liability, physical damage, theft, medical payments, uninsured motorists, and other insurance coverages written in connection with the sale of such insurance, as may be advisable to inform the public of insurance premium differentials and of the nature and types of coverages provided. The explanations of coverages provided for in this section must comply with the provisions of Article 38 of this Chapter.

(9) Repealed by Session Laws 2000, ch. 19, s. 3, effective on or after April 1, 1998. (1899, c. 54, s. 8; 1905, c. 430, s. 3; Rev., s. 4689; C.S., s. 6269; 1945, c. 383; 1947, c. 721; 1965, c. 127, s. 1; 1971, c. 757, s. 1; 1977, c. 376, s. 1; 1979, c. 755, s. 19; c. 881, s. 1; 1981, c. 846, s. 2; 1989, c. 485, s. 29; 1991, c. 644, s. 26; 1997-392, s. 3; 2000-19, s. 3.)

Cross References. — For the Readable Insurance Policies Act, see G.S. 58-38-1 et seq. As to certain duties of Commissioner with regard to fire inspection and prevention, see Article 79 of this Chapter. As to Commissioner's duties with regard to the Firemen's Relief Fund, see Articles 84 to 88 of this Chapter.

Editor's Note. — Session Laws 2000-19, s. 22, as amended by Session Laws 2001-265, s. 4, provides: "This act constitutes a recent act of the General Assembly within the meaning of G.S. 150B-21.1. The Environmental Manage-ment Commission and the Commission on Health Services may adopt temporary rules to implement the provisions of this act until 1 July 2002."

Session Laws 2000-19, s. 20, contains a severability clause.

Legal Periodicals. — For survey of 1979 administrative law, see 58 N.C.L. Rev. 1185 (1980).

For article discussing limitations on ad hoc adjudicatory rulemaking by an administrative agency, see 61 N.C.L. Rev. 67 (1982).

CASE NOTES

Rate-making authority, as distinguished from purely administrative functions, must be derived from a clear statutory enactment granting the Commissioner of Insurance such power. State ex rel. Comm'r of Ins. v. Integon Life Ins. Co., 28 N.C. App. 7, 220 S.E.2d 409 (1975).

The Commissioner of Insurance has no authority to prescribe or regulate premium rates except insofar as that authority has been conferred upon him by statute. State ex rel. Comm'r of Ins. v. North Carolina Auto. Rate Admin. Office, 24 N.C. App. 223, 210 S.E.2d 441 (1974), cert. denied, 286 N.C. 412, 211 S.E.2d 801 (1975).

Commissioner Has No Express or Implied Power to Set Rates. — Clearly, subdi-vision (1) contains no express grant of authority to set rates and it is not such an implied power as is reasonably necessary for the Commissioner's proper functioning. State ex rel. Comm'r of Ins. v. Integon Life Ins. Co., 28 N.C. App. 7, 220 S.E.2d 409 (1975).

The Commissioner's power to make "rules and regulations" can in no way grant him the authority to carry out the "legislative power" of setting rates. State ex rel. Comm'r of Ins. v. Integon Life Ins. Co., 28 N.C. App. 7, 220 S.E.2d 409 (1975).

Insurance Commissioner's approval of a requested rate increase conditioned upon a delayed implementation date and one-year guarantee was within his statutory scope of authority. Golden Rule Ins. Co. v. Long, 113

N.C. App. 187, 439 S.E.2d 599 (1993).

Or to Make Substantive Law. — An administrative agency has no power to promulgate rules and regulations which alter or add to the law it was set up to administer or which have the effect of substantive law. State ex rel. Comm'r of Ins. v. Integon Life Ins. Co., 28 N.C. App. 7, 220 S.E.2d 409 (1975).

Nothing in § 58-63-10 grants authority to the Commissioner of Insurance to take any action whatsoever. It merely prohibits unfair methods of competition or unfair or deceptive acts or practices in the insurance industry, which are exhaustively defined in G.S. 58-63-15. State ex rel. Comm'r of Ins. v. Integon Life Ins. Co., 28 N.C. App. 7, 220 S.E.2d 409 (1975).

Clearly Article 63 of this Chapter, G.S. 58-63-1 et seq., generally and G.S. 58-63-10 specifically contain no authority to issue orders setting premium rates. State ex rel. Comm'r of Ins. v. Integon Life Ins. Co., 28 N.C. App. 7, 220 S.E.2d 409 (1975).

Power to Remedy Unfair Trade Practices Under §§ 58-63-20 et seq. Limited. — Sections 58-63-20 and 58-63-25 and former G.S. 58-63-30, which provide for the Commissioner's power to act in regard to "any unfair method of competition or in any unfair or deceptive act or practice prohibited by G.S. 58-63-10 ...," grant no remedial power to the Commissioner to remedy unfair trade practices, other than the power to investigate, bring charges and issue cease and desist orders. State ex rel. Comm'r of Ins. v. Integon Life Ins. Co., 28 N.C. App. 7, 220 S.E.2d 409 (1975).

Commissioner's Power Under Plan of Operation. — The Commissioner, not the superior court, was vested with the power to determine if an insurer was entitled, under plan of operation, to a retroactive amendment of its ceding expense allowance; however, the powers given to the Commission by G.S. 58-37-40 do not permit the Commissioner to make findings of fact which are not supported by material and substantial evidence. North Carolina Reinsurance Facility v. Long, 98 N.C. App. 41, 390 S.E.2d 176 (1990).

Effect of Companies' Acquiescence in Rating Setting. — Commissioner's contention that acquiescence by companies writing credit life insurance in rates set by prior Commissioners of Insurance gave present Commissioner the authority to fix credit life rates was untenable. State ex rel. Comm'r of Ins. v. Integon Life Ins. Co., 28 N.C. App. 7, 220 S.E.2d 409 (1975).

Commissioner of Insurance had no au- **thority to enjoin an insurance company from entering into an agreement to lease property** owned by the company's president and treasurer. Charlotte Liberty Mut. Ins. Co. v. State ex rel. Lanier, 16 N.C. App. 381, 192 S.E.2d 57 (1972).

Applicability of Rule-Making Provisions of Administrative Procedure Act. — A requirement by the Commissioner of Insurance that audited data be submitted in a ratemaking case was a legislative rule and therefore subject to the rule making provisions of the North Carolina Administrative Procedure Act, G.S. 150B-1 et seq. State ex rel. Comm'r of Ins. v. North Carolina Rate Bureau, 300 N.C. 381, 269 S.E.2d 547, rehearing denied, 301 N.C. 107, 273 S.E.2d 300 (1980).

Anti-subrogation Rule. — Commissioner's promulgation of 11 N.C.A.C. 12.0319, prohibiting subrogation provisions in life or accident and health insurance contracts, supported by this section (right to limit practices injurious to the public) and G.S. 58-50-15(a) (prohibiting provisions less favorable to the insured), did not exceed his statutory authority, even though it may have changed state substantive law, and did not amount to an unconstitutional delegation of legislative powers because statutory provisions (this section and G.S. 58-51-15 and 58-50-15) and judicial review (available under Chapter 150B) offer adequate procedural safeguards and support the delegation of power to the Commissioner. In re Ruling by N. C. Comm'r of Ins., 134 N.C. App. 22, 517 S.E.2d 134, 1999 N.C. App. LEXIS 665 (1999), cert. denied, appeal dismissed, 351 N.C. 105, 540 S.E.2d 356 (1999).

Applied in State ex rel. Comm'r of Ins. v. North Carolina Auto. Rate Admin. Office, 287 N.C. 192, 214 S.E.2d 98 (1975); State ex rel. Comm'r of Ins. v. North Carolina Fire Ins. Rating Bureau, 292 N.C. 70, 231 S.E.2d 882 (1977).

Cited in Allstate Ins. Co. v. Lanier, 242 F. Supp. 73 (E.D.N.C. 1965); State ex rel. Lanier v. Vines, 274 N.C. 486, 164 S.E.2d 161 (1968); State ex rel. Lanier v. Vines, 1 N.C. App. 208, 161 S.E.2d 35 (1968); In re North Carolina Auto. Rate Admin. Office, 278 N.C. 302, 180 S.E.2d 155 (1971); Marks v. Thompson, 282 N.C. 174, 192 S.E.2d 311 (1972); State v. Felts, 79 N.C. App. 205, 339 S.E.2d 99 (1986); North Carolina Life & Accident & Health Ins. Guar. Ass'n v. Alcatel, 876 F. Supp. 748 (E.D.N.C. 1995).

§ 58-2-45. Orders of Commissioner; when writing required.

Whenever by any provision of Articles 1 through 64 of this Chapter, the Commissioner is authorized to grant any approval, authorization or permission or to make any other order affecting any insurer, insurance agent, insurance broker or other person or persons subject to the provisions of Articles 1 through 64 of this Chapter, such order shall not be effective unless made in writing and signed by the Commissioner or by his authority. (1945, c. 383.)

CASE NOTES

Cited in Allstate Ins. Co. v. Lanier, 242 F. Supp. 73 (E.D.N.C. 1965).

§ 58-2-50. Examinations, hearings, and investigations.

All examinations, hearings, and investigations provided for by this Chapter may be conducted by the Commissioner personally or by one or more deputies, investigators, actuaries, examiners or employees designated for the purpose. If the Commissioner or any investigator appointed to conduct the investigations is of the opinion that there is evidence to charge any person or persons with a criminal violation of any provision of this Chapter, the Commissioner may arrest with warrant or cause the person or persons to be arrested. All hearings shall, unless otherwise specially provided, be held in accordance with this Article and Article 3A of Chapter 150B of the General Statutes and at a time and place designated in a written notice given by the Commissioner to the person cited to appear. The notice shall state the subject of inquiry and the specific charges, if any. (1945, c. 383; 1969, c. 1009; 1995, c. 193, s. 6; 1999-219, s. 1.1.)

Legal Periodicals. — For article discussing limitations on ad hoc adjudicatory rulemaking by an administrative agency, see 61 N.C.L. Rev. 67 (1982).

CASE NOTES

For discussion of respective powers and duties of the Commissioner and his designated hearing officer in the review of filed rates and entry of a final agency decision in a contested insurance rate case, see State ex rel. Comm'r of Ins. v. North Carolina Rate Bureau, 61 N.C. App. 506, 300 S.E.2d 845 (1983).

Arbitrary and Capricious Procedure. — Where no notice whatever was given by the Commissioner to the Rating Bureau of his intent to convert contemplated hearing on the Bureau's motion to vacate "letter order" into an independent investigation of the reasonableness of existing premium rates for extended coverage insurance pursuant to former G.S. 58-131.2, Commissioner's action in proceeding without such notice and an adequate opportunity to the Bureau to present evidence as to the merits of the existing premium rate level would be deemed arbitrary and capricious. State ex rel. Comm'r of Ins. v. North Carolina Fire Ins. Rating Bureau, 291 N.C. 55, 229 S.E.2d 268 (1976).

Cited in Allstate Ins. Co. v. Lanier, 242 F. Supp. 73 (E.D.N.C. 1965); In re North Carolina Auto. Rate Admin. Office, 278 N.C. 302, 180 S.E.2d 155 (1971); State ex rel. Comm'r of Ins. v. North Carolina Rate Bureau, 61 N.C. App. 262, 300 S.E.2d 586 (1983).

§ 58-2-52. Appeals and rate-making hearings before the Commissioner.

(a) The Commissioner may adopt rules for the hearing of appeals by the Commissioner or the Commissioner's designated hearing officer under G.S. 58-36-35, 58-37-65, 58-45-50, 58-46-30, 58-48-40(c)(7), 58-48-42, and 58-62-51(c). These rules may provide for prefiled evidence and testimony of the parties, prehearing statements and conferences, settlement conferences, discovery, subpoenas, sanctions, motions, intervention, consolidation of cases, continuances, rights and responsibilities of parties, witnesses, and evidence.

(b) Notwithstanding G.S. 150B-38(h), hearing procedures for rate filings made by the North Carolina Rate Bureau shall be governed by the provisions of Article 36 of this Chapter and G.S. 150B-39 through G.S. 150B-41. The Commissioner may adopt rules for those hearings.

(c) Appeals under the statutes cited in subsection (a) of this section are not contested cases within the meaning of G.S. 150B-2(2). (1993, c. 409, s. 23; 1995, c. 193, s. 7.)

§ 58-2-53. Filing approvals and disapprovals; clarification of law.

Whenever any provision of this Chapter requires a person to file rates, forms, classification plans, rating plans, plans of operation, the Safe Driver Incentive Plan, or any other item with the Commissioner or Department for approval, the approval or disapproval of the filing is an agency decision under Chapter 150B of the General Statutes only with respect to the person making the filing or any person that intervenes in the filing. (2001-423, s. 2.)

Editor's Note. — Session Laws 2001-423, s. 4, made this section effective September 22, 2001.

§ 58-2-55. Designated hearing officers.

In any contested case under this Chapter or Article 9A or Article 9B of Chapter 143 of the General Statutes, the Commissioner may designate a member of his staff to serve as a hearing officer. When the Commissioner is unable or elects not to hear a contested case and elects not to designate a hearing officer to hear a contested case, he shall apply to the director of the Office of Administrative Hearings for the designation of an administrative law judge to preside at the hearing of a contested case. Upon receipt of the application, the Director shall, without undue delay, assign an administrative law judge to hear the case. (1989, c. 485, s. 30; 1999-393, s. 4.)

§ 58-2-60. Restraining orders; criminal convictions.

(a) Whenever it appears to the Commissioner that any person has violated, is violating, or threatens to violate any provision of Articles 1 through 64, 65 and 66, 67, 69, 70, or 71 of this Chapter, or Article 9A of Chapter 143 of the General Statutes, he may apply to the superior court of any county in which the violation has occurred, is occurring, or may occur for a restraining order and injunction to restrain such violation. If upon application the court finds that any provision of said statutes has been violated, is being violated, or a violation thereof is threatened, the court shall issue an order restraining and enjoining such violations; and such relief may be granted regardless of whether criminal prosecution is instituted under any provision of law.

(b) The conviction in any court of competent jurisdiction of any licensee for any criminal violation of the statutes referred to in subsection (a) of this section automatically has the effect of suspending the license of that person until such time that the license is reinstated by the Commissioner. As used in this subsection, "conviction" includes an adjudication of guilt, a plea of guilty, and a plea of nolo contendere. (1989, c. 485, s. 30.)

§ 58-2-65. License surrenders.

This section applies to persons or entities licensed under Articles 1 through 64, 65 and 66, 67, 69, 70, or 71 of this Chapter, or Article 9A of Chapter 143 of the General Statutes. When a licensee is accused of any act, omission, or misconduct that would subject the license to suspension or revocation, the licensee, with the consent and approval of the Commissioner, may surrender the license for a period of time established by the Commissioner. A person or entity who surrenders a license shall not thereafter be eligible for or submit any application for licensure during the period of license surrender. (1989, c. 485, s. 30.)

§ 58-2-69. Notification of criminal convictions and changes of address; service of notice.

(a) As used in this section:
    (1) "License" includes any license, certificate, registration, or permit issued under this Chapter.
    (2) "Licensee" means any person who holds a license.
(b) Every applicant for a license shall inform the Commissioner of the applicant's residential address. Every licensee shall give written notification to the Commissioner of any change of the licensee's residential address within 10 business days after the licensee moves into the licensee's new residence. This requirement applies if the change of residential address is by governmental action and there has been no actual change of residence location; in which case the licensee must notify the Commissioner within 10 business days after the effective date of the change. A violation of this subsection is not a ground for revocation, suspension, or nonrenewal of the license or for the imposition of any other penalty by the Commissioner.
(c) If a licensee is convicted in any court of competent jurisdiction for any crime or offense other than a motor vehicle infraction, the licensee shall notify the Commissioner within 10 days after the date of the conviction. As used in this subsection, "conviction" includes an adjudication of guilt, a plea of guilty, or a plea of nolo contendere.
(d) Notwithstanding any other provision of law, whenever the Commissioner is authorized or required to give any notice under this Chapter to a licensee, the notice may be given personally or by sending the notice by first-class mail to the licensee at the address that the licensee has provided to the Commissioner under subsection (b) of this section.
(e) The giving of notice by mail under subsection (d) of this section is complete upon the expiration of four days after the deposit of the notice in the post office. Proof of the giving of notice by mail may be made by the certificate of any employee of the Department. (1998-211, s. 16.)

§ 58-2-70. Civil penalties or restitution for violations; administrative procedure.

(a) This section applies to any person who is subject to licensure or certification under this Chapter.

(b) Whenever the Commissioner has reason to believe that any person has violated any of the provisions of this Chapter, and the violation subjects the license or certification of that person to suspension or revocation, the Commissioner may, after notice and opportunity for a hearing, proceed under the appropriate subsections of this section.

(c) If, under subsection (b) of this section, the Commissioner finds a violation of this Chapter, the Commissioner may, in addition to or instead of suspending or revoking the license or certification, order the payment of a monetary penalty as provided in subsection (d) of this section or petition the Superior Court of Wake County for an order directing payment of restitution as provided in subsection (e) of this section, or both. Each day during which a violation occurs constitutes a separate violation.

(d) If the Commissioner orders the payment of a monetary penalty pursuant to subsection (c) of this section, the penalty shall not be less than one hundred dollars ($100.00) nor more than one thousand dollars ($1,000). In determining the amount of the penalty, the Commissioner shall consider the degree and extent of harm caused by the violation, the amount of money that inured to the benefit of the violator as a result of the violation, whether the violation was committed willfully, and the prior record of the violator in complying or failing to comply with laws, rules, or orders applicable to the violator. The clear proceeds of the penalty shall be remitted to the Civil Penalty and Forfeiture Fund in accordance with G.S. 115C-457.2. Payment of the civil penalty under this section shall be in addition to payment of any other penalty for a violation of the criminal laws of this State.

(e) Upon petition of the Commissioner the court may order the person who committed a violation specified in subsection (c) of this section to make restitution in an amount that would make whole any person harmed by the violation. The petition may be made at any time and also in any appeal of the Commissioner's order.

(f) Restitution to any State agency for extraordinary administrative expenses incurred in the investigation and hearing of the violation may also be ordered by the court in such amount that would reimburse the agency for the expenses.

(g) Nothing in this section prevents the Commissioner from negotiating a mutually acceptable agreement with any person as to the status of the person's license or certificate or as to any civil penalty or restitution.

(h) Unless otherwise specifically provided for, all administrative proceedings under this Chapter are governed by Chapter 150B of the General Statutes. Appeals of the Commissioner's orders under this section shall be governed by G.S. 58-2-75. (1985, c. 666, s. 35; 1987, c. 752, ss. 3-5; c. 864, s. 1; 1989, c. 485, s. 46; 1998-211, s. 15; 1998-215, s. 83(a).)

Legal Periodicals. — For a survey of 1996 developments in constitutional law, see 75 N.C.L. Rev. 2252 (1997).

CASE NOTES

The General Assembly specifically provided for penalties for violations of Chapter 58 in this section and G.S. 58-3-100. Home Indem. Co. v. Hoechst Celanese Corp., 128 N.C. App. 226, 494 S.E.2d 768, 1998 N.C. App. LEXIS 23 (1998), cert. denied, 505 S.E.2d 869 (1998).

Cited in In re Appeal from Civil Penalty Assessed for Violations of Sedimentation Pollu-tion Control Act, 92 N.C. App. 1, 373 S.E.2d 572 (1988); North Carolina Steel, Inc. v. National Council on Comp. Ins., 123 N.C. App. 163, 472 S.E.2d 578 (1996), aff'd in part and rev'd in part, 347 N.C. 627, 496 S.E.2d 369 (1998); North Carolina Steel, Inc. v. National Council Comp. Ins., 347 N.C. 627, 496 S.E.2d 369 (1998).

§ 58-2-75. Court review of orders and decisions.

(a) Any order or decision made, issued or executed by the Commissioner, except an order to make good an impairment of capital or surplus or a deficiency in the amount of admitted assets and except an order or decision that the premium rates charged or filed on all or any class of risks are excessive, inadequate, unreasonable, unfairly discriminatory or are otherwise not in the public interest or that a classification assignment is unwarranted, unreasonable, improper, unfairly discriminatory, or not in the public interest, shall be subject to review in the Superior Court of Wake County on petition by any person aggrieved filed within 30 days from the date of the delivery of a copy of the order or decision made by the Commissioner upon such person. A copy of such petition for review as filed with and certified to by the clerk of said court shall be served upon the Commissioner or in his absence upon someone in active charge of the Department within five days after the filing thereof. If such petition for review is not filed within the said 30 days, the parties aggrieved shall be deemed to have waived the right to have the merits of the order or decision reviewed and there shall be no trial of the merits thereof by any court to which application may be made by petition or otherwise, to enforce or restrain the enforcement of the same.

(b) The Commissioner shall within 30 days, unless the time be extended by order of court, after the service of the copy of the petition for review as provided in subsection (a) of this section, prepare and file with the clerk of the Superior Court of Wake County a complete transcript of the record of the hearing, if any, had before him, and a true copy of the order or decision duly certified. The order or decision of the Commissioner if supported by substantial evidence shall be presumed to be correct and proper. The court may change the place of hearing,

    (1) Upon consent of the parties; or

    (2) When the convenience of witnesses and the ends of justice would be promoted by the change; or

    (3) When the judge has at any time been interested as a party or counsel.

The cause shall be heard by the trial judge as a civil case upon transcript of the record for review of findings of fact and errors of law only. It shall be the duty of the trial judge to hear and determine such petition with all convenient speed and to this end the cause shall be placed on the calendar for the next succeeding term for hearing ahead of all other cases except those already given priority by law. If on the hearing before the trial judge it shall appear that the record filed by the Commissioner is incomplete, he may by appropriate order direct the Commissioner to certify any or all parts of the record so omitted.

(c) The trial judge shall have jurisdiction to affirm or to set aside the order or decision of the Commissioner and to restrain the enforcement thereof.

(d) Appeals from all final orders and judgments entered by the superior court in reviewing the orders and decisions of the Commissioner may be taken to the appellate division of the General Court of Justice by any party to the action as in other civil cases.

(e) The commencement of proceedings under this section shall not operate as a stay of the Commissioner's order or decision, unless otherwise ordered by the court. (1945, c. 383; 1947, c. 721; 1969, c. 44, s. 55; 1971, c. 703, s. 1.)

Legal Periodicals. — For comment on the 1947 amendment which rewrote subsection (b), see 25 N.C.L. Rev. 439 (1947).

For survey of 1976 case law on insurance, see 55 N.C.L. Rev. 1052 (1977).

For article discussing limitations on ad hoc adjudicatory rulemaking by an administrative agency, see 61 N.C.L. Rev. 67 (1982).

For article analyzing the scope of the North Carolina Insurance Commissioner's rate-making authority, see 61 N.C.L. Rev. 97 (1982).

CASE NOTES

Differentiation Between This Section and § 58-2-80. — This section omits any grant to the Commissioner of the authority to seek judicial review, whereas G.S. 58-2-80 expressly grants him such authority, which indicates a clear legislative intent to differentiate between these two sections. State Farm Mut. Auto. Ins. Co. v. Ingram, 288 N.C. 381, 218 S.E.2d 364 (1975).

The powers of the Commissioner are not to be construed broadly so as to include a right of appeal under this section. State Farm Mut. Auto. Ins. Co. v. Ingram, 288 N.C. 381, 218 S.E.2d 364 (1975).

The Commissioner was not intended to be the representative of the public or to be deemed an aggrieved person so as to permit him to appeal pursuant to the provisions of this section. State Farm Mut. Auto. Ins. Co. v. Ingram, 288 N.C. 381, 218 S.E.2d 364 (1975).

Or Under § 58-37-35. — The Commissioner is not expressly granted the power to appeal by G.S. 58-37-35. State Farm Mut. Auto. Ins. Co. v. Ingram, 288 N.C. 381, 218 S.E.2d 364 (1975).

Commissioner's Power Under Plan of Operation. — The Commissioner, not the superior court, was vested with the power to determine if an insurer was entitled, under plan of operation, to a retroactive amendment of its ceding expense allowance; however, the powers given to the Commission by G.S. 58-37-40 do not permit the Commissioner to make findings of fact which are not supported by material and substantial evidence. North Carolina Reinsurance Facility v. Long, 98 N.C. App. 41, 390 S.E.2d 176 (1990).

Applicability of This Section and § 150B-51. — Although this section and G.S. 150B-51 are comparable, G.S. 150B-51 is the controlling judicial review statute; however, to the extent that G.S. 58-2-75 added to and was consistent with the judicial review function of G.S. 150B-51, the court would apply the review standards articulated in both statutes. North Carolina Reinsurance Facility v. Long, 98 N.C. App. 41, 390 S.E.2d 176 (1990).

Section Applies to Appeals in the Court of Appeals. — Cases involving judicial review before a court other than the Wake County Superior Court, by statutory interpretation and implication extend the application of this section to higher appeals, particularly, appeals to North Carolina Court of Appeals. North Carolina Reinsurance Facility v. Long, 98 N.C. App. 41, 390 S.E.2d 176 (1990).

Applicability of Standing Requirement in Court of Appeals. — Where a case involves the right of the Commissioner to seek review before the Court of Appeals and not before the superior court, this section is not expressly applicable. However, since by statutory interpretation and implication this section would extend its application to the analogous, higher appeal to the Court of Appeals, its requirement that the person must be aggrieved in order to appeal still applies. State Farm Mut. Auto. Ins. Co. v. Ingram, 288 N.C. 381, 218 S.E.2d 364 (1975).

Order Not Excepted from Review. — An order by the Commissioner in which, without notice or hearing, he abruptly directed that the Automobile Rate Administrative Office could not follow the standard rule of application for placing into effect changes, whether increases or decreases, in insurance premium rates was not such a decision as is described in G.S. 58-2-80, nor did it fall within any of the categories excepted from review by petition to the Superior Court of Wake County under this section. North Carolina Auto. Rate Admin. Office v. Ingram, 35 N.C. App. 578, 242 S.E.2d 205 (1978).

Issuance of Mandatory Injunction Requiring Commissioner to Approve Reorganization. — The trial court did not exceed its power and authority by issuing its mandatory injunction requiring the Commissioner of Insurance to approve a domestic insurance corporation's plan to reorganize under a holding company structure where the Commissioner acted arbitrarily and capriciously when he disapproved the plan. Occidental Life Ins. Co. v. Ingram, 34 N.C. App. 619, 240 S.E.2d 460 (1977).

Review Under Article 4 of Chapter 150B. — Since the scope of review provided in Art. 4, Ch. 150B is substantially broader than that provided by this section, the scope of judicial review applicable to a denial by the Commissioner of Insurance of a plan by a domestic insurance company to reorganize under a holding company structure is that provided for in Art. 4 of Ch. 150B. Occidental Life Ins. Co. v. Ingram, 34 N.C. App. 619, 240 S.E.2d 460 (1977).

Presumption Favoring Commissioner's Future Projections. — The Commissioner's projection of past experience and present conditions into the future is presumed to be correct and proper if supported by substantial evidence and if he has taken into account all of the relevant facts which he is directed by statute to consider. In re North Carolina Fire Ins. Rating Bureau, 275 N.C. 15, 165 S.E.2d 207 (1969).

Applied in In re Blue Bird Taxi Co., 237 N.C. 373, 75 S.E.2d 156 (1953); In re North Carolina Fire Ins. Rating Bureau, 245 N.C. 444, 96 S.E.2d 344 (1957); State ex rel. Comm'r of Ins. v. Integon Life Ins. Co., 28 N.C. App. 7, 220 S.E.2d 409 (1975); North Carolina Fire Ins.

Rating Bureau v. Ingram, 29 N.C. App. 338, 224 S.E.2d 229 (1976); Unigard Mut. Ins. Co. v. Ingram, 71 N.C. App. 725, 323 S.E.2d 442 (1984).

Cited in Allstate Ins. Co. v. Lanier, 242 F. Supp. 73 (E.D.N.C. 1965); State ex rel. N.C. Utils. Comm'n v. Old Fort Finishing Plant, 264 N.C. 416, 142 S.E.2d 8 (1965); Elmore v. Lanier, 270 N.C. 674, 155 S.E.2d 114 (1967); In re North Carolina Fire Ins. Rating Bureau, 2 N.C. App. 10, 162 S.E.2d 671 (1968); State ex rel. Lanier v. Vines, 1 N.C. App. 208, 161 S.E.2d 35 (1968); In re North Carolina Auto. Rate Admin. Office, 278 N.C. 302, 180 S.E.2d 155 (1971); In re Hardware Mut. Ins. Co., 278 N.C. 670, 180 S.E.2d 840 (1971); American Guarantee & Liab. Ins. Co. v. Ingram, 32 N.C. App. 552, 233 S.E.2d 398 (1977); In re McCrary, 112 N.C. App. 161, 435 S.E.2d 359 (1993); North Carolina Life & Accident & Health Ins. Guar. Ass'n v. Alcatel, 876 F. Supp. 748 (E.D.N.C. 1995); North Carolina Steel, Inc. v. National Council on Comp. Ins., 123 N.C. App. 163, 472 S.E.2d 578 (1996), aff'd in part and rev'd in part, 347 N.C. 627, 496 S.E.2d 369 (1998); St. Paul Fire & Marine Ins. Co. v. North Carolina Motor Vehicle Reinsurance Facility, 124 N.C. App. 450, 476 S.E.2d 897 (1996); North Carolina Steel, Inc. v. National Council Comp. Ins., 347 N.C. 627, 496 S.E.2d 369 (1998); Lupton v. Blue Cross & Blue Shield of N.C., 139 N.C. App. 421, 533 S.E.2d 270, 2000 N.C. App. LEXIS 909 (2000), cert. denied, 353 N.C. 266, 546 S.E.2d 105 (2000).

§ 58-2-80. Court review of rates and classification.

Any order or decision of the Commissioner that the premium rates charged or filed on all or any class of risks are excessive, inadequate, unreasonable, unfairly discriminatory or are otherwise not in the public interest or that a classification or classification assignment is unwarranted, unreasonable, improper, unfairly discriminatory or not in the public interest may be appealed to the North Carolina Court of Appeals by any party aggrieved thereby. Any such order shall be based on findings of fact, and if applicable, findings as to trends related to the matter under investigation, and conclusions of law based thereon. Any order or decision of the Commissioner, if supported by substantial evidence, shall be presumed to be correct and proper. For the purposes of the appeal the Insurance Commissioner, who shall be represented by his general counsel, shall be deemed an aggrieved party. (1971, c. 703, s. 2.)

Cross References. — As to jurisdiction of the Court of Appeals to review orders or decisions of the Commissioner of Insurance, see G.S. 7A-250.

Legal Periodicals. — For article discussing limitations on ad hoc adjudicatory rulemaking by an administrative agency, see 61 N.C.L. Rev. 67 (1982).

For article analyzing the scope of the North Carolina Insurance Commissioner's rate-making authority, see 61 N.C.L. Rev. 97 (1982).

CASE NOTES

Differentiation Between § 58-2-75 and This Section. — Section 58-2-75 omits any grant to the Commissioner of the authority to seek judicial review, whereas this section expressly grants him such authority. This indicates a clear legislative intent to differentiate between these two sections. State Farm Mut. Auto. Ins. Co. v. Ingram, 288 N.C. 381, 218 S.E.2d 364 (1975).

This section applies only to orders affecting premium rates on any class of risks or the propriety of a given classification or classification assignment. State Farm Mut. Auto. Ins. Co. v. Ingram, 288 N.C. 381, 218 S.E.2d 364 (1975).

Inapplicability to Appointment of Agent Representative. — Where a case involves the appointment of an agent to represent an insurance company, neither this section nor the exceptions to G.S. 58-2-75, other than that for an order covered by this section, are applicable. State Farm Mut. Auto. Ins. Co. v. Ingram, 288 N.C. 381, 218 S.E.2d 364 (1975).

Construction of This Section with Article 12B (now Article 36) of This Chapter. — Prior to the 1977 legislation enacting Article 12B (now Article 36) of Chapter 58, it was held that the reviewing court had no inherent authority to fix rates nor to continue them in effect pending a hearing on remand. Under the 1977 legislative scheme, however, the Court of Appeals is not setting a workers' compensation rate when it reverses Commissioner's order of disapproval. The rate is set by the Commissioner in failing to carry the burden of showing affirmatively and specifically that the filing does not comply with statutory standards. State ex rel. Comm'r of Ins. v. North Carolina Rate Bureau, 40 N.C. App. 85, 252 S.E.2d 811, cert. denied, 297 N.C. 452, 256 S.E.2d 810 (1979).

Rate Bureau was a "party aggrieved" within the meaning of this section; accordingly, it could challenge orders and decisions of the Commissioner of Insurance that disapproved premium rates, and there was no reason to conclude that the Rate Bureau had standing in this context but not in the context of challenging the distribution of funds under G.S. 58-36-25. State ex rel. Comm'r of Ins. v. North Carolina Rate Bureau, 102 N.C. App. 809, 403 S.E.2d 597 (1991).

Burden on Commissioner in Disapproving Rate Filing. — The Commissioner can no longer effectively disapprove a rate filing by inaction or a bare assertion that the Rate Bureau has not carried its burden of proof. Though the new statutory scheme does not shift the ultimate burden of proof from the Rate Bureau to the Commissioner, it does place on the Commissioner, in disapproving a filing, the burden of affirmatively and specifically showing how the bureau has not carried its burden of proof, and, if the Commissioner fails to do so by substantial evidence, the presumption of prima facie correctness given to an order of the Commissioner by this section and G.S. 58-2-90 is rebutted. State ex rel. Comm'r of Ins. v. North Carolina Rate Bureau, 40 N.C. App. 85, 252 S.E.2d 811, cert. denied, 297 N.C. 452, 256 S.E.2d 810 (1979).

Duty of Court of Appeals on Appeal from Commissioner's Order of Disapproval of Rate Filing. — If the Commissioner fails to perform the affirmative duties imposed upon him by Article 12B (now Article 36) of Chapter 58 after a filing by the Rate Bureau, the filing shall be deemed to be approved, just as there is a deemed approval upon his failure to give notice of hearing within 30 days under G.S. 58-36-20(b). If the Court of Appeals, on appeal from the Commissioner's order of disapproval, finds that the order is not supported by material and substantial evidence, it is then the duty of the court to determine whether the filing complies with the statutory standards and methods and is supported by substantial evidence. If no such compliance is found the disapproval order will be vacated and the filing approved, and this will constitute a final determination under G.S. 58-36-25, which will require an order distributing the escrowed funds to the members of the Rate Bureau. State ex rel. Comm'r of Ins. v. North Carolina Rate Bureau, 40 N.C. App. 85, 252 S.E.2d 811, cert. denied, 297 N.C. 452, 256 S.E.2d 810 (1979).

Findings of Fact Prerequisite to Review. — Without appropriate findings of fact, as required by this section, an order of the Commissioner cannot be judicially reviewed by an appellate court. State ex rel. Comm'r of Ins. v. Compensation Rating & Inspection Bureau, 30 N.C. App. 332, 228 S.E.2d 264 (1976), rev'd on other grounds, 292 N.C. 471, 234 S.E.2d 720 (1977).

Order Not Excepted from Review. — An order by the Commissioner in which, without notice or hearing, he abruptly directed that the Automobile Rate Administrative Office could not follow the standard rule of application for placing into effect changes, whether increases or decreases, in insurance premium rates was not such a decision as is described in this section, nor did it fall within any of the categories excepted from review by petition to the Superior Court of Wake County under G.S. 58-2-75(a). North Carolina Auto. Rate Admin. Office v. Ingram, 35 N.C. App. 578, 242 S.E.2d 205 (1978).

Meaning of "Substantial Evidence." — Substantial evidence has been described as such relevant evidence as a reasonable mind might accept as adequate to support a conclusion. State ex rel. Comm'r of Ins. v. North Carolina Auto. Rate Admin. Office, 30 N.C. App. 427, 227 S.E.2d 603 (1976), aff'd in part, rev'd in part, 292 N.C. 1, 231 S.E.2d 867 (1977); State ex rel. Comm'r of Ins. v. North Carolina Rate Bureau, 44 N.C. App. 191, 261 S.E.2d 671 (1979), modified and aff'd, 300 N.C. 485, 269 S.E.2d 602 (1980).

Substantial evidence is more than a scintilla or a permissible inference. State ex rel. Comm'r of Ins. v. North Carolina Auto. Rate Admin. Office, 30 N.C. App. 427, 227 S.E.2d 603 (1976), aff'd in part, rev'd in part, 292 N.C. 1, 231 S.E.2d 867 (1977); State ex rel. Comm'r of Ins. v. North Carolina Rate Bureau, 44 N.C. App. 191, 261 S.E.2d 671 (1979), modified and aff'd, 300 N.C. 485, 269 S.E.2d 602 (1980).

Application of "Substantial Evidence" Standard. — In the application of the "substantial evidence" standard, courts will generally defer to the expertise of the administrator in his specialized field if there is reasonable evidence to support his decision. State ex rel. Comm'r of Ins. v. State ex rel. Att'y Gen., 19 N.C. App. 263, 198 S.E.2d 575, appeal dismissed, 284 N.C. 252, 200 S.E.2d 659 (1973).

Calculation of Profit Provisions. — There was substantial and material evidence to support the Commissioner's use of the more conservative statutory accounting principles (SAP) in calculating the profit provisions. State ex rel. Comm'r of Ins. v. North Carolina Rate Bureau, 124 N.C. App. 674, 478 S.E.2d 794 (1996), cert. denied, 346 N.C. 184, 486 S.E.2d 217 (1997).

Premium-to-Surplus Ratio. — There was substantial evidence to support the Commissioner's selection of the traditional standard 2 to 1 for the premium-to-surplus ratio. State ex rel. Comm'r of Ins. v. North Carolina Rate Bureau, 124 N.C. App. 674, 478 S.E.2d 794 (1996), cert. denied, 346 N.C. 184, 486 S.E.2d 217 (1997).

Findings Must Be Clear and Specific. — In reaching his ultimate determination, the Commissioner must make findings which clearly and specifically indicate the facts on which he bases his order, the resolution of conflicting evidence, and the consideration he has given to the material and substantial evidence that has been offered. State ex rel. Comm'r of Ins. v. North Carolina Rate Bureau, 95 N.C. App. 157, 381 S.E.2d 801 (1989), appeal dismissed, State ex rel. Comm'r of Ins. v. North Carolina Rate Bureau, 102 N.C. App. 809, 403 S.E.2d 597 (1991).

As to the statutory scheme for Workers' Compensation rate-making, see State ex rel. Comm'r of Ins. v. North Carolina Rate Bureau, 40 N.C. App. 85, 252 S.E.2d 811, cert. denied, 297 N.C. 452, 256 S.E.2d 810 (1979).

Applied in State ex rel. Comm'r of Ins. v. State ex rel. Att'y Gen., 16 N.C. App. 279, 192 S.E.2d 138 (1972); State ex rel. Comm'r of Ins. v. North Carolina Auto. Rate Admin. Office, 19 N.C. App. 548, 199 S.E.2d 479 (1973); State ex rel. Comm'r of Ins. v. North Carolina Auto. Rate Admin. Office, 287 N.C. 192, 214 S.E.2d 98 (1975); State ex rel. Comm'r of Ins. v. Integon Life Ins. Co., 28 N.C. App. 7, 220 S.E.2d 409 (1975); North Carolina Fire Ins. Rating Bureau v. Ingram, 29 N.C. App. 338, 224 S.E.2d 229 (1976); State ex rel. Comm'r of Ins. v. North Carolina Fire Ins. Rating Bureau, 292 N.C. 70, 231 S.E.2d 882 (1977).

Cited in State ex rel. Comm'r of Ins. v. North Carolina Rate Bureau, 129 N.C. App. 662, 501 S.E.2d 681 (1998).

§ 58-2-85. Procedure on appeal under § 58-2-80.

Appeals to the North Carolina Court of Appeals pursuant to G.S. 58-2-80 shall be subject to the following provisions:

(1) No party to a proceeding before the Commissioner may appeal from any final order or decision of the Commissioner unless within 30 days after the entry of such final order or decision, or within such time thereafter as may be fixed by the Commissioner, by order made within 30 days, the party aggrieved by such decision or order shall file with the Commissioner notice of appeal and exceptions which shall set forth specifically the ground or grounds on which the aggrieved party considers said decision or order to be unlawful, unjust, unreasonable or unwarranted, and including errors alleged to have been committed by the Commissioner.

(2) Any party may appeal from all or any portion of any final order or decision of the Commissioner in the manner herein provided. Copy of the notice of appeal shall be mailed by the appealing party at the time of filing with the Commissioner, to each party to the proceeding to the addresses as they appear in the files of the Commissioner in the proceeding. The failure of any party, other than the Commissioner, to be served with or to receive a copy of the notice of appeal shall not affect the validity or regularity of the appeal.

(3) The Commissioner may on motion of any party to the proceeding or on its own motion set the exceptions to the final order upon which such appeal is based for further hearing before the Commissioner.

(4) The appeal shall lie to the Court of Appeals as provided in G.S. 7A-29. The procedure for the appeal shall be as provided by the rules of appellate procedure.

(5), (6) Repealed by Session Laws 1975, c. 391, s. 11.

(7) The Court of Appeals shall hear and determine all matters arising on such appeal, as in this Article provided, and may in the exercise of its discretion assign the hearing of said appeal to any panel of the Court of Appeals.

(8) Unless otherwise provided by the rules of appellate procedure, the cause on appeal from the Commissioner of Insurance shall be entitled "State of North Carolina ex rel. Commissioner of Insurance (here add any additional parties in support of the Commissioner's order and

their capacity before the Commissioner). Appellee(s) v. (here insert name of appellant and his capacity before the Commissioner), Appellant." Appeals from the Insurance Commissioner pending in the superior courts on January 1, 1972, shall remain on the civil issue docket of such superior court and shall have priority over other civil actions. Appeals to the Court of Appeals under G.S. 7A-29 shall be docketed in accordance with the rules of appellate procedure.

(9) In any appeal to the Court of Appeals, the complainant in the original complaint before the Commissioner shall be a party to the record and each of the parties to the proceeding before the Commissioner shall have a right to appear and participate in said appeal.

(10) An appeal under this section shall operate as a stay of the Commissioner's order or decision until said appeal has been dismissed or the questions raised by the appeal determined according to law. (1971, c. 703, s. 3; 1975, c. 391, s. 11.)

Legal Periodicals. — For survey of 1976 case law on insurance, see 55 N.C.L. Rev. 1052 (1977).

For article discussing limitations on ad hoc adjudicatory rulemaking by an administrative agency, see 61 N.C.L. Rev. 67 (1982).

CASE NOTES

Applicability of §§ 58-2-40 Through 58-2-200 to Judicial Review of Ratemaking Procedures. — While the North Carolina Administrative Procedure Act, G.S. 150B-1 et seq., controls judicial review of insurance ratemaking procedures, the review provisions of G.S. 58-2-40 through 58-2-200 should also apply insofar as those provisions are compatible with the act. State ex rel. Comm'r of Ins. v. North Carolina Rate Bureau, 300 N.C. 460, 269 S.E.2d 538 (1980).

Applied in State ex rel. Comm'r of Ins. v. North Carolina Auto. Rate Admin. Office, 19 N.C. App. 548, 199 S.E.2d 479 (1973); State ex rel. Comm'r of Ins. v. North Carolina Auto. Rate Admin. Office, 287 N.C. 192, 214 S.E.2d 98 (1975); North Carolina Fire Ins. Rating Bureau v. Ingram, 29 N.C. App. 338, 224 S.E.2d 229 (1976).

§ 58-2-90. Extent of review under § 58-2-80.

(a) On appeal the court shall review the record and the exceptions and assignments of error in accordance with the rules of the Court of Appeals, and any alleged irregularities in procedures before the Commissioner, not shown in the record, shall be considered under the rules of the Court of Appeals.

(b) So far as necessary to the decision and where presented, the court shall decide all relevant questions of law, interpret constitutional and statutory provisions, and determine the meaning and applicability of the terms of any action of the Commissioner. The court may affirm or reverse the decision of the Commissioner, declare the same null and void, or remand the case for further proceedings; or it may reverse or modify the decision if the substantial rights of the appellants have been prejudiced because the Commissioner's findings, inferences, conclusions or decisions are:

(1) In violation of constitutional provisions, or

(2) In excess of statutory authority or jurisdiction of the Commissioner, or

(3) Made upon unlawful proceedings, or

(4) Affected by other errors of law, or

(5) Unsupported by material and substantial evidence in view of the entire record as submitted, or

(6) Arbitrary or capricious.

(c) In making the foregoing determinations, the court shall review the whole record or such portions thereof as may be cited by any party and due account shall be taken of the rule of prejudicial error. The appellant shall not be permitted to rely upon any grounds for relief on appeal which were not set forth specifically in his notice of appeal filed with the Commissioner.

(d) The court shall also compel action of the Commissioner unlawfully withheld or unlawfully or unreasonably delayed.

(e) Upon any appeal, the rates fixed or any rule, regulation, finding, determination, or order made by the Commissioner under the provisions of Articles 1 through 64 of this Chapter shall be prima facie correct. (1971, c. 703, s. 4.)

Legal Periodicals. — For survey of 1979 administrative law, see 58 N.C.L. Rev. 1185 (1980).

For survey of 1980 administrative law, see 59 N.C.L. Rev. 1017 (1981).

For article discussing limitations on ad hoc adjudicatory rulemaking by an administrative agency, see 61 N.C.L. Rev. 67 (1982).

For article analyzing the scope of the North Carolina Insurance Commissioner's rate-making authority, see 61 N.C.L. Rev. 97 (1982).

CASE NOTES

Applicability of Review Standards to Ratemaking Cases. — Section 150B-51 is the controlling judicial review statute in insurance ratemaking cases. However, to the extent that subsection (b) of this section adds to the judicial review function and in light of the virtually identical thrust of the two statutes, the Supreme Court applied the review standards of both this section and G.S. 150B-51, where those standards could be construed as being consistent with each other. State ex rel. Comm'r of Ins. v. North Carolina Rate Bureau, 300 N.C. 381, 269 S.E.2d 547, rehearing denied, 301 N.C. 107, 273 S.E.2d 300 (1980).

Subdivision (b)(1) and § 150B-51(b)(1) do not contemplate constitutional review where appellants, the rate bureau and member companies make no assertion that their rights have been prejudiced because any of the findings or conclusions of the Commissioner of Insurance were in violation of any constitutional provisions. State ex rel. Comm'r of Ins. v. North Carolina Rate Bureau, 300 N.C. 381, 269 S.E.2d 547, rehearing denied, 301 N.C. 107, 273 S.E.2d 300 (1980).

Prohibitions in Subdivisions (b)(2) and (b)(3) Distinguished. — The prohibition against agency action "in excess of statutory authority" under subdivision (b)(2) of this section and G.S. 150B-51(b)(2) refers to the general authority of an administrative agency properly to discharge its statutorily assigned responsibilities, while the prohibition against agency action "made upon unlawful procedure" under subdivision (b)(3) and G.S. 150B-51(b)(3) refers to the procedures employed by the agency in discharging its statutorily authorized acts. State ex rel. Comm'r of Ins. v. North Carolina Rate Bureau, 300 N.C. 381, 269 S.E.2d 547, rehearing denied, 301 N.C. 107, 273 S.E.2d 300 (1980).

The **"whole record" test is applicable to judicial review of administrative decisions** in North Carolina, and both subdivision (b)(5) of this section and G.S. 150B-51(b)(5) put forth that test as a proper standard of judicial review of insurance ratemaking proceedings. State ex rel. Comm'r of Ins. v. North Carolina Rate Bureau, 300 N.C. 381, 269 S.E.2d 547, rehearing denied, 301 N.C. 107, 273 S.E.2d 300 (1980).

When evidence is conflicting, the standard for judicial review of administrative decisions in North Carolina is that of the "whole record" test. State ex rel. Comm'r of Ins. v. North Carolina Rate Bureau, 300 N.C. 381, 269 S.E.2d 547, rehearing denied, 301 N.C. 107, 273 S.E.2d 300 (1980).

"Whole Record" Test Explained. — The "whole record" test requires the reviewing court to consider the record evidence supporting the commissioner's order, to also consider the record evidence contradicting the commissioner's findings, and to determine if the commissioner's decision had a rational basis in the material and substantial evidence offered. State ex rel. Comm'r of Ins. v. North Carolina Rate Bureau, 75 N.C. App. 201, 331 S.E.2d 124, cert. denied, 314 N.C. 547, 335 S.E.2d 319 (1985).

Construction with Article 12B (now Article 36) of This Chapter. — Prior to the 1977 legislation enacting Article 12B (now Article 36) of Chapter 58, it was held that the reviewing court had no inherent authority to fix rates nor to continue them in effect pending a hearing on remand. Under the 1977 legislative scheme, however, the Court of Appeals is not setting a workers' compensation rate when it reverses the Commissioner's order of disapproval. The rate is set by the Commissioner in failing to carry the burden of showing affirmatively and specifically that the filing does not comply with statutory standards. State ex rel. Comm'r of Ins. v. North Carolina Rate Bureau, 40 N.C. App. 85, 252 S.E.2d 811, cert. denied, 297 N.C. 452, 256 S.E.2d 810 (1979).

Burden of Proof on Rate Bureau. — While the commissioner's order must be based on material and substantial evidence in the record, the ultimate burden of proof to justify a rate adjustment and its amount is on the rate bureau. State ex rel. Comm'r of Ins. v. North Carolina Rate Bureau, 75 N.C. App. 201, 331 S.E.2d 124, cert. denied, 314 N.C. 547, 335 S.E.2d 319 (1985).

Burden on Commissioner in Disapproving Rate Filing. — The Commissioner can no longer effectively disapprove a rate filing by inaction or a bare assertion that the Rate Bureau has not carried its burden of proof. Though the new statutory scheme does not shift the ultimate burden of proof from the Rate Bureau to the Commissioner, it does place on the Commissioner, in disapproving a filing, the burden of affirmatively and specifically showing how the bureau has not carried its burden of proof, and, if the Commissioner fails to do so by substantial evidence, the presumption of prima facie correctness given to an order of the Commissioner by G.S. 58-2-80 and this section is rebutted. State ex rel. Comm'r of Ins. v. North Carolina Rate Bureau, 40 N.C. App. 85, 252 S.E.2d 811, cert. denied, 297 N.C. 452, 256 S.E.2d 810 (1979).

Duty of Court of Appeals on Appeal from Commissioner's Order of Disapproval of Rate Filing. — If the Commissioner fails to perform the affirmative duties imposed upon him by Article 12B (now Article 36) of Chapter 58 after a filing by the Rate Bureau, the filing shall be deemed to be approved, just as there is a deemed approval upon his failure to give notice of hearing within 30 days under G.S. 58-36-20(b). If the Court of Appeals, on appeal from the Commissioner's order of disapproval, finds that the order is not supported by material and substantial evidence, it is then the duty of the court to determine whether the filing complies with the statutory standards and methods and is supported by substantial evidence. If no such compliance is found the disapproval order will be vacated and the filing approved, and this will constitute a final determination under G.S. 58-36-25, which will require an order distributing the escrowed funds to the members of the Rate Bureau. State ex rel. Comm'r of Ins. v. North Carolina Rate Bureau, 40 N.C. App. 85, 252 S.E.2d 811, cert. denied, 297 N.C. 452, 256 S.E.2d 810 (1979).

Sufficiency of Evidence Is for Agency to Determine. — It is for the administrative agency to determine the weight and sufficiency of the evidence and the credibility of the witnesses, to draw inferences from the facts, and to appraise conflicting and circumstantial evidence. State ex rel. Comm'r of Ins. v. North Carolina Rate Bureau, 300 N.C. 381, 269 S.E.2d 547, rehearing denied, 301 N.C. 107, 273 S.E.2d 300 (1980).

Meaning of "Substantial Evidence." — Substantial evidence is such relevant evidence as a reasonable mind might accept as adequate to support a conclusion. State ex rel. Comm'r of Ins. v. North Carolina Auto. Rate Admin. Office, 287 N.C. 192, 214 S.E.2d 98 (1975); State ex rel. Comm'r of Ins. v. North Carolina Auto. Rate Admin. Office, 30 N.C. App. 427, 227 S.E.2d 603 (1976), modified, 292 N.C. 1, 231 S.E.2d 867 (1977); State ex rel. Comm'r of Ins. v. North Carolina Fire Ins. Rating Bureau, 292 N.C. 70, 231 S.E.2d 882 (1977); State ex rel. Comm'r of Ins. v. North Carolina Rate Bureau, 41 N.C. App. 310, 255 S.E.2d 557 (1979), aff'd in part and rev'd in part, 300 N.C. 381, 269 S.E.2d 547 (1980).

A finding that a fact is true because the fact finder finds no reason to believe it is not true is not supported by "material and substantial evidence." State ex rel. Comm'r of Ins. v. North Carolina Auto. Rate Admin. Office, 24 N.C. App. 223, 210 S.E.2d 441 (1974), cert. denied, 286 N.C. 412, 211 S.E.2d 801 (1975).

Substantial evidence is more than a scintilla or a permissible inference. State ex rel. Comm'r of Ins. v. North Carolina Auto. Rate Admin. Office, 287 N.C. 192, 214 S.E.2d 98 (1975); State ex rel. Comm'r of Ins. v. North Carolina Auto. Rate Admin. Office, 30 N.C. App. 427, 227 S.E.2d 603 (1976), aff'd in part, rev'd in part, 292 N.C. 1, 231 S.E.2d 867 (1977).

The weight and credibility of conflicting evidence in a rate making hearing was for the commissioner to decide. State ex rel. Comm'r of Ins. v. North Carolina Rate Bureau, 75 N.C. App. 201, 331 S.E.2d 124, cert. denied, 314 N.C. 547, 335 S.E.2d 319 (1985).

Order Held Not in Excess of Statutory Powers. — An order of the Commissioner of Insurance that data submitted in a ratemaking case be audited was not in excess of his statutory powers as contemplated by subdivision (b)(2) of this section or G.S. 150B-51(b)(2). State ex rel. Comm'r of Ins. v. North Carolina Rate Bureau, 300 N.C. 381, 269 S.E.2d 547, rehearing denied, 301 N.C. 107, 273 S.E.2d 300 (1980).

Ad Hoc Rulemaking Held Improper. — Though administrative agencies can establish rules through the case-by-case process of administrative adjudication, ad hoc rulemaking requiring audited data was not proper where: (1) the lack of unaudited data was not a problem unforeseen by the Commissioner, (2) absence of a relevant general rule did not prohibit this ratemaking, (3) the Commissioner had sufficient experience with the problem, and (4) the problem of auditing was not so specialized and varying in nature as to be impossible of capture within the boundaries of a general rule. State ex rel. Comm'r of Ins. v. North Carolina Rate Bureau, 300 N.C. 381, 269 S.E.2d 547, rehearing denied, 301 N.C. 107, 273 S.E.2d 300 (1980).

Commissioner's attempt to establish a rule requiring audited data in an insurance ratemaking hearing was "made upon unlawful procedure" as contemplated by subdivision (b)(3) of this section and G.S. 150B-51(b)(3) where the Commissioner sought to establish the rule on an ad hoc adjudication basis rather than following normal North Carolina Administrative Procedure Act rulemaking requirements, since the process of rulemaking would have presented no danger that its use would frustrate the effective accomplishment of the agency's functions. State ex rel. Comm'r of Ins. v. North Carolina Rate Bureau, 300 N.C. 381, 269 S.E.2d 547, rehearing denied, 301 N.C. 107, 273 S.E.2d 300 (1980).

Methods of Analysis Upheld. — Commissioner's reliance on market to book ratio analysis, a discounted cash flow analysis, and a comparable earnings analysis as methods of analysis of the profit to which insurance companies were entitled lay entirely within his discretion. State ex rel. Comm'r of Ins. v. North Carolina Rate Bureau, 96 N.C. App. 220, 385 S.E.2d 510 (1989).

Action Held Arbitrary and Capricious. — Where the Commissioner of Insurance did nothing more, in adopting a complicated and novel formula for determining underwriting profit, than listen to one employee of an insurance department in a sister state, such an approach was a clear example of an arbitrary and capricious action by an administrative agency as contemplated by the North Carolina legislature in establishing that criterion for judicial review in subdivision (b)(6) of this section and G.S. 150B-51(b)(6). State ex rel. Comm'r of Ins. v. North Carolina Rate Bureau, 300 N.C. 381, 269 S.E.2d 547, rehearing denied, 301 N.C. 107, 273 S.E.2d 300 (1980).

The Commissioner's action ordering audited data in a ratemaking case was arbitrary and capricious as contemplated by subdivision (b)(6) of this section and G.S. 150B-51(b)(6), where: (1) the order was vague and uncertain in that it did not establish the extent to which examination of "original source documents" was required; (2) it did not make clear whether the auditing must be performed by certified public accountants, other accountants, or actuaries; (3) it did not specify the degree of precision and reliability required of "statistical sampling"; (4) it generally did not provided adequate guidelines for compliance with the general conclusion that data in a ratemaking hearing be audited; (5) it included no determination by the Commissioner as to the possibil-

ity of performance of his new rule nor whether implementation of the rule would be economically feasible; (6) it included no determination whether the statutory time limits could be complied with in face of the new rule; and (7) it included no determination whether the "original source data" contemplated by the new rule was even available for the past years involved in the filing or whether such data, if available, was located in North Carolina or outside the State in the case of the several hundred companies writing insurance in this State. State ex rel. Comm'r of Ins. v. North Carolina Rate Bureau, 300 N.C. 381, 269 S.E.2d 547, rehearing denied, 301 N.C. 107, 273 S.E.2d 300 (1980).

Speculative Statements as Inadequate for Rates. — The effects on automobile liability insurance costs in this State, if any, of the so-called "energy crisis" and economic conditions, including the unemployment rate, are difficult, if not impossible, to quantify. Rates cannot be based upon such speculative statements. Hence, order of the Commissioner was not based on material and substantial evidence and would be reversed. State ex rel. Comm'r of Ins. v. North Carolina Auto. Rate Admin. Office, 30 N.C. App. 427, 227 S.E.2d 603 (1976), aff'd in part, rev'd in part, 292 N.C. 1, 231 S.E.2d 867 (1977).

It is proper for the Commissioner to consider investment earnings on capital invested by insurers in reviewing the ratemaking formula. State ex rel. Comm'r of Ins. v. North Carolina Rate Bureau, 41 N.C. App. 310, 255 S.E.2d 557 (1979), aff'd in part and rev'd in part, 300 N.C. 381, 269 S.E.2d 547 (1980).

As to the statutory scheme for workers' compensation ratemaking, see State ex rel. Comm'r of Ins. v. North Carolina Rate Bureau, 40 N.C. App. 85, 252 S.E.2d 811, cert. denied, 297 N.C. 452, 256 S.E.2d 810 (1979).

Unlawful Delegation of Power to Make Final Agency Decision. — Where the Commissioner of Insurance delegated to his appointed hearing officer the power to make the final agency decision, the commissioner made an unlawful delegation of his powers. State ex rel. Comm'r of Ins. v. North Carolina Rate Bureau, 61 N.C. App. 262, 300 S.E.2d 586, cert. denied, 308 N.C. 392, 301 S.E.2d 702; 308 N.C. 548, 304 S.E.2d 242 (1983).

For discussion of respective powers and duties of the Commissioner and his designated hearing officer in the review of filed rates and entry of a final agency decision in a contested insurance rate case, see State ex rel. Comm'r of Ins. v. North Carolina Rate Bureau, 61 N.C. App. 506, 300 S.E.2d 845 (1983).

Applied in State ex rel. Comm'r of Ins. v. North Carolina Auto. Rate Admin. Office, 19 N.C. App. 548, 199 S.E.2d 479 (1973); State ex rel. Comm'r of Ins. v. North Carolina Auto. Rate Admin. Office, 24 N.C. App. 228, 210 S.E.2d 439 (1974); State ex rel. Comm'r of Ins. v. North Carolina Fire Ins. Rating Bureau, 291 N.C. 55, 229 S.E.2d 268 (1976); Foremost Ins. Co. v. Ingram, 292 N.C. 244, 232 S.E.2d 414 (1977); State ex rel. Comm'r of Ins. v. North Carolina Auto. Rate Admin. Office, 293 N.C. 365, 239 S.E.2d 48 (1977); State ex rel. Comm'r of Ins. v. North Carolina Rate Bureau, 43 N.C. App. 715, 295 S.E.2d 922 (1979); State ex rel. Comm'r of Ins. v. North Carolina Rate Bureau, 300 N.C. 460, 269 S.E.2d 538 (1980); State ex rel. Comm'r of Ins. v. North Carolina Rate Bureau, 300 N.C. 474, 269 S.E.2d 595 (1980); State ex rel. Comm'r of Ins. v. North Carolina Rate Bureau, 300 N.C. 485, 269 S.E.2d 602 (1980);

State ex rel. Comm'r of Ins. v. North Carolina Rate Bureau, 129 N.C. App. 662, 501 S.E.2d 681 (1998).

Cited in State ex rel. Comm'r of Ins. v. State ex rel. Att'y Gen., 19 N.C. App. 263, 198 S.E.2d 575 (1973); State ex rel. Comm'r of Ins. v. North Carolina Rate Bureau, 44 N.C. App. 191, 261 S.E.2d 671 (1979); State ex rel. Comm'r of Ins. v. North Carolina Rate Bureau, 54 N.C. App. 601, 284 S.E.2d 339 (1981); State ex rel. Comm'r of Ins. v. North Carolina Rate Bureau, 61 N.C. App. 262, 300 S.E.2d 586 (1983); State ex rel. Comm'r of Ins. v. North Carolina Rate Bureau, 124 N.C. App. 674, 478 S.E.2d 794 (1996), cert. denied, 346 N.C. 184, 486 S.E.2d 217 (1997).

§ 58-2-95. Commissioner to supervise local inspectors.

The Commissioner shall exercise general supervision over local investigators of fires and fire prevention inspectors. Whenever the Commissioner has reason to believe that the local inspectors are not doing their duty, he or his deputy shall make special trips of inspection and take proper steps to have all the provisions of the law relative to the investigation of fires and the prevention of fire waste enforced. (1905, c. 506, s. 6; Rev., s. 4690; C.S., s. 6270; 1925, c. 89; 1969, c. 1063, s. 2.)

Legal Periodicals. — For article discussing limitations on ad hoc adjudicatory rulemaking by an administrative agency, see 61 N.C.L. Rev. 67 (1982).

§ 58-2-100. Office of Commissioner a public office; records, etc., subject to inspection.

The office of the Commissioner shall be a public office and the records, reports, books and papers thereof on file therein shall be accessible to the inspection of the public, except that the records compiled as a part of an investigation for the crime of arson, that of unlawful burning, or of fraud, shall not be considered as public records and may be made available to the public only upon an order of court of competent jurisdiction. Provided that such records shall upon request be made available to the district attorney of any district if the same concerns persons or investigations in his district. (1899, c. 54, ss. 9, 77; Rev., s. 4683; 1907, c. 1000, s. 1; C.S., s. 6271; 1945, c. 383; 1951, c. 781, s. 11; 1955, c. 456; 1973, c. 47, s. 2.)

Cross References. — As to reports and affidavits of surplus lines licensees not being public records, see G.S. 58-21-35.

Legal Periodicals. — For brief comment on the 1951 amendment, see 29 N.C.L. Rev. 398 (1951).

CASE NOTES

The General Assembly specifically provided for penalties for violations of Chapter 58 in G.S. 58-2-70 and this section. Home Indem. Co. v. Hoechst Celanese Corp., 128 N.C. App. 226, 494 S.E.2d 768, 1998 N.C. App. LEXIS 23 (1998), cert. denied, 505 S.E.2d 869 (1998).

§ 58-2-105. Confidentiality of medical and credentialing records.

(a) All patient medical records in the possession of the Department are confidential and are not public records pursuant to G.S. 58-2-100 or G.S. 132-1. As used in this section, "patient medical records" includes personal information that relates to an individual's physical or mental condition, medical history, or medical treatment, and that has been obtained from the individual patient, a health care provider, or from the patient's spouse, parent, or legal guardian.

(b) Under Part 4 of Article 50 of this Chapter, the Department may disclose patient medical records to an independent review organization, and the organization shall maintain the confidentiality of those records as required by this section, except as allowed by G.S. 58-39-75 and G.S. 58-39-76.

(c) Under Part 4 of Article 50 of this Chapter, all information related to the credentialing of medical professionals that is in the possession of the Commissioner is confidential and is a public record neither under this section nor under Chapter 132 of the General Statutes. (1989 (Reg. Sess., 1990), c. 1021, s. 4; 1993 (Reg. Sess., 1994), c. 678, s. 3; 2001-446, s. 5(a); 2002-187, s. 3.4.)

Editor's Note. — Session Laws 2001-446, s. 8 provides: "Nothing in this act obligates the General Assembly to appropriate funds to implement this act."

Session Laws 2001-446, s. 7 is a severability clause.

Effect of Amendments. — Session Laws 2001-446, s. 5(a), effective July 1, 2002, and applicable to health benefit plans that are in effect, delivered, issued for delivery, or renewed on or after that date, added subsection (b) and designated the existing provisions of this section as subsection (a).

Session Laws 2002-187, s. 3.4, effective October 31, 2002, in the catchline inserted "and credentialing"; and added subsection (c).

§ 58-2-110. Original documents and certified copies as evidence.

Every certificate, assignment, or conveyance executed by the Commissioner, in pursuance of any authority conferred on him by law and sealed with his seal of office, may be used as evidence and may be recorded in the proper recording offices, in the same manner and with like effect as a deed regularly acknowledged or proved before an officer authorized by law to take the probate of deeds; and all copies of papers in the office of the Commissioner, certified by him and authenticated by his official seal, shall be evidence as the original. (1899, c. 54, s. 11; Rev., s. 4684; C.S., s. 6272.)

§ 58-2-115. Admissibility of certificate as evidence of agent's authority.

In any case or controversy arising in any court of original jurisdiction within this State wherein it is necessary to establish the question as to whether any insurance or other corporation or agent thereof is or has been licensed by the Department to do business in this State, the certificate of the Commissioner under the seal of his office shall be admissible in evidence as proof of such corporation or agent's authority as conferred by the Department. (1929, c. 289, s. 1; 1991, c. 720, ss. 4, 5.)

§ 58-2-120. Reports of Commissioner to the Governor and General Assembly.

The Commissioner shall, from time to time, report to the Governor and the General Assembly any change or changes that in the Commissioner's opinion should be made in the laws relating to insurance and other subjects pertaining to the Department. (1899, c. 54, ss. 6, 7, 10; 1901, c. 391, s. 2; Rev., ss. 4687, 4688; 1911, c. 211, s. 2; C.S., s. 6273; 1927, c. 217, s. 5; 1945, c. 383; 1999-219, s. 8.)

§ 58-2-125. Authority over all insurance companies; no exemptions from license.

Every insurance company must be licensed and supervised by the Commissioner, and must pay all licenses, taxes, and fees as prescribed in the insurance laws of the State for the class of company, association, or order to which it belongs. No provision in any statute, public or private, may relieve any company, association, or order from the supervision prescribed for the class of companies, associations, or orders of like character, or release it from the payment of the licenses, taxes, and fees prescribed for companies, associations, and orders of the same class; and all such special provisions or exemptions are hereby repealed. It is unlawful for the Commissioner to grant or issue a license to any company, association, or order, or agent for them, claiming such exemption from supervision by his Department and release for the payment of license, fees, and taxes. (1903, c. 594, ss. 1, 2, 3; Rev., s. 4691; C.S., s. 6274; 1945, c. 383; 1991, c. 720, s. 4.)

CASE NOTES

A fraternal insurance order incorporated under the laws of another state, but with branch offices in this State, comes within the meaning of this section and must be licensed and supervised by the Commissioner of Insurance. State v. Arlington, 157 N.C. 640, 73 S.E. 122 (1911).

Cited in Fuller v. Lockhart, 209 N.C. 61, 182 S.E. 733 (1935).

§ 58-2-128. Interagency consultation.

(a) Purpose. — It is the stated intention of the Congress in P.L. 106-102, the Gramm-Leach-Bliley Act, that the Board of Governors of the Federal Reserve System, as the umbrella supervisor for financial holding companies, and the Commissioner, as the functional regulator of persons engaged in insurance activities, coordinate efforts to supervise persons that control both a depository institution and a person engaged in insurance activities regulated under State law. In particular, Congress believes that the Board and the Commissioner should share, on a confidential basis, information relevant to the supervision of persons that control both a depository institution and a person engaged in insurance activities, including information regarding the financial health of the consolidated organization and information regarding transactions and relationships between persons engaged in insurance activities and affiliated depository institutions. The purpose of this section is to encourage this coordination and confidential sharing of information and to thereby improve both the efficiency and the quality of the supervision of financial holding companies and their affiliated depository institutions and persons engaged in insurance activities.

(b) Commissioner's Authority. — Upon the request of the Board or the appropriate federal banking agency, the North Carolina Secretary of State, or the North Carolina Commissioner of Banks, the Commissioner may provide any examination or other reports, records, or other information to which the Commissioner has access with respect to a person that:

  (1) Is engaged in insurance activities and regulated by the Commissioner.
  (2) Is an affiliate of a depository institution or financial holding company.

Upon the request of the Board or the appropriate federal banking agency, the North Carolina Secretary of State, or the North Carolina Commissioner of Banks, the Commissioner may provide any examination or other reports, records, or other information to which the Commissioner has access with respect to any insurance producer.

(c) Privilege. — The provision of information or material under this section by the Commissioner does not constitute a waiver of, or otherwise affect, any privilege to which the information or material is otherwise subject.

(d) Definitions. — As used in this section, the terms:

    (1) "Appropriate federal banking agency" and "depository institution" have the same meanings as in section 3 of the Federal Deposit Insurance Act, 12 U.S.C. § 1813.

    (2) "Board" and "financial holding company" have the same meanings as in section 2 of the Bank Holding Company Act of 1956, 12 U.S.C. § 1841, et seq.

    (3) "Insurance producer" or "producer" means a person required to be licensed under this Article to sell, solicit, or negotiate insurance. "Insurance producer" or "producer" includes an agent, a broker, and a limited representative. (2001-215, s. 1.)

§ 58-2-130: Repealed by Session Laws 1991, c. 681, s. 3.

§ 58-2-131. Examinations to be made; authority, scope, scheduling, and conduct of examinations.

(a) This section and G.S. 58-2-132 through G.S. 58-2-134 shall be known and may be cited as the Examination Law. The purpose of the Examination Law is to provide an effective and efficient system for examining the activities, operations, financial condition, and affairs of all persons transacting the business of insurance in this State and all persons otherwise subject to the Commissioner's jurisdiction; and to enable the Commissioner to use a flexible system of examinations that directs resources that are appropriate and necessary for the administration of the insurance statutes and rules of this State.

(b) As used in this section and G.S. 58-2-132 through G.S. 58-2-134, unless the context clearly indicates otherwise:

    (1) "Commissioner" includes an authorized representative or designee of the Commissioner.

    (2) "Examination" means an examination conducted under the Examination Law.

    (3) "Examiner" means any person authorized by the Commissioner to conduct an examination.

    (4) "Insurance regulator" means the official or agency of another jurisdiction that is responsible for the regulation of a foreign or alien insurer.

    (5) "Person" includes a trust or any affiliate of a person.

(c) Before licensing any person to write insurance in this State, the Commissioner shall be satisfied, by such examination and evidence as the Commissioner decides to make and require, that the person is otherwise duly qualified under the laws of this State to transact business in this State.

(d) The Commissioner may conduct an examination of any entity whenever the Commissioner deems it to be prudent for the protection of policyholders or the public, but shall at a minimum conduct a financial examination of every domestic insurer not less frequently than once every five years. In scheduling and determining the nature, scope, and frequency of examinations, the Commissioner shall consider such matters as the results of financial statement analyses and ratios, changes in management or ownership, actuarial opinions, reports of independent certified public accountants, and other criteria as set forth in the NAIC Examiners' Handbook.

(e) To complete an examination of any entity, the Commissioner may authorize an examination or investigation of any person, or the business of any person, insofar as the examination or investigation is necessary or material to the entity under examination.

(f) Instead of examining any foreign or alien insurer licensed in this State, the Commissioner may accept an examination report on that insurer prepared by the insurer's domiciliary insurance regulator. In making a determination to accept the domiciliary insurance regulator's report, the Commissioner may consider whether (i) the insurance regulator was at the time of the examination accredited under NAIC Financial Regulation Standards and Accreditation Program, or (ii) the examination is performed under the supervision of an NAIC-accredited insurance regulator or with the participation of one or more examiners who are employed by the regulator and who, after a review of the examination work papers and report, state under oath that the examination was performed in a manner consistent with the standards and procedures required by the regulator.

(g) If it appears that the insurer is of good financial and business standing and is solvent, and it is certified in writing and attested by the seal, if any, of the insurer's insurance regulator that it has been examined by the regulator in the manner prescribed by its laws, and was by the examination found to be in sound condition, that there is no reason to doubt its solvency, and that it is still permitted under the laws of such jurisdiction to do business therein, then, in the Commissioner's discretion, further examination may be dispensed with, and the obtained information and the furnished certificate may be accepted as sufficient evidence of the solvency of the insurer.

(h) Upon determining that an examination should be conducted, the Commissioner shall issue a notice of examination appointing one or more examiners to perform the examination and instructing them about the scope of the examination. In conducting the examination, an examiner shall observe the guidelines and procedures in the NAIC Examiners' Handbook. The Commissioner may also use such other guidelines or procedures as the Commissioner deems to be appropriate.

(i) Every person from whom information is sought and its officers, directors, and agents must provide to the Commissioner timely, convenient, and free access, at all reasonable hours at its offices, to all data relating to the property, assets, business, and affairs of the entity being examined. The officers, directors, employees, and agents of the entity must facilitate and aid in the examination. The refusal of any entity, by its officers, directors, employees, or agents, to submit to examination or to comply with any reasonable written request of the Commissioner or to knowingly or willfully make any false statement in regard to the examination or written request, is grounds for revocation, suspension, refusal, or nonrenewal of any license or authority held by the entity to engage in an insurance or other business subject to the Commissioner's jurisdiction.

(j) The Commissioner may issue subpoenas, administer oaths, and examine under oath any person about any matter pertinent to the examination. Upon the failure or refusal of any person to obey a subpoena, the Commissioner may petition the Superior Court of Wake County, and upon proper showing the Court may enter any order compelling the witness to appear and testify or produce documentary evidence. Failure to obey the Court order is punishable as contempt of court.

(k) **(Effective until June 30, 2004)** When making an examination, the Commissioner may retain attorneys, appraisers, independent actuaries, inde-

G.S. 58-2-131(k) is set out twice. See notes.

pendent certified public accountants, or other professionals and specialists as examiners. In the case of an examination of an insurer, the insurer shall bear the cost of retaining those persons.

(k) **(Effective June 30, 2004)** When making an examination, the Commissioner may retain attorneys, appraisers, independent actuaries, independent certified public accountants, or other professionals and specialists as examiners.

(*l*) Pending, during, and after the examination of any entity, the Commissioner shall not make public the financial statement, findings, or examination report, or any report affecting the status or standing of the entity examined, until the entity examined has either accepted and approved the final examination report or has been given a reasonable opportunity to be heard on the report and to answer or rebut any statements or findings in the report. The hearing, if requested, shall be informal and private.

(m) Nothing in the Examination Law limits the Commissioner's authority to terminate or suspend any examination in order to pursue other legal or regulatory action under the laws and rules of this State and to use any final or preliminary examination report, any examiner or insurer work papers or other documents, or any other information discovered or developed during any examination in the furtherance of any legal or regulatory action that the Commissioner may consider to be appropriate. Findings of fact and conclusions made pursuant to any examination are prima facie evidence in any legal or regulator action. (1991, c. 681, s. 2; 1995, c. 360, s. 2(c); c. 517, s. 1; 1998-212, s. 26B(b), (c), (f); 2001-180, ss. 1, 2, 3; 2002-144, s. 6; 2002-187, ss. 2.1, 2.2; 2003-284, s. 22.2.)

Subsection (k) Set Out Twice. — The first version of subsection (k) set out above is effective until June 30, 2004. The second version of subsection (k) set out above is effective June 30, 2004.

Editor's Note. — Session Laws 2002-144, s. 11, contains a severability clause.

Session Laws 2003-284, s. 1.2, provides: "This act shall be known as the 'Current Operations and Capital Improvements Appropriations Act of 2003'."

Session Laws 2003-284, s. 49.3, provides: "Except for statutory changes or other provisions that clearly indicate an intention to have effects beyond the 2003-2005 fiscal biennium, the textual provisions of this act apply only to funds appropriated for, and activities occurring during, the 2003-2005 fiscal biennium."

Session Laws 2003-284, s. 49.5 is a severability clause.

Effect of Amendments. — Session Laws 2002-144, s. 6, as amended by Session Laws 2003-284, s. 22.2, effective July 1, 2002 and expiring June 30, 2004, added the second sentence of subsection (k).

Session Laws 2002-187, ss. 2.1 and 2.2, effective October 31, 2002, in the first sentence of subsection (d) substituted "financial examination" for "regular examination"; in the second sentence of subsection (i) substituted "entity" for "person"; and substituted "entity" for "insurer" throughout.

§ 58-2-132. Examination reports.

(a) All examination reports shall comprise only facts appearing upon the books, records, or other documents of the entity, its agents or other persons examined, or as ascertained from the testimony of its officers or agents or other persons examined concerning its affairs, and conclusions and recommendations that the examiners find reasonably warranted from the facts.

(b) No later than 60 days following completion of an examination, the examiners shall file with the Department a verified written examination report under oath. Upon receipt of the verified report, the Department shall send the report to the entity examined, together with a notice that affords the entity examined a reasonable opportunity of not more than 30 days to make a written submission or rebuttal with respect to any matters contained in the examination report. Within 30 days after the date of the examination report, the entity examined shall file affidavits executed by each of its directors stating under oath that they have received and read a copy of the report.

(c) At the end of the 30 days provided for the receipt of written submissions or rebuttals, the Commissioner shall fully consider and review the report, together with any written submissions or rebuttals and any relevant parts of the examiners' work papers and enter an order:

(1) Adopting the examination report as filed or with modifications or corrections. If the examination report reveals that the entity examined is operating in violation of any law, rule, or prior order of the Commissioner, the Commissioner may order the entity examined to take any action the Commissioner considers necessary and appropriate to cure the violation; or

(2) Rejecting the examination report with directions to the examiners to reopen the examination to obtain additional data, documentation of the information, and refiling under subdivision (1) of this subsection; or

(3) Calling for an investigatory hearing with no less than 20 days' notice to the insurer for purposes of obtaining additional documentation, data, and testimony.

(d) All orders entered under subdivision (c)(1) of this section shall be accompanied by findings and conclusions resulting from the Commissioner's consideration and review of the examination report, relevant examiner work papers, and any written submissions or rebuttals. Any such order shall be considered a final administration decision and shall be served upon the entity examined by certified mail. Any hearing conducted under subdivision (c)(3) of this section shall be conducted as a nonadversarial confidential investigatory proceeding as necessary for the resolution of any inconsistencies, discrepancies, or disputed issues apparent on the face of the filed examination report or raised by or as a result of the Commissioner's review of relevant work papers or by the written submission or rebuttal of the entity examined. Within 20 days after the conclusion of any such hearing, the Commissioner shall enter an order under subdivision (c)(1) of this section. The Commissioner may not appoint a member of the Department's examination staff as an authorized representative to conduct the hearing. The hearing shall proceed expeditiously with discovery by the entity examined limited to the examiner's work papers that tend to substantiate any assertions set forth in any written submission or rebuttal. The Commissioner may issue subpoenas for the attendance of any witnesses or the production of any documents the Commissioner considers to be relevant to the investigation, whether they are under the control of the Department, the entity examined, or other persons. The documents produced shall be included in the record, and testimony taken by the Commissioner shall be under oath and preserved for the record. Nothing in this section requires the Department to disclose any information or records that would show the existence or content of any investigation or activity of any federal or state criminal justice agency. In the hearing, the Commissioner shall question the persons subpoenaed. Thereafter the entity examined and the Department may present testimony relevant to the investigation. Cross-examination shall be conducted only by the Commissioner. The entity examined and the Department may make closing statements and may be represented by counsel of their choice.

(e) Upon completion of the examination report under subdivision (c)(1) of this section, the Commissioner shall hold the content of the examination report as private and confidential information for the 30-day period provided for written submissions or rebuttals. If after 30 days after the examination report has been submitted to it, the entity examined has neither notified the

Commissioner of its acceptance and approval of the report nor requested to be heard on the report, the report shall then be filed as a public document and shall be open to public inspection, as long as no court of competent jurisdiction has stayed its publication. Nothing in the Examination Law prohibits the Commissioner from disclosing the content of the examination report, preliminary examination report or results, or any related matter, to an insurance regulator or to law enforcement officials of this or any other state or country or of the United States government at any time, as long as the person or agency receiving the report or related matters agrees in writing and is authorized by law to hold it confidential and in a manner consistent with this section. If the Commissioner determines that further regulatory action is appropriate as a result of any examination, the Commissioner may initiate such proceedings or actions as provided by law.

(f) All working papers, information, documents, and copies thereof produced by, obtained by, or disclosed to the Commissioner or any other person in connection with an examination or financial analysis shall be given confidential treatment, are not subject to subpoena, and shall not be made public by the Commissioner or any other person. The Commissioner may use the documents, materials, or other information in the furtherance of any regulatory or legal action brought as part of the Commissioner's official duties.

(g) In order to assist in the performance of the Commissioner's duties, the Commissioner may:

    (1) Share documents, materials, or other information, including the confidential and privileged documents, materials, or information subject to subsection (f) of this section, with other state, federal, and international regulatory agencies, with the NAIC, and with state, federal, and international law enforcement authorities, provided that the recipient agrees to maintain the confidentiality and privileged status of the document, material, communication, or other information.

    (2) Receive documents, materials, communications, or information, including otherwise confidential and privileged documents, materials, or information, from the NAIC, and from regulatory and law enforcement officials of other foreign or domestic jurisdictions, and shall maintain as confidential or privileged any document, material, or information received with notice or the understanding that it is confidential or privileged under the laws of the jurisdiction that is the source of the document, material, or information.

    (3) Enter into agreements governing sharing and use of information consistent with this section.

(h) No waiver of an existing privilege or claim of confidentiality in the documents, materials, or information shall occur as a result of disclosure to the Commissioner under this section or as a result of sharing as authorized in subsection (g) of this section.

(i) A privilege established under the law of any state or jurisdiction that is substantially similar to the privilege established under this section shall be available and enforced in any proceeding in, and in any court of, this State.

(j) In this section, "department," "insurance regulator," "law enforcement official or authority," "NAIC," and "regulatory official or agency" include employees, agents, consultants, and contractors of those entities. (1991, c. 681, s. 2; 2001-180, s. 4.)

§ 58-2-133. Conflict of interest; cost of examinations; immunity from liability.

(a) No person may be appointed as an examiner by the Commissioner if that person, either directly or indirectly, has a conflict of interest or is affiliated with the management of or owns a pecuniary interest in any person subject to examination. This section does not preclude an examiner from being:

(1) A policyholder or claimant under an insurance policy;

(2) A grantor of a mortgage or similar instrument on the examiner's residence to an insurer if done under customary terms and in the ordinary course of business;

(3) An investment owner in shares of regulated diversified investment companies; or

(4) A settler or beneficiary of a blind trust into which any otherwise nonpermissible holdings have been placed.

(b) **(Effective until June 30, 2004)** Notwithstanding the requirements of G.S. 58-2-131, the Commissioner may retain from time to time, on an individual basis, qualified actuaries, certified public accountants, or other similar individuals who are independently practicing their professions, even though they may from time to time be similarly employed or retained by persons subject to examination under the Examination Law. In the case of an examination of an insurer, the insurer shall bear the cost of retaining those persons.

(b) **(Effective June 30, 2004)** Notwithstanding the requirements of G.S. 58-2-131, the Commissioner may retain from time to time, on an individual basis, qualified actuaries, certified public accountants, or other similar individuals who are independently practicing their professions, even though they may from time to time be similarly employed or retained by persons subject to examination under the Examination Law.

(c) The refusal of any insurer to submit to examination is grounds for the revocation, suspension, or refusal of a license. The Commissioner may make public any such revocation, suspension, or refusal of license and may give reasons for that action.

(d) The provisions of G.S. 58-2-160 apply to examinations conducted under the Examination Law. (1991, c. 681, s. 2; 1995, c. 360, s. 2(d); 2002-144, s. 7; 2003-284, s. 22.2.)

Subsection (b) Set Out Twice. — The first version of subsection (b) set out above is effective until June 30, 2004. The second version of subsection (b) set out above is effective June 30, 2004.

Editor's Note. — Session Laws 2002-144, s. 11, contains a severability clause.

Session Laws 2003-284, s. 1.2, provides: "This act shall be known as the 'Current Operations and Capital Improvements Appropriations Act of 2003'."

Session Laws 2003-284, s. 49.3, provides: "Except for statutory changes or other provisions that clearly indicate an intention to have effects beyond the 2003-2005 fiscal biennium, the textual provisions of this act apply only to funds appropriated for, and activities occurring during, the 2003-2005 fiscal biennium."

Session Laws 2003-284, s. 49.5 is a severability clause.

Effect of Amendments. — Session Laws 2002-144, s. 7, as amended by Session Laws 2003-284, s. 22.2, effective July 1, 2002 and expiring June 30, 2004, added the second sentence of subsection (b).

§ 58-2-134. Cost of certain examinations.

(a) An insurer shall reimburse the State Treasurer for the actual expenses incurred by the Department in any examination of those records or assets conducted under G.S. 58-2-131, 58-2-132, or 58-2-133 under any of the following circumstances:

(1) The insurer maintains part of its records or assets outside this State under G.S. 58-7-50 or G.S. 58-7-55 and the examination is of the records or assets outside this State.

(2) The insurer requests an examination of its records or assets.

(3) The Commissioner examines an insurer that is impaired or insolvent or is unlikely to be able to meet obligations with respect to known or anticipated claims or to pay other obligations in the normal course of business.

(4) The examination involves analysis of the company's investment portfolio, a material portion of which comprises a sophisticated derivatives program, material holdings of collateralized mortgage obligations with high flux scores, unusual real estate or limited partnership holdings, high or unusual portfolio turnover, material asset movement between related parties, or unusual securities lending activities.

(b) The amount paid by an insurer for an examination of records or assets under this section shall not exceed one hundred thousand dollars ($100,000), unless the insurer and the Commissioner agree on a higher amount. The State Treasurer shall deposit all funds received under this section in the Insurance Regulatory Fund established under G.S. 58-6-25. Funds received under this section shall be used by the Department for offsetting the actual expenses incurred by the Department for examinations under this section. (1998-212, s. 26B(d); 1999-435, s. 7; 2002-187, s. 2.3.)

Effect of Amendments. — Session Laws 2002-187, s. 2.3, effective October 31, 2002, in subsection (a) substituted "under any of the following circumstances" for "when"; and added subdivision (a)(4).

§ **58-2-135:** Repealed by Session Laws 1991, c. 681, s. 3.

§ 58-2-136. (Expires June 30, 2004) Insurer records sent to Department for examination; expenses.

(a) As used in this section, "records" means all data relating to the property, assets, business, and affairs of the insurer being examined.

(b) In addition to the Commissioner's authority in G.S. 58-2-185 through G.S. 58-2-200 to compel the production of records, in lieu of sending examiners to the location of an insurer's records to conduct an examination under the Examination Law, the Commissioner may require the insurer to send copies of its records to the Department. The chief executive or financial officer of the insurer shall certify under oath that the copies are true and accurate copies of the insurer's records. The insurer being examined shall pay all expenses associated with the examination. The insurer is not liable for the salaries and benefits of Department employees. The refusal by an insurer to pay for expenses under this subsection is grounds for the suspension, revocation, or refusal of a license.

(c) If the Commissioner sends examiners to the location of an insurer's records to conduct an examination under the Examination Law, the insurer shall pay for the travel and subsistence expenses and other administrative expenses associated with the examination. The insurer is not liable for the salaries and benefits of Department employees. The refusal by an insurer to pay for expenses under this subsection is grounds for the suspension, revocation, or refusal of a license. (2002-144, s. 8; 2003-284, s. 22.2.)

Editor's Note. — Session Laws 2002-144, s. 12, as amended by Session Laws 2003-284, s. 22.2, made this section effective July 1, 2002, and provided that this section shall expire on June 30, 2004.

Session Laws 2002-144, s. 11, contains a severability clause.

Session Laws 2003-284, s. 1.2, provides: "This act shall be known as the 'Current Operations and Capital Improvements Appropriations Act of 2003'."

Session Laws 2003-284, s. 49.3, provides: "Except for statutory changes or other provisions that clearly indicate an intention to have effects beyond the 2003-2005 fiscal biennium, the textual provisions of this act apply only to funds appropriated for, and activities occurring during, the 2003-2005 fiscal biennium." Session Laws 2003-284, s. 49.5 is a severability clause.

§ 58-2-140: Repealed by Session Laws 1991, c. 681, s. 3.

§ 58-2-145: Repealed by Session Laws 1997-362, s. 7.

§ 58-2-150. Oath required for compliance with law.

Before issuing license to any insurance company to transact the business of insurance in this State, the Commissioner shall require, in every case, in addition to the other requirements provided for by law, that the company file with him the affidavit of its president or other chief officer that it has not violated any of the provisions of Articles 1 through 64 of this Chapter for the space of 12 months last past, and that it accepts the terms and obligations of Articles 1 through 64 of this Chapter as a part of the consideration of the license. (1899, c. 54, s. 110; 1901, c. 391, s. 8; Rev., s. 4693; C.S., s. 6276; 1991, c. 720, s. 4.)

§ 58-2-155. Investigation of charges.

Upon his own motion or upon complaint being filed by a citizen of this State that a company authorized to do business in the State has violated any of the provisions of Articles 1 through 64 of this Chapter, the Commissioner shall investigate the matter, and, if necessary, examine, under oath, by himself or his accredited representatives the president and such other officer or agents of such companies as may be deemed proper; also all books, records, and papers of the same. In case the Commissioner shall find upon substantial evidence that any complaint against a company is justified, said company, in addition to such penalties as are imposed for violation of any of the provisions of Articles 1 through 64 of this Chapter, shall be liable for the expenses of the investigation, and the Commissioner shall promptly present said company with a statement of such expenses. If the company refuses or neglects to pay, the Commissioner is authorized to bring a civil action for the collection of these expenses. (1899, c. 54, s. 111; 1903, c. 438, s. 11; Rev., s. 4694; C.S., s. 6277; 1921, c. 136, s. 4; 1925, c. 275, s. 6; 1945, c. 383.)

Legal Periodicals. — For article discussing limitations on ad hoc adjudicatory rulemaking by an administrative agency, see 61 N.C.L. Rev. 67 (1982).

§ 58-2-160. Reporting and investigation of insurance and reinsurance fraud and the financial condition of licensees; immunity from liability.

(a) As used in this section, "Commissioner" includes an employee, agent, or designee of the Commissioner. A person, or an employee or agent of that person, acting without actual malice, is not subject to civil liability for libel, slander, or any other cause of action by virtue of furnishing to the Commissioner under the requirements of law or at the direction of the Commissioner reports or other information relating to (i) any known or suspected fraudulent insurance or reinsurance claim, transaction, or act or (ii) the financial condition of any licensee. In the absence of actual malice, members of the NAIC, their duly authorized committees, subcommittees, task forces, delegates, and employees, and all other persons charged with the responsibility of collecting, reviewing, analyzing, or disseminating the information developed from filings of financial statements or examinations of licensees are not subject to civil liability for libel, slander, or any other cause of action by virtue of their collection, review, analysis, or dissemination of the data and information collected from such filings or examinations.

(b) The Commissioner, acting without actual malice, is not subject to civil liability for libel or slander by virtue of an investigation of (i) any known or suspected fraudulent insurance or reinsurance claim, transaction, or act or (ii) the financial condition of any licensee; or by virtue of the publication or dissemination of any official report related to any such investigation, which report is published or disseminated in the absence of fraud, bad faith, or actual malice on the part of the Commissioner. The Commissioner is not subject to civil liability in relation to the collecting, reviewing, analyzing, or dissemination of information that is developed by the NAIC from the filing of financial statements with the NAIC or from the examination of insurers by the NAIC and that is communicated to the Commissioner, including any investigation or publication or dissemination of any report or other information in relation thereto, which report is published or disseminated in the absence of fraud, bad faith, negligence, or actual malice on the part of the Commissioner.

(c) During the course of an investigation of (i) a known or suspected fraudulent insurance or reinsurance claim, transaction, or act or (ii) the financial condition of any licensee, the Commissioner may request any person to furnish copies of any information relative to the (i) known or suspected claim, transaction, or act or (ii) financial condition of the licensee. The person shall release the information requested and cooperate with the Commissioner pursuant to this section. (1985 (Reg. Sess., 1986), c. 1013, s. 3; 1987, c. 864, s. 43; 1987 (Reg. Sess., 1988), c. 975, s. 3; 1989 (Reg. Sess., 1990), c. 1054, s. 1.)

Legal Periodicals. — For note, "Utmost Good Faith in Reinsurance: A Tradition in Need of Adjustment," see 1992 Duke L.J. 41.

§ 58-2-161. False statement to procure or deny benefit of insurance policy or certificate.

(a) For the purposes of this section:

  (1) "Insurer" has the same meaning as in G.S. 58-1-5(3) and also includes:

    a. Any hull insurance and protection and indemnity club operating under Article 20 of this Chapter.

    b. Any surplus lines insurer operating under Article 21 of this Chapter.

    c. Any risk retention group or purchasing group operating under Article 22 of this Chapter.

    d. Any local government risk pool operating under Article 23 of this Chapter.

    e. Any risk-sharing plan operating under Article 42 of this Chapter.

    f. The North Carolina Insurance Underwriting Association operating under Article 45 of this Chapter.

    g. The North Carolina Joint Insurance Underwriting Association operating under Article 46 of this Chapter.

    h. The North Carolina Insurance Guaranty Association operating under Article 48 of this Chapter.

    i. Any multiple employer welfare arrangement operating under Article 49 of this Chapter.

    j. The North Carolina Life and Health Insurance Guaranty Association operating under Article 62 of this Chapter.

    k. Any service corporation operating under Article 65 of this Chapter.

    l. Any health maintenance organization operating under Article 67 of this Chapter.

    m. The Teachers' and State Employees' Comprehensive Major Medical Plan operating under Chapter 135 of the General Statutes.

    n. A group of employers self-insuring their workers' compensation liabilities under Article 47 of this Chapter.

    o. An employer self-insuring its workers' compensation liabilities under Article 5 of Chapter 97 of the General Statutes.

    p. The North Carolina Self-Insurance Guaranty Association under Article 4 of Chapter 97 of the General Statutes.

    q. Any reinsurer licensed or accredited under this Chapter.

  (2) "Statement" includes any application, notice, statement, proof of loss, bill of lading, receipt for payment, invoice, account, estimate of property damages, bill for services, diagnosis, prescription, hospital or doctor records, X rays, test result, or other evidence of loss, injury, or expense.

(b) Any person who, with the intent to injure, defraud, or deceive an insurer or insurance claimant:

  (1) Presents or causes to be presented a written or oral statement, including computer-generated documents as part of, in support of, or in opposition to, a claim for payment or other benefit pursuant to an insurance policy, knowing that the statement contains false or misleading information concerning any fact or matter material to the claim, or

  (2) Assists, abets, solicits, or conspires with another person to prepare or make any written or oral statement that is intended to be presented to an insurer or insurance claimant in connection with, in support of, or in opposition to, a claim for payment or other benefit pursuant to an insurance policy, knowing that the statement contains false or misleading information concerning a fact or matter material to the claim

is guilty of a Class H felony. Each claim shall be considered a separate count. Upon conviction, if the court imposes probation, the court may order the defendant to pay restitution as a condition of probation. In determination of the amount of restitution pursuant to G.S. 15A-1343(d), the reasonable costs and attorneys' fees incurred by the victim in the investigation of, and efforts to recover damages arising from, the claim, may be considered part of the damage caused by the defendant arising out of the offense.

    In a civil cause of action for recovery based upon a claim for which a defendant has been convicted under this section, the conviction may be entered into evidence against the defendant. The court may award the prevailing party compensatory damages, attorneys' fees, costs, and reasonable investigative costs. If the prevailing party can demonstrate that the defendant has engaged in a pattern of violations of this section, the court may award treble damages. (1899, c. 54, s. 60; Rev., s. 3487; 1913, c. 89, s. 28; C.S., s. 4369; 1937, c. 248; 1967, c. 1088, s. 1; 1979, c. 760, s. 5; 1989 (Reg. Sess., 1990), c. 1054, s. 2; 1995, c. 43, s. 1; 1999-294, s. 3.)

Editor's Note. — This section was enacted by Session Laws 1989 (Reg. Sess., 1990), c. 1054, which repealed G.S. 14-214, relating to a similar subject matter. The historical citation and annotations to repealed G.S. 14-214 have been placed under this section.

Legal Periodicals. — For article discussing "reverse bad faith," the concept of allowing an insurer to assert a counterclaim for affirmative relief against an insured who brings a frivolous, bad faith action, see 19 Campbell L. Rev. 43 (1996).

CASE NOTES

Editor's Note. — *Many of the cases below were decided under former G.S. 14-214, which contained language similar to this section.*

"Fraudulent" Claim Defined. — Where the filing of a false claim is coupled with a knowing intent for the purposes of conviction under the statute, the filing of a "false" claim is tantamount to the filing of a "fraudulent" claim. State v. Carroll, 101 N.C. App. 691, 401 S.E.2d 114, cert. denied, 329 N.C. 501, 407 S.E.2d 543 (1991).

Meaning of "Willfully" and "Knowingly". — The word "willfully" as used in former G.S. 14-214 meant something more than an intention to commit the offense. It implied committing the offense purposely and designedly in violation of law. The word "knowingly" as so used meant that defendant knew what he was about to do, and with such knowledge, proceeded to do the act charged. These words combined in the phrase "willfully and knowingly," in reference to violation of the statute, meant intentionally and consciously. One does not "willfully and knowingly" violate a statute when he does that which he believes he has a bona fide right to do. State v. Fraylon, 240 N.C. 365, 82 S.E.2d 400 (1954).

"Willful" and "Knowing" Required Elements. — The North Carolina Supreme Court has stated that conviction under this section always requires an element of "willful" and "knowing" submission of a false claim. State v. Carroll, 101 N.C. App. 691, 401 S.E.2d 114, cert. denied, 329 N.C. 501, 407 S.E.2d 543 (1991).

Incorrect Use of "False" and "Fraudulent" Not Plain Error. — Where judge, in his instructions to the jury asked them to decide whether the defendant had filed a "false or fraudulent" claim and submitted a verdict sheet which used only the word "false" and the indictment used only the word "fraudulent", such did not constitute plain error even though "false" and "fraudulent" do have different though overlapping meanings, because either is sufficient for conviction under the statute. In addition, trial court specifically and correctly instructed the jury that it must find that the defendant "willfully and knowingly" made a false claim. State v. Carroll, 101 N.C. App. 691, 401 S.E.2d 114, cert. denied, 329 N.C. 501, 407 S.E.2d 543 (1991).

The existence of unreported liens or other insurance upon property was a civil matter governed by Chapter 58, and would not tend to show criminal intent in connection with the filing of proofs of claim within the meaning of former G.S. 14-214. State v. Fraylon, 240 N.C. 365, 82 S.E.2d 400 (1954).

The filing of an insurance claim based on an accident admittedly staged with the intent to defraud the insurance company was a violation of former G.S. 14-214. State v. Walker, 22 N.C. App. 291, 206 S.E.2d 395 (1974).

Burden on the State. — The gravamen of the offense defined by former G.S. 14-214 was willfully and knowingly presenting a false or fraudulent proof of claim for a loss upon a contract of insurance; and in the prosecution thereunder the burden was upon the State to prove that the claim for loss was false, that defendant knew it was false, and that, with such knowledge, he proceeded to make the claim for payment of insurance thereon. State v. Stephenson, 218 N.C. 258, 10 S.E.2d 819 (1940).

In a prosecution under former G.S. 14-214, the burden was upon the State to prove that defendant "willfully and knowingly" presented a false and fraudulent claim and presented proof in support of such claim, and when the evidence, considered in the light most favorable to the State, raised no more than a suspicion or conjecture of defendant's guilt of the charge under the statute, defendant's motion to nonsuit would be allowed. State v. Fraylon, 240 N.C. 365, 82 S.E.2d 400 (1954).

Broker as Competent Witness. — It was not necessary that a broker have the authority to contract directly with the insurance company in order to be a competent witness with regard to the contract of insurance in a prosecution under former G.S. 14-214 where his testimony relating to the insurance contract did not extend beyond his personal knowledge and observation of the facts so as to render his testimony incompetent or hearsay. State v. Moose, 36 N.C. App. 202, 243 S.E.2d 425 (1978).

Evidence of Prior Claims Held Relevant. — Evidence concerning two previous insurance claims made by defendant on other stores owned by her after purchasing theft policies are relevant insofar as they tend to show intent, absence of mistake and a pattern by which defendant made and then exaggerated claims resulting from commercial burglary. State v. Carroll, 101 N.C. App. 691, 401 S.E.2d 114, cert. denied, 329 N.C. 501, 407 S.E.2d 543 (1991).

Evidence Sufficient to Show Conspiracy to Procure Insurance by Means of False Claim. — Evidence held sufficient to be submitted to jury in prosecution for conspiracy to procure insurance benefits by means of false claim. State v. Hedrick, 236 N.C. 727, 73 S.E.2d 904 (1953).

Where defendant claimed $46,461.00 in losses from 700-800 items from showroom floor, and showroom floor still appeared stocked to near capacity and defendant could not produce invoices for these items, this, in conjunction with prior instances of defendant's similar exaggerated claims was sufficient to sustain conviction for making fraudulent statements to insurance company. State v. Carroll, 101 N.C. App. 691, 401 S.E.2d 114, cert. denied, 329 N.C. 501, 407 S.E.2d 543 (1991).

Evidence held insufficient to show that defendant willfully and knowingly presented fraudulent claim for insurance loss and proofs in support thereof. State v. Fraylon, 240 N.C. 365, 82 S.E.2d 400 (1954).

Aggravation of Sentence. — Fact that insurance fraud involved property of great monetary value was not an element of the offense, and could therefore be used to aggravate defendant's sentence. State v. Payne, 149 N.C. App. 421, 561 S.E.2d 507, 2002 N.C. App. LEXIS 218 (2002).

Criminal Actions as Guidance in Civil Actions. — Although criminal actions under former G.S. 14-214 could not establish the standard for judging misrepresentation in civil actions, they did provide guidance. Shields v. Nationwide Mut. Fire Ins. Co., 61 N.C. App. 365, 301 S.E.2d 439, cert. denied, 308 N.C. 678, 304 S.E.2d 759 (1983).

§ 58-2-162. Embezzlement by insurance agents, brokers, or administrators.

If any insurance agent, broker, or administrator embezzles or fraudulently converts to his own use, or, with intent to use or embezzle, takes, secretes, or otherwise disposes of, or fraudulently withholds, appropriates, lends, invests, or otherwise uses or applies any money, negotiable instrument, or other consideration received by him in his performance as an agent, broker, or administrator, he shall be guilty of a felony. If the value of the money, negotiable instrument, or other consideration is one hundred thousand dollars ($100,000) or more, violation of this section is a Class C felony. If the value of the money, negotiable instrument, or other consideration is less than one hundred thousand dollars ($100,000), violation of this section is a Class H felony. (1889, c. 54, s. 103; Rev., s. 3489; 1911, c. 196, s. 8; C.S., s. 4274; 1989 (Reg. Sess., 1990), c. 1054, s. 2; 1997-443, s. 19.25(n).)

Editor's Note. — This section was enacted by Session Laws 1989 (Reg. Sess., 1990), c. 1054, which repealed G.S. 14-96, relating to a similar subject matter. The historical citation for repealed G.S. 14-96 has been placed under this section.

§ 58-2-163. Report to Commissioner.

Whenever any insurance company, or employee or representative of such company, or any other person licensed or registered under Articles 1 through 67 of this Chapter knows or has reasonable cause to believe that any other person has violated G.S. 58-2-161, 58-2-162, 58-2-180, 58-8-1, or 58-24-180(e), or whenever any insurance company, or employee or representative of such company, or any other person licensed or registered under Articles 1 through 67 of this Chapter knows or has reasonable cause to believe that any entity licensed by the Commissioner is financially impaired, it is the duty of such person, upon acquiring such knowledge, to notify the Commissioner and provide the Commissioner with a complete statement of all of the relevant facts and circumstances. Such report is a privileged communication, and when made without actual malice does not subject the person making the same to any liability whatsoever. The Commissioner may suspend, revoke, or refuse to renew the license of any licensee who willfully fails to comply with this section. (1945, c. 382; 1987, c. 752, s. 2; 1989 (Reg. Sess., 1990), c. 1054, s. 2.)

Editor's Note. — This section was enacted by Session Laws 1989 (Reg. Sess., 1990), c. 1054, which repealed G.S. 14-96.1, relating to a similar subject matter. The historical citation for repealed G.S. 14-96.1 has been placed under this section.

§ 58-2-165. Annual, semiannual, monthly, or quarterly statements to be filed with Commissioner.

(a) Except as provided in subsection (a1) of this section, every insurance company shall file in the Commissioner's office, on or before March 1 of each year, a statement showing the business standing and financial condition of the company, association, or order on the preceding December 31, signed and sworn to by the chief managing agent or officer thereof, before the Commissioner or some officer authorized by law to administer oaths. Provided, the Commissioner may, for good and sufficient cause shown by an applicant company, extend the filing date of the company's annual statement, for a reasonable period of time, not to exceed 30 days. In addition, except as provided in subsection (a1) of this section, the Commissioner may require any insurance company, association, or order to file its statement semiannually, quarterly, or monthly.

(a1) A town or county mutual, organized under G.S. 58-7-75(5)d., is required to file only an annual statement or an audited financial statement that was prepared by a certified public accountant if for the preceding year it had a direct written premium of less than one hundred fifty thousand dollars ($150,000) and fewer than 400 policyholders. The Commissioner shall not require those mutuals to file statements semiannually, quarterly, or monthly.

(b) The Commissioner may require statements under this section, G.S. 58-2-170, and G.S. 58-2-190 to be filed in a format that can be read by electronic data processing equipment, provided that this subsection does not apply to an audited financial statement prepared by a certified public accountant that is submitted by a town or county mutual pursuant to subsection (a1) of this section.

(c) Except as provided herein, all statements filed under this section must be prepared in accordance with the appropriate NAIC Annual Statement Instructions Handbook and pursuant to the NAIC Accounting Practices and Procedures Manual and on the NAIC Model Financial Statement Blank, unless further modified by the Commissioner as the Commissioner considers to be appropriate. This subsection does not apply to statements filed by a town or county mutual organized under G.S. 58-7-75(5)d. if for the preceding year it had a direct written premium of less than one hundred fifty thousand dollars ($150,000) and fewer than 400 policyholders. (1899, c. 54, ss. 72, 73, 83, 90, 97; 1901, c. 706, s. 2; 1903, c. 438, s. 9; Rev., s. 4698; C.S., s. 6280; 1945, c. 383; 1957, c. 407; 1985, c. 666, ss. 50, 51; 1985 (Reg. Sess., 1986), c. 1013, s. 11; 1991, c. 681, s. 7; 1993, c. 504, s. 1; 1998-211, s. 22; 1999-192, s. 1.)

CASE NOTES

Cited in In re North Carolina Auto. Rate Admin. Office, 278 N.C. 302, 180 S.E.2d 155 (1971); State ex rel. Comm'r of Ins. v. North Carolina Rate Bureau, 44 N.C. App. 191, 261 S.E.2d 671 (1979); State ex rel. Comm'r of Ins. v. North Carolina Rate Bureau, 124 N.C. App. 674, 478 S.E.2d 794 (1996), cert. denied, 346 N.C. 184, 486 S.E.2d 217 (1997).

§ 58-2-170. Annual statements by professional liability insurers; medical malpractice claim reports.

(a) In addition to the financial statements required by G.S. 58-2-165, every insurer, self-insurer, and risk retention group that provides professional liability insurance in the State shall file with the Commissioner, on or before the first day of February in each year, in form and detail as the Commissioner prescribes, a statement showing the items set forth in subsection (b) of this section, as of the preceding 31st day of December. The annual statement shall not be reported or disclosed to the public in a manner or format which identifies or could reasonably be used to identify any individual health care provider or medical center. The statement shall be signed and sworn to by the chief managing agent or officer of the insurer, self-insurer, or risk retention group, before the Commissioner or some officer authorized by law to administer oaths. The Commissioner shall, in December of each year, furnish to each such person that provides professional liability insurance in the State forms for the annual statements. The Commissioner may, for good cause, authorize an extension of the report due date upon written application of any person required to file. An extension is not valid unless the Commissioner's authorization is in writing and signed by the Commissioner or one of his deputies.

(b) The statement required by subsection (a) of this section shall contain:
(1) Number of claims pending at beginning of year;
(2) Number of claims pending at end of year;
(3) Number of claims paid;
(4) Number of claims closed no payment;
(5) Number and amounts of claims in court in which judgment paid:
    a. Highest amount
    b. Lowest amount
    c. Average amount
    d. Median amount;
(6) Number and amounts of claims out of court in which settlement paid:
    a. Highest amount
    b. Lowest amount
    c. Average amount
    d. Median amount;
(7) Average amount per claim set up in reserve;
(8) Total premium collection;
(9) Total expenses less reserve expenses; and
(10) Total reserve expenses.

(c) Every insurer, self-insurer, and risk retention group that provides professional liability insurance to health care providers in this State shall file, within 90 days following the request of the Commissioner, a report containing information for the purpose of allowing the Commissioner to analyze claims. The report shall be in the form prescribed by the Commissioner. The form prescribed by the Commissioner shall be a form that permits the public inspection, examination, or copying of any information contained in the report: Provided, however, that any data or other characteristics that identify or could be used to identify the names or addresses of the claimants or the names or addresses of the individual health care provider or medical center against whom the claims are or have been asserted or any data that could be used to identify the dollar amounts involved in such claims shall be treated as privileged information and shall not be made available to the public. The Commissioner shall analyze these reports and shall file statistical and other summaries based on these reports with the General Assembly as soon as practicable after receipt of the reports. The Commissioner shall assess a penalty against any person that willfully fails to file a report required by this subsection. Such penalty shall be one thousand dollars ($1,000) for each day after the due date of the report that the person willfully fails to file: Provided, however, the penalty for an individual who self insures shall be two hundred dollars ($200.00) for each day after the due date of the report that the person willfully fails to file: Provided, however, that upon the failure of a person to file the report as required by this subsection, the Commissioner shall send by certified mail, return receipt requested, a notice to that person informing him that he has 10 business days after receipt of the notice to either request an extension of time or file the report. The Commissioner may, for good cause, authorize an extension of the report due date upon written application of any person required to file. An extension is not valid unless the Commissioner's authorization is in writing and signed by the Commissioner or one of his deputies.

(d) Every person that self-insures against professional liability in this State shall provide the Commissioner with written notice of such self-insurance, which notice shall include the name and address of the person self-insuring. This notice shall be filed with the Commissioner each year for the purpose of apprising the Commissioner of the number and locations of persons that self-insure against professional liability. (1975, 2nd Sess., c. 977, s. 6; 1985, c. 666, s. 53; 1987, c. 343.)

§ 58-2-171. Qualifications of actuaries.

The Commissioner may adopt rules setting forth requisite qualifications of consulting actuaries for the sole purpose of qualifying them to certify financial statements filed and rate filings made by entities under this Chapter as to the actuarial validity of those filings. The qualifications shall be commensurate with the degree of complexity of the actuarial principles applicable to the various statements filed or rate filings made. Nothing in this section affects the scope of practice or the professional qualifications of actuaries. (1995, c. 517, s. 2.)

§ 58-2-175: Repealed by Session Laws 1993, c. 452, s. 65.

§ 58-2-180. Punishment for making false statement.

If any person in any financial or other statement required by this Chapter willfully misstates information, that person making oath to or subscribing the statement is guilty of a Class I felony; and the entity on whose behalf the person made the oath or subscribed the statement is subject to a fine imposed by the court of not less than two thousand dollars ($2,000) nor more than ten thousand dollars ($10,000). (1899, c. 54, s. 97; Rev., s. 3493; C.S., s. 6281; 1985, c. 666, s. 13; 1989 (Reg. Sess., 1990), c. 1054, s. 5; 1993 (Reg. Sess., 1994), c. 767, s. 23.)

CASE NOTES

Cited in State ex rel. Comm'r of Ins. v. North Carolina Rate Bureau, 44 N.C. App. 191, 261 S.E.2d 671 (1979).

§ 58-2-185. Record of business kept by companies and agents; Commissioner may inspect.

All companies, agents, or brokers doing any kind of insurance business in this State must make and keep a full and correct record of the business done by them, showing the number, date, term, amount insured, premiums, and the persons to whom issued, of every policy or certificate or renewal. Information from these records must be furnished to the Commissioner on demand, and the original books of records shall be open to the inspection of the Commissioner when demanded. (1899, c. 54, s. 108; 1903, c. 438, s. 11; Rev., s. 4696; C.S., s. 6284; 1945, c. 383; 1991, c. 720, s. 4.)

Cited in State ex rel. Comm'r of Ins. v. North Carolina Rate Bureau, 44 N.C. App. 191, 261 S.E.2d 671 (1979).

§ 58-2-190. Commissioner may require special reports.

The Commissioner may also address to any authorized insurer, rating organization, advisory organization, joint underwriting or joint reinsurance organization, or the North Carolina Rate Bureau or Motor Vehicle Reinsurance Facility, or its officers any inquiry in relation to its transactions or condition or any matter connected therewith. Every corporation or person so addressed shall reply in writing to such inquiry promptly and truthfully, and such reply shall be verified, if required by the Commissioner, by such individual, or by such officer or officers of a corporation, as he shall designate. (1945, c. 383; 1985 (Reg. Sess., 1986), c. 1027, s. 8.)

Cited in State ex rel. Comm'r of Ins. v. North Carolina Rate Bureau, 44 N.C. App. 191, 261 S.E.2d 671 (1979).

§ 58-2-195. Commissioner may require records, reports, etc., for agencies, agents and others.

(a) The Commissioner is empowered to make and promulgate reasonable rules and regulations governing the recording and reporting of insurance business transactions by insurance agencies, agents, brokers and producers of record, any of which agencies, agents, brokers or producers of record are licensed in this State or are transacting insurance business in this State to the end that such records and reports will accurately and separately reflect the insurance business transactions of such agency, agent, broker or producer of record in this State. Information from records required to be kept pursuant to the provisions of this section must be furnished the Commissioner on demand and the original records required to be kept pursuant to the provisions of this section shall be open to the inspection for the Commissioner or any other authorized employee described in G.S. 58-2-25 when demanded.

(b) Every insurance agency transacting insurance business in this State shall at all times have appointed some person employed or associated with such agency who shall have the responsibility of seeing that such records and reports as are required pursuant to the provisions of this section are kept and maintained.

(c) Any person subject to the provisions of subsection (a) of this section who violates the provisions of this section or the rules and regulations prescribed by the Commissioner pursuant to the provisions of this section may after notice and hearing: for the first offense have his license or licenses (in case license be issued for more than one company in such person's case) suspended or revoked for not less than one month nor more than six months and for the second offense shall have his license or licenses (in case license be issued from more than one company in his case) suspended or revoked for the period of one year and such person shall not thereafter be licensed for one year from the date said revocation or suspension first became effective.

(d) For the purpose of enforcing the provisions of this section the Commissioner or any other authorized employee described in G.S. 58-2-25 is authorized and empowered to examine persons, administer oaths and require production of papers and records relative to this section.

(e) Whenever the Commissioner deems it to be prudent for the protection of policyholders in this State, he or any other authorized employee described in G.S. 58-2-25 shall visit and examine any insurance agency, agent, broker, adjuster, motor vehicle damage appraiser, or producer of record. The refusal of any agency, agent, broker, adjuster, motor vehicle damage appraiser, or producer of record to submit to examination is grounds for the revocation or refusal of a license. (1971, c. 948, s. 1; 1987, c. 629, ss. 14, 15; c. 752, s. 1; 1995, c. 360, s. 2(e).)

§ 58-2-200. Books and papers required to be exhibited.

It is the duty of any person having in his possession or control any books, accounts, or papers of any company licensed under Articles 1 through 64 of this Chapter, to exhibit the same to the Commissioner or to any deputy, actuary, accountant, or persons acting with or for the Commissioner. Any person who shall refuse, on demand, to exhibit the books, accounts, or papers, as above provided, or who shall knowingly or willfully make any false statement in regard to the same, shall be subject to suspension or revocation of his license under Articles 1 through 64 of this Chapter; and shall be deemed guilty of a Class 1 misdemeanor. (1899, c. 54, s. 76; Rev., ss. 3494, 4697; 1907, c. 1000, s. 3; C.S., s. 6286; 1945, c. 383; 1985 (Reg. Sess., 1986), c. 1013, s. 6; 1991, c. 720, s. 4; 1993, c. 539, s. 445; 1994, Ex. Sess., c. 24, s. 14(c).)

§ 58-2-205. CPA audits of financial statements.

The Commissioner may adopt rules to provide for audits and opinions of insurers' financial statements by certified public accountants. These rules shall be substantially similar to the NAIC model rule that requires audited financial reports, as amended. The Commissioner may adopt, amend, or repeal provisions of these rules under G.S. 150B-21.1 in order to keep these rules current with the NAIC model rule. (1989, c. 485, s. 38; 1998-212, s. 26B(g).)

§ 58-2-210. Rules for mortgage insurance consolidations.

The Commissioner is authorized to adopt rules governing mortgage insurance consolidations and related rules concerning unfair rate discrimination. In the event the Commissioner adopts such rules, while such rules are in effect the unfair rate discrimination provisions of G.S. 58-58-35 and G.S. 58-63-15(7) will not apply to mortgage insurance consolidations to the extent those provisions are inconsistent with such rules. For purposes of this section, "mortgage insurance consolidation" means any transaction in which a mortgage loan servicer makes its premium collection services available to mortgage debtors in connection with an insurer's offer of mortgage insurance, which offer is made to debtors who, immediately prior to the offer, had mortgage insurance with another insurer and were paying premiums for that insurance with their monthly mortgage payments. (1989, c. 341, s. 1.)

§ 58-2-215. Consumer Protection Fund.

(a) A special fund is created in the Office of the State Treasurer, to be known as the Department of Insurance Consumer Protection Fund. The Fund shall be placed in an interest bearing account and any interest or other income derived from the Fund shall be credited to the Fund. Moneys in the Fund shall only be spent pursuant to warrants drawn by the Commissioner on the Fund through the State Treasurer. The Fund shall be subject to the provisions of the Executive Budget Act; except that the provisions of Article 3C of Chapter 143 of the General Statutes do not apply to subdivision (b)(1) of this section.

(b) All moneys credited to the Fund shall be used only to pay the following expenses incurred by the Department:

(1) For the purpose of retaining outside actuarial and economic consultants, legal counsel, and court reporting services in the review and analysis of rate filings, in conducting all hearings, and through any final adjudication.

(2) In connection with any delinquency proceeding under Article 30 of this Chapter, for the purpose of locating and recovering the assets of or any other obligations or liabilities owed to or due an insurer that has been placed under such proceeding.

(3) In connection with any civil litigation, other than under Chapter 150B of the General Statutes or any appeal from an order of the Commissioner or his deputies, that is commenced against the Commissioner or his deputies and that arises out of the performance of their official duties, for the purpose of retaining outside consultants, legal counsel, and court reporting services to defend such litigation.

(c) Moneys appropriated by the General Assembly shall be deposited in the Fund and shall become a part of the continuation budget of the Department of Insurance. Such continuation budget amount shall equal the actual expenditures drawn from the Fund during the prior fiscal year plus the official inflation rate designated by the Director of the Budget in the preparation of the State Budget for each ensuing fiscal year; provided that if interest income on the Fund exceeds the amount yielded by the application of the official inflation rate, such continuation budget amount shall be the actual expenditures drawn from the Fund, except that the appropriation for the 1995-96 fiscal year shall not exceed the sum of seven hundred fifty thousand dollars ($750,000) and for the 1996-97 fiscal year shall not exceed the sum of two hundred fifty thousand dollars ($250,000). In the event the amount in the Fund exceeds two hundred fifty thousand dollars ($250,000) at the end of any fiscal year, beginning with the 1995-96 fiscal year, such excess shall revert to the General Fund.

(d) Repealed by Session Laws 1996, c. 507, s. 11A(a), (b). (1989 (Reg. Sess., 1990), c. 1069, s. 22; 1993 (Reg. Sess., 1994), c. 769, s. 14.1; 1995, c. 507, s. 11A(a), (b), (c).)

§ 58-2-220. Insurance Regulatory Information System and similar program test data not public records.

Except as provided in G.S. 58-4-25, financial test ratios, data, or information generated by the Commissioner pursuant to the NAIC Insurance Regulatory Information System, any successor program, or any similar program developed by the Commissioner, are not public records and are not subject to Chapter 132 of the General Statutes or G.S. 58-2-100. (1985 (Reg. Sess., 1986), c. 1013, s. 9; 1989 (Reg. Sess., 1990), c. 1021, s. 7; 1991, c. 681, s. 14.)

Editor's Note. — This section was formerly G.S. 58-4-20. It was recodified as G.S. 58-2-215 by Session Laws 1989 (Reg. Sess., 1990), c. 1021, s. 7, effective July 27, 1990, and renumbered as G.S. 58-2-220 at the direction of the Revisor of Statutes.

§ 58-2-225: Repealed by Session Laws 1995, c. 193, s. 8.

§ 58-2-230. Commissioner to share information with Department of Labor.

The Commissioner shall provide or cause to be provided to the Department of Labor, on an annual basis, the name and business address of every employer that is self-insured for workers' compensation. Information provided or caused to be provided by the Commissioner to the Department of Labor under this section is confidential and not open for public inspection under G.S. 132-6. (1991 (Reg. Sess., 1992), c. 894, s. 5.)

§ 58-2-235. Expired.

Expired. (1999-184, s. 1.)

Editor's Note. — This section was enacted by Session Laws 1999, c. 184, s. 1, and pursuant to s. 3 of that act, expired on December 31, 2000.

ARTICLE 3.

General Regulations for Insurance.

§ 58-3-1. State law governs insurance contracts.

All contracts of insurance on property, lives, or interests in this State shall be deemed to be made therein, and all contracts of insurance the applications for which are taken within the State shall be deemed to have been made within this State and are subject to the laws thereof. (1899, c. 54, s. 2; 1901, c. 705, s. 1; Rev., s. 4806; C.S., s. 6287.)

Legal Periodicals. — For note on validity of statutes localizing insurance contracts, see 13 N.C.L. Rev. 213 (1935).

For comment, "Insurance Contract and Policy in General as It Relates to North Carolina," see 3 N.C. Cent. L.J. 259 (1972).

For article, "Statutes of Limitations in the Conflict of Laws," see 52 N.C.L. Rev. 489 (1974).

CASE NOTES

This section is constitutional. Williams v. Mutual Reserve Fund Life Ass'n, 145 N.C. 128, 28 S.E. 802 (1907).

Regulation of insurance is a function of the states rather than the federal government. State ex rel. Comm'r of Ins. v. North Carolina Rate Bureau, 300 N.C. 381, 269 S.E.2d 547, rehearing denied, 301 N.C. 107, 273 S.E.2d 300 (1980).

And Is Constitutional. — The insurance business is charged with a public interest, and its regulation is constitutional. State ex rel. Comm'r of Ins. v. North Carolina Rate Bureau, 300 N.C. 381, 269 S.E.2d 547, rehearing denied, 301 N.C. 107, 273 S.E.2d 300 (1980).

Policies Made in North Carolina. — For a policy "made" in North Carolina, where insured resided in this state, North Carolina substantive law governs construction of the policy and its terms. Beavers v. Federal Ins. Co., 113 N.C. App. 254, 437 S.E.2d 881, cert. denied, 336 N.C. 602, 447 S.E.2d 384 (1994).

An insurance contract was deemed to have been made in North Carolina and would be interpreted under North Carolina law, even though plaintiff was a Delaware corporation with its principal place of business in California, with its transportation division located in North Carolina, and the policy was procured by a broker in California. North Carolina had a close connection with the interests insured, since most of plaintiff's trucks were located and titled in North Carolina and the accident occurred in North Carolina. Collins & Aikman Corp. v. Hartford Accident & Indem. Co., 335 N.C. 91, 436 S.E.2d 243 (1993).

Applications Taken Within State. — Policies of insurance issued by a foreign company, the applications for which are taken in this State, are to be construed in accordance with the laws of this State, even though the insurance company may under its charter be allowed privileges which are contrary to statutes of this State. Wilson v. Supreme Conclave, Improved Order of Heptasophs, 174 N.C. 628, 94 S.E. 443 (1917), appeal dismissed, 249 U.S. 583, 39 S. Ct. 287, 63 L. Ed. 787 (1919). See also, Horton v. Life Ins. Co., 122 N.C. 498, 29 S.E. 944 (1898); Cordell v. Brotherhood of Locomotive Firemen, 208 N.C. 632, 182 S.E. 141 (1935).

A contract of insurance, based upon the application of insured made while residing in this State, must be construed in accordance with the laws of this State rather than the laws in force at the time of the inception of the contract in the state in which the insurer is incorporated. Pace v. New York Life Ins. Co., 219 N.C. 451, 14 S.E.2d 411 (1941).

Applications Taken Out of State. — When neither party was a resident of the State at the time of the contract of insurance and the application was taken out of State the rule of lex loci contractu will apply. Keesler v. Mutual Benefit Life Ins. Co., 177 N.C. 394, 99 S.E. 97 (1919).

Where insurance policies were applied for, countersigned and delivered in New Jersey, they would be governed by the law of New Jersey as regards interpretation and effect, and this section would not operate to make them North Carolina contracts merely because the insured property, a tractor, was property in this State, and because of driver's coverage under the omnibus clauses of the policies. Turner v. Liberty Mut. Ins. Co., 105 F. Supp. 723 (E.D.N.C. 1952).

Even though a policy application for liability insurance was not "taken" in North Carolina, where the policy insured "property, lives, or interests in this State," the policy must be construed in accordance with the laws of North Carolina. Collins & Aikman Corp. v. Hartford Accident & Indem. Co., 106 N.C. App. 357, 416 S.E.2d 591 (1992), aff'd, 355 N.C. 91, 436 S.E.2d 243 (1993).

North Carolina law applied to determination of an insurer's defense obligations under a professional liability insurance policy in connection with a lawsuit brought in North Carolina; although the policy was delivered to the insured in Ohio, four of the insured's approximately 50 weight-loss center franchises were located in North Carolina, and between 2,000 and 5,000 North Carolina citizens were customers of the centers, so North Carolina had much more than a casual connection with the substance of the insurance policy. Cont'l Cas. Co. v. Physicians Weight Loss Ctrs. of Am., Inc., — F.3d —, 2003 U.S. App. LEXIS 6024 (4th Cir. Mar. 31, 2003).

Effect of Stipulation Making Policy a Foreign Contract. — A provision in a contract of insurance that "This contract shall be governed by, subject to, and construed only according to the laws of the State of New York, the home office of said association" is void, insofar as the courts of this State are concerned. Blackwell v. Life Ass'n, 141 N.C. 117, 53 S.E. 833 (1906). See Cordell v. Brotherhood of Locomotive Firemen, 208 N.C. 632, 182 S.E. 141 (1935).

Provision in Policy That Its Terms Are Controlled by State Statute. — Where the policy itself provides that its terms are controlled by a statute of the state wherein the property is located, which conflicts with a policy provision and does not conflict with federal law, the courts may apply state statutory law in appropriate circumstances by virtue of such policy provision, but never merely because it is the law of the forum. Dixie Whse. v. Federal Emergency Mgt. Agency, 547 F. Supp. 81 (M.D.N.C. 1982).

An automobile accident did not, in and of itself, constitute a sufficient interest or connection between the insurer and North Carolina under this section to warrant application of North Carolina law where the policy was issued in Florida, the insured vehicle had a Florida identification number and a Florida license plate, and the insured had a Florida driver's license. Fortune Ins. Co. v. Owens, 351 N.C. 424, 526 S.E.2d 463, 2000 N.C. LEXIS 240 (2000).

Laws in Force Become Part of Insurance Contract. — Laws in force at the time of executing a policy of insurance are binding on the insurer and become a part of the insurance contract. Fuller v. Lockhart, 209 N.C. 61, 182 S.E. 733 (1935).

North Carolina Choice-of-Law Rules Control. — The provision of this section that all contracts of insurance on lives in North Carolina shall be subject to the law of North Carolina seems to mean the whole law of North Carolina, including choice-of-law rules. Lowe's N. Wilkesboro Hdwe., Inc. v. Fidelity Mut. Life Ins. Co., 206 F. Supp. 427 (M.D.N.C. 1962), aff'd, 319 F.2d 469 (4th Cir. 1963).

Workers' Compensation When Lex Loci Inapplicable. — Traditionally, North Carolina has adhered to the conflict of laws rule that the lex loci determines matters affecting substantial rights. Where a plaintiff is injured in another state, the law of that state will determine substantive issues in a negligence action. However, in dealing with conflicting workers' compensation laws, the lex loci principle did not apply where the interests and public policy of North Carolina were overriding. Braxton v. Anco Elec., Inc., 100 N.C. App. 635, 397 S.E.2d 640 (1990), aff'd, 330 N.C. 124, 409 S.E.2d 914 (1991).

Same Injury in Virginia. — Plaintiff sought and received workers' compensation benefits pursuant to the North Carolina Workers' Compensation Act for injury caused by third-party subcontractor. All parties were North Carolina citizens and North Carolina was the state with the greatest interest in the matter. Thus, the choice of law would not be based on the fortuitous circumstance that an injury occurred in Virginia. North Carolina was the place of plaintiff's residence, the location of defendant's business, and the place of the initial hiring. Thus, North Carolina had significant interests in applying its own law based on the employment relationship and its connection with North Carolina. Braxton v. Anco Elec., Inc., 100 N.C. App. 635, 397 S.E.2d 640 (1990), aff'd, 330 N.C. 124, 409 S.E.2d 914 (1991).

Pursuant to this statute it is sound public policy of North Carolina to provide for a right of action on behalf of an injured employee against a third-party tortfeasor (even a fellow subcontractor) even though the injured employee applied for and received workers' compensation benefits. Virginia law which violated this policy was not applied even though injury occurred in Virginia. Braxton v. Anco Elec., Inc., 100 N.C. App. 635, 397 S.E.2d 640 (1990), aff'd, 330 N.C. 124, 409 S.E.2d 914 (1991).

Application of State Law to Federal Flood Insurance Issues. — To determine if state statutory law where the property is located should apply to federal flood insurance issues, three factors must be considered: (1) the terms of the policy; (2) applicable state statutory law; and (3) applicable federal statutory or decisional law. Where no term in the policy addresses an issue in dispute, federal law is applied. If no decisional or statutory federal law exists the federal courts may apply the traditional common-law technique of decision by drawing upon standard insurance law principles. Dixie Whse. v. Federal Emergency Mgt. Agency, 547 F. Supp. 81 (M.D.N.C. 1982).

Applied in Fountain & Herrington, Inc. v. Mutual Life Ins. Co., 55 F.2d 120 (4th Cir. 1932); Wells v. Jefferson Std. Life Ins. Co., 211 N.C. 427, 190 S.E. 744 (1937); Petty v. Pacific Mut. Life Ins. Co., 212 N.C. 157, 193 S.E. 228 (1937); Rossman v. New York Life Ins. Co., 19 N.C. App. 651, 199 S.E.2d 681 (1973); St. Paul Fire & Marine Ins. Co. v. Hanover Ins. Co., 187 F. Supp. 2d 584, 2000 U.S. Dist. LEXIS 2783 (E.D.N.C. 2000).

Cited in Hartford Accident & Indem. Co. v. United States Fire Ins. Co., 710 F. Supp. 164 (E.D.N.C. 1989); Harrison Agency, Inc. v. Pacific Mut. Life Ins. Co., 703 F. Supp. 441 (W.D.N.C. 1989); Martin v. Continental Ins. Co., 123 N.C. App. 650, 474 S.E.2d 146 (1996).

§ 58-3-5. No insurance contracts except under Articles 1 through 64 of this Chapter.

Except as provided in G.S. 58-3-6, it is unlawful for any company to make any contract of insurance upon or concerning any property or interest or lives in this State, or with any resident thereof, or for any person as insurance agent or insurance broker to make, negotiate, solicit, or in any manner aid in the transaction of such insurance, unless and except as authorized under the provisions of Articles 1 though 64 of this Chapter. (1899, c. 54, s. 2; Rev., s. 4807; C.S., s. 6288; 1998-211, s. 1(a).)

Legal Periodicals. — For comment, "Insurance Contract and Policy in General as It Relates to North Carolina," see 3 N.C. Cent. L.J. 259 (1972).

CASE NOTES

Recovery by Insured Where Contract Void as to Insurer. — The statute does not impose on the insured the duty of showing the authority of the company or its agent, as the statute is for the protection of the policyholder, and a recovery can be had by the insured although as to the insurer the contract may be void. Gazzam v. German Union Fire Ins. Co., 155 N.C. 330, 71 S.E. 434 (1911).

When a statute or valid regulation in restraint only of the company's action is made for protection of the policyholder, a recovery may ordinarily be had, though the contract is in breach of the regulation. Blount v. Royal Fraternal Ass'n, 163 N.C. 167, 79 S.E. 299 (1913); Robinson v. Security Life & Annuity Co., 163 N.C. 415, 79 S.E. 681 (1913); Morgan v. Royal Fraternal Ass'n, 170 N.C. 75, 86 S.E. 975 (1915).

Exclusion Not Void Despite Failure to Obtain Approval. — Surplus insurer's failure to get advance form approval did not result in the absolute pollution exclusion being void. Home Indem. Co. v. Hoechst Celanese Corp., 128 N.C. App. 226, 494 S.E.2d 768, 1998 N.C. App. LEXIS 23 (1998), cert. denied, 505 S.E.2d 869 (1998).

Resident Process Agent Held Not Re-

quired. — The issuance of one or more policies of fire insurance by a corporation created and existing under the laws of another state, not by or through any agent, did not constitute "doing business" in the State of North Carolina, so as to require a resident process agent. Ivy River Land & Timber Co. v. National Fire & Marine Ins. Co., 192 N.C. 115, 133 S.E. 424 (1926).

Applied in Wells v. Jefferson Std. Life Ins.

Co., 211 N.C. 427, 190 S.E. 744 (1937); Glover v. Rowan Mut. Fire Ins. Co., 228 N.C. 195, 45 S.E.2d 45 (1947).

Cited in Charleston & W. Carolina Ry. v. Robert G. Lassiter & Co., 207 N.C. 408, 177 S.E. 9 (1934); Petty v. Pacific Mut. Life Ins. Co., 212 N.C. 157, 193 S.E. 228 (1937); Miller Brewing Co. v. Morgan Mechanical Contractors, 90 N.C. App. 310, 368 S.E.2d 438 (1988).

§ 58-3-6. Charitable gift annuities.

(a) A charitable organization as described in section 501(c)(3) or section 170(c) of the Internal Revenue Code or an educational institution may receive a transfer of property from a donor in exchange for an annuity payable over one or two lives, under which the actuarial value of the annuity is less than the value of the property transferred and the difference in value constitutes a charitable deduction for federal tax purposes. The issuance of the annuity by a charitable organization does not constitute engaging in the business of insurance if the organization, when the annuity agreement is issued:

   (1) Has a minimum of $100,000 in unrestricted cash, cash equivalents, or publicly-traded securities, exclusive of the assets contributed by the donor in return for the annuity agreement;

   (2) Has been in active, continuous operation for at least three years or is a successor to or affiliate of a charitable organization that has been in active operation for at least three years; and

   (3) Includes the following disclosure clause in each annuity agreement issued on or after November 1, 1998: "This annuity is not issued by an insurance company, is not subject to regulation by the State of North Carolina, and is not protected or otherwise guaranteed by any government agency or insurance guaranty fund."

Subdivisions (1) and (2) of this subsection do not apply to an educational institution that was issuing annuity agreements prior to October 30, 1998 nor to an organization formed solely to support an educational institution in active operation at least three years prior to October 30, 1998.

(b) A charitable organization or educational institution that issues a charitable annuity shall notify the Department by January 1, 1999, or within 90 days of issuing its first annuity, whichever is later. The notice shall be signed by an officer or director of the organization or educational institution, identify the organization or institution, and certify that the organization or institution is a charitable organization or educational institution and that its annuities are issued in compliance with the applicable provisions of subsection (a) of this section.

(c) A charitable organization that issues charitable annuities must make available to the Commissioner, upon request, a copy of its Internal Revenue Service Form 990 or Form 990-EZ for the most recent fiscal year for which the due date has passed. If the organization was not required to file either form with the Internal Revenue Service for the preceding fiscal year, or was allowed to submit the form in abbreviated format, it shall make available to the Commissioner, upon request, the same information that would have been required to have been filed under the Form 990, in a similar format as specified by the Commissioner. A copy of the Form 990, or corresponding substitute information as authorized by the Commissioner, shall be made available to the prospective annuitant at the time of the initial solicitation of the contribution, and updated information shall be made available at the time of execution of the annuity agreement.

(d) The Department may enforce performance of the requirements of this section by notifying the organization or institution and demanding that it comply with the requirements of this section. The Department may fine an organization or educational institution, up to $1,000 per annuity agreement, for failure to comply after notice and demand from the Commissioner.

(e) A charitable gift annuity issued by a charitable organization or educational institution prior to October 30, 1998 does not constitute engaging in the business of insurance.

(f) For purposes of this section, an "educational institution" means a public or private college, university, or community college that maintains a faculty to provide instruction to students. (1998-211, s. 1(b).)

§ 58-3-10. Statements in application not warranties.

All statements or descriptions in any application for a policy of insurance, or in the policy itself, shall be deemed representations and not warranties, and a representation, unless material or fraudulent, will not prevent a recovery on the policy. (1901, c. 705, s. 2; Rev., s. 4808; C.S., s. 6289.)

Legal Periodicals. — For note, "Life Insurance Applications: Opinion Answers or Material Misrepresentations," see 49 N.C.L. Rev. 560 (1971).

CASE NOTES

I. In General.
II. Particular Representations.

I. IN GENERAL.

The purpose of this section is to prevent insurance companies from escaping the payment of honest losses upon technicalities and strict construction of contracts. Cottingham v. Maryland Motor Car Ins. Co., 168 N.C. 259, 84 S.E. 274 (1915); Garvey v. Old Colony Ins. Co., 153 F. Supp. 755 (E.D.N.C. 1957), aff'd, 253 F.2d 299 (4th Cir. 1958).

Section Superseded with Respect to Automobile Liability Insurance. — Section 58-3-10, adopted in 1901, falls within Chapter 58, Insurance, Article 3, General Regulations for Insurance. As an earlier and more general statement of insurance law, it is superseded with respect to automobile liability insurance by Chapter 20, Motor Vehicles, specifically by Article 9A, the Motor Vehicle Safety and Financial Responsibility Act of 1953, and Article 13, the Vehicle Financial Responsibility Act of 1957. Chapter 20 represents a complete and comprehensive legislative scheme for the regulation of motor vehicles and as such, its insurance provisions regarding automobiles prevail over the more general insurance regulations of Chapter 58. Odum v. Nationwide Mut. Ins. Co., 101 N.C. App. 627, 401 S.E.2d 87, cert. denied, 329 N.C. 499, 407 S.E.2d 539 (1991).

Applicability of Section to Fraternal Benefit Associations and Fraternal Orders. — Fraternal benefit associations fall within the provision of this section as to representations, but fraternal orders as defined in former G.S. 58-264 do not. Gay v. Woodmen of World, 179 N.C. 210, 102 S.E. 195 (1920).

What Representations Are Material. — In an application for a policy of life insurance every fact stated will be deemed material which would materially influence the judgment of the insurance company, either in accepting the risk or in fixing the premium rate. Bryant v. Metropolitan Life Ins. Co., 147 N.C. 181, 60 S.E. 983 (1908); Gardner v. North State Mut. Life Ins. Co., 163 N.C. 367, 79 S.E. 806 (1913); Garvey v. Old Colony Ins. Co., 153 F. Supp. 755 (E.D.N.C. 1957), aff'd, 253 F.2d 299 (4th Cir. 1958).

The materiality of the representation depends on whether it was such as would naturally and reasonably have influenced the insurance company with respect to the contract or risk. Carroll v. Carolina Cas. Ins. Co., 227 N.C. 456, 42 S.E.2d 607 (1947); Walker v. Philadelphia Life Ins. Co., 127 F. Supp. 26 (E.D.N.C. 1954); Old Colony Ins. Co. v. Garvey, 253 F.2d 299 (4th Cir. 1958); Cockerham v. Pilot Life Ins. Co., 92 N.C. App. 218, 374 S.E.2d 174 (1988).

A representation in an application for insurance that influences the insurance company to accept the risk and enter into the contract is a material representation. Whether such representations are material depends upon the circumstances in each case and is usually, though not always, a question of fact for the jury. Michael v. St. Paul Fire & Marine Ins. Co., 65 N.C. App. 50, 308 S.E.2d 727 (1983).

Written Questions and Answers Relating to Health Deemed Material as Matter of Law. — In an application for a policy of life insurance, written questions relating to health and written answers thereto are deemed material as a matter of law. Tedder v. Union Fid. Life Ins. Co., 436 F. Supp. 847 (E.D.N.C. 1977).

A representation in an application for a policy of life insurance is deemed material if the knowledge or ignorance of it would naturally influence the judgment of insurer in making the contract, and written questions relating to health and their answers in an application are deemed material as a matter of law. Tolbert v. Mutual Benefit Life Ins. Co., 236 N.C. 416, 72 S.E.2d 915 (1952).

A statement in an application for reinstatement of an insurance policy that applicant, in the year previous, had not had any injury, sickness, or ailment of any kind, and had not required the services of a physician, being a statement of fact within the knowledge of applicant, is a material representation as a matter of law. Petty v. Pacific Mut. Life Ins. Co., 212 N.C. 157, 193 S.E. 228 (1937).

Answer to Ambiguous Yes or No Question Cannot Be False. — An answer to a question in an application for life insurance that is ambiguous and calls for a yes or no answer cannot be false as a matter of law. Cockerham v. Pilot Life Ins. Co., 92 N.C. App. 218, 374 S.E.2d 174 (1988).

Interpretation of Ambiguous Question Issue for Jury. — Question in an application of whether insured had within the preceding two years consulted or been treated by a physician for any condition other than a routine physical examination was ambiguous and required a yes or no answer; therefore, the issue of how the insured interpreted the question was one for the jury. Cockerham v. Pilot Life Ins. Co., 92 N.C. App. 218, 374 S.E.2d 174 (1988).

Where Company and Agents Were Unaware of the Truth. — Where application declares that the statements the applicant makes are true and there is no evidence that the company or its agents were aware of any facts to the contrary, all of the misrepresentations made as to the prior attendance of physicians, diseases, surgical operations, and the like are deemed material. Alexander v. Metropolitan Life Ins. Co., 150 N.C. 536, 64 S.E. 432 (1909); Mutual Life Ins. Co. v. Leaksville Woolen Mills, 172 N.C. 534, 90 S.E. 574 (1916).

But treatment for a mere temporary indisposition may well be regarded as immaterial where an applicant fully discloses medical treatment for a serious ailment administered at or about the same time. Jeffress v. New York Life Ins. Co., 74 F.2d 874 (4th Cir. 1935).

Relationship Between Insured and Beneficiary Immaterial. — The false representation of the relationship between insured and beneficiary is, as a matter of law, immaterial.

Howell v. American Nat'l Ins. Co., 189 N.C. 212, 126 S.E. 603 (1925).

Answers as to Other Applications Material Where Offered as Inducement. — Answers made in response to questions in the application as to applications for other insurance, where the applicant declares that they are true and offers them as an inducement to the issuance of the policy, are deemed material as a matter of law. Fountain & Herrington, Inc. v. Mutual Life Ins. Co., 55 F.2d 120 (4th Cir. 1932).

Verbal Answers Made to Agent by Applicant for Fire Policy Not Material as Matter of Law. — There is nothing in the law of this State, or anywhere else, which requires that the rule with respect to the effect to be given to written answers to written questions in an application for a life insurance policy which is attached to and made a part of the policy be applied to verbal answers made by an applicant for a fire policy to an agent asking questions for the purpose of obtaining information upon which to describe the insured property in the policy. To hold that such answers are to be deemed material as a matter of law would be to give them the status of warranties in contravention of this section. Old Colony Ins. Co. v. Garvey, 253 F.2d 299 (4th Cir. 1958).

Misrepresentation Need Not Contribute to Loss. — It is not necessary, to defeat recovery, that a material misrepresentation by the applicant must contribute in some way to the loss for which indemnity is claimed. Bryant v. Metropolitan Life Ins. Co., 147 N.C. 181, 60 S.E. 983 (1908).

As Materiality Is Judged in Terms of Effect on Insurer's Decision. — The materiality of the misrepresentation is judged in terms of its effect upon the insurer's decision to underwrite the risk and therefore, the actual cause of death does not have to be related to the health matters misrepresented. Tedder v. Union Fid. Life Ins. Co., 436 F. Supp. 847 (E.D.N.C. 1977).

Policy Avoided by False Material Representations. — A material representation shall avoid the policy if it is also false and is calculated to influence the company, if without notice of its falsity, in making the contract at all, in estimating the degree and character of the risk, or in fixing the premiums. Gardner v. North State Mut. Life Ins. Co., 163 N.C. 367, 79 S.E. 806 (1913).

Misrepresentations admitted, of which the court will take judicial notice, must be deemed material as a matter of law; and their making is sufficient ground for canceling of the policy, whatever may be proved in extenuation of the conduct of insured in making them. Jeffress v. New York Life Ins. Co., 74 F.2d 874 (4th Cir. 1935).

It is well settled that a material representation which is false will constitute sufficient ground upon which to avoid the policy. Tolbert v. Mutual Benefit Life Ins. Co., 236 N.C. 416, 72 S.E.2d 915 (1952).

Answers to questions in application for life insurance were material, and being also false, the contract of insurance was vitiated and there could be no recovery. Walker v. Philadelphia Life Ins. Co., 127 F. Supp. 26 (E.D.N.C. 1954).

An insurer's duty under an insurance contract may be avoided by a showing that the insured made representations in his insurance application which were material and false. Willetts v. Integon Life Ins. Corp., 45 N.C. App. 424, 263 S.E.2d 300, cert. denied, 300 N.C. 562, 270 S.E.2d 116 (1980); Sauls v. Charlotte Liberty Mut. Ins. Co., 62 N.C. App. 533, 303 S.E.2d 358 (1983).

Even if Misrepresentations were Unintentional. — The company is entitled to have the policy canceled on bringing suit within the proper time, especially where, even if the misrepresentations are not intentional, the policy, when delivered, plainly discloses the untruthfulness of the representations. Mutual Life Ins. Co. v. Leaksville Woolen Mills, 172 N.C. 534, 90 S.E. 574 (1916).

The North Carolina law is that a fraudulent or material misrepresentation in the application for insurance, even though innocently made, will prevent recovery on the policy. Garvey v. Old Colony Ins. Co., 153 F. Supp. 755 (E.D.N.C. 1957), aff'd, 253 F.2d 299 (4th Cir. 1958).

A material false representation in an application for insurance renders a policy voidable by the insurance company, and a policy may be declared voidable even in the absence of any intentional or fraudulent misrepresentation. Galindo v. John Hancock Variable Life Ins. Co., — F. Supp. 2d —, 2000 U.S. Dist. LEXIS 5108 (E.D.N.C. Mar. 13, 2000).

Misrepresentations Need Not Be Fraudulent to Prevent Recovery. — Where representations were material to the issuance of an insurance certificate, the certificate was void, notwithstanding the evidence tended to show that the representations, although false, were not fraudulent. Inman v. Sovereign Camp, W.O.W., 211 N.C. 179, 189 S.E. 496 (1937).

Fraud is not essential under this section, since as a general rule recovery will not be allowed if the statements made and accepted as inducements to the contract of insurance are false and material. Wells v. Jefferson Std. Life Ins. Co., 211 N.C. 427, 190 S.E. 744 (1937).

An instruction of the court which tended to leave the impression that it was not only necessary that insurer show that representations were false and material but also that they were fraudulently made with intent to deceive would be held prejudicial. Tolbert v. Mutual Benefit Life Ins. Co., 236 N.C. 416, 72 S.E.2d 915 (1952).

Clearly a representation which is material and false will prevent recovery, even though not fraudulent. Walker v. Philadelphia Life Ins. Co., 127 F. Supp. 26 (E.D.N.C. 1954).

If a representation is material and false, it is not necessary for avoidance of the policy that such misrepresentation be intentional. Tedder v. Union Fid. Life Ins. Co., 436 F. Supp. 847 (E.D.N.C. 1977).

But if the insurance company knew that the representations made by the insured were false, it cannot set the policy aside on the grounds that they were material or fraudulent. Gardner v. North State Mut. Life Ins. Co., 163 N.C. 367, 79 S.E. 806 (1913).

An insurance company cannot avoid liability on a life insurance policy on the basis of facts known to it at the time the policy went into effect. Willetts v. Integon Life Ins. Corp., 45 N.C. App. 424, 263 S.E.2d 300 (1980), cert. denied, 300 N.C. 562, 270 S.E.2d 116 (1980).

Imputation of Agents' Knowledge to Insurer. — Where, in an application for a double indemnity life insurance policy which was completed for the insured by defendant insurer's agent, only a charge of speeding 60 mph in a 45 mph zone was listed in answer to a question as to whether insured had been charged with any motor vehicle moving violations or had had his license revoked within the past three years, but insured discussed with the agent the possibility that a charge against him for driving under the influence might have occurred within the past three years and was told by the agent that he should not worry about whether the charge was within three years because insurer would obtain a copy of insured's driving record and would notify insured if there was a problem, the agent had notice of insured's conviction within the past three years for driving under the influence which further inquiry would have revealed; such notice was imputed to defendant insurer and precluded defendant from avoiding the policy on the ground that such conviction was not listed in the application, notwithstanding the application contained a provision that knowledge of an agent did not constitute knowledge of the insurer. Willetts v. Integon Life Ins. Corp., 45 N.C. App. 424, 263 S.E.2d 300, cert. denied, 300 N.C. 562, 270 S.E.2d 116 (1980).

Burden on Insurer to Prove Misrepresentation. — By offering in evidence the policy of insurance and the insurer's admission of its execution and delivery and of the death of the insured, the beneficiaries made out a prima facie case, and the burden was then upon the insurer to rebut it by proof of the alleged misrepresentation. And though the beneficiaries, in anticipation of the defense, elected to offer testimony as to misrepresentations, this did not change the rule as to the burden of proof. Wells v. Jefferson Std. Life Ins. Co., 211 N.C. 427, 190 S.E. 744 (1937).

Evidence of Misrepresentations Admissible in Action on Policy. — After a contract of life insurance has become effective, its terms may not be contradicted so as to affect its continued validity; but it may be shown that the delivery of the policy was made upon false representations in the application therefor as to the health of the insured and as to his not having been subjected to contagious diseases for a prior period of one year, and the like, for such matters bear upon the question as to whether the policy had ever taken effect as a contract of insurance. Gardner v. North State Mut. Life Ins. Co., 163 N.C. 367, 79 S.E. 806 (1913).

A representation by insured that he had never consulted a physician or been in a hospital was material, and testimony of physicians that insured was not in sound health at the date of the delivery of the policy was competent on the issue of fraud. Potts v. Life Ins. Co., 206 N.C. 257, 174 S.E. 123 (1934).

Identification of Insured Vehicle. — A vehicle covered by a policy of liability insurance may be identified as between the parties not only by the motor and serial numbers entered on the policy, but also by descriptive insignia resorted to in the policy, or, in case of an ambiguous description, by evidence aliunde, and this without resort to the equitable doctrine of reformation for mutual mistake or fraud. Ratliff v. Virginia Sur. Co., 232 N.C. 166, 59 S.E.2d 609 (1950).

Questions for Jury. — Although it has occasionally been held that the materiality of the misrepresentation is a question of fact for the jury, these cases are exceptional and usually involve a dispute as to whether the insured actually had a disease or infirmity at the time of the application or the question of whether the insured's opinion as to his good health was truthful, at least to the insured's knowledge, at the time he applied. Tedder v. Union Fid. Life Ins. Co., 436 F. Supp. 847 (E.D.N.C. 1977).

Whether a misrepresentation is made with fraudulent intent by insured, or whether it is material, so that insurer would not have issued the policy had it known the truth, are ordinarily questions for the jury. Harrison v. Metropolitan Life Ins. Co., 207 N.C. 487, 177 S.E. 423 (1934).

Where the evidence tended to show that in her application for hospital insurance plaintiff inadvertently misrepresented that she did not have hernia, and that subsequent to the issuance of the policy she was hospitalized for appendicitis, a charge to the effect that the misrepresentation would bar recovery if the hernia in any way contributed to the hospitalization or materially affected the acceptance of the risk by insurer, so that the insurer would

not have written the policy in the form it was issued if the existence of the hernia had been known, was without error, as the question of materiality of the misrepresentation was for the jury upon the evidence. Carroll v. Carolina Cas. Ins. Co., 227 N.C. 456, 42 S.E.2d 607 (1947), discussed in 26 N.C.L. Rev. 78 (1948).

Where the insured had hernia at the time of his application, and, without specific question as to this, stated he was in sound physical and mental condition, with "no exceptions," and there was evidence tending to show that the hernia did not affect the soundness of his health, it was for the jury to determine whether his representation was false and material. Hines v. New England Cas. Co., 172 N.C. 225, 90 S.E. 131 (1916).

Effect of "Binding Slip." — Where an insurance company has given a "binding slip" to an applicant for insurance, it only protects the applicant against the contingency of his sickness intervening its date and the delivery of the policy, if the applicant for insurance is accepted, and as such slip does not insure of itself, it does not affect the right of the insurer to avail itself of all defenses it may have, under the policy, after its delivery, to avoid payment thereof by reason of material misrepresentation made in the application for it. Gardner v. North State Mut. Life Ins. Co., 163 N.C. 367, 79 S.E. 806 (1913).

Applied in Tharrington v. Sturdivant Life Ins. Co., 115 N.C. App. 123, 443 S.E.2d 797 (1994).

Cited in Jones v. Home Sec. Life Ins. Co., 254 N.C. 407, 119 S.E.2d 215 (1961); In re McCrary, 112 N.C. App. 161, 435 S.E.2d 359 (1993); Metropolitan Property & Cas. Ins. Co. v. Dillard, 126 N.C. App. 795, 487 S.E.2d 157 (1997); Crawford v. Commercial Union Midwest Ins. Co., 147 N.C. App. 455, 556 S.E.2d 30, 2001 N.C. App. LEXIS 1183 (2001), cert. denied, 356 N.C. 160, 568 S.E.2d 190 (2002).

II. PARTICULAR REPRESENTATIONS.

Failure of insured to disclose treatment by a physician within five years prior to the application was held not a suppression of a material fact in light of the evidence, and was not adequate cause for cancellation of the policy. Anthony v. Teachers Protective Union, 206 N.C. 7, 173 S.E. 6 (1934).

Where insured stated she was not pregnant and died of childbirth in less than nine months, her statement did not preclude recovery, in view of the evidence that insurer issued its policy on the life of the insured when it knew she was 33 years of age, had been married about a year, and that ordinarily pregnancy might be expected, and it required an additional premium on that account. Wells v.

Jefferson Std. Life Ins. Co., 211 N.C. 427, 190 S.E. 744 (1937).

Incurable Disease Unknown to Insured. — Where the evidence showed that insured was suffering with an incurable disease, but that he was ignorant of this fact, and that he had been assured by a physician, whom he had consulted, that there was nothing the matter with him at the date of application, there was no evidence from which the jury could have found that the statement made by the applicant in the application was fraudulent, and this section was applicable. Missouri State Life Ins. Co. v. Hardin, 208 N.C. 22, 179 S.E. 2 (1935).

Failure to Disclose Mild Bout of Malaria. — Under this section, a failure to disclose the fact that insured had had, at some time previous to her application, one-half degree of fever due to a mild form of malaria from which she had entirely recovered, taken in connection with the further fact that she was at the time of the application in sound health and otherwise insurable, was held not material. Wells v. Jefferson Std. Life Ins. Co., 211 N.C. 427, 190 S.E. 744 (1937).

Unoccupancy of Insured House. — Evidence was held insufficient to show that knowledge of the unoccupancy of insured house would have influenced the company naturally and materially on the question of risk. Garvey v. Old Colony Ins. Co., 153 F. Supp. 755 (E.D.N.C. 1957), aff'd, 253 F.2d 299 (4th Cir. 1958).

Malignancy for Which Surgery Had Been Scheduled. — Application for group insurance held to contain material misrepresentations justifying insurer's denial of coverage, where applicant failed to disclose that she had had a lump on her hand for about a year and a half, had seen three physicians about the lump within that year and a half, and was scheduled to have the lump surgically excised, although the exact date of surgery had not been established, and where surgery subsequently revealed that applicant had a rare form of cancer. Cary Family Medicine v. Prudential Ins. Co. of Am., 88 N.C. App. 760, 364 S.E.2d 737 (1988).

§ 58-3-15. Additional or coinsurance clause.

No insurance company or agent licensed to do business in this State may issue any policy or contract of insurance covering property in this State that contains any clause or provision requiring the insured to take or maintain a larger amount of insurance than that expressed in the policy, nor in any way provide that the insured shall be liable as a coinsurer with the company issuing the policy for any part of the loss or damage to the property described in the policy, and any such clause or provision shall be null and void, and of no effect: Provided, the coinsurance clause or provision may be written in or attached to a policy or policies issued when there is printed or stamped on the declarations page of the policy or on the form containing the clause the words "coinsurance contract," and the Commissioner may, in the Commissioner's discretion, determine the location of the words "coinsurance contract" and the size of the type to be used. If there is a difference in the rate for the insurance with and without the coinsurance clause, the rates for each shall be furnished the insured upon request. (1915, c. 109, s. 5; C.S., s. 6441; 1925, c. 70, s. 4; 1945, c. 377; 1947, c. 721; 1999-132, s. 7.1.)

Cross References. — As to standard policy and permissible variations, see G.S. 58-44-20.

CASE NOTES

Replacement cost provisions under which the insureds could only collect the full cost of repair or replacement of their dwelling for at least 80% of its full replacement cost and under which they would become coinsurers or self-insurers for the difference between the amount of coverage and 80% of the full replacement cost, if the insurance maintained on the property was for less than 80% of its full replacement cost, are essentially coinsurance provisions. Surrant v. Grain Dealers Mut. Ins. Co., 74 N.C. App. 288, 328 S.E.2d 16 (1985).

§ 58-3-20. Group plans other than life, annuity or accident and health.

No policy of insurance other than life, annuity or accident and health may be written in North Carolina on a group plan which insures a group of individuals under a master policy at rates lower than those charged for individual policies covering similar risks. The master policy and certificates, if any, shall be first approved by the Commissioner and the rate, premiums or other essential information shall be shown on the certificate. (1945, c. 377.)

CASE NOTES

Cited in First Nat'l Bank v. Nationwide Ins. Co., 303 N.C. 203, 278 S.E.2d 507 (1981).

§ 58-3-25. Discriminatory practices prohibited.

(a) No insurer shall after September 1, 1975, base any standard or rating plan for private passenger automobiles or motorcycles, in whole or in part, directly or indirectly, upon the age or sex of the persons insured.

(b) No insurer shall refuse to insure or refuse to continue to insure an individual, limit the amount, extent, or kind of coverage available to an individual, or charge an individual a different rate for the same coverage, solely because of blindness or partial blindness or deafness or partial deafness. With respect to all other physical conditions, including the underlying cause of the blindness or partial blindness or deafness or partial deafness, individuals who are blind or partially blind shall be subject to the same standards of sound actuarial principles or actual or reasonably anticipated experience as are sighted individuals or individuals whose hearing is not impaired. Refusal to insure or refusal to continue to insure includes denial by an insurer providing disability insurance on the grounds that the policy defines disability as being presumed in the event that the insured loses his eyesight or hearing: Provided that an insurer providing disability insurance may except disability coverage for blindness, partial blindness, deafness, or partial deafness when those conditions existed at the time the application was made for the disability insurance policy. The provisions of this subsection shall be construed to supplement the provisions of G.S. 58-63-15(7) and G.S. 168-10. This subsection shall apply only to the underwriting of life insurance, accident, health, or accident and health insurance under Articles 1 through 66 of this Chapter, and annuities.

(c) No insurer shall refuse to insure or refuse to continue to insure an individual; limit the amount, extent, or kind of coverage available to an individual; or charge an individual a different rate for the same coverage, because of the race, color, or national or ethnic origin of that individual. This subsection supplements the provisions of G.S. 58-3-120, 58-33-80, 58-58-35, and 58-63-15(7). (1975, c. 666, s. 1; 1985, c. 267, s. 1; 1989, c. 485, s. 22; 1991, c. 720, s. 67.)

Legal Periodicals. — For survey of 1978 administrative law, see 57 N.C.L. Rev. 831 (1979).

For comment, "Patients' Bill of Rights; Legislative Cure-All or Prescription for Disaster?," see 81 N.C.L. Rev. 653 (2003).

CASE NOTES

Purpose of This Section and Former § 58-30.4. — This section and former G.S. 58-30.4 were designed to eliminate primary classifications utilizing sex or age as a criterion and to give safe drivers a premium reduction to be offset by increasing the premiums to be paid by inexperienced drivers and those drivers with motor vehicle offenses or chargeable accidents on their records. State ex rel. Comm'r of Ins. v. North Carolina Auto. Rate Admin. Office, 293 N.C. 365, 239 S.E.2d 48 (1977).

The primary purpose of this section and former G.S. 58-30.4 was to abolish age and sex as criteria for classifying motor vehicle insurance, both automobile and motorcycle. State ex rel. Comm'r of Ins. v. North Carolina Auto. Rate Admin. Office, 294 N.C. 60, 241 S.E.2d 324 (1978).

The new classification plan required by former § 58-30.4 was intended to put into effect this section, ending classifications based on age or sex. State ex rel. Comm'r of Ins. v. North Carolina Rate Bureau, 41 N.C. App. 310, 255 S.E.2d 557 (1979), aff'd in part and rev'd in part, 300 N.C. 381, 269 S.E.2d 547 (1980).

Both this section and former § 58-30.4 apply to private passenger automobiles and motorcycles. State ex rel. Comm'r of Ins. v. North Carolina Auto. Rate Admin. Office, 30 N.C. App. 477, 227 S.E.2d 621 (1976), aff'd, 294 N.C. 60, 241 S.E.2d 324 (1978).

Motorcycles Not Removed from Plans Applicable to Motor Vehicles. — The General Assembly did not intend, by enacting this section and former G.S. 58-30.4, to remove motorcycles from the primary and subclassification plans applicable to motor vehicles generally. State ex rel. Comm'r of Ins. v. North Carolina Auto. Rate Admin. Office, 294 N.C. 60, 241 S.E.2d 324 (1978).

The legislature intended to classify and subclassify motorcycles in the same manner as automobiles for insurance ratemaking purposes. State ex rel. Comm'r of Ins. v. North Carolina Auto. Rate Admin. Office, 294 N.C. 60, 241 S.E.2d 324 (1978).

A new filing was mandated by this section and former § 58-30.4, and a review of the 1970 filing could serve no present purpose. The request of the former Automobile Rate Office to be allowed to withdraw the 1970 filing should have been granted. State ex rel. Comm'r of Ins. v. North Carolina Auto. Rate Admin. Office, 30 N.C. App. 477, 227 S.E.2d 621 (1976), aff'd, 294 N.C. 60, 241 S.E.2d 324 (1978).

Cited in State ex rel. Comm'r of Ins. v. Motors Ins. Corp., 294 N.C. 360, 241 S.E.2d 332 (1978).

§ 58-3-30. Meaning of terms "accident", "accidental injury", and "accidental means".

(a) This section applies to the provisions of all group life, group accident, group health, and group accident and health insurance policies and group annuities under Articles 1 through 64 of this Chapter that are issued on or after October 1, 1989, and preferred provider arrangements under Articles 1 through 64 of this Chapter that are entered into on or after October 1, 1989.

(b) "Accident", "accidental injury", and "accidental means" shall be defined to imply "result" language and shall not include words that establish an accidental means test. (1989, c. 485, s. 10.)

§ 58-3-33. Insurer conditionally required to provide information.

(a) A person who claims to have been physically injured or to have incurred property damage where such injury or damage is subject to a policy of nonfleet private passenger automobile insurance may request by certified mail directed to the insurance adjuster or to the insurance company (Attention Corporate Secretary) at its last known principal place of business that the insurance company provide information regarding the policy's limits of coverage under the applicable policy. Upon receipt of such a request, which shall include the policyholder's name, and, if available, policy number, the insurance company shall notify that person within 15 business days, on a form developed by the Department, that the insurer is required to provide this information prior to litigation only if the person seeking the information satisfies all of the following conditions:

(1) The person seeking the information submits to the insurer the person's written consent to the person's physicians to release to the insurer the person's medical records for the three years prior to the date on which the claim arose.

   (2) The person seeking the information submits to the insurer the person's written consent to participate in mediation of the person's claim under G.S. 7A-38.3A.

   (3) The person seeking the information submits to the insurer a copy of the accident report required under G.S. 20-166.1 and a description of the events at issue with sufficient particularity to permit the insurer to make an initial determination of the potential liability of its insured.

  (b) Within 30 days of receiving the person's written documents required under subsection (a) of this section, the insurer shall provide the policy limits.

  (c) Disclosure of the policy limits under this section shall not constitute an admission that the alleged injury or damage is subject to the policy.

  (d) This section does not apply to claims seeking recovery for medical malpractice or claims for which an insurer intends to deny coverage under any policy of insurance. (2003-307, s. 1.)

Editor's Note. — Session Laws 2003-307, s. 3, made this section effective January 1, 2004, and applicable to claims regarding physical injury or property damage that arise on or after that date.

§ 58-3-35. Stipulations as to jurisdiction and limitation of actions.

  (a) No insurer, self-insurer, service corporation, HMO, or MEWA licensed under this Chapter shall make any condition or stipulation in its insurance contracts or policies concerning the court or jurisdiction in which any suit or action on the contract may be brought.

  (b) No insurer, self-insurer, service corporation, HMO, or MEWA licensed under this Chapter shall limit the time within which any suit or action referred to in subsection (a) of this section may be commenced to less than the period prescribed by law.

  (c) All conditions and stipulations forbidden by this section are void. (1899, c. 54, ss. 23, 106; 1901, c. 391, s. 8; Rev., s. 4809; C.S., s. 6290; 2001-334, s. 1.)

Legal Periodicals. — For article, "Statutes of Limitations in the Conflict of Laws," see 52 N.C.L. Rev. 489 (1974).

CASE NOTES

Editor's Note. — *The cases below were decided prior to the 2001 amendment which rewrote this section.*

Section Repealed to Extent of Conflict with Contractual Limitation in Standard Form of Fire Insurance Policy. — This section was repealed by c. 378, Session Laws of 1945 (G.S. 58-44-15) insofar as it is in conflict with the contractual limitation in standard fire insurance policy form that suit on the policy be instituted within one year of the inception of loss. Boyd v. Bankers & Shippers Ins. Co., 245 N.C. 503, 96 S.E.2d 703 (1957).

Validity of Limitation Not in Conflict with Statute. — A stipulation in a policy as to time of bringing action is a contractual limitation, and has been held by the Supreme Court to be valid when it does not conflict with any provision of the statute. Parker v. Insurance Co., 143 N.C. 339, 55 S.E. 717 (1906). See also Muse v. London Assurance Corp., 108 N.C. 240, 13 S.E. 94 (1891); Dibbrell v. Georgia Home Ins. Co., 110 N.C. 193, 14 S.E. 783 (1892).

Provision Requiring Joinder of Person Allegedly Responsible for Damage Held Void. — Provision of an automobile liability policy which required the insured, in an action against the insurer, to join as a party defendant the person or organization allegedly responsible for the damage to the insured, was held void as a violation of this section, where the party defendant was a nonresident uninsured motorist and not amenable to the jurisdiction of this State. Dildy v. Southeastern Fire Ins. Co., 13 N.C. App. 66, 185 S.E.2d 272 (1971).

   The standard policy is not regulated by

the statute of limitations, and the disabilities which stop the running of the statute have no effect upon it. Hence, the imprisonment of the insured will not give him the right to recover when he has delayed his action for more than a year. This rule applies likewise to minors. Holly v. London Assurance Co., 170 N.C. 4, 86 S.E. 694 (1915).

Stipulations in accident insurance policies that proceedings shall not be begun until 90 days after proof of loss do not contravene this section, when the policy also states that the insured may bring his action within 12 months after the accident, this being construed to mean that he will have 12 months after the cause of action accrues. Heilig v. Aetna Life Ins. Co., 152 N.C. 358, 67 S.E. 927 (1910).

Waiver of Stipulation of Standard Policy. — As the stipulation of the standard policy is a contract, and not a statute of limitations, it may be waived, or the party for whose benefit it was provided may be estopped by his conduct from insisting upon its enforcement. Dibbrell v. Georgia Home Ins. Co., 110 N.C. 193, 14 S.E. 783 (1892).

Contracts of indemnity against loss or surety bonds for the faithful performance of a building contract are regarded in the nature of contracts of insurance and any conflicting restrictions in such contracts as to the time of bringing an action to recover damages for breach thereof are void. Guilford Lumber Mfg. Co. v. Johnson, 177 N.C. 44, 97 S.E. 732 (1919).

Provisions of the constitution and by-laws of a fraternal insurance order, that suits shall not be brought or maintained for any cause or claim arising out of the benefit certificate of a member unless within one year from the time the right of action accrues, are valid. Faulk v. Fraternal Mystic Circle, 171 N.C. 301, 88 S.E. 431 (1916).

Presumption as to Entry of Nonsuit. — Where a nonsuit is entered and it does not appear on record when the nonsuit was entered, it will be presumed that it was within six months prior to the date on which action was commenced. Parker v. Insurance Co., 143 N.C. 339, 55 S.E. 717 (1906).

Limitation in Surety Bond Must Be Pleaded. — A limitation in a surety bond as to the time in which an action may be maintained against the surety thereon, after notice of default, is contractual, and affects the remedy, and it is necessary that the surety plead it in the action for it to be available as a defense. Ideal Brick Co. v. Gentry, 191 N.C. 636, 132 S.E. 800 (1926).

For history of this section, see Boyd v. Bankers & Shippers Ins. Co., 245 N.C. 503, 96 S.E.2d 703 (1957).

Applied in F & D Co. v. Aetna Ins. Co., 53 N.C. App. 92, 280 S.E.2d 34 (1981); F & D Co. v. Aetna Ins. Co., 305 N.C. 256, 287 S.E.2d 867 (1982).

Cited in Lowe v. United States Mut. Accident Ass'n, 115 N.C. 18, 20 S.E. 169 (1894); Gerringer v. North Carolina Home Ins. Co., 133 N.C. 407, 45 S.E. 773 (1903); Modlin v. Atlantic Fire Ins. Co., 151 N.C. 35, 65 S.E. 605 (1909).

§ 58-3-40. Proof of loss forms required to be furnished.

When any company under any insurance policy requires a written proof of loss after notice of such loss has been given by the insured or beneficiary, the company or its representative shall furnish a blank to be used for that purpose. If such forms are not so furnished within 15 days after the receipt of such notice the claimant shall be deemed to have complied with the requirements of this policy as to proof of loss, upon submitting within the time fixed in the policy for filing proofs of loss, written proof covering the occurrence, character, and extent of the loss for which claim is made. (1945, c. 377.)

CASE NOTES

Section places burden upon insurer to provide proof of loss form to insured. If the insurer fails to do so, the insured need only provide written proof of the occurrence, character and extent of loss. Dixie Whse. v. Federal Emergency Mgt. Agency, 547 F. Supp. 81 (M.D.N.C. 1982).

No Conflict with Federal Rule of Substantial Compliance. — There is no conflict between the federal rule of substantial compliance and the North Carolina rule requiring proof of occurrence, character and extent of loss. In order to substantially comply the proof must at least supply enough information to satisfy the reason behind the rule. Proof of loss supplies evidence of the particulars of the occurrence and enables the insurer to determine its liability and the amount thereof. Both the federal authority and state statute promote this general policy. Dixie Whse. v. Federal Emergency Mgt. Agency, 547 F. Supp. 81 (M.D.N.C. 1982).

No Conflict with Federal Insurance Programs. — Federal case authority most closely addressing the issue of sufficiency of proof of loss under a federal insurance program does not conflict with this section. Dixie Whse. v. Federal Emergency Mgt. Agency, 547 F. Supp. 81 (M.D.N.C. 1982).

Waiver of Policy Provision Requiring Proof of Loss. — The insurer waived policy provision requiring proof of loss to be furnished within 60 days, where (1) The insured went to the insurer's agent, who had sold him the policy, and notified him of the loss; (2) The insured notified the insurer in writing of his loss; and (3) The insurer failed to furnish proof of loss forms to the insured. McElrath v. State Capital Ins. Co., 13 N.C. App. 211, 184 S.E.2d 912 (1971), cert. denied, 280 N.C. 722, 186 S.E.2d 924 (1972).

Applied in Avis v. Hartford Fire Ins. Co., 283 N.C. 142, 195 S.E.2d 545 (1973).

Cited in Northern Assurance Co. of Am. v. Spencer, 246 F. Supp. 730 (W.D.N.C. 1965).

§ 58-3-45. Insurance as security for a loan by the company.

Where an insurance company, as a condition for a loan by such company, of money upon mortgage or other security, requires that the borrower insure either his life or that of another, or his property, or the title to his property, with the company, and assign or cause to be assigned to it a policy of insurance as security for the loan, and agree to pay premiums thereon during the continuance of the loan, whether the premium is paid annually, semiannually, quarterly, or monthly, such premiums shall not be considered as interest on such loans, nor will any loan be rendered usurious by reason of any such requirements, where the rate of interest charged for the loan does not exceed the legal rate and where the premiums charged for the insurance do not exceed the premiums charged to other persons for similar policies who do not obtain loans. (1915, c. 8; 1917, c. 61; C.S., s. 6291.)

Legal Periodicals. — For comment on usury law in North Carolina, see 47 N.C.L. Rev. 761 (1969).

CASE NOTES

Insurance Companies Not Exempted from Usury Laws. — This section does not exempt insurance companies from the provisions of G.S. 24-1 and G.S. 24-2, relating to usury; the purport and effect of the section is merely to allow insurance companies to require as a condition precedent to the loan of money that the borrower take out a policy of insurance and assign same as security for the loan. If this section did provide that insurance companies should be exempt from G.S. 24-1 and G.S. 24-2, it would be void as in violation of former Art. I, § 7, of the State Constitution (see now N. C. Const., Art. I, § 32). Cowan v. Security Life & Trust Co., 211 N.C. 18, 188 S.E. 812 (1936).

A 10-year endowment policy came within the provisions of this section, when such endowment policy provided that the face amount thereof would be paid to the beneficiary if the insured died during the 10-year period while the policy was in force. Cowan v. Security Life & Trust Co., 211 N.C. 18, 188 S.E. 812 (1936).

Cited in Huski-Bilt, Inc. v. First-Citizens Bank & Trust Co., 271 N.C. 662, 157 S.E.2d 352 (1967).

§ 58-3-50. Companies must do business in own name; emblems, insignias, etc.

Every insurance company or group of companies must conduct its business in the State in, and the policies and contracts of insurance issued by it shall be headed or entitled only by, its proper or corporate name or names. There shall not appear on the policy anything that would indicate that it is the obligation of any other than the company or companies responsible for the payment of losses under the policy, though it will be permissible to stamp or print on the policy, the name or names of the department or general agency issuing the same, and the group of companies with which the company is financially affiliated. The use of any emblem, insignia, or anything other than the true and proper corporate name of the company or group of companies shall be permitted only with the approval of the Commissioner. (1899, c. 54, s. 18; Rev., s. 4811; C.S., s. 6292; 1945, c. 377; 1951, c. 781, s. 10; 1995, c. 193, s. 9.)

Legal Periodicals. — For brief comment on the 1951 amendment, see 29 N.C.L. Rev. 398 (1951).

§ 58-3-55. Must not pay death benefits in services.

No insurance company now doing business in this State or that may hereafter be authorized to do business in this State issuing contracts providing benefits in the event of death shall issue any contract providing for the payment of benefits in merchandise or service to be rendered to such policyholder or his beneficiary. (1945, c. 377.)

§ 58-3-60. Publication of assets and liabilities; penalty for failure.

When any company publishes its assets, it must in the same connection and with equal conspicuousness publish its liabilities computed on the basis allowed for its annual statements; and any publications purporting to show its capital must exhibit only the amount of such capital as has been actually paid in cash. Any company or agent thereof who violates this section shall be guilty of a Class 3 misdemeanor and, upon conviction, shall be punished only by a fine of not less than five hundred dollars ($500.00) nor more than one thousand dollars ($1,000). (1899, c. 54, ss. 18, 96; Rev., ss. 3492, 4812; C.S., s. 6293; 1985, c. 666, s. 14; 1993, c. 539, s. 446; 1994, Ex. Sess., c. 24, s. 14(c).)

§ 58-3-65. Publication of financial information.

Notwithstanding any other provision of the laws of this State an insurer may, subject to requirements set forth by regulation promulgated by the Commissioner, publish financial statements or information based on financial statements prepared on a basis which is in accordance with requirements of a competent authority and which differs from the basis of the statements which have been filed with the Commissioner. Such differing financial statements or information based on financial statements shall not be made the basis for the application of provisions of any laws of this State not relating solely to the publication of financial information unless such provisions specifically so require. (1973, c. 1130; 1991, c. 720, s. 5.)

§ 58-3-70: Repealed by Session Laws 1993, c. 452, s. 65.

Cross References. — As to unearned premium reserves, see G.S. 58-3-71.

§ 58-3-71. Unearned premium reserves.

(a) Every insurance company, other than a life or real estate title insurance company, shall maintain reserves equal to the unearned portions of the gross premiums charged on unexpired or unterminated risks and policies.

(b) No deductions may be made from the gross premiums in force except for original premiums canceled on risks terminated or reduced before expiration, or except for premiums paid or credited for risks reinsured with other solvent assuming insurers authorized to transact business in this State.

(c) Premiums charged for bulk or portfolio reinsurance assumed from other insurers shall be included as premiums in force on the basis of the original premiums and original terms of the policies of the ceding insurer.

(d) Reinsurance ceded to an authorized assuming insurer may be deducted on the basis of original premiums and original terms, except in the case of excess loss or catastrophe reinsurance, which may be deducted only on the basis of actual reinsurance premiums and actual reinsurance terms.

(e) The reserve for unearned premiums shall be computed on an actual basis or may be computed on the monthly pro rata fractional basis if in the opinion of the Commissioner this method produces an adequate reserve.

(f) With respect to marine insurance, premiums on trip risks not terminated shall be deemed unearned; and the Commissioner may require a reserve to be carried thereon equal to one hundred percent (100%) of the premiums on trip risks written during the month ended as of the statement date.

(g) The Commissioner may adopt rules for the unearned premium reserve computation for premiums covering indefinite terms. (1993, c. 452, s. 1.)

CASE NOTES

Editor's Note. — *The case cited below was decided under former G.S. 58-3-70.*

Constitutionality. — Former G.S. 58-3-70 in no way impinged on the Constitution. Hardware Mut. Fire Ins. Co. v. Stinson, 210 N.C. 69, 185 S.E. 449 (1936).

Unearned premiums are a liability of the company. Hardware Mut. Fire Ins. Co. v. Stinson, 210 N.C. 69, 185 S.E. 449 (1936).

§ 58-3-72. Premium deficiency reserves.

(a) In determining the financial condition of any casualty, fidelity, and surety company and any fire and marine company referred to in G.S. 58-7-75, and in any financial statement or report of the company, there shall be included in the liabilities of the company premium deficiency reserves at least equal to the amounts required under this section. The date as of which the determination, statement, or report is made is known as the "date of determination."

(b) For all recorded unearned premium reserves, a premium deficiency reserve shall be calculated to include the amount by which the anticipated losses, loss adjustment expenses, commissions and other acquisition costs, and maintenance costs exceed the sum of those unearned premium reserves and any related expected future installment premiums as of the date of determination.

(c) Except as provided in subsection (f) of this section, commissions, other acquisition costs, and premium taxes do not have to be considered in the determination of the premium deficiency reserve, to the extent that they have previously been incurred.

(d) Except as provided in subsection (f) of this section, no reduction shall be taken for anticipated investment income in the determination of the premium deficiency reserve.

(e) For purposes of determining if a premium deficiency exists, insurance contracts shall be grouped in a manner consistent with the way in which such policies are marketed or serviced.

(f) If the Commissioner determines that the premium deficiency reserves of any company that have been calculated in accordance with this section are inadequate or excessive, the Commissioner may prescribe any other basis that will produce adequate and reasonable reserves. (2001-223, s. 1.1.)

Editor's Note. — Session Laws 2001-223, s. 28 made this section effective June 15, 2001.

Session Laws 2001-223, s. 27 is a severability clause.

§ 58-3-75. Loss and loss expense reserves of fire and marine insurance companies.

In any determination of the financial condition of any fire or marine or fire and marine insurance company authorized to do business in this State, such company shall be charged, in addition to its unearned premium liability as prescribed in G.S. 58-3-71, with a liability for loss reserves in an amount equal to the aggregate of the estimated amounts payable on all outstanding claims reported to it which arose out of any contract of insurance or reinsurance made by it, and in addition thereto an amount fairly estimated as necessary to provide for unreported losses incurred on or prior to the date of such determination, as defined in G.S. 58-3-81(a), and including, both as to reported and unreported claims, an amount estimated as necessary to provide for the expense of adjusting such claims, and there shall be deducted, in determining such liability for loss reserves, the amount of reinsurance recoverable by such company, in respect to such claims, from assuming insurers in accordance with G.S. 58-7-21. Such loss and loss expense reserves shall be calculated in accordance with any method adopted or approved by the NAIC, unless the Commissioner determines that another more conservative method is appropriate. (1945, c. 377; 1993, c. 452, s. 2; 1993 (Reg. Sess., 1994), c. 678, s. 4.)

§ 58-3-80: Repealed by Session Laws 1993, c. 452, s. 65.

Cross References. — As to loss and loss expense reserves of casualty insurance and surety companies, G.S. 58-3-80.

§ 58-3-81. Loss and loss expense reserves of casualty insurance and surety companies.

(a) In determining the financial condition of any casualty insurance or surety company and in any financial statement or report of any such company, there shall be included in the liabilities of that company loss reserves and loss expense reserves at least equal to the amounts required under this section. The amount of those reserves shall be diminished by an allowance or credit for reinsurance recoverable from assuming reinsurers in accordance with G.S. 58-7-21 or G.S. 58-7-26. The date as of which the determination, statement, or report is made is known as the date of determination.

(b) For all outstanding losses and loss expenses, the reserves shall be valued as of the date of determination and shall include the following:

    (1) The aggregate estimated amounts due for losses and loss adjustment expenses on account of all known claims.

    (2) The aggregate estimated amounts due for losses and loss adjustment expenses on account of all unknown, incurred but not reported claims.

(c) Except as provided in subsection (e) of this section, the minimum loss and loss expense reserves for workers' compensation insurance shall be determined as follows:

    (1) In the case of indemnity benefits where tabular reserves are prescribed for the reporting of such benefits under the Workers' Compensation Statistical Plan (WCSP) of the National Council on Compensation Insurance, the minimum reserve shall be the result obtained by the application of the appropriate pension table in the WCSP, unless

the reserve required by any method adopted or approved by the NAIC is greater, in which case that greater reserve shall be used.

   (2) In all other cases, including other indemnity benefits, medical benefits, and loss adjustment expense, the reserve shall be determined by subsection (b) of this section, unless the reserve required by any method adopted or approved by the NAIC is greater, in which case that greater reserve shall be used.

   (d) Repealed by Session Laws 2001-223, s. 1.2, effective June 15, 2001.

   (e) Whenever in the judgment of the Commissioner the loss and loss expense reserves of any casualty or surety company doing business in this State calculated in accordance with the foregoing provisions are inadequate or excessive, he may prescribe any other basis that will produce adequate and reasonable reserves.

   (f) Every casualty insurance and every surety company doing business in this State shall keep a complete and itemized record showing all losses and claims on which it has received notices, including all notices received by it of the occurrence of any event that may result in a loss. (1993, c. 452, s. 3; 2001-223, s. 1.2.)

§ 58-3-85. Corporation or association maintaining office in State required to qualify and secure license.

Any corporation or voluntary association, other than an association of companies, the members of which are licensed in this State, issuing contracts of insurance and maintaining a principal, branch, or other office within this State, whether soliciting business in this State or in foreign states, shall qualify under the insurance laws of this State applicable to the type of insurance written by such corporation or association and secure license from the Commissioner as provided under Articles 1 through 64 of this Chapter on insurance, as amended, and the officers and agents of any such corporation or association maintaining offices within this State and failing to qualify and secure license as herein provided shall be deemed guilty of a Class 1 misdemeanor. (1937, c. 39; 1991, c. 720, s. 4; 1993, c. 539, s. 447; 1994, Ex. Sess., c. 24, s. 14(c).)

§ 58-3-90: Repealed by Session Laws 2001-223, s. 2.1, effective July 1, 2001.

§ 58-3-95: Repealed by Session Laws 1991, c. 720, s. 71.

§ 58-3-100. Insurance company licensing provisions.

   (a) The Commissioner may, after notice and opportunity for a hearing, revoke, suspend, or restrict the license of any insurer if:
   (1) The insurer fails or refuses to comply with any law, order or rule applicable to the insurer.
   (2) The insurer's financial condition is unsound, or its assets above its liabilities, exclusive of capital, are less than the amount of its capital or required minimum surplus.
   (3) The insurer has published or made to the Department or to the public any false statement or report.
   (4) The insurer or any of the insurer's officers, directors, employees, or other representatives refuse to submit to any examination authorized by law or refuse to perform any legal obligation in relation to an examination.

(5) The insurer is found to make a practice of unduly engaging in litigation or of delaying the investigation of claims or the adjustment or payment of valid claims.

(b) Any suspension, revocation or refusal to renew an insurer's license under this section may also be made applicable to the license or registration of any individual regulated under this Chapter who is a party to any of the causes for licensing sanctions listed in subsection (a) of this section.

(c) The Commissioner may impose a civil penalty under G.S. 58-2-70 if an HMO, service corporation, MEWA, or insurer fails to acknowledge a claim within 30 days after receiving written or electronic notice of the claim, but only if the notice contains sufficient information for the insurer to identify the specific coverage involved. Acknowledgement of the claim shall be one of the following:

(1) A statement made to the claimant or to the claimant's legal representative advising that the claim is being investigated.

(2) Payment of the claim.

(3) A bona fide written offer of settlement.

(4) A written denial of the claim.

A claimant includes an insured, a health care provider, or a health care facility that is responsible for directly making the claim with an insurer, HMO, service corporation, or MEWA. With respect to a claim under an accident, health, or disability policy, if the acknowledgement sent to the claimant indicates that the claim remains under investigation, within 45 days after receipt by the insurer of the initial claim, the insurer shall send a claim status report to the insured and every 45 days thereafter until the claim is paid or denied. The report shall give details sufficient for the insured to understand why processing of the claim has not been completed and whether the insurer needs additional information to process the claim. If the claim acknowledgement includes information about why processing of the claim has not been completed and indicates whether additional information is needed, it may satisfy the requirement for the initial claim status report. This subsection does not apply to HMOs, service corporations, MEWAs or insurers subject to G.S. 58-3-225.

(d) If a foreign insurance company's license is suspended or revoked, the Commissioner shall cause written notification of the suspension or revocation to be given to all of the company's agents in this State. Until the Commissioner restores the company's license, the company shall not write any new business in this State.

(e) The Commissioner may, after considering the standards under G.S. 58-30-60(b), restrict an insurer's license by prohibiting or limiting the kind or amount of insurance written by that insurer. For a foreign insurer, this restriction relates to the insurer's business conducted in this State. The Commissioner shall remove any restriction under this subsection once the Commissioner determines that the operations of the insurer are no longer hazardous to the public or the insurer's policyholders or creditors. As used in this subsection, "insurer" includes an HMO, service corporation, and MEWA. (1899, c. 54, ss. 66, 75, 112; 1901, c. 391, s. 5; Rev., ss. 4703, 4705; C.S., s. 6297; 1947, c. 721; 1963, c. 1234; 1993, c. 409, s. 1; 1995, c. 193, s. 10; 1999-294, s. 9; 2000-162, s. 4(b); 2001-223, s. 2.2; 2001-334, s. 15; 2003-212, s. 26(a).)

Effect of Amendments. — Session Laws 2003-212, s. 26.(a), effective January 1, 2004, and applicable to all company licenses issued or otherwise eligible for renewal or continuation after that date, substituted "revoke, suspend, or restrict" for "revoke, suspend, restrict, or refuse to renew" in subsection (a).

§ 58-3-102. Request for determination of coverage for transplants under health benefit payment mechanisms; required response time; penalties.

(a) As used in this section, "insurer" means any payer of health benefits that is subject to Articles 1 through 66 of this Chapter.

(b) When a person or that person's health care provider or representative requests that person's insurer to determine whether a transplant is eligible for benefits under that person's health benefit coverage, the insurer shall, within 10 business days after receipt of the request and medical documentation necessary to determine if there is coverage, inform the requesting person as to whether there is coverage; provided coverage exists at the time of the transplant. (1991, c. 644, s. 14.)

§ 58-3-105. Limitation of risk.

Except as otherwise provided in Articles 1 through 64 of this Chapter, no insurer doing business in this State shall expose itself to any loss on any one risk in an amount exceeding ten percent (10%) of its surplus to policyholders. Any risk or portion of any risk which shall have been reinsured shall be deducted in determining the limitation of risk prescribed in this section. This section shall not apply to life insurance or to the insurance of marine risks, or marine protection and indemnity risks, or workers' compensation or employer's liability risks, or to certificates of title or guaranties of title or policies of title insurance. For the purpose of determining the limitation of risk under any provision of Articles 1 through 64 of this Chapter, "surplus to policyholders" shall

(1) Be deemed to include any voluntary reserves, or any part thereof, which are not required by or pursuant to law, and

(2) Be determined from the last sworn statement of such insurer on file with the Commissioner pursuant to law, or by the last report on examination filed by the Commissioner, whichever is more recent at the time of assumption of such risk.

In applying the limitation of risk under any provision of Articles 1 through 64 of this Chapter to alien insurers, such provision shall be deemed to refer to the exposure to risk and to the surplus to policyholders of the United States branch of such alien insurer. (1945, c. 377; 1991, c. 636, s. 3.)

§ 58-3-110. Limitation of liability assumed.

(a) No company transacting fidelity or surety business in this State shall expose itself to any loss on any one fidelity or surety risk or hazard in an amount exceeding ten per centum (10%) of its policyholders' surplus, unless it shall be protected in excess of that amount by:

(1) Reinsurance in such form as to enable the obligee or beneficiary to maintain an action thereon against the company reinsured jointly with such reinsurer and, upon recovering judgment against such reinsured, to have recovery against such reinsurer for payment to the extent in which it may be liable under such reinsurance and in discharge thereof; or

(2) The cosuretyship of such a company similarly authorized; or

(3) By deposit with it in pledge or conveyance to it in trust for its protection of property; or

(4) By conveyance or mortgage for its protection; or

(5) In case a suretyship obligation was made on behalf or on account of a fiduciary holding property in a trust capacity, by deposit or other disposition of a portion of the property so held in trust that no future sale, mortgage, pledge or other disposition can be made thereof without the consent of such company; except by decree or order of a court of competent jurisdiction;

(b) Provided:

(1) That such company may execute what are known as transportation or warehousing bonds for United States internal revenue taxes to an amount equal to fifty per centum (50%) of its policyholders' surplus;

(2) That, when the penalty of the suretyship obligation exceeds the amount of a judgment described therein as appealed from and thereby secured, or exceeds the amount of the subject matter in controversy or of the estate in the hands of the fiduciary for the performance of whose duties it is conditioned, the bond may be executed if the actual amount of the judgment or the subject matter in controversy or estate not subject to the supervision or control of the surety is not in excess of such limitation; and

(3) That, when the penalty of the suretyship obligation executed for the performance of a contract exceeds the contract price, the latter shall be taken as the basis for estimating the limit of risk within the meaning of this section.

(c) No such company shall, anything to the contrary in this section notwithstanding, execute suretyship obligations guaranteeing the deposits of any single financial institution in an aggregate amount in excess of ten per centum (10%) of the policyholders' surplus of such surety, unless it shall be protected in excess of that amount by credits in accordance with subdivisions (1), (2), (3) or (4) of subsection (a) of this section: Provided, nothing in this section shall be construed to make invalid any contract entered into by such company with another person, firm, corporation or municipal corporation, notwithstanding any provisions of this section. (1911, c. 28; C.S., s. 6382; 1931, c. 285; 1945, c. 377.)

CASE NOTES

As to joint-control agreements between fiduciaries and their sureties, see Pierce v. Pierce, 197 N.C. 348, 148 S.E. 438 (1929); State ex rel. Leonard v. York, 202 N.C. 704, 163 S.E. 878 (1932).

§ 58-3-115. Twisting with respect to insurance policies; penalties.

No insurer shall make or issue, or cause to be issued, any written or oral statement that willfully misrepresents or willfully makes an incomplete comparison as to the terms, conditions, or benefits contained in any policy of insurance for the purpose of inducing or attempting to induce a policyholder in any way to terminate or surrender, exchange, or convert any insurance policy. Any person who violates this section is subject to the provisions of G.S. 58-2-70 or G.S. 58-3-100. (1961, c. 823; 1987, c. 629, s. 4; c. 787, s. 2; c. 864, ss. 3(a), 74; 1989, c. 485, s. 25; 1999-132, s. 1.3.)

CASE NOTES

Applicability of Former § 143-318. — Former G.S. 143-318, relating to evidence in administrative proceedings, in light of former G.S. 143-317(3), was intended to apply only to hearings which might result in a loss by a specific party of some legal right, duty or privilege, such as hearings relating to the revocation of the license of a specified insurance agent or of a specified insurance company or to the imposition of a fine or penalty upon an insurance agent or insurance company for violation of the insurance law. Such hearings involve the essential elements of a court trial, and the Attorney General, as legal advisor to the Commissioner, can provide counsel as to whether proffered evidence complies with the applicable rules of evidence. In re North Carolina Auto. Rate Admin. Office, 278 N.C. 302, 180 S.E.2d 155 (1971).

§ 58-3-120. Discrimination forbidden.

(a) No company doing the business of insurance as defined in G.S. 58-7-15 shall make any discrimination in favor of any person.

(b) Discrimination between individuals of the same class in the amount of premiums or rates charged for any policy of insurance covered by Articles 50 through 55 of this Chapter, or in the benefits payable thereon, or in any of the terms or conditions of such policy, or in any other manner whatsoever, is prohibited. (1903, c. 488, s. 2; 1905, c. 170, s. 2; Rev., s. 4766; C.S., s. 6430; 1923, c. 4, s. 70; 1925, c. 70, s. 6; 1945, c. 458; 1987, c. 629, s. 5; 2001-297, s. 4.)

CASE NOTES

Purpose and Applicability. — The statutory provisions which prohibit an insurer or insurance agent from "discrimination" in setting rates for any person — G.S. 58-3-120, former 58-44.5, and 58-63-15 — are obviously designed to prohibit an insurance agent or company from charging reduced or excessive insurance rates contrary to the established rating rules applicable to the risk, and are not applicable to rate making. State ex rel. Comm'r of Ins. v. North Carolina Rate Bureau, 75 N.C. App. 201, 331 S.E.2d 124, cert. denied, 314 N.C. 547, 335 S.E.2d 319 (1985).

The prohibition against discrimination in rates is directed to insurers, agents, brokers and other representatives of insurers. Hyde Ins. Agency, Inc. v. Dixie Leasing Corp., 26 N.C. App. 138, 215 S.E.2d 162 (1975).

The sanctions provided by statutes for violations of the antirebate provisions are directed to the insurers, agents, brokers or other representatives, and the statutes do not declare that contracts in violation of the antirebate provision are void. Hyde Ins. Agency, Inc. v. Dixie Leasing Corp., 26 N.C. App. 138, 215 S.E.2d 162 (1975).

Applicability of Former § 143-318. — Former G.S. 143-318, relating to evidence in administrative proceedings, in light of former G.S. 143-317(3), was intended to apply only to hearings which might result in a loss by a specific party of some legal right, duty or privilege, such as hearings relating to the revocation of the license of a specified insurance agent or of a specified insurance company or to the imposition of a fine or penalty upon an insurance agent or insurance company for violation of the insurance law. Such hearings involve the essential elements of a court trial, and the Attorney General, as legal advisor to the Commissioner, can provide counsel as to whether proffered evidence complies with the applicable rules of evidence. In re North Carolina Auto. Rate Admin. Office, 278 N.C. 302, 180 S.E.2d 155 (1971).

§ 58-3-121. Discrimination against coverage of certain bones and joints prohibited.

(a) Discrimination against coverage of procedures involving bones or joints of the jaw, face, or head is prohibited in any health benefit plan. Whenever a health benefit plan provides coverage on a group or individual basis for diagnostic, therapeutic, or surgical procedures involving bones or joints of the human skeletal structure, that plan may not exclude or deny the same coverage for procedures involving any bone or joint of the jaw, face, or head, so long as the procedure is medically necessary to treat a condition which prevents normal functioning of the particular bone or joint involved and the condition is caused by congenital deformity, disease, or traumatic injury. The coverage required by this section involving bones or joints of the jaw, face, or head shall be subject to the same conditions and limitations as are applicable to coverage of procedures involving other bones and joints of the human skeletal structure.

(b) For purposes of this section, in providing coverage for the treatment of conditions of the jaw (temporomandibular joint), authorized therapeutic procedures shall include splinting and use of intraoral prosthetic appliances to reposition the bones. Payment for these therapeutic procedures, and for procedures involved in any other nonsurgical treatment of temporomandibular joint dysfunction, may be subjected to a reasonable lifetime maximum dollar amount. Nothing in this subsection shall require a health benefit plan to cover orthodontic braces, crowns, bridges, dentures, treatment for periodontal disease, dental root form implants, or root canals.

(c) For purposes of this section, "health benefit plan" means accident and health insurance policies or certificates; nonprofit hospital or medical service corporation contracts; health, hospital, or medical service corporation plan contracts; health maintenance (HMO) subscriber contracts; and plans provided by a MEWA or plans provided by other benefit arrangements, to the extent permitted by ERISA. (1995, c. 483, s. 1.)

§ 58-3-122. Anesthesia and hospital charges necessary for safe and effective administration of dental procedures for young children, persons with serious mental or physical conditions, and persons with significant behavioral problems; coverage in health benefit plans.

(a) All health benefit plans shall provide coverage for payment of anesthesia and hospital or facility charges for services performed in a hospital or ambulatory surgical facility in connection with dental procedures for children below the age of nine years, persons with serious mental or physical conditions, and persons with significant behavioral problems, where the provider treating the patient involved certifies that, because of the patient's age or condition or problem, hospitalization or general anesthesia is required in order to safely and effectively perform the procedures. The same deductibles, coinsurance, network requirements, medical necessity provisions, and other limitations as apply to physical illness benefits under the health benefit plan shall apply to coverage for anesthesia and hospital or facility charges required to be covered under this section.

(b) As used in this section, the term:

(1) "Health benefit plan" means an accident and health insurance policy or certificate; a nonprofit hospital or medical service corporation contract; a health maintenance organization subscriber contract; a plan provided by a multiple employer welfare arrangement; or a plan provided by another benefit arrangement, to the extent permitted by the Employee Retirement Income Security Act of 1974, as amended, or by any waiver of or other exception to that Act provided under federal law or regulation. "Health benefit plan" does not mean any plan implemented or administered by the North Carolina Department of Health and Human Services or the United States Department of Health and Human Services, or any successor agency, or its representatives. "Health benefit plan" also does not mean any of the following kinds of insurance:

a. Accident.

b. Credit.

c. Disability income.

d. Long-term care or nursing home care.

  e. Medicare supplement.
  f. Specified disease.
  g. Dental or vision.
  h. Coverage issued as a supplement to liability insurance.
  i. Workers' compensation.
  j. Medical payments under automobile or homeowners.
  k. Hospital income or indemnity.
  l. Insurance under which benefits are payable with or without regard to fault and that is statutorily required to be contained in any liability policy or equivalent self-insurance.
 (2) "Insurer" includes an insurance company subject to this Chapter, a service corporation organized under Article 65 of this Chapter, a health maintenance organization organized under Article 67 of this Chapter, or a multiple employer welfare arrangement subject to Article 49 of this Chapter. (1999-134, s. 1.)

Editor's Note. — Session Laws 1999-134, s. 2 provides that this section is effective January 1, 2000 and applies to health benefit plans that are delivered, issued for delivery, or renewed on and after January 1, 2000. For purposes of Session Laws 1999-134, renewal of a health benefit policy, contract, or plan is presumed to occur on each anniversary of the date on which coverage was first effective on the person or persons covered by the health benefit plan.

§ **58-3-125:** Repealed by Session Laws 1999-132, s. 1.1.

§ **58-3-130. Agent, adjuster, etc., acting without a license or violating insurance law.**

If any person shall assume to act either as principal, agent, broker, limited representative, adjuster or motor vehicle damage appraiser without license as is required by law or, pretending to be a principal, agent, broker, limited representative, adjuster or licensed motor vehicle damage appraiser, shall solicit, examine or inspect any risk, or shall examine into, adjust, or aid in adjusting any loss, investigate or advise relative to the nature and amount of damages to motor vehicles or the amount necessary to effect repairs thereto, or shall receive, collect, or transmit any premium of insurance, or shall do any other act in the soliciting, making or executing any contract of insurance of any kind otherwise than the law permits, or as principal or agent shall violate any provision of law contained in Articles 1 through 64 of this Chapter, the punishment for which is not elsewhere provided for, he shall be deemed guilty of a Class 1 misdemeanor. (1899, c. 54, s. 115; Rev., s. 3490; C.S., s. 6310; 1945, c. 458; 1949, c. 958, s. 1; 1951, c. 105, s. 1; 1971, c. 757, s. 7; 1985, c. 666, s. 20; 1987, c. 629, s. 9; 1993, c. 539, s. 448; 1994, Ex. Sess., c. 24, s. 14(c).)

CASE NOTES

Statute of Limitations. — A negligence action against attorneys by the liquidator of a life insurer was barred where more than three years elapsed since the last negligent act of defendants and, where the complaint did not allege "continuous representation" by defen- dants connected with the original negligent act, that doctrine did not apply to toll running of the statute. State ex rel. Long v. Petree Stockton, 129 N.C. App. 432, 499 S.E.2d 790 (1998), cert. granted, 349 N.C. 240, 516 S.E.2d 607 (1998).

§ 58-3-135. Certain insurance activities by lenders with customers prohibited.

No lender shall require the purchase of insurance from such lender or subsidiary or affiliate of such lender as a condition to the making, renewing or refinancing of any loan or to the establishing of any of the terms or conditions of such loan. Lenders shall not include organizations of the Farm Credit System. (1985, c. 679, s. 1.)

§ 58-3-140. Temporary contracts of insurance permitted.

A lender engaged in making or servicing real estate mortgage or deed of trust loans on one to four family residences shall accept as evidence of insurance a temporary written contract of insurance meeting the requirements of G.S. 58-44-20(4) and issued by any duly licensed insurance agent, broker, or insurance company.

Nothing herein prohibits the lender from refusing to accept a binder or from disapproving such insurer or agent provided such refusal or disapproval is reasonable.

Such lender need not accept a binder unless such binder:
 (1) Includes:
     a. The name and address of the insured;
     b. The name and address of the mortgagee;
     c. A description of the insured collateral;
     d. A provision that it may not be cancelled within a term of the binder except upon 10 days' written notice to the mortgagee; and
     e. The amount of insurance bound.
 (2) Is accompanied by a paid receipt for one year's premium, except in the case of the renewal of a policy subsequent to the closing of a loan; and
 (3) Includes an undertaking of agent to use his best efforts to have the insurance company issue a policy.

The Department may require binders to contain any additional information to permit the binders to comply with the reasonable requirements of Fannie Mae, the Government National Mortgage Association, or the Federal Home Loan Mortgage Corporation for purchase of mortgage loans. (1989, c. 459, s. 1; 1991, c. 720, s. 4; 2001-487, s. 14(f).)

§ 58-3-145. Solicitation, negotiation or payment of premiums on insurance policies.

An insurer, agent, or broker may accept payment of an insurance premium by credit card if the insurer accepting payment by credit card meets the following conditions:
 (1) The insurer makes payment by credit card available to all existing and prospective insureds and does not limit the use of credit card payments to certain persons.
 (2) The insurer pays the fees charged by the credit card company for the payment of premiums by credit card. (1967, c. 1245; 1979, c. 528; 1991, c. 720, s. 7; 1999-365, s. 1.)

OPINIONS OF ATTORNEY GENERAL

The 1979 amendment to this section permitted insurance premiums to be charged to a credit card facility respecting travel accident insurance as to both public and private modes of transportation. See opinion of Attorney General to Joseph E. Johnson, Representative, 15th District, 49 N.C.A.G. 116 (1980).

§ 58-3-147. Credit card guaranty or collateral prohibited.

No insurer, representative of any insurer, or insurance broker shall enter into any arrangement that involves the sale of insurance or the pledging of existing insurance as guaranty or collateral for the issuance of any credit card. (1993, c. 226, s. 9; c. 504, s. 40.)

Editor's Note. — Session Laws 1993, c. 504, s. 40, effective July 24, 1993, recodified this section as G.S. 58-3-147.

§ 58-3-150. Forms to be approved by Commissioner.

(a) It is unlawful for any insurance company licensed and admitted to do business in this State to issue, sell, or dispose of any policy, contract, or certificate, or use applications in connection therewith, until the forms of the same have been submitted to and approved by the Commissioner, and copies filed in the Department. If a policy form filing is disapproved by the Commissioner, the Commissioner may return the filing to the filer. As used in this section, "policy form" includes endorsements, riders, or amendments to policies that have already been approved by the Commissioner.

(b) With respect to group and blanket accident and health insurance, group life insurance, and group annuity policies issued and delivered to a trust or to an association outside of this State and covering persons resident in this State, the group certificates to be delivered or issued for delivery in this State shall be filed with and approved by the Commissioner pursuant to subsection (a) of this section.

(c) If not submitted electronically, all contracts, literature, advertising materials, letters, and other documents submitted to the Department to comply with the filing requirements of this Chapter or an administrative rule adopted pursuant to this Chapter shall be submitted on paper eight and one-half inches by eleven inches. Brochures and pamphlets shall not be stapled or bound. (1907, c. 879; 1913, c. 139; C.S., s. 6312; 1945, c. 377; 1987, c. 752, s. 7; 1989, c. 485, s. 9; 1991, c. 720, ss. 5, 51; 1993, c. 506, s. 1; 1998-211, s. 37.3(a); 2003-290, s. 3.)

Effect of Amendments. — Session Laws 2003-290, s. 3, effective October 1, 2003, added subsection (c).

CASE NOTES

Validity of Unapproved Policy. — The statute does not purport to deal with the validity of the contract of insurance, but with the insurance company. It does not say a policy shall be void unless approved by the Commissioner, but that it shall be unlawful for the company to issue such policy. Blount v. Royal Fraternal Ass'n, 163 N.C. 167, 79 S.E. 299 (1913).

Exclusion Not Void Despite Failure to Obtain Approval. — Surplus insurer's failure to get advance form approval did not result in the absolute pollution exclusion being void.

Home Indem. Co. v. Hoechst Celanese Corp., 128 N.C. App. 226, 494 S.E.2d 768, 1998 N.C. App. LEXIS 23 (1998), cert. denied, 505 S.E.2d 869 (1998).

Nowhere does this section declare that all unapproved policy provisions are void and unenforceable. Home Indem. Co. v. Hoechst Celanese Corp., 128 N.C. App. 226, 494 S.E.2d 768, 1998 N.C. App. LEXIS 23 (1998), cert. denied, 505 S.E.2d 869 (1998).

Cited in North Carolina Life & Accident & Health Ins. Guar. Ass'n v. Alcatel, 876 F. Supp. 748 (E.D.N.C. 1995).

§ 58-3-151. Deemer provisions.

No entity subject to the Commissioner's jurisdiction and regulation shall be fined or penalized by the Commissioner for using forms, contracts, schedules of premiums, or other documents required to be filed and approved under this Chapter or for executing contracts required to be filed and approved under this Chapter if those forms, contracts, schedules of premiums, or other documents have been by law deemed to have been approved, and the entity has notified the Commissioner before using the filing or executing the contract that the law has deemed the filing or the contract to be approved. (2001-334, s. 14.)

Editor's Note. — Session Laws 2001-334, s. 21 makes this section effective August 3, 2001.

Session Laws 2001-334, s. 19 is a severability clause.

§ 58-3-152. Excess liability policies; uninsured and underinsured motorist coverages.

With respect to policy forms that provide excess liability coverage, an insurer may limit or exclude coverage for uninsured motorists as provided in G.S. 20-279.21(b)(3) and for underinsured motorists as provided in G.S. 20-279.21(b)(4). (1997-396, s. 1.)

CASE NOTES

Applied in Progressive Am. Ins. Co. v. Vasquez, 350 N.C. 386, 515 S.E.2d 8 (1999).

§ 58-3-155. Business transacted with insurer-controlled brokers.

(a) As used in this section:
  (1) "Broker" means a person who, being a licensed agent, obtains insurance for another party through a duly authorized agent of an insurer that is licensed to do business in this State but for which the broker is not authorized to act as agent.
  (2) "Control" or "controlled" means the direct or indirect possession of the power to direct or cause the direction of the management and policies of a person, whether through the ownership of voting securities, by contract other than a commercial contract for goods or nonmanagement services, or otherwise, unless the power is the result of an official position with or a corporate office held by the person. Control is presumed to exist if any person directly or indirectly owns, controls, holds with the power to vote, or holds proxies representing ten percent (10%) or more of the voting securities of any other person.
(b) The Commissioner may determine, after furnishing all persons in interest notice and opportunity to be heard and making specific findings of fact to support that determination, that control exists in fact, notwithstanding the absence of a presumption to that effect. The Commissioner may determine upon application that any person does not or will not upon the taking of some proposed action control another person. The Commissioner may prospectively revoke or modify that determination, after notice and opportunity to be heard whenever in the Commissioner's judgment revocation or modification is consistent with this section.
(c) No licensed property or casualty insurer that has control of a broker may accept insurance from the broker in any transaction in which the broker, when the insurance is placed, is acting as such on behalf of the insured for any

compensation, commission, or thing of value unless the broker, before the effective date of the coverage, delivers written notice to the prospective insured disclosing the relationship between the insurer and broker. The disclosure must be signed by the insured and must be retained in the insurer's underwriting file until the completion and release of the examination report under G.S. 58-2-131 through G.S. 58-2-134 for the period in which the coverage is in effect. If the insurance is placed through a subbroker that is not a controlled broker, the controlling insurer shall retain in its records a signed commitment from the subbroker that the subbroker is aware of the relationship between the insurer and the broker and that the subbroker has notified or will notify the insured.

(d) This section does not affect the rights of policyholders, claimants, creditors, or other third parties. (1991, c. 681, s. 9; 1999-132, s. 11.1.)

§ 58-3-160. Sale of company or major reorganization; license to be restricted.

The Commissioner shall restrict the license by prohibiting new or renewal insurance business transacted in this State by any licensed insurer that, in anticipation of a sale of the insurer to new owners or a major reorganization of the business or management of the insurer, transfers all of its existing insurance business to another insurer through an assumption reinsurance agreement or does not write any new insurance business for over one year. The restriction shall remain in force until after the insurer has filed the following information with the Commissioner and the Commissioner has granted approval:

(1) Biographical information in a form acceptable to the Commissioner for each new owner, director, or management person;

(2) A detailed and complete plan of operation describing the kinds of insurance to be written and the method in which the reorganized insurer will perform its various functions;

(3) Financial projections of the anticipated operational results of the reorganized insurer for the succeeding three years based on the capitalization of the reorganized insurer and its plan of operation, which must be prepared by a properly qualified individual, be in sufficient detail for a complete analysis to be performed, and be accompanied by a list of the assumptions used in making the projections; and

(4) Any other information the Commissioner considers to be pertinent for a proper analysis of the reorganized insurer. (1991, c. 681, s. 10.)

§ 58-3-165. Business transacted with producer-controlled property or casualty insurers.

(a) As used in this section:

(1) "Accredited state" means a state in which the insurance department or regulatory agency has qualified as meeting the minimum financial regulatory standards promulgated and established from time to time by the NAIC.

(2) "Captive insurer" means an insurance company that is owned by another organization and whose exclusive purpose is to insure risks of the parent organization and affiliated companies. In the case of groups and associations, "captive insurer" means an insurance organization that is owned by the insureds, and whose exclusive purpose is to insure risks of member organizations or group members and their affiliates.

 (3) "Control" and its cognates mean the direct or indirect possession of the power to direct or cause the direction of the management and policies of a person, whether through the ownership of voting securities, by contract other than a commercial contract for goods or nonmanagement services, or otherwise, unless the power is the result of an official position with or corporate office held by the person. Control is presumed to exist if any person directly or indirectly owns, controls, holds with the power to vote, or holds proxies representing ten percent (10%) or more of the voting securities of any other person.

 (4) "Controlled insurer" means an insurer that is controlled, directly or indirectly, by a producer.

 (5) "Controlling producer" means a producer who, directly or indirectly, controls an insurer.

 (6) "Insurer" means any person licensed to write property or casualty insurance in this State. "Insurer" does not mean a risk retention group under Article 22 of this Chapter, residual market mechanism, joint underwriting authority, nor captive insurer.

 (7) "Producer" means an insurance broker or brokers or any other person, when, for any compensation, commission, or other thing of value, that person acts or aids in any manner in soliciting, negotiating, or procuring the making of any insurance contract on behalf of an insured other than that person. "Producer" does not mean an exclusive agent or any independent agent acting on behalf of a controlled insurer, including any subagent or representative of the agent, who acts as such in the solicitation of, negotiation for, or procurement or making of an insurance contract, if the agent is not also acting in the capacity of an insurance broker in the transaction in question.

(b) The Commissioner may determine, after furnishing all persons in interest notice and opportunity to be heard and making specific findings of fact to support the determination, that control exists in fact, notwithstanding the absence of a presumption to that effect. The Commissioner may determine upon application that any person does not or will not upon the taking of some proposed action control another person. The Commissioner may prospectively revoke or modify that determination, after notice and opportunity to be heard, whenever in the Commissioner's judgment revocation or modification is consistent with this section.

(c) This section applies to insurers that are either domiciled in this State or domiciled in a state that is not an accredited state having in effect a substantially similar law. The provisions of Article 19 of this Chapter, to the extent they are not superseded by this section, apply to all parties within holding company systems subject to this section.

(d) The provisions of this section apply if, in any calendar year, the aggregate amount of gross written premiums on business placed with a controlled insurer by a controlling producer is equal to or greater than five percent (5%) of the admitted assets of the controlled insurer, as reported in the controlled insurer's most recent annual statement or its quarterly statement filed as of September 30 of the prior year. The provisions of this section do not apply if:

 (1) The controlling producer places insurance only with the controlled insurer, or only with the controlled insurer and a member or members of the controlled insurer's holding company system, or the controlled insurer's parent, affiliate, or subsidiary and receives no compensation based upon the amount of premiums written in connection with that insurance; and the controlling producer accepts insurance placements only from nonaffiliated subproducers, and not directly from insureds; and

(2) The controlled insurer, except for insurance business written through a residual market mechanism, accepts insurance business only from a controlling producer, a producer controlled by the controlled insurer, or a producer that is a subsidiary of the controlled insurer.

(e) A controlled insurer shall not accept business from a controlling producer and a controlling producer shall not place business with a controlled insurer unless there is a written contract between the producer and the insurer specifying the responsibilities of each party, and unless the contract has been approved by the board of directors of the insurer and contains all of the following minimum provisions:

(1) The insurer may terminate the contract for cause, upon written notice to the producer. The insurer shall suspend the producer's authority to write business during the pendency of any dispute regarding the cause for the termination.

(2) The producer shall render accounts to the insurer detailing all material transactions, including information necessary to support all commissions, charges, and other fees received by, or owing to, the producer.

(3) The producer shall remit all funds due under the contract terms to the insurer on at least a monthly basis. The due date shall be fixed so that premiums or installments of premiums collected shall be remitted no later than 90 days after the effective date of any policy placed with the insurer under this contract.

(4) The producer shall hold all funds collected for the insurer's account in a fiduciary capacity, in one or more appropriately identified bank accounts in banks that are members of the Federal Reserve System, in accordance with the provisions of this Chapter as applicable. Funds of a producer who is not required to be licensed in this State shall be maintained in compliance with the requirements of the producer's domiciliary jurisdiction.

(5) The producer shall maintain separately identifiable records of business written for the insurer.

(6) The producer shall not assign the contract in whole or in part.

(7) The insurer shall provide the producer with its underwriting standards, rules and procedures, the manual setting forth the rates to be charged, and the conditions for the acceptance or rejection of risks. The producer shall adhere to the standards, rules, procedures, rates, and conditions. The standards, rules, procedures, rates, and conditions shall be the same as those applicable to comparable business placed with the insurer by a producer other than a controlling producer.

(8) The rates and terms of the producer's commissions, charges, or other fees and the purposes for the charges or fees. The rates of the commissions, charges, and other fees shall be no greater than those applicable to comparable business placed with the insurer by producers other than controlling producers. For the purposes of this subdivision and subdivision (7) of this subsection, "comparable business" includes the same lines of insurance, same kinds of insurance, same kinds of risks, similar policy limits, and similar quality of business.

(9) If the contract provides that the producer, on insurance business placed with the insurer, is to be compensated contingent upon the insurer's profits on that business, then the compensation shall not be determined and paid until at least five years after the premiums on liability insurance are earned and at least one year after the premiums are earned on any other insurance. In no event shall the commissions be paid until the adequacy of the insurer's reserves on

remaining claims has been independently verified under subsection (g) of this section.

(10) A limit on the producer's writings in relation to the insurer's surplus and total writings. The insurer may establish a different limit for each line or subline of business. The insurer shall notify the producer when the applicable limit is approached and shall not accept business from the producer if the limit is reached. The producer shall not place business with the insurer if it has been notified by the insurer that the limit has been reached.

(11) The producer may negotiate but shall not bind reinsurance on behalf of the insurer on business the producer places with the insurer; however, the producer may bind facultative reinsurance contracts under obligatory facultative agreements if the producer's contract with the insurer contains underwriting guidelines including, for both reinsurance assumed and ceded, a list of reinsurers with which the automatic agreements are in effect, the coverages and amounts or percentages that may be reinsured, and commission schedules.

(f) Every controlled insurer shall have an audit committee, consisting of independent directors, of the insurer's board of directors. The audit committee shall meet annually with the insurer's management, the insurer's independent certified public accountants, and an independent casualty actuary or another independent loss reserve specialist acceptable to the Commissioner, to review the adequacy of the insurer's loss reserves.

(g) In addition to any other required loss reserve certification, the controlled insurer shall, on or before April 1 of each year, file with the Commissioner an opinion of an independent casualty actuary or of another independent loss reserve specialist acceptable to the Commissioner, reporting loss ratios for each kind of insurance written and attesting to the adequacy of loss reserves established for losses incurred and outstanding and for incurred but not reported losses as of the end of the prior calendar year on business placed by the producer.

(h) The controlled insurer shall report annually to the Commissioner the amount of commissions paid to the controlling producer, the percentage that amount represents of the net premiums written, and comparable amounts and percentages paid to noncontrolling producers for placements of the same kinds of insurance.

(i) The controlling producer, before the effective date of any policy, shall deliver written notice to the prospective insured disclosing the relationship between the producer and the controlled insurer: However, if the business is placed through a subproducer who is not a controlling producer, the controlling producer shall retain in the controlling producer's records a signed commitment from the subproducer that the subproducer is aware of the relationship between the insurer and the producer and that the subproducer has or will notify the prospective insured.

(j) If the Commissioner believes that a controlling producer or any other person has not materially complied with this section or with any rule adopted or order issued under this section, after notice and opportunity to be heard, the Commissioner may order the controlling producer to stop placing business with the controlled insurer. If it is found that, because of the material noncompliance, the controlled insurer or any policyholder of the controlled insurer has suffered any loss or damage, the Commissioner may maintain a civil action or intervene in an action brought by or on behalf of the insurer or policyholder for recovery of compensatory damages for the benefit of the insurer or policyholder or other appropriate relief.

(k) If an order for liquidation or rehabilitation of the controlled insurer has been entered under Article 30 of this Chapter, and the receiver appointed under that order believes that the controlling producer or any other person has not materially complied with this section or any rule adopted or order issued under this section, and the insurer suffered any loss or damage therefrom, the receiver may maintain a civil action for recovery of damages or other appropriate sanctions for the benefit of the insurer.

(*l*) In addition to any other remedies provided in this section, whenever the Commissioner believes that a person has not materially complied with this section, the Commissioner may institute a proceeding under G.S. 58-2-60 or under G.S. 58-2-70. In addition to the civil penalty or restitution proceedings provided for in G.S. 58-2-70, the Commissioner may issue a cease and desist order against the person.

(m) This section does not affect the Commissioner's right to impose any other penalties provided for in this Chapter nor the rights of policyholders, claimants, creditors, or other third parties.

(n) Controlled insurers and controlling producers who are not in compliance with subsection (e) of this section on October 1, 1991, have until December 1, 1991, to come into compliance and shall comply with subsection (i) of this section beginning with all policies written or renewed on or after December 1, 1991. (1991, c. 681, s. 28; c. 720, s. 92.)

§ 58-3-167. Applicability of acts of the General Assembly to health benefit plans.

(a) As used in this section:

(1) "Health benefit plan" means an accident and health insurance policy or certificate; a nonprofit hospital or medical service corporation contract; a health maintenance organization subscriber contract; a plan provided by a multiple employer welfare arrangement; or a plan provided by another benefit arrangement, to the extent permitted by the Employee Retirement Income Security Act of 1974, as amended, or by any waiver of or other exception to that act provided under federal law or regulation. "Health benefit plan" does not mean any plan implemented or administered by the North Carolina or United States Department of Health and Human Services, or any successor agency, or its representatives. "Health benefit plan" does not mean any of the following kinds of insurance:

a. Accident.
b. Credit.
c. Disability income.
d. Long-term or nursing home care.
e. Medicare supplement.
f. Specified disease.
g. Dental or vision.
h. Coverage issued as a supplement to liability insurance.
i. Workers' compensation.
j. Medical payments under automobile or homeowners.
k. Hospital income or indemnity.
l. Insurance under which benefits are payable with or without regard to fault and that is statutorily required to be contained in any liability policy or equivalent self-insurance.
m. Short-term limited duration health insurance policies as defined in Part 144 of Title 45 of the Code of Federal Regulations.

(2) "Insurer" includes an insurance company subject to this Chapter, a service corporation organized under Article 65 of this Chapter, a health maintenance organization organized under Article 67 of this Chapter, and a multiple employer welfare arrangement subject to Article 49 of this Chapter.

(b) Whenever a law is enacted by the General Assembly on or after October 1, 1999 that applies to a health benefit plan, the term "health benefit plan" shall be defined for purposes of that law as provided in subsection (a) of this section unless that law provides a different definition or otherwise expressly provides that the definition in this section is not applicable.

(c) Whenever a law is enacted by the General Assembly that applies to health benefit plans that are delivered, issued for delivery, or renewed on and after a certain date, the renewal of a health benefit plan is presumed to occur on each anniversary of the date on which coverage was first effective on the person or persons covered by the health benefit plan. (1999-294, s. 5; 1999-456, s. 16.)

§ 58-3-168. Coverage for postmastectomy inpatient care.

(a) Every entity providing a health benefit plan that provides coverage for mastectomy, including coverage for postmastectomy inpatient care, shall ensure that the decision whether to discharge the patient following mastectomy is made by the attending physician in consultation with the patient, and shall further ensure that the length of postmastectomy hospital stay is based on the unique characteristics of each patient taking into consideration the health and medical history of the patient.

(b) As used in this section, "health benefit plans" means accident and health insurance policies or certificates; nonprofit hospital or medical service corporation contracts; health, hospital, or medical service corporation plan contracts; health maintenance organization (HMO) subscriber contracts; and plans provided by a MEWA or plans provided by other benefit arrangements, to the extent permitted by ERISA.

(c) As used in this section, "mastectomy" means the surgical removal of all or part of a breast as a result of breast cancer or breast disease. (1997-440, s. 1.)

Editor's Note. — Session Laws 1997-440, s. 1, enacted as G.S. 58-3-171.1, was codified as this section at the direction of the Revisor of Statutes.

§ 58-3-169. Required coverage for minimum hospital stay following birth.

(a) Definitions. — As used in this section:
  (1) "Attending providers" includes:
    a. The obstetrician-gynecologists, pediatricians, family physicians, and other physicians primarily responsible for the care of a mother and newborn; and
    b. The nurse midwives and nurse practitioners primarily responsible for the care of a mother and her newborn child in accordance with State licensure and certification laws.
  (2) "Health benefit plan" means an accident and health insurance policy or certificate; a nonprofit hospital or medical service corporation contract; a health maintenance organization subscriber contract; a plan provided by a multiple employer welfare arrangement; or a plan provided by another benefit arrangement, to the extent permitted by the Employee Retirement Income Security Act of 1974, as amended, or by any waiver of or other exception to that Act provided under federal law or regulation. "Health benefit plan" does not mean any of the following kinds of insurance:
    a. Accident,
    b. Credit,

  c. Disability income,

  d. Long-term or nursing home care,

  e. Medicare supplement,

  f. Specified disease,

  g. Dental or vision,

  h. Coverage issued as a supplement to liability insurance,

  i. Workers' compensation,

  j. Medical payments under automobile or homeowners, and

  k. Insurance under which benefits are payable with or without regard to fault and that is statutorily required to be contained in any liability policy or equivalent self-insurance.

  l. Hospital income or indemnity.

 (3) "Insurer" means an insurance company subject to this Chapter, a service corporation organized under Article 65 of this Chapter, a health maintenance organization organized under Article 67 of this Chapter, and a multiple employer welfare arrangement subject to Article 49 of this Chapter.

(b) In General. — Except as provided in subsection (c) of this section, an insurer that provides a health benefit plan that contains maternity benefits, including benefits for childbirth, shall ensure that coverage is provided with respect to a mother who is a participant, beneficiary, or policyholder under the plan and her newborn child for a minimum of 48 hours of inpatient length of stay following a normal vaginal delivery, and a minimum of 96 hours of inpatient length of stay following a cesarean section, without requiring the attending provider to obtain authorization from the insurer or its representative.

(c) Exception. — Notwithstanding subsection (b) of this section, an insurer is not required to provide coverage for postdelivery inpatient length of stay for a mother who is a participant, beneficiary, or policyholder under the insurer's health benefit plan and her newborn child for the period referred to in subsection (b) of this section if:

 (1) A decision to discharge the mother and her newborn child before the expiration of the period is made by the attending provider in consultation with the mother; and

 (2) The health benefit plan provides coverage for postdelivery follow-up care as described in subsections (d) and (e) of this section.

(d) Postdelivery Follow-Up Care. — In the case of a decision to discharge a mother and her newborn child from the inpatient setting before the expiration of 48 hours following a normal vaginal delivery or 96 hours following a cesarean section, the health benefit plan shall provide coverage for timely postdelivery care. This health care shall be provided to a mother and her newborn child by a registered nurse, physician, nurse practitioner, nurse midwife, or physician assistant experienced in maternal and child health in:

 (1) The home, a provider's office, a hospital, a birthing center, an intermediate care facility, a federally qualified health center, a federally qualified rural health clinic, or a State health department maternity clinic; or

 (2) Another setting determined appropriate under federal regulations promulgated under Title VI of Public Law 104-204.

The attending provider in consultation with the mother shall decide the most appropriate location for follow-up care.

(e) Timely Care. — As used in subsection (d) of this section, "timely postdelivery care" means health care that is provided:

 (1) Following the discharge of a mother and her newborn child from the inpatient setting; and

 (2) In a manner that meets the health care needs of the mother and her newborn child, that provides for the appropriate monitoring of the

conditions of the mother and child, and that occurs not later than the 72-hour period immediately following discharge.

(f) Prohibitions. — An insurer shall not:

    (1) Deny enrollment, renewal, or continued coverage with respect to its health benefit plan to a mother and her newborn child who are participants, beneficiaries, or policyholders, based on compliance with this section;

    (2) Provide monetary payments or rebates to mothers to encourage the mothers to request less than the minimum coverage required under this section;

    (3) Penalize or otherwise reduce or limit the reimbursement of an attending provider because the provider provided treatment to an individual policyholder, participant, or beneficiary in accordance with this section; or

    (4) Provide monetary or other incentives to an attending provider to induce the provider to provide treatment to an individual policyholder, participant, or beneficiary in a manner inconsistent with this section.

(g) Effect on Mother. — Nothing in this section requires that a mother who is a participant, beneficiary, or policyholder covered under this section:

    (1) Give birth in a hospital; or

    (2) Stay in the hospital for a fixed period of time following the birth of her child.

(h) Level and Type of Reimbursements. — Nothing in this section prevents an insurer from negotiating the level and type of reimbursement with an attending provider for care provided in accordance with this section. (1997-259, s. 19.)

Legal Periodicals. — For article, "Drive-Through Deliveries: Is 'Consumer Protection' Just What the Doctor Ordered?" see 78 N.C.L. Rev. 5 (1999).

§ 58-3-170. Requirements for maternity coverage.

(a) Every entity providing a health benefit plan that provides maternity coverage in this State shall provide benefits for the necessary care and treatment related to maternity that are no less favorable than benefits for physical illness generally.

(a1) Repealed by Session Laws 1997-259, s. 20.

(b) As used in this section, "health benefit plans" means accident and health insurance policies or certificates; nonprofit hospital or medical service corporation contracts; health, hospital, or medical service corporation plan contracts; health maintenance organization (HMO) subscriber contracts; and plans provided by a MEWA or plans provided by other benefit arrangements, to the extent permitted by ERISA. (1993, c. 506, s. 2; 1995, c. 517, s. 3.1; 1997-259, s. 20.)

Editor's Note. — The subsection (a1) designation was assigned at the direction of the Revisor of Statutes, the designation in Session Laws 1995, c. 517, s. 3.1 having been (b).

§ 58-3-171. Uniform claim forms.

(a) All claims submitted by health care providers to health benefit plans shall be submitted on a uniform form or format that shall be developed by the Department and approved by the Commissioner. Additional information beyond that contained on the uniform form or format may be collected subject to rules adopted by the Commissioner. This section applies to the submission of claims in writing and by electronic means.

(b) After consultation with the North Carolina Industrial Commission, the Commissioner may include workers' compensation insurance policies as "health benefit plans" for the purpose of administering the provisions of this section.

(c) For purposes of this section, "health benefit plans" means accident and health insurance policies or certificates; nonprofit hospital or medical service corporation contracts; health maintenance organization (HMO) subscriber contracts and other plans provided by managed-care organizations; plans provided by a MEWA or plans provided by other benefit arrangements, to the extent permitted by ERISA; the Teachers' and State Employees' Comprehensive Major Medical Plan; and medical payment coverages under homeowners and automobile insurance policies. (1993, c. 529, s. 4.2.)

§ 58-3-172. Notice of claim denied.

(a) For all claims denied for health care provider services under health benefit plans, written notification of the denied claim shall be given to the insured and to the health care provider submitting the claim if the health care provider would otherwise be eligible for payment. This subsection does not apply to insurers subject to G.S. 58-3-225.

(b) For purposes of this section, "health benefit plans" means accident and health insurance policies or certificates; nonprofit hospital or medical service corporation contracts; health, hospital, or medical service corporation plan contracts; health maintenance organization (HMO) subscriber contracts and other plans provided by managed-care organizations; plans provided by a MEWA or plans provided by other benefit arrangements, to the extent permitted by ERISA; and the Teachers' and State Employees' Comprehensive Major Medical Plan. (1993, c. 529, s. 4.2; 1993 (Reg. Sess., 1994), c. 678, s. 6; 2000-162, s. 4(c).)

§ 58-3-173: Repealed by Session Laws 1997-259, s. 24.

§ 58-3-174. Coverage for bone mass measurement for diagnosis and evaluation of osteoporosis or low bone mass.

(a) Every entity providing a health benefit plan shall provide coverage for a qualified individual for scientifically proven and approved bone mass measurement for the diagnosis and evaluation of osteoporosis or low bone mass. The same deductibles, coinsurance, and other limitations as apply to similar services covered under the plan shall apply to coverage for bone mass measurement.

(b) A health benefit plan may provide that bone mass measurement will be covered if at least 23 months have elapsed since the last bone mass measurement was performed, except that a plan must provide coverage for follow-up bone mass measurement performed more frequently than every 23 months if the follow-up measurement is medically necessary. Conditions under which more frequent bone mass measurement coverage may be medically necessary include, but are not limited to:

    (1) Monitoring beneficiaries on long-term glucocorticoid therapy of more than three months.

    (2) Allowing for a central bone mass measurement to determine the effectiveness of adding an additional treatment regimen for a quali-

fied individual who is proven to have low bone mass so long as the bone mass measurement is performed 12 to 18 months from the start date of the additional regimen.

(c) Nothing in this section shall be construed to require health benefit plans to cover screening for nonqualified individuals.

(d) As used in this section, the term:

(1) "Bone mass measurement" means a scientifically proven radiologic, radioisotopic, or other procedure performed on a qualified individual to identify bone mass or detect bone loss for the purpose of initiating or modifying treatment.

(2) "Health benefit plan" means an accident and health insurance policy or certificate; a nonprofit hospital or medical service corporation contract; a health maintenance organization subscriber contract; a plan provided by a multiple employer welfare arrangement; or a plan provided by another benefit arrangement, to the extent permitted by the Employee Retirement Income Security Act of 1974, as amended, or by any waiver of or other exception to that act provided under federal law or regulation. "Health benefit plan" does not mean any plan implemented or administered by the North Carolina Department of Health and Human Services or the United States Department of Health and Human Services, or any successor agency, or its representatives. "Health benefit plan" also does not mean any of the following kinds of insurance:

a. Accident

b. Credit

c. Disability income

d. Long-term care or nursing home care

e. Medicare supplement

f. Specified disease

g. Dental or vision

h. Short-term limited duration coverage

i. Coverage issued as a supplement to liability insurance

j. Workers' compensation

k. Medical payments under automobile or homeowners

l. Hospital income or indemnity

m. Insurance under which benefits are payable with or without regard to fault and that is statutorily required to be contained in any liability policy or equivalent self-insurance.

(3) "Insurer" includes an insurance company subject to this Chapter, a service corporation organized under Article 65 of this Chapter, a health maintenance organization organized under Article 67 of this Chapter, and a multiple employer welfare arrangement subject to Article 49 of this Chapter.

(4) "Qualified individual" means any one or more of the following:

a. An individual who is estrogen-deficient and at clinical risk of osteoporosis or low bone mass.

b. An individual with radiographic osteopenia anywhere in the skeleton.

c. An individual who is receiving long-term glucocorticoid (steroid) therapy.

d. An individual with primary hyperparathyroidism.

e. An individual who is being monitored to assess the response to or efficacy of commonly accepted osteoporosis drug therapies.

f. An individual who has a history of low-trauma fractures.

g. An individual with other conditions or on medical therapies known to cause osteoporosis or low bone mass. (1999-197, s. 1.)

Editor's Note. — Session Laws 1999-197, s. 1, made this section effective January 1, 2000 and applicable to health benefit plans that are delivered, issued for delivery, or renewed on and after January 1, 2000. For purposes of this act, renewal of a health benefit plan is presumed to occur on each anniversary of the date on which coverage was first effective on the person or persons covered by the health benefit plan.

§ 58-3-175. Direct payment to government agencies.

(a) As used in this section, "health benefit plan" has the same meaning as in G.S. 58-50-110(11) and includes the Teachers' and State Employees' Comprehensive Major Medical Plan.

(b) Every entity providing or administering a health benefit plan covering persons in this State shall make payment for health care services covered by the health benefit plan that are provided by any State, county, or city agency, directly to the agency providing the services.

(c) This section does not apply to the extent the agency providing the services has been paid for the services by or on behalf of the person receiving the services.

(d) Nothing in this section shall require any entity providing or administering a health benefit plan covering persons in this State to pay any agency directly:

(1) If the agency is outside of the health benefit plan's service area;

(2) If the entity operates a program by which it only pays the health care provider directly upon the acceptance of certain rates and the agency does not accept said rates; or

(3) If the entity operates a program by which it provides, authorizes, or arranges for a covered person to receive health care from a designated provider or refers the covered person to a designated provider, and the agency is not a designated provider. (1993, c. 41, s. 1.)

Editor's Note. — The number of this section was assigned by the Revisor of Statutes, the number in Session Laws 1993, c. 41, s. 1 having been 58-3-170.

§ 58-3-176. Treatment discussions not limited.

(a) An insurer shall not limit either of the following:

(1) The participating plan provider's ability to discuss with an enrollee the clinical treatment options medically available, the risks associated with the treatments, or a recommended course of treatment.

(2) The participating plan provider's professional obligations to patients as specified under the provider's professional license.

(b) Nothing in this section shall be construed to expand or revise the scope of benefits covered by a health benefit plan.

(c) As used in this section:

(1) "Health benefit plan" means any of the following if written by an insurer: an accident and health insurance policy or certificate; a nonprofit hospital or medical service corporation contract; a health maintenance organization subscriber contract; or a plan provided by a multiple employer welfare arrangement. "Health benefit plan" does not mean any plan implemented or administered through the Department of Health and Human Services or its representatives. "Health benefit plan" also does not mean any of the following kinds of insurance:

a. Accident.

b. Credit.

c. Disability income.

d. Long-term or nursing home care.

      e. Medicare supplement.
      f. Specified disease.
      g. Dental or vision.
      h. Coverage issued as a supplement to liability insurance.
      i. Workers' compensation.
      j. Medical payments under automobile or homeowners insurance.
      k. Hospital income or indemnity.
      l. Insurance under which benefits are payable with or without regard to fault and that is statutorily required to be contained in any liability policy or equivalent self-insurance.

  (2) "Insurer" means an entity that writes a health benefit plan and that is an insurance company subject to this Chapter, a service corporation under Article 65 of this Chapter, a health maintenance organization under Article 67 of this Chapter, or a multiple employer welfare arrangement under Article 49 of this Chapter. (1997-443, s. 11A.122; 1997-474, s. 1.)

§ 58-3-177. Uniform prescription drug identification cards.

  (a) Every health benefit plan that provides coverage for prescription drugs or devices and that issues a prescription drug card, shall issue to its insureds a uniform prescription drug identification card. The uniform prescription drug identification card shall contain the information listed in subdivisions (1) through (7) of this subsection in the following order beginning at the top left margin of the card:

  (1) The health benefit plan's name and/or logo.
  (2) The American National Standards Institute assigned Issuer Identification Number.
  (3) The processor control number.
  (4) The insured's group number.
  (5) The health benefit plan's card issuer identifier.
  (6) The insured's identification number.
  (7) The insured's name.

  (b) In addition to the information required under subsection (a), the uniform prescription drug card shall contain, in one of the lower-most elements on the back side of the card, the following information:

  (1) The health benefit plan's claims submission name and address.
  (2) The health benefit plan's help desk telephone number and name.

Nothing in this section shall require a health benefit plan to violate a contractual agreement, service mark agreement, or trademark agreement.

  (c) A new uniform prescription drug identification card as required under subsection (a) of this section shall be issued annually by a health benefit plan if there has been any change in the insured's coverage in the previous 12 months. A change in the insured's coverage shall include, but is not limited to, the addition or deletion of a dependent of the insured covered by a health benefit plan.

  (d) Not later than January 1, 2003, the uniform prescription drug identification card provided under subsection (a) of this section shall contain one of the following mediums capable of the processing or adjudicating of a claim through electronic verification:

  (1) A magnetic strip.
  (2) A bar code.
  (3) Any new technology available that is capable of processing or adjudicating a claim by electronic verification.

  (e) As used in this section, "health benefit plan" means an accident and health insurance policy or certificate; a nonprofit hospital or medical service corporation contract; a health maintenance organization subscriber contract; a plan provided by a multiple employer welfare arrangement; or a plan provided by another benefit arrangement, to the extent permitted by the Employee Retirement Income Security Act of 1974, as amended, or by any waiver of or other exception to that Act provided under federal law or regulation. "Health benefit plan" does not mean any of the following kinds of insurance:

    (1) Accident.

    (2) Credit.

    (3) Disability income.

    (4) Long-term or nursing home care.

    (5) Medicare supplement.

    (6) Specified disease.

    (7) Dental or vision.

    (8) Coverage issued as a supplement to liability insurance.

    (9) Workers' compensation.

    (10) Medical payments under automobile or homeowners.

    (11) Insurance under which benefits are payable with or without regard to fault and that is statutorily required to be contained in any liability policy or equivalent self-insurance.

    (12) Hospital income or indemnity.

(f) This section shall not apply to an entity that has its own facility and employs or contracts with physicians, pharmacists, nurses, and other health care personnel, to the extent that the entity dispenses prescription drugs or devices from its own pharmacies to its employees and to enrollees of its health benefit plan. This section does not apply to a health benefit plan that issues a single identification card to its insureds for all services covered under the plan. (1999-343, s. 1.)

Editor's Note. — Session Laws 1999-343, s. 2, makes this section effective July 22, 1999, and, except as provided in G.S. 58-3-177(c) (now subsection (d)) as enacted in s. 1, applicable to health benefit plans that are delivered, issued for delivery, or renewed on and after July 1, 2000. For purposes of this act, renewal of a health benefit policy, contract, or plan is presumed to occur on each anniversary of the date on which coverage was first effective on the person or persons covered by the health benefit plan.

    Subsections (b) to (f) were designated as such at the direction of the Revisor of Statutes, the designations in Session Laws 1999-343, s. 1 having been (a1) to (e).

§ 58-3-178. Coverage for prescription contraceptive drugs or devices and for outpatient contraceptive services; exemption for religious employers.

(a) Except as provided in subsection (e) of this section, every insurer providing a health benefit plan that provides coverage for prescription drugs or devices shall provide coverage for prescription contraceptive drugs or devices. Coverage shall include coverage for the insertion or removal of and any medically necessary examination associated with the use of the prescribed contraceptive drug or device. Except as otherwise provided in this subsection, the same deductibles, coinsurance, and other limitations as apply to prescription drugs or devices covered under the health benefit plan shall apply to coverage for prescribed contraceptive drugs or devices. A health benefit plan may require that the total coinsurance, based on the useful life of the drug or device, be paid in advance for those drugs or devices that are inserted or prescribed and do not have to be refilled on a periodic basis.

(b) Every insurer providing a health benefit plan that provides coverage for outpatient services provided by a health care professional shall provide coverage for outpatient contraceptive services. The same deductibles, coinsurance, and other limitations as apply to outpatient services covered under the health benefit plan shall apply to coverage for outpatient contraceptive services.

(c) As used in this section, the term:

(1) "Health benefit plan" means an accident and health insurance policy or certificate; a nonprofit hospital or medical service corporation contract; a health maintenance organization subscriber contract; a plan provided by a multiple employer welfare arrangement; or a plan provided by another benefit arrangement, to the extent permitted by the Employee Retirement Income Security Act of 1974, as amended, or by any waiver of or other exception to that Act provided under federal law or regulation. "Health benefit plan" does not mean any plan implemented or administered by the North Carolina Department of Health and Human Services or the United States Department of Health and Human Services, or any successor agency, or its representatives. "Health benefit plan" also does not mean any of the following kinds of insurance:

   a. Accident.

   b. Credit.

   c. Disability income.

   d. Long-term care or nursing home care.

   e. Medicare supplement.

   f. Specified disease.

   g. Dental or vision.

   h. Coverage issued as a supplement to liability insurance.

   i. Workers' compensation.

   j. Medical payments under automobile or homeowners.

   k. Hospital income or indemnity.

   l. Insurance under which benefits are payable with or without regard to fault and that is statutorily required to be contained in any liability policy or equivalent self-insurance.

   m. Short-term limited duration health insurance policies as defined in Part 144 of Title 45 of the Code of Federal Regulations.

(2) "Insurer" includes an insurance company subject to this Chapter, a service corporation organized under Article 65 of this Chapter, a health maintenance organization organized under Article 67 of this Chapter, and a multiple employer welfare arrangement subject to Article 49 of this Chapter.

(3) "Outpatient contraceptive services" means consultations, examinations, procedures, and medical services provided on an outpatient basis and related to the use of contraceptive methods to prevent pregnancy.

(4) "Prescribed contraceptive drugs or devices" means drugs or devices that prevent pregnancy and that are approved by the United States Food and Drug Administration for use as contraceptives and obtained under a prescription written by a health care provider authorized to prescribe medications under the laws of this State. Prescription drugs or devices required to be covered under this section shall not include:

   a. The prescription drug known as "RU-486" or any "equivalent drug product" as defined in G.S. 90-85.27(1).

   b. The prescription drug marketed under the name "Preven" or any "equivalent drug product" as defined in G.S. 90-85.27(1).

(d) A health benefit plan subject to this section shall not do any of the following:

(1) Deny eligibility or continued eligibility to enroll or to renew coverage under the terms of the health benefit plan, solely for the purpose of avoiding the requirements of this section.

    (2) Provide monetary payments or rebates to an individual participant or beneficiary to encourage the individual participant or beneficiary to accept less than the minimum protections available under this section.

    (3) Penalize or otherwise reduce or limit the reimbursement of an attending provider because the provider prescribed contraceptive drugs or devices, or provided contraceptive services in accordance with this section.

    (4) Provide incentives, monetary or otherwise, to an attending provider to induce the provider to withhold from an individual participant or beneficiary contraceptive drugs, devices, or services.

  (e) A religious employer may request an insurer providing a health benefit plan to provide to the religious employer a health benefit plan that excludes coverage for prescription contraceptive drugs or devices that are contrary to the employer's religious tenets. Upon request, the insurer shall provide the requested health benefit plan. An insurer providing a health benefit plan requested by a religious employer pursuant to this section shall provide written notice to each person covered under the health benefit plan that prescription contraceptive drugs or devices are excluded from coverage pursuant to this section at the request of the employer. The notice shall appear, in not less than 10-point type, in the health benefit plan, application, and sales brochure for the health benefit plan. Nothing in this subsection authorizes a health benefit plan to exclude coverage for prescription drugs ordered by a health care provider with prescriptive authority for reasons other than contraceptive purposes, or for prescription contraception that is necessary to preserve the life or health of a person covered under the plan. As used in this subsection, the term "religious employer" means an entity for which all of the following are true:

    (1) The entity is organized and operated for religious purposes and is tax exempt under section 501(c)(3) of the U.S. Internal Revenue Code.

    (2) The inculcation of religious values is one of the primary purposes of the entity.

    (3) The entity employs primarily persons who share the religious tenets of the entity. (1999-231, s. 1; 1999-456, s. 15(a).)

Editor's Note. — Session Laws 1999-231, s. 3, contains a severability clause.

  Session Laws 1999-231, s. 4, made this section effective January 1, 2000 and applicable to health benefit plans that are delivered, issued for delivery, or renewed on and after that date. For purposes of this act, renewal of a health benefit policy, contract, or plan is presumed to occur on each anniversary of the date on which coverage was first effective on the person or persons covered by the health benefit plan.

  Legal Periodicals. — For note, "Controversy Aroused: North Carolina Mandates Insurance Coverage of Contraceptives in the Wake of Viagra," see 79 N.C.L. Rev. 779 (2001).

§ 58-3-179. Coverage for colorectal cancer screening.

  (a) Every health benefit plan, as defined in G.S. 58-3-167, shall provide coverage for colorectal cancer examinations and laboratory tests for cancer, in accordance with the most recently published American Cancer Society guidelines or guidelines adopted by the North Carolina Advisory Committee on Cancer Coordination and Control for colorectal cancer screening, for any nonsymptomatic covered individual who is:

    (1) At least 50 years of age, or

    (2) Less than 50 years of age and at high risk for colorectal cancer according to the most recently published colorectal cancer screening guidelines of the American Cancer Society or guidelines adopted by

the North Carolina Advisory Committee on Cancer Coordination and Control.

The same deductibles, coinsurance, and other limitations as apply to similar services covered under the plan apply to coverage for colorectal examinations and laboratory tests required to be covered under this section.

(b) Reserved for future codification purposes. (2001-116, s. 1.)

Editor's Note. — Session Laws 2001-116, s. 3, which enacted this section, provided: "This act becomes effective January 1, 2002, and applies to all health benefit plans that are delivered, issued for delivery, or renewed on and after that date. For the purposes of this act, renewal of a health benefit plan is presumed to occur on each anniversary of the date on which coverage was first effective on the person or persons covered by the health benefit plan."

§ 58-3-180. Motor vehicle repairs; selection by claimant.

(a) A policy covering damage to a motor vehicle shall allow the claimant to select the repair service or source for the repair of the damage.

(b) The amount determined by the insurer to be payable under a policy covering damage to a motor vehicle shall be paid regardless of the repair service or source selected by the claimant.

(b1) No insurer or insurer representative shall recommend the use of a particular motor vehicle repair service without clearly informing the claimant that (i) the claimant is under no obligation to use the recommended repair service, (ii) the claimant may use the repair service of the claimant's choice, (iii) the amount determined by the insurer to be payable under the policy will be paid regardless of whether or not the claimant uses the recommended repair service, and (iv) that the insurer or insurer representative has, at the time the recommendations are made, a financial interest in the recommended motor vehicle repair service. No insurer shall require that the insured or claimant must have a damaged vehicle repaired at an insurer-owned motor vehicle repair service.

(b2) The provisions of subsection (b1) of this section shall be included in nonfleet private passenger motor vehicle insurance policy forms promulgated by the Bureau and approved by the Commissioner.

(c) Any person who violates this section is subject to the applicable provisions of G.S. 58-2-70 and G.S. 58-33-46, provided that the maximum civil penalty that can be assessed under G.S. 58-2-70(d) for a violation of this section is two thousand dollars ($2,000).

(d) As used in this section, "insurer representative" includes an insurance agent, limited representative, broker, adjuster, and appraiser. (1993, c. 525, s. 2; 2001-203, s. 26; 2001-451, s. 1; 2003-395, s. 1.)

Editor's Note. — The number of this section was assigned by the Revisor of Statutes, the number in Session Laws 1993, c. 506, s. 2 having been 58-3-170.

Session Laws 2001-203, s. 31, contains a severability clause.

Effect of Amendments. — Session Laws 2001-203, s. 26, effective July 1, 2002, substituted "G.S. 58-33-46" for "G.S. 58-33-45" in subsection (c).

Session Laws 2001-451, s. 1, effective April 1, 2002, and applicable to policies issued or renewed on and after that date, in this section as amended by Session Laws 2001-203, s. 26, added subsections (b1), (b2) and (d).

Session Laws 2003-395, s. 1, effective August 7, 2003, in subsection (b1), added clause (iv), and made minor stylistic and punctuation changes.

§ 58-3-185. Lien created for payment of past-due child support obligations.

(a) In the event that the Department of Health and Human Services or any other obligee, as defined in G.S. 110-129, provides written notification to an insurance company authorized to issue policies of insurance pursuant to this Chapter that a claimant or beneficiary under a contract of insurance owes past-due child support and accompanies this information with a certified copy of the court order ordering support together with proof that the claimant or beneficiary is past due in meeting this obligation, there is created a lien upon any insurance proceeds in favor of the Department or obligee. This section shall apply only in those instances in which there is a nonrecurring payment of a lump-sum amount equal to or in excess of three thousand dollars ($3,000) or periodic payments with an aggregate amount that equals or exceeds three thousand dollars ($3,000).

(b) Liens arising under this section shall be subordinate to liens upon insurance proceeds for personal injuries arising under Article 9 of Chapter 44 of the General Statutes and valid health care provider claims covered by health benefit plans as defined in G.S. 58-3-172. As used in this section, the term health benefit plans does not include disability income insurance. (1995, c. 538, s. 6(a); 1995 (Reg. Sess., 1996), c. 674, ss. 1, 2; 1997-443, s. 11A.118(a).)

Editor's Note. — Session Laws 1995, c. 485, s. 6(a) was codified as this section at the direction of the Revisor of Statutes, the number in the 1995 act having been G.S. 44-49.1.

§ 58-3-190. Coverage required for emergency care.

(a) Every insurer shall provide coverage for emergency services to the extent necessary to screen and to stabilize the person covered under the plan and shall not require prior authorization of the services if a prudent layperson acting reasonably would have believed that an emergency medical condition existed. Payment of claims for emergency services shall be based on the retrospective review of the presenting history and symptoms of the covered person.

(b) With respect to emergency services provided by a health care provider who is not under contract with the insurer, the services shall be covered if:

    (1) A prudent layperson acting reasonably would have believed that a delay would worsen the emergency, or

    (2) The covered person did not seek services from a provider under contract with the insurer because of circumstances beyond the control of the covered person.

(c) An insurer that has given prior authorization for emergency services shall cover the services and shall not retract the authorization after the services have been provided unless the authorization was based on a material misrepresentation about the covered person's health condition made by the provider of the emergency services or the covered person.

(d) Coverage of emergency services shall be subject to coinsurance, co-payments, and deductibles applicable under the health benefit plan. An insurer shall not impose cost-sharing for emergency services provided under this section that differs from the cost-sharing that would have been imposed if the physician or provider furnishing the services were a provider contracting with the insurer.

(e) Both the emergency department and the insurer shall make a good faith effort to communicate with each other in a timely fashion to expedite postevaluation or poststabilization services in order to avoid material deterioration of the covered person's condition within a reasonable clinical confidence, or with respect to a pregnant woman, to avoid material deterioration of the condition of the unborn child within a reasonable clinical confidence.

(f) Insurers shall provide information to their covered persons on all of the following:

(1) Coverage of emergency medical services.

(2) The appropriate use of emergency services, including the use of the "911" system and other telephone access systems utilized to access prehospital emergency services.

(3) Any cost-sharing provisions for emergency medical services.

(4) The process and procedures for obtaining emergency services, so that covered persons are familiar with the location of in-plan emergency departments and with the location and availability of other in-plan settings at which covered persons may receive medical care.

(g) As used in this section, the term:

(1) "Emergency medical condition" means a medical condition manifesting itself by acute symptoms of sufficient severity, including, but not limited to, severe pain, or by acute symptoms developing from a chronic medical condition that would lead a prudent layperson, possessing an average knowledge of health and medicine, to reasonably expect the absence of immediate medical attention to result in any of the following:

a. Placing the health of an individual, or with respect to a pregnant woman, the health of the woman or her unborn child, in serious jeopardy.

b. Serious impairment to bodily functions.

c. Serious dysfunction of any bodily organ or part.

(2) "Emergency services" means health care items and services furnished or required to screen for or treat an emergency medical condition until the condition is stabilized, including prehospital care and ancillary services routinely available to the emergency department.

(3) "Health benefit plan" means any of the following if written by an insurer: an accident and health insurance policy or certificate; a nonprofit hospital or medical service corporation contract; a health maintenance organization subscriber contract; or a plan provided by a multiple employer welfare arrangement. "Health benefit plan" does not mean any plan implemented or administered through the Department of Health and Human Services or its representatives. "Health benefit plan" also does not mean any of the following kinds of insurance:

a. Accident.

b. Credit.

c. Disability income.

d. Long-term or nursing home care.

e. Medicare supplement.

f. Specified disease.

g. Dental or vision.

h. Coverage issued as a supplement to liability insurance.

i. Workers' compensation.

j. Medical payments under automobile or homeowners insurance.

k. Hospital income or indemnity.

l. Insurance under which benefits are payable with or without regard to fault and that is statutorily required to be contained in any liability policy or equivalent self-insurance.

(4) "Insurer" means an entity that writes a health benefit plan and that is an insurance company subject to this Chapter, a service corporation under Article 65 of this Chapter, a health maintenance organization

under Article 67 of this Chapter, or a multiple employer welfare arrangement under Article 49 of this Chapter.

(5) "To stabilize" means to provide medical care that is appropriate to prevent a material deterioration of the person's condition, within reasonable medical probability, in accordance with the HCFA (Health Care Financing Administration) interpretative guidelines, policies and regulations pertaining to responsibilities of hospitals in emergency cases (as provided under the Emergency Medical Treatment and Labor Act, section 1867 of the Social Security Act, 42 U.S.C.S. 1395dd), including medically necessary services and supplies to maintain stabilization until the person is transferred. (1997-443, s. 11A.122; 1997-474, s. 2)

Legal Periodicals. — For 1997 legislative survey, see 20 Campbell L. Rev. 469.

§ 58-3-191. Managed care reporting and disclosure requirements.

(a) Each health benefit plan shall annually, on or before the first day of March of each year, file in the office of the Commissioner the following information for the previous calendar year:

(1) The number of and reasons for grievances received from plan participants regarding medical treatment. The report shall include the number of covered lives, total number of grievances categorized by reason for the grievance, the number of grievances referred to the second level grievance review, the number of grievances resolved at each level and their resolution, and a description of the actions that are being taken to correct the problems that have been identified through grievances received. Every health benefit plan shall file with the Commissioner, as part of its annual grievance report, a certificate of compliance stating that the carrier has established and follows, for each of its lines of business, grievance procedures that comply with G.S. 58-50-62.

(2) The number of participants and groups who terminated coverage under the plan for any reason. The report shall include the number of participants who terminated coverage because the group contract under which they were covered was terminated, the number of participants who terminated coverage for reasons other than the termination of the group under which they were enrolled, and the number of group contracts terminated.

(3) The number of provider contracts that were terminated and the reasons for termination. This information shall include the number of providers leaving the plan and the number of new providers. The report shall show voluntary and involuntary terminations separately.

(4) Data relating to the utilization, quality, availability, and accessibility of services. The report shall include the following:

a. Information on the health benefit plan's program to determine the level of network availability, as measured by the numbers and types of network providers, required to provide covered services to covered persons. This information shall include the plan's methodology for:

1. Establishing performance targets for the numbers and types of providers by specialty, area of practice, or facility type, for each of the following categories: primary care physicians, specialty care physicians, nonphysician health care providers, hospitals, and nonhospital health care facilities.

    2. Determining when changes in plan membership will necessitate changes in the provider network.

The report shall also include: the availability performance targets for the previous and current years; the numbers and types of providers currently participating in the health benefit plan's provider network; and an evaluation of actual plan performance against performance targets.

    b. The health benefit plan's method for arranging or providing health care services from nonnetwork providers, both within and outside of its service area, when network providers are not available to provide covered services.

    c. Information on the health benefit plan's program to determine the level of provider network accessibility necessary to serve its membership. This information shall include the health benefit plan's methodology for establishing performance targets for member access to covered services from primary care physicians, specialty care physicians, nonphysician health care providers, hospitals, and nonhospital health care facilities. The methodology shall establish targets for:

      1. The proximity of network providers to members, as measured by member driving distance, to access primary care, specialty care, hospital-based services, and services of nonhospital facilities.

      2. Expected waiting time for appointments for urgent care, acute care, specialty care, and routine services for prevention and wellness.

The report shall also include: the accessibility performance targets for the previous and current years; data on actual overall accessibility as measured by driving distance and average appointment waiting time; and an evaluation of actual plan performance against performance targets. Measures of actual accessibility may be developed using scientifically valid random sample techniques.

    d. A statement of the health benefit plan's methods and standards for determining whether in-network services are reasonably available and accessible to a covered person, for the purpose of determining whether a covered person should receive the in-network level of coverage for services received from a nonnetwork provider.

    e. A description of the health benefit plan's program to monitor the adequacy of its network availability and accessibility methodologies and performance targets, plan performance, and network provider performance.

    f. A summary of the health benefit plan's utilization review program activities for the previous calendar year. The report shall include the number of: each type of utilization review performed, noncertifications for each type of review, each type of review appealed, and appeals settled in favor of covered persons. The report shall be accompanied by a certification from the carrier that it has established and follows procedures that comply with G.S. 58-50-61.

  (5) Aggregate financial compensation data, including the percentage of providers paid under a capitation arrangement, discounted fee-for-service or salary, the services included in the capitation payment, and the range of compensation paid by withhold or incentive payments. This information shall be submitted on a form prescribed by the Commissioner.

The name, or group or institutional name, of an individual provider may not be disclosed pursuant to this subsection. No civil liability shall arise from compliance with the provisions of this subsection, provided that the acts or omissions are made in good faith and do not constitute gross negligence, willful or wanton misconduct, or intentional wrongdoing.

(b) Disclosure requirements. — Each health benefit plan shall provide the following applicable information to plan participants and bona fide prospective participants upon request:

    (1) The evidence of coverage (G.S. 58-67-50), subscriber contract (G.S. 58-65-60, 58-65-140), health insurance policy (G.S. 58-51-80, 58-50-125, 58-50-55), or the contract and benefit summary of any other type of health benefit plan;

    (2) An explanation of the utilization review criteria and treatment protocol under which treatments are provided for conditions specified by the prospective participant. This explanation shall be in writing if so requested;

    (3) If denied a recommended treatment, written reasons for the denial and an explanation of the utilization review criteria or treatment protocol upon which the denial was based;

    (4) The plan's formularies, restricted access drugs or devices as defined in G.S. 58-3-221, or prior approval requirements for obtaining prescription drugs, whether a particular drug or therapeutic class of drugs is excluded from its formulary, and the circumstances under which a nonformulary drug may be covered; and

    (5) The plan's procedures and medically based criteria for determining whether a specified procedure, test, or treatment is experimental.

(b1) Effective March 1, 1998, insurers shall make the reports that are required under subsection (a) of this section and that have been filed with the Commissioner available on their business premises and shall provide any insured access to them upon request.

(c) For purposes of this section, "health benefit plan" or "plan" means (i) health maintenance organization (HMO) subscriber contracts and (ii) insurance company or hospital and medical service corporation preferred provider benefit plans as defined in G.S. 58-50-56. (1997-480, s. 1; 1997-519, s. 1.1; 2001-334, s. 2.2; 2001-446, s. 2.1.)

Editor's Note. — Section 58-50-55, referred to in subdivision (b)(1), has been repealed.

Section 58-65-140, referred to in subdivision (b)(1), has been repealed.

This section was enacted as G.S. 58-3-190 by Session Laws 1997-480, s. 1. It was renumbered as 58-3-191 by Session Laws 1997-519, s. 1.1.

Session Laws 2001-446, s. 8 provides: "Nothing in this act obligates the General Assembly to appropriate funds to implement this act."

Session Laws 2001-446, s. 7 is a severability clause.

Effect of Amendments. — Session Laws 2001-446, s. 2.1, effective March 1, 2002, and applicable to health benefit plans that are in effect, delivered, issued for delivery, or renewed on or after that date, substituted "The plan's formularies, restricted access drugs or devices as defined in G.S. 58-3-221, or" for "The plan's restrictive formularies or" at the beginning of subdivision (b)(4).

Legal Periodicals. — For 1997 legislative survey, see 20 Campbell L. Rev. 469.

For comment, "Managed Care Organizations in North Carolina: Tort Liability Theories and Defenses," see 23 N.C. Cent. L.J. 58 (1997).

§ 58-3-200. Miscellaneous insurance and managed care coverage and network provisions.

(a) Definitions. — As used in this section:

    (1) "Health benefit plan" means any of the following if written by an insurer: an accident and health insurance policy or certificate; a

nonprofit hospital or medical service corporation contract; a health maintenance organization subscriber contract; or a plan provided by a multiple employer welfare arrangement. "Health benefit plan" does not mean any plan implemented or administered through the Department of Health and Human Services or its representatives. "Health benefit plan" also does not mean any of the following kinds of insurance:

  a. Accident.
  b. Credit.
  c. Disability income.
  d. Long-term or nursing home care.
  e. Medicare supplement.
  f. Specified disease.
  g. Dental or vision.
  h. Coverage issued as a supplement to liability insurance.
  i. Workers' compensation.
  j. Medical payments under automobile or homeowners insurance.
  k. Hospital income or indemnity.
  l. Insurance under which benefits are payable with or without regard to fault and that is statutorily required to be contained in any liability policy or equivalent self-insurance.

  (2) "Insurer" means an entity that writes a health benefit plan and that is an insurance company subject to this Chapter, a service corporation under Article 65 of this Chapter, a health maintenance organization under Article 67 of this Chapter, or a multiple employer welfare arrangement under Article 49 of this Chapter.

(b) Medical Necessity. — An insurer that limits its health benefit plan coverage to medically necessary services and supplies shall define "medically necessary services or supplies" in its health benefit plan as those covered services or supplies that are:

  (1) Provided for the diagnosis, treatment, cure, or relief of a health condition, illness, injury, or disease; and, except as allowed under G.S. 58-3-255, not for experimental, investigational, or cosmetic purposes.

  (2) Necessary for and appropriate to the diagnosis, treatment, cure, or relief of a health condition, illness, injury, disease, or its symptoms.

  (3) Within generally accepted standards of medical care in the community.

  (4) Not solely for the convenience of the insured, the insured's family, or the provider.

For medically necessary services, nothing in this subsection precludes an insurer from comparing the cost-effectiveness of alternative services or supplies when determining which of the services or supplies will be covered.

(c) Coverage Determinations. — If an insurer or its authorized representative determines that services, supplies, or other items are covered under its health benefit plan, including any determination under G.S. 58-50-61, the insurer shall not subsequently retract its determination after the services, supplies, or other items have been provided, or reduce payments for a service, supply, or other item furnished in reliance on such a determination, unless the determination was based on a material misrepresentation about the insured's health condition that was knowingly made by the insured or the provider of the service, supply, or other item.

(d) Services Outside Provider Networks. — No insurer shall penalize an insured or subject an insured to the out-of-network benefit levels offered under the insured's approved health benefit plan, including an insured receiving an extended or standing referral under G.S. 58-3-223, unless contracting health care providers able to meet health needs of the insured are reasonably available to the insured without unreasonable delay.

(e) Nondiscrimination Against High-Risk Populations. — No insurer shall establish provider selection or contract renewal standards or procedures that are designed to avoid or otherwise have the effect of avoiding enrolling high-risk populations by excluding providers because they are located in geographic areas that contain high-risk populations or because they treat or specialize in treating populations that present a risk of higher-than-average claims or health care services utilization. This subsection does not prohibit an insurer from declining to select a provider or from not renewing a contract with a provider who fails to meet the insurer's selection criteria.

(f) Continuing Care Retirement Community Residents. — As used in this subsection, "Medicare benefits" means medical and health products, benefits, and services used in accordance with Title XVIII of the Social Security Act. If an insured with coverage for Medicare benefits or similar benefits under a plan for retired federal government employees is a resident of a continuing care retirement community regulated under Article 64 of this Chapter, and the insured's primary care physician determines that it is medically necessary for the insured to be referred to a skilled nursing facility upon discharge from an acute care facility, the insurer shall not require that the insured relocate to a skilled nursing facility outside the continuing care retirement community if the continuing care retirement community:

    (1) Is a Medicare-certified skilled nursing facility.

    (2) Agrees to be reimbursed at the insurer's contract rate negotiated with similar providers for the same services and supplies.

    (3) Agrees not to bill the insured for fees over and above the insurer's contract rate.

    (4) Meets all guidelines established by the insurer related to quality of care, including:

       a. Quality assurance programs that promote continuous quality improvement.

       b. Standards for performance measurement for measuring and reporting the quality of health care services provided to insureds.

       c. Utilization review, including compliance with utilization management procedures.

       d. Confidentiality of medical information.

       e. Insured grievances and appeals from adverse treatment decisions.

       f. Nondiscrimination.

    (5) Agrees to comply with the insurer's procedures for referral authorization, risk assumption, use of insurer services, and other criteria applicable to providers under contract for the same services and supplies.

A continuing care retirement community that satisfies subdivisions (1) through (5) of this subsection shall not be obligated to accept, as a skilled nursing facility, any patient other than a resident of the continuing care retirement community, and neither the insurer nor the retirement community shall be allowed to list or otherwise advertise the skilled nursing facility as a participating network provider for Medicare benefits for anyone other than residents of the continuing care retirement community. (1997-443, s. 11A.122; 1997-519, s. 2.1; 2001-446, ss. 5(b), 1.2A.)

Editor's Note. — Session Laws 2001-446, s. 8 provides: "Nothing in this act obligates the General Assembly to appropriate funds to implement this act."

Session Laws 2001-446, s. 7 is a severability clause.

Effect of Amendments. — Session Laws 2001-446, ss. 1.2A and 5(b), effective March 1, 2002, and applicable to health benefit plans that are in effect, delivered, issued for delivery, or renewed on or after that date, inserted "except as allowed under G.S. 58-2-255" in subdivision (b)(1); and inserted "including an insured receiving an extended or standing referral under G.S. 58-3-223" in subsection (d).

Legal Periodicals. — For 1997 legislative

survey, see 20 Campbell L. Rev. 469.   in North Carolina: Tort Liability Theories and
    For comment, "Managed Care Organizations   Defenses," see 23 N.C. Cent. L.J. 58 (1997).

§ 58-3-215. Genetic information in health insurance.

(a) Definitions. — As used in this section:

(1) "Genetic information" means information about genes, gene products, or inherited characteristics that may derive from an individual or a family member. "Genetic information" does not include the results of routine physical measurements, blood chemistries, blood counts, urine analyses, tests for abuse of drugs, and tests for the presence of human immunodeficiency virus.

(2) "Health benefit plan" means an accident and health insurance policy or certificate; a nonprofit hospital or medical service corporation contract; a health maintenance organization subscriber contract; a plan provided by a multiple employer welfare arrangement; or a plan provided by another benefit arrangement, to the extent permitted by the Employee Retirement Income Security Act of 1974, as amended, or by any waiver of or other exception to that Act provided under federal law or regulation. "Health benefit plan" does not mean any plan implemented or administered through the Department of Health and Human Services or its representatives. "Health benefit plan" also does not mean any of the following kinds of insurance:

a. Accident

b. Credit

c. Disability income

d. Long-term or nursing home care

e. Medicare supplement

f. Specified disease

g. Dental or vision

h. Coverage issued as a supplement to liability insurance

i. Workers' compensation

j. Medical payments under automobile or homeowners

k. Hospital income or indemnity

l. Insurance under which benefits are payable with or without regard to fault and that is statutorily required to be contained in any liability policy or equivalent self-insurance

m. Blanket accident and sickness.

(3) "Insurer" means an insurance company subject to this Chapter; a service corporation organized under Article 65 of this Chapter; a health maintenance organization organized under Article 67 of this Chapter; or a multiple employer welfare arrangement subject to Article 49 of this Chapter.

(b) For the purpose of this section, routine physical measurements, blood chemistries, blood counts, urine analyses, tests for abuse of drugs, and tests for the presence of human immunodeficiency virus are not to be considered genetic tests.

(c) No insurer shall:

(1) Raise the premium or contribution rates paid by a group for a group health benefit plan on the basis of genetic information obtained about an individual member of the group.

(2) Refuse to issue or deliver a health benefit plan because of genetic information obtained about any person to be insured by the health benefit plan.

(3) Charge a higher premium rate or charge for a health benefit plan because of genetic information obtained about any person to be

insured by the health benefit plan. (1997-350, s. 1; 1997-443, s. 11A.118(b).)

Editor's Note. — Session Laws 1997-350, s. 4, provides: "Nothing in this act applies to specified accident, specified disease, hospital indemnity, disability, or long-term care health insurance policies."

§ 58-3-221. Access to nonformulary and restricted access prescription drugs.

(a) If an insurer maintains one or more closed formularies for or restricts access to covered prescription drugs or devices, then the insurer shall do all of the following:

(1) Develop the formulary or formularies and any restrictions on access to covered prescription drugs or devices in consultation with and with the approval of a pharmacy and therapeutics committee, which shall include participating physicians who are licensed to practice medicine in this State.

(2) Make available to participating providers, pharmacists, and enrollees the complete drugs or devices formulary or formularies maintained by the insurer including a list of the devices and prescription drugs on the formulary by major therapeutic category that specifies whether a particular drug or device is preferred over other drugs or devices.

(3) Establish and maintain an expeditious process or procedure that allows an enrollee or the enrollee's physician acting on behalf of the enrollee to obtain, without penalty or additional cost-sharing beyond that provided for in the health benefit plan, coverage for a specific nonformulary drug or device determined to be medically necessary and appropriate by the enrollee's participating physician without prior approval from the insurer, after the enrollee's participating physician notifies the insurer that:

a. Either (i) the formulary alternatives have been ineffective in the treatment of the enrollee's disease or condition, or (ii) the formulary alternatives cause or are reasonably expected by the physician to cause a harmful or adverse clinical reaction in the enrollee; and

b. Either (i) the drug is prescribed in accordance with any applicable clinical protocol of the insurer for the prescribing of the drug, or (ii) the drug has been approved as an exception to the clinical protocol pursuant to the insurer's exception procedure.

(4) Provide coverage for a restricted access drug or device to an enrollee without requiring prior approval or use of a nonrestricted formulary drug if an enrollee's physician certifies in writing that the enrollee has previously used an alternative nonrestricted access drug or device and the alternative drug or device has been detrimental to the enrollee's health or has been ineffective in treating the same condition and, in the opinion of the prescribing physician, is likely to be detrimental to the enrollee's health or ineffective in treating the condition again.

(b) An insurer may not void a contract or refuse to renew a contract between the insurer and a prescribing provider because the prescribing provider has prescribed a medically necessary and appropriate nonformulary or restricted access drug or device as provided in this section.

(c) As used in this section:

(1) "Closed formulary" means a list of prescription drugs and devices reimbursed by the insurer that excludes coverage for drugs and devices not listed.

(1a) "Health benefit plan" has definition provided in G.S. 58-3-167.

(2) "Insurer" has the meaning provided in G.S. 58-3-167.

(3) "Restricted access drug or device" means those covered prescription drugs or devices for which reimbursement by the insurer is conditioned on the insurer's prior approval to prescribe the drug or device or on the provider prescribing one or more alternative drugs or devices before prescribing the drug or device in question.

(d) Nothing in this section requires an insurer to pay for drugs or devices or classes of drugs or devices related to a benefit that is specifically excluded from coverage by the insurer. (1999-178, s. 1; 1999-294, s. 14(a), (b); 2001-446, s. 1.5.)

Editor's Note. — Session Laws 1999-178, s. 2, makes this section effective June 14, 1999, and applicable to health benefit plans that are delivered, issued for delivery, or renewed on and after January 1, 2000. Section 2 further provides that for purposes of this act, renewal of a health benefit policy, contract, or plan is presumed to occur on each anniversary of the date on which coverage was first effective on the person or persons covered by the health benefit plan.

Subdivisions (c)(1a) and (c)(2) were designated as such at the direction of the Revisor of Statutes, having been designated (c)(2) and (c)(3) by Session Laws 1999-294, s. 14(a).

Session Laws 2001-446, s. 8 provides: "Nothing in this act obligates the General Assembly to appropriate funds to implement this act."

Session Laws 2001-446, s. 7 is a severability clause.

Effect of Amendments. — Session Laws 2001-446, s. 1.5, effective March 1, 2002, and applicable to health benefit plans that are in effect, delivered, issued for delivery, or renewed on or after that date, inserted "and restricted access" in the section catchline; in subsection (a), inserted "or restricts access to covered" in the introductory paragraph; in subdivision (a)(1), inserted "and any restrictions on access to covered prescription drugs or devices," and substituted "physicians who are licensed to practice medicine in this State" for "providers who are licensed to prescribe prescription drugs or devices"; substituted "providers, pharmacists, and enrollees" for "providers and pharmacists" in subdivision (a)(2); in subdivision (a)(3), in the introductory paragraph, inserted "or the enrollee's physician acting on behalf of the enrollee" and inserted "enrollee's" preceding "participating physician" in two places; added subdivision (a)(4); inserted "or restricted access" in subsection (b); and in subsection (c), rewrote subdivisions (c)(1a) and (c)(2) and added subdivision (c)(3).

§ 58-3-223. Managed care access to specialist care.

(a) Each insurer offering a health benefit plan that does not allow direct access to all in-plan specialists shall develop and maintain written policies and procedures by which an insured may receive an extended or standing referral to an in-plan specialist. The insurer shall provide for an extended or standing referral to a specialist if the insured has a serious or chronic degenerative, disabling, or life-threatening disease or condition, which in the opinion of the insured's primary care physician, in consultation with the specialist, requires ongoing specialty care. The extended or standing referral shall be for a period not to exceed 12 months and shall be made under a treatment plan coordinated with the insurer in consultation with the primary care physician, the specialist, and the insured or the insured's designee.

(b) As used in this section:

(1) "Health benefit plan" has the meaning applied in G.S. 58-3-167.

(2) "Insurer" has the meaning applied in G.S. 58-3-167.

(3) "Serious or chronic degenerative, disabling, or life-threatening disease or condition" means a disease or condition, which in the opinion of the patient's treating primary care physician and specialist, requires frequent and periodic monitoring and consultation with the specialist on an ongoing basis.

(4) "Specialist" includes a subspecialist. (1999-168, s. 1; 2001-446, s. 1.2.)

Editor's Note. — Session Laws 1999-168, s. 2, made this section effective June 8, 1999, and applicable to health benefit plans that are delivered, issued for delivery, or renewed on and after January 1, 2000. For purposes of this act, renewal of a health benefit policy, contract, or plan is presumed to occur on each anniversary of the date on which coverage was first effective on the person or persons covered by the health benefit plan.

Session Laws 2001-446, s. 8 provides: "Nothing in this act obligates the General Assembly to appropriate funds to implement this act."

Session Laws 2001-446, s. 7 is a severability clause.

Effect of Amendments. — Session Laws 2001-446, s. 1.2, effective March 1, 2002, and applicable to health benefit plans that are in effect, delivered, issued for delivery, or renewed on or after that date, substituted "The insurer" for "The procedure" at the beginning of second sentence in subsection (a); and in subsection (b), rewrote subdivisions (b)(1) and (b)(2), and added subdivision (b)(4).

Legal Periodicals. — For comment, "Managed Care Organizations in North Carolina: Tort Liability Theories and Defenses," see 23 N.C. Cent. L.J. 58 (1997).

§ 58-3-225. Prompt claim payments under health benefit plans.

(a) As used in this section:
(1) "Claimant" includes a health care provider or facility that is responsible or permitted under contract with the insurer or by valid assignment of benefits for directly making the claim with an insurer.
(2) "Health benefit plan" means an accident and health insurance policy or certificate; a nonprofit hospital or medical service corporation contract; a health maintenance organization subscriber contract; a plan provided by a multiple employer welfare arrangement; or a plan provided by another benefit arrangement, to the extent permitted by the Employee Retirement Income Security Act of 1974, as amended, or by any waiver of or other exception to that act provided under federal law or regulation. "Health benefit plan" does not mean any plan implemented or administered by the North Carolina or United States Department of Health and Human Services, or any successor agency, or its representatives. "Health benefit plan" also does not mean any of the following kinds of insurance:
a. Credit.
b. Disability income.
c. Coverage issued as a supplement to liability insurance.
d. Hospital income or indemnity.
e. Insurance under which benefits are payable with or without regard to fault and that is statutorily required to be contained in any liability policy or equivalent self-insurance.
f. Long-term or nursing home care.
g. Medical payments under motor vehicle or homeowners' insurance policies.
h. Medicare supplement.
i. Short-term limited duration health insurance policies as defined in Part 144 of Title 45 of the Code of Federal Regulations.
j. Workers' compensation.
(3) "Health care facility" means a facility that is licensed under Chapter 131E or Chapter 122C of the General Statutes or is owned or operated by the State of North Carolina in which health care services are provided to patients.
(4) "Health care provider" means an individual who is licensed, certified, or otherwise authorized under Chapter 90 or 90B of the General Statutes or under the laws of another state to provide health care services in the ordinary course of business or practice of a profession or in an approved education or training program.

(5) "Insurer" includes an insurance company subject to this Chapter, a service corporation organized under Article 65 of this Chapter, a health maintenance organization organized under Article 67 of this Chapter, or a multiple employer welfare arrangement subject to Article 49 of this Chapter, that writes a health benefit plan.

(b) An insurer shall, within 30 calendar days after receipt of a claim, send by electronic or paper mail to the claimant:

(1) Payment of the claim.

(2) Notice of denial of the claim.

(3) Notice that the proof of loss is inadequate or incomplete.

(4) Notice that the claim is not submitted on the form required by the health benefit plan, by the contract between the insurer and health care provider or health care facility, or by applicable law.

(5) Notice that coordination of benefits information is needed in order to pay the claim.

(6) Notice that the claim is pending based on nonpayment of fees or premiums.

For purposes of this section, an insurer is presumed to have received a written claim five business days after the claim has been placed first-class postage prepaid in the United States mail addressed to the insurer or an electronic claim transmitted to the insurer or a designated clearinghouse on the day the claim is electronically transmitted. The presumption may be rebutted by sufficient evidence that the claim was received on another day or not received at all.

(c) If the claim is denied, the notice shall include all of the specific good faith reason or reasons for the denial, including, without limitation, coordination of benefits, lack of eligibility, or lack of coverage for the services provided. If the claim is contested or cannot be paid because the proof of loss is inadequate or incomplete, or not paid pending receipt of requested coordination of benefits information, the notice shall contain the specific good faith reason or reasons why the claim has not been paid and an itemization or description of all of the information needed by the insurer to complete the processing of the claim. If all or part of the claim is contested or cannot be paid because of the application of a specific utilization management or medical necessity standard is not satisfied, the notice shall contain the specific clinical rationale for that decision or shall refer to specific provisions in documents that are made readily available through the insurer which provide the specific clinical rationale for that decision; however, if a notice of noncertification has already been provided under G.S. 58-50-61(h), then the specific clinical rationale for the decision is not required under this subsection. If the claim is contested or cannot be paid because of nonpayment of premiums, the notice shall contain a statement advising the claimant of the nonpayment of premiums. If a claim is not paid pending receipt of requested coordination of benefits information, the notice shall so specify. If a claim is denied or contested in part, the insurer shall pay the undisputed portion of the claim within 30 calendar days after receipt of the claim and send the notice of the denial or contested status within 30 days after receipt of the claim. If a claim is contested or cannot be paid because the claim was not submitted on the required form, the notice shall contain the required form, if the form is other than a UB or HCFA form, and instructions to complete that form. Upon receipt of additional information requested in its notice to the claimant, the insurer shall continue processing the claim and pay or deny the claim within 30 days after receiving the additional information.

(d) If an insurer requests additional information under subsection (c) of this section and the insurer does not receive the additional information within 90 days after the request was made, the insurer shall deny the claim and send the notice of denial to the claimant in accordance with subsection (c) of this section.

The insurer shall include the specific reason or reasons for denial in the notice, including the fact that information that was requested was not provided. The insurer shall inform the claimant in the notice that the claim will be reopened if the information previously requested is submitted to the insurer within one year after the date of the denial notice closing the claim.

(e) Health benefit plan claim payments that are not made in accordance with this section shall bear interest at the annual percentage rate of eighteen percent (18%) beginning on the date following the day on which the claim should have been paid. If additional information was requested by the insurer under subsection (b) of this section, interest on health benefit claim payments shall begin to accrue on the 31st day after the insurer received the additional information. A payment is considered made on the date upon which a check, draft, or other valid negotiable instrument is placed in the United States Postal Service in a properly addressed, postpaid envelope, or, if not mailed, on the date of the electronic transfer or other delivery of the payment to the claimant. This subsection does not apply to claims for benefits that are not covered by the health benefit plan; nor does this subsection apply to deductibles, co-payments, or other amounts for which the insurer is not liable.

(f) Insurers may require that claims be submitted within 180 days after the date of the provision of care to the patient by the health care provider and, in the case of health care provider facility claims, within 180 days after the date of the patient's discharge from the facility. However, an insurer may not limit the time in which claims may be submitted to fewer than 180 days. Unless otherwise agreed to by the insurer and the claimant, failure to submit a claim within the time required does not invalidate or reduce any claim if it was not reasonably possible for the claimant to file the claim within that time, provided that the claim is submitted as soon as reasonably possible and in no event, except in the absence of legal capacity of the insured, later than one year from the time submittal of the claim is otherwise required.

(g) If a claim for which the claimant is a health care provider or health care facility has not been paid or denied within 60 days after receipt of the initial claim, the insurer shall send a claim status report to the insured. Provided, however, that the claims status report is not required during the time an insurer is awaiting information requested under subsection (c) of this section. The report shall indicate that the claim is under review and the insurer is communicating with the health care provider or health care facility to resolve the matter. While a claim remains unresolved, the insurer shall send a claim status report to the insured with a copy to the provider 30 days after the previous report was sent.

(h) To the extent permitted by the contract between the insurer and the health care provider or health care facility, the insurer may recover overpayments made to the health care provider or health care facility by making demands for refunds and by offsetting future payments. Any such recoveries may also include related interest payments that were made under the requirements of this section. Recoveries by the insurer must be accompanied by the specific reason and adequate information to identify the specific claim. To the extent permitted by the contract between the insurer and the health care provider or health care facility, the health care provider or health care facility may recover underpayments or nonpayments by the insurer by making demands for refunds. Any such recoveries by the health care provider or health care facility of underpayments or nonpayment by the insurer may include applicable interest under this section. The period for which such recoveries may be made may be specified in the contract between the insurer and health care provider or health care facility.

(i) Every insurer shall maintain written or electronic records of its activities under this section, including records of when each claim was received, paid, denied, or pended, and the insurer's review and handling of each claim under this section, sufficient to demonstrate compliance with this section.

(j) A violation of this section by an insurer subjects the insurer to the sanctions in G.S. 58-2-70. The authority of the Commissioner under this subsection does not impair the right of a claimant to pursue any other action or remedy available under law. With respect to a specific claim, an insurer paying statutory interest in good faith under this section is not subject to sanctions for that claim under this subsection.

(k) An insurer is not in violation of this section nor subject to interest payments under this section if its failure to comply with this section is caused in material part by (i) the person submitting the claim, or (ii) by matters beyond the insurer's reasonable control, including an act of God, insurrection, strike, fire, or power outages. In addition, an insurer is not in violation of this section or subject to interest payments to the claimant under this section if the insurer has a reasonable basis to believe that the claim was submitted fraudulently and notifies the claimant of the alleged fraud.

(*l*) Expired January 1, 2003.

(m) Nothing in this section limits or impairs the patient's liability under existing law for payment of medical expenses. (2000-162, s. 4(a); 2001-417, s. 1.)

Editor's Note. — The definitions in subdivisions (a)(1) and (a)(2) were enacted by Session Laws 2000-162, s. 4(a) in reverse order, and were redesignated at the direction of the Revisor of Statutes to preserve alphabetical order.

Session Laws 2000-162, s. 5, made this section effective July 1, 2001 and applicable to claims received on or after that date.

§ 58-3-227. (See Editor's note for effective date and applicability) Health plans fee schedules.

(a) Definitions. — As used in this section, the following terms mean:
  (1) Claim submission policy. — The procedure adopted by an insurer and used by a provider or facility to submit to the insurer claims for services rendered and to seek reimbursement for those services.
  (2) Health care facility or facility. — A facility that is licensed under Chapter 131E or Chapter 122C of the General Statutes or is owned or operated by the State of North Carolina in which health care services are provided to patients.
  (3) Health care provider or provider. — An individual who is licensed, certified, or otherwise authorized under Chapter 90 or Chapter 90B of the General Statutes or under the laws of another state to provide health care services in the ordinary course of business or practice of a profession or in an approved education or training program.
  (4) Insurer. — An entity that writes a health benefit plan and that is an insurance company subject to this Chapter, a service corporation under Article 65 of this Chapter, a health maintenance organization under Article 67 of this Chapter, or a multiple employer welfare arrangement under Article 49 of this Chapter, except it does not include an entity that writes stand alone dental insurance.
  (5) Reimbursement policy. — Information relating to payment of providers and facilities including policies on the following:
    a. Claims bundling and other claims editing processes.
    b. Recognition or nonrecognition of CPT code modifiers.
    c. Downcoding of services or procedures.
    d. The definition of global surgery periods.
    e. Multiple surgical procedures.
    f. Payment based on the relationship of procedure code to diagnosis code.

   (6) Schedule of fees. — CPT, HCPCS, ICD-9- CM codes, ASA codes, modifiers, and other applicable codes for the procedures billed for that class of provider.

  (b) Purpose. — The purpose of this section is to establish the minimum required provisions for the disclosure and notification of an insurer's schedule of fees, claims submission, and reimbursement policies to health care providers and health care facilities. Nothing in this section shall supercede (i) the schedule of fees, claim submission, and reimbursement policy terms in an insurer's contract with a provider or facility that exceed the minimum requirements of this section nor (ii) any contractual requirement for mutual written consent of changes to reimbursement policies, claims submission policies, or fees. Nothing in this section shall prevent an insurer from requiring that providers and facilities keep confidential, and not disclose to third parties, the information that an insurer must provide under this section.

  (c) **(See Editor's note)** Disclosure of Fee Schedules. — An insurer shall make available to contracted providers the following information:

   (1) The insurer's schedule of fees associated with the top 30 services or procedures most commonly billed by that class of provider, and, upon request, the full schedule of fees for services or procedures billed by that class of provider, in accordance with subdivision (3) of this subsection.

   (2) In the case of a contract incorporating multiple classes of providers, the insurer's schedule of fees associated with the top 30 services or procedures most commonly billed for each class of provider, and, upon request, the full schedule of fees for services or procedures billed for each class of provider, in accordance with subdivision (3) of this subsection.

   (3) If a provider requests fees for more than 30 services and procedures, the insurer may require the provider to specify the additional requested services and procedures and may limit the provider's access to the additional schedule of fees to those associated with services and procedures performed by or reasonably expected to be performed by the provider. The insurer may also limit the frequency of requests for the additional codes by each provider, provided that such additional codes will be made available upon request at least annually and at any time there are changes for which notification is required pursuant to subsection (f) of this section.

  (d) Disclosure of Policies. — An insurer shall make available to contracted providers and facilities a description of the insurer's claim submission and reimbursement policies.

  (e) Availability of Information. — Insurers shall notify contracted providers and facilities in writing of the availability of information required or authorized to be provided under this section. An insurer may satisfy this requirement by indicating in the contract with the provider the availability of this information or by providing notice in a manner authorized under subsection (f) of this section for notification of changes.

  (f) Notification of Changes. — Insurers shall provide advance notice to providers and facilities of changes to the information that insurers are required to provide under this section. The notice period for a change in the schedule of fees, reimbursement policies, or submission of claims policies shall be the contractual notice period, but in no event shall the notices be given less than 30 days prior to the change. An insurer is not required to provide advance notice of changes to the information required under this section if the change has the effect of increasing fees, expanding health benefit plan coverage, or is made for patient safety considerations, in which case, notification of the changes may be made concurrent with the implementation of the changes.

Information and notice of changes may be provided in the medium selected by the insurer, including an electronic medium. However, the insurer must inform the affected contracted provider or facility of the notification method to be used by the insurer and, if the insurer uses an electronic medium to provide notice of changes required under this section, the insurer shall provide clear instructions regarding how the provider or facility may access the information contained in the notice.

(g) Reference Information. — If an insurer references source information that is the basis for a schedule of fees, reimbursement policy, or claim submission policy, and the source information is developed independently of the insurer, the insurer may satisfy the requirements of this section by providing clear instructions regarding how the provider or facility may readily access the source information or by providing for actual access if agreed to in the contract between the insurer and the provider.

(h) Contract Negotiations. — When an insurer offers a contract to a provider, the insurer shall also make available its schedule of fees associated with the top 30 services or procedures most commonly billed by that class of provider. Upon the request of a provider, the insurer shall also make available the full schedule of fees for services or procedures billed by that class of provider or for each class of provider in the case of a contract incorporating multiple classes of providers. If a provider requests fees for more than 30 services and procedures, the insurer may require the provider to specify the additional requested services and procedures and may limit the provider's access to the additional schedule of fees to those associated with services and procedures performed by or reasonably expected to be performed by the provider.

(i) **(See Editor's note)** Exemptions. — Except for the information required to be provided under subsection (c) of this section, this section does not apply to:

(1) Claims processed by an insurer on a claims adjudication system that was implemented prior to January 1, 1982, provided that the insurer (i) verifies with the Commissioner that its claims adjudication system qualified under this subsection, (ii) is implementing a new claims adjudication software system, and (iii) is proceeding in good faith to move all insured claims to the new system as soon as possible and in any event no later than December 31, 2004; or

(2) Information that the insurer verifies with the Commissioner is required to be provided by the terms of a national settlement agreement between the insurer and trade associations representing certain providers, provided that the agreement is approved prior to March 1, 2004, by the court having jurisdiction over the settlement. The exemption provided in this subdivision shall be limited to those terms of the agreement that are required to be implemented no later than December 31, 2004. Nothing in this subdivision shall be construed to relieve the insurer of complying with any terms and deadlines as set out in the agreement. (2003-369, s. 1.)

Editor's Note. — Session Laws 2003-369, s. 3, makes this section effective March 1, 2004, except that subsection (c) becomes effective January 1, 2004, and applies to the earlier of the following: (i) a contract issued, renewed, or modified on or after January 1, 2004; or (ii) any fee schedule request made on or after July 1, 2004. Subsection (i) expires on January 1, 2005.

Session Laws 2003-369, s. 2, provides: "On or before the applicable effective dates, each insurer shall provide to the Commissioner of Insurance a written description of the policies and procedures to be used by the insurer to comply with this act."

§ 58-3-230. Uniform provider credentialing.

(a) An insurer that provides a health benefit plan and that credentials providers for its networks shall maintain a process to assess and verify the qualifications of a licensed health care practitioner, or applicant for licensure as a health care practitioner, within 60 days of receipt of a completed provider credentialing application form approved by the Commissioner. When a health care practitioner joins a practice that is under contract with an insurer to participate in a health benefit plan, the effective date of the health care practitioner's participation in the health benefit plan network shall be the date the insurer approves the practitioner's credentialing application.

(b) The Commissioner shall by rule adopt a uniform provider credentialing application form that will provide health benefit plans with the information necessary to adequately assess and verify the qualifications of an applicant. The Commissioner may update the uniform provider credentialing application form, as necessary. No insurer that provides a health benefit plan may require an applicant to submit information that is not required by the uniform provider credentialing application form.

(c) As used in this section, the terms "health benefit plan" and "insurer" shall have the meaning provided under G.S. 58-3-167. (2001-172, s. 1; 2002-126, s. 6.9(a).)

Editor's Note. — Session Laws 2002-126, s. 1.2, provides: "This act shall be known as 'The Current Operations, Capitol Improvements, and Finance Act of 2002'."

Session Laws 2002-126, s. 31.6 is a severability clause.

Effect of Amendments. — Session Laws 2002-126, s. 6.9(a), effective October 1, 2002, added the last sentence of subsection (a).

§ 58-3-235. Selection of specialist as primary care provider.

(a) Each insurer that offers a health benefit plan shall have a procedure by which an insured diagnosed with a serious or chronic degenerative, disabling, or life-threatening disease or condition, either of which requires specialized medical care may select as his or her primary care physician a specialist with expertise in treating the disease or condition who shall be responsible for and capable of providing and coordinating the insured's primary and specialty care. If the insurer determines that the insured's care would not be appropriately coordinated by that specialist, the insurer may deny access to that specialist as a primary care provider.

(b) The selection of the specialist shall be made under a treatment plan approved by the insurer, in consultation with the specialist and the insured or the insured's designee and after notice to the insured's primary care provider, if any. The specialist may provide ongoing care to the insured and may authorize such referrals, procedures, tests, and other medical services as the insured's primary care provider would otherwise be allowed to provide or authorize, subject to the terms of the treatment plan. Services provided by a specialist who is providing and coordinating primary and specialty care remain subject to utilization review and other requirements of the insurer, including its requirements for primary care providers. (2001-446, s. 1.3.)

Editor's Note. — Session Laws 2001-446, s. 8, makes this section effective March 1, 2002, and applicable to health benefit plans that are in effect, delivered, issued for delivery, or renewed on or after that date.

Session Laws 2001-446, s. 8 provides: "Nothing in this act obligates the General Assembly to appropriate funds to implement this act."

Session Laws 2001-446, s. 7 is a severability clause.

Legal Periodicals. — For comment, "Patients' Bill of Rights; Legislative Cure-All or Prescription for Disaster?," see 81 N.C.L. Rev. 653 (2003).

§ 58-3-240. Direct access to pediatrician for minors.

Each insurer offering a health benefit plan that uses a network of contracting health care providers shall allow an insured to choose a contracting pediatrician in the network as the primary care provider for the insured's children under the age of 18 and covered under the policy. (2001-446, s. 1.4.)

Editor's Note. — Session Laws 2001-446, s. 8, makes this section effective March 1, 2002, and applicable to health benefit plans that are in effect, delivered, issued for delivery, or renewed on or after that date.

Session Laws 2001-446, s. 8 provides: "Nothing in this act obligates the General Assembly to appropriate funds to implement this act."

Session Laws 2001-446, s. 7 is a severability clause.

Legal Periodicals. — For comment, "Patients' Bill of Rights; Legislative Cure-All or Prescription for Disaster?," see 81 N.C.L. Rev. 653 (2003).

§ 58-3-245. Provider directories.

(a) Every health benefit plan utilizing a provider network shall maintain a provider directory that includes a listing of network providers available to insureds and shall update the listing no less frequently than once a year. In addition, every health benefit plan shall maintain a telephone system and may maintain an electronic or on-line system through which insureds can access up-to-date network information. If the health benefit plan produces printed directories, the directories shall contain language disclosing the date of publication, frequency of updates, that the directory listing may not contain the latest network information, and contact information for accessing up-to-date network information.

(b) Each directory listing shall include the following network information:

   (1) The provider's name, address, telephone number, and, if applicable, area of specialty.

   (2) Whether the provider may be selected as a primary care provider.

   (3) To the extent known to the health benefit plan, an indication of whether the provider:

      a. Is or is not currently accepting new patients.

      b. Has any other restrictions that would limit an insured's access to that provider.

(c) The directory listing shall include all of the types of participating providers. Upon a participating provider's written request, the insurer shall also list in the directory, as part of the participating provider's listing, the names of any allied health professionals who provide primary care services under the supervision of the participating provider and whose services are covered by virtue of the insurer's contract with the supervising participating provider and whose credentials have been verified by the supervising participating provider. These allied health professionals shall be listed as a part of the directory listing for the participating provider upon receipt of a certification by the supervising participating provider that the credentials of the allied health professional have been verified consistent with the requirements for the type of information required to be verified under G.S. 58-3-230. (2001-446, s. 2.2.)

Editor's Note. — Session Laws 2001-446, s. 8, makes this section effective March 1, 2002, and applicable to health benefit plans that are in effect, delivered, issued for delivery, or renewed on or after that date.

Session Laws 2001-446, s. 8 provides: "Nothing in this act obligates the General Assembly to appropriate funds to implement this act."

Session Laws 2001-446, s. 7 is a severability clause.

§ 58-3-250. Payment obligations for covered services.

(a) If an insurer calculates a benefit amount for a covered service under a health benefit plan through a method other than a fixed dollar co-payment, the insurer shall clearly explain in its evidence of coverage and plan summaries how it determines its payment obligations and the payment obligations of the insured. The explanation shall include:

    (1) An example of the steps the insurer would take in calculating the benefit amount and the payment obligations of each party.

    (2) Whether the insurer has obtained the agreement of health care providers not to bill an insured for any amounts by which a provider's charge exceeds the insurer's recognized charge for a covered service and whether the insured may be liable for paying any excess amount.

    (3) Which party is responsible for filing a claim or bill with the insurer.

(b) If an insured is liable for an amount that differs from a stated fixed dollar co-payment or may differ from a stated coinsurance percentage because the coinsurance amount is based on a plan allowance or other such amount rather than the actual charges and providers are permitted to balance bill the insured, the evidence of coverage, plan summaries, and marketing and advertising materials that include information on benefit levels shall contain the following statement: "NOTICE: Your actual expenses for covered services may exceed the stated [coinsurance percentage or co-payment amount] because actual provider charges may not be used to determine [plan/insurer or similar term] and [insured/member/enrollee or similar term] payment obligations." (2001-446, s. 2.3.)

Editor's Note. — Session Laws 2001-446, s. 8, makes this section effective March 1, 2002, and applicable to health benefit plans that are in effect, delivered, issued for delivery, or renewed on or after that date.

Session Laws 2001-446, s. 8 provides: "Nothing in this act obligates the General Assembly to appropriate funds to implement this act."

Session Laws 2001-446, s. 7 is a severability clause.

§ 58-3-255. Coverage of clinical trials.

(a) As used in this section:

    (1) "Covered clinical trials" means phase II, phase III, and phase IV patient research studies designed to evaluate new treatments, including prescription drugs, and that: (i) involve the treatment of life-threatening medical conditions, (ii) are medically indicated and preferable for that patient compared to available noninvestigational treatment alternatives, and (iii) have clinical and preclinical data that shows the trial will likely be more effective for that patient than available noninvestigational alternatives. Covered clinical trials must also meet the following requirements:

    a. Must involve determinations by treating physicians, relevant scientific data, and opinions of experts in relevant medical specialties.

    b. Must be trials approved by centers or cooperative groups that are funded by the National Institutes of Health, the Food and Drug Administration, the Centers for Disease Control, the Agency for Health Care Research and Quality, the Department of Defense, or the Department of Veterans Affairs. The health benefit plan may also cover clinical trials sponsored by other entities.

    c. Must be conducted in a setting and by personnel that maintain a high level of expertise because of their training, experience, and volume of patients.

    (2) "Health benefit plan" is defined by G.S. 58-3-167.

(3) "Insurer" is defined by G.S. 58-3-167.

(b) Each health benefit plan shall provide coverage for participation in phase II, phase III, and phase IV covered clinical trials by its insureds or enrollees who meet protocol requirements of the trials and provide informed consent.

(c) Only medically necessary costs of health care services, as defined in G.S. 58-50-61, associated with participation in a covered clinical trial, including those related to health care services typically provided absent a clinical trial, the diagnosis and treatment of complications, and medically necessary monitoring, are required to be covered by the health benefit plan and only to the extent that such costs have not been or are not funded by national agencies, commercial manufacturers, distributors, or other research sponsors of participants in clinical trials. Nothing in this section shall be construed to require a health benefit plan to pay or reimburse for non-FDA approved drugs provided or made available to a patient who received the drug during a covered clinical trial after the clinical trial has been discontinued.

(d) Clinical trial costs not required to be covered by a health benefit plan include the costs of services that are not health care services, those provided solely to satisfy data collection and analysis needs, those related to investigational drugs and devices, and those that are not provided for the direct clinical management of the patient. In the event a claim contains charges related to services for which coverage is required under this section, and those charges have not been or cannot be separated from costs related to services for which coverage is not required under this section, the health benefit plan may deny the claim. (2001-446, s. 3.1.)

Editor's Note. — Session Laws 2001-446, s. 8, makes this section effective March 1, 2002, and applicable to health benefit plans that are in effect, delivered, issued for delivery, or renewed on or after that date.

Session Laws 2001-446, s. 8 provides: "Nothing in this act obligates the General Assembly to appropriate funds to implement this act."

Session Laws 2001-446, s. 7 is a severability clause.

Legal Periodicals. — For comment, "Patients' Bill of Rights; Legislative Cure-All or Prescription for Disaster?," see 81 N.C.L. Rev. 653 (2003).

§ 58-3-260. Insurance coverage for newborn hearing screening mandated.

(a) As used in this section, the terms "health benefit plan" and "insurer" have the meanings applied under G.S. 58-3-167.

(b) Each health benefit plan shall provide coverage for newborn hearing screening ordered by the attending physician pursuant to G.S. 130A-125. The same deductibles, coinsurance, reimbursement methodologies, and other limitations and administrative procedures as apply to similar services covered under the health benefit plan shall apply to coverage for newborn hearing screening. (2001-446, s. 3.2.)

Editor's Note. — Session Laws 2001-446, s. 8, makes this section effective March 1, 2002, and applicable to health benefit plans that are in effect, delivered, issued for delivery, or renewed on or after that date.

Session Laws 2001-446, s. 8 provides: "Nothing in this act obligates the General Assembly to appropriate funds to implement this act."

Session Laws 2001-446, s. 7 is a severability clause.

Legal Periodicals. — For comment, "Patients' Bill of Rights; Legislative Cure-All or Prescription for Disaster?," see 81 N.C.L. Rev. 653 (2003).

§ 58-3-265. Prohibition on managed care provider incentives.

An insurer offering a health benefit plan may not offer or pay any type of material inducement, bonus, or other financial incentive to a participating provider to deny, reduce, withhold, limit, or delay specific medically necessary and appropriate health care services covered under the health benefit plan to a specific insured or enrollee. This section does not prohibit insurers from paying a provider on a capitated basis or withholding payment or paying a bonus based on the aggregate services rendered by the provider or the insurer's financial performance. (2001-446, s. 1.8.)

Editor's Note. — Session Laws 2001-446, s. 8, makes this section effective March 1, 2002, and applicable to health benefit plans that are in effect, delivered, issued for delivery, or renewed on or after that date.

Session Laws 2001-446, s. 8 provides: "Nothing in this act obligates the General Assembly to appropriate funds to implement this act."

Session Laws 2001-446, s. 7 is a severability clause.

Legal Periodicals. — For comment, "Patients' Bill of Rights; Legislative Cure-All or Prescription for Disaster?," see 81 N.C.L. Rev. 653 (2003).

§ 58-3-270. Coverage for surveillance tests for women at risk for ovarian cancer.

(a) Every health benefit plan, as defined in G.S. 58-3-167, shall provide coverage for surveillance tests for women age 25 and older at risk for ovarian cancer. As used in this section:
   (1) "At risk for ovarian cancer" means either:
      a. Having a family history:
         1. With at least one first-degree relative with ovarian cancer; and
         2. A second relative, either first-degree or second-degree, with breast, ovarian, or nonpolyposis colorectal cancer; or
      b. Testing positive for a hereditary ovarian cancer syndrome.
   (2) "Surveillance tests" mean annual screening using:
      a. Transvaginal ultrasound; and
      b. Rectovaginal pelvic examination.
(b) The same deductibles, coinsurance, and other limitations as apply to similar services covered under the plan apply to coverage for transvaginal ultrasound and rectovaginal pelvic examinations required to be covered under this section. (2003-223, s. 1.)

Editor's Note. — This section was originally enacted by Session Laws 2003-223, s. 1, as G.S. 58-3-266. It was renumbered as G.S. 58-3-270 at the direction of the Revisor of Statutes.

Session Laws 2003-223, s. 3, made this section effective January 1, 2004, and applicable to all health benefit plans that are delivered, issued for delivery, or renewed on and after that date. For purposes of this act, renewal of a health benefit plan is presumed to occur on each anniversary of the date on which coverage was first effective on the person or persons covered by the health benefit plan.

ARTICLE 4.

NAIC Filing Requirements.

§ 58-4-1. Scope.

The provisions of this Article shall apply to all domestic, foreign, and alien insurers who are authorized to transact business in this State. (1985, c. 305, s. 1.)

§ 58-4-5. Filing requirements.

(a) Each domestic, foreign, and alien insurer that is authorized to transact insurance in this State shall file with the NAIC a copy of its financial statements required by G.S. 58-2-165, applicable rules, and legal directives and bulletins issued by the Department. The statements shall, in the Commissioner's discretion, be filed annually, semiannually, quarterly, or monthly and shall be filed in a form or format prescribed or permitted by the Commissioner. The Commissioner may require the statements to be filed in a format that can be read by electronic data processing equipment. Any amendments and addenda to the financial statement that are subsequently filed with the Commissioner shall also be filed with the NAIC.

(b) Foreign insurers that are domiciled in a state that has a law or regulation substantially similar to this Article shall be deemed to be in compliance with this section. (1985, c. 305, s. 1; 1991, c. 681, s. 11; 1993, c. 504, s. 2.)

§ 58-4-10. Immunity.

In the absence of actual malice, or gross negligence, members of the NAIC, their duly authorized committees, subcommittees, and task forces, their delegates, NAIC employees, and all others charged with the responsibility of collecting, reviewing, analyzing, and disseminating the information developed from the filings made pursuant to G.S. 58-4-10 shall be acting as agents of the Commissioner under the authority of this Article and shall not be subject to civil liability for libel, slander, or any other cause of action by virtue of their collection, review, and analysis or dissemination of the data and information collected from the filings required under this Article. (1985, c. 305, s. 1.)

§ 58-4-15. Revocation or suspension of license.

The Commissioner may suspend or revoke the license of any insurer failing to file its financial statement when due or within any extension of time that the Commissioner, for good cause, may have granted. (1985, c. 305, s. 1; 1991, c. 681, s. 12; 1999-132, s. 9.1; 2003-212, s. 26(b).)

Effect of Amendments. — Session Laws 2003-212, s. 26.(b), effective January 1, 2004, and applicable to all company licenses issued or otherwise eligible for renewal or continuation after that date, inserted "or suspension" in the section heading; and in the text of the section, substituted "suspend or revoke" for "suspend, revoke, or refuse to renew."

§ 58-4-20: Recodified as § 58-2-220 pursuant to Session Laws 1989 (Regular Session, 1990), c. 1021, s. 7.

§ 58-4-25. Insurance Regulatory Information System and similar program test data records.

Financial test ratios, data, or information generated by the NAIC Insurance Regulatory Information System, any successor program, or any similar program shall be disseminated by the Commissioner consistent with procedures established by the NAIC. (1991, c. 681, s. 13.)

ARTICLE 5.

Deposits and Bonds by Insurance Companies.

§ 58-5-1. Deposits; use of master trust.

Notwithstanding any other provision of law, the Commissioner is authorized to select a bank or trust company as master trustee to hold cash or securities to be pledged to the State when deposited with him pursuant to statute. Securities may be held by the master trustee in any form which, in fact, perfects the security interest of the State in the securities. The Commissioner shall by rule establish the manner in which the master trust shall operate. The master trustee may charge the person making the deposit reasonable fees for services rendered in connection with the operation of the trust. (1985, c. 666, s. 55; 1987, c. 864, s. 23.)

§ 58-5-5. Amount of deposits required of foreign or alien fire and/or marine insurance companies.

Unless otherwise provided in this Article, every fire, marine, or fire and marine insurance company chartered by any other state or foreign government shall make and maintain deposits of securities with the Commissioner in the amount of one hundred thousand dollars ($100,000) market value. (1909, c. 923, s. 1; 1911, c. 164, s. 1; Ex. Sess. 1913, c. 62, ss. 1, 2, 3; 1915, c. 166, s. 6; C.S., s. 6442; 1933, c. 60; 1945, c. 384; 1991, c. 681, s. 15; 2003-212, s. 1.)

Effect of Amendments. — Session Laws 2003-212, s. 1, effective October 1, 2003, substituted "one hundred thousand dollars ($100,000)" for "twenty-five thousand dollars ($25,000)."

Legal Periodicals. — For discussion of the 1933 amendment, see 11 N.C.L. Rev. 234 (1933).

CASE NOTES

Cited in State ex rel. Ingram v. Reserve Ins. Co., 303 N.C. 623, 281 S.E.2d 16 (1981); Underwriters Nat'l Assurance Co. v. North Carolina Life & Accident & Health Ins. Guar. Ass'n, 455 U.S. 691, 102 S. Ct. 1357, 71 L. Ed. 2d 558 (1982).

§ 58-5-10. Amount of deposits required of foreign or alien fidelity, surety and casualty insurance companies.

Unless otherwise provided in this Article, every fidelity, surety or casualty insurance company chartered by any other state or foreign government shall make and maintain deposits of securities with the Commissioner in the amount of two hundred thousand dollars ($200,000) market value. (1945, c. 384; 1991, c. 681, s. 16; 2003-212, s. 2.)

Effect of Amendments. — Session Laws 2003-212, s. 2, effective October 1, 2003, substituted "two hundred thousand dollars ($200,000)" for "fifty thousand dollars ($50,000)."

Title and Rights to Deposited Securities. — It is the manifest intention of the North Carolina legislature that the title and rights to securities deposited in accord with this section and G.S. 58-5-20, 58-5-30, 58-5-35 and 58-5-110 be vested in the Commissioner, the Treasurer, and the State. Continental Bank & Trust Co. v. Gold, 140 F. Supp. 252 (E.D.N.C. 1956).

Federal Receiver of Foreign Insurance Company Not Entitled to Recover Deposit. — A federal receiver of a foreign insurance company, who pursuant to an order of the federal court appointing him filed a petition and motion to recover the deposit of the com-pany from State officials, was not entitled to recover the deposit, since such a deposit was not the property of the foreign insurance company, but was held in trust by the State Treasurer for payment of qualified claimants against the foreign insurance company. Continental Bank & Trust Co. v. Gold, 140 F. Supp. 252 (E.D.N.C. 1956).

Cited in Resolute Ins. Co. v. North Carolina, 276 F. Supp. 660 (E.D.N.C. 1967); State ex rel. Ingram v. Reserve Ins. Co., 303 N.C. 623, 281 S.E.2d 16 (1981); North Carolina Reinsurance Facility v. North Carolina Ins. Guar. Ass'n, 67 N.C. App. 359, 313 S.E.2d 253 (1984).

§ 58-5-15. Minimum deposit required upon admission.

Upon admission to do business in the State of North Carolina every foreign or alien fire, marine, or fire and marine, fidelity, surety or casualty company shall deposit with the Commissioner securities in the amounts required under G.S. 58-5-5 and G.S. 58-5-10. (1945, c. 384; 1991, c. 681, s. 17; 2001-487, s. 18.)

Cited in State ex rel. Ingram v. Reserve Ins. Co., 303 N.C. 623, 281 S.E.2d 16 (1981).

§ 58-5-20. Type of deposits.

The deposits required to be made under G.S. 58-5-5, 58-5-10, and 58-5-50 shall be composed of:
  (a) Interest-bearing bonds of the United States of America;
  (b) Interest-bearing bonds of the State of North Carolina, or of its cities or counties; or
  (c) Certificates of deposit issued by any solvent bank domesticated in the State of North Carolina. (1945, c. 384; 1989, c. 485, s. 34; 1991, c. 681, s. 18.)

Cited in Continental Bank & Trust Co. v. Gold, 140 F. Supp. 252 (E.D.N.C. 1956); State ex rel. Ingram v. Reserve Ins. Co., 303 N.C. 623, 281 S.E.2d 16 (1981).

§ 58-5-25. Replacements upon depreciation of securities.

Whenever any of the securities deposited by companies under the provisions of G.S. 58-5-5, 58-5-10, and 58-5-50 shall be depreciated or reduced in value, such company shall forthwith increase the deposit in order to maintain the required deposit in accordance with the amounts required by the said sections. (1945, c. 384; 1989, c. 485, s. 34.)

§ 58-5-30. Power of attorney.

With the securities deposited in accordance with G.S. 58-5-5, 58-5-10, and 58-5-50 the company shall at the same time deliver to the Commissioner a power of attorney executed by its president and secretary or other proper officers authorizing the sale or transfer of said securities or any part thereof for the purpose of paying any of the liabilities provided for in this Article. (1945, c. 384; 1989, c. 485, s. 34; 1991, c. 720, s. 4.)

CASE NOTES

Cited in Continental Bank & Trust Co. v. Gold, 140 F. Supp. 252 (E.D.N.C. 1956); State ex rel. Ingram v. Reserve Ins. Co., 303 N.C. 623, 281 S.E.2d 16 (1981).

§ 58-5-35. Securities held by Treasurer; faith of State pledged therefor; nontaxable.

Unless a master trustee is selected by the Commissioner pursuant to G.S. 58-5-1, the securities required to be deposited by each insurance company in this Article shall be delivered for safekeeping by the Commissioner to the Treasurer of the State who shall receipt him therefor. For the securities so deposited the faith of the State is pledged that they shall be returned to the companies entitled to receive them or disposed of as herein provided for. The securities deposited by any company under this Article shall not, on account of such securities being in this State, be subjected to taxation but shall be held exclusively and solely for the protection of contract holders. (1945, c. 384; 1985, c. 666, s. 56.)

CASE NOTES

Plaintiff's complaint should not have been dismissed for failure to state a claim since the court did not see an absence of law or fact to support plaintiff's claim or disclosure of a fact that necessarily defeated plaintiff's claim, and plaintiff's complaint concerning the loss of the bearer bonds deposited with the Commissioner of Insurance presented a basis for declaratory relief. Selective Ins. Co. v. NCNB Nat'l Bank, 91 N.C. App. 597, 372 S.E.2d 876 (1988), rev'd on other grounds, 324 N.C. 560, 380 S.E.2d 521 (1989).

Cited in Continental Bank & Trust Co. v. Gold, 140 F. Supp. 252 (E.D.N.C. 1956); State ex rel. Ingram v. Reserve Ins. Co., 303 N.C. 623, 281 S.E.2d 16 (1981); North Carolina Reinsurance Facility v. North Carolina Ins. Guar. Ass'n, 67 N.C. App. 359, 313 S.E.2d 253 (1984).

§ 58-5-40. Authority to increase deposit.

When, in the Commissioner's opinion, it is necessary for the protection of the public interest to increase the amount of deposits specified in G.S. 58-5-5, 58-5-10, 58-5-50, and 58-5-55, the companies described in those sections shall, upon demand, make additional deposits in such sums as the Commissioner may require, and those additional deposits shall be held in accordance with and for the purposes set out in this Article, and shall comprise:

(a) Interest-bearing bonds of the United States of America;
(b) Interest-bearing bonds of the State of North Carolina or of its cities or counties;
(c) Certificates of deposit issued by any solvent bank domesticated in the State of North Carolina;
(d) Interest-bearing AA or better rated corporate bonds and classified as investment grade in the latest NAIC Securities Valuation Manual; or
(e) Other interest-bearing bonds or notes considered to be acceptable by the Commissioner on a case by case basis. (1945, c. 384; 1989, c. 485, s. 34; 1991, c. 681, s. 19.)

§ **58-5-45:** Repealed by Session Laws 1991, c. 681, s. 21.

§ 58-5-50. Deposits of foreign life insurance companies.

In addition to other requirements of Articles 1 through 64 of this Chapter, all foreign life insurance companies shall deposit securities, as specified in G.S. 58-5-20, having a market value of four hundred thousand dollars ($400,000) as a prerequisite of doing business in this State. All foreign life insurance companies shall deposit an additional two hundred thousand dollars ($200,000) where such companies cannot show three years of net operational gains prior to admission. Foreign life insurance companies that are licensed on or before the effective date of this section shall have one year from that date to comply with this section. (1989, c. 485, s. 35; 2003-212, s. 3.)

Effect of Amendments. — Session Laws 2003-212, s. 3, effective October 1, 2003, in the first sentence, substituted "four hundred thousand dollars ($400,000)" for "one hundred thousand dollars ($100,000)"; and in the second sentence, substituted "two hundred thousand dollars ($200,000)" for "one hundred thousand dollars ($100,000)."

§ 58-5-55. Deposits of capital and surplus by domestic insurance companies.

(a) In addition to other requirements of Articles 1 through 64 of this Chapter, all domestic stock insurance companies shall deposit their required statutory capital with the Department. Such deposits shall be under the exclusive control of the Department, for the protection of policyholders.

(b) In addition to other requirements of Articles 1 through 64 of this Chapter, all domestic mutual insurance companies shall deposit at least fifty percent (50%) of their minimum required surplus with the Department, with the amount of the deposit to be determined by the Commissioner. Such deposits shall be under the exclusive control of the Department, for the protection of policyholders.

(c) Deposits fulfilling the requirements of this section shall comprise:
(1) Interest-bearing bonds of the United States of America;
(2) Interest-bearing bonds of the State of North Carolina or of its cities or counties; or
(3) Certificates of deposit issued by any solvent bank domesticated in the State of North Carolina. (1989, c. 485, s. 35; 1991, c. 681, s. 20; 1993, c. 504, s. 3.)

§ **58-5-60:** Repealed by Session Laws 1995, c. 193, s. 8.

§ 58-5-63. Interest; liquidation of deposits for liabilities.

(a) All insurance companies making deposits under this Article are entitled to interest on those deposits. The right to interest is subject to a company paying its insurance policy liabilities. If any company fails to pay those liabilities, interest accruing after the failure is payable to the Commissioner for the payment of those liabilities under subsection (b) of this section.

(b) If any company fails to pay its insurance policy liabilities after those liabilities have been established by settlement or final adjudication, the Commissioner may liquidate the amount of the company's deposit and accrued interest specified in subsection (a) of this section that will satisfy the company's policy liabilities and make payment to the person to whom the liability is owed. After payment has been made, the Commissioner may require the company to deposit the amount paid out under this subsection. As used in this section, "insurance policy" includes a policy written by a surety bondsman under Article 71 of this Chapter.

(c) Notwithstanding the provisions of G.S. 58-5-70, if any company that is or has been the subject of supervision or rehabilitation proceedings fails to pay its liabilities for temporary disability payments or emergency medical expenses under policies of workers' compensation insurance, the Commissioner shall liquidate the company's deposits and accrued interest and shall use the proceeds to pay such liabilities until that company becomes the subject of a final order of liquidation with a finding of insolvency that has not been stayed or been the subject of a writ of supersedeas or other comparable order. The Commissioner also may enter into one or more contracts to handle the administration of the identification and payment of such liabilities, and to the extent such a contract is entered into, the contractor and its employees, agents, and attorneys, shall have immunity of the same scope and extent as an employee of the State acting in the course and scope of the public duties of such employment. After an order of liquidation with a finding of insolvency has been entered by a court of competent jurisdiction that has not been stayed or been the subject of a writ of supersedeas or other comparable order, then the balance of the proceeds, if any, shall be delivered to the North Carolina Insurance Guaranty Association in accordance with G.S. 58-48-95. To the extent that any payment made hereunder reduces the ratable amount payable to policyholders under G.S. 58-5-70, the liens obtained by the North Carolina Insurance Guaranty Association pursuant to Article 48 of this Chapter shall be reduced to such extent as necessary to permit the policyholders to be paid the ratable share that would have been due but for such payments. (1995, c. 193, s. 11; 1999-294, s. 8; 2001-223, s. 23.2; 2002-185, s. 8.)

Effect of Amendments. — Session Laws 2002-185, s. 8, effective October 31, 2002, added subsection (c).

§ **58-5-65:** Repealed by Session Laws 1995, c. 193, s. 8.

§ **58-5-70. Lien of policyholders; action to enforce.**

Upon the securities deposited with the Commissioner by any foreign or alien insurance company, the holders of all contracts of the company who are citizens or residents of this State at the time, or who hold policies issued upon property in the State, shall have a lien for amounts in excess of fifty dollars ($50.00) due them, respectively, under or in consequence of the contracts for losses, equitable values, return premiums, or otherwise, and shall be entitled to be paid ratably out of the proceeds of the securities, if the proceeds are not sufficient to pay all of the contract holders. When any foreign or alien insurance company depositing securities under this Article becomes insolvent or bankrupt or makes an assignment for the benefit of its creditors, any holder of the contract may begin an action in the Superior Court of the County of Wake to enforce the lien for the benefit of all the holders of the contracts. The Commissioner shall be a party to the suit, and the funds shall be distributed by the court, but the cost of the action shall not be adjudged against the Commissioner. (1909, c. 923, s. 4; C.S., s. 6445; 1991, c. 720, s. 4; 1995, c. 193, s. 12; 2001-223, s. 24.1; 2001-487, s. 103(a).)

CASE NOTES

Lien Rights Not Lost by Operation of § 58-48-95. — The Quick Access Statute, G.S. 58-48-95, which requires that deposits made by an insolvent casualty insurer be paid to the North Carolina Insurance Guaranty Association for use in paying claims against the insolvent insurer, is to be applied retroactively to deposits made before the date of its enactment and to the holders of policies issued prior to that date. However, claimants against the deposit of a foreign insurer under this section will retain their lien rights after payment of the deposit to the Guaranty Association, and may proceed against the Guaranty Association to the extent of the deposit for any claims they have under this section which are not paid by the Guaranty Association pursuant to Article 48 of this Chapter, G.S. 58-48-1 et seq. State ex rel. Ingram v. Reserve Ins. Co., 48 N.C. App. 643, 269 S.E.2d 757 (1980), modified and aff'd, 303 N.C. 623, 281 S.E.2d 16 (1981).

All deposit funds under § 58-48-95 must be paid to claimants pro rata as provided by this section, and if all claimants are satisfied either directly by the Guaranty Association or by the Commissioner of Insurance (if the claim is under $100.00) and deposit funds remain, then and only then are such funds to be permanently credited to the Guaranty Association for its expenses. State ex rel. Ingram v. Reserve Ins. Co., 303 N.C. 623, 281 S.E.2d 16 (1981).

The federal receiver of a foreign insurance company would be entitled to appear and contest any doubtful claim in an action brought under this section to subject the insurance company's deposit to the payment of unsatisfied claims of State claimants. Continental Bank & Trust Co. v. Gold, 140 F. Supp. 252 (E.D.N.C. 1956).

Cited in State ex rel. Boney v. Central Mut. Ins. Co., 213 N.C. 470, 196 S.E. 837, 117 A.L.R. 231 (1938); North Carolina Reinsurance Facility v. North Carolina Ins. Guar. Ass'n, 67 N.C. App. 359, 313 S.E.2d 253 (1984); Barclays American/Leasing, Inc. v. North Carolina Ins. Guar. Ass'n, 99 N.C. App. 290, 392 S.E.2d 772 (1990).

§ 58-5-71. Liens of policyholders; subordination.

Liens against the deposit of a foreign insurer under G.S. 58-5-70 shall be subordinated to the reasonable and necessary expenses of the Commissioner in liquidating the deposit and paying the special deposit claims. (1993 (Reg. Sess., 1994), c. 678, s. 7.)

§ 58-5-75. Substitution for securities paid.

Where the principal of any of the securities so deposited is paid to the Commissioner, he shall notify the company or its agent in this State, and pay the money so received to the company upon receiving other securities of the character named in this Article to an equal amount, or, upon the failure of the company for 30 days after receiving notice to deliver such securities to an equal amount to the Commissioner, he may invest the money in any such securities and hold the same as he held those which were paid. (1909, c. 923, s. 5; C.S., s. 6446; 1991, c. 720, s. 4.)

§ 58-5-80. Return of deposits.

If such company ceases to do business in this State and its liabilities, whether fixed or contingent upon its contracts, to persons residing in this State or having policies upon property situated in this State have been satisfied or have been terminated, or have been fully reinsured, with the approval of the Commissioner, in a solvent company licensed to do an insurance business in North Carolina approved by the Commissioner, upon satisfactory evidence of this fact to the Commissioner, the State Treasurer or the trustee selected pursuant to G.S. 58-5-1 shall deliver to such company, upon the order of the Commissioner, the securities in his possession belonging to it, or such of them as remain after paying the liabilities aforesaid. (1909, c. 923, s. 6; C.S., s. 6447; 1951, c. 781, s. 1; 1985, c. 666, s. 57; 1991, c. 720, s. 4.)

Legal Periodicals. — For a brief comment on the 1951 amendment, see 29 N.C.L. Rev. 398 (1951).

§ 58-5-85: Repealed by Session Laws 1991, c. 681, s. 21.

§ 58-5-90. Deposits held in trust by Commissioner or Treasurer.

(a) Deposits by Domestic Company. — The Commissioner or the Treasurer, in his official capacity, shall take and hold in trust deposits made by any domestic insurance company for the purpose of complying with the laws of any other state to enable the company to do business in that state. The company making the deposits is entitled to the income thereof, and may, from time to time, with the consent of the Commissioner or Treasurer, and when not forbidden by the law under which the deposit was made, change in whole or in part the securities which compose the deposit for other solvent securities of equal par value. Upon request of any domestic insurance company such officer may return to the company the whole or any portion of the securities of the company held by him on deposit, when he is satisfied that they are subject to no liability and are not required to be longer held by any provision of law or purpose of the original deposit.

(b) Deposits by Foreign or Alien Company. — The Commissioner or Treasurer may return to the trustees or other representatives authorized for that purpose any deposit made by a foreign or alien insurance company, when it appears that the company has ceased to do business in the State and is under no obligation to policyholders or other persons in the State for whose benefit the deposit was made.

(c) Action to Enforce or Terminate the Trust. — An insurance company which has made a deposit in this State pursuant to Articles 1 through 64 of this Chapter, or its trustees or resident managers in the United States, or the Commissioner, or any creditor of the company, may at any time bring an action in the Superior Court of Wake County against the State and other parties properly joined therein, to enforce, administer, or terminate the trust created by the deposit. The process in this action shall be served on the officer of the State having the deposit, who shall appear and answer in behalf of the State and perform such orders and judgments as the court may make in such action. (1899, c. 54, s. 17; 1901, c. 391, s. 2; 1903, c. 438, s. 1; c. 536, s. 4; Rev., s. 4709; C.S., s. 6313; 1945, c. 384; 1991, c. 720, s. 4.)

CASE NOTES

Plaintiff's complaint should not have been dismissed for failure to state a claim, since the court did not see an absence of law or fact to support plaintiff's claim or disclosure of a fact that necessarily defeated plaintiff's claim, and plaintiff's complaint concerning the loss of the bearer bonds deposited with the Commissioner of Insurance presented a basis for declaratory relief. Selective Ins. Co. v. NCNB Nat'l Bank, 91 N.C. App. 597, 372 S.E.2d 876 (1988), rev'd on other grounds, 324 N.C. 560, 380 S.E.2d 521 (1989).

Cited in State ex rel. Ingram v. Reserve Ins. Co., 303 N.C. 623, 281 S.E.2d 16 (1981).

§ 58-5-95. Deposits subject to approval and control of Commissioner.

The deposits of securities required to be made by any insurance company of this State shall be approved by the Commissioner of the State, and he may examine them at all times, and may order all or any part thereof changed for better security, and no change or transfer of the same may be made without his assent. (1903, c. 536, s. 5; Rev., s. 4710; C.S., s. 6314; 1945, c. 384; 1991, c. 720, s. 4.)

§ 58-5-100. Deposits by alien companies required and regulated.

An alien company, other than life, shall not be admitted to do business in this State until, in addition to complying with the conditions by law prescribed for the licensing and admission of such companies to do business in this State, it has made a deposit with the Treasurer or Commissioner, or with the financial officer of some other state of the United States, of a sum not less than the capital required of like companies under Articles 1 through 64 of this Chapter. This deposit must be in exclusive trust for the benefit and security of all the company's policyholders and creditors in the United States, and may be made in the securities, but subject to the limitations, specified in Articles 1 through 64 of this Chapter with regard to the investment of the capital of domestic companies formed and organized under the provisions of Articles 1 through 64 of this Chapter. The deposit shall be deemed for all purposes of the insurance law the capital of the company making it. (1899, c. 54, s. 64; 1903, c. 438, s. 6; Rev., s. 4711; C.S., s. 6315; 1945, c. 384; 1991, c. 720, s. 52.)

§ 58-5-105. Deposits by life companies not chartered in United States.

Every alien life insurance company organized under the laws of any other country than the United States must have and keep on deposit with some state insurance department or in the hands of trustees, in exclusive trust for the security of its contracts with policyholders in the United States, funds of an amount equal to the net value of all its policies in the United States and not less than three hundred thousand dollars ($300,000). (1899, c. 54, s. 56; Rev., s. 4712; C.S., s. 6316; 1945, c. 384.)

§ 58-5-110. Registration of bonds deposited in name of Treasurer or Commissioner.

The Commissioner is hereby empowered, upon the written consent of any insurance company depositing with the Commissioner or the State Treasurer under any law of this State, any state, county, city, or town bonds or notes which are payable to bearer, to cause such bonds or notes to be registered as to the principal thereof in lawful books of registry kept by or in behalf of the issuing state, county, city or town, such registration to be in the name of the Treasurer of North Carolina or the Commissioner in trust for the company depositing the notes or bonds and the State of North Carolina, as their respective interest may appear, and is further empowered to require of any and all such companies the filing of written consent to such registration as a condition precedent to the right of making any such deposit or right to continue any such deposit heretofore made. (1925, c. 145, s. 2; 1945, c. 384; 1985, c. 666, s. 58; 1991, c. 720, s. 4.)

CASE NOTES

Title and rights to securities deposited in accord with this section are vested in the Commissioner of Insurance, the Treasurer and the State. North Carolina Life & Accident & Health Ins. Guar. Ass'n v. Underwriters Nat'l Assurance Co., 48 N.C. App. 508, 269 S.E.2d 688, cert. denied and appeal dismissed, 301 N.C. 527, 273 S.E.2d 453 (1980), rev'd on other grounds, 455 U.S. 691, 102 S. Ct. 1357, 71 L. Ed. 558 (1982).

Cited in Continental Bank & Trust Co. v. Gold, 140 F. Supp. 252 (E.D.N.C. 1956).

§ 58-5-115. Notation of registration; release.

Bonds or notes so registered shall bear notation of such registration on the reverse thereof, signed by the registering officer or agent, and may be released from such registration and may be transferred on such books of registry by the signature of the State Treasurer or Commissioner. (1925, c. 145, s. 3; 1945, c. 384; 1985, c. 666, s. 59.)

§ 58-5-120. Expenses of registration.

The necessary expenses of procuring such registration and any transfer thereof shall be paid by the company making the deposits. (1925, c. 145, s. 4; 1945, c. 384.)

§ 58-5-125: Repealed by Session Laws 1991, c. 681, s. 21.

ARTICLE 6.

License Fees and Taxes.

§ 58-6-1. Commissioner to report taxes and fees and pay monthly.

On or before the 10th day of each month the Commissioner shall furnish to the Auditor a statement in detail of the taxes and fees received during the previous month, and shall pay the amounts received to the Treasurer. Except as otherwise provided, the amounts shall be credited to the General Fund. The Auditor may examine the accounts of the Commissioner and check them up with said statement. (1899, c. 54, s. 82; 1901, c. 391, s. 7; 1905, c. 430, s. 4; Rev., s. 4714; C.S., s. 6317; 1991, c. 720, s. 4; 1991 (Reg. Sess., 1992), c. 1014, s. 4; 1998-215, s. 83(b).)

CASE NOTES

Payment of Penalty Imposed by Former § 58-44.6 to State Treasurer. — By clear implication of this section and G.S. 58-6-5, the amount of any monetary civil penalty imposed and collected as authorized by former G.S. 58-44.6 should have been paid over to the State Treasurer. State ex rel. Lanier v. Vines, 1 N.C. App. 208, 161 S.E.2d 35, rev'd on other grounds, 274 N.C. 486, 164 S.E.2d 161 (1968).

§ 58-6-5. Schedule of fees and charges.

The Commissioner shall collect and pay into the State treasury fees and charges as follows:

(1) For filing and examining an insurance company application for admission, a nonrefundable fee of two hundred fifty dollars ($250.00), to be submitted with such filing; for filing and auditing annual statement, one hundred dollars ($100.00); for filing any other papers required by law, twenty-five dollars ($25.00); for each certificate of examination, condition, or qualification of company or association, fifteen dollars ($15.00); for each seal when required, ten dollars ($10.00); for a list of licensed insurance companies, ten dollars ($10.00).

(2) Repealed by Session Laws 1977, c. 376, s. 2.

(3) The Commissioner shall receive for copy of any record or paper in his office fifty cents (50¢) per copy sheet and ten dollars ($10.00) for certifying same, or any fact or data from the records of his office and for the examination and approval of charters of companies, twenty-five dollars ($25.00).

(4) He shall collect all other fees and charges due and payable into the State treasury by any company, association, order, or individual under his Department.

(5) Repealed by Session Laws 1999-435, s. 1, effective August 10, 1999. (1899, c. 54, ss. 50, 68, 80, 81, 82, 87, 90, 92; 1901, c. 391, s. 7; c. 706, s. 2; 1903, c. 438, ss. 7, 8; c. 536, s. 4; cc. 680, 774; 1905, c. 588, s. 68; Rev., s. 4715; 1913, c. 140, s. 1; 1919, c. 186, s. 6; C.S., s. 6318; 1921, c. 218; 1935, c. 334; 1939, c. 158, s. 208; 1945, c. 386; 1947, c. 721; 1957, cc. 133, 1047; 1959, c. 911; 1963, c. 692; 1977, c. 376, s. 2; c. 802, s. 50; 1983, c. 790, s. 6; 1989 (Reg. Sess., 1990), c. 1069, s. 2; 1991, c. 720, s. 4; 1995, c. 360, s. 2(f); c. 507, s. 11A(c); 1999-435, s. 1.)

CASE NOTES

Payment of Penalty Imposed by Former § 58-44.6 to State Treasurer. — By clear implication of this section and G.S. 58-6-1, the amount of any monetary civil penalty imposed and collected as authorized by former G.S. 58-44.6 should have been paid over to the State Treasurer. State ex rel. Lanier v. Vines, 1 N.C. App. 208, 161 S.E.2d 35, rev'd on other grounds, 274 N.C. 486, 164 S.E.2d 161 (1968).

§ 58-6-7. Licenses; perpetual licensing; annual license continuation fees for insurance companies.

(a) In order to do business in this State, an insurance company shall apply for and obtain a license from the Commissioner. The license shall be perpetual and shall continue in full force and effect, subject to timely payment of the annual license continuation fee in accordance with this Chapter and subject to any other applicable provision of the insurance laws of this State. Except as provided in subsection (b) of this section, the insurance company shall pay a fee for each year the license is in effect, as follows:

For each domestic farmer's mutual assessment fire insurance company .... $ 25.00
For each fraternal order 100.00
For each of all other insurance companies, except mutual burial associations taxed under G.S. 105-121.1 .... 1,000.00

The fees levied in this subsection are in addition to those specified in G.S. 58-6-5.

(b) When the paid-in capital stock or surplus, or both, of an insurance company, other than a farmer's mutual assessment company or a fraternal order, does not exceed one hundred thousand dollars ($100,000), the fee levied in this section shall be one-half the amount specified.

(c) Upon payment of the fee specified above and the fees and taxes elsewhere specified each insurance company, exchange, bureau, or agency, shall be entitled to do the types of business specified in Chapter 58, of the General Statutes of North Carolina as amended, to the extent authorized therein, except that: Insurance companies authorized to do either the types of business specified for (i) life insurance companies, or (ii) for fire and marine companies, or (iii) for casualty and fidelity and surety companies, in G.S. 58-7-75, which shall also do the types of business authorized in one or both of the other of the above classifications shall in addition to the fees above specified pay one hundred dollars ($100.00) for each such additional classification of business done. All fees and charges collected by the Commissioner under this Chapter are nonrefundable.

(d) Any rating bureau established by action of the General Assembly of North Carolina shall be exempt from the fees in this section. (1945, c. 752, s. 2; 1947, c. 501, s. 8; 1955, c. 179, s. 5; 1989 (Reg. Sess., 1990), c. 1069, s. 4; 1993, c. 495, s. 4; 1993 (Reg. Sess., 1994), c. 745, s. 12; 1995, c. 193, s. 65; c. 360, s. 1(c); c. 507, s. 11A(c); 1999-435, s. 2; 2003-212, s. 26(c).)

Editor's Note. — This section is former G.S. 105-228.4, as recodified by Session Laws 1995, c. 360, s. 1(c). The historical citation from the former section has been added to this section as recodified.

Effect of Amendments. — Session Laws 2003-212, s. 26.(c), effective January 1, 2004, and applicable to all company licenses issued or otherwise eligible for renewal or continuation after that date, rewrote the section heading, which formerly read "Annual license fees for insurance companies"; and rewrote subsection (a).

§ **58-6-10:** Repealed by Session Laws 1999-132, s. 1.1, effective June 4, 1999.

§ 58-6-15. Annual license continuation fee definition; requirements.

For purposes of this Chapter only, "annual license continuation fee means" the fee specified in G.S. 58-6-7 submitted to the Commissioner for each year the license is in effect after the company's year of initial licensing. The annual license continuation fee must be submitted on or before the first day of March on a form to be supplied by the Commissioner each year the license is to remain in effect. If the Commissioner is satisfied that the company has met all requirements of law and appears to be financially solvent, the Commissioner shall not revoke or suspend the license of the company, and the company shall be authorized to do business in this State, subject to all other applicable provisions of the insurance laws of this State. Nothing contained in this section shall be interpreted as applying to licenses issued to individual representatives of insurance companies. (1899, c. 54, s. 78; Rev., s. 4718; C.S., s. 6321; 1955, c. 179, s. 1; 1987, c. 629, s. 16; 1989 (Reg. Sess., 1990), c. 1069, s. 3; 1995, c. 507, s. 11A(c); 2003-212, s. 26(d).)

Editor's Note. — Session Laws 1991, c. 720, s. 4 directed that this section be amended by substituting "Commissioner" for "Commissioner of Insurance." However, the phrase "Commissioner of Insurance" does not occur in this section.

Effect of Amendments. — Session Laws 2003-212, s. 26.(d), effective January 1, 2004, and applicable to all company licenses issued or otherwise eligible for renewal or continuation after that date, rewrote the section heading, which formerly read "Licenses run from July 1"; and rewrote the section.

CASE NOTES

Cited in National Home Life Assurance Co. v. Ingram, 21 N.C. App. 591, 205 S.E.2d 313 (1974).

§ 58-6-20. Policyholders to furnish information.

Every corporation, firm, or individual doing business in the State shall, upon request of the Commissioner, furnish the Commissioner any information the Commissioner considers necessary to enable the Commissioner to enforce the payment of a tax levied in this Chapter. (1899, c. 54, s. 79; 1901, c. 391, s. 7; 1903, c. 438, s. 8; Rev., s. 4720; C.S., s. 6323; 1987, c. 864, s. 38; 1991, c. 720, s. 4; 1995 (Reg. Sess., 1996), c. 747, s. 11.)

Editor's Note. — Session Laws 1995 (Reg. Sess., 1996), c. 747, s. 16, provides: "This act does not obligate the General Assembly to appropriate funds."

§ 58-6-25. Insurance regulatory charge.

(a) **(See Editor's note)** Charge Levied. — There is levied on each insurance company an annual charge for the purposes stated in subsection (d) of this section. The charge levied in this section is in addition to all other fees and taxes. The percentage rate of the charge is established pursuant to subsection (b) of this section. For each insurance company that is not a health maintenance organization, the rate is applied to the company's premium tax liability for the taxable year. For health maintenance organizations, the rate is applied to a premium tax liability for the taxable year calculated as if the corporation or organization were paying tax at the rate in G.S. 105-228.5(d)(2). In determining an insurance company's premium tax liability for a taxable year, the following shall be disregarded:

(1) Additional taxes imposed by G.S. 105-228.8.

(2) The additional local fire and lightning tax imposed by G.S. 105-228.5(d)(4).

(3) Any tax credits for guaranty or solvency fund assessments under G.S. 105-228.5A or G.S. 97-133(a).

(4) Any tax credits allowed under Chapter 105 of the General Statutes other than tax payments made by or on behalf of the taxpayer.

(b) Rates. — The rate of the charge for each taxable year shall be the percentage rate established by the General Assembly. When the Department prepares its budget request for each upcoming fiscal year, the Department shall propose a percentage rate of the charge levied in this section. The Governor shall submit that proposed rate to the General Assembly each fiscal year. The General Assembly shall set by law the percentage rate of the charge levied in this section. The percentage rate may not exceed the rate necessary to generate funds sufficient to defray the estimated cost of the operations of the Department for each upcoming fiscal year, including a reasonable margin for a reserve fund. The amount of the reserve may not exceed one-third of the estimated cost of operating the Department for each upcoming fiscal year. In calculating the amount of the reserve, the General Assembly shall consider all relevant factors that may affect the cost of operating the Department or a possible unanticipated increase or decrease in North Carolina premiums or other charge revenue.

(c) Returns; When Payable. — The charge levied on each insurance company is payable at the time the insurance company remits its premium tax. If the insurance company is required to remit installment payments of premiums tax under G.S. 105-228.5 for a taxable year, it shall also remit installment payments of the charge levied in this section for that taxable year at the same time and on the same basis as the premium tax installment payments. Each installment payment shall be equal to at least thirty-three and one-third percent (33.3%) of the insurance company's regulatory charge liability incurred in the immediately preceding taxable year.

Every insurance company shall, on or before the date the charge levied in this section is due, file a return on a form prescribed by the Secretary of Revenue. The return shall state the company's total North Carolina premiums or presumed premiums for the taxable year and shall be accompanied by any supporting documentation that the Secretary of Revenue may by rule require.

(d) Use of Proceeds. — The Insurance Regulatory Fund is created in the State treasury, under the control of the Office of State Budget and Management. The proceeds of the charge levied in this section and all fees collected under Articles 69 through 71 of this Chapter and under Articles 9 and 9C of Chapter 143 of the General Statutes shall be credited to the Fund. The Fund shall be placed in an interest-bearing account and any interest or other income derived from the Fund shall be credited to the Fund. Moneys in the Fund may be spent only pursuant to appropriation by the General Assembly and in accordance with the line item budget enacted by the General Assembly. The Fund is subject to the provisions of the Executive Budget Act, except that no unexpended surplus of the Fund shall revert to the General Fund. All money credited to the Fund shall be used to reimburse the General Fund for the following:

(1) Money appropriated to the Department of Insurance to pay its expenses incurred in regulating the insurance industry and other industries in this State.

(2) Money appropriated to State agencies to pay the expenses incurred in regulating the insurance industry, in certifying statewide data processors under Article 11A of Chapter 131E of the General Statutes, and in purchasing reports of patient data from statewide data processors certified under that Article.

(3) Money appropriated to the Department of Revenue to pay the expenses incurred in collecting and administering the taxes on insurance companies levied in Article 8B of Chapter 105 of the General Statutes.

(4) Money appropriated for the office of Managed Care Patient Assistance Program established under G.S. 143-730 to pay the actual costs of administering the program.

(5) Money appropriated to the Department of Insurance for the implementation and administration of independent external review procedures required by Part 4 of Article 50 of this Chapter.

(6) Money appropriated to the Department of Justice to pay its expenses incurred in representing the Department of Insurance in its regulation of the insurance industry and other related programs and industries in this State that fall under the jurisdiction of the Department of Insurance.

(7) **(Effective until June 30, 2004)** Money appropriated to the Department of Insurance to pay its expenses incurred in connection with providing staff support for State boards and commissions, including the North Carolina Manufactured Housing Board, State Fire and Rescue Commission, North Carolina Building Code Council, North Carolina Code Officials Qualification Board, Public Officers and Employees Liability Insurance Commission, North Carolina Home Inspector Licensure Board, and the Volunteer Safety Workers' Compensation Board.

(8) **(Effective until June 30, 2004)** Money appropriated to the Department of Insurance to pay its expenses incurred in connection with continuing education programs under Article 33 of this Chapter and in connection with the purchase and sale of copies of the North Carolina State Building Code.

(e) **(See Editor's note)** Definitions. — The following definitions apply in this section:

(1) **(Effective for taxable years beginning before January 1, 2004)** Article 65 corporation. — Defined in G.S. 105-228.3.

(1) **(Effective for taxable years beginning on or after January 1, 2004)** Repealed by Session Laws 2003-284, s. 43.2, effective for taxable years beginning on or after January 1, 2004.

(2) Insurance company. — A company that pays the gross premiums tax levied in G.S. 105-228.5 and G.S. 105-228.8.

(3) Insurer. — Defined in G.S. 105-228.3. (1991, c. 689, s. 289; 1991 (Reg. Sess., 1992), c. 812, s. 6(e); 1995, c. 360, ss. 1(i), 3(a); c. 517, s. 39(f), (g); 1995 (Reg. Sess., 1996), c. 646, s. 19; c. 747, s. 3; 1997-443, s. 26.1; 1997-475, s. 2.2; 1998-212, s. 29A.7(b); 1999-413, s. 4; 2000-140, s. 93.1(a); 2001-424, ss. 12.2(b), 14E.1(a), 34.22(b), 34.22(c); 2001-489, s. 2(d); 2002-72, s. 9(a); 2002-126, s. 15.5; 2002-144, s. 1; 2002-159, s. 66.5; 2003-284, ss. 22.2, 43.2.)

Subdivision (e)(1) Set Out Twice. — The first version of subdivision (e)(1) set out above is effective for taxable years beginning before January 1, 2004. The second version of subdivision (e)(1) set out above is effective for taxable years beginning on or after January 1, 2004.

Editor's Note. — Session Laws 1995 (Reg. Sess., 1996), c. 747, s. 16, provides: "This act does not obligate the General Assembly to appropriate funds."

Session Laws 2003-284, s. 33.1(a), provides: "The percentage rate to be used in calculating the insurance regulatory charge under G.S. 58-6-25 is five percent (5%) for the 2003 calendar year."

Session Laws 1995, c. 178, s. 1(a); 1995 (Reg. Sess., 1996), c. 670, s. 1(a); 1997-475, s. 2.1; 1998-212, s. 29A.7(a); 1999-413, s. 3; 2000-109, s. 3; 2001-427, s. 1(a); and 2002-126, s. 30E(a), contained similar provisions for calendar years 1995 through 2002, providing for percentage rates of 7.25% for 1995 and 1996, 8.75% for 1997, 6% for 1998, 7% for 1999 and 2000, and 6.5% for 2001 and 2002.

Session Laws 2002-126, s. 1.2, provides: "This act shall be known as 'The Current Operations, Capitol Improvements, and Finance Act of 2002'."

Session Laws 2002-126, s. 2.(i), provides: "The reimbursement from the Insurance Regulatory Fund to the General Fund includes an increase of six hundred thousand dollars ($600,000) for the 2002-2003 fiscal year for the costs and expenses incurred by the Department of Justice as provided in Section 15.5 of this act."

Session Laws 2002-126, s. 31.3, provides: "Except for statutory changes or other provisions that clearly indicate an intention to have effects beyond the 2002-2003 fiscal year, the textual provisions of this act apply only to funds appropriated for, and activities occurring during, the 2002-2003 fiscal year. For example, uncodified provisions of this act relating to the Medicaid program apply only to the 2002-2003 fiscal year."

Session Laws 2002-126, s. 31.6 contains a severability clause.

Session Laws 2002-144, s. 11, contains a severability clause.

Session Laws 2003-284, s. 1.2, provides: "This act shall be known as the 'Current Operations and Capital Improvements Appropriations Act of 2003'."

Session Laws 2003-284, s. 43.4, provides in part: "The Commissioner of Insurance must make a certification to the Secretary of Revenue and to the Revisor of Statutes when there are no Article 65 corporations that offer medical service plans or hospital service plans. This part [Part XLIII of Session Laws 2003-284] is repealed effective for taxable years beginning on or after the January 1 immediately following the certification required by this section."

Session Laws 2003-284, s. 48.1, provides: "Parts 32 through 47 of this act do not affect the rights or liabilities of the State, a taxpayer, or another person arising under a statute amended or repealed by those parts before the effective date of its amendment or repeal; nor do they affect the right to any refund or credit of a tax that accrued under the amended or repealed statute before the effective date of its amendment or repeal."

Session Laws 2003-284, s. 49.3, provides: "Except for statutory changes or other provisions that clearly indicate an intention to have effects beyond the 2003-2005 fiscal biennium, the textual provisions of this act apply only to funds appropriated for, and activities occurring during, the 2003-2005 fiscal biennium."

Session Laws 2003-284, s. 49.5 is a severability clause.

Effect of Amendments. — Session Laws 2001-424, ss. 34.22(b) and (c), as amended by 2001-489, s. 2(d), effective for taxable years beginning on or after January 1, 2003, in the next to last sentence of subsection (a), deleted "presumed" preceding "premium tax liability" and substituted "paying tax at the rate in G.S. 105-228.5(d)(2)" for "an insurer providing health insurance"; and in subsection (e), deleted "or a health maintenance organization" at the end of subdivision (2).

Session Laws 2002-72, s. 9(a), effective for taxable years beginning on or after January 1, 2003, in subsection (c), deleted the former first sentence, which read "The charge levied on each health maintenance organization is payable March 15 following the end of each calendar year," and deleted "other than a health maintenance organization" following "levied on each insurance company" in the present first sentence.

Session Laws 2002-126, ss. 15.5, effective July 1, 2002, added subdivision (d)(6).

Session Laws 2002-144, s. 1, as amended by Session Laws 2003-284, s. 22.2, effective July 1, 2002 and expiring June 30, 2004, added subdivisions (d)(6) and (d)(7) (subsequently recodified as (d)(7) and (d)(8)).

Session Laws 2002-159, s. 66.5, effective October 11, 2002, recodified subdivisions (d)(6) and (d)(7), as added by Session Laws 2002-144, s. 1, as subdivisions (d)(7) and (d)(8), respectively.

Session Laws 2003-284, s. 43.2, effective for taxable years beginning on or after January 1, 2004, and repealed effective for taxable years beginning on or after the January 1 immediately following the certification required by s. 43.4, in subsection (a), deleted "an Article 65 corporation nor" following "company this is not," deleted "Article 65 corporations and" following "For" at the beginning of the fifth sentence; and deleted subdivision (e)(1).

Legal Periodicals. — For 1997 legislative survey, see 20 Campbell L. Rev. 481.

CASE NOTES

Regulatory Charge. — The regulatory charge imposed by this section is not a tax. State Farm Mut. Auto. Ins. Co. v. Long, 129 N.C. App. 164, 497 S.E.2d 451 (1998), aff'd, 350 N.C. 84, 511 S.E.2d 303 (1999).

ARTICLE 7.

General Domestic Companies.

§ 58-7-1. Application of Articles 1 through 64 of this Chapter and general laws.

The general provisions of law relative to the powers, duties, and liabilities of corporations apply to all incorporated domestic insurance companies where pertinent and not in conflict with other provisions of law relative to such companies or with their charters. All insurance companies of this State shall be governed by Articles 1 through 64 of this Chapter, notwithstanding anything in their special charters to the contrary, provided notice of the acceptance of Articles 1 through 64 of this Chapter is filed with the Commissioner. (1899, c. 54, s. 19; Rev., s. 4721; C.S., s. 6324; 1991, c. 720, s. 4.)

§ 58-7-5. Extension of existing charters.

Domestic insurance companies incorporated by special acts, whose charters are subject to limitation of time, shall, after the limitation expires, and upon filing statement and paying the taxes and fees required for an amendment of the charter, continue to be bodies corporate, subject to all general laws applicable to such companies. (1899, c. 54, s. 20; Rev., s. 4722; C.S., s. 6325.)

§ 58-7-10. Certificate required before issuing policies.

No domestic insurance company may issue policies until upon examination of the Commissioner, his deputy or examiner, it is found to have complied with the laws of the State, and until it has obtained from the Commissioner a certificate setting forth that fact and authorizing it to issue policies. The issuing of policies in violation of this section renders the company liable to the forfeiture prescribed by law, but such policies are binding upon the company. (1899, c. 54, ss. 21, 99; 1903, c. 438, s. 10; Rev., s. 4723; C.S., s. 6326; 1991, c. 720, s. 4.)

§ 58-7-15. Kinds of insurance authorized.

The kinds of insurance that may be authorized in this State, subject to the other provisions of Articles 1 through 64 of this Chapter, are set forth in this section. Except to the extent an insurer participates in a risk sharing plan under Article 42 of this Chapter, nothing in this section requires any insurer to insure every kind of risk that it is authorized to insure. Except to the extent an insurer participates in a risk sharing plan under Article 42 of this Chapter, no insurer may transact any other business than that specified in its charter and articles of association or incorporation. The power to do any kind of insurance against loss of or damage to property includes the power to insure all lawful interests in the property and to insure against loss of use and occupancy and rents and profits resulting therefrom; but no kind of insurance includes life insurance or insurance against legal liability for personal injury or death unless specified in this section. In addition to any power to engage in any other kind of business than an insurance business that is specifically conferred by the provisions of Articles 1 through 64 of this Chapter, any insurer authorized to do business in this State may engage in such other kinds of business to the extent necessarily or properly incidental to the kinds of insurance business that it is authorized to do in this State. Each of the following indicates the scope of the kind of insurance business specified:

   (1) "Life insurance", meaning every insurance upon the lives of human beings and every insurance appertaining thereto. The business of life insurance includes the granting of endowment benefits; additional benefits in the event of death by accident or accidental means; additional benefits operating to safeguard the contract from lapse, or to provide a special surrender value, in the event of total and permanent disability of the insured, including industrial sick benefit; and optional modes of settlement of proceeds.

   (2) "Annuities", meaning all agreements to make periodical payments, whether in fixed or variable dollar amounts, or both, at specified intervals.

   (3) "Accident and health insurance", meaning:
      a. Insurance against death or personal injury by accident or by any specified kinds of accident and insurance against sickness, ailment or bodily injury except as specified in paragraph b following; and
      b. "Noncancelable disability insurance," meaning insurance against disability resulting from sickness, ailment or bodily injury (but not including insurance solely against accidental injury), under any contract that does not give the insurer the option to cancel or otherwise terminate the contract at or after one year from its effective date or renewal date.

   (4) "Fire insurance", meaning insurance against loss of or damage to any property resulting from fire, including loss or damage incident to the extinguishment of a fire or to the salvaging of property in connection therewith.

   (5) "Miscellaneous property insurance", meaning loss of or damage to property resulting from:

    a. Lightning, smoke or smudge, windstorm, tornado, cyclone, earth-quake, volcanic eruption, rain, hail, frost and freeze, weather or climatic conditions, excess or deficiency of moisture, flood, the rising of the waters of the ocean or its tributaries, or

    b. Insects, or blights, or from disease of such property other than animals, or

    c. Electrical disturbance causing or concomitant with a fire or an explosion in public service or public utility property, or

    d. Bombardment, invasion, insurrection, riot, civil war or commotion, military or usurped power, any order of a civil authority made to prevent the spread of a conflagration, epidemic or catastrophe, vandalism or malicious mischief, strike or lockout, or explosion; but not including any kind of insurance specified in subdivision (9), except insurance against loss or damage to property resulting from:

       1. Explosion of pressure vessels (except steam boilers of more than 15 pounds pressure) in buildings designed and used solely for residential purposes by not more than four families,

       2. Explosion of any kind originating outside of the insured building or outside of the building containing the property insured,

       3. Explosion of pressure vessels that do not contain steam or that are not operated with steam coils or steam jackets,

       4. Electrical disturbance causing or concomitant with an explosion in public service or public utility property.

(6) "Water damage insurance," meaning insurance against loss or damage by water or other fluid or substance to any property resulting from the breakage or leakage of sprinklers, pumps, or other apparatus erected for extinguishing fires or of water pipes or other conduits or containers; or resulting from casual water entering through leaks or openings in buildings or by seepage through building walls; but not including loss or damage resulting from flood or the rising of the waters of the ocean or its tributaries; and including insurance against accidental injury of such sprinklers, pumps, fire apparatus, conduits, or containers.

(7) "Burglary and theft insurance," meaning:

    a. Insurance against loss of or damage to any property resulting from burglary, theft, larceny, robbery, forgery, fraud, vandalism, malicious mischief, confiscation, or wrongful conversion, disposal or concealment by any person or persons, or from any attempt at any of the foregoing, and

    b. Insurance against loss of or damage to moneys, coins, bullion, securities, notes, drafts, acceptances, or any other valuable papers or documents, resulting from any cause, except while in the custody or possession of and being transported by any carrier for hire or in the mail.

(8) "Glass insurance," meaning insurance against loss of or damage to glass and its appurtenances resulting from any cause.

(9) "Boiler and machinery insurance," meaning insurance against loss of or damage to any property of the insured, resulting from the explosion of or injury to:

    a. Any boiler, heater or other fired pressure vessel;

    b. Any unfired pressure vessel;

    c. Pipes or containers connected with any of said boilers or vessels;

    d. Any engine, turbine, compressor, pump or wheel;

    e. Any apparatus generating, transmitting or using electricity;

    f. Any other machinery or apparatus connected with or operated by any of the previously named boilers, vessels or machines;

and including the incidental power to make inspections of and to issue certificates of inspection upon, any such boilers, apparatus, and machinery, whether insured or otherwise.

(10) "Elevator insurance," meaning insurance against loss of or damage to any property of the insured, resulting from the ownership, maintenance or use of elevators, except loss or damage by fire.

(11) "Animal insurance," meaning insurance against loss of or damage to any domesticated or wild animal resulting from any cause.

(12) "Collision insurance," meaning insurance against loss of or damage to any property of the insured resulting from collision of any other object with the property, but not including collision to or by elevators or to or by vessels, craft, piers or other instrumentalities of ocean or inland navigation.

(13) "Personal injury liability insurance," meaning insurance against legal liability of the insured, and against loss, damage, or expense incident to a claim of such liability; including personal excess liability or personal "umbrella" insurance; and including an obligation of the insurer to pay medical, hospital, surgical, or funeral benefits; and in the case of motor vehicle liability insurance including also disability and death benefits to injured persons, irrespective of legal liability of the insured, arising out of the death or injury of any person, or arising out of injury to the economic interests of any person as a result of negligence in rendering expert, fiduciary, or professional service; but not including any kind of insurance specified in subdivision (15) of this section.

(14) "Property damage liability insurance," meaning insurance against legal liability of the insured, and against loss, damage or expense incident to a claim of such liability, arising out of the loss or destruction of, or damage to, the property of any other person, but not including any kind of insurance specified in subdivision (13) or (15).

(15) "Workers' compensation and employer's liability insurance," meaning insurance against the legal liability, whether imposed by common law or by statute or assumed by contract, of any employer for the death or disablement of, or injury to, the employer's employee.

(16) "Fidelity and surety insurance," meaning:

    a. Guaranteeing the fidelity of persons holding positions of public or private trust;

    b. Becoming surety on, or guaranteeing the performance of, any lawful contract except the following:

        1. A contract of indebtedness secured by title to, or mortgage upon, or interest in, real or personal property;

        2. Any insurance contract except reinsurance;

    c. Becoming surety on, or guaranteeing the performance of, bonds and undertakings required or permitted in all judicial proceedings or otherwise by law allowed, including surety bonds accepted by states and municipal authorities in lieu of deposits as security for the performance of insurance contracts;

    d. Guaranteeing contracts of indebtedness secured by any title to, or interest in, real property, only to the extent required for the purpose of refunding, extending, refinancing, liquidating or salvaging obligations heretofore lawfully made and guaranteed;

    e. Indemnifying banks, bankers, brokers, financial or moneyed corporations or associations against loss resulting from any cause of bills of exchange, notes, bonds, securities, evidences of debts, deeds, mortgages, warehouse receipts, or other valuable papers, documents, money, precious metals and articles made therefrom, jewelry, watches, necklaces, bracelets, gems, precious and semi-precious stones, including any loss while the same are being transported in armored motor vehicles, or by messenger; but not including any other risks of transportation or navigation; also against loss or damage to such an insured's premises, or to the insured's furnishings, fixtures, equipment, safes and vaults therein, caused by burglary, robbery, theft, vandalism or malicious mischief, or any attempt thereat.

(17) "Credit insurance," meaning indemnifying merchants or other persons extending credit against loss or damage resulting from the nonpayment of debts owed to them; and including the incidental power to acquire and dispose of debts so insured, and to collect any debts owed to the insurer or to any person so insured by the insurer including without limiting the foregoing, mortgage guaranty insurance that is insurance against financial loss by reason of the nonpayment of principal, interest and other sums agreed to be paid under the terms of any note or bond, or other evidence of indebtedness secured by a security interest, mortgage, deed of trust, or other instrument constituting a lien or charge on real estate, or on such personal property as the Commissioner may from time to time approve.

(18) "Title insurance," meaning insuring the owners of real property and chattels real and other persons lawfully interested therein against loss by reason of defective titles and encumbrances thereon and insuring the correctness of searches for all instruments, liens or charges affecting the title to that property, including the power to procure and furnish information relative thereto, and other incidental powers that are specifically granted in Articles 1 through 64 of this Chapter.

(19) "Motor vehicle or aircraft insurance," meaning insurance against loss of or damage resulting from any cause to motor vehicles or aircraft and their equipment, and against legal liability of the insured for loss or damage to another's property resulting from the ownership, maintenance or use of motor vehicles or aircraft and against loss, damage or expense incident to a claim of such liability. This subdivision does not apply to commercial aircraft as defined in G.S. 58-1-5.

(20) "Marine insurance," meaning insurance against any and all kinds of loss or damage to:

    a. Vessels, craft, aircraft, cars, automobiles and vehicles of every kind, as well as all goods, freights, cargoes, merchandise, effects, disbursements, profits, moneys, bullion, precious stones, securities, choses in action, evidences of debt, valuable papers, bottomry and respondentia interests and all other kinds of property and interests therein, in respect to, appertaining to or in connection with any and all risks or perils of navigation, transit, or transportation, including war risks, on or under any seas or other waters, on land or in the air, or while being assembled, packed, crated, baled, compressed or similarly prepared for shipment or while awaiting the same or during any delays, storage, transshipment, or reshipment incident thereto, including marine builder's risks and all personal property floater risks, and

    b. Person or to property in connection with or appertaining to a marine, inland marine, transit or transportation insurance, including liability for loss of or damage to either, arising out of or in connection with the construction, repair, operation, maintenance or use of the subject matter of the insurance (but not including life insurance or surety bonds nor insurance against loss because of bodily injury to the person arising out of the ownership, maintenance or use of automobiles), and

c. Precious stones, jewels, jewelry, gold, silver and other precious metals, whether used in business or trade or otherwise and whether the same be in course of transportation or otherwise, and

d. Bridges, tunnels and other instrumentalities of transportation and communication (excluding buildings, their furniture and furnishings, fixed contents and supplies held in storage) unless fire, tornado, sprinkler leakage, hail, explosion, earthquake, riot and/or civil commotion are the only hazards to be covered; piers, wharves, docks and slips, excluding the risks of fire, tornado, sprinkler leakage, hail, explosion, earthquake, riot and/or civil commotion; other aids to navigation and transportation, including dry docks and marine railways against all risks.

(21) "Marine protection and indemnity insurance," meaning insurance against, or against legal liability of the insured for, loss, damage or expense arising out of, or incident to, the ownership, operation, chartering, maintenance, use, repair or construction of any vessel, craft or instrumentality in use in ocean or inland waterways, including liability of the insured for personal injury, illness or death or for loss of or damage to the property of another person.

(22) "Miscellaneous insurance," meaning insurance against any other casualty authorized by the charter of the company, not included in subdivisions (1) to (21) of this section, which is a proper subject of insurance. (1899, c. 54, ss. 24, 26; 1903, c. 438, s. 1; Rev., s. 4726; 1911, c. 111, s. 1; C.S., s. 6327; 1945, c. 386; 1947, c. 721; 1953, c. 992; 1967, c. 624, s. 1; 1969, c. 616, s. 1; 1979, c. 714, s. 2; 1986, Ex. Sess., c. 7, ss. 2, 3; 1987, c. 731, s. 1, c. 864, ss. 39, 40; 1991, c. 644, s. 7; 1999-219, s. 5.1; 2001-236, s. 3; 2001-423, s. 3.)

Effect of Amendments. — Session Laws 2001-236, s. 3, as amended by Session Laws 2001-423, s. 3, effective January 1, 2002, in subdivision (13), inserted "including personal excess liability or personal 'umbrella' insurance," substituted "motor vehicle" for "automobile" preceding "liability insurance," and added "of this section" at the end thereof.

CASE NOTES

No public policy of this State precludes liability insurance coverage for punitive damages in medical malpractice cases. This section appears to authorize insurers to provide coverage for punitive damages. The modern trend and better reasoned decisions in other jurisdictions are to the effect that it is not against public policy to insure against punitive damages. Thus, in North Carolina, punitive damages may be awarded in negligence cases for wanton or gross acts. Mazza v. Medical Mut. Ins. Co., 311 N.C. 621, 319 S.E.2d 217 (1984).

A contract to pay on behalf of its insured "... all sums which the insured shall become legally obligated to pay as damages ..." as part of a physician's liability insurance policy is so broad that it must be interpreted to provide coverage for punitive damages for medical malpractice. Mazza v. Medical Mut. Ins. Co., 311 N.C. 621, 319 S.E.2d 217 (1984).

Punitive Damages for Intentional Conduct. — In the absence of an explicit public policy, the terms of an insurance contract covering punitive damages are controlling with respect to the award of punitive damages for intentional conduct. St. Paul Mercury Ins. Co. v. Duke Univ., 849 F.2d 133 (4th Cir. 1988).

Cited in Hartford Accident & Indem. Co. v. Ingram, 290 N.C. 457, 226 S.E.2d 498 (1976).

§ 58-7-16. Funding agreements authorized.

(a) As used in this section, "funding agreement" means an agreement that authorizes a licensed life insurer to accept funds and that provides for an accumulation of funds for the purpose of making one or more payments at future dates in amounts that are not based on mortality or morbidity contingencies. A "funding agreement" is not an "annuity" as defined in G.S. 58-7-15; and is not a "security" as defined in G.S. 78A-2.

(b) Any insurer that is licensed to write life insurance or annuities in this State may deliver, or issue for delivery, funding agreements in this State.

(c) Funding agreements may be issued to persons authorized by a state or foreign country to engage in an insurance business or to their affiliates, including affiliates of the issuer. Issuance to an affiliate of an issuer is not subject to the provisions of Article 19 of this Chapter. Funding agreements may be issued to persons other than those licensed to write life insurance and annuities or their affiliates in order to fund one or more of the following:

    (1) Benefits under any employee benefit plan as defined in the federal Employee Retirement Income Security Act of 1974, 29 U.S.C. § 1001 et seq., maintained in the United States or in a foreign country.

    (2) The activities of an organization exempt from taxation under section 501(c) of the Internal Revenue Code or of any similar organization in a foreign country.

    (3) A program of the government of the United States, the government of a state, foreign country, or political subdivision, agency, or instrumentality thereof.

    (4) An agreement providing for one or more payments in satisfaction of a claim or liability.

    (5) A program of an institution that has assets in excess of twenty-five million dollars ($25,000,000).

(d) Amounts shall not be guaranteed or credited under a funding agreement except upon reasonable assumptions as to investment income and expenses and on a basis equitable to all holders of funding agreements of a given class.

(e) Amounts paid to the insurer and proceeds applied under optional modes of settlement under funding agreements may be allocated by the insurer to one or more separate accounts pursuant to G.S. 58-7-95.

(f) The Commissioner has sole authority to regulate the issuance and sale of funding agreements on behalf of insurers. In addition to the authority in G.S. 58-2-40, the Commissioner may adopt rules relating to:

    (1) Standards to be followed in the approval of forms of funding agreements.

    (2) Reserves to be maintained by and valuation rules for insurers issuing funding agreements.

    (3) Accounting and reporting of funds credited under funding agreements.

    (4) Disclosure of information to be given to holders and prospective holders of funding agreements.

    (5) Qualification and compensation of persons selling funding agreements on behalf of insurers.

In determining minimum valuation reserves to be maintained by and valuation rules for insurers issuing funding agreements, the Commissioner may use any relevant actuarial guideline, regulation, interpretation, or paper published by the Society of Actuaries or the American Academy of Actuaries that the Commissioner considers reasonable. (1993 (Reg. Sess., 1994), c. 600, s. 1; 1998-212, s. 26B(e); 2001-334, s. 17.2.)

§ 58-7-20: Repealed by Session Laws 1991, c. 681, s. 23.

§ 58-7-21. Credit allowed a domestic ceding insurer.

(a) The purpose of this section and G.S. 58-7-26 is to protect the interest of insureds, claimants, ceding insurers, assuming insurers, and the public generally. The General Assembly declares its intent is to ensure adequate regulation of insurers and reinsurers and adequate protection for those to whom they owe obligations. In furtherance of that interest, the General Assembly provides a mandate that upon the insolvency of an alien insurer or reinsurer that provides security to fund its United States obligations in accordance with this section and G.S. 58-7-26, the assets representing the security shall be maintained in the United States and claims shall be filed with and valued by the state insurance commissioner with regulatory oversight, and the assets shall be distributed, in accordance with the insurance laws of the state in which the trust is domiciled that are applicable to the liquidation of domestic United States insurance companies. The General Assembly declares that the matters contained in this section and G.S. 58-7-26 are fundamental to the business of insurance in accordance with 15 U.S.C. §§ 1011-1012.

(b) Credit for reinsurance shall be allowed a domestic ceding insurer as either an asset or a reduction from liability on account of reinsurance ceded only when the reinsurer meets the requirements of subdivisions (1), (2), (3), (4), or (5) of this subsection. Credit shall be allowed under subdivision (1), (2), or (3) of this subsection only with regard to cessions of those kinds or classes of business in which the assuming insurer is licensed or otherwise permitted to write or assume in its state of domicile or, in the case of a United States branch of an alien assuming insurer, in the state through which it is entered and licensed to transact insurance or reinsurance. Credit shall be allowed under subdivision (3) or (4) of this subsection only if the applicable requirements of subdivision (6) of this section have been satisfied.

    (1) Credit shall be allowed when the reinsurance is ceded to an assuming insurer that is licensed to transact insurance or reinsurance in this State.

    (2) Credit shall be allowed when the reinsurance is ceded to an assuming insurer that is accredited as a reinsurer in this State. An accredited reinsurer is one that:

        a. Files with the Commissioner evidence of its submission to this State's jurisdiction;

        b. Submits to this State's authority to examine its books and records;

        c. Is licensed to transact insurance or reinsurance in at least one state, or in the case of a United States branch of an alien assuming insurer is entered through and licensed to transact insurance or reinsurance in at least one state;

        d. Files annually with the Commissioner a copy of its annual statement filed with the insurance regulator of its state of domicile, a copy of its most recent audited financial statement, and a fee of five hundred dollars ($500.00); and either

           1. Maintains a policyholders' surplus in an amount that is not less than twenty million dollars ($20,000,000) and whose accreditation has not been denied by the Commissioner within 90 days after its submission; or

           2. Maintains a policyholders' surplus in an amount less than twenty million dollars ($20,000,000) and whose accreditation has been approved by the Commissioner.

        Credit shall not be allowed a domestic ceding insurer if the assuming insurer's accreditation has been revoked by the Commissioner after notice and opportunity for a hearing.

(3) Credit shall be allowed when the reinsurance is ceded to an assuming insurer that is domiciled in, or in the case of a United States branch of an alien assuming insurer is entered through, a state that uses standards regarding credit for reinsurance substantially similar to those applicable under this section and the assuming insurer or United States branch of an alien assuming insurer:

    a. Maintains a policyholders' surplus in an amount not less than twenty million dollars ($20,000,000); and

    b. Submits to the authority of this State to examine its books and records.

The requirement in sub-subdivision (3)a. of this subsection does not apply to reinsurance ceded and assumed under pooling arrangements among insurers in the same holding company system.

(4)a. Credit shall be allowed when the reinsurance is ceded to an assuming insurer that maintains a trust fund in a qualified United States financial institution, as defined in G.S. 58-7-26(b), for the payment of the valid claims of its United States ceding insurers, their assigns and successors in interest. The assuming insurer shall report annually to the Commissioner information substantially the same as that required to be reported on the NAIC Annual Statement form by licensed insurers to enable the Commissioner to determine the sufficiency of the trust fund. The assuming insurer shall submit to examination of its books and records by the Commissioner and bear the expense of examination.

    b. Repealed by Session Laws 2001-223, s. 3.1. For applicability, see note.

    b1. Credit for reinsurance shall not be granted under this subdivision unless the form of the trust and any amendments to the trust have been approved by:

        1. The insurance regulator of the state where the trust is domiciled; or

        2. The insurance regulator of another state who, pursuant to the terms of the trust instrument, has accepted principal regulatory oversight of the trust.

    b2. The form of the trust and any trust amendments also shall be filed with the insurance regulator of every state in which the ceding insurer beneficiaries of the trust are domiciled. The trust instrument shall provide that contested claims shall be valid and enforceable upon the final order of any court of competent jurisdiction in the United States. The trust shall vest legal title to its assets in its trustees for the benefit of the assuming insurer's United States ceding insurers, their assigns, and successors in interest. The trust and the assuming insurer shall be subject to examination as determined by the Commissioner.

    b3. The trust shall remain in effect for as long as the assuming insurer has outstanding obligations due under the reinsurance agreements subject to the trust. No later than February 28 of each year, the trustees of the trust shall report to the Commissioner in writing the balance of the trust, shall list the trust's investments at the end of the preceding year, and shall certify the date of termination of the trust, if so planned, or shall certify that the trust will not expire before the following December 31.

    c. The following requirements apply to the following categories of assuming insurer:

        1. The trust fund for a single assuming insurer shall consist of funds in trust in an amount not less than the assuming

insurer's liabilities attributable to reinsurance ceded by United States ceding insurers, and, in addition, the assuming insurer shall maintain a surplus in trust of not less than twenty million dollars ($20,000,000).

2. In the case of a group including incorporated and individual unincorporated underwriters:

I. For reinsurance ceded under reinsurance agreements with an inception, amendment, or renewal date on or after August 1, 1995, the trust shall consist of an account in trust in an amount not less than the group's several liabilities attributable to business ceded by United States domiciled ceding insurers to any member of the group.

II. For reinsurance ceded under reinsurance agreements with an inception date on or before July 31, 1995, and not amended or renewed after that date, notwithstanding the other provisions of this section and G.S. 58-7-26, the trust shall consist of an account in trust in an amount not less than the group's several insurance and reinsurance liabilities attributable to business written in the United States.

In addition to these trusts, the group shall maintain in trust a surplus of which one hundred million dollars ($100,000,000) shall be held jointly for the benefit of the United States domiciled ceding insurers of any member of the group for all years of account. Each incorporated member of the group shall not be engaged in any business other than underwriting as a member of the group and shall be subject to the same level of regulation and solvency control by the group's domiciliary insurance regulator as are the unincorporated members. Within 90 days after its financial statements are due to be filed with the group's domiciliary insurance regulator, the group shall provide to the Commissioner an annual certification by the group's domiciliary insurance regulator of the solvency of each underwriter member or, if a certification is unavailable, financial statements prepared by independent public accountants of each underwriter member of the group.

d. Repealed by Session Laws 2001-223, s. 3.1. For applicability, see note.

(5) Credit shall be allowed when the reinsurance is ceded to an assuming insurer not meeting the requirements of subdivisions (1), (2), (3), or (4) of this subsection, but only with respect to the insurance of risks located in jurisdictions where the reinsurance is required by applicable law or regulation of that jurisdiction.

(6) If the assuming insurer is not licensed or accredited to transact insurance or reinsurance in this State, the credit permitted by subdivisions (3) and (4) of this subsection shall not be allowed unless the assuming insurer agrees in the reinsurance agreements:

a. That if the assuming insurer fails to perform its obligations under the terms of the reinsurance agreement, the assuming insurer, at the ceding insurer's request, shall submit to the jurisdiction of any court of competent jurisdiction in any state of the United States, shall comply with all requirements necessary to give the court jurisdiction, and shall abide by the final decision of the court or of any appellate court if there is an appeal; and

   b. To designate the Commissioner or a designated attorney as its true and lawful attorney upon whom may be served any lawful process in any action, suit, or proceeding begun by or on behalf of the ceding company.

This subdivision does not affect the obligation of the parties to a reinsurance agreement to arbitrate their disputes, if the obligation is created in the agreement.

(7) If the assuming insurer does not meet the requirements of subdivision (1), (2), or (3) of this subsection, the credit permitted by subdivision (4) of this subsection shall not be allowed unless the assuming insurer agrees in the trust agreements to the following conditions:

   a. Notwithstanding any other provisions in the trust instrument, if the trust fund is inadequate because it contains an amount less than the amount required by sub-subdivision of this subsection, or if the grantor of the trust has been declared insolvent or placed into receivership, rehabilitation, liquidation, or similar proceedings under the laws of its state or country of domicile, the trustee shall comply with an order of the public official with regulatory oversight over the trust or with an order of a court of competent jurisdiction directing the trustee to transfer to the public official with regulatory oversight all of the assets of the trust fund.

   b. The assets shall be distributed by, and claims shall be filed with and valued by, the public official with regulatory oversight in accordance with the laws of the state in which the trust is domiciled that are applicable to the liquidation of domestic insurance companies.

   c. If the public official with regulatory oversight determines that the assets of the trust fund or any part thereof are not necessary to satisfy the claims of the United States ceding insurers of the grantor of the trust, those assets shall be returned by the public official with regulatory oversight to the trustee for distribution in accordance with the trust agreement.

   d. The grantor shall waive any right otherwise available to it under United States law that is inconsistent with this provision.

(c) This section applies to all reinsurance cessions made on or after January 1, 1992, under reinsurance agreements that have an inception, anniversary, or renewal date on or after January 1, 1992. (1991, c. 681, s. 22; 1993, c. 452, s. 42; 1993 (Reg. Sess., 1994), c. 678, s. 8; 1995, c. 193, s. 13; c. 360, s. 2(g); 2001-223, s. 3.1.)

Editor's Note. — Session Laws 2001-223, s. 27 is a severability clause.

Effect of Amendments. — Session Laws 2001-223, s. 3.1, applicable to all reinsurance cessions made on or after January 1, 2002, under reinsurance agreements that have an inception, anniversary, or renewal date on or after January 1, 2002, rewrote subsection (a) and the introductory paragraph of subsection (b); substituted "Credit shall not" for "No credit" at the beginning of the last sentence of subdivision (b)(2)d; in subdivision (b)(3), deleted "and licensed" following "domiciled" in the first sentence, and substituted "The" for "However, the" at the beginning of the last sentence; in subdivision (b)(4)a, deleted "policyholders and" preceding "ceding insurers" in the first sentence, deleted the former last two sentences, and inserted the current last sentence; deleted former subdivision (d)(4)b; added subdivisions (d)(4)b1 through (d)(4)b3; rewrote subdivision (d)(4)c; deleted former subdivision (d)(4)d, relating to an annual report by the trustees of the trust; inserted "or a designated attorney" in subdivision (d)(6)b; and added subdivision (b)(7).

§ **58-7-25:** Repealed by Session Laws 1991, c. 681, s. 23.

§ 58-7-26. Asset or reduction from liability for reinsurance ceded by a domestic insurer to an assuming insurer not meeting the requirements of G.S. 58-7-21.

(a) An asset or a reduction from liability for reinsurance ceded by a domestic insurer to an assuming insurer not meeting the requirements of G.S. 58-7-21 shall be allowed in an amount not exceeding the liabilities carried by the ceding insurer. The reduction shall be in the amount of funds held by or on behalf of the ceding insurer, including funds held in trust for the ceding insurer, under a reinsurance contract with the assuming insurer as security for the payment of obligations thereunder, if the security is held in the United States subject to withdrawal solely by, and under the exclusive control of, the ceding insurer; or, in the case of a trust, held in a qualified United States financial institution as defined in subsection (c) of this section. This security may be in the form of:

    (1) Cash;

    (2) Securities that are listed by the Securities Valuation Office of the NAIC and qualifying as admitted assets;

    (3) Clean, irrevocable, unconditional letters of credit, issued or confirmed by a qualified United States financial institution, as defined in subsection (b) of this section, no later than December 31 of the year for which the filing is being made, and in the possession of, or in trust for, the ceding company on or before the filing date of its annual statement. Letters of credit meeting applicable standards of issuer acceptability as of the dates of their issuance (or confirmation) shall, notwithstanding the issuing (or confirming) institution's subsequent failure to meet applicable standards of issuer acceptability, continue to be acceptable as security until their expiration, extension, renewal, modification or amendment, whichever occurs first; or

    (4) Any other form of security acceptable to the Commissioner.

(b) For purposes of subdivision (a)(3) of this section, a "qualified United States financial institution" means an institution that:

    (1) Is organized, or in the case of a United States office of a foreign banking organization licensed, under the laws of the United States or any of its states;

    (2) Is regulated, supervised, and examined by United States federal or state authorities having regulatory authority over banks and trust companies; and

    (3) Has been determined by either the Commissioner or the Securities Valuation Office of the NAIC to meet such standards of financial condition and standing as are considered necessary and appropriate to regulate the quality of financial institutions whose letters of credit will be acceptable to the Commissioner.

(c) A "qualified United States financial institution" means, for purposes of those provisions of this section specifying those institutions that are eligible to act as a fiduciary of a trust, an institution that:

    (1) Is organized, or in the case of a United States branch or agency office of a foreign banking organization licensed, under the laws of the United States or any of its states and has been granted authority to operate with fiduciary powers; and

    (2) Is regulated, supervised, and examined by federal or state authorities having regulatory authority over banks and trust companies.

(d) This section applies to all reinsurance cessions made on or after January 1, 1992, under reinsurance agreements that have an inception, anniversary, or renewal date on or after January 1, 1992. (1991, c. 681, s. 22; 2001-223, s. 3.2.)

Editor's Note. — Session Laws 2001-223, s. 27 is a severability clause.

Effect of Amendments. — Session Laws 2001-223, s. 3.2, applicable to all reinsurance cessions made on or after January 1, 2002, under reinsurance agreements that have an inception, anniversary, or renewal date on or after January 1, 2002, inserted "Asset or" at the beginning of the section heading, and added "not meeting the requirements of G.S. 58-7-21" at the end thereof; in subsection (a), divided the former first sentence into the present first two sentences, added "An asset or" at the beginning of the present first sentence, and substituted "The" for "and such" at the beginning of the present second sentence; and added "or in trust for" in the first sentence of subdivision (a)(3).

§ 58-7-30. Insolvent ceding insurer.

(a) Notwithstanding any other provision of this Article, no credit shall be allowed, as an admitted asset or as a reduction from liability, to any ceding insurer for reinsurance, unless the reinsurance is payable by the assuming insurer, on the basis of reported claims allowed by the court overseeing the liquidation against the ceding insurer under the contract or contracts reinsured without diminution because of the insolvency of the ceding insurer, directly to the ceding insurer or to its domiciliary receiver except (1) where the contract or other written agreement specifically provides for another payee of the reinsurance in the event of the insolvency of the ceding insurer or (2) where the assuming insurer, with the consent of the direct insured or insureds, has assumed the policy obligations of the ceding insurer as direct obligations of the assuming insurer to the payees under the policies and in substitution of the obligations of the ceding insurer to the payees.

(b) No credit shall be allowed, as an admitted asset or as a reduction from liability, to any ceding insurer for reinsurance, unless the reinsurance is documented by a policy, certificate, treaty, or other form of agreement that is properly executed by an authorized officer of the assuming insurer. If the reinsurance is ceded through an underwriting manager or agent, the manager or agent shall provide to the domestic ceding insurer evidence of the manager or agent's authority to assume reinsurance for and on behalf of the assuming insurer. The evidence shall consist of either an acceptable letter of authority executed by an authorized officer of the assuming insurer or a copy of the actual agency agreement between the underwriting manager or agent and the assuming insurer; and the evidence shall be specific as to the classes of business within the authority and as to the term of the authority. If there is any conflict between this subsection and Article 9 of this Chapter, the provisions of Article 9 govern.

(c) The reinsurance agreement may provide that the domiciliary liquidator of an insolvent ceding insurer shall give written notice to the assuming insurer of the pendency of a claim against the ceding insurer on the contract reinsured within a reasonable time after the claim is filed in the liquidation proceeding. During the pendency of the claim, any assuming insurer may investigate the claim and interpose at its own expense in the proceeding where the claim is to be adjudicated, any defenses which it deems available to the ceding insurer or its liquidator. The expense may be filed as a claim against the insolvent ceding insurer to the extent of a proportionate share of the benefit which may accrue to the ceding insurer solely as a result of the defense undertaken by the assuming insurer. Where two or more assuming insurers are involved in the same claim and a majority in interest elect to interpose a defense to the claim, the expense shall be apportioned in accordance with the terms of the reinsurance agreement as though the expense had been incurred by the ceding insurer. (1985, c. 572, s. 1; 1995, c. 193, s. 14; c. 517, s. 4; 2001-223, s. 3.3.)

§ 58-7-31. Life and health reinsurance agreements.

(a) Notwithstanding any other provision of this Article, this section applies to every domestic life and accident and health insurer, to every other licensed life and accident and health insurer that is not subject to a substantially similar statute or administrative rule in its domiciliary state, and to every licensed property and casualty insurer with respect to its accident and health business. This section does not apply to assumption reinsurance, yearly renewable term reinsurance, nor to certain nonproportional reinsurance, such as stop loss or catastrophe reinsurance.

(b) No insurer shall, for reinsurance ceded, reduce any liability or establish any asset in any financial statement filed with the Commissioner if, by the terms of the reinsurance agreement, in substance or effect, any of the following conditions exist:

    (1) Renewal expense allowances provided or to be provided to the ceding insurer by the reinsurer in any accounting period, are not sufficient to cover anticipated allocable renewal expenses of the ceding insurer on the portion of the business reinsured, unless a liability is established for the present value of the shortfall, using assumptions equal to the applicable statutory reserve basis on the business reinsured. Those expenses include commissions, premium taxes, and direct expenses including, but not limited to, billing, valuation, claims, and maintenance expected by the company at the time the business is reinsured.

    (2) The ceding insurer can be deprived of surplus or assets at the reinsurer's option or automatically upon the occurrence of some event, such as the insolvency of the ceding insurer; except that termination of the reinsurance agreement by the reinsurer for nonpayment of reinsurance premiums or other amounts due, such as modified coinsurance reserve adjustments, interest, and adjustments on funds withheld, and tax reimbursements, are not a deprivation of surplus or assets.

    (3) The ceding insurer is required to reimburse the reinsurer for negative experience under the reinsurance agreement; except that neither offsetting experience refunds against current and prior years' losses under the reinsurance agreement nor payment by the ceding insurer of an amount equal to the current and prior years' losses under the reinsurance agreement upon voluntary termination of in-force reinsurance by the ceding insurer are a reimbursement to the reinsurer for negative experience. Voluntary termination does not include situations where termination occurs because of unreasonable provisions that allow the reinsurer to reduce its risk under the reinsurance agreement.

    (4) The ceding insurer must, at specific points in time scheduled in the reinsurance agreement, terminate or automatically recapture all or part of the reinsurance ceded.

    (5) The reinsurance agreement involves the possible payment by the ceding insurer to the reinsurer of amounts other than from income realized from the reinsured policies. No ceding company shall pay reinsurance premiums or other fees or charges to a reinsurer that are greater than the direct premiums collected by the ceding company.

    (6) The treaty does not transfer all of the significant risk inherent in the business being reinsured. The following table identifies for a representative sampling of products or type of business, the risks that are considered to be significant. For products not specifically included, the risks determined to be significant shall be consistent with this table.

Risk Categories:

a.=   Morbidity.

b.=   Mortality.

c.=   Lapse. (This is the risk that a policy will voluntarily terminate before the recoupment of a statutory surplus strain experienced at issue of the policy.)

d.=   Credit Quality (C1). (This is the risk that invested assets supporting the reinsured business will decrease in value. The main hazards are that assets will default or that there will be a decrease in earning power. It excludes market value declines due to changes in interest rate.)

e.=   Reinvestment (C3). (This is the risk that interest rates will fall and funds reinvested [coupon payments or monies received upon asset maturity or call] will therefore earn less than expected. If asset durations are less than liability durations, the mismatch will increase.)

f.=   Disintermediation (C3). (This is the risk that interest rates will rise and policy loans and surrenders increase or maturing contracts do not renew at anticipated rates of renewal. If asset durations are greater than the liability durations, the mismatch will increase. Policyholders will move their funds into new products offering higher rates. The company may have to sell assets at a loss to provide for these withdrawals.)

+=   Significant   0 = Insignificant

RISK CATEGORY

	a	b	c	d	e	f
Health Insurance — other than LTC/LTD*	+	0	+	0	0	0
Health Insurance — LTC/LTD*	+	0	+	+	+	0
Immediate Annuities	0	+	0	+	+	0
Single Premium Deferred Annuities	0	0	+	+	+	+
Flexible Premium Deferred Annuities	0	0	+	+	+	+
Guaranteed Interest Contracts	0	0	0	+	+	+
Other Annuity Deposit Business	0	0	+	+	+	+
Single Premium Whole Life	0	+	+	+	+	+
Traditional Non-Par Permanent	0	+	+	+	+	+
Traditional Non-Par Term	0	+	+	0	0	0
Traditional Par Permanent	0	+	+	+	+	+
Traditional Par Term	0	+	+	0	0	0
Adjustable Premium Permanent	0	+	+	+	+	+
Indeterminate Premium Permanent	0	+	+	+	+	+
Universal Life Flexible Premium	0	+	+	+	+	+
Universal Life Fixed Premium	0	+	+	+	+	+
Universal Life Fixed Premium (dump-in premiums allowed)	0	+	+	+	+	+

*LTC = Long-Term Care Insurance

*LTD = Long-Term Disability Insurance

(7)a. The credit quality, reinvestment, or disintermediation risk is significant for the business reinsured and the ceding company does not (other than for the classes of business excepted in subdivision (7)b. of this section) either transfer the underlying assets to the reinsurer or legally segregate such assets in a trust or escrow account or otherwise establish a mechanism satisfactory to the Commissioner that legally segregates, by contract or contractual provisions, the underlying assets.

 b. Notwithstanding the requirements of subdivision (7)a. of this section, the assets supporting the reserves for the following classes of business and any classes of business that do not have a significant credit quality, reinvestment, or disintermediation risk may be held by the ceding company without segregation of those assets:

  — Health Insurance — LTC/LTD
  — Traditional Non-Par Permanent
  — Traditional Par Permanent
  — Adjustable Premium Permanent
  — Indeterminate Premium Permanent
  — Universal Life Fixed Premium
  (no dump-in premiums allowed)

The associated formula for determining the reserve interest rate adjustment must use a formula that reflects the ceding company's investment earnings and incorporates all realized and unrealized gains and losses reflected in the statutory statement. The following is an acceptable formula:

$$\text{Rate} = \frac{2 \ (I + CG)}{X \ + \ Y - I - CG}$$

Where: I is the net investment income.

 CG is capital gains less capital losses.

 X is the current year cash and invested assets plus investment income due and accrued less borrowed money.

 Y is the same as X but for the prior year.

 (8) Settlements are made less frequently than quarterly or payments due from the reinsurer are not made in cash within 90 days after the settlement date.

 (9) The ceding insurer is required to make representations or warranties not reasonably related to the business being reinsured.

 (10) The ceding insurer is required to make representations or warranties about future performance of the business being reinsured.

 (11) The reinsurance agreement is entered into for the principal purpose of producing significant surplus aid for the ceding insurer, typically on a temporary basis, while not transferring all of the significant risks inherent in the business reinsured and, in substance or effect, the expected potential liability to the ceding insurer remains basically unchanged.

(c) Notwithstanding subsection (b) of this section, an insurer may, with the prior approval of the Commissioner, take such reserve credit or establish such asset as the Commissioner deems to be consistent with the insurance laws or rules of this State, including actuarial interpretations or standards adopted by the Commissioner.

 (d)(1) Reinsurance agreements entered into after October 1, 1993, that involve the reinsurance of business issued prior to the effective date of the reinsurance agreements, along with any subsequent amendments thereto, shall be filed by the ceding company with the Commissioner within 30 days after its date of execution. Each filing shall include data detailing the financial impact of the transaction. The ceding insurer's actuary who signs the financial statement actuarial opinion with respect to valuation of reserves shall consider this statute and any applicable actuarial standards of practice when determining the proper credit in financial statements filed with the Commissioner. The actuary should maintain adequate documentation and be prepared upon request to describe the actuarial work performed for inclusion in the financial statements and to demonstrate that such work conforms to this statute.

(2) Any increase in surplus net of federal income tax resulting from arrangements described in subdivision (d)(1) of this section shall be identified separately on the insurer's statutory financial statement as a surplus item (aggregate write-ins for gains and losses in surplus in the Capital and Surplus Account, page 4 of the Annual Statement) and recognition of the surplus increase as income shall be reflected on a net of tax basis in the "Reinsurance Ceded" line, page 4 of the Annual Statement as earnings emerge from the business reinsured.

(e) No reinsurance agreement or amendment to any reinsurance agreement may be used to reduce any liability or to establish any asset in any financial statement filed with the Commissioner, unless the reinsurance agreement, amendment, or a binding letter of intent has been duly executed by both parties no later than the "as of date" of the financial statement.

(f) In the case of a letter of intent, a reinsurance agreement or an amendment to a reinsurance agreement must be executed within a reasonable period of time, not exceeding 90 days after the execution date of the letter of intent, in order for credit to be granted for the reinsurance ceded.

(g) The reinsurance agreement shall contain provisions that provide that:

(1) The reinsurance agreement shall constitute the entire reinsurance agreement between the parties with respect to the business being reinsured thereunder and that there are no understandings between the parties other than as expressed in the reinsurance agreement; and

(2) Any change or modification to the reinsurance agreement shall be null and void unless made by amendment to the reinsurance agreement and signed by both parties.

(h) Insurers subject to this section shall reduce to zero by December 31, 1994, any reserve credits or assets established with respect to reinsurance agreements entered into prior to October 1, 1993, that, under the provisions of this section, would not be entitled to recognition of such reserve credits or assets; provided, however, that such reinsurance agreements shall have been in compliance with laws or regulations in existence immediately preceding October 1, 1993. (1993, c. 452, s. 4; 1993 (Reg. Sess., 1994), c. 678, s. 9; 1995, c. 193, ss. 15, 16; 2001-223, ss. 3.4, 3.5.)

§ **58-7-32:** Repealed by Session Laws 1993, c. 452, s. 65.

Cross References. — As to life and health reinsurance agreements, see G.S. 58-7-31.

§ 58-7-33. Minimum policyholders' surplus to assume property or casualty reinsurance.

(a) Notwithstanding any other provision of law, no domestic property or casualty insurer with less than ten million dollars ($10,000,000) in policyholders' surplus may, without the Commissioner's prior written approval, assume reinsurance on any risk that it is otherwise permitted to assume except where the reinsurance is:

(1) Required by applicable law or regulation; or

(2) Assumed under pooling arrangement among members of the same holding company system.

(b) This section applies to reinsurance contracts entered into or renewed on or after July 13, 1991.

(c) This section does not invalidate any reinsurance contract that was entered into before July 13, 1991, as between the parties to the contract. (1991, c. 681, s. 26.)

§ 58-7-35. Manner of creating such corporations.

The procedure for organizing such corporations is as follows: The proposed incorporators, not less than 10 in number, a majority of whom must be residents of the State, shall subscribe articles of association setting forth their intention to form a corporation; its proposed name, which must not so closely resemble the name of an existing corporation doing business under the laws of this State as to be likely to mislead the public, and must be approved by the Commissioner; the class of insurance it proposes to transact and on what business plan or principle; the place of its location within the State, and if on the stock plan, the amount of its capital stock. The words "insurance company," "insurance association," or "insurance society" or "life" or "casualty" or "indemnity," or an acceptable alternative approved by the Commissioner, must be a part of the title of any such corporation. The certificate of incorporation must be subscribed and sworn to by the incorporators before an officer authorized to take acknowledgment of deeds, who shall forthwith certify the certificate of incorporation, as so made out and signed, to the Commissioner at his office in the City of Raleigh. The Commissioner shall examine the certificate, and if he approves of it and finds that the requirements of the law have been complied with, shall certify such facts, by certificate on such articles, to the Secretary of State. Upon the filing in the office of the Secretary of State of the certificate of incorporation and attached certificates, and the payment of a charter fee in the amount required for private corporations, and the same fees to the Secretary of State, the Secretary of State shall cause the certificate and accompanying certificates to be recorded in his office, and shall issue a certificate in the following form:

Be it known that, whereas (here the names of the subscribers to the articles of association shall be inserted) have associated themselves with the intention of forming a corporation under the name of (here the name of the corporation shall be inserted), for the purpose (here the purpose declared in the articles of association shall be inserted), with a capital (or with a permanent fund) of (here the amount of capital or permanent fund fixed in the articles of association shall be inserted), and have complied with the provisions of the statute of this State in such case made and provided, as appears from the following certified articles of association: (here copy articles of association and accompanying certificates). Now, therefore, I (here the name of the Secretary shall be inserted), Secretary of State, hereby certify that (here the names of the subscribers to the articles of association shall be inserted), their associates and successors, are legally organized and established as, and are hereby made, an existing corporation under the name of (here the name of the corporation shall be inserted), with such articles of association, and have all the powers, rights, and privileges and are subject to the duties, liabilities, and restrictions which by law appertain thereto.

Witness my official signature hereunto subscribed, and the seal of the State of North Carolina hereunto affixed, this the _____ day of _____, in the year _____ (in these blanks the day, month, and year of execution of this certificate shall be inserted; and in the case of purely mutual companies, so much as relates to capital stock shall be omitted).

The Secretary of State shall sign the certificate and cause the seal of the State to be affixed to it, and such certificate of incorporation and certificate of the Secretary of State has the effect of a special charter and is conclusive evidence of the organization and establishment of the corporation. The

Secretary of State shall also cause a record of his certificate to be made, and a certified copy of this record may be given in evidence with the same effect as the original certificate.

Subject to G.S. 58-8-5, any proposed change in the articles of incorporation shall be filed with the Commissioner, who shall examine the change. If the Commissioner approves the change, the Commissioner shall place a certificate of approval on the change, and forward it to the Secretary of State. (1899, c. 54, s. 25; 1903, c. 438, ss. 2, 3; Rev., s. 4727; C.S., s. 6328; 1957, c. 98; 1987 (Reg. Sess., 1988), c. 975, s. 15; 1989, c. 485, s. 50; 1991, c. 720, ss. 4, 53; 1993, c. 504, s. 4.)

§ 58-7-37. Background of incorporators and proposed management personnel.

(a) Before a license is issued to a new domestic insurance company, each key person must furnish the Commissioner a complete set of the applicant's fingerprints and a recent passport size full-face photograph of the applicant. The applicant's fingerprints shall be certified by an authorized law enforcement officer. The fingerprints of every applicant shall be forwarded to the State Bureau of Investigation for a search of the applicant's criminal history record file, if any. If warranted, the State Bureau of Investigation shall forward a set of the fingerprints to the Federal Bureau of Investigation for a national criminal history record check. An applicant shall pay the cost of the State and any national criminal history record check of the applicant.

(b) As used in this section, 'key person' means a proposed officer, director, or any other individual who will be in a position to influence the operating decisions of a domestic insurance company.

(c) The Commissioner may refuse to approve the formation or initial license of a new domestic insurance company under this Article if, after notice to the applicant and an opportunity for a hearing, the Commissioner finds as to the incorporators or other key person any one or more of the following conditions:

    (1) Any untrue material statement regarding the background or experience of any incorporator or other key person;

    (2) Violation of, or noncompliance with, any insurance laws, or of any rule or order of the Commissioner or of a commissioner of another state by any incorporator or other key person;

    (3) Obtaining or attempting to obtain the license through misrepresentation or fraud;

    (4) An incorporator or other key person has been convicted of a felony;

    (5) An incorporator or other key person has been found to have committed any unfair trade practice or fraud;

    (6) An incorporator or other key person has used fraudulent, coercive, or dishonest practices, or has acted in a manner that is incompetent, untrustworthy, or financially irresponsible; or

    (7) An incorporator or other key person has held such a position in another insurance company that has had its license suspended or revoked by any state.

(d) If the Commissioner disapproves of the formation or initial license, the Commissioner shall notify the applicant and advise the applicant in writing of the reasons for the disapproval. Within 30 days after receipt of notification, the applicant may make written demand upon the Commissioner for a hearing to determine the reasonableness of the Commissioner's action. The hearing shall be scheduled within 30 days after the date of receipt of the written demand.

(e) For the purposes of investigation under this section, the Commissioner shall have all the power conferred by G.S. 58-2-50 and other applicable provisions of this Chapter.

(f) The Commissioner may adopt rules to set standards for obtaining background information on each incorporator or other key person of a proposed new domestic insurance company. (2001-223, s. 4.1.)

§ 58-7-40. First meeting; organization; license.

The first meeting for the purpose of organization under such charter shall be called by a notice signed by one or more of the subscribers to the certificate of incorporation, stating the time, place, and purpose of the meeting; and at least seven days before the appointed time a copy of this notice shall be given to each subscriber, left at his usual place of business or residence, or duly mailed to his post-office address, unless the signers waive notice in writing. Whoever gives the notice must make affidavit thereof, which affidavit shall include a copy of the notice and be entered upon the records of the corporation. At the first meeting, or any adjournment thereof, an organization shall be effected by the choice of a temporary clerk, who shall be sworn; by the adoption of bylaws; and by the election of directors and such other officers as the bylaws require; but at this meeting no person may be elected director who has not signed the certificate of incorporation. The temporary clerk shall record the proceedings until the election and qualification of the secretary. The directors so chosen shall elect a president, secretary, and other officers which under the bylaws they are so authorized to choose. The president, secretary, and a majority of the directors shall forthwith make, sign, and swear to a certificate setting forth a copy of the certificate of incorporation, with the names of the subscribers thereto, the date of the first meeting and of any adjournments thereof, and shall submit such certificate and the records of the corporation to the Commissioner of Insurance, who shall examine the same, and who may require such other evidence as he deems necessary. If upon his examination the Commissioner of Insurance approves of the bylaws and finds that the requirements of the law have been complied with, he shall issue a license to the company to do business in the State, as is provided for in this Chapter. (1899, c. 54, s. 25; 1903, c. 438, ss. 2, 3; Rev., s. 4728; C.S., s. 6329.)

§ 58-7-45. Bylaws; classification and election of directors; amendments.

(a) A domestic company may adopt bylaws for the conduct of its business that are not repugnant to law or its articles of incorporation and therein provide for the division of its board of directors into two, three, or four classes, and the election thereof at its annual meetings so that the members of one class only shall retire and their successors be chosen each year. Vacancies in any such class may be filled by election by the board for the unexpired term.

(b) Any change in the bylaws of a domestic company shall be promptly filed with the Commissioner. (1899, c. 54, s. 22; Rev., s. 4724; C.S., s. 6330; 1993, c. 504, s. 5.)

§ 58-7-50. Maintenance and removal of records and assets.

(a) Every domestic insurer shall maintain its home or principal office in this State and keep therein complete records of its assets, transactions, and affairs, specifically including:

    (1) Financial records;
    (2) Corporate records;
    (3) Reinsurance documents;
    (4) All accounting transactions;
    (5) Claim files; and

   (6) Payment of claims, in accordance with such methods and systems as are customary or suitable as to the kind or kinds of insurance transacted.

  (b) Every domestic insurer shall have and maintain its assets in this State, except as to:

   (1) Real property and personal property appurtenant thereto lawfully owned by the insurer and located outside this State; and

   (2) Such property of the insurer as may be customary, necessary, and convenient to enable and facilitate the operation of its branch offices, regional home offices, and operations offices, located outside this State as referred to in G.S. 58-7-55.

  (c) The removal from this State of all or a part of the records or assets of a domestic insurer except pursuant to a plan of merger or consolidation approved by the Commissioner or for such reasonable purposes and periods of time as may be approved by the Commissioner in writing in advance of such removal, or concealment of such records or assets or part thereof from the Commissioner is prohibited. Any person who, without the prior approval of the Commissioner, removes or attempts to remove such records or assets or part thereof from the office or offices in which they are required to be kept and maintained under subsection (a) of this section or who conceals or attempts to conceal such records from the Commissioner, in violation of this subsection, shall be guilty of a Class I felony. Upon any removal or attempted removal of such records or assets or upon retention of such records or assets or part thereof outside this State, beyond the period therefor specified in the consent of the Commissioner under which consent the records were so removed thereat, or upon concealment of or attempt to conceal records or assets in violation of this section, the Commissioner may institute delinquency proceedings against the insurer pursuant to the provisions of Article 30 of this Chapter.

  (d) This section is subject to the exceptions provided in G.S. 58-7-55. The Commissioner may allow a domestic insurer to maintain certain records or assets outside this State.

  (e) Every domestic insurer that has its home or principal office in a location outside this State on October 1, 1993, shall petition the Commissioner for approval to continue to operate in that manner. The Commissioner, in determining whether to approve or disapprove the petition, shall consider the exceptions of G.S. 58-7-55, as well as any other factors that might affect the Commissioner's ability to regulate the insurer, or that might affect the insurer's ability to service or protect its policyholders. (1985 (Reg. Sess., 1986), c. 1013, s. 7; 1989, c. 452, s. 3; 1993, c. 452, s. 5; c. 539, s. 1270; 1994, Ex. Sess., c. 24, s. 14(c); 1998-212, s. 26B(a).)

Editor's Note. — The designation of subsection (e) was assigned by the Revisor of Statutes, the designation in Session Laws 1993, c. 452, s. 5 having been (d).

§ 58-7-55. Exceptions to requirements of G.S. 58-7-50.

  The provisions of G.S. 58-7-50 shall not be deemed to prohibit or prevent an insurer from:

   (1) Establishing and maintaining branch offices or regional home offices in other states where necessary or convenient to the transaction of its business and keeping therein the detailed records and assets customary and reasonably necessary for the servicing of its insurance in force and affairs in the territory served by such an office, as long as such records and assets are made readily available at such office for examination by the Commissioner at his request.

(2) Having, depositing, or transmitting funds and assets of the insurer in or to jurisdictions outside this State as required by other jurisdictions as a condition of transacting insurance in such jurisdictions reasonably and customarily required in the regular course of its business.

(3) Establishing and maintaining its principal operations offices, its usual operations records, and such of its assets as may be necessary or convenient for the purpose, in another state in which the insurer is authorized to transact insurance in order that general administration of its affairs may be combined with that of an affiliated insurer or insurers, but subject to the following conditions:

    a. That the Commissioner consents in writing to such removal of offices, records, and assets from this State upon evidence satisfactory to him that the same will facilitate and make more economical the operations of the insurer, and will not unreasonably diminish the service or protection thereafter to be given the insurer's policyholders in this State and elsewhere;

    b. That the insurer will continue to maintain in this State its principal corporate office or place of business, and maintain therein available to the inspection of the Commissioner complete records of its corporate proceedings and a copy of each financial statement of the insurer current within the preceding five years, including a copy of each interim financial statement prepared for the information of the insurer's officers or directors;

    c. That, upon the written request of the Commissioner, the insurer will with reasonable promptness produce at its principal corporate offices in this State for examination or for subpoena, its records or copies thereof relative to a particular transaction or transactions of the insurer as designated by the Commissioner in his request; and

    d. That if at any time the Commissioner finds that the conditions justifying the maintenance of such offices, records, and assets outside of this State no longer exist, or that the insurer has willfully and knowingly violated any of the conditions stated in sub-subdivisions b. and c., the Commissioner may order the return of such offices, records, and assets to this State within such reasonable time, not less than six months, as may be specified in the order; and that for failure to comply with such order, as thereafter modified or extended, if any, the Commissioner shall suspend or revoke the insurer's license.

(4) Placing its investment assets in one or more custodial accounts inside or outside of this State with banks, trust companies, or other similar institutions pursuant to custodial agreements approved by the Commissioner.

(5) Permitting policyholder and certificate holder records and claims and other information to be kept and maintained by agents, general agents, third-party administrators, creditors, employers, associations, and others in the ordinary course of business in a manner customary or suitable to the kind or kinds of insurance transacted; provided, however, that the insurer shall, upon reasonable notice, make available to the Commissioner or his designee any records or other information permitted by this subsection to be maintained outside this State. (1985 (Reg. Sess., 1986), c. 1013, s. 7; 1999-132, s. 9.1.)

§ 58-7-60. Approval as a domestic insurer.

Any insurer that is organized under the laws of any other state and is licensed to transact the business of insurance in this State may become a domestic insurer by (i) complying with laws and regulations regarding the organization and licensing of a domestic insurer of the same type; (ii) designating its principal place of business at a place in this State; and (iii) obtaining the approval of the Commissioner. Such domestic insurer shall be entitled to like certificates of authority to transact business in this State and shall be subject to the authority and jurisdiction of this State. Articles of Incorporation of such domestic insurer may be amended to provide that the corporation is a continuation of the corporate existence of the original foreign corporation through adoption of this State as its corporate domicile and that the original date of incorporation in its original domicilliary state is the date of incorporation of such domestic insurer. (1987, c. 752, s. 10.)

§ 58-7-65. Conversion to foreign insurer.

Any domestic insurer may, upon the approval of the Commissioner, transfer its domicile to any other state in which it is licensed to transact the business of insurance. Upon such a transfer such insurer shall cease to be a domestic insurer and shall be licensed in this State, if qualified, as a foreign insurer. The Commissioner shall approve any such proposed transfer unless he determines that such transfer is not in the interest of the policyholders of this State. (1987, c. 752, s. 10.)

§ 58-7-70. Effects of redomestication.

The license, agent appointments and licenses, rates, and other items that the Commissioner authorizes or grants, in his discretion, that are in existence at the time any insurer licensed by the Commissioner transfers its corporate domicile to this or any other state by merger, consolidation, or any other lawful method, shall continue in full force and effect upon the transfer if the insurer remains duly licensed by the Commissioner. All outstanding policies of any transferring insurer shall remain in full force and effect and need not be endorsed as to any new name of the insurer or its new location unless so ordered by the Commissioner. Every transferring insurer shall file new policy forms with the Commissioner on or before the effective date of the transfer, but may use existing policy forms with appropriate endorsements if allowed by, and under such conditions as approved by, the Commissioner: Provided, however, every such transferring insurer shall (i) notify the Commissioner of the details of the proposed transfer and (ii) promptly file any resulting amendments to corporate documents filed or required to be filed with the Commissioner. (1987, c. 752, s. 10; 1999-132, s. 9.1; 2000-140, s. 11; 2001-223, s. 4.2.)

§ 58-7-73. Dissolutions of insurers.

Upon reaching a determination of intent to dissolve and before filing articles of dissolution with the Office of the Secretary of State, a domestic insurer organized under this Chapter shall file a plan of dissolution for approval by the Commissioner. At such time the Commissioner may restrict the license of the insurer. In order to proceed with a dissolution, the plan must be approved by the Commissioner. (2002-187, s. 2.4.)

Editor's Note. — Session Laws 2002-187, s. 9, makes this section effective October 31, 2002.

§ 58-7-75. Amount of capital and/or surplus required; impairment of capital or surplus.

The amount of capital and/or surplus requisite to the formation and organization of companies under the provisions of Articles 1 through 64 of this Chapter shall be as follows:

    (1) Stock Life Insurance Companies. — A stock corporation may be organized in the manner prescribed in this Chapter and licensed to do the business of life insurance, only when it has paid-in capital of at least six hundred thousand dollars ($600,000) and a paid-in initial surplus of at least nine hundred thousand dollars ($900,000), and it may in addition do the kind of business specified in G.S. 58-7-15(2), without having additional capital or surplus. Every such company shall at all times thereafter maintain a minimum capital of not less than six hundred thousand dollars ($600,000) and a minimum surplus of at least one hundred fifty thousand dollars ($150,000). Provided that, any such corporation may do either or both of the kinds of insurance authorized for stock accident and health insurance companies, as set out in G.S. 58-7-15(3)a. and b., where its charter so permits, and only as long as it maintains a minimum capital and surplus equal to the sum of the minimum capital and surplus requirements of this subdivision and the minimum capital and surplus requirements of subdivision (2) of this section.

    (2) Stock Accident and Health Insurance Companies.

        a. A stock corporation may be organized in the manner prescribed in this Chapter and licensed to do only the kind of insurance specified in G.S. 58-7-15(3)a, when it has paid-in capital of not less than four hundred thousand dollars ($400,000), and a paid-in initial surplus of at least six hundred thousand dollars ($600,000). Every such company shall at all times thereafter maintain a minimum capital of not less than four hundred thousand dollars ($400,000) and a minimum surplus of at least one hundred thousand dollars ($100,000).

        b. Any company organized under the provisions of paragraph a of this subdivision may, by the provisions of its original charter or any amendment thereto, acquire the power to do the kind of business specified in G.S. 58-7-15(3)b, if it has a paid-in capital of at least six hundred thousand dollars ($600,000) and a paid-in initial surplus of at least nine hundred thousand dollars ($900,000). Every such company shall at all times maintain a minimum capital of not less than six hundred thousand dollars ($600,000) and a minimum surplus of at least one hundred fifty thousand dollars ($150,000).

    (3) Stock Fire and Marine Companies. — A stock corporation may be organized in the manner prescribed in this Chapter and licensed to do one or more of the kinds of insurance specified in G.S. 58-7-15 (4), (5), (6), (7), (8), (11), (12), (19), (20), (21) and (22) only when it has a paid-in capital of not less than eight hundred thousand dollars ($800,000) and a paid-in initial surplus of not less than one million two hundred thousand dollars ($1,200,000). Every such company shall at all times thereafter maintain a minimum capital of not less than eight hundred thousand dollars ($800,000) and a minimum surplus of at least two hundred thousand dollars ($200,000). Provided that, any such corporation may do all the kinds of insurance authorized for casualty, fidelity and surety companies, as set out in subdivision (4) of this section where its charter so permits, and when and so long as it meets

and thereafter maintains a minimum capital and surplus equal to the sum of the minimum capital and surplus requirements of this subdivision and the minimum capital and surplus requirements of subdivision (4) of this section.

(4) Stock Casualty and Fidelity and Surety Companies. — A stock corporation may be organized in the manner prescribed in this Chapter and licensed to do one or more of the kinds of insurance specified in G.S. 58-7-15 (3), (6), (7), (8), (9), (10), (11), (12), (13), (14), (15), (16), (17), (18), (19), (21) and (22) only when it has a paid-in capital of not less than one million dollars ($1,000,000) and a paid-in initial surplus of not less than one million five hundred thousand dollars ($1,500,000). Every such company shall at all times thereafter maintain a minimum capital of not less than one million dollars ($1,000,000) and a minimum surplus of at least two hundred fifty thousand dollars ($250,000).

(5) Mutual Fire and Marine Companies.

   a. Limited assessment companies. — A limited assessment mutual company may be organized in the manner prescribed in this Chapter and licensed to do one or more kinds of insurance specified in G.S. 58-7-15 (4), (5), (6), (7), (8), (11), (12), (19), (20), (21) and (22) only when it has no less than five hundred thousand dollars ($500,000) of insurance in not fewer than 500 separate risks subscribed with a paid-in initial surplus of at least three hundred thousand dollars ($300,000), which surplus shall at all times be maintained. The assessment liability of a policyholder of a company organized in accordance with the provisions of this sub-subdivision shall not be limited to less than five annual premiums; provided, the limited assessment company may reduce the assessment liability of its policyholders from such five annual premiums to one additional annual premium when the free surplus of the company amounts to not less than three hundred thousand dollars ($300,000), which surplus shall at all times be maintained.

   b. Assessable mutual companies. — An assessable mutual company may be organized in the manner prescribed in this Chapter and licensed to do one or more of the kinds of insurance specified in G.S. 58-7-15 (4), (5) and (6), with an unlimited assessment liability of its policyholders only when it has not less than five hundred thousand dollars ($500,000) of insurance in not fewer than 500 separate risks subscribed with a paid-in initial surplus equal to twice the amount of the maximum net retained liability under the largest policy of insurance issued by the company; but not less than sixty thousand dollars ($60,000); which surplus shall at all times be maintained. Provided the company, when its charter so permits, in addition may be licensed to do one or more of the kinds of insurance specified in G.S. 58-7-15 (7), (8), (11), (12), (19), (20), (21) and (22), with an unlimited assessment liability of its policyholders, when its free surplus amounts to not less than sixty thousand dollars ($60,000), which surplus shall at all times be maintained.

   c. Nonassessable mutual companies. — A nonassessable mutual company may be organized in the manner prescribed in this Chapter and licensed to do one or more of the kinds of insurance specified in G.S. 58-7-15 (4), (5), (6), (7), (8), (11), (12), (19), (20), (21) and (22) and may be authorized to issue policies under the terms of which a policyholder is not liable for any assessments in addition to the premium set out in the policy only when it has not less than five hundred thousand dollars ($500,000) of insurance in not fewer than 500 separate risks subscribed with a paid-in initial surplus of not less than eight hundred thousand dollars ($800,000), which surplus shall at all times be maintained.

    d. Town or county mutual insurance companies. — A town or county mutual insurance company with unlimited assessment liability may be organized in the manner prescribed in this Chapter and licensed to do the kinds of insurance specified in G.S. 58-7-15(4) only when it has not less than fifty thousand dollars ($50,000) of insurance in force in not fewer than 50 separate risks subscribed with a paid-in initial surplus of not less than fifteen thousand dollars ($15,000), which surplus shall at all times be maintained. A town or county mutual insurance company may, in addition to writing the business specified in G.S. 58-7-15(4) cover in the same policy the hazards usually insured against under an extended coverage endorsement when the company has not less than five hundred thousand dollars ($500,000) of insurance in force in not fewer than 500 separate risks and maintains a surplus at all times of not less than one hundred twenty thousand dollars ($120,000): Provided, that the company may not operate in more than six adjacent counties in this State. Any company authorized under this section before July 1, 1991, shall be permitted to continue to do the same kinds of business that it was authorized to do prior to July 1, 1991, without being required to increase its surplus; however, the insurer shall increase its surplus to the required amounts on or before July 1, 1992. The requirements of this sub-subdivision as to surplus shall apply to such companies as a prerequisite to writing additional lines of business, and to such companies as a prerequisite to commencing business if unlicensed prior to July 1, 1991.

(6) Mutual Life, Accident and Health Insurance Companies. — A nonassessable mutual insurance company may be organized in the manner prescribed in this Chapter, and licensed to do only one or more of the kinds of insurance specified in G.S. 58-7-15 (1), (2) and (3) when it has complied with the requirements of this Chapter and with those set forth in sub-subdivisions a through d of this subdivision, inclusive, whichever shall be applicable.

    a. If organized to do only the kinds of insurance specified in G.S. 58-7-15 (1) and (2) the company shall have not less than 500 bona fide applications for life insurance in an aggregate amount not less than five hundred thousand dollars ($500,000), and shall have received from each such applicant in cash the full amount of one annual premium on the policy for which the applicant applied, in an aggregate amount at least equal to ten thousand dollars ($10,000), and shall in addition have a paid-in initial surplus of two hundred thousand dollars ($200,000), and shall have and maintain at all times a minimum surplus of one hundred thousand dollars ($100,000).

    b. If organized to do only the kind of insurance specified in paragraph a of G.S. 58-7-15(3) the company shall have not less than 250 bona fide applications for that insurance, and shall have received from each applicant in cash the full amount of one annual premium on the policy for which the applicant applied, in an aggregate amount of at least ten thousand dollars ($10,000), and shall have a paid-in initial surplus of two hundred thousand dollars ($200,000) and shall have and maintain at all times a minimum surplus of one hundred thousand dollars ($100,000).

    c. If organized to do the kinds of insurance specified in G.S. 58-7-15 (1) and (3)a, the company shall have complied with the provisions of sub-subdivisions a and b of this subdivision.

    d. If organized to do the kind of insurance specified in G.S. 58-7-15(3)b, in addition to the kind or kinds of insurance designated in any one of the preceding sub-subdivisions of this subdivision, the company shall have a paid-in initial surplus of at least five hundred thousand dollars ($500,000) and shall maintain a minimum surplus of at least three hundred thousand dollars ($300,000).

(7) Organization of Mutual Casualty, Fidelity and Surety Companies.

    a. Nonassessable, mutual companies. — A mutual insurance company with no assessment liability provided for its policyholders may be organized in the manner prescribed in this Chapter and licensed to do one or more of the kinds of insurance specified in G.S. 58-7-15 (3), (6), (7), (8), (9), (10), (11), (12), (13), (14), (15), (16), (17), (18), (19), (21) and (22) when it has a minimum paid-in initial surplus of one million dollars ($1,000,000) and not less than five hundred thousand dollars ($500,000) in insurance subscribed in not less than 500 separate risks. The surplus of the company shall at all times be maintained at or above that amount.

    b. Assessable mutual companies. — A mutual insurance company with assessment liability provided for its policyholders may be organized in the manner prescribed in this Chapter and licensed to do one or more of the kinds of insurance specified in G.S. 58-7-15 (3), (6), (7), (8), (9), (10), (11), (12), (13), (14), (15), (16), (17), (18), (19), (21) and (22) when it has a minimum paid-in initial surplus of four hundred thousand dollars ($400,000) and not less than five hundred thousand dollars ($500,000) of insurance subscribed in not less than 500 separate risks. The company shall at all times maintain a surplus in an amount not less than four hundred thousand dollars ($400,000). The assessment liability of a policyholder of the company shall not be limited to less than one annual premium.

(8) Organization of Mutual Multiple Line Companies.

    a. Assessable mutual companies. — A company may do all the kinds of insurance authorized to be done by a company organized under the provisions of sub-subdivision (5)a, and sub-subdivision (7)b of this subdivision, where its charter so permits when and if it meets the combined minimum requirements of those sub-subdivisions. The assessment liability of policyholders of such a company shall not be limited to less than one annual premium within any one policy year.

    b. Nonassessable mutual companies. — A company may do all the kinds of insurance authorized to be done by a company organized under the provisions of sub-subdivision (5)c, and sub-subdivision (7)a of this subdivision, where its charter so permits when and if it meets the combined minimum requirements of those paragraphs. The policyholders of such a company shall not be subject to any assessment liability.

(9) Repealed by Session Laws 1991, c. 644, s. 32.

(10) Impairment of Capital and/or Surplus. — Whenever the Commissioner finds from a financial statement made by any company, or from

a report of examination of any company, that its admitted assets are less than the aggregate amount of its liabilities and its outstanding capital stock, required minimum surplus, or both, the Commissioner shall determine, in accordance with G.S. 58-2-165 and other applicable provisions of this Chapter, the amount of the impairment of capital, surplus, or both and issue an order in writing requiring the company to eliminate the impairment within such period of not more than 90 days as the Commissioner shall designate. The Commissioner may, by order served upon the company, prohibit the company from issuing any new policies while the impairment exists. If at the expiration of the designated period the company has not satisfied the Commissioner that the impairment has been eliminated, an order for the rehabilitation or liquidation of the company may be entered as provided in Article 30 of this Chapter.

(11) The Commissioner may require an insurer to have and maintain a larger amount of capital or surplus than prescribed in this section, based upon the volume and kinds of insurance transacted by the insurer and on the principles of risk-based capital as determined by the NAIC or the Commissioner. (1899, c. 54, s. 26; 1903, c. 438, s. 4; Rev., s. 4729; 1907, c. 1000, s. 5; 1913, c. 140, s. 2; C.S., s. 6332; 1929, c. 284, s. 1; 1945, c. 386; 1947, c. 721; 1963, c. 943; 1965, c. 947; 1967, c. 300; 1971, c. 536; 1973, c. 686; 1979, c. 421, s. 1; 1983, c. 472; 1985, c. 666, s. 75; 1985 (Reg. Sess., 1986), c. 1013, s. 10; 1989, c. 485, s. 53; 1991, c. 644, s. 32; c. 681, s. 27; 1995, c. 193, s. 17; 2001-223, s. 5.1.)

CASE NOTES

Cited in American Equitable Assurance Co. v. Gold, 249 N.C. 461, 106 S.E.2d 875 (1959).

§ 58-7-80. Capital stock fully paid in cash.

The capital stock shall be paid in cash within 12 months from the date of the charter or certificate of organization, and no certificate of full shares and no policies may be issued until the whole capital is paid in. A majority of the directors shall certify on oath that the money has been paid by the stockholders for their respective shares and is held as the capital of the company invested or to be invested as required by G.S. 58-7-75. (1899, c. 54, s. 27; Rev., s. 4730; C.S., s. 6333; 1945, c. 386.)

§§ 58-7-85, 58-7-90: Repealed by Session Laws 1991, c. 681, s. 30.

§ 58-7-95. Establishment of separate accounts by life insurance companies.

(a) When used in this section, "variable contract" shall mean any individual or group contract issued by an insurance company providing for life insurance or annuity benefits or contractual payments or values which vary so as to reflect investment results of any segregated portfolio of investments or of a designated separate account or accounts in which amounts received or retained in connection with any of such contracts have been placed.

(b) Any domestic life insurance company may, pursuant to resolution of its board of directors, establish one or more separate accounts and may allocate to such account or accounts amounts (including without limitation proceeds applied under optional modes of settlement or under dividend options) to provide for life insurance, guaranteed investment contracts, or annuities (and benefits incidental thereto) payable in fixed or variable amounts or both.

(c) In addition to the amounts allocated under subsection (b), such company may allocate from its general accounts to such separate account or accounts additional amounts, which may include an initial allocation to establish such account; provided, that such company shall be entitled to withdraw at any time, in whole or in part, its participation in any separate account to which funds have been allocated as provided in this subsection (c), and to receive, upon withdrawal, its proportionate share of the value of the assets of the separate account at the time of withdrawal.

(d) Except as hereinafter provided, the amounts allocated to any separate account and accumulations thereon may be invested and reinvested without regard to any requirements or limitations prescribed by the laws of this State governing the investments of life insurance companies; provided, that to the extent that the company's reserve liability with regard to (i) benefits guaranteed as to amount and duration, and (ii) funds guaranteed as to principal amount or stated rate of interest is maintained in any separate account, a portion of the assets of such separate account at least equal to such reserve liability shall be, except as the Commissioner may otherwise approve, invested in accordance with the laws of this State governing the investments of life insurance companies. The investments in such separate account or accounts shall not be taken into account in applying the investment limitations applicable to other investments of the company.

(e) Repealed by Session Laws 2001-223, s. 6.3, effective June 15, 2001.

(f) Repealed by Session Laws 2001-223, s. 6.3, effective June 15, 2001.

(g) The life insurance company shall maintain in each separate account assets with a value at least equal to the reserves and other contract liabilities with respect to the account, except as may otherwise be approved by the Commissioner.

(h) The income, if any, and gains and losses, realized or unrealized, from assets allocated to each account shall be credited to or charged against the account without regard to other income, gains or losses of the company.

(i) Unless otherwise approved by the Commissioner, assets allocated to a separate account shall be valued at their market value on the date of valuation, or if there is no readily available market, then as provided under the terms of the contract or the rules or other written agreement applicable to such separate account; provided, that unless otherwise approved by the Commissioner that portion of the assets of such separate account equal to the company's reserve liability with regard to the guaranteed benefits and funds referred to in subsection (d) hereof, if any, shall be valued in accordance with the rules otherwise applicable to the company's assets. The reserve liability for variable contracts shall be determined in accordance with actuarial procedures that recognize the variable nature of the benefits provided and any mortality guarantees.

(j) If and to the extent so provided under the applicable contracts, that portion of the assets of any such separate account equal to the reserves and other contract liabilities with respect to such account shall not be chargeable with liabilities arising out of any other business the company may conduct.

(k) The life insurance company shall have the power and the company's charter shall be deemed amended to authorize such company to do all things necessary under any applicable state or federal law in order that variable contracts may be lawfully sold or offered for sale. To the extent such company deems it necessary to comply with any applicable federal or state laws, such company, with respect to any separate account, including without limitation any separate account which is a management investment company or a unit investment trust, may provide, for persons having an interest therein, appropriate voting and other rights and special procedures for the conduct of the business of such account, including without limitation special rights and procedures relating to investment policy, investment advisory services, selection of independent public accountants, and the selection of a committee, the members of which need not be otherwise affiliated with such company, to manage the business of such account. This provision shall not affect existing laws pertaining to the voting rights of the life insurance company's policyholders.

(*l*) Amounts allocated to a separate account in the exercise of the power granted by this section shall be owned by the company, and the company shall not be, or hold itself out to be, a trustee with respect to such amounts.

(m) The company shall not, in connection with the allocation of investments or expenses, or in any other respect, discriminate unfairly between separate accounts or between separate and other accounts, but this provision shall not require the company to follow uniform investment policies for its accounts.

(n) No sale, exchange or other transfer of assets may be made by a company between any of its separate accounts or between any other investment account and one or more of its separate accounts unless, in case of a transfer into a separate account, such transfer is made solely to establish the account or to support the operation of the contracts with respect to the separate account to which the transfer is made, and unless such transfer, whether into or from a separate account, is made (i) by a transfer of cash, or (ii) by a transfer of securities having a readily determinable market value, provided that such transfer of securities is approved by the Commissioner. The Commissioner may approve other transfers among such accounts if, in his opinion, such transfers would not be inequitable.

(o) Any contract providing benefits payable in variable amounts delivered or issued for delivery in this State shall contain a statement of the essential features of the procedure to be followed by the company in determining the dollar amount of such variable benefits. Any such contract under which the benefits vary to reflect investment experience, including a group contract and any certificate in evidence of variable benefits issued thereunder, shall state that such dollar amount will so vary and shall contain on its first page a statement to the effect that the benefits thereunder are on a variable basis.

(p) Any variable annuity contract providing benefits payable in variable amounts issued under this section may include as an incidental benefit provision for payment on death during the deferred period of an amount not in excess of the greater of the sum of the premiums or stipulated payments paid under the contract or the value of the contract at time of death or any other incidental amount approved by the Commissioner; such contracts will be deemed not to be contracts of life insurance and therefore not subject to the provisions of the insurance law governing life insurance contracts. Provision for any other benefit on death during the deferred period will be subject to such insurance provisions.

(q) No domestic life insurance company and no other life insurance company shall deliver or issue for delivery within this State any contracts under this section unless it is licensed or organized to do a life insurance or annuity business in this State, and the Commissioner is satisfied that its financial condition and its methods of operation in connection with the issuance of such contracts will not render its operation hazardous to the public or its policyholders in this State. In determining the qualification of a company requesting authority to deliver such contracts within this State, the Commissioner shall consider, among other things:

    (1) The history and financial condition of the company;

    (2) The character, responsibility and general fitness of the officers and directors of the company; and

(3) The law and regulations under which the company is authorized in the state of domicile to issue variable annuity contracts. The state of entry of an alien company shall be deemed its place of domicile for this purpose.

If the company is a subsidiary of an admitted life insurance company, or affiliated with such company through common management or ownership, it may be deemed by the Commissioner to have met the provisions of this subsection if either it or the parent or affiliated company meets the requirements hereof.

(r) The Commissioner shall have sole and exclusive authority to regulate the issuance by life insurance companies and the sale of such contracts and to issue such reasonable rules and regulations as may be necessary to carry out the purposes and provisions of this section, and such contracts and the life insurance companies which issue them shall not be subject to the Securities Law of North Carolina nor to the jurisdiction of the Secretary of State thereunder.

(s) **(Effective until October 1, 2004)** Except for G.S. 58-58-60 and 58-58-120 in the case of a variable annuity contract and G.S. 58-58-55, 58-58-120, and 58-58-140(1) in the case of a variable life insurance policy and except as otherwise provided in this section, all pertinent provisions of the insurance laws of this State shall apply to separate accounts and contracts issued in connection therewith. Any individual variable life insurance contract, delivered or issued for delivery within this State, shall contain reinstatement and nonforfeiture provisions appropriate to such a contract. Any group variable life insurance contract, delivered or issued for delivery within this State, shall contain grace provisions appropriate to such a contract. Any individual variable annuity contract, delivered or issued for delivery within this State, shall contain reinstatement provisions appropriate to such a contract.

(s) **(Effective October 1, 2004)** Except for G.S. 58-58-61 and G.S. 58-58-120 in the case of a variable annuity contract, G.S. 58-58-55, 58-58-120, and 58-58-140(1) in the case of a variable life insurance policy, and except as otherwise provided in this section, all pertinent provisions of this Chapter apply to separate accounts and contracts issued in connection with separate accounts. Any individual variable life insurance contract, delivered or issued for delivery within this State, shall contain reinstatement and nonforfeiture provisions appropriate to that contract. Any group variable life insurance contract, delivered or issued for delivery within this State, shall contain grace provisions appropriate to that contract. Any individual variable annuity contract, delivered or issued for delivery within this State, shall contain reinstatement provisions appropriate to that contract. (1965, c. 166; 1969, c. 616, s. 2; 1971, c. 831, s. 2; 1973, c. 490; 1979, c. 409, s. 10; 1991, c. 720, s. 4; 1991 (Reg. Sess., 1992), c. 837, s. 7; 2001-223, ss. 6.1, 6.2, 6.3, 6.4; 2003-144, s. 3.)

Subsection (s) Set Out Twice. — The first version of subsection (s) set out above is effective until October 1, 2004. The second version of subsection (s) set out above is effective October 1, 2004.

Effect of Amendments. — Session Laws 2003-144, s. 3, effective October, 1, 2004, in subsection (s), substituted "G.S. 58-58-61 and G.S. 58-58-120" for "G.S. 58-58-60 and 58-58-120," "this Chapter" for "the insurance laws of this State shall," and "with separate accounts" for "therewith" in the first sentence, substituted "that contract" for "such a contract" in the second, third, and last sentences, and made minor stylistic and punctuation changes.

§ 58-7-100: Repealed by Session Laws 1991, c. 681, s. 30.

§ 58-7-105. Authority to increase or reduce capital stock.

The Commissioner shall, upon application, examine the proceedings of domestic companies to increase or reduce their capital stock, and when found conformable to law shall issue certificates of authority to such companies to transact business upon such increased or reduced capital: Provided, that in no event shall the said capital stock be reduced to an amount less than that required upon organization of such company in G.S. 58-7-75. He shall not allow stockholders' obligations of any description as part of the assets or capital of any stock insurance company unless the same are secured by competent collateral. (1899, c. 54, s. 15; Rev., s. 4732; C.S., s. 6335; 1945, c. 386; 1991, c. 720, s. 4.)

§ 58-7-110. Assessment of shares; revocation of license.

When the net assets of a company organized under this Article do not amount to more than the amount required in G.S. 58-7-75 for its original capital, it may make good its capital to the original amount by assessment of its stock. Shares on which such an assessment is not paid within 60 days after demand shall be forfeitable and may be canceled by vote of the directors and new shares issued to make up the deficiency. If such company does not, within three months after notice from the Commissioner to that effect, make good its capital or reduce the same, as allowed by this Article, its authority to transact new business of insurance shall be revoked by the Commissioner. (1899, c. 54, s. 28; 1903, c. 438, s. 4; Rev., s. 4733; C.S., s. 6336; 1945, c. 386; 1991, c. 720, s. 4.)

§ 58-7-115. Increase of capital stock.

Any company organized under the provisions of Articles 1 through 64 of this Chapter may issue pro rata to its stockholders certificates of any portion of its surplus which shall be considered an increase of its capital to the amount of such certificates. As used in this section, "surplus" means earned surplus; provided, however, issuance of certificates out of paid-in and contributed surplus will be permitted on a case-by-case basis, with the prior approval of the Commissioner. The issuance of those certificates shall not lower the total surplus of the insurer to an amount less than that required to be maintained by G.S. 58-7-75. The company may, at a meeting called for the purpose, vote to increase the amount and number of shares of its capital stock, and to issue certificates therefor when paid for in full. In whichever method the increase is made, the company shall, within 30 days after the issue of such certificates, submit to the Commissioner a certificate setting forth the amount of the increase and the facts of the transaction, signed and sworn to by its president and secretary and a majority of its directors. If the Commissioner finds that the facts conform to the law, he shall endorse his approval thereof; and upon filing such certificate so endorsed with the Secretary of State, and the payment of a fee of five dollars ($5.00) for filing the same, the company may transact business upon the capital as increased, and the Commissioner shall issue his certificate to that effect. (1899, c. 54, s. 29; Rev., s. 4734; C.S., s. 6337; 1945, c. 386; 1991, c. 720, s. 4; 1993, c. 452, s. 6.)

§ 58-7-120. Reduction of capital stock.

When the capital stock of a company organized under this Article is impaired, the company may, upon a vote of the majority of the stock represented at a meeting legally called for that purpose, reduce its capital stock and the number of shares thereof to an amount not less than the minimum sum required by law, but no part of its assets and property shall be distributed to its stockholders. Within 10 days after such meeting the company must submit to the Commissioner a certificate setting forth the proceedings thereof and the amount of the reduction and the assets and liabilities of the company, signed and sworn to by its president, secretary, and a majority of its directors. The Commissioner shall examine the facts in the case, and if they conform to law, and in his judgment the proposed reduction may be made without prejudice to the public, he shall endorse his approval upon the certificate. Upon filing the certificate so endorsed with the Secretary of State and paying a filing fee of five dollars ($5.00), the company may transact business upon the basis of the reduced capital as though it were original capital, and its charter shall be deemed to be amended to conform thereto, and the Commissioner shall issue his certificate to that effect. The company may, by a majority vote of its directors, after the reduction, require the return of the original certificates of stock held by each stockholder in exchange for new certificates it may issue in lieu thereof for such number of shares as each stockholder is entitled to in the proportion that the reduced capital bears to the original capital. (1899, c. 54, s. 30; Rev., s. 4735; C.S., s. 6338; 1991, c. 720, s. 4.)

§ 58-7-125. Dividends not payable when capital stock impaired; liability of stockholders for unlawful dividends.

No dividend shall be paid by any company incorporated in this State when its capital stock is impaired, or when such payment would have the effect of impairing its capital stock; and any dividend so paid subjects the stockholders receiving it to a joint and several liability to the creditors of said company to the extent of the dividend so paid. (1899, c. 54, s. 31; 1903, c. 536, s. 3; Rev., s. 4736; C.S., s. 6339; 1945, c. 386.)

§ 58-7-130. Dividends and distributions to stockholders.

(a) Each domestic insurance company in North Carolina shall be restricted by the Commissioner from the payment of any dividends or other distributions to its stockholders whenever the Commissioner determines from examination of the company's financial condition that the payment of future dividends or other distributions would cause a hazardous financial condition, impair the financial soundness of the company or be detrimental to its policyholders, and those restrictions shall continue in force until the Commissioner specifically permits the payment of dividends or other distributions to stockholders by the company through a written authorization.

(b) No domestic stock insurance company shall declare or pay dividends to its stockholders except from the unassigned surplus of the company as reflected in the company's most recent financial statement filed with the Commissioner under G.S. 58-2-165.

(c) A transfer out of paid-in and contributed surplus to common or preferred capital stock will be permitted on a case-by-case basis, with the Commissioner's prior approval, depending on the necessity for a company to make the transfer.

(d) Nothing in this section and no action taken by the Commissioner in any way restricts the liability of stockholders under G.S. 58-7-125.

(e) Dividends and other distributions paid to stockholders are subject to the requirements and limitations of G.S. 58-19-25(d) and G.S. 58-19-30(c). (1945, c. 386; 1991, c. 720, s. 9; 2001-223, s. 5.2; 2002-187, s. 2.5.)

Effect of Amendments. — Session Laws 2002-187, s. 2.5, effective October 31, 2002, inserted "or pay" following "declare" in subsection (b).

§ **58-7-135:** Repealed by Session Laws 1993, c. 452, s. 65.

Cross References. — As to life and health reinsurance agreements, see G.S. 58-7-31.

§ 58-7-140. Certain officers debarred from commissions.

No officer or other person whose duty it is to determine the character of the risk, and upon whose decision the application shall be accepted or rejected by an insurance company, shall receive as any part of his compensation a commission upon the premiums, but his compensation shall be a fixed salary and such share in the net profits as the directors may determine. Nor shall such officer or person be an employee of any officer or agent of the company. (1899, c. 54, s. 32; 1903, c. 438, s. 4; Rev., s. 4738; C.S., s. 6347; 1945, c. 386.)

§ 58-7-145. Restrictions on purchase and sale of equity securities of domestic companies.

(a) Statement of Ownership of Equity Securities. — Every person who is directly or indirectly the beneficial owner of more than ten percent (10%) of any class of any equity security of a domestic stock insurance company or who is a director or an officer of such company shall file in the office of the Commissioner on or before the first day of June, 1966, or within 10 days after he becomes such beneficial owner, director or officer, a statement, in such form as the Commissioner may prescribe, of the amount of all equity securities of such company of which he is the beneficial owner, and within 10 days after the close of each calendar month thereafter if there has been a change in such ownership during such month, shall file in the office of the Commissioner a statement, in such form as the Commissioner may prescribe, indicating his ownership at the close of the calendar month and such changes in his ownership as have occurred during such calendar month.

(b) Profit Made from Sale of Equity Security Held Less than Six Months. — For the purpose of preventing the unfair use of information which may have been obtained by such beneficial owner, director, or officer by reason of his relationship to such company, any profit realized by him from any purchase and sale, or any sale and purchase, of any equity security of such company within a period of less than six months, unless such security was acquired in good faith in connection with a debt previously contracted, shall inure to and be recoverable by the company, irrespective of any intention on the part of such beneficial owner, director or officer in entering into such transaction of holding the security purchased or of not repurchasing the security sold for a period exceeding six months. Suit to recover such profit may be instituted at law or in equity in any court of competent jurisdiction by the company, or by the owner of any equity security of the company in the name and in behalf of the company, if the company shall fail or refuse to bring such suit within 60 days after request or shall fail diligently to prosecute the same thereafter; but no such suit shall be brought more than two years after the date such profit was realized. This section shall not be construed to cover any transaction where such beneficial owner was not such both at the time of the purchase and sale, or the sale and purchase, of the equity security involved, or any transaction or transactions which the Commissioner by rules and regulations may exempt as not comprehended within the purpose of this section.

(c) Delivery of Security Sold. — It shall be unlawful for any such beneficial owner, director or officer, directly or indirectly, to sell any equity security of such company if the person selling the security or his principal (i) does not own the security sold, or (ii) if owning the security, does not deliver it against such sale within 20 days thereafter, or does not within five days after such sale deposit it in the mails or other usual channels of transportation; but no person shall be deemed to have violated this section if he proves that notwithstanding the exercise of good faith he was unable to make such delivery or deposit within such time, or that to do so would cause undue inconvenience or expense.

(d) Sales by Dealers. — The provisions of subsection (b) shall not apply to any purchase and sale, or sale and purchase, and the provisions of subsection (c) shall not apply to any sale, of an equity security of a domestic stock insurance company not then or theretofore held by him in an investment account, by a dealer in the ordinary course of his business and incident to the establishment or maintenance by him of a primary or secondary market (otherwise than on an exchange as defined in the Securities Exchange Act of 1934) for such security. The Commissioner may, by such rules and regulations as he deems necessary or appropriate in the public interest, define and prescribe terms and conditions with respect to securities held in an investment account and transactions made in the ordinary course of business and incident to the establishment or maintenance of a primary or secondary market.

(e) Arbitrage Transactions. — The provisions of subsections (a), (b) and (c) of this section shall not apply to foreign or domestic arbitrage transactions unless made in contravention of such rules and regulations as the Commissioner may adopt in order to carry out the purposes of this section.

(f) "Equity Security" Defined. — The term "equity security" when used in this section means any stock or similar security; or any security convertible, with or without consideration, into such a security, or carrying any warrant or right to subscribe to or purchase such a security; or any such warrant or right; or any other security which the Commissioner shall deem to be of similar nature and consider necessary or appropriate, by such rules and regulations as he may prescribe in the public interest or for the protection of investors, to treat as an equity security.

(g) Exemptions from Requirements of Section. — The provisions of subsections (a), (b) and (c) hereof shall not apply to equity securities of a domestic stock insurance company if

    (1) Such securities shall be registered, or shall be required to be registered, pursuant to section 12 of the Securities Exchange Act of 1934, as amended, or if

    (2) Such domestic stock insurance company shall not have any class of its equity securities held of record by 100 or more persons on the last business day of the year next preceding the year in which equity securities of the company would be subject to the provisions of subsections (a), (b) and (c) hereof except for the provisions of this subdivision (2).

(h) Rules and Regulations of Commissioner. — The Commissioner shall have the power to make such rules and regulations as may be necessary for the execution of the functions vested in him by subsections (a) through (g) hereof, and may for such purpose classify domestic stock insurance companies, securities, and other persons or matters within his jurisdiction. No provision of subsections (a), (b) and (c) hereof imposing any liability shall apply to any act done or omitted in good faith in conformity with any rule or regulation of the

Commissioner, notwithstanding that such rule or regulation may, after such act or omission, be amended or rescinded or determined by judicial or other authority to be invalid for any reason.

(i) Severability. — If any part or provision of this section or the application thereof to any person or circumstance be adjudged invalid by any court of competent jurisdiction, such judgment shall be confined in its operation to the part, provision or application directly involved in the controversy in which such judgment shall have been rendered and shall not affect or impair the validity of the remainder of this section or the application thereof to other persons or circumstances. (1965, c. 127, s. 2.)

§ 58-7-150. Consolidation.

(a) A domestic insurer may consolidate with another insurer, subject to the following conditions:

(1) The plan of consolidation must be submitted to and be approved by the Commissioner before the consolidation.

(2) The Commissioner shall not approve the plan unless the Commissioner finds that it is fair, equitable to policyholders, consistent with law, and will not conflict with the public interest. If the Commissioner disapproves the plan, the Commissioner shall state the reasons for the disapproval and call for a hearing.

(3) No director, officer, member or subscriber of any such insurer, except as is expressly provided by the plan of consolidation, shall receive any fee, commission, other compensation or valuable consideration whatever, for in any manner aiding, promoting or assisting in the consolidation.

(4) Any consolidation as to an incorporated domestic insurer shall in other respects be governed by the general laws of this State relating to business corporations. The consolidation of a domestic mutual insurer may be effected by vote of two thirds of the members voting thereon pursuant to such notice and procedure as the Commissioner may prescribe.

(b) Reinsurance of all or substantially all of the insurance obligations or risks of existing or in-force policies of a domestic insurer by another insurer under an assumption reinsurance agreement, as defined in G.S. 58-10-25(a)(2), shall be deemed a consolidation for the purposes of this section. This section does not apply to consolidations to the extent regulated by Article 19 or other Articles of this Chapter.

(c) An application for consolidation under this section shall be accompanied by a nonrefundable fee of two hundred fifty dollars ($250.00). (1947, c. 923; 1955, c. 905; 1985, c. 572, s. 4; 1989 (Reg. Sess., 1990), c. 1069, s. 10; 1993, c. 452, s. 7; 1993 (Reg. Sess., 1994), c. 678, s. 10; 1995, c. 193, s. 18; c. 507, s. 11A(c); 2001-223, ss. 7.1, 7.2.)

Editor's Note. — Session Laws 1989, c. 452, s. 8 changed the title of former Article 17A of Chapter 58, of which this section was the first section, to "Mergers of Insurance Companies." However, most of Article 17A was repealed by Session Laws 1989, c. 452, and due to the recodification of this Chapter, the amendment by c. 452, s. 8 was not effectuated. Session Laws 1989, c. 452 also enacted an Article 46 of Chapter 58, containing similar provisions to those contained in the repealed sections of former Article 17A. Article 46 has been recodified as Article 30 of this Chapter.

Legal Periodicals. — For discussion of this Article, see 25 N.C.L. Rev. 429 (1947).

Cited in Long v. Beacon Ins. Co., 87 N.C.
App. 171, 360 S.E.2d 134 (1987).

§ 58-7-155. Application fee.

Every application for redomestication under G.S. 58-7-60 and G.S. 58-7-65 shall be accompanied by a nonrefundable fee of two hundred dollars ($200.00). (1989 (Reg. Sess., 1990), c. 1069, s. 9; 1995, c. 507, s. 11A(c).)

§ 58-7-160. Investments unlawfully acquired.

Whenever it appears by examination as authorized by law that a domestic insurer has acquired any assets in violation of the law in force on the date of the acquisition, the Commissioner shall disallow the amount of the assets, if wholly ineligible, or the amount of the value thereof in excess of any limitation prescribed by this Chapter and shall deduct that amount as a nonadmitted asset of the insurer. (1991, c. 681, s. 29.)

§ 58-7-162. Allowable or admitted assets.

In any determination of the financial condition of an insurer, there shall be allowed as assets only those assets owned by an insurer and that consist of:
  (1) Cash in the possession of the insurer, or in transit under its control, and including the true balance of any deposit in a solvent United States bank, savings and loan association, or trust company, and the balance of any such deposit in an insolvent United States bank, savings and loan association, or trust company, to the extent insured by a federal agency.
  (2) Investments, securities, properties, and loans acquired or held in accordance with this Chapter.
  (3) Premium notes, policy loans, and other policy assets and liens on policies and certificates of life insurance and annuity contracts and accrued interest thereon, in an amount not exceeding the legal reserve and other policy liabilities carried on each individual policy.
  (4) The net amount of uncollected and deferred premiums and annuity considerations in the case of a life insurer.
  (5) Repealed by Session Laws 2003-212, s. 5, effective October 1, 2003.
  (6) All premiums in the course of collection not more than 90 days past due, excluding commissions payable thereon, due from any person that solely or in combination with the person's affiliates owes the insurer an amount that equals or exceeds five percent (5%) of the insurer's surplus as regards policyholders, but only if:
    a. The premiums collected by the person or affiliates and not remitted to the insurer are held in a trust account with a bank or other depository approved by the Commissioner. The funds shall be held as trust funds and may not be commingled with any other funds of the person or affiliates. Disbursements from the trust account may be made only to the insurer, the insured, or, for the purpose of returning premiums, a person that is entitled to returned premiums on behalf of the insured. A written copy of the trust agreement shall be filed with and approved by the Commissioner before becoming effective. The Commissioner shall disapprove any trust agreement filed under this sub-subdivision that does not assure the safety of the premiums collected. The invest-

ment income derived from the trust may be allocated as the parties consider to be proper. The person or affiliates shall deposit premiums collected into the trust account within 15 business days after collection; or

b. The person or affiliates shall provide to the insurer, and the insurer shall maintain in its possession, an unexpired, clean, irrevocable letter of credit, payable to the insurer, issued for a term of no less than one year and in conformity with the requirements set forth in this sub-subdivision, the amount of which equals or exceeds the liability of the person or affiliates to the insurer, at all times during the period that the letter of credit is in effect, for premiums collected by the person or affiliates. The letter of credit shall be issued under arrangements satisfactory to the Commissioner and the letter shall be issued by a banking institution that is a member of the Federal Reserve System and that has a financial standing satisfactory to the Commissioner; or

c. The person or affiliates shall provide to the insurer, and the insurer shall maintain in its possession, evidence that the person or affiliates have purchased and have currently in effect a financial guaranty bond, payable to the insurer, issued for a term of not less than one year and that is in conformity with the requirements set forth in this sub-subdivision, the amount of which equals or exceeds the liability of the person or affiliates to the insurer, at all times during which the financial guaranty bond is in effect, for the premiums collected by the person or persons. The financial guaranty bond shall be issued under an arrangement satisfactory to the Commissioner and the financial guaranty bond shall be issued by an insurer that is authorized to transact that business in this State, that has a financial standing satisfactory to the Commissioner, and that is neither controlled nor controlling in relation to either the insurer or the person or affiliates for whom the bond is purchased.

Premiums receivable under this subdivision will not be allowed as an admitted asset if a financial evaluation by the Commissioner indicates that the person or affiliates are unlikely to be able to pay the premiums as they become due. The financial evaluation shall be based on a review of the books and records of the controlling or controlled person.

(7) Repealed by Session Laws 2003-212, s. 5, effective October 1, 2003.

(8) Notes and like written obligations not past due, taken for premiums other than life insurance premiums, on policies permitted to be issued on that basis, to the extent of the unearned premium reserves carried thereon.

(9) The full amount of reinsurance which is recoverable by a ceding insurer from a solvent reinsurer and is authorized under G.S. 58-7-21.

(10) Amounts receivable by an assuming insurer representing funds withheld by a solvent ceding insurer under a reinsurance treaty.

(11) Deposits or equities recoverable from underwriting associations, syndicates, and reinsurance funds, or from any suspended banking institution, to the extent considered by the Commissioner to be available for the payment of losses and claims and at values to be determined by the Commissioner.

(12) Electronic and mechanical machines, including operating and system software constituting a management information system.

(13) Other assets, not inconsistent with the provisions of this section, considered by the Commissioner to be available for the payment of

losses and claims, at values to be determined by the Commissioner. (1991, c. 681, s. 29; 1993, c. 452, s. 8; 1995 (Reg. Sess., 1996), c. 659, s. 1; 2003-212, ss. 4-6.)

Effect of Amendments. — Session Laws 2003-212, ss. 4-6, effective October 1, 2003, rewrote subdivisions (2) and (12); and repealed subdivisions (5) and (7).

§ 58-7-163. Assets not allowed.

In addition to assets impliedly excluded by the provisions of G.S. 58-7-162, the following expressly shall not be allowed as assets in any determination of the financial condition of an insurer:

(1) Repealed by Session Laws 2003-212, s. 7, effective October 1, 2003.

(2) Advances (other than policy loans) to officers, directors, and controlling stockholders, whether secured or not, and advances to employees, agents, and other persons on personal security only.

(3) Stock of the insurer or any material equity therein or loans secured thereby, or any material proportionate interest in the stock acquired or held through the ownership by the insurer of an interest in another firm, corporation, or business unit.

(4) Repealed by Session Laws 2003-212, s. 7, effective October 1, 2003.

(5) The amount, if any, by which the aggregate book value of investments as carried in the ledger assets of the insurer exceeds the aggregate value of the investments as determined under this Chapter.

(6) Bonds, notes, or other evidences of indebtedness that are secured by mortgages or deeds of trust that are in default, to the extent of the cost or carrying value that is in excess of the value as determined pursuant to other provisions of this Chapter.

(7) Repealed by Session Laws 2003-212, s. 7, effective October 1, 2003.

(8) Certificates of contribution, surplus notes, or other similar evidences of indebtedness, to the extent that admission of these investments results in the double counting of these investments in the reporting entity's balance sheet.

(9) Any asset that is encumbered in any manner unless the asset is authorized under G.S. 58-7-187 or G.S. 58-7-162(13). (1991, c. 681, s. 29; 1993, c. 452, s. 9; 1993 (Reg. Sess., 1994), c. 678, s. 11; 2003-212, s. 7.)

Effect of Amendments. — Session Laws 2003-212, s. 7, effective October 1, 2003, deleted subdivisions (1), (4), and (7); and in subdivision (8), inserted "surplus notes" and added "to the extent that admission of these investments results in the double counting of these investments in the reporting entity's balance sheet" at the end.

§ 58-7-165. Eligible investments.

(a) Insurers shall invest in or lend their funds on the security of, and shall hold as invested assets, only eligible investments as prescribed in this Chapter.

(b) Any particular investment held by an insurer on December 31, 1991, that was a legal investment when it was made, and that the insurer was legally entitled to possess immediately before January 1, 1992, is an eligible investment.

(c) Eligibility of an investment shall be determined as of the date of its making or acquisition, except as stated otherwise in this Chapter.

(d) Any investment limitation based upon the amount of the insurer's assets or particular funds shall relate to those assets or funds shown by the insurer's annual statement as of the December 31 preceding the date of acquisition of the investment by the insurer, or, if applicable, as shown by the most current quarterly financial statement filed by the insurer. (1991, c. 681, s. 29.)

§ 58-7-167. General qualifications.

(a) No security or investment, other than real or personal property acquired under G.S. 58-7-187, is eligible for acquisition unless it is interest-bearing or interest-accruing, is entitled to receive dividends if and when declared and paid, or is otherwise income-producing, is not then in default in any respect, and the insurer is entitled to receive for its exclusive account and benefit the interest or income accruing thereon.

(b) No security or investment shall be eligible for purchase at a price above its market value unless it is approved by the Commissioner and is valued in accordance with valuation procedures of the NAIC that have been adopted by the Commissioner.

(c) This Chapter does not prohibit the acquisition by an insurer of other or additional securities or property if received as a dividend, as a lawful distribution of assets, or under a lawful and bona fide agreement of bulk reinsurance, merger, or consolidation. Any investment so acquired that is not otherwise eligible under this Chapter shall be disposed of under G.S. 58-7-188 if the investment is in property or securities. (1991, c. 681, s. 29.)

§ 58-7-168. Authorization of investment.

An insurer shall not make any investment or loan, other than a policy loan or annuity contract loan of a life insurer, unless the investment or loan is authorized or approved by the insurer's board of directors or by a committee authorized by the board and charged with the supervision or making of the investment or loan. The minutes of any such committee shall be recorded and regular reports of the committee shall be submitted to the board of directors. (1991, c. 681, s. 29.)

§ 58-7-170. Diversification.

(a) Every insurer must maintain an amount equal to its entire policyholder-related liabilities and the minimum capital and surplus required to be maintained by the insurer under this Chapter invested in coin or currency of the United States and in investments authorized under this Chapter, other than the investments authorized under G.S. 58-7-183 or G.S. 58-7-187, except G.S. 58-7-187(b)(1).

(b) Investments eligible under subsection (a), except investments acquired under G.S. 58-7-183, are subject to the following limitations, other limitations of this section, and any other limitations that are expressly provided for in any provision under which the investment is authorized:

    (1) The cost of investments made by insurers in stock authorized by G.S. 58-7-173 shall not exceed twenty-five percent (25%) of the insurer's admitted assets, provided that no more than twenty percent (20%) of the insurer's admitted assets shall be invested in common stock; and the cost of an investment in stock of any one corporation shall not exceed three percent (3%) of the insurer's admitted assets. Notwithstanding any other provision in this Chapter, the financial statement carrying value of all stock investments shall be used for the purpose of determining the asset value against which the percentage limitations are to be applied. Investments in the voting securities of a depository institution, or any company that controls a depository institution, shall not exceed five percent (5%) of the insurer's admitted

assets. As used in this subdivision, "depository institution" has the same meaning as in section 3 of the Federal Deposit Insurance Act, 12 U.S.C. § 1813; and includes any foreign bank that maintains a branch, an agency, or a commercial lending company in the United States.

(2) The cost of Canadian investments authorized by G.S. 58-7-173 shall not exceed forty percent (40%) of the insurer's admitted assets in the aggregate, provided that no more than twenty-five percent (25%) of the insurer's admitted assets shall be invested in Canadian investments authorized by G.S. 58-7-173(11).

(c) The cost of investments made by an insurer in mortgage loans authorized by G.S. 58-7-179 with any one person, or in mortgage pass-through securities and derivatives of mortgage pass-through securities authorized by G.S. 58-7-173(1), (2), (8), or (17), and backed by a single collateral package, shall not exceed three percent (3%) of the insurer's admitted assets. An insurer shall not invest in additional mortgage loans or mortgage pass-through securities and derivatives of mortgage pass-through securities without the Commissioner's consent if the admitted value of all those investments held by the insurer exceeds an aggregate of sixty percent (60%) of the admitted assets of the insurer. Within the aggregate sixty percent (60%) limitation, the admitted value of all mortgage pass-through securities and derivatives of mortgage pass-through securities permitted by G.S. 58-7-173(17) shall not exceed thirty-five percent (35%) of the admitted assets of the insurer. The admitted value of other mortgage loans permitted by G.S. 58-7-179 shall not exceed forty percent (40%) of the admitted assets of the insurer. Mortgage pass-through securities authorized by G.S. 58-7-173(1), (2), or (8) shall only be subject to the single collateral package limitation and the sixty percent (60%) aggregate limitation. No later than January 31, 1999, an insurer that has mortgage investments that exceed the limitations specified in this subsection shall submit to the Commissioner a plan to bring the amount of mortgage investments into compliance with the specified limitations by January 1, 2004.

(d) Without the Commissioner's prior written approval, the cost of investments permitted under G.S. 58-7-173 and G.S. 58-7-178, and that are classified as medium to lower quality obligations, other than obligations of subsidiaries or affiliated corporations as that term is defined in G.S. 58-19-5, shall be limited to:

(1) No more than twenty percent (20%) of an insurer's admitted assets;

(2) No more than ten percent (10%) of an insurer's admitted assets in obligations that have been given a rating of 4, 5, or 6 by the Securities Valuation Office of the NAIC;

(3) No more than three percent (3%) of an insurer's admitted assets in obligations that have been given a rating of 5 or 6 by the Securities Valuation Office of the NAIC; and

(4) No more than one percent (1%) of an insurer's admitted assets in obligations that have been given a rating of 6 by the Securities Valuation Office of the NAIC.

(5), (6). Repealed by Session Laws 1993, c. 452, s. 11.

(e) As used in subsections (d), (f), (g), and (h) of this section, "medium to lower quality obligations" means obligations that have been given a rating of 3, 4, 5, or 6 by the Securities Valuation Office of the NAIC.

(f) Each insurer shall possess and maintain adequate documentation to establish that its investments in medium to lower quality obligations do not exceed the limitations under subsection (d).

(g) The provisions of subsections (d), (e), and (f) of this section apply to any investment made after December 31, 1991. If an insurer's investments in medium to lower quality obligations equal or exceed the maximum amounts permitted by subsection (d) as of December 31, 1991, the insurer shall not acquire any additional medium to lower quality obligations without the Commissioner's prior written approval. An insurer that is not in compliance with subsection (d) of this section as of December 31, 1991, may hold until maturity or until December 31, 1995, whichever is sooner, only those medium to lower quality obligations it owns on that date, if the obligations were obtained in compliance with the law in effect when the investments were made. If the insurer sells, transfers, or otherwise disposes of the securities before maturity, the insurer may not acquire any medium to lower quality obligations as substitutions or replacements without the Commissioner's prior approval.

(h) An insurer that is not in compliance with subsection (d) of this section on December 31, 1991, shall file with its annual statement a separate schedule of the medium to lower quality obligations it owns on December 31, 1991. Until it is in compliance with subsection (d) of this section, the insurer shall file with each succeeding annual and quarterly statement a separate schedule of the medium to lower quality obligations it owns as of the reporting date of the filed statement.

(i) Failure to obtain the Commissioner's prior written approval shall result in any investments in excess of those permitted by subsection (d) of this section not being allowed as an asset of the insurer.

(j) The Commissioner may limit the extent of an insurer's deposits with any financial institution if the Commissioner determines that the financial solvency of the insurer is threatened by a deposit in excess of insured limits.

(k) The provisions of this section supersede any inconsistent provision of section 106 of the Secondary Mortgage Market Enhancement Act of 1984, 15 U.S.C. § 77r-1, to the extent permitted by that Act. (1991, c. 681, s. 29; 1993, c. 452, ss. 10-13; c. 504, s. 43; 1993 (Reg. Sess., 1994), c. 678, s. 12; 1998-212, s. 26B(i); 2001-215, s. 3; 2001-223, ss. 8.1, 8.2.)

§ 58-7-172. Cash and deposits.

An insurer may have funds in coin or currency of the United States on hand or on deposit in any solvent national or state bank, savings and loan association, or trust company. (1991, c. 681, s. 29.)

§ 58-7-173. Permitted insurer investments.

An insurer may invest in:
   (1) Bonds, notes, warrants, and other evidences of indebtedness that are direct obligations of the U.S. Government or for which the full faith and credit of the U.S. Government is pledged for the payment of principal and interest.
   (2) Loans insured or guaranteed as to principal and interest by the U.S. Government or by any agency or instrumentality of the U.S. Government to the extent of the insurance or guaranty.
   (3) Student loans insured or guaranteed as to principal by the U.S. Government or by any agency or instrumentality of the U.S. Government to the extent of the insurance or guaranty.
   (4) Bonds, notes, warrants, and other securities not in default that are the direct obligations of any state or United States territory or the government of Canada or any Canadian province, or for which the full faith and credit of such state, government, or province has been pledged for the payment of principal and interest.
   (5) Bonds, notes, warrants, and other securities not in default of any county, district, incorporated city, or school district in any state of the

United States, or the District of Columbia, or in any Canadian province, that are the direct obligations of the county, district, city, or school district and for payment of the principal and interest of which the county, district, city, or school district has lawful authority to levy taxes or make assessments.

(6) Bonds, notes, certificates of indebtedness, warranties, or other evidences of indebtedness that are payable from revenues or earnings specifically pledged therefor of any public toll bridge, structure, or improvement owned by any state, incorporated city, or legally constituted public corporation or commission, all within the United States or Canada, for the payment of the principal and interest of which a lawful sinking fund has been established and is being maintained and if no default by the issuer in payment of principal or interest has occurred on any of its bonds, notes, warrants, or other securities within five years prior to the date of investment therein.

(7) Bonds, notes, certificates of indebtedness, warrants, or other evidences of indebtedness that are valid obligations issued, assumed, or guaranteed by the United States, any state, any county, city, district, political subdivision, civil division, or public instrumentality of any such government or unit thereof, or in any province of Canada; if by statute or other legal requirements the obligations are payable as to both principal and interest from revenues or earnings from the whole or any part of any utility supplying water, gas, a sewage disposal facility, electricity, or any other public service, including but not limited to a toll road or toll bridge.

(8) Bonds, debentures, or other securities of the following agencies, whether or not those obligations are guaranteed by the U.S. Government:

    a. Fannie Mae, and stock thereof when acquired in connection with the sale of mortgage loans to the Association.

    b. Any federal land bank, when the securities are issued under the Farm Loan Act;

    c. Any federal home loan bank, when the securities are issued under the Home Loan Bank Act;

    d. The Home Owners' Loan Corporation, created by the Home Owners' Loan Act of 1933;

    e. Any federal intermediate credit bank, created by the Agricultural Credits Act;

    f. The Central Bank for Cooperatives and regional banks for cooperatives organized under the Farm Credit Act of 1933, or by any of such banks; and any notes, bonds, debentures, or other similar obligations, consolidated or otherwise, issued by farm credit institutions under the Farm Credit Act of 1971;

    g. Any other similar agency of the U.S. Government that is of similar financial quality.

(9) Bonds, debentures, or other securities of public housing authorities, issued under the Housing Act, of 1949, the Municipal Housing Commission Act, or the Rural Housing Commission Act, or issued by any public housing authority or agency in the United States, if the bonds, debentures, or other securities are secured by a pledge of annual contributions to be paid by the United States or any United States agency.

(10) Obligations issued, assumed, or guaranteed by the International Bank for Reconstruction and Development, the International Finance Corporation, the Inter-American Development Bank, the Asian Development Bank, or the African Development Bank; and the cost of

investments made under this subdivision in any one institution shall not exceed three percent (3%) of the insurer admitted assets.

(11) Bonds, notes, or other interest-bearing or interest-accruing obligations of any solvent institution organized under the laws of the United States, of any state, Canada or any Canadian province; provided such instruments are rated and valued by the Securities Valuation Office of the NAIC. The cost of investments made under this subdivision in any one issuer shall not exceed three percent (3%) of an insurer's admitted assets.

(12) Secured obligations of duly constituted churches and of church-holding companies; and the cost of investments made under this subdivision shall not exceed three percent (3%) of the insurer's admitted assets.

(13) Equipment trust obligations or certificates adequately secured and evidencing an interest in transportation equipment, wholly or in part within the United States, and the right to receive determined portions of rental, purchase, or other fixed obligatory payments for the use or purchase of that transportation equipment; and the cost of investments made under this subdivision shall not exceed twenty percent (20%) of the insurer's admitted assets.

(14) Share or savings accounts of savings and loan associations or building and loan associations.

(15) Loans with a maturity not in excess of 12 years from the date thereof that are secured by the pledge of securities eligible for investment under this Chapter or by the pledge or assignment of life insurance policies issued by other insurers authorized to transact insurance in this State. On the date made, no such loan shall exceed in amount seventy-five percent (75%) of the market value of the collateral pledged, except that loans upon the pledge of U.S. Government bonds and loans upon the pledge or assignment of life insurance policies shall not exceed ninety-five percent (95%) of the market value of the bonds or the cash surrender value of the policies pledged. The market value of the collateral pledge shall at all times during the continuance of the loans meet or exceed the miminum percentages herein. Loans made under this section shall not be renewable beyond a period of 12 years from the date of the loan.

(16) Stocks, common or preferred, of any corporation created or existing under the laws of the United States, any U.S. territory, Canada or any Canadian province, or of any state. An insurer may invest in stocks, common or preferred, of any corporation created or existing under the laws of any foreign country other than Canada subject to the provisions of G.S. 58-7-178.

(17) Mortgage pass-through securities and derivatives thereof, that have been rated as investment grade by the Securities Valuation Office of the NAIC including, without limitation, collateral mortgage obligations backed by a pool of mortgages of the kind, class, and investment quality as those eligible for investment under G.S. 58-7-179. (1991, c. 681, s. 29; 1993, c. 105, s. 1; c. 452, s. 14; c. 504, s. 44; 2001-223, ss. 8.3, 8.4, 8.5, 8.6, 8.7, 8.8; 2001-487, s. 14(g).)

CASE NOTES

There was no requirement in former § 58-7-90 that insurance companies invest in risk-free ventures; rather, the statute provided that insurance companies could engage in a variety of investments. State ex rel. Comm'r of Ins. v. North Carolina Rate Bureau, 40 N.C. App. 85, 252 S.E.2d 811, cert. denied, 297 N.C. 452, 256 S.E.2d 810 (1979).

§ 58-7-175. Policy loans.

A life insurer may lend to its policyholder, upon pledge of the policy as collateral security, any sum not exceeding the cash loan value of the policy; or may lend against pledge or assignment of any of its supplementary contracts or other contracts or obligations, as long as the loan is adequately secured by the pledge or assignment. Loans so made are eligible investments of the insurer. (1991, c. 681, s. 29.)

§ 58-7-177: Repealed by Session Laws 2001-223, s. 8.9, effective June 15, 2001.

§ 58-7-178. Foreign or territorial investments.

(a) An insurer authorized to transact insurance in a foreign country or any U.S. territory may have funds invested in securities that may be required for that authority and for the transaction of that business, provided the funds and securities are substantially of the same kinds, classes, and investment grades as those otherwise eligible for investment under this Chapter. The aggregate amount of investments under this subsection shall not exceed the amount that the insurer is required by law to invest in the foreign country or United States territory, or one and one-half times the amount of reserves and other obligations under the contracts, whichever is greater.

(b) An insurer, whether or not it is authorized to do business or has outstanding insurance contracts on lives or risks in any foreign country, may invest in bonds, notes, or stocks of any foreign country or alien corporation that are substantially of the same kinds, classes, and investment grades as those otherwise eligible for investment under this Chapter. The aggregate cost of investments under this subsection shall not exceed ten percent (10%) of the insurer's admitted assets, provided that the cost of investments in any foreign country under this subsection shall not exceed three percent (3%) of the insurer's admitted assets.

(c) Canadian securities eligible for investment under other provisions of this Chapter are not subject to this section. (1991, c. 681, s. 29; 2001-223, s. 8.11; 2001-487, s. 103(b); 2002-187, s. 2.6.)

Effect of Amendments. — Session Laws 2002-187, s. 2.6, effective October 31, 2002, substituted "cost" for "amount" in the second sentence of subsection (b).

§ 58-7-179. Mortgage loans.

(a) An insurer may invest any of its funds in bonds, notes, or other evidences of indebtedness that are secured by first mortgages or deeds of trust upon improved real property located in the United States, any U.S. territory, or Canada, or that are secured by first mortgages or deeds of trust upon leasehold estates having an unexpired term of not less than 30 years, inclusive of the terms that may be provided by enforceable options of renewal, as long as the loan matures at least 20 years before the expiration of such lease, in improved real property located in the United States, any U.S. territory, or Canada. In all cases the security for the loan must be a first lien upon the real property, and there must not be any condition or right of reentry or forfeiture not insured against under which, in the case of real property other than leaseholds, the lien can be cut off or subordinated or otherwise disturbed, or under which, in the case of leaseholds, the insurer cannot continue the lease in force for the duration of the loan. Nothing herein prohibits any investment because of the existence of any prior lien for ground rents, taxes, assessments, or other similar charges not yet delinquent. This section does not prohibit investment in mortgages or similar obligations when made under G.S. 58-7-180.

(b) "Improved real property" means all farmlands used for tillage, crops, or pasture; timberlands; and all real property on which permanent improvements, and improvements under construction or in process of construction, suitable for residential, institutional, commercial, or industrial use are situated.

(c) No such mortgage loan or loans made or acquired by an insurer on any one property shall, at the time of investment by the insurer, exceed the larger of the following amounts, as applicable:

(1) Ninety-five percent (95%) of the value of the real property or leasehold securing the real property in the case of a mortgage on a dwelling primarily intended for occupancy by not more than four families if they insure down to seventy-five percent (75%) with a licensed mortgage insurance company, or seventy-five percent (75%) of the value in the case of other real estate mortgages;

(2) The amount of any insurance or guaranty of the loan by the United States or by an agency or instrumentality thereof; or

(3) The percentage-of-value limit on the amount of the loan applicable under subdivision (1) of this subsection, plus the amount by which the excess of the loan over the percentage-of-value limit is insured or guaranteed by the United States or by any agency or instrumentality thereof.

(d) In the case of a purchase money mortgage given to secure the purchase price of real estate sold by the insurer, the amount lent or invested shall not exceed the unpaid part of the purchase price.

(e) Nothing in this section prohibits an insurer from renewing or extending a loan for the original or a lesser amount where a shrinkage in value of the real estate securing the loan would cause its value to be less than the amount otherwise required in relation to the amount of the loan. (1991, c. 681, s. 29; 2003-212, s. 11.)

Effect of Amendments. — Session Laws 2003-212, s. 11, effective October 1, 2003, deleted "and shall be valued in accordance with G.S. 58-7-195" following "part of the purchase price" at the end of subsection (d).

§ 58-7-180. Chattel mortgages.

(a) In connection with a mortgage loan on the security of real estate designed and used primarily for residential purposes only, where the mortgage loan was acquired under G.S. 58-7-179, an insurer may lend or invest an amount not exceeding twenty percent (20%) of the amount lent on or invested in such real estate mortgage on the security of a chattel mortgage to be amortized by regular periodic payments with a term of not more than five years, and representing a first and prior lien, except for taxes not then delinquent, on personal property constituting durable equipment owned by the mortgagor and kept and used in the mortgaged premises.

(b) For the purposes of this section, the term "durable equipment" includes only mechanical refrigerators, air-conditioning equipment, mechanical laundering machines, heating and cooking stoves and ranges, and, in addition, in the case of apartment houses and hotels, room furniture and furnishings.

(c) Before the acquisition of a chattel mortgage under this section, items of property to be included therein shall be separately appraised by a qualified appraiser and the fair market value determined. No such chattel mortgage loan shall exceed in amount the same ratio of loan to the value of the property as is applicable to the companion loan on the real property.

(d) This section does not prohibit an insurer from taking liens on personal property as additional security for any investment otherwise eligible under this Chapter. (1991, c. 681, s. 29.)

§ 58-7-182. Special investments by title insurers.

In addition to other investments eligible under this Chapter, a title insurer may invest and have invested an amount not exceeding the greater of three hundred thousand dollars ($300,000) or fifty percent (50%) of that part of its policyholders' surplus that exceeds the minimum surplus required by G.S. 58-7-75 in its abstract plant and equipment, in loans secured by mortgages on abstract plants and equipment, and, with the Commissioner's consent, in stocks of abstract companies. (1991, c. 681, s. 29.)

§ 58-7-183. Special consent investments.

(a) After satisfying the requirements of this Chapter, any funds of an insurer in excess of its reserves and policyholders' surplus required to be maintained may be invested:
   (1) Without limitation in any investments otherwise authorized by this Chapter; or
   (2) In such other investments not specifically authorized by this Chapter as long as any single interest investment does not exceed two percent (2%) of admitted assets and the aggregate of the investments does not exceed the lesser of five percent (5%) of the insurer's total admitted assets or sixty percent (60%) of the amount by which the insurer's policyholders' surplus exceeds the minimum required to be maintained.
The limitations in subdivision (2) of this subsection may be exceeded if approved in writing by the Commissioner.
   (b) In no case shall the investments authorized under this section being held by an insurer be greater than the amount by which the insurer's policyholders' surplus exceeds the minimum required to be maintained.
   (c) Notwithstanding the provisions of this section, an insurer may not invest in investments prohibited by this Chapter. (1991, c. 681, s. 29; 1993, c. 452, s. 14.1; c. 504, s. 6.)

§ 58-7-185. Prohibited investments and investment underwriting.

(a) In addition to investments excluded under other provisions of this Chapter, except with prior approval by the Commissioner, an insurer shall not directly or indirectly invest in or lend its funds upon the security of:
   (1) Issued shares of its own capital stock, except in connection with a plan for purchase of the shares by the insurer's officers, employees, or agents. No such stock shall, however, constitute an asset of the insurer in any determination of its financial condition.
   (2) Except with the Commissioner's consent, securities issued by any corporation or enterprise, the controlling interest of which is or will after acquisition by the insurer be held directly or indirectly by the insurer or any combination of the insurer and the insurer's directors, officers, parent corporation, subsidiaries, or controlling stockholders. Investments in subsidiaries under G.S. 58-19-10 are not subject to this provision.
   (3) Repealed by Session Laws 2001-223, s. 8.13, effective June 15, 2001.
   (b) No insurer shall underwrite or participate in the underwriting of an offering of securities or property by any other person. (1991, c. 681, s. 29; 2001-223, ss. 8.12, 8.13.)

§ 58-7-187. Real estate, in general.

(a) An insurer shall not directly or indirectly acquire or hold real estate except as authorized in this section.

(b) An insurer may acquire and hold:

(1) Land and buildings thereon used or acquired for use as its principal home office and branch offices, or used in conjunction with such offices, for the convenient transaction of its own business.

(2) Real property acquired in satisfaction in whole or in part of loans, mortgages, liens, judgments, decrees, or debts previously owing to the insurer, in the course of its business.

(3) Real property acquired in part payment of the consideration on the sale of other real property owned by it, if the transaction effects a net reduction in the insurer's investment in real estate.

(4) Real property acquired by gift or devise or through merger, consolidation, or bulk reinsurance of another insurer under this Chapter.

(5) Additional real property and equipment incident to real property, if necessary or convenient for the enhancement of the marketability or sale value of real property previously acquired or held by it under subdivisions (2) through (4) of this subsection.

(c) An insurer may acquire and hold real property for investment, subject to the following conditions:

(1) The amount shall not exceed in the aggregate the lesser of five percent (5%) of the insurer's admitted assets or fifteen percent (15%) of the insurer's capital and surplus.

(2) The amount in any one property shall not exceed one percent (1%) of the insurer's admitted assets.

(3) The amount in unimproved land shall not exceed one-half of one percent (0.5%) of the insurer's admitted assets.

(4) There shall be no time limit for the disposal of investment real estate.

(d) The amount in real property acquired and held by an insurer shall not exceed fifteen percent (15%) of the insurer's admitted assets; but the Commissioner may permit an insurer to invest in real property in such increased amount as the Commissioner considers to be proper. (1991, c. 681, s. 29.)

CASE NOTES

Reserve Investment Can Consist of Real Estate. — Former G.S. 58-7-90(c)(8) provided that a company's reserve investment could consist of real estate, but only if used for the company's principal office or for its convenient accommodation in the transaction of its business. In re Hdwe. Mut. Ins. Co., 278 N.C. 670, 180 S.E.2d 840 (1971).

Value of Property. — Under former G.S. 58-7-90(e), a company could not even acquire real property for the purposes stated in former G.S. 58-7-90(c)(8)a and b if the value of the acquired property, together with all the real property held by the company, exceeded 10% of its total admitted assets. In re Hdwe. Mut. Ins. Co., 278 N.C. 670, 180 S.E.2d 840 (1971).

§ 58-7-188. Time limit for disposal of ineligible property and securities; effect of failure to dispose.

(a) Any property or securities lawfully acquired by an insurer that it could not otherwise have invested in or lent its funds upon at the time of the acquisition shall be disposed of within three years from the date of acquisition, unless within that period the security has attained to the standard of eligibility; except that any security or property acquired under any agreement of bulk reinsurance, merger, or consolidation may be retained for a longer period if so provided in the plan for the reinsurance, merger, or consolidation as approved by the Commissioner under this Chapter. Upon application by the insurer and proof that forced sale of any such property or security would materially injure the insurer's interests, the Commissioner may extend the disposal period for an additional reasonable time.

(b) Any property or securities lawfully acquired and held by an insurer after expiration of the period for their disposal or any extension of the period granted by the Commissioner shall not be allowed as an asset of the insurer. (1991, c. 681, s. 29.)

§ **58-7-190:** Repealed by Session Laws 1993, c. 452, s. 65.

§ 58-7-192. Valuation of securities and investments.

(a) through (c) Repealed by Session Laws 2003-212, s. 8, effective October 1, 2003.

(d) No valuations shall be greater than any applicable valuation or method contained in the latest edition of the NAIC publications entitled "Purposes and Procedures Manual of the NAIC Securities Valuation Office" or the "Accounting Practices and Procedures Manual", unless the Commissioner determines that another valuation method is appropriate when it results in a more conservative valuation.

(e) Repealed by Session Laws 2003-212, s. 8, effective October 1, 2003. (1991, c. 681, s. 29; 1993, c. 452, ss. 15, 16; 2001-223, s. 8.14; 2003-212, s. 8.)

Effect of Amendments. — Session Laws 2003-212, s. 8, effective October 1, 2003, repealed subsections (a) through (c) and (e); and in subsection (d), substituted "Purposes and Procedures Manual of the NAIC Securities Valuation Office" for "Valuations of Securities."

§ 58-7-193. Valuation of property.

(a), (b) Repealed by Session Laws 2003-212, s. 9, effective October 1, 2003.

(c) Personal property acquired pursuant to chattel mortgages made in accordance with G.S. 58-7-180 shall not be valued at an amount greater than the unpaid balance of principal on the defaulted loan at the date of acquisition, or the fair market value of the property, whichever amount is less.

(d) If the Commissioner and an insurer do not agree on the value of real or personal property of an insurer, in carrying out the Commissioner's responsibilities under this section, the Commissioner may retain the services of a qualified real or personal property appraiser. The insurer shall reimburse the Commissioner for the costs of the services of any appraiser incurred with respect to the Commissioner's responsibilities under this section. (1991, c. 681, s. 29; 2003-212, s. 9.)

Effect of Amendments. — Session Laws 2003-212, s. 9, effective October 1, 2003, repealed subsections (a) and (b).

§ **58-7-195:** Repealed by Session Laws 2003-212, s. 10, effective October 1, 2003.

§ 58-7-197. Replacing certain assets; reporting certain liabilities.

(a) The Commissioner, upon determining that an insurer's asset has not been valued according to this Chapter or that it does not qualify as an asset, shall require the insurer to properly revalue an improperly valued asset or replace a nonadmitted asset with an asset suitable to the Commissioner within 90 days after the determination.

(b) The Commissioner, upon determining that an insurer has failed to report certain liabilities that should have been reported, shall require that the insurer report those liabilities to the Commissioner within 90 days after notice to the insurer.

(c) When the Commissioner determines that an admitted asset held by any insurer is of doubtful value or is without ascertainable value on a public exchange, unless the insurer establishes a value by placing the asset upon the market and obtaining a bona fide offer for the asset, the Commissioner may have the asset appraised, and the appraisal shall be the true value of the asset. No asset may be carried in an insurer's financial statement under G.S. 58-2-165 at an appraised value established by the insurer unless the Commissioner's prior written approval is obtained.

(d) When any admitted asset defaults as to principal or in the payment of interest or dividends after it has been purchased by an insurer, the asset shall subsequently be carried at its market value or, after notice and opportunity for hearing, at a value determined by the Commissioner.

(e) Whenever it appears to the Commissioner that an insurer has acquired any asset in violation of this Chapter, the Commissioner shall disallow, in whole or in part, the amount of the asset that is prohibited by this Chapter. In any determination of the financial position of the insurer, that amount shall be deducted as a nonadmitted asset of the insurer. (1991, c. 681, s. 29.)

§ 58-7-198. Assets of foreign or alien insurers.

The Commissioner may refuse a new or renewal license to any foreign or alien insurer upon finding that its assets do not comply in substance with the investment requirements and limitations imposed by this Chapter upon like domestic insurers whenever authorized to do the same kinds of insurance business. (1991, c. 681, s. 29.)

§ 58-7-200. Investment transactions.

(a) The transactions specified in subsections (b) through (e) of this section are expressly allowed or prohibited as provided in this section and to the extent they are not in conflict with other provisions of this Chapter.

(b) An insurer may engage in derivative transactions under the provisions and limitations of G.S. 58-7-205.

(c) No insurer shall directly or indirectly invest in, or lend its funds to, any of its directors, officers, controlling stockholders, or any other person in which an officer, director, or controlling stockholder is substantially interested, nor shall any director, officer, or controlling stockholder directly or indirectly accept the funds.

(d) No director, officer, or controlling stockholder of any insurer shall receive any money or valuable thing, either directly or indirectly or through any substantial interest in any other person, for negotiating, procuring, recommending, or aiding in any purchase or sale of property or loan from the insurer; or be monetarily interested either as principal, corporation, agent, or beneficiary, in any such purchase, sale, or loan; and no financial obligation of any such director, officer, or stockholder shall be guaranteed by the insurer. "Substantial interest in any other person" means an interest equivalent to ownership or control by a director, officer, or controlling stockholder or the aggregate ownership or control by all directors, officers, and controlling stockholders of the same insurer of those percentages or more of the stock of the person, as defined under "control" in G.S. 58-19-5(2).

(e) Nothing in this section prohibits:
(1) A director or officer of any insurer from receiving the usual salary, compensation, or emoluments for services rendered in the ordinary course of that person's duties as a director or officer, if the salary, compensation, or emolument is authorized by vote of the board of directors of the insurer;
(2) Any insurer in connection with the relocation of the place of employment of an officer, including any relocation in connection with the initial employment of the officer, from (i) making, or the officer from accepting therefrom, a mortgage loan to the officer on real property owned by the officer that is to serve as the officer's residence or (ii) acquiring, or the officer from selling thereto, at not more than its fair market value, the officer's prior residence;
(3) The payment to a director or officer of any such insurer who is a licensed attorney-at-law of fees in connection with loans made by the insurer if and when the fees are paid by the borrower and do not constitute a charge against the insurer; or
(4) An insurer from making a loan upon a policy held therein by the borrower not in excess of the policy's net value. (1991, c. 681, s. 29; 2001-223, ss. 8.15, 8.16.)

§ 58-7-205. Derivative transactions.

(a) As used in this section, the following terms have the following meanings:
(1) "Business entity" includes a sole proprietorship, corporation, limited liability company, association, partnership, joint stock company, joint venture, mutual fund, trust, joint tenancy or other similar form of business organization, whether for-profit or not-for-profit.
(2) "Counterparty exposure" amount means:
a. The amount of credit risk attributable to a derivative instrument entered into with a business entity other than through a qualified exchange, qualified foreign exchange, or cleared through a qualified clearinghouse ("over-the-counter derivative instrument"). The amount of credit risk equals:
1. The market value of the over-the-counter derivative instrument if the liquidation of the derivative instrument would result in a final cash payment to the insurer; or
2. Zero if the liquidation of the derivative instrument would not result in a final cash payment to the insurer.
b. If over-the-counter derivative instruments are entered into under a written master agreement which provides for netting of payments owed by the respective parties and the domicile of the counterparty is either within the United States or, if not within the United States, within a foreign jurisdiction listed in the Purposes and Procedures of the Securities Valuation Office of the NAIC as eligible for netting, the net amount of credit risk shall be the greater of zero or the net sum of:
1. The market value of the over-the-counter derivative instruments entered into under the agreement, the liquidation of which would result in a final cash payment to the insurer; and
2. The market value of the over-the-counter derivative instruments entered into under the agreement, the liquidation of which would result in a final cash payment by the insurer to the business entity.
c. For open transactions, market value shall be determined at the end of the most recent quarter of the insurer's fiscal year and shall be

323

reduced by the market value of acceptable collateral held by the insurer or placed in escrow by one or both parties.

(3) "Derivative instrument" means an agreement, option, instrument, or a series or combination thereof:

    a. To make or take delivery of, or assume or relinquish, a specified amount of one or more underlying interests, or to make a cash settlement in lieu thereof; or

    b. That has a price, performance, value, or cash flow based primarily upon the actual or expected price level, performance, value, or cash flow of one or more underlying interests.

Derivative instruments include options, warrants used in a hedging transaction and not attached to another financial instrument, caps, floors, collars, swaps, forwards, futures, and any other agreements, options, or instruments substantially similar thereto or any series or combination thereof. Derivative instruments shall additionally include any agreements, options, or instruments permitted under rules adopted under subsection (c) of this section. Derivative instruments shall not include an investment authorized by G.S. 58-7-173, 58-7-175, 58-7-178, 58-7-179, 58-7-180, and 58-7-187.

(4) "Derivative transaction" means any transaction involving the use of one or more derivative instruments.

(5) "Qualified clearinghouse" means a clearinghouse for, and subject to the rules of, a qualified exchange or a qualified foreign exchange. The clearinghouse provides clearing services, including acting as a counterparty to each of the parties to a transaction such that the parties no longer have credit risk as to each other.

(6) "Qualified exchange" means:

    a. A securities exchange registered as a national securities exchange, or a securities market regulated under the Securities Exchange Act of 1934 (15 U.S.C. §§ 78, et seq.), as amended;

    b. A board of trade or commodities exchange designated as a contract market by the Commodity Futures Trading Commission, or any successor thereof;

    c. Private Offerings, Resales and Trading through Automated Linkages (PORTAL);

    d. A designated offshore securities market as defined in Securities Exchange Commission Regulation S, 17 C.F.R. Part 230, as amended; or

    e. A qualified foreign exchange.

(7) "Qualified foreign exchange" means a foreign exchange, board of trade, or contract market located outside the United States, its territories or possessions:

    a. That has received regulatory comparability relief under Commodity Futures Trading Commission Rule 30.10 (as set forth in Appendix C to Part 30 of the CFTC's Regulations, 17 C.F.R. Part 30);

    b. That is, or its members are, subject to the jurisdiction of a foreign futures authority that has received regulatory comparability relief under Commodity Futures Trading Commission Rule 30.10 (as set forth in Appendix C to Part 30 of the CFTC's Regulations, 17 C.F.R. Part 30) as to futures transactions in the jurisdiction where the exchange, board of trade, or contract market is located; or

    c. Upon which foreign stock index futures contracts are listed that are the subject of no-action relief issued by the CFTC's Office of General Counsel, but an exchange, board of trade, or contract market that qualifies as a "qualified foreign exchange" only under this paragraph shall only be a "qualified foreign exchange" as to foreign stock index futures contracts that are the subject of the no-action relief under this paragraph.

(8) "Replication transaction" means a derivative transaction that is intended to replicate the investment in one or more assets that an insurer is authorized to acquire or sell under this section or G.S. 58-7-165. A derivative transaction that is entered into as a hedging transaction shall not be considered a replication transaction.

(b) An insurer may, directly or indirectly through an investment subsidiary, engage in derivative transactions under this section under the following conditions:

(1) An insurer may use derivative instruments under this section to engage in hedging transactions and certain income generation transactions as may be further defined by rules adopted by the Commissioner.

(2) An insurer shall be able to demonstrate to the Commissioner the intended hedging characteristics and the ongoing effectiveness of the derivative transaction or combination of the transactions through cash flow testing or other appropriate analyses.

(c) The Commissioner may adopt reasonable rules for investments and transactions under this section including, but not limited to, rules which impose financial solvency standards, valuation standards, and reporting requirements.

(d) An insurer may enter into hedging transactions under this section if, as a result of and after giving effect to the transaction:

(1) The aggregate statement value of options, caps, floors, and warrants not attached to another financial instrument purchased and used in hedging transactions then engaged in by the insurer does not exceed seven and one-half percent (7.5%) of its admitted assets;

(2) The aggregate statement value of options, caps, and floors written in hedging transactions then engaged in by the insurer does not exceed three percent (3%) of its admitted assets; and

(3) The aggregate potential exposure of collars, swaps, forwards, and futures used in hedging transactions then engaged in by the insurer does not exceed six and one-half percent (6.5%) of its admitted assets.

(e) An insurer may enter into the following types of income generation transactions if, as a result of and after giving effect to the transactions, the aggregate statement value of the fixed income assets that are subject to call or that generate the cash flows for payments under the caps or floors, plus the face value of fixed income securities underlying a derivative instrument subject to call, plus the amount of the purchase obligations under the puts, does not exceed ten percent (10%) of its admitted assets:

(1) Sales of covered call options on noncallable fixed-income securities, callable fixed-income securities if the option expires by its terms before the end of the noncallable period, or derivative instruments based on fixed income securities;

(2) Sales of covered call options on equity securities, if the insurer holds in its portfolio, or can immediately acquire through the exercise of options, warrants, or conversion rights already owned, the equity securities subject to call during the complete term of the call option sold;

(3) Sales of covered puts on investments that the insurer is permitted to acquire under this Chapter, if the insurer has escrowed or entered into a custodian agreement segregating cash or cash equivalents with a market value equal to the amount of its purchase obligations under the put during the complete term of the put option sold; or

    (4) Sales of covered caps or floors, if the insurer holds in its portfolio the investments generating the cash flow to make the required payments under the caps or floors during the complete term that the cap or floor is outstanding.

  (f) An insurer shall include all counterparty exposure amounts in determining compliance with the limitations of G.S. 58-7-170.

  (g) Under rules that may be adopted by the Commissioner, additional transactions involving the use of derivative instruments in excess of the limits of subsection (d) of this section or for other risk management purposes may be approved by the Commissioner.

  (h) An insurer shall establish guidelines and internal procedures as follows:

    (1) Before engaging in a derivative transaction, an insurer shall establish written guidelines that shall be used for effecting and maintaining the transactions. The guidelines shall:

      a. Address investment or, if applicable, underwriting objectives, and risk constraints such as credit risk limits;

      b. Address permissible transactions and the relationship of those transactions to its operations, such as a precise identification of the risks being hedged by a derivative transaction; and

      c. Require compliance with internal control procedures.

    (2) An insurer shall have a system for determining whether a derivative instrument used for hedging has been effective.

    (3) An insurer shall have a credit risk management system for over-the-counter derivative transactions that measures credit risk exposure using the counterparty exposure amount.

    (4) An insurer's board of directors shall, in accordance with G.S. 58-7-168:

      a. Approve the guidelines required by subdivision (1) of this subsection and the systems required by subdivisions (2) and (3) of this subsection; and

      b. Determine whether the insurer has adequate professional personnel, technical expertise and systems to implement investment practices involving derivatives.

  (i) An insurer shall maintain documentation and records relating to each derivative transaction, such as:

    (1) The purpose or purposes of the transaction;

    (2) The assets or liabilities to which the transaction relates;

    (3) The specific derivative instrument used in the transaction;

    (4) For over-the-counter derivative instrument transactions, the name of the counterparty and counterparty exposure amount; and

    (5) For exchange-traded derivative instruments, the name of the exchange and the name of the firm that handled the trade.

  (j) Each derivative instrument shall be:

    (1) Traded on a qualified exchange;

    (2) Entered into with, or guaranteed by, a business entity;

    (3) Issued or written by or entered into with the issuer of the underlying interest on which the derivative instrument is based; or

    (4) Entered into with a qualified foreign exchange. (2001-223, s. 8.17.)

ARTICLE 8.

Mutual Insurance Companies.

§ 58-8-1. Mutual insurance companies organized; requisites for doing business.

No policy may be issued by a mutual company until the president and the secretary of the company have certified under oath that every subscription for

326

insurance in the list presented to the Commissioner for approval is genuine, and made with an agreement with every subscriber for insurance that he will take the policies subscribed for by him within 30 days after the granting of a license to the company by the Commissioner to issue policies. Any person making a false oath in respect to the certificate is guilty of a Class I felony. (1899, c. 54, ss. 25, 32, 34; 1901, c. 391, s. 3; 1903, c. 438, s. 4; Rev., s. 4738; 1911, c. 93; C.S., s. 6346; 1945, c. 386; 1989 (Reg. Sess., 1990), c. 1054, s. 4; 1993 (Reg. Sess., 1994), c. 767, s. 24.)

CASE NOTES

Cited in Warren v. Jackson, 125 N.C. App. 96, 479 S.E.2d 278 (1997).

§ 58-8-5. Manner of amending charter.

(a) A domestic mutual insurance company may hereafter amend its charter in the following manner only:
 (1) A meeting of the board of directors shall be called in accordance with the bylaws, specifying the amendment to be voted upon at such meeting;
 (2) If at such meeting two thirds of the directors present vote in favor of the proposed amendment, then the president and secretary shall under oath make a certificate to this effect, which certificate shall set forth the call for such meeting, the service of such call upon all directors, and the minutes of the meeting relating to the adoption of the proposed amendment;
 (3) If the meeting at which the proposed amendment is to be considered is a special meeting, rather than a regular annual meeting of policyholders, such special meeting can be called only after the Commissioner has given his approval in writing;
 (4) If at such policyholders' meeting two thirds of those voting in person or by proxy shall vote in favor of any proposed amendment, the president and secretary shall make a certificate under oath setting forth such fact together with the full text of the amendment thus approved. Said certificate shall, within 30 days after such meeting, be submitted to the Commissioner for his approval as conforming to the requirements of law, and it shall be the duty of the Commissioner to act upon all proposed amendments within 10 days after the filing of such certificate with him.

(b) All charter amendments heretofore issued upon application of the board of directors of any domestic mutual insurance company are hereby validated, if otherwise legally adopted. (1943, c. 170; 1947, c. 721; 1991, c. 720, s. 4; 2001-223, s. 9.1.)

Legal Periodicals. — For comment on this section, see 25 N.C.L. Rev. 441 (1947).

§ 58-8-10. Policyholders are members of mutual companies.

Every person insured by a mutual insurance company is a member while that person's policy is in force, entitled to one vote for each policy that person holds, and must be notified of the time and place of holding the company's meetings by a written notice or by an imprint upon the back of each policy, receipt, or certificate of renewal, as follows:

The insured is hereby notified that by virtue of this policy the insured is a member of the _____ insurance company, and that the annual meetings of the company are held at its home office on the _____ day of _____, in each year, at _____ o'clock.

The blanks shall be duly filled in print and are a sufficient notice. A corporation that becomes a member of a mutual insurance company may authorize any person to represent the corporation; and this representative has all the rights of an individual member. A person holding property in trust may insure it in a mutual insurance company, and as trustee assume the liability and be entitled to the rights of a member; but is not personally liable upon the contract of insurance. Members may vote by proxies, dated and executed within one year after receipt, and returned and recorded on the books of the company three days or more before the meeting at which they are to be used. (1899, c. 54, s. 33; Rev., s. 4739; C.S., s. 6348; 1945, c. 386; 1947, c. 721; 1998-211, s. 37.1(a).)

CASE NOTES

This section is an enabling statute to protect a trustee from liability. Fuller v. Lockhart, 209 N.C. 61, 182 S.E. 733 (1935).

Policyholders in a mutual fire insurance company are not liable for its debts beyond the contingent liability fixed in the policy. Fuller v. Lockhart, 209 N.C. 61, 182 S.E. 733 (1935). See §§ 58-8-30 through 58-8-40.

As to county boards of education as policyholders, see Fuller v. Lockhart, 209 N.C. 61, 182 S.E. 733 (1935).

§ 58-8-15. Directors in mutual companies.

Every mutual insurance company shall elect by ballot a board of not less than seven directors, who shall manage and conduct its business and hold office for one year or for such term as the bylaws provide and until their successors are qualified. The directors need not be residents of this State or members of the company. In companies with a guaranty capital, no more than one-half of the directors shall be elected by the holders of guaranty capital, except where guaranty capital holders are policyholders. Policyholders which are holders of guaranty capital shall be entitled to one vote for each policy that person holds and one vote for each unit of guaranty capital that person holds. (1899, c. 54, s. 33; Rev., s. 4739; C.S., s. 6349; 1945, c. 386; 1971, c. 751; 2003-212, s. 14.)

Effect of Amendments. — Session Laws 2003-212, s. 14, effective October 1, 2003, in the third sentence, substituted "no more than one-half" for "one half" and substituted "elected by the holders of guaranty capital, except where guaranty capital holders are policyholders" for "chosen by and from the stockholders"; and added the last sentence.

§ 58-8-20. Mutual companies with a guaranty capital.

(a) A mutual insurance company formed as provided in Articles 1 through 64 of this Chapter, in lieu of the contributed surplus required for the organization of mutual companies under the provisions of G.S. 58-7-75, or a mutual insurance company now existing, may, with the prior approval of the Commissioner, tender a guaranty capital offering of not less than fifty thousand dollars ($50,000), divided into units of one hundred dollars ($100.00) each, which shall be invested in the same manner as is provided in this Chapter for the investment of the capital stock of insurance companies.

(a1) Guaranty capital may be issued by an existing domestic mutual insurance company only under the following terms and conditions:

(1) To aid and assist a financially troubled domestic mutual insurance company which otherwise faces rehabilitation or liquidation by this Department; or

(2) For any other reason as presented in a petition to the Commissioner and which is found by the Commissioner to be reasonable, justifiable, and in the best interest of all the policyholders of the company.

Guaranty capital issued under subdivision (2) of this subsection shall require written notification of the action proposed by the board of directors of the company to be mailed to the policyholders of the company not less than 30 days before the meeting when the action may be taken. The written notification shall be advertised in two newspapers of general circulation, approved by the Commissioner, not less than three times a week for a period of not less than four weeks before the meeting. The written notification to policyholders shall include a proxy statement to allow policyholders to vote on the proposed action without personal attendance at the meeting, and the Commissioner shall approve both the written notification and the proxy statement. The proposed action shall be effected by a vote of two-thirds of the policyholders voting thereon in person or by proxy.

(b) The board of directors of a company may distribute interest to the holders of guaranty capital in accordance with the guaranty capital filing approved by the Department.

(c) Guaranty capital shall be applied to the payment of losses only when the company has exhausted its cash in hand and the invested assets, exclusive of uncollected premiums, and when thus impaired, the directors may make good the whole or any part of it by assessments upon the contingent funds of the company at the date of such impairment.

(d) Guaranty capital holders are entitled to one vote per unit of guaranty capital. Guaranty capital holders who are not policyholders are not entitled to participate in the policyholder votes prescribed under subdivision (a1)(2) and subsection (e) of this section.

(e) Guaranty capital may be reduced or retired by vote of the policyholders of the company and the assent of the Commissioner, if the net assets of the company above its reserve and all other claims and obligations, exclusive of guaranty capital, for two years immediately preceding and including the date of its last annual statement, is not less than twenty-five percent (25%) of the guaranty capital. Due notice of such proposed action on the part of the company must be mailed to each policyholder of the company not less than 30 days before the meeting when the action may be taken, and must also be advertised in two papers of general circulation, approved by the Commissioner, not less than three times a week for a period of not less than four weeks before such meeting.

(f) No insurance company with guaranty capital shall distribute to its holders of guaranty capital its assets, except as provided in the guaranty capital filing as approved by the Commissioner.

(g) In the event of a merger, demutualization, or other event where the entity ceases to exist, guaranty capital shall only be returned or repaid to the holders of guaranty capital to the extent that the guaranty capital has been contributed together with accrued interest as specified in the filing approved by the Commissioner. (1899, c. 54, s. 34; Rev., s. 4740; 1911, c. 196, s. 3; C.S., s. 6350; 1945, c. 386; 1971, c. 752; 1981, c. 723; 1989, c. 320; 1991, c. 720, s. 10; 1993, c. 452, s. 17; 2003-212, s. 15.)

Effect of Amendments. — Session Laws 2003-212, s. 15, effective October 1, 2003, in subsection (a), substituted "tender a guaranty capital offering" for "establish a guaranty capital," and substituted "divided into units" for "divided into shares"; added subsections (a1), (f), and (g); and rewrote subsections (b), (c), (d), and (e).

Income from guaranty fund investments does not accrue solely to benefit of guaranty fund shareholders. See opinion of Attorney General to Ron Raxter, Staff Attorney, Dep't of Insurance, 49 N.C.A.G. 207 (1980).

§ 58-8-25. Dividends to policyholders.

(a) Any participating or dividend-paying company, stock or mutual or foreign or domestic, that writes other than life insurance or workers' compensation insurance and employers' liability insurance in connection therewith, may declare and pay a dividend to policyholders from its unassigned surplus, as reflected in the company's most recent annual or quarterly statement filed with the Commissioner under G.S. 58-2-165, which shall include only its surplus in excess of any required minimum surplus. No such dividend shall be paid unless it is fair and equitable and for the best interest of the company and its policyholders. In declaring any dividend to its policyholders, any such company may make reasonable classifications of policies expiring during a fixed period, upon the basis of each general kind of insurance covered by those policies and by territorial divisions of the location of risks by states, except that in fixing the amount of dividends to be paid on each general kind of insurance, the dividends shall be uniform in rate and applicable to the majority of risks within that general kind of insurance, and exceptions may be made as to any class or classes of risk and a different rate or amount of dividends paid on the class or classes if the conditions applicable to the class or classes differ substantially from the condition applicable to the kind of insurance as a whole. Every such company shall have an equal rate of dividend for the same term on all policies insuring risks in the same classification. The payment of dividends to policyholders shall not be contingent upon the maintenance or renewal of the policy. All dividends shall be paid to the policyholder unless a written assignment of those dividends is executed. Neither the payment of dividends nor the rate of the dividends may be guaranteed by any company, or its agent, before the declaration of the dividend by the board of directors of the company. The holders of policies of insurance issued by a company in compliance with the orders of any public official, bureau or committee, in conformity with any statutory requirement or voluntary arrangement, for the issuance of insurance to risks not otherwise acceptable to the company, may be established as a separate class of risks.

(b) Any participating or dividend-paying company, stock or mutual or foreign or domestic, that writes workers' compensation insurance and employers' liability insurance in connection therewith may declare and pay a dividend to policyholders from its unassigned surplus, as reflected in the company's most recent statement filed with the Commissioner under G.S. 58-2-165, which shall include only its surplus in excess of any required minimum surplus. No such dividend shall be paid unless it is fair and equitable and for the best interest of the company and its policyholders. In declaring any dividend to its policyholders, any such company may make reasonable classifications of policies expiring during a fixed period. The payment of dividends to policyholders shall not be contingent upon the maintenance or renewal of the policy. All dividends shall be paid to the policyholder unless a written assignment of those dividends is executed. Neither the payment of dividends nor the rate of the dividends may be guaranteed by any company, or its agent, before the declaration of the dividend by the board of directors of the company. The holders of policies of insurance issued by a company in compliance with the orders of any public official, bureau, or committee, in conformity with any statutory requirement or voluntary arrangement, for the issuance of insurance to risks not otherwise acceptable to the company, may be established as a separate class of risks. (1899, c. 54, s. 35; Rev., s. 4741; C.S., s. 6351; 1935, c. 89; 1945, c. 386; 1947, c. 721; 1955, c. 645; 1983, c. 374, ss. 2, 3; 2001-223, s. 9.2.)

For case upholding contract between county board of education and mutual fire insurance corporations, see Fuller v. Lockhart, 209 N.C. 61, 182 S.E. 733 (1935).
Cited in Paramore v. Farmers' Mut. Fire Ins. Ass'n, 207 N.C. 300, 176 S.E. 585 (1934).

§ 58-8-30. Contingent liability of policyholders.

Every insurance company shall in its bylaws and policies prescribe the contingent liability, if any, of its members for the payment of losses, reserves and expenses not provided for by its assets, which contingent liability shall be in accordance with the provisions of G.S. 58-7-75. Each member is liable for the payment of his proportionate share of any assessments made by the company in accordance with the law, his contract and the bylaws of the company on account of losses incurred while he was a member, if he is notified of such assessment within one year after the expiration of his policy. When any reduction is made in the contingent liability of members, it shall apply proportionately to all policies in force. (1945, c. 386.)

For case upholding contract between county board of education and mutual fire insurance corporations, see Fuller v. Lockhart, 209 N.C. 61, 182 S.E. 733 (1935).

§ 58-8-35. Contingent liability printed on policy.

Every insurance company licensed to do business in this State shall print on each policy in clear and explicit language the full contingent liability of its members. (1945, c. 386; 1991, c. 644, s. 1; 1991 (Reg. Sess., 1992), c. 837, s. 2.)

§ 58-8-40. Nonassessable policies; foreign or alien companies.

No foreign or alien insurance company shall be licensed to issue in this State nonassessable policies unless it has a free surplus equal in amount to that required of a domestic insurance company, writing the same kind or kinds of insurance, and in addition thereto has fully complied with the requirements of the government under which it was organized; and no foreign or alien insurance company may be licensed to do business in this State to issue assessable policies if it issues nonassessable policies in any other state or country unless all policies shall state that any assessment shall be for the exclusive benefit of holders of policies which provide for such contingent liability and the holders of policies subject to assessment shall not be liable to assessment in an amount greater in proportion to the total deficiency than the ratio that the deficiency attributable to the assessable business bears to the total deficiency. (1945, c. 386.)

§ 58-8-45. Waiver of forfeiture in policies assigned or pledged; notice of assignment; payment of assessment or premium by assignee or mortgagee.

When any policy of insurance is issued by any mutual insurance company or association other than life, organized under the laws of this State and such policy is assigned or pledged as collateral security for the payment of a debt, such company or association, by its president and secretary or other managing officers, may insert in such policy so assigned or pledged, or attach thereto as a rider thereon, a provision or provisions to be approved by the Commissioner, whereby any or all conditions of the policy which work a suspension or forfeiture and especially the provisions of the statute which limits such corporation to insure only property of its members, may be waived in such case for the benefit of the assignee or mortgagee. In case any such company or association shall consent to such assignment of any policy or policies, or the proceeds thereof, it may nevertheless at any time thereafter, by its president and secretary or such other officer as may be authorized by the board of directors, cancel such policy by giving the assignee or mortgagee not less than 10 days' notice in writing: Provided, however, a longer period may be agreed upon by the company or association and such assignee or mortgagee. And the president and secretary of such company or association, with the approval of the Commissioner, may agree with the assignee or mortgagee upon an assessment or premium to be paid to the insurer in case the insured shall not pay the same, which shall not be less than such a rate or sum of money as may be produced by the average assessments or premiums made or charged by like company or association during a period of five years next preceding the year of such agreement and assignment. When an assignment is made as herein provided the policy or policies so assigned or pledged, subject to the conditions herein, shall remain in full force and effect for the benefit of the assignee or mortgagee, notwithstanding the title or ownership of the assured to the property insured, or to any interest therein, shall be in any manner changed, transferred or encumbered. (Ex. Sess., 1920, c. 79; C.S., s. 6351(a); 1945, c. 386; 1991, c. 720, s. 4.)

§ 58-8-50. Guaranty against assessments prohibited.

If any director, officer, or agent of a mutual insurance company, either officially or privately, gives a guarantee to a policyholder of the company against an assessment to which that policyholder would otherwise be liable, the director, officer, or agent shall be punished by a fine not exceeding one thousand dollars ($1,000) for each offense. (1899, c. 54, s. 100; Rev., s. 3496; C.S., s. 6352; 1945, c. 386; 2003-212, s. 16.)

Effect of Amendments. — Session Laws 2003-212, s. 16, effective October 1, 2003, substituted "gives a guarantee to a policyholder of the company" for "shall give a guarantee to a policyholder thereof"; substituted "that policy-holder" for "such policyholder"; substituted "the director, officer, or agent shall be punished" for "he shall be punished"; and substituted "one thousand dollars ($1,000)" for "one hundred dollars ($100)."

CASE NOTES

Cited in Paramore v. Farmers' Mut. Fire Ins. Ass'n, 207 N.C. 300, 176 S.E. 585 (1934).

§ 58-8-55. Manner of making assessments; rights and liabilities of policyholders.

When a mutual insurance company is not possessed of cash funds above its reserve sufficient for the payment of insured losses and expenses, it must make an assessment for the amount needed to pay such losses and expenses upon its members liable to assessment therefor in proportion to their several liabilities. The company shall cause to be recorded in a book kept for that purpose the order for the assessment, together with a statement which must set forth the condition of the company at the date of the order, the amount of its cash assets and deposits, notes, or other contingent funds liable to the assessment, the amount the assessment calls for, and the particular losses or liabilities it is made to provide for. This record must be made and signed by the directors who voted for the order before any part of the assessment is collected, and any person liable to the assessment may inspect and take a copy of the same. When, by reason of depreciation or loss of its funds or otherwise, the cash assets of such company, after providing for its other debts, are less than the required premium reserve upon its policies, it must make good the deficiency by assessment in the manner above provided. If the directors are of the opinion that the company is liable to become insolvent they may, instead of such assessment, make two assessments, the first determining what each policyholder must equitably pay or receive in case of withdrawal from the company and having his policy canceled; the second, what further sum each must pay in order to reinsure the unexpired term of his policy at the same rate as the whole was insured at first. Each policyholder must pay or receive according to the first assessment, and his policy shall be cancelled unless he pays the sum further determined by the second assessment, in which case his policy continues in force; but in neither case may a policyholder receive or have credited to him more than he would have received on having his policy canceled by a vote of the directors under the bylaws. (1899, c. 54, ss. 36, 37; Rev., s. 4742; C.S., s. 6353; 1945, c. 386.)

CASE NOTES

Waiver of Forfeiture. — Failure to pay assessments, in accordance with the terms of a contract of insurance, works a forfeiture of the policy, but the insurance company may by acts of unequivocal character waive such forfeiture. Perry v. Farmers Mut. Life Ins. Co., 132 N.C. 283, 43 S.E. 837 (1903).

An acceptance of an overdue assessment by a fire insurance company, after the property is burned, the company having notice thereof, is a waiver of the forfeiture of the policy. Perry v. Farmers Mut. Life Ins. Co., 132 N.C. 283, 43 S.E. 837 (1903).

Where mutual fire insurance company relies on failure to pay assessment in order to defeat recovery on policy, it must show that the assessment was legally made in conformity with the provisions of this section; hence, where it failed to so show and plaintiff insurer testified that she did not get notice of the assessment or of the cancellation of the policy, peremptory instructions against insurer on the affirmative defense were without error. Abernethy v. Mecklenburg Farmers' Mut. Fire Ins. Co., 213 N.C. 23, 195 S.E. 30 (1938).

Right of Insured to Withdraw. — Where the members of mutual insurance companies have enjoyed the protection which membership affords, they cannot, after a loss has been sustained, withdraw and refuse to pay their portion of the loss. Perry v. Farmers Mut. Fire Ass'n, 139 N.C. 374, 51 S.E. 1025 (1905).

No Claim on Amount Paid to Another Policyholder. — The right of each policyholder in the defendant company is to have an assessment made to pay his loss, and he has no claim upon an amount paid to another policyholder. Perry v. Farmers Mut. Fire Ass'n, 139 N.C. 374, 51 S.E. 1025 (1905).

§ 58-8-60. Independent charters for members of the Farmers Mutual Fire Insurance Association of North Carolina.

(a) Each branch of the Farmers Mutual Fire Insurance Association of North Carolina ("Association"), created by Chapter 343 of the 1893 Private Laws of North Carolina, as amended, shall adopt articles of incorporation by a majority vote of its board of directors.

(b) The articles of incorporation shall provide for the name of the corporation, to be approved by the Commissioner; the kinds of insurance it proposes to transact and on what business plan or principle; and the place of its location in the State. The certificate of incorporation must be subscribed and sworn to by a majority of the board of directors before an officer authorized to take acknowledgement of deeds, who shall certify the certificate to the Commissioner. The Commissioner shall review the certificate and articles of incorporation and file them with the Secretary of State in accordance with G.S. 58-7-35 upon payment of the required fees.

(c) The independently chartered former branches of the Association shall transact the same kinds of insurance and operate under the same business plan as they did as members of the Association. The assets of each independently chartered former branch shall remain the assets of the corporation to which the branch is converted pursuant to this section.

(d) The independently chartered former branches of the Association may change their methods of operation upon compliance with G.S. 58-8-5 and applicable provisions of this Chapter.

(e) The corporations created under this section are subject to applicable provisions of this Chapter.

(f) The corporations created under this section shall enjoy the same rights, privileges, and exemptions as enjoyed by the former Association.

(g) No officer nor member of the board of directors of an independently chartered former branch shall incur any liability for actions taken in good faith pursuant to this section. (1993, c. 495, s. 1.)

Editor's Note. — Session Laws 1993, c. 495, s. 2, provides: "Chapter 343 of the 1893 Private Laws of North Carolina, Chapter 15 of the 1895 Private Laws of North Carolina, Chapter 123 of the 1897 Private Laws of North Carolina, Chapter 18 of the 1903 Private Laws of North Carolina, Chapter 212 of the 1909 Private Laws of North Carolina, Chapter 445 of the 1911 Private Laws of North Carolina, Chapter 187 of the 1921 Private Laws of North Carolina, Chapter 285 of the 1945 Session Laws of North Carolina, and Chapter 674 of the 1949 Session Laws of North Carolina are repealed; and the Farmers Mutual Fire Insurance Association of North Carolina is hereby abolished."

Session Laws 1993, c. 495, s. 3 provides: "Nothing in this act affects any policy that was written or issued by any branch of the Farmers Mutual Fire Insurance Association of North Carolina."

ARTICLE 9.

Reinsurance Intermediaries.

§ 58-9-1: Repealed by Session Laws 1993, c. 452, s. 65.

Cross References. — As to acquisition of control of, or merger with, domestic insurer, see G.S. 58-19-15.

§ 58-9-2. Reinsurance intermediaries.

(a) As used in this Article:

    (1) "Actuary" means a person who meets the standards of a qualified actuary, as specified in the NAIC Annual Statement Instructions, as amended or clarified by rule or order of the Commissioner, for the type of insurer for which an intermediary is establishing loss reserves.

    (2) "Broker" means any person, other than an officer or employee of a ceding insurer, who solicits, negotiates, or places reinsurance cessions or retrocessions on behalf of a ceding insurer without the authority or power to bind reinsurance on behalf of the ceding insurer.

    (3) "Commissioner" includes the Commissioner's authorized deputies and employees.

    (4) "Controlling person" means any person who directly or indirectly has the power to direct or cause to be directed the management, control, or activities of an intermediary.

    (5) "Intermediary" means any person who acts as a broker, as defined in G.S. 58-33-10(3), in soliciting, negotiating, or procuring the making of any reinsurance contract or binder on behalf of a ceding insurer; or acts as a broker, as defined in G.S. 58-33-10(3), in accepting any reinsurance contract on behalf of an assuming insurer. "Intermediary" includes a broker or a manager, as those terms are defined in this section.

    (6) "Manager" means any person who has authority to bind or manages all or part of the assumed reinsurance business of a reinsurer (including the management of a separate division, department, or underwriting office) and acts as an agent for the reinsurer. The following persons are not managers, with respect to a reinsurer:

        a. An employee of a reinsurer;

        b. A United States manager of the United States branch of an alien reinsurer;

        c. An underwriting manager who, pursuant to contract, manages all the reinsurance operations of a reinsurer, is under common control with the reinsurer under Article 19 of this Chapter, and whose compensation is not based on the volume of premiums written;

        d. The manager of a group, association, pool, or organization of insurers that engages in joint underwriting or joint reinsurance and that is subject to examination by the insurance regulator of the state in which the manager's principal business office is located.

    (7) "Producer" means an insurance agent or insurance broker licensed under Article 33 of this Chapter or an intermediary licensed under this Article.

    (8) "Qualified United States financial institution" means a bank that:

        a. Is organized, or in the case of a United States office of a foreign banking organization is licensed, under the laws of the United States or any state;

        b. Is regulated, supervised, and examined by federal or state authorities having regulatory authority over banks and trust companies; and

        c. Has been determined by the Securities Valuation Office of the NAIC to meet its standards of financial condition and standing in order to issue letters of credit.

    (9) "Reinsurer" means any insurer that is licensed by the Commissioner and that is authorized to assume reinsurance.

(b) No person shall act as a broker in this State if the broker maintains an office either directly, as a member or employee of a noncorporate entity, or as an officer, director, or employee of a corporation:

    (1) In this State, unless the broker is a producer in this State; or

    (2) In another state, unless the broker is a producer in this State or another state having a law or rule substantially similar to this Article or unless the broker is licensed under this Article as a nonresident intermediary.

(c) No person shall act as a manager:

    (1) For a reinsurer domiciled in this State, unless the manager is a producer in this State;

    (2) In this State, if the manager maintains an office directly, as a member or employee of a noncorporate entity, or as an officer, director, or employee of a corporation in this State, unless the manager is a producer in this State;

    (3) In another state for a foreign insurer, unless the manager is a producer in this State or another state having a law or rule substantially similar to this Article, or the manager is licensed in this State as a nonresident intermediary.

(d) Every manager subject to subsection (c) of this section shall demonstrate to the Commissioner that he has evidence of financial responsibility in the form of fidelity bonds or liability insurance to cover the manager's contractual obligations. If any manager cannot demonstrate this evidence, the Commissioner shall require the manager to:

    (1) Maintain a separate fidelity bond in favor of each reinsurer represented in an amount that will cover those obligations and which bond is issued by an authorized insurer; or

    (2) Maintain an errors and omissions liability insurance policy in an amount that will cover those obligations and which policy is issued by a licensed insurer. (1993, c. 452, s. 19; 1995, c. 193, s. 20; 2001-203, s. 27; 2002-187, s. 2.7.)

Editor's Note. — Session Laws 2001-203, s. 31, contains a severability clause.

Effect of Amendments. — Session Laws 2001-203, s. 27, effective July 1, 2002, substituted "G.S. 58-33-10(3)" for "G.S. 58-33-10(c)" twice in subdivision (5).

Session Laws 2002-187, s. 2.7, effective October 31, 2002, rewrote subdivision (a)(9).

§ **58-9-5:** Repealed by Session Laws 1993, c. 452, s. 65.

Cross References. — As to acquisition of control of or merger with domestic insurer, see G.S. 58-19-15.

§ **58-9-6. Licensing.**

(a) The Commissioner shall issue an intermediary license or an exemption from the license, subject to G.S. 58-9-2(b)(2) or G.S. 58-9-2(c)(3), to any person who has complied with the requirements of this Article. A license issued to a non corporate entity authorizes all of the members of the entity and any designated employees to act as intermediaries under the license, and those persons shall be named in the application and any supplements. A license issued to a corporation authorizes all of the officers and any designated employees and directors of the corporation to act as intermediaries on behalf of the corporation, and those persons shall be named in the application and any supplements.

(b) If an applicant for an intermediary license is a nonresident, the applicant, before receiving a license, shall designate the Commissioner as his agent for service of legal process and shall furnish the Commissioner with the name and address of a resident of this State upon whom notices or orders of the Commissioner or process affecting the nonresident intermediary may be served. The licensee shall notify the Commissioner in writing of every change in his designated agent for service of process within five business days after the change, and the change shall not become effective until acknowledged by the Commissioner.

(c) The Commissioner shall refuse to issue an intermediary license if:

    (1) The applicant, anyone named on the application, or any member, principal, officer, or director of the applicant is not trustworthy;

    (2) Any controlling person of the applicant is not trustworthy to act as an intermediary; or

    (3) Any of the persons in subdivisions (1) and (2) of this subsection has given cause for revocation or suspension of the license or has failed to comply with any prerequisite for the issuance of the license.

Upon written request, the Commissioner shall furnish a summary of the basis for refusal to issue a license.

(d) Attorneys-at-law licensed by this State are exempt from this section when they are acting in their professional capacities. (1993, c. 452, s. 20; 2001-223, s. 10.1.)

§ 58-9-10: Repealed by Session Laws 1993, c. 452, s. 65.

Cross References. — As to acquisition of control of or merger with domestic insurer, see G.S. 58-19-15.

§ 58-9-11. Broker and insurer transactions.

(a) Transactions between a broker and the insurer it represents as a broker shall only be entered into pursuant to a written authorization, specifying the responsibilities of each party. The authorization shall include provisions to the effect that:

    (1) The insurer may terminate the broker's authority at any time.

    (2) The broker will render accounts to the insurer that accurately detail all material transactions, including information necessary to support all commissions, charges, and other fees received by or owing to the broker and will remit all funds due to the insurer within 30 days after receipt by the broker.

    (3) All funds collected for the insurer's account will be held by the broker in a fiduciary capacity in a qualified United States financial institution.

    (4) The broker will comply with this Article.

    (5) The broker will comply with the written standards established by the insurer for the cession or retrocession of all risks.

    (6) The broker will disclose to the insurer any relationship with any reinsurer to which business will be ceded or retroceded.

    (7) The broker will annually provide the insurer with an audited statement of the broker's financial condition, which statement will be prepared by an independent certified public accountant.

    (8) The insurer will have access and the right to copy and audit all accounts and records maintained by the broker related to its business, in a form usable by the insurer.

(9) For at least 10 years after the expiration of each contract of reinsurance transacted by the broker, the broker will keep a complete record for each transaction showing:
    a. The type of contract, limits, underwriting restrictions, classes or risks, and territory;
    b. Period of coverage, including effective and expiration dates, cancellation provisions, and notice required of cancellation;
    c. Reporting and settlement requirements of balances;
    d. Rate or rates used to compute the reinsurance premium;
    e. Names and addresses of assuming reinsurers;
    f. Rates of all reinsurance commissions, including the commissions on any retrocession handled by the broker;
    g. Related correspondence and memoranda;
    h. Proof of placement;
    i. Details regarding retrocessions handled by the broker, including the identity of retrocessionaires and percentage of each contract assumed or ceded;
    j. Financial records, including premium and loss accounts; and
    k. When the broker procures a reinsurance contract on behalf of a licensed ceding insurer:
        1. Directly from any assuming reinsurer, written evidence that the assuming reinsurer has agreed to assume the risk; or
        2. If placed through a representative of the assuming reinsurer, other than an employee, written evidence that the reinsurer has delegated binding authority to the representative.
 (b) An insurer shall not engage the services of any person to act as a broker on its behalf unless the person is licensed under G.S. 58-9-6 or exempted under this Article. An insurer shall not employ an individual who is employed by a broker with which it transacts business, unless the broker is under common control with the insurer under Article 19 of this Chapter. (1993, c. 452, s. 21; 2001-223, s. 10.2.)

§ **58-9-15:** Repealed by Session Laws 1993, c. 452, s. 65.

§ **58-9-16. Manager and reinsurer transactions.**

(a) Transactions between a manager and the reinsurer it represents as a manager shall only be entered into pursuant to a written contract, specifying the responsibilities of each party, which shall be approved by the reinsurer's board of directors. At least 30 days before the reinsurer assumes or cedes business through the manager, a certified copy of the approved contract shall be filed with the Commissioner for approval. The contract shall include provisions to the effect that:
    (1) The reinsurer may terminate the contract for cause upon written notice to the manager. The reinsurer may immediately suspend the authority of the manager to assume or cede business during the pendency of any dispute regarding the cause for termination.
    (2) The manager will render accounts to the reinsurer accurately detailing all material transactions, including information necessary to support all commissions, charges, and other fees received by or owing to the manager and will remit all funds due under the contract to the reinsurer at least once every month.
    (3) All funds collected for the reinsurer's account will be held by the manager in a fiduciary capacity in a qualified United States financial institution. The manager may retain no more than three months' estimated claims payments and allocated loss adjustment expenses.

The manager shall maintain a separate bank account for each reinsurer that it represents.

(4) For at least 10 years after the expiration of each contract of reinsurance transacted by the manager, the manager will keep a complete record for each transaction showing:

    a. The type of contract, limits, underwriting restrictions, classes or risks, and territory;

    b. Period of coverage, including effective and expiration dates, cancellation provisions and notice required of cancellation, and disposition of outstanding reserves on covered risk;

    c. Reporting and settlement requirements of balances;

    d. Rate used to compute the reinsurance premium;

    e. Names and addresses of reinsurers;

    f. Rates of all reinsurance commissions, including the commissions on any retrocessions handled by the manager;

    g. Related correspondence and memoranda;

    h. Proof of placement;

    i. Details regarding retrocessions handled by the manager, as permitted by G.S. 58-9-21, including the identity of retrocessionaires and percentage of each contract assumed or ceded;

    j. Financial records, including, but not limited to, premium and loss accounts; and

    k. When the manager places a reinsurance contract on behalf of a ceding insurer:

        1. Directly from any assuming reinsurer, written evidence that the assuming reinsurer has agreed to assume the risk; or

        2. If placed through a representative of the assuming reinsurer, other than an employee, written evidence that the reinsurer has delegated binding authority to the representative.

(5) The reinsurer will have access and the right to copy all accounts and records maintained by the manager related to its business in a form usable by the reinsurer.

(6) The contract cannot be assigned in whole or in part by the manager.

(7) The manager will comply with the written underwriting and rating standards established by the insurer for the acceptance, rejection, or cession of all risks.

(8) The rates, terms, and purposes of commissions, charges, and other fees that the manager may levy against the reinsurer shall be set forth.

(9) If the contract permits the manager to settle claims on behalf of the reinsurer:

    a. All claims will be reported to the reinsurer in a timely manner;

    b. A copy of the claim file will be sent to the reinsurer at its request or as soon as it becomes known that the claim:

        1. Has the potential to exceed an amount set by the reinsurer and approved by the Commissioner;

        2. Involves a coverage dispute;

        3. May exceed the manager's claims settlement authority;

        4. Is open for more than six months; or

        5. Is closed by payment of an amount set by the reinsurer and approved by the Commissioner.

    c. All claim files will be the joint property of the reinsurer and manager. However, upon an order of liquidation of the reinsurer, the files shall become the sole property of the reinsurer or its estate; the manager shall have reasonable access to and the right to copy the files on a timely basis; and

    d. Any settlement authority granted to the manager may be terminated for cause upon the reinsurer's written notice to the manager or upon the termination of the contract. The reinsurer may suspend the settlement authority during the pendency of the dispute regarding the cause of termination.

(10) If the contract provides for a sharing of interim profits by the manager, the interim profits will not be paid until one year after the end of each underwriting period for property business and five years after the end of each underwriting period for casualty business and not until the adequacy of reserves on remaining claims has been verified pursuant to G.S. 58-9-21.

(11) The manager will annually provide the reinsurer with an audited statement of its financial condition prepared by an independent certified public accountant.

(12) The reinsurer shall at least semiannually conduct an on-site review of the underwriting and claims processing operations of the manager.

(13) The manager will disclose to the reinsurer any relationship it has with any insurer before ceding or assuming any business with the insurer pursuant to this contract.

(14) Within the scope of its actual or apparent authority, the acts of the manager shall be deemed to be the acts of the reinsurer on whose behalf it is acting.

(b) A manager shall not:

(1) Cede retrocessions on behalf of the reinsurer, except that the manager may cede facultative retrocessions pursuant to obligatory facultative agreements if the contract with the reinsurer contains reinsurance underwriting guidelines for the retrocessions. The guidelines shall include a list of reinsurers with which the automatic agreements are in effect, and for each reinsurer, the coverages and amounts or percentages that may be reinsured, and commission schedules.

(2) Commit the reinsurer to participate in reinsurance syndicates.

(3) Appoint any producer without assuring that the producer is duly licensed to transact the type of reinsurance for which he is appointed.

(4) Without prior approval of the reinsurer, pay or commit the reinsurer to pay a claim settlement with a retrocessionaire, without prior approval of the reinsurer. If prior approval is given, a report must be promptly forwarded to the reinsurer.

(5) Collect any payment from a retrocessionaire or commit the reinsurer to any claim settlement with a retrocessionaire, without prior approval of the reinsurer. If prior approval is given, a report must be promptly forwarded to the reinsurer.

(6) Jointly employ an individual who is employed by the reinsurer unless the manager is under common control with the reinsurer under Article 19 of this Chapter.

(7) Appoint a submanager. (1993, c. 452, s. 22.)

§ **58-9-20:** Repealed by Session Laws 1993, c. 452, s. 65.

§ **58-9-21. Miscellaneous provisions.**

(a) A reinsurer shall not engage the services of any person to act as a manager on its behalf unless the person is licensed under G.S. 58-9-6 or exempted under this Article.

(b) If a manager establishes loss reserves, the reinsurer shall annually obtain the opinion of an actuary attesting to the adequacy of loss reserves established for losses incurred and outstanding on business produced by the manager. This opinion shall be in addition to any other required loss reserve certification.

(c) Binding authority for all retrocessional contracts or participation in reinsurance syndicates shall be given to an officer of the reinsurer who is not affiliated with the manager.

(d) Within 30 days after termination of a contract with a manager, the reinsurer shall provide written notification of the termination to the Commissioner.

(e) A reinsurer shall not appoint to its board of directors any officer, director, employee, controlling person, or subproducer of its manager. This Article does not apply to relationships governed by Article 19 of this Chapter or G.S. 58-3-165.

(f) An intermediary is subject to examination by the Commissioner. The Commissioner shall have access to all books, bank accounts, and records of an intermediary in a form usable to the Commissioner. A manager may be examined as if it were the reinsurer. (1993, c. 452, s. 23; 2001-223, s. 10.3.)

§ **58-9-25:** Repealed by Session Laws 1993, c. 452, s. 65.

§ **58-9-26. Sanctions.**

(a) If the Commissioner determines that any person has not materially complied with this Article or with any rule adopted or order issued under this Article, after notice and opportunity to be heard, the Commissioner may order:

(1) For each separate violation, a civil penalty under the procedures in G.S. 58-2-70(d); or

(2) Revocation or suspension of the person's license.

If the Commissioner finds that because of a material noncompliance that an insurer or reinsurer has suffered any loss or damage, the Commissioner may maintain a civil action brought by or on behalf of the insurer or reinsurer and its policyholders and creditors for recovery of compensatory damages for the benefit of the insurer or reinsurer and its policyholders and creditors or for other appropriate relief.

(b) If an order of rehabilitation or liquidation of the insurer has been entered under Article 30 of this Chapter, and the receiver appointed under that order determines that any person has not materially complied with this Article, or any rule adopted or order issued under this Article, and the insurer suffered any loss or damage from the material noncompliance, the receiver may maintain a civil action for recovery of damages or other appropriate sanctions for the benefit of the insurer. (1993, c. 452, s. 24.)

§ **58-9-30:** Repealed by Session Laws 1993, c. 452, s. 65.

ARTICLE 10.

Miscellaneous Insurer Financial Provisions.

Part 1. Conversion of Stock and Mutual Insurers.

§ **58-10-1. Stock to mutual insurer conversion.**

Any domestic stock life insurance corporation may become a mutual life insurance corporation, and to that end may carry out a plan for the acquisition of shares of its capital stock: Provided, however, that such plan (i) shall have been adopted by a vote of a majority of the directors of such corporation; (ii) shall have been approved by a vote of the holders of two thirds of the stock outstanding at the time of issuing the call for a meeting for that purpose; (iii) shall have been submitted to the Commissioner and shall have been approved by him in writing, and (iv) shall have been approved by a majority vote of the policyholders (including, for the purpose of this Part, the employer or the president, secretary or other executive officer of any corporation or association to which a master group policy has been issued, but excluding the holders of certificates or policies issued under or in connection with a master group policy) voting at said meeting, called for that purpose, at which meeting only such policyholders whose insurance shall then be in force and shall have been in force for at least one year prior to such a meeting shall be entitled to vote; notice of such a meeting shall be given by mailing such notice, postage prepaid, from the home office of such corporation at least 30 days prior to such meeting to such policyholders at their last known post-office addresses: Provided, that personal delivery of such written notice to any policyholder may be in lieu of mailing the same; and such meeting shall be otherwise provided for and conducted in such a manner as shall be provided in such plan: Provided, however, that policyholders may vote in person, by proxy, or by mail; that all such votes shall be cast by ballot, and a representative of the Commissioner shall supervise and direct the methods and procedure of said meeting and appoint an adequate number of inspectors to conduct the voting at said meeting who shall have power to determine all questions concerning the verification of the ballots, the ascertainment of the validity thereof, the qualifications of the voters, and the canvass of the vote, and who shall certify to the said representative and to the corporation the results thereof, and with respect thereto shall act under such rules and regulations as shall be prescribed by the Commissioner; that all necessary expenses incurred by the Commissioner or his representative shall be paid by the corporation as certified to by said Commissioner. Every payment for the acquisition of any shares of the capital stock of such corporation, the purchase price of which is not fixed by such plan, shall be subject to the approval of the Commissioner: Provided, that neither such plan, nor any payment thereunder, nor any payment not fixed by such plan, shall be approved by the Commissioner, if the making of such payment shall reduce the assets of the corporation to an amount less than the entire liabilities of the corporation, including therein the net values of its outstanding contracts according to the standard adopted by the Commissioner, and also all other funds, contingent reserves and surplus which the corporation is required by order or direction of the Commissioner to maintain, save so much of the surplus as shall have been appropriated or paid under such plan. (1937, c. 231, s. 1; 1991, c. 720, s. 4; 1995, c. 318, s. 1; 2001-223, s. 9.3.)

Editor's Note. — Session Laws 2001-223, s. 9.4, effective June 15, 2001, rewrote the heading for Part 1.

Session Laws 2001-223, s. 27 is a severability clause.

Session Laws 2001-387, s. 154(b), provides that nothing in this act shall supersede the provisions of Article 10 or 65 of Chapter 58 of the General Statutes, and this act does not create an alternate means for an entity governed by Article 65 of Chapter 58 of the General Statutes to convert to a different business form.

Legal Periodicals. — For discussion of the 1937 act from which this Article was codified, see 15 N.C.L. Rev. 359 (1937).

§ 58-10-5. Stock acquired to be turned over to voting trust until all stock acquired; dividends repaid to corporation for beneficiaries.

If a domestic stock life insurance corporation shall determine to become a mutual life insurance corporation it may, in carrying out any plan to that end under the provisions of G.S. 58-10-1, acquire any shares of its own stock by gift, bequest or purchase. And until all such shares are acquired, any shares so acquired shall be acquired in trust for the policyholders of the corporation as hereinafter provided, and shall be assigned and transferred on the books of the corporation to not less than three nor more than five trustees, and be held by them in trust and be voted by such trustees at all corporate meetings at which stockholders have the right to vote until all of the capital stock of such corporation is acquired, when the entire capital stock shall be retired and canceled; and thereupon, unless sooner incorporated as such, the corporation shall be and become a mutual life insurance corporation without capital stock. Said trustees shall be appointed and vacancies shall be filled as provided in the plan adopted under G.S. 58-10-1. Said trustees shall file with the corporation and with the Commissioner a verified acceptance of their appointments and declaration that they will faithfully discharge their duties as such trustees. After the payment of such dividends to stockholders or former stockholders as may have been provided in the plan adopted under G.S. 58-10-1, all dividends and other sums received by said trustees on said shares of stock so acquired, after paying the necessary expenses of executing said trust, shall be immediately repaid to said corporation for the benefit of all who are or may become policyholders of said corporation and entitled to participate in the profits thereof, and shall be added to and become a part of the surplus earned by said corporation, and be apportionable accordingly as a part of said surplus among said policyholders. (1937, c. 231, s. 2; 1991, c. 720, s. 4.)

§ 58-10-10. Mutual to stock insurer conversion.

(a) A domestic mutual insurer may convert to a domestic stock insurer under a plan that is approved in advance by the Commissioner.

(b) The Commissioner shall not approve the plan unless:

(1) It is fair and equitable to the insurer's policyholders.

(2) It is adopted by the insurer's board of directors in accordance with the insurer's bylaws and approved by a vote of not less than two-thirds of the insurer's members voting on it in person, by proxy, or by mail at a meeting called for the purpose of voting on the plan, pursuant to reasonable notice and procedure as approved by the Commissioner. If the company is a life insurer, the right to vote may be limited, as its bylaws provide, to members whose policies are other than term or group policies and have been in effect for more than one year.

(3) Each policyholder's equity in the insurer is determinable under a fair and reasonable formula approved by the Commissioner. The equity shall be based upon the insurer's entire statutory surplus after deducting certificates of contribution, guaranty capital certificates, and similar evidences of indebtedness included in an insurer's statutory surplus.

(4) The policyholders entitled to vote on the plan and participate in the purchase of stock and distribution of assets include all policyholders on the date the plan was adopted by the insurer's board of directors.

(5) The plan provides that each policyholder specified in subdivision (4) of this subsection receives a preemptive right to acquire a proportionate part of all of the proposed capital stock of the insurer or of all of the stock of a corporation affiliated with the insurer within a designated reasonable period as the part is determinable under the plan of conversion; and to apply toward the purchase of the stock the amount of the policyholder's equity in the insurer under subdivision (3) of this subsection. The plan must provide for an equitable distribution of fractional interests.

(6) The plan provides for payment to each policyholder of the policyholder's entire equity in the insurer; with that payment to be applied toward the purchase of stock to which the policyholder is entitled preemptively or to be made in cash, or both. The cash payment may not exceed fifty percent (50%) of each policyholder's equity. The stock purchased, together with the cash payment, if any, shall constitute full payment and discharge of the policyholder's equity as an owner of the mutual insurer.

(7) Shares are to be offered to policyholders at a price not greater than that of shares to be subsequently offered to others.

(8) The Commissioner finds that the insurer's management has not, through reduction of volume of new business written, through policy cancellations, or through any other means, sought to (i) reduce, limit, or affect the number or identity of the insurer's members entitled to participate in the plan or (ii) secure for the individuals constituting management any unfair advantage through the plan.

(9) The plan, when completed, provides that the insurer's capital and surplus are not less than the minimum required of a domestic stock insurer transacting the same kinds of insurance, are reasonable in relation to the insurer's outstanding liabilities, and are adequate to meet its financial needs.

(c) With respect to an insurer with a guaranty capital, the conversion plan shall be approved by a vote of not less than two-thirds of the insurer's guaranty capital shareholders and policyholders as provided for in subdivision (b)(2) of this section. The plan may provide for the issuance of stock in exchange for outstanding guaranty capital shares at their redemption value subject to the conditions in subsection (b) of this section.

(d) The Commissioner may schedule a public hearing on the proposed conversion plan.

(e) The Commissioner may retain, at the mutual insurer's expense, any attorneys, actuaries, economists, accountants, or other experts not otherwise a part of the Commissioner's staff as may be reasonably necessary to assist the Commissioner in reviewing the proposed conversion plan.

(f) The corporate existence of the mutual company continues in the stock company created under this section. All assets, rights, franchises, and interests of the former mutual insurer, in and to real or personal property, are deemed to be transferred to and vested in the stock insurer, without any other deed or transfer; and the stock insurer simultaneously assumes all of the obligations and liabilities of the former mutual insurer.

(g) No director, officer, or employee of the insurer shall receive:

(1) Any fee, commission, compensation, or other valuable consideration for aiding, promoting, or assisting in the conversion of the mutual insurer to a domestic stock insurer, other than compensation paid to any director, officer, or employee of the insurer in the ordinary course of business; or

(2) Any distribution of the assets, surplus, or capital of the insurer as part of a conversion.

(h) The Commissioner may adopt rules to carry out the provisions of this section. (1999-369, s. 6; 2001-223, s. 9.5.)

Legal Periodicals. — For "Legislative Survey: Business & Banking," see 22 Campbell L. Rev. 253 (2000).

§ 58-10-12. Conversion plan requirements.

(a) As used in this section:

(1) "Closed block" means an allocation of assets for a defined group of in-force policies which, together with the premiums of those policies and related investment earnings, are expected to be sufficient to maintain the payments of guaranteed benefits, certain expenses, and continuation of the current dividend scale on the closed block, if experience does not change.

(2) "Converting mutual" means a domestic mutual insurance company that has adopted a plan of conversion and an amendment to its articles of incorporation under this section that will, upon consummation, result in the domestic mutual insurance company converting into a domestic stock insurance company.

(3) "Eligible member" means a person who:

    a. Is a member of the converting mutual on the date the converting mutual's board of directors adopts a resolution proposing a plan of conversion and an amendment to the articles of incorporation; and

    b. Continues to be a member of the converting mutual on the effective date of the conversion.

(4) "Former mutual" means the domestic stock insurance company resulting from the conversion of a converting mutual to a stock insurance company under a plan of conversion and an amendment to its articles of incorporation under this section.

(5) "Member" means a person that, according to the records, articles of incorporation, and bylaws of a converting mutual, is a member of the converting mutual.

(6) "Membership interests" means:

    a. The voting rights of members of a domestic mutual insurance company as provided by law and by the company's articles of incorporation and bylaws; and

    b. The rights of members of a domestic mutual insurance company to receive cash, stock, or other consideration in the event of a conversion to a stock insurance company under this section or a dissolution as provided by the company's articles of incorporation and bylaws.

(7) "Parent company" means a corporation that, upon the effective date of a conversion, owns all of the stock of the former mutual.

(8) "Plan of conversion" means the plan of conversion described in subsection (b) of this section.

(b) The plan of conversion under G.S. 58-10-10 shall:

(1) Describe the manner in which the proposed conversion will occur and the insurance and any other companies that will result from or be directly affected by the conversion, including the former mutual and any parent company.

(2) Provide that the membership interests in the converting mutual will be extinguished as of the effective date of the conversion.

(3) Require the distribution to the eligible members, upon the extinguishing of their membership interests, of aggregate consideration equal to the fair value of the converting mutual.

(4) Describe the manner in which the fair value of the converting mutual has been or will be determined.

(5) Describe the form or forms and amount, if known, of consideration to be distributed to the eligible members.

(6) Specify relevant classes, categories, or groups of eligible members and describe and explain any differences in the form or forms and amount of consideration to be distributed to or among the eligible members.

(7) Require and describe the method or formula for the fair and equitable allocation of the consideration among the eligible members.

(8) Provide for the determination and preservation of the reasonable dividend expectations of eligible members and other policyholders with policies that provide for the distribution of policy dividends, through establishment of a closed block or other method acceptable to the Commissioner.

(9) Provide that each member and other policyholder of the converting mutual will receive notification of the address and telephone number of the converting mutual and the former mutual, if different, along with the notice of hearing as approved by the Commissioner.

(10) Include other provisions as the converting mutual determines to be necessary.

(c) After the adoption by the board of directors of the resolution proposing the plan of conversion under G.S. 58-10-10 and the amendment to its articles of incorporation, the converting mutual shall file with the Commissioner an application for approval of the plan and amendment. The application must contain the following information, together with any additional information as the Commissioner may require:

(1) The plan of conversion and a certificate of the secretary of the converting mutual certifying the adoption of the plan by the board of directors.

(2) A statement of the reasons for the proposed conversion and why the conversion is in the best interests of the converting mutual, the eligible members, and the other policyholders. The statement must include an analysis of the risks and benefits to the converting mutual and its members of the proposed conversion and a comparison of the risks and benefits of the conversion with the risks and benefits of reasonable alternatives to a conversion.

(3) A five-year business plan and at least two years of financial forecasts of the former mutual and any parent company.

(4) Any plans that the former mutual or any parent company may have to:
   a. Raise additional capital through the issuance of stock or otherwise;
   b. Sell or issue stock to any person, including any compensation or benefit plan for directors, officers, or employees under which stock may be issued;
   c. Liquidate or dissolve any company or sell any material assets;
   d. Merge or consolidate or pursue any other form of reorganization with any person; or
   e. Make any other material change in investment policy, business, corporate structure, or management.

(5) Any plans for a delayed distribution of consideration to eligible members or restrictions on sale or transfer of stock or other securities.

(6) A copy of the form of trust agreement, if a distribution of consideration is to be delayed by more than six months after the effective date of the conversion.

(7) A plan of operation for a closed block, if a closed block is used for the preservation of the reasonable dividend expectations of eligible members and other policyholders with policies that provide for the distribution of policy dividends.

(8) Copies of the amendment to the articles of incorporation proposed by the board of directors and proposed bylaws of the former mutual and copies of the existing and any proposed articles of incorporation and bylaws of any parent company.

(9) A list of all individuals who are or have been selected to become directors or officers of the former mutual and any parent company, or

the individuals who perform or will perform duties customarily performed by a director or officer, and the following information concerning each individual on the list unless the information is already on file with the Commissioner:

a. The individual's principal occupation.

b. All offices and positions the individual has held in the preceding five years.

c. Any crime of which the individual has been convicted (other than traffic violations) in the preceding 10 years.

d. Information concerning any personal bankruptcy of the individual or the individual's spouse during the previous seven years.

e. Information concerning the bankruptcy of any corporation or other entity of which the individual was an officer or director during the previous seven years.

f. Information concerning allegations of state or federal securities law violations made against the individual that within the previous 10 years resulted in (i) a determination that the individual violated state or federal securities laws; (ii) a plea of nolo contendere; or (iii) a consent decree.

g. Information concerning the suspension, revocation, or other disciplinary action during the previous 10 years of any state or federal license issued to the individual.

h. Information as to whether the individual was refused a bond during the previous 10 years.

(10) A fairness opinion addressed to the board of directors of the converting mutual from a qualified, independent financial adviser asserting:

a. That the provision of stock, cash, policy benefits, or other forms of consideration upon the extinguishing of the converting mutual's membership interests under the plan of conversion and the amendment to the articles of incorporation is fair to the eligible members, as a group, from a financial point of view; and

b. Whether the total consideration under sub-subdivision a. of this subdivision is equal to or greater than the surplus of the converting mutual.

The Commissioner may waive the fairness opinion in situations involving a straightforward issuance of stock to members of the former mutual.

(11) An actuarial opinion as to the following:

a. The reasonableness and appropriateness of the methodology or formulas used to allocate consideration among eligible members, consistent with this Article.

b. The reasonableness of the plan of operation and sufficiency of the assets allocated to the closed block, if a closed block is used for the preservation of the reasonable dividend expectations of eligible members and other policyholders with policies that provide for the distribution of policy dividends.

(12) If any of the consideration to be distributed to eligible members consists of stock or other securities, subject to the limitations of G.S. 58-10-10(b)(6), a description of the plans made by the former mutual or its parent company to assure that an active public trading market for the stock or other securities will develop within a reasonable amount of time after the effective date of the plan of conversion and that eligible members who receive stock or other securities will be able to sell their stock or other securities, subject to any delayed distribution or transfer restrictions, at reasonable cost and effort.

(13) Any additional information, documents, or materials that the converting mutual determines to be necessary.

(d) Distribution of all or part of the consideration to some or all of the eligible members may be delayed, or restrictions on sale or transfer of any stock or other securities to be distributed to eligible members may be required, for a reasonable period of time following the effective date of the conversion. However, the period of time shall not exceed six months unless otherwise approved by the Commissioner.

(e) Except as specifically provided in a plan of conversion, for five years following the effective date of the conversion, no person or persons acting in concert (other than the former mutual, any parent company, or any employee benefit plans or trusts sponsored by the former mutual or a parent company) shall directly or indirectly acquire, or agree or offer to acquire, in any manner the beneficial ownership of five percent (5%) or more of the outstanding shares of any class of a voting security of the former mutual or any parent company without the prior approval of the Commissioner of a statement filed by that person with the Commissioner. The statement shall contain the information required by G.S. 58-19-15(b) and any other information required by the Commissioner. The Commissioner shall not approve an acquisition under this subsection unless the Commissioner finds that:

(1) The requirements of G.S. 58-19-15(e) will be satisfied.

(2) The acquisition will not frustrate the plan of conversion or the amendment to the articles of incorporation as approved by the members and the Commissioner.

(3) The boards of directors of the former mutual and any parent company have approved the acquisition.

(4) The acquisition would be in the best interest of the present and future policyholders of the former mutual without regard to any interest of policyholders as shareholders of the former mutual or any parent company. (2001-223, s. 9.6.)

Editor's Note. — Session Laws 2001-223, s. 28, makes this section effective June 15, 2001.   Session Laws 2001-223, s. 27 is a severability clause.

Part 2. Assumption Reinsurance.

§ 58-10-20. Scope.

(a) This Part applies to any licensed insurer that either assumes or transfers the obligations or risks on policies under an assumption reinsurance agreement that is entered into on or after January 1, 1996.

(b) This Part does not apply to:

(1) Any reinsurance agreement or transaction in which the ceding insurer continues to remain directly liable for its insurance obligations or risks under the policies subject to the reinsurance agreement.

(2) The substitution of one insurer for another upon the expiration of insurance coverage under statutory or contractual requirements and the issuance of a new policy by another insurer.

(3) The transfer of policies under mergers or consolidations of two or more insurers to the extent that those transactions are regulated by statute.

(4) Any insurer subject to a judicial order of liquidation or rehabilitation.

(5) Any reinsurance agreement or transaction to which a state insurance guaranty association is a party, provided that policyholders do not lose any rights or claims afforded under their original policies under Articles 48 or 62 of this Chapter.

(6) The transfer of liabilities from one insurer to another under a single group policy upon the request of the group policyholder. (1995, c. 318, s. 1.)

§ 58-10-25. Definitions.

(a) As used in this Part:
  (1) Assuming insurer. — The insurer that acquires an insurance obligation or risk from the transferring insurer under an assumption reinsurance agreement.
  (2) Assumption reinsurance agreement. — Any contract, arrangement, or plan that:
      a. Transfers insurance obligations or risks of existing or in-force policies from a transferring insurer to an assuming insurer.
      b. Is intended to effect a novation of transferred policies with the result that the assuming insurer becomes directly liable to the policyholders of the transferring insurer and the transferring insurer's insurance obligations or risks under the policies are extinguished.
  (3) Home service business. — Insurance business on which premiums are collected on a weekly or monthly basis by an agent of the insurer.
  (4) Policy. — A contract of insurance as defined in G.S. 58-1-10.
  (5) Policyholder. — Any person that has the right to terminate or otherwise alter the terms of a policy. It includes any group policy certificate holder whose certificate is in force on the proposed effective date of the assumption, if the certificate holder has the right to keep the certificate in force without any change in benefits after termination of the group policy. The right to keep the certificate in force referred to in this subdivision does not include the right to elect individual coverage under the Consolidated Omnibus Budget Reconciliation Act ("COBRA"), section 601, et seq., of the Employee Retirement Income Security Act of 1974, as amended, 29 U.S.C. § 1161, et seq.
  (6) Transferring insurer. — The insurer that transfers an insurance obligation or risk to an assuming insurer under an assumption reinsurance agreement.
(b) For the purposes of this Part, a "novation" does not require the formation of a new policy or the amendment of an existing policy between the assuming insurer and the policyholder. (1995, c. 318, s. 1; 1995 (Reg. Sess., 1996), c. 752, s. 2.)

Editor's Note. — The subsection (a) designation was added at the direction of the Revisor of Statutes.

§ 58-10-30. Notice requirements.

(a) The transferring insurer shall provide or cause to be provided to each policyholder a notice of transfer by first-class mail, addressed to the policyholder's last known address or to the address to which premium notices or other policy documents are sent; or with respect to home service business, by personal delivery with acknowledged receipt. A notice of transfer shall also be sent to the transferring insurer's agents or brokers of record on the affected policies.

(b) The notice of transfer shall be in a form identical or substantially similar to Appendix A of the NAIC Assumption Reinsurance Model Act, as amended by the NAIC and shall state or provide:

(1) The date on which the transfer and novation of the policyholder's policy is proposed to take place.

(2) The names, addresses, and telephone numbers of the assuming and transferring insurers.

(3) That the policyholder has the right to either consent to or reject the transfer and novation.

(4) The procedures and time limit for consenting to or rejecting the transfer and novation.

(5) A summary of any effect that consenting to or rejecting the transfer and novation will have on the policyholder's rights.

(6) A statement that the assuming insurer is licensed to write the type of business being assumed in the state where the policyholder resides, or is otherwise authorized, as provided in this Part, to assume that business.

(7) The name and address of the person at the transferring insurer to whom the policyholder should send the policyholder's written statement of acceptance or rejection of the transfer and novation.

(8) The address and telephone number of the insurance department where the policyholder resides so that the policyholder may write or call that insurance department for further information about the financial condition of the assuming insurer.

(9) The following financial data for both insurers:

   a. Ratings for the last five years, if available, or for any shorter period that is available, from two nationally recognized insurance rating services acceptable to the Commissioner, including the rating services' explanations of the meanings of their ratings. If ratings are unavailable for any year of the five-year period, this shall also be disclosed.

   b. A balance sheet as of December 31 for the previous three years, if available, or for any shorter period that is available, and as of the date of the most recent quarterly statement.

   c. A copy of the Management's Discussion and Analysis that was filed as a supplement to the previous year's annual statement.

   d. An explanation of the reason for the transfer.

(c) The notice of transfer shall include a preaddressed, postage-paid response card that the policyholder may return as the policyholder's written statement of acceptance or rejection of the transfer and novation.

(d) The notice of transfer shall be filed as part of the prior approval requirement set forth in subsection (e) of this section.

(e) Prior approval by the Commissioner is required for any transaction in which a domestic insurer assumes or transfers obligations or risks on policies under an assumption reinsurance agreement. No insurer licensed in this State shall transfer obligations or risks on policies issued to or owned by residents of this State to any insurer that is not licensed in this State. A domestic insurer shall not assume obligations or risks on policies issued to or owned by policyholders residing in any other state unless it is licensed in the other state, or the insurance regulator of that state has approved the assumption.

(f) Any licensed foreign insurer that enters into an assumption reinsurance agreement that transfers the obligations or risks on policies issued to or owned by residents of this State shall file with the Commissioner the assumption certificate, a copy of the notice of transfer, and an affidavit that the transaction is subject to substantially similar requirements in the states of domicile of both the transferring and assuming insurers. If those requirements do not exist in the state of domicile of either the transferring or assuming insurer, the requirements of subsection (g) of this section apply.

(g) Any licensed foreign insurer that enters into an assumption reinsurance agreement that transfers the obligations or risks on policies issued to or owned by residents of this State shall obtain prior approval of the Commissioner and be subject to all other requirements of this Part with respect to residents of this State, unless the transferring and assuming insurers are subject to assumption reinsurance requirements adopted by statute or administrative rule in the states of their domicile that are substantially similar to those contained in this Part and in any administrative rules adopted under this Part.

(h) The following factors, along with any other factors the Commissioner deems to be appropriate under the circumstances, shall be considered by the Commissioner in reviewing a request for approval:

(1) The financial condition of the transferring and assuming insurers and the effect the transaction will have on the financial condition of each company.

(2) The competence, experience, and integrity of those persons who control the operation of the assuming insurer.

(3) The plans or proposals the assuming insurer has with respect to the administration of the policies subject to the proposed transfer.

(4) Whether the transfer is fair and reasonable to the policyholders of both insurers.

(5) Whether the notice of transfer to be provided by the insurer is fair, adequate, and not misleading. (1995, c. 318, s. 1.)

§ 58-10-35. Policyholder rights.

(a) Policyholders may reject the transfer and novation of their policies by indicating on the response card that the assumption is rejected and returning the card to the transferring insurer.

(b) Payment of any premium to the assuming company during the 24-month period after the notice of transfer has been received indicates the policyholder's acceptance of the transfer to the assuming insurer; and a novation shall occur only if the premium notice clearly states that payment of the premium to the assuming insurer constitutes acceptance of the transfer. The premium notice shall also provide a method for the policyholder to pay the premium while reserving the right to reject the transfer. With respect to any home service business or any other business not using premium notices, the disclosures and procedural requirements of this subsection are to be set forth in the notice of transfer required by G.S. 58-10-30 and in the assumption certificate.

(c) After no fewer than 24 months after the mailing of the initial notice of transfer required under G.S. 58-10-30, if positive consent to, or rejection of, the transfer and assumption has not been received or consent has occurred under subsection (b) of this section, the transferring insurer shall send to the policyholder a second and final notice of transfer as specified in G.S. 58-10-30. If the policyholder does not accept or reject the transfer during the one-month period immediately after the date on which the transferring insurer mailed the second and final notice of transfer, the policyholder's consent and novation of the contract will occur. With respect to the home service business, or any other business not using premium notices, the 24-month and one-month periods shall be measured from the date of delivery of the notice of transfer under G.S. 58-10-30.

(d) The transferring insurer shall be deemed to have received the response card on the date it is postmarked. A policyholder may also send the response card by facsimile, other electronic transmission, registered mail, express delivery, or courier service; in which case the response card shall be deemed to have been received by the transferring insurer on the date of actual receipt by the transferring insurer. (1995, c. 318, s. 1.)

§ 58-10-40. Effect of consent.

If a policyholder consents to the transfer under G.S. 58-10-35 or if the transfer is effected under G.S. 58-10-45, there shall be a novation of the policy, subject to the assumption reinsurance agreement, with the result that the transferring insurer is thereby relieved of all insurance obligations or risks transferred under the assumption reinsurance agreement and the assuming insurer is directly and solely liable to the policyholder for those insurance obligations or risks. (1995, c. 318, s. 1.)

§ 58-10-45. Commissioner's discretion.

If a domestic insurer or a foreign insurer from a state having a substantially similar law is deemed by its domiciliary insurance regulator to be in hazardous financial condition or a proceeding has been instituted against it for the purpose of reorganizing or conserving the insurer, and the transfer of the policies is in the best interest of the policyholders, as determined by the domiciliary insurance regulator, a transfer and novation may be effected notwithstanding the provisions of this Part. This may include a form of implied consent and adequate notification to the policyholders of the circumstances requiring the transfer as approved by the Commissioner. (1995, c. 318, s. 1.)

Part 3. Disclosure of Material Transactions.

§ 58-10-55. Report.

(a) This Part applies only to domestic insurers. Effective October 1, 1995, every insurer shall file a report with the Commissioner disclosing material acquisitions and dispositions of assets or material nonrenewals, cancellations, or revisions of ceded reinsurance agreements, unless the acquisitions and dispositions of assets or material nonrenewals, cancellations, or revisions of ceded reinsurance agreements have been submitted to the Commissioner for review, approval, or informational purposes under any other provisions of this Chapter or the North Carolina Administrative Code. This report is due within 15 days after the end of the calendar month in which any of these transactions occurred. A copy of the report, including any filed exhibits or other attachments, shall also be filed with the NAIC.

(b) All reports obtained by or disclosed to the Commissioner under this Part are confidential and are not subject to subpoena. No report shall be made public by the Commissioner, the NAIC, or any other person, except to insurance regulators of other states, without the prior written consent of the reporting insurer, unless the Commissioner, after giving the insurer notice and an opportunity to be heard, determines that the interest of policyholders, shareholders, or the public will be served by the publication of the report. In that event, the Commissioner may publish all or any part of the report in a manner the Commissioner considers appropriate. (1995, c. 318, s. 1.)

§ 58-10-60. Acquisitions and dispositions of assets.

(a) Insurers do not have to report acquisitions or dispositions under G.S. 58-10-55 if they are not material. For the purposes of this Part, a material acquisition or the aggregate of any series of related acquisitions during any 30-day period, or a material disposition or the aggregate of any series of related dispositions during any 30-day period, is one that is nonrecurring, not in the ordinary course of business, and involves more than five percent (5%) of the insurer's total admitted assets as reported in its most recent financial statement filed with the Department.

(b) Asset acquisitions subject to this Part include every purchase, lease, exchange, merger, consolidation, succession, or other acquisition, other than the construction or development of real property by or for the insurer or the acquisition of materials for that purpose. Asset dispositions subject to this Part include every sale, lease, exchange, merger, consolidation, mortgage, hypothecation, assignment for the benefit of creditors or otherwise, abandonment, destruction, or other disposition.

(c) The following information shall be disclosed in any report under this section:

(1) Date of the transaction.
(2) Manner of acquisition or disposition.
(3) Description of the assets involved.
(4) Nature and amount of the consideration given or received.
(5) Purpose of, or reason for, the transaction.
(6) Manner by which the amount of consideration was determined.
(7) Gain or loss recognized or realized as a result of the transaction.
(8) Name of each person from whom the assets were acquired or to whom they were disposed.

(d) Every insurer shall report material acquisitions and dispositions on a nonconsolidated basis unless the insurer is part of a consolidated group of insurers that uses a pooling arrangement or one hundred percent (100%) reinsurance agreement that affects the solvency and integrity of the insurer's reserves and the insurer ceded substantially all of its direct and assumed business to the pool. An insurer cedes substantially all of its direct and assumed business to a pool if the insurer has less than one million dollars ($1,000,000) total direct plus assumed written premiums during a calendar year that are not subject to a pooling arrangement and the net income of the business not subject to the pooling arrangement represents less than five percent (5%) of the insurer's capital and surplus. (1995, c. 318, s. 1.)

§ 58-10-65. Nonrenewals, cancellations, or revisions of ceded reinsurance agreements.

(a) Insurers do not have to report nonrenewals, cancellations, or revisions of ceded reinsurance agreements under G.S. 58-10-55 if they are not material. For the purposes of this Part, a nonrenewal, cancellation, or revision of a ceded reinsurance agreement is considered material and must be reported if:

(1) It is for property and casualty business, including accident and health business written by a property and casualty insurer and affects:
   a. More than fifty percent (50%) of the insurer's total ceded written premium; or
   b. More than fifty percent (50%) of the insurer's total ceded indemnity and loss adjustment reserves.
(2) It is for life, annuity, and accident and health business and affects more than fifty percent (50%) of the total reserve credit taken for business ceded, on an annualized basis, as indicated in the insurer's most recent annual statement.
(3) It is for either property and casualty, or life, annuity, and accident and health business, and:
   a. An authorized reinsurer representing more than ten percent (10%) of a total cession is replaced by one or more unauthorized reinsurers; or

    b. Previously established collateral requirements have been reduced or waived with respect to one or more unauthorized reinsurer's representing collectively more than ten percent (10%) of a total cession.

(b) No filing is required if:

    (1) For property and casualty business, including accident and health business written by a property and casualty insurer, the insurer's total ceded written premium represents, on an annualized basis, less than ten percent (10%) of its total written premium for direct and assumed business.

    (2) For life, annuity, and accident and health business, the total reserve credit taken for business ceded represents, on an annualized basis, less than ten percent (10%) of the statutory reserve requirement before any cession.

(c) The following information shall be disclosed in any report under this section:

    (1) Effective date of the nonrenewal, cancellation, or revision.

    (2) Description of the transaction, with an identification of the initiator of the transaction.

    (3) Purpose of, or reason for, the transaction.

    (4) If applicable, identity of the replacement reinsurers.

(d) Every insurer shall report all material nonrenewals, cancellations, or revisions of ceded reinsurance agreements on a nonconsolidated basis unless the insurer is part of a consolidated group of insurers that uses a pooling arrangement or one hundred percent (100%) reinsurance agreement that affects the solvency and integrity of the insurer's reserves and the insurer ceded substantially all of its direct and assumed business to the pool. An insurer cedes substantially all of its direct and assumed business to a pool if the insurer has less than one million dollars ($1,000,000) total direct plus assumed written premiums during a calendar year that are not subject to the pooling arrangement and the net income of the business not subject to the pooling arrangement represents less than five percent (5%) of the insurer's capital and surplus. (1995, c. 318, s. 1.)

Part 4. Protected Cell Companies.

§ 58-10-75. Purpose and legislative intent.

This Part provides a basis for the creation of protected cells by a domestic insurer as one means of accessing alternative sources of capital and achieving the benefits of insurance securitization. Investors in fully funded insurance securitization transactions provide funds that are available to pay the insurer's insurance obligations or to repay the investors or both. The creation of protected cells is intended to be a means to achieve more efficiencies in conducting insurance securitizations. (2001-223, s. 25.)

Editor's Note. — Session Laws 2001-223, s. 28, makes this Part effective June 15, 2001. Session Laws 2001-223, s. 27 is a severability clause.

§ 58-10-80. Definitions.

As used in this Part, unless the context requires otherwise, the following terms have the following meanings:

    (1) "Domestic insurer" means an insurer domiciled in the State of North Carolina.

(2) "Fair value" means the amount at which that asset (or liability) could be bought (or incurred) or sold (or settled) in a current transaction between willing parties, that is, other than in a forced or liquidation sale. Quoted marked prices in active markets are the best evidence of fair value and shall be used as the basis for the measurement, if available. If a quoted market price is available, the fair value is the product of the number of trading units times market price. If quoted market prices are not available, the estimate of fair value shall be based on the best information available. The estimate of fair value shall consider prices for similar assets and liabilities and the results of valuation techniques to the extent available in the circumstances. Examples of valuation techniques include the present value of estimated expected future cash flows using a discount rate commensurate with the risks involved, option-pricing models, matrix pricing, option-adjusted spread models, and fundamental analysis. Valuation techniques for measuring financial assets and liabilities and servicing assets and liabilities shall be consistent with the objective of measuring fair value. Those techniques shall incorporate assumptions that market participants would use in their estimates of values, future revenues, and future expenses, including assumptions about interest rates, default, prepayment, and volatility. In measuring financial liabilities and servicing liabilities at fair value by discounting estimated future cash flows, an objective is to use discount rates at which those liabilities could be settled in an arm's-length transaction. Estimates of expected future cash flows, if used to estimate fair value, shall be the best estimate based on reasonable and supportable assumptions and projections. All available evidence shall be considered in developing estimates of expected future cash flows. The weight given to the evidence shall be commensurate with the extent to which the evidence can be verified objectively. If a range is estimated for either the amount or timing of possible cash flows, the likelihood of possible outcomes shall be considered in determining the best estimate of future cash flows.

(3) "Fully funded" means that, with respect to any exposure attributed to a protected cell, the market value of the protected cell assets, on the date on which the insurance securitization is effected, equals or exceeds the maximum possible exposure attributable to the protected cell with respect to the exposures.

(4) "General account" means the assets and liabilities of a protected cell company other than protected cell assets and protected cell liabilities.

(5) "Indemnity trigger" means a transaction term by which relief of the issuer's obligation to repay investors is triggered by its incurring a specified level of losses under its insurance or reinsurance contracts.

(6) "Nonindemnity trigger" means a transaction term by which relief of the issuer's obligation to repay investors is triggered solely by some event or condition other than the individual protected cell company incurring a specified level of losses under its insurance or reinsurance contracts.

(7) "Protected cell" means an identified pool of assets and liabilities of a protected cell company segregated and insulated by means of this Chapter from the remainder of the protected cell company's assets and liabilities.

(8) "Protected cell account" means a specifically identified bank or custodial account established by a protected cell company for the purpose of segregating the protected cell assets of one protected cell from the protected cell assets of other protected cells and from the assets of the protected cell company's general account.

(9) "Protected cell assets" means all assets, contract rights, and general intangibles, identified with and attributable to a specific protected cell of a protected cell company.

(10) "Protected cell company" means a domestic insurer that has one or more protected cells.

(11) "Protected cell company insurance securitization" means the issuance of debt instruments, the proceeds from which support the exposures attributed to the protected cell, by a protected cell company where repayment of principal or interest, or both, to investors under the transaction terms is contingent upon the occurrence or nonoccurrence of an event with respect to which the protected cell company is exposed to loss under insurance or reinsurance contracts it has issued.

(12) "Protected cell liabilities" means all liabilities and other obligations identified with and attributable to a specific protected cell of a protected cell company. (2001-223, s. 25.)

Editor's Note. — The definitions in this section were redesignated at the direction of the Revisor of Statutes to preserve alphabetical order.

Session Laws 2001-223, s. 27 contains a severability clause.

§ 58-10-85. Establishment of protected cells.

(a) A protected cell company may establish one or more protected cells with the prior written approval of the Commissioner of a plan of operation or amendments submitted by the protected cell company with respect to each protected cell in connection with an insurance securitization. Upon the Commissioner's written approval of the plan of operation, which plan shall include the specific business objectives and investment guidelines of the protected cell, the protected cell company, in accordance with the approved plan of operation, may attribute to the protected cell insurance obligations with respect to its insurance business and obligations relating to the insurance securitization and assets to fund the obligations. A protected cell shall have its own distinct name or designation, which shall include the words "protected cell." The protected cell company shall transfer all assets attributable to a protected cell to one or more separately established and identified protected cell accounts bearing the name or designation of that protected cell. Protected cell assets must be held in the protected cell accounts for the purpose of satisfying the obligations of that protected cell.

(b) All attributions of assets and liabilities between a protected cell and the general account must be in accordance with the plan of operation approved by the Commissioner. A protected cell company may make no other attribution of assets or liabilities between the protected cell company's general account and its protected cells. Any attribution of assets and liabilities between the general account and a protected cell, or from investors in the form of principal on a debt instrument issued by a protected cell company in connection with a protected cell company securitization, must be in cash or in readily marketable securities with established market values.

(c) The creation of a protected cell does not create, with respect to that protected cell, a legal person separate from the protected cell company. Amounts attributed to a protected cell under this Chapter, including assets transferred to a protected cell account, are owned by the protected cell company, and the protected cell company may not be, or may not hold itself out to be, a trustee with respect to those protected cell assets of that protected cell account. Notwithstanding the provisions of this subsection, the protected cell company may allow for a security interest to attach to protected cell assets or a protected cell account when in favor of a creditor of the protected cell and otherwise allowed under applicable law.

(d) This Part does not prohibit the protected cell company from contracting with or arranging for an investment advisor, commodity trading advisor, or other third party to manage the protected cell assets of a protected cell, if all remuneration, expenses, and other compensation of the third-party advisor or manager are payable from the protected cell assets of that protected cell and not from the protected cell assets of other protected cells or the assets of the protected cell company's general account.

(e) A protected cell company shall establish administrative and accounting procedures necessary to properly identify the one or more protected cells of the protected cell company and the protected cell assets and protected cell liabilities attributable to the protected cells. It shall be the duty of the directors of a protected cell company to keep protected cell assets and protected cell liabilities:

    (1) Separate and separately identifiable from the assets and liabilities of the protected cell company's general account; and

    (2) Attributable to one protected cell separate and separately identifiable from protected cell assets and protected cell liabilities attributable to other protected cells. Notwithstanding the provisions of this subsection, if this subsection is violated, the remedy of tracing is applicable to protected cell assets when commingled with protected cell assets of other protected cells or the assets of the protected cell company's general account. The remedy of tracing is not an exclusive remedy.

(f) When establishing a protected cell, the protected cell company shall attribute to the protected cell assets a value at least equal to the reserves and other insurance liabilities attributed to that protected cell. (2001-223, s. 25.)

Editor's Note. — Session Laws 2001-223, s. 27 contains a severability clause.

§ 58-10-90. Use and operation of protected cells.

(a) The protected cell assets of a protected cell may not be charged with liabilities arising out of any other business the protected cell company may conduct. All contracts or other documentation reflecting protected cell liabilities shall clearly indicate that only the protected cell assets are available for the satisfaction of those protected cell liabilities.

(b) The income, gains and losses, realized or unrealized, from protected cell assets and protected cell liabilities must be credited to or charged against the protected cell without regard to other income, gains or losses of the protected cell company, including income, gains or losses of other protected cells. Amounts attributed to any protected cell and accumulations on the attributed amounts may be invested and reinvested without regard to any requirements or limitations of this Chapter and the investments in a protected cell or cells may not be taken into account in applying the investment limitations otherwise applicable to the investments of the protected cell company.

(c) Assets attributed to a protected cell must be valued at their fair value on the date of valuation.

(d) A protected cell company, with respect to any of its protected cells, shall engage in fully funded indemnity triggered insurance securitization to support in full the protected cell exposures attributable to that protected cell. A protected cell company insurance securitization that is nonindemnity triggered shall qualify as an insurance securitization under the terms of this Chapter only after the Commissioner adopts rules addressing the methods of funding of the portion of this risk that is not indemnity based and addressing accounting, disclosure, risk-based capital treatment, and assessing risks associated with the securitizations. A protected cell company insurance securitization that is not fully funded, whether indemnity triggered or nonindemnity triggered, is prohibited. Protected cell assets may be used to pay interest or other consideration on any outstanding debt or other obligation attributable to that protected cell, and nothing in this subsection may be construed or interpreted to prevent a protected cell company from entering into a swap agreement or other transaction for the account of the protected cell that has the effect of guaranteeing interest or other consideration.

(e) In all protected cell company insurance securitizations, the contracts or other documentation effecting the transaction shall contain provisions identifying the protected cell to which the transaction will be attributed. In addition, the contracts or other documentation shall clearly disclose that the assets of that protected cell, and only those assets, are available to pay the obligations of that protected cell. Notwithstanding the provisions of this subsection and subject to the provisions of this Chapter and any other applicable law or rule, the failure to include such language in the contracts or other documentation may not be used as the sole basis by creditors, reinsurers, or other claimants to circumvent the provisions of this Part.

(f) A protected cell company shall only be authorized to attribute to a protected cell account the insurance obligations relating to the protected cell company's general account. Under no circumstances may a protected cell be authorized to issue insurance or reinsurance contracts directly to policyholders or reinsureds or have any obligation to the policyholders or reinsureds of the protected cell company's general account.

(g) At the cessation of business of a protected cell in accordance with the plan approved by the Commissioner, the protected cell company voluntarily shall close out the protected cell account. (2001-223, s. 25.)

Editor's Note. — Session Laws 2001-223, s. 27 contains a severability clause.

§ 58-10-95. Reach of creditors and other claimants.

(a) Protected cell assets shall only be available to the creditors of the protected cell company that are creditors with respect to that protected cell and, accordingly, are entitled, in conformity with this Chapter, to have recourse to the protected cell assets attributable to that protected cell and are absolutely protected from the creditors of the protected cell company that are not creditors with respect to that protected cell and who, accordingly, are not entitled to have recourse to the protected cell assets attributable to that protected cell. Creditors with respect to a protected cell are not entitled to have recourse against the protected cell assets of other protected cells or the assets or the protected cell company's general account. Protected cell assets are only available to creditors of a protected cell company after all protected cell liabilities have been extinguished or otherwise provided for in accordance with the plan of operation relating to that protected cell.

(b) When an obligation of a protected cell company to a person arises from a transaction, or is otherwise imposed, with respect to a protected cell:

(1) That obligation of the protected cell company extends only to the protected cell assets attributable to that protected cell, and the person, with respect to that obligation, is entitled to have recourse only to the protected cell assets attributable to that protected cell; and

(2) That obligation of the protected cell company does not extend to the protected cell assets of any other protected cell or the assets of the protected cell company's general account, and that person, with respect to that obligation, is not entitled to have recourse to the

protected cell assets of any other protected cell or the assets of the protected cell company's general account.

(c) When an obligation of a protected cell company relates solely to the general account, the obligation of the protected cell company extends only to, and that creditor, with respect to that obligation, is entitled to have recourse only to the assets of the protected cell company's general account.

(d) The activities, assets, and obligations relating to a protected cell are not subject to the provisions of Articles 48 and 62 of this Chapter, and neither a protected cell nor a protected cell company may be assessed by, or otherwise be required to contribute to, any guaranty fund or guaranty association in this State with respect to the activities, assets, or obligations of a protected cell. Nothing in this subsection affects the activities or obligations of an insurer's general account.

(e) The establishment of one or more protected cells alone does not constitute a fraudulent conveyance, an intent by the protected cell company to defraud creditors, or the carrying out of business by the protected cell company for any other fraudulent purpose. (2001-223, s. 25.)

Editor's Note. — Session Laws 2001-223, s. 27 contains a severability clause.

§ 58-10-100. Conservation, rehabilitation, or liquidation of protected cell companies.

(a) Notwithstanding any other provision of law or rule, upon an order of conservation, rehabilitation, or liquidation of a protected cell company, the receiver shall deal with the protected cell company's assets and liabilities, including protected cell assets and protected cell liabilities, in accordance with the requirements set forth in this Part.

(b) With respect to amounts recoverable under a protected cell company insurance securitization, the amount recoverable by the receiver may not be reduced or diminished as a result of the entry of an order of conservation, rehabilitation, or liquidation with respect to the protected cell company, notwithstanding any provisions to the contrary in the contracts or other documentation governing the protected cell company insurance securitization. (2001-223, s. 25.)

Editor's Note. — Session Laws 2001-223, s. 27 contains a severability clause.

§ 58-10-105. No transaction of an insurance business.

A protected cell company insurance securitization may not be deemed to be an insurance or reinsurance contract. An investor in a protected cell company insurance securitization, by sole means of this investment, may not be deemed to be conducting an insurance business in this State. The underwriters or selling agents and their partners, directors, officers, members, managers, employees, agents, representatives, and advisors involved in a protected cell company insurance securitization may not be deemed to be conducting an insurance or reinsurance agency, brokerage, intermediary, advisory, or consulting business by virtue of their activities in connection with that business. (2001-223, s. 25.)

Editor's Note. — Session Laws 2001-223, s. 27 contains a severability clause.

§ 58-10-110. Authority to adopt rules.

The Commissioner may adopt rules necessary to effectuate the purposes of this Part. (2001-223, s. 25.)

Editor's Note. — Session Laws 2001-223, s. 27 contains a severability clause.

Part 5. Mortgage Guaranty Insurance.

§ 58-10-120. Definitions.

As used in this Part:
  (1) "Mortgage guaranty insurers report of policyholders position" means the annual supplementary report required by the Commissioner.
  (2) "Policyholders position" means the contingency reserve established under G.S. 58-10-135 and policyholders' surplus. "Minimum policyholders position" is calculated as described in G.S. 58-10-125.
  (3) "Policyholders surplus" means an insurer's net worth; the difference between its assets and liabilities, as reported in its annual statement. (2001-223, s. 11.)

Editor's Note. — Session Laws 2001-233, s. 28 makes this Part effective June 15, 2001.

Session Laws 2001-223, s. 27 is a severability clause.

§ 58-10-125. Minimum policyholders position.

(a) For the purpose of complying with G.S. 58-7-75, a mortgage guaranty insurer shall maintain at all times a minimum policyholders position in the amount required by this section. The policyholders position shall be net of reinsurance ceded but shall include reinsurance assumed.

(b) If a mortgage guaranty insurer does not have the minimum amount of policyholders position required by this section it shall cease transacting new business until the time that its policyholders position is in compliance with this section.

(c) If a policy of mortgage guaranty insurance insures individual loans with a percentage claim settlement option on those loans, a mortgage guaranty insurer shall maintain a policyholders position based on each one hundred dollars ($100.00) of the face amount of the mortgage, the percentage coverage, and the loan-to-value category. The minimum amount of policyholders position shall be calculated in the following manner:
  (1) If the loan-to-value is greater than seventy-five percent (75%), the minimum policyholders position per one hundred dollars ($100.00) of the face amount of the mortgage for the specific percent coverage shall be as shown in the schedule below:
  (2) If the loan-to-value is at least fifty percent (50%) and not more than seventy-five percent (75%), the minimum amount of the policyholders position shall be fifty percent (50%) of the minimum of the amount calculated under subdivision (c)(1) of this section.
  (3) If the loan-to-value is less than fifty percent (50%), the minimum amount of policyholders position shall be twenty-five percent (25%) of the amount calculated under subdivision (c)(1) of this section.

(d) If a policy of mortgage guaranty insurance provides coverage on a group of loans subject to an aggregate loss limit, the policyholders position shall be:
  (1) If the equity is not more than fifty percent (50%) and is at least twenty percent (20%), or equity plus prior insurance or a deductible is at least

360

twenty-five percent (25%) and not more than fifty-five percent (55%), the minimum amount of policyholders position shall be calculated as follows:

(2) If the equity is less than twenty percent (20%), or the equity plus prior insurance or a deductible is less than twenty-five percent (25%), the minimum amount of policyholders position shall be two hundred percent (200%) of the amount required by subdivision (d)(1) of this section.

(3) If the equity is more than fifty percent (50%) or the equity plus prior insurance or a deductible is more than fifty-five percent (55%), the minimum amount of policyholders position shall be fifty percent (50%) of the amount required by subdivision (d)(1) of this section.

(e) If a policy of mortgage guaranty insurance provides for layers of coverage, deductibles, or excess reinsurance, the minimum amount of policyholders position shall be computed by subtraction of the minimum position for the lower percentage coverage limit from the minimum position for the upper or greater coverage limit.

(f) If a policy of mortgage guaranty insurance provides for coverage on loans secured by junior liens, the policyholders position shall be:

(1) If the policy provides coverage on individual loans, the minimum amount of policyholders position shall be calculated as in subsection (c) of this section as follows:

a. The loan-to-value percent is the entire loan indebtedness on the property divided by the value of the property;

b. The percent coverage is the insured portion of the junior loan divided by the entire loan indebtedness on the collateral property; and

c. The face amount of the insured mortgage is the entire loan indebtedness on the property.

(2) If the policy provides coverage on a group of loans subject to an aggregate loss limit, the policyholders position shall be calculated according to subsection (d) of this section as follows:

a. The equity is the complement of the loan-to-value percent calculated as in subdivision (d)(1) of this section;

b. The percent coverage is calculated as in subdivision (d)(1) of this section; and

c. The face amount of the insured mortgage is the entire loan indebtedness on the property.

(g) If a policy of mortgage guaranty insurance provides for coverage on leases, the policyholders position shall be four dollars ($4.00) for each one hundred dollars ($100.00) of the insured amount of the lease.

(h) If a policy of mortgage guaranty insurance insures loans with a percentage loss settlement option coverage between any of the entries in the schedules in this section, then the factor for policyholders position per one hundred dollars ($100.00) of the face amount of the mortgage shall be prorated between the factors for the nearest percent coverage listed. (2001-223, s. 11.)

Editor's Note. — Session Laws 2001-223, s. 27 contains a severability clause.

§ 58-10-130. Unearned premium reserve.

(a) The unearned premium reserve shall be computed as follows:

(1) The unearned premium reserve for premiums paid in advance annually shall be calculated on the monthly pro rata fractional basis.

(2) Premiums paid in advance for 10-year coverage shall be placed in the unearned premium reserve and shall be released from this reserve as follows:

    a. 1st month — $\frac{1}{132}$;

    b. 2nd through 12th month — $\frac{2}{132}$ each month;

    c. 13th month — $\frac{3}{264}$;

    d. 14th through 120th month — $\frac{1}{132}$ per month;

    e. 121st month — $\frac{1}{264}$

(3) Premiums paid in advance for periods in excess of 10 years. During the first 10 years of coverage the unearned portion of the premium shall be the premium collected minus an amount equal to the premium that would have been earned had the applicable premium for 10 years of coverage been received. The premium remaining after 10 years shall be released from the unearned premium reserve monthly pro rata over the remaining term of coverage.

(b) Repealed by Session Laws 2001-334, s. 16.1, effective August 3, 2001.

(c) The case basis method shall be used to determine the loss reserve which shall include a reserve for claims reported and unpaid and a reserve for claims incurred but not reported. (2001-223, s. 11; 2001-334, s. 16.1.)

Editor's Note. — Session Laws 2001-223, s. 27, contains a severability clause.

§ 58-10-135. Contingency reserve.

(a) Subject to G.S. 58-7-21, a mortgage guaranty insurer shall make an annual contribution to the contingency reserve which in the aggregate shall be the greater of:

(1) Fifty percent (50%) of the net earned premium reported in the annual statement; or

(2) The sum of:

    a. The policyholders position established under G.S. 58-10-125 on residential buildings designed for occupancy by not more than four families divided by seven;

    b. The policyholders position established under G.S. 58-10-125 on residential buildings designed for occupancy by five or more families divided by five;

    c. The policyholders position established under G.S. 58-10-125 on buildings occupied for industrial or commercial purposes divided by three; and

    d. The policyholders position established under G.S. 58-10-125 for leases divided by 10.

(b) If the mortgage guaranty coverage is not expressly provided for in this section, the Commissioner may establish a rate formula factor that will produce a contingency reserve adequate for the risk assumed.

(c) The contingency reserve established by this section shall be maintained for 120 months and reported in the financial statements as a liability. That portion of the contingency reserve established and maintained for more than 120 months shall be released and shall no longer constitute part of the contingency reserve.

(d) With the approval of the Commissioner, withdrawals may be made from the contingency reserve when incurred losses and incurred loss expenses exceed the greater of either thirty-five percent (35%) of the net earned premium or seventy percent (70%) of the amount which subsection (a) of this section requires to be contributed to the contingency reserve in such year. On a quarterly basis, provisional withdrawals may be made from the contingency reserve in an amount not to exceed seventy-five percent (75%) of the withdrawal calculated in accordance with this subsection.

(e) With the approval of the Commissioner, a mortgage guaranty insurer may withdraw from the contingency reserve any amounts which are in excess of the minimum policyholders position as filed with the most recently filed annual statement. In reviewing a request for withdrawal pursuant to this subsection, the Commissioner may consider loss development and trends. If any portion of the contingency reserve for which withdrawal is requested pursuant to this subsection is maintained by a reinsurer, the Commissioner may also consider the financial condition of the reinsurer. If any portion of the contingency reserve for which withdrawal is requested pursuant to this subsection is maintained in a segregated account or segregated trust and such withdrawal would result in funds being removed from the segregated account or segregated trust, the Commissioner may also consider the financial condition of the reinsurer.

(f) Releases and withdrawals from the contingency reserve shall be accounted for on a first-in-first-out basis as prescribed by the Commissioner.

(g) The calculations to develop the contingency reserve shall be made in the following sequence:

(1) The additions required by subsections (a) and (b) of this section;

(2) The releases permitted by subsection (c) of this section;

(3) The withdrawals permitted by subsection (d) of this section; and

(4) The withdrawals permitted by subsection (e) of this section.

(h) Whenever the laws or regulations of another jurisdiction in which a mortgage guaranty insurer, subject to the requirements of this Part is licensed, require a larger unearned premium reserve or a larger contingency reserve in the aggregate than that set forth in this Part, the establishment and maintenance of the larger unearned premium reserve or contingency reserve shall be deemed to be in compliance with this Part. (2001-223, s. 11; 2001-334, ss. 16.2, 16.3.)

Editor's Note. — Session Laws 2001-223, s. 28, made this section effective June 15, 2001. Session Laws 2001-223, s. 27, is a severability clause.

ARTICLE 11.

Assessment Companies.

§ 58-11-1. Copies of charter and bylaws filed.

Every corporation, society, or organization of this or any other state or country, transacting business upon the cooperative or assessment plan, must file with the Commissioner, before beginning to do business in this State, a copy of its charter or articles of association, and the bylaws, rules, or regulations referred to in its policies or certificates and made a part of such contract. Bylaws or regulations not so filed with the Commissioner will not avoid or affect any policy or certificate issued by such company or association. (1899, c. 54, s. 86; Rev., s. 4790; C.S., s. 6356; 1991, c. 720, ss. 4, 66.)

Cross References. — As to mutual insurance companies generally, see G.S. 58-8-1 through 58-8-55. As to fraternal orders and societies, see G.S. 58-24-1 et seq., and G.S. 58-25-1 et seq.

§ 58-11-5. Contracts must accord with charter and bylaws.

Every policy or certificate or renewal receipt issued to a resident of this State by any corporation, association, or order transacting therein the business of insurance upon the assessment plan must be in accord with the provisions of the charter and bylaws of such corporation, association, or order, as filed with the Commissioner. It is unlawful for any such domestic or foreign insurance company or fraternal order to transact or offer to transact any business not authorized by the provisions of its charter and terms of its bylaws, or, through an agent or otherwise, to offer or issue any policy, renewal certificate, or other contract whose terms are not in clear accord with the powers, terms, and stipulations of its charter and bylaws. (1899, c. 54, s. 84; 1903, c. 438, s. 9; Rev., s. 4791; C.S., s. 6357; 1991, c. 720, s. 4.)

CASE NOTES

The contract of insurance must conform to the charter and bylaws, and these are as authorized by the state of its origin. Hollingsworth v. Supreme Council of Royal Arcanum, 175 N.C. 615, 96 S.E. 81 (1918), distinguishing Caldwell Land & Lumber Co. v. Commissioners of Caldwell County, 174 N.C. 634, 94 S.E. 406 (1917).

Assessment companies are prohibited from issuing policies or transacting business not authorized by their charters.

Brenizer v. Royal Arcanum, 141 N.C. 409, 53 S.E. 835 (1906).

Duty and Liability Under Bylaws. — The bylaws of an assessment association, when assented to by the members, as provided in the statute, constitute the measure of duty and liability of the parties, provided they are reasonable and not in violation of any principle of public law. Duffy v. Fidelity Mut. Life Ins. Co., 142 N.C. 103, 55 S.E. 79 (1906).

§ 58-11-10. "Assessment plan" printed on application and policy.

Every policy or certificate issued to a resident of the State by any corporation transacting in the State the business of life insurance upon the assessment plan, or admitted to do business in this State on the assessment plan, shall print in bold type near the top of the front page of the policy, upon every policy or certificate issued upon the life of any such resident of the State, the words "issued upon the assessment plan"; and the words "assessment plan" shall be printed conspicuously upon every application, circular, card, and any and all printed documents issued, circulated, or caused to be circulated by such corporation within the State. (1913, c. 159, s. 1; C.S., s. 6358; 1929, c. 93, s. 1; 1933, c. 34; 1945, c. 386.)

§ 58-11-15. Revocation for noncompliance.

If any corporation or association transacting insurance business in this State on the assessment plan or issuing any policy upon the life of a resident of North Carolina upon the assessment plan shall fail or refuse to comply with G.S. 58-11-10, the Commissioner shall forthwith suspend or revoke all authority of such corporation or association and of its agents to do business in this State. (1913, c. 159, s. 2; C.S., s. 6359; 1991, c. 720, ss. 4, 13.)

§ 58-11-20. Deposits and advance assessments required.

Every domestic insurance company, association, order, or fraternal benefit society doing business on the assessment plan shall collect and keep at all times in its treasury one regular loss assessment sufficient to pay one regular average loss; and no such company, association, order, or fraternal benefit society shall be licensed by the Commissioner unless it makes and maintains with him for the protection of its obligations at least five thousand dollars ($5,000) in United States or North Carolina bonds, in farm loan bonds issued by federal loan banks, or in the bonds of some city, county, or town of North Carolina to be approved by the Commissioner, or deposit with him a good and sufficient bond, secured by a deed of trust on real estate situated in North Carolina and approved by him, or by depositing with the Commissioner a bond in an amount of not less than five thousand dollars ($5,000), issued by any corporate surety company authorized to do business in this State. The Commissioner may increase the amount of deposit to the amount of reserve on the contracts of the association or society. The provisions of this section shall not apply to the farmers mutual fire insurance associations now doing business in the State and restricting their activities to not more than six adjacent counties. (Rev., s. 4792; 1913, c. 119, s. 1; 1917, c. 191, s. 2; C.S., s. 6360; 1933, c. 47; 1945, c. 386; 1991, c. 720, ss. 4, 87.)

§ 58-11-25. Deposits by foreign assessment companies or orders.

Each foreign insurance company, association, order, or fraternal benefit society doing business in this State on the assessment plan shall keep at all times deposited with the Commissioner or in its head office in this State, or in some responsible banking or trust company, one regular assessment sufficient to pay the average loss or losses occurring among its members in this State during the time allowed by it for the collection of assessments and payment of losses. It shall notify the Commissioner of the place of deposit and furnish him at all times such information as he requires in regard thereto; and no such company, association, order, or fraternal benefit society shall be licensed by the Commissioner unless it makes and maintains with him for the protection of its obligations at least five thousand dollars ($5,000) in United States or North Carolina bonds, in farm loan bonds issued by federal land banks, or in the bonds of some county, city, or town in North Carolina to be approved by the Commissioner, or a good and sufficient bond or note, secured by deed of trust on real estate situate in North Carolina, and approved by the Commissioner. (1899, c. 54, s. 84; 1903, c. 438, s. 9; Rev., s. 4713; 1913, c. 119, ss. 2, 3; 1917, c. 191, s. 2; C.S., s. 6361; 1945, c. 386; 1991, c. 720, s. 4.)

§ 58-11-30. Revocation of license.

If any such corporation, association, or order at any time fails to comply with the provisions of G.S. 58-11-20 and 58-11-25 or shall issue policies or certificates not in accord with its charter and bylaws, as provided in this Article, the Commissioner shall forthwith suspend or revoke all authority to it, and of all its agents or officers, to do business in this State, and shall publish such revocation in some newspaper published in this State. (1899, c. 54, s. 85; Rev., s. 4793; C.S., s. 6362; 1991, c. 720, s. 4.)

§ 58-11-35. Mutual life insurance companies; assessments prohibited.

No domestic mutual life insurance company shall, after March 6, 1945, be organized to issue any policy of life insurance or any annuity contract which provides for the payment of any assessment by any policyholder or member in addition to the regular premium charged for such insurance; nor shall any such company have power to levy or collect any such assessment. No foreign or alien life insurance company shall be permitted to do business in this State if it does business, in this State or elsewhere, on such or any other assessment plan. (1945, c. 386.)

ARTICLE 12.

Risk-Based Capital Requirements.

§ **58-12-1:** Repealed by Session Laws 1993, c. 452, s. 65.

Cross References. — As to mutual companies with a guaranty capital, see G.S. 58-8-20.

§ **58-12-2. Definitions.**

As used in this Article, the following terms have the following meanings:
  (1) Adjusted risk-based capital report. — A risk-based capital report that has been adjusted by the Commissioner under G.S. 58-12-6.
  (2) Corrective order. — An order issued by the Commissioner specifying corrective actions that the Commissioner has determined are required.
  (3) Domestic insurer. — Any insurance company or health organization organized in this State under Article 7, 15, 65, or 67 of this Chapter.
  (4) Foreign insurer. — Any insurance company or health organization that is admitted to do business in this State under Article 16 or 67 of this Chapter but is not domiciled in this State.
  (4a) Health organization. — Any health maintenance organization, limited health service organization, dental or vision plan, hospital, medical, or dental indemnity or service corporation, or other organization licensed under Article 65 or 67 of this Chapter. "Health organization" does not include an insurer that is licensed as either a life or health insurer or a property or casualty insurer under this Chapter and that is otherwise subject to either the life or property and casualty risk-based capital requirements.
  (4b) Life or health insurer. — Any insurance company licensed to write the kinds of insurance specified in G.S. 58-7-15(1), (2), or (3); or a licensed property and casualty insurer writing only the kinds of insurance specified in G.S. 58-7-15(3).
  (5) Negative trend. — A negative trend, with respect to a life or health insurer, over a period of time, as determined in accordance with the "trend test calculation" included in the risk-based capital instructions.
  (5a) Property or casualty insurer. — Any insurance company licensed to write the kinds of insurance specified in G.S. 58-7-15(4) through (22); but not monoline mortgage guaranty insurers, financial guaranty insurers, or title insurers.
  (6) Risk-based capital instructions. — The risk-based capital report including risk-based capital instructions adopted by the NAIC, as those risk-based capital instructions may be amended by the NAIC from time to time in accordance with the procedures adopted by the NAIC.
  (7) Risk-based capital level. — An insurer's company action level risk-based capital, regulatory action level risk-based capital, authorized control level risk-based capital, or mandatory control level risk-based capital where:
    a. "Company action level risk-based capital" means, with respect to any insurer, the product of 2.0 and its authorized control level risk-based capital.

    b. "Regulatory action level risk-based capital" means the product of 1.5 and its authorized control level risk-based capital.

    c. "Authorized control level risk-based capital" means the number determined under the risk-based capital formula in accordance with the risk-based capital instructions.

    d. "Mandatory control level risk-based capital" means the product of .70 and the authorized control level risk-based capital.

(8) Risk-based capital plan. — A comprehensive financial plan containing the elements specified in G.S. 58-12-11(b). If the Commissioner rejects the risk-based capital plan, and it is revised by the insurer, with or without the Commissioner's recommendation, the plan shall be called the "revised risk-based capital plan".

(9) Risk-based capital report. — The report required in G.S. 58-12-6.

(10) Total adjusted capital. — The sum of:

    a. An insurer's statutory capital and surplus, as determined in accordance with the statutory accounting applicable to the annual financial statements required under G.S. 58-2-165; and

    b. Such other items, if any, as the risk-based capital instructions may provide. (1993 (Reg. Sess., 1994), c. 678, s. 1; 1995, c. 318, s. 2; 2001-223, ss. 12.1, 12.2, 12.3.)

Editor's Note. — The definitions in this section were redesignated at the direction of the Revisor of Statutes to preserve alphabetical order.

§ 58-12-4. Finding; endorsement of additional capital.

The General Assembly finds that an excess of capital over the amount produced by the risk-based capital requirements contained in this Article and in the formulas, schedules, and instructions referenced in this Article is desirable in the business of insurance. Accordingly, the General Assembly encourages insurers to seek to maintain capital above the risk-based capital levels required by this Article. Additional capital is used and useful in the insurance business and helps to secure an insurer against various risks inherent in or affecting the business of insurance but not accounted for or only partially measured by the risk-based capital requirements contained in this Article. (1995, c. 318, s. 3.)

§ 58-12-5: Repealed by Session Laws 1993, c. 452, s. 65.

§ 58-12-6. Risk-based capital reports.

(a) Every domestic insurer shall, on or before each March 1 (the "filing date"), prepare and submit to the Commissioner a report of its risk-based capital levels as of the end of the calendar year just ended, in a form and containing such information as is required by the risk-based capital instructions. In addition, every domestic insurer shall file its risk-based capital report:

(1) With the NAIC in accordance with the risk-based capital instructions; and

(2) With the insurance regulator in any state in which the insurer is authorized to do business, if the Commissioner has notified the insurer of its request in writing, in which case the insurer shall file its risk-based capital report not later than the later of:

    a. Fifteen days after the receipt of notice to file its risk-based capital report with that state; or

    b. The filing date.

(b) A life or health insurer's risk-based capital shall be determined in accordance with the formula set forth in the risk-based capital instructions.

The formula shall take into account (and may adjust for the covariance between):

 (1) The risk with respect to the insurer's assets;

 (2) The risk of adverse insurance experience with respect to the insurer's liabilities and obligations;

 (3) The interest rate risk with respect to the insurer's business; and

 (4) All other business risks and such other relevant risks as are set forth in the risk-based capital instructions.

These risks shall be determined in each case by applying the factors in the manner set forth in the risk-based capital instructions.

 (c) If a domestic insurer files a risk-based capital report that in the judgment of the Commissioner is inaccurate, the Commissioner shall adjust the risk-based capital report to correct the inaccuracy and shall notify the insurer of the adjustment. The notice shall contain a statement of the reason for the adjustment. A risk-based capital report as adjusted is referred to as an "adjusted risk-based capital report".

 (d) A property or casualty insurer's risk-based capital and a health organization's risk-based capital shall be determined in accordance with the formula set forth in the risk-based capital instructions. The formula shall take into account (and may adjust for the covariance between):

 (1) Asset risk;

 (2) Credit risk;

 (3) Underwriting risk; and

 (4) All business and other relevant risks set forth in the risk-based capital instructions, determined in each case by applying the factors in the manner set forth in the risk-based capital instructions. (1993 (Reg. Sess., 1994), c. 678, s. 1; 1995, c. 318, s. 4; 2001-223, s. 12.4.)

§ 58-12-10: Repealed by Session Laws 1993, c. 452, s. 65.

§ 58-12-11. Company action level event.

 (a) "Company action level event" means any of the following events:

 (1) The filing of a risk-based capital report by an insurer that indicates that:

  a. The insurer's total adjusted capital is greater than or equal to its regulatory action level risk-based capital but less than its company action level risk-based capital, if the insurer is a property or casualty insurer or a health organization; or

  b. The insurer has total adjusted capital that is greater than or equal to its company action level risk-based capital but less than the product of its authorized control level risk-based capital and 2.5 and has a negative trend, if the insurer is a life or health insurer.

 (2) The notification by the Commissioner to the insurer of an adjusted risk-bases capital report that indicates the event in sub-subdivision (1)a. or b. of this subsection if the insurer does not challenge the adjusted risk-based capital report under G.S. 58-12-30.

 (3) If the insurer challenges an adjusted risk-based capital report that indicates the event in sub-subdivision (1)a. or b. of this subsection under G.S. 58-12-30, the notification by the Commissioner to the insurer that the Commissioner has rejected the insurer's challenge.

 (b) In the event of a company action level event, the insurer shall prepare and submit to the Commissioner a comprehensive financial plan that:

 (1) Identifies the conditions in the insurer that contribute to the company action level event.

   (2) Contains proposals of corrective actions that the insurer intends to take and would be expected to result in the elimination of the company action level event.

   (3) Provides forecasts of the insurer's financial results in the current year and at least the four succeeding years, both in the absence of proposed corrective actions and giving effect to the proposed corrective actions, including forecasts of statutory operating income, net income, capital, or surplus (the forecasts for both new and renewal business should include separate forecasts for each major line of business and separately identify each significant income, expense, and benefit component). For a health organization, the forecasted financial results shall be for the current year and at least two succeeding years and shall include statutory balance sheets, operating income, net income, capital and surplus, and risk-based capital levels.

   (4) Identifies the key assumptions affecting the insurer's forecasts and the sensitivity of the forecasts to the assumptions.

   (5) Identifies the quality of, and problems associated with, the insurer's business, including its assets, anticipated business growth and associated surplus strain, extraordinary exposure to risk, mix of business, and use of reinsurance in each case, if any.

(c) The risk-based capital plan shall be submitted:

   (1) Within 45 days after the company action level event; or

   (2) If the insurer challenges an adjusted risk-based capital report pursuant to G.S. 58-12-30, within 45 days after notification to the insurer that the Commissioner has rejected the insurer's challenge.

(d) Within 60 days after the submittal by an insurer of a risk-based capital plan to the Commissioner, the Commissioner shall notify the insurer whether the risk-based capital plan shall be implemented or is, in the judgment of the Commissioner, unsatisfactory. If the Commissioner determines the risk-based capital plan is unsatisfactory, the notification to the insurer shall set forth the reasons for the determination, and may set forth proposed revisions that will render the risk-based capital plan satisfactory, in the judgment of the Commissioner. Upon notification from the Commissioner, the insurer shall prepare a revised risk-based capital plan, which may incorporate by reference any revisions proposed by the Commissioner, and shall submit the revised risk-based capital plan to the Commissioner:

   (1) Within 45 days after notification from the Commissioner; or

   (2) If the insurer challenges the notification from the Commissioner under G.S. 58-12-30, within 45 days after a notification to the insurer that the Commissioner has rejected the insurer's challenge.

(e) In the event of a notification by the Commissioner to an insurer that the insurer's risk-based capital plan or revised risk-based capital plan is unsatisfactory, the Commissioner may, subject to the insurer's right to a hearing under G.S. 58-12-30, specify in the notification that the notification constitutes a regulatory action level event.

(f) Every domestic insurer that files a risk-based capital plan or revised risk-based capital plan with the Commissioner shall file a copy of the risk-based capital plan or revised risk-based capital plan with the insurance regulator in any state in which the insurer is authorized to do business if:

   (1) That state has a risk-based capital provision substantially similar to G.S. 58-12-21(a); and

   (2) The insurance regulator of that state has notified the insurer of its request for the filing in writing, in which case the insurer shall file a copy of the risk-based capital plan or revised risk-based capital plan in that state no later than the later of:

      a. Fifteen days after the receipt of notice to file a copy of its risk-based capital plan or revised risk-based capital plan with the state; or

      b. The date on which the risk-based capital plan or revised risk-based capital plan is filed under subsection (c) or (d) of this section. (1993 (Reg. Sess., 1994), c. 678, s. 1; 1995, c. 193, s. 21; c. 318, s. 5; 2001-223, ss. 12.5, 12.6.)

§ **58-12-15:** Repealed by Session Laws 1993, c. 452, s. 65.

§ 58-12-16. Regulatory action level event.

(a) "Regulatory action level event" means, with respect to any insurer, any of the following events:

    (1) The filing of a risk-based capital plan report by the insurer that indicates that the insurer's total adjusted capital is greater than or equal to its authorized control level risk-based capital but less than its regulatory action level risk-based capital.

    (2) The notification by the Commissioner to an insurer of an adjusted risk-based capital report that indicates the event in subdivision (1) of this subsection, if the insurer does not challenge the adjusted risk-based capital report under G.S. 58-12-30.

    (3) If the insurer challenges an adjusted risk-based capital report that indicates the event in subdivision (1) of this subsection under G.S. 58-12-30, the notification by the Commissioner to the insurer that the Commissioner has rejected the insurer's challenge.

    (4) The failure of the insurer to file a risk-based capital report by the filing date, unless the insurer has provided an explanation for the failure that is satisfactory to the Commissioner and has cured the failure within 10 days after the filing date.

    (5) The failure of the insurer to submit a risk-based capital plan to the Commissioner within the time period set forth in G.S. 58-12-11(c).

    (6) Notification by the Commissioner to the insurer that:

      a. The risk-based capital plan or revised risk-based capital plan submitted by the insurer is, in the judgment of the Commissioner, unsatisfactory; and

      b. The notification constitutes a regulatory action level event with respect to the insurer, provided the insurer has not challenged the determination under G.S. 58-12-30.

    (7) If the insurer challenges a determination by the Commissioner under subdivision (6) of this subsection pursuant to G.S. 58-12-30, the notification by the Commissioner to the insurer that the Commissioner has rejected the challenge.

    (8) Notification by the Commissioner to the insurer that the insurer has failed to adhere to its risk-based capital plan or revised risk-based capital plan; but only if the failure has a substantial adverse effect on the ability of the insurer to eliminate the company action level event in accordance with its risk-based capital plan or revised risk-based capital plan and the Commissioner has so stated in the notification, provided the insurer has not challenged the determination under G.S. 58-12-30.

    (9) If the insurer challenges a determination by the Commissioner under subdivision (8) of this subsection pursuant to G.S. 58-12-30, the notification by the Commissioner to the insurer that the Commissioner has rejected the challenge (unless the failure of the insurer to adhere to its risk-based capital plan or revised risk-based capital plan has no substantial adverse effect on the ability of the insurer to eliminate the regulatory action level event with respect to the insurer).

(b) In the event of a regulatory action level event the Commissioner shall:

    (1) Require the insurer to prepare and submit a risk-based capital plan or, if applicable, a revised risk-based capital plan.

    (2) Perform such examination or analysis, as the Commissioner deems necessary, of the assets, liabilities, and operations of the insurer, including a review of its risk-based capital plan or revised risk-based capital plan.

    (3) After the examination or analysis, issue an order specifying such corrective actions as the Commissioner shall determine are required (a "Corrective Order").

(c) In determining corrective actions, the Commissioner may take into account such factors as are deemed relevant with respect to the insurer based upon the Commissioner's examination or analysis of the assets, liabilities, and operations of the insurer, including, but not limited to, the results of any sensitivity tests undertaken pursuant to risk-based capital instructions. The risk-based capital plan or revised risk-based capital plan shall be submitted:

    (1) Within 45 days after the occurrence of the regulatory action level event;

    (2) If the insurer challenges an adjusted risk-based capital report pursuant to G.S. 58-12-30 and the challenge is not in the judgment of the Commissioner frivolous, within 45 days after the notification to the insurer that the Commissioner has, after a hearing, rejected the insurer's challenge; or

    (3) If the insurer challenges a revised risk-based capital plan under G.S. 58-12-30, within 45 days after notification to the insurer that the Commissioner has rejected the challenge.

(d) The Commissioner may retain actuaries and investment experts and other consultants as may be necessary in the judgment of the Commissioner to review the insurer's risk-based capital plan or revised risk-based capital plan, examine or analyze the assets, liabilities, and operations of the insurer and formulate the Corrective Order with respect to the insurer. The fees, costs, and expenses relating to consultants shall be borne by the affected insurer or such other party as directed by the Commissioner. (1993 (Reg. Sess., 1994), c. 678, s. 1.)

§ **58-12-20:** Repealed by Session Laws 1993, c. 452, s. 65.

§ **58-12-21. Authorized control level event.**

(a) "Authorized control level event" means any of the following events:

    (1) The filing of a risk-based capital report by the insurer that indicates that the insurer's total adjusted capital is greater than or equal to its mandatory control level risk-based capital but less than its authorized control level risk-based capital.

    (2) The notification by the Commissioner to the insurer of an adjusted risk-based capital report that indicates the event in subdivision (1) of this subsection if the insurer does not challenge the adjusted risk-based capital report under G.S. 58-12-30.

    (3) If the insurer challenges an adjusted risk-based capital report that indicates the event in subdivision (1) of this subsection under G.S. 58-12-30, notification by the Commissioner to the insurer that the Commissioner has rejected the challenge.

    (4) The failure of the insurer to respond, in a manner satisfactory to the Commissioner, to a Corrective Order if the insurer has not challenged the Corrective Order under G.S. 58-12-30.

    (5) If the insurer has challenged a Corrective Order under G.S. 58-12-30 and the Commissioner has rejected the challenge or modified the Corrective Order, the failure of the insurer to respond, in a manner satisfactory to the Commissioner, to the Corrective Order after the rejection or modification by the Commissioner.

  (b) In the event of an authorized control level event with respect to an insurer, the Commissioner shall:

    (1) Take such actions as are required under G.S. 58-12-30 regarding an insurer with respect to which a regulatory action level event has occurred; or

    (2) If the Commissioner deems it to be in the best interests of the policyholders and creditors of the insurer and of the public, take such actions as are necessary to cause the insurer to be placed under regulatory control under Article 30 of this Chapter. If the Commissioner takes such actions, the authorized control level event shall be deemed sufficient grounds for the Commissioner to take action under Article 30 of this Chapter, and the Commissioner shall have the rights, powers, and duties with respect to the insurer as are set forth in Article 30 of this Chapter. If the Commissioner takes actions under this subdivision pursuant to an adjusted risk-based capital report, the insurer shall be entitled to such protections as are afforded to insurers under the provisions of Article 30 of this Chapter pertaining to summary proceedings. (1993 (Reg. Sess., 1994), c. 678, s. 1.)

§ 58-12-25. Mandatory control level event.

  (a) "Mandatory control level event" means any of the following events:

    (1) The filing of a risk-based capital report that indicates that the insurer's total adjusted capital is less than its mandatory control level risk-based capital.

    (2) Notification by the Commissioner to the insurer of an adjusted risk-based capital report that indicates the event in subdivision (1) of this subsection if the insurer does not challenge the adjusted risk-based capital report under G.S. 58-12-30.

    (3) If the insurer challenges an adjusted risk-based capital report that indicates the event in subdivision (1) of this subsection under G.S. 58-12-30, notification by the Commissioner to the insurer that the Commissioner has rejected the challenge.

  (b) In the event of a mandatory control level event with respect to a life insurer or a health organization, the Commissioner shall take actions as are necessary to cause the insurer to be placed under regulatory control under Article 30 of this Chapter. The mandatory control level event is sufficient grounds for the Commissioner to take action under Article 30 of this Chapter, and the Commissioner shall have the rights, powers, and duties with respect to the insurer as are set forth in Article 30 of this Chapter. If the Commissioner takes actions pursuant to an adjusted risk-based capital report, the insurer shall be entitled to such protections as are afforded to insurers under the provisions of Article 30 of this Chapter pertaining to summary proceedings. Notwithstanding any of the foregoing, the Commissioner may forego action for up to 90 days after the mandatory control level event if the Commissioner finds there is a reasonable expectation that the mandatory control level event may be eliminated within the 90-day period.

  (c) In the event of a mandatory control level event with respect to a property and casualty insurer, the Commissioner shall take actions as are necessary to cause the insurer to be placed under regulatory control under Article 30 of this Chapter, or, in the case of an insurer which is writing no business and which is running off its existing business, may allow the insurer to continue its runoff under the supervision of the Commissioner. In either event, the mandatory control level event is sufficient grounds for the Commissioner to take action under Article 30 of this Chapter, and the Commissioner shall have the rights, powers, and duties with respect to the insurer as are set forth in Article 30 of this Chapter. If the Commissioner takes actions under an adjusted risk-based capital report, the insurer shall be entitled to such protections as are afforded to insurers under the provisions of Article 30 of this Chapter pertaining to summary proceedings. Notwithstanding any of the foregoing, the Commissioner may forego action for up to 90 days after the mandatory control level event if the Commissioner finds there is a reasonable expectation that the mandatory control level event may be eliminated within the 90-day period. (1993 (Reg. Sess., 1994), c. 678, s. 1; 2001-223, ss. 12.7, 12.8.)

§ 58-12-30. Hearings.

Upon (i) notification to an insurer by the Commissioner of an adjusted risk-based capital report; or (ii) notification to an insurer by the Commissioner that the insurer's risk-based capital plan or revised risk-based capital plan is unsatisfactory, and the notification constitutes a regulatory action level event with respect to the insurer; or (iii) notification to any insurer by the Commissioner that the insurer has failed to adhere to its risk-based capital plan or revised risk-based capital plan and that the failure has a substantial adverse effect on the ability of the insurer to eliminate the company action level event with respect to the insurer in accordance with its risk-based capital plan or revised risk-based capital plan; or (iv) notification to an insurer by the Commissioner of a corrective order with respect to the insurer, the insurer has a right to a confidential hearing, at which the insurer may challenge any determination or action by the Commissioner. The insurer shall notify the Commissioner of its request for a hearing within five days after the notification by the Commissioner under this section. Upon receipt of the insurer's request for a hearing, the Commissioner shall set a date for the hearing; the date shall be no less than 10 days nor more than 30 days after the date of the insurer's request. (1993 (Reg. Sess., 1994), c. 678, s. 1; 1995, c. 517, s. 5.)

§ 58-12-35. Confidentiality and prohibition on announcements.

(a) All risk-based capital reports, to the extent the information therein is not required to be set forth in a publicly available annual statement schedule, and the risk-based capital plans, including the results or report of any examination or analysis of an insurer performed pursuant hereto and any corrective order issued by the Commissioner pursuant to examination or analysis, with respect to any domestic insurer or foreign insurer that are filed with the Commissioner constitute confidential information that shall be kept confidential by the Commissioner. This information shall not be made public or be subject to subpoena, other than by the Commissioner, and then only for the purpose of enforcement actions taken by the Commissioner under this Article or any other provision of this Chapter.

(b) The General Assembly finds that the comparison of an insurer's total adjusted capital to any of its risk-based capital levels is a regulatory tool that may indicate the need for possible corrective action with respect to the insurer, and is not intended as a means to rank insurers generally. Therefore, except as otherwise required under this Article, the making, publishing, disseminating, circulating, or placing before the public, or causing, directly or indirectly, to be made, published, disseminated, circulated, or placed before the public, in a newspaper, magazine, or other publication, or in the form of a notice, circular, pamphlet, letter, or poster, or over any radio or television station, or in any other way, an advertisement, announcement, or statement containing an assertion, representation, or statement with regard to the risk-based capital levels of any insurer, or of any component derived in the calculation by any insurer, agent, broker, or other person engaged in any manner in the insurance business is prohibited; provided, however, that if any materially false statement with respect to the comparison regarding an insurer's total adjusted capital to its risk-based capital levels (or any of them) or an inappropriate comparison of any other amount to the insurers' risk-based capital levels is published in any written publication and the insurer is able to demonstrate to the Commissioner, with substantial proof, the falsity of the statement, or the inappropriateness, as the case may be, then the insurer may publish an announcement in a written publication if the sole purpose of the announcement is to rebut the materially false statement. (1993 (Reg. Sess., 1994), c. 678, s. 1; 1995, c. 193, s. 22.)

§ 58-12-40. Supplemental provisions; rules; exemptions.

(a) The provisions of this Article are supplemental to any other provisions of the laws of this State, and do not preclude or limit any other powers or duties of the Commissioner under those laws, including Article 30 of this Chapter.

(b) Risk-based capital instructions, risk-based capital reports, adjusted risk-based capital reports, risk-based capital plans, and revised risk-based capital plans are solely for use by the Commissioner in monitoring the solvency of insurers and the need for possible corrective action with respect to insurers. The Commissioner shall not use any of these reports or plans for rate making nor consider or introduce them as evidence in any rate proceeding. The Commissioner shall not use these reports or plans to calculate or derive any elements of an appropriate premium level or rate of return for any kind of insurance that an insurer or any affiliate is authorized to write.

(c) The Commissioner may exempt from the application of this Article any domestic property or casualty insurer that does all of the following:
  (1) Writes direct business only in this State.
  (2) Writes direct annual premiums of one thousand dollars ($1,000) or less.
  (3) Assumes no reinsurance in excess of five percent (5%) of direct written premiums. (1993 (Reg. Sess., 1994), c. 678, s. 1; 1995, c. 318, s. 6.)

§ 58-12-45. Foreign insurers.

(a) Any foreign insurer shall, upon written request of the Commissioner, submit to the Commissioner a risk-based capital report as of the end of the calendar year just ended the later of:
  (1) The date a risk-based capital report would be required to be filed by a domestic insurer under this Article; or
  (2) Fifteen days after the request is received by the foreign insurer.
Any foreign insurer shall, at the written request of the Commissioner, promptly submit to the Commissioner a copy of any risk-based capital plan that is filed with the insurance regulator of any other state.

(b) In the event of a company action level event, regulatory action level event, or authorized control level event with respect to any foreign insurer as determined under the risk-based capital statute or rule applicable in the state of domicile of the insurer, or if no risk-based capital statute or rule is in force in that state under the provisions of this Article, if the insurance regulator of the state of domicile of the foreign insurer fails to require the foreign insurer to file a risk-based capital plan in the manner specified under the risk-based capital statute or, if no risk-based capital provision is in force in that state, under G.S. 58-12-11, the Commissioner may require the foreign insurer to file a risk-based capital plan with the Commissioner. In that event the failure of the foreign insurer to file a risk-based capital plan with the Commissioner is grounds to order the insurer to cease and desist from writing new insurance business in this State.

(c) In the event of a mandatory control level event with respect to any foreign insurer, if no domiciliary receiver has been appointed with respect to the foreign insurer under the rehabilitation or liquidation statutes of the state of domicile of the foreign insurer, the Commissioner may make application to the Superior Court of Wake County as permitted under Article 30 of this Chapter with respect to the liquidation of property of foreign insurers found in this State; and the occurrence of the mandatory control level event is an adequate ground for the application. (1993 (Reg. Sess., 1994), c. 678, s. 1; 1995, c. 193, s. 23.)

§ 58-12-50. Notices.

All notices by the Commissioner to an insurer that may result in regulatory action under this Article are effective upon dispatch if transmitted by registered or certified mail; or in the case of any other transmission are effective upon the insurer's receipt of the notice. (1993 (Reg. Sess., 1994), c. 678, s. 1.)

§ 58-12-55. Phase-in provision.

For risk-based capital reports required to be filed with respect to 1994, the following requirements apply in lieu of the provisions of G.S. 58-12-11:

    (1) In the event of a company action level event with respect to a domestic insurer, the Commissioner shall take no regulatory action hereunder.

    (2) In the event of a regulatory action level event under G.S. 58-12-16(a)(1), (2), or (3) the Commissioner shall take the actions required under G.S. 58-12-11.

    (3) In the event of a regulatory action level event under G.S. 58-12-16(a)(4), (5), (6), (7), (8), or (9) or an authorized control level event, the Commissioner shall take the actions required under G.S. 58-12-16 with respect to the insurer.

    (4) In the event of a mandatory control level event with respect to an insurer, the Commissioner shall take the actions required under G.S. 58-12-21 with respect to the insurer. (1993 (Reg. Sess., 1994), c. 678, s. 1.)

§ 58-12-60. Property or casualty phase-in provision.

For risk-based capital reports required to be filed by property or casualty insurers with respect to 1995, the following requirements apply in lieu of the provisions of G.S. 58-12-11, 58-12-16, 58-12-21, and 58-12-25:

    (1) In the event of a company action level event with respect to a domestic insurer, the Commissioner shall take no regulatory action under this Article.

    (2) In the event of a regulatory action level event under G.S. 58-12-16(a)(1), (2), or (3), the Commissioner shall take the actions required under G.S. 58-12-11.

    (3) In the event of a regulatory action level event under G.S. 58-12-16(a)(4), (5), (6), (7), (8), or (9), or an authorized control level event, the Commissioner shall take the actions required under G.S. 58-12-16 with respect to the insurer.

(4) In the event of a mandatory control level event with respect to an insurer, the Commissioner shall take the actions required under G.S. 58-12-21 with respect to the insurer. (1995, c. 318, s. 7.)

§ 58-12-65. Health organization phase-in provision.

For risk-based capital reports required to be filed by health organizations with respect to calendar year 2001, the following requirements apply in lieu of the provisions of G.S. 58-12-11, 58-12-16, 58-12-21, and 58-12-25:

(1) In the event of a company action level event with respect to a domestic insurer, the Commissioner shall take no regulatory action under this Article.

(2) In the event of a regulatory action level event under G.S. 58-12-16(a)(1), (2), or (3), the Commissioner shall take the actions required under G.S. 58-12-11.

(3) In the event of a regulatory action level event under G.S. 58-12-16(a)(4), (5), (6), (7), (8) or (9), or an authorized control level event, the Commissioner shall take the actions required under G.S. 58-12-16 with respect to the insurer.

(4) In the event of a mandatory control level event with respect to an insurer, the Commissioner shall take the actions required under G.S. 58-12-21 with respect to the insurer. (2001-223, s. 12.9.)

Editor's Note. — Session Laws 2001-223, s. 28, makes this section effective June 15, 2001.

Session Laws 2001-223, s. 27 is a severability clause.

§ 58-12-70. HMO net worth requirements.

The Commissioner may require an HMO to have and maintain a larger amount of net worth than prescribed in G.S. 58-67-110, based upon the principles of risk-based capital as determined by the NAIC or the Commissioner. (2001-223, s. 12.10.)

Editor's Note. — Session Laws 2001-223, s. 28, makes this section effective June 15, 2001.

Session Laws 2001-223, s. 27 is a severability clause.

ARTICLE 13.

Asset Protection Act.

§ 58-13-1. Title.

This Article shall be known and may be cited as the "Asset Protection Act." (1985, c. 327, s. 1.)

§ 58-13-5. Purposes.

The purposes of this Article are to require insurers to maintain unencumbered assets in amounts equal to policyholder-related liabilities and minimum required capital and minimum required surplus; to provide preferential claims against insurers' assets in favor of owners, beneficiaries, assignees, and holders of insurance policies and certificates; and to prevent the pledging, hypothecation, or encumbrance of assets without a prior written order of the Commissioner. (1985, c. 327, s. 1; 1991, c. 681, s. 30.1; 1993, c. 504, s. 7.)

§ 58-13-10. Scope.

This Article applies to all domestic insurers and to all kinds of insurance written by those insurers under Articles 1 through 68 of this Chapter. Foreign insurers shall comply in substance with the requirements and limitations of this Article. This Article does not apply to the following:

   (1) Variable contracts or guaranteed investment contracts for which separate accounts are required to be maintained.

   (2) Statutory deposits that are required by insurance regulatory agencies to be maintained as a requirement for doing business in such jurisdictions.

   (3) Real estate, authorized under G.S. 58-7-187, encumbered by a mortgage loan with a first lien. (1985, c. 327, s. 1; 1991, c. 681, s. 30.2; 1993, c. 452, s. 25; 1993 (Reg. Sess., 1994), c. 678, s. 13; 1999-244, s. 4; 2001-223, s. 13.1; 2002-187, s. 2.8.)

Effect of Amendments. — Session Laws 2002-187, s. 2.8, effective October 31, 2002, inserted "Articles 1 through 68 of" in the introductory paragraph.

§ 58-13-15. Definitions.

As used in this Article:

   (1) "Assets" means all property, real or personal, tangible or intangible, legal or equitable, owned by an insurer.

   (2) "Claimants" means any owners, beneficiaries, assignees, certificate holders, or third-party beneficiaries of any insurance benefit or right arising out of and within the coverage of an insurance policy covered by this Article.

   (3) "Reserve assets" means those assets of an insurer that are authorized investments for policy reserves in accordance with this Chapter.

   (4) "Policyholder-related liabilities" means those liabilities that are required to be established by an insurer for all of its outstanding insurance policies in accordance with this Chapter. (1985, c. 327, s. 1; 1993, c. 504, s. 8; 2001-223, ss. 13.2, 13.3.)

§ 58-13-20. Exception.

(a) This Article does not apply to those reserve assets of an insurer that are held, deposited, pledged, hypothecated, or otherwise encumbered as provided in this section to secure, offset, protect, or meet those policyholder-related liabilities of the insurer that are established, incurred, or required under the provisions of a reinsurance agreement whereby the insurer has reinsured the insurance policy liabilities of a ceding insurer, provided:

   (1) The ceding insurer and the reinsurer are both licensed to transact business in this State;

   (2) Pursuant to a written agreement between the ceding insurer and the reinsurer, reserve assets substantially equal to the policyholder-related liabilities required to be established by the reinsurer on the reinsured business are either (i) deposited by or are withheld from the reinsurer and are in the custody of the ceding insurer as security for the payment of the reinsurer's obligations under the reinsurance agreement, and such assets are held subject to withdrawal by and under the separate or joint control of the ceding insurer, or (ii) deposited and held in trust account for that purpose and under those conditions with a State or national bank domiciled in this State.

(b) The Commissioner has the right to examine any of such assets, reinsurance agreements, or deposit arrangements at any time in accordance with his authority to make examinations of insurers as conferred by other provisions of this Chapter. (1985, c. 327, s. 1; 1993, c. 504, s. 9; 2001-223, s. 13.4.)

§ 58-13-25. Prohibition of hypothecation.

(a) Every insurer subject to this Article shall at all times have and maintain free and unencumbered reserve assets equal to an amount that is the total of its policyholder-related liabilities and its required minimum capital and minimum surplus and shall not pledge, hypothecate, or otherwise encumber those reserve assets. The Commissioner, upon application made to the Commissioner, may issue a written order approving the pledging, hypothecation, or encumbrance of any of the assets of an insurer not otherwise prohibited upon a finding that the pledging, hypothecation, or encumbrance will not adversely affect the insurer's solvency.

(b) Every insurer shall file, along with any statement filed under G.S. 58-2-165, a statement sworn to by the chief executive officer of the insurer that: (i) Title to assets in an amount equal to the policyholder-related liabilities and minimum required capital and minimum required surplus of the insurer that are not pledged, hypothecated, or otherwise encumbered is vested in the insurer; (ii) the only assets of the insurer that are pledged, hypothecated, or otherwise encumbered are as identified and reported in the sworn statement and no other assets of the insurer are pledged, hypothecated, or otherwise encumbered; and (iii) the terms and provisions of the transaction of the pledge, hypothecation, or encumbrance are as reported in the sworn statement.

(c) Any person that accepts a pledge, hypothecation, or encumbrance of any asset of an insurer, as security for a debt or other obligation of the insurer, not in accordance with this Article, is deemed to have accepted the asset subject to a superior, preferential, and automatically perfected lien in favor of claimants: Provided, that said lien does not apply to the assets of an insurer in a delinquency proceeding under Article 30 of this Chapter if the Commissioner or the court, whichever is appropriate, approves the pledge, hypothecation, or encumbrance of the assets.

(d) In the event of the liquidation of any insurer subject to this Article, claimants of the insurer shall have a prior and preferential claim against all assets of the insurer except those that have been pledged, hypothecated, or encumbered in accordance with this Article. Subject to Article 30 of this Chapter, all claimants have equal status; and their prior and preferential claims are superior to any claim or cause of action against the insurer by any other person. (1985, c. 327, s. 1; 1989, c. 452, s. 4; 1991, c. 681, s. 30.3; 1993, c. 504, s. 10; 2002-187, s. 2.9.)

Effect of Amendments. — Session Laws 2002-187, s. 2.9, effective October 31, 2002, deleted "at least ten percent (10%) more than" following "amount that is" in the first sentence of subsection (a).

ARTICLE 14.

Unauthorized Insurance by Domestic Companies.

§ 58-14-1. Purpose of Article.

It is the purpose of this Article to effectively control and regulate the activities of domestic insurance companies so as to prevent them from engaging in and transacting insurance business in states and jurisdictions in which they are not authorized to do a business of insurance. The General

Assembly recognizes that insofar as domestic companies of this State engage in transacting insurance business in states and jurisdictions in which they are not authorized to do business that such activity subjects the domestic companies of this State to the penalties for such unlawful activities in other states and jurisdictions, and that such activities tend to substantially impair the effectiveness of the domestic companies in this State. The General Assembly also recognizes that the practices of unauthorized insurers could be largely corrected if each state would effectively regulate the activities of its domestic companies. The provisions of this Article are in addition to all other statutory provisions designed to control the activities of domestic companies and nothing herein shall be construed to amend, modify or repeal the provisions of existing laws. (1967, c. 935, s. 1.)

§ 58-14-5. Domestic insurers prohibited from transacting business in foreign states without authorization; exceptions.

Except as hereinafter provided, no domestic insurer organized under the laws of this State shall transact or attempt to transact or solicit business in any manner or accept risks in any jurisdiction in which such insurer is not licensed in accordance with the laws of such jurisdiction. There is excepted from the terms of this section the following acts and transactions:

    (1) Contracts entered into by a domestic company insuring a risk within a foreign state or jurisdiction, where the law of the foreign state or jurisdiction permits an unauthorized insurer to so contract;

    (2) Contracts entered into where the prospective insured is personally present in the state in which the insurer is authorized to transact business when he signs the application;

    (3) Contracts of reinsurance between a licensed insurer of the foreign state or jurisdiction and a domestic company;

    (4) The issuance of certificates under a lawfully transacted group life or group disability policy, where the master policy was entered into in a state in which the insurer was then authorized to transact business;

    (5) The renewal or continuance in force, with or without modification, of contracts otherwise lawful and which were not originally executed in violation of this section. (1967, c. 935, s. 1.)

§ 58-14-10. Domestic insurers; advertising; exceptions.

No domestic insurer shall knowingly solicit or advertise its insurance business in a state or jurisdiction in which it is not licensed as an authorized insurer. Provided, however, that this section shall not prohibit a domestic insurer from advertising through publications, radio or television if such advertising is not expressly directed toward the residents or subjects of insurance in a foreign state or other jurisdiction. Nor shall this section apply to trade journals or directories. (1967, c. 935, s. 1.)

§ 58-14-15. Penalties provided for unauthorized acts.

When any domestic insurer knowingly engages in the practice of soliciting, advertising or making contracts for insurance in states or jurisdictions in which it is not licensed, the Commissioner may issue an order requiring the company to cease and desist from engaging in such activities and, for the purposes of this section, the acts prohibited by G.S. 58-14-10 and the foregoing sections, are declared to be an unfair trade practice within the meaning of G.S. 58-63-15 and G.S. 58-63-40. When the Commissioner has reason to believe that any domestic company has been engaged or is engaging in the practice of knowingly soliciting, advertising or writing contracts of insurance on risks within a state or jurisdiction in which it is not licensed, the Commissioner shall serve the company with notice of hearing and the hearing shall conform with the hearing procedure set forth in G.S. 58-63-25. Any action taken by the Commissioner after the hearing shall comply with G.S. 58-63-32, and any company aggrieved by an order of the Commissioner is entitled to the judicial review provided in G.S. 58-63-35. (1967, c. 935, s. 1; 1991, c. 720, ss. 4, 54; 1995, c. 193, s. 24; 1995 (Reg. Sess., 1996), c. 742, s. 23.)

ARTICLE 15.

Reciprocal Insurance.

Part 1. General Provisions.

§ 58-15-1. Scope.

This Article applies to all reciprocals and reciprocal insurance. (1989, c. 425, s. 1.)

§ 58-15-5. Definitions.

As used in this Article:
(1) "Attorney" means the person designated and authorized by subscribers as the attorney-in-fact having authority to obligate them on reciprocal and other insurance contracts.
(2) "License" means a license to transact the business of insurance in this State, issued by the Commissioner.
(3) In addition to the meaning of the term as defined in G.S. 12-3(6) and G.S. 58-1-5(9), "person" means any county, city, school board, hospital authority, or any other local governmental authority or local agency or public service corporation owned, operated or controlled by a local government or local government authority, that has the power to enter into contractual undertakings within or without the State.
(4) "Reciprocal" means an aggregation of subscribers under a common name.
(5) "Reciprocal insurance" means insurance resulting from the mutual exchange of insurance contracts among persons in an unincorporated association under a common name through an attorney-in-fact having authority to obligate each person both as insured and insurer.
(6) "Subscriber" means a person obligated under a reciprocal insurance agreement. (1989, c. 425, s. 1; 1991, c. 720, s. 15; 1999-132, s. 9.1.)

§ 58-15-10. Kinds of insurance.

A reciprocal licensed in this State may write the kinds of insurance enumerated in G.S. 58-7-15, except life insurance, annuities, and title insurance. (1989, c. 425, s. 1.)

§ 58-15-15. Risk limitations.

(a) Except for Article 11 of this Chapter and as otherwise specifically provided, all the provisions of Articles 1 through 64 of this Chapter relating to insurers generally, and those relating to insurers writing the same kinds of insurance that reciprocals are permitted to write, are applicable to reciprocals.

(b) A reciprocal shall be deemed to comply with G.S. 58-3-105 if:

    (1) It issues policies containing a contingent assessment liability, provided for in G.S. 58-15-60; and

    (2) It maintains reinsurance in an amount that the Commissioner considers adequate to reasonably limit the reciprocal's aggregate losses to the lesser of:

        a. Ten percent (10%) of the surplus to policyholders of the reciprocal multiplied by the number of subscribers;

        b. The surplus to policyholders of the reciprocal multiplied by three; or

        c. Five million dollars ($5,000,000). (1989, c. 425, s. 1.)

§ 58-15-20. Eligible contracting persons.

(a) Persons of this State may enter into reciprocal insurance contracts with each other and with persons of other states and countries.

(b) For any corporation now existing or subsequently organized under the laws of this State, the authority to enter into reciprocal insurance contracts is in addition to the authority conferred upon it in its charter and is incidental to the purposes for which the corporation is organized. (1989, c. 425, s. 1.)

§ 58-15-25. Business name.

Every reciprocal shall have and use an appropriate business name that includes the word or words "reciprocal," "interinsurer," "interinsurance," or "exchange". (1989, c. 425, s. 1.)

§ 58-15-30. License, surplus, and deposit requirements.

(a) No reciprocal shall engage in any insurance transaction in this State until it has obtained a license to do so in accordance with the applicable provisions of Articles 1 through 64 of this Chapter. Such license shall expire on the last day of June of each year.

(b) No domestic or foreign reciprocal shall be licensed in this State unless it has a surplus to policyholders of at least eight hundred thousand dollars ($800,000); and no alien reciprocal shall be licensed unless it has a trusteed surplus of at least eight hundred thousand dollars ($800,000).

(c) Each domestic, foreign, or alien reciprocal licensed in this State must maintain a minimum deposit with the Commissioner of at least one hundred thousand dollars ($100,000) in cash or in value of securities of the kind specified in G.S. 58-5-15, which shall be subject to the same conditions as contained in Article 5 of this Chapter. (1989, c. 425, s. 1.)

Editor's Note. — Session Laws 2003-212, s. 26.(e), effective January 1, 2004, and applicable to all company licenses issued or otherwise eligible for renewal or continuation after that date, amended G.S. 58-6-30(a) by rewriting the last sentence to read as follows: "The license shall continue in full force and effect, subject to timely payment of an annual license continuation fee in accordance with G.S. 58-6-7 and subject to any other applicable provisions of the insurance laws of this state." There is no G.S. 58-6-30, and the apparent intent of the General Assembly was to amend G.S. 58-15-30(a). Subsection (a) has been set out in the form above at the direction of the Revisor of Statutes.

§ 58-15-35. Continuation of business under prior requirements.

(a) Notwithstanding other provisions of Articles 1 through 64 of this Chapter regarding minimum required surplus, any reciprocal that was licensed to write and was writing any kind of insurance in this State on January 1, 1990 may continue to write that kind of insurance under the appropriate license from the Commissioner. Such reciprocal shall maintain at all times the minimum surplus, and the minimum trusteed surplus if an alien reciprocal, that was required before January 1, 1990.

(b) Before any reciprocal obtains a license to write in this State any kind of insurance that it was not licensed to write and writing in this State on January 1, 1990, it shall comply with all the requirements of this Part regarding surplus. (1989, c. 425, s. 1.)

§ 58-15-40. Certification of foreign and alien reciprocals.

No foreign reciprocal shall be licensed in this State until it files with the Commissioner a certificate of the insurance regulator of the state in which it is organized. The certificate shall show that the foreign reciprocal is licensed to write and is writing actively in that state the kind of insurance it proposes to write in this State. No alien reciprocal shall be licensed in this State until it files with the Commissioner a certificate of the insurance regulator of (i) the state through which it entered the United States or (ii) the alien reciprocal's domiciliary country. The certificate shall show that the alien reciprocal is licensed to write and is writing actively in that state or country the kind of insurance it proposes to write in this State. Foreign and alien reciprocals must also satisfy the appropriate provisions of Article 16 of this Chapter pertaining to admission requirements. (1989, c. 425, s. 1.)

§ 58-15-45. Attorney's domicile.

Nothing in Articles 1 through 64 of this Chapter regarding the admission and licensing of foreign and alien insurers requires that the attorney of a foreign or alien reciprocal be resident or domiciled in this State, or that the principal office of the attorney be maintained in this State. The office or offices of the attorney shall be determined by the subscribers through the power of attorney. (1989, c. 425, s. 1.)

§ 58-15-50. Contracts and property.

A reciprocal may enter into contracts and acquire, hold title to, and convey property in its business name. All contracts of a reciprocal, including its insurance contracts, shall be executed on behalf of the reciprocal by the attorney of the reciprocal. (1989, c. 425, s. 1.)

§ 58-15-55. Agent's license.

No person shall act in this State as an agent of a reciprocal in the solicitation or procurement of applications for insurance, subscriber's agreements, or powers of attorney, or in the collection of premiums in connection with the reciprocal, without first procuring an agent's license from the Commissioner pursuant to Article 33 of this Chapter. An agent shall be appointed by each reciprocal the agent represents. (1989, c. 425, s. 1.)

§ 58-15-60. Subscribers' contingent liability.

(a) Each subscriber insured under an assessable policy has a contingent assessment liability for payment of actual losses and expenses incurred by the reciprocal while his policy was in force. This liability is in the amount provided for in the power of attorney or subscriber's agreement.

(b) The contingent assessment liability on any one policy in any one calendar year equals the premiums earned, as defined in G.S. 58-15-135, on the policy for that year multiplied by not more than ten.

(c) The contingent assessment liability is several and not joint.

(d) Each assessable policy issued by the reciprocal shall plainly set forth a statement of the contingent assessment liability on the front of the policy in capital letters, in contrasting color, and in no less than ten-point type. (1989, c. 425, s. 1.)

§ 58-15-65. Nonassessable policies.

(a) The Commissioner may issue a certificate authorizing the reciprocal to reduce or extinguish the contingent assessment liability of subscribers under its policies then in force in this State and to omit provisions imposing contingent assessment liability in all policies delivered or issued for delivery in this State for as long as all such surplus to policyholders remains unimpaired. The certificate may be issued if (i) a reciprocal has surplus to policyholders of at least two million dollars ($2,000,000), and (ii) an application of the attorney has been approved by the subscribers' advisory committee.

(b) The Commissioner shall issue this certificate if the conditions of subsection (a) of this section are met and if he determines that the reciprocal's surplus to policyholders is reasonable in relation to the reciprocal's outstanding liabilities and is adequate to meet its financial needs. In making that determination the following factors, among others, shall be considered:

    (1) The size of the reciprocal as measured by its assets, capital and surplus, reserves, premium writings, insurance in force, and other appropriate criteria;

    (2) The extent to which the reciprocal's business is diversified among different kinds of insurance;

    (3) The number and size of risks insured in each kind of insurance;

    (4) The extent of the geographic dispersion of the reciprocal's insured risks;

    (5) The nature and extent of the reciprocal's reinsurance program;

    (6) The quality, diversification, and liquidity of the reciprocal's investment portfolio;

    (7) The recent past and trend in the size of the reciprocal's surplus to policyholders;

    (8) The surplus to policyholders maintained by other comparable insurers; and

    (9) The adequacy of the reciprocal's reserves.

(c) Upon impairment of the surplus to policyholders as described in subsection (a) of this section, the Commissioner shall revoke the certificate. After revocation, the reciprocal shall not issue or renew any policy without providing for the contingent assessment liability of subscribers.

(d) The Commissioner shall not authorize a domestic reciprocal to extinguish the contingent assessment liability of any of its subscribers or in any of its policies to be issued, unless it has the required surplus to policyholders and extinguishes the contingent assessment liability of all of its subscribers and in all policies to be issued for all kinds of insurance it writes. However, if required by the laws of another state in which the domestic reciprocal is transacting the business of insurance as a licensed insurer, it may issue policies providing for the contingent assessment liability of its subscribers that acquire policies in that state and need not extinguish the contingent assessment liability applicable to policies already in force in that state. (1989, c. 425, s. 1.)

§ 58-15-70. Distribution to subscribers.

A reciprocal may return to its subscribers any savings or credits accruing to their accounts. Any such distribution shall not unfairly discriminate between classes of risks or policies or between subscribers. However, the distribution may vary for classes of subscribers based upon the experience of those classes. (1989, c. 425, s. 1.)

§ 58-15-75. Reserves.

Each reciprocal shall maintain the same unearned premium and loss or claim reserves required for stock and mutual companies writing the same kinds of insurance. (1989, c. 425, s. 1.)

§ 58-15-80: Reserved for future codification purposes.

§ 58-15-85. Service of process.

(a) Each attorney of a domestic reciprocal who files the declaration required by G.S. 58-15-100, and each attorney of a foreign or alien reciprocal that applies for a license, shall file with the Commissioner a written power of attorney executed in duplicate by the attorney that appoints the Commissioner as agent of the reciprocal. Upon the appointment, the Commissioner may be served all legal process against such reciprocal pursuant to G.S. 58-16-30. A copy of the power of attorney, duly certified by the Commissioner, is admissible as evidence in the courts of this State.

(b) Whenever any such process is served upon the Commissioner, G.S. 58-16-45 is applicable, except that the process shall be directed to the attorney at the address shown on the power of attorney. Nothing in this section limits the right to serve any process upon any reciprocal in any other manner permitted by law. (1989, c. 425, s. 1.)

§ 58-15-90. Legal proceedings.

(a) Any reciprocal doing business in this State may sue or be sued in its business name.

(b) Any action or suit against a reciprocal may be brought in any county (i) where its principal office is located, or (ii) where the cause of action or any part of the cause of action arose. If the action or suit is to recover a loss under a policy of property insurance, it may also be brought in the county where the property insured was situated at the date of the policy. Any action or suit against a foreign or alien reciprocal may also be brought in any county of this State in which it has any debts owed to it.

(c) In an action against a reciprocal, process against the reciprocal may be served upon the Commissioner. If the defendant in the action is a domestic reciprocal, process against that domestic reciprocal shall be served upon the attorney for that domestic reciprocal unless service upon that attorney is not feasible. (1989, c. 425, s. 1.)

§ 58-15-95. Liability on judgments.

Any judgment against a reciprocal based upon legal process duly served as provided in this Article is binding upon the reciprocal and upon each of the reciprocal's subscribers as their respective interests may appear, in an amount not exceeding their respective contingent assessment liabilities. There is no derivative liability on the part of the attorney, officers, employees, agents, or subscribers' advisory committee of the reciprocal arising merely by reason of the status of such persons. (1989, c. 425, s. 1.)

Part 2. Domestic Reciprocals.

§ 58-15-100. Declaration for license.

(a) One hundred or more persons domiciled in this State and designated as subscribers may organize a domestic reciprocal and apply to the Commissioner for a license to transact the business of insurance. The Commissioner may authorize such a reciprocal to form with a lesser number of subscribers upon being satisfied that the risks are adequately spread and financial projections indicate that such a reciprocal will have a reasonable potential to succeed in its business with such a lesser number of subscribers. The original subscribers and the proposed attorney shall execute and file with the Commissioner a declaration setting forth:

    (1) The name of the attorney and the business name of the reciprocal;

    (2) The location of the reciprocal's principal office, which shall be the same as that of the attorney and shall be in this State;

    (3) The kinds of insurance proposed to be written;

    (4) The names and addresses of the original subscribers;

    (5) The designation and appointment of the attorney, and a copy of the power of attorney and subscriber's agreement;

    (6) The names and addresses of the officers and directors of the attorney, if a corporation, or of its members if not a corporation;

    (7) The powers of the subscribers' advisory committee, and the names and terms of office of its members;

    (8) A statement that each of the original subscribers has in good faith applied for insurance of the kind proposed to be written and that the reciprocal has received from each original subscriber the anticipated premium or premium deposit for a term of not less than six months for the policy for which application is made;

    (9) A statement of the financial condition of the reciprocal, including a schedule of its assets;

    (10) A statement that the reciprocal has the surplus to policyholders required by G.S. 58-15-30;

    (11) A copy of each policy, endorsement, and application form it proposes to issue or use; and

    (12) Financial projections of the anticipated operational results of the reciprocal for a five-year period based upon the initial surplus of the proposed reciprocal and its plan of operation.

(b) The declaration shall be acknowledged by each original subscriber and by the attorney. (1989, c. 425, s. 1.)

§ 58-15-105. Attorney's bond.

(a) Concurrent with the filing of the declaration provided for in G.S. 58-15-100, the attorney of a domestic reciprocal shall file with the Commissioner a fidelity bond payable to this State. The bond shall be executed by the attorney and by a licensed insurer and is subject to the approval of the Commissioner.

(b) The bond shall be in an amount established in the discretion of the Commissioner, which amount shall be at least fifty thousand dollars ($50,000). The bond shall be on the condition that the attorney faithfully accounts for all moneys and other property of the reciprocal coming into the attorney's control and that the attorney does not withdraw or appropriate for his own use from the funds of the reciprocal any moneys or property to which he is not entitled under the power of attorney.

(c) The bond is not subject to cancellation unless 30-days' written notice of intent to cancel is given to the attorney and the Commissioner. (1989, c. 425, s. 1.)

§ 58-15-110. Deposit in lieu of bond.

Instead of filing the bond required by G.S. 58-15-105, the attorney may maintain on deposit with the Commissioner an equal amount in cash or in value of securities of the kind specified in G.S. 58-5-20 and subject to the same conditions as the bond. (1989, c. 425, s. 1.)

§ 58-15-115. Advisory committee.

The advisory committee exercising the subscribers' rights in a domestic reciprocal shall be selected under rules adopted by the subscribers. At least three-fourths of the committee shall comprise subscribers or their representatives other than the attorney or any person employed by, representing, or having a financial interest in the attorney. The committee shall supervise the finances of the reciprocal and the reciprocal's operations to the extent required to assure their conformity with the subscriber's agreement and power of attorney and shall exercise any other powers conferred on it by the subscriber's agreement. (1989, c. 425, s. 1.)

§ 58-15-120. Subscriber's agreement and power of attorney.

(a) Every subscriber of a domestic reciprocal shall execute a subscriber's agreement and power of attorney setting forth the rights, privileges, and obligations of the subscriber as an underwriter and as a policyholder, and the powers and duties of the attorney. The subscriber's agreement and power of attorney shall contain in substance the following provisions:

    (1) A designation and appointment of the attorney to act for and bind the subscriber in all transactions relating to or arising out of the operations of the reciprocal;

    (2) A provision empowering the attorney (i) to accept service of legal process on behalf of the reciprocal and (ii) to appoint the Commissioner agent of the reciprocal upon whom may be served all legal process against the reciprocal;

    (3) Except for nonassessable policies, a provision for a contingent assessment liability of each subscriber in a specified amount in accordance with G.S. 58-15-60; and

    (4) The maximum amount to be deducted from advance premiums or deposits to be paid the attorney, and the items of expense, in addition to losses, to be paid by the reciprocal.

(b) The subscriber's agreement may:

    (1) Provide for the right of substitution of the attorney and revocation of the power of attorney;

(2) Impose any restrictions upon the exercise of the power agreed upon by the subscribers;

(3) Provide for the exercise of any right reserved to the subscribers directly or through an advisory committee;

(4) Provide for indemnification of the attorney, officers, employees, agents, and subscribers' advisory committee of the reciprocal against liability and litigation expenses to the extent permitted in the case of domestic business corporations; or

(5) Contain other lawful provisions considered advisable. (1989, c. 425, s. 1.)

§ 58-15-125. Modification of subscriber's agreement and power of attorney.

Modification of the terms of the subscriber's agreement and the power of attorney of a domestic reciprocal shall be made jointly by the attorney and the subscriber's advisory committee. No modification is retroactive nor does it affect any insurance contract issued prior to the modification. (1989, c. 425, s. 1.)

§ 58-15-130. Advance of funds.

The attorney or other interested persons may advance to a domestic reciprocal any funds required for its operations. The funds advanced shall not be treated as a liability of the reciprocal and shall not be withdrawn or repaid except out of the reciprocal's earned surplus in excess of its minimum required surplus. This section does not apply to loans made by commercial lenders in the ordinary course of their businesses. (1989, c. 425, s. 1.)

§ 58-15-135. Assessments.

(a) Assessments may be levied upon the subscribers of a domestic reciprocal by the attorney in accordance with G.S. 58-15-60. The assessments shall be approved in advance by the subscribers' advisory committee.

(b) Each domestic reciprocal subscriber's share of an assessment shall be computed by multiplying the premiums earned on the subscriber's policies during the period to be covered by the assessment by the ratio of the total assessment to the total premiums earned during the period upon all policies subject to the assessment. However, no assessment shall exceed the aggregate contingent assessment liability computed in accordance with G.S. 58-15-60. For the purposes of this section, the premiums earned on the subscriber's policies are the gross premiums charged by the reciprocal for the policies minus any charges not recurring upon the renewal or extension of the policies. No subscriber shall have an offset against any assessment for which he is liable on account of any claim for unearned premium or losses payable. (1989, c. 425, s. 1.)

§ 58-15-140. Duration of liability for assessment.

Every subscriber of a domestic reciprocal having contingent assessment liability shall be liable for and shall pay his share of any assessment computed in accordance with this Part, if, while the policy is in force or for such period after its termination as the Commissioner may establish by rule, the subscriber is notified (i) by the attorney of his intention to levy the assessment or (ii) that delinquency proceedings have been commenced against the reciprocal under the provisions of Article 30 of this Chapter, and the Commissioner or receiver intends to levy an assessment. In adopting such rules the Commissioner may take into account factors including the kinds of insurance issued by such reciprocals. (1989, c. 425, s. 1; c. 770, s. 70; 1989 (Reg. Sess., 1990), c. 1021, s. 1.)

§ 58-15-145. Distribution of assets after liquidation.

Upon the liquidation of a domestic reciprocal, the assets remaining after (i) discharge of its indebtedness and policy obligations, (ii) the return of any contributions of the attorney or other person made as provided in G.S. 58-15-130, and (iii) the return of any unused deposits, savings, or credits, shall be distributed. The distribution shall be according to a formula approved by the Commissioner or the Court to the persons who were its subscribers within the 12 months prior to the final termination of its license. (1989, c. 425, s. 1.)

§ 58-15-150. Financial impairment; assessment; liquidation.

(a) If (i) the assets of a domestic reciprocal are at any time insufficient to settle the sum of its liabilities, except those on account of funds contributed by the attorney or other parties, and its required surplus to policyholders, and (ii) the deficiency is not cured from other sources, its attorney shall levy an assessment upon subscribers made subject to assessment by the terms of their policies for the amount needed to make up the deficiency. However, the assessment shall be subject to G.S. 58-15-60.

(b) If the attorney fails to make the assessment within 30 days after the Commissioner orders him to do so, or if the deficiency is not fully made up within 60 days after the date the assessment is made, delinquency proceedings may be instituted and conducted against the insurer as provided in Article 30 of this Chapter.

(c) If liquidation of the reciprocal is ordered, an assessment shall be levied upon the subscribers for the amount the Commissioner or the Court, as the case may be, determines to be necessary to discharge all liabilities of the reciprocal. This assessment shall exclude any funds contributed by the attorney or other persons, but shall include the reasonable cost of the liquidation. However, the assessment is subject to G.S. 58-15-60. (1989, c. 425, s. 1; c. 770, s. 71.)

ARTICLE 16.

Foreign or Alien Insurance Companies.

§ 58-16-1. Admitted to do business.

Foreign or alien insurance companies, upon complying with the conditions of Articles 1 through 64 of this Chapter applicable to them, may be admitted to transact in this State any class of insurance authorized by the laws in force relative to the duties, obligations, prohibitions, and penalties of insurance companies, and subject to all laws applicable to the transaction of such business by foreign or alien insurance companies and their agents. (1899, c. 54, s. 61; Rev., s. 4746; C.S., s. 6410; 1945, c. 384; 1987, c. 629, s. 17.)

When a foreign insurance company has complied with all the laws of the State, the courts thereof are open to it for the purpose of enforcing the liabilities of policyholders.

Commonwealth Mut. Fire Ins. Co. v. Edwards & Broughton, 124 N.C. 116, 32 S.E. 404 (1899).

Cited in Hodges v. Home Ins. Co., 232 N.C. 475, 61 S.E.2d 372 (1950).

§ 58-16-5. Conditions of licensure.

A foreign or alien insurance company may be licensed to do business when it:

(1) Deposits with the Commissioner a certified copy of its charter or certificate of organization and a statement of its financial condition and business, in the form and detail that the Commissioner requires, signed and sworn to by its president and secretary or other proper officer, and pays for the filing of this statement the sum required by law.

(2) Satisfies the Commissioner that it is fully and legally organized under the laws of its state or government to do the business it proposes to transact as direct insurance or assumed reinsurance, and that it has been successful in the conduct of the business; that it has, if a stock company, a free surplus and a fully paid-up and unimpaired capital, exclusive of stockholders' obligations of any description of an amount not less than that required for the organization of a domestic company writing the same kinds of business; and if a mutual company that its free surplus is not less than that required for the organization of a domestic company writing the same kind of business, and that the capital, surplus, and other funds are invested substantially in accordance with the requirements of this Chapter.

(3) Repealed by Session Laws 1995, c. 517, s. 6.

(4) Repealed by Session Laws 1987, c. 629, s. 20.

(5) Files with the Commissioner a certificate that it has complied with the laws of the state or government under which it was organized and is authorized to make contracts of insurance.

(6) Satisfies the Commissioner that it is in substantial compliance with G.S. 58-7-21, 58-7-26, 58-7-30, and 58-7-31 and Article 13 of this Chapter.

(7) Satisfies the Commissioner that it is in compliance with the company name requirements of G.S. 58-7-35.

(8) Satisfies the Commissioner that the operation of the company in this State would not be hazardous to prospective policyholders, creditors, or the general public.

(9) Satisfies the Commissioner that it is in substantial compliance with the requirements of G.S. 58-7-37 pertaining to the background of its officers and directors.

(10) Files with the Commissioner an instrument appointing the Commissioner as the company's agent on whom any legal process under G.S. 58-16-30 may be served. This appointment is irrevocable as long as any liability of the company remains outstanding in this State. A copy of this instrument, certified by the Commissioner, is sufficient evidence of this appointment; and service upon the Commissioner is sufficient service upon the company. (1899, c. 54, s. 62; 1901, c. 391, s. 5; 1903, c. 438, s. 6; Rev., s. 4747; C.S., s. 6411; 1945, c. 384; 1951, c. 781, s. 3; 1985 (Reg. Sess., 1986), c. 1027, s. 32; 1987, c. 629, s. 20; 1987 (Reg. Sess., 1988), c. 975, s. 16; 1991, c. 681, s. 24; 1995, c. 193, s. 25; c. 517, s. 6; 1999-294, s. 7; 2001-223, s. 14.1.)

Cross References. — As to deposits required of foreign companies, see G.S. 58-5-5 et seq. and 58-11-25.

Legal Periodicals. — For brief comment on the 1951 amendment, see 29 N.C.L. Rev. 398 (1951).

CASE NOTES

This section prescribes the conditions for a foreign insurance company to be admitted and authorized to do business in North Carolina. Crain & Denbo, Inc. v. Harris & Harris Constr. Co., 250 N.C. 106, 108 S.E.2d 122 (1959).

Statement Setting Forth Principal Place of Business, etc., Not Required. — This section does not require a foreign insurance corporation desiring to be admitted and authorized to do business in North Carolina to file a statement in the office of the Commissioner of Insurance setting forth its "principal place of business" or "principal office" or "a registered office." Crain & Denbo, Inc. v. Harris & Harris Constr. Co., 250 N.C. 106, 108 S.E.2d 122 (1959).

Effect of Appointment of Commissioner as Attorney for Service of Process. — When an insurance company, pursuant to this section, designates the Commissioner of Insurance its true and lawful attorney upon whom all lawful processes in any action against it may be served, it creates "a passive agency" for the service of lawful process alone, and the statute gives no authority to the Commissioner even to accept service of process. It provides residents of this State a simple procedure to be followed in obtaining service of lawful process upon foreign insurance companies doing business here, and nothing more. Crain & Denbo, Inc. v. Harris & Harris Constr. Co., 250 N.C. 106, 108 S.E.2d 122 (1959).

The Commissioner of Insurance is not authorized to accept service for foreign insurance companies under the provisions of this section, the passive agency under this section being solely for the purpose of constituting him an agent upon whom service on foreign insurance companies may be made in the statutory manner. Hodges v. Homes Ins. Co., 232 N.C. 475, 61 S.E.2d 372 (1950).

Irrevocability of Power of Attorney for Service of Process. — This section requires the power of attorney executed to the Commissioner of Insurance to be irrevocable as long as "any liability of the company remains outstanding" in this State. Biggs v. Life Ass'n, 128 N.C. 5, 37 S.E. 955 (1901); Insurance Co. v. Scott, 136 N.C. 157, 48 S.E. 581 (1904).

Service of process upon the Commissioner of Insurance was valid notwithstanding the insurance company attempted to annul the power of attorney conferred upon him under this section. Biggs v. Life Ass'n, 128 N.C. 5, 37 S.E. 955 (1901).

Service on the Commissioner is not valid when the insurance company has ceased doing business in the State and has no further liabilities therein. Williams v. Mutual Reserve Fund Life Ins. Ass'n, 145 N.C. 128, 58 S.E. 802 (1907).

Broker as Agent. — Where a citizen of this State applied for a policy in a foreign company through a broker here, and the application was accepted and the policy was delivered, the broker would be deemed to be the agent of the company, and the contract to be made here, subject to the laws of this State. Commonwealth Mut. Fire Ins. Co. v. Edwards & Broughton, 124 N.C. 116, 32 S.E. 404 (1899).

Power of Corporation to Sue and Be Sued. — Where a foreign insurance corporation has fully complied with the provisions of this section, and has moved its head office to this State and has domesticated here, it acquires the right to sue and be sued in the courts of this State as a domestic corporation. Occidental Life Ins. Co. v. Lawrence, 204 N.C. 707, 169 S.E. 636 (1933).

When an insurance company complies with the provisions of this section, it acquires the right to sue and be sued in the State courts, under the rules and statutes which apply to domestic corporations. Crain & Denbo, Inc. v. Harris & Harris Constr. Co., 250 N.C. 106, 108 S.E.2d 122 (1959).

General rule is that a domesticated foreign corporation is treated like a domestic corporation for venue purposes. Travelers Indem. Co. v. Marshburn, 91 N.C. App. 271, 371 S.E.2d 310 (1988).

Cited in Fuller v. Lockhart, 209 N.C. 61, 182 S.E. 733 (1935).

§ 58-16-6. Conditions of continued licensure.

In order for a foreign insurance company to continue to be licensed, it shall report any changes in the documents filed under G.S. 58-16-5(1) or G.S. 58-16-5(5), maintain the amounts of capital and surplus specified in G.S. 58-16-5(2), and remain in substantial compliance with the statutes listed in G.S. 58-16-5(6), (7), and (8). (1995, c. 517, s. 7; 2001-223, s. 14.2.)

§ 58-16-10. Limitation as to kinds of insurance.

Any foreign or alien company admitted to do business in this State shall be limited with respect to doing kinds of insurance in this State in the same manner and to the same extent as are domestic companies, provided that any foreign insurance company which has been licensed to do the business of life insurance in this State continuously during a period of 20 years next preceding March 6, 1945, may continue to be licensed, in the discretion of the Commissioner, to do the kind or kinds of insurance business which it was authorized to do immediately prior to March 6, 1945. (1899, c. 44, s. 65; 1901, c. 391, s. 5; 1903, c. 438, s. 6; Rev., s. 4748; 1911, c. 111, s. 2; C.S., s. 6412; 1945, c. 384; 1985 (Reg. Sess., 1986), c. 1027, s. 53; 1987 (Reg. Sess., 1988), c. 975, s. 17.)

§ 58-16-15. Foreign companies; requirements for admission.

A company organized under the laws of any other of these United States for the transaction of life insurance may be admitted to do business in this State if it complies with the other provisions of Articles 1 through 64 of this Chapter regulating the terms and conditions upon which foreign life insurance companies may be admitted and authorized to do business in this State, and, in the opinion of the Commissioner, is in sound financial condition and has policies in force upon not less than 500 lives for an aggregate amount of not less than five hundred thousand dollars ($500,000). Any life company organized under the laws of any other country than the United States, in addition to the above requirements, must make and maintain the deposit required of such companies by Article 5 of this Chapter. (1899, c. 54, s. 56; Rev., s. 4774; C.S., s. 6456; 1945, c. 379; 1991, c. 720, ss. 4, 16.)

§ 58-16-20. Company owned or controlled by foreign government prohibited from doing business.

(a) Any insurance company or other insurance entity that is owned or controlled by any foreign government outside the continental limits of the United States or the territories of the United States is prohibited from doing any kind of insurance business in the State of North Carolina. For the purposes of this section, "foreign government" means any foreign government or any state, province, municipality, or political subdivision of any foreign government, and shall not be construed to apply to any insurance company organized under the laws of a foreign nation that is owned or controlled by the private citizens or private business interest of that foreign nation.

(b) The Commissioner shall not license any insurance company or other insurance entity that is owned or controlled by any foreign government outside the continental limits of the United States or the territories of the United States, nor shall the Commissioner authorize any such company or entity to transact any kind of insurance business in the State of North Carolina.

(c) Any insurance company or other insurance entity that is owned or controlled by any foreign government outside the continental limits of the United States or the territories of the United States, or any representative or agent of any such company or entity that violates the provisions of this section, is guilty of a Class 3 misdemeanor.

(d) This section does not apply to the operating subsidiary of any insurance company or other insurance entity, where the company or entity is owned or controlled by any foreign government outside the continental limits of the United States or the territories of the United States, as long as the operating subsidiary is domesticated in and licensed by another state of the United

States as an insurer or reinsurer and as a separate subsidiary. (1955, c. 449; 1991, c. 720, s. 4; 1993, c. 539, s. 449; 1994, Ex. Sess., c. 24, s. 14(c); 1997-179, s. 1.)

§ 58-16-25. Retaliatory laws.

When, by the laws of any other state or nation, any fines, penalties, licenses, fees, deposits of money or of securities, or other obligations or prohibitions are imposed upon insurance companies of this State doing business in such other state or nation or upon their agents therein greater than those imposed by this State upon insurance companies of such other state, then, so long as such laws continue in force, the same fines, penalties, licenses, fees, deposits, obligations and prohibitions, of whatever kind, may in the discretion of the Commissioner be imposed upon all such insurance companies of such other state or nation doing business within this State and upon their agents here. Nothing herein repeals or reduces the license, fees, taxes, and other obligations now imposed by the laws of this State or to go into effect with the companies of any other state or nation unless some company of this State is actually doing or seeking to do business in such state or nation. When an insurance company organized under the laws of any state or country is prohibited by the laws of such state or country or by its charter from investing its assets other than capital stock in the bonds of this State, then and in such case the Commissioner is authorized and directed to refuse to grant a license to transact business in this State to such insurance company. (1899, c. 54, s. 71; 1903, c. 536, s. 11; Rev., s. 4749; C.S., s. 6413; 1927, c. 32; 1945, c. 384; 1987, c. 814, s. 3; 1991, c. 720, s. 4.)

CASE NOTES

This section was not impliedly repealed by the Revenue Acts of 1923 or 1925 (Public Laws 1923, c. 4, G.S. 903; 1925, c. 101, G.S. 903). The 1927 amendment was legislative recognition that it was still in force. Atlantic Life Ins. Co. v. Wade, 195 N.C. 424, 142 S.E. 474 (1928).

Cited in State Farm Mut. Auto. Ins. Co. v. Long, 129 N.C. App. 164, 497 S.E.2d 451 (1998), aff'd, 350 N.C. 84, 511 S.E.2d 303 (1999).

§ 58-16-30. Service of legal process upon Commissioner.

As an alternative to service of legal process under G.S. 1A-1, Rule 4, the service of such process upon any insurance company or any foreign or alien entity licensed or admitted and authorized to do business in this State under the provisions of this Chapter may be made by the sheriff or any other person delivering and leaving a copy of the process in the office of the Commissioner with a deputy or any other person duly appointed by the Commissioner for that purpose; or acceptance of service of the process may be made by the Commissioner or a duly appointed deputy or person. Service may also be made by mailing a copy of the summons and of the complaint, registered or certified mail, return receipt requested, addressed to the Commissioner. As a condition precedent to a valid service of process under this section, the party obtaining such service shall pay to the Commissioner at the time of service or acceptance of service the sum of ten dollars ($10.00), which the party shall recover as part of the taxable costs if the party prevails in the action. (1899, c. 54, ss. 16, 62; 1903, c. 438, s. 6; Rev., s. 4750; C.S., s. 6414; 1927, c. 167, s. 1; 1931, c. 287; 1951, c. 781, s. 9; 1971, c. 421, s. 1; 1985, c. 666, s. 5; 1989, c. 645, s. 2; 1991, c. 720, s. 4; 1995, c. 517, s. 8.)

Cross References. — As to service on foreign corporations, see G.S. 55-15-10.

Legal Periodicals. — For brief comment on the 1951 amendment, see 29 N.C.L. Rev. 398 (1951).

CASE NOTES

Appointment of Commissioner as Attorney to Receive Process as Condition Precedent to Doing Business. — One of the conditions precedent upon which a foreign insurance company is authorized to do business in this State is that such company will file a duly executed instrument with the Commissioner of Insurance appointing him its attorney, upon whom all lawful process against said company can be served. Biggs v. Life Ass'n, 128 N.C. 5, 37 S.E. 955 (1901). See § 58-16-5.

Irrevocability of Power of Attorney. — The service of a licensed insurance company made upon the Commissioner was valid even though the insurance company may have attempted to annul the power of attorney, for the statute requires power of attorney to be irrevocable so long as the insurance company has any liabilities in the State. Biggs v. Life Ass'n, 128 N.C. 5, 37 S.E. 955 (1901); Moore v. Mutual Reserve Fund Life Ass'n, 129 N.C. 31, 39 S.E. 637 (1901); Hinton v. Mutual Reserve Fund Life Ass'n, 135 N.C. 314, 47 S.E. 474 (1904).

To serve legal process under this section, an insurance company must be licensed or admitted and authorized to do business in this State. Parris v. Garner Com. Disposal, Inc., 40 N.C. App. 282, 253 S.E.2d 29, cert. denied, 297 N.C. 455, 256 S.E.2d 808 (1979).

Service can be made under this section only on licensed insurance companies. Parker v. Insurance Co., 143 N.C. 339, 55 S.E. 717 (1906).

A foreign insurance company that has no process agent in this State and is not licensed or transacting business here cannot be served with process under this section. Ivy River Land & Timber Co. v. National Fire & Marine Ins. Co., 192 N.C. 115, 133 S.E. 424 (1926).

Fraternal Society. — In an action against a foreign fraternal insurance society doing business in this State, service of summons on the Commissioner of Insurance would bring the corporation into court. Brenizer v. Royal Arcanum, 141 N.C. 409, 53 S.E. 835 (1906).

Applied in Fulton v. Mickle, 134 N.C. App. 620, 518 S.E.2d 518 (1999).

Cited in Hodges v. Home Ins. Co., 232 N.C. 475, 61 S.E.2d 372 (1950); Hodges v. Carter, 239 N.C. 517, 80 S.E.2d 144 (1954).

§ 58-16-35. Unauthorized Insurers Process Act.

(a) Purpose of Section. — The purpose of this section is to subject certain insurers to the jurisdiction of courts of this State in suits by or on behalf of insureds or beneficiaries under insurance contracts. The General Assembly declares that it is a subject of concern that many residents of this State hold policies of insurance issued by insurers not authorized to do business in this State, thus presenting to such residents the often insuperable obstacle of resorting to distant forums for the purpose of asserting legal rights under such policies. In furtherance of such State interest, the General Assembly herein provides a method of substituted service of process upon such insurers and declares that in so doing it exercises its power to protect its residents and to define, for the purpose of this statute, what constitutes doing business in this State, and also exercises powers and privileges available to the State by virtue of Public Law 15, 79th Congress of the United States, Chapter 20, 1st Session, s. 340, as amended, which declares that the business of insurance and every person engaged therein shall be subject to the laws of the several states.

(b) Service of Process upon Unauthorized Insurer. —

(1) Any of the following acts in this State, effected by mail or otherwise, by an unauthorized foreign or alien insurer:

a. The issuance or delivery of contracts of insurance to residents of this State or to corporations authorized to do business therein,

b. The solicitation of applications for such contracts,

c. The collection of premiums, membership fees, assessments or other considerations for such contracts, or

d. Any other transaction of business,

is equivalent to and shall constitute an appointment by such insurer of the Commissioner and his successor or successors in office, to be its true and lawful attorney, upon whom may be served all lawful process in any action, suit, or proceeding instituted by or on behalf of an insured or beneficiary arising out of any such contract of insurance, and any such act shall be signification of its agreement that such service of process is of the same legal force and validity as personal service of process in this State upon such insurer.

(2) Such service of process shall be made by delivering to and leaving with the Commissioner or some person in apparent charge of his office two copies thereof and the payment to him of ten dollars ($10.00). The Commissioner shall within four business days mail by certified or registered mail one of the copies of such process to the defendant at its last known principal place of business, and shall keep a record of all process so served upon him. Such service of process is sufficient, provided notice of such service and a copy of the process are sent within 10 days thereafter by certified or registered mail by plaintiff or plaintiff's attorney to the defendant at its last known principal place of business, and the defendant's receipt, or receipt issued by the transmitting post office, showing the name of the sender of the letter and the name and address of the person to whom the letter is addressed, and the affidavit of the plaintiff or plaintiff's attorney showing a compliance herewith are filed with the clerk of the court in which such action is pending on or before the date the defendant is required to appear, or within such further time as the court may allow.

(3) Service of process in any such action, suit or proceeding shall in addition to the manner provided in subdivision (2) of this subsection be valid if:

a. It is served on a person within this State who is in the State on behalf of the insurer to solicit insurance, make, issue, or deliver a contract of insurance, or collect or receive a premium, membership fee, assessment, or other consideration for insurance;

b. A copy of the process is sent within 10 days after service by certified or registered mail by the plaintiff or plaintiff's attorney to the defendant at the defendant's last known principal place of business; and

c. The defendant's receipt, or the receipt issued by the transmitting post office, showing the name of the sender of the letter and the name and address of the person to whom the letter is addressed, and the affidavit of the plaintiff or plaintiff's attorney showing a compliance herewith are filed with the clerk of the court in which such action is pending on or before the date the defendant is required to appear, or within such further time as the court may allow.

(4) No plaintiff or complainant shall be entitled to a judgment by default under this section until the expiration of 30 days from the date of the filing of the affidavit of compliance.

(5) Nothing in this section contained shall limit or abridge the right to serve any process, notice or demand upon any insurer in any other manner now or hereafter permitted by law.

(c) Defense of Action by Unauthorized Insurer. —

(1) Before any unauthorized foreign or alien insurer shall file or cause to be filed any pleading in any action, suit or proceeding instituted against it, such unauthorized insurer shall either

a. Deposit with the clerk of the court in which such action, suit or proceeding is pending cash or securities or file with such clerk a bond with good and sufficient sureties, to be approved by the court, in an amount to be fixed by the court sufficient to secure the payment of any final judgment which may be rendered in such action; or

    b. Procure a license to transact the business of insurance in this State.

(2) The court in any action, suit, or proceeding, in which service is made in the manner provided in subdivisions (2) or (3) of subsection (b) may, in its discretion, order such postponement as may be necessary to afford the defendant reasonable opportunity to comply with the provisions of subdivision (1) of this subsection and to defend such action.

(3) Nothing in subdivision (1) of this subsection is to be construed to prevent an unauthorized foreign or alien insurer from filing a motion to quash a writ or to set aside service thereof made in the manner provided in subdivisions (2) or (3) of subsection (b) on the ground either

    a. That such unauthorized insurer has not done any of the acts enumerated in subdivision (1) of subsection (b), or

    b. That the person on whom service was made pursuant to subdivision (3) of subsection (b) was not doing any of the acts therein enumerated.

(d) Attorney Fees. — In any action against an unauthorized foreign or alien insurer upon a contract of insurance issued or delivered in this State to a resident thereof or to a corporation authorized to do business therein, if the insurer has failed for 30 days after demand prior to the commencement of the action to make payment in accordance with the terms of the contract, and it appears to the court that such refusal was vexatious and without reasonable cause, the court may allow to the plaintiff a reasonable attorney fee and include such fee in any judgment that may be rendered in such action; providing, however, that the fee or portion of fee included in the judgment shall be not less than twenty-five dollars ($25.00) nor more than twelve and one-half percent (12 ½%) of the amount which the court or jury finds the plaintiff is entitled to recover against the insurer. Failure of an insurer to defend any such action shall be deemed prima facie evidence that its failure to make payment was vexatious and without reasonable cause.

(e) Short Title. — This section may be cited as the Unauthorized Insurers Process Act. (1955, c. 1040; 1985, c. 666, ss. 5, 8; 1987, c. 752, s. 11; 1989, c. 645, s. 3; 1991, c. 720, s. 4; 1999-132, s. 9.1.)

CASE NOTES

Former subdivision (e)(1) of § 58-28-45 has been superseded by this section and is no longer in effect. Safeway Trails, Inc. v. Stuyvesant Ins. Co., 211 F. Supp. 227 (M.D.N.C. 1962), aff'd, 316 F.2d 234 (4th Cir. 1963).

The purpose of this section is to protect residents of this State who are insureds or beneficiaries of insurance contracts. Safeway Trails, Inc. v. Stuyvesant Ins. Co., 211 F. Supp. 227 (M.D.N.C. 1962), aff'd, 316 F.2d 234 (4th Cir. 1963).

The primary purpose of this section is to protect residents of this State, and to prevent the necessity of North Carolina residents resorting to distant forums to assert rights under insurance policies. Safeway Trails, Inc. v. Stuyvesant Ins. Co., 211 F. Supp. 227 (M.D.N.C. 1962), aff'd, 316 F.2d 234 (4th Cir. 1963).

Nonresident Reinsurers Licensed to Do Business in State. — Nonresident reinsurers were subject to the jurisdiction of the United States District Court in North Carolina by reason of the fact that they were licensed to do business in North Carolina. Safeway Trails, Inc. v. Stuyvesant Ins. Co., 211 F. Supp. 227 (M.D.N.C. 1962), aff'd, 316 F.2d 234 (4th Cir. 1963).

Nonresident Plaintiffs. — Where none of the plaintiffs are residents of North Carolina they are not entitled to take advantage of this section. Safeway Trails, Inc. v. Stuyvesant Ins. Co., 211 F. Supp. 227 (M.D.N.C. 1962), aff'd, 316 F.2d 234 (4th Cir. 1963).

A substitute service statute would be inequitable where a nonresident seeks to take advantage of it to sue on a foreign cause of action unrelated to the State. Under such circumstances, a showing of substantial business activity in the State by the defendants would be required. In fact, unless such statutes are construed to make these requirements, there is considerable doubt of their constitutionality. Safeway Trails, Inc. v. Stuyvesant Ins. Co., 211 F. Supp. 227 (M.D.N.C. 1962), aff'd, 316 F.2d 234 (4th Cir. 1963).

Holders of public liability policies were neither "residents" nor "insureds or beneficiaries" within the meaning of this section; therefore, this section was inapplicable in their declaratory judgment action against nonresident reinsurers who did not transact business in North Carolina, and service of process attempted under this section on such defendants was ineffectual and invalid. Safeway Trails, Inc. v. Stuyvesant Ins. Co., 211 F. Supp. 227 (M.D.N.C. 1962), aff'd, 316 F.2d 234 (4th Cir. 1963).

Applied in Parris v. Garner Com. Disposal, Inc., 40 N.C. App. 282, 253 S.E.2d 29 (1979).

Cited in Home Indem. Co. v. Hoechst Celanese Corp., 128 N.C. App. 226, 494 S.E.2d 768, 1998 N.C. App. LEXIS 23 (1998), cert. denied, 505 S.E.2d 869 (1998).

§ 58-16-40. Alternative service of process on insurers.

In addition to the procedures set out in Articles 1 through 64 of this Chapter, insurers may be served with process and subjected to the jurisdiction of the courts of this State pursuant to applicable provisions of Chapter 1 and Chapter 1A of the General Statutes. (1967, c. 954, s. 3.)

§ 58-16-45. Commissioner to notify company of service or acceptance of service of process.

When service of legal process is made in the manner provided in G.S. 58-16-30, the Commissioner or his duly appointed deputy shall within four business days thereafter notify the company served of such service or acceptance of service by registered or certified mail directed to its secretary, or its resident manager in the case of a foreign company having no secretary in the United States. Such notification shall be accompanied by a copy of the process served or accepted and any pleading or order accompanying the process. The Commissioner shall keep a record which shall show the day and hour of such service or acceptance of service of process and whether any pleading or order accompanied the process. When service is made under the provisions of G.S. 58-16-30, the time within which to file a responsive pleading, as provided by Chapter 1A of the General Statutes, shall be deemed extended by 12 days. (1899, c. 54, s. 16; Rev., s. 4751; C.S., s. 6415; 1927, c. 167, s. 2; 1971, c. 421, s. 2; 1985, c. 666, s. 7; 1987, c. 752, s. 11; 1991, c. 720, s. 4.)

CASE NOTES

Cited in Ivy River Land & Timber Co. v. National Fire & Marine Ins. Co., 192 N.C. 115, 133 S.E. 424 (1926).

§ 58-16-50. Action to enforce compliance with this Chapter.

Compliance with the provisions of Articles 1 through 64 of this Chapter as to deposits, obligations, and prohibitions, and the payment of taxes, fines, fees, and penalties by foreign or alien insurance companies, may be enforced in the ordinary course of legal procedure by action brought in the Superior Court of Wake County by the Attorney General in the name of the State upon the relation of the Commissioner of Insurance. (1899, c. 54, s. 102; 1903, c. 438, s. 10; Rev., s. 4752; C.S., s. 6416; 1945, c. 384.)

§ 58-16-55. Amendments to documents.

Any change in or amendment to any document required to be filed under G.S. 58-16-5 shall be promptly filed with the Commissioner. (1989, c. 485, s. 49.)

ARTICLE 17.

"Lloyds" Insurance Associations.

§ 58-17-1. "Lloyds" insurance associations may transact business of insurance other than life, on certain conditions.

Associations of individuals, whether organized within the State or elsewhere, formed upon the plan known as "Lloyds" — whereby each associate underwriter becomes liable for a proportionate part of the whole amount insured by policy — may be authorized to transact business of insurance, other than life, in this State, in like manner and upon the same terms and conditions as are required of and imposed upon insurance companies regularly organized; but all such "Lloyds" whether organized within the State or elsewhere, shall make the same deposit, and upon the same terms and conditions as required by Articles 5 and 16 of this Chapter for foreign or alien insurance companies incorporated under the laws of any government or state other than the United States or one of the several states of the Union. Provided, such associations shall be subject to all of the laws and regulations of the State of North Carolina relating to the transaction of insurance business within this State. (1967, c. 844.)

ARTICLES 18.

§§ 58-18-1 through 58-18-25: Repealed by Session Laws 2001-223, s. 15, effective June 15, 2001.

ARTICLE 19.

Insurance Holding Company System Regulatory Act.

§ 58-19-1. Findings; purpose; legislative intent.

(a) The General Assembly finds that the public interest and the interests of policyholders are or may be adversely affected when any of the following occur:
   (1) Control of an insurer is sought by persons who would utilize such control adversely to the interests of policyholders.
   (2) Acquisition of control of an insurer would substantially lessen competition or create a monopoly in the insurance business in this State.
   (3) An insurer that is part of a holding company system is caused to enter into transactions or relationships with affiliated companies on terms that are not fair and reasonable.
   (4) An insurer pays dividends to shareholders that jeopardize the financial condition of such insurer.
(b) The General Assembly declares that the policies and purposes of this Article are to promote the public interest by doing all of the following:

(1) Requiring disclosure of pertinent information relating to changes in control of an insurer.
(2) Requiring disclosure by an insurer of material transactions and relationships between the insurer and its affiliates, including certain dividends to shareholders paid by the insurer.
(3) Providing standards governing material transactions between an insurer and its affiliates. (1989, c. 722, s. 1.)

§ 58-19-2. Compliance with federal law.

(a) As used in this section, "depository institution" has the same meaning as in section 3 of the Federal Deposit Insurance Act, 12 U.S.C. § 1813, and includes any foreign bank that maintains a branch, an agency, or a commercial lending company in the United States.

(b) With respect to affiliations between a depository institution or any affiliate of a depository institution and any insurer, the provisions of section 104(c) of the Gramm-Leach-Bliley Act, P.L. 106-102, shall apply to this Article. (2001-215, s. 2.)

§ 58-19-5. Definitions.

As used in this Article, unless the context requires otherwise, the following terms have the following meanings:

(1) An "affiliate" of or person "affiliated" with a specific person is a person that indirectly through one or more intermediaries or directly controls, is controlled by, or is under common control with the person specified.
(2) "Control", including the terms "controlling", "controlled by", and "under common control with", means the direct or indirect possession of the power to direct or cause the direction of the management and policies of a person, whether through the ownership of voting securities, by contract other than a commercial contract for goods or nonmanagement services, or otherwise. Control is presumed to exist if any person directly or indirectly owns, controls, holds with the power to vote, or holds proxies representing, ten percent (10%) or more of the voting securities of any other person. This presumption may be rebutted by a showing made in the manner provided by G.S. 58-19-25(j) that control does not exist in fact. The Commissioner may determine, after furnishing all persons in interest notice and opportunity to be heard and making specific findings of fact to support such determination, that control exists in fact, notwithstanding the absence of a presumption to that effect.
(3) "Insurance holding company system" means an entity comprising two or more affiliated persons, one or more of which is an insurer.
(4) "Insurer" includes a person subject to Articles 65 and 66 or 67 of this Chapter. "Insurer" does not include (1) an agency, authority, or instrumentality of the United States; any of its possessions and territories; the Commonwealth of Puerto Rico; the District of Columbia; nor a state or political subdivision of a state; nor (2) fraternal benefit societies or fraternal orders.
(5) "Person" means an individual, corporation, partnership, limited liability company, association, joint stock company, trust, unincorporated organization, or any similar entity or any combination of the foregoing acting in concert.
(6) A "security holder" of a specified person is one who owns any security of such person, including common stock, preferred stock, debt obliga-

tions, or any other security convertible into or evidencing the right to acquire any of the foregoing.

(7) A "subsidiary" of a specified person is an affiliate controlled by such person indirectly through one or more intermediaries or directly.

(8) "Voting security" includes any security convertible into or evidencing a right to acquire a voting security. (1989, c. 722, s. 1; 1995, c. 517, ss. 9, 10; 2001-223, s. 16.1.)

§ 58-19-10. Subsidiaries of insurers.

(a) Any domestic insurer, either by itself or in cooperation with one or more persons, may organize or acquire one or more subsidiaries engaged in the following kinds of business:

(1) Any kind of insurance business authorized by the jurisdiction in which it is incorporated.

(2) Acting as an insurance broker or as an insurance agent for its parent or for any of its parent's insurer subsidiaries.

(3) Investing, reinvesting, or trading in securities for its own account, that of its parent, any subsidiary of its parent, or any affiliate or subsidiary.

(4) Management of any investment company subject to or registered pursuant to the federal Investment Company Act of 1940, as amended, including related sales and services.

(5) Acting as a broker-dealer subject to or registered pursuant to the federal Securities Exchange Act of 1934, as amended.

(6) Rendering investment advice to governments, government agencies, corporations, or other organizations or groups.

(7) Rendering other services related to the operations of an insurance business, including actuarial, loss prevention, safety engineering, data processing, accounting, claims, appraisal, and collection services.

(8) Ownership and management of assets that the parent corporation could itself own or manage.

(9) Acting as an administrative agent for a governmental instrumentality that is performing an insurance function.

(10) Financing of insurance premiums, agents, and other forms of consumer financing.

(11) Any other business activity that is reasonably ancillary to an insurance business.

(12) Owning a corporation or corporations engaged or organized to engage exclusively in one or more of the businesses specified in this section.

(b) In addition to investments in common stock, preferred stock, debt obligations, and other securities permitted under this Chapter, a domestic insurer may also:

(1) Invest, in common stock, preferred stock, debt obligations, and other securities of one or more subsidiaries, amounts that do not exceed the lesser of ten percent (10%) of the insurer's admitted assets or fifty percent (50%) of the insurer's policyholders' surplus, provided that after those investments, the insurer's policyholders' surplus will be reasonable in relation to the insurer's outstanding liabilities and adequate to its financial needs. In calculating the amount of the investments, investments in domestic or foreign insurance subsidiaries and health maintenance organizations shall be excluded, and there shall be included: (i) total net monies or other consideration expended and obligations assumed in the acquisition or formation of a subsidiary, including all organizational expenses and contributions to capital and surplus of the subsidiary whether or not represented by

the purchase of capital stock or issuance of other securities; and (ii) all amounts expended in acquiring additional common stock, preferred stock, debt obligations, and other securities, and all contributions to the capital or surplus, of a subsidiary subsequent to its acquisition or formation;

(2) Invest any amount in common stock, preferred stock, debt obligations and other securities of one or more subsidiaries engaged or organized to engage exclusively in the ownership and management of assets authorized as investments for the insurer; provided that such subsidiary agrees to limit its investments in any asset so that such investments will not cause the amount of the total investment of the insurer to exceed any of the investment limitations specified in subdivision (b)(1) of this section or in Article 7 of this Chapter applicable to the insurer. For the purposes of this section, "the total investment of the insurer" includes: (i) any direct investment by the insurer in an asset; and (ii) the insurer's proportionate share of any investment in an asset by any subsidiary of the insurer, which shall be calculated by multiplying the amount of the subsidiary's investment by the percentage of the ownership of such subsidiary.

(3) With the approval of the Commissioner, invest any greater amount in common stock, preferred stock, debt obligations, or other securities of one or more subsidiaries; provided that after such investment the insurer's policyholders' surplus will be reasonable in relation to the insurer's outstanding liabilities and adequate to its financial needs.

(c) Investments in common stock, preferred stock, debt obligations, or other securities of subsidiaries made pursuant to subsection (b) of this section are not subject to any of the otherwise applicable restrictions or prohibitions contained in this Chapter applicable to such investments of insurers.

(d) Whether any investment pursuant to subsection (b) of this section meets the applicable requirements of that subsection is to be determined, before such investment is made, by calculating the applicable investment limitations as though the investment had already been made, taking into account the then outstanding principal balance on all previous investments in debt obligations, and the value of all previous investments in equity securities as of the day they were made, net of any return of capital invested, not including dividends.

(e) If an insurer ceases to control a subsidiary, it shall dispose of any investment therein made pursuant to this section within three years from the time of the cessation of control or within such further time as the Commissioner may prescribe, (i) unless after cessation of control such investment meets the requirements for investment under any other provision of Articles 1 through 64 of this Chapter, or (ii) unless the Commissioner authorizes the insurer to continue the investment. (1989, c. 722, s. 1; 1993, c. 504, s. 11; 2001-223, ss. 16.2, 16.3, 16.4.)

§ 58-19-15. Acquisition of control of or merger with domestic insurer.

(a) No person other than the issuer shall make a tender offer for or a request or invitation for tenders of, or enter into any agreement to exchange securities, or seek to acquire, or acquire, in the open market or otherwise, any voting security of a domestic insurer, if, after the consummation thereof, the person would, directly or indirectly (or by conversion or by exercise of any right to acquire), be in control of the insurer, and no person shall enter into an agreement to merge with or otherwise to acquire control of a domestic insurer or any person controlling a domestic insurer unless the offer, request, invitation, agreement, or acquisition is conditioned upon the approval of the

Commissioner under this section. No such merger or other acquisition of control is effective until a statement containing the information required by this section has been filed with the Commissioner and all other provisions of this section have been complied with and the merger or acquisition of control has been approved by the Commissioner under this section. The statement containing the information required by this section shall also be filed with the domestic insurer when it is filed with the Commissioner.

(a1) For the purposes of this section a "domestic insurer" includes any person controlling a domestic insurer. Further, for the purposes of this section, "person" does not include any securities broker holding, in the usual and customary broker's function, less than twenty percent (20%) of the voting securities of an insurance company or of any person that controls an insurance company.

(a2) Any acquisition of control of a domestic insurer must be completed not later than 90 days after the date of the Commissioner's order approving the acquisition under this section, unless the Commissioner grants an extension in writing on a showing of good cause for the delay. Any increase in a company's capital and surplus required under this Article as a result of the change of control of a domestic insurer must be completed not later than 90 days after the date of the Commissioner's order approving the change of control and before the company writes any new insurance business.

(a3) If the deadlines for completion in subsection (a2) of this section are not met, the person seeking to acquire control of the domestic insurer must resubmit the statement required by subsection (b) of this section, and the Commissioner may reconsider approval of acquisition of control under this section.

(b) The statement to be filed with the Commissioner under subsection (a) of this section shall be made under oath or affirmation and shall contain the following information:

    (1) The name and address of each person by whom or on whose behalf the merger or other acquisition of control referred to in subsection (a) of this section is to be effected (hereinafter called "acquiring party"), and: (i) if such person is an individual, his principal occupation and all offices and positions held during the past five years, and any conviction of crimes other than minor traffic violations during the past 10 years; (ii) if such person is not an individual, a report of the nature of its business operations during the past five years or for such lesser period as such person and any predecessors thereof shall have been in existence; an informative description of the business intended to be done by such person and such person's subsidiaries; and a list of all individuals who are or who have been selected to become directors or executive officers of such person, or who perform or will perform functions appropriate to such positions. Such list shall include for each such individual the information required by sub-subdivision (1)(i) of this subsection.

    (2) The source, nature, and amount of the consideration used or to be used in effecting the merger or other acquisition of control; a description of any transaction wherein funds were or are to be obtained for any such purpose, including any pledge of the insurer's stock, or the stock of any of its subsidiaries or controlling affiliates; and the identity of persons furnishing such consideration; provided, however, that where a source of such consideration is a loan made in the lender's ordinary course of business, the identity of the lender shall remain confidential, if the person filing such statement so requests.

    (3) Fully audited financial information as to the earnings and financial condition of each acquiring party for the preceding five fiscal years of

each such acquiring party, or for such lesser period as such acquiring party and any predecessors thereof have been in existence; and similar unaudited information as of a date not earlier than 90 days prior to the filing of the statement.

(4) Any plans or proposals that each acquiring party may have to liquidate such insurer, to sell its assets or merge or consolidate it with any person, or to make any other material change in its business or corporate structure or management.

(5) The number of shares of any security referred to in subsection (a) of this section that each acquiring party proposes to acquire; the terms of the offer, request, invitation, agreement, or acquisition referred to in subsection (a) of this section; and a statement as to the method by which the fairness of the proposal was arrived at.

(6) The amount of each class of any security referred to in subsection (a) of this section that is beneficially owned or concerning which there is a right to acquire beneficial ownership by each acquiring party.

(7) A full description of any contracts, arrangements, or understandings with respect to any security referred to in subsection (a) of this section in which any acquiring party is involved, including transfer of any of the securities, joint ventures, loan or option arrangements, puts or calls, guarantees of loans, guarantees against loss or guarantees of profits, division of losses or profits, or the giving or withholding of proxies. Such description shall identify the persons with whom such contracts, arrangements, or understandings have been entered into.

(8) A description of the purchase of any security referred to in subsection (a) of this section during the 12 calendar months preceding the filing of the statement, by any acquiring party, including the dates of purchase, names of the purchasers, and consideration paid or agreed to be paid therefor.

(9) A description of any recommendations to purchase any security referred to in subsection (a) of this section made during the 12 calendar months preceding the filing of the statement, by any acquiring party, or by anyone based upon interviews or at the suggestion of such acquiring party.

(10) Copies of all tender offers for, requests, or invitations for tenders of, exchange offers for, and agreements to acquire or exchange any securities referred to in subsection (a) of this section, and any related additional soliciting material that has been distributed.

(11) The term of any agreement, contract, or understanding made with or proposed to be made with any third party in connection with any acquisition of control of or merger with a domestic insurer, and the amount of any fees, commissions, or other compensation to be paid to the third party with regard thereto.

(12) Such additional information as the Commissioner may by rule prescribe as necessary or appropriate for the protection of policyholders of the insurer or in the public interest.

If the person required to file the statement referred to in subsection (a) of this section is a partnership, limited partnership, syndicate, or other group, the Commissioner shall require that the information called for by subdivisions (1) through (12) of this subsection be given with respect to each partner of such partnership or limited partnership, each member of such syndicate or group, and each person who controls such partner or member. If any such partner, member, or person is a corporation or the person required to file the statement referred to in subsection (a) of this section is a corporation, the Commissioner shall require that the information called for by subdivisions (1) through (12) of this subsection be given with respect to such corporation, each officer and director of such corporation, and each person who is, directly or indirectly, the beneficial owner of more than ten percent (10%) of the outstanding voting securities of such corporation.

If any material change occurs in the facts set forth in the statement filed with the Commissioner and sent to such insurer pursuant to this section, an amendment setting forth such change, together with copies of all documents and other material relevant to such change, shall be filed with the Commissioner and sent to such insurer by the filer within two business days after the person learns of such change.

(c) If any offer, request, invitation, agreement, or acquisition referred to in subsection (a) of this section is proposed to be made by means of a registration statement under the Federal Securities Act of 1933, in circumstances requiring the disclosure of similar information under the Federal Securities Exchange Act of 1934, or under any State law requiring similar registration or disclosure, the person required to file the statement referred to in subsection (a) may utilize such documents in furnishing the information called for by that statement.

(d) The Commissioner shall approve any merger or other acquisition of control referred to in subsection (a) of this section unless, after a public hearing thereon, he finds any of the following:

(1) After the change of control, the domestic insurer referred to in subsection (a) of this section would not be able to satisfy the requirements for the issuance of a license to write the kind or kinds of insurance for which it is presently licensed.

(2) The effect of the merger or other acquisition of control would be substantially to lessen competition in insurance or tend to create a monopoly in this State.

(3) The financial condition of any acquiring party might jeopardize the financial stability of the insurer or prejudice the interest of its policyholders.

(4) Any plans or proposals that the acquiring party has to liquidate the insurer, sell its assets or consolidate or merge it with any person, or to make any other material change in its business or corporate structure or management, are unfair and unreasonable to policyholders of the insurer and not in the public interest.

(5) The competence, experience, and integrity of those persons who would control the operation of the insurer are such that it would not be in the interests of policyholders of the insurer and of the public to permit the merger or other acquisition of control.

(6) The acquisition is likely to be hazardous or prejudicial to the insurance-buying public.

(e) The public hearing referred to in subsection (d) of this section shall be held within 120 days after the statement required by subsection (a) of this section is filed, and the Commissioner shall give at least 30 days notice of the hearing to the person filing the statement, to the insurer, and to such other persons as may be designated by the Commissioner. The Commissioner shall make a determination as expeditiously as is reasonably practicable after the conclusion of the hearing. At the hearing, the person filing the statement, the insurer, any person to whom notice of hearing was sent, and any other person whose interest may be affected by the hearing shall have the right to present evidence, examine and cross-examine witnesses, and offer oral or written arguments; and in connection therewith shall be entitled to conduct discovery proceedings at any time after the statement is filed with the Commissioner under this section and in the same manner as is presently allowed in the superior courts of this State. In connection with discovery proceedings authorized by this section, the Commissioner may issue such protective orders and other orders governing the timing and scheduling of discovery proceedings as might otherwise have been issued by a superior court of this State in connection with a civil proceeding. If any party fails to make reasonable and adequate response to discovery on a timely basis or fails to comply with any order of the Commissioner with respect to discovery, the Commissioner on the Commissioner's own motion or on motion of any other party or person may order that the hearing be postponed, recessed, convened, or reconvened, as the case may be, following proper completion of discovery and reasonable notice to the person filing the statement, to the insurer, and to such other persons as may be designated by the Commissioner.

(f) The Commissioner may retain, at the acquiring person's expense, any attorneys, actuaries, economists, accountants, or other experts not otherwise a part of the Commissioner's staff as may be reasonably necessary to assist the Commissioner in reviewing the proposed acquisition of control.

(g) The expenses of mailing any notices and other materials required by this section shall be borne by the person making the filing. As security for the payment of such expenses, such person shall file with the Commissioner an acceptable bond or other deposit in an amount to be determined by the Commissioner.

(h) The provisions of this section do not apply to any offer, request, invitation, agreement, or acquisition that the Commissioner by order exempts therefrom as (i) not having been made or entered into for the purpose and not having the effect of changing or influencing the control of a domestic insurer, or (ii) as otherwise not comprehended within the purposes of this section. Any acquisition of stock of a former domestic mutual insurer by a parent company that occurs in connection with the conversion of a mutual insurer to a stock insurer under G.S. 58-10-10 is not subject to this section, provided that no person acquires control of the parent company.

(i) The following are violations of this section:

    (1) The failure to file any statement, amendment, or other material required to be filed pursuant to subsection (a) or (b) of this section; or

    (2) The effectuation or any attempt to effectuate an acquisition of control of or merger with a domestic insurer, unless the Commissioner has given his approval thereto.

(j) The courts of this State are vested with jurisdiction over every person not resident, domiciled, or authorized to do business in this State who files a statement with the Commissioner under this section; and each such person is deemed to have performed acts equivalent to and constituting an appointment by such person of the Commissioner to be his true and lawful attorney upon whom may be served all legal process in any action, suit, or proceeding arising out of violations of this section. Copies of all such process shall be handled in accordance with the provisions of G.S. 58-16-30, 58-16-35, and 58-16-45. (1989, c. 722, s. 1; 1991, c. 681, ss. 31, 32; c. 720, s. 17; 1993, c. 452, ss. 26-29; c. 504, s. 12; c. 553, s. 16; 1995, c. 517, ss. 11, 12; 2001-223, s. 16.5.)

CASE NOTES

Editor's Note. — *Most of the cases below were decided under former G.S. 58-9-5 prior to its repeal.*

Propriety of Insurance Company Having Holding Company Structure. — By enacting former Article 6A of Chapter 58 (see now this Article), the General Assembly recognized, and in so doing established as the public policy of this State, that it was entirely proper for a domestic insurance company and its stockhold-

ers to enjoy the benefits of a corporate reorganization so as to bring their company under a holding company structure, provided the protective procedures prescribed were followed. Occidental Life Ins. Co. v. Ingram, 34 N.C. App. 619, 240 S.E.2d 460 (1977).

Notice and Hearing Required. — Because there may be circumstances in which a corporate reorganization might work to the detriment of the domestic insurance company or its shareholders or policyholders, the corporate reorganization could be accomplished only after notice was given to all shareholders and to the public of a public hearing which the Commissioner of Insurance was directed to hold. Occidental Life Ins. Co. v. Ingram, 34 N.C. App. 619, 240 S.E.2d 460 (1977).

Commissioner Must Act in Good Faith. — A clearly implied condition upon the powers conferred upon the Commissioner by former G.S. 58-9-9 was that he will exercise them in good faith. Occidental Life Ins. Co. v. Ingram, 34 N.C. App. 619, 240 S.E.2d 460 (1977).

And Not Arbitrarily. — The powers conferred upon the Commissioner of Insurance were not so broad as to permit him arbitrarily to refuse to make findings favorable to petitioners when all of the evidence supported such findings and there was no competent evidence to the contrary. Occidental Life Ins. Co. v. Ingram, 34 N.C. App. 619, 240 S.E.2d 460 (1977).

The Commissioner of Insurance abused the powers granted to him by the General Assembly when he arbitrarily and capriciously denied a domestic insurance company's plan to reorganize under a holding company structure where all of the competent evidence showed it was clearly entitled to reorganization. Occidental Life Ins. Co. v. Ingram, 34 N.C. App. 619, 240 S.E.2d 460 (1977).

Relief from Commissioner's Arbitrary Action. — If the Commissioner acts arbitrarily, petitioners are not left helpless, nor are the courts powerless to grant them adequate relief. Occidental Life Ins. Co. v. Ingram, 34 N.C. App. 619, 240 S.E.2d 460 (1977).

Issuance of Mandatory Injunction Requiring Commissioner to Act Upheld. — The trial court did not exceed its power and authority by issuing its mandatory injunction requiring the Commissioner of Insurance to approve a domestic insurance corporation's plan to reorganize under a holding company structure where the Commissioner acted arbitrarily and capriciously when he disapproved the plan. Occidental Life Ins. Co. v. Ingram, 34 N.C. App. 619, 240 S.E.2d 460 (1977).

OPINIONS OF ATTORNEY GENERAL

Contracts negotiated pursuant to G.S. 58-19-15(f) are not exempt from the requirements of Article 3C of Chapter 143. See opinion of Attorney General to Peter A. Kolbe, General Counsel, North Carolina Department of Insurance, 2001 N.C. AG LEXIS 29 (10/3/01).

Retention of Experts to Assist in Reviewing Proposed Acquisition of Control. — The Commissioner of Insurance is not required to adhere to a bid process in retaining experts to assist in reviewing a proposed acquisition of control if either of two conditions is met: (1) the Division of Purchase and Contract and the Governor have determined that performance or price competition is not available; and (2) the Division of Purchase and Contract and the Governor have determined that the contract price is too small to justify soliciting competitive proposals. See opinion of Attorney General to Peter A. Kolbe, General Counsel, North Carolina Department of Insurance, 2001 N.C. AG LEXIS 29 (10/3/01).

Prior to granting written approval for a contract for the Commissioner of Insurance to retain an expert to assist in reviewing a proposed acquisition of control, the Governor must find that the estimated cost is reasonable as compared with the likely benefits or results. See opinion of Attorney General to Peter A. Kolbe, General Counsel, North Carolina Department of Insurance, 2001 N.C. AG LEXIS 29 (10/3/01).

Payment of Travel Allowances to Experts Retained by Commissioner of Insurance. — Experts retained by the Commissioner of Insurance under G.S. 58-19-15(f) are not state employees and, therefore, G.S. 38-6 does not control the payment of travel allowances to such experts. See opinion of Attorney General to Peter A. Kolbe, General Counsel, North Carolina Department of Insurance, 2001 N.C. AG LEXIS 29 (10/3/01).

§ 58-19-17. Foreign or alien insurer's report of change of control.

(a) As used in this section, "controlling capital stock" means enough of an insurer's shares of the issued and outstanding stock, as defined in G.S. 58-19-5(2), to give its owner the power to exercise a controlling influence over the management or policies of the insurer.

(b) If there is a change in the controlling capital stock or a change of twenty-five percent (25%) or more of the assets of a foreign or alien insurer, the insurer shall report the change in writing to the Commissioner within 30 days after the effective date of the change. The report shall be in a form prescribed by the Commissioner and shall contain the name and address of the new owners of the controlling stock or assets, the nature and value of the new assets, and other relevant information that the Commissioner requires. (1991, c. 681, s. 38.)

§ **58-19-20:** Repealed by Session Laws 1993, c. 452, s. 65.

§ 58-19-25. Registration of insurers.

(a) Every insurer that is licensed to do business in this State and that is a member of an insurance holding company system shall register with the Commissioner, except a foreign insurer subject to the registration requirements and standards adopted by statute or regulation in the jurisdiction of its domicile that are substantially similar to those contained in:

(1) This section.

(2) G.S. 58-19-30(a), G.S. 58-19-30(c), and G.S. 58-19-30(d).

(3) G.S. 58-19-30(b) or a statutory or regulatory provision such as the following: Each registered insurer shall keep current the information required to be disclosed in its registration statement by reporting all material changes or additions within 15 days after the end of the month in which it learns of each change or addition. The insurer shall also file a copy of its registration statement and any amendments to the statement in each state in which that insurer is authorized to do business, if requested by the insurance regulator of that state.

Any insurer that is subject to registration under this section shall register within 30 days after it becomes subject to registration, and an amendment to the registration statement shall be filed by April 1 of each year for the previous calendar year; unless the Commissioner for good cause shown extends the time for registration or filing, and then within the extended time. All registration statements shall contain a summary, on a form prescribed by the Commissioner, outlining all items in the current registration statement representing changes from the prior registration statement. The Commissioner may require any insurer that is a member of a holding company system that is not subject to registration under this section to furnish a copy of the registration statement or other information filed by the insurance company with the insurance regulator of its domiciliary jurisdiction.

(b) Every insurer subject to registration shall file the registration statement on a form prescribed by the Commissioner, which shall contain the following current information:

(1) The bylaws, capital structure, general financial condition, ownership, and management of the insurer and any person controlling the insurer.

(2) The identity and relationship of every member of the insurance holding company system.

(3) The following agreements in force, and transactions currently outstanding or that have occurred during the last calendar year between such insurer and its affiliates:

a. Loans, other investments, or purchases, sales or exchanges of securities of the affiliates by the insurer or of the insurer by its affiliates.

b. Purchases, sales, or exchange of assets.

c. Transactions not in the ordinary course of business.

d. Guarantees or undertakings for the benefit of an affiliate that result in an actual contingent exposure of the insurer's assets to liability, other than insurance contracts entered into in the ordinary course of the insurer's business.

 e. All management agreements, service contracts, and cost-sharing arrangements.

 f. Reinsurance agreements.

 g. Dividends and other distributions to shareholders.

 h. Consolidated tax allocation agreements.

 (4) Any pledge of the insurer's stock, including stock of any subsidiary or controlling affiliate, for a loan made to any member of the insurance holding company system.

 (5) Other matters concerning transactions between registered insurers and any affiliates as may be included from time to time in any registration forms adopted or approved by the Commissioner.

(c) No information need be disclosed on the registration statement filed pursuant to subsection (b) of this section if such information is not material for the purposes of this section. Unless the Commissioner by rule or order provides otherwise, all sales, purchases, exchanges, loans or extensions of credit, investments, or guarantees involving one-half of one percent (1/2%) or less of an insurer's admitted assets as of the preceding December 31 are not material for the purposes of this section.

(d) Subject to G.S. 58-19-30(c), each domestic insurer shall report to the Commissioner all dividends and other distributions to shareholders within 15 business days following the declaration thereof. The Commissioner may prescribe the form to be used to report that information.

(e) Any person within an insurance holding company system subject to registration shall provide complete and accurate information to an insurer, where such information is reasonably necessary to enable the insurer to comply with the provisions of this Article.

(f) The Commissioner shall terminate the registration of any insurer that demonstrates that it no longer is a member of an insurance holding company system.

(g) The Commissioner may require or allow two or more affiliated insurers subject to registration under this section to file a consolidated registration statement.

(h) The Commissioner may allow an insurer that is authorized to do business in this State and that is part of an insurance holding company system to register on behalf of any affiliated insurer that is required to register under subsection (a) of this section and to file all information and material required to be filed under this section.

(i) The provisions of this section do not apply to any insurer, information, or transaction if and to the extent that the Commissioner by rule or order exempts the same from the provisions of this section.

(j) Any person may file with the Commissioner a disclaimer of affiliation with any authorized insurer, or such a disclaimer may be filed by such insurer or any member of an insurance holding company system. The disclaimer shall fully disclose all material relationships and bases for affiliation between such person and such insurer as well as the basis for disclaiming such affiliation. After a disclaimer has been filed, the insurer shall be relieved of any duty to register or report under this section that may arise out of the insurer's relationship with such person unless the Commissioner disallows such a disclaimer. The Commissioner shall disallow such a disclaimer only after furnishing all parties in interest with notice and opportunity to be heard and after making specific findings of fact to support such disallowance.

(k) The failure to file a registration statement or any summary of the registration statement thereto required by this section within the time specified for such filing is a violation of this section. (1989, c. 722, s. 1; 1991, c.

681, ss. 33, 34; 1993, c. 452, ss. 30-32; c. 504, s. 13; 1993 (Reg. Sess., 1994), c. 678, s. 14; 1995, c. 193, s. 26; 2001-223, s. 16.6.)

§ 58-19-30. Standards and management of an insurer within a holding company system.

(a) Transactions within a holding company system to which an insurer subject to registration is a party are subject to all of the following standards:

(1) The terms shall be fair and reasonable.

(2) Charges or fees for services performed shall be reasonable.

(3) Expenses incurred and payment received shall be allocated to the insurer in conformity with customary insurance accounting practices consistently applied.

(4) The books, accounts, and records of each party to all such transactions shall be so maintained as to clearly and accurately disclose the nature and details of the transactions, including such accounting information as is necessary to support the reasonableness of the charges or fees to the respective parties.

(5) The insurer's surplus as regards policyholders following any dividends or distributions to shareholder affiliates shall be reasonable in relation to the insurer's outstanding liabilities and adequate to its financial needs.

(b) The following transactions involving a domestic insurer and any person in its holding company system may not be entered into unless the insurer has notified the Commissioner in writing of its intention to enter into the transaction at least 30 days before the transaction, or such shorter period as the Commissioner permits, and the Commissioner has not disapproved it within that period:

(1) Sales, purchases, exchanges, loans or extensions of credit, guarantees, or investments, provided the transactions equal or exceed: (i) with respect to nonlife insurers, the lesser of three percent (3%) of the insurer's admitted assets or twenty-five percent (25%) of surplus as regards policyholders; (ii) with respect to life insurers, three percent (3%) of the insurer's admitted assets; each as of the preceding December 31.

(2) Loans or extensions of credit to any person who is not affiliated, where the insurer makes the loans or extensions of credit with the agreement or understanding that the proceeds of the transactions, in whole or in substantial part, are to be used to make loans or extensions of credit to, to purchase assets of, or to make investments in, any affiliate of the insurer making the loans or extensions of credit provided the transactions equal or exceed: (i) with respect to nonlife insurers, the lesser of three percent (3%) of the insurer's admitted assets or twenty-five percent (25%) of surplus as regards policyholders; (ii) with respect to life insurers, three percent (3%) of the insurer's admitted assets; each as of the preceding December 31.

(3) Reinsurance agreements or modifications to the agreements in which the reinsurance premium or a change in the insurer's liabilities equals or exceeds five percent (5%) of the insurer's surplus as regards policyholders, as of the preceding December 31, including those agreements that may require as consideration the transfer of assets from an insurer to a nonaffiliate, if an agreement or understanding exists between the insurer and nonaffiliate that any portion of the assets will be transferred to one or more affiliates of the insurer.

(4) All management agreements, service contracts, guarantees, or cost-sharing arrangements.

(5) Any material transactions, specified by rule, that the Commissioner determines may adversely affect the interests of the insurer's policyholders.

Nothing in this section authorizes or permits any transactions that, in the case of an insurer, not a member of the same holding company system, would be otherwise contrary to law. A domestic insurer may not enter into transactions that are part of a plan or series of like transactions with persons within the holding company system if the purpose of those separate transactions is to avoid the statutory threshold amount and thus avoid the review that would otherwise occur. If the Commissioner determines that such separate transactions were entered into over any 12-month period for that purpose, the Commissioner may exercise the Commissioner's authority under G.S. 58-19-50. The Commissioner, in reviewing transactions pursuant to this subsection, shall consider whether the transactions comply with the standards set forth in subsection (a) of this section and whether they may adversely affect the interests of policyholders. The Commissioner shall be notified within 30 days after any investment of a domestic insurer in any one corporation if, as a result of the investment, the total investment in the corporation by the insurance holding company system exceeds ten percent (10%) of the corporation's voting securities.

(c) No domestic insurer shall pay any extraordinary dividend or make any other extraordinary distribution to its shareholders until (i) 30 days after the Commissioner has received notice of the declaration thereof and has not within that period disapproved the payment or (ii) the Commissioner has approved the payment within the 30-day period.

For the purposes of this section, an "extraordinary dividend" or "extraordinary distribution" includes any dividend or distribution of cash or other property, whose fair market value together with that of other dividends or distributions made within the preceding 12 months exceeds the lesser of (i) ten percent (10%) of the insurer's surplus as regards policyholders as of the preceding December 31, or (ii) the net gain from operations of the insurer, if the insurer is a life insurer, or the net income, if the insurer is not a life insurer, not including realized capital gains, for the 12-month period ending the preceding December 31; but does not include pro rata distributions of any class of the insurer's own securities. In determining whether a dividend or distribution is extraordinary, an insurer other than a life insurer may carry forward net income from the previous two calendar years that has not already been paid out as dividends. This carryforward shall be computed by taking the net income from the second and third preceding calendar years, not including realized capital gains, less dividends paid in the second and immediate preceding calendar years.

Notwithstanding any other provision of law, an insurer may declare an extraordinary dividend or distribution that is conditional upon the Commissioner's approval, and the declaration shall confer no rights upon shareholders until (i) the Commissioner has approved the payment of the dividend or distribution or (ii) the Commissioner has not disapproved the payment within the 30-day period referred to above.

(d) For the purposes of this Article, in determining whether an insurer's surplus as regards policyholders is reasonable in relation to the insurer's outstanding liabilities and adequate to its financial needs, all of the following factors, among others, shall be considered:

(1) The size of the insurer as measured by its assets, capital and surplus, reserves, premium writings, insurance in force, and other appropriate criteria.

(2) The extent to which the insurer's business is diversified among the several kinds of insurance.

(3) The number and size of risks insured in each kind of insurance.
(4) The extent of the geographic dispersion of the insurer's insured risks.
(5) The nature and extent of the insurer's reinsurance program.
(6) The quality, diversification, and liquidity of the insurer's investment portfolio.
(7) The recent past and projected future trend in the size of the insurer's surplus as regards policyholders.
(8) The surplus as regards policyholders maintained by other comparable insurers.
(9) The adequacy of the insurer's reserves.
(10) The quality and liquidity of investments in affiliates. The Commissioner may treat any such investment as a disallowed asset for purposes of determining the adequacy of surplus as regards policyholders whenever in his judgment such investment so warrants. (1989, c. 722, s. 1; 1991, c. 681, ss. 35, 36; c. 720, s. 18; 1993, c. 452, s. 33; 2001-223, s. 16.7.)

CASE NOTES

Applicability. — This section required approval by the Commissioner of Insurance of a $2.5 million loan by an insolvent insurer, where the loan was more than 3% of the $75 million in admitted assets and 25% of surplus. State ex rel. Long v. ILA Corp., 132 N.C. App. 587, 513 S.E.2d 812 (1999).

§ 58-19-35. Examination.

(a) Subject to the limitation contained in this section and in addition to the powers that the Commissioner has under other provisions of Articles 1 through 64 of this Chapter relating to the examination of insurers, the Commissioner also has the power to order any insurer registered under G.S. 58-19-25 or any acquiring party to produce such records, books, or other information in the possession of the insurer or its affiliates or the acquiring party as are reasonably necessary to ascertain the financial condition of such insurer or acquiring party or to determine compliance with Articles 1 through 64 of this Chapter. In the event such insurer or acquiring party fails to comply with such order, the Commissioner shall have the power to examine such insurer or its affiliates or such acquiring party to obtain such information.

(b) The Commissioner may retain, at the expense of the registered insurer or acquiring party that is being examined, such attorneys, actuaries, economists, accountants, and other experts not otherwise a part of the Commissioner's staff as are reasonably necessary to assist in the conduct of the examination under subsection (a) of this section. Any persons so retained shall be under the direction and control of the Commissioner and shall act in a purely advisory capacity.

(c) Repealed by Session Laws 1995, c. 360, s. 2(h).

(d) The Commissioner shall exercise his power under subsection (a) of this section only if the examination of the insurer or acquiring party under other provisions of Articles 1 through 64 of this Chapter is inadequate or the interests of the policyholders of such insurer may be adversely affected. (1989, c. 722, s. 1; 1995, c. 193, s. 27; c. 360, s. 2(h).)

§ 58-19-40. Confidential treatment.

All information, documents, and copies thereof obtained by or disclosed to the Commissioner or any other person in the course of an examination or investigation made pursuant to G.S. 58-19-35, and all information reported pursuant to G.S. 58-19-25 and G.S. 58-19-30, shall be given confidential treatment; shall not be subject to subpoena; and shall not be made public by the Commissioner, the NAIC, or any other person, except to insurance regulators of other states, without the prior written consent of the insurer or acquiring party to which it pertains unless the Commissioner, after giving the insurer and its affiliates or the acquiring party that would be affected thereby notice and opportunity to be heard, determines that the interest of the insurer's policyholders or the public will be served by the publication thereof, in which event he may publish all or any part thereof in such manner as he considers appropriate. (1989, c. 722, s. 1.)

§ 58-19-45. Injunctions; prohibitions against the voting of securities; sequestration of voting securities.

(a) Whenever it appears to the Commissioner that any person has committed or is about to commit a violation of this Article or of any rule or order of the Commissioner under this Article, the Commissioner may apply to the Superior Court of Wake County for an order enjoining such person from violating or continuing to violate this Article or any such rule or order; and for such other equitable relief as the nature of the case and the interest of the domestic insurer's policyholders or the public may require.

(b) No security that is the subject of any agreement or arrangement regarding acquisition, or that is acquired or to be acquired, in contravention of the provisions of this Article or of any rule or order of the Commissioner under this Article, may be voted at any shareholder's meeting nor may be counted for quorum purposes; and any action of shareholders requiring the affirmative vote of a percentage of shares may be taken as though such securities were not issued and outstanding. No action taken at any such meeting shall be invalidated by the voting of such securities, unless the action would materially affect control of the insurer or unless the courts of this State have so ordered. If an insurer or the Commissioner has reason to believe that any security of the insurer has been or is about to be acquired in contravention of the provisions of this Article or of any rule or order issued by the Commissioner under this Article, the insurer or the Commissioner may apply to the Superior Court of Wake County to enjoin any offer, request, invitation, agreement, or acquisition made in contravention of G.S. 58-19-15 or any rule or order of the Commissioner under that section to enjoin the voting of any security so acquired, to void any vote of such security already cast at any meeting of shareholders, and for such other equitable relief as the nature of the case and the interest of the insurer's policyholders or the public may require.

(c) In any case where a person has acquired or is proposing to acquire any voting securities in violation of this Article or any rule or order of the Commissioner under this Article, the Superior Court of Wake County may, on such notice as the court considers appropriate and upon the application of the insurer or the Commissioner, seize or sequester any voting securities of the insurer owned directly or indirectly by the person, and issue an order with respect thereto as may be appropriate to effectuate the provisions of this Article. Notwithstanding any other provision of law, for the purposes of this Article the sites of the ownership of the securities of domestic insurers are in this State. (1989, c. 722, s. 1; 1991, c. 681, s. 37; 1993, c. 452, s. 34.)

§ 58-19-50. Sanctions.

(a) Any person failing, without just cause, to file any registration statement as required in this Article shall pay, after notice and hearing, a civil penalty of one hundred dollars ($100.00) for each day's delay, not to exceed a total penalty of one thousand dollars ($1,000), to the Commissioner. The clear proceeds of civil penalties provided for in this section shall be remitted to the Civil Penalty and Forfeiture Fund in accordance with G.S. 115C-457.2.

(b) Every director or officer of an insurance holding company system who knowingly and willfully violates, participates in, or assents to, or who knowingly and willfully permits any of the officers or agents of the insurer to engage in transactions or make investments that have not been properly reported or submitted pursuant to G.S. 58-19-25(a), 58-19-30(b), or 58-19-30(c), or that violate this Article, shall pay, in his individual capacity, after notice and hearing, a civil penalty of one hundred dollars ($100.00) per violation, not to exceed a total penalty of one thousand dollars ($1,000), to the Commissioner, who shall forward the clear proceeds to the General Fund of this State.

(c) Whenever it appears to the Commissioner that any insurer subject to this Article or any director, officer, employee, or agent thereof has engaged in any transaction or entered into a contract that is subject to G.S. 58-19-30 and that would not have been approved had such approval been requested, the Commissioner may order the insurer to immediately cease and desist from any further activity under that transaction or contract. After notice and hearing the Commissioner may also order the insurer to void any such contracts and restore the status quo if such action is in the best interest of the policyholders, creditors, or the public.

(d) Whenever it appears to the Commissioner that any insurer or any director, officer, employee, or agent thereof has knowingly and willfully committed a violation of this Article, the Commissioner may cause criminal proceedings to be instituted by the Superior Court of Wake County against such insurer or the responsible director, officer, employee, or agent thereof. Any insurer that knowingly and willfully violates this Article may be fined not more than one thousand dollars ($1,000). Any individual who knowingly and willfully violates this Article is guilty of a Class I felony.

(e) Any officer, director, or employee of an insurance holding company system who knowingly and willfully subscribes to or makes or causes to be made any false statements or false reports or false filings with the intent to deceive the Commissioner in the performance of his duties under this Article, is guilty of a Class I felony. Any fines imposed shall be paid by the officer, director, or employee in his individual capacity. (1989, c. 722, s. 1; 1993, c. 504, s. 14; c. 539, ss. 1271, 1272; 1994, Ex. Sess., c. 24, s. 14(c); 1998-215, s. 84.)

§ 58-19-55. Receivership.

Whenever it appears to the Commissioner that any person has committed a violation of this Article that so impairs the financial condition of a domestic insurer as to threaten insolvency or make the further transaction of business by it hazardous to its policyholders, creditors, shareholders, or the public, then the Commissioner may proceed as provided in Article 30 of this Chapter. (1989, c. 722, s. 1.)

§ 58-19-60. Recovery.

(a) If an order for liquidation or rehabilitation of a domestic insurer has been entered, the receiver appointed under such order has a right to recover on behalf of the insurer, (i) from any parent corporation or holding company or person or affiliate who otherwise controlled the insurer, the amount of distributions (other than distributions of shares of the same class of stock) paid by the insurer on its capital stock, or (ii) any payment in the form of a bonus, termination settlement, or extraordinary lump sum salary adjustment made by the insurer or its subsidiary or subsidiaries to a director, officer, or employee, where the distribution or payment pursuant to (i) or (ii) above is made at any time during the one year preceding the petition for liquidation or rehabilitation, as the case may be, subject to the limitations of subsections (b), (c), and (d) of this section.

(b) No such distribution is recoverable if the parent or affiliate shows that when paid such distribution was lawful and reasonable, and that the insurer did not know and could not reasonably have known that such distribution might adversely affect the ability of the insurer to fulfill its contractual obligations.

(c) Any person that was a parent corporation or holding company or a person that otherwise controlled the insurer or affiliate at the time such distributions were paid is liable up to the amount of distributions or payments under subsection (a) of this section such person received. Any person who otherwise controlled the insurer at the time such distributions were declared is liable up to the amount of distributions he would have received if they had been paid immediately. If two or more persons are liable with respect to the same distributions, they are jointly and severally liable.

(d) The maximum amount recoverable under this section is the amount needed in excess of all other available assets of the insurer to pay its contractual obligations and to reimburse any guaranty funds.

(e) To the extent that any person liable under subsection (c) of this section is insolvent or otherwise fails to pay claims due from it pursuant to that subsection, its parent corporation, holding company, or person who otherwise controlled it at the time that the distribution was paid, are jointly and severally liable for any resulting deficiency in the amount recovered from such parent corporation or holding company or person who otherwise controlled it. (1989, c. 722, s. 1.)

§ 58-19-65. Revocation or suspension of insurer's license.

Whenever it appears to the Commissioner that any person has committed a violation of this Article that makes the continued operation of an insurer contrary to the interests of policyholders or the public, the Commissioner may, after giving notice and an opportunity to be heard, suspend or revoke such insurer's license to do business in this State for such period as he finds is required for the protection of policyholders or the public. Any such determination shall be accompanied by specific findings of fact and conclusions of law. (1989, c. 722, s. 1; 2003-212, s. 26(f).)

Effect of Amendments. — Session Laws 2003-212, s. 26.(f), effective January 1, 2004, and applicable to all company licenses issued or otherwise eligible for renewal or continuation after that date, substituted "Revocation or suspension" for "Revocation, suspension, or nonrenewal" in the section heading; and in the first sentence, substituted "suspend or revoke" "for suspend, revoke, or refuse to renew."

§ 58-19-70. Judicial review; mandatory injunction or writ of mandamus.

(a) Any person aggrieved by any order made by the Commissioner pursuant to this Article may appeal in accordance with G.S. 58-2-75.

(b) Any person aggrieved by any failure of the Commissioner to act or make a determination required by this Article may petition the Superior Court of Wake County for a mandatory injunction or a writ of mandamus directing the Commissioner to act or make such determination forthwith. (1989, c. 722, s. 1.)

ARTICLE 20.

Hull Insurance, and Protection and Indemnity Clubs.

§ 58-20-1. Short title.

This Article may be cited as the "Commercial Fishermen's Hull Insurance, and Protection and Indemnity Club Act". (1987, c. 330, s. 1.)

§ 58-20-5. Definitions.

For purposes of this Article:
  (1) "Association" means a trade or professional association that has been in existence for at least five years, and has adopted a written constitution, and a written set of bylaws, and was created for purposes other than for participating in a club.
  (2) "Club" means a commercial fishermen's hull insurance and protection and indemnity club created under this Article.
  (3) "Commercial fisherman" means any individual, corporation, or other business entity whose earned income is at least fifty percent (50%) derived from taking and selling food resources living in any ocean, bay, river, gulf, estuary, tidal wetlands, spoil area, estuation exit or entrance, or any other body of water or tidal wetlands from which a commercial harvest of fish may be taken.
  (4) "Hull Insurance and Protection and Indemnity" means:
    a. Insurance against loss or damage to a vessel's hull, lifeboats, rafts, and other operating equipment of the vessel other than its electrical machinery; and
    b. Insurance against loss of life, personal injury, or illness to the master, the crew, and other third parties, and against damage to any other vessel or property, such as cargo, for which the insured is legally liable. (1987, c. 330, s. 1.)

§ 58-20-10. Commercial Fishermen Hull Insurance, and Protection and Indemnity Clubs authorized.

In addition to other authority granted under Articles 1 through 64 of this Chapter, ten or more commercial fishermen who are members of an association may enter into contracts or agreements under this Article for the joint protection and retention of their risk for Hull Insurance, and Protection and Indemnity, and for the payment of losses or claims made against any member. Any group of commercial fishermen intending to organize and operate a Club under this Article shall give the Commissioner 30 days' advance written notification of its intention in a form prescribed by the Commissioner. (1987, c. 330, s. 1.)

§ 58-20-15. Board of trustees.

(a) A Club shall be operated by a board of trustees. Each trustee shall also be a member of an association. The trustees shall be selected by the Club members under the rules of organization of the Club. The board of trustees shall:
  (1) Establish the terms and conditions of hull insurance and protection and indemnity coverage within the Club, including underwriting and exclusions of coverage;
  (2) Ensure that all valid claims are paid promptly;

(3) Take all necessary precautions to safeguard the assets of the Club;

(4) Maintain minutes of its meeting and make those minutes available to the Commissioner;

(5) Designate an administrator to carry out the policies established by the trustees; and

(6) Establish guidelines for membership in the Club.

(b) The board of trustees shall not:

(1) Extend credit to an individual member for payment of a premium, except under a payment plan approved by the Commissioner; or

(2) Borrow money from the Club, or in the name of the Club, except in the ordinary course of business.

Whenever the board of trustees borrow money from the Club as authorized by this subdivision it shall first advise the Commissioner of the nature and purpose of the loan, and shall obtain his prior approval of such loan. (1987, c. 330, s. 1.)

§ 58-20-20. Mutual agreement for indemnification.

(a) An agreement made under this Article shall contain provisions for:

(1) A system or program of loss control;

(2) The termination of membership;

(3) The payment by the Club of all claims for which a member incurred liability during the period of his membership;

(4) The non-payment of claims where a member has individually retained the risk, or where the risk is not specifically covered, or where the amount of the claim exceeds the coverage provided by the Club;

(5) The assessment of members;

(6) The payment of contributions from members to satisfy deficiencies;

(7) The maintenance of claim reserves equal to known incurred losses and loss adjustment expenses and to an estimate of incurred but not reported losses; and

(8) Final accounting and settlement of the obligations or refunds to a terminating member when all incurred claims are settled.

(b) The agreement required by this section may also include provisions authorizing the Club to:

(1) To establish offices where necessary in this State, and employ necessary staff to carry out its purposes;

(2) Retain legal counsel, actuaries, claims adjusters, auditors, engineers, private consultants, and advisors, and other persons as the board of trustees or the administrator deem to be necessary;

(3) Amend or repeal its bylaws;

(4) Purchase, lease, or rent real and personal property as it deems necessary; and

(5) Enter into agreements with financial institutions that permit it to issue checks or other negotiable instruments in its own name. (1987, c. 330, s. 1.)

§ 58-20-25. Termination of Club membership; notice.

If a member fails to pay his contributions calls, or assessment, or other property required by the board of trustees as authorized by this Article, he shall not be entitled to any hull insurance and protection and indemnity coverage under this Article, and the Club may terminate his membership upon giving the member at least 10 days' notice. The Club may terminate a membership for any other reason upon giving the member at least 90 days' written notice of the termination. A member may terminate his membership with the Club upon giving at least 90 days' written notice of the termination. (1987, c. 330, s. 1.)

§ 58-20-30. Financial monitoring and evaluation of clubs.

Each club shall be audited annually, at the Club's expense, by a certified public accounting firm. A copy of the audit report shall be furnished to each member, and to the Commissioner. The trustees shall obtain an appropriate actuarial evaluation of the loss and loss adjustment expenses reserves of the Club, including estimate of losses and loss adjustment expenses incurred but not reported. The provisions of G.S. 58-2-131 through G.S. 58-2-134, G.S. 58-2-150, 58-2-160, 58-2-165, 58-2-180, 58-2-185, 58-2-190, 58-2-200, and G.S. 58-6-5 apply to each Club and to persons that administer the Clubs. (1987, c. 330, s. 1; 1991, c. 681, s. 5; 1999-132, s. 11.2.)

§ 58-20-35. Insolvency or impairment of Club.

(a) If an annual audit or an examination by the Commissioner reveals that the assets of a Club are insufficient to discharge its legal liabilities and other obligations, the Commissioner shall notify the administrator and board of trustees of the Club's deficiency; and he shall recommend the measures to be taken in order to abate the deficiency. He may recommend that the Club refrain from adding new members until the deficiency is abated. If the Club fails to comply with the recommendations within 30 days after the date of the notice, the Commissioner may apply to the Superior Court of Wake County for an order requiring the Club to abate the deficiency and authorizing the Commissioner to appoint one or more special deputy commissioners, counsel, clerks, or assistants to oversee the implementation of the Court's order. The compensation and expenses of such persons shall be fixed by the Commissioner, subject to the approval of the Court, and shall be paid out of the funds or assets of the Club.

(b) If a Club is determined to be insolvent, financially impaired, or is otherwise unable to discharge its legal liabilities and other obligations, each member shall be assessed on a pro rata basis as provided under G.S. 58-20-15. (1987, c. 330, s. 1.)

§ 58-20-40. Immunity of administrators and boards of trustees.

There is no liability on the part of and no cause of action arises against any board of trustees established under this Article, or against any administrator appointed as their representative, or any Club, its members or its employees, agents, contractors, or subcontractors for any good faith action taken by them in the performance of their powers and duties in creating or administering any Club under this Article. (1987, c. 330, s. 1.)

ARTICLE 21.

Surplus Lines Act.

§ 58-21-1. Short title.

This Article shall be known and may be cited as the "Surplus Lines Act". (1985, c. 688, s. 1.)

§ 58-21-2. Relationship to other insurance laws.

Unless surplus lines insurance, surplus lines licensees, or nonadmitted insurers are specifically referenced in a particular section of this Chapter, no sections contained in Articles of this Chapter other than this Article apply to surplus lines insurance, surplus lines licensees, or nonadmitted insurers. (1999-219, s. 6.2.)

§ 58-21-5. Purposes; necessity for regulation.

This Article shall be liberally construed and applied to promote its underlying purposes, which include:

(1) Protecting persons in this State seeking insurance;
(2) Permitting surplus lines insurance to be placed with reputable and financially sound nonadmitted insurers and exported from this State pursuant to this Article;
(3) Establishing a system of regulation that will permit orderly access to surplus lines insurance in this State and encourage admitted insurers to provide new and innovative types of insurance available to consumers in this State; and
(4) Protecting revenues of this State. (1985, c. 688, s. 1.)

§ 58-21-10. Definitions.

As used in this Article:

(1) "Admitted insurer" means an insurer licensed to do an insurance business in this State.
(2) "Capital", as used in the financial requirements of G.S. 58-21-20, means funds paid in for stock or other evidence of ownership.
(3) "Eligible surplus lines insurer" means a nonadmitted insurer with which a surplus lines licensee may place surplus lines insurance under G.S. 58-21-20.
(4) "Export" means to place surplus lines insurance with a nonadmitted insurer.
(5) "Nonadmitted insurer" means an insurer not licensed to do an insurance business in this State. This definition includes insurance exchanges authorized under the laws of various states.
(6) "Producing broker" means an agent or broker licensed under Article 33 of this Chapter who deals directly with the party seeking insurance and who may also be a surplus lines licensee.
(7) "Surplus", as used in the financial requirements of G.S. 58-21-20, means funds over and above liabilities and capital of the company for the protection of policyholders.
(8) "Surplus lines insurance" means any insurance in this State of risks resident, located, or to be performed in this State, permitted to be placed through a surplus lines licensee with a nonadmitted insurer eligible to accept such insurance, other than reinsurance, commercial aircraft insurance, wet marine and transportation insurance, insurance independently procured pursuant to G.S. 58-28-5, life and accident or health insurance, and annuities.

(9) "Surplus lines licensee" means a person licensed under G.S. 58-21-65 to place insurance on risks resident, located, or to be performed in this State with nonadmitted insurers eligible to accept such insurance.

(10) "Wet marine and transportation insurance" means:

    a. Insurance upon vessels, crafts, hulls and of interests therein or with relation thereto;

    b. Insurance of marine builder's risks, marine war risks and contracts of marine protection and indemnity insurance;

    c. Insurance of freights and disbursements pertaining to a subject of insurance coming within this subsection; and

    d. Insurance of personal property and interests therein, in the course of exportation from or importation into any country, or in the course of transportation coastwise or on inland waters including transportation by land, water, or air from point of origin to final destination, in connection with any and all risks or perils of navigation, transit or transportation, and while being prepared for and while awaiting shipment, and during any delays, transshipment, or reshipment incident thereto. (1985, c. 688, s. 1; 1985 (Reg. Sess., 1986), c. 1027, s. 45; 1987, c. 629, s. 19; c. 727, s. 6; c. 864, s. 73; 1998-211, s. 3; 1999-219, s. 5.3.)

§ 58-21-15. Placement of surplus lines insurance.

Insurance may be procured through a surplus lines licensee from nonadmitted insurers if:

(1) Each insurer is an eligible surplus lines insurer;

(2) The full amount or kind of insurance cannot be obtained from insurers who are admitted to do business in this State. Such full amount or kind of insurance may be procured from eligible surplus lines insurers, provided that a diligent search is made among the insurers who are admitted to transact and are actually writing the particular kind and class of insurance in this State; and

(3) All other requirements of this Article are met. (1985, c. 688, s. 1; 1985 (Reg. Sess., 1986), c. 1013, s. 5.)

§ 58-21-20. Eligible surplus lines insurers required.

(a) No surplus lines licensee shall place any coverage with a nonadmitted insurer, unless at the time of placement, such nonadmitted insurer:

(1) Has established satisfactory evidence of good repute and financial integrity; and

(2) Qualifies under one of the following subdivisions:

    a. Has capital and surplus or its equivalent under the laws of its domiciliary jurisdiction, which equals either:

        1. This State's minimum capital and surplus requirements under G.S. 58-7-75, or

        2. Fifteen million dollars ($15,000,000),

    whichever is greater, except that nonadmitted insurers already qualified under this Article must have ten million dollars ($10,000,000) by December 31, 1991, twelve million five hundred thousand dollars ($12,500,000) by December 31, 1992, and fifteen million dollars ($15,000,000) by December 31, 1993. The requirements of this sub-subdivision may be satisfied by an insurer possessing less than the commitment capital and surplus upon an affirmative finding of acceptability by the Commissioner. The finding shall be based upon such factors as quality of management, capital and surplus of any parent company, company underwriting profit and investment income trends, and the insurer's record and reputation within the industry. In no event shall the Commissioner make an affirmative finding of acceptability when the insurer's capital and surplus is less than four million five hundred thousand dollars ($4,500,000).

In addition, an alien insurer qualifies under this subdivision if it complies with the capital and surplus requirements of this subdivision and maintains in the United States an irrevocable trust fund in either a national bank or a member of the Federal Reserve System, in an amount not less than five million four hundred thousand dollars ($5,400,000) for the protection of all of its policyholders in the United States, and the trust fund consists of cash, securities, letters of credit, or of investment of substantially the same character and quality as those which are eligible investments for the capital and statutory reserves of admitted insurers authorized to write like kinds of insurance in this State. The trust fund, which shall be included in any calculation of capital and surplus or its equivalent, shall have an expiration date which at no time shall be less than five years; or

b. In the case of any Lloyd's plans or other similar group of insurers, which consists of unincorporated individual insurers, or a combination of both unincorporated and incorporated insurers, maintains a trust fund in an amount of not less than one hundred million dollars ($100,000,000) as security to the full amount thereof for all policyholders and creditors in the United States of each member of the group, and the trust shall likewise comply with the terms and conditions established in subdivision (2)a. of this section for alien insurers; and

c. In the case of an "insurance exchange" created by the laws of individual states, maintain capital and surplus, or the substantial equivalent thereof, of not less than seventy-five million dollars ($75,000,000) in the aggregate. For insurance exchanges which maintain funds in an amount of not less than fifteen million dollars ($15,000,000) for the protection of all insurance exchange policyholders, each individual syndicate shall maintain minimum capital and surplus, or the substantial equivalent thereof, of not less than five million dollars ($5,000,000). If the insurance exchange does not maintain funds in an amount of not less than fifteen million dollars ($15,000,000) for the protection of all insurance exchange policyholders, each individual syndicate shall meet the minimum capital and surplus requirements of subdivision (2)a. of this section.

d. In the case of a group of incorporated insurers under common administration, which has continuously transacted an insurance business outside the United States for at least three years immediately before this time, and which submits to this State's authority to examine its books and records and bears the expense of the examination, and maintains an aggregate policyholders' surplus of not less than ten billion dollars ($10,000,000,000), and maintains in trust a surplus of not less than one hundred million dollars ($100,000,000) for the benefit of United States surplus lines policyholders of any member of the group, and each insurer maintains capital and surplus of not less than twenty-five million dollars ($25,000,000) per company.

(3) Has caused to be provided to the Commissioner a copy of its current annual statement certified by such insurer; such statement to be

provided no more than two months, and for alien insurers six months, after the close of the period reported upon and that is either:

    a. Filed with and approved by the regulatory authority in the domicile of the nonadmitted insurer; or

    b. Certified by an accounting or auditing firm licensed in the jurisdiction of the insurer's domicile; or

    c. In the case of an insurance exchange, the statement may be an aggregate combined statement of all underwriting syndicates operating during the period reported.

(b) In addition to meeting the requirements in subdivisions (a)(1) through (a)(3) of this section, an insurer shall be an eligible surplus lines insurer if it appears on the most recent list of eligible surplus lines insurers published by the Commissioner. Nothing in this subsection shall require the Commissioner to place or maintain the name of any nonadmitted insurer on the list of eligible surplus lines insurers. There shall be no liability on the part of, and no cause of action of any nature shall arise against, the Commissioner or his employees or representatives for any action taken or not taken by them in the performance of their powers and duties under this subsection.

(c) Every surplus lines insurer that applies for eligibility under this section shall pay a nonrefundable fee of two hundred fifty dollars ($250.00). In order to renew eligibility, such insurer shall pay a nonrefundable renewal fee of five hundred dollars ($500.00) on or before January 1 of each year thereafter. Such fees shall not be prorated. (1985, c. 688, s. 1; c. 793; 1985 (Reg. Sess., 1986), c. 1027, s. 46; 1989 (Reg. Sess., 1990), c. 1069, s. 13; 1991, c. 681, s. 39; 1993 (Reg. Sess., 1994), c. 678, s. 15; 1995, c. 507, s. 11A(c); 2001-223, s. 17.1.)

§ 58-21-25. Other nonadmitted insurers.

Only that portion of any risk eligible for export for which the full amount of coverage is not procurable from eligible surplus lines insurers may be placed with any other nonadmitted insurer that does not appear on the list of eligible surplus lines insurers published by the Commissioner pursuant to G.S. 58-21-20(b), but nonetheless meets the requirements set forth in G.S. 58-21-20(a)(1) through (a)(3) and any regulations of the Commissioner. The surplus lines licensee seeking to provide coverage through an unlisted nonadmitted insurer shall make a filing specifying the amount and percentage of each risk to be placed, and naming the nonadmitted insurer with which placement is intended. Within 30 days after the coverage has been placed, the producing broker or surplus lines licensee shall send written notice to the insured that the insurance, or a portion thereof, has been placed with such nonadmitted insurer. (1985, c. 688, s. 1.)

§ 58-21-30. Withdrawal of eligibility from a surplus lines insurer.

If at any time the Commissioner has reason to believe that an eligible surplus lines insurer:

    (1) Is in unsound financial condition or has acted in an untrustworthy manner,

    (2) Is no longer eligible under G.S. 58-21-20,

    (3) Has willfully violated the laws of this State, or

    (4) Does not make reasonably prompt payment of just losses and claims in this State or elsewhere, the Commissioner may declare it ineligible. The Commissioner shall promptly mail notice of all such declarations to each surplus lines licensee. (1985, c. 688, s. 1; 2001-223, s. 17.2.)

§ 58-21-35. Duty to file reports and retain affidavits.

(a) Within 30 days after the placing of any surplus lines insurance, the surplus lines licensee shall file with the Commissioner a report in a format prescribed by the Commissioner regarding the insurance and including the following information:

(1) The name of the insured.

(2) The identity of the insurer or insurers.

(3) A description of the subject and location of the risk.

(4) The amount of premium charged for the insurance.

(5) The amount of premium tax for the insurance.

(6) The policy period.

(7) The policy number.

(8) The name, address, telephone number, facsimile telephone number, and electronic mail address of the licensee, as applicable.

(9) Any other relevant information the Commissioner may reasonably require.

(b) The licensee shall complete and retain an affidavit as to the efforts to place the coverage with admitted insurers and the results of the efforts, in accordance with G.S. 58-21-15. The report and affidavit required by this section and the quarterly report required by G.S. 58-21-80 shall be completed on a standardized form or forms prescribed by the Commissioner and are not public records under G.S. 132-1 or G.S. 58-2-100. (1985, c. 688, s. 1; 1987, c. 864, s. 35; 1993 (Reg. Sess., 1994), c. 678, s. 16; 1999-219, s. 6.1.)

§ 58-21-40. Surplus lines regulatory support organization.

(a) A surplus lines regulatory support organization of surplus lines licensees shall be formed to:

(1) Facilitate and encourage compliance by resident and nonresident surplus lines licensees with the laws of this State and the rules and regulations of the Commissioner relative to surplus lines insurance;

(2) Communicate with organizations of admitted insurers with respect to the proper use of the surplus lines market;

(3) Receive and disseminate to surplus lines licensees information about surplus lines insurance, including, without limitation, new electronic filing procedures approved by the Commissioner, changes in the list of eligible surplus lines insurers, and modifications in coverages, procedures, and requirements as may be requested by the Commissioner; and

(4) Countersign nonresident produced surplus lines coverages and remit premium taxes for those coverages under G.S. 58-21-70 by means satisfactory to the Commissioner; and charge the nonresident surplus lines licensee a fee for the certification and countersignature as approved by the Commissioner.

(b) The regulatory support organization shall file with the Commissioner:

(1) A copy of its constitution, articles of agreement or association, or certificate of incorporation;

(2) A copy of its bylaws and rules governing its activities;

(3) An annually updated list of resident and nonresident licensees;

(4) The name and address of a resident of this State upon whom notices or orders of the Commissioner or processes issued at his direction may be served; and

(5) An agreement that the Commissioner may examine the regulatory support organization in accordance with subsection (c) of this section.

(c) The Commissioner may, at times deemed appropriate, make or cause to be made an examination of each regulatory support organization; in which case the provisions of G.S. 58-2-131, 58-2-132, 58-2-133, 58-2-134, 58-2-150, 58-2-155, 58-2-180, 58-2-185, 58-2-190, 58-2-195, and 58-2-200 shall apply. If the Commissioner finds the regulatory support organization or any surplus lines licensee, whether resident or nonresident, to be in violation of this Article, the Commissioner may issue an order requiring the discontinuance of the violation.

(d) Each resident surplus lines licensee shall maintain active membership in a regulatory support organization as a condition of continued licensure under this Article. (1985, c. 688, s. 1; 1987 (Reg. Sess., 1988), c. 975, s. 13; 1995, c. 193, s. 28; 1999-132, s. 11.3; 2001-203, s. 28; 2001-451, ss. 2.1, 2.2; 2001-487, s. 63.)

Editor's Note. — Session Laws 2001-203, s. 31, contains a severability clause.

Session Laws 2001-451, s. 2.1, effective October 28, 2001, changed the effective date of Session Laws 2001-203, s. 28, from October 1, 2001, to January 1, 2002.

Effect of Amendments. — Session Laws 2001-203, s. 28, as amended by 2001-451, s. 2.1, effective January 1, 2002, substituted "regulatory support organization" for "advisory organizations" in the section catchline, and rewrote the section.

Session Laws 2001-203, s. 28, as amended by Session Laws 2001-451, s. 2.2, effective January 1, 2002, in subdivision (a)(4) of this section substituted "Countersign" for "Certify satisfactory evidence of current nonresident surplus lines licensure in this State by countersigning" and inserted "remit premium taxes for those coverages under G.S. 58-21-70."

Session Laws 2001-487, s. 63, effective January 1, 2002, in subdivision (a)(4), as amended by Session Laws 2001-203, s. 28, and by Session Laws 2001-451, s. 2.2, inserted "and" preceding "remit premium taxes."

§ 58-21-45. Evidence of the insurance; changes; penalty.

(a) As soon as surplus lines insurance has been placed, the producing broker or surplus lines licensee shall promptly deliver the policy to the insured. If the policy is not then available, the broker or licensee shall promptly deliver to the insured a certificate described in subsection (d) of this section, cover note, binder, or other evidence of insurance. The certificate described in subsection (d), cover note, binder, or other evidence of insurance shall be executed by the surplus lines licensee and shall show the description and location of the subject of the insurance, coverages including any material limitations other than those in standard forms, a general description of the coverages of the insurance, the premium and rate charged and taxes to be collected from the insured, and the name and address of the insured and surplus lines insurer or insurers and proportion of the entire risk assumed by each, and the name of the surplus lines licensee and the licensee's license number.

(b) No producing broker or surplus lines licensee shall issue or deliver any evidence of insurance or purport to insure or represent that insurance will be or has been written by any eligible surplus lines insurer, or a nonadmitted insurer pursuant to G.S. 58-21-25, unless he has authority from the insurer to cause the risk to be insured, or has received information from the insurer in the regular course of business that such insurance has been granted.

(c) If, after delivery of any such evidence of insurance there is any change in the identity of the insurers, or the proportion of the risk assumed by any insurer, or any other material change in coverage as stated in the producing broker's or surplus lines licensee's original evidence of insurance, or in any other material as to the insurance coverage so evidenced, the producing broker or surplus lines licensee shall promptly issue and deliver to the insured an appropriate substitute for or endorsement of the original document, accurately showing the current status of the coverage and the insurers responsible thereunder.

(d) As soon as reasonably possible after the placement of any such insurance the producing broker or surplus lines licensee shall deliver a copy of the policy or, if not available, a certificate of insurance to the insured to replace any evidence of insurance previously issued. Each certificate or policy of insurance shall contain or have attached thereto a complete record of all policy insuring agreements, conditions, exclusions, clauses, endorsements, or any other material facts that would regularly be included in the policy.

(e) Any surplus lines licensee or producing broker who fails to comply with the requirements of this section shall be subject to the penalties provided in G.S. 58-21-105.

(f) Every evidence of insurance negotiated, placed, or procured under the provisions of this Article issued by the surplus lines licensee shall bear the name of the licensee and the following legend in 10 point type and in contrasting color: "The insurance company with which this coverage has been placed is not licensed by the State of North Carolina and is not subject to its supervision. In the event of the insolvency of the insurance company, losses under this policy will not be paid by any State insurance guaranty or solvency fund." (1985, c. 688, s. 1.)

§ 58-21-50. Duty to notify insured.

No contract of insurance placed by a surplus lines licensee under this Article shall be binding upon the insured and no premium charged therefor shall be due and payable until the producing broker or surplus lines licensee notifies the insured in writing, a copy of which shall be maintained by the broker or licensee with the records of the contract and available for possible examination, that:

(1) The insurer with which the coverage has been placed is not licensed by this State and is not subject to its supervision; and

(2) In the event of the insolvency of the surplus lines insurer, losses will not be paid by any State insurance guaranty or solvency fund.

Nothing in this section shall nullify any agreement by any insurer to provide insurance. (1985, c. 688, s. 1.)

§ 58-21-55. Valid surplus lines insurance.

Insurance contracts procured under this Article shall be valid and enforceable as to all parties. (1985, c. 688, s. 1.)

§ 58-21-60. Effect of payment to surplus lines licensee.

A payment of premium to a surplus lines licensee acting for a person other than himself in negotiating, continuing, or reviewing any policy of insurance under this Article shall be deemed to be payment to the insurer, notwithstanding any conditions or stipulations inserted in the policy or contract. (1985, c. 688, s. 1.)

§ 58-21-65. Licensing of surplus lines licensee.

(a) No agent or broker licensed by the Commissioner shall procure any contract of surplus lines insurance with any nonadmitted insurer, unless he possesses a current surplus lines insurance license issued by the Commissioner.

(b) The Commissioner shall issue a surplus lines license to any qualified holder of a current fire and casualty broker's or agent's license, but only when the broker or agent has:

(1) Remitted the fifty dollars ($50.00) annual fee to the Commissioner;

(2) Submitted a completed license application on a form supplied by the Commissioner, and the application has been approved by the Commissioner;

(3) Passed a qualifying examination approved by the Commissioner; except that all holders of a license prior to July 11, 1985 shall be deemed to have passed such an examination; and

(4) Filed with the Commissioner, and maintains during the term of the license, in force and unimpaired a bond in favor of this State in the sum of ten thousand dollars ($10,000), aggregate liability, with corporate sureties approved by the Commissioner. The bond shall be conditioned that the surplus lines licensee will conduct business in accordance with the provisions of this Article and will promptly remit the taxes as provided by law. No bond shall be terminated unless at least 30 days prior written notice is given to the licensee and Commissioner. A person required by this subdivision to maintain a bond may, in lieu of that bond, deposit with the Commissioner the equivalent amount in cash, in certificates of deposit issued by banks organized under the laws of the State of North Carolina, or any national bank having its principal office in North Carolina, or securities, which shall be held in accordance with Article 5 of this Chapter. Securities may only be obligations of the United States or of federal agencies listed in G.S. 147-69.1(c)(2) guaranteed by the United States, obligations of the State of North Carolina, or obligations of a city or county of this State. Any proposed deposit of an obligation of a city or county of this State is subject to the prior approval of the Commissioner.

(c) Corporations shall be eligible to be resident surplus lines licensees, upon the following conditions:

(1) The corporate licensee shall list individuals within the corporation who have satisfied all requirements of this Article to become surplus lines licensees; and

(2) Only those individuals listed on the corporate license and who are surplus lines licensees shall transact surplus lines business.

(d) Each surplus lines license shall be issued on September 1 of each year and expire August 31 of the following year unless renewed. Application for renewal shall be made 30 days before the expiration date. The license shall be renewed upon payment of the annual license fee and compliance with the other applicable provisions of this section. Any person who places surplus lines insurance without a valid surplus lines license in effect shall pay a penalty of one thousand dollars ($1,000) and be subject to such other penalties as provided by law.

The clear proceeds of civil penalties provided for in this subsection shall be remitted to the Civil Penalty and Forfeiture Fund in accordance with G.S. 115C-457.2.

(e) Any person who does not renew a surplus lines license and applies for another surplus lines license more than two years after the expiration date of the previous license shall be required to satisfy every condition in this section, including the written exam, before the Commissioner issues another surplus lines license to that person.

(f) A person licensed as a surplus lines licensee under the laws of a state bordering this State may be licensed as a surplus lines licensee under this Article, if: (i) the laws of the bordering state are substantially similar to the provisions of this Article and (ii) the bordering state has a law or regulation substantially similar to this subsection that permits surplus lines licensees licensed under this Article to be licensed by the bordering state and (iii) the person complies with all requirements of this Article and submits himself or herself to the Commissioner's jurisdiction. (1985, c. 688, s. 1; 1985 (Reg. Sess., 1986), c. 928, s. 6; c. 1013, ss. 4, 16; 1987, c. 629, s. 18; c. 752, s. 6; 1987 (Reg. Sess., 1988), c. 975, s. 14; 1991, c. 212, s. 1; c. 644, s. 41; 1998-215, s. 85.)

§ 58-21-70. Surplus lines licensees may accept business from other agents or brokers; countersignatures required; remittance of premium tax.

(a) A surplus lines licensee may originate surplus lines insurance or accept such insurance from any other duly licensed agent or broker, and the surplus lines licensee may compensate such agent or broker therefor.

(b) Every report filed by a nonresident licensee under G.S. 58-21-35(a) shall, before being filed with the Commissioner, be countersigned by a resident licensee or by a regulatory support organization. The resident licensee or regulatory support organization may charge the nonresident licensee a countersignature fee.

(c) Every resident licensee and regulatory support organization that countersigns a report under subsection (b) of this section is responsible for remitting the premium tax for the coverage, as specified in G.S. 58-21-85, to the Commissioner. (1985, c. 688, s. 1; 2001-451, s. 2.)

Effect of Amendments. — Session Laws 2001-451, s. 2, effective January 1, 2002, added "countersignatures required; remittance of premium tax" at the end of the section catchline; designated the existing provision of the section as subsection (a); and added subsections (b) and (c).

§ 58-21-75. Records of surplus lines licensee.

Each surplus lines licensee shall keep in his or her office in this State a full and true record of each surplus lines insurance contract placed by or through the licensee, including a copy of the policy, certificate, cover note, or other evidence of insurance. The record shall include the following items:

(1) Amount of the insurance and perils insured;

(2) Brief description of the property insured and its location;

(3) Gross premium charged;

(4) Any return premium paid;

(5) Rate of premium charged upon the several items of property;

(6) Effective date of the contract, and the terms of the contract;

(7) Name and address of the insured;

(8) Name and address of the insurer;

(9) Amount of tax and other sums to be collected from the insured; and

(10) Identity of the producing broker, any confirming correspondence from the insurer or its representative, and the application.

The record of each contract shall be kept open at all reasonable times to examination by the Commissioner without notice for a period not less than three years following termination of the contract. (1985, c. 688, s. 1; 1991, c. 644, s. 42.)

§ 58-21-80. Quarterly reports; summary of exported business.

On or before the end of January, April, July, and October of each year, each surplus lines licensee shall file with the Commissioner, on a form prescribed by the Commissioner, a verified report of all surplus lines insurance transacted during the preceding three months showing:

(1) Aggregate gross premiums written;

(2) Aggregate return premiums; and

(3) Amount of aggregate tax to be remitted. (1985, c. 688, s. 1; 1987, c. 864, s. 36.)

§ 58-21-85. Surplus lines tax.

(a) Gross premiums charged, less any return premiums, for surplus lines insurance are subject to a premium receipts tax of five percent (5%), which shall be collected by the surplus lines licensee as specified by the Commissioner, in addition to the full amount of the gross premium charged by the insurer for the insurance. The tax on any portion of the premium unearned at termination of insurance having been credited by the State to the licensee shall be returned to the policyholder directly by the surplus lines licensee or through the producing broker, if any. The surplus lines licensee is prohibited from absorbing such tax and from rebating for any reason, any part of such tax.

(b) At the same time that he files his quarterly report as set forth in G.S. 58-21-80, each surplus lines licensee shall pay the premium receipts tax due for the period covered by the report.

(c) This section does not apply to risks of State government agencies nor to risks of local government risk pools created and operating under Article 23 of this Chapter.

(d) The surplus lines licensee placing the insurance and claiming the exemption in subsection (c) of this section shall affirmatively show in writing to the Commissioner that the risk qualifies for the exemption. (1985, c. 688, s. 1; 1985 (Reg. Sess., 1986), c. 928, s. 11; 1987, c. 727, ss. 2, 3; c. 864, s. 37.)

§ 58-21-90. Collection of tax.

All provisions of Chapter 105 of the General Statutes, not inconsistent with this Article, relating to administration, auditing and making returns, the imposition and collection of tax and the lien thereon, assessments, refunds, and penalties, shall be applicable to the tax imposed by this Article; and with respect thereto, the Commissioner has the same power and authority as is given to the Secretary of Revenue under the provisions of Chapter 105 of the General Statutes. (1985, c. 688, s. 1; 1985 (Reg. Sess., 1986), c. 928, s. 7.)

§ 58-21-95. Suspension, revocation or nonrenewal of surplus lines licensee's license.

The Commissioner may suspend, revoke, or refuse to renew the license of a surplus lines licensee after notice and hearing as provided under G.S. 58-2-70 upon any one or more of the following grounds:

    (1) Removal of the surplus lines licensee's office from this State;

    (2) Removal of the surplus lines licensee's office accounts and records from this State during the period during which such accounts and records are required to be maintained under G.S. 58-21-75;

    (3) Closing of the surplus lines licensee's office for a period of more than 30 business days, unless permission is granted by the Commissioner;

    (4) Failure to make and file required reports;

    (5) Failure to transmit the required tax on surplus lines premiums;

    (6) Failure to maintain the required bond;

    (7) Violation of any provision of this Article; or

    (8) For any other cause for which an insurance license could be denied, revoked, suspended, or renewal refused under the Insurance Law. (1985, c. 688, s. 1.)

§ 58-21-100. Actions against surplus lines insurer; service of process.

(a) A surplus lines insurer may be sued upon any cause of action arising in this State, under any surplus lines insurance contract made by it or evidence of insurance issued or delivered by the surplus lines licensee, pursuant to the procedure provided in G.S. 58-16-30. Any such policy issued by the surplus lines licensee shall contain a provision stating the substance of this section and designating the person to whom the Commissioner shall mail process.

(b) Each surplus lines insurer engaging in surplus lines insurance shall be deemed thereby to have subjected itself to this Article.

(c) The remedies and procedures provided in this section are in addition to any other methods provided by law for service of process upon insurers. (1985, c. 688, s. 1; 1991, c. 720, s. 43.)

§ 58-21-105. Penalties.

(a) Any surplus lines licensee who in this State represents or aids a nonadmitted insurer in violation of this Article shall be guilty of a Class 1 misdemeanor.

(b) In addition to any other penalty provided for in this section or otherwise provided by law, including any suspension, revocation, or refusal to renew a license, any person violating any provision of this Article shall be subject to a civil penalty, payment of restitution, or both, in accordance with G.S. 58-2-70. (1985, c. 688, s. 1; 1993, c. 539, s. 450; 1994, Ex. Sess., c. 24, s. 14(c).)

ARTICLE 22.

Liability Risk Retention.

§ 58-22-1. Purpose.

The purpose of this Article is to regulate the formation and operation of risk retention and purchasing groups in this State that are formed pursuant to the provisions of the Product Liability Risk Retention Act of 1981, as amended by the Risk Retention Amendments of 1986 (15 U.S.C. § 3901 et seq.). (1985 (Reg. Sess., 1986), c. 1013, s. 8; 1987, c. 310, s. 1.)

§ 58-22-5: Reserved for future codification purposes.

§ 58-22-10. Definitions.

As used in this Article:
  (1) "Completed operations liability" means liability arising out of the installation, maintenance, or repair of any product at a site that is not owned or controlled by:
    a. Any person who performs that work; or
    b. Any person who hires an independent contractor to perform that work;
    but includes liability for activities that are completed or abandoned before the date of the occurrence giving rise to the liability.
  (2) "Domicile", for purposes of determining the state in which a purchasing group is domiciled, means:
    a. For a corporation, the state in which the purchasing group is incorporated; and
    b. For an unincorporated entity, the state of its principal place of business.
  (3) "Hazardous financial condition" means that, based on its present or reasonably anticipated financial condition, a risk retention group is

insolvent or, although not yet financially impaired or insolvent, is unlikely to be able:

    a. To meet obligations to policyholders with respect to known claims and reasonably anticipated claims; or

    b. To pay other obligations in the normal course of business.

(4) "Insurance" means primary insurance, excess insurance, reinsurance, surplus lines insurance, and any other arrangement for shifting and distributing risk that is determined to be insurance under the laws of this State.

(5) "Liability" means legal liability for damages, including costs of defense, legal costs and fees, and other claims expenses, because of injuries to other persons, damage to their property, or other damage or loss to such other persons resulting from or arising out of any profit or nonprofit business, trade, product, professional or other services, premises, or operations; or any activity of any state or local government, or any agency or political subdivision thereof. Liability does not include personal risk liability or an employer's liability with respect to its employees other than legal liability under the Federal Employers' Liability Act (45 U.S.C. § 51 et seq.).

(6) "Personal risk liability" means liability for damage because of injury to any person, damage to property, or other loss or damage resulting from any personal, familial, or household responsibilities or activities. Personal risk liability does not include liability as defined in subdivision (5) of this section.

(7) "Plan of operation" or "feasibility study" means an analysis that presents the expected activities and results of a risk retention group including, at a minimum:

    a. For each state in which the group intends to do business, the coverages, deductibles, coverage limits, rates, and rating classification systems for each kind of insurance the group intends to offer;

    b. Historical and expected loss experience of the proposed members and national experience of similar exposures;

    c. Prospective financial statements and projections;

    d. Appropriate opinions by a qualified, independent casualty actuary, including a determination of minimum premium or participation levels required to commence operations and to prevent a hazardous financial condition;

    e. Identification of management, underwriting and claim procedures, marketing methods, managerial oversight methods, reinsurance agreements, and investment policies;

    f. Identification of each state in which the group has obtained, or sought to obtain, a charter and license, and a description of its status in each such state;

    g. Information sufficient to verify that the group's members are engaged in businesses or activities similar or related with respect to the liability to which those members are exposed by virtue of any related, similar, or common business, trade, product, services, premises, or operations; and

    h. Such other matters that are prescribed by the Commissioner for liability insurance companies authorized by this Chapter.

(8) "Product liability" means liability for damages because of any personal injury, death, emotional harm, consequential economic damage, or property damage, including damages resulting from the loss of use of property, arising out of the manufacture, design, importation, distribution, packaging, labeling, lease, or sale of a product; but does not

include the liability of any person for those damages if the product involved was in the possession of such person when the incident giving rise to the claim occurred.

(9) "Purchasing group" means any group that:

    a. Has as one of its purposes the purchase of liability insurance on a group basis;

    b. Purchases such insurance only for its group members and only to cover their similar or related liability exposure, as described in sub-subdivision c. of this subdivision;

    c. Is composed of members whose businesses or activities are similar or related with respect to the liability to which the members are exposed by virtue of any related, similar, or common business, trade, product, services, premises, or operations; and

    d. Is domiciled in any state.

(10) "Risk retention group" means any corporation or other limited liability association:

    a. Whose primary activity consists of assuming and spreading all or any portion of the liability exposure of its group members;

    b. That is organized for the primary purpose of conducting the activity described under sub-subdivision a. of this subdivision;

    c. That

        (i) Is chartered and licensed as a liability insurance company and authorized to engage in the business of insurance under the laws of any state; or

        (ii) Before January 1, 1985, was chartered or licensed and authorized to engage in the business of insurance under the laws of Bermuda or the Cayman Islands and, before that date, had certified to the insurance regulator of at least one state that it satisfied the capitalization requirements of such state; except that any such group shall be considered to be a risk retention group only if it has been engaged in business continuously since that date and only for the purpose of continuing to provide insurance to cover product liability or completed operations liability, as such terms were defined in the Product Liability Risk Retention Act of 1981 before the effective date of the Risk Retention Act of 1986;

    d. That does not exclude any person from membership in the group solely to provide for members of such a group a competitive advantage over such person;

    e. That

        (i) Has as its members only persons who have an ownership interest in the group and that has as its owners only persons who are members who are provided insurance by the risk retention group; or

        (ii) Has as its sole member and sole owner an organization that is owned by persons who are provided insurance by the risk retention group;

    f. Whose members are engaged in businesses or activities similar or related with respect to the liability of which such members are exposed by virtue of any related, similar, or common business trade, product, services, premises, or operations;

    g. Whose activities do not include the provision of insurance other than:

        (i) Liability insurance for assuming and spreading all or any portion of the liability of its group members; and

        (ii) Reinsurance with respect to the liability of any other risk retention group, or any members of such other group, that is engaged in businesses or activities so that such group or member meets the requirement described in sub-subdivision f. of this subdivision from membership in the risk retention group that provides such reinsurance; and

   h. The name of which includes the phrase "Risk Retention Group". (1985 (Reg. Sess., 1986), c. 1013, s. 8; 1987, c. 310, s. 1; 1993, c. 452, s. 35; 2001-223, s. 18.)

§ 58-22-15. Risk retention groups chartered in this State.

(a) A risk retention group seeking to be chartered in this State must be chartered and licensed as a liability insurance company under Article 7 of this Chapter and, except as provided elsewhere in this Article, must comply with all of the laws and rules applicable to such insurers chartered and licensed in this State and with G.S. 58-22-20 to the extent such requirements are not a limitation on laws, administrative rules, or requirements of this State. As a chartered and licensed liability insurance company, the group is subject to the taxes imposed in Article 8B of Chapter 105 of the General Statutes.

(b) Before it may offer insurance in any state, each risk retention group shall also submit for approval to the Commissioner of this State a plan of operation or feasibility study. The risk retention group shall submit an appropriate revision in the event of any subsequent material change in any item of the plan of operation or feasibility study, within 10 days after any such change. The group shall not offer any additional kinds of liability insurance, in this State or in any other state, until a revision of such plan or study is approved by the Commissioner.

(c) At the time of filing its application for a charter, the risk retention group shall provide to the Commissioner in summary form the following information: the identity of the initial members of the group, the identity of those individuals who organized the group or who will provide administrative services or otherwise influence or control the activities of the group, the amount and nature of initial capitalization, the coverages to be afforded, and the states in which the group intends to operate. Upon receipt of this information, the Commissioner shall forward such information to the NAIC. Providing notification to the NAIC is in addition to and shall not be sufficient to satisfy the requirements of G.S. 58-22-20 or any other sections of this Article. (1985 (Reg. Sess., 1986), c. 1013, s. 8; 1987, c. 310, s. 1; c. 727, s. 13; 1993, c. 452, s. 36; 1995 (Reg. Sess., 1996), c. 747, s. 8.)

    Editor's Note. — Session Laws 1995 (Reg. Sess., 1996), c. 747, s. 16, provides: "This act does not obligate the General Assembly to appropriate funds."

§ 58-22-20. Risk retention groups not chartered in this State.

Risk retention groups that have been chartered in states other than this State and that seek to do business as risk retention groups in this state must observe and abide by the laws of this State as follows:

   (1) Notice of Operations and Designation of Commissioner as Agent. — Before offering insurance in this State, a risk retention group shall submit to the Commissioner:

      a. A statement identifying the state or states in which the risk retention group is chartered and licensed as a liability insurance company, date of chartering, its principal place of business, and such other information including information on its membership, as the Commissioner may require to verify that the risk retention group is qualified under G.S. 58-22-10(10);

b. A copy of its plan of operations or a feasibility study and revisions of such plan or study submitted to its state of domicile; provided, however, that the provision relating to the submission of a plan of operation or a feasibility study shall not apply with respect to any line or classification of liability insurance that (i) was defined in the Product Liability Risk Retention Act of 1981 before October 27, 1986, and (ii) was offered before that date by any risk retention group that had been chartered and operating for not less than three years before that date;

c. The risk retention group shall submit a copy of any revision to its plan of operation or feasibility study required by G.S. 58-22-15(b) at the same time that such revision is submitted to the Commissioner of its chartering state; and

d. A statement of registration that designates the Commissioner as its agent for the purpose of receiving service of legal process.

(2) Financial Condition. — A risk retention group doing business in this State shall file with the Commissioner:

a. A copy of the group's financial statement submitted to its state of domicile, which shall be certified by an independent public accountant and contain a statement of opinion on loss and loss adjustment expense reserves made by a member of the American Academy of Actuaries or a qualified loss reserve specialist, under criteria established by the NAIC or by the Commissioner;

b. A copy of each examination of the risk retention group as certified by the State insurance regulator or public official conducting the examination;

c. Upon request by the Commissioner, a copy of any audit performed with respect to the risk retention group; and

d. Such information as may be required to verify its continuing qualification as a risk retention group under G.S. 58-22-10(10).

(3) Taxation.

a. All premiums paid for coverages within this State to risk retention groups shall be subject to taxation at the same rate and subject to the same payment procedures and to the same interest, fines, and penalties for nonpayment as those applicable to surplus lines insurance under Article 21 of this Chapter. Premiums paid by purchasing groups are, however, taxed as provided in G.S. 58-22-35(b).

b. To the extent licensed agents or brokers are utilized pursuant to G.S. 58-22-60, they shall report and pay the taxes for the premiums for risks that they have placed with or on behalf of a risk retention group not chartered in this State. Such agent or broker shall keep a complete and separate record of all policies procured from each such risk retention group, which record shall be open to examination by the Commissioner, as provided in G.S. 58-2-185. These records shall, for each policy and each kind of insurance provided thereunder, include the following:

1. The limit of liability;
2. The time period covered;
3. The effective date;
4. The name of the risk retention group that issued the policy;
5. The gross premium charged; and
6. The amount of return premiums, if any.

c. To the extent that insurance agents or brokers are not utilized or fail to pay the tax, each risk retention group shall pay the tax for risks insured within the State. Each risk retention group shall report to the Commissioner all premiums paid to it for risks insured within the State.

(4) Compliance With Unfair Claims Settlement Practices Law. — A risk retention group and its agents and representatives shall comply with G.S. 58-3-100(5) and G.S. 58-63-15(11).

(5) Deceptive, False, or Fraudulent Practices. — A risk retention group shall comply with the provisions of Article 63 of this Chapter and Chapter 75 of the General Statutes regarding deceptive, false, or fraudulent acts or practices.

(6) Examination Regarding Financial Condition. — A risk retention group must submit to an examination by the Commissioner to determine its financial condition if the insurance regulator of the jurisdiction in which the group is chartered has not initiated an examination or does not initiate an examination within 60 days after a request by the Commissioner. This examination shall be coordinated to avoid unjustified repetition and conducted in an expeditious manner and in accordance with the Examiner Handbook of the NAIC.

(7) Notice to Purchasers. — Any policy issued by a risk retention group shall contain in 10 point type and contrasting color on the front page and the declaration page, the following notice:

"NOTICE

This policy is issued by your risk retention group. Your risk retention group is not subject to all of the insurance laws and regulations of your state. In the event of the insolvency of your risk retention group, losses under this policy will not be paid by any insurance insolvency or guaranty fund in this State."

(8) Prohibited Acts Regarding Solicitation or Sale. — The following acts by a risk retention group are prohibited:
a. The solicitation or sale of insurance by a risk retention group to any person who is not eligible for membership in such group; and
b. The solicitation or sale of insurance by, or operation of, a risk retention group that is in a hazardous financial condition or is financially impaired.

(9) Prohibition of Ownership By An Insurance Company. — No risk retention group shall be allowed to do business in this State if an insurance company is directly or indirectly a member or owner of such risk retention group, other than in the case of a risk retention group all of whose members are insurance companies.

(10) Prohibited Coverage. — No risk retention group may offer insurance policy coverage prohibited or not authorized by this Chapter or declared unlawful by the appellate courts of this State.

(11) Delinquency Proceedings. — A risk retention group not chartered in this State and doing business in this State must comply with a lawful order issued in a voluntary dissolution proceeding or in a delinquency proceeding commenced by a state insurance commissioner if there has been a finding of financial impairment after an examination under G.S. 58-22-20(6).

(12) Penalties. — A risk retention group that violates any provision of this Article is subject to G.S. 58-2-70. (1985 (Reg. Sess., 1986), c. 1013, s. 8; 1987, c. 310, s. 1; c. 727, ss. 1, 2; 1993, c. 452, s. 37; 1995 (Reg. Sess., 1996), c. 747, s. 9.)

Editor's Note. — Session Laws 1995 (Reg. Sess., 1996), c. 747, s. 16, provides: "This act does not obligate the General Assembly to appropriate funds."

§ 58-22-25. Compulsory association.

(a) No risk retention group is required to join or contribute financially to any insurance insolvency or guaranty fund or similar mechanism in this State; nor shall any risk retention group or its insureds receive any benefit from any such fund for claims arising out of the operations of such risk retention group.

(b) A risk retention group may be required to participate in residual market mechanisms under Articles 37 and 42 of this Chapter. (1987, c. 310, s. 1.)

§ 58-22-30. Countersignature not required.

A policy of insurance issued to a risk retention group or any member of that group is not required to be countersigned as otherwise provided in Articles 1 through 64 of this Chapter. (1985 (Reg. Sess., 1986), c. 1013, s. 8; 1987, c. 310, s. 1.)

§ 58-22-35. Purchasing groups; exemption from certain laws relating to the group purchase of insurance.

(a) Any purchasing group meeting the criteria established under the provisions of 15 U.S.C. § 3901 et seq. is exempt from any law of this State relating to the creation of groups for the purchase of insurance, prohibition of group purchasing, or any law that discriminates against a purchasing group or its members. In addition, an insurer is exempt from any law of this State that prohibits providing, or offering to provide, to a purchasing group or its members, advantages based on their loss and expense experience not afforded to other persons with respect to rates, policy forms, coverages, or other matters. A purchasing group is subject to all other applicable laws of this State.

(b) Taxes on premiums paid for coverage of risks resident or located in this State by a purchasing group or any members of the purchasing group shall be:

   (1) Imposed at the same rate and subject to the same interest, fines, and penalties as those applicable to premium taxes on similar coverage from a similar insurance source by other insureds. For example, coverage provided by a surplus lines licensee is taxed under Article 21 of this Chapter, coverage provided by an insurance company is taxed under Article 8B of Chapter 105 of the General Statutes, and coverage provided by an unlicensed insurer is taxed under G.S. 58-28-5(b).

   (2) Paid first by such insurance source, and if not by such source then by the agent or broker for the purchasing group, and if not by such agent or broker then by the purchasing group, and if not by such group then by each of its members. (1987, c. 310, s. 1; c. 727, s. 9; 1995 (Reg. Sess., 1996), c. 747, s. 10.)

Editor's Note. — Session Laws 1995 (Reg. Sess., 1996), c. 747, s. 16, provides: "This act does not obligate the General Assembly to appropriate funds."

§ 58-22-40. Notice and registration requirements of purchasing groups.

(a) A purchasing group that intends to do business in this State shall, before doing business, furnish notice to the Commissioner that shall:

   (1) Identify the state in which the group is domiciled;

    (2) Specify the lines and classifications of liability insurance that the purchasing group intends to purchase;

    (3) Identify the insurer from which the group intends to purchase its insurance and the domicile of such insurer;

    (4) Identify the principal place of business of the group;

    (5) Provide such other information as may be required by the Commissioner to verify that the purchasing group is qualified under G.S. 58-22-10(9);

    (6) Specify the method by which and the person or persons, if any, through whom insurance will be offered to its members whose risks are resident or located in this State; and furnish such information as may be required by the Commissioner to determine the appropriate premium tax treatment; and

    (7) Identify all other states in which the group intends to do business.

  (b) The purchasing group shall register with and designate the Commissioner as its agent solely for the purpose of receiving service of legal documents or process, except that such requirement does not apply in the case of a purchasing group:

    (1) That
      a. Was domiciled before April 2, 1986, in any state of the United States; and
      b. Is domiciled on and after October 27, 1986, in any state of the United States;

    (2) That before October 27, 1986, purchased insurance from an insurer licensed in any state; and since October 27, 1986, purchased its insurance from an insurer licensed in any state;

    (3) That was a purchasing group under the requirements of the Product Liability Retention Act of 1981 before October 27, 1986; and

    (4) That does not purchase insurance that was not authorized for purposes of an exemption under that act, as in effect before October 27, 1986.

  (c) A purchasing group shall notify the Commissioner of any changes in any of the items in subsection (a) of this section within 10 days after those changes.

  (d) Each purchasing group that is required to give notice under subsection (a) of this section shall also furnish such information as may be required by the Commissioner to:

    (1) Verify that the entity qualifies as a purchasing group;

    (2) Determine where the purchasing group is located; and

    (3) Determine appropriate tax treatment. (1987, c. 310, s. 1; c. 727, s. 10; 1993, c. 452, s. 38.)

§ 58-22-45. Restriction on insurance purchased by purchasing groups.

  (a) A purchasing group may not purchase insurance from a risk retention group that is not chartered in a state nor from an insurer not admitted in the state in which the purchasing group is located, unless the purchase is effected through a licensed agent or broker acting pursuant to the surplus lines laws and regulations of such state.

  (b) A purchasing group that obtains liability insurance from a nonadmitted insurer or from a risk retention group shall provide each member of the purchasing group that has a risk resident or located in this State with the notice specified in G.S. 58-21-45(f) or G.S. 58-22-20(7), whichever is applicable.

  (c) No purchasing group may purchase insurance that provides for a deductible or for a self-insured retention applicable to the group as a whole; provided, however, that coverage may provide for a deductible or for self-insured retention applicable to members of the group. (1987, c. 310, s. 1; c. 727, s. 11.)

§ 58-22-50. Administrative and procedural authority regarding risk retention groups and purchasing groups.

The Commissioner is authorized to make use of any of the powers established under Articles 1 through 64 of this Chapter to enforce the laws of this State as long as those powers are not specifically preempted by the Product Liability Risk Retention Act of 1981, as amended by the Risk Retention Act of 1986. This includes, but is not limited to, the Commissioner's administrative authority to investigate, issue subpoenas, conduct depositions and hearings, issue orders, and seek or impose penalties. With regard to any investigation, administrative proceeding, or litigation, the Commissioner can rely on the procedural law and regulations of the State. The injunctive authority of the Commissioner in regard to risk retention groups is restricted by the requirement that any injunction be issued by a court of competent jurisdiction. (1987, c. 310, s. 1.)

§ 58-22-55. Penalties.

A risk retention group that violates any provision of this Article is subject to G.S. 58-2-70. (1985 (Reg. Sess., 1986), c. 1013, s. 8; 1987, c. 310, s. 1.)

§ 58-22-60. Duty of agents or brokers to obtain license.

Any person acting, or offering to act, as an agent or broker for a risk retention group or purchasing group, that solicits members, sells insurance coverage, purchases coverage for its members located within the State, or otherwise does business in this State shall, before commencing any such activity, obtain a license from the Commissioner. (1987, c. 310, s. 1.)

§ 58-22-65. Binding effect of orders issued in U.S. District Court.

An order issued by any district court of the United States enjoining a risk retention group from soliciting or selling insurance, or operating, in any state, or in all states or in any territory or possession of the United States, upon a finding that such a group is in a hazardous financial condition, is enforceable in the courts of this State. (1987, c. 310, s. 1.)

§ 58-22-70. Registration and renewal fees.

Every risk retention group and purchasing group that registers with the Commissioner under this Article shall pay the following fees:

    Risk retention group registration $250.00
    Purchasing group registration 50.00
    Risk retention group renewal 1,000.00
    Purchasing group renewal 50.00

Registration fees shall not be prorated and must be submitted with the application for registration. Renewal fees shall not be prorated and shall be paid on or before January 1 of each year. (1989 (Reg. Sess., 1990), c. 1069, s. 12; 1995, c. 507, s. 11A(c); 1999-435, s. 3.)

ARTICLE 23.

Local Government Risk Pools.

§ 58-23-1. Short title; definition.

This Article shall be known and may be cited as the Local Government Risk Pool Act. As used in this Article, "local government" means any county, city, or housing authority located in this State. (1985 (Reg. Sess., 1986), c. 1027, s. 26; 1987, c. 864, s. 30.)

Local Modification. — Town of Tarboro: 1987 (Reg. Sess., 1988), c. 1083.

CASE NOTES

Board of Education could not join a risk pool pursuant to this section. Lyles v. City of Charlotte, 344 N.C. 676, 477 S.E.2d 150 (1996).

Counties, Cities, and Housing Authorities. — Only counties, cities, and housing authorities are defined as local governments for purposes of joining a local government risk pool. Lyles v. City of Charlotte, 344 N.C. 676, 477 S.E.2d 150 (1996).

Governmental Immunity And Risk Pools. — The City and two police officers in their official capacities were entitled to partial summary judgment on the grounds of governmental immunity for damages of $600,000 or less, and for damages greater than $7,000,000 where the City was insured above $7,000,000 and where the plaintiff, mistaken for a hit-and-run car operator, failed to show that a fund in which the City participated constituted a local government risk pool to the extent that the City had to reimburse claims up to $600,000 although the reimbursement of claims exceeding $600,000 and up to and including $2,000,000 might well result in the classification of the fund as a local government risk pool. Schlossberg v. Goins, 141 N.C. App. 436, 540 S.E.2d 49, 2000 N.C. App. LEXIS 1296 (2000).

§ 58-23-5. Local government pooling of property, liability and workers' compensation coverages.

(a) In addition to other authority granted to local governments under Chapters 153A and 160A of the General Statutes to jointly purchase insurance or pool retention of their risks, two or more local governments may enter into contracts or agreements under this Article for the joint purchasing of insurance or to pool retention of their risks for property losses and liability claims and to provide for the payment of such losses of or claims made against any member of the pool on a cooperative or contract basis with one another, or may enter into a trust agreement to carry out the provisions of this Article.

(b) In addition to other authority granted to local governments under Chapters 153A and 160A of the General Statutes or under G.S. 97-7 to jointly purchase insurance or pool retention of their risks, two or more local governments may enter into contracts or agreements pursuant to this Article to establish a separate workers' compensation pool to provide for the payment of workers' compensation claims under Chapter 97 of the General Statutes.

(c) In addition to other authority granted to local governments under Chapters 153A and 160A of the General Statutes to pool retention of their risks, two or more local governments may enter into contracts or agreements under this Article to establish pools providing for life or accident and health insurance for their employees on a cooperative or contract basis with one another; or may enter into a trust agreement to carry out the provisions of this Article.

(d) A workers' compensation pool established under this Article may only provide coverage for workers' compensation, employers' liability, and occupational disease claims.

(e) Local governments that intend to operate under this Article shall give the Commissioner 30 days' advance written notification, in a form prescribed by the Commissioner, that they intend to organize and operate risk pools pursuant to this Article. Local governments that jointly purchase insurance or pool retention of their risks under authority granted to them in Chapters 153A and 160A of the General Statutes or under G.S. 97-7 and that do not provide the Commissioner with the notification prescribed by this subsection shall not be subject to regulation by the Commissioner and shall not be under the jurisdiction of the Commissioner. (1985 (Reg. Sess., 1986), c. 1027, s. 26; 1987, c. 441, s. 14; 2001-334, s. 18.3.)

Legal Periodicals. — For a survey of 1996 developments in tort law, see 75 N.C.L. Rev. 2468 (1997).

For note, "Searching for Limits on a Municipality's Retention of Governmental Immunity," see 76 N.C.L. Rev. 269 (1997).

CASE NOTES

Risk management program in which city participated fell within the scope of the statute. Lyles v. City of Charlotte, 120 N.C. App. 96, 461 S.E.2d 347 (1995).

Counties, Cities, and Housing Authorities. — Only counties, cities, and housing authorities are defined as local governments for purposes of joining a local government risk pool. Lyles v. City of Charlotte, 344 N.C. 676, 477 S.E.2d 150 (1996).

Claim Not Paid If Reimbursed. — A local government risk pool agreement must contain a provision that the pool pay all claims for which a member incurs liability; the pool has not paid a claim if it is reimbursed for it. Lyles v. City of Charlotte, 344 N.C. 676, 477 S.E.2d 150 (1996).

The risks of the parties must be put in one pool for the payment of claims in order to have a local government risk pool. Lyles v. City of Charlotte, 344 N.C. 676, 477 S.E.2d 150 (1996).

The city did not waive governmental immunity by participating in a local gov-ernment **excess liability fund;** the fund was not a local government risk pool under this Article because two members of the fund were not "local governments," no notice was given to the commissioner of insurance that the participating entities intended to organize and operate a risk pool pursuant to statute, and the fund did not contain a provision for a system or program of loss control as required by this section. Dobrowolska v. Wall, 138 N.C. App. 1, 530 S.E.2d 590, 2000 N.C. App. LEXIS 539 (2000).

Rules of Construction. — Policies or coverage documents issued by local government risk retention pools to their members are subject to the same standard rules of construction as traditional insurance policies issued by insurance companies to their customers. Washington Hous. Auth. v. North Carolina Hous. Authorities Risk Retention Pool, 130 N.C. App. 279, 502 S.E.2d 626 (1998).

Applied in Schlossberg v. Goins, 141 N.C. App. 436, 540 S.E.2d 49, 2000 N.C. App. LEXIS 1296 (2000).

§ 58-23-10. Board of trustees.

(a) Each pool will be operated by a board of trustees consisting of at least five persons who are elected officials or employees of local governments within this State. The board of trustees of each pool will:
  (1) Establish terms and conditions of coverage within the pool, including underwriting criteria and exclusions of coverage;
  (2) Ensure that all valid claims are paid promptly;
  (3) Take all necessary precautions to safeguard the assets of the pool;
  (4) Maintain minutes of its meeting and make those minutes available to the Commissioner;
  (5) Designate an administrator to carry out the policies established by the board of trustees and to provide day to day management of the group

and delineate in written minutes of its meetings the areas of authority it delegates to the administrator; and

(6) Establish guidelines for membership in the pool.

(b) The board of trustees may not:

(1) Extend credit to individual members for payment of a premium, except pursuant to payment plans approved by the Commissioner.

(2) Borrow any moneys from the pool or in the name of the pool, except in the ordinary course of business, without first advising the Commissioner of the nature and purpose of the loan and obtaining prior approval from the Commissioner. (1985 (Reg. Sess., 1986), c. 1027, s. 26.)

Legal Periodicals. — For note, "Searching for Limits on a Municipality's Retention of Governmental Immunity," see 76 N.C.L. Rev. 269 (1997).

CASE NOTES

Cited in Lyles v. City of Charlotte, 344 N.C. 676, 477 S.E.2d 150 (1996); Washington Hous. Auth. v. North Carolina Hous. Authorities Risk Retention Pool, 130 N.C. App. 279, 502 S.E.2d 626 (1998).

§ 58-23-15. Contract.

A contract or agreement made pursuant to this Article must contain provisions:

(1) For a system or program of loss control;

(2) For termination of membership including either:

a. Cancellation of individual members of the pool by the pool; or

b. Election by an individual member of the pool to terminate its participation;

(3) Requiring the pool to pay all claims for which each member incurs liability during each member's period of membership, except where a member has individually retained the risk, where the risk is not covered, and except for amount of claims above the coverage provided by the pool.

(4) For the maintenance of claim reserves equal to known incurred losses and loss adjustment expenses and to an estimate of incurred but not reported losses;

(5) For a final accounting and settlement of the obligations of or refunds to a terminating member to occur when all incurred claims are concluded, settled, or paid;

(6) That the pool may establish offices where necessary in this State and employ necessary staff to carry out the purposes of the pool;

(7) That the pool may retain legal counsel, actuaries, claims adjusters, auditors, engineers, private consultants, and advisors, and other persons as the board of trustees or the administrator deem to be necessary;

(8) That the pool may make and alter bylaws and rules pertaining to the exercise of its purpose and powers;

(9) That the pool may purchase, lease, or rent real and personal property it deems to be necessary; and

(10) That the pool may enter into financial services agreements with financial institutions and that it may issue checks in its own name. (1985 (Reg. Sess., 1986), c. 1027, s. 26.)

Legal Periodicals. — For note, "Searching for Limits on a Municipality's Retention of Governmental Immunity," see 76 N.C.L. Rev. 269 (1997).

CASE NOTES

The risks of the parties must be put in one pool for the payment of claims in order to have a local government risk pool. Lyles v. City of Charlotte, 344 N.C. 676, 477 S.E.2d 150 (1996).

Applied in Dobrowolska v. Wall, 138 N.C. App. 1, 530 S.E.2d 590, 2000 N.C. App. LEXIS 539 (2000); Schlossberg v. Goins, 141 N.C. App. 436, 540 S.E.2d 49, 2000 N.C. App. LEXIS 1296 (2000).

§ 58-23-20. Termination.

A pool or a terminating member must provide at least 90 days' written notice of the termination or cancellation. A workers' compensation pool must notify the Commissioner of the termination or cancellation of a member within 10 days after notice of termination or cancellation is received or issued. (1985 (Reg. Sess., 1986), c. 1027, s. 26.)

§ 58-23-25: Repealed by Session Laws 1993, c. 452, s. 65.

Cross References. — As to financial monitoring and evaluation of pools, see G.S. 58-23-26.

§ 58-23-26. Financial monitoring and evaluation of pools.

(a) Each pool shall have an annual audit by an independent certified public accountant, at the expense of the pool, and shall make a copy of the audit available to the governing body or chief executive officer of each member of the pool. A copy of the audit shall be filed with the Commissioner within 130 days after the end of the pool's fiscal year, unless that time is extended by the Commissioner. The annual audit shall report the financial position of the pool in conformity with statutory accounting practices prescribed or permitted by the Commissioner.

(b) Each pool shall have an actuarial evaluation of its loss and loss adjustment expense reserves, including reserves for loss and loss adjustment expenses incurred but not reported, performed annually by a qualified actuary. A copy of the evaluation shall be filed with the Commissioner along with the annual audit submitted pursuant to subsection (a) of this section. A "qualified actuary" shall be as defined or prescribed by the Commissioner.

(c) Each pool is subject to G.S. 58-2-131, 58-2-132, 58-2-133, 58-2-134, 58-2-150, 58-2-155, 58-2-165, 58-2-180, 58-2-185, 58-2-190, 58-2-200, 58-3-71, 58-3-75, 58-3-81, 58-3-105, 58-6-5, 58-7-21, 58-7-26, 58-7-30, 58-7-31, 58-7-50, 58-7-55, 58-7-140, 58-7-160, 58-7-162, 58-7-163, 58-7-165, 58-7-167, 58-7-168, 58-7-170, 58-7-172, 58-7-173, 58-7-175, 58-7-179, 58-7-180, 58-7-183, 58-7-185, 58-7-187, 58-7-188, 58-7-192, 58-7-193, 58-7-197, 58-7-200, and Articles 13, 19, and 34 of this Chapter. Annual financial statements required by G.S. 58-2-165 shall be filed by each pool within 60 days after the end of the pool's fiscal year, subject to extension by the Commissioner. (1993, c. 452, s. 39; c. 504, s. 45; 1999-132, s. 11.4; 2001-223, s. 8.10; 2003-212, s. 12.)

Effect of Amendments. — Session Laws 2003-212, s. 12, effective October 1, 2003, deleted "58-7-195" following "58-7-193" in subsection (c).

Legal Periodicals. — For note, "Searching for Limits on a Municipality's Retention of Governmental Immunity," see 76 N.C.L. Rev. 269 (1997).

§ 58-23-30. Insolvency or impairment of pool.

(a) If, as a result of the annual audit or an examination by the Commissioner, it appears that the assets of a pool are insufficient to enable the pool to discharge its legal liabilities and other obligations, the Commissioner must notify the administrator and the board of trustees of the pool of the deficiency and his list of recommendations to abate the deficiency, including a recommendation not to add any new members until the deficiency is abated. If the pool fails to comply with the recommendations within 30 days after the date of the notice, the Commissioner may apply to the Superior Court of Wake County for an order requiring the pool to abate the deficiency and authorizing the Commissioner to appoint one or more special deputy commissioners, counsel, clerks, or assistants to oversee the implementation of the Court's order. The compensation and expenses of such persons shall be fixed by the Commissioner, subject to the approval of the Court, and shall be paid out of the funds or assets of the pool.

(b) If a pool is determined to be insolvent, financially impaired, or is otherwise found to be unable to discharge its legal liabilities and other obligations, each pool contract will provide that the members of the pool shall be assessed on a pro rata basis as calculated by the amount of each member's average annual contribution in order to satisfy the amount of deficiency. Members of a pool may, by contract, agree to limit the assessment to the amount of each member's annual contribution to the pool. Such a contractual agreement shall not impair the authority granted the Commissioner by this section. (1985 (Reg. Sess., 1986), c. 1027, s. 26; 1987, c. 441, ss. 16, 17.)

§ 58-23-35. Immunity of administrators and boards of trustees.

There is no liability on the part of and no cause of action arises against any board of trustees established or administrator appointed pursuant to G.S. 58-23-10, their representatives, or any pool, its members, or its employees, agents, contractors, or subcontractors for any good faith action taken by them in the performance of their powers and duties in creating or administering any pool under this Article. (1985 (Reg. Sess., 1986), c. 1027, s. 26.)

§ 58-23-40. Pools not covered by guaranty associations.

The provisions of Articles 48 and 62 of this Chapter and of Article 4 of Chapter 97 of the General Statutes do not apply to any risks retained by local governments pursuant to this Article. (1985 (Reg. Sess., 1986), c. 1027, s. 26; 1987, c. 441, s. 18; 1993, c. 504, s. 16.)

§ 58-23-45. Relationship to other insurance laws.

Unless local government risk pools are specifically referenced in a particular section of this Chapter, no provisions in this Chapter other than this Article apply to local government risk pools. (1999-351, s. 6.)

Article 24.

Fraternal Benefit Societies.

§ 58-24-1. Fraternal benefit societies.

Any incorporated society, order or supreme lodge, without capital stock, including one exempted under the provisions of G.S. 58-24-185(a)(2) whether incorporated or not, conducted solely for the benefit of its members and their beneficiaries and not for profit, operated on a lodge system with ritualistic form of work, having a representative form of government, and which provides benefits in accordance with this Article, is hereby declared to be a fraternal benefit society. (1987, c. 483, s. 2.)

§ 58-24-5. Lodge system.

(a) A society is operating on the lodge system if it has a supreme governing body and subordinate lodges into which members are elected, initiated or admitted in accordance with its laws, rules and ritual. Subordinate lodges shall be required by the laws of the society to hold regular meetings periodically in furtherance of the purposes of the society.

(b) A society may, at its option, organize and operate lodges for children under the minimum age for adult membership. Membership and initiation in local lodges shall not be required of such children, nor shall they have a voice or vote in the management of the society. (1987, c. 483, s. 2.)

§ 58-24-10. Representative form of government.

A society has a representative form of government when:

(a) It has a supreme governing body constituted in one of the following ways:

(1) Assembly. — The supreme governing body is an assembly composed of delegates elected directly by the members or at intermediate assemblies or conventions of members or their representatives, together with other delegates as may be prescribed in the society's laws. A society may provide for election of delegates by mail. The elected delegates shall constitute a majority in number and shall not have less than two-thirds of the votes and not less than the number of votes required to amend the society's laws. The assembly shall be elected and shall meet at least once every four years and shall elect a board of directors to conduct the business of the society between meetings of the assembly. Vacancies on the board of directors between elections may be filled in the manner prescribed by the society's laws.

(2) Direct Election. — The supreme governing body is a board composed of persons elected by the members, either directly or by their representatives in intermediate assemblies, and any other persons prescribed in the society's laws. A society may provide for election of the board by mail. Each term of a board member may not exceed four years. Vacancies on the board between elections may be filled in the manner prescribed by the society's laws. Those persons elected to the board shall constitute a majority in number and not less than the number of votes required to amend the society's laws. A person filling the unexpired term of an elected board member shall be considered to be an elected member. The board shall meet at least quarterly to conduct the business of the society.

(b) The officers of the society are elected either by the supreme governing body or by the board of directors;

(c) Only benefit members are eligible for election to the supreme governing body, the board of directors or any intermediate assembly; and

(d) Each voting member shall have one vote; no vote may be cast by proxy. (1987, c. 483, s. 2; 1989, c. 364, s. 1.)

§ 58-24-15. Terms used.

Whenever used in this Article:
- (a) "Benefit contract" shall mean the agreement for provision of benefits authorized by G.S. 58-24-75, as that agreement is described in G.S. 58-24-90(a).
- (b) "Benefit member" shall mean an adult member who is designated by the laws or rules of the society to be a benefit member under a benefit contract.
- (c) "Certificate" shall mean the document issued as written evidence of the benefit contract.
- (d) "Premiums" shall mean premiums, rates, dues or other required contributions by whatever name known, which are payable under the certificate.
- (e) "Laws" shall mean the society's articles of incorporation, constitution and bylaws, however designated.
- (f) "Rules" shall mean all rules, regulations or resolutions adopted by the supreme governing body or board of directors which are intended to have general application to the members of the society.
- (g) "Society" shall mean fraternal benefit society, unless otherwise indicated.
- (h) "Lodge" shall mean subordinate member units of the society, known as camps, courts, councils, branches or by any other designation. (1987, c. 483, s. 2.)

§ 58-24-20. Purposes and powers.

(a) A society shall operate for the benefit of members and their beneficiaries by:
- (1) Providing benefits as specified in G.S. 58-24-75; and
- (2) Operating for one or more social, intellectual, educational, charitable, benevolent, moral, fraternal, patriotic or religious purposes for the benefit of its members, which may also be extended to others.

Such purposes may be carried out directly by the society, or indirectly through subsidiary corporations or affiliated organizations.

(b) Every society shall have the power to adopt laws and rules for the government of the society, the admission of its members, and the management of its affairs. It shall have the power to change, alter, add to or amend such laws and rules and shall have such other powers as are necessary and incidental to carrying into effect the objects and purposes of the society. (1987, c. 483, s. 2.)

§ 58-24-25. Qualifications for membership.

(a) A society shall specify in its laws or rules:
- (1) Eligibility standards for each and every class of membership, provided that if benefits are provided on the lives of children, the minimum age for adult membership shall be set at not less than age 15 and not greater than age 21;
- (2) The process for admission to membership for each membership class; and
- (3) The rights and privileges of each membership class, provided that only benefit members shall have the right to vote on the management of the insurance affairs of the society.

(b) A society may also admit social members who shall have no voice or vote in the management of the insurance affairs of the society.

(c) Membership rights in the society are personal to the member and are not assignable. (1987, c. 483, s. 2.)

§ 58-24-30. Location of office, meetings, communications to members, grievance procedures.

(a) The principal office of any domestic society shall be located in this State. The meetings of its supreme governing body may be held in any state, district, province or territory wherein such society has at least one subordinate lodge, or in such other location as determined by the supreme governing body, and all business transacted at such meetings shall be as valid in all respects as if such meetings were held in this State. The minutes of the proceedings of the supreme governing body and of the board of directors shall be in the English language.

(b) A society may provide in its laws for an official publication in which any notice, report, or statement required by law to be given to members, including notice of election, may be published. Such required reports, notices and statements shall be printed conspicuously in the publication. If the records of a society show that two or more members have the same mailing address, an official publication mailed to one member is deemed to be mailed to all members at the same address unless a member requests a separate copy.

(c) Not later than June 1 of each year, a synopsis of the society's annual statement providing an explanation of the facts concerning the condition of the society thereby disclosed shall be printed and mailed to each benefit member of the society or, in lieu thereof, such synopsis may be published in the society's official publication.

(d) A society may provide in its laws or rules for grievance or complaint procedures for members. (1987, c. 483, s. 2.)

§ 58-24-35. No personal liability.

(a) The officers and members of the supreme governing body or any subordinate body of a society shall not be personally liable for any benefits provided by a society.

(b) Any person may be indemnified and reimbursed by any society for expenses reasonably incurred by, and liabilities imposed upon, such person in connection with or arising out of any action, suit or proceeding, whether civil, criminal, administrative or investigative, or threat thereof, in which the person may be involved by reason of the fact that he or she is or was a director, officer, employee or agent of the society or of any firm, corporation or organization which he or she served in any capacity at the request of the society. A person shall not be so indemnified or reimbursed (1) in relation to any matter in such action, suit or proceeding as to which he or she shall finally be adjudged to be or have been guilty of breach of a duty as a director, officer, employee or agent of the society or (2) in relation to any matter in such action, suit or proceeding, or threat thereof, which has been made the subject of a compromise settlement; unless in either such case the person acted in good faith for a purpose the person reasonably believed to be in or not opposed to the best interests of the society and, in a criminal action or proceeding, in addition, had no reasonable cause to believe that his or her conduct was unlawful. The determination whether the conduct of such person met the standard required in order to justify indemnification and reimbursement in relation to any matter described in subpoints (1) or (2) of the preceding sentence may only be made by the supreme governing body or board of directors by a majority vote of a quorum consisting of persons who were not parties to such action, suit or proceeding or by a court of competent jurisdiction. The termination of any action, suit or proceeding by judgment, order, settlement, conviction, or upon a plea of no contest, as to such person shall not in itself create a conclusive presumption that the person did not meet the standard of conduct required in order to justify indemnification and reimbursement. The foregoing right of indemnification and reimbursement shall not be exclusive of other rights to which such person may be entitled as a matter of law and shall inure to the benefit of his or her heirs, executors and administrators.

(c) A society shall have power to purchase and maintain insurance on behalf of any person who is or was a director, officer, employee or agent of the society, or who is or was serving at the request of the society as a director, officer, employee or agent of any other firm, corporation, or organization against any liability asserted against such person and incurred by him or her in any such capacity or arising out of his or her status as such, whether or not the society would have the power to indemnify the person against such liability under this section.

(d) A person serving as an officer or a member of a supreme governing body of a society shall be immune individually from civil liability for monetary damages, except to the extent covered by insurance, for any act or failure to act, except where the person:

(1) Is compensated for his services beyond reimbursement for expenses,
(2) Was not acting within the scope of his official duties,
(3) Was not acting in good faith,
(4) Committed gross negligence or willful or wanton misconduct that resulted in the damage or injury,
(5) Derived an improper personal financial benefit from the transaction,
(6) Incurred the liability from the operation of a motor vehicle, or
(7) Is sued in an action that would qualify as a derivative action if the organization were a for-profit corporation or as a member's or director's derivative action under G.S. 55A-28.1 or G.S. 55A-28.2 if the organization were a nonprofit corporation.

The immunity in this subsection is personal to the individual officers and members of the supreme governing body and does not immunize the organization for the acts or omissions of those officers or members. (1987, c. 483, s. 2; c. 799, s. 2.)

§ 58-24-40. Waiver.

The laws of the society may provide that no subordinate body, nor any of its subordinate officers or members shall have the power or authority to waive any of the provisions of the laws of the society. Such provision shall be binding on the society and every member and beneficiary of a member. (1987, c. 483, s. 2.)

CASE NOTES

Editor's Note. — *The case below was decided under prior statutory provisions.*

For case distinguishing between waiver by local agents, prohibited by former § 58-276, and a custom of dealing established over a period of years to the knowledge of the home office, see Shackelford v. Sovereign Camp of Woodmen of World, 209 N.C. 633, 184 S.E. 691 (1936).

§ 58-24-45. Organization.

A domestic society organized on or after January 1, 1988 shall be formed as follows:

(a) Ten or more citizens of the United States, a majority of whom are citizens of this State, who desire to form a fraternal benefit society, may make, sign and acknowledge before some officer competent to take acknowledgement of deeds, articles of incorporation, in which shall be stated:

(1) The proposed corporate name of the society, which shall not so closely resemble the name of any society or insurance company as to be misleading or confusing;

(2) The purposes for which it is being formed and the mode in which its corporate powers are to be exercised. Such purposes shall not include more liberal powers than are granted by this Article;

(3) The names and residences of the incorporators and the names, residences and official titles of all the officers, trustees, directors, or other persons who are to have and exercise the general control of the management of the affairs and funds of the society for the first year or until the ensuing election at which all such officers shall be elected by the supreme governing body, which election shall be held not later than one year from the date of issuance of the permanent license.

(b) Such articles of incorporation, duly certified copies of the society's bylaws and rules, copies of all proposed forms of certificates, applications therefor, and circulars to be issued by the society and a bond conditioned upon the return to applicants of the advanced payments if the organization is not completed within one year shall be filed with the Commissioner, who may require such further information as the Commissioner deems necessary. The bond with sureties approved by the Commissioner shall be in such amount, not less than three hundred thousand dollars ($300,000) nor more than one million five hundred thousand dollars ($1,500,000), as required by the Commissioner. All documents filed are to be in the English language. If the purposes of the society conform to the requirements of this chapter and all provisions of the law have been complied with, the Commissioner shall so certify, retain and file the articles of incorporation and furnish the incorporators a preliminary license authorizing the society to solicit members as hereinafter provided.

(c) No preliminary license granted under the provisions of this section shall be valid after one year from its date or after such further period, not exceeding one year, as may be authorized by the Commissioner upon cause shown, unless the 500 applicants hereinafter required have been secured and the organization has been completed as herein provided. The articles of incorporation and all other proceedings thereunder shall become null and void in one year from the date of the preliminary license, or at the expiration of the extended period, unless the society shall have completed its organization and received a license to do business as hereinafter provided.

(d) Upon receipt of a preliminary license from the Commissioner, the society may solicit members for the purpose of completing its organization, shall collect from each applicant the amount of not less than one regular monthly premium in accordance with its table of rates, and shall issue to each such applicant a receipt for the amount so collected. No society shall incur any liability other than for the return of such advance premium, nor issue any certificate, nor pay, allow, or offer or promise to pay or allow, any benefit to any person until:

(1) Actual bona fide applications for benefits have been secured on not less than 500 applicants, and any necessary evidence of insurability has been furnished to and approved by the society;

(2) At least 10 subordinate lodges have been established into which the 500 applicants have been admitted;

(3) There has been submitted to the Commissioner, under oath of the president or secretary, or corresponding officer of the society, a list

of such applicants, giving their names, addresses, date each was admitted, name and number of the subordinate lodge of which each applicant is a member, amount of benefits to be granted and premiums therefor; and

(4) It shall have been shown to the Commissioner, by sworn statement of the treasurer, or corresponding officer of such society, that at least 500 applicants have each paid in cash at least one regular monthly premium as herein provided, which premiums in the aggregate shall amount to at least one hundred and fifty thousand dollars ($150,000). Said advance premiums shall be held in trust during the period of organization and if the society has not qualified for a license within one year, as herein provided, such premiums shall be returned to said applicants.

(e) The Commissioner may make such examination and require such further information as the Commissioner deems advisable. Upon presentation of satisfactory evidence that the society has complied with all the provisions of law, the Commissioner shall issue to the society a license to that effect and that the society is authorized to transact business pursuant to the provisions of this Article. The license shall be prima facie evidence of the existence of the society at the date of such certificate. The Commissioner shall cause a record of such license to be made. A certified copy of such record may be given in evidence with like effect as the original license.

(f) Any incorporated society authorized to transact business in this State at the time this Article becomes effective shall not be required to reincorporate. (1987, c. 483, s. 2; 1991, c. 720, s. 4; 1999-132, s. 9.1.)

§ 58-24-50. Amendments to laws.

(a) A domestic society may amend its laws in accordance with the provisions thereof by action of its supreme governing body at any regular or special meeting thereof or, if its laws so provide, by referendum. Such referendum may be held in accordance with the provisions of its laws by the vote of the voting members of the society, by the vote of delegates or representatives of voting members or by the vote of local lodges. A society may provide for voting by mail. No amendment submitted for adoption by referendum shall be adopted unless, within six months from the date of submission thereof, a majority of the members voting shall have signified their consent to such amendment by one of the methods herein specified.

(b) No amendment to the laws of any domestic society shall take effect unless approved by the Commissioner who shall approve such amendment if the Commissioner finds that it has been duly adopted and is not inconsistent with any requirement of the laws of this State or with the character, objects and purposes of the society. Unless the Commissioner shall disapprove any such amendment within 60 days after the filing of same, such amendment shall be considered approved. The approval or disapproval of the Commissioner shall be in writing and mailed to the secretary or corresponding officer of the society at its principal office. In case the Commissioner disapproves such amendment, the reasons therefor shall be stated in such written notice.

(c) Within 90 days from the approval thereof by the Commissioner, all such amendments, or a synopsis thereof, shall be furnished to all members of the society either by mail or by publication in full in the official publication of the society. The affidavit of any officer of the society or of anyone authorized by it to mail any amendments or synopsis thereof, stating facts which show that same have been duly addressed and mailed, shall be prima facie evidence that such amendments or synopsis thereof, have been furnished the addressee.

(d) Every foreign or alien society authorized to do business in this State shall file with the Commissioner a duly certified copy of all amendments of, or additions to, its laws within 90 days after the enactment of same.

(e) Printed copies of the laws as amended, certified by the secretary or corresponding officer of the society shall be prima facie evidence of the legal adoption thereof. (1987, c. 483, s. 2; 1991, c. 720, s. 4.)

CASE NOTES

Editor's Note. — *The case below was decided under prior statutory provisions.*

Failure to File Copy of Amendments. — As to suspension of member where copy of amendments not filed, see Wilson v. Supreme Conclave, Improved Order of Heptasophs, 174 N.C. 628, 94 S.E. 443 (1917), appeal dismissed, 249 U.S. 583, 39 S. Ct. 287, 63 L. Ed. 787 (1919).

§ 58-24-55. Institutions.

A society may create, maintain and operate, or may establish organizations to operate, not for profit institutions to further the purposes permitted by G.S. 58-24-20(a)(2). Such institutions may furnish services free or at a reasonable charge. Any real or personal property owned, held or leased by the society for this purpose shall be reported in every annual statement. (1987, c. 483, s. 2.)

§ 58-24-60. Reinsurance.

(a) A domestic society may, by a reinsurance agreement, cede any individual risk or risks in whole or in part to an insurer (other than another fraternal benefit society) having the power to make such reinsurance and authorized to do business in this State, or if not so authorized, one which is approved by the Commissioner, but no such society may reinsure substantially all of its insurance in force without the written permission of the Commissioner. It may take credit for the reserves on such ceded risks to the extent reinsured, but no credit shall be allowed as an admitted asset or as a deduction from liability, to a ceding society for reinsurance made, ceded, renewed, or otherwise becoming effective after January 1, 1988, unless the reinsurance is payable by the assuming insurer on the basis of the liability of the ceding society under the contract or contracts reinsured without diminution because of the insolvency of the ceding society.

(b) Notwithstanding the limitation in subsection (a), a society may reinsure the risks of another society in a consolidation or merger approved by the Commissioner under G.S. 58-24-65. (1987, c. 483, s. 2; 1991, c. 720, s. 4.)

§ 58-24-65. Consolidations and mergers.

(a) A domestic society may consolidate or merge with any other society by complying with the provisions of this section. It shall file with the Commissioner:
  (1) A certified copy of the written contract containing in full the terms and conditions of the consolidation or merger;
  (2) A sworn statement by the president and secretary or corresponding officers of each society showing the financial condition thereof on a date fixed by the Commissioner but not earlier than December 31, next preceding the date of the contract;
  (3) A certificate of such officers, duly verified by their respective oaths, that the consolidation or merger has been approved by a two-thirds vote of the supreme governing body of each society, such vote being

conducted at a regular or special meeting of each such body, or, if the society's laws so permit, by mail; and

(4) Evidence that at least 60 days prior to the action of the supreme governing body of each society, the text of the contract has been furnished to all members of each society either by mail or by publication in full in the official publication of each society.

(b) If the Commissioner finds that the contract is in conformity with the provisions of this section, that the financial statements are correct and that the consolidation or merger is just and equitable to the members of each society, the Commissioner shall approve the contract and issue a certificate to such effect. Upon such approval, the contract shall be in full force and effect unless any society which is a party to the contract is incorporated under the laws of any other state or territory. In such event the consolidation or merger shall not become effective unless and until it has been approved as provided by the laws of such state or territory and a certificate of such approval filed with the Commissioner of this State or, if the laws of such state or territory contain no such provision, then the consolidation or merger shall not become effective unless and until it has been approved by the Commissioner of such state or territory and a certificate of such approval filed with the Commissioner of this State. In case such contract is not approved it shall be inoperative, and the fact of the submission and its contents shall not be disclosed by the Commissioner.

(c) Upon the consolidation or merger becoming effective as herein provided, all the rights, franchises and interests of the consolidated or merged societies in and to every species of property, real, personal or mixed, and things in action thereunto belonging shall be vested in the society resulting from or remaining after the consolidation or merger without any other instrument, except that conveyances of real property may be evidenced by proper deeds, and the title to any real estate or interest therein, vested under the laws of this State in any of the societies consolidated or merged, shall not revert or be in any way impaired by reason of the consolidation or merger, but shall vest absolutely in the society resulting from or remaining after such consolidation or merger.

(d) The affidavit of any officer of the society or of anyone authorized by it to mail any notice or document, stating that such notice or document has been duly addressed and mailed, shall be prima facie evidence that such notice or document has been furnished the addressees.

(e) All necessary and actual expenses and compensation incident to the proceedings provided in this section shall be paid as provided by such contract of consolidation or merger: Provided, however, that no brokerage or commission shall be included in such expenses and compensation or shall be paid to any person by either of the parties to any such contract in connection with the negotiation therefor or execution thereof, nor shall any compensation be paid to any officer or employee of either of the parties to such contract for directly or indirectly aiding in effecting such contract of consolidation or merger. An itemized statement of all such expenses shall be filed with the Commissioner, subject to approval, and when approved the same shall be binding on the parties thereto. Except as fully expressed in the contract of consolidation or merger, or itemized statement of expenses, as approved by the Commissioner, or commissioners, as the case may be, no compensation shall be paid to any person or persons, and no officer or employee of the State shall receive any compensation, directly or indirectly, for in any manner aiding, promoting, or assisting any such consolidation or merger. (1987, c. 483, s. 2; 1991, c. 720, s. 4.)

§ 58-24-70. Conversion of fraternal benefit society into mutual life insurance company.

Any domestic fraternal benefit society may be converted and licensed as a mutual life insurance company by compliance with all the requirements of the general insurance laws for mutual life insurance companies. A plan of conversion shall be prepared in writing by the board of directors setting forth in full the terms and conditions of conversion. The affirmative vote of two-thirds of all members of the supreme governing body at a regular or special meeting shall be necessary for the approval of such plan. No such conversion shall take effect unless and until approved by the Commissioner who may give such approval if the Commissioner finds that the proposed change is in conformity with the requirements of law and not prejudicial to the certificateholders of the society. (1987, c. 483, s. 2; 1991, c. 720, s. 4.)

§ 58-24-75. Benefits.

(a) A society may provide the following contractual benefits in any form:
(1) Death benefits;
(2) Endowment benefits;
(3) Annuity benefits;
(4) Temporary or permanent disability benefits;
(5) Hospital, medical or nursing benefits;
(6) Monument or tombstone benefits to the memory of deceased members; and
(7) Such other benefits as authorized for life insurers and which are not inconsistent with this Article.

(b) A society shall specify in its rules those persons who may be issued, or covered by, the contractual benefits in subsection (a), consistent with providing benefits to members and their dependents. A society may provide benefits on the lives of children under the minimum age for adult membership upon application of an adult person. (1987, c. 483, s. 2.)

§ 58-24-80. Beneficiaries.

(a) The owner of a benefit contract shall have the right at all times to change the beneficiary or beneficiaries in accordance with the laws or rules of the society unless the owner waives this right by specifically requesting in writing that the beneficiary designation be irrevocable. A society may, through its laws or rules, limit the scope of beneficiary designations and shall provide that no revocable beneficiary shall have or obtain any vested interest in the proceeds of any certificate until the certificate has become due and payable in conformity with the provisions of the benefit contract.

(b) A society may make provision for the payment of funeral benefits to the extent of such portion of any payment under a certificate as might reasonably appear to be due to any person equitably entitled thereto by reason of having incurred expense occasioned by the burial of the member.

(c) If, at the death of any person insured under a benefit contract, there is no lawful beneficiary to whom the proceeds shall be payable, the amount of such benefit, except to the extent that funeral benefits may be paid as hereinbefore provided, shall be payable to the personal representative of the deceased insured, provided that if the owner of the certificate is other than the insured, such proceeds shall be payable to such owner. (1987, c. 483, s. 2.)

CASE NOTES

Editor's Note. — *The cases below were decided under prior statutory provisions.*

Where assured named wife as beneficiary and afterwards substituted the name of another, disqualified to take under the statute, such attempted change was not a revocation of the provisions of the policy first issued and left it in force. Andrews v. Most Worshipful Grand Lodge Free & Accepted Order of Masons, 189 N.C. 697, 128 S.E. 4 (1925).

Annulment of Beneficiary Designation by Absolute Divorce. — Although the legislature has provided in this section that absolute divorce automatically annuls the designation of a husband or wife as beneficiary in a policy issued by a fraternal order or society, policies of that type are sui generis. There is no similar provision applicable to insurance policies generally. DeVane v. Travelers Ins. Co., 8 N.C. App. 247, 174 S.E.2d 146 (1970).

Bigamous Wife's Right to Recover. — A fraternal assessment benefit association having a representative form of government may, by its contract and constitution, confine the beneficiaries to certain blood relatives, wife, affianced wife, persons dependent upon the member, etc., in conformity with the laws of the state wherein it has its head organization; and where such beneficiary sues upon a policy, claiming as the wife of the deceased member, and it appears that in fact the marriage was bigamous, she may not recover, though the certificate states she was his wife. Applebaum v. Order of United Com. Travelers of Am., 171 N.C. 435, 88 S.E. 722 (1916).

Nature of Right of Beneficiary. — Within the restrictions of this section, the beneficiary may be changed by the mere will of the member and without the beneficiary's consent. In such case, the right of the beneficiary is not property, but a mere expectancy, dependent on the will of the member to whom the certificate is issued. For this reason the beneficiary's interest in the certificate and contract evidenced thereby differs totally from the interest of a beneficiary named in an ordinary life insurance policy containing no provision for the designation of a new beneficiary. Pollick v. Household of Hardy,

150 N.C. 211, 63 S.E. 940 (1909).

The right of the insured to change the beneficiary is declared and guaranteed by this section. Hence, anyone named as beneficiary has, during the life of the insured, no vested right in the certificate. It is a mere expectancy. Widows Fund of Sudan Temple v. Umphlett, 246 N.C. 555, 99 S.E.2d 791 (1957).

Insured's Brother Held Entitled to Proceeds to Exclusion of Insured's Wife's Nephew. — Where insured's wife was named beneficiary, and after her death insured's brother, who became the beneficiary under the terms of the certificate as insured's nearest blood relation, kept the certificate in force until the death of the insured a short time thereafter, it was held that under the terms of the certificate the insured's brother was entitled to the proceeds thereof, to the exclusion of the wife's nephew who claimed under the will of the wife, the payment of dues or premiums alone being insufficient to create a lien against the certificate, or the proceeds thereof, and the wife at no time having any vested interest as the named beneficiary which she could bequeath by will. Sorrell v. Sovereign Camp, Woodmen of World, 209 N.C. 226, 183 S.E. 400 (1936).

Trustee as Beneficiary. — Prior to the 1937 amendment, an incorporated trust company, authorized by a trust agreement to collect the proceeds of life insurance policies on the life of the trustor upon his death, could not be named beneficiary in a fraternal benefit contract on the trustor's life. Equitable Trust Co. v. Widows' Fund of Oasis & Omar Temples, 207 N.C. 534, 177 S.E. 799 (1935).

§ 58-24-85. Benefits not attachable.

No money or other benefit, charity, relief or aid to be paid, provided or rendered by any society, shall be liable to attachment, garnishment or other process, or to be seized, taken, appropriated or applied by any legal or equitable process or operation of law to pay any debt or liability of a member or beneficiary, or any other person who may have a right thereunder, either before or after payment by the society. (1987, c. 483, s. 2.)

CASE NOTES

Cited in Sara Lee Corp. v. Carter, 351 N.C. 27, 519 S.E.2d 308 (1999).

§ 58-24-90. The benefit contract.

(a) Every society authorized to do business in this State shall issue to each owner of a benefit contract a certificate specifying the amount of benefits provided thereby. The certificate, together with any riders or endorsements attached thereto, the laws of the society, the application for membership, the application for insurance and declaration of insurability, if any, signed by the applicant, and all amendments to each thereof, shall constitute the benefit contract, as of the date of issuance, between the society and the owner, and the certificate shall so state. A copy of the application for insurance and declaration of insurability, if any, shall be endorsed upon or attached to the certificate. All statements on the application shall be representations and not warranties. Any waiver of this provision shall be void.

(b) Any changes, additions or amendments to the laws of the society duly made or enacted subsequent to the issuance of the certificate, shall bind the owner and the beneficiaries, and shall govern and control the benefit contract in all respects the same as though such changes, additions or amendments had been made prior to and were in force at the time of the application for insurance, except that no change, addition or amendment shall destroy or diminish benefits which the society contracted to give the owner as of the date of issuance.

(c) Any person upon whose life a benefit contract is issued prior to attaining the age of majority shall be bound by the terms of the application and certificate and by all the laws and rules of the society to the same extent as though the age of majority had been attained at the time of application.

(d) A society shall provide in its laws that if its reserves as to all or any class of certificates become impaired its board of directors or corresponding body may require that there shall be paid by the owner to the society the amount of the owner's equitable proportion of such deficiency as ascertained by its board, and that if the payment is not made either (1) it shall stand as an indebtedness against the certificate and draw interest not to exceed the rate specified for certificate loans under the certificates; or (2) in lieu of or in combination with (1), the owner may accept a proportionate reduction in benefits under the certificate. The society may specify the manner of the election and which alternative is to be presumed if no election is made.

(e) Copies of any of the documents mentioned in this section, certified by the secretary or corresponding officer of the society, shall be received in evidence of the terms and conditions thereof.

(f) No certificate shall be delivered or issued for delivery in this State unless a copy of the form has been filed with and approved by the Commissioner in the manner provided for like policies issued by life insurers in this State. Every life, accident, health, or disability insurance certificate and every annuity certificate issued on or after one year from the effective date of this Article shall meet the standard contract provision requirements not inconsistent with this Article for like policies issued by life insurers in this State, except that a society may provide for a grace period for payment of premiums of one full month in its certificates. The certificate shall also contain a provision stating the amount of premiums which are payable under the certificate and a provision reciting or setting forth the substance of any sections of the society's laws or rules in force at the time of issuance of the certificate which, if violated, will result in the termination or reduction of benefits payable under the certificate. If the laws of the society provide for expulsion or suspension of a member, the certificate shall also contain a provision that any member so expelled or suspended, except for nonpayment of a premium or within the contestable period for material misrepresentation in the application for membership or insurance, shall have the privilege of maintaining the certificate in force by continuing payment of the required premium.

(g) Benefit contracts issued on the lives of persons below the society's minimum age for adult membership may provide for transfer of control of ownership to the insured at an age specified in the certificate. A society may require approval of an application for membership in order to effect this transfer, and may provide in all other respects for the regulation, government and control of such certificates and all rights, obligations and liabilities incident thereto and connected therewith. Ownership rights prior to such transfer shall be specified in the certificate.

(h) A society may specify the terms and conditions on which benefit contracts may be assigned. (1987, c. 483, s. 2; 1991, c. 720, s. 4.)

CASE NOTES

Editor's Note. — *The cases below were decided under prior statutory provisions.*

Alteration of Constitution or Bylaws Impairing Vested Rights. — A general consent of a policyholder in an assessment fraternal benefit society that the society may thereafter alter or amend its constitution or bylaws does not authorize the society to make such changes therein as will impair the vested right of its members and policyholders arising under their contract of insurance with the society. Wilson v. Supreme Conclave, Improved Order of Heptasophs, 174 N.C. 628, 94 S.E. 443 (1917), appeal dismissed, 249 U.S. 583, 39 S. Ct. 287, 63 L. Ed. 787 (1919).

Where a fraternal benefit society has issued a policy to a member, and has changed its plan of business so as to impair the vested rights of the insured under his contract, and refuses to accept the proper premium, and declares the policy void, the insured may maintain his action to recover of the insurer the principal sum of money he has paid on his policy, and simple interest thereon. Wilson v. Supreme Conclave, Improved Order of Heptasophs, 174 N.C. 628, 94 S.E. 443 (1917), appeal dismissed, 249 U.S. 583, 39 S. Ct. 287, 63 L. Ed. 787 (1919).

Suspension of Members Where Changes in Bylaws Not Filed. — Where a fraternal benefit insurance society was required to file a certified copy of changes made in its constitution and bylaws with the Insurance Commissioner within 90 days and failed to do so, it could not, while thus in default, suspend a member for noncompliance therewith. Wilson v. Supreme Conclave, Improved Order of Heptasophs, 174 N.C. 628, 94 S.E. 443 (1917), appeal dismissed, 249 U.S. 583, 39 S. Ct. 287, 63 L. Ed. 787 (1919).

Proof of Forfeiture of Benefits. — A stipulation in an endowment policy in a fraternal order requiring the member to be in good standing at the time of his death must be construed in reference to provisions in the charter and bylaws of the order, that the member can only be suspended for failure to pay his dues for six months of which notice shall be given him; and an order of suspension made in his absence will not have the effect of suspending him from benefits when there is no evidence that he had failed to pay his dues for the stated period or that notice had been given in accordance with the constitution and bylaws. Lyons v. Grand Lodge of Knights of Pythias, 172 N.C. 408, 90 S.E. 423 (1916).

Burden of Showing Nonpayment of Dues. — In an action upon a life insurance certificate in a fraternal order, the burden of proof is upon the defendant to show nonpayment of dues or other matters to avoid the certificate, when the certificate has been put in evidence and the death has been shown. Wilkie v. National Council, J.O.U.A.M., 147 N.C. 637, 61 S.E. 580 (1908); Harris v. National Council, J.O.U.A.M., 168 N.C. 357, 84 S.E. 405 (1915).

False Representations of Insured. — Where an insurance policy in a fraternal order was issued in violation of certain restrictions contained in its constitution and bylaws, and there was evidence tending to show that this fact was known at the time to the applicant, and the policy was issued by reason of false and material statements on the part of the applicant, the order was not estopped, as a conclusion of law, from resisting payment of the policy because of the fact that its agent also knew that the applicant's statements were false. Robinson v. Brotherhood of Locomotive Firemen, 170 N.C. 545, 87 S.E. 537 (1916).

Waiver of Defects in Policy. — A policy in the insurance department of a fraternal order cannot be recovered on when issued by a local agent contrary to its rules and regulations as contained in its constitution and bylaws, unless the defect has been waived by the order or it is in some way estopped from insisting on the forfeiture. Robinson v. Brotherhood of Locomotive Firemen, 170 N.C. 545, 87 S.E. 537 (1916).

§ 58-24-95. Nonforfeiture benefits, cash surrender values, certificate loans and other options.

(a) For certificates issued prior to one year after January 1, 1988, the value of every paid-up nonforfeiture benefit and the amount of any cash surrender value, loan or other option granted shall comply with the provisions of law applicable immediately prior to January 1, 1988.

(b) For certificates issued on or after one year from January 1, 1988 for which reserves are computed on the Commissioner's 1941 Standard Ordinary Mortality Table, the Commissioner's 1941 Standard Industrial Table or the

Commissioner's 1958 Standard Ordinary Mortality Table, or the Commissioner's 1980 Standard Mortality Table, or any more recent table made applicable to life insurers, every paid-up nonforfeiture benefit and the amount of any cash surrender value, loan or other option granted shall not be less than the corresponding amount ascertained in accordance with the laws of this State applicable to life insurers issuing policies containing like benefits based upon such tables. (1987, c. 483, s. 2.)

§ 58-24-100. Investments.

A society shall invest its funds only in investments that are authorized by the laws of this State for the investment of assets of life insurers and subject to the limitations thereon. Any foreign or alien society permitted or seeking to do business in this State must comply in substance with the investment requirements and limitations imposed by Article 7 of this Chapter and applicable to life insurers; provided, that any society that invests its funds in accordance with the laws of the state, district, territory, country, or province in which it is incorporated, shall thereby be deemed to be in compliance with the investment requirements and limitations for a period of two years from January 1, 1988. (1987, c. 483, s. 2; 1995, c. 193, s. 29.)

§ 58-24-105. Funds.

(a) All assets shall be held, invested and disbursed for the use and benefit of the society and no member or beneficiary shall have or acquire individual rights therein or become entitled to any apportionment on the surrender of any part thereof, except as provided in the benefit contract.

(b) A society may create, maintain, invest, disburse and apply any special fund or funds necessary to carry out any purpose permitted by the laws of such society.

(c) A society may, pursuant to resolution of its supreme governing body, establish and operate one or more separate accounts and issue contracts on a variable basis, subject to the provisions of law regulating life insurers establishing such accounts and issuing such contracts. To the extent the society deems it necessary in order to comply with any applicable federal or State laws, or any rules issued thereunder, the society may adopt special procedures for the conduct of the business and affairs of a separate account, may, for persons having beneficial interests therein, provide special voting and other rights, including without limitation special rights and procedures relating to investment policy, investment advisory services, selection of certified public accountants, and selection of a committee to manage the business and affairs of the account, and may issue contracts on a variable basis to which G.S. 58-24-90(b) and G.S. 58-24-90(d) shall not apply. (1987, c. 483, s. 2.)

§ 58-24-110. Exemptions.

Except as herein provided, societies shall be governed by this Article and shall be exempt from all other provisions of the general insurance laws of this State unless they be expressly designated therein, or unless it is specifically made applicable by this Article. (1987, c. 483, s. 2.)

§ 58-24-115. Taxation.

Every society organized or licensed under this Article is hereby declared to be a charitable and benevolent institution, and all of its funds shall be exempt from all and every State, county, district, municipal and school tax other than taxes on real estate not occupied by such society in carrying on its business. (1987, c. 483, s. 2.)

§ 58-24-120. Valuation.

(a) Standards of valuation for certificates issued prior to one year after the effective date of this Article shall be those provided by the laws applicable immediately prior to January 1, 1988.

(b) The minimum standards of valuation for certificates issued on or after one year from January 1, 1988, shall be based on the following tables:

    (1) For certificates of life insurance — the Commissioner's 1941 Standard Ordinary Mortality Table, the Commissioner's 1941 Standard Industrial Mortality Table, the Commissioner's 1958 Standard Ordinary Mortality Table, the Commissioner's 1980 Standard Ordinary Mortality Table or any more recent table made applicable to life insurers;

    (2) For annuity and pure endowment certificates, for total and permanent disability benefits, for accidental death benefits and for non-cancellable accident and health benefits — such tables as are authorized for use by life insurers in this State.

All of the above shall be under valuation methods and standards (including interest assumptions) in accordance with the laws of this State applicable to life insurers issuing policies containing like benefits.

(c) The Commissioner may, in his or her discretion, accept other standards for valuation if the Commissioner finds that the reserves produced thereby will not be less in the aggregate than reserves computed in accordance with the minimum valuation standard herein prescribed. The Commissioner may, in his or her discretion, vary the standards of mortality applicable to all benefit contracts on substandard lives or other extra hazardous lives by any society authorized to do business in this State.

(d) Any society, with the consent of the Commissioner of the state of domicile of the society and under such conditions, if any, which the Commissioner may impose, may establish and maintain reserves on its certificates in excess of the reserves required thereunder, but the contractual rights of any benefit member shall not be affected thereby. (1987, c. 483, s. 2; 1991, c. 720, s. 4.)

§ 58-24-125. Reports.

Reports shall be filed in accordance with the provisions of this section.

    (a) Every society transacting business in this State shall annually, on or before the first day of March, unless for cause shown such time has been extended by the Commissioner, file with the Commissioner a true statement of its financial condition, transactions and affairs for the preceding calendar year and pay the fee specified in G.S. 58-6-5 for filing same. The statement shall be in general form and context as approved by the NAIC for fraternal benefit societies and as supplemented by additional information required by the Commissioner.

    (b) As part of the annual statement herein required, each society shall, on or before the first day of March, file with the Commissioner a valuation of its certificates in force on December 31st last preceding, provided the Commissioner may, in his or her discretion for cause shown, extend the time for filing such valuation for not more than two calendar months. Such valuation shall be done in accordance with the standards specified in G.S. 58-24-120. Such valuation and underlying data shall be certified by a qualified actuary or, at the expense of the society, verified by the actuary of the Department of the state of domicile of the society.

(c) A society neglecting to file the annual statement in the form and within the time provided by this section shall forfeit one hundred dollars ($100.00) for each day during which such neglect continues, and, upon notice by the Commissioner to that effect, its authority to do business in this State shall cease while such default continues. (1987, c. 483, s. 2; 1991, c. 720, ss. 4, 19.)

§ 58-24-130. Perpetual license.

Subject to timely payment of the annual license continuation fee and subject to any other applicable provisions of the insurance laws of this State, a license, other than a preliminary license, to a fraternal benefit society under this Article shall continue in full force and effect. For each license the society shall pay the Commissioner the fee specified in G.S. 58-6-5. The society shall pay the Commissioner, as an annual license continuation fee and a condition of the continuation of the license, the fee specified in G.S. 58-6-7 on or before the first day of March on a form to be supplied by the Commissioner. A duly certified copy or duplicate of the license shall be prima facie evidence that the licensee is a fraternal benefit society within the meaning of Articles 1 through 64 of this Chapter. (1987, c. 483, s. 2; 1991, c. 720, s. 4; 2003-212, s. 26(g).)

Effect of Amendments. — Session Laws 2003-212, s. 26.(g), effective January 1, 2004, and applicable to all company licenses issued or otherwise eligible for renewal or continuation after that date, rewrote the section heading, which formerly read "Annual license"; and rewrote the section.

§ 58-24-135. Examination of societies; no adverse publications.

(a) The Commissioner, or any person he or she may appoint, may examine any domestic, foreign or alien society transacting or applying for admission to transact business in this State in the same manner as authorized for examination of domestic, foreign or alien insurers. Requirements of notice and an opportunity to respond before findings are made public as provided in the laws regulating insurers shall also be applicable to the examination of societies.

(b) Repealed by Session Laws 1995, c. 360, s. 2(i). (1987, c. 483, s. 2; 1991, c. 720, s. 4; 1995, c. 360, s. 2(i).)

Editor's Note. — This section is set out in the form above at the direction of the Revisor of Statutes.

§ 58-24-140. Foreign or alien society — Admission.

No foreign or alien society shall transact business in this State without a license issued by the Commissioner. Any such society desiring admission to this State shall comply substantially with the requirements and limitations of this Article applicable to domestic societies. Any such society may be licensed to transact business in this State upon filing with the Commissioner:

(a) A duly certified copy of its Articles of Incorporation;
(b) A copy of its bylaws, certified by its secretary or corresponding officer;
(c) A power of attorney to the Commissioner as prescribed in G.S. 58-24-170;
(d) A statement of its business under oath of its president and secretary or corresponding officers in a form prescribed by the Commissioner, duly

verified by an examination made by the supervising insurance official of its home state or other state, territory, province or country, satisfactory to the Commissioner of this State;

(e) Certification from the proper official of its home state, territory, province or country that the society is legally incorporated and licensed to transact business therein;

(f) Copies of its certificate forms; and

(g) Such other information as the Commissioner may deem necessary; and upon a showing that its assets are invested in accordance with the provisions of Articles 1 through 64 of this Chapter. (1987, c. 483, s. 2; 1991, c. 720, ss. 4, 20.)

§ 58-24-145. Injunction — Liquidation — Receivership of domestic society.

(a) When the Commissioner upon investigation finds that a domestic society:

(1) Has exceeded its powers;

(2) Has failed to comply with any provision of this Article;

(3) Is not fulfilling its contracts in good faith;

(4) Has a membership of less than 400 after an existence of one year or more; or

(5) Is conducting business fraudulently or in a manner hazardous to its members, creditors, the public or the business;

the Commissioner shall notify the society of such deficiency or deficiencies and state in writing the reasons for his or her dissatisfaction. The Commissioner shall at once issue a written notice to the society requiring that the deficiency or deficiencies which exist are corrected. After such notice the society shall have a 30 day period in which to comply with the Commissioner's request for correction, and if the society fails to comply the Commissioner shall notify the society of such findings of noncompliance and require the society to show cause on a date named why it should not be enjoined from carrying on any business until the violation complained of shall have been corrected, or why an action under Article 41 of Chapter 1 of the General Statutes (quo warranto) should not be commenced against the society.

(b) If on such date the society does not present good and sufficient reasons why it should not be so enjoined or why such action should not be commenced, the Commissioner may present the facts relating thereto to the Attorney General who shall, if he or she deems the circumstances warrant, commence an action to enjoin the society from transacting business or under Article 41 of Chapter 1 of the General Statutes (quo warranto).

(c) The court shall thereupon notify the officers of the society of a hearing. If after a full hearing it appears that the society should be so enjoined or liquidated or a receiver appointed, the court shall enter the necessary order. No society so enjoined shall have the authority to do business until:

(1) The Commissioner finds that the violation complained of has been corrected;

(2) The costs of such action shall have been paid by the society if the court finds that the society was in default as charged;

(3) The court has dissolved its injunction; and

(4) The Commissioner has reinstated the license.

(d) If the court orders the society liquidated, it shall be enjoined from carrying on any further business, whereupon the receiver of the society shall proceed at once to take possession of the books, papers, money and other assets of the society and, under the direction of the court, proceed forthwith to close the affairs of the society and to distribute its funds to those entitled thereto.

(e) No action under this section shall be recognized in any court of this State unless brought by the Attorney General upon request of the Commissioner. Whenever a receiver is to be appointed for a domestic society, the court shall appoint the Commissioner as such receiver.

(f) The provisions of this section relating to hearing by the Commissioner, action by the Attorney General at the request of the Commissioner, hearing by the court, injunction and receivership shall be applicable to a society which shall voluntarily determine to discontinue business. (1987, c. 483, s. 2; 1991, c. 720, s. 4; 1999-132, s. 9.1.)

§ 58-24-150. Suspension, revocation or refusal of license of foreign or alien society.

(a) When the Commissioner upon investigation finds that a foreign or alien society transacting or applying to transact business in this State:
   (1) Has exceeded its powers;
   (2) Has failed to comply with any of the provisions of this Article;
   (3) Is not fulfilling its contracts in good faith; or
   (4) Is conducting its business fraudulently or in a manner hazardous to its members or creditors or the public;
the Commissioner shall notify the society of such deficiency or deficiencies and state in writing the reasons for his or her dissatisfaction. The Commissioner shall at once issue a written notice to the society requiring that the deficiency or deficiencies which exist are corrected. After such notice the society shall have a 30 day period in which to comply with the Commissioner's request for correction, and if the society fails to comply the Commissioner shall notify the society of such findings of noncompliance and require the society to show cause on a date named why its license should not be suspended, revoked or refused. If on such date the society does not present good and sufficient reason why its authority to do business in this State should not be suspended, revoked or refused, the Commissioner may suspend or refuse the license of the society to do business in this State until satisfactory evidence is furnished to the Commissioner that such suspension or refusal should be withdrawn or the Commissioner may revoke the authority of the society to do business in this State.

(b) Nothing contained in this section shall be taken or construed as preventing any such society from continuing in good faith all contracts made in this State during the time such society was legally authorized to transact business herein. (1987, c. 483, s. 2; 1991, c. 720, s. 4.)

§ 58-24-155. Injunction.

No application or petition for injunction against any domestic, foreign or alien society, or lodge thereof, shall be recognized in any court of this State unless made by the Attorney General upon request of the Commissioner. (1987, c. 483, s. 2; 1991, c. 720, s. 4.)

§ 58-24-160. Licensing of agents.

(a) Agents of societies shall be licensed in accordance with the provisions of the general insurance laws regulating the licensing, revocation, suspension or termination of license of resident and nonresident agents; provided that agents licensed pursuant to former G.S. 58-268 as of July 1, 1977, shall be exempt from examination.

(b) No examination or license shall be required of any regular salaried officer, employee or member of a licensed society who devotes substantially all of his or her services to activities other than the solicitation of fraternal insurance contracts from the public, and who receives for the solicitation of such contracts no commission or other compensation directly dependent upon the amount of business obtained. (1987, c. 483, s. 2.)

§ 58-24-165. Unfair methods of competition and unfair and deceptive acts and practices.

Every society authorized to do business in this State shall be subject to the provisions of Article 63 of this Chapter relating to unfair methods of competition and unfair or deceptive acts or practices; provided, however, that nothing in such provisions shall be construed as applying to or affecting the right of any society to determine its eligibility requirements for membership, or be construed as applying to or affecting the offering of benefits exclusively to members or persons eligible for membership in the society by a subsidiary corporation or affiliated organization of the society. (1987, c. 483, s. 2.)

§ 58-24-170. Service of process.

(a) Every society authorized to do business in this State shall appoint in writing the Commissioner and each successor in office to be its true and lawful attorney upon whom all lawful process in any action or proceeding against it shall be served, and shall agree in such writing that any lawful process against it which is served on said attorney shall be of the same legal force and validity as if served upon the society, and that the authority shall continue in force so long as any liability remains outstanding in this State. Copies of such appointment, certified by said Commissioner, shall be deemed sufficient evidence thereof and shall be admitted in evidence with the same force and effect as the original thereof might be admitted.

(b) Service shall only be made upon the Commissioner, or if absent, upon the person in charge of the Commissioner's office. It shall be made in duplicate and shall constitute sufficient service upon the society. When legal process against a society is served upon the Commissioner, the Commissioner shall forthwith forward one of the duplicate copies by certified or registered mail, prepaid, directed to the secretary or corresponding officer. No such service shall require a society to file its answer, pleading or defense in less than 30 days from the date of mailing the copy of the service to a society. Legal process shall not be served upon a society except in the manner herein provided. At the time of serving any process upon the Commissioner, the plaintiff or complainant in the action shall pay to the Commissioner a fee in the amount set in G.S. 58-16-30. (1987, c. 483, s. 2; 1989, c. 645, s. 4; 1991, c. 720, s. 4.)

§ 58-24-175. Review.

All decisions and findings of the Commissioner made under the provisions of this Article shall be subject to review under G.S. 58-2-75. (1987, c. 483, s. 2; 1991, c. 720, ss. 4, 21.)

§ 58-24-180. Penalties.

(a) Any person, officer, member, or examining physician of any society authorized to do business under this Article who shall knowingly or willfully make any false or fraudulent statement or representation in or with reference to any application for membership, or for the purpose of obtaining money from or benefit in any society transacting business under this Article, shall be guilty of a Class 1 misdemeanor.

(b) Any person who shall solicit membership for, or in any manner assist in procuring membership in any fraternal benefit society not licensed to do business in this State, or who shall solicit membership for, or in any manner assist in procuring membership in any such society not authorized as herein provided to do business as herein defined in this State, shall be guilty of a Class 3 misdemeanor and upon conviction thereof shall be punished only by a fine of not less than one thousand dollars ($1,000) nor more than five thousand dollars ($5,000).

(c) Any society, or any officer, agent, or employee thereof, neglecting or refusing to comply with, or violating, any of the provisions of this Article, the penalty for which neglect, refusal, or violation is not specified in this section, shall be guilty of a Class 3 misdemeanor, and upon conviction shall be punished only by a fine not to exceed five thousand dollars ($5,000).

(d) Any person violating the provisions of G.S. 58-24-65 shall be guilty of a Class I felony.

(e) Any person who willfully makes any false statement under oath in any verified report or declaration that is required by law from fraternal benefit societies, is guilty of a Class I felony. (1987, c. 483, s. 2; 1989 (Reg. Sess., 1990), c. 1054, s. 3; 1993, c. 539, ss. 451, 1273; 1994, Ex. Sess., c. 24, s. 14(c); 1993 (Reg. Sess., 1994), c. 767, s. 25.)

§ 58-24-185. Exemption of certain societies.

(a) Nothing contained in this Article shall be so construed as to affect or apply to:

    (1) Grand or subordinate lodges of societies, orders or associations now doing business in this State which provide benefits exclusively through local or subordinate lodges;

    (2) Orders, societies or associations which admit to membership only persons engaged in one or more crafts or hazardous occupations, in the same or similar lines of business, insuring only their own members and their families, and the ladies' societies or ladies' auxiliaries to such orders, societies or associations;

    (3) Domestic societies which limit their membership to employees of a particular city or town, designated firm, business house or corporation which provide for a death benefit of not more than five hundred dollars ($500.00) or disability benefits of not more than three hundred fifty dollars ($350.00) to any person in any one year, or both;

    (4) Domestic societies or associations of a purely religious, charitable or benevolent description, which provide for a death benefit of not more than five hundred dollars ($500.00) or for disability benefits of not more than three hundred fifty dollars ($350.00) to any one person in any one year, or both; or

    (5) An association of local lodges of a society now doing business in this State which provides death benefits not exceeding five hundred dollars ($500.00) to any one person, provided, that the Commissioner may authorize the payment of death benefits not exceeding three thousand dollars ($3,000) to any one person, or may authorize disability benefits not exceeding three hundred dollars ($300.00), or may authorize both payments, in any one year to any one person.

(b) Any such society or association described in subsections (a)(3) or (a)(4) supra which provides for death or disability benefits for which benefit certificates are issued, and any such society or association included in subsection (a)(4) which has more than 1000 members, shall not be exempted from the provisions of this Article but shall comply with all requirements thereof.

(c) No society which, by the provisions of this section, is exempt from the requirements of this Article, except any society described in subsection (a)(2) supra, shall give or allow, or promise to give or allow to any person any compensation for procuring new members.

(d) Every society which provides for benefits in case of death or disability resulting solely from accident, and which does not obligate itself to pay natural death or sick benefits shall have all of the privileges and be subject to all the applicable provisions and regulations of this Article except that the provisions thereof relating to medical examination, valuations of benefit certificates, and incontestability, shall not apply to such society.

(e) The Commissioner may require from any society or association, by examination or otherwise, such information as will enable the Commissioner to determine whether such society or association is exempt from the provisions of this Article.

(f) Societies, exempted under the provisions of this section, shall also be exempt from all other provisions of the general insurance laws of this State. (1987, c. 483, s. 2; 1989, c. 364, s. 2; c. 485, s. 2; 1991, c. 476, s. 1; c. 720, ss. 4, 45, 55.)

CASE NOTES

Editor's Note. — *The case below was decided under prior statutory provisions.*

Service on Resident Secretary Held Valid. — Personal service on resident secretary of fraternal insurance association allowed to do business in the State without a license under former G.S. 58-291, G.S. 58-2-125 and former G.S. 58-251 held valid service on the association in action on policy. Winchester v. Grand Lodge of Bhd. of R.R. Trainmen, 203 N.C. 735, 167 S.E. 49 (1932).

§ 58-24-190. Severability.

If any provision of this Article or the application of such provision to any circumstance is held invalid, the remainder of the Article or the application of the provision to other circumstances, shall not be affected thereby. (1987, c. 483, s. 2.)

ARTICLE 25.

Fraternal Orders.

§ 58-25-1. General insurance law not applicable.

Nothing in the general insurance laws, except such as apply to fraternal orders shall be construed to extend to benevolent associations incorporated under the laws of this State that only levy an assessment on the members to create a fund to pay the family of a deceased member and make no profit therefrom, and do not solicit business through agents. (1987, c. 483, s. 2.)

§ 58-25-5. Fraternal orders defined.

Every incorporated association, order, or society doing business in this State on the lodge system, with ritualistic form of work and representative form of government, for the purpose of making provision for the payment of benefits of three hundred dollars ($300.00) or less in case of death, sickness, temporary or permanent physical disability, either as the result of disease, accident, or old age, formed and organized for the sole benefit of its members and their beneficiaries, and not for profit, is hereby declared to be a "fraternal order". Societies and orders which do not make insurance contracts or collect dues or assessments therefor, but simply pay burial or other benefits out of the treasury of their orders, and use their funds for the purpose of building homes or asylums for the purpose of caring for and educating orphan children and aged and infirm people in this State, shall not be considered as "fraternal orders"; and such order or association paying death or disability benefits may also create, maintain, apply, or disburse among its membership a reserve or emergency fund as may be provided in its constitution or bylaws; but no profit or gain may be added to the payments made by a member. (1987, c. 483, s. 2.)

§ 58-25-10. Funds derived from assessments and dues.

The fund from which the payment of benefits, as provided for in G.S. 58-25-5, shall be made, and the fund from which the expenses of such association, order or society shall be defrayed, shall be derived from assessments or dues collected from its members. Such societies or associations shall be governed by the laws of the State governing fraternal orders or societies, and are exempt from the provisions of all general insurance laws of this State, and no law hereafter passed shall apply to such orders or societies unless fraternal orders or societies are designated therein. (1987, c. 483, s. 2.)

CASE NOTES

Editor's Note. — *The cases below were decided under prior statutory provisions.*

Assessments Governed by Charter and Bylaws. — A fraternal society or association is governed by its own charter and bylaws and an assessment in accordance with its own laws is valid. Hollingsworth v. Supreme Council of Royal Arcanum, 175 N.C. 615, 96 S.E. 81 (1918).

Funds Held Not Subject to Attachment. — Where the constitution of a foreign fraternal insurance society provided for the creation of a fund to be raised from assessments upon its members for the benefit of widows and orphans of deceased members, any money paid to such fund was impressed with the qualities of a trust for the special purposes expressed, and such fund in the hands of a local collector, which he was bound to pay over to the society's treasurer, was not subject to an attachment by a creditor of the society. Brenizer v. Royal Arcanum, 141 N.C. 409, 53 S.E. 835 (1906).

§ 58-25-15. Appointment of member as receiver or collector; appointee as agent for order or society; rights of members.

Assessments and dues referred to in G.S. 58-25-5 and G.S. 58-25-10 may be collected, receipted, and remitted by a member or officer of any local or subordinate lodge of any fraternal order or society when so appointed or designated by any grand, district, or subordinate lodge or officer, deputy, or representative of the same, there being no regular licensed agent or deputy of said grand lodge charged with said duties; but any person so collecting said dues or assessments shall be the agent or representative of such fraternal order or society, or any department thereof, and shall bind them by their acts in collecting and remitting said amounts so collected. Under no circumstances, regardless of any agreement, bylaws, contract, or notice, shall said officer or collector be the agent or representative of the individual member from whom any such collection is made; nor shall said member be responsible for the failure of such officer or collector to safely keep, handle, or remit said dues or assessments so collected, in accordance with the rules, regulations, or bylaws of said order or society; nor shall said member, regardless of any rules, regulations, or bylaws to the contrary, forfeit any rights under his certificate of membership in said fraternal order or society by reason of any default or misconduct of any said officer or member so acting. (1987, c. 483, s. 2.)

CASE NOTES

Editor's Note. — The case below was decided under prior statutory provisions.

Waiver of Provisions of Certificate and Bylaws. — Where plaintiff's evidence showed that it had been the custom of defendant mutual benefit association's collecting agents to collect dues within 30 days after the due date, that defendant's home office knew of this custom, and that insured made payment of the dues for the preceding month within 30 days of the due date and died prior to the customary time for the collection of dues for the following month, it was held that the evidence was sufficient to be submitted to the jury on the question of defendant's waiver of the provisions of its certificate and bylaws, requiring a certificate of good health before reinstating a policy upon payment of premium after the due date, and upon the verdict of the jury plaintiff was entitled to judgment for the amount of the policy, less the dues for the month not paid. Shackelford v. Sovereign Camp of Woodmen of World, 209 N.C. 633, 184 S.E. 691 (1936).

§ 58-25-20. Meetings of governing body; principal office.

Any such order or society incorporated and organized under the laws of this State may provide for the meeting of its supreme legislative or governing body in any other state, province, or territory wherein such order or society has subordinate lodges, and all business transacted at such meetings is as valid in all respects as if the meetings were held in this State; but the principal business office of such order or society shall always be kept in this State. (1987, c. 483, s. 2.)

§ 58-25-25. Conditions precedent to doing business.

Any such fraternal order, society, or association as defined by this Article, chartered and organized in this State or organized and doing business under the laws of any other state, district, province, or territory, having the qualifications required of domestic societies of like character, upon satisfying the Commissioner that its business is proper and legitimate and so conducted, may be admitted to transact business in this State upon the same conditions as are prescribed by Articles 1 through 64 of this Chapter for admitting and authorizing foreign insurance companies to do business in this State, except that such fraternal orders shall not be required to have the capital required of such insurance companies. Organizers or agents shall be licensed without requiring an examination; provided, organizers or agents who are engaged in or intend to engage in the sale of individual policies of life insurance shall take the examination required of life insurance agents. Those organizers or agents licensed for the sale of insurance pursuant to former G.S. 58-268 as of July 1, 1977, shall be exempt from examination. (1987, c. 483, s. 2; 1991, c. 720, s. 4.)

§ 58-25-30. Certain lodge systems exempt.

The following beneficial orders or societies shall be exempt from the requirements of this Article, and shall not be required to pay any license tax or fees nor make any report to the Commissioner, unless the assessments collected for death benefits by the supreme lodge amount to at least three hundred dollars ($300.00) in one year: Beneficial fraternal orders, or societies incorporated under the laws of this State, which are conducted under the lodge system which have the supreme lodge or governing body located in this State, and which are so organized that the membership consists of members of subordinate lodges; that the subordinate lodges accept for membership only residents of the county in which such subordinate lodge is located; that each subordinate lodge issues certificates, makes assessments, and collects a fund to pay benefits to the widows and orphans of its own deceased members and their families, each lodge independently of the others, for itself and independently of the supreme lodge; that each lodge controls the fund for this purpose; that in addition to the benefits paid by each subordinate lodge to its own members, the supreme lodge provides for an additional benefit for such of the members of the subordinate lodges as are qualified, at the option of the subordinate lodge members; that such organization is not conducted for profit, has no capital stock, and has been in operation for 10 years in this State.

The Commissioner may require the chief or presiding officer, or the secretary, to file annually an affidavit that such organization is entitled to this exemption. (1987, c. 483, s. 2; 1991, c. 720, s. 4.)

§ 58-25-35. Insurance on children.

Any fraternal order or society authorized pursuant to this Article to do business in this State and operating on the lodge plan may provide in its constitution and bylaws, in addition to other benefits provided for therein, for the payment of death or annuity benefits upon the lives of children between the ages of one and 16 years at next birthday, for whose support and maintenance a member of such order or society is responsible. The order or society may at its option organize and operate branches for such children and membership in local lodges, and initiation therein shall not be required of such children, nor shall they have any voice in the management of the order or society. The total benefits payable as above provided shall in no case exceed the following amounts at ages at next birthday at time of death, respectively, as follows: one year, twenty dollars ($20.00); two years, fifty dollars ($50.00); three years, seventy-five dollars ($75.00); four years, one hundred dollars ($100.00); five years, one hundred twenty-five dollars ($125.00); six years, one hundred fifty dollars ($150.00); seven years, two hundred dollars ($200.00); eight years, two hundred fifty dollars ($250.00); nine years, three hundred dollars ($300.00); 10 years, four hundred dollars ($400.00); 11 years, five hundred dollars ($500.00); 12 years, six hundred dollars ($600.00); 13 years, seven hundred dollars ($700.00); 14 years, eight hundred dollars ($800.00); 15 years, nine hundred dollars ($900.00); 16 years, one thousand dollars ($1,000). (1987, c. 483, s. 2.)

§ 58-25-40. Medical examination; certificates and contributions.

No benefit certificate as to any child shall take effect until after medical examination or inspection by a licensed medical practitioner, in accordance with the laws of the order or society, nor shall any such benefit certificate be issued unless the order or society shall simultaneously put in force at least 500 such certificates, on each of which at least one assessment has been paid, nor where the number of lives represented by such certificate falls below 500. The death benefit contributions to be made upon such certificate shall be based upon the "Standard Mortality Table" or the "English Life Table Number Six," and a rate of interest not greater than four percent (4%) per annum, upon a higher standard or upon such mortality, morbidity, and interest standards permitted by the laws of this State for use by life insurance companies; but contributions may be waived or returns may be made from any surplus held in excess of reserve and other liabilities, as provided in the bylaws; and extra contributions shall be made if the reserves hereafter provided for become impaired. (1987, c. 483, s. 2.)

§ 58-25-45. Reserve fund; exchange of certificates.

Any order or society entering into such insurance agreements shall maintain on all such contracts the reserve required by the standard of mortality and interest adopted by the order or society for computing contributions as provided in G.S. 58-25-35, and the funds representing the benefit contributions and all accretions thereon shall be kept as separate and distinct funds, independent of the other funds of the order or society, and shall not be liable for nor used for the payment of the debts and obligations of the order or society other than the benefits herein authorized. An order or society may provide that when a child reaches the minimum age for initiation into membership in such order or society, any benefit certificate issued hereunder may be surrendered for cancellation and exchanged for any other form of certificate issued by the order or society: Provided, that such surrender will not reduce the number of lives insured below 500; and upon the issuance of such new certificate any reserve upon the original certificate herein provided for shall be transferred to the credit of the new certificate. Neither the person who originally made application for benefits on account of such child, nor the beneficiary named in such original certificate, nor the person who paid the contributions, shall have any vested right in such new certificate, the free nomination of a beneficiary under the new certificate being left to the child so admitted to benefit membership. (1987, c. 483, s. 2.)

§ 58-25-50. Separation of funds.

An entirely separate financial statement of the business transactions and of assets and liabilities arising therefrom shall be made in its annual report to the Commissioner by an order or society availing itself of the provisions hereof. The separation of assets, funds, and liabilities required hereby shall not be terminated, rescinded, or modified, nor shall the funds be diverted for any use other than as specified in the preceding section, as long as any certificates issued hereunder remain in force, and this requirement shall be recognized and enforced in any liquidation, reinsurance, merger, or other change in the condition or the status of the order or society. (1987, c. 483, s. 2; 1991, c. 720, s. 4.)

§ 58-25-55. Payments to expense or general fund.

Any order or society shall have the right to provide in its laws and the certificate issued hereunder for specified payments on account of the expense or general fund, which payments shall or shall not be mingled with the general fund of the order or society, as its constitution and bylaws may provide. (1987, c. 483, s. 2.)

§ 58-25-60. Continuation of certificates.

In the event of the termination of membership in the order or society by the person responsible for the support of any child on whose account a certificate may have been issued as provided herein, the certificate may be continued for the benefit of the estate of the child, provided the contributions are continued, or for the benefit of any other person responsible for the support and maintenance of such child who shall assume the payment of the required contributions. (1987, c. 483, s. 2.)

§ 58-25-65. Appointment of trustees to hold property.

The lodges of Masons, Odd Fellows, Knights of Pythias, camps of Woodmen of the World, councils of the Junior Order of United American Mechanics, orders of the Elks, Young Men's Christian Associations, Young Women's Christian Associations and other benevolent or fraternal orders and societies may appoint from time to time suitable persons trustees of their bodies or societies, in such manner as they deem proper, which trustees, and their successors, shall have power to receive, purchase, take, and hold property, real and personal, in trust for such society or body. The trustees shall have power, when instructed so to do by resolution adopted by the order, society or body which they represent, to mortgage or sell and convey in fee simple any real or personal property owned by the order, society or body; and the conveyances so made by the trustees shall be effective to pass the property in fee simple to the purchaser or to the mortgagee or trustee for the purposes in such conveyance or mortgage expressed. If there shall be no trustee, then any real or personal property which could be held by such trustees shall vest in and be held by such charitable, benevolent, religious, or fraternal orders and societies, respectively, according to such intent. (1987, c. 483, s. 2.)

§ 58-25-70. Unauthorized wearing of badges, etc.

Any person who fraudulently and willfully wears the badge or button of any fraternal organization or society, either in the identical form or in such near resemblance thereto as to be a colorable imitation thereof, or who fraudulently and willfully uses the name of any such order, society or organization, the titles of its officers, or its insignia, ritual, or ceremonies, unless entitled to wear or use the same under the constitution and bylaws, rules and regulations of such fraternal organization, society, or order, shall be deemed guilty of a Class 3 misdemeanor. (1987, c. 483, s. 2; 1993, c. 539, s. 452; 1994, Ex. Sess., c. 24, s. 14(c).)

ARTICLE 26.

Real Estate Title Insurance Companies.

§ 58-26-1. Purpose of organization; formation; insuring closing services; premium rates; combined premiums for lenders' coverages.

(a) Companies may be formed in the manner provided in this Article for the purpose of furnishing information in relation to titles to real estate and of insuring owners and others interested therein against loss by reason of encumbrances and defective title; provided, however, that no such information shall be so furnished nor shall such insurance be so issued as to North Carolina real property unless and until the title insurance company has obtained the opinion of an attorney, licensed to practice law in North Carolina and not an employee or agent of the company, who has conducted or caused to be conducted under the attorney's direct supervision a reasonable examination of the title. The company shall cause to be made a determination of insurability of title in accordance with sound underwriting practices for title insurance companies. A company may also insure the proper performance of services necessary to conduct a real estate closing performed by an approved attorney licensed to practice in North Carolina. Provided, however, nothing in this section shall be construed to prohibit or preclude a title insurance company from insuring proper performance by its issuing agents.

(b) Repealed by Session Laws 2002-187, s. 7.1.

(b1) Domestic and foreign title insurance companies are subject to the same capital, surplus, and investment requirements that govern the formation and operation of domestic stock casualty companies. Domestic title insurance companies are subject to the same deposit requirements that govern the operation of other domestic casualty companies in this State. Foreign or alien title insurance companies are subject to an initial deposit pursuant to G.S. 58-26-31(b), based on the forecasted statutory premium reserve and the supplemental reserve for the first full year of operation in this State, but not less than two hundred thousand dollars ($200,000).

(c) This Article shall not be interpreted so as to imply the repeal or amendment of any of the provisions of Chapter 84 of the General Statutes of North Carolina nor of any other provisions of common law or statutory law governing the practice of law.

(d) The premium rates charged for insuring against loss by reason of encumbrances and defective title and for insuring real estate closing services shall be based on the purchase price of the real estate being conveyed or the loan amount and shall not be established as flat fees. If a title insurer has also issued title insurance protecting a lender or owner against loss by reason of encumbrances and defective title, the insurer shall charge one undivided premium for the combination of the title insurance and the closing services insurance.

(e) If the premium stated upon a policy of title insurance has been understated or overstated due to inadvertence, mistake, or miscalculation of the closing attorney or his employees, and the incident is not purposeful or part of a pattern, the Commissioner of Insurance shall not be required to impose a civil penalty or other sanction for the inadvertence, mistake, or miscalculation. (1899, c. 54, s. 38; 1901, c. 391, s. 3; Rev., s. 4745; C.S., s. 6395; 1923, c. 71; 1973, c. 128; 1985, c. 666, s. 43; 1987, c. 625, ss. 1-3; 1993, c. 129, s. 1; c. 504, s. 15; 2002-187, ss. 7.1, 7.2.)

Effect of Amendments. — Session Laws 2002-187, ss. 7.1 and 7.2, effective October 31, 2002, repealed former subsection (b), providing conditions for real estate title insurance companies, and added subsection (b1).

CASE NOTES

Ethical Obligation of Attorney. — Where attorney knew that a particular lot was mistakenly included in the deed, he was under an ethical obligation to disclose this information to the title insurance company in order to prevent the possible perpetuation of a fraud. Lawyers Title Ins. Co. v. Golf Links Dev. Corp., 87 F. Supp. 2d 505, 1999 U.S. Dist. LEXIS 21315 (W.D.N.C. 1999).

Cited in Gardner v. North Carolina State Bar, 316 N.C. 285, 341 S.E.2d 517 (1986).

§ 58-26-5. Certificate of authority to do business.

Before any such company may issue any policy or make any contract or guarantee of insurance, it shall file with the Commissioner a certified copy of the record or the certificate of its organization in the office of the Secretary of State, and obtain from the Commissioner his certificate that it has complied with the laws applicable to it and that it is authorized to do business. (1899, c. 54, s. 38; 1901, c. 391, s. 3; Rev., s. 4745; C.S., s. 6396; 1991, c. 720, s. 4.)

§ 58-26-10. Financial statements and licenses required.

Title insurance companies are subject to G.S. 58-2-131, 58-2-132, 58-2-133, 58-2-134, 58-2-165, 58-2-180, and 58-6-5. The Commissioner may require title insurance companies to separately report their experience in insuring titles and in insuring closing services. The license to do business in this State issued to a title insurance company shall continue in full force and effect, subject to timely payment of the annual license continuation fee in accordance with G.S. 58-6-7 and subject to any other applicable provisions of the insurance laws of this State. The Commissioner shall annually license the agents of title insurance companies. (1899, c. 54, s. 38; 1901, c. 391, s. 3; Rev., s. 4745; C.S., s. 6397; 1987, c. 625, ss. 4, 5; 1991, c. 720, s. 4; 1993, c. 504, s. 17; 1999-132, s. 11.5; 2003-212, s. 26(h).)

Effect of Amendments. — Session Laws 2003-212, s. 26.(h), effective January 1, 2004, and applicable to all company licenses issued or otherwise eligible for renewal or continuation after that date, inserted the second sentence, and at the end of the last sentence, substituted "the agents of title insurance companies" for "such companies and their agents."

§ 58-26-15. Limitation of risk.

No real estate title insurance company shall guarantee or insure in any one risk on real property located in North Carolina more than forty percent (40%) of its combined capital and surplus without first having the approval of the Commissioner, which approval shall be endorsed upon the policy. (1945, c. 386; 1967, c. 936; 1993, c. 504, s. 18.)

Legal Periodicals. — For article, "Transferring North Carolina Real Estate Part I: How the Present System Functions," see 49 N.C.L. Rev. 413 (1971).

§ 58-26-20. Statutory premium reserve.

Every domestic title insurance company shall, in addition to other reserves, establish and maintain a reserve to be known as the "statutory premium reserve" for title insurance, which shall at all times and for all purposes be considered and constitute a reserve liability of the title insurance company in determining its financial condition. (1969, c. 897; 1973, c. 1035, s. 1; 1993, c. 504, s. 19; 2002-187, s. 7.3.)

Effect of Amendments. — Session Laws 2002-187, s. 7.3, effective October 31, 2002, rewrote the section, which formerly pertained to unearned premium reserves.

§ 58-26-25. Amount of unearned [statutory] premium reserve.

(a) The statutory premium reserve of every domestic title insurance company shall consist of the aggregate of:
   (1) The amount of the unearned premium reserve held as of December 31, 1998.
   (2) The amount of all additions required to be made to such reserve by this section, less the reduction of the aggregate amount required by this section.

(b) A domestic title insurance company on and after January 1, 1999, shall reserve initially as a statutory premium reserve a sum equal to ten percent (10%) of the following items set forth in the title insurer's most recent annual statement on file with the Commissioner:
   (1) Direct premiums written.
   (2) Premiums for reinsurance assumed less premiums for reinsurance ceded during the year.

(c) The aggregate of the amounts set aside in statutory premium reserves in any calendar year, under subsection (b) of this section, shall be reduced annually at the end of each calendar year following the year in which the policy is issued, over a period of 20 years, pursuant to the following: twenty percent (20%) the first year; ten percent (10%) for years two and three; five percent

(5%) for years four through 10; three percent (3%) for years 11 through 15; and two percent (2%) for years 16 through 20.

(d) The entire amount of the unearned premium reserve held as of December 31, 1998, shall be accorded a fresh start and shall be released from said reserve and restored to net profits in accordance with the percentages set forth in subsection (c) of this section.

(e) A supplemental reserve shall be established in accordance with the instructions of the annual statement required by G.S. 58-2-165 and G.S. 58-26-10 consisting of the reserves necessary, when taken in combination with the reserves required by subsections (a) through (d) of this section to cover the company's liabilities with respect to all losses, claims, and loss adjustment expenses.

(f) Each title insurer subject to the provisions of this Article shall file with its annual statement required by G.S. 58-2-165 and G.S. 58-26-10 a certification of a member in good standing of the American Academy of Actuaries. The actuarial certification required of a title insurer must conform to the annual statement instructions for title insurers of the National Association of Insurance Commissioners. (1969, c. 897; 1973, c. 1035, ss. 2-4; 1999-383, s. 1; 2002-187, ss. 7.4, 7.5, 7.6.)

Editor's Note. — The word "[statutory]" has been inserted in the section heading at the direction of the Revisor of the Statutes.

Effect of Amendments. — Session Laws 2002-187, ss. 7.4 to 7.6, effective October 31, 2002, in subsections (a), (b) and (c), substituted "statutory" for "unearned"; and made stylistic changes.

§ **58-26-30:** Repealed by Session Laws 2002-187, s. 7.7, effective October 31, 2002.

Cross References. — As to statutory premium reserve held in trust or as a deposit, see § 58-26-31.

§ 58-26-31. Statutory premium reserve held in trust or as a deposit.

(a) Each domestic title insurance company shall withdraw from use funds to be used by the Commissioner in the event of the insurer's insolvency, the funds being equal to the statutory premium reserve and the supplemental reserve pursuant to G.S. 58-26-25. The amount shall be held in a trust account, as approved by the Commissioner. The trust account will be held in favor of the holders of title policies in the event of the insolvency of the insurer, and is not subject to G.S. 41-15. Nothing in this section precludes the insurer from investing the reserve in investments authorized by law for that insurer, and the income from the invested reserve shall be included in the general income of the insurer to be used by the insurer for any lawful purpose.

(b) Each foreign or alien title insurance company shall withdraw from use funds to be used by the Commissioner in the event of the insurer's insolvency, the funds being equal to the statutory premium reserve and the supplemental reserve as calculated under G.S. 58-26-25 for North Carolina risks. The Commissioner shall hold the funds as a deposit in accordance with G.S. 58-5-20. Annually, the company shall file a statement of actuarial opinion consistent with the annual statement instructions for North Carolina risks, issued by a qualified actuary, in support of this deposit.

(c) A title insurance company shall have 30 days after notification by the Commissioner to increase the amounts held on deposit. If the amount held on deposit is greater than the amount required under subsection (b) of this section, the Commissioner shall release the excess within 30 days after a request by the insurer. (2002-187, s. 7.8; 2003-221, s. 2.)

Editor's Note. — Session Laws 2002-187, s. 9, makes this section effective October 31, 2002.
Effect of Amendments. — Session Laws

2003-221, s. 2, effective June 19, 2003, inserted "and is not subject to G.S. 41-15" in subsection (a).

§ 58-26-35. Maintenance of the statutory premium reserve.

If the amount of the assets of a title insurance company held in trust or held by the Commissioner under G.S. 58-26-31 should on any date be less than the amount required to be maintained, and the deficiency is not promptly cured, the title insurance company shall immediately give written notice of the deficiency to the Commissioner and shall not write or assume any title insurance until the deficiency has been eliminated and until it has received written approval from the Commissioner authorizing it to again write and assume title insurance. (1969, c. 897; 2002-187, s. 7.9.)

Effect of Amendments. — Session Laws 2002-187, s. 7.9, effective October 31, 2002,

rewrote the section, which formerly pertained to maintenance of unearned premium reserves.

§ 58-26-40: Repealed by Session Laws 2002-187, s. 7.10, effective October 31, 2002.

ARTICLE 27.

Title Insurance Companies and Land Mortgage Companies Issuing Collateral Loan Certificates.

§ 58-27-1. Issuance of collateral loan certificates; security.

Any domestic land mortgage company or title insurance company having a paid-in capital and surplus of at least two hundred thousand dollars ($200,000), may, under the supervision and control of the Commissioner, issue collateral loan certificates, or other certificates of indebtedness secured by the deposit of first mortgages on real estate with the Commissioner, or under his direction, or secured by the deposit with the Commissioner, or under his direction, of collateral trust bonds secured by first mortgages, the principal and interest of which said mortgages is guaranteed by a surety company having assets of at least ten million dollars ($10,000,000), upon a basis not to exceed one hundred dollars ($100.00) for each one hundred dollars ($100.00) of liability under the collateral loan certificates or other certificates of indebtedness outstanding and secured by such first mortgages or collateral trust bonds. (1927, c. 204, s. 1; 1991, c. 720, s. 4.)

§ 58-27-5. Prohibition against payment or receipt of title insurance kickbacks, rebates, commissions and other payments.

(a) No person or entity selling real property, or performing services as a real estate agent, attorney or lender, which services are incident to or a part of any real estate settlement or sale, shall pay or receive, directly or indirectly, any kickback, rebate, commission or other payment in connection with the issuance of title insurance for any real property which is a part of such sale or settlement; nor shall any title insurance company, agency or agent make any such payment.

(b) Any person or entity violating the provisions of this section shall be guilty of a Class 2 misdemeanor which may include a fine of not more than five thousand dollars ($5,000).

(c) No persons or entity shall be in violation of this section solely by reason of ownership of stock in a bona fide title insurance company, agency, or agent. For purposes of this section, and in addition to any other statutory or regulatory requirements, a bona fide title insurance company, agency or agent is defined to be a company, agency or agent that passes upon and makes title insurance underwriting decisions on title risks, including the issuance of title insurance policies, binders and endorsements, and that maintains a separate and distinct staff and office or offices for such purposes. (1973, c. 1336, s. 1; 1985, c. 666, s. 24; 1993, c. 504, s. 41; c. 539, s. 453; 1994, Ex. Sess., c. 24, s. 14(c).)

§ 58-27-10. Licenses.

Any domestic land mortgage company, or title insurance company, wishing to do business under the provisions of this Article upon making written application and submitting proof satisfactory to the Commissioner that its business, capital and other qualifications comply with the provisions of this Article, upon paying to the Commissioner, the sum of five hundred dollars ($500.00) as a license fee and all other fees assessed against such company may be licensed to do business in this State under the provisions of this Article until the first day of the following July, and may have its license renewed for each year thereafter so long as it complies with the provisions of this Article and such rules adopted by the Commissioner. For each such renewal such company shall pay to the Commissioner the sum of one thousand dollars ($1,000), and all other fees assessed against such company and such renewal shall continue in force and effect until a new license be issued or specifically refused, unless revoked for good cause. The Commissioner, or any person appointed by him, shall have the power and authority to make such rules and regulations and examinations not inconsistent with the provisions of this Article, as may be in his discretion necessary or proper to enforce the provisions hereof and secure compliance with the terms of this Article. For any examination made hereunder the Commissioner shall charge the land mortgage companies or title insurance companies examined with the actual expense of such examination. (1927, c. 204, s. 2; 1955, c. 179, s. 3; 1991, c. 720, s. 4; c. 721, s. 1; 1999-435, s. 4.)

§ 58-27-15. Annual statements furnished.

Every such domestic land mortgage company or title insurance company doing business in this State under this Article shall annually file with the Commissioner on or before the first day of March in each year a full and complete sworn statement of its financial condition on the thirty-first day of December next preceding. Such statement shall plainly exhibit all real and contingent assets and liabilities and a complete account of its income and disbursements during the year, and shall also exhibit the amount of real estate mortgages deposited by such land mortgage company or title insurance company for the protection of the certificates issued under this Article. The Commissioner is hereby empowered to require such further information as may be reasonably necessary to satisfy him that the statements contained in the sworn statements are true and correct. (1927, c. 204, s. 3; 1991, c. 720, s. 4.)

Article 28.

Unauthorized Insurers.

§ 58-28-1. Purpose of Article.

It is the purpose of this Article to abate and prevent the practices of unauthorized insurers within the State of North Carolina, and to provide methods for effectively enforcing the laws of this State against such practices. The General Assembly finds that there is within this State a substantial amount of insurance business being transacted by insurers who have not complied with the laws of this State and have not been authorized by the Commissioner to do business. These practices by unauthorized insurers are deemed to be harmful and contrary to public welfare of the citizens of this State. The difficulties which arise from the acts and practices of unauthorized insurers are compounded by the fact that such companies may be licensed in foreign jurisdictions and conduct a long-range business without having personal representatives or agents in proximity to insureds. The General Assembly further declares that it is a subject of vital public interest to the State that unlicensed and unauthorized companies have been and are now engaged in soliciting by way of direct mail and other advertising media, insurance risks within this State, and that such companies enjoy the many benefits and privileges provided by the State as well as the protection afforded to citizens under exercise of the police powers of the State, without themselves being subject to the laws designed to protect the insurance consuming public. The provisions of this Article are in addition to all other statutory provisions of Articles 1 through 64 of this Chapter relating to unauthorized insurers and do not replace, alter, modify or repeal such existing provisions. (1967, c. 909, s. 1; 1987, c. 864, s. 46; 1991, c. 720, s. 4.)

CASE NOTES

The purpose of §§ 58-28-1 through 58-28-15 is to protect unwary North Carolinians against the overreaching machinations and solicitations of unauthorized out-of-state insurers in selling insurance policies; certainly, their purpose is not to immunize from liability indemnitors who travel to other states and induce foreign sureties to bond fledgling North Carolina building contractors that have no credit of their own and that require bonds to stay in business. Henry Angelo & Sons v. Property Dev. Corp., 63 N.C. App. 569, 306 S.E.2d 162 (1983).

§ 58-28-5. Transacting business without certificate of authority prohibited; exceptions.

(a) Except as otherwise provided in this section, it is unlawful for any company to enter into a contract of insurance as an insurer or to transact insurance business in this State as set forth in G.S. 58-28-10, without a license issued by the Commissioner. This section does not apply to the following acts or transactions:

    (1) The procuring of a policy of insurance upon a risk within this State where the applicant is unable to procure coverage in the open market with admitted companies and is otherwise in compliance with Article 21 of this Chapter.

(2) Contracts of reinsurance; but not including assumption reinsurance transactions, whereby the reinsuring company succeeds to all of the liabilities of and supplants the ceding company on the insurance contracts that are the subject of the transaction, unless prior approval has been obtained from the Commissioner.

(3) Transactions in this State involving a policy lawfully solicited, written and delivered outside of this State covering only subjects of insurance not resident, located or expressly to be performed in this State at the time of issuance, and which transactions are subsequent to the issuance of such policy.

(4) Transactions in this State involving group life insurance, group annuities, or group, blanket, or franchise accident and health insurance where the master policy for the insurance was lawfully issued and delivered in a state in which the company was authorized to transact business.

(5) Transactions in this State involving all policies of insurance issued before July 1, 1967.

(6) The procuring of contracts of insurance issued to a nuclear insured. As used in this subdivision, "nuclear insured" means a public utility procuring insurance against radioactive contamination and other risks of direct physical loss at a nuclear electric generating plant.

(7) Insurance independently procured, as specified in subsection (b) of this section.

(8) Insurance on vessels or craft, their cargoes, marine builders' risks, marine protection and indemnity, or other risks commonly insured under marine insurance policies, as distinguished from inland marine insurance policies.

(9) Transactions in this State involving commercial aircraft insurance, meaning insurance against (i) loss of or damage resulting from any cause to commercial aircraft and its equipment, (ii) legal liability of the insured for loss or damage to another person's property resulting from the ownership, maintenance, or use of commercial aircraft, and (iii) loss, damage, or expense incident to a liability claim.

(b) Any person in this State may directly procure or directly renew insurance with an unlicensed insurer without the involvement of an agent, broker, or surplus lines licensee, on a risk located or to be performed, in whole or in part, in this State. The person shall, within 30 days after the date the insurance is procured or renewed, file a written report with the Commissioner on forms prescribed by the Commissioner. The report must contain the name and address of the insured; name and address of the insurer; the subject of insurance; a general description of the coverage; the amount of premium currently charged; and any additional information requested by the Commissioner. The report must also contain an affidavit of the insured that states that the full amount or kind of insurance cannot be obtained from insurers that are admitted to do business in this State; and that the insured has made a diligent search among the insurers that are admitted to transact and are actually writing the particular kind and class of insurance in this State. Gross premiums charged for the insurance, less any return premiums, are subject to a tax at the rate of five percent (5%). At the time of filing the report required by this subsection, the insured shall pay the tax to the Commissioner. The Commissioner has the powers specified in G.S. 58-21-90 with respect to the tax levied by this subsection.

(c) This section does not apply to any surviving nonprofit corporation that results from a merger between the nonprofit corporation established by the North Carolina State Bar Council pursuant to Chapter 707 of the 1975 Session Laws of North Carolina and another domestic nonprofit corporation; provided, however, that any such surviving corporation shall register with the North Carolina State Bar Council under G.S. 84-23.1. (1967, c. 909, s. 1; 1971, c. 510, s. 3; 1985, c. 688, s. 2; 1987, c. 727, ss. 4, 5; c. 864, ss. 47, 70; 1991, c. 644, s. 6; 1993, c. 409, s. 26; c. 504, s. 20; 1995, c. 193, s. 30; 1999-219, s. 5.4.)

CASE NOTES

The purpose of §§ 58-28-1 through 58-28-15 is to protect unwary North Carolinians against the overreaching machinations and solicitations of unauthorized out-of-state insurers in selling insurance policies; certainly, their purpose is not to immunize from liability indemnitors who travel to other states and induce foreign sureties to bond fledgling North Carolina building contractors that have no credit of their own and that require bonds to stay in business. Henry Angelo & Sons v. Property Dev. Corp., 63 N.C. App. 569, 306 S.E.2d 162 (1983).

Cited in Blackwelder v. City of Winston-Salem, 332 N.C. 319, 420 S.E.2d 432 (1992).

§ 58-28-10. Acts or transactions deemed to constitute transacting insurance business in this State.

The following acts, if performed in this State, shall be included among those deemed to constitute transacting insurance business in this State:

  (1)a. Maintaining any agency or office where any acts in furtherance of an insurance business are transacted, including, but not limited to the execution of contracts of insurance with citizens of this or any other state;

    b. Maintaining files or records of contracts of insurance; or

    c. Receiving payments of premiums for contracts of insurance.

  (2) Likewise, any of the following acts in this State, whether effected by mail or otherwise by an unauthorized insurer, is included among those deemed to constitute transacting insurance business in this State:

    a. The issuance or delivery of contracts of insurance to residents of this State or to corporations authorized to do business therein;

    b. The soliciting of applications for contracts of insurance through the use of the United States mail or any other media, method or device;

    c. The collections of premiums, membership fees, assessments or other considerations for such contracts; or

    d. The transaction of any matters prior to or subsequent to the execution of such contracts in contemplation thereof or arising out of them.

Any company violating any of the provisions of this section, by doing any of the foregoing acts or transactions while not authorized to do business within this State, shall be subject to penalty of not less than one thousand dollars ($1,000) nor more than five thousand dollars ($5,000) for each offense; such penalty shall be payable to the Commissioner, who shall in turn forward the same to the county or counties wherein the violation or violations occur, for the use of the public schools of such county or counties: Provided, that each day in which a violation occurs shall constitute a separate offense. The Attorney General of the State of North Carolina at the request of and upon information from the Commissioner shall initiate a civil action in behalf of the Commissioner in any county of the State wherein a violation under this section occurs to recover the penalty provided. Service of process upon the unauthorized insurer shall be had as is provided in G.S. 58-28-40. (1967, c. 909, s. 1; 1985, c. 666, s. 22; 1991, c. 720, s. 4.)

CASE NOTES

The purpose of §§ 58-28-1 through 58-28-15 is to protect unwary North Carolinians against the overreaching machinations and solicitations of unauthorized out-of-state insurers in selling insurance policies; certainly, their purpose is not to immunize from liability indemnitors who travel to other states and induce foreign sureties to bond fledgling North Carolina building contractors that have no credit of their own and that require bonds to stay in business. Henry Angelo & Sons v. Property Dev. Corp., 63 N.C. App. 569, 306 S.E.2d 162 (1983).

Cited in Blackwelder v. City of Winston-Salem, 332 N.C. 319, 420 S.E.2d 432 (1992).

§ 58-28-15. Validity of acts or contracts of unauthorized company shall not impair obligation of contract as to the company; maintenance of suits; right to defend.

The failure of a company to obtain a license shall not impair the validity of any acts or contracts of the company. Any person or insured holding contracts of insurance of an unauthorized insurer may bring an action in the courts of this State under the provisions of G.S. 58-16-35 for the enforcement of any rights pursuant to the contract of insurance. The failure of the insurance company to obtain a license shall not prevent such company from defending any action at law or suit in equity in any court of this State so long as the said company fully complies with the provisions of G.S. 58-16-35(c), but no company transacting insurance business in this State without a license shall be permitted to maintain an action at law or in equity in any court of this State to enforce any right, claim or demand arising out of the transaction of such business until such company shall have obtained a license. Nor shall an action at law or in equity be maintained in any court of this State by any successor or assignee of such company on any such right, claim or demand originally held by such company until a license shall have been obtained by the company or by a company which has acquired all or substantially all of its assets. Nothing in this section shall be construed to abrogate the conditions of admission into this State nor to impair the authority of the Commissioner with respect to the issuance of licenses. The Commissioner in considering the issuance of a license shall take into consideration the acts or transactions which an unauthorized company has engaged in in this State prior to its application for a license. (1967, c. 909, s. 1; 1991, c. 720, ss. 4, 56; 1999-132, s. 9.1; 2000-140, s. 12.)

CASE NOTES

The purpose of §§ 58-28-1 through 58-28-15 is to protect unwary North Carolinians against the overreaching machinations and solicitations of unauthorized out-of-state insurers in selling insurance policies; certainly, their purpose is not to immunize from liability indemnitors who travel to other states and induce foreign sureties to bond fledgling North Carolina building contractors that have no credit of their own and that require bonds to stay in business. Henry Angelo & Sons v. Property Dev. Corp., 63 N.C. App. 569, 306 S.E.2d 162 (1983).

The phrase "action at law or in equity" cannot be interpreted to prevent cross-claims among defendants sued by others. Henry Angelo & Sons v. Property Dev. Corp., 63 N.C. App. 569, 306 S.E.2d 162 (1983).

This section deprives unauthorized insurers only of the right "to maintain an action at law or in equity" in regard to their prohibited business; it says nothing at all about maintaining cross-claims against codefendants. Henry Angelo & Sons v. Property Dev. Corp., 63 N.C. App. 569, 306 S.E.2d 162 (1983).

This section will not be extended beyond its express terms. Henry Angelo & Sons v. Property Dev. Corp., 63 N.C. App. 569, 306 S.E.2d 162 (1983).

§ 58-28-20. Cease and desist orders.

(a) Whenever the Commissioner, from evidence satisfactory to him, has reasonable grounds to believe that any person is violating or is about to violate G.S. 58-28-5, he may, after notice and opportunity for hearing, reduce his findings to writing and issue and cause to be served upon such person an order to cease and desist from violating G.S. 58-28-5.

(b) Until the expiration of the time allowed under G.S. 58-28-25(a) for filing a petition for review, if no such petition has been duly filed within such time; or if a petition for review has been filed within such time, then until the transcript of the record in the proceeding has been filed in the Court, the Commissioner may at any time, upon such notice and in such manner as he considers proper, modify or set aside in whole or in part any order issued by him under this section.

(c) After the expiration of the time allowed for filing a petition for review, if no such petition has been duly filed within such time, the Commissioner may at any time, after notice and opportunity for hearing, reopen and alter, modify, or set aside, in whole or in part, any order issued by him under this section, whenever in his opinion conditions of fact or of law have so changed as to require such action or if the public interest requires.

(d) Whenever the Commissioner has evidence that any person has or is violating G.S. 58-28-5, or has or is violating any order or requirement of the Commissioner issued or promulgated by the Commissioner under this Article, and that the interests of policyholders, creditors, or the public may be irreparably harmed by delay, the Commissioner may issue a cease and desist order. Notice of the cease and desist order and notice of hearing shall be delivered by first-class mail. (1967, c. 909, s. 1; 1987, c. 864, s. 61; 1989, c. 485, s. 14; 1999-294, s. 6.)

§ 58-28-25. Judicial review of cease and desist orders.

(a) Any person required by an order of the Commissioner under G.S. 58-28-20 to cease and desist may obtain a review of such order by filing in the Superior Court of Wake County, within 30 days from the date of the service of such order, a written petition praying that the order of the Commissioner be set aside. A copy of such petition shall be immediately served upon the Commissioner, and the Commissioner shall then immediately certify and file in the court a transcript of the entire record in the proceeding, including all the evidence taken, and the order of the Commissioner. Upon such filing of the petition and transcript the court has jurisdiction of the proceeding and of the question determined therein, shall determine whether the filing of such petition shall operate as a stay of such order of the Commissioner, and has the power to make and enter upon the pleadings, evidence, and proceedings set forth in such transcript a decree modifying, affirming, or reversing the order of the Commissioner, in whole or in part. The findings of the Commissioner as to the facts, if supported by substantial evidence, shall be conclusive.

(b) To the extent that the order of the Commissioner is affirmed, the court shall thereupon issue its own order commanding obedience to the terms of such order of the Commissioner. If either party applies to the court for leave to adduce additional evidence, and satisfies the court that such additional evidence is material and that there were reasonable grounds for the failure to adduce such evidence in the proceeding before the Commissioner, the court may order such additional evidence to be taken before the Commissioner and to be adduced upon the hearing in such manner and upon such terms and conditions as the court considers proper. The Commissioner may modify his findings of fact, or make new findings by reason of the additional evidence so taken; and he shall file such modified or new findings which, if supported by substantial evidence, shall be conclusive; or shall file his recommendations, if any, for the modification or setting aside of his original order, with the return of such additional evidence.

(c) A cease and desist order issued by the Commissioner under G.S. 58-28-20 shall become final:

(1) Upon the expiration of the time allowed for filing a petition for review if no such petition has been duly filed within such time; except that the Commissioner may thereafter modify or set aside his order to the extent provided in G.S. 58-28-20(b); or

(2) Upon the final decision of the court if the court directs that the order of the Commissioner be affirmed or the petition for review dismissed.

(d) No order of the Commissioner under this Article or order of a court to enforce the same shall in any way relieve or absolve any person affected by such order from any liability under any other laws of this State. (1989, c. 485, s. 15.)

§ 58-28-30. Penalty.

Any person who willfully violates a cease and desist order of the Commissioner under G.S. 58-28-20, after it has become final, and while such order is in effect, is subject to the provisions of G.S. 58-2-70. (1989, c. 485, s. 15.)

§ 58-28-35. Provisions of Article additional to existing law; application.

The powers vested in the Commissioner by this Article are additional to any other powers to enforce any penalties, fines, or forfeitures authorized by law with respect to transacting the business of insurance without authority. This Article applies to all kinds of insurance, including service corporations that would be subject to Article 65 of this Chapter, HMOs that would be subject to Article 67 of this Chapter, MEWAs that would be subject to Article 49 of this Chapter, and self-insured workers compensation operations that would be subject to Article 47 of this Chapter or Article 4 of Chapter 97 of the General Statutes. (1989, c. 485, s. 15; 1999-244, s. 9.)

§ 58-28-40. Service of process on Secretary of State as agent for unauthorized company.

(a) Any act of entering into a contract of insurance as an insurer or transacting insurance business in this State, as set forth in G.S. 58-28-10 by an unauthorized, foreign or alien company, shall be equivalent to and shall constitute an appointment by such company of the Secretary of State to be its true and lawful attorney upon whom may be served all lawful process in any action or proceeding against it arising out of a violation of G.S. 58-28-5, and any of said acts shall be a signification of its agreement that any such process against it, which is so served, shall be of the same legal force and validity as if in fact served upon the company.

(b) Service of process on the Secretary of State shall be made by the sheriff delivering to and leaving with the Secretary of State duplicate copies of such process, notice or demand. Service shall be deemed complete when the Secretary of State is so served. The Secretary of State shall endorse upon both copies the time of receipt and shall forthwith send one of such copies by registered mail, with return receipt requested, to such insurer at its last known principal place of business as shown on the process, notice or demand served on the Secretary of State. The Commissioner and the Attorney General shall see that such address is included on the process, notice or demand which is served upon the Secretary of State. A copy of the complaint or order of the clerk extending the time for filing the complaint must be mailed to the insurer with the copy of the summons. When a copy of the complaint is not mailed with the summons, the Secretary of State shall mail a copy of the complaint when it is served on him in the same manner as the copy of summons is required to be mailed.

(c) Upon the return to the Secretary of State of the requested return receipt showing delivery and acceptance of such registered mail, or upon the return of such registered mail showing refusal thereof by such unauthorized insurer, the Secretary of State shall note thereon the date of such return to him and shall attach either the return receipt or such refused mail including the envelope, as the case may be, to the copy of the process, notice or demand theretofore retained by him and shall mail the same to the clerk of the court in which such action or proceeding is pending and in respect of which such process, notice or demand was issued. Such mailing, in addition to the return by the sheriff, shall constitute the due return required by law. The clerk of the court shall thereupon file the same as a paper in such action or proceeding.

(d) Service made under this section shall have the same legal force and validity as if the service had been made personally in this State. The refusal of any such unauthorized insurer to accept delivery of the registered mail provided for in subsection (b) of this section or the refusal to sign the return receipt shall not affect the validity of such service; and any foreign or alien insurer refusing to accept delivery of such registered mail shall be charged with knowledge of the contents of any process, notice or demand contained therein.

(e) Whenever service of process is made upon the Secretary of State as herein provided the defendant unauthorized insurer shall have 30 days from the date when the defendant receives or refuses to accept the registered mail containing the copy of the complaint sent as in this section provided in which to appear and answer the complaint in the action or proceeding so instituted. Entries on the defendant's return receipt or the refused registered mail shall be sufficient evidence of such date. If the date of acceptance or refusal to accept the registered mail cannot be determined from the entries on the return receipt or from notations of the postal authorities on the envelope, then the date when the defendant accepted or refused to accept the registered mail shall be deemed to be the date that the return receipt or the registered mail was received back by the Secretary of State.

(f) The court in any action or proceeding in which service is made in the manner provided in the above paragraph may, in its discretion, order such postponement as may be necessary to afford such company reasonable opportunity to defend such action or proceeding.

(g) The Secretary of State shall keep a summarized record of all processes, notices and demands served upon him under this section, and shall record therein the time of such service and his action with reference thereto.

(h) Nothing herein contained shall limit or affect the right to serve any process, notice or demand to be served upon an insurer in any other manner now or hereafter permitted by law.

(i) No judgment by default shall be entered in any such action or proceeding until the expiration of 30 days from the date of the filing of the affidavit of compliance. (1967, c. 909, s. 1; 1987, c. 864, ss. 62-64; 1991, c. 720, s. 4.)

§ 58-28-45. Uniform Unauthorized Insurers Act.

(a) No person, corporation, association or partnership shall in this State act as agent for any insurer not authorized to transact business in this State, or negotiate for or place or aid in placing insurance coverage in this State for another with any such insurer.

(b) No person, corporation, association or partnership shall in this State aid any unauthorized insurer in effecting insurance or in transacting insurance business in this State, either by fixing rates, by adjusting or investigating losses, by inspecting or examining risks, by acting as attorney-in-fact or as attorney for service for process, or otherwise, except as provided in subsection (e) hereof.

(c) No person, corporation, association or partnership shall make, negotiate for or place, or aid in negotiating or placing any insurance contract in this State for another who is an applicant for insurance covering any property or risk in another state, territory or district of the United States with any insurer not authorized to transact insurance business in the state, territory or district wherein such property or risk or any part thereof is located.

(d) The provisions of the three foregoing subsections do not apply to contracts of reinsurance, or to contracts of insurance made through surplus lines licensees as provided in Article 21 of this Chapter, nor do they apply to any insurer not authorized in this State, or its representatives, in investigating, adjusting losses or otherwise complying in this State with the terms of its insurance contracts made in a state wherein the insurer was authorized; provided, the property or risk insured under such contracts at the time such contract was issued was located in such other state. A motor vehicle used and kept garaged principally in another state shall be deemed to be located in such state.

(e)(1) Repealed by Session Laws 1985, c. 666, s. 40.

(2) Such service of process shall be made by delivering and leaving with the Commissioner or to some person in apparent charge of his office two copies thereof and the payment to him of such fees as may be prescribed by law. The Commissioner shall forthwith mail by registered mail one of the copies of such process to the defendant at its last known principal place of business, and shall keep a record of all such process so served upon him. Such service of process is sufficient provided notice of such service and a copy of the process are sent within 10 days thereafter by registered mail by plaintiff's attorney to the defendant at its last known principal place of business, and the defendant's receipt, or receipt issued by the post office with which the letter is registered, showing the name of the sender of the letter and the name and address of the person to whom the letter is addressed, and the affidavit of plaintiff's attorney showing a compliance herewith are filed with the clerk of the court in which such action is pending on or before the date the defendant is required to appear, or within such further time as the court may allow. However, no plaintiff or complainant shall be entitled to a judgment by default under this subdivision (2) until the expiration of 30 days from the date of the filing of the affidavit of compliance.

(3) Service of process in any such action, suit or proceeding shall be in addition to the manner provided in the preceding subdivision (2) be valid if served upon any person within this State who, in this State on behalf of such insurer, is

a. Soliciting insurance, or

b. Making any contract of insurance or issuing or delivering any policies or written contracts of insurance, or

c. Collecting or receiving any premium for insurance; and a copy of such process is sent within 10 days thereafter by registered mail by plaintiff's attorney to the defendant at the last known principal place of business of the defendant, and the defendant's receipt, or the receipt issued by the post office with which the letter is registered, showing the name of the sender of the letter and the name and address of the person to whom the letter is addressed, and the affidavit of plaintiff's attorney showing a compliance herewith are filed with the clerk of the court in which such action is pending on or before the date the defendant is required to appear, or within such further time as the court may allow.

    d. Nothing in this subsection (e) shall limit or abridge the right to serve process, notice or demand upon any insurer in any other manner now or hereafter permitted by law.

(f) No unauthorized insurer shall institute or file, or cause to be instituted or filed, any suit, action or proceeding in this State to enforce any right, claim or demand arising out of the transaction of business in this State until such insurer shall have obtained a license to transact insurance business in this State. Nothing in this subsection shall be construed to require an unauthorized insurance company to obtain a license before instituting or filing, or causing to be instituted or filed, any suit, action or proceeding either in connection with any of its investments in this State or in connection with any contract issued by it at a time when it was authorized to do business in the state where such contract was issued.

(g)(1) Before any unauthorized insurer shall file or cause to be filed any pleading in any action, suit or proceeding instituted against it, such unauthorized insurer shall either

    a. File with the clerk of the court in which such action, suit or proceeding is pending a bond with good and sufficient sureties, to be approved by the court, in an amount to be fixed by the court sufficient to secure the payment of any final judgment which may be rendered in such action or

    b. Procure a license to transact the business of insurance in this State.

(2) The court in any action, suit or proceeding in which service is made in the manner prescribed in subdivisions (2) and (3) of subsection (e) may order such postponement as may be necessary to afford the defendant reasonable opportunity to comply with the provisions of subdivision (1) of this subsection (g) and to defend such action.

(3) Nothing in subdivision (1) of this subsection (g) shall be construed to prevent an unauthorized insurer from filing a motion to quash a writ or to set aside service thereof made in the manner provided in subdivisions (2) and (3) of subsection (e) on the ground either

    a. That no policy or contract of insurance has been issued or delivered to a citizen or resident of this State or to a corporation authorized to do business therein, or

    b. That such insurer has not been transacting business in this State, or

    c. That the person on whom service was made pursuant to subdivision (3) of subsection (e) was not doing any of the acts enumerated therein.

(h) Any person, corporation, association or partnership violating any of the provisions of this section shall be guilty of a Class 3 misdemeanor and shall only be fined not less than one thousand dollars ($1,000) nor more than five thousand dollars ($5,000).

(i) This section shall be so interpreted and construed as to effectuate its general purpose to make uniform the law of those states which enact it.

(j) This section may be cited as the Uniform Unauthorized Insurers Act. (1899, c. 54, s. 105; Rev., s. 4763; C.S., s. 6424; 1945, c. 386; 1985, c. 666, ss. 20,

40; 1987, c. 864, s. 17; 1993, c. 539, s. 454; 1994, Ex. Sess., c. 24, s. 14(c); 1999-132, s. 9.1.)

CASE NOTES

Subdivision (e)(1) of this section is no longer in effect and has been superseded by G.S. 58-16-35. Safeway Trails, Inc. v. Stuyvesant Ins. Co., 211 F. Supp. 227 (M.D.N.C. 1962), aff'd, 316 F.2d 234 (4th Cir. 1963).

This section applies only to fire insurance. Safeway Trails, Inc. v. Stuyvesant Ins. Co., 211 F. Supp. 227 (M.D.N.C. 1962), aff'd, 316 F.2d 234 (4th Cir. 1963).

This section does not make the policy void in the hands of the assured, and the company issuing a policy in violation of this section may not receive the premiums and rely upon the statute to invalidate the policy, for this would permit it to take advantage of its own wrong. T.T. Hay & Bro. v. Union Fire Ins. Co., 167 N.C. 82, 83 S.E. 241 (1914).

Applied in Suits v. Old Equity Life Ins. Co., 241 N.C. 483, 85 S.E.2d 602 (1955).

ARTICLE 29.

Unauthorized Insurers False Advertising Process Act.

§ 58-29-1. Purpose; construction.

(a) The purpose of this Article is to subject to the jurisdiction of the Commissioner and to the jurisdiction of the courts of this State, insurers not authorized to transact business in this State which place in or send into this State any false advertising designed to induce residents of this State to purchase insurance from insurers not authorized to transact business in this State. The General Assembly declares it is in the interest of the citizens of this State who purchase insurance from insurers which solicit insurance business in this State in the manner set forth in the preceding sentence that such insurers be subject to the provisions of this Article. In furtherance of such interest, the General Assembly in this Article provides a method of substituted service of process upon such insurers and declares in so doing, it exercises its power to protect its residents and also exercises powers and privileges available to the State by virtue of Public Law 15, 79th Congress of the United States, Chapter 20, 1st Session, section 340, which declares that the business of insurance and every person engaged therein shall be subject to the laws of the several states; the authority provided herein to be in addition to any existing powers of this State.

(b) The provisions of this Article shall be liberally construed. (1965, c. 910; 1991, c. 720, s. 4.)

§ 58-29-5. Definitions.

As used in this Article:
    (1) "Residents" shall mean and include person, partnership or corporation, domestic, alien or foreign.
    (2) "Unfair Trade Practice Act" shall mean Article 63 of this Chapter. (1965, c. 910.)

§ 58-29-10. Unlawful advertising; notice to unauthorized insurer and domiciliary insurance supervisory official.

No unauthorized foreign or alien insurer shall make, issue, circulate or cause to be made, issued or circulated, to residents of this State any estimate, illustration, circular, pamphlet, or letter, or cause to be made in any newspaper, magazine or other publication or over any radio or television station, any announcement or statement to such residents misrepresenting its financial condition or the terms of any contracts issued or to be issued or the benefits or advantages promised thereby, or the dividends or share of the surplus to be received thereon in violation of the Unfair Trade Practice Act, and whenever the Commissioner shall have reason to believe that any such insurer is engaging in such unlawful advertising, it shall be his duty to give notice of such fact by registered mail to such insurer and to the insurance supervisory official of the domiciliary state of such insurer. For the purpose of this section, the domiciliary state of an alien insurer shall be deemed to be the state of entry or the state of the principal office in the United States. (1965, c. 910.)

§ 58-29-15. Action by Commissioner under Unfair Trade Practice Act.

If after 30 days following the giving of the notice mentioned in G.S. 58-29-10 such insurer has failed to cease making, issuing, or circulating such false misrepresentations or causing the same to be made, issued or circulated in this State, and if the Commissioner has reason to believe that a proceeding by him in respect to such matters would be to the interest of the public, and that such insurer is issuing or delivering contracts of insurance to residents of this State or collecting premiums on such contracts or doing any of the acts enumerated in G.S. 58-29-20, he shall take action against such insurer under the Unfair Trade Practice Act. (1965, c. 910.)

§ 58-29-20. Acts appointing Commissioner as attorney for service of statement of charges, notices and process; manner of service; limitation on entry of order or judgment.

(a) Any of the following acts in this State, effected by mail or otherwise, by any such unauthorized foreign or alien insurer:
  (1) The issuance or delivery of contracts of insurance to residents of this State,
  (2) The solicitation of applications for such contracts,
  (3) The collection of premiums, membership fees, assessments or other considerations for such contracts, or
  (4) Any other transaction of insurance business,
Is equivalent to and shall constitute an appointment by such insurer of the Commissioner and his successor or successors in office, to be its true and lawful attorney, upon whom may be served all statements of charges, notices and lawful process in any proceeding instituted in respect to the misrepresentations set forth in G.S. 58-29-10 under the provisions of the Unfair Trade Practice Act, or in any action, suit or proceeding for the recovery of any penalty therein provided, and any such act shall be signification of its agreement that such service of statement of charges, notices or process is of the same legal force and validity as personal service of such statement of charges, notices or process in this State, upon such insurer.
(b) Service of a statement of charges and notices under said Unfair Trade Practice Act shall be made by any deputy or employee of the Department delivering to and leaving with the Commissioner or some person in apparent charge of his office, two copies thereof. Service of process issued by any court in any action, suit or proceeding to collect any penalty under said act provided, shall be made by delivering and leaving with the Commissioner, or some

person in apparent charge of his office, two copies thereof. The Commissioner shall forthwith cause to be mailed by registered mail one of the copies of such statement of charges, notices or process to the defendant at its last known principal place of business, and shall keep a record of all statements, charges, notices and process so served. Such service of statement of charges, notices or process shall be sufficient provided they shall have been so mailed and the defendant's receipt or receipt issued by the post office with which the letter is registered, showing the name of the sender of the letter and the name and address of the person to whom the letter is addressed, and the affidavit of the person mailing such letter showing a compliance herewith are filed with the Commissioner in the case of any statement of charges or notices, or with the clerk of the court in which such action is pending in the case of any process, on or before the date the defendant is required to appear or within such further time as may be allowed.

(c) Service of statement of charges, notices and process in any such proceeding, action or suit shall in addition to the manner provided in subsection (b) of this section be valid if served upon any person within this State who on behalf of such insurer is

(1) Soliciting insurance, or

(2) Making, issuing or delivering any contract of insurance, or

(3) Collecting or receiving in this State any premium for insurance;

And a copy of such statement of charges, notices or process is sent within 10 days thereafter by registered mail by or on behalf of the Commissioner to the defendant at the last known principal place of business of the defendant, and the defendant's receipt, or the receipt issued by the post office with which the letter is registered, showing the name of the sender of the letter, the name and address of the person to whom the letter is addressed, and the affidavit of the person mailing the same showing a compliance herewith, are filed with the Commissioner in the case of any statement of charges or notices, or with the clerk of the court in which such action is pending in the case of any process, on or before the date the defendant is required to appear or within such further time as the court may allow.

(d) No cease or desist order or default judgment under this section shall be entered until the expiration of 30 days from the date of the filing of the affidavit of compliance.

(e) Service of process and notice under the provisions of this Article shall be in addition to all other methods of service provided by law, and nothing in this Article shall limit or prohibit the right to serve any statement of charges, notices or process upon any insurer in any other manner now or hereafter permitted by law. (1965, c. 910; 1991, c. 720, ss. 4, 5, 57.)

§ 58-29-25. Short title.

This Article may be cited as the Unauthorized Insurers False Advertising Process Act. (1965, c. 910.)

ARTICLE 30.

Insurers Supervision, Rehabilitation, and Liquidation.

§ 58-30-1. Construction and purpose.

(a) This Article does not limit powers granted to the Commissioner by any other provision of law. To the extent practicable, the Commissioner may supplement the provisions of this Article with those of Part 2 of Article 38 of Chapter 1 of the General Statutes.

(b) This Article shall be liberally construed to effect the purpose stated in subsection (c) of this section.

(c) The purpose of this Article is to protect the interests of policyholders, claimants, creditors, and the public generally with minimum interference with the normal prerogatives of the owners and managers of insurers, through:

    (1) Early detection of any potentially dangerous condition in an insurer, and prompt application of appropriate corrective measures;

    (2) Improved methods for rehabilitating insurers, involving the cooperation and management expertise of the insurance industry;

    (3) Enhanced efficiency and economy of liquidation, through clarification of the law, to minimize legal uncertainty and litigation;

    (4) Equitable apportionment of any unavoidable loss;

    (5) Lessening the problems of interstate rehabilitation and liquidation by facilitating cooperation between states in the liquidation process, and by extending the scope of personal jurisdiction over debtors of the insurer outside this State; and

    (6) Regulation of the insurance business by the impact of the law relating to delinquency procedures and substantive rules on the entire insurance business. (1989, c. 452, s. 1.)

CASE NOTES

Federal abstention under Burford v. Sun Oil Co., 319 U.S. 315, 63 S. Ct. 1098, 87 L. Ed. 1424 (1943), was inappropriate where the case raised no questions of uniquely federal jurisdiction; although North Carolina's liquidation laws attempt to minimize legal uncertainty and litigation and to promote efficiency and economy of liquidation, as federal court decisionmaking of the kind that exists along-side state insurance liquidation proceedings do not significantly disrupt state regulatory frameworks. American Sec. Life Assurance Co. v. Mason, 836 F. Supp. 333 (E.D.N.C. 1993).

Cited in State ex rel. Long v. Interstate Cas. Ins. Co., 106 N.C. App. 470, 417 S.E.2d 296 (1992); State ex rel. Long v. ILA Corp., 132 N.C. App. 587, 513 S.E.2d 812 (1999).

§ 58-30-5. Persons covered.

The proceedings authorized by this Article may be applied to:

    (1) All insurers that are doing, or have done, an insurance business in this State, and against whom claims arising from that business may exist now or in the future.

    (2) All insurers that purport to do an insurance business in this State.

    (3) All insurers that have insureds resident in this State.

    (4) All persons organized or in the process of organizing with the intent to do an insurance business in this State.

    (5) All persons subject to Articles 64, 65 and 66, or 67 of this Chapter; except to the extent there is a conflict between the provisions of this Article and the provisions of those Articles, in which case those Articles will govern.

    (6) Self-insured group workers' compensation funds subject to Article 47 of this Chapter. (1989, c. 452, s. 1; 1995, c. 471, s. 3; 1995 (Reg. Sess., 1996), c. 582, s. 1; 1999-132, s. 7.2.)

§ 58-30-10. Definitions.

As used in this Article, unless the context clearly indicates otherwise:

    (1) "Alien country" means any other jurisdiction not in any state.

    (2) "Ancillary state" means any state other than a domiciliary state.

    (3) "Court" means the Superior Court of Wake County.

(4) "Creditor" means a person having any claim, whether matured or unmatured, liquidated or unliquidated, secured or unsecured, absolute, fixed, or contingent.

(5) "Delinquency proceeding" means any proceeding instituted against an insurer for the purpose of supervising, rehabilitating, conserving, or liquidating such insurer.

(6) "Doing business" includes any of the following acts by insurers, whether effected by mail or otherwise:

    a. The issuance or delivery of contracts of insurance to persons resident in this State;

    b. The solicitation of applications for such contracts, or other negotiations preliminary to the execution of such contracts;

    c. The collection of premiums, membership fees, assessments, or other consideration for such contracts;

    d. The transaction of matters subsequent to execution of such contracts and arising out of them;

    e. Operating as an insurer under a license issued by the Department; or

    f. The purchase of contracts of insurance issued to persons in this State by an assumption agreement.

(7) "Domestic guaranty association" means the Postassessment Insurance Guaranty Association in Article 48 of this Chapter, as amended; the North Carolina Self-Insurance Guaranty Association in Article 4 of Chapter 97 of the General Statutes; the Life and Accident and Health Insurance Guaranty Association in Article 62 of this Chapter, as amended; or any other similar entity hereafter created by the General Assembly for the payment of claims of insolvent insurers.

(8) "Domiciliary state" means the state in which an insurer is incorporated or organized; or, in the case of an alien insurer, its state of entry.

(9) "Fair consideration" is given for property or obligation when:

    a. In exchange for such property or obligation, as a fair equivalent therefor, and in good faith, property is conveyed or services are rendered or an obligation is incurred or an antecedent debt is satisfied; or

    b. Such property or obligation is received in good faith to secure a present advance or antecedent debt in amount not disproportionately small as compared to the value of the property or obligation obtained.

(10) "Foreign guaranty association" means a guaranty association now in existence in or hereafter created by the legislature of any other state.

(11) "Formal delinquency proceeding" means any liquidation or rehabilitation proceeding.

(12) "General assets" means all real, personal, or other property that is not specifically mortgaged, pledged, hypothecated, deposited, or otherwise encumbered for the security or benefit of specified persons or classes of persons. As to specifically encumbered property, "general assets" includes all such property or its proceeds in excess of the amount necessary to discharge the sum or sums secured thereby. Assets that are held in trust and on deposit for the security or benefit of all policyholders in more than one state or all policyholders and creditors in more than one state shall be treated as "general assets". No person shall have a claim against general assets unless that claim is in an amount in excess of fifty dollars ($50.00).

(13) "Insolvency" or "insolvent" means that an insurer is unable to pay its obligations when they are due, or that its admitted assets do not exceed its liabilities plus the greater of (i) any capital and surplus

required by law for its organization; or (ii) the total par or stated value of its authorized and issued capital stock. For the purposes of this subdivision, "liabilities" includes reserves required by statute, by Department rules, or by specific requirements imposed by the Commissioner upon a subject company at the time of admission or subsequent thereto, except those reserves that are an allocation of surplus as specified in G.S. 58-65-95.

(14) "Insurer" means any entity that is or should be licensed under Articles 7, 16, 26, 47, 49, 65, or 67 of this Chapter or under Article 5 of Chapter 97 of the General Statutes. For the purposes of this Article, "insurer" also includes continuing care retirement communities that are or should be licensed under Article 64 of this Chapter.

(15) "Preferred claim" means any claim with respect to which the provisions of this Article accord priority of payment from the general assets of the insurer.

(16) "Receiver" includes a liquidator, rehabilitator, or conservator, as the context requires.

(17) "Reciprocal state" means any state other than this State in which in substance and effect the provisions of G.S. 58-30-105(a), 58-30-270, 58-30-275, and 58-30-285 through 58-30-295 are in force, and in which provisions are in force requiring that the insurance regulator of that state be the receiver of a delinquent insurer; and in which provisions exist for the avoidance of fraudulent conveyances and preferential transfers.

(18) "Secured claim" means any claim secured by mortgage, trust deed, pledge, deposit as security, escrow, or otherwise; and includes any claim that has become a lien upon specific assets by reason of judicial process. "Secured claim" does not include a special deposit claim or a claim against general assets.

(19) "Special deposit claim" means any claim in excess of fifty dollars ($50.00) secured by a deposit made pursuant to statute for the security or benefit of a limited class or classes of persons, but does not include any claim secured by general assets.

(20) "Transfer" includes the sale and every other and different mode, whether direct or indirect, of disposing of or of parting with property, an interest therein, or the possession thereof; or of voluntarily fixing a lien upon property or an interest therein, whether absolutely or conditionally, by or without judicial proceedings. The retention of a security title to property delivered to a debtor is a transfer suffered by the debtor. (1989, c. 452, s. 1; 1995, c. 471, ss. 4, 5; 1995 (Reg. Sess., 1996), c. 582, s. 2; c. 742, s. 24; 1999-132, ss. 2.1, 7.3, 9.1; 1999-294, s. 11(a), (b); 2000-140, s. 13; 2001-223, ss. 24.2, 24.3; 2001-487, s. 103(a).)

Effect of Amendments. — Session Laws 2001-223, ss. 24.2 and 24.3, effective June 15, 2001, as amended by 2001-487, s. 103(a), and applicable to estates that are pending, added the last sentence of subdivision (12), and inserted "in excess of fifty dollars ($50.00)" in subdivision (19).

CASE NOTES

Cited in State ex rel. Long v. American Sec. Life Assurance Co., 109 N.C. App. 530, 428 S.E.2d 200 (1993).

§ 58-30-12. Duty to report insurer impairment; violations; penalties.

(a) As used in this section:

    (1) "Chief executive officer", as used in subsection (b) of this section, means the person, irrespective of title, designated by the board of directors or trustees of an insurer as the person charged with administering and implementing an insurer's policies and procedures.

    (2) "Impaired", as used in subsections (b) and (c) of this section, means a financial condition in which the assets of an insurer are less than the sum of the insurer's minimum required capital, minimum required surplus, and all liabilities as determined in accordance with the requirements for the preparation and filing of a financial statement under G.S. 58-2-165 and under other provisions of this Chapter.

    (3) "Insolvent", as used in subsection (c) of this section, has the same meaning as set forth in G.S. 58-30-10(13).

(b) Whenever an insurer is impaired, its chief executive officer shall, as soon as is reasonably possible, notify the Commissioner in writing of the impairment and shall at the same time notify in writing all of the members of the board of directors or trustees of the insurer, if the chief executive officer knows or has reason to know of the impairment. An officer, director, or trustee of an insurer shall notify the chief executive officer of the impairment of the insurer if the officer, director, or trustee knows or has reason to know that the insurer is impaired. Any person who knowingly violates this subsection shall, upon conviction, be guilty of a Class 1 misdemeanor.

(c) Any person who willfully:

    (1) Conceals any property belonging to an insurer; or

    (2) Transfers or conceals in contemplation of a delinquency proceeding the person's own property or property belonging to an insurer; or

    (3) Conceals, destroys, mutilates, alters, or makes a false entry in any document that affects or relates to the property of an insurer or withholds any such document from a receiver, trustee, or other officer of a court entitled to its possession; or

    (4) Gives, obtains, or receives a thing of value for acting or forbearing to act in any court proceedings;

and any such act results in or contributes to an insurer becoming impaired or insolvent; shall be guilty of a Class H felony. (1991, c. 681, s. 40; 1993, c. 539, s. 455; 1994, Ex. Sess., c. 24, s. 14(c).)

§ 58-30-15. Jurisdiction and venue.

(a) No delinquency proceeding shall be commenced by anyone other than the Commissioner and no other court has jurisdiction to entertain, hear, or determine any proceeding commenced by any other person.

(b) Except as provided in this Article, no court of this State has jurisdiction to entertain, hear, or determine any complaint praying for the dissolution, liquidation, rehabilitation, sequestration, conservation, or receivership of any insurer; or praying for an injunction or restraining order or other relief preliminary to, incidental to, or relating to such proceedings.

(c) In addition to other grounds for jurisdiction provided by the laws of this State, the Court has jurisdiction over a person served pursuant to Chapter 1A of the General Statutes or other applicable provisions of law in an action brought by the receiver of a domestic insurer or an alien insurer domiciled in this State:

    (1) If the person served is obligated to the insurer in any way as an incident to any agency or brokerage arrangement that may exist or

has existed between the insurer and the agent or broker, in any action on or incident to the obligation; or

(2) If the person served is a reinsurer who has at any time entered into a contract of reinsurance with an insurer against which a rehabilitation or liquidation order is in effect when the action is commenced, or is an agent or broker of or for the reinsurer, in any action on or incident to the reinsurance contract; or

(3) If the person served is or has been an officer, manager, trustee, organizer, promoter, or person in a position of comparable authority or influence, in an insurer against which a rehabilitation or liquidation order is in effect when the action is commenced, in any action resulting from such a relationship with the insurer; or

(4) If the person served is or was, when the delinquency proceeding was begun against the insurer, holding assets in which the receiver claims an interest on behalf of the insurer, in any action concerning the assets; or

(5) If the person served is obligated to the insurer in any way whatsoever, in any action on or incident to the obligation.

(d) All actions authorized in this Article shall be brought in the Superior Court of Wake County.

(e) The provisions of Chapter 150B of the General Statutes do not apply to this Article. (1989, c. 452, s. 1; 1991, c. 681, s. 41.)

CASE NOTES

Federal abstention under Burford v. Sun Oil Co., 319 U.S. 315, 63 S. Ct. 1098, 87 L. Ed. 1424 (1943), was inappropriate where the case raised no questions of uniquely federal jurisdiction; although North Carolina's liquidation laws attempt to minimize legal uncertainty and litigation and to promote efficiency and economy of liquidation, as federal court decisionmaking of the kind that exists alongside state insurance liquidation proceedings do not significantly disrupt state regulatory frameworks. American Sec. Life Assurance Co. v. Mason, 836 F. Supp. 333 (E.D.N.C. 1993).

§ 58-30-20. Injunctions and orders.

(a) Any receiver appointed in a proceeding under this Article may at any time apply for, and any court of general jurisdiction may grant, such restraining orders, preliminary and permanent injunctions, and other orders as may be deemed to be necessary and proper to prevent:

(1) The transaction of further business;

(2) The transfer of property;

(3) Interference with the receiver or with a proceeding under this Article;

(4) Waste of the insurer's assets;

(5) Dissipation and transfer of bank accounts;

(6) The institution or further prosecution of any actions or proceedings;

(7) The obtaining of preferences, judgments, attachments, garnishments, or liens against the insurer, its assets or its policyholders;

(8) The levying of execution against the insurer, its assets, or its policyholders;

(9) The making of any sale or deed for nonpayment of taxes or assessments that would lessen the value of the assets of the insurer;

(10) The withholding from the receiver of books, accounts, documents, or other records relating to the business of the insurer; or

(11) Any other threatened or contemplated action that might lessen the value of the insurer's assets or prejudice the rights of policyholders, creditors, or shareholders, or the administration of any proceeding under this Article.

(b) The receiver may apply to any court outside of this State for the relief described in subsection (a) of this section. (1989, c. 452, s. 1.)

The Commissioner as liquidator is entitled to seek an injunction when necessary to prevent the withholding of all documents and records related to the business of the insurer.

Eastern Appraisal Servs., Inc. v. State, 118 N.C. App. 692, 457 S.E.2d 312, appeal dismissed, cert. denied, 341 N.C. 648, 462 S.E.2d 509 (1995).

§ 58-30-22. Powers of Commissioner and receiver to examine or audit books or records.

(a) As used in this section, "person" includes an agent of the insurer; a broker, ceding or assuming reinsurer, or reinsurance intermediary that has done business with the insurer; or any affiliate of the insurer.

(b) In addition to other powers granted under this Chapter, the Commissioner in any supervision proceeding under this Article and a receiver in any delinquency proceeding under this Article has the power to examine or audit the books or records of any person insofar as those books or records relate to the business activities of the insurer that is under supervision or subject to a delinquency proceeding.

(c) Repealed by Session Laws 1995, c. 360, s. 2(a). (1991, c. 681, s. 42; 1995, c. 360, s. 2(a).)

§ 58-30-25. Cooperation of officers, owners and employees.

(a) Any officer, manager, director, trustee, owner, employee, or agent of any insurer, and any other person with authority over or in charge of any segment of the insurer's affairs, shall cooperate with the Commissioner in any proceeding under this Article or any investigation preliminary to the proceeding. As used in this section, "person" includes any person who exercises direct or indirect control over activities of an insurer through any holding company or other affiliate of the insurer. "Cooperate" includes replying promptly in writing to any inquiry from the Commissioner requesting such a reply and making available to the Commissioner any books, accounts, documents, or other records or information or property of or pertaining to the insurer and in his possession, custody, or control.

(b) No person shall obstruct or interfere with the Commissioner in the conduct of any delinquency proceeding or any investigation preliminary or incidental thereto.

(c) This section does not abridge otherwise existing legal rights, including the right to resist a petition for any delinquency proceeding or other order.

(d) Any person described in subsection (a) of this section who fails to cooperate with the Commissioner, or any person who obstructs or interferes with the Commissioner in the conduct of any delinquency proceeding or any investigation preliminary or incidental thereto, or any person who knowingly and willfully violates any order the Commissioner issued validly under this Article is subject to the civil penalty and restitution provisions of G.S. 58-2-70 and is subject further to the revocation or suspension of any licenses issued by the Commissioner. (1989, c. 452, s. 1.)

Cited in Eastern Appraisal Servs., Inc. v. State, 118 N.C. App. 692, 457 S.E.2d 312 (1995).

§ 58-30-30. Bonds.

In any proceeding under this Article, the Commissioner and his deputies shall be responsible on their official bonds for the faithful performance of their duties. (1989, c. 452, s. 1.)

§ 58-30-35. Executory contracts and unexpired leases.

(a) Except as provided in subsections (b), (c), and (d) of this section, the receiver, subject to the Court's approval, may assume or reject any executory contract or unexpired lease of the insurer.

(b)(1) If there has been a default in an executory contract or unexpired lease of the insurer, the receiver may not assume such contract or lease unless, at the time of assumption of such contract or lease, the receiver:

a. Cures, or provides adequate assurance that the receiver will promptly cure, such default;

b. Compensates, or provides adequate assurance that the receiver will promptly compensate, a party, other than the insurer to such contract or lease, for any actual pecuniary loss to such party resulting from such default; and

c. Provides adequate assurance of future performance under such contract or lease.

(2) Subdivision (1) of this subsection does not apply to a default that is a breach of a provision relating to;

a. The insolvency or financial condition of the insurer at any time before the closing of the case;

b. The commencement of a proceeding under this Article; or

c. The appointment of or taking possession by a receiver in a proceeding under this Article or a custodian before such commencement.

(3) Notwithstanding any other provision of this section, if there has been a default in an unexpired lease of the insurer, other than a default of a kind specified in subdivision (2) of this subsection, the receiver may not require a lessor to provide services or supplies incidental to such lease before assumption of such lease unless the lessor is compensated under the terms of such lease for any services and supplies provided under such lease before assumption of such lease.

(c) The receiver may not assume or assign an executory contract or unexpired lease of the insurer, whether or not such contract or lease prohibits or restricts assignment of rights or delegation of duties, if:

(1)a. Applicable law excuses a party, other than the insurer, to such contract or lease from accepting performance from or rendering performance to the receiver or an assignee of such contract or lease, whether or not such contract or lease prohibits or restricts assignment of rights or delegation of duties; and

b. Such party does not consent to such assumption or assignment; or

(2) Such contract is a contract to make a loan, or extend other debt financing or financial accommodations, to or for the benefit of the insurer, or to issue a security of the insurer.

(d)(1) In a proceeding under G.S. 58-30-105, if the receiver does not assume or reject an executory contract or unexpired lease of the insurer within 60 days after the order for liquidation, or within such additional time as the Court, for cause, within such 60-day period, fixes, then such contract or lease is deemed to be rejected.

(2) In a proceeding under G.S. 58-30-80 the receiver may assume or reject an executory contract or unexpired lease of the insurer at any time

before the order for a plan of rehabilitation, but the Court, on request of any party to such contract or lease, may order the receiver to determine within a specified period of time whether to assume or reject such contract or lease.

(e)(1) Notwithstanding a provision in an executory contract or unexpired lease, or in applicable law, an executory contract or unexpired lease of the insurer may not be terminated or modified, and any right or obligation under such contract or lease may not be terminated or modified, at any time after the commencement of the proceeding solely because of a provision in such contract or lease that is conditioned on:

    a. The insolvency or financial condition of the insurer at any time before the closing of the proceeding;

    b. The commencement of a proceeding under this Article; or

    c. The appointment of or taking possession by a receiver in a proceeding under this Article or a custodian before such commencement.

(2) Subdivision (1) of this subsection does not apply to an executory contract or unexpired lease of the insurer, whether or not such contract or lease prohibits or restricts assignment of rights or delegation of duties, if:

    a. Applicable law excused a party, other than the insurer, to such contract or lease from accepting performance from or rendering performance to the receiver or to an assignee of such contract or lease, whether or not such contract or lease prohibits or restricts assignment of rights or delegation of duties and such party does not consent to such assumption or assignment; or

    b. Such contract is a contract to make a loan, or extend other debt financing or financial accommodations, to or for the benefit of the insurer, or to issue a security of the insurer.

(f)(1) Except as provided in subsection (c) of this section, notwithstanding a provision in an executory contract or unexpired lease of the insurer, or in applicable law, that prohibits, restricts, or conditions the assignment of such contract or lease, the receiver may assign such contract or lease under subdivision (2) of this subsection.

(2) The receiver may assign an executory contract or unexpired lease of the insurer only if:

    a. The receiver assumes such contract or lease in accordance with the provisions of this section; and

    b. Adequate assurance of future performance by the assignee of such contract or lease is provided, whether or not there has been a default in such contract or lease.

(3) Notwithstanding a provision in an executory contract or unexpired lease of the insurer, or in applicable law that terminates or modifies, or permits a party other than the insurer to terminate or modify, such contract or lease or a right or obligation under such contract or lease on account of an assignment of such contract or lease, such contract, lease, right, or obligation may not be terminated or modified under such provision because of the assumption or assignment of such contract or lease by the receiver.

(g) Except as provided in subdivisions (h)(2) and (i)(2) of this section, the rejection of an executory contract or unexpired lease of the insurer constitutes a breach of such contract or lease:

(1) If such contract or lease has not been assumed under this section or under a plan of rehabilitation under G.S. 58-30-80, immediately before the date of the filing of the petition; or

(2) If such contract or lease has been assumed under this section or under a plan of rehabilitation under G.S. 58-30-80:

    a. If before such rejection the proceeding has not been converted to a proceeding under G.S. 58-30-105 at the time of such rejection; or

    b. If before such rejection the case has been converted to a proceeding under G.S. 58-30-105: (i) immediately before the date of such conversion, if such contract or lease was assumed before such conversion; or (ii) at the time of such rejection, if such contract or lease was assumed after such conversion.

(h)(1) If the receiver rejects an unexpired lease of real property of the insurer under which the insurer is the lessor, the lessee under such lease may treat the lease as terminated by such rejection, or, in the alternative, may remain in possession for the balance of the term of such lease and any renewal or extension of such term that is enforceable by such lessee under applicable provision of law outside of this Article.

(2) If such lessee remains in possession, such lessee may offset against the rent reserved under such lease for the balance of the term after the date of the rejection of such lease, and any such renewal or extension, any damages occurring after such date caused by the nonperformance of any obligation of the insurer after such date, but such lessee does not have any rights against the estate on account of any damages arising after such date from such rejection, other than such offset.

(i)(1) If the receiver rejects an executory contract of the insurer for the sale of real property under which the purchaser is in possession, such purchaser may treat such contract as terminated, or, in the alternative, may remain in possession of such real property.

(2) If such purchaser remains in possession:

    a. Such purchaser shall continue to make all payments due under such contract but may offset against such payments any damages occurring after the date of the rejection of such contract caused by the nonperformance of any obligation of the insurer after such date, but such purchaser does not have any rights against the estate on account of any damages arising after such date from such rejection, other than such offset; and

    b. The receiver shall deliver title to such purchaser in accordance with the provisions of such contract, but is relieved of all other obligations to perform under such contract.

(j) A purchaser that treats an executory contract as terminated under subsection (i) of this section, or a party whose executory contract to purchase real property from the insurer is rejected and under which such party is not in possession, has a lien on the interest of the insurer in such property for the recovery of any portion of the purchase price that such purchaser or party has paid.

(k) Assignment by the receiver to a person of a contract or lease assumed under this section relieves the receiver and the estate from any liability for any breach of such contract or lease occurring after such assignment. (1989, c. 452, s. 1.)

§ 58-30-40. Turnover of property by a custodian.

(a) As used in this section "custodian" means:

(1) A receiver or trustee of any of the property of the insurer, appointed in a case or proceeding not under this Article;

(2) An assignee under a general assignment for the benefit of the insurer's creditors; or

 (3) A trustee, receiver, or agent under applicable law, or under a contract, that is appointed or authorized to take charge of property of the insurer for the purpose of enforcing a lien against such property, or for the purpose of general administration of such property for the benefit of the insurer's creditors.

 (b) A custodian with knowledge of the commencement of a proceeding under this Article may not make any disbursement from, or take any action in the administration of property of the insurer, proceeds of such property, or property of the estate, in the possession, custody, or control of such custodian, except such action as is necessary to preserve such property.

 (c) A custodian shall:

  (1) Deliver to the receiver any property of the insurer transferred to such custodian, or proceeds of such property, that is in such custodian's possession, custody, or control on the date that such custodian acquires knowledge of the commencement of the proceeding; and

  (2) File an accounting of any property of the insurer, or proceeds of such property, that, at any time, came into the possession, custody, or control of such custodian.

 (d) The Court, after notice and a hearing, shall:

  (1) Protect all entities to which a custodian has become obligated with respect to such property;

  (2) Provide for the payment of reasonable compensation for services rendered and costs and expenses incurred by such custodian; and

  (3) Surcharge such custodian, other than an assignee for the benefit of the insurer's creditors that was appointed or took possession more than 120 days before the date of the filing of the petition, for any improper excessive disbursement, other than a disbursement that has been made in accordance with applicable law or approved, after notice and a hearing, by a court of competent jurisdiction before the commencment of the proceeding under this Article.

 (e) The Court may, after notice and a hearing, excuse compliance with subsection (a), (b), or (c) of this section, if the interests of policyholders, creditors, and any equity security holders would be better served by permitting a custodian to continue in possession, custody, or control of such property. (1989, c. 452, s. 1.)

§ 58-30-45. Utility service.

 (a) Except as provided in subsection (b) of this section, a utility may not alter, refuse, or discontinue service to, or discriminate against, the receiver or the insurer solely on the basis that a debt owed by the insurer to such utility for service rendered before an order of rehabilitation or liquidation was not paid when due.

 (b) Such utility may alter, refuse, or discontinue service if neither the receiver nor the insurer, within 20 days after the date of an order of rehabilitation or liquidation, furnishes adequate assurance of payment, in the form of a deposit or other security, for services after such date. On request of a party in interest and after notice and a hearing, the Court may order reasonable modification of the amount of the deposit or other security necessary to provide adequate assurance of payment. (1989, c. 452, s. 1.)

§ 58-30-50. Continuation of delinquency proceedings.

 Every proceeding that was commenced under the laws in effect before June 26, 1989, is deemed to have been commenced under this Article for the purpose of conducting the proceeding; except that in the discretion of the Commissioner the proceeding may be continued, in whole or in part, as it would have been continued had this Article not been enacted. (1989, c. 452, s. 1.)

§ 58-30-55. Condition on release from delinquency proceedings.

No insurer that is subject to any delinquency proceedings, whether formal or informal, administrative or judicial, shall:

    (1) Be released from such proceeding, unless such proceeding is converted into a judicial rehabilitation or liquidation proceeding;

    (2) Be permitted to solicit or accept new business or request or accept the restoration of any suspended or revoked license;

    (3) Be returned to the control of its shareholders or private management; or

    (4) Have any of its assets returned to the control of its shareholders or private management;

until all payments of or on account of the insurer's contractual obligations by all guaranty associations, along with all expenses thereof and interest on all such payments and expenses, have been repaid to the guaranty associations or a plan of repayment by the insurer shall have been approved by the guaranty associations. (1989, c. 452, s. 1; 1999-132, s. 9.1; 2000-140, s. 14.)

Effect of Amendments. — Session Laws 2000-140, s. 14, effective July 21, 2000, deleted "license or" preceding "license" at the end of subdivision (2).

§ 58-30-60. Commissioner's summary orders and supervision proceedings.

(a) Whenever the Commissioner has reasonable cause to believe, and determines after a hearing held under subsection (e) of this section, that any domestic insurer has committed or is engaged in, or is about to commit or engage in, any act, practice, or transaction that would subject it to delinquency proceedings under this Article, he may make and serve upon the insurer and any other persons involved, such orders as are reasonably necessary to correct, eliminate, or remedy such conduct, condition, or ground.

(b) The Commissioner may consider any or all of the following standards to determine whether the continued operation of any licensed insurer is hazardous to its policyholders, creditors, or the general public:

    (1) Adverse findings reported in financial condition and market conduct examination reports;

    (2) The NAIC Insurance Regulatory Information System and its related reports;

    (3) The ratios of commission expense, general insurance expense, policy benefits, and reserve increases as to annual premium and net investment income that could lead to an impairment of capital and surplus;

    (4) Whether an insurer's asset portfolio, when viewed in light of current economic conditions, is not of sufficient value, liquidity, or diversity to assure the insurer's ability to meet its outstanding obligations as they mature;

    (5) The ability of an assuming reinsurer to perform and whether the ceding insurer's reinsurance program provides sufficient protection for the insurer's remaining surplus, after taking into account the insurer's cash flow and the classes of business written as well as the financial condition of the assuming reinsurer;

    (6) Whether an insurer's operating loss in the last 12-month period or any shorter time, including net capital gain or loss, changes in

nonadmitted assets, and cash dividends paid to shareholders, is greater than fifty percent (50%) of the insurer's remaining policyholders' surplus in excess of the minimum required;

(7) Whether any affiliate, subsidiary, or reinsurer is insolvent, threatened with insolvency, or delinquent in payment of its monetary or any other obligation;

(8) Contingent liabilities, pledges, or guaranties that either individually or collectively involve a total amount that in the Commissioner's opinion may affect an insurer's solvency;

(9) Whether any controlling person of an insurer is delinquent in the transmitting to or payment of net premiums to the insurer;

(10) The age and collectibility of receivables;

(11) Whether the management of an insurer, including officers, directors, or any other person who directly or indirectly controls the operation of the insurer, fails to possess or demonstrate the competence, fitness, or reputation considered by the Commissioner to be necessary to serve the insurer in that position;

(12) Whether the management of an insurer has failed to respond to the Commissioner's inquiries about the condition of the insurer or has furnished false and misleading information in response to an inquiry by the Commissioner;

(13) Whether the management of an insurer has filed any false or misleading sworn financial statement, has released a false or misleading financial statement to a lending institution or to the general public, or has made a false or misleading entry or omitted an entry of material amount in the insurer's books;

(14) Whether the insurer has grown so rapidly and to such an extent that it lacks adequate financial and administrative capacity to meet its obligations in a timely manner; or

(15) Whether the insurer has experienced or will experience in the foreseeable future cash flow or liquidity problems.

To determine an insurer's financial condition under this Article, the Commissioner may: disregard any credit or amount receivable resulting from transactions with a reinsurer that is insolvent, impaired, or otherwise subject to a delinquency proceeding; make appropriate adjustments to asset values attributable to investments in or transactions with parents, subsidiaries, or affiliates of an insurer; refuse to recognize the stated value of accounts receivable if the insurer's ability to collect receivables is highly speculative in view of the age of the account or the financial condition of the debtor; or increase the insurer's liability in an amount equal to any contingent liability, pledge, or guarantee not otherwise included if there is a substantial risk that the insurer will be called upon to meet the obligation undertaken within the next 12-month period.

If upon examination or at any other time the Commissioner has reasonable cause to believe that any domestic insurer is in such condition as to render the continuance of its business hazardous to the public or to holders of its policies or certificates of insurance, or if the domestic insurer gives its consent, then the Commissioner shall upon the Commissioner's determination:

(1) Notify the insurer of that determination; and

(2) Furnish to the insurer a written list of the Commissioner's requirements to abate that determination.

The written list may include requirements that the insurer: reduce the total amount of present and potential liability for policy benefits by reinsurance; reduce, suspend, or limit the volume of insurance being accepted or renewed; reduce general insurance and commission expenses by specified methods; increase its capital and surplus; suspend or limit its declaration and payment of dividends to its stockholders or policyholders; file reports in a form acceptable to the Commissioner concerning the market value of its assets; limit or withdraw from certain investments or discontinue certain investment practices to the extent the Commissioner considers to be necessary; document the adequacy of premium rates in relation to the risks insured; or file, in addition to regular annual financial statements, interim financial reports on the form adopted by the NAIC or on such format prescribed by the Commissioner. Notwithstanding any other provision of law limiting the frequency or amount of premium rate adjustments, the Commissioner may include in the list of requirements any rate adjustments for any kinds of insurance written by the insurer that the Commissioner considers necessary to improve the financial condition of the insurer.

(c) If the Commissioner makes a determination to supervise an insurer subject to an order under subsections (a) or (b) of this section, he shall notify the insurer that it is under the supervision of the Commissioner. During the period of supervision, the Commissioner may appoint a supervisor to supervise such insurer. The order appointing a supervisor shall direct the supervisor to enforce orders issued under subsections (a) and (b) of this section and may also require that the insurer may not do any of the following things during the period of supervision, without the prior approval of the Commissioner or his supervisor:

    (1) Dispose of, convey, or encumber any of its assets or its business in force;

    (2) Withdraw from any of its bank accounts;

    (3) Lend any of its funds;

    (4) Invest any of its funds;

    (5) Transfer any of its property;

    (6) Incur any debt, obligation, or liability;

    (7) Merge or consolidate with another company; or

    (8) Enter into any new reinsurance contract or treaty.

(d) Any insurer subject to an order under this section shall comply with the lawful requirements of the Commissioner and, if placed under supervision, shall comply with the requirements of the Commissioner within such period of time established by the Commissioner. The Commissioner may in his discretion extend the time for compliance beyond such period of time for cause. In the event of such insurer's failure to comply within such period of time, the Commissioner may institute proceedings under this Article to have a rehabilitator or liquidator appointed, or extend the period of supervision.

(e) The notice of hearing under subsection (a) of this section and any order issued pursuant to that subsection shall be served upon the insurer pursuant to the applicable rules of civil procedure. The notice of hearing shall state the time and place of hearing, and the conduct, condition, or ground upon which the Commissioner would base his order. Unless mutually agreed upon between the Commissioner and the insurer, the hearing shall occur not less than 10 days nor more than 30 days after notice is served and shall be either in Wake County or in some other place designated by the Commissioner. The Commissioner shall hold all hearings under subsection (a) of this section privately unless the insurer requests a public hearing, in which case the hearing shall be public.

(f) Any insurer subject to an order under subsection (b) of this section may request an administrative hearing before the Commissioner or his designee to review that order. Such hearing shall be held as provided in subsection (e) of this section, but the request for a hearing shall not stay the effect of the order. If the Commissioner issues an order under subsection (b) of this section, the insurer may, at any time, waive the hearing and apply for immediate judicial relief by means of any remedy afforded by law without first exhausting its administrative remedies. Subsequent to an administrative hearing, any party to the proceedings whose interests are substantially affected is entitled to judicial review of any order issued by the Commissioner.

(g) During the period of supervision the insurer may request the Commissioner to review any action taken or proposed to be taken by the supervisor, specifying wherein the action complained of is believed not to be in the best interest of the insurer.

(h) If any person violates any supervision order issued under this section that as to him is then still in effect, he shall be liable to pay a civil penalty imposed by the Court not to exceed ten thousand dollars ($10,000). The clear proceeds of civil penalties imposed pursuant to this subsection shall be remitted to the Civil Penalty and Forfeiture Fund in accordance with G.S. 115C-457.2.

(i) The Commissioner may apply for, and any court of general jurisdiction may grant, such restraining orders, preliminary and permanent injunctions, and other orders as may be deemed to be necessary and proper to enforce a supervision order.

(j) In the event that any person subject to the provisions of this Article, including any person described in G.S. 58-30-25(a), knowingly and willfully violates any valid order of the Commissioner issued under the provisions of this section and, as a result of such violation, the net worth of the insurer is reduced or the insurer suffers loss that it would not otherwise have suffered, said person shall become personally liable to the insurer for the amount of any such reduction or loss. The Commissioner or supervisor is authorized to bring an action on behalf of the insurer in the Court to recover the amount of the reduction or loss together with any costs. (1989, c. 452, s. 1; 1989 (Reg. Sess., 1990), c. 1021, s. 6; 1991, c. 681, s. 43; 1998-215, s. 86.)

§ 58-30-62. Administrative supervision of insurers.

(a) As used in this section, an insurer has "exceeded its powers" when it: has refused to permit examination of its books, papers, accounts, records or affairs by the Commissioner; has in violation of G.S. 58-7-50 removed from this State books, papers, accounts or records necessary for an examination of the insurer; has failed to comply promptly with applicable financial reporting statutes or rules and related Department requests; continues to transact the business of insurance after its license has been revoked or suspended by the Commissioner; by contract or otherwise, has unlawfully, or has in violation of an order of the Commissioner, or has without first having obtained any legally required written approval of the Commissioner, totally reinsured its entire outstanding business or merged or consolidated substantially its entire property or business with another insurer; has engaged in any transaction in which it is not authorized to engage under the laws of this State; has not complied with G.S. 58-7-73; or has refused to comply with a lawful order of the Commissioner. As used in this section, "Commissioner" includes an authorized representative or designee of the Commissioner.

(b) This section applies to all domestic insurers and any other insurer doing business in this State whose state of domicile has asked the Commissioner to apply the provisions of this section to that insurer.

(c) An insurer may be subject to administrative supervision by the Commissioner if upon examination or at any other time it appears to the Commissioner that the insurer: has exceeded its powers; has failed to comply with applicable provisions of this Chapter; is conducting its business in a manner that is hazardous to the public or to its insureds; or consents to administrative supervision.

(d) If the Commissioner determines that the conditions set forth in subsection (c) of this section exist, the Commissioner shall: notify the insurer of that determination; furnish to the insurer a written list of the requirements to abate those conditions; and notify the insurer that it is under the supervision of the Commissioner and that the Commissioner is applying and effectuating the provisions of this section.

(e) If placed under administrative supervision, the insurer shall have 60 days, or a different period of time determined by the Commissioner, to comply with the requirements of the Commissioner under this section. If the Commissioner determines after notice and hearing that the conditions giving rise to the supervision still exist at the end of the supervision period specified in this subsection, the Commissioner may extend the period; or if the Commissioner determines that none of the conditions giving rise to the supervision exist, the Commissioner shall release the insurer from supervision.

(f) Notwithstanding any other provision of law and except as set forth in this section, all proceedings, hearings, notices, correspondence, reports, records, and other information in the possession of the Commissioner or the Department relating to the supervision of any insurer are confidential. The Department shall have access to such proceedings, hearings, notices, correspondence, reports, records, or other information as permitted by the Commissioner. The Commissioner may open the proceedings or hearings, or disclose the notices, correspondence, reports, records, or information to a department, agency or instrumentality of this or another state of the United States if the Commissioner determines that the disclosure is necessary or proper for the enforcement of the laws of this or another state of the United States. The Commissioner may open the proceedings or hearings or make public the notices, correspondence, reports, records, or other information if the Commissioner considers that it is in the best interest of the insurer, its insureds or creditors, or the general public. This section does not apply to hearings, notices, correspondence, reports, records, or other information obtained upon the appointment of a receiver for the insurer by a court of competent jurisdiction.

(g) During the period of supervision, the Commissioner shall serve as the administrative supervisor. The Commissioner may provide that the insurer shall not do any of the following during the period of supervision, without the Commissioner's prior approval: dispose of, convey, or encumber any of its assets or its business in force; withdraw from any of its bank accounts; lend or invest any of its funds; transfer any of its property; incur any debt, obligation, or liability; merge or consolidate with another company; establish new premiums or renew any policies; enter into any new reinsurance contract or treaty; terminate, surrender, forfeit, convert, or lapse any insurance coverage, except for nonpayment of premiums due; release, pay, or refund premium deposits, accrued cash, or loan values, unearned premiums, or other reserves on any insurance coverage; make any material change in management; increase salaries or benefits of officers or directors or make preferential payment of bonuses, dividends, or other payments considered preferential; or make any other change in its operations that the Commissioner considers to be material.

(h) During the period of supervision the insurer may contest an action taken or proposed to be taken by the Commissioner, specifying why the action being complained of would not result in improving the insurer's condition.

(i) This section does not limit powers granted to the Commissioner by any other provision of law. This section does not preclude the Commissioner from initiating judicial proceedings to place an insurer in a delinquency proceeding under this Article, regardless of whether the Commissioner has previously initiated administrative supervision proceedings under this section or under G.S. 58-30-60 against the insurer. The determination as to actions under this section is in the Commissioner's discretion.

(j) Notwithstanding any other provision of law, the Commissioner may meet with a supervisor appointed under this section and with the attorney or other

497

representative of the supervisor, without the presence of any other person, at the time of any proceeding or during the pendency of any proceeding held under the authority of this section, to carry out the Commissioner's duties under this section or for the supervisor to carry out the supervisor's duties under this section.

(k) There is no liability by, and no cause of action of any nature arises against, the Commissioner for any acts or omissions by the Commissioner in the performance of the Commissioner's powers and duties under this section. (1991, c. 681, s. 44; 2002-187, s. 2.10; 2003-212, s. 26(i).)

Effect of Amendments. — Session Laws 2002-187, s. 2.10, effective October 31, 2002, inserted "has not complied with G.S. 58-7-73" near the end of subsection (a).

Session Laws 2003-212, s. 26.(i), effective January 1, 2004, and applicable to all company licenses issued or otherwise eligible for renewal or continuation after that date, in subsection (a), substituted "revoked or suspended" for "revoked, suspended, or not renewed."

§ 58-30-65. Court's seizure order.

(a) The Commissioner may file in the Court a petition alleging, with respect to a domestic insurer:

    (1) That there exist grounds that justify a judicial order for a formal delinquency proceeding against an insurer under this Article;

    (2) That the interests of policyholders, creditors, or the public will be endangered by delay; and

    (3) The contents of an order deemed by the Commissioner to be necessary.

(b) Upon a filing under subsection (a) of this section, the Court may issue forthwith, ex parte, the requested order, that directs the Commissioner to take possession and control of all or a part of the property, books, accounts, documents, and other records of an insurer, and of the premises occupied by it for transaction of its business, and that, until further order of the Court, enjoins the insurer and its officers, managers, agents, and employees from disposing of its property and from transacting its business except with the written consent of the Commissioner.

(c) The Court shall specify in the order what its duration shall be, which shall be such time as the Court considers necessary for the Commissioner to ascertain the condition of the insurer. On motion of either party or on its own motion, the Court may from time to time hold such hearings as it considers desirable after such notice as it considers appropriate; and may extend, shorten, or modify the terms of the seizure order. The Court shall vacate the seizure order if the Commissioner fails to commence a formal proceeding under this Article after having a reasonable opportunity to do so. An order of the Court pursuant to a formal proceeding under this Article shall ipso facto vacate the seizure order.

(d) Entry of a seizure order under this section does not constitute an anticipatory breach of any contract of the insurer.

(e) An insurer subject to an ex parte order under this section may petition the Court at any time after the issuance of such order for a hearing and review of the order. The Court shall hold such a hearing and review not more than 15 days after the request. A hearing under this subsection may be held privately in chambers, and it shall be so held if the insurer proceeded against so requests.

(f) If, at any time after the issuance of such an order, it appears to the Court that any person whose interest is or will be substantially affected by the order did not appear at the hearing and has not been served, the Court may order that notice be given. An order that notice be given does not stay the effect of any order previously issued by the Court. (1989, c. 452, s. 1.)

§ 58-30-70. Confidentiality of hearings.

In all proceedings and judicial reviews thereof under G.S. 58-30-60 and G.S. 58-30-65, all records of the insurer, other documents, and all Department files and Court records and papers, insofar as they pertain to or are a part of the record of the proceedings, shall be and remain confidential except as is necessary to obtain compliance therewith, unless the Court, after hearing arguments from the parties in chambers, orders otherwise; or unless the insurer requests that the matter be made public. Until such Court order, all papers filed with the clerk of the Court shall be held by him in a confidential file. (1989, c. 452, s. 1.)

§ 58-30-71. Immunity and indemnification of the receiver and employees.

(a) For the purposes of this section, the persons entitled to protection under this section are:

    (1) All receivers responsible for the conduct of a delinquency proceeding under this Article, including present and former receivers; and

    (2) Their employees meaning all present and former special deputies and assistant special deputies appointed by the Commissioner, staff assigned to the delinquency proceeding employed by the Attorney General's Office, and all persons whom the Commissioner, special deputies, or assistant special deputies have employed to assist in a delinquency proceeding under this Article. Attorneys, accountants, auditors, and other professional persons or firms, who are retained by the receiver as independent contractors and their employees are not employees of the receiver for purposes of this section.

(b) The receiver and his employees have official immunity and are immune from suit and liability, both personally and in their official capacities, for any claim for damage to or loss of property or personal injury or other civil liability caused by or resulting from any alleged act, error, or omission of the receiver or any employee arising out of or by reason of their duties or employment; provided that nothing in this section holds the receiver or any employee immune from suit or liability for any damage, loss, injury, or liability caused by the intentional or willful and wanton misconduct of the receiver or any employee or for any bodily injury caused by the operation of a motor vehicle.

(c) If any legal action is commenced against the receiver or any employee, whether against him personally or in his official capacity, alleging property damage, property loss, personal injury, or other civil liability caused by or resulting from any alleged act, error, or omission of the receiver or any employee arising out of or by reason of their duties or employment, the receiver and any employee shall be indemnified from the assets of the insurer for all expenses, attorneys' fees, judgments, settlements, decrees, or amounts due and owing or paid in satisfaction of or incurred in the defense of such legal action; unless it is determined upon a final adjudication on the merits that the alleged act, error, or omission of the receiver or employee giving rise to the claim did not arise out of or by reason of his duties or employment, or was caused by intentional or willful and wanton misconduct.

(d) Attorneys' fees and all related expenses incurred in defending a legal action for which immunity or indemnity is available under this section shall be paid from the assets of the insurer, as they are incurred, before the final disposition of the action, upon receipt of any agreement by or on behalf of the receiver or employee to repay the attorneys' fees and expenses if it is ultimately determined upon a final adjudication on the merits that the receiver or employee is not entitled to immunity or indemnity under this section.

(e) Any indemnification for expense payments, judgments, settlements, decrees, attorneys' fees, surety bond premiums, or other amounts paid or to be paid from the insurer's assets under this section shall be an administrative expense of the insurer.

(f) In the event of any actual or threatened litigation against a receiver or any employee for which immunity or indemnity may be available under this section, a reasonable amount of funds, that in the judgment of the Commissioner may be needed to provide immunity or indemnity, shall be segregated and reserved from the assets of the insurer as security for the payment of indemnity until all applicable statutes of limitation have run, all actual or threatened actions against the receiver or any employee have been completely and finally resolved, and all obligations of the insurer and the Commissioner under this section have been satisfied.

(g) In lieu of segregation and reserving of funds, the Commissioner may, in his discretion, obtain a surety bond or make other arrangements that will enable the Commissioner to fully secure the payment of all obligations under this section.

(h) If any legal action against an employee for which indemnity may be available under this section is settled before final adjudication on the merits, the insurer must pay the settlement amount on behalf of the employee, or indemnify the employee for the settlement amount, unless the Commissioner determines:

(1) That the claim did not arise out of or by reason of the employee's duties or employment; or

(2) That the claims were caused by the intentional or willful and wanton misconduct of the employee.

(i) In any legal action in which the receiver is a defendant, that portion of any settlement relating to the alleged act, error, or omission of the receiver is subject to the approval of the court before which the delinquency proceeding is pending. The court shall not approve that portion of the settlement if it determines:

(1) That the claim did not arise out of or by reason of the receiver's duties or employment; or

(2) That the claim was caused by the intentional or willful and wanton misconduct of the receiver.

(j) Nothing in this section deprives the receiver or any employee of any immunity, indemnity, benefits of law, rights, or any defense otherwise available.

(k) Subsection (b) of this section applies to any suit based in whole or in part on any alleged act, error, or omission that occurs on or after October 1, 1993.

(l) No legal action shall lie against the receiver or any employee based in whole or in part on any alleged act, error, or omission that occurred before October 1, 1993, unless suit is filed and valid service of process is obtained within 12 months after October 1, 1993.

(m) Subsections (c), (h), and (i) of this section apply to any suit that is pending on or filed after October 1, 1993, without regard to when the alleged act, error, or omission took place. (1993, c. 452, s. 40.)

§ 58-30-75. Grounds for rehabilitation.

The Commissioner may petition the Court for an order authorizing him to rehabilitate a domestic insurer or an alien insurer domiciled in this State on any one or more of the following grounds:

(1) The insurer is in such condition that the further transaction of business would be hazardous financially to its policyholders, creditors, or the public.

(2) There is reasonable cause to believe that there has been embezzlement from the insurer, wrongful sequestration or diversion of the insurer's assets, forgery or fraud affecting the insurer, or other illegal conduct in, by, or with respect to the insurer that if established would endanger assets in an amount threatening the solvency of the insurer.

(3) The insurer has failed to remove any person who in fact has executive authority in the insurer, whether an officer, manager, general agent, employee, or other person; if the person has been found after notice and hearing by the Commissioner to be dishonest or untrustworthy in a way affecting the insurer's business.

(4) Control of the insurer, whether by stock ownership or otherwise, and whether direct or indirect, is in a person or persons found after notice and hearing to be untrustworthy.

(5) Any person who in fact has executive authority in the insurer, whether an officer, manager, general agent, director or trustee, employee, or other person, has refused to be examined under oath by the Commissioner concerning its affairs, whether in this State or elsewhere; and after reasonable notice of the fact, the insurer has failed promptly and effectively to terminate the employment and status of the person and all his influence on management.

(6) After demand by the Commissioner the insurer has failed to promptly make available for examination any of its own property, books, accounts, documents, or other records; those of any subsidiary or related company within the control of the insurer; or those of any person having executive authority in the insurer insofar as they pertain to the insurer.

(7) Without first obtaining the written consent of the Commissioner, the insurer has (i) transferred, or attempted to transfer, in a manner contrary to Article 19 of this Chapter, substantially its entire property or business, or (ii) has entered into any transaction, the effect of which is to merge, consolidate, or reinsure substantially its entire property or business in or with the property or business of any other person.

(8) The insurer or its property has been or is the subject of an application for the appointment of a receiver, trustee, custodian, conservator, or sequestrator or similar fiduciary of the insurer or its property otherwise than as authorized under Articles 1 through 64 of this Chapter, and such appointment has been made or is imminent, and such appointment might oust the courts of this State of jurisdiction or might prejudice orderly delinquency proceedings under this Article.

(9) Within the previous four years the insurer has willfully violated its charter or articles of incorporation, its bylaws, Articles 1 through 67 of this Chapter, or any valid order of the Commissioner under G.S. 58-30-60.

(10) The insurer has failed to pay within 60 days after due any obligation to any state or any subdivision thereof or any judgment entered in any state, if the court in which such judgment was entered has jurisdiction over such subject matter; except that such nonpayment is not a ground until 60 days after any good faith effort by the insurer to contest the obligation has been terminated, whether it is before the Commissioner or in the courts, or the insurer has systematically attempted to compromise or renegotiate previously agreed settlements with its creditors on the ground that it is financially unable to pay its obligations in full.

(11) The insurer has failed to file its annual report or any other financial report required by statute within the time allowed by law and, after written demand by the Commissioner, has failed to immediately give an adequate explanation.

(12) The board of directors or the holders of a majority of the shares entitled to vote, or a majority of those individuals entitled to the control of those persons specified in G.S. 58-30-5, request or consent to rehabilitation under this Article. (1989, c. 452, s. 1; c. 770, s. 72.1; 1995, c. 193, s. 31; 2001-223, s. 19.)

Editor's Note. — Session Laws 1991, c. 720, s. 23, directed that G.S. 58-30-175 be amended by substituting "67" for "64" in subdivision (9). However, there is no subdivision (9) in G.S. 58-30-175. The Legislature probably intended the amendment to be for G.S. 58-30-75. Such a correction was subsequently made to G.S. 58-30-75 by Session Laws 1995, c. 193, s. 31.

CASE NOTES

Editor's Note. — *The cases below were decided under prior statutory provisions.*
The commissioner as rehabilitator has discretionary as well as ministerial powers. State ex rel. Ingram v. All Am. Assurance Co., 34 N.C. App. 517, 239 S.E.2d 474 (1977).
Commissioner as Rehabilitator Loses Immunity of State. — Where insurance company, an insolvent North Carolina corporation, was placed in voluntary rehabilitation by order of the North Carolina superior court and where action was subsequently brought by the North Carolina Commissioner of Insurance in his capacity as company's rehabilitator, defendant's counterclaims could not be dismissed on the basis that U.S. Const., Amend. XI and sovereign immunity barred them; the commissioner as rehabilitator loses his identity as the State, and with it his immunity as an officer of the State, by assuming the identity of the insurer in actions brought for and against the insurer. North Carolina ex rel. Long v. Alexander & Alexander Servs., Inc., 711 F. Supp. 257 (E.D.N.C. 1989).

§ 58-30-80. Rehabilitation orders.

(a) An order to rehabilitate the business of a domestic insurer or an alien insurer domiciled in this State, shall appoint the Commissioner and his successors in office as the rehabilitator, and shall direct the rehabilitator forthwith to take possession of the assets of the insurer and to administer them under the general supervision of the Court. The filing or recording of the order with the clerk of the Court or register of deeds of the county in which the principal business of the insurer is conducted, or the county in which its principal office or place of business is located, shall impart the same notice as a deed, bill of sale, or other evidence of title duly filed or recorded with that register of deeds would have imparted. The order to rehabilitate the insurer shall by operation of law vest title to all assets of the insurer in the rehabilitator.

(b) Any order issued under this section shall require accounting to the Court by the rehabilitator. Accountings shall be at such intervals as the Court specifies in its order.

(c) Entry of an order of rehabilitation shall not constitute an anticipatory breach of any contract of the insurer. (1989, c. 452, s. 1.)

§ 58-30-85. Powers and duties of the rehabilitator.

(a) The rehabilitator has the power:
  (1) To appoint a special deputy to act for him under this Article, and to determine his reasonable compensation. The special deputy has all powers of the rehabilitator granted by this section. The special deputy serves at the pleasure of the rehabilitator.
  (2) To employ employees and agents, legal counsel, actuaries, accountants, appraisers, consultants, and such other personnel as he may deem to be necessary to assist in the rehabilitation.

(3) To fix the reasonable compensation of employees and agents, legal counsel, actuaries, accountants, appraisers, and consultants, with the approval of the Court.

(4) To pay reasonable compensation to persons appointed; and to defray from the funds or assets of the insurer all expenses of taking possession of, conserving, conducting, rehabilitating, disposing of, or otherwise dealing with the business and property of the insurer.

(5) To hold hearings, to subpoena witnesses to compel their attendance, to administer oaths, to examine any person under oath, and to compel any person to subscribe to this testimony after it has been correctly reduced to writing; and in connection therewith to require the production of any books, papers, records, or other documents that he considers relevant to the inquiry.

(6) To collect all debts and moneys due and claims belonging to the insurer, wherever located, and for this purpose:

   a. To institute timely action in other jurisdictions, in order to forestall garnishment and attachment proceedings against such debts;

   b. To do such other acts that are necessary or expedient to collect, conserve, or protect its assets or property, including the power to sell, compound, compromise, or assign debts for purposes of collection upon such terms and conditions as he deems to be best; and

   c. To pursue any creditor's remedies available to enforce his claims.

(7) To conduct public and private sales of the property of the insurer.

(8) To use assets of the estate of an insurer under a rehabilitation order to transfer policy obligations to a solvent assuming insurer, if the transfer can be arranged without prejudice to applicable priorities under G.S. 58-30-220.

(9) To acquire, hypothecate, encumber, lease, improve, sell, transfer, abandon, or otherwise dispose of or deal with, any property of the insurer at its market value or upon such terms and conditions that are fair and reasonable. He also has the power to execute, acknowledge, and deliver any and all deeds, assignments, releases and other instruments necessary or proper to effectuate any sale of property or other transaction in connection with the rehabilitation.

(10) To borrow money on the security of the insurer's assets or without security and to execute and deliver all documents necessary to that transaction for the purpose of facilitating the rehabilitation.

(11) To enter into such contracts that are necessary to carry out the order to rehabilitate, and to affirm or disavow any contracts to which the insurer is a party.

(12) To continue to prosecute and to institute in the name of the insurer or in his own name any and all suits and other legal proceedings, in this State or elsewhere, and to abandon the prosecution of claims he deems unprofitable to pursue further.

(13) To prosecute any action that may exist in behalf of the creditors, members, policyholders, or shareholders of the insurer against any officer of the insurer or against any other person.

(14) To remove any or all records and property of the insurer to the offices of the Commissioner or to such other place as may be convenient for the purposes of efficient and orderly execution of the rehabilitation.

(15) To deposit in one or more banks in this State such sums as are required for meeting current administration expenses and dividend distributions.

(16) To invest all sums not currently needed, unless the Court orders otherwise.

(17) To file any necessary documents for recording in the office of any register of deeds in this State or elsewhere where property of the insurer is located.

(18) To assert all defenses available to the insurer as against third persons, including statutes of limitation, statutes of frauds, and the defense of usury. A waiver of any defense by the insurer after a petition in rehabilitation has been filed shall not bind the rehabilitator.

(19) To exercise and enforce all rights, remedies, and powers of any creditor, shareholder, policyholder, or member; including any power to avoid any transfer or lien that may be given by law and that is not included within G.S. 58-30-140 through 58-30-150.

(20) To intervene in any proceeding wherever instituted that might lead to the appointment of a receiver or trustee, and to act as the receiver or trustee whenever the appointment is offered.

(21) To enter into agreements with any receiver or insurance regulator of any other state relating to the rehabilitation, liquidation, conservation, or dissolution of an insurer doing business in both states.

(22) To exercise all powers now held or subsequently conferred upon receivers by laws of this State not inconsistent with the provisions of this Article.

(b) The enumeration in this section of the powers and authority of the rehabilitator shall not be construed as a limitation upon him, nor shall it exclude in any manner his right to do such other acts not specifically enumerated in this section or otherwise provided for, as may be necessary or appropriate for the accomplishment of or in aid of the purpose of rehabilitation.

(c) The rehabilitator may take such action as he considers necessary or appropriate to reform and revitalize the insurer. He shall have all the powers of the directors, officers, and managers, whose authority shall be suspended, except to the extent they may be redelegated by the rehabilitator. He shall have full power to direct, manage, hire, and discharge employees, subject to any contract rights they may have, and to deal with the property and business of the insurer.

(d) If it appears to the rehabilitator that there has been criminal or tortious conduct, or breach of any contractual or fiduciary obligation detrimental to the insurer by any officer, manager, agent, broker, employee or other person, he may pursue all available legal remedies on behalf of the insurer.

(e) If the rehabilitator determines that reorganization, consolidation, conversion, reinsurance, merger, or other transformation of the insurer is appropriate, he shall prepare a plan to effect such changes. Upon application of the rehabilitator for approval of the plan, and after such notice and hearings as the Court may prescribe, the Court may either approve or disapprove the plan proposed, or may modify it and approve it as modified. Any plan approved under this section shall be, in the opinion of the Court, fair and equitable to all parties concerned. If the plan is approved, the rehabilitator shall carry out the plan. In the case of a life insurer, the plan proposed may include the imposition of liens upon the policies of the insurer, if all rights of shareholders are first relinquished. A plan for a life insurer may also propose imposition of a moratorium upon loan and cash surrender rights under policies, for such period and to such an extent as may be necessary.

(f) The rehabilitator shall have the power under G.S. 58-30-140 and G.S. 58-30-145 to avoid fraudulent transfers. (1989, c. 452, s. 1.)

Editor's Note. — *Most of the cases below were decided under prior statutory provisions.*

Settlement of an outstanding debt by the rehabilitator is clearly a step "toward removal of the causes and conditions which have made rehabilitation necessary as the court may direct." State ex rel. Ingram v. All Am. Assurance Co., 34 N.C. App. 517, 239 S.E.2d 474 (1977).

Commissioner as Rehabilitator Loses Immunity of State. — Where insurance company, an insolvent North Carolina corporation, was placed in voluntary rehabilitation by order of the North Carolina superior court and action was subsequently brought by the North Caro-

lina Commissioner of Insurance in his capacity as company's rehabilitator, defendant's counterclaims could not be dismissed on the basis that U.S. Const., Amend. XI and sovereign immunity barred them; the Commissioner as rehabilitator loses his identity as the State, and with it his immunity as an officer of the State, by assuming the identity of the insurer in actions brought for and against the insurer. North Carolina ex rel. Long v. Alexander & Alexander Servs., Inc., 711 F. Supp. 257 (E.D.N.C. 1989).

Cited in State ex rel. Long v. American Sec. Life Assurance Co., 109 N.C. App. 530, 428 S.E.2d 200 (1993).

§ 58-30-90. Actions by and against rehabilitator.

(a) When a rehabilitation order against an insurer is entered, every court in this State, before which any pending action or proceeding in which the insurer is a party or is obligated to defend a party, shall stay the action or proceeding for 120 days and such additional time that is necessary for the rehabilitator to obtain proper representation and prepare for further proceedings. The rehabilitator may take such action respecting pending litigation as he deems necessary in the interests of justice and for the protection of creditors, policyholders, and the public. The rehabilitator may immediately consider all litigation pending outside this State and may petition the courts having jurisdiction over that litigation for stays whenever necessary to protect the estate of the insurer.

(b) No statute of limitations or defense of laches shall run with respect to any action by or against an insurer between the filing of a petition for appointment of a rehabilitator for that insurer and the order granting or denying that petition.

(c) Any domestic or foreign guaranty association has standing to appear in any Court proceeding concerning the rehabilitation of an insurer if such association is or may become liable to act as a result of the rehabilitation. (1989, c. 452, s. 1.)

§ 58-30-95. Termination of rehabilitation.

(a) Whenever the rehabilitator believes further attempts to rehabilitate an insurer would substantially increase the risk of loss to creditors, policyholders or the public, or would be futile, the rehabilitator may petition the Court for an order of liquidation. A petition under this subsection shall have the same effect as a petition under G.S. 58-30-100. The Court may make such findings and issue such orders at any time upon its own motion. The Court shall permit the directors of the insurer to take such actions as are reasonably necessary to defend against the petition and may order payment from the estate of the insurer of such costs and other expenses of defense as justice may require. The court may allow the payment of costs and expenses incurred in defending against the petition for an order of liquidation only upon a specific finding that the defense was conducted, and the costs and expenses were incurred, in good faith. The directors shall have the burden of proving good faith. Evidence of good faith shall be the existence of a reasonable basis to conclude that the insurer is actually solvent or that there exists a viable means to accomplish rehabilitation without jeopardizing the remaining assets of the insurer and that continued operation of the insurer is in the best interest of the policy-holders, stockholders, and creditors.

(b) The rehabilitator may at any time petition the Court for an order terminating rehabilitation of an insurer. The Court shall also permit the directors of the insurer to petition the Court for an order terminating rehabilitation of the insurer and may order payment from the estate of the insurer of such costs and other expenses of such petition as justice may require. The court may allow the payment of costs and expenses incurred in defending against the petition for an order terminating rehabilitation only upon a specific finding that the defense was conducted, and the costs and expenses were incurred, in good faith. The directors shall have the burden of proving good faith. Evidence of good faith shall be the existence of a reasonable basis to conclude that the insurer is actually solvent or that there exists a viable means to accomplish rehabilitation without jeopardizing the remaining assets of the insurer and that continued operation of the insurer is in the best interest of the policyholders, stockholders, and creditors. If the Court finds that rehabilitation has been accomplished and that grounds for rehabilitation under G.S. 58-30-75 no longer exist, it shall order that the insurer be restored to possession of its property and the control of the business. The Court may also make that finding and issue that order at any time upon its own motion. (1989, c. 452, s. 1; 1993, c. 452, s. 41.)

CASE NOTES

Considerations in Defense to Liquidation. — The directors of an insolvent company are not, as a matter of law, disallowed from defending against a petition for liquidation; rather, all of the facts and circumstances of a particular case should be examined in determining whether the defense to liquidation was brought in good faith, with the solvency of the company examined as one of many factors, and not as the sole factor, in the ultimate decision to award fees and costs. State ex rel. Long v. American Sec. Life Assurance Co., 109 N.C. App. 530, 428 S.E.2d 200 (1993).

Award of Costs and Fees. — The trial court has been granted broad discretion to award the fees and costs incurred in defending against a petition for liquidation. State ex rel. Long v. American Sec. Life Assurance Co., 109 N.C. App. 530, 428 S.E.2d 200 (1993).

Standard of Review on Appeal. — Because of the discretionary nature of this section, the standard of review on appeal is whether a trial court's award of fees and costs constitutes an abuse of discretion. State ex rel. Long v. American Sec. Life Assurance Co., 109 N.C. App. 530, 428 S.E.2d 200 (1993).

§ 58-30-100. Grounds for liquidation.

The Commissioner may petition the Court for an order directing him to liquidate a domestic insurer or an alien insurer domiciled in this State on the basis:

(1) Of any ground for an order of rehabilitation as specified in G.S. 58-30-75, whether or not there has been a prior order directing the rehabilitation of the insurer;

(2) That the insurer is insolvent; or

(3) That the insurer is in such condition that the further transaction of business would be hazardous, financially or otherwise, to its policy-holders, its creditors, or the public. (1989, c. 452, s. 1.)

§ 58-30-105. Liquidation orders.

(a) An order to liquidate the business of a domestic insurer shall appoint the Commissioner and his successors in office liquidator and shall direct the liquidator forthwith to take possession of the assets of the insurer and to administer them under the general supervision of the Court. The liquidator is vested by operation of law with the title to all of the property, contracts, and rights of action, and all of the books and records of the insurer ordered liquidated, wherever located, as of the entry of the final order of liquidation. The filing or recording of the order with the clerk of the superior court and the register of deeds of the county in which its principal office or place of business is located; or, in the case of real estate, with the register of deeds of the county where the property is located, shall impart the same notice as a deed, bill of sale, or other evidence of title duly filed or recorded with that register of deeds would have imparted.

(b) Upon issuance of the order, the rights and liabilities of any such insurer and of its creditors, policyholders, shareholders, members and all other persons interested in its estate shall become fixed as of the date of entry of the order of liquidation, except as provided in G.S. 58-30-110 and G.S. 58-30-195.

(c) An order to liquidate the business of an alien insurer domiciled in this State shall be in the same terms and have the same legal effect as an order to liquidate a domestic insurer; except that the assets and the business in the United States shall be the only assets and business included therein.

(d) At the time of petitioning for an order of liquidation or at any time thereafter the Commissioner, after making appropriate findings of an insurer's insolvency, may petition the Court for a judicial declaration of such insolvency. After providing such notice and hearing as it deems to be proper, the Court may make the declaration.

(e) Any order issued under this section requires accounting to the Court by the liquidator. Accountings shall be at such intervals as the Court specifies in its order. (1989, c. 452, s. 1.)

CASE NOTES

Editor's Note. — *One of the cases below was decided under prior statutory provisions.*

The trial court has broad supervisory powers and must also be held to have broad initiative powers as well, so as to effect the mandate of such provisions as former G.S. 58-155.18, which directed the court after full hearing to deny or grant the application for rehabilitation "together with such other relief as the nature of the case and the interests of policyholders, creditors, stockholders, members, subscribers or the public may require." State ex. rel. Ingram. v. All Am. Assurance Co., 34 N.C. App. 517, 239 S.E.2d 474 (1977).

Authority to Order Payment of Fair Compensation to Counsel. — The supervisory power of the trial court in a rehabilitation suit includes the authority to order that the insurer pay fair and reasonable compensation to its counsel of record for legal services rendered. State ex rel. Ingram v. All Am. Assurance Co., 34 N.C. App. 517, 239 S.E.2d 474 (1977).

Cited in State ex rel. Long v. Interstate Cas. Ins. Co., 106 N.C. App. 470, 417 S.E.2d 296 (1992).

§ 58-30-110. Continuance of coverage.

(a) All policies, other than life or health insurance or annuities, that are in effect at the time of the issuance of an order of liquidation shall continue in force only for the lesser of:

    (1) A period of 30 days from the date of entry of the liquidation orders;

    (2) The expiration of the policy coverage;

    (3) The date when the insured has replaced the insurance coverage with equivalent insurance in another insurer or otherwise terminated the policy; or

    (4) The liquidator has effected a transfer of the policy obligation pursuant to G.S. 58-30-120(a)(8).

(b) An order of liquidation under G.S. 58-30-105 terminates coverages at the time specified in subsection (a) of this section for the purposes of any other statute.

507

(c) Policies of life or health insurance or annuities shall continue in force for such period and under such terms as is provided for by any applicable domestic or foreign guaranty association.

(d) Policies of life or health insurance or annuities or any period of coverage of such policies that are not covered by a domestic or foreign guaranty association shall terminate under subsections (a) and (b) of this section. (1989, c. 452, s. 1.)

§ 58-30-115. Dissolution of insurer.

The Commissioner may petition for an order dissolving the corporate existence of a domestic insurer or the United States branch of an alien insurer domiciled in this State at the time he applies for a liquidation order. The Court shall order dissolution of the corporation upon petition by the Commissioner upon or after the granting of a liquidation order. If the dissolution has not previously been ordered, it shall be effected by operation of law upon the discharge of the liquidator if the insurer is under a liquidation order for some other reason. (1989, c. 452, s. 1.)

§ 58-30-120. Powers of liquidator.

(a) The liquidator has the power:
   (1) To appoint a special deputy to act for him under this Article, and to determine his reasonable compensation. The special deputy has all powers of the liquidator granted by this section. The special deputy serves at the pleasure of the liquidator.
   (2) To employ employees and agents, legal counsel, actuaries, accountants, appraisers, consultants, and such other personnel as he may deem to be necessary to assist in the liquidation.
   (3) To fix the reasonable compensation of employees and agents, legal counsel, actuaries, accountants, appraisers, and consultants, with the approval of the Court.
   (4) To pay reasonable compensation to persons appointed; and to defray from the funds or assets of the insurer all expenses of taking possession of, conserving, conducting, liquidating, disposing of, or otherwise dealing with the business and property of the insurer. In the event that the property of the insurer does not contain sufficient cash or liquid assets to defray the costs incurred, the Commissioner may advance the costs so incurred out of any appropriation for the maintenance of the Department. Any amounts so advanced for expenses of administration shall be repaid to the Commissioner for the use of the Department out of the first available moneys of the insurer.
   (5) To hold hearings, to subpoena witnesses to compel their attendance, to administer oaths, to examine any person under oath, and to compel any person to subscribe to this testimony after it has been correctly reduced to writing; and in connection therewith to require the production of any books, papers, records, or other documents that he considers relevant to the inquiry.
   (6) To collect all debts and moneys due and claims belonging to the insurer, wherever located, and for this purpose:
      a. To institute timely action in other jurisdictions, in order to forestall garnishment and attachment proceedings against such debts;
      b. To do such other acts that are necessary or expedient to collect, conserve, or protect its assets or property, including the power to sell, compound, compromise, or assign debts for purposes of collection upon such terms and conditions as he deems to be best; and

     c. To pursue any creditor's remedies available to enforce his claims.

(7) To conduct public and private sales of the property of the insurer.

(8) To use assets of the estate of an insurer under a liquidation order to transfer policy obligations to a solvent assuming insurer, if the transfer can be arranged without prejudice to applicable priorities under G.S. 58-30-220.

(9) To acquire, hypothecate, encumber, lease, improve, sell, transfer, abandon, or otherwise dispose of or deal with, any property of the insurer at its market value or upon such terms and conditions that are fair and reasonable. He also has the power to execute, acknowledge, and deliver any and all deeds, assignments, releases and other instruments necessary or proper to effectuate any sale of property or other transaction in connection with the liquidation.

(10) To borrow money on the security of the insurer's assets or without security and to execute and deliver all documents necessary to that transaction for the purpose of facilitating the liquidation.

(11) To enter into such contracts that are necessary to carry out the order to liquidate, and to affirm or disavow any contracts to which the insurer is a party.

(12) To continue to prosecute and to institute in the name of the insurer or in his own name any and all suits and other legal proceedings, in this State or elsewhere, and to abandon the prosecution of claims he deems unprofitable to pursue further. If the insurer is dissolved under G.S. 58-30-115, he shall have the power to apply to any court in this State or elsewhere for leave to substitute himself for the insurer as plaintiff.

(13) To prosecute any action that may exist in behalf of the creditors, members, policyholders, or shareholders of the insurer against any officer of the insurer or against any other person.

(14) To remove any or all records and property of the insurer to the offices of the Commissioner or to such other place as may be convenient for the purposes of efficient and orderly execution of the liquidation. Domestic and foreign guaranty associations shall have such reasonable access to the records of the insurer as is necessary for them to carry out their statutory obligations.

(15) To deposit in one or more banks in this State such sums as are required for meeting current administration expenses and dividend distributions.

(16) To invest all sums not currently needed, unless the Court orders otherwise.

(17) To file any necessary documents for recording in the office of any register of deeds in this State or elsewhere where property of the insurer is located.

(18) To assert all defenses available to the insurer as against third persons, including statutes of limitation, statutes of frauds, and the defense of usury. A waiver of any defense by the insurer after a petition in liquidation has been filed shall not bind the liquidator. Whenever a domestic or foreign guaranty association has an obligation to defend any suit, the liquidator shall give precedence to such obligation and may defend only in the absence of a defense by such guaranty associations.

(19) To exercise and enforce all rights, remedies, and powers of any creditor, shareholder, policyholder, or member; including any power to avoid any transfer or lien that may be given by law and that is not included within G.S. 58-30-140 through G.S. 58-30-150.

(20) To intervene in any proceeding wherever instituted that might lead to the appointment of a receiver or trustee, and to act as the receiver or trustee whenever the appointment is offered.

(21) To enter into agreements with any receiver or insurance regulator of any other state relating to the rehabilitation, liquidation, conservation, or dissolution of an insurer doing business in both states.

(22) To exercise all powers now held or subsequently conferred upon receivers by laws of this State not inconsistent with the provisions of this Article.

(b) The enumeration in this section of the powers and authority of the liquidator shall not be construed as a limitation upon him, nor shall it exclude in any manner his right to do such other acts not specifically enumerated in this section or otherwise provided for, as may be necessary or appropriate for the accomplishment of or in aid of the purpose of liquidation. (1989, c. 452, s. 1.)

CASE NOTES

Applicability. — Because alleged acts of misconduct by the director and chief executive officer of an insolvent insurer occurred within three years prior to the order appointing the Commissioner of Insurance as liquidator and because the Commissioner filed actions against the defendant within two years of his appointment, such claims were protected by the two-year extension of this section. State ex rel. Long v. ILA Corp., 132 N.C. App. 587, 513 S.E.2d 812 (1999).

Standing. — This section conferred standing on the Commissioner of Insurance to assert the claims of an insolvent insurer for breach of fiduciary duties to and negligent mismanagement of the insurer. State ex rel. Long v. ILA Corp., 132 N.C. App. 587, 513 S.E.2d 812 (1999).

Cited in State ex rel. Long v. Interstate Cas. Ins. Co., 106 N.C. App. 470, 417 S.E.2d 296 (1992).

§ 58-30-125. Notice to creditors and others.

(a) Unless the Court otherwise directs, the liquidator shall give or cause to be given notice of the liquidation order as soon as possible:

(1) By first-class mail and either by telecopier, telegram, or telephone to the insurance regulator of each jurisdiction in which the insurer is doing business;

(2) By first-class mail to any domestic or foreign guaranty association that is or may become obligated as a result of the liquidation;

(3) By first-class mail to all insurance agents of the insurer;

(4) By first-class mail to all persons known or reasonably expected to have claims against the insurer, including all policyholders, at their last known addresses indicated by the records of the insurer; and

(5) By publication in a newspaper of general circulation in the county in which the insurer has its principal place of business and in such other locations as the liquidator deems to be appropriate.

(b) Notice to potential claimants under subsection (a) of this section shall require claimants to file with the liquidator their claims, together with proper proofs thereof under G.S. 58-30-190, on or before a date the liquidator specifies in the notice. The liquidator need not require persons claiming cash surrender values or other investment values in life insurance and annuities to file claims. All claimants have a duty to keep the liquidator informed of any changes of address.

(c) If notice is given in accordance with this section, the distribution of assets of the insurer under this Article shall be conclusive with respect to all claimants, whether or not they receive notice. (1989, c. 452, s. 1.)

§ 58-30-127. Duties of agents.

(a) Every person who receives notice in the form prescribed in G.S. 58-30-125 that an insurer that person represents as an agent is the subject of a liquidation order shall, upon request of the liquidator and within 60 days after receipt of the request, provide to the liquidator the information in the agent's records related to any policy issued by the insurer through the agent; and if the agent is a general agent, the information in the general agent's records related to any policy issued by the insurer through a subagent under contract with the general agent, including the name and address of the subagent.

(b) For the purpose of this section, a policy is issued through an agent if the agent has a property interest in the expiration of the policy or if the agent has had in the agent's possession a copy of the declarations of the policy at any time during the life of the policy, except where the ownership of the expiration of the policy has been transferred to another person.

(c) Any agent failing to provide information to the liquidator as required by this section is to be subject to G.S. 58-2-70.

(d) The provisions of this section are in addition to any other duties in this Chapter that are placed on agents. (1991, c. 681, s. 45.)

§ 58-30-130. Actions by and against liquidator.

(a) Upon the issuance of an order appointing a liquidator of a domestic insurer or of an alien insurer domiciled in this State, no action at law or equity shall be brought against the insurer or liquidator, whether in this State or elsewhere, nor shall any such existing actions be maintained or further presented after issuance of such order. The Court shall give full faith and credit to injunctions against the liquidator or the insurer or the continuation of existing actions against the liquidator or the insurer, when such injunctions are included in an order to liquidate an insurer issued pursuant to corresponding provisions in other states. Whenever, in the liquidator's judgement, protection of the estate of the insurer necessitates intervention in an action against the insurer that is pending outside this State, he may intervene in the action. The liquidator may defend any action in which he intervenes under this section at the expense of the estate of the insurer.

(b) The liquidator may, upon or after an order for liquidation, within two years or such subsequent time period as applicable law may permit, institute an action or proceeding on behalf of the estate of the insurer upon any cause of action against which the period of limitation fixed by applicable law has not expired at the time of the filing of the petition upon which such order is entered. Where (i) by any agreement, a period of limitation is fixed for instituting a suit or proceeding upon any claim, or for filing any claim, proof of claim, proof of loss, demand, notice, or the like; or (ii) in any proceeding, judicial or otherwise, a period of limitation is fixed, either in the proceeding or by applicable law, for taking any action, filing any claim or pleading, or doing any act; and (iii) in any such case the period had not expired at the date of the filing of the petition; the liquidator may, for the benefit of the estate, take any such action or do any such act, required of or permitted to the insurer, within a period of 180 days subsequent to the entry of an order for liquidation, or within such further period as is shown to the satisfaction of the Court not to be unfairly prejudicial to the other party.

(c) Any domestic or foreign guaranty association has standing to appear in any Court proceeding concerning the liquidation of an insurer if such association is or may become liable to act as a result of the liquidation. (1989, c. 452, s. 1.)

CASE NOTES

The doctrine that the statute of limitations cannot run against the state did not apply in the case of a negligence action brought by the state as liquidator of a life insurer against attorneys for the insurer. State ex rel. Long v. Petree Stockton, 129 N.C. App. 432, 499 S.E.2d 790 (1998), cert. granted, 349 N.C. 240, 516 S.E.2d 607 (1998).

§ 58-30-135. Collection and list of assets.

(a) As soon as practicable after the liquidation order but not later than 120 days thereafter, the liquidator shall prepare in duplicate a list of the insurer's assets. The list shall be amended or supplemented from time to time as the liquidator determines. One copy shall be filed in the office of the clerk of the Court and one copy shall be retained for the liquidator's files. All amendments and supplements shall be similarly filed.

(b) The liquidator shall reduce the assets to a degree of liquidity that is consistent with the effective execution of the liquidation.

(c) A submittal to the Court for disbursement of assets in accordance with G.S. 58-30-180 fulfills the requirements of subsection (a) of this section. (1989, c. 452, s. 1.)

§ 58-30-140. Fraudulent transfers prior to petition.

(a) Every transfer made or suffered and every obligation incurred by an insurer within one year prior to the filing of a successful petition for rehabilitation or liquidation under this Article is fraudulent as to then existing and future creditors if made or incurred without fair consideration or if made or incurred with actual intent to hinder, delay, or defraud either existing or future creditors. A transfer made or an obligation incurred by an insurer ordered to be rehabilitated or liquidated under this Article, that is fraudulent under this section, may be avoided by the receiver, except as to a person who in good faith is a purchaser, lienor, or obligee, for a present fair equivalent value; and except that any purchaser, lienor, or obligee, who in good faith has given a consideration less than fair for such transfer, lien, or obligation, may retain the property, lien, or obligation as security for repayment. The Court may, on due notice, order any such transfer or obligation to be preserved for the benefit of the estate, and in that event, the receiver shall succeed to and may enforce the rights of the purchaser, lienor, or obligee.

(b) A transfer of property other than real property is made or suffered when it becomes so far perfected that no subsequent lien obtainable by legal or equitable proceedings on a simple contract could become superior to the rights of the transferee under G.S. 58-30-150(c). A transfer of real property is made or suffered when it becomes so far perfected that no subsequent bona fide purchaser from the insurer could obtain rights superior to the rights of the transferee. A transfer that creates an equitable lien is not perfected if there are available means by which a legal lien could be created. Any transfer that is not perfected prior to the filing of a petition for liquidation shall be deemed to be made immediately before the filing of the successful petition. The provisions of this subsection apply whether or not there are or were creditors who might have obtained any liens or persons who might have become bona fide purchasers.

(c) Any transaction of the insurer with a reinsurer is fraudulent and may be avoided by the receiver under subsection (a) of this section if:

    (1) The transaction consists of the termination, adjustment, or settlement of a reinsurance contract in which the reinsurer is released from any part of its duty to pay the originally specified share of losses that had occurred prior to the time of the transaction, unless the reinsurer gives a present fair equivalent value for the release; and

    (2) Any part of the transaction took place within one year prior to the date of filing of the petition through which the receivership was commenced.

(d) Every person receiving any property from the insurer or any benefit thereof as the result of a fraudulent transfer under subsection (a) of this section is personally liable therefor and is bound to account to the liquidator. (1989, c. 452, s. 1; 1991, c. 681, s. 46.)

CASE NOTES

Federal abstention under Burford v. Sun Oil Co., 319 U.S. 315, 63 S. Ct. 1098, 87 L. Ed. 1424 (1943), was inappropriate where the case raised no questions of uniquely federal jurisdiction; although North Carolina's liquidation laws attempt to minimize legal uncertainty and litigation and to promote efficiency and econ- omy of liquidation, as federal court decisionmaking of the kind that exists alongside state insurance liquidation proceedings do not significantly disrupt state regulatory frameworks. American Sec. Life Assurance Co. v. Mason, 836 F. Supp. 333 (E.D.N.C. 1993).

§ 58-30-145. Fraudulent transfer after petition.

(a) After a petition for rehabilitation or liquidation has been filed, a transfer of any of the real property of the insurer made to a person acting in good faith shall be valid against the receiver if made for a present fair equivalent value; or, if not made for a present fair equivalent value, then to the extent of the present consideration actually paid therefor, for which amount the transferee shall have a lien on the property so transferred. The commencement of a proceeding in rehabilitation or liquidation shall be constructive notice upon the recording of a copy of the petition for or order of rehabilitation or liquidation with the register of deeds in the county in which any real property in question is located. The exercise by a court of the United States or any state to authorize or effect a judicial sale of real property of the insurer within any county in any state is not impaired by the pendency of such a proceeding unless the copy is recorded in the county prior to the consummation of the judicial sale.

(b) After a petition for rehabilitation or liquidation has been filed and before either the receiver takes possession of the property of the insurer or an order of rehabilitation or liquidation is granted:

(1) A transfer of any of the property of the insurer, other than real property, made to a person acting in good faith is valid against the receiver if made for a present fair equivalent value; or, if not made for a present fair equivalent value, then to the extent of the present consideration actually paid therefor, for which amount the transferee shall have a lien on the property so transferred.

(2) A person indebted to the insurer or holding property of the insurer may, if acting in good faith, pay the indebtedness or deliver the property, or any part thereof, to the insurer or upon his order, with the same effect as if the petition were not pending.

(3) A person having actual knowledge of the pending rehabilitation or liquidation shall be deemed not to act in good faith.

(4) A person asserting the validity of a transfer under this section has the burden of proof. Except as elsewhere provided in this section, no transfer by or on behalf of the insurer after the date of the petition for liquidation by any person other than the liquidator is valid as against the liquidator.

(c) Nothing in this Article impairs the validity of currency or the negotiability of any instrument. (1989, c. 452, s. 1.)

§ 58-30-150. Voidable preferences and liens.

(a) A preference is a transfer of any of the property of an insurer to or for the benefit of a creditor, for or on account of an antecedent debt, made or suffered by the insurer within one year before the filing of a successful petition for liquidation under this Article, the effect of which transfer may be to enable the creditor to obtain a greater percentage of this debt than another creditor of the same class would receive. If a liquidation order is entered while the insurer is already subject to a rehabilitation order, then such transfers shall be deemed to be preferences if made or suffered within one year before the filing of the successful petition for rehabilitation, or within two years before the filing of the successful petition for liquidation, whichever time is shorter. Any preference may be avoided by the liquidator if:

    (1) The insurer was insolvent at the time of the transfer;

    (2) The transfer was made within four months before the filing of the petition;

    (3) The creditor receiving it or to be benefited thereby or his agent acting with reference thereto had, at the time the transfer was made, reasonable cause to believe that the insurer was insolvent or was about to become insolvent; or

    (4) The creditor receiving it was an officer, or any employee, attorney, or other person who was in fact in a position of comparable influence in the insurer to an officer, whether or not he held such position, or any shareholder holding directly or indirectly more than five percent (5%) of any class of any equity security issued by the insurer, or any other person, firm, corporation, association, or aggregation of persons with whom the insurer did not deal at arm's length.

Where the preference is voidable, the liquidator may recover the property or, if it has been converted, its value from any person who has received or converted the property; except where a bona fide purchaser or lienor has given less than fair equivalent value, he shall have a lien upon the property to the extent of the consideration actually given by him. Where a preference by way of lien or security title is voidable, the Court may on due notice order the lien or title to be preserved for the benefit of the estate, in which event the lien or title shall pass to the liquidator.

(b) A transfer of property other than real property shall be deemed to be made or suffered when it becomes so far perfected that no subsequent lien obtainable by legal or equitable proceedings on a simple contract could become superior to the rights of the transferee. A transfer of real property shall be deemed to be made or suffered when it becomes so far perfected that no subsequent bona fide purchaser from the insurer could obtain rights superior to the rights of the transferee. A transfer that creates an equitable lien shall not be deemed to be perfected if there are available means by which a legal lien could be created. A transfer not perfected prior to the filing of a petition for liquidation shall be deemed to be made immediately before the filing of the successful petition. The provisions of this subsection apply whether or not there are or were creditors who might have obtained liens or persons who might have become bona fide purchasers.

(c) A lien obtainable by legal or equitable proceedings upon a simple contract is one arising in the ordinary course of such proceedings upon the entry or docketing of a judgment or decree, or upon attachment, garnishment, execution, or like process, whether before, upon, or after judgment or decree and whether before or upon levy. It does not include liens that under applicable law are given a special priority over other liens that are prior in time. A lien obtainable by legal or equitable proceedings could become superior to the rights of a transferee, or a purchaser could obtain rights superior to the rights of a transferee within the meaning of subsection (b) of this section, if such consequences would follow only from the lien or purchase itself, or from the lien or purchase followed by any step wholly within the control of the respective lienholder or purchaser, with or without the aid of ministerial action by public officials. Such a lien could not, however, become superior and such a purchase could not create superior rights for the purpose of subsection (b) of this section through any acts subsequent to the obtaining of such a lien or subsequent to such a purchase that require the agreement or concurrence of any third party or that require any further judicial action or ruling.

(d) A transfer of property for or on account of a new and contemporaneous consideration that is deemed under subsection (b) of this section to be made or suffered after the transfer because of delay in perfecting it does not thereby become a transfer for or on account of any antecedent debt if any acts required by the applicable law to be performed in order to perfect the transfer as against liens or bona fide purchasers' rights are performed within 21 days or any period expressly allowed by the law, whichever is less. A transfer to secure a future loan, if such a loan is actually made, or a transfer that becomes security for a future loan, shall have the same effect as a transfer for or on account of a new and contemporaneous consideration.

(e) If any lien deemed to be voidable under subdivision (a)(2) of this section has been dissolved by the furnishing of a bond or other obligation, the surety on which has been indemnified directly or indirectly by the transfer of or the creation of a lien upon any property of an insurer before the filing of a petition under this Article that results in a liquidation order, the indemnifying transfer or lien shall also be deemed to be voidable.

(f) The property affected by any lien deemed to be voidable under subsections (a) and (e) of this section shall be discharged from such lien, and that property and any of the indemnifying property transferred to or for the benefit of a surety shall pass to the liquidator; except that the Court may on due notice order any such lien to be preserved for the benefit of the estate, and the Court may direct that such conveyance be executed as may be proper or adequate to evidence the title of the liquidator.

(g) The Court shall have summary jurisdiction of any proceeding by the liquidator to hear and determine the rights of any parties under this section. Reasonable notice of any hearing in the proceeding shall be given to all parties in interest, including the obligee of a releasing bond or other like obligation. Where an order is entered for the recovery of indemnifying property in kind or for the avoidance of an indemnifying lien, the Court, upon application of any party in interest, shall in the same proceeding ascertain the value of the property or lien. If such value is less than the amount for which the property is indemnity or than the amount of the lien, the transferee or lienholder may elect to retain the property or lien upon payment of its value, as ascertained by the Court, to the liquidator, within such reasonable times as the Court shall fix.

(h) The liability of the surety under a releasing bond or other like obligation shall be discharged to the extent of the value of the indemnifying property recovered or the indemnifying lien nullified and avoided by the liquidator; or where the property is retained under subsection (g) of this section to the extent of the amount paid to the liquidator.

(i) If a creditor has been preferred and afterward in good faith gives the insurer further credit, without security of any kind, for property that becomes a part of the insurer's estate, the amount of the new credit remaining unpaid at the time of the petition may be set off against the preference that would otherwise be recoverable from him.

(j) If an insurer, within four months before the filing of a successful petition for liquidation under this Article, or at any time in contemplation of a proceeding to liquidate it, directly or indirectly pays money or transfers property to an attorney at law for services rendered or to be rendered, such transactions may be examined by the Court on its own motion or on petition of the liquidator, and shall be held valid only to the extent of a reasonable amount to be determined by the Court. Any excess may be recovered by the liquidator for the benefit of the estate; provided that where the attorney is in a position of influence in the insurer or an affiliate thereof, payment of any money or the transfer of any property to the attorney at law for services rendered or to be rendered shall be governed by the provision of subdivision (a)(4) of this section.

(k) Every officer, manager, employee, shareholder, member, subscriber, attorney, or any other person acting on behalf of the insurer who knowingly participates in giving any preference, when he has reasonable cause to believe the insurer is or is about to become insolvent at the time of the preference, shall be personally liable to the liquidator for the amount of the preference. It is permissible to infer that there is a reasonable cause to so believe if the transfer was made within four months before the date of filing of the successful petition for liquidation. Every person receiving any property from the insurer or the benefit thereof as a preference voidable under subsection (a) of this section shall be personally liable therefor and shall be bound to account to the liquidator. Nothing in this subsection prejudices any other claim by the liquidator against any person. (1989, c. 452, s. 1.)

§ 58-30-155. Claims of holders of void or voidable rights.

(a) No claims of a creditor who has received or acquired a preference, lien, conveyance, transfer, assignment, or encumbrance voidable under this Article shall be allowed unless he surrenders the preference, lien, conveyance, transfer, assignment or encumbrance. If the avoidance is effected by a proceeding in which a final judgment has been entered, the claim shall not be allowed unless the money is paid or the property is delivered to the liquidator within 30 days from the date of the entering of the final judgment; except that the Court having jurisdiction over the liquidation may allow further time if there is an appeal or other continuation of the proceeding.

(b) A claim allowable under subsection (a) of this section by reason of the avoidance, whether voluntary or involuntary, of a preference, lien, conveyance, transfer, assignment, or encumbrance, may be filed as an excused late filing under G.S. 58-30-185 if filed within 30 days from the date of the avoidance, or within the further time allowed by the Court under subsection (a) of this section. (1989, c. 452, s. 1.)

§ 58-30-160. Setoffs.

(a) Mutual debts or mutual credits, whether arising out of one or more contracts between the insurer and another person in connection with any action or proceeding under this Article shall be set off and the balance only shall be allowed or paid, except as provided in subsections (b), (d), and (e) of this section and in G.S. 58-30-175.

(b) No setoff shall be allowed in favor of any person where:
  (1) The obligation of the insurer to the person would not at the date of the filing of a petition for liquidation entitle the person to share as a claimant in the assets of the insurer;
  (2) The obligation of the insurer to the person was purchased by or transferred to the person with a view to its being used as a setoff;
  (3) The obligation of the person is to pay an assessment levied against the members or subscribers of the insurer, or is to pay a balance upon a subscription to the capital stock of the insurer, or is in any other way in the nature of a capital contribution;
  (4) Repealed by Session Laws 1995 (Regular Session, 1996), c. 658, s. 1, effective October 1, 1996.
  (5) The obligation of the insurer is owed to an affiliate of the person, or to any other entity or association other than the person;

    (6) The obligation of the person is owed to an affiliate of the insurer, or to any other entity or association other than the insurer;

    (7) The obligations between the person and the insurer arise out of transactions where either the person or the insurer has assumed risks and obligations from the other party and then has ceded back to that party substantially the same risks and obligations;

    (8) The obligation of the person is to pay to the insurer sums held in a fiduciary capacity for the insurer; or

    (9) The person alone or together with any other member of its insurance company holding system owns fifty percent (50%) or more of the voting stock of the insurer.

  (c) A setoff shall be permitted to local agents against agents' balances otherwise payable to the domiciliary or ancillary receiver for the amount expended by the agents to replace insurance coverage of their insureds and the reasonable expenses incident thereto as a result of any domestic, foreign or alien insurer being placed in delinquency proceedings. Agents claiming a setoff shall within 60 days of replacing coverage provide a verified accounting of the replacement of the insurance to the domiciliary receiver, the ancillary receiver, if any, and the North Carolina Insurance Guaranty Association or similar organization in the state of residence of the policyholder. The verified accounting shall include the name of the agent, the name of the insured, the policy number, the replacement policy number, the cost of the replacement policy, the amount of unearned premium under each policy as to which setoff is claimed, any claimed expenses and a verification that the accounting has been provided to each of the persons and entities described herein. Unearned premiums set off as provided above in any amount shall be deemed paid in full by the insurer and no person shall have a claim for the unearned premiums against the North Carolina Insurance Guaranty Association or similar organization in the state of residence of the policyholder.

  (d) The receiver shall provide persons with accounting statements identifying debts which are currently due and payable. Where a person owes to the insurer currently due and payable balances, against which the person asserts setoff of mutual credits which may become due and payable from the insurer in the future, the person shall promptly pay to the receiver the currently due and payable amount; provided that, notwithstanding any other provision of this Article, the receiver shall promptly and fully refund, to the extent of the person's prior payments, any mutual credits that become due and payable to the person by the insurer.

  (e) Notwithstanding any other provision of this section, a setoff of sums due on obligations in the nature of those set forth in subdivision (b)(7) of this section shall be allowed for those sums accruing from business written where the contracts were entered into, renewed, or extended with the express written approval of the insurance regulator of the state of domicile of the now insolvent insurer, when in the judgment of the regulator it was necessary to provide reinsurance in order to prevent or mitigate a threatened impairment or insolvency of the insurer in connection with the exercise of the regulator's official responsibilities. (1989, c. 452, s. 1; 1991, c. 681, s. 47; 1995 (Reg. Sess., 1996), c. 658, s. 1.)

§ 58-30-165. Assessments.

  (a) As soon as practicable but not more than two years from the date of an order of liquidation under G.S. 58-30-105 of an insurer issuing assessable policies, the liquidator shall make a report to the Court setting forth:

    (1) The reasonable value of the assets of the insurer;

    (2) The insurer's probable total liabilities;

    (3) The probable aggregate amount of the assessment necessary to pay all claims of creditors and expenses in full, including expenses of administration and costs of collecting the assessment; and

    (4) A recommendation as to whether an assessment should be made and in what amount.

  (b) Upon the basis of the report provided in subsection (a) of this section, including any supplements and amendments thereto, the Court may levy one or more assessments against all members of the insurer who are subject to assessment. Subject to any applicable legal limits on assessability, the aggregate assessment shall be for the amount that the sum of the probable liabilities, the expenses of administration, and the estimated cost of collection of the assessment, exceeds the value of existing assets, with due regard given to assessments that cannot be collected economically.

  (c) After a levy of assessment under subsection (b) of this section, the liquidator shall issue an order directing each member who has not paid the assessment pursuant to the order, to show cause why the liquidator should not pursue a judgment therefor.

  (d) The liquidator shall give notice of the order to show cause by publication and by first class mail to each member liable thereunder mailed to his last known address as it appears on the insurer's records, at least 20 days before the return day of the order to show cause.

  (e) If a member does not appear and serve duly verified objections upon the liquidator on or before the return day of the order to show cause under subsection (c) of this section, the Court shall make an order adjudging the member liable for the amount of the assessment against him pursuant to subsection (c) of this section, together with costs, and the liquidator shall have a judgment against the member therefor. If on or before such return day, the member appears and serves duly verified objections upon the liquidator, the Commissioner may hear and determine the matter or may appoint a referee to hear it and make such order as the facts warrant. In the event that the Commissioner determines that such objections do not warrant relief from assessment, the member may request the Court to review the matter and vacate the order to show cause.

  (f) The liquidator may enforce any order or collect any judgment under subsection (e) of this section by any lawful means. (1989, c. 452, s. 1.)

§ 58-30-170. Reinsurer's liability.

  The amount recoverable by the liquidator from reinsurers shall not be reduced as a result of the delinquency proceedings, regardless of any provision in the reinsurance contract or other agreement. Payment made directly to an insured or other creditor does not diminish the reinsurer's obligation to the insurer's estate except;

    (1) Where the contract specifically provides for another payee of the reinsurance in the event of the insolvency of the ceding insurer or

    (2) Where the assuming insurer, with the consent of the direct insured or insureds, has assumed the policy obligations of the ceding insurer as direct obligations of the assuming insurer to the payees under policies and in substitution of the obligations of the ceding insurer to the payees. (1989, c. 452, s. 1.)

§ 58-30-175. Recovery of premiums owed.

  (a) An agent, broker, premium finance company, or any other person, other than the insured, responsible for the payment of a premium is obligated to pay an unpaid premium for the full policy term due the insurer at the time of the declaration of insolvency, whether earned or unearned, as shown on the records of the insurer. The liquidator also has the right to recover from such person any part of an unearned premium that represents commission of such person. Except as provided in G.S. 58-30-160, credits or setoffs or both are not allowed to an agent, broker, or premium finance company for any amounts advanced to the insurer by the agent, broker, or premium finance company on behalf of, but in the absence of a payment by, the insured.

(b) An insured is obligated to pay any unpaid premium due the insurer at the time of the declaration of insolvency, as shown on the records of the insurer. (1989, c. 452, s. 1.)

Editor's Note. — Session Laws 1991, c. 720, s. 23, directed that G.S. 58-30-175 be amended by substituting "67" for "64" in subdivision (9). However, there is no subdivision (9) in G.S. 58-30-175. The Legislature probably intended the act to amend G.S. 58-30-75. Such a correction was subsequently made to G.S. 58-30-75 by Session Laws 1995, c. 193, s. 31.

§ 58-30-180. Domiciliary liquidator's proposal to distribute assets.

(a) Within 120 days of a final determination of insolvency of an insurer by the Court, the liquidator shall make application to the Court for approval of a proposal to disburse assets out of marshalled assets, from time to time as such assets become available, to a domestic or foreign guaranty association having obligations because of such insolvency. If the liquidator determines that there are insufficient assets to disburse, the application required by this section shall be considered satisfied by a filing by the liquidator stating the reasons for this determination.

(b) Such proposal shall at least include provisions for:

(1) Reserving amounts for the payment of expenses of administration and the payment of claims of secured creditors, to the extent of the value of the security held, and claims falling within the priorities established in G.S. 58-30-220(1) and (4);

(2) Disbursement of the assets marshalled to date and subsequent disbursement of assets as they become available;

(3) Equitable allocation of disbursements to each of the domestic and foreign guaranty associations entitled thereto;

(4) The securing by the liquidator from each of the associations entitled to disbursements pursuant to this section of an agreement to return to the liquidator such assets, together with income earned on assets previously disbursed, as may be required to pay claims of secured creditors and claims falling within the priorities established in G.S. 58-30-220 in accordance with such priorities. No bond shall be required of any such association; and

(5) A full report to be made by each association to the liquidator accounting for all assets so disbursed to the association, all disbursements made therefrom, any interest earned by the association on such assets and any other matter as the Court directs.

(c) The liquidator's proposal shall provide for disbursements to the associations in amounts estimated at least equal to the claim payments made or to be made thereby for which such associations could assert a claim against the liquidator; and shall further provide that if the assets available for disbursement from time to time do not equal or exceed the amount of such claim payments made or to be made by the association then disbursements shall be in the amount of available assets.

(d) The liquidator's proposal shall, with respect to an insolvent insurer writing life or health insurance or annuities, provide for disbursements of assets to any domestic or foreign guaranty association covering life or health insurance or annuities or to any other entity reinsuring, assuming, or guaranteeing policies or contracts of insurance under the acts creating such associations.

(e) Notice of such application shall be given to the association in and to the insurance regulators of each of the states. Any such notice shall be deemed to have been given when deposited in United States certified mail, first class postage prepaid, at least 30 days prior to submission of such application to the Court. Action on the application may be taken by the Court provided the above required notice has been given and provided further that the liquidator's proposal complies with subdivisions (b)(1) and (b)(2) of this section. (1989, c. 452, s. 1; 1995, c. 517, s. 13.)

§ 58-30-185. Filing of claims.

(a) Proof of all claims shall be filed with the liquidator in the form required by G.S. 58-30-190 on or before the last day for filing specified in the notice required under G.S. 58-30-125, except that proof of claims for cash surrender values or other investment values in life insurance and annuities need not be filed unless the liquidator expressly so requires.

(b) The liquidator may permit a claimant making a late filing to share in distributions, whether past or future, as if he were not late, to the extent that any such payment will not prejudice the orderly administration of the liquidation, under the following circumstances:

(1) The existence of the claim was not known to the claimant and that he filed his claim as promptly thereafter as reasonably possible after learning of it;

(2) A transfer to a creditor was avoided under G.S. 58-30-140 through 58-30-150, or was voluntarily surrendered under G.S. 58-30-155, and that the filing satisfies the conditions of G.S. 58-30-155; and

(3) The valuation under G.S. 58-30-215, of security held by a secured creditor shows a deficiency, that is filed within 30 days after the valuation.

(c) The liquidator shall permit late filing claims to share in distributions, whether past or future, as if they were not late, if such claims are claims of a guaranty association or foreign guaranty association for reimbursement of covered claims paid or expenses incurred, or both, subsequent to the last day for filing where such payments were made and expenses incurred as provided by law. Claims of domestic and foreign guaranty associations for reimbursement of covered claims paid or expenses incurred shall be deemed to be absolute.

(d) The liquidator may consider any claim filed late that is not covered by subsection (b) of this section, and permit it to receive distributions that are subsequently declared on any claims of the same or lower priority if the payment does not prejudice the orderly administration of the liquidation. The late-filing claimant shall receive, at each distribution, the same percentage of the amount allowed on his claim as is then being paid to claimants of any lower priority. This shall continue until his claim has been paid in full. (1989, c. 452, s. 1.)

§ 58-30-190. Proof of claim.

(a) Proof of claim shall consist of a statement signed by the claimant that includes all of the following that are applicable:

(1) The particulars of the claim, including the consideration given for it;

(2) The identity and amount of the security on the claim;

   (3) The payments made on the debt, if any;

   (4) That the sum claimed is justly owing and that there is no setoff, counterclaim, or defense to the claim;

   (5) Any right of priority of payment or other specific right asserted by the claimant;

   (6) A copy of the written instrument that is the foundation of the claim; and

   (7) The name and address of the claimant and any attorney who represents him.

  (b) No claim need be considered or allowed if it does not contain all the information in subsection (a) of this section that may be applicable. The liquidator may require that a prescribed form be used, and may require that other information and documents be included.

  (c) At any time the liquidator may request the claimant to present information or evidence supplementary to that required under subsection (a) of this section; and may take testimony under oath, require production of affidavits or depositions, or otherwise obtain additional information or evidence.

  (d) No judgment or order against an insured or the insurer entered after the date of filing of a successful petition for liquidation, and no judgment or order against an insured or the insurer entered at any time by default or by collusion, need be considered as evidence of liability or of amount of damages. No judgment or order against an insured or the insurer entered within four months before the filing of the petition need be considered as evidence of liability or of the amount of damages.

  (e) All claims of a guaranty association or foreign guaranty association shall be in such form and contain such substantiation as may be agreed to by the association and the liquidator; and failing such agreement as ordered by the Court. (1989, c. 452, s. 1.)

CASE NOTES

  Cited in State ex rel. Long v. Interstate Cas. Ins. Co., 106 N.C. App. 470, 417 S.E.2d 296 (1992).

§ 58-30-195. Special claims.

  (a) No contingent claim shall share in a distribution of the assets of an insurer that has been adjudicated to be insolvent by an order made pursuant to G.S. 58-30-105; except that such claims shall be considered, if properly presented, and may be allowed to share where:

   (1) Such claim becomes absolute against the insurer on or before the last day fixed for filing of proofs of claim against the assets of such insurer, or

   (2) There is a surplus and the liquidation is thereafter conducted upon the basis that such insurer is solvent.

  (b) Where an insurer has been so adjudicated to be insolvent, any person who has a cause of action against an insured of such insurer under a liability insurance policy issued by such insurer, has the right to file a claim in the liquidation proceedings, regardless of the fact that such claim may be contingent, and such claim may be allowed:

   (1) If it may be reasonably inferred from the proof presented upon such claim that such person would be able to obtain a judgment upon such cause of action against such insured; and

   (2) If such person furnishes suitable proof, unless the Court for good cause shown otherwise directs, that no further valid claims against such

insurer arising out of his cause of action other than those already presented can be made; and

   (3) If the total liability of such insurer to all claimants arising out of the same act of its insured is no greater than its total liability would be were it not in liquidation.

No judgment against such an insured taken after the date of the entry of the liquidation order shall be considered in the liquidation proceedings as evidence of liability or of the amount of damages, and no judgment against an insured taken by default, inquest, or by collusion prior to the entry of the liquidation order shall be considered as conclusive evidence in the liquidation proceeding, either of the liability of such insured to such person upon such cause of action or of the amount of damages to which such person is therein entitled.

   (c) No claim of any secured claimant shall be allowed at a sum greater than the difference between the value of the claim without security and the value of the security itself as of the date of entry of the order of liquidation or such other date set by the Court for fixation of rights and liabilities as provided in G.S. 58-30-105 unless the claimant surrenders his security to the Commissioner, in which event the claim shall be allowed in the full amount for which it is valued.

   (d) Claims that are due but for the passage of time, including any structured settlements or judgments involving periodic payments, shall be treated the same as absolute claims, except that such claims may be discounted at the legal rate of interest.

   (e) Claims made under employment contracts by directors, principal officers, or persons in fact performing similar functions or having similar powers, are limited to payment for services rendered prior to the issuance of any order of rehabilitation or liquidation under this Article. (1989, c. 452, s. 1.)

§ 58-30-200. Special provisions for third party claims.

   (a) Whenever any third party asserts a cause of action against an insured of an insurer in liquidation, the third party may file a claim with the liquidator.

   (b) Whether or not the third party files a claim, the insured may file a claim on his own behalf in the liquidation. If the insured fails to file a claim by the date for filing claims specified in the order of liquidation or within 60 days after mailing of the notice required by G.S. 58-30-125, whichever is later, he is an unexcused late filer.

   (c) The liquidator shall make his recommendations to the Court under G.S. 58-30-225 for the allowance of an insured's claim under subsection (b) of this section after consideration of the probable outcome of any pending action against the insured on which the claim is based, the probable damages recoverable in the action, and the probable costs and expenses of defense. After allowance by the Court, the liquidator shall withhold any dividends payable on the claim, pending the outcome of litigation and negotiation with the insured. Whenever it seems appropriate, he shall reconsider the claim on the basis of additional information and amend his recommendations to the Court. The insured shall be afforded the same notice and opportunity to be heard on all changes in the recommendation as in its initial determination. The Court may amend its allowance as it thinks appropriate. As claims against the insured are settled or barred, the insured shall be paid from the amount withheld the same percentage dividend as was paid on other claims of like property, based on the lesser of (i) the amount actually recovered from the insured by action or paid by agreement plus the reasonable costs and expense of defense, or (ii) the amount allowed on the claims by the Court. After all claims are settled or barred, any sum remaining from the amount withheld shall revert to the undistributed assets of the insurer. Delay in final payment under this subsection shall not be a reason for unreasonable delay of final distribution and discharge of the liquidator.

(d) No claim may be presented under this section if it is or may be covered by any domestic or foreign guaranty association. (1989, c. 452, s. 1; 2003-221, s. 14.)

Effect of Amendments. — Session Laws 2003-221, s. 14, effective June 19, 2003, substituted "G.S. 58-30-225" for "G.S. 58-30-125" in the first sentence of subsection (c).

§ 58-30-205. Disputed claims.

(a) When a claim is denied in whole or in part by the liquidator, written notice of the determination shall be given to the claimant or his attorney by first class mail at the address shown in the proof of claim. Within 60 days from the mailing of the notice, the claimant may file his objections with the liquidator. If no such filing is made, the claimant may not further object to the determination.

(b) Whenever objections are filed with the liquidator and the liquidator does not alter his denial of the claim as a result of the objections, the liquidator shall ask the Court for a hearing as soon as practicable and give notice of the hearing by first class mail to the claimant or his attorney and to any other persons directly affected, not less than 10 nor more than 30 days before the date of the hearing. The matter may be heard by the Court or by a court-appointed referee who shall submit findings of fact along with his recommendation. (1989, c. 452, s. 1.)

CASE NOTES

Cited in State ex rel. Long v. Interstate Cas. Ins. Co., 106 N.C. App. 470, 417 S.E.2d 296 (1992).

§ 58-30-210. Claims of surety.

Whenever a creditor, whose claim against an insurer is secured in whole or in part by the undertaking of another person, fails to prove and file that claim, the other person may do so in the creditor's name and shall be subrogated to the rights of the creditor, whether the claim has been filed by the creditor or by the other person in the creditor's name, to the extent that he discharges the undertaking. In the absence of an agreement with the creditor to the contrary, the other person shall not be entitled to any distribution until the amount paid to the creditor on the undertaking plus the distributions paid on the claim from the insurer's estate to the creditor equals the amount of the entire claim of the creditor. Any excess received by the creditor shall be held by him in trust for such other person. As used in this section, "other person" does not mean a guaranty association or foreign guaranty association. (1989, c. 452, s. 1.)

§ 58-30-215. Secured creditor's claims.

(a) The value of any security held by a secured creditor shall be determined in one of the following ways, as the Court may direct:

    (1) By converting the same into money according to the terms of the agreement pursuant to which the security was delivered to such creditors; or

    (2) By agreement, arbitration, compromise or litigation between the creditor and the liquidator.

(b) The determination shall be under the supervision and control of the Court with due regard for the recommendation of the liquidator. The amount so determined shall be credited upon the secured claim, and any deficiency shall be treated as an unsecured claim. If the claimant surrenders his security to the liquidator, the entire claim shall be allowed as if unsecured. (1989, c. 452, s. 1; 1991, c. 720, s. 68.)

§ 58-30-220. Priority of distribution.

The priority of distribution of claims from the insurer's estate shall be in accordance with the order in which each class of claims is set forth in this section. Every claim in each class shall be paid in full or adequate funds shall be retained for payment before the members of the next class receive any payment. No subcategories shall be established within the categories in a class. The order of distribution of claims shall be:

(1) The receiver's expenses for the administration and conservation of assets of the insurer.

(2) Claims or portions of claims for benefits under policies and for losses incurred, including claims of third parties under liability policies; claims of HMO enrollees and HMO enrollees' beneficiaries; claims for unearned premiums; claims for funds or consideration held under funding agreements, as defined in G.S. 58-7-16; claims under life insurance and annuity policies, whether for death proceeds, annuity proceeds, or investment values; and claims of domestic and foreign guaranty associations, including claims for the reasonable adminis-trative expenses of domestic and foreign guaranty associations; but excluding claims of insurance pools, underwriting associations, or those arising out of reinsurance agreements, claims of other insurers for subrogation, and claims of insurers for payments and settlements under uninsured and underinsured motorist coverages.

(2a) For HMOs, claims of providers and participating providers, as defined in G.S. 58-67-5(h) and G.S. 58-67-5(1)[(*l*)], who are obligated by statute, agreement, or court order to hold enrollees harmless from liability for services provided and covered by an HMO.

(3) Claims of the federal or any state or local government or taxing authority, including claims for taxes.

(4) Compensation actually owing to employees other than officers of the insurer for services rendered within three months before the com-mencement of a delinquency proceeding against the insurer under this Article, but not exceeding one thousand dollars ($1,000) for each employee. In the discretion of the Commissioner, this compensation may be paid as soon as practicable after the proceeding has been commenced. This priority is in lieu of any other similar priority that may be authorized by law as to wages or compensation of those employees.

(5) Claims of general creditors, including claims of insurance pools, underwriting associations, or those arising out of reinsurance agree-ments; claims of other insurers for subrogation; and claims of insurers for payments and settlements under uninsured and underinsured motorist coverages. (1989, c. 452, s. 1; 1993 (Reg. Sess., 1994), c. 600, s. 2; 1995, c. 517, s. 14; 1998-211, s. 4.)

CASE NOTES

Editor's Note. — *Some of the cases below were decided under prior statutory provisions.*

"Reinsurers" Defined. — The legislature did not intend, by its use of the word "reinsurers" in former G.S. 58-155.15, to de-scribe only those insurers to whom a risk is ceded by reinsurance. Instead, the General Assembly intended the word "reinsurers" as a comprehensive term, referring to all parties involved in reinsurance transactions, whether as ceding insurers or as assuming insurers. State ex rel. Long v. Beacon Ins. Co., 87 N.C. App. 72, 359 S.E.2d 508 (1987), cert. denied, 321 N.C. 480, 364 S.E.2d 671 (1988).

The conclusion that "reinsurers" was intended by the legislature as a comprehensive term, including all parties to a contract of reinsurance, was reinforced by the provisions of 1987 Sess. Laws, c. 864, which implicitly acknowledged that the word "reinsurers" was inaptly used in the original enactment of the statute and expressed an unequivocal legislative intent that all claims arising out of contracts of reinsurance were to be excluded from the priority created by subdivision (a)(3) of former G.S. 58-155.15 and were to be treated the same as claims of general creditors pursuant to subdivision (a)(5) of that section. State ex rel. Long v. Beacon Ins. Co., 87 N.C. App. 72, 359 S.E.2d 508 (1987), cert. denied, 321 N.C. 480, 364 S.E.2d 671 (1988).

Claims growing out of contracts of reinsurance with insolvent insurer are entitled to no higher priority than the claims of general creditors for the purposes of subsection (a) of former G.S. 58-155.15. State ex rel. Long v. Beacon Ins. Co., 87 N.C. App. 72, 359 S.E.2d 508 (1987), cert. denied, 321 N.C. 480, 364 S.E.2d 671 (1988).

Common Fund Doctrine Precluded. — The comprehensive nature of this section precludes the application of any equitable doctrine — including the common fund doctrine — to alter the Class 5 priority assigned to attorneys' claims for fees in insurance company liquidation. State ex rel. Long v. Interstate Cas. Ins. Guar. Ass'n, 120 N.C. App. 743, 464 S.E.2d 73 (1995).

Assets Must Be Part of the Insurer's Estate. — "Assets," as used in subsection (1), must refer to items listed by the liquidator which become part of the "insurer's estate." Class 1 priority, therefore, is awarded only to entities which conserve or administer assets of the insurer after the items have become part of the "insurer's estate." State ex rel. Long v. Interstate Cas. Ins. Guar. Ass'n, 120 N.C. App. 743, 464 S.E.2d 73 (1995).

§ 58-30-225. Liquidator's recommendations to the Court.

(a) The liquidator shall review all claims duly filed in the liquidation and shall make such further investigation as necessary. He may compound, compromise, or in any other manner negotiate the amount for which claims will be recommended to the Court except where he is required by law to accept claims as settled by any person or organization, including any domestic or foreign guaranty association. Unresolved disputes shall be determined under G.S. 58-30-205. As soon as practicable, the liquidator shall present to the Court a report of the claims against the insurer with his recommendations. The report shall include the name and address of each claimant and the amount of any claim finally recommended. If the insurer has issued annuities or life insurance policies, the liquidator shall report the persons to whom, according to the records of the insurer, amounts are owed as cash surrender values or other investment values and the amounts owed.

(b) The Court may approve, disapprove, or modify the report on claims by the liquidator. Such reports that are not modified by the Court within a period of 60 days following submission by the liquidator shall be treated by the liquidator as allowed claims, subject thereafter to later modification or to rulings made by the Court pursuant to G.S. 58-30-205. No claim under a policy of insurance shall be allowed for an amount in excess of the applicable policy benefits. (1989, c. 452, s. 1.)

CASE NOTES

Because of the discretionary nature of subsection (b), the trial court's decision regarding priority should not be disturbed absent an abuse of discretion. State ex rel. Long v. Interstate Cas. Ins. Guar. Ass'n, 120 N.C. App. 743, 464 S.E.2d 73 (1995).

§ 58-30-230. Distribution of assets.

(a) Under the direction of the Court, the liquidator shall pay distributions in a manner that will assure the proper recognition of priorities and a reasonable balance between the expeditious completion of the liquidation and the protection of unliquidated and undetermined claims, including third party claims. Distribution of assets in kind may be made at valuations set by agreement between the liquidator and the creditor and approved by the Court.

(b) Interest on claims shall be paid only after all claims have been paid under subsection (a) of this section. This subsection does not apply to interest awarded as part of a judgment. (1989, c. 452, s. 1.)

§ 58-30-235. Unclaimed and withheld funds.

(a) All unclaimed funds subject to distribution remaining in the liquidator's hands when he is ready to apply to the Court for discharge, including the amount distributable to any creditor, shareholder, member, or other person who is unknown or cannot be found, shall be deposited with the State Treasurer, and shall be paid without interest except in accordance with G.S. 58-30-220 to the person entitled thereto or his legal representative upon proof satisfactory to the State Treasurer of his right thereto. Any amount on deposit not claimed within six years from the discharge of the liquidator shall be considered abandoned and shall be escheated without formal escheat proceedings.

(b) All funds withheld under G.S. 58-30-195 and not distributed shall upon discharge of the liquidator be deposited with the State Treasurer and paid by him in accordance with G.S. 58-30-220. Any sums remaining that under G.S. 58-30-220 would revert to the undistributed assets of the insurer shall be transferred to the State Treasurer and become the property of the State under subsection (a) of this section, unless the Commissioner in his discretion petitions the Court to reopen the liquidation under G.S. 58-30-245. (1989, c. 452, s. 1.)

§ 58-30-240. Termination of proceedings.

(a) When all assets justifying the expense of collection and distribution have been collected and distributed under this Article, the liquidator shall apply to the Court for discharge. The Court may grant the discharge and make any other orders, including an order to transfer any remaining funds that are uneconomic to distribute, as may be deemed appropriate.

(b) Any other person may apply to the Court at any time for an order under subsection (a) of this section. If the application is denied, the applicant shall pay the costs and expenses of the liquidator in resisting the application, including reasonable attorney fees. (1989, c. 452, s. 1.)

§ 58-30-245. Reopening liquidation.

After the liquidation proceeding has been terminated and the liquidator discharged, the Commissioner or other interested party may at any time petition the Court to reopen the proceedings for good cause, including the discovery of additional assets. If the Court is satisfied that there is justification for reopening, it shall so order. (1989, c. 452, s. 1.)

§ 58-30-250. Disposition of records during and after termination of liquidation.

Whenever it appears to the Commissioner that the records of any insurer in process of liquidation or completely liquidated are no longer useful, he may recommend to the Court and the Court shall direct what records should be retained for future reference and what should be destroyed. (1989, c. 452, s. 1.)

§ 58-30-255. External audit of the receiver's books.

The Court may, as it deems to be desirable, cause audits to be made of the books of the Commissioner relating to any receivership established under this Article, and a report of each audit shall be filed with the Commissioner and with the Court. The books, records, and other documents of the receivership shall be made available to any auditor at any time without notice. The expense of each audit shall be considered a cost of administration of the receivership. (1989, c. 452, s. 1.)

§ 58-30-260. Conservation of property of foreign or alien insurers found in this State.

(a) If a domiciliary liquidator has not been appointed, the Commissioner may apply to the Court by verified petition for an order directing him to act as conservator to conserve the property of an alien insurer not domiciled in this State or a foreign insurer on any one or more of the following grounds:

(1) Any of the grounds in G.S. 58-30-75;
(2) That any of its property has been sequestered by official action in its domiciliary state, or in any other state;
(3) That enough of its property has been sequestered in an alien country to give reasonable cause to fear that the insurer is or may become insolvent;
(4) That its license to do business in this State has been revoked or that none was ever issued; and that there are residents of this State with outstanding claims or outstanding policies.

(b) When an order is sought under subsection (a) of this section, the Court shall cause the insurer to be given such notice and time to respond thereto as is reasonable under the circumstances.

(c) The Court may issue the order in whatever terms it shall deem appropriate. The filing or recording of the order with the clerk of court or the register of deeds of the county in which the principal business of the company is located, shall impart the same notice as a deed, bill of sale or other evidence of title duly filed or recorded with that register of deeds would have imparted.

(d) The conservator may at any time petition for and the Court may grant an order under G.S. 58-30-265 to liquidate assets of a foreign or alien insurer under conservation, or, if appropriate, for an order under G.S. 58-30-275, to be appointed ancillary receiver.

(e) The conservator may at any time petition the Court for an order terminating conservation of an insurer. If the Court finds that the conservation is no longer necessary, it shall order that the insurer be restored to possession of its property and the control of its business. The Court may also make such finding and issue such order at any time upon motion of any interested party, but if such motion is denied all costs shall be assessed against such party. (1989, c. 452, s. 1; 1999-132, s. 9.1.)

CASE NOTES

Editor's Note. — The case below was decided under prior statutory provisions.

Creditors in nondomiciliary states are at liberty to prefer themselves by commencing attachment or similar proceedings against such property as may be found in their respective states. This, of course, results in inequity as to other creditors. North Carolina Reinsurance Facility v. North Carolina Ins. Guar. Ass'n, 67 N.C. App. 359, 313 S.E.2d 253 (1984).

Wasteful conflicts are likely to arise be-

tween the domiciliary and the ancillary receivers during the administration of the assets since each receiver feels bound to seize as much of the company's property as possible in order that he may protect local creditors to the greatest possible extent. By requiring consolidation of general assets with the domiciliary receiver, while allowing local general creditors to prove their claims locally, the Uniform Insurers Liquidation Act resolved problems both of unfair preferences for local creditors and of unnecessary hardship to them in participating in the domiciliary proceedings. North Carolina Reinsurance Facility v. North Carolina Ins. Guar. Ass'n, 67 N.C. App. 359, 313 S.E.2d 253 (1984).

§ 58-30-265. Liquidation of property of foreign or alien insurers found in this State.

(a) If no domiciliary receiver has been appointed, the Commissioner may apply to the Court by verified petition for an order directing him to liquidate the assets found in this State of a foreign insurer or an alien insurer not domiciled in this State, on any of the following grounds:

(1) Any of the grounds in G.S. 58-30-75 or G.S. 58-30-100; or

(2) Any of the grounds specified in G.S. 58-30-260(a)(2) through (4).

(b) When an order is sought under subsection (a) of this section, the Court shall cause the insurer to be given such notice and time to respond thereto as is reasonable under the circumstances.

(c) If it appears to the Court that the best interests of creditors, policyholders, and the public require, the Court may issue an order to liquidate in whatever terms it deems to be appropriate. The filing or recording of the order with the clerk of the Court or the register of deeds of the county in which the principal business of the insurer is located or the county in which its principal office or place of business is located, shall impart the same notice as a deed, bill of sale, or other evidence of title duly filed or recorded with that register of deeds would have imparted.

(d) If a domiciliary liquidator is appointed in a reciprocal state while a liquidation is proceeding under this section, the liquidator under this section shall thereafter act as ancillary receiver under G.S. 58-30-275. If a domiciliary liquidator is appointed in a nonreciprocal state while a liquidation is proceeding under this section, the liquidator under this section, may petition the court for permission to act as ancillary receiver under G.S. 58-30-275.

(e) On the same grounds as are specified in subsection (a) of this section, the Commissioner may petition any appropriate federal district court to be appointed receiver to liquidate that portion of the insurer's assets and business over which that court will exercise jurisdiction, or any lesser part thereof that the Commissioner considers desirable for the protection of the policyholders and creditors in this State.

(f) The Court may order the Commissioner, when he has liquidated the assets of a foreign or alien insurer under this section, to pay claims of residents of this State against the insurer under such rules as to the liquidation of insurers under this Article as are otherwise compatible with the provisions of this section. (1989, c. 452, s. 1.)

§ 58-30-270. Domiciliary liquidators in other states.

(a) The domiciliary liquidator of an insurer domiciled in a reciprocal state is, except as to special deposits and security on secured claims under G.S. 58-30-275(c), vested by operation of law with the title to all of the assets, property, contracts and rights of action, agents' balances, and all of the books, accounts, and other records of the insurer located in this State. The date of vesting shall be the date of the filing of the petition, if that date is specified by the domiciliary law for the vesting of property in the domiciliary state. Otherwise, the date of vesting shall be the date of entry of the order directing possession to be taken. The domiciliary liquidator shall have the immediate right to recover the balances due from agents and to obtain possession of the books, accounts, and other records of the insurer located in this State. He also shall have the right to recover all other assets of the insurer located in this State, subject to G.S. 58-30-275.

(b) If a domiciliary liquidator is appointed for an insurer not domiciled in a reciprocal state, the Commissioner shall be vested by operation of law with the title to all of the property, contracts, and rights of action, and all of the books, accounts and other records of the insurer located in this State, at the same time that the domiciliary liquidator is vested with title in the domicile. The Commissioner may petition for a conservation or liquidation order under G.S. 58-30-260 and G.S. 58-30-265, or for an ancillary receivership under G.S. 58-30-275, or after approval by the Court may transfer title to the domiciliary liquidator, as the interests of justice and the equitable distribution of the assets require.

(c) Claimants residing in this State may file claims with the liquidator or ancillary receiver, if any, in this State or with the domiciliary liquidator, if the domiciliary law permits. The claims must be filed on or before the last date fixed for the filing of claims in the domiciliary liquidation proceedings. (1989, c. 452, s. 1.)

§ 58-30-275. Ancillary formal proceedings.

(a) If a domiciliary liquidator has been appointed for an insurer not domiciled in this State, the Commissioner may file a petition with the Court requesting appointment as ancillary receiver in this State:

    (1) If he finds that there are sufficient assets of the insurer located in this State to justify the appointment of an ancillary receiver;

    (2) If the protection of creditors or policyholders in this State so requires.

(b) The Court may issue an order appointing an ancillary receiver in whatever terms it deems to be appropriate, including provisions for payment of the reasonable and necessary expenses of the proceedings. The filing or recording of the order with a register of deeds in this State imparts the same notice as a deed, bill of sale, or other evidence of title duly filed or recorded with that register of deeds.

(c) When a domiciliary liquidator has been appointed in a reciprocal state, then the ancillary receiver appointed in this State, may, whenever necessary, aid and assist the domiciliary liquidator in recovering assets of the insurer located in this State. The ancillary receiver shall, as soon as practicable, liquidate from their respective securities those special deposit claims and secured claims which are proved and allowed in the ancillary proceedings in this State, and shall pay the necessary expenses of the proceedings. He shall promptly transfer all remaining assets, books, accounts, and records to the domiciliary liquidator. Subject to this section, the ancillary receiver and his deputies shall have the same powers and be subject to the same duties with respect to the administration of assets as a liquidator of an insurer domiciled in this State.

(d) When a domiciliary liquidator has been appointed in this State, ancillary receivers appointed in reciprocal states shall have, as to assets and books, accounts, and other records in their respective states, corresponding rights, duties and powers to those provided in subsection (c) of this section for ancillary receivers appointed in this State. (1989, c. 452, s. 1; 1993 (Reg. Sess., 1994), c. 678, s. 17.)

§ 58-30-280. Ancillary summary proceedings.

The Commissioner in his sole discretion may institute proceedings under G.S. 58-30-60 through 58-30-70 at the request of the insurance regulator of the domiciliary state of any foreign or alien insurer having property located in this State. (1989, c. 452, s. 1.)

§ 58-30-285. Claims of nonresidents against insurers domiciled in this State.

(a) In a liquidation proceeding begun in this State against an insurer domiciled in this State, claimants residing in foreign countries or in states not reciprocal states must file claims in this State, and claimants residing in reciprocal states may file claims either with the ancillary receivers, if any, in their respective states, or with the domiciliary liquidator. Claims must be filed on or before the last date fixed for the filing of claims in the domiciliary liquidation proceeding.

(b) Claims belonging to claimants residing in reciprocal states may be proved either in the liquidation proceeding in this State as provided in this Article, or in ancillary proceedings, if any, in the reciprocal states. If notice of the claims and opportunity to appear and be heard is afforded the domiciliary liquidator of this State as provided in G.S. 58-30-290(b) with respect to ancillary proceedings, the final allowance of claims by the courts in ancillary proceedings in reciprocal states shall be conclusive as to amount and as to priority against special deposits or other security located in such ancillary states, but shall not be conclusive with respect to priorities against general assets under G.S. 58-30-220. (1989, c. 452, s. 1.)

§ 58-30-290. Claims of residents against insurers domiciled in reciprocal states.

(a) In a liquidation proceeding in a reciprocal state against an insurer domiciled in that state, claimants against the insurer who reside within this State may file claims either with the ancillary receiver, if any, in this State, or with the domiciliary liquidator. Claims must be filed on or before the last dates fixed for the filing of claims in the domiciliary proceeding.

(b) Claims belonging to claimants residing in this State may be proved either in the domiciliary state under the law of that state, or in ancillary proceedings, if any, in this State. If a claimant elects to prove his claim in this State, he shall file his claim with the liquidator in the manner provided in G.S. 58-30-185 and G.S. 58-30-190. The ancillary receiver shall make his recommendation to the Court as under G.S. 58-30-225. He shall also arrange a date for hearing if necessary under G.S. 58-30-205 and shall give notice to the liquidator in the domiciliary state, either by certified mail or by personal service at least 40 days prior to the date set for hearing. If the domiciliary liquidator, within 30 days after the giving of such notice, gives notice in writing to the ancillary receiver and to the claimant, either by certified mail or by personal service, of his intention to contest the claim, he shall be entitled to appear or to be represented in any proceedings in this State involving the adjudication of the claim.

(c) The final allowance of the claim by the courts of this State shall be accepted as conclusive as to amount and as to priority against special deposits or other security located in this State. (1989, c. 452, s. 1.)

CASE NOTES

Creditors in nondomiciliary states are at liberty to prefer themselves by commencing attachment or similar proceedings against such property as may be found in their respective states. This, of course, results in inequity as to other creditors. North Carolina Reinsurance Facility v. North Carolina Ins. Guar. Ass'n, 67 N.C. App. 359, 313 S.E.2d 253 (1984).

Wasteful conflicts are likely to arise between the domiciliary and the ancillary receivers during the administration of the assets since each receiver feels bound to seize as much of the company's property as possible in order that he may protect local creditors to the greatest possible extent. By requiring consolidation of general assets with the domiciliary receiver, while allowing local general creditors to prove their claims locally, the Uniform Insurers Liquidation Act resolved problems both of unfair preferences for local creditors and of unnecessary hardship to them in participating in the domiciliary proceedings. North Carolina Reinsurance Facility v. North Carolina Ins. Guar. Ass'n, 67 N.C. App. 359, 313 S.E.2d 253 (1984).

§ 58-30-295. Attachment, garnishment and levy of execution.

During the pendency in this or any other state of a liquidation proceeding, whether called by that name or not, no action or proceeding in the nature of an attachment, garnishment, or levy of execution shall be commenced or maintained in this State against the delinquent insurer or its assets. (1989, c. 452, s. 1.)

§ 58-30-300. Interstate priorities.

(a) In a liquidation proceeding in this State involving one or more reciprocal states, the order of distribution of the domiciliary state shall control as to all claims of residents of this and reciprocal states. All claims of residents of reciprocal states shall be given equal priority of payment from general assets regardless of where such assets are located.

(b) The owners of special deposit claims against an insurer for which a liquidator is appointed in this or any other state shall be given priority against the special deposits in accordance with the statutes governing the creation and maintenance of the deposits. If there is a deficiency in any deposit, so that the claims secured by it are not fully discharged from it, the claimants may share in the general assets, but the sharing shall be deferred until general creditors, and also claimants against other special deposits who have received smaller percentages from their respective special deposits, have been paid percentages of their claims equal to the percentage paid from the special deposit.

(c) The owner of a secured claim against an insurer for which a liquidator has been appointed in this or any other state may surrender the owner's security and file the claim as a general creditor, or the claim may be discharged by resort to the security in accordance with G.S. 58-30-215 in which case the deficiency, if any, shall be treated as a claim against the general assets of the insurer on the same basis as claims of unsecured creditors. (1989, c. 452, s. 1; 1995, c. 193, s. 32.)

§ 58-30-305. Subordination of claims for noncooperation.

If an ancillary receiver in another state or foreign country, whether called by that name or not, fails to transfer to the domiciliary liquidator in this State any assets within his control other than special deposits, diminished only by the expenses of the ancillary receivership, if any, the claims filed in the ancillary receivership, other than special deposit claims or secured claims shall be placed in the class of claims under G.S. 58-30-220(5). (1989, c. 452, s. 1.)

§ 58-30-310. Exemption from filing fees.

As used in this section, "Commissioner" includes the Commissioner's deputies, employees, or attorneys of record. The Commissioner is not required to pay any fee to any public officer in this State for filing, recording, issuing a transcript or certificate, or authenticating any paper or instrument pertaining to the exercise by the Commissioner of any of the powers or duties conferred upon him under this Article. This section applies whether or not the paper or instrument is connected with the commencement of an action or proceeding by or against the Commissioner or with the subsequent conduct of an action or proceeding. (1989 (Reg. Sess., 1990), c. 1069, s. 15.)

ARTICLE 31.

Insuring State Property, Officials and Employees.

§ 58-31-1. State Property Fire Insurance Fund created.

Upon the expiration of all existing policies of fire insurance upon state-owned buildings, fixtures, furniture, and equipment, including all such property the title to which may be in any State department, institution, or agency, the State of North Carolina shall not reinsure any of such properties.

There is hereby created a "State Property Fire Insurance Fund," which shall be as a special fund in the State treasury, for the purpose of providing a reserve against loss from fire at State departments and institutions. The State Treasurer shall be the custodian of the "State Property Fire Insurance Fund" and shall invest its assets in accordance with the provisions of G.S. 147-69.2 and 147-69.3. The unexpended appropriations of State departments and institutions for fire insurance premiums for the fiscal year 1944-1945 and the appropriations for fire insurance premiums made for the biennium 1945-1947 or that may thereafter be made for this purpose shall be transferred to the "State Property Fire Insurance Fund." (1945, c. 1027, s. 1; 1963, c. 462; 1975, c. 519, s. 1; 1979, c. 467, s. 4.)

§ 58-31-5. Appropriations; fund to pay administrative expenses.

Upon the expiration of the existing fire insurance policies on said properties and in making appropriations for any biennium after the next biennium, the Commissioner shall file with the Department of Administration his estimate of the appropriations which will be necessary in order to set up and maintain an adequate reserve to provide a fund sufficient to protect the State, its departments, institutions, and agencies from loss or damage to any of said properties up to fifty per centum (50%) of the value thereof. Appropriations made for the creating of such fire insurance reserves against property of the Department of Agriculture and Consumer Services, or the Department of Transportation or any special operating fund shall be charged against the funds of such departments.

The State Property Fire Insurance Fund is authorized and empowered to pay all the administrative expenses occasioned by the administration of Article 31 of Chapter 58 of the General Statutes. (1945, c. 1027, s. 2; 1957, c. 65, s. 11; c. 269, s. 1; 1959, c. 182, s. 1; 1973, c. 507, s. 5; 1977, c. 464, s. 34; 1991, c. 720, s. 4; 1997-261, s. 109.)

§ 58-31-10. Payment of losses on basis of actual cost of restoration or replacement; rules; insurance and reinsurance; sprinkler leakage insurance.

(a) In the case of total or partial loss of any property of any State agency or institution, the Commissioner shall determine the amount of loss and certify that amount to the agency or institution concerned and to the Director of the Budget and Council of State. The Director of the Budget and Council of State may authorize transfers from the Fund to the agency or institution that suffered the loss in amounts that are necessary to pay for the actual cost of restoration or replacement of the property. In the event there is not a sufficient amount in the Fund to pay for the actual cost of restoration or replacement, the Director of the Budget and the Council of State may supplement the Fund by transferring amounts from the Contingency and Emergency Fund.

(b) The Commissioner, with the approval of the Council of State, is authorized to adopt rules necessary to carry out the purpose of this Article, which rules shall be binding on all State agencies and institutions. The Commissioner, with the approval of the Director of the Budget and the Council of State, is authorized to purchase from qualified insurers insurance or reinsurance necessary to protect the Fund against loss on any one building and its contents in excess of fifty thousand dollars ($50,000), and the premiums for this coverage shall be paid from the Fund.

(c) Upon the request of any State agency or institution, sprinkler leakage insurance shall be provided on designated property of the agency or institution that is insured by the Fund. Premiums for this coverage shall be paid by the requesting agency or institution in accordance with rates fixed by the Commissioner. Losses covered by this insurance may be paid out of the Fund in the same manner as other losses. The Commissioner, with the approval of the Director of the Budget and the Council of State, is authorized to purchase from qualified insurers insurance or reinsurance necessary to protect the Fund against loss with respect to sprinkler leakage insurance coverage. (1945, c. 1027, s. 3; 1951, c. 802; 1959, c. 182, s. 2; 1983, c. 913, s. 7; 1985, c. 786.)

§ 58-31-12. Policy forms.

The Commissioner, with the approval of the Council of State, may adopt insurance forms for coverages provided by the State Property Fire Insurance Fund under this Article. (1993, c. 409, s. 13.)

§ 58-31-13. Hazardous conditions in State-owned buildings.

If the Commissioner determines that an undue hazard to life, safety, or property exists because of a condition or the use of a building owned by the State, the Commissioner shall advise the proper agency how to limit or prohibit use of the building until the hazard is abated. (1993, c. 409, s. 13.)

§ 58-31-15. Extended coverage insurance.

Upon request of any State department, agency or institution, extended coverage insurance, and other property insurance, may be provided on designated state-owned property of such department, agency or institution which is insured by the State Property Fire Insurance Fund. Premiums for such insurance coverage shall be paid by each requesting department, agency or institution in accordance with rates fixed by the Commissioner. Losses covered by such insurance may be paid for out of the State Property Fire Insurance

Fund in the same manner as fire losses. The Commissioner, with the approval of the Governor and Council of State, is authorized and empowered to purchase from insurers admitted to do business in North Carolina such insurance or reinsurance as may be necessary to protect the State Property Fire Insurance Fund against loss with respect to such insurance coverage. The words "extended coverage insurance," as used in this section, mean insurance against loss or damage caused by windstorm, hail, explosion, riot, riot attending a strike, civil commotion, aircraft, vehicles or smoke. (1957, c. 67; 1975, c. 519, s. 2; 1991, c. 720, s. 4.)

§ 58-31-20. Use and occupancy and business interruption insurance.

Upon request of any State department, agency or institution, use and occupancy and business interruption insurance shall be provided on state-owned property of such department, agency or institution which is insured by the State Property Fire Insurance Fund. Premiums for such insurance coverage shall be paid by each requesting department, agency or institution in accordance with rates fixed by the Commissioner. Losses covered by such insurance may be paid for out of the State Property Fire Insurance Fund in the same manner as fire losses. The Commissioner, with the approval of the Governor and Council of State, is authorized and empowered to purchase from insurers admitted to do business in North Carolina such insurance or reinsurance as may be necessary to protect the State Property Fire Insurance Fund against loss with respect to such insurance coverage. (1957, c. 67; 1991, c. 720, s. 4.)

§ 58-31-25. Professional liability insurance for officials and employees of the State.

The Commissioner may acquire professional liability insurance covering the officers and employees of any State department, institution or agency upon the request of such State department, institution or agency. Premiums for such insurance coverage shall be paid by the requesting department, institution or agency at rates fixed by the Commissioner from funds made available to it for the purpose. The Commissioner, in placing a contract for such insurance is authorized to place such insurance through the Public Officers and Employees' Liability Insurance Commission, and shall exercise all efforts to place such insurance through the said commission prior to attempting to procure such insurance through any other source.

The Commissioner, pursuant to this section, may acquire professional liability insurance covering the officers and employees of a department, institution or agency of State government only if the coverage to be provided by such policy is coverage of claims in excess of the protection provided by Articles 31 and 31A of Chapter 143 of the General Statutes.

The purchase, by any State department, institution or agency of professional liability insurance covering the law-enforcement officers, officers or employees of such department, institution or agency shall not be construed as a waiver of any defense of sovereign immunity by such department, institution or agency. The purchase of such insurance shall not be deemed a waiver by any employee of the defense of sovereign immunity to the extent that such defense may be available to him.

The payment, by any State department, institution or agency of funds as premiums for professional liability insurance through the plan provided herein, covering the law-enforcement officers or officials or employees of such department, institution or agency is hereby declared to be for a public purpose. (1979, c. 206, s. 1; 1987, c. 864, s. 53; 1991, c. 720, s. 4.)

§ 58-31-30: Expired at the end of the 1993-94 fiscal year by its own terms.

Editor's Note. — This section expired at the end of the 1993-94 fiscal year pursuant to its own terms. See Session Laws 1989 (Reg. Sess., 1990), c. 1069, ss. 25, 26.

§ 58-31-35. Information furnished Commissioner by officers in charge.

It is the duty of the different officers or boards having in their custody any property belonging to the State to inform the Commissioner, giving him in detail a full description of same, and to keep him informed of any changes in such property or its location or surroundings. (1901, c. 710, ss. 1, 2; 1903, c. 771, s. 2; Rev., s. 4828; C.S., s. 6452.)

§ 58-31-40. Commissioner to inspect State property; plans submitted.

(a) The Commissioner shall, at least once every year or more often if the Commissioner considers it necessary, visit, inspect, and thoroughly examine every State property to analyze and determine its protection from fire, including the property's occupants or contents. The Commissioner shall notify the agency or official in charge of the property of any defect noted by the Commissioner or any improvement considered by the Commissioner to be necessary.

(b) No agency or other person authorized or directed by law to select a plan and erect a building for the use of the State or any State institution shall receive and approve of the plan until it is submitted to and approved by the Commissioner as to the safety of the proposed building from fire, including the property's occupants or contents. No agency or person authorized or directed by law to select a plan or erect a building comprising 10,000 square feet or more for the use of any county, city, or school district shall receive and approve of the plan until it is submitted to and approved by the Commissioner as to the safety of the proposed building from fire, including the property's occupants or contents.

(c) The Commissioner shall review a plan subject to subsection (b) of this section within 30 days of submission, provided that the Commissioner may require one additional 30-day extension if necessary to complete the review. If the Commissioner has neither approved nor denied the plan during the initial 30-day review period, the owner may proceed with the building site preparation, the building foundation, and any structural components of the building that are not subject to inspection for the purposes set forth in subsection (b) of this section. If the Commissioner has neither approved nor denied the plan within 60 days of submission, the owner may request review and final approval under subsection (b) of this section by the Department of Administration, State Construction Office, pursuant to rules adopted under G.S. 143-135.26. (1901, c. 710, ss. 1, 2; 1903, c. 771, s. 3; Rev., s. 4829; 1909, c. 880; 1919, c. 186, s. 3; C.S., s. 6453; 2000-122, s. 10; 2001-487, s. 19; 2001-496, s. 11.1.)

Editor's Note. — This section was amended by Session Laws 2000-122, s. 10 in the coded bill drafting format. The act inadvertently failed to strike through an extra "or", which was later deleted by Session Laws 2001-487, s. 19.

Session Laws 2001-496, s. 13.1 is a severability clause.

Effect of Amendments. — Session Laws 2001-496, s. 11.1, effective March 1, 2002, added subsection (c).

§ 58-31-45. Report required of Commissioner.

The Commissioner must submit to the Governor a full report of his official action under this Article, with such recommendations as commend themselves to him, and it shall be embodied in or attached to his biennial report to the General Assembly. (1901, c. 710, ss. 1, 2; 1903, c. 771, s. 4; Rev., s. 4830; C.S., s. 6454; 1945, c. 386; 1991, c. 720, s. 4.)

§ 58-31-50. Liability insurance required for state-owned vehicles.

Every department, agency or institution of the State shall acquire motor vehicle liability insurance on all state-owned motor vehicles under its control. (1959, c. 1248; 1983, c. 717, s. 10.)

§ 58-31-52. State motor vehicle safety program.

(a) Findings, Policy, and Purpose. — Motor vehicle accidents exact a terrible toll of human tragedy and suffering as well as national resources within the United States. The same is true, on a smaller scale, within North Carolina State government. Every year State employees or members of the general public are killed or injured, and a significant portion of the State's financial resources is expended as a direct result of accidents involving State-owned vehicles. Accordingly, it is North Carolina policy that the State-owned motor vehicle fleet and vehicles used on behalf of the State be operated and maintained in such a manner as to minimize deaths, injuries, and costs. The purpose of this section is to direct the Commissioner of Insurance to develop a program to provide policy, requirements, procedures, technical information, and standards for administering a State vehicle safety program which will apply to all State personnel involved in the administration and operation of vehicles on behalf of the State.

(b) The Commissioner shall develop and adopt a State motor vehicle safety program to assure that State-owned motor vehicles are operated and maintained in a safe manner.

(c) In developing the program, the Commissioner shall include the following:

(1) Basic criteria concerning qualifications, screening, and education of drivers.

(2) Required and prohibited driving practices.

(3) Safety maintenance requirements.

(4) Accident reporting and review procedures.

(d) The requirements and procedures established under the program apply to all agencies and persons operating vehicles on behalf of the State, unless specifically exempted by the Commissioner. Agencies may adopt more stringent requirements and procedures than those adopted by the Commissioner under this section. The administration of the program in each agency is the responsibility of each agency head or that person's designee.

(e) The provisions of Chapter 150B of the General Statutes do not apply to the program developed and adopted under this section. (1995, c. 517, s. 15.)

§ 58-31-55. Insurance and official fidelity bonds for State agencies to be placed by Department; exception; costs of placement.

Except as provided in G.S. 58-32-15, all insurance and all official fidelity and surety bonds authorized for State departments, institutions, and agencies shall be effected and placed by the Department, and the cost of such placement shall be paid by the State department, institution, or agency involved upon bills rendered to and approved by the Commissioner. (1975, c. 875, s. 11; 1981, c. 1109, s. 4; 1993, c. 504, s. 21.)

§ 58-31-60. Competitive selection of payroll deduction insurance products paid for by State employees.

(a) Employee Insurance Committee. — The head of each State government employee payroll unit offering payroll deduction insurance products to employees shall appoint an Employee Insurance Committee for the following purposes:

(1) To review insurance products currently offered through payroll deduction to the State employees in the Employee Insurance Committee's payroll unit to determine if those products meet the needs and desires of employees in the Employee Insurance Committee's payroll unit.

(2) To select the types of insurance products that reflect the needs and desires of employees in the Employee Insurance Committee's payroll unit.

(3) To competitively select the best insurance products of the types determined by the Employee Insurance Committee to reflect the needs and desires of the employees of that payroll unit.

As used in this section, "insurance product" includes a prepaid legal services plan registered under G.S. 84-23.1.

(b) Appointment of Employee Insurance Committee Members. — The members of the Employee Insurance Committee shall be appointed by the head of the payroll unit. The Committee shall consist of not less than five or more than nine individuals a majority of whom have been employed in the payroll unit for at least one year. The committee members shall, except where necessary initially to establish the rotation herein prescribed, serve three-year terms with approximately one-third of the terms expiring annually. Committee membership make-up shall fairly represent the work force in the payroll unit and be selected without regard to any political or other affiliations. It shall be the duty of the payroll unit head to assure that the Employee Insurance Committee is completely autonomous in its selection of insurance products and insurance companies and that no member of the Employee Insurance Committee has any conflict of interest in serving on the Committee. A committee on employee benefits elected or appointed by the faculty representative body of a constituent institution of The University of North Carolina shall be deemed constituted and functioning as an employee insurance committee in accordance with this section. Any decision rendered by the Employee Insurance Committee where the autonomy of the Committee or a conflict of interest is questioned shall be subject to appeal pursuant to the Administrative Procedure Act, or in the case of departments, boards and commissions which are specifically exempt from the Administrative Procedure Act, pursuant to the appeals procedure prescribed for such department, board or commission.

(c) Payroll Deduction Slots. — Each payroll unit shall be entitled to not less than four payroll deduction slots to be used for payment of insurance premiums for products selected by the Employee Insurance Committee and offered to the employees of the payroll unit. The Employee Insurance Committee shall select only one company per payroll deduction slot. The Company selected by the Employee Insurance Committee shall be permitted to sell through payroll deduction only the products specifically approved by the Employee Insurance Committee. The assignment by the Employee Insurance Committee of a payroll deduction slot shall be for a period of not less than two years unless the insurance company shall be in violation of the terms of the written agreement specified in this subsection. The insurance company awarded a payroll deduction slot shall, pursuant to a written agreement setting out the rights and duties of the insurance company, be afforded an adequate opportunity to solicit employees of the payroll unit by making such employees aware that a representative of the company will be available at a specified time and at a location convenient to the employees.

Notwithstanding any other provision of the General Statutes, once an employee has selected an insurance product for payroll deduction, that product may not be removed from payroll deduction for that employee without his or her specific written consent.

When an employee retires from State employment and payroll deduction under this section is no longer available, the insurance company may not terminate life insurance products purchased under the payroll deduction plan without the retiree's specific written consent solely because the premium is no longer deducted from payroll.

(c1) Procedure for Selection of Insurance Product Proposals. — All insurance product proposals shall be sealed. The Committee shall open all proposals in public and record them in the minutes of the Committee, at which time the proposals become public records open to public inspection.

After the public opening, the Committee shall review the proposals, examining the cost and quality of the products, the reputation and capabilities of the insurance companies submitting the proposals, and other appropriate criteria. The Committee shall determine which proposal, if any, would meet the needs and desires of the employees of that Committee's payroll unit and shall award a payroll deduction slot to the company submitting the proposal that meets those needs and desires. The Committee may reject any or all proposals.

A company may seek to modify or withdraw a proposal only after the public opening and only on the basis that the proposal contains an unintentional clerical error as opposed to an error in judgment. A company seeking to modify or withdraw a proposal shall submit to the Committee a written request, with facts and evidence in support of its position, prior to the award of the payroll deduction slot, but not later than two days after the public opening of the proposals. The Committee shall promptly review the request, examine the nature of the error, and determine whether to permit or deny the request.

(d) Criminal Penalty. — It shall be a Class 3 misdemeanor for any State employee, who has supervisory authority over any member of the Employee Insurance Committee, to attempt to influence the autonomy of any Employee Insurance Committee either in the appointment of members to such Committee or in the operation of such Committee; or for anyone to open a sealed insurance product proposal or disclose or exhibit the contents of a sealed insurance product proposal, prior to the public opening of the proposal. The Commissioner of Insurance shall have the authority to investigate complaints alleging acts subject to the criminal penalty and shall report his findings to the Attorney General of North Carolina. (1985, c. 213, s. 1; 1985 (Reg. Sess., 1986), c. 1013, s. 15; 1987, c. 752, s. 12; c. 864, s. 92; 1989, c. 299; 1991, c. 644, s. 3.1; 1993, c. 539, s. 456; 1994, Ex. Sess., c. 24, s. 14(c); 1995, c. 193, s. 33; 1998-187, s. 1.)

Editor's Note. — Session Laws 1998-187, s. 2 provides: "Effective January 1, 1999, the employee insurance committees of the Department of Health and Human Services are abolished and shall be replaced with a single employee insurance committee, appointed by the Secretary of the Department of Health and

Human Services, to represent all employees of that Department."

OPINIONS OF ATTORNEY GENERAL

Adoption of Rules. — When Employee Insurance Committees establish procedures that affect the rights or procedures of others, they must be codified as rules. Should the committees elect to operate by the procedural process established in the enabling statutes, no rule adoptions are necessary. See opinion of Attorney General to Elizabeth H. Drury, Director, Office of Legislative and Legal Affairs, Department of Human Resources, 56 N.C.A.G. 25 (1986).

Employee Insurance Committees have rule-making and limited quasi-judicial powers pursuant to G.S. 58-31-60(b) and are "agencies" within the meaning of G.S. 150B-2(1). See opinion of Attorney General to Elizabeth H. Drury, Director, Office of Legislative and Legal Affairs, Department of Human Resources, 56 N.C.A.G. 25 (1986).

§ 58-31-65. Owner-controlled or wrap-up insurance authorized.

(a) To the extent it is determined necessary and in the best interest of this State, the Department may obtain design and construction insurance or provide for self-insurance against property damage caused by this State, its departments, agencies, boards, and commissions and all officers and employees of this State in connection with the construction of public works projects. Workers' compensation and general liability insurance may be purchased to cover both general contractors and subcontractors doing work on a specific contracted work site. In connection with the construction of public works projects, the Department may also use an owner-controlled or wrap-up insurance program if all of the following conditions are met:

(1) The total cost of the project or group of projects is over fifty million dollars ($50,000,000).

(2) The program maintains completed operations coverage for a term during which coverage is reasonably commercially available as determined by the Commissioner, but in no event for fewer than three years.

(3) Bid specifications clearly specify for all bidders the insurance coverage provided under the program and the minimum safety requirements that shall be met.

(4) The program does not prohibit a contractor or subcontractor from purchasing any additional insurance coverage that a contractor believes is necessary for protection from any liability arising out of the contract. The cost of the additional insurance shall not be passed through to this State on a contract bid.

(5) The program does not include surety insurance.

(6) The State may purchase an owner-controlled or wrap-up policy that has a deductible or self-insured retention as long as the deductible or self-insured retention does not exceed one million dollars ($1,000,000).

(b) For the purposes of subsection (a) of this section:

(1) "Owner-controlled or wrap-up insurance" means a series of insurance policies issued to cover this State and all of the construction managers, contractors, subcontractors, architects, and engineers on a specified contracted work site or work sites for purposes of general liability, property damage, and workers' compensation. A State agency or the State may be a secondary insured under owner-controlled or wrap-up insurance.

(2) "Specific contracted work site" means construction being performed at one site or a series of contiguous sites separated only by a street, roadway, waterway, or railroad right-of-way, or along a continuous system for the provision of water and power. (2001-167, s. 1.)

§ 58-31-66. Public construction contract surety bonds.

(a) Neither the State nor any county, city, or other political subdivision of the State, or any officer, employee, or other person acting on behalf of any such entity shall, with respect to any public building or construction contract, require any contractor, bidder, or proposer to procure a bid bond, payment bond, or performance bond from a particular surety, agent, producer, or broker.

(b) Nothing in this section prohibits an officer or employee acting on behalf of the State or a county, city, or other political subdivision of the State from:

(1) Approving the form, sufficiency, or manner of execution of the surety bonds furnished by the surety selected by the bidder to underwrite the bonds.

(2) Disapproving, on a reasonable, nondiscriminatory basis, the surety selected by the bidder to underwrite the bonds because of the financial condition of the surety.

(c) A violation of this section renders the public building or construction contract void ab initio. (2003-212, s. 27.)

Editor's Note. — Session Laws 2003-212, s. 28, made this section effective October 1, 2003.

ARTICLE 32.

Public Officers and Employees Liability Insurance Commission.

§ 58-32-1. Commission created; membership.

There is hereby created within the Department a Public Officers and Employees Liability Insurance Commission. The Commission shall consist of 11 members who shall be appointed as follows: the Commissioner shall appoint six members as follows: two members who are members of the insurance industry who may be chosen from a list of six nominees submitted to the Commissioner by the Independent Insurance Agents of North Carolina, Inc.; one member who is employed by a police department who may be chosen from a list of three nominees submitted to the Commissioner jointly by the North Carolina Police Chiefs Association and North Carolina Police Executives Association, and one member who is employed by a sheriff's department who may be chosen from a list of three nominees submitted to the Commissioner by the North Carolina Sheriff's Association; one member representing city government who may be chosen from a list of three nominees submitted to the Commissioner by the North Carolina League of Municipalities; and one member representing county government who may be chosen from a list of three nominees submitted to the Commissioner by the North Carolina Association of County Commissioners; and the General Assembly shall appoint two persons, one upon the recommendation of the Speaker of the House of Representatives, and one upon the recommendation of the President Pro Tempore of the Senate. The Commissioner or the Commissioner's designate shall be an ex officio member. Appointments by the General Assembly shall be made in accordance with G.S. 120-121, and vacancies in those appointments shall be filled in accordance with G.S. 120-122. The terms of the initial appointees by the General Assembly shall expire on June 30, 1983. The

Secretary of the Department of Crime Control and Public Safety or the Secretary's designate shall be an ex officio member. The Attorney General or the Attorney General's designate shall be an ex officio member. One insurance industry member appointed by the Commissioner shall be appointed to a term of two years and one insurance industry member shall be appointed to a term of four years. The police department member shall be appointed to a term of two years and the sheriff's department member shall be appointed to a term of four years. The representative of county government shall be appointed to a term of two years and the representative of city government to a term of four years. Beginning July 1, 1983, the appointment made by the General Assembly upon the recommendation of the Speaker shall be for two years, and the appointment made by the General Assembly upon the recommendation of the President Pro Tempore of the Senate shall be for four years. Except as provided in this section, if any vacancy occurs in the membership of the Commission, the appointing authority shall appoint another person to fill the unexpired term of the vacating member. After the initial terms established herein have expired, all appointees to the Commission shall be appointed to terms of four years.

The Commission members shall elect the chair and vice-chair of the Commission. The Commission may, by majority vote, remove any member of the Commission for chronic absenteeism, misfeasance, malfeasance or other good cause. (1979, c. 325, s. 1; 1981 (Reg. Sess., 1982), c. 1191, ss. 24-26; 1983, c. 543, ss. 1, 2; 1985, c. 666, ss. 76, 77, 79; 1991, c. 720, s. 4; 1995, c. 490, s. 41; 1999-132, s. 6.1.)

§ 58-32-5. Meetings of Commission; compensation.

The Commission shall meet at least four times per year, on or about January 15, April 15, July 15, October 15 and upon call of the chairman. The members shall receive no compensation for attendance at meetings, except a per diem expense reimbursement. Members of the Commission who are not officers or employees of the State shall receive reimbursement for subsistence and travel expenses at rates set out in G.S. 138-5 from funds made available to the Commission. Members of the Commission who are officers or employees of the State shall be reimbursed for travel and subsistence at the rates set out in G.S. 138-6 from funds made available to the Commission. (1979, c. 325, s.1; 1981 (Reg. Sess., 1982), c. 1191, s. 27; 1985, c. 666, s. 79.)

§ 58-32-10. Powers and duties of Commission.

The Commission may acquire from an insurance company or insurance companies a group plan of professional liability insurance covering the law-enforcement officers and/or public officers and employees of any political subdivision of the State. The Commission shall have full authority to negotiate with insurance companies submitting bids or proposals and shall award its group plan master contract on the basis of the company or companies found by it to offer maximum coverage at the most reasonable premium. The Commission is authorized to enter into a master policy contract of such term as it finds to be in the best interests of the law-enforcement officers and/or public officers and employees of the political subdivisions of the State, not to exceed five years. The Commission, in negotiating for such contract, is not authorized to pledge or offer the credit of the State of North Carolina. The insurance premiums shall be paid by the political subdivisions whose employees are covered by the professional liability insurance. Any political subdivision may elect coverage for any or all of its employees on a departmental basis; provided all employees in a department must be covered if coverage is elected for that department. Nothing contained herein shall be construed to require any political subdivision to participate in any group plan of professional liability insurance.

The Commission may, in its discretion, employ professional and clerical staff whose salaries shall be as established by the State Personnel Commission.

Should the Commission determine that reasonable coverage is not available at a reasonable cost, the Commission may undertake such studies and inquiries into the situation and alternatives, including self insurance and State administered funds, as the Commission deems appropriate. The Commission shall then bring before the General Assembly such recommendations as it deems appropriate.

The Commission may acquire information regarding loss ratios, loss factors, loss experience and other such facts and figures from any agency or company issuing professional liability insurance covering public officers, employees or law-enforcement officers in the State of North Carolina. Such information shall not be deemed a public record within the meaning of Chapter 132 of the General Statutes where it names the company divulging such information, but the Commission may make public such information to show aggregate statistics in respect to the experience of the State as a whole. The information shall be provided to the Commission upon its written demand and shall be submitted to the Commission by such company or companies upon sworn affidavit. If any agency or company shall fail or refuse to supply such information to the Commission within a reasonable time following receipt of the demand, the Commission may apply to the Superior Court sitting in Wake County for appropriate orders to enforce the demand.

For purposes of this section, the term "political subdivision" includes any county, city, town, incorporated village, sanitary district, metropolitan water district, county water and sewer district, water and sewer authority, hospital authority, parking authority, local ABC boards, special airport district, airport authority, soil and water conservation district created pursuant to G.S. 139-5, fire district, volunteer or paid fire department, rescue squads, city or county parks and recreation commissions, area mental health boards, area mental health, mental retardation and substance abuse authority as described in G.S. 122C-117, domiciliary home community advisory committees, county and district boards of health, nursing home advisory committees, county boards of social services, local school administrative units, local boards of education, community colleges, and all other persons, bodies, or agencies authorized or regulated by Chapters 108A, 115C, 115D, 118, 122C, 130A, 131A, 131D, 131E, 153A, 160A, and 160B of the General Statutes. (1979, c. 325, s. 1; 1983, c. 543, s. 3; 1985, c. 666, s. 79; 1985 (Reg. Sess., 1986), c. 1027, s. 30; 1987, c. 564, s. 9.)

Editor's Note. — Chapter 118, referred to in this section, has been recodified as Articles 84 to 88 of Chapter 58.

§ 58-32-15. Professional liability insurance for State officials.

(a) The Commission may acquire professional liability insurance covering the officers and employees, or any group thereof, of any State department, institution or agency or any community college or technical college. Premiums for such insurance shall be paid by the requesting department, institution, agency, community college or technical college at rates established by the Commission, from funds made available to such department, institution, agency, community college or technical college for the purpose.

(b) The Commission, pursuant to this section, may acquire professional liability insurance covering the officers and employees, or any group thereof, of a department, institution or agency of State government or a community college or technical college only if the coverage to be provided by the insurance policy is in excess of the protection provided by Articles 31 and 31A of Chapter 143 of the General Statutes, other than the protection provided by G.S. 143-300.9.

(c) The purchase, by any State department, institution, agency, community college or technical college of professional liability insurance covering the law-enforcement officers, officers or employees of such department, institution, agency, community college or technical college shall not be construed as a waiver of any defense of sovereign immunity by such department, institution, agency, community college or technical college. The purchase of such insurance shall not be deemed a waiver by any employee of the defense of sovereign immunity to the extent that such defense may be available to him.

(d) The payment, by any State department, institution, agency, community college or technical college of funds as premiums for professional liability insurance through the plan provided herein, covering the law-enforcement officers or officials or employees of such department, institution, agency, community college or technical college is hereby declared to be for a public purpose. (1981, c. 1109, s. 3; 1985, c. 666, s. 79; 1987, c. 301; 1991, c. 674, s. 3.)

Editor's Note. — Session Laws 1997-443, s. 32.20(m), provides: "Upon ownership of all voting stock in the North Carolina Railroad Company by the State of North Carolina, and upon the request of the Board of Directors of the North Carolina Railroad Company, the Public Officers and Employees Liability Insurance Commission shall effect and place coverage for the officers, directors, and employees of the North Carolina Railroad under G.S. 58-32-15. The North Carolina Railroad Company shall pay the premiums for this insurance at rates established by the Commission, and shall make any other payments required by G.S. 143-300.6. Coverage of the officers, directors, and employees of the North Carolina Railroad company under this subsection shall not be construed as defining the North Carolina Railroad Company as a public body or as defining its officers, directors, or employees as public officials or employees for any other purpose."

Session Laws 2001-505, s. 3, as amended by Session Laws 2002-159, s. 60, provides: "The Public Officers and Employees Liability Insurance Commission in the Department of Insurance shall effect and place professional liability insurance coverage under G.S. 58-32-15 for local health department sanitarians defended by the State under G.S. 143-300.8. For insurance purposes only under G.S. 58-32-15, local health department sanitarians are considered to be employees of the Department of Environment and Natural Resources."

§ 58-32-20. Commission to act as liaison; meetings of Commission.

The Commission shall act as liaison between the insurance company or companies with which it contracts, their servicing agent and the insureds. The Commission shall give notice of its meetings to the company or companies and to all insureds. The Commission shall attempt to resolve such difficulties as arise in the servicing and administration of the program of insurance between the company and insureds. (1979, c. 325, s. 1; 1985, c. 666, s. 79.)

§ 58-32-25. Contract conditions.

The Commission, in procuring and negotiating for the contract of insurance herein described shall include in any procurement document the following conditions, which are not subject to negotiation and which are deemed a part of the said contract when entered into:

(1) The master policy shall be issued in the name of the Commission and shall include all governmental entities for which coverage was requested in the procurement document.

(2) The company or companies selected must name a servicing agent resident in North Carolina who shall issue all certificates, collect all premiums, process all claims, and be responsible for all processing, service and administration of the program of insurance provided. (1979, c. 325, s. 1; 1985, c. 666, s. 79.)

§ 58-32-30. Payment a public purpose.

The payment by any county or municipality of funds as premiums for professional liability insurance through the plan provided herein, covering the law-enforcement officers or public officials or employees of such subdivision of government, is declared to be for a public purpose. (1979, c. 325, s. 1; 1985, c. 666, s. 79.)

ARTICLE 33.

Licensing of Agents, Brokers, Limited Representatives, and Adjusters.

§ 58-33-1. Scope.

This Article governs the qualifications and procedures for the licensing of agents, brokers, limited representatives, adjusters, and motor vehicle damage appraisers. This Article applies to any and all kinds of insurance and insurers under this Chapter. For purposes of this Article, all references to insurance include annuities, unless the context otherwise requires. (1987, c. 629, s. 1; 2001-203, s. 1.)

Editor's Note. — Session Laws 2001-203, s. 31, contains a severability clause.
Effect of Amendments. — Session Laws 2001-203, s. 1, effective July 1, 2002, deleted "Articles 1 through 67 of" preceding "this chapter" in the second sentence and deleted the former third sentence, which read: "Except as provided in G.S. 58-33-125, this Article does not apply to the licensing of surplus lines licensees under Article 21 of this Chapter."

§ 58-33-5. License required.

A person shall not sell, solicit, or negotiate insurance in this State unless the person is licensed for that kind of insurance in accordance with this Article. (2001-203, s. 2.)

Editor's Note. — Session Laws 2001-203, s. 31, contains a severability clause.
Session Laws 2001-203, s. 32, made this section effective July 1, 2002.

§ 58-33-10. Definitions.

As used in this Article, the following definitions apply:
(1) "Agent" means a person licensed to solicit applications for, or to negotiate a policy of, insurance. A person not duly licensed who solicits or negotiates a policy of insurance on behalf of an insurer is an agent within the intent of this Article, and thereby becomes liable for all the duties, requirements, liabilities and penalties to which an agent of such company is subject, and such company by compensating such person through any of its officers, agents or employees for soliciting

policies of insurance shall thereby accept and acknowledge such person as its agent in such transaction.

(2) "Adjuster" means any individual who, for salary, fee, commission, or other compensation of any nature, investigates or reports to his principal relative to claims arising under insurance contracts other than life or annuity. An attorney at law who adjusts insurance losses from time to time incidental to the practice of his profession or an adjuster of marine losses is not deemed to be an adjuster for purposes of this Article. An individual may not simultaneously hold an agent's and an adjuster's license in this State.

(3) "Broker" means a person who, being a licensed agent, procures insurance for a party other than himself through a duly authorized agent of an insurer that is licensed to do business in this State but for which the broker is not authorized to act as agent. A person not duly licensed who procures insurance for a party other than himself is a broker within the intent of this Article, and thereby becomes liable for all the duties, requirements, liabilities and penalties to which such licensed brokers are subject.

(4) "Business entity" means a corporation, association, partnership, limited liability company, limited liability partnership, or other legal entity. "Business entity" does not mean a sole proprietorship.

(5) "Home state" means the District of Columbia and any state or territory of the United States in which an insurance producer maintains his or her principal place of residence or principal place of business and is licensed to act as an insurance producer.

(6) "Insurance" means any of the kinds of insurance in G.S. 58-7-15.

(7) "Insurance producer" or "producer" means a person required to be licensed under this Article to sell, solicit, or negotiate insurance. "Insurance producer" or "producer" includes an agent, broker, and limited representative.

(8) "License" means a document issued by the Commissioner authorizing a person to act as an insurance producer for the kinds of insurance specified in the document. The license itself does not create any authority, actual, apparent, or inherent, in the holder to represent or commit an insurance carrier.

(9) "Limited line credit insurance" includes any type of credit insurance written under Article 57 of this Chapter, mortgage life, mortgage guaranty, mortgage disability, automobile dealer gap insurance, and any other form of insurance offered in connection with an extension of credit that is limited to partially or wholly extinguishing that credit obligation and that the Commissioner determines should be designated a form of limited line credit insurance.

(10) "Limited line credit insurance producer" means a person who sells, solicits, or negotiates one or more forms of limited line credit insurance coverage to individuals through a master, corporate, group, or individual policy.

(11) "Limited lines insurance" means motor vehicle physical damage insurance and title insurance, or any other kind of insurance that the Commissioner considers necessary to recognize for the purposes of complying with G.S. 58-33-32(f).

(12) "Limited lines producer" means a person authorized by the Commissioner to sell, solicit, or negotiate limited lines insurance.

(13) "Limited representative" means a person who is authorized by the Commissioner to solicit or negotiate contracts for the particular kinds of insurance identified in G.S. 58-33-26(g) and which kinds of insurance are restricted in the scope of coverage afforded.

(14) "Motor vehicle damage appraiser" means an individual who, for salary, fee, commission, or other compensation of any nature, regularly investigates or advises relative to the nature and amount of damage to motor vehicles located in this State or the amount of money deemed necessary to effect repairs thereto and who is not:

    a. An adjuster licensed to adjust insurance claims in this State;

    b. An agent for an insurance company who is not required by law to be licensed as an adjuster;

    c. An attorney at law who is not required by law to be licensed as an adjuster; or

    d. An individual who, incident to his regular employment in the business of repairing defective or damaged motor vehicles, investigates and advises relative to the nature and amount of motor vehicle damage or the amount of money deemed necessary to effect repairs thereto.

(15) "Negotiate" means the act of conferring directly with, or offering advice directly to, a purchaser or prospective purchaser of a particular contract of insurance concerning any of the substantive benefits, terms, or conditions of the contract, only if the person engaged in that act either sells insurance or obtains insurance from insurers for purchasers. "Negotiate" does not mean a referral to a licensed insurance agent or broker that does not include a discussion of specific insurance policy terms and conditions.

(16) "Person" means an individual or a business entity, but does not mean a county, city, or other political subdivision of the State of North Carolina.

(17) "Sell" means to exchange a contract of insurance by any means, for money or its equivalent, on behalf of an insurance company. "Sell" does not mean a referral to a licensed insurance agent or broker that does not include a discussion of specific insurance policy terms and conditions.

(18) "Solicit" means attempting to sell insurance or asking or urging a person to apply for a particular kind of insurance from a particular company. "Solicit" does not mean a referral to a licensed insurance agent or broker that does not include a discussion of specific insurance policy terms and conditions.

(19) "Terminate" means the cancellation of the relationship between an insurance producer and the insurer or the termination of a producer's authority to transact insurance.

(20) "Uniform Business Entity Application" means the current version of the NAIC Uniform Business Entity Application for resident and nonresident business entities.

(21) "Uniform Application" means the current version of the NAIC Uniform Application for resident and nonresident producer licensing. (1987, c. 629, s. 1; c. 864, ss. 76, 77; 1987 (Reg. Sess., 1988), c. 975, s. 8; 2001-203, s. 3.)

Editor's Note. — Session Laws 2001-203, s. 31, contains a severability clause.

Effect of Amendments. — Session Laws 2001-203, s. 3, effective July 1, 2002, substituted the present subdivision designations (1) through (3), (13) and (14) for former subsection designations (a) through (e); added present subdivisions (4) through (12) and (15) through (21); substituted "G.S. 58-33-26(g)" for "G.S. 58-33-25(e)" in present subdivision (13); and substituted the present designations a. through d. for former designations (1) through (4) in present subdivision (14).

CASE NOTES

Editor's Note. — The cases below were decided prior to the enactment of this section.

An insurance agent is within the Employment Security Law, Chapter 96. Unemployment Comp. Comm'n v. Jefferson Std. Life Ins. Co., 215 N.C. 479, 2 S.E.2d 584 (1939).

Insurance Broker as Agent of Insured. — An insurance broker is primarily the agent of the person who first employs him; hence, he is the agent of the insured as to all matters within the scope of his employment, and the acts or knowledge of such broker or agent will be binding on, or imputed to, the insured and not to the company. Williams v. Canal Ins. Co., 21 N.C. App. 658, 205 S.E.2d 331 (1974).

§ 58-33-15. Restricted license for overseas military agents.

Notwithstanding any other provision of this Article, an individual may be licensed by the Commissioner as a foreign military sales agent to represent a life insurance company domiciled in this State, provided the agent represents the insurance company only in a foreign country or territory and either on a United States military installation or with United States military personnel. The Commissioner may, upon request of the insurance company on application forms furnished by the Commissioner and upon payment of the fee specified in G.S. 58-33-125, issue to the applicant a restricted license which will be valid only for the representation of the insurance company in a foreign country or territory and either on a United States military installation or with United States military personnel. The insurance company shall certify to the Commissioner that the applicant has the necessary training to hold himself out as a life insurance agent, and that the insurance company is willing to be bound by the acts of the applicant within the scope of his employment. A restricted license issued under this section shall be renewed annually as provided in G.S. 58-33-25(n). (1987, c. 629, s. 1; 1987 (Reg. Sess., 1988), c. 975, s. 9.)

§ 58-33-17. Limited license for rental car companies.

(a) As used in this section:
(1) "Limited licensee" means a person authorized to sell certain coverages relating to the rental of motor vehicles pursuant to the provisions of this section and Article 28 of Chapter 66 of the General Statutes.
(2) "Rental agreement" means any written agreement setting forth the terms and conditions governing the use of a vehicle provided by the rental car company.
(3) "Rental car company" means any person in the business of providing vehicles to the public.
(4) "Renter" means any person obtaining the use of a vehicle from a rental car company under the terms of a rental agreement.
(5) "Vehicle" means a motor vehicle of the private passenger type including passenger vans and minivans that are primarily intended for the transport of persons.
(b) The Commissioner may issue to a rental car company, or to a franchisee of a rental car company, that has complied with the requirements of this section, a limited license authorizing the licensee, known as a "limited licensee" for the purpose of this Article, to act as agent, with reference to the kinds of insurance specified in this section, of any insurer authorized to write such kinds of insurance in this State.
(c) The prerequisites for issuance of a limited license under this section are the filing with the Commissioner of the following:
(1) A written application, signed by an officer of the applicant, for the limited license in such form or forms, and supplements thereto, and containing such information, as the Commissioner may prescribe; and

(2) A certificate by the insurer that is to be named in such limited license, stating that it has satisfied itself that the named applicant is trustworthy and competent to act as its insurance agent for this limited purpose and that the insurer will appoint such applicant to act as the agent in reference to the doing of such kind or kinds of insurance as are permitted by this section, if the limited license applied for is issued by the Commissioner. Such certificate shall be subscribed by an officer or managing agent of such insurer and affirmed as true under the penalties of perjury.

(d) In the event that any provision of this section is violated by a limited licensee, the Commissioner may:

(1) Revoke or suspend a limited license issued under this section in accordance with the provisions of G.S. 58-33-46; or

(2) After notice and hearing, impose such other penalties, including suspending the transaction of insurance at specific rental locations where violations of this Article have occurred, as the Commissioner deems to be necessary or convenient to carry out the purposes of this section.

(e) The rental car company or franchisee licensed pursuant to subsection (b) of this section may act as agent for an authorized insurer only in connection with the rental of vehicles and only with respect to the following kinds of insurance:

(1) Excess liability insurance that provides coverage to the rental car company or franchisee and renters and other authorized drivers of rental vehicles, in excess of the standard liability limits provided by the rental car company in its rental agreement, for liability arising from the negligent operation of the rental vehicle;

(2) Accident and health insurance that provides coverage to renters and other vehicle occupants for accidental death or dismemberment and for medical expenses resulting from an accident that occurs during the rental period;

(3) Personal effects insurance that provides coverage to renters and other vehicle occupants for the loss of, or damage to, personal effects that occurs during the rental period; or

(4) Any other coverage that the Commissioner may approve as meaningful and appropriate in connection with the rental of vehicles.

(f) No insurance may be issued pursuant to this section unless:

(1) The rental period of the rental agreement does not exceed 30 consecutive days; and

(2) At every rental car location where rental car agreements are executed, brochures or other written materials are readily available to the prospective renter that:

a. Summarize, clearly and correctly, the material terms of insurance coverage, including the identity of the insurer, offered to renters;

b. Disclose that these policies offered by the rental car company may provide a duplication of coverage already provided by a renter's personal automobile insurance policy, homeowner's insurance policy, personal liability insurance policy, or other source of coverage;

c. State that the purchase by the renter of the kinds of insurance specified in this section is not required in order to rent a vehicle;

d. Describe the process for filing a claim in the event the renter elects to purchase coverage and in the event of a claim; and

e. Contain any additional information on the price, benefits, exclusions, conditions or other limitations of such policies as the Commissioner may by regulation prescribe; and

    (3) Evidence of coverage is provided to every renter who elects to purchase such coverage.

    (g) Any limited license issued under this section shall also authorize any salaried employee of the licensee who, pursuant to subsection (h) of this section, is trained to act individually on behalf, and under the supervision, of the licensee with respect to the kinds of insurance specified in this section.

    (h) Each rental car company or franchisee licensed pursuant to this section shall conduct a training program which shall be submitted to the commissioner for approval prior to use and which shall meet the following minimum standards:

    (1) Each trainee shall receive basic instruction about the kinds of insurance specified in this section offered for purchase by prospective renters of rental vehicles;

    (2) Each trainee shall be instructed to acknowledge to a prospective renter of a rental vehicle that purchase of any such insurance specified in this section is not required in order for the renter to rent a vehicle; and

    (3) Each trainee shall be instructed to acknowledge to a prospective renter of a rental vehicle that the renter may have insurance policies that already provide the coverage being offered by the rental car company pursuant to this section.

    (i) Limited licensees acting pursuant to and under the authority of this section shall comply with all applicable provisions of this Article, except that notwithstanding any other provision of this Article, or any rule adopted by the Commissioner, a limited licensee pursuant to this section shall not be required to treat premiums collected from renters purchasing such insurance when renting vehicles as funds received in a fiduciary capacity, provided that:

    (1) The insurer represented by the limited licensee has consented in writing, signed by the insurer's officer, that premiums need not be segregated from funds received by the rental car company on account of vehicle rental; and

    (2) The charges for insurance coverage are itemized but not billed to the renter separately from the charges for rental vehicles.

    (j) No limited licensee under this section shall advertise, represent, or otherwise hold itself or any of its employees themselves out as licensed insurance agents or brokers. (1991, c. 139, s. 1; 2001-203, s. 4.)

Editor's Note. — Session Laws 2001-203, s. 31, contains a severability clause.

Effect of Amendments. — Session Laws 2001-203, s. 4, effective July 1, 2002, substituted "G.S.58-33-46" for "G.S. 58-33-45" in subdivision (d)(1).

§ 58-33-18. Limited license for self-service storage companies.

    (a) As used in this section:

    (1) "Limited licensee" means a person authorized to sell certain coverages relating to the rental of self-service storage units pursuant to the provisions of this section and Article 39 of Chapter 66 of the General Statutes.

    (2) "Rental agreement" means any written agreement setting forth the terms and conditions governing the use of a storage unit provided by the owner of a self-service storage facility company.

    (3) "Self-service storage company" means any person in the business of renting storage units to the public.

   (4) "Renter" or "occupant" means any person obtaining the use of a storage unit from a self-service storage company under the terms of a rental agreement.
   (5) "Storage unit" means a semienclosed or fully enclosed area, room, or space that is primarily intended for the storage of personal property and which shall be accessible by the renter of the unit pursuant to the terms of the rental agreement.

(b) The Commissioner may issue to a self-service storage company, or to a franchisee of a self-service storage company, that has complied with the requirements of this section a limited license authorizing the licensee, known as a "limited licensee" for the purpose of this Article, to act as agent, with reference to the kinds of insurance specified in this section of any insurer authorized to write such kinds of insurance in this State.

(c) The prerequisites for issuance of a limited license under this section are the filing with the Commissioner of the following:
   (1) A written application, signed by an officer of the applicant, for the limited license in such form or forms, and supplements thereto, and containing such information as the Commissioner may prescribe; and
   (2) A certificate by the insurer that is to be named in such limited license, stating that it has satisfied itself that the named applicant is trustworthy and competent to act as its insurance agent for this limited purpose and that the insurer will appoint such applicant to act as the agent in reference to the doing of such kind or kinds of insurance as are permitted by this section if the limited license applied for is issued by the Commissioner. Such certificate shall be subscribed by an officer or managing agent of such insurer and affirmed as true under the penalties of perjury.

(d) In the event that any provision of this section is violated by a limited licensee, the Commissioner may:
   (1) Revoke or suspend a limited license issued under this section in accordance with the provisions of G.S. 58-33-46; or
   (2) After notice and hearing, impose such other penalties, including suspending the transaction of insurance at specific rental locations where violations of this Article have occurred, as the Commissioner deems to be necessary or convenient to carry out the purposes of this section.

(e) The self-service storage company or franchisee licensed pursuant to subsection (b) of this section may act as agent for an authorized insurer only in connection with the rental of storage units and only with respect to the following kinds of insurance:
   (1) Personal effects insurance that provides coverage to renters of storage units at the same facility for the loss of, or damage to, personal effects that occurs at the same facility during the rental period; or
   (2) Any other coverage that the Commissioner may approve as meaningful and appropriate in connection with the rental of storage units.

(f) No insurance may be issued pursuant to this section unless:
   (1) The rental period of the rental agreement does not exceed two years; and
   (2) At every self-service storage location where self-service storage agreements are executed, brochures or other written materials are readily available to the prospective renter that:
     a. Summarize, clearly and correctly, the material terms of insurance coverage, including the identity of the insurer, offered to renters;
     b. Disclose that these policies offered by the self-service storage company may provide a duplication of coverage already provided by a renter's homeowners' insurance policy, personal liability insurance policy, or other source of coverage;

  c. State that the purchase by the renter of the kinds of insurance specified in this section is not required in order to rent a storage unit;

  d. Describe the process for filing a claim in the event the renter elects to purchase coverage and in the event of a claim; and

  e. Contain any additional information on the price, benefits, exclusions, conditions, or other limitations of such policies as the Commissioner may by regulation prescribe; and

 (3) Evidence of coverage is provided to every renter who elects to purchase such coverage.

(g) Any limited license issued under this section shall also authorize any employee of the licensee who is trained, pursuant to subsection (h) of this section, to act individually on behalf, and under the supervision, of the licensee with respect to the kinds of insurance specified in this section.

(h) Each self-service storage company or franchisee licensed pursuant to this section shall conduct a training program which shall be submitted to the Commissioner for approval prior to use and which shall meet the following minimum standards:

 (1) Each trainee shall receive basic instruction about the kinds of insurance specified in this section offered for purchase by prospective renters of storage units;

 (2) Each trainee shall be instructed to acknowledge to a prospective renter of a storage unit that purchase of any such insurance specified in this section is not required in order for the renter to rent a storage unit; and

 (3) Each trainee shall be instructed to acknowledge to a prospective renter of a storage unit that the renter may have insurance policies that already provide the coverage being offered by the self-service storage company pursuant to this section.

(i) Limited licensees acting pursuant to and under the authority of this section shall comply with all applicable provisions of this Article, except that notwithstanding any other provision of this Article, or any rule adopted by the Commissioner, a limited licensee pursuant to this section shall not be required to treat premiums collected from renters purchasing such insurance when renting storage units as funds received in a fiduciary capacity, provided that:

 (1) The insurer represented by the limited licensee has consented in writing, signed by the insurer's officer, that premiums need not be segregated from funds received by the self-service storage company on account of storage unit rental; and

 (2) The charges for insurance coverage are itemized but not billed to the renter separately from the charges for storage units.

(j) No limited licensee under this section shall advertise, represent, or otherwise hold itself or any of its employees out as licensed insurance agents or brokers. No renter or occupant may be required to obtain insurance under this section as a condition of obtaining a rental agreement for a storage unit. The renter shall be informed that the insurance offered under this section is not required as a condition for obtaining a rental agreement for a storage unit. (2003-290, s. 5.)

Editor's Note. — Session Laws 2003-290, s. 6, made this section effective July 4, 2003.

§ 58-33-20. Representation.

(a) Every agent or limited representative who solicits or negotiates an application for insurance of any kind, in any controversy between the insured or his beneficiary and the insurer, is regarded as representing the insurer and not the insured or his beneficiary. This provision does not affect the apparent authority of an agent.

(b) Every broker who solicits an application for insurance of any kind, in any controversy between the insured or his beneficiary and the insurer issuing any policy upon such application, is regarded as representing the insured or his beneficiary and not the insurer; except any insurer that directly or through its agents delivers in this State to any insurance broker a policy of insurance pursuant to the application or request of such broker, acting for an insured other than himself, is deemed to have authorized such broker to receive on its behalf payment of any premium that is due on such policy of insurance at the time of its issuance or delivery. (1987, c. 629, s. 1.)

CASE NOTES

Cited in Webster Enters., Inc. v. Selective Ins. Co., 125 N.C. App. 36, 479 S.E.2d 243 (1996).

§ 58-33-25: Repealed by Session Laws 2001-203, s. 5, effective July 1, 2002.

Cross References. — For present provisions covering the subject matter of the repealed section, see G.S. 58-33-26.

§ 58-33-26. General license requirements.

(a) No person shall act as or hold himself or herself out to be an agent, broker, limited representative, adjuster, or motor vehicle damage appraiser unless duly licensed.

(b) No agent, broker, or limited representative shall make application for, procure, negotiate for, or place for others, any policies for any kinds of insurance as to which that person is not then qualified and duly licensed.

(c) An agent or broker may be licensed for the following kinds of insurance:
    (1) Life and health insurance, meaning:
        a. Life-insurance coverage on human lives, including benefits of endowment and annuities, and may include benefits in the event of death or dismemberment by accident and benefits for disability income.
        b. Variable life and variable annuity products-insurance coverage provided under variable life insurance contracts and variable annuities.
        c. Accident and health or sickness-insurance coverage for sickness, bodily injury, or accidental death and may include benefits for disability income.
    (2) Property and liability insurance, meaning:
        a. Coverage for the direct or consequential loss or damage to property of every kind.
        b. Coverage against legal liability, including that for death, injury, or disability or damage to real or personal property.
    (3) Personal lines, meaning property and liability insurance coverage sold to individuals and families for primarily noncommercial purposes.

    (4) Medicare supplement insurance and long-term care insurance, as a supplement to a license for the kinds of insurance listed in subdivision (1) of this subsection.

  (d) A property and liability insurance license does not authorize an agent to sell accident and health insurance. An agent must hold a life and health insurance license to sell accident and health insurance.

  (e) A life and health insurance license authorizes a resident agent to sell variable contracts if the agent satisfies the Commissioner that the agent has met the National Association of Securities Dealers requirements of the Secretary of State of North Carolina.

  (f) A life and health insurance license authorizes a resident agent to sell Medicare supplement and long-term care insurance policies as defined respectively in Articles 54 and 55 of this Chapter, provided that the licensee takes and passes a supplemental written examination for the insurance as provided in G.S. 58-33-30(e) and pays the supplemental registration fee provided in G.S. 58-33-125(c).

  (g) A limited representative may receive qualification for one or more licenses without examination for the following kinds of insurance:

    (1) Dental services.

    (2) Limited line credit insurance.

    (3) Limited lines insurance.

    (4) Motor club.

    (5) Prearrangement insurance, as defined in G.S. 58-60-35(a)(2), when offered or sold by a preneed sales licensee licensed under Article 13D of Chapter 90 of the General Statutes.

    (6) Travel accident and baggage.

    (7) Vehicle service agreements and mechanical breakdown insurance.

  (h) No licensed agent, broker, or limited representative shall solicit anywhere in the boundaries of this State, or receive or transmit an application or premium of insurance, for a company not licensed to do business in this State, except as provided in G.S. 58-28-5 and Article 21 of this Chapter.

  (i) No agent shall place a policy of insurance with any insurer unless the agent has a current appointment as agent for the insurer in accordance with G.S. 58-33-40 or has a valid temporary license issued in accordance with G.S. 58-33-66.

  (j) A business entity that sells, negotiates, or solicits insurance shall be licensed in accordance with G.S. 58-33-31(b). Every member of the partnership and every officer, director, stockholder, and employee of the business entity personally engaged in this State in soliciting or negotiating policies of insurance shall qualify as an individual licensee.

  (k) The license shall state the name and social security number, or other identifying number of the licensee, date of issue, kind or kinds of insurance covered by the license, and any other information as the Commissioner deems to be proper.

  (l) A license issued to an agent authorizes him to act until his license is otherwise suspended or revoked. Upon the suspension or revocation of a license, the licensee or any person having possession of such license shall return it to the Commissioner.

  (m) A license of a broker, limited representative, adjuster, or motor vehicle damage appraiser shall be renewed on April 1 each year, and renewal fees shall be paid. The Commissioner is not required to print licenses for the purpose of renewing licenses. The Commissioner may establish for licenses "staggered" license renewal dates that will apportion renewals throughout each calendar year. If the system of staggered licensing is adopted, the Commissioner may extend the licensure period for some licensees. License renewal fees prescribed by G.S. 58-33-125 shall be prorated to the extent they are commensurate with extensions.

(n) A license as an insurance producer is not required of the following:

(1) An officer, director, or employee of an insurer or of an insurance producer, provided that the officer, director, or employee does not receive any commission on policies written or sold to insure risks residing, located, or to be performed in this State, except for indirect receipt of proceeds of commissions in the form of salary, benefits, or distributions, and:

    a. The officer, director, or employee's activities are executive, administrative, managerial, clerical, or a combination of these, and are only indirectly related to the sale, solicitation, or negotiation of insurance; or

    b. The officer, director, or employee's function relates to underwriting, loss control, inspection, or the processing, adjusting, investigating, or settling of a claim on a contract of insurance; or

    c. The officer, director, or employee is acting in the capacity of a special agent or agency supervisor assisting insurance producers where the person's activities are limited to providing technical advice and assistance to licensed insurance producers and do not include the sale, solicitation, or negotiation of insurance.

(2) A person who secures and furnishes information for the purpose of group life insurance, group property and casualty insurance, group annuities, group or blanket accident and health insurance; or for the purpose of enrolling individuals under plans; issuing certificates under plans or otherwise assisting in administering plans; or performs administrative services related to mass-marketed property and casualty insurance; where no commission is paid to the person for the service.

(3) An employer or association or its officers, directors, employees, or the trustees of an employee trust plan, to the extent that the employers, officers, employees, director, or trustees are engaged in the administration or operation of a program of employee benefits for the employer's or association's own employees or the employees of its subsidiaries or affiliates, which program involves the use of insurance issued by an insurer, as long as the employers, associations, officers, directors, employees, or trustees are not in any manner compensated, directly or indirectly, by the company issuing the contracts.

(4) Employees of insurers or organizations employed by insurers who are engaging in the inspection, rating, or classification of risks, or in the supervision of the training of insurance producers and who are not individually engaged in the sale, solicitation, or negotiation of insurance.

(5) A person whose activities in this State are limited to advertising without the intent to solicit insurance in this State through communications in printed publications or other forms of electronic mass media whose distribution is not limited to residents of this State, provided that the person does not sell, solicit, or negotiate insurance that would insure risks residing, located, or to be performed in this State.

(6) A person who is not a resident of this State who sells, solicits, or negotiates a contract of insurance for commercial property and casualty risks to an insured with risks located in more than one state insured under that contract, provided that that person is otherwise licensed as an insurance producer to sell, solicit, or negotiate that insurance in the state where the insured maintains its principal place of business and the contract of insurance insures risks located in that state.

(7) A salaried full-time employee who counsels or advises his or her employer relative to the insurance interests of the employer or of the subsidiaries or business affiliates of the employer provided that the employee does not sell or solicit insurance or receive a commission.

(8) Licensed insurers authorized to write the kinds of insurance described in G.S. 58-7-15(1) through G.S. 58-7-15(3) that do business without the involvement of a licensed agent.

(9) A person indirectly receiving proceeds of commissions as part of the transfer of insurance business or in the form of retirement or similar benefits.

(o) Nothing in this Article requires an insurer to obtain an insurance producer license. In this subsection, "insurer" does not include an insurer's officers, directors, employees, subsidiaries, or affiliates. (2001-203, s. 6.)

Editor's Note. — Session Laws 2001-203, s. 32, made this section effective July 1, 2002.

Session Laws 2001-203, s. 31, contains a severability clause.

§ 58-33-30. License requirements.

The Commissioner shall not issue or continue any license of an agent, broker, limited representative, adjuster, or motor vehicle damage appraiser except as follows:

(a) Application. — The applicable license application requirements of G.S. 58-33-31 shall be satisfied.

(b) Repealed by Session Laws 2001-203, s. 7, effective July 1, 2002

(c) Repealed by Session Laws 2001-203, s. 7, effective July 1, 2002

(d) Education and Training. —

(1) Each applicant must have had special education, training, or experience of sufficient duration and extent reasonably to satisfy the Commissioner that the applicant possesses the competence necessary to fulfill the responsibilities of an agent, broker, limited representative, adjuster, or motor vehicle damage appraiser.

(2) All individual applicants for licensing as life and health agents or as property and liability agents shall furnish evidence satisfactory to the Commissioner of successful completion of at least 40 hours of instruction, which shall in all cases include the general principles of insurance and any other topics that the Commissioner establishes by regulation; and which shall, in the case of life and health insurance applicants, include the principles of life, accident, and health insurance and, in the case of property and liability insurance applicants, shall include instruction in property and liability insurance. Any applicant who submits satisfactory evidence of having successfully completed an agent training course that has been approved by the Commissioner and that is offered by or under the auspices of a property or liability or life or health insurance company admitted to do business in this State or a professional insurance association shall be deemed to have satisfied the educational requirements of this subdivision. The requirement in this subdivision for completion of 40 hours of instruction applies only to applicants for life and health or property and liability insurance licenses.

(3) Each resident applicant for a Medicare supplement and long-term care insurance license shall furnish evidence satisfactory to the Commissioner of successful completion of 10 hours of instruction, which shall in all cases include the principles of Medicare supplement and long-term care insurance and federal and North

Carolina law relating to such insurance. A resident applicant who submits satisfactory evidence of having successfully completed an agent training course that has been approved by the Commissioner and that is offered by or under the auspices of a licensed life or health insurer or a professional insurance association satisfies the educational requirements of this subdivision.

(e) Examination.

(1) After completion and filing of the application with the Commissioner, except as provided in G.S. 58-33-35, the Commissioner shall require each applicant for license as an agent or an adjuster to take an examination as to the applicant's competence to be licensed. The applicant must take and pass the examination according to requirements prescribed by the Commissioner.

(2) The Commissioner may require any licensed agent, adjuster, or motor vehicle damage appraiser to take and successfully pass an examination in writing, testing his competence and qualifications as a condition to the continuance or renewal of his license, if the licensee has been found guilty of any violation of any provision of this Chapter. If an individual fails to pass such an examination, the Commissioner shall revoke all licenses issued in his name and no license shall be issued until such individual has passed an examination as provided in this Article.

(3) Each examination shall be as the Commissioner prescribes and shall be of sufficient scope to test the applicant's knowledge of:

a. The terms and provisions of the policies or contracts of insurance the applicant proposes to effect; or

b. The types of claims or losses the applicant proposes to adjust; and

c. The duties and responsibilities of the license; and

d. The current laws of this State applicable to the license.

(4) The answers of the applicant to the examination shall be provided by the applicant under the Commissioner's supervision. The Commissioner shall give examinations at such times and places within this State as the Commissioner considers necessary reasonably to serve the convenience of both the Commissioner and applicants: Provided that the Commissioner may contract directly with persons for the processing of examination application forms and for the administration and grading of the examinations required by this section; the Commissioner may charge a reasonable fee in addition to the registration fee charged under G.S. 58-33-125, to offset the cost of the examination contract authorized by this subsection; and such contracts shall not be subject to Article 3 of Chapter 143 of the General Statutes.

(5) The Commissioner shall collect in advance the examination and registration fees provided in G.S. 58-33-125 and in subsection (4) of this section. The Commissioner shall make or cause to be made available to all applicants, for a reasonable fee to offset the costs of production, materials that he considers necessary for the applicants' proper preparation for examinations. The Commissioner may contract directly with publishers and other suppliers for the production of the preparatory materials, and contracts so let by the Commissioner shall not be subject to Article 3 of Chapter 143 of the General Statutes.

(6) In addition to the examinations for the kinds of insurance specified in G.S. 58-33-25(c)(1) and (2), before any resident may sell Medicare supplement or long-term care insurance policies defined

respectively in Articles 54 and 55 of this Chapter, the resident must take and pass a supplemental written examination according to requirements prescribed by the Commissioner.

(7) An individual who fails to appear for the examination as scheduled or fails to pass the examination shall reapply for an examination and remit all required fees and forms before being rescheduled for another examination.

(f) Brokers.

(1) Bond. — Prior to issuance of a license as a broker, the applicant shall file with the Commissioner and thereafter, for as long as the license remains in effect, shall keep in force a bond in favor of the State of North Carolina for the use of aggrieved parties in the sum of not less than fifteen thousand dollars ($15,000), executed by an authorized corporate surety approved by the Commissioner. The aggregate liability of the surety for any and all claims on any such bond shall in no event exceed the sum thereof. The bond shall be conditioned on the accounting by the broker (i) to any person requesting the broker to obtain insurance for moneys or premiums collected in connection therewith, (ii) to any licensed insurer or agent who provides coverage for such person with respect to any such moneys or premiums, and (iii) to any premium finance company or to any association of insurers under any plan or plans for the placement of insurance under the laws of North Carolina which afforded coverage for such person with respect to any such moneys or premiums. No such bond shall be terminated unless at least 30 days' prior written notice thereof is given by the surety to the licensee and the Commissioner. Upon termination of the license for which the bond was in effect, the Commissioner shall notify the surety within 10 business days. A person required by this subdivision to maintain a bond may, in lieu of that bond, deposit with the Commissioner the equivalent amount in cash, in certificates of deposit issued by banks organized under the laws of the State of North Carolina, or any national bank having its principal office in North Carolina, or securities, which shall be held in accordance with Article 5 of this Chapter. Securities may only be obligations of the United States or of federal agencies listed in G.S. 147-69.1(c)(2) guaranteed by the United States, obligations of the State of North Carolina, or obligations of a city or county of this State. Any proposed deposit of an obligation of a city or county of this State is subject to the prior approval of the Commissioner.

(2) Other Requirements. — An applicant must hold a valid agent's license at the time of application for the broker's license and throughout the duration of the broker's license. A broker's license shall be issued to cover only those kinds of insurance authorized by his agent's license. Suspension or revocation of the agent's license shall cause immediate revocation of the broker's license.

(g) Denial of License. — If the Commissioner finds that the applicant has not fully met the requirements for licensing, he shall refuse to issue the license and shall notify in writing the applicant and the appointing insurer, if any, of such denial, stating the grounds therefor. The application may also be denied for any reason for which a license may be suspended or revoked or not renewed under G.S. 58-33-46. Within 30 days after service of the notification, the applicant may make a written demand upon the Commissioner for a review to determine the reasonableness of the Commissioner's action. The review shall be completed without undue delay, and the applicant shall be notified promptly in writing as to the outcome of the review. Within 30 days after service of the notification as to the outcome, the applicant may make a written demand upon the Commissioner for a hearing under Article 3A of Chapter 150B of the General Statutes if the applicant disagrees with the outcome.

(h) Resident-Nonresident Licenses. — The Commissioner shall issue a resident or nonresident license to an agent, broker, limited representative, adjuster, or motor vehicle damage appraiser as follows:

(1) Resident.

An individual may qualify for a license as a resident if he resides in this State. Any license issued pursuant to an application claiming residency in this State shall be void if the licensee, while holding a resident license in this State, also holds or makes application for a resident license in, or thereafter claims to be a resident of, any other state, or ceases to be a resident of this State; provided, however, if the applicant is a resident of a county in another state, the border of which county is contiguous with the state line of this State, the applicant may qualify as a resident for licensing purposes in this State.

(2) Nonresident.

a. An individual may qualify for a license under this Article as a nonresident if he holds a like license in another state or territory of the United States. An individual may qualify for a license as a nonresident motor vehicle damage appraiser or a nonresident adjuster if the applicant's state of residency does not offer such licenses and such applicant meets all other requirements for licensure of a resident. A license issued to a nonresident of this State shall grant the same rights and privileges afforded a resident licensee, except as provided in subsection (i) of this section.

b. Except as provided in G.S. 58-33-32, a nonresident of this State may be licensed without taking an otherwise required written examination if the insurance regulator of the state of the applicant's residence certifies that the applicant has passed a similar written examination or has been a continuous holder, prior to the time such written examination was required, of a license like the license being applied for in this State.

c. Notwithstanding other provisions of this Article, no new bond shall be required for a nonresident broker if the Commissioner is satisfied that an existing bond covers his insurance business in this State.

d. Process Against Nonresident Licensees.

1. Each licensed nonresident agent, broker, adjuster, limited representative, or motor vehicle damage appraiser shall by the act of acquiring such license be deemed to appoint the Commissioner as his attorney to receive service of legal process issued against the agent, broker, adjuster, limited representative, or motor vehicle damage appraiser in this State upon causes of action arising within this State.

2. The appointment shall be irrevocable for as long as there could be any cause of action against the nonresident arising out of his insurance transactions in this State.

3. Duplicate copies of such legal process against such nonresident licensee shall be served upon the Commissioner

either by a person competent to serve a summons, or through certified or registered mail. At the time of such service the plaintiff shall pay to the Commissioner a fee in the amount set in G.S. 58-16-30, taxable as costs in the action to defray the expense of such service.

4. Upon receiving such service, the Commissioner or his duly appointed deputy shall within three business days send one of the copies of the process, by registered or certified mail, to the defendant nonresident licensee at his last address of record as filed with the Commissioner.

5. The Commissioner shall keep a record of the day and hour of service upon him of all such legal process. No proceedings shall be had against the defendant nonresident licensee, and such defendant shall not be required to appear, plead or answer until the expiration of 40 days after the date of service upon the Commissioner.

e. If the Commissioner revokes or suspends any nonresident's license through a formal proceeding under this Article, he shall promptly notify the appropriate Commissioner of the licensee's residence of such action and of the particulars thereof.

(i) Retaliatory Provision. — Whenever, by the laws or regulations of any other state or jurisdiction, any limitation of rights and privileges, conditions precedent, or any other requirements are imposed upon residents of this State who are nonresident applicants or licensees of such other state or jurisdiction in addition to, or in excess of, those imposed on nonresidents under this Article, the same such requirements shall be imposed upon such residents of such other state or jurisdiction. This subsection does not apply to fees charged to insurance producers.

(j) Reciprocity Provision. — To the extent that other states that provide for the licensing and regulation of and payment of commissions to agents, limited representatives, or brokers, waive restrictions on the basis of reciprocity with respect to North Carolina licensees applying for or holding nonresident licenses in those states, the same restrictions on licensees from those states applying for or holding North Carolina nonresident licenses shall be waived. (1987, c. 629, s. 1; c. 864, ss. 80, 86; 1987 (Reg. Sess., 1988), c. 975, s. 30; 1989, c. 485, s. 21; c. 645, s. 5; c. 657, s. 1.1; 1989 (Reg. Sess., 1990), c. 941, ss. 3, 7; 1991, c. 212, s. 2; c. 476, s. 3; 1993, c. 409, s. 2; c. 504, ss. 26, 37; 1998-211, s. 18; 2000-122, s. 3; 2001-203, ss. 7, 8, 9, 10, 11, 29.)

Editor's Note. — Session Laws 2001-203, s. 31, contains a severability clause.

Effect of Amendments. — Session Laws 2001-203, ss. 7 to 11 and 29, effective July 1, 2002, rewrote subsection (a), which read: "Application shall be made to the Commissioner by the applicant on a form prescribed by the Commissioner"; repealed subsections (b) and (c), regarding age and character; in subdivision (d)(3), inserted "resident" in the first sentence, deleted "An" and inserted "resident" thereafter at the beginning of the second sentence, and in that sentence substituted "a licensed life" for "an admitted life"; substituted "an examination as to the applicant's competence" for "a written examination as his competence" in subdivision

(e)(1); deleted "Articles 1 through 67 of" preceding "this Chapter" at the end of the first sentence of subdivision (e)(2); made stylistic and gender neutral changes in subdivision (e)(3); in subdivision (e)(4), substituted "the examination shall be provided" for "any such examination shall be written," substituted "the Commissioner considers" for "he deems," and substituted "may" for "is authorized" in two places; in subdivision (e)(5) substituted "considers" for "deems," substituted "examinations" for "such exams," substituted "may contract" for "is empowered to contract," and substituted "the" for "such"; inserted the subdivision (6) designation to precede the former final sentence of subdivision (5), and in subdivision (6) substituted "resident" for "person" and substituted "the resident" for "he"; substituted "G.S. 58-33-46" for "G.S. 58-33-45(a)" in subsection (g); and added the last sentence of subsection (i).

§ 58-33-31. Application for license.

(a) A person applying for a resident insurance producer license shall make application to the Commissioner on the Uniform Application and declare under penalty of denial, suspension, or revocation of the license that the statements made in the application are true, correct, and complete to the best of the individual's knowledge and belief. Before approving the application, the Commissioner shall find that the individual:

(1) Is at least 18 years of age.
(2) Has not committed any act that is a ground for probation, suspension, nonrenewal, or revocation set forth in G.S. 58-33-46.
(3) Has satisfied any applicable requirements of G.S. 58-33-30(d).
(4) Has paid the applicable fees set forth in G.S. 58-33-125.
(5) Has successfully passed any examinations required by G.S. 58-33-30(e).

(b) A business entity selling, soliciting, or negotiating insurance shall obtain an insurance producer license. Application shall be made using the Uniform Business Entity Application. Before approving the application, the Commissioner shall find that:

(1) The business entity has paid the applicable fees set forth in G.S. 58-33-125.
(2) The business entity has designated a licensed producer, who is a natural person, responsible for the business entity's compliance with the insurance laws and administrative rules of this State and orders of the Commissioner.

(c) The Commissioner may require any documents reasonably necessary to verify the information contained in an application. (2001-203, s. 12.)

Editor's Note. — Session Laws 2001-203, s. 32 made this section effective July 1, 2002. Session Laws 2001-203, s. 31, contains a severability clause.

§ 58-33-32. Interstate reciprocity in producer licensing.

(a) The purpose of this section is to make North Carolina insurance producer licensing comply with the reciprocity requirements in the federal Gramm-Leach-Bliley Act, Public Law 106-102. This section does not apply to surplus lines licensees in Article 21 of this Chapter, except as provided in subsections (c) and (d) of this section.

(b) Repealed by Session Laws 2001-203, s. 13, effective July 1, 2002.

(c) Unless denied licensure under G.S. 58-33-30 or G.S. 58-33-50, a nonresident person shall receive a nonresident producer license if:

(1) The person is currently licensed as a resident and in good standing in that person's home state;
(2) The person has submitted the request for licensure in the form prescribed by the Commissioner and has paid the applicable fees required by G.S. 58-33-125;
(3) The person has submitted or transmitted to the Commissioner a copy of the application for licensure that the person submitted to that person's home state, or in lieu of the same, a completed Uniform Application or Uniform Business Entity Application; and
(4) The person's home state awards nonresident producer licenses to residents of this State on a reciprocal basis.

The Commissioner may verify the producer's licensing status through the producer database maintained by the NAIC or affiliates or subsidiaries of the NAIC.

(d) A person licensed as a surplus lines producer in that person's home state shall receive a nonresident surplus lines license under subsection (c) of this section. Except for the licensure provisions of this section, nothing in this section otherwise amends or supersedes any provision of Article 21 of this Chapter.

(e) A person licensed or registered as a viatical settlement broker or provider, as defined in G.S. 58-58-205, in that person's home state shall receive a nonresident viatical settlement broker or provider license under subsection (c) of this section. Except for the licensure provisions of this section, nothing in this section otherwise amends or supersedes any provision of Part 5 of Article 58 of this Chapter.

(f) A person licensed as a limited line credit insurance producer or other type of limited lines producer in that person's home state may, under subsection (c) of this section, receive a nonresident limited lines producer license granting the same scope of authority as granted under the license issued by the producer's home state. For the purposes of this subsection, limited lines insurance is any authority granted by the home state that restricts the authority of the license to less than the total authority prescribed in the associated major lines under G.S. 58-33-26(c)(1), 58-33-26(c)(2), 58-33-26(c)(3), and 58-33-26(c)(4).

(g) An individual who applies for an insurance producer license in this State who was previously licensed for the same kinds of insurance in that individual's home state shall not be required to complete any prelicensing education or examination. This exemption is available only if:

(1) The applicant is currently licensed in the applicant's home state; or

(2) The application is received within 90 days after the cancellation of the applicant's previous license and the applicant's home state issues a certification that, at the time of cancellation, the applicant was in good standing in that state; or

(3) The home state's producer database records, maintained by the NAIC or affiliates or subsidiaries of the NAIC, indicate that the producer is or was licensed in good standing for the kind of insurance requested.

A person licensed as an insurance producer in another state who moves to this State and who wants to be licensed as a resident under G.S. 58-33-31 shall apply within 90 days after establishing legal residence.

(h) The Commissioner shall not assess a greater fee for an insurance license or related service to a nonresident producer based solely on the fact that the producer does not reside in this State.

(i) The Commissioner shall waive any license application requirements for a nonresident license applicant with a valid license from the applicant's home state, except the requirements imposed by subsection (c) of this section, if the applicant's home state awards nonresident licenses to residents of this State on the same basis.

(j) A nonresident producer's satisfaction of the nonresident producer's home state's continuing education requirements for licensed insurance producers shall constitute satisfaction of this State's continuing education requirements if the nonresident producer's home state recognizes the satisfaction of its continuing education requirements imposed upon producers from this State on the same basis.

(k) A producer shall report to the Commissioner any administrative action taken against the producer in another state or by another governmental agency in this State within 30 days after the final disposition of the matter. This report shall include a copy of the order or consent order and other information or documents filed in the proceeding necessary to describe the action.

(*l*) Within 30 days after the initial pretrial hearing date or similar proceeding, a producer shall report to the Commissioner any criminal prosecution of the producer. The report shall include a copy of the initial complaint filed, the order resulting from the hearing or similar proceeding, and any other information or documents filed in the proceeding necessary to describe the prosecution. (2000-122, s. 2; 2001-203, s. 13; 2001-436, s. 4.)

Editor's Note. — Session Laws 2001-203, s. 31, contains a severability clause.

Session Laws 2001-436, s. 17 is a severability clause.

Effect of Amendments. — Session Laws 2001-203, s. 13, effective July 1, 2002, deleted subsection (b), which contained definitions; substituted "the request for licensure in the form prescribed by the Commissioner" for "the proper request for licensure" and inserted "applicable" in subdivision (c)(2); inserted "a copy of" in subdivision (c)(3); substituted "a reciprocal basis" preceding "the same basis" at the end of subdivision (c)(4); deleted "Notwithstanding any other provision of this section" at the beginning of the first sentence of subsection (d), and substituted "under subsection (c)" for "pursuant to the provisions" in that sentence; rewrote subsection (e); rewrote the first sentence of subsection (f), and added the second sentence of that subsection; substituted "information or documents filed in the proceeding necessary to

describe the action" for "relevant legal documents" at the end of subsection (k); and in subsection (*l*), inserted "or similar proceeding" following "date" and deleted "taken in any state" following "producer" in the first sentence, and in the second sentence, inserted "or similar proceeding" following "hearing" and substituted "information or documents filed in the proceeding necessary to describe the prosecution."

Session Laws 2001-436, s. 4, effective April 1, 2002, in subsection (e), substituted "viatical settlement broker or provider as defined in G.S. 58-58-205" for "broker, viatical settlement provider, or viatical settlement representative, as defined in G.S. 58-58-42(a)," and substituted "viatical settlement broker or provider" for "viatical settlement broker, viatical settlement provider, or viatical settlement representative" in the first sentence, and substituted "Part 5 of Article 58 of this Chapter" for "G.S. 58-58-42" in the second sentence.

§ 58-33-35. Exemption from examination.

The following are exempt from the requirement for a written examination:
   (1) Repealed by Session Laws 1993, c. 409, s. 3.
   (2) Repealed by Session Laws 1989, c. 485, s. 66.
   (3) An applicant who has attained the designation of Chartered Life Underwriter (CLU), Chartered Financial Consultant (ChFC), Life Underwriter Training Council Fellow (LUTCF) or Fellow of Life Management Institute (FLMI), shall be exempt from the examination for licenses in G.S. 58-33-25(c)(1).
   (4) An applicant who has attained the designation of Chartered Property and Casualty Underwriter (CPCU) shall be exempt from the examination for licenses in G.S. 58-33-25(c)(3) and (7).
   (5) Applicants for license as limited representatives or as motor vehicle damage appraisers.
   (6) Applicants for license as agents for companies or associations specified in G.S. 58-36-50; provided that with respect to town or county farmers mutual fire insurance companies, this exemption applies only to those agents who solicit and sell only those kinds of insurance specified in G.S. 58-7- 75(5)d for such companies. (1987, c. 629, s. 1; c. 864, s. 81; 1989, c. 485, s. 66; 1989 (Reg. Sess., 1990), c. 1021, s. 8; 1993, c. 409, s. 3.)

§ 58-33-40. Appointment of agents.

(a) No individual who holds a valid insurance agent's license issued by the Commissioner shall, either directly or for an insurance agency, solicit, negotiate, or otherwise act as an agent for an insurer by which the individual has not been appointed.

(b) Any insurer authorized to transact business in this State may appoint as its agent any individual who holds a valid agent's license issued by the Commissioner. Upon the appointment, the individual shall be authorized to act as an agent for the appointing insurer for all kinds of insurance for which the insurer is authorized in this State and for which the appointed agent is licensed in this State, unless specifically limited.

(c) Within 30 days the insurer shall file in a form prescribed by the Commissioner the names, addresses, and other information required by the Commissioner for its newly-appointed agents.

(d) Every insurer shall remit in a manner prescribed by the Commissioner the appointment fee specified in G.S. 58-33-125 for each appointed agent.

(e) An appointment shall continue in effect as long as the appointed agent is properly licensed and the appointing insurer is authorized to transact business in this State, unless the appointment is cancelled.

(f) Prior to April 1 of each year, every insurer shall remit in a manner prescribed by the Commissioner the renewal appointment fee specified in G.S. 58-33-125.

(g) Any agent license in effect on February 1, 1988, shall be deemed to be an appointment for the unexpired term of that license.

(h) No insurer shall accept an insurance application from an individual who is not currently appointed by the insurer. (1987, c. 629, s. 1; 2001-203, s. 14.)

Editor's Note. — Session Laws 2001-203, s. 31, contains a severability clause.
Effect of Amendments. — Session Laws 2001-203, s. 14, effective July 1, 2002, deleted the last two sentences of subsection (e), regarding the cancellation of an appointment.

§ **58-33-45:** Repealed by Session Laws 2001-203, s. 15, effective July 1, 2002.

Cross References. — For present provisions covering the subject matter of the repealed section, see G.S. 58-33-46.

CASE NOTES

Editor's Note. — The case below was decided under prior statutory provisions.
Motions for Continuance and Bill of Particulars Addressed to Commissioner's Discretion. — In a hearing before the Commissioner of Insurance in proceedings for the revocation of an agent's license, where the agent was given more than the 10-day statutory notice, motions for a continuance and for a bill of particulars were addressed to the sound discretion of the Commissioner, and the denial of the motions would not be disturbed in the absence of a showing of abuse. Elmore v. Lanier, 270 N.C. 674, 155 S.E.2d 114 (1967).

§ **58-33-46. Suspension, probation, revocation, or nonrenewal of licenses.**

(a) The Commissioner may place on probation, suspend, revoke, or refuse to renew any license issued under this Article, in accordance with the provisions of Article 3A of Chapter 150B of the General Statutes, for any one or more of the following causes:

    (1) Providing materially incorrect, misleading, incomplete, or materially untrue information in the license application.

(2) Violating any insurance laws, or violating any administrative rule, subpoena, or order of the Commissioner or of another state's insurance regulator.

(3) Obtaining or attempting to obtain a license through misrepresentation or fraud.

(4) Improperly withholding, misappropriating, or converting any monies or properties received in the course of doing insurance business.

(5) Intentionally misrepresenting the terms of an actual or proposed insurance contract or application for insurance.

(6) Having been convicted of a felony or of a misdemeanor involving dishonesty or a breach of trust.

(7) Having admitted or been found to have committed any insurance unfair trade practice or fraud.

(8) Using fraudulent, coercive, or dishonest practices, or demonstrating incompetence, untrustworthiness, or financial irresponsibility in the conduct of business in this State or elsewhere.

(9) Having an insurance producer license, or its equivalent, denied, suspended, or revoked in any other jurisdiction for reasons substantially similar to those listed in this subsection.

(10) Forging another's name to an application for insurance or to any document related to an insurance transaction.

(11) Willfully failing to provide the notification required by subsection (c) of this section.

(12) Knowingly accepting brokered insurance business from an individual who is not licensed to broker that kind of insurance.

(13) Failing to comply with an administrative or court order imposing a child support obligation, after entry of a final judgment or order finding the violation to have been willful.

(14) Failing to pay State income tax or comply with any administrative or court order directing payment of State income tax, after entry of a final judgment or order finding the violation to have been willful.

(15) Cheating on an examination for an insurance license or for a prelicensing or continuing education course, including improperly using notes or any other reference material to complete an examination for an insurance license or for a prelicensing or continuing education course.

(16) Willfully overinsuring property.

(17) Any cause for which issuance of the license could have been refused had it then existed and been known to the Commissioner at the time of issuance.

(b) G.S. 58-2-50 applies to any investigation under this section. G.S. 58-2-70 applies to any person subject to licensure under this Article.

(c) Any person licensed under this Article shall notify the Commissioner of the commencement of any bankruptcy, insolvency, or receivership proceeding affecting the person licensed, or upon making an assignment for the benefit of creditors of the person licensed. Each owner, manager, or officer of a business entity that is a licensed person shall be responsible for providing this notification. Any person responsible for notifying the Commissioner shall provide the notice within three business days after the commencement of the proceeding or the making of the assignment.

(d) If the Commissioner refuses to grant a license, or suspends or revokes a license, any appointment of the applicant or licensee shall likewise be revoked. No individual whose license is revoked shall be issued another license without first complying with all requirements of this Article.

(e) No person shall be issued a license or appointment to enter the employment of any other person, which other person is at that time found by the Commissioner to be in violation of any of the insurance laws of this State, or which other person has been in any manner disqualified under any state or federal law to engage in the insurance business.

(f) The Commissioner shall retain the authority to enforce the provisions of, and impose any penalty or remedy authorized by, this Chapter against any person who is under investigation for or charged with a violation of this Chapter even if the person's license or registration has been surrendered or has lapsed by operation of law. (2001-203, s. 16.)

Editor's Note. — Session Laws 2001-203, s. 32, made this section effective July 1, 2002.

Session Laws 2001-203, s. 31, contains a severability clause.

CASE NOTES

Editor's Note. — *The case below was decided under prior statutory provisions.*

Motions for Continuance and Bill of Particulars Addressed to Commissioner's Discretion. — In a hearing before the Commissioner of Insurance in proceedings for the revocation of an agent's license, where the agent was given more than the 10-day statutory notice, motions for a continuance and for a bill of particulars were addressed to the sound discretion of the Commissioner, and the denial of the motions would not be disturbed in the absence of a showing of abuse. Elmore v. Lanier, 270 N.C. 674, 155 S.E.2d 114 (1967).

§ 58-33-50. Notices; loss of residency; duplicate licenses.

(a) The Commissioner shall notify every appointing insurer about any suspension, revocation, or nonrenewal of a license by the Commissioner and about any surrender of a license by a licensee, whether by consent order or otherwise.

(b) Upon suspension, revocation, nonrenewal, surrender, or reinstatement of any license, the Commissioner shall notify the Central Office of the NAIC.

(c) Any licensee who ceases to maintain his residency in this State shall deliver his insurance license or licenses to the Commissioner by personal delivery or by mail within 30 days after terminating residency.

(d) The Commissioner may issue a duplicate license for any lost, stolen, or destroyed license issued pursuant to this Article upon a written request from the licensee and payment of appropriate fees. (1987, c. 629, s. 1; 1993, c. 504, s. 29.)

§ 58-33-55: Repealed by Session Laws 2001-203, s. 17, effective July 1, 2002.

§ 58-33-56. Notification to Commissioner of termination.

(a) An insurer or authorized representative of the insurer that terminates the appointment, employment, contract, or other insurance business relationship with a producer shall notify the Commissioner within 30 days after the effective date of the termination, using a form prescribed by the Commissioner, if the reason for termination is for or related to one of the causes listed in G.S. 58-33-46(a) or the insurer has knowledge the producer was found by a court, government body, or self-regulatory organization authorized by law to have engaged in any of the activities in G.S. 58-33-46(a). Upon the written request of the Commissioner, the insurer shall provide additional information, documents, records, or other data pertaining to the termination or activity of the producer.

(b) An insurer or authorized representative of the insurer that terminates the appointment, employment, or contract with a producer for any reason that is not for or related to one of the causes listed in G.S. 58-33-46(a) shall notify the Commissioner within 30 days after the effective date of the termination, using a form prescribed by the Commissioner. Upon written request of the Commissioner, the insurer shall provide additional information, documents, records, or other data pertaining to the termination.

(c) The insurer or the authorized representative of the insurer shall promptly notify the Commissioner in a form acceptable to the Commissioner if, upon further review or investigation, the insurer discovers additional information that would have been reportable to the Commissioner in accordance with subsection (a) of this section had the insurer then known of its existence.

(d) Within 15 days after making the notification required by subsections (a), (b), and (c) of this section, the insurer shall mail a copy of the notification to the producer at the producer's last known address. If the producer is terminated for cause for any of the reasons listed in G.S. 58-33-46(a), the insurer shall provide a copy of the notification to the producer at the producer's last known address by certified mail, return receipt requested, postage prepaid, or by overnight delivery using a nationally recognized carrier.

(e) Within 30 days after the producer has received the original or additional notification, the producer may file written comments concerning the substance of the notification with the Commissioner. The producer shall, by the same means, simultaneously send a copy of the comments to the reporting insurer, and the comments shall become a part of the Commissioner's file and accompany every copy of a report distributed or disclosed for any reason about the producer as permitted under subsection (h) of this section.

(f) In the absence of actual malice, neither an insurer, the authorized representative of the insurer, a producer, the Commissioner, an organization of which the Commissioner is a member, nor the respective employees and agents of such persons acting on behalf of such persons shall be subject to civil liability as a result of any statement or information provided pursuant to this section.

(g) In any action brought against a person that may have immunity under subsection (f) of this section for making any statement required by this section or for providing any information relating to any statement that may be requested by the Commissioner, the party bringing the action shall plead specifically in any allegation that subsection (f) of this section does not apply because the person making the statement or providing the information did so with actual malice. Subsections (f) and (g) of this section do not abrogate or modify any existing statutory or common law privileges or immunities.

(h) Notwithstanding any other provision of this Chapter, any documents, materials, or other information in the control or possession of the Commissioner or any organization of which the Commissioner is a member that is (i) furnished by an insurer, producer, or an employee or agent thereof acting on behalf of the insurer or producer under this section, or (ii) obtained by the Commissioner in an investigation under this section shall be confidential by law and privileged, shall not be subject to or public records under G.S. 58-2-100 or Chapter 132 of the General Statutes, shall not be subject to subpoena, and shall not be subject to discovery in any civil action other than a proceeding brought by the Commissioner against a person to whom such documents, materials, or other information relate. However, the Commissioner is authorized to use the documents, materials, or other information in the furtherance of any regulatory or legal action brought as a part of the Commissioner's duties. Neither the Commissioner nor any person who received documents, materials, or other information while acting under the authority of the Commissioner shall be permitted or required to testify in any civil action other than a proceeding brought by the Commissioner against a person to whom such documents, materials, or other information relate concerning any such documents, materials, or information.

(i) In order to assist in the performance of the Commissioner's duties under this Article, the Commissioner may:

(1) Share documents, materials, or other information, including the confidential documents, materials, or information described in this section, with other state, federal, and international regulatory agencies, with the NAIC, its affiliates or subsidiaries, and with state, federal, and international law enforcement authorities. The Commissioner may condition such sharing on an agreement by the recipient to maintain the confidentiality and privileged status of the document, material, or other information;

(2) Receive documents, materials, or information, including otherwise confidential and privileged documents, materials, or information from other state, federal, and international regulatory agencies, from the NAIC, its affiliates or subsidiaries, and from state, federal, and international law enforcement authorities, and may agree to maintain the confidential and privileged status of the document, material, or other information received under the laws of the jurisdiction that is the source of the document, material, or information; and

(3) Enter into agreements governing sharing and use of information consistent with this subsection.

(j) No waiver of any applicable privilege or claim of confidentiality in the documents, materials, or information shall occur as a result of disclosure to the Commissioner under this section or as a result of sharing as authorized in subsection (i) of this section.

(k) Nothing in this Article prohibits the Commissioner from releasing final, adjudicated actions including for cause terminations that are open to public inspection under G.S. 58-2-100, to a database or other clearinghouse service maintained by the NAIC, its affiliates, or subsidiaries of the NAIC.

(*l*) An insurer, the authorized representative of the insurer, or producer that fails to report as required under this section or that is found to have reported with actual malice by a court of competent jurisdiction may, after notice and hearing, have its license suspended or revoked and may be fined in accordance with G.S. 58-2-70. (2001-203, s. 18.)

Editor's Note. — Session Laws 2001-203, s. 32, made this section effective July 1, 2002.

Session Laws 2001-203, s. 31, contains a severability clause.

§ 58-33-60. Countersignature and related laws.

Subject to the retaliatory provisions of G.S. 58-33-30(i), there shall be no requirement that a licensed resident agent or broker must countersign, solicit, transact, take, accept, deliver, record, or process in any manner an application, policy, contract, or any other form of insurance on behalf of a nonresident agent or broker or an authorized insurer; or share in the payment of commissions, if any, related to such business. (1987, c. 629, s. 1.)

§ 58-33-65: Repealed by Session Laws 2001-203, s. 19, effective July 1, 2002.

Cross References. — For present provisions covering the subject matter of this repealed section, see G.S. 58-33-66.

§ 58-33-66. Temporary licensing.

(a) The Commissioner may issue a temporary insurance producer license for a period not to exceed 180 days or longer, for good cause, without requiring an examination if the Commissioner deems that the temporary license is necessary for the servicing of an insurance business in any of the following cases:

(1) To the spouse or surviving spouse or court-appointed personal representative or guardian of a licensed insurance producer who dies or becomes mentally or physically disabled to allow adequate time for the transfer of the insurance business owned by the producer, for the recovery or return of the producer to the business, or for the training and licensing of new personnel to operate the producer's business.

(2) To a member or employee of a business entity licensed as an insurance producer, upon the death or disability of an individual designated in the business entity application or the license.

(3) To the designee of a licensed insurance producer entering active service in the armed forces of the United States of America.

(4) In any other circumstance where the Commissioner deems that the public interest will be served best by the issuance of this license.

(b) The Commissioner may by order limit the authority of any temporary licensee in any way deemed necessary to protect insureds and the public. The Commissioner may require the temporary licensee to have a suitable sponsor who is a licensed producer or insurer and who assumes responsibility for all acts of the temporary licensee and may impose other similar requirements designed to protect insureds and the public. The Commissioner may by order revoke a temporary license if the interest of insureds or the public are endangered. A temporary license terminates upon the transfer of the business.

(c) An individual requesting a temporary license on account of death or disability of an agent or broker shall be licensed to represent only those insurers that had appointed such agent at the time of death or commencement of disability. (2001-203, s. 20.)

Editor's Note. — Session Laws 2001-203, s. 32 makes this section effective July 1, 2002.

Session Laws 2001-203, s. 31, contains a severability clause.

§ 58-33-70. Special provisions for adjusters and motor vehicle damage appraisers.

(a) It shall be unlawful and cause for revocation of license for a licensed adjuster to engage in the practice of law.

(b) On behalf and on request of an insurer by which an agent or limited representative is appointed, the agent or limited representative may from time to time act as an adjuster and investigate and report upon claims without being licensed as an adjuster. No agent or limited representative shall adjust any losses where the agent's or representative's remuneration for the sale of insurance is in any way dependent upon the adjustment of those losses.

(c) Upon the filing of the application for an adjuster's license, the advance payment of the examination fee, and the filing with the Commissioner of a certificate signed by the applicant's employer, the Commissioner may issue a learner's permit authorizing the applicant to act as an adjuster for a learning period of 90 days without a requirement of any other license. Not more than one learner's permit shall ever be issued to one individual. The employer's certificate required by this subsection shall certify that:

(1) The applicant is an individual of good character.

(2) The applicant is employed by the signer of the certificate.

(3) The applicant will operate as a student or learner under the instruction and general supervision of a licensed adjuster.

(4) The employer will be responsible for the adjustment acts of the applicant during the learning period.

(d) Repealed by Session Laws 1998-211, s. 19, effective November 1, 1998.

(e) The Commissioner may permit an experienced adjuster, who regularly adjusts in another state and who is licensed in the other state (if that state requires a license), to act as an adjuster in this State without a North Carolina license only for an insurance company authorized to do business in this State, for emergency insurance adjustment work, for a period to be determined by the Commissioner, done for an employer who is an adjuster licensed by this State or who is a regular employer of one or more adjusters licensed by this State; provided that the employer shall furnish to the Commissioner a notice in writing immediately upon the beginning of any such emergency insurance adjustment work. As used in this subsection, "emergency insurance adjustment work" includes, but is not limited to, (i) adjusting of a single loss or losses arising out of an event or catastrophe common to all of those losses or (ii) adjusting losses in any area declared to be a state of disaster by the Governor under G.S. 166A-6 or by the President of the United States under applicable federal law.

(f) The Commissioner may permit an experienced motor vehicle damage appraiser who is regularly appraising in another state and who is licensed in such other state (if that state requires a license) to act as a motor vehicle damage appraiser in this State without a North Carolina license for emergency motor vehicle damage appraisal work for a period not exceeding 30 days done for an employer who notifies the Commissioner, in writing, at the beginning of the period of emergency appraisal work and who is:

(1) An insurance adjuster licensed by this State;

(2) A motor vehicle damage appraiser licensed by this State;

(3) A regular employer of one or more insurance adjusters licensed by this State; or

(4) A regular employer of one or more motor vehicle damage appraisers licensed by this State. (1987, c. 629, s. 1; 1998-211, s. 19.)

§ 58-33-75. Twisting with respect to insurance policies; penalties.

No licensee shall make or issue, or cause to be issued, any written or oral statement that willfully misrepresents or willfully makes an incomplete comparison as to the terms, conditions, or benefits contained in any policy of insurance for the purpose of inducing or attempting to induce a policyholder in any way to terminate or surrender, exchange, or convert any insurance policy. Any person who violates this section is subject to the provisions of G.S. 58-2-70 and G.S. 58-33-46. (1987, c. 629, s. 1; c. 864, s. 75; 2001-203, s. 21.)

Editor's Note. — Session Laws 2001-203, s. 31, contains a severability clause.

Effect of Amendments. — Session Laws 2001-203, s. 21, effective July 1, 2002, substituted "G.S. 58-33-46" for "G.S. 58-33-45" at the end of the section.

§ 58-33-76. Referral of business to repair source; prohibitions.

(a) No insurance company, agent, adjuster or appraiser or any person employed to perform their service shall recommend the use of a particular service or source for the repair of property damage without clearly informing the claimant that the claimant is under no obligation to use the recommended repair service.

(b) No insurance company, agent, adjuster or appraiser or any person employed to perform their service shall accept any gratuity or other form of remuneration from a repair service for recommending that repair service to a claimant. Provided, however, discounts agreed to by repair services shall not violate this section.

(c) Any person who violates this section is subject to the provisions of G.S. 58-2-70 and G.S. 58-33-46. (1991, c. 386, s. 1; 1993, c. 525, s. 1; 2001-203, s. 22.)

Editor's Note. — Session Laws 2001-203, s. 31, contains a severability clause.

Effect of Amendments. — Session Laws 2001-203, s. 22, effective July 1, 2002, substituted "G.S. 58-33-46" for "G.S. 58-33-45" in subsection (c).

§ 58-33-80. Discrimination forbidden.

No agent or representative of any company doing the business of insurance as defined in G.S. 58-7-15 shall make any discrimination in favor of any person. (1987, c. 629, s. 1.)

CASE NOTES

Editor's Note. — *The case below was decided prior to the enactment of this section.*

The prohibition against discrimination in rates is directed to insurers, agents, brokers and other representatives of insurers. Hyde Ins. Agency, Inc. v. Dixie Leasing Corp., 26 N.C. App. 138, 215 S.E.2d 162 (1975).

§ 58-33-82. Commissions.

(a) An insurance company or insurance producer shall not pay a commission, service fee, or other valuable consideration to a person for selling, soliciting, or negotiating insurance in this State if that person is required to be licensed under this Article and is not so licensed.

(b) A person shall not accept a commission, service fee, brokerage, or other valuable consideration for selling, soliciting, or negotiating insurance in this State if that person is required to be licensed under this Article and is not so licensed.

(c) Renewal or other deferred commissions may be paid to a person for selling, soliciting, or negotiating insurance in this State if the person was required to be licensed under this Article at the time of the sale, solicitation, or negotiation and was so licensed at that time.

(d) Except as provided in subsection (e) of this section, only agents who are duly licensed with appropriate company appointments, licensed brokers, licensed limited lines producers, or licensed limited representatives may accept, directly or indirectly, any commission, fee, or other valuable consideration for the sale, solicitation, or negotiation of insurance.

(e) Commissions, fees, or other valuable consideration for the sale, solicitation, or negotiation of insurance may be assigned or directed to be paid in the following circumstances:

    (1) To a business entity by a person who is an owner, shareholder, member, partner, director, employee, or agent of that business entity.

    (2) To a producer in connection with renewals of insurance business originally sold by or through the licensed person or for other deferred commissions.

    (3) In connection with the indirect receipt of commissions in circumstances in which a license is not required under G.S. 58-33-26(m). (2001-203, s. 23.)

Editor's Note. — Session Laws 2001-203, s. 32, made this section effective July 1, 2002.

Session Laws 2001-203, s. 31, contains a severability clause.

§ 58-33-83. Assumed names.

An insurance producer doing business under any name other than the producer's legal name shall notify the Commissioner before using the assumed name. (2001-203, s. 24; 2003-221, s. 13.)

Editor's Note. — Session Laws 2001-203, s. 32, made this section effective July 1, 2002.

Session Laws 2001-203, s. 31, contains a severability clause.

Effect of Amendments. — Session Laws 2003-221, s. 13, effective June 19, 2003, substituted "notify the Commissioner" for "notify the Commission."

§ 58-33-85. Rebates and charges in excess of premium prohibited; exceptions.

(a) No insurer, agent, broker or limited representative shall knowingly charge, demand or receive a premium for any policy of insurance except in accordance with the applicable filing approved by the Commissioner. No insurer, agent, broker or limited representative shall pay, allow, or give, or offer to pay, allow, or give, directly or indirectly, as an inducement to insurance, or after insurance has been effected, any rebate, discount, abatement, credit, or reduction of the premium named in a policy of insurance, or any special favor or advantage in the dividends or other benefits to accrue thereon, or any valuable consideration or inducement whatever, not specified in the policy of insurance. No insured named in a policy of insurance, nor any employee of such insured, shall knowingly receive or accept, directly or indirectly, any such rebate, discount, abatement or reduction of premium, or any special favor or advantage or valuable consideration or inducement. Nothing herein contained shall be construed as prohibiting the payment of commissions or other compensation to duly licensed agents, brokers and limited representatives, nor as prohibiting any participating insurer from distributing to its policyholders dividends, savings or the unused or unabsorbed portion of premiums and premium deposits. As used in this section the word "insurance" includes suretyship and the word "policy" includes bond.

(b) No insurer, agent, broker, or limited representative shall knowingly charge to or demand or receive from an applicant for insurance any money or other consideration in return for the processing of applications or other forms or for the rendering of services associated with a contract of insurance, which money or other consideration is in addition to the premium for such contract, unless the applicant consents in writing before any services are rendered. This subsection does not apply to the charging or collection of any fees otherwise provided for by law. (1987, c. 629, s. 1; c. 864, ss. 49, 89; 1989, c. 485, s. 52; 1991, c. 720, s. 4; 2001-203, s. 25.)

Editor's Note. — Session Laws 2001-203, s. 31, contains a severability clause.

Effect of Amendments. — Session Laws

2001-203, s. 25, effective June 15, 2001, added the last sentence of subsection (b).

CASE NOTES

Editor's Note. — *The case below was decided under prior statutory provisions.*

The sanctions provided by statutes for violations of the antirebate provisions are directed to the insurers, agents, brokers or

other representatives. The statutes do not declare that contracts in violation of the antirebate provision are void. Hyde Ins. Agency, Inc. v. Dixie Leasing Corp., 26 N.C. App. 138, 215 S.E.2d 162 (1975).

§ 58-33-90. Rebate of premiums on credit life and credit accident and health insurance; retention of funds by agent.

It shall be unlawful for any insurance carrier, or officer, agent or representative of an insurance company writing credit life and credit accident and health insurance, as defined in G.S. 58-58-10 and G.S. 58-51-100, or combination credit life, accident and health, hospitalization and disability insurance in connection with loans, to permit any agent or representative of such company to retain any portion of funds received for the payment of losses incurred, or to be incurred, under such policies of insurance issued by such company, or to pay, allow, permit, give or offer to pay, allow, permit or give, directly or indirectly, as an inducement to insurance, or after insurance has been effected, any rebate, discount, abatement, credit or reduction of the premium, to any loan agency, insurance agency or broker, or to any creditor of the debtor on whose account the insurance was issued, or to any person, firm or corporation which received a commission or fee in connection with the issuance of such insurance: Provided, that this section shall not prohibit the payment of commissions to a licensed insurance agent or agency or limited representative on the sale of a policy of credit life and credit accident and health insurance, or combination credit life, accident and health, hospitalization and disability insurance in connection with loans.

It shall be unlawful for any agent, agency, broker, limited representative, or insured named in any such policy, or for any loan agency or broker, or any agent, officer or employee of any loan agency or broker to receive or accept, directly or indirectly, any such rebate, discount, abatement, credit or reduction of the premium as set out in this section. (1987, c. 629, s. 1.)

§ 58-33-95. Agents personally liable; representing unlicensed company prohibited; penalty.

Any person representing an insurer is personally liable on all contracts of insurance unlawfully made by or through him, directly or indirectly, for any company not authorized to do business in the State. A person or citizen of the State who fills up or signs any open policy, certificate, blank or coupon of, or furnished by, an unlicensed company, agent, broker or limited representative, the effect of which is to bind any insurance in an unlicensed company on property in this State, is the representative of such company, and personally liable for all licenses and taxes due on account of such transaction. If any person shall unlawfully solicit, negotiate for, collect or transmit a premium for a contract of insurance or act in any way in the negotiation or transaction of any unlawful insurance with an insurance company not licensed to do an insurance business in North Carolina, he shall be guilty of a Class 1 misdemeanor. (1987, c. 629, s. 1; 1993, c. 539, s. 457; 1994, Ex. Sess., c. 24, s. 14(c).)

§ 58-33-100. Payment of premium to agent valid; obtaining by fraud a crime.

(a) Any agent, broker or limited representative who acts for a person other than himself negotiating a contract of insurance is, for the purpose of receiving the premium therefor, the company's agent, whatever conditions or stipulations may be contained in the policy or contract. This subsection does not apply to the Insurance Underwriting Association established under Article 45 of this Chapter or the Joint Underwriting Association established under Article 46 of this Chapter.

(b) Any agent, broker or limited representative knowingly procuring by fraudulent representations payment, or the obligation for the payment, of a premium of insurance, shall be guilty of a Class 1 misdemeanor. (1987, c. 629, s. 1; 1993, c. 539, s. 458; 1994, Ex. Sess., c. 24, s. 14(c); 1997-498, s. 4.)

§ 58-33-105. False statements in applications for insurance.

If any agent, examining physician, applicant, or other person shall knowingly or willfully make any false or fraudulent statement or representation in or with reference to any application for insurance, or shall make any such statement for the purpose of obtaining any fee, commission, money or benefit from any company engaged in the business of insurance in this State, he shall be guilty of a Class 1 misdemeanor. This section shall also apply to contracts and certificates issued under Articles 65 through 67 of this Chapter. (1987, c. 629, s. 1; 1993, c. 539, s. 459; 1994, Ex. Sess., c. 24, s. 14(c).)

§ 58-33-110. Agents signing certain blank policies.

Any agent or limited representative who signs any blank contract or policy of insurance is guilty of a Class 3 misdemeanor and, upon conviction, shall be punished only by a fine of not less than one thousand dollars ($1,000) nor more than five thousand dollars ($5,000); provided, however, that transportation ticket policies of accident insurance and baggage insurance policies may be countersigned in blank for issuance only through coin-operated machines, subject to regulations prescribed by the Commissioner. (1987, c. 629, s. 1; 1993, c. 539, s. 460; 1994, Ex. Sess., c. 24, s. 14(c).)

§ 58-33-115. Adjuster acting for unauthorized company.

If any person shall act as adjuster on a contract made otherwise than as authorized by the laws of this State, or by any insurance company or other person not regularly licensed to do business in this State, or shall adjust or aid in the adjustment, either directly or indirectly, of a claim arising under a contract of insurance not authorized by the laws of the State, he shall be deemed guilty of a Class 1 misdemeanor. (1987, c. 629, s. 1; 1993, c. 539, s. 461; 1994, Ex. Sess., c. 24, s. 14(c).)

§ 58-33-120. Agent, adjuster, etc., acting without a license or violating insurance law.

If any person shall assume to act either as principal, agent, broker, limited representative, adjuster or motor vehicle damage appraiser without license as is required by law or pretending to be a principal, agent, broker, limited representative, adjuster or licensed motor vehicle damage appraiser, shall solicit, examine or inspect any risk, or shall examine into, adjust, or aid in adjusting any loss, investigate or advise relative to the nature and amount of damages to motor vehicles or the amount necessary to effect repairs thereto, or shall receive, collect, or transmit any premium of insurance, or shall do any other act in the soliciting, making or executing any contract of insurance of any kind otherwise than the law permits, or as principal or agent shall violate any provision of law contained in Articles 1 through 64 of this Chapter, the punishment for which is not elsewhere provided for, he shall be deemed guilty of a Class 1 misdemeanor. (1987, c. 629, s. 1; 1987 (Reg. Sess., 1988), c. 975, s. 11; 1993, c. 539, s. 462; 1994, Ex. Sess., c. 24, s. 14(c).)

§ 58-33-125. Fees.

(a) The following table indicates the annual fees that are required for the respective licenses issued, renewed, or cancelled under this Article and Article 21 of this Chapter:

Adjuster	$75.00
Adjuster, crop hail only	20.00
Agent appointment cancellation (paid by insurer)	10.00
Agent appointment, individual	20.00
Agent appointment, nonindividual	50.00
Agent appointment, Medicare supplement and long-term care, individual	10.00
Agent appointment, Medicare supplement and long-term care, nonindividual	20.00
Agent, overseas military	20.00
Broker, nonresident	50.00
Broker, resident	50.00
Limited representative	20.00
Limited representative cancellation (paid by insurer)	10.00
Motor vehicle damage appraiser	75.00
Recertification, continuing education	5.00
Surplus lines licensee, corporate	50.00
Surplus lines licensee, individual	50.00

These fees are in lieu of any other license fees. Fees paid by an insurer on behalf of a person who is licensed or appointed to represent the insurer shall be paid to the Commissioner on a quarterly or monthly basis, in the discretion of the Commissioner. The recertification fee in this subsection shall be paid by persons subject to G.S. 58-33-130 at the time they renew their licenses or appointments under G.S. 58-33-130(c).

(b) Whenever a temporary license may be issued pursuant to this Article, the fee shall be at the same rate as provided in subsection (a) of this section; and any amounts so paid for a temporary license may be credited against the fee required for an appointment by the sponsoring company.

(c) Any person not registered who is required by law or administrative rule to secure a license shall, upon application for registration, pay to the Commissioner a fee of thirty dollars ($30.00). In the event additional licensing for other kinds of insurance is requested, a fee of thirty dollars ($30.00) shall be paid to the Commissioner upon application for registration for each additional kind of insurance.

In addition to the fees prescribed by this subsection, any person applying for a supplemental license to sell Medicare supplement and long-term care insurance policies shall pay an additional fee of thirty dollars ($30.00) upon application for registration for those kinds of insurance.

(d) The requirement for an examination, prelicensing education, continuing education, or a registration fee does not apply to agents for domestic farmers' mutual assessment fire insurance companies or associations who solicit and sell only those kinds of insurance specified in G.S. 58-7-75(5)d for such companies or associations.

(e) In the event a license issued under this Article is lost, stolen, or destroyed, the Commissioner may issue a duplicate license upon a written request from the licensee and payment of a fee of five dollars ($5.00).

(f) Whenever a printed record of an agent's file is requested, the fee shall be ten dollars ($10.00) for each copy whether or not the agent is currently licensed, previously licensed, or no record of that agent exists.

(g) All fees prescribed by this section are nonrefundable. (1987, c. 629, s. 1; c. 864, ss. 84, 85; 1989 (Reg. Sess., 1990), c. 941, ss. 4-5; c. 1021, s. 9; c. 1069, s. 14; 1991, c. 476, s. 3; c. 721, s. 7; 1991 (Reg. Sess., 1992), c. 837, s. 3; 2000-122, s. 1.)

§ 58-33-130. Continuing education program for licensees.

(a) The Commissioner may adopt rules to provide for a program of continuing education requirements for the purpose of enhancing the professional competence and professional responsibility of adjusters and motor vehicle damage appraisers. The rules may include criteria for:

    (1) The content of continuing education courses;

    (2) Accreditation of continuing education sponsors and programs;

    (3) Accreditation of videotape or other audiovisual programs;

    (4) Computation of credit;

    (5) Special cases and exemptions;

    (6) General compliance procedures; and

    (7) Sanctions for noncompliance.

(b) The Commissioner may adopt rules to provide for the continuing professional education of all agents and brokers, including fraternal field marketers, but excluding limited representatives. In adopting the rules, the Commissioner may use the same criteria as specified in subsection (a) of this section and shall provide that agents holding more than one license under G.S. 58-33-25(c) are required to complete no more than 18 credit hours per year.

(c) The license of any person who fails to comply with the continuing education requirements under this section shall lapse. The Commissioner may, for good cause shown, grant extensions of time to licensees to comply with these requirements.

(d) Annual continuing professional education hour requirements shall be determined by the Commissioner, but shall not be more than 12 credit hours.

(e) No more than seventy-five percent (75%) of the requirement relating to life or health insurance agents or brokers may be met by taking courses offered by licensed life or health insurance companies with which those agents or brokers have appointments.

(f) Repealed by Session Laws 1993 (Reg. Sess., 1994), c. 678, s. 18, effective July 5, 1994.

(g) The Commissioner shall permit any licensee to carry over to a subsequent calendar year up to seventy-five percent (75%) of the required annual hours of continuing professional education.

(h) Any licensee who, after obtaining an extension under subsection (c) of this section, offers evidence satisfactory to the Commissioner that the licensee has satisfactorily completed the required continuing professional education courses is in compliance with this section.

(i) The Commissioner is authorized to approve continuing professional education courses.

(j) **(Effective until June 30, 2004)** Repealed by Session Laws 2002-144, s. 3, effective July 1, 2002.

(j) **(Effective June 30, 2004)** The Commissioner is authorized to establish fees to be paid to the Commissioner by licensees who are required to comply with this section or by course vendors for the purpose of offsetting the cost of

G.S. 58-33-130(j) is set out twice. See notes.

additional staff and resources to administer the program authorized by this section. To assure continued and proper administration of the program, any unexpended revenue from the fees shall not revert to the General Fund.

(k) Repealed by Session Laws 1993, c. 409, s. 4, effective July 1, 1993. (1989, c. 657, s. 1; 1989 (Reg. Sess., 1990), c. 941, s. 6; 1991, c. 476, s. 2; c. 554, s. 1; c. 720, s. 22; 1993, c. 409, s. 4; 1993 (Reg. Sess., 1994), c. 678, s. 18; 1998-211, ss. 20, 21; 2002-144, s. 3; 2003-284, s. 22.2.)

Subsection (j) Set Out Twice. — Subsection (j) is repealed effective July 1, 2002, and expiring June 30, 2004, by Session Laws 2002-144, s. 3, as amended by Session Laws 2003-284, s. 22.2. The second version of subsection (j) is effective June 30, 2004.

Editor's Note. — Session Laws 2002-144, s. 11, contains a severability clause.

Session Laws 2003-284, s. 1.2, provides: "This act shall be known as the 'Current Operations and Capital Improvements Appropriations Act of 2003'."

Session Laws 2003-284, s. 49.3, provides:

"Except for statutory changes or other provisions that clearly indicate an intention to have effects beyond the 2003-2005 fiscal biennium, the textual provisions of this act apply only to funds appropriated for, and activities occurring during, the 2003-2005 fiscal biennium."

Session Laws 2003-284, s. 49.5 is a severability clause.

Effect of Amendments. — Session Laws 2002-144, s. 3, as amended by Session Laws 2003-284, s. 22.2, effective July 1, 2002 and expiring on June 30, 2004, repealed subsection (j).

§ 58-33-132. Qualifications of instructors.

(a) The Commissioner may adopt rules to establish requisite qualifications for and issuance, renewal, summary suspension, and termination of provider, presenter, and instructor authority for prelicensing and continuing insurance education courses. During any suspension, the instructor shall not engage in any instruction of prelicensing or continuing insurance education courses prior to an administrative review. No person shall provide, present, or instruct any course unless that person has been qualified and possesses a license from the Commissioner.

(b) The Commissioner may summarily suspend or terminate the authority of an instructor, course provider, or presenter if the course presentation:

(1) Is determined to be inaccurate; or
(2) Receives an evaluation of poor from any Department monitor and a majority of attendees responding to Department questionnaires about the presentation. (1995, c. 517, s. 17; 1999-132, s. 9.1.)

§ 58-33-133. (Expires June 30, 2004) Continuing education course provider fees.

(a) Each course provider shall submit a fee of one dollar ($1.00) per approved credit hour per individual who successfully completes a course under G.S. 58-33-130.

(b) At the time a course provider submits an application to the Commissioner for approval of a course under G.S. 58-33-130, the provider shall pay to the Commissioner a filing fee of one hundred dollars ($100.00) per course up to a two thousand five hundred dollars ($2,500) per calendar year maximum.

(c) Fees collected by the Commissioner under this section shall be credited to the Insurance Regulatory Fund created under G.S. 58-6-25. (2002-144, s. 2; 2003-221, s. 5; 2003-284, s. 22.2.)

Editor's Note. — Session Laws 2002-144, s. 12, as amended by Session Laws 2003-284, s. 22.2, made this section effective July 1, 2002, and provided that this section shall expire on June 30, 2004.

Session Laws 2002-144, s. 11, contains a severability clause.

Session Laws 2003-284, s. 1.2, provides: "This act shall be known as the 'Current Operations and Capital Improvements Appropriations Act of 2003'."

Session Laws 2003-284, s. 49.3, provides:

"Except for statutory changes or other provisions that clearly indicate an intention to have effects beyond the 2003-2005 fiscal biennium, the textual provisions of this act apply only to funds appropriated for, and activities occurring during, the 2003-2005 fiscal biennium."

Session Laws 2003-284, s. 49.5 is a severability clause.

Effect of Amendments. — Session Laws 2003-221, s. 5, effective June 19, 2003, in subsection (c), substituted "Insurance Regulatory Fund" for "Department of Insurance Fund."

§ 58-33-135. Continuing education advisory committee.

(a) The Commissioner shall appoint, in accordance with G.S. 58-2-30, one advisory committee for fire and casualty insurance licensees and one advisory committee for life and health insurance licensees. The advisory committees shall recommend reasonable rules to the Commissioner for promulgation under G.S. 58-33-130. The Commissioner may adopt, reject, or modify such recommendations. After the promulgation of rules under G.S. 58-33-130, the committees may from time to time make further recommendations to the Commissioner for additional rules or changes in existing rules.

(b) The property and liability advisory committee shall comprise:

   (1) Two employees of the Department of Insurance;

   (2) Two representatives from a list of four nominees submitted by the Independent Insurance Agents of North Carolina;

   (3) Repealed by Session Laws 1999-132, s 6.3, effective June 4, 1999.

   (4) One representative of a licensed property and liability insurance company writing business in this State that operates through an exclusive agency force;

   (5) One representative from a list of two nominees submitted by the North Carolina Adjusters Association;

   (6) One representative of property and liability insurers from a list of two nominees submitted by the Association of North Carolina Property and Casualty Insurance Companies; and

   (7) One representative from a list of two nominees submitted by the Community Colleges System Office.

(c) The life and health advisory committee shall comprise:

   (1) Two employees of the Department of Insurance, which may be the same persons appointed under subsection (b) of this section;

   (2) One representative from a list of two nominees submitted by the North Carolina Association of Life Underwriters;

   (3) One representative of life and health insurers from a list of two nominees submitted by the Association of North Carolina Life Insurance Companies;

   (4) One representative from a list of two nominees submitted by the General Agents and Managers Conference;

   (5) One representative from a licensed medical or hospital service corporation;

   (6) One licensed health insurance agent from a list of two nominees submitted by the North Carolina Association of Health Underwriters;

   (7) One representative of a licensed life or health insurer writing business in this State that operates through an exclusive agency force;

   (8) One representative from a list of two nominees submitted by the North Carolina Fraternal Congress; and

(9) One representative from a list of two nominees submitted by the Community Colleges System Office. (1989, c. 657, s. 1; 1999-84, ss. 17, 18; 1999-132, s. 6.3.)

ARTICLE 34.

Agency and Management Contracts.

§ **58-34-1:** Repealed by Session Laws 1991, c. 681, s. 50.

Editor's Note. — Session Laws 1991, c. 681, s. 49, substituted "Agency and Management Contracts" for "Managing General Agents" as the title of Article 34 of Chapter 58.

§ 58-34-2. Managing general agents.

(a) As used in this Article:

(1) "Control", including the terms "controlling", "controlled by", and "under common control", means the direct or indirect possession of the power to direct or cause the direction of the management and policies of a person, whether through the ownership of voting securities, by contract other than a commercial contract for goods or nonmanagement services, or otherwise, unless the power is the result of an official position with or corporate office held by the person.

(1a) "Custodial agreement" means any agreement or contract under which any person is delegated authority to safekeep assets of the insurer.

(2) "Insurer" means a domestic insurer but does not mean a reciprocal regulated under Article 15 of this Chapter.

(2a) "Management contract" means any agreement or contract under which any person is delegated management duties or control of an insurer or transfers a substantial part of any major function of an insurer, such as adjustment of losses, production of business, investment of assets, or general servicing of the insurer's business.

(3) "Managing general agent" or "MGA" means any person who manages all or part of the insurance business of an insurer (including the management of a separate division, department, or underwriting office) and acts as an agent for the insurer, whether known as a managing general agent, manager, or other similar term, who, with or without the authority, either separately or together with persons under common control, produces, directly or indirectly, and underwrites an amount of gross direct written premium equal to or more than five percent (5%) of the policyholder surplus as reported in the last annual statement of the insurer in any one quarter or year together with one or more of the following activities related to the business produced: (i) adjusts or pays any claims, or (ii) negotiates reinsurance on behalf of the insurer. "MGA" does not mean an employee of the insurer; an underwriting manager who, pursuant to contract, manages all or part of the insurance operations of the insurer, is under common control with the insurer, is subject to Article 19 of this Chapter, and whose compensation is not based on the volume of premiums written; a person who, under Article 15 of this Chapter, is designated and authorized by subscribers as the attorney-in-fact for a reciprocal having authority to obligate them on reciprocal and other insurance contracts; or a U.S. Manager of the United States branch of an alien insurer.

    (4) "Qualified actuary" means a person who meets the standards of a qualified actuary as specified in the NAIC Annual Statement Instructions, as amended or clarified by rule, order, directive, or bulletin of the Department, for the type of insurer for which the MGA is establishing loss reserves.

    (5) "Underwrite" means the authority to accept or reject risk on behalf of the insurer.

  (b) Control is presumed to exist if any person directly or indirectly owns, controls, holds with the power to vote, or holds proxies representing ten percent (10%) or more of the voting securities of any other person. The Commissioner may determine, after furnishing all persons in interest notice and opportunity to be heard and making specific findings of fact to support the determination, that control exists in fact, notwithstanding the absence of a presumption to that effect. The Commissioner may determine upon application that any person does not or will not upon the taking of some proposed action control another person. The Commissioner may prospectively revoke or modify that determination, after the notice and opportunity to be heard, whenever, in the Commissioner's judgment, revocation, or modification is consistent with this Article.

  (c) No person shall act as an MGA with respect to risks located in this State for an insurer unless that person is a licensed agent in this State. No person shall act as an MGA representing an insurer with respect to risks located outside of this State unless that person is licensed as an agent in this State; and the license may be a nonresident license. The Commissioner may require a bond in an amount acceptable to the Commissioner for the protection of the insurer. The Commissioner may require the MGA to maintain an errors and omissions policy.

  (d) No person acting as an MGA shall place business with an insurer unless there is in force a written contract between the MGA and the insurer that sets forth the responsibilities of each party and, where both parties share responsibility for a particular function, specifies the division of such responsibilities, and that contains the following minimum provisions:

    (1) The insurer may terminate the contract for cause upon written notice to the MGA. The insurer may suspend the underwriting authority of the MGA during the pendency of any dispute regarding the cause for termination.

    (2) The MGA will render accounts to the insurer detailing all transactions and remit all funds due under the contract to the insurer on not less than a monthly basis.

    (3) All funds collected for the account of an insurer will be held by the MGA in a fiduciary capacity in a bank that is a member of the Federal Reserve System. This account shall be used for all payments on behalf of the insurer. The MGA may retain no more than three months estimated claims payments and allocated loss adjustment expenses.

    (4) Separate records of business written by the MGA will be maintained. The insurer shall have access to and right to copy all accounts related to its business in a form usable by the insurer, and the Commissioner shall have access to all books, bank accounts, and records of the MGA in a form usable to the Commissioner. The records shall be retained according to the provisions of 11 NCAC 11C.0105.

    (5) The contract may not be assigned in whole or part by the MGA.

    (6) Appropriate underwriting guidelines, including: the maximum annual premium volume; the basis of the rates to be charged; the types of risks that may be written; maximum limits of liability; applicable exclusions; territorial limitations; policy cancellation provisions; and the maximum policy period. The insurer shall have the right to cancel

or nonrenew any policy of insurance subject to applicable laws and rules.

(7) If the contract permits the MGA to settle claims on behalf of the insurer:

    a. All claims must be reported to the insurer in a timely manner.

    b. A copy of the claim file will be sent to the insurer at its request or as soon as it becomes known that the claim: has the potential to exceed an amount determined by the insurer and approved by the Commissioner; involves a coverage dispute; may exceed the MGA's claims settlement authority; is open for more than six months; or is closed by payment of an amount set by the insurer and approved by the Commissioner.

    c. All claim files will be the joint property of the insurer and MGA. However, upon an order of liquidation of the insurer the files shall become the sole property of the insurer or its estate; the MGA shall have reasonable access to and the right to copy the files on a timely basis.

    d. Any settlement authority granted to the MGA may be terminated for cause upon the insurer's written notice to the MGA or upon the termination of the contract. The insurer may suspend the settlement authority during the pendency of any dispute regarding the cause for termination.

(8) Where electronic claims files are in existence, the contract must address the timely transmission of the data.

(9) If the contract provides for a sharing of interim profits by the MGA, and the MGA has the authority to determine the amount of the interim profits by establishing loss reserves, controlling claim payments, or by any other manner, interim profits will not be paid to the MGA until one year after they are earned for property insurance business and five years after they are earned on casualty business and not until the profits have been verified under subsection (f) of this section.

(10) The MGA shall not:

    a. Bind reinsurance or retrocessions on behalf of the insurer, except that the MGA may bind facultative reinsurance contracts pursuant to obligatory facultative agreements if the contract with the insurer contains reinsurance underwriting guidelines including, for both reinsurance assumed and ceded, a list of reinsurers with which such automatic agreements are in effect, the coverages and amounts or percentages that may be reinsured, and commission schedules;

    b. Commit the insurer to participate in insurance or reinsurance syndicates;

    c. Appoint any producer without assuring that the producer is lawfully licensed to transact the type of insurance for which the producer is appointed;

    d. Without prior approval of the insurer, pay or commit the insurer to pay a claim over a specified amount, net of reinsurance, which shall not exceed one percent (1%) of the insurer's policyholder's surplus as of the preceding December 31;

    e. Collect any payment from a reinsurer or commit the insurer to any claim settlement with a reinsurer, without the insurer's prior approval. If prior approval is given, a report must be promptly forwarded to the insurer;

    f. Permit its subproducer to serve on the insurer's board of directors;

     g. Jointly employ an individual who is employed with the insurer; or

     h. Appoint a sub-MGA.

(e) An insurer shall have on file by June 1 of each year an audited financial report of each MGA with which it is doing business. The report shall include the opinion of an independent certified public accountant, report the financial position of the MGA as of the most recent year-end and the results of its operations and cash flows, and include appropriate notes to financial statements. The insurer shall provide a copy of the report to the Commissioner within 15 days of receipt by the insurer.

(f) If an MGA establishes loss reserves, the insurer shall provide with its annual statement, in addition to any other required statement of actuarial opinion, the statement of a qualified actuary attesting to the adequacy of loss reserves established on business produced by the MGA. The statement shall comply in all respects with the NAIC Annual Statement Instructions regarding the Statement of Actuarial Opinion.

(g) The insurer shall periodically, at least semiannually, conduct an on-site review of the underwriting and claims processing operations of the MGA. The insurer shall prepare and maintain a written report on the review and make it available to the Commissioner upon the Commissioner's request.

(h) Binding authority for all reinsurance contracts, except those contracts expressly permitted under sub-subdivision (d)(10)a. of this section, or participation in insurance or reinsurance syndicates, shall rest with an officer of the insurer, who shall not be affiliated with the MGA.

(i) Within 15 days after entering into or termination of a contract with an MGA, the insurer shall provide written notification of the appointment or termination to the Commissioner. Notices of appointment of an MGA shall include a copy of the contract, a statement of duties that the MGA is expected to perform on behalf of the insurer, the lines of insurance for which the MGA is to be authorized to act, whether any affiliation exists between the insurer and the MGA and the basis for the affiliation, NAIC biographical affidavit for each officer, director, and each person who owns ten percent (10%) or more of the outstanding voting stock of the MGA, and any other information the Commissioner may request. The Commissioner may prescribe the form to be used for notification of the information required by this item.

(j) The Commissioner shall disapprove any such contract that:

    (1) Does not contain the required contract provisions specified in subsection (d) of this section;

    (2) Subjects the insurer to excessive charges for expenses or commission;

    (3) Vests in the MGA any control over the management of the affairs of the insurer to the exclusion of the board of directors of the insurer;

    (4) Is entered into with any person if the person or its officers and directors are of known bad character or have been affiliated directly or indirectly through ownership, control, management, reinsurance transactions, or other insurance or business relationships with any person known to have been involved in the improper manipulation of assets, accounts, or reinsurance; or

    (5) Is determined by the Commissioner to contain provisions that are not fair and reasonable to the insurer.

Failure of the Commissioner to disapprove any such contract within 30 days after the contract has been filed with the Commissioner constitutes the Commissioner's approval of the contract. An insurer may continue to accept business from the person until the Commissioner disapproves the contract. Any disapproval shall be in writing. The Commissioner may withdraw approval of any contract the Commissioner has previously approved if the Commissioner determines that the basis of the original approval no longer exists or that the contract has, in actual operation, shown itself to be subject to disapproval on any of the grounds in this subsection. If the Commissioner withdraws approval of a contract, the Commissioner shall give the insurer notice of, and written reasons for, the withdrawal of approval. The Commissioner shall grant any party to the contract a hearing upon request.

(k) An insurer shall review its books and records each quarter to determine if any agent has become an MGA. If the insurer determines that an agent has become an MGA, the insurer shall promptly notify the agent of that determination and the insurer and agent must fully comply with the provisions of this Article within 15 days.

(*l*) An insurer shall not appoint to its board of directors an officer, director, employee, subagent, or controlling shareholder of its MGAs. This subsection does not apply to relationships governed by Article 19 of this Chapter or, if applicable, G.S. 58-3-165.

(m) The acts of an MGA are considered to be the acts of the insurer on whose behalf it is acting. An MGA may be examined by the Commissioner under G.S. 58-2-131 through G.S. 58-2-134 as if it were an insurer.

(n) If the Commissioner determines that an MGA or any other person has not materially complied with this section or with any rule adopted or order issued under this section, after notice and opportunity to be heard, the Commissioner may order:

    (1) For each separate violation, a civil penalty under the procedures in G.S. 58-2-70(d); or

    (2) Revocation or suspension of the person's license.

    (3) Repealed by Session Laws 1993, c. 452, s. 47.

If the Commissioner finds that because of a material noncompliance that an insurer has suffered any loss or damage, the Commissioner may maintain a civil action brought by or on behalf of the insurer and its policyholders and creditors for recovery of compensatory damages for the benefit of the insurer and its policyholders and creditors or for other appropriate relief.

(o) Nothing in this section affects the Commissioner's right to impose any other penalties provided for in this Chapter. Nothing in this Article limits or restricts the rights of policyholders, claimants, and creditors.

(p) If an order of rehabilitation or liquidation of the insurer has been entered under Article 30 of this Chapter, and the receiver appointed under that order determines that the MGA or any other person has not materially complied with this section, or any regulation or order promulgated thereunder, and the insurer suffered any loss or damage therefrom, the receiver may maintain a civil action for recovery of damages or other appropriate sanctions for the benefit of the insurer. (1991, c. 681, s. 51; 1993, c. 452, ss. 43-48; 1993 (Reg. Sess., 1994), c. 678, s. 19; 1995, c. 193, s. 34; 1999-132, s. 11.6; 2001-223, ss. 20.1, 20.2.)

§ 58-34-5. Retrospective compensation agreements.

(a) Retrospective compensation agreements for business written under Articles 1 through 64 of this Chapter must be filed with the Commissioner for his approval.

(b) "Retrospective compensation agreement" means any such arrangement, agreement, or contract having as its purpose the actual or constructive retention by a domestic insurer of a fixed proportion of the gross premiums, with the balance of the premiums, retained actually or constructively by the agent or the producer of the business, who assumes to pay therefrom all losses, all subordinate commissions, loss adjustment expenses and his profit, if any, with other provisions of such arrangement, agreement, or contract auxiliary or incidental to such purpose.

(c) The standards for approval shall be as set forth under G.S. 58-34-2(d)(5). (1987, c. 752, s. 8; 1989, c. 485, s. 60; 1991, c. 681, s. 52.)

§ 58-34-10. Management contracts.

(a) Subject to G.S. 58-19-30(b)(4), any domestic insurer that enters into a management contract or custodial agreement must file that contract or agreement with the Commissioner on or before its effective date.

(b) Any domestic insurer that has a management contract or custodial agreement shall file a statement with the initial filing of that contract that discloses (i) criteria on which charges to the insurer are based for that contract; (ii) whether management personnel or other employees of the insurer are to be performing management functions and receiving any remuneration therefor through that contract in addition to the compensation by way of salary received directly from the insurer for their services; (iii) whether the contract transfers substantial control of the insurer or any of the powers vested in the board of directors, by statute, articles of incorporation, or bylaws, or substantially all of the basic functions of the insurer's management; (iv) biographical information for each officer and director of the management firm; and (v) other information concerning the contract or the management or custodian firm as may be included from time to time in any registration forms adopted or approved by the Commissioner. The statement shall be filed on a form prescribed by the Commissioner.

(c) Any domestic insurer that amends or cancels a management contract or custodial agreement filed under subsection (a) of this section shall notify the Commissioner within 15 business days after the amendment or cancellation. If the contract is amended, the notice shall provide a copy of the amended contract and shall disclose if the amendment affects any of the items in subsection (b) of this section. The Commissioner may prescribe a form to be used to provide notice under this subsection.

(d) Any domestic insurer that has a management contract or custodial agreement shall file a statement on or before March 1 of each year, for the preceding calendar year, disclosing (i) total charges incurred by the insurer under the contract; (ii) any salaries, commissions, or other valuable consideration paid by the insurer directly to any officer, director, or shareholder of the management or custodian firm; and (iii) other information concerning the contract or the management or custodian firm as may be included from time to time in any registration forms adopted or approved by the Commissioner. The Commissioner may prescribe a form to be used to provide the information required by this subsection.

(e) Any domestic insurer that has a management contract may request an exemption from the filing requirements of this section if the contract is for a group of affiliated insurers on a pooled funds basis or service company management basis, where costs to the individual member insurers are charged on an actually incurred or closely estimated basis. The request for an exemption must be in writing, must explain the basis for the exemption, and must be received by the Commissioner on or before the effective date of the contract. As used in this subsection, "affiliated" has the same meaning as in G.S. 58-19-5(1). Management contracts exempted under this subsection must still be reduced to written form. (1987, c. 752, s. 8; 1989, c. 485, s. 61; 1991, c. 681, s. 53; 1993, c. 452, s. 49; 2001-223, s. 20.3.)

§ 58-34-15. Grounds for disapproval.

(a) The Commissioner must disapprove any management contract or custodial agreement filed under G.S. 58-34-10 if, at any time, the Commissioner finds:

    (1) That the service or management charges are based upon criteria unrelated either to the managed insurer's profits or to the reasonable

customary and usual charges for the services or are based on factors unrelated to the value of the services to the insurer; or

(2) That management personnel or other employees of the insurer are to be performing management functions and receiving any remuneration for those functions through the management or service contract in addition to the compensation by way of salary received directly from the insurer for their services; or

(3) That the contract would transfer substantial control of the insurer or any of the powers vested in the board of directors, by statute, articles of incorporation, or bylaws, or substantially all of the basic functions of the insurance company management; or

(4) That the contract contains provisions that would be clearly detrimental to the best interest of policyholders, stockholders, or members of the insurer; or

(5) That the officers and directors of the management or custodial firm are of known bad character or have been affiliated, directly or indirectly, through ownership, control, management, reinsurance transactions, or other insurance or business relations with any person known to have been involved in the improper manipulation of assets, accounts, or reinsurance.

(6) That the custodial agreement is not substantially the same as the form adopted by the Commissioner.

(b) If the Commissioner disapproves any management contract or custodial agreement, notice of the disapproval shall be given to the insurer stating the reasons for the disapproval in writing. The Commissioner shall grant any party to the contract a hearing if the party requests a hearing. (1987, c. 752, s. 8; 1991, c. 681, s. 54; 1993, c. 452, s. 50; 2001-223, s. 20.4.)

§ **58-34-20:** Repealed by Session Laws 1993, c. 452, s. 65.

Cross References. — As to management contracts, see G.S. 58-34-10.

ARTICLE 35.

Insurance Premium Financing.

§ **58-35-1. Definitions.**

When used in this Article:

(1) An insurance premium finance company is hereby defined to be:
   a. Any person engaged, in whole or in part, in the business of entering into insurance premium finance agreements with insureds; or
   b. Any person engaged, in whole or in part, in the business of acquiring insurance premium finance agreements from other insurance premium finance companies.

(2) "Insurance premium finance agreement" means a promissory note or other written agreement by which an insured promises or agrees to pay to, or to the order of, an insurance premium finance company the amount advanced or to be advanced under the agreement to an insurer or to an insurance agent, in payment of premiums on an insurance contract, together with a service charge as authorized and limited by this Article. (1963, c. 1118.)

CASE NOTES

Law Governing Premium Finance Agreements. — The North Carolina Insurance Premium Financing Act, governs secured transactions involving premium finance agreements. In re Universal Motor Express, Inc., 72 Bankr. 208 (Bankr. W.D.N.C. 1987).

Cited in Northcutt v. Clayton, 269 N.C. 428, 152 S.E.2d 471 (1967).

§ 58-35-5. License required; fees.

(a) No person except an authorized insurer shall engage in the business of an insurance premium finance company without obtaining a license from the Commissioner, as provided in this Article.

(b) Application for license required under this Article shall be in writing, and in the form prescribed by the Commissioner.

(c) When an applicant has more than one office, separate applications for license shall be made for each such office.

(d) At the time of filing an application for a license, the applicant shall pay to the Commissioner the license fee. Upon original application or upon application subsequent to denial of application, or revocation, suspension or surrender of a license, an examination fee may be required.

(e) There shall be two types of licenses issued to an insurance premium finance company:

(1) An "A" type license shall be issued to insurance premium finance companies whose business of insurance premium financing is limited to the financing of insurance premiums of one insurance agent or agency and whose primary function is to finance only the insurance premium of such agent or agency. The license fee for an "A" type license shall be three hundred dollars ($300.00) for each license year or part thereof.

(2) A "B" type license shall be issued to an insurance premium finance company whose business of insurance premium financing is not limited to the financing of insurance premiums of one insurance agent or agency and whose primary function is to finance the insurance premiums of more than one insurance agent or agency. The license fee for a "B" type license shall be one thousand two hundred dollars ($1,200) for each license year or part thereof.

A branch office license may be issued for either an "A" type or "B" type license. The fee for the branch office license shall be fifty dollars ($50.00) for each license year or part thereof. The examination fee when required by this section shall be two hundred fifty dollars ($250.00) per application. (1963, c. 1118; 1967, c. 1232, s. 1; 1989 (Reg. Sess., 1990), c. 1069, s. 7; 1995, c. 507, s. 11A(c).)

Cross References. — As to exemption of insurance premium finance companies licensed under this Article from the license tax on loan agencies or brokers, see G.S. 105-88(b).

CASE NOTES

Fees Intended to Pay Expenses of Supervision. — The fees exacted of insurance premium financiers by this section and of persons engaged in business under the Consumers Finance Act by G.S. 53-167 are intended to pay the necessary expenses of licensing, regulating, and supervising the business. Although any surplus collected under this section reverts to the general treasury of the State under G.S. 58-35-95, this is merely an incidental budgetary provision. Northcutt v. Clayton, 269 N.C. 428, 152 S.E.2d 471 (1967).

§ 58-35-10. Exceptions to license requirements.

(a) Any person, firm or corporation doing business under the authority of any law of this State or of the United States relating to banks, trust companies, installment paper dealers, auto finance companies, savings and loan associations, cooperative credit unions, agricultural credit corporations or associations, organized under the laws of North Carolina or any person, firm or corporation subject to the provisions of the North Carolina Consumer Finance Act and the North Carolina Motor Vehicle Dealers and Manufacturers Licensing Law, Article 12, Chapter 20, of the General Statutes of North Carolina are exempt from the provisions of this Article.

(b) An insurance company duly licensed in this State may make an installment payment charge as set forth in the rate filings and approved by the Commissioner and is thereby exempt from the provisions of this Article.

(c) A fire and casualty insurance agent or an insurance broker duly licensed in this State who extends credit to and only to his own policyholders may charge and collect finance charges or other fees at a periodic (monthly) rate as provided in G.S. 24-11(a), after said amount has been outstanding for 30 days, and is hereby exempt from the provisions of this Article. Notwithstanding the exceptions set forth in subsections (a), (b) and (c) of this section, when any person, firm, or corporation shall exercise a power of attorney taken in connection with the financing of an insurance premium, such person, firm or corporation shall comply with the requirements of G.S. 58-35-85, as if it were an insurance premium financing company. (1963, c. 1118; 1967, c. 942, s. 1; 1971, c. 1186, ss. 1, 2; 1995 (Reg. Sess., 1996), c. 742, s. 25.)

Legal Periodicals. — For survey of 1976 case law on insurance, see 55 N.C.L. Rev. 1052 (1977).

CASE NOTES

Those Subject to This Article Not Intended to Be Subject to Consumer Finance Act. — Had the legislature intended to subject to the provisions of the Consumer Finance Act, G.S. 53-164 et seq., those who make loans solely to finance insurance premiums, surely it would not have enacted this Article in the first instance, since it exempts from its provisions those subject to the Consumer Finance Act. The legislature did not deem it necessary for both the Commissioner of Banks and the Commissioner of Insurance to supervise an insurance premium financing company. Northcutt v. Clayton, 269 N.C. 428, 152 S.E.2d 471 (1967).

Agent May Impose Finance Charge. — Section 24-11 and this section authorize an insurance agent who extends customer credit on an open account to impose a finance charge on his own customers in an amount not to exceed an aggregate annual rate of 18 percent. Hyde Ins. Agency, Inc. v. Noland, 30 N.C. App. 503, 227 S.E.2d 169 (1976).

Providing Notice Is Given at Time Credit Is Extended. — The creditor could collect a finance charge on an open insurance account under the provisions of G.S. 24-11(a) provided the person to whom the credit was extended had been notified by the creditor when the credit was extended of all the details and circumstances pertaining to the imposition of finance charges. Hyde Ins. Agency, Inc. v. Noland, 30 N.C. App. 503, 227 S.E.2d 169 (1976).

It was the intention of the legislature to authorize the imposition of finance charges on an open insurance account, even though there had not been any prior express agreement between the parties regarding such charges. Such charges could not be imposed unless the debtor was given proper notice that the creditor intended to impose such finance charges. Hyde Ins. Agency, Inc. v. Noland, 30 N.C. App. 503, 227 S.E.2d 169 (1976).

§ 58-35-15. Issuance or refusal of license; bond; duration of license; renewal; one office per license; display of license; notice of change of location.

(a) Within 60 days after the filing of an application for a license accompanied by payment of the fees for license and examination, the Commissioner shall issue the license or may refuse to issue the license and so advise the applicant. The applicant shall submit with such application any and all information which the Commissioner may require to assist him in determining the financial condition, business integrity, method of operation and protection to the public offered by the person filing such application. The Commissioner may require a bond not to exceed twenty-five thousand dollars ($25,000) on applications and any renewal thereof. Such license to engage in business in accordance with the provisions of this Article at the location specified in the application shall be executed in duplicate by the Commissioner and he shall transmit one copy to the applicant and retain a copy on file. A person required by this subsection to maintain a bond may, in lieu of that bond, deposit with the Commissioner the equivalent amount in cash, in certificates of deposit issued by banks organized under the laws of the State of North Carolina, or any national bank having its principal office in North Carolina, or securities, which shall be held in accordance with Article 5 of this Chapter. Securities may only be obligations of the United States or of federal agencies listed in G.S. 147-69.1(c)(2) guaranteed by the United States, obligations of the State of North Carolina, or obligations of a city or county of this State. Any proposed deposit of an obligation of a city or county of this State is subject to the prior approval of the Commissioner.

(b) Whenever the Commissioner denies an initial application for a license, he shall notify the applicant and advise, in writing, the applicant of the reasons for the denial of the license. Within 30 days of receipt of notification the applicant may make written demand upon the Commissioner for a hearing to determine the reasonableness of the Commissioner's action. Such hearing shall be scheduled within 30 days from the date of receipt of the written demand.

(c) Each license issued hereunder shall remain in full force and effect until the last day of June unless earlier surrendered, suspended, or revoked pursuant to this Article, and may be renewed for the ensuing license year upon the filing of an application and conforming with G.S. 58-35-5, but subject to all of the provisions of this Article. If an application for a renewal of a license is filed with the Commissioner before July 1 of any year, the license sought to be renewed shall be continued in full force and effect either until the issuance by the Commissioner of the renewal license applied for or until five days after the Commissioner refuses to issue such renewal license under the provisions of this Article.

(d) Only one office may be maintained under each license, but more than one license may be issued to the same licensee pursuant to this Article.

(e) Such license shall state the name and address of the licensee and shall at all times be prominently displayed in the office of the licensee and shall not be transferable or assignable.

(f) Before any licensee changes any office of his to another location, he shall give written notice thereof to the Commissioner. (1963, c. 1118; 1965, c. 1039; 1989, c. 485, s. 47; 1991, c. 212, s. 3.)

§ 58-35-20. Grounds for refusal, suspension or revocation of licenses; surrender of licenses; reinstatement.

(a) The Commissioner may forthwith deny, suspend, revoke, or refuse to renew or continue any license hereunder if he shall find that:

(1) The licensee has failed to pay the annual license fee or any sum of money lawfully demanded under authority of any section of this Article or has violated or failed to comply with any demand, ruling, provision or requirement of the Commissioner lawfully made pursuant to or within the authority of this Article.

(2) Any fact or condition exists which, if it had been known to exist at the time of the original application, would have caused the original license to have been refused.

(b) The Commissioner may revoke or suspend only the particular license with respect to which grounds for revocation or suspension may occur or exist; or if he shall find that such grounds for revocation or suspension are of general application to all offices, or to more than one office, operated by such licensee, he shall revoke or suspend all of the licenses issued to such licensee or such number of licenses as such grounds apply to, as the case may be.

(1) Any licensee may surrender any license by delivering to the Commissioner written notice that he thereby surrenders such license, but such surrender shall not affect such licensee's civil or criminal liability for acts committed prior to such surrender.

(2) No revocation or suspension or surrender of any license shall impair or affect the obligation of any insured under any lawful insurance premium finance agreement previously acquired or held by the licensee.

(3) Every license issued hereunder shall remain in force and effect until the same shall have been surrendered, revoked, suspended, or expires in accordance with the provisions of this Article; but the Commissioner shall have authority to reinstate suspended licenses or to issue new licenses to a licensee whose license or licenses shall have been revoked, if no fact or condition then exists which clearly would have warranted the Commissioner in refusing originally to issue such license under this Article. (1963, c. 1118.)

§ 58-35-25. Investigations; hearings.

For the purpose of conducting investigations and holding hearings on insurance premium finance companies, the Commissioner shall have the same authority as that vested in him by G.S. 58-2-50 and 58-2-70. (1963, c. 1118; 1987, c. 864, s. 3(b).)

§ 58-35-30. Licensee's books and records; reports; refusing to exhibit records; making false statements.

(a) The licensee shall keep and use in his business any books, accounts, and records that will enable the Commissioner to determine whether the licensee is complying with the provisions of this Article and with the rules and regulations lawfully made by the Commissioner hereunder. Every licensee shall preserve such books, accounts, and records, including cards used in a card system, if any, for at least three years after making the final entry in respect to any insurance premium finance agreement recorded therein; provided, however, the preservation of photographic reproductions thereof or records in photographic, imaging, microfilm, or microfiche form shall constitute compliance with this requirement by any licensee. The Commissioner may require of licensees under oath and in the form prescribed by him regular or special reports as he may deem necessary to the proper supervision of licensees under this Article.

(b) Any person who shall refuse, on demand, to exhibit to the Commissioner or to any deputy, or person acting with or for the Commissioner, the books, accounts or records as above provided, or who shall knowingly or willfully make any false statement in regard to the same shall be deemed guilty of a Class 1 misdemeanor. (1963, c. 1118; 1991, c. 720, s. 4; 1993, c. 539, s. 463; 1994, Ex. Sess., c. 24, s. 14(c); 1999-157, s. 1.)

§ 58-35-35. Excessive insurance premium finance charges; penalty.

The knowingly taking, receiving, reserving, [or] charging a greater insurance premium finance charge than that authorized in this Article shall be held and adjudged a forfeiture of the entire insurance premium finance charge which the insurance premium finance agreement carries with it, or which has been agreed to be paid thereon; and if a greater insurance premium finance charge has been paid, the person paying the same or his legal representative may recover from the insurance premium finance company twice the entire amount of the insurance premium finance thus paid if action therefor is brought within two years from the time of such payment. (1963, c. 1118.)

§ 58-35-40. Rebates and inducements prohibited; assignment of insurance premium finance agreements.

(a) No insurance premium finance company shall pay, allow, or offer to pay or allow payment to an insurance agent, and no insurance agent shall accept from a company, a rebate as an inducement to the financing of an insurance policy with the company. No insurance premium finance company shall give or offer to give to an insurance agent, and no insurance agent shall accept from a company, any valuable consideration or inducement of any kind, directly or indirectly, other than an article of merchandise not exceeding one dollar ($1.00) in value which shall have thereon the advertisement of the insurance premium finance company. An insurance premium finance company may purchase or otherwise acquire an insurance premium finance agreement from another insurance premium finance company with recourse against the insurance premium finance company on such terms and conditions as may be mutually agreed upon by the parties, if the agreement complies with the requirements of this Article. The terms and conditions of the agreement shall be subject to the approval of the Commissioner.

(b) No filing of the assignment or notice thereof to the insured shall be necessary to the validity of the written assignment of an insurance premium finance agreement as against creditors or subsequent purchases, pledges, or encumbrancers of the assignor.

(c) As used in this section, the term "insurance premium finance company" includes employees of the company; the term "insurance agent" includes employees of the insurance agent; and the word "company" means an insurance premium finance company. (1963, c. 1118; 1989, c. 485, s. 64; 1991 (Reg. Sess., 1992), c. 837, s. 1; 1999-157, s. 7.)

CASE NOTES

Filing Unnecessary for Initial Assignment of Unearned Premiums to Premium Finance Company. — As no filing is necessary for the validity of a subsequent assignment by the insurance premium finance company, no filing is necessary for the validity of the initial assignment of unearned premiums to insurance premium finance company, possession of the documents themselves being all that is required. In re Universal Motor Express, Inc., 72 Bankr. 208 (Bankr. W.D.N.C. 1987).

§ 58-35-45. Filing and approval of forms and service charges.

(a) No insurance premium finance agreement form or related form shall be used in this State unless it has been filed with and written approval given by the Commissioner.

(b) In addition each insurance premium finance company shall file with the Commissioner the service charge rate plan to be used in insurance premium financing including all modifications of service charges to be paid by the insured or others under the insurance premium finance agreement. Such filings shall not be used in this State until written approval has been given by the Commissioner. (1963, c. 1118.)

§ 58-35-50. Form, contents and execution of insurance premium finance agreements.

(a) An insurance premium finance agreement shall be in writing, dated, signed by the insured, and the printed portion thereof shall be in type that is legible, as determined by rule. It shall contain the entire agreement of the parties with respect to the insurance contract, the premiums for which are advanced or to be advanced under it, and the following:

"INSURANCE PREMIUM FINANCE AGREEMENT
NOTICE

Do not sign this agreement before you read it.
You are entitled to a copy of this agreement.
Under the law, you have the right to pay off in advance the full amount due and under certain conditions to obtain a partial refund of the service charge."

(b) An insurance premium finance agreement shall:
  (1) Contain the following:
    a. The name and place of business of the insurance agent or broker negotiating the related insurance contract;
    b. The name of the insured and the residence, the place of business, or any other mailing address of the insured as specified by the insured;
    c. The name and place of business of the insurance premium finance company to which installments or other payments are to be made;
    d. A brief description of the insurance contract;
    e. The premiums for which are advanced or to be advanced under the agreement; and
    f. The amount of the premiums for such insurance contract; and
  (2) Set forth the following items where applicable:
    a. The total amount of the premiums;
    b. The amount of the down payment;
    c. The principal balance, which is the difference between items a and b;

  d. The amount of the service charge;

  e. The balance payable by the insured, meaning the sum of the amounts stated under items c. and d. of this subdivision.

  f. The number of installments required, the amount of each installment expressed in dollars and the due date or period thereof.

(c) The items set forth in subsection (b) of this section need not be stated in the sequence or order in which they appear in that subsection, and additional items may be included to explain the computations made in determining the amount to be paid by the insured.

(d) No insurance premium finance agreement shall be signed by an insured when it contains any blank space to be filled in after it has been signed; however, if the insurance contract, the premiums for which are advanced or to be advanced under the agreement, has not been issued at the time of its signature by the insured and it so provides, the name of the authorized insurer by whom such insurance contract is issued and the policy number and the due date of the first installment may be left blank and later inserted in the original of the agreement after it has been signed by the insured. (1963, c. 1118; 1999-157, s. 2.)

CASE NOTES

Cited in Northcutt v. Clayton, 269 N.C. 428, 152 S.E.2d 471 (1967).

§ 58-35-55. Limitations on service charges; computation; minimum charges.

(a) An insurance premium finance company shall not directly or indirectly except as otherwise provided by law, impose, take, receive from, reserve, contract for, or charge an insured greater service charges than are permitted by this Article. No insurance premium finance company shall be permitted to charge or finance any membership fees, dues, registration fees, or any other charges except the service charges provided for in this Article for financing insurance premiums on policies of insurance lawfully placed in this State.

(b) An insurance premium finance company may, in an insurance premium finance agreement, contract for, charge, receive, and collect a service charge for financing the premiums under the agreement computed as provided in subsection (c).

(c) The service charge provided for in this section shall be computed on the principal balance of the insurance premium finance agreement from the inception date of the insurance contract, the premiums for which are advanced or to be advanced under the agreement unless otherwise provided under rules and regulations prescribed by the Commissioner, to and including the date when the final installment of the insurance premium finance agreement is payable, at a rate not exceeding twelve dollars ($12.00) per one hundred dollars ($100.00) per annum; plus a nonrefundable origination fee which shall not exceed fifteen dollars ($15.00) per premium finance agreement.

(d) The provisions of subsection (c) of this section pertaining to the time from which the service charge is calculated apply if the premiums under only one insurance contract are advanced or are to be advanced under an insurance premium finance agreement. If premiums under more than one insurance contract are advanced or are to be advanced under an insurance premium finance agreement, the service charge shall be computed from the earlier of the following:

  (1) The date that the premium is advanced on behalf of the insured.

  (2) The inception date of any insurance contract financed on the premium finance agreement.

Only one minimum service charge shall apply to each insurance premium finance agreement.

(e) No insurance agent or insurance premium finance company shall induce an insured to become obligated under more than one insurance premium finance agreement for the purpose of or with the effect of obtaining service charges in excess of those authorized by this Article.

(f) A premium service agreement may provide for the payment by the insured of a delinquency and collection charge on each installment in default for a period of not less than five days in an amount of one dollar ($1.00) or a maximum of five percent (5%) of such installment, whichever is greater, provided that only one such delinquency and collection charge may be collected on any such installment regardless of the period during which it remains in default. (1963, c. 1118; 1967, c. 824; 1979, 2nd Sess., c. 1083, ss. 1, 2; 1981, c. 394, s. 1; 1999-157, s. 3.)

§ 58-35-60. Prohibited provisions in insurance premium finance agreements.

No insurance premium finance agreement shall contain any provisions by which:
  (1) In the absence of default of the insured, the insurance premium finance company holding the agreement may, arbitrarily and without reasonable cause, accelerate the maturity of any part or all of the amount owing thereunder;
  (2) A power of attorney is given to confess judgment in this State; or
  (3) The insured relieves the insurance agent or the insurance premium finance company holding the agreement from liability for any legal rights or remedies which the insured may otherwise have against him. (1963, c. 1118.)

§ 58-35-65. Delivery of copy of insurance premium finance agreement to insured.

Before the due date of the first installment payable under an insurance premium finance agreement, the insurance premium finance company holding the agreement or the insurance agent shall cause to be delivered to the insured, or mail to the insured at the insured's address as shown in the agreement, a copy of the agreement. (1963, c. 1118; 1999-157, s. 4.)

§ 58-35-70. Payments by insured without notice of assignment of agreement.

Unless the insured has notice of actual or intended assignment of the insurance premium finance agreement, payment thereunder by him to the last known holder of the agreement shall be binding upon all subsequent holders or assignees. (1963, c. 1118.)

§ 58-35-75. Statement of account; release on payment in full.

(a) At any time after its execution, but not later than one year after the last payment thereunder, an insurance premium finance company holding an insurance premium finance agreement shall, upon written request of the insured, give or mail to him a written statement of the dates and amounts of payments and the total amount, if any, unpaid thereunder.

(b) After the payment of all sums for which an insured is obligated under an insurance premium finance agreement, and upon his written demand, the insurance premium finance company holding the agreement shall deliver, or mail to the insured at his last known address, such one or more good and sufficient instruments as may be necessary to acknowledge payment in full and to release all interest in or rights to the insurance contracts, the premiums for which were advanced or are to be advanced under the agreement. (1963, c. 1118.)

§ 58-35-80. Credit upon anticipation of payments.

(a) Notwithstanding the provisions of any insurance premium finance agreement to the contrary, any insured may pay it in full at any time before the maturity of the final installment of the balance thereof; and, if he does so and the agreement included an amount for service charge, he shall receive and be entitled to receive for such anticipation a refund credit thereon.

(b) The amount of any such refund credit shall represent at least as great proportion of the service charge, if any, as the sum of the periodic balances after the month in which prepayment is made bears to the sum of all periodic balances under the schedule of installments in the agreement. Where the amount of the refund credit for anticipation of payment is less than one dollar ($1.00), no refund need be made. This section does not relieve the premium finance company of its duty to report and deliver these unrefunded monies to the State Treasurer in accordance with G.S. 116B-29(b). (1963, c. 1118; 1981, c. 394, s. 2; 1999-157, s. 5.)

Editor's Note. — Section 116B-29(b), referred to in subsection (8) above, has been repealed. See now G.S. 116B-60(b).

§ 58-35-85. Procedure for cancellation of insurance contract upon default; return of unearned premiums; collection of cash surrender value.

When an insurance premium finance agreement contains a power of attorney or other authority enabling the insurance premium finance company to cancel any insurance contract or contracts listed in the agreement, the insurance contract or contracts shall not be cancelled unless the cancellation is effectuated in accordance with the following provisions:

(1) Not less than 10 days' written notice is sent by personal delivery, first-class mail, electronic mail, or facsimile transmission to the last known address of the insured or insureds shown on the insurance premium finance agreement of the intent of the insurance premium finance company to cancel his or their insurance contract or contracts unless the defaulted installment payment is received. Notification thereof shall also be provided to the insurance agent.

(2) After expiration of the 10-day period, the insurance premium finance company shall send the insurer a request for cancellation and shall send notice of the requested cancellation to the insured by personal delivery, first-class mail, electronic mail, electronic transmission, or facsimile transmission at his last known address as shown on the records of the insurance premium finance company and to the agent. Upon written request of the insurance company, the premium finance company shall furnish a copy of the power of attorney to the insurance company. The written request shall be sent by mail, personal delivery, electronic mail, or facsimile transmission.

(3) Upon receipt of a copy of the request for cancellation notice by the insurer, the insurance contract shall be cancelled with the same force and effect as if the request for cancellation had been submitted by the insured, without requiring the return of the insurance contract or contracts.

(4) All statutory, regulatory, and contractual restrictions providing that the insured may not cancel the insurance contract unless the insurer first satisfies the restrictions by giving a prescribed notice to a governmental agency, the insurance carrier, an individual, or a person designated to receive the notice for said governmental agency, insurance carrier, or individual shall apply where cancellation is effected under the provisions of this section.

(4a) If an insurer receives notification from an insurance agent or premium finance company that the initial down payment for the premium being financed has been dishonored by a financial institution, or otherwise unpaid, there is no valid contract for insurance and the policy will be voided.

(5) When an insurance contract is cancelled in accordance with this section, the insurer shall promptly return the gross unearned premiums that are due under the contract to the insurance premium finance company effecting the cancellation, for the benefit of the insured or insureds, no later than 30 days after the effective date of cancellation. When the return premium is more than the amount the insured owes the insurance premium finance company under the agreement, the excess shall be promptly remitted to the order of the insured, as provided in subdivision (8) of this section, subject to the minimum service charge provided for in this Article. If a premium is subject to an audit to determine the final premium amount, the amount to be refunded to the premium finance company shall be calculated upon the deposit premium, and the insurer shall return that amount to the premium finance company no later than 90 days after the effective date of cancellation. This subdivision does not limit any other remedies the insurer may have against the insured for additional premiums.

(6) The provisions of this section relating to request for cancellation by the insurance premium finance company of an insurance contract and the return by an insurer of unearned premiums to the insurance premium finance company, also apply to the surrender by the insurance premium finance company of an insurance contract providing life insurance and the payment by the insurer of the cash value of the contract to the insurance premium finance company, except that the insurer may require the surrender of the insurance contract.

(7) The insurer shall not deduct from any return premiums any amount owed to the insurer for any other indebtedness owed to the insurer by the insured on any policy or policies other than those being financed under the premium finance agreement.

(8) In the event that the crediting of return premiums to the account of the insured results in a surplus over the amount due from the insured, the premium finance company shall refund the excess to the insured as soon as possible, but in no event later than 30 days of receipt of the return premium, provided that no refund shall be required if it is in an amount less than one dollar ($1.00). This subdivision does not relieve the premium finance company of its duty to report and deliver these unrefunded monies to the State Treasurer in accordance with G.S. 116B-29(b).

(9) In the event that a balance due the premium finance company remains on the account after the cancellation of the agreement, the outstand-

ing balance may earn interest at the rate stated in the agreement until paid in full.

(10) If a mortgagee or other loss payee is shown on the insurance contract, the insurer shall notify the mortgagee or loss payee of the cancellation. The written notice shall be sent by mail, personal delivery, electronic mail, or facsimile transmission to the designated mortgagee's or loss payee's last known address. Proof of mailing is sufficient proof of notice. Failure to send this notice to any designated mortgagee or loss payee shall not give rise to any claim on the part of the insured. (1963, c. 1118; 1967, c. 825; 1969, c. 941; 1987, c. 864, s. 22; 1995, c. 121, s. 1; 1999-157, s. 6; 2002-187, s. 6.)

Editor's Note. — Section 116B-29(b), referred to in subsection (b) above, has been repealed. See now 116B-60(b).

Effect of Amendments. — Session Laws 2002-187, s. 6, effective October 31, 2002, in subdivision (5), substituted "90 days" for "30 days," and made stylistic changes.

CASE NOTES

Filing of Premium Finance Agreement Unnecessary. — Since the purpose of any filing is to give notice to other potential creditors, there is no need for notice of a premium finance agreement, as the debtor cannot assign its unearned premiums to any other parties. In re Universal Motor Express, Inc., 72 Bankr. 208 (Bankr. W.D.N.C. 1987).

As no filing is necessary for the validity of a subsequent assignment by the insurance premium finance company, no filing is necessary for the validity of the initial assignment of unearned premiums to insurance premium finance company, possession of the documents themselves being all that is required. In re Universal Motor Express, Inc., 72 Bankr. 208 (Bankr. W.D.N.C. 1987).

No Requirement of Perfection of Right to Unearned Premiums. — Under North Carolina law, there is no requirement that any right to unearned premiums in a premium financing agreement be perfected in any manner. In re Universal Motor Express, Inc., 72 Bankr. 208 (Bankr. W.D.N.C. 1987).

Authority to Cancel Policy and Collect Unearned Premium as Security. — The authority given by a borrower to an insurance premium finance company to cancel the policy and collect the unearned premium upon the borrower's default is security analogous to a chattel mortgage or a conditional sale. Northcutt v. Clayton, 269 N.C. 428, 152 S.E.2d 471 (1967).

The burden is upon the insurance company to show that all statutory requirements have been complied with, including the 10 days' written notice by the premium finance company to the insured, together with said notice to the insurance agent, prior to the premium finance company requesting cancellation of the policy. Grant v. State Farm Mut.

Auto. Ins. Co., 1 N.C. App. 76, 159 S.E.2d 368 (1968).

The burden of proving cancellation by the insured or his agent is on the insurance company. Ingram v. Nationwide Mut. Ins. Co., 5 N.C. App. 255, 168 S.E.2d 224 (1969).

To avoid liability to a third-party beneficiary of an assigned risk automobile insurance policy, the insurer must allege and prove cancellation and termination of the policy in accordance with the applicable statutes. Grant v. State Farm Mut. Auto. Ins. Co., 1 N.C. App. 76, 159 S.E.2d 368 (1968).

Insurance policy was cancelled the day insurance company received the cancellation request from a premium financing company requesting cancellation because the insured defaulted on his payments. Unisun Ins. Co. v. Goodman, 117 N.C. App. 454, 451 S.E.2d 4 (1994).

Redress of Insurance Company Where Finance Company Wrongfully Requests Cancellation. — If the premium finance company misleads the insurance company wrongfully by requesting cancellation of the policy, the insurance company can seek redress from the premium finance company. Ingram v. Nationwide Mut. Ins. Co., 5 N.C. App. 255, 168 S.E.2d 224 (1969).

Compliance Shown. — Appellants complied with the cancellation provisions of a finance agreement with appellee tractor-trailer owner, which provisions track the language of this section, where the uncontradicted evidence indicated that the appellee was given more than 10 days' notice before his policy was cancelled. Cahoon v. Canal Ins. Co., 140 N.C. App. 577, 537 S.E.2d 538, 2000 N.C. App. LEXIS 1247 (2000).

Compliance Not Shown. — While insurance premium finance company did comply with the requirement that cancellation notice have the wording "Notice of Cancellation" in bold print at the top, company did not comply with this section's requirements since it failed to mail the insurer a request for cancellation, including a copy of the power of attorney, and to mail a copy of the request for cancellation to the insured. GEICO v. New South Ins. Co., 119 N.C. App. 700, 459 S.E.2d 817 (1995).

This section does not require an insurance company to obtain a copy of a policy holder's power of attorney from a finance company; it requires the finance company to furnish such upon "written request of the insurance company." Cahoon v. Canal Ins. Co., 140 N.C. App. 577, 537 S.E.2d 538, 2000 N.C. App. LEXIS 1247 (2000).

Regarding the Time for Mailing the Notice of Cancellation. — The court disagreed with the plaintiff tractor-trailer owner's con-

tention that the defendant insurer prematurely sent the Notice of Cancellation to the finance company. Cahoon v. Canal Ins. Co., 140 N.C. App. 577, 537 S.E.2d 538, 2000 N.C. App. LEXIS 1247 (2000).

The cancellation of plaintiff tractor-trailer owner's insurance policy complied with regulations promulgated pursuant to this section, specifically the North Carolina Administrative Code title 11, r. 13.0317. Cahoon v. Canal Ins. Co., 140 N.C. App. 577, 537 S.E.2d 538, 2000 N.C. App. LEXIS 1247 (2000).

Applied in Graves v. ABC Roofing Co., 55 N.C. App. 252, 284 S.E.2d 718 (1981).

Cited in Hayes v. Hartford Accident & Indem. Co., 274 N.C. 73, 161 S.E.2d 552 (1968); Paris v. Woolard, 128 N.C. App. 416, 497 S.E.2d 283 (1998), cert. denied, 348 N.C. 283, 502 S.E.2d 843 (1998).

§ 58-35-90. Violations; penalties.

Any person who shall engage in the business referred to in this Article without first receiving a license, or who shall fail to secure a renewal of his license upon the expiration of the license year, or shall engage in the business herein referred to after the license has been suspended or revoked as herein provided, or who shall fail or refuse to furnish the information required of the Commissioner, or who shall willfully and knowingly enter false information on an insurance premium finance agreement, or who shall fail to observe the rules and regulations made by the Commissioner pursuant to this Article, shall be deemed guilty of a Class 1 misdemeanor. (1963, c. 1118; 1965, c. 1040; 1985, c. 666, s. 20; 1993, c. 539, s. 464; 1994, Ex. Sess., c. 24, s. 14(c).)

§ 58-35-95. Disposition of fees.

All fees collected hereunder shall be credited to the account of the Commissioner for the specific purpose of providing the personnel, equipment and supplies necessary to enforce this Article, but the Director of the Budget shall have the right to budget the revenues received in accordance with the requirements of the Commissioner for the purposes herein required, and at the end of the fiscal year, if any sum whatever shall remain to the credit of the Commissioner, derived from the sources herein referred to, the same shall revert to the general treasury of the State to be appropriated as other funds. (1963, c. 1118; 1991, c. 720, s. 5.)

CASE NOTES

Cited in Northcutt v. Clayton, 269 N.C. 428, 152 S.E.2d 471 (1967).

§ 58-35-100. Fees are nonrefundable.

All fees that are imposed and collected under this Article are nonrefundable. (1993 (Reg. Sess., 1994), c. 678, s. 20.)

ARTICLE 36.

North Carolina Rate Bureau.

§ 58-36-1. North Carolina Rate Bureau created.

There is hereby created a Bureau to be known as the "North Carolina Rate Bureau," with the following objects and functions:

(1) To assume the functions formerly performed by the North Carolina Fire Insurance Rating Bureau, the North Carolina Automobile Rate Administrative Office, and the Compensation Rating and Inspection Bureau of North Carolina, with regard to the promulgation of rates, for insurance against loss to residential real property with not more than four housing units located in this State and any contents thereof and valuable interest therein and other insurance coverages written in connection with the sale of such property insurance; except as provided in G.S. 58-36-3(a)(6), for theft of and physical damage to nonfleet private passenger motor vehicles; for liability insurance for such motor vehicles, automobile medical payments insurance, uninsured motorists coverage and other insurance coverages written in connection with the sale of such liability insurance; and for workers' compensation and employers' liability insurance written in connection therewith except for insurance excluded from the Bureau's jurisdiction in G.S. 58-36-1(3).

(2) The Bureau shall provide reasonable means to be approved by the Commissioner whereby any person affected by a rate or loss costs made by it may be heard in person or by the person's authorized representative before the governing committee or other proper executive of the Bureau.

(3) The Bureau shall promulgate and propose rates for insurance against loss to residential real property with not more than four housing units located in this State and any contents thereof or valuable interest therein and other insurance coverages written in connection with the sale of such property insurance; for insurance against theft of or physical damage to nonfleet private passenger motor vehicles; for liability insurance for such motor vehicles, automobile medical payments insurance, uninsured and underinsured motorists coverage and other insurance coverages written in connection with the sale of such liability insurance; and, as provided in G.S. 58-36-100, for loss costs and residual market rate filings for workers' compensation and employers' liability insurance written in connection therewith. This subdivision does not apply to motor vehicles operated under certificates of authority from the Utilities Commission, the Interstate Commerce Commission, or their successor agencies, where insurance or other proof of financial responsibility is required by law or by regulations specifically applicable to such certificated vehicles.

(4) Agreements may be made between or among members with respect to equitable apportionment among them of insurance which may be afforded applicants who are in good faith entitled to but who are unable to procure such insurance through ordinary methods. The members may agree between or among themselves on the use of reasonable rate modifications for such insurance, agreements, and rate modifications to be subject to the approval of the Commissioner.

(5)a. It is the duty of every insurer that writes workers' compensation insurance in this State and is a member of the Bureau, as defined in this section and G.S. 58-36-5 to insure and accept any workers'

597

compensation insurance risk that has been certified to be "difficult to place" by any fire and casualty insurance agent who is licensed in this State. When any such risk is called to the attention of the Bureau by receipt of an application with an estimated or deposit premium payment and it appears that the risk is in good faith entitled to such coverage, the Bureau will bind coverage for 30 days and will designate a member who must issue a standard workers' compensation policy of insurance that contains the usual and customary provisions found in those policies. Multiple coordinated policies, as defined by the Bureau and approved by the Commissioner, may be used for the issuance of coverage under this subdivision for risks involved in employee leasing arrangements. Coverage will be bound at 12:01 A.M. on the first day following the postmark time and date on the envelope in which the application is mailed including the estimated annual or deposit premium, or the expiration of existing coverage, whichever is later. If there should be no postmark, coverage will be effective 12:01 A.M. on the date of receipt by the Bureau unless a later date is requested. Those applications hand delivered to the Bureau will be effective as of 12:01 A.M. of the date following receipt by the Bureau unless a later date is requested. The Bureau will make and adopt such rules as are necessary to carry this section into effect, subject to final approval of the Commissioner. As a prerequisite to the transaction of workers' compensation insurance in this State, every member of the Bureau that writes such insurance must file with the Bureau written authority permitting the Bureau to act in its behalf, as provided in this section, and an agreement to accept risks that are assigned to the member by the Bureau, as provided in this section.

b. The Bureau shall maintain a compendium of employers refused voluntary coverage, which shall be made available by the Bureau to all insurers, licensed agents, and self-insureds' administrators doing business in this State. It shall be stored and indexed to allow access to information by industry, primary classifications of employees, geography, experience modification, and in any other manner the Bureau determines is commercially useful to facilitate voluntary coverage of listed employers. The Bureau shall be immune from civil liability for erroneous information released by the Bureau pursuant to this section, provided that the Bureau acted in good faith and without malicious or willful intent to harm in releasing the erroneous information.

c. Failure or refusal by any assigned employer risk to make full disclosure to the Bureau, servicing carrier, or insurer writing a policy of information regarding the employer's true ownership, change of ownership, operations, or payroll, or any other failure to disclose fully any records pertaining to workers' compensation insurance shall be sufficient grounds for the termination of the policy of that employer.

(6) The Bureau shall maintain and furnish to the Commissioner on an annual basis the statistics on earnings derived by member companies from the investment of unearned premium, loss, and loss expense reserves on nonfleet private passenger motor vehicle insurance policies written in this State. Whenever the Bureau proposes rates under this Article, it shall prepare a separate exhibit for the experience years in question showing the combined earnings realized from the

investment of such reserves on policies written in this State. The amount of earnings may in an equitable manner be included in the ratemaking formula to arrive at a fair and equitable rate. The Commissioner may require further information as to such earnings and may require calculations of the Bureau bearing on such earnings.

(7) Member companies shall furnish, upon request of any person carrying nonfleet private passenger motor vehicle insurance in the State upon whose risk a rate has been promulgated, information as to rating, including the method of calculation. (1977, c. 828, s. 6; 1981, c. 888, ss. 1-3; 1983, c. 416, s. 5; 1985 (Reg. Sess., 1986), c. 1027, s. 5.1; 1991, c. 339, s. 1; 1993, c. 409, s. 27; 1993 (Reg. Sess., 1994), c. 679, s. 8.5; 1995, c. 505, s. 1; c. 517, s. 18; 1999-132, ss. 3.1, 3.2; 1999-219, s. 11; 2001-236, s. 2; 2001-389, ss. 1, 2; 2001-423, s. 3.)

Cross References. — As to the regulation of insurance rates, see G.S. 58-40-1 et seq.

Editor's Note. — Session Laws 2001-389, s. 6, provides: "This act becomes effective January 1, 2002. Rates, rating systems, territories, classifications, and policy forms lawfully in use on January 1, 2002, may continue to be used thereafter."

Effect of Amendments. — Session Laws 2001-236, s. 2, as amended by Session Laws 2001-423, s. 3, effective January 1, 2002, inserted "personal excess liability or personal "umbrella" insurance" in the third sentence of subdivision (3).

Session Laws 2001-389, ss. 1 and 2, effective January 1, 2002, in subdivision (1), added "except as provided in G.S. 58-36-3(a)(6)," and substituted "nonfleet private passenger motor vehicles" for "private passenger (nonfleet) mo-

tor vehicles as the same are defined under Article 40 of this Chapter"; and in subdivision (3), as amended by Session Laws 2001-236, deleted the final sentence, regarding exclusions to the Bureau's jurisdiction.

Legal Periodicals. — For note discussing compulsory rating bureaus and the antitrust laws, see 54 N.C.L. Rev. 481 (1967).

For a survey of 1977 law on insurance, see 56 N.C.L. Rev. 1084 (1978).

For survey of 1980 administrative law, see 59 N.C.L. Rev. 1017 (1981).

For note discussing changes in automobile rate regulation and the role of the Insurance Commissioner in North Carolina, see 17 Wake Forest L. Rev. 822 (1981).

For article discussing limitations on ad hoc adjudicatory rulemaking by an administrative agency, see 61 N.C.L. Rev. 67 (1982).

CASE NOTES

Editor's Note. — *Some of the cases cited below were decided under former statutory provisions.*

Legislative Intent. — It was the legislative intent in enacting this Article to eliminate unfair and unnecessary delay in the ratemaking process. State ex rel. Comm'r of Ins. v. North Carolina Rate Bureau, 40 N.C. App. 85, 252 S.E.2d 811, cert. denied, 297 N.C. 452, 256 S.E.2d 810 (1979).

Purpose of former Article relating to the North Carolina Fire Insurance Rating Bureau was to provide for the public, at reasonable cost, insurance in financially responsible companies. Not only fair play, but the accomplishment of this legislative purpose as well, required that the premium be fixed at a level which would enable the insuring company, i.e., the entire insurance industry in this State treated as if it were one company, (1) to pay the losses which will be incurred during the life of the policies to be issued under such rates, (2) to pay other operating expenses, and (3) to retain a "fair and reasonable profit" and no more. In re

North Carolina Fire Ins. Rating Bureau, 275 N.C. 15, 165 S.E.2d 207 (1969).

Statutory plan of former Article relating to the North Carolina Fire Insurance Rating Bureau contemplated a uniform premium rate schedule for all companies operating in the State. In re North Carolina Fire Ins. Rating Bureau, 275 N.C. 15, 165 S.E.2d 207 (1969).

In the statutory plan, the State has undertaken to make available to its people the economic necessity of fire insurance policies which actually insure by authorizing the Bureau to propose premium rates just as would a single company having a monopoly of the fire insurance business in North Carolina. To protect the public against the danger of exorbitant rates for this economic necessity, which danger is inherent in monopolistic price fixing, the legislature has vested in the Commissioner its own authority to withhold approval of such rates proposed by the Bureau and to fix rates which are fair and reasonable. In re North Carolina Fire Ins. Rating Bureau, 275 N.C. 15, 165 S.E.2d 207 (1969).

The Bureau is not a State agency. The rating bureau is a body separate and apart from the State, in that it is composed of private citizens as to its employees and governing committee, but it is also answerable to the Commissioner at every turn. Allstate Ins. Co. v. Lanier, 242 F. Supp. 73 (E.D.N.C. 1965), cer. denied, 385 U.S. 930, 87 S. Ct. 290, 17 L. Ed. 2d 212 (1966), aff'd, 361 F.2d 870 (4th Cir.)

The North Carolina Rate Bureau is charged with promulgating rates for insurance against loss, including fire loss, to residential real property with not more than four housing units located in North Carolina. Bentley v. North Carolina Ins. Guar. Ass'n, 107 N.C. App. 1, 418 S.E.2d 705 (1992).

The Bureau is to be regarded as if it were the only insurance company operating in North Carolina, for ratemaking purposes, and as if it had an earned premium experience, an incurred loss experience and an operating expense experience equivalent to the composite of those of the companies actually in operation. In re North Carolina Fire Ins. Rating Bureau, 275 N.C. 15, 165 S.E.2d 207 (1969); State ex rel. Comm'r of Ins. v. North Carolina Fire Ins. Rating Bureau, 291 N.C. 55, 229 S.E.2d 268 (1976).

For ratemaking purposes, the Bureau is treated as if it were the only insurance company writing policies upon the risks over which it has jurisdiction. The Bureau is regarded as having an earned premium experience, an incurred loss experience and an operating expense experience equivalent to the composite of all those companies over which it has jurisdiction. This is proper since all companies writing policies covering the risks over which the Bureau has jurisdiction are members of the Bureau. Foremost Ins. Co. v. Ingram, 292 N.C. 244, 232 S.E.2d 414 (1977).

Scope of Commissioner's Authority. — The authority of the commissioner to review, approve, modify, or disapprove insurance rates promulgated by the rate bureau is limited to that authority granted by the General Assembly. State ex rel. Comm'r of Ins. v. North Caro-

lina Rate Bureau, 75 N.C. App. 201, 331 S.E.2d 124, cert. denied, 314 N.C. 547, 335 S.E.2d 319 (1985).

The commissioner did not have the statutory authority to withhold approval of an 11.7% rate increase for farmowner insurance coverages subject to the rate bureau's jurisdiction on the condition that the insurance service office file for a rate decrease for farmowner insurance coverages not subject to the rate bureau's jurisdiction. State ex rel. Comm'r of Ins. v. North Carolina Rate Bureau, 75 N.C. App. 201, 331 S.E.2d 124, cert. denied, 314 N.C. 547, 335 S.E.2d 319 (1985).

Use of Rate Bureau Form Does Not Confer Jurisdiction over Fleet Policy. — By requiring rejection of under-insured motorist (UIM) coverage to be accomplished by use of a specific Rate Bureau form, G.S. 20-279.21(b)(4) does not effectively confer additional jurisdictional authority to the Rate Bureau, but is merely concerned with avoiding confusion and ambiguity through the use of a single standard and approved form, and mandating use of a Rate Bureau form for rejection of UIM coverage within a fleet policy does not necessarily conflict with this section. Hendrickson v. Lee, 119 N.C. App. 444, 459 S.E.2d 275 (1995).

Applied in State ex rel. Comm'r of Ins. v. North Carolina Rate Bureau, 44 N.C. App. 191, 261 S.E.2d 671 (1979).

Cited in State ex rel. Comm'r of Ins. v. North Carolina Rate Bureau, 300 N.C. 381, 269 S.E.2d 547 (1980); State ex rel. Hunt v. North Carolina Reinsurance Facility, 49 N.C. App. 206, 271 S.E.2d 302 (1980); State ex rel. Comm'r of Ins. v. North Carolina Rate Bureau, 52 N.C. App. 79, 277 S.E.2d 844 (1981); Doud v. K & G Janitorial Servs., 69 N.C. App. 205, 316 S.E.2d 664 (1984); State ex rel. Comm'r of Ins. v. North Carolina Rate Bureau, 97 N.C. App. 644, 389 S.E.2d 574 (1990); North Carolina Steel, Inc. v. National Council Comp. Ins., 347 N.C. 627, 496 S.E.2d 369 (1998); State ex rel. Commissioner of Ins. v. North Carolina Rate Bureau, 350 N.C. 539, 516 S.E.2d 150 (1999).

§ 58-36-2. Private passenger motor vehicles; number of nonfleet policies.

Notwithstanding the definition of "nonfleet" in G.S. 58-40-10(2), the Bureau shall adopt rules, subject to the Commissioner's approval, that specify the circumstances under which more than four private passenger motor vehicles may be covered under a nonfleet private passenger motor vehicle policy that is subject to this Article. (1995 (Reg. Sess., 1996), c. 730, s. 2.)

§ 58-36-3. Limitation of scope; motorcycle endorsements allowed; Department of Insurance report.

(a) The Bureau has no jurisdiction over:

(1) Excess workers' compensation insurance for employers qualifying as self-insurers as provided in Article 47 of this Chapter or Article 5 of Chapter 97 of the General Statutes.

(2) Farm buildings, farm dwellings, and their appurtenant structures; farm personal property or other coverages written in connection with farm real or personal property.

(3) Travel or camper trailers designed to be pulled by private passenger motor vehicles, unless insured under policies covering nonfleet private passenger motor vehicles.

(4) Mechanical breakdown insurance covering nonfleet private passenger motor vehicles and other incidental coverages written in connection with this insurance, including emergency road service assistance, trip interruption reimbursement, rental car reimbursement, and tire coverage.

(5) Residential real and personal property insured in multiple line insurance policies covering business activities as the primary insurable interest; and marine, general liability, burglary and theft, glass, and animal collision insurance, except when such coverages are written as an integral part of a multiple line insurance policy for which there is an indivisible premium.

(6) Insurance against theft of or physical damage to motorcycles, as defined in G.S. 20-4.01(27)d.

(7) Personal excess liability or personal "umbrella" insurance.

(b) Member companies writing motorcycle liability insurance under this Article and writing insurance against theft of or physical damage to motorcycles under Article 40 of this Chapter may incorporate motorcycle theft and physical damage coverage as an endorsement to the liability policy issued under this Article.

(c) Beginning on February 1, 2003, and annually thereafter, the Department of Insurance shall report to the President Pro Tempore of the Senate and the Speaker of the House of Representatives on the effectiveness of S.L. 2001-389 in assuring the provision of insurance coverage to motorcyclists at fair and economical rates. (2001-389, ss. 3, 5.1.)

Editor's Note. — Session Laws 2001-389, s. 5.1 was codified as subsection (c) of this section at the direction of the Revisor of Statutes.

Session Laws 2001-389, s. 6, provides: "This act becomes effective January 1, 2002. Rates, rating systems, territories, classifications, and policy forms lawfully in use on January 1, 2002, may continue to be used thereafter."

§ 58-36-5. Membership as a prerequisite for writing insurance; governing committee; rules and regulations; expenses.

(a) Before the Commissioner shall grant permission to any stock, nonstock, or reciprocal insurance company or any other insurance organization to write in this State insurance against loss to residential real property with not more than four housing units located in this State or any contents thereof or valuable interest therein or other insurance coverages written in connection with the sale of such property insurance; or insurance against theft of or physical damage to private passenger (nonfleet) motor vehicles; or liability insurance for such motor vehicles, automobile medical payments insurance, uninsured motorists coverage or other insurance coverage written in connection with the sale of such liability insurance; or workers' compensation and employers' liability insurance written in connection therewith; except for insurance excluded from the Bureau's jurisdiction in G.S. 58-36-1(3); it shall be a requisite that they shall subscribe to and become members of the Bureau.

(b) Each member of the Bureau writing any one or more of the above lines of insurance in North Carolina shall, as a requisite thereto, be represented in the Bureau and shall be entitled to one representative and one vote in the administration of the affairs of the Bureau. They shall, upon organization, elect a governing committee which governing committee shall be composed of equal representation by stock and nonstock members. The governing committee of the Bureau shall also have as nonvoting members two persons who are not employed by or affiliated with any insurance company or the Department and who are appointed by the Governor to serve at his pleasure.

(c) The Bureau, when created, shall adopt such rules and regulations for its orderly procedure as shall be necessary for its maintenance and operation. No such rules and regulations shall discriminate against any type of insurer because of its plan of operation, nor shall any insurer be prevented from returning any unused or unabsorbed premium, deposit, savings or earnings to its policyholders or subscribers. The expense of such Bureau shall be borne by its members by quarterly contributions to be made in advance, such contributions to be made in advance by prorating such expense among the members in accordance with the amount of gross premiums derived from the above lines of insurance in North Carolina during the preceding year and members entering the Bureau since that date to advance an amount to be fixed by the governing committee. After the first fiscal year of operation of the Bureau the necessary expense of the Bureau shall be advanced by the members in accordance with rules and regulations to be established and adopted by the governing committee. The Bureau shall be empowered to subscribe for or purchase any necessary service, and employ and fix the salaries of such personnel and assistants as are necessary.

(d) The Commissioner is hereby authorized to compel the production of all books, data, papers and records and any other data necessary to compile statistics for the purpose of determining the underwriting experience of lines of insurance referred to in this Article, and this information shall be available and for the use of the Bureau for the capitulation and promulgation of rates on lines of insurance as are subject to the ratemaking authority of the Bureau. (1977, c. 828, s. 6; 1981, c. 888, s. 4; 1985 (Reg. Sess., 1986), c. 1027, s. 6; 1991, c. 720, s. 4.)

Legal Periodicals. — For article analyzing the scope of the North Carolina Insurance Commissioner's rate-making authority, see 61 N.C.L. Rev. 97 (1982).

CASE NOTES

Editor's Note. — *The cases below were decided under former statutory provisions.*

Membership Required. — Every company engaged in the writing of fire insurance policies, including extended coverage endorsements attached thereto, is required to be a member of the Bureau. State ex rel. Comm'r of Ins. v. North Carolina Fire Ins. Rating Bureau, 291 N.C. 55, 229 S.E.2d 268 (1976) (decided under former statutory provisions).

Power to Require Audited Data in Ratemaking Case. — An order of the Commissioner of Insurance that data submitted in a ratemaking case be audited was not in excess of his statutory powers as contemplated by G.S. 58-2-90(b)(2) or G.S. 150B-51(b)(2). State ex rel. Comm'r of Ins. v. North Carolina Rate Bureau, 300 N.C. 381, 269 S.E.2d 547, rehearing denied, 301 N.C. 107, 273 S.E.2d 300 (1980).

Applied in State ex rel. Comm'r of Ins. v. North Carolina Rate Bureau, 40 N.C. App. 85, 252 S.E.2d 811 (1979).

Cited in Doud v. K & G Janitorial Servs., 69 N.C. App. 205, 316 S.E.2d 664 (1984); State ex rel. Commissioner of Ins. v. North Carolina Rate Bureau, 350 N.C. 539, 516 S.E.2d 150 (1999); Prentiss v. Allstate Ins. Co., 87 F. Supp. 2d 514, 1999 U.S. Dist. LEXIS 21397 (W.D.N.C. 1999).

§ 58-36-10. Method of rate making; factors considered.

The following standards shall apply to the making and use of rates:

(1) Rates or loss costs shall not be excessive, inadequate or unfairly discriminatory.

(2) Due consideration shall be given to actual loss and expense experience within this State for the most recent three-year period for which that information is available; to prospective loss and expense experience within this State; to the hazards of conflagration and catastrophe; to a reasonable margin for underwriting profit and to contingencies; to dividends, savings, or unabsorbed premium deposits allowed or returned by insurers to their policyholders, members, or subscribers; to investment income earned or realized by insurers from their unearned premium, loss, and loss expense reserve funds generated from business within this State; to past and prospective expenses specially applicable to this State; and to all other relevant factors within this State: Provided, however, that countrywide expense and loss experience and other countrywide data may be considered only where credible North Carolina experience or data is not available.

(3) In the case of property insurance rates under this Article, consideration may be given to the experience of property insurance business during the most recent five-year period for which that experience is available. In the case of property insurance rates under this Article, consideration shall be given to the insurance public protection classifications of fire districts established by the Commissioner. The Commissioner shall establish and modify from time to time insurance public protection districts for all rural areas of the State and for cities with populations of 100,000 or fewer, according to the most recent annual population estimates certified by the State Planning Officer. In establishing and modifying these districts, the Commissioner shall use standards at least equivalent to those used by the Insurance Services Office, Inc., or any successor organization. The standards developed by the Commissioner are subject to Article 2A of Chapter 150B of the General Statutes. The insurance public protection classifications established by the Commissioner issued pursuant to the provisions of this Article shall be subject to appeal as provided in G.S. 58-2-75, et seq. The exceptions stated in G.S. 58-2-75(a) do not apply.

(4) Risks may be grouped by classifications and lines of insurance for establishment of rates, loss costs, and base premiums. Classification rates may be modified to produce rates for individual risks in accordance with rating plans that establish standards for measuring variations in hazards or expense provisions or both. Those standards may measure any differences among risks that can be demonstrated to have a probable effect upon losses or expenses. The Bureau shall establish and implement a comprehensive classification rating plan for motor vehicle insurance under its jurisdiction. No such classification plans shall base any standard or rating plan for private passenger (nonfleet) motor vehicles, in whole or in part, directly or indirectly, upon the age or gender of the persons insured. The Bureau shall at least once every three years make a complete review of the filed classification rates to determine whether they are proper and supported by statistical evidence, and shall at least once every 10 years make a complete review of the territories for nonfleet private passenger motor vehicle insurance to determine whether they are proper and reasonable.

(5) In the case of workers' compensation insurance and employers' liability insurance written in connection therewith, due consideration shall

603

be given to the past and prospective effects of changes in compensation benefits and in legal and medical fees that are provided for in General Statutes Chapter 97. (1977, c. 828, s. 6; 1979, c. 824, s. 1; 1981, c. 521, s. 5; c. 790; 1987, c. 632, s. 1; 1991, c. 644, s. 39; 1999-132, s. 3.3; 2000-176, s. 1.)

Editor's Note. — Session Laws 2000-176, s. 3, makes the act is effective August 2, 2000, and provides that any changes to classifications of insurance public protection districts issued by the Commissioner pursuant to the act shall become effective no sooner than 90 days after the standards for public protection district classifications are adopted by the Department and shall apply to insurance policies issued or renewed on or after that date.

Legal Periodicals. — For survey of 1979 administrative law, see 58 N.C.L. Rev. 1185 (1980).

For survey of 1981 administrative law, see 60 N.C.L. Rev. 1165 (1982).

For article analyzing the scope of the North Carolina Insurance Commissioner's rate-making authority, see 61 N.C.L. Rev. 97 (1982).

CASE NOTES

Editor's Note. — *Many of the cases cited below were decided under former statutory provisions.*

Fixing of Premium Rate as Exercise of Legislative Power. — In fixing by law the premium rate, it is the legislative power of the State which is being exercised. In re North Carolina Fire Ins. Rating Bureau, 275 N.C. 15, 165 S.E.2d 207 (1969).

The power to fix rates effective from a specified future date is a legislative power, and this is no less true because its exercise is preceded by investigations and hearings. In re North Carolina Auto. Rate Admin. Office, 278 N.C. 302, 180 S.E.2d 155 (1971).

Subdivision (1) of this section applies only to insurance coverages subject to the rate bureau's jurisdiction. State ex rel. Comm'r of Ins. v. North Carolina Rate Bureau, 75 N.C. App. 201, 331 S.E.2d 124, cert. denied, 314 N.C. 547, 335 S.E.2d 319 (1985).

"Inadequate" and "Excessive" Rates. — In enacting the provisions of subdivision (1), the legislative intent was that the term "inadequate" should operate to protect the interest of insurance companies in achieving rate levels which are sufficient for them to earn a reasonable profit, while the term "excessive" should operate to protect the interest of consumers in being offered rates which will not enable insurance companies to earn unreasonable profits. State ex rel. Comm'r of Ins. v. North Carolina Rate Bureau, 54 N.C. App. 601, 284 S.E.2d 339 (1981), appeal dismissed, 305 N.C. 298, 290 S.E.2d 708 (1982); State ex rel. Comm'r of Ins. v. North Carolina Rate Bureau, 75 N.C. App. 201, 331 S.E.2d 124, cert. denied, 314 N.C. 547, 335 S.E.2d 319 (1985).

Filed rate doctrine, as adopted in North Carolina, precludes a claim for damages measured by the difference between the rates as approved by the commissioner and the rates which would have been approved but for the illegal conduct of the defendants; thus, the doctrine forbids the recalculation of commissioner-approved rates by a jury. North Carolina Steel, Inc. v. National Council on Comp. Ins., 123 N.C. App. 163, 472 S.E.2d 578 (1996), aff'd in part and rev'd in part, 347 N.C. 627, 496 S.E.2d 369 (1998).

Filed rate doctrine does not act to bar any claims which involve damages other than inflated rates. North Carolina Steel, Inc. v. National Council on Comp. Ins., 123 N.C. App. 163, 472 S.E.2d 578 (1996), aff'd in part and rev'd in part, 347 N.C. 627, 496 S.E.2d 369 (1998).

Plaintiff may not claim damages on the grounds that a rate filed with and approved by a regulator as reasonable was nonetheless excessive or inadequate because it was the product of an anticompetitive conspiracy or other unlawful conduct by the defendants. North Carolina Steel, Inc. v. National Council on Comp. Ins., 123 N.C. App. 163, 472 S.E.2d 578 (1996), aff'd in part and rev'd in part, 347 N.C. 627, 496 S.E.2d 369 (1998).

Discrimination Prohibited. — Former section prevented discrimination between unprotected farm and unprotected nonfarm properties similar in location, construction and hazards, and having substantially the same degree of protection. In re North Carolina Fire Ins. Rating Bureau, 245 N.C. 444, 96 S.E.2d 344 (1957).

The prohibition against discrimination in rates is directed to insurers, agents, brokers and other representatives of insurers. Hyde Ins. Agency, Inc. v. Dixie Leasing Corp., 26 N.C. App. 138, 215 S.E.2d 162 (1975).

Separate Classes of Property May Have Same Rate. — Properties need not necessarily be included in the same class in order for them to have the same fire insurance rate, but separate classes may have the same rate provided the location, construction and degree of protection are substantially the same for both. In re North Carolina Fire Ins. Rating Bureau, 245 N.C. 444, 96 S.E.2d 344 (1957).

There is no requirement that the Rate Bureau must always use the same rate-making formulas. State ex rel. Comm'r of Ins. v. North Carolina Rate Bureau, 40 N.C. App. 85, 252 S.E.2d 811, cert. denied, 297 N.C. 452, 256 S.E.2d 810 (1979).

Rates are made prospectively, not retroactively; therefore, the entire procedure of ratemaking contemplates a looking to the future. State ex rel. Hunt v. North Carolina Reinsurance Facility, 302 N.C. 274, 275 S.E.2d 399 (1981).

It is not only impractical to fix premium rates retroactively, but is expressly required that premium rates fixed in accordance with the statutory plan be applied only to policies issued after the rates are so established. Consequently, the entire procedure contemplates a looking to the future. In re North Carolina Fire Ins. Rating Bureau, 275 N.C. 15, 165 S.E.2d 207 (1969).

As Distinguished from Surcharge Assessments. — Ratemaking is a prospective process, while surcharge assessments involve recoupment for losses already incurred. State ex rel. Hunt v. North Carolina Reinsurance Facility, 302 N.C. 274, 275 S.E.2d 399 (1981).

There is no presumption that a rate filing by the Bureau is correct and proper. In re North Carolina Fire Ins. Rating Bureau, 275 N.C. 15, 165 S.E.2d 207 (1969).

The burden is upon the Bureau to show that the rate schedule proposed by it is fair and reasonable and that it does not discriminate unfairly between risks. In re North Carolina Fire Ins. Rating Bureau, 275 N.C. 15, 165 S.E.2d 207 (1969).

There is no statute or decision that makes a request of the Bureau for an increase or decrease in rates presumptively correct and proper. The burden is upon the Bureau to establish that the proposed rate is fair and reasonable and that it does not "unfairly discriminate between risks involving essentially the same construction and hazards, and having substantially the same degree of protection." In re North Carolina Fire Ins. Rating Bureau, 245 N.C. 444, 96 S.E.2d 344 (1957).

Fair and Reasonable Profit as Ultimate Question. — The ultimate question for the Commissioner's determination is whether the proposed rates will, after provision for reasonably anticipated losses and operating expenses, leave for the insurers (considered as if the Bureau were a single company with the composite experience of all companies issuing homeowners insurance in North Carolina) a fair and reasonable profit and no more. State ex rel. Comm'r of Ins. v. North Carolina Fire Ins.

Rating Bureau, 292 N.C. 471, 234 S.E.2d 720 (1977).

The ultimate question to be determined by the Commissioner is whether an increase in premium rates is necessary in order to yield a "fair and reasonable profit" in the immediate future (i.e., treating the Bureau as if it were an operating company whose experience in the past is the composite of the experiences of all of the operating companies), and if so, how much increase is required for that purpose. This cannot be determined without specific findings of fact, upon substantial evidence, as to: (1) The reasonably anticipated loss experience during the life of the policies to be issued in the near future; (2) The reasonably anticipated operating expenses in the same period; and (3) The percent of earned premiums which will constitute a "fair and reasonable profit" in that period. In re North Carolina Fire Ins. Rating Bureau, 275 N.C. 15, 165 S.E.2d 207 (1969); State ex rel. Comm'r of Ins. v. State ex rel. Att'y Gen., 16 N.C. App. 724, 193 S.E.2d 432 (1972).

Calculation of Rate Level. — The Commissioner provided for the appropriate amount for dividends and deviations in the profit provision by calculating the amount that was provided in his prospective rate level based on evidence in the record on existing levels. State ex rel. Comm'r of Ins. v. North Carolina Rate Bureau, 124 N.C. App. 674, 478 S.E.2d 794 (1996), cert. denied, 346 N.C. 184, 486 S.E.2d 217 (1997).

Where the established rate level was not inadequate, excessive, or unfairly discriminatory, the Commissioner of Insurance, in the exercise of his sound discretion and expertise, gave "due consideration" to dividends and deviations as required under this section. State ex rel. Commissioner of Ins. v. North Carolina Rate Bureau, 350 N.C. 539, 516 S.E.2d 150 (1999).

Investment Income Improperly Considered. — The Commissioner erred as a matter of law in considering investment income from capital and surplus in his ratemaking calculations. State ex rel. Comm'r of Ins. v. North Carolina Rate Bureau, 124 N.C. App. 674, 478 S.E.2d 794 (1996), cert. denied, 346 N.C. 184, 486 S.E.2d 217 (1997).

Premium-to-Surplus Ratio. — There was substantial evidence to support the Commissioner's selection of the traditional standard 2 to 1 for the premium-to-surplus ratio. State ex rel. Comm'r of Ins. v. North Carolina Rate Bureau, 124 N.C. App. 674, 478 S.E.2d 794 (1996), cert. denied, 346 N.C. 184, 486 S.E.2d 217 (1997).

Hypothetical Ratio. — There was nothing to preclude the Commissioner's use of a hypothetical normative premium-to-surplus ratio as opposed to the actual ratio where there was substantial evidence to support the Commissioner's selection. State ex rel. Comm'r of Ins. v. North Carolina Rate Bureau, 124 N.C. App. 674, 478 S.E.2d 794 (1996), cert. denied, 346 N.C. 184, 486 S.E.2d 217 (1997).

Criteria for Determining Rates Designed to Earn Fair and Reasonable Profit. — What rates are necessary to entitle the companies to earn a fair and reasonable profit, and no more, cannot be determined without specific findings of fact, upon substantial evidence, as to: (1) The reasonably anticipated loss experience during the life of the policies to be issued in the near future; (2) The reasonably anticipated operating expenses in the same period; and (3) The percent of earned premiums which will constitute a fair and reasonable profit in that period. State ex rel. Comm'r of Ins. v. North Carolina Fire Ins. Rating Bureau, 292 N.C. 471, 234 S.E.2d 720 (1977).

The problem for the rate maker is to determine what amount, collected as premiums at the inception of the policies hereafter to be issued, will enable the company (1) to pay losses to be incurred during the life of such policies, at replacement costs prevailing at the time of such losses, (2) to pay other proper operating expenses of the company, and (3) to retain a "fair and reasonable profit." In re North Carolina Fire Ins. Rating Bureau, 275 N.C. 15, 165 S.E.2d 207 (1969).

Proposed rates will be proper for future use in North Carolina if they provide for anticipated losses, loss adjustment expenses, and other expenses of the companies attributable to that line of insurance business and include in the formula an amount which would provide for a fair and reasonable underwriting profit to the companies. State ex rel. Att'y Gen., 16 N.C. App. 279, 192 S.E.2d 138 (1972).

A "fair and reasonable profit" varies from time to time, like construction costs and consumer prices. In re North Carolina Fire Ins. Rating Bureau, 275 N.C. 15, 165 S.E.2d 207 (1969); State ex rel. Comm'r of Ins. v. State ex rel. Att'y Gen., 16 N.C. App. 724, 193 S.E.2d 432 (1972).

A "reasonable profit" cannot be determined until there is first a determination of reasonable expenses attributable to the business operated in this State. In re North Carolina Fire Ins. Rating Bureau, 275 N.C. 15, 165 S.E.2d 207 (1969).

"Prospective Loss Experience" and "Loss Trend". — "Prospective loss experience" and the present "loss trend" relate not only to the number of fires and to the extent of the physical destruction thereby, but also to the cost of replacement of the destroyed property. In re North Carolina Fire Ins. Rating Bureau, 275 N.C. 15, 165 S.E.2d 207 (1969).

Adjustment of Past Loss Experience. — The past loss experience should be adjusted to take into account any newly discovered practi-

cable procedures and devices for reducing the risk of fire. In re North Carolina Fire Ins. Rating Bureau, 275 N.C. 15, 165 S.E.2d 207 (1969).

The use of past experience to estimate future needs involves, of necessity, a projection of known data into the unknown future. In re North Carolina Fire Ins. Rating Bureau, 275 N.C. 15, 165 S.E.2d 207 (1969).

Evidence that present conditions are not those which prevailed during former experience is relevant to the translation of the past experience into an informed judgment concerning the future. In re North Carolina Fire Ins. Rating Bureau, 275 N.C. 15, 165 S.E.2d 207 (1969).

Evidence, otherwise competent, of a cost trend, upward or downward, which continues from the past into the present, and expert testimony, otherwise competent, that such trend may reasonably be expected to continue into the future, so that future costs will be higher or lower than present costs, was evidence of "reasonable and related factors" which former section required the Commissioner to consider in making his own projection into the future. It was not a proper ground for the rejection of such evidence that such projection of an upward or downward cost trend into the future had never before been used in the rate-making process. The section did not contemplate that procedures and methods for determining replacement costs for the future be frozen. In re North Carolina Fire Ins. Rating Bureau, 275 N.C. 15, 165 S.E.2d 207 (1969).

Evidence of Change After Date of Filing. — While former statute required that a hearing by the Commissioner upon a filing by the Bureau be held promptly, it was well within the bounds of possibility that, between the filing and the hearing, experience might be had which would be most relevant to the determination of the direction of a projection of the present "loss trend" into the future. Such change in conditions after the date of the filing might indicate a sharply downward trend in construction costs or in fire hazard. The statute did not contemplate that the Commissioner should shut his eyes to such a change in conditions after the date of the filing. Moreover, the Bureau could offer evidence of more recent experience which corroborated its allegations in the filing. In re North Carolina Fire Ins. Rating Bureau, 275 N.C. 15, 165 S.E.2d 207 (1969).

This section requires that the Commissioner consider certain rating factors, including a reasonable margin for underwriting profit and to contingencies as well as dividends, savings, or unabsorbed premium deposits allowed or returned by insurers to their policyholders, members, or subscribers. State ex rel. Comm'r of Ins. v. North Carolina Rate Bureau,

97 N.C. App. 644, 389 S.E.2d 574 (1990).

Factors for Consideration When Figuring Underwriting Profit. — Although the payment of dividends and rate deviations are by nature the result of business decisions, the Commissioner of Insurance was required to consider these factors when figuring underwriting profit. State ex rel. Comm'r of Ins. v. North Carolina Rate Bureau, 97 N.C. App. 644, 389 S.E.2d 574 (1990).

This section lists the factors considered in ratemaking, and makes no provision for consideration of investment income from capital and surplus; the Court of Appeals therefore correctly concluded that the Commissioner of Insurance cannot order rates based on underwriting profit provisions that require the consideration of such income. State ex rel. Commissioner of Ins. v. North Carolina Rate Bureau, 350 N.C. 539, 516 S.E.2d 150 (1999).

Statistical evidence which becomes available at any time during a public hearing for the establishment of fire insurance rates and the use of which will produce no unreasonable delay should be admitted and taken into consideration in fixing rates. In re North Carolina Fire Ins. Rating Bureau, 2 N.C. App. 10, 162 S.E.2d 671 (1968), modified, 275 N.C. 15, 165 S.E.2d 207 (1969).

Fire Insurance Rate Not to Be Fixed upon Consideration of Hazard Alone. — The General Assembly has never authorized a fire insurance rate to be fixed upon a consideration of hazard alone. In re North Carolina Fire Ins. Rating Bureau, 245 N.C. 444, 96 S.E.2d 344 (1957).

Consideration of Fire Rate Based on Not Less Than Five Years' Experience. — Upon hearing of a petition of the former Fire Insurance Rating Bureau for review of fire insurance rates on a particular classification, the Commissioner had no right to consider a rate which was not based on experience for a period of not less than five years next preceding the year in which the review is requested. In re North Carolina Fire Ins. Rating Bureau, 245 N.C. 444, 96 S.E.2d 344 (1957).

Income from Invested Capital Not Considered in Ratemaking Cases. — It has never been the law in this jurisdiction that income from invested capital is to be considered in an insurance ratemaking case. State ex rel. Comm'r of Ins. v. North Carolina Rate Bureau, 300 N.C. 381, 269 S.E.2d 547, rehearing denied, 301 N.C. 107, 273 S.E.2d 300 (1980).

The Commissioner of Insurance erred as a matter of law in concluding that the law of this jurisdiction allowed consideration of income from invested capital in an insurance ratemaking case. State ex rel. Comm'r of Ins. v. North Carolina Rate Bureau, 300 N.C. 460, 269 S.E.2d 538 (1980).

The commissioner had to consider evidence tending to show that the insurance department's expert witness based part of his calculations on investment income from capital and surplus, because investment income from these sources may not be considered in insurance rate making. State ex rel. Comm'r of Ins. v. North Carolina Rate Bureau, 75 N.C. App. 201, 331 S.E.2d 124, cert. denied, 314 N.C. 547, 335 S.E.2d 319 (1985).

Figures from Companies' Reports as Competent Evidence. — In a proceeding initiated by the Commissioner to consider the propriety of a reduction in the premium rate because of excessive profits accruing to the companies under existing rates, figures taken from the companies' reports to him would qualify as competent evidence of the "experience of the fire insurance business" within the meaning of this section and could be given "consideration" by him. Such evidence is equally competent in consideration of a filing by the Bureau. State ex rel. Comm'r of Ins. v. North Carolina Fire Ins. Rating Bureau, 292 N.C. 471, 234 S.E.2d 720 (1977).

Where countrywide data was used only to supplement North Carolina evidence, filing was not in violation of this section. State ex rel. Comm'r of Ins. v. North Carolina Rate Bureau, 40 N.C. App. 85, 252 S.E.2d 811, cert. denied, 297 N.C. 452, 256 S.E.2d 810 (1979).

Application for Increase Properly Denied. — Application for an increase in insurance rates on unprotected farm dwellings, which would result in a higher rate from that applicable to unprotected nonfarm dwellings, similar in location, construction and hazards, and having substantially the same degree of protection, was properly denied by the Commissioner of Insurance, since former G.S. 58-131 proscribed such discrimination. In re North Carolina Fire Ins. Rating Bureau, 245 N.C. 444, 96 S.E.2d 344 (1957).

Increase of Automobile Insurance Rates Upheld. — Though information which was more current might have been available to the Commissioner, the record supported a conclusion that automobile insurance rates should be increased and that substantial justice had been done to all parties concerned, both affected insurance companies and the consuming public. State ex rel. Comm'r of Ins. v. State ex rel. Att'y Gen., 18 N.C. App. 23, 195 S.E.2d 572, cert. denied, 283 N.C. 585, 196 S.E.2d 811 (1973).

As to the statutory scheme for workers' compensation rate-making, see State ex rel. Comm'r of Ins. v. North Carolina Rate Bureau, 40 N.C. App. 85, 252 S.E.2d 811, cert. denied, 297 N.C. 452, 256 S.E.2d 810 (1979).

In a workers' compensation rate hearing, the Commissioner of Insurance could properly consider investment income in determining whether a certain margin for underwriting was reasonable; however, the Commissioner erred in requiring the investment income to be considered at a risk-free rate of return rather than the rate of return actually experienced by the companies, since such requirement would limit the range of investments by insurance companies contrary to the provisions of former G.S. 58-7-90. State ex rel. Comm'r of Ins. v. North Carolina Rate Bureau, 40 N.C. App. 85, 252 S.E.2d 811, cert. denied, 297 N.C. 452, 256 S.E.2d 810 (1979).

The commissioner was not required to approve rates which provided a positive underwriting profit as a matter of law, but was only required to give "due consideration" to this criteria. Consequently, the commissioner properly ordered a rate level that produced an underwriting loss while providing for an overall adequate profit. State ex rel. Comm'r of Ins. v. North Carolina Rate Bureau, 75 N.C. App. 201, 331 S.E.2d 124, cert. denied, 314 N.C. 547, 335 S.E.2d 319 (1985).

The commissioner was not required to approve an underwriting profit greater than that requested by the rate bureau. State ex rel. Comm'r of Ins. v. North Carolina

Rate Bureau, 75 N.C. App. 201, 331 S.E.2d 124, cert. denied, 314 N.C. 547, 335 S.E.2d 319 (1985).

The commissioner's order of a five percent "excess multiplier" (i.e., computation providing premium against catastrophic losses) was based on evidence that was not material or substantial, that was fact speculation, and was rejected by the court. State ex rel. Comm'r of Ins. v. North Carolina Rate Bureau, 75 N.C. App. 201, 331 S.E.2d 124, cert. denied, 314 N.C. 547, 335 S.E.2d 319 (1985).

Applied in State ex rel. Comm'r of Ins. v. North Carolina Rate Bureau, 41 N.C. App. 310, 255 S.E.2d 557 (1979); State ex rel. Comm'r of Ins. v. North Carolina Rate Bureau, 43 N.C. App. 715, 295 S.E.2d 922 (1979); State ex rel. Comm'r of Ins. v. North Carolina Rate Bureau, 44 N.C. App. 191, 261 S.E.2d 671 (1979); Unigard Mut. Ins. Co. v. Ingram, 71 N.C. App. 725, 323 S.E.2d 442 (1984).

Cited in State ex rel. Comm'r of Ins. v. North Carolina Rate Bureau, 44 N.C. App. 191, 261 S.E.2d 671 (1979); North Carolina Steel, Inc. v. National Council Comp. Ins., 347 N.C. 627, 496 S.E.2d 369 (1998).

§ 58-36-15. Filing loss costs, rates, plans with Commissioner; public inspection of filings.

(a) The Bureau shall file with the Commissioner copies of the rates, loss costs, classification plans, rating plans and rating systems used by its members. Each rate or loss costs filing shall become effective on the date specified in the filing, but not earlier than 210 days from the date the filing is received by the Commissioner: Provided that (1) rate or loss costs filings for workers' compensation insurance and employers' liability insurance written in connection therewith shall not become effective earlier than 210 days from the date the filing is received by the Commissioner or on the date as provided in G.S. 58-36-100, whichever is earlier; and (2) any filing may become effective on a date earlier than that specified in this subsection upon agreement between the Commissioner and the Bureau.

(b) A filing shall be open to public inspection immediately upon submission to the Commissioner.

(c) The Bureau shall maintain reasonable records, of the type and kind reasonably adapted to its method of operation, of the experience of its members and of the data, statistics or information collected or used by it in connection with the rates, rating plans, rating systems, loss costs and other data as specified in G.S. 58-36-100, underwriting rules, policy or bond forms, surveys or inspections made or used by it.

(d) With respect to the filing of rates for nonfleet private passenger motor vehicle insurance, the Bureau shall, on or before February 1 of each year, or later with the approval of the Commissioner, file with the Commissioner the experience, data, statistics, and information referred to in subsection (c) of this section and any proposed adjustments in the rates for all member companies of the Bureau. The filing shall include, where deemed by the Commissioner to be necessary for proper review, the data specified in subsections (c), (e), (g) and (h) of this section. Any filing that does not contain the data required by this subsection may be returned to the Bureau and not be deemed a proper filing.

Provided, however, that if the Commissioner concludes that a filing does not constitute a proper filing he shall promptly notify the Bureau in writing to that effect, which notification shall state in reasonable detail the basis of the Commissioner's conclusion. The Bureau shall then have a reasonable time to remedy the defects so specified. An otherwise defective filing thus remedied shall be deemed to be a proper and timely filing, except that all periods of time specified in this Article will run from the date the Commissioner receives additional or amended documents necessary to remedy all material defects in the original filing.

(e) The Commissioner may require the filing of supporting data including:

(1) The Bureau's interpretation of any statistical data relied upon;

(2) Descriptions of the methods employed in setting the rates;

(3) Analysis of the incurred losses submitted on an accident year or policy year basis into their component parts; to wit, paid losses, reserves for losses and loss expenses, and reserves for losses incurred but not reported;

(4) The total number and dollar amount of paid claims;

(5) The total number and dollar amount of case basis reserve claims;

(6) Earned and written premiums at current rates by rating territory;

(7) Earned premiums and incurred losses according to classification plan categories; and

(8) Income from investment of unearned premiums and loss and loss expense reserves generated by business within this State.

Provided, however, that with respect to business written prior to January 1, 1980, the Commissioner shall not require the filing of such supporting data which has not been required to be recorded under statistical plans approved by the Commissioner.

(f) On or before September 1 of each calendar year, or later with the approval of the Commissioner, the Bureau shall submit to the Commissioner the experience, data, statistics, and information referred to in subsection (c) of this section and required under G.S. 58-36-100 and a residual market rate or prospective loss costs review based on those data for workers' compensation insurance and employers' liability insurance written in connection therewith. Any rate or loss costs increase for that insurance that is implemented under this Article shall become effective solely to insurance with an inception date on or after the effective date of the rate or loss costs increase.

(g) The following information must be included in policy form, rule, and rate or loss costs filings under this Article and under Article 37 of this Chapter:

(1) A detailed list of the rates, loss costs, rules, and policy forms filed, accompanied by a list of those superseded; and

(2) A detailed description, properly referenced, of all changes in policy forms, rules, prospective loss costs, and rates, including the effect of each change.

(h) Except to the extent the Commissioner determines that this subsection is inapplicable to filings made under G.S. 58-36-100 and except for filings made under G.S. 58-36-30, all policy form, rule, prospective loss costs, and rate filings under this Article and Article 37 of this Chapter that are based on statistical data must be accompanied by the following properly identified information:

(1) North Carolina earned premiums at the actual and current rate level; losses and loss adjustment expenses, each on paid and incurred bases without trending or other modification for the experience period, including the loss ratio anticipated at the time the rates were promulgated for the experience period;

(2) Credibility factor development and application;

(3) Loss development factor derivation and application on both paid and incurred bases and in both numbers and dollars of claims;

(4) Trending factor development and application;

(5) Changes in premium base resulting from rating exposure trends;

(6) Limiting factor development and application;

(7) Overhead expense development and application of commission and brokerage, other acquisition expenses, general expenses, taxes, licenses, and fees;

(8) Percent rate or prospective loss costs change;

(9) Final proposed rates;

(10) Investment earnings, consisting of investment income and realized plus unrealized capital gains, from loss, loss expense, and unearned premium reserves;

(11) Identification of applicable statistical plans and programs and a certification of compliance with them;

(12) Investment earnings on capital and surplus;

(13) Level of capital and surplus needed to support premium writings without endangering the solvency of member companies; and

(14) Such other information that may be required by any rule adopted by the Commissioner.

Provided, however, that no filing may be returned or disapproved on the grounds that such information has not been furnished if insurers have not been required to collect such information pursuant to statistical plans or programs or to report such information to the Bureau or to statistical agents, except where the Commissioner has given reasonable prior notice to the insurers to begin collecting and reporting such information, or except when the information is readily available to the insurers.

(i) The Bureau shall file with and at the time of any rate or prospective loss costs filing all testimony, exhibits, and other information on which the Bureau will rely at the hearing on the rate filing. The Department shall file all testimony, exhibits, and other information on which the Department will rely at the hearing on the rate filing 20 days in advance of the convening date of the hearing. Upon the issuance of a notice of hearing the Commissioner shall hold a meeting of the parties to provide for the scheduling of any additional testimony, including written testimony, exhibits or other information, in response to the notice of hearing and any potential rebuttal testimony, exhibits, or other information. This subsection also applies to rate filings made by the North Carolina Motor Vehicle Reinsurance Facility under Article 37 of this Chapter. (1977, c. 828, s. 6; 1979, c. 824, s. 2; 1981, c. 521, s. 1; 1985, c. 666, s. 3; 1985 (Reg. Sess., 1986), c. 1027, ss. 2, 3; 1993, c. 409, s. 10; 1995, c. 505, s. 2; 1999-132, ss. 3.4-3.6; 2002-187, s. 4.1.)

Effect of Amendments. — Session Laws 2002-187, s. 4.1, effective October 31, 2002, substituted "210 days" for "105 days" and "120 days" in subsection (a).

Legal Periodicals. — For survey of 1979 administrative law, see 58 N.C.L. Rev. 1185 (1980).

CASE NOTES

Editor's Note. — *Some of the cases below were decided under prior statutory provisions.*

"Reasonable Records". — The term "reasonable records," as used in this section, does not require, absent evidence of possible error, that data from all companies be presented in a rate filing. State ex rel. Comm'r of Ins. v. North Carolina Rate Bureau, 300 N.C. 474, 269 S.E.2d 595 (1980).

The Bureau must maintain reasonable records of the policy or bond forms made or used by it. Bentley v. North Carolina Ins. Guar. Ass'n, 107 N.C. App. 1, 418 S.E.2d 705 (1992).

Power to Require Audited Data in Ratemaking Case. — An order of the Commissioner of Insurance requiring that data submitted in a ratemaking case be audited was not in excess of his statutory powers as contemplated by G.S. 58-2-90(b)(2) or former G.S. 150A-51(2). State ex rel. Comm'r of Ins. v.

North Carolina Rate Bureau, 300 N.C. 381, 269 S.E.2d 547, rehearing denied, 301 N.C. 107, 273 S.E.2d 300 (1980).

Right of Bureau to Amend Filing. — When the Bureau makes a filing in which it proposes an increase in the premium rates, unquestionably, the Bureau may amend its filing so as to purpose a smaller increase in premium rates than that proposed in the original filing. State ex rel. Comm'r of Ins. v. North Carolina Fire Ins. Rating Bureau, 291 N.C. 55, 229 S.E.2d 268 (1976).

Withdrawal of Filing. — Nothing in this section relating to filings by the Bureau supports the contention that a filing, once made, cannot be withdrawn for any reason satisfactory to the Bureau. In this respect, there is no basis for making a distinction between a filing which proposes an increase in the premium rate and a filing which proposes a decrease in such rate. State ex rel. Comm'r of Ins. v. North Carolina Fire Ins. Rating Bureau, 291 N.C. 55, 229 S.E.2d 268 (1976).

When a revised classification and rate plan change is filed, the last sentence in former G.S. 58-30.4 provided that "the filing, hearing, disapproval, review and appeal procedures before the Commissioner and the courts" shall be subject to the procedures as provided for rates and classification plans in G.S. 58-36-15, 58-36-20, and 58-36-25. Of these statutes, only G.S. 58-36-20(a) speaks to any duty of the commissioner relevant to the subject. The statute declares that once there has been a filing and once there has been notice given by the commissioner, there must be a hearing. State ex rel. Comm'r of Ins. v. North Carolina Rate Bureau, 61 N.C. App. 262, 300 S.E.2d 586, cert. denied, 308 N.C. 392, 301 S.E.2d 702, 308 N.C. 548, 304 S.E.2d 242 (1983).

The controlling statutes do not require the rate bureau to provide justification of classification changes in the rate filing itself. State ex rel. Comm'r of Ins. v. North Carolina Rate Bureau, 75 N.C. App. 201, 331 S.E.2d 124, cert. denied, 314 N.C. 547, 335 S.E.2d 319 (1985).

Underlying burden of proving the need and reasonableness of a rate increase rests upon the Rate Bureau. State ex rel. Comm'r of Ins. v. North Carolina Rate Bureau, 300 N.C. 381, 269 S.E.2d 547, rehearing denied, 301 N.C. 107, 273 S.E.2d 300 (1980).

But the Commissioner can no longer effectively disapprove a rate filing by inaction or a bare assertion that the Rate Bureau has not carried its burden of proof. Though the new statutory scheme does not shift the ultimate burden of proof from the Rate Bureau to the Commissioner, it does place on the Commissioner, in disapproving a filing, the burden of affirmatively and specifically showing how the Bureau has not carried its burden

of proof, and, if the Commissioner fails to do so by substantial evidence, the presumption of prima facie correctness given to an order of the Commissioner by G.S. 58-2-80 and 58-2-90 is rebutted. State ex rel. Comm'r of Ins. v. North Carolina Rate Bureau, 40 N.C. App. 85, 252 S.E.2d 811, cert. denied, 297 N.C. 452, 256 S.E.2d 810 (1979).

Deemed Approval of Filing. — If the Commissioner fails to perform the affirmative duties imposed upon him by this Article after a filing by the Rate Bureau, the filing shall be deemed to be approved, just as there is a deemed approval upon his failure to give notice of hearing within 30 days under G.S. 58-36-20(b). State ex rel. Comm'r of Ins. v. North Carolina Rate Bureau, 40 N.C. App. 85, 252 S.E.2d 811, cert. denied, 297 N.C. 452, 256 S.E.2d 810 (1979).

Consideration of Effect of Disapproval. — Where the rate bureau's separate filing requesting to write farmowner policies on a one-year rather than a three-year basis did not note that disapproval of the filing would require increases in premium trends in its farmowner filing upon the separate filing being disapproved, the commissioner was not required to consider the effect of this disapproval on farmowner insurance rates. State ex rel. Comm'r of Ins. v. North Carolina Rate Bureau, 75 N.C. App. 201, 331 S.E.2d 124, cert. denied, 314 N.C. 547, 335 S.E.2d 319 (1985).

Review of Order of Disapproval. — If the Court of Appeals, on appeal from Commissioner's order of disapproval, finds that the order is not supported by material and substantial evidence, it is then the duty of the court to determine whether the filing complies with the statutory standards and methods and is supported by substantial evidence. If no such compliance is found, the disapproval order will be vacated and the cause remanded for proceedings as directed. If such compliance is found, the disapproval order will be vacated and the filing approved, and this will constitute a final determination under G.S. 58-36-25, which will require an order distributing the escrowed funds to the members of the Rate Bureau. State ex rel. Comm'r of Ins. v. North Carolina Rate Bureau, 40 N.C. App. 85, 252 S.E.2d 811, cert. denied, 297 N.C. 452, 256 S.E.2d 810 (1979).

Where the rate bureau's filing specifically requested a rate adjustment for the reclassification of masonry veneer structures, having failed to give the rate bureau notice of the alleged deficiency in supporting data, the commissioner was precluded from raising the classification change at the hearing and was required to permit a rate adjustment on this basis because of the material and substantial evidence offered by the bureau. State ex rel. Comm'r of Ins. v. North Carolina Rate Bureau, 75 N.C. App. 201, 331 S.E.2d 124, cert. denied,

314 N.C. 547, 335 S.E.2d 319 (1985).

Use of Rate Making Data Beyond That Provided by ISO. — Although the rate bureau was not required by statute to base a rate filing on data from all insurance companies comprising its membership, instead of only data from the Insurance Service Office (ISO), there was no error in the commissioner relying on rate making data beyond that compiled by the ISO. State ex rel. Comm'r of Ins. v. North Carolina Rate Bureau, 75 N.C. App. 201, 331 S.E.2d 124, cert. denied, 314 N.C. 547, 335 S.E.2d 319 (1985).

As to the statutory scheme for workers'

compensation rate-making, see State ex rel. Comm'r of Ins. v. North Carolina Rate Bureau, 40 N.C. App. 85, 252 S.E.2d 811, cert. denied, 297 N.C. 452, 256 S.E.2d 810 (1979).

Cited in State ex rel. Comm'r of Ins. v. North Carolina Rate Bureau, 44 N.C. App. 191, 261 S.E.2d 671 (1979); State ex rel. Comm'r of Ins. v. North Carolina Rate Bureau, 52 N.C. App. 79, 277 S.E.2d 844 (1981); State ex rel. Hunt v. North Carolina Reinsurance Facility, 302 N.C. 274, 275 S.E.2d 399 (1981); North Carolina Steel, Inc. v. National Council Comp. Ins., 347 N.C. 627, 496 S.E.2d 369 (1998).

§ 58-36-16. Bureau to share information with Department of Labor.

The Bureau shall provide to the Department of Labor information from the Bureau's records indicating each employer's experience rate modifier established for the purpose of setting premium rates for workers' compensation insurance and the name and business address of each employer whose workers' compensation coverage is provided through the assigned-risk pool pursuant to G.S. 58-36-1. Information provided to the Department of Labor with respect to experience rate modifiers shall include the name of the employer and the employer's most current intrastate or interstate experience rate modifier. The information provided to the Department under this section shall be confidential and not open for public inspection. The Bureau shall be immune from civil liability for erroneous information released by the Bureau pursuant to this section, provided that the Bureau acted in good faith and without malicious or wilful intent to harm in releasing the erroneous information. (1991 (Reg. Sess., 1992), c. 894, s. 4.)

§ 58-36-20. Disapproval; hearing, order; adjustment of premium, review of filing.

(a) At any time within 50 days after the date of any filing, the Commissioner may give written notice to the Bureau specifying in what respect and to what extent the Commissioner contends the filing fails to comply with the requirements of this Article and fixing a date for hearing not less than 30 days from the date of mailing of such notice. At the hearing the factors specified in G.S. 58-36-10 shall be considered. If the Commissioner after hearing finds that the filing does not comply with the provisions of this Article, he may issue his order determining wherein and to what extent such filing is deemed to be improper and fixing a date thereafter, within a reasonable time, after which the filing shall no longer be effective. Any order of disapproval under this section must be entered within 210 days after the date the filing is received by the Commissioner.

(b) In the event that no notice of hearing shall be issued within 50 days from the date of any such filing, the filing shall be deemed to be approved. If the Commissioner disapproves such filing pursuant to subsection (a) as not being in compliance with G.S. 58-36-10, he may order an adjustment of the premium to be made with the policyholder either by collection of an additional premium or by refund, if the amount exceeds five dollars ($5.00). The Commissioner may thereafter review any filing in the manner provided; but if so reviewed, no adjustment of any premium on any policy then in force may be ordered.

(c) For workers' compensation insurance and employers' liability insurance written in connection therewith, the period between the date of any filing and the date the Commissioner may give written notice as described in subsection (a) of this section and the period between the date of any filing and the deadline for giving notice of hearing as described in subsection (b) of this section shall be 60 days. (1977, c. 828, s. 6; 1979, c. 824, s. 3; 1985, c. 666, s. 2; 1993, c. 409, s. 12; 2002-187, s. 4.2.)

Effect of Amendments. — Session Laws 2002-187, s. 4.2, effective October 31, 2002, in subsection (a), substituted "210 days" for "105 days," deleted the proviso at the end, pertaining to entry of an order of disapproval, and made stylistic changes.

Legal Periodicals. — For survey of 1979 administrative law, see 58 N.C.L. Rev. 1185 (1980).

For article analyzing the scope of the North Carolina Insurance Commissioner's rate-making authority, see 61 N.C.L. Rev. 97 (1982).

CASE NOTES

Editor's Note. — *Many of the cases cited below were decided under former statutory provisions.*

When a revised classification and rate plan change is filed, the last sentence in former G.S. 58-30.4 provided that "the filing, hearing, disapproval, review and appeal procedures before the Commissioner and the courts" shall be subject to the procedures as provided for rates and classification plans in G.S. 58-36-15, 58-36-20, and 58-36-25. Of these statutes, only subsection (a) of this section speaks to any duty of the commissioner relevant to the subject. The statute declares that once there has been a filing and once there has been notice given by the commissioner, there must be a hearing. State ex rel. Comm'r of Ins. v. North Carolina Rate Bureau, 61 N.C. App. 262, 300 S.E.2d 586, cert. denied, 308 N.C. 392, 301 S.E.2d 702; 308 N.C. 548, 304 S.E.2d 242 (1983).

For rate-making purposes, the Bureau is to be regarded as if it were the only insurance company operating in North Carolina, and as if it had an earned premium experience, an incurred loss experience and an operating experience equivalent to the composite of those of the companies actually in operation. State ex rel. Comm'r of Ins. v. North Carolina Fire Ins. Rating Bureau, 292 N.C. 471, 234 S.E.2d 720 (1977).

For discussion of respective powers and duties of the Commissioner and his designated hearing officer in the review of filed rates and entry of a final agency decision in a contested insurance rate case, see State ex rel. Comm'r of Ins. v. North Carolina Rate Bureau, 61 N.C. App. 262, 300 S.E.2d 845, cert. denied, 308 N.C. 392, 301 S.E.2d 702; 308 N.C. 548, 304 S.E.2d 242 (1983).

Unlawful Delegation of Power to Make Final Agency Decision. — Where the Commissioner of Insurance delegated to his appointed hearing officer the power to make the final agency decision, the commissioner made an unlawful delegation of his powers. State ex rel. Comm'r of Ins. v. North Carolina Rate Bureau, 61 N.C. App. 262, 300 S.E.2d 586, cert. denied, 308 N.C. 392, 301 S.E.2d 702; 308 N.C. 548, 304 S.E.2d 242 (1983).

Purpose of Notice. — The purpose of the provision of this section that when a filing is made "the Commissioner may give written notice to the Bureau specifying in what respect and to what extent he contends such filing fails to comply" with the law is to provide the Bureau a reasonable opportunity to prepare and offer evidence, and to prevent surprise at the hearing. State ex rel. Comm'r of Ins. v. North Carolina Rate Bureau, 41 N.C. App. 310, 255 S.E.2d 557 (1979), aff'd in part and rev'd in part, 300 N.C. 381, 269 S.E.2d 547 (1980).

Purpose of Hearing. — The purpose of the hearing before the Commissioner is to determine whether the proposed rates are unreasonable, excessive or discriminatory. State ex rel. Comm'r of Ins. v. North Carolina Rate Bureau, 40 N.C. App. 85, 252 S.E.2d 811, cert. denied, 297 N.C. 452, 256 S.E.2d 810 (1979).

When Public Hearing Required. — Approval or disapproval of the Commissioner under former G.S. 58-131.1 necessarily contemplated action by the Commissioner, and a public hearing under former G.S. 58-27.2 was required prior to such action upon a proposed material rate change. State ex rel. Comm'r of Ins. v. North Carolina Fire Ins. Rating Bureau, 292 N.C. 70, 231 S.E.2d 882 (1977).

Commissioner to Comply with Statutory Procedures and Standards. — The Commissioner of Insurance has no authority to prescribe or regulate premium rates except insofar as that authority has been conferred upon him by statute. In exercising that authority he must comply with the statutory procedures and standards. In re North Carolina Fire Ins. Bureau, 275 N.C. 15, 165 S.E.2d 207 (1969); State ex rel. Comm'r of Ins. v. North Carolina Fire Ins. Rating Bureau, 291 N.C. 55, 229 S.E.2d 268 (1976).

Specificity Required in Notice of Hearing. — When the Commissioner of Insurance knows prior to the giving of public notice in what respect and to what extent he contends such filing fails to comply with the requirements of the statutes, he must give the specifics in his notice of public hearing. State ex rel. Comm'r of Ins. v. North Carolina Rate Bureau, 300 N.C. 381, 269 S.E.2d 547, rehearing denied, 301 N.C. 107, 273 S.E.2d 300 (1980).

Where the Commissioner gave no notice of his intention to challenge the weighting process utilized in a filing which was set forth clearly and prominently in the filing, such omission clearly violated subsection (a) of this section. State ex rel. Comm'r of Ins. v. North Carolina Rate Bureau, 300 N.C. 474, 269 S.E.2d 595 (1980).

Mathematical Specificity Required in Rejecting Proposed Increases. — This section requires the Commissioner of Insurance to be mathematically specific in rejecting proposed rate increases, and orders of the Commissioner should specify "wherein and to what extent" proposed filings are deemed improper. State ex rel. Comm'r of Ins. v. North Carolina Rate Bureau, 300 N.C. 381, 269 S.E.2d 547, rehearing denied, 301 N.C. 107, 273 S.E.2d 300 (1980).

Notice of Alleged Deficiency. — Clearly, the commissioner knew, prior to the notice of hearing, that the rate bureau, based on its filing, had used fire and extended coverage data in calculating its "excess multiplier" (i.e., computation providing premium against catastrophic losses). This section and fundamental fairness required the commissioner to give notice of the nature and extent of any alleged deficiency in the use of this data. Having failed to give such notice, the commissioner was prohibited from disapproving the rate bureau's excess multiplier on that basis. State ex rel. Comm'r of Ins. v. North Carolina Rate Bureau, 75 N.C. App. 201, 331 S.E.2d 124, cert. denied, 314 N.C. 547, 335 S.E.2d 319 (1985).

Failure to Give Notice of Alleged Deficiency. — Where the rate bureau's filing specifically requested a rate adjustment for the reclassification of masonry veneer structures, having failed to give the rate bureau notice of alleged deficiency in supporting data, the commissioner was precluded from raising the classification change at the hearing and was required to permit a rate adjustment on this basis because of the material and substantial evidence offered by the bureau. State ex rel. Comm'r of Ins. v. North Carolina Rate Bureau, 75 N.C. App. 201, 331 S.E.2d 124, cert. denied, 314 N.C. 547, 335 S.E.2d 319 (1985).

Notice Held Adequate. — The commissioner's notice of hearing specifically providing that investment income had not been considered and that the rate bureau had failed to justify the profit and contingency margin requested was adequate notice of the alleged deficiencies in the bureau's profit determination. The commissioner was not required to provide in his notice the manner in which profitability would be determined, there being no evidence to indicate that he knew the precise rating methodology that he would propose at the hearing before the notice of hearing was required. State ex rel. Comm'r of Ins. v. North Carolina Rate Bureau, 75 N.C. App. 20, 331 S.E.2d 124, cert. denied, 314 N.C. 547, 335 S.E.2d 319 (1985).

Burden of Proof on Rate Bureau. — The burden of proof, as that term is ordinarily understood in civil litigation, rests with the Rate Bureau in a ratemaking hearing. State ex rel. Comm'r of Ins. v. North Carolina Rate Bureau, 300 N.C. 474, 269 S.E.2d 595 (1980); State ex rel. Comm'r of Ins. v. North Carolina Rate Bureau, 300 N.C. 485, 269 S.E.2d 602 (1980).

The underlying burden of proving the need and reasonableness of a rate increase rests upon the Rate Bureau. State ex rel. Comm'r of Ins. v. North Carolina Rate Bureau, 300 N.C. 381, 269 S.E.2d 547, rehearing denied, 301 N.C. 107, 273 S.E.2d 300 (1980).

The burden of proving the need and reasonableness of a rate increase rests upon the Rate Bureau. State ex rel. Comm'r of Ins. v. North Carolina Rate Bureau, 300 N.C. 460, 269 S.E.2d 538 (1980).

Basis for Commissioner's Disapproval. — The fact that the Commissioner personally disapproves of a proposed rate revision does not, standing alone, warrant disapproval of the filing. The Commissioner's disapproval must be based on an affirmative showing that the proposed filing (1) fails to comply with statutory standards, or (2) is not supported by substantial evidence, or both. State ex rel. Comm'r of Ins. v. North Carolina Fire Ins. Rating Bureau, 30 N.C. App. 487, 228 S.E.2d 261 (1976), aff'd in part, rev'd in part, 292 N.C. 70, 231 S.E.2d 882 (1977).

The Commissioner's disapproval must be based on an affirmative showing that the proposed filing fails to comply with statutory standards. State ex rel. Comm'r of Ins. v. North Carolina Rate Bureau, 40 N.C. App. 85, 252 S.E.2d 811, cert. denied, 297 N.C. 452, 256 S.E.2d 810 (1979).

Burden on Commissioner to Make Affirmative Showing. — The Commissioner can no longer effectively disapprove a rate filing by inaction or a bare assertion that the Rate Bureau has not carried its burden of proof. Though the new statutory scheme does not shift the ultimate burden of proof from the Rate Bureau to the Commissioner, it does place on the Commissioner, in disapproving a filing, the burden of affirmatively and specifically showing how the bureau has not carried its burden of proof, and, if the Commissioner fails to do so by substantial evidence, the presumption of prima facie correctness given to an order of the Commissioner by G.S. 58-2-80 and 58-2-90 is rebutted. State ex rel. Comm'r of Ins. v. North Carolina Rate Bureau, 40 N.C. App. 85, 252 S.E.2d 811, cert. denied, 297 N.C. 452, 256 S.E.2d 810 (1979).

Material and Substantial Evidence Must Support Commissioner's Findings. — The enactment of this section did not transfer the burden of proof to the Commissioner, and there is no burden upon the Commissioner to disprove the filing; the burden upon him is that of being certain that material and substantial evidence exists in the record to support his findings. State ex rel. Comm'r of Ins. v. North Carolina Rate Bureau, 41 N.C. App. 310, 255 S.E.2d 557 (1979), aff'd in part and rev'd in part, 300 N.C. 381, 269 S.E.2d 547 (1980).

Commissioner is not required to approve or disapprove filing in toto, and may approve it in part. State ex rel. Comm'r of Ins. v. North Carolina Fire Ins. Rating Bureau, 292 N.C. 471, 234 S.E.2d 720 (1977).

The Commissioner need not approve or disapprove a filing by the Bureau in its entirety. In re North Carolina Fire Ins. Rating Bureau, 275 N.C. 15, 165 S.E.2d 207 (1969).

The Commissioner may not submit his own proposals, whether they be deemed "modifications" or "substitutions," nor may he order his scheme into effect. State ex rel. Comm'r of Ins. v. North Carolina Rate Bureau, 43 N.C. App. 715, 259 S.E.2d 922 (1979), cert. denied, 299 N.C. 735, 267 S.E.2d 670 (1980).

Credibility of Evidence. — The credibility of evidence, whether offered by the Bureau, the Department of Insurance or a protestant, and the weight to be given such evidence, are to be determined by the Commissioner. However, in this determination, as in other aspects of such rate-making proceeding, the Commissioner may not act arbitrarily, rejecting as untrustworthy, for no stated or apparent reason, uncontradicted testimony or data submitted through competent and unimpeached witnesses. State ex rel. Comm'r of Ins. v. North Carolina Fire Ins. Rating Bureau, 292 N.C. 471, 234 S.E.2d 720 (1977).

The Commissioner may not reject as untrustworthy evidence that is uncontradicted or unimpeached. State ex rel. Comm'r of Ins. v. North Carolina Rate Bureau, 40 N.C. App. 85, 252 S.E.2d 811, cert. denied, 297 N.C. 452, 256 S.E.2d 810 (1979).

Deemed Approval of Filing. — If the Commissioner fails to perform the affirmative duties imposed upon him by this Article after a filing by the Rate Bureau, the filing shall be deemed to be approved, just as there is a deemed approval upon his failure to give notice of hearing within 30 days under G.S. 58-36-20(b). State ex rel. Comm'r of Ins. v. North Carolina Rate Bureau, 40 N.C. App. 85, 252 S.E.2d 811, cert. denied, 297 N.C. 452, 256 S.E.2d 810 (1979).

Consideration of Effect of Disapproval. — Where the rate bureau's separate filing requesting to write farmowner policies on a one-year rather than a three-year basis did not note that disapproval of the filing would require increases in premium trends in its farmowner filing upon the separate filing being disapproved, the commissioner was not required to consider the effect of this disapproval on farmowner insurance rates. State ex rel. Comm'r of Ins. v. North Carolina Rate Bureau, 75 N.C. App. 201, 331 S.E.2d 124, cert. denied, 314 N.C. 547, 335 S.E.2d 319 (1985).

Review of Order of Disapproval. — If the Court of Appeals, on appeal from the Commissioner's order of disapproval, finds that the order is not supported by material and substantial evidence, it is then the duty of the court to determine whether the filing complies with the statutory standards and methods and is supported by substantial evidence. If no such compliance is found the disapproval order will be vacated and the cause remanded for proceedings as directed. If such compliance is found, the disapproval order will be vacated and the filing approved, and this will constitute a final determination under G.S. 58-36-25, which will require an order distributing the escrowed funds to the members of the Rate Bureau. State ex rel. Comm'r of Ins. v. North Carolina Rate Bureau, 40 N.C. App. 85, 252 S.E.2d 811, cert. denied, 297 N.C. 452, 256 S.E.2d 810 (1979).

The Bureau may amend its filing so as to propose a smaller increase in premium rates than that proposed in the original filing; in the absence of such amendment, the Commissioner, upon proper findings of fact supported by substantial evidence, may fix premium rates at a level such as to allow part but not all of the increase proposed by the Bureau. In re North Carolina Fire Ins. Rating Bureau, 275 N.C. 15, 165 S.E.2d 207 (1969).

Effect of Withdrawal of Voluntary Filing on Order Subsequently Entered by Commissioner. — The Rate Bureau may withdraw a voluntary filing for dwelling fire and extended coverage rates after the Commissioner of Insurance sets the filing for a public hearing; hence, an order entered by the Commissioner of Insurance after such withdrawal, disapproving the fire insurance filing and approving a decrease in extended coverage rates, was null and void. State ex rel. Comm'r of Ins. v. North Carolina Rate Bureau, 52 N.C. App. 79, 277 S.E.2d 844 (1981).

As to the statutory scheme for workers' compensation rate-making, see State ex rel. Comm'r of Ins. v. North Carolina Rate Bureau, 40 N.C. App. 85, 252 S.E.2d 811, cert. denied, 297 N.C. 452, 256 S.E.2d 810 (1979).

In a workers' compensation rate hear-

ing, the Commissioner of Insurance could properly consider investment income in determining whether a certain margin for underwriting was reasonable; however, the Commissioner erred in requiring the investment income to be considered at a risk-free rate of return rather than the rate of return actually experienced by the companies, since such requirement would limit the range of investments by insurance companies, contrary to the provisions of former G.S. 58-7-90. State ex rel. Comm'r of Ins. v. North Carolina Rate Bureau,

40 N.C. App. 85, 252 S.E.2d 811, cert. denied, 297 N.C. 452, 256 S.E.2d 810 (1979).

Applied in Unigard Mut. Ins. Co. v. Ingram, 71 N.C. App. 725, 323 S.E.2d 442 (1984).

Cited in State ex rel. Comm'r of Ins. v. North Carolina Auto. Rate Admin. Office, 294 N.C. 60, 241 S.E.2d 324 (1978); State ex rel. Comm'r of Ins. v. North Carolina Rate Bureau, 44 N.C. App. 191, 261 S.E.2d 671 (1979); State ex rel. Hunt v. North Carolina Reinsurance Facility, 302 N.C. 274, 275 S.E.2d 399 (1981).

§ 58-36-25. Appeal of Commissioner's order.

(a) Any order or decision of the Commissioner shall be subject to judicial review as provided in Article 2 of this Chapter.

(b) Whenever a Bureau rate is held to be unfairly discriminatory or excessive and no longer effective by order of the Commissioner issued under G.S. 58-36-20, the members of the Bureau, in accordance with rules and regulations established and adopted by the governing committee, shall have the option to continue to use such rate for the interim period pending judicial review of such order, provided each such member shall place in escrow account the purportedly unfairly discriminatory or excessive portion of the premium collected during such interim period. Upon a final determination by the Court, or upon a consent agreement or consent order between the Bureau and the Commissioner, the Commissioner shall order the escrowed funds to be distributed appropriately. If refunds are to be made to policyholders, the Commissioner shall order that the members of the Bureau refund the difference between the total premium per policy using the rate levels finally determined and the total premium per policy collected during the interim period pending judicial review, except that refund amounts that are five dollars ($5.00) or less per policy shall not be required. The court may also require that purportedly excess premiums resulting from an adjustment of premiums ordered pursuant to G.S. 58-36-20(b) be placed in such escrow account pending judicial review. If refunds made to policyholders are ordered under this subsection, the amounts refunded shall bear interest at the rate determined under this subsection. That rate, to be computed by the Bureau, shall be the average of the prime rates on the effective date of the filing and each anniversary of that date occurring prior to the date of the Commissioner's order requiring refunds, with the prime rate on each of the dates being the average of the prime rates of the four largest banking institutions domiciled in this State as of that date, plus three percent (3%). (1977, c. 828, s. 6; 1979, c. 824, s. 4; 1985 (Reg. Sess., 1986), c. 1027, ss. 3.1, 4; 1995, c. 517, s. 19.)

CASE NOTES

Editor's Note. — Some of the cases below were decided under prior statutory provisions.

Final determination as used in this section means all proceedings arising out of a disapproval order in a rate filing, including proceedings on remand. State ex rel. Comm'r of Ins. v. North Carolina Rate Bureau, 102 N.C. App. 809, 403 S.E.2d 597 (1991).

Insurance rate making is a technical, complicated and involved procedure carried on by trained men, but not an exact science, and judgment based upon a thorough knowledge of the problem must be applied. While courts cannot abdicate their duty to examine the evidence and the adjudication, and to interpret and apply the law, they must recognize the value of the judgment of an insurance commissioner who is specializing in the field of insurance and the efficacy of an adjudication supported by evidence of experts who have devoted a lifetime of service to rate making. In re North Carolina Fire Ins. Rating Bureau, 2 N.C. App. 10, 162 S.E.2d 671 (1968), modified, 275 N.C. 15, 165 S.E.2d 207 (1969).

When a revised classification and rate plan change is filed, the last sentence in former G.S. 58-30.4 provided that "the filing, hearing, disapproval, review and appeal procedures before the Commissioner and the courts" shall be subject to the procedures as provided for rates and classification plans in G.S. 58-36-15, 58-36-20, and 58-36-25. Of these statutes, only G.S. 58-36-20(a) speaks to any duty of the commissioner relevant to the subject. The statute declares that once there has been a filing and once there has been notice given by the commissioner, there must be a hearing. State ex rel. Comm'r of Ins. v. North Carolina Rate Bureau, 61 N.C. App. 262, 300 S.E.2d 586, cert. denied, 308 N.C. 392, 301 S.E.2d 702; 308 N.C. 548, 304 S.E.2d 242 (1983).

Review of Order of Disapproval. — If the Court of Appeals, on appeal from the Commissioner's order of disapproval, finds that the order is not supported by material and substantial evidence, it is then the duty of the court to determine whether the filing complies with the statutory standards and methods and is supported by substantial evidence. If no such compliance is found the disapproval order will be vacated and the cause remanded for proceedings as directed. If compliance is found, the disapproval order will be vacated and the filing approved, and this will constitute a final determination under G.S. 58-36-25, which will require an order distributing the escrowed funds to the members of the Rate Bureau. State ex rel. Comm'r of Ins. v. North Carolina Rate Bureau, 40 N.C. App. 85, 252 S.E.2d 811, cert. denied, 297 N.C. 452, 256 S.E.2d 810 (1979).

Neither the Court of Appeals nor the Supreme Court has the inherent power to fix rates of insurance premiums, nor to continue them in effect pending a hearing on remand. State ex rel. Comm'r of Ins. v. North Carolina Fire Ins. Rating Bureau, 292 N.C. 471, 234 S.E.2d 720 (1977).

Deemed Approval. — If the Commissioner fails to perform the affirmative duties imposed upon him by this Article after a filing by the Rate Bureau, the filing shall be deemed to be approved, just as there is a deemed approval

upon his failure to give notice of hearing within 30 days under G.S. 58-36-20(b). State ex rel. Comm'r of Ins. v. North Carolina Rate Bureau, 40 N.C. App. 85, 252 S.E.2d 811, cert. denied, 297 N.C. 452, 256 S.E.2d 810 (1979).

Rate Bureau was a "party aggrieved" within the meaning of G.S. 58-2-80; accordingly, it could challenge orders and decisions of the Commissioner of Insurance that disapproved premium rates, and there was no reason to conclude that the Rate Bureau had standing in this context but not in the context of challenging the distribution of funds under this section. State ex rel. Comm'r of Ins. v. North Carolina Rate Bureau, 102 N.C. App. 809, 403 S.E.2d 597 (1991).

As to the statutory scheme for workers' compensation rate-making, see State ex rel. Comm'r of Ins. v. North Carolina Rate Bureau, 40 N.C. App. 85, 252 S.E.2d 811, cert. denied, 297 N.C. 452, 256 S.E.2d 810 (1979).

Applied in State ex rel. Comm'r of Ins. v. North Carolina Rate Bureau, 41 N.C. App. 310, 255 S.E.2d 557 (1979); State ex rel. Comm'r of Ins. v. North Carolina Rate Bureau, 300 N.C. 381, 269 S.E.2d 547 (1980); State ex rel. Comm'r of Ins. v. North Carolina Rate Bureau, 300 N.C. 460, 269 S.E.2d 538 (1980); State ex rel. Comm'r of Ins. v. North Carolina Rate Bureau, 300 N.C. 474, 269 S.E.2d 595 (1980); State ex rel. Comm'r of Ins. v. North Carolina Rate Bureau, 300 N.C. 485, 269 S.E.2d 602 (1980); State ex rel. Comm'r of Ins. v. North Carolina Rate Bureau, 50 N.C. App. 304, 272 S.E.2d 923 (1980); State ex rel. Comm'r of Ins. v. North Carolina Rate Bureau, 75 N.C. App. 201, 331 S.E.2d 124 (1985); State ex rel. Comm'r of Ins. v. North Carolina Rate Bureau, 104 N.C. App. 211, 408 S.E.2d 868 (1991).

Cited in State ex rel. Comm'r of Ins. v. North Carolina Rate Bureau, 44 N.C. App. 191, 261 S.E.2d 671 (1979); State ex rel. Hunt v. North Carolina Reinsurance Facility, 302 N.C. 274, 275 S.E.2d 399 (1981); State ex rel. Comm'r of Ins. v. North Carolina Rate Bureau, 61 N.C. App. 506, 300 S.E.2d 845 (1983); North Carolina Ins. Guar. Ass'n v. Burnette, 131 N.C. App. 840, 508 S.E.2d 837 (1998).

§ 58-36-30. Deviations.

(a) Except as permitted by G.S. 58-36-100 for workers' compensation loss costs filings, no insurer and no officer, agent, or representative of an insurer shall knowingly issue or deliver or knowingly permit the issuance or delivery of any policy of insurance in this State that does not conform to the rates, rating plans, classifications, schedules, rules and standards made and filed by the Bureau. An insurer may deviate from the rates promulgated by the Bureau if the insurer has filed the proposed deviation with the Bureau and the Commissioner, if the proposed deviation is based on sound actuarial principles, and if the proposed deviation is approved by the Commissioner. Amendments to deviations are subject to the same requirements as initial filings. An insurer may terminate a deviation only if the deviation has been in effect for a period of six months before the effective date of the termination and the insurer notifies the Commissioner of the termination no later than 15 days before the effective date of the termination.

(b) A rate in excess of that promulgated by the Bureau may be charged by an insurer on any specific risk if the higher rate is charged in accordance with rules adopted by the Commissioner and with the knowledge and written consent of the insured. The insurer is not required to obtain the written consent of the insured on any renewal of or endorsement to the policy if the policy renewal or endorsement states that the rates are greater than those rates that are applicable in the State of North Carolina. The insurer shall retain the signed consent form and other policy information for each insured and make this information available to the Commissioner, upon request of the Commissioner. This subsection may be used to provide motor vehicle liability coverage limits above those required under Article 9A of Chapter 20 of the General Statutes and above those cedable to the Facility under Article 37 of this Chapter to persons whose personal excess liability insurance policies require that they maintain specific higher liability coverage limits. Any data obtained by the Commissioner under this subsection is proprietary and confidential and is not a public record under G.S. 132-1 or G.S. 58-2-100.

(c) Any approved rate under subsection (b) of this section with respect to workers' compensation and employers' liability insurance written in connection therewith shall be furnished to the Bureau.

(d) Notwithstanding any other provision of law prohibiting insurance rate differentials based on age, with respect to nonfleet private passenger motor vehicle insurance under the jurisdiction of the Bureau, any member of the Bureau may apply for and use in this State, subject to the Commissioner's approval, a downward deviation in the rates for insureds who are 55 years of age or older. A member of the Bureau may condition a deviation under this subsection or a deviation under subsection (a) of this section on the successful completion of a motor vehicle accident prevention course that has been approved by the Commissioner of Motor Vehicles, as designated in the deviation. (1977, c. 828, s. 6; 1983, c. 162, ss. 1, 2; 1985, c. 666, s. 1; 1987, c. 869, s. 1; 1993, c. 409, s. 25; 1995, c. 517, ss. 20, 21; 1995 (Reg. Sess., 1996), c. 668, s. 1; 1999-132, ss. 3.7, 3.8; 2001-423, s. 1.)

Legal Periodicals. — For article, "North Carolina's Cautious Approach Toward the Imposition of Extracontract Liability on Insurers for Bad Faith," see 21 Wake Forest L. Rev. 957 (1986).

CASE NOTES

Section 75-5 is concerned with protecting competitors from predatory business practices, including the fixing of unreasonably low prices with the purpose of lessening competition. On the other hand, G.S. 58-36-30(b) is concerned with protecting the insurance consumer from excessive rates. In responding to deviations from approved rates, the commissioner makes no attempt to determine whether the rates are being charged with anticompetitive purpose or effect. His determination is restricted solely to seeing that the rates do not exceed the approved ceiling. Phillips v. Integon Corp., 70 N.C. App. 440, 319 S.E.2d 673 (1984).

Applied in Unigard Mut. Ins. Co. v. Ingram, 71 N.C. App. 725, 323 S.E.2d 442 (1984).

§ 58-36-35. Appeal to Commissioner from decision of Bureau.

(a) Any member of the Bureau may appeal to the Commissioner from any decision of the Bureau, except for a decision made under G.S. 58-36-1(2). After a hearing held on not fewer than 10 days' written notice to the appellant and to the Bureau, the Commissioner shall issue an order approving the decision or directing the Bureau to reconsider the decision. If the Commissioner directs the Bureau to reconsider the decision and the Bureau fails to take action satisfactory to the Commissioner, the Commissioner shall make such order as the Commissioner may see fit.

(b) No later than 20 days before the hearing, the appellant shall file with the Commissioner or the Commissioner's designated hearing officer and shall serve on the appellee a written statement of his case and any evidence the appellant intends to offer at the hearing. No later than five days before such hearing, the appellee shall file with the Commissioner or the Commissioner's designated hearing officer and shall serve on the appellant a written statement of the appellee's case and any evidence the appellee intends to offer at the hearing. Each such hearing shall be recorded and transcribed. The cost of the recording and transcribing shall be borne equally by the appellant and appellee; provided that upon any final adjudication the prevailing party shall be reimbursed for his share of such costs by the other party. Each party shall, on a date determined by the Commissioner or the Commissioner's designated hearing officer, but not sooner than 15 days after delivery of the completed transcript to the party, submit to the Commissioner or the Commissioner's designated hearing officer and serve on the other party, a proposed order. The Commissioner or the Commissioner's designated hearing officer shall then issue an order. (1977, c. 828, s. 6; 1989, c. 485, s. 28; 1989 (Reg. Sess., 1990), c. 1069, s. 16; 2001-232, s. 3.)

§ 58-36-40. Existing rates, rating systems, territories, classifications and policy forms.

Rates, rating systems, territories, classifications and policy forms lawfully in use on September 1, 1977, may continue to be used thereafter, notwithstanding any provision of this Article. (1977, c. 828, s. 6.)

CASE NOTES

Territories are not "classifications," and their use in a filing was therefore not prohibited by former G.S. 58-30.4 which concerned revised classifications and rates. State ex rel. Comm'r of Ins. v. North Carolina Rate Bureau, 300 N.C. 460, 269 S.E.2d 538 (1980).

§ 58-36-41. Development of policy endorsement for exclusive use of original equipment manufactured crash parts.

The Rate Bureau shall develop an optional policy endorsement to be filed with the Commissioner for approval that permits policyholders to elect nonfleet private passenger motor vehicle physical damage coverage specifying the exclusive use of original equipment manufactured crash parts. (2003-395, s. 3.)

Editor's Note. — Session Laws 2003-395, s. 4, made this section effective January 1, 2004.

§ 58-36-45. Notice of coverage or rate change.

Whenever an insurer changes the coverage other than at the request of the insured or changes the premium rate, it shall give the insured written notice of such coverage change or premium rate change at least 15 days in advance of the effective date of such change or changes with a copy of such notice to the agent. This section shall apply to all policies and coverages subject to the provisions of this Article except workers' compensation insurance and employers' liability insurance written in connection therewith. (1977, c. 828, s. 6; 1985, c. 666, s. 4.)

§ 58-36-50. Limitation.

Nothing in this Article shall apply to any town or county farmers mutual fire insurance association restricting its operations to not more than six adjacent counties in this State, or to domestic insurance companies, associations, orders or fraternal benefit societies now doing business in this State on the assessment plan. (1977, c. 828, s. 6; 1985 (Reg. Sess., 1986), c. 1013, s. 10.1; 1989, c. 485, s. 53.)

§ 58-36-55. Policy forms.

No policy form applying to insurance on risks or operations covered by this Article may be delivered or issued for delivery unless it has been filed with the Commissioner by the Bureau and either he has approved it, or 90 days have elapsed and he has not disapproved it. (1979, c. 824, s. 6.)

CASE NOTES

Filing Requirement. — No policy form applying to insurance on risks covered by this Article, including risk of loss by fire, may be issued for delivery unless filed by the Bureau with the Commissioner of Insurance and approved explicitly or through default as provided by statute. Bentley v. North Carolina Ins. Guar. Ass'n, 107 N.C. App. 1, 418 S.E.2d 705 (1992).

§ 58-36-60. Payment of dividends not prohibited or regulated; plan for payment into rating system.

Nothing in this Article will be construed to prohibit or regulate the payment of dividends, savings, or unabsorbed premium deposits allowed or returned by insurers to their policyholders, members, or subscribers. Individual policyholder loss experience may be considered as a factor in determining dividends for workers' compensation insurance and employers' liability insurance written in connection therewith. A plan for the payment of dividends, savings, or unabsorbed premium deposits allowed or returned by insurers to their policyholders, members, or subscribers will not be deemed a rating plan or system. (1979, c. 824, s. 6; 1983, c. 374, s. 1.)

§ 58-36-65. Classifications and Safe Driver Incentive Plan for nonfleet private passenger motor vehicle insurance.

(a) The Bureau shall file, subject to review, modification, and promulgation by the Commissioner, such rate classifications, schedules, or rules that the Commissioner deems to be desirable and equitable to classify drivers of nonfleet private passenger motor vehicles for insurance purposes. Subsequently, the Commissioner may require the Bureau to file modifications of the classifications, schedules, or rules. If the Bureau does not file the modifications within a reasonable time, the Commissioner may promulgate the modifications. In promulgating or modifying these classifications, schedules, or rules, the Commissioner may give consideration to the following:

    (1) Uses of vehicles, including without limitation to farm use, pleasure use, driving to and from work, and business use;

    (2) Principal and occasional operation of vehicles;

    (3) Years of driving experience of insureds as licensed drivers;

    (4) The characteristics of vehicles; or

    (5) Any other factors, not in conflict with any law, deemed by the Commissioner to be appropriate.

(b) The Bureau shall file, subject to review, modification, and promulgation by the Commissioner, a Safe Driver Incentive Plan ("Plan") that adequately and factually distinguishes among various classes of drivers that have safe driving records and various classes of drivers that have a record of at-fault accidents; a record of convictions of major moving traffic violations; a record of convictions of minor moving traffic violations; or a combination thereof; and that provides for premium differentials among those classes of drivers. Subsequently, the Commissioner may require the Bureau to file modifications of the Plan. If the Bureau does not file the modifications within a reasonable time, the Commissioner may promulgate the modifications. The Commissioner is authorized to structure the Plan to provide for surcharges above and discounts below the rate otherwise charged.

(c) The classifications and Plan filed by the Bureau shall be subject to the filing, hearing, modification, approval, disapproval, review, and appeal procedures provided by law; provided that the 210-day disapproval period in G.S. 58-36-20(a) and the 50-day deemer period in G.S. 58-36-20(b) do not apply to filings or modifications made under this section. The classifications or Plan filed by the Bureau and promulgated by the Commissioner shall of itself not be designed to bring about any increase or decrease in the overall rate level.

(d) Whenever any policy loses any safe driver discount provided by the Plan or is surcharged due to an accumulation of points under the Plan, the insurer shall, pursuant to rules adopted by the Commissioner, prior to or simultaneously with the billing for additional premium, inform the named insured of the surcharge or loss of discount by mailing to such insured a notice that states the basis for the surcharge or loss of discount, and that advises that upon receipt of a written request from the named insured it will promptly mail to the named insured a statement of the amount of increased premium attributable to the surcharge or loss of discount. The statement of the basis of the surcharge or loss of discount is privileged, and does not constitute grounds for any cause of action for defamation or invasion of privacy against the insurer or its representatives, or against any person who furnishes to the insurer the information upon which the insurer's reasons are based, unless the statement or furnishing of information is made with malice or in bad faith.

(e) Records of convictions for moving traffic violations to be considered under this section shall be obtained at least annually from the Division of Motor Vehicles and applied by the Bureau's member companies in accordance with rules to be established by the Bureau.

(f) The Bureau is authorized to establish reasonable rules providing for the exchange of information among its member companies as to chargeable accidents and similar information involving persons to be insured under policies. Neither the Bureau, any employee of the Bureau, nor any company or individual serving on any committee of the Bureau has any liability for defamation or invasion of privacy to any person arising out of the adoption, implementation, or enforcement of any such rule. No insurer or individual requesting, furnishing, or otherwise using any information that such insurer or person reasonably believes to be for purposes authorized by this section has any liability for defamation or invasion of privacy to any person on account of any such requesting, furnishing, or use. The immunity provided by this subsection does not apply to any acts made with malice or in bad faith.

(g) If an applicant for the issuance or renewal of a nonfleet private passenger motor vehicle insurance policy knowingly makes a material misrepresentation of the years of driving experience or the driving record of any named insured or of any other operator who resides in the same household and who customarily operates a motor vehicle to be insured under the policy, the insurer may:

(1) Cancel or refuse to renew the policy;

(2) Surcharge the policy in accordance with rules to be adopted by the Bureau and approved by the Commissioner; or

(3) Recover from the applicant the appropriate amount of premium or surcharge that would have been collected by the insurer had the applicant furnished the correct information.

(h) If an insured disputes his insurer's determination that the operator of an insured vehicle was at fault in an accident, such dispute shall be resolved pursuant to G.S. 58-36-1(2), unless there has been an adjudication or admission of negligence of such operator.

(i) As used in this section, "conviction" means a conviction as defined in G.S. 20-279.1 and means an infraction as defined in G.S. 14-3.1.

(j) Subclassification plan surcharges shall be applied to a policy for a period of not less nor more than three policy years.

(k) The subclassification plan may provide for premium surcharges for insureds having less than three years' driving experience as licensed drivers.

(*l*) Except as provided in G.S. 58-36-30(d), no classification or subclassification plan for nonfleet private passenger motor vehicle insurance shall be based, in whole or in part, directly or indirectly, upon the age or gender of insureds.

(m) Notwithstanding any other provision of law, with respect to motorcycle insurance under the jurisdiction of the Bureau, any member of the Bureau may apply for and use in this State, subject to the Commissioner's approval, a downward deviation in the rates of insureds who show proof of satisfactory completion of the Motorcycle Safety Instruction Program. (1985 (Reg. Sess., 1986), c. 1027, s. 1; 1987, c. 864, ss. 28, 33; c. 869, s. 9; 1987 (Reg. Sess., 1988), c. 975, ss. 4, 5; 1989, c. 755, s. 3; 1993, c. 320, s. 5; 2002-187, s. 4.3.)

Effect of Amendments. — Session Laws 2002-187, s. 4.3, effective October 31, 2002, substituted "210-day" for "105 day" in the first sentence of subsection (c).

CASE NOTES

Challenge to Regulatory Scheme to be Decided in State Court. — The court declined to make a declaratory judgment where plaintiffs sought a declaration in state court that the delegation of adjudicative power to an automobile insurer is unconstitutional under the North Carolina constitution, because the State of North Carolina's interest in having this challenge to its regulatory scheme decided in state court was compelling. Prentiss v. Allstate Ins. Co., 87 F. Supp. 2d 514, 1999 U.S. Dist. LEXIS 21397 (W.D.N.C. 1999).

Cited in State ex rel. Commissioner of Ins. v. North Carolina Rate Bureau, 350 N.C. 539, 516 S.E.2d 150 (1999); Prentiss v. Allstate Ins. Co., 144 N.C. App. 404, 548 S.E.2d 557, 2001 N.C. App. LEXIS 441 (2001).

§ 58-36-70. Rate filings and hearings for motor vehicle insurance.

(a) With respect to nonfleet private passenger motor vehicle insurance, except as provided in G.S. 58-36-25, a filing made by the Bureau under G.S. 58-36-15(d) is not effective until approved by the Commissioner or unless 60 days have elapsed since the making of a proper filing under that subsection and the Commissioner has not called for a hearing on the filing. If the Commissioner calls for a hearing, he must give written notice to the Bureau, specify in the notice in what respect the filing fails to comply with this Article, and fix a date for the hearing that is not less than 30 days from the date the notice is mailed.

(b) At least 15 days before the date set for the convening of the hearing the respective staffs and consultants of the Bureau and Commissioner shall meet at a prehearing conference to review the filing and discuss any points of disagreement that are likely to be in issue at the hearing. At the prehearing conference, the parties shall list the names of potential witnesses and, where possible, stipulate to their qualifications as expert witnesses, stipulate to the sequence of appearances of witnesses, and stipulate to the relevance of proposed exhibits to be offered by the parties. Minutes of the prehearing conference shall be made and reduced to writing and become part of the hearing record. Any agreements reached as to preliminary matters shall be set forth in writing and consented to by the Bureau and the Commissioner. The purpose of this subsection is to avoid unnecessary delay in the rate hearings.

(c) Once begun, hearings must proceed without undue delay. At the hearing the burden of proving that the proposed rates are not excessive, inadequate, or unfairly discriminatory is on the Bureau. The Commissioner may disregard at the hearing any exhibits, judgments, or conclusions offered as evidence by the Bureau that were developed by or available to or could reasonably have been obtained or developed by the Bureau at or before the time the Bureau made its proper filing and which exhibits, judgments, or conclusions were not included and supported in the filing; unless the evidence is offered in response to inquiries made at the hearing by the Department, the notice of hearing, or as rebuttal to the Department's evidence. If relevant data becomes available after the filing has been properly made, the Commissioner may consider such data as evidence in the hearing. The order of presenting evidence shall be (1) by the Bureau; (2) by the Department; (3) any rebuttal evidence by the Bureau regarding the Department's evidence; and (4) any rebuttal evidence by the Department regarding the Bureau's rebuttal evidence. Neither the Bureau nor the Department shall present repetitious testimony or evidence relating to the same issues.

(d) If the Commissioner finds that a filing complies with the provisions of this Article, either after the hearing or at any other time after the filing has been properly made, he may issue an order approving the filing. If the Commissioner after the hearing finds that the filing does not comply with the provisions of this Article, he may issue an order disapproving the filing, determining in what respect the filing is improper, and specifying the appropriate rate level or levels that may be used by the members of the Bureau instead of the rate level or levels proposed by the Bureau filing, unless there has not been data admitted into evidence in the hearing that is sufficiently credible for arriving at the appropriate rate level or levels. Any order issued after a hearing shall be issued within 45 days after the completion of the hearing. If no order is issued within 45 days after the completion of the hearing, the filing shall be deemed to be approved. The Commissioner may thereafter review any filing in the manner provided; but if so reviewed, no adjustment of any premium on any policy then in force may be ordered. The escrow provisions of G.S. 58-36-25(b) apply to any order of the Commissioner under this subsection.

(e) No person shall willfully withhold information required by this Article from or knowingly furnish false or misleading information to the Commissioner, any statistical agency designated by the Commissioner, any rating or advisory organization, the Bureau, the North Carolina Motor Vehicle Reinsurance Facility, or any insurer, which information affects the rates, rating plans, classifications, or policy forms subject to this Article or Article 37 of this Chapter. (1985 (Reg. Sess., 1986), c. 1027, s. 5; 1987, c. 864, s. 65; 1987 (Reg. Sess., 1988), c. 975, s. 6; 1989 (Reg. Sess., 1990), c. 1069, s. 23; 1995, c. 507, s. 11A(c).)

CASE NOTES

Applied in State ex rel. Comm'r of Ins. v. North Carolina Rate Bureau, 97 N.C. App. 644, 389 S.E.2d 574 (1990).

Cited in State ex rel. Comm'r of Ins. v. North Carolina Rate Bureau, 95 N.C. App. 157, 381 S.E.2d 801 (1989); State ex rel. Comm'r of Ins. v. North Carolina Rate Bureau, 104 N.C. App. 211, 408 S.E.2d 868 (1991); State ex rel. Comm'r of Ins. v. North Carolina Rate Bureau, 124 N.C. App. 674, 478 S.E.2d 794 (1996), cert. denied, 346 N.C. 184, 486 S.E.2d 217 (1997).

§ 58-36-75. At-fault accidents and certain moving traffic violations under the Safe Driver Incentive Plan.

(a) The subclassification plan promulgated pursuant to G.S. 58-36-65(b) may provide for separate surcharges for major, intermediate, and minor accidents. A "major accident" is an at-fault accident that results in either (i) bodily injury or death or (ii) only property damage of three thousand dollars ($3,000) or more. An "intermediate accident" is an at-fault accident that results in only property damage of more than one thousand eight hundred dollars ($1,800) but less than three thousand dollars ($3,000). A minor accident" is an at-fault accident that results in only property damage of one thousand eight hundred dollars ($1,800) or less. The subclassification plan may also exempt certain minor accidents from the Facility recoupment surcharge. The Bureau shall assign varying Safe Driver Incentive Plan point values and surcharges for bodily injury in at-fault accidents that are commensurate with the severity of the injury, provided that the point value and surcharge assigned for the most severe bodily injury shall not exceed the point value and surcharge assigned to a major accident involving only property damage.

(a1) The subclassification plan shall provide that there shall be no premium surcharge, increase in premium on account of cession to the Reinsurance Facility, or assessment of points against an insured where: (i) the insured is involved and is at fault in a "minor accident," as defined in subsection (a) of this section; (ii) the insured is not convicted of a moving traffic violation in connection with the accident; (iii) neither the vehicle owner, principal operator, nor any licensed operator in the owner's household has a driving record consisting of one or more convictions for a moving traffic violation or one or more at-fault accidents during the three-year period immediately preceding the date of the application for a policy or the date of the preparation of the renewal of a policy; and (iv) the insured has been covered by liability insurance with the same company or company group continuously for at least the six months immediately preceding the accident. Notwithstanding (iv) of this subsection, if the insured has been covered by liability insurance with the same company or company group for at least six continuous months, some or all of which were after the accident, the insurance company shall remove any premium surcharge or assessment of points against the insured if requirements (i), (ii), and (iii) of this subsection are met. Also notwithstanding (iv) of this subsection, an insurance company may choose not to assess a premium surcharge or points against an insured who has been covered by liability insurance with that company or with the company's group for less than six months immediately preceding the accident, if requirements (i), (ii), and (iii) are met.

(a2) The subclassification plan shall provide that there shall be no premium surcharge or assessment of points against an insured where (i) the insured's driver's license has been revoked under G.S. 20-16.5; and (ii) the insured is subsequently acquitted of the offense involving impaired driving, as defined in G.S. 20-4.01(24a), that is related to the revocation, or the charge for that offense is dismissed. In addition, no insurer shall use, for rating, underwriting, or classification purposes, including ceding any risk to the Facility or writing any kind of coverage subject to this Article, any license revocation under G.S. 20-16.5 if the insured is acquitted or the charge is dismissed as described in this subsection.

(b) Repealed by Session Laws 1999-294, s. 12(a), effective July 14, 1999.

(c) Repealed by Session Laws 1999-132, s. 8.1, effective June 4, 1999.

(d) There shall be no Safe Driver Incentive Plan surcharges under G.S. 58-36-65 for accidents occurring when only operating a firefighting, rescue squad, or law enforcement vehicle in accordance with G.S. 20-125(b) and in response to an emergency if the operator of the vehicle at the time of the accident was a paid or volunteer member of any fire department, rescue squad, or any law enforcement agency. This exception does not include an accident occurring after the vehicle ceases to be used in response to the emergency and the emergency ceases to exist.

(e) Repealed by Session Laws 1999-294, s. 12(a), effective July 14, 1999.

(f) The subclassification plan shall provide that with respect to a conviction for a "violation of speeding 10 miles per hour or less over the speed limit" there shall be no premium surcharge nor any assessment of points unless there is a driving record consisting of a conviction or convictions for a moving traffic violation or violations, except for a prayer for judgment continued for any moving traffic violation, during the three years immediately preceding the date of application or the preparation of the renewal. The subclassification plan shall also provide that with respect to a prayer for judgment continued for any moving traffic violation, there shall be no premium surcharge nor any assessment of points unless the vehicle owner, principal operator, or any licensed operator in the owner's household has a driving record consisting of a prayer or prayers for judgment continued for any moving traffic violation or violations during the three years immediately preceding the date of application or the preparation of the renewal. For the purpose of this subsection, a "prayer for judgment continued" means a determination of guilt by a jury or a court though no sentence has been imposed. For the purpose of this subsection, a "violation of speeding 10 miles per hour or less over the speed limit" does not include the offense of speeding in a school zone in excess of the posted school zone speed limit.

(f1) The subclassification plan shall provide that in the event an insured is at fault in an accident and is convicted of a moving traffic violation in connection with the accident, only the higher plan premium surcharge between the accident and the conviction shall be assessed on the policy.

(g) As used in this section "conviction" means a conviction as defined in G.S. 20-279.1 and means an infraction as defined in G.S. 14-3.1. (1987, c. 869, s. 6; 1991, c. 101, s. 1; c. 713, s. 1; c. 720, s. 90; 1991 (Reg. Sess., 1992), c. 837, s. 11; c. 997, s. 1; 1993, c. 285, s. 11; 1995 (Reg. Sess., 1996), c. 730, s. 3; 1997-332, s. 1; 1997-443, s. 19.26(d); 1999-132, s. 8.1; 1999-294, s. 12(a), (b); 2003-137, s. 1.)

Cross References. — As to funeral processions, see G.S. 20-157.1.

Effect of Amendments. — Session Laws 2003-137, s. 1, effective January 1, 2004, and applicable to accidents occurring on and after that date, in subsection (a), substituted "three thousand dollars ($3,000)" for "two thousand five hundred dollars ($2,500)" in the second and third sentences, and substituted "one thousand eight hundred dollars $1,800)" for "one thousand five hundred dollars ($1,500)" in the third and fourth sentences.

§ 58-36-80. Coverage for damage to rental vehicles authorized.

As used in this section, "property damage" means damage or loss to a rented vehicle in excess of two hundred fifty dollars ($250.00), including loss of use and any costs or expenses incident to the damage or loss, for which the renter is legally obligated to pay; and "rented" means rented on a daily rate basis for a period of 21 consecutive days or less. The Bureau is authorized to promulgate rates and policy forms for insurance against property damage to rented private passenger motor vehicles. Such coverage may be offered at the option of the individual member companies of the Bureau. (1989, c. 631, s. 1; 1989 (Reg. Sess., 1990), c. 1021, s. 10.)

§ 58-36-85. Termination of a nonfleet private passenger motor vehicle insurance policy.

(a) Definitions. — The following definitions apply in this section:
   (1) Policy. — A nonfleet private passenger motor vehicle liability insurance policy, including a policy that provides medical payments, uninsured motorist, or underinsured motorist coverage, whose named insured is one individual or two or more individuals who reside in the same household.
   (2) Terminate. — To cancel or refuse to renew a policy.

(b) Termination Restrictions. — An insurer shall not terminate a policy for a reason that is not specified in G.S. 58-37-50(1) through (5) or G.S. 58-36-65(g). A termination of a policy is not effective unless the insurer either has notified a named insured of the termination by sending a written termination notice by first class mail to the insured's last known address or is not required by this subsection to send a written termination notice. Proof of mailing of a written termination notice is proof that the notice was sent.

An insurer is not required to send a written termination notice if any of the following applies:
   (1) The insurer has manifested its willingness to renew the policy by issuing or offering to issue a renewal policy, a certificate, or other evidence of renewal.
   (2) The insurer has manifested its willingness to renew the policy by any means not described in subdivision (1) of this subsection, including mailing a premium notice or expiration notice by first class mail to the named insured and the failure of the insured to pay the required premium on or before the premium due date.
   (3) A named insured has given written notification to the insurer or its agent that the named insured wants the policy to be terminated.

(c) Contents of Notice. — The form of a written termination notice used by an insurer must be approved by the Commissioner before it is used. A written termination notice must state the reason for the termination and the date the termination is effective. If the policy is terminated for nonpayment of the premium, the effective date may be 15 days from the date the notice is mailed. If the policy is terminated for any other reason, the effective date must be at least 60 days after the notice is mailed. A written termination notice must include or be accompanied by a statement that advises the insured of the penalty for driving a vehicle without complying with Article 13 of Chapter 20 of the General Statutes and that the insured has the right to request the Department to review the termination.

(d) Request for Review. — An insured who receives from an insurer a written termination notice may obtain review of the termination by filing with the Department a written request for review within 10 days after receiving a termination notice that complies with subsection (c) of this section. An insured who does not file a request within the required time waives the right to a review.

(e) Administrative Review. — When the Department receives a written request to review a termination, it must investigate and determine the reason for the termination. The Department shall issue a letter requiring one of the following upon completing its review:

(1) Approval of the termination, if it finds the termination complies with the law.

(2) Renewal or reinstatement of the policy, if it finds the termination does not comply with the law.

(3) Renewal or reinstatement of the policy and payment by the insurer of the costs of the Department's review, not to exceed one thousand dollars ($1,000), if it finds the termination does not comply with the law and the insurer willfully violated this section.

The Department shall mail the letter to the insured and the insurer. An insured or an insurer who disagrees with the determination of the Department in the letter may file a petition for a contested case under Article 3A of Chapter 150B of the General Statutes and the rules adopted by the Commissioner to implement that Article. The petition must be filed within 30 days after receiving the copy of the letter.

(f) Delegation. — The Commissioner shall designate an employee or a deputy to conduct the departmental review of a termination. The Commissioner may designate a deputy to conduct a contested case hearing concerning a termination. The Commissioner may not designate a deputy who conducted the departmental review of a termination to conduct a contested case hearing concerning the same termination.

(g) Effect of Review on Policy. — A policy shall remain in effect during administrative and judicial review of an insurer's action to terminate the policy.

(h) Liability Limit. — There is no liability on the part of and no cause of action for defamation or invasion of privacy arises against an insurer, an insurer's authorized representatives, agents, or employees, or a licensed insurance agent or broker for a communication or statement made concerning a written notice of termination.

(i) Records. — An insurer shall keep a record of a termination for three years. (1993 (Reg. Sess., 1994), c. 761, s. 30; 1995, c. 517, s. 22.)

CASE NOTES

Editor's Note. — *The cases cited below were decided under former G.S. 20-310, which was repealed by Session Laws 1993 (Reg. Sess., 1994), c. 761, s. 29, effective February 1, 1995.*

Legislative Intent. — The legislature intended for insurers to meet the requirements of former G.S. 20-310(f) in all cases of termination by the insurer, including those situations in which the insured fails to pay the premium when due. Former section 20-310(g) was not rendered superfluous by this interpretation. Rather such subsection retained its purpose to allow an insured to avoid the requirements of subsection (f) where the insurer had manifested its willingness to renew and the insured unequivocally rejected the renewal by acts such as obtaining an insurance policy from another company or by notifying the insurer or its agent in writing that he did not wish the policy to be renewed. Smith v. Nationwide Mut. Ins. Co., 72

N.C. App. 400, 324 S.E.2d 868, rev'd on other grounds, 315 N.C. 262, 337 S.E.2d 569 (1985).

All of the provisions of former G.S. 20-310(f) had to be complied with before an insurer could refuse to renew an insurance policy pursuant to former G.S. 20-310(e)(4). Compliance meant substantial compliance with former G.S. 20-310 in order for an insurer to effectively cancel, or fail to renew, an automobile liability policy for nonpayment of premium. Smith v. Nationwide Mut. Ins. Co., 72 N.C. App. 400, 324 S.E.2d 868, rev'd on other grounds, 315 N.C. 262, 337 S.E.2d 569 (1985).

It was the intent of this Article (former § 20-310) that motor vehicle owners maintain financial responsibility continuously and that the law enforce this purpose. Crisp v. State Farm Mut. Auto. Ins. Co., 256 N.C. 408, 124 S.E.2d 149 (1962).

The primary intent of the General Assembly was that every motorist maintain continuously proof of financial responsibility. Perkins v. American Mut. Fire Ins. Co., 274 N.C. 134, 161 S.E.2d 536 (1968).

Operation without Such Maintenance Is Crime. — Operation of a motor vehicle without insurance or deposit for the protection of those injured as a result of its use is a crime. Levinson v. Travelers Indem. Co., 258 N.C. 672, 129 S.E.2d 297 (1963).

Article Must Be Read into Policy and Construed Liberally. — A policy having been issued pursuant to the assigned risk plan (former G.S. 20-279.34) and for the purpose of fulfilling the requirement of the Financial Responsibility Act of 1957 (G.S. 20-309 et seq.), the provisions of that act, relative to the cancellation of such policies, must be read into this policy and construed liberally so as to effectuate the purpose of the act. Harrelson v. State Farm Mut. Auto. Ins. Co., 272 N.C. 603, 158 S.E.2d 812 (1968).

Statutes Control Policy Provisions as to Cancellation. — The provisions of this Article (former G.S. 20-310) and Article 9A, liberally construed to effectuate the legislative policy, control any provision written into a policy which otherwise would give an insurance company a greater right to cancel than is provided by the statute. Harrelson v. State Farm Mut. Auto. Ins. Co., 272 N.C. 603, 158 S.E.2d 812 (1968).

Section 20-279.22 Does Not Apply to Policies Issued Under This Article. — This Article (former G.S. 20-310) had separate, distinct and specific provisions for notice of termination of a policy issued thereunder. Thus G.S. 20-279.22, relating to notice of termination of policies issued under Article 9A of this Chapter, has no application to insurance policies issued pursuant to this Article (former G.S. 20-310). Faizan v. Grain Dealers Mut. Ins. Co., 254 N.C. 47, 118 S.E.2d 303 (1961).

Former § 20-310 governed only termination of liability coverage; collision coverage was not governed by this section. Scott v. Allstate Ins. Co., 57 N.C. App. 357, 291 S.E.2d 277 (1982).

Former § 20-310 was intended to protect insured from the acts of the insurer, not from his own intentional acts. Levinson v. Travelers Indem. Co., 258 N.C. 672, 129 S.E.2d 297 (1963).

As to the interrelationship between subdivision (d)(1) and subsection (f) of former G.S. 20-310, see Peerless Ins. Co. v. Freeman, 78 N.C. App. 774, 338 S.E.2d 570, aff'd, 317 N.C. 145, 343 S.E.2d 539 (1986).

Substantial Compliance with Former § 20-310 Required. — In order to effectively cancel a policy an insurer had to substantially comply with the requirements of former G.S. 20-310. Crisp v. State Farm Mut. Auto. Ins. Co., 256 N.C. 408, 124 S.E.2d 149 (1962).

In order to be effective, a purported cancellation had to comply with the provisions of G.S. 20-309(e) and former G.S. 20-310. Redmon v. United States Fid. & Guar. Co., 21 N.C. App. 704, 206 S.E.2d 298, cert. denied, 285 N.C. 661, 207 S.E.2d 755 (1974).

Strict Compliance with Subdivision (f)(2) of Former § 20-310 Required. — As to stating the date and giving the statutorily required 15 days from the date of mailing of the notice, the insurer had to strictly comply with the statute. Pearson v. Nationwide Mut. Ins. Co., 325 N.C. 246, 382 S.E.2d 745 (1989).

Subdivision (f)(2) of former § 20-310 was not a substantial compliance statute; rather, it was established as a strict requirement. The language was plain. The statute simply did not contemplate a notice of less than 15 days. Pearson v. Nationwide Mut. Ins. Co., 90 N.C. App. 295, 368 S.E.2d 406, aff'd, 325 N.C. 246, 382 S.E.2d 745 (1989).

Subdivision (f)(2) of Former § 20-310 Did Not Create Exception to Requirement to State Date. — It was not reasonable to construe subdivision (f)(2) of former G.S. 20-310 to eliminate the requirement of stating the date when cancellation is for nonpayment of premium; subdivision (f)(2) did not create an exception to the requirement to state the date, but rather, created an exception only to the period of time required to be given in the notice. Pearson v. Nationwide Mut. Ins. Co., 325 N.C. 246, 382 S.E.2d 745 (1989).

Strict Statutory Compliance Required for Cancellation of Compulsory Policy. — Mid-term cancellation by the insurer of a compulsory insurance policy for nonpayment of premium installments was not effective unless and until the insurer had strictly complied with the provisions of subsection (f) of former G.S. 20-310. Pearson v. Nationwide Mut. Ins. Co., 90 N.C. App. 295, 368 S.E.2d 406, aff'd, 325 N.C.

246, 382 S.E.2d 745 (1989).

Cancellation Dates Must Be Specified with Certainty. — For the protection of both the motoring public and the insured, automobile insurance cancellation dates must be expressly and carefully specified with certainty; they should not be left to the possible vagaries of date calculations, nor to the uncertainties which result when less than the statutorily prescribed period of time has been given; when accidents occur and questions of insurance coverage arise it becomes essential to know the precise date and time at which a policy, which might otherwise provide coverage, was in fact and in law cancelled. Pearson v. Nationwide Mut. Ins. Co., 325 N.C. 246, 382 S.E.2d 745 (1989).

Regardless of Reason for Cancellation. — The legislature intended the requirement to state the date to apply to cancellation notices when cancellation was either for nonpayment of premium or for some other reason; because automobile insurance cancellation has the effect of rendering the insured and third parties without automobile insurance protection, there was a need to establish the cancellation date with precision, and because the effect of cancellation, insofar as it deprives the insured and third parties of insurance protection, was the same whether the cancellation was for nonpayment of premium or for some other reason, the need for precision in establishing the cancellation date remained the same in both instances. Pearson v. Nationwide Mut. Ins. Co., 325 N.C. 246, 382 S.E.2d 745 (1989).

Termination Before End of Policy Period Governed by Section. — An insurer could terminate automobile liability coverage before the end of a policy period only for the reasons stated in and in compliance with procedural requirements of former G.S. 20-310. Peerless Ins. Co. v. Freeman, 78 N.C. App. 774, 338 S.E.2d 570, aff'd, 317 N.C. 145, 343 S.E.2d 539 (1986).

Former § 20-310 applied both to termination by cancellation and to termination by failure to renew. Robinson v. Nationwide Ins. Co., 273 N.C. 391, 159 S.E.2d 896 (1968).

Subsection (f) of former G.S. 20-310 related to the notice and warning that had to be given the policyholder in the event his policy was terminated by the insurer, whether the termination was by cancellation or by failure to renew. Perkins v. American Mut. Fire Ins. Co., 274 N.C. 134, 161 S.E.2d 536 (1968); Nationwide Mut. Ins. Co. v. Davis, 7 N.C. App. 152, 171 S.E.2d 601 (1970).

Nonrenewal for Nonpayment of Premiums. — Provisions of former G.S. 20-310 were not intended to apply to the situation in which the policy was simply not renewed for nonpayment of premiums, where the insurer's "Premium Notice" put the insured on notice of the need

to renew and afforded him an opportunity to do so. Smith v. Nationwide Mut. Ins. Co., 315 N.C. 262, 337 S.E.2d 569 (1985).

Where insurer's "Premium Notice" constituted a manifestation of its willingness to renew insured's policy, subdivision (g)(1) of former G.S. 20-310 was invoked and the requirements of subsection (f) of former G.S. 20-310 did not apply. Smith v. Nationwide Mut. Ins. Co., 315 N.C. 262, 337 S.E.2d 569 (1985).

By sending a "Premium Notice" to insured, insurance company manifested its willingness to renew the policy and the failure to pay the premium by the due date was a termination of the policy by the insured not by the insurer. Zenns v. Hartford Accident & Indem. Co., 115 N.C. App. 482, 444 S.E.2d 692, cert. denied, 337 N.C. 699, 448 S.E.2d 541 (1994).

An insurer could not cancel for nonpayment of premiums without following the provisions of former § 20-310 and G.S. 20-309(e). Nationwide Mut. Ins. Co. v. Davis, 7 N.C. App. 152, 171 S.E.2d 601 (1970).

Insurer Required to Give Notice to Insured Where It Cancels Policy. — Where circumstances known to the insurer indicated a definite desire on the part of the insured to renew a policy, a termination of the policy was "by the insurer," necessitating the giving to the insured by the insurer of the notice of termination required by former G.S. 20-310. Nationwide Mut. Ins. Co. v. Cotten, 280 N.C. 20, 185 S.E.2d 182 (1971).

Notice in Premium Notice Required. — Where the premium notice neither expressly informed plaintiff that his policy was about to expire nor apprised him of the date of expiration, the notice was simply a statement of an account that will be due on the date indicated and failed to constitute a manifestation of the insurance company's willingness to renew within the meaning of subsection (g). Hales v. North Carolina Ins. Guar. Ass'n, 337 N.C. 329, 445 S.E.2d 590 (1994).

Notice and Opportunity for a Hearing Required. — The provisions of former G.S. 20-310 required the carrier to give the policyholder specific notice and in addition provided the insured with the opportunity for a hearing and the right to apply to the Insurance Commissioner for a review of the actions of the insurer in cancelling or refusing to renew the policy. Pearson v. Nationwide Mut. Ins. Co., 90 N.C. App. 295, 368 S.E.2d 406, aff'd, 325 N.C. 246, 382 S.E.2d 745 (1989).

A Policy Continues After Expiration Until Notice Is Given. — Many common-law contractual rights were restricted by former G.S. 20-310. Thus, for example, there was, at common law, the absolute right to refuse to renew a policy upon the expiration of its term, but this was restricted by the statute so that the policy continued in force after its expiration date without a renewal, unless and until notice of termination was given in accordance with former G.S. 20-310. Pearson v. Nationwide Mut. Ins. Co., 90 N.C. App. 295, 368 S.E.2d 406, aff'd, 325 N.C. 246, 382 S.E.2d 745 (1989).

In order to cancel a policy the carrier must comply with the procedural requirements of the statute or the attempt at cancellation fails and the policy will continue in effect despite the insured's failure to pay in full the required premium. Hales v. North Carolina Ins. Guar. Ass'n, 337 N.C. 329, 445 S.E.2d 590 (1994).

Purpose of Notice. — The notice gives insured reasonable opportunity to procure other insurance. Levinson v. Travelers Indem. Co., 258 N.C. 672, 129 S.E.2d 297 (1963).

If the notice failed to conform to former § 20-310, the contract remained in force. Levinson v. Travelers Indem. Co., 258 N.C. 672, 129 S.E.2d 297 (1963).

Where the insurer failed to give the insured the required notice and warning prior to terminating a policy of automobile liability insurance, the policy continued in force and effect notwithstanding the insured's failure to pay in full the required premium. Perkins v. American Mut. Fire Ins. Co., 274 N.C. 134, 161 S.E.2d 536 (1968).

Fifteen-Day Notice Rule Applied. — Where the cancellation of an automobile insurance policy was based on failure to pay premiums, the 15-day notice rule under subdivision (f)(2) of former G.S. 20-310 applied. Pearson v. Nationwide Mut. Ins. Co., 90 N.C. App. 295, 368 S.E.2d 406, aff'd, 325 N.C. 246, 382 S.E.2d 745 (1989).

Twelve-Day Notice Held Defective. — Defendant's notice of cancellation of automobile insurance policy was defective because it provided only a 12-day period between notice and the computed effective date of cancellation. Pearson v. Nationwide Mut. Ins. Co., 90 N.C. App. 295, 368 S.E.2d 406, aff'd, 325 N.C. 246, 382 S.E.2d 745 (1989).

Statement Reminding Vehicle Owner of Requirements of Law. — The statement required by former G.S. 20-310 was not merely formal and directory. It was intended as a firm reminder to vehicle owners of the requirements of the law, and as a notice that failure to comply constitutes a criminal offense. It was to be given at the very time when insurance protection and financial responsibility were being withdrawn. Crisp v. State Farm Mut. Auto. Ins. Co., 256 N.C. 408, 124 S.E.2d 149 (1962).

Is Essential to Valid Cancellation or Termination. — In the absence of circumstances in a civil action which might constitute a waiver or an estoppel, or render harmless the failure to include a statement that proof of financial responsibility must be maintained, it is essential to a valid cancellation or termination, especially when the suit is by a member of the class the act is designed to protect. Crisp v. State Farm Mut. Auto. Ins. Co., 256 N.C. 408, 124 S.E.2d 149 (1962).

Insurer Is Not Required to Notify Insured Where Insured Himself Terminates Policy. — Former G.S. 20-310 did not require the insurer to notify the insured where the insured himself terminated the policy. Nationwide Mut. Ins. Co. v. Davis, 7 N.C. App. 152, 171 S.E.2d 601 (1970).

Where there is a cancellation by insured, insurer is not required to give notice of such cancellation to the insured. Underwood v. National Grange Mut. Liab. Co., 258 N.C. 211, 128 S.E.2d 577 (1962); Daniels v. Nationwide Mut. Ins. Co., 258 N.C. 660, 129 S.E.2d 314 (1963).

Repeal by Implication of Requirement as to Notice of Plan. — While the legislature effectively abolished the North Carolina Automobile Insurance Plan with passage of the Reinsurance Facility Act (G.S. 58-248.26 et seq.) (see now G.S. 58-37-1 et seq.), notification of the Plan under subdivision (f)(5) of former G.S. 20-310 was not specifically repealed until 1985, by Sess. L. 1985, c. 666, s. 67. However, since the legislature repealed the former Plan system, subdivision (f)(5) of former G.S. 20-310 was also thereby repealed by implication, to the extent that it required notification of the defunct Plan. Coleman v. Interstate Cas. Ins. Co., 84 N.C. App. 268, 352 S.E.2d 249 (1987).

As the Reinsurance Facility Act (G.S. 58-248.26 et seq.) (see now G.S. 58-37-1 et seq.) operated to repeal by implication that portion of subdivision (f)(5) of former G.S. 20-310 requiring notice of the defunct North Carolina Automobile Insurance Plan, cancellation notice which did not advise insured of the Plan was nevertheless valid. Colemen v. Interstate Cas. Ins. Co., 84 N.C. App. 268, 352 S.E.2d 249 (1987).

Insured May Cancel Policy by Agent. — There is nothing in the Vehicle Financial Responsibility Act which expressly or impliedly forbids the cancellation of a policy by insured through a duly authorized agent. Daniels v. Nationwide Mut. Ins. Co., 258 N.C. 660, 129 S.E.2d 314 (1963).

Cancellation of the policy by the insured is not an act so personal in its nature that it cannot be delegated to an agent. Daniels v. Nationwide Mut. Ins. Co., 258 N.C. 660, 129 S.E.2d 314 (1963).

Certification of Financial Responsibility by Insured Does Not Show Intent to Renew Policy. — Certification by an insured to the Department (now Division) of Motor Vehicles that he had financial responsibility as required by the Vehicle Financial Responsibility Act and his giving the name of his insurer in that certification are for the purpose of getting a license plate for his automobile and do not show his intent to renew the policy so as to extend its coverage. Nationwide Mut. Ins. Co. v. Cotten, 280 N.C. 20, 185 S.E.2d 182 (1971).

Substitution of Vehicle at Insured's Request Is Not Cancellation as to Original Vehicle. — Where insured requests insurer to substitute another vehicle for the vehicle insured, and insurer in compliance with the request endorses the policy and issues form FS-1, there is no cancellation of the policy but the policy does not thereafter cover the original vehicle, and no liability can attach to insurer for any injuries inflicted in the negligent operation of the original vehicle by insured or by another with insured's permission. Levinson v. Travelers Indem. Co., 258 N.C. 672, 129 S.E.2d 297 (1963).

Notice to Insured Held Sufficient Under Former Law. — See Faizan v. Grain Dealers Mut. Ins. Co., 254 N.C. 47, 118 S.E.2d 303 (1961).

Notice to Commissioner of Motor Vehicles Under Former Law. — As to notice of termination of policy required to be given to the Commissioner of Motor Vehicles before the 1963 amendment to former G.S. 20-310, see Nixon v. Liberty Mut. Ins. Co., 258 N.C. 41, 127 S.E.2d 892 (1962); Levinson v. Travelers Indem. Co., 258 N.C. 672, 129 S.E.2d 297 (1963); Allstate Ins. Co. v. Hale, 270 N.C. 195, 154

S.E.2d 79 (1967). See now § 20-309(e).

Cancellation Notice Held Not to Comply with Former § 20-310. — Cancellation notice sent by insurer to insured for nonpayment of premium, which stated when the premium was due and that the policy would be terminated 20 days after the due date, but failed to state the date upon which cancellation would become effective, as required by statute, and failed to give by its terms the statutorily required 15 days from the date of mailing of the notice, did not comply, even substantially, with former G.S. 20-310. Pearson v. Nationwide Mut. Ins. Co., 325 N.C. 246, 382 S.E.2d 745 (1989).

Failure to Comply with Former § 20-310. — Where the insured had accepted the insurance company's offer to renew when insured sent and insurer accepted partial payment in August, the insurer's attempted cancellation two months after renewal could only be deemed an act of the insurer, thereby invoking this former G.S. 20-310; and where insurer did not fulfill its obligations in conformity with former G.S. 20-310, it did not effectively cancel insured's liability policy prior to the accident in question. Peerless Ins. Co. v. Freeman, 78 N.C. App. 774, 338 S.E.2d 570, aff'd, 317 N.C. 145, 343 S.E.2d 539 (1986).

OPINIONS OF ATTORNEY GENERAL

Editor's Note. — *The opinions below were rendered under prior statutory law.*

Termination of Policy in Effect for 60 Days. — Where a policy of automobile liability insurance had been in effect for 60 days, it could not be terminated by cancellation except for the statutory reasons set forth in former G.S. 20-310 even though the insurer prior to the expiration of 60 days had given notice of intent to cancel. See opinion of Attorney General to Honorable Edwin S. Lanier, Commissioner of Insurance, 40 N.C.A.G. 326 (1969). 315 N.C. 262, 337 S.E.2d 569 (1985), rev'd on other grounds.

Forty-Eight Consecutive Months of Coverage Excluding Policy from Application of Former § 20-310. — No period of continuous automobile liability insurance coverage prior to Jan. 1, 1972, written either voluntarily or under automobile assigned risk plan, would count toward completion of period of 48 consecutive months of coverage necessary to exclude a policy from provisions of former G.S. 20-310. See opinion of Attorney General to Honorable Edwin S. Lanier, Commissioner of Insurance, 42 N.C.A.G. 22 (1972).

§ 58-36-90. Prohibitions on using credit scoring to rate noncommercial private passenger motor vehicle and residential property insurance; exceptions.

(a) Definitions. — As used in this section:

   (1) "Adverse action" has the same meaning as in section 1681a(k) of the federal Fair Credit Reporting Act and includes a denial or cancellation of, an increase in any charge for, or a reduction or other adverse or unfavorable change in the terms of coverage or amount of any insurance, existing or applied for, in connection with the underwriting of insurance.

    (2) "Credit report" means any written, oral, or other communication of any information by a consumer reporting agency that bears on a consumer's credit worthiness, credit standing, or credit capacity. Credit report does not include accident or traffic violation records as maintained by the North Carolina Division of Motor Vehicles or any other law enforcement agency, a property loss report or claims history that does not include information that bears on a consumer's credit worthiness, credit standing, or credit capacity, or any report containing information solely as to transactions or experiences between the consumer and the person making the report.

    (3) "Credit score" means a score that is derived by utilizing data from an individual's credit report in an algorithm, computer program, model, or other process that reduces the data to a number or rating.

    (4) "Noncommercial private passenger motor vehicle" means a "private passenger motor vehicle," as defined by G.S. 58-40-10, that is neither insured under a commercial policy nor used for commercial purposes.

    (5) "Private passenger motor vehicle" has the same meaning as set forth in G.S. 58-40-10.

    (6) "Residential property" means real property with not more than four housing units located in this State, the contents thereof and valuable interest therein, and insurance coverage written in connection with the sale of that property. It also includes mobile homes, modular homes, townhomes, condominiums, and insurance on contents of apartments and rental property used for residential purposes.

  (b) Prohibitions; Exceptions. — In the rating and underwriting of noncommercial private passenger motor vehicle and residential property insurance coverage, insurers shall not use credit scoring as the sole basis for terminating an existing policy or any coverage in an existing policy or subjecting a policy to consent to rate as specified in G.S. 58-36-30(b) without consideration of any other risk factors, but insurers may use credit scoring as the sole basis for discounting rates. For purposes of this subsection only, "existing policy" means a policy that has been in effect for more than 60 days.

  (c) Notification. — If a credit report is used in conjunction with other criteria to take an adverse action, the insurer shall provide the applicant or policyholder with written notice of the action taken, in a form approved by the Commissioner. The notification shall include, in easily understandable language:

    (1) The specific reason for the adverse action and, if the adverse action was based upon a credit score, a description of the factors that were the primary influence on the score.

    (2) The name, address, and toll-free telephone number of the credit bureau that provided the insurer with the credit-based information.

    (3) The fact that the consumer has the right to obtain a free copy of the consumer's credit report from the appropriate credit bureau.

    (4) The fact that the consumer has the right to challenge information contained in the consumer's credit report.

  (d) Disputed Credit Report Information. — If it is determined through the dispute resolution process set forth in the federal Fair Credit Reporting Act, 15 U.S.C. § 1681i(a)(5), that the credit information of a current insured was incorrect or incomplete and if the insurer receives notice of such determination from either the consumer reporting agency or from the insured, the insurer shall re-underwrite or re-rate the consumer within 30 days of receiving the notice. After re- underwriting or re-rating the insured, the insurer shall make any adjustments necessary, consistent with its underwriting guidelines. If an insurer determines the insured has overpaid premium, the insurer shall refund to the insured the amount of overpayment calculated back to the shorter of either the last 12 months of coverage or the actual policy period.

(e) Indemnification. — An insurer shall indemnify, defend, and hold agents harmless from and against all liability, fees, and costs arising out of or relating to the actions, errors, or omissions of an agent who obtains or uses credit information or insurance scores for an insurer, provided the agent follows the instructions or procedures established by the insurer and complies with any applicable law or regulation. Nothing in this subsection shall be construed to provide a consumer or other insured with a cause of action that does not exist in the absence of this subsection.

(f) Filing. — Insurers that use insurance scores to underwrite and rate risks shall file their scoring models, or other scoring processes, with the Department. A filing that includes insurance scoring may include loss experience justifying the applicable surcharge or credit. A filer may request that its credit score data be considered a trade secret and may designate parts of its filings accordingly. (2003-216, s. 1.)

Editor's Note. — Session Laws 2003-216, s. 2, made this section effective January 1, 2004, and applicable to policies issued or renewed on or after that date and to applications for coverage made on or after that date.

§ 58-36-95. Use of nonoriginal crash repair parts.

(a) As used in this section, the following definitions apply:
　(1) "Insurer" includes any person authorized to represent an insurer with respect to a claim.
　(2) "Nonoriginal crash repair part" refers to sheet metal and/or plastic parts — generally components of the exterior of a motor vehicle — that are not manufactured by or for the original equipment manufacturer of the vehicle.

(b) An insurer shall disclose to a claimant in writing, either on the estimate or on a separate document attached to the estimate, the following in no smaller than ten point type: "THIS ESTIMATE HAS BEEN PREPARED BASED ON THE USE OF AUTOMOBILE PARTS NOT MADE BY THE ORIGINAL MANUFACTURER. PARTS USED IN THE REPAIR OF YOUR VEHICLE MADE BY OTHER THAN THE ORIGINAL MANUFACTURER ARE REQUIRED TO BE AT LEAST EQUIVALENT IN TERMS OF FIT, QUALITY, PERFORMANCE, AND WARRANTY TO THE ORIGINAL MANUFACTURER PARTS THEY ARE REPLACING."

(c) It is a violation of G.S. 58-2-180 for an automobile repair facility or parts person to place a nonoriginal crash repair part, nonoriginal windshield, or nonoriginal auto glass on a motor vehicle and to submit an invoice for an original repair part.

(d) Any insurer or other person who has reason to believe that fraud has occurred under this section shall report that fraud to the Commissioner for further action pursuant to G.S. 58-2-160. (2003-395, s. 2.)

Editor's Note. — Session Laws 2003-395, s. 4, made this section effective January 1, 2004.

§ 58-36-100. Prospective loss costs filings and final rate filings for workers' compensation and employers' liability insurance.

(a) Except as provided in subsections (k) and (m) of this section, the Bureau shall no longer develop or file any minimum premiums, minimum premium formulas, or expense constants. If an insurer wishes to amend minimum premium formulas or expense constants, it must file the minimum premium rules, formulas, or amounts it proposes to use. A copy of each filing submitted to the Commissioner under subsections (e) and (g) of this section shall also be sent to the Bureau.

(b) Definitions. As used in this section, the following terms have the following meanings:

(1) "Expenses". — That portion of a rate attributable to acquisition, field supervision, collection expenses, any tax levied by the State or by any political subdivision of the State, licensing costs, fees, and general expenses, as determined by the insurer.

(2) "Developed losses". — Losses (including loss adjustment expenses) adjusted, using standard actuarial techniques, to eliminate the effect of differences between current payment or reserve estimates and those needed to provide actual ultimate loss (including loss adjustment expense) payments.

(3) "Insurer". — A member insurer or group.

(4) "Loss trending". — Any procedure for projecting developed losses to the average date of loss for the period during which the policies are to be effective.

(5) "Multiplier". — An insurer's determination of the expenses, other than loss expense and loss adjustment expense, associated with writing workers' compensation and employers' liability insurance, which shall be expressed as a single nonintegral number to be applied equally and uniformly to the prospective loss costs approved by the Commissioner in making rates for each classification of risks utilized by that insurer.

(6) "Prospective loss costs". — That portion of a rate that does not include provisions for expenses (other than loss adjustment expenses) or profit; and that are based on historical aggregate losses and loss adjustment expenses adjusted through development to their ultimate value and projected through trending to a future point in time.

(7) "Rate". — The cost of insurance per exposure unit, whether expressed as a single number or as a prospective loss cost with an adjustment to account for the treatment of expenses, profit, and variations in loss experience, prior to any application of individual risk variations based on loss or expense considerations, and does not include minimum premiums.

(8) "Supplementary rating information". — Includes any manual or plan of rates, classification, rating schedule, minimum premium, policy fee, rating rule, rate-related underwriting rule, experience rating plan, statistical plan and any other similar information needed to determine the applicable rate in effect or to be in effect.

(c) Except as provided in subsection (m) of this section, for workers' compensation and employers' liability insurance written in connection with workers' compensation insurance, the Bureau shall no longer develop or file advisory final rates that contain provisions for expenses (other than loss adjustment expenses) and profit. The Bureau shall instead develop and file for approval with the Commissioner, in accordance with this section, reference filings containing advisory prospective loss costs and the underlying loss data and other supporting statistical and actuarial information for any calculations or assumptions underlying these loss costs. Loss-based assessments will be included in prospective loss costs.

(d) After a reference filing has been filed with the Commissioner and approved, the Bureau shall provide its member insurers with a copy of the approved reference filing. The Bureau may print and distribute manuals of prospective loss costs as well as rules and other supplementary rating information described in subsection (k) of this section.

(e) Each insurer shall independently and individually determine the final rates it will file and the effective date of any rate changes. If an insurer decides to use the prospective loss costs in the approved reference filing in support of its own filing, the insurer shall make a filing using the reference filing adoption form. The insurer's rates shall be the combination of the prospective loss costs and the loss multiplier contained in the reference filing adoption form. Insurers may file modifications of the prospective loss costs in the approved reference filing based on their own anticipated experience. Supporting documentation is required for any upward or downward modifications of the prospective loss costs in the approved reference filing.

(f) The summary of supporting information form shall contain a reference to examples of how to apply an insurer's loss cost modification factor to the Bureau's prospective loss costs. Insurers may vary expense loads by individual classification or grouping. Insurers may use variable or fixed expense loads or a combination of these to establish their expense loadings. Each filing that varies the expense load by class shall specify the expense factor applicable to each class and shall include information supporting the justification for the variation. However, insurers shall file data in accordance with the uniform statistical plan approved by the Commissioner. Insurers may offer premium discount plans.

(g) An insurer may request to have its loss multiplier remain on file and reference all subsequent prospective loss costs reference filings. Upon receipt of subsequent approved Bureau reference filings, the insurer's rates shall be the combination of the prospective loss costs and the loss multiplier contained in the reference filing adoption form on file with the Commissioner, and will be effective on or after the effective date of the prospective loss costs. The insurer need not file anything further with the Commissioner. If an insurer that has filed to have its loss multiplier remain on file with the Department intends to delay, modify, or not adopt a particular Bureau reference filing, the insurer must make an appropriate filing with the Commissioner. The insurer's filed loss multiplier shall remain in effect until the insurer withdraws it or files a revised reference filing adoption form. The provisions of G.S. 58-40-20, 58-40-30, 58-40-35, and 58-40-45 apply to filings made by insurers under this section.

(h) An insurer may file such other information that the insurer considers relevant and shall provide such other information as may be requested by the Commissioner. When a filing is not accompanied by the information required under this section, the Commissioner shall inform the filer within 30 days after the initial filing that the filing is incomplete and describe what additional information is required. A filing is complete when the required information is furnished or when the filer certifies to the Commissioner that the additional information required by the Commissioner is not maintained or cannot be provided.

(i) To the extent that an insurer's final rates are determined solely by applying its loss multiplier, as presented in the reference filing adoption form, to the prospective loss costs contained in the Bureau's reference filing and printed in the Bureau's rating manual, the insurer need not develop or file its final rate pages with the Commissioner. If an insurer chooses to print and distribute final rate pages for its own use, based solely upon the application of its filed loss costs, the insurer need not file those pages with the Commissioner. If the Bureau does not print the loss costs in its manual, the insurer must submit its rates to the Commissioner.

(j) For reference filings filed by the Bureau:
    (1) If the insurer has filed to have its loss multiplier remain on file, applicable to subsequent reference filings, and a new reference filing is filed and approved and if:
        a. The insurer decides to use the revision of the prospective loss costs and effective date as filed, then the insurer does not file anything

with the Commissioner. Rates are the combination of the prospective loss costs and the on-file loss multiplier and become effective on the effective date of the loss costs.

    b. The insurer decides to use the prospective loss costs as filed but with a different effective date, then the insurer must notify the Commissioner of its effective date before the effective date of the loss costs.

    c. The insurer decides to use the revision of the prospective loss costs, but wishes to change its loss multiplier, then the insurer must file a revised reference filing adoption form before the effective date of the reference filing.

    d. The insurer decides not to revise its rates using the prospective loss costs, then the insurer must notify the Commissioner before the effective date of the loss costs.

(2) If an insurer has not elected to have its loss multiplier remain on file, applicable to future prospective loss costs reference filings, and a new reference filing is filed and approved, and if:

    a. The insurer decides to use the prospective loss costs to revise its rates, then the insurer must file a reference filing adoption form including its effective date.

    b. The insurer decides not to use the revisions, then the insurer does not file anything with the Commissioner.

    c. The insurer decides to change its multiplier, then the insurer must file a reference filing adoption form referencing the current approved prospective loss costs, including its effective date and, if applicable, its loss costs modification factor and supporting documentation. The insurer shall not make a change to its loss costs multiplier based on any reference filing other than the current approved reference filing.

(k) The Bureau shall file with the Commissioner, for approval, filings containing a revision of rules and supplementary rating information. This includes policy-writing rules, rating plans, classification codes and descriptions, and rules that include factors or relativities, such as increased limits factors and related minimum premiums classification relativities, or similar factors. The Bureau may print and distribute manuals of rules and supplementary rating information.

(*l*) If a new filing of rules, relativities, and supplementary rating information is filed by the Bureau and approved and if:

(1) The insurer decides to use the revisions and effective date as filed together with the loss multiplier on file with the Commissioner, then the insurer shall not file anything with the Commissioner.

(2) The insurer decides to use the revisions as filed but with a different effective date, then the insurer must notify the Commissioner of its effective date before the approved Bureau filing's effective date.

(3) The insurer decides not to use the revision, then the insurer must notify the Commissioner before the Bureau filing's effective date.

(4) The insurer decides to use the revision with modifications, then the insurer must file the modification with the Commissioner, specifying the basis for the modification and the insurer's proposed effective date if different than the Bureau filing's effective date.

(m) The Bureau shall file all of the following with the Commissioner:

(1) Final workers' compensation rates and rating plans for the residual market.

(2) The uniform classification plan and rules.

(3) The uniform experience rating plan and rules.

(4) A uniform policy form to be used by member insurers for voluntary and residual market business.

(5) Advisory manual workers' compensation rates to be used for the sole purpose of computing the premium tax liability of self-insurers under G.S. 105-228.5.

(n) The rates filed under subdivision (m)(1) of this section shall be set at levels to self-fund the residual market, provide adequate premiums to pay losses and expenses, establish appropriate reserves, and provide a reasonable margin for underwriting profit and contingencies.

(o) Every insurer shall adhere to the uniform classification plan, experience rating plan, and policy form filed by the Bureau. (1995, c. 505, ss. 3-8; 1999-132, ss. 3.9-3.12; 2001-232, s. 2.)

Editor's Note. — Session Laws 1995, c. 505, which enacted this section, also amended sub- sections (a), (e), (g), (j), and (*l*) of this section, effective September 1, 1997.

§ 58-36-105. Certain workers' compensation insurance policy cancellations prohibited.

(a) No policy of workers' compensation insurance or employers' liability insurance written in connection with a policy of workers' compensation insurance shall be cancelled by the insurer before the expiration of the term or anniversary date stated in the policy and without the prior written consent of the insured, except for any one of the following reasons:

(1) Nonpayment of premium in accordance with the policy terms.

(2) An act or omission by the insured or the insured's representative that constitutes material misrepresentation or nondisclosure of a material fact in obtaining the policy, continuing the policy, or presenting a claim under the policy.

(3) Increased hazard or material change in the risk assumed that could not have been reasonably contemplated by the parties at the time of assumption of the risk.

(4) Substantial breach of contractual duties, conditions, or warranties that materially affects the insurability of the risk.

(5) A fraudulent act against the company by the insured or the insured's representative that materially affects the insurability of the risk.

(6) Willful failure by the insured or the insured's representative to institute reasonable loss control measures that materially affect the insurability of the risk after written notice by the insurer.

(7) Loss of facultative reinsurance or loss of or substantial changes in applicable reinsurance as provided in G.S. 58-41-30.

(8) Conviction of the insured of a crime arising out of acts that materially affect the insurability of the risk.

(9) A determination by the Commissioner that the continuation of the policy would place the insurer in violation of the laws of this State.

(10) The named insured fails to meet the requirements contained in the corporate charter, articles of incorporation, or bylaws of the insurer, when the insurer is a company organized for the sole purpose of providing members of an organization with insurance coverage in this State.

(b) Any cancellation permitted by subsection (a) of this section is not effective unless written notice of cancellation has been given by registered or certified mail, return receipt requested, to the insured not less than 15 days before the proposed effective date of cancellation. The notice shall be given by registered or certified mail, return receipt requested, to the insured and any other person designated in the policy to receive notice of cancellation at their addresses shown in the policy or, if not indicated in the policy, at their last known addresses. The notice shall state the precise reason for cancellation.

Whenever notice of intention to cancel is required to be given by registered or certified mail, no cancellation by the insurer shall be effective unless and until such method is employed and completed. Failure to send this notice, as provided in this section, to any other person designated in the policy to receive notice of cancellation invalidates the cancellation only as to that other person's interest.

(c) This section does not apply to any policy that has been in effect for fewer than 60 days and is not a renewal of a policy. That policy may be cancelled for any reason by giving at least 30 days' prior written notice of and reasons for cancellation to the insured by registered or certified mail, return receipt requested.

(d) Cancellation for nonpayment of premium is not effective if the amount due is paid before the effective date set forth in the notice of cancellation.

(e) Copies of the notice required by this section shall also be sent to the agent or broker of record though failure to send copies of the notice to those persons shall not invalidate the cancellation. Mailing copies of the notice by regular first-class mail to the agent or broker of record satisfies the requirements of this subsection. (2001-241, s. 2.)

Editor's Note. — Session Laws 2001-241, s. 3, makes this section effective October 1, 2001, and applicable to policies issued, renewed or subject to renewal, or amended on or after that date.

§ 58-36-110. Notice of nonrenewal, premium rate increase, or change in workers' compensation insurance coverage required.

(a) No insurer shall refuse to renew a policy of workers' compensation insurance or employers' liability insurance written in connection with a policy of workers' compensation insurance except in accordance with the provisions of this section, and any nonrenewal attempted or made that is not in compliance with this section is not effective. This section does not apply if the policyholder has obtained insurance elsewhere, has accepted replacement coverage, or has requested or agreed to nonrenewal.

(b) An insurer may refuse to renew a policy that has been written for a term of one year or less at the policy's expiration date by mailing written notice of nonrenewal to the insured not less than 45 days prior to the expiration date of the policy.

(c) An insurer may refuse to renew a policy that has been written for a term of more than one year or for an indefinite term at the policy anniversary date by mailing written notice of nonrenewal to the insured not less than 45 days prior to the anniversary date of the policy.

(d) Whenever an insurer lowers coverage limits, raises deductibles, or raises premium rates for reasons within the exclusive control of the insurer or other than at the request of the policyholder, the insurer shall mail to the policyholder written notice of the change at least 30 days in advance of the effective date of the change. As used in this subsection, the phrase, "reasons within the exclusive control of the insurer" does not mean experience modification changes, exposure changes, or loss cost rate changes.

(e) The notice required by this section shall be given by mail to the insured and any other person designated in the policy to receive this notice at their addresses shown in the policy or, if not indicated in the policy, at their last known addresses. The notice of nonrenewal shall state the precise reason for nonrenewal. Failure to send this notice, as provided in this section, to any other person designated in the policy to receive this notice invalidates the nonrenewal only as to that other person's interest.

(f) Copies of the notice required by this section shall also be sent to the agent or broker of record, though failure to send copies of the notice to such persons shall not invalidate the nonrenewal.

(g) Mailing copies of the notice by regular first-class mail satisfies the notice requirements of this section. (2001-241, s. 2.)

Editor's Note. — Session Laws 2001-241, s. 3, makes this section effective October 1, 2001, and applicable to policies issued, renewed or subject to renewal, or amended on or after that date.

ARTICLE 37.

North Carolina Motor Vehicle Reinsurance Facility.

§ 58-37-1. Definitions.

As used in this Article:

(1) "Cede" or "cession" means the act of transferring the risk of loss from the individual insurer to all insurers through the operation of the facility.

(2) Repealed by Session Laws 1991, c. 720, s. 6.

(3) "Company" means each member of the Facility.

(4) "Eligible risk" means a person who is a resident of this State who owns a motor vehicle registered or principally garaged in this State or who has a valid driver's license in this State or who is required to file proof of financial responsibility pursuant to Article 9A or 13 of the North Carolina Motor Vehicle Code in order to register his motor vehicle or obtain a driver's license in this State; or a nonresident of this State who owns a motor vehicle registered or principally garaged in this State, or the State and its agencies and cities, counties, towns and municipal corporations in this State and their agencies, provided, however, that no person shall be deemed an eligible risk if timely payment of premium is not tendered or if there is a valid unsatisfied judgment of record against such person for recovery of amounts due for motor vehicle insurance premiums and such person has not been discharged from paying said judgment, or if such person does not furnish the information necessary to effect insurance.

(5) "Facility" means the North Carolina Motor Vehicle Reinsurance Facility established pursuant to the provisions of this Article.

(6) "Motor vehicle" means every self-propelled vehicle that is designed for use upon a highway, including trailers and semitrailers designed for use with such vehicles (except traction engines, road rollers, farm tractors, tractor cranes, power shovels, and well drillers). "Motor vehicle" also means a motorcycle, as defined in G.S. 20-4.01(27)d.

(7) "Motor vehicle insurance" means direct insurance against liability arising out of the ownership, operation, maintenance or use of a motor vehicle for bodily injury including death and property damage and includes medical payments and uninsured and underinsured motorist coverages.

With respect to motor carriers who are subject to the financial responsibility requirements established under the Motor Carrier Act of 1980, the term, "motor vehicle insurance" includes coverage with respect to environmental restoration. As used in this subsection the term, "environmental restoration" means restitution for the loss, damage, or destruction of natural resources arising out of the accidental discharge, dispersal, release, or escape into or upon the land, atmosphere, water course, or body of water of any commodity transported by a motor carrier. Environmental restoration includes the cost of removal and the cost of necessary measures taken to minimize or mitigate damage to human health, the natural environment, fish, shellfish, and wildlife.

(8) "Person" means every natural person, firm, partnership, association, trust, limited liability company, firm, corporation, government, or governmental agency.

(9) "Plan of operation" means the plan of operation approved pursuant to the provisions of this Article.

(10) Repealed by Session Laws 1977, c. 828, s. 10. (1973, c. 818, s. 1; 1977, c. 828, s. 10; 1981, c. 776, s. 1; 1985, c. 666, s. 48; 1989, c. 485, s. 48; 1991, c. 720, s. 6; 1999-132, s. 8.2; 2001-389, s. 4; 2002-187, s. 1.1.)

Cross References. — For provisions relating to motor vehicle financial responsibility, referenced in subdivision (4) above, see G.S. 20-279.1 et seq. and 20-309 et seq.

Editor's Note. — Session Laws 2001-389, s. 6, provides: "This act becomes effective January 1, 2002. Rates, rating systems, territories, classifications, and policy forms lawfully in use on January 1, 2002, may continue to be used thereafter."

Effect of Amendments. — Session Laws 2001-389, s. 4, effective January 1, 2002, added the final sentence of subdivision (6).

Session Laws 2002-187, s. 1.1, effective October 31, 2002, rewrote subdivision (8).

Legal Periodicals. — For survey of 1977 law on insurance, see 56 N.C.L. Rev. 1084 (1978).

For survey of 1979 administrative law, see 58 N.C.L. Rev. 1185 (1980).

For note discussing changes in automobile rate regulation and the role of the Insurance Commissioner in North Carolina, see 17 Wake Forest L. Rev. 822 (1981).

For survey of 1981 administrative law, see 60 N.C.L. Rev. 1165 (1982).

For 1984 survey, "Employee Exclusion Clauses in Automobile Liability Insurance Policies," see 63 N.C.L. Rev. 1228 (1985).

For 1984 survey, "Application of the Tate Test to Notice Requirements in Reinsurance Contracts," see 63 N.C.L. Rev. 1240 (1985).

For note as to terminating an insurance policy according to North Carolina's financial responsibility legislation, in light of Peerless Ins. Co. v. Freeman, 78 N.C. App. 774, 338 S.E.2d 570, aff'd per curiam, 317 N.C. 145, 343 S.E.2d 539 (1986), see 65 N.C.L. Rev. 1409 (1987).

CASE NOTES

Editor's Note. — *Most of the cases below were decided under former G.S. 20-279.34, the North Carolina Automobile Insurance Plan.*

Effect on § 20-310(f)(5). — While the legislature effectively abolished the North Carolina Automobile Insurance Plan with passage of this article, the Reinsurance Facility Act, notification of the Plan under G.S. 20-310(f)(5) was not specifically repealed until 1985, by Session Laws 1985, c. 666, s. 67. However, since the legislature repealed the former Plan system, G.S. 20-310(f)(5) was also thereby repealed by implication, to the extent that it required notification of the defunct Plan. Coleman v. Interstate Cas. Ins. Co., 84 N.C. App. 268, 352 S.E.2d 249 (1987).

Purpose of Assigned Risk Plan. — The assigned risk plan authorized by former G.S. 20-279.34 was for the equitable apportionment among insurance carriers licensed to write motor vehicle insurance in this State of those applicants for motor vehicle liability policies who were required to file proof of financial responsibility under the Financial Responsibility Act but who were unable to secure such insurance through ordinary methods. Jones v. State Farm Mut. Auto. Ins. Co., 270 N.C. 454, 155 S.E.2d 118 (1967).

Former G.S. 20-279.34 was incorporated by reference into the Financial Responsibility Act of 1957 by G.S. 20-314. Harrelson v. State Farm Mut. Auto. Ins. Co., 272 N.C. 603, 158 S.E.2d 812 (1968).

Restriction of Right to Cancel. — The right of an insurer to cancel policies issued under the assigned risk plan was restricted by former G.S. 20-279.34. Griffin v. Hartford Accident & Indem. Co., 264 N.C. 212, 141 S.E.2d 300 (1965).

And This Requirement Did Not Constitute Denial of Due Process. — The fact that an insurance company is required to issue assigned risk motor vehicle liability policies as a condition of transacting liability insurance business in North Carolina did not constitute a denial of due process in violation of State and federal constitutional provisions. Jones v. State Farm Mut. Auto. Ins. Co., 270 N.C. 454, 155 S.E.2d 118 (1967); Beasley v. Hartford Accident & Indem. Co., 11 N.C. App. 34, 180 S.E.2d 381, aff'd, 280 N.C. 177, 184 S.E.2d 841 (1971).

Liberal Construction. — Interpreting former G.S. 20-279.34 liberally, in order to accomplish the legislative purpose of maintenance of financial responsibility throughout the period of registration of the vehicle, it was construed to mean that, notwithstanding provisions in the policy, an insurance carrier could cancel an assigned risk policy, issued to fulfill the requirements of either Article 9A or Article 13 of Chapter 20, only when it was shown both that (1) there had been a nonpayment of premium or a suspension of the driver's license of the insured, and (2) the Commissioner of Insurance had approved the cancellation, which he could apparently do by the issuance of general rules and regulations with reference thereto. Harrelson v. State Farm Mut. Auto. Ins. Co., 272 N.C. 603, 158 S.E.2d 812 (1968).

Insurance Carriers Required to Subscribe to and Participate in Assigned Risk Plan. — All insurance carriers, as a prerequisite to engaging and writing motor vehicle insurance in this State, had to subscribe to, and participate in, the plans and procedures constituting the assigned risk plan. Jones v. State Farm Mut. Auto. Ins. Co., 270 N.C. 454, 155 S.E.2d 118 (1967).

Assigned risk insurance was compulsory both as to the insurer and the insured, made so by law. Grant v. State Farm Mut. Auto. Ins. Co., 1 N.C. App. 76, 159 S.E.2d 368, cert. denied, 273 N.C. 657 (1968).

Insurance supplied by a policy issued under the assigned risk plan was compulsory both as to the insured owner and as to the insurance carrier. Harrelson v. State Farm Mut. Auto. Ins. Co., 272 N.C. 603, 158 S.E.2d 812 (1968).

Act Must Be Read into Policy and Construed Liberally. — A policy having been issued pursuant to the assigned risk plan and for the purpose of fulfilling the requirement of the Financial Responsibility Act of 1957 (G.S. 20-309 et seq.), the provisions of that act, relative to the cancellation of such policies, must be read into this policy and construed liberally so as to effectuate the purpose of the act. Harrelson v. State Farm Mut. Auto. Ins. Co., 272 N.C. 603, 158 S.E.2d 812 (1968); Grant v. State Farm Mut. Auto. Ins. Co., 1 N.C. App. 76, 159 S.E.2d 368, cert. denied, 273 N.C. 657 (1968).

To avoid liability to a third party beneficiary of an assigned risk automobile insurance policy, the insurer had to allege and prove cancellation and termination of the policy in accordance with the applicable statutes. Grant v. State Farm Mut. Auto. Ins. Co., 1 N.C. App. 76, 159 S.E.2d 368, cert. denied, 273 N.C. 657 (1968).

Coverage Not Extended to Replacement Vehicle Owned by Person Other Than Named Insured. — Nothing in former G.S. 20-279.34 required any carrier to extend the coverage of an assigned risk policy to a replacement vehicle owned by and registered to a person other than the original named insured owner of the vehicle originally described and insured. Beasley v. Hartford Accident & Indem. Co., 11 N.C. App. 34, 180 S.E.2d 381, aff'd, 280 N.C. 177, 184 S.E.2d 841 (1971).

Nonpayment of Fee for Filing Form SR-22. — The failure of an insured under the assigned risk plan to pay his insurer a fee for filing a certificate of financial responsibility (Form SR-22) with the Department of Motor Vehicles was not a nonpayment of premium within the purview of former G.S. 20-279.34 for which the insurer could cancel a policy of automobile liability insurance. Harrelson v. State Farm Mut. Auto. Ins. Co., 272 N.C. 603, 158 S.E.2d 812 (1968).

Cited in State ex rel. Comm'r of Ins. v. North Carolina Rate Bureau, 300 N.C. 381, 269 S.E.2d 547 (1980); State ex rel. Hunt v. North Carolina Reinsurance Facility, 49 N.C. App. 206, 271 S.E.2d 302 (1980); State ex rel. Hunt v. North Carolina Reinsurance Facility, 302 N.C. 274, 275 S.E.2d 399 (1981); North Carolina Reinsurance Facility v. North Carolina Ins. Guar. Ass'n, 67 N.C. App. 359, 313 S.E.2d 253 (1984).

§ 58-37-5. North Carolina Motor Vehicle Reinsurance Facility; creation; membership.

There is created a nonprofit unincorporated legal entity to be known as the North Carolina Motor Vehicle Reinsurance Facility consisting of all insurers licensed to write and engaged in writing within this State motor vehicle insurance or any component thereof. Every such insurer, as a prerequisite to further engaging in writing such insurance in this State, shall be a member of the Facility and shall be bound by the rules of operation thereof as provided for in this Article and as promulgated by the Board of Governors. No company may withdraw from membership in the Facility unless it ceases to write motor vehicle insurance in this State or ceases to be licensed to write such insurance. (1973, c. 818, s. 1; 1983, c. 416, s. 6.)

Legal Periodicals. — For article discussing limitations on ad hoc adjudicatory rulemaking by an administrative agency, see 61 N.C.L. Rev. 67 (1982).

For article analyzing the scope of the North Carolina Insurance Commissioner's ratemaking authority, see 61 N.C.L. Rev. 97 (1982).

CASE NOTES

Applied in State ex rel. Comm'r of Ins. v. North Carolina Rate Bureau, 300 N.C. 381, 269 S.E.2d 547 (1980); North Carolina Reinsurance Facility v. North Carolina Ins. Guar. Ass'n, 67 N.C. App. 359, 313 S.E.2d 253 (1984).

§ 58-37-10. Obligations after termination of membership.

Any company whose membership in the Facility has been terminated by withdrawal shall, nevertheless, with respect to its business prior to midnight of the effective date of such termination continue to be governed by this Article. (1973, c. 818, s. 1.)

CASE NOTES

Applied in North Carolina Reinsurance Facility v. North Carolina Ins. Guar. Ass'n, 67 N.C. App. 359, 313 S.E.2d 253 (1984).

§ 58-37-15. Insolvency.

Any unsatisfied net liability to the Facility of any insolvent member shall be assumed by and apportioned among the remaining members in the Facility in the same manner in which assessments are apportioned by the Facility. The Facility shall have all rights allowed by law in behalf of the remaining members against the estate or funds of such insolvent for sums due the Facility in accordance with this Article. (1973, c. 818, s. 1; 1977, c. 828, s. 12.)

CASE NOTES

Cited in North Carolina Reinsurance Facility v. North Carolina Ins. Guar. Ass'n, 67 N.C. App. 359, 313 S.E.2d 253 (1984).

§ 58-37-20. Merger, consolidation or cession.

When a member has been merged or consolidated into another insurer, or has reinsured its entire motor vehicle liability insurance business in the State with another insurer, such company or its successor in interest shall remain liable for all obligations hereunder and such company and its successor in interest and the other insurers with which it has been merged or consolidated shall continue to participate in the Facility according to the rules of operation. (1973, c. 818, s. 1; 1977, c. 828, s. 13.)

§ 58-37-25. General obligations of insurers.

(a) Except as otherwise provided in this Article all insurers as a prerequisite to the further engaging in this State in the writing of motor vehicle insurance or any component thereof shall accept and insure any otherwise unacceptable applicant therefor who is an eligible risk if cession of the particular coverage and coverage limits applied for are permitted in the Facility. All such insurers shall equitably share the results of such otherwise unacceptable business through the Facility and shall be bound by the acts of their agents in accordance with the provisions of this Article. No insurer shall impose upon any of its agents, solely on account of ceded business received from such agents, any quota or matching requirement for any other insurance as a condition for further acceptance of ceded business from such agents.

(b) Each insurer will provide the same type of service to ceded business that it provides for its voluntary market. Records provided to agents and brokers will include an indication that the business is ceded. When an insurer cedes a policy or renewal thereof to the Facility and the Facility premium for such policy is higher than the premium that the insurer would normally charge for such policy if retained by the insurer, the policyholder will be informed that (i) his policy is ceded, (ii) the coverages are written at the Facility rate, which rate differential must be specified, (iii) the reason or reasons for the cession to the Facility, (iv) the specific reason or reasons for the cession to the Facility will be provided upon the written request of the policyholder to the insurer, and (v) the policyholder may seek insurance through other insurers who may elect not to cede his policy. If such policyholder obtains motor vehicle liability insurance through another insurer who elects not to cede his policy to the Facility and the policyholder cancels his ceded policy within 45 days of the effective date of such ceded policy, the earned premium for such ceded policy shall be calculated on the pro rata basis, except that the pro rata calculation shall not apply to a cancellation by any insurance premium finance company as provided in G.S. 58-35-85.

(c) Upon the written request of any eligible risk who has been notified pursuant to subsection (b) of this section that his motor vehicle insurance policy has been ceded to the Facility, the insurer ceding the insurance policy must provide in writing to that eligible risk the specific reason or reasons for the decision to cede that policy to the Facility. Proof of mailing of the written reason or reasons is sufficient proof of compliance with this obligation. With regard to any notice of cession or any written or oral communications specifying the reason or reasons for cession, there will be no liability on the part of, and no cause of action of any nature will arise against, (i) any insurer or its authorized representatives, agents, or employees, or (ii) any licensed agent, broker, or persons who furnish to the insurer information as to the reason or reasons for the cession, for any communications or statements made by them, unless the communications or statements are shown to have been made in bad faith with malice in fact. (1973, c. 818, s. 1; 1979, c. 732.)

Legal Periodicals. — For survey of 1979 administrative law, see 58 N.C.L. Rev. 1185 (1980).

CASE NOTES

Use of Own Policy Forms Not Permitted. — An insurer writing automobile insurance in North Carolina is not permitted to use its own policy forms on insurance policies ceded to the Facility. St. Paul Fire & Marine Ins. Co. v. North Carolina Motor Vehicle Reinsurance Facility, 124 N.C. App. 450, 476 S.E.2d 897 (1996).

As the legislature has specifically stated in another statute that policy forms are to be determined by the Facility, and the more spe-

cific statute prevails, there is no violation of the anti-discrimination provision of subsection (b) when the Facility mandates the uniform use of policy forms for all ceded motor vehicle insurance business. St. Paul Fire & Marine Ins. Co. v. North Carolina Motor Vehicle Reinsurance Facility, 124 N.C. App. 450, 476 S.E.2d 897 (1996).

Cited in State ex rel. Comm'r of Ins. v. North Carolina Rate Bureau, 300 N.C. 381, 269

S.E.2d 547 (1980); State ex rel. Hunt v. North
Carolina Reinsurance Facility, 49 N.C. App.
206, 271 S.E.2d 302 (1980); State ex rel. Hunt v.
North Carolina Reinsurance Facility, 302 N.C.
274, 275 S.E.2d 399 (1981); Coleman v. Interstate Cas. Ins. Co., 84 N.C. App. 268, 352
S.E.2d 249 (1987).

§ 58-37-30. General obligations of agents.

(a) Except as otherwise provided in this Article, no licensed agent of an
insurer authorized to solicit and accept premiums for motor vehicle insurance
or any component thereof by the company he represents shall refuse on behalf
of said company to accept any application from an eligible risk for such
insurance and to immediately bind the coverage applied for and for a period of
not less than six months if cession of the particular coverage and coverage
limits applied for are permitted in the Facility, provided the application is
submitted during the agent's normal business hours, at his customary place of
business and in accordance with the agent's customary practices and procedures. The commission paid on the insurance coverages provided in this Article
shall not be less than the commission on insurance coverage written through
the North Carolina Insurance Plan on May 1, 1973. The same commission
shall apply uniformly statewide.

(b) It shall be the responsibility of the agent to write the coverage applied for
at what he believes to be the appropriate rate level. If coverage is written at the
Facility rate level and the company elects not to cede, the policy shall be rated
at a rate under Article 36 of this Chapter. Coverage written at a rate under
Article 36 of this Chapter that is not acceptable to the company must either be
placed with another company or rated at the Facility rate level by the agent.
(1973, c. 818, s. 1; 1977, c. 828, s. 11; 1995, c. 517, s. 23.)

CASE NOTES

**Facility rates can be higher than those
for the voluntary market if** a higher facility
rate is actuarially indicated. State ex rel.
Comm'r of Ins. v. North Carolina Rate Bureau,
300 N.C. 381, 269 S.E.2d 547, rehearing denied, 301 N.C. 107, 273 S.E.2d 300 (1980).

Cited in State ex rel. Hunt v. North Carolina
Reinsurance Facility, 302 N.C. 274, 275 S.E.2d
399 (1981).

§ 58-37-35. The Facility; functions; administration.

(a) The operation of the Facility shall assure the availability of motor
vehicle insurance to any eligible risk and the Facility shall accept all placements made in accordance with this Article, the plan of operation adopted
pursuant thereto, and any amendments to either.

(b) The Facility shall reinsure for each coverage available in the Facility to
the standard percentage of one hundred percent (100%) or lesser equitable
percentage established in the Facility's plan of operation as follows:

(1) For the following coverages of motor vehicle insurance and in at least
the following amounts of insurance:
a. Bodily injury liability: thirty thousand dollars ($30,000) each
person, sixty thousand dollars ($60,000) each accident;
b. Property damage liability: twenty-five thousand dollars ($25,000)
each person;
c. Medical payments: one thousand dollars ($1,000) each person;
except that this coverage shall not be available for motorcycles;
d. Uninsured motorist: thirty thousand dollars ($30,000) each person;
sixty thousand dollars ($60,000) each accident for bodily injury;
twenty-five thousand dollars ($25,000) each accident property
damage (one hundred dollars ($100.00) deductible);

      e. Any other motor vehicle insurance or financial responsibility limits in the amounts required by any federal law or federal agency regulation; by any law of this State; or by any rule duly adopted under Chapter 150B of the General Statutes or by the North Carolina Utilities Commission.

  (2) Additional ceding privileges for motor vehicle insurance shall be provided by the Board of Governors up to the following:

      a. Bodily injury liability: one hundred thousand dollars ($100,000) each person, three hundred thousand dollars ($300,000) each accident;

      b. Property damage liability: fifty thousand dollars ($50,000) each accident;

      c. Medical payments: two thousand dollars ($2,000) each person; except that this coverage shall not be available for motorcycles;

      d. Underinsured motorist: one million dollars ($1,000,000) each person and each accident for bodily injury liability; and

      e. Uninsured motorist: one million dollars ($1,000,000) each person and each accident for bodily injury and fifty thousand dollars ($50,000) each accident for property damage (one hundred dollars ($100.00) deductible).

  (2a) For persons who must maintain liability coverage limits above those available under subdivision (2) of this subsection in order to obtain or continue coverage under personal excess liability or personal "umbrella" insurance policies, additional ceding privileges for motor vehicle insurance shall be provided by the Board of Governors up to the following:

      a. Bodily injury liability: two hundred fifty thousand dollars ($250,000) each person, five hundred thousand dollars ($500,000) each accident.

      b. Property damage liability: one hundred thousand dollars ($100,000) each accident.

      c. Medical payments: five thousand dollars ($5,000) each person; except that this coverage shall not be available for motorcycles.

      d. Uninsured motorist: one hundred thousand dollars ($100,000) each accident for property damage (one hundred dollars ($100.00) deductible).

  (3) Whenever the additional ceding privileges are provided as in G.S. 58-37-35(b)(2) for any component of motor vehicle insurance, the same additional ceding privileges shall be available to "all other" types of risks subject to the rating jurisdiction of the North Carolina Rate Bureau.

(c) The Facility shall require each member to adjust losses for ceded business fairly and efficiently in the same manner as voluntary business losses are adjusted and to effect settlement where settlement is appropriate.

(d) The Facility shall be administered by a Board of Governors. The Board of Governors shall consist of 12 members having one vote each from the classifications specified in this subsection and the Commissioner, who shall serve ex officio without vote. Each Facility insurance company member serving on the Board shall be represented by a senior officer of the company. Not more than one company in a group under the same ownership or management shall be represented on the Board at the same time. Five members of the Board shall be selected by the member insurers, which members shall be fairly representative of the industry. To insure representative member insurers, one each shall be selected from the following trade associations: the American Insurance Association (or its successors), the Alliance of American Insurers (or its successors), the National Association of Independent Insurers (or its successors), all other stock insurers not affiliated with those trade associations, and all other nonstock insurers not affiliated with those trade associations. The Commissioner shall appoint two members of the Board who are Facility insurance company members domiciled in this State. The Commissioner shall appoint five members of the Board who shall be fire and casualty insurance agents licensed in this State and actively engaged in writing motor vehicle insurance in this State. The initial term of office of the Board members shall be two years. Following completion of initial terms, successors to the members of the original Board of Governors shall be selected to serve three years. All members of the Board of Governors shall serve until their successors are selected and qualified and the Commissioner may fill any vacancy on the Board from any of the classifications specified in this subsection until the vacancies are filled in accordance with this Article. The Board of Governors of the Facility shall also have as nonvoting members two persons who are not employed by or affiliated with any insurance company or the Department and who are appointed by the Governor to serve at the Governor's pleasure.

(e) The Commissioner and member companies shall provide for a Board of Governors. The Board of Governors shall elect from its membership a chair and shall meet at the call of the chair or at the request of four members of the Board of Governors. The chair shall retain the right to vote on all issues. Seven members of the Board of Governors shall constitute a quorum. The same member may not serve as chair for more than two consecutive years; provided, however, that a member may continue to serve as chair until a successor chair is elected and qualified.

(f) The Board of Governors shall have full power and administrative responsibility for the operation of the Facility. Such administrative responsibility shall include but not be limited to:

(1) Proper establishment and implementation of the Facility.
(2) Employment of a manager who shall be responsible for the continuous operation of the Facility and such other employees, officers and committees as it deems necessary.
(3) Provision for appropriate housing and equipment to assure the efficient operation of the Facility.
(4) Promulgation of reasonable rules and regulations for the administration and operation of the Facility and delegation to the manager of such authority as it deems necessary to insure the proper administration and operation thereof.

(g) Except as may be delegated specifically to others in the plan of operation or reserved to the members, power and responsibility for the establishment and operation of the Facility is vested in the Board of Governors, which power and responsibility include but is not limited to the following:

(1) To sue and be sued in the name of the Facility. No judgment against the Facility shall create any direct liability in the individual member companies of the Facility.
(2) To receive and record cessions.
(3) To assess members on the basis of participation ratios established in the plan of operation to cover anticipated or incurred costs of operation and administration of the Facility at such intervals as are established in the plan of operation.
(4) To contract for goods and services from others to assure the efficient operation of the Facility.
(5) To hear and determine complaints of any company, agent or other interested party concerning the operation of the Facility.
(6) Upon the request of any licensed fire and casualty agent meeting any two of the standards set forth below as determined by the Commissioner within 10 days of the receipt of the application, the Facility

shall contract with one or more members within 20 days of receipt of the determination to appoint such licensed fire and casualty agent as designated agents in accordance with reasonable rules as are established by the plan of operation. The standards shall be:

a. Whether the agent's evidence establishes that he has been conducting his business in a community for a period of at least one year;

b. Whether the agent's evidence establishes that he had a gross premium volume during the 13 months next preceding the date of his application of at least twenty thousand dollars ($20,000) from motor vehicle insurance;

c. Whether the agent's evidence establishes that the number of eligible risks served by him during the 13 months next preceding the date of application was 200 or more;

d. Whether the agent's evidence establishes a growth in eligible risks served and premium volume during his years of service as an agent;

e. Whether the agent's evidence establishes that he made available to eligible risks premium financing or any other plan for deferred payment of premiums.

With respect to business produced by designated agents, adequate provision shall be made by the Facility to assure that such business is rated using Facility rates. All business produced by designated agents may be ceded to the Facility, except designated agents appointed before September 1, 1987, may place liability insurance policies with a voluntary carrier, provided that all policies written by the voluntary carrier are retained by the voluntary carrier unless ceded to the Facility using Facility rates. Designated agents must provide the Facility with a list of such policies written by the voluntary carrier at least annually, or as requested by the Facility, on a form approved by the Facility. If no insurer is willing to contract with any such agent on terms acceptable to the Board, the Facility shall license such agent to write directly on behalf of the Facility. However, for this purpose the Facility does not act as an insurer, but acts only as the statutory agent of all of the members of the Facility, which shall be bound on risks written by the Facility's appointed agent. The Facility may contract with one or more servicing carriers and shall promulgate fair and reasonable underwriting procedures to require that business produced by Facility agents and written through those servicing carriers shall be rated using Facility rates. All business produced by Facility agents may be ceded to the Facility. Any designated agent who is disabled or retiring or the estate of any deceased designated agent may transfer the designation and the book of business to some other licensed fire and casualty agent meeting the requirements of this section and under rules established by the Facility, and a transfer from a designated agent appointed before September 1, 1987, shall entitle the transferee designated agent to place liability insurance policies with a voluntary carrier.

The Commissioner shall require, as a condition precedent to the issuance, renewal, or continuation of a resident agent's license to any designated agent to act for the company appointing such designated agent under contract with the Facility, that the designated agent file and thereafter maintain in force while so licensed a bond in favor of the State of North Carolina executed by an authorized corporate surety approved by the Commissioner, cash, mortgage on real property, or other securities approved by the Commissioner, in the amount of ten thousand dollars ($10,000) for the use of aggrieved persons. Such bond, cash, mortgage, or other securities shall be conditioned on the accounting by the designated agent (i) to any person requesting the designated agent to obtain motor vehicle insurance for moneys or premiums collected in connection therewith, and (ii) to the company providing coverage with respect to any such moneys or premiums under contract with the Facility. Any such bond shall remain in force until the surety is released from liability by the Commissioner, or until the bond is cancelled by the surety. Without prejudice to any liability accrued prior to such cancellation, the surety may cancel the bond upon 30 days' advance notice in writing filed with the Commissioner.

No agent may be designated under this subdivision to any insurer that does not actively write voluntary market business.

(7) To maintain all loss, expense, and premium data relative to all risks reinsured in the Facility, and to require each member to furnish such statistics relative to insurance reinsured by the Facility at such times and in such form and detail as may be required.

(8) To establish fair and reasonable procedures for the sharing among members of any loss on Facility business that cannot be recouped under G.S. 58-37-40(e) and other costs, charges, expenses, liabilities, income, property and other assets of the Facility and for assessing or distributing to members their appropriate shares. The shares may be based on the member's premiums for voluntary business for the appropriate category of motor vehicle insurance or by any other fair and reasonable method.

(9) To receive or distribute all sums required by the operation of the Facility.

(10) To accept all risks submitted in accordance with this Article.

(11) To establish procedures for reviewing claims practices of member companies to the end that claims to the account of the Facility will be handled fairly and efficiently.

(12) To adopt and enforce all rules and to do anything else where the Board is not elsewhere herein specifically empowered which is otherwise necessary to accomplish the purpose of the Facility and is not in conflict with the other provisions of this Article.

(h) Each member company shall authorize the Facility to audit that part of the company's business which is written subject to the Facility in a manner and time prescribed by the Board of Governors.

(i) The Board of Governors shall fix a date for an annual meeting and shall annually meet on that date. Twenty days' notice of such meeting shall be given in writing to all members of the Board of Governors.

(j) There shall be furnished to each member an annual report of the operation of the Facility in such form and detail as may be determined by the Board of Governors.

(k) Each member shall furnish statistics in connection with insurance subject to the Facility as may be required by the Facility. Such statistics shall be furnished at such time and in such form and detail as may be required but at least will include premiums charged, expenses and losses.

(l) The classifications, rules, rates, rating plans and policy forms used on motor vehicle insurance policies reinsured by the Facility may be made by the Facility or by any licensed or statutory rating organization or bureau on its behalf and shall be filed with the Commissioner. The Board of Governors shall establish a separate subclassification within the Facility for "clean risks". For the purpose of this Article, a "clean risk" is any owner of a nonfleet private passenger motor vehicle as defined in G.S. 58-40-10, if the owner, principal operator, and each licensed operator in the owner's household have two years' driving experience as licensed drivers and if none of the persons has been assigned any Safe Driver Incentive Plan points under Article 36 of this Chapter during the three-year period immediately preceding either (i) the date of application for a motor vehicle insurance policy or (ii) the date of preparation of a renewal of a motor vehicle insurance policy. The filings may incorporate by reference any other material on file with the Commissioner. Rates shall be neither excessive, inadequate nor unfairly discriminatory. If the Commissioner finds, after a hearing, that a rate is either excessive, inadequate or unfairly discriminatory, the Commissioner shall issue an order specifying in what respect it is deficient and stating when, within a reasonable period thereafter, the rate is no longer effective. The order is subject to judicial review as set out in Article 2 of this Chapter. Pending judicial review of said order, the filed classification plan and the filed rates may be used, charged and collected in the same manner as set out in G.S. 58-40-45 of this Chapter. The order shall not affect any contract or policy made or issued before the expiration of the period set forth in the order. All rates shall be on an actuarially sound basis and shall be calculated, insofar as is possible, to produce neither a profit nor a loss. However, the rates made by or on behalf of the Facility with respect to "clean risks" shall not exceed the rates charged "clean risks" who are not reinsured in the Facility. The difference between the actual rate charged and the actuarially sound and self-supporting rates for "clean risks" reinsured in the Facility may be recouped in similar manner as assessments under G.S. 58-37-40(f). Rates shall not include any factor for underwriting profit on Facility business, but shall provide an allowance for contingencies. There shall be a strong presumption that the rates and premiums for the business of the Facility are neither unreasonable nor excessive.

(m) In addition to annual premiums, the rules of the Facility shall allow semiannual and quarterly premium terms. (1973, c. 818, s. 1; 1977, c. 710; c. 828, ss. 14-19; 1977, 2nd Sess., c. 1135; 1979, c. 676, ss. 1, 2; 1981, c. 776, ss. 2, 3; c. 776, ss. 2, 3; 1983, c. 416, ss. 3, 4; c. 690; 1985, c. 666, s. 49; 1985 (Reg. Sess., 1986), c. 1027, ss. 7, 19, 33, 43; 1987, c. 869, ss. 3, 4(1), (2), 15; 1989, c. 67; 1991, c. 469, s. 7; c. 562, s. 2; c. 709, s. 1; c. 720, s. 4; 1999-132, ss. 6.2, 8.3, 8.4, 8.7, 8.8; 1999-228, s. 8; 2001-236, s. 1; 2001-423, s. 3; 2002-185, s. 6; 2002-187, ss. 1.2, 1.3.)

Effect of Amendments. — Session Laws 2002-185, s. 6, effective October 31, 2002, rewrote subsection (d), substituting "trade associations" for "groups" throughout, deleting provisions that members be appointed from the Auto Insurance Agents of North Carolina, Inc., and the Independent Insurance Agents of North Carolina, Inc., increasing the number of fire and casualty insurance agent members to five, and making sytlistic changes.

Session Laws 2002-187, ss. 1.2 and 1.3, effective October 31, 2002, in subdivision (b)(2)c added "except that this coverage shall not be available for motorcycles"; in subdivision (b)(2)e inserted "each accident" following "($50,000)"; in subdivision (b)(2a)c added "except that this coverage shall not be available for motorcycles"; and added subdivision (b)(2a)d.

Legal Periodicals. — For survey of 1979 administrative law, see 58 N.C.L. Rev. 1185 (1980).

For survey of 1981 administrative law, see 60 N.C.L. Rev. 1165 (1982).

CASE NOTES

Subdivision (g)(1) makes the Board of Governors of the Facility the public's representative, to the exclusion of all others, except where the facility act expressly provides otherwise. State Farm Mut. Auto Ins. Co. v. Ingram, 288 N.C. 381, 218 S.E.2d 364 (1975).

The Commissioner was not intended to be the representative of the public or to be deemed an aggrieved person so as to permit him to appeal pursuant to the provisions of G.S. 58-2-75. State Farm Mut. Auto. Ins. Co. v. Ingram, 288 N.C. 381, 218 S.E.2d 364 (1975).

Thus the Commissioner is not expressly granted the power to appeal by this sec-

tion. State Farm Mut. Auto. Ins. Co. v. Ingram, 288 N.C. 381, 218 S.E.2d 364 (1975).

Recoupment Surcharges. — The legislature's concern that the Facility operate on a no profit-no loss basis, together with the statutory cap on rates, indicates that the legislature intended recoupment surcharges to be separate and apart from rates. State ex rel. Hunt v. North Carolina Reinsurance Facility, 302 N.C. 274, 275 S.E.2d 399 (1981), decided prior to the 1981 amendment to § 58-37-40(e).

Surcharges on automobile liability insurance coverages ceded to the North Carolina Reinsurance Facility to recoup past facility losses and on all automobile liability coverages to recoup anticipated losses on ceded "clean risks" do not constitute rates, and no filing with or approval by the Commissioner of Insurance is required by law with respect to the surcharges. State ex rel. Hunt v. North Carolina Reinsurance Facility, 302 N.C. 274, 275 S.E.2d 399 (1981), decided prior to 1981 amendment to § 58-37-40(e).

Use of Own Policy Forms Prohibited. — An insurer writing automobile insurance in North Carolina is not permitted to use its own policy forms on insurance policies ceded to the Facility. St. Paul Fire & Marine Ins. Co. v. North Carolina Motor Vehicle Reinsurance Facility, 124 N.C. App. 450, 476 S.E.2d 897 (1996).

Subsection (l) is unambiguous in stating that insurers are required to use, in the writing of motor vehicle insurance policies ceded to the Facility, only those policy forms made by the Facility or those made by any licensed or statutory rating organization or bureau and filed with the Commissioner. St. Paul Fire & Marine Ins. Co. v. North Carolina Motor Vehicle Reinsurance Facility, 124 N.C. App. 450, 476 S.E.2d 897 (1996).

As the legislature has specifically stated in another statute that policy forms are to be determined by the Facility, and the more specific statute prevails, there is no violation of the anti-discrimination provision of G.S. 58-37-25 (b) when the Facility mandates the uniform use of policy forms for all ceded motor vehicle insurance business. St. Paul Fire & Marine Ins. Co. v. North Carolina Motor Vehicle Reinsurance Facility, 124 N.C. App. 450, 476 S.E.2d 897 (1996).

Applied in State ex rel. Comm'r of Ins. v. North Carolina Rate Bureau, 300 N.C. 381, 269 S.E.2d 547 (1980); Unigard Mut. Ins. Co. v. Ingram, 71 N.C. App. 725, 323 S.E.2d 442 (1984).

Cited in North Carolina Reinsurance Facility v. North Carolina Ins. Guar. Ass'n, 67 N.C. App. 359, 313 S.E.2d 253 (1984).

§ 58-37-40. Plan of operation.

(a) Within 60 days after the initial organizational meeting, the Facility shall submit to the Commissioner, for his approval, a proposed plan of operation, consistent with the provisions of this Article, which shall provide for economical, fair and nondiscriminating administration and for the prompt and efficient provision of motor vehicle insurance to eligible risks. Should no plan be submitted within the aforesaid 60-day period, then the Commissioner of Insurance shall formulate and place into effect a plan consistent with the provisions of this Article.

(b) The plan of operation, unless sooner approved in writing, shall be deemed to meet the requirements of the Article if it is not disapproved by order of the Commissioner within 30 days from the date of filing. Prior to the disapproval of all or any part of the proposed plan of operation the Commissioner shall notify the Facility in what respect the plan of operation fails to meet the specific requirements of this Article. The Facility shall, within 30 days thereafter, submit for his approval a revised plan of operation which meets the specific requirements of this Article. In the event the Facility fails to submit a revised plan of operation which meets the specific requirements of this Article within the aforesaid 30-day period, the Commissioner shall enter an order accordingly and shall immediately thereafter formulate and place into effect a plan consistent with the provisions of this Article.

(c) Any revision of the proposed plan of operation or any subsequent amendments to an approved plan of operation shall be subject to approval or disapproval by the Commissioner in the manner herein provided in subsection (b) with respect to the initial plan of operation.

(d) Any order of the Commissioner with respect to the plan of operation or any revision or amendment thereof shall be subject to court review as provided in G.S. 58-2-75.

(e) Upon approval of the Commissioner of the plan so submitted or promulgation of a plan deemed approved by the Commissioner, all insurance companies licensed to write motor vehicle insurance in this State or any component thereof as a prerequisite to further engaging in writing the insurance shall formally subscribe to and participate in the plan so approved.

The plan of operation shall provide for, among other matters, (i) the establishment of necessary facilities; (ii) the management of the Facility; (iii) the preliminary assessment of all members for initial expenses necessary to commence operations; (iv) the assessment of members if necessary to defray losses and expenses; (v) the distribution of gains to defray losses incurred since September 1, 1977; (vi) the distribution of gains by credit or reduction of recoupment surcharges to policies subject to recoupment surcharges pursuant to this Article (the Facility may apportion the distribution of gains among the coverages eligible for cession pursuant to this Article); (vii) the recoupment of losses sustained by the Facility since September 1, 1977, pursuant to this Article, which losses may be recouped by equitable pro rata assessment of companies or by way of a surcharge on motor vehicle policies issued by member companies or through the Facility; (viii) the standard amount (one hundred percent (100%) or any equitable lesser amount) of coverage afforded on eligible risks which a member company may cede to the Facility; and (ix) the procedure by which reinsurance shall be accepted by the Facility. The plan shall further provide that:

(1) Members of the Board of Governors shall receive reimbursement from the Facility for their actual and necessary expenses incurred on Facility business, en route to perform Facility business, and while returning from Facility business plus a per diem allowance of twenty-five dollars ($25.00) a day which may be waived.

(2) In order to obtain a transfer of business to the Facility effective when the binder or policy or renewal thereof first becomes effective, the company must within 30 days of the binding or policy effective date notify the Facility of the identification of the insured, the coverage and limits afforded, classification data, and premium. The Facility shall accept risks at other times on receipt of necessary information, but acceptance shall not be retroactive. The Facility shall accept renewal business after the member on underwriting review elects to again cede the business.

(f) The plan of operation shall provide that every member shall, following payment of any pro rata assessment, begin recoupment of that assessment by way of a surcharge on motor vehicle insurance policies issued by the member or through the Facility until the assessment has been recouped. Any surcharge under this subsection or under subsection (e) of this section shall be a percentage of premium adopted by the Board of Governors of the Facility; and the charges determined on the basis of the surcharge shall be combined with and displayed as a part of the applicable premium charges. Recoupment of losses sustained by the Facility since September 1, 1977, with respect to nonfleet private passenger motor vehicles may be made only by surcharging nonfleet private passenger motor vehicle insurance policies. If the amount collected during the period of surcharge exceeds assessments paid by the member to the Facility, the member shall pay over the excess to the Facility on a date specified by the Board of Governors. If the amount collected during the period of surcharge is less than the assessments paid by the member to the Facility, the Facility shall pay the difference to the member. Except as otherwise provided in this Article, the amount of recoupment shall not be considered or treated as a rate or premium for any purpose. The Board of Governors shall adopt and implement a plan for compensation of agents of Facility members when recoupment surcharges are imposed; that compensation shall not exceed the compensation or commission rate normally paid to the agent for the issuance or renewal of the automobile liability policy issued through the North Carolina Reinsurance Facility affected by the surcharge. However, the surcharge shall include an amount necessary to recover the amount of the assessment to member companies and the compensation paid by each member, under this section, to agents.

(g) The plan of operation shall provide that all investment income from the premium on business reinsured by the Facility shall be retained by or paid over to the Facility. In determining the cost of operation of the Facility, all investment income shall be taken into consideration.

(h) The plan of operation shall provide for audit of the annual statement of the Facility by independent auditor approved by the Legislative Services Commission.

(i) The Facility shall file with the Commissioner revisions in the Facility plan of operation for his approval or modification. Such revisions shall be made for the purpose of revising the classification and rating plans for other than nonfleet private passenger motor vehicle insurance ceded to the Facility. (1973, c. 818, s. 1; 1975, c. 19, s. 18; 1977, c. 828, ss. 20, 21; 1981, c. 590; c. 916, ss. 2, 3; 1985 (Reg. Sess., 1986), c. 1027, s. 34; 1987, c. 869, s. 5(1)—5(3); 1989, c. 424, s. 1; 1991, c. 720, s. 4; 1995, c. 517, s. 24; 1999-132, ss. 8.5, 8.6.)

Legal Periodicals. — For survey of 1979 administrative law, see 58 N.C.L. Rev. 1185 (1980).

For survey of 1980 administrative law, see 59 N.C.L. Rev. 1017 (1981).

For survey of 1981 administrative law, see 60 N.C.L. Rev. 1165 (1982).

For article analyzing the scope of the North Carolina Insurance Commissioner's ratemaking authority, see 61 N.C.L. Rev. 97 (1982).

CASE NOTES

Recoupment Surcharges. — The legislature's concern that the Facility operate on a no profit-no loss basis, together with the statutory cap on rates, indicates that the legislature intended recoupment surcharges to be separate and apart from rates. State ex rel. Hunt v. North Carolina Reinsurance Facility, 302 N.C. 274, 275 S.E.2d 399 (1981), decided prior to 1981 amendment to subsection (e).

Surcharges on automobile liability insurance coverages ceded to the North Carolina Reinsurance Facility to recoup past facility losses and on all automobile liability coverages to recoup anticipated losses on ceded "clean risks" do not constitute rates, and no filing with or approval by the Commissioner of Insurance is required by law with respect to the surcharges. State ex rel. Hunt v. North Carolina Reinsurance Facility, 302 N.C. 274, 275 S.E.2d 399 (1981), decided prior to 1981 amendment to subsection (e).

Commissioner's Findings of Fact Must Be Supported by Material and Substantial Evidence. — The Commissioner, not the superior court, was vested with the power to determine if an insurer was entitled, under plan of operation, to a retroactive amendment of its ceding expense allowance; however, the powers given to the Commission by this section do not permit the Commissioner to make findings of fact which are not supported by material and substantial evidence. North Carolina Reinsurance Facility v. Long, 98 N.C. App. 41, 390 S.E.2d 176 (1990).

Cited in State Farm Mut. Auto. Ins. Co. v. Ingram, 288 N.C. 381, 218 S.E.2d 364 (1975); State ex rel. Comm'r of Ins. v. North Carolina Rate Bureau, 300 N.C. 381, 269 S.E.2d 547 (1980).

§ 58-37-45. Procedure for cession provided in plan of operation.

Upon receipt by the company of a risk which it does not elect to retain, the company shall follow such procedures for ceding the risk as are established by the plan of operation. (1973, c. 818, s. 1; 1977, c. 828, s. 22.)

Legal Periodicals. — For survey of 1979 administrative law, see 58 N.C.L. Rev. 1185 (1980).

CASE NOTES

Applied in State ex rel. Comm'r of Ins. v. North Carolina Rate Bureau, 41 N.C. App. 310, 255 S.E.2d 557 (1979).

Cited in State ex rel. Comm'r of Ins. v. North Carolina Rate Bureau, 300 N.C. 381, 269 S.E.2d 547 (1980); State ex rel. Hunt v. North Carolina Reinsurance Facility, 49 N.C. App. 206, 271 S.E.2d 302 (1980).

§ 58-37-50. Termination of insurance.

No member may terminate insurance to the extent that cession of a particular type of coverage and limits is available under the provisions of this Article except for the following reasons:

    (1) Nonpayment of premium when due to the insurer or producing agent.

    (2) The named insured has become a nonresident of this State and would not otherwise be entitled to insurance on submission of new application under this Article.

    (3) A member company has terminated an agency contract for reasons other than the quality of the agent's insureds or the agent has terminated the contract and such agent represented the company in taking the original application for insurance.

    (4) When the insurance contract has been cancelled pursuant to a power of attorney given a company licensed pursuant to the provisions of G.S. 58-35-5.

    (5) The named insured, at the time of renewal, fails to meet the requirements contained in the corporate charter, articles of incorporation, and/or bylaws of the insurer, when the insurer is a company organized for the sole purpose of providing members of an organization with insurance policies in North Carolina. (1973, c. 818, s. 1; 1979, c. 497.)

§ 58-37-55. Exemption from requirements of this Article of companies and their agents.

The Board of Governors may exempt a company and its agents from the requirements of this Article, insofar as new business is concerned. The Board may further exempt a company and its agents from the requirements of this Article regarding the selling and servicing a particular category of business, if the company is not qualified to service the business. (1973, c. 818, s. 1; 1977, c. 828, s. 23.)

§ 58-37-60. Physical damage insurance availability.

No physical damage insurer shall refuse to make physical damage coverage available to any applicant for the reason that such applicant has, or may acquire, auto liability insurance through the Facility plan as provided herein; further that no such insurer may levy a surcharge or increased rate for such physical damage coverage on the basis that such applicant has, or may acquire, auto liability insurance through the Facility plan as provided herein.

Any insurer or representative thereof who fails to comply with or violates this section shall be subject to suspension or revocation of his certificate or license and shall be subject to the provisions of G.S. 58-2-70. (1973, c. 818, s. 1; 1985, c. 666, s. 37.)

§ 58-37-65. Hearings; review.

(a) Any applicant for a policy from any carrier, any person insured under such a policy, any member of the Facility and any agent duly licensed to write motor vehicle insurance, may request a formal hearing and ruling by the Board of Governors of the Facility on any alleged violation of or failure to comply with the plan of operation or the provisions of this Article or any alleged improper act or ruling of the Facility directly affecting him as to coverage or premium or in the case of a member directly affecting its assessment, and in the case of an agent, any matter affecting his appointment to a carrier or his account therewith. The request for hearing must be made within 15 days after the date of the alleged violation or improper act or ruling. The hearing shall be held within 15 days after the receipt of the request. The hearing may be held by any panel of the Board of Governors consisting of not less than three members thereof, and the ruling of a majority of the panel shall be deemed to be the formal ruling of the Board, unless the full Board on its own motion shall modify or rescind the action of the panel.

(b) Any formal ruling by the Board of Governors may be appealed to the Commissioner by filing notice of appeal with the Facility and Commissioner within 30 days after issuance of the ruling.

(c) The Commissioner shall, after a hearing held on not less than 30 days written notice to the appellant and to the Board, (i) issue an order approving the decision of the Board or (ii) after setting out the findings and conclusions as to how the action of the Board is not in accordance with the plan of operation, the Standard Practice Manual, or other provisions of this Article, direct the Board to reconsider its decision. In the event the Commissioner directs the Board to reconsider its decision and the Board fails to take action in accordance with the plan of operation, the Standard Practice Manual, or other provisions of this Article, the Commissioner may issue an order modifying the action of the Board to the extent necessary to comply with the plan of operation, the Standard Practice Manual, or other provisions of this Article.

No later than 20 days before each hearing, the appellant shall file with the Commissioner or his designated hearing officer and shall serve on the appellee a written statement of his case and any evidence he intends to offer at the hearing. No later than five days before such hearing, the appellee shall file with the Commissioner or his designated hearing officer and shall serve on the appellant a written statement of his case and any evidence he intends to offer at the hearing. Each such hearing shall be recorded and transcribed. The cost of such recording and transcribing shall be borne equally by the appellant and appellee; provided that upon any final adjudication the prevailing party shall be reimbursed for his share of such costs by the other party. Each party shall, on a date determined by the Commissioner or his designated hearing officer, but not sooner than 15 days after delivery of the completed transcript to the party, submit to the Commissioner or his designated hearing officer and serve on the other party, a proposed order. The Commissioner or his designated hearing officer shall then issue an order.

(d) Any aggrieved person or organization, any member of the Facility or the Facility may request a public hearing and ruling by the Commissioner on the provisions of the plan of operation, rules, regulations or policy forms approved by the Commissioner. The request for hearing shall specify the matter or matters to be considered. The hearing shall be held within 30 days after receipt of the request. The Commissioner shall give public notice of the hearing and the matter or matters to be considered not less than 15 days in advance of the hearing date.

(e) In any hearing held pursuant to this section by the Board of Governors or the Commissioner, the Board or the Commissioner as the case may be, shall issue a ruling or order within 30 days after the close of the hearing.

(f) All rulings or orders of the Commissioner under this section shall be subject to judicial review as approved in G.S. 58-2-75. (1973, c. 818, s. 1; 1989, c. 424, s. 3; 1989 (Reg. Sess., 1990), c. 1069, s. 17.)

Legal Periodicals. — For article discussing limitations on ad hoc adjudicatory rulemaking by an administrative agency, see 61 N.C.L. Rev. 67 (1982).

For article analyzing the scope of the North Carolina Insurance Commissioner's rate-making authority, see 61 N.C.L. Rev. 97 (1982).

CASE NOTES

Commissioner's Findings Must Be Supported by Material and Substantial Evidence. — The Commissioner, not the superior court, was vested with the power to determine if an insurer was entitled, under plan of operation, to a retroactive amendment of its ceding expense allowance; however, the powers given to the Commission by G.S. 58-37-40 do not permit the Commissioner to make findings of fact which are not supported by material and substantial evidence. North Carolina Reinsurance Facility v. Long, 98 N.C. App. 41, 390 S.E.2d 176 (1990).

Cited in State Farm Mut. Auto. Ins. Co. v. Ingram, 288 N.C. 381, 218 S.E.2d 364 (1975); St. Paul Fire & Marine Ins. Co. v. North Carolina Motor Vehicle Reinsurance Facility, 124 N.C. App. 450, 476 S.E.2d 897 (1996).

§ 58-37-70: Repealed by Session Laws 1991, c. 720, s. 6.

§ 58-37-75: Repealed by Session Laws 1999-132, s. 8.9.

ARTICLE 38.

Readable Insurance Policies.

§ 58-38-1. Title.

This Article is known and may be cited as the "Readable Insurance Policies Act." (1979, c. 755, s. 1.)

Legal Periodicals. — For survey of 1979 administrative law, see 58 N.C.L. Rev. 1185 (1980).

§ 58-38-5. Purpose.

The purpose of this Article is to provide that insurance policies and contracts be readable by a person of average intelligence, experience, and education. All insurers are required by this Article to use policy and contract forms and, where applicable, benefit booklets that are written in simple and commonly used language, that are logically and clearly arranged, and that are printed in a legible format. (1979, c. 755, s. 1.)

§ 58-38-10. Scope of application.

(a) Except as provided in subsection (b) of this section, the provisions of this Article apply to the policies and contracts of direct insurance that are described in G.S. 58-38-35(a).

(b) Nothing in this Article applies to:

(1) Any policy that is a security subject to federal jurisdiction;

(2) Any group policy covering a group of 1,000 or more lives at date of issue, other than a group credit life insurance policy, nor any group

policy delivered or issued for delivery outside of this State; however, this does not exempt any certificate issued pursuant to a group policy delivered or issued for delivery in this State;

(3) Any group annuity contract that serves as a funding vehicle for pension, profit-sharing, or deferred compensation plans;

(4) Any form used in connection with, as a conversion from, as an addition to, or in exchange pursuant to a contractual provision for, a policy delivered or issued for delivery on a form approved or permitted to be issued prior to the dates such forms must be approved under this Article;

(5) The renewal of a policy delivered or issued for delivery prior to the date such policy must be approved under this Article; nor

(6) Insurers who issue benefit booklets on group and nongroup bases for the policies described in G.S. 58-38-35(a)(2). In such cases, the provisions of this Article apply to the benefit booklets furnished to the persons insured.

(7) Insurance on farm buildings (other than farm dwellings and their appurtenant structures); farm personal property; travel or camper trailers designed to be pulled by private passenger motor vehicles unless insured under policies covering nonfleet private passenger motor vehicles; nonfleet private passenger motor vehicles insured under a commercial motor vehicle insurance policy when combined with a commercial risk; residential real and personal property insured in multiple line insurance policies covering business activities as the primary insurable interest; and marine, general liability, burglary and theft, glass, and animal collision insurance except when such coverages are written as an integral part of a multiple line insurance policy for which there is an indivisible premium.

(c) No other provision of the General Statutes setting language simplification standards shall apply to any policy forms covered by this Article.

(d) Any non-English language policy delivered or issued for delivery in this State shall be deemed to be in compliance with this Article if the insurer certifies that such policy is translated from an English language policy which does comply with this Article. (1979, c. 755, s. 1; 1981, c. 888, s. 6; 1983, c. 393, s. 1.)

Legal Periodicals. — For survey of 1979 administrative law, see 58 N.C.L. Rev. 1185 (1980).

§ 58-38-15. Definitions.

As used in this Article, unless the context clearly indicates otherwise:

(1) "Benefit booklet" means any written explanation of insurance coverages or benefits issued by an insurer and which is supplemental to and not a part of an insurance policy or contract.

(2) Repealed by Session Laws 1991, c. 720, s. 6.

(3) "Flesch scale analysis readability score" means a measurement of the ease of readability of an insurance policy or contract made pursuant to the procedures described in G.S. 58-38-35.

(4) "Insurance policy or contract" or "policy" means an agreement as defined by G.S. 58-1-10.

(5) "Insurer" means every person entering insurance policies or contracts as a principal, as described in G.S. 58-1-5(3).

(6) "Person" means any individual, corporation, partnership, association, business trust, or voluntary organization. (1979, c. 755, s. 1; 1987, c. 864, s. 10; 1991, c. 720, s. 6.)

§ 58-38-20. Format requirements.

(a) All insurance policies and contracts covered by G.S. 58-38-35 must be printed in a typeface at least as large as 10 point modern type, one point leaded, be written in a logical and clear order and form, and contain the following items:

    (1) On the cover, first, or insert page of the policy a statement that the policy is a legal contract between the policy owner and the insurer and the statement, printed in larger or other contrasting type or color, "Read your policy carefully";

    (2) An index of the major provisions of the policy, which may include the following items:

        a. The person or persons insured by the policy;

        b. The applicable events, occurrences, conditions, losses, or damages covered by the policy;

        c. The limitations or conditions on the coverage of the policy;

        d. Definitional sections of the policy;

        e. Provisions governing the procedure for filing a claim under the policy;

        f. Provisions governing cancellation, renewal, or amendment of the policy by either the insurer or the policyholder;

        g. Any options under the policy; and

        h. Provisions governing the insurer's duties and powers in the event that suit is filed against the insured.

(b) In determining whether or not a policy is written in a logical and clear order and form the Commissioner must consider the following factors:

    (1) The extent to which sections or provisions are set off and clearly identified by titles, headings, or margin notations;

    (2) The use of a more readable format, such as narrative or outline forms;

    (3) Margin size and the amount and use of space to separate sections of the policy; and

    (4) Contrast and legibility of the colors of the ink and paper and the use of contrasting titles or headings for sections. (1979, c. 755, s. 1.)

Legal Periodicals. — For survey of 1979 administrative law, see 58 N.C.L. Rev. 1185 (1980).

§ 58-38-25. Flesch scale analysis readability score; procedures.

(a) A Flesch scale analysis readability score will be measured as provided in this section.

(b) For policies containing 10,000 words or less of text, the entire policy must be analyzed. For policies containing more than 10,000 words, the readability of two 200-word samples per page may be analyzed in lieu of the entire policy. The samples must be separated by at least 20 printed lines. For the purposes of this subsection a word will be counted as five printed characters or spaces between characters.

(c) The number of words and sentences in the text must be counted and the total number of words divided by the total number of sentences. The figure obtained must be multiplied by a factor of 1.015. The total number of syllables must be counted and divided by the total number of words. The figure obtained must be multiplied by a factor of 84.6. The sum of the figures computed under this subsection subtracted from 206.835 equals the Flesch scale analysis readability score for the policy.

(d) For the purposes of subsection (c) of this section the following procedures must be used:

    (1) A contraction, hyphenated word, or numbers and letters, when separated by spaces, will be counted as one word;

    (2) A unit of words ending with a period, semicolon, or colon, but excluding headings and captions, will be counted as a sentence; and

    (3) A syllable means a unit of spoken language consisting of one or more letters of a word as divided by an accepted dictionary. Where the dictionary shows two or more equally acceptable pronunciations of a word, the pronunciation containing fewer syllables may be used.

(e) The term "text" as used in this section includes all printed matter except the following:

    (1) The name and address of the insurer; the name, number or title of the policy; the table of contents or index; captions and subcaptions; specification pages, schedules or tables; and

    (2) Any policy language that is drafted to conform to the requirements of any law, regulation, or agency interpretation of any state or the federal government; any policy language required by any collectively bargained agreement; any medical terminology; and any words that are defined in the policy: Provided, however, that the insurer submits with his filing under G.S. 58-38-30 a certified document identifying the language or terminology that is entitled to be excepted by this subdivision. (1979, c. 755, s. 1.)

Legal Periodicals. — For survey of 1979 administrative law, see 58 N.C.L. Rev. 1185 (1980).

§ 58-38-30. Filing requirements; duties of the Commissioner.

(a) No insurer may make, issue, amend, or renew any insurance policy or contract after the dates specified in G.S. 58-38-35 for the applicable type of insurance unless the policy is in compliance with the provisions of G.S. 58-38-20 and G.S. 58-38-25 and unless the policy is filed with the Commissioner for his approval. The policy will be deemed approved 90 days after filing unless disapproved within the 90-day period. The Commissioner may not unreasonably withhold his approval. Any disapproval must be delivered to the insurer in writing and must state the grounds for disapproval. Any policy filed with the Commissioner must be accompanied by a certified Flesch scale readability analysis and test score and by the insurer's certification that the policy is, in the insurer's judgment, readable based on the factors specified in G.S. 58-38-20 and G.S. 58-38-25.

(b) The Commissioner must disapprove any policy covered by subsection (a) of this section if he finds that:

    (1) It is not accompanied by a certified Flesch scale analysis readability score of 50 or more.

    (2) It is not accompanied by the insurer's certification that the policy is, in the judgment of the insurer, readable under the standards of this Article; or

    (3) It does not comply with the format requirements of G.S. 58-38-20. (1979, c. 755, s. 1; 1979, 2nd Sess., c. 1161, s. 2.)

Legal Periodicals. — For survey of 1979 administrative law, see 58 N.C.L. Rev. 1185 (1980).

§ 58-38-35. Application to policies; dates; duties of the Commissioner.

(a) The filing requirements of G.S. 58-38-30 apply as follows:
  (1) As described in Article 36 of this Chapter, to all policies of private passenger nonfleet motor vehicle insurance except as excluded by G.S. 58-38-10(b)(7), to all policies of insurance against loss to residential real property with not more than four housing units located in this State and any contents thereof and valuable interest therein, and other insurance coverages written in connection with the sale of such property insurance except as excluded in G.S. 58-38-10(b)(7), that are made, issued, amended, or renewed after March 1, 1981; and
  (2) To all policies of life insurance as described in Article 58 of this Chapter, to all benefit certificates issued by fraternal orders and societies as described in Articles 24 and 25 of this Chapter, to all policies of accident and health insurance as described in Articles 50 through 55 of this Chapter, to all subscribers' contracts of hospital, medical, and dental service corporations as described in Articles 65 and 66 of this Chapter, and to all health maintenance organization evidences of coverage as described in Article 67 of this Chapter, that are made, issued, amended, or renewed after July 1, 1983.
(b) Repealed by Session Laws 1991, c. 720, s. 6. (1979, c. 755, s. 1; 1979, 2nd Sess., c. 1161, s. 3; 1981, c. 888, s. 7; 1983, c. 393, s. 2; 1987, c. 864, s. 11; 1991, c. 720, ss. 6, 42.)

§ 58-38-40. Construction.

(a) The provisions of this Article will not operate to relieve any insurer from any provision of law regulating the contents or provisions of insurance policies or contracts nor operate to reduce an insured's or beneficiary's rights or protection granted under any statute or provision of law.

(b) The provisions of this Article shall not be construed to mandate, require, or allow alteration of the legal effect of any provision of any insurance policy or contract.

(c) In any action brought by a policyholder or claimant arising out of a policy approved pursuant to this Article, the policyholder or claimant may base such an action on either or both (i) the substantive language prescribed by such other statute or provision of law or (ii) the wording of the approved policy. (1979, c. 755, s. 1.)

ARTICLE 39.

Consumer and Customer Information Privacy.

Part 1. Insurance Information and Privacy Protection.

§ 58-39-1. Short titles.

This Article may be cited as the Consumer and Customer Information Privacy Act. Part 1 of this Article may be cited as the Insurance Information and Privacy Protection Act. Part 3 of this Article may be cited as the Customer Information Safeguards Act. (1981, c. 846, s. 1; 2003-262, s. 3.)

Editor's Note. — Session Laws 2003-262, s. 1, effective June 26, 2003, rewrote the Article 39 heading, which formerly read "Insurance Information and Privacy Protection Act."

Sessions Laws 2003-262, s. 2(1), effective June 26, 2003, redesignated G.S. 58-39-1 through 58-39-76 as Part 1 of Article 39 of Chapter 58, under the heading "Insurance Information and Privacy Protection."

Legal Periodicals. — For survey of 1981 administrative law, see 60 N.C.L. Rev. 1165 (1982).

Effect of Amendments. — Session Laws 2003-262, s. 3, effective June 26, 2003, substituted "Short titles" for "Short title" in the section heading; and rewrote the section.

§ 58-39-5. Purpose.

The purpose of this Article is to establish standards for the collection, use, and disclosure of information gathered in connection with insurance transactions by insurance institutions, agents, or insurance-support organizations; to maintain a balance between the need for information by those conducting the business of insurance and the public's need for fairness in insurance information practices, including the need to minimize intrusiveness; to establish a regulatory mechanism to enable natural persons to ascertain what information is being or has been collected about them in connection with insurance transactions and to have access to such information for the purpose of verifying or disputing its accuracy; to limit the disclosure of information collected in connection with insurance transactions; and to enable insurance applicants and policyholders to obtain the reasons for any adverse underwriting decision. (1981, c. 846, s. 1; 2003-262, s. 2(1).)

Editor's Note. — Sessions Laws 2003-262, s. 2(1), effective June 26, 2003, redesignated G.S. 58-39-1 through 58-39-76 as Part 1 of Article 39 of Chapter 58, under the heading "Insurance Information and Privacy Protection."

§ 58-39-10. Scope.

(a) The obligations imposed by this Article shall apply to those insurance institutions, agents, or insurance-support organizations that:
  (1) In the case of life, health, or disability insurance:
    a. Collect, receive, or maintain information in connection with insurance transactions that pertains to natural persons who are residents of this State; or
    b. Engage in insurance transactions with applicants, individuals, or policyholders who are residents of this State; and
  (2) In the case of property or casualty insurance:
    a. Collect, receive, or maintain information in connection with insurance transactions involving policies, contracts, or certificates of insurance delivered, issued for delivery, or renewed in this State;
    b. Engage in insurance transactions involving policies, contracts, or certificates of insurance delivered, issued for delivery, or renewed in this State; or
    c. Engage in transactions involving mortgage guaranty insurance where the mortgage guaranty policies, contracts, or certificates of insurance are delivered, issued for delivery, or renewed in this State.
(b) The rights granted by this Article shall extend to:
  (1) In the case of life, health, or disability insurance, the following persons who are residents of this State:
    a. Natural persons who are the subject of information collected, received, or maintained in connection with insurance transactions; and
    b. Applicants, individuals, or policyholders who engage in or seek to engage in insurance transactions;
  (2) In the case of property or casualty insurance, the following persons:

  a. Natural persons who are the subject of information collected, received, or maintained in connection with insurance transactions involving policies, contracts, or certificates of insurance delivered, issued for delivery, or renewed in this State; and

  b. Applicants, individuals, or policyholders who engage in or seek to engage in (i) insurance transactions involving policies, contracts, or certificates of insurance delivered, issued for delivery, or renewed in this State; or (ii) mortgage guaranty insurance transactions involving policies, contracts, or certificates of insurance delivered, issued for delivery, or renewed in this State.

(c) For purposes of this section, a person shall be considered a resident of this State if the person's last known mailing address, as shown in the records of the insurance institution, agent, or insurance-support organization, is located in this State.

(d) Notwithstanding subsections (a) and (b) of this section, this Article shall not apply to information collected from the public records of a governmental authority and maintained by an insurance institution or its representatives for the purpose of insuring the title to real property located in this State.

(e) This Article applies to credit insurance that is subject to Article 57 of this Chapter. (1981, c. 846, s. 1; 2001-351, s. 1; 2003-262, s. 2(1).)

Editor's Note. — Session Laws 2001-351, s. 13, contains a severability clause.

Session Laws 2001-351, s. 14, provides: "This act becomes effective January 1, 2002, and applies to policies and contracts newly issued or renewed on and after that date. For the purposes of the application of this act to policies or contracts renewed on and after January 1, 2002, the renewal of a policy or contract is presumed to occur on each anniversary of the date on which coverage was first effective on the person or persons covered by the policy or contract."

Effect of Amendments. — Session Laws 2001-351, s. 1, effective January 1, 2002, deleted "on or after July 1, 1982" following "organizations" in the introductory paragraph of subsection (a); substituted "life, health, or disability insurance" for "life or accident and health insurance" in the first sentence of subdivisions (a)(1) and (b)(1); inserted "or" at the end of subdivision (a)(2)b; added subdivision (a)(2)c; in subdivision (b)(2)b, inserted "(1)," added "or" at the end of subdivision (b)(2)b(i), and inserted subdivision (b)(2)b(ii); and added subsection (e). See editor's note for applicability.

Editor's Note. — Sessions Laws 2003-262, s. 2(1), effective June 26, 2003, redesignated G.S. 58-39-1 through 58-39-76 as Part 1 of Article 39 of Chapter 58, under the heading "Insurance Information and Privacy Protection."

§ 58-39-15. Definitions.

As used in this Article:

 (1) "Adverse underwriting decision" means:

  a. Any of the following actions with respect to insurance transactions involving insurance coverage that is individually underwritten:

   1. A declination of insurance coverage;

   2. A termination of insurance coverage;

   3. Failure of an agent to apply for insurance coverage with a specific insurance institution that an agent represents and that is requested by an applicant;

   4. In the case of a property or casualty insurance coverage:

    I. Placement by an insurance institution or agent of a risk with a residual market mechanism, an unauthorized insurer, or an insurance institution that specializes in substandard risks; or

    II. The charging of a higher rate on the basis of information that differs from that which the applicant or policyholder furnished; or

     5. In the case of a life, health, or disability insurance coverage, an offer to insure at higher than standard rates.

   b. Notwithstanding subdivision (1)a. of this section, the following actions shall not be considered adverse underwriting decisions, but the insurance institution or agent responsible for their occurrence shall nevertheless provide the applicant or policyholder with the specific reason or reasons for their occurrence:

     1. The termination of an individual policy form on a class or statewide basis;

     2. A declination of insurance coverage solely because such coverage is not available on a class or statewide basis; or

     3. The rescission of a policy.

(2) "Affiliate" or "affiliated" means a person that directly, or indirectly through one or more intermediaries, controls, is controlled by, or is under common control with another person.

(3) "Agent" has the meaning as set forth in G.S. 58-33-10, and includes limited representatives, limited line credit insurance producers, limited lines producers, insurance producers, and surplus lines licensees.

(4) "Applicant" means any person who seeks to contract for insurance coverage other than a person seeking group insurance that is not individually underwritten.

(5) "Consumer report" means any written, oral, or other communication of information bearing on a natural person's credit worthiness, credit standing, credit capacity, character, general reputation, personal characteristics, or mode of living that is used or expected to be used in connection with an insurance transaction.

(6) "Consumer reporting agency" means any person who:

   a. Regularly engages, in whole or in part, in the practice of assembling or preparing consumer reports for a monetary fee;

   b. Obtains information primarily from sources other than insurance institutions; and

   c. Furnishes consumer reports to other persons.

(7) "Control," including the terms "controlled by" or "under common control with," means the possession, direct or indirect, of the power to direct or cause the direction of the management and policies of a person, whether through the ownership of voting securities, by contract other than a commercial contract for goods or nonmanagement services, or otherwise, unless the power is the result of an official position with or corporate office held by the person.

(8) "Declination of insurance coverage" means a denial, in whole or in part, by an insurance institution or agent of requested insurance coverage.

(9) "Individual" means any natural person who:

   a. In the case of property or casualty insurance, is a past, present, or proposed named insured or certificate holder;

   b. In the case of life, health, or disability insurance, is a past, present, or proposed principal insured or certificate holder;

   c. Is a past, present or proposed policy owner;

   d. Is a past or present applicant;

   e. Is a past or present claimant;

   f. Derived, derives, or is proposed to derive insurance coverage under an insurance policy or certificate subject to this Article; or

   g. Is the subject of personal information collected or maintained by an insurance institution, agent, or insurance-support organization in connection with mortgage guaranty insurance.

(10) "Institutional source" means any person or governmental entity that provides information about an individual to an agent, insurance institution, or insurance-support organization, other than:

a. An agent;

b. The individual who is the subject of the information; or

c. A natural person acting in a personal capacity rather than in a business or professional capacity.

(11) "Insurance institution" means any corporation, association, partnership, reciprocal exchange, inter-insurer, Lloyd's insurer, fraternal benefit society, or other person engaged in the business of insurance, including health maintenance organizations and medical, surgical, hospital, dental, and optometric service plans, governed by Articles 65 through 67 of this Chapter. "Insurance institution" shall not include agents or insurance-support organizations.

(12) "Insurance-support organization" means any person who regularly engages, in whole or in part, in the practice of assembling or collecting information about natural persons for the primary purpose of providing the information to an insurance institution or agent for insurance transactions, including: (i) the furnishing of consumer reports or investigative consumer reports to an insurance institution or agent for use in connection with an insurance transaction; or (ii) the collection of personal information from insurance institutions, agents, or other insurance-support organizations for the purpose of detecting or preventing fraud, material misrepresentation, or material nondisclosure in connection with insurance underwriting or insurance claim activity; provided, however, the following persons shall not be considered "insurance-support organizations" for purposes of this Article: agents, governmental institutions, insurance institutions, medical-care institutions, and medical professionals.

(13) "Insurance transaction" means any transaction involving insurance primarily for personal, family, or household needs rather than business or professional needs that entails:

a. The determination of an individual's eligibility for an insurance coverage, benefit, or payment; or

b. The servicing of an insurance application, policy, contract, or certificate.

(14) "Investigative consumer report" means a consumer report or portion thereof in which information about a natural person's character, general reputation, personal characteristics, or mode of living is obtained through personal interviews with the person's neighbors, friends, associates, acquaintances, or others who may have knowledge concerning such items of information.

(15) "Life insurance" includes annuities.

(16) "Medical-care institution" means any facility or institution that is licensed to provide health care services to natural persons, including but not limited to, hospitals, skilled nursing facilities, home-health agencies, medical clinics, rehabilitation agencies, public health agencies, or health-maintenance organizations.

(17) "Medical professional" means any person licensed or certified to provide health care services to natural persons, including but not limited to, a physician, dentist, nurse, chiropractor, optometrist, physical or occupational therapist, licensed clinical social worker, clinical dietitian, clinical psychologist, pharmacist, or speech therapist.

(18) "Medical-record information" means personal information that:

a. Relates to an individual's physical or mental condition, medical history, or medical treatment; and

b. Is obtained from a medical professional or medical-care institution, from the individual, or from the individual's spouse, parent, or legal guardian.

(19) "Personal information" means any individually identifiable information gathered in connection with an insurance transaction from which judgments can be made about an individual's character, habits, avocations, finances, occupation, general reputation, credit, health, or any other personal characteristics. "Personal information" includes an individual's name and address and medical-record information, but does not include privileged information.

(20) "Policyholder" means any person who:
   a. In the case of individual property or casualty insurance, is a present named insured;
   b. In the case of individual life or accident and health insurance, is a present policy owner; or
   c. In the case of group insurance that is individually underwritten, is a present group certificate holder.

(21) "Pretext interview" means an interview whereby a person, in an attempt to obtain information about a natural person, performs one or more of the following acts:
   a. Pretends to be someone he is not;
   b. Pretends to represent a person he is not in fact representing;
   c. Misrepresents the true purpose of the interview; or
   d. Refuses to identify himself upon request.

(22) "Privileged information" means any individually identifiable information that (i) relates to a claim for insurance benefits or a civil or criminal proceeding involving an individual, and (ii) is collected in connection with or in reasonable anticipation of a claim for insurance benefits or civil or criminal proceeding involving an individual: Provided, however, information otherwise meeting the requirements of this subsection shall nevertheless be considered personal information under this Article if it is disclosed in violation of G.S. 58-39-75.

(23) "Residual market mechanism" means any reinsurance facility, joint underwriting association, assigned risk plan, or other similar plan established under the laws of this State.

(24) "Termination of insurance coverage" or "termination of an insurance policy" means either a cancellation or nonrenewal of an insurance policy, in whole or in part, for any reason other than the failure to pay a premium as required by the policy.

(25) "Unauthorized insurer" means an insurance institution that has not been granted a license by the Commissioner to transact the business of insurance in this State. (1981, c. 846, s. 1; 1987, c. 629, s. 13; 1993, c. 464, s. 1; 2001-203, s. 30; 2001-351, ss. 2, 3; 2001-487, s. 40(f); 2003-262, s. 2(1).)

Editor's Note. — Session Laws 2001-351, s. 13, contains a severability clause.

Session Laws 2001-351, s. 14, provides: "This act becomes effective January 1, 2002, and applies to policies and contracts newly issued or renewed on and after that date. For the purposes of the application of this act to policies or contracts renewed on and after January 1, 2002, the renewal of a policy or contract is presumed to occur on each anniversary of the date on which coverage was first effective on the person or persons covered by the policy or contract."

Sessions Laws 2003-262, s. 2(1), effective June 26, 2003, redesignated G.S. 58-39-1 through 58-39-76 as Part 1 of Article 39 of Chapter 58, under the heading "Insurance Information and Privacy Protection."

Effect of Amendments. — Session Laws 2001-351, ss. 2 and 3, effective January 1, 2002, in subdivision (1)a.4.I., deleted "or" preceding "an unauthorized insurer" and inserted "or an insurance institution that specializes in substandard risks" thereafter; substituted "life, health, or disability insurance" for "life or accident and health insurance" in subdivisions (1)a.5. and (9)b.; deleted "or" at the end of subdivision (9)f.; addded subdivision (9)g.; and made minor stylistic changes. See editor's note for applicability.

§ 58-39-20. Pretext interviews.

No insurance institution, agent, or insurance-support organization shall use or authorize the use of pretext interviews to obtain information in connection with an insurance transaction: Provided, however, a pretext interview may be undertaken to obtain information from a person or institution that does not have a generally or statutorily recognized privileged relationship with the person about whom the information relates for the purpose of investigating a claim where, based upon specific information available for review by the Commissioner, there is a reasonable basis for suspecting criminal activity, fraud, material misrepresentation, or material nondisclosure in connection with the claim. (1981, c. 846, s. 1; 2003-262, s. 2(1).)

Editor's Note. — Sessions Laws 2003-262, s. 2(1), effective June 26, 2003, redesignated G.S. 58-39-1 through 58-39-76 as Part 1 of Article 39 of Chapter 58, under the heading "Insurance Information and Privacy Protection."

§ 58-39-25. Notice of insurance information practices.

(a) An insurance institution or agent shall provide a notice of information practices to all applicants or policyholders in connection with insurance transactions as provided in this section:

   (1) In the case of an application for insurance a notice shall be provided no later than:

      a. At the time of the delivery of the insurance policy or certificate when personal information is collected only from the applicant or from public records; or

      b. At the time the collection of personal information is initiated when personal information is collected from a source other than the applicant or public records;

   (2) In the case of a policy renewal, a notice shall be provided no later than the policy renewal date, except that no notice shall be required in connection with a policy renewal if:

      a. Personal information is collected only from the policyholder or from public records; or

      b. A notice meeting the requirements of this section has been given within the previous 24 months; or

   (3) In the case of a policy reinstatement or change in insurance benefits, a notice shall be provided no later than the time a request for a policy reinstatement or change in insurance benefits is received by the insurance institution, except that no notice shall be required if personal information is collected only from the policyholder or from public records.

(b) The notice required by subsection (a) of this section shall be in writing and shall state:

   (1) Whether personal information may be collected from persons other than the individual or individuals proposed for coverage;

   (2) The types of personal information that may be collected and the types of sources and investigative techniques that may be used to collect such information;

   (3) The types of disclosures identified in subsections (2), (3), (4), (5), (6), (9), (11), (12), and (14) of G.S. 58-39-75 and the circumstances under which such disclosures may be made without prior authorization: Provided, however, only those circumstances need be described that occur with such frequency as to indicate a general business practice;

   (4) A description of the rights established under G.S. 58-39-45 and 58-39-50 and the manner in which such rights may be exercised; and

    (5) That information obtained from a report prepared by an insurance-support organization may be retained by the insurance-support organization and disclosed to other persons.

  (c) In lieu of the notice prescribed in subsection (b) of this section, the insurance institution or agent may provide an abbreviated notice informing the applicant or policyholder that:

    (1) Personal information may be collected from persons other than the individual or individuals proposed for coverage;

    (2) Such information, as well as other personal or privileged information subsequently collected by the insurance institution or agent, in certain circumstances, may be disclosed to third parties without authorization;

    (3) A right of access and correction exists with respect to all personal information collected; and

    (4) The notice prescribed in subsection (b) of this section will be furnished to the applicant or policyholder upon request.

  (d) The obligations imposed by this section upon an insurance institution or agent may be satisfied by another insurance institution or agent authorized to act on its behalf. (1981, c. 846, s. 1; 2003-262, s. 2(1).)

Editor's Note. — Sessions Laws 2003-262, s. 2(1), effective June 26, 2003, redesignated G.S. 58-39-1 through 58-39-76 as Part 1 of Article 39 of Chapter 58, under the heading "Insurance Information and Privacy Protection."

§ 58-39-26. Federal privacy disclosure notice requirements.

  (a) Disclosure Required. — In addition to the notice requirements of G.S. 58-39-25, an insurance institution or agent shall provide, to all applicants and policyholders no later than (i) before the initial disclosure of personal information under G.S. 58-39-75(11) or (ii) the time of the delivery of the insurance policy or certificate, a clear and conspicuous notice, in written or electronic form, of the insurance institution or agent's policies and practices with respect to:

    (1) Disclosing nonpublic personal information to affiliates and nonaffiliated third parties, consistent with section 502 of Public Law 106-102, including the categories of information that may be disclosed.

    (2) Disclosing nonpublic personal information of persons who have ceased to be customers of the financial institution.

    (3) Protecting the nonpublic personal information of consumers.

These disclosures shall be made in accordance with the regulations prescribed under section 505 of Public Law 106-102.

  (b) Information to Be Included. — The disclosure required by subsection (a) of this section shall include:

    (1) The policies and practices of the insurance institution or agent with respect to disclosing nonpublic personal information to nonaffiliated third parties, other than agents of the insurance institution or agent, consistent with section 502 of Public Law 106-102, and including:

      a. The categories of persons to whom the information is or may be disclosed, other than the persons to whom the information may be provided under section 502(e) of Public Law 106-102.

      b. The policies and practices of the insurance institution or agent with respect to disclosing of nonpublic personal information of persons who have ceased to be customers of the insurance institution or agent.

    (2) The categories of nonpublic personal information that are collected by the insurance institution or agent.

(3) The policies that the insurance institution or agent maintains to protect the confidentiality and security of nonpublic personal information in accordance with section 501 of Public Law 106-102.

(4) The disclosures required, if any, under section 603(d)(2)(A) (iii) of the Fair Credit Reporting Act.

(c) In the case of a policyholder, the notice required by this section shall be provided not less than annually during the continuation of the policy. As used in this subsection, "annually" means at least once in any period of 12 consecutive months during which the policy is in effect. (2001-351, s. 4; 2003-262, s. 2(1).)

Editor's Note. — Session Laws 2001-351, s. 13, contains a severability clause.

Session Laws 2001-351, s. 14, provides: "This act becomes effective January 1, 2002, and applies to policies and contracts newly issued or renewed on and after that date. For the purposes of the application of this act to policies or contracts renewed on and after January 1, 2002, the renewal of a policy or contract is presumed to occur on each anniversary of the date on which coverage was first effective on the person or persons covered by the policy or contract."

Sessions Laws 2003-262, s. 2(1), effective June 26, 2003, redesignated G.S. 58-39-1 through 58-39-76 as Part 1 of Article 39 of Chapter 58, under the heading "Insurance Information and Privacy Protection."

§ 58-39-27. Privacy notice and disclosure requirement exceptions.

(a) Under G.S. 58-39-25 and G.S. 58-39-26, an insurance institution or agent may provide a joint notice from the insurance institution or agent and one or more of its affiliates or other financial institutions, as defined in the notice, as long as the notice is accurate with respect to the insurance institution or agent and the other institutions.

(b) An insurance institution or agent may satisfy the notice requirements of G.S. 58-39-25 and G.S. 58-39-26 by providing a single notice if two or more applicants or policyholders jointly obtain or apply for an insurance product.

(c) An insurance institution or agent may satisfy the notice requirements of G.S. 58-39-25 and G.S. 58-39-26 through the use of separate or combined notices.

(d) An insurance institution or agent is not required to provide the notices required by G.S. 58-39-25 and G.S. 58-39-26 to:

(1) Any applicant or policyholder whose last known address, according to the insurance institution's or agent's records is deemed invalid. The applicant's or policyholder's last known address shall be deemed invalid if mail sent to that address has been returned by the postal authorities as undeliverable and if subsequent reasonable attempts to obtain a current valid address for the applicant or policyholder have been unsuccessful; or

(2) Any policyholder whose policy is lapsed, expired, or otherwise inactive or dormant under the insurance institution's business practices, and the insurance institution has not communicated with the policyholder about the relationship for a period of 12 consecutive months, other than annual privacy notices, material required by law or regulation, or promotional materials.

(e) If an agent does not share information with any person other than the agent's principal or an affiliate of the principal, and if the principal provides all notices required by G.S. 58-39-25 and G.S. 58-39-26, the agent is not required to provide the notices required by G.S. 58-39-25 and G.S. 58-39-26. G.S. 58-39-75 applies to the sharing of information with an affiliate under this subsection.

(f) When an agent discloses a policyholder's personal information, other than medical information, to an insurance institution solely for the purposes of renewal, transfer, replacement, reinstatement, or modification of an existing policy, the agent is not required to provide the notices required by G.S. 58-39-25 and G.S. 58-39-26.

(g) For the purposes of G.S. 58-39-26 only, the terms "applicant" or "policyholder" include respectively a person who applies for, or a certificate holder who obtains, insurance coverage under a group or blanket insurance contract, employee benefit plan, or group annuity contract, regardless of whether the coverage is individually underwritten. An insurance institution or agent that does not disclose personal information about an applicant or policyholder under a group or blanket insurance contract, employee benefit plan, or group annuity contract, except as permitted under G.S. 58-39-75(1) through (10) and G.S. 58-39-75(12) through (21), may satisfy any notice requirement that otherwise exists under G.S. 58-39-26 with respect to that applicant or policyholder by providing a notice of information practices to the holder of the group or blanket insurance or annuity contract or the employee benefit plan sponsor. If an insurance institution or agent discloses personal information about an applicant or policyholder as permitted by G.S. 58-39-75(11), it shall provide the notice required by G.S. 58-39-26 to the applicant or policyholder not less than 30 days before the information is disclosed, and it may satisfy any other notice requirement that otherwise exists under this section with respect to that applicant or policyholder by providing a notice of information practices to the holder of the group or blanket insurance or annuity contract or employee benefit plan sponsor. (2001-351, s. 5; 2003-262, s. 2(1).)

Editor's Note. — Session Laws 2001-351, s. 13, contains a severability clause.

Session Laws 2001-351, s. 14, provides: "This act becomes effective January 1, 2002, and applies to policies and contracts newly issued or renewed on and after that date. For the purposes of the application of this act to policies or contracts renewed on and after January 1, 2002, the renewal of a policy or contract is presumed to occur on each anniversary of the date on which coverage was first effective on the person or persons covered by the policy or contract."

Sessions Laws 2003-262, s. 2(1), effective June 26, 2003, redesignated G.S. 58-39-1 through 58-39-76 as Part 1 of Article 39 of Chapter 58, under the heading "Insurance Information and Privacy Protection."

§ 58-39-28. Exception for title and mortgage guaranty insurance.

(a) A title insurance company shall give notice of its insurance information practices under G.S. 58-39-25 and G.S. 58-39-26 only at the time the final policy of title insurance is issued and is not subject to any annual notice requirement thereafter.

(b) In the case of mortgage guaranty insurance, the notice required by G.S. 58-39-25 and G.S. 58-39-26 shall be provided at the time a master policy is issued and thereafter only if there is a material change in the insurer's policies and practices regarding the use or disclosure of personal information. (2001-351, s. 6; 2003-262, s. 2(1).)

Editor's Note. — Session Laws 2001-351, s. 13, contains a severability clause.

Session Laws 2001-351, s. 14, provides: "This act becomes effective January 1, 2002, and applies to policies and contracts newly issued or renewed on and after that date. For the purposes of the application of this act to policies or contracts renewed on and after January 1, 2002, the renewal of a policy or contract is presumed to occur on each anniversary of the date on which coverage was first effective on the person or persons covered by the policy or contract."

Sessions Laws 2003-262, s. 2(1), effective June 26, 2003, redesignated G.S. 58-39-1 through 58-39-76 as Part 1 of Article 39 of Chapter 58, under the heading "Insurance Information and Privacy Protection."

§ 58-39-30. Marketing and research surveys.

An insurance institution or agent shall clearly specify those questions designed to obtain information solely for marketing or research purposes from an individual in connection with an insurance transaction. (1981, c. 846, s. 1; 2003-262, s. 2(1).)

Editor's Note. — Sessions Laws 2003-262, s. 2(1), effective June 26, 2003, redesignated G.S. 58-39-1 through 58-39-76 as Part 1 of Article 39 of Chapter 58, under the heading "Insurance Information and Privacy Protection."

§ 58-39-35. Content of disclosure authorization forms.

Notwithstanding any other provision of law of this State, no insurance institution, agent, or insurance-support organization shall utilize as its disclosure authorization form in connection with insurance transactions involving insurance policies or contracts issued after July 1, 1982, a form or statement that authorizes the disclosure of personal or privileged information about an individual to the insurance institution, agent, or insurance-support organization unless the form or statement:

(1) Complies with the provisions of Article 38 of this Chapter;
(2) Is dated;
(3) Specifies the types of persons authorized to disclose information about the individual;
(4) Specifies the nature of the information authorized to be disclosed;
(5) Names the insurance institution or agent and identifies by generic reference representatives of the insurance institution to whom the individual is authorizing information to be disclosed;
(6) Specifies the purposes for which the information is collected;
(7) Specifies the length of time such authorization shall remain valid, which shall be no longer than:
   a. In the case of authorizations signed for the purpose of collecting information in connection with an application for an insurance policy, a policy reinstatement, or a request for change in policy benefits:
     1. Thirty months from the date the authorization is signed if the application or request involves life, health, or disability insurance; or
     2. One year from the date the authorization is signed if the application or request involves property or casualty insurance;
   b. In the case of authorizations signed for the purpose of collecting information in connection with a claim for benefits under an insurance policy:
     1. The term of coverage of the policy if the claim is for a health insurance benefit; or
     2. The duration of the claim if the claim is not for a health insurance benefit; and
(8) Advises the individual or a person authorized to act on behalf of the individual that the individual or the individual's authorized representative is entitled to receive a copy of the authorization form. (1981, c. 846, s. 1; c. 1127, s. 56; 2003-262, s. 2(1).)

Editor's Note. — Sessions Laws 2003-262, s. 2(1), effective June 26, 2003, redesignated G.S. 58-39-1 through 58-39-76 as Part 1 of Article 39 of Chapter 58, under the heading "Insurance Information and Privacy Protection."

§ 58-39-40. Investigative consumer reports.

(a) No insurance institution, agent, or insurance-support organization may prepare or request an investigative consumer report about an individual in connection with an insurance transaction involving an application for insurance, a policy renewal, a policy reinstatement, or a change in insurance benefits unless the insurance institution or agent informs the individual:

    (1) That he may request to be interviewed in connection with the preparation of the investigative consumer report; and

    (2) That upon a request pursuant to G.S. 58-39-45 he is entitled to receive a copy of the investigative consumer report.

(b) If an investigative consumer report is to be prepared by an insurance institution or agent, the insurance institution or agent shall institute reasonable procedures to conduct a personal interview requested by an individual.

(c) If an investigative consumer report is to be prepared by an insurance-support organization, the insurance institution or agent desiring such report shall inform the insurance-support organization whether a personal interview has been requested by the individual. The insurance-support organization shall institute reasonable procedures to conduct such interviews, if requested. (1981, c. 846, s. 1; 2003-262, s. 2(1).)

Editor's Note. — Sessions Laws 2003-262, s. 2(1), effective June 26, 2003, redesignated G.S. 58-39-1 through 58-39-76 as Part 1 of Article 39 of Chapter 58, under the heading "Insurance Information and Privacy Protection."

§ 58-39-45. Access to recorded personal information.

(a) If any individual, after proper identification, submits a written request to an insurance institution, agent, or insurance-support organization for access to recorded personal information about the individual that is reasonably described by the individual and reasonably locatable and retrievable by the insurance institution, agent, or insurance-support organization, the insurance institution, agent, or insurance-support organization shall within 30 business days from the date such request is received:

    (1) Inform the individual of the nature and substance of such recorded personal information in writing, by telephone, or by other oral communication, whichever the insurance institution, agent, or insurance-support organization prefers;

    (2) Permit the individual to see and copy, in person, such recorded personal information pertaining to him or to obtain a copy of such recorded personal information by mail, whichever the individual prefers, unless such recorded personal information is in coded form, in which case an accurate translation in plain language shall be provided in writing;

    (3) Disclose to the individual the identity, if recorded, of those persons to whom the insurance institution, agent, or insurance-support organization has disclosed such personal information within two years prior to such request, and if the identity is not recorded, the names of those insurance institutions, agents, insurance-support organizations or other persons to whom such information is normally disclosed; and

    (4) Provide the individual with a summary of the procedures by which he may request correction, amendment, or deletion of recorded personal information.

(b) Any personal information provided pursuant to subsection (a) of this section shall identify the source of the information if such source is an institutional source.

(c) Medical-record information supplied by a medical-care institution or medical professional and requested under subsection (a) of this section together with the identity of the medical professional or medical-care institution that provided such information, shall be supplied either directly to the individual or to a medical professional designated by the individual and licensed to provide medical care with respect to the condition to which the information relates, whichever the insurance institution, agent, or insurance-support organization prefers. If it elects to disclose the information to a medical professional designated by the individual, the insurance institution, agent, or insurance-support organization shall notify the individual, at the time of the disclosure, that it has provided the information to the medical professional.

(d) Except for personal information provided under G.S. 58-39-55, an insurance institution, agent, or insurance-support organization may charge a reasonable fee to cover the costs incurred in providing a copy of recorded personal information to individuals.

(e) The obligations imposed by this section upon an insurance institution or agent may be satisfied by another insurance institution or agent authorized to act on its behalf. With respect to the copying and disclosure of recorded personal information pursuant to a request under subsection (a) of this section, an insurance institution, agent, or insurance-support organization may make arrangements with an insurance-support organization or a consumer reporting agency to copy and disclose recorded personal information on its behalf.

(f) The rights granted to individuals in this section shall extend to all natural persons to the extent information about them is collected and maintained by an insurance institution, agent, or insurance-support organization in connection with an insurance transaction. The rights granted to all natural persons by this subsection shall not extend to information about them that relates to and is collected in connection with or in reasonable anticipation of a claim or civil or criminal proceeding involving them.

(g) For purposes of this section, the term, "insurance-support organization" does not include the term, "consumer reporting agency." (1981, c. 846, s. 1; 2003-262, s. 2(1).)

Editor's Note. — Sessions Laws 2003-262, s. 2(1), effective June 26, 2003, redesignated G.S. 58-39-1 through 58-39-76 as Part 1 of Article 39 of Chapter 58, under the heading "Insurance Information and Privacy Protection."

§ 58-39-50. Correction, amendment, or deletion of recorded personal information.

(a) Within 30 business days from the date of receipt of a written request from an individual to correct, amend, or delete any recorded personal information about the individual within its possession, an insurance institution, agent, or insurance-support organization shall either:

    (1) Correct, amend, or delete the portion of the recorded personal information in dispute; or

    (2) Notify the individual of:

        a. Its refusal to make such correction, amendment, or deletion;

        b. The reasons for the refusal; and

        c. The individual's right to file a statement as provided in subsection (c) of this section.

(b) If the insurance institution, agent, or insurance-support organization corrects, amends, or deletes recorded personal information in accordance with subdivision (a)(1) of this section, the insurance institution, agent, or insurance-support organization shall so notify the individual in writing and furnish the correction, amendment, or fact of deletion to:

(1) Any person specifically designated by the individual who, within the preceding two years, may have received such recorded personal information;

(2) Any insurance-support organization whose primary source of personal information is insurance institutions if the insurance-support organization has systematically received such recorded personal information from the insurance institution within the preceding seven years. The correction, amendment, or fact of deletion need not be furnished if the insurance-support organization no longer maintains recorded personal information about the individual; and

(3) Any insurance-support organization that furnished the personal information that has been corrected, amended, or deleted.

(c) Whenever an individual disagrees with an insurance institution's, agent's, or insurance-support organization's refusal to correct, amend, or delete recorded personal information, the individual shall be permitted to file with the insurance institution, agent, or insurance-support organization:

(1) A concise statement setting forth what the individual thinks is the correct, relevant, or fair information; and

(2) A concise statement of the reasons why the individual disagrees with the insurance institution's, agent's, or insurance-support organization's refusal to correct, amend, or delete recorded personal information.

(d) In the event an individual files either statement as described in subsection (c) of this section, the insurance institution, agent, or support organization shall:

(1) File the statement with the disputed personal information and provide a means by which anyone reviewing the disputed personal information will be made aware of the individual's statement and have access to it; and

(2) In any subsequent disclosure by the insurance institution, agent, or support organization of the recorded personal information that is the subject of disagreement, clearly identify the matter or matters in dispute and provide the individual's statement along with the recorded personal information being disclosed; and

(3) Furnish the statement to the persons and in the manner specified in subsection (b) of this section.

(e) The rights granted to individuals in this section shall extend to all natural persons to the extent information about them is collected and maintained by an insurance institution, agent, or insurance-support organization in connection with an insurance transaction. The rights granted to all natural persons by this subsection shall not extend to information about them that relates to and is collected in connection with or in reasonable anticipation of a claim or civil or criminal proceeding involving them.

(f) For purposes of this section, the term, "insurance-support organization" does not include the term, "consumer reporting agency." (1981, c. 846, s. 1; 1991, c. 720, s. 74; 2003-262, s. 2(1).)

Editor's Note. — Sessions Laws 2003-262, s. 2(1), effective June 26, 2003, redesignated G.S. 58-39-1 through 58-39-76 as Part 1 of Article 39 of Chapter 58, under the heading "Insurance Information and Privacy Protection."

§ 58-39-55. Reasons for adverse underwriting decisions.

(a) In the event of an adverse underwriting decision, the insurance institution or agent responsible for the decision shall give a written notice in a form approved by the Commissioner that:

  (1) Either provides the applicant, policyholder, or individual proposed for coverage with the specific reason or reasons for the adverse underwriting decision in writing or advises such person that upon written request he may receive the specific reason or reasons in writing; and

  (2) Provides the applicant, policyholder, or individual proposed for coverage with a summary of the rights established under subsection (b) of this section and G.S. 58-39-45 and 58-39-50.

(b) Upon receipt of a written request within 90 business days from the date of the mailing of notice or other communication of an adverse underwriting decision to an applicant, policyholder or individual proposed for coverage, the insurance institution or agent shall furnish to such person within 21 business days from the date of receipt of such written request:

  (1) The specific reason or reasons for the adverse underwriting decision, in writing, if such information was not initially furnished in writing pursuant to subdivision (a)(1) of this section;

  (2) The specific items of personal and privileged information that support those reasons: Provided, however:

    a. The insurance institution or agent shall not be required to furnish specific items of privileged information if it has a reasonable suspicion, based upon specific information available for review by the Commissioner, that the applicant, policyholder, or individual proposed for coverage has engaged in criminal activity, fraud, material misrepresentation, or material nondisclosure, and

    b. Specific items of medical-record information supplied by a medical-care institution or medical professional shall be disclosed either directly to the individual about whom the information relates or to the medical professional designated by the individual and licensed to provide medical care with respect to the condition to which the information relates, whichever the insurance institution or agent prefers; and

  (3) The names and addresses of the institutional sources that supplied the specific items of information given pursuant to subdivision (b)(2) of this section: Provided, however, the identity of any medical professional or medical-care institution shall be disclosed either directly to the individual or to the designated medical professional, whichever the insurance institution or agent prefers.

(c) The obligations imposed by this section upon an insurance institution or agent may be satisfied by another insurance institution or agent authorized to act on its behalf.

(d) When an adverse underwriting decision results solely from an oral request or inquiry, the explanation of reasons and summary of rights required by this section may be given orally. (1981, c. 846, s. 1; 2003-262, s. 2(1).)

Editor's Note. — Sessions Laws 2003-262, s. 2(1), effective June 26, 2003, redesignated G.S. 58-39-1 through 58-39-76 as Part 1 of Article 39 of Chapter 58, under the heading "Insurance Information and Privacy Protection."

§ 58-39-60. Information concerning previous adverse underwriting decisions.

No insurance institution, agent, or insurance-support organization may seek information in connection with an insurance transaction concerning: (i) any previous adverse underwriting decision experienced by an individual; or (ii) any previous insurance coverage obtained by an individual through a residual market mechanism, unless such inquiry also requests the reasons for any previous adverse underwriting decision or the reasons why insurance coverage was previously obtained through a residual market mechanism. (1981, c. 846, s. 1; 2003-262, s. 2(1).)

Editor's Note. — Sessions Laws 2003-262, s. 2(1), effective June 26, 2003, redesignated G.S. 58-39-1 through 58-39-76 as Part 1 of Article 39 of Chapter 58, under the heading "Insurance Information and Privacy Protection."

§ 58-39-65. Previous adverse underwriting decisions.

No insurance institution or agent may base an adverse underwriting decision in whole or in part:

(1) On the fact of a previous adverse underwriting decision or on the fact that an individual previously obtained insurance coverage through a residual market mechanism: Provided, however, an insurance institution or agent may base an adverse underwriting decision on further information obtained from an insurance institution or agent responsible for a previous adverse underwriting decision;

(2) On personal information received from an insurance-support organization whose primary source of information is insurance institutions: Provided, however, an insurance institution or agent may base an adverse underwriting decision on further personal information obtained as the result of information received from such insurance-support organization. (1981, c. 846, s. 1; 2003-262, s. 2(1).)

Editor's Note. — Sessions Laws 2003-262, s. 2(1), effective June 26, 2003, redesignated G.S. 58-39-1 through 58-39-76 as Part 1 of Article 39 of Chapter 58, under the heading "Insurance Information and Privacy Protection."

§ 58-39-70: Recodified as G.S. 58-39-125 by Session Laws 2003-262, s. 2(3), effective June 26, 2003.

Editor's Note. — Sessions Laws 2003-262, s. 2(1), effective June 26, 2003, redesignated G.S. 58-39-1 through 58-39-76 as Part 1 of Article 39 of Chapter 58, under the heading "Insurance Information and Privacy Protection." Session Laws 2003-262, s. 2(3), effective June 26, 2003, recodified former G.S. 58-39-70 as present 58-39-125."

§ 58-39-75. Disclosure limitations and conditions.

An insurance institution, agent, or insurance-support organization shall not disclose any personal or privileged information about an individual collected or received in connection with an insurance transaction unless the disclosure is:

(1) With the written authorization of the individual, provided:

     a. If such authorization is submitted by another insurance institution, agent, or insurance-support organization, the authorization meets the requirements of G.S. 58-39-35; or

    b. If such authorization is submitted by a person other than an insurance institution, agent, or insurance-support organization, the authorization meets the requirements of G.S. 58-39-35 and is:
       1. Dated;
       2. Signed by the individual; and
       3. Obtained one year or less before the date a disclosure is sought pursuant to this paragraph; or

(2) To a person other than an insurance institution, agent, or insurance-support organization, provided such disclosure is reasonably necessary:

    a. To enable that person to perform a business, professional, or insurance function for the disclosing insurance institution, agent, or insurance-support organization, including, but not limited to, performing marketing functions and other functions regarding the provision of information concerning the disclosing institution's own products, services, and programs, and that person agrees not to disclose the information further without the individual's written authorization unless the further disclosure:
       1. Would otherwise be permitted by this section if made by an insurance institution, agent, or insurance-support organization; or
       2. Is reasonably necessary for that person to perform its function for the disclosing insurance institution, agent, or insurance-support organization; or
    b. To enable that person to provide information to the disclosing insurance institution, agent, or insurance-support organization for the purpose of:
       1. Determining an individual's eligibility for an insurance benefit or payment; or
       2. Detecting or preventing criminal activity, fraud, material misrepresentation, or material nondisclosure in connection with an insurance transaction; or

(3) To an insurance institution, agent, insurance-support organization, or self-insurer, provided the information disclosed is limited to that which is reasonably necessary:

    a. To detect or prevent criminal activity, fraud, material misrepresentation, or material nondisclosure in connection with insurance transactions; or
    b. For either the disclosing or receiving insurance institution, agent, or insurance-support organization to perform its function in connection with an insurance transaction involving the individual; or

(4) To a medical-care institution or medical professional for the purpose of (i) verifying insurance coverage or benefits, (ii) informing an individual of a medical problem of which the individual may not be aware, or (iii) conducting an operations or services audit, provided only such information is disclosed as is reasonably necessary to accomplish the foregoing purposes; or

(5) To an insurance regulatory authority; or

(6) To a law-enforcement or other government authority:

    a. To protect the interests of the insurance institution, agent, or insurance-support organization in preventing or prosecuting the perpetration of fraud upon it; or
    b. If the insurance institution, agent, or insurance-support organization reasonably believes that illegal activities have been conducted by the individual; or

(7) Otherwise permitted or required by law; or

(8) In response to a facially valid administrative or judicial order, including a search warrant or subpoena; or

(9) Made for the purpose of conducting actuarial or research studies, provided:

    a. No individual may be identified in any actuarial or research report;

    b. Materials allowing the individual to be identified are returned or destroyed as soon as they are no longer needed; and

    c. The actuarial or research organization agrees not to disclose the information unless the disclosure would otherwise be permitted by this section if made by an insurance institution, agent, or insurance-support organization; or

(10) To a party or a representative of a party to a proposed or consummated sale, transfer, merger, or consolidation of all or part of the business of the insurance institution, agent, or insurance-support organization, provided:

    a. Prior to the consummation of the sale, transfer, merger, or consolidation only such information is disclosed as is reasonably necessary to enable the recipient to make business decisions about the purchase, transfer, merger, or consolidation, and

    b. The recipient agrees not to disclose the information unless the disclosure would otherwise be permitted by this section if made by an insurance institution, agent or insurance-support organization; or

(11) To a person whose only use of such information will be in connection with the marketing of a product or service, provided:

    a. No medical-record information, privileged information, or personal information relating to an individual's character, personal habits, mode of living, or general reputation is disclosed, and no classification derived from such information is disclosed;

    b. The individual has been given an opportunity to indicate that he does not want personal information disclosed for marketing purposes and has given no indication that such individual does not want the information disclosed; and

    c. The person receiving such information agrees not to use it except in connection with the marketing of a product or service; or

(12) To an affiliate whose only use of the information will be in connection with an audit of the insurance institution or agent or the marketing of an insurance product or service, provided the affiliate agrees not to disclose the information for any other purpose or to unaffiliated persons; and further provided that no medical record information may be disclosed to the affiliate for the marketing of an insurance product or service; or

(13) By a consumer reporting agency, provided the disclosure is to a person other than an insurance institution or agent; or

(14) To a group policyholder for the purpose of reporting claims experience or conducting an audit of the insurance institution's or agent's operations or services, provided the information disclosed is reasonably necessary for the group policyholder to conduct the review or audit; or

(15) To a professional peer review organization for the purpose of reviewing the service or conduct of a medical-care institution or medical professional; or

(16) To a governmental authority for the purpose of determining the individual's eligibility for health benefits for which the governmental authority may be liable; or

(17) To a certificate holder or policyholder for the purpose of providing information regarding the status of an insurance transaction; or

(18) To a lienholder, mortgagee, assignee, lessor, or other person shown on the records of an insurance institution or agent as having a legal or beneficial interest in a policy of insurance only if:

    a. No medical record information is disclosed unless the disclosure would otherwise be permitted by this section; and

    b. The information disclosed is limited to that which is reasonably necessary to permit such person to protect its interest in such policy; or

(19) To authorized personnel of the Division of Motor Vehicles upon requests pursuant to G.S. 20-309(c) or G.S. 20-309(f).

(20) To the Department of Health and Human Services and the information disclosed is immunization information described in G.S. 130A-153.

(21) To a person whose only use of an applicant's or policyholder's personal information, but not including medical record information, will be in connection with the marketing of a financial product or service intended to be provided by participants in a marketing program where the program participants and the types of information to be shared are identified to the applicant or policyholder when the applicant or policyholder is first offered the financial product or service. As used in this subdivision:

    a. "Financial institution" means any institution the business of which is engaging in activities that are financial in nature or incidental to such financial activities as described in section 4(k) of the Bank Holding Company Act of 1956 (12 U.S.C. § 1843(k)).

    b. "Financial product or service" means any product or service that a financial holding company could offer by engaging in an activity that is financial in nature or incidental to such financial activity under section 4(k) of the Bank Holding Company Act of 1956 (12 U.S.C. § 1843(k)).

    c. "Marketing program" includes only those programs established by written agreement by the insurance institution and one or more financial institutions under which they jointly offer, endorse, or sponsor a financial product or service. (1981, c. 846, s. 1; 1985, c. 666, s. 68; 1993, c. 134, s. 2; 1997-443, s. 11A.20A; 2001-351, ss. 7, 8, 10, 11, 12; 2003-262, s. 2(1).)

Editor's Note. — Session Laws 2001-351, s. 14, provides: "This act becomes effective January 1, 2002, and applies to policies and contracts newly issued or renewed on and after that date. For the purposes of the application of this act to policies or contracts renewed on and after January 1, 2002, the renewal of a policy or contract is presumed to occur on each anniversary of the date on which coverage was first effective on the person or persons covered by the policy or contract."

Session Laws 2001-351, s. 13, contains a severability clause.

Sessions Laws 2003-262, s. 2(1), effective June 26, 2003, redesignated G.S. 58-39-1 through 58-39-76 as Part 1 of Article 39 of Chapter 58, under the heading "Insurance Information and Privacy Protection."

Effect of Amendments. — Session Laws 2001-351, ss. 7, 8, 10, 11 and 12, effective January 1, 2002, inserted "meets the requirements of G.S. 58-39-35 and" in the introductory paragraph of subdivision (1)b.; substituted "before" for "prior to" preceding "the date" in subdivision (1)b.3.; inserted "including, but not limited to. . . services and programs" in subdivision (2)a.; added "and further provided. . . product or service" preceding "or" at the end of subdivision (12); in subdivision (18) substituted "policy of insurance only if" for "policy of insurance; provided that" at the end of the introductory language, added subdivision (18)a., and inserted the subdivision b. designation; added subdivision (21); and made minor stylistic changes. See editor's note for applicability.

Cited in Romig v. Jefferson-Pilot Life Ins. Co., 132 N.C. App. 682, 513 S.E.2d 598, 1999 N.C. App. LEXIS 285 (1999), cert. denied, 350 N.C. 836, 539 S.E.2d 294 (1999), aff'd, 351 N.C. 349, 524 S.E.2d 804 (2000).

§ 58-39-76. Limits on sharing account number information for marketing purposes.

(a) General Prohibition on Disclosure of Account Numbers. — An insurance institution, insurance agent, or insurance-support organization shall not disclose, other than to a consumer reporting agency, an account number or similar form of access number or access code for a credit card account, deposit account, or transaction account of a consumer to any nonaffiliated third party for use in telemarketing, direct mail marketing, or other marketing through electronic mail to the consumer.

(b) Definitions. — As used in this section:

 (1) "Account number" means an account number, or similar form of access number or access code, but does not include a number or code in an encrypted form, as long as the insurance institution, insurance agent, or insurance-support organization does not provide the recipient with a means to decode the number or code.

 (2) "Transaction account" means an account other than a deposit account or credit card account. A transaction account does not include an account to which third parties cannot initiate charges.

(c) Exceptions. — Subsection (a) of this section does not apply if an insurance institution, insurance agent, or insurance-support organization discloses an account number or similar form of access number or access code:

 (1) To the insurance institution's, insurance agent's, or insurance-support organization's agent or service provider solely in order to perform marketing for the insurance institution's, insurance agent's, or insurance-support organization's own products or services, as long as the agent or service provider is not authorized to directly initiate charges to the account; or

 (2) To a participant in a private label credit card program or an affinity or similar program where the participants in the program are identified to the customer when the customer enters into the program. (2001-351, s. 9; 2003-262, s. 2(1).)

Editor's Note. — Session Laws 2001-351, s. 14, provides: "This act becomes effective January 1, 2002, and applies to policies and contracts newly issued or renewed on and after that date. For the purposes of the application of this act to policies or contracts renewed on and after January 1, 2002, the renewal of a policy or contract is presumed to occur on each anniversary of the date on which coverage was first effective on the person or persons covered by the policy or contract."

Session Laws 2001-351, s. 13, contains a severability clause.

Sessions Laws 2003-262, s. 2(1), effective June 26, 2003, redesignated G.S. 58-39-1 through 58-39-76 as Part 1 of Article 39 of Chapter 58, under the heading "Insurance Information and Privacy Protection."

Part 2. Enforcement, Sanctions, Remedies, and Rights.

§ 58-39-80. Hearings and procedures.

(a) Whenever the Commissioner has reason to believe that an insurance institution, agent, or insurance-support organization has been or is engaged in conduct in this State that violates this Article, or whenever the Commissioner has reason to believe that an insurance-support organization has been or is engaged in conduct outside this State that has an effect on a person residing in this State and that violates this Article, the Commissioner may issue and serve upon such insurance institution, agent, or insurance-support organization a statement of charges and notice of hearing to be held at a time and place fixed in the notice. The date for such hearing shall be not less than 10 days after the date of service.

(b) At the time and place fixed for such hearing the insurance institution, agent, or insurance-support organization charged shall have an opportunity to answer the charges against it and present evidence on its behalf. Upon good cause shown, the Commissioner shall permit any adversely affected person to intervene, appear, and be heard at such hearing by counsel or in person. (1981, c. 846, s. 1; 2003-262, s. 2(2).)

Editor's Note. — Sessions Laws 2003-262, s. 2(2), effective June 26, 2003, redesignated G.S. 58-39-80 through 58-39-125 as Part 2 of Article 39 of Chapter 58, under the heading "Enforcement, Sanctions, Remedies, and Rights."

§ 58-39-85. Service of process; insurance-support organizations.

For the purpose of this Article, an insurance-support organization transacting business outside this State that has an effect on a person residing in this State shall be deemed to have appointed the Commissioner to accept service of process on its behalf. The provisions of G.S. 58-16-30 and 58-16-45 shall apply to service of process under this section, except that such service shall be mailed to the insurance-support organization at its last known principal place of business. (1981, c. 846, s. 1; 1985, c. 666, s. 9; 2003-262, s. 2(2).)

Editor's Note. — Sessions Laws 2003-262, s. 2(2), effective June 26, 2003, redesignated G.S. 58-39-80 through 58-39-125 as Part 2 of Article 39 of Chapter 58, under the heading "Enforcement, Sanctions, Remedies, and Rights."

§ 58-39-90. Cease and desist orders.

If, after a hearing pursuant to G.S. 58-39-80, the Commissioner determines that the insurance institution, agent, or insurance-support organization charged has engaged in conduct or practices in violation of this Article, he may issue an order requiring such insurance institution, agent, or insurance-support organization to cease and desist from the conduct or practices constituting a violation of this Article. (1981, c. 846, s. 1; 2003-262, s. 2(2).)

Editor's Note. — Sessions Laws 2003-262, s. 2(2), effective June 26, 2003, redesignated G.S. 58-39-80 through 58-39-125 as Part 2 of Article 39 of Chapter 58, under the heading "Enforcement, Sanctions, Remedies, and Rights."

§ 58-39-95. Penalties.

(a) In any case where a hearing pursuant to G.S. 58-39-80 results in the findings of a violation of this Article, the Commissioner, in addition to the issuance of a cease and desist order as prescribed in G.S. 58-39-90, may levy a civil penalty under G.S. 58-2-70.

(b) Any person who violates a cease and desist order of the Commissioner under G.S. 58-39-90, after notice and hearing and upon order of the court, may be subject to one or more of the following penalties, at the discretion of the court:

(1) A monetary fine of not more than ten thousand dollars ($10,000) for each violation; or

(2) A monetary fine of not more than fifty thousand dollars ($50,000) if the court finds that violations have occurred with such frequency as to constitute a general business practice; or

(3) Suspension or revocation of an insurance institution's or agent's license.

(c) The clear proceeds of any civil penalties levied pursuant to this section shall be remitted to the Civil Penalty and Forfeiture Fund in accordance with G.S. 115C-457.2. (1981, c. 846, s. 1; 1991, c. 720, s. 73; 1998-215, s. 89(b); 2003-262, s. 2(2).)

Editor's Note. — Sessions Laws 2003-262, s. 2(2), effective June 26, 2003, redesignated G.S. 58-39-80 through 58-39-125 as Part 2 of Article 39 of Chapter 58, under the heading "Enforcement, Sanctions, Remedies, and Rights."

§ 58-39-100. Appeal of right.

From any final order of the Commissioner issued pursuant to the provisions of this Article there shall be an appeal as provided in G.S. 58-2-75. (1981, c. 846, s. 1; 2003-262, s. 2(2).)

Editor's Note. — Sessions Laws 2003-262, s. 2(2), effective June 26, 2003, redesignated G.S. 58-39-80 through 58-39-125 as Part 2 of Article 39 of Chapter 58, under the heading "Enforcement, Sanctions, Remedies, and Rights."

§ 58-39-105. Individual remedies.

(a) If any insurance institution, agent, or insurance-support organization fails to comply with G.S. 58-39-45, 58-39-50, or 58-39-55 with respect to the rights granted under those sections, any person whose rights are violated may apply to the superior court in the county in which such person resides for appropriate equitable relief.

(b) An insurance institution, agent, or insurance-support organization that discloses information in violation of G.S. 58-39-75 shall be liable for damages sustained by the individual to whom the information relates. No individual, however, shall be entitled to a monetary award that exceeds the actual damages sustained by the individual as a result of a violation of G.S. 58-39-75.

(c) In any action brought pursuant to this section, the court may award the cost of the action and reasonable attorney's fees to the prevailing party.

(d) An action under this section must be brought within two years from the date the alleged violation is or should have been discovered.

(e) Except as specifically provided in this section, there shall be no remedy or recovery available to individuals for any occurrence that constitutes a violation of any provision of this Article. (1981, c. 846, s. 1; 2003-262, s. 2(2).)

Editor's Note. — Sessions Laws 2003-262, s. 2(2), effective June 26, 2003, redesignated G.S. 58-39-80 through 58-39-125 as Part 2 of Article 39 of Chapter 58, under the heading "Enforcement, Sanctions, Remedies, and Rights."

§ 58-39-110. Immunity.

No cause of action in the nature of defamation, invasion of privacy, or negligence shall arise against any person for disclosing personal or privileged information in accordance with this Article, nor shall such a cause of action arise against any person for furnishing personal or privileged information to an insurance institution, agent, or insurance-support organization: Provided, however, this section shall provide no immunity for disclosing or furnishing false information with malice or willful intent to injure any person. (1981, c. 846, s. 1; 2003-262, s. 2(2).)

Editor's Note. — Sessions Laws 2003-262, s. 2(2), effective June 26, 2003, redesignated G.S. 58-39-80 through 58-39-125 as Part 2 of Article 39 of Chapter 58, under the heading "Enforcement, Sanctions, Remedies, and Rights."

§ 58-39-115. Obtaining information under false pretenses.

Any person who knowingly and willfully obtains information about an individual from an insurance institution, agent, or insurance-support organization under false pretenses shall, upon conviction, be guilty of a Class 1 misdemeanor. (1981, c. 846, s. 1; 1985, c. 666, s. 33; 1993, c. 539, s. 465; 1994, Ex. Sess., c. 24, s. 14(c); 2003-262, s. 2(2).)

Editor's Note. — Sessions Laws 2003-262, s. 2(2), effective June 26, 2003, redesignated G.S. 58-39-80 through 58-39-125 as Part 2 of Article 39 of Chapter 58, under the heading "Enforcement, Sanctions, Remedies, and Rights."

§ 58-39-120. Rights.

The rights granted under G.S. 58-39-45, 58-39-50, and 58-39-75 shall take effect on July 1, 1982, regardless of the date of the collection or receipt of the information that is the subject of such sections. (1981, c. 846, s. 1; c. 1127, s. 56; 2003-262, s. 2(2).)

Editor's Note. — Sessions Laws 2003-262, s. 2(2), effective June 26, 2003, redesignated G.S. 58-39-80 through 58-39-125 as Part 2 of Article 39 of Chapter 58, under the heading "Enforcement, Sanctions, Remedies, and Rights."

§ 58-39-125. Powers of the Commissioner.

(a) The Commissioner shall have the power to examine and investigate into the affairs of every insurance institution or agent doing business in this State to determine whether the insurance institution or agent has been or is engaged in any conduct in violation of this Article.

(b) The Commissioner shall have the power to examine and investigate the affairs of every insurance-support organization that acts on behalf of an insurance institution or agent and that either (i) transacts business in this State, or (ii) transacts business outside this State and has an effect on a person residing in this State in order to determine whether such insurance-support organization has been or is engaged in any conduct in violation of this Article. (1981, c. 846, s. 1; 2003-262, ss. 2(1), 2(3).)

Editor's Note. — Session Laws 2003-262, s. 2(3), effective June 26, 2003, recodified former G.S. 58-39-70 as present 58-39-125.

Session Laws 2003-262, s. 2(2), effective June 26, 2003, redesignated G.S. 58-39-80 through 58-39-125 as Part 2 of Article 39 of Chapter 58, under the heading "Enforcement, Sanctions, Remedies, and Rights."

Part 3. Customer Information Safeguards.

§ 58-39-130. Purpose.

The purpose of this Part is to establish standards for developing and implementing administrative, technical, and physical safeguards to protect the security, confidentiality, and integrity of customer information, as required by sections 501, 505(b), and 507 of the federal Gramm-Leach-Bliley Act (Public Law 106-102), codified as 15 U.S.C. §§ 6801, 6805(b), and 6807. The purpose of this Part is also to provide privacy and security protection consistent with federal regulations governing the privacy and security of medical records when this Part is consistent with those federal regulations. In those instances in which this Part and the federal regulations are inconsistent and this Part provides privacy and security protection beyond that offered by the federal regulations, the purpose of this Part is to provide that additional privacy and security protection. (2003-262, s. 4.)

Editor's Note. — Session Laws 2003-262, s. 5, made this Part effective June 26, 2003.

§ 58-39-135. Scope.

The safeguards established under this Part apply to all customer information as defined in G.S. 58-39-140. (2003-262, s. 4.)

§ 58-39-140. Definitions.

As used in this Part, in addition to the definitions in G.S. 58-39-15:
    (1) "Customer" means an applicant with or policyholder of a licensee.
    (2) "Customer information" means nonpublic personal information about a customer, whether in paper, electronic, or other form that is maintained by or on behalf of the licensee.
    (3) "Customer information systems" means the electronic or physical methods used to access, collect, store, use, transmit, protect, or dispose of customer information.
    (4) "Licensee" means any producer, as defined in G.S. 58-33-10(7), insurer, MEWA, HMO, or service corporation governed by this Chapter. "Licensee" does not mean:
        a. An insurance-support organization.
        b. A licensee who is a natural person operating within the scope of the licensee's employment by or affiliation with an insurer or producer.
        c. A surplus lines insurer or licensee under Article 21 of this Chapter.
    (5) "Service provider" means a person that maintains, processes, or otherwise is permitted access to customer information through its provision of services directly to the licensee and includes an insurance support organization. (2003-262, s. 4.)

§ 58-39-145. Information security program.

Each licensee shall implement a comprehensive written information security program that includes administrative, technical, and physical safeguards for the protection of customer information. The administrative, technical, and physical safeguards included in the information security program shall be appropriate to the size and complexity of the licensee and the nature and scope of its activities. (2003-262, s. 4.)

§ 58-39-150. Objectives of information security program.

A licensee's information security program shall be designed to:
  (1) Ensure the security and confidentiality of customer information;
  (2) Protect against any anticipated threats or hazards to the security or integrity of the information; and
  (3) Protect against unauthorized access to or use of the information that could result in substantial harm or inconvenience to any customer. (2003-262, s. 4.)

§ 58-39-155. Rules.

The Commissioner may adopt rules that the Commissioner deems necessary to carry out the purposes of this Part, including rules that govern licensee oversight of service providers with which it contracts or has a relationship. (2003-262, s. 4.)

§ 58-39-160. Violation.

A violation of G.S. 58-39-145 or G.S. 58-39-150 subjects the violator to Part 2 of this Article. (2003-262, s. 4.)

§ 58-39-165. Effective date.

Each licensee shall establish an information security program, including appropriate policies and systems under this Part by April 1, 2005. (2003-262, s. 4.)

ARTICLE 40.

Regulation of Insurance Rates.

§ 58-40-1. Purposes.

The purposes of this Article are
  (1) To promote the public welfare by regulating rates to the end that they shall not be excessive, inadequate, or unfairly discriminatory;
  (2) To authorize the existence and operation of qualified rating organizations and advisory organizations and require that specified rating services of such rating organizations be generally available to all admitted insurers;
  (3) To encourage, as the most effective way to produce rates that conform to the standards of subsection (1) of this section, independent action by and reasonable price competition among insurers;
  (4) To authorize cooperative action among insurers in the rate-making process, and to regulate such cooperation in order to prevent practices that tend to bring about monopoly or to lessen or destroy competition; and
  (5) To encourage the most efficient and economic marketing practices. (1977, c. 828, s. 2.)

Cross References. — As to the North Carolina Rate Bureau, see G.S. 58-36-1 et seq.
Legal Periodicals. — For a survey of 1977 law on insurance, see 56 N.C.L. Rev. 1084 (1978).

The prohibition against discrimination in rates is directed to insurers, agents, brokers and other representatives of insurers. Hyde Ins. Agency, Inc. v. Dixie Leasing Corp., 26 N.C. App. 138, 215 S.E.2d 162 (1975) (decided under former statutory provisions).

Scope of Commissioner's Authority. — The authority of the commissioner to review, approve, modify, or disapprove insurance rates promulgated by the rate bureau is limited to that authority granted by the General Assembly. State ex rel. Comm'r of Ins. v. North Carolina Rate Bureau, 75 N.C. App. 201, 331 S.E.2d 124, cert. denied, 314 N.C. 547, 335 S.E.2d 319 (1985).

Cited in State ex rel. Comm'r of Ins. v. North Carolina Rate Bureau, 300 N.C. 381, 269 S.E.2d 547 (1980); Wysong & Miles Co. v. Employers of Wausau, 4 F. Supp. 2d 421 (M.D.N.C. 1998).

§ 58-40-5. Definitions.

As used in this Article:

(1) "Advisory organization" means every person, other than an admitted insurer, whether located within or outside this State, who prepares policy forms or makes underwriting rules incident to but not including the making of rates, or rating plans or rating systems, or which collects and furnishes to admitted insurers or rating organizations loss or expense statistics or other statistical information and data and acts in an advisory, as distinguished from a rate-making, capacity. No duly authorized attorney-at-law acting in the usual course of his profession shall be deemed to be an advisory organization.

(2) Repealed by Session Laws 1991, c. 720, s. 6.

(3) "Inland marine insurance" shall be deemed to include insurance now or hereafter defined by statute, or by interpretation thereof, or if not so defined or interpreted, by ruling of the Commissioner or as established by general custom of the business, as inland marine insurance.

(4) "Member," unless otherwise apparent from the context, means an insurer who participates in or is entitled to participate in the management of a rating, advisory or other organization.

(5) "Rating organization" means every person, other than an admitted insurer, whether located within or outside this State, who has as his object or purpose the making of rates, rating plans, or rating systems. Two or more insurers which act in concert for the purpose of making rates, rating plans, or rating systems, and which do not operate within the specific authorizations contained in G.S. 58-40-60, 58-40-65, 58-40-70 and 58-40-75, shall be deemed to be a rating organization. No single insurer shall be deemed to be a rating organization.

(6) "Subscriber," unless otherwise apparent from the context, means an insurer which is furnished at its request (i) with rates and rating manuals by a rating organization of which it is not a member, or (ii) with advisory services by an advisory organization of which it is not a member.

(7) "Willful" means in relation to an act or omission which constitutes a violation of this Article with actual knowledge or belief that such act or omission constitutes such violation and with specific intent to commit such violation.

(8), (9) Repealed by Session Laws 1987, c. 864, s. 66. (1977, c. 828, s. 2; 1987, c. 864, s. 66; 1991, c. 720, s. 6.)

Cited in State ex rel. Comm'r of Ins. v. North Carolina Auto. Rate Admin. Office, 294 N.C. 60, 241 S.E.2d 324 (1978).

§ 58-40-10. Other definitions.

As used in this Article and in Articles 36 and 37 of this Chapter:
  (1) "Private passenger motor vehicle" means:
    a. A motor vehicle of the private passenger or station wagon type that is owned or hired under a long-term contract by the policy named insured and that is neither used as a public or livery conveyance for passengers nor rented to others without a driver; or
    b. A motor vehicle that is a pickup truck or van that is owned by an individual or by husband and wife or individuals who are residents of the same household if it:
      1. Has a gross vehicle weight as specified by the manufacturer of less than 10,000 pounds; and
      2. Is not used for the delivery or transportation of goods or materials unless such use is (i) incidental to the insured's business of installing, maintaining, or repairing furnishings or equipment, or (ii) for farming or ranching.
      Such vehicles owned by a family farm copartnership or a family farm corporation shall be considered owned by an individual for the purposes of this section; or
    c. A motorcycle, motorized scooter or other similar motorized vehicle not used for commercial purposes.
  (2) "Nonfleet" motor vehicle means a motor vehicle not eligible for classification as a fleet vehicle for the reason that the motor vehicle is one of four or fewer motor vehicles hired under a long-term contract or owned by the insured named in the policy. (1987, c. 864, s. 67; 1989, c. 789, s. 1; 1995, c. 517, s. 25; 1995 (Reg. Sess., 1996), c. 730, s. 1.)

Private Passenger Motor Vehicle. — Low-boy trailer and Mack truck were not private passenger motor vehicles as they did not have a pickup body and were not delivery sedans nor panel trucks. Nationwide Mut. Ins. Co. v. Mabe, 342 N.C. 482, 467 S.E.2d 34 (1996).

"Nonfleet." — Fire vehicles listed in policy were private passenger vehicles not used in insured's business and hence "nonfleet" vehicles to which the exception to intrapolicy stacking of G.S. 20-279.21(b)(4) as it read prior to 1991 did not apply. McCaskill v. Pennsylvania Nat'l Mut. Cas. Ins. Co., 118 N.C. App. 320, 454 S.E.2d 842 (1995).

Summary judgment was inappropriate where a genuine issue of material fact existed as to the whether the policy covering a dump truck met any of the statutory definitions of a "private passenger motor vehicle" under this section and could be stacked with the other policies under G.S. 20-279.21(b)(4); the parties disputed the characteristics and weight of the truck. Erwin v. Tweed, 142 N.C. App. 643, 544 S.E.2d 803, 2001 N.C. App. LEXIS 175 (2001), review denied, 353 N.C. 724, 551 S.E.2d 437 (2001).

Vehicles owned by a family farm trust shall be treated as individually owned for insurance purposes. Erwin v. Tweed, 142 N.C. App. 643, 544 S.E.2d 803, 2001 N.C. App. LEXIS 175 (2001), review denied, 353 N.C. 724, 551 S.E.2d 437 (2001).

Cited in Sutton v. Aetna Cas. & Sur. Co., 325 N.C. 259, 382 S.E.2d 759 (1989); Aetna Cas. & Sur. Co. v. Fields, 105 N.C. App. 563, 414 S.E.2d 69 (1992); Hendrickson v. Lee, 119 N.C. App. 444, 459 S.E.2d 275 (1995).

§ 58-40-15. Scope of application.

The provisions of this Article shall apply to all insurance on risks or on operations in this State, except:

(1) Reinsurance, other than joint reinsurance to the extent stated in G.S. 58-40-60;

(2) Any policy of insurance against loss or damage to or legal liability in connection with property located outside this State, or any motor vehicle or aircraft principally garaged and used outside of this State, or any activity wholly carried on outside this State;

(3) Insurance of vessels or craft, their cargoes, marine builders' risks, marine protection and indemnity, or other risks commonly insured under marine, as distinguished from inland marine, insurance policies;

(4) Accident, health, or life insurance;

(5) Annuities;

(6) Repealed by Session Laws 1985, c. 666, s. 43.

(7) Mortgage guaranty insurance;

(8) Workers' compensation and employers' liability insurance written in connection therewith;

(9) For private passenger (nonfleet) motor vehicle liability insurance, automobile medical payments insurance, uninsured motorists' coverage and other insurance coverages written in connection with the sale of such liability insurance;

(10) Theft of or physical damage to nonfleet private passenger motor vehicles; except this Article applies to insurance against theft of or physical damage to motorcycles, as defined in G.S. 20-4.01(27)d.; and

(11) Insurance against loss to residential real property with not more than four housing units located in this State or any contents thereof or valuable interest therein and other insurance coverages written in connection with the sale of such property insurance. Provided, however, that this Article shall apply to insurance against loss to farm dwellings, farm buildings and their appurtenant structures, farm personal property and other coverages written in connection with farm real or personal property; travel or camper trailers designed to be pulled by private passenger motor vehicles unless insured under policies covering nonfleet private passenger motor vehicles; residential real and personal property insured in multiple line insurance policies covering business activities as the primary insurable interest; and marine, general liability, burglary and theft, glass, and animal collision insurance except when such coverages are written as an integral part of a multiple line insurance policy for which there is an indivisible premium.

The provisions of this Article shall not apply to hospital service or medical service corporations, investment companies, mutual benefit associations, or fraternal beneficiary associations. (1977, c. 828, s. 2; 1979, c. 714, s. 2; 1981, c. 888, s. 5; 1985, c. 666, s. 43; 1991, c. 339, s. 2; 2001-389, s. 5.)

Editor's Note. — Session Laws 2001-389, s. 6, provided: "This act becomes effective January 1, 2002. Rates, rating systems, territories, classifications, and policy forms lawfully in use on January 1, 2002, may continue to be used thereafter."

Effect of Amendments. — Session Laws 2001-389, s. 5, effective January 1, 2002, in subdivision (10), substituted "nonfleet private passenger" for "private passenger (nonfleet)," and added "except this Article applies to insurance against theft of or physical damage to motorcycles, as defined in G.S. 20-4.01(27)d."

The Commissioner did not have the statutory authority to withhold approval of an 11.7% rate increase for farmowner insurance coverages subject to the rate bureau's jurisdiction on the condition that the insurance service office file for a rate decrease for farmowner insurance coverages not subject to the rate bureau's jurisdiction. State ex rel. Comm'r of Ins. v. North Carolina Rate Bureau, 75 N.C. App. 201, 331 S.E.2d 124, cert. denied, 314 N.C. 547, 335 S.E.2d 319 (1985).

Cited in Harleysville Mut. Ins. Co. v. Packer, 60 F.3d 1116 (4th Cir. 1995).

§ 58-40-20. Rate standards.

(a) In order to serve the public interest, rates shall not be excessive, inadequate, or unfairly discriminatory.

(b), (c) Repealed by Session Laws 1985 (Regular Session, 1986), c. 1027, s. 10.

(d) No rate is inadequate unless the rate is unreasonably low for the insurance provided and the use or continued use of the rate by the insurer has had or will have the effect of:

(1) Endangering the solvency of the insurer; or

(2) Destroying competition; or

(3) Creating a monopoly; or

(4) Violating actuarial principles, practices, or soundness.

(e) A rate is not unfairly discriminatory in relation to another in the same class if it reflects equitably the differences in expected losses and expenses. Rates are not unfairly discriminatory because different premiums result for policyholders with like loss exposures but different expense factors, or like expense factors but different loss exposures, as long as the rates reflect the differences with reasonable accuracy. Rates are not unfairly discriminatory if they are averaged broadly among persons insured under a group, franchise, or blanket policy. (1977, c. 828, s. 2; 1985 (Reg. Sess., 1986), c. 1027, ss. 9.1, 10, 11.)

Cited in State ex rel. Comm'r of Ins. v. North Carolina Rate Bureau, 300 N.C. 381, 269 S.E.2d 547 (1980); Mackey v. Nationwide Ins. Cos., 724 F.2d 419 (4th Cir. 1984); Wysong & Miles Co. v. Employers of Wausau, 4 F. Supp. 2d 421 (M.D.N.C. 1998).

§ 58-40-25. Rating methods.

In determining whether rates comply with the standards under G.S. 58-40-20, the following criteria shall be applied:

(1) Due consideration shall be given to past and prospective loss and expense experience within this State, to catastrophe hazards, to a reasonable margin for underwriting profit and contingencies, to trends within this State, to dividends or savings to be allowed or returned by insurers to their policyholders, members, or subscribers, and to all other relevant factors, including judgment factors; however, regional or countrywide expense or loss experience and other regional or countrywide data may be considered only when credible North Carolina expense or loss experience or other data is not available.

(2) Risks may be grouped by classifications for the establishment of rates and minimum premiums. Classification rates may be modified to produce rates for individual risks in accordance with rating plans which establish standards for measuring variations in hazards or expense provisions, or both. Those standards may measure any

differences among risks that have probable effect upon losses or expenses. Classifications or modifications of classifications of risks may be established based upon size, expense, management, individual experience, location or dispersion of hazard, or any other reasonable considerations. Those classifications and modifications shall apply to all risks under the same or substantially the same circumstances or conditions.

(3) The expense provisions included in the rates to be used by an insurer may reflect the operating methods of the insurer and, as far as it is credible, its own expense experience.

(4) In the case of property insurance rates under this Article, consideration shall be given to the insurance public protection classifications of fire districts established by the Commissioner. The Commissioner shall establish and modify from time to time insurance public protection districts for all rural areas of the State and for cities with populations of 100,000 or fewer, according to the most recent annual population estimates certified by the State Planning Officer. In establishing and modifying these districts, the Commissioner shall use standards at least equivalent to those used by the Insurance Services Office, Inc., or any successor organization. The standards developed by the Commissioner are subject to Article 2A of Chapter 150B of the General Statutes. The insurance public protection classifications established by the Commissioner issued pursuant to the provisions of this Article shall be subject to appeal as provided in G.S. 58-2-75, et seq. The exceptions stated in G.S. 58-2-75(a) do not apply. (1977, c. 828, s. 2; 1985 (Reg. Sess., 1986), c. 1027, s. 16; 1991, c. 644, s. 40; 2000-176, s. 2.)

Editor's Note. — Session Laws 2000-176, s. 3, makes the act is effective August 2, 2000, and provides that any changes to classifications of insurance public protection districts issued by the Commissioner pursuant to this act shall become effective no sooner than 90 days after the standards for public protection district classifications are adopted by the Department and shall apply to insurance policies issued or renewed on or after that date.

CASE NOTES

Editor's Note. — *The cases below were decided under prior statutory provisions.*

Consideration of Past Experience. — When a filing is made the ratemaker must, of necessity, estimate what will happen in the future. The natural guide is past experience, and former G.S. 58-248 specifically provided for consideration of factors relating to past experience. State ex rel. Comm'r of Ins. v. North Carolina Auto. Rate Admin. Office, 292 N.C. 1, 231 S.E.2d 867 (1977).

Former § 58-248 contemplated a trending method which, on the basis of trends in past loss experience, projected the losses to be anticipated during the future period in which the proposed rates would be in effect. State ex rel. Comm'r of Ins. v. North Carolina Auto. Rate Admin. Office, 292 N.C. 1, 231 S.E.2d 867 (1977).

§ 58-40-30. Filing of rates and supporting data.

(a) With the exception of inland marine insurance that is not written according to manual rates and rating plans, every admitted insurer and every licensed rating organization, which has been designated by any insurer for the filing of rates under G.S. 58-40-40, shall file with the Commissioner all rates and all changes and amendments thereto made by it for use in this State prior to the time they become effective.

(b) The Commissioner may require the filing of supporting data including:

(1) The experience and judgment of the filer, and to the extent the filer wishes or the Commissioner requires, of other insurers or rating organizations;

(2) The filer's interpretation of any statistical data relied upon; and

(3) Descriptions of the methods employed in setting the rates.

(c) Upon written consent of the insured stating the insured's reasons, a rate or deductible or both in excess of that provided by an otherwise applicable filing may be used on a specific risk, in accordance with rules adopted by the Commissioner. The insurer is not required to obtain the written consent of the insured on any renewal of or endorsement to the policy if the policy renewal or endorsement states that the rates or deductible, or both, are greater than those rates or deductibles, or both, that are applicable in the State of North Carolina. The insurer shall retain the signed consent form and other policy information for each insured and make this information available to the Commissioner, upon request of the Commissioner.

(d) This section and G.S. 58-41-50 shall be construed in pari materia. (1977, c. 828, s. 2; 1985 (Reg. Sess., 1986), c. 1027, s. 17; 1987, c. 441, s. 8; 1995 (Reg. Sess., 1996), c. 668, s. 2.)

CASE NOTES

Cited in State ex rel. Comm'r of Ins. v. North Carolina Rate Bureau, 300 N.C. 381, 269 S.E.2d 547 (1980); Wysong & Miles Co. v. Employers of Wausau, 4 F. Supp. 2d 421 (M.D.N.C. 1998).

§ 58-40-35. Filing open to inspection.

Each filing and supporting data filed under this Article shall, as soon as filed, be open to public inspection at any reasonable time. Copies may be obtained by any person on request and upon payment of a reasonable charge therefor. (1977, c. 828, s. 2.)

§ 58-40-40. Delegation of rate making and rate filing obligation.

(a) An insurer may itself establish rates based on the factors in G.S. 58-40-25 or it may use rates prepared by a rating organization, with average expense factors determined by the rating organization or with such modification for its own expense and loss experience as the credibility of that experience allows.

(b) An insurer may discharge its obligation under G.S. 58-40-30 by giving notice to the Commissioner that it uses rates prepared by a designated rating organization, with such information about modifications thereof as are necessary to fully inform the Commissioner. The insurer's rates shall be those filed from time to time by the rating organization, including any amendments thereto as filed, subject, however, to the modifications filed by the insurer. (1977, c. 828, s. 2.)

CASE NOTES

Cited in State ex rel. Comm'r of Ins. v. North Carolina Rate Bureau, 300 N.C. 381, 269 S.E.2d 547 (1980); Hendrickson v. Lee, 119 N.C. App. 444, 459 S.E.2d 275 (1995).

§ 58-40-45. Disapproval of rates; interim use of rates.

(a) If, after a hearing, the Commissioner disapproves a rate, he must issue an order specifying in what respects the rate fails to meet the requirements of G.S. 58-40-20. If the Commissioner finds a rate to be excessive, he shall order the excess premium, plus interest at a rate determined in the same manner as in G.S. 58-36-25(b) as of the dates such rates were effective for policyholders, to be refunded to those policyholders who have paid the excess premium. If the Commissioner finds a rate to be unfairly discriminatory, he shall order an appropriate adjustment for policyholders who have paid the unfairly discriminatory premium. The order must be issued within 30 business days after the close of the hearing.

(b) Whenever a rate of an insurer is held to be unfairly discriminatory or excessive and the rate is deemed no longer effective by order of the Commissioner issued under subsection (a) of this section, the insurer shall have the option to continue to use the rate for the interim period pending judicial review of the order, provided that the insurer shall place in an escrow account approved by the Commissioner the purported unfairly discriminatory or excessive portion of the premium collected during the interim period. The court, upon a final determination, shall order the escrowed funds or any overcharge in the interim rates to be distributed appropriately, except that refunds to policyholders that are de minimis shall not be required.

(c) No person shall willfully withhold information required by this Article from or knowingly furnish false or misleading information to the Commissioner, any statistical agency designated by the Commissioner, any rating or advisory organization, or any insurer, which information will affect the rates, rating plans, classifications, or policy forms subject to this Article. (1977, c. 828, s. 2; 1985 (Reg. Sess., 1986), c. 1027, ss. 12, 12.1.)

CASE NOTES

Editor's Note. — *Some of the cases below were decided under prior statutory provisions.*

The Rate Office and the Commissioner possess only such respective powers as are granted by the General Assembly. State ex rel. Comm'r of Ins. v. North Carolina Auto. Rate Admin. Office, 292 N.C. 1, 231 S.E.2d 867 (1977).

The Commissioner has the duty to consider rate proposals in accordance with statutory standards and has no authority merely to accept a proposal as being true and accurate for purposes of entering an interim order. State ex rel. Comm'r of Ins. v. North Carolina Auto. Rate Admin. Office, 287 N.C. 192, 214 S.E.2d 98 (1975).

Cited in State ex rel. Comm'r of Ins. v. North Carolina Auto. Rate Admin. Office, 294 N.C. 60, 241 S.E.2d 324 (1978); State ex rel. Comm'r of Ins. v. North Carolina Rate Bureau, 300 N.C. 381, 269 S.E.2d 547 (1980); Wysong & Miles Co. v. Employers of Wausau, 4 F. Supp. 2d 421 (M.D.N.C. 1998).

§ 58-40-50. Rating organizations.

(a) No rating organization shall provide any service relating to rates subject to this Article and no insurer shall utilize the service of such organization for such purpose unless the organization has obtained a license from the Commissioner.

(b) No rating organization shall refuse to supply any services for which it is licensed in this State to any insurer admitted to do business in this State and offering to pay the fair and usual compensation for the services.

(c) A rating organization applying for a license shall include with its application:

(1) A copy of its constitution, charter, articles of organization, agreement, association, or incorporation, and a copy of its bylaws, plan of

operation, and any other rules or regulations governing the conduct of its business;

(2) A list of its members and subscribers;

(3) The name and address of one or more residents of this State upon whom notices, process affecting it, or orders of the Commissioner may be served;

(4) A statement showing its technical qualifications for acting in the capacity for which it seeks a license; and

(5) Any other relevant information and documents that the Commissioner may require.

(d) If the Commissioner finds that the applicant and the natural persons through whom it acts are qualified to provide the services proposed, and that all requirements of law are met, he shall issue a license specifying the authorized activity of the applicant. He shall not issue a license if the proposed activity would tend to create a monopoly or to lessen or to destroy price competition. Licenses issued pursuant to this section shall remain in effect until the licensee withdraws from the State or until the license is suspended or revoked.

(e) Any change in or amendment to any document required to be filed under this section shall be promptly filed with the Commissioner.

(f) Every rating organization providing services in this State on September 1, 1977, may continue to provide services thereafter as a rating organization, subject to the provisions of this Article and pending its application to the Commissioner for a license to provide services as a rating organization, which application shall be made within 30 days after September 1, 1977. (1977, c. 828, s. 2.)

§ 58-40-55. Advisory organizations.

(a) No advisory organization shall conduct its operations in this State unless and until it has obtained a license from and filed with the Commissioner:

(1) A copy of its constitution, articles of incorporation, agreement, or association, and of its bylaws, or rules and regulations governing its activities, all duly certified by the custodian of the originals thereof;

(2) A list of its members and subscribers; and

(3) The name and address of a resident of this State upon whom notices, process affecting it, or orders of the Commissioner may be served.

(b) Any change in or amendment to any document required to be filed under this section shall be promptly filed with the Commissioner.

(c) No advisory organization shall engage in any unfair or unreasonable practice with respect to its activities. (1977, c. 828, s. 2; 1985 (Reg. Sess., 1986), c. 1027, s. 47; 1987, c. 441, s. 11.)

§ 58-40-60. Joint underwriting and joint reinsurance organizations.

(a) Every group, association, or other organization of insurers which engages in joint underwriting or joint reinsurance through such group, association, or organization, or by standing agreement among the members thereof, shall obtain a license from and file with the Commissioner:

(1) A copy of its constitution, articles of incorporation, agreement, or association, and bylaws;

(2) A list of its members; and

(3) The name and address of a resident of this State upon whom notices, process affecting it, or orders of the Commissioner may be served.

(b) Any change in or amendment to any document required to be filed under this section shall be promptly filed with the Commissioner.

(c) If after a hearing, the Commissioner finds that any activity or practice of any such group, association, or other organization is unfair, unreasonable, or otherwise inconsistent with the provisions of this Article, he may issue a written order specifying in what respects the activity or practice is unfair, unreasonable, or otherwise inconsistent with the provisions of this Article, and requiring the discontinuance of the activity or practice. (1977, c. 828, s. 2; 1985 (Reg. Sess., 1986), c. 1027, s. 48; 1987, c. 441, s. 12; c. 864, s. 71.)

§ 58-40-65. Insurers authorized to act in concert.

Subject to and in compliance with the provisions of Articles 1 through 64 of this Chapter authorizing insurers to be members or subscribers of rating or advisory organizations or to engage in joint underwriting or joint reinsurance, two or more insurers may act in concert with each other and with others with respect to any matters pertaining to the making of rates or rating systems, the preparation or making of insurance policy or bond forms, underwriting rules, surveys, inspections and investigations, the furnishing of loss or expense statistics or other information and data, the creation, administration, or termination of a market assistance program, or carrying on of research. (1977, c. 828, s. 2; 1986, Ex. Sess., c. 7, s. 9; 1987, c. 731, s. 1.)

§ 58-40-70. Insurers authorized to act in concert; admitted insurers with common ownership or management; matters relating to co-surety bonds.

With respect to any matters pertaining to the making of rates or rating systems, the preparation or making of insurance policy or bond forms, underwriting rules, surveys, inspections and investigations, the furnishing of loss or expense statistics or other information and data, or carrying on of research, two or more admitted insurers having a common ownership or operating in this State under common management or control, are hereby authorized to act in concert between or among themselves the same as if they constituted a single insurer. To the extent that such matters relate to co-surety bonds, two or more admitted insurers executing co-surety bonds are authorized to act in concert between or among themselves the same as if they constituted a single insurer. (1977, c. 828, s. 2.)

§ 58-40-75. Agreements to adhere.

No insurer shall assume any obligation to any person, other than a policyholder or other insurers with which it is under common control or management or is a member of a market assistance program or of a joint underwriting or joint reinsurance organization, to use or adhere to certain rates or rules; and no other person shall impose any penalty or other adverse consequence for failure of an insurer to adhere to certain rates or rules. This section does not apply to mandatory or voluntary risk sharing plans established under Article 42 of this Chapter or apportionment agreements among insurers approved by the Commissioner pursuant to G.S. 58-40-95. Provided, however, that members and subscribers of rating or advisory organizations may use the rates, rating systems, underwriting rules, or policy or bond forms of such organizations either consistently or intermittently. The fact that two or more admitted insurers, whether or not members or subscribers of a rating or advisory organization, consistently or intermittently use the rates or rating systems made or adopted by a rating organization, or the underwriting rules or policy or bond forms prepared by a rating or advisory organization, shall not be sufficient in itself to support a finding that an agreement to so adhere exists, and it may be used only for the purpose of supplementing or explaining direct evidence of the existence of any such agreement. (1977, c. 828, s. 2; 1986, Ex. Sess., c. 7, ss. 10, 11; 1987, c. 731, s. 1.)

§ 58-40-80. Exchange of information or experience data; consultation with rating organizations and insurers.

Rating organizations licensed pursuant to G.S. 58-40-50 and admitted insurers are authorized to exchange information and experience data between and among themselves in this State and with rating organizations and insurers in other states and may consult with them with respect to rate making and the application of rating systems. (1977, c. 828, s. 2.)

§ 58-40-85. Recording and reporting of experience.

The Commissioner shall promulgate or approve reasonable rules, including rules providing statistical plans, for use thereafter by all insurers in the recording and reporting of loss and expense experience, in order that the experience of such insurers may be made available to him. No insurer shall be required to record or report its experience on a classification basis inconsistent with its own rating system. The Commissioner may designate one or more rating organizations to assist him in gathering and making compilations of such experience. (1977, c. 828, s. 2.)

§ 58-40-90. Examination of rating, joint underwriting, and joint reinsurance organizations.

The Commissioner shall, at least once every three years, make or cause to be made an examination of each rating organization licensed pursuant to G.S. 58-40-50 and each advisory organization licensed pursuant to G.S. 58-40-55. The Commissioner may, as often as deemed expedient, make or cause to be made, an examination of each group, association, or other organization referred to in G.S. 58-40-60. This examination shall relate only to the activities conducted pursuant to this Article and to the organizations licensed under this Article. The officers, manager, agents and employees of any such organization may be examined at any time under oath and shall exhibit all books, records, accounts, documents or agreements governing its method of operation. In lieu of any such examination, the Commissioner may accept the report of an examination made by the insurance advisory official of another state, pursuant to the laws of that state. (1977, c. 828, s. 2; 1995, c. 360, s. 2(b); 1995 (Reg. Sess., 1996), c. 742, s. 26.)

§ 58-40-95. Apportionment agreements among insurers.

Agreements may be made between or among insurers with respect to equitable apportionment among them of insurance which may be afforded applicants who are in good faith entitled to but who are unable to procure such insurance through ordinary methods. The insurers may agree between or among themselves on the use of reasonable rate modifications for such insurance, agreements, and rate modifications to be subject to the approval of the Commissioner. (1977, c. 828, s. 2.)

§ 58-40-100. Request for review of rate, rating plan, rating system or underwriting rule.

(a) Any person aggrieved by any rate charged, rating plan, rating system, or underwriting rule followed or adopted by an insurer or rating organization may request the insurer or rating organization to review the manner in which the rate, plan, system, or rule has been applied with respect to insurance afforded him. Such request may be made by his authorized representative, and shall be in writing. If the request is not granted within 30 days after it is made, the requestor may treat it as rejected. Any person aggrieved by the action of an insurer or rating organization in refusing the review requested or in failing or refusing to grant all or part of the relief requested, may file a written complaint and request for hearing with the Commissioner, and shall specify the grounds relied upon. If the Commissioner has information concerning a similar complaint he may deny the hearing. If the Commissioner believes that probable cause for the complaint does not exist or that the complaint is not made in good faith, he shall deny the hearing. If the Commissioner finds that the complaint charges a violation of this Article and that the complainant would be aggrieved if the violation is proven, he shall proceed as provided in G.S. 58-2-50 or 58-2-70.

(b) Repealed by Session Laws 1985 (Regular Session, 1986), c. 1027, s. 15. (1977, c. 828, s. 2; 1985, c. 733, s. 3; 1985 (Reg. Sess., 1986), c. 1027, s. 15; 1987, c. 441, s. 13.)

§ 58-40-105. Hearing and judicial review.

(a) Any insurer, person, or organization to which the Commissioner has directed an order or decision made without a hearing may, within 30 days after notice to it of the order or decision, make written request to the Commissioner for a hearing thereon. The Commissioner shall hear the party or parties within 20 days after receipt of the request and shall give not less than 10 days' written notice of the time and place of hearing. Within 15 days after the hearing, the Commissioner shall affirm, reverse, or modify his previous action, and specify his reasons therefor. Pending such hearing and decision thereon, the Commissioner may suspend or postpone the effective date of his previous action.

(b) Any order or decision of the Commissioner shall be subject to judicial review as provided in Article 2 of this Chapter. (1977, c. 828, s. 2.)

CASE NOTES

Cited in State ex rel. Comm'r of Ins. v. North Carolina Rate Bureau, 300 N.C. 381, 269 S.E.2d 547 (1980).

§ 58-40-110. Suspension of license.

(a) Repealed by Session Laws 1985, c. 666, s. 36.

(b) The Commissioner may suspend the license of any rating organization or insurer that fails to comply with an order of the Commissioner within the time limited by such order, or within any extension thereof that the Commissioner may grant. The Commissioner shall not suspend the license of any rating organization or insurer for failure to comply with an order until the time prescribed for an appeal therefrom has expired or, if an appeal has been taken, until such order has been affirmed. The Commissioner may determine when a suspension of a license shall become effective, and such suspension shall remain in effect for the period fixed by him unless he modifies or rescinds such suspension, or until the order upon which such suspension is based is modified, rescinded, or reversed.

(c) No license shall be suspended except upon a written order of the Commissioner stating his findings, made after a hearing held upon not less than 10 days' written notice to such person or organization, and specifying the alleged violation. (1977, c. 828, s. 2; 1985, c. 666, s. 36.)

§ 58-40-115. Existing rates, rating systems, territories, classifications and policy forms.

Rates, rating systems, territories, classifications, and policy forms lawfully in use on September 1, 1977, may continue to be used thereafter, notwithstanding any provision of this Article. (1977, c. 828, s. 2.)

§ 58-40-120. Payment of dividends not prohibited or regulated; plan for payment into rating system.

Nothing in this Article shall be construed to prohibit or regulate the payment of dividends, savings, or unabsorbed premium deposits allowed or returned by insurers to their policyholders, members, or subscribers. A plan for the payment of dividends, savings, or unabsorbed premium deposits allowed or returned by insurers to their policyholders, members, or subscribers shall not be deemed a rating plan or system. (1977, c. 828, s. 2.)

§ 58-40-125. Limitation.

Nothing in this Article shall apply to any town or county farmers mutual fire insurance association restricting its operations to not more than six adjacent counties in this State, or to domestic insurance companies, associations, orders or fraternal benefit societies now doing business in this State on the assessment plan. (1977, c. 828, s. 2; 1985 (Reg. Sess., 1986), c. 1013, s. 10.1; 1989, c. 485, s. 53.)

§ 58-40-130. Financial disclosure; rate modifications; reporting requirements.

(a) The Commissioner may require each insurer subject to this Article to report, on a form prescribed by the Commissioner, its loss and expense experience, investment income, administrative expenses, and other data that he may require, for kinds of insurance or classes of risks that he designates. These reports are in addition to financial or other statements required by Articles 1 through 64 of this Chapter.

(b) The Commissioner may designate one or more rating organizations or advisory organizations to gather and compile the experience and data referred to in subsection (a) of this section for their member companies.

(c) Whereas the provisions enacted by the General Assembly in 1986 regarding modifications in North Carolina civil law may have a prospective effect upon the loss experience of insurers subject to this Article, the Commissioner is authorized to review each company's rates by type of insurance that are in effect on and after January 1, 1987, and, when and where appropriate, require modification of such rates.

(d) Each insurer subject to this Article shall record the experience and data referred to in subsection (a) of this section arising from causes of action arising against its insureds on and after January 1, 1987. Such experience and data shall be reported to the Commissioner by March 31, 1988, which report shall be on a form prescribed by the Commissioner reflecting such experience and data for the one-year period beginning on January 1, 1987. Subsequently, such experience and data shall be reported to the Commissioner by March 31 of each year for each one-year period ending on December 31 of the previous year.

(e) On or before July 1, 1988, and annually thereafter, the Commissioner shall report to the General Assembly the effects, if any, of changes in North Carolina civil law statutes on the experience of insurers subject to this section. (1985 (Reg. Sess., 1986), c. 1027, c. 13.)

§ 58-40-135. Good faith immunity for operation of market assistance programs.

There is no liability on the part of and no cause of action of any nature arises against any director, administrator, or employee of a market assistance program, or the Commissioner or his representatives, for any acts or omissions taken by them in creation or operation of a market assistance program. The immunity established by this section does not extend to willful neglect, malfeasance, bad faith, fraud, or malice that would otherwise make an act or omission actionable. (1985 (Reg. Sess., 1986), c. 1027, s. 28.)

§ 58-40-140. Extended reporting.

(a) Any policy for commercial general liability coverage or professional liability insurance wherein the insurer offers, and the insured elects to purchase, an extended reporting period for claims arising during the expiring policy period must provide:

(1) That in the event of a cancellation permitted by G.S. 58-41-15 or nonrenewal effective under G.S. 58-41-20, there shall be a 30-day period after the effective date of the cancellation or nonrenewal during which the insured may elect to purchase coverage for the extended reporting period.

(2) That the limit of liability in the policy aggregate for the extended reporting period shall be one hundred percent (100%) of the expiring policy aggregate that was in effect at the inception of the policy.

(3) Within 45 days after the mailing or delivery of the written request of the insured, the insurer shall mail or deliver the following loss information covering a three-year period:

    a. Aggregate information on total closed claims, including date and description of occurrence, and any paid losses;

    b. Aggregate information on total open claims, including date and description of occurrence, and amounts of any payments;

    c. Information on notice of any occurrence, including date and description of occurrence.

(b) In the event of a cancellation or nonrenewal of a health care provider's professional liability insurance policy by the insured or by the insurer, as permitted by G.S. 58-41-15 or G.S. 58-41-20, except for nonpayment of premium, there shall be a 30-day period after the effective date of the cancellation or nonrenewal during which the insured may elect to obtain an endorsement providing an extended reporting period of unlimited duration covering claims first reported during the extended reporting period and arising from the acts, errors, or omissions committed during the policy period and otherwise covered by the policy.

(c) An unlimited extended reporting period for health care provider professional liability claims must be provided if the insured: (i) dies; (ii) becomes permanently disabled and is unable to carry out his or her profession or practice; or (iii) retires permanently from his or her profession or practice after attaining the age of 65 and accumulating five or more consecutive years of claims-made coverage. (1985 (Reg. Sess., 1986), c. 1013, s. 17; c. 1027, s. 29; 1993, c. 409, s. 9; 1993 (Reg. Sess., 1994), c. 678, s. 21; 1999-294, s. 2.)

ARTICLE 41.

Insurance Regulatory Reform Act.

§ 58-41-1. Short title.

This Article is known and may be cited as the Insurance Regulatory Reform Act. (1985 (Reg. Sess., 1986), c. 1027, s. 14.)

§ 58-41-5. Legislative findings and intent.

(a) Due to conditions in national and international property and liability insurance markets, insureds in the United States have experienced unprecedented in-term cancellations of existing policies for entire books of business, have been afforded little or no notice that existing policies would not be renewed at their expiration dates, or would be renewed only at substantially higher rates or on less favorable terms. The General Assembly finds that such conditions pose an imminent peril to the public welfare for the following reasons:

(1) In-term cancellations of insurance coverages erode insureds' confidence and breach insureds' trust; unfairly and prematurely terminate the promised coverage; force persons to go without needed insurance protection or force the procurement of substitute insurance at greater cost; and create marketplace confusion resulting in product unavailability.

(2) Failures to provide timely notices of nonrenewals or of renewals with altered terms deprive persons of adequate opportunities to secure affordable replacement coverages or require persons to go without needed insurance protection.

(b) The General Assembly finds that there is no uniform requirement for the notice of cancellation, renewal, or nonrenewal for commercial property and liability insurance and that it should adopt reasonable requirements for such notices and should regulate in-term cancellations of entire books of business by companies. (1985 (Reg. Sess., 1986), c. 1027, s. 14.)

§ 58-41-10. Scope.

(a) Except as otherwise provided, this Article applies to all kinds of insurance authorized by G.S. 58-7-15(4) through (14) and G.S. 58-7-15(18) through (22), and to all insurance companies licensed by the Commissioner to write those kinds of insurance. This Article does not apply to insurance written under Articles 21, 26, 36, 37, 45 or 46 of this Chapter; insurance written for residential risks in conjunction with insurance written under Article 36 of this Chapter; to marine insurance as defined in G.S. 58-40-15(3); to personal inland marine insurance; to commercial aircraft insurance; to policies issued in this State covering risks with multistate locations, except with respect to coverages applicable to locations within this State; to any town or county farmers mutual fire insurance association restricting its operations to not more than six adjacent counties in this State; nor to domestic insurance companies, associations, orders, or fraternal benefit societies doing business in this State on the assessment plan.

(b) This Article is not exclusive, and the Commissioner may also consider other provisions of Articles 1 through 64 of this Chapter to be applicable to the circumstances or situations addressed in this Article. Policies may provide terms more favorable to insureds than are required by this Article. The rights provided by this Article are in addition to and do not prejudice any other rights the insured may have at common law, under statutes, or under administrative rules. (1985 (Reg. Sess., 1986), c. 1027, s. 14; 1987, c. 441, ss. 1, 2; 1989 c. 485, s. 53; 1993, c. 409, s. 21; 1993 (Reg. Sess., 1994), c. 678, s. 22; 1999-219, s. 5.2; 1999-294, s. 1.)

§ 58-41-15. Certain policy cancellations prohibited.

(a) No insurance policy or renewal thereof may be cancelled by the insurer prior to the expiration of the term or anniversary date stated in the policy and without the prior written consent of the insured, except for any one of the following reasons:

    (1) Nonpayment of premium in accordance with the policy terms;

    (2) An act or omission by the insured or his representative that constitutes material misrepresentation or nondisclosure of a material fact in obtaining the policy, continuing the policy, or presenting a claim under the policy;

    (3) Increased hazard or material change in the risk assumed that could not have been reasonably contemplated by the parties at the time of assumption of the risk;

    (4) Substantial breach of contractual duties, conditions, or warranties that materially affects the insurability of the risk;

    (5) A fraudulent act against the company by the insured or his representative that materially affects the insurability of the risk;

    (6) Willful failure by the insured or his representative to institute reasonable loss control measures that materially affect the insurability of the risk after written notice by the insurer;

    (7) Loss of facultative reinsurance, or loss of or substantial changes in applicable reinsurance as provided in G.S. 58-41-30;

    (8) Conviction of the insured of a crime arising out of acts that materially affect the insurability of the risk; or

    (9) A determination by the Commissioner that the continuation of the policy would place the insurer in violation of the laws of this State;

   (10) The named insured fails to meet the requirements contained in the corporate charter, articles of incorporation, or bylaws of the insurer, when the insurer is a company organized for the sole purpose of providing members of an organization with insurance coverage in this State.

(b) Any cancellation permitted by subsection (a) of this section is not effective unless written notice of cancellation has been delivered or mailed to the insured, not less than 15 days before the proposed effective date of cancellation. The notice must be given or mailed to the insured, and any designated mortgagee or loss payee at their addresses shown in the policy or, if not indicated in the policy, at their last known addresses. The notice must state the precise reason for cancellation. Proof of mailing is sufficient proof of notice. Failure to send this notice to any designated mortgagee or loss payee invalidates the cancellation only as to the mortgagee's or loss payee's interest.

(c) This section does not apply to any insurance policy that has been in effect for less than 60 days and is not a renewal of a policy. That policy may be cancelled for any reason by furnishing to the insured at least 15 days prior written notice of and reasons for cancellation.

(d) Cancellation for nonpayment of premium is not effective if the amount due is paid before the effective date set forth in the notice of cancellation.

(e) Copies of the notice required by this section shall also be sent to the agent or broker of record; however, failure to send copies of the notice to such persons shall not invalidate the cancellation. (1985 (Reg. Sess., 1986), c. 1027, s. 14.)

The plaintiff/lender was not entitled to notice pursuant to this section because the defendant/insurer did not cancel the policy within the meaning of this section where the policy expired at the end of its term as a result of the insured's failure to pay the premium. Associates Fin. Servs. of Am., Inc. v. North Carolina Farm Bureau Mut. Ins. Co., 137 N.C. App. 526, 528 S.E.2d 621, 2000 N.C. App. LEXIS 421 (2000).

§ 58-41-20. Notice of nonrenewal, premium rate increase, or change in coverage required.

(a) No insurer may refuse to renew an insurance policy except in accordance with the provisions of this section, and any nonrenewal attempted or made that is not in compliance with this section is not effective. This section does not apply if the policyholder has insured elsewhere, has accepted replacement coverage, or has requested or agreed to nonrenewal.

(b) An insurer may refuse to renew a policy that has been written for a term of one year or less at the policy's expiration date by giving or mailing written notice of nonrenewal to the insured not less than 45 days prior to the expiration date of the policy.

(c) An insurer may refuse to renew a policy that has been written for a term of more than one year or for an indefinite term at the policy anniversary date by giving or mailing written notice of nonrenewal to the insured not less than 45 days prior to the anniversary date of the policy.

(d) Except as provided in G.S. 58-41-25, whenever an insurer lowers coverage limits or raises deductibles or premium rates other than at the request of the policyholder, the insurer shall give the policyholder written notice of such change at least 30 days in advance of the effective date of the change.

(e) The notice required by this section must be given or mailed to the insured and any designated mortgagee or loss payee at their addresses shown in the policy or, if not indicated in the policy, at their last known addresses. Proof of mailing is sufficient proof of notice. The notice of nonrenewal must state the precise reason for nonrenewal. Failure to send this notice to any designated mortgagee or loss payee invalidates the nonrenewal only as to the mortgagee's or loss payee's interest.

(f) Copies of the notice required by this section shall also be sent the agent or broker of record; however, failure to send copies of the notice to such persons shall not invalidate the nonrenewal. (1985 (Reg. Sess., 1986), c. 1027, s. 14; 1987, c. 441, ss. 3, 4.)

The notice requirements of this section did not apply, and defendant was not required to provide plaintiff with notification of the policy's expiration where the undisputed facts showed that defendant mailed two renewal declarations to the insureds, that these renewal declarations demonstrated defendant's willingness to renew the policy, and that the failure of the policy holders to pay the premium was a rejection of defendant's offer to renew the policy. Associates Fin. Servs. of Am., Inc. v. North Carolina Farm Bureau Mut. Ins. Co., 137 N.C. App. 526, 528 S.E.2d 621, 2000 N.C. App. LEXIS 421 (2000).

§ 58-41-25. Notice of renewal of policies with premium rate or coverage changes.

(a) If an insurer intends to renew a policy, the insurer must furnish to the insured the renewal terms and a statement of the amount of premium due for the renewal policy period. This section applies only if the insurer intends to decrease coverage, increase deductibles, impose any kind of surcharge, or increase the premium rate in the renewal policy.

(b) If the policy being renewed was written for a term of one year or less, the renewal terms and statement of premium due must be given or mailed not less than 45 days before the expiration date of that policy. If the policy being renewed was written for a term of more than one year or for an indefinite term, the renewal terms and statement of premium due must be given or mailed not less than 45 days before the anniversary date of that policy. The renewal terms and statement of premium due must be given or mailed to the insured and any designated mortgagee or loss payee at their addresses shown in the policy, or, if not indicated in the policy, at their last known addresses.

(c) If the insurer fails to furnish the renewal terms and statement of premium due in the manner required by this section, the insured may cancel the renewal policy within the 30-day period following receipt of the renewal terms and statement of premium due. For refund purposes, earned premium for any period of coverage shall be calculated pro rata upon the premium applicable to the policy being renewed instead of the renewal policy. If an insurer fails to comply with the 45-day notice requirement of this section, the insured is entitled to the option of coverage under the policy being renewed and at the same cost of that policy until 45 days have elapsed after the insurer has provided the insured with the notice.

(d) If a policy has been issued for a term longer than one year, and for additional consideration a premium has been guaranteed for the entire term, it is unlawful for the insurer to increase that premium or require policy deductibles or other policy or coverage provisions less favorable to the insured during the term of the policy.

(e) Copies of the notice required by this section shall also be given or mailed to any designated mortgagee or loss payee and may also be given or mailed to the agent or broker of record. (1985 (Reg. Sess., 1986), c. 1027, s. 14; 1987, c. 441, ss. 5, 6; 1989, c. 485, ss. 5, 6.)

§ 58-41-30. Loss of reinsurance.

An insurer may cancel or refuse to renew a kind of insurance when the cancellation or nonrenewal is necessary because of a loss of or substantial reduction in applicable reinsurance, by filing a plan with the Commissioner pursuant to the requirements of this section. The insurer's plan must be filed with the Commissioner at least 15 business days prior to the issuance of any notice of cancellation or nonrenewal. The insurer may implement its plan upon the approval of the Commissioner, which shall be granted or denied in writing, with the reasons for his actions, within 15 business days of the Commissioner's receipt of the plan. Any plan submitted for approval shall contain a certification by an elected officer of the company:

    (1) That the loss or substantial change in applicable reinsurance necessitates the cancellation or nonrenewal action;

    (2) That the insurer has made a good faith effort to obtain replacement reinsurance but was unable to do so because of the unavailability or unaffordability of replacement reinsurance;

    (3) Identifying the category of risks, the total number of risks written by the company in that category, and the number of risks intended to be cancelled or not renewed;

(4) Identifying the total amount of the insurer's net retention for the risks intended to be cancelled or not renewed;

(5) Identifying the total amount of risk ceded to each reinsurer and the portion of that total that is no longer available;

(6) Explaining how the loss of or reduction in reinsurance affects the insurer's risks throughout the kind of insurance proposed for cancellation or nonrenewal;

(7) Explaining why cancellation or nonrenewal is necessary to cure the loss of or reduction in reinsurance; and

(8) Explaining how the cancellations or nonrenewals, if approved, will be implemented and the steps that will be taken to ensure that the cancellation or nonrenewal decisions will not be applied in an arbitrary, capricious, or unfairly discriminatory manner. (1985 (Reg. Sess., 1986), c. 1027, s. 14.)

§ **58-41-35:** Repealed by Session Laws 1999-219, s. 9.

§ 58-41-40. No liability for statements or communications made in good faith; prior notice to agents or brokers.

(a) There is no liability on the part of and no cause of action for defamation or invasion of privacy arises against any insurer or its authorized representatives, agents, or employees, or any licensed insurance agent or broker, for any communication or statement made, unless shown to have been made in bad faith with malice, in any of the following:

(1) A written notice of cancellation under G.S. 58-41-15 or of nonrenewal under G.S. 58-41-20, specifying the reasons for cancellation.

(2) Communications providing information pertaining to the cancellation or nonrenewal.

(3) Evidence submitted at any court proceeding, administrative hearing, or informal inquiry in which the cancellation or nonrenewal is an issue.

(b) With respect to the notices that must be given or mailed to agents or brokers under G.S. 58-41-15, 58-41-20, and 58-41-25, the insurer may give or mail that notice at the same time or prior to giving or mailing the notice to the insured. (1985 (Reg. Sess., 1986), c. 1027, s. 14; 1987 (Reg. Sess., 1988), c. 975, s. 31; 1999-219, s. 9.1.)

§ 58-41-45. Termination of writing kind of insurance.

(a) Except as provided in G.S. 58-41-30, no insurer may terminate, by nonrenewals, an entire book of business of any kind of insurance without 60 days prior written notice to the Commissioner; unless the Commissioner determines that continuation of the line of business would impair the solvency of the insurer or unless the Commissioner determines that such termination is effected under a plan that minimizes disruption in the marketplace or that makes provisions for alternative coverage at comparable rates and terms.

(b) Except as provided in G.S. 58-41-30, in-term cancellation by an insurer of an entire book of business of any kind of insurance is presumed to be unfair, inequitable, and contrary to the public interest, unless the Commissioner determines that continuation of the line of business would impair the solvency of the insurer or unless the Commissioner determines that such termination is effected under a plan that minimizes disruption in the marketplace or that makes provisions for alternative coverage at comparable rates and terms. (1985 (Reg. Sess., 1986), c. 1027, s. 14.)

§ 58-41-50. Policy form and rate filings; punitive damages; data required to support filings.

(a) With the exception of inland marine insurance that is not written according to manual rates and rating plans, all policy forms must be filed with and either approved by the Commissioner or 90 days have elapsed and he has not disapproved the form before they may be used in this State. With respect to liability insurance policy forms, an insurer may exclude or limit coverage for punitive damages awarded against its insured.

(b) With the exception of inland marine insurance that is not written according to manual rates and rating plans, all rates or prospective loss cost multipliers by licensed fire and casualty companies or their designated rating organizations must be filed with the Commissioner at least 60 days before they may be used in this State. Any filing may become effective on a date earlier than that specified in this subsection upon agreement between the Commissioner and the filer.

(c) A filing that does not include the statistical and rating information required by subsections (d) and (e) of this section is not a proper filing, and will be returned to the filing insurer or organization. The filer may then remedy the defects in the filing. An otherwise defective filing thus remedied shall be deemed to be a proper filing, except that all periods of time specified in this Article will run from the date the Commissioner receives additional or amended documents necessary to remedy all material defects in the filing.

(d) The following information must be included in each policy form, rule, and rate filing:

    (1) A detailed list of the rates, rules, and policy forms filed, accompanied by a list of those superseded; and

    (2) A detailed description, properly referenced, of all changes in policy forms, rules, and rates, including the effect of each change.

(e) Each policy form, rule, and rate filing that is based on statistical data must be accompanied by the following properly identified information:

    (1) North Carolina earned premiums at the actual and current rate level; losses and loss adjustment expenses, each on paid and incurred bases without trending or other modification for the experience period, including the loss ratio anticipated at the time the rates were promulgated for the experience period;

    (2) Credibility factor development and application;

    (3) Loss development factor derivation and application on both paid and incurred bases and in both numbers and dollars of claims;

    (4) Trending factor development and application;

    (5) Changes in premium base resulting from rating exposure trends;

    (6) Limiting factor development and application;

    (7) Overhead expense development and application of commission and brokerage, other acquisition expenses, general expenses, taxes, licenses, and fees;

    (8) Percent rate change;

    (9) Final proposed rates;

    (10) Investment earnings, consisting of investment income and realized plus unrealized capital gains, from loss, loss expense, and unearned premium reserves;

    (11) Identification of applicable statistical plans and programs and a certification of compliance with them;

    (12) Investment earnings on capital and surplus;

    (13) Level of capital and surplus needed to support premium writings without endangering the solvency of the company or companies involved; and

(14) Such other information that may be required by any rule adopted by the Commissioner.

Provided, however, that no filing may be returned or disapproved on the grounds that such information has not been furnished if the filer has not been required to collect such information pursuant to statistical plans or programs or to report such information to statistical agents, except where the Commissioner has given reasonable prior notice to the filer to begin collecting and reporting such information or except when the information is readily available to the filer.

(f) It is unlawful for an insurer to charge or collect, or attempt to charge or collect, any premium for insurance except in accordance with filings made with the Commissioner under this section and Article 40 of this Chapter.

(g) An insurer subject to this Article may develop and use an individual form or rate as a result of the uniqueness of a particular risk. The form or rate shall be developed, filed, and used in accordance with rules adopted by the Commissioner. (1985 (Reg. Sess., 1986), c. 1027, s. 14; 1987, c. 441, ss. 7, 9, 10; 1991, c. 644, s. 4; 1995, c. 193, s. 37.)

§ 58-41-55. Penalties; restitution.

In addition to criminal penalties for acts declared unlawful by this Article, any violation of this Article subjects an insurer to revocation or suspension of its license, or monetary penalties or payment of restitution as provided in G.S. 58-2-70. (1985 (Reg. Sess., 1986), c. 1027, s. 14; 1999-132, s. 9.1.)

ARTICLE 42.

Mandatory or Voluntary Risk Sharing Plans.

§ 58-42-1. Establishment of plans.

(a) If the Commissioner finds, after a hearing held in accordance with Article 3A of Chapter 150B of the General Statutes, that in all or any part of this State, any amount or kind of insurance authorized by G.S. 58-7-15(4) through G.S. 58-7-15(22) is not readily available in the voluntary market and that the public interest requires the availability of that insurance, he may either:

(1) Promulgate plans to provide insurance coverage for any risks in this State that are, based on reasonable underwriting standards, entitled to obtain but are otherwise unable to obtain coverage; or

(2) Call upon insurers to prepare plans for his approval.

(b) Consistent with G.S. 58-42-5(a)(2), the Commissioner shall at least annually reevaluate a plan promulgated pursuant to this section and shall terminate the plan upon determining that the insurance coverage is readily available in the voluntary market or that the public interest no longer requires the operation of the plan. (1986, Ex. Sess., c. 7, s. 1; 1999-114, ss. 1, 2.)

Editor's Note. — Session Laws 1999-114, s. 2, effective May 28, 1999, reenacted this Article, which had expired July 1, 1997, pursuant to Session Laws 1995, c. 517, s. 26. Session Laws 2001-122, s. 1, effective June 30, 2001, repealed G.S. 58-42-55, which had provided for expiration of this section on July 1, 2001.

Session Laws 1999-114, s. 8, contains a severability clause.

OPINIONS OF ATTORNEY GENERAL

General Assembly Can Extend Statute. — There is no reason that the General Assembly cannot extend this article. See opinion of Attorney General to The Honorable E. David Redwine, North Carolina House of Representatives and The Honorable Patrick J. Ballantine, Senate Minority Leader, 2001 N.C. AG LEXIS 19 (6/18/2001).

§ 58-42-5. Purposes, contents, and operation of risk sharing plans.

(a) Each plan promulgated or prepared pursuant to G.S. 58-42-1 shall:
  (1) Give consideration to:
    a. The need for adequate and readily accessible coverage;
    b. Optional methods of improving the market affected;
    c. The inherent limitations of the insurance mechanism;
    d. The need for reasonable underwriting standards; and
    e. The requirement of reasonable loss prevention measures;
  (2) Establish procedures that will create minimum interference with the voluntary market;
  (3) Distribute the obligations imposed by the plan, and any profits or losses experienced by the plan, equitably and efficiently among the participating insurers; and
  (4) Establish procedures for applicants and participants to have their grievances reviewed by an impartial body. The filing and processing of a grievance pursuant to this subdivision does not stay the requirement for participation in a plan mandated by G.S. 58-42-10.
(b) Each plan may, on behalf of its participants:
  (1) Issue policies of insurance to eligible applicants;
  (2) Underwrite, adjust, and pay losses on insurance issued by the plan;
  (3) Appoint a service company or companies to perform the functions enumerated in this subsection; and
  (4) Obtain reinsurance for any part or all of its risks. (1986, Ex. Sess., c. 7, s. 1; 1999-114, s. 1.)

§ 58-42-10. Persons required to participate.

(a) Each plan shall require participation:
  (1) By all insurers licensed in this State to write the kinds of insurance covered by the specific plan;
  (2) By all agents licensed to represent those insurers for that kind of insurance; and
  (3) By every rating organization that makes rates for that kind of insurance.
(b) The Commissioner shall exclude from each plan any person if participation would impair the solvency of that person. (1986, Ex. Sess., c. 7, s. 1; 1999-114, s. 1.)

§ 58-42-15. Voluntary participation.

Each plan may provide for participation by:
  (1) Insurers that are not required to participate by G.S. 58-42-10;
  (2) Eligible surplus lines insurers as defined in G.S. 58-21-10(3); or
  (3) Reinsurers approved by the Commissioner. (1986, Ex. Sess., c. 7, s. 1; 1999-114, s. 1.)

§ 58-42-20. Classification and rates.

Each plan shall provide for:
(1) The method of classifying risks;
(2) The making and filing of rates that are not excessive, inadequate, or unfairly discriminatory and that are calculated on an actuarially sound basis and policy forms applicable to the various risks insured by the plan;
(3) The adjusting and processing of claims;
(4) The commission rates to be paid to agents or brokers for coverages written by the plan; and
(5) Any other insurance or investment functions that are necessary for the purpose of providing adequate and readily accessible coverage. (1986, Ex. Sess., c. 7, s. 1; 1999-114, s. 1.)

§ 58-42-25. Basis for participation.

Each plan shall specify the basis for participation by insurers, agents, rating organizations, and other participants and shall specify the conditions under which risks shall be accepted and underwritten by the plan. (1986, Ex. Sess., c. 7, s. 1; 1999-114, s. 1.)

§ 58-42-30. Duty to provide information.

Every participating insurer and agent shall provide to any person seeking the insurance available in each plan, information about the services prescribed in the plan, including full information on the requirements and procedures for obtaining insurance under the plan, whenever the insurance is not readily available in the voluntary market. (1986, Ex. Sess., c. 7, s. 1; 1999-114, s. 1.)

§ 58-42-35. Provision of marketing facilities.

If the Commissioner finds that the lack of participating insurers or agents in a geographic area makes the functioning of a plan difficult, he may order that the plan appoint agents on such terms as he designates or that the plan take other appropriate steps to guarantee that service is available. (1986, Ex. Sess., c. 7, s. 1; 1999-114, s. 1.)

§ 58-42-40. Voluntary risk sharing plans.

Insurers doing business within this State or reinsurers approved by the Commissioner may prepare voluntary plans that will provide any specific amount or kind of insurance or component thereof for all or any part of this State in which that insurance is not readily available in the voluntary market and in which the public interest requires the availability of the coverage. These plans shall be submitted to the Commissioner and, if approved by him, may be put into operation. (1986, Ex. Sess., c. 7, s. 1; 1999-114, s. 1.)

§ 58-42-45. Article subject to Administrative Procedure Act; legislative oversight of plans.

(a) The provisions of Chapter 150B of the General Statutes shall apply to this Article.
(b) At the same time the Commissioner issues a notice of hearing under G.S. 150B-38, the Commissioner shall provide copies of the notice to the Joint Legislative Administrative Procedure Oversight Committee and to the Joint

Legislative Commission on Governmental Operations. The Commissioner shall provide the Committee and Commission with copies of any plan promulgated by or approved by the Commissioner under G.S. 58-42-1(1) or (2). (1986, Ex. Sess., c. 7, s. 1; 1999-114, s. 1; 2000-140, s. 15.)

§ 58-42-50. Immunity of Commissioner and plan participants.

There shall be no liability on the part of, and no cause of action shall arise against the Commissioner, his representatives, or any plan, its participants, or its employee for any good faith action taken by them in the performance of their powers and duties in creating any plan pursuant to this Article. (1986, Ex. Sess., c. 7, s. 1; 1999-114, s. 1.)

§ 58-42-55: Repealed by Session Laws 2001-122, s. 1, effective June 30, 2001.

ARTICLE 43.

General Regulations of Business—Fire Insurance.

§ 58-43-1. Performance of contracts as to devices not prohibited.

Nothing contained in Articles 1 through 64 of this Chapter shall be construed as prohibiting the performance of any contract hereafter made for the introduction or installation of automatic sprinklers or other betterments or improvements for reducing the risk by fire or water on any property located in this State, and containing provisions for obtaining insurance against loss or damage by fire or water, for a specified time at a fixed rate; provided, every policy issued under such contract shall be as provided by law. (1929, c. 145, s. 1.)

§ 58-43-5. Limitation as to amount and term; indemnity contracts for difference in actual value and cost of replacement; functional replacement.

No insurance company or agent shall knowingly issue any fire insurance policy upon property within this State for an amount which, together with any existing insurance thereon, exceeds the fair value of the property, nor for a longer term than seven years: Provided, any fire insurance company authorized to transact business in this State may, by appropriate riders or endorsements or otherwise, provide insurance indemnifying the insured for the difference between the actual value of the insured property at the time any loss or damage occurs, and the amount actually expended to repair, rebuild or replace on the premises described in the policy, or some other location within the State of North Carolina with new materials of like size, kind and quality, property that has been damaged or destroyed by fire or other perils insured against: Provided further, that the Commissioner may approve forms that permit functional replacement by the insurance company, at the insured's option. Functional replacement means to replace the property with property that performs the same function when replacement with materials of like size, kind, and quality is not possible, necessary, or less costly than obsolete, antique, or custom construction materials and methods. Forms and rating plans may also provide for credits when functional replacement cost coverage is provided. Policies issued in violation of this section are binding upon the company issuing them, but the company is liable for the forfeitures by law prescribed for such violation. (1899, c. 54, ss. 39, 99; 1903, c. 438, s. 10; Rev., s. 4755; C.S., s. 6418; 1949, c. 295, s. 1; 1991, c. 644, s. 5.)

Cross References. — As to punishment prescribed, see § 58-43-35.

CASE NOTES

Replacement Cost Not Recoverable Where No Repair Performed. — In an action to recover fire insurance for loss of a home under a homeowner's policy which included a replacement cost provision, plaintiffs were entitled to recover only the actual cash value of the home at the time of the fire, rather than the replacement cost of the home, where they did not repair or rebuild the home, but bought another home, and they were not entitled to recover anything more from defendant insurer where they failed to show that the actual cash value of the property destroyed was greater than the amount they had been paid by defendant. Edmund v. Firemen's Fund Ins. Co., 42 N.C. App. 237, 256 S.E.2d 268 (1979).

Construction of Policy in Light of Premium Charged. — Where insurer contended that policy covered only one of three stores contained in plaintiffs' building and not the entire building, and the amount of the policy was greatly in excess of the value of the one store but was about the value of the entire building, and insured paid the premium based upon the amount for which the policy was issued, it was held that in construing the policy it would not be presumed that the insurer charged a premium based upon a valuation greatly in excess of the value of the property insured in violation of this section and G.S. 58-44-5, but that the policy covered the entire building. Williams v. Greensboro Fire Ins. Co., 209 N.C. 765, 185 S.E. 21 (1936).

Competency of Agent's Statement in Determining Amount of Loss. — A statement of an agent acting for his company in writing fire insurance, made after an inspection of the property to be insured, is competent upon the question of the amount of the loss, in an action brought by the insured to recover upon the policy issued, especially as this section requires that the insurer should know the true value of the property, etc., to be insured before issuing the policy thereon. Queen v. Dixie Fire Ins. Co., 177 N.C. 34, 97 S.E. 741 (1919).

The total amount of insurance payments made on a particular loss cannot exceed the value of the loss itself. This is a longstanding rule that cannot be violated lest the insurance industry be turned into a lottery. State Farm Fire & Cas. Co. v. Folger, 677 F. Supp. 844 (E.D.N.C. 1988).

Proof of First Mortgagee's Interest by Second Mortgagee. — Normally, a second mortgagee would not have to prove the amount of the first mortgage in order to recover under the policy if the first mortgagee was not insured. However, where the first mortgagee is covered by a separate insurance policy, the second mortgagee must prove the amount of the first mortgagee's interest in order for the court to prevent total insurance payments from exceeding the value of the loss. State Farm Fire & Cas. Co. v. Folger, 677 F. Supp. 844 (E.D.N.C. 1988).

Applied in Surrant v. Grain Dealers Mut. Ins. Co., 74 N.C. App. 288, 328 S.E.2d 16 (1985).

Cited in Bentley v. North Carolina Ins. Guar. Ass'n, 107 N.C. App. 1, 418 S.E.2d 705 (1992).

§ 58-43-10. Limit of liability on total loss.

Subject to the provisions of G.S. 58-43-5, when buildings insured against loss by fire and situated within the State are totally destroyed by fire, the company is not liable beyond the actual cash value of the insured property at the time of the loss or damage; and if it appears that the insured has paid a premium on a sum in excess of the actual value, he shall be reimbursed the proportionate excess of premium paid on the difference between the amount named in the policy and the ascertained values, with interest at six per centum (6%) per annum from the date of issue. (1899, c. 54, s. 40; Rev., s. 4756; C.S., s. 6419; 1949, c. 295, s. 2.)

Replacement Cost Not Recoverable Where No Repair Performed. — In an action to recover fire insurance for loss of a home under a homeowner's policy which included a replacement cost provision, plaintiffs were entitled to recover only the actual cash value of the home at the time of the fire, rather than the replacement cost of the home, where they did not repair or rebuild the home, but bought another home, and they were not entitled to recover anything more from defendant insurer where they failed to show that the actual cash value of the property destroyed was greater than the amount they had been paid by defendant. Edmund v. Firemen's Fund Ins. Co., 42 N.C. App. 237, 256 S.E.2d 268 (1979).

§ 58-43-15. Policies for the benefit of mortgagees.

Where by an agreement with the insured, or by the terms of a fire insurance policy taken out by a mortgagor, the whole or any part of the loss thereon is payable to a mortgagee of the property for his benefit, the company shall, upon satisfactory proof of the rights and title of the parties, in accordance with such terms or agreement, pay all mortgagees protected by such policy in the order of their priority of claim, as their claims appear, not beyond the amount for which the company is liable, and such payments are, to the extent thereof, payment and satisfaction of the liabilities of the company under the policy. Any payment due by the insuring company to mortgagees or loss payees under the terms of the policy shall be made within 90 days of the loss or within 60 days of the filing of proof of loss, whichever is the longer period; provided, the payment of or settlement of the claim of the mortgagee or loss payee under the policy shall in no way constitute an admission of liability as to the insured and the fact of such payment or settlement shall be inadmissible in any action at law. (1899, c. 54, s. 41; Rev., s. 4757; C.S., s. 6420; 1969, c. 1077, s. 1.)

Priority Between Mortgagees. — Where the owner of lands borrows money thereon under two separate mortgages from different persons, one registered prior to the other, and the mortgagor contracts with each to take out certain policies of fire insurance for their benefit, the rights of the mortgagees to the proceeds under the policies will be determined by the contracts as executed in the loss payable clauses in the policies; hence, where the policies were of the New York standard form, made payable to the mortgagees "as interest may appear," the mortgagee under the prior registered mortgage had a superior lien on the proceeds to the one having the later registered security. Wayne Nat'l Bank v. National Bank, 197 N.C. 68, 147 S.E. 691 (1929).

Where a mortgagor procured insurance for the benefit of first mortgagee, whose mortgage was registered December 14, 1920, and for the benefit of subsequent mortgagee, whose mortgage was not executed until May 11, 1925, the claim of the first mortgagee would first be paid out of funds derived from the policy under this section, providing that where, by terms of a fire policy taken out by a mortgagor, loss is payable to a mortgagee for his benefit, the company shall pay all mortgages in order of their priority of claim, and in view of G.S. 47-20, by which priority is given to the mortgage which was first recorded. Wayne Nat'l Bank v. National Bank, 197 N.C. 68, 147 S.E. 691 (1929).

Division of Proceeds Where Neither Mortgagee Has Claim to Priority. — If neither of two mortgagees for whom insurance has been procured has any priority of claim or of liens, the proceeds of the policies will ordinarily be divided between them in proportion to their respective claims. Wayne Nat'l Bank v. National Bank, 197 N.C. 68, 147 S.E. 691 (1929).

The standard mortgage clause is designed to protect the mortgagee from acts of the mortgagor that would invalidate the coverage and leave the mortgagee without security. Under the clause there is nothing a mortgagor can do that will diminish the mortgagee's right to receive under the policy. The clause creates an independent contract between the mortgagee and the insurer. State Farm Fire & Cas. Co. v. Folger, 677 F. Supp. 844 (E.D.N.C. 1988).

Requirement that mortgagees be paid off in the order of their priority only applies where more than one mortgagee is named on the same policy. State Farm Fire & Cas. Co. v. Folger, 677 F. Supp. 844 (E.D.N.C. 1988).

Proof of First Mortgagee's Interest by

Second Mortgagee. — Normally, a second mortgagee would not have to prove the amount of the first mortgage in order to recover under the policy if the first mortgagee was not insured. However, where the first mortgagee is covered by a separate insurance policy, the second mortgagee must prove the amount of the first mortgagee's interest in order for the court to prevent total insurance payments from exceeding the value of the loss. State Farm Fire & Cas. Co. v. Folger, 677 F. Supp. 844 (E.D.N.C. 1988).

Cited in Peeler v. United States Cas. Co., 197 N.C. 286, 148 S.E. 261 (1929).

§ 58-43-20: Repealed by Session Laws 1995 (Regular Session, 1996), c. 752, s. 1.

§ 58-43-25. Limitation of fire insurance risks.

No insurer authorized to do in this State the business of fire insurance shall expose itself to any loss on any one fire risk, whether located in this State or elsewhere, in an amount exceeding ten percent (10%) of its surplus to policyholders, except that in the case of risks adequately protected by automatic sprinklers or risks principally of noncombustible construction and occupancy such insurer may expose itself to any loss on any one risk in an amount not exceeding twenty-five percent (25%) of the sum of (i) its unearned premium reserve and (ii) its surplus to policyholders. Any risk or portion of any risk which shall have been reinsured shall be deducted in determining the limitation of risk prescribed in this section. (1945, c. 378.)

§ 58-43-30. Agreements restricting agent's commission; penalty.

It is unlawful for any insurance company doing the business of insurance as defined in subdivisions (3) to (22), inclusive, of G.S. 58-7-15 and employing an agent representing another such company, either directly or through any organization or association, to enter into, make or maintain any stipulation or agreement in anywise limiting the compensation such agent may receive from any such other company or forbidding or prohibiting reinsurance of the risks of any such domestic company in whole or in part by any other company holding membership in or cooperating with such organization or association. The penalty for any violation of this section shall be a fine of not less than one thousand dollars ($1,000) nor more than five thousand dollars ($5,000), and the forfeiture of license to do business in this State for a period of 12 months following conviction. (1905, c. 424; Rev., ss. 3491, 4768; 1915, c. 166, ss. 2, 3; C.S., s. 6432; 1945, c. 458; 1985, c. 666, s. 26.)

§ 58-43-35. Punishment for issuing fire policies contrary to law.

Any insurance company or agent who makes, issues, or delivers a policy of fire insurance in willful violation of the provisions of Articles 1 through 64 of this Chapter that prohibit a domestic insurance company from issuing policies before obtaining a license from the Commissioner; or that prohibit the issuing of a fire insurance policy for more than the fair value of the property or for a longer term than seven years; or that prohibit stipulations in insurance contracts restricting the jurisdiction of courts, or limiting the time within which an action may be brought to less than one year after the cause of action accrues or to less than six months after a nonsuit by the plaintiff, shall be guilty of a Class 3 misdemeanor and shall, upon conviction, be punished only by a fine of not less than one thousand dollars ($1,000) nor more than five thousand dollars ($5,000); but the policy shall be binding upon the company issuing it. (1899, c. 54, s. 99; 1903, c. 438, s. 10; Rev., s. 4832; C.S., s. 6433; 1985, c. 666, s. 27; 1993, c. 539, s. 466; 1994, Ex. Sess., c. 24, s. 14(c); 1999-132, s. 9.2.)

§ 58-43-40: Expired pursuant to Session Laws 1997-438, s. 1, effective January 1, 2000.

Editor's Note. — Session Laws 1997-438, s. 2, made this section effective October 1, 1997, and applicable to insurance policies issued or renewed on or after January 1, 1998, and provided that this section would expire January 1, 2000.

ARTICLE 44.

Fire Insurance Policies.

§ 58-44-1. Terms and conditions must be set out in policy.

In all insurance against loss by fire the conditions of insurance must be stated in full, and the rules and bylaws of the company are not a warranty or a part of the contract, except as incorporated in full into the policy. (1899, c. 54, s. 42; Rev., s. 4758; C.S., s. 6434.)

§ 58-44-5. Items to be expressed in policies.

Upon request there shall be printed, stamped, or written on each fire policy issued in this State the basis rate, deficiency charge, the credit for improvements, and the rate at which written, and whenever a rate is made or changed on any property situated in this State upon request a full statement thereof showing in detail the basis rate, deficiency charges and credits, as well as rate proposed to be made, shall be delivered to the owner or his representative having the insurance on the property in charge, by the company, association, their agent or representative. (1915, c. 109, s. 3; C.S., s. 6435; 1925, c. 70, s. 3; 1945, c. 378.)

§ 58-44-10: Repealed by Session Laws 1995, c. 517, s. 27.

§ 58-44-15. Fire insurance contract; standard policy provisions.

(a) The printed form of a policy on fire insurance, as set forth in subsection (c) shall be known and designated as the "Standard Fire Insurance Policy for North Carolina."

(b) No policy or contract of fire insurance except contracts of automobile fire, theft, comprehensive and collision, marine and inland marine insurance shall be made, issued or delivered by any insurer or by any agent or representative thereof, on any property in this State, unless it conforms in substance with all of the provisions, stipulations, agreements, and conditions of the policy form in subsection (c) of this section.

There shall be printed at the head of said policy the name of the insurer or insurers issuing the policy; the location of the home office thereof; a statement whether said insurer or insurers are stock or mutual corporations or are reciprocal insurers. No provisions of this section limit a company to the use of any particular size or manner of folding the paper upon which the policy is printed; provided, however, that any company organized under special charter provisions may so indicate upon its policy, and may add a statement of the plan under which it operates in this State.

The standard fire insurance policy provided for herein need not be used for effecting reinsurance between insurers.

(c) The form of the standard fire insurance policy for North Carolina (with permission to substitute for the word "company" a more accurate descriptive term for the type of insurer and with permission to change the manner of folding the policy and arrangement of the pages and the arrangement of the wording of page 1, page 3, and the back of the policy and relocation of the signatures, and any other relocations or rearrangement of the contents of the policy, with the approval of the Commissioner) shall be in substance as follows: (See the three following pages for a form photographically reproduced.)

STANDARD FIRE INSURANCE POLICY for Alabama, Alaska, Arizona, Arkansas, Colorado, Connecticut, Delaware, District of Columbia, Florida, Georgia, Hawaii, Idaho, Illinois, Indiana, Iowa, Kansas, Kentucky, Louisiana, Maryland, Michigan, Mississippi, Missouri, Montana, Nebraska, Nevada, New Hampshire, New Jersey, New Mexico, New York, North Carolina, North Dakota, Ohio, Oklahoma, Oregon, Pennsylvania, Rhode Island, South Carolina, South Dakota, Tennessee, Utah, Vermont, Virginia, Washington, West Virginia, Wisconsin and Wyoming.

No.   **TYPE OF COMPANY**

RENEWAL OF NUMBER

SPACE FOR COMPANY NAME, INSIGNIA, AND LOCATION

Insured's Name and Mailing Address

Policy Term:

SPACE FOR PRODUCER'S NAME AND MAILING ADDRESS

Inception (Mo. Day Yr.)   Expiration (Mo. Day Yr.)   Years

It is important that the written portions of all policies covering the same property read exactly alike. If they do not, they should be made uniform at once.

INSURANCE IS PROVIDED AGAINST ONLY THOSE PERILS AND FOR ONLY THOSE COVERAGES INDICATED BELOW BY A PREMIUM CHARGE AND AGAINST OTHER PERILS AND FOR OTHER COVERAGES ONLY WHEN ENDORSED HEREON OR ADDED HERETO.

Item No.	DESCRIPTION AND LOCATION OF PROPERTY COVERED — Show address (No., Street, City, County, State, Zip Code), construction, type of roof and occupancy of building(s) covered or containing property covered. If occupied as a dwelling state if building is a seasonal or farm dwelling. If commercial state exact nature of product (and whether manufacturer, wholesaler or retailer) or the service or activity involved.	Protection Class	Dwelling Business Only			
			No. of Families	Feet From Hydrant	Miles From Fire Dept.	Zone
1.						

Item No.	PERIL(S) INSURED AGAINST AND COVERAGE(S) PROVIDED (INSERT NAME OF EACH)	Per Cent of Co-Insurance Applicable	Deductible Amount	Amount of Insurance	Rate	Prepaid or Installment Premium Due At Inception	Installment Premium Due At Each Anniversary
1.	FIRE AND LIGHTNING			$		$	$
	EXTENDED COVERAGE			x x x x x x x			
				TOTAL(S) $			$

TOTAL PREMIUM FOR POLICY TERM PAID IN INSTALLMENTS $

Subject to Form No(s).   **attached hereto.**

INSERT FORM NUMBER(S) AND EDITION DATE(S)

Mortgage Clause: Subject to the provisions of the mortgage clause attached hereto, loss, if any, on building items, shall be payable to:

INSERT NAME(S) OF MORTGAGEE(S) AND MAILING ADDRESS(ES)

Countersignature Date   Agency at   Agent

IN CONSIDERATION OF THE PROVISIONS AND STIPULATIONS HEREIN OR ADDED HERETO AND OF the premium above specified, this Company, for the term of years specified above from inception date shown above At Noon (Standard Time) to expiration date shown above At Noon (Standard Time) at location of property involved, to an amount not exceeding the amount(s) above specified, does insure the insured named above and legal representatives, to the extent of the actual cash value of the property at the time of loss, but not exceeding the amount which it would cost to repair or replace the property with material of like kind and quality within a reasonable time after such loss, without allowance for any increased cost of repair or reconstruction by reason of any ordinance or law regulating construction or repair, and without compensation for loss resulting from interruption of business or manufacture, nor in any event for more than the interest of the insured, against all **DIRECT LOSS BY FIRE, LIGHTNING AND BY REMOVAL FROM PREMISES ENDANGERED BY THE PERILS INSURED AGAINST IN THIS POLICY, EXCEPT AS HEREINAFTER PROVIDED,** to the property described herein while located or contained as described in this policy, or pro rata for five days at each proper place to which any of the property shall necessarily be removed for preservation from the perils insured against in this policy, but not elsewhere.

Assignment of this policy shall not be valid except with the written consent of this Company.

This policy is made and accepted subject to the foregoing provisions and stipulations and those hereinafter stated, which are hereby made a part of this policy, together with such other provisions, stipulations and agreements as may be added hereto, as provided in this policy.

—————————————————ATTACH FORM BELOW THIS LINE—————————————

1 **Concealment,** This entire policy shall be void if, whether
2 **fraud.** before or after a loss, the insured has wil-
3 fully concealed or misrepresented any ma-
4 terial fact or circumstance concerning this insurance or the
5 subject thereof, or the interest of the insured therein, or in case
6 of any fraud or false swearing by the insured relating thereto.
7 **Uninsurable** This policy shall not cover accounts, bills,
8 **and** currency, deeds, evidences of debt, money or
9 **excepted property.** securities; nor, unless specifically named
10 hereon in writing, bullion or manuscripts.
11 **Perils not** This Company shall not be liable for loss by
12 **included.** fire or other perils insured against in this
13 policy caused, directly or indirectly, by: (a)
14 enemy attack by armed forces, including action taken by mili-
15 tary, naval or air forces in resisting an actual or an immediately
16 impending enemy attack; (b) invasion; (c) insurrection; (d)
17 rebellion; (e) revolution; (f) civil war; (g) usurped power; (h)
18 order of any civil authority except acts of destruction at the time
19 of and for the purpose of preventing the spread of fire, provided
20 that such fire did not originate from any of the perils excluded
21 by this policy; (i) neglect of the insured to use all reasonable
22 means to save and preserve the property at and after a loss, or
23 when the property is endangered by fire in neighboring prem-
24 ises; (j) nor shall this Company be liable for loss by theft.
25 **Other Insurance.** Other insurance may be prohibited or the
26 amount of insurance may be limited by en-
27 dorsement attached hereto.
28 **Conditions suspending or restricting insurance. Unless other-**
29 **wise provided in writing added hereto this Company shall not**
30 **be liable for loss occurring**
31 (a) while the hazard is increased by any means within the con-
32 trol or knowledge of the insured; or
33 (b) while a described building, whether intended for occupancy
34 by owner or tenant, is vacant or unoccupied beyond a period of
35 sixty consecutive days; or
36 (c) as a result of explosion or riot, unless fire ensue, and in
37 that event for loss by fire only.
38 **Other perils** Any other peril to be insured against or sub-
39 **or subjects.** ject of insurance to be covered in this policy
40 shall be by endorsement in writing hereon or
41 added hereto.
42 **Added provisions.** The extent of the application of insurance
43 under this policy and of the contribution to
44 be made by this Company in case of loss, and any other pro-
45 vision or agreement not inconsistent with the provisions of this
46 policy, may be provided for in writing added hereto, but no pro-
47 vision may be waived except such as by the terms of this policy
48 is subject to change.
49 **Waiver** No permission affecting this insurance shall
50 **provisions.** exist, or waiver of any provision be valid,
51 unless granted herein or expressed in writing
52 added hereto. No provision, stipulation or forfeiture shall be
53 held to be waived by any requirement or proceeding on the part
54 of this Company relating to appraisal or to any examination
55 provided for herein.
56 **Cancellation** This policy shall be cancelled at any time
57 **of policy.** at the request of the insured, in which case
58 this Company shall, upon demand and sur-
59 render of this policy, refund the excess of paid premium above
60 the customary short rates for the expired time. This pol-
61 icy may be cancelled at any time by this Company by giving
62 to the insured a five days' written notice of cancellation with
63 or without tender of the excess of paid premium above the pro
64 rata premium for the expired time, which excess, if not ten-
65 dered, shall be refunded on demand. Notice of cancellation shall
66 state that said excess premium (if not tendered) will be re-
67 funded on demand.
68 **Mortgage** If loss hereunder is made payable, in whole
69 **interests and** or in part, to a designated mortgagee not
70 **obligations.** named herein as the insured, such interest in
71 this policy may be cancelled by giving to such
72 mortgagee a ten days' written notice of can-
73 cellation.
74 If the insured fails to render proof of loss such mortgagee, upon
75 notice, shall render proof of loss in the form herein specified
76 within sixty (60) days thereafter and shall be subject to the pro-
77 visions hereof relating to appraisal and time of payment and of
78 bringing suit. If this Company shall claim that no liability ex-
79 isted as to the mortgagor or owner, it shall, to the extent of pay-
80 ment of loss to the mortgagee, be subrogated to all the mort-
81 gagee's rights of recovery, but without impairing mortgagee's
82 right to sue; or it may pay off the mortgage debt and require
83 an assignment thereof and of the mortgage. Other provisions

84 relating to the interests and obligations of such mortgagee may
85 be added hereto by agreement in writing.
86 **Pro rata liability.** This Company shall not be liable for a greater
87 proportion of any loss than the amount
88 hereby insured shall bear to the whole insurance covering the
89 property against the peril involved, whether collectible or not.
90 **Requirements in** The insured shall give immediate written
91 **case loss occurs.** notice to this Company of any loss, protect
92 the property from further damage, forthwith
93 separate the damaged and undamaged personal property, put
94 it in the best possible order, furnish a complete inventory of
95 the destroyed, damaged and undamaged property, showing in
96 detail quantities, costs, actual cash value and amount of loss
97 claimed; **and within sixty days after the loss, unless such time**
98 **is extended in writing by this Company, the insured shall render**
99 **to this Company a proof of loss,** signed and sworn to by the
100 insured, stating the knowledge and belief of the insured as to
101 the following: the time and origin of the loss, the interest of the
102 insured and of all others in the property, the actual cash value of
103 each item thereof and the amount of loss thereto, all encum-
104 brances thereon, all other contracts of insurance, whether valid
105 or not, covering any of said property, any changes in the title,
106 use, occupation, location, possession or exposures of said prop-
107 erty since the issuing of this policy, by whom and for what
108 purpose any building herein described and the several parts
109 thereof were occupied at the time of loss and whether or not it
110 then stood on leased ground, and shall furnish a copy of all the
111 descriptions and schedules in all policies and, if required, verified
112 plans and specifications of any building, fixtures or machinery
113 destroyed or damaged. The insured, as often as may be reason-
114 ably required, shall exhibit to any person designated by this
115 Company all that remains of any property herein described, and
116 submit to examinations under oath by any person named by this
117 Company, and subscribe the same; and, as often as may be
118 reasonably required, shall produce for examination all books of
119 account, bills, invoices and other vouchers, or certified copies
120 thereof if originals be lost, at such reasonable time and place as
121 may be designated by this Company or its representative, and
122 shall permit extracts and copies thereof to be made.
123 **Appraisal.** In case the insured and this Company shall
124 fail to agree as to the actual cash value or
125 the amount of loss, then, on the written demand of either, each
126 shall select a competent and disinterested appraiser and notify
127 the other of the appraiser selected within twenty days of such
128 demand. The appraisers shall first select a competent and dis-
129 interested umpire; and failing for fifteen days to agree upon
130 such umpire, then, on request of the insured or this Company,
131 such umpire shall be selected by a judge of a court of record in
132 the state in which the property covered is located. The ap-
133 praisers shall then appraise the loss, stating separately actual
134 cash value and loss to each item; and, failing to agree, shall
135 submit their differences, only, to the umpire An award in writ-
136 ing, so itemized, of any two when filed with this Company shall
137 determine the amount of actual cash value and loss. Each
138 appraiser shall be paid by the party selecting him and the ex-
139 penses of appraisal and umpire shall be paid by the parties
140 equally.
141 **Company's** It shall be optional with this Company to
142 **options.** take all, or any part, of the property at the
143 agreed or appraised value, and also to re-
144 pair, rebuild or replace the property destroyed or damaged with
145 other of like kind and quality within a reasonable time, on giv-
146 ing notice of its intention so to do within thirty days after the
147 receipt of the proof of loss herein required.
148 **Abandonment.** There can be no abandonment to this Com-
149 pany of any property.
150 **When loss** The amount of loss for which this Company
151 **payable.** may be liable shall be payable sixty days
152 after proof of loss, as herein provided, is
153 received by this Company and ascertainment of the loss is made
154 either by agreement between the insured and this Company or
155 pressed in writing or by the filing with this Company of an
156 award as herein provided.
157 **Suit.** No suit or action on this policy for the recov-
158 ery of any claim shall be sustainable in any
159 court of law or equity unless all the requirements of this policy
160 shall have been complied with, and unless commenced within
161 twelve months next after inception of the loss.
162 **Subrogation.** This Company may require from the insured
163 an assignment of all right of recovery against
164 any party for loss to the extent that payment therefor is made
165 by this Company.

In Witness Whereof, this Company has executed and attested these presents; but this policy shall not be valid unless countersigned by the duly authorized Agent of this Company at the agency hereinbefore mentioned.

INSERT SIGNATURES AND
TITLES OF PROPER OFFICERS

(1899, c. 54, s. 43; 1901, c. 391, s. 4; Rev., s. 4760; 1915, c. 109, s. 9; C.S., s. 6437; 1945, c. 378; 1951, c. 767; 1955, c. 622; c. 807, s. 2; 1971, c. 476, s. 1; 1977, c. 828, s. 3; 1979, c. 755, ss. 2-4; 1989, c. 485, s. 8.)

Cross References. — As to limitation of actions, see G.S. 58-3-35. For the Readable Insurance Policies Act, see G.S. 58-38-1 et seq. As to the standard fire insurance policy and permissible variations, see G.S. 58-44-20.

Editor's Note. — In the sample fire insurance policy form reproduced at the end of subsection (c) of this section, the time for commencement of suit reflected in the next to last paragraph, headed "Suit," should be three years, not twelve months. See § 1-52 (12).

Legal Periodicals. — For article, "Statutes of Limitations in the Conflict of Laws," see 52 N.C.L. Rev. 489 (1974).

For survey of 1979 property law, see 58 N.C.L. Rev. 1509 (1980).

For note discussing interpretation of notice provisions in insurance contracts, in light of Great Am. Ins. Co. v. C.G. Tate Constr. Co., 303 N.C. 387, 279 S.E.2d 769 (1981), see 61 N.C.L. Rev. 167 (1982).

For an article discussing "reverse bad faith," the concept of allowing an insurer to assert a counterclaim for affirmative relief against an insured who brings a frivolous, bad faith action, see 19 Campbell L. Rev. 43 (1996).

CASE NOTES

I. IN GENERAL.

For history of legislation in respect to the "standard fire insurance policy", see Boyd v. Bankers & Shippers Ins. Co., 245 N.C. 503, 96 S.E.2d 703 (1957).

Legislative Intent. — The legislature did not intend that a claimant on a fire insurance policy should be denied coverage if he or she executes the proof of loss before a notary without raising his or her hand and swearing to the truth of the statements in the proof of loss. Thompson v. Home Ins. Co., 62 N.C. App. 562, 303 S.E.2d 209, cert. denied, 309 N.C. 324, 307 S.E.2d 169 (1983).

Applicability. — In the context of a fire/homeowners policy, G.S. 58-44-15 is the controlling statute and any misrepresentation or concealment made in the insurance application process is governed by that statute, not G.S. 58-3-10. Crawford v. Commercial Union Midwest Ins. Co., 147 N.C. App. 455, 556 S.E.2d 30, 2001 N.C. App. LEXIS 1183 (2001), cert. denied, 356 N.C. 160, 568 S.E.2d 190 (2002).

An insurance policy is but a special kind of contract and the terms agreed to therein, unless forbidden by law, are binding on insurer and insured alike. Payne v. Buffalo Reinsurance Co., 69 N.C. App. 551, 317 S.E.2d 408 (1984).

Provisions of Standard Form Are Those of the Law. — The material provisions of the standard form of a fire insurance policy written in accordance with this section are those of the law. Greene v. Aetna Ins. Co., 196 N.C. 335, 145 S.E. 616 (1928).

Statutory standard fire insurance policy is incorporated into every policy of fire insurance issued in North Carolina. Star Varifoam Corp. of Am. v. Buffalo Reinsurance Co., 64 N.C. App. 306, 307 S.E.2d 194 (1983), cert. denied, 310 N.C. 154, 311 S.E.2d 294 (1984).

Commissioner has no power to authorize or acquiesce in issuance of policies unauthorized or forbidden by statute. Glover v. Rowan Mut. Fire Ins. Co., 228 N.C. 195, 45 S.E.2d 45 (1947).

Agreements in a policy contrary to statutory provisions are void. Buckner v. United States Fire Ins. Co., 209 N.C. 640, 184 S.E. 520 (1936).

The provisions of the standard form of fire insurance policy are valid. Zibelin v. Pawtucket Mut. Fire Ins. Co., 229 N.C. 567, 50 S.E.2d 290 (1948); Boyd v. Bankers & Shippers Ins. Co., 245 N.C. 503, 96 S.E.2d 703 (1957).

And Binding on the Parties. — The terms and conditions of the standard form of a fire insurance policy, and the stipulations as to a valid waiver thereof, are valid and binding on the parties. Midkiff v. North Carolina Home Ins. Co., 197 N.C. 139, 147 S.E. 812 (1929).

And Rights and Liabilities of Both Parties Must Be Determined in Accordance

Therewith. — The provisions of the standard form of fire insurance policy are valid, and the rights and liabilities of both parties under the policy must be ascertained and determined in accordance with its terms. Gardner v. Carolina Ins. Co., 230 N.C. 750, 55 S.E.2d 694 (1949).

The rights and liabilities of both insurer and insured must be determined in accordance with the terms of the standard form of fire insurance policy. Zibelin v. Pawtucket Mut. Fire Ins. Co., 229 N.C. 567, 50 S.E.2d 290 (1948).

The rights of the parties under a loss-payable clause in a policy of fire insurance will be determined in accordance with the terms and provisions of the contract, which derive no extra validity by reason of the fact that the form is prescribed by law. Atlantic Joint Stock Land Bank v. Foster, 217 N.C. 415, 8 S.E.2d 235 (1940).

When a policy of insurance, in the form prescribed by this section, has been issued by an insurance company and accepted by the insured, and has thereby become effective for all purposes as their contract, the rights and liabilities of both the insurer and the insured, under the policy, must be ascertained and determined in accordance with its terms and provisions. These terms and provisions have been prescribed by statute, and are valid in all respects; they are just both to the insurer and to the insured. Both are presumed to know all the terms, provisions and conditions which are included in the policy, and both are ordinarily bound by them. Lancaster v. Southern Ins. Co., 153 N.C. 285, 69 S.E. 214 (1910); Midkiff v. North Carolina Home Ins. Co., 197 N.C. 139, 147 S.E. 812 (1929). See Boyd v. Bankers & Shippers Ins. Co., 245 N.C. 503, 96 S.E.2d 703 (1957).

To prevail in an affirmative defense of misrepresentation, the insurance company must prove that the insured made statements that were: 1) false, 2) material, and 3) knowingly and willfully made. Bryant v. Nationwide Mut. Fire Ins. Co., 313 N.C. 362, 329 S.E.2d 333 (1985); Pittman v. Nationwide Mut. Fire Ins. Co., 79 N.C. App. 431, 339 S.E.2d 441, cert. denied, 316 N.C. 733, 345 S.E.2d 391 (1986).

To void a fire insurance policy, the insurer must prove that the insured knowingly and willfully made statements that were false and material. Harris v. North Carolina Farm Bureau Mut. Ins. Co., 91 N.C. App. 147, 370 S.E.2d 700 (1988).

Defendants did not make material misrepresentations where they "inflated" the estimated losses by submitting their bids for repairs based on the assumption of a "worst case" scenario and were forthright in revealing what they sought recovery for. Westchester Fire Ins. Co. v. Johnson, — F. Supp. 2d —, 2000 U.S. Dist. LEXIS 5001 (M.D.N.C. Jan. 6, 2000).

Binders Not Contrary to Law. — Our statute, by establishing a standard form of fire insurance, does not prevent the binding effect of a parol agreement of insurance, looking to the delivery of the policy according to the form prescribed and evidenced by a written memorandum thereof, called a binder; and when such binder is shown to have been made in a manner to bind the company, it is in force from that time, and thereafter the insured is responsible for the loss in accordance with the terms of the statutory form of policy. Lea & Adcock v. Atlantic Fire Ins. Co., 168 N.C. 478, 84 S.E. 813 (1915). See § 58-44-20(4).

Waivers Making Policy More Restrictive Are Void. — Waivers inserted in or attached to a policy of fire insurance which have the effect of making the provisions of the standard fire form more restrictive are void under this section and G.S. 58-44-20. Glover v. Rowan Mut. Fire Ins. Co., 228 N.C. 195, 45 S.E.2d 45 (1947).

A waiver attached to a policy of fire insurance which provided that the policy should not cover loss caused by fire originating on the property of a neighbor if the insured property was situated within a stipulated distance of the combustible property of a neighbor was restrictive of the provisions of the standard policy form and was therefore void. Glover v. Rowan Mut. Fire Ins. Co., 228 N.C. 195, 45 S.E.2d 45 (1947).

Knowledge of Insurer as Waiver. — A breach of a condition in the policy will not avoid it, if the insurer has knowledge thereof, and does not object, in which case the breach is considered as waived. Argall v. Old N. State Ins. Co., 84 N.C. 355 (1881); Scottish Fire Ins. Co. v. Stuyvesant Ins. Co., 161 N.C. 485, 76 S.E. 728 (1913).

Sending a check in payment of the claim may constitute a waiver, whether received or not, of unfulfilled conditions. Roper v. National Fire Ins. Co., 161 N.C. 151, 76 S.E. 869 (1912).

Waiver by or Estoppel Against Insurer from Act or Omission of Agent. — A waiver by, or an estoppel against, an insurer may arise from the act, conduct, omission, or knowledge of a duly authorized representative of the insurer acting within the scope of his actual or apparent authority. Northern Assurance Co. of Am. v. Spencer, 246 F. Supp. 730 (W.D.N.C. 1965), aff'd, 373 F.2d 35 (4th Cir. 1966).

When Knowledge of Agent Imputed to Company. — In the absence of fraud or collusion between the insured and the agent, the knowledge of the agent when acting within the scope of the powers entrusted to him will be imputed to the company, even though a direct stipulation to the contrary appears in the policy or the application. Faircloth v. Ohio Farmers Ins. Co., 253 N.C. 522, 117 S.E.2d 404 (1960).

In the absence of fraud or collusion, and when acting within the scope of his authority, the agent's knowledge is in law the knowledge of the insurer, even though it is not in fact communicated to the insurer. Northern Assurance Co. of Am. v. Spencer, 246 F. Supp. 730 (W.D.N.C. 1965), aff'd, 373 F.2d 35 (4th Cir. 1966).

Limitations on Agent's Authority as to Conditions Arising After Issuance of Policy and Loss. — Limitations on the agent's authority expressed in unambiguous language in the policy must be held binding on the insured. And while provisions in the policy restricting the local agent's power to waive conditions as a general rule do not include conditions existing at the inception of the contract, the rule is otherwise as to those arising after the policy has been issued and loss has occurred. Zibelin v. Pawtucket Mut. Fire Ins. Co., 229 N.C. 567, 50 S.E.2d 290 (1948).

At the time of issuing the policy the local agent pro hac vice represents the company and his knowledge is ordinarily held to be notice to his principal. But this rule does not apply to authorize extension of time for the performance of conditions precedent to establishing liability after the loss has occurred, and in direct contradiction of the terms of the written contract of insurance. Zibelin v. Pawtucket Mut. Fire Ins. Co., 229 N.C. 567, 50 S.E.2d 290 (1948).

The provision restricting the agent's power to waive conditions does not, as a general rule, refer to or include conditions existing at the inception of the contract, but those arising after the policy is issued. Conditions which form a part of the contract of insurance at its inception may be waived by the agent of the insurer, although they are embraced in the policy when it is delivered; and the local agent's knowledge of such conditions is deemed to be the knowledge of his principal. Bullard v. Pilot Fire Ins. Co., 189 N.C. 34, 126 S.E. 179 (1925). See Hayes v. United States Fire Ins. Co., 132 N.C. 702, 44 S.E. 404 (1903); Weddington v. Piedmont Fire Ins. Co., 141 N.C. 234, 54 S.E. 271 (1906); Johnson v. Rhode Island Ins. Co., 172 N.C. 142, 90 S.E. 124 (1916); Fireman's Fund Ins. Co. v. Rowland Lumber Co., 186 N.C. 269, 119 S.E. 362 (1923); Smith v. National Ben Franklin Fire Ins. Co., 193 N.C. 446, 137 S.E. 310 (1927).

Agent May Not Alter Terms of Policy After Loss. — Suggestions made by the local agent to the insured after loss are not within the scope of his authority, nor may he alter the terms of the policy after its issue and loss thereunder has been reported. Zibelin v. Pawtucket Mut. Fire Ins. Co., 229 N.C. 567, 50 S.E.2d 290 (1948).

An agent of a fire insurance company, whether general or local, cannot waive the requirements of a standard policy except in the form prescribed by the statute. Roper v. National Fire Ins. Co., 161 N.C. 151, 76 S.E. 869 (1912).

Effect of Agent's Parol Contract Inconsistent with Standard Form. — In the absence of fraud, an insurance company cannot be held liable upon a parol contract alleged to have been made by its agent, which is contradictory of and totally inconsistent with the standard form prescribed by statute. Hardin v. Liverpool & London & Globe Ins. Co., 189 N.C. 423, 127 S.E. 353 (1925).

Liability of Agent and Insurer Due to Apparent Authority of Employee. — One dealing with an insurance agency under ordinary circumstances need not concern himself with the extent of the authority of an employee in the agent's office who undertakes to act for the agent; the apparent authority with which such employee is clothed by the agent renders him and his principal liable regardless of the actual limits of the authority of the employee. Northern Assurance Co. of Am. v. Spencer, 246 F. Supp. 730 (W.D.N.C. 1965), aff'd, 373 F.2d 35 (4th Cir. 1966).

Liability of Agent for Loss Occasioned Insured by Negligence. — Where the general agent of a fire insurance company for a limited territory, through the negligence of an employee, fails to write into the policy a statement required to make it valid, the agents are liable in damages to the insured for loss by fire, in an action based solely on the ground of negligence and not upon the invalid contract of insurance negligently issued by them. Case v. Ewbanks, Ewbanks & Co., 194 N.C. 775, 140 S.E. 709 (1927).

The inception of the risk is not delayed until the policy is countersigned. Pruitt v. Great Am. Ins. Co., 241 N.C. 725, 86 S.E.2d 401 (1955).

When a loss occurs the rights of the parties to a fire insurance policy become fixed. Baysdon v. Nationwide Mut. Fire Ins. Co., 259 N.C. 181, 130 S.E.2d 311 (1963).

The standard fire policy does not provide for automatic termination of the insurance upon default in the payment of premium installments. Baysdon v. Nationwide Mut. Fire Ins. Co., 259 N.C. 181, 130 S.E.2d 311 (1963).

When Policy May Be Rescinded or Terminated. — An insurance policy is a contract; a contract may be rescinded for fraud or mutual mistake, it may be terminated in accordance with the provisions thereof or by mutual consent, a meeting of the minds, but one of the parties may not terminate it without the assent of the other unless the contract so provides. Baysdon v. Nationwide Mut. Fire Ins. Co., 259 N.C. 181, 130 S.E.2d 311 (1963).

Either party to the contract may cancel the standard form policies without the consent of the other, by following the applicable provisions of the policy. Roberta Mfg. Co. v. Royal Exch. Assurance Co., 161 N.C. 88, 76 S.E. 865 (1912).

Provision in a policy that insurer must

give notice to insured as a condition precedent to cancellation is for insured's benefit and may be waived by him. Baysdon v. Nationwide Mut. Fire Ins. Co., 259 N.C. 181, 130 S.E.2d 311 (1963).

The provision for five days' notice before cancellation is for the protection of the insured, and the insurer cannot effect cancellation until the expiration of five days from the receipt of the written notice by plaintiff; whether plaintiff intends to waive this provision and does waive it by returning the policy as requested is for the determination of the jury. Wilson v. National Union Fire Ins. Co., 206 N.C. 635, 174 S.E. 745 (1934).

And Must Be Strictly Complied With. — To effect a cancellation by insurer, the five days' notice provision must be strictly complied with. Baysdon v. Nationwide Mut. Fire Ins. Co., 259 N.C. 181, 130 S.E.2d 311 (1963).

Unless Waived by Insured. — Unless the requirement is waived by insured, an insurer must comply with the terms of the policy or statute that it give notice of its intention to cancel. Baysdon v. Nationwide Mut. Fire Ins. Co., 259 N.C. 181, 130 S.E.2d 311 (1963).

The burden is on insurer to show a waiver by the insured, and it must appear clearly that the insured expressly or impliedly waived notice of cancellation if he is to be held bound by such waiver. Baysdon v. Nationwide Mut. Fire Ins. Co., 259 N.C. 181, 130 S.E.2d 311 (1963).

Communication of Insured's Intent to Cancel. — To effect a cancellation by the insured a definite and unconditional request therefor must be communicated to the insurer by the insured or his authorized agent. Baysdon v. Nationwide Mut. Fire Ins. Co., 259 N.C. 181, 130 S.E.2d 311 (1963).

A mere intention to cancel, not communicated to insurer, is not sufficient to effect a cancellation by the insured. Baysdon v. Nationwide Mut. Fire Ins. Co., 259 N.C. 181, 130 S.E.2d 311 (1963).

Procuring additional insurance without requesting original insurer to cancel does not terminate the policy. Baysdon v. Nationwide Mut. Fire Ins. Co., 259 N.C. 181, 130 S.E.2d 311 (1963).

Substitution of One Policy for Another Must Be by Mutual Consent. — In order for cancellation to take place by the substitution of one policy for another it must be done by mutual consent or agreement. Baysdon v. Nationwide Mut. Fire Ins. Co., 259 N.C. 181, 130 S.E.2d 311 (1963).

Mere procuring of substituted insurance with the intent to replace existing insurance and without the intent to thereby acquire additional insurance does not per se work a cancelling of the existing insurance. Baysdon v. Na-

tionwide Mut. Fire Ins. Co., 259 N.C. 181, 130 S.E.2d 311 (1963).

Language insuring property located in a building occupied by the insured is expressly authorized by this section. It is a material part of the contract, and cannot be ignored. Parker v. Worcester Mut. Fire Ins. Co., 264 N.C. 339, 141 S.E.2d 466 (1965).

Where a policy insured the contents of a building occupied by the insured, it meant the building occupied by insured when the policy was issued, and not elsewhere. Parker v. Worcester Mut. Fire Ins. Co., 264 N.C. 339, 141 S.E.2d 466 (1965).

Effect of Standard or Union Mortgage Clause. — When the standard or union mortgage clause is attached to or inserted in a policy insuring property against loss, it operates as a distinct and independent contract between the insurance company and the mortgagee, effecting a separate insurance of the mortgage interest. Shores v. Rabon, 251 N.C. 790, 112 S.E.2d 556 (1960).

A standard loss-payable clause in a policy of fire insurance issued to the mortgagor constitutes a separate contract insuring the mortgage interest, and loss paid by insurer thereunder must be applied to the reduction of the mortgage debt. Employers' Fire Ins. Co. v. British Am. Assurance Co., 259 N.C. 485, 131 S.E.2d 36 (1963).

Limitation on Mortgagee's Interest. — The clause in the standard policy that provides the insured shall not collect "in any event for more than the interest of the insured" limits a mortgagee's interest to the debt due him. Employers' Fire Ins. Co. v. British Am. Assurance Co., 259 N.C. 485, 131 S.E.2d 36 (1963).

Deed to mortgagee upon foreclosure of mortgage does not defeat mortgagee's right under a standard or union mortgage clause. Shores v. Rabon, 251 N.C. 790, 112 S.E.2d 556 (1960).

When Insurer Subrogated to Rights of Mortgagee. — When a mortgagee purchases with his funds insurance solely for his protection, the insurer, upon payment of the mortgagee's loss as provided in the policy, is subrogated to the rights of the mortgagee against the mortgagor; but where the insurance is procured by the mortgagee pursuant to the authorization and at the expense of the mortgagor, no right of subrogation exists and the amount paid by the insurer must be applied to discharge or reduce mortgagor's obligation to mortgagee. Employers' Fire Ins. Co. v. British Am. Assurance Co., 259 N.C. 485, 131 S.E.2d 36 (1963).

Where the mortgagee has insured the mortgaged property for his own benefits, and where the mortgagor has assumed the risk of loss under his contract of purchase, the insurer, having paid the loss, is subrogated to the rights of the mortgagee. Stuyvesant Ins. Co. v. Reid,

171 N.C. 513, 88 S.E. 779 (1916).

Insurer Held Not Entitled to Subrogation to Mortgagee's Rights. — Where, pursuant to the terms of a deed of trust, the mortgagee insured the property and added the amount of the premiums to the mortgage debt, and the contract of insurance provided that in case of loss the insurer should be subrogated to the rights of the mortgagee, and that in case of conflict between the contract of insurance and the standard policy set out in this section the standard policy should prevail, and the mortgagor had no notice of the subrogation agreement, it was held that the insurer had no right to subrogation, either under the terms of the policy or on any equitable principle, and that the mortgagor was entitled to have the amount paid by the insurer applied on the mortgage debt. Buckner v. United States Fire Ins. Co., 209 N.C. 640, 184 S.E. 520 (1936).

Mortgagee Held Not Liable for Premiums. — Provision in the loss-payable clause of a fire insurance policy taken out by a mortgagor that the mortgagee would pay the premium on demand should the mortgagor not do so was held to be a condition upon which the mortgagee might receive the benefit of the protection afforded by the policy as a special contract made in his favor, and not as a covenant that he would pay the premium on demand of the insurer upon the mortgagor's default; and upon the mortgagee's refusal or neglect to pay the premiums in default upon the insurer's demand, the latter might after 10 days' written notice cancel the policy. Whitehead v. Wilson Knitting Mills, 194 N.C. 281, 139 S.E. 456, 56 A.L.R. 674 (1927).

Proration of Loss Between Insurers. — Where property destroyed by fire was insured by two policies, one issued to the mortgagee under authority of the mortgagor, the mortgagor being liable for the premiums thereon, and one issued to the mortgagor both containing a standard loss-payable clause, it was proper to prorate the loss between the insurers. Employers' Fire Ins. Co. v. British Am. Assurance Co., 259 N.C. 485, 131 S.E.2d 36 (1963).

Insurer Subrogated to Rights of Insured Against Tort-Feasor. — Upon paying the loss by fire, the insurer is entitled to subrogation to the rights of insured against the third person tort-feasor causing the loss, to the extent of the amount paid, both by provision of this section and under equitable principles. Fidelity Ins. Co. v. Atlantic C.L.R.R., 165 N.C. 136, 80 S.E. 1069 (1914); Powell & Powell, Inc. v. Wake Water Co., 171 N.C. 290, 88 S.E. 426 (1916); Lumberman's Mut. Ins. Co. v. Southern Ry., 179 N.C. 255, 102 S.E. 417 (1920); Buckner v. United States Fire Ins. Co., 209 N.C. 640, 184 S.E. 520 (1936); Winkler v. Appalachian Amusement Co., 238 N.C. 589, 79 S.E.2d 185 (1953);

General Ins. Co. of Am. v. Faulkner, 259 N.C. 317, 130 S.E.2d 645 (1963); Dixie Fire & Cas. Co. v. Esso Standard Oil Co., 265 N.C. 121, 143 S.E.2d 279 (1965).

Evidence Sufficient to Support Finding of Insurable Interest. — Evidence that the owner of property advised insurer's agent that he was giving the property in question to his son, that he requested the agent to change the insurance so as to name his son as insured, that the owner thereafter died and that the son remained in exclusive possession of the property and continued the insurance in force, was sufficient to support the conclusion that the son had an insurable interest in the property so as to be entitled to recover on the policy. King v. National Union Fire Ins. Co., 258 N.C. 432, 128 S.E.2d 849 (1963).

Applied in Pettit v. Wood-Owen Trailer Co., 214 N.C. 335, 199 S.E. 279 (1938); Gower v. Aetna Ins. Co., 281 N.C. 577, 189 S.E.2d 165 (1972); Knapp v. Pennsylvania Nat'l Mut. Cas. Ins. Co., 17 N.C. App. 455, 194 S.E.2d 572 (1973); Andrews v. North Carolina Farm Bureau Mut. Ins. Co., 26 N.C. App. 163, 215 S.E.2d 373 (1975); Collins v. Quincy Mut. Fire Ins. Co., 297 N.C. 680, 256 S.E.2d 718 (1979); Kinlaw v. North Carolina Farm Bureau Mut. Ins. Co., 98 N.C. App. 13, 389 S.E.2d 840 (1990).

Cited in Cuthrell v. Milwaukee Mechanics Ins. Co., 234 N.C. 137, 66 S.E.2d 649 (1951); Crowell v. Eastern Air Lines, 240 N.C. 20, 81 S.E.2d 178 (1954); Firemen's Mut. Ins. Co. v. High Point Sprinkler Co., 266 N.C. 134, 146 S.E.2d 53 (1966); In re North Carolina Fire Ins. Rating Bureau, 2 N.C. App. 10, 162 S.E.2d 671 (1968); Greenway v. North Carolina Farm Bureau Mut. Ins. Co., 35 N.C. App. 308, 241 S.E.2d 339 (1978); Collins v. Quincy Mut. Fire Ins. Co., 39 N.C. App. 38, 249 S.E.2d 461 (1978); F & D Co. v. Aetna Ins. Co., 305 N.C. 256, 287 S.E.2d 867 (1982); Durham v. Quincy Mut. Fire Ins. Co., 311 N.C. 361, 317 S.E.2d 372 (1984); Hawkins v. State Capital Ins. Co., 79 N.C. App. 449, 328 S.E.2d 793 (1985); McMillan v. State Farm Fire & Cas. Co., 93 N.C. App. 748, 379 S.E.2d 88 (1989).

II. CONDITIONS.

A. In General.

Validity of "Additional Insurance" Clauses. — This section does not prohibit the inclusion of other insurance clauses in policies written in this State. The statute clearly permits such a clause to be included in a policy by endorsement. It merely declines to make the clause a standard policy provision as it was formerly. Allstate Ins. Co. v. Old Republic Ins. Co., 49 N.C. App. 32, 270 S.E.2d 510 (1980).

The condition against additional insurance on the property, formerly appearing in the standard policy, was valid and enforceable.

Black v. Atlantic Home Ins. Co., 148 N.C. 169, 61 S.E. 672 (1908).

When the standard fire insurance policy under this section provided that the policy should be void if the insured procured other contemporaneous insurance on the same property during the term covered, unless the insurer agreed thereto and a writing to that effect was attached to the policy contract, the provision was valid and binding. Johnson v. Aetna Ins. Co., 201 N.C. 362, 160 S.E. 454 (1931).

Where defendant included a provision against additional insurance in all its policies, its binders were also governed thereby. Allstate Ins. Co. v. Old Republic Ins. Co., 49 N.C. App. 32, 270 S.E.2d 510 (1980).

Avoidance of Policy for Breach of "Additional Insurance" Prohibition. — This section does not change prior law that if a valid other insurance clause is breached, the insurer may void the entire policy. Allstate Ins. Co. v. Old Republic Ins. Co., 49 N.C. App. 32, 270 S.E.2d 510 (1980).

Where insured obtains other insurance contrary to the provisions of his policy, the insurer may avoid liability for breach of the provision prohibiting other insurance, since breach of the provision against additional insurance, both before and after the 1945 amendment to this section, does not merely limit the amount of insurer's liability, but is a breach of condition defeating recovery. Hiatt v. American Ins. Co., 250 N.C. 553, 109 S.E.2d 185 (1959).

When the insured had violated the provision of the former standard policy by placing more concurrent insurance on the property than the policy permitted, the policy was invalid. Roper v. National Fire Ins. Co., 161 N.C. 151, 76 S.E. 869 (1912).

Waiver of "Additional Insurance" Provision by Agent. — Where the insured, before taking out additional insurance, mentioned his intention to the insurer's subagent who had issued its policy to the insured, and was told that it was all right, this constituted a waiver of the condition. Grubbs v. North Carolina Home Ins. Co., 108 N.C. 472, 13 S.E. 236 (1891).

Right of Insurer to Have Other Coverage Determined and Maintained. — Provision of an insurance contract providing that the insurer "shall not be liable for a greater portion of any loss than the amount hereby insured shall bear to the whole insurance covering the property against the peril involved," gives it the right to have determined whether there was at the time of the loss other coverage, what its liability is, and to insist that other coverage not be extinguished after the loss by acts of the insured which will cast the entire loss on it. Baysdon v. Nationwide Mut. Fire Ins. Co., 259 N.C. 181, 130 S.E.2d 311 (1963).

"Additional Insurance" Provision Held Inapplicable. — Where a policy of fire insurance was issued to devisee of the fee in property subject to a charge in favor of other beneficiaries under the will, and thereafter the guardian of such other beneficiaries took out a policy, following the former standard form, to protect the interest of his wards, the insurer issuing the policy to the guardian could not avoid liability thereon on the ground of the additional insurance issued to the owner of the fee, since such additional insurance was not issued to or for the benefit of those insured under its policy. Bryan v. Old Colony Ins. Co., 213 N.C. 391, 196 S.E. 345 (1938).

Condition or Use of Property Provision May Be Waived. — An insurance company may waive, or be estopped to rely on, a provision or condition in a policy of insurance relating to use or condition of property. Northern Assurance Co. of Am. v. Spencer, 246 F. Supp. 730 (W.D.N.C. 1965), aff'd, 373 F.2d 35 (4th Cir. 1966).

Permit When House Unoccupied. — Provision in the standard fire insurance policy requiring a permit in writing from the insurer when insured house is unoccupied for more than 10 (now 60) days must be complied with to make the insurer liable for damages by fire occurring after such vacancy, and after the policy has been issued and is in binding effect the local agent of the insurer is without authority to bind his principal by acts and parol representations made contrary to the terms of this provision. Greene v. Aetna Ins. Co., 196 N.C. 335, 145 S.E. 616 (1928).

As to validity of the "iron-safe clause" in policies of insurance, see Coggins v. Aetna Ins. Co., 144 N.C. 7, 56 S.E. 506 (1907). See also, § 58-44-20(3).

A substantial compliance with an "iron-safe" provision will suffice. Arnold v. Indemnity Fire Ins. Co., 152 N.C. 232, 67 S.E. 574 (1910).

Waiver of "Iron-Safe" Provision. — If the company, knowing the insured has not complied with the "iron-safe" clause, collects the premiums and recognizes the validity and binding force and effect of the policy it has issued, it should not be heard to insist upon the introduction of records, the keeping of which it has thus tacitly waived. Bullard v. Pilot Fire Ins. Co., 189 N.C. 34, 126 S.E. 179 (1925).

Inventory. — An inventory of a stock of general merchandise containing the number of articles and cost of each class at a certain date, made about one month before the fire, and testified to as being practically the same as on the date of the fire, was a substantial compliance with the inventory provision in the standard form of a fire insurance policy, and was competent as evidence upon the trial. Mortt v. Liverpool & London & Globe Ins. Co., 192 N.C. 8, 133 S.E. 337 (1926). See also Coggins v. Aetna Ins. Co., 144 N.C. 7, 56 S.E. 506 (1907).

Violation Which Ceased Three Months Prior to Loss. — Where an insured mill was operated at night, in violation of the former standard policy, but under a permit from the insurance agent, such operation was no defense to an action on the policy for a loss happening three months after the violation had ceased. Strause v. Palatine Ins. Co., 128 N.C. 64, 38 S.E. 256 (1901).

Willful Concealment or Misrepresentation. — The provisions of this section pertaining to willful concealment or misrepresentation are inserted in the insurance contract by this section as a part of the public policy of the State, and the rights and liabilities of the parties under the policy must be ascertained and determined in accordance with its terms. Hanks v. Nationwide Mut. Fire Ins. Co., 47 N.C. App. 393, 267 S.E.2d 409 (1980).

Summary judgment was improperly granted to insurance company that had claimed the insurance policy was void, following the destruction of the homeowner's property in a fire, because of homeowner's material misrepresentations; there was no evidence the homeowner knowingly or willfully made misrepresentations about encumbrances on his property to an insurance agent in applying for the homeowners policy. Crawford v. Commercial Union Midwest Ins. Co., 147 N.C. App. 455, 556 S.E.2d 30, 2001 N.C. App. LEXIS 1183 (2001), cert. denied, 356 N.C. 160, 568 S.E.2d 190 (2002).

Effect of "Forfeiture Clause" Where Both Personal and Real Property Involved. — Where a fire insurance policy contained a forfeiture clause for willful misrepresentation of a material fact and contained one basic premium in payment for the coverage of both plaintiffs' house and their personal property therein, and the risk to the real and personal property was identical, both being subject to the same fire, the policy was not divisible; therefore, where plaintiffs willfully misrepresented material facts in swearing to their proof of loss with respect to their personal property, the policy was void with respect to their real property as well. Dale v. Iowa Mut. Ins. Co., 40 N.C. App. 715, 254 S.E.2d 41, cert. denied, 297 N.C. 609, 257 S.E.2d 217 (1979).

B. Former Conditions as to Title or Interest of Insured.

Editor's Note. — The cases under this analysis line were decided before the 1945 amendments to this section and G.S. 58-44-20. Most of them construe provisions in the former standard policy to the effect that the policy should be void if the interest of the insured was other than unconditional and sole ownership, if, with the knowledge of the insured, foreclosure proceedings were commenced or notice given of sale of the property under any mortgage or deed of trust, or if any change, other than by the death of an insured, took place in the interest, title or possession of the property.

Requirement of "unconditional and sole ownership" in a policy of fire insurance in the former standard form as required by this section was statutory as well as contractual. Roberts v. American Alliance Ins. Co., 212 N.C. 1, 192 S.E. 873, 113 A.L.R. 310 (1937).

Title under Executory Contract. — A vendee of land occupying it under an executory contract, on which he had paid a portion of the price and on which he had erected a building, was an "unconditional and sole owner" in fee simple within the conditions of a fire policy providing that it should be void if the interest of the insured was other than sole ownership of the fee simple title. Jordan v. Hanover Fire Ins. Co., 151 N.C. 341, 66 S.E. 206 (1909).

Existence of Lien Did Not Violate Provision. — The stipulation in a fire policy for sole and unconditional ownership was not violated by the existence of a lien on the property. Lancaster v. Southern Ins. Co., 153 N.C. 285, 69 S.E. 214 (1910).

Misrepresentations as to Title. — Misrepresentations as to title of part of the premises insured avoided the entire contract of insurance. Cuthbertson v. North Carolina Home Ins. Co., 96 N.C. 480, 2 S.E. 258 (1887).

Policy Invalidated by Mortgage. — Where the insured failed to state that the property was mortgaged, when in fact it was mortgaged, and the policy provided that the contract of insurance would be void if the insured property was mortgaged, the policy was invalid though the omission was made without the intent to deceive. Hayes v. United States Fire Ins. Co., 132 N.C. 702, 44 S.E. 404 (1903).

Execution of a mortgage on the insured property so affected title as to void an insurance policy then existing thereon and forfeit its benefit, if the mortgage was made without the knowledge or consent of the insurance company and not attested as prescribed by the policy contract, unless the company thereafter, by its acts, conduct and statements had waived the effect of the mortgage and was estopped to assert the forfeiture. Modlin v. Atlantic Fire Ins. Co., 151 N.C. 35, 65 S.E. 605 (1909).

Assignment for Creditors. — Making an assignment for creditors avoided a policy containing an unconditional ownership clause. Roper v. National Fire Ins. Co., 161 N.C. 151, 76 S.E. 869 (1912).

Right of Insurer to Know of Encumbrances. — The validity of a provision in a policy of insurance against the creating of encumbrances without the consent of the insurer can hardly be contested at this late day. The facts in regard to title, ownership, encumbrances, and possession of the insured property are all important to be known by the insurer, as the character of the hazard is often affected by these circumstances. Weddington v. Piedmont Fire Ins. Co., 141 N.C. 234, 54 S.E. 271 (1906); Watson v. North Carolina Home Ins. Co., 159 N.C. 638, 75 S.E. 1105 (1912).

Removal of Encumbrance Before Loss. — Where the owner of an unencumbered automobile insured it under a statutory form of policy stipulating, among other things, that the policy would be void if the interest of the assured was other than unconditional or sole ownership, or if the property was or became encumbered by a chattel mortgage, and thereafter gave a mortgage thereon which was canceled four days before the destruction of the machine by fire, this loss coming within the terms of the policy, the cancellation of the mortgage revived the original status of the policy, the temporary violation of the stipulation being immaterial, and put the policy again in force, the effect of the mortgage being to invalidate the policy during the continuance of the lien, or to suspend the obligation of the insurance company during the violation of the stipulation. Cottingham v. Maryland Motor Car Ins. Co., 168 N.C. 259, 84 S.E. 274 (1915).

Commencement of foreclosure against insured property terminated the policy where there was a provision in the policy to that effect. Hayes v. United States Fire Ins. Co., 132 N.C. 702, 44 S.E. 404 (1903).

Waiver of Sole Ownership Provision. — Where agent issued a policy with full knowledge of the state of the title, the condition of sole ownership was waived. Gerringer v. North Carolina Home Ins. Co., 133 N.C. 407, 45 S.E. 773 (1903).

Where a policy of fire insurance was issued under the former statutory standard form, the condition therein of sole and unconditional ownership of the insured could not be held to have been waived by the insurer or its agent in the absence of knowledge that the insured's ownership was otherwise than as stated in the policy contract. Hardin v. Liverpool & London & Globe Ins. Co., 189 N.C. 423, 127 S.E. 353 (1925).

The condition that the policy should be void if the insured had not the sole and unconditional title was valid and enforceable by the company without the necessity of disclaiming liability upon notice or knowledge of its infraction, and the company's inaction in this respect was not a waiver of the condition. Smith v. National Ben Franklin Fire Ins. Co., 193 N.C. 446, 137 S.E. 310 (1927).

The provision in a policy of fire insurance written in accordance with the former standard statutory form, that the policy should be void if the insured was not the unconditional owner of the property in fee simple, was not waived by a written agreement providing that the agreement was solely for the purpose of determining the loss and to save time to the parties and that it should not operate as a waiver of any conditions or provisions of the policy. Sasser v. Pilot Fire Ins. Co., 203 N.C. 232, 165 S.E. 684 (1932).

III. PROOF OF LOSS AND LIMITATION OF SUIT.

The burden is on plaintiff to offer evidence in support of all essential elements to establish his claim. The occurrence of a condition precedent is an essential element of plaintiff's case, and it is therefore incumbent upon plaintiff to offer proof of compliance with the terms of the contract. Chavis v. State Farm Fire & Cas. Co., 79 N.C. App. 213, 338 S.E.2d 787, rev'd on other grounds, 317 N.C. 683, 346 S.E.2d 496 (1986).

Filing of Proof of Loss Within Prescribed Period Required. — Under the terms of the standard fire insurance policy in effect in this State, no action may be maintained on a policy unless proof of loss shall be filed within the prescribed period. Boyd v. Bankers & Shippers Ins. Co., 245 N.C. 503, 96 S.E.2d 703 (1957). See now § 58-44-50.

Insurer's denial of liability upon fire insurance policy is a waiver of its right to require proof of loss therein specified. Profitt Mercantile Co. v. State Mut. Fire Ins. Co., 176 N.C. 545, 97 S.E. 476 (1918).

A misrepresentation by an insured constitutes a breach of cooperation clause only when the misrepresentation results in some actual detriment to the insured. Bryant v. Nationwide Mut. Fire Ins. Co., 67 N.C. App. 616, 313 S.E.2d 803, aff'd in part and rev'd in part, 313 N.C. 362, 329 S.E.2d 333 (1985).

A misrepresentation during a loss investigation is material within the meaning of subsection (c) of this section only when the misrepresentation prejudices the insurer. Bryant v. Nationwide Mut. Fire Ins. Co., 67 N.C. App. 616, 313 S.E.2d 803; 311 N.C. 399, 319 S.E.2d 267 (1984).

Object of provisions requiring insured to submit to examination under oath is to enable insurance company to obtain information to determine the extent of its obligation and to protect itself from false claims, and the provision requiring the production of documents is designed to serve the same purpose. While these provisions do not give the insurer license to harass plaintiff with aimless questions and demands for documents, questions asked and documents sought which relate to the validity of the insured's claim are material and relevant. Chavis v. State Farm Fire & Cas. Co., 79 N.C. App. 213, 338 S.E.2d 787, rev'd on other grounds, 317 N.C. 683, 346 S.E.2d 496 (1986).

Insufficient Demand for Examination under Oath. — Insurer's demand for an examination under oath, which failed to designate a date, time and place for the examination and the person before whom the examination was to be taken, was insufficient, and under these circumstances, the refusal of plaintiff insured to submit to an examination did not give rise to a defense under the policy. Huggins v. Hartford Ins. Co., 650 F. Supp. 38 (E.D.N.C. 1986).

Failure to Submit to Examination. — Where a fire insurance policy required plaintiff to submit to an examination under oath when reasonably requested before suit was filed and she refused to be so examined, her willingness to be examined after suit was filed did not meet the requirement of the policy and her suit was properly dismissed. Baker v. Independent Fire Ins. Co., 103 N.C. App. 424, 405 S.E.2d 779 (1991).

Production of Documents as Condition Precedent to Suit. — Compliance with provisions of an insurance policy requiring the insured to produce documents "as often as may be reasonably required" at a "reasonable time and place" is a condition precedent to bringing suit where the insurer notifies the insured of the time and place for production. The "reasonable time and place" clause ordinarily means that a demand must be made within a reasonable period of time and that the location must be in the locality of the insured property. Chavis v. State Farm Fire & Cas. Co., 79 N.C. App. 213, 338 S.E.2d 787, rev'd on other grounds, 317 N.C. 683, 346 S.E.2d 496 (1986).

Insurer's Request for Production of Documents Must Be Specific. — In order to carry out the reasonable and relevant requirements in the statutory "production of documents" provision, the standard fire insurance policy requires the insurer's request to be specific. Chavis v. State Farm Fire & Cas. Co., 317 N.C. 683, 346 S.E.2d 496 (1986).

And Reasonable. — The statutory "production of documents" clause in the standard fire insurance policy does not expressly authorize the insurer's unlimited access to any and all of the insured's business and financial records. Rather, the language of the statutory provision assumes that the insurer's requests for documents will be reasonable and will relate to the insured property. The provision does not grant to the insurer an unlimited right to roam at will through all of the insureds' financial records, without the restriction of reasonableness and specificity. Chavis v. State Farm Fire & Cas. Co., 317 N.C. 683, 346 S.E.2d 496 (1986).

What Documents to Be Produced. — The "production of documents" provision in the statutory standard fire insurance policy only expressly provides that the insured shall produce for examination "all books of account, bills, invoices, and other vouchers." Chavis v. State Farm Fire & Cas. Co., 317 N.C. 683, 346 S.E.2d 496 (1986).

Request for Production of Documents Held Overbroad. — Release form which insurer required insureds who had suffered a fire loss to sign in connection with the statutory "production of documents" provision of their standard fire insurance policy, requesting access to "any and all records" in connection with "all banks and/or any type of lending institution" with which plaintiffs had done "any business," was unreasonably broad, and insureds were justified as a matter of law in refusing to sign this overbroad release. Chavis v. State Farm Fire & Cas. Co., 317 N.C. 683, 346 S.E.2d 496 (1986).

Refusal to Produce Documents. — Where insurer's second request for production of documents at county courthouse specifically provided that insured should produce them in "whatever status the records are presently in," and insured expressly refused to bring the requested records to either the first or second examination, maintaining that he did not have time to compile them, but admitted at trial that he need only have transported his files in "a bunch of bags" from his store to the courthouse to comply with defendant's second request for production, the evidence was insufficient to create a jury question as to the reasonableness of the time or place for the production of these documents; and the court erred in failing to grant defendant's motion for directed verdict on plaintiff's contractual claims. Moore v. North Carolina Farm Bureau Mut. Ins. Co., 82 N.C. App. 616, 347 S.E.2d 489 (1986), cert. denied, 318 N.C. 696, 351 S.E.2d 749 (1987).

The financial condition of the insured is relevant to an arson defense in a suit upon a fire insurance policy. Chavis v. State Farm Fire & Cas. Co., 79 N.C. App. 213, 338 S.E.2d 787, rev'd on other grounds, 317 N.C. 683, 346 S.E.2d 496 (1986).

Waiver by Inducing Delay in Filing. — An insurance company which causes or induces the insured to delay in furnishing sufficient notice and proofs of loss thereby waives such delay. Northern Assurance Co. of Am. v. Spencer, 246 F. Supp. 730 (W.D.N.C. 1965), aff'd, 373 F.2d 35 (4th Cir. 1966).

Violation of Provision Held Not a Forfeiture. — A clause in a policy requiring proof of loss and forbidding the bringing of any suit upon the policy until 60 days thereafter is a continuing one, and does not mean that failure to file proof within 60 days of the fire works a forfeiture of the policy. Higson v. North River Ins. Co., 152 N.C. 206, 67 S.E. 509 (1910).

Good Cause Failure to Comply with Proof of Loss Requirements. — The failure of an insured to comply with the proof of loss requirements, if it was for "good cause" and did not prejudice the insurer, will not relieve the insurer of its obligation to pay on the policy. Smith v. North Carolina Farm Bureau Mut.

Ins. Co., 84 N.C. App. 120, 351 S.E.2d 774, aff'd, 321 N.C. 60, 361 S.E.2d 571 (1987).

The insured under a fire insurance policy must bear the burden of proof as to "good cause" for the failure to give timely proof of loss, and the insurer must bear the burden of proof as to prejudice. Smith v. North Carolina Farm Bureau Mut. Ins. Co., 321 N.C. 60, 361 S.E.2d 571 (1987).

Limitations on Bringing Suit. — The provisions of the limitation of suit, "and unless commenced within twelve months next after the inception of the loss," are used conjunctively, so that there must be compliance with all the requirements of the policy, and the suit or action must be commenced within 12 months next after inception of the loss. Boyd v. Bankers & Shippers Ins. Co., 245 N.C. 503, 96 S.E.2d 703 (1957).

Effect of § 58-44-50 was to alter earlier holdings which had dictated that a defect in the proof of loss under the terms of a fire insurance policy operates as a strict forfeiture of the right to recover for loss. Smith v. North Carolina Farm Bureau Mut. Ins., Co., 321 N.C. 60, 361 S.E.2d 571 (1987).

Effect of § 1-52(12). — By enacting G.S. 1-52(12), the General Assembly intended only to include the standard fire insurance policy limitation period in the comprehensive list of actions which are generally subject to three-year periods of limitation and to provide a cross-reference between general statutory periods of limitation contained in G.S. 1-52, and the more specific limitation provisions of the Standard Fire Insurance Policy for North Carolina set out in subsection (c) of this section. Marshburn v. Associated Indem. Corp., 84 N.C. App. 365, 353 S.E.2d 123, cert. denied, 319 N.C. 673, 356 S.E.2d 779 (1987).

The Standard Fire Insurance Policy limitation provision, contained in G.S. 1-52(12) and subsection (c) of this section, and reproduced in plaintiffs' policy of homeowners' insurance, constituted a limitation period "otherwise provided by statute," which precluded the applicability of G.S. 1-52(16) to the case. Marshburn v. Associated Indem. Corp., 84 N.C. App. 365, 353 S.E.2d 123, cert. denied, 319 N.C. 673, 356 S.E.2d 779 (1987).

Construction with § 58-3-35. — The provisions of a standard fire insurance policy, as set out in this section, must be construed with the provisions of G.S. 58-3-35, and when the action is brought within the time therein prescribed it will not be barred. Modlin v. Atlantic Fire Ins. Co., 151 N.C. 35, 65 S.E. 605 (1909).

Under the standard policy and G.S. 58-3-35, the insured has 60 days to file his proof of loss, and then he has 12 months within which to commence his suit. Muse v. London Assurance Corp., 108 N.C. 240, 13 S.E. 94 (1891); Dibbrell v. Georgia Home Ins. Co., 110 N.C. 193, 14 S.E.

783 (1892); Lowe v. United States Mut. Accident Ass'n, 115 N.C. 18, 20 S.E. 169 (1894); Gerringer v. North Carolina Home Ins. Co., 133 N.C. 407, 45 S.E. 773 (1903).

The word "inception" means "act or process of beginning; commencement; initiation." Hence, "inception" necessarily means that the beginning, the commencement, the initiation of the loss was that caused by the fire. Boyd v. Bankers & Shippers Ins. Co., 245 N.C. 503, 96 S.E.2d 703 (1957).

Noncompliance with Time Limitation Bars Action. — If, in an action upon a fire insurance policy, the judge sustained a demurrer to the complaint and a new complaint was filed more than 12 months "after the inception of the loss," nothing else appearing, the action would be barred for failure to comply with this section. Gaskins v. Hartford Fire Ins. Co., 260 N.C. 122, 131 S.E.2d 872 (1963).

In an action upon a policy of fire insurance in the standard form, judgment of nonsuit was proper when the record disclosed that more than 12 months elapsed between the inception of the loss and the commencement of the suit. Boyd v. Bankers & Shippers Ins. Co., 245 N.C. 503, 96 S.E.2d 703 (1957).

Where, after the occurrence of loss, insurer's local agent advised insured to defer filing formal claim until such time as materials could be obtained for repairs, and insured failed to file proof of loss within the time specified in the policy and did not institute action on the policy until after the expiration of the time limited therein, insurer's demurrer should have been sustained. Zibelin v. Pawtucket Mut. Fire Ins. Co., 229 N.C. 567, 50 S.E.2d 290 (1948).

A claim filed after the contractual time limitation has expired is barred, regardless of its merit, unless the insurer, by its conduct, waives or is estopped from relying upon the limitation provision of the policy. Marshburn v. Associated Indem. Corp., 84 N.C. App. 365, 353 S.E.2d 123, cert. denied, 319 N.C. 673, 356 S.E.2d 779 (1987).

Exception Where Longer Time Agreed Upon. — Statutory requirement that an action on a fire insurance policy must be instituted within 12 months after the loss unless a longer time to institute suit is agreed upon between the parties and such agreement appears on the face of the policy is binding upon the parties in the absence of waiver or estoppel; and where insured, instituting action more than 12 months after the loss, relies upon such statutory exception, he must plead facts bringing himself thereunder. Meekins v. Aetna Ins. Co., 231 N.C. 452, 57 S.E.2d 777, 15 A.L.R.2d 949 (1950); Boyd v. Bankers & Shippers Ins. Co., 245 N.C. 503, 96 S.E.2d 703 (1957).

Time Stipulation Is Not Construed as Statute of Limitations. — As the stipulation of the standard policy is a contract, and not a statute of limitations, it may be waived, or the party for whose benefit it was provided may be estopped by his conduct from insisting upon its enforcement. Dibbrell v. Georgia Home Ins. Co., 110 N.C. 193, 14 S.E. 783 (1892). See Meekins v. Aetna Ins. Co., 231 N.C. 452, 57 S.E.2d 777, 15 A.L.R.2d 949 (1950).

The standard policy is not regulated by the statute of limitations, and the disabilities which stop the running of the statute have no effect upon it. Hence, the imprisonment of the insured will not give him a right to recover when he has delayed his action for more than a year. This rule applies likewise to minors. Holly v. London Assurance Co., 170 N.C. 4, 86 S.E. 694 (1915).

And Is Subject to Waiver or Estoppel. — A provision in a standard fire insurance policy that action on it must be commenced within 12 months after inception of the loss is contractual. It is, therefore, subject to waiver or estoppel. Gaskins v. Hartford Fire Ins. Co., 260 N.C. 122, 131 S.E.2d 872 (1963).

Waiver of Time Provision. — Where insurer enters into negotiations with insured and promises that the claim will be paid or satisfactorily adjusted upon completion of investigation, and thereafter insurer demands additional proof of loss without denying the claim after it is too late for suit to be brought within the 12 months' period, insurer waives the policy provision requiring action to be instituted within 12 months next after loss. Meekins v. Aetna Ins. Co., 231 N.C. 452, 57 S.E.2d 777, 15 A.L.R.2d 949 (1950).

Where insured filed a complaint stating an enforceable cause of action within 12 months of the loss by fire, and after the expiration of the 12-month period the parties consented that defendant's demurrer should be sustained, and thereafter an amended complaint was filed in accordance with the consent order, defendant insurer was not permitted to assert the provision of the policy that action be instituted within 12 months after loss, since the provision was contractual and subject to waiver or estoppel. Gaskins v. Hartford Fire Ins. Co., 260 N.C. 122, 131 S.E.2d 872 (1963).

The valid provision of a standard fire insurance policy, approved by statute, limiting to 12 months from the time of loss by fire the time within which an action might be maintained, was not waived by the time taken under an agreement for an appraisal and award for the damage sustained by the insured. John Tatham & Co. v. Liverpool, London & Globe Ins. Co., 181 N.C. 434, 107 S.E. 450 (1921).

Time Limitation Provision Held Valid. — Provision of insurance policy that no suit or action on the policy for the recovery of any claim would be sustainable unless all requirements of the policy had been complied with, and unless commenced within three years next

after inception of the loss, complied with the "Standard Fire Insurance Policy for North Carolina" prescribed by this section and was a valid contractual limitation, binding upon and enforceable between the parties. Marshburn v. Associated Indem. Corp., 84 N.C. App. 365, 353 S.E.2d 123, cert. denied, 319 N.C. 673, 356 S.E.2d 779 (1987).

The phrase "inception of the loss," when used in a policy of insurance, means that the policy limitation period runs from the date of the occurrence of the event out of which the claim for recovery arose. Marshburn v. Associated Indem. Corp., 84 N.C. App. 365, 353 S.E.2d 123, cert. denied, 319 N.C. 673, 356 S.E.2d 779 (1987).

Discovery of Damage After Running of Limitations Period. — The insured's failure or inability to discover damage resulting from the casualty insured against until after the contractual limitations period has run is immaterial and does not operate to toll or restart the limitations period. Marshburn v. Associated Indem. Corp., 84 N.C. App. 365, 353 S.E.2d 123, cert. denied, 319 N.C. 673, 356 S.E.2d 779 (1987).

IV. APPRAISAL AND RECOVERY.

Constitutionality of Appraisal Clause. — The appraisal clause did not deprive plaintiff of his right to due process under the North Carolina Constitution. Bentley v. North Carolina Ins. Guar. Ass'n, 107 N.C. App. 1, 418 S.E.2d 705 (1992).

Plaintiff's right under the North Carolina Constitution to trial by jury was not abridged by the appraisal clause. Bentley v. North Carolina Ins. Guar. Ass'n, 107 N.C. App. 1, 418 S.E.2d 705 (1992).

The policy appraisal procedure is analogous to an arbitration proceeding; thus, errors of law or fact are insufficient to invalidate an award fairly and honestly made. Enzor v. North Carolina Farm Bureau Mut. Ins. Co., 123 N.C. App. 544, 473 S.E.2d 638 (1996).

Trial court did not err by failing to instruct the appraisers and umpire on the proper method for determining actual cash value. Enzor v. North Carolina Farm Bureau Mut. Ins. Co., 123 N.C. App. 544, 473 S.E.2d 638 (1996).

Appraisal procedure was not followed where report was signed only by the umpire as the umpire's signature alone failed to demonstrate that at least one other appraiser concurred in the award; thus, the appraisal award was invalid. Enzor v. North Carolina Farm Bureau Mut. Ins. Co., 123 N.C. App. 544, 473 S.E.2d 638 (1996).

Option to Repair, Rebuild, or Replace Property as Contract Between Insurer and Insured. — A provision in a policy of fire insurance by which, in case of loss, it is made optional with the insurer to repair, rebuild, or replace the property destroyed, by giving notice within a certain time, constitutes a contract exclusively between insurer and insured; and neither a judgment creditor nor a mortgagee can interpose to prevent its performance. Moreover, if the insurer has not given notice of an intention to repair, etc., within the time specified, no one but the insured can take advantage of it and require the payment of the insurance money instead. Stamps v. Commercial Fire Ins. Co., 77 N.C. 209, 24 Am. R. 443 (1877).

Cost of Replacement at Time of Fire Determinative. — The amount which the company is obligated to pay is measured not by the cost of such replacement at the inception of the policy but by the cost of such replacement at the time of the fire. In re North Carolina Fire Ins. Rating Bureau, 275 N.C. 15, 165 S.E.2d 207 (1969).

Appointment of Umpire Is Not Judgment of Court. — The appointment of an umpire pursuant to the "appraisal" clause is not the judgment of a court, but a mere ministerial act pursuant to contract, albeit authorized by statute. In re Roberts Co., 258 N.C. 184, 128 S.E.2d 137 (1962).

No Notice or Hearing Required for Appointment of Umpire. — The appointment of an umpire is made at the request of either the insurer or insured; no notice to the other is required and no hearing is contemplated. In re Roberts Co., 258 N.C. 184, 128 S.E.2d 137 (1962).

Appointment Need Not Be Made at Any Particular Time or Place. — There is no requirement that the appointment of an umpire be made in term or at any particular time

or place. In re Roberts Co., 258 N.C. 184, 128 S.E.2d 137 (1962).

Challenge to Validity of Appointment of Umpire. — The validity of the appointment of an umpire by a judge may be adjudicated when the question is raised in a properly instituted civil action. Bentley v. North Carolina Ins. Guar. Ass'n, 107 N.C. App. 1, 418 S.E.2d 705 (1992).

The appointment of an umpire may be challenged only by an action instituted for that purpose. In re Roberts Co., 258 N.C. 184, 128 S.E.2d 137 (1962).

The legal effect of the appointment of an umpire and any acts done pursuant thereto may be challenged in any action in which they arise. In re Roberts Co., 258 N.C. 184, 128 S.E.2d 137 (1962).

Damage by Water. — In an early case decided prior to enactment of this section, it was held that an insurance company was liable on a fire insurance policy for damages done to goods by water used in saving them from destruction by fire. Whitehurst v. Fayetteville Mut. Ins. Co., 51 N.C. 352 (1859).

Loss by theft is excluded from the standard policy set out in this section. However, it was formerly held that such loss consequent on the removal of goods in case of fire was fairly within a contract to insure against fire. Whitehurst v. Fayetteville Mut. Ins. Co., 51 N.C. 352 (1859).

For cases decided prior to the enactment of this statute, holding that the amount the insured was entitled to recover was the "fair" cash value of the property at the time and place of the loss, see Fowler v. Old N. State Ins. Co., 74 N.C. 89 (1876); Grubbs v. North Carolina Home Ins. Co., 108 N.C. 472, 13 S.E. 236, 23 Am. St. R. 62 (1891); Boyd v. Royal Ins. Co., 111 N.C. 372, 16 S.E. 389 (1892).

§ 58-44-20. Standard policy; permissible variations.

No fire insurance company shall issue fire insurance policies, except policies of automobile fire, theft, comprehensive and collision, marine and inland marine insurance, on property in this State other than those of the substance of the standard form as set forth in G.S. 58-44-15 except as follows:

(1) A company may print on or in its policies the date of incorporation, the amount of its paid-up capital stock, the names of its officers, and to the words at the top of the back of said policy, "Standard Fire Insurance Policy for" may be added after or before the words "North Carolina" the names of any states or political jurisdiction in which the said policy form may be standard when the policy is used.

(2) A company may print in its policies or use in its policies written or printed forms of description and specification of the property insured.

(3) A company may write or print upon the margin or across the face of a policy, in unused spaces or upon separate slips or riders to be attached thereto, provisions adding to or modifying those contained in the standard form, and all such slips, riders, and provisions must be signed by an officer or agent of the company so using them. Provided, however, such provisions shall not have the effect of making the provisions of the standard policy form more restrictive except for such

restrictions as are provided for in the charter or bylaws of a domestic mutual fire insurance company doing business in no more than three adjacent counties of the State and chiefly engaged in writing policies of insurance on rural properties upon an assessment or nonpremium basis, provided all such restrictions contained in the charter and bylaws of such domestic mutual fire insurance company shall be actually included within the printed terms of the policy contract so affected as a condition precedent to their being effective and binding on any policyholder. The iron safe or any similar clause requiring the taking of inventories, the keeping of books and producing the same in the adjustment of any loss, shall not be used or operative in the settlement of losses on buildings, furniture and fixtures, or any property not subject to any change in bulk and value.

(4) Binders or other contracts for temporary insurance may be made, orally or in writing, for a period which shall not exceed 60 days, and shall be deemed to include all the terms of such standard fire insurance policy and all such applicable endorsements, approved by the Commissioner, as may be designated in such contract of temporary insurance; except that the cancellation clause of such standard fire insurance policy, and the clause thereof specifying the hour of the day at which the insurance shall commence, may be superseded by the express terms of such contract of temporary insurance.

(5) Two or more companies authorized to do in this State the business of fire insurance, may, with the approval of the Commissioner, issue a combination standard form of fire insurance policy which shall contain the following provisions:

a. A provision substantially to the effect that the insurers executing such policy shall be severally liable for the full amount of any loss or damage, according to the terms of the policy, or for specified percentages or amounts thereof, aggregating the full amount of such insurance under such policy.

b. A provision substantially to the effect that service of process, or of any notice or proof of loss required by such policy, upon any of the companies executing such policy, shall be deemed to be service upon all such insurers.

(6) Appropriate forms of supplemental contract or contracts or extended coverage endorsements and other endorsements whereby the interest in the property described in such policy shall be insured against one or more of the perils which the company is empowered to assume, in addition to the perils covered by said standard fire insurance policy may be approved by the Commissioner, and their use in connection with a standard fire insurance policy may be authorized by him. In his discretion the Commissioner may authorize the printing of such supplemental contract or contracts or extended coverage endorsements and other endorsements in the substance of the form of the standard fire insurance policy. The first page of the policy may in form approved by the Commissioner be arranged to provide space for listing of amounts of insurance, rates and premiums, description of construction, occupancy and location of property covered for the basic coverages insured under the standard form of policy and for additional coverages or perils insured under endorsements attached or printed therein, and such other data as may be conveniently included for duplication on daily reports for office records.

(7) A company may print on or in its policy, with the approval of the Commissioner, any provisions which it is required by law to insert in its policies not in conflict with the substance of provisions of such

standard form. Such provisions shall be printed apart from the other provisions, agreements, or conditions of the policy, under a separate title, as follows: "Provisions Required by Law to Be Inserted in This Policy." (1899, c. 54, s. 43; 1901, c. 391, s. 4; Rev., s. 4759; 1907, c. 800, s. 1; 1915, c. 109, s. 10; C.S., s. 6436; 1925, c. 70, s. 5; 1945, c. 378; 1949, c. 418; 1951, c. 767; c. 781, s. 5; 1955, c. 807, s. 3; 1979, c. 755, ss. 5-7.)

Cross References. — For the Readable Insurance Policies Act, see G.S. 58-38-1 et seq.

Legal Periodicals. — For brief comment on the second 1951 amendment, see 29 N.C.L. Rev. 398 (1951).

For note discussing interpretation of notice provisions in insurance contracts, in light of Great Am. Ins. Co. v. C.G. Tate Constr. Co., 303 N.C. 387, 279 S.E.2d 769 (1981), see 61 N.C.L. Rev. 167 (1982).

CASE NOTES

Legislative Intent. — The wording of the statute is unambiguous, reflecting a clear legislative intent that binders and contracts for temporary insurance be enforceable for only 60 days. Hornby v. Pennsylvania Nat'l Mut. Cas. Ins. Co., 62 N.C. App. 419, 303 S.E.2d 332, cert. denied, 309 N.C. 461, 307 S.E.2d 364, 307 S.E.2d 365 (1983).

The word "restrictive" in subdivision (3) of this section, construed in light of the statutory object and not in a narrow or technical sense, was intended to cover any clause or provision included in or appended to the standard fire policy whereby an essential provision of the standard fire policy, materially influencing the rights of the insured, is limited or modified. Greenway v. North Carolina Farm Bureau Mut. Ins. Co., 35 N.C. App. 308, 241 S.E.2d 339 (1978).

Limiting Provisions. — An insurer may insure only such properties as are situated outside the limits set out in a limiting provision, which provision is descriptive, not restrictive, of the standard coverage. What an insurer may not do is promise general coverage, receive appropriate premium payment and then restrict coverage by a restrictively limiting provision. Greenway v. North Carolina Farm Bureau Mut. Ins. Co., 35 N.C. App. 308, 241 S.E.2d 339 (1978).

"Binder". — In insurance parlance, a "binder" is insurer's bare acknowledgment of its contract to protect the insured against casualty of a specified kind until a formal policy can be issued, or until insured gives notice of its election to terminate. Mayo v. American Fire & Cas. Co., 15 N.C. App. 309, 190 S.E.2d 398, vacated on other grounds, 282 N.C. 346, 192 S.E.2d 828 (1972).

No specific form is necessary to constitute a binder as a valid contract of insurance. Mayo v. American Fire & Cas. Co., 282 N.C. 346, 192 S.E.2d 828 (1972).

Binder Not Required to Set Forth All Terms of Contract. — It is not required that the writing, or oral communication, intended as a binder set forth all the terms of the contemplated contract of insurance. Mayo v. American Fire & Cas. Co., 282 N.C. 346, 192 S.E.2d 828 (1972).

The statutory fire insurance provisions are read into all binders, whether oral or written. Allstate Ins. Co. v. Old Republic Ins. Co., 49 N.C. App. 32, 270 S.E.2d 510 (1980).

An extension of credit to the insured for the premium does not destroy the validity of the binder. Mayo v. American Fire & Cas. Co., 282 N.C. 346, 192 S.E.2d 828 (1972).

Binders are void beyond the 60-day statutory period. Hornby v. Pennsylvania Nat'l Mut. Cas. Ins. Co., 62 N.C. App. 419, 303 S.E.2d 332, cert. denied, 309 N.C. 461, 307 S.E.2d 364, 307 S.E.2d 365 (1983).

Negligent Conduct by Insurance Company on Binder Application. — Where the evidence showed only that the insurance company negligently delayed in acting upon plaintiff's application for insurance, even if such conduct constituted a violation of subdivision (4) of this section, such a violation did not justify an award of punitive damages. Hornby v. Pennsylvania Nat'l Mut. Cas. Ins. Co., 62 N.C. App. 419, 303 S.E.2d 332, cert. denied, 309 N.C. 461, 307 S.E.2d 364, 307 S.E.2d 365 (1983).

Getting a rating from the Rating Bureau is not a prerequisite to entering into a contract of insurance. Mayo v. American Fire & Cas. Co., 282 N.C. 346, 192 S.E.2d 828 (1972).

Applied in Faircloth v. Ohio Farmers Ins. Co., 253 N.C. 522, 117 S.E.2d 404 (1960).

Cited in Hodges v. Home Ins. Co., 233 N.C. 289, 63 S.E.2d 819 (1951); Cuthrell v. Milwaukee Mechanics Ins. Co., 234 N.C. 137, 66 S.E.2d 649 (1951); Pruitt v. Great Am. Ins. Co., 241 N.C. 725, 86 S.E.2d 401 (1955); Boyd v. Bankers & Shippers Ins. Co., 245 N.C. 503, 96 S.E.2d 703 (1957); Webster Enters., Inc. v. Selective

Ins. Co., 125 N.C. App. 36, 479 S.E.2d 243 (1996).

§ 58-44-25. Optional provisions as to loss or damage from nuclear reaction, nuclear radiation or radioactive contamination.

Insurers issuing the standard fire insurance policy pursuant to G.S. 58-44-15, or any permissible variation thereof, and policies issued pursuant to G.S. 58-44-20 and Article 36 of this Chapter, are hereby authorized to affix thereto or include therein a written statement that the policy does not cover loss or damage caused by nuclear reaction or nuclear radiation or radioactive contamination, all whether directly or indirectly resulting from an insured peril under said policy; provided, however, that nothing herein contained shall be construed to prohibit the attachment to any such policy of an endorsement or endorsements specifically assuming coverage for loss or damage caused by nuclear reaction or nuclear radiation or radioactive contamination. (1963, c. 1148; 1987, c. 864, s. 7.)

§ 58-44-30. Notice by insured or agent as to increase of hazard, unoccupancy and other insurance.

If notice in writing signed by the insured, or his agent, is given before loss or damage by any peril insured against under the standard fire insurance policy to the agent of the company of any fact or condition stated in paragraphs (a), (b) or with respect to "other insurance" of the standard form of policy set out in G.S. 58-44-15 it is equivalent to an agreement in writing added thereto, and has the force of the agreement in writing referred to in the foregoing form of policy with respect to the liability of the company and the waiver; but this notice does not affect the right of the company to cancel the policy as therein stipulated. (1899, c. 54, s. 43; Rev., s. 4761; 1907, c. 578, s. 1; 1915, c. 109, s. 11; C.S., s. 6438; 1929, c. 60, s. 1; 1945, c. 378.)

CASE NOTES

Cited in State v. Fraylon, 240 N.C. 365, 82 S.E.2d 400 (1954).

§ 58-44-35. Judge to select umpire.

The resident judge of the superior court of the district in which the property insured is located is designated as the judge of the court of record to select the umpire referred to in the standard form of policy. (1945, c. 378.)

§ 58-44-40. Effect of failure to give notice of encumbrance.

No policy of insurance issued upon any property shall be held void because of the failure to give notice to the company of a mortgage or deed of trust existing thereon or thereafter placed thereon, except during the life of the mortgage or deed of trust. (1915, c. 109, s. 4; C.S., s. 6440.)

CASE NOTES

Cited in State v. Fraylon, 240 N.C. 365, 82 S.E.2d 400 (1954).

§ 58-44-45. Policy issued to husband or wife on joint property.

Any policy of fire insurance issued to husband or wife, on buildings and household furniture owned by the husband and wife, either by entirety, in common, or jointly, either name of one of the parties in interest named as the insured or beneficiary therein, shall be sufficient and the policy shall not be void for failure to disclose the interest of the other, unless it appears that in the procuring of the issuance of such policy, fraudulent means or methods were used by the insured or owner thereof. (1945, c. 378.)

Legal Periodicals. — For article on tenancy by the entirety in North Carolina, see 41 N.C.L. Rev. 67 (1962).

For survey of 1979 property law, see 58 N.C.L. Rev. 1509 (1980).

For note on innocent spouse's right to recover after husband's arson, see 17 Wake Forest L. Rev. 1022 (1981).

CASE NOTES

Right of Wife to Proceeds of Policy Issued to Husband Alone. — A policy of fire insurance issued to a husband on a house held by the entirety but occupied by him alone while separated from his wife inured to the benefit of the entire estate as owned by both husband and wife, and where the entire estate, as so insured, was severed by absolute divorce after fire, the wife was entitled to receive half the proceeds of the insurance moneys paid into court. Carter v. Continental Ins. Co., 242 N.C. 578, 89 S.E.2d 122 (1955), commented on in 35 N.C.L. Rev. 134 (1956).

Where husband and wife sell lands held by entireties and take a note secured by a deed of trust in part payment of the purchase price, the wife's interest in the note is personalty and she owns no interest in the dwelling on the land so as to bring her within the purview of this section; therefore, she is not covered by the mortgage clause in a policy of fire insurance on the premises in which she is not named. Shores v. Rabon, 251 N.C. 790, 112 S.E.2d 556 (1960).

Recovery by Wife Where Husband Burns Property. — An innocent wife can recover under an insurance policy issued to her husband which insures property owned by them as tenants by the entirety, when the loss by fire resulted from intentional burning of the property by the husband. Lovell v. Rowan Mut. Fire Ins. Co., 302 N.C. 150, 274 S.E.2d 170 (1981).

Cited in Worrells v. North Carolina Farm Bureau Mut. Ins. Co., 103 N.C. App. 69, 404 S.E.2d 188 (1991).

§ 58-44-50. Bar to defense of failure to render timely proof of loss.

In any action brought to enforce an insurance policy subject to the provisions of this Article, any party claiming benefit under the policy may reply to the pleading of any other party against whom liability is sought which asserts as a defense, the failure to render timely proof of loss as required by the terms of the policy that such failure was for good cause and that the failure to render timely proof of loss has not substantially harmed the party against whom liability is sought in his ability to defend. The issues raised by such reply shall be determined by the jury if jury trial has been demanded. (1973, c. 1391.)

CASE NOTES

This section was intended to benefit the insured, and not the insurer, by relieving the hardship which had resulted from the courts' strict contractual approach. Smith v. North Carolina Farm Bureau Mut. Ins. Co., 84 N.C. App. 120, 351 S.E.2d 774, aff'd, 321 N.C. 20, 361 S.E.2d 571 (1987).

The failure of an insured to comply with proof of loss requirements, if it was for "good cause" and did not prejudice the insurer, will not relieve the insurer of its obligation to pay on the policy. Smith v. North Carolina Farm Bureau Mut. Ins. Co., 84 N.C. App. 120, 351 S.E.2d 774, aff'd, 321 N.C. 60, 361 S.E.2d 571 (1987).

The effect of G.S. 58-44-50 was to alter earlier holdings which had dictated that a defect in the proof of loss under the terms of a fire insurance policy operated as a strict forfeiture of the right to recover for loss. Smith v. North Carolina Farm Bureau Mut. Ins. Co., 321 N.C. 60, 361 S.E.2d 571 (1987).

Insured Must Prove Good Cause. — Before the burden of showing substantial harm may be placed on the insurer, the insured must prove to the jury that his actions were for "good cause." Smith v. North Carolina Farm Bureau Mut. Ins. Co., 84 N.C. App. 120, 351 S.E.2d 774, aff'd, 321 N.C. 60, 361 S.E.2d 571 (1987).

The burden of showing prejudice is on the insurance company, once the insured carries the burden of showing "good faith" in his failure to properly notify the insurance company. Smith v. North Carolina Farm Bureau Mut. Ins. Co., 84 N.C. App. 120, 351 S.E.2d 774, aff'd, 321 N.C. 60, 361 S.E.2d 571 (1987).

What Pleadings Required. — This section requires no more technical pleadings than the principles of notice pleading would otherwise require. Smith v. North Carolina Farm Bureau Mut. Ins. Co., 84 N.C. App. 120, 351 S.E.2d 774, aff'd, 321 N.C. 60, 361 S.E.2d 571 (1987).

Complaint Held Sufficient. — Plaintiff insured's complaint against insurers sufficiently alleged the provisions of this section, where he alleged that he submitted a sworn proof of loss statement which set forth that his losses were in excess of the policy limits, although he failed to include on the proof of loss statement, among other things, the actual cash value of the prop-

erty at the time of the loss, the "whole loss and damage," and the "amount claimed," as plaintiff's allegation that his losses exceeded the policy limits would suggest that plaintiff believed that the omitted information was irrelevant since defendant, if liable, was obligated to pay only up to those limits if, in fact, the losses did exceed them, and thus plaintiff's allegations were sufficient to bring the issue of substantial harm before the trial court. Smith v. North Carolina Farm Bureau Mut. Ins. Co., 84 N.C. App. 120, 351 S.E.2d 774, aff'd, 321 N.C. 60, 361 S.E.2d 571 (1987).

Where plaintiff insured testified that he filled out proof of loss form according to the instructions he received, this was sufficient to enable a jury to find that plaintiff, at least subjectively, had good cause for failing to properly file the proof of loss statement. Therefore, lack of good cause on the part of plaintiff could not have been a basis for granting a directed verdict. Smith v. North Carolina Farm Bureau Mut. Ins. Co., 84 N.C. App. 120, 351 S.E.2d 774, aff'd, 321 N.C. 60, 361 S.E.2d 571 (1987).

Facts held sufficient to require the court to charge the jury under the provisions of this section. Brandon v. Nationwide Mut. Fire Ins. Co., 46 N.C. App. 472, 265 S.E.2d 497, modified and aff'd, 301 N.C. 366, 271 S.E.2d 380 (1980).

Applied in Brandon v. Nationwide Mut. Fire Ins. Co., 301 N.C. 366, 271 S.E.2d 380 (1980).

§ 58-44-55. Farmowners' and other property policies; ice, snow, or sleet damage.

Under any policy of farmowners' or other property insurance that insures against all direct loss by fire, lightning, or other perils that may be delivered or issued for delivery in this State with respect to any farm dwellings, appurtenant private structures, barns, or other farm buildings or farm structures located in this State, coverage shall be available for inclusion therein or supplemental thereto to include direct loss caused by weight of ice, snow, or sleet that results in physical damage to such buildings or structures, and shall be offered to all insureds requesting these policies. (1981, c. 550, s. 1.)

Legal Periodicals. — For survey of 1981 administrative law, see 60 N.C.L. Rev. 1165 (1982).

ARTICLE 45.

Essential Property Insurance for Beach Area Property.

§ 58-45-1. Declarations and purpose of Article.

(a) It is hereby declared by the General Assembly of North Carolina that an adequate market for essential property insurance is necessary to the economic welfare of the beach and coastal areas of the State of North Carolina and that without such insurance the orderly growth and development of those areas would be severely impeded; that furthermore, adequate insurance upon property in the beach and coastal areas is necessary to enable homeowners and commercial owners to obtain financing for the purchase and improvement of their property; and that while the need for such insurance is increasing, the market for such insurance is not adequate and is likely to become less adequate in the future; and that the present plans to provide adequate insurance on property in the beach and coastal areas, while deserving praise, have not been sufficient to meet the needs of this area. It is further declared that the State has an obligation to provide an equitable method whereby every licensed insurer writing essential property insurance in North Carolina is required to meet its public responsibility instead of shifting the burden to a few willing and public-spirited insurers. It is the purpose of this Article to accept this obligation and to provide a mandatory program to assure an adequate market for essential property insurance in the beach and coastal areas of North Carolina.

(b) The General Assembly further declares that it is its intent in creating and, from time to time, amending this Article that the market provided by this Article not be the first market of choice, but the market of last resort. (1967, c. 1111, s. 1; 1969, c. 249; 1979, c. 601, s. 1; 1997-498, s. 9.)

Editor's Note. — Session Laws 2002-185, s. 1, effective October 31, 2002, provides:

"The General Assembly of North Carolina finds that:

"(1) An adequate market for property insurance is necessary to the economic welfare of the beach and coastal counties of North Carolina.

"(2) The establishment of the North Carolina Insurance Underwriting Association ("Beach Plan") was designed to provide a residual property insurance market in our State's beach and coastal counties.

"(3) Despite the availability of property protection through the Beach Plan, the availability of homeowners' insurance policies continues to be inadequate in beach and coastal counties.

"(4) In an effort to address this ongoing problem, the Commissioner of Insurance has requested the Board of Directors of the Beach Plan to offer homeowners' insurance to residents in beach and coastal counties.

"(5) The Board of Directors of the Beach Plan has developed a homeowners' policy and has submitted this policy to the Commissioner of Insurance for approval.

"(6) The Commissioner of Insurance has the authority under G.S. 58-45-30 to direct and approve the offering of a homeowners' insurance policy through the Beach Plan.

"(7) The availability of a homeowners' insurance policy offered through the Beach Plan will assist in alleviating the lack of homeowners' insurance currently available in beach and coastal counties.

"(8) The General Assembly will await further recommendations by the Commissioner of Insurance on other options to increase the availability of homeowners' insurance both in beach and coastal counties and statewide, as directed in Section 3 of this act." (see Editor's Notes, G.S. 58-45-1 and 58-46-1)

Session Laws 2002-185, s. 3, effective October 31, 2002, provides: "The Commissioner of Insurance, in consultation with other governmental bodies specified below, shall study the provisions of Articles 45 and 46 of Chapter 58 of the General Statutes, other relevant portions of the General Statutes, and the plans and operations of the North Carolina Insurance Underwriting Association ('Beach Plan') and the North Carolina Joint Underwriting Association ('FAIR Plan'). In this study, the Commissioner may consider all issues and potential remedies related to the availability of homeowners' insurance coverage statewide, and specifically in the beach and coastal counties of the State. In conducting this study, the Commissioner may call upon any department, agency, institution, or officer of the State or of any political subdivision of the State, and the North Carolina Rate Bureau, the North Carolina Insurance Underwriting Association ('Beach Plan'), the North Carolina Joint Underwriting Association ('FAIR Plan'), and the North Carolina Motor Vehicle Reinsurance Facility, and representatives of property and casualty insurers and reinsurers, for such assistance and information, and these departments, agencies, institutions, officers, and other entities shall cooperate with the Commissioner to the fullest possible extent. The Commissioner shall report to the 2003 General Assembly on or before April 1, 2003, on the Commissioner's findings and may make any legislative or other recommendations he considers appropriate."

Cited in Gray v. North Carolina Ins. Underwriting Ass'n, 352 N.C. 61, 529 S.E.2d 676,
2000 N.C. LEXIS 437 (2000).

§ 58-45-5. Definition of terms.

As used in this Article, unless the context clearly otherwise requires:
  (1) "Association" means the North Carolina Insurance Underwriting Association established under this Article;
  (2) "Beach area" means all of that area of the State of North Carolina south and east of the inland waterway from the South Carolina line to Fort Macon (Beaufort Inlet); thence south and east of Core, Pamlico, Roanoke and Currituck sounds to the Virginia line, being those portions of land generally known as the Outer Banks;
  (2a) "Coastal area" means all of that area of the State of North Carolina comprising the following counties: Beaufort, Brunswick, Camden, Carteret, Chowan, Craven, Currituck, Dare, Hyde, Jones, New Hanover, Onslow, Pamlico, Pasquotank, Pender, Perquimans, Tyrrell, and Washington. "Coastal area" does not include the portions of these counties that lie within the beach area.
  (3) Repealed by Session Laws 1991, c. 720, s. 6.
  (3a) "Crime insurance" means insurance against losses resulting from robbery, burglary, larceny, and similar crimes, as more specifically defined and limited in the various crime insurance policies, or their successor forms of coverage, approved by the Commissioner and issued by the Association. Such policies shall not be more restrictive than those issued under the Federal Crime Insurance Program authorized by Public Law 91-609.
  (3b) "Directors" means the Board of Directors of the Association.
  (4) "Essential property insurance" means insurance against direct loss to property as defined in the standard statutory fire policy and extended coverage, vandalism and malicious mischief endorsements thereon, or their successor forms of coverage, as approved by the Commissioner;
  (5) "Insurable property" means real property at fixed locations in the beach and coastal area, including travel trailers when tied down at a fixed location, or the tangible personal property located therein, but shall not include insurance on motor vehicles; which property is determined by the Association, after inspection and under the criteria specified in the plan of operation, to be in an insurable condition. However, any one and two family dwellings built in substantial accordance with the Federal Manufactured Home Construction and Safety Standards, any predecessor or successor federal or State construction or safety standards, and any further construction or safety standards promulgated by the association and approved by the Commissioner, or the North Carolina Uniform Residential Building Code and any structure or building built in substantial compliance with the North Carolina State Building Code, including the design-wind requirements, which is not otherwise rendered uninsurable by reason of use or occupancy, shall be an insurable risk within the meaning of this Article. However, none of the following factors shall be considered in determining insurable condition: neighborhood, area, location, environmental hazards beyond the control of the applicant or owner of the property. Also, any structure begun on or after January 1, 1970, not built in substantial compliance with the Federal Manu-

factured Home Construction and Safety Standards, any predecessor or successor federal or State construction or safety standards, and any further construction or safety standards promulgated by the association and approved by the Commissioner, or the North Carolina Uniform Residential Building Code or the North Carolina State Building Code, including the design-wind requirements therein, shall not be an insurable risk. The owner or applicant shall furnish with the application proof in the form of a certificate from a local building inspector, contractor, engineer or architect that the structure is built in substantial accordance with the Federal Manufactured Home Construction and Safety Standards, any predecessor or successor federal or State construction or safety standards, and any further construction or safety standards promulgated by the association and approved by the Commissioner, or the North Carolina Uniform Residential Building Code or the North Carolina State Building Code; however, an individual certificate shall not be necessary where the structure is located within a political subdivision which has certified to the Association on an annual basis that it is enforcing the North Carolina Uniform Residential Building Code or the North Carolina State Building Code and has no plans to discontinue enforcing these codes during that year.

(6) Repealed by Session Laws 1995 (Regular Session, 1996), c. 592, s. 2.

(6a) "Net direct premiums" means gross direct premiums (excluding reinsurance assumed and ceded) written on property in this State for essential property insurance, farmowners insurance, homeowners insurance, and the property portion of commercial multiple peril insurance policies as computed by the Commissioner, less:
　　a. Return premiums on uncancelled contracts;
　　b. Dividends paid or credited to policyholders; and
　　c. The unused or unabsorbed portion of premium deposits.

(7) "Plan of operation" or "plan" means the plan of operation of the Association approved or promulgated by the Commissioner under this Article. (1967, c. 1111, s. 1; 1969, c. 249; 1979, c. 601, ss. 2, 3; 1985, c. 516, s. 1; 1985 (Reg. Sess., 1986), c. 1027, ss. 21, 25; 1987 (Reg. Sess., 1988), c. 975, ss. 18, 19; 1991, c. 720, ss. 4, 6; 1991 (Reg. Sess., 1992), c. 784, s. 4; 1995 (Reg. Sess., 1996), c. 592, s. 2; 1997-498, s. 1.)

§ 58-45-6. Persons who can be insured by the Association.

As used in this Article, "person" includes the State of North Carolina and any county, city, or other political subdivision of the State of North Carolina. (2000-122, s. 5; 2002-187, s. 1.4.)

Effect of Amendments. — Session Laws 2002-187, s. 1.4, effective October 31, 2002, inserted "the State of North Carolina and."

§ 58-45-10. North Carolina Insurance Underwriting Association created.

There is hereby created the North Carolina Insurance Underwriting Association, consisting of all insurers authorized to write and engage in writing within this State, on a direct basis, essential property insurance, except town and county mutual insurance associations and assessable mutual companies as authorized by G.S. 58-7-75(5)b, 58-7-75(5)d, and 58-7-75(7)b and except an insurer who only writes insurance in this State on property exempted from taxation by the provisions of G.S. 105-278.1 through G.S. 105-278.8. Every such insurer shall be a member of the Association and shall remain a member of the Association so long as the Association is in existence as a condition of its authority to continue to transact the business of insurance in this State. (1967, c. 1111, s. 1; 1969, c. 249; 1971, c. 1067, s. 2; 1987 (Reg. Sess., 1988), c. 975, s. 20; 1998-211, s. 6.)

CASE NOTES

Cited in Gray v. North Carolina Ins. Underwriting Ass'n, 352 N.C. 61, 529 S.E.2d 676, 2000 N.C. LEXIS 437 (2000).

§ 58-45-15. Powers and duties of Association.

The Association shall, pursuant to the provisions of this Article and the plan of operation, and with respect to the insurance coverages authorized in this Article, have the power on behalf of its members:

    (1) To cause to be issued policies of insurance to applicants;

    (2) To assume reinsurance from its members;

    (3) To cede reinsurance to its members and to purchase reinsurance in behalf of its members. (1967, c. 1111, s. 1; 1969, c. 249; 1999-114, s. 7.)

§ 58-45-20. Temporary directors of Association.

Within 10 days after April 17, 1969, the Commissioner shall appoint a temporary board of directors of this Association, which shall consist of 11 representatives of members of the Association. Such temporary board of directors shall prepare and submit a plan of operation in accordance with G.S. 58-45-30 and shall serve until the permanent board of directors shall take office in accordance with said plan of operation. (1967, c. 1111, s. 1; 1969, c. 249.)

§ 58-45-25. Each member of Association to participate in its expenses, profits, and losses.

(a) Each member of the Association shall participate in the expenses, profits, and losses of the Association in the proportion that its net direct premium written in this State during the preceding calendar year for residential and commercial properties outside of the beach and coastal areas bears to the aggregate net direct premiums written in this State during the preceding calendar year for residential and commercial properties outside of the beach and coastal areas by all members of the Association, as certified to the Association by the Commissioner. The Commissioner shall certify each member's participation after review of annual statements and any other reports and data necessary to determine participation and may obtain any necessary information or data from any member of the Association for this purpose. Any insurer that is authorized to write and that is engaged in writing any insurance, the writing of which requires the insurer to be a member of the Association under G.S. 58-45-10, shall become a member of the Association on the first day of January after authorization. The determination of the insurer's participation in the Association shall be made as of the date of membership of the insurer in the same manner as for all other members of the Association.

(b) All member companies shall receive credit each year for essential property insurance, farmowners insurance, homeowners insurance, and the property portion of commercial multiple peril policies voluntarily written in the beach and coastal areas in accordance with guidelines and procedures to be submitted by the Directors to the Commissioner for approval. The participation of each member company in the expenses, profits, and losses of the Association shall be reduced accordingly; provided, no credit shall be given where coverage for the peril of wind has been excluded. The guidelines and procedures for granting credit shall encourage and assist each member company to voluntarily write these coverages in the beach and coastal areas for commercial and residential properties.

(c) The North Carolina Insurance Underwriting Association shall use the "take out" program, as filed with and approved by the Commissioner, in the coastal area. (1967, c. 1111, s. 1; 1969, c. 249; 1991, c. 720, s. 58; 1995 (Reg. Sess., 1996), c. 592, s. 1; 1997-498, s. 2.)

Editor's Note. — Session Laws 1997-498, s. 13, was codified as subsection (c) of this section at the direction of the Revisor of Statutes.

Subsection (c) became effective September 11, 1997.

§ 58-45-30. Directors to submit plan of operation to Commissioner; review and approval; amendments.

(a) The Directors shall submit to the Commissioner for his review and approval, a proposed plan of operation. The plan shall set forth the number, qualifications, terms of office, and manner of election of the members of the board of directors, and shall grant proper credit annually to each member of the Association for essential property insurance, farmowners, homeowners insurance, and the property portion of commercial multiple peril policies voluntarily written in the beach and coastal areas and shall provide for the efficient, economical, fair and nondiscriminatory administration of the Association and for the prompt and efficient provision of essential property insurance in the beach and coastal areas of North Carolina to promote orderly community development in those areas and to provide means for the adequate maintenance and improvement of the property in those areas. The plan may include the establishment of necessary facilities; management of the Association; the assessment of members to defray losses and expenses; underwriting standards; procedures for the acceptance and cession of reinsurance; procedures for determining the amounts of insurance to be provided to specific risks; time limits and procedures for processing applications for insurance; and any other provisions that are considered necessary by the Commissioner to carry out the purposes of this Article.

(b) The proposed plan shall be reviewed by the Commissioner and approved by him if he finds that such plan fulfills the purposes provided by G.S. 58-45-1. In the review of the proposed plan the Commissioner may, in his discretion, consult with the directors of the Association and may seek any further information which he deems necessary to his decision. If the Commissioner approves the proposed plan, he shall certify such approval to the directors and the plan shall become effective 10 days after such certification. If the Commissioner disapproves all or any part of the proposed plan of operation he shall return the same to the directors with his written statement for the reasons for disapproval and any recommendations he may wish to make. The directors may alter the plan in accordance with the Commissioner's recommendation or may within 30 days from the date of disapproval return a new plan to the Commissioner. Should the directors fail to submit a proposed plan of operation within 90 days of April 17, 1969, or a new plan which is acceptable to the Commissioner, or accept the recommendations of the Commissioner within 30 days after his disapproval of the plan, the Commissioner shall promulgate and place into effect a plan of operation certifying the same to the directors of the

Association. Any such plan promulgated by the Commissioner shall take effect 10 days after certification to the directors: Provided, however, that until a plan of operation is in effect, pursuant to the provisions of this Article, any existing temporary placement facility may be continued in effect on a mandatory basis on such terms as the Commissioner may determine.

(c) The directors of the Association may, subject to the approval of the Commissioner, amend the plan of operation at any time. The Commissioner may review the plan of operation at any time the Commissioner deems expedient or prudent, but not less than once in each calendar year. After review of the plan the Commissioner may amend the plan after consultation with the directors and upon certification to the directors of the amendment.

(d) As used in this subsection, "homeowners' insurance policy" means a multiperil policy providing full coverage of residential property similar to the coverage provided under an HO-2, HO-3, HO-4, or HO-6 policy under Article 36 of this Chapter. The Association shall issue, for principal residences, homeowners' insurance policies approved by the Commissioner. Homeowners' insurance policies shall be available to persons who reside in the beach and coastal areas who meet the Association's underwriting standards and who are unable to obtain homeowners' insurance policies from insurers that are authorized to transact and are actually writing homeowners' insurance policies in this State. The Association shall file for approval by the Commissioner underwriting standards to determine whether property is insurable. The standards shall reflect underwriting standards commonly used in the voluntary homeowners' insurance business. The terms and conditions of the homeowners' insurance policies available under this subsection shall not be more favorable than those of homeowners' insurance policies available in the voluntary market in beach and coastal counties.

(e) The Association shall, subject to the Commissioner's approval or modification, provide in the plan of operation for coverage for appropriate classes of manufacturing risks.

(f) As used in this section, "plan of operation" includes all written rules, practices, and procedures of the Association, except for staffing and personnel matters. (1967, c. 1111, s. 1; 1969, c. 249; 1986, Ex. Sess., c. 7, s. 8; 1987, c. 731, s. 1; c. 864, s. 41; 1991, c. 720, s. 59; 1991 (Reg. Sess., 1992), c. 784, s. 5; 1997-498, s. 3; 2002-185, s. 2; 2003-158, ss. 1, 3.1.)

Effect of Amendments. — Session Laws 2002-185, s. 2, as amended by Session Laws 2003-158, s. 3.1, effective July 1, 2003, rewrote subsection (d).

Session Laws 2003-158, s. 1, effective June 5, 2003, in subsection (d), inserted "who meet the Association's underwriting standards" in the third sentence, added the present fourth and fifth sentences, and deleted the former last sentence, which read: "Rates for the homeowners' insurance policies authorized by this subsection shall be set pursuant to rate standards set forth in G.S. 58-40-20(a), and the provisions of G.S. 58-45-45(a) shall not apply."

§ 58-45-35. Persons eligible to apply to Association for coverage; contents of application.

(a) Any person having an insurable interest in insurable property, may, on or after the effective date of the plan of operation, be entitled to apply to the Association for such coverage and for an inspection of the property. A broker or agent authorized by the applicant may apply on the applicant's behalf. Each application shall contain a statement as to whether or not there are any unpaid premiums due from the applicant for essential property insurance on the property.

The term "insurable interest" as used in this subsection shall include any lawful and substantial economic interest in the safety or preservation of property from loss, destruction or pecuniary damage.

(b) If the Association determines that the property is insurable and that there is no unpaid premium due from the applicant for prior insurance on the property, the Association, upon receipt of the premium, or part of the premium, as is prescribed in the plan of operation, shall cause to be issued a policy of essential property insurance and shall offer additional extended coverage, optional perils endorsements, business income and extra expense coverage, crime insurance, separate policies of windstorm and hail insurance, or their successor forms of coverage, for a term of one year or three years. Short term policies may also be issued. Any policy issued under this section shall be renewed, upon application, as long as the property is insurable property.

(b1) If the Association determines that the property, for which application for a homeowners' policy is made, is insurable, that there is no unpaid premium due from the applicant for prior insurance on the property, and that the underwriting guidelines established by the Association and approved by the Commissioner are met, the Association, upon receipt of the premium, or part of the premium, as is prescribed in the plan of operation, shall cause to be issued a homeowners' insurance policy.

(c) If the Association, for any reason, denies an application and refuses to cause to be issued an insurance policy on insurable property to any applicant or takes no action on an application within the time prescribed in the plan of operation, the applicant may appeal to the Commissioner and the Commissioner, or the Commissioner's designee from the Commissioner's staff, after reviewing the facts, may direct the Association to issue or cause to be issued an insurance policy to the applicant. In carrying out the Commissioner's duties under this section, the Commissioner may request, and the Association shall provide, any information the Commissioner deems necessary to a determination concerning the reason for the denial or delay of the application.

(d) An agent who is licensed under Article 33 of this Chapter as an agent of a company which is a member of the Association established under this Article shall not be deemed an agent of the Association. The foregoing notwithstanding, an agent of a company which is a member of the Association shall have the authority, subject to the underwriting guidelines established by the Association, to temporarily bind coverage with the Association. The Association shall establish rules and procedures, including any limitations for binding authority, in the plan of operation.

Any unearned premium on the temporary binder shall be returned to the policyholder if the Association refuses to issue a policy. Nothing in this section shall prevent the Association from suspending binding authority in accordance with its plan of operation.

(e) Policies of windstorm and hail insurance provided for in subsection (b) of this section are available only for risks in the beach and coastal areas for which essential property insurance has been written by licensed insurers. Whenever such other essential property insurance written by licensed insurers includes replacement cost coverage, the Association shall also offer replacement cost coverage. In order to be eligible for a policy of windstorm and hail insurance, the applicant shall provide the Association, along with the premium payment for the windstorm and hail insurance, a certificate that the essential property insurance is in force. The policy forms for windstorm and hail insurance shall be filed by the Association with the Commissioner for the Commissioner's approval before they may be used. Catastrophic losses, as determined by the Association and approved by the Commissioner, that are covered under the windstorm an1 hail coverage in the beach and coastal areas shall be adjusted by the licensed insurer that issued the essential property insurance and not by the Association. The Association shall reimburse the insurer for reasonable expenses incurred by the insurer in adjusting windstorm and hail losses. (1967, c. 1111, s. 1; 1969, c. 249; 1985, c. 516, s. 2; 1985 (Reg. Sess., 1986), c.

1027, s. 22; 1987, c. 421, ss. 1, 2; c. 629, s. 11; c. 864, s. 24; 1987 (Reg. Sess., 1988), c. 975, ss. 21-23; 1989, c. 376; c. 485, s. 26; 1991, c. 720, s. 25; 1991 (Reg. Sess., 1992), c. 784, s. 1; 1995, c. 517, s. 28; 1995 (Reg. Sess., 1996), c. 740, s. 1; 1997-498, ss. 5, 6; 2001-421, s. 4.1; 2002-185, s. 4.1; 2003-158, s. 2.)

Effect of Amendments. — Session Laws 2002-185, s. 4.1, effective January 1, 2002, in subsection (d), added the last two sentences in the first paragraph and added the last paragraph.

Session Laws 2003-158, s. 2, effective June 5, 2003, inserted subsection (b1).

§ 58-45-36. Temporary contracts of insurance.

Consistent with G.S. 58-45-35(d), the Association shall be temporarily bound by a written temporary binder of insurance issued by any duly licensed insurance agent or broker. Coverage shall be effective upon payment to the agent or broker of the entire premium or part of the premium, as prescribed by the Association's plan of operation. Nothing in this section shall impair or restrict the rights of the Association under G.S. 58-45-35(b) to decline to issue a policy based upon a lack of insurability as determined by the Association or the existence of an unpaid premium due from the applicant. (2002-185, s. 4.2.)

Editor's Note. — Session Laws 2002-185, s. 9, makes the section effective January 1, 2003.

§ 58-45-40. Association members may cede insurance to Association.

Any member of the Association may cede to the Association essential property insurance written on insurable property, to the extent, if any, and on the terms and conditions set forth in the plan of operation. (1967, c. 1111, s. 1; 1969, c. 249.)

§ 58-45-45. Rates, rating plans, rating rules, and forms applicable.

(a) Except as provided in subsection (b) of this section, the rates, rating plans, rating rules, and forms applicable to the insurance written by the Association shall be in accordance with the most recent manual rates or adjusted loss costs and forms that are legally in effect in the State. Except as provided in subsection (c) of this section, no special surcharge, other than those presently in effect, may be applied to the property insurance rates of properties located in the beach and coastal areas.

(b) The rates, rating plans, and rating rules for the separate policies of windstorm and hail insurance described in G.S. 58-45-35(b) shall be filed by the Association with the Commissioner for the Commissioner's approval, disapproval, or modification. The provisions of Articles 40 and 41 of this Chapter shall govern the filings. Policy deductible plans, consistent with G.S. 58-45-1(b), may be filed by the Association with the Commissioner for the Commissioner's approval, disapproval, or modification.

(c) Notwithstanding subsection (a) of this section, the Association may, subject to the prior approval of the Commissioner, adopt a schedule of special surcharges relating to homeowners' insurance policies issued by the Association pursuant to G.S. 58-45-30(d). Such schedule may reflect any differences in risk that can be demonstrated to have a probable effect on losses or expenses. Notwithstanding subsections (a) and (b) of this section, the provisions of G.S.

58-36-10(1), 36-15(a), 58-36-20, and 58-36-25 shall apply to such filings. (1967, c. 1111, s. 1; 1969, c. 249; 1979, c. 601, s. 4; 1987 (Reg. Sess., 1988), c. 975, s. 24; 1991 (Reg. Sess., 1992), c. 784, s. 2; 1997-498, ss. 7, 8; 1999-114, s. 7.1; 2003-158, s. 3.)

Editor's Note. — Session Laws 1997-498, s. 14, is a severability clause.

Session Laws 1999-114, s. 8, contains a severability clause.

Effect of Amendments. — Session Laws 1997-498, s. 8, as amended by Session Laws 1999-114, s. 7.1, effective January 1, 2002, deleted the third sentence of subsection (b),

relating to windstorm and hail policies.

Session Laws 2003-158, s. 3, effective June 5, 2003, in subsection (a), substituted "Except as provided in subsection (c) of this section, no" for "No" at the beginning of the second sentence, and substituted "and coastal areas" for "area" at the end of the second sentence; and added subsection (c).

§ 58-45-46. Unearned premium, loss, and loss expense reserves.

The Association shall make provisions for reserving unearned premiums and reserving for losses, including incurred but not reported losses, and loss expenses, in accordance with G.S. 58-3-71, 58-3-75, and 58-3-81. (2002-185, s. 5.1.)

Editor's Note. — Session Laws 2002-185, s. 9, makes the section effective October 31, 2002.

Session Laws 2002-185, s. 5.3, directs the North Carolina Joint Underwriting Association and the North Carolina Insurance Underwriting Association to request from the United States Internal Revenue Service a ruling as to

whether or not the reserves required by Sections 5.1 and 5.2 of this act are subject to federal taxation. If the ruling states that the reserves are subject to federal taxation, in whole or in part, the Associations is to pursue ways and means for an exemption from federal taxation.

§ 58-45-50. Appeal from acts of Association to Commissioner; appeal from Commissioner to superior court.

(a) Any person or any insurer who may be aggrieved by an act, ruling, or decision of the Association other than an act, ruling, or decision relating to (i) the cause or amount of a claimed loss or (ii) the reasonableness of expenses incurred by an insurer in adjusting windstorm and hail losses, may, within 30 days after the ruling, appeal to the Commissioner. Any hearings held by the Commissioner under the appeal shall be in accordance with rules adopted by the Commissioner: Provided, however, the Commissioner is authorized to appoint a member of the Commissioner's staff as deputy commissioner for the purpose of hearing those appeals and a ruling based upon the hearing shall have the same effect as if heard by the Commissioner. All persons or insureds aggrieved by any order or decision of the Commissioner may appeal as is provided in G.S. 58-2-75.

(b) No later than 10 days before each hearing, the appellant shall file with the Commissioner or the Commissioner's designated hearing officer and shall serve on the appellee a written statement of the appellant's case and any evidence that the appellant intends to offer at the hearing. No later than five days before the hearing, the appellee shall file with the Commissioner or the designated hearing officer and shall serve on the appellant a written statement of the appellee's case and any evidence that the appellee intends to offer at the hearing. Each hearing shall be recorded and may be transcribed. If the matter is between an insurer and the Association, the cost of the recording and transcribing shall be borne equally by the appellant and appellee; provided that upon any final adjudication the prevailing party shall be reimbursed for his share of such costs by the other party. If the matter is between an insured and the Association, the cost of transcribing shall be borne equally by the appellant and appellee; provided that the Commissioner may order the Association to pay recording or transcribing costs for which the insured is financially unable to pay. Each party shall, on a date determined by the Commissioner or the designated hearing officer, but not sooner than 15 days after delivery of the completed transcript to the party, submit to the Commissioner or the designated hearing officer and serve on the other party, a proposed order. The Commissioner or the designated hearing officer shall then issue an order. (1967, c. 1111, s. 1; 1969, c. 249; 1985, c. 516, s. 3; 1989 (Reg. Sess., 1990), c. 1069, s. 18; 1991, c. 720, s. 4; 1999-219, s. 1.2; 2001-421, s. 4.2.)

§ 58-45-55. Reports of inspection made available.

All reports of inspection performed by or on behalf of the Association shall be made available to the members of the Association, applicants, agent or broker, and the Commissioner. (1967, c. 1111, s. 1; 1969, c. 249.)

§ 58-45-60. Association and Commissioner immune from liability.

There shall be no liability on the part of and no cause of action of any nature shall arise against any member insurer, the Association or its agents or employees, the board of directors, or the Commissioner or his representatives for any action taken by them in good faith in the performance of their powers and duties under this Article. (1967, c. 1111, s. 1; 1969, c. 249; 1991, c. 720, s. 4; 1999-114, s. 5.)

§ 58-45-65. Association to file annual report with Commissioner.

The Association shall file in the office of the Commissioner on an annual basis on or before January 1 a statement which shall summarize the transactions, conditions, operations and affairs of the Association during the preceding year. Such statement shall contain such matters and information as are prescribed by the Commissioner and shall be in such form as is approved by him. The Commissioner may at any time require the Association to furnish to him any additional information with respect to its transactions or any other matter which the Commissioner deems to be material to assist him in evaluating the operation and experience of the Association. (1967, c. 1111, s. 1; 1969, c. 249; 1987 (Reg. Sess., 1988), c. 975, s. 27.)

§ 58-45-70. Commissioner may examine affairs of Association.

The Commissioner may from time to time make an examination into the affairs of the Association when he deems it to be prudent and in undertaking such examination he may hold a public hearing pursuant to the provisions of G.S. 58-2-50. The expenses of such examination shall be borne and paid by the Association. (1967, c. 1111, s. 1; 1969, c. 249.)

§ 58-45-75. Commissioner authorized to promulgate reasonable rules and regulations.

The Commissioner shall have authority to make reasonable rules and regulations, not inconsistent with law, to enforce, carry out and make effective the provisions of this Article. The Commissioner shall not be liable for any act or omission in connection with the administration of the duties imposed upon him by the provisions of this Article. (1967, c. 1111, s. 1; 1969, c. 249; 1991, c. 720, s. 4.)

§ 58-45-80. Premium taxes to be paid through Association.

All premium taxes due on insurance written under this Article shall be remitted by each insurer to the Association; and the Association, as collecting agent for its member companies, shall forward all such taxes to the Secretary of Revenue as provided in Article 8B of Chapter 105 of the General Statutes. (1985 (Reg. Sess., 1986), c. 928, s. 10; 1995 (Reg. Sess., 1996), c. 747, s. 12.)

Editor's Note. — Session Laws 1995 (Reg. Sess., 1996), c. 747, s. 16, provides: "This act does not obligate the General Assembly to appropriate funds."

§ 58-45-85. Assessment; inability to pay.

If any insurer fails, by reason of insolvency, to pay any assessment as provided in this Article, the amount assessed each insurer shall be immediately recalculated, excluding the insolvent insurer, so that its assessment is assumed and redistributed among the remaining insurers. Any assessment against an insolvent insurer shall not be a charge against any special deposit fund held under the provisions of Article 5 of this Chapter for the benefit of policyholders. (1991 (Reg. Sess., 1992), c. 784, s. 7.)

§ 58-45-90. Open meetings.

The Association is subject to the Open Meetings Act, Article 33C of Chapter 143 of the General Statutes, as amended. (2002-185, s. 7.1.)

Editor's Note. — Session Laws 2002-185, s. 9, makes this section effective October 31, 2002.

Article 46.

Fair Access to Insurance Requirements.

§ 58-46-1. Purpose and geographic coverage of Article.

(a) It is the purpose of this Article to provide a program whereby adequate basic property insurance may be made available to property owners having insurable property in the State. It is further the purpose of this Article to encourage the improvement of properties located in the State and to arrest the decline of properties located in the State. It is the intent of the General Assembly in creating and, from time to time, amending this Article that the market provided by this Article not be the first market of choice, but the market of last resort.

(b) This Article shall apply to all geographic areas of the State except the "Beach Area" defined in G.S. 58-45-5(2).

(c) As used in this Article, "crime insurance" means insurance against losses resulting from robbery, burglary, larceny, and similar crimes, as more specifically defined and limited in the various crime insurance policies, or their successor forms of coverage, approved by the Commissioner and issued by the Association. Such policies shall not be more restrictive than those issued under the Federal Crime Insurance Program authorized by Public Law 91-609.

(1969, c. 1284; 1985, c. 519, s. 1; 1986, Ex. Sess., c. 7, s. 4; 1985 (Reg. Sess., 1986), c. 1027, s. 24; 1987, c. 731, s. 1; 1987 (Reg. Sess., 1988), c. 975, s. 18; 1997-498, s. 10.)

Editor's Note. — Session Laws 2002-185, s. 3, effective October 31, 2002, provides: "The Commissioner of Insurance, in consultation with other governmental bodies specified below, shall study the provisions of Articles 45 and 46 of Chapter 58 of the General Statutes, other relevant portions of the General Statutes, and the plans and operations of the North Carolina Insurance Underwriting Association ('Beach Plan') and the North Carolina Joint Underwriting Association ('FAIR Plan'). In this study, the Commissioner may consider all issues and potential remedies related to the availability of homeowners' insurance coverage statewide, and specifically in the beach and coastal counties of the State. In conducting this study, the Commissioner may call upon any department, agency, institution, or officer of the State or of any political subdivision of the State, and the North Carolina Rate Bureau, the North Carolina Insurance Underwriting Association ('Beach Plan'), the North Carolina Joint Underwriting Association ('FAIR Plan'), and the North Carolina Motor Vehicle Reinsurance Facility, and representatives of property and casualty insurers and reinsurers, for such assistance and information, and these departments, agencies, institutions, officers, and other entities shall cooperate with the Commissioner to the fullest possible extent. The Commissioner shall report to the 2003 General Assembly on or before April 1, 2003, on the Commissioner's findings and may make any legislative or other recommendations he considers appropriate."

§ 58-46-2. Persons who can be insured by the Association.

As used in this Article, "person" includes the State of North Carolina and any county, city, or other political subdivision of the State of North Carolina. (2000-122, s. 6; 2002-187, s. 1.5.)

Editor's Note. — Session Laws 2000-122, s. 11, made this section effective July 14, 2000.
Effect of Amendments. — Session Laws 2002-187, s. 1.5, effective October 31, 2002, inserted "the State of North Carolina and."

§ 58-46-5. Organization of underwriting association.

All insurers licensed to write and writing property insurance in this State on a direct basis are authorized, subject to the approval and regulation by the Commissioner, to establish and maintain a FAIR Plan (Fair Access to Insurance Requirements) and to establish and maintain an underwriting association and to formulate, and from time to time, to amend the plans and articles of the association and rules and regulations in connection therewith, and to assess and share on a fair and equitable basis all expenses, income and losses incident to such FAIR Plan and underwriting association in a manner consistent with the provisions of this Article. (1969, c. 1284; 1985, c. 519, s. 2.)

§ 58-46-10. Participation in association.

(a) Every insurer authorized to write basic property insurance in this State except town and county mutual insurance associations and assessable mutual companies as authorized by G.S. 58-7-75(5)b, 58-7-75(5)d and 58-7-75(7)b and except an insurer who only writes insurance on property exempted from taxation by the provisions of G.S. 105-278.1 through 105-278.8 shall be required to become and remain a member of the Plan and underwriting association and comply with the requirements thereof as a condition of its authority to transact basic property insurance business in the State of North Carolina.

(b) An agent who is licensed under Article 33 of this Chapter as an agent of a company which is a member of the Association established under this Article shall not be deemed an agent of the Association. (1969, c. 1284; 1971, c. 1067, s. 1; 1985, c. 519, s. 3; 1987, c. 629, s. 12; 1991, c. 720, s. 24.)

The credit referred to in this section is to be accumulated by the Federal Insurance Development Fund and is available to pay reinsured riot-caused losses. It is not a credit which accrues to the benefit of the individual participating insurers in the State, but it does reduce the possibility of a call upon the State. See opinion of the Attorney General to the Honorable Edwin S. Lanier, Commissioner of Insurance, 40 N.C.A.G. 333 (1969).

§ 58-46-15. Requirements of Plan and authority of Association.

The Association formed pursuant to the provisions of this Article shall have authority on behalf of its members to cause to be issued basic property insurance policies, including coverage for farm risks; and shall offer additional extended coverage, optional perils endorsements, and crime insurance policies, or their successor forms of coverage; to reinsure in whole or in part, any such policies; and to cede any such reinsurance. The Plan adopted, pursuant to the provision of this Article, shall provide, among other things, for the perils to be covered, compensation and commissions, assessments of members, the sharing of expenses, income and losses on an equitable basis, cumulative weighted voting for the board of directors of the Association, the administration of the Plan and Association and any other matter necessary or convenient for the purpose of assuring fair access to insurance requirements. The directors of the Association may, subject to the approval of the Commissioner, amend the plan of operation at any time. The Commissioner may review the plan of operation at any time he deems to be expedient or prudent, but not less than once in each calendar year. After review of such plan the Commissioner may amend the plan after consultation with the directors and upon certification to the directors of such amendment. (1969, c. 1284; 1985, c. 519, s. 4; 1986, Ex. Sess., c. 7, ss. 5, 6; 1985 (Reg. Sess., 1986), c. 1027, s. 23; 1987, c. 731, s. 1; c. 864, s. 24; 1987 (Reg. Sess., 1988), c. 975, ss. 25, 29.)

§ 58-46-20. Authority of Commissioner.

(a) Within 90 days following July 2, 1969, and before August 1, 1969, the directors of the association shall submit to the Commissioner for his review, a proposed FAIR Plan and articles of the association consistent with the provisions of this Article.

(b) The FAIR Plan and articles of association shall be subject to approval by the Commissioner and shall take effect 10 days after having been approved by him. If the Commissioner disapproves all or any part of the proposed Plan and articles, the directors of the association shall within 30 days submit for review an appropriately revised Plan and articles and if the directors fail to do so, the Commissioner shall thereafter promulgate such Plan and articles not inconsistent with the provisions of this Article.

(c) The Commissioner may designate the kinds of property insurance policies on principal residences to be offered by the association, including insurance policies under Article 36 of this Chapter, and the commission rates to be paid to agents or brokers for these policies, if he finds, after a hearing held in accordance with G.S. 58-2-50, that the public interest requires the designation. The provisions of Chapter 150B do not apply to any procedure under this subsection, except that G.S. 150B-39 and G.S. 150B-41 shall apply to a hearing under this subsection. Within 30 days after the receipt of notification from the Commissioner of a change in designation pursuant to this subsection, the association shall submit a revised plan and articles of association for approval in accordance with subsection (b) of this section.

(d) As used in this section and in G.S. 58-46-15, "FAIR Plan", "plan of operation", and "articles of association" include all written rules, practices, and procedures of the Association, except for staffing and personnel matters. (1969, c. 1284; 1986, Ex. Sess., c. 7, s. 7; 1987, c. 731, s. 1; 1991, c. 720, s. 4; 1991 (Reg. Sess., 1992), c. 784, s. 6.)

§ 58-46-25. Temporary directors of association.

Within 10 days after July 2, 1969, the Commissioner shall appoint a temporary board of directors of the association, which temporary board of directors may prepare and submit a Plan of operation and articles of association in accordance with G.S. 58-46-20. (1969, c. 1284.)

§ 58-46-30. Appeals; judicial review.

The association shall provide reasonable means, to be approved by the Commissioner, whereby any person or insurer affected by any act or decision of the administrators of the Plan or underwriting association, other than an act or decision relating to the cause or amount of a claimed loss, may be heard in person or by an authorized representative, before the governing board of the association or a designated committee. Any person or insurer aggrieved by any decision of the governing board or designated committee, may be appealed to the Commissioner within 30 days after the date of the ruling or decision. The Commissioner, after a hearing held under rules adopted by the Commissioner, shall issue an order approving or disapproving the act or decision with respect to the matter that is the subject of appeal. The Commissioner may appoint a member of the Commissioner's staff as deputy commissioner for the purpose of hearing the appeals and a ruling based on the hearing has the same effect as if heard by the Commissioner. All persons or insurers or their representatives aggrieved by any order or decision of the Commissioner may appeal as provided in G.S. 58-2-75.

No later than 10 days before each hearing, the appellant shall file with the Commissioner or the designated hearing officer and shall serve on the appellee a written statement of the appellant's case and any evidence that the appellant intends to offer at the hearing. No later than five days before the hearing, the appellee shall file with the Commissioner or the designated hearing officer and shall serve on the appellant a written statement of the appellee's case and any evidence that the appellee intends to offer at the hearing. Each hearing shall be recorded and may be transcribed. If the matter is between an insurer and the Association, the cost of the recording and transcribing shall be borne equally by the appellant and appellee; provided that upon any final adjudication the prevailing party shall be reimbursed for his share of such costs by the other party. If the matter is between an insured and the Association, the cost of transcribing shall be borne equally by the appellant and appellee; provided that the Commissioner may order the Association to pay recording or transcribing costs for which the insured is financially unable to pay. Each party shall, on a date determined by the Commissioner or the designated hearing officer, but not sooner than 15 days after delivery of the completed transcript to the party, submit to the Commissioner or the designated hearing officer and serve on the other party, a proposed order. The Commissioner or the designated hearing officer shall then issue an order. (1969, c. 1284; 1985, c. 519, s. 5; 1989 (Reg. Sess., 1990), c. 1069, s. 19; 1999-219, s. 1.3.)

§ 58-46-35. Reports of inspection made available; immunity from liability.

All reports of inspection performed by or on behalf of the association shall be made available to the members of the association, applicants and the Commissioner. There shall be no liability on the part of and no cause of action of any nature shall arise against any member insurer, the Association or its agents or employees, the board of directors, or the Commissioner or his representatives for any action taken by them in good faith in the performance of their powers and duties under this Article. (1969, c. 1284; 1999-114, s. 6.)

§ 58-46-40. Assessment; inability to pay.

In the event any insurer fails by reason of insolvency to pay any assessment as provided herein, the amount assessed each insurer shall be immediately recalculated excluding therefrom the insolvent insurer so that its assessment is, in effect, assumed and redistributed among the remaining insurers. Such an assessment against an insolvent insurer shall not be a charge against any special deposit fund held under the provisions of Article 5 of this Chapter for the benefit of policyholders. (1969, c. 1284; 1985, c. 519, s. 7; 1991, c. 720, s. 26.)

§ 58-46-41. Unearned premium, loss, and loss expense reserves.

The Association shall make provisions for reserving unearned premiums and reserving for losses, including incurred but not reported losses, and loss expenses, in accordance with G.S. 58-3-71, 58-3-75, and 58-3-81. (2002-185, s. 5.2.)

Editor's Note. — Session Laws 2002-185, s. 9, makes the section effective October 31, 2002.

Session Laws 2002-185, s. 5.3, directs the North Carolina Joint Underwriting Association and the North Carolina Insurance Underwriting Association to request from the United States Internal Revenue Service a ruling as to whether or not the reserves required by Sections 5.1 and 5.2 of this act are subject to federal taxation. If the ruling states that the reserves are subject to federal taxation, in whole or in part, the Associations is to pursue ways and means for an exemption from federal taxation.

§ 58-46-45. Premium taxes to be paid through Association.

All premium taxes due on insurance written under this Article shall be remitted by each insurer to the Association; and the Association, as collecting agent for its member companies, shall forward all such taxes to the Secretary of Revenue as provided in Article 8B of Chapter 105 of the General Statutes. (1985 (Reg. Sess., 1986), c. 928, s. 10; 1995 (Reg. Sess., 1996), c. 747, s. 13.)

Editor's Note. — Session Laws 1995 (Reg. Sess., 1996), c. 747, s. 16, provides: "This act does not obligate the General Assembly to appropriate funds."

§ 58-46-50. Annual reports.

On or before January 1 of each year the association shall file with the Commissioner a statement that summarizes the transactions, conditions, operations, and affairs of the association during the preceding year. The statement shall contain such matters and information as are prescribed by the Commissioner and shall be in such form as is approved by him. The Commissioner may at any time require the association to furnish him with any additional information with respect to its transactions or any other matter that the Commissioner deems to be material to assist him in evaluating the operation and experience of the association. (1987 (Reg. Sess., 1988), c. 975, s. 26.)

§ 58-46-55. Rates, rating plans, rating rules, and forms applicable.

The rates, rating plans, rating rules, and forms applicable to the insurance written by the association shall be in accordance with the most recent manual rates or adjusted loss costs and forms that are legally in effect in this State. No special surcharge, other than those presently in effect, may be applied to the property insurance rates of properties located in the geographic areas to which this Article applies. (1987 (Reg. Sess., 1988), c. 975, s. 28; 1991 (Reg. Sess., 1992), c. 784, s. 3.)

§ 58-46-60. Open meetings.

The Association is subject to the Open Meetings Act, Article 33C of Chapter 143 of the General Statutes, as amended. (2002-185, s. 7.2.)

Editor's Note. — Session Laws 2002-185, s. 9, makes this section effective October 31, 2002.

ARTICLE 47.

Workers' Compensation Self-Insurance.

§§ **58-47-1 through 58-47-50:** Repealed by Session Laws 1997-362, s. 2.

Part 1. Employer Groups.

§ 58-47-60. Definitions.

As used in this part:
  (1) "Act" means the Workers' Compensation Act in Article 1 of Chapter 97 of the General Statutes, as amended.
  (2) "Affiliate" has the same meaning as in G.S. 58-19-5(1).
  (3) "Annual statement filing" means the most recent annual filing made with the Commissioner under G.S. 58-2-165.
  (4) "Board" means the board of trustees or other governing body of a group.
  (5) "Books and records" means all files, documents, and databases in a paper form, electronic medium, or both.
  (6) "Control" means "control" as defined in G.S. 58-19-5(2).
  (7) "GAAP financial statement" means a financial statement as defined by generally accepted accounting principles.
  (8) "Group" means two or more employers who agree to pool their workers' compensation liabilities under the Act and are licensed under this Part.
  (9) "Hazardous financial condition" means that, based on its present or reasonably anticipated financial condition, a person is insolvent or, although not financially impaired or insolvent, is unlikely to be able:
    a. To meet obligations for known claims and reasonably anticipated claims; or
    b. To pay other obligations in the normal course of business.
  (10) "Member" means an employer that participates in a group.
  (11) "Qualified actuary" means a member in good standing of the Casualty Actuarial Society or a member in good standing of the American

Academy of Actuaries, who has been approved as qualified for signing casualty loss reserve opinions by the Casualty Practice Council of the American Academy of Actuaries, and is in compliance with G.S. 58-2-171.

(12) "Rate" means the cost of insurance per exposure unit, whether expressed as a single number or as a prospective loss cost with an adjustment to account for the treatment of expenses, profit, and variations in loss experience, before any application of individual risk variations based on loss or expense considerations, and does not include minimum premiums.

(13) "Service company" means an entity that has contracted with an employer or group for the purpose of providing any services related to claims adjustment, loss control, or both.

(14) "Third-party administrator" or "TPA" means a person engaged by a board to execute the policies established by the board and to provide day-to-day management of the group. "Third-party administrator" or "TPA" does not mean:

   a. An employer acting on behalf of its employees or the employees of one or more of its affiliates.

   b. An insurer that is licensed under this Chapter or that is acting as an insurer with respect to a policy lawfully issued and delivered by it and under the laws of a state in which the insurer is licensed to write insurance.

   c. An agent or broker who is licensed by the Commissioner under Article 33 of this Chapter whose activities are limited exclusively to the sale of insurance.

   d. An adjuster licensed by the Commissioner under Article 33 of this Chapter whose activities are limited to adjustment of claims.

   e. An individual who is an officer, a member, or an employee of a board.

(15) "Underwriting" means the process of selecting risks and classifying them according to their degrees of insurability so that the appropriate rates may be assigned. The process also includes rejection of those risks that do not qualify. (1997-362, s. 3; 2001-223, s. 21.1.)

§ 58-47-65. Licensing; qualification for approval.

(a) No group shall self-insure its workers' compensation liabilities under the Act unless it is licensed by the Commissioner under this Part. This subsection does not apply to a group that was organized and approved under the North Carolina law before July 1, 1995, and whose authority to self-insure its workers' compensation liabilities under the Act has not terminated after that date.

(b) An applicant for a license shall file with the Commissioner the information required by subsection (f) of this section on a form prescribed by the Commissioner at least 90 days before the proposed licensing date. The applicant shall furnish to the Commissioner satisfactory proof of the proposed group's financial ability, through its members, to comply with the Act. No application is complete until the Commissioner has received all required information.

(c) The group shall comprise two or more employers who are members of and are sponsored by a single bona fide trade or professional association. The association shall (i) comprise members engaged in the same or substantially similar business or profession within the State, (ii) have been incorporated in North Carolina, (iii) have been in existence for at least five years before the date of application to the Commissioner to form a group, and (iv) submit a written determination from the Internal Revenue Service that it is exempt from taxation under 26 U.S.C. § 501(c). This subsection does not apply to a group that was organized and approved under North Carolina law before July 1, 1995.

(d) Only an applicant whose members' employee base is actuarially sufficient in numbers and provides an actuarially appropriate spreading of risk may apply for a license. The Commissioner shall consider (i) the financial strength and liquidity of the applicant relative to its ability to comply with the Act, (ii) the applicant's criteria and procedures regarding the review and monitoring of members' financial strength, (iii) reliability of the financial information, (iv) workers' compensation loss history, (v) underwriting guidelines, (vi) claims administration, (vii) excess insurance or reinsurance, and (viii) access to excess insurance or reinsurance.

(e) Before issuing a license to any applicant, the Commissioner shall require, in addition to the other requirements provided by law, that the applicant file an affidavit signed by the association's board members that it has not violated any of the applicable provisions of this Part or the Act during the last 12 months, and that it accepts the provisions of this Part and the Act in return for the license.

(f) The license application shall comprise the following information:

   (1) Biographical affidavits providing the education, prior occupation, business experience, and other supplementary information submitted for each promoter, incorporator, director, trustee, proposed management personnel, and other persons similarly situated.

   (2) A forecast for a five-year period based on the initial capitalization of the proposed group and its plan of operation. The forecast shall be prepared by a certified public accountant, a qualified actuary, or both, be in sufficient detail for a complete analysis to be performed, and be accompanied by a list of the assumptions utilized in making the forecast.

   (3) An individual application, under G.S. 58-47-125, of each member applying for coverage in the proposed group on the inception date of the proposed group, with a current GAAP financial statement of each member. The financial statements are confidential, but the Commissioner may use them in any judicial or administrative proceeding.

   (4) A breakdown of all forecasted administrative expenses for the proposed group's fiscal year in a dollar amount and as a percentage of the estimated annual premium.

   (5) The proposed group's procedures for evaluating the current and continuing financial strength of members.

   (6) Evidence of the coverage required by G.S. 58-47-95.

   (7) Demonstration provided by the board, satisfactory to the Commissioner, that the proposed group's member employee base is actuarially sufficient in numbers and provides an actuarially appropriate spreading of risk.

   (8) An assessment plan under G.S. 58-47-135(a).

   (9) A listing of the estimated premium to be developed for each member individually and in total for the proposed group. Payroll data for each of the three preceding years shall be furnished by risk classification.

   (10) An executed agreement by each member showing the member's obligation to pay to the proposed group not less than twenty-five percent (25%) of the member's estimated annual premium not later than the first day of coverage afforded by the proposed group.

   (11) Composition of the initial board.

   (12) An indemnity agreement on a form prescribed by the Commissioner.

   (13) Proof, satisfactory to the Commissioner, that either the applicant has within its own organization ample facilities and competent personnel

to service its program for underwriting, claims, and industrial safety engineering, or that the applicant will contract for any of these services. If the applicant is to perform any servicing, biographical affidavits of those persons who will be responsible for or performing servicing shall be included with the information in subdivision (1) of this subsection. If a group contracts with a service company or TPA to administer and adjust claims, the group shall provide proof of compliance with the other provisions of this Part.

(14) A letter stipulating the applicant's acceptance of membership in the North Carolina Self-Insurance Guaranty Association under Article 4 of Chapter 97 of the General Statutes.

(15) Any other specific information the Commissioner considers relevant to the organization of the proposed group.

(g) Every applicant shall execute and file with the Commissioner an agreement, as part of the application, in which the applicant agrees to deposit with the Commissioner cash or securities acceptable to the Commissioner. (1997-362, s. 3; 1999-132, s. 13.1; 2003-212, s. 24.)

Effect of Amendments. — Session Laws 2003-212, s. 24, effective October 1, 2003, added the last sentence in subsection (a).

Legal Periodicals. — For 1997 legislative survey, see 20 Campbell L. Rev. 487.

OPINIONS OF ATTORNEY GENERAL

Application of Grandfather Clause of Subsection (c). — Grandfather clause set forth in subsection (c) applied to a particular worker's compensation self-insurance fund. See opinion of Attorney General to the Honorable Edd Nye, North Carolina General Assembly, 2002 NC AG LEXIS 18 (6/20/02).

§ 58-47-70. License denial; termination; revocation; restrictions.

(a) If the Commissioner denies a license, the Commissioner shall inform the applicant of the reasons for the denial. The Commissioner may issue a license to an applicant that remedies the reasons for a denial within 60 days after the Commissioner's notice. The Commissioner may grant additional time to an applicant to remedy any deficiencies in its application. A request for an extension of time shall be made in writing by the applicant within 30 days after the Commissioner's notice. If the applicant fails to remedy the reasons for the denial, the application shall be withdrawn or denied.

(b) A group shall not terminate its license or cease the writing of renewal business without obtaining prior written approval from the Commissioner. The Commissioner shall not grant the request of any group to terminate its license unless the group has closed or reinsured all of its incurred workers' compensation obligations and has settled all of its other legal obligations, including known and unknown claims and associated expenses.

(c) No group shall transfer its workers' compensation obligations under an assumption reinsurance agreement without complying with Part 2 of Article 10 of this Chapter.

(d) Every group is subject to Article 19 of this Chapter. No group shall merge with another group unless both groups are engaged in the same or a similar type of business. (1997-362, s. 3.)

§ 58-47-75. Reporting and records.

(a) As used in this section:

(1) "Audited financial report" has the same meaning as in the NAIC Model Rule Requiring Annual Audited Financial Reports, as specified in G.S. 58-2-205.

(2) "Duplicate record" means a counterpart produced by the same impression as the original record, or from the same matrix, or by mechanical or electronic rerecording or by chemical reproduction, or by equivalent techniques, such as imaging or image processing, that accurately reproduce the original record.

(3) "Original record" means the writing or recording itself or any counterpart intended to have the same effect by a person executing or issuing it, in the normal and ordinary course of business, or data stored in a computer or similar device, the printout or other output readable by sight, shown to reflect the data accurately. An "original" of a photograph includes the negative or any print from the negative.

(b) Each group shall file with the Commissioner the following:

(1) A statement in accordance with G.S. 58-2-165.

(2) An audited financial report.

(3) Annual payroll information within 90 days after the close of its fiscal year. The report shall summarize the payroll by annual amount paid and by classifications using the rules, classifications, and rates set forth in the most recently approved Workers' Compensation and Employers' Liability Insurance Manual governing audits of payrolls and adjustments of premiums. Each group shall maintain true and accurate payroll records. The payroll records shall be maintained to allow for verification of the completeness and accuracy of the annual payroll report.

(c) Each group shall make its financial statement and audited financial report available to its members upon request.

(d) All records shall be maintained by the group for the years during which an examination under G.S. 58-2-131 has not yet been completed.

(e) All records that are required to be maintained by this section shall be either original or duplicate records.

(f) If only duplicate records are maintained, the following requirements apply:

(1) The data shall be accessible to the Commissioner in legible form, and legible, reproduced copies shall be available.

(2) Before the destruction of any original records, the group in possession of the original records shall:

a. Verify that the records stored consist of all information contained in the original records, and that the original records can be reconstructed therefrom in a form acceptable to the Commissioner; and

b. Implement disaster preparedness or disaster recovery procedures that include provisions for the maintenance of duplicate records at an off-site location.

(3) Adequate controls shall be established with respect to the transfer and maintenance of data.

(g) Each group shall maintain its records under G.S. 58-7-50, G.S. 58-7-55, and the Act.

(h) All books of original entry and corporate records shall be retained by the group or its successor for a period of 15 years after the group ceases to exist. (1997-362, s. 3.)

§ 58-47-80. Assets and invested assets.

Funds shall be held and invested by the board under G.S. 58-7-160, 58-7-162, 58-7-163, 58-7-165, 58-7-167, 58-7-168, 58-7-170, 58-7-172, 58-7-173, 58-7-178,

58-7-179, 58-7-180, 58-7-183, 58-7-185, 58-7-187, 58-7-188, 58-7-192, 58-7-193, 58-7-197, 58-7-200, and 58-19-10. (1997-362, s. 3; 2001-223, s. 21.2; 2003-212, s. 13.)

Effect of Amendments. — Session Laws 2003-212, s. 13, effective October 1, 2003, deleted "58-7-195" following "58-7-193."

§ 58-47-85. Surplus requirements.

Every group shall maintain minimum surplus under one of the options in subdivision (1), (2), or (3) of this section:

(1) Maintain minimum surplus in accordance with Article 12 of this Chapter. A group organized and authorized before the effective date of this section shall comply with this section under the following schedule:

   a. Forty percent (40%) of the surplus, in accordance with Article 12, by January 1, 1999.

   b. Fifty-five percent (55%) of the surplus, in accordance with Article 12, by January 1, 2000.

   c. Seventy percent (70%) of the surplus, in accordance with Article 12, by January 1, 2001.

   d. Eighty-five percent (85%) of the surplus, in accordance with Article 12, by January 1, 2002.

   e. One hundred percent (100%) of the surplus, in accordance with Article 12, by January 1, 2003.

The Commissioner shall not approve any dividend request that results in a surplus that is less than one hundred percent (100%) of the minimum surplus required by Article 12 of this Chapter.

(2) Maintain minimum surplus at an amount equal to ten percent (10%) of the group's total undiscounted outstanding claim liability, according to the group's annual statement filing, or such other amount as the Commissioner prescribes based on, but not limited to, the financial condition of the group and the risk retained by the group. In addition, the group shall:

   a. Maintain specific excess insurance or reinsurance that provides the coverage limits in G.S. 58-47-95(a). The group shall retain no specific risk greater than five percent (5%) of the group's total annual earned premium according to the group's annual statement filing.

   b. Maintain aggregate excess insurance or reinsurance with a coverage limit being the greater of two million dollars ($2,000,000) or twenty percent (20%) of the group's annual earned premium, according to the group's annual statement filing. The aggregate excess attachment point shall be one hundred ten percent (110%) of the annual earned premium, according to the group's annual statement filing. The required attachment point shall be reduced by each point, or fraction of a point, that a group's expense ratio exceeds thirty percent (30%). Conversely, the required attachment point may be increased by each point, or fraction of a point, that a group's expense ratio is less than thirty percent (30%), but in no event shall the attachment point be greater than one hundred fifteen percent (115%) of the annual earned premium.

   c. Adopt a policy whereby every member:

      1. Pays a deposit to the group of twenty-five percent (25%) of the member's estimated annual earned premium, or another

amount that the Commissioner prescribes based on, but not limited to, the financial condition of the group and the risk retained by the group; or

2. Once every year files with the group the member's most recent year-end balance sheet, which, at a minimum, is compiled by an independent certified public accountant. The balance sheet shall demonstrate that the member's financial position does not show a deficit equity and is appropriate for membership in the group. At the request of the Commissioner, the group shall make these filings available for review. These filings shall be kept confidential; provided that the Commissioner may use that information in any judicial or administrative proceeding.

(3) Maintain minimum surplus at an amount equal to three hundred thousand dollars ($300,000). The group shall immediately assess its members if, at any time, the group's surplus is less than the minimum surplus amount. In addition, the group shall maintain:

a. Specific excess insurance or reinsurance that provides coverage limits pursuant to G.S. 58-47-95(a). The group shall retain no specific risk greater than five percent (5%) of the group's total annual earned premium according to the group's annual statement filing.

b. Aggregate excess insurance or reinsurance with a coverage limit being the greater of two million dollars ($2,000,000) or twenty percent (20%) of the group's annual earned premium, according to the group's annual statement filing. The aggregate excess attachment point shall be one hundred ten percent (110%) of the annual earned premium, according to the group's annual statement filing. The required attachment point shall be reduced by each point, or fraction of a point, that a group's expense ratio exceeds thirty percent (30%). Conversely, the required attachment point may be increased by each point, or fraction of a point, that a group's expense ratio is less than thirty percent (30%), but in no event shall the attachment point be greater than one hundred fifteen percent (115%) of the annual earned premium.

The Commissioner may require different levels, or waive the requirement, of specific and aggregate excess loss coverage consistent with the market availability of excess loss coverage, the group's claims experience, and the group's financial condition. (1997-362, s. 3; 1999-132, s. 13.2.)

Legal Periodicals. — For 1997 legislative survey, see 20 Campbell L. Rev. 487.

§ 58-47-90. Deposits.

(a) Each group shall deposit with the Commissioner an amount equal to ten percent (10%) of the group's total annual earned premium, according to the group's annual statement filing, but not less than six hundred thousand dollars ($600,000), or another amount that the Commissioner prescribes based on, but not limited to, the financial condition of the group and the risk retained by the group.

(b) G.S. 58-5-1, 58-5-20, 58-5-25, 58-5-30, 58-5-35, 58-5-40, 58-5-63, 58-5-75, 58-5-80, 58-5-90(a) and (c), 58-5-95, 58-5-110, 58-5-115, and 58-5-120 apply to groups.

(c) A group organized and authorized before January 1, 1998, has until January 1, 2001, to comply with subsection (b) of this section. However, a dividend request shall not be approved by the Commissioner until the group has replaced its surety bonds with the deposit required by subsection (b) of this section.

(d) No judgment creditor, other than a claimant entitled to benefits under the Act, may levy upon any deposits made under this section.

(e) Surety bonds shall be in a form prescribed by the Commissioner and issued by an insurer authorized by the Commissioner to write surety business in North Carolina.

(f) Any surety bond may be exchanged or replaced with another surety bond that meets the requirements of this section if 90 days' advance written notice is provided to the Commissioner. An endorsement to a surety bond shall be filed with the Commissioner within 30 days after its effective date.

(g) If a group ceases to self-insure, dissolves, or transfers its workers' compensation obligations under an assumption reinsurance agreement, the Commissioner shall not release any deposits until the group has fully discharged all of its obligations under the Act. (1997-362, s. 3.)

Legal Periodicals. — For 1997 legislative survey, see 20 Campbell L. Rev. 487.

§ 58-47-95. Excess insurance and reinsurance.

(a) Each group, on or before its effective date of operation and on a continuing basis thereafter, shall maintain specific and aggregate excess loss coverage through an insurance policy or reinsurance contract. Groups shall maintain limits and retentions commensurate with their exposures. A group's retention shall be the lowest retention suitable for groups with similar exposures and annual premium. The Commissioner may require different levels, or waive the requirement, of specific and aggregate excess loss coverage consistent with the market availability of excess loss coverage, the group's claims experience, and the group's financial condition.

(b) Any excess insurance policy or reinsurance contract under this section shall be issued by a licensed insurance company, an approved surplus lines insurance company, or an accredited reinsurer, and shall:

(1) Provide for at least 30 days' written notice of cancellation by certified mail, return receipt requested, to the group and to the Commissioner.

(2) Be renewable automatically at its expiration, except upon 30 days' written notice of nonrenewal by certified mail, return receipt requested, to the group and to the Commissioner.

(c) Every group shall provide to the Commissioner evidence of its excess insurance or reinsurance coverage, and any amendments, within 30 days after their effective dates. Every group shall, at the request of the Commissioner, furnish copies of any excess insurance policies or reinsurance contracts and any amendments. (1997-362, s. 3.)

§ 58-47-100. Examinations.

G.S. 58-2-131 through G.S. 58-2-134 apply to groups. (1997-362, s. 3; 1999-132, s. 11.7.)

§ 58-47-105. Dividends and other distributions.

(a) Group dividends and other distributions shall be made in accordance with G.S. 58-7-130, 58-8-25(b), and 58-19-30. A group shall be in compliance with this Part before payment of dividends or other distributions to its members. No group shall pay dividends or other distributions to its members until two years after the group's licensing date.

(b) Payment of dividends to the members of any group shall not be contingent upon the maintenance or continuance of membership in the group. (1997-362, s. 3.)

§ 58-47-110. Premium rates.

(a) As used in this section:
  (1) "Bureau" means the North Carolina Rate Bureau in Article 36 of this Chapter.
  (2) "Expenses" means that portion of a premium rate attributable to acquisition, field supervision, collection expenses, and general expenses, as determined by the group.
  (3) "Multiplier" means a group's determination of the expenses, other than loss expense and loss adjustment expense, associated with writing workers' compensation and employers' liability insurance, which shall be expressed as a single nonintegral number to be applied equally and uniformly to the prospective loss costs approved by the Commissioner in making rates for each classification of risks utilized by that group.
  (4) "Prospective loss costs" means that portion of a rate that does not include provisions for expenses (other than loss adjustment expenses) or profit and that is based on historical aggregate losses and loss adjustment expenses adjusted through development to their ultimate value and forecasted through trending to a future point in time.
  (5) "Supplementary rating information" means any manual or plan of rates, classification, rating schedule, minimum premium, policy fee, rating rule, rate-related underwriting rule, experience rating plan, statistical plan, and any other similar information needed to determine the applicable rate in effect or to be in effect.
(b) Rates and the effective date shall be submitted by the group to the Commissioner for prior approval in the form of a rate filing. The rate filing:
  (1) Shall be on a form prescribed by the Commissioner and shall be supported by competent analysis, prepared by an actuary who is a member in good standing of the Casualty Actuarial Society or the American Academy of Actuaries, demonstrating that the resulting rates meet the standards of not being excessive, inadequate, or unfairly discriminatory;
  (2) Shall have the final rates and the effective date determined independently and individually by the group;
  (3) Shall have manual rates that are the combination of the prospective loss costs and the multiplier;
  (4) Shall file any other information that the group considers relevant and shall provide any other information requested by the Commissioner;
  (5) Shall be considered complete when the required information and all additional information requested by the Commissioner is received by the Commissioner. When a filing is not accompanied by the information required under this section, the Commissioner shall inform the group within 30 days after the initial filing that the filing is incomplete and shall note the deficiencies. If information required by a rate filing or requested by the Commissioner is not maintained or cannot be provided, the group shall certify that to the Commissioner;
  (6) May include deviations to the prospective loss cost based on the group's anticipated experience. Sufficient documentation supporting the deviations and the impact of the deviation shall be included in the rate filing. Expense loads, whether variable, fixed, or a combination of variable and fixed, may vary by individual classification or grouping.

Each filing that varies the expense load by class shall specify the expense factor applicable to each class and shall include information supporting the justification for the variation;

(7) Shall include any proposed use of a premium-sized discount program, a schedule rating program, a small deductible credit program or an expense constant or minimum premium, and the use shall be supported in the rate filing; and

(8) Shall be deemed approved, unless disapproved by the Commissioner in writing, within 60 days after the rate filing is made in its entirety. A group is not required to refile rates previously approved until two years after the effective date of this Part.

(c) At the time of the rate filing, a group may request to have its approved multiplier remain in effect and continue to use either the prospective loss cost filing in effect at the time of the rate filing or the prospective loss cost filing in effect at the time of the filing, along with all other subsequent prospective loss cost filings, as approved.

(d) To the extent that a group's manual rates are determined solely by applying its multiplier, as presented and approved in the rate filing, to the prospective loss costs contained in the Bureau's reference filing and printed in the Bureau's rating manual, the group need not develop or file its final rate pages with the Commissioner. If a group chooses to print and distribute final rate pages for its own use, based solely upon the application of its filed prospective loss costs, the group need not file those pages with the Commissioner. If the Bureau does not print the prospective loss costs in its manual, the group shall submit its rates to the Commissioner.

(e) If a new filing of rules, relativities, and supplementary rating information is filed by the Bureau and approved:

(1) The group shall not file anything with the Commissioner if the group decides to use the revisions as filed, with the effective date as filed together with the prospective loss multiplier on file with the Commissioner.

(2) The group shall notify the Commissioner of its effective date before the Bureau filing's effective date if the group decides to use the revisions as filed but with a different effective date.

(3) The group shall notify the Commissioner before the Bureau filing's effective date if the group decides not to use the revision or revisions.

(4) The group shall file the modification with the Commissioner, for approval, specifying the basis for the modification and the group's proposed effective date if different from the Bureau filing's effective date, if the group decides to use the revision with deviations.

(f) Every group shall adhere to the uniform classification plan and experience rating plan filed by the Bureau.

(g) Groups shall maintain data in accordance with the uniform statistical plan approved by the Commissioner.

(h) Each group shall submit annually a rate certification, signed by an actuary who is a member in good standing of the Casualty Actuarial Society or the American Academy of Actuaries, which states that the group's prospective rates are not excessive, inadequate, or unfairly discriminatory. The certification is to accompany the group's rate filing. If a rate filing is not required, the actuarial rate certification is to be submitted by the end of the calendar year. (1997-362, s. 3.)

§ 58-47-115. Premium payment requirements.

Groups shall collect members' premiums for each policy period in a manner so that at no time the sum of a member's premium payments is less than the total estimated earned premium for that member. (1997-362, s. 3.)

§ 58-47-120. Board; composition, powers, duties, and prohibitions.

(a) Each group shall be governed by a board or other governing body comprising no fewer than three persons, elected for stated terms of office, and subject to the Commissioner's approval. All board members shall be residents of this State or members of the group. At least two-thirds of the board shall comprise employees, officers, or directors of members; provided that the Commissioner may waive this requirement for good cause. The group's TPA, service company, or any owner, officer, employee, or agent of, or any other person affiliated with, the TPA or service company shall not serve as a board member. The board shall ensure that all claims are paid promptly and take all necessary precautions to safeguard the assets of the group.

(b) The board shall be responsible for the following:

    (1) Maintaining minutes of its meetings and making the minutes available to the Commissioner.

    (2) Providing for the execution of its policies, including providing for day-to-day management of the group and delineating in the minutes of its meetings the areas of authority it delegates.

    (3) Designating a chair to facilitate communication between the group and the Commissioner.

    (4) Adopting a policy of reimbursement from the assets of the group for out-of-pocket expenses incurred as board members, if so desired.

(c) The board shall not:

    (1) Be compensated by the group, TPA, or service company except for out-of-pocket expenses incurred as board members.

    (2) Extend credit to members for payment of a premium, except under payment requirements set forth in this Part.

    (3) Borrow any money from the group or in the name of the group, except in the ordinary course of business, without first informing the Commissioner of the nature and purpose of the loan and obtaining the Commissioner's approval.

(d) The board shall adopt bylaws to govern the operation of the group. The bylaws shall comply with the provisions of this section and shall include:

    (1) The method for selecting the board members, including terms of office.

    (2) The method for amending the bylaws and the plans of operation and assessment.

    (3) The method for establishing and maintaining the group.

    (4) The procedures and requirements for dissolving the group.

(e) Each group shall file a copy of its bylaws with the Commissioner. Any changes to the bylaws shall be filed with the Commissioner no later than 30 days before their effective dates. The Commissioner may order the group to rescind or revoke any bylaw if it violates this section or any other applicable law or administrative rule.

(f) The board shall adopt and administer a plan of operation to assure the fair, reasonable, and equitable administration of the group. All members shall comply with the plan. The plan shall comply with this section and include:

    (1) Procedures for administering the assets of the group.

    (2) A plan of assessment.

    (3) Loss control services to be provided to the members.

    (4) Rules for payment and collection of premium.

    (5) Basis for dividends.

    (6) Reimbursement of board members.

    (7) Intervals for meetings of the board, which shall be held at least semiannually.

    (8) Procedures for the maintenance of records of all transactions of the group.

(9) Procedures for the selection of the board members.
(10) Additional provisions necessary or proper for the execution of the powers and duties of the group.
(11) Qualifications for group membership, including underwriting guidelines and procedures to identify any member that is in a hazardous financial condition.

(g) The plan and any amendments become effective upon approval in writing by the Commissioner.

(h) Each year the board shall review:
(1) The performance evaluation of the TPA or service company, if applicable.
(2) Loss control services.
(3) Investment policies.
(4) Delinquent debts.
(5) Membership cancellation procedures.
(6) Admission of new members.
(7) Claims administration and reporting.
(8) Payroll audits and findings.
(9) Excess insurance or reinsurance coverage.

The board's findings from its review shall be documented in the board's minutes.

(i) G.S. 58-7-140 applies to board members. (1997-362, s. 3; 1999-132, s. 13.3.)

Legal Periodicals. — For 1997 legislative survey, see 20 Campbell L. Rev. 487.

§ 58-47-125. Admission and termination of group members.

(a) Prospective group members shall submit applications for membership to the board. The board, a designated employee of the group, or TPA shall approve an application for membership under the bylaws of the group. Members shall have bona fide offices in this State and members' employees shall be primarily engaged in business activities within this State. Members shall receive certificates of coverage from the board on a form acceptable to the Commissioner.

(b) The group shall make available to the Commissioner properly executed applications and indemnity agreements for all members, on forms prescribed by the Commissioner. If the applications and indemnity agreements are not executed properly and maintained, the Commissioner may order the group to cease writing all new business until all of the agreements are executed properly and obtained.

(c) Members may elect to terminate their participation in a group and may be terminated by the group under subsection (d) of this section and the bylaws of the group.

(d) A group may terminate a member's participation in the group on 30 days' written notice to the member. A group may terminate a member's participation in the group for nonpayment of premium on 10 days' written notice to the member. A member may terminate its participation in the group on 10 days' written notice to the group. Notices under this subsection shall be given by certified mail, return receipt requested. No termination by the group is effective until the notice is received by the member. (1997-362, s. 3; 2001-451, s. 3.)

§ 58-47-130. Disclosure.

Every group through its board, TPA, service company, agents, or other representatives shall require, before accepting an application, each applicant for membership to acknowledge in writing that the applicant has received the following:

(1) A document disclosing that the members are jointly and severally liable for the obligations of the group.

(2) A copy of the group's plan of assessment.

(3) The amount of specific and aggregate stop loss or excess insurance or reinsurance carried by the group, the amount and kind of risk retained by the group, and the name and rating of the insurer providing stop loss, excess insurance, or reinsurance. (1997-362, s. 3.)

§ 58-47-135. Assessment plan and indemnity agreement.

(a) Each group shall establish an assessment plan that provides for a reasonable and equitable mechanism for assessing its members. The plan and any amendments shall be approved by the Commissioner. The plan shall include descriptions of the circumstances that initiate an assessment, basis, and allocation to members of the amount being assessed, and collection of the assessment.

(b) The board shall notify the Commissioner of an assessment no fewer than 60 days before an assessment.

(c) The Commissioner shall impose an assessment on members if the board or third-party administrator fails to take action to correct a hazardous financial condition.

(d) Every group shall file an indemnity agreement on a form prescribed by the Commissioner, which jointly and severally binds the members of the group to comply with the provisions of the act and pay obligations imposed by the Act. (1997-362, s. 3.)

§ 58-47-140. Other provisions of this Chapter.

G.S. 58-1-10, 58-2-45, 58-2-50, 58-2-70, 58-2-100, 58-2-105, 58-2-155, 58-2-161, 58-2-180, 58-2-185, 58-2-190, 58-2-200, 58-3-71, 58-3-81, 58-3-100, 58-3-120, 58-3-125, 58-6-25, 58-7-21, 58-7-26, 58-7-30, 58-7-33, and Articles 13, 19, 30, 33, 34, and 63 of this Chapter apply to groups. (1997-362, s. 3.)

Editor's Note. — Section 58-3-125, referred to in this Section, has been repealed.

Part 2. Third-Party Administrators and Service Companies For Individual And Group Self-insurers.

§ 58-47-150. Definitions.

As used in this Part:

(1) "Books and records" means all files, documents, and databases in a paper form, electronic medium, or both.

(2) "Self-insurer" means a group of employers licensed by the Commissioner under Part 1 of this Article or a single employer licensed by the Commissioner under Article 5 of Chapter 97 of the General Statutes to retain its liability under the Workers' Compensation Act and to pay directly the compensation in the amount and manner and when due as provided for in the Act.

(3) "Service company" means an entity that has contracted with a self-insurer for the purpose of providing any services related to claims adjustment, loss control, or both.

(4) "Third-party administrator" or "TPA" means a person engaged by a self-insurer to execute the policies established by the self-insurer and to provide day-to-day management of the self-insurer. "Third-Party Administrator" and "TPA" does not mean:

    a. A self-insurer acting on behalf of its employees or the employees of one or more of its affiliates.

    b. An insurer that is licensed under this Chapter or that is acting as an insurer with respect to a policy lawfully issued and delivered by it and under the laws of a state in which the insurer is licensed to write insurance.

    c. An agent or broker who is licensed by the Commissioner under Article 33 of this Chapter whose activities are limited exclusively to the sale of insurance.

    d. An adjuster licensed by the Commissioner under Article 33 of this Chapter whose activities are limited to adjustment of claims.

    e. An individual who is an officer, a member, or an employee of a board.

(5) "Underwriting" means the process of selecting risks and classifying them according to their degrees of insurability so that the appropriate rates may be assigned. The process also includes rejection of those risks that do not qualify. (1997-362, s. 3.)

Legal Periodicals. — For 1997 legislative survey, see 20 Campbell L. Rev. 487.

§ 58-47-155. TPAs and service companies; authority; qualifications.

(a) No person shall act as, offer to act as, or hold himself or herself out as a TPA or a service company with respect to risks located in this State for a self-insurer unless that person complies with this Article.

(b) A TPA or service company shall post with the self-insurer a fidelity bond or other appropriate coverage, issued by an authorized insurer, in a form acceptable to the Commissioner, in an amount commensurate with the risk, and with the governing board of the self-insurer as obligee or beneficiary.

(c) A TPA or service company shall maintain errors and omissions coverage or other appropriate liability insurance in a form acceptable to the Commissioner and in an amount commensurate with the risk. The governing body of the self-insurer shall be obligee or beneficiary of the coverage or insurance.

(d) If the Commissioner determines that a TPA or service company or any other person has not materially complied with this Article or with any rule adopted or order issued under this Article, after notice and opportunity to be heard, the Commissioner may order for each separate violation a civil penalty under G.S. 58-2-70(d).

(e) If the Commissioner finds that because of a material noncompliance that a self-insurer has suffered any loss or damage, the Commissioner may maintain a civil action brought by or on behalf of the self-insurer and its covered members or persons and creditors for recovery of compensatory damages for the benefit of the self-insurer and its covered members or persons and creditors, or for other appropriate relief.

(f) Nothing in this Article affects the Commissioner's right to impose any other penalties provided for in this Chapter or limits or restricts the rights of covered members or persons, claimants, and creditors.

(g) If an order of rehabilitation or liquidation of the self-insurer has been entered under Article 30 of this Chapter, and the receiver appointed under that order determines that the TPA or service company or any other person has not materially complied with this Article or any rule adopted or order issued under this Article, and the self-insurer suffered any loss or damage from the noncompliance, the receiver may maintain a civil action for recovery of damages or other appropriate sanctions for the benefit of the self-insurer. (1997-362, s. 3.)

§ 58-47-160. Written agreement; composition; restrictions.

(a) No person may act as a TPA or service company without a written agreement between the TPA or service company and the self-insurer. The written agreement shall be retained by the self-insurer and the TPA or service company for the duration of the agreement and for five years thereafter. The agreement shall contain all provisions required by this Article, to the extent those requirements apply to the functions performed by the TPA or service company.

(b) Groups shall file with the Commissioner the written agreement, and any amendments to the agreement, within 30 days after execution. Single employers shall furnish the Commissioner, upon request, the written agreement and any amendments to the agreement. The information required by this section, including any trade secrets, shall be kept confidential; provided that the Commissioner may use that information in any judicial or administrative proceeding instituted against the TPA or service company.

(c) The written agreement shall set forth the duties and powers of the TPA or service company and the self-insurer. The Commissioner shall disapprove any such written agreement that:

    (1) Subjects the self-insurer to excessive charges for expenses or commission.

    (2) Vests in the TPA or service company any control over the management of the affairs of the self-insurer to the exclusion of the governing board of the self-insurer.

    (3) Is entered into with any TPA or service company if the person acting as the TPA or service company, or any of the officers or directors of the TPA or service company, is of known bad character or has been affiliated directly or indirectly through ownership, control, management, reinsurance transactions, or other insurance or business relationships with any person known to have been involved in the improper manipulation of assets, accounts, or reinsurance.

    (4) Is determined by the Commissioner to contain provisions that are not fair and reasonable to the self-insurer.

(d) The self-insurer, TPA, or service company may, by written notice, terminate the agreement as provided in the agreement. The self-insurer may suspend the underwriting authority of the TPA during the pendency of any dispute regarding the cause for termination of the agreement. The self-insurer shall fulfill any lawful obligations with respect to policies affected by the agreement, regardless of any dispute between the self-insurer and the TPA or service company.

(e) The contract may not be assigned in whole or part by the TPA or service company without prior approval by the governing board of the self-insurer and the Commissioner. (1997-362, s. 3.)

§ 58-47-165. Books and records.

(a) Every TPA or service company shall maintain and make available to the self-insurer complete books and records of all transactions performed on behalf of the self-insurer. The books and records shall be maintained by the self-insurer, TPA, or service company in accordance with G.S. 58-47-180.

(b) The Commissioner shall have access to books and records maintained by a TPA or service company for the purposes of examination, audit, or inspection. The Commissioner shall keep confidential any trade secrets contained in those books and records, including the identity and addresses of the covered members of a self-insurer, except that the Commissioner may use the information in any judicial or administrative proceeding instituted against the TPA or service company.

(c) The Commissioner may use the TPA or service company as an intermediary in the Commissioner's dealings with the self-insurer if the Commissioner determines that this will result in a more rapid and accurate flow of information from the self-insurer and will aid in the self-insurer's compliance with this Article and the Workers' Compensation Act.

(d) The self-insurer shall own the books and records generated by the TPA or service company pertaining to the self-insurer's business.

(e) The self-insurer shall have access to and rights to duplicate all books and records related to its business.

(f) If the self-insurer and the TPA or service company cancel their agreement, notwithstanding the provisions of subsection (a) of this section, the TPA or service company, shall transfer all books and records to the new TPA, service company, or the self-insurer in a form acceptable to the Commissioner. The new TPA or service company shall acknowledge, in writing, that it is responsible for retaining the books and records of the previous TPA, service company, or the self-insurer as required in subsection (a) of this section. (1997-362, s. 3.)

§ 58-47-170. Payments to TPA or service company.

If a self-insurer uses the services of a TPA, the payment to the TPA of any premiums or charges for insurance by or on behalf of the insured party is considered payment to the self-insurer. The payment of return premiums or claim payments forwarded by the self-insurer to the TPA or service company is not considered payment to the insured party or claimant until the payments are received by the insured party or claimant. This section does not limit any right of the self-insurer against the TPA or service company resulting from the failure of the TPA or service company to make payments to the self-insurer, insured parties, or claimants. (1997-362, s. 3.)

§ 58-47-175. Approval of advertising.

A TPA or service company may use only the advertising pertaining to or affecting the business underwritten by a self-insurer that has been approved in writing by the self-insurer before its use. (1997-362, s. 3.)

§ 58-47-180. Premium collection and payment of claims.

(a) The TPA or service company, at a minimum, shall:
   (1) Periodically render an accounting to the self-insurer detailing all transactions performed by the TPA or service company pertaining to the business underwritten, premium or other charges collected, and claims paid by the self-insurer, when applicable.
   (2) Deposit all receipts directly into an account maintained in the name of the self-insurer.
   (3) Pay claims on drafts or checks of and authorized by the self-insurer.
   (4) Not withdraw from the self-insurer's account except for authority limited to pay claims and refund premiums.

(5) Remit return premium, directly from the self-insurer's account, to the person entitled to the return premium.

(b) Any check disbursement authority granted to the TPA or service company may be terminated upon the self-insurer's written notice to the TPA or service company or upon termination of the agreement. The self-insurer may suspend the check disbursement authority during the pendency of any dispute regarding the cause for termination. (1997-362, s. 3.)

§ 58-47-185. Notices; disclosure.

(a) When the services of a TPA are used, the TPA shall provide a written notice approved by the self-insurer to covered members advising them of the identity of, and relationship among, the TPA, the member, and the self-insurer.

(b) When a TPA collects funds, the reason for collection of each item shall be identified to the member and each item shall be shown separately from any premium. Additional charges may not be made for services to the extent the services have been paid for by the self-insurer.

(c) The TPA shall disclose to the self-insurer all charges, fees, and commissions received from all services in connection with the provision of administrative services for the self-insurer, including any fees or commissions paid by self-insurers for obtaining reinsurance.

(d) The TPA or service company shall disclose to the self-insurer the nature of other business in which it is involved. (1997-362, s. 3.)

§ 58-47-190. Compensation.

A TPA or service company shall not enter into any agreement or understanding with a self-insurer that makes the amount of the TPA's or service company's commissions, fees, or charges contingent upon savings affected in the adjustment, settlement, and payment of losses covered by the self-insurer's obligations. This section does not prohibit a TPA or service company from receiving performance-based compensation for providing medical services through a physician-based network or auditing services and does not prevent the compensation of a TPA or service company from being based on premiums or charges collected or the number of claims paid or processed. (1997-362, s. 3.)

§ 58-47-195. Examinations.

TPAs and service companies may be examined under G.S. 58-2-131 through G.S. 58-2-134. (1997-362, s. 3; 1999-132, s. 11.8.)

§ 58-47-200. Unfair trade practices.

TPAs and service companies are subject to Article 63 of this Chapter. (1997-362, s. 3.)

§ 58-47-205. Other requirements.

(a) A TPA or service company, or any owner, officer, employee, or agent of a TPA or service company, or any other person affiliated with or related to the TPA or service company shall not serve as a trustee of a self-insurer.

(b) Each TPA or service company shall make available for inspection by the Commissioner copies of all contracts with persons using the services of the TPA. (1997-362, s. 3.)

Part 3. Third-Party Administrators for Groups.

§§ 58-47-210 through 58-47-220: Repealed by Session Laws 2001-223, s. 21.3, effective January 1, 2002.

ARTICLE 48.

Postassessment Insurance Guaranty Association.

§ 58-48-1. Short title.

This Article shall be known and may be cited as the "Insurance Guaranty Association Act." (1971, c. 670, s. 1.)

CASE NOTES

Summary Judgment Affirmed. — Defendant's motion for summary judgment was affirmed where there was no genuine issue of material fact as to whether defendant had a duty to defend and indemnify plaintiff corporation on the underlying discrimination actions. Fieldcrest Cannon, Inc. v. Fireman's Fund Ins. Co., 127 N.C. App. 729, 493 S.E.2d 658, 1996 N.C. App. LEXIS 1062 (1997), cert. denied, 348 N.C. 497, 510 S.E.2d 383 (1998).

Applied in City of Greensboro v. Reserve Ins. Co., 70 N.C. App. 651, 321 S.E.2d 232 (1984).

Cited in Newton v. United States Fire Ins. Co., 98 N.C. App. 619, 391 S.E.2d 837 (1990); North Carolina Ins. Guar. Ass'n v. State Farm Mut. Auto. Ins. Co., 115 N.C. App. 666, 446 S.E.2d 364 (1994).

§ 58-48-5. Purpose of Article.

The purpose of this Article is to provide a mechanism for the payment of covered claims under certain insurance policies, to avoid excessive delay in payment, and to avoid financial loss to claimants or policyholders because of the insolvency of an insurer, to assist in the detection and prevention of insurer insolvencies, and to provide an association to assess the cost of such protection among insurers. (1971, c. 670, s. 1.)

CASE NOTES

The determination of whether a particular policy of insurance is one of indemnity or liability depends upon the intention of the parties as evinced by the phraseology of the agreement in the policy. City of Greensboro v. Reserve Ins. Co., 70 N.C. App. 651, 321 S.E.2d 232 (1984).

The fundamental distinction between a policy of indemnity insurance and one of liability involves when the obligation of the insurer to the insured first attaches. City of Greensboro v. Reserve Ins. Co., 70 N.C. App. 651, 321 S.E.2d 232 (1984).

The general distinction between indemnity insurance and liability insurance is that if the policy is one against liability, the coverage thereunder attaches when the liability attaches, regardless of actual loss at that time; but if the policy is one of indemnity only, an action against the insurer does not lie until an actual loss in the discharge of the liability is sustained by the insured. City of Greensboro v. Reserve Ins. Co., 70 N.C. App. 651, 321 S.E.2d 232 (1984).

Cited in North Carolina Ins. Guar. Ass'n v. Century Indem. Co., 115 N.C. App. 175, 444 S.E.2d 464, cert. denied, 337 N.C. 696, 448 S.E.2d 532 (1994); State ex rel. Ingram v. Reserve Ins. Co., 303 N.C. 623, 281 S.E.2d 16 (1981); North Carolina Reinsurance Facility v. North Carolina Ins. Guar. Ass'n, 67 N.C. App. 359, 313 S.E.2d 253 (1984); Rinehart v. Hartford Cas. Ins. Co., 91 N.C. App. 368, 371 S.E.2d 788 (1988); Bentley v. North Carolina Ins. Guar. Ass'n, 107 N.C. App. 1, 418 S.E.2d 705 (1992); Hales v. North Carolina Ins. Guar. Ass'n, 337 N.C. 329, 445 S.E.2d 590 (1994).

§ 58-48-10. Scope.

This Article shall apply to all kinds of direct insurance, but shall not be applicable to:
    (1) Life, annuity, accident and health or disability insurance;

(2) Mortgage guaranty, financial guaranty or other forms of insurance offering protection against investment risks;

(3) Fidelity or surety bonds, or any other bonding obligations;

(4) Credit insurance, vendors' single interest insurance, collateral protection insurance, or any similar insurance protecting the interests of a creditor arising out of a creditor-debtor transaction;

(5) Insurance of warranties or service contracts;

(6) Title insurance;

(7) Ocean marine insurance;

(8) Repealed by Session Laws 1991 (Regular Session, 1992), c. 802, s. 1, effective January 1, 1993.

(9) Any transaction or combination of transactions between a person (including affiliates of such person) and an insurer (including affiliates of such insurer) which involves the transfer of investment or credit risk unaccompanied by transfer of insurance risk;

(10) Insurance written on a retroactive basis to cover known or unknown losses which have resulted from an event with respect to which a claim has already been made, and the claim is known to the insurer at the time the insurance is bound. (1971, c. 670, s. 1; 1989, c. 206, s. 1; 1991 (Reg. Sess., 1992), c. 802, s. 1.)

CASE NOTES

Cited in State ex rel. Ingram v. Reserve Ins. Co., 303 N.C. 623, 281 S.E.2d 16 (1981).

§ 58-48-15. Construction.

This Article shall be liberally construed to effect the purpose under G.S. 58-48-5 which shall constitute an aid and guide to interpretation. (1971, c. 670, s. 1.)

§ 58-48-20. Definitions.

As used in this Article:

(1) "Account" means any one of the three accounts created by G.S. 58-48-25.

(1a) "Affiliate" means a person who directly, or indirectly, through one or more intermediaries, controls, is controlled by, or is under common control with an insolvent insurer on December 31 of the year next preceding the date the insurer becomes an insolvent insurer.

(2) "Association" means the North Carolina Insurance Guaranty Association created under G.S. 58-48-25.

(2a) "Claimant" means any insured making a first party claim or any person instituting a liability claim; provided that no person who is an affiliate of the insolvent insurer may be a claimant.

(3) Repealed by Session Laws 1991, c. 720, s. 6.

(3a) "Control" means the possession, direct or indirect, of the power to direct or cause the direction of the management and policies of a person, whether through the ownership of voting securities, by contract, other than a commercial contract for goods or nonmanagement services, or otherwise, unless the power is the result of an official position with or corporate office held by the person. Control shall be presumed to exist if any person, directly or indirectly owns, controls, holds with the power to vote, or holds proxies representing ten percent (10%) or more of the voting securities of any other person. This presumption may be rebutted by a showing that control does not exist in fact.

(4) "Covered claim" means an unpaid claim, including one of unearned premiums, which is in excess of fifty dollars ($50.00) and arises out of and is within the coverage and not in excess of the applicable limits of an insurance policy to which this Article applies as issued by an insurer, if such insurer becomes an insolvent insurer after the effective date of this Article and (i) the claimant or insured is a resident of this State at the time of the insured event; or (ii) the property from which the claim arises is permanently located in this State. "Covered claim" shall not include any amount awarded (i) as punitive or exemplary damages; (ii) sought as a return of premium under any retrospective rating plan; or (iii) due any reinsurer, insurer, insurance pool, or underwriting association, as subrogation or contribution recoveries or otherwise. "Covered claim" also shall not include fines or penalties, including attorneys fees, imposed against an insolvent insurer or its insured or claims of any claimant whose net worth exceeds fifty million dollars ($50,000,000) on December 31 of the year preceding the date the insurer becomes insolvent.

(5) "Insolvent insurer" means (i) an insurer licensed and authorized to transact insurance in this State either at the time the policy was issued or when the insured event occurred and (ii) against whom an order of liquidation with a finding of insolvency has been entered after the effective date of this Article by a court of competent jurisdiction in the insurer's state of domicile or of this State under the provisions of Article 30 of this Chapter, and which order of liquidation has not been stayed or been the subject of a writ of supersedeas or other comparable order.

(6) "Member insurer" means any person who (i) writes any kind of insurance to which this Article applies under G.S. 58-48-10, including the exchange of reciprocal or interinsurance contracts, and (ii) is licensed and authorized to transact insurance in this State.

(7) "Net direct written premiums" means direct gross premiums written in this State on insurance policies to which this Article applies, less return premiums thereon and dividends paid or credited to policyholders on such direct business. "Net direct written premiums" does not include premiums on contracts between insurers or reinsurers.

(7a) "Ocean marine insurance" includes (i) marine insurance as defined in G.S. 58-7-15(20)a., except for inland marine, (ii) marine protection and indemnity insurance as defined in G.S. 58-7-15(21), and (iii) any other form of insurance, regardless of the name, label, or marketing designation of the insurance policy, which insures against maritime perils or risks and other related perils or risks, which are usually insured by traditional marine insurance such as hull and machinery, marine builders' risks, and marine protection and indemnity. The perils and risks insured against include loss, damage, or expense, or legal liability of the insured for loss, damage, or expense, arising out of, or incident to, ownership, operation, chartering, maintenance, use, repair, or construction of any vessel, craft, or instrumentality in use in ocean or inland waterways, including liability of the insured for personal injury, illness, death, or for loss or damage to the property of the insured or another person. "Ocean marine insurance" does not include insurance on vessels or vehicles under five tons gross weight.

(8) "Person" means any individual, corporation, partnership, association or voluntary organization.

(9) "Policyholder" means the person to whom an insurance policy to which this Article applies was issued by an insurer which has become an insolvent insurer.

(10) "Resident" means:

    a. An individual domiciled in this State;

    b. An individual formerly domiciled in this State at the time the applicable policy was issued or renewed and the term of the policy had not expired at the time of the insured event, and who at the time of the insured event had complied with the laws of the current domicile necessary to allow maintenance in force and effect of the applicable policy; or

    c. In the case of a corporation or other entity that is not a natural person, a corporation or entity whose principal place of business is located in this State at the time of the insured event. (1971, c. 670, s. 1; 1985, c. 613, ss. 1-3; 1989, c. 206, s. 2; c. 770, s. 72; 1991, c. 720, s. 6; 1991 (Reg. Sess., 1992), c. 802, s. 2; 1993, c. 452, s. 51; 2003-167, s. 1.)

Effect of Amendments. — Session Laws 2003-167, s. 1, effective June 10, 2003, and applicable to claims associated with insurers that become insolvent on or after that date, made a minor punctuation change in subdivision (3a); in subdivision (4), added the third sentence; and added subdivision (7a).

CASE NOTES

North Carolina Guaranty Association Not Required to Assume Insurer's Obligation Where Claim Not Covered by Policy. — Where orders entered by bankruptcy court required adjusters, pursuant to plaintiff's allegations of default by insurer, to return all vehicles that were subject of lease between plaintiff and rental company, which necessarily included 300 cars enrolled under residual value policy issued by insurer, and plaintiff was required to dispose of all vehicles and apply proceeds to indebtedness of rental company, with company retaining no rights whatsoever in any vehicles, undeniable effect of relief afforded to plaintiff in bankruptcy court was to extinguish lease with respect to the cars that were enrolled under residual value policy. Consequently, by express terms of residual value policy issued by insurer, plaintiff's claim pertaining to such vehicles was not covered. Thus North Carolina Guaranty Association defendant, as a matter of law, was not required under this Article to assume insurer's obligation. Barclays American/Leasing, Inc. v. North Carolina Ins. Guar. Ass'n, 99 N.C. App. 290, 392 S.E.2d 772 (1990), discretionary review denied, 328 N.C. 328, 402 S.E.2d 829 (1991), decided prior to 1989 amendments.

Association Not Vicariously Liable for Insolvent Insurers' Torts or Unfair Practices. — The North Carolina Insurance Guaranty Association is not subject to vicarious liability for the tortious conduct of insolvent insurers. Bentley v. North Carolina Ins. Guar. Ass'n, 107 N.C. App. 1, 418 S.E.2d 705 (1992).

Since, as a matter of law, defendant Association was not vicariously liable for the torts or unfair practices of insurer, the trial court did not err in granting summary judgment for defendant Association on these claims. Bentley v. North Carolina Ins. Guar. Ass'n, 107 N.C. App. 1, 418 S.E.2d 705 (1992).

Subrogation and Contribution. — Because subrogation and contribution are contractual or tort based forms of remedies and equitable subrogation is a judicially imposed remedy grounded in equity, the phrase "or otherwise" as used in subsection (4) does not encompass the purely equitable remedy. North Carolina Ins. Guar. Ass'n v. Century Indem. Co., 115 N.C. App. 175, 444 S.E.2d 464, cert. denied, 337 N.C. 696, 448 S.E.2d 532 (1994).

Punitive Damages. — North Carolina cases permit recovery of punitive damages for breach of contract only for identifiable torts accompanied by aggravation. The plain language of this Article both speaks of contracts and precludes recovery of punitive damages. Bentley v. North Carolina Ins. Guar. Ass'n, 107 N.C. App. 1, 418 S.E.2d 705 (1992).

Under the plain language of this section, punitive damages cannot be recovered from the North Carolina Insurance Guaranty Association. Bentley v. North Carolina Ins. Guar. Ass'n, 107 N.C. App. 1, 418 S.E.2d 705 (1992).

Applied in State ex rel. Ingram v. Reserve Ins. Co., 48 N.C. App. 643, 269 S.E.2d 757 (1980).

Cited in Hales v. North Carolina Ins. Guar. Ass'n, 337 N.C. 329, 445 S.E.2d 590 (1994).

§ 58-48-25. Creation of the Association.

There is created a nonprofit, unincorporated legal entity to be known as the North Carolina Insurance Guaranty Association. All insurers defined as member insurers in G.S. 58-48-20(6) shall be and remain members of the Association as a condition of their authority to transact insurance in this State. The Association shall perform its functions under a plan of operation established and approved under G.S. 58-48-40 and shall exercise its powers through a board of directors established under G.S. 58-48-30. For purposes of administration and assessment, the Association shall be divided into three separate accounts: (i) the automobile insurance account; (ii) the workers' compensation account; and (iii) the account for all other insurance to which the Article applies. Each person becoming a member insurer after October 1, 1985, shall pay to the Association upon demand a nonrefundable initial membership fee of fifty dollars ($50.00). (1971, c. 670, s. 1; 1985, c. 613, s. 4; 1991 (Reg. Sess., 1992), c. 802, s. 3.)

CASE NOTES

Waiver Not Negated by Insolvency of Municipality's Insurance Carrier. — If there had been a waiver of immunity by the purchase of insurance under G.S. 160A-485 it would not have been negated by the insolvency of municipality's insurance carrier, even though by purchasing liability insurance a municipality waives its immunity only to the extent that it is indemnified by the insurance contract from tort liability, since in this state behind every licensed liability insurance company that becomes insolvent is an agency created by this section that, to some extent and under certain conditions, takes over the insolvent's obligations to indemnify its insureds by paying legally entitled claimants. McDonald v. Village of Pinehurst, 91 N.C. App. 633, 372 S.E.2d 733 (1988).

Applied in North Carolina Reinsurance Facility v. North Carolina Ins. Guar. Ass'n, 67 N.C. App. 359, 313 S.E.2d 253 (1984).

Cited in State ex rel. Ingram v. Reserve Ins. Co., 303 N.C. 623, 281 S.E.2d 16 (1981); Rinehart v. Hartford Cas. Ins. Co., 91 N.C. App. 368, 371 S.E.2d 788 (1988).

§ 58-48-30. Board of directors.

(a) The board of directors of the Association shall consist of not less than five nor more than nine persons serving terms as established in the plan of operation. One non-voting member of the board shall be a property and casualty insurance agent authorized to write insurance for a member insurer, and appointed by the Commissioner; and the remaining members shall be selected by member insurers subject to the approval of the Commissioner. Vacancies of the Board shall be filled for the remaining period of the term in the same manner as initial appointments. If no members are selected within 60 days after June 25, 1971, the Commissioner may appoint the initial members of the board of directors.

(b) In approving selections to the board, the Commissioner shall consider among other things whether all member insurers are fairly represented.

(c) Members of the board may be reimbursed from the assets of the Association for expenses incurred by them as members of the board of directors. (1971, c. 670, s. 1; 1987, c. 864, s. 60.)

§ 58-48-35. Powers and duties of the Association.

(a) The Association shall:

(1) Be obligated to the extent of the covered claims existing prior to the determination of insolvency and arising within 30 days after the determination of insolvency, or before the policy expiration date if less than 30 days after the determination, or before the insured replaces

the policy or causes its cancellation, if he does so within 30 days of the determination. This obligation includes only the amount of each covered claim that is in excess of fifty dollars ($50.00) and is less than three hundred thousand dollars ($300,000). However, the Association shall pay the full amount of a covered claim for benefits under a workers' compensation insurance coverage, and shall pay an amount not exceeding ten thousand dollars ($10,000) per policy for a covered claim for the return of unearned premium. The Association has no obligation to pay a claimant's covered claim, except a claimant's workers' compensation claim, if:

a. The insured had primary coverage at the time of the loss with a solvent insurer equal to or in excess of three hundred thousand dollars ($300,000) and applicable to the claimant's loss; or

b. The insured's coverage is written subject to a self-insured retention equal to or in excess of three hundred thousand dollars ($300,000).

If the primary coverage or the self-insured retention is less than three hundred thousand dollars ($300,000), the Association's obligation to the claimant is reduced by the coverage and the retention. The Association shall pay the full amount of a covered claim for benefits under a workers' compensation insurance coverage to a claimant notwithstanding any self-insured retention, but the Association has the right to recover the amount of the self-insured retention from the employer.

In no event shall the Association be obligated to a policyholder or claimant in an amount in excess of the obligation of the insolvent insurer under the policy from which the claim arises. Notwithstanding any other provision of this Article, a covered claim shall not include any claim filed with the Association after the final date set by the court for the filing of claims against the liquidator or receiver of an insolvent insurer.

(2) Be deemed the insurer to the extent of the Association's obligation on the covered claims and to such extent shall have all rights, duties, and obligations of the insolvent insurer as if the insurer had not become insolvent. However, the Association has the right but not the obligation to defend an insured who is not a resident of this State at the time of the insured event unless the property from which the claim arises is permanently located in this State in which instance the Association does have the obligation to defend the matter in accordance with policy.

(3) Allocate claims paid and expenses incurred among the two accounts separately, and assess member insurers separately for each account amounts necessary to pay the obligation of the Association under subsection (a) above subsequent to an insolvency, the expenses of handling covered claims subsequent to an insolvency, the cost of examinations under G.S. 58-48-60 and other expenses authorized by this Article. The assessments of each member insurer shall be in the proportion that the net direct written premiums of the member insurer for the preceding calendar year on the kinds of insurance in the account bears to the net direct written premiums of all member insurers for the preceding calendar year on the kinds of insurance in the account; provided, for purposes of assessment only, premiums otherwise reportable by a servicing insurer under any plan of operation approved by the Commissioner of Insurance under Articles 45 or 46 of this Chapter shall not be deemed to be the net direct written premiums of such servicing insurer or association, but shall be

deemed to be the net direct written premiums of the individual insurers to the extent provided for in any such plan of operation. Each member insurer shall be notified of the assessment not later than 30 days before it is due. No member insurer may be assessed in any year on any account an amount greater than two percent (2%) of that member insurer's net direct written premiums for the preceding calendar year on the kinds of insurance in the account. If the maximum assessment, together with the other assets of the Association in any account, does not provide in any one year in any account an amount sufficient to make all necessary payments from that account, the funds available shall be prorated and the unpaid portion shall be paid as soon thereafter as funds become available. The Association may exempt or defer, in whole or in part, the assessment of any member insurer, if the assessment would cause the member insurer's financial statement to reflect amounts of capital or surplus less than the minimum amounts required for a license by any jurisdiction in which the member insurer is authorized to transact insurance. Each member insurer may set off against any assessment, authorized payments made on covered claims and expenses incurred in the payment of such claims by the member insurer if they are chargeable to the account for which the assessment is made.

(4) Investigate claims brought against the Association and adjust, compromise, settle, and pay covered claims to the extent of the Association's obligation and deny all other claims and may review settlements, releases and judgments to which the insolvent insurer or its insureds were parties to determine the extent to which such settlements, releases and judgments may be properly contested.

(5) Notify such persons as the Commissioner directs under G.S. 58-48-45(b)(1).

(6) Handle claims through its employees or through one or more insurers or other persons designated as servicing facilities. Designation of a servicing facility is subject to the approval of the Commissioner, but such designation may be declined by a member insurer.

(7) Reimburse each servicing facility for obligations of the Association paid by the facility and for expenses incurred by the facility while handling claims on behalf of the Association and shall pay the other expenses of the Association authorized by this Article.

(b) The Association may:

(1) Employ or retain such persons as are necessary to handle claims and perform other duties of the Association.

(2) Borrow funds necessary to effect the purposes of this Article in accord with the plan of operation.

(3) Sue or be sued.

(4) Negotiate and become a party to such contracts as are necessary to carry out the purpose of this Article.

(5) Perform such other acts as are necessary or proper to effectuate the purpose of this Article.

(6) Refund to the member insurers in proportion to the contribution of each member insurer to that account that amount by which the assets of the account exceed the liabilities if, at the end of any calendar year, the board of directors finds that the assets of the Association in any account exceed the liabilities of that account as estimated by the board of directors for the coming year. (1971, c. 670, s. 1; 1977, c. 343; 1979, c. 295, s. 1; 1985, c. 613, ss. 5, 6; 1989, c. 206, s. 3; 1991 (Reg. Sess., 1992), c. 802, s. 4; 1999-132, s. 9.1.)

CASE NOTES

The legislature intended that the equivalent of the association have a direct right to facility proceeds. North Carolina Reinsurance Facility v. North Carolina Ins. Guar. Ass'n, 67 N.C. App. 359, 313 S.E.2d 253 (1984).

The General Assembly did not intend for the term "subrogation" to encompass equitable subrogation, particularly in a context in which plaintiff failed to fulfill its statutory obligation under subdivision (a)(1), based upon its misreading of the insurance contract. North Carolina Ins. Guar. Ass'n v. Century Indem. Co., 115 N.C. App. 175, 444 S.E.2d 464, cert. denied, 337 N.C. 696, 448 S.E.2d 532 (1994).

The determination of whether a particular policy of insurance is one of indemnity or liability depends upon the intention of the parties as evinced by the phraseology of the agreement in the policy. City of Greensboro v. Reserve Ins. Co., 70 N.C. App. 651, 321 S.E.2d 232 (1984).

The fundamental distinction between a policy of indemnity insurance and one of liability involves when the obligation of the insurer to the insured first attaches. City of Greensboro v. Reserve Ins. Co., 70 N.C. App. 651, 321 S.E.2d 232 (1984).

The general distinction between indemnity insurance and liability insurance is that if the policy is one against liability, the coverage thereunder attaches when the liability attaches, regardless of actual loss at that time; but if the policy is one of indemnity only, an action against the insurer does not lie until an actual loss in the discharge of the liability is sustained by the insured. City of Greensboro v. Reserve Ins. Co., 70 N.C. App. 651, 321 S.E.2d 232 (1984).

Police Power of Commissioner. — Where, in order to determine which claims to pursue and which to abandon, it was necessary for the Commissioner and the Association to review plaintiff's claim files, the Commissioner seeking custody of the files was well within the usual scope of police power activity conducted to protect the general welfare. Eastern Appraisal Servs., Inc. v. State, 118 N.C. App. 692, 457 S.E.2d 312, appeal dismissed, cert. denied, 341 N.C. 648, 462 S.E.2d 509 (1995).

The Association Is An Insurer over Which Industrial Commission Has Jurisdiction. — Trial court lacked subject matter jurisdiction under N.C. R. Civ. P. 12(b)(1) over whether the insurance guaranty association was required by amendments to the Insurance Guaranty Association Act, G.S. 58-48-1 et seq., and the North Carolina Workers' Compensation Act, G.S. 97-1 et seq., to defend and indemnify the workers' compensation claims against the insolvent insurers, as the industrial commission had jurisdiction over the matter; not only was the association an insurer under G.S. 58-48-35(a)(2) over which the industrial commission had jurisdiction, but also, under G.S. 97-91, the industrial commission had jurisdiction to hear all questions arising under the Workers' Compensation Act. N.C. Ins. Guar. Ass'n v. Int'l Paper Co., 152 N.C. App. 224, 569 S.E.2d 285, 2002 N.C. App. LEXIS 1092 (2002).

Prejudgment Interest Assessed Against Guaranty Association. — Although North Carolina allows prejudgment interest to be awarded in a breach of contract action, whether prejudgment interest may be assessed against an insurance guaranty association where the insolvent insurer might have been liable for it is a question not yet encountered by North Carolina courts. City of Greensboro v. Reserve Ins. Co., 70 N.C. App. 651, 321 S.E.2d 232 (1984).

Association Not Vicariously Liable. — The North Carolina Insurance Guaranty Association is not subject to vicarious liability for the tortious conduct of insolvent insurers. Bentley v. North Carolina Ins. Guar. Ass'n, 107 N.C. App. 1, 418 S.E.2d 705 (1992).

Since, as a matter of law, defendant Association was not vicariously liable for the torts or unfair practices of insurer, the trial court did not err in granting summary judgment for defendant Association on these claims. Bentley v. North Carolina Ins. Guar. Ass'n, 107 N.C. App. 1, 418 S.E.2d 705 (1992).

North Carolina Guaranty Association Not Required to Assume Insurer's Obligation Where Claim Not Covered by Policy. — Where orders entered by bankruptcy court required adjusters, pursuant to plaintiff's allegations of default by insurer, to return all vehicles that were subject matter of lease between plaintiff and rental company, which necessarily included 300 cars enrolled under the residual value policy issued by insurer, and plaintiff was required to dispose of all vehicles and apply the proceeds to indebtedness of rental company, with company retaining no rights whatsoever in any vehicles, undeniable effect of the relief afforded to plaintiff in bankruptcy court was to extinguish lease with respect to the cars that were enrolled under residual value policy. Consequently, by the express terms of the residual value policy issued by insurer, plaintiff's claim pertaining to such vehicles was not covered. Thus North Carolina Guaranty Association defendant, as a matter of law, was not required under this Article to assume insurer's obligation. Barclays American/Leasing, Inc. v. North Carolina Ins. Guar. Ass'n, 99 N.C. App. 290, 392 S.E.2d 772 (1990) discretionary review denied, 328 N.C. 328, 402 S.E.2d 829 (1991), decided prior to 1989 amendments.

Defendant's Umbrella Coverage Did Not "Drop Down" to Primary Coverage. — Where there was no ambiguity as to the term "amount recoverable" or as to the scope of coverage and the primary insurer's insolvency did not constitute an occurrence as that term was defined in the policy, defendant's umbrella coverage did not "drop down" to become primary coverage. North Carolina Ins. Guar. Ass'n v. Century Indem. Co., 115 N.C. App. 175, 444 S.E.2d 464, cert. denied, 337 N.C. 696, 448 S.E.2d 532 (1994).

Liability Limited for Single Covered Claim. — The Insurance Guaranty Association's limit of liability was $300,000 for a single covered claim, notwithstanding that the school board had two separate policies with the insolvent insurer for primary and excess liability coverage, and this limit was subject to a $25,000 set-off. North Carolina Ins. Guar. Ass'n v. Burnette, 131 N.C. App. 840, 508 S.E.2d 837 (1998).

Defendant insurer was entitled to be paid by the association an amount up to the statutory cap, as stated in subdivision (a)(1). North Carolina Ins. Guar. Ass'n v. Century Indem. Co., 115 N.C. App. 175, 444 S.E.2d 464, cert. denied, 337 N.C. 696, 448 S.E.2d 532 (1994).

Punitive Damages. — North Carolina cases permit recovery of punitive damages for breach of contract only for identifiable torts accompanied by aggravation. The plain language of Article 48 both speaks of contracts and precludes recovery of punitive damages. Bentley v. North Carolina Ins. Guar. Ass'n, 107 N.C. App. 1, 418 S.E.2d 705 (1992).

Applied in Newton v. United States Fire Ins. Co., 98 N.C. App. 619, 391 S.E.2d 837 (1990).

Cited in State ex rel. Ingram v. Reserve Ins. Co., 303 N.C. 623, 281 S.E.2d 16 (1981); Rinehart v. Hartford Cas. Ins. Co., 91 N.C. App. 368, 371 S.E.2d 788 (1988); Hales v. North Carolina Ins. Guar. Ass'n, 111 N.C. App. 892, 433 S.E.2d 468 (1993); Hales v. North Carolina Ins. Guar. Ass'n, 337 N.C. 329, 445 S.E.2d 590 (1994).

§ 58-48-40. Plan of operation.

(a) The Association shall submit to the Commissioner a plan of operation and any amendment thereto necessary or suitable to assure the fair, reasonable, and equitable administration of the Association. The plan of operation and any amendments thereto shall become effective upon approval in writing by the Commissioner.

If the Association fails to submit a suitable plan of operation within 90 days following June 25, 1971, or if at any time thereafter the Association fails to submit suitable amendments to the plan, the Commissioner shall, after notice and hearing, adopt and promulgate such reasonable rules as are necessary or advisable to effectuate the provisions of this Article. Such rules shall continue in force until modified by the Commissioner or superseded by a plan submitted by the Association and approved by the Commissioner.

(b) All member insurers shall comply with the plan of operation.

(c) The plan of operation shall:

(1) Establish the procedures whereby all the powers and duties of the Association under G.S. 58-48-35 will be performed.

(2) Establish procedures for handling assets of the Association.

(3) Establish the amount and method of reimbursing members of the board of directors under G.S. 58-48-30.

(4) Establish procedures by which claims may be filed with the Association and establish acceptable forms of proof of covered claims. Notice of claims to the receiver or liquidator of the insolvent insurer shall be deemed notice to the Association or its agent and a list of such claims shall be periodically submitted to the Association or similar organization in another state by the receiver or liquidator.

(5) Establish regular places and times for meetings of the board of directors.

(6) Establish procedures for records to be kept of all financial transactions of the Association, its agents, and the board of directors.

(7) Provide that any member insurer aggrieved by any final action or decision of the Association may appeal to the Commissioner within 30 days after the action or decision.

(8) Establish the procedures whereby selections for the board of directors will be submitted to the Commissioner.

(9) Contain additional provisions necessary or proper for the execution of the powers and duties of the Association.

(d) The plan of operation may provide that any or all powers and duties of the Association, except those under G.S. 58-48-35(a)(3) and G.S. 58-48-35(b)(2), are delegated to a corporation, association, or other organization which performs or will perform functions similar to those of this Association, or its equivalent, in two or more states. Such a corporation, association or organization shall be reimbursed as a servicing facility would be reimbursed and shall be paid for its performance of any other functions of the Association. A delegation under this subsection shall take effect only with the approval of both the board of directors and the Commissioner, and may be made only to a corporation, association, or organization which extends protection not substantially less favorable and effective than that provided by this Article. (1971, c. 670, s. 1; 1973, c. 1446, s. 2.)

§ 58-48-42. Procedure for appeal to Commissioner from decision of Association.

In any hearing called by the Commissioner for an appeal made pursuant to G.S. 58-48-40(c)(7) no later than 20 days before the hearing the appellant shall file with the Commissioner or the Commissioner's designated hearing officer and shall serve on the appellee a written statement of the appellant's case and any evidence the appellant intends to offer at the hearing. No later than five days before the hearing, the appellee shall file with the Commissioner or the Commissioner's designated hearing officer and shall serve on the appellant a written statement of the appellee's case and any evidence the appellee intends to offer at the hearing. Each hearing shall be recorded and transcribed. The cost of the recording and transcribing shall be borne equally by the appellant and the appellee. However, upon any final adjudication the prevailing party shall be reimbursed for that party's share of the costs by the other party. Each party shall, on a date determined by the Commissioner or the Commissioner's designated hearing officer, but not sooner than 15 days after delivery of the completed transcript to the party, submit to the Commissioner or the Commissioner's designated hearing officer and serve on the other party, a proposed order. The Commissioner or the Commissioner's designated hearing officer shall then issue an order. (1991, c. 644, s. 31; 1993, c. 504, s. 42.)

§ 58-48-45. Duties and powers of the Commissioner.

(a) The Commissioner shall:

(1) Notify the Association of the existence of an insolvent insurer not later than three days after he receives notice of the determination of the insolvency.

(2) Upon request of the board of directors, provide the Association with a statement of the net direct written premiums of each member insurer.

(b) The Commissioner may:

(1) Require that the Association notify the insureds of the insolvent insurer and any other interested parties of the determination of insolvency and of their rights under this Article. Such notification shall be by mail at their last known address, where available, but if sufficient information for notification by mail is not available, notice

by publication in a newspaper of general circulation shall be sufficient.

(2) Suspend or revoke, after notice and hearing, the license to transact insurance in this State of any member insurer which fails to pay an assessment when due or fails to comply with the plan of operation. As an alternative, the Commissioner may levy a fine on any member insurer which fails to pay an assessment when due. Such fine shall not exceed five percent (5%) of the unpaid assessment per month, except that no fine shall be less than one hundred dollars ($100.00) per month.

(3) Revoke the designation of any servicing facility if he finds claims are being handled unsatisfactorily.

(c) Any final action or order of the Commissioner under this Article shall be subject to judicial review in accordance with the provisions of G.S. 58-2-75. (1971, c. 670, s. 1; 1999-132, s. 9.1.)

§ 58-48-50. Effect of paid claims.

(a) Any person recovering under this Article shall be deemed to have assigned his rights under the policy or at law to the Association to the extent of his recovery from the Association. Every insured or claimant seeking the protection of this Article shall cooperate with the Association to the same extent as such person would have been required to cooperate with the insolvent insurer. The Association shall have no cause of action against the insured of the insolvent insurer for any sums it has paid out except such causes of action as the insolvent insurer would have had if such sums had been paid by the insolvent insurer. In the case of an insolvent insurer operating on a plan with assessment liability, payments of claims of the Association shall not operate to reduce the liability of insureds to the receiver, liquidator, or statutory successor for unpaid assessments.

(a1) The Association shall have the right to recover from the following persons the amount of any "covered claim" paid and any and all expenses incurred, including attorneys' fees and costs of defense, in connection with any claim against the person or the person's affiliate pursuant to this Article:

(1) Any insured whose net worth on December 31 of the year next preceding the date the insurer becomes insolvent exceeds fifty million dollars ($50,000,000) and whose liability obligations to other persons are satisfied in whole or in part by payments under this Article; or

(2) Any person who is an affiliate of the insolvent insurer and whose liability obligations to other persons are satisfied in whole or in part by payments made under this Article.

(b) The receiver, liquidator, or statutory successor of an insolvent insurer shall be bound by settlements of covered claims by the Association or a similar organization in another state. The court having jurisdiction shall grant such claims priority equal to that to which the claimant would have been entitled in the absence of this Article against the assets of the insolvent insurer. The expenses of the Association or similar organization in handling claims shall be accorded the same priority as the liquidator's expenses.

(c) The Association shall periodically file with the receiver or liquidator of the insolvent insurer statements of the covered claims paid by the Association and estimates of anticipated claims on the Association which shall preserve the rights of the Association against the assets of the insolvent insurer. (1971, c. 670, s. 1; 1989, c. 206, ss. 4, 5; 2003-167, s. 2.)

Effect of Amendments. — Session Laws 2003-167, s. 2, effective June 10, 2003, and applicable to claims associated with insurers that become insolvent on or after that date, substituted "and any and all expenses incurred, including attorneys' fees and costs of defense, in connection with any claim against the person or the person's affiliate" for "on behalf of such person" in subsection (a1).

CASE NOTES

Cited in State ex rel. Ingram v. Reserve Ins. Co., 303 N.C. 623, 281 S.E.2d 16 (1981); North Carolina Reinsurance Facility v. North Carolina Ins. Guar. Ass'n, 67 N.C. App. 359, 313 S.E.2d 253 (1984).

§ 58-48-55. Nonduplication of recovery.

(a) Any person having a right to a defense or a claim against an insurer under any provision in an insurance policy other than a policy of an insolvent insurer which is also a covered claim, shall be required to exhaust first his rights under such policy. Any amount payable on a covered claim under this Article shall be reduced by the amount of any recovery under that insurance policy. For purposes of this section, a claim under an insurance policy shall include a claim under or covered by any kind of insurance, whether it is a first-party or a third-party claim, and whether it is a policy covering the policyholder or another person liable to the claimant, and shall include, without limitation, policies of accident and health insurance, workers' compensation insurance, medical expense coverage, and all other coverage except for policies of an insolvent insurer.

(a1) Any person having a claim or legal right of recovery under any governmental insurance or guaranty program which is also a covered claim shall be required to exhaust first his right under such program. Any amount payable on a covered claim under this Article shall be reduced by the amount of any recovery under such program.

(b) Any person having a claim which may be recovered under more than one insurance guaranty association or its equivalent shall seek recovery first from the association of the place of residence of the policyholder except that if it is a first party claim for damage to property with a permanent location, he shall seek recovery first from the association of the location of the property, and if it is a workers' compensation claim, he shall seek recovery first from the association of the residence of the claimant. Any recovery under this Article shall be reduced by the amount of recovery from any other insurance guaranty association or its equivalent.

(c) No claim held by an insurer, reinsurer, insurance pool, or underwriting association, whether the claim is:

(1) based on an assignment, or

(2) based on rights of subrogation or contribution, or

(3) based on any other grounds,

nor any claim of lien, may be asserted in any legal action against a person insured under a policy issued by an insolvent insurer except to the extent the amount of such claim exceeds the obligation of the Association under G.S. 58-48-35(a)(1).

(d) Any person that has liquidated by settlement or judgment a claim against an insured under a policy issued by an insolvent insurer, which claim is a covered claim and is also a claim within the coverage of any policy issued by a solvent insurer, shall be required to exhaust first his rights under such policy issued by the solvent insurer before execution, levy, or any other proceedings are commenced to enforce any judgment obtained against or the settlement with the insured of the insolvent insurer. Any amount so recovered from a solvent insurer shall be credited against the amount of the judgment or settlement. (1971, c. 670, s. 1; 1985, c. 613, ss. 7, 8; 1989, c. 206, s. 6; 1991 (Reg. Sess., 1992), c. 802, s. 5; 2003-167, s. 3.)

Effect of Amendments. — Session Laws 2003-167, s. 3, effective June 10, 2003, and applicable to claims associated with insurers that become insolvent on or after that date, in subsection (a), inserted "a right to a defense or" in the first sentence, substituted "that insurance policy" for "such insurance policy" in the second sentence, and added the third sentence.

CASE NOTES

This statute applies only to claims that are concurrently covered by both a policy of an insolvent insurer and a policy of a solvent insurer. City of Greensboro v. Reserve Ins. Co., 70 N.C. App. 651, 321 S.E.2d 232 (1984).

Any liability under the Insurance Guaranty Association Act is reduced by the amount of "any recovery" under any policy of a solvent insurer. This statute does not distinguish between primary and secondary coverage or between an operator's policy and an uninsured motorists provision. Rinehart v. Hartford Cas. Ins. Co., 91 N.C. App. 368, 371 S.E.2d 788 (1988).

Prejudgment Interest Assessed Against Guaranty Association. — Although North Carolina allows prejudgment interest to be awarded in a breach of contract action, whether prejudgment interest may be assessed against an insurance guaranty association where the insolvent insurer might have been liable for it is a question not yet encountered by North Carolina courts. City of Greensboro v. Reserve Ins. Co., 70 N.C. App. 651, 321 S.E.2d 232 (1984).

Cited in Patel v. Stone, 138 N.C. App. 693, 531 S.E.2d 879, 2000 N.C. App. LEXIS 788 (2000).

§ 58-48-60. Prevention of insolvencies.

(a) Repealed by Session Laws 1989, c. 206, s. 7.

(b) To aid in the detection and prevention of insurer insolvencies, the board of directors may, upon majority vote, request that the Commissioner order an examination of any member insurer which the board in good faith believes may be in a financial condition hazardous to the policyholders or the public. Within 30 days of the receipt of such request, the Commissioner shall begin such examination. The examination may be conducted as an NAIC examination or may be conducted by such persons as the Commissioner designates. The examination report shall be treated as are other examination reports. In no event shall such examination report be released to the board of directors prior to its release to the public, but this shall not preclude the Commissioner from complying with subsection (c) below. The Commissioner shall notify the board of directors when the examination is completed. The request for an examination shall be kept on file by the Commissioner but it shall not be open to public inspection prior to the release of the examination report to the public.

(c) It shall be the duty of the Commissioner to report to the board of directors when he has reasonable cause to believe that any member insurer examined or being examined at the request of the board of directors may be insolvent or in a financial condition hazardous to the policyholders or the public.

(d) The board of directors may, upon majority vote, make reports and recommendations to the Commissioner upon any matter germane to the solvency, liquidation, rehabilitation or conservation of any member insurer. Such reports and recommendations shall not be considered public documents.

(e) The board of directors may, upon majority vote, make recommendations to the Commissioner for the detection and prevention of insurer insolvencies.

(f) The board of directors may, at the conclusion of any domestic insurer insolvency in which the Association was obligated to pay covered claims, prepare a report on the history and causes of such insolvency, based on the information available to the Association, and submit such report to the Commissioner. (1971, c. 670, s. 1; 1989, c. 206, s. 7; 1991, c. 720, s. 27; 1995, c. 360, s. 2(j).)

§ 58-48-65. Examination of the Association.

The Association shall be subject to examination and regulation by the Commissioner. The board of directors shall submit, not later than March 30 of each year, a financial report for the preceding calendar year in a form approved by the Commissioner. (1971, c. 670, s. 1.)

§ 58-48-70. Tax exemption.

The Association shall be exempt from payment of all fees and all taxes levied by this State or any of its subdivisions except taxes levied by its subdivisions on real or personal property. (1971, c. 670, s. 1.)

§ 58-48-75: Repealed by Session Laws 1991, c. 689, s. 299.

§ 58-48-80. Immunity.

There shall be no liability on the part of and no cause of action of any nature shall arise against any member insurer, the Association or its agents or employees, the board of directors, or the Commissioner or his representatives for any action taken by them in the performance of their powers and duties under this Article. (1971, c. 670, s. 1.)

§ 58-48-85. Stay of proceedings; reopening of default judgments.

All proceedings in which the insolvent insurer is a party or is obligated to defend a party in any court or before any administrative agency or the North Carolina Industrial Commission shall be stayed automatically for 120 days and such additional time thereafter as may be determined by the court from the date the insolvency is determined or any ancillary proceedings are initiated in this State, whichever is later, to permit proper defense by the Association of all pending causes of action. Any party to any proceeding which is stayed pursuant to this section shall have the right, upon application and notice, to seek a vacation or modification of such stay. Any covered claims arising from any judgment under any decision, verdict or finding based on the default of the insolvent insurer or its failure to defend an insured, shall, upon application and notice by the Association be vacated and set aside by the same court in which such judgment, order, decision, verdict, or finding is entered and the Association either on its own behalf or on behalf of any insured or an insolvent insurer, shall be permitted to defend against such claim on the merits. Any party who has obtained any such judgment or order shall have the right, upon application and notice, to have the judgment or order restored if within 90 days following the entry of the judgment or order the Association has not notified such party and the court that it intends to defend the matter on the merits. (1971, c. 670, s. 1; 1989, c. 206, s. 8; 2003-167, s. 4.)

Effect of Amendments. — Session Laws 2003-167, s. 4, effective June 10, 2003, and applicable to claims associated with insurers that become insolvent on or after that date, substituted "court or before any administrative agency or the North Carolina Industrial Commission" for "court in this State" in the first sentence.

§ 58-48-90. Termination; distribution of funds.

(a) The Commissioner shall by order terminate the operation of the North Carolina Insurance Guaranty Association as to any kind of insurance covered by this Article with respect to which he has found, after hearing, that there is in effect a statutory or voluntary plan which:

(1) Is a permanent plan which is adequately funded or for which adequate funding is provided; and

(2) Extends, or will extend to the North Carolina policyholders and residents protection and benefits with respect to insolvent insurers not substantially less favorable and effective to such policyholders and residents than the protection and benefits provided with respect to such kinds of insurance under this Article.

(b) The Commissioner shall by the same such order authorize discontinuance of future payments by insurers to the North Carolina Insurance Guaranty Association with respect to the same kinds of insurance; provided, the assessments and payments shall continue, as necessary, to liquidate covered claims of insurers adjudged insolvent prior to said order and the related expenses not covered by such other plan.

(c) In the event the operation of the North Carolina Insurance Guaranty Association shall be so terminated as to all kinds of insurance otherwise within its scope, the Association as soon as possible thereafter shall distribute the balance of moneys and assets remaining (after discharge of the functions of the Association with respect to prior insurer insolvencies not covered by such other plan, together with related expenses) to the insurers which are then writing in this State policies of the kinds of insurance covered by this Article and which had made payments to the Association, pro rata upon the basis of the aggregate of such payments made by the respective insurers during the period of five years next preceding the date of such order. Upon completion of such distribution with respect to all of the kinds of insurance covered by this Article, this Article shall be deemed to have expired. (1971, c. 670, s. 1.)

§ 58-48-95. Use of deposits made by insolvent insurer.

(a) Notwithstanding any other provision of this Chapter pertaining to the use of deposits made by insurance companies for the protection of policyholders, the Association shall receive, upon its request, from the Commissioner and may expend, any deposit or deposits made, whether or not required by statute, by an insolvent insurer to the extent those deposits are needed by the Association first to pay the covered claims as required by this Article and then to the extent those deposits are needed to pay all expenses of the Association relating to the insurer: Provided that the Commissioner may retain and use an amount of the deposit up to ten thousand dollars ($10,000) to defray administrative costs to be incurred by the Commissioner in carrying out his powers and duties with respect to the insolvent insurer, notwithstanding G.S. 58-5-70.

(b) In, however the case of a deposit made by an insolvent domestic insurer, the Association shall receive, upon its request, from the Commissioner, the portions of the deposit made for the protection of policyholders having covered claims. As for the general deposit, those portions shall be in the proportions that the insolvent domestic insurer's domestic net direct written premiums for the preceding calendar year on the kinds of insurance in the account bears to its total net direct written premiums for the preceding calendar year on the kinds of insurance in the account.

(c) The Association shall account to the Commissioner and the insolvent insurer for all deposits received from the Commissioner under this section. After the deposits of the insolvent insurer received by the Association under this section have been expended by the Association for the purposes set out in this section, the member insurers shall be assessed as provided by this Article to pay any remaining liabilities of the Association arising under this Article. (1979, c. 628; 1985, c. 613, s. 10; c. 666, s. 41; 1987, c. 864, s. 6; 1989, c. 206, s. 9; c. 452, s. 5; 1993 (Reg. Sess., 1994), c. 678, s. 23; 2001-223, s. 24.4; 2001-487, s. 103(a).)

Legal Periodicals. — For survey of 1981 administrative law, see 60 N.C.L. Rev. 1165 (1982).

CASE NOTES

This section is to be read in conjunction with former § 58-155.25, which is now repealed. North Carolina Reinsurance Facility v. North Carolina Ins. Guar. Ass'n, 67 N.C. App. 359, 313 S.E.2d 253 (1984).

Section to Be Applied Retroactively. — This section, the Quick Access Statute, which requires that deposits made by an insolvent casualty insurer be paid to the North Carolina Insurance Guaranty Association for use in paying claims against the insolvent insurer, is to be applied retroactively to deposits made before the date of its enactment and to the holders of policies issued prior to that date. State ex rel. Ingram v. Reserve Ins. Co., 48 N.C. App. 643, 269 S.E.2d 757 (1980), modified and aff'd, 303 N.C. 623, 281 S.E.2d 16 (1981).

However, claimants against the deposit of a foreign insurer under § 58-5-70 will retain their lien rights after payment of the deposit to the Guaranty Association and may proceed against the Guaranty Association the extent of the deposit for any claims they have under G.S. 58-5-70 which are not paid by the Guaranty Association pursuant to this article. State ex rel. Ingram v. Reserve Ins. Co., 48 N.C. App. 643, 269 S.E.2d 757 (1980), modified and aff'd, 303 N.C. 623, 281 S.E.2d 16 (1981).

When Deposit Funds to Be Permanently Credited to Association. — While the Guaranty Association has the initial right to use deposit funds to cover operating expenses incident to the insolvent insurer, all deposit funds must be paid to claimants pro rata as provided by G.S. 58-5-70, and if all claimants are satisfied either directly by the Guaranty Association or by the Commissioner of Insurance (if the claim is under $100.00) and deposit funds remain, then and only then are such funds to be permanently credited to the Guaranty Association for its expenses. State ex rel. Ingram v. Reserve Ins. Co., 303 N.C. 623, 281 S.E.2d 16 (1981).

Cited in Barclays American/Leasing, Inc. v. North Carolina Ins. Guar. Ass'n, 99 N.C. App. 290, 392 S.E.2d 772 (1990).

§ 58-48-100. Statute of repose; guardians ad litem; notice.

(a) Notwithstanding any other provision of law, a covered claim with respect to which settlement is not effected with the Association, or suit is not instituted against the insured of an insolvent insurer or the Association, within five years after the date of entry of the order by a court of competent jurisdiction determining the insurer to be insolvent, shall thenceforth be barred forever as a claim against the Association.

(b) As to any person under a disability described in G.S. 1-17, the Association may not invoke the bar of the period of repose provided in subsection (a) of this section unless the Association has petitioned for the appointment of a guardian ad litem for such person and the disposition of that petition has become final. If a guardian ad litem is appointed pursuant to this subsection more than four years after the date of entry of the order by a court of competent jurisdiction determining the insurer to be insolvent, the period of repose under subsection (a) of this section shall be extended for such person one year after the date of the appointment.

(c) Within six months after the Association has been activated as to an insolvent insurer, the Commissioner may request that the Association submit an amendment to the plan of operation in accordance with G.S. 58-48-40, which amendment shall be applicable only to that insolvent insurer and shall prescribe a fair, reasonable, and equitable procedure for notice to insureds and to the public. (1985, c. 613, s. 9.)

§ 58-48-105. Transfer of balance of security funds.

(a) All moneys received and paid into the Stock Workers' Compensation Security Fund under former G.S. 97-107, together with all property and securities acquired by and through the use of moneys belonging to this Fund, including interest earned upon moneys in this Fund, shall be transferred and deposited into a new account with the Association created pursuant to G.S. 58-48-115. This account shall be separate and apart from any other accounts similarly created and from all other Association funds. The Association shall be the custodian of the account, and shall administer the account in accordance with the provisions of this Article.

(b) All moneys received and paid into the Mutual Workers' Compensation Security Fund under former G.S. 97-114, together with all property and securities acquired by and through the use of moneys belonging to this Fund, including interest earned upon moneys in this Fund, shall be transferred and deposited into a new account with the Association created pursuant to G.S. 58-48-120. This account shall be separate and apart from any other accounts similarly created and from all other Association accounts. The Association shall be the custodian of the account, and shall administer the account in accordance with the provisions of this Article. (1991 (Reg. Sess., 1992), c. 802, s. 6.)

§ 58-48-110. Purpose of the accounts.

The purpose of the accounts created in the Association pursuant to G.S. 58-48-115 and G.S. 58-48-120 of this Article shall be solely to:
  (1) Receive the balance from the accounts created under former G.S. 97-107 and G.S. 97-114;
  (2) Receive assessment moneys from member companies as provided in G.S. 58-48-115(a)(3), 58-48-120(b), and 58-48-120(c);
  (3) Receive interest on moneys in the accounts;
  (4) Pay stock or mutual carrier claims made against the security funds established under G.S. 97-107 and G.S. 97-114, but only for claims existing before January 1, 1993; and
  (5) Refund to the contributing stock companies in accordance with G.S. 58-48-115 the excess moneys in the stock fund account as set forth in G.S. 58-48-115(a)(2). (1991 (Reg. Sess., 1992), c. 802, s. 7.)

§ 58-48-115. Creation of Stock Fund Account; maintenance of Stock Fund Account; and distribution of Stock Fund.

(a) The moneys received by the Association pursuant to G.S. 58- 48-105(a) shall be distributed as follows:
  (1) An amount equivalent to one and one-half times the contingent liabilities of the Stock Workers' Compensation Security Fund created pursuant to former G.S. 97-107 existing on December 31, 1992, shall be deposited in a separate reserve account to be maintained by the Association which shall be designated as the "Stock Reserve Account." The amount of the Fund's contingent liabilities and the amount to be deposited in this Stock Reserve Account shall be determined and approved by the Department.

(2) The balance of the moneys received from the Stock Workers' Compensation Security Fund created pursuant to former G.S. 97-107 shall be refunded by the Association to member insurers that were contributing stock carriers during calendar year 1989 in accordance with the determination of the Department under this subdivision. The amount to be refunded to each stock carrier shall be in proportion to the contributions paid in by each stock carrier. The Department shall, as nearly as practicable, determine this amount under generally accepted accounting principles and the determination of the Department shall be final and not subject to appeal.

(3) Should the balance of the moneys in the Stock Reserve Account be reduced to less than one and one-half times the contingent liabilities of the account, the Association shall assess all member insurers that are stock carriers writing workers' compensation in this State at the time of the assessment in an amount equivalent to one and one-half times the contingent liabilities of said account. The assessment under this subdivision shall be made in accordance with the provisions of G.S. 58-48-35(a)(3). (1991 (Reg. Sess., 1992), c. 802, s. 8.)

§ 58-48-120. Creation of Mutual Fund Account; maintenance of Mutual Fund Account.

(a) The moneys received by the Association pursuant to G.S. 58-48-105(b) shall be deposited in a separate reserve account to be maintained by the Association which shall be designated as the Mutual Reserve Account. The amount in this account shall be equivalent to one and one-half times the contingent liabilities of the Mutual Workers' Compensation Security Fund created pursuant to former G.S. 97-114 existing on December 31, 1992. The amount of this Fund's contingent liabilities and the amount to be deposited into this Mutual Reserve Account shall be determined and approved by the Department.

(b) If the amount received by the Association from the former Mutual Workers' Compensation Security Fund created pursuant to G.S. 97-114 and received by the Association pursuant to G.S. 58-48-105(b) is insufficient to equal one and one-half times the contingent liabilities of the Fund existing on December 31, 1992, the Association shall, over the five years following January 1, 1993, assess the member insurers that are mutual carriers writing workers' compensation insurance in this State at the time of the assessment in the amount it determines necessary to make up the difference between the money received by the Association pursuant to G.S. 58-48-105(b) and one and one-half times the contingent liabilities of the Fund as determined by the Department of Insurance pursuant to G.S. 58-48-120(a). The assessment under this subsection shall be made in accordance with the provisions of G.S. 58-48-35(a)(3).

(c) After December 31, 1997, should the balance of the moneys in the Mutual Reserve Account be reduced to less than one and one-half times the contingent liabilities of the account, the Association shall assess all member insurers that are mutual carriers writing workers' compensation insurance in this State at the time of the assessment in an amount necessary to raise the account to an amount equivalent to one and one-half times the contingent liabilities of said account. The assessment under this subsection shall be made in accordance with the provisions of G.S. 58-48-35(a)(3). (1991 (Reg. Sess., 1992), c. 802, s. 9.)

§ 58-48-125. Payments by the Association.

The accounts created in G.S. 58-48-115 and G.S. 58-48-120 shall be used to pay the claims against insolvent stock workers' compensation insurers and insolvent mutual workers' compensation insurers, respectively, pursuant to G.S. 58-48-110(4) where the insolvency occurred prior to January 1, 1993. The expenses of administering these accounts, including loss adjustment expenses, shall be paid out of the respective accounts. (1991 (Reg. Sess., 1992), c. 802, s. 10; 1993, c. 504, s. 30.)

§ 58-48-130. Termination.

The account created in G.S. 58-48-115 shall be dissolved when all liabilities of the Stock Workers' Compensation Security Fund, under former G.S. 97-107 have been satisfied. Any excess moneys in the Stock Reserve Account shall be refunded to the member insurers that were stock workers' compensation carriers during the preceding calendar year. The amount to be refunded to each stock carrier shall be in proportion to the assessments paid by each stock carrier. The account created in G.S. 58-48-120 shall be dissolved when the liabilities of the Mutual Workers' Compensation Security Fund, under former G.S. 97-114, have been satisfied. Any excess moneys in the mutual reserve account shall be refunded to the member insurers that were mutual workers' compensation carriers during the preceding calendar year. The amount to be refunded to each mutual carrier shall be in proportion to the assessments paid by each mutual carrier. (1991 (Reg. Sess., 1992), c. 802, s. 11.)

ARTICLE 49.

Determination of Jurisdiction Over Providers of Health Care Benefits; Regulation of Multiple Employer Welfare Arrangements.

§ 58-49-1. Purposes.

The purposes of this section and G.S. 58-49-5 through G.S. 58-49-25 are: To give the State jurisdiction over providers of health care benefits; to indicate how each provider of health care benefits may show under what jurisdiction it falls; to allow for examinations by the State if the provider of health care benefits is unable to show it is subject to the exclusive jurisdiction of another governmental agency; to make such a provider of health care benefits subject to the laws of the State if it cannot show that it is subject to the exclusive jurisdiction of another governmental agency; and to disclose the purchasers of such health care benefits whether or not the plans are fully insured. As used in G.S. 58-49-5 through G.S. 58-49-20, "person" does not mean the State of North Carolina or any county, city, or other political subdivision of the State of North Carolina. (1985, c. 304, s. 1; 1993 (Reg. Sess., 1994), c. 569, s. 1; 2001-334, s. 18.1.)

Editor's Note. — Session Laws 1991, c. 611, s. 2 amended the title of Article 49, which formerly read "Determination of Jurisdiction Over Providers of Health Care Benefits."

§ 58-49-5. Authority and jurisdiction of Commissioner.

Notwithstanding any other provision of law, and except as provided in this Article, any person that provides coverage in this State for medical, surgical, chiropractic, physical therapy, speech pathology, audiology, professional mental health, dental, hospital, or optometric expenses, whether the coverage is by direct payment, reimbursement, or otherwise, shall be presumed to be subject to the jurisdiction of the Commissioner, unless the person shows that while providing the services it is subject to the exclusive jurisdiction of another agency or subdivision of this State or of the federal government. (1985, c. 304, s. 1; 1993 (Reg. Sess., 1994), c. 569, s. 2; 1995, c. 193, s. 40.)

§ 58-49-10. How to show jurisdiction.

A person may show that it is subject to the exclusive jurisdiction of another agency or subdivision of this State or the federal government, by providing to the Commissioner the appropriate certificate, license, or other document issued by the other governmental agency that permits or qualifies it to provide those services. If no documentation is issued by that other agency, the person may provide a certification by an official of that agency that states that the person is under the exclusive jurisdiction of that agency. (1985, c. 304, s. 1; 1993 (Reg. Sess., 1994), c. 569, s. 3.)

§ 58-49-15. Examination.

Any person that is unable to show under G.S. 58-49-10 that it is subject to the exclusive jurisdiction of another agency or subdivision of this State or of the federal government, shall submit to an examination by the Commissioner to determine the organization and solvency of the person, and to determine whether or not such person complies with the applicable provisions of this Chapter. (1985, c. 304, s. 1; 1993 (Reg. Sess., 1994), c. 569, s. 4.)

§ 58-49-20. Subject to State laws.

Any person unable to show that it is subject to the exclusive jurisdiction of another agency or subdivision of this State or the federal government, shall be subject to all appropriate provisions of this Chapter regarding the conduct of its business. (1985, c. 304, s. 1; 1993 (Reg. Sess., 1994), c. 569, s. 5.)

§ 58-49-25. Disclosure.

(a) Any production agency or administrator that advertises, sells, transacts, or administers the coverage in this State described in G.S. 58-49-5 and that is required to submit to an examination by the Commissioner under G.S. 58-49-15, shall, if said coverage is not fully insured or otherwise fully covered by an admitted life, accident, health, accident and health, or disability insurer, nonprofit hospital, medical, or dental service plan, or nonprofit health care plan, clearly and distinctly advise every purchaser, prospective purchaser, and covered person of such lack of insurance or other coverage.

(b) Any administrator that advertises or administers the coverage in this State described in G.S. 58-49-5 and that is required to submit to an examination by the Commissioner under G.S. 58-49-15, shall advise any production agency of the elements of the coverage, including the amount of "stop-loss" insurance in effect. (1985, c. 304, s. 1.)

§ 58-49-30. Multiple employer welfare arrangements; definition; administrators.

(a) As used in this section, the term "multiple employer welfare arrangement" or "MEWA" means that term as defined in Section 3 of the Employee Retirement Income Security Act of 1974, 29 U.S.C. § 1002(40)(A), as amended, that meets either or both of the following criteria:

   (1) One or more of the employer members of the MEWA is either domiciled in this State or has its principal headquarters or principal administrative office in this State.

   (2) The MEWA solicits an employer that is domiciled in this State or that has its principal headquarters or principal administrative office in this State.

(b) Repealed by Session Laws 1991, c. 611, s. 3.

(c) Each insurer licensed to do business in this State that administers a MEWA shall, at the request of the Commissioner, provide the Commissioner with such information regarding the insurer's administrative services contract or contracts with such MEWA or MEWAs that the Commissioner requires. No unlicensed insurer shall administer any MEWA.

(d), (e) Repealed by Session Laws 1991, c. 611, s. 3. (1989 (Reg. Sess., 1990), c. 1055, s. 1; 1991, c. 611, s. 3.)

§ 58-49-35. Multiple employer welfare arrangements; license required; penalty.

(a) It is unlawful to operate, maintain, or establish a MEWA unless the MEWA has a valid license issued by the Commissioner. Any MEWA operating in this State without a valid license is an unauthorized insurer.

(b) G.S. 58-49-30 through 58-49-65 do not apply to a MEWA that offers or provides benefits that are fully insured by an authorized insurer or to a MEWA that is exempt from state insurance regulation in accordance with the Employee Retirement Income Security Act of 1974, Public Law Number 43-406. (1991, c. 611, s. 1.)

§ 58-49-40. Qualifications for licensure.

(a) To meet the requirements for issuance of a license and to maintain a MEWA, a MEWA must be:

   (1) Nonprofit;

   (2) Established by a trade association, industry association, or professional association of employers or professionals that has a constitution or bylaws and that has been organized and maintained in good faith for a continuous period of five years for purposes other than that of obtaining or providing insurance;

   (3) Operated pursuant to a trust agreement by a board of trustees that has complete fiscal control over the MEWA and that is responsible for all operations of the MEWA. Except as provided in this subdivision, the trustees must be owners, partners, officers, directors, or employees of one or more employers in the MEWA. With the Commissioner's approval, a person who is not such an owner, partner, officer, director, or employee may serve as a trustee if that person possesses the expertise required for such service. A trustee may not be an owner, officer or employee of the administrator or service company of the MEWA. The trustees have the authority to approve applications of association members for participation in the MEWA and to contract with an authorized administrator or service company to administer the operations of the MEWA;

   (4) Neither offered nor advertised to the public generally; and

   (5) Operated in accordance with sound actuarial principles.

(b) The MEWA shall issue to each covered employee a policy, contract, certificate, summary plan description, or other evidence of the benefits and coverages provided. The evidence of benefits and coverages provided shall contain, in boldface print in a conspicuous location, the following statement:

"THE BENEFITS AND COVERAGES DESCRIBED HEREIN ARE PRO-VIDED THROUGH A TRUST FUND ESTABLISHED BY A GROUP OF EMPLOYERS [name of MEWA]. EXCESS INSURANCE IS PROVIDED BY A LICENSED INSURANCE COMPANY TO COVER HIGH AMOUNT MEDI-CAL CLAIMS. THE TRUST FUND IS NOT SUBJECT TO ANY INSURANCE GUARANTY ASSOCIATION, ALTHOUGH THE TRUST FUND IS MONI-TORED BY THE NORTH CAROLINA DEPARTMENT OF INSURANCE. OTHER RELATED FINANCIAL INFORMATION IS AVAILABLE FROM YOUR EMPLOYER OR FROM THE [name of MEWA]." If applicable, the same documents shall contain, in boldface print in a conspicuous location, the following statement: "PARTICIPATING EMPLOYERS WILL BE RESPONSI-BLE FOR FUNDING ALL CLAIMS INCURRED BY EMPLOYEES COV-ERED UNDER THE TRUST." Any statement required by this subsection is not required on identification cards issued to covered employees or other insureds.

(c) Each MEWA shall maintain excess insurance written by an insurer authorized to do business in this State with a retention level determined in accordance with sound actuarial principles. Such contracts must be filed with the Commissioner and contain notification provisions requiring at least 60 days' notice to the Commissioner from the insurer issuing such coverage prior to the termination or modification of such coverage. The Commissioner may by rule prescribe net retentions levels for MEWAs in accordance with the number of risks insured.

(d) Each MEWA shall establish and maintain appropriate loss reserves determined in accordance with sound actuarial principles.

(e) The Commissioner shall not grant or continue a license to any MEWA if the Commissioner deems that any trustee, manager, or administrator is incompetent, untrustworthy, or so lacking in insurance expertise as to make the operations of the MEWA hazardous to the potential and existing insureds; that any trustee, manager, or administrator has been found guilty of or has pled guilty or no contest to a felony, a crime involving moral turpitude, or a crime punishable by imprisonment of one year or more under the law of any state or country, whether or not a judgment or conviction has been entered; that any trustee, manager, or administrator has had any type of insurance license revoked in this or any other state; or that the business operations of the MEWA are or have been characterized, to the detriment of the employers participating in the MEWA, of persons receiving benefits from the MEWA, or of creditors or the public, by the improper manipulation of assets, accounts, or excess insurance or by bad faith.

(f) To qualify for and retain a license, a MEWA shall file all contracts with administrators or service companies with the Commissioner, and report any changes to such contracts to the Commissioner in advance of their implementation.

(g) Failure to maintain compliance with the eligibility requirements established by this section is a ground for denial, suspension, or revocation of the license of a MEWA. (1991, c. 611, s. 1.)

§ 58-49-45. Certain words prohibited in name of MEWA.

No licensed MEWA shall use in its name, contracts, literature, advertising in any medium, or any other printed matter the words "insurance", "casualty", "surety", "mutual", or any other words descriptive of the insurance business or deceptively similar to the name or description of any insurer doing business in this State. (1991, c. 611, s. 1.)

§ 58-49-50. Filing of application.

An association sponsoring a MEWA shall file with the Commissioner an application for a license on a form prescribed by the Commissioner and signed under oath by officers of the association. The application shall include or have attached the following:

  (1) A copy of the articles of incorporation, constitution, and bylaws of the association;

  (2) A list of the names, addresses, and official capacities with the MEWA of the individuals who will be responsible for the management and conduct of the affairs of the MEWA, including all trustees, officers, and directors. Such individuals shall fully disclose the extent and nature of any contracts or arrangements between them and the MEWA, including possible conflicts of interest.

  (3) A copy of the articles of incorporation, bylaws, or trust agreement that governs the operation of the MEWA.

  (4) A copy of the policy, contract, certificate, summary plan description, or other evidence of the benefits and coverages provided to covered employees, including a table of the rates charged or proposed to be charged for each form of such contract. An actuary who is a member of the American Academy of Actuaries or the Society of Actuaries and has experience in establishing rates for a self-insured trust and health services being provided, shall certify that:

    a. The rates are neither inadequate, nor excessive, nor unfairly discriminatory.

    b. The rates are appropriate for the classes of risks for which they have been computed.

    c. An adequate description of the rating methodology has been filed with the Commissioner and such methodology follows consistent and equitable actuarial principles.

  (5) A copy of a fidelity bond, in an amount determined by rules adopted by the Commissioner, issued in the name of the MEWA and covering any individuals managing or handling the funds or assets of the MEWA. In no case may the bond be less than fifty thousand dollars ($50,000) or more than five hundred thousand dollars ($500,000).

  (6) A copy of the MEWA's excess insurance agreement.

  (7) A feasibility study, made by an independent qualified actuary and an independent certified public accountant with an opinion acceptable to the Commissioner, that addresses market potential, market penetration, market competition, operating expenses, gross revenues, net income, total assets and liabilities, cash flow, and other items as the Commissioner requires. The study shall be for the greater of three years or until the MEWA has been projected to be profitable for 12 consecutive months. The study must show that the MEWA would not, at any month end of the projection period, have less than the reserves as required by G.S. 58-49-40(d).

  (8) A copy of an audited financial statement of the MEWA reflecting the minimum statutory reserve as required by G.S. 58-49-40(d).

  (9) Evidence satisfactory to the Commissioner showing that the MEWA will be operated in accordance with sound actuarial principles. The Commissioner shall not approve the MEWA unless it is determined that the MEWA is designed to provide sufficient revenues to pay current and future liabilities, as determined in accordance with sound actuarial principles.

  (10) A copy of every contract between the MEWA and any administrator or service company.

  (11) Such additional information as the Commissioner may require. (1991, c. 611, s. 1.)

§ 58-49-55. Examinations; deposits; solvency regulation.

(a) The provisions of Articles 2, 5, and 30 of this Chapter regarding examinations, deposits, and supervision and receivership respectively apply to MEWAs. The provisions of Article 62 of this Chapter and of Article 8B of Chapter 105 of the General Statutes do not apply to MEWAs.

(b) An audit or examination of a MEWA shall be conducted only when there are circumstances to support a reasonable belief of a MEWA's noncompliance with this Article. (1991, c. 611, s. 1.)

§ 58-49-60. Annual reports; actuarial certifications; quarterly reports.

(a) Every MEWA shall, within 150 days after the end of each of its fiscal years or within any such extension of time that the Commissioner for good cause grants, file a report with the Commissioner, on forms prescribed by the Commissioner and verified by the oath of a member of the board of trustees and by an administrative executive appointed by the board, showing its financial condition on the last day of the preceding fiscal year. The report shall contain an audited financial statement of the MEWA prepared in accordance with statutory accounting principles, including its balance sheet and a statement of the operations for the preceding fiscal year certified by an independent certified public accountant. The report shall also include an analysis of the adequacy of reserves and contributions or premiums charged, based on a review of past and projected claims and expenses.

(b) In addition to the information called for and furnished in connection with the annual report, if reasonable grounds exist, the Commissioner may request information that summarizes paid and incurred expenses and contributions or premiums received; and may request evidence satisfactory to the Commissioner that the MEWA is actuarially sound. That information and evidence shall be furnished by the MEWA not later than 30 days after the request, unless the Commissioner, for good cause, grants an extension.

(c) Annually, in conjunction with the annual report required in subsection (a) of this section, the MEWA shall submit an actuarial certification prepared by an independent qualified actuary that indicates:

   (1) The MEWA is actuarially sound, with the certification considering the rates, benefits, and expenses of, and any other funds available for the payment of obligations of, the MEWA;

   (2) The rates being charged and to be charged for contracts are actuarially adequate to the end of the period for which rates have been guaranteed;

   (3) Incurred but not reported claims and claims reported but not fully paid have been adequately provided for; and

   (4) Such other information relating to the performance of the MEWA that is required by the Commissioner.

(d) If reasonable grounds exist, the Commissioner may require a MEWA to file quarterly, within 45 days after the end of each of its fiscal quarters, an unaudited financial statement on a form prescribed by the Commissioner, verified by the oath of a member of the board of trustees and an administrative executive appointed by the board, showing its financial condition on the last day of the preceding quarter.

(e) Any MEWA that fails to file a report as required by this section is subject to G.S. 58-2-70; and after notice and opportunity for hearing, the Commissioner may suspend the MEWA's authority to enroll new insureds or to do business in this State while the failure continues. (1991, c. 611, s. 1.)

§ 58-49-65. Denial, suspension, or revocation of license.

(a) The Commissioner shall deny, suspend, or revoke a MEWA's license if the Commissioner finds that the MEWA:

(1) Is insolvent;

(2) Is using such methods and practices in the conduct of its business as to render its further transaction of business in this State hazardous or injurious to its participating employers, covered employees and dependents, or to the public;

(3) Has failed to pay any final judgment rendered against it in a court of competent jurisdiction within 60 days after the judgment became final;

(4) Is or has been in violation of or threatens to violate any provision of this Article;

(5) Is no longer actuarially sound; or

(6) Is charging rates that are excessive, inadequate, or unfairly discriminatory.

(b) The Commissioner may deny, suspend, or revoke the license of any MEWA if the Commissioner determines that the MEWA:

(1) Has violated any lawful order or rule of the Commissioner; or any applicable provision of this Article; or

(2) Has refused to produce its accounts, records, or files for examination under G.S. 58-49-55 or through any of its officers has refused to give information with respect to its affairs or to perform any other legal obligation as to an examination.

(c) Whenever the financial condition of the MEWA is such that, if not modified or corrected, its continued operation would result in impairment or insolvency, in addition to any provisions in Article 30 of this Chapter, the Commissioner may order the MEWA to file with the Commissioner and implement a corrective action plan designed to do one or more of the following:

(1) Reduce the total amount of present potential liability for benefits by reinsurance or other means.

(2) Reduce the volume of new business being accepted.

(3) Reduce the expenses of the MEWA by specified methods.

(4) Suspend or limit the writing of new business for a period of time.

If the MEWA fails to submit a plan within the time specified by the Commissioner or submits a plan that is insufficient to correct the MEWA's financial condition, the Commissioner may order the MEWA to implement one or more of the corrective actions listed in this subsection.

(d) The Commissioner shall, in the order suspending the authority of a MEWA to enroll new insureds, specify the period during which the suspension is to be in effect and the conditions, if any, that must be met prior to reinstatement of its authority to enroll new insureds. The order of suspension is subject to rescission or modification by further order of the Commissioner before the expiration of the suspension period. Reinstatement shall not be made unless requested by the MEWA; however, the Commissioner shall not grant reinstatement if it is found that the circumstances for which suspension occurred still exist. (1991, c. 611, s. 1.)

ARTICLE 50.

General Accident and Health Insurance Regulations.

Part 1. Miscellaneous Provisions.

§ 58-50-1. Waiver by insurer.

The acknowledgment by any insurer of the receipt of notice given under any policy covered by Articles 49, 50 through 55, 65, or 67 of this Chapter, or the furnishing of forms for filing proofs of loss, or the acceptance of such proofs, or the investigation of any claim under the policy, shall not operate as a waiver of any of the rights of the insurer in defense of any claim arising under the policy. (1913, c. 91, s. 7; C.S., s. 6484; 1991, c. 720, s. 28; 1999-244, s. 10; 2000-140, s. 16.)

Editor's Note. — Session Laws 2001-446, s. 4.1, effective July 1, 2002, and applicable to health benefit plans that are in effect, delivered, issued for delivery, or renewed on or after that date, rewrote the title of this article, which formerly read: "General Insurance Regulations."

Session Laws 2001-446, s. 4.2(1), effective July 1, 2002, and applicable to health benefit plans that are in effect, delivered, issued for delivery, or renewed on or after that date, designates G.S. 58-50-1 through 58-50-45 as Part 1 of Article 50, with the heading "Miscellaneous Provisions."

§ 58-50-5. Application.

(a) On and after January 1, 1956, each individual or family accident, health, hospitalization policy, certificate or service plan of hospitalization and medical and/or dental service corporations shall be issued only on application in writing signed by the insured or the head of the household or guardian. Any application or enrollment form that is taken by a resident agent shall also contain the certificate of the agent that he has truly and accurately recorded on the application or enrollment form the information supplied by the insured. Every policy subject to the provisions of this section shall contain as a part of such policy the original or a reproduction of the application required by this section. This section shall not apply to travel or dread disease policies or to policies issued pursuant to a group insurance conversion privilege. If any such policy delivered or issued for delivery to any person in this State shall be reinstated or renewed, and the insured or the beneficiary or assignee of such policy shall make written request to the insurer for a copy of the application, if any, for such reinstatement or renewal, the insurer shall within 15 days after the receipt of such request at his home office or any branch office of the insurer, deliver or mail to the person making such request, a copy of such application. If such copy shall not be so delivered or mailed, the insurer shall be precluded from introducing such application as evidence in any action or proceeding based upon or involving such policy or its reinstatement or renewal.

(b) No alteration of any written application for any such policy shall be made by any person other than the applicant without his written consent, except that insertions may be made by the insurer, for administrative purposes only, in such manner as to indicate clearly that such insertions are not to be ascribed to the applicant.

(c) The falsity of any statement in the application for any policy covered by Articles 50 through 55 of this Chapter may not bar the right to recover thereunder unless such false statement materially affected either the acceptance of the risk or the hazard assumed by the insurer. (1913, c. 91, s. 8; C.S.,

s. 6485; 1953, c. 1095, s. 9; 1955, c. 850, s. 6; 1961, c. 1149; 1985, c. 484, s. 4.2; 1991, c. 720, s. 29.)

Editor's Note. — Section 12 of the 1955 amendatory act made the act applicable to hospital and medical service corporations under former Chapter 57 (now Articles 65 and 66 of Chapter 58) to the same extent as to insurers under Articles 1 through 64 of this Chapter.

§ **58-50-10:** Repealed by Session Laws 1993, c. 529, s. 4.1.

§ 58-50-15. Conforming to statute.

(a) Other Policy Provisions. — No policy provision which is not subject to G.S. 58-51-15 shall make a policy, or any portion thereof, less favorable in any respect to the insured or the beneficiary than the provisions thereof which are subject to Articles 50 through 55 of this Chapter.

(b) Policy Conflicting with Articles 50 through 55 of this Chapter. — A policy delivered or issued for delivery to any person in this State in violation of Articles 50 through 55 of this Chapter shall be held valid but shall be construed as provided in Articles 50 through 55 of this Chapter. When any provision in a policy subject to Articles 50 through 55 of this Chapter is in conflict with any provision of Articles 50 through 55 of this Chapter, the rights, duties and obligations of the insurer, the insured and the beneficiary shall be governed by the provisions of Articles 50 through 55 of this Chapter. (1913, c. 91, s. 9; C.S., s. 6486; 1953, c. 1095, s. 10; 1991, c. 720, s. 29.)

CASE NOTES

Anti-subrogation Rule. — Commissioner's promulgation of 11 N.C.A.C. 12.0319, prohibiting subrogation provisions in life or accident and health insurance contracts, supported by G.S. 58-2-40 (right to limit practices injurious to the public) and subsection (a) of this section (prohibiting provisions less favorable to the insured), did not exceed his statutory authority, even though it may have changed state substantive law, and did not amount to an unconstitutional delegation of legislative powers because statutory provisions (G.S. 58-2-40 and 58-51-15, and this section) and judicial review (available under Chapter 150B) offer adequate procedural safeguards and support the delegation of power to the Commissioner. In re Ruling by N. C. Comm'r of Ins., 134 N.C. App. 22, 517 S.E.2d 134, 1999 N.C. App. LEXIS 665 (1999), cert. denied, appeal dismissed, 351 N.C. 105, 540 S.E.2d 356 (1999).

Applied in Stainback v. Investor's Consol. Ins. Co., 64 N.C. App. 197, 306 S.E.2d 532 (1983).

Cited in Harrison Agency, Inc. v. Pacific Mut. Life Ins. Co., 703 F. Supp. 441 (W.D.N.C. 1989).

§ 58-50-20. Age limit.

If any such policy contains a provision establishing, as an age limit or otherwise, a date after which the coverage provided by the policy will not be effective, and if such date falls within a period for which premium is accepted by the insurer or if the insurer accepts a premium after such date, the coverage provided by the policy will continue in force subject to any right of cancellation until the end of the period for which premium has been accepted. In the event the age of the insured has been misstated and if, according to the correct age of the insured, the coverage provided by the policy would not have become effective, or would have ceased prior to the acceptance of such premium or premiums, then the liability of the insurer shall be limited to the refund, upon request, of all premiums paid for the period not covered by the policy. (1953, c. 1095, s. 11.)

CASE NOTES

Misrepresentation as to Age. — Where a policy provides that in the event of misrepresentation as to age the contract will be adjusted so as to pay the amount actually due under the insured's correct age, it is generally held that this provision relates not to the efficacy of the contract, but to the benefits due, and is not affected by an incontestable clause. Wall v. Diamond State Life Ins. Co., 9 N.C. App. 231, 175 S.E.2d 602 (1970).

§ 58-50-25. Nurses' services.

(a) No agency, institution or physician providing a service for which payment or reimbursement is required to be made under a policy governed by Articles 1 through 64 of this Chapter shall be denied such payment or reimbursement on account of the fact that such services were rendered through a registered nurse acting under authority of rules and regulations adopted by the North Carolina Medical Board and the Board of Nursing pursuant to G.S. 90-6 and 90-171.23.

(b) A licensed registered nurse who has successfully completed a program established under G.S. 90-171.38(b) may receive direct payment for conducting medical examinations or medical procedures for the purpose of collecting evidence from victims of offenses described in that subsection if the payment would have otherwise been permitted. (1973, c. 437; 1991, c. 720, s. 37; 1993, c. 347, s. 1; 1995, c. 94, s. 2; 1997-197, s. 1; 1997-375, s. 3.)

§ 58-50-26. Physician services provided by physician assistants.

No agency, institution, or physician providing a service for which payment or reimbursement is required to be made under a policy governed by Articles 1 through 64 of this Chapter shall be denied the payment or reimbursement on account of the fact that the services were rendered through a physician assistant acting under the authority of rules adopted by the North Carolina Medical Board pursuant to G.S. 90-18.1. (1999-210, s. 1.)

Editor's Note. — Session Laws 1999-210, s. 9, made this section effective January 1, 2000, and applicable to treatment or services rendered on or after that date.

§ 58-50-30. Right to choose services of optometrist, podiatrist, licensed clinical social worker, certified substance abuse professional, licensed professional counselor, dentist, chiropractor, psychologist, pharmacist, certified fee-based practicing pastoral counselor, advanced practice nurse, licensed marriage and family therapist, or physician assistant.

(a) Repealed by Session Laws 2001-297, s. 1, effective January 1, 2001.

(a1) Whenever any health benefit plan, subscriber contract, or policy of insurance issued by a health maintenance organization, hospital or medical service corporation, or insurer governed by Articles 1 through 67 of this Chapter provides for coverage for, payment of, or reimbursement for any service rendered in connection with a condition or complaint that is within the scope of practice of a duly licensed optometrist, a duly licensed podiatrist, a duly licensed dentist, a duly licensed chiropractor, a duly licensed clinical social worker, a duly certified substance abuse professional, a duly licensed professional counselor, a duly licensed psychologist, a duly licensed pharmacist, a duly certified fee-based practicing pastoral counselor, a duly licensed physician assistant, a duly licensed marriage and family therapist, or an advanced practice registered nurse, the insured or other persons entitled to benefits under the policy shall be entitled to coverage of, payment of, or reimbursement for the services, whether the services be performed by a duly licensed physician, or a provider listed in this subsection, notwithstanding any provision contained in the plan or policy limiting access to the providers. The policyholder, insured, or beneficiary shall have the right to choose the provider of services notwithstanding any provision to the contrary in any other statute, subject to the utilization review, referral, and prior approval requirements of the plan that apply to all providers for that service; provided that:

    (1) In the case of plans that require the use of network providers as a condition of obtaining benefits under the plan or policy, the policyholder, insured, or beneficiary must choose a provider of the services within the network; and

    (2) In the case of plans that require the use of network providers as a condition of obtaining a higher level of benefits under the plan or policy, the policyholder, insured, or beneficiary must choose a provider of the services within the network in order to obtain the higher level of benefits.

(a2) Whenever any policy of insurance governed by Articles 1 through 64 of this Chapter provides for certification of disability that is within the scope of practice of a duly licensed physician, a duly licensed physician assistant, a duly licensed optometrist, a duly licensed podiatrist, a duly licensed dentist, a duly licensed chiropractor, a duly licensed clinical social worker, a duly certified substance abuse professional, a duly licensed professional counselor, a duly licensed psychologist, a duly certified fee-based practicing pastoral counselor, a duly licensed marriage and family therapist, or an advanced practice registered nurse, the insured or other persons entitled to benefits under the policy shall be entitled to payment of or reimbursement for the disability whether the disability be certified by a duly licensed physician, or a provider listed in this subsection, notwithstanding any provisions contained in the policy. The policyholder, insured, or beneficiary shall have the right to choose the provider of the services notwithstanding any provision to the contrary in any other statute; provided that for plans that require the use of network providers either as a condition of obtaining benefits under the plan or policy or to access a higher level of benefits under the plan or policy, the policyholder, insured, or beneficiary must choose a provider of the services within the network, subject to the requirements of the plan or policy.

(a3) Whenever any health benefit plan, subscriber contract, or policy of insurance issued by a health maintenance organization, hospital or medical service corporation, or insurer governed by Articles 1 through 67 of this Chapter provides coverage for medically necessary treatment, the insurer shall not impose any limitation on treatment or levels of coverage if performed by a duly licensed chiropractor acting within the scope of the chiropractor's practice as defined in G.S. 90-151 unless a comparable limitation is imposed on the medically necessary treatment if performed or authorized by any other duly licensed physician.

(b) For the purposes of this section, a "duly licensed psychologist" is a:

    (1) Licensed psychologist who holds permanent licensure and certification as a health services provider psychologist issued by the North Carolina Psychology Board; or

    (2) Licensed psychological associate who holds permanent licensure.

(c) For the purposes of this section, a "duly licensed clinical social worker" is a "licensed clinical social worker " as defined in G.S. 90B-3(2) and licensed by the North Carolina Social Work Certification and Licensure Board pursuant to Chapter 90B of the General Statutes.

(c1) For purposes of this section, a "duly certified fee-based practicing pastoral counselor" shall be defined only to include fee-based practicing pastoral counselors certified by the North Carolina State Board of Examiners of Fee-Based Practicing Pastoral Counselors pursuant to Article 26 of Chapter 90 of the General Statutes.

(c2) For purposes of this section, a "duly certified substance abuse professional" is a person certified by the North Carolina Substance Abuse Professional Certification Board pursuant to Article 5C of Chapter 90 of the General Statutes.

(c3) For purposes of this section, a "duly licensed professional counselor" is a person licensed by the North Carolina Board of Licensed Professional Counselors pursuant to Article 24 of Chapter 90 of the General Statutes.

(c4) For purposes of this section, a "duly licensed marriage and family therapist" is a person licensed by the North Carolina Marriage and Family Therapy Licensure Board pursuant to Article 18C of Chapter 90 of the General Statutes.

(d) Payment or reimbursement is required by this section for a service performed by an advanced practice registered nurse only when:

    (1) The service performed is within the nurse's lawful scope of practice;

    (2) The policy currently provides benefits for identical services performed by other licensed health care providers;

    (3) The service is not performed while the nurse is a regular employee in an office of a licensed physician;

    (4) The service is not performed while the registered nurse is employed by a nursing facility (including a hospital, skilled nursing facility, intermediate care facility, or home care agency); and

    (5) Nothing in this section is intended to authorize payment to more than one provider for the same service.

No lack of signature, referral, or employment by any other health care provider may be asserted to deny benefits under this provision, unless these plan requirements apply to all providers for that service.

For purposes of this section, an "advanced practice registered nurse" means only a registered nurse who is duly licensed or certified as a nurse practitioner, clinical specialist in psychiatric and mental health nursing, or nurse midwife.

(e) Payment or reimbursement is required by this section for a service performed by a duly licensed pharmacist only when:

    (1) The service performed is within the lawful scope of practice of the pharmacist;

    (2) The service performed is not initial counseling services required under State or federal law or regulation of the North Carolina Board of Pharmacy;

    (3) The policy currently provides reimbursement for identical services performed by other licensed health care providers; and

    (4) The service is identified as a separate service that is performed by other licensed health care providers and is reimbursed by identical payment methods.

Nothing in this subsection authorizes payment to more than one provider for the same service.

(f) Payment or reimbursement is required by this section for a service performed by a duly licensed physician assistant only when:

    (1) The service performed is within the lawful scope of practice of the physician assistant in accordance with rules adopted by the North Carolina Medical Board pursuant to G.S. 90-18.1;

    (2) The policy currently provides reimbursement for identical services performed by other licensed health care providers; and

(3) The reimbursement is made to the physician, clinic, agency, or institution employing the physician assistant.

Nothing in this subsection is intended to authorize payment to more than one provider for the same service. For the purposes of this section, a "duly licensed physician assistant" is a physician assistant as defined by G.S. 90-18.1.

(g) A health maintenance organization, hospital or medical service corporation, or insurer governed by Articles 1 through 67 of this Chapter shall not exclude from participation in its provider network or from eligibility to provide particular covered services under the plan or policy any duly licensed physician or provider listed in subsection (a1) of this section, acting within the scope of the provider's license or certification under North Carolina law, solely on the basis of the provider's license or certification. Any health maintenance organization, hospital or medical service corporation, or insurer governed by Articles 1 through 67 of this Chapter that offers coverage through a network plan may condition participation in the network on satisfying written participation criteria, including credentialing, quality, and accessibility criteria. The participation criteria shall be developed and applied in a like manner consistent with the licensure and scope of practice for each type of provider. Any health maintenance organization, hospital or medical service corporation, or insurer governed by Articles 1 through 67 of this Chapter that excludes a provider listed in subsection (a1) of this section from participation in its network or from eligibility to provide particular covered services under the plan or policy shall provide the affected listed provider with a written explanation of the basis for its decision. A health maintenance organization, hospital or medical service corporation, or insurer governed by Articles 1 through 67 of this Chapter shall not exclude from participation in its provider network a provider listed in subsection (a1) of this section acting within the scope of the provider's license or certification under North Carolina law solely on the basis that the provider lacks hospital privileges, unless use of hospital services by the provider on behalf of a policy holder, insured, or beneficiary reasonably could be expected.

(h) Nothing in this section shall be construed as expanding the scope of practice of any duly licensed physician or provider listed in subsection (a1) of this section. (1913, c. 91, s. 11; C.S., s. 6488; 1965, c. 396, s. 2; c. 1169, s. 2; 1967, c. 690, s. 2; 1969, c. 679; 1973, c. 610; 1977, c. 601, ss. 2, 31/2; 1991, c. 720, s. 29; 1993, c. 347, s. 2; c. 375, s. 3; c. 464, s. 2; c. 554, s. 1; 1995, 193, s. 41, c. 223, s. 1; c. 406, s. 3; 1997-197, ss. 1, 2; 1999-186, s. 1; 1999-199, s. 1; 1999-210, s. 2; 2001-297, s. 1; 2001-446, s. 1.7; 2001-487, s. 40(g); 2003-117, s. 1; 2003-368, s. 1.)

Cross References. — As to prohibition against discrimination between individuals of the same class in premiums or rates charged for policies covered by Articles 50 through 53 of Chapter 58, or any other matter, see G.S. 58-3-120(b).

Editor's Note. — Session Laws 1965, c. 396, which amended this section, provided in s. 4 that the act should not be construed to equate optometrists with physicians except to the extent that each must be duly licensed.

Session Laws 1967, c. 690, which amended this section, provided in s. 4: "Nothing in this act shall be construed to equate podiatrists with physicians except to the extent that each must be duly licensed."

This section was amended by Session Laws 1993, c. 347, s. 2; c. 375, s. 3; c. 464, s. 2 and c.

554, s. 1 in the coded bill drafting format provided by G.S. 120-20.1. It has been set out in the form above at the direction of the Revisor of Statutes. Present subsection (b) was so designated at the direction of the Revisor of Statutes. The subsection designated as subsection (b) by Session Laws 1993, c. 464, s. 2 was redesignated as subsection (d).

Session Laws 2001-446, s. 8 provides: "Nothing in this act obligates the General Assembly to appropriate funds to implement this act."

Session Laws 2001-446, s. 7 is a severability clause.

Effect of Amendments. — Session Laws 2001-446, s. 1.7, effective March 1, 2002, and applicable to health benefit plans that are in effect, delivered, issued for delivery, or renewed on or after that date, in this section as amended by Session Laws 2001-297, s. 1, in the first sentence of subsection (a1), substituted "any health benefit plan, subscriber contract, or policy of insurance issued by a health maintenance organization, hospital or medical service corporation, or insurer" for "any policy of insurance governed," substituted "67" for "65," substituted "coverage for, payment of, or" for "payment of or" preceding "reimbursement for any service," substituted "coverage of, payment of, or" for "payment of or" preceding "reimbursement for the services," and substituted "plan or policy limiting access to the providers" for "policy"; added the second sentence of subdivision (a1); added subdivisions (a1)(1) and (a1)(2); in subdivision (a2) substituted "64" for "65" near the beginning thereof, and added the proviso at the end of the subsection; substituted the language "any health benefit plan ... of this Chapter" for "any policy of insurance" in subsection (a3); added "unless these plan requirements apply to all providers for that service" at the end of the sentence of subsection (d) following subdivision (d)(5); and added subsections (g) and (h).

Session Laws 2003-117, s. 1, effective October 1, 2003, and applicable to claims for payment or reimbursement for services rendered on or after that date, in the section heading and in the first sentence of subsections (a1) and (a2), inserted "licensed marriage and family therapist"; inserted subsection (c4); and made minor punctuation changes.

Session Laws 2003-368, s. 1, effective January 1, 2004, and applicable to services rendered by psychological associates on and after that date, rewrote subsection (b).

Legal Periodicals. — For note, "ERISA Preemption of State Mandated-Provider Laws," see 6 Duke L. Rev. 1194 (1985).

For comment, "Patients' Bill of Rights; Legislative Cure-All or Prescription for Disaster?," see 81 N.C.L. Rev. 653 (2003).

§ 58-50-35. Notice of nonpayment of premium required before forfeiture.

No insurance company doing business in this State and issuing health and/or accident insurance policies, other than contracts of group insurance or disability and/or accidental death benefits in connection with policies of life insurance, the premium for which is to be collected in weekly, monthly, or other periodical installments by authority of a payroll deduction order executed by the assured and delivered to such insurance company or the assured's employer authorizing the deduction of such premium installments from the assured's salary or wages, shall, during the period for which such policy is issued, declare forfeited or lapsed any such policy hereafter issued or renewed until and unless a written or printed notice of the failure of the employer to remit said premium or installment thereof stating the amount or portion thereof due on such policy and to whom it must be paid, has been duly addressed and mailed to the person who is insured under such policy at least 15 days before said policy is canceled or lapsed. (1909, c. 884; C.S., s. 6465; 1929, c. 308, s. 1; 1931, c. 317; 1945, c. 379.)

§ 58-50-40. Willful failure to pay group insurance premiums; willful termination of a group health plan; notice to persons insured; penalty; restitution; examination of insurance transactions.

(a) As used in this section and in G.S. 58-50-45:
  (1) "Group health insurance" means any policy described in G.S. 58-51-75, 58-51-80, or 58-51-90; any group insurance certificate or group subscriber contract issued by a service corporation pursuant to Articles 65 and 66 of this Chapter; any health care plan provided or arranged by a health maintenance organization pursuant to Article 67 of this Chapter; or any multiple employer welfare arrangement as defined in G.S. 58-49-30(a).
  (2) "Group health plan" means a single employer self-insured group health plan as defined in section 607(1) of the Employee Retirement Income Security Act of 1974, 29 U.S.C. § 1167(1), as amended.

(3) "Insurance fiduciary" means any person, employer, principal, agent, trustee, or third-party administrator who is responsible for the payment of group health or group life insurance premiums or who is responsible for funding a group health plan.

(4) "Premiums" includes contributions to a group health plan or to a multiple employer welfare arrangement.

(b) No insurance fiduciary shall:

(1) Cause the cancellation or nonrenewal of group health or group life insurance and the consequential loss of the coverages of the persons insured by willfully failing to pay such premiums in accordance with the terms of a group health or group life insurance contract; or, in the case of a group health plan to which there are no premiums contributed, terminate the plan by willfully failing to fund the plan; and

(2) Willfully fail to deliver, at least 45 days before the termination of the group health or group life insurance or group health plan, to all persons covered by the group policy or group health plan a written notice of the insurance fiduciary's intention to stop payment of premiums for the group life or health insurance or the insurance fiduciary's intention to cease funding of a group health plan.

(c) Any insurance fiduciary who violates subsection (b) of this section shall be guilty of a Class H felony.

(d) Repealed by Session Laws 1991, c. 644, s. 37.

(e) Upon conviction under subsection (c) of this section the court shall order the insurance fiduciary to make full restitution to persons insured who incurred expenses that would have been covered by the group health insurance or group health plan or full restitution to beneficiaries of the group life insurance for death benefits that would have been paid if the coverage had not been terminated.

(f) Insurance fiduciaries subject to this section shall be subject to the provisions of G.S. 58-2-200 with respect only to transactions involving group health or life insurance.

(g) In the notice required by subsection (b) of this section, the insurance fiduciary shall also notify those persons of their rights to health insurance conversion policies under Article 53 of this Chapter and their rights to purchase individual policies under the federal Health Insurance Portability and Accountability Act of 1996 (HIPAA), Public Law 104-191, as amended, and Article 68 of this Chapter.

(h) In the event of the insolvency of an employer or insurance fiduciary who has violated this section, any person specified in subsection (e) of this section shall have a lien upon the assets of the employer or insurance fiduciary for the expenses or benefits specified in subsection (e) of this section. With respect to personal property within the estate of the insolvent employer or insurance fiduciary, the lien shall have priority over unperfected security interests.

(i) Upon the termination of a group health insurance contract by the insurer, the insurer shall notify every subscriber and certificate holder under the contract of the termination of the contract along with the certification required to be provided under G.S. 58-68-30(e).

(j) This section shall not apply to the cessation of individual contributions made by any person covered by a group health or group life insurance policy or group health plan. (1985, c. 507, s. 1; 1989, c. 485, s. 51; 1989 (Reg. Sess., 1990), c. 1055, ss. 2, 3.1; 1991, c. 644, s. 37; 1993, c. 539, s. 1274; 1994, Ex. Sess., c. 24, s. 14(c); 2001-422, s. 1.)

§ 58-50-45. Group health or life insurers to notify insurance fiduciaries of obligations.

(a) Upon the issuance or renewal of any policy, contract, certificate, or evidence of coverage of group health or life insurance, the insurer, corporation, or health maintenance organization shall give written notice to the insurance fiduciary of the provisions of G.S. 58-50-40.

(b) The notice required by subsection (a) of this section shall be printed in 10 point type and shall read as follows:

"UNDER NORTH CAROLINA GENERAL STATUTE SECTION 58-50-40, NO PERSON, EMPLOYER, PRINCIPAL, AGENT, TRUSTEE, OR THIRD PARTY ADMINISTRATOR, WHO IS RESPONSIBLE FOR THE PAYMENT OF GROUP HEALTH OR LIFE INSURANCE OR GROUP HEALTH PLAN PREMIUMS, SHALL: (1) CAUSE THE CANCELLATION OR NONRENEWAL OF GROUP HEALTH OR LIFE INSURANCE, HOSPITAL, MEDICAL, OR DENTAL SERVICE CORPORATION PLAN, MULTIPLE EMPLOYER WELFARE ARRANGEMENT, OR GROUP HEALTH PLAN COVERAGES AND THE CONSEQUENTIAL LOSS OF THE COVERAGES OF THE PERSONS INSURED, BY WILLFULLY FAILING TO PAY THOSE PREMIUMS IN ACCORDANCE WITH THE TERMS OF THE INSURANCE OR PLAN CONTRACT, AND (2) WILLFULLY FAIL TO DELIVER, AT LEAST 45 DAYS BEFORE THE TERMINATION OF THOSE COVERAGES, TO ALL PERSONS COVERED BY THE GROUP POLICY A WRITTEN NOTICE OF THE PERSON'S INTENTION TO STOP PAYMENT OF PREMIUMS. THIS WRITTEN NOTICE MUST ALSO CONTAIN A NOTICE TO ALL PERSONS COVERED BY THE GROUP POLICY OF THEIR RIGHTS TO HEALTH INSURANCE CONVERSION POLICIES UNDER ARTICLE 53 OF CHAPTER 58 OF THE GENERAL STATUTES AND THEIR RIGHTS TO PURCHASE INDIVIDUAL POLICIES UNDER THE FEDERAL HEALTH INSURANCE PORTABILITY AND ACCOUNTABILITY ACT AND UNDER ARTICLE 68 OF CHAPTER 58 OF THE GENERAL STATUTES. VIOLATION OF THIS LAW IS A FELONY. ANY PERSON VIOLATING THIS LAW IS ALSO SUBJECT TO A COURT ORDER REQUIRING THE PERSON TO COMPENSATE PERSONS INSURED FOR EXPENSES OR LOSSES INCURRED AS A RESULT OF THE TERMINATION OF THE INSURANCE." (1985, c. 507, s. 1; 1989 (Reg. Sess., 1990), c. 1055, s. 3; 1991, c. 644, s. 38; 2001-422, s. 2.)

Part 2. PPOs, Utilization Review and Grievances.

§ 58-50-50: Repealed by Session Laws, 1997-519, s. 3.17.

Cross References. — For present provisions regarding preferred providers, see G.S. 58-55-56.

Editor's Note. — Session Laws 1997-519, s. 3.19, as amended by Session Laws 1999-132, s. 4.8, effective June 4, 1999, provides: "Except as modified by G.S. 58-50-56(i), as enacted in this Part, any administrative rules that were adopted by the Commissioner under the authority of G.S. 58-65-140, 58-50-50 or 58-50-55 and that were effective before January 1, 1998, are not affected by the repeals in Section 3.16 or 3.17 of this act." Sections 3.16 and 3.17 of the act provided for the repeal of G.S. 58-50-50, 58-50-55, and 58-65-140.

Session Laws 2001-446, s. 4.2(2), effective July 1, 2002, and applicable to health benefit plans that are in effect, delivered, issued for delivery, or renewed on or after that date, designates G.S. 58-50-50 through 58-50-64 as Part 2 of Article 50, with the heading "PPOs, Utilization Review and Grievances."

§ 58-50-55: Repealed by Session Laws 1997-519, s. 3.17.

Editor's Note. — Session Laws 1997-519, s. 3.19, as amended by Session Laws 1999-132, s. 4.8, effective June 4, 1999, provides: "Except as modified by G.S. 58-50-56(i), as enacted in this Part, any administrative rules that were adopted by the Commissioner under the authority of G.S. 58-65-140, 58-50-50 or 58-50-55 and that were effective before January 1, 1998, are not affected by the repeals in Section 3.16 or 3.17 of this act." Sections 3.16 and 3.17 of the

act provided for the repeal of G.S. 58-50-50,
58-50-55, and 58-65-140.

§ 58-50-56. Insurers, preferred provider organizations, and preferred provider benefit plans.

(a) Definitions. — As used in this section:
  (1) "Insurer" means an insurer or service corporation subject to this Chapter.
  (2) "Preferred provider" means a health care provider who has agreed to accept special reimbursement or other terms for health care services from an insurer for health care services on a fee-for-service basis. A "preferred provider" is not a health care provider participating in any prepaid health service or capitation arrangement implemented or administered by the Department of Health and Human Services or its representatives.
  (3) "Preferred provider benefit plan" means a health benefit plan offered by an insurer in which covered services are available from health care providers who are under a contract with the insurer in accordance with this section and in which enrollees are given incentives through differentials in deductibles, coinsurance, or copayments to obtain covered health care services from contracted health care providers.
  (4) "Preferred provider organization" or "PPO" means an insurer holding contracts with preferred providers to be used by or offered to insurers offering preferred provider benefit plans.

(b) Insurers may enter into preferred provider contracts or enter into other cost containment arrangements approved by the Commissioner to reduce the costs of providing health care services. These contracts or arrangements may be entered into with licensed health care providers of all kinds without regard to specialty of services or limitation to a specific type of practice. A preferred provider contract or other cost containment arrangement that is not disapproved by the Commissioner within 90 days of its filing by the insurer shall be deemed to be approved.

(c) At the initial offering of a preferred provider plan to the public, health care providers may submit proposals for participation in accordance with the terms of the preferred provider plan within 30 days after that offering. After that time period, any health care provider may submit a proposal, and the insurer offering the preferred provider benefit plan shall consider all pending applications for participation and give reasons for any rejections or failure to act on an application on at least an annual basis. Any health care provider seeking to participate in the preferred provider benefit plan, whether upon the initial offering or subsequently, may be permitted to do so in the discretion of the insurer offering the preferred provider benefit plan. G.S. 58-50-30 applies to preferred provider benefit plans.

(d) Any provision of a contract between an insurer offering a preferred provider benefit plan and a health care provider that restricts the provider's right to enter into preferred provider contracts with other persons is prohibited, is void ab initio, and is not enforceable. The existence of that restriction does not invalidate any other provision of the contract.

(e) Except where specifically prohibited either by this section or by rules adopted by the Commissioner, the contractual terms and conditions for special reimbursements shall be those that the parties find mutually agreeable.

(f) Every insurer offering a preferred provider benefit plan and contracting with a PPO shall require by contract that the PPO shall provide all of the preferred providers with whom it holds contracts information about the insurer and the insurer's preferred provider benefit plans. This information shall include for each insurer and preferred provider benefit plan the benefit designs and incentives that are used to encourage insureds to use preferred providers.

(g) The Commissioner may adopt rules applicable to insurers offering preferred provider benefit plans under this section. These rules shall provide for:

(1) Accessibility of preferred provider services to individuals within the insured group.

(2) The adequacy of the number and locations of health care providers.

(3) The availability of services at reasonable times.

(4) Financial solvency.

(h) Each insurer offering a preferred provider benefit plan shall provide the Commissioner with summary data about the financial reimbursements offered to health care providers. All such insurers shall disclose annually the following information:

(1) The name by which the preferred provider benefit plan is known and its business address.

(2) The name, address, and nature of any PPO or other separate organization that administers the preferred provider benefit plan for the insurer.

(3) The terms of the agreements entered into by the insurer with preferred providers.

(4) Any other information necessary to determine compliance with this section, rules adopted under this section, or other requirements applicable to preferred provider benefit plans.

(i) A person enrolled in a preferred provider benefit plan may obtain covered health care services from a provider who does not participate in the plan. In accordance with rules adopted by the Commissioner and subject to G.S. 58-3-200(d), the preferred provider benefit plan may limit coverage for health care services obtained from a nonparticipating provider. The Commissioner shall adopt rules on product limitations, including payment differentials for services rendered by nonparticipating providers. These rules shall be similar in substance to rules governing HMO point-of-service products.

(j) A list of the current participating providers in the geographic area in which a substantial portion of health care services will be available shall be provided to insureds and contracting parties. The list shall include participating physician assistants and their supervising physician.

(k) Publications or advertisements of preferred provider benefit plans or organizations shall not refer to the quality or efficiency of the services of nonparticipating providers. (1997-443, s. 11A.122; 1997-519, s. 3.1; 1998-211, s. 2; 1999-210, s. 3; 2001-297, s. 3; 2001-334, s. 2.1.)

Editor's Note. — Session Laws 1997-519, s. 3.19, as amended by Session Laws 1999-132, s. 4.8, effective June 4, 1999, provides: "Except as modified by G.S. 58-50-56(i), as enacted in this Part, any administrative rules that were adopted by the Commissioner under the authority of G.S. 58-65-140, 58-50-50 or 58-50-55 and that were effective before January 1, 1998, are not affected by the repeals in Section 3.16 or 3.17 of this act. Sections 3.16 and 3.17 of the act provided for the repeal of G.S. 58-50-50, 58-50-55, and 58-65-140.

Legal Periodicals. — For 1997 legislative survey, see 20 Campbell L. Rev. 469.

§ 58-50-57. Offsets against provider reimbursement for workers' compensation payments forbidden.

(a) An insurer that provides a health benefit plan as defined in G.S. 58-3-167 shall not offset or reverse a health plan payment against a provider reimbursement for other medical charges unless the health plan payment was for a specific medical charge for which the employee, employer, or carrier is liable or responsible according to a final adjudication of the claim under the Workers' Compensation Act, Article 1 of Chapter 97 of the General Statutes or an order of the North Carolina Industrial Commission approving a settlement agreement entered into under that Article.

(b) No contract between an insurer that provides a health benefit plan as defined in G.S. 58-3-167 and a medical provider shall contain a provision that authorizes the insurer to offset or reverse a health plan payment against a provider reimbursement for other medical charges unless the health plan payment was for a specific medical charge for which the employee, employer, or carrier is liable or responsible according to a final adjudication of the claim under the Workers' Compensation Act, Article 1 of Chapter 97 of the General Statutes or an order of the North Carolina Industrial Commission approving a settlement agreement entered into under that Article. (2001-216, s. 5; 2001-487, s. 102(b).)

Editor's Note. — Session Laws 2001-216, s. 6, provides: "The North Carolina Industrial Commission shall adopt any rules needed to implement this act."

Session Laws 2001-216, s. 6.1, as added by Session Laws 2001-487, s. 102(a), contains a severability clause.

Session Laws 2001-216, s. 7, as rewritten by 2001-487, s. 102(b), makes the section effective June 15, 2001, and applicable to cases pending on or after that date except those cases in which a health benefit plan has intervened prior to that date.

§§ 58-50-58, 58-50-59: Reserved for future codification purposes.

§ 58-50-60: Repealed by Session Laws 1997-519, s. 4.4, effective January 1, 1998.

Editor's Note. — Session Laws 1997-519, s. 5, provides: "This act becomes effective January 1, 1998. Part II of this act [which added G.S. 58-3-200] applies to all health benefit plans that are delivered, issued for delivery, or renewed on or after January 1, 1998. For the purposes of this act, renewal of a health benefit plan is presumed to occur on each anniversary of the date on which coverage was first effective on the person or persons covered by the health benefit plan. Insurers other than health maintenance organizations that are subject to Part

IV of this act [which added G.S. 58-50-61, 58-50-62 and 90-21.22A and repealed G.S. 58-50-60] have until July 1, 1998, to implement the procedures for grievances that are contained in Section 4.2 of Part IV of this act [which added G.S. 58-50-62]; provided, however, that insurers other than health maintenance organizations shall comply with the second-level grievance review procedures in Section 4.2 of Part IV of this act for appeals of noncertifications effective January 1, 1998."

§ 58-50-61. Utilization review.

(a) Definitions. — As used in this section, in G.S. 58-50-62, and in Part 4 of this Article, the term:

   (1) "Clinical peer" means a health care professional who holds an unrestricted license in a state of the United States, in the same or similar specialty, and routinely provides the health care services subject to utilization review.

   (2) "Clinical review criteria" means the written screening procedures, decision abstracts, clinical protocols, and practice guidelines used by an insurer to determine medically necessary services and supplies.

   (3) "Covered person" means a policyholder, subscriber, enrollee, or other individual covered by a health benefit plan. "Covered person" includes another person, other than the covered person's provider, who is authorized to act on behalf of a covered person.

(4) "Emergency medical condition" means a medical condition manifesting itself by acute symptoms of sufficient severity including, but not limited to, severe pain, or by acute symptoms developing from a chronic medical condition that would lead a prudent layperson, possessing an average knowledge of health and medicine, to reasonably expect the absence of immediate medical attention to result in any of the following:

   a. Placing the health of an individual, or with respect to a pregnant woman, the health of the woman or her unborn child, in serious jeopardy.

   b. Serious impairment to bodily functions.

   c. Serious dysfunction of any bodily organ or part.

(5) "Emergency services" means health care items and services furnished or required to screen for or treat an emergency medical condition until the condition is stabilized, including prehospital care and ancillary services routinely available to the emergency department.

(6) "Grievance" means a written complaint submitted by a covered person about any of the following:

   a. An insurer's decisions, policies, or actions related to availability, delivery, or quality of health care services. A written complaint submitted by a covered person about a decision rendered solely on the basis that the health benefit plan contains a benefits exclusion for the health care service in question is not a grievance if the exclusion of the specific service requested is clearly stated in the certificate of coverage.

   b. Claims payment or handling; or reimbursement for services.

   c. The contractual relationship between a covered person and an insurer.

   d. The outcome of an appeal of a noncertification under this section.

(7) "Health benefit plan" means any of the following if offered by an insurer: an accident and health insurance policy or certificate; a nonprofit hospital or medical service corporation contract; a health maintenance organization subscriber contract; or a plan provided by a multiple employer welfare arrangement. "Health benefit plan" does not mean any plan implemented or administered through the Department of Health and Human Services or its representatives. "Health benefit plan" also does not mean any of the following kinds of insurance:

   a. Accident.

   b. Credit.

   c. Disability income.

   d. Long-term or nursing home care.

   e. Medicare supplement.

   f. Specified disease.

   g. Dental or vision.

   h. Coverage issued as a supplement to liability insurance.

   i. Workers' compensation.

   j. Medical payments under automobile or homeowners.

   k. Hospital income or indemnity.

   l. Insurance under which benefits are payable with or without regard to fault and that is statutorily required to be contained in any liability policy or equivalent self-insurance.

(8) "Health care provider" means any person who is licensed, registered, or certified under Chapter 90 of the General Statutes or the laws of another state to provide health care services in the ordinary care of business or practice or a profession or in an approved education or

training program; a health care facility as defined in G.S. 131E-176(9b) or the laws of another state to operate as a health care facility; or a pharmacy.

(9) "Health care services" means services provided for the diagnosis, prevention, treatment, cure, or relief of a health condition, illness, injury, or disease.

(10) "Insurer" means an entity that writes a health benefit plan and that is an insurance company subject to this Chapter, a service corporation under Article 65 of this Chapter, a health maintenance organization under Article 67 of this Chapter, or a multiple employer welfare arrangement under Article 49 of this Chapter.

(11) "Managed care plan" means a health benefit plan in which an insurer either (i) requires a covered person to use or (ii) creates incentives, including financial incentives, for a covered person to use providers that are under contract with or managed, owned, or employed by the insurer.

(12) "Medically necessary services or supplies" means those covered services or supplies that are:
   a. Provided for the diagnosis, treatment, cure, or relief of a health condition, illness, injury, or disease.
   b. Except as allowed under G.S. 58-3-255, not for experimental, investigational, or cosmetic purposes.
   c. Necessary for and appropriate to the diagnosis, treatment, cure, or relief of a health condition, illness, injury, disease, or its symptoms.
   d. Within generally accepted standards of medical care in the community.
   e. Not solely for the convenience of the insured, the insured's family, or the provider.
   For medically necessary services, nothing in this subdivision precludes an insurer from comparing the cost-effectiveness of alternative services or supplies when determining which of the services or supplies will be covered.

(13) "Noncertification" means a determination by an insurer or its designated utilization review organization that an admission, availability of care, continued stay, or other health care service has been reviewed and, based upon the information provided, does not meet the insurer's requirements for medical necessity, appropriateness, health care setting, level of care or effectiveness, or does not meet the prudent layperson standard for coverage of emergency services in G.S. 58-3-190, and the requested service is therefore denied, reduced, or terminated. A "noncertification" is not a decision rendered solely on the basis that the health benefit plan does not provide benefits for the health care service in question, if the exclusion of the specific service requested is clearly stated in the certificate of coverage. A "noncertification" includes any situation in which an insurer or its designated agent makes a decision about a covered person's condition to determine whether a requested treatment is experimental, investigational, or cosmetic, and the extent of coverage under the health benefit plan is affected by that decision.

(14) "Participating provider" means a provider who, under a contract with an insurer or with an insurer's contractor or subcontractor, has agreed to provide health care services to covered persons in return for direct or indirect payment from the insurer, other than coinsurance, copayments, or deductibles.

(15) "Provider" means a health care provider.

(16) "Stabilize" means to provide medical care that is appropriate to prevent a material deterioration of the person's condition, within reasonable medical probability, in accordance with the HCFA (Health Care Financing Administration) interpretative guidelines, policies, and regulations pertaining to responsibilities of hospitals in emergency cases (as provided under the Emergency Medical Treatment and Labor Act, section 1867 of the Social Security Act, 42 U.S.C.S. § 1395dd), including medically necessary services and supplies to maintain stabilization until the person is transferred.

(17) "Utilization review" means a set of formal techniques designed to monitor the use of or evaluate the clinical necessity, appropriateness, efficacy or efficiency of health care services, procedures, providers, or facilities. These techniques may include:

a. Ambulatory review. — Utilization review of services performed or provided in an outpatient setting.

b. Case management. — A coordinated set of activities conducted for individual patient management of serious, complicated, protracted, or other health conditions.

c. Certification. — A determination by an insurer or its designated URO that an admission, availability of care, continued stay, or other service has been reviewed and, based on the information provided, satisfies the insurer's requirements for medically necessary services and supplies, appropriateness, health care setting, level of care, and effectiveness.

d. Concurrent review. — Utilization review conducted during a patient's hospital stay or course of treatment.

e. Discharge planning. — The formal process for determining, before discharge from a provider facility, the coordination and management of the care that a patient receives after discharge from a provider facility.

f. Prospective review. — Utilization review conducted before an admission or a course of treatment including any required preauthorization or precertification.

g. Retrospective review. — Utilization review of medically necessary services and supplies that is conducted after services have been provided to a patient, but not the review of a claim that is limited to an evaluation of reimbursement levels, veracity of documentation, accuracy of coding, or adjudication for payment. Retrospective review includes the review of claims for emergency services to determine whether the prudent layperson standard in G.S. 58-3-190 has been met.

h. Second opinion. — An opportunity or requirement to obtain a clinical evaluation by a provider other than the provider originally making a recommendation for a proposed service to assess the clinical necessity and appropriateness of the proposed service.

(18) "Utilization review organization" or "URO" means an entity that conducts utilization review under a managed care plan, but does not mean an insurer performing utilization review for its own health benefit plan.

(b) Insurer Oversight. — Every insurer shall monitor all utilization review carried out by or on behalf of the insurer and ensure compliance with this section. An insurer shall ensure that appropriate personnel have operational responsibility for the conduct of the insurer's utilization review program. If an insurer contracts to have a URO perform its utilization review, the insurer shall monitor the URO to ensure compliance with this section, which shall include:

(1) A written description of the URO's activities and responsibilities, including reporting requirements.

(2) Evidence of formal approval of the utilization review organization program by the insurer.

(3) A process by which the insurer evaluates the performance of the URO.

(c) Scope and Content of Program. — Every insurer shall prepare and maintain a utilization review program document that describes all delegated and nondelegated review functions for covered services including:

(1) Procedures to evaluate the clinical necessity, appropriateness, efficacy, or efficiency of health services.

(2) Data sources and clinical review criteria used in decision making.

(3) The process for conducting appeals of noncertifications.

(4) Mechanisms to ensure consistent application of review criteria and compatible decisions.

(5) Data collection processes and analytical methods used in assessing utilization of health care services.

(6) Provisions for assuring confidentiality of clinical and patient information in accordance with State and federal law.

(7) The organizational structure (e.g., utilization review committee, quality assurance, or other committee) that periodically assesses utilization review activities and reports to the insurer's governing body.

(8) The staff position functionally responsible for day-to-day program management.

(9) The methods of collection and assessment of data about underutilization and overutilization of health care services and how the assessment is used to evaluate and improve procedures and criteria for utilization review.

(d) Program Operations. — In every utilization review program, an insurer or URO shall use documented clinical review criteria that are based on sound clinical evidence and that are periodically evaluated to assure ongoing efficacy. An insurer may develop its own clinical review criteria or purchase or license clinical review criteria. Criteria for determining when a patient needs to be placed in a substance abuse treatment program shall be either (i) the diagnostic criteria contained in the most recent revision of the American Society of Addiction Medicine Patient Placement Criteria for the Treatment of Substance-Related Disorders or (ii) criteria adopted by the insurer or its URO. The Department, in consultation with the Department of Health and Human Services, may require proof of compliance with this subsection by a plan or URO.

Qualified health care professionals shall administer the utilization review program and oversee review decisions under the direction of a medical doctor. A medical doctor licensed to practice medicine in this State shall evaluate the clinical appropriateness of noncertifications. Compensation to persons involved in utilization review shall not contain any direct or indirect incentives for them to make any particular review decisions. Compensation to utilization reviewers shall not be directly or indirectly based on the number or type of noncertifications they render. In issuing a utilization review decision, an insurer shall: obtain all information required to make the decision, including pertinent clinical information; employ a process to ensure that utilization reviewers apply clinical review criteria consistently; and issue the decision in a timely manner pursuant to this section.

(e) Insurer Responsibilities. — Every insurer shall:

(1) Routinely assess the effectiveness and efficiency of its utilization review program.

(2) Coordinate the utilization review program with its other medical management activity, including quality assurance, credentialing, pro-

vider contracting, data reporting, grievance procedures, processes for assessing satisfaction of covered persons, and risk management.

(3) Provide covered persons and their providers with access to its review staff by a toll-free or collect call telephone number whenever any provider is required to be available to provide services which may require prior certification to any plan enrollee. Every insurer shall establish standards for telephone accessibility and monitor telephone service as indicated by average speed of answer and call abandonment rate, on at least a month-by-month basis, to ensure that telephone service is adequate, and take corrective action when necessary.

(4) Limit its requests for information to only that information that is necessary to certify the admission, procedure or treatment, length of stay, and frequency and duration of health care services.

(5) Have written procedures for making utilization review decisions and for notifying covered persons of those decisions.

(6) Have written procedures to address the failure or inability of a provider or covered person to provide all necessary information for review. If a provider or covered person fails to release necessary information in a timely manner, the insurer may deny certification.

(f) Prospective and Concurrent Reviews. — As used in this subsection, "necessary information" includes the results of any patient examination, clinical evaluation, or second opinion that may be required. Prospective and concurrent determinations shall be communicated to the covered person's provider within three business days after the insurer obtains all necessary information about the admission, procedure, or health care service. If an insurer certifies a health care service, the insurer shall notify the covered person's provider. For a noncertification, the insurer shall notify the covered person's provider and send written or electronic confirmation of the noncertification to the covered person. In concurrent reviews, the insurer shall remain liable for health care services until the covered person has been notified of the noncertification.

(g) Retrospective Reviews. — As used in this subsection, "necessary information" includes the results of any patient examination, clinical evaluation, or second opinion that may be required. For retrospective review determinations, an insurer shall make the determination within 30 days after receiving all necessary information. For a certification, the insurer may give written notification to the covered person's provider. For a noncertification, the insurer shall give written notification to the covered person and the covered person's provider within five business days after making the noncertification.

(h) Notice of Noncertification. — A written notification of a noncertification shall include all reasons for the noncertification, including the clinical rationale, the instructions for initiating a voluntary appeal or reconsideration of the noncertification, and the instructions for requesting a written statement of the clinical review criteria used to make the noncertification. An insurer shall provide the clinical review criteria used to make the noncertification to any person who received the notification of the noncertification and who follows the procedures for a request. An insurer shall also inform the covered person in writing about the availability of assistance from the Managed Care Patient Assistance Program, including the telephone number and address of the Program.

(i) Requests for Informal Reconsideration. — An insurer may establish procedures for informal reconsideration of noncertifications and, if established, the procedures shall be in writing. After a written notice of noncertification has been issued in accordance with subsection (h) of this section, the reconsideration shall be conducted between the covered person's provider and a medical doctor licensed to practice medicine in this State designated by the insurer. An insurer shall not require a covered person to participate in an informal reconsideration before the covered person may appeal a noncertification under subsection (j) of this section. If, after informal reconsideration, the insurer upholds the noncertification decision, the insurer shall issue a new notice in accordance with subsection (h) of this section. If the insurer is unable to render an informal reconsideration decision within 10 business days after the date of receipt of the request for an informal reconsideration, it shall treat the request for informal reconsideration as a request for an appeal; provided that the requirements of subsection (k) of this section for acknowledging the request shall apply beginning on the day the insurer determines an informal reconsideration decision cannot be made before the tenth business day after receipt of the request for an informal reconsideration.

(j) Appeals of Noncertifications. — Every insurer shall have written procedures for appeals of noncertifications by covered persons or their providers acting on their behalves, including expedited review to address a situation where the time frames for the standard review procedures set forth in this section would reasonably appear to seriously jeopardize the life or health of a covered person or jeopardize the covered person's ability to regain maximum function. Each appeal shall be evaluated by a medical doctor licensed to practice medicine in this State who was not involved in the noncertification.

(k) Nonexpedited Appeals. — Within three business days after receiving a request for a standard, nonexpedited appeal, the insurer shall provide the covered person with the name, address, and telephone number of the coordinator and information on how to submit written material. For standard, nonexpedited appeals, the insurer shall give written notification of the decision, in clear terms, to the covered person and the covered person's provider within 30 days after the insurer receives the request for an appeal. If the decision is not in favor of the covered person, the written decision shall contain:

    (1) The professional qualifications and licensure of the person or persons reviewing the appeal.

    (2) A statement of the reviewers' understanding of the reason for the covered person's appeal.

    (3) The reviewers' decision in clear terms and the medical rationale in sufficient detail for the covered person to respond further to the insurer's position.

    (4) A reference to the evidence or documentation that is the basis for the decision, including the clinical review criteria used to make the determination, and instructions for requesting the clinical review criteria.

    (5) A statement advising the covered person of the covered person's right to request a second-level grievance review and a description of the procedure for submitting a second-level grievance under G.S. 58-50-62.

    (6) Notice of the availability of assistance from the Managed Care Patient Assistance Program, including the telephone number and address of the Program.

(l) Expedited Appeals. — An expedited appeal of a noncertification may be requested by a covered person or his or her provider acting on the covered person's behalf only when a nonexpedited appeal would reasonably appear to seriously jeopardize the life or health of a covered person or jeopardize the covered person's ability to regain maximum function. The insurer may require documentation of the medical justification for the expedited appeal. The insurer shall, in consultation with a medical doctor licensed to practice medicine in this State, provide expedited review, and the insurer shall communicate its decision in writing to the covered person and his or her provider as soon as possible, but not later than four days after receiving the information justifying expedited review. The written decision shall contain the provisions specified in subsection (k) of this section. If the expedited review is a concurrent review determination, the insurer shall remain liable for the coverage of health care services until the covered person has been notified of the determination. An insurer is not required to provide an expedited review for retrospective noncertifications.

(m) Disclosure Requirements. — In the certificate of coverage and member handbook provided to covered persons, an insurer shall include a clear and comprehensive description of its utilization review procedures, including the procedures for appealing noncertifications and a statement of the rights and responsibilities of covered persons, including the voluntary nature of the appeal process, with respect to those procedures. An insurer shall also include in the certificate of coverage and the member handbook information about the availability of assistance from the Managed Care Patient Assistance Program, including the telephone number and address of the Program. An insurer shall include a summary of its utilization review procedures in materials intended for prospective covered persons. An insurer shall print on its membership cards a toll-free telephone number to call for utilization review purposes.

(n) Maintenance of Records. — Every insurer and URO shall maintain records of each review performed and each appeal received or reviewed, as well as documentation sufficient to demonstrate compliance with this section. The maintenance of these records, including electronic reproduction and storage, shall be governed by rules adopted by the Commissioner that apply to insurers. These records shall be retained by the insurer and URO for a period of three years or until the Commissioner has adopted a final report of a general examination that contains a review of these records for that calendar year, whichever is later.

(o) Violation. — A violation of this section subjects an insurer to G.S. 58-2-70. (1997-443, s. 11A.122; 1997-519, s. 4.1; 1999-116, s. 1; 1999-391, ss. 1-4; 2001-417, ss. 2-7; 2001-416, ss. 4.4, 5; 2003-105, s. 1.)

Cross References. — As to right of a managed care entity to indemnity with regard to certain noncertification decisions, see G.S. 90-21.52(c).

Editor's Note. — Session Laws 1997-519, s. 5, provides: "This act becomes effective January 1, 1998. Part II of this act [which added G.S. 58-3-200] applies to all health benefit plans that are delivered, issued for delivery, or renewed on or after January 1, 1998. For the purposes of this act, renewal of a health benefit plan is presumed to occur on each anniversary of the date on which coverage was first effective on the person or persons covered by the health benefit plan. Insurers other than health maintenance organizations that are subject to Part IV of this act [which added G.S. 58-50-61, 58-50-62 and 90-21.22A and repealed G.S. 58-50-60] have until July 1, 1998, to implement the procedures for grievances that are contained in Section 4.2 of Part IV of this act [which added G.S. 58-50-62] ; provided, however, that insurers other than health maintenance organizations shall comply with the second-level grievance review procedures in Section 4.2 of Part IV of this act for appeals of noncertifications effective January 1, 1998."

Session Laws 2001-446, s. 7 is a severability clause.

Session Laws 2001-446, s. 8 provides: "Nothing in this act obligates the General Assembly to appropriate funds to implement this act."

Session Laws 2003-105, s. 4, provides in part: "G.S. 58-50-61, as amended by this act, applies to member handbooks printed after October 1, 2003."

Effect of Amendments. — Session Laws, 2001-446, s. 5(c), effective March 1, 2002, and applicable to health benefit plans that are in effect, delivered, issued for delivery, or renewed on or after that date, added the language "Except as allowed under G.S. 58-3-255" at the beginning of subdivision (a)(12)b.

Session Laws 2001-446, s. 4.4, effective July 1, 2002, and applicable to health benefit plans that are in effect, delivered, issued for delivery, or renewed on or after that date, substituted "this section, G.S. 58-50-62, and in Part 4 of this Article," for "this section and in G.S. 58-50-62" in the introductory paragraph of subsection (a).

Session Laws 2003-105, s. 1, effective October 1, 2003, and applicable to actions taken by the insurer under the subsections of G.S. 58-50-

61, 58-50-62, and 58-50-80 amended by this act, on and after that date, in subsection (h), added the last sentence; added subdivision (k)(6); and in subsection (m), inserted the present second sentence.

Legal Periodicals. — For 1997 legislative survey, see 20 Campbell L. Rev. 469.

§ 58-50-62. Insurer grievance procedures.

(a) Purpose and Intent. — The purpose of this section is to provide standards for the establishment and maintenance of procedures by insurers to assure that covered persons have the opportunity for appropriate resolutions of their grievances.

(b) Availability of Grievance Process. — Every insurer shall have a grievance process whereby a covered person may voluntarily request a review of any decision, policy, or action of the insurer that affects that covered person. A decision rendered solely on the basis that the health benefit plan does not provide benefits for the health care service in question is not subject to the insurer's grievance procedures, if the exclusion of the specific service requested is clearly stated in the certificate of coverage. The grievance process may provide for an immediate informal consideration by the insurer of a grievance. If the insurer does not have a procedure for informal consideration or if an informal consideration does not resolve the grievance, the grievance process shall provide for first- and second-level reviews of grievances. Appeal of a noncertification that has been reviewed under G.S. 58-50-61 shall be reviewed as a second-level grievance under this section.

(b1) Informal Consideration of Grievances. — If the insurer provides procedures for informal consideration of grievances, the procedures shall be in writing, and the following requirements apply:

(1) If the grievance concerns a clinical issue and the informal consideration decision is not in favor of the covered person, the insurer shall treat the request as a request for a first-level grievance review, except that the requirements of subdivision (e)(1) of this section apply on the day the decision is made or on the tenth business day after receipt of the request for informal consideration, whichever is sooner;

(2) If the grievance concerns a nonclinical issue and the informal consideration decision is not in favor of the covered person, the insurer shall issue a written decision that includes the information set forth in subsection (c) of this section; or

(3) If the insurer is unable to render an informal consideration decision within 10 business days after receipt of the grievance, the insurer shall treat the request as a request for a first-level grievance review, except that the requirements of subdivision (e)(1) of this section apply beginning on the day the insurer determines an informal consideration decision cannot be made before the tenth business day after receipt of the grievance.

(c) Grievance Procedures. — Every insurer shall have written procedures for receiving and resolving grievances from covered persons. A description of the grievance procedures shall be set forth in or attached to the certificate of coverage and member handbook provided to covered persons. The description shall include a statement informing the covered person that the grievance procedures are voluntary and shall also inform the covered person about the availability of the Commissioner's office for assistance, including the telephone number and address of the office. The description shall also inform the covered person about the availability of assistance from the Managed Care Patient Assistance Program, including the telephone number and address of the Program.

(d) Maintenance of Records. — Every insurer shall maintain records of each grievance received and the insurer's review of each grievance, as well as documentation sufficient to demonstrate compliance with this section. The maintenance of these records, including electronic reproduction and storage, shall be governed by rules adopted by the Commissioner that apply to insurers. The insurer shall retain these records for three years or until the Commissioner has adopted a final report of a general examination that contains a review of these records for that calendar year, whichever is later.

(e) First-Level Grievance Review. — A covered person or a covered person's provider acting on the covered person's behalf may submit a grievance.

    (1) The insurer does not have to allow a covered person to attend the first-level grievance review. A covered person may submit written material. Except as provided in subdivision (3) of this subsection, within three business days after receiving a grievance, the insurer shall provide the covered person with the name, address, and telephone number of the coordinator and information on how to submit written material.

    (2) An insurer shall issue a written decision, in clear terms, to the covered person and, if applicable, to the covered person's provider, within 30 days after receiving a grievance. The person or persons reviewing the grievance shall not be the same person or persons who initially handled the matter that is the subject of the grievance and, if the issue is a clinical one, at least one of whom shall be a medical doctor with appropriate expertise to evaluate the matter. Except as provided in subdivision (3) of this subsection, if the decision is not in favor of the covered person, the written decision issued in a first-level grievance review shall contain:

        a. The professional qualifications and licensure of the person or persons reviewing the grievance.

        b. A statement of the reviewers' understanding of the grievance.

        c. The reviewers' decision in clear terms and the contractual basis or medical rationale in sufficient detail for the covered person to respond further to the insurer's position.

        d. A reference to the evidence or documentation used as the basis for the decision.

        e. A statement advising the covered person of his or her right to request a second-level grievance review and a description of the procedure for submitting a second-level grievance under this section.

        f. Notice of the availability of assistance from the Managed Care Patient Assistance Program, including the telephone number and address of the Program.

    (3) For grievances concerning the quality of clinical care delivered by the covered person's provider, the insurer shall acknowledge the grievance within 10 business days. The acknowledgement shall advise the covered person that (i) the insurer will refer the grievance to its quality assurance committee for review and consideration or any appropriate action against the provider and (ii) State law does not allow for a second-level grievance review for grievances concerning quality of care.

(f) Second-Level Grievance Review. — An insurer shall establish a second-level grievance review process for covered persons who are dissatisfied with the first-level grievance review decision or a utilization review appeal decision. A covered person or the covered person's provider acting on the covered person's behalf may submit a second-level grievance.

    (1) An insurer shall, within 10 business days after receiving a request for a second-level grievance review, make known to the covered person:

      a. The name, address, and telephone number of a person designated to coordinate the grievance review for the insurer.

      b. A statement of a covered person's rights, which include the right to request and receive from an insurer all information relevant to the case; attend the second-level grievance review; present his or her case to the review panel; submit supporting materials before and at the review meeting; ask questions of any member of the review panel; and be assisted or represented by a person of his or her choice, which person may be without limitation to: a provider, family member, employer representative, or attorney. If the covered person chooses to be represented by an attorney, the insurer may also be represented by an attorney.

      c. The availability of assistance from the Managed Care Patient Assistance Program, including the telephone number and address of the Program.

  (2) An insurer shall convene a second-level grievance review panel for each request. The panel shall comprise persons who were not previously involved in any matter giving rise to the second-level grievance, are not employees of the insurer or URO, and do not have a financial interest in the outcome of the review. A person who was previously involved in the matter may appear before the panel to present information or answer questions. All of the persons reviewing a second-level grievance involving a noncertification or a clinical issue shall be providers who have appropriate expertise, including at least one clinical peer. Provided, however, an insurer that uses a clinical peer on an appeal of a noncertification under G.S. 58-50-61 or on a first-level grievance review panel under this section may use one of the insurer's employees on the second-level grievance review panel in the same matter if the second-level grievance review panel comprises three or more persons.

  (g) Second-Level Grievance Review Procedures. — An insurer's procedures for conducting a second-level grievance review shall include:

    (1) The review panel shall schedule and hold a review meeting within 45 days after receiving a request for a second-level review.

    (2) The covered person shall be notified in writing at least 15 days before the review meeting date.

    (3) The covered person's right to a full review shall not be conditioned on the covered person's appearance at the review meeting.

  (h) Second-Level Grievance Review Decisions. — An insurer shall issue a written decision to the covered person and, if applicable, to the covered person's provider, within seven business days after completing the review meeting. The decision shall include:

    (1) The professional qualifications and licensure of the members of the review panel.

    (2) A statement of the review panel's understanding of the nature of the grievance and all pertinent facts.

    (3) The review panel's recommendation to the insurer and the rationale behind that recommendation.

    (4) A description of or reference to the evidence or documentation considered by the review panel in making the recommendation.

    (5) In the review of a noncertification or other clinical matter, a written statement of the clinical rationale, including the clinical review criteria, that was used by the review panel to make the recommendation.

    (6) The rationale for the insurer's decision if it differs from the review panel's recommendation.

(7) A statement that the decision is the insurer's final determination in the matter. In cases where the review concerned a noncertification and the insurer's decision on the second-level grievance review is to uphold its initial noncertification, a statement advising the covered person of his or her right to request an external review and a description of the procedure for submitting a request for external review to the Commissioner of Insurance.

(8) Notice of the availability of the Commissioner's office for assistance, including the telephone number and address of the Commissioner's office.

(9) Notice of the availability of assistance from the Managed Care Patient Assistance Program, including the telephone number and address of the Program.

(i) Expedited Second-Level Procedures. — An expedited second-level review shall be made available where medically justified as provided in G.S. 58-50-61(l), whether or not the initial review was expedited. The provisions of subsections (f), (g), and (h) of this section apply to this subsection except for the following timetable: When a covered person is eligible for an expedited second-level review, the insurer shall conduct the review proceeding and communicate its decision within four days after receiving all necessary information. The review meeting may take place by way of a telephone conference call or through the exchange of written information.

(j) No insurer shall discriminate against any provider based on any action taken by the provider under this section or G.S. 58-50-61 on behalf of a covered person.

(k) Violation. — A violation of this section subjects an insurer to G.S. 58-2-70. (1997-519, s. 4.2; 2001-417, ss. 8-11; 2001-446, s. 4.6; 2003-105, s. 2(a)-(d).)

Editor's Note. — Session Laws 1997-519, s. 5, provides: "This act becomes effective January 1, 1998. Part II of this act [which added G.S. 58-3-200] applies to all health benefit plans that are delivered, issued for delivery, or renewed on or after January 1, 1998. For the purposes of this act, renewal of a health benefit plan is presumed to occur on each anniversary of the date on which coverage was first effective on the person or persons covered by the health benefit plan. Insurers other than health maintenance organizations that are subject to Part IV of this act [which added G.S. 58-50-61, 58-50-62 and 90-21.22A and repealed G.S. 58-50-60] have until July 1, 1998, to implement the procedures for grievances that are contained in Section 4.2 of Part IV of this act [which added G.S. 58-50-62]; provided, however, that insurers other than health maintenance organizations shall comply with the second-level grievance review procedures in

Section 4.2 of Part IV of this act for appeals of noncertifications effective January 1, 1998."

Session Laws 2001-446, s. 8 provides: "Nothing in this act obligates the General Assembly to appropriate funds to implement this act."

Session Laws 2001-446, s. 7 is a severability clause.

Effect of Amendments. — Session Laws 2001-446, s. 4.6, effective July 1, 2002, and applicable to health benefit plans that are in effect, delivered, issued for delivery, or renewed on or after that date, added the last sentence in subdivision (h)(7).

Session Laws 2003-105, s. 2(a)-(d), effective October 1, 2003, and applicable to actions taken by the insurer under the subsections of G.S. 58-50-61, 58-50-62, and 58-50-80 amended by this act, on and after that date, in subsection (c), added the last sentence; and added subdivisions (e)(2)f., (f)(1)c., and (h)(9).

§ 58-50-63. (Effective until July 1, 2005) Additional coverage mandates prohibited; exception.

(a) Notwithstanding any other provision of law to the contrary, except as otherwise provided in this section, an insurer shall not deliver, issue, or renew a health benefit plan after July 1, 2003, that includes any additional coverage requirements beyond those requirements in effect for health benefit plans on June 30, 2003.

(b) Nothing in this section shall be construed to prohibit an employer from electing to expand coverage on any group or individual health benefit plan or policy covering the employer and the employees of the employer.

(c) As used in this section, the terms "insurer" and "health benefit plan" have the meaning applied in G.S. 58-3-167. (2001-453, s. 1.)

Editor's Note. — Session Laws 2001-453, s. 2, provides: "The Legislative Research Commission may study the issue of health insurance mandated benefits and the cost to employers and individuals of unfunded health insurance mandates. In conducting the study, the Commission shall consider cost-benefit analysis to determine the cost-efficiency of mandated benefits, including any cost-benefit analysis performed by the Department of Insurance. The Commission shall make a progress report to the 2001 General Assembly upon its reconvening in 2002, and shall make its final report to the 2003 General Assembly. Progress and final reports of the Commission may include recommended legislation."

Session Laws 2001-453, s. 3, makes this section effective October 28, 2001, and provides that it will expire on July 1, 2005.

§ **58-50-64:** Reserved for future codification purposes.

Part 3. Scope and Sanctions.

§ **58-50-65. Certain policies of insurance not affected.**

(a) Nothing in Articles 50 through 55 of this Chapter applies to or affects any policy of liability or workers' compensation insurance, except that the provisions of G.S. 58-50-56(g) and (h) apply to policies of workers' compensation insurance and to individual and group self-funded workers' compensation insurance plans. If there is any conflict between managed care provisions of this Chapter and managed care provisions of Chapter 97 of the General Statutes with respect to workers' compensation insurance, the provisions of Chapter 97 govern.

(b) Nothing in Articles 50 through 55 of this Chapter shall apply to or in any way affect contracts supplemental to contracts of life or endowment insurance where such supplemental contracts contain no provisions except such as operate to safeguard such insurance against lapse or to provide special benefits therefor in the event that the insured shall be totally, or totally and permanently disabled by reason of accidental bodily injury or by sickness, nor to contracts issued as supplements to life insurance contracts or contracts of endowment insurance, and intended to increase the amount insured by such life or endowment contracts in the event that the death or disability of the insured shall result from accidental bodily injuries: Provided, that no such supplemental contracts shall be issued or delivered to any person in this State unless and until a copy of the form thereof has been submitted to and approved by the Commissioner under such reasonable rules and regulations as he shall make concerning the provisions in such contracts, and their submission to and approval by him.

(c) Nothing in Articles 50 through 55 of this Chapter shall apply to or in any way affect fraternal benefit societies.

(d) The provisions of G.S. 58-51-5(5) and G.S. 58-51-15(a)(1), (4), and (10) may be omitted from railroad ticket policies sold only at railroad stations or at railroad ticket offices by railroad employees. (1911, c. 209, s. 5; 1913, c. 91, s. 12; C.S., s. 6489; 1921, c. 136, s. 5; 1945, c. 385; 1947, c. 721; 1991, c. 636, s. 3; c. 720, ss. 4, 42; 1993 (Reg. Sess., 1994), c. 679, s. 10.4; 1995, c. 193, s. 42; 1999-219, s. 4.1.)

Editor's Note. — The reference in subsection (d) of this section to subdivision (5) of G.S. 58-51-5 initially referred to subdivision (5) of former G.S. 58-250 (now G.S. 58-51-5) as enacted in 1913, which required that a brief description of the policy be printed on its first page and on its filing back in at least 14 point typeface.

Session Laws 2001-446, s. 4.2(3), effective July 1, 2002, and applicable to health benefit plans that are in effect, delivered, issued for delivery, or renewed on or after that date, designates G.S. 58-50-65 through 58-50-70 as Part 3 of Article 50, with the heading "Scope and Sanctions."

§ 58-50-70. Punishment for violation.

Any company, association, society, or other insurer or any officer or agent thereof, which or who issues or delivers to any person in this State any policy in willful violation of Articles 50 through 55 of this Chapter, shall be guilty of a Class 3 misdemeanor and, upon conviction, shall be punished only by a fine of not more than five thousand dollars ($5,000) for each offense; and the Commissioner may revoke the license of any company, corporation, association, society, or other insurer of another state or country, or of the agent thereof, which or who willfully violates any provision of Articles 50 through 55 of this Chapter. (1911, c. 209, s. 6; 1913, c. 91, s. 13; C.S., s. 6490; 1985, c. 666, s. 28; 1991, c. 720, ss. 4, 42; 1993, c. 539, s. 467; 1994, Ex. Sess., c. 24, s. 14(c).)

CASE NOTES

Applicability of Former Rules of Evidence. — Former G.S. 143-317(3) showed that former G.S. 143-318 was intended to apply only to hearings which result in a loss by a specific party of some legal right, duty or privilege, such as hearings relating to the revocation of the license of a specified insurance agent or of a specified insurance company or to the imposition of a fine or penalty upon an insurance agent or insurance company for violation of the Insurance Law. In re North Carolina Auto. Rate Admin. Office, 278 N.C. 302, 180 S.E.2d 155 (1971).

Part 4. Health Benefit Plan External Review.

§ 58-50-75. Purpose, scope, and definitions.

(a) The purpose of this Part is to provide standards for the establishment and maintenance of external review procedures to assure that covered persons have the opportunity for an independent review of an appeal decision upholding a noncertification or a second-level grievance review decision upholding a noncertification, as defined in this Part.

(b) This Part applies to all insurers that offer a health benefit plan and that provide or perform utilization review pursuant to G.S. 58-50-61, the Teachers' and State Employees' Comprehensive Major Medical Plan, and the Health Insurance Program for Children. With respect to second-level grievance review decisions, this Part applies only to second-level grievance review decisions involving noncertification decisions.

(c) In addition to the definitions in G.S. 58-50-61(a), as used in this Part:

(1) "Covered benefits" or "benefits" means those benefits consisting of medical care, provided directly through insurance or otherwise and including items and services paid for as medical care, under the terms of a health benefit plan.

(2) "Covered person" means a policyholder, subscriber, enrollee, or other individual covered by a health benefit plan. "Covered person" includes another person, including the covered person's health care provider, acting on behalf of the covered person. Nothing in this subdivision shall require the covered person's health care provider to act on behalf of the covered person.

(3) "Independent review organization" or "organization" means an entity that conducts independent external reviews of appeals of noncertifications and second-level grievance review decisions. (2001-446, s. 4.5.)

Editor's Note. — Session Laws 2001-446, s. 4.2(4), effective July 1, 2002, and applicable to health benefit plans that are in effect, delivered, issued for delivery, or renewed on or after that date, designates G.S. 58-50-75 through 58-50-95 as Part 4 of Article 50, with the heading "Health Benefit Plan External Review."

Session Laws 2001-446, s. 7 is a severability clause.

Session Laws 2001-446, s. 8, makes this Part effective July 1, 2002, and applicable to health benefit plans that are in effect, delivered, issued for delivery, or renewed on or after that date.

Session Laws 2001-446, s. 8 provides: "Nothing in this act obligates the General Assembly to appropriate funds to implement this act."

§ 58-50-76: Reserved for future codification purposes.

Editor's Note. — Session Laws 2001-446, s. 4.5, reserves this section for future codification purposes.

§ 58-50-77. Notice of right to external review.

(a) An insurer shall notify the covered person in writing of the covered person's right to request an external review and include the appropriate statements and information set forth in this section at the time the insurer sends written notice of:

(1) A noncertification decision under G.S. 58-50-61;

(2) An appeal decision under G.S. 58-50-61 upholding a noncertification; and

(3) A second-level grievance review decision under G.S. 58-50-62 upholding the original noncertification.

(b) The insurer shall include in the notice required under subsection (a) of this section for a notice related to a noncertification decision under G.S. 58-50-61, a statement informing the covered person that if the covered person has a medical condition where the time frame for completion of an expedited review of an appeal decision involving a noncertification decision under G.S. 58-50-61 would reasonably be expected to seriously jeopardize the life or health of the covered person or jeopardize the covered person's ability to regain maximum function, then the covered person may file a request for an expedited external review under G.S. 58-50-82 at the same time the covered person files a request for an expedited review of an appeal involving a noncertification decision under G.S. 58-50-61, but that the Commissioner will determine whether the covered person shall be required to complete the expedited review of the grievance before conducting the expedited external review.

(c) The insurer shall include in the notice required under subsection (a) of this section for a notice related to an appeal decision under G.S. 58-50-61, a statement informing the covered person that:

(1) If the covered person has a medical condition where the time frame for completion of an expedited review of a grievance involving an appeal decision under G.S. 58-50-61 would reasonably be expected to seriously jeopardize the life or health of the covered person or jeopardize the covered person's ability to regain maximum function, the covered person may file a request for an expedited external review under G.S. 58-50-82 at the same time the covered person files a request for an expedited review of a grievance involving an appeal decision under

G.S. 58-50-62, but that the Commissioner will determine whether the covered person shall be required to complete the expedited review of the grievance before conducting the expedited external review.

(2) If the covered person has not received a written decision from the insurer within 60 days after the date the covered person files the second- level grievance with the insurer pursuant to G.S. 58-50-62 and the covered person has not requested or agreed to a delay, the covered person may file a request for external review under G.S. 58-50-80 and shall be considered to have exhausted the insurer's internal grievance process for purposes of G.S. 58-50-79.

(d) The insurer shall include in the notice required under subsection (a) of this section for a notice related to a final second-level grievance review decision under G.S. 58-50-62, a statement informing the covered person that:

(1) If the covered person has a medical condition where the time frame for completion of a standard external review under G.S. 58-50-80 would reasonably be expected to seriously jeopardize the life or health of the covered person or jeopardize the covered person's ability to regain maximum function, the covered person may file a request for an expedited external review under G.S. 58-50-82; or

(2) If the second-level grievance review decision concerns an admission, availability of care, continued stay, or health care service for which the covered person received emergency services but has not been discharged from a facility, the covered person may request an expedited external review under G.S. 58-50-82.

(e) In addition to the information to be provided under this section, the insurer shall include a copy of the description of both the standard and expedited external review procedures the insurer is required to provide under G.S. 58-50-93, including the provisions in the external review procedures that give the covered person the opportunity to submit additional information. (2001-446, s. 4.5.)

§ 58-50-78: Reserved for future codification purposes.

Editor's Note. — Session Laws 2001-446, s. 4.5, reserves this section for future codification purposes.

§ 58-50-79. Exhaustion of internal grievance process.

(a) Except as provided in G.S. 58-50-82, a request for an external review under G.S. 58-50-80 or G.S. 58-50-82 shall not be made until the covered person has exhausted the insurer's internal appeal and grievance processes under G.S. 58-50-61 and G.S. 58-50-62.

(b) A covered person shall be considered to have exhausted the insurer's internal grievance process for purposes of this section, if the covered person:

(1) Has filed a second-level grievance involving a noncertification appeal decision under G.S. 58-50-61 and G.S. 58-50-62, and

(2) Except to the extent the covered person requested or agreed to a delay, has not received a written decision on the grievance from the insurer within 60 days since the date the covered person filed the grievance with the insurer.

(c) Notwithstanding subsection (b) of this section, a covered person may not make a request for an external review of a noncertification involving a retrospective review determination made under G.S. 58-50-61 until the covered person has exhausted the insurer's internal grievance process.

(d) A request for an external review of a noncertification may be made before the covered person has exhausted the insurer's internal grievance and appeal procedures under G.S. 58-50-61 and G.S. 58-50-62 whenever the insurer agrees to waive the exhaustion requirement. If the requirement to exhaust the insurer's internal grievance procedures is waived, the covered person may file a request in writing for a standard external review as set forth in G.S. 58-50-80 or may make a request for an expedited external review as set forth in G.S. 58-50-82. In addition, the insurer may choose to eliminate the second-level grievance review under G.S. 58-50-62. In such case, the covered person may file a request in writing for a standard external review under G.S. 58-50-80 or may make a request for an expedited external review as set forth in G.S. 58-50-82 within 60 days after receiving notice of an appeal decision upholding a noncertification. (2001-446, s. 4.5.)

Legal Periodicals. — For comment, "Patients' Bill of Rights; Legislative Cure-All or Prescription for Disaster?," see 81 N.C.L. Rev. 653 (2003).

§ 58-50-80. Standard external review.

(a) Within 60 days after the date of receipt of a notice under G.S. 58-50-77, a covered person may file a request for an external review with the Commissioner.

(b) Upon receipt of a request for an external review under subsection (a) of this section, the Commissioner shall, within 10 business days, complete all of the following:

(1) Notify and send a copy of the request to the insurer that made the decision which is the subject of the request. The notice shall include a request for any information that the Commissioner requires to conduct the preliminary review under subdivision (2) of this subsection and require that the insurer deliver the requested information to the Commissioner within three business days of receipt of the notice.

(2) Conduct a preliminary review of the request to determine whether:

a. The individual is or was a covered person in the health benefit plan at the time the health care service was requested or, in the case of a retrospective review, was a covered person in the health benefit plan at the time the health care service was provided.

b. The health care service that is the subject of the noncertification appeal decision or the second-level grievance review decision upholding a noncertification reasonably appears to be a covered service under the covered person's health benefit plan.

c. The covered person has exhausted the insurer's internal appeal and grievance processes under G.S. 58-50-61 and G.S. 58-50-62, unless the covered person is considered to have exhausted the insurer's internal appeal or grievance process under G.S. 58-50-79, or unless the insurer has waived its right to conduct an expedited review of the appeal decision.

d. The covered person has provided all the information and forms required by the Commissioner that are necessary to process an external review.

(3) Notify in writing the covered person and the covered person's provider who performed or requested the service whether the request is complete and whether the request has been accepted for external review. If the request is complete and accepted for external review, the notice shall include a copy of the information that the insurer provided to the Commissioner pursuant to subdivision (b)(1) of this section, and inform the covered person that the covered person may

submit to the assigned independent review organization in writing, within seven days after the receipt of the notice, additional information and supporting documentation relevant to the initial denial for the organization to consider when conducting the external review. If the covered person chooses to send additional information to the assigned independent review organization, then the covered person shall at the same time and by the same means, send a copy of that information to the insurer. The Commissioner shall also notify the covered person in writing of the availability of assistance from the Managed Care Patient Assistance Program, including the telephone number and address of the Program.

(4) Notify the insurer in writing whether the request for external review has been accepted. If the request has been accepted, the notice shall direct the insurer or its designee utilization review organization to provide to the assigned organization, within seven days of receipt of the notice, the documents and any information considered in making the noncertification appeal decision or the second-level grievance review decision.

(5) Assign the review to an independent review organization approved under G.S. 58-50-85. The assignment shall be made using an alphabetical list of the independent review organizations, systematically assigning reviews on a rotating basis to the next independent review organization on that list capable of performing the review to conduct the external review. After the last organization on the list has been assigned a review, the Commissioner shall return to the top of the list to continue assigning reviews.

(6) Forward to the review organization that was assigned by the Commissioner any documents that were received relating to the request for external review.

(c) If the finding of the preliminary review under subdivision (b)(2) of this section is that the request is not complete, the Commissioner shall request from the covered person the information or materials needed to make the request complete. The covered person shall furnish the Commissioner with the requested information or materials within 90 days after the date of the insurer's decision for which external review is requested.

(d) If the finding of the preliminary review under subdivision (b)(2) of this section is that the request is not accepted for external review, the Commissioner shall inform the covered person, the covered person's provider who performed or requested the service, and the insurer in writing of the reasons for its nonacceptance.

(e) Failure by the insurer or its designee utilization review organization to provide the documents and information within the time specified in this subsection shall not delay the conduct of the external review. However, if the insurer or its utilization review organization fails to provide the documents and information within the time specified in subdivision (b)(4) of this section, the assigned organization may terminate the external review and make a decision to reverse the noncertification appeal decision or the second-level grievance review decision. Within one business day of making the decision under this subsection, the organization shall notify the covered person, the insurer, and the Commissioner.

(f) If the covered person submits additional information to the Commissioner pursuant to subdivision (b)(3) of this section, the Commissioner shall forward the information to the assigned review organization within two business days of receiving it and shall forward a copy of the information to the insurer.

(g) Upon receipt of the information required to be forwarded under subsection (f) of this section, the insurer may reconsider its noncertification appeal decision or second-level grievance review decision that is the subject of the external review. Reconsideration by the insurer of its noncertification appeal decision or second-level grievance review decision under this subsection shall not delay or terminate the external review. The external review shall be terminated if the insurer decides, upon completion of its reconsideration, to reverse its noncertification appeal decision or second-level grievance review decision and provide coverage or payment for the requested health care service that is the subject of the noncertification appeal decision or second-level grievance review decision.

(h) Upon making the decision to reverse its noncertification appeal decision or second-level grievance review decision under subsection (g) of this section, the insurer shall notify the covered person, the organization, and the Commissioner in writing of its decision. The organization shall terminate the external review upon receipt of the notice from the insurer sent under this subsection.

(i) The assigned organization shall review all of the information and documents received under subsections (b) and (f) of this section that have been forwarded to the organization by the Commissioner and the insurer. In addition, the assigned review organization, to the extent the documents or information are available, shall consider the following in reaching a decision:

    (1) The covered person's medical records.

    (2) The attending health care provider's recommendation.

    (3) Consulting reports from appropriate health care providers and other documents submitted by the insurer, covered person, or the covered person's treating provider.

    (4) The most appropriate practice guidelines that are based on sound clinical evidence and that are periodically evaluated to assure ongoing efficacy.

    (5) Any applicable clinical review criteria developed and used by the insurer or its designee utilization review organization.

    (6) Medical necessity, as defined in G.S. 58-3-200(b).

    (7) Any documentation supporting the medical necessity and appropriateness of the provider's recommendation.

The assigned organization shall review the terms of coverage under the covered person's health benefit plan to ensure that the organization's decision shall not be contrary to the terms of coverage under the covered person's health benefit plan with the insurer.

The assigned organization's determination shall be based on the covered person's medical condition at the time of the initial noncertification decision.

(j) Within 45 days after the date of receipt by the Commissioner of the request for external review, the assigned organization shall provide written notice of its decision to uphold or reverse the noncertification appeal decision or second-level grievance review decision to the covered person, the insurer, the covered person's provider who performed or requested the service, and the Commissioner. In reaching a decision, the assigned review organization is not bound by any decisions or conclusions reached during the insurer's utilization review process or the insurer's internal grievance process under G.S. 58-50-61 and G.S. 58-50-62.

(k) The organization shall include in the notice sent under subsection (j) of this section:

    (1) A general description of the reason for the request for external review.

    (2) The date the organization received the assignment from the Commissioner to conduct the external review.

    (3) The date the organization received information and documents submitted by the covered person and by the insurer.

    (4) The date the external review was conducted.

    (5) The date of its decision.

(6) The principal reason or reasons for its decision.

(7) The clinical rationale for its decision.

(8) References to the evidence or documentation, including the practice guidelines, considered in reaching its decision.

(9) The professional qualifications and licensure of the clinical peer reviewers.

(10) Notice to the covered person that he or she is not liable for the cost of the external review.

(*l*) Upon receipt of a notice of a decision under subsection (k) of this section reversing the noncertification appeal decision or second-level grievance review decision, the insurer shall within three business days reverse the noncertification appeal decision or second-level grievance review decision that was the subject of the review and shall provide coverage or payment for the requested health care service or supply that was the subject of the noncertification appeal decision or second-level grievance review decision. In the event the covered person is no longer enrolled in the health benefit plan when the insurer receives notice of a decision under subsection (k) of this section reversing the noncertification appeal decision or second-level grievance review decision, the insurer that made the noncertification appeal decision or second-level grievance review decision shall be responsible under this section only for the costs of those services or supplies the covered person received or would have received prior to disenrollment if the service had not been denied when first requested.

(m) For the purposes of this section, a person is presumed to have received a written notice two days after the notice has been placed, first-class postage prepaid, in the United States mail addressed to the person. The presumption may be rebutted by sufficient evidence that the notice was received on another day or not received at all. (2001-446, s. 4.5; 2002-187, ss. 3.1, 3.2; 2003-105, s. 3.)

Effect of Amendments. — Session Laws 2002-187, ss. 3.1 and 3.2, effective October 31, 2002, in the second sentence of subdivision (b)(3) substituted "receipt of the notice" for "date of the notice"; and added subsection (m). Session Laws 2003-105, s. 3, effective October 1, 2003, and applicable to actions taken by the insurer under the subsections of G.S. 58-50-61, 58-50-62, and 58-50-80 amended by this act, on and after that date, added the last sentence in subdivision (b)(3).

§ **58-50-81:** Reserved for future codification purposes.

Editor's Note. — Session Laws 2001-446, s. 4.5, reserves this section for future codification purposes.

§ **58-50-82. Expedited external review.**

(a) Except as provided in subsection (g) of this section, a covered person may make a written or oral request for an expedited external review with the Commissioner at the time the covered person receives:

(1) A noncertification decision under G.S. 58-50-61(f) if:

a. The covered person has a medical condition where the time frame for completion of an expedited review of an appeal involving a noncertification set forth in G.S. 58-50-61(l) would be reasonably expected to seriously jeopardize the life or health of the covered person or would jeopardize the covered person's ability to regain maximum function; and

b. The covered person has filed a request for an expedited appeal under G.S. 58-50-61(l).

(2) An appeal decision under G.S. 58-50-61(k) or (l) upholding a noncertification if:

   a. The noncertification appeal decision involves a medical condition of the covered person for which the time frame for completion of an expedited second-level grievance review of a noncertification set forth in G.S. 58-50-62(i) would reasonably be expected to seriously jeopardize the life or health of the covered person or jeopardize the covered person's ability to regain maximum function; and

   b. The covered person has filed a request for an expedited second-level review of a noncertification as set forth in G.S. 58-50-61(i); or

(3) A second-level grievance review decision under G.S. 58-60-62(h) or (i) upholding a noncertification:

   a. If the covered person has a medical condition where the time frame for completion of a standard external review under G.S. 58-50-80 would reasonably be expected to seriously jeopardize the life or health of the covered person or jeopardize the covered person's ability to regain maximum function; or

   b. If the second-level grievance concerns a noncertification of an admission, availability of care, continued stay, or health care service for which the covered person received emergency services, but has not been discharged from a facility.

(b) Within three days of receiving a request for an expedited external review, the Commissioner shall complete all of the following:

(1) Notify the insurer that made the noncertification, noncertification appeal decision, or second-level grievance review decision which is the subject of the request that the request has been received and provide a copy of the request or verbally convey all of the information included in the request. The Commissioner shall also request any information from the insurer necessary to make the preliminary review set forth in G.S. 58-50-80(b)(2) and require the insurer to deliver the information not later than one day after the request was made.

(2) Determine whether the request is eligible for external review and, if it is eligible, determine whether it is eligible for expedited review.

   a. For a request made pursuant to subdivision (a)(1) of this section that the Commissioner has determined meets the reviewability requirements set forth in G.S. 58-50-80(b)(2), determine, based on medical advice from a medical professional who is not affiliated with the organization that will be assigned to conduct the external review of the request, whether the request should be reviewed on an expedited basis because the time frame for completion of an expedited review under G.S. 58-50-61(1) would reasonably be expected to seriously jeopardize the life or health of the covered person or would jeopardize the covered person's ability to regain maximum function. The Commissioner shall then inform the covered person, the covered person's provider who performed or requested the service, and the insurer whether the Commissioner has accepted the covered person's request for an expedited external review. If the Commissioner has accepted the covered person's request for an expedited external review, then the Commissioner shall, in accordance with G.S. 58-50-80, assign an organization to conduct the review within the appropriate time frame. If the Commissioner has not accepted the covered person's request for an expedited external review, then the covered person shall be informed by the Commissioner that the covered person must exhaust, at a minimum, the insurer's internal appeal process under G.S. 58-50-61(1) before making another request for an external review with the Commissioner.

b. For a request made pursuant to subdivision (a)(2) of this section that the Commissioner has determined meets the reviewability requirements set forth in G.S. 58-50-80(b)(2), the Commissioner shall determine, based on medical advice from a medical professional who is not affiliated with the organization that will be assigned to conduct the external review of the request, whether the request should be reviewed on an expedited basis because the time frame for completion of an expedited review under G.S. 58-50-62 would reasonably be expected to seriously jeopardize the life or health of the covered person or would jeopardize the covered person's ability to regain maximum function. The Commissioner shall then inform the covered person, the covered person's provider who performed or requested the service, and the insurer whether the Commissioner has accepted the covered person's request for an expedited external review. If the Commissioner has accepted the covered person's request for an expedited external review, then the Commissioner shall, in accordance with G.S. 58-50-80, assign an organization to conduct the review within the appropriate time frame. If the Commissioner has not accepted the covered person's request for an expedited external review, then the covered person shall be informed by the Commissioner that the covered person must exhaust the insurer's internal grievance process under G.S. 58-50-62 before making another request for an external review with the Commissioner.

c. For a request made pursuant to sub-subdivision (a)(3)a. of this section that the Commissioner has determined meets the reviewability requirements set forth in G.S. 58-50-80(b)(2), the Commissioner shall determine, based on medical advice from a medical professional who is not affiliated with the organization that will be assigned to conduct the external review of the request, whether the request should be reviewed on an expedited basis because the time frame for completion of a standard external review under G.S. 58-50-80 would reasonably be expected to seriously jeopardize the life or health of the covered person or would jeopardize the covered person's ability to regain maximum function. The Commissioner shall then inform the covered person, the covered person's provider who performed or requested the service, and the insurer whether the review will be conducted using an expedited or standard time frame and shall, in accordance with G.S. 58-50-80, assign an organization to conduct the review within the appropriate time frame.

d. For a request made pursuant to sub-subdivision (a)(3)b. of this section, that the Commissioner has determined meets the reviewability requirements set forth in G.S. 58-50-80(b)(2), the Commissioner shall, in accordance with G.S. 58-50-80, assign an organization to conduct the expedited review and inform the covered person, the covered person's provider who performed or requested the service, and the insurer of its decision.

(c) As soon as possible, but within the same day of receiving notice under subdivision (b)(2) of this section that the request has been assigned to a review organization, the insurer or its designee utilization review organization shall provide or transmit all documents and information considered in making the noncertification appeal decision or the second-level grievance review decision to the assigned review organization electronically or by telephone or facsimile or any other available expeditious method.

(d) In addition to the documents and information provided or transmitted under subsection (c) of this section, the assigned organization, to the extent the information or documents are available, shall consider the following in reaching a decision:

(1) The covered person's pertinent medical records.

(2) The attending health care provider's recommendation.

(3) Consulting reports from appropriate health care providers and other documents submitted by the insurer, covered person, or the covered person's treating provider.

(4) The most appropriate practice guidelines that are based on sound clinical evidence and that are periodically evaluated to assure ongoing efficacy.

(5) Any applicable clinical review criteria developed and used by the insurer or its designee utilization review organization in making noncertification decisions.

(6) Medical necessity, as defined in G.S. 58-3-200(b).

(7) Any documentation supporting the medical necessity and appropriateness of the provider's recommendation.

The assigned organization shall review the terms of coverage under the covered person's health benefit plan to ensure that the organization's decision shall not be contrary to the terms of coverage under the covered person's health benefit plan.

The assigned organization's determination shall be based on the covered person's medical condition at the time of the initial noncertification decision.

(e) As expeditiously as the covered person's medical condition or circumstances require, but not more than four days after the date of receipt of the request for an expedited external review, the assigned organization shall make a decision to uphold or reverse the noncertification, noncertification appeal decision, or second-level grievance review decision and notify the covered person, the covered person's provider who performed or requested the service, the insurer, and the Commissioner of the decision. In reaching a decision, the assigned organization is not bound by any decisions or conclusions reached during the insurer's utilization review process or internal grievance process under G.S. 58-50-61 and G.S. 58-50-62.

(f) If the notice provided under subsection (e) of this section was not in writing, within two days after the date of providing that notice, the assigned organization shall provide written confirmation of the decision to the covered person, the covered person's provider who performed or requested the service, the insurer, and the Commissioner and include the information set forth in G.S. 58-50-80(m). Upon receipt of the notice of a decision under subsection (e) of this section that reverses the noncertification, noncertification appeal decision, or second-level grievance review decision, the insurer shall within one day reverse the noncertification, noncertification appeal decision, or second-level grievance review decision that was the subject of the review and shall provide coverage or payment for the requested health care service or supply that was the subject of the noncertification, noncertification appeal decision, or second-level grievance review decision.

(g) An expedited external review shall not be provided for retrospective noncertifications. (2001-446, s. 4.5.)

§ **58-50-83:** Reserved for future codification purposes.

Editor's Note. — Session Laws 2001-446, s. 4.5, reserves this section for future codification purposes.

§ 58-50-84. Binding nature of external review decision.

(a) An external review decision is binding on the insurer.

(b) An external review decision is binding on the covered person except to the extent the covered person has other remedies available under applicable federal or State law.

(c) A covered person may not file a subsequent request for external review involving the same noncertification appeal decision or second-level grievance review decision for which the covered person has already received an external review decision under this Part. (2001-446, s. 4.5.)

§ 58-50-85. Approval of independent review organizations.

(a) The Commissioner shall approve independent review organizations eligible to be assigned to conduct external reviews under this Part to ensure that an organization satisfies the minimum qualifications established under G.S. 58-50-87. The Commissioner shall develop an application form for initially approving and for reapproving organizations to conduct external reviews.

(b) Any organization wishing to be approved to conduct external reviews under this Part shall submit the application form and include with the form all documentation and information necessary for the Commissioner to determine if the organization satisfies the minimum qualifications established under G.S. 58-50-87. Applicants must submit pricing information sufficient to demonstrate that if selected, the applicant's total fee per review will not exceed commercially reasonable fees charged for similar services in the industry. The Commissioner shall not approve any independent review organization that either fails to provide sufficient pricing information or has fees that do not meet the guidelines established under this subsection.

(c) The Commissioner may determine that accreditation by a nationally recognized private accrediting entity with established and maintained standards for independent review organizations that meet the minimum qualifications established under G.S. 58-50-87 will cause an independent review organization to be deemed to have met, in whole or in part, the requirements of this section and G.S. 58-50-87. A decision by the Commissioner to recognize an accreditation program for the purpose of granting deemed status may be made only after reviewing the accreditation standards and program information submitted by the accrediting body. An independent review organization seeking deemed status due to its accreditation shall submit original documentation issued by the accrediting body to demonstrate its accreditation.

(d) An approval is effective for two years, unless the Commissioner determines before expiration of the approval that the independent review organization is not satisfying the minimum qualifications established under G.S. 58-50-87.

(e) Whenever the Commissioner determines that an independent review organization no longer satisfies the minimum requirements established under G.S. 58-50-87, the Commissioner shall terminate the approval of the independent review organization. (2001-446, s. 4.5.)

§ 58-50-86: Reserved for future codification purposes.

Editor's Note. — Session Laws 2001-446, s. 4.5, reserves this section for future codification purposes.

§ 58-50-87. Minimum qualifications for independent review organizations.

(a) As a condition of approval under G.S. 58-50-85 to conduct external reviews, an independent review organization shall have and maintain written policies and procedures that govern all aspects of both the standard external review process and the expedited external review process set forth in G.S. 58-50-80 and G.S. 58-50-82 that include, at a minimum:

    (1) A quality assurance mechanism in place that ensures:

        a. That external reviews are conducted within the specified time frames and required notices are provided in a timely manner.

        b. The selection of qualified and impartial clinical peer reviewers to conduct external reviews on behalf of the independent review organization and suitable matching of reviewers to specific cases.

        c. The confidentiality of medical and treatment records and clinical review criteria.

        d. That any person employed by or under contract with the independent review organization adheres to the requirements of this Part.

        e. The independence and impartiality of the independent review organization and the external review process and limits the ability of any person to improperly influence the external review decision.

    (2) A toll-free telephone service to receive information on a 24-hour-day, seven-day-a-week basis related to external reviews that is capable of accepting or recording inquiries or providing appropriate instruction to incoming telephone callers during other than normal business hours.

    (3) An agreement to maintain and provide to the Commissioner the information set out in G.S. 58-50-90.

    (4) A program for credentialing clinical peer reviewers.

    (5) An agreement to contractual terms or written requirements established by the Commissioner regarding the procedures for handling a review.

    (6) That the independent review organization consult with a medical doctor licensed to practice in North Carolina to advise the independent review organization on issues related to the standard of practice, technology, and training of North Carolina physicians with respect to the organization's North Carolina business.

(b) All clinical peer reviewers assigned by an independent review organization to conduct external reviews shall be medical doctors or other appropriate health care providers who meet the following minimum qualifications:

    (1) Be an expert in the treatment of the covered person's injury, illness, or medical condition that is the subject of the external review.

    (2) Be knowledgeable about the recommended health care service or treatment through recent or current actual clinical experience treating patients with the same or similar injury, illness, or medical condition of the covered person.

    (3) If the covered person's treating provider is a medical doctor, hold a nonrestricted license and, if a specialist medical doctor, a current certification by a recognized American medical specialty board in the area or areas appropriate to the subject of the external review.

    (4) If the covered person's treating provider is not a medical doctor, hold a nonrestricted license, registration, or certification in the same allied health occupation as the covered person's treating provider.

    (5) Have no history of disciplinary actions or sanctions, including loss of staff privileges or participation restrictions, that have been taken or

are pending by any hospital, governmental agency or unit, or regulatory body that raise a substantial question as to the clinical peer reviewer's physical, mental, or professional competence or moral character.

(c) In addition to the requirements set forth in subsection (a) of this section, an independent review organization may not own or control, be a subsidiary of, or in any way be owned or controlled by, or exercise control with a health benefit plan, a national, State, or local trade association of health benefit plans, or a national, State, or local trade association of health care providers.

(d) In addition to the requirements set forth in subsections (a), (b), and (c) of this section, to be approved under G.S. 58-50-85 to conduct an external review of a specified case, neither the independent review organization selected to conduct the external review nor any clinical peer reviewer assigned by the independent organization to conduct the external review may have a material professional, familial, or financial conflict of interest with any of the following:

(1) The insurer that is the subject of the external review.

(2) The covered person whose treatment is the subject of the external review or the covered person's authorized representative.

(3) Any officer, director, or management employee of the insurer that is the subject of the external review.

(4) The health care provider, the health care provider's medical group, or independent practice association recommending the health care service or treatment that is the subject of the external review.

(5) The facility at which the recommended health care service or treatment would be provided.

(6) The developer or manufacturer of the principal drug, device, procedure, or other therapy being recommended for the covered person whose treatment is the subject of the external review.

(e) In determining whether an independent review organization or a clinical peer reviewer of the independent review organization has a material professional, familial, or financial conflict of interest for purposes of subsection (d) of this section, the Commissioner shall take into consideration situations where the independent review organization to be assigned to conduct an external review of a specified case or a clinical peer reviewer to be assigned by the independent review organization to conduct an external review of a specified case may have an apparent professional, familial, or financial relationship or connection with a person described in subsection (d) of this section, but that the characteristics of that relationship or connection are such that they are not a material professional, familial, or financial conflict of interest that results in the disapproval of the independent review organization or the clinical peer reviewer from conducting the external review. (2001-446, s. 4.5.)

§ 58-50-88: Reserved for future codification purposes.

Editor's Note. — Session Laws 2001-446, s. 4.5, reserves this section for future codification purposes.

§ 58-50-89. Hold harmless for Commissioner, medical professionals, and independent review organizations.

Neither the Commissioner, a medical professional rendering advice to the Commissioner under G.S. 58-50-82(b)(2), an independent review organization, nor a clinical peer reviewer working on behalf of an organization shall be liable for damages to any person for any opinions rendered during or upon completion of an external review conducted under this Part, unless the opinion was rendered in bad faith or involved gross negligence. (2001-446, s. 4.5; 2002-187, s. 3.3.)

Effect of Amendments. — Session Laws 2002-187, s. 3.3, effective October 31, 2002, inserted "a medical professional rendering ad- vice to the Commissioner under G.S. 58-50-82(b)(2)," made a corresponding change in the catchline, and made stylistic changes.

§ 58-50-90. External review reporting requirements.

(a) An organization assigned under G.S. 58-50-80 or G.S. 58-50-82 to conduct an external review shall maintain written records in the aggregate and by insurer on all requests for external review for which it conducted an external review during a calendar year and submit a report to the Commissioner, as required under subsection (b) of this section.

(b) Each organization required to maintain written records on all requests for external review under subsection (a) of this section for which it was assigned to conduct an external review shall submit to the Commissioner, at least annually, a report in the format specified by the Commissioner.

(c) The report shall include in the aggregate and for each insurer:

(1) The total number of requests for external review.

(2) The number of requests for external review resolved and, of those resolved, the number resolved upholding the noncertification appeal decision or second-level grievance review decision and the number resolved reversing the noncertification appeal decision or second-level grievance review decision.

(3) The average length of time for resolution.

(4) A summary of the types of coverages or cases for which an external review was sought, as provided in the format required by the Commissioner.

(5) The number of external reviews under G.S. 58-50-80 that were terminated as the result of a reconsideration by the insurer of its noncertification appeal decision or second-level grievance review decision after the receipt of additional information from the covered person.

(6) Any other information the Commissioner may request or require.

(d) The organization shall retain the written records required under this section for at least three years.

(e) Each insurer shall maintain written records in the aggregate and for each type of health benefit plan offered by the insurer on all requests for external review of which the insurer receives notice from the Commissioner under this Part. The insurer shall retain the written records required under this section for at least three years. (2001-446, s. 4.5.)

§ 58-50-91: Reserved for future codification purposes.

Editor's Note. — Session Laws 2001-446, s. 4.5, reserves this section for future codification purposes.

§ 58-50-92. Funding of external review.

The insurer against which a request for a standard external review or an expedited external review is filed shall reimburse the Department of Insurance for the fees charged by the organization in conducting the external review, including work actually performed by the organization for a case that was terminated due to the insurer's decision to reconsider a request and reverse its noncertification decision, prior to the insurer notifying the organization of the reversal pursuant to G.S. 58-50-80(j), or when a review is terminated pursuant to G.S. 58-50-80(h) because the insurer failed to provide information to the review organization. (2001-446, s. 4.5.)

§ 58-50-93. Disclosure requirements.

(a) Each insurer shall include a description of the external review procedures in or attached to the policy, certificate, membership booklet, outline of coverage, or other evidence of coverage it provides to covered persons.

(b) The description required under subsection (a) of this section shall include a statement that informs the covered person of the right of the covered person to file a request for an external review of a noncertification, noncertification appeal decision or a second-level grievance review decision upholding a noncertification with the Commissioner. The statement shall include the telephone number and address of the Commissioner.

(c) In addition to subsection (b) of this section, the statement shall inform the covered person that, when filing a request for an external review, the covered person will be required to authorize the release of any medical records of the covered person that may be required to be reviewed for the purpose of reaching a decision on the external review. (2001-446, s. 4.5.)

§ 58-50-94. Selection of independent review organizations.

(a) At least every two years, or more frequently if the Commissioner determines is needed to secure adequate selection of independent review organizations, the Commissioner shall prepare and publish requests for proposals from independent review organizations that want to be approved under G.S. 58-50-85. All proposals shall be sealed. The Commissioner shall open all proposals in public.

(b) After the public opening, the Commissioner shall review the proposals, examining the costs and quality of the services offered by the independent review organizations, the reputation and capabilities of the independent review organizations submitting the proposals, and the provisions in G.S. 58-50-85 and G.S. 58-50-87. The Commissioner shall determine which proposal or proposals would satisfy the provisions of this Part. The Commissioner shall make his determination in consultation with an evaluation committee whose membership includes representatives of insurers subject to Part 4 of Article 50 of Chapter 58 of the General Statutes, health care providers, and insureds. In selecting the review organizations, in addition to considering cost, quality, and adherence to the requirements of the request for proposals, the Commissioner shall consider the desirability and feasibility of contracting with multiple review organizations and shall ensure that, for any given type of case involving highly specialized services and treatments, at least one review organization is available and capable of reviewing the case.

(c) An independent review organization may seek to modify or withdraw a proposal only after the public opening and only on the basis that the proposal contains an unintentional clerical error as opposed to an error in judgment. An independent review organization seeking to modify or withdraw a proposal shall submit to the Commissioner a written request, with facts and evidence in support of its position, before the determination made by the Commissioner under subsection (b) of this section, but not later than two days after the public opening of the proposals. The Commissioner shall promptly review the request, examine the nature of the error, and determine whether to permit or deny the request.

(d) The provisions of Article 3C of Chapter 143 of the General Statutes do not apply to this Part. (2001-446, s. 4.5.)

§ 58-50-95. Report by Commissioner.

The Commissioner shall report semiannually to the Joint Legislative Health Care Oversight Committee regarding the nature and appropriateness of reviews conducted under this Part. The report, which shall be provided to the public upon request, should include the number of reviews, underlying issues in dispute, character of the reviews, dollar amounts in question, whether the review was decided in favor of the covered person or the health benefit plan, the cost of review, and any other information relevant to the evaluation of the effectiveness of this Part. (2001-446, s. 4.5.)

Part 5. Small Employer Group Health Insurance Reform.

§ 58-50-100. Title and reference.

This section and G.S. 58-50-105 through G.S. 58-50-150 are known and may be cited as the North Carolina Small Employer Group Health Coverage Reform Act, referred to in those sections as "this Act". (1991, c. 630, s. 1.)

Editor's Note. — Session Laws 2001-446, s. 4.2(5), effective July 1, 2002, and applicable to health benefit plans that are in effect, delivered, issued for delivery, or renewed on or after that date, designates G.S. 58-50-100 through 58-50-156 as Part 5 of Article 50, with the heading "Small Employer Group Health Insurance Reform."

§ 58-50-105. Purpose and intent.

The purpose and intent of this Act is to promote the availability of accident and health insurance coverage to small employers, to prevent abusive rating practices, to require disclosure of rating practices to purchasers, to establish rules for continuity of coverage for employers and covered individuals, and to improve the efficiency and fairness of the small group accident and health insurance marketplace. (1991, c. 630, s. 1.)

Editor's Note. — For meaning of the words "this Act" see G.S. 58-50-100.

§ 58-50-110. Definitions.

As used in this Act:
(1) Repealed by Session Laws 2001-334, s. 12.1, effective August 3, 2001.
(1a) "Actuarial certification" means a written statement by a member of the American Academy of Actuaries or other individual acceptable to the Commissioner that a small employer carrier is in compliance with the provisions of G.S. 58-50-130, and to the extent applicable, the provisions of Article 68 of this Chapter, based upon the person's examination, including a review of the appropriate records and of the actuarial assumptions and methods used by the small employer carrier in establishing premium rates for applicable health benefit plans.
(1b) "Adjusted community rating" means a method used to develop carrier premiums which spreads financial risk across a large population and allows adjustments for the following demographic factors: age, gender,

family composition, and geographic areas, as determined pursuant to G.S. 58-50-130(b).

(2) Repealed by Session Laws 1993, c. 529, s. 3.3.

(3) "Basic health care plan" means a health care plan for small employers that is lower in cost than a standard health care plan and is required to be offered by all small employer carriers pursuant to G.S. 58-50-125 and approved by the Commissioner in accordance with G.S. 58-50-125.

(4) "Board" means the board of directors of the Pool.

(5) "Carrier" means any person that provides one or more health benefit plans in this State, including a licensed insurance company, a prepaid hospital or medical service plan, a health maintenance organization (HMO), and a multiple employer welfare arrangement.

(5a) "Case characteristics" means the demographic factors age, gender, family size, and geographic location.

(6), (7) Repealed by Session Laws 1993, c. 529, s. 3.3.

(8) "Committee" means the Small Employer Carrier Committee as created by G.S. 58-50-120.

(9) "Dependent" means the spouse or child of an eligible employee, subject to applicable terms of the health care plan covering the employee.

(10) "Eligible employee" means an employee who works for a small employer on a full-time basis, with a normal work week of 30 or more hours, including a sole proprietor, a partner or a partnership, or an independent contractor, if included as an employee under a health care plan of a small employer; but does not include employees who work on a part-time, temporary, or substitute basis.

(11) "Health benefit plan" means any accident and health insurance policy or certificate; nonprofit hospital or medical service corporation contract; health, hospital, or medical service corporation plan contract; HMO subscriber contract; plan provided by a MEWA or plan provided by another benefit arrangement, to the extent permitted by ERISA, subject to G.S. 58-50-115. Health benefit plan does not include benefits described in G.S. 58-68-25(b).

(12) "Impaired insurer" has the same meaning as prescribed in G.S. 58-62-20(6) or G.S. 58-62-16(8).

(13) Repealed by Session Laws 1993, c. 529, s. 3.3.

(14) "Late enrollee" has the same meaning as defined in G.S. 58-68-30(b)(2); provided that the initial enrollment period shall be a period of at least 30 consecutive calendar days. In addition to the special enrollment provisions in G.S. 58-68-30(f), an eligible employee or dependent shall not be considered a late enrollee under a small employer health benefit plan if:

a. Repealed by Session Laws 1998-211, s. 9, effective November 1, 1998.

    1, 2. Repealed by Session Laws 1998-211, s. 9, effective November 1, 1998.

    3, 4. Repealed by Session Laws 1993, c. 529, s. 3.3.

b. The individual elects a different health benefit plan offered by the small employer during an open enrollment period;

c. Repealed by Session Laws 1998-211, s. 9, effective November 1, 1998.

d. A court has ordered coverage be provided for a spouse or minor child under a covered employee's health benefit plan and the request for enrollment for a spouse is made within 30 days after issuance of the court order. A minor child shall be enrolled in accordance with the requirements of G.S. 58-51-120; or

     e. Repealed by Session Laws 1998-211, s. 9, effective November 1, 1998.

(15) Repealed by Session Laws 1993, c. 529, s. 3.3.

(16) "Pool" means the North Carolina Small Employer Health Reinsurance Pool created in G.S. 58-50-150.

(17) "Preexisting-conditions provision" means a preexisting-condition provision as defined in G.S. 58-68-30.

(18) "Premium" includes insurance premiums or other fees charged for a health benefit plan, including the costs of benefits paid or reimbursements made to or on behalf of persons covered by the plan.

(19) "Rating period" means the calendar period for which premium rates established by a small employer carrier are assumed to be in effect, as determined by the small employer carrier.

(20) "Risk-assuming carrier" means a small employer carrier electing to comply with the requirements set forth in G.S. 58-50-140.

(21) "Reinsuring carrier" means a small employer carrier electing to comply with the requirements set forth in G.S. 58-50-145.

(21a) "Self-employed individual" means an individual or sole proprietor who derives a majority of his or her income from a trade or business carried on by the individual or sole proprietor which results in taxable income as indicated on IRS form 1040, Schedule C or F and which generated taxable income in one of the two previous years.

(22) "Small employer" means any individual actively engaged in business that, on at least fifty percent (50%) of its working days during the preceding calendar quarter, employed no more than 50 eligible employees, the majority of whom are employed within this State, and is not formed primarily for purposes of buying health insurance and in which a bona fide employer-employee relationship exists. In determining the number of eligible employees, companies that are affiliated companies, or that are eligible to file a combined tax return for purposes of taxation by this State, shall be considered one employer. Subsequent to the issuance of a health benefit plan to a small employer and for the purpose of determining eligibility, the size of a small employer shall be determined annually. Except as otherwise specifically provided, the provisions of this Act that apply to a small employer shall continue to apply until the plan anniversary following the date the small employer no longer meets the requirements of this definition. For purposes of this Act, the term small employer includes self-employed individuals.

(23) "Small employer carrier" means any carrier that offers health benefit plans covering eligible employees of one or more small employers.

(24) "Standard health care plan" means a health care plan for small employers required to be offered by all small employer carriers under G.S. 58-50-125 and approved by the Commissioner in accordance with G.S. 58-50-125. (1991, c. 630, s. 1; 1993, c. 408, ss. 1, 2; c. 529, s. 3.3; 1993 (Reg. Sess., 1994), c. 569, s. 6; 1997-259, s. 2; 1998-211, s. 9; 2001-334, ss. 12.1, 12.2.)

Editor's Note. — For meaning of the words "this Act" see G.S. 58-50-100.

§ 58-50-112. Affiliated companies; HMOs.

For the purposes of this Act, companies that are affiliated companies or that are eligible to file a consolidated tax return shall be treated as one carrier except that any insurance company, hospital service plan, or medical service plan that is an affiliate of an HMO located in North Carolina or any HMO located in North Carolina that is an affiliate of an insurance company, a health service corporation, or a medical service corporation may treat the HMO as a separate carrier and each HMO that operates only one HMO in a service area of North Carolina may be considered a separate carrier. (1991, c. 630, s. 1.)

Editor's Note. — For meaning of the words "this Act" see G.S. 58-50-100.

§ 58-50-113: Repealed by Session Laws 1993, c. 529, s. 3.4.

§ 58-50-115. Health benefit plans subject to Act.

(a) A health benefit plan is subject to this Act if it provides health benefits for small employers or self-employed individuals and if any of the following conditions are met:

(1) Any part of the premiums or benefits is paid by a small employer or any covered individual is reimbursed, whether through wage or adjustments or otherwise, by a small employer for any portion of the premium;

(2) The health benefit plan is treated by the employer or any of the covered self-employed individuals as part of a plan or program for the purpose of sections 106, 125, or 162 of the United States Internal Revenue Code; or

(3) The small employer or self-employed individuals have permitted payroll deductions for the eligible enrollees for the health benefit plans.

(b) Repealed by Session Laws 1993, c. 529, s. 3.5, effective January 1, 1995. (1991, c. 630, s. 1; 1993, c. 529, s. 3.5.)

Editor's Note. — For meaning of the words "this Act" see G.S. 58-50-100.

Subsection (a) of this section was amended by Session Laws 1993, c. 529, s. 3.5, in the coded bill drafting format provided by G.S. 120-20.1. It has been set out in the form above at the direction of the Revisor of Statutes.

§ 58-50-120. Small Employer Carrier Committee.

(a) The Commissioner shall appoint the Small Employer Carrier Committee with fair representation of (i) risk-assuming carriers and reinsuring carriers; (ii) the insurance agent and small employer communities; and (iii) consumers who are served by plans covered by this Act. Two-thirds of the Committee shall be appointed from among representatives of small employer carriers.

(b) Subject to the Commissioner's approval, the Committee shall recommend the form and level of coverages to be made available by small employer carriers in accordance with the provisions of G.S. 58-50-125(a). The Committee shall recommend benefit levels, cost-sharing factors, exclusions, and limitations for the basic and standard health care plans. One basic health care plan and one standard health care plan shall contain benefit and cost-sharing levels that are consistent with the basic method of operation and the benefit plans of HMOs, including any restrictions imposed by federal law. The Committee shall submit the plans to the Commissioner for approval within 180 days after the Committee's appointment according to this section. The plans may include cost containment features such as: utilization review of health care services, including review of medical necessity of hospital and physician services; case management benefit alternatives; selective contracting with hospitals, physicians, and other health care providers; reasonable benefit differentials applicable to participating and nonparticipating providers; and other managed care provisions.

(c) To assure the broadest availability of health benefit plans to small employers, the Committee shall recommend for the Commissioner's approval, market conduct and other requirements for carriers, agents, brokers, and third-party administrators, including requirements developed as a result of a request by the Commissioner, relating to the following:

(1) Registration by each carrier with the Department of its intention to be a small employer carrier under this act.

(2) Publication by the Department, the Committee, or the Pool of a list of all small employer carriers, including a potential requirement applicable to agents, brokers, third-party administrators, and carriers that no health benefit plan may be sold to a small employer by a carrier not so identified as a small employer carrier.

(3) The availability of a broadly publicized toll-free telephone number for access by small employers to information concerning this Act.

(4) To the extent deemed to be necessary by the Committee to assure the fair distribution of high-risk individuals and groups among carriers, periodic reports by carriers, agents, brokers, and third-party administrators about health benefit plans issued; provided that reporting requirements shall be limited to information concerning case characteristics and numbers of health benefit plans in various categories marketed or issued to small employers.

(5) Registration by agents, brokers, and third-party administrators of their intention to be such for health benefit plans marketed to small employers under this Act.

(6) Methods concerning periodic demonstration by small employer carriers, agents, brokers, and third-party administrators that they are marketing and issuing health benefit plans to small employers in fulfillment of the purposes of this Act.

(7) Establishing standards for those conditions under which a carrier would not be required to write business received from a particular agent or broker.

(d) Within three years after September 1, 1991, the Committee shall conduct a study of the effectiveness of the provisions of this Act, recommend further improvements to achieve greater stability, accessibility, and affordability in the small employer marketplace, and submit it to the Commissioner. (1991, c. 630, s. 1.)

Editor's Note. — For meaning of the words "this Act" see G.S. 58-50-100.

§ 58-50-125. Health care plans; formation; approval; offerings.

(a) To improve the availability and affordability of health benefits coverage for small employers, the Committee shall recommend to the Commissioner two plans of coverage, one of which shall be a basic health care plan and the second of which shall be a standard health care plan. Each plan of coverage shall be in two forms, one of which shall be in the form of insurance and the second of which shall be consistent with the basic method of operation and benefit plans of HMOs, including federally qualified HMOs. On or before January 1, 1992, the Committee shall file a progress report with the Commissioner. The Committee shall submit the recommended plans to the Commissioner for approval within 180 days after the appointment of the Committee under G.S. 58-50-120. The Committee shall take into consideration the levels of health benefit plans provided in North Carolina, and appropriate medical and economic factors, and shall establish benefit levels, cost sharing, exclusions, and limitations. Notwithstanding subsection (c) of this section, in developing and approving the plans, the Committee and the Commissioner shall give due consideration to cost-effective and life-saving health care services and to cost-effective health care providers. The Committee shall file with the Commissioner its findings and recommendations, and reasons for the findings and recommendations, if it does not provide for coverage by any type of health care provider specified in G.S. 58-50-30. The recommended plans may include cost containment features such as, but not limited to: preferred provider provisions; utilization review of medical necessity of hospital and physician services; case management benefit alternatives; or other managed care provisions.

(b) After the Commissioner's approval of the plans submitted by the Committee under subsection (a) of this section and in lieu of any contrary procedure established by this Chapter, any small employer carrier may certify to the Commissioner, in the form and manner prescribed by the Commissioner, that the basic and standard health care plans filed by the carrier are in substantial compliance with the provisions of the corresponding approved Committee plans. Upon receipt by the Commissioner of the certification, the carrier may use the certified plans unless their use is disapproved by the Commissioner.

(c) Except as provided under Article 68 of this Chapter, the plans developed under this section are not required to provide coverage that meets the requirements of other provisions of this Chapter that mandate either coverage or the offer of coverage by the type or level of health care services or health care provider.

(d) Within 180 days after the Commissioner's approval under subsection (b) of this section, every small employer carrier shall, as a condition of transacting business in this State, offer small employers at least one basic and one standard health care plan. Every small employer that elects to be covered under such a plan and agrees to make the required premium payments and to satisfy the other provisions of the plan shall be issued such a plan by the small employer carrier. The premium payment requirements used in connection with basic and standard health care plans may address the potential credit risk of small employers that elect coverage in accordance with this subsection by means of payment security provisions that are reasonably related to the risk and are uniformly applied.

If a small employer carrier offers coverage to a small employer, the small employer carrier shall offer coverage to all eligible employees of a small employer and their dependents. A small employer carrier shall not offer coverage to only certain individuals in a small employer group except in the case of late enrollees as provided in G.S. 58-50-130(a)(4). A small employer carrier shall not modify any health benefit plan with respect to a small employer, any eligible employee, or dependent through riders, endorsements, or otherwise, in order to restrict or exclude coverage for certain diseases or medical conditions otherwise covered by the health benefit plan. In the case of an eligible employee or dependent of an eligible employee who, before the effective date of the plan, was excluded from coverage or denied coverage by a small employer carrier in the process of providing a health benefit plan to an eligible small employer, the small employer carrier shall provide an opportunity for the eligible employee or dependent of an eligible employee to enroll in the health benefit plan currently held by the small employer.

(e) No small employer carrier is required to offer coverage or accept applications under subsection (d) of this section:

    (1) From a group already covered under a health benefit plan except for coverage that is to begin after the group's anniversary date, but this

subsection shall not be construed to prohibit a group from seeking coverage or a small employer carrier from issuing coverage to a group before its anniversary date; or

(2) If the Commissioner determines that acceptance of an application or applications would result in the carrier being declared an impaired insurer.

(3) Repealed by Session Laws 1993, c. 529, s. 3.6.

(f) Every small employer carrier shall fairly market the basic and standard health care plan to all small employers in the geographic areas in which the carrier makes coverage available or provides benefits.

(g) No HMO operating as either a risk-assuming carrier or a reinsuring carrier is required to offer coverage or accept applications under subsection (d) of this section in the case of any of the following:

(1) To a group that is not physically located in the HMO's approved service areas;

(2) To an employee who does not reside within the HMO's approved service areas;

(3) Within an area, where the HMO can reasonably anticipate, and demonstrate, to the Commissioner's satisfaction, that it will not have the capacity within that area and its network of providers to deliver services adequately to the enrollees of those groups because of its obligations to existing group contract holders and enrollees.

An HMO that does not offer coverage pursuant to subdivision (3) of this subsection may not offer coverage in the applicable area to new employer groups with more than 49 eligible employees until the later of 90 days after that closure or the date on which the carrier notifies the Commissioner that it has regained capacity to deliver services to small employers.

(h) The provisions of subsections (b), (d), and (g) and subdivision (e)(2) of this section apply to every health benefit plan delivered, issued for delivery, renewed, or continued in this State or covering persons residing in this State on or after the date the plan becomes operational, as determined by the Commissioner. For purposes of this subsection, the date a health benefit plan is continued is the anniversary date of the issuance of the health benefit plan. (1991, c. 630, s. 1; c. 761, s. 10; 1993, c. 529, s. 3.6; 1997-259, ss. 3, 4.)

§ 58-50-130. Required health care plan provisions.

(a) Health benefit plans covering small employers are subject to the following provisions:

(1) to (4) Repealed by Session Laws 1997-259, s. 5, effective July 14, 1997.

(4a) A carrier may continue to enforce reasonable employer participation and contribution requirements on small employers applying for coverage; however, participation and contribution requirements may vary among small employers only by the size of the small employer group and shall not differ because of the health benefit plan involved. In applying minimum participation requirements to a small employer, a small employer carrier shall not consider employees or dependents who have qualifying existing coverage in determining whether an applicable participation level is met. "Qualifying existing coverage" means benefits or coverage provided under: (i) Medicare, Medicaid, and other government funded programs; or (ii) an employer-based health insurance or health benefit arrangement, including a self-insured plan, that provides benefits similar to or in excess of benefits provided under the basic health care plan.

(4b) Late enrollees may only be excluded from coverage for the greater of 18 months or an 18-month preexisting-condition exclusion; however, if both a period of exclusion from coverage and a preexisting-condition exclusion are applicable to a late enrollee, the combined period shall not exceed 18 months. If a period of exclusion from coverage is applied, a late enrollee shall be enrolled at the end of that period in the health benefit plan held at the time by the small employer.

(5) Notwithstanding any other provision of this Chapter, no small employer carrier, insurer, subsidiary of an insurer, or controlled individual of an insurance holding company shall act as an administrator or claims paying agent, as opposed to an insurer, on behalf of small groups which, if they purchased insurance, would be subject to this section. No small employer carrier, insurer, subsidiary of an insurer, or controlled individual of an insurance holding company shall provide stop loss, catastrophic, or reinsurance coverage to small employers that does not comply with the underwriting, rating, and other applicable standards in this Act.

(6) If a small employer carrier offers coverage to a small employer, the small employer carrier shall offer coverage to all eligible employees of a small employer and their dependents. A small employer carrier shall not offer coverage to only certain individuals in a small employer group except in the case of late enrollees as provided in G.S. 58-50-130(a)(4).

(7), (8) Repealed by Session Laws 1997-259, s. 5.

(9) The health benefit plan must meet the applicable requirements of Article 68 of this Chapter.

(b) For all small employer health benefit plans that are subject to this section, premium rates for health benefit plans subject to this section are subject to the following provisions:

(1) Small employer carriers shall use an adjusted-community rating methodology in which the premium for each small employer can vary only on the basis of the eligible employee's or dependent's age as determined in accordance with subdivision (6) of this subsection, the gender of the eligible employee or dependent, number of family members covered, or geographic area as determined under subdivision (7) of this subsection. Premium rates charged during a rating period to small employers with similar case characteristics for same coverage shall not vary from the adjusted community rate by more than twenty percent (20%) for any reason, including differences in administrative costs and claims experience.

(2) Rating factors related to age, gender, number of family members covered, or geographic location may be developed by each carrier to reflect the carrier's experience. The factors used by carriers are subject to the Commissioner's review;

(3) A small employer carrier shall not modify the premium rate charged to a small employer or a small employer group member, including changes in rates related to the increasing age of a group member, for 12 months from the initial issue date or renewal date, unless the group is composite rated and composition of the group changed by twenty percent (20%) or more or benefits are changed. The percentage increase in the premium rate charged to a small employer for a new rating period shall not exceed the sum of the following:

    a. The percentage change in the adjusted community rate as measured from the first day of the prior rating period to the first day of the new rating period, and

    b. Any adjustment, not to exceed fifteen percent (15%) annually, due to claim experience, health status, or duration of coverage of the employees or dependents of the small employer, and

    c. Any adjustment because of change in coverage or change in case characteristics of the small employer group.

(4), (5) Repealed by Session Laws 1995, c. 238, s. 1.

(6) For the purposes of subsection (b) of this section, a small employer carrier shall, unless the small employer carrier uses composite rating, use the following age brackets:

    a. Younger than 15 years;

    b. 15 to 19 years;

    c. 20 to 24 years;

    d. 25 to 29 years;

    e. 30 to 34 years;

    f. 35 to 39 years;

    g. 40 to 44 years;

    h. 45 to 49 years;

    i. 50 to 54 years;

    j. 55 to 59 years;

    k. 60 to 64 years;

    l. 65 years.

Carriers may combine, but shall not split, complete age brackets for the purposes of determining rates under subsection (b) of this section. Small employer carriers shall be permitted to develop separate rates for individuals aged 65 years and older for coverage for which Medicare is the primary payor and coverage for which Medicare is not the primary payor.

(7) For the purposes of subsection (b) of this section, a carrier shall not apply different geographic rating factors to the rates of small employers located within the same county; and

(8) The Department may adopt rules to administer this subsection and to assure that rating practices used by small employer carriers are consistent with the purposes of this subsection. Those rules shall include consideration of differences based on the following:

    a. Health benefit plans that use different provider network arrangements may be considered separate plans for the purposes of determining the rating in subdivision (1) of this subsection, provided that the different arrangements are expected to result in substantial differences in claims costs;

    b. Except as provided for in sub-subdivision a. of this subdivision, differences in rates charged for different health benefit plans shall be reasonable and reflect objective differences in plan design, but shall not permit differences in premium rates because of the case characteristics of groups assumed to select particular health benefit plans; and

    c. Small employer carriers shall apply allowable rating factors consistently with respect to all small employers.

(c) Repealed by Session Laws 1993, c. 529, s. 3.7.

(d) In connection with the offering for sale of any health benefit plan to a small employer, each small employer carrier shall make a reasonable disclosure, as part of its solicitation and sales materials, of the following and shall provide this information to the small employer upon request:

(1) Repealed by Session Laws 1993, c. 529, s. 3.7.

(2) Provisions concerning the small employer carrier's right to change premium rates and the factors other than claims experience that affect changes in premium rates.

(3) Provisions relating to renewability of policies and contracts.

(4) Provisions affecting any preexisting conditions provision.

(5) The benefits available and premiums charged under all health benefit plans for which the small employer is eligible.

(e) Each small employer carrier shall maintain at its principal place of business a complete and detailed description of its rating practices and renewal underwriting practices, including information and documentation that demonstrate that its rating methods and practices are based upon commonly accepted actuarial assumptions and are in accordance with sound actuarial principles.

(f) Each small employer carrier shall file with the Commissioner annually on or before March 15 an actuarial certification certifying that it is in compliance with this Act and that its rating methods are actuarially sound. The small employer carrier shall retain a copy of the certification at its principal place of business.

(g) A small employer carrier shall make the information and documentation described in subsection (e) of this section available to the Commissioner upon request. Except in cases of violations of this Act, the information is proprietary and trade secret information and is not subject to disclosure by the Commissioner to persons outside of the Department except as agreed to by the small employer carrier or as ordered by a court of competent jurisdiction. Nothing in this section affects the Commissioner's authority to approve rates before their use under G.S. 58-65-60(e) or G.S. 58-67-50(c).

(h) The provisions of subdivisions (a)(1), (3), and (5) and subsections (b) through (g) of this section apply to health benefit plans delivered, issued for delivery, renewed, or continued in this State or covering persons residing in this State on or after January 1, 1992. The provisions of subdivisions (a)(2) and (4) of this section apply to health benefit plans delivered, issued for delivery, renewed, or continued in this State or covering persons residing in this State on or after the date the plan becomes operational, as designated by the Commissioner. For purposes of this subsection, the date a health benefit plan is continued is the anniversary date of the issuance of the health benefit plan. (1991, c. 630, s. 1; 1993, c. 408, s. 6; c. 529, ss. 3.2, 3.7; 1993 (Reg. Sess., 1994), c. 569, ss. 7, 8; c. 678, ss. 24, 25; 1995, c. 238, s. 1; c. 507, s. 23A.1(b); 1995 (Reg. Sess., 1996), c. 669, s. 1; 1997-259, ss. 5, 6; 1998-211, ss. 9.1, 10; 1999-132, s. 4.1; 2001-334, ss. 3, 12.3.)

Editor's Note. — For meaning of the words "this Act" see G.S. 58-50-100.

§ 58-50-135. Elections by carriers.

(a) Every small employer carrier shall elect either to become a risk-assuming carrier and comply with the provisions of G.S. 58-50-140 or become a reinsuring carrier and comply with the provisions of G.S. 58-50-145. The election shall be binding for a five-year period except that a newly licensed carrier's initial election shall be made for two years. The Commissioner may, for good cause, permit a carrier to modify its election during the five-year period. All carriers under common ownership or control must make the same election in this State; provided, however, that the Commissioner may, for good cause, permit an affiliated carrier to make a separate election.

(b) A small employer carrier that elects to stop participating as a reinsuring carrier and to become a risk-assuming carrier shall not reinsure or continue to reinsure any small employer health benefit plans under G.S. 58-50-145 and G.S. 58-50-150 as soon as the carrier becomes a risk-assuming carrier; however, a reinsuring carrier electing to become a risk-assuming carrier shall pay a prorated assessment based upon business issued as a reinsuring carrier for any part of the year that the business was reinsured. A small employer carrier that elects to stop participating as a risk-assuming carrier and to become a reinsuring carrier may reinsure small employer health benefit plans under the provisions of G.S. 58-50-145 and G.S. 58-50-150.

(c) Any small employer carrier that stops writing, administering, or otherwise providing health benefit plans to employers in this State shall continue to be governed by this Act with respect to business conducted under this Act that was transacted before the effective date of termination and that remains in force. (1991, c. 630, s. 1; 1998-211, s. 11.)

Editor's Note. — For meaning of the words "this Act" see G.S. 58-50-100.

§ 58-50-140. Risk-assuming carriers.

(a) Any small employer carrier may elect to become a risk-assuming carrier upon application to and approval by the Commissioner. A small employer carrier shall not be approved as a risk-assuming carrier if the Commissioner finds that the carrier is not capable of assuming that status under the criteria set forth in subsection (b) of this section. The carrier shall provide public notice of its application to become a risk-assuming carrier. A small employer carrier's application to be a risk-assuming carrier shall be approved unless disapproved by the Commissioner within 60 days after the carrier's application. A small employer carrier that has had its application to be a risk-assuming carrier disapproved may request and shall be granted a public hearing within 60 days after the disapproval.

(b) In determining whether or not to approve an application by a small employer carrier to become a risk-assuming carrier, the Commissioner shall consider the carrier's financial condition and the financial condition of its parent or guaranteeing corporation, if any; its history of assuming and managing risk; its ability to assume and manage the risk of enrolling small employers without the protection of the reinsurance provided in G.S. 58-50-150; and its commitment to market fairly to all small employers in its service area. (1991, c. 630, s. 1.)

§ 58-50-145. Reinsuring carriers.

(a) Any small employer carrier may elect to operate under the provisions of this section and G.S. 58-50-150 as a reinsuring carrier.

(b) Each reinsuring carrier shall conduct business with its members and subscribers, and administer claims for coverage reinsured by the Pool, in the same manner as it would administer health claims that it writes without reinsurance. (1991, c. 630, s. 1.)

§ 58-50-149. Limit on cessions to the Reinsurance Pool.

In addition to any individual or group previously reinsured in accordance with G.S. 58-50-150(g)(1), the Pool shall only reinsure a health benefit plan issued or delivered for original issue by a reinsuring carrier on or after October 1, 1995, if the health benefit plan provides coverage to a small employer with no more than 25 eligible employees, including self-employed individuals. (1995, c. 517, s. 29.)

§ 58-50-150. North Carolina Small Employer Health Reinsurance Pool.

(a) There is created a nonprofit entity to be known as the North Carolina Small Employer Health Reinsurance Pool. All carriers issuing or providing health benefit plans in this State on and after January 1, 1992, except any small employer carrier electing to be a risk-assuming carrier, are members of the Pool.

(b) Within 30 days after January 1, 1992, the Commissioner shall give notice to all carriers of the time and place for the initial organizational meeting, which shall take place within 90 days after the notice from the Commissioner. The members shall select the initial Board, subject to the Commissioner's approval. The Board shall consist of nine members. There shall be no more than two members of the Board representing any one carrier. In determining voting rights at the organizational meeting, each member shall be entitled to vote in person or by proxy. The voting rights to determine initial Board membership shall be weighted based upon net group health benefit plan premium derived from this State in the previous calendar year. Thereafter, voting rights shall be based on net group health benefit plan premium derived from small employer business. The Board shall at all times, to the extent possible, include at least one domestic insurance company licensed to transact accident and health insurance, one HMO, one nonprofit hospital or medical service plan. Six of the members of the Board shall be small employer carriers. In approving selection of the Board, the Commissioner shall assure that all members are fairly represented.

(c) If the initial Board is not elected at the organizational meeting, the Commissioner shall appoint the initial Board within 30 days of the organizational meeting.

(d) As used in this section, "plan of operation" includes articles, bylaws, and operating rules of the Pool. Within 180 days after the appointment of the initial Board, the Board shall submit to the Commissioner a plan of operation and any amendments necessary or suitable to assume the fair, reasonable, and equitable administration of the Pool. The Commissioner shall approve the plan of operation if it assures the fair, reasonable, and equitable administration of the Pool and provides for the proportionate basis in accordance with the provisions of subsections (h) through (o) of this section. The plan of operation shall become effective upon approval in writing by the Commissioner consistent with the date on which the coverage under this section shall be made available. If the Board fails to submit a suitable plan of operation within 180 days after its appointment, or at any time thereafter fails to submit suitable amendments to the plan of operation, the Commissioner shall adopt and promulgate a plan of operation or amendment, as appropriate. The Commissioner shall amend any plan of operation he adopts, as necessary, after a plan of operation is submitted by the Board and approved by the Commissioner.

(e) The plan of operation shall establish procedures for, among other things:

(1) Handling and accounting of assets and moneys of the Pool, and for an annual financial reporting to the Commissioner.

(2) Filling vacancies on the Board, subject to the Commissioner's approval.

(3) Selecting an administering carrier and setting forth the powers and duties of the administering carrier.

(4) Reinsuring risks in accordance with the provisions of this Act.

(5) Collecting assessments from members subject to assessment to provide for claims reinsured by the Pool and for administrative expenses incurred or estimated to be incurred during the period for which the assessment is made.

(6) Any additional matters in the Board's discretion.

(f) The Pool has the general powers and authority granted under the laws of this State to insurance companies licensed to transact accident and health insurance except the power to issue coverage directly to enrollees, and, in addition, the specific authority to do all of the following:

(1) Enter into contracts that are necessary or proper to carry out the provisions and purposes of this Act, including the authority, with the Commissioner's approval, to enter into contracts with similar pools of

other states for the joint performance of common administrative functions, or with persons or other organizations for the performance of administrative functions.

(2) Sue or be sued, including taking any legal actions necessary or proper for recovery of any assessments for, on behalf of, or against members.

(3) Take any legal action necessary to avoid the payment of improper, incorrect, or fraudulent claims against the Pool or the coverage reinsured by the Pool.

(4) Issue various reinsurance policies in accordance with the requirements of this section.

(5) Establish rules, conditions, and procedures pertaining to the reinsurance of members' risks by the Pool.

(6) Establish appropriate rates, rate schedules, rate adjustments, rate classifications, and any other actuarial functions appropriate to the Pool's operation.

(7) Assess members in accordance with the provisions of subsections (h) through (o) of this section; and make advance interim assessments that are reasonable and necessary for organizational and interim operating expenses. Any interim assessments shall be credited as offsets against any regular assessments due following the close of the Pool's fiscal year.

(8) Appoint from among members appropriate legal, actuarial, and other committees that are necessary to provide technical assistance in the operation of the Pool, policy, and other contract design, and any other function within the Pool's authority.

(9) Borrow money to effect the purposes of the Pool. Any notes or other evidence of indebtedness of the Pool not in default are legal investments for members and may be carried as admitted assets.

(g) Any member that elects to be a reinsuring carrier may cede, and the Pool shall reinsure the reinsuring carrier, subject to all of the following:

(1) The Pool shall reinsure any basic and standard health care plan originally issued or delivered for original issue by a reinsuring carrier on or after January 1, 1992, under the requirements in G.S. 58-50-125(d). With respect to a basic or standard health care plan, the Pool shall reinsure the level of coverage provided and, with respect to other plans, the Pool shall reinsure the level of coverage provided in the basic or standard health care plan up to, but not exceeding, the level of coverage provided under either the basic or standard health care plans. Small group business of reinsuring carriers in force before January 1, 1992, may not be ceded to the Pool until January 1, 1995, and then only if and when the Board determines that sufficient funding sources are available.

(2) The Pool shall reinsure eligible employees or their dependents or entire small employer groups according to the following:

a. With respect to eligible employees and their dependents who either (i) are employed by a small employer as of the date such employer's coverage by the member begins or (ii) are hired after the beginning of the employer's coverage by the member: The coverage may be reinsured within 60 days after the beginning of the eligible employees' or dependents' coverage under the plan.

b. With respect to eligible employees and their dependents, when the entire employer group is eligible for reinsurance: A small employer carrier may reinsure the entire employer group within 60 days after the beginning of the group's coverage under the plan.

c. With respect to any person reinsured, no reinsurance may be provided for a reinsured employee or dependent until five thousand dollars ($5,000) in benefit payments have been made for services provided during a calendar year for that reinsured employee or dependent, which payments would have been reimbursed through the reinsurance in the absence of the five thousand dollar ($5,000) deductible. The Boards shall review periodically the amount of the deductible and adjust it for inflation. In addition, the member shall retain ten percent (10%) of the next fifty thousand dollars ($50,000) of benefit payments during a calendar year and the Pool shall reinsure the remainder; provided that the members' liability under this section shall not exceed ten thousand dollars ($10,000) in any one calendar year with respect to any one person reinsured. The amount of the member's maximum liability shall be periodically reviewed by the Board and adjusted for inflation, as determined by the Board.

  d. Reinsurance may be terminated for each reinsured employee or dependent on any plan anniversary.

  e. Premium rates charged for reinsurance by the program to an HMO that is approved by the Secretary of Health and Human Services as a federally qualified health maintenance organization under 42 U.S.C. § 300 et seq., shall be reduced to reflect the restrictions and requirements of 42 U.S.C. § 300 et seq.

  f. Every carrier subject to G.S. 58-50-130 shall apply its case management and claims handling techniques, including but not limited to utilization review, individual case management, preferred provider provisions, other managed care provisions or methods of operation, consistently with both reinsured and non-reinsured business.

  g. Except as otherwise provided in this section, premium rates charged by the Pool for coverage reinsured by the Pool for that classification or group with similar case characteristics and coverage shall be established as follows:

    1. One and one-half times the rate established by the Pool with respect to the eligible employees and their dependents of a small employer, all of whose coverage is reinsured with the Pool and who are reinsured in accordance with this section.

    2. Five times the rate established by the Pool with respect to an eligible employee or dependent who is reinsured in accordance with this section.

  (3) The Pool shall reinsure no more than the level of benefits provided in either the basic or standard health care plan established in accordance with G.S. 58-50-125.

  (4) The Pool may issue different types and levels of reinsurance coverage, including stop-loss coverage; and the reinsurance premium shall be adjusted to reflect the type and level of reinsurance coverage issued.

  (5) The reinsurance premium shall also be adjusted to reflect cost containment features of the plan of operation that have proven to be effective including, but not limited to: preferred provider provisions, utilization review of medical necessity of hospital and physician services, case management benefit alternatives, and other managed care provisions or methods of operation.

  (h) Following the close of each fiscal year, the administering carrier shall determine the net premiums, the Pool expenses of administration, and the incurred losses for the year, taking into account investment income and other appropriate gains and losses. Health benefit plan premiums and benefits paid by a member that are less than an amount determined by the Board to justify the cost of collection shall not be considered for purposes of determining assessments. As used in this section, "net premiums" means health benefit plan premiums for insured plans but does not mean premiums or revenue received by a carrier for Medicare and Medicaid contracts.

(i) Any net losses for the year shall be recouped by assessments of members as follows:

(1) The Board shall determine an equitable assessment formula to recoup assessments of members that takes into consideration both overall market share of small employer carriers that are members of the Pool and the share of new business of the small employer carriers assumed during the preceding calendar year. For the first three years of operation of the Pool, if an assessment is based on an adjustment made, the assessment shall not be less than fifty percent (50%) nor more than one hundred fifty percent (150%) of the amount it would have been if the assessment were based on the proportional relationship of the small employer carrier's total premiums for small employer coverage written in the year to the total premiums of small employer coverage written by all small employer carriers in this State in the year. The Board shall also determine whether the assessment base used to determine assessments shall be made on a transitional basis or shall be permanent. In no event shall assessments exceed four percent (4%) of the total health benefit plan premium earned in this State from health benefit plans covering small employers of members during the calendar year coinciding or ending during the fiscal year of the Pool. The Board may change the assessment formula, including an assessment adjustment formula, if applicable, from time to time as appropriate.

(2) Health benefit plan premiums and benefits paid by a member that are less than an amount determined by the Board to justify the cost of collection shall not be considered for purposes of determining assessments. For the purposes of this section, health benefit plan premiums earned by MEWAs and other benefit arrangements, to the extent permitted by ERISA, shall be established by adding paid health losses and administrative expenses.

(j) If the assessment level is inadequate, the Board may adjust reinsurance thresholds, retention levels, or consider other forms of reinsurance. After the first three full years of operations the Board shall report to the Commissioner on its experience, the effect on reinsurance and small group rates of individual ceding, and recommendations on additional funding sources, if needed. If legislative or other broader funding alternatives are not found, the Board may enter into negotiations with representatives of health care providers to resolve any deficit through reductions in future years' payment levels for reinsured plans. Any such recommendations shall take into account the findings of the actuarial study provided for in this subsection. An actuarial study shall be undertaken within the first three years of the Pool's operation to evaluate and measure the relative risks being assumed by differing types of small employer carriers as a result of this Act. The study shall be developed by three actuaries appointed by the Commissioner, with one representing risk assuming carriers, one representing reinsuring carriers, and one from within the Department.

(k) Subject to the approval of the Commissioner, the Board may make an adjustment to the assessment formula for any reinsuring carrier that is an HMO approved as a federally qualified HMO by the Secretary of Health and Human Services under 42 U.S.C. § 300 for restrictions placed on them other than those for which an adjustment has already been made in subsection (b)(2) or (b)(5) of this section that are not imposed on other small group carriers.

(l) If assessments exceed actual losses and administrative expenses of the Pool, the excess shall be held at interest and used by the Board to offset future losses or to reduce Pool premiums. As used in this subsection, "future losses" includes reserves for incurred but not reported claims.

(m) The Board shall determine annually each member's proportion of participation in the Pool based on financial statements and other reports that the Board considers to be necessary and requires that the member files with the Board. All carriers shall report, to the Board, claims payments made and administrative expenses incurred in this State on an annual basis and on a form prescribed by the Commissioner.

(n) The plan of operation shall provide for the imposition of an interest penalty for late payment of assessments.

(o) The Board may abate or defer, in whole or in part, the assessment of a member if, in the Board's opinion, payment of the assessment would endanger the member's ability to fulfill its contractual obligations. In the event an assessment against a member is abated or deferred in whole or in part, the amount by which the assessment is abated or deferred may be assessed against the other members in a manner consistent with the basis for assessments set forth in this section. The member receiving the abatement or deferment shall remain liable to the Pool for the deficiency.

(p) Neither the participation in the Pool as members, the establishment of rates, forms, or procedures, nor any other joint or collective action required by this Act shall be the basis of any legal action, criminal or civil liability, or penalty against the Pool or any of its members.

(q) Any person or member made a party to any action, suit, or proceeding because the person or member serves or served on the Board or on a committee or is or was an officer or employee of the Pool shall be held harmless and be indemnified by the Pool against all liability and costs, including the amounts of judgments, settlements, fines, or penalties, and expenses and reasonable attorneys' fees incurred in connection with the action, suit, or proceeding. However, the indemnification shall not be provided on any matter in which the person or member is finally adjudged in the action, suit, or proceeding to have committed a breach of duty involving gross negligence, dishonesty, willful misfeasance, or reckless disregard of the responsibilities of service or office. Costs and expenses of the indemnification shall be prorated among and paid for by all members.

(r) The Pool is exempt from the taxes imposed by Article 8B of Chapter 105 of the General Statutes. (1991, c. 630, s. 1; 1993, c. 408, s. 7.)

Editor's Note. — For meaning of the words "this Act" see G.S. 58-50-100.

Legal Periodicals. — For article, "Toward Full Participation and Protection of the Worker with Illness: The Failure of Federal Health Law After McGann v. H & H Music Co.," see 29 Wake Forest L. Rev. 781 (1994).

§ 58-50-151: Recodified as G.S. 58-51-116 by Session Laws 2001-446, s. 4.3, effective July 1, 2002.

§ 58-50-155. Standard and basic health care plan coverages.

(a) Notwithstanding G.S. 58-50-125(c), the standard health plan developed and approved under G.S. 58-50-125 shall provide coverage for all of the following:

   (1) Mammograms and examinations and laboratory tests for the screening for the early detection of cervical cancer at least equal to the coverage required by G.S. 58-51-57.

(2) Prostate-specific antigen (PSA) tests or equivalent tests for the presence of prostate cancer at least equal to the coverage required by G.S. 58-51-58.

(3) Reconstructive breast surgery resulting from a mastectomy at least equal to the coverage required by G.S. 58-51-62.

(4) For a qualified individual, scientifically proven bone mass measurement for the diagnosis and evaluation of osteoporosis or low bone mass at least equal to the coverage required by G.S. 58-3-174.

(5) Prescribed contraceptive drugs or devices that prevent pregnancy and that are approved by the United States Food and Drug Administration for use as contraceptives, or outpatient contraceptive services at least equal to the coverage required by G.S. 58-3-178, if the plan covers prescription drugs or devices, or outpatient services, as applicable. The same exceptions and exclusions as are provided under G.S. 58-3-178 apply to standard plans developed and approved under G.S. 58-50-125.

(6) Colorectal cancer examinations and laboratory tests at least equal to the coverage required by G.S. 58-3-179.

(7) Surveillance tests at least equal to coverage required by G.S. 58-3-266.

(a1), (a2) Repealed by Session Laws 1999-197, s. 2.

(b) Notwithstanding G.S. 58-50-125(c), in developing and approving the plans under G.S. 58-50-125, the Committee and Commissioner shall give due consideration to cost-effective and life-saving health care services and to cost-effective health care providers. (1991, c. 490, s. 5; 1993, c. 269, s. 4; 1997-312, s. 4; 1997-456, s. 40(b); 1999-197, s. 2; 1999-231, ss. 2, 2.1; 1999-456, s. 15(b)-(d); 2001-116, s. 2; 2003-186, s. 1; 2003-223, s. 2.)

Editor's Note. — Session Laws 1997-312, s. 6, provides: "Nothing in this act shall apply to specified accident, specified disease, hospital indemnity, or long-term care health insurance policies."

Session Laws 1999-197, s. 3, provided that this act applies to health benefit plans that are delivered, issued for delivery, or renewed on and after January 1, 2000. For purposes of Session Laws 1999-197, renewal of a health benefit plan is presumed to occur on each anniversary of the date on which coverage was first effective on the person or persons covered by the health benefit plan.

Session Laws 1999-231, s. 3, contains a severability clause.

Session Laws 1999-231, s. 4, provides that this act applies to health benefit plans that are delivered, issued for delivery, or renewed on and after January 1, 2000. For purposes of Session Laws 1999-231, renewal of a health benefit policy, contract, or plan is presumed to occur on each anniversary of the date on which coverage was first effective on the person or persons covered by the health benefit plan.

Session Laws 2001-116, s. 3, provides that: "This act becomes effective January 1, 2002, and applies to all health benefit plans that are delivered, issued for delivery, or renewed on and after that date. For the purposes of this act, renewal of a health benefit plan is presumed to occur on each anniversary of the date on which

coverage was first effective on the person or persons covered by the health benefit plan."

Session Laws 2003-186, s. 6, provides, in part, that for the purposes of this act, renewal of a health benefit plan is presumed to occur on each anniversary of the date on which coverage was first effective on the person or persons covered by the health benefit plan.

Session Laws 2003-223, s. 3, provides that the amendment to this section by s. 2 of the act is applicable to all health benefit plans that are delivered, issued for delivery, or renewed on and after that date. For the purposes of this act, renewal of a health benefit plan is presumed to occur on each anniversary of the date on which coverage was first effective on the person or persons covered by the health benefit plan.

Effect of Amendments. — Session Laws 2001-116, s. 2, effective January 1, 2002, added subdivision (a)(6). See editor's note for applicability.

Session Laws 2003-186, s. 1, effective January 1, 2004, and applicable to all health benefit plans that are delivered, issued for delivery, or renewed on and after that date, substituted "examinations and laboratory tests for the screening for the early detection of cervical cancer" for "pap smears" in subdivision (a)(1).

Session Laws 2003-223, s. 2, effective January 1, 2004, added subdivision (a)(7). See editor's note for applicability.

§ 58-50-156. Coverage of certain prescribed drugs for cancer treatment.

Notwithstanding G.S. 58-50-125(c), if the standard health plan developed and approved under G.S. 58-50-125 provides coverage for prescribed drugs approved by the federal Food and Drug Administration for the treatment of certain types of cancer, then coverage may not be excluded for any drug on the basis that the drug has been prescribed for the treatment of a type of cancer for which the drug has not been approved by the federal Food and Drug Administration. Coverage for such drugs shall be as required under G.S. 58-51-59. (1993, c. 506, s. 4.4.)

Editor's Note. — As enacted, this section contained a subsection (a) but no (b). This section has been set out in the form above at the direction of the Revisor of Statutes.

ARTICLE 51.

Nature of Policies.

§ 58-51-1. Form, classification and rates to be approved by Commissioner.

No policy of insurance against loss or damage from the sickness or the bodily injury or death of the insured by accident shall be issued or delivered to any person in this State until a copy of the form thereof and of the classification of risks and the premium rates pertaining thereto have been filed with, and the forms approved by, the Commissioner. If the Commissioner shall notify, in writing, the company or other insurer which has filed such form that it does not comply with the requirements of law, specifying the reasons for his opinion, it shall be unlawful thereafter for any such insurer to issue any policy in such form. The action of the Commissioner in this regard shall be subject to review by any court of competent jurisdiction; but nothing in this Article shall be construed to give jurisdiction to any court not already having jurisdiction. (1911, c. 209, s. 1; 1913, c. 91, s. 1; C.S., s. 6477; 1945, c. 385; 1991, c. 720, s. 4.)

§ 58-51-5. Form of policy.

(a) No policy of accident and health insurance shall be delivered or issued for delivery to any person in this State unless:

(1) The entire money and other considerations therefor are expressed therein; and

(2) The time at which the insurance takes effect and terminates is expressed therein; and

(3) It purports to insure only one person, except that a policy may insure, originally or by subsequent amendment, upon the application of an adult member of a family who shall be deemed the policyholder, any two or more eligible members of that family, including husband, wife, dependent children or any children under a specified age which shall not exceed 19 years and any other persons dependent upon the policyholder; and

(4) The style, arrangement, and overall appearance of the policy, any endorsements, or attached papers give no undue prominence to any portion of the text. For the purpose of this subdivision, "text" includes all printed matter except the name and address of the insurer, the name or title of the policy, and captions and subcaptions.

(5) The exceptions and reductions of indemnity are set forth in the policy and, except those which are set forth in G.S. 58-51-15, are printed, at the insurer's option, either included with the benefit provision to which they apply, or under an appropriate caption such as "EXCEPTIONS," or "EXCEPTIONS AND REDUCTIONS," provided that if an exception or reduction specifically applies only to a particular benefit of the policy, a statement of such exception or reduction shall be included with the benefit provision to which it applies; and

(6) Each such form, including riders and endorsements, shall be identified by a form number in the lower left-hand corner of the first page thereof; and

(7) It contains no provision purporting to make any portion of the charter, rules, constitution, or bylaws of the insurer a part of the policy unless such portion is set forth in full in the policy, except in the case of the incorporation of, or reference to, a statement of rates or classification of risks, or short-rate table filed with the Commissioner.

(8) It contains no provision excluding from coverage claims that are subject to the Workers' Compensation Act, Article 1 of Chapter 97 of the General Statutes, unless the exclusion extends to only specific medical charges for which the employee, employer, or carrier is liable or responsible according to a final adjudication of the claim under that Article or an order of the North Carolina Industrial Commission approving a settlement agreement entered into under that Article.

(b) If any policy is issued by an insurer domiciled in this State for delivery to a person residing in another state, and if the official having responsibility for the administration of the insurance laws of such other state shall have advised the Commissioner that any such policy is not subject to approval or disapproval by such official, the Commissioner may by ruling require that such policy meet the standards set forth in subsection (a) of this section and in G.S. 58-51-15. (1913, c. 91, s. 2; C.S., s. 6478; 1945, c. 385; 1953, c. 1095, s. 1; 1979, c. 755, s. 8; 2001-216, s. 4; 2001-487, s. 102(b).)

Cross References. — For the Readable Insurance Policies Act, see G.S. 58-38-1 et seq.

Editor's Note. — Session Laws 2001-216, s. 6, provides: "The North Carolina Industrial Commission shall adopt any rules needed to implement this act."

Session Laws 2001-216, s. 6.1, as added by Session Laws 2001-487, s. 102(a), contains a severability clause.

Session Laws 2001-216, s. 7, as rewritten by 2001-487, s. 102(b), makes the amendment to this section by Session Laws 2001-216, s. 4, effective June 15, 2001, and applicable to cases pending on or after that date except those cases in which a health benefit plan has intervened prior to that date.

§ 58-51-10. Right to return policy and have premium refunded.

Every individual or family hospitalization policy, certificate, contract or plan issued for delivery in the State of North Carolina on and after July 1, 1961, must have printed thereon or attached thereto a notice stating substantially: "YOUR POLICY MAY NOT BE IN FORCE WHEN YOU HAVE A CLAIM! PLEASE READ! Your policy was issued based on the information entered in your application, a copy of which is attached to the policy. If, to the best of your knowledge and belief, there is any misstatement in your application or if any information concerning the medical history of any insured person has been omitted, you should advise the Company immediately regarding the incorrect or omitted information; otherwise, your policy may not be a valid contract. RIGHT TO RETURN POLICY WITHIN 10 DAYS. If for any reason you are not satisfied with your policy, you may return it to the Company within 10 days of the date you received it and the premium you paid will be promptly refunded." If a policyholder or certificate holder or purchaser of a contract or plan returns same pursuant to such notice, coverage under such policy, certificate, contract or plan shall become void immediately upon the mailing or delivery of the contract, certificate, policy or plan to the insurance company at its home or branch office or to the agent through whom it was purchased. Coverage shall exist under such policy, certificate, contract or plan within said 10-day period until said mailing or delivery of the contract. (1955, c. 850, s. 10; 1961, c. 962.)

Editor's Note. — Section 12 of Session Laws 1955, c. 850, which enacted this section, made it applicable to hospital and medical service corporations under Chapter 57 (now Articles 65 and 66 of Chapter 58) to the same extent as to insurers under Articles 1 through 64 of this Chapter.

§ 58-51-15. Accident and health policy provisions.

(a) Required Provisions. — Except as provided in subsection (c) of this section each such policy delivered or issued for delivery to any person in this State shall contain the provisions specified in this subsection in the substance of the words that appear in this section. Such provisions shall be preceded individually by the caption appearing in this subsection or, at the option of the insurer, by such appropriate individual or group captions or subcaptions as the Commissioner may approve.

(1) A provision in the substance of the following language:

ENTIRE CONTRACT; CHANGES: This policy, including the endorsements and the attached papers, if any, constitutes the entire contract of insurance. No change in this policy shall be valid until approved by an executive officer of the insurer and unless such approval be endorsed hereon or attached hereto. No agent has authority to change this policy or waive any of its provisions.

(2) A provision in the substance of the following language:

TIME LIMIT ON CERTAIN DEFENSES:

a. After two years from the date of issue or reinstatement of this policy no misstatements except fraudulent misstatements made by the applicant in the application for such policy shall be used to void the policy or deny a claim for loss incurred or disability (as defined in the policy) commencing after the expiration of such two-year period.

The foregoing policy provision may be used in its entirety only in major or catastrophe hospitalization policies and major medical policies each affording benefits of five thousand dollars ($5,000) or more for any one sickness or injury; disability income policies affording benefits of one hundred dollars ($100.00) or more per month for not less than 12 months; and franchise policies. Other policies to which this section applies must delete the words "except fraudulent misstatements."

(The foregoing policy provision shall not be so construed as to affect any legal requirement for avoidance of a policy or denial of a claim during such initial two-year period, nor to limit the application of G.S. 58-51-15(b), (1), (2), (3), (4) and (5) in the event of misstatement with respect to age or occupation or other insurance.)

(A policy which the insured has the right to continue in force subject to its terms by the timely payment of premium:

1. Until at least age 50 or,

2. In the case of a policy issued after age 44, for at least five years from its date of issue, may contain in lieu of the foregoing the

following provisions (from which the clause in parentheses may be omitted at the insurer's option) under the caption "INCONTESTABLE."

After this policy has been in force for a period of two years during the lifetime of the insured (excluding any period during which the insured is disabled), it shall become incontestable as to the statements contained in the application.)

b. This policy contains a provision limiting coverage for preexisting conditions. Preexisting conditions are covered under this policy _____ (insert number of months or days, not to exceed one year) after the effective date of coverage. Preexisting conditions mean "those conditions for which medical advice, diagnosis, care, or treatment was received or recommended within the one-year period immediately preceding the effective date of the person's coverage." Credit for having satisfied some or all of the preexisting condition waiting periods under previous health benefits coverage shall be given in accordance with G.S. 58-68-30.

(3) A provision in the substance of the following language:

GRACE PERIOD: A grace period of _____ (insert a number not less than "7" for weekly premium policies, "10" for monthly premium policies and "31" for all other policies) days will be granted for the payment of each premium falling due after the first premium, during which grace period the policy shall continue in force.

(A policy which contains a cancellation provision may add, at the end of the above provision, subject to the right of the insurer to cancel in accordance with the cancellation provision hereof.

A policy in which the insurer reserves the right to refuse any renewal shall have, at the beginning of the above provision,

Unless not less than five days prior to the premium due date the insurer has delivered to the insured or has mailed to his last address as shown by the record of the insurer written notice of its intention not to renew this policy beyond the period for which the premium has been accepted.)

(4) A provision in the substance of the following language:

REINSTATEMENT: If any renewal premium be not paid within the time granted the insured for payment, a subsequent acceptance of premium by the insurer or by any agent duly authorized by the insurer to accept such premium, without requiring in connection therewith an application for reinstatement, shall reinstate the policy; provided, however, that if the insurer or such agent requires an application for reinstatement and issues a conditional receipt for the premium tendered, the policy will be reinstated upon approval of such application by the insurer, or, lacking such approval, upon the forty-fifth day following the date of such conditional receipt unless the insurer has previously notified the insured in writing of its disapproval of such application. The reinstated policy shall cover only loss resulting from such accidental injury as may be sustained after the date of reinstatement and loss due to such sickness as may begin more than 10 days after such date. In all other respects the insured and insurer shall have the same rights thereunder as they had under the policy immediately before the due date of the defaulted premium, subject to any provisions endorsed hereon or attached hereto in connection with the reinstatement. Any premium accepted in connection with a reinstatement shall be applied to a period for which premium has not been previously paid, but not to any period more than 60 days prior to the date of reinstatement.

(The last sentence of the above provision may be omitted from any policy which the insured has the right to continue in force subject to its terms by the timely payment of premiums:

a. Until at least age 50 or,

b. In the case of a policy issued after age 44, for at least five years from its date of issue.)

(5) A provision in the substance of the following language:

NOTICE OF CLAIM: Written notice of claim must be given to the insurer within 20 days after the occurrence or commencement of any loss covered by the policy, or as soon thereafter as is reasonably possible. Notice given by or on behalf of the insured or the beneficiary to the insurer at _____ (insert the location of such office as the insurer may designate for the purpose), or to any authorized agent of the insurer, with information sufficient to identify the insured, shall be deemed notice to the insurer.

(In a policy providing a loss-of-time benefit which may be payable for at least two years, an insurer may at its option insert the following between the first and second sentences of the above provision:

Subject to the qualifications set forth below, if the insured suffers loss of time on account of disability for which indemnity may be payable for at least two years, he shall, at least once in every six months after having given notice of claim, give to the insurer notice of continuance of said disability, except in the event of legal incapacity. The period of six months following any filing of proof by the insured or any payment by the insurer on account of such claim or any denial of liability in whole or in part by the insurer shall be excluded in applying this provision. Delay in the giving of such notice shall not impair the insured's right to any indemnity which would otherwise have accrued during the period of six months preceding the date on which such notice is actually given.)

(6) A provision in the substance of the following language:

CLAIM FORMS: The insurer, upon receipt of a notice of claim, will furnish to the claimant such forms as are usually furnished by it for filing proofs of loss. If such forms are not furnished within 15 days after the giving of such notice the claimant shall be deemed to have complied with the requirements of this policy as to proof of loss upon submitting, within the time fixed in the policy for filing proofs of loss, written proof covering the occurrence, the character and the extent of the loss for which claim is made.

(7) A provision in the substance of the following language:

PROOFS OF LOSS: Written proof of loss must be furnished to the insurer at its said office in the case of a claim for loss for which this policy provides any periodic payment contingent upon continuing loss within 180 days after the termination of the period for which the insurer is liable and in case of a claim for any other loss within 180 days after the date of such loss. Failure to furnish such proof within the time required shall not invalidate nor reduce any claim if it was not reasonably possible to give proof within such time, provided such proof is furnished as soon as reasonably possible and in no event, except in the absence of legal capacity of the insured, later than one year from the time proof is otherwise required.

(8) A provision in the substance of the following language:

TIME OF PAYMENT OF CLAIMS: Indemnities payable under this policy for any loss other than loss for which this policy provides any period payment will be paid immediately upon receipt of due written proof of such loss. Subject to due written proof of loss, all accrued indemnities for loss for which this policy provides periodic payment will be paid _____ (insert period for payment which must not be less frequently than monthly) and any balance remaining unpaid upon the termination of liability will be paid immediately upon receipt of due written proof.

(9) A provision in the substance of the following language:

PAYMENT OF CLAIMS: Indemnity for loss of life will be payable in accordance with the beneficiary designation and the provisions respecting such payment which may be prescribed herein and effective at the time of payment. If no such designation or provision is then effective, such indemnity shall be payable to the estate of the insured. Any other accrued indemnities unpaid at the insured's death may, at the option of the insurer, be paid either to such beneficiary or to such estate. All other indemnities will be payable to the insured.

(The following provisions, or either of them, may be included with the foregoing provision at the option of the insurer:

If any indemnity of this policy shall be payable to the estate of the insured, or to an insured or beneficiary who is a minor or otherwise not competent to give a valid release, the insurer may pay such indemnity, up to an amount not exceeding $ _____ (insert an amount which shall not exceed three thousand dollars ($3,000)), to any relative by blood or connection by marriage of the insured or beneficiary who is deemed by the insurer to be equitably entitled thereto. Any payment made by the insurer in good faith pursuant to this provision shall fully discharge the insurer to the extent of such payment.

Subject to any written direction of the insured in the application or otherwise all or a portion of any indemnities provided by this policy on account of hospital, nursing, medical, or surgical services, may at the insurer's option and unless the insured requests otherwise in writing not later than the time of filing proofs of such loss, be paid directly to the hospital or person rendering such services; but it is not required that the service be rendered by a particular hospital or person.)

(10) A provision in the substance of the following language:

PHYSICAL EXAMINATIONS AND AUTOPSY: The insurer at its own expense shall have the right and opportunity to examine the person of the insured when and as often as it may reasonably require during the pendency of a claim hereunder and to make an autopsy in case of death where it is not forbidden by law.

(11) A provision in the substance of the following language:

LEGAL ACTIONS: No action at law or in equity shall be brought to recover on this policy prior to the expiration of 60 days after written proof of loss has been furnished in accordance with the requirements of this policy. No such action shall be brought after the expiration of three years after the time written proof of loss is required to be furnished.

(12) A provision in the substance of the following language:

CHANGE OF BENEFICIARY: Unless the insured makes an irrevocable designation of beneficiary, the right to change of beneficiary is reserved to the insured and the consent of the beneficiary or beneficiaries shall not be requisite to surrender or assignment of this policy or to any change of beneficiary or beneficiaries, or to any other changes in this policy.

(The first clause of this provision, relating to the irrevocable designation of beneficiary, may be omitted at the insurer's option.)

(b) Other Provisions. — Except as provided in subsection (c) of this section, no such policy delivered or issued for delivery to any person in this State shall contain provisions respecting the matters set forth below unless such provisions are in the substance of the words that appear in this section. Any such provision contained in the policy shall be preceded individually by the appropriate caption appearing in this subsection or, at the option of the insurer, by such appropriate individual or group captions or subcaptions as the Commissioner may approve.

(1) A provision in the substance of the following language:

CHANGE OF OCCUPATION: If the insured be injured or contract sickness after having changed his occupation to one classified by the insurer as more hazardous than that stated in this policy or while doing for compensation anything pertaining to an occupation so classified, the insurer will pay only such portion of the indemnities provided in this policy as the premium paid would have purchased at the rates and within the limits fixed by the insurer for such more hazardous occupation. If the insured changes his occupation to one classified by the insurer as less hazardous than that stated in this policy, the insurer, upon receipt of proof of such change of occupation, will reduce the premium rate accordingly, and will return the excess pro rata unearned premium from the date of change of occupation or from the policy anniversary date immediately preceding receipt of such proof, whichever is the more recent. In applying this provision, the classification of occupational risk and the premium rates shall be such as have been last filed by the insurer prior to the occurrence of the loss for which the insurer is liable or prior to date of proof of change in occupation with the state official having supervision of insurance in the state where the insured resided at the time this policy was issued; but if such filing was not required, then the classification of occupational risk and the premium rates shall be those last made effective by the insurer in such state prior to the occurrence of the loss or prior to the date of proof of change in occupation.

(2) A provision in the substance of the following language:

MISSTATEMENT OF AGE: If the age of the insured has been misstated, all amounts payable under this policy shall be such as the premium paid would have purchased at the correct age.

(3) A provision in the substance of the following language:

OTHER INSURANCE IN THIS INSURER: If an accident or health or accident and health policy or policies previously issued by the insurer to the insured be in force concurrently herewith, making the aggregate indemnity for _____ (insert type of coverage or coverages) in excess of $ _____ (insert maximum limit of indemnity or indemnities) the excess insurance shall be void and all premiums paid for such excess shall be returned to the insured or to his estate.

Or, in lieu thereof:

Insurance effective at any one time on the insured under a like policy or policies in this insurer is limited to the one such policy elected by the insured, his beneficiary or his estate, as the case may be, and the insurer will return all premiums paid for all other such policies.

(4) A provision in the substance of the following language:

INSURANCE WITH OTHER INSURERS: If there be other valid coverage, not with this insurer, providing benefits for the same loss on a provision of service basis or on an expense incurred basis and of which this insurer has not been given written notice prior to the occurrence or commencement of loss, the only liability under any expense incurred coverage of this policy shall be for such proportion of the loss as the amount which would otherwise have been payable hereunder plus the total of the like amounts under all such other valid coverages for the same loss of which this insurer had notice bears to the total like amounts under all valid coverages for such loss, and for the return of such portion of the premiums paid as shall exceed the pro rata portion for the amount so determined. For the purpose of applying this provision when other coverage is on a provision of service basis, the "like amount" of such other coverage shall be taken as the amount which the services rendered would have cost in the absence of such coverage.

(If the foregoing policy provision is included in a policy which also contains the next following policy provision there shall be added to the caption of the foregoing provision the phrase "_____ EXPENSE INCURRED BENEFITS." The insurer may, at its option, include in this provision a definition of "other valid coverage," approved as to form by the Commissioner, which definition shall be limited in subject matter to coverage provided by organizations subject to regulation by insurance law or by insurance authorities of this or any other state of the United States or any province of Canada, and by hospital or medical service organizations, and to any other coverage the inclusion of which may be approved by the Commissioner. In the absence of such definition such term shall not include group insurance, automobile medical payments insurance, or coverage provided by hospital or medical service organizations or by union welfare plans or employer or employee benefit organizations. For the purpose of applying the foregoing policy provision with respect to any insured, any amount of benefit provided for such insured pursuant to any compulsory benefit statute (including any workers' compensation or employer's liability statute) whether provided by a governmental agency or otherwise shall in all cases be deemed to be "other valid coverage" of which the insurer has had notice. In applying the foregoing policy provisions no third-party liability coverage shall be included as "other valid coverage.")

(5) A provision in the substance of the following language:

INSURANCE WITH OTHER INSURERS: If there be other valid coverage, not with this insurer, providing benefits for the same loss on other than an expense incurred basis and of which this insurer has not been given written notice prior to the occurrence or commencement of loss, the only liability for such benefits under this policy shall be for such proportion of the indemnities otherwise provided hereunder for such loss as the like indemnities of which the insurer had notice (including the indemnities under this policy) bear to the total amount of all like indemnities for such loss, and for the return of such portion of the premium paid as shall exceed the pro rata portion for the indemnities thus determined.

(If the foregoing policy provision is included in a policy which also contains the next preceding policy provision there shall be added to the caption of the foregoing provision the phrase "_____ OTHER BENEFITS." The insurer may, at its option, include in this provision a definition of "other valid coverage," approved as to form by the Commissioner, which definition shall be limited in subject matter to coverage provided by organizations subject to regulation by insurance law or by insurance authorities of this or any other state of the United States or any province of Canada, and to any other coverage the inclusion of which may be approved by the Commissioner. In the absence of such definition such term shall not include group insurance, or benefits provided by union welfare plans or by employer or employee benefit organizations. For the purpose of applying the foregoing policy provision with respect to any insured, any amount of benefit provided for such insured pursuant to any compulsory benefit statute (including any workers' compensation or employer's liability statute) whether provided by a governmental agency or otherwise shall in all cases be deemed to be "other valid coverage" of which the insurer has had notice. In applying the foregoing policy provision no third-party liability coverage shall be included as "other valid coverage.")

(6) A provision in the substance of the following language:

RELATION OF EARNINGS TO INSURANCE: If the total monthly amount of loss of time benefits promised for the same loss under all valid loss of time coverage upon the insured, whether payable on a weekly or monthly basis, shall exceed the monthly earnings of the insured at the time disability commenced or his average monthly earnings for the period of two years immediately preceding a disability for which claim is made, whichever is the greater, the insurer will be liable only for such proportionate amount of such benefits under this policy as the amount of such monthly earnings or such average monthly earnings of the insured bears to the total amount of monthly benefits for the same loss under all such coverage upon the insured at the time such disability commences and for the return of such part of the premiums paid during such two years as shall exceed the pro rata amount of the premiums for the benefits actually paid hereunder; but this shall not operate to reduce the total monthly amount of benefits payable under all such coverage upon the insured below the sum of two hundred dollars ($200.00) or the sum of the monthly benefits specified in such coverages, whichever is the lesser, nor shall it operate to reduce benefits other than those payable for loss of time.

(The foregoing policy provision may be inserted only in a policy which the insured has the right to continue in force subject to its terms by the timely payment of premiums:

a. Until at least age 50 or,

b. In the case of a policy issued after age 44, for at least five years from its date of issue.

The insurer may, at its option, include in this provision a definition of "valid loss of time coverage," approved as to form by the Commissioner, which definition shall be limited in subject matter to coverage provided by governmental agencies or by organizations subject to regulation by insurance law or by insurance authorities of this or any other state of the United States or any province of Canada, or to any other coverage the inclusion of which may be approved by the Commissioner or any combination of such coverages. In the absence of such definition such term shall not include any coverage provided for such insured pursuant to any compulsory benefit statute (including any workers' compensation or employer's liability statute), or benefits provided by union welfare plans or by employer or employee benefit organizations.)

(7) A provision in the substance of the following language:

UNPAID PREMIUM: Upon the payment of a claim under this policy, any premium then due and unpaid or covered by any note or written order may be deducted therefrom.

(8) Repealed by Session Laws 1955, c. 886, s. 1.

(9) A provision in the substance of the following language:

CONFORMITY WITH STATE STATUTES: Any provision of this policy which, on its effective date, is in conflict with the statutes of the state in which the insured resides on such date is hereby amended to conform to the minimum requirements of such statutes.

(10) A provision in the substance of the following language:

ILLEGAL OCCUPATION: The insurer shall not be liable for any loss to which a contributing cause was the insured's commission of or attempt to commit a felony or to which a contributing cause was the insured's being engaged in an illegal occupation.

(11) Repealed by Session Laws 2001-334, s. 4.1, effective October 1, 2001.

(c) Inapplicable or Inconsistent Provisions. — If any provision of this section is in whole or in part inapplicable to or inconsistent with the coverage provided by a particular form of policy the insurer, with the approval of the Commissioner, shall omit from such policy any inapplicable provision or part of a provision, and shall modify any inconsistent provision or part of the provision in such manner as to make the provision as contained in the policy consistent with the coverage provided by the policy.

(d) Order of Certain Policy Provisions. — The provisions which are the subject of subsections (a) and (b) of this section, or any corresponding provisions which are used in lieu thereof in accordance with such subsections, shall be printed in the consecutive order of the provisions in such subsections or, at the option of the insurer, any such provision may appear as a unit in any part of the policy, with other provisions to which it may be logically related, provided the resulting policy shall not be in whole or in part unintelligible, uncertain, ambiguous, abstruse, or likely to mislead a person to whom the policy is offered, delivered or issued.

(e) Third-Party Ownership. — The word "insured," as used in Articles 50 through 55 of this Chapter shall not be construed as preventing a person other than the insured with a proper insurable interest from making application for and owning a policy covering the insured or from being entitled under such a policy to any indemnities, benefits and rights provided therein.

(f) Requirements of Other Jurisdictions.

(1) Any policy of a foreign or alien insurer, when delivered or issued for delivery to any person in this State, may contain any provision which is not less favorable to the insured or the beneficiary than the provisions of Articles 50 through 55 of this Chapter and which is prescribed or required by the law of the state under which the insurer is organized.

(2) Any policy of a domestic insurer may, when issued for delivery in any other state or country, contain any provision permitted or required by the laws of such other state or country.

(g) Filing Procedure. — The Commissioner may make such reasonable rules and regulations concerning the procedure for the filing or submission of policies subject to Articles 50 through 55 of this Chapter as are necessary, proper or advisable to the administration of Articles 50 through 55 of this Chapter. This provision shall not abridge any other authority granted the Commissioner by law.

(h) Preexisting Condition Exclusion Clarification. — Sub-subdivision (a)(2) b. of this section does not apply to:

(1) Policies issued to eligible individuals under G.S. 58-68-60.

(2) Excepted benefits as described in G.S. 58-68-25(b). (1953, c. 1095, s. 2; 1955, c. 850, s. 8; c. 886, s. 1; 1961, c. 432; 1979, c. 755, ss. 9-12; 1983 (Reg. Sess., 1984), c. 1110, s. 13; 1987, c. 864, s. 42; 1987 (Reg. Sess., 1988), c. 975, s. 2; 1991, c. 636, s. 3; c. 720, s. 35; 1993, c. 506, s. 4; c. 553, s. 17; 1995, c. 507, s. 23A.1(g); 1995 (Reg. Sess., 1996), c. 742, s. 27; 1997-259, ss. 7, 7.1; 1999-351, s. 1; 2000-162, s. 4(d); 2001-334, s. 4.1; 2002-187, s. 5.2.)

Cross References. — For the Readable Insurance Policies Act, see G.S. 58-38-1 et seq. As to liability of insurer for loss sustained in consequence of being intoxicated or under the influence, see G.S. 58-51-16.

Effect of Amendments. — Session Laws 2002-187, s. 5.2, effective October 31, 2002, substituted "G.S. 58-68-25(b)" for "G.S. 58-68-25(b)(1), (2), and (4)" in subdivision (h)(2).

Legal Periodicals. — For comment on the 1955 amendments, see 33 N.C.L. Rev. 555 (1955).

For note discussing interpretation of notice provisions in insurance contracts, in light of Great Am. Ins. Co. v. C.G. Tate Constr. Co., 303 N.C. 387, 279 S.E.2d 769 (1981), see 61 N.C.L. Rev. 167 (1982).

CASE NOTES

Anti-subrogation Rule. — Commissioner's promulgation of 11 N.C.A.C. 12.0319, prohibiting subrogation provisions in life or accident and health insurance contracts, supported by G.S. 58-2-40 (right to limit practices injurious to the public) and G.S. 58-50-15(a) (prohibiting provisions less favorable to the insured), did not exceed his statutory authority, even though it may have changed state substantive law, and did not amount to an unconstitutional delegation of legislative powers because statutory provisions (G.S. 58-2-40 and 58-50-15 and this section) and judicial review (available under Chapter 150B) offer adequate procedural safeguards and support the delegation of power to the Commissioner. In re Ruling by N. C. Comm'r of Ins., 134 N.C. App. 22, 517 S.E.2d 134, 1999 N.C. App. LEXIS 665 (1999), cert. denied, appeal dismissed, 351 N.C. 105, 540 S.E.2d 356 (1999).

As to clause excluding from coverage death caused by intentional act of any person, see Patrick v. Pilot Life Ins. Co., 241 N.C. 614, 86 S.E.2d 201 (1955), citing former § 58-253(6).

Accident did not occur "in the course of" the insured's employment, where he had left the work area and had gone off to another area, totally unused in his business, to sleep for 45 minutes and was injured by a falling ceiling fan. The fact that he also owned the sleeping area appears merely fortuitous and does not affect the result. Therefore, he was not excluded from coverage by a policy provision excluding treatment of bodily injuries arising from or in the course of any employment. Dayal v. Provident Life & Accident Ins. Co., 71 N.C. App. 131, 321 S.E.2d 452 (1984).

Applied in Hooks v. Colonial Life & Accident Ins. Co., 43 N.C. App. 606, 259 S.E.2d 567 (1979).

Cited in F & D Co. v. Aetna Ins. Co., 305 N.C. 256, 287 S.E.2d 867 (1982); Johnston County v. McCormick, 65 N.C. App. 63, 308 S.E.2d 872 (1983).

§ 58-51-16. Intoxicants and narcotics.

(a) Except for the payment of benefits for the necessary care and treatment of chemical dependency as provided by law, an accident and health insurer shall not be liable for any loss sustained or contracted in consequence of the insured's being intoxicated or under the influence of any narcotic unless administered on the advice of a physician.

(b) The provision in subsection (a) of this section may not be used with respect to a medical expense policy.

(c) For purposes of this section, "medical expense policy" means an accident and health insurance policy that provides hospital, medical, and surgical expense coverage. (2001-334, s. 4.2.)

Editor's Note. — Session Laws 2001-334, s. 21 makes this section effective October 1, 2001.

Session Laws 2001-334, s. 19 is a severability clause.

§ 58-51-20. Renewability of individual and blanket hospitalization and accident and health insurance policies.

(a) Every individual or blanket family hospitalization policy and accident and health policy, other than noncancelable or nonrenewable policies but including group, blanket and franchise policies, as defined in Articles 1 through 64 of this Chapter, covering less than 10 persons, issued in North Carolina after January 1, 1956, shall include in substance the following provision:

Renewability: This policy is renewable at the option of the policyholder unless sufficient notice of nonrenewal is given the policyholder in writing by the insurer.

Sufficient notice shall be, during the first year of any policy, or during the first year following any lapse and reinstatement, a period of 30 days before the premium due date. After one continuous year of coverage and acceptance of premium for any portion of the second or subsequent year sufficient notice shall be a number of full months most nearly equivalent to one fourth the number of months of continuous coverage from the inception date of the policy, to the date of mailing of the notice: Provided no period of required notice shall exceed two years.

(b) No insurance company issuing individual or blanket family hospitalization or accident and health policies of insurance shall have the right to unilaterally restrict coverage, reduce benefits or increase rates upon any contract of hospitalization or accident and health insurance which is subject to the provisions of this section except as provided herein.

(c) Any hospitalization or accident and health policy reissued or renewed in the name of the insured during the grace period shall be construed to be a continuation of the policy first issued.

(d) The requirements of this section do not apply to a refusal or renewal because of a change of occupation of an insured to one classified by the insurer as uninsurable nor to an increase in rate due to a change of occupation of an insured to a more hazardous occupation. (1955, c. 886, s. 2; 1957, c. 1085, s. 2; 1979, c. 755, s. 13; 1985, c. 666, s. 71; 1989, c. 485, s. 55; 1991, c. 644, s. 27.)

Cross References. — For the Readable Insurance Policies Act, see G.S. 58-38-1 et seq.

CASE NOTES

Constitutionality. — See American Nat'l Ins. Co. v. Ingram, 63 N.C. App. 38, 303 S.E.2d 649, cert. denied, 309 N.C. 819, 310 S.E.2d 348 (1983).

Purpose of Section. — This act was designed to curb the abuse, at that time, of companies collecting premiums, then mass canceling of policies. In order to prevent companies from being locked in on inadequate rates, however, the General Assembly provided a method whereby the company, after giving the proper notice of nonrenewal, could seek a rate increase. American Nat'l Ins. Co. v. Ingram, 63 N.C. App. 38, 303 S.E.2d 649, cert. denied, 309 N.C. 819, 310 S.E.2d 348 (1983).

§ 58-51-25. Policy coverage to continue as to mentally retarded or physically handicapped children.

An individual or group accident and health insurance policy, hospital service policy, or medical service plan policy, delivered or issued for delivery in this State after July 1, 1969, which provides that coverage of a dependent child shall terminate upon attainment of the limiting age for dependent children specified in the policy or contract, shall also provide in substance that attainment of such limiting age shall not operate or terminate the coverage of such child while the child is and continues to be (i) incapable of self-sustaining employment by reason of mental retardation or physical handicap; and (ii) chiefly dependent upon the policyholder or subscriber for support and maintenance: Provided, proof of such incapacity and dependency is furnished to the insurer, hospital service plan corporation, or medical service plan corporation by the policyholder or subscriber within 31 days of the child's attainment of the limiting age and subsequently as may be required by the insurer or corporation, but not more frequently than annually after the child's attainment of the limiting age. (1969, c. 745, s. 1; 1971, c. 1126, s. 1.)

§ 58-51-30. Policies to cover newborn infants, foster children, and adopted children.

(a) As used in this section:

    (1) "Foster child" means a minor (i) over whom a guardian has been appointed by the clerk of superior court of any county in North Carolina; or (ii) the primary or sole custody of whom has been assigned by order of a court of competent jurisdiction;

    (2) "Placement in the foster home" means physically residing with a person appointed as guardian or custodian of a foster child as long as that guardian or sustodian has assumed the legal obligation for total or partial support of the foster child with the intent that the foster child reside with the guardian or custodian on more than a temporary or short-term basis.

    (3) "Placement for adoption" has the same meaning as defined in G.S. 58-51-125(a)(2).

(b) Every health benefit plan, as defined in G.S. 58-3-167, that provides benefits for any sickness, illness, or disability of any minor child or that provides benefits for any medical treatment or service furnished by a health care provider or institution to any minor child shall provide the benefits for those occurrences beginning with the moment of the child's birth if the birth occurs while the plan is in force. Every health benefit plan shall extend coverage to a newborn child without requirements for prior notification unless an additional premium charge to add the dependent is due. If an additional premium charge is due to cover the dependent, the health benefit plan shall cover the newborn child from the moment of birth if the newborn is enrolled within 30 days after the date of birth. Foster children and adopted children shall be treated the same as newborn infants and eligible for coverage on the same basis upon placement in the foster home or placement for adoption. Every health benefit plan shall extend coverage to a foster child or adopted child without requirements for prior notification unless an additional premium charge to add the foster child or adopted child is due. If an additional premium charge is due to cover the foster child or adopted child, the health benefit plan shall cover the foster child or adopted child upon placement in the foster home or placement for adoption if the foster child or adopted child is enrolled within 30 days after the placement in the foster home or placement for adoption.

(c) Benefits in such plans shall be the same for congenital defects or anomalies as are provided for most sicknesses or illnesses suffered by minor children that are covered by the plans. Benefits for congenital defects or anomalies shall specifically include, but not be limited to, all necessary treatment and care needed by individuals born with cleft lip or cleft palate.

(d) No plan shall be approved by the Commissioner under this Chapter that does not comply with this section.

(e) This section applies to insurers governed by Articles 1 through 63 of this Chapter and to corporations governed by Articles 65, 66, and 67 of this Chapter.

(f) This section and G.S. 58-51-125 shall be construed in pari materia. (1973, c. 345, ss. 1, 2; 1981 (Reg. Sess., 1982), c. 1349; 1991, c. 644, s. 12; 1993, c. 504, s. 32; c. 553, s. 18; 1993 (Reg. Sess., 1994), c. 644, s. 2; 2001-334, s. 5.)

Effect of Application for Policy After Birth. — Where a hospital, medical and surgical expense policy issued to a named insured was in effect when she gave birth to a son, and the insured applied after the birth of her son to have the coverage of the policy extended to the son, and the policy was thereafter endorsed to extend coverage to the son, and the premium increased to reflect this new coverage, the provisions of this section did not cause the policy to extend coverage to insured's son back to the moment of his birth, since this section applies only where there is a policy in effect at the birth of a child which provides coverage for the child. Norris v. Home Sec. Life Ins. Co., 42 N.C. App. 719, 257 S.E.2d 647 (1979), decided prior to the 2001 amendment.

§ 58-51-35. Insurers and others to afford coverage to mentally retarded and physically handicapped children.

(a) No insurance company licensed in this State pursuant to the provisions of Articles 1 through 64 of this Chapter and no corporation governed by the provisions of Articles 65 and 66 of this Chapter shall refuse to issue or deliver any individual or group accident and health insurance policy of hospital or medical service plan policy in this State which it is currently issuing for delivery in this State and which affords benefits or coverage for minor children of the applicant, by reason of the physical handicap or mental retardation of any minor children of the applicant; nor shall any such policy issued and delivered in this State carry a higher premium rate or charge or restrict or exclude coverage or benefits by reason of said mental retardation or physical handicap. Provided, however, such policy may exclude benefits, otherwise payable for disability, hospitalization, or medical or other therapeutic expense directly and solely attributable to such mental retardation or such physical handicap.

(b) The Commissioner shall revoke the license of any insurer or any corporation governed by the provisions of Articles 65 and 66 of this Chapter if it fails to comply with the provisions of this section.

(c) The provisions of this section shall apply to corporations governed by the provisions of Articles 65 and 66 of this Chapter. (1973, c. 754, ss. 1, 2; 1991, c. 720, s. 4.)

Cited in Johnston County v. McCormick, 65 N.C. App. 63, 308 S.E.2d 872 (1983).

§ 58-51-37. Pharmacy of choice.

(a) This section shall apply to all health benefit plans providing pharmaceutical services benefits, including prescription drugs, to any resident of North Carolina. This section shall also apply to insurance companies and health maintenance organizations that provide or administer coverages and benefits for prescription drugs. This section shall not apply to any entity that has its own facility, employs or contracts with physicians, pharmacists, nurses, and other health care personnel, and that dispenses prescription drugs from its own pharmacy to its employees and to enrollees of its health benefit plan; provided, however, this section shall apply to an entity otherwise excluded that contracts with an outside pharmacy or group of pharmacies to provide prescription drugs and services. This section shall not apply to any federal program, clinical trial program, hospital or other health care facility licensed pursuant to Chapter 131E or Chapter 122C of the General Statutes, when dispensing prescription drugs to its patients.

(b) As used in this section:

    (1) "Copayment" means a type of cost sharing whereby insured or covered persons pay a specified predetermined amount per unit of service with their insurer paying the remainder of the charge. The copayment is incurred at the time the service is used. The copayment may be a fixed or variable amount.

    (2) "Contract provider" means a pharmacy granted the right to provide prescription drugs and pharmacy services according to the terms of the insurer.

    (3) "Health benefit plan" is as that term is defined in G.S. 58-50-110(11).

    (4) "Insurer" means any entity that provides or offers a health benefit plan.

    (5) "Pharmacy" means a pharmacy registered with the North Carolina Board of Pharmacy.

(c) The terms of a health benefit plan shall not:

    (1) Prohibit or limit a resident of this State, who is eligible for reimbursement for pharmacy services as a participant or beneficiary of a health benefit plan, from selecting a pharmacy of his or her choice when the pharmacy has agreed to participate in the health benefit plan according to the terms offered by the insurer;

    (2) Deny a pharmacy the opportunity to participate as a contract provider under a health benefit plan if the pharmacy agrees to provide pharmacy services that meet the terms and requirements, including terms of reimbursement, of the insurer under a health benefit plan, provided that if the pharmacy is offered the opportunity to participate, it must participate or no provisions of G.S. 58-51-37 shall apply;

    (3) Impose upon a beneficiary of pharmacy services under a health benefit plan any copayment, fee, or condition that is not equally imposed upon all beneficiaries in the same benefit category, class, or copayment level under the health benefit plan when receiving services from a contract provider;

    (4) Impose a monetary advantage or penalty under a health benefit plan that would affect a beneficiary's choice of pharmacy. Monetary advantage or penalty includes higher copayment, a reduction in reimbursement for services, or promotion of one participating pharmacy over another by these methods.

    (5) Reduce allowable reimbursement for pharmacy services to a beneficiary under a health benefit plan because the beneficiary selects a pharmacy of his or her choice, so long as that pharmacy has enrolled with the health benefit plan under the terms offered to all pharmacies in the plan coverage area; or

    (6) Require a beneficiary, as a condition of payment or reimbursement, to purchase pharmacy services, including prescription drugs, exclusively through a mail-order pharmacy.

(d) A pharmacy, by or through a pharmacist acting on its behalf as its employee, agent, or owner, may not waive, discount, rebate, or distort a copayment of any insurer, policy, or plan, or a beneficiary's coinsurance portion of a prescription drug coverage or reimbursement and if a pharmacy, by or through a pharmacist's acting on its behalf as its employee, agent or owner, provides a pharmacy service to an enrollee of a health benefit plan that meets the terms and requirements of the insurer under a health benefit plan, the pharmacy shall provide its pharmacy services to all enrollees of that health benefit plan on the same terms and requirements of the insurer. A violation of this subsection shall be a violation of the Pharmacy Practice Act subjecting the pharmacist as a licensee to disciplinary authority of the North Carolina Board of Pharmacy pursuant to G.S. 90-85.38.

(e) At least 60 days before the effective date of any health benefit plan providing reimbursement to North Carolina residents for prescription drugs, which restricts pharmacy participation, the entity providing the health benefit plan shall notify, in writing, all pharmacies within the geographical coverage area of the health benefit plan, and offer to the pharmacies the opportunity to participate in the health benefit plan. All pharmacies in the geographical coverage area of the plan shall be eligible to participate under identical reimbursement terms for providing pharmacy services, including prescription drugs. The entity providing the health benefit plan shall, through reasonable means, on a timely basis, and on regular intervals in order to effectuate the purposes of this section, inform the beneficiaries of the plan of the names and locations of pharmacies that are participating in the plan as providers of pharmacy services and prescription drugs. Additionally, participating pharmacies shall be entitled to announce their participation to their customers through a means acceptable to the pharmacy and the entity providing the health benefit plans. The pharmacy notification provisions of this section shall not apply when an individual or group is enrolled, but when the plan enters a particular county of the State.

(f) If rebates or marketing incentives are allowed to pharmacies or other dispensing entities providing services or benefits under a health benefit plan, these rebates or marketing incentives shall be offered on an equal basis to all pharmacies and other dispensing entities providing services or benefits under a health benefit plan when pharmacy services, including prescription drugs, are purchased in the same volume and under the same terms of payment. Nothing in this section shall prevent a pharmaceutical manufacturer or wholesale distributor of pharmaceutical products from providing special prices, marketing incentives, rebates, or discounts to different purchasers not prohibited by federal and State antitrust laws.

(g) Any entity or insurer providing a health benefit plan is subject to G.S. 58-2-70. A violation of this section shall subject the entity providing a health benefit plan to the sanctions of revocation, suspension, or refusal to renew license in the discretion of the Commissioner pursuant to G.S. 58-3-100.

(h) A violation of this section creates a civil cause of action for damages or injunctive relief in favor of any person or pharmacy aggrieved by the violation.

(i) The Commissioner shall not approve any health benefit plan providing pharmaceutical services which does not conform to this section.

(j) Any provision in a health benefit plan which is executed, delivered, or renewed, or otherwise contracted for in this State that is contrary to any provision of this section shall, to the extent of the conflict, be void.

(k) It shall be a violation of this section for any insurer or any person to provide any health benefit plan providing for pharmaceutical services to residents of this State that does not conform to the provisions of this section. (1993, c. 293, s. 1.)

Editor's Note. — The number of this section was assigned by the Revisor of Statutes, the number in Session Laws 1993, c. 293, s. 1 having been 58-51-58.

§ 58-51-38. Direct access to obstetrician-gynecologists.

(a) Each health benefit plan shall allow each female plan participant or beneficiary age 13 or older direct access within the health benefit plan, without prior referral, to the health care services of an obstetrician-gynecologist participating in the health benefit plan, within the benefits provided under that health benefit plan pertaining to obstetrician-gynecologist services.

For purposes of this section:
  (1) "Health benefit plan" means an HMO subscriber contract or any preferred provider, exclusive provider, or other managed care arrangement offered under a health benefit plan, as defined in G.S. 58-50-110(11).
  (2) "Health care services" means the full scope of medically necessary services provided by the participating obstetrician-gynecologist in the care of or related to the female reproductive system and breasts, and in performing annual screening, counseling, and immunization for disorders and diseases in accordance with the most current published recommendations of the American College of Obstetricians and Gynecologists, and includes services provided by nurse practitioners, physician's assistants, and certified nurse midwives in collaboration with the obstetrician-gynecologist in the care of the participant or beneficiary.
  (3) "Benefits" are those medical services or other items to which an individual is entitled under the terms of her contract with a health benefit plan, as approved by the Department of Insurance.

(b) Each health benefit plan shall inform female participants and beneficiaries in writing of the provisions of this section. The information shall be provided in benefit handbooks and materials and enrollment materials. (1995, c. 63, s. 1.)

§ 58-51-40. Insurers and others to afford coverage for active medical treatment in tax-supported institutions.

(a) Whenever any policy of insurance governed by Articles 1 through 64 of this Chapter provides for benefits for charges of hospitals or physicians, the policy shall provide for payments of benefits for charges made for medical care rendered in or by duly licensed State tax-supported institutions, including charges for medical care of cerebral palsy, other orthopedic and crippling disabilities, mental and nervous diseases or disorders, mental retardation, alcoholism and drug or chemical dependency, and respiratory illness, on a basis no less favorable than the basis which would apply had the medical care been rendered in or by any other public or private institution or provider. The term "State tax-supported institutions" shall include community mental health centers and other health clinics which are certified as Medicaid providers.

(b) No policy shall exclude payment for charges of a duly licensed State tax-supported institution because of its being a specialty facility for one particular type of illness nor because it does not have an operating room and related equipment for the performance of surgery, but it is not required that benefits be payable for domiciliary or custodial care, rehabilitation, training, schooling, or occupational therapy.

(c) The restrictions and regulations of this section shall not apply to any policy which is individually underwritten or provided for a specific individual and the members of his family as a nongroup policy but shall apply to any group policy of insurance governed by Articles 1 through 64 of this Chapter. (1975, c. 345, s. 1; 1981, c. 816, ss. 1, 2.)

CASE NOTES

Cited in Johnston County v. McCormick, 65 N.C. App. 63, 308 S.E.2d 872 (1983).

§ 58-51-45. Policies to be issued to any person possessing the sickle cell trait or hemoglobin C trait.

No insurance company licensed in this State pursuant to the provisions of Articles 1 through 64 of this Chapter shall refuse to issue or deliver any policy (regardless of whether any of such policies shall be defined as individual, family, group, blanket, franchise, industrial or otherwise) which is currently being issued for delivery in this State, and which affords benefits or coverage for any medical treatment or service authorized or permitted to be furnished by a hospital, clinic, family health plan, neighborhood health plan, health maintenance organization, physician, physician's assistant, nurse practitioner or any medical service facility or personnel by reason of the fact that the person to be insured possesses sickle cell trait or hemoglobin C trait, nor shall any such policy issued and delivered in this State carry a higher premium rate or charge by reason of the fact that the person to be insured possesses said trait. (1975, c. 599, s. 1.)

§ 58-51-50. Coverage for chemical dependency treatment.

(a) As used in this section, the term "chemical dependency" means the pathological use or abuse of alcohol or other drugs in a manner or to a degree that produces an impairment in personal, social or occupational functioning and which may, but need not, include a pattern of tolerance and withdrawal.

(b) Every insurer that writes a policy or contract of group or blanket health insurance or group or blanket accident and health insurance that is issued, renewed, or amended on or after January 1, 1985, shall offer to its insureds benefits for the necessary care and treatment of chemical dependency that are not less favorable than benefits for physical illness generally. Except as provided in subsection (c) of this section, benefits for treatment of chemical dependency shall be subject to the same durational limits, dollar limits, deductibles, and coinsurance factors as are benefits for physical illness generally.

(c) Every group policy or group contract of insurance that provides benefits for chemical dependency treatment and that provides total annual benefits for all illnesses in excess of eight thousand dollars ($8,000) is subject to the following conditions:

    (1) The policy or contract shall provide, for each 12-month period, a minimum benefit of eight thousand dollars ($8,000) for the necessary care and treatment of chemical dependency.

    (2) The policy or contract shall provide a minimum benefit of sixteen thousand dollars ($16,000) for the necessary care and treatment of chemical dependency for the life of the policy or contract.

(d) Provisions for benefits for necessary care and treatment of chemical dependency in group policies or group contracts of insurance shall provide benefit payments for the following providers of necessary care and treatment of chemical dependency:

    (1) The following units of a general hospital licensed under Article 5 of General Statutes Chapter 131E:

        a. Chemical dependency units in facilities licensed after October 1, 1984;

        b. Medical units;

        c. Psychiatric units; and

    (2) The following facilities or programs licensed after July 1, 1984, under Article 2 of General Statutes Chapter 122C:

        a. Chemical dependency units in psychiatric hospitals;

        b. Chemical dependency hospitals;

      c. Residential chemical dependency treatment facilities;

      d. Social setting detoxification facilities or programs;

      e. Medical detoxification or programs; and

  (3) Duly licensed physicians and duly licensed practicing psychologists and certified professionals working under the direct supervision of such physicians or psychologists in facilities described in (1) and (2) above and in day/night programs or outpatient treatment facilities licensed after July 1, 1984, under Article 2 of General Statutes Chapter 122C.

Provided, however, that nothing in this subsection shall prohibit any policy or contract of insurance from requiring the most cost effective treatment setting to be utilized by the person undergoing necessary care and treatment for chemical dependency.

  (e) Coverage for chemical dependency treatment as described in this section shall not be applicable to any group policy holder or group contract holder who rejects the coverage in writing. (1983 (Reg. Sess., 1984), c. 1110, s. 7; 1985, c. 589, s. 43(a), (b); 1989, c. 175, s. 1; 1991, c. 720, s. 64.)

§ 58-51-55. No discrimination against the mentally ill and chemically dependent.

  (a) Definitions. — As used in this section, the term:

  (1) "Mental illness" has the same meaning as defined in G.S. 122C-3(21); and

  (2) "Chemical dependency" has the same meaning as defined in G.S. 58-51-50

with a diagnosis found in the Diagnostic and Statistical Manual of Mental Disorders DSM-3-R or the International Classification of Diseases ICD/9/CM, or a later edition of those manuals.

  (b) Coverage of Physical Illness. — No insurance company licensed in this State under this Chapter shall, solely because an individual to be insured has or had a mental illness or chemical dependency:

  (1) Refuse to issue or deliver to that individual any policy that affords benefits or coverages for any medical treatment or service for physical illness or injury;

  (2) Have a higher premium rate or charge for physical illness or injury coverages or benefits for that individual; or

  (3) Reduce physical illness or injury coverages or benefits for that individual.

  (c) Mental Illness or Chemical Dependency Coverage Not Required. — Nothing in this section requires an insurer to offer coverage for mental illness or chemical dependency, except as provided in G.S. 58-51-50.

  (d) Applicability. — Subsection (b1) of this section applies only to group health insurance contracts, other than excepted benefits as defined in G.S. 58-68-25, covering more than 50 employees. The remainder of this section applies only to group health insurance contracts covering 20 or more employees. For purposes of this section, "group health insurance contracts" include MEWAs, as defined in G.S. 58-49-30(a). (1989, c. 369, s. 3; 1991, c. 720, s. 81; 1997-259, s. 21; 1999-132, s. 4.2.)

Editor's Note. — Subdivision (b1) expired by its own terms on October 1, 2001, and concerned restrictions on policies imposing lesser lifetime or annual dollar limitations on mental health benefits compared to physical illness or injury benefits.

§ 58-51-57. Coverage for mammograms and cervical cancer screening.

(a) Every policy or contract of accident or health insurance, and every preferred provider benefit plan under G.S. 58-50-56, that is issued, renewed, or amended on or after January 1, 1992, shall provide coverage for examinations and laboratory tests for the screening for the early detection of cervical cancer and for low-dose screening mammography. The same deductibles, coinsurance, and other limitations as apply to similar services covered under the policy, contract, or plan shall apply to coverage for examinations and laboratory tests for the screening for the early detection of cervical cancer and low-dose screening mammography.

(a1) As used in this section, "examinations and laboratory tests for the screening for the early detection of cervical cancer" means conventional PAP smear screening, liquid-based cytology, and human papilloma virus (HPV) detection methods for women with equivocal findings on cervical cytologic analysis that are subject to the approval of and have been approved by the United States Food and Drug Administration.

(b) As used in this section, "low-dose screening mammography" means a radiologic procedure for the early detection of breast cancer provided to an asymptomatic woman using equipment dedicated specifically for mammography, including a physician's interpretation of the results of the procedure.

(c) Coverage for low-dose screening mammography shall be provided as follows:

    (1) One or more mammograms a year, as recommended by a physician, for any woman who is at risk for breast cancer. For purposes of this subdivision, a woman is at risk for breast cancer if any one or more of the following is true:

        a. The woman has a personal history of breast cancer;

        b. The woman has a personal history of biopsy-proven benign breast disease;

        c. The woman's mother, sister, or daughter has or has had breast cancer; or

        d. The woman has not given birth prior to the age of 30;

    (2) One baseline mammogram for any woman 35 through 39 years of age, inclusive;

    (3) A mammogram every other year for any woman 40 through 49 years of age, inclusive, or more frequently upon recommendation of a physician; and

    (4) A mammogram every year for any woman 50 years of age or older.

(d) Reimbursement for a mammogram authorized under this section shall be made only if the facility in which the mammogram was performed meets mammography accreditation standards established by the North Carolina Medical Care Commission.

(e) Coverage for the screening for the early detection of cervical cancer shall be in accordance with the most recently published American Cancer Society guidelines or guidelines adopted by the North Carolina Advisory Committee on Cancer Coordination and Control. Coverage shall include the examination, the laboratory fee, and the physician's interpretation of the laboratory results. Reimbursements for laboratory fees shall be made only if the laboratory meets accreditation standards adopted by the North Carolina Medical Care Commission. (1991, c. 490, s. 1; 1997-519, s. 3.3; 2003-186, s. 2.)

Cervical Cancer Elimination Task Force. — Session Laws 2003-176, ss. 1(a) through 1(k), establish a standing ad hoc task force on cervical cancer elimination to serve the

Advisory Committee on Cancer Coordination and Control. The ad hoc task force shall be called the Cervical Cancer Elimination Task Force (Task Force). For full text of note pertaining to the Task Force, see G.S. 130A-33.50.

Session Laws 2003-186, s. 6, provides, in part, that for the purposes of this act, renewal of a health benefit plan is presumed to occur on each anniversary of the date on which coverage was first effective on the person or persons covered by the health benefit plan.

Effect of Amendments. — Session Laws 2003-186, s. 2, effective January 1, 2004, and applicable to all health benefit plans that are delivered, issued for delivery, or renewed on and after that date, in the section heading, substituted "cervical cancer screening" for "pap smears"; in the first and last sentences of subsection (a), substituted "examinations and laboratory tests for the screening for the early detection of cervical cancer" for "pap smears"; added subsection (a1); and rewrote subsections (d) and (e).

§ 58-51-58. Coverage for prostate-specific antigen (PSA) tests.

(a) Every policy or contract of accident and health insurance, and every preferred provider benefit plan under G.S. 58-50-56, that is issued, renewed, or amended on or after January 1, 1994, shall provide coverage for prostate-specific antigen (PSA) tests or equivalent tests for the presence of prostate cancer. The same deductibles, coinsurance, and other limitations as apply to similar services covered under the policy, contract, or plan shall apply to coverage for prostate-specific antigen (PSA) tests or equivalent tests for the presence of prostate cancer.

(b) As used in this section, "prostate-specific antigen (PSA) tests or equivalent tests for the presence of prostate cancer" means serological tests for determining the presence of prostate cytoplasmic protein (PSA) and the generation of antibodies to it, as a novel marker for prostatic disease.

(c) Coverage for prostate-specific antigen (PSA) tests or equivalent tests for the presence of prostate cancer shall be provided when recommended by a physician. (1993, c. 269, s. 1; 1997-519, s. 3.4.)

§ 58-51-59. Coverage of certain prescribed drugs for cancer treatment.

(a) No policy or contract of accident or health insurance, and no preferred provider benefit plan under G.S. 58-50-56, that is issued, renewed, or amended on or after January 1, 1994, and that provides coverage for prescribed drugs approved by the federal Food and Drug Administration for the treatment of certain types of cancer shall exclude coverage of any drug on the basis that the drug has been prescribed for the treatment of a type of cancer for which the drug has not been approved by the federal Food and Drug Administration. The drug, however, must be approved by the federal Food and Drug Administration and must have been proven effective and accepted for the treatment of the specific type of cancer for which the drug has been prescribed in any one of the following established reference compendia:

(1) The American Medical Association Drug Evaluations;
(2) The American Hospital Formulary Service Drug Information; or
(3) The United States Pharmacopeia Drug Information.

(b) Notwithstanding subsection (a) of this section, coverage shall not be required for any experimental or investigational drugs or any drug that the federal Food and Drug Administration has determined to be contraindicated for treatment of the specific type of cancer for which the drug has been prescribed.

(c) This section shall apply only to cancer drugs and nothing in this section shall be construed, expressly or by implication, to create, impair, alter, limit, notify, enlarge, abrogate, or prohibit reimbursement for drugs used in the treatment of any other disease or condition. (1993, c. 506, s. 4.1; 1997-519, s. 3.5.)

Editor's Note. — The number of this section was assigned by the Revisor of Statutes, the number in Session Laws 1993, c. 506, s. 4 having been 58-51-58.

§ 58-51-60. Meaning of term "preexisting conditions" in certain policies.

At the time of issuing any new policy of individual or family hospitalization insurance or individual accident and health insurance to insureds over age 65, the term "preexisting conditions," or its equivalent in said policy shall include only conditions specifically eliminated by rider. (1955, c. 850, s. 5.)

Editor's Note. — Section 12 of Session Laws 1955, c. 850, made this section applicable to hospital and medical service corporations under Chapter 57 (now Articles 65 and 66 of Chapter 58) to the same extent as to insurers under Articles 1 through 64 of this Chapter.

§ 58-51-61. Coverage for certain treatment for diabetes.

(a) Every policy or contract of accident or health insurance, and every preferred provider benefit plan under G.S. 58-50-56, that is issued, renewed, or amended on or after October 1, 1997, shall provide coverage for medically appropriate and necessary services, including diabetes outpatient self-management training and educational services, and equipment, supplies, medications, and laboratory procedures used to treat diabetes. Diabetes outpatient self-management training and educational services shall be provided by a physician or a health care professional designated by the physician. The insurer shall determine who shall provide and be reimbursed for the diabetes outpatient self-management training and educational services. The same deductibles, coinsurance, and other limitations as apply to similar services covered under the policy, contract, or plan shall apply to the diabetes coverage required under this section.

(b) For the purposes of this section, "physician" is a person licensed to practice in this State under Article 1 or Article 7 of Chapter 90 of the General Statutes. (1997-225, s. 1; 1997-519, s. 3.11.)

Editor's Note. — Session Laws 1997-225, s. 4, provides: "Nothing in this act shall apply to specified accident, specified disease, hospital indemnity, or long-term care health insurance policies."

Legal Periodicals. — For 1997 legislative survey, see 20 Campbell L. Rev. 469.

§ 58-51-62. Coverage for reconstructive breast surgery following mastectomy.

(a) Every policy or contract of accident and health insurance, and every preferred provider benefit plan under G.S. 58-50-56 that provides coverage for mastectomy shall provide coverage for reconstructive breast surgery following a mastectomy. The coverage shall include coverage for all stages and revisions of reconstructive breast surgery performed on a nondiseased breast to establish symmetry if reconstructive surgery on a diseased breast is performed, as well as coverage for prostheses and physical complications in all stages of mastectomy, including lymphademas. The same deductibles, coinsurance, and other limitations as apply to similar services covered under the policy, contract, or plan shall apply to coverage for reconstructive breast surgery. Reconstruction of the nipple/areolar complex following a mastectomy is covered without regard to the lapse of time between the mastectomy and the reconstruction, subject to the approval of the treating physician.

(b) As used in this section, the following terms have the meanings indicated:

(1) "Mastectomy" means the surgical removal of all or part of a breast as a result of breast cancer or breast disease.

(2) "Reconstructive breast surgery" means surgery performed as a result of a mastectomy to reestablish symmetry between the two breasts, and includes reconstruction of the mastectomy site, creation of a new breast mound, and creation of a new nipple/areolar complex. "Reconstructive breast surgery" also includes augmentation mammoplasty, reduction mammoplasty, and mastopexy of the nondiseased breast.

(c) A policy, contract, or plan subject to this section shall not:

(1) Deny coverage described in subsection (a) of this section on the basis that the coverage is for cosmetic surgery;

(2) Deny to a woman eligibility or continued eligibility to enroll or to renew coverage under the terms of the contract, policy, or plan, solely for the purpose of avoiding the requirements of this section;

(3) Provide monetary payments or rebates to a woman to encourage her to accept less than the minimum protections available under this section;

(4) Penalize or otherwise reduce or limit the reimbursement of an attending provider because the provider provided care to an individual participant or beneficiary in accordance with this section; or

(5) Provide incentives, monetary or otherwise, to an attending provider to induce the provider to provide care to an individual participant or beneficiary in a manner inconsistent with this section.

(d) Written notice of the availability of the coverage provided by this section shall be delivered to every policyholder under an individual policy, contract, or plan and to every certificate holder under a group policy, contract, or plan upon initial coverage under the policy, contract, or plan and annually thereafter. The notice required by this subsection may be included as a part of any yearly informational packet sent to the policyholder or certificate holder. (1997-312, s. 1; 1997-456, s. 40(a); 1997-519, s. 3.9; 1999-351, s. 3.1; 2001-334, s. 13.1.)

Editor's Note. — Session Laws 1997-312, s. 6, provides: "Nothing in this act shall apply to specified accident, specified disease, hospital indemnity, or long-term care health insurance policies."

§ 58-51-65. Industrial sick benefit insurance defined.

Industrial sick benefit insurance is hereby defined as that form of insurance for which premiums are payable weekly and which provides for the payment of a weekly indemnity on account of sickness or accident in addition to a benefit in case of death. Such death benefit shall not exceed one hundred and fifty dollars ($150.00). There shall be a provision for the payment of weekly premium, eighty percent (80%) of which shall be allocated for the purchase of sick and accident coverages and twenty percent (20%) thereof for the purchase of death benefits. (1945, c. 385.)

CASE NOTES

Cited in Johnston County v. McCormick, 65 N.C. App. 63, 308 S.E.2d 872 (1983).

§ 58-51-70. Industrial sick benefit insurance; provisions.

Policies issued under the industrial sick benefit plan shall contain the substance of provisions contained in G.S. 58-51-15 and in addition shall contain the following:

    (1) A provision for grace for the payment of the additional premium or assessment or proportion thereof for such death benefits of not less than four weeks during which period the death benefit shall continue in force;

    (2) A provision for incontestability of the death benefit coverage after not more than two years except for

        a. Nonpayment of premiums, and

        b. Misstatement of age;

    (3) A provision that the death benefit is noncancellable by the company except for nonpayment of premium.

The Commissioner may approve any form of certificate to be issued under the industrial sick benefit plan which omits or modifies any of the provisions hereinbefore required, if he deems such omission or modification suitable for the character of such insurance and not unjust to the persons insured thereunder. (1945, c. 385; 1953, c. 1095, s. 4; 1979, c. 755, s. 14.)

Cross References. — For the Readable Insurance Policies Act, see G.S. 58-38-1 et seq.

Legal Periodicals. — For note discussing interpretation of notice provisions in insurance contracts, in light of Great Am. Ins. Co. v. C.G. Tate Constr. Co., 303 N.C. 387, 279 S.E.2d 769 (1981), see 61 N.C.L. Rev. 167 (1982).

CASE NOTES

Cited in Johnston County v. McCormick, 65 N.C. App. 63, 308 S.E.2d 872 (1983).

§ 58-51-75. Blanket accident and health insurance defined.

(a) Any policy or contract of insurance against death or injury resulting from accident or from accidental means which insures a group of persons conforming to the requirements of one of the following subdivisions (1) to (7), inclusive, shall be deemed a blanket accident policy. Any policy or contract which insures a group of persons conforming to the requirements of one of the following subdivisions (3), (5), (6) or (7) against total or partial disability, excluding such disability from accident or from accidental means, shall be deemed a blanket health insurance policy. Any policy or contract of insurance which combines the coverage of blanket accident insurance and of blanket health insurance on such a group of persons shall be deemed a blanket accident and health insurance policy:

    (1) Under a policy or contract issued to any railroad, steamship, motorbus or airplane carrier of passengers, which shall be deemed the policyholder, a group defined as all persons who may become such passengers may be insured against death or bodily injury either while, or as a result of, being such passengers.

    (2) Under a policy or contract issued to an employer, or the trustee of a fund established by the employer, who shall be deemed the policyholder, covering any group of employees defined by reference to exceptional hazards incident to such employment, insuring such employee against death or bodily injury resulting while, or from, being exposed to such exceptional hazard.

(3) Under a policy or contract issued to a college, school or other institution of learning or to the head or principal thereof, who or which shall be deemed the policyholder.

(4) Under a policy or contract issued in the name of any volunteer fire department, which shall be deemed the policyholder, covering all of the members of such department.

(5) Under a policy or contract issued to and in the name of an incorporated or unincorporated association of persons having a common interest or calling, which association shall be deemed the policyholder, having not less than 25 members, and formed for purposes other than obtaining insurance, covering all of the members of such association.

(6) Under a policy or contract issued to the head of a family, who shall be deemed the policyholder, whereunder the benefits thereof shall provide for the payment by the insurer of amounts for expenses incurred by the policyholder on account of hospitalization or medical or surgical aid for himself, his spouse, his child or children, or other persons chiefly dependent on him for support and maintenance.

(7) Under a policy or contract issued in the name of any municipal or county recreation commission or department which shall be deemed the policyholder.

(b) All benefits under any blanket accident, blanket health or blanket accident and health insurance policy shall be payable to the person insured, or to his designated beneficiary or beneficiaries, or to his estate, except that if the person insured be a minor, such benefits may be made payable to his parent, guardian, or other person actually supporting him, or to a person or persons chiefly dependent upon him for support and maintenance.

(c) Nothing contained in this section shall be deemed to affect the legal liability of policyholders for the death of or injury to, any such member of such group. (1945, c. 385; 1947, c. 721; 1953, c. 1095, s. 5; 1961, c. 603.)

Legal Periodicals. — For comment on the 1947 amendment, see 25 N.C.L. Rev. 437 (1947).

§ 58-51-80. Group accident and health insurance defined.

(a) Any policy or contract of insurance against death or injury resulting from accident or from accidental means which covers more than one person except blanket accident policies as defined in G.S. 58-51-75, shall be deemed a group accident insurance policy. Any policy or contract which insures against disablement, disease or sickness of the insured (excluding disablement which results from accident or from accidental means) and which covers more than one person, except blanket health insurance policies as defined in G.S. 58-51-75, shall be deemed a group health insurance policy or contract. Any policy or contract of insurance which combines the coverage of group accident insurance and of group health insurance shall be deemed a group accident and health insurance policy. No policy or contract of group accident, group health or group accident and health insurance, and no certificates thereunder, shall be delivered or issued for delivery in this State unless it conforms to the requirements of subsection (b).

(b) No policy or contract of group accident, group health or group accident and health insurance shall be delivered or issued for delivery in this State unless the group of persons thereby insured conforms to the requirements of the following subdivisions:

(1) Under a policy issued to an employer, principal, or to the trustee of a fund established by an employer or two or more employers in the same industry or kind of business, or by a principal or two or more

principals in the same industry or kind of business, which employer, principal, or trustee shall be deemed the policyholder, covering, except as hereinafter provided, only employees, or agents, of any class or classes thereof determined by conditions pertaining to employment, or agency, for amounts of insurance based upon some plan which will preclude individual selection. The premium may be paid by the employer, by the employer and the employees jointly, or by the employee; and where the relationship of principal and agent exists, the premium may be paid by the principal, by the principal and agents, jointly, or by the agents. If the premium is paid by the employer and the employees jointly, or by the principal and agents jointly, or by the employees, or by the agents, the group shall be structured on an actuarially sound basis.

(1a) Under a policy issued to an association or to a trust or to the trustee or trustees of a fund established, created, or maintained for the benefit of members of one or more associations. The association or associations shall have at the outset a minimum of 500 persons and shall have been organized and maintained in good faith for purposes other than that of obtaining insurance; shall have been in active existence for at least five years; and shall have a constitution and bylaws that provide that (i) the association or associations hold regular meetings not less than annually to further purposes of the members; (ii) except for credit unions, the association or associations collect dues or solicit contributions from members; and (iii) the members, other than associate members, have voting privileges and representation on the governing board and committees. The policy is subject to the following requirements:

　　a. The policy may insure members of the association or associations, employees of the association or associations, or employees of members, or one or more of the preceding or all of any class or classes for the benefit of persons other than the employee's employer.

　　b. The premium for the policy shall be paid from funds contributed by the association or associations, or by employer members, or by both, or from funds contributed by the covered persons or from both the covered persons and the association, associations, or employer members.

　　c. Repealed by Session Laws 1997-259, s. 8.

(1b) Under a policy issued to a creditor as defined in G.S. 58-57-5 who shall be deemed the policyholder, to insure debtors as defined in G.S. 58-57-5 of the creditor to provide indemnity for payments becoming due on a specific loan or other credit transaction as defined in G.S. 58-51-100, with or without insurance against death by accident, subject to the following requirements:

　　a. The debtors eligible for insurance under the policy shall be all of the debtors of the creditor whose indebtedness is repayable in installments, or all of any class or classes thereof determined by conditions pertaining to the indebtedness or to the purchase giving rise to the indebtedness. The policy may provide that the term "debtors" shall include the debtors of one or more subsidiary corporations, and the debtors of one or more affiliated corporations, proprietors or partnerships if the business of the policyholder and of such affiliated corporations, proprietors or partnerships is under common control through stock ownership, contract or otherwise.

　　b. The premium for the policy shall be paid from the creditor's funds, from charges collected from the insured debtors, or from both. A policy on which part or all of the premium is to be derived from the collection from the insured debtors or identifiable charges not required of uninsured debtors shall not include, in the class or classes of debtors eligible for insurance, debtors under obligations outstanding at its date of issue without evidence of individual insurability unless the group is structured on an actuarially sound basis. A policy on which no part of the premium is to be derived from the collection of such identifiable charges must insure all eligible debtors, or all except any as to whom evidence of individual insurability is not satisfactory to the insurer.

    c. The policy may be issued only if the group of eligible debtors is then receiving new entrants at the rate of at least 100 persons yearly, or may reasonably be expected to receive at least 100 new entrants during the first policy year, and only if the policy reserves to the insurer the right to require evidence of individual insurability if less than seventy-five percent (75%) of the new entrants become insured.

    d. Premiums for this coverage shall be actuarially equivalent to the rates authorized under Article 57 of Chapter 58 of the General Statutes for credit accident and health insurance.

  (2), (3) Repealed by Session Laws 1997-259, s. 8.

  (c) The term "employees" as used in this section shall be deemed to include, for the purposes of insurance hereunder, employees of a single employer, the officers, managers, and employees of the employer and of subsidiary or affiliated corporations of a corporation employer, and the individual proprietors, partners, and employees of individuals and firms of which the business is controlled by the insured employer through stock ownership, contract or otherwise. With the exception of disability income insurance, employees shall be added to the group coverage no later than 90 days after their first day of employment. Employment shall be considered continuous and not be considered broken except for unexcused absences from work for reasons other than illness or injury. The term "employee" is defined as a nonseasonal person who works on a full-time basis, with a normal work week of 30 or more hours and who is otherwise eligible for coverage, but does not include a person who works on a part-time, temporary, or substitute basis. The term "employer" as used herein may be deemed to include the State of North Carolina, any county, municipality or corporation, or the proper officers, as such, of any unincorporated municipality or any department or subdivision of the State, county, such corporation, or municipality determined by conditions pertaining to the employment.

  (d) The term "agents" as used in this section shall be deemed to include, for the purposes of insurance hereunder, agents of a single principal who are under contract to devote all, or substantially all, of their time in rendering personal services for such principal, for a commission or other fixed or ascertainable compensation.

  (e) The benefits payable under any policy or contract of group accident, group health and group accident and health insurance shall be payable to the employees, or agents, or to some beneficiary or beneficiaries designated by the employee or agent, other than the employer or principal, but if there is no designated beneficiary as to all or any part of the insurance at the death of the employee or agent, then the amount of insurance payable for which there is no designated beneficiary shall be payable to the estate of the employee or agent, except that the insurer may in such case, at its option, pay such insurance to any one or more of the following surviving relatives of the employee or agent: wife, husband, mother, father, child, or children, brothers or sisters; and except that payment of benefits for expenses incurred on account of hospitalization or medical or surgical aid, as provided in subsection (f), may be made by the insurer to the hospital or other person or persons furnishing such aid. Payment so made shall discharge the insurer's obligation with respect to the amount of insurance so paid.

(f) Any policy or contract of group accident, group health or group accident and health insurance may include provisions for the payment by the insurer of benefits to the employee or agent of the insured group, on account of hospitalization or medical or surgical aid for himself, his spouse, his child or children, or other persons chiefly dependent upon him for support and maintenance.

(g) Any policy or contract of group accident, group health or group accident and health insurance may provide for readjustment of the rate of premium based on the experience thereunder at the end of the first year, or at any time during any subsequent year based upon at least 12 months of experience: Provided that any such readjustment after the first year shall not be made any more frequently than once every six months. Any rate adjustment must be preceded by a 45-day notice to the contract holder before the effective date of any rate increase or any policy benefit revision. A notice of nonrenewal shall be given to the contract holder 45 days prior to termination. Any refund under any plan for readjustment of the rate of premium based on the experience under group policies and any dividend paid under the policies may be used to reduce the employer's or principal's contribution to group insurance for the employees of the employer, or the agents of the principal, and the excess over the contribution by the employer, or principal, shall be applied by the employer, or principal, for the sole benefit of the employees or agents.

(h) Nothing contained in this section applies to any contract issued by any corporation defined in Article 65 of this Chapter. (1945, c. 385; 1947, c. 721; 1951, c. 282; 1953, c. 1095, ss. 6, 7; 1987, c. 752, s. 19; 1989, c. 485, s. 41; c. 775, ss. 1, 2; 1991, c. 644, s. 11; c. 720, s. 88; 1991 (Reg. Sess., 1992), c. 837, s. 4; 1993, c. 408, ss. 3, 3.1; c. 409, s. 14; 1995, c. 507, ss. 23A.1(c), 23A.1(d); 1997-259, ss. 8, 9; 2000-132, s. 1; 2003-221, s. 12.)

Effect of Amendments. — Session Laws 2003-221, s. 12, effective June 19, 2003, added "With the exception of disability income insurance," at the beginning of the second sentence of subsection (c).

Legal Periodicals. — For comment on the 1947 amendment, see 25 N.C.L. Rev. 437 (1947).

CASE NOTES

Applied in Stainback v. Investor's Consol. Ins. Co., 64 N.C. App. 197, 306 S.E.2d 532 (1983).

Cited in Johnston County v. McCormick, 65 N.C. App. 63, 308 S.E.2d 872 (1983).

§ 58-51-81. Group accident and health insurance for public school students.

(a) Notwithstanding G.S. 58-51-80, a policy of group accident, health, or accident and health insurance may be delivered or issued to a local board of education or to any of its schools, as policyholder, covering only students for amounts of insurance based upon some plan that will preclude individual selection. The premium may be paid by the board, jointly by the board and the students or any other persons on behalf of the students, or by the students and any other persons on behalf of the students. In addition to the authority granted in G.S. 115C-47(6), any board may establish fees for the payment of premiums by or on behalf of the covered students.

(b) Entities subject to Articles 65 and 67 of this Chapter may provide their products in the same manner described in subsection (a) of this section. (1993 (Reg. Sess., 1994), c. 716, s. 1.)

§ 58-51-85. Group or blanket accident and health insurance; approval of forms and filing of rates.

No policy of group or blanket accident, health or accident and health insurance shall be delivered or issued for delivery in this State unless the form of the policy contracts including the master policy contract, the individual certificates thereunder, the applications for the contract, and a schedule of the premium rates pertaining to such form or forms, have been filed with and the forms approved by the Commissioner. (1945, c. 385; 1991, c. 720, s. 34.)

§ 58-51-90. Definition of franchise accident and health insurance.

Accident and health insurance on a franchise plan is hereby declared to be that form of accident and health insurance issued to five or more employees of any corporation, copartnership or individual employer or any governmental corporation, agency or department thereof, or 10 or more members of any trade or professional association or of a labor union or of any other association where such association or union has a constitution or bylaws and is formed in good faith for purposes other than that of obtaining insurance, where such persons, with or without their dependents, are issued the same form of an individual policy varying only as to amounts and kinds of coverage applied for by such persons, under an arrangement whereby the premiums on such policies may be paid to the insurer periodically by the employer, with or without payroll deductions, or by the association for its members, or by some designated person acting on behalf of such employer or association. The provisions of this section shall not be construed so as to repeal G.S. 58-51-75 and 58-51-80 or any parts thereof. (1947, c. 721; 1961, c. 646.)

Legal Periodicals. — For brief comment on this section, see 25 N.C.L. Rev. 438 (1947).

§ 58-51-95. Approval by Commissioner of forms, classification and rates; hearing; exceptions.

(a) No policy of insurance against loss or expense from the sickness, or from the bodily injury or death by accident of the insured shall be issued or delivered to any person in this State nor shall any application, rider or endorsement be used in connection therewith until a copy of the form thereof and of the classification of risks and the premium rates, or, in the case of cooperatives or assessment companies the estimated cost pertaining thereto, have been filed with the Commissioner.

(b) No such policy shall be issued, nor shall any application, rider or endorsement be used in connection therewith, until the expiration of 90 days after it has been so filed unless the Commissioner shall sooner give his written approval thereto.

(c) The Commissioner may within 90 days after the filing of any such form, disapprove such form

    (1) If the benefits provided therein are unreasonable in relation to the premium charged, or

(2) If it contains a provision or provisions which are unjust, unfair, inequitable, misleading, deceptive or encourage misrepresentation of such policy.

(d) If the Commissioner shall notify the insurer which has filed any such form that it does not comply with the provisions of this section or sections, it shall be unlawful thereafter for such insurer to issue such form or use it in connection with any policy. In such notice the Commissioner shall specify the reasons for his disapproval and state that a hearing will be granted within 20 days after request in writing by the insurer.

(e) The Commissioner may at any time, after a hearing of which not less than 20 days' written notice shall have been given to the insurer, withdraw his approval of any such form on any of the grounds stated in this section. It shall be unlawful for the insurer to issue such form or use it in connection with any policy after the effective date of such withdrawal of approval. The notice of any hearing called under this paragraph shall specify the matters to be considered at such hearing and any decision affirming disapproval or directing withdrawal of approval under this section shall be in writing and shall specify the reasons therefor: Provided, that the provisions of this section shall not apply to workers' compensation insurance, accidental death or disability benefits issued supplementary to life insurance or annuity contracts, medical expense benefits under liability policies or to group accident and health insurance.

(f) An insurer may increase rates chargeable on policies subject to this section, other than noncancellable policies, with the approval of the Commissioner if the Commissioner finds that the rates are not excessive, not inadequate, and not unfairly discriminatory; and exhibit a reasonable relationship to the benefits provided by the policies. The approved rates shall be guaranteed by the insurer, as to the policyholders affected by the rates, for a period of not less than 12 months; or as an alternative to the insurer giving the guarantee, the approved rates may be applicable to all policyholders at one time if the insurer chooses to apply for that relief with respect to those policies no more frequently than once in any 12-month period. The rates shall be applicable to all policies of the same type; provided that no rate increase may become effective for any policy unless the insurer has given the policyholder written notice of the rate revision 45 days before the effective date of the revision. The policyholder must then pay the revised rate in order to continue the policy in force. The Commissioner may adopt reasonable rules, after notice and hearing, to require the submission of supporting data and such information as the Commissioner considers necessary to determine whether the rate revisions meet these standards. In adopting the rules under this subsection, the Commissioner may require identification of the types of rating methodologies used by filers and may also address issue age or attained age rating, or both; policy reserves used in rating; and other recognized actuarial principles of the NAIC, the American Academy of Actuaries, and the Society of Actuaries. (1951, c. 784; 1979, c. 755, s. 15; 1989, c. 485, s. 56; 1991, c. 636, s. 3; c. 720, s. 4; 2001-334, s. 17.3.)

Cross References. — For the Readable Insurance Policies Act, see G.S. 58-38-1 et seq.

Legal Periodicals. — For brief comment on this section, see 29 N.C.L. Rev. 398 (1951).

§ 58-51-100. Credit accident and health insurance.

Credit accident and health insurance is declared to be insurance against death or personal injury by accident or by any specified kind or kinds of accident, and insurance against sickness, ailment, or bodily injury of a debtor who may be indebted to any person, firm, or corporation extending credit to such debtor. The amount of credit accident and health insurance written shall not exceed the installment payment. (1953, c. 1096, s. 2; 1961, c. 1071.)

CASE NOTES

Legislative Intent. — The legislature intended to provide for uniformity of coverage by requiring that all policies of "credit accident and health insurance" issued in the State of North Carolina cover "death or personal injury by accident" as well as "sickness, ailment or bodily injury." Newbold v. Globe Life Ins. Co., 50 N.C. App. 628, 274 S.E.2d 905 (1981).

One Type of Insurance Defined by Section. — The phrase "against death or personal injury by accident" and the phrase "against sickness, ailment or bodily injury" are conjunctive and together define one type of insurance. Newbold v. Globe Life Ins. Co., 50 N.C. App. 628, 274 S.E.2d 905 (1981).

Coverage of Credit, Accident and Health Insurance Policies. — In an action to recover on a policy of credit life and disability insurance issued by defendant, where defendant alleged that no charge was made for life insurance but only for disability insurance and therefore that the death of plaintiff's decedent was not the event against which the policy insured, the trial court properly entered judgment for plaintiff, since all policies of "credit, accident and health insurance" issued in the State of North Carolina cover "death or personal injury by accident" as well as "sickness, ailment or bodily injury." Newbold v. Globe Life Ins. Co., 50 N.C. App. 628, 274 S.E.2d 905 (1981).

Applied in Community Bank v. McKenzie, 32 N.C. App. 68, 230 S.E.2d 788 (1977).

Cited in State ex rel. Comm'r of Ins. v. Integon Life Ins. Co., 28 N.C. App. 7, 220 S.E.2d 409 (1975).

§ 58-51-105. Hospitalization insurance defined.

Hospitalization insurance is declared to be any form of accident and health insurance which provides indemnity or payment for expenses incurred due to or in connection with hospitalization of the insured, or his dependents. (1953, c. 1096, s. 3.)

§ 58-51-110. Renewal, discontinuance, or replacement of group health insurance.

(a) This section applies to group accident, group health, or group accident and health policies or certificates that are delivered, issued for delivery, renewed, or used in this State which provide hospital, surgical, or major medical expense insurance, or any combination of these coverages, on an expense incurred or service basis. It specifically includes a certificate issued under a policy that was issued to a trust located out of this State, but which includes participating employers located in this State. Renewal of these policies or certificates is presumed to occur on the anniversary date that the coverage was first effective on the employees of the employer.

(b) Whenever a contract described in subsection (a) of this section is replaced by another group contract within 15 days of termination of coverage of the previous group contract, the liability of the succeeding insurer for insuring persons covered under the previous group contract is:

 (1) Each person who is eligible for coverage in accordance with the succeeding insurer's plan of benefits, regardless of any other provisions of the new group contract relating to active employment or hospital confinement or pregnancy, shall be covered by the succeeding insurer's plan of benefits; and

 (2) Each person not covered under the succeeding insurer's plan of benefits in accordance with subdivision (b)(1) of this section must nevertheless be covered by the succeeding insurer if that person was validly covered, including benefit extension, under the prior plan on the date of discontinuance and if the person is a member of the class of persons eligible for coverage under the succeeding insurer's plan.

875

(1989, c. 775, s. 3; 1991, c. 720, s. 88; 1991 (Reg. Sess., 1992), c. 837, s. 4; 2001-334, s. 6.)

§ 58-51-115. Coordination of benefits with Medicaid.

(a) As used in this section and in G.S. 58-51-120 and G.S. 58-51-125:
  (1) "Health benefit plan" means any accident and health insurance policy or certificate; a nonprofit hospital or medical service corporation contract; a health maintenance organization subscriber contract; a plan provided by a multiple employer welfare arrangement; the Teachers' and State Employees' Comprehensive Major Medical Plan under Chapter 135 of the General Statutes; or a plan provided by another benefit arrangement. "Health benefit plan" does not mean a Medicare supplement policy as defined in G.S. 58-54-1(5).
  (2) "Health insurer" means any health insurance company subject to Articles 1 through 63 of this Chapter, including a multiple employee welfare arrangement, and any corporation subject to Articles 65 and 67 of this Chapter; a group health plan, as defined in section 607(1) of the Employee Retirement Income Security Act of 1974; and the Teachers' and State Employees' Comprehensive Major Medical Plan under Chapter 135 of the General Statutes.

(b) No health insurer shall take into account that an individual is eligible for or is provided medical assistance in this or any other state under 42 U.S.C. § 1396a (section 1902 of the Social Security Act) in insuring that individual or making payments under its health benefit plan for benefits to that individual or on that individual's behalf. (1993 (Reg. Sess., 1994), c. 644, s. 1; 1995, c. 193, s. 43; 1999-293, s. 9.)

OPINIONS OF ATTORNEY GENERAL

Medical Child Support Provisions. — The medical child support enforcement provisions of House Bill 1563, 1993 (Reg. Sess. 1994) N.C. Session Laws Ch. 644, are inapplicable to the North Carolina Teachers' and State Employees' Comprehensive Major Medical Plan and the governmental entities whose employees and retirees, along with their dependents, are eligible for coverage under the Plan or its HMO option. Medical child support orders nonetheless may be enforced directly against State employees and retirees who fail to enroll, or maintain coverage for, their eligible dependent children under the State Health Plan in accordance with the provisions of G.S. 50-13.4(f), 50-13.9 and 50-13.11. See opinion of Attorney General to Patricia Crawford, Associate General Counsel, University of North Carolina at Chapel Hill, — N.C.A.G. — (August 10, 1995).

§ 58-51-116. ERISA plans may not require Medicaid to pay first.

An employee benefit plan as defined in ERISA shall not include any provision which, because an individual is provided or is eligible for benefits or service pursuant to a State plan under Title XIX of the Social Security Act (Medicaid), has the effect of limiting or excluding coverage or payment for any health care for that individual under the terms of the employee benefit plan, provided that the individual is one who would otherwise be covered or entitled to benefits or services under the employee benefit plan. (1993, c. 321, s. 238.1; 2001-446, s. 4.3.)

Editor's Note. — This section was formerly numbered G.S. 58-50-151. It was recodified as G.S. 58-51-116 by Session Laws 2001-446, s. 4.3, effective July 1, 2002, and applicable to health benefit plans that are in effect, delivered, issued for delivery, or renewed on or after that date.

Session Laws 2001-446, s. 7, is a severability clause.

Session Laws 2001-446, s. 8, provides that nothing in this act obligates the General Assembly to appropriate funds to implement this act.

§ 58-51-120. Coverage of children.

(a) No health insurer shall deny enrollment of a child under the health benefit plan of the child's parent on any of the following grounds:

(1) The child was born out of wedlock.

(2) The child is not claimed as a dependent on the parent's federal income tax return.

(3) The child does not reside with the parent or in the insurer's service area.

(b) If a parent is required by a court or administrative order to provide health benefit plan coverage for a child, and the parent is eligible for family health benefit plan coverage through a health insurer, the health insurer:

(1) Must allow the parent to enroll, under the family coverage, a child who is otherwise eligible for the coverage without regard to any enrollment season restrictions.

(2) Must enroll the child under family coverage upon application of the child's other parent or the Department of Health and Human Services in connection with its administration of the Medical Assistance or Child Support Enforcement Program if the parent is enrolled but fails to make application to obtain coverage for the child.

(3) May not disenroll or eliminate coverage of the child unless the health insurer is provided satisfactory written evidence that:

a. The court or administrative order is no longer in effect; or

b. The child is or will be enrolled in comparable health benefit plan coverage through another health insurer, which coverage will take effect not later than the effective date of disenrollment.

(c) If a child has health benefit plan coverage through the health insurer of a noncustodial parent, that health insurer shall do all of the following:

(1) Provide such information to the custodial parent as may be necessary for the child to obtain benefits through that coverage.

(2) Permit the custodial parent (or the health care provider, with the custodial parent's approval) to submit claims for covered services without the approval of the noncustodial parent.

(3) Make payments on claims submitted in accordance with subdivision (2) of this subsection directly to the custodial parent, the provider, or the Department of Health and Human Services.

(d) No health insurer may impose requirements on any State agency that has been assigned the rights of an individual eligible for medical assistance under Medicaid and covered for health benefits from the insurer that are different from requirements applicable to an agent or assignee of any other individual so covered. (1993 (Reg. Sess., 1994), c. 644, s. 1; 1997-443, s. 11A.118(a).)

§ 58-51-125. Adopted child coverage.

(a) Definitions. — As used in this section:

(1) "Child" means, in connection with any adoption or placement for adoption of the child, an individual who has not attained 18 years of age as of the date of the adoption or placement for adoption.

(2) "Placement for adoption" means the assumption and retention by a person of a legal obligation for total or partial support of a child in

anticipation of the adoption of the child. The child's placement with a person terminates upon the termination of such legal obligations.

(b) Coverage Effective Upon Placement for Adoption. — If a health benefit plan provides coverage for dependent children of persons covered by the plan, the plan shall provide benefits to dependent children placed with covered persons for adoption under the same terms and conditions that apply to the natural, dependent children of covered persons, irrespective of whether the adoption has become final.

(c) Restrictions Based on Preexisting Conditions at Time of Placement for Adoption Prohibited. — A health benefit plan may not restrict coverage under the plan of any dependent child adopted by a covered person, or placed with a covered person for adoption, solely on the basis of any preexisting condition of the child at the time that the child would otherwise become eligible for coverage under the plan, if the adoption or placement for adoption occurs while the covered person is eligible for coverage under the plan. (1993 (Reg. Sess., 1994), c. 644, s. 1.)

§ 58-51-130. Standards for disability income insurance policies.

(a) Definitions. — As used in this section:
  (1) "Disability income insurance policy" or "policy" means a policy of accident and health insurance that provides payments when the insured is unable to work because of illness, disease, or injury.
  (2) "Policy" includes the certificates referred to in subsection (b) of this section.

(b) Applicability. — This section applies to all policies used in this State, including certificates issued under group policies that are used in this State. This section also applies to a certificate issued under a policy issued and delivered to a trust or to an association outside of this State and covering persons residing in this State.

(c) Disclosure Standards. — Every disability income insurance policy shall include provisions, where applicable, addressing:
  (1) Terms of renewability.
  (2) Initial and subsequent conditions of eligibility.
  (3) Nonduplication of coverage.
  (4) Preexisting conditions.
  (5) Probationary periods.
  (6) Elimination periods.
  (7) Requirements for replacement.
  (8) Recurrent conditions.
  (9) Definitions of terms.

(d) Preexisting Conditions. — If an insurer does not seek a prospective insured's medical history in the application or enrollment process, the insurer shall not deny a claim for disabilities that commence more than 24 months after the effective date of the insured person's coverage on the grounds the disability is caused by a preexisting condition. A policy shall not define a preexisting condition more restrictively than "a condition for which medical advice, diagnosis, care, or treatment was received or recommended within the 24-month period immediately preceding the effective date of coverage of the insured person."

(e) Exceptions. — Nothing in this section prohibits an insurer from:
  (1) Using an application or enrollment form designed to elicit the medical history of a prospective insured.
  (2) Underwriting based on answers on the form according to the insurer's established standards.

(3) Contesting the answers in accordance with G.S. 58-51-15(a)(2)a.

(f) Required Provisions. — Each policy shall include:

    (1) A description of the principal benefits and coverage provided in the policy.

    (2) A statement of the exceptions, reductions, and limitations contained in the policy.

    (3) A statement of the renewal provisions, including any reservation by the insurer of a right to change premiums.

(g) Other Applicable Provisions. — G.S. 58-51-95(f) applies to individual policies and G.S. 58-51-80(g) applies to group policies.

(h) Other Income Sources. — If a policy contains a provision that provides for integration of benefits with other income sources, it shall include a definition of what is considered other income sources and a complete description of how benefits will be reduced by other income sources, if at all. No disability income policy shall provide that the amount of any disability benefit paid to the insured shall be reduced by reason of any cost-of-living increase, designated as such under the federal Social Security Act, if the cost-of-living increase occurs during the period for which benefits are payable. (1999-351, s. 2.)

ARTICLE 52.

Joint Action to Insure Elderly.

§ 58-52-1. Definitions.

Wherever used in this Article, the following terms shall have the respective meanings hereinafter set forth or indicated, unless the context otherwise requires:

    (1) "Association" means a voluntary unincorporated association formed for the sole purpose of enabling joint and cooperative action to provide accident and health insurance in accordance with this Article in this or any other State having legislation enabling the issuance of insurance of the type provided in this Article.

    (2) "Insurer" means any insurance company which is authorized under Articles 1 through 64 of this Chapter to transact accident and health insurance business in this State. (1963, c. 1125.)

§ 58-52-5. Joint action to insure persons 65 years of age or over and their spouses permitted; associations of insurers; individual and group policies.

Notwithstanding any other provisions of Articles 1 through 64 of this Chapter or any other law which may be inconsistent herewith, any insurer may join with one or more other insurers to plan, develop, underwrite, offer, sell and provide to or for any resident person of this State, or of another state if permitted by the laws of such other state, who is 65 years of age or over and to the spouse of such person, insurance against financial loss from accident or sickness, or both. Such insurance may also cover an employer's nonresident employees and nonresident retired employees 65 years of age or older and their spouses, provided such employees are regularly employed within this State or were so employed at the time of their retirement. Such insurance may be offered, issued and administered through an association of two or more insurers which association is formed for the purpose of offering, selling, issuing and administering such insurance, and may be in the form of a policy insuring a resident who is 65 years of age or older, and the spouse of such resident, if any, or in the form of a group policy insuring residents 65 years of age or older and the spouses of such residents, or in both forms. On such insurance each insurer shall be severally liable for a percentage of the risks determined under the articles of association of the association. The insurer members of such association may agree with respect to premium rates, policy provisions, commission rates and other matters within the scope of this Article. (1963, c. 1125; 1965, c. 677; 1991, c. 720, s. 72.)

§ 58-52-10. Regional plans authorized.

If "over 65" accident and health insurance plans exist or hereafter come into existence in other states pursuant to legislative authority similar to that herein given, North Carolina insurers may jointly participate with insurers of such other states in forming a regional plan to carry out the purposes of this Article. Any association formed for the operation of a regional plan shall be exempt from the provisions of G.S. 58-3-85 and may engage in business in North Carolina through its insurer members only, without being separately licensed. (1963, c. 1125.)

§ 58-52-15. Forms and rate manuals subject to § 58-51-1; disapproval of rates.

The forms of the policies, applications, certificates or other evidence of insurance coverage and the rate manual showing rates, rules and classification of risks applicable thereto shall be subject to the applicable provisions of G.S. 58-51-1. The Commissioner may disapprove the premium rates for such insurance, or any class thereof, if he finds that such rates are by reasonable assumptions excessive in relation to the benefits provided. In determining whether such rates by reasonable assumptions are excessive in relation to the benefits provided, the Commissioner shall give due consideration to past and prospective claim experience on such insurance, or other comparable insurance, within and outside this State, and to fluctuations in such claim experience, to a reasonable risk charge, to contribution to surplus and contingency funds, to past and prospective expenses, both within and outside this State, and to all other relevant factors within and outside this State, including any differing operating methods of the insurers joining in the issue of such insurance. In the event of any such disapproval, the decision of the Commissioner shall be subject to review under G.S. 58-2-75. In exercising the powers conferred by this section, the Commissioner shall not be bound by any other requirements of Articles 1 through 64 of this Chapter with respect to standard provisions required to be included in the forms of the policies, applications, certificates or other evidence of insurance coverage filed with the Commissioner. (1963, c. 1125.)

§ 58-52-20. Organization of associations of insurers; powers; annual statements; mutual insurers may participate.

An association formed for the purposes of this Article shall adopt articles of association for the organization, administration and regulation of its affairs, which articles of association and any amendments thereto shall be filed within 30 days of adoption of same with the Commissioner. Such association may establish requirements for membership of insurers, hold title to property, incur expenses for advertising, soliciting and administering such insurance, including payment of salary or compensation to persons employed by it, enter into contracts, limit the liability of and among its members, and shall be subject to the provisions of G.S. 1-69.1.

Such association shall file annually with the Commissioner, on such date and in such form as the Commissioner may prescribe, a statement with respect to its operations.

For the purpose of implementing joint action of insurers in furnishing accident and health insurance coverage to persons 65 years of age and older and their spouses, in accordance with the intent of this Article as expressed herein, insurers operating on a mutual plan, or on any other membership basis, may participate in such a plan, and the persons insured through the plan shall not be entitled to membership in any such insurer nor shall they be entitled to any dividend rights, voting rights, or any other rights peculiar to mutual insurance policyholders and participants in membership insurance plans. (1963, c. 1125; 1991, c. 720, s. 4.)

§ 58-52-25. No additional licensing required.

Accident and health insurance authorized by this Article and offered by or through an association formed for the purpose of this Article may be solicited and offered directly by such association, any insurer member of such association, and by or through any person authorized by the Department to sell accident and health insurance in this State, without any additional license being required. (1963, c. 1125; 1991, c. 720, s. 60.)

ARTICLE 53.

Group Health Insurance Continuation and Conversion Privileges.

Part 1. Continuation.

§ 58-53-1. Definitions.

As used in this Article, the following terms have the meanings specified:
  (1) "Group policy" means a group accident and health insurance policy issued by an insurance company and a group contract issued by a service corporation or health maintenance organization or similar corporation or organization.
  (2) "Individual policy" or "converted policy" means an individual health insurance policy issued by an insurance company or an individual contract issued by a service corporation or health maintenance organization or similar corporation or organization.
  (3) "Insurance" and "insured" refer to coverage under a group policy, individual policy or converted policy on a premium-paying basis, and do not include coverage provided by reason of a disability extension.
  (4) "Insurer" means the entity issuing a group policy or an individual or converted policy.
  (5) "Medicare" means Title XVIII of the United States Social Security Act as added by the Social Security Amendments of 1965 or as later amended or superseded.
  (5a) "Member" or "employee" includes an insured spouse or dependent of a member or of an employee.
  (6) "Premium" includes any premium or other consideration payable for coverage under a group or individual policy.

(7) "Reasonable and customary" means the most frequently used level of charge made for the supplies or for a specific service in the geographic subarea in which such supplies or services are received, of like kind or by physicians, or other practitioners, with similar qualifications. (1981, c. 706, s. 1; 1983, c. 142, s. 1; 1997-259, s. 10.)

§ 58-53-5. Continuation of group hospital, surgical, and major medical coverage after termination of employment or membership.

A group policy delivered or issued for delivery in this State that insures employees or members for hospital, surgical or major medical insurance on an expense incurred or service basis under this Chapter, other than for specific diseases or for accidental injuries only, shall provide that employees or members whose coverage under the group policy would otherwise terminate because of termination of active employment or membership, or termination of membership in the eligible class or classes under the policy, shall be entitled to continue their hospital, surgical, and medical insurance under that group policy, for themselves and their eligible spouses and dependents with respect to whom they were insured on the date of termination, subject to all of the group policy's terms and conditions and to the conditions specified in this Part. Provided, the terms and conditions set forth in this Part are intended as minimum requirements and shall not be construed to impose additional or different requirements upon those group hospital, surgical, or major medical plans that provide continuation benefits equal to or better than those required in this Part. (1981, c. 706, s. 1; 1997-259, s. 11.)

§ 58-53-10. Eligibility.

Continuation shall only be available to an employee or member who has been continuously insured under the group policy, or for similar benefits under any other group policy that it replaced, during the period of three consecutive months immediately before the date of termination. The employee or member may elect continuation for a period of not fewer than 60 days after the date of termination or loss of eligibility. The employee or member shall make the first contribution upon the election to continue coverage, and the coverage shall be retroactive to the date of termination or loss of eligibility. (1981, c. 706, s. 1; 2001-334, s. 7.1.)

§ 58-53-15. Exception.

Continuation shall not be available for any person who is or could be covered by any other arrangement of hospital, surgical, or medical coverage for individuals in a group, whether insured or uninsured, within 31 days immediately following the date of termination; or whose insurance terminated because he failed to pay any required contribution for the insurance. (1981, c. 706, s. 1.)

§ 58-53-20. Benefits not included.

Continuation is not required to include dental, vision care, or prescription drug benefits, or any other benefits provided under the group policy in addition to its hospital, surgical, or major medical benefits. (1981, c. 706, s. 1.)

§ 58-53-25. Notification to employee.

In addition to the notification requirement set forth in G.S. 58-53-40, notification may be included on insurance identification cards or may be given by the employer, orally or in writing as a part of the exit process from the employment. (1981, c. 706, s. 1.)

§ 58-53-30. Payment of premiums.

An employee or member electing continuation must pay to the group policyholder or his employer, in advance, the amount of contribution required by the policyholder or employer, but not more than one hundred two percent (102%) of the full group rate for the insurance applicable under the group policy on the due date of each payment. The employee or member may not be required to pay the amount of the contribution less often than monthly. In order to be eligible for continuation of coverage, the employee or member must make a written election of continuation, on a form furnished by the group policyholder or by the insurer. (1981, c. 706, s. 1; 1999-273, s. 1; 2001-334, s. 7.2.)

§ 58-53-35. Termination of continuation.

(a) Continuation of insurance under the group policy for any person shall terminate on the earliest of the following dates:
   (1) The date 18 months after the date the employee's or member's insurance under the policy would otherwise have terminated because of termination of employment or members;
   (2) The date ending the period for which the employee or member last makes his required contribution, if he discontinues his contributions;
   (3) The date the employee or member becomes or is eligible to become covered for similar benefits under any arrangement of coverage for individuals in a group, whether insured or uninsured;
   (4) The date on which the group policy is terminated or, in the case of a multiple employer plan, the date his employer terminates participation under the group master policy. When this occurs the employee or member shall have the privilege described in G.S. 58-53-45 if the date of termination precedes that on which his actual continuation of insurance under that policy would have terminated. The insurer that insured the group before the date of termination shall make a converted policy available to the employee or member.
(b) Notwithstanding subdivision (a)(4) of this section, if the employer replaces the group policy with another group policy, the employee is entitled to continue under the successor group policy for any unexpired period of continuation to which the employee is entitled. (1981, c. 706, s. 1; 1983, c. 142, s. 2; 1993, c. 529, s. 3.8; 1997-259, s. 12.)

Legal Periodicals. — For survey of 1981 administrative law, see 60 N.C.L. Rev. 1165 (1982).

§ 58-53-40. Notification.

A notification of the continuation privilege shall be included in each individual certification of coverage. (1981, c. 706, s. 1.)

Part 2. Conversion.

§ 58-53-45. Right to obtain individual policy upon termination of group hospital, surgical or major medical coverage.

A group policy delivered or issued for delivery in this State that insures employees or members for hospital, surgical, or medical insurance on an expense incurred or service basis under Articles 1 through 67 of this Chapter other than for specific diseases or for accidental injuries only, shall provide that an employee or member whose insurance under the group policy has been terminated shall be entitled to have a converted policy issued to him by the insurer under whose group policy he was last insured, without evidence of insurability, subject to the terms and conditions specified in this Part. Provided, the terms and conditions set forth in this Part are intended as minimum requirements and shall not be construed to impose additional or different requirements upon those group hospital, surgical, or major medical plans already in force, or hereafter placed into effect, that provide conversion benefits equal to or better than those required in this Part. (1981, c. 706, s. 1.)

§ 58-53-50. Restrictions.

A converted policy shall not be available to an employee or member if termination of his insurance under the group policy occurred because:
 (1) Of termination of employment or membership and either he was not entitled to continuation of group coverage under Part 1 of this Article or failed to elect such continuation;
 (2) He failed to make timely payment of any required contribution for the cost of continuation of insurance;
 (3) He had not been continuously covered under the group policy or for similar benefits under any other group policy that it replaced during the period of three consecutive months immediately prior to termination of active employment ending with such termination;
 (4) The group policy terminated or an employer's participation terminated, and the insurance is replaced by similar coverage under another group policy within 31 days of date of termination; or
 (5) He failed to continue his insurance for the entire maximum period of 18 months following termination of active employment as provided for in Part 1 of this Article, unless that failure to continue was because of change of insurer by the employer and the change of insurer was consummated during the one year continuation period. In that event the employee or member shall be entitled to be issued a converted policy by the insurer that provided the group policy to the employer before the change of insurer. (1981, c. 706, s. 1; 1983, c. 142, s. 3; 1993 (Reg. Sess., 1994), c. 569, s. 9; 1997-259, s. 13.)

§ 58-53-55. Time limit.

In order to be eligible for conversion, written application and the first premium payment for the converted policy must be made to the insurer not later than 31 days after the date of termination of insurance provided under Part 1 of this Article. The effective date of the converted policy shall be the day following the later of:
 (1) The termination of insurance under the group policy when it is not replaced by one providing similar coverage within 31 days of the termination date of the immediately prior group plan; or

(2) The termination of the period of continued coverage under the group policy or policies. (1981, c. 706, s. 1; 1993 (Reg. Sess., 1994), c. 569, s. 10; 1997-259, s. 14.)

§ 58-53-60. Premium.

(a) The premium for the converted policy or group conversion trust certificate shall be determined in accordance with the insurer's table of premium rates applicable to the age and class of risk to be covered under that policy and to the type and amount of insurance provided.

(b) All insurers licensed to do business in this State, who issue conversion policies or group conversion trust certificates under this Part, have the right to increase that element of the premium that applies to hospital room and board benefit increases provided for in G.S. 58-53-95(5) by an amount proportionate to the increase promulgated by the Commissioner. Such premium increases shall be filed with the Commissioner.

(c) All premium rates and adjustments to premium rates for converted policies or group conversion trust certificates shall be reasonable and must be filed with and approved by the Commissioner prior to use. A premium rate shall be deemed to be reasonable if the insurer demonstrates that the premium charged is expected to produce an incurred loss ratio to earned premiums of not less than sixty percent (60%) for all policies or group conversion trust certificates providing similar benefits offered and issued by the insurer. If an insurer experiences an incurred loss ratio of greater than eighty percent (80%) for all such policies, it shall be deemed reasonable for that insurer to increase premium rates to a level that will produce a prospective incurred loss ratio of no greater than eighty percent (80%), and the insurer shall file such new rates with the Commissioner not more often than once a year. (1981, c. 706, s. 1; 1983, c. 669; 1995, c. 517, s. 30.)

§ 58-53-65. Coverage.

The converted policy shall cover the employee or member and his eligible dependents who were covered by the group policy on the date of termination of insurance. At the option of the insurer, a separate converted policy may be issued to cover any such eligible dependent. (1981, c. 706, s. 1.)

§ 58-53-70. Exclusions.

An insurer shall not be required to issue a converted policy covering any person if such person is or can be covered by Medicare. Furthermore, an insurer shall not be required to issue a converted policy covering any person if:

    (1)a. Such person is covered for similar benefits by another hospital, surgical, medical or major medical expense insurance policy, or hospital or medical service subscriber contract or medical practice or other prepayment plan, or by any other plan or program;

        b. Such person is or could be covered for similar benefits, whether or not covered for such benefits, under any arrangement of coverage for individuals in a group, whether insured or uninsured; or

        c. Similar benefits are provided for or available to such person, whether or not covered for such benefits, by reason of any State or federal law; and

    (2) The benefits under sources of the kind referred to in subdivision (1)a of this section for such person, or benefits provided or available under sources of the kind referred to in subdivisions (1)b and (1)c of this section for such person, together with the converted policy's benefits

would result in overinsurance according to the insurer's standards for overinsurance; or

(3) An enrollee's enrollment in a health maintenance organization has been terminated for cause in accord with the terms of the enrollee's evidence of coverage or the health maintenance organization's contract with the group. (1981, c. 706, s. 1; 1991, c. 195, s. 2.)

§ 58-53-75. Information.

A converted policy may provide that an insurer may at any time request information of an insured policyholder with respect to any person covered thereunder as to whether he is covered for the similar benefits described in G.S. 58-53-70(1)a or is or could be covered for the similar benefits described in G.S. 58-53-70(1)b and 58-53-70(1)c. The converted policy may provide that as of any premium due date an insurer may refuse to renew the policy or the coverage of any insured person for the following reasons only:

(1) Either those similar benefits for which such person is or could be covered, together with the converted policy's benefits, would result in overinsurance according to the insurer's standards for overinsurance, or the policyholder of the converted policy fails to provide the requested information;

(2) Fraud or material misrepresentation in applying for any benefits under the converted policy;

(3) Eligibility of any insured person for coverage under Medicare, or under any other State or federal law providing benefits substantially similar to those provided by the converted policy; or

(4) Termination of an enrollee's enrollment in a health maintenance organization for cause in accord with the terms of the enrollee's evidence of coverage or the health maintenance organization's contract with the group. (1981, c. 706, s. 1; 1991, c. 195, s. 3.)

§ 58-53-80. Excess benefits.

An insurer shall not be required to issue a converted policy providing benefits in excess of the equivalent value of hospital, surgical, or major medical insurance under the group policy from which conversion is made. (1981, c. 706, s. 1.)

§ 58-53-85. Preexisting conditions.

The converted policy shall not exclude, as a preexisting condition, any condition covered by the group policy. However, the converted policy may provide for a reduction of its hospital, surgical or medical benefits by the amount of any such benefits payable under the group policy after the individual's insurance terminates thereunder. The converted policy may also provide that during the first policy year the benefits payable under the converted policy, together with the benefits payable under the group policy, shall not exceed those that would have been payable had the individual's insurance under the group policy remained in force and effect. (1981, c. 706, s. 1.)

§ 58-53-90. Basic coverage plans.

(a) Subject to the provisions of this Article, if the group insurance policy from which conversion is made insures the employee or member for basic hospital and surgical expense insurance, the employee or member shall be entitled to obtain a converted policy providing, at his option, coverage on an expense incurred basis under any of the following plans:

    (1) Plan A:

        a. Hospital room and board daily expense benefits in a maximum dollar amount approximating the average semiprivate rate charged in the major metropolitan area of this State, for a maximum duration of 70 days;

        b. Miscellaneous hospital expense benefits up to a maximum amount of 10 times the hospital room and board daily expense benefits; and

        c. Surgical expense benefits according to a surgical procedures schedule consistent with those customarily offered by the insurer under group or individual health insurance policies and providing a maximum benefit of eight hundred dollars ($800.00).

    (2) Plan B:

        Identical to Plan A, except that (i) the maximum hospital room and board daily expense benefit is seventy-five percent (75%) of the corresponding Plan A maximum and (ii) the surgical schedule maximum is six hundred dollars ($600.00).

    (3) Plan C:

        Identical to Plan A, except that (i) the maximum hospital room and board daily expense benefit is fifty percent (50%) of the corresponding Plan A maximum and (ii) the surgical schedule maximum is four hundred dollars ($400.00).

  (b) The maximum dollar amount for the maximum hospital room and board daily expense benefit of Plan A shall be determined by the Commissioner and may be redetermined by him from time to time as to converted policies issued subsequent to such redetermination. Such redetermination shall not be made more often than once in three years. The Plan A maximum, and the corresponding maximums in Plans B and C, shall be rounded to the nearest multiple ten dollars ($10.00), provided that rounding may be to the next higher or lower multiple of ten dollars ($10.00) if otherwise exactly midway between. (1981, c. 706, s. 1.)

§ 58-53-95. Major medical plans.

Subject to the provisions of this Article, if the group policy from which conversion is made insures the employee or member for major medical expense insurance, the employee or member shall be entitled to obtain a converted policy providing catastrophic or major medical coverage under a plan meeting the following requirements:

    (1) A maximum benefit at least equal to either, at the option of the insurer,

        a. A maximum payment per covered person for all covered medical expenses incurred during that person's lifetime, equal to the lesser of the maximum benefit provided under the group policy or one hundred thousand dollars ($100,000); or

        b. A maximum payment for each unrelated injury or sickness, equal to the lesser of the maximum benefit provided under the group policy or one hundred thousand dollars ($100,000).

    (2) Payment of benefits at the rate of eighty percent (80%) of covered medical expenses that are in excess of the deductible, until twenty percent (20%) of such expenses in a benefit period reaches one thousand dollars ($1,000), after which benefits will be paid at the rate of one hundred percent (100%) during the remainder of such benefit period. Payment of benefits for outpatient treatment of mental illness, if provided in the converted policy, may be at a lesser rate but not less than fifty percent (50%).

(3) A deductible for each benefit period which, at the option of the insurer, shall be (i) the sum of the benefits deductible and one hundred dollars ($100.00), or (ii) the corresponding deductible in the group policy. The term "benefits deductible," as used in this Part, means the value of any benefits provided on an expense incurred basis that are provided with respect to covered medical expenses by any other group or individual hospital, surgical, or medical insurance policy or medical practice or other prepayment plan, or any other plan, or program whether insured or uninsured, or by reason of any State or federal law and if, pursuant to G.S. 58-53-100, the converted policy provides both basic hospital or surgical coverage and major medical coverage, the value of such basic benefits.

If the maximum benefit is determined by subdivision (1)a of this section, the insurer may require that the deductible be satisfied during a period of not less than three months if the deductible is one hundred dollars ($100.00) or less, and not less than six months if the deductible exceeds one hundred dollars ($100.00).

(4) The benefit period shall be each calendar year when the maximum benefit is determined by subdivision (1)a of this section or 24 months when the maximum benefit is determined by subdivision (1)b of this section.

(5) The term "covered medical expenses," as used in this Part, shall include, in the case of hospital room and board charges, at a minimum the lesser of the dollar amount in G.S. 58-53-90(a)(1) and the average semiprivate room and board rate for the hospital in which the individual is confined, and at a minimum twice such amount for charges in an intensive care unit. Any surgical procedures schedule shall be consistent with those customarily offered by the insurer under group or individual health insurance policies and must provide at least a one thousand two hundred dollar ($1,200) maximum. (1981, c. 706, s. 1.)

§ 58-53-100. Alternative plans.

At the option of the insurer, such plans of benefits set forth in G.S. 58-53-90 and 58-53-95 may be provided under one policy. Instead of providing the plans of benefits set forth in G.S. 58-53-90 and 58-53-95, the insurer may elect to provide a policy of comprehensive medical expense benefits without first dollar coverage. Said policy shall conform to the requirements of G.S. 58-53-95; provided, however, that an insurer electing to provide such a policy shall make available the following deductible options: one hundred dollars ($100.00), five hundred dollars ($500.00), and one thousand dollars ($1,000). Alternatively, such a policy may provide for deductible options equal to the greater of the benefits deductible and the amount specified in the preceding sentence. (1981, c. 706, s. 1.)

§ 58-53-105. Insurer option.

The insurer may, at its option, offer alternative plans for group health conversion in addition to those required by this Part. Furthermore, if any insurer customarily offers individual policies on a service basis, that insurer may, in lieu of converted policies on an expense incurred basis, make available converted policies on a service basis which, in the opinion of the Commissioner satisfy the intent of this Part. (1981, c. 706, s. 1.)

§ 58-53-110. Other conversion provisions.

(a) If coverage would in any event have been continued under the group policy on an employee following his retirement prior to the time he is or could be covered by Medicare and provided he would have been eligible for continuation under the group policy as specified in G.S. 58-53-10, the employee or member may elect, in lieu of such continuation of group insurance, to have the same conversion rights as would apply had that insurance terminated at retirement.

(b) The converted policy may provide for reduction or termination of coverage of any person upon his eligibility for coverage under Medicare or under any other State or federal law providing for benefits similar to those provided by the converted policy.

(c) Subject to the conditions set forth in this subsection, the conversion privilege shall also be available (i) to the surviving spouse, if any, at the death of the employee or member, with respect to the spouse and any eligible children whose coverage under the group policy terminates by reason of such death, or if the group policy provides for continuation of dependents' coverage following the employee's or member's death, at the end of such continuation, or (ii) to the spouse of the employee or member upon termination of coverage of the spouse because the spouse becomes ineligible because of divorce, separation, or otherwise, while the employee or member remains insured under the group policy, with respect to the spouse and such children whose coverage under the group policy terminates at the same time, or (iii) to a child solely with respect to himself upon termination of his coverage by reason of ceasing to be an eligible family member under the group policy, if a conversion privilege is not otherwise provided above with respect to such termination.

(d) The insurer may elect to provide group insurance coverage in lieu of the issuance of a converted individual policy, notwithstanding the maximum period of group continuation specified in G.S. 58-53-35(1).

(e) A notification of the conversion privilege shall be included in each certificate of coverage.

(f) A converted policy which is delivered outside this State may be on a form which could be delivered in such other jurisdiction as a converted policy had the group policy been issued in that jurisdiction. (1981, c. 706, s. 1; 1983, c. 668, s. 1.)

§ 58-53-115. Article inapplicable to certain plans.

The provisions of this article shall not apply to hospital, surgical or major medical plans offered by employers on a self-insured basis. (1981, c. 706, s. 2.)

ARTICLE 54.

Medicare Supplement Insurance Minimum Standards.

§ 58-54-1. Definitions.

Unless the context clearly indicates otherwise, the following words, as used in this Article, have the following meanings:

(1) "Applicant" means (i) in the case of an individual Medicare supplement policy or subscriber contract, the person who seeks to contract for insurance benefits; and (ii) in the case of a group Medicare supplement policy or subscriber contract, the proposed certificate holder.

(2) "Certificate" means any certificate issued under a group Medicare supplement policy, which certificate has been delivered or issued for delivery in this State.

(3) "Insurer" includes entities subject to Articles 65 through 67 of this Chapter.

(4) "Medicare" means the "Health Insurance for the Aged Act", Title XVIII of the Social Security Amendments of 1965, as then constituted or later amended.

(5) "Policy" means a Medicare supplement policy, which is a group or individual policy of accident and health insurance under Articles 1 through 64 of this Chapter, a subscriber contract under Articles 65 and 66 of this Chapter, or an evidence of coverage under Article 67 of this Chapter, other than a policy issued pursuant to a contract under section 1876 or section 1833 of the federal Social Security Act (42 U.S.C. § 1395 et seq.), or an issued policy under a demonstration project authorized pursuant to amendments to the federal Social Security Act, that is advertised, marketed, or designed primarily as a supplement to reimbursements under Medicare for the hospital, medical, or surgical expenses of persons eligible for Medicare. (1989, c. 729, s. 1; 1991 (Reg. Sess., 1992), c. 815, s. 1; 1993, c. 553, s. 19.)

§ 58-54-5. Applicability and scope.

(a) Except as otherwise specifically provided, this Article, applies to:
(1) All policies delivered or issued for delivery in this State on or after August 7, 1989; and
(2) All certificates issued under group policies that have been delivered or issued for delivery in this State on or after August 7, 1989.

(b) This Article does not apply to an insurance contract of one or more employers or labor organizations, or of the trustees of a fund established by one or more employers or labor organizations, or combination thereof, for employees or former employees or a combination thereof, or for members or former members, or a combination thereof, of the labor organizations.

(c) This Article does not prohibit or apply to insurance contracts or health care benefit plans, including group conversion policies, that are provided to Medicare eligible persons and that are not marketed or held out to be Medicare supplement policies or benefit plans. (1989, c. 729, s. 1.)

§ 58-54-10. Standards for policy provisions.

(a) No policy in force in this State shall contain benefits that duplicate benefits provided by Medicare.

(b) The Commissioner shall adopt rules to establish specific standards for provisions of policies. Such standards shall be in addition to and in accordance with applicable State law. No requirement of State law relating to minimum required policy benefits, other than the minimum standards contained in this Article, applies to policies. The standards may include without limitation to: terms of renewability; initial and subsequent conditions of eligibility; nonduplication of coverage; probationary periods; benefit limitations, exceptions, and reductions; elimination periods; requirements for replacement; recurrent conditions; and definitions of terms.

(c) The Commissioner may adopt rules that specify prohibited policy provisions not otherwise specifically authorized by State law that, in the opinion of the Commissioner, are unjust, unfair, or unfairly discriminatory to any person insured or proposed for coverage under a policy.

(d) Notwithstanding any other provision of State law, a policy may not deny a claim for losses incurred more than six months from the effective date of coverage for a preexisting condition. A policy may not define a preexisting condition more restrictively than a condition for which medical advice was given or treatment was recommended by or received from a physician within six months before the effective date of coverage.

(e) Repealed by Session Laws 1991 (Regular Session, 1992), c. 815, s. 3. (1989, c. 729, s. 1; 1991, c. 490, s. 6; 1991 (Reg. Sess., 1992), c. 815, s. 3.)

§ 58-54-15. Minimum standards for benefits, marketing practices, compensation arrangements, reporting practices, and claims payments.

The Commissioner shall adopt rules to establish minimum standards for benefits, marketing practices, compensation arrangements, reporting practices, and claims payments under policies. (1989, c. 729, s. 1; 1989 (Reg. Sess., 1990), c. 941, s. 8; 1993, c. 504, s. 38.)

§ 58-54-20. Loss ratio standards and filing requirements.

(a) Every insurer providing group Medicare supplement insurance benefits to a resident of this State pursuant to G.S. 58-54-5 shall file a copy of the master policy and any certificate used in this State in accordance with the filing requirements and procedures applicable to group policies issued in this State.

(b) Policies shall return to policyholders benefits that are reasonable in relation to the premium charged. The Commissioner shall adopt rules to establish minimum standards for loss ratios of policies on the basis of incurred claims experience, or incurred health care expenses where coverage is provided by a health maintenance organization on a service rather than reimbursement basis, and earned premiums in accordance with accepted actuarial principles and practices. Every insurer providing policies or certificates in this State shall annually file its rates, rating schedules, and supporting documentation to demonstrate that it is in compliance with the applicable loss ratio standards of this State. All filings of rates and rating schedules shall demonstrate that the actual and expected losses in relation to premiums comply with the requirements of this Article.

(c) No insurer shall provide compensation to its agents or other producers that is greater than the renewal compensation that would have been paid on an existing policy if the existing policy is replaced by another policy with the same insurer where the new policy benefits are substantially similar to the benefits under the old policy and the old policy was issued by the same insurer or insurer group. (1989, c. 729, s. 1; 1991 (Reg. Sess., 1992), c. 815, s. 4.)

§ 58-54-25. Disclosure standards.

(a) In order to provide for full and fair disclosure in the sale of policies, no policy or certificate shall be delivered in this State unless an outline of coverage is delivered to the applicant at the time application is made.

(b) The Commissioner shall prescribe the format and content of the outline of coverage required by subsection (a) of this section. For purposes of this section, "format" means style, arrangement, and overall appearance, including such items as the size, color, and prominence of type and arrangement of text and captions. Such outline of coverage shall include:

(1) A description of the principal benefits and coverage provided in the policy;

(2) A statement of the exceptions, reductions, and limitations contained in the policy;

   (3) A statement of the renewal provisions, including any reservation by the insurer of a right to change premiums; and

   (4) A statement that the outline of coverage is a summary of the policy issued or applied for and that the policy should be consulted to determine governing contractual provisions.

(c) The Commissioner may prescribe by rule a standard form and the contents of an informational brochure for persons eligible for Medicare, which is intended to improve the buyer's ability to select the most appropriate coverage and improve the buyer's understanding of Medicare. Except in the case of direct response insurance policies, the Commissioner may require by rule that the information brochure be provided to any prospective insured eligible for Medicare concurrently with delivery of the outline of coverage. With respect to direct response insurance policies, the Commissioner may require by rule that the prescribed brochure be provided upon request to any prospective insured eligible for Medicare, but in no event later than the time of policy delivery.

(d) The Commissioner may adopt rules for captions or notice requirements, determined to be in the public interest and designed to inform prospective insureds that particular insurance coverages are not Medicare supplement coverages, for all accident and health insurance policies sold to persons eligible for Medicare, other than: Medicare supplement policies; disability income policies; basic, catastrophic, or major medical expense policies; or single premium, nonrenewable policies.

(e) The Commissioner may further adopt rules to govern the full and fair disclosure of the information in connection with the replacement of accident and health insurance policies, subscriber contracts, or certificates by persons eligible for Medicare.

(f) No insurer shall use attained age as a structure or methodology for its Medicare supplement insurance rates unless the structure or methodology is fully disclosed to the applicant at the time of application or to the insured at the time of delivery if the purchase is by mail order. All types of solicitation materials shall clearly indicate that the premiums are based on attained age, which means that those premiums will increase each year. The Commissioner shall prescribe by rule the format and content of the attained age rating disclosure notice. The notice shall include:

   (1) A statement that attained age rating means that rates increase as the insured ages or by the age group in which the insured is.

   (2) An illustration based on actual attained age that states the dollar amount of premium increase for the insured over a period of not less than 10 policy years and that displays the life expectancy of the insured at the beginning of the period.

   (3) A statement that premiums for other Medicare supplement policies that are on issue age bases do not increase as the insured ages.

   (4) A statement that other Medicare supplement policies that are on issue age bases should be compared to policies on attained age bases. (1989, c. 729, s. 1; 1991 (Reg. Sess., 1992), c. 815, s. 2; 1998-211, s. 12.)

§ 58-54-30. Notice of free examination.

Policies or certificates shall have a notice prominently printed on the first page of the policy or certificate or attached thereon stating in substance that the applicant has the right to return the policy or certificate within 30 days of its delivery and to have the premium refunded if, after examination of the policy or certificate, the applicant is not satisfied for any reason. Any refund made pursuant to this section shall be paid directly to the applicant by the insurer in a timely manner. (1989, c. 729, s. 1.)

§ 58-54-35. Filing requirements for advertising.

Every insurer providing Medicare supplement insurance or benefits in this State shall provide a copy of any Medicare supplement advertisement intended for use in this State whether through written, radio, or television medium to the Commissioner for review or approval by the Commissioner. (1989, c. 729, s. 1.)

§ 58-54-40. Penalties.

In addition to any other applicable penalties for violations of Articles 1 through 64 or 65 and 66 or 67 of this Chapter, the Commissioner may require any person that has violated or is violating any provision of this Article or any rule adopted under this Article to either (i) cease marketing any policy or certificate in this State that is related directly or indirectly to a violation or (ii) take such actions as are necessary to comply with this Article or such rules. (1989, c. 729, s. 1.)

§ 58-54-45. By reason of disability.

(a) In addition to any rule adopted under this Article that is directly or indirectly related to open enrollment, an insurer shall at least make standardized Medicare Supplement Plans A, C, and J available to persons eligible for Medicare by reason of disability before age 65. This action shall be taken without regard to medical condition, claims experience, or health status. To be eligible, a person must submit an application during the six-month period beginning with the first month the person first enrolls in Medicare Part B.

(b) Persons eligible for Medicare by reason of disability before age 65 who are enrolled in a managed care plan and whose coverage under the managed care plan is terminated through cancellation, nonrenewal, or disenrollment have the guaranteed right to purchase Medicare Supplement Plans A and C from any insurer within 63 days after the date of termination or disenrollment.

(c) An insurer may develop premium rates specific to the disabled population. No insurer shall discriminate in the pricing of the Medicare supplement plans referred to in this section because of the health status, claims experience, receipt of health care, or medical condition of an applicant where an application for the plan is submitted during an open enrollment or is submitted within 63 days after the managed care plan is terminated. The rates and any applicable rating factors for the Medicare supplement plans referred to in this section shall be filed with and approved by the Commissioner. (1998-211, s. 13; 2001-334, ss. 10.1, 10.2.)

Editor's Note. — Session Laws 1998-211, s. 39, made this section effective November 1, 1998, and provided that this section would expire on November 1, 2001. Session Laws 2001-334, s. 10.2 deleted the sunset provision.

§ 58-54-50. Rules for compliance with federal law and regulations.

The Commissioner may adopt temporary rules necessary to conform Medicare supplement policies and certificates to the requirements of federal law and regulations, including:

(1) Requiring refunds or credits if the policies or certificates do not meet loss ratio requirements.

(2) Establishing a uniform methodology for calculating and reporting loss ratios.

   (3) Assuring public access to policies, premiums, and loss ratio informa-
       tion of issuers of Medicare supplement insurance.
   (4) Establishing standards for Medicare Select policies and certificates.
   (5) Any other changes required by Congress or the U.S. Department of
       Health and Human Services, or any successor agency. (1998-211, s. 13;
       2001-334, s. 11.1.)

ARTICLE 55.

Long-Term Care Insurance.

§ 58-55-1. Short title.

   This Article may be cited as the "Long-Term Care Insurance Act". (1987, c.
331, s. 1.)

§ 58-55-5. Dual options.

   (a) No policy that conditions the eligibility of benefits on prior hospitalization may be delivered or issued for delivery in this State unless the insurer or
other entity offering that policy also offers a policy that does not condition
eligibility of benefits on such a requirement.
   (b) Policies that were delivered, issued for delivery, or renewed on and after
October 1, 1989, that did not condition the eligibility of benefits on prior
hospitalizations shall be amended, upon the insured's written request, to
condition eligibility of benefits on prior hospitalization, provided that the
insured receives the appropriate reduction in premium. (1991, c. 644, s. 24.)

§ 58-55-10. Purposes.

   The purposes of this Article are to promote the public interest, to promote
the availability of long-term care insurance policies, to protect applicants for
long-term care insurance from unfair or deceptive sales or enrollment practices, to establish standards for long-term care insurance, to facilitate public
understanding and comparison of long-term care insurance policies, and to
facilitate flexibility and innovation in the development of long-term care
insurance coverage. (1987, c. 331, s. 1.)

§ 58-55-15. Scope.

   This Article applies to long-term care insurance policies in this State. This
Article does not supersede the obligations of any person subject to its
provisions to comply with other applicable laws and rules if those laws and
rules do not conflict with this Article. The laws and rules established to govern
Medicare supplement insurance policies shall not apply to long-term care
insurance. A policy that is not advertised, marketed, or offered as long-term
care insurance or nursing home insurance is not subject to this Article. (1987,
c. 331, s. 1; 1991, c. 720, s. 84.)

§ 58-55-20. Definitions.

   As used in this Article:
   (1) "Applicant" means:
       a. In the case of an individual long-term care insurance policy, the
          person who seeks to contract for benefits; and

   b. In the case of a group long-term care insurance policy, the proposed certificate holder.
(2) "Certificate" means any certificate issued under a group long-term care insurance policy, which policy has been delivered or issued for delivery in this State.
(3) "Group long-term care insurance" means a long-term care insurance policy that is delivered or issued for delivery in this State and issued to:
   a. One or more employers or labor organizations, or to a trust or to the trustees of a fund established by one or more employers or labor organizations, or both, for employees or former employees or both, or for members or former members or both, of the employers or labor organizations; or
   b. Any professional, trade, or occupational association for its members or former or retired members, or all, if such association:
      (i) Comprises individuals all of whom are or were actively engaged in the same profession, trade, or occupation; and
      (ii) Has been maintained in good faith for purposes other than obtaining insurance; or
   c. An association or to a trust or to the trustee or trustees of a fund established, created, or maintained for the benefit of members of one or more associations. Prior to advertising, marketing, or offering such policy within this State, the association or associations, or the insurer of the association or associations, shall file evidence with the Commissioner that the association or associations have at the outset a minimum of 100 persons and have been organized and maintained in good faith for purposes other than that of obtaining insurance; have been in active existence for at least one year; and have a constitution and bylaws which provide that (i) the association or associations hold regular meetings not less than annually to further purposes of the members, (ii) except for credit unions, the association or associations collect dues or solicit contributions from members, and (iii) the members have voting privileges and representation on the governing board and committees. Ninety days after such filing the association or associations will be deemed to have satisfied such organizational requirements, unless the Commissioner makes a finding that the association or associations do not satisfy those organizational requirements.
   d. A group other than as described in subdivisions (3)a., (3)b., and (3)c. of this section, subject to a finding by the Commissioner that:
      (i) The issuance of the group policy is not contrary to the best interest of the public;
      (ii) The issuance of the group policy would result in economies of acquisition or administration; and
      (iii) The benefits are reasonable in relation to the premiums charged.
(4) "Long-term care insurance" means any policy or certificate advertised, marketed, offered, or designed to provide coverage for not less than 12 consecutive months for each covered person on an expense incurred, indemnity, prepaid, or other basis, for one or more necessary or medically necessary diagnostic, preventive, therapeutic, rehabilitative, maintenance, or personal care services, provided in a setting other than an acute care unit of a hospital. "Long-term care insurance" includes group and individual policies whether issued by insurers, fraternal benefit societies, nonprofit health, hospital, and

medical service corporations, prepaid health plans, health maintenance organizations, or any similar organization. "Long-term care
insurance" does not include any policy that is offered primarily to
provide basic Medicare supplement coverage, basic hospital expense
coverage, basic medical-surgical expense coverage, hospital confinement indemnity coverage, major medical expense coverage, disability
income protection coverage, accident only coverage, specified disease
or specified accident coverage, or limited benefit health coverage.

(5) "Policy" means any policy, contract, certificate, subscriber agreement,
rider, or endorsement delivered or issued for delivery in this State by
an insurer, fraternal benefit society, nonprofit health, hospital or
medical service corporation, prepaid health plan, health maintenance
organization, or any similar organization. (1987, c. 331, s. 1; c. 864, s.
68.)

§ 58-55-25. Limits of group long-term care insurance.

No group long-term care insurance coverage may be offered to a resident of
this State under a group policy issued in another state to a group described in
G.S. 58-55-20(3)d, unless the Commissioner or the insurance regulator of the
other state having statutory and regulatory long-term care insurance requirements substantially similar to those adopted in this State has made a
determination that such requirements have been met. (1987, c. 331, s. 1; 1991,
c. 720, s. 44.)

§ 58-55-30. Disclosure and performance standards for long-term care insurance.

(a) The Commissioner may adopt rules that include standards for full and
fair disclosure setting forth the manner, content, and required disclosures for
the sale of long-term care insurance policies, terms of renewability, initial and
subsequent conditions of eligibility, nonduplication of coverage provisions,
coverage of dependents, pre-existing conditions, termination of insurance,
probationary periods, limitations, exceptions, reductions, elimination periods,
requirements for replacement, recurrent conditions, and definitions of terms.

(b) No long-term care insurance policy may:

(1) Be cancelled, nonrenewed, or otherwise terminated on the grounds of
the age or the deterioration of the mental or physical health of the
insured individual or certificate holder; or

(2) Contain a provision establishing a new waiting period in the event
existing coverage is converted to or replaced by a new or other form
within the same company, except with respect to an increase in
benefits voluntarily selected by the insured individual or group
policyholder; or

(3) Provide coverage for skilled nursing care only or provide significantly
more coverage for skilled care in a facility than coverage for lower
levels of care.

(c) Pre-existing condition:

(1) No long-term care insurance policy, other than that issued to a group
defined in G.S. 58-55-20(3)a, shall use a definition of "pre-existing
condition" that is more restrictive than the following: "pre-existing
condition" means a condition for which medical advice or treatment
was recommended by, or received from a provider of health care
services, within six months preceding the effective date of coverage of
an insured person.

(2) No long-term care insurance policy, other than that issued to a group
defined in G.S. 58-55-20(3)a, shall exclude coverage for a loss or

confinement that is the result of a pre-existing condition unless such loss or confinement begins within six months following the effective date of coverage of an insured person.

(d) Except as provided in G.S. 58-55-5, no long-term care insurance policy may be delivered or issued for delivery in this State if it:

    (1) Conditions eligibility for any benefits on a prior hospitalization requirement; or

    (2) Conditions eligibility for benefits provided in an institutional care setting on the receipt of a higher level of institutional care.

(d1) Except as provided in G.S. 58-55-5, any long-term care insurance policy containing any limitations or conditions for eligibility other than those prohibited by law shall describe in a separate paragraph of the policy, to be entitled "Limitations or Conditions on Eligibility for Benefits", the limitations or conditions, including any required number of days of confinement.

(d2) A long-term care insurance policy that contains a benefit advertised, marketed, or offered as home health care or a home care benefit may not condition receipt of benefits on a prior institutionalization requirement.

(d3) A long-term care insurance policy that conditions eligibility for noninstitutional benefits on the prior receipt of institutional care shall not require a prior institutional stay of more than 30 days for which benefits are paid.

(e) The Commissioner may adopt rules establishing loss ratio standards for long-term care insurance policies, provided that a specific reference to long-term care insurance policies is contained in the rules.

(f) An individual long-term care insurance policy holder has the right to return the policy within 30 days of its delivery and to have the premium refunded if, after examination of the policy, the policyholder is not satisfied for any reason. Individual long-term care insurance policies shall have a notice prominently printed on the first page of the policy or attached thereto stating in substance that unless the policyholder has received benefits under the policy, the policyholder has the right to return the policy within 30 days of its delivery and to have the premium refunded if, after examination of the policy, the policyholder is not satisfied for any reason.

(g) A person insured under a long-term care insurance policy issued pursuant to a direct response has the right to return the policy within 30 days of its delivery and to have the premium refunded if, after examination, the insured person is not satisfied for any reason. Long-term care insurance policies issued pursuant to a direct response solicitation shall have a notice prominently printed on the first page or attached thereto stating in substance that unless the insured person has received benefits under the policy, the insured person shall have the right to return the policy within 30 days of its delivery and to have the premium refunded if after examination the insured person is not satisfied for any reason.

(h) An outline of coverage shall be delivered to an applicant for an individual long-term care insurance policy at the time of application for an individual policy. In the case of direct response solicitations, the insurer shall deliver the outline of coverage upon the applicant's request; but regardless of request shall make such delivery no later than at the time of policy delivery. Such outline of coverage shall include:

    (1) A description of the principal benefits and coverage provided in the policy;

    (2) A statement of the principal exclusions, reductions, and limitations contained in the policy;

    (3) A statement of the renewal provisions, including any reservation in the policy of a right to change premiums; and

    (4) A statement that the outline of coverage is a summary of the policy issued or applied for, and that the policy should be consulted to determine governing contractual provisions.

(i) A certificate issued pursuant to a group long-term care insurance policy, which policy is delivered or issued for delivery in this State, shall include:

    (1) A description of the principal benefits and coverage provided in the policy;

    (2) A statement of the principal exclusions, reductions, and limitations contained in the policy; and

    (3) A statement that the group master policy determines governing contractual provisions.

(j) No policy or certificate may be advertised, marketed, or offered as long-term care or nursing home insurance unless it complies with the provisions of this Article.

(k) The Commissioner shall adopt rules to establish minimum standards for marketing practices and compensation arrangements for long-term care insurance. (1987, c. 331, s. 1; 1989, c. 207, ss. 1-4; 1989 (Reg. Sess., 1990), c. 941, s. 9; 1991, c. 720, ss. 45, 86; c. 721, s. 85; 1993, c. 504, s. 39; c. 553, s. 20.)

§ 58-55-31. Additional requirements.

(a) No policy shall be used in this State unless it provides for an offer of nonforfeiture, which shall not be less than an offer of reduced paid-up insurance benefits, extended term insurance benefits, or a shortened benefit period. No policy shall pay a cash surrender value unless the dividends or refunds are applied as a reduction of future premiums or an increase in future benefits.

(b) The Commissioner shall adopt rules to provide for annual reports by insurers of the number of claims denied, number of rescissions, and the percentage of sales involving the replacement of policies.

(c) No policy shall be used in this State unless the insurer has developed a financial or personal asset suitability test to determine whether or not issuing long-term care insurance to an applicant is appropriate. For purposes of this section:

    (1) All insurers except those issuing life insurance that accelerates the death benefit for long-term care shall use the financial or suitability form and format standards as developed and adopted by the NAIC. A personal long-term care worksheet and disclosure notice of issues an applicant should know before buying long-term care insurance shall be completed and provided before an application is taken.

    (2) Each applicant that does not meet the recommended financial or personal asset suitability test criteria shall receive a letter of notification and shall be given an option to waive the results of the financial suitability test and proceed with the purchase of the policy.

(d) The Commissioner shall adopt standards to handle consumer complaints about noncompliance with State requirements. (1997-259, s. 15.)

§ 58-55-35. Facilities, services, and conditions defined.

(a) Whenever long-term care insurance provides coverage for the facilities, services, or physical or mental conditions listed below, unless otherwise defined in the policy and certificate, and approved by the Commissioner, such facilities, services, or conditions are defined as follows:

    (1) "Adult care home" shall be defined in accordance with the terms of G.S. 131D-2(a)(3).

    (1a) "Adult day care program" shall be defined in accordance with the provisions of G.S. 131D-6(b).

    (2) "Chore" services include the performance of tasks incidental to activities of daily living that do not require the services of a trained

homemaker or other specialist. Such services are provided to enable individuals to remain in their own homes and may include such services as: assistance in meeting basic care needs such as meal preparation; shopping for food and other necessities; running necessary errands; providing transportation to essential service facilities; care and cleaning of the house, grounds, clothing, and linens.

(3) "Combination home" shall be defined in accordance with the terms of G.S. 131E-101(1).

(4) Repealed by Session Laws 1995, c. 535, s. 3.

(5) "Family care home" shall be defined in accordance with the terms of G.S. 131D-2(a)(5).

(6) Renumbered.

(7) Repealed by Session Laws 1995, c. 535, s. 3.

(8) "Home health services" shall be defined in accordance with the terms of G.S. 131E-136(3).

(9) "Homemaker services" means supportive services provided by qualified para-professionals who are trained, equipped, assigned, and supervised by professionals within the agency to help maintain, strengthen, and safeguard the care of the elderly in their own homes. These standards must, at a minimum, meet standards established by the North Carolina Division of Social Services and may include: Providing assistance in management of household budgets; planning nutritious meals; purchasing and preparing foods; housekeeping duties; consumer education; and basic personal and health care.

(10) "Hospice" shall be defined in accordance with the terms of G.S. 131E-176(13a).

(11) "Intermediate care facility" shall be defined in accordance with the terms of G.S. 131E-176(14b).

(12) "Nursing home" shall be defined in accordance with the terms of G.S. 131E-101(6).

(13) "Respite care, institutional" means provision of temporary support to the primary caregiver of the aged, disabled, or handicapped individual by taking over the tasks of that person for a limited period of time. The insured receives care for the respite period in an institutional setting, such as a nursing home, family care home, rest home, or other appropriate setting.

(14) "Respite care, non-institutional" means provision of temporary support to the primary caregiver of the aged, disabled, or handicapped individual by taking over the tasks of that person for a limited period of time in the home of the insured or other appropriate community location.

(15) "Skilled Nursing Facility" shall be defined in accordance with the terms of G.S. 131E-176(23).

(16) "Supervised living facility for developmentally disabled adults" means a residential facility, as defined in G.S. 122C-3(14), which has two to nine developmentally disabled adult residents.

(b) Whenever long-term care insurance provides coverage for organic brain disorder syndrome, progressive dementing illness, or primary degenerative dementia, such phrases shall be interpreted to include Alzheimer's Disease. Clinical diagnosis of "organic brain disorder syndrome", "progressive dementing illness", and "primary degenerative dementia" must be accepted as evidence that such conditions exist in an insured when a pathological diagnosis cannot be made; provided that such medical evidence substantially documents the diagnosis of the condition and the insured received treatment for such condition.

(c) All long-term care insurance policies must be filed with and approved by the Commissioner before they can be used in this State and are subject to the provisions of Article 38 of this Chapter. (1987, c. 331, s. 1; 1989, c. 207, ss. 5, 6; 1991, c. 721, s. 85; 1995, c. 535, s. 3; 2001-209, s. 4.)

Editor's Note. — The subdivision (a)(1a) designation and the order of subdivisions in subsection (a) were assigned by the Revisor of Statutes.

Section 131D-2(a)(3), referred to in subdivision (a)(1), was repealed by Session Laws 1995, c. 535, s. 8.

The reference in subdivision (a)(15) above to G.S. 131E-176(23) should probably now be G.S. 131E-176(17a).

§ 58-55-50. Rules for compliance with federal law and regulations.

The Commissioner may adopt temporary rules necessary to conform long-term care policies and certificates to the requirements of federal law and regulations, including any changes required by Congress or the U.S. Department of Health and Human Services, or any successor agencies. (2001-334, s. 11.2.)

Editor's Note. — Session Laws 2001-334, s. 21, makes this section effective August 3, 2001.

Session Laws 2001-334, s. 19 is a severability clause.

ARTICLE 56.

Third Party Administrators.

§ 58-56-1: Repealed by Session Laws 1991, c. 627, s. 2.

§ 58-56-2. Definitions.

The following definitions apply in this Article:
  (1) Affiliate. Any person who, directly or indirectly, through one or more intermediaries, controls, is controlled by, or is under common control with a specified entity or person.
  (2) Control. Defined in G.S. 58-19-5(2).
  (3) Insurance. Any coverage offered or provided by an insurer.
  (4) Insurer. A person who undertakes to provide life or health insurance or benefits in this State that are subject to this Chapter. The term "insurer" does not include a bona fide employee benefit plan established by an employer, an employee organization, or both, for which the insurance laws of this State are preempted pursuant to the Employee Retirement Income Security Act of 1974.
  (5) Third party administrator. A person who directly or indirectly solicits or effects coverage of, underwrites, collects charges or premiums from, or adjusts or settles claims on residents of this State, or residents of another state from offices in this State, in connection with life or health insurance or annuities, except any of the following:
    a. An employer on behalf of its employees or the employees of one or more of its affiliates.
    b. A union on behalf of its members.
    c. An insurer that is licensed under Articles 1 through 67 of this Chapter or that is acting as an insurer with respect to a policy lawfully issued and delivered by it and pursuant to the laws of a state in which the insurer is licensed to write insurance.
    d. An agent or broker who is licensed by the Commissioner to sell life or health insurance and whose activities are limited exclusively to the sale of insurance.

     e. A creditor on behalf of its debtors with respect to insurance covering a debt between the creditor and its debtors.

     f. A trust and its trustees, agents, and employees acting pursuant to the trust established in conformity with 29 U.S.C. § 186.

     g. A trust exempt from taxation under section 501(a) of the Internal Revenue Code and its trustees and employees acting pursuant to the trust, or a custodian and the custodian's agents or employees acting pursuant to a custodian account that meets the requirements of section 401(f) of the Internal Revenue Code.

     h. A financial institution subject to supervision or examination by federal or state banking authorities, or a mortgage lender, to the extent the financial institution or mortgage lender collects and remits premiums to licensed insurance agents or authorized insurers in connection with loan payments.

     i. An attorney-at-law who adjusts or settles claims in the normal course of business as an attorney-at-law and who does not collect charges or premiums in connection with life or health insurance or annuities.

     j. An adjuster licensed by the Commissioner whose activities are limited to adjustment of claims.

     k. A person who acts solely as a TPA of one or more bona fide employee benefit plans established by an employer, an employee organization, or both, for which the insurance laws of this State are preempted pursuant to the Employee Income Security Act of 1974. The person shall comply with the requirements of G.S. 58-56-51(f).

     l. A person licensed as a managing general agent in this State, whose activities are limited exclusively to the scope of activities conveyed under the license.

    (6) TPA. A third party administrator.

    (7) Underwriting. This term includes the acceptance of employer or individual applications for coverage of individuals in accordance with the written rules of the insurer, the planning and coordination of an insurance program, and the ability to procure bonds and excess insurance. (1991, c. 627, s. 1.)

§ **58-56-5:** Reserved for future codification purposes.

§ **58-56-6. Written agreement necessary.**

    (a) No TPA may act as a TPA without a written agreement between the TPA and the insurer. The written agreement shall be retained as part of the official records of both the insurer and the TPA for the duration of the agreement and for five years thereafter. The agreement shall contain all provisions required by this Article, to the extent those requirements apply to the functions performed by the TPA.

    (b) The agreement shall include a statement of duties that the TPA is expected to perform on behalf of the insurer and the kinds of insurance the TPA is to be authorized to administer. The agreement shall provide for underwriting or other standards pertaining to the business underwritten by the insurer.

    (c) The insurer or TPA may, with written notice, terminate the agreement for cause as provided in the agreement. The insurer may suspend the underwriting authority of the TPA during the pendency of any dispute regarding the cause for termination of the agreement. The insurer must fulfill any lawful obligations with respect to policies affected by the agreement, regardless of any dispute between the insurer and the TPA. (1991, c. 627, s. 1.)

§ **58-56-10:** Repealed by Session Laws 1991, c. 627, s. 2.

§ 58-56-11. Payment to TPA.

If an insurer uses the services of a TPA, the payment to the TPA of any premiums or charges for insurance by or on behalf of the insured party is considered payment to the insurer. The payment of return premiums or claim payments forwarded by the insurer to the TPA is not considered payment to the insured party or claimant until the payments are received by the insured party or claimant. This section does not limit any right of the insurer against the TPA resulting from the failure of the TPA to make payments to the insurer, insured parties, or claimants. (1991, c. 627, s. 1.)

§ **58-56-15:** Repealed by Session Laws 1991, c. 627, s. 2.

§ 58-56-16. Records to be kept.

(a) Every TPA shall maintain and make available to the insurer complete books and records of all transactions performed on behalf of the insurer. The books and records shall be maintained in accordance with prudent standards of insurance record keeping and must be maintained for a period of at least five years after the date of their creation.

(b) The Commissioner shall have access to books and records maintained by a TPA for the purposes of examination, audit, and inspection. The Commissioner shall keep confidential any trade secrets contained in those books and records, including the identity and addresses of policyholders and certificate holders, except that the Commissioner may use the information in any judicial or administrative proceeding instituted against the TPA.

(c) The insurer shall own the records generated by the TPA pertaining to the insurer, but the TPA shall retain the right to continuing access to books and records to permit the TPA to fulfill all of its contractual obligations to insured parties, claimants, and the insurer.

(d) In the event the insurer and the TPA cancel their agreement, notwithstanding the provisions of subsection (a) of this section, the TPA may, by written agreement with the insurer, transfer all records to a new TPA rather than retain them for five years. In this case, the new TPA shall acknowledge, in writing, that it is responsible for retaining the records of the prior TPA as required in subsection (a) of this section. (1991, c. 627, s. 1.)

§ **58-56-20:** Repealed by Session Laws 1991, c. 627, s. 2.

§ 58-56-21. Approval of advertising.

A TPA may use only the advertising pertaining to the business underwritten by an insurer that has been approved in writing by the insurer in advance of its use. (1991, c. 627, s. 1.)

§ **58-56-25:** Repealed by Session Laws 1991, c. 627, s. 2.

§ 58-56-26. Responsibilities of the insurer.

(a) If an insurer uses the services of a TPA, the insurer is responsible for determining the benefits, premium rates, underwriting criteria, and claims payment procedures applicable to the coverage and for securing reinsurance, if any. The rules pertaining to these matters must be provided, in writing, by the insurer to the TPA. The responsibilities of the TPA as to any of these matters shall be set forth in the agreement between the TPA and the insurer.

(b) It is the sole responsibility of the insurer to provide for competent administration of its programs.

(c) In cases where a TPA administers benefits for more than 100 certificate holders on behalf of an insurer, the insurer shall, at least semiannually, conduct a review of the operations of the TPA. At least one semiannual review shall be an on-site audit of the operations of the TPA. (1991, c. 627, s. 1.)

§ 58-56-30: Repealed by Session Laws 1991, c. 627, s. 2.

§ 58-56-31. Premium collection and payment of claims.

(a) All insurance charges or premiums collected by a TPA on behalf of or for an insurer, and the return of premiums received from that insurer, shall be held by the TPA in a fiduciary capacity. These funds shall be immediately remitted to the person entitled to them or shall be deposited promptly in a fiduciary account established and maintained by the TPA in a federally or State insured financial institution. The agreement between the TPA and the insurer shall require the TPA to periodically render an accounting to the insurer detailing all transactions performed by the TPA pertaining to the business underwritten by the insurer.

(b) If charges or premiums deposited in a fiduciary account have been collected on behalf of or for one or more insurers, the TPA shall keep records clearly recording the deposits in and withdrawals from the account on behalf of each insurer. The TPA shall keep copies of all the records and, upon request of an insurer, shall furnish the insurer with copies of the records pertaining to the deposits and withdrawals.

(c) The TPA shall not pay any claim by withdrawals from a fiduciary account in which premiums or charges are deposited. Withdrawals from this account shall be made only as provided in the agreement between the TPA and the insurer. The agreement shall address, but not be limited to, the following:

(1) Remittance to an insurer entitled to remittance.

(2) Deposit in an account maintained in the name of the insurer.

(3) Transfer to and deposit in a claims-paying account, with claims to be paid as provided in subsection (d) of this section.

(4) Payment to a group policyholder for remittance to the insurer entitled to the remittance.

(5) Payment to the TPA of its commissions, fees, or charges.

(6) Remittance of a return premium to the person entitled to the return premium.

(d) All claims paid by the TPA from funds collected on behalf of or for an insurer shall be paid only on drafts or checks of and as authorized by the insurer. (1991, c. 627, s. 1.)

§ 58-56-35: Repealed by Session Laws 1991, c. 627, s. 2.

§ 58-56-36. Compensation to the TPA.

A TPA shall not enter into any agreement or understanding with an insurer that makes the amount of the TPA's commissions, fees, or charges contingent upon savings effected in the adjustment, settlement, and payment of losses covered by the insurer's obligations. This section does not prohibit a TPA from receiving performance-based compensation for providing hospital or other auditing services and does not prevent the compensation of a TPA from being based on premiums or charges collected or the number of claims paid or processed. (1991, c. 627, s. 1.)

§ **58-56-40:** Repealed by Session Laws 1991, c. 627, s. 2.

§ 58-56-41. Notice to covered individuals; disclosure of charges and fees.

(a) When the services of a TPA are used, the TPA shall provide a written notice approved by the insurer to covered individuals advising them of the identity of, and relationship among, the TPA, the policyholder, and the insurer.

(b) When a TPA collects funds, the reason for collection of each item must be identified to the insured party and each item must be shown separately from any premium. Additional charges may not be made for services to the extent the services have been paid for by the insurer.

(c) The TPA shall disclose to the insurer all charges, fees and commissions received from all services in connection with the provision of administrative services for the insurer, including any fees or commissions paid by insurers providing reinsurance. (1991, c. 627, s. 1.)

§ **58-56-45:** Repealed by Session Laws 1991, c. 627, s. 2.

§ 58-56-46. Delivery of materials to covered individuals.

Any policies, certificates, booklets, termination notices, and other written communications delivered by the insurer to the TPA for delivery to insured parties or covered individuals shall be delivered by the TPA promptly after receipt of instructions from the insurer to deliver them. (1991, c. 627, s. 1.)

§ **58-56-50:** Repealed by Session Laws 1991, c. 627, s. 2.

§ 58-56-51. License required.

(a) No person shall act as, offer to act as, or hold himself or herself out as a TPA in this State without a valid TPA license issued by the Commissioner. Licenses shall be renewed annually.

(b) Each application for the issuance or renewal of a license shall be made upon a form prescribed by the Commissioner and shall be accompanied by a nonrefundable filing fee of one hundred dollars ($100.00) and evidence of maintenance of a fidelity bond, errors and omissions liability insurance, or other security, of a type and in an amount to be determined by rules of the Commissioner. Applications for issuance of licenses shall include or be accompanied by the following information and documents:

    (1) All organizational documents of the TPA, including any articles of incorporation, articles of association, partnership agreement, trade name certificate, or trust agreement, any other applicable documents, and all amendments to these documents.

    (2) The bylaws, rules, regulations, or similar documents regulating the internal affairs of the TPA.

    (3) The names, addresses, official positions, and professional qualifications of the individuals who are responsible for the conduct of affairs

of the TPA, including all (i) members of the board of directors, board of trustees, executive committee, or other governing board or committee, (ii) the principal officers in the case of a corporation or the partners or members in the case of a partnership or association, (iii) all shareholders holding directly or indirectly ten percent (10%) or more of the voting securities of the TPA, and (iv) any other person who exercises control or influence over the affairs of the TPA.

(4) Annual financial statements or reports for the two most recent years that prove that the applicant is solvent and any other information the Commissioner may require in order to review the current financial condition of the applicant.

(5) A general description of the business operations, including information on staffing levels and activities proposed in this State and nationwide. The description must provide details setting forth the TPA's capability for providing a sufficient number of experienced and qualified personnel in the areas of claims processing, record keeping, and underwriting.

(6) If the applicant will be managing the solicitation of new or renewal business, evidence that it employs or has contracted with an agent licensed by this State for soliciting and taking applications. Any applicant that intends to directly solicit insurance contracts or to otherwise act as an insurance agent must provide proof of having a license as an insurance agent in this State.

(7) Any other pertinent information required by rules of the Commissioner.

The information required by subdivisions (1) through (7) of this subsection, including any trade secrets, shall be kept confidential; provided that the Commissioner may use that information in any judicial or administrative proceeding instituted against the TPA. Applications for renewals of licenses shall include or be accompanied by any changes in the information required by subdivisions (1) through (7) of this subsection.

(c) Each applicant shall make available for inspection by the Commissioner copies of all contracts with insurers or other persons using the services of the TPA.

(d) The Commissioner may refuse to issue a license if the Commissioner determines that the TPA, or any individual responsible for the conduct of affairs of the TPA as defined in subdivision (b)(3) of this section, is not competent, trustworthy, financially responsible in accordance with subsection (b) of this section, or of good personal and business reputation, or has had an insurance or a TPA license denied, suspended, or revoked for cause by any state.

(e) A TPA is not required to be licensed as a TPA in this state if all of the following conditions are met:

(1) The TPA's principal place of business is in another state.

(2) The TPA is not soliciting business as a TPA in this State.

(3) In the case of any group policy or plan of insurance serviced by the TPA, no more than either five percent (5%) or 100 certificate holders, whichever is fewer, reside in this State.

(f) A person is not required to be licensed as a TPA in this State if the person provides services exclusively to one or more bona fide employee benefit plans each of which is established by an employer, an employee organization, or both, and for which the insurance laws of this State are preempted pursuant to the Employee Retirement Income Security Act of 1974. Persons who are not required to be licensed shall register with the Commissioner annually, verifying their status as described in this subsection.

(g) A TPA shall notify the Commissioner of any material change in its ownership, control, or other fact or circumstance affecting its qualification for a license in this State, within 10 business days after the change.

(h) No bonding shall be required by the Commissioner of any TPA whose business is restricted solely to benefit plans that are either fully insured by an authorized insurer or that are bona fide employee benefit plans established by an employer, any employee organization, or both, for which the insurance laws of this State are preempted pursuant to the Employee Retirement Income Security Act of 1974. (1991, c. 627, s. 1.)

§ **58-56-55:** Repealed by Session Laws 1991, c. 627, s. 2.

§ 58-56-56. Waiver of application for license.

Upon request from a TPA, the Commissioner may waive the application requirements of G.S. 58-56-51(b) if the TPA has a valid license as a TPA issued in a state that has standards for TPAs that are at least as stringent as those contained in this Article. (1991, c. 627, s. 1.)

§ **58-56-60:** Repealed by Session Laws 1991, c. 627, s. 2.

§ **58-56-61:** Reserved for future codification purposes.

§ 58-56-65. Committee on Third Party Administrators.

The Commissioner is authorized to appoint a Committee on Third Party Administrators in conformance with the provisions of G.S. 58-2-30. (1987, c. 676, s. 1.)

§ 58-56-66. Grounds for suspension or revocation of license.

(a) The Commissioner shall, after notice and opportunity for hearing, suspend or revoke the license of a TPA if the Commissioner finds that either of the following apply to the TPA:

    (1) The TPA is using methods or practices in the conduct of its business that render its further transaction of business in this State hazardous or injurious to insured persons or the public.

    (2) The TPA has failed to pay any judgment rendered against it in this State within 60 days after the judgment has become final.

(b) The Commissioner may, after notice and opportunity for hearing, suspend or revoke the license of a TPA if the Commissioner finds that any of the following apply to the TPA:

    (1) The TPA has violated a rule or an order of the Commissioner or any provision of this Chapter.

    (2) The TPA has refused to be examined or to produce its accounts, records, and files for examination, or any of its officers has refused to give information with respect to its affairs or has refused to perform any other legal obligation as to that examination, when required by the Commissioner.

    (3) The TPA has, without just cause, refused to pay proper claims or perform services arising under its contracts or has, without just cause, caused covered individuals to accept less than the amount due them or caused covered individuals to employ attorneys or bring suit against the TPA to secure full payment or settlement of the claims.

    (4) The TPA is an affiliate of or under the same general management, interlocking directorate, or ownership as another TPA or insurer that unlawfully transacts business in this State without having a license.

(5) The TPA at any time fails to meet any qualification for which issuance of the license could have been refused had the failure then existed and been known to the Commissioner at the time of the application.

(6) The TPA has been convicted of, or has entered a plea of guilty or **nolo contendere** to, a felony without regard to whether judgment was withheld.

(7) The TPA is under suspension or revocation in another state.

(c) The Commissioner may without advance notice or hearing immediately suspend the license of any TPA if the Commissioner finds that any of the following apply to the TPA:

(1) The TPA is insolvent or financially impaired. "Financially impaired" means that the TPA is unable or potentially unable to fulfill its contractual obligations.

(2) A proceeding for receivership, conservatorship, rehabilitation, or other delinquency proceeding regarding the TPA has been commenced in any state.

(3) The financial condition or business practices of the TPA otherwise pose an imminent threat to the public health, safety, or welfare of the residents of this State. (1991, c. 627, s. 1.)

ARTICLE 57.

Regulation of Credit Insurance.

§ 58-57-1. Application of Article.

All credit life insurance, all credit accident and health insurance, all credit property insurance, all credit insurance on credit card balances, all family leave credit insurance, and all credit unemployment insurance written in connection with direct loans, consumer credit installment sale contracts of whatever term permitted by G.S. 25A-33, leases, or other credit transactions shall be subject to the provisions of this Article, except credit insurance written in connection with direct loans of more than 15 years' duration. The provisions of this Article shall be controlling as to such insurance and no other provisions of Articles 1 through 64 of this Chapter shall be applicable unless otherwise specifically provided; nor shall such insurance be subject to the provisions of this Article where the issuance of such insurance is an isolated transaction on the part of the insurer not related to an agreement or a plan for insuring debtors of the creditor. (1975, c. 660, s. 1; 1987, c. 826, ss. 1, 12; 1993, c. 226, s. 1; 1999-351, s. 5.2.)

CASE NOTES

Applied in Newbold v. Globe Life Ins. Co., 50 N.C. App. 628, 274 S.E.2d 905 (1981).

§ 58-57-5. Definitions.

As used in this Article, unless the context requires otherwise, the following words or terms shall have the meanings herein ascribed to them, respectively:

(1) Repealed by Session Laws 1991, c. 720, s. 6.

(2) "Credit accident and health insurance" means insurance on a debtor to provide indemnity for payments becoming due on a specific loan or other credit transaction as defined in G.S. 58-51-100, with or without insurance against death by accident.

(2a) "Credit insurance agent" means an agent of an insurance company licensed in this State who is authorized to solicit, negotiate or effect credit life insurance, credit accident and health insurance, credit unemployment insurance, credit property insurance, or any of them, but only to the extent as is authorized and limited in this Article.

(3) "Credit life insurance" means insurance on the life of a debtor pursuant to or in connection with a specific loan or other credit transaction as defined in G.S. 58-58-10.

(4) Recodified as G.S. § 58-57-5(2a) (See Note.)

(4a) "Credit transaction" means any transaction by the terms of which the repayment of money loaned or loan commitment made, or payment for goods, services, or properties sold or leased, is to be made at a future date or dates.

(4b) "Credit unemployment insurance" means insurance on a debtor in connection with a specified loan or other credit transaction to provide payment to a creditor of the debtor for the installment payments or other periodic payment becoming due while the debtor is involuntarily unemployed as defined in the policy.

(5) "Creditor" means any lender of money or vendor or lessor of goods, services, property, rights or privileges, including any person that directly or indirectly provides credit in connection with any such sale or lease, for which payment is arranged through a credit-related transaction; or any successor to the right, title or interest of any such lender, vendor, lessor, or person extending credit, and an affiliate, associate, or subsidiary of any of them, or any director, officer, or employee of any of them or any other person in any way associated with any of them.

(6) "Debtor" means a borrower of money or a purchaser or lessee of goods, services, property, rights or privileges for which payment is arranged through a credit transaction.

(6a) "Family leave credit insurance" means insurance on a debtor in connection with a specified loan or other credit transaction to provide payment to a creditor of the debtor for the installment payments or other periodic payments becoming due when the debtor suffers a loss of income because of a voluntary, employer-approved leave of absence for qualifying events specified in G.S. 58-57-115(d).

(7) "Indebtedness" means the total amount payable for the term of the loan by debtor to creditor in connection with a loan or other credit transaction, including principal, interest, allowable charges, and any premiums authorized hereunder.

(7a) "Joint accident and health coverage" means credit accident and health insurance covering two or more debtors; provided that only one monthly benefit, as defined in G.S. 58-57-15(b), shall be payable each month on a specific indebtedness regardless of the number of debtors insured.

(8) "Joint life coverage" means credit life insurance covering two or more lives, the entire amount of insurance being payable upon the death of the first insured debtor to die.

(9) "Lease" means a contract whereby the lessee of a "motor vehicle," as defined in G.S. 20-4.01(23), contracts to pay as compensation for use a sum substantially equivalent to or in excess of the aggregate value of the property, but not exceeding the term of years in G.S. 58-57-1.

(10) "Open-end credit" means credit extended by a creditor under an agreement in which:

a. The creditor reasonably contemplates repeated transactions;

b. The creditor imposes a finance charge from time to time on an outstanding unpaid balance; and

    c. The amount of credit that may be extended to the debtor during the term of the agreement (up to any limit set by the creditor) is generally made available to the extent that any outstanding balance is repaid.

     "Open-end credit" includes credit card balances.

  (11) "Truncated coverage" means a credit insurance benefit with a term of insurance coverage that is less than the term of the credit transaction. (1975, c. 660, s. 1; 1987, c. 826, ss. 2, 3; 1991, c. 720, s. 6; 1993, c. 226, s. 2; 1995, c. 193, s. 45; c. 208, s. 1; 1999-351, s. 5.3.)

Editor's Note. — The number of subsections (2a), (10) and (11) were assigned by the Revisor of Statutes to preserve alphabetical order, the numbers previously having been (4), (11) and (10), respectively.

CASE NOTES

Coverage of Credit Accident and Health Insurance. — The legislature intended to provide for uniformity of coverage by requiring that all policies of "credit accident and health insurance" issued in the State of North Carolina cover "death or personal injury by accident" as well as "sickness, ailment or bodily injury." Newbold v. Globe Life Ins. Co., 50 N.C. App. 628, 274 S.E.2d 905 (1981).

In an action to recover on a policy of credit life and disability insurance issued by defendant, where defendant alleged that no charge was made for life insurance but only for disability insurance and therefore that the death of plaintiff's decedent was not the event against which the policy insured, the trial court properly entered judgment for plaintiff, since all policies of "credit, accident and health insurance" issued in the State of North Carolina cover "death or personal injury by accident" as well as "sickness, ailment or bodily injury." Newbold v. Globe Life Ins. Co., 50 N.C. App. 628, 274 S.E.2d 905 (1981).

§ 58-57-10. Forms of insurance which are authorized.

Credit life insurance and credit accident and health insurance shall be issued only in the following forms:

  (1) Individual policies of life insurance issued to debtors on the term plan;

  (2) Individual policies of accident and health insurance issued to debtors on a term plan or disability benefit provisions in individual policies of credit life insurance;

  (3) Group policies of life insurance issued to creditors providing insurance upon the lives of debtors on the term plan;

  (4) Group policies of accident and health insurance issued to creditors on a term plan insuring debtors or disability benefit provisions in group credit life insurance policies to provide such coverage. (1975, c. 660, s. 1.)

CASE NOTES

Applied in Newbold v. Globe Life Ins. Co., 50 N.C. App. 628, 274 S.E.2d 905 (1981).

§ 58-57-15. Amount.

(a) Credit Life Insurance. —

  (1) The amount of credit life insurance shall not exceed the amount of unpaid indebtedness as it exists from time to time, less any unearned interest or finance charges; provided, however, that if the amount of credit insurance is based on a predetermined schedule, the amount of credit insurance shall not exceed the scheduled amount of unpaid

indebtedness, less any unearned interest or finance charges, plus an amount equal to three monthly installments or the equivalent thereof.

(2) Notwithstanding the provisions of the above subdivision, insurance on seasonal credit line commitments (such as may be found in agricultural credit transactions) not exceeding one year in duration may be written up to the amount of the loan commitment on a nondecreasing or level term plan.

(3) Notwithstanding this or any other section, insurance on education credit transaction commitments may be written for the amount of such commitment.

(b) Credit Accident and Health and Credit Unemployment Insurance. — The total amount of indemnity payable by credit accident and health or credit unemployment insurance in the event of disability or unemployment, as defined in the policy, shall not exceed the indebtedness; and the amount of each monthly benefit shall not exceed the indebtedness divided by the number of months in the term of the loan. A daily benefit equal in amount to one thirtieth of the scheduled monthly payment is permissible. For open-end credit transactions, the total amount of indemnity payable shall not exceed the amount of unpaid indebtedness at the time disability or unemployment begins, including interest and insurance charges that would accrue on that indebtedness using the creditor's minimum payment schedule. The periodic indemnity may exceed the creditor's minimum payment amount. (1975, c. 660, s. 1; 1981, c. 759, s. 1; 1993, c. 226, s. 3; c. 553, s. 75.)

§ 58-57-20. Term; termination prior to scheduled maturity.

Except as otherwise provided in this section, the term of any credit life insurance or credit accident and health insurance shall, subject to acceptance by the insurer, commence on the date when the debtor becomes obligated to the creditor, except that, where a group policy provides coverage with respect to existing obligations, the insurance on a debtor with respect to such indebtedness shall commence on the effective date of the policy. For credit insurance offered to the debtor subsequent to the date the debtor becomes obligated to the creditor, the term of the insurance shall, subject to the acceptance by the insurer, commence not more than 30 days following the insurer's receipt of the debtor's request for the insurance. The term of such insurance shall not extend more than 15 days beyond the maturity date of the indebtedness or final installment thereof; but the term of the insurance may be less than the term of the indebtedness to provide truncated coverage in connection with transactions having initial terms of more than 60 months or consistent with any age or other termination provisions contained in the policy. If the indebtedness is discharged due to prepayment, the insurance in force shall be terminated unless otherwise requested by the insured in writing. If the indebtedness is discharged due to renewal or refinancing prior to such maturity date, the insurance in force shall be terminated before any new insurance may be issued in connection with the renewed or refinanced indebtedness. In all cases of termination prior to scheduled maturity, a refund shall be paid or credited as provided in G.S. 58-57-50. (1975, c. 660, s. 1; 1991, c. 720, s. 30; 1993, c. 226, s. 4.)

§ 58-57-25. Insurance to be evidenced by individual policy; notice of proposed insurance or certificate; required and prohibited provisions; when debtor to receive copy.

(a) All individual credit insurance sold shall be evidenced by an individual policy. All group insurance sold where any part of the premium is paid by the debtors or by the creditors from identifiable charges collected from the insured debtors shall be evidenced by a certificate of insurance.

(b) Each individual policy or certificate of credit insurance shall set forth the name and home-office address of the insurer, the identity of the insured debtor by name or otherwise, the premium or amount of payment, if any, by the debtor separately for each type of credit insurance if not disclosed in other documents furnished to the debtor, a description of the coverage including the amount and term thereof, and any exceptions, limitations or restrictions, and shall state that the benefits shall be paid to the creditor to reduce or extinguish the unpaid indebtedness, and wherever the amount of insurance may exceed the unpaid indebtedness, that any such excess shall be payable to a beneficiary other than the creditor named by the debtor, or to his estate. For open-end credit, the premium shall be disclosed as the monthly amount charged for each one hundred dollars ($100.00) or one thousand dollars ($1,000) of outstanding indebtedness.

(c) No individual policy of credit insurance and no group policy of credit insurance shall be delivered or issued for delivery in this State unless each contains in substance all of the following provisions:

(1) In each policy there shall be a provision that the policy, or the policy and application therefor, if any, or if a copy of the application is endorsed upon or attached to the policy when issued, shall constitute the entire insurance contract between the parties, and that all statements made by the creditor or by the individual debtors shall, in the absence of fraud, be deemed representations and not warranties.

(2) In each such policy there shall be a provision that the validity of the policy shall not be contested, except for nonpayment of premiums, after it has been in force for two years from its date of issue; and that no statement made by any person insured under the policy relating to his insurability shall be used in contesting the validity of the insurance with respect to which such statement was made after such insurance has been in force on such insured for a period of two years during such person's lifetime, and prior to the date on which the claim thereunder arose. Provided, however, that unless the insured writes his own age on the form and signs a statement that he has done so, there shall be no denial of claims grounded on the debtor's age. Provided further, if the indebtedness is paid by renewal or refinancing prior to the scheduled maturity date, the effective date of the coverage with respect to any policy provision shall be deemed to be the first date on which the debtor became insured under the policy covering the original prior indebtedness that was renewed or refinanced, at least to the extent of the amount and term of the coverage outstanding at the time of renewal and refinancing of the debt.

(3) In each such policy there shall be a provision that when a claim for the death, disability, or unemployment of the insured arises thereunder, settlement shall be made upon receipt of due proof of such death, disability, or unemployment.

(4) On the face of each such policy there shall be placed a title which shall briefly and accurately describe the nature and form of the policy.

(5) Each such policy, including rider and endorsement, shall be identified by a form number in the lower left-hand corner of the first page thereof, and no restriction, condition or provision in or endorsed on such policy shall be valid unless such provision or condition is printed in type as large as 10-point type, one-point leaded.

(6) In each such policy there shall be a provision that the insured debtor shall have the right to rescind the insurance policy or certificate of insurance upon giving written notice to the insurer within 30 days from the date the insured debtor received such policy or certificate.

(d) No individual policy of credit insurance and no group policy of credit insurance shall be delivered or issued for delivery in this State if it contains any provision:

    (1) Limiting the time within which any action at law or in equity may be commenced to less than three years after the cause of action accrues; or

    (2) To the effect that the agent soliciting the insurance is the agent of the person insured under the policy, or making the acts or representations of such agent binding upon the person so insured under the policy.

(e) If said individual policy or certificate of group insurance is not delivered to the debtor at the time the debtor requests credit insurance or mailed to the debtor within 30 days thereafter, a written notification must be furnished to the debtor within the 30-day period, which notification shall set forth the following:

    (1) The name and home-office address of the insurer;

    (2) The identity of the debtor, by name or otherwise;

    (3) The premium or identifiable charge to the debtor, if any, separately for each type of credit insurance;

    (4) The amount and term of the coverage provided, if possible, otherwise a clear description of the means of determining the amount and time of expiry;

    (5) A brief description of the coverage provided;

    (6) A statement that, if the insurance is declined by the insurer or otherwise does not become effective, any premium or identifiable charge will be refunded or credited to the debtor; and

    (7) A statement that, upon acceptance by the insurer, the insurance coverage provided shall become effective as specified in G.S. 58-57-20.

Any portion of the information required in said notification may be furnished by other documents, if copies of such documents are attached to said notification. If an insurance policy or certificate of insurance is not delivered to the insured debtor at the time the debtor requests credit insurance, the debtor shall be given the right to rescind the insurance policy or certificate of insurance upon giving written notice to the insurer within 30 days from the date the insured debtor receives such policy or certificate. (1975, c. 660, s. 1; 1981, c. 759, s. 3; 1993, c. 226, s. 5.)

§ 58-57-30. Forms to be filed with Commissioner; approval or disapproval by Commissioner.

(a) All forms of policies, certificates of insurance, notices of proposed insurance, endorsements and riders intended for use in this State shall be filed with the Commissioner.

(b) The Commissioner shall, within 90 days after the filing of any such policies, certificates of insurance, notices of proposed insurance, endorsements and riders, disapprove any such form if it contains provisions which are contrary to, or not in accordance with, any provision of this Article, Article 38 of this Chapter, or of any rule or regulation promulgated thereunder. Unless disapproved in writing within such 90 days, a form shall be deemed approved.

(c) If the Commissioner notifies the insurer that the form is disapproved, it is unlawful thereafter for such insurer to issue or use such form for a period of 60 days, or until the Commissioner has issued a final order after hearing, whichever is earlier. In such notice, the Commissioner shall specify the reason for his disapproval and state that a hearing will be granted within 20 days after request in writing by the insurer. No such policy, certificate of insurance, notice of proposed insurance, endorsement or rider shall be issued or used until the expiration of 30 days after it has been so filed, unless the Commissioner shall give his prior written approval thereto.

(d) The Commissioner may, at any time after a hearing held not less than 20 days after written notice to the insurer, withdraw his approval of any such form on any ground set forth in subsection (b) above. The written notice of such hearing shall state the reason for the proposed withdrawal.

(e) No insurer shall issue such forms or use them after the effective date of such withdrawal. (1975, c. 660, s. 1; 1979, c. 755, s. 16.)

Cross References. — For the Readable Insurance Policies Act, see G.S. 58-38-1 et seq.

§ 58-57-35. General premium rate standard.

(a) Benefits provided by credit life, credit accident and health and credit unemployment insurance written under this Article shall be reasonable in relation to the premium charge. This requirement is conclusively presumed to be satisfied if the premium rates to be charged for credit life and credit accident and health insurance are no greater than those premium rates set forth in G.S. 58-57-40, 58-57-45, and 58-57-105 for benefits as described in those sections. If an insurer files premium rates for all or part of its business that are greater than those premium rates to which this conclusive presumption applies, the greater rates may be disapproved by the Commissioner if the insurer fails to demonstrate that the benefits are reasonable in relation to the premium rates filed for the group or groups of insureds to which the premium rates would apply and which groups shall meet credibility standards established by the Commissioner. In making this determination, the Commissioner shall give due consideration to the past and prospective loss experience of the group or groups of insureds to which the rates would apply, to reasonable costs and expenses attributable to the insurer and creditor making the coverage available and to other relevant factors, including a fair return to the insurer and creditor. These premium rates shall be allowed to be applied only to the group or groups with respect to which the rate filing is made and approved. The premium rates for credit unemployment insurance shall be filed with and approved by the Commissioner. The amount charged to a debtor for any credit life, credit accident and health, or credit unemployment insurance shall not exceed the premiums charged by the insurer, as computed at the time the charge to the debtor is determined.

(b) The premium or cost of credit life, disability, or unemployment insurance, when written by or through any lender or other creditor, its affiliate, associate or subsidiary shall not be deemed as interest or charges or consideration or an amount in excess of permitted charges in connection with the loan or credit transaction and any gain or advantage to any lender or other creditor, its affiliate, associate or subsidiary, arising out of the premium or commission or dividend from the sale or provision of such insurance shall not be deemed a violation of any other law, general or special, civil or criminal, of this State, or of any rule, regulation or order issued by any regulatory authority of this State.

(c) If premiums are to be determined according to the age of the insured debtor or by age brackets, an insurer may determine premium rates on a basis actuarially equivalent with the rates provided in G.S. 58-57-35, but such rates shall be filed with and approved by the Commissioner. (1975, c. 660, s. 1; 1993, c. 226, s. 6.)

§ 58-57-40. Credit life insurance rate standards.

(a) The premium rate standards set forth below are applicable to plans of credit life insurance with or without requirements for evidence of insurability:

(1) Which contain no exclusions or no exclusions other than suicide; and

(2) Which contain no age restrictions, or only age restrictions not making ineligible for the coverage

    a. Debtors under 65 at the time the indebtedness is incurred; or

    b. Debtors who will not have attained age 66 on the maturity date of the indebtedness.

(b) Rates for use with forms which are more restrictive in any material respect shall reflect such variations in the form or lower rates to the extent that a significant difference in claim cost can reasonably be anticipated unless the insurer demonstrates that such lower rate is not appropriate.

(c) If premiums are payable in one sum in advance, for decreasing term life insurance on indebtedness repayable in substantially equal monthly install-ments, a premium rate not exceeding sixty-five cents (65¢) per one hundred dollars ($100.00) of initial insured indebtedness per year is authorized. Effective January 1, 1995, a premium rate not exceeding sixty cents (60¢) per one hundred dollars ($100.00) of indebtedness per year is authorized. Effective January 1, 1996, a premium rate not exceeding fifty-five cents (55¢) per one hundred dollars ($100.00) of indebtedness per year is authorized. Effective January 1, 1997, a premium rate not exceeding fifty cents (50¢) per one hundred dollars ($100.00) of indebtedness per year is authorized.

(d) The premium rate of joint life coverage shall not exceed one and two-thirds (1 ⅔) the permitted single life rate.

(e) For level term life insurance, a premium rate of one dollar and twenty-five cents ($1.25) per one hundred dollars ($100.00) per year is authorized. Effective January 1, 1995, a premium rate of one dollar and twenty cents ($1.20) per one hundred dollars ($100.00) per year is authorized. Effective January 1, 1996, a premium rate of one dollar and fifteen cents ($1.15) per one hundred dollars ($100.00) per year is authorized. Effective January 1, 1997, a premium rate of one dollar and ten cents ($1.10) per one hundred dollars ($100.00) per year is authorized.

(f) For policies for which monthly premiums are charged on a basis of the then-outstanding balances, a monthly premium per one thousand dollars ($1,000) of outstanding balances is authorized, based on the following formula:

$$Op_n = \frac{20 \quad SP_n}{n + 1}$$

where SP_n = Single premium rate per one hundred dollars ($100.00) of initial insured indebtedness repayable in n equal monthly installments.

Op_n = Monthly outstanding balance premium rate per one thousand dollars ($1,000).

    n = Original repayment period, in months.

(f1) Notwithstanding the premium rates otherwise set forth in this section for credit life insurance, the premium rates for such insurance written in connection with direct loans with contractual commitments of more than 10 years' duration shall be filed with and approved by the Commissioner. Such premium rates shall exhibit a reasonable relationship to the benefits provided.

(g) For credit life insurance on a basis other than the foregoing, premiums charged shall be actuarially equivalent.

(h) In addition to the premium rate authorized, a charge may also be made for a nonrefundable origination fee per credit life insurance transaction as set forth below:

Insured Indebtedness	Fee Permitted
less than $250.00	none
$250.00 or more but less than $500.00	$1.00
$500.00 or more	$3.00

No third or subsequent origination fee may be charged in connection with a third or subsequent refinancing within any twelve-month period. (1975, c. 660, s. 1; 1987, c. 826, ss. 4, 5, 13; 1991, c. 720, s. 91; 1993, c. 226, s. 7.)

§ 58-57-45. Credit accident and health insurance rate standards.

(a) The rate standards set forth below shall be applicable for contracts which contain a provision excluding or denying claim for disability resulting from preexisting illness, disease or physical condition, for which the debtor received medical advice, consultation, or treatment within the six-month period immediately preceding the effective date of the debtor's coverage and if said disability occurs within the six-month period immediately following such date, but contain no other provision which excludes or restricts liability in the event of disability caused in a certain specified manner, except that they may contain provisions excluding or restricting coverage in the event of normal pregnancy; intentionally self-inflicted injuries; sickness resulting from intoxication, addiction to alcohol or narcotics, or from the use thereof unless administered on the advice of a physician; flight in nonscheduled aircraft; war; military service; and may contain the same age restrictions as those mentioned for credit life insurance in G.S. 58-57-40. Provided, if the indebtedness is paid by renewal or refinancing prior to the scheduled maturity date, the effective date of the coverage with respect to any policy provision shall be deemed to be the first date on which the debtor became insured under the policy covering the original prior indebtedness that was renewed or refinanced, at least to the extent of the amount and term of the coverage outstanding at the time of renewal and refinancing of the debt.

(b) A policy of credit accident and health insurance shall include a definition of "disability" providing that during the first 12 months of disability the insured shall be unable to perform the duties of his occupation at the time the disability occurred (or his previous occupation if the person is unemployed or retired at the time the disability occurs), and thereafter the duties of any occupation for which the insured is reasonably fitted by education, training, or experience.

(c) Any policy to which the rates below apply may require the debtor to be gainfully employed on the effective date of the insurance. Provided, however, that unless the insured writes the name of his employer on the application and signs a statement that he is employed, there shall be no denial of claims grounded on the insured's failure to be employed on the effective date of the insurance.

(d) If premiums are payable in one sum in advance for the entire duration of the indebtedness, for insurance with a preexisting exclusion as defined above, the following premiums are authorized:

Single Premium Rates per $100.00 of
Initial Insured Indebtedness

No. of Months in which Indebtedness is Repayable	Nonretroactive Benefits		Retroactive Benefits		
	14-Day	30-Day	7-Day	14-Day	30-Day
12	1.40	.95	2.60	2.10	1.40

915

No. of Months in which Indebtedness is Repayable	Nonretroactive Benefits		Retroactive Benefits		
	14-Day	30-Day	7-Day	14-Day	30-Day
24	1.90	1.40	3.50	2.85	1.90
36	2.40	1.90	4.35	3.65	2.40
48	2.85	2.40	5.25	4.40	2.85
60	3.35	2.85	6.10	5.20	3.35
72	3.85	3.35		5.95	3.85
84	4.30	3.85		6.70	4.30
96	4.80	4.30		7.50	4.80
108	5.25	4.80		8.25	5.25
120	5.75	5.25		9.00	5.75

For terms other than the above, premiums shall be prorated.

(e) For policies for which monthly premiums are charged on a basis of the then-outstanding balances, a monthly premium per one thousand dollars ($1,000) of outstanding balances is authorized, based on the following formula:

$$Op_n = \frac{20 \; SP_n}{n + 1}$$

where SP_n = Single premium rate per one hundred dollars ($100.00) of initial indebtedness repayable in n equal monthly installments.

Op_n = Monthly outstanding balance premium rate per one thousand dollars ($1,000).

n = Original repayment period, in months.

(e1) Notwithstanding the premium rates otherwise set forth in this section for credit accident and health insurance, the premium rates for such insurance written in connection with direct loans with contractual commitments of more than 10 years' duration shall be filed with and approved by the Commissioner. Such premium rates shall exhibit a reasonable relationship to the benefits provided.

(f) Premium rate standards for other benefit plans and for indebtedness repayable in installments other than as indicated above shall be actuarially consistent with the above rate standards.

(g) In addition to the premium rate authorized, a charge may also be made for a nonrefundable origination fee per credit accident and health insurance transaction as set forth below:

Insured Indebtedness	Fee Permitted
less than $250.00	none
$250.00 or more but less than $500.00	$1.00
$500.00 or more	$3.00

No third or subsequent origination fee may be charged in connection with a third or subsequent refinancing within any twelve-month period.

(h) The premium rates for joint accident and health coverage shall not exceed one and two-thirds (1 ⅔) times the permitted single accident and health rate. (1975, c. 660, s. 1; 1981, c. 759, ss. 2, 4-6, 9; 1987, c. 826, ss. 6, 7, 14; 1993, c. 226, s. 8.)

§ 58-57-50. Premium refunds or credits.

(a) Each individual policy or group certificate shall provide that in the event of termination of the insurance prior to the scheduled maturity date of indebtedness, any refund of an amount paid by the debtor for insurance shall be paid or credited promptly to the person entitled thereto.

(b) The refund of premiums for decreasing term credit life insurance in transactions of 60 months duration or less and the refund of premiums for single interest credit property insurance and single interest physical damage insurance shall be equal to the amount computed by the sum of digits formula known as the "Rule of 78." The refund of premiums for decreasing term credit life insurance in transactions of more than 60 months duration shall be equal to the premium that would be charged for the remaining term and amount of coverage in the policy. The refund of premiums for level term credit life insurance and dual interest credit property insurance and dual interest physical damage insurance shall be equal to the pro rata unearned gross premiums.

(c) The refund of premiums in the case of credit accident and health insurance shall be equal to one-half the amount computed by the sum-of-digits formula commonly known as the "Rule of 78" plus one-half the amount of the pro rata unearned gross premium.

In lieu thereof the refund may be computed by the "Pure Premium" method. The refund is computed from the schedule of credit accident and health premiums and is equal to the premium from that schedule which would be charged for such insurance in the amount of the total remaining benefits for the remaining term of the indebtedness outstanding on the date of termination.

(d) No refund need be made if the amount thereof is less than one dollar ($1.00).

(e) If a creditor requires a debtor to make any payment for credit life insurance or credit accident and health insurance and an individual policy or group certificate of insurance is not issued, the creditor shall immediately give written notice to such debtor and shall promptly make an appropriate credit to the account. (1975, c. 660, s. 1; 1981, c. 759, s. 8; 1989, c. 485, s. 7.)

§ 58-57-55. Issuance of policies.

All policies of credit life insurance and credit accident and health insurance shall be delivered or issued for delivery in this State only by an insurer authorized to do an insurance business therein, and shall be issued only through holders of licenses or authorizations issued by the Commissioner. The enrollment of debtors under a group policy issued to a creditor and authorized under this Article shall not constitute the issuance of a policy of insurance. (1975, c. 660, s. 1.)

§ 58-57-60. Claims.

(a) All claims shall be promptly reported to the insurer or its designated claim representative, and the insurer shall maintain adequate claim files. All claims shall be settled as soon as possible and in accordance with the terms of the insurance contract.

(b) All claims shall be paid either by draft drawn upon the insurer or by check of the insurer or by electronic funds transfer or be paid by such other specified method upon the direction of the beneficiary who is entitled thereto pursuant to the policy provisions.

(c) No plan or arrangement shall be used whereby any person, firm or corporation other than the insurer or its designated claim representative shall be authorized to settle or adjust claims. The creditor shall not be designated as claim representative for the insurer in adjusting claims; provided, that a group policyholder may, by arrangement with the group insurer, draw drafts, electronic funds transfers, or checks in payment of claims due to the group policyholder subject to audit and review by the insurer. (1975, c. 660, s. 1; 1993, c. 226, s. 10.)

§ 58-57-65. Existing insurance; choice of insurer.

Credit life insurance and credit accident and health insurance may not be required of any borrower by any creditor. When credit property insurance is required for any indebtedness, the debtor shall be notified in writing of the option of furnishing the required amount of insurance through existing policies owned or controlled by him or of procuring and furnishing the required coverage through any insurer authorized to transact an insurance business within this State. (1975, c. 660, s. 1; 1987, c. 826, s. 8.)

§ 58-57-70. Enforcement.

The Commissioner may, after notice and hearing, issue rules and regulations necessary for the implementation of this Article. Whenever the Commissioner finds that there has been a violation of this Article or any rules or regulations issued pursuant thereto, and after written notice thereof and hearing given to the insurer or other person authorized or licensed by the Commissioner, he shall set forth the details of his findings together with an order for compliance by a specified date. Such order shall be binding on the insurer and other person authorized or licensed by the Commissioner on the date specified unless sooner withdrawn by the Commissioner or a stay thereof has been ordered by a court of competent jurisdiction. The provisions of G.S. 58-57-20 through 58-57-50 shall not be operative until 90 days after June 18, 1975, and the Commissioner in his discretion may extend by not more than an additional 90 days the initial period within which the provisions of said sections shall not be operative. (1975, c. 660, s. 1.)

§ 58-57-75. Judicial review.

Any party to the proceeding affected by an order of the Commissioner shall be entitled to judicial review by following the procedure set forth in G.S. 58-2-75 through 58-2-90. (1975, c. 660, s. 1.)

§ 58-57-80. Penalties.

In addition to any other penalty provided by law, any person, firm or corporation which willfully violates an order of the Commissioner after it has become final, and while such order is in effect, shall, upon proof thereof to the satisfaction of the court, forfeit and pay to the State of North Carolina a sum not to exceed one thousand dollars ($1,000) which may be recovered in a civil action, except that if such violation is found to be willful, the amount of such penalty shall be a sum not to exceed five thousand dollars ($5,000). The Commissioner, in his discretion, may revoke or suspend the license of the person, firm or corporation guilty of such willful violation. Such order for suspension or revocation shall be upon notice and hearing, and shall be subject to judicial review as provided in G.S. 58-57-75. Any creditor who requires credit life insurance or credit accident and health insurance, or both, in excess of the amounts set forth in G.S. 58-57-15 or who violates the provisions of G.S. 58-57-65 shall be guilty of a Class 3 misdemeanor, the penalty for which shall only be a fine of two thousand dollars ($2,000) for each such occurrence or violation. (1975, c. 660, s. 1; 1985, c. 666, s. 32; 1993, c. 539, s. 468; 1994, Ex. Sess., c. 24, s. 14(c); 1998-215, s. 87; 1999-132, s. 9.3.)

§ 58-57-85: Repealed by Session Laws 2001-223, s. 3.6, effective June 15, 2001.

§ 58-57-90. Credit property insurance; personal household property coverage.

(a) As used in this Article, the term "single interest credit property" insurance means insurance of the personal household property of the debtor against loss, with the creditor as sole beneficiary; and the term "dual credit property" insurance means insurance of personal household property of the debtor, with the creditor as primary beneficiary and the debtor as beneficiary of proceeds not paid to the creditor. For the purpose of this Article, "personal household property" means household furniture, furnishings and appliances designed for household use and not used by the debtor in a business trade or profession.

(b) Premium rates charged shall not exceed eighty-seven cents (87¢) per year per one hundred dollars ($100.00) of insured value for single interest credit property insurance and shall not exceed one dollar and thirty-one cents ($1.31) per year per one hundred dollars ($100.00) of insured value for dual interest credit property insurance. The insured value shall not exceed the lesser of the value of the property or the amount of the initial indebtedness.

In addition to the premium rate authorized, a charge may also be made for a nonrefundable origination fee per credit property insurance transaction as set forth below:

Insured Value	*Fee Permitted*
less than $250.00	none
$250.00 or more but less than $500.00	$1.00
$500.00 or more	$3.00

No third or subsequent origination fee may be charged in connection with the third or subsequent refinancing within any twelve-month period.

The Department shall collect data on credit property insurance written in North Carolina, including but not limited to: the amount of coverage written, direct premiums, earned premiums, dividends and retrospective rate credits paid, direct losses paid, direct losses incurred, commissions paid, loss ratios and policy provisions. (1981, c. 759, s. 7; 1987, c. 826, s. 9; 1993, c. 226, s. 11; 1993 (Reg. Sess., 1994), c. 720, s. 2.)

§ 58-57-95. Rebate of premiums on credit life and credit accident and health insurance; retention of funds by agent.

It shall be unlawful for any insurance carrier, or officer, agent or representative of an insurance company writing credit life and credit accident and health insurance, as defined in G.S. 58-58-10 and G.S. 58-51-100, or combination credit life, accident and health, hospitalization and disability insurance in connection with loans, to permit any agent or representative of such company to retain any portion of funds received for the payment of losses incurred, or to be incurred, under such policies of insurance issued by such company, or to pay, allow, permit, give or offer to pay, allow, permit or give, directly or indirectly, as an inducement to insurance, or after insurance has been effected, any rebate, discount, abatement, credit or reduction of the premium, to any loan agency, insurance agency or broker, or to any creditor of the debtor on whose account the insurance was issued, or to any person, firm or corporation which received a commission or fee in connection with the issuance of such insurance: Provided, that this section shall not prohibit the payment of commissions to a licensed insurance agent or agency or limited representative on the sale of a policy of credit life and credit accident and health insurance, or combination credit life, accident and health, hospitalization and disability insurance in connection with loans. (1955, c. 1341, s. 1; 1987, c. 629, s. 8.)

CASE NOTES

A bank could not have legally made a refund of money which had gone, even through its hands, to an insurance company as premiums on credit life insurance. It is unlawful for an insurance company writing credit life insurance in connection with a loan to permit any agent to pay any rebate or to refund any premiums without the consent of the policyholders. Huski-Bilt, Inc. v. First-Citizens Bank & Trust Co., 271 N.C. 662, 157 S.E.2d 352 (1967).

§ 58-57-100. Credit property insurance; automobile physical damage insurance.

(a) Single interest or dual interest physical damage insurance may be written on nonfleet private passenger motor vehicles, as defined in G.S. 58-40-10, that are used as collateral for loans made under Article 15 of Chapter 53 of the General Statutes. Automobile physical damage insurance as described in this section is a form of credit property insurance, as referred to in G.S. 53-189. It is subject to the following conditions:

    (1) Such insurance may be written only on a motor vehicle on which there is a valid inspection sticker.

    (2) If a motor vehicle is already insured and the lender is named loss payee and that insurance continues in force, then no other physical damage insurance may be written.

    (3) Notification must be given orally and in writing to the borrower that he has the option to provide his own insurance coverage at any point during the term of the loan.

    (4) The creditor must have either a first or second lien on the motor vehicle to be insured.

    (5) The amount of insurance coverage may not exceed the lesser of (i) the principal amount of the loan plus allowable charges, excluding interest, plus two scheduled installment payments or (ii) the actual fair market value of the collateral at the time the insurance is written.

    (6) When a creditor accepts other collateral in addition to a motor vehicle as herein defined, the combined insurance on all collateral may not exceed the initial indebtedness of the loan.

(b) Policy forms, rates, rating plans, and classifications for single or dual interest nonfleet private passenger motor vehicle physical damage insurance shall be filed with the Commissioner in accordance with Articles 40 and 41 of this Chapter. Every insurer writing such insurance shall, on or before April 1 of each year, file a supplemental financial statement in such form and detail that the Commissioner prescribes that will enable the Commissioner to review and analyze the filings made under this subsection. (1989, c. 485, s. 13; 1989 (Reg. Sess., 1990), c. 1021, s. 2; 1993 (Reg. Sess., 1994), c. 720, s. 1.)

§ 58-57-105. Credit insurance on credit card balances.

(a) Credit card facilities may be used for the solicitation, negotiation, or payment of premiums for credit insurance on the unpaid balance of any credit card account pursuant to G.S. 58-3-145. Solicitation or negotiation for credit insurance on credit card account balances may not be made by unsolicited telephone calls or facsimile transmissions.

(b) If credit life insurance premiums are charged through a credit card facility or if credit life insurance premiums are payable on the then outstanding balances on revolving charge account contracts defined in G.S. 25A-11, a premium not exceeding seventy-four cents (74¢) per one thousand dollars ($1,000) of insured indebtedness per month is authorized. The premium rate for joint credit life insurance may not exceed one and two-thirds (12/3) the permitted single credit life insurance premium rate. (1993, c. 226, s. 9; c. 504, s. 46; 1999-365, s. 2.)

§ 58-57-107: Recodified as § 58-3-147 by Session Laws 1993, c. 504, s. 40.

Editor's Note. — Session Laws 1993, c. 226, s. 9, effective June 28, 1993, added new G.S. 58-57-107, which was recodified as G.S. 58-3-147 by Session Laws 1993, c. 504, s. 40, effective July 24, 1993.

§ 58-57-110. Credit unemployment insurance rate standards; policy provisions.

(a) Each year the Commissioner shall prescribe a minimum incurred loss ratio standard requirement to develop a premium rate reasonable in relation to the benefits provided by credit unemployment insurance coverage. The following requirements must be met:
   (1) Coverage is provided or offered, with or without underwriting, to all debtors regardless of age who are working for salary, wages, or other employment income for at least 30 hours per week and have done so for 12 consecutive months;
   (2) Coverage sets forth a definition of involuntary unemployment as a loss of employment income that may include, but is not limited to, loss caused by layoff, general strike, termination of employment, or lockout;
   (3) Coverage does not contain any exclusion except: debts with irregular monthly payments; voluntary forfeiture of salary, wages, or other employment income; resignation; retirement; sickness, disease, or normal pregnancy; or loss of income due to termination as a result of willful misconduct that is a violation of some established, definite rule of conduct, a forbidden act, or willful dereliction of duty, or criminal misconduct.

(b) The Commissioner may approve other policy provisions and coverages consistent with the purposes of unemployment coverage.

(c) Joint coverage rates for credit unemployment insurance shall be one and two-thirds (1 ⅔) times the approved single rate of coverage. (1993, c. 226, s. 9.)

§ 58-57-115. Family leave credit insurance standards; policy provisions.

(a) Definitions. — As used in this section:
   (1) "Foster child" means a minor (i) over whom a guardian has been appointed by the clerk of superior court of any county in North Carolina; or (ii) the primary or sole custody of whom has been assigned by order of a court of competent jurisdiction.

(2) "Immediate family member" means a spouse, child (natural, adopted, or foster), or parent of the insured person.

(3) "Placement in the foster home" means physically residing with the insured person appointed as the guardian or custodian of a foster child or children as long as the insured person has assumed the legal obligation for total or partial support of the foster child or children with the intent that the foster child or children reside with the insured person on more than a temporary or short-term basis.

(b) Coverage. — Insurers may provide coverage for loss of income because of a voluntary, employer-approved leave of absence granted upon the occurrence of any of the qualifying events in subsection (d) of this section. The insured person shall not be required to meet any federal requirements in order to qualify for benefits provided by this coverage. Benefits shall be paid to the creditor to reduce the insured person's indebtedness.

(c) Eligibility. — Coverage may be provided or offered to any debtor who has not yet reached his or her 71st birthday and has been working for wages for at least 30 hours per week for the past five consecutive weeks.

(d) Qualifying Events. — Benefits shall be paid only for the following qualifying events:

(1) An accident involving sickness of, or incapacitation of, an immediate family member that requires the insured person to attend to the family member's needs.

(2) Birth of a child or children of the insured person.

(3) Adoption of a child or children of the insured person.

(4) Placement in the foster home of a foster child or children.

(5) The insured person's principal residence is in a federally declared disaster area.

(6) The insured person is called to active military duty.

(7) The insured person is called to petit or grand jury duty.

(e) Exclusions. — Coverage shall not contain any exclusions except:

(1) Retirement of the insured person from employment.

(2) Voluntary resignation of the insured person from employment.

(3) Seasonal unemployment of the insured person.

(4) Involuntary unemployment of the insured person.

(5) Disability of the insured person.

(6) Employment termination because of willful or criminal misconduct of the insured person.

(f) Notice. — The insurer shall send a notice to the insured person at the insured person's home address to inform the insured person that benefits have been paid, including the dates and the amount of payment. The notice shall be sent to the insured person within 60 days after the last day of the benefit period.

(g) Minimum Amounts. — The minimum monthly benefit amount shall be level for the entire benefit period. The minimum monthly benefit amount shall equal or exceed the minimum monthly payment required by the creditor, plus the premium charge for the coverage attributable to the benefit period.

(h) Miscellaneous Provisions. — Any waiting period for benefits shall not exceed 30 days. The insured shall provide satisfactory evidence of employer approval of qualified leave. Lump-sum benefits may be paid. Refunds of unearned single premiums shall be equal to the pro rata unearned gross premium.

(i) Rates. — Premium rates shall be actuarially demonstrated to generate a sixty percent (60%) incurred loss ratio. Joint coverage rates shall be one and two-thirds (1 ⅔) times the approved single rate. Rates shall be filed for approval before they can be used.

(j) Reports. — By March 31 of each year every insurer writing family leave coverage shall file a statistical report of the past calendar year's actuarial experience for that coverage. The report shall demonstrate the actual experience loss ratio for the calendar year and shall include the: number of insureds, total earned premium, total number of incurred claims, total incurred claims, total number of incurred claims for each qualifying event, average monthly benefit per claim for each qualifying event, and premium refunds. (1999-351, s. 5.1.)

ARTICLE 58.

Life Insurance and Viatical Settlements.

Part 1. General Provisions.

§ 58-58-1. Definitions; requisites of contract.

All corporations or associations doing business in this State, under any charter or statute of this or any other state, involving the payment of money or other thing of value to families or representatives of policy and certificate holders or members, conditioned upon the continuance or cessation of human life, or involving an insurance, guaranty, contract, or pledge for the payment of endowments or annuities, or who employ agents to solicit such business, are life insurance companies, in all respects subject to the laws herein made and provided for the government of life insurance companies, and shall not make any such insurance, guaranty, contract, or pledge in this State with any citizen, or resident thereof, which does not distinctly state the amount of benefits payable, the manner of payment, the consideration therefor and such other provisions as the Commissioner may require. (1899, c. 54, s. 55; Rev., s. 4773; C.S., s. 6455; 1945, c. 379.)

Editor's Note. — Session Laws 2001-436, s. 1, effective April 1, 2002, rewrote the heading to Article 58, which formerly read: "General Regulations of Business Life Insurance."

Session Laws 2001-436, s. 2, effective April 1, 2002, divided Article 58 into Parts 1 to 4, assigning a Part head to each Part, with G.S. 58-58-1 to 58-58-40 in Part 1, G.S. 58-58-45 to 58-58-65 in Part 2, G.S. 58-58-70 to 58-58-120 in Part 3, and G.S. 58-58-125 to 58-58-170 in Part 4, reserving G.S. 58-58-175 to 58-58-195 for future codification purposes.

Session Laws 2001-436, s. 17, is a severability clause.

§ 58-58-5. Industrial life insurance defined.

Industrial life insurance is hereby declared to be that form of life insurance under which the premiums are payable monthly or oftener, provided the face amount of insurance stated in the policy does not exceed one thousand dollars ($1,000) and the words "Industrial Policy" are printed upon the policy as a part of the descriptive matter. (1945, c. 379; 1947, c. 721.)

§ 58-58-10. Credit life insurance defined.

Credit life insurance is declared to be insurance upon the life of a debtor who may be indebted to any person, firm, or corporation extending credit to said debtor. Credit life insurance may include the granting of additional benefits in the event of total and permanent disability of the debtor. (1953, c. 1096, s. 1.)

CASE NOTES

Insurable Interest Requirement as Public Policy. — The long established public policy of this State prevents one who lacks a legally recognized insurable interest in the life of another from taking out and enforcing for his own benefit a policy of insurance on such other person's life. Newsome v. Prudential Ins. Co. of Am., 4 N.C. App. 161, 166 S.E.2d 487 (1969).

Creditor has an insurable interest in debtor's life. Hatley v. Johnston, 265 N.C. 73, 143 S.E.2d 260 (1965).

Credit life insurance, as between creditor and insured debtor, is collateral security. Hatley v. Johnston, 265 N.C. 73, 143 S.E.2d 260 (1965).

And Payment of Debt with Credit Life Insurance Is Payment by Debtor. — Credit life insurance, as between the creditor and insured debtor, is collateral security. Consequently, payment of the debt with credit life insurance, when the insured authorizes the creditor to procure the policy and pays the premium himself, is payment by the insured debtor, just as payment with any collateral security is payment by the owner thereof. Newsome v. Prudential Ins. Co. of Am., 4 N.C. App. 161, 166 S.E.2d 487 (1969).

Payment of the debt with credit life insurance, when the insured authorizes the creditor to procure the policy and pays the premium himself, is payment by the insured debtor, just as payment with any collateral security is payment by the owner thereof. The presence of an assuming grantee, who has no right to change the beneficiary under the policy, and therefore no claim of ownership, would not alter that result. Hatley v. Johnston, 265 N.C. 73, 143 S.E.2d 260 (1965).

Insurer Not Secondarily Liable on Debt. — As between the creditor and the insured debtor the credit life insurance is collateral security, but this does not place the defendant insurance company in the position of a surety or in any sense render it secondarily liable on the debt. Newsome v. Prudential Ins. Co. of Am., 4 N.C. App. 161, 166 S.E.2d 487 (1969).

Credit life insurance, as between the creditor and the insured debtor, is collateral security, but this does not place the insurance company in the position of a surety or in any sense render it secondarily liable on the debt, the insurance company becoming liable solely because, for a premium paid to it, it assumed the risk of the debtor's continued life and his death occurs while the insurance policy is in effect. Newsome v. Prudential Ins. Co. of Am., 4 N.C. App. 161, 166 S.E.2d 487 (1969).

When Liability Established. — Liability of the insurer under a credit life insurance policy is established at the moment of the insured debtor's death, and payment thereafter of the debt to the creditor, thereby terminating the creditor's insurable interest in the life of the debtor, does not terminate the insurer's liability under its policy of insurance. Newsome v. Prudential Ins. Co. of Am., 4 N.C. App. 161, 166 S.E.2d 487 (1969).

Insurer is liable upon its policy of credit life insurance where the creditor repossesses the mortgaged chattel subsequent to the insured debtor's death, notwithstanding the policy provided that it should terminate automatically upon repossession of the chattel, since insurer's liability under the policy became fixed when the debtor died before repossession of the chattel occurred. Newsome v. Prudential Ins. Co. of Am., 4 N.C. App. 161, 166 S.E.2d 487 (1969).

Beneficiary May Enforce Terms of Contract. — North Carolina has long recognized the right of one for whose benefit a contract has been made to sue to enforce its terms, even though he is not directly a party to the contract. Newsome v. Prudential Ins. Co. of Am., 4 N.C. App. 161, 166 S.E.2d 487 (1969).

When a creditor named as beneficiary of a credit life insurance policy effects payment of its indebtedness after the death of the insured debtor by repossessing the chattel purchased by the debtor under a conditional sales contract, thereby giving up its rights in the proceeds of the policy, the credit life insurance policy becomes one for the benefit of the insured, collectible by his executors or administrators. Newsome v. Prudential Ins. Co. of Am., 4 N.C. App. 161, 166 S.E.2d 487 (1969).

The creditor who is named as beneficiary loses all interest in the proceeds of the policy upon payment of the indebtedness, and the policy then becomes one for the benefit of the insured, collectible by his executors or administrators. Newsome v. Prudential Ins. Co. of Am., 4 N.C. App. 161, 166 S.E.2d 487 (1969).

Action by Debtor's Administratrix to Recover Policy Proceeds. — The fact that the insured debtor's estate is not named directly as beneficiary in a credit life insurance policy is no bar to the right of the insured's administratrix to maintain an action upon the policy, since one for whose benefit a contract has been made may sue to enforce its terms even though he is not directly a party to the contract, the credit life insurance being for the benefit of insured's estate in that the proceeds of the policy are, by contractual and statutory provision, to be applied to discharge an indebtedness of the estate. Newsome v. Prudential Ins. Co. of Am., 4 N.C. App. 161, 166 S.E.2d 487 (1969).

When the debt to the creditor is satisfied subsequent to the insured debtor's death by repossession of the mortgaged chattel, the debtor's estate becomes subrogated to the rights of the creditor as beneficiary under the credit life insurance policy as against the insurer, and the debtor's administratrix may maintain an action against the insurer to recover the proceeds of the policy. Newsome v. Prudential Ins. Co. of Am., 4 N.C. App. 161, 166 S.E.2d 487 (1969).

Creditor Not Entitled to Proceeds Following Repossession After Debtor's Death. — Creditor relinquished its rights in the proceeds of a credit life insurance policy when, following the death of the insured debtor, it effected payment of its indebtedness by repossession of the chattel purchased by debtor under a conditional sales contract, and the creditor could not thereafter collect and retain for its own account the proceeds of the credit life insurance policy, since it no longer had an insurable interest in the life of the debtor. Newsome v. Prudential Ins. Co. of Am., 4 N.C. App. 161, 166 S.E.2d 487 (1969).

Nothing in statutes grants to Commissioner express or implied authority to set rates for credit life insurance. State ex rel. Comm'r of Ins. v. Integon Life Ins. Co., 28 N.C. App. 7, 220 S.E.2d 409 (1975).

The conspicuous absence of express rate-making authority with regard to credit life insurance, when such authority existed with regard to credit accident and health insurance, manifests the fact that no such authority has been conferred. State ex rel. Comm'r of Ins. v. Integon Life Ins. Co., 28 N.C. App. 7, 220 S.E.2d 409 (1975).

Nor Does Companies' Acquiescence Raise Such Authority. — Contention that acquiescence by companies writing credit life insurance in rates set by prior Commissioners of Insurance gave present Commissioner the authority to fix credit life rates was untenable. State ex rel. Comm'r of Ins. v. Integon Life Ins. Co., 28 N.C. App. 7, 220 S.E.2d 409 (1975).

Former Statute Inapplicable. — Since former G.S. 54-260.2 applied only to credit accident and health insurance as defined in G.S. 58-51-100, it had no application to credit life insurance, and could not be seen as granting implied authority to set credit life rates. State ex rel. Comm'r of Ins. v. Integon Life Ins. Co., 28 N.C. App. 7, 220 S.E.2d 409 (1975).

Cited in Newbold v. Globe Life Ins. Co., 50 N.C. App. 628, 274 S.E.2d 905 (1981).

§ 58-58-15. Any type of survivorship fund in life insurance contract prohibited.

No life insurance company shall hereafter deliver in this State, as a part of or in combination with any insurance, endowment or annuity contract, any agreement or plan, additional to the rights, dividends, and benefits arising out of any such insurance, endowment or annuity contract, which provides for the accumulation of profits over a period of years and for payment of all or any part of such accumulated profits only to members or policyholders of a designated group or class who continue as members or policyholders until the end of a specified period of years. Nor shall any such company deliver in this State any individual life insurance policy which provides that on the death of anyone not specifically named therein, the owner or beneficiary of the policy shall receive the payment or granting of anything of value. (1955, c. 492.)

§ 58-58-20. Tie-in sales with life insurance prohibited.

No life insurance company shall hereafter deliver in this State, as a part of or in combination with any insurance, endowment or annuity contract, any agreement or plan, additional to the rights, dividends, and benefits arising out of any such insurance, endowment, or annuity contract which provides for the sale, solicitation, or delivery of any stock or shares of stock in the company issuing the policy or in any other insurance company or other corporation, or benefit certificate, securities, or any special advisory board contract, or other contracts or resolutions of any kind promising returns and profits, or dividends equivalent to stock dividends as an inducement to or in connection with the sale of the insurance or to the taking of the policy. Nothing herein contained shall be construed as prohibiting any participating insurer from distributing to its policyholders dividends, savings or the unused or unabsorbed portion of premiums and premium deposits. (1957, c. 752.)

§ 58-58-22. Individual policy standard provisions.

No policy of individual life insurance shall be delivered in this State unless it contains in substance the following provisions, or provisions that in the Commissioner's opinion are more favorable to the person insured:

    (1) Grace period. — A provision that the insured is entitled to a grace period of 31 days for the payment of any premium due except the first, during which grace period the death benefit coverage shall continue in force. The policy may provide that if a claim arises under the policy during the grace period, the amount of any premium due or overdue may be deducted from any amount payable under the policy in settlement.

    (2) Incontestability. — A provision that the validity of the policy shall not be contested, except for nonpayment of premium, once it has been in force for two years after its date of issue; and that no statement made by any person insured under the policy about that person's insurability shall be used during the person's lifetime to contest the validity of the policy after the insurance has been in force for two years.

    (3) Misstatement of age or gender. — A provision specifying an equitable adjustment of premiums or benefits, or both, to be made if the age or gender of the person insured has been misstated; the provision to contain a clear statement of the method of adjustment to be used.

    (4) Suicide. — A provision that may not limit payment of benefits for a period more than two years after the date of issue of the policy because of suicide and that provides for at least the return of premiums paid on the policy if there is suicide during the two-year period.

    (5) Reinstatement. — A provision that, unless the policy has been surrendered for its cash surrender value, or its cash surrender value has been exhausted, the policy will be reinstated at any time within five years after the date of premium default upon written application therefor, the production of evidence of insurability satisfactory to the insurer, the payment of all overdue premiums, and the payment of reinstatement of any other indebtedness to the insurer upon the policy, all with interest at the rate specified. (1995, c. 517, s. 31(a).)

§ 58-58-23. Standard provisions for annuity and pure endowment contracts.

No annuity or pure endowment contract, except a reversionary or survivorship annuity and except a group annuity contract, shall be delivered or issued for delivery in this State unless it contains in substance the following provisions or provisions that in the opinion of the Commissioner are more favorable to the holders of the contracts:

    (1) Grace period. — A provision for a grace period of not less than 31 days within which any stipulated payment to the insurer falling due after the first payment may be made. During the grace period, the contract shall continue in full force. If a claim arises under the contract because of death before the expiration of the grace period and before the overdue payment to the insurer is made, the amount of the payments, with interest on any overdue payments, may be deducted from any amount payable under the contract.

    (2) Incontestability. — If any statements are required as a condition of issue, there shall be a provision that the contract shall be incontestable during the lifetime of the person or of each of the persons as to whom the statements are required after it has been in force for a period of two years after its date of issue, except for nonpayment of stipulated payments to the insurer.

    (3) Misstatements of age or gender. — A provision that if the age or gender of any person upon whose life the contract is made has been misstated, the amount payable or benefits accruing under the contract shall be such as the stipulated payment or payments to the insurer

would have been according to the correct age or gender; and if the insurer makes an overpayment because of the misstatement, that amount with interest at the rate specified in the contract may be charged against any current or subsequent payment by the insurer under the contract.

(4) Reinstatement. — A provision that the contract may be reinstated at any time within one year after a default in making stipulated payments to the insurer, unless the cash surrender value has been paid; but all overdue stipulated payments and any indebtedness to the insurer on the contract shall be paid or reinstated with interest at a rate specified in the contract. When applicable, the insurer may also require evidence of insurability satisfactory to the insurer. (1995, c. 517, s. 31(a).)

§ 58-58-25. Policies to be issued to any person possessing the sickle cell trait or hemoglobin C trait.

No insurance company licensed in this State pursuant to the provisions of Articles 1 through 64 of this Chapter shall refuse to issue or deliver any policy of life insurance authorized thereunder solely by reason of the fact that the person to be insured possesses sickle cell trait or hemoglobin C trait; nor shall any such policy issued and delivered in this State carry a higher premium rate or charge by reason of the fact that the person to be insured possesses said traits. The term "sickle cell trait" is defined as the condition wherein the major natural hemoglobin components present in the blood of the individual are hemoglobin A (normal) and hemoglobin S (sickle hemoglobin) as defined by standard chemical and physical analytic techniques, including electrophoresis, and the proportion of hemoglobin A is greater than the proportion of hemoglobin S or one natural parent of the individual is shown to have only normal hemoglobin components (hemoglobin A, hemoglobin A2, hemoglobin F) in the normal proportions by standard chemical and physical analytic tests. The term "hemoglobin C trait" is defined as the condition wherein the major natural hemoglobin components present in the blood of the individual are hemoglobin A (normal) and hemoglobin C as defined by standard chemical and physical analytic techniques, including electrophoresis, and the proportion of hemoglobin A is greater than the proportion of hemoglobin C or one natural parent of the individual is shown to have only normal hemoglobin components (hemoglobin A, hemoglobin A2, hemoglobin F) in the normal proportions by standard chemical and physical analytic tests. (1975, c. 600, s. 1.)

§ 58-58-30. Soliciting agent represents the company.

A person who solicits an application for insurance upon the life of another, in any controversy relating thereto between the insured or his beneficiary and the company issuing a policy upon such application, is the agent of the company and not of the insured. (1907, c. 958, s. 1; C.S., s. 6457.)

CASE NOTES

Legislative Intent. — This section was enacted by the General Assembly as a protective measure for consumers of insurance services. Its import is obviously to expand the class of persons capable of binding insurers to enforceable insurance obligations, and to prevent insurers who obtain consideration from persons solicited on their behalf, from relying on the purportedly ultra vires actions of their agents to deny liability to beneficiaries. Northern Nat'l Life Ins. Co. v. Lacy J. Miller Mach. Co., 63 N.C. App. 424, 305 S.E.2d 568 (1983), aff'd, 311 N.C. 62, 316 S.E.2d 256 (1984).

This section establishes a conclusive presumption of an agency relationship once "solicitation" on the part of the agent is found.

Northern Nat'l Life Ins. Co. v. Lacy J. Miller Mach. Co., 63 N.C. App. 424, 305 S.E.2d 568 (1983), aff'd, 311 N.C. 62, 316 S.E.2d 256 (1984).

"Solicit" Defined. — The word "solicit" is not defined in G.S. 58-1-5; nor does the term appear to have been authoritatively construed in the reported decisions of the appellate courts of this State. Its meaning must be discerned, therefore, by application of fundamental principles of statutory construction. Northern Nat'l Life Ins. Co. v. Lacy J. Miller Mach. Co., 63 N.C. App. 424, 305 S.E.2d 568 (1983), aff'd, 311 N.C. 62, 316 S.E.2d 256 (1984).

The term "solicit" must be interpreted to further the intent of the Legislature and, absent a special definition, must be given its ordinary meaning. Northern Nat'l Life Ins. Co. v. Lacy J. Miller Mach. Co., 311 N.C. 62, 316 S.E.2d 256 (1984).

Where there is evidence that a person actively participated in the placement of a life insurance policy by approaching corporate officers with information about the policy, obtaining and completing blank applications for the policy, collecting premiums, distributing policies, and collecting a commission, there is ample evidence that the person has "solicited" an application for insurance upon the life of another within the meaning of this section. Northern Nat'l Life Ins. Co. v. Lacy J. Miller Mach. Co., 311 N.C. 62, 316 S.E.2d 256 (1984).

This section does not attempt to prescribe the extent of the agent's authority or to convert a special or limited agency into one with general powers. Fountain & Herrington, Inc. v. Mutual Life Ins. Co., 55 F.2d 120 (4th Cir. 1932). See also Provident Mut. Life Ins. Co. v. Parsons, 70 F.2d 863 (4th Cir. 1934), cert. denied, 293 U.S. 582, 55 S. Ct. 95, 79 L. Ed. 678 (1934).

Broker as Agent of Insurer. — Where a broker "solicits" within the meaning of this section, he is deemed an agent of the insurer in situations covered by that statute. Northern Nat'l Life Ins. Co. v. Lacy J. Miller Mach. Co., 311 N.C. 62, 316 S.E.2d 256 (1984).

Liability of Insurer for Delay of Agent. — If defendant's agent wrongfully failed to deliver policy within a reasonably short time after its receipt, during which time plaintiff's intestate was in good health and ready, able, and willing to pay the premium on delivery, as stipulated, and plaintiff's intestate thereafter became ill, the defendant could not withhold delivery so as to release it from responsibility. American Trust Co. v. Life Ins. Co., 173 N.C. 558, 92 S.E. 706 (1917); Fox v. Volunteer State Life Ins. Co., 185 N.C. 121, 116 S.E. 266 (1923).

When Knowledge of Agent Imputed to Company. — In the absence of fraud or collusion between the insured and the agent, the knowledge of the agent when acting within the scope of the powers entrusted to him will be imputed to the company, even though a direct stipulation to the contrary appears in the policy or the application for the same. However, when it clearly appears that an insurance agent and the insured participated in a fraud by inserting false answers with respect to material facts in an application for insurance, the knowledge of the agent will not be imputable to his principal. Thomas-Yelverton Co. v. State Capital Life Ins. Co., 238 N.C. 278, 77 S.E.2d 692 (1953); Faircloth v. Ohio Farmers Ins. Co., 253 N.C. 522, 117 S.E.2d 404 (1960); McCrimmon v. North Carolina Mut. Life Ins. Co., 69 N.C. App. 683, 317 S.E.2d 709, cert. denied, 312 N.C. 84, 322 S.E.2d 175 (1984).

Responsibility of Insured for False Answers Inserted by Agent in Application. — The rule that the insured is not responsible for false answers in the application where they have been inserted by the agent through mistake, negligence, or fraud is not absolute, and applies only if the insured is justifiably ignorant of the untrue answers, has no actual or implied knowledge thereof, and has been guilty of no bad faith or fraud. Jones v. Home Sec. Life Ins. Co., 254 N.C. 407, 119 S.E.2d 215 (1961).

When the agent of the insurance company answers questions for the applicant on an application for insurance, without the applicant having reason to know what answers the agent is supplying, the insurance company will be equitably estopped to rely on the falsity or inaccuracy supplied by its own agent in any effort to defeat liability on the policy. Northern Nat'l Life Ins. Co. v. Lacy J. Miller Mach. Co., 63 N.C. App. 424, 305 S.E.2d 568 (1983), aff'd, 311 N.C. 62, 316 S.E.2d 256 (1984).

If an application for insurance containing material misrepresentations is filled in by the agent before being signed by the applicant, these are material misrepresentations of the applicant which bar recovery. McCrimmon v. North Carolina Mut. Life Ins. Co., 69 N.C. App. 683, 317 S.E.2d 709, cert. denied, 312 N.C. 84, 322 S.E.2d 175 (1984).

§ 58-58-35. Discrimination between insurants forbidden.

A life insurance company doing business in this State shall not make any distinction or discrimination in favor of individuals between insurants of the same class and equal expectation of life in the amount of payment of premiums or rates charged for policies of life or endowment insurance, or in the dividends or other benefits payable thereon, or in any of the terms and conditions of the contracts it makes; nor shall any such company or any agent thereof make any contract of insurance or agreement as to such contract other than as plainly expressed in the policy issued thereon, nor pay or allow as inducement to insurance any rebate of premium payable on the policy, or any special favor or advantage in the dividends or other benefit to accrue thereon, or any valuable consideration or inducement whatever not specified in the policy contract of insurance; nor give, sell, or purchase, or offer to give, sell, or purchase as inducement to insurance or in connection therewith any stocks, bonds, or other securities of any insurance company or other corporation, association, or partnership, or any dividends or profits to accrue therein, or anything of value whatsoever not specified in the policy. (1899, c. 54, s. 57; 1903, c. 438, ss. 5, 10; Rev., s. 4775; 1911, c. 196, s. 7; C.S., s. 6458.)

CASE NOTES

Purpose of Section. — The purpose of this section is to prevent discrimination among policyholders of like class and expectancy, and, in aid and furtherance of this desirable purpose, to secure publicity by requiring that all the stipulations of the contract and all agreements between the insurant and the company in reference thereto shall be plainly expressed in the policy. Smathers v. Bankers Life Ins. Co., 151 N.C. 98, 65 S.E. 746 (1909).

The purpose of this section is to require all of the contract between the parties to be set forth in the policy and to afford protection to the policyholder. The purpose is to require the parties to incorporate in the insurance contract anything pertaining to its validity at the time it is written. New York Life Ins. Co. v. Guyes, 22 F. Supp. 454 (M.D.N.C. 1938), aff'd, 99 F.2d 303 (4th Cir. 1938).

The prohibition of discrimination is a restriction applicable to the insurer, and the statute purports to operate upon insurance companies alone. Robinson v. Security Life & Annuity Co., 163 N.C. 415, 79 S.E. 681 (1913).

Exercise of an option given by a mutual life insurance company to one of its policyholders of greater value than that given to the others was an illegal and void discrimination, prohibited by our statute and general principles of law. Graham v. Mutual Life Ins. Co., 176 N.C. 313, 97 S.E. 6 (1918).

This section does not invalidate contracts of insurance made in violation of its provisions. Security Life & Annuity Co. v. Costner, 149 N.C. 293, 63 S.E. 304 (1908); Robinson v. Security Life & Annuity Co., 163 N.C. 415, 79 S.E. 681 (1913).

And Insured May Recover for Cancellation of Policy. — Where the insured has, in good faith, entered into a policy contract with the company whereby he has secured a policy at a reduced rate of premium, the parties are not in pari delicto; and he may recover damages, upon the cancellation by the company of his policy, for its discrimination forbidden by the statute. Robinson v. Security Life & Annuity Co., 163 N.C. 415, 79 S.E. 681 (1913).

Transactions up to the issuance of a life policy merge therein upon its issuance and acceptance by the insured. Floars v. Aetna Life Ins. Co., 144 N.C. 232, 56 S.E. 915 (1907); Graham v. Mutual Life Ins. Co., 176 N.C. 313, 97 S.E. 6 (1918); New York Life Ins. Co. v. Guyes, 22 F. Supp. 454 (M.D.N.C. 1938), aff'd, 99 F.2d 303 (4th Cir. 1938).

And Collateral Agreements Are Not Binding Unless Included in Policy. — Under this section, the terms and conditions of the insurance must be plainly expressed in the policy as issued, and collateral agreements with local agents are not binding unless included in the policy. Graham v. Mutual Life Ins. Co., 176 N.C. 313, 97 S.E. 6 (1918).

Prohibited Collateral Agreement Not Enforceable. — A policyholder cannot enforce against the insurance company a severable collateral agreement to his policy contract of life insurance which is prohibited by this statute, upon the principle that the law was not passed for the benefit of the company resisting recovery, but for the protection of the policyholders, when it appears that the agreement was executory in character and gave him a preference over the general body of policyholders for whose benefit the statute was passed. In such cases, the parties are in pari delicto. Smathers v. Bankers Life Ins. Co., 151 N.C. 98, 65 S.E. 746 (1909).

When a collateral agreement delivered to insured with his policy provided for the reduction of premiums to be paid thereon, and was claimed to be the sole inducement moving him to take the policy, it was necessary for these inducements so claimed to be specified in the policy contract. Otherwise the collateral agreement would be prohibited by the statute and not enforceable. Smathers v. Bankers Life Ins. Co., 151 N.C. 98, 65 S.E. 746 (1909).

Agreement for Earlier Effective Date. — It would seem that an agreement by a local agent that the policy would be in effect from the date of application and payment of the first premium, where the policy provided it would be effective from delivery, would be in contravention of this section. Jones v. Gate City Life Ins. Co., 216 N.C. 300, 4 S.E.2d 848 (1939).

A valid policy of life insurance is severable from an invalid collateral agreement made at one and the same time, respecting a benefit prohibited by the statute. Security Life & Annuity Co. v. Costner, 149 N.C. 293, 63 S.E. 304 (1908).

And Insurer May Recover on Note Given in Payment of Policy. — When the insured has given his note for the premiums on his life insurance policy, and has received for one year, in this manner, the benefits of the insurance, he cannot avoid paying his note upon the ground of his having collaterally contracted with the company for the deduction of a certain amount by way of renewal commissions in violation of the provisions of this section. Security Life & Annuity Co. v. Costner, 149 N.C. 293, 63 S.E. 304 (1908); Smathers v. Bankers Life Ins. Co., 151 N.C. 98, 65 S.E. 746 (1909).

§ 58-58-40. Misrepresentations of policy forbidden.

No life insurance company doing business in this State, and no officer, director, solicitor, or other agent thereof, shall make, issue, or circulate, or cause to be made, issued, or circulated any estimate, illustration, circular, or statement of any sort misrepresenting the terms of the policy issued by it or the dividends or share of surplus to be received thereon, or shall use any name or title of any policy or class of policies misrepresenting the true nature thereof. Nor shall any such company, agent, or broker make any misrepresentation to any person insured in said company or in any other insurer or governmental agency for the purpose of inducing or tending to induce such person to lapse, forfeit, or surrender his said insurance. (1913, c. 95; C.S., s. 6459; 1947, c. 721.)

Legal Periodicals. — For survey of 1979 administrative law, see 58 N.C.L. Rev. 1185 (1980).

§ 58-58-42: Repealed by Session Laws 2001-436, s. 5, effective April 1, 2002.

Cross References. — As to viatical settlements, see now G.S. 58-58-200 et seq.

Part 2. Financial Provisions.

§ 58-58-45. Financial Provisions.

The valuation of the reserves on the policies and bonds of every life insurance company incorporated by the laws of this State shall be based upon any recognized standard of valuation and mortality table as the Commissioner should deem best for the security of the business and the safety of the persons insured. The Commissioner shall annually value or cause to be valued the reserves on all policies and annuities of each domestic company and may accept the valuation of such reserves made by the company upon such evidence of its correctness as he may require. Upon this valuation being made by the Commissioner and a certificate thereof furnished by him, each company shall pay to such officer, to defray the expenses thereof, the sum of one cent (1¢) for every thousand dollars ($1,000) of the whole amount insured by its policies so valued. The reserve fund hereinbefore provided for shall not be available for or used for any other purpose than the discharge of policy obligations, but is a trust fund to be held and expended only for the benefit of policyholders. In case of the insolvency of the company, the reserve on outstanding policies may, with the consent of the Commissioner, be used for the reinsurance of its policies to the extent of their pro rata part thereof. (1903, c. 536, s. 4; 1905, c. 410; Rev., s. 4777; 1907, c. 1000, s. 7; C.S., s. 6461; 1945, c. 379.)

Editor's Note. — Session Laws 2001-436, s. 2, effective April 1, 2002, divided Article 58 into Parts 1 to 4, assigning a Part head to each Part, with G.S. 58-58-1 to 58-58-40 in Part 1, G.S. 58-58-45 to 58-58-65 in Part 2, G.S. 58-58-70 to 58-58-120 in Part 3, and G.S. 58-58-125 to 58-58-170 in Part 4, reserving G.S. 58-58-175 to 58-58-195 for future codification purposes.

Session Laws 2001-436, s. 17, is a severability clause.

§ 58-58-50. Standard Valuation Law.

(a) This section shall be known as the Standard Valuation Law.

(b) The Commissioner shall annually value, or cause to be valued, the reserve liabilities (hereinafter called reserves) for all outstanding life insurance policies and annuity and pure endowment contracts of every life insurance company doing business in this State, except that in the case of an alien company, such valuation shall be limited to its United States business, and may certify the amount of such reserves, specifying the mortality table or tables, rate or rates of interest and methods (net level premium method or other) used in the calculation of such reserves. Group methods and approximate averages for fractions of a year or otherwise may be used in calculating such reserves and the valuation made by the company may be accepted by the Commissioner upon such evidence of its correctness as the Commissioner may require. In lieu of the valuation of the reserves herein required of any foreign or alien company, he may accept any valuation made, or caused to be made, by the insurance supervisory official of any state or other jurisdiction when such valuation complies with the minimum standard herein provided and if the official of such state or jurisdiction accepts as sufficient and valid for all legal purposes the certificate of valuation of the Commissioner when such certificate states the valuation to have been made in a specified manner according to which the aggregate reserves would be at least as large as if they had been computed in the manner prescribed by the law of that state or jurisdiction.

(c)(1) Except as otherwise provided in subdivisions (3) and (4) of this subsection, the minimum standard for the valuation of all such policies and contracts issued before the effective date of this section shall be that provided by the laws in effect immediately before that date, except that the minimum standard for the valuation of annuities and pure endowments purchased under group annuity and pure endowment contracts issued before that date shall be that provided by the laws in effect immediately before that date but replacing the interest rates specified in such laws by an interest rate of five percent (5%) per annum, and five and one-half percent (5 ½%) interest for single premium life insurance policies.

(2) Except as otherwise provided in subdivisions (3) and (4) of this subsection, the minimum standards for the valuation of all such policies and contracts issued on or after the effective date of this section shall be the Commissioner's reserve valuation methods defined in subsections (d), (d-1) and (g), five percent (5%) interest for group annuity and pure endowment contracts and three and one-half percent (3 ½%) interest for all other policies and contracts, or, in the case of policies and contracts other than annuity and pure endowment contracts, issued on or after July 1, 1975, four percent (4%) interest for such policies issued prior to April 19, 1979, and four and one-half percent (4 ½%) interest for such policies issued on or after April 19, 1979, and the following tables:

    a. For all ordinary policies of life insurance issued on the standard basis, excluding any disability and accidental death benefits in such policies — the Commissioner's 1941 Standard Ordinary Mortality Table for such policies issued prior to the operative date of subdivision (e)(2) of G.S. 58-58-55, the Commissioner's 1958 Standard Ordinary Mortality Table for such policies issued on or after the operative date of subdivision (e)(2) of G.S. 58-58-55 prior to the operative date of subdivision (e)(4) of G.S. 58-58-55, provided that for any category of such policies issued on female risks, all modified net premiums and present values referred to in this section may be calculated according to an age not more than six years younger than the actual age of the insured; and, for such policies issued on or after the operative date of subdivision (e)(4) of G.S. 58-58-55, (i) the Commissioner's 1980 Standard Ordinary Mortality Table, or (ii) at the election of the company for any one or more specified plans of life insurance, the Commissioner's 1980 Standard Ordinary Mortality Table with Ten-Year Select Mortality Factors, or (iii) any ordinary mortality table, adopted after 1980 by the NAIC, that is approved by regulation promulgated by the Commissioner for use in determining the minimum standard of valuation for such policies;

    b. For all industrial life insurance policies issued on the standard basis, excluding any disability and accidental death benefits in such policies — the 1941 Standard Industrial Mortality Table for such policies issued prior to the operative date of subdivision (e)(3) of G.S. 58-58-55 and for such policies issued on or after such operative date the Commissioner's 1961 Standard Industrial Mortality Table or any industrial mortality table, adopted after 1980 by the NAIC, that is approved by regulation promulgated by the Commissioner for use in determining the minimum standard of valuation for such policies;

    c. For individual annuity and pure endowment contracts, excluding any disability and accidental death benefits in such policies — the 1937 Standard Annuity Mortality Table or, at the option of the company, the Annuity Mortality Table for 1949, Ultimate, or any modification of either of these tables approved by the Commissioner;

    d. For group annuity and pure endowment contracts, excluding any disability and accidental death benefits in such policies — the Group Annuity Mortality Table for 1951, any modification of such table approved by the Commissioner, or, at the option of the company, any of the tables or modifications of tables specified for individual annuity and pure endowment contracts;

    e. For total and permanent disability benefits in or supplementary to ordinary policies or contracts — for policies or contracts issued on or after January 1, 1966, the tables of Period 2 disablement rates and the 1930 to 1950 termination rates of the 1952 Disability Study of the Society of Actuaries, with due regard to the type of benefit or any tables of disablement rates and termination rates, adopted after 1980 by the NAIC, that are approved by regulation promulgated by the Commissioner for use in determining the minimum standard of valuation for such policies; for policies or contracts issued on or after January 1, 1961, and prior to January 1, 1966, either such tables or, at the option of the company, the Class (3) Disability Table (1926); and for policies issued prior to January 1, 1961, the Class (3) Disability Table (1926). Any such table shall, for active lives, be combined with a mortality table permitted for calculating the reserves for life insurance policies;

f. For accidental death benefits in or supplementary to policies — for policies issued on or after January 1, 1966, the 1959 Accidental Death Benefits Table or any accidental death benefits table, adopted after 1980 by the NAIC, that is approved by regulation promulgated by the Commissioner for use in determining the minimum standard of valuation for such policies; for policies issued on or after January 1, 1961, and prior to January 1, 1966, either such table or, at the option of the company, the Inter-Company Double Indemnity Mortality Table; and for policies issued prior to January 1, 1961, the Inter-Company Double Indemnity Mortality Table. Either table shall be combined with a mortality table permitted for calculating the reserves for life insurance policies;

g. For group life insurance, life insurance issued on the substandard basis and other special benefits — such tables as may be approved by the Commissioner.

(3) Except as provided in subdivision (4) of this subsection, the minimum standard for the valuation of all individual annuity and pure endowment contracts issued on or after the operative date of this subdivision (3), as defined herein, and for all annuities and pure endowments purchased on or after such operative date under group annuity and pure endowment contracts, shall be the Commissioner's reserve valuation methods defined in subsections (d) and (d-1) and the following tables and interest rates:

a. For individual annuity and pure endowment contracts issued prior to April 19, 1979, excluding any disability and accidental death benefits in such contracts — the 1971 Individual Annuity Mortality Table, or any modification of this table approved by the Commissioner, and six percent (6%) interest for single premium immediate annuity contracts, and four percent (4%) interest for all other individual annuity and pure endowment contracts;

b. For individual single premium immediate annuity contracts issued on or after April 19, 1979, excluding any disability and accidental death benefits in such contracts — the 1971 Individual Annuity Mortality Table or any individual annuity mortality table, adopted after 1980 by the NAIC, that is approved by regulation promulgated by the Commissioner for use in determining the minimum standard of valuation for such contracts, or any modification of these tables approved by the Commissioner, and seven and one-half percent (7 ½%) interest;

c. For individual annuity and pure endowment contracts issued on or after April 19, 1979, other than single premium immediate annuity contracts, excluding any disability and accidental death benefits in such contracts — the 1971 Individual Annuity Mortality Table or any individual annuity mortality table, adopted after 1980 by the NAIC, that is approved by regulation promulgated by the Commissioner for use in determining the minimum standard of valuation for such contracts, or any modification of these tables approved by the Commissioner, and five and one-half percent (5 ½%) interest for single premium deferred annuity and pure endowment contracts and four and one-half percent (4 ½%) interest for all other such individual annuity and pure endowment contracts;

d. For all annuities and pure endowments purchased prior to April 19, 1979, under group annuity and pure endowment contracts, excluding any disability and accidental death benefits purchased under such contracts — the 1971 Group Annuity Mortality Table, or any modification of this table approved by the Commissioner, and six percent (6%) interest;

e. For all annuities and pure endowments purchased on or after April 19, 1979, under group annuity and pure endowment contracts, excluding any disability and accidental death benefits purchased under such contracts — the 1971 Group Annuity Mortality Table or any group annuity mortality table, adopted after 1980 by the NAIC, that is approved by regulation promulgated by the Commissioner for use in determining the minimum standard of valuation for such annuities and pure endowments, or any modification of these tables approved by the Commissioner, and seven and one-half percent (7 ½%) interest.

After July 1, 1975, any company may file with the Commissioner a written notice of its election to comply with the provisions of this subdivision (3) after a specified date before January 1, 1979, which shall be the operative date of this subdivision for such company, provided, a company may elect a different operative date for individual annuity and pure endowment contracts from that elected for group annuity and pure endowment contracts. If a company makes no such election, the operative date of this subdivision for such company shall be January 1, 1979.

(4) a. Applicability of This Subdivision. The interest rates used in determining the minimum standard for the valuation of:

1. All life insurance policies issued in a particular calendar year, on or after the operative date of subdivision (e)(4) of G.S. 58-58-55,

2. All individual annuity and pure endowment contracts issued in a particular calendar year on or after January 1, 1982,

3. All annuities and pure endowments purchased in a particular calendar year on or after January 1, 1982, under group annuity and pure endowment contracts, and

4. The net increase, if any, in a particular calendar year after January 1, 1982, in amounts held under guaranteed interest contracts

shall be the calendar year statutory valuation interest rates as defined in this subdivision.

b. Calendar Year Statutory Valuation Interest Rates.

1. The calendar year statutory valuation interest rates, I shall be determined as follows and the results rounded to the nearer one-quarter of one percent (¼ of 1%):

I. For life insurance,

$$I = .03 \text{ plus } W (R_1 - .03) \text{ plus } \frac{W}{2}(R_2 - .09);$$

II. For single premium immediate annuities and for annuity benefits involving life contingencies arising from other annuities with cash settlement options and from guaranteed interest contracts with cash settlement options,

$$I = .03 \text{ plus } W (R - .03)$$

where R_1 is the lesser of R and .09,

R_2 is the greater of R and .09,

R is the reference interest rate defined in this subdivision, and W is the weighting factor defined in this subdivision,

III. For other annuities with cash settlement options and guaranteed interest contracts with cash settlement options, valued on an issue year basis, except as stated in II above, the formula for life insurance stated in I above shall apply to annuities and guaranteed interest contracts with guarantee durations in excess of 10 years and the formula for single premium immediate annuities stated in II above shall apply to annuities and guaranteed interest contracts with guarantee duration of 10 years or less,

IV. For other annuities with no cash settlement options and for guaranteed interest contracts with no cash settlement options, the formula for single premium immediate annuities stated in II above shall apply,

V. For other annuities with cash settlement options and guaranteed interest contracts with cash settlement options, valued on a change in fund basis, the formula for single premium immediate annuities stated in II above shall apply.

2. However, if the calendar year statutory valuation interest rate for any life insurance policies issued in any calendar year determined without reference to this sentence differs from the corresponding actual rate for similar policies issued in the immediately preceding calendar year by less than one-half of one percent (½ of 1%), the calendar year statutory valuation interest rate for such life insurance policies shall be equal to the corresponding actual rate for the immediately preceding calendar year. For purposes of applying the immediately preceding sentence, the calendar year statutory valuation interest rate for life insurance policies issued in a calendar year shall be determined for 1980 (using the reference interest rate defined for 1979) and shall be determined for each subsequent calendar year regardless of when subdivision (e)(4) of G.S. 58-58-55 becomes operative.

c. Weighting Factors.

1. The weighting factors referred to in the formulas stated above are given in the following tables:

I. Weighting Factors for Life Insurance:

Guarantee Duration (Years)	Weighting Factors
10 or less	.50
More than 10, but not more than 20	.45
More than 20	.35

For life insurance, the guarantee duration is the maximum number of years the life insurance can remain in force on a basis guaranteed in the policy or under options to convert to plans of life insurance with premium rates or nonforfeiture values or both which are guaranteed in the original policy;

II. Weighting factor for single premium immediate annuities and for annuity benefits involving life contingencies arising from other annuities with cash settlement options and guaranteed interest contracts with cash settlement options:

.80

III. Weighting factors for other annuities and for guaranteed interest contracts, except as stated in II. above, shall be

935

as specified in tables (i), (ii), and (iii) below, according to the rules and definitions in (iv), (v) and (vi) below:

(i) For annuities and guaranteed interest contracts valued on an issue year basis:

Guarantee Duration (Years)	Weighting Factor For Plan Type		
	A	B	C
5 or less:	.80	.60	.50
More than 5, but not more than 10:	.75	.60	.50
More than 10, but not more than 20:	.65	.50	.45
More than 20:	.45	.35	.35

(ii) For annuities and guaranteed interest contracts valued on a change in fund basis, the factors shown in (i) above increased by:

Plan Type		
A	B	C
.15	.25	.05

(iii) For annuities and guaranteed interest contracts valued on an issue year basis (other than those with no cash settlement options) which do not guarantee interest on considerations received more than one year after issue or purchase and for annuities and guaranteed interest contracts valued on a change in fund basis which do not guarantee interest rates on considerations received more than 12 months beyond the valuation date, the factors shown in (i) or derived in (ii) increased by:

Plan Type		
A	B	C
.05	.05	.05

(iv) For other annuities with cash settlement options and guaranteed interest contracts with cash settlement options, the guarantee duration is the number of years for which the contract guarantees interest rates in excess of the calendar year statutory valuation interest rate for life insurance policies with guarantee duration in excess of 20 years. For other annuities with no cash settlement options and for guaranteed interest contracts with no cash settlement options, the guarantee duration is the number of years from the date of issue or date of purchase to the date annuity benefits are scheduled to commence.

(v) Plan type as used in the above tables is defined as follows:

Plan Type A: At any time policyholder may withdraw funds only (1) with an adjustment to reflect changes in interest rates or asset values since receipt of the funds by the insurance company, or (2) without such adjustment but in installments over five years or more, or (3) as an immediate life annuity, or (4) no withdrawal permitted.

Plan Type B: Before expiration of the interest rate guarantee, policyholder may withdraw funds only (1) with an adjustment to reflect changes in interest rates or asset values since receipt of the funds by the insurance company, or (2) without such adjustment but in installments over five years or more, or (3) no withdrawal permitted. At the end of interest rate guarantee, funds may be withdrawn without such adjustment in a single sum or installments over less than five years.

Plan Type C: Policyholder may withdraw funds before expiration of interest rate guarantee in a single sum or installments over less than five years either (1) without adjustment to reflect changes in interest rates or asset values since receipt of the funds by the insurance company, or (2) subject only to a fixed surrender charge stipulated in the contract as a percentage of the fund.

(vi) A company may elect to value guaranteed interest contracts with cash settlement options and annuities with cash settlement options on either an issue year basis or on a change in fund basis. Guaranteed interest contracts with no cash settlement options and other annuities with no cash settlement options must be valued on an issue year basis. As used in this section, an issue year basis of valuation refers to a valuation basis under which the interest rate used to determine the minimum valuation standard for the entire duration of the annuity or guaranteed interest contract is the calendar year valuation interest rate for the year of issue or year of purchase of the annuity or guaranteed interest contract, and the change in fund basis of valuation refers to a valuation basis under which the interest rate used to determine the minimum valuation standard applicable to each change in the fund held under the annuity or guaranteed interest contract is the calendar year valuation interest rate for the year of the change in the fund.

d. Reference Interest Rate.
  1. The reference interest rate referred to in paragraph b of this
     subdivision shall be defined as follows:
      I. For all life insurance, the lesser of the average over a
         period of 36 months and the average over a period of 12
         months, ending on June 30 of the calendar year next
         preceding the year of issue, of Moody's Corporate Bond
         Yield Average — Monthly Average Corporates, as pub-
         lished by Moody's Investors Service, Inc.
     II. For single premium immediate annuities and for annuity
         benefits involving life contingencies arising from other
         annuities with cash settlement options and guaranteed
         interest contracts with cash settlement options, the
         average over a period of 12 months, ending on June 30 of
         the calendar year of issue or year of purchase, of Moody's
         Corporate Bond Yield Average — Monthly Average
         Corporates, as published by Moody's Investors Service,
         Inc.
    III. For other annuities with cash settlement options and
         guaranteed interest contracts with cash settlement op-
         tions, valued on a year of issue basis, except as stated in
         II above, with guarantee duration in excess of 10 years,
         the lesser of the average over a period of 36 months and
         the average over a period of 12 months, ending on June
         30 of the calendar year of issue or purchase, of Moody's
         Corporate Bond Yield Average — Monthly Average
         Corporates, as published by Moody's Investors Service,
         Inc.
     IV. For other annuities with cash settlement options and
         guaranteed interest contracts with cash settlement op-
         tions, valued on a year of issue basis, except as stated in
         II above, with guarantee duration of 10 years or less, the
         average over a period of 12 months, ending on June 30 of
         the calendar year of issue or purchase, of Moody's Cor-
         porate Bond Yield Average — Monthly Average
         Corporates, as published by Moody's Investors Service,
         Inc.
      V. For other annuities with no cash settlement options and
         for guaranteed interest contracts with no cash settle-
         ment options, the average over a period of 12 months,
         ending on June 30 of the calendar year of issue or
         purchase, of Moody's Corporate Bond Yield Average —
         Monthly Average Corporates, as published by Moody's
         Investors Service, Inc.
     VI. For other annuities with cash settlement options and
         guaranteed interest contracts with cash settlement op-
         tions, valued on a change in fund basis, except as stated
         in II above, the average over a period of 12 months,
         ending on June 30 of the calendar year of the change in
         the fund, of Moody's Corporate Bond Yield Average —
         Monthly Average Corporates, as published by Moody's
         Investors Service, Inc.
e. Alternative Method for Determining Reference Interest Rates.
  1. In the event that Moody's Corporate Bond Yield Average —
     Monthly Average Corporates is no longer published by
     Moody's Investors Service, Inc., or in the event that the NAIC

determines that Moody's Corporate Bond Yield Average — Monthly Average Corporates as published by Moody's Investors Service, Inc., is no longer appropriate for the determination of the reference interest rate, than an alternative method for determination of the reference interest rate, which is adopted by the NAIC and approved by regulation promulgated by the Commissioner, may be substituted.

(d) Except as otherwise provided in subsections (d-1) and (g), reserves according to the Commissioner's reserve valuation method, for the life insurance and endowment benefits of policies providing for a uniform amount of insurance and requiring the payment of uniform premiums, shall be the excess, if any, of the present value, at the date of valuation, of such future guaranteed benefits provided for by such policies, over the then present value of any future modified net premiums therefor. The modified net premiums for any such policy shall be such uniform percentage of the respective contract premiums for such benefits that the present value, at the date of issue of the policy, of all such modified net premiums shall be equal to the sum of the then present value of such benefits provided for by the policy and the excess of (1) and (2), as follows:

    (1) A net level annual premium equal to the present value, at the date of issue, of such benefits provided for after the first policy year, divided by the present value, at the date of issue, of an annuity of one per annum payable on the first and each subsequent anniversary of such policy on which a premium falls due; provided, however, that such net level annual premium shall not exceed the net level annual premium on the 19-year premium whole life plan for insurance of the same amount at an age one year higher than the age at issue of such policy.

    (2) A net one year term premium for such benefits provided for in the first policy year.

Provided that for any life insurance policy issued on or after January 1, 1985, for which the contract premium in the first policy year exceeds that of the second year and for which no comparable additional benefits are provided in the first year for such excess and which provides an endowment benefit or a cash surrender value of a combination thereof in an amount greater than such excess premium, the reserve according to the Commissioner's reserve valuation method as of any policy anniversary occurring on or before the assumed ending date defined herein as the first policy anniversary on which the sum of any endowment benefit and any cash surrender value then available is greater than such excess premium shall, except as otherwise provided in subsection (g), be the greater of the reserve as of such policy anniversary calculated as described in the first paragraph of this subsection and the reserve as of such policy anniversary calculated as described in that paragraph, but with (i) the value defined in subparagraph (1) of that paragraph being reduced by fifteen percent (15%) of the amount of such excess first year premium, (ii) all present values of benefits and premiums being determined without reference to premiums or benefits provided for by the policy after the assumed ending date, (iii) the policy being assumed to mature on such date as an endowment, and (iv) the cash surrender value provided on such date being considered as an endowment benefit. In making the above comparison the mortality and interest bases stated in subdivisions (2) and (4) of subsection (c) shall be used.

Reserves according to the Commissioner's reserve valuation method for: (i) life insurance policies providing for a varying amount of insurance or requiring the payment of varying premiums; (ii) group annuity and pure endowment contracts purchased under a retirement plan or plan of deferred compensation, established or maintained by an employer (including a partnership or sole proprietorship) or by an employee organization, or by both, other than a plan providing individual retirement accounts or individual retirement annuities under section 408 of the Internal Revenue Code, as now or hereafter amended; (iii) disability and accidental death benefits in all policies and contracts; and (iv) all other benefits, except life insurance and endowment benefits in life insurance policies and benefits provided by all other annuity and pure endowment contracts, shall be calculated by a method consistent with the principles of this subsection except that any extra premiums charged because of impairments or special hazards shall be disregarded in the determination of modified net premiums.

(d-1) This subsection shall apply to all annuity and pure endowment contracts other than group annuity and pure endowment contracts purchased under a retirement plan or plan of deferred compensation, established or maintained by an employer (including a partnership or sole proprietorship) or by an employee organization, or by both, other than a plan providing individual retirement accounts or individual retirement annuities under section 408 of the Internal Revenue Code, as now or hereafter amended.

Reserves according to the Commissioner's annuity reserve method for benefits under annuity or pure endowment contracts, excluding any disability and accidental death benefits in such contracts, shall be the greatest of the respective excesses of the present values, at the date of valuation, of the future guaranteed benefits, including guaranteed nonforfeiture benefits, provided for by such contracts at the end of each respective contract year, over the present value, at the date of valuation, of any future valuation considerations derived from future gross considerations, required by the terms of such contract, that become payable prior to the end of such respective contract year. The future guaranteed benefits shall be determined by using the mortality table, if any, and the interest rate, or rates, specified in such contracts for determining guaranteed benefits. The valuation considerations are the portions of the respective gross considerations applied under the terms of such contracts to determine nonforfeiture values.

(e) In no event shall a company's aggregate reserves for all life insurance policies, excluding disability and accidental death benefits, issued on or after the effective date of this section, be less than the aggregate reserves calculated in accordance with the methods set forth in subsections (d), (d-1), (g) and (h) of this section and the mortality table or tables and rate or rates of interest used in calculating nonforfeiture benefits for such policies. In no event shall the aggregate reserves for all policies, contracts, and benefits be less than the aggregate reserves determined by the qualified actuary to be necessary to render the opinion required by subsection (i) of this section.

(f) Reserves for all policies and contracts issued before the effective date of this section may be calculated, at the option of the company, according to any standards that produce greater aggregate reserves for those policies and contracts than the minimum reserves required by the laws in effect immediately before that date.

Reserves for any category of policies, contracts or benefits as established by the Commissioner, issued on or after the effective date of this section may be calculated, at the option of the company, according to any standards that produce greater aggregate reserves for such category than those calculated according to the minimum standard herein provided, but the rate or rates of interest used for policies and contracts, other than annuity and pure endowment contracts, shall not be higher than the corresponding rate or rates of interest used in calculating any nonforfeiture benefits provided for therein.

Any such company that adopts any standard of valuation producing greater aggregate reserves than those calculated according to the minimum standard herein provided may, with the approval of the Commissioner, adopt any lower standard of valuation, but not lower than the minimum herein provided.

Provided, however, that for the purposes of this section, the holding of additional reserves previously determined by a qualified actuary to be necessary to render the opinion required by subsection (c) of this section shall not be deemed to be the adoption of a higher standard of valuation.

(g) If in any contract year the gross premium charged by any life insurance company on any policy or contract is less than the valuation net premium for the policy or contract calculated by the method used in calculating the reserve thereon but using the minimum valuation standards of mortality and rate of interest, the minimum reserve required for such policy or contract shall be the greater of either the reserve calculated according to the mortality table, rate of interest, and method actually used for such policy or contract, or the reserve calculated by the method actually used for such policy or contract but using the minimum valuation standards of mortality and rate of interest and replacing the valuation net premium by the actual gross premium in each contract year for which the valuation net premium exceeds the actual gross premium. The minimum valuation standards of mortality and rate of interest referred to in this subsection are those standards stated in subdivisions (1), (2) and (4) of subsection (c).

Provided that for any life insurance policy issued on or after January 1, 1985, for which the gross premium in the first policy year exceeds that of the second year and for which no comparable additional benefit is provided in the first year for such excess and which provides an endowment benefit or a cash surrender value or a combination thereof in an amount greater than such excess premium, the foregoing provisions of this subsection (g) shall be applied as if the method actually used in calculating the reserve for such policy were the method described in subsection (d), ignoring the second paragraph of subsection (d). The minimum reserve at each policy anniversary of such a policy shall be the greater of the minimum reserve calculated in accordance with subsection (d), including the second paragraph of that subsection, and the minimum reserve calculated in accordance with this subsection (g).

(h) In the case of any plan of life insurance which provides for future premium determination, the amounts of which are to be determined by the insurance company based on then estimates of future experience, or in the case of any plan of life insurance or annuity which is of such a nature that the minimum reserves cannot be determined by the methods described in subsections (d), (d-1), and (g), the reserves which are held under any such plan must:

(1) Be appropriate in relation to the benefits and the pattern of premiums for that plan, and

(2) Be computed by a method which is consistent with the principles of this Standard Valuation Law, as determined by regulations promulgated by the Commissioner.

(i) Every life insurance company doing business in this State shall annually submit the opinion of a qualified actuary as to whether the reserves and related actuarial items held in support of the policies and contracts specified by the Commissioner by rule are computed appropriately, are based on assumptions that satisfy contractual provisions, are consistent with previously reported amounts, and comply with applicable laws of this State. The Commissioner by rule shall define the specifics of this opinion and add any other items deemed to be necessary to its scope. Every life insurance company, except as exempted by or pursuant to rule, shall also annually include in the opinion required by this subsection, an opinion of the same qualified actuary as to whether the reserves and related actuarial items held in support of the policies and contracts specified by the Commissioner by rule, when considered in light of the assets held by the company with respect to the reserves and related actuarial items, including but not limited to the investment earnings on the assets and the considerations anticipated to be received and retained under

941

the policies and contracts, make adequate provision for the company's obligations under the policies and contracts, including but not limited to the benefits under and expenses associated with the policies and contracts. The Commissioner may provide by rule for a transition period for establishing any higher reserves that the qualified actuary may deem to be necessary in order to render the opinion required by this subsection.

(j) Each opinion required by subsection (i) of this section shall be governed by the following provisions:

(1) A memorandum, in form and substance acceptable to the Commissioner as specified by rule, shall be prepared to support each actuarial opinion.

(2) If the insurance company fails to provide a supporting memorandum at the request of the Commissioner within a period specified by rule or the Commissioner determines that the supporting memorandum provided by the insurance company fails to meet the standards prescribed by the rules or is otherwise unacceptable to the Commissioner, the Commissioner may engage a qualified actuary at the expense of the company to review the opinion and the basis for the opinion and prepare such supporting memorandum as is required by the Commissioner.

(3) The opinion shall be submitted with the annual statement reflecting the valuation of such reserve liabilities for each year ending on or after December 31, 1994.

(4) The opinion shall apply to all business in force including individual and group health insurance plans, in form and substance acceptable to the Commissioner as specified by rule.

(5) The opinion shall be based on standards adopted from time to time by the actuarial standards board and on such additional standards as the Commissioner may by rule prescribe.

(6) In the case of an opinion required to be submitted by a foreign or alien company, the Commissioner may accept the opinion filed by that company with the insurance supervisory official of another state if the Commissioner determines that the opinion reasonably meets the requirements applicable to a company domiciled in this State.

(7) For the purposes of this section, "qualified actuary" means a member in good standing of the American Academy of Actuaries who meets the requirement set forth in such rules.

(8) Except in cases of fraud or willful misconduct, the qualified actuary shall not be liable for damages to any person (other than the insurance company and the Commissioner) for any act, error, omission, decision, or conduct with respect to the actuary's opinion.

(9) Disciplinary action by the Commissioner against the company or the qualified actuary shall be defined in rules by the Commissioner.

(10) Any memorandum in support of the opinion, and any other material provided by the company to the Commissioner in connection therewith, shall be kept confidential by the Commissioner and shall not be made public and shall not be subject to subpoena, other than for the purpose of defending an action seeking damages from any person by reason of any action required by this section or by rules adopted under this section; provided, however, that the memorandum or other material may otherwise be released by the Commissioner (i) with the written consent of the company or (ii) to the American Academy of Actuaries upon request stating the memorandum or other material is required for the purpose of professional disciplinary proceedings and setting forth procedures satisfactory to the Commissioner for preserving the confidentiality of the memorandum or other material. Once

any portion of the confidential memorandum is cited by the company in its marketing or is cited before any governmental agency other than a state insurance department or is released by the company to the news media, all portions of the confidential memorandum shall be no longer confidential.

(k) The Commissioner shall adopt rules containing the minimum standards applicable to the valuation of health plans. The Commissioner may also adopt rules for the purpose of recognizing new annuity mortality tables for use in determining reserve liabilities for annuities and may adopt rules that govern minimum valuation standards for reserves of life insurance companies. In adopting these rules, the Commissioner may consider model laws and regulations promulgated and amended from time to time by the NAIC.

(*l*) The Commissioner may adopt rules for life insurers for the following matters:

(1) Reserves for contracts issued by insurers.
(2) Optional smoker/nonsmoker mortality tables permitted for use in determining minimum reserve liabilities and nonforfeiture benefits.
(3) Optional blended gender mortality tables permitted for use in determining nonforfeiture benefits for individual life policies.
(4) Optional tables acceptable for use in determining reserves and minimum cash surrender values and amounts of paid-up nonforfeiture benefits.

In adopting these rules, the Commissioner may consider model laws and regulations promulgated and amended from time to time by the NAIC. (1945, c. 379; 1959, c. 484, s. 1; 1961, c. 255, ss. 1-3; 1963, c. 791, ss. 1, 2; 1975, c. 603, s. 1; 1979, c. 409, ss. 1-6; 1981, c. 761, ss. 1-5; 1985, c. 666, s. 46; 1991, c. 720, s. 19; 1993, c. 452, ss. 52-56; 1999-219, s. 10; 2001-334, s. 17.1.)

§ 58-58-55. Standard nonforfeiture provisions.

(a) This section shall be known as the Standard Nonforfeiture Law for Life Insurance.

(b) In the case of policies issued on or after the operative date of this section, as defined in subsection (h), no policy of life insurance, except as stated in subsection (g), shall be delivered or issued for delivery in this State unless it shall contain in substance the following provisions, or corresponding provisions which in the opinion of the Commissioner are at least as favorable to the defaulting or surrendering policyholder as are the minimum requirements hereinafter specified and are essentially in compliance with subsection (f1) of this section:

(1) That, in the event of default in any premium payment after premiums have been paid for at least one full year in the case of ordinary insurance or three full years in the case of industrial insurance, the company will grant, upon proper request not later than 60 days after the due date of the premium in default, a paid-up nonforfeiture benefit on a plan stipulated in the policy, effective as of such due date, of such amount as may be hereinafter specified. In lieu of such stipulated paid-up nonforfeiture benefit, the company may substitute, upon proper request not later than 60 days after the due date of the premium in default, an actuarially equivalent alternative paid-up nonforfeiture benefit which provides a greater amount or longer period of death benefits or, if applicable, a greater amount or earlier payment of endowment benefits.

(2) That, upon surrender of the policy within 60 days after the due date of any premium payment in default after premiums have been paid for at least three full years in the case of ordinary insurance or five full

years in the case of industrial insurance, the company will pay, in lieu of any paid-up nonforfeiture benefit, a cash surrender value of such amount as may be hereinafter specified.

(3) That a specified paid-up nonforfeiture benefit shall become effective as specified in the policy unless the person entitled to make such election elects another available option not later than 60 days after the due date of the premium in default. Nothing herein shall prevent the use of an automatic premium loan provision.

(4) That, if the policy shall have become paid up by completion of all premium payments or if it is continued under any paid-up nonforfeiture benefit which became effective on or after the third policy anniversary in the case of ordinary insurance or the fifth policy anniversary in the case of industrial insurance, the company will pay, upon surrender of the policy within 30 days after any policy anniversary, a cash surrender value of such amount as may be hereinafter specified.

(5) In the case of policies which cause on a basis guaranteed in the policy unscheduled changes in benefits or premiums, or which provide an option for changes in benefits or premiums other than a change to a new policy, a statement of the mortality table, interest rate, and method used in calculating cash surrender values and the paid-up nonforfeiture benefits available under the policy. In the case of all other policies, a statement of the mortality table and interest rate used in calculating the cash surrender values and the paid-up nonforfeiture benefits available under the policy, together with a table showing the cash surrender value, if any, and paid-up nonforfeiture benefit, if any available under the policy on each policy anniversary either during the first 20 policy years or during the term of the policy, whichever is shorter, such values and benefits to be calculated upon the assumption that there are no dividends or paid-up additions credited to the policy and that there is no indebtedness to the company on the policy.

(6) A statement that the cash surrender values and the paid-up nonforfeiture benefits available under the policy are not less than the minimum values and benefits required by or pursuant to the insurance law of the state in which the policy is delivered; an explanation of the manner in which the cash surrender values and the paid-up nonforfeiture benefits are altered by the existence of any paid-up additions credited to the policy or any indebtedness to the company on the policy; if a detailed statement of the method of computation of the values and benefits shown in the policy is not stated therein, a statement that such method of computation has been filed with the Commissioner in which the policy is delivered; and a statement of the method to be used in calculating the cash surrender value and paid-up nonforfeiture benefit available under the policy on any policy anniversary beyond the last anniversary for which such values and benefits are consecutively shown in the policy.

Any of the foregoing provisions or portions thereof not applicable by reason of the plan of insurance may, to the extent inapplicable, be omitted from the policy.

The company shall reserve the right to defer the payment of any cash surrender value for a period of six months after demand therefor with surrender of the policy.

(c) Any cash surrender value available under the policy in the event of default in a premium payment due on any policy anniversary, whether or not required by subsection (b), shall be an amount not less than the excess, if any, of the present value, on such anniversary, of the future guaranteed benefits which would have been provided for by the policy, including any existing paid-up additions, if there had been no default, over the sum of (i) the then present value of the adjusted premiums as defined in subsection (e), corresponding to premiums which would have fallen due on and after such anniversary, and (ii) the amount of any indebtedness to the company on the policy.

Provided, however, that for any policy issued on or after the operative date of subdivision (4) of subsection (e) as defined therein, which provides supplemental life insurance or annuity benefits at the option of the insured and for an identifiable additional premium by rider or supplemental policy provision, the cash surrender value referred to in the first paragraph of this subsection shall be an amount not less than the sum of the cash surrender value as defined in such paragraph for an otherwise similar policy issued at the same age without such rider or supplemental policy provision and the cash surrender value as defined in such paragraph for a policy which provides only the benefits otherwise provided by such rider or supplemental policy provision.

Provided, further, that for any family policy issued on or after the operative date of subdivision (4) of subsection (e) as defined therein, which defines a primary insured and provides term insurance on the life of the spouse of the primary insured expiring before the spouse's age 71, the cash surrender value referred to in the first paragraph of this subsection shall be an amount not less than the sum of the cash surrender value as defined in such paragraph for an otherwise similar policy issued at the same age without such term insurance on the life of the spouse and cash surrender value as defined in such paragraph for a policy which provides only the benefits otherwise provided by such term insurance on the life of the spouse.

Any cash surrender value available within 30 days after any policy anniversary under any policy paid up by completion of all premium payments or any policy continued under any paid-up nonforfeiture benefit, whether or not required by subsection (b), shall be an amount not less than the present value, on such anniversary, of the future guaranteed benefits provided for by the policy, including any existing paid-up additions, decreased by any indebtedness to the company on the policy.

(d) Any paid-up nonforfeiture benefit available under the policy in the event of default in a premium payment due on any policy anniversary shall be such that its present value as of such anniversary shall be at least equal to the cash surrender value then provided for by the policy or, if none is provided for, at least equal to that cash surrender value which would have been required by this section in the absence of the condition that premiums shall have been paid for at least a specified period.

(e)(1) This subdivision (1) of subsection (e) shall not apply to policies issued on or after the operative date of subdivision (4) of subsection (e) as defined therein. Except as provided in the third paragraph of this subdivision, the adjusted premiums for any policy shall be calculated on an annual basis and shall be such uniform percentage of the respective premiums specified in the policy for each policy year, excluding any extra premiums charged because of impairments or special hazards, that the present value, at the date of issue of the policy, of all such adjusted premiums shall be equal to the sum of (i) the then present value of the future guaranteed benefits provided for by the policy; (ii) two percent (2%) of the amount of insurance, if the insurance be uniform in amount, or of the equivalent uniform amount, as hereinafter defined, if the amount of insurance varies with duration of the policy; (iii) forty percent (40%) of the adjusted premium for the first policy year; (iv) twenty-five percent (25%) of either the adjusted premium for the first policy year or the adjusted premium for a whole life policy of the same uniform or equivalent uniform amount with uniform premiums for the whole of life issued at the same age for the same amount of insurance, whichever is less. Provided, however, that in applying the percentages specified in (iii) and (iv) above, no adjusted premium shall be deemed to exceed four percent (4%) of the amount of insurance or uniform amount equivalent thereto. The date of issue of a policy for the purpose of this subsection shall be the date as of which the rated age of the insured is determined.

In the case of a policy providing an amount of insurance varying with duration of the policy, the equivalent uniform amount thereof for the purpose of this section shall be deemed to be the uniform amount of insurance provided by an otherwise similar policy containing the same endowment benefit or benefits, if any, issued at the same age and for the same term, the amount of which does not vary with duration and the benefits under which have the same present value at the date of issue as the benefits under the policy, provided, however, that in the case of a policy providing a varying amount of insurance issued on the life of a child under age 10, the equivalent uniform amount may be computed as though the amount of insurance provided by the policy prior to the attainment of age 10 were the amount provided by such policy at age 10.

The adjusted premiums for any policy providing term insurance benefits by rider or supplemental policy provision shall be equal to (i) the adjusted premiums for an otherwise similar policy issued at the same age without such term insurance benefits, increased, during the period for which premiums for such term insurance benefits are payable, by (ii) the adjusted premiums for such term insurance, the foregoing items (i) and (ii) being calculated separately and as specified in the first two paragraphs of this subsection except that, for the purposes of (ii), (iii) and (iv) of the first such paragraph, the amount of insurance or equivalent uniform amount of insurance used in the calculation of the adjusted premiums referred to in (ii) of this paragraph shall be equal to the excess of the corresponding amount determined for the entire policy over the amount used in the calculation of the adjusted premiums in (i).

Except as otherwise provided in subdivisions (2) and (3) of this subsection, all adjusted premiums and present values referred to in this section shall for all policies of ordinary insurance be calculated on the basis of the Commissioner's 1941 Standard Ordinary Mortality Table, provided that for any category of ordinary insurance issued on female risks, adjusted premiums and present values may be calculated according to an age not more than three years younger than the actual age of the insured, and such calculations for all policies of industrial insurance shall be made on the basis of the 1941 Standard Industrial Mortality Table. All calculations shall be made on the basis of the rate of interest, not exceeding three and one-half percent (3 ½%) per annum, specified in the policy for calculating cash surrender values and paid-up nonforfeiture benefits. Provided, however, that in calculating the present value of any paid-up term insurance with accompanying pure endowment, if any, offered as a nonforfeiture benefit, the rates of mortality assumed may not be more than one hundred and thirty percent (130%) of the rates of mortality according to such applicable table. Provided, further, that for insurance issued on a substandard basis, the calculation of any such adjusted premiums and present values may be based on such other table of mortality as may be specified by the company and approved by the Commissioner.

(2) This subdivision (2) of subsection (e) shall not apply to ordinary policies issued on or after the operative date of subdivision (4) of subsection (e) as defined therein. In the case of ordinary policies issued on or after the operative date of this subdivision (2) as defined herein, all adjusted premiums and present values referred to in this section shall be calculated on the basis of the Commissioner's 1958 Standard Ordinary Mortality Table and the rate of interest specified in the policy for calculating cash surrender values and paid-up nonforfeiture benefits, provided that such rate of interest shall not exceed three and one-half percent (3 ½%) per annum except that a rate of interest not exceeding four percent (4%) per annum may be used for policies issued on or after July 1, 1975, and prior to April 19, 1979, and a rate of interest not exceeding five and one-half percent (5 ½%) per annum may be used for policies issued on or after April 19, 1979, and, provided that for any category of ordinary insurance issued on female risks, adjusted premiums and present values may be calculated according to an age not more than six years younger than the actual age of the insured; provided, however, that in calculating the present value of any paid-up term insurance with accompanying pure endowment, if any, offered as a nonforfeiture benefit, the rates of mortality assumed may be not more than those shown in the Commissioner's 1958 Extended Term Insurance Table. Provided, further, that for insurance issued on a substandard basis, the calculation of any such adjusted premiums and present values may be based on such other table of mortality as may be specified by the company and approved by the Commissioner.

After May 12, 1959, any company may file with the Commissioner a written notice of its election to comply with the provisions of this subdivision (2) after a specified date before January 1, 1966. After the filing of such notice, then upon such specified date (which shall be the operative date of this subdivision (2) for such company), this subdivision (2) shall become operative with respect to the ordinary policies thereafter issued by such company. If a company makes no such election, the operative date of this subdivision (2) for such company shall be January 1, 1966.

(3) This subdivision (3) of subsection (e) shall not apply to industrial policies issued on or after the operative date of subdivision (4) of subsection (e) as defined therein. In the case of industrial policies issued on or after the operative date of this subdivision (3) as defined herein, all adjusted premiums and present values referred to in this section shall be calculated on the basis of the Commissioner's 1961 Standard Industrial Mortality Table and the rate of interest specified in the policy for calculating cash surrender values and paid-up nonforfeiture benefits, provided that such rate of interest shall not exceed three and one-half percent (3 ½%) per annum except that a rate of interest not exceeding four percent (4%) per annum may be used for policies issued on or after July 1, 1975, and prior to April 19, 1979, and a rate of interest not exceeding five and one-half percent (5 ½%) per annum may be used for policies issued on or after April 19, 1979; provided, however, that in calculating the present value of any paid-up term insurance with accompanying pure endowment, if any, offered as a nonforfeiture benefit, the rates of mortality assumed may be not more than those shown in the Commissioner's 1961 Industrial Extended Term Insurance Table. Provided, further, that for insurance

issued on a substandard basis, the calculation of any such adjusted premiums and present values may be based on such other table of mortality as may be specified by the company and approved by the Commissioner.

After June 11, 1963, any company may file with the Commissioner a written notice of its election to comply with the provisions of this subdivision (3) after a specified date before January 1, 1968. After the filing of such notice, then upon such specified date (which shall be the operative date of this subdivision (3) for such company), this subdivision (3) shall become operative with respect to the industrial policies thereafter issued by such company. If a company makes no such election, the operative date of this subdivision (3) for such company shall be January 1, 1968.

(4)a. This subdivision shall apply to all policies issued on or after the operative date of this subdivision (4) of subsection (e) as defined herein. Except as provided in paragraph g of this subdivision, the adjusted premiums for any policy shall be calculated on an annual basis and shall be such uniform percentage of the respective premiums specified in the policy for each policy year, excluding amounts payable as extra premiums to cover impairments or special hazards and also excluding any uniform annual contract charge or policy fee specified in the policy in a statement of the method to be used in calculating the cash surrender values and paid-up nonforfeiture benefits, that the present value, at the date of issue of the policy, of all adjusted premiums shall be equal to the sum of (i) the then present value of the future guaranteed benefits provided for by the policy; (ii) one percent (1%) of either the amount of insurance, if the insurance be uniform in amount, or the average amount of insurance at the beginning of each of the first 10 policy years; and (iii) one hundred twenty-five percent (125%) of the nonforfeiture net level premium as hereinafter defined. Provided, however, that in applying the percentage specified in (iii) above no nonforfeiture net level premium shall be deemed to exceed four percent (4%) of either the amount of insurance, if the insurance be uniform in amount, or the average amount of insurance at the beginning of each of the first 10 policy years. The date of issue of a policy for the purpose of this subdivision shall be the date as of which the rated age of the insured is determined.

b. The nonforfeiture net level premium shall be equal to the present value, at the date of issue of the policy, of the guaranteed benefits provided for by the policy divided by the present value, at the date of issue of the policy, of an annuity of one per annum payable on the date of issue of the policy and on each anniversary of such policy on which a premium falls due.

c. In the case of policies which cause on a basis guaranteed in the policy unscheduled changes in benefits or premiums, or which provide an option for changes in benefits or premiums other than a change to a new policy, the adjusted premiums and present values shall initially be calculated on the assumption that future benefits and premiums do not change from those stipulated at the date of issue of the policy. At the time of any such change in the benefits or premiums the future adjusted premiums, nonforfeiture net level premiums and present values shall be recalculated on the assumption that future benefits and premiums do not change from those stipulated by the policy immediately after the change.

d. Except as otherwise provided in paragraph g of this subdivision, the recalculated future adjusted premiums for any such policy shall be such uniform percentage of the respective future premiums specified in the policy for each policy year, excluding amounts payable as extra premiums to cover impairments and special hazards, and also excluding any uniform annual contract charge or policy fee specified in the policy in a statement of the method to be used in calculating the cash surrender values and paid-up nonforfeiture benefits, that the present value, at the time of change to the newly defined benefits or premiums, of all such future adjusted premiums shall be equal to the excess of (A) the sum of (i) the then present value of the then future guaranteed benefits provided for by the policy and (ii) the additional expense allowance, if any, over (B) the then cash surrender value, if any, or present value of any paid-up nonforfeiture benefit under the policy.

e. The additional expense allowance, at the time of the change to the newly defined benefits or premiums, shall be the sum of (i) one percent (1%) of the excess, if positive, of the average amount of insurance at the beginning of each of the first 10 policy years subsequent to the change over the average amount of insurance prior to the change at the beginning of each of the first 10 policy years subsequent to the time of the most recent previous change, or, if there has been no previous change, the date of issue of the policy; and (ii) one hundred twenty-five percent (125%) of the increase, if positive, in the nonforfeiture net level premium.

f. The recalculated nonforfeiture net level premium shall be equal to the result obtained by dividing (A) by (B) where

(A) Equals the sum of

(i) The nonforfeiture net level premium applicable prior to the change times the present value of an annuity of one per annum payable on each anniversary of the policy on or subsequent to the date of the change on which a premium would have fallen due had the change not occurred, and

(ii) The present value of the increase in future guaranteed benefits provided for by the policy, and

(B) Equals the present value of an annuity of one per annum payable on each anniversary of the policy on or subsequent to the date of change on which a premium falls due.

g. Notwithstanding any other provisions of this subdivision to the contrary, in the case of a policy issued on a substandard basis which provides reduced graded amounts of insurance so that, in each policy year, such policy has the same tabular mortality cost as an otherwise similar policy issued on the standard basis which provides higher uniform amounts of insurance, adjusted premiums and present values for such substandard policy may be calculated as if it were issued to provide such higher uniform amounts of insurance on the standard basis.

h. All adjusted premiums and present values referred to in this section shall for all policies of ordinary insurance be calculated on the basis of (i) the Commissioner's 1980 Standard Ordinary Mortality Table or (ii) at the election of the company for any one or more specified plans of life insurance, the Commissioner's 1980 Standard Ordinary Mortality Table with Ten-Year Select Mortality Factors; shall for all policies of industrial insurance be calculated on the basis of the Commissioner's 1961 Standard Industrial Mortality Table; and shall for all policies issued in a particular calendar year be calculated on the basis of a rate of interest not exceeding the nonforfeiture interest rate as defined in this subdivision for policies issued in that calendar year. Provided, however, that:

1. At the option of the company, calculations for all policies issued in a particular calendar year may be made on the basis of a rate of interest not exceeding the nonforfeiture interest rate, as defined in this subdivision, for policies issued in the immediately preceding calendar year.

2. Under any paid-up nonforfeiture benefit, including any paid-up dividend additions, any cash surrender value available, whether or not required by subsection (b), shall be calculated on the basis of the mortality table and rate of interest used in determining the amount of such paid-up nonforfeiture benefit and paid-up dividend additions, if any.

3. A company may calculate the amount of any guaranteed paid-up nonforfeiture benefit including any paid-up additions under the policy on the basis of an interest rate no lower than that specified in the policy for calculating cash surrender values.

4. In calculating the present value of any paid-up term insurance with accompanying pure endowment, if any, offered as a nonforfeiture benefit, the rates of mortality assumed may be not more than those shown in the Commissioner's 1980 Extended Term Insurance Table for policies of ordinary insurance and not more than the Commissioner's 1961 Industrial Extended Term Insurance Table for policies of industrial insurance.

5. For insurance issued on a substandard basis, the calculation of any such adjusted premiums and present values may be based on appropriate modifications of the aforementioned tables.

6. Any ordinary mortality tables, adopted after 1980 by the NAIC, that are approved by regulation promulgated by the Commissioner for use in determining the minimum nonforfeiture standard may be substituted for the Commissioner's 1980 Standard Ordinary Mortality Table with or without Ten-Year Select Mortality Factors or for the Commissioner's 1980 Extended Term Insurance Table.

7. Any industrial mortality tables, adopted after 1980 by the NAIC, that are approved by regulation promulgated by the Commissioner for use in determining the minimum nonforfeiture standard may be substituted for the Commissioner's 1961 Standard Industrial Mortality Table or the Commissioner's 1961 Industrial Extended Term Insurance Table.

i. The nonforfeiture interest rate per annum for any policy issued in a particular calendar year shall be equal to one hundred and twenty-five percent (125%) of the calendar year statutory valuation interest rate for such policy as defined in the Standard Valuation Law, rounded to the nearer one quarter of one percent (¼ of 1%).

j. Notwithstanding any other provision in this Chapter to the contrary, any refiling of nonforfeiture values or their methods of computation for any previously approved policy form which involves only a change in the interest rate or mortality table used to compute nonforfeiture values shall not require refiling of any other provisions of that policy form.

k. After the effective date of this subdivision (4) of subsection (e), any company may file with the Commissioner a written notice of its election to comply with the provisions of this subdivision after a specified date before January 1, 1989, which shall be the operative date of this subdivision for such company. If a company makes no such election, the operative date of this subdivision for such company shall be January 1, 1989.

(e1) In the case of any plan of life insurance which provides for future premium determination, the amounts of which are to be determined by the insurance company based on then estimates of future experience, or in the case of any plan of life insurance which is of such a nature that minimum values cannot be determined by the methods described in subsections (b), (c), (d), or (e) herein, then:

(1) The Commissioner must be satisfied that the benefits provided under the plan are substantially as favorable to policyholders and insureds as the minimum benefits otherwise required by subsections (b), (c), (d), or (e) herein;

(2) The Commissioner must be satisfied that the benefits and the pattern of premiums of that plan are not such as to mislead prospective policyholders or insureds;

(3) The cash surrender values and paid-up nonforfeiture benefits provided by such plan must not be less than the minimum values and benefits required for the plan computed by a method consistent with the principles of this Standard Nonforfeiture Law, as determined by regulations promulgated by the Commissioner;

(4) Notwithstanding any other provision in the laws of this State, any policy, contract, or certificate providing life insurance under any such plan must be affirmatively approved by the Commissioner before it can be marketed, issued, delivered, or used in this State.

(f) Any cash surrender value and any paid-up nonforfeiture benefit, available under the policy in the event of default in a premium payment due at any time other than on the policy anniversary, shall be calculated with allowance for the lapse of time and the payment of fractional premiums beyond the last preceding policy anniversary. Any values referred to in subsections (c), (d) and (e) may be calculated upon the assumption that any death benefit is payable at the end of the policy year of death. The net value of any paid-up additions, other than paid-up term additions, shall be not less than the amounts used to provide such additions. Notwithstanding the provisions of Section 3 [subsection (c)], additional benefits payable (i) in the event of death or dismemberment by accident or accidental means, (ii) in the event of total and permanent disability, (iii) as reversionary annuity or deferred reversionary annuity benefits, (iv) as term insurance benefits provided by a rider or supplemental policy provision to which, if issued as a separate policy, this section would not apply, (v) as term insurance on the life of a child or on the lives of children provided in a policy on the life of a parent of the child, if such term insurance expires before the child's age is 26, is uniform in amount after the child's age is one, and has not become paid up by reason of the death of a parent of the child, and (vi) as other policy benefits additional to life insurance and endowment benefits, and premiums for all such additional benefits, shall be disregarded in ascertaining cash surrender values and nonforfeiture benefits required by this section, and no such additional benefits shall be required to be included in any paid-up nonforfeiture benefits.

(f1) This subsection, in addition to all other applicable subsections of this section, shall apply to all policies issued on or after January 1, 1985. Any cash surrender value available under the policy in the event of default in a premium payment due on any policy anniversary shall be in an amount which does not differ by more than two-tenths of one percent (²⁄₁₀ of 1%) of either the amount of insurance, if the insurance be uniform in amount, or the average amount of insurance at the beginning of each of the first 10 policy years, from the sum of (1) the greater of zero and the basic cash value hereinafter specified and (2) the present value of any existing paid-up additions less the amount of any indebtedness to the company under the policy.

The basic cash value shall be equal to the present value, on such anniversary, of the future guaranteed benefits which would have been provided for by the policy, excluding any existing paid-up additions and before deduction of any indebtedness to the company, if there had been no default, less the then present value of the nonforfeiture factors, as hereinafter defined, corresponding to premiums which would have fallen due on and after such anniversary. Provided, however, that the effects on the basic cash value of supplemental life insurance or annuity benefits or of family coverage, as described in subsection (c) or (e)(1), whichever is applicable, shall be the same as are the effects specified in subsection (c) or (e)(1), whichever is applicable, on the cash surrender values defined in that subsection.

The nonforfeiture factor for each policy year shall be an amount equal to a percentage of the adjusted premium for the policy year, as defined in subsection (e)(1) or (e)(4), whichever is applicable. Except as is required by the next succeeding sentence of this paragraph, such percentage:

(1) Must be the same percentage for each policy year between the second policy anniversary and the later of (i) the fifth policy anniversary and (ii) the first policy anniversary at which there is available under the policy a cash surrender value in an amount, before including any paid-up additions and before deducting any indebtedness, of at least two-tenths of one percent (²⁄₁₀ of 1%) of either the amount of insurance, if the insurance be uniform in amount, or the average amount of insurance at the beginning of each of the first 10 policy years; and

(2) Must be such that no percentage after the later of the two policy anniversaries specified in the preceding item (1) may apply to fewer than five consecutive policy years.

Provided, that no basic cash value may be less than the value which would be obtained if the adjusted premiums for the policy, as defined in subsection (e)(1) or (e)(4), whichever is applicable, were substituted for the nonforfeiture factors in the calculation of the basic cash value.

All adjusted premiums and present values referred to in this subsection shall for a particular policy be calculated on the same mortality and interest bases as are used in demonstrating the policy's compliance with the other subsections of this section. The cash surrender values referred to in this subsection shall include any endowment benefits provided for by the policy.

Any cash surrender value available other than in the event of default in a premium payment due on a policy anniversary, and the amount of any paid-up nonforfeiture benefit available under the policy in the event of default in a premium payment shall be determined in manners consistent with the manners specified for determining the analogous minimum amounts in subsections (b), (c), (d), (e)(4), and (f). The amounts of any cash surrender values and of any paid-up nonforfeiture benefits granted in connection with additional benefits such as those listed as items (i) through (vi) in subsection (f) shall conform with the principles of this subsection (f1).

(g) The provisions of this section shall not apply to any of the following:

(1) Industrial sick benefit insurance as defined in Articles 1 through 64 of this Chapter,

(2) Reinsurance,

(3) Group insurance,

(4) Pure endowment,

(5) Annuity or reversionary annuity contract,

(6) Term policy of uniform amount, which provides no guaranteed nonforfeiture or endowment benefits, or renewal thereof, of 20 years or less, for which uniform premiums are payable during the entire term of the policy,

(7) Term policy of decreasing amount, which provides no guaranteed nonforfeiture or endowment benefits, on which each adjusted premium, calculated as specified in subsection (e), is less than the adjusted premium so calculated, on a term policy of uniform amount, or renewal thereof, which provides no guaranteed nonforfeiture or endowment benefits, issued at the same age and for the same initial amount of insurance and for a term of 20 years or less expiring before age 71, for which uniform premiums are payable during the entire term of the policy,

(8) Policy, which provides no guaranteed nonforfeiture or endowment benefits, for which no cash surrender value, if any, or present value of any paid-up nonforfeiture benefit, at the beginning of any policy year, calculated as specified in subsections (c), (d) and (e), exceeds two and one-half percent (2 ½%) of the amount of insurance at the beginning of the same policy year, nor

(9) Policy which shall be delivered outside this State through an agent or other representative of the company issuing the policy.

For purposes of determining the applicability of this section, the age at expiry for a joint term life insurance policy shall be the age at expiry of the oldest life.

(h) After March 6, 1945, any company may file with the Commissioner a written notice of its election to comply with the provisions of this section after a specified date before January 1, 1950. After the filing of such notice then upon such specified date (which shall be the operative date for such company) this section shall become operative with respect to the policies thereafter issued by such company. If a company makes no such election, the operative date of this section for such company shall be January 1, 1950.

(i) For any single premium whole life or endowment insurance policy subject to subdivisions (e)(2) and (e)(3) of this section, a rate of interest not exceeding six and one-half percent (6 ½%) per annum may be used. (1945, c. 379; 1959, c. 484, s. 2; 1961, c. 255, ss. 4-7; 1963, c. 791, ss. 3, 4; 1975, c. 603, ss. 2, 3; 1979, c. 409, ss. 7-9; 1981, c. 761, ss. 6-14; 1991, c. 720, ss. 19, 31; 1993, c. 452, ss. 57-59.)

§ 58-58-60. (Repealed effective October 1, 2004 — See editor's note) Standard Nonforfeiture Law for Individual Deferred Annuities.

(a) This section shall be known as the Standard Nonforfeiture Law for Individual Deferred Annuities.

(b) This section shall not apply to any reinsurance, group annuity purchased under a retirement plan or plan of deferred compensation established or maintained by an employer (including a partnership or sole proprietorship) or by an employee organization, or by both, other than a plan providing individual retirement accounts or individual retirement annuities under section 408 of the Internal Revenue Code, as now or hereafter amended, premium deposit fund, variable annuity, investment annuity, immediate annuity, any deferred annuity contract after annuity payments have commenced, or reversionary annuity, nor to any contract which shall be delivered outside this State through an agent or other representative of the company issuing the contract.

(c) In the case of contracts issued on or after the operative date of this section as defined in subsection (1), no contract of annuity, except as stated in subsection (b), shall be delivered or issued for delivery in this State unless it contains in substance the following provisions, or corresponding provisions which in the opinion of the Commissioner are at least as favorable to the contract holder, upon cessation of payment of considerations under the contract.

    (1) That upon cessation of payment of considerations under a contract, the company will grant a paid-up annuity benefit on a plan stipulated in the contract of such value as is specified in subsections (e), (f), (g), (h) and (j).

    (2) If a contract provides for a lump sum settlement at maturity, or at any other time, that upon surrender of the contract at or prior to the commencement of any annuity payments, the company will pay in lieu of any paid-up annuity benefit a cash surrender benefit of such amount as is specified in subsections (e), (f), (h) and (j). The company shall reserve the right to defer the payment of such cash surrender benefit for a period of six months after demand therefor with surrender of the contract.

    (3) A statement of the mortality table, if any, and interest rates used in calculating any minimum paid-up annuity, cash surrender or death benefits that are guaranteed under the contract, together with sufficient information to determine the amounts of such benefits.

    (4) A statement that any paid-up annuity, cash surrender or death benefits that may be available under the contract are not less than the minimum benefits required by any statute of the state in which the contract is delivered and an explanation of the manner in which such benefits are altered by the existence of any additional amounts credited by the company to the contract, any indebtedness to the company on the contract or any prior withdrawals from or partial surrenders of the contract.

Notwithstanding the requirements of this section, any deferred annuity contract may provide that if no considerations have been received under a contract for a period of two full years and the portion of the paid-up annuity benefit at maturity on the plan stipulated in the contract arising from considerations paid prior to such period would be less than twenty dollars ($20.00) monthly, the company may at its option terminate contract by payment in cash of the then present value of such portion of the paid-up annuity benefit, calculated on the basis of the mortality table, if any, and interest rate specified in the contract for determining the paid-up annuity benefit, and by such payment shall be relieved of any further obligation under such contract.

(d) The minimum values as specified in subsections (e), (f), (g), (h) and (j) of any paid-up annuity, cash surrender or death benefits available under an annuity contract shall be based upon minimum nonforfeiture amounts as defined in this section.

    (1) With respect to contracts providing for flexible considerations, the minimum nonforfeiture amount at any time at or prior to the commencement of any annuity payments shall be equal to an accumulation up to such time at a rate of interest of one and one-half percent (1½%) per annum of percentages of the net considerations (as hereinafter defined) paid prior to such time, decreased by the sum of:

        (i) Any prior withdrawals from or partial surrenders of the contract accumulated at a rate of interest of one and one-half percent (1½%) per annum; and

(ii) The amount of any indebtedness to the company on the contract, including interest due and accrued, and increased by any existing additional amounts credited by the company to the contract.

The net considerations for a given contract year used to define the minimum nonforfeiture amount shall be an amount not less than zero and shall be equal to the corresponding gross considerations credited to the contract during that contract year less an annual contract charge of thirty dollars ($30.00) and less a collection charge of one dollar and twenty-five cents ($1.25) per consideration credited to the contract during that contract year. The percentages of net considerations shall be sixty-five percent (65%) of the net consideration for the first contract year and eighty-seven and one-half (87 ½%) of the net considerations for the second and later contract years. Notwithstanding the provisions of the preceding sentence, the percentage shall be sixty-five percent (65%) of the portion of the total net consideration for any renewal contract year which exceeds by not more than two times the sum of those portions of the net considerations in all prior contract years for which the percentage was sixty-five percent (65%).

(2) With respect to contracts providing for fixed scheduled considerations, minimum nonforfeiture amounts shall be calculated on the assumption that considerations are paid annually in advance and shall be defined as for contracts with flexible considerations which are paid annually with two exceptions:

(i) The portion of the net consideration for the first contract year to be accumulated shall be the sum of sixty-five percent (65%) of the net consideration for the first contract year plus twenty-two and one-half percent (22 ½%) of the excess of the net consideration for the first contract year over the lesser of the net considerations for the second and third contract years.

(ii) The annual contract charge shall be the lesser of (i) thirty dollars ($30.00) or (ii) ten percent (10%) of the gross annual considerations.

(3) With respect to contracts providing for a single consideration, minimum nonforfeiture amounts shall be defined as for contracts with flexible considerations except that the percentage of net consideration used to determine the minimum nonforfeiture amount shall be equal to ninety percent (90%) and the net consideration shall be the gross consideration less a contract charge of seventy-five dollars ($75.00).

(e) Any paid-up annuity benefit available under a contract shall be such that its present value on the date annuity payments are to commence is at least equal to the minimum nonforfeiture amount on that date. Such present value shall be computed using the mortality table, if any, and the interest rate specified in the contract for determining the minimum paid-up annuity benefits guaranteed in the contract.

(f) For contracts which provide cash surrender benefits, such cash surrender benefits available prior to maturity shall not be less than the present value as of the date of surrender of that portion of the maturity value of the paid-up annuity benefit which would be provided under the contract at maturity arising from considerations paid prior to the time of cash surrender reduced by the amount appropriate to reflect any prior withdrawals from or partial surrenders of the contract, such present value being calculated on the basis of an interest rate not more than one percent (1%) higher than the interest rate specified in the contract for accumulating the net considerations to determine such maturity value, decreased by the amount of any indebtedness to the company on the contract, including interest due and accrued, and increased by any existing additional amounts credited by the company to the contract. In no event shall any cash surrender benefit be less than the minimum nonforfeiture amount at that time. The death benefit under such contracts shall be at least equal to the cash surrender benefit.

(g) For contracts which do not provide cash surrender benefits, the present value of any paid-up annuity benefit available as a nonforfeiture option at any time prior to maturity shall not be less than the present value of that portion of the maturity value of the paid-up annuity benefit provided under the contract arising from considerations paid prior to the time the contract is surrendered in exchange for, or changed to, a deferred paid-up annuity, such present value being calculated for the period prior to the maturity date on the basis of the interest rate specified in the contract for accumulating the net considerations to determine such maturity value, and increased by any existing additional amounts credited by the company to the contract. For contracts which do not provide any death benefits prior to the commencement of any annuity payments, such present values shall be calculated on the basis of such interest rate and the mortality table specified in the contract for determining the maturity value of the paid-up annuity benefit. However, in no event shall the present value of a paid-up annuity benefit be less than the minimum nonforfeiture amount at that time.

(h) For the purpose of determining the benefits calculated under subsections (f) and (g), in the case of annuity contracts under which an election may be made to have annuity payments commence at optional maturity dates, the maturity date shall be deemed to be the latest date for which election shall be permitted by the contract, but shall not be deemed to be later than the anniversary of the contract next following the annuitant's seventieth birthday or the tenth anniversary of the contract, whichever is later.

(i) Any contract which does not provide cash surrender benefits or does not provide death benefits at least equal to the minimum nonforfeiture amount prior to the commencement of any annuity payments shall include a statement in a prominent place in the contract that such benefits are not provided.

(j) Any paid-up annuity, cash surrender or death benefits available at any time, other than on the contract anniversary under any contract with fixed scheduled considerations, shall be calculated with allowance for the lapse of time and the payment of any scheduled considerations beyond the beginning of the contract year in which cessation of payment of considerations under the contract occurs.

(k) For any contract which provides, within the same contract by rider or supplemental contract provision, both annuity benefits and life insurance benefits that are in excess of the greater of cash surrender benefits or a return of the gross considerations with interest, the minimum nonforfeiture benefits shall be equal to the sum of the minimum nonforfeiture benefits for the annuity portion and the minimum nonforfeiture benefits, if any, for the life insurance portion computed as if each portion were a separate contract. Notwithstanding the provisions of subsections (e), (f), (g), (h) and (j), additional benefits payable (1) in the event of total and permanent disability, (2) as reversionary annuity or deferred reversionary annuity benefits, or (3) as other policy benefits additional to life insurance, endowment and annuity benefits, and considerations for all such additional benefits, shall be disregarded in ascertaining the minimum nonforfeiture amounts, paid-up annuity, cash surrender and death benefits that may be required by this section. The inclusion of such additional benefits shall not be required in any paid-up benefits, unless such additional benefits separately would require minimum nonforfeiture amounts, paid-up annuity, cash surrender and death benefits.

(l) After April 19, 1979, any company may file with the Commissioner a written notice of its election to comply with the provisions of this section after a specified date before the second anniversary of the effective date of this section. After the filing of such notice, then upon such specified date, which shall be the operative date of this section for such company, this section shall become operative with respect to annuity contracts thereafter issued by such company. If a company makes no such election, the operative date of this section for such company shall be the second anniversary of the effective date of this section. (1979, c. 409, s. 11; 2002-187, s. 8; 2003-144, s. 2.)

Editor's Note. — Session Laws 2003-144, s. 2, provides that G.S. 58-58-60 is repealed effective October 1, 2004.

§ 58-58-61. Standard nonforfeiture law for individual deferred annuities.

(a) Title. — This section is and may be cited as the Standard Nonforfeiture Law for Individual Deferred Annuities.

(b) Applicability. — This section does not apply to any:

(1) Reinsurance.

(2) Group annuity purchased under a retirement plan or plan of deferred compensation established or maintained by an employer, including a partnership or sole proprietorship, or by an employee organization, or by both, other than a plan providing individual retirement accounts or individual retirement annuities under section 408 of the Internal Revenue Code, as amended.

(3) Premium deposit fund.

(4) Variable annuity.

(5) Investment annuity.

(6) Immediate annuity.

(7) Deferred annuity contract after annuity payments have commenced.

(8) Reversionary annuity.

(9) Contract delivered outside this State through an agent or other representative of the company issuing the contract.

(c) Nonforfeiture Requirements. — In the case of contracts issued on or after the operative date of this section as defined in subsection (o) of this section, no contract of annuity, except as stated in subsection (b) of this section, shall be delivered or issued for delivery in this State unless it contains in substance the following provisions, or corresponding provisions that in the opinion of the Commissioner are at least as favorable to the contract holder, upon cessation of payment of considerations under the contract:

(1) That upon cessation of payment of considerations under a contract, or upon the written request of the contract owner, the company shall grant a paid-up annuity benefit on a plan stipulated in the contract of the value specified in subsections (g), (h), (i), (j), and (l) of this section.

(2) If a contract provides for a lump sum settlement at maturity or at any other time, that upon surrender of the contract at or before the commencement of any annuity payments, the company shall pay in lieu of a paid-up annuity benefit a cash surrender benefit of the amount specified in subsections (g), (h), (j), and (l) of this section. The company may reserve the right to defer the payment of the cash surrender benefit for a period not to exceed six months after demand for the payment with surrender of the contract after making written request and receiving written approval of the Commissioner. The request shall address the necessity and equitability to all policyholders of the deferral.

(3) A statement of the mortality table, if any, and interest rates used in calculating any minimum paid-up annuity, cash surrender, or death

957

benefits that are guaranteed under the contract, together with sufficient information to determine the amounts of the benefits.

(4) A statement that any paid-up annuity, cash surrender, or death benefits that may be available under the contract are not less than the minimum benefits required by any statute of the state in which the contract is delivered and an explanation of the manner in which the benefits are altered by the existence of any additional amounts credited by the company to the contract, any indebtedness to the company on the contract, or any prior withdrawals from or partial surrenders of the contract.

Notwithstanding the requirements of this subsection, a deferred annuity contract may provide that if no considerations have been received under the contract for a period of two full years and the portion of the paid-up annuity benefit at maturity on the plan stipulated in the contract arising from prior considerations paid would be less than twenty dollars ($20.00) monthly, the company may at its option terminate the contract by payment in cash of the then-present value of the portion of the paid-up annuity benefit, calculated on the basis of the mortality table, if any, and interest rate specified in the contract for determining the paid-up annuity benefit, and by this payment shall be relieved of any further obligation under the contract.

(d) Minimum Values. — The minimum values specified in subsections (g), (h), (i), (j), and (l) of this section of any paid-up annuity, cash surrender, or death benefits available under an annuity contract shall be based upon minimum nonforfeiture amounts as defined in this section. The minimum nonforfeiture amount at any time at or before the commencement of any annuity payments shall be equal to an accumulation up to that time at rates of interest as indicated in subsection (e) of this section of the net considerations, as hereinafter defined, paid before that time, decreased by the sum of the following:

(1) Any prior withdrawals from or partial surrenders of the contract accumulated at rates of interest as indicated in subsection (e) of this section.

(2) An annual contract charge of fifty dollars ($50.00), accumulated at rates of interest as indicated in subsection (e) of this section.

(3) Any premium tax paid by the company for the contract, accumulated at rates of interest as indicated in subsection (e) of this section.

(4) The amount of any indebtedness to the company on the contract, including interest due and accrued.

The net considerations for a given contract year used to define the minimum nonforfeiture amount shall be an amount equal to eighty-seven and one-half percent (87 1/2%) of the gross considerations credited to the contract during that contract year.

(e) The interest rate used in determining minimum nonforfeiture amounts shall be an annual rate of interest determined as the lesser of three percent (3%) per annum and the following, which shall be specified in the contract if the interest rate will be reset:

(1) The five-year Constant Maturity Treasury Rate reported by the Federal Reserve as of a date, or average over a period, rounded to the nearest one-twentieth of one percent (0.05%), specified in the contract no longer than 15 months before the contract issue date or redetermination date under subdivision (4) of this subsection.

(2) Reduced by 125 basis points.

(3) Where the resulting interest guarantee is not less than one percent (1%).

(4) The interest rate shall apply for an initial period and may be redetermined for additional periods. The redetermination date, basis,

and period, if any, shall be stated in the contract. The basis is the date or average over a specified period that produces the value of the five-year Constant Maturity Treasury Rate to be used at each redetermination date.

(f) During the period or term that a contract provides substantive participation in an equity indexed benefit, it may increase the reduction described in subdivision (e)(2) of this section by up to an additional 100 basis points to reflect the value of the equity index benefit. The present value at the contract issue date, and at each subsequent redetermination date, of the additional reduction shall not exceed the market value of the benefit. The Commissioner may require a demonstration that the present value of the additional reduction does not exceed the market value of the benefit. Absent a demonstration that is acceptable to the Commissioner, the Commissioner may disallow or limit the additional reduction. The Commissioner may adopt rules to implement the provisions of this subsection and to provide for further adjustments to the calculation of minimum nonforfeiture amounts for contracts that provide substantive participation in an equity index benefit and for other contracts for which the Commissioner determines adjustments are justified.

(g) Computation of Present Value. — Any paid-up annuity benefit available under a contract shall be such that its present value on the date annuity payments are to commence is at least equal to the minimum nonforfeiture amount on that date. Present value shall be computed using the mortality table, if any, and the interest rates specified in the contract for determining the minimum paid-up annuity benefits guaranteed in the contract.

(h) Calculation of Cash Surrender Value. — For contracts that provide cash surrender benefits, the cash surrender benefits available before maturity shall not be less than the present value as of the date of surrender of that portion of the maturity value of the paid-up annuity benefit that would be provided under the contract at maturity arising from considerations paid before the time of cash surrender reduced by the amount appropriate to reflect any prior withdrawals from or partial surrenders of the contract, such present value being calculated on the basis of an interest rate not more than one percent (1%) higher than the interest rate specified in the contract for accumulating the net considerations to determine maturity value, decreased by the amount of any indebtedness to the company on the contract, including interest due and accrued, and increased by any existing additional amounts credited by the company to the contract. In no event shall any cash surrender benefit be less than the minimum nonforfeiture amount at that time. The death benefit under such contracts shall be at least equal to the cash surrender benefit.

(i) Calculation of Paid-Up Annuity Benefits. — For contracts that do not provide cash surrender benefits, the present value of any paid-up annuity benefit available as a nonforfeiture option at any time before maturity shall not be less than the present value of that portion of the maturity value of the paid-up annuity benefit provided under the contract arising from considerations paid before the time the contract is surrendered in exchange for, or changed to, a deferred paid-up annuity, the present value being calculated for the period before the maturity date on the basis of the interest rate specified in the contract for accumulating the net considerations to determine maturity value, and increased by any additional amounts credited by the company to the contract. For contracts that do not provide any death benefits before the commencement of any annuity payments, present values shall be calculated on the basis of the interest rate and the mortality table specified in the contract for determining the maturity value of the paid-up annuity benefit. However, in no event shall the present value of a paid-up annuity benefit be less than the minimum nonforfeiture amount at that time.

(j) Maturity Date. — For the purpose of determining the benefits calculated under subsections (h) and (i) of this section, in the case of annuity contracts under which an election may be made to have annuity payments commence at optional maturity dates, the maturity date shall be the latest date for which election is permitted by the contract but not later than the anniversary of the contract next following the annuitant's seventieth birthday or the tenth anniversary of the contract, whichever is later.

(k) Disclosure of Limited Death Benefits. — A contract that does not provide cash surrender benefits or does not provide death benefits at least equal to the minimum nonforfeiture amount before the commencement of any annuity payments shall include a statement in a prominent place in the contract that those benefits are not provided.

(*l*) Inclusion of Lapse of Time Considerations. — Any paid-up annuity, cash surrender, or death benefits available at any time, other than on the contract anniversary under any contract with fixed scheduled considerations, shall be calculated with allowance for the lapse of time and the payment of any scheduled considerations beyond the beginning of the contract year in which cessation of payment of considerations under the contract occurs.

(m) Proration of Values; Additional Benefits. — For a contract that provides within the same contract, by rider or supplemental contract provision, both annuity benefits and life insurance benefits that are in excess of the greater of cash surrender benefits or a return of the gross considerations with interest, the minimum nonforfeiture benefits shall be equal to the sum of the minimum nonforfeiture benefits for the annuity portion and the minimum nonforfeiture benefits, if any, for the life insurance portion computed as if each portion were a separate contract. Notwithstanding the provisions of subsections (g), (h), (i), (j), and (l) of this section, additional benefits payable in the event of total and permanent disability, as reversionary annuity or deferred reversionary annuity benefits, or as other policy benefits additional to life insurance, endowment, and annuity benefits, and considerations for all such additional benefits, shall be disregarded in ascertaining the minimum nonforfeiture amounts, paid-up annuity, cash surrender, and death benefits that may be required by this section. The inclusion of those benefits shall not be required in any paid-up benefits, unless the additional benefits separately would require minimum nonforfeiture amounts, paid-up annuity, cash surrender, and death benefits.

(n) Rules. — The Commissioner may adopt rules to implement the provisions of this section.

(o) Effective Date. — On and after October 1, 2003, a company may elect to apply the provisions of this section to annuity contracts on a contract form-by-contract form basis before October 1, 2004. In all other instances, this section shall become operative with respect to annuity contracts issued by the company on and after October 1, 2004. (2003-144, s. 1.)

Editor's Note. — Session Laws 2003-144, s. 4, made this section effective October 1, 2003.

§ 58-58-65. Reinsurance of companies regulated.

The receiver of any life insurance company organized under the laws of this State, when the assets of the company are sufficient for that purpose, and the consent of two thirds of its policyholders has been secured in writing, may reinsure all the policy obligations of such company in some other solvent life insurance company, or, when the assets are insufficient to secure the reinsurance of all the policies in full, he may reinsure such a percentage of each and every policy outstanding as the assets will secure; but there must be no preference or discrimination as against any policyholder, and the contract for such reinsurance by the receiver must be approved by the Commissioner before it has effect. (1899, c. 54, s. 58; 1903, c. 536, s. 9; Rev., s. 4778; C.S., s. 6462; 1945, c. 379; 1991, c. 720, s. 61.)

Part 3. Insurable Interests and Other Rights.

§ 58-58-70. Insurable interest as between stockholders, partners, etc.

Where two or more persons have heretofore contracted or hereafter contract with one another for the purchase, at the death of one, by the survivor or survivors, of the stock, share or interest of the deceased in any corporation, partnership or business association of any kind, the person or persons making the contract of purchase shall be deemed to have, and are hereby declared to have, an insurable interest in the life or lives of the person or persons contracting to sell. (1941, c. 201; 1969, c. 751, s. 44.)

Editor's Note. — Session Laws 2001-436, s. 2, effective April 1, 2002, divided Article 58 into Parts 1 to 4, assigning a Part head to each Part, with G.S. 58-58-1 to 58-58-40 in Part 1, G.S. 58-58-45 to 58-58-65 in Part 2, G.S. 58-58-70 to 58-58-120 in Part 3, and G.S. 58-58-125 to 58-58-170 in Part 4, reserving G.S. 58-58-175 to 58-58-195 for future codification purposes.

Session Laws 2001-436, s. 17, is a severability clause.

Legal Periodicals. — For comment on this section, see 19 N.C.L. Rev. 490 (1941).

§ 58-58-75. Insurable interest in life and physical ability of employee or agent.

An employer, whether a partnership, joint venture, business trust, mutual association, corporation, any other form of business organization, or one or more individuals, or any religious, educational, or charitable corporation, institution or body, has an insurable interest in and the right to insure the physical ability or the life, or both the physical ability and the life, of an employee for the benefit of such employer. Any principal shall have a life insurable interest in and the right to insure the physical ability or the life, or both the physical ability and the life, of an agent for the benefit of such principal. (1951, c. 283, s. 1; 1957, c. 1086.)

Legal Periodicals. — For brief comment on this section and G.S. 58-58-80 through 58-58-90, see 29 N.C.L. Rev. 401 (1951).

§ 58-58-80. Insurable interest in life and physical ability of partner.

Any partner has an insurable interest in and the right to insure the physical ability or the life, or both the physical ability and the life, of any other partner or partners who are members of the same partnership for his benefit, either alone or jointly with another partner or partners of the same partnership. A partnership has a like insurable interest in and the right to insure the physical ability or the life, or both the physical ability and the life, of one or more partners of the partnership. (1951, c. 283, s. 2.)

§ 58-58-85. Insurable interest in life of person covered by pension plan.

A trustee under a written document providing for a pension plan for payments of money or delivery of other benefits to be made to persons eligible to receive them under the terms and provisions of such written document shall be deemed to have and is hereby declared to have an insurable interest in the lives of any person or persons covered by the pension plan, to the extent that contracts or policies of insurance are in conformity with and in furtherance of the purposes of the pension plan. (1951, c. 283, s. 21/2.)

CASE NOTES

Cited in Allgood v. Wilmington Sav. & Trust Co., 242 N.C. 506, 88 S.E.2d 825 (1955).

§ 58-58-86. Insurable interest of charitable organizations.

If an organization described in section 501(c)(3) of the Internal Revenue Code purchases or receives by assignment, before, on, or after the effective date of this section, life insurance on an insured who consents to the purchase or assignment, the organization is deemed to have an insurable interest in the insured person's life. (1991, c. 644, s. 2.)

§ 58-58-90. Construction.

G.S. 58-58-75, 58-58-80, 58-58-85, and 58-58-86 do not limit or abridge any insurable interest or right to insure now existing at common law or by statute, and shall be construed liberally to sustain insurable interest, whether as a declaration of existing law or as an extension of or addition to existing law. (1951, c. 283, s. 3; 1991, c. 644, s. 3.)

§ 58-58-95. Rights of beneficiaries.

When a policy of insurance is effected by any person on his own life, or on another life in favor of some person other than himself having an insurable interest therein, the lawful beneficiary thereof, other than himself or his legal representatives, is entitled to its proceeds against the creditors and representatives of the person effecting the insurance. The person to whom a policy of life insurance is made payable may maintain an action thereon in his own name. A person may insure his or her own life for the sole use and benefit of his or her spouse, or children, or both, and upon his or her death the proceeds from the insurance shall be paid to or for the benefit of the spouse, or children, or both, or to a guardian, free from all claims of the representatives or creditors of the insured or his or her estate. Any insurance policy which insures the life of a person for the sole use and benefit of that person's spouse, or children, or both, shall not be subject to the claims of creditors of the insured during his or her lifetime, whether or not the policy reserves to the insured during his or her lifetime any or all rights provided for by the policy and whether or not the policy proceeds are payable to the estate of the insured in the event the beneficiary or beneficiaries predecease the insured. (Const., Art. X, s. 7; 1899, c. 54, s. 59; Rev., ss. 4771, 4772; C.S., s. 6464; 1977, c. 518, s. 1.)

Cross References. — As to freedom of life insurance for the benefit of one's spouse or children or both from the claims of creditors, see N.C. Const., Art. X, § 5. As to receipt and disbursement of insurance for minors and incapacitated adults, see G.S. 7A-111. For provision depriving creditors of benefits of life insurance in favor of beneficiary other than the insured, except in cases of fraud, see G.S. 58-58-115.

CASE NOTES

Section 58-58-115 is actually an amendment of this section. In re Wolfe, 249 F. Supp. 784 (M.D.N.C. 1966), decided prior to the 1977 amendment to this section, and commented on in 45 N.C.L. Rev. 696 (1967).

Section 58-58-115 supersedes this section where there are variations or conflicts. Home Sec. Life Ins. Co. v. McDonald, 277 N.C. 275, 177 S.E.2d 291 (1970), decided prior to the 1977 amendment to this section.

Change of Beneficiary Not Fraudulent. — A beneficiary in a policy of life insurance has only a contingent interest therein, and where the insured retains the right to change the beneficiary by the terms of the policy, he may do so; hence, where, upon the death of the beneficiary, the insured changed the beneficiary, in accordance with the terms of the policy, to a trustee for the use of certain creditors and heirs at law of the insured, the other creditors could not claim that the change in the beneficiary was void as being fraudulent as to them. Teague v. Pilot Life Ins. Co., 200 N.C. 450, 157 S.E. 421 (1931).

Where the insured in a policy of life insurance, payable at his death to his estate, procured a change of beneficiary in said policy in accordance with its provisions, by which his wife became the beneficiary, such change was not void as against creditors, even though at the date the change was made the insured was insolvent. Pearsall v. Bloodworth, 194 N.C. 628, 140 S.E. 303 (1927); Teague v. Pilot Life Ins. Co., 200 N.C. 450, 157 S.E. 421 (1931); Meadows Fertilizer Co. v. Godley, 204 N.C. 243, 167 S.E. 816 (1933).

Change of Beneficiary Given Effect. — Where a policy of life insurance reserves the right in the insured to change the beneficiary therein named, the named beneficiary has only a contingent interest therein, and the insured may change the beneficiary in accordance with the terms of the policy at any time; moreover, where the insured has done all that is possible under the circumstances to change the beneficiary in accordance with the terms of the policy, such change of beneficiary will be given effect under the principle that equity regards as done that which ought to have been done. Hence, where the insured's wife was thus made the beneficiary, the proceeds inured to her sole benefit, free from the claims of insured's creditors. Meadows Fertilizer Co. v. Godley, 204 N.C. 243, 167 S.E. 816 (1933).

Change of Beneficiary Not Effected. — Where deceased had expressed an intention to change the beneficiary in a policy of insurance on his life, but had taken no affirmative act to effect such change, the court's judgment that no change of beneficiary had been effected was upheld. Meadows Fertilizer Co. v. Godley, 204 N.C. 243, 167 S.E. 816 (1933).

When individual insured his life for the benefit of his wife and children, and at the time had no wife, but did have two children, one of whom died before him, it was held that upon his death the money due on the policy should be divided between the surviving child and the administrator of the dead child. The insertion of his "wife" as a beneficiary, when he had no wife living, was a nullity. Hooker v. Sugg, 102 N.C. 115, 8 S.E. 919 (1889).

Applied in Russell v. Owen, 203 N.C. 262, 165 S.E. 687 (1932).

Cited in Philadelphia Life Ins. Co. v. Crosland-Cullen Co., 234 F.2d 780 (4th Cir. 1956).

§ 58-58-100. Minors may enter into insurance or annuity contracts and have full rights, powers and privileges thereunder.

All minors in North Carolina of the age of 15 years and upwards shall have full power and authority to make contracts of insurance or annuity with any life insurance company authorized to do business in the State of North Carolina, either domestic or foreign, and to exercise all the powers, rights, and privileges of ownership conferred upon them under the terms of any and all such contracts applied for by and issued to them, and with full power to surrender, assign, modify, pledge, or change such contracts, and to receive any dividends thereon and generally to have the full power and authority in the premises that persons 18 years and upwards could and would have relative to any and all such contracts. (1945, c. 379; 1947, c. 721; 1971, c. 1231, s. 1.)

Legal Periodicals. — For article, "The Contracts of Minors Viewed from the Perspective of Fair Exchange," see 50 N.C.L. Rev. 571 (1972).

Cited in Gastonia Personnel Corp. v. Rogers, 276 N.C. 279, 172 S.E.2d 19 (1970).

§ 58-58-105. Renunciation.

A beneficiary of a life insurance policy who did not possess the incidents of ownership under the policy at the time of death of the insured may renounce as provided in Chapter 31B of the General Statutes. (1975, c. 371, s. 5.)

§ 58-58-110. Interest payments on death benefits.

(a) Each insurer admitted to transact insurance in this State which, without the written consent of the beneficiary, fails or refuses to pay the death proceeds or death benefits in accordance with the terms of any policy providing a death benefit issued by it in this State within 30 days after receipt of satisfactory proof of loss because of the death, whether accidental or otherwise, of the insured shall pay interest, at a rate not less than the then current rate of interest on death proceeds left on deposit with the insurer computed from the date of the insured's death, on any moneys payable and unpaid after the expiration of the 30-day period. As used in this subsection, the phrase "satisfactory proof of loss because of the death" includes, but is not limited to, a certified copy of the death certificate; or a written statement by the attending physician at the time of death that contains the following information: (i) the name and address of the physician, who must be duly licensed to practice medicine in the United States; (ii) the name of the deceased; (iii) the date, time, and place of the death; and (iv) the immediate cause of the death.

(b) Within the meaning of this section, payment of proceeds or benefits shall be deemed to have been made on the date upon which a check, draft or other valid instrument equivalent to the payment of money was placed in the United States mails in a properly addressed, postpaid envelope, or, if not so posted, on the date of delivery of such instrument to the beneficiary.

(c) This section does not allow an insurer to withhold payment of money payable under any policy providing a death benefit to any beneficiary for a period longer than reasonably necessary to determine whether benefits are payable and to transmit the payment.

(d) This section shall not apply to policies of insurance issued prior to the effective date of this section to the extent that such policies contain specific provisions in conflict with this section. (1977, c. 395, s. 1; 1983, c. 749; 1985, c. 666, s. 45; 1991, c. 644, s. 8; 1995, c. 193, s. 46.)

Applied in Fedoronko v. American Defender Life Ins. Co., 69 N.C. App. 655, 318 S.E.2d 244 (1984).

§ 58-58-115. Creditors deprived of benefits of life insurance policies except in cases of fraud.

If a policy of insurance is effected by any person on his own life or on another life in favor of a person other than himself, or, except in cases of transfer with intent to defraud creditors, if a policy of life insurance is assigned or in any way made payable to any such person, the lawful beneficiary or assignee thereof, other than the insured or the person so effecting such insurance or the executor or administrator of such insured or of the person effecting such insurance, shall be entitled to its proceeds and avails against creditors and representatives of the insured and of the person effecting same, whether or not the right to change the beneficiary is reserved or permitted, and whether or not the policy is made payable to the person whose life is insured if the beneficiary or assignee shall predecease such person: Provided, that subject to the statute of limitations, the amount of any premiums for said insurance paid with the intent to defraud creditors, with interest thereon, shall inure to their benefit from the proceeds of the policy; but the company issuing the policy shall be discharged of all liability thereon by payment of its proceeds in accordance with its terms unless, before such payment, the company shall have written notice by or in behalf of the creditor, of a claim to recover for transfer made or premiums paid with intent to defraud creditors, with specifications of the amount claimed. (1931, c. 179, s. 1; 1947, c. 721.)

Cross References. — As to freedom of life insurance for the benefit of one's spouse or children or both from the claims of creditors, see N.C. Const., Art. X, § 5. As to the rights of life insurance beneficiaries, see G.S. 58-58-95.

CASE NOTES

Constitutionality. — This section exempts the cash surrender values of policies of life insurance in which the "wife and/or children" of the insured (bankrupt) are designated beneficiaries; and N.C. Const., Art. X, § 5, does not conflict with and nullify this section in those instances where the "wife and/or children" are designated beneficiaries, but on the contrary is in accord therewith. Home Sec. Life Ins. Co. v. McDonald, 277 N.C. 275, 177 S.E.2d 291 (1970).

N.C. Const., Art. X, § 5, was adopted for the express purpose of protecting insurance for wives and children from creditors during the life of the insured. The intent of the General Assembly and of the electorate would be thwarted if § 5 were construed as providing a lesser benefit than that provided by this section for the "wife and/or children." Home Sec. Life Ins. Co. v. McDonald, 277 N.C. 275, 177 S.E.2d 291 (1970).

This section is actually an amendment of § 58-58-95. In re Wolfe, 249 F. Supp. 784 (M.D.N.C. 1966), decided prior to the 1977 amendment to § 58-58-95, and commented on in 45 N.C.L. Rev. 696 (1967).

This section supersedes § 58-58-95 where there are variations or conflicts. Home Sec. Life Ins. Co. v. McDonald, 277 N.C. 275, 177 S.E.2d 291 (1970), decided prior to the 1977 amendment to § 58-58-95.

Construction of Section. — The significance of this section is to be considered in the light of the general rule of statutory construction that where the terms used in a statute have acquired a settled meaning through judicial interpretation, and the same terms are used in a subsequent statute upon the same subject matter, they are to be understood in the same sense, unless by qualifying or explanatory addition the contrary intent of the legislature is made clear. Home Sec. Life Ins. Co. v. McDonald, 277 N.C. 275, 177 S.E.2d 291 (1970).

Meaning of "Proceeds" or "Proceeds and Avails". — The words "proceeds" or "proceeds and avails," when used in life insurance exemption statutes, comprehend the protection of cash surrender values and other values built up during the life of the policies, as well as the death benefits. Home Sec. Life Ins. Co. v. McDonald, 277 N.C. 275, 177 S.E.2d 291 (1970).

Exemption of Cash Surrender Value. — This section exempts the cash surrender values of policies of life insurance in which the "wife and/or children" of the insured (bankrupt) are the designated beneficiaries, notwithstanding insured's reservation of the right to change beneficiaries. Home Sec. Life Ins. Co. v. McDonald, 277 N.C. 275, 177 S.E.2d 291 (1970). But see, In re Wolfe, 249 F. Supp. 784 (M.D.N.C. 1966), commented on in 45 N.C.L. Rev. 696, (1967).

Wives and children of bankrupts are protected from claims of the bankrupt's creditors, both during his life and at his death, if life insurance policies are for their sole benefit. In re Wolfe, 249 F. Supp. 784 (M.D.N.C. 1966), commented on in 45 N.C.L. Rev. 696, (1967).

Protection of Third-Party Beneficiaries. — The protection afforded by this section is not limited to any particular class of beneficiaries. It relates to a policy on the life of the insured payable to any third-party beneficiary. Home Sec. Life Ins. Co. v. McDonald, 277 N.C. 275, 177 S.E.2d 291 (1970).

**This section cannot affect policies written before the effective date of the statute. Commissioner of Banks ex rel. Goldsboro Sav. & Trust Co. v. Yelverton, 204 N.C. 441, 168 S.E. 505 (1933).

Applied in First Nat'l Bank v. Dixon, 38 N.C. App. 430, 248 S.E.2d 416 (1978).

Cited in Meadows Fertilizer Co. v. Godley, 204 N.C. 243, 167 S.E. 816 (1933); Philadelphia Life Ins. Co. v. Crosland-Cullen Co., 234 F.2d 780 (4th Cir. 1956).

§ 58-58-120. Notice of nonpayment of premium required before forfeiture.

No life insurance corporation doing business in this State shall, within one year after the default in payment of any premium, installment, or interest, declare forfeited or lapsed any policy hereafter issued or renewed, except policies on which premiums are payable monthly or at shorter intervals and except group insurance contracts and term insurance contracts for one year or less, nor shall any such policy be forfeited or lapsed by reason of nonpayment, when due, of any premium, interest, or installment or any portion thereof required by the terms of the policy to be paid, within one year from the failure to pay such premium, interest, or installment, unless a written or printed notice stating the amount of such premium, interest, installment, or portion thereof due on such policy, the place where it shall be paid, and the person to whom the same is payable has been duly addressed and mailed, postage paid, to the person whose life is insured, or to the assignee or owner of the policy, or to the person designated in writing by such insured, assignee or owner, if notice of the assignment has been given to the corporation, at his or her last known post-office address in this State, by the corporation or by any officer thereof or person appointed by it to collect such premium, at least 15 and not more than 45 days prior to the day when the same is payable, as regards policies which do not contain a provision for grace or are not entitled to grace in the payment of premiums and at least five and not more than 45 days prior to the day when the same is payable as regards policies which do contain a provision for grace or are entitled to grace in the payment of premiums. The notice shall also state that unless such premium, interest, installment, or portion thereof then due shall be paid to the corporation or to the duly appointed agent or person authorized to collect such premium, by or before the day it falls due, the policy and all payments thereon will become forfeited and void, except as to the right to a surrender value or paid-up policy, as in the contract provided. If the payment demanded by such notice shall be made within its time limit therefor, it shall be taken to be in full compliance with the requirements of the policy in respect to the time of such payment; and no such policy shall in any case be forfeited or declared forfeited or lapsed until the expiration of 30 days after the mailing of such notice. The affidavit of any officer, clerk, or agent of the corporation, or of anyone authorized to mail such notice, that the notice required by this section has been duly addressed and mailed by the corporation issuing such policy, shall be presumptive evidence that such notice has been duly given. No action shall be maintained to recover under a forfeited policy unless the same is instituted within three years from the day upon which default was made in paying the premium, installment, interest, or portion thereof for which it is claimed that forfeiture ensued. (1909, c. 884; C.S., s. 6465; 1929, c. 308, s. 1; 1931, c. 317; 1945, c. 379.)

CASE NOTES

When Policy Subject to Forfeiture. — The insurance company must give notice that the premiums are due and the policy is not subject to forfeiture until the statutory time after such notice is given. Aiken v. Atlantic Life Ins. Co., 173 N.C. 400, 92 S.E. 184 (1917).

Notice as Prerequisite to Forfeiture Unless Premiums Are Payable Monthly. — Notice that any premium or premiums are in default is a prerequisite to forfeiture of the policy under this section, except as to policies on which premiums are payable monthly. Wiles v. Nationwide Life Ins. Co., 334 F.2d 296 (4th Cir. 1964).

Notice as to Extension Notes Not Required. — Where there has been a default and forfeiture and the insured has furnished a health certificate and secured a reinstatement and an extension of time for payment, it is not necessary to again give the statutory notice of the time when the extension notes will become due. Philadelphia Life Ins. Co. v. Hayworth, 296 F. 339 (4th Cir. 1924).

Notice of Next Premium Not Waiver of Forfeiture. — Where a policy of life insurance was forfeited for failure to pay at maturity a note given for extension of payment of premium, the mailing of notice of the next regular quarterly premium by the insurer in compliance with this section, which notice did not demand payment of the balance due on the extended premium, was not a waiver by the insurer of forfeiture. Sellers v. Life Ins. Co., 205 N.C. 355, 171 S.E. 328 (1933).

Notice of Consequences of Non-Payment of Premiums. — Although the insurer paid out the amount of an extended term policy rider, because the trustee of the deceased insured was not provided with notice of the consequences of non-payment of the premium (namely that the subject whole life policy and all payments thereon would become forfeited and void) the insurer had not complied with the statutory notice requirements of G.S. 58-58-120. Cent. Carolina Bank & Trust Co. v. Sec. Life of Denver Ins. Co., 247 F. Supp. 2d 791, 2003 U.S. Dist. LEXIS 3098 (M.D.N.C. 2003).

Insured Need Not Keep Tender Open. — After tender and failure of insurer to accept the tender, the insured does not have to keep the tender open. An application for reinstatement does not alter the insured's rights, if the policy has not been forfeited. Aiken v. Atlantic Life Ins. Co., 173 N.C. 400, 92 S.E. 184 (1917).

Action for Recovery of Premiums Held Barred. — In an action for the recovery of premiums paid on forfeited policies issued on the lives of relatives, where the evidence was to the effect that these policies were canceled for the nonpayment of premiums on March 19, 1936, and that summons was issued February 17, 1942, the action was barred by this section and G.S. 1-52. Bynum v. Life Ins. Co., 222 N.C. 742, 24 S.E.2d 613 (1943).

Applicability of Section After Withdrawal of Old Policy and Issuance of New Policy. — Where an old policy which was issued before enactment of this section was withdrawn and a new policy was issued after such enactment, notice had to be given in accordance with the statute in order to have a legal forfeiture. Garland v. Jefferson Std. Life Ins. Co., 179 N.C. 67, 101 S.E. 616 (1919).

Cited in Felts v. Shenandoah Life Ins. Co., 221 N.C. 148, 19 S.E.2d 259 (1942); Abrams v. Metropolitan Life Ins. Co., 223 N.C. 500, 27 S.E.2d 148 (1943); Abrams v. Metropolitan Life Ins. Co., 224 N.C. 1, 29 S.E.2d 130 (1944).

Part 4. Miscellaneous Provisions.

§ 58-58-125. Minimum premium rates for assessment life insurance companies.

No assessment life insurance corporation, organization or association of any kind issuing policies or contracts upon the life of any resident of this State shall hereafter be organized or licensed by the Commissioner unless such corporation, organization or association adopt premium rates based upon the attained age of the assured at the time of issuance of the contract and such rates shall not be less than those fixed by the American Experience Table of Mortality or any other recognized table of mortality approved by the Commissioner. Nothing contained in this section shall be construed to affect burial associations regulated under G.S. 90-210.80 through 90-210.106 or railroad burial associations. (1939, c. 161; 1991, c. 720, ss. 4, 32.)

Editor's Note. — Section 143B-472 referred to in this section has been repealed.

Session Laws 2001-436, s. 2, effective April 1, 2002, divided Article 58 into Parts 1 to 4, assigning a Part head to each part, with G.S. 58-58-1 to 58-58-40 in Part 1, G.S. 58-58-45 to 58-58-65 in Part 2, G.S. 58-58-70 to 58-58-120 in Part 3, and G.S. 58-58-125 to 58-58-170 in Part 4, reserving G.S. 58-58-175 to 58-58-195 for future codification purposes.

Session Laws 2001-436, s. 17, is a severability clause.

Legal Periodicals. — For comment on this section, see 17 N.C.L. Rev. 362 (1939).

§ 58-58-130. Distribution of surplus in mutual companies.

Every life insurance company doing business in this State upon the principle of mutual insurance, or the members of which are entitled to share in the surplus funds thereof, may distribute the surplus annually, or once in two, three, four, or five years, as its directors determine. No payments shall be made to policyholders by way of dividends unless the company possesses admitted assets in the amount of such payments in excess of its capital and/or minimum required surplus and all other liabilities. (1903, c. 536, s. 10; Rev., s. 4776; C.S., s. 6466; 1945, c. 379.)

§ 58-58-135. "Group life insurance" defined.

No policy of group life insurance shall be delivered in this State unless it conforms to one of the following descriptions:

(1) A policy issued to an employer, or to the trustee of a fund established by an employer, which employer or trustee shall be deemed the policyholder, to insure employees of the employer for the benefit of persons other than the employer subject to the following requirements:

a. The employees eligible for insurance under the policy shall be all of the employees of the employer, or all of any class or classes thereof determined by conditions pertaining to their employment. The policy may provide that the term "employees" shall include the employees of one or more subsidiary corporations, and the employees, individual proprietors, and partners of one or more affiliated corporations, proprietors or partnerships if the business of the employer and of such affiliated corporations, proprietors or partnerships is under common control through stock ownership, contract, or otherwise. The policy may provide that the term "employees" shall include the individual proprietor or partners if the employer is an individual proprietor or a partnership. The policy may provide that the term "employees" shall include retired employees. The term "employer" as used herein may be deemed to include any county, municipality, or the proper officers, as such, of any unincorporated municipality or any department, division, agency, instrumentality or subdivision of a county, unincorporated municipality or municipality. In all cases where counties, municipalities or unincorporated municipalities or any officer, agent, division, subdivision or agency of the same have heretofore entered into contracts and purchased group life insurance for their employees, such transactions, contracts and insurance and the purchase of the same is hereby approved, authorized and validated.

b. The premium for the policy shall be paid either wholly or partly from the employer's funds or funds contributed by him, or wholly or partly from funds contributed by the insured employees, or by both. A policy on which all or part of the premium is to be derived from funds contributed by the insured employees may be placed in force provided the group is structured on an actuarially sound basis. A policy on which no part of the premium is to be derived from funds contributed by the insured employees must insure all eligible employees, or all except any as to whom evidence of individual insurability is not satisfactory to the insurer.

c. The policy must cover at least 10 employees at date of issue.

d. Repealed by Session Laws 1991 (Regular Session, 1992), c. 837, s. 6.

(2) A policy issued to a creditor, who shall be deemed the policyholder, to insure debtors of the creditor, subject to the following requirements:

a. The debtors eligible for insurance under the policy shall be all of the debtors of the creditor whose indebtedness is repayable in installments, or all of any class or classes thereof determined by conditions pertaining to the indebtedness or to the purchase giving rise to the indebtedness. The policy may provide that the term "debtors" shall include the debtors of one or more subsidiary corporations, and the debtors of one or more affiliated corporations, proprietors or partnerships if the business of the policyholder and of such affiliated corporations, proprietors or partnerships is under common control through stock ownership, contract or otherwise.

b. The premium for the policy shall be paid from the creditor's funds, from charges collected from the insured debtors, or from both. A policy on which part or all of the premium is to be derived from the collection from the insured debtors or identifiable charges not required of uninsured debtors shall not include, in the class or classes of debtors eligible for insurance, debtors under obligations outstanding at its date of issue without evidence of individual insurability unless the group is structured on an actuarially sound basis. A policy on which no part of the premium is to be derived from the collection of such identifiable charges must insure all eligible debtors, or all except any as to whom evidence of individual insurability is not satisfactory to the insurer.

c. The policy may be issued only if the group of eligible debtors is then receiving new entrants at the rate of at least 100 persons yearly, or may reasonably be expected to receive at least 100 new entrants during the first policy year, and only if the policy reserves to the insurer the right to require evidence of individual insurability if less than seventy-five percent (75%) of the new entrants become insured.

d, e. Repealed by Session Laws 1975, c. 660, s. 4.

(3) A policy issued to a labor union, which shall be deemed the policyholder, to insure members of such union for the benefit of persons other than the union or any of its officials, representatives or agents, subject to the following requirements:

a. The members eligible for insurance under the policy shall be all of the members of the union, or all of any class or classes thereof determined by conditions pertaining to their employment, or to membership in the union, or both.

b. The premium for the policy shall be paid either wholly or partly from the union's funds, or wholly or partly from funds contributed by the insured members specifically for their insurance, or by both. A policy on which all or part of the premium is to be derived from funds contributed by the insured members specifically for their insurance may be placed in force provided the group is structured on an actuarially sound basis. A policy on which no part of the premium is to be derived from funds contributed by the insured members specifically for their insurance must insure all eligible members, or all except any as to whom evidence of individual insurability is not satisfactory to the insurer.

c. The policy must cover at least 25 members at date of issue.

d. Repealed by Session Laws 1991 (Regular Session, 1992), c. 837, s. 6.

(4) A policy issued to the trustee of a fund established by two or more employers in the same industry or kind of business or by two or more

labor unions, which trustee shall be deemed the policyholder, to insure employees of the employers or members of the unions for the benefit of persons other than the employers or the unions, subject to the following requirements:

  a. The persons eligible for insurance shall be all of the employees of the employers or all of the members of the unions, or all of any class or classes thereof determined by conditions pertaining to their employment, or to memberships in the unions, or to both. The policy may provide that the term "employees" shall include the individual proprietor or partners if an employer is an individual proprietor or a partnership. The policy may provide that the term "employees" shall include the trustee or the employees of the trustee, or both, if their duties are principally connected with such trusteeship. The policy may provide that the term "employees" shall include retired employees.

  b. The premium for the policy shall be paid wholly or partly from funds contributed by the participating employer, labor union, or the insured persons.

    If none of the premium paid by the participating employer or labor union is to be derived from funds contributed by the insured persons specifically for the insurance, all eligible employees of that particular participating employer or labor union must be insured, or all except any as to whom evidence of insurability is not satisfactory to the insurer.

    If part of the premium paid by the participating employer or labor union is to be derived from funds contributed by the insured persons specifically for their insurance, coverage may be placed in force on employees of a participating employer or on members of a participating labor union provided the group is structured on an actuarially sound basis.

  c. The policy must cover at least 100 persons at date of issue.

  d. Repealed by Session Laws 1991 (Regular Session, 1992), c. 837, s. 6.

(5) A policy issued to an association of persons having a common professional or business interest, which association shall be deemed the policyholder, to insure members of such association for the benefit of persons other than the association or any of its officials, representatives or agents, subject to the following requirements:

  a. Such association shall have had an active existence for at least two years immediately preceding the purchase of such insurance, was formed for purposes other than procuring insurance and does not derive its funds principally from contributions of insured members toward the payment of premiums for the insurance.

  b. The members eligible for insurance under the policy shall be all of the members of the association or all of any class or classes thereof determined by conditions pertaining to their employment, or the membership in the association, or both. The policy may provide that the term "members" shall include the employees of members, if their duties are principally connected with the member's business or profession.

  c. The premium for the policy shall be paid either wholly or partly from the association's funds, or wholly or partly from funds contributed by the insured members specifically for their insurance, or by both. No policy may be issued if the Commissioner finds that the rate of insured members' contributions will exceed the maximum rate customarily charged employees insured under like group life insurance policies issued in accordance with the provisions of subdivision (1). A policy on which all or part of the premium is to be derived from funds contributed by the insured members specifically for their insurance may be placed in force provided the group is structured on an actuarially sound basis. A policy on which no part of the premium is to be derived from funds contributed by the insured members specifically for their insurance must insure all eligible members, or all except any as to whom evidence of individual insurability is not satisfactory to the insurer.

d. The policy must cover at least 25 members at date of issue.

e. Repealed by Session Laws 1991 (Regular Session, 1992), c. 837, s. 6.

(6) Notwithstanding the provisions of this section, or any other provisions of law to the contrary, a policy may be issued to the employees of the State or any other political subdivision where the entire amount of premium therefor is paid by such employees. (1925, c. 58, s. 1; 1931, c. 328; 1943, c. 597, s. 1; 1947, c. 834; 1951, c. 800; 1955, c. 1280; 1957, c. 998; 1959, c. 287; 1965, c. 869; 1971, c. 516; 1973, c. 249; 1975, c. 660, s. 4; 1977, c. 192, ss. 1-4; c. 835; 1987, c. 752, ss. 14-18; 1991 (Reg. Sess., 1992), c. 837, s. 6.)

Legal Periodicals. — For comments on former section and amendments thereto, see 3 N.C.L. Rev. 145 (1925); 12 N.C.L. Rev. 167 (1934); 21 N.C.L. Rev. 355 (1943).

For comment on the 1947 amendment, see 25 N.C.L. Rev. 432 (1947).

CASE NOTES

Cited in Newsome v. Prudential Ins. Co. of Am., 4 N.C. App. 161, 166 S.E.2d 487 (1969); Clayton v. Prudential Ins. Co. of Am., 4 N.C. App. 43, 165 S.E.2d 763 (1969); First Nat'l Bank v. Nationwide Ins. Co., 303 N.C. 203, 278 S.E.2d 507 (1981).

OPINIONS OF ATTORNEY GENERAL

As to inapplicability of statutory limit on amount of group life insurance, see opinion of Attorney General to Mr. A.C. Barefoot, Jr., Chairman, Teachers' and State Employees' Benefits Study Commission, 40 N.C.A.G. 631 (1970).

§ 58-58-140. Group life insurance standard provisions.

No policy of group life insurance shall be delivered in this State unless it contains in substance the following provisions, or provisions which in the Commissioner's opinion are more favorable to the persons insured, or at least as favorable to the persons insured and more favorable to the policyholder, provided, however, (i) that subdivisions (6) through (10) of this section do not apply to policies issued to a creditor to insure the creditor's debtors; (ii) that the standard provisions required for individual life insurance policies do not apply to group life insurance policies; and (iii) that if the group life insurance policy is on a plan of insurance other than the term plan, it shall contain a nonforfeiture provision or provisions that in the Commissioner's opinion is or are equitable to the insured persons and to the policyholder, but nothing in this section requires group life insurance policies to contain the same nonforfeiture provisions that are required for individual life insurance policies:

(1) A provision that the policyholder is entitled to a grace period of 31 days for the payment of any premium due except the first, during which grace period the death benefit coverage shall continue in force, unless the policyholder has given the insurer written notice of discontinu-

ance before the date of discontinuance and in accordance with the terms of the policy. The policy may provide that the policyholder shall be liable to the insurer for the payment of a pro rata premium for the time the policy was in force during the grace period.

(2) A provision that the validity of the policy shall not be contested, except for nonpayment of premiums, after it has been in force for two years from its date of issue; and that no statement made by any person insured under the policy relating to that person's insurability shall be used in contesting the validity of the insurance with respect to which the statement was made after the insurance has been in force before the contest for a period of two years during the person's lifetime nor unless it is contained in a written instrument signed by the person.

(3) A provision that a copy of the application, if any, of the policyholder shall be attached to the policy when issued, that all statements made by the policyholder or by the persons insured shall be considered representations and not warranties; and that no statement made by any person insured shall be used in any contest unless a copy of the instrument containing the statement is or has been furnished to the person or to the person's beneficiary.

(4) A provision setting forth the conditions, if any, under which the insurer reserves the right to require a person eligible for insurance to furnish evidence of individual insurability satisfactory to the insurer as a condition to part or all of the person's coverage.

(5) A provision specifying an equitable adjustment of premiums or benefits, or both, to be made if the age of a person insured has been misstated; the provision to contain a clear statement of the method of adjustment to be used.

(6) A provision that any sum becoming due because of the death of the person insured shall be payable to the beneficiary designated by the person insured, subject to the provisions of the policy if there is no designated beneficiary as to all or any part of the sum living at the death of the person insured, and subject to any right reserved by the insurer in the policy and set forth in the certificate to pay at its option a part of the sum not exceeding two hundred fifty dollars ($250.00) to any person appearing to the insurer to be equitably entitled thereto by having incurred funeral or other expenses incident to the last illness or death of the person insured.

(7) A provision that the insurer will issue to the policyholder, for delivery to each person insured, an individual certificate setting forth a statement as to the insurance protection to which the person is entitled, to whom the insurance benefits are payable, and the rights and conditions set forth in subdivisions (8), (9) and (10) of this section.

(8) A provision that if the insurance, or any portion of it, on a person covered under the policy ceases because of termination of employment or of membership in the classes eligible for coverage under the policy, the person shall be entitled to be issued by the insurer, without evidence of insurability, an individual policy of life insurance without disability or other supplementary benefits, provided application for the individual policy shall be made, and the first premium paid to the insurer, within 31 days after such termination, and provided further that,

a. The individual policy shall, at the option of the person, be on any one of the forms, except term insurance, then customarily issued by the insurer at the age and for the amount applied for;

b. The individual policy shall be in an amount not in excess of the amount of life insurance which ceases because of the termination, provided that any amount of insurance which shall have matured on or before the date of the termination as an endowment payable to the person insured, whether in one sum or in installments or in the form of an annuity, shall not, for the purposes of this provision, be included in the amount which is considered to cease because of the termination; and

c. The premium on the individual policy shall be at the insurer's then customary rate applicable to the form and amount of the individual policy, to the class of risk to which the person then belongs, and to the person's age on the effective date of the individual policy.

(9) A provision that if the group policy terminates or is amended so as to terminate the insurance of any class of insured persons, every person insured under the policy at the date of the termination whose insurance terminates and who has been so insured for at least five years before the termination date shall be entitled to be issued by the insurer an individual policy of life insurance, subject to the conditions and limitations in (8) above, except that the group policy may provide that the amount of the individual policy shall not exceed the smaller of (i) the amount of the person's life insurance protection ceasing because of the termination or amendment of the group policy, less the amount of any life insurance for which the person is or becomes eligible under any group policy issued or reinstated by the same or another insurer within 31 days after termination, and (ii) ten thousand dollars ($10,000).

(10) A provision that if a person insured under the group policy dies during the period within which the person would have been entitled to have been issued an individual policy in accordance with (8) or (9) above and before such an individual policy shall have become effective, the amount of life insurance which the person would have been entitled to have been issued under the individual policy shall be payable as a claim under the group policy, whether or not application for the individual policy or the payment of the first premium therefor has been made. (1925, c. 58, s. 2; 1943, c. 597, s. 2; 1947, c. 834; 1991, c. 644, s. 9.)

Legal Periodicals. — For comment on the 1943 amendment, see 21 N.C.L. Rev. 355 (1943).

For comment on the 1947 amendment, see 25 N.C.L. Rev. 435 (1947).

CASE NOTES

This section relates to a policy of life insurance delivered in this State. Clayton v. Prudential Ins. Co. of Am., 4 N.C. App. 43, 165 S.E.2d 763 (1969).

Grace Period Does Not Extend Period of Coverage. — The provision in this section that the policyholder of a group life insurance policy is entitled to a grace period of 31 days for the payment of any premium due except the first only extends the time in which a premium may be paid; it does not extend the period of coverage. Conner v. Occidental Life Ins. Co., 41 N.C. App. 610, 255 S.E.2d 420, cert. denied, 298 N.C. 295, 267 S.E.2d 658 (1979).

Where group life insurance policy had

expired at the time of insured's death, and the policy contained no provisions for extension or renewal, no payment for any premium was or could have been due after that date and no extension of the period of coverage arose; although the insured died within 31 days of the expiration of the policy, the policy was not in effect on and after that date of expiration, notwithstanding the provisions of this section. Conner v. Occidental Life Ins. Co., 41 N.C. App. 610, 255 S.E.2d 420, cert. denied, 298 N.C. 295, 267 S.E.2d 658 (1979).

Applied in Haneline v. Turner White Casket Co., 238 N.C. 127, 76 S.E.2d 372 (1953).

Cited in Conger v. Travelers Ins. Co., 266

N.C. 496, 146 S.E.2d 462 (1966); Newsome v.
Prudential Ins. Co. of Am., 4 N.C. App. 161, 166
S.E.2d 487 (1969).

§ 58-58-145. Group annuity contracts defined; requirements.

Any policy or contract, except a joint, reversionary or survivorship annuity contract, whereby annuities are payable to more than one person, is a group annuity contract. The person, firm or corporation to whom or to which such contract is issued, as herein provided, is the holder of the contract. The term "annuitant" means any person to whom or which payments are made under the group annuity contract. No authorized insurer shall deliver or issue for delivery in this State any group annuity contract except upon a group of annuitants that conforms to the following: under a contract issued to an employer, or to the trustee of a fund established by an employer or two or more employers in the same industry or kind of business, the stipulated payments on which shall be paid by the holder of such contract either wholly from the employer's funds or funds contributed by him, or partly from such funds and partly from funds contributed by the employees covered by such contract, and providing a plan of retirement annuities under a plan which permits all of the employees of such employer or of any specified class or classes thereof to become annuitants. Any such group of employees may include retired employees, and may include officers and managers as employees, and may include the employees of subsidiary or affiliated corporations of a corporation employer, and may include the individual proprietors, partners and employees of affiliated individuals and firms controlled by the holders through stock ownership, contract or otherwise. (1947, c. 721; 1993, c. 506, s. 3.)

Legal Periodicals. — For comment on this
section, see 25 N.C.L. Rev. 437 (1947).

§ 58-58-150. Employee life insurance defined.

Employee life insurance is hereby declared to be that plan of life insurance other than salary savings life insurance under which individual policies are issued to the employees of any employer where such policies are issued on the life of more than one employee at date of issue. Premiums for such policies shall be paid by the employer or the trustee of a fund established by the employer either wholly from the employer's funds, or funds contributed by him, or partly from such funds and partly from funds contributed by the insured employees. (1947, c. 721; 1957, c. 1008.)

Legal Periodicals. — For comment on this
section, see 25 N.C.L. Rev. 436 (1947).

§ 58-58-155. Assignment of interest in group policies and annuity contracts.

Any individual insured under a group insurance policy or group annuity contract shall have the right, unless expressly prohibited under the terms of the policy or contract of insurance, to assign to any other person his rights and benefits under the policy or contract, including, but not limited to the right to designate the beneficiary or beneficiaries and the right of conversion guaranteed by G.S. 58-58-140, and, subject to the provisions of the policy relating to assignments thereunder, any such assignment, made either before or after

April 28, 1969, shall be valid for the purpose of vesting in the assignee all such rights and benefits so assigned. (1969, c. 319.)

§ 58-58-160. Voting power under policies of group life insurance.

In every group policy issued by a domestic life insurance company, the employer shall be deemed to be the policyholder for all purposes within the meaning of Articles 1 through 64 of this Chapter, and, if entitled to vote at meetings of the company, shall be entitled to one vote thereat. (1925, c. 58, s. 3.)

§ 58-58-165. Exemption from execution.

No policy of group insurance, nor the proceeds thereof, when paid to any employee or employees thereunder, shall be liable to attachment, garnishment, or other process, or to be seized, taken, appropriated or applied by any legal or equitable process or operation of law, to pay any debt or liability of such employee, or his beneficiary, or any other person who may have a right thereunder, either before or after payment; but the proceeds thereof, when made payable to the estate of the employee insured, shall constitute a part of the estate of such employee available for the payment of debts. (1925, c. 58, s. 4; 1957, c. 1361.)

Legal Periodicals. — For article analyzing North Carolina's exemptions law, see 18 Wake Forest L. Rev. 1025 (1982).

CASE NOTES

Applied in First Nat'l Bank v. Dixon, 38 N.C. App. 430, 248 S.E.2d 416 (1978).

§ 58-58-170. Contestability after reinstatement.

A reinstated policy of life insurance or annuity contract may be contested on account of fraud or misrepresentation of facts material to the reinstatement only for the same period following reinstatement and with the same conditions and exceptions as the policy provides with respect to contestability after original issuance. The reinstatement application shall be deemed to be a part of the policy whether or not attached thereto. (1987, c. 752, s. 13.)

§§ 58-58-175 through 58-58-195: Reserved for future codification purposes.

Part 5. Viatical Settlements.

§ 58-58-200. Short title.

This Part may be cited as the Viatical Settlements Act. (2001-436, s. 3.)

Editor's Note. — Session Laws 2001-436, s. 18, makes this Part effective April 1, 2002.

Session Laws 2001-436, s. 17 is a severability clause.

§ 58-58-205. Definitions.

As used in this Article:

    (1) "Advertising" means any written, electronic, or printed communication or any communication by means of recorded telephone messages or transmitted on radio, television, the Internet, or similar communications media, including filmstrips, motion pictures, and videos, published, disseminated, circulated, or placed before the public, directly or indirectly, for the purpose of creating an interest in or inducing a person to sell a life insurance policy under a viatical settlement contract.

    (2) "Business of viatical settlements" means an activity involved in, but not limited to, the offering, solicitation, negotiation, procurement, effectuation, purchasing, investing, financing, monitoring, tracking, underwriting, selling, transferring, assigning, pledging, hypothecating, or in any other manner, of viatical settlement contracts. "Business of viatical settlements" does not include an activity involving viatical settlement contracts as investments as regulated by Chapter 78A of the General Statutes.

    (3) "Chronically ill" means:

        a. Being unable to perform at least two activities of daily living (i.e., eating, toileting, transferring, bathing, dressing, or continence);

        b. Requiring substantial supervision to protect the individual from threats to health and safety due to severe cognitive impairment; or

        c. Having a level of disability similar to that described in subsubdivision a. of this subdivision as determined by the Secretary of Health and Human Services.

    (4) "Financing entity" means an underwriter, placement agent, lender, purchaser of securities, purchaser of a policy from a viatical settlement provider, credit enhancer, or any entity that has a direct ownership in a policy that is the subject of a viatical settlement contract, but:

        a. Whose principal activity related to the transaction is providing funds to effect the viatical settlement or purchase of one or more viaticated policies; and

        b. Who has an agreement in writing with one or more licensed viatical settlement providers to finance the acquisition of viatical settlement contracts.

"Financing entity" does not include a nonaccredited investor or viatical settlement purchaser.

    (5) "Fraudulent viatical settlement act" includes:

        a. Acts or omissions committed by any person who, knowingly and with intent to defraud, for the purpose of depriving another of property or for pecuniary gain, commits, or permits its employees or its agents to engage in acts including:

            1. Presenting, causing to be presented, or preparing with knowledge or belief that it will be presented to or by a viatical settlement provider, viatical settlement broker, viatical settlement purchaser, financing entity, insurer, insurance producer, viator, insured or any other person false material information, or concealing material information, as part of, in support of, or concerning a fact material to one or more of the following:

                I. An application for the issuance of a viatical settlement contract or insurance policy.

II. The underwriting of a viatical settlement contract or insurance policy.

III. A claim for payment or benefit under a viatical settlement contract or insurance policy.

IV. Premiums paid on an insurance policy.

V. Payments and changes in ownership or beneficiary made in accordance with the terms of a viatical settlement contract or insurance policy.

VI. The reinstatement or conversion of an insurance policy.

VII. The solicitation, offer, effectuation, or sale of a viatical settlement contract or insurance policy.

VIII. The issuance of written evidence of viatical settlement contract or insurance.

IX. A financing transaction.

2. Employing any device, scheme, or artifice to defraud related to viaticated policies.

b. In the furtherance of a fraud or to prevent the detection of a fraud, any person commits or permits the person's employees or agents to:

1. Remove, conceal, alter, destroy, or sequester from the Commissioner the assets or records of a licensee or other person engaged in the business of viatical settlements;

2. Misrepresent or conceal the financial condition of a licensee, financing entity, insurer, or other person;

3. Transact the business of viatical settlements in violation of laws requiring a license, certificate of authority, or other legal authority for the transaction of the business of viatical settlements; or

4. File with the Commissioner or the insurance regulator of another jurisdiction a document containing false information or otherwise conceal information about a material fact from the Commissioner.

c. Embezzlement, theft, misappropriation, or conversion of monies, funds, premiums, credits, or other property of a viatical settlement provider, insurer, insured, viator, insurance policy owner, or any other person engaged in the business of viatical settlements or insurance; or

d. Attempting to commit, assisting, aiding, or abetting in the commission of, or conspiracy to commit, the acts or omissions specified in this subdivision.

(6) "Policy" means an individual or group life insurance policy, group life insurance certificate, group life insurance contract, or any other arrangement of life insurance affecting the rights of a resident of this State or bearing a reasonable relation to this State, regardless of whether delivered or issued for delivery in this State.

(7) "Related provider trust" means a titling trust or other trust established by a licensed viatical settlement provider or a financing entity for the sole purpose of holding the ownership or beneficial interest in purchased policies in connection with a financing transaction.

(8) "Special purpose entity" means a corporation, partnership, trust, limited liability company, or other similar entity formed solely to provide either directly or indirectly access to institutional capital markets for a financing entity or licensed viatical settlement provider.

(9) "Terminally ill" means having an illness or sickness that can reasonably be expected to result in death in 24 months or fewer.

(10) "Viatical settlement broker" or "broker" means a person that on behalf of a viator and for a fee, commission, or other valuable

977

consideration offers or attempts to negotiate viatical settlement contracts between a viator and one or more viatical settlement providers. The term does not include an attorney, certified public accountant, or a financial planner accredited by a nationally recognized accreditation agency who is retained to represent the viator and whose compensation is not paid directly or indirectly by the viatical settlement provider or purchaser.

(11) "Viatical settlement contract" means a written agreement establishing the terms under which compensation or anything of value will be paid, which compensation or value is less than the expected death benefit of the policy, in return for the viator's assignment, transfer, sale, devise, or bequest of the death benefit or ownership of any portion of the policy. A viatical settlement contract also includes a contract for a loan or other financing transaction with a viator secured primarily by a policy, other than a loan by a life insurance company under the terms of the life insurance contract, or a loan secured by the cash value of a policy. A viatical settlement contract includes an agreement with a viator to transfer ownership or change the beneficiary designation at a later date regardless of the date that compensation is paid to the viator.

(12) "Viatical settlement provider" or "provider" means a person, other than a viator, that enters into or effectuates a viatical settlement contract. Viatical settlement provider does not include:

a. A bank, savings bank, savings and loan association, credit union, or other licensed lending institution that takes an assignment of a life insurance policy as collateral for a loan;

b. The issuer of a life insurance policy providing accelerated benefits under rules adopted by the Commissioner and under the contract;

c. An authorized or eligible insurer that provides stop-loss coverage to a viatical settlement provider, purchaser, financing entity, special purpose entity, or related provider trust;

d. A natural person who enters into or effectuates no more than one agreement in a calendar year for the transfer of life insurance policies for any value less than the expected death benefit;

e. A financing entity;

f. A special purpose entity;

g. A related provider trust;

h. A viatical settlement purchaser; or

i. An accredited investor or qualified institutional buyer as defined respectively in Regulation D, Rule 501 or Rule 144A of the Federal Securities Act of 1933, as amended, and who purchases a viaticated policy from a viatical settlement provider.

(13) "Viatical settlement purchase agreement" or "purchase agreement" means an agreement, entered into by a viatical settlement purchaser, to which the viator is not a party, to purchase a life insurance policy or an interest in a life insurance policy, that is entered into for the purpose of deriving an economic benefit.

(14) "Viatical settlement purchaser" or "purchaser" means a person who gives a sum of money as consideration for a life insurance policy or an interest in the death benefits of a life insurance policy or a person who owns or acquires or is entitled to a beneficial interest in a trust that owns a viatical settlement contract or is the beneficiary of a life insurance policy that has been or will be the subject of a viatical settlement contract for the purpose of deriving an economic benefit. "Viatical settlement purchaser" does not include:

a. A licensee under this Part;

      b. An accredited investor or qualified institutional buyer as defined respectively in Regulation D, Rule 501 or Rule 144A of the Federal Securities Act of 1933, as amended;

      c. A financing entity;

      d. A special purpose entity; or

      e. A related provider trust.

  (15) "Viaticated policy" means a policy that has been acquired by a viatical settlement provider under a viatical settlement contract.

  (16) "Viator" means the owner of a policy or a certificate holder under a group policy who enters or seeks to enter into a viatical settlement contract. For the purposes of this Part, a viator shall not be limited to an owner of a life insurance policy or a certificate holder under a group policy insuring the life of an individual with a terminal or chronic illness or condition except where specifically addressed. "Viator" does not include:

      a. A licensee under this Part;

      b. An accredited investor or qualified institutional buyer as defined respectively in Regulation D, Rule 501 or Rule 144A of the Federal Securities Act of 1933, as amended;

      c. A financing entity;

      d. A special purpose entity; or

      e. A related provider trust. (2001-436, s. 3.)

§ 58-58-210. License requirements.

(a) No person shall operate as a provider or broker without first obtaining a license from the insurance regulator of the state of residence of the viator. If there is more than one viator on a single policy and the viators are residents of different states, the viatical settlement shall be governed by the law of the state in which the viator having the largest percentage ownership resides or, if the viators hold equal ownership, the state of residence of one viator agreed upon in writing by all viators.

(b) Application for a provider or broker license shall be made to the Commissioner by the applicant on a form prescribed by the Commissioner, and these applications shall be accompanied by a fee of one hundred dollars ($100.00).

(c) Licenses may be renewed from year to year on the anniversary date upon payment of the annual renewal fee of one hundred dollars ($100.00). Failure to pay the fees by the renewal date results in expiration of the license.

(d) The applicant shall provide information on forms required by the Commissioner. The Commissioner may require the applicant to fully disclose the identity of all stockholders, partners, officers, members, and employees; and the Commissioner may refuse to issue a license in the name of a legal entity if not satisfied that any officer, employee, stockholder, partner, or member of the legal entity who may materially influence the applicant's conduct meets the standards of this Part.

(e) A license issued to a legal entity authorizes all partners, officers, members, and designated employees to act as providers or brokers, as applicable, under the license; and all those persons shall be named in the application and any supplements to the application.

(f) Upon the filing of an application and the payment of the license fee, the Commissioner shall investigate each applicant and issue a license if the Commissioner finds that the applicant:

  (1) If a provider, has provided a detailed plan of operation.

  (2) Is competent and trustworthy and intends to act in good faith in the capacity involved by the license applied for.

(3) Has a good business reputation and has had experience, training, or education so as to be qualified in the business for which the license is applied.

(4) If a legal entity, provides a certificate of good standing from the state of its domicile.

(g) The Commissioner shall not issue a license to a nonresident applicant unless a written designation of an agent for service of process is filed and maintained with the Commissioner or the applicant has filed with the Commissioner the applicant's written irrevocable consent that any action against the applicant may be commenced against the applicant by service of process on the Commissioner.

(h) A provider or broker shall provide to the Commissioner new or revised information about officers, ten percent (10%) or more stockholders, partners, directors, members, or designated employees within 20 days after any change in the constituent membership of that respective category of persons. (2001-436, s. 3.)

§ 58-58-215. License revocation and denial.

The Commissioner may suspend, revoke, or refuse to issue or renew the license of a provider or broker if the Commissioner finds that:

(1) There was any material misrepresentation in the application for the license;

(2) The licensee or any officer, partner, member, or key management personnel has been convicted of fraudulent or dishonest practices, is subject to a final administrative action, or is otherwise shown to be untrustworthy or incompetent;

(3) The provider demonstrates a pattern of unreasonable payments to viators;

(4) The licensee or any officer, partner, member, or key management personnel has been found guilty of, or has pleaded guilty or nolo contendere to, any felony, or to a misdemeanor involving fraud or moral turpitude, regardless of whether a judgment of conviction has been entered by the court;

(5) The provider has entered into any viatical settlement contract that has not been approved pursuant to this Part;

(6) The provider has failed to honor contractual obligations set out in a viatical settlement contract;

(7) The licensee no longer meets the requirements for initial licensure;

(8) The provider has assigned, transferred, or pledged a viaticated policy to a person other than a provider licensed in this State, viatical settlement purchaser, an accredited investor, or qualified institutional buyer as defined respectively in Regulation D, Rule 501 or Rule 144A of the Federal Securities Act of 1933, as amended, financing entity, special purpose entity, or related provider trust; or

(9) The licensee or any officer, partner, member, or key management personnel has violated any provision of this Part. (2001-436, s. 3.)

§ 58-58-220. Approval of viatical settlement contracts and disclosure statements.

A person shall not use a contract or provide to a viator a disclosure statement form in this State unless filed with and approved by the Commissioner. The Commissioner shall disapprove a contract form or disclosure statement form if, in the Commissioner's opinion, the contract or provisions contained therein are unreasonable, contrary to the interests of the public, or otherwise misleading or unfair to the viator. The Commissioner may also require the submission of advertising material. (2001-436, s. 3.)

§ 58-58-225. Reporting requirements and privacy.

(a) Each licensee shall file with the Commissioner on or before June 1 of each year an annual statement containing such information as the Commissioner prescribes by administrative rule.

(b) Except as otherwise allowed or required by law, a provider, broker, insurance company, insurance producer, information bureau, rating agency or company, or any other person with actual knowledge of an insured's identity shall not disclose that identity as an insured, or the insured's financial or medical information, to any other person unless the disclosure:

    (1) Is necessary to effect a viatical settlement between the viator and a provider and the viator and insured have provided prior written consent to the disclosure;

    (2) Is provided in response to an investigation or examination by the Commissioner or any other governmental officer or agency or pursuant to the requirements of G.S. 58-58-270;

    (3) Is a term of or condition to the transfer of a policy by one provider to another provider;

    (4) Is necessary to permit a financing entity, related provider trust, or special purpose entity to finance the purchase of policies by a provider and the viator and insured have provided prior written consent to the disclosure;

    (5) Is necessary to allow the provider or broker or its authorized representatives to make contacts for the purpose of determining health status; or

    (6) Is required to purchase stop-loss coverage. (2001-436, s. 3.)

§ 58-58-230. Examinations.

(a) The Commissioner may conduct an examination of a licensee as often as the Commissioner considers appropriate.

(b) An examination under this Part shall be conducted in accordance with the Examination Law.

(c) In lieu of an examination of any foreign or alien person licensed under this Part, the Commissioner may accept an examination report on the licensee prepared by the appropriate viatical settlement regulator for the licensee's state of domicile or port-of-entry state.

(d) When making an examination under this Part, the Commissioner may retain attorneys, appraisers, independent actuaries, independent certified public accountants, or other professionals and specialists as examiners, the reasonable cost of which shall be borne by the licensee that is the subject of the examination. (2001-436, s. 3.)

§ 58-58-235. Record retention requirements.

(a) A person licensed under this Part shall retain copies for five years of all:

    (1) Proposed, offered, or executed contracts, purchase agreements, underwriting documents, policy forms, and applications from the date of the proposal, offer, or execution of the contract or purchase agreement, whichever is later.

    (2) Checks, drafts, or other evidence and documentation related to the payment, transfer, deposit, or release of funds from the date of the transaction.

(3) Other records and documents related to the requirements of this Part.

(b) This section does not relieve a person of the obligation to produce these documents to the Commissioner after the retention period has expired if the person has retained the documents.

(c) Records required to be retained by this section must be legible and complete and may be retained in paper, photograph, microprocessor, magnetic, mechanical, or electronic media, or by any process that accurately reproduces or forms a durable medium for the reproduction of a record. (2001-436, s. 3.)

§ 58-58-240. Investigative authority of the Commissioner.

The Commissioner may investigate suspected fraudulent viatical settlement acts and persons engaged in the business of viatical settlements. (2001-436, s. 3.)

§ 58-58-245. Disclosure.

(a) With each application for a viatical settlement, the provider or broker shall provide the viator with at least the following disclosures no later than the time the application for the contract is signed by all parties. The disclosures shall be provided in a separate document that is signed by the viator and the provider or broker and shall provide the following information:

  (1) There are possible alternatives to contracts including any accelerated death benefits or policy loans offered under the viator's policy.
  (2) Some or all of the proceeds of the viatical settlement may be taxable under federal income tax and state franchise and income taxes, and assistance should be sought from a professional tax advisor.
  (3) Proceeds of the viatical settlement could be subject to the claims of creditors.
  (4) Receipt of the proceeds of a viatical settlement may adversely affect the viator's eligibility for Medicaid or other government benefits or entitlements, and advice should be obtained from the appropriate government agencies.
  (5) The viator has the right to rescind a contract for 10 business days after the receipt of the viatical settlement proceeds by the viator, as provided in G.S. 58-58-250(h). If the insured dies during the rescission period, the settlement contract shall be deemed to have been rescinded, subject to repayment of all viatical settlement proceeds and any premiums, loans, and loan interest to the provider or purchaser.
  (6) Funds will be sent to the viator within three business days after the provider has received the insurer or group administrator's acknowledgment that ownership of the policy or interest in the certificate has been transferred and the beneficiary has been designated.
  (7) Entering into a contract may cause other rights or benefits, including conversion rights and waiver of premium benefits that may exist under the policy, to be forfeited by the viator. Assistance should be sought from a financial adviser.
  (8) Disclosure to a viator shall include distribution of a brochure describing the process of viatical settlements. The NAIC's form for the brochure shall be used unless the Commissioner develops one.
  (9) The disclosure document shall contain the following language: "All medical, financial, or personal information solicited or obtained by a provider or broker about an insured, including the insured's identity or the identity of family members, a spouse or a significant other may be disclosed as necessary to effect the viatical settlement between the viator and the provider. If you are asked to provide this information,

you will be asked to consent to the disclosure. The information may be provided to someone who buys the policy or provides funds for the purchase. You may be asked to renew your permission to share information every two years.

   (10) The insured may be contacted by either the provider or broker or its authorized representative for the purpose of determining the insured's health status. This contact is limited to once every three months if the insured has a life expectancy of more than one year, and no more than once per month if the insured has a life expectancy of one year or less.

  (b) A provider shall provide the viator with at least the following disclosures no later than the date the contract is signed by all parties. The disclosures shall be conspicuously displayed in the contract or in a separate document signed by the viator and the provider or broker, and provide the following information:

   (1) State the affiliation, if any, between the provider and the issuer of the insurance policy to be viaticated.

   (2) The document shall include the name, address, and telephone number of the provider.

   (3) A broker shall disclose to a prospective viator the amount and method of calculating the broker's compensation. The term "compensation" includes anything of value paid or given to a broker for the placement of a policy.

   (4) If an insurance policy to be viaticated has been issued as a joint policy or involves family riders or any coverage of a life other than the insured under the policy to be viaticated, the viator shall be informed of the possible loss of coverage on the other lives under the policy and shall be advised to consult with his or her insurance producer or the insurer issuing the policy for advice on the proposed viatical settlement.

   (5) State the dollar amount of the current death benefit payable to the provider under the policy. If known, the provider shall also disclose the availability of any additional guaranteed insurance benefits, the dollar amount of any accidental death and dismemberment benefits under the policy, and the provider's interest in those benefits.

   (6) State the name, business address, and telephone number of the independent third-party escrow agent and the fact that the viator or owner may inspect or receive copies of the relevant escrow or trust agreements or documents.

  (c) If the provider transfers ownership or changes the beneficiary of the insurance policy, the provider shall communicate the change in ownership or beneficiary to the insured within 20 days after the change. (2001-436, s. 3.)

§ 58-58-250. General rules.

  (a) A provider entering into a contract shall first obtain:

   (1) If the viator is the insured, a written statement from a licensed attending physician that the viator is of sound mind and under no constraint or undue influence to enter into a contract.

   (2) A document in which the insured consents to the release of his or her medical records to a provider or broker and, if the policy being viaticated has been in effect for less than five years, to the insurance company that issued the policy covering the life of the insured.

  (b) Within 20 days after a viator executes documents necessary to transfer any rights under a policy or within 20 days after entering any agreement, option, promise, or any other form of understanding, expressed or implied, to viaticate the policy, the provider shall give written notice to the insurer that issued that policy that the policy has or will become a viaticated policy. The notice shall be accompanied by the documents required by subsection (c) of this section.

(c) If the policy being viaticated has been in effect for less than five years, the viatical provider shall deliver a copy of the medical release required under subdivision (a)(2) of this section, a copy of the viator's application for the contract, the notice required under subsection (b) of this section, and a request for verification of coverage to the insurer that issued the policy that is the subject of the viatical settlement. The NAIC's form for verification shall be used unless the Commissioner develops standards for verification.

(d) The insurer shall respond to a request for verification of coverage submitted on an approved form by a provider within 30 days after the date the request is received and shall indicate whether, based on the medical evidence and documents provided, the insurer intends to pursue an investigation at this time regarding the validity of the policy.

(e) Before or at the time of execution of the contract, the provider shall obtain a witnessed document in which the viator consents to the contract, represents that the viator has a full and complete understanding of the contract, that he or she has a full and complete understanding of the benefits of the policy, acknowledges that he or she is entering into the contract freely and voluntarily and, for persons with a terminal or chronic illness or condition, acknowledges that the insured has a terminal or chronic illness or condition and that the terminal or chronic illness or condition was first diagnosed after the policy was issued.

(f) If a broker performs any of these activities required of the provider, the provider is deemed to have fulfilled the requirements of this section.

(g) All medical information solicited or obtained by any licensee is subject to the applicable provisions of federal and North Carolina law relating to confidentiality of medical information.

(h) All contracts entered into in this State shall provide the viator with an unconditional right to rescind the contract for at least 10 business days after the receipt of the viatical settlement proceeds. If the insured dies during the rescission period, the contract shall be deemed to have been rescinded, subject to repayment to the provider or purchaser of all viatical settlement proceeds, and any premiums, loans, and loan interest that have been paid by the provider or purchaser.

(i) The provider shall instruct the viator to send the executed documents required to effect the change in ownership, assignment, or change in beneficiary directly to the independent escrow agent. Within three business days after the date the escrow agent receives the documents, or from the date the provider receives the documents, if the viator erroneously provides the documents directly to the provider, the provider shall pay or transfer the proceeds of the viatical settlement into an escrow or trust account maintained in a state or federally chartered financial institution, the deposits of which are insured by the Federal Deposit Insurance Corporation (FDIC) or any successor entity. Upon payment of the settlement proceeds into the escrow account, the escrow agent shall deliver the original change in ownership, assignment, or change in beneficiary forms to the provider or related provider trust. Upon the escrow agent's receipt of the acknowledgment of the properly completed transfer of ownership, assignment, or designation of beneficiary from the insurance company, the escrow agent shall pay the settlement proceeds to the viator.

(j) Failure to tender consideration to the viator for the contract within the time required under G.S. 58-58-245(a)(6) renders the contract voidable by the viator for lack of consideration until the time consideration is tendered to and accepted by the viator.

(k) Contacts with the insured for the purpose of determining the health status of the insured by the provider or broker after the viatical settlement has occurred shall only be made by the provider or broker licensed in this State or its authorized representatives and shall be limited to once every three months for insureds with a life expectancy of more than one year, and to no more than once per month for insureds with a life expectancy of one year or less. The provider or broker shall explain the procedure for these contacts at the time the contract is entered into. The limitations set forth in this subsection shall not apply to any contacts with an insured for reasons other than determining the insured's health status. Providers and brokers shall be responsible for the actions of their authorized representatives.

(l) Every related provider trust shall have a written agreement with the licensed viatical settlement provider under which the licensed viatical settlement provider is responsible for ensuring compliance with all statutory and regulatory requirements and under which the trust agrees to make all records and files related to viatical settlement transactions available to the Commissioner as if those records and files were maintained directly by the licensed viatical settlement provider.

(m) Notwithstanding the manner in which a viatical settlement broker is compensated, a broker is deemed to represent only the viator and owes a fiduciary duty to the viator to act according to the viator's instructions and in the best interest of the viator. (2001-436, s. 3.)

§ 58-58-255. Prohibited practices.

(a) It is a violation of this Part for any person to enter into a contract within a two-year period commencing with the date of issuance of the policy unless the viator certifies to the provider that one or more of the following conditions have been met within the two-year period:

(1) The policy was issued upon the viator's exercise of conversion rights arising out of a policy, provided the total time covered under the conversion policy plus the time covered under the prior policy is at least 24 months, or the contestability and suicide time periods have been waived by the insurer. The time covered under a group policy shall be calculated without regard to any change in insurance carriers, provided the coverage has been continuous and under the same group sponsorship.

(2) The viator is a charitable organization exempt from taxation under 26 U.S.C. § 501(c)(3).

(3) The viator is not a natural person (e.g., the owner is a corporation, limited liability company, partnership, etc.).

(4) The viator submits independent evidence to the provider that one or more of the following conditions have been met within the two-year period:

a. The viator or insured is terminally or chronically ill.

b. The viator's spouse dies.

c. The viator divorces his or her spouse.

d. The viator retires from full-time employment.

e. The viator becomes physically or mentally disabled and a physician determines that the disability prevents the viator from maintaining full-time employment.

f. The viator was the insured's employer at the time the policy was issued and the employment relationship terminated.

g. A final order, judgment, or decree is entered by a court of competent jurisdiction, on the application of a creditor of the viator, adjudicating the viator bankrupt or insolvent, or approving a petition seeking reorganization of the viator or appointing a receiver, trustee, or liquidator to all or a substantial part of the viator's assets.

    h. The viator experiences a significant decrease in income that is unexpected and that impairs the viator's reasonable ability to pay the policy premium.

    i. The viator or insured disposes of his or her ownership interests in a closely held corporation.

(b) Copies of the independent evidence described in subdivision (a)(4) of this section and documents required by G.S. 58-58-250(a) shall be submitted to the insurer when the provider submits a request to the insurer for verification of coverage. The copies shall be accompanied by a letter of attestation from the provider that the copies are true and correct copies of the documents received by the provider.

(c) If the provider submits to the insurer a copy of the owner or insured's certification described in subdivision (a)(4) and subsection (b) of this section when the provider submits a request to the insurer to effect the transfer of the policy to the provider, the copy shall be deemed to conclusively establish that the contract satisfies the requirements of this section, and the insurer shall timely respond to the request. (2001-436, s. 3.)

§ 58-58-260. Advertising for viatical settlements.

(a) The purpose of this section is to provide prospective viators with clear and unambiguous statements in the advertisement of viatical settlements and to assure the clear, truthful, and adequate disclosure of the benefits, risks, limitations, and exclusions of any contract. This purpose is intended to be accomplished by the establishment of guidelines and standards of permissible and impermissible conduct in the advertising of viatical settlements to assure that product descriptions are presented in a manner that prevents unfair, deceptive, or misleading advertising and is conducive to accurate presentation and description of viatical settlements through the advertising media and material used by viatical settlement licensees.

(b) This section shall apply to any advertising of contracts or related products or services intended for dissemination in this State, including Internet advertising viewed by persons located in this State. Where disclosure requirements are established pursuant to federal regulation, this section shall be interpreted so as to minimize or eliminate conflict with federal regulation wherever possible.

(c) Every viatical settlement licensee shall establish and at all times maintain a system of control over the content, form, and method of dissemination of all advertisements of its contracts, products, and services. All advertisements, regardless of by whom written, created, designed, or presented, shall be the responsibility of the viatical settlement licensee, as well as the individual who created or presented the advertisement. A system of control shall include regular routine notification, at least once a year, to agents and others, authorized by the viatical settlement licensee, who disseminate advertisements of the requirements and procedures for approval before the use of any advertisements not furnished by the viatical settlement licensee.

(d) Advertisements shall be truthful and not misleading in fact or by implication. The form and content of an advertisement of a contract shall be sufficiently complete and clear so as to avoid deception. It shall not have the capacity or tendency to mislead or deceive. Whether an advertisement has the capacity or tendency to mislead or deceive shall be determined by the Commissioner from the overall impression that the advertisement may be reasonably expected to create upon a person of average education or intelligence within the segment of the public to which it is directed.

(e) All information required to be disclosed under this Part shall be set out conspicuously and in close conjunction with the statements to which such information relates or under appropriate captions of such prominence that it shall not be minimized, rendered obscure, or presented in an ambiguous fashion or intermingled with the context of the advertisement so as to be confusing or misleading.

(f) An advertisement shall not:

(1) Omit material information or use words, phrases, statements, references, or illustrations if the omission or use has the capacity, tendency, or effect of misleading or deceiving viators as to the nature or extent of any benefit, loss covered, premium payable, or state or federal tax consequence. The fact that the contract offered is made available for inspection before consummation of the sale, or an offer is made to refund the payment if the viator is not satisfied or that the contract includes a "free look" period that satisfies or exceeds legal requirements, does not remedy misleading statements.

(2) Use the name or title of a life insurance company or a policy unless the insurer has approved the advertisement.

(3) State or imply that interest charged on an accelerated death benefit or a policy loan is unfair, inequitable, or in any manner an incorrect or improper practice.

(4) State or imply that a contract, benefit, or service has been approved or endorsed by a group of individuals, society, association, or other organization unless that is the fact and unless any relationship between an organization and the viatical settlement licensee is disclosed. If the entity making the endorsement or testimonial is owned, controlled, or managed by the viatical settlement licensee, or receives any payment or other consideration from the viatical settlement licensee for making an endorsement or testimonial, that fact shall be disclosed in the advertisement.

(5) Contain statistical information unless it accurately reflects recent and relevant facts. The source of all statistics used in an advertisement shall be identified.

(6) Disparage insurers, providers, brokers, insurance producers, policies, services, or methods of marketing.

(7) Use a trade name, group designation, name of the parent company of a viatical settlement licensee, name of a particular division of the viatical settlement licensee, service mark, slogan, symbol, or other device or reference without disclosing the name of the viatical settlement licensee, if the advertisement would have the capacity or tendency to mislead or deceive as to the true identity of the viatical settlement licensee, or to create the impression that a company other than the viatical settlement licensee would have any responsibility for the financial obligation under a contract.

(8) Use any combination of words, symbols, or physical materials that by their content, phraseology, shape, color, or other characteristics are so similar to a combination of words, symbols, or physical materials used by a government program or agency or otherwise appear to be of such a nature that they tend to mislead prospective viators into believing that the solicitation is in some manner connected with a government program or agency.

(9) Create the impression that the provider, its financial condition or status, the payment of its claims, or the merits, desirability, or advisability of its contracts are recommended or endorsed by any government entity.

(g) The words "free", "no cost", "without cost", "no additional cost", "at no extra cost", or words of similar import shall not be used with respect to any benefit or service unless true. An advertisement may specify the charge for a benefit or a service, may state that a charge is included in the payment, or use other appropriate language.

(h) Testimonials, appraisals, or analyses used in advertisements must be genuine; represent the current opinion of the author; be applicable to the contract, product, or service advertised, if any; and be accurately reproduced with sufficient completeness to avoid misleading or deceiving prospective viators as to the nature or scope of the testimonials, appraisals, analyses, or endorsements. In using testimonials, appraisals, or analyses, the viatical settlement licensee makes as its own all the statements contained therein, and the statements are subject to all the provisions of this section.

(i) If the individual making a testimonial, appraisal, analysis, or an endorsement has a financial interest in the provider or related entity as a stockholder, director, officer, employee, or otherwise, or receives any benefit directly or indirectly other than required union scale wages, that fact shall be prominently disclosed in the advertisement.

(j) When an endorsement refers to benefits received under a contract, all pertinent information shall be retained for a period of five years after its use.

(k) The name of the viatical settlement licensee shall be clearly identified in all advertisements about the licensee or its contracts, products, or services, and if any specific contract is advertised, the contract shall be identified either by form number or some other appropriate description. If an application is part of the advertisement, the name of the provider or broker shall be shown on the application.

(l) An advertisement may state that a viatical settlement licensee is licensed in the state where the advertisement appears, provided it does not exaggerate that fact or suggest or imply that a competing viatical settlement licensee may not be so licensed. The advertisement may ask the audience to consult the licensee's web site or contact the Department to find out if the state requires licensing and, if so, whether the provider or broker is licensed.

(m) The name of the actual licensee shall be stated in all of its advertisements. An advertisement shall not use a trade name, any group designation, name of any affiliate or controlling entity of the licensee, service mark, slogan, symbol, or other device in a manner that would have the capacity or tendency to mislead or deceive as to the true identity of the actual licensee or create the false impression that an affiliate or controlling entity would have any responsibility for the financial obligation of the licensee.

(n) An advertisement shall not directly or indirectly create the impression that any state or federal governmental agency endorses, approves, or favors:

(1) Any viatical settlement licensee or its business practices or methods of operation;

(2) The merits, desirability, or advisability of any contract;

(3) Any contract; or

(4) Any policy or life insurance company.

(o) If the advertiser emphasizes the speed with which the viatication will occur, the advertising must disclose the average time frame from completed application to the date of offer and from acceptance of the offer to receipt of the funds by the viator.

(p) If the advertising emphasizes the dollar amounts available to viators, the advertising shall disclose the average purchase price as a percent of face value obtained by viators contracting with the licensee during the past six months. (2001-436, s. 3.)

§ 58-58-265. Fraudulent viatical settlement acts, interference, and participation of convicted felons prohibited.

(a) A person who commits a fraudulent viatical settlement act is guilty of a Class H felony.

(b) A person shall not knowingly or intentionally interfere with the enforcement of the provisions of this Part or investigations of suspected or actual violations of this Part.

(c) A person in the business of viatical settlements shall not knowingly or intentionally permit any person convicted of a felony involving dishonesty or breach of trust to participate in the business of viatical settlements. (2001-436, s. 3.)

§ 58-58-267. Fraud warning required.

(a) Viatical settlement contracts and purchase agreement forms and applications for viatical settlements, regardless of the form of transmission, shall contain the following statement or a substantially similar statement:

"Any person who knowingly presents false information in an application for insurance or viatical settlement contract or a viatical settlement purchase agreement is guilty of a felony and may be subject to fines and confinement in prison."

(b) The lack of a statement as required in subsection (a) of this section does not constitute a defense in any prosecution for a fraudulent viatical settlement act. (2001-436, s. 3.)

§ 58-58-268. Viatical settlement antifraud initiatives.

(a) Viatical settlement providers and viatical settlement brokers shall have in place antifraud initiatives reasonably calculated to detect, prosecute, and prevent fraudulent viatical settlement acts. At the discretion of the Commissioner, the Commissioner may order, or a licensee may request and the Commissioner may grant, such modifications of the following required initiatives as necessary to ensure an effective antifraud program. The modifications may be more or less restrictive than the required initiatives so long as the modifications may reasonably be expected to accomplish the purpose of this section.

(b) Antifraud initiatives shall include:

    (1) Fraud investigators, who may be viatical settlement provider employees or viatical settlement broker employees or independent contractors; and

    (2) An antifraud plan, which shall be submitted to the Commissioner. The antifraud plan shall include, but not be limited to:

        a. A description of the procedures for detecting and investigating possible fraudulent viatical settlement acts and procedures for resolving material inconsistencies between medical records and insurance applications;

        b. A description of the procedures for reporting possible fraudulent viatical settlement acts to the Commissioner;

        c. A description of the plan for antifraud education and training of underwriters and other personnel; and

        d. A description or chart outlining the organizational arrangement of the antifraud personnel who are responsible for the investigation and reporting of possible fraudulent viatical settlement acts and investigating unresolved material inconsistencies between medical records and insurance applications.

(c) Antifraud plans submitted to the Commissioner are privileged and confidential, are not public records, and are not subject to discovery or subpoena in a civil or criminal action. (2001-436, s. 3.)

§ 58-58-270. Report to Commissioner.

Whenever any person licensed under this Part knows or has reasonable cause to believe that any other person has violated any provision of this Part, it is the duty of that person, upon acquiring the knowledge, to notify the Commissioner and provide the Commissioner with a complete statement of all of the relevant facts and circumstances. The report is a privileged communication and when made without actual malice does not subject the person making the report to any liability whatsoever. The Commissioner may suspend, revoke, or refuse to renew the license of any person who willfully fails to comply with this section. (2001-436, s. 3.)

§ 58-58-275. Reporting and investigation of suspected viatical settlement fraudulent acts; immunity from liability.

(a) As used in this section, "Commissioner" includes an employee, agent, or designee of the Commissioner. A person, or an employee or agent of that person, acting without actual malice, is not subject to civil liability for libel, slander, or any other cause of action by virtue of furnishing to the Commissioner, under the requirements of law or at the direction of the Commissioner, reports or other information relating to any known or suspected viatical settlement fraudulent act.

(b) The Commissioner, acting without actual malice, is not subject to civil liability for libel or slander by virtue of an investigation of any known or suspected viatical settlement fraudulent act; or by virtue of the publication or dissemination of any official report related to any such investigation, which report is published or disseminated in the absence of fraud, bad faith, or actual malice on the part of the Commissioner.

(c) During the course of an investigation of a known or suspected viatical settlement fraudulent act, the Commissioner may request any person to furnish copies of any information relative to the known or suspected viatical settlement fraudulent act. The person shall release the information requested and cooperate with the Commissioner under this section. (2001-436, s. 3.)

§ 58-58-280. Confidentiality.

(a) Information and evidence provided under G.S. 58-58-270 or G.S. 58-58-275 or obtained by the Commissioner in an investigation of suspected or actual fraudulent viatical settlement acts shall be privileged and confidential, is not a public record, and is not subject to discovery or subpoena in a civil or criminal action.

(b) Subsection (a) of this section does not prohibit release by the Commissioner of documents and evidence obtained in an investigation of suspected or actual fraudulent viatical settlement acts:

(1) In administrative or judicial proceedings to enforce laws administered by the Commissioner;

(2) To federal, state, or local law enforcement or regulatory agencies, to an organization established for the purpose of detecting and preventing fraudulent viatical settlement acts, or to the NAIC; or

(3) At the discretion of the Commissioner, to a person in the business of viatical settlements that is aggrieved by a fraudulent viatical settlement act.

(c) Release of documents and evidence under subsection (b) of this section does not abrogate or modify the privilege granted in subsection (a) of this section. (2001-436, s. 3.)

§ 58-58-285. Other law enforcement or regulatory authority.

This Part does not:
(1) Preempt the authority or relieve the duty of other law enforcement or regulatory agencies to investigate, examine, and prosecute suspected violations of law.
(2) Prevent or prohibit a person from disclosing voluntarily information concerning viatical settlement fraud to a law enforcement or regulatory agency other than the Commissioner.
(3) Limit the powers granted elsewhere by the laws of this State to the Commissioner to investigate and examine possible violations of law and to take appropriate action against wrongdoers. (2001-436, s. 3.)

§ 58-58-290. Injunctions; civil remedies; cease and desist orders.

(a) In addition to the penalties and other enforcement provisions of this Part, if any person violates this Part or any rule implementing this Part, the Commissioner may seek an injunction in a court of competent jurisdiction and may apply for temporary and permanent orders that the Commissioner determines are necessary to restrain the person from committing the violation.

(b) Any person damaged by the acts of a person in violation of this Part may bring a civil action against the person committing the violation in a court of competent jurisdiction.

(c) The Commissioner may issue, in accordance with G.S. 58-63-32, a cease and desist order upon a person that violates any provision of this Part, any rule or order adopted by the Commissioner, or any written agreement entered into with the Commissioner. The cease and desist order may be subject to judicial review under G.S. 58-63-35.

(d) When the Commissioner finds that an activity in violation of this Part presents an immediate danger to the public that requires an immediate final order, the Commissioner may issue an emergency cease and desist order reciting with particularity the facts underlying the findings. The emergency cease and desist order is effective immediately upon service of a copy of the order on the respondent and remains effective for 90 days. If the Commissioner begins nonemergency cease and desist proceedings, the emergency cease and desist order remains effective, absent an order by a court of competent jurisdiction in accordance with G.S. 58-63-35.

(e) In addition to the penalties and other enforcement provisions of this Part, any person who violates this Part is subject to G.S. 58-2-70. (2001-436, s. 3.)

§ 58-58-295. Unfair trade practices.

A violation of this Part is an unfair trade practice under Article 63 of this Chapter. (2001-436, s. 3.)

§ 58-58-300. Authority to adopt rules.

The Commissioner may:
 (1) Adopt rules implementing this Part.
 (2) Establish standards for evaluating reasonableness of payments under contracts for persons who are terminally or chronically ill, including standards for the amount paid in exchange for assignment, transfer, sale, devise, or bequest of a benefit under a policy.
 (3) Establish appropriate licensing requirements, fees, and standards for continued licensure for providers.
 (4) Require a bond or other mechanism for financial accountability for providers and brokers.
 (5) Adopt rules governing the relationship and responsibilities of insurers, providers, and brokers during the viatication of a policy. (2001-436, s. 3.)

§ 58-58-305. Jurisdictional limitations.

Nothing in this Part affects the North Carolina Securities Act or the jurisdiction of the North Carolina Secretary of State. (2001-436, s. 3.)

§ 58-58-310. Effective date.

A provider or broker transacting business in this State, pursuant to G.S. 58-58-42, on the effective date of this Part may continue to do so pending approval of the provider's or broker's application for a license as long as the application is filed with the Commissioner no later than July 1, 2002. If the application is disapproved, then the provider or broker shall cease transacting viatical business in this State. (2001-436, s. 3.)

Editor's Note. — Section 58-58-42 referred to in the above 58-58-310 was repealed by Session Laws 2001-436, s. 5.

ARTICLE 59.

Registered Policies.

§ 58-59-1. Deposits to secure registered policies.

Any life insurance company, incorporated under the laws of this State, may deposit with the Commissioner securities of the kind authorized for the investment of the funds of life insurance companies, which shall be legally transferred by it to him as Commissioner and his successors for the common benefit of all the holders of its "registered" policies and annuity bonds issued under the provisions of this Article; and these securities shall be held by him and his successors in office in trust for the purposes and objects specified herein.

All securities offered to the Commissioner for deposit under this section shall be received and held pursuant to regulations promulgated by the Commissioner. (1905, c. 504, s. 12; Rev., s. 4780; 1909, c. 920, ss. 1, 2; 1911, c. 140, s. 1; 1917, c. 191, s. 2; C.S., s. 6467; 1945, c. 379.)

Cross References. — As to investments in bonds guaranteed by the United States, see G.S. 53-44. As to investments in bonds and notes secured by mortgages insured by the Secretary of Housing and Urban Development, etc., see G.S. 53-45. As to investments in federal

farm loan bonds, see G.S. 53-60. As to investments in refunding bonds of North Carolina,
see G.S. 142-29.1 et seq.

§ 58-59-5. Additional deposits may be required.

Each company which has made deposits herein provided for shall make additional deposits from time to time, as the Commissioner prescribes, in amounts of not less than five thousand dollars ($5,000) and of such securities as are described in the preceding section [G.S. 58-59-1], so that the admitted value of the securities deposited shall equal the net value of the registered policies and annuity bonds issued by the company, less such liens not exceeding such value as the company has against it. The Commissioner shall annually value or cause to be valued such policies and shall prepare an estimate based upon probable changes in the minimum amounts to be kept on deposit for each month of the ensuing year. (1905, c. 504, s. 15; Rev., s. 4781; 1909, c. 920, s. 3; 1911, c. 140, s. 2; 1917, c. 191, s. 3; C.S., s. 6468; 1945, c. 379; 1991, c. 720, s. 4.)

§ 58-59-10. Withdrawal of deposits.

Any such company whose deposits exceed the net value of all registered policies and annuity bonds it has in force, less such liens not exceeding such value as the company holds against them, may withdraw such excess or it may withdraw any of such securities at any time by depositing in their place others of equal value and of the character authorized by law; and as long as such company remains solvent and keeps up its deposits, as herein required, it may collect the interest and coupons on the securities deposited as they accrue; and any life insurance company may withdraw such securities by and with the consent of the policyholder only; and in case of such withdrawal, the certificate of registration in each case must be surrendered for cancellation, or a receipt from the policyholder, satisfactory to the Commissioner, must be produced before such withdrawal of deposits shall be allowed. (1905, c. 504, s. 18; Rev., s. 4782; 1911, c. 134; C.S., s. 6469; 1991, c. 720, s. 4.)

§ 58-59-15. Record of securities kept by Commissioner; deficit made good.

The Commissioner shall keep a careful record of the securities deposited by each company, and when furnishing the annual certificates of value required in this Article, he may enter thereon the face and market value of the securities deposited by such company. If at any time it appears from such certificate or otherwise that the value of securities held on deposit is less than the net value of the registered policies and annuity bonds issued by such companies, it is not lawful for the Commissioner to execute the certificate on any additional policies or annuity bonds of such company until it has made good the deficit. If any company fails or neglects to make such deposits for 60 days the Commissioner may suspend its license to do business until such deposit be made. (1905, c. 504, s. 16; Rev., s. 4784; C.S., s. 6471; 1945, c. 379; 1991, c. 720, s. 4.)

§ 58-59-20. Registered policies certified.

After making the deposits provided for in this Article no company may issue a policy of insurance or endowment or an annuity bond known or designated as "registered" unless it has upon its face a certificate in the following words: "This policy or annuity bond is registered and secured by pledge of bonds, stocks, or securities deposited with this Department as provided by law," which certificate shall be signed by the Commissioner and sealed with the seal of his office. Such policies and bonds shall be known as "registered" policies and annuity bonds, and a sample copy of such kind, class, and issue shall be kept in the office of the Commissioner. All policies and bonds of each kind and class issued, and the copies thereof, filed in the office of the Commissioner must have imprinted thereon some appropriate designating letter, combination of letters or terms identifying the special forms of contract, together with the year of adoption of such form, and whenever any change or modification is made in the form of contracts, policy, or bond, the designating letters or terms and year of adoption thereon shall be changed accordingly. (1905, c. 504, s. 13; Rev., s. 4785; C.S., s. 6472; 1991, c. 720, s. 4.)

§ 58-59-25. Power of Commissioner in case of insolvency.

If at any time the affairs of a life insurance company which has deposited securities under the provisions of this Article, in the opinion of the Commissioner, appear in such condition as to render the issuing of additional policies and annuity bonds by such company injurious to the public interest, the Commissioner may take such proceedings against the company as are authorized by law to be taken against other insolvent companies, and said companies are in all respects subject to the provisions of law affecting other companies. (1905, c. 504, s. 20; Rev., s. 4788; C.S., s. 6475; 1991, c. 720, s. 4.)

§ 58-59-30. Fees for registering policies.

Every company making deposits under the provisions of this Article must pay to the Commissioner for each certificate on registered policies or annuity bonds, including seal, a fee of fifty cents (50¢) for those exceeding ten thousand dollars ($10,000) in amount and twenty-five cents (25¢) for all under ten thousand dollars ($10,000) in amount, except policies for one hundred dollars ($100.00) and not exceeding five hundred dollars ($500.00) the fee shall be fifteen cents (15¢); for policies of one hundred dollars ($100.00) or less the fee shall be ten cents (10¢). (1905, c. 504, s. 21; Rev., s. 4789; C.S., s. 6476; 1945, c. 379; 1991, c. 720, s. 4.)

§ 58-59-35. Registration of policies.

After January 1, 1947, the Commissioner shall not register any new policies that are issued by any company, nor accept any deposits covering reserves on business thereafter written. (1945, c. 379.)

ARTICLE 60.

Regulation of Life Insurance Solicitation.

§ 58-60-1. Purpose of Article.

The purpose of this Article is to require insurers to deliver to purchasers of life insurance, information which will improve the buyer's ability to select the most appropriate plan of life insurance for their needs, improve the buyer's understanding of the basic features of the policy which has been purchased or which is under consideration and to improve the ability of the buyer to evaluate the relative costs of similar plans of life insurance.

This Article does not prohibit an insurer to use additional material which is not in violation of Articles 1 through 64 of this Chapter nor any other statute or regulation. (1979, c. 447.)

Legal Periodicals. — For survey of 1979 administrative law, see 58 N.C.L. Rev. 1185 (1980).

§ 58-60-5. Scope of Article; exemptions.

(a) Except as otherwise provided in this Article, this Article applies to any solicitation, negotiation or procurement of life insurance occurring within this State. This Article applies to any issuer of a life insurance contract, including fraternal benefit societies.

(b) Unless otherwise specifically included, this Article does not apply to:

    (1) Annuities,

    (2) Credit life insurance,

    (3) Group life insurance,

    (4) Life insurance policies issued in connection with pension and welfare plans as defined by and that are subject to the federal Employee Retirement Income Security Act of 1974 (ERISA),

    (5) Variable life insurance under which the death benefits and cash values vary in accordance with unit values of investments held in a separate account.

(c) The policy summary in this Article is not required for policies that are sold subject to rules adopted by the Commissioner for life insurance illustrations. (1979, c. 447; 1998-211, s. 14.)

Legal Periodicals. — For survey of 1979 administrative law, see 58 N.C.L. Rev. 1185 (1980).

§ 58-60-10. Definitions.

Unless the context of use indicates a different meaning, for the purposes of this Article, the following definitions shall apply:

    (1) Buyer's Guide. — A Buyer's Guide is a document furnished pursuant to G.S. 58-60-15, which shall contain all the requirements of and be in substantial compliance with G.S. 58-60-25.

    (2) Cash Dividend. — A Cash Dividend is the current illustrated dividend which can be applied toward payment of gross premium.

    (3) Equivalent Level Annual Dividend. — The Equivalent Level Annual Dividend is calculated by applying the following steps:

        a. Accumulate the annual cash dividends at five percent (5%) interest compounded annually to the end of the 10th and 20th policy years;

        b. Divide each accumulation of paragraph a of this subdivision by an interest factor that converts it into one equivalent level annual amount that, if paid at the beginning of each year, would accrue to the values in paragraph a of this subdivision over the respective periods stipulated in paragraph a of this subdivision. If the period is 10 years, the factor is 13.207 and if the period is 20 years, the factor is 34.719.

        c. Divide the results of paragraph b of this subdivision by the number of thousands of the Equivalent Level Death Benefit to arrive at the Equivalent Level Annual Dividend.

    (4) Equivalent Level Death Benefit. — The Equivalent Level Death Benefit of a policy or term life insurance rider is an amount calculated as follows:

        a. Accumulate the guaranteed amount payable upon death, regardless of the cause of death, at the beginning of each policy year for

10 and 20 years at five percent (5%) interest compounded annually to the end of the 10th and 20th policy years respectively;

b. Divide each accumulation of paragraph a of this subdivision by an interest factor that converts it into one equivalent level annual amount that, if paid at the beginning of each year, would accrue to the value in paragraph a of this subdivision over the respective periods stipulated in paragraph a of this subdivision. If the period is 10 years, the factor is 13.207 and if the period is 20 years, the factor is 34.719.

(5) Generic Name. — Generic Name means a short title which is descriptive of the premium and benefit patterns of a policy or a rider.

(6) Life Insurance Cost Indexes. —

a. Life Insurance Surrender Cost Index. The Life Insurance Surrender Cost Index is calculated by applying the following steps:

1. Determine the guaranteed cash surrender value, if any, available at the end of the 10th and 20th policy years;

2. For participating policies, add the terminal dividend payable upon surrender, if any, to the accumulation of the annual Cash Dividends at five percent (5%) interest compounded annually to the end of the period selected and add this sum to the amount determined in subdivision a;

3. Divide the result of subparagraph 2 (subparagraph 1 for guaranteed-cost policies) by an interest factor that converts it into an equivalent level annual that, if paid at the beginning of each year, would accrue to the value in subparagraph 2 (subparagraph 1 for guaranteed-cost policies) over the respective periods stipulated in subparagraph 1. If the period is 10 years, the factor is 13.207 and if the period is 20 years, the factor is 34.719;

4. Determine the equivalent level premium by accumulating each annual premium payable for the basic policy or rider at five percent (5%) interest compounded annually to the end of the period stipulated in subparagraph 1 and dividing the result by the respective factors stated in subparagraph 3 (this amount is the annual premium payable for a level premium plan);

5. Subtract the result of subparagraph 3 from subparagraph 4;

6. Divide the result of subparagraph 5 by the number of thousands of the Equivalent Level Death Benefit to arrive at the Life Insurance Surrender Cost Index.

b. Life Insurance Net Payment Cost Index. The Life Insurance Net Payment Cost Index is calculated in the same manner as the comparable Life Insurance Cost Index except that the cash surrender value and any terminal dividend are set at zero.

(7) Policy Summary. — Policy Summary means a written statement describing the elements of the policy including but not limited to:

a. A prominently placed title in at least 10-point boldface capital letters as follows: STATEMENT OF POLICY COST AND BENEFIT INFORMATION;

b. The name and address of the insurance agent, or, if no agent is involved, a statement of the procedure to be followed in order to receive responses to inquiries regarding the Policy Summary;

c. The full name and home office or administrative office address of the company in which the life insurance policy is to be or has been written;

d. The Generic Name of the basic policy and each rider;

e. The following amounts, where applicable, for the first five policy years and representative policy years thereafter sufficient to clearly illustrate the premium and benefit patterns, including, but not necessarily limited to, the years for which Life Insurance Cost Indexes are displayed and at least one age from 60 through 65 or maturity, whichever is earlier:

1. The annual premium for the basic policy;
2. The annual premium for each optional rider;
3. Guaranteed amount payable upon death, at the beginning of the policy year regardless of the cause of death other than suicide, or other specifically enumerated exclusions, which is provided by the basic policy and each optional rider, with benefits provided under the basic policy and each rider shown separately;
4. Total guaranteed cash surrender values at the end of the year with values shown separately for the basic policy and each rider;
5. Cash Dividends payable at the end of the year with values shown separately for the basic policy and each rider. (Dividends need not be displayed beyond the 20th policy year);
6. Guaranteed endowment amounts payable under the policy which are not included under guaranteed cash surrender values above.

f. The effective policy loan annual percentage interest rate, if the policy contains this provision, specifying whether this rate is applied in advance or in arrears. If the policy loan interest rate is variable, the Policy Summary includes the maximum annual percentage rate;

g. Life Insurance Cost Indexes for 10 and 20 years but in no case beyond the premium paying period. Separate indexes must be displayed for the basic policy and for each optional term life insurance rider. Such indexes need not be included for optional riders which are limited to benefits such as accidental death benefits, disability waiver of premium, preliminary term life insurance coverage of less than 12 months and guaranteed insurability benefits nor for basic policies or optional riders covering more than one life;

h. The Equivalent Level Annual Dividend, in the case of participating policies and participating optional term life insurance riders, under the same circumstances and for the same durations at which Life Insurance Cost Indexes are displayed;

i. A Policy Summary which includes dividends shall also include a statement that dividends are based on the company's current dividend scale and are not guaranteed in addition to a statement in close proximity to the Equivalent Level Annual Dividend as follows: An explanation of the intended use of the Equivalent Level Annual Dividend is included in the Life Insurance Buyer's Guide;

j. A statement in close proximity to the Life Insurance Cost Indexes as follows: An explanation of the intended use of these indexes is provided in the Life Insurance Buyer's Guide.

k. The date on which the Policy Summary is prepared.

The Policy Summary must consist of a separate document. All information required to be disclosed must be set out in such a manner as to not minimize or render any portion thereof obscure. Any amounts which remain level for two or more years of the policy may be represented by a single number if it is clearly indicated what amounts are applicable for each policy year. Amounts in subparagraph e of this paragraph shall be listed in total, not on a per thousand nor per unit basis. If more than one insured is covered under one policy or rider, guaranteed death benefits shall be displayed separately for each insured or for each class of insureds if death benefits do not differ within the class. Zero amounts shall be displayed as zero and shall not be displayed as a blank space. (1979, c. 447.)

Legal Periodicals. — For survey of 1979 administrative law, see 58 N.C.L. Rev. 1185 (1980).

§ 58-60-15. Disclosure requirements.

(a) The insurer shall provide to all prospective purchasers a Buyer's Guide and a Policy Summary prior to accepting any applicant's initial premium deposit, unless the policy for which application is made contains an unconditional refund provision of at least 10 days or unless the Policy Summary contains such an unconditional refund offer, in which event the Buyer's Guide and Policy Summary must be delivered with the policy or prior to delivery of the policy.

(b) The insurer shall provide a Buyer's Guide and a Policy Summary to any prospective purchaser upon request.

(c) In the case of policies whose Equivalent Level Death Benefit does not exceed five thousand dollars ($5,000), the requirement for providing a Policy Summary will be satisfied by delivery of a written statement containing the information described in G.S. 58-60-10(7), subdivisions b, c, d, e1, e2, e3, f, g, j, and k. (1979, c. 447; 1993, c. 553, s. 21.)

Legal Periodicals. — For survey of 1979 administrative law, see 58 N.C.L. Rev. 1185 (1980).

§ 58-60-20. General rules relating to solicitation.

(a) Each insurer subject to this Article shall maintain at its home office or principal office a complete file containing one copy of each document authorized by the insurer for use pursuant to this Article. Such file shall contain one copy of each authorized form for a period of three years following the date of its last authorized use.

(b) An agent shall inform the prospective purchaser, prior to commencing a life insurance sales presentation, that he is acting as a life insurance agent and inform the prospective purchaser of the full name of the insurance company which he is representing to the buyer. In sales situations in which an agent is not involved, the insurer shall identify its full name.

(c) Terms such as financial planner, investment advisor, financial consultant, or financial counseling shall not be used in such a way as to imply that the insurance agent is generally engaged in an advisory business in which compensation is unrelated to sales unless such is actually the case.

(d) Any reference to policy dividends must include a statement that dividends are not guaranteed.

(e) A system or presentation which does not recognize the time value of money through the use of appropriate interest adjustments shall not be used for comparing the cost of two or more life insurance policies. Such a system may be used for the purpose of demonstrating the cash-flow pattern of a policy if such presentation is accompanied by a statement disclosing that the presentation does not recognize that, because of interest, a dollar in the future has less value than a dollar today.

(f) A presentation of benefits shall not display guaranteed and nonguaranteed benefits as a single sum unless they are shown separately in close proximity thereto.

(g) A statement regarding the use of the Life Insurance Cost Indexes shall include an explanation to the effect that the indexes are useful only for the comparison of the relative costs of two or more similar policies.

(h) A Life Insurance Cost Index which reflects dividends or an Equivalent Level Annual Dividend shall be accompanied by a statement that it is based on the insurer's current dividend scale and is not guaranteed.

(i) For the purposes of this Article, the annual premium for a basic policy or rider, for which the insurer reserves the right to change the premium, shall be the maximum annual premium. (1979, c. 447.)

Legal Periodicals. — For survey of 1979 administrative law, see 58 N.C.L. Rev. 1185 (1980).

§ 58-60-25. Adoption of Buyer's Guide; requirements.

Any insurer soliciting life insurance in this State on or after December 1, 1979, shall adopt and use a Buyer's Guide, and the adoption and use by an insurer of the Buyer's Guide promulgated by the National Association of Insurance Commissioners in the NAIC Model Life Insurance Solicitation Regulations shall be in compliance with the requirements of this Article. (1979, c. 447.)

Legal Periodicals. — For survey of 1979 administrative law, see 58 N.C.L. Rev. 1185 (1980).

§ 58-60-30. Failure to comply.

The failure of an insurer to provide or deliver a Buyer's Guide, or a Policy Summary as provided in G.S. 58-60-15(a) and (b) shall constitute an omission which misrepresents the benefits, advantages, conditions or terms of an insurance policy within the meaning of G.S. 58-58-40 and Article 63 (Unfair Trade Practice Act) of this Chapter. (1979, c. 447.)

Legal Periodicals. — For survey of 1979 administrative law, see 58 N.C.L. Rev. 1185 (1980).

§ 58-60-35. Disclosure of prearrangement insurance policy provisions.

(a) As used in this section:

(1) "Prearrangement" means any contract, agreement, or mutual under-
standing, or any series or combination of contracts, agreements or mutual understandings, whether funded by trust deposits or prear-
rangement insurance policies, or any combination thereof, which has for a purpose the furnishing or performance of specific funeral services, or the furnishing or delivery of specific personal property, merchandise, or services of any nature in connection with the final

disposition of a dead human body, to be furnished or delivered at a time determinable by the death of the person whose body is to be disposed of, but does not mean the furnishing of a cemetery lot, crypt, niche, mausoleum, grave marker or monument.

(2) "Prearrangement insurance policy" means a life insurance policy, annuity contract, or other insurance contract, or any series of contracts or agreements in any form or manner, issued on a group or individual basis by an insurance company authorized by law to do business in this State, which, whether by assignment or otherwise, has for its sole purpose the funding of a specific preneed funeral contract or a specific insurance-funded funeral or burial prearrangement, the insured being the person for whose service the funds were paid.

(b) The following information shall be adequately disclosed by the insurance agent or limited representative at the time an application is made, prior to accepting the applicant's initial premium, for a prearrangement insurance policy:

(1) The fact that a prearrangement insurance policy is involved or being used to fund a prearrangement;

(2) The nature of the relationship among the insurance agent or limited representative, the provider of the funeral or cemetery merchandise or services, the administrator, and any other person;

(3) The relationship of the prearrangement insurance policy to the funding of the prearrangement and the nature and existence of any guarantees relating to the prearrangement;

(4) The effect on the prearrangement of (i) any changes in the prearrangement insurance policy, including but not limited to, changes in the assignment, beneficiary designation, or use of the policy proceeds; (ii) any penalties to be incurred by the insured as a result of failure to make premium payments; and (iii) any penalties to be incurred or monies to be received as a result of cancellation or surrender of the prearrangement insurance policy;

(5) All relevant information concerning what occurs and whether any entitlements or obligations arise if there is a difference between the policy proceeds and the amount actually needed to fund the prearrangement; and

(6) Any penalties or restrictions, including geographic restrictions or the inability of the provider to perform, on the delivery of merchandise, services, or the prearrangement guarantee. (1989, c. 738, s. 1; 1991, c. 644, s. 10; 1995, c. 517, s. 32.)

ARTICLE 61.

Regulation of Interest Rates on Life Insurance Policy Loans.

§ 58-61-1. Purpose.

The purpose of this Article is to permit and set guidelines for life insurers to include in life insurance policies issued after the effective date of this Article a provision for periodic adjustment of policy loan interest rates. Nothing in this Article shall be construed to prohibit a life insurer from issuing a policy that contains only the provision specified in G.S. 58-61-10(a)(1) with respect to policy loan interest rates. (1981, c. 841, s. 1.)

Legal Periodicals. — For survey of 1981 administrative law, see 60 N.C.L. Rev. 1165 (1982).

§ 58-61-5. Definitions.

For purposes of this Article the "Published Monthly Average" means:
   (1) The Monthly Average of the Composite Yield on Seasoned Corporate Bonds as published by Moody's Investors Service, Inc., or any successor thereto; or
   (2) In the event that the Monthly Average of the Composite Yield on Seasoned Corporate Bonds is no longer published, a substantially similar average, established by regulation issued by the Commissioner. (1981, c. 841, s. 1.)

§ 58-61-10. Maximum rate of interest on policy loans.

(a) Policies issued on or after September 1, 1981 shall provide for policy loan interest rates as follows:
   (1) A provision permitting a maximum interest rate of not more than eight percent (8%) per annum; or
   (2) A provision permitting an adjustable maximum interest rate established from time to time by the life insurer as permitted by law.
(b) The rate of interest on a policy loan made under subsection (a)(2) shall not exceed the higher of the following:
   (1) The published monthly average for the calendar month ending two months before the date on which the rate is determined; or
   (2) The rate used to compute the cash surrender values under the policy during the applicable period plus one percent (1%) per annum.
(c) If the maximum rate of interest is determined pursuant to subsection (a)(2), the policy shall contain a provision setting forth the frequency at which the rate is to be determined for that policy.
(d) The maximum rate for each policy must be determined at regular intervals at least once every 12 months, but not more frequently than once in any three-month period. At the intervals specified in the policy:
   (1) The rate being charged may be increased whenever such increase as determined under subsection (b) would increase that rate by one-half percent (½%) or more per annum;
   (2) The rate being charged must be reduced whenever such reduction as determined under subsection (b) would decrease that rate by one-half percent (½%) or more per annum.
(e) The life insurer shall:
   (1) Notify the policyholder at the time a cash loan is made of the initial rate of interest on the loan;
   (2) Notify the policyholder with respect to premium loans of the initial rate of interest on the loan as soon as it is reasonably practical to do so after making the initial loan. Notice need not be given to the policyholder when a further premium loan is added, except as provided in (3) below;
   (3) Send to policyholders with loans reasonable advance notice of any increase in the rate; and
   (4) Include in the notices required above the substance of the pertinent provisions of subsections (a) and (c).
(f) No policy shall terminate in a policy year as the sole result of change in the interest rate during that policy year, and the life insurer shall maintain coverage during that policy year until the time at which it would otherwise have terminated if there had been no change during that policy year.

(g) The substance of the pertinent provisions of subsections (a) and (c) shall be set forth in the policies to which they apply.

(h) For purposes of this section:

(1) The rate of interest on policy loans permitted under this section includes the interest rate charged on reinstatement of policy loans for the period during and after any lapse of a policy.

(2) The term "policy loan" includes any premium loan made under a policy to pay one or more premiums that were not paid to the life insurer as they fell due.

(3) The term "policyholder" includes the owner of the policy or the person designated to pay premiums as shown on the records of the life insurer.

(4) The term "policy" includes certificates issued by a fraternal benefit society and annuity contracts which provide for policy loans.

(i) No other provision of law shall apply to policy loan interest rates unless made specifically applicable to such rates. (1981, c. 841, s. 1.)

§ 58-61-15. Applicability to existing policies.

The provisions of this Article shall not apply to any insurance contract issued before September 1, 1981. (1981, c. 841, s. 1.)

ARTICLE 62.

Life and Health Insurance Guaranty Association.

§ 58-62-1: Repealed by Session Laws 1991, c. 681, s. 57.

§ 58-62-2. Title.

This Article shall be known and may be cited as the North Carolina Life and Health Insurance Guaranty Association Act. (1991, c. 681, s. 56.)

Editor's Note. — Session Laws 1991, c. 681, s. 58 provides: "The Commissioner and the Commissioner's staff shall maintain close relations with the insurance regulators of other states and shall actively participate in the activities and affairs of the National Association of Insurance Commissioners, the National Conference of Insurance Legislators, and other organizations or successor organizations insofar as it will, in the Commissioner's judgment, enhance the purposes of the regulation of insurance. The actual and necessary travel and related expenses incurred by the Commissioner and members of the Commissioner's staff in attending meetings of such organizations, their committees, subcommittees, hearings, and other official activities, as well as the general expenses of participation in such organizations shall be a charge on available funds and the appropriation of the Department."

§ 58-62-5: Repealed by Session Laws 1991, c. 681, s. 57.

§ 58-62-6. Purpose.

(a) The purpose of this Article is to protect, subject to certain limitations, the persons specified in G.S. 58-62-21(a) against failure in the performance of contractual obligations, under life and health insurance policies and annuity contracts specified in G.S. 58-62-21(b), because of the delinquency of the member insurer that issued the policies.

(b) To provide this protection, an association of insurers is created to pay benefits and to continue coverages as limited herein, and members of the

Association are subject to assessment to provide funds to carry out the purpose of this Article. (1991, c. 681, s. 56.)

§ **58-62-10:** Repealed by Session Laws 1991, c. 681, s. 57.

§ 58-62-11. Construction.

This Article shall be liberally construed to effect the purpose under G.S. 58-62-6, which shall constitute an aid and guide to interpretation. (1991, c. 681, s. 56.)

§ **58-62-15:** Repealed by Session Laws 1991, c. 681, s. 57.

§ 58-62-16. Definitions.

As used in this Article:
  (1) "Account" means any of the two accounts created under G.S. 58-62-26.
  (2) "Association" means the North Carolina Life and Health Insurance Guaranty Association created under G.S. 58-62-26.
  (3) "Board" means the board of directors of the Association established under G.S. 58-62-31.
  (4) "Contractual obligation" means any obligation under a policy or certificate under a group policy, or part thereof, for which coverage is provided under G.S. 58-62-21.
  (5) "Covered policy" means any policy within the scope of this Article under G.S. 58-62-21.
  (6) "Delinquent insurer" means an impaired insurer or an insolvent insurer; and "delinquency" means an insurer impairment or insolvency.
  (7) "Health insurance" includes hospital or medical service corporation contracts, accident and health insurance, accident insurance, and disability insurance.
  (8) "Impaired insurer" means a member insurer that, after the effective date of this Article, is not an insolvent insurer, and (i) is deemed by the Commissioner to be potentially unable to fulfill its contractual obligations or (ii) is placed under an order of rehabilitation or conservation by a court of competent jurisdiction.
  (9) "Insolvent insurer" means a member insurer that, after the effective date of this Article, is placed under an order of liquidation with a finding of insolvency by a court of competent jurisdiction.
  (10) "Insurance regulator" means the official or agency of another state that is responsible for the regulation of a foreign insurer.
  (11) "Member insurer" means any insurer and any hospital or medical service corporation that is governed by Article 65 of this Chapter and that is licensed or that holds a license to transact in this State any kind of insurance for which coverage is provided under G.S. 58-62-21; and includes any insurer whose license in this State may have been suspended, revoked, not renewed or voluntarily withdrawn, but does not include an entity governed by Article 67 of this Chapter; fraternal order or fraternal benefit society; mandatory State pooling plan; mutual assessment company or any entity that operates on an assessment basis; insurance exchange; or any entity similar to any of the foregoing.
  (12) "Moody's Corporate Bond Yield Average" means the Monthly Average Corporates as published by Moody's Investors Service, Inc., or any successor thereto.

(13) "Person" includes an individual, corporation, company, partnership, association, or aggregation of individuals.
(14) "Plan" means the plan of operation established under G.S. 58-62-46.
(15) "Policy" includes a master group contract and subscriber contract under Article 65 of this Chapter, a contract of insurance and an annuity contract.
(16) "Premiums" means amounts received in any calendar year on covered policies less premiums, considerations, and deposits returned thereon, and less dividends and experience credits thereon. "Premiums" does not include any amounts received for any policies or for the parts of any policies for which coverage is not provided under G.S. 58-62-21(b); except that assessable premium shall not be reduced on account of G.S. 58-62-21(c)(3) relating to interest limitations and G.S. 58-62-21(d)(2) relating to limitations with respect to any one individual, any one participant, and any one contract holder.
(17) "Resident" means any person who resides in this State when a member insurer is determined to be a delinquent insurer and to whom a contractual obligation is owed. A person may be a resident of only one state, which in the case of a person other than a natural person shall be its principal place of business. "Resident" also means a U.S. citizen residing outside of the United States who owns a covered policy that was purchased from a member insurer while that person resided in this State.
(18) "Unallocated annuity contract" means any annuity contract or group annuity certificate that is not issued to and owned by an individual, except to the extent of any annuity benefits guaranteed to an individual by an insurer under the contract or certificate. (1991, c. 681, s. 56; 1993, c. 452, s. 60; 1995, c. 177, s. 1.)

§ **58-62-20:** Repealed by Session Laws 1991, c. 681, s. 57.

§ **58-62-21. Coverage and limitations.**

(a) This Article provides coverage for the policies and contracts specified in subsection (b) of this section:
(1) To persons who, regardless of where they reside (except for nonresident certificate holders under group policies), are the beneficiaries, assignees, or payees of the persons covered under subdivision (2) of this subsection, and
(2) To persons who are owners or certificate holders under the policies, or in the case of unallocated annuity contracts to the persons who are the contract holders, and who are residents of this State, or who are not residents of this State, but only under all of the following conditions: (i) the insurers that issued the policies are domiciled in this State; (ii) the insurers never held a license in the states in which the persons reside; (iii) the states have associations similar to the association created by this Article; and (iv) the persons are not eligible for coverage by the associations.

(b) This Article provides coverage to the persons specified in subsection (a) of this section for direct, nongroup life, health, annuity, and supplemental policies, for certificates under direct group policies and contracts, and for unallocated annuity contracts issued by member insurers, except as limited by this Article. Annuity contracts and certificates under group annuity contracts include guaranteed investment contracts, deposit administration contracts, unallocated funding agreements, allocated funding agreements, structured settlement agreements, lottery contracts, and any immediate or deferred annuity contracts.

(c) This Article does not provide coverage for:

(1) Any part of a policy not guaranteed by the insurer, or under which the risk is borne by the policyholder;

(2) Any policy or contract of reinsurance, unless assumption certificates have been issued;

(3) Any part of a policy to the extent that the rate of interest on which it is based:

a. Averaged over the period of four years before the date on which the Association becomes obligated with respect to the policy, exceeds a rate of interest determined by subtracting two percentage points from Moody's Corporate Bond Yield Average averaged for that same four-year period or for a lesser period if the policy was issued less than four years before the Association became obligated; and

b. On and after the date on which the Association becomes obligated with respect to the policy, exceeds the rate of interest determined by subtracting three percentage points from Moody's Corporate Bond Yield Average as most recently available;

(4) Any plan or program of an employer, association, or similar entity to provide life, health, or annuity benefits to its employees or members to the extent that the plan or program is self-funded or uninsured, including benefits payable by an employer, association, or similar entity under:

a. A multiple employer welfare arrangement as defined in section 514 of the Employee Retirement Income Security Act of 1974, as amended;

b. A minimum premium group insurance plan;

c. A stop-loss group insurance plan; or

d. An administrative services only contract;

(5) Any part of a policy to the extent that it provides dividends or experience-rating credits, or provides that any fees or allowances be paid to any person, including the policyholder, in connection with the service to or administration of the policy;

(6) Any policy issued in this State by a member insurer at a time when it was not licensed to issue the policy in this State;

(7) Any unallocated annuity contract issued to an employee benefit plan protected under the federal Pension Benefit Guaranty Corporation; and

(8) Any part of any unallocated annuity contract that is not issued to or in connection with a specific employee, union, or association of natural persons benefit plan or a government lottery.

(d) The benefits for which the Association is liable do not, in any event, exceed the lesser of:

(1) The contractual obligations for which the insurer is liable or would have been liable if it were not a delinquent insurer; or

(2) With respect to any one individual, regardless of the number of policies, three hundred thousand dollars ($300,000) for all benefits, including cash values; or

(3) With respect to each individual participating in a governmental retirement plan established under section 401, 403(b), or 457 of the Internal Revenue Code covered by an unallocated annuity contract, or the beneficiaries of each individual if deceased, in the aggregate, three hundred thousand dollars ($300,000) in present value annuity benefits, including net cash surrender and net cash withdrawal values; or

(4) With respect to any one contract holder covered by any unallocated annuity contract not included in subdivision (3) of this subsection, five million dollars ($5,000,000) in benefits, regardless of the number of such contracts held by that contract holder.

(e) In no event is the Association liable to expend more than three hundred thousand dollars ($300,000) in the aggregate with respect to any one individual under this section. (1991, c. 681, s. 56; c. 720, s. 93; 1993, c. 452, s. 61.)

§ **58-62-25:** Repealed by Session Laws 1991, c. 681, s. 57.

§ **58-62-26. Creation of the Association.**

(a) There is created a nonprofit legal entity to be known as the North Carolina Life and Health Insurance Guaranty Association. All member insurers shall be and remain members of the Association as a condition of their authority to transact insurance in this State. The Association shall perform its functions under the Plan established and approved under G.S. 58-62-46 and shall exercise its powers through the Board established under G.S. 58-62-31. For purposes of administration and assessment, the Association shall maintain two accounts:

(1) The life insurance and annuity account, which includes the following subaccounts:
    a. Life insurance account;
    b. Annuity account.
(2) The health insurance account.

(b) The Association is under the immediate supervision of the Commissioner and is subject to the applicable provisions of this Chapter. Meetings or records of the Association may be opened to the public upon majority vote of the Board. (1991, c. 681, s. 56.)

§ **58-62-30:** Repealed by Session Laws 1991, c. 681, s. 57.

§ **58-62-31. Board of directors.**

(a) The Board shall consist of not less than five nor more than nine member insurers serving terms as established in the Plan. The members of the Board shall be selected by member insurers, subject to the Commissioner's approval. Vacancies on the Board shall be filled for the remaining period of the term by a majority vote of the remaining Board members, subject to the Commissioner's approval. To select the initial Board, and initially organize the Association, the Board's predecessor shall notify all member insurers of the time and place of the organizational meeting. In determining voting rights at the organizational meeting, each member insurer is entitled to one vote in person or by proxy. If the Board is not selected within 60 days after notice of the organizational meeting, the Commissioner may appoint the initial members.

(b) In approving selections or in appointing members to the Board, the Commissioner shall consider, among other things, whether all member insurers are fairly represented.

(c) Members of the Board may be reimbursed from the assets of the Association for expenses they incur as members of the Board, but they shall not otherwise be compensated by the Association for their services. (1991, c. 681, s. 56.)

§ **58-62-35:** Repealed by Session Laws 1991, c. 681, s. 57.

§ 58-62-36. Powers and duties of the Association.

(a) If a member insurer is an impaired domestic insurer, the Association may, subject to any conditions imposed by the Association and approved by the Commissioner that do not impair the contractual obligations of the impaired insurer and that are, except in cases of court-ordered conservation or rehabilitation, also approved by the impaired insurer:

    (1) Guarantee, assume, or reinsure, or cause to be guaranteed, assumed, or reinsured, any or all of the policies of the impaired insurer;

    (2) Provide such monies, pledges, notes, guarantees, or other means as are proper to carry out subdivision (1) of this subsection and assure payment of the contractual obligations of the impaired insurer pending action under subdivision (1) of this subsection; or

    (3) Lend money to the impaired insurer.

(b) If a member insurer is an impaired insurer, whether domestic, foreign, or alien, and the insurer is not paying claims in a timely manner, then subject to the preconditions specified in subsection (c) of this section, the Association shall, in its discretion, either:

    (1) Take any of the actions specified in subsection (a) of this section, subject to the conditions therein; or

    (2) Provide substitute benefits in lieu of the contractual obligations of the impaired insurer solely for health claims, periodic annuity benefit payments, death benefits, supplemental benefits, and cash withdrawals for policyowners who petition therefor under claims of emergency or hardship in accordance with standards proposed by the Association and approved by the Commissioner.

(c) The Association is subject to the requirements of subsection (b) of this section only if:

    (1) The laws of the impaired insurer's state of domicile provide that until all payments of or on account of the impaired insurer's contractual obligations by all guaranty associations, along with all expenses thereof and interest on all the payments and expenses, have been repaid to the guaranty associations or a plan of repayment by the impaired insurer has been approved by the guaranty associations, the delinquency proceeding shall not be dismissed; neither the impaired insurer nor its assets may be returned to the control of its shareholders or private management; and the impaired insurer may not solicit or accept new business or have any suspended or revoked license restored; and

    (2) The impaired insurer is a domestic insurer that has been placed under an order of rehabilitation by a court of competent jurisdiction in this State; or the impaired insurer is a foreign or alien insurer that has been prohibited from soliciting or accepting new business in this State, its license has been suspended or revoked in this State, and a petition for rehabilitation or liquidation has been filed in a court of competent jurisdiction in its state of domicile by that state's insurance regulator.

(d) If a member insurer is an insolvent insurer, the Association shall, in its discretion, either:

    (1) Guarantee, assume or reinsure, or cause to be guaranteed, assumed, or reinsured, the policies of the insolvent insurer; or

    (2) Assure payment of the contractual obligations of the insolvent insurer; and

    (3) Provide such monies, pledges, guarantees, or other means as are reasonably necessary to discharge those duties; or

    (4) With respect only to life and health insurance policies, provide benefits and coverages in accordance with subsection (e) of this section.

(e) When proceeding under subdivision (b)(2) or (d)(4) of this section, the Association shall, with respect to only life and health insurance policies:

(1) Assure payment of benefits for premiums identical to the premiums and benefits (except for terms of conversion and renewability) that would have been payable under the policies of the insolvent insurer, for claims incurred:

    a. With respect to group policies, not later than the earlier of the next renewal date under the policies or 45 days, but in no event less than 30 days after the date on which the Association becomes obligated with respect to the policies;

    b. With respect to individual policies, not later than the earlier of the next renewal date (if any) under the policies or one year, but in no event less than 30 days from the date on which the Association becomes obligated with respect to the policies;

(2) Make diligent efforts to provide all known insureds or group policyholders with respect to group policies 30 days' notice of the termination of the benefits provided; and

(3) With respect to individual policies, make available to each known insured, or owner if other than the insured, and with respect to an individual formerly insured under a group policy who is not eligible for replacement group coverage, make available substitute coverage on an individual basis in accordance with the provisions of subsection (f) of this section, if the insured had a right under law or the terminated policy to convert coverage to individual coverage or to continue an individual policy in force until a specified age or for a specified time, during which the insurer had no right unilaterally to make changes in any provision of the policy or had a right only to make changes in premium by class.

(f) In providing the substitute coverage required under subdivision (e)(3) of this section, the Association may offer either to reissue the terminated coverage or to issue an alternative policy. An alternative or reissued policy shall be offered without requiring evidence of insurability, and shall not provide for any waiting period or exclusion that would not have applied under the terminated policy. The Association may reinsure any alternative or reissued policy.

(g) Alternative life or health insurance policies adopted by the Association are subject to the Commissioner's approval. The Association may adopt alternative policies of various types for future issuance without regard to any particular delinquency. Alternative policies shall contain at least the minimum statutory provisions required in this State and provide benefits that are not unreasonable in relation to the premium charged. The Association shall set the premium in accordance with a table of rates, which it shall adopt. The premium shall reflect the amount of insurance to be provided and the age and class of risk of each insured, but it shall not reflect any changes in the health of the insured after the original policy was last underwritten. Any alternative policy issued by the Association shall provide coverage of a type similar to that of the policy issued by the delinquent insurer, as determined by the Association.

(h) If the Association elects to reissue terminated coverage at a premium rate different from that charged under the terminated life or health insurance policy, the premium shall be set by the Association in accordance with the amount of insurance provided and the age and class of risk, subject to the approval of the Commissioner or by a court of competent jurisdiction.

(i) The Association's obligations with respect to coverage under any life or health insurance policy of the delinquent insurer or under any reissued or alternative policy cease on the date the coverage or policy is replaced by another similar policy by the policyholder, the insured, or the Association.

(j) When proceeding under subdivision (b)(2) of this section or under subsection (c) of this section with respect to any policy carrying guaranteed minimum interest rates, the Association shall assure the payment or crediting of a rate of interest consistent with G.S. 58-62-21(c)(3).

(k) Nonpayment of premiums within 31 days after the date required under the terms of any guaranteed, assumed, alternative, or reissued policy or substitute coverage terminates the Association's obligations under the policy or coverage under this Article with respect to the policy or coverage, except with respect to any claims incurred or any net cash surrender value that may be due under this Article.

(l) Premiums due for coverage after an entry of an order of liquidation of an insolvent insurer belong to and are payable at the direction of the Association; and the Association is liable for unearned premiums owed to policyowners arising after the entry of the order.

(m) The protection provided by this Article does not apply where any similar guaranty protection is provided to residents of this State by the laws of the domiciliary state or jurisdiction of a delinquent foreign or alien insurer.

(n) In carrying out its duties under subsections (b) through (d) of this section, the Association may, subject to approval by the court:

    (1) Impose permanent policy liens in connection with any guarantee, assumption, or reinsurance agreement, if the Association finds that the amounts that can be assessed under this Article are less than the amounts needed to assure full and prompt performance of the Association's duties under this Article, or that the economic or financial conditions as they affect member insurers are sufficiently adverse to render the imposition of the permanent policy liens to be in the public interest;

    (2) Impose temporary moratoria or liens on payments of cash values and policy loans, or any other right to withdraw funds held in conjunction with policies, in addition to any contractual provisions for deferral of cash or policy loan value.

(o) If the Association fails to act within a reasonable period of time as provided in subdivision (b)(2) of this section and subsections (d) and (e) of this section, the Commissioner has the powers and duties of the Association under this Article with respect to delinquent insurers.

(p) The Association may render assistance and advice to the Commissioner, upon the Commissioner's request concerning rehabilitation, payment of claims, continuance of coverage, or the performance of other contractual obligations of any delinquent insurer.

(q) The Association has standing to appear before any court in this State with jurisdiction over a delinquent insurer for which the Association is or may become obligated under this Article. This standing extends to all matters germane to the powers and duties of the Association, including, but not limited to, proposals for reinsuring, modifying, or guaranteeing the policies of the delinquent insurer and the determination of the policies and contractual obligations. The Association also has the right to appear or intervene before a court in another state with jurisdiction over a delinquent insurer for which the Association is or may become obligated or with jurisdiction over a third party against whom the Association may have rights through subrogation of the insurer's policyholders.

(r) Any person receiving benefits under this Article is considered to have been assigned the rights under, and any causes of action relating to, the covered policy to the Association to the extent of the benefits received because of this Article, whether the benefits are payments of or on account of contractual obligations, continuance of coverage, or provision of substitute or alternative coverages. The Association may require an assignment to it of such rights and cause of action by any payee, policyowner, beneficiary, insured or annuitant as a condition precedent to the receipt of any right or benefits conferred by this Article upon the person. The subrogation rights of the Association under this subsection have the same priority against the delinquent insurer's assets as that possessed by the person entitled to receive benefits under this Article. In addition to other provisions of this subsection, the Association has all common-law rights of subrogation and any other equitable or legal remedy that would have been available to the delinquent insurer or holder of a policy with respect to the policy.

(s) The Association may:

    (1) Enter into contracts that are necessary or proper to carry out the provisions and purposes of this Article;

    (2) Sue or be sued, including taking any legal actions necessary or proper to recover any unpaid assessments under G.S. 58-62-41 and to settle claims or potential claims against it;

    (3) Borrow money to effect the purposes of this Article; any notes or other evidence of indebtedness of the Association not in default shall be legal investments for domestic insurers and may be carried as admitted assets;

    (4) Employ or retain persons that are necessary to handle the financial transactions of the Association, and to perform other functions that become necessary or proper under this Article;

    (5) Take legal action that may be necessary to avoid payment of improper claims;

    (6) Exercise, for the purposes of this Article and to the extent approved by the Commissioner, the powers of a domestic life or health insurer, but in no case may the Association issue insurance policies or annuity contracts other than those issued to perform its obligations under this Article.

(t) The Association may join an organization of one or more other state associations of similar purposes, in order to further the purposes of this Article and administer the powers and duties of the Association. (1991, c. 681, s. 56; c. 720, s. 94.)

§ 58-62-40: Repealed by Session Laws 1991, c. 681, s. 57.

§ 58-62-41. Assessments.

(a) To provide the funds necessary to carry out the powers and duties of the Association, the Board shall assess the member insurers, separately for each account, at such time and for such amounts as the Board finds necessary. Assessments are due not less than 30 days after prior written notice to the member insurers and shall accrue interest at the rate of one percent (1%) per month, or any part thereof, after the due date.

(b) There shall be two classes of assessments, as follows:

    (1) Class A assessments shall be made for the purpose of meeting administrative and legal costs and other expenses and examinations conducted under the authority of G.S. 58-62-56(e). Class A assessments may be made whether or not they are related to a particular delinquent insurer.

    (2) Class B assessments shall be made to the extent necessary to carry out the powers and duties of the Association under G.S. 58-62-36 with regard to a delinquent insurer.

(c) The amount of any Class A assessment shall be determined by the Board and may or may not be prorated. If prorated, the Board may provide that it be credited against future Class B assessments. If not prorated, the assessment shall not exceed one hundred fifty dollars ($150.00) per member insurer in any one calendar year. The amount of any Class B assessment shall be allocated for assessment purposes among the accounts pursuant to an allocation formula, which may be based on the premiums or reserves of the delinquent insurer or any other standard considered by the Board in its sole discretion to be fair and reasonable under the circumstances.

(d) Class B assessments against member insurers for each account and subaccount shall be in the proportion that the premiums received on business in this State by each assessed member insurer or policies covered by each account for the three most recent calendar years for which information is available preceding the year in which the insurer became delinquent, as the case may be, bears to the premiums received on business in this State for those calendar years by all assessed member insurers.

(e) Assessments for funds to meet the requirements of the Association with respect to a delinquent insurer shall not be made until necessary to implement the purposes of this Article. Classification of assessments under subsection (b) of this section and computation of assessments under this subsection shall be made with a reasonable degree of accuracy, recognizing that exact determinations may not always be possible.

(f) The Association may abate or defer, in whole or in part, the assessment of a member insurer if, in the Board's opinion, payment of the assessment would endanger the member insurer's ability to fulfill its contractual obligations. If an assessment against a member insurer is abated, or deferred in whole or in part, the amount by which the assessment is abated or deferred may be assessed against the other member insurers in a manner consistent with the basis for assessments set forth in this section.

(g) The total of all assessments upon a member insurer for the life and annuity account and for each subaccount thereunder shall not in any one calendar year exceed two percent (2%) and for the health account shall not in any one calendar year exceed two percent (2%) of the insurer's average premiums received in this State on the policies and contracts covered by the account during the three calendar years preceding the year in which an insurer became a delinquent insurer. If the maximum assessment, together with the other assets of the Association in any account, does not provide in any one year in either account an amount sufficient to carry out the Association's responsibilities, the necessary additional funds shall be assessed as soon thereafter as permitted by this Article.

(h) The Board may provide in the Plan a method of allocating funds among claims, whether relating to one or more delinquent insurers, when the maximum assessment will be insufficient to cover anticipated claims.

(i) If a one percent (1%) assessment for any subaccount of the life and annuity account in any one year does not provide an amount sufficient to carry out the Association's responsibilities, then under subsection (d) of this section, the Board shall assess all subaccounts of the life and annuity account for the necessary additional amount, subject to the maximum stated in subsection (g) of this section.

(j) The Board may, by an equitable method as established in the Plan, refund to member insurers, in proportion to the contribution of each insurer to that account, the amount by which the assets of the account exceed the amount the Board finds is necessary to carry out during the coming year the obligations of the Association with regard to that account, including assets accruing from assignment, subrogation, net realized gains, and income from investments. A reasonable amount may be retained in any account to provide funds for the continuing expenses of the Association and for future losses.

(k) It is proper for any member insurer, in determining its premium rates and policyowner dividends as to any kind of insurance within the scope of this

Article, to consider the amount reasonably necessary to meet its assessment obligations under this Article.

(*l*) The Association shall issue to each insurer paying an assessment under this Article, other than a Class A assessment, a certificate of contribution, in a form prescribed by the Commissioner, for the amount of the assessment so paid. All outstanding certificates shall be of equal dignity and priority without reference to amounts or dates of issue. (1991, c. 681, s. 56; 1993, c. 452, ss. 61.1, 62; 1995, c. 193, ss. 47, 48.)

§ **58-62-45:** Repealed by Session Laws 1991, c. 681, s. 57.

§ **58-62-46. Plan of operation.**

(a) The Association shall submit to the Commissioner a Plan and any amendments necessary or suitable to assure the fair, reasonable, and equitable administration of the Association. The Plan and any amendments shall become effective upon the Commissioner's written approval or unless the Commissioner has not disapproved it within 30 days.

(b) If the Association fails to submit a suitable Plan within 120 days after the effective date of this Article or if at any time thereafter the Association fails to submit suitable amendments to the Plan, the Commissioner shall, after notice and hearing, adopt rules that are necessary or advisable to carry out the provisions of this Article. The rules shall continue in force until modified by the Commissioner or superseded by a Plan submitted by the Association and approved by the Commissioner.

(c) All member insurers shall comply with the Plan.

(d) The Plan shall, in addition to other requirements specified in this Article, establish:

    (1) Procedures for handling the assets of the Association;

    (2) The amount and method of reimbursing members of the Board under G.S. 58-62-31;

    (3) Regular places and times for meetings, including telephone conference calls, of the Board;

    (4) Procedures for records to be kept of all financial transactions of the Association, its agents, and the Board;

    (5) The procedures whereby selections for the Board will be made and submitted to the Commissioner;

    (6) Any additional procedures for assessments under G.S. 58-62-41;

    (7) Additional provisions necessary or proper for the execution of the powers and duties of the Association.

(e) The Plan may provide that any or all powers and duties of the Association, except those under G.S. 58-62-36(r) and G.S. 58-62-41, may be delegated to a corporation, association, or other organization that performs or will perform functions similar to those of the Association, or its equivalent, in two or more states. Such a corporation, association, or organization shall be reimbursed for any payments made on behalf of the Association and shall be paid for its performance of any function of the Association. A delegation under this subsection is effective only with the approval of both the Board and the Commissioner, and may be made only to a corporation, association, or organization that extends protection not substantially less favorable and effective than that provided by this Article. (1991, c. 681, s. 56.)

§ **58-62-50:** Repealed by Session Laws 1991, c. 681, s. 57.

§ 58-62-51. Duties and powers of the Commissioner.

(a) In addition to other duties and powers specified in this Article, the Commissioner shall:

    (1) Upon request of the Board, provide the Association with a statement of the premiums in this State and any other appropriate states for each member insurer;

    (2) When an impairment is declared and the amount of the impairment is determined, serve a demand upon the impaired insurer to make good the impairment within a reasonable time; notice to the impaired insurer shall constitute notice to its shareholders, if any; the failure of the insurer to comply promptly with the demand does not excuse the Association from the performance of its powers and duties under this Article; and

    (3) In any liquidation or rehabilitation proceeding involving a domestic insurer, be appointed as the liquidator or rehabilitator as provided in Article 30 of this Chapter.

(b) The Commissioner may suspend or revoke, after notice and hearing, the license to transact insurance in this State of any member insurer that fails to pay an assessment when due or fails to comply with the Plan. As an alternative the Commissioner may levy a forfeiture on any member insurer that fails to pay an assessment when due. The forfeiture shall not exceed five percent (5%) of the unpaid assessment per month, but no forfeiture shall be less than one hundred dollars ($100.00) per month.

(c) Any action of the Board or the Association may be appealed to the Commissioner by any member insurer if the appeal is taken within 60 days of the final action being appealed. If a member company is appealing an assessment, the amount assessed shall be paid to the Association and available to meet Association obligations during the pendency of an appeal. If the appeal on the assessment is upheld, the amount paid in error or excess shall be returned to the member company. No later than 20 days before each hearing, the appellant shall file with the Commissioner or the Commissioner's designated hearing officer and shall serve on the appellee a written statement of the appellant's case and any evidence the appellant intends to offer at the hearing. No later than five days before the hearing, the appellee shall file with the Commissioner or the Commissioner's designated hearing officer and shall serve on the appellant a written statement of the appellee's case and any evidence the appellee intends to offer at the hearing. Each hearing shall be recorded and transcribed. The cost of the recording and transcribing shall be borne equally by the appellant and appellee; however, upon any final adjudication the prevailing party shall be reimbursed for that party's share of the costs by the other party. Each party shall, on a date determined by the Commissioner or the Commissioner's designated hearing officer, but not sooner than 15 days after delivery of the completed transcript to the party, submit to the Commissioner or the Commissioner's designated hearing officer and serve on the other party, a proposed order. The Commissioner or the Commissioner's designated hearing officer shall then issue an order. Any final action or order of the Commissioner or the Commissioner's designated hearing officer is subject to judicial review under G.S. 58-2-75.

(d) The liquidator, rehabilitator, or conservator of any impaired insurer may notify all interested persons of the effect of this Article. (1991, c. 681, s. 56.)

§ **58-62-55:** Repealed by Session Laws 1991, c. 681, s. 57.

§ 58-62-56. Prevention of delinquencies.

(a) To aid in the detection and prevention of insurer delinquencies, it is the Commissioner's duty to:

(1) Notify insurance regulators when revoking or suspending the license of a member insurer, or making any formal order that the insurer restrict its premium writing, obtain additional contributions to surplus, withdraw from this State, reinsure all or any part of its business, or increase capital, surplus, or any other account for the security of policyholders or creditors. That notice shall be sent electronically through the NAIC headquarters and mailed to all insurance regulators within 30 days following the action taken or the date on which the action occurs.

(2) Report to the Board when the Commissioner has taken any of the actions in subdivision (1) of this subsection or has received a report from another insurance regulator indicating that any such action has been taken in another state. The report to the Board shall contain all significant details of the action taken or the report received from another insurance regulator.

(3) Report to the Board when the Commissioner has reasonable cause to believe from any examination, whether completed or in process, of any member insurer that the insurer may be delinquent.

(4) Furnish the Board with the NAIC Insurance Regulatory Information System financial test ratios and a listing of companies that are not included in the ratios developed by the NAIC; and the Board may use that data in carrying out its duties and responsibilities under this section. The data shall be kept confidential by the Board until it is made public by the Commissioner or another lawful authority.

(b) The Commissioner may seek the advice and recommendations of the Board concerning any matter affecting the Commissioner's duties and responsibilities regarding the financial condition of member insurers and other entities seeking admission to transact insurance business in this State.

(c) The Board may, upon majority vote, make reports and recommendations to the Commissioner upon any matter germane to the solvency, liquidation, rehabilitation, or conservation of any member insurer or germane to the solvency of any company seeking to do an insurance business in this State. The reports and recommendations are not public records.

(d) The Board shall, upon majority vote, notify the Commissioner of any information indicating that any member insurer may be delinquent.

(e) The Board may, upon majority vote, request that the Commissioner order an examination of any member insurer that the Board in good faith believes may be delinquent. Within 30 days of the receipt of the request, the Commissioner shall begin the examination. The examination may be conducted as an NAIC examination or may be conducted by persons the Commissioner designates. The examination report shall be treated as are other examination reports. In no event shall the examination report be released to the Board before its release to the public; but this does not preclude the Commissioner from complying with subsection (a) of this section. The Commissioner shall notify the Board when the examination is completed. The request for an examination shall be kept on file by the Commissioner, but shall not be open to public inspection before the release of the examination report to the public.

(f) The Board may, upon majority vote, make recommendations to the Commissioner for the detection and prevention of insurer delinquencies.

(g) The Board shall, at the conclusion of any insurer insolvency in which the Association was obligated to pay covered claims, prepare a report to the

Commissioner containing any information that it has in its possession bearing on the history and causes of the insolvency. The Board shall cooperate with the boards of directors of guaranty associations in other states in preparing a report on the history and causes of insolvency of a particular insurer, and the Board may adopt by reference any report prepared by such other associations. (1991, c. 681, s. 56; 1995, c. 360, s. 2(k).)

§ **58-62-60:** Repealed by Session Laws 1991, c. 681, s. 57.

§ 58-62-61. Miscellaneous provisions.

(a) Nothing in this Article reduces the liability for unpaid assessments of the insureds of a delinquent insurer operating under an insurance plan with assessment liability.

(b) Records shall be kept of all negotiations and meetings in which the Association or its representatives are involved and in which the activities of the Association in carrying out its powers and duties under G.S. 58-62-36 are discussed. Records of those negotiations or meetings shall be made public only upon the termination of a liquidation, rehabilitation, or conservation proceeding involving the delinquent insurer, upon the termination of the delinquency of the insurer, or upon the order of a court of competent jurisdiction. Nothing in this subsection limits the duty of the Association to render a report of its activities under G.S. 58-62-66.

(c) For the purpose of carrying out its obligations under this Article, the Association is a creditor of the delinquent insurer to the extent of assets attributable to covered policies reduced by any amounts to which the Association is entitled as subrogee under G.S. 58-62-36(r). Assets of the delinquent insurer attributable to covered policies shall be used to continue all covered policies and pay all contractual obligations of the delinquent insurer as required by this Article. Assets attributable to covered policies, as used in this subsection, are that proportion of the assets that the reserves that should have been established for the policies bear to the reserves that should have been established for all policies of insurance written by the delinquent insurer.

(d) Before the termination of any liquidation, rehabilitation, or conservation proceeding, the court may take into consideration the contributions of the respective parties, including the Association, the shareholders, and policyowners of the insolvent insurer, and any other party with a bona fide interest, in making an equitable distribution of the ownership rights of the insolvent insurer. In making such a determination, consideration shall be given to the welfare of the policyholders of the continuing or successor insurer.

(e) No distribution to stockholders, if any, of a delinquent insurer shall be made until and unless the Association has fully recovered the total amount of its valid claims with interest thereon for funds expended in carrying out its powers and duties under G.S. 58-62-36 with respect to the insurer.

(f) If an order for liquidation or rehabilitation of an insurer domiciled in this State has been entered, the receiver appointed under the order has a right to recover on behalf of the insurer, from any affiliate that controlled it, the amount of distributions, other than stock dividends paid by the insurer on its capital stock, made at any time during the five years preceding the petition for liquidation or rehabilitation subject to the limitations of subsections (g) through (i) of this section.

(g) No such distribution is recoverable if the insurer shows that when paid the distribution was lawful and reasonable, and that the insurer did not know and could not reasonably have known that the distribution might adversely affect the insurer's ability to fulfill its contractual obligations.

(h) Any person who was an affiliate that controlled the insurer when the distributions were paid is liable up to the amount of distributions it received. Any person who was an affiliate that controlled the insurer when the distributions were declared is liable up to the amount of distributions it would have received if they had been paid immediately. If two or more persons are liable with respect to the same distributions, they are jointly and severally liable.

(i) The maximum amount recoverable under this subsection is the amount needed in excess of all other available assets of the insolvent insurer to pay the insolvent insurer's contractual obligations.

(j) If any person liable under subsection (h) of this section is insolvent, all of its affiliates that controlled it when the distribution was paid are jointly and severally liable for any resulting deficiency in the amount recovered from the insolvent affiliate. (1991, c. 681, s. 56.)

§ **58-62-65:** Repealed by Session Laws 1991, c. 681, s. 57.

§ **58-62-66. Examination of the Association; annual report.**

The Association is subject to examination and regulation by the Commissioner. The Board shall submit to the Commissioner each year, not later than 120 days after the Association's fiscal year, a financial report in a form approved by the Commissioner and a report of its activities during the preceding fiscal year. (1991, c. 681, s. 56.)

§ **58-62-70:** Repealed by Session Laws 1991, c. 681, s. 57.

§ **58-62-75. Tax exemptions.**

The Association shall be exempt from payment of all fees and all taxes levied by this State or any of its subdivisions, except taxes levied on real property. (1973, c. 1438, s. 1.)

§ **58-62-76. Immunity.**

There is no liability by, and no cause of action of any nature arises against, any member insurer or its agents or employees, the Association or its agents or employees, members of the Board, the Commissioner or the Commissioner's representatives, or insurance regulators or their representatives, for any act or omission by them in the performance of their powers and duties under this Article. This immunity extends to the participation in any organization of one or more other state associations of similar purposes and to any such organization and its agents or employees. (1991, c. 681, s. 56.)

§ **58-62-77. Actions not precluded.**

Nothing in this Article precludes any resident from bringing any action against the Association in any court of competent jurisdiction with respect to any contractual obligation arising under covered policies. (1993 (Reg. Sess., 1994), c. 678, s. 26.)

§ **58-62-80:** Repealed by Session Laws 1991, c. 681, s. 57.

§ 58-62-81. Stay of proceedings; reopening default judgments.

All proceedings in which the insolvent insurer is a party in any court in this State shall be stayed 60 days from the date an order of liquidation, rehabilitation, or conservation is final to permit proper legal action by the Association on any matters germane to its powers or duties. As to a judgment under any decision, order, verdict or finding based on default, the Association may apply to have the judgment set aside by the same court that made the judgment and may defend against such suit on the merits. (1991, c. 681, s. 56.)

§ 58-62-85: Repealed by Session Laws 1991, c. 681, s. 57.

§ 58-62-86. Prohibited advertisement of Article in insurance sales; notice to policyholders.

(a) No person shall make, publish, disseminate, circulate, or place before the public, or cause directly or indirectly to be made, published, disseminated, circulated, or placed before the public, in any newspaper, magazine, or other publication, or in the form of a notice, circular, pamphlet, letter, or poster, or over any radio station or television station, or in any other way, any oral or written advertisement, announcement, or statement that uses the existence of the Association or this Article for the purpose of sale or solicitation of or inducement to purchase any kind of insurance covered by this Article. However, this subsection does not apply to the Association or any other person who does not sell or solicit insurance.

(b) Within 180 days after the effective date of this Article, the Association shall prepare a summary document that describes the general purposes and current limitations of this Article and that complies with subsection (c) of this section. This document shall be submitted to the Commissioner for the Commissioner's approval. Sixty days after receiving approval, no insurer may deliver a policy described in G.S. 58-62-21(b) to any person unless the document is delivered to that person before or at the time of delivery of the policy, unless subsection (d) of this section applies. The document shall also be available upon request by a policyholder. The distribution, delivery, contents, or interpretation of this document does not mean that either the policy or the policyholder would be covered in the event of the delinquency of a member insurer. The document shall be revised by the Association as amendments to this Article require. Failure to receive this document does not give any person greater rights than those stated in this Article.

(c) The document prepared under subsection (b) of this section shall contain a clear and conspicuous disclaimer on its face. The Commissioner shall prescribe the form and content of the disclaimer. The disclaimer shall:

(1) State the name and addresses of the Association and Department;
(2) Prominently warn the policyholder that the Association may not cover the policy or, if coverage is available, it will be subject to substantial limitations and exclusions and conditioned on continued residence in this State;
(3) State that the insurer and its agents are prohibited by law from using the existence of the Association for the purpose of sale or solicitation of or inducement to purchase any kind of insurance;
(4) Emphasize that the applicant or policyholder should not rely on coverage under the Association when selecting an insurer; and
(5) Provide other information as directed by the Commissioner.

(d) No insurer or agent may deliver a policy described in G.S. 58-62-21(b) and excluded under G.S. 58-62-21(c) from coverage under this Article unless the insurer or agent, before or at the time of delivery, gives the policyholder a separate written notice that clearly and conspicuously discloses that the policy is not covered by the Association. The Commissioner shall prescribe the form and content of the notice. (1991, c. 681, s. 56.)

§ **58-62-90:** Repealed by Session Laws 1991, c. 681, s. 57.

§ **58-62-92:** Repealed by Session Laws 1993 (Reg. Sess., 1994), c. 678, s. 27.

§ 58-62-95. Use of deposits made by impaired insurer.

Notwithstanding any other provision of this Chapter pertaining to the use of deposits made by insurance companies for the protection of policyholders, the Association shall receive, upon its request, from the Commissioner and may expend, any deposit or deposits made, whether or not made pursuant to statute, by an insurer determined to be impaired under this Article to the extent those deposits are needed by the Association to pay contractual obligations of that impaired insurer owed under covered policies as required by this Article, and to the extent those deposits are needed to pay all expenses of the Association relating to the impaired insurer: Provided that the Commissioner may retain and use an amount of the deposit up to ten thousand dollars ($10,000) to defray administrative costs to be incurred by the Commissioner in carrying out his powers and duties with respect to the insolvent insurer, notwithstanding G.S. 58-5-70. The Association shall account to the Commissioner and the impaired insurer for all deposits received from the Commissioner under this section. After the deposits of the impaired insurer received by the Association under this section have been expended by the Association for the purposes set out in this section, the member insurers shall be assessed as provided by this Article to pay any remaining liabilities of the Association arising under this Article. (1979, c. 418; 1985, c. 666, s. 42; 1989, c. 452, s. 6; 1993 (Reg. Sess., 1994), c. 678, s. 28.)

ARTICLE 63.

Unfair Trade Practices.

§ 58-63-1. Declaration of purpose.

The purpose of this Article is to regulate trade practices in the business of insurance in accordance with the intent of Congress as expressed in the Act of Congress of March 9, 1945 (Public Law 15, 79th Congress), by defining, or providing for the determination of, all such practices in this State which constitute unfair methods of competition or unfair or deceptive acts or practices and by prohibiting the trade practices so defined or determined. (1949, c. 1112.)

Legal Periodicals. — For brief discussion of this Article, see 27 N.C.L. Rev. 461 (1949).

For survey of 1979 administrative law, see 58 N.C.L. Rev. 1185 (1980).

For note, "Consumer Protection—The Unfair Trade Practice Act and the Insurance Code: Does Per Se Necessarily Preempt?" see 10 Campbell L. Rev. 487 (1988).

For article, "The Learned Profession Exemption of the North Carolina Deceptive Trade Practices Act: The Wrong Bright Line?," see 15 Campbell L. Rev. 223 (1993).

CASE NOTES

The purpose of this Article is not to make these sections the exclusive North Carolina remedy for unfair trade practices in the insurance industry. Ray v. United Family Life Ins. Co., 430 F. Supp. 1353 (W.D.N.C. 1977).

No action will lie against the North Carolina Insurance Guaranty Association for an insolvent insurer's violation of the Unfair or Deceptive Trade Practice Act. Bentley v. North Carolina Ins. Guar. Ass'n, 107 N.C. App. 1, 418 S.E.2d 705 (1992).

Federal Anti-Trust Law. — This Article was enacted to regulate trade practices in the insurance business in accordance with directives from federal anti-trust law. State ex rel. Comm'r of Ins. v. Integon Life Ins. Co., 28 N.C. App. 7, 220 S.E.2d 409 (1975).

This Article does not so comprehensively regulate unfair trade practices in the business of insurance in North Carolina as to preclude subjecting the acts complained of to the Sherman Anti-Trust Act, 15 U.S.C.A. § 1 et seq. Ray v. United Family Life Ins. Co., 430 F. Supp. 1353 (W.D.N.C. 1977).

Claims based on tortious acts arising from this article are unassignable personal torts. Horton v. New South Ins. Co., 122 N.C. App. 265, 468 S.E.2d 856, 1996 N.C. App. LEXIS 240 (1996), cert. denied, 472 S.E.2d 8 (1996).

Recovery Under § 75-1.1. — Plaintiff can recover damages under G.S. 75-1.1 even though unfair methods of competition perpetrated by persons engaged in the business of insurance are regulated by the insurance statutes which do not provide for civil damage actions. Ray v. United Family Life Ins. Co., 430 F. Supp. 1353 (W.D.N.C. 1977).

Unfair and deceptive acts and practices in the insurance industry are not regulated exclusively by this Article and may constitute the basis of recovery under G.S. 75-1.1. Ellis v. Smith-Broadhurst, Inc., 48 N.C. App. 180, 268 S.E.2d 271 (1980).

Recovery Under § 75-1.1. — Although it is true that jurisdiction under the Insurance Unfair Trade Practices Act lies in the Commissioner's office, unfair and deceptive acts in the insurance area are not regulated exclusively by this article, but are also actionable under G.S. 75-1.1. Golden Rule Ins. Co. v. Long, 113 N.C. App. 187, 439 S.E.2d 599 (1993).

No Rate Setting Authority. — This Article generally, and G.S. 58-63-10 specifically, contain no authority to issue orders setting premium rates. State ex rel. Comm'r of Ins. v. Integon Life Ins. Co., 28 N.C. App. 7, 220 S.E.2d 409 (1975).

Applied in Sharpe v. Nationwide Mut. Fire Ins. Co., 62 N.C. App. 564, 302 S.E.2d 893 (1983); First Fin. Sav. Bank, Inc. v. American Bankers Ins. Co., 783 F. Supp. 963 (E.D.N.C. 1991).

Cited in Pearce v. American Defender Life Ins. Co., 74 N.C. App. 620, 330 S.E.2d 9 (1985); Winston Realty Co. v. G.H.G., Inc., 314 N.C. 90, 331 S.E.2d 677 (1985).

§ 58-63-5. Definitions.

When used in this Article:
(1) Repealed by Session Laws 1991, c. 720, s. 6.
(2) "Person" means any individual, corporation, association, partnership, reciprocal exchange, interinsurer, Lloyds insurer, fraternal benefit society, and any other legal entity engaged in the business of insurance under this Chapter; and includes agents, brokers, limited representatives, and adjusters. (1949, c. 1112; 1987, c. 629, s. 10; 1991, c. 720, s. 6; 1999-244, s. 13.)

CASE NOTES

Business of Insurance Includes Interstate Securities Transactions. — The purpose of North Carolina Unfair and Deceptive Trade Practice Act would be frustrated if persons who serve as vital links in the marketing chain are not considered to be within the scope of these statutes. Accordingly, the phrase "engaged in the business of insurance" should be construed to include persons who engaged in interstate securities transactions. First Fin. Sav. Bank, Inc. v. American Bankers Ins. Co., 699 F. Supp. 1158 (E.D.N.C. 1988).

§ 58-63-10. Unfair methods of competition or unfair and deceptive acts or practices prohibited.

No person shall engage in this State in any trade practice which is defined in this Article as or determined pursuant to this Article to be an unfair method of competition or an unfair or deceptive act or practice in the business of insurance. (1949, c. 1112.)

Legal Periodicals. — For survey of 1979 administrative law, see 58 N.C.L. Rev. 1185 (1980).

For note, "Consumer Protection—The Unfair Trade Practice Act and the Insurance Code: Does Per Se Necessarily Preempt?" see 10 Campbell L. Rev. 487 (1988).

CASE NOTES

Nothing in this section grants authority to the Commissioner of Insurance to take any action whatsoever. It merely prohibits unfair methods of competition or unfair or deceptive acts or practices in the insurance industry, which are exhaustively defined in G.S. 58-63-15. State ex rel. Comm'r of Ins. v. Integon Life Ins. Co., 28 N.C. App. 7, 220 S.E.2d 409 (1975).

Limited Remedial Powers. — Moreover, G.S. 58-63-20 and 58-63-25 and former G.S. 58-63-30, which provide for the Commissioner's power to act in regard to "any unfair method of competition or in any unfair or deceptive act or practice prohibited by G.S. 58-63-10 ...," grant no remedial power to the Commissioner to remedy unfair trade practices other than the power to investigate, bring charges and issue cease and desist orders. State ex rel. Comm'r of Ins. v. Integon Life Ins. Co., 28 N.C. App. 7, 220 S.E.2d 409 (1975).

Charging of Excessive Rates Not within Prohibition of This Section. — Nothing in G.S. 58-63-15 declares the charging of excessive rates to be an act or practice within the prohibition of this section. State ex rel. Comm'r of Ins. v. Integon Life Ins. Co., 28 N.C. App. 7, 220 S.E.2d 409 (1975).

No Rate Setting Authority. — Clearly this Article generally, and this section specifically, contain no authority to issue orders setting premium rates. State ex rel. Comm'r of Ins. v. Integon Life Ins. Co., 28 N.C. App. 7, 220 S.E.2d 409 (1975).

Cited in Gray v. North Carolina Ins. Underwriting Ass'n, 132 N.C. App. 63, 510 S.E.2d 396 (1999); Anderson v. Lancaster Aviation, Inc., 220 F. Supp. 2d 524, 2002 U.S. Dist. LEXIS 18423 (M.D.N.C. 2002).

§ 58-63-15. Unfair methods of competition and unfair or deceptive acts or practices defined.

The following are hereby defined as unfair methods of competition and unfair and deceptive acts or practices in the business of insurance:

    (1) Misrepresentations and False Advertising of Policy Contracts. — Making, issuing, circulating, or causing to be made, issued or circulated, any estimate, illustration, circular or statement misrepresenting the terms of any policy issued or to be issued or the benefits or advantages promised thereby or the dividends or share of the surplus to be received thereon, or making any false or misleading statement as to the dividends or share or surplus previously paid on similar policies, or making any misleading representation or any misrepresentation as to the financial condition of any insurer, or as to the legal reserve system upon which any life insurer operates, or using any name or title of any policy or class of policies misrepresenting the true nature thereof, or making any misrepresentation to any policyholder insured in any company for the purpose of inducing or tending to induce such policyholder to lapse, forfeit, or surrender his insurance.

    (2) False Information and Advertising Generally. — Making, publishing, disseminating, circulating, or placing before the public, or causing,

directly or indirectly, to be made, published, disseminated, circulated, or placed before the public, in a newspaper, magazine or other publication, or in the form of a notice, circular, pamphlet, letter or poster, or over any radio station, or in any other way, an advertisement, announcement or statement containing any assertion, representation or statement with respect to the business of insurance or with respect to any person in the conduct of his insurance business, which is untrue, deceptive or misleading.

(3) Defamation. — Making, publishing, disseminating, or circulating, directly or indirectly, or aiding, abetting or encouraging the making, publishing, disseminating or circulating of any oral or written statement or any pamphlet, circular, article or literature which is false, or maliciously critical of or derogatory to the financial condition of an insurer, and which is calculated to injure any person engaged in the business of insurance.

(4) Boycott, Coercion and Intimidation. — Entering into any agreement to commit, or by any concerted action committing, any act of boycott, coercion or intimidation resulting in or tending to result in unreasonable restraint of, or monopoly in, the business of insurance.

(5) False Financial Statements. — Filing with any supervisory or other public official, or making, publishing, disseminating, circulating or delivering to any person, or placing before the public, or causing directly or indirectly, to be made, published, disseminated, circulated, delivered to any person, or placed before the public, any false statement of financial condition of an insurer with intent to deceive.

Making any false entry in any book, report or statement of any insurer with intent to deceive any agent or examiner lawfully appointed to examine into its condition or into any of its affairs, or any public official to whom such insurer is required by law to report, or who has authority by law to examine into its condition or into any of its affairs, or, with like intent, willfully omitting to make a true entry of any material fact pertaining to the business of such insurer in any book, report or statement of such insurer.

(6) Stock Operations and Insurance Company Advisory Board Contracts. — Issuing or delivering or permitting agents, officers, or employees to issue or deliver, agency company stock or other capital stock, or benefit certificates or shares in any common-law corporation, or securities or any special or any insurance company advisory board contracts or other contracts of any kind promising returns and profit as an inducement to insurance.

(7) Unfair Discrimination.

a. Making or permitting any unfair discrimination between individuals of the same class and equal expectation of life in the rates charged for any contract of life insurance or of life annuity or in the dividends or other benefits payable thereon, or in any other of the terms and conditions of such contract.

b. Making or permitting any unfair discrimination between individuals of the same class and of essentially the same hazard in the amount of premium, policy fees, or rates charged for any policy or contract of accident or health insurance or in the benefits payable thereunder, or in any of the terms or conditions of such contract, or in any other manner whatever.

c. Making or permitting any unfair discrimination between or among individuals or risks of the same class and of essentially the same hazard by refusing to issue, refusing to renew, cancelling, or limiting the amount of insurance coverage on a property or casualty risk because of the geographic location of the risk, unless:

    1. The refusal or limitation is for the purpose of preserving the solvency of the insurer and is not a mere pretext for unfair discrimination, or

    2. The refusal, cancellation, or limitation is required by law.

  d. Making or permitting any unfair discrimination between or among individuals or risks of the same class and of essentially the same hazard by refusing to issue, refusing to renew, cancelling, or limiting the amount of insurance coverage on a residential property risk, or the personal property contained therein, because of the age of the residential property, unless:

    1. The refusal or limitation is for the purpose of preserving the solvency of the insurer and is not a mere pretext for unfair discrimination, or

    2. The refusal, cancellation, or limitation is required by law.

(8) Rebates.

  a. Except as otherwise expressly provided by law, knowingly permitting or offering to make or making any contract of life insurance, life annuity or accident and health insurance, or agreement as to such contract other than as plainly expressed in the contract issued thereon, or paying or allowing, or giving or offering to pay, allow, or give, directly or indirectly, as inducement to such insurance, or annuity, any rebate of premiums payable on the contract, or any special favor or advantage in the dividends or other benefits thereon, or any valuable consideration or inducement whatever not specified in the contract; or giving, or selling, or purchasing or offering to give, sell, or purchase as inducement to such insurance or annuity or in connection therewith, any stocks, bonds, or other securities of any insurance company or other corporation, association, or partnership, or any dividends or profits accrued thereon, or anything of value whatsoever not specified in the contract.

  b. Nothing in subdivision (7) or paragraph a of subdivision (8) of this section shall be construed as including within the definition of discrimination or rebates any of the following practices:

    1. In the case of any contract of life insurance or life annuity, paying bonuses to policyholders or otherwise abating their premiums in whole or in part out of surplus accumulated from nonparticipating insurance, provided, that any such bonuses or abatement of premiums shall be fair and equitable to policyholders and for the best interests of the company and its policyholders;

    2. In the case of life insurance policies issued on the industrial debit plan, making allowance to policyholders who have continuously for a specified period made premium payments directly to an office of the insurer in an amount which fairly represents the saving in collection expense;

    3. Readjustment of the rate of premium for a group insurance policy based on the loss or expense experienced thereunder, at the end of the first or any subsequent policy year of insurance thereunder, which may be made retroactive only for such policy year.

  c. No insurer or employee thereof, and no broker or agent shall pay, allow, or give, or offer to pay, allow, or give, directly or indirectly, as an inducement to insurance, or after insurance has been effected, any rebate, discount, abatement, credit or reduction of the premium named in a policy of insurance, or any special favor or advantage in the dividends or other benefits to accrue thereon, or any valuable consideration or inducement whatever, not specified in the policy of insurance. Nothing herein contained shall be construed as prohibiting the payment of commissions or other compensation to regularly appointed and licensed agents and to brokers duly licensed by this State; nor as prohibiting any participating insurer from distributing to its policyholders dividends, savings or the unused or unabsorbed portion of premiums and premium deposits.

(9) Advertising of Health, Accident or Hospitalization Insurance. — In all advertising of policies, certificates or service plans of health, accident or hospitalization insurance, except those providing group coverage, where details of benefits provided by a particular policy, certificate or plan are set forth in any advertising material, such advertising material shall contain reference to the major exceptions or major clauses limiting or voiding liability contained in the policy, certificate or plan so advertised. The references to such exceptions or clauses shall be printed in a type no smaller than that used to set forth the benefits of the policy, certificate or plan. In all advertising of such policies, certificates or plans which contain a cancellation provision or a provision that the policies, certificates or plans may be renewed at the option of the company or medical service corporation only, such advertising material shall contain clear and definite reference to the fact that the policies, certificates or plans are cancellable or that the same may be renewed at the option of the company only.

In advertising, sale, or solicitation for sale of any insurance policy represented or advertised to afford coverages and benefits supplemental to or in addition to Medicare coverage, all such advertising materials, except for advertisements which have as their objective the creation of a desire to inquire further about an insurance product and do nothing more than generally describe the product and invite inquiries for costs and further details of the coverage, including limitations, exclusions, reductions or limitations and terms under which the policy may be continued in force, in whatever medium, and all solicitation and presentations for the sale of such policies, shall contain specific references to major exclusions or major exceptions that may result in voiding liability or in a reduction of benefits below those primarily advertised. When such policies contain a coordination of benefits clause whereby benefits are limited by or prorated with other outstanding coverages, such provision shall be called to the attention of the prospective purchaser by conspicuously printed type no smaller than 10 point type. When such policies are advertised to provide coverage above Medicare payments, but contain provisions limiting benefits to those approved for payment by Medicare under Part B, such limitation in benefits shall be called to the attention of the prospective purchaser regardless of the advertising medium; and when policies containing such provisions are delivered, there shall be incorporated therein the language or affixed thereto a sticker in conspicuously printed type no smaller than 10 point type stating: CAUTION: POLICY BENEFITS ARE LIMITED TO THOSE APPROVED BY MEDICARE FOR PAYMENT. Any person engaged in the solicitation or sale of such supplemental Medicare policies in this State shall, as a part of the application, determine and list on the application all policies of Medicare supplement or other health insurance currently in force that cover the prospective insured. In compiling such information, the person is entitled to rely upon information furnished by the prospective purchaser or insured.

(10) Soliciting, etc., Unauthorized Insurance Contracts in Other States. — Soliciting, advertising or entering into insurance contracts in foreign states and any other jurisdiction in which such domestic insurer is not licensed in accordance with the laws of such state or jurisdiction, except as provided in G.S. 58-14-5.

(11) Unfair Claim Settlement Practices. — Committing or performing with such frequency as to indicate a general business practice of any of the following: Provided, however, that no violation of this subsection shall of itself create any cause of action in favor of any person other than the Commissioner:

   a. Misrepresenting pertinent facts or insurance policy provisions relating to coverages at issue;

   b. Failing to acknowledge and act reasonably promptly upon communications with respect to claims arising under insurance policies;

   c. Failing to adopt and implement reasonable standards for the prompt investigation of claims arising under insurance policies;

   d. Refusing to pay claims without conducting a reasonable investigation based upon all available information;

   e. Failing to affirm or deny coverage of claims within a reasonable time after proof-of-loss statements have been completed;

   f. Not attempting in good faith to effectuate prompt, fair and equitable settlements of claims in which liability has become reasonably clear;

   g. Compelling [the] insured to institute litigation to recover amounts due under an insurance policy by offering substantially less than the amounts ultimately recovered in actions brought by such insured;

   h. Attempting to settle a claim for less than the amount to which a reasonable man would have believed he was entitled;

   i. Attempting to settle claims on the basis of an application which was altered without notice to, or knowledge or consent of, the insured;

   j. Making claims payments to insureds or beneficiaries not accompanied by [a] statement setting forth the coverage under which the payments are being made;

   k. Making known to insureds or claimants a policy of appealing from arbitration awards in favor of insureds or claimants for the purpose of compelling them to accept settlements or compromises less than the amount awarded in arbitration;

   l. Delaying the investigation or payment of claims by requiring an insured claimant, or the physician, of [or] either, to submit a preliminary claim report and then requiring the subsequent submission of formal proof-of-loss forms, both of which submissions contain substantially the same information;

   m. Failing to promptly settle claims where liability has become reasonably clear, under one portion of the insurance policy coverage in order to influence settlements under other portions of the insurance policy coverage; and

   n. Failing to promptly provide a reasonable explanation of the basis in the insurance policy in relation to the facts or applicable law for denial of a claim or for the offer of a compromise settlement.

(12) Misuse of borrowers' confidential information. Soliciting, accepting, or using any information from a lender concerning policies of insurance held by such lender as a mortgagee of real property, except from

a lender who is an insurer where the loan has been made by or sold or held for sale to such insurer. Provided, however, this subdivision shall not apply to the use of such information by a lender for the solicitation of life or accident and health insurance.

(13) Overinsurance in Credit or Loan Transactions. — In connection with a loan or extension of credit secured by real or personal property or both, requiring the applicant to procure property and casualty insurance against any one risk which results in coverage which exceeds the replacement value of the secured property at the time of the loan or extension of credit. In connection with a secured or unsecured loan or extension of credit, requiring the applicant to procure life or health insurance against any one risk which exceeds the amount of the loan. In connection with a loan secured by both real and personal property, requiring credit property insurance, as defined in G.S. 58-57-90, on the personal property. For the purposes of this subsection "amount of loan" shall be deemed to be the amount of principal and accrued interest to be paid by the debtor including other allowable charges. (1949, c. 1112; 1955, c. 850, s. 3; 1967, c. 935, s. 2; 1975, c. 668; 1983, c. 831; 1985 (Reg. Sess., 1986), c. 1027, ss. 18, 20; 1987, c. 787, ss. 1, 3.)

Editor's Note. — Session Laws 1955, c. 850, which added subdivision (9), provided in s. 12 that the amendment would be applicable to hospital and medical service corporations under Chapter 57 (now Articles 65 and 66 of Chapter 58) to the same extent as to insurers under Articles 1 through 64 of this Chapter.

Legal Periodicals. — For survey of 1979 administrative law, see 58 N.C.L. Rev. 1185 (1980).

For note, "Bad Faith Refusal to Pay First-Party Insurance Claims: A Growing Recognition of Extra-Contract Damages," see 64 N.C.L. Rev. 1421 (1986).

For article, "North Carolina's Cautious Approach Toward the Imposition of Extracontract Liability on Insurers for Bad Faith," see 21 Wake Forest L. Rev. 957 (1986).

CASE NOTES

Purpose and Applicability. — The statutory provisions which prohibit an insurer or insurance agent from "discrimination" in setting rates for any person are obviously designed to prohibit an insurance agent or company from charging reduced or excessive insurance rates contrary to the established rating rules applicable to the risk and are not applicable to rate making. State ex rel. Comm'r of Ins. v. North Carolina Rate Bureau, 75 N.C. App. 201, 331 S.E.2d 124, cert. denied, 314 N.C. 547, 335 S.E.2d 319 (1985).

Claims based on tortious acts arising from this article are unassignable personal torts. Horton v. New South Ins. Co., 122 N.C. App. 265, 468 S.E.2d 856, 1996 N.C. App. LEXIS 240 (1996), cert. denied, 472 S.E.2d 8 (1996).

A private right of action under this section and G.S. 75-1.1 may not be asserted by a third-party claimant against the insurer of an adverse party. Wilson v. Wilson, 121 N.C. App. 662, 468 S.E.2d 495 (1996).

Third-Party Action. — Allowing a third-party action because of a violation of this section would require the insurer to act in the best interests of the party adverse to its insured and would likely put the insurer in a position of conflict with its insured. Wilson v. Wilson, 121 N.C. App. 662, 468 S.E.2d 495 (1996).

North Carolina does not recognize any cause of action under either this section or G.S. 75-1.1 for unfair or deceptive trade practices by third-party claimants against the insurance company of an adverse party. Lee v. Mutual Cmty. Sav. Bank, 136 N.C. App. 808, 525 S.E.2d 854, 2000 N.C. App. LEXIS 156 (2000).

A third party who was not the insured and who was not in privity with the insurer did not have a cause of action against the insurer under G.S. 75-1.1, based upon G.S. 58-63-15(11). Anderson v. Lancaster Aviation, Inc., 220 F. Supp. 2d 524, 2002 U.S. Dist. LEXIS 18423 (M.D.N.C. 2002).

The prohibition against discrimination in rates is directed to insurers, agents, brokers and other representatives of insurers. Hyde Ins. Agency, Inc. v. Dixie Leasing Corp., 26 N.C. App. 138, 215 S.E.2d 162 (1975).

The sanctions provided by statutes for violations of the antirebate provisions are directed to the insurers, agents, brokers or other representatives. The statutes do not declare that contracts in violation of the antirebate provision are void. Hyde Ins. Agency, Inc. v. Dixie Leasing Corp., 26 N.C. App. 138, 215 S.E.2d 162 (1975).

Nothing in this section declares the charging of excessive rates to be an act or practice within the prohibition of § 58-63-5. State ex rel. Comm'r of Ins. v. Integon Life Ins. Co., 28 N.C. App. 7, 220 S.E.2d 409 (1975).

A violation of this section as a matter of law constitutes an unfair or deceptive trade practice in violation of G.S. 75-1.1. Pearce v. American Defender Life Ins. Co., 316 N.C. 461, 343 S.E.2d 174 (1986); Miller v. Nationwide Mut. Ins. Co., 112 N.C. App. 295, 435 S.E.2d 537 (1993), cert. denied, 335 N.C. 770, 442 S.E.2d 519 (1994).

A violation of this section is, as a matter of law, a violation of G.S. 75-1.1. North Carolina Chiropractic Ass'n v. Aetna Cas. & Sur. Co., 89 N.C. App. 1, 365 S.E.2d 312 (1988).

This section governs unfair methods of competition or deceptive acts or practices in the insurance industry; however, the insurance commissioner's enforcement of this Chapter is not the exclusive state remedy for unfair trade practices in the insurance industry, as this chapter does not create a private right of action, but a violation of this section as a matter of law constitutes a violation of G.S. 75-1.1. United States Fire Ins. Co. v. Nationwide Mut. Ins. Co., 735 F. Supp. 1320 (E.D.N.C. 1990).

Violation of any form of conduct listed operates as a per se instance of unfair and deceptive trade practice under G.S. 75-1.1. Murray v. Nationwide Mut. Ins. Co., 123 N.C. App. 1, 472 S.E.2d 358 (1996).

Subsection (11) enumerates a list of practices which are, as a matter of law, instances of unfair and deceptive conduct. Murray v. Nationwide Mut. Ins. Co., 123 N.C. App. 1, 472 S.E.2d 358 (1996).

Unfair and deceptive acts in the insurance area are not regulated exclusively by Article 63 of Chapter 58, but are also actionable under G.S. 75-1.1; there is no requirement that a party bringing a claim for unfair or deceptive trade practices against an insurance company allege a violation of G.S. 58-63-15 in order to bring a claim pursuant to G.S. 75-1.1. Country Club of Johnston County, Inc. v. U.S. Fid. & Guar. Co., 150 N.C. App. 231, 563 S.E.2d 269, 2002 N.C. App. LEXIS 499 (2002).

General Business Practice Need Not Be Shown Under G.S. 75-1.1. — Acts listed in G.S. 58-63-15(11) constitute a violation of G.S. 75-1.1 without the necessity of an additional showing of frequency indicating a "general business practice," as is required under G.S. 58-63-15(11)(f). Country Club of Johnston County, Inc. v. U.S. Fid. & Guar. Co., 150 N.C.

App. 231, 563 S.E.2d 269, 2002 N.C. App. LEXIS 499 (2002).

This Section Furnishes Examples of Unfair and Deceptive Acts or Practices. — In order to establish a violation of G.S. 75-1.1, a plaintiff must show: (1) an unfair or deceptive act or practice, (2) in or affecting commerce, and (3) which proximately caused injury to plaintiffs; a court may look to the types of conduct prohibited by G.S. 58-63-15(11) for examples of conduct which would constitute an unfair and deceptive act or practice. Country Club of Johnston County, Inc. v. U.S. Fid. & Guar. Co., 150 N.C. App. 231, 563 S.E.2d 269, 2002 N.C. App. LEXIS 499 (2002).

Failure to Settle Insurance Claim Violates Both § 75-1.1 And This Section. — Defendant/Insurer violated G.S. 75-1.1 by "not attempting in good faith to effectuate prompt, fair and equitable settlements of claims in which liability has become reasonably clear" as well as the provisions of this section. Gray v. North Carolina Ins. Underwriting Ass'n, 352 N.C. 61, 529 S.E.2d 676, 2000 N.C. LEXIS 437 (2000).

Failure to Prove Unfair Claims Practices Does Not Necessitate Judgment Against a Related Claim. — Award of treble damages and attorney fees under the North Carolina Unfair and Deceptive Trade Practices Act was not precluded by earlier summary judgment for the insurer on insured's claim under the North Carolina Unfair Claims Settlement Practices Act; failure to prove unfair claims practices does not independently necessitate judgment as a matter of law against a related claim for unfair trade practices. High Country Arts & Craft Guild v. Hartford Fire Ins. Co., 126 F.3d 629 (4th Cir. 1997).

Showing of General Business Practice. — Before there is a violation of this statute, a plaintiff must allege that a defendant has engaged in the prohibited practice with such frequency as to indicate a general business practice. Whiteville Oil Co. v. Federated Mut. Ins. Co., 889 F. Supp. 241 (E.D.N.C. 1995); aff'd, 87 F.3d 1310 (4th Cir. 1996); Gray v. North Carolina Ins. Underwriting Ass'n, 132 N.C. App. 63, 510 S.E.2d 396 (1999).

Where plaintiff in underlying action failed to allege specific facts indicating that defendant engaged in any prohibited practice with sufficient frequency, as required by statute, and because North Carolina case law does not place a duty on the insurer to interpret policies for the insured, plaintiff's claim against insurer for unfair and deceptive trade practices would not be allowed to go forward. Whiteville Oil Co. v. Federated Mut. Ins. Co., 889 F. Supp. 241 (E.D.N.C. 1995), aff'd, 87 F.3d 1310 (4th Cir. 1996).

Insured failed to allege that the commercial general liability insurer engaged in any prohibited practices with sufficient frequency to constitute a general business practice for purposes of a claim for unfair and deceptive trade practices. Wake Stone Corp. v. Aetna Cas. & Sur. Co., 995 F. Supp. 612 (E.D.N.C. 1998).

Article Violation Was Not Required to Show Violation of Consumer Protection Chapter. — Excess and umbrella insurers were not required to prove a violation of Article 3A of this Chapter, The Unfair Trade Practices Article of the Insurance Statutes, in order to show a violation of Chapter 75. United States Fire Ins. Co. v. Nationwide Mut. Ins. Co., 735 F. Supp. 1320 (E.D.N.C. 1990), decided under law in effect prior to the 1985 amendment.

Misrepresentation Within Scope of Section. — Misrepresentation of the nature of the insurance coverage by defendants clearly placed their conduct within the scope of this section. First Fin. Sav. Bank, Inc. v. American Bankers Ins. Co., 699 F. Supp. 1158 (E.D.N.C. 1988).

Misrepresentation of Owner and Beneficiary. — Misrepresentation to policy holder by the insurance carrier as to who was the owner and who was the beneficiary of the policy did not constitute an unfair practice; subsection (1) is directed at false statements connected with sale of insurance policies and an insurance company gains no advantage if it incorrectly advises a person as to who is the owner or beneficiary of a policy. Jefferson-Pilot Life Ins. Co. v. Spencer, 336 N.C. 49, 442 S.E.2d 316 (1994).

Failure to disclose information may be tantamount to misrepresentation and thus an unfair or deceptive practice. Kron Medical Corp. v. Collier Cobb & Assocs., 107 N.C. App. 331, 420 S.E.2d 192, cert. denied, 333 N.C. 168, 424 S.E.2d 910 (1992), appeal dismissed, 333 N.C. 345, 426 S.E.2d 706 (1993).

Prohibited Act Under Subsection (11) Must Be Alleged as General Practice. — In order to establish a claim for relief under subsection (11) of this section, plaintiff must allege not only that defendant engaged in the prohibited acts under the statute, but also, that defendant engaged in the prohibited acts with such frequency as to indicate a general practice. von Hagel v. Blue Cross & Blue Shield, 91 N.C. App. 58, 370 S.E.2d 695 (1988).

"With Such Frequency as to Indicate General Business Practice." — Where plaintiffs did not allege that defendant's insurance agency and agent violated any of the acts prohibited by subdivision (11) "with such frequency as to indicate a general business practice," they failed to establish a claim premised on violation of that statute, and judgment dismissing their claim was properly entered as to that issue. Belmont Land & Inv. Co. v. Standard Fire Ins. Co., 102 N.C. App. 745, 403 S.E.2d 924 (1991).

Arbitrary Requirement of Unnecessary Medical Reports. — Arbitrarily requiring, under a mortgage payment disability policy, costly, difficult to obtain medical reports that are clearly unnecessary and serve no legitimate purpose, as when the insurer already has proof from a doctor, or the circumstances clearly indicate that the insured's disability is not episodic but will extend beyond the current period benefits are applied for, is an unfair trade practice. Douglas v. Pennamco, Inc., 75 N.C. App. 644, 331 S.E.2d 298, cert. denied, 314 N.C. 664, 336 S.E.2d 399 (1985).

Monthly Proof of Disability. — The requirement, under a mortgage payment disability policy, that the insured, whose injury was of uncertain duration and subject to improvement, submit proof of his disability each month benefits were applied for, did not constitute an unfair and deceptive trade practice. Douglas v. Pennamco, Inc., 75 N.C. App. 644, 331 S.E.2d 298, cert. denied, 314 N.C. 664, 336 S.E.2d 399 (1985).

The average consumer would not have understood the below-quoted statement, included in a letter written by an employee of an insurer in response to an inquiry by an agent of the insured as to the extent of the insured's coverage while he was in military service, to mean that the remaining exceptions to coverage, including an "air craft except," set out in the "accidental death rider" would no longer be applied: "However, in addition to the basic policy, this accidental death rider would also be payable should his death occur while in the Armed Forces but not as a result of an act of war." Pearce v. American Defender Life Ins. Co., 74 N.C. App. 620, 330 S.E.2d 9, aff'd in part and rev'd in part, 316 N.C. 461, 343 S.E.2d 174 (1986).

Refusal of Insurers to Cover Chiropractors for Workers' Compensation Purposes. — Plaintiff chiropractors, alleging that defendant insurance companies had interfered with their contractual rights by refusing to honor employers' choices of chiropractors as providers of health care treatment to employees under the Workers' Compensation Act, that defendants had misrepresented to employer insureds that their workers' compensation policies did not provide coverage for chiropractic treatment, that said misrepresentations were unfair and deceptive trade practices in violation of G.S. 75-1.1, and that defendants had conspired among themselves and with members of the medical profession to deprive plaintiffs of business opportunities by refusing to pay for chiropractic services provided in compliance with the act, an illegal restraint of trade in violation of G.S. 75-1 and federal law, could not maintain their action in superior court without first seeking relief from the Industrial Commission. North Carolina Chiropractic Ass'n v.

Aetna Cas. & Sur. Co., 89 N.C. App. 1, 365 S.E.2d 312 (1988), remanding case to the trial court for entry of an order staying plaintiffs' action pending a determination of the underlying workers' compensation issues by the Commission.

Failure to allege more than a single refusal by insurance company to settle a claim is fatal to a cause of action under subdivision (11) of this section. Marshburn v. Associated Indem. Corp., 84 N.C. App. 365, 353 S.E.2d 123, cert. denied, 319 N.C. 673, 356 S.E.2d 779 (1987).

Insurer Not Entitled to Motion for Summary Judgment. — Since failing to adopt and implement reasonable standards for the prompt investigation of claims arising under insurance policies and not attempting in good faith to effectuate prompt, fair and equitable settlements of claims in which liability has become reasonably clear and which are prohibited by this Chapter with regard to first party claims, these practices, if found by the jury, could support a finding of unfair or deceptive acts or practices under Chapter 75; therefore, there was a genuine issue as to material fact and primary insurer was not entitled to motion for summary judgment on unfair trade practices claim of excess and umbrella insurers. United States Fire Ins. Co. v. Nationwide Mut. Ins. Co., 735 F. Supp. 1320 (E.D.N.C. 1990), decided under law in effect prior to 1985 amendment.

Material Issue of Fact Existed That Underinsurance Coverage Was Worthless. — Where plaintiff paid additional annual premiums for underinsured motorist coverage to defendant insurance company, where plaintiff subsequently was involved in automobile accident which caused him serious injuries resulting in medical expenses exceeding $100,000, and where after plaintiff settled with driver of other automobile for $25,000, defendant denied liability for any additional expenses by claiming its responsibility under the $25,000 underinsurance coverage was reduced by plaintiff's $25,000 settlement with the other driver, insurers' renewal of plaintiff's minimum limits underinsurance, without disclosing its true value, was evidence of an unfair trade practice. Davidson v. Knauff Ins. Agency, Inc., 93 N.C. App. 20, 376 S.E.2d 488, cert. denied, 324 N.C. 577, 381 S.E.2d 772 (1989).

Evidence held insufficient to show a violation of subsections (2) or (4) of this section. Dull v. Mutual of Omaha Ins. Co., 85 N.C. App. 310, 354 S.E.2d 752, cert. denied, 320 N.C. 512, 358 S.E.2d 518 (1987).

Bad Faith Refusal to Settle. — No abuse of discretion was found where a jury awarded $225,000.00 against an insurance company for bad faith refusal to settle. Lovell v. Nationwide Mut. Ins. Co., 108 N.C. App. 416, 424 S.E.2d

181, aff'd in part; discretionary review improvidently granted in part, 334 N.C. 682, 435 S.E.2d 71 (1993).

Dismissal of Claim Upheld. — Where plaintiff failed to allege any facts supporting a violation of subdivision (11) of this section, and failed to plead that alleged violations occurred "with such frequency as to indicate a general business practice," the court did not err in dismissing a claim under this section. Beasley v. National Sav. Life Ins. Co., 75 N.C. App. 104, 330 S.E.2d 207, cert. improvidently allowed, 316 N.C. 372, 341 S.E.2d 338 (1986).

Because a necessary element of a claim for unfair or deceptive practices in the business of insurance which must be alleged is that the forbidden act complained of was done "with such frequency as to indicate a general business practice," and the only factual allegation bearing thereon in plaintiff's claim was that defendants "knowingly misrepresented the plaintiff's insurance coverage and failed to act with reasonable promptness in response to plaintiff's claim," the trial judge did not err in dismissing the claim. Alexvale Furn., Inc. v. Alexander & Alexander, 93 N.C. App. 478, 378 S.E.2d 436, cert. denied, 325 N.C. 228, 381 S.E.2d 783 (1989).

Plaintiff who sued defendant/insurance company for unfair and deceptive practices and acts, when it raised his insurance premiums after paying a claim which he repeatedly informed the insurer was fraudulent, failed to state facts sufficient to survive summary judgment under this section. Where the defendant's advertising claimed that it did not want to pay false claims, the plaintiff should have alleged that it did want to, not merely that it did, and where the defendant failed to adequately investigate the claim, the plaintiff should have alleged that the defendant did not act promptly in doing so. Cash v. State Farm Mut. Auto. Ins. Co., 137 N.C. App. 192, 528 S.E.2d 372, 2000 N.C. App. LEXIS 312 (2000).

Parents' complaint that alleged that an insurer's failure to pay medical claims submitted on their son constituted unfair claim handling under G.S. 58-63-15 was preempted by the Employee Retirement Income Security Act because the parents' claim did not bear upon the "business of insurance." Voelske v. Mid-South Ins. Co., 154 N.C. App. 704, 572 S.E.2d 841, 2002 N.C. App. LEXIS 1533 (2002).

Statute of limitations on defendant's unfair trade practice claim, based upon a violation of subdivision (1) of this section, did not begin to run until her deceased husband could no longer make alternative financial arrangements to provide for defendant. Whether defendant's claim was barred by the statute of limitations, then, was dependent upon the resolution of the factual issue of her deceased husband's financial status from the time of the misrepresentations made by insurance company as to the identity of the beneficiary of decedent's insurance policies until his death. Jefferson-Pilot Life Ins. Co. v. Spencer, 110 N.C. App. 194, 429 S.E.2d 583 (1993), rev'd on other grounds, 336 N.C. 49, 442 S.E.2d 316 (1994).

Showing of Bad Faith, etc., Creates Jury Question on Punitive Damages. — Where claimant forecasts evidence that insurance company's delay in payment has no good faith basis in fact and is accompanied by aggravated conduct, the claimant is entitled to take his case of punitive damages to the jury. Robinson v. North Carolina Farm Bureau Ins. Co., 86 N.C. App. 44, 356 S.E.2d 392 (1987), cert. denied, 321 N.C. 592, 364 S.E.2d 140 (1988).

Facts Sufficient to State Claim for Punitive Damages. — Plaintiff's allegations that defendant had violated subdivision (11) of this section did not alone determine the validity of his claim for punitive damages; rather, the facts pleaded in the complaint determined whether the complaint stated a claim upon which relief could be granted. Thus, plaintiff's complaint stated a claim for punitive damages based on aggravated and oppressive tortious conduct, and the trial court erred in dismissing plaintiff's cause of action for those damages. Smith v. Nationwide Mut. Fire Ins. Co., 96 N.C. App. 215, 385 S.E.2d 152 (1989), cert. denied, 326 N.C. 365, 389 S.E.2d 816 (1990).

Punitive Damages Not Precluded by Eventual Payment Where Bad Faith Present. — An action for punitive damages from tortious conduct of an insurance company is not precluded when the company eventually pays, if bad faith delay and aggravating conduct is present. Robinson v. North Carolina Farm Bureau Ins. Co., 86 N.C. App. 44, 356 S.E.2d 392 (1987), cert. denied, 321 N.C. 592, 364 S.E.2d 140 (1988).

The plaintiffs's claim of unfair and deceptive trade practices failed where defendants stood to gain very little from misleading the plaintiffs by expanding their existing insurance policy to cover inventory in a basement that was uninsurable under the policy; where the effect of defendants' actions in the marketplace would be negligible; and where the flood insurance sought by plaintiffs was not available among competing insurers so that no unfair advantage was or could be gained from defendants' actions. Erler v. Aon Risks Servs., Inc., 141 N.C. App. 312, 540 S.E.2d 65, 2000 N.C. App. LEXIS 1400 (2000).

Where an insurer's liability for a full death benefit to the insured was not reasonably clear because a legitimate issue existed as to whether the premium notice complied with the statutory notice requirements of G.S. 58-58-120, the insurer's advocating a position that was ultimately determined to be incorrect did not necessarily demonstrate a lack of good faith in attempting to settle the insured's claim. Cent. Carolina Bank & Trust Co. v. Sec. Life of Denver Ins. Co., 247 F. Supp. 2d 791, 2003 U.S. Dist. LEXIS 3098 (M.D.N.C. 2003).

Applied in Smith v. King, 52 N.C. App. 158, 277 S.E.2d 875 (1981).

Cited in Hooper v. Liberty Mut. Ins. Co., 84 N.C. App. 549, 353 S.E.2d 248 (1987); Pelican Watch v. United States Fire Ins. Co., 90 N.C. App. 150, 367 S.E.2d 351 (1988); Pelican Watch v. United States Fire Ins. Co., 323 N.C. 700, 375 S.E.2d 161 (1989); First Fin. Sav. Bank, Inc. v. American Bankers Ins. Co., 783 F. Supp. 963 (E.D.N.C. 1991); Isenhour v. Universal Underwriters Ins. Co., 341 N.C. 597, 461 S.E.2d 317 (1995); Braddy v. Nationwide Mut. Liab. Ins. Co., 122 N.C. App. 402, 470 S.E.2d 820 (1996); North Carolina Steel, Inc. v. National Council on Comp. Ins., 123 N.C. App. 163, 472 S.E.2d 578 (1996), aff'd in part and rev'd in part, 347 N.C. 627, 496 S.E.2d 369 (1998); Members Interior Constr., Inc. v. Leader Constr. Co., 124 N.C. App. 121, 476 S.E.2d 399 (1996); Wake County Hosp. Sys. v. Safety Nat'l Cas. Corp., 127 N.C. App. 33, 487 S.E.2d 789 (1997), cert. denied, 347 N.C. 410, 494 S.E.2d 600 (1997); Westchester Fire Ins. Co. v. Johnson, — F. Supp. 2d —, 2000 U.S. Dist. LEXIS 5001 (M.D.N.C. Jan. 6, 2000); Anderson v. Lancaster Aviation, Inc., 220 F. Supp. 2d 524, 2002 U.S. Dist. LEXIS 18423 (M.D.N.C. 2002); Cialino v. Wal-Mart Stores, 156 N.C. App. 463, 577 S.E.2d 345, 2003 N.C. App. LEXIS 203 (2003).

§ 58-63-20. Power of Commissioner.

The Commissioner shall have power to examine and investigate into the affairs of every person engaged in the business of insurance in this State in order to determine whether such person has been or is engaged in any unfair method of competition or in any unfair or deceptive act or practice prohibited by G.S. 58-63-10. (1949, c. 1112; 1991, c. 720, s. 62.)

Legal Periodicals. — For note, "Consumer Protection—The Unfair Trade Practice Act and the Insurance Code: Does Per Se Necessarily Preempt?" see 10 Campbell L. Rev. 487 (1988).

Limited Remedial Power. — Section 58-63-25 and former G.S. 58-63-30 and this section, which provide for the Commissioner's power to act in regard to "any unfair method of competition or in any unfair or deceptive act or practice prohibited by G.S. 58-63-10 ...," grant no remedial power to the Commissioner to remedy unfair trade practices other than the power to investigate, bring charges and issue cease and desist orders. State ex rel. Comm'r of Ins. v. Integon Life Ins. Co., 28 N.C. App. 7, 220 S.E.2d 409 (1975).

Cited in North Carolina Chiropractic Ass'n v. Aetna Cas. & Sur. Co., 89 N.C. App. 1, 365 S.E.2d 312 (1988).

§ 58-63-25. Hearings, witnesses, appearances, production of books and service of process.

(a) When the Commissioner has reason to believe that any person has been engaged or is engaging in this State in any unfair method of competition or any unfair or deceptive act or practice defined in G.S. 58-63-15 or under G.S. 58-63-65, and that a proceeding by the Commissioner on the matter would be in the interest of the public, the Commissioner shall issue and serve upon the person a statement of the charges in that respect and a notice of the hearing on the matter to be held at the time and place fixed in the notice, which shall not be less than 10 days after the date of the service of the notice.

(b) At the time and place fixed for such hearing, such person shall have an opportunity to be heard and to show cause why an order should not be made by the Commissioner requiring such person to cease and desist from the acts, methods or practices so complained of. Upon good cause shown, the Commissioner shall permit any person to intervene, appear and be heard at such hearing by counsel or in person.

(c) Nothing contained in this Article shall require the observance at any such hearing of formal rules of pleading or evidence.

(d) The Commissioner, upon such hearing, may administer oaths, examine and cross-examine witnesses, receive oral and documentary evidence, and shall have the power to subpoena witnesses, compel their attendance, and require the production of books, papers, records, correspondence, or other documents which he deems relevant to the inquiry. The Commissioner, upon such hearing, may, and upon the request of any party shall, cause to be made a stenographic record of all the evidence and all the proceedings had at such hearing. If no stenographic record is made and if a judicial review is sought, the Commissioner shall prepare a statement of the evidence and proceeding for use on review. In case of a refusal of any person to comply with any subpoena issued hereunder or to testify with respect to any matter concerning which he may be lawfully interrogated, the Superior Court of Wake County, on application of the Commissioner, may issue an order requiring such person to comply with such subpoena and to testify; and any failure to obey any such order of the court may be punished by the court as a contempt thereof.

(e) Statements of charges, notices, orders, and other processes of the Commissioner under this Article may be served by anyone duly authorized by the Commissioner, either in the manner provided by law for service of process in civil actions, or by registering and mailing a copy thereof to the person affected by such statement, notice, order, or other process at his or its residence or principal office or place of business. The verified return by the person so serving such statement, notice, order, or other process, setting forth the manner of such service, shall be proof of the same, and the return postcard receipt for such statement, notice, order, or other process, registered and mailed as aforesaid, shall be proof of the service of the same. (1949, c. 1112; 1995, c. 193, s. 49.)

Legal Periodicals. — For note, "Consumer Protection—The Unfair Trade Practice Act and the Insurance Code: Does Per Se Necessarily Preempt?" see 10 Campbell L. Rev. 487 (1988).

CASE NOTES

Limited Remedial Power. — Section 58-63-20 and former G.S. 58-63-30 and this section, which provide for the Commissioner's power to act in regard to "any unfair method of competition or in any unfair or deceptive act or practice prohibited by G.S. 58-63-10 …," grant no remedial power to the Commissioner to remedy unfair trade practices other than the power to investigate, bring charges and issue cease and desist orders. State ex rel. Comm'r of Ins. v. Integon Life Ins. Co., 28 N.C. App. 7, 220 S.E.2d 409 (1975).

Cited in State ex rel. Lanier v. Vines, 1 N.C. App. 208, 161 S.E.2d 35 (1968).

§ 58-63-30: Repealed by Session Laws 1991, c. 644, s. 29.

§ 58-63-32. Cease and desist order.

(a) If, after a hearing under G.S. 58-63-25, the Commissioner determines that the method of competition or the act or practice in question is defined in G.S. 58-63-15 and that the person complained of has engaged in the method of competition, act, or practice in violation of this Article, the Commissioner shall reduce his finding to writing and shall issue and cause to be served upon the person charged with the violation an order requiring the person to cease and desist from engaging in the method, act, or practice.

(b) Until the expiration of the time allowed under G.S. 58-63-35(a) for filing a petition for review, if no such petition has been duly filed within that time, then until the transcript of the record in the proceeding has been filed in court, the Commissioner may at any time, upon such notice and in such manner as the Commissioner considers proper, modify or set aside in whole or in part any order issued by the Commissioner under this section.

(c) After the expiration of the time allowed for filing a petition for review, if no such petition has been duly filed within that time, the Commissioner may at any time, after notice and opportunity for hearing, reopen and alter, modify, or set aside, in whole or in part, any order issued by the Commissioner under this section, whenever in the Commissioner's opinion conditions of fact or of law have so changed as to require the action or if the public interest requires. (1991, c. 644, s. 28.)

§ 58-63-35. Judicial review of cease and desist orders.

(a) Any person required by an order of the Commissioner under G.S. 58-63-32 to cease and desist from engaging in any unfair method of competition or any unfair or deceptive act or practice defined in G.S. 58-63-15 may obtain a review of the order by filing in the Superior Court of Wake County, within 30 days from the date of the service of such order, a written petition praying that the order of the Commissioner be set aside. A copy of the petition shall be immediately served upon the Commissioner, and at that time the Commissioner immediately shall certify and file in the court a transcript of the entire record in the proceeding, including all the evidence taken and the report and order of the Commissioner. Upon the filing of the petition and transcript, the court has jurisdiction of the proceeding and of the question determined therein, shall determine whether the filing of the petition shall operate as a stay of the Commissioner's order, and has power to make and enter upon the pleadings, evidence, and proceedings set forth in the transcript a decree modifying, affirming or reversing the order of the Commissioner, in whole or in part. The findings of the Commissioner as to the facts, if supported by substantial evidence, are conclusive.

(b) To the extent that the order of the Commissioner is affirmed, the court shall thereupon issue its own order commanding obedience to the terms of such order of the Commissioner. If either party shall apply to the court for leave to adduce additional evidence, and shall show to the satisfaction of the court that such additional evidence is material and that there were reasonable grounds for the failure to adduce such evidence in the proceeding before the Commissioner, the court may order such additional evidence to be taken before the Commissioner and to be adduced upon the hearing in such manner and upon such terms and conditions as to the court may seem proper. The Commissioner may modify his findings of fact, or make new findings by reason of the additional evidence so taken, and he shall file such modified or new findings which, if supported by substantial evidence shall be conclusive, and his recommendations, if any, for the modification or setting aside of his original order, with the return of such additional evidence.

(c) A cease and desist order issued by the Commissioner under G.S. 58-63-30 shall become final:

    (1) Upon the expiration of the time allowed for filing a petition for review if no such petition has been duly filed within such time; except that the Commissioner may thereafter modify or set aside his order to the extent provided in G.S. 58-63-30(b); or

    (2) Upon the final decision of the court if the court directs that the order of the Commissioner be affirmed or the petition for review dismissed.

(d) No order of the Commissioner under this Article or order of a court to enforce the same shall in any way relieve or absolve any person affected by such order from any liability under any other laws of this State. (1949, c. 1112; 1995, c. 193, s. 50.)

CASE NOTES

Applied in North Carolina Steel, Inc. v. National Council on Comp. Ins., 123 N.C. App. 163, 472 S.E.2d 578 (1996), aff'd in part and rev'd in part, 347 N.C. 627, 496 S.E.2d 369 (1998).

§ 58-63-40. Procedure as to unfair methods of competition and unfair or deceptive acts or practices which are not defined.

(a) Whenever the Commissioner shall have reason to believe that any person engaged in the business of insurance is engaging in this State in any method of competition or in any act or practice in the conduct of such business which is not defined in G.S. 58-63-15, that such method of competition is unfair or that such act or practice is unfair or deceptive and that a proceeding by him in respect thereto would be to the interest of the public, he may issue and serve upon such person a statement of the charges in that respect and a notice of a hearing thereon to be held at a time and place fixed in the notice, which shall not be less than 10 days after the date of the service thereof. Each such hearing shall be conducted in the same manner as the hearings provided for in G.S. 58-63-25. The Commissioner shall, after such hearing, make a report in writing in which he shall state his findings as to the facts, and he shall serve a copy thereof upon such person.

(b) If such report charges a violation of this Article and if such method of competition, act or practice has not been discontinued, the Commissioner may, through the Attorney General of this State, at any time after 10 days after the service of such report cause a petition to be filed in the superior court of this State of the county wherein the person resides or has his principal place of business, to enjoin and restrain such person from engaging in such method, act or practice. The court shall have jurisdiction of the proceeding and shall have power to make and enter appropriate orders in connection therewith and to issue such writs as are ancillary to its jurisdiction or are necessary in its judgment to prevent injury to the public pendente lite. To the extent that the order of the Commissioner is affirmed, the court shall thereupon issue its order commanding obedience to the terms of such order of the Commissioner.

(c) A transcript of the proceedings before the Commissioner including all evidence taken and the report and findings shall be filed with such petition. If either party shall apply to the court for leave to adduce additional evidence and shall show, to the satisfaction of the court, that such additional evidence is material and there were reasonable grounds for the failure to adduce such evidence in the proceeding before the Commissioner, the court may order such additional evidence to be taken before the Commissioner and to be adduced upon the hearing in such manner and upon such terms and conditions as to the court may seem proper. The Commissioner may modify his findings of fact or make new findings by reason of the additional evidence so taken, and he shall file such modified or new findings with the return of such additional evidence.

(d) If the court finds that the method of competition complained of is unfair or that the act or practice complained of is unfair or deceptive, that the proceeding by the Commissioner with respect thereto is to the interest of the public and that the findings of the Commissioner are supported by the weight of the evidence, it shall issue its order enjoining and restraining the continuance of such method of competition, act or practice. (1949, c. 1112.)

CASE NOTES

Recovery Under § 75-1.1. — Although it is true that jurisdiction under the Insurance Unfair Trade Practices Act lies in the Commissioner's office, unfair and deceptive acts in the insurance area are not regulated exclusively by this article, but are also actionable under G.S. 75-1.1. Golden Rule Ins. Co. v. Long, 113 N.C. App. 187, 439 S.E.2d 599 (1993).

§ 58-63-45. Judicial review by intervenor.

If the report of the Commissioner does not charge a violation of this Article, then any intervenor in the proceedings may within 10 days after the service of such report, cause a notice of appeal to be filed in the Superior Court of Wake County for a review of such report. Upon such review, the court shall have authority to issue appropriate orders and decrees in connection therewith, including, if the court finds that it is to the interest of the public, orders enjoining and restraining the continuance of any method of competition, act or practice which it finds, notwithstanding such report of the Commissioner, constitutes a violation of this Article. (1949, c. 1112.)

§ 58-63-50. Penalty.

Any person who willfully violates a cease and desist order of the Commissioner under G.S. 58-63-32, after it has become final, and while the order is in effect, shall forfeit and pay to the Commissioner the sum of not less than one thousand dollars ($1,000) nor more than five thousand dollars ($5,000) for each violation, which if not paid shall be recovered in a civil action instituted in the name of the Commissioner in the Superior Court of Wake County. The clear proceeds of forfeitures provided for in this section shall be remitted to the Civil Penalty and Forfeiture Fund in accordance with G.S. 115C-457.2. (1949, c. 1112; 1985, c. 666, s. 21; 1991, c. 720, ss. 33, 63; 1995, c. 193, s. 51; 1998-215, s. 88.)

Legal Periodicals. — For survey of 1979 administrative law, see 58 N.C.L. Rev. 1185 (1980).

For note, "Consumer Protection—The Unfair Trade Practice Act and the Insurance Code: Does Per Se Necessarily Preempt?" see 10 Campbell L. Rev. 487 (1988).

§ 58-63-55. Provisions of Article additional to existing law.

The powers vested in the Commissioner by this Article shall be additional to any other powers to enforce any penalties, fines or forfeitures authorized by law with respect to the methods, acts and practices hereby declared to be unfair or deceptive. (1949, c. 1112.)

Legal Periodicals. — For survey of 1979 administrative law, see 58 N.C.L. Rev. 1185 (1980).

CASE NOTES

Applied in Ray v. United Family Life Ins. Co., 430 F. Supp. 1353 (W.D.N.C. 1977).

§ 58-63-60. Immunity from prosecution.

If any person shall ask to be excused from attending and testifying or from producing any books, papers, records, correspondence or other documents at any hearing on the ground that the testimony or evidence required of him may tend to incriminate him or subject him to a penalty or forfeiture, and shall notwithstanding be directed to give such testimony or produce such evidence, he must nonetheless comply with such direction, but he shall not thereafter be prosecuted or subjected to any penalty or forfeiture for or on account of any transaction, matter or thing concerning which he may testify or produce evidence pursuant thereto, and no testimony so given or evidence produced shall be received against him upon any criminal action, investigation or proceeding, provided, however, that no such individual so testifying shall be exempt from prosecution or punishment for any perjury committed by him while so testifying and the testimony or evidence so given or produced shall be admissible against him upon any criminal action, investigation or proceeding concerning such perjury, nor shall he be exempt from the refusal, revocation or suspension of any license, permission or authority conferred, or to be conferred, pursuant to the insurance law of this State. Any such individual may execute, acknowledge and file in the office of the Commissioner a statement expressly waiving such immunity or privilege in respect to any transaction, matter or thing specified in such statement and thereupon the testimony of such person or such evidence in relation to such transaction, matter or thing may be received or produced before any judge or justice, court, tribunal, grand jury or otherwise, and if so received or produced such individual shall not be entitled to any immunity or privilege on account of any testimony he may so give or evidence so produced. (1949, c. 1112.)

§ 58-63-65. Rule-making authority.

The Commissioner may adopt rules to carry out the provisions of this Article, including rules that define unfair methods of competition or unfair or deceptive acts or practices in the business of insurance, in addition to those defined in G.S. 58-63-15 and determined under G.S. 58-63-40. (1993, c. 409, s. 15.)

§§ 58-63-66 through 58-63-69: Reserved for future codification purposes.

§ 58-63-70. Health care service discount practices by insurers and service corporations.

(a) It is an unfair trade practice for any insurer or service corporation subject to this Chapter to make an intentional misrepresentation to a health care provider to the effect that the insurer or service corporation is entitled to a certain preferred provider or other discount off the fees charged for medical services, procedures, or supplies provided by the health care provider, when the insurer or service corporation is not entitled to any discount or is entitled to a lesser discount from the provider on those fees.

(b) It is an unfair trade practice for any person with knowledge that an insurer or service corporation intends to make the type of misrepresentation prohibited in subsection (a) of this section to provide substantial assistance to that insurer or service corporation in accomplishing that misrepresentation. (1997-519, s. 3.2.)

Legal Periodicals. — For 1997 legislative survey, see 20 Campbell L. Rev. 469.

ARTICLE 64.

Continuing Care Retirement Communities.

§ 58-64-1. Definitions.

As used in this Article, unless otherwise specified:
(1) "Continuing care" means the furnishing to an individual other than an individual related by blood, marriage, or adoption to the person furnishing the care, of lodging together with nursing services, medical services, or other health related services, under an agreement effective for the life of the individual or for a period longer than one year.
(2) "Entrance fee" means a payment that assures a resident a place in a facility for a term of years or for life.
(3) "Facility" means the retirement community or communities in which a provider undertakes to provide continuing care to an individual.
(4) "Health related services" means, at a minimum, nursing home admission or assistance in the activities of daily living, exclusive of the provision of meals or cleaning services.
(5) "Living unit" means a room, apartment, cottage, or other area within a facility set aside for the exclusive use or control of one or more identified residents.
(6) "Provider" means the promoter, developer, or owner of a facility, whether a natural person, partnership, or other unincorporated association, however organized, trust, or corporation, of an institution, building, residence, or other place, whether operated for profit or not, or any other person, that solicits or undertakes to provide continuing care under a continuing care facility contract, or that represents himself, herself, or itself as providing continuing care or "life care."
(7) "Resident" means a purchaser of, a nominee of, or a subscriber to, a continuing care contract.
(8) "Hazardous financial condition" means a provider is insolvent or in eminent danger of becoming insolvent. (1989, c. 758, s. 1; 1989 (Reg. Sess., 1990), c. 1024, s. 45; 1991, c. 720, ss. 2, 39; 1999-132, ss. 2.2, 2.3.)

Editor's Note. — Session Laws 1989, c. 758, s. 3 initially provided that the act should not be construed to obligate the General Assembly to make any appropriations to implement the provisions of the act, and would not become effective unless monies necessary to implement this act were appropriated. The necessary appropriations were made in Session Laws 1989, c. 752, s. 3.

Furthermore, Session Laws 1989, c. 758, s. 5, as amended by Session Laws 1989 (Reg. Sess., 1990), c. 1024, s. 45, provided that nothing in the act would be construed to affect the authority of the Department of Human Resources otherwise provided by law to license or regulate any health service facility or domiciliary service facility.

However, Session Laws 1991, c. 720, s. 2, repealed ss. 3 and 5 of Chapter 758 and s. 45 of Chapter 1024 of the 1989 Session Laws.

§ 58-64-5. License.

(a) No provider shall engage in the business of offering or providing continuing care in this State without a license to do so obtained from the Commissioner as provided in this Article. It is a Class 1 misdemeanor for any person, other than a provider licensed under this Article, to advertise or market to the general public any product similar to continuing care through the use of such terms as "life care", "continuing care", or "guaranteed care for life", or similar terms, words, or phrases. The licensing process may involve a series of steps pursuant to rules adopted by the Commissioner under this Article.

(b) The application for a license shall be filed with the Department by the provider on forms prescribed by the Department and within a period of time prescribed by the Department; and shall include all information required by the Department pursuant to rules adopted by it under this Article including, but not limited to, the disclosure statement meeting the requirements of this Article and other financial and facility development information required by the Department. The application for a license must be accompanied by an application fee of two hundred dollars ($200.00).

(c) Upon receipt of the complete application for a license in proper form, the Department shall, within 10 business days, issue a notice of filing to the applicant. Within 90 days of the notice of filing, the Department shall enter an order issuing the license or rejecting the application.

(d) If the Commissioner determines that any of the requirements of this Article have not been met, the Commissioner shall notify the applicant that the application must be corrected within 30 days in such particulars as designated by the Commissioner. If the requirements are not met within the time allowed, the Commissioner may enter an order rejecting the application, which order shall include the findings of fact upon which the order is based and which shall not become effective until 20 days after the end of the 30-day period. During the 20-day period, the applicant may petition for reconsideration and is entitled to a hearing.

(e) Repealed by Session Laws 2003-193, s. 1, effective June 12, 2003.

(f) The Commissioner may, on an annual basis or on a more frequent basis if he deems it to be necessary, in addition to the annual disclosure statement revision required by G.S. 58-64-30, require every licensed provider to file with the Department any of the information provided by G.S. 58-64-5(b) for new licensure that the Commissioner, pursuant to rules adopted by him under this Article, determines is needed for review of licensed providers.

(g) The Commissioner may require a provider to: (i) provide the report of an actuary that estimates the capacity of the provider to meet its contractual obligation to the resident, or (ii) give consideration to expected rates of mortality and morbidity, expected refunds, and expected capital expenditures in accordance with standards promulgated by the American Academy of Actuaries, within the five-year forecast statements, as required by G.S. 58-64-20(a)(12). (1989, c. 758, s. 1; 1991, c. 196, ss. 1, 2; 2001-223, s. 22.1; 2003-193, ss. 1, 2.)

Editor's Note. — Session Laws 2003-193, s. 16, is a severability clause.
Effect of Amendments. — Session Laws

2003-193, ss. 1 and 2, effective June 12, 2003, repealed subsection (e); and in subsection (g), substituted "provider" for "facility."

§ 58-64-10. Revocation of license.

(a) The license of a provider shall remain in effect until revoked after notice and hearing, upon written findings of fact by the Commissioner, that the provider has:

    (1) Willfully violated any provision of this Article or of any rule or order of the Commissioner;

    (2) Failed to file an annual disclosure statement or standard form of contract as required by this Article;

    (3) Failed to deliver to prospective residents the disclosure statements required by this Article;

    (4) Delivered to prospective residents a disclosure statement that makes an untrue statement or omits a material fact and the provider, at the time of the delivery of the disclosure statement, had actual knowledge of the misstatement or omission;

    (5) Failed to comply with the terms of a cease and desist order; or

    (6) Has been determined by the Commissioner to be in a hazardous financial condition.

(b) Findings of fact in support of revocation shall be accompanied by an explicit statement of the underlying facts supporting the findings.

(c) If the Commissioner has good cause to believe that the provider is guilty of a violation for which revocation could be ordered, the Commissioner may first issue a cease and desist order. If the cease and desist order is not or cannot be effective in remedying the violation, the Commissioner may, after notice and hearing, order that the license be revoked and surrendered. Such a cease and desist order may be appealed to the Superior Court of Wake County in the manner provided by G.S. 58-63-35. The provider shall accept no new applicant funds while the revocation order is under appeal. (1989, c. 758, s. 1.)

§ 58-64-15. Sale or transfer of ownership.

No license is transferable, and no license issued pursuant to this Article has value for sale or exchange as property. No provider or other owning entity shall sell or transfer ownership of the facility, or enter into a contract with a third-party provider for management of the facility, unless the Commissioner approves such transfer or contract. (1989, c. 758, s. 1.)

§ 58-64-20. Disclosure statement.

(a) At the time of, or prior to, the execution of a contract to provide continuing care, or at the time of, or prior to, the transfer of any money or other property to a provider by or on behalf of a prospective resident, whichever occurs first, the provider shall deliver a current disclosure statement to the person with whom the contract is to be entered into, the text of which shall contain at least:

    (1) The name and business address of the provider and a statement of whether the provider is a partnership, corporation, or other type of legal entity.

    (2) The names and business addresses of the officers, directors, trustees, managing or general partners, any person having a ten percent (10%) or greater equity or beneficial interest in the provider, and any person who will be managing the facility on a day-to-day basis, and a

description of these persons' interests in or occupations with the provider.

(3) The following information on all persons named in response to subdivision (2) of this section:

    a. A description of the business experience of this person, if any, in the operation or management of similar facilities;

    b. The name and address of any professional service firm, association, trust, partnership, or corporation in which this person has, or which has in this person, a ten percent (10%) or greater interest and which it is presently intended shall currently or in the future provide goods, leases, or services to the facility, or to residents of the facility, of an aggregate value of five hundred dollars ($500.00) or more within any year, including a description of the goods, leases, or services and the probable or anticipated cost thereof to the facility, provider, or residents or a statement that this cost cannot presently be estimated; and

    c. A description of any matter in which the person (i) has been convicted of a felony or pleaded nolo contendere to a felony charge, or been held liable or enjoined in a civil action by final judgment, if the felony or civil action involved fraud, embezzlement, fraudulent conversion, or misappropriation of property; or (ii) is subject to a currently effective injunctive or restrictive court order, or within the past five years, had any State or federal license or permit suspended or revoked as a result of an action brought by a governmental agency or department, if the order or action arose out of or related to business activity of health care, including actions affecting a license to operate a foster care facility, nursing home, retirement home, home for aged, or facility subject to this Article or a similar law in another state.

(4) A statement as to whether the provider is, or is not affiliated with, a religious, charitable, or other nonprofit organization, the extent of the affiliation, if any, the extent to which the affiliate organization will be responsible for the financial and contract obligations of the provider, and the provision of the Federal Internal Revenue Code, if any, under which the provider or affiliate is exempt from the payment of income tax.

(5) The location and description of the physical property or properties of the facility, existing or proposed, and to the extent proposed, the estimated completion date or dates, whether construction has begun, and the contingencies subject to which construction may be deferred.

(6) The services provided or proposed to be provided pursuant to contracts for continuing care at the facility, including the extent to which medical care is furnished, and a clear statement of which services are included for specified basic fees for continuing care and which services are made available at or by the facility at extra charge.

(7) A description of all fees required of residents, including the entrance fee and periodic charges, if any. The description shall include:

    a. A statement of the fees that will be charged if the resident marries while at the facility, and a statement of the terms concerning the entry of a spouse to the facility and the consequences if the spouse does not meet the requirements for entry;

    b. The circumstances under which the resident will be permitted to remain in the facility in the event of possible financial difficulties of the resident;

    c. The terms and conditions under which a contract for continuing care at the facility may be canceled by the provider or by the resident, and the conditions, if any, under which all or any portion of the entrance fee or any other fee will be refunded in the event of cancellation of the contract by the provider or by the resident or in the event of the death of the resident prior to or following occupancy of a living unit;

    d. The conditions under which a living unit occupied by a resident may be made available by the provider to a different or new resident other than on the death of the prior resident; and

    e. The manner by which the provider may adjust periodic charges or other recurring fees and the limitations on these adjustments, if any; and, if the facility is already in operation, or if the provider or manager operates one or more similar continuing care locations within this State, tables shall be included showing the frequency and average dollar amount of each increase in periodic charges, or other recurring fees at each facility or location for the previous five years, or such shorter period as the facility or location may have been operated by the provider or manager.

(8) The health and financial condition required for an individual to be accepted as a resident and to continue as a resident once accepted, including the effect of any change in the health or financial condition of a person between the date of entering into a contract for continuing care and the date of initial occupancy of a living unit by that person.

(9) The provisions that have been made or will be made, including, but not limited to, the requirements of G.S. 58-64-33 and G.S. 58-64-35, to provide reserve funding or security to enable the provider to perform its obligations fully under contracts to provide continuing care at the facility, including the establishment of escrow accounts, trusts, or reserve funds, together with the manner in which these funds will be invested, and the names and experience of any individuals in the direct employment of the provider who will make the investment decisions.

(10) Financial statements of the provider certified to by an independent public accountant as of the end of the most recent fiscal year or such shorter period of time as the provider shall have been in existence. If the provider's fiscal year ended more than 120 days prior to the date the disclosure statement is recorded, interim financial statements as of a date not more than 90 days prior to the date of recording the statement shall also be included, but need not be certified to by an independent certified public accountant.

(11) In the event the provider has had an actuarial report prepared within the prior two years, the summary of a report of an actuary that estimates the capacity of the provider to meet its contractual obligations to the residents.

(12) Forecasted financial statements for the provider of the next five years, including a balance sheet, a statement of operations, a statement of cash flows, and a statement detailing all significant assumptions, compiled by an independent certified public accountant. Reporting routine, categories, and structure may be further defined by regulations or forms adopted by the Commissioner.

(13) The estimated number of residents of the facility to be provided services by the provider pursuant to the contract for continuing care.

(14) Proposed or development stage facilities shall additionally provide:

    a. The summary of the report of an actuary estimating the capacity of the provider to meet its contractual obligation to the residents;

    b. Narrative disclosure detailing all significant assumptions used in the preparation of the forecasted financial statements, including:

1. Details of any long-term financing for the purchase or construction of the facility including interest rate, repayment terms, loan covenants, and assets pledged;
2. Details of any other funding sources that the provider anticipates using to fund any start-up losses or to provide reserve funds to assure full performance of the obligations of the provider under contracts for the provision of continuing care;
3. The total life occupancy fees to be received from or on behalf of, residents at, or prior to, commencement of operations along with anticipated accounting methods used in the recognition of revenues from and expected refunds of life occupancy fees;
4. A description of any equity capital to be received by the facility;
5. The cost of the acquisition of the facility or, if the facility is to be constructed, the estimated cost of the acquisition of the land and construction cost of the facility;
6. Related costs, such as financing any development costs that the provider expects to incur or become obligated for prior to the commencement of operations;
7. The marketing and resident acquisition costs to be incurred prior to commencement of operations; and
8. A description of the assumptions used for calculating the estimated occupancy rate of the facility and the effect on the income of the facility of government subsidies for health care services.

(15) Any other material information concerning the facility or the provider which, if omitted, would lead a reasonable person not to enter into this contract.

(b) The cover page of the disclosure statement shall state, in a prominent location and in boldface type, the date of the disclosure statement, the last date through which that disclosure statement may be delivered if not earlier revised, and that the delivery of the disclosure statement to a contracting party before the execution of a contract for the provision of continuing care is required by this Article but that the disclosure statement has not been reviewed or approved by any government agency or representative to ensure accuracy or completeness of the information set out.

(c) A copy of the standard form of contract for continuing care used by the provider shall be attached to each disclosure statement.

(d) The Commissioner, by rules adopted by him under this Article, may prescribe a standardized format for the disclosure statement required by this section.

(e) The disclosure statement shall be in plain English and in language understandable by a layperson and combine simplicity and accuracy to fully advise residents of the items required by this section.

(f) The Department may require a provider to alter or amend its disclosure statement in order to provide full and fair disclosure to prospective residents. The Department may also require the revision of a disclosure statement which it finds to be unnecessarily complex, confusing or illegible. (1989, c. 758, s. 1; 1991, c. 196, s. 3; c. 720, s. 89; 1993, c. 452, s. 63; 2001-223, s. 22.2; 2003-193, ss. 3, 4, 5, 6.)

Editor's Note. — Session Laws 2003-193, s. 16, is a severability clause.

Effect of Amendments. — Session Laws 2003-193, ss. 3 through 6, effective June 12, 2003, in subdivisions (a)(7)d., (a)(11), and in the first sentence of subdivision (a)(12), substituted "provider" for "facility"; in the first sentence of subdivision (a)(12), substituted "Forecasted" for "Forecast"; and in subdivision (a)(14)b., substituted "forecasted" for "forecast."

§ 58-64-25. Contract for continuing care; specifications.

(a) Each contract for continuing care shall provide that:
(1) The party contracting with the provider may rescind the contract within 30 days following the later of the execution of the contract or the receipt of a disclosure statement that meets the requirements of this section, and the resident to whom the contract pertains is not required to move into the facility before the expiration of the 30-day period; and
(2) If a resident dies before occupying a living unit in the facility, or if, on account of illness, injury, or incapacity, a resident would be precluded from occupying a living unit in the facility under the terms of the contract for continuing care, the contract is automatically canceled; and
(3) For rescinded or canceled contracts under this section, the resident or the resident's legal representative shall receive a refund of all money or property transferred to the provider, less (i) periodic charges specified in the contract and applicable only to the period a living unit was actually occupied by the resident; (ii) those nonstandard costs specifically incurred by the provider or facility at the request of the resident and described in the contract or any contract amendment signed by the resident; (iii) nonrefundable fees, if set out in the contract; and (iv) a reasonable service charge, if set out in the contract, not to exceed the greater of one thousand dollars ($1,000) or two percent (2%) of the entrance fee.
(b) Each contract shall include provisions that specify the following:
(1) The total consideration to be paid;
(2) Services to be provided;
(3) The procedures the provider shall follow to change the resident's accommodation if necessary for the protection of the health or safety of the resident or the general and economic welfare of the residents;
(4) The policies to be implemented if the resident cannot pay the periodic fees;
(5) The terms governing the refund of any portion of the entrance fee in the event of discharge by the provider or cancellation by the resident;
(6) The policy regarding increasing the periodic fees;
(7) The description of the living quarters;
(8) Any religious or charitable affiliations of the provider and the extent, if any, to which the affiliate organization will be responsible for the financial and contractual obligations of the provider;
(9) Any property rights of the resident;
(10) The policy, if any, regarding fee adjustments if the resident is voluntarily absent from the facility; and
(11) Any requirement, if any, that the resident apply for Medicaid, public assistance, or any public benefit program. (1989, c. 758, s. 1; 1991, c. 196, s. 4.)

§ 58-64-30. Annual disclosure statement revision.

(a) Within 150 days following the end of each fiscal year, the provider shall file with the Commissioner a revised disclosure statement setting forth current information required pursuant to G.S. 58-64-20. The provider shall also make this revised disclosure statement available to all the residents of the facility. This revised disclosure statement shall include a narrative describing any material differences between (i) the forecasted statements of revenues and expenses and cash flows or other forecasted financial data filed pursuant to

G.S. 58-64-20 as a part of the disclosure statement recorded most immediately subsequent to the start of the provider's most recently completed fiscal year and (ii) the actual results of operations during that fiscal year, together with the revised forecasted statements of revenues and expenses and cash flows or other forecasted financial data being filed as a part of the revised disclosure statement. A provider may also revise its disclosure statement and have the revised disclosure statement recorded at any other time if, in the opinion of the provider, revision is necessary to prevent an otherwise current disclosure statement from containing a material misstatement of fact or omitting a material fact required to be stated therein. Only the most recently recorded disclosure statement, with respect to a facility, and in any event, only a disclosure statement dated within one year plus 150 days prior to the date of delivery, shall be considered current for purposes of this Article or delivered pursuant to G.S. 58-64-20.

(b) The annual disclosure statement required to be filed with the Commissioner under this section shall be accompanied by an annual filing fee of one hundred dollars ($100.00). (1989, c. 758, s. 1; 2003-193, s. 7.)

Editor's Note. — Session Laws 2003-193, s. 16, is a severability clause.

Effect of Amendments. — Session Laws

2003-193, s. 7, effective June 12, 2003, substituted "forecasted" for "forecast" in four places in the second sentence of subsection (a).

§ 58-64-33. Operating reserves.

(a) A provider shall maintain after the opening of a facility: an operating reserve equal to fifty percent (50%) of the total operating costs of the facility forecasted for the 12-month period following the period covered by the most recent disclosure statement filed with the Department. The forecast statements as required by G.S. 58-64-20(a)(12) shall serve as the basis for computing the operating reserve. In addition to total operating expenses, total operating costs will include debt service, consisting of principal and interest payments along with taxes and insurance on any mortgage loan or other long-term financing, but will exclude depreciation, amortized expenses, and extraordinary items as approved by the Commissioner. If the debt service portion is accounted for by way of another reserve account, the debt service portion may be excluded. If a facility maintains an occupancy level in excess of ninety percent (90%), a provider shall only be required to maintain a twenty-five percent (25%) operating reserve upon approval of the Commissioner, unless otherwise instructed by the Commissioner. The operating reserve must be funded by cash, by cash equivalents, or by investment grade securities, including bonds, stocks, U.S. Treasury obligations, or obligations of U.S. government agencies.

(b) A provider that has begun construction or has permanent financing in place or is in operation on the effective date of this section has up to five years to meet the operating reserve requirements.

(c) An operating reserve shall only be released upon the submittal of a detailed request from the provider or facility and must be approved by the Commissioner. Such requests must be submitted in writing for the Commissioner to review at least 10 business days prior to the date of withdrawal. (1991, c. 196, s. 5; c. 720, s. 89; 1993, c. 452, s. 64; 1993 (Reg. Sess., 1994), c. 678, s. 29; 1995, c. 193, s. 52; 2003-193, s. 8.)

Editor's Note. — Session Laws 2003-193, s. 16, is a severability clause.

Effect of Amendments. — Session Laws 2003-193, s. 8, effective June 12, 2003, in subsection (a), substituted "A provider shall main-

tain after the opening of a facility: an operating reserve" for "All continuing care facilities shall maintain after opening: operating reserves," substituted "operating costs of the facility forecasted" for "operating costs projected," and substituted "recent disclosure statement" for "recent annual statement" in the first sentence, in the fifth sentence, substituted "If a facility maintains" for "Facilities that maintain," inserted "a provider", and made a minor stylistic change; and in the first sentence of subsection (c), substituted "An operating reserve" for "Operating reserves."

§ 58-64-35. Escrow, collection of deposits.

(a) Where escrow accounts are required by this Article, a provider shall establish an escrow account with (i) a bank, (ii) a trust company, or (iii) another independent person or entity agreed upon by the provider and the resident, unless such account arrangement is prohibited by the Commissioner. The terms of this escrow account shall provide that the total amount of any entrance fee, or any other fee or deposit that may be applied toward the entrance fee, received by the provider be placed in this escrow account. These funds may be released only as follows:

(1) The first twenty-five percent (25%) of escrowed monies can be released when: (i) the provider has presold at least fifty percent (50%) of the independent living units, having received a minimum ten percent (10%) deposit on the presold units; (ii) the provider has received a commitment for any permanent mortgage loan or other long-term financing, and any conditions of the commitment prior to disbursement of funds thereunder have been substantially satisfied; and (iii) aggregate entrance fees received or receivable by the provider pursuant to binding continuing care contracts, plus the anticipated proceeds of any first mortgage loan or other long-term financing commitment are equal to not less than ninety percent (90%) of the aggregate cost of constructing or purchasing, equipping, and furnishing the facility plus not less than ninety percent (90%) of the funds estimated in the statement of cash flows submitted by the provider as that part of the disclosure statement required by G.S. 58-64-20, to be necessary to fund start-up losses and assure full performance of the obligations of the provider pursuant to continuing care contracts.

(2) The remaining seventy-five percent (75%) of escrowed monies can be released when:

a. (i) the provider has presold a minimum of seventy-five percent (75%) of the independent living units, having received a minimum ten percent (10%) deposit on the presold units, or has maintained an independent living unit occupancy minimum of seventy-five percent (75%) for at least 60 days; (ii) construction or purchase of the independent living unit has been completed and an occupancy permit, if applicable, has been issued by the local government having authority to issue such permits; and (iii) the living unit becomes available for occupancy by the new resident; or

b. the provider submits a plan of reorganization that is accepted and approved by the Commissioner.

(b) Upon receipt by the escrow agent of a request by the provider for the release of these escrow funds, the escrow agent shall approve release of the funds within five working days unless the escrow agent finds that the requirements of subsection (a) of this section have not been met and notifies the provider of the basis for this finding. The request for release of the escrow funds shall be accompanied by any documentation the fiduciary requires.

(b1) Release of any escrowed funds that may be due to the subscriber or resident shall occur upon: five working days' notice of death, nonacceptance by the facility, or voluntary cancellation. If voluntary cancellation occurs after construction has begun, the refund may be delayed until a new subscriber is obtained for that specific unit, provided it does not exceed a period of two years.

(c) If the provider fails to meet the requirements for release of funds held in this escrow account within a time period the escrow agent considers reasonable, these funds shall be returned by the escrow agent to the persons who have made payment to the provider. The escrow agent shall notify the provider of the length of this time period when the provider requests release of the funds.

(d) Facilities that currently meet the seventy-five percent (75%) presales or the seventy-five percent (75%) occupancy requirements, as outlined in subdivision (a)(2) of this section, are not required to escrow entrance fees, unless otherwise required by the Commissioner. (1989, c. 758, s. 1; 1991, c. 196, s. 6; c. 720, s. 8; c. 761, ss. 11, 12.)

§ 58-64-40. Right to organization.

(a) A resident living in a facility operated by a provider licensed under this Article has the right of self-organization, the right to be represented by an individual of the resident's own choosing, and the right to engage in concerted activities to keep informed on the operation of the facility in which the resident resides or for other mutual aid or protection.

(b) The board of directors or other governing body of a provider or its designated representative shall hold semiannual meetings with the residents of each facility operated by the provider for free discussions of subjects including, but not limited to, income, expenditures, and financial trends and problems as they apply to the facility and discussions of proposed changes in policies, programs, and services. Upon request of the most representative residents' organization, a member of the governing body of the provider, such as a board member, a general partner, or a principal owner shall attend such meetings. Residents shall be entitled to at least seven days advance notice of each meeting. An agenda and any materials that will be distributed by the governing body at the meetings shall remain available upon request to residents. (1989, c. 758, s. 1; 1999-132, s. 2.4; 2001-223, s. 22.3; 2003-193, s. 9.)

Editor's Note. — Session Laws 2003-193, s. 16, is a severability clause.

Effect of Amendments. — Session Laws 2003-193, s. 9, effective June 12, 2003, in subsection (a), substituted "operated by a provider licensed under this Article" for "registered under this Article," "the resident's" for "his," and "the resident resides" for "he is a resident"; and in the first sentence of subsection (b), substituted "provider" for "facility" and "each facility operated by the provider" for "the facility."

§ 58-64-45. Supervision, rehabilitation, and liquidation.

(a) If, at any time, the Commissioner determines, after notice and an opportunity for the provider to be heard, that:

(1) A portion of an entrance fee escrow account required to be maintained under this Article has been or is proposed to be released in violation of this Article;

(2) A provider has been or will be unable, in such a manner as may endanger the ability of the provider, to fully perform its obligations pursuant to contracts for continuing care, to meet the forecasted financial data previously filed by the provider;

(3) A provider has failed to maintain the escrow account required under this Article; or

(4) A provider is bankrupt or insolvent, or in imminent danger of becoming bankrupt or insolvent;

the Commissioner may commence a supervision proceeding pursuant to Article 30 of this Chapter or may apply to the Superior Court of Wake County or to the federal bankruptcy court that may have previously taken jurisdiction over the provider or facility for an order directing the Commissioner or authorizing the Commissioner to rehabilitate or to liquidate a facility in accordance with Article 30 of this Chapter.

(b) The definition of "insolvency" or "insolvent" in G.S. 58-30-10(13) shall not apply to providers under this Article. Rules adopted by the Commissioner shall define and describe "insolvency" or "hazardous financial condition" for providers under this Article. G.S. 58-30-12 shall not apply to facilities under this Article.

(c) If, at any time, the Court finds, upon petition of the Commissioner or provider, or on its own motion, that the objectives of an order to rehabilitate a provider have been accomplished and that the facility or facilities owned by, or operated by, the provider can be returned to the provider's management without further jeopardy to the residents of the facility or facilities, the Court may, upon a full report and accounting of the conduct of the provider's affairs during the rehabilitation and of the provider's current financial condition, terminate the rehabilitation and, by order, return the facility or facilities owned by, or operated by, the provider, along with the assets and affairs of the provider, to the provider's management.

(d), (e) Repealed by Session Laws 1995 (Regular Session, 1996), c. 582, s. 3.

(f) In applying for an order to rehabilitate or liquidate a provider, the Commissioner shall give due consideration in the application to the manner in which the welfare of persons who have previously contracted with the provider for continuing care may be best served.

(g) An order for rehabilitation shall be refused or vacated if the provider posts a bond, by a recognized surety authorized to do business in this State and executed in favor of the Commissioner on behalf of persons who may be found entitled to a refund of entrance fees from the provider or other damages in the event the provider is unable to fulfill its contracts to provide continuing care at the facility or facilities, in an amount determined by the Court to be equal to the reserve funding that would otherwise need to be available to fulfill such obligations. (1989, c. 758, s. 1; 1995 (Reg. Sess., 1996), c. 582, s. 3; 2003-193, s. 10.)

Editor's Note. — Session Laws 2003-193, s. 16, is a severability clause.

Effect of Amendments. — Session Laws 2003-193, s. 10, effective June 12, 2003, in subdivision (a)(2), substituted "forecasted" for "projected"; in subdivision (a)(4) and subsections (c) and (f), substituted "provider" for "facility"; in the first and last sentences of subsection (b), substituted "providers" for "facilities"; in subsection (c), inserted "or facilities owned by, or operated by, the provider," substituted "facility or facilities" for "facility," "provider's" for "facility's" in two places, and "or facilities owned by, or operated by, the provider, along with the" for "and its"; and in subsection (g), substituted "facility or facilities" for "facility."

§ 58-64-46. Receiverships; exception for facility beds.

When the Commissioner has been appointed as a receiver under Article 30 of this Chapter for a provider or facility subject to this Article, the Department of Health and Human Services may, notwithstanding any other provision of law, accept and approve the addition of adult care home beds for a facility owned by, or operated by, the provider, if it appears to the court, upon petition of the Commissioner or the provider, or on the court's own motion, that (i) the best interests of the provider or (ii) the welfare of persons who have previously contracted with the provider or may contract with the provider, may be best served by the addition of adult care home beds. (1999-219, s. 2; 2003-193, s. 11.)

Editor's Note. — Session Laws 2003-193, s. 16, is a severability clause.

Effect of Amendments. — Session Laws 2003-193, s. 11, effective June 12, 2003, substituted "for a facility owned by, or operated by, the provider" for "for that facility"; substituted

"provider" for "facility" in two places; and made
a minor punctuation change.

§ 58-64-50. Investigations and subpoenas.

(a) The Commissioner may make such public or private investigations
within or outside of this State as necessary (i) to determine whether any person
has violated or is about to violate any provision of this Article, (ii) to aid in the
enforcement of this Article, or (iii) to verify statements contained in any
disclosure statement filed or delivered under this Article.

(b) For the purpose of any investigation or proceeding under this Article, the
Commissioner may require or permit any person to file a statement in writing,
under oath or otherwise, as to any of the facts and circumstances concerning
the matter to be investigated.

(c) For the purpose of any investigation or proceeding under this Article, the
Commissioner or his designee has all the powers given to him for insurance
companies. He may administer oaths and affirmations, subpoena witnesses,
compel their attendance, take evidence, and require the production of any
books, papers, correspondence, memoranda, agreements, or other documents
or records deemed relevant or material to the inquiry, all of which may be
enforced in the Superior Court of Wake County. (1989, c. 758, s. 1.)

§ 58-64-55. Examinations; financial statements.

The Commissioner or the Commissioner's designee may, in the Commissioner's discretion, visit a provider offering continuing care in this State to examine
its books and records. Expenses incurred by the Commissioner in conducting
examinations under this section shall be paid by the provider examined. The
provisions of G.S. 58-2-131, 58-2-132, 58-2-133, 58-2-134, 58-2-155, 58-2-165,
58-2-180, 58-2-185, 58-2-190, and 58-6-5 apply to this Article and are hereby
incorporated by reference. (1989, c. 758, s. 1; 1995, c. 193, s. 53; 1999-132, s.
11.9; 2003-193, s. 12.)

Editor's Note. — Session Laws 2003-193, s.
16, is a severability clause.
Effect of Amendments. — Session Laws

2003-193, s. 12, effective June 12, 2003, substituted "provider" for "facility" in the first and
second sentences.

§ 58-64-60. Contracts as preferred claims on liquidation.

In the event of liquidation of a provider, all contracts for continuing care
executed by the provider shall be deemed preferred claims against all assets
owned by the provider; provided, however, such claims shall be subordinate to
the liquidator's cost of administration or any secured claim. (1989, c. 758, s. 1;
1995 (Reg. Sess., 1996), c. 582, s. 4; 2003-193, s. 13.)

Editor's Note. — Session Laws 2003-193, s.
16, is a severability clause.
Effect of Amendments. — Session Laws
2003-193, s. 13, effective June 12, 2003, in the

section heading, substituted "Contracts" for
"Agreements"; and substituted "contracts for
continuing care" for "continuing care agreements."

§ 58-64-65. Rule-making authority; reasonable time to comply with rules.

(a) The Commissioner is authorized to promulgate rules to carry out and
enforce the provisions of this Article.

(b) Any provider who is offering continuing care may be given a reasonable time, not to exceed one year from the date of publication of any applicable rules promulgated pursuant to this Article, within which to comply with the rules. (1989, c. 758, s. 1; 2003-193, s. 14.)

Editor's Note. — Session Laws 2003-193, s. 16, is a severability clause.

Effect of Amendments. — Session Laws 2003-193, s. 14, effective June 12, 2003, deleted "and to obtain a license" at the end of subsection (b).

§ 58-64-70. Civil liability.

(a) A provider who enters into a contract for continuing care at a facility without having first delivered a disclosure statement meeting the requirements of G.S. 58-64-20 to the person contracting for this continuing care, or enters into a contract for continuing care at a facility with a person who has relied on a disclosure statement that omits to state a material fact required to be stated therein or necessary in order to make the statements made therein, in light of the circumstances under which they are made, not misleading, shall be liable to the person contracting for this continuing care for actual damages and repayment of all fees paid to the provider violating this Article, less the reasonable value of care and lodging provided to the resident by or on whose behalf the contract for continuing care was entered into prior to discovery of the violation, misstatement, or omission or the time the violation, misstatement, or omission should reasonably have been discovered, together with interest thereon at the legal rate for judgments, and court costs and reasonable attorney fees.

(b) Liability under this section exists regardless of whether the provider had actual knowledge of the misstatement or omission.

(c) A person may not file or maintain an action under this section if the person, before filing the action, received a written offer of a refund of all amounts paid the provider, together with interest at the rate established monthly by the Commissioner of Banks pursuant to G.S. 24-1.1(c), less the current contractual value of care and lodging provided prior to receipt of the offer, and if the offer recited the provisions of this section and the recipient of the offer failed to accept it within 30 days of actual receipt.

(d) An action may not be maintained to enforce a liability created under this Article unless brought before the expiration of three years after the execution of the contract for continuing care that gave rise to the violation. (1989, c. 758, s. 1; 1995, c. 193, s. 54; 2003-193, s. 15.)

Editor's Note. — Session Laws 2003-193, s. 16, is a severability clause.

Effect of Amendments. — Session Laws 2003-193, s. 15, effective June 12, 2003, in subsection (a), deleted "facility, or person" preceding "violating this Article" and made a minor punctuation change; in subsection (b), deleted "or person liable" following "the provider"; and in subsection (c), deleted "facility, or person violating this Article" following "paid the provider."

§ 58-64-75. Criminal penalties.

Any person who willfully and knowingly violates any provision of this Article is guilty of a Class 1 misdemeanor. The Commissioner may refer such evidence as is available concerning violation of the Article or of any rule or order hereunder to the Attorney General or a district attorney who may, with or without such reference institute the appropriate criminal proceedings under this Article. Nothing in this Article limits the power of the State to punish any person for any conduct that constitutes a crime under any other statute. (1989, c. 758, s. 1; 1993, c. 539, s. 469; 1994, Ex. Sess., c. 24, s. 14(c).)

§ 58-64-80. Advisory Committee.

There shall be a nine member Continuing Care Advisory Committee appointed by the Commissioner. The Committee shall consist of at least two residents of facilities, two representatives of the North Carolina Association of Nonprofit Homes for the Aging, one individual who is a certified public accountant and is licensed to practice in this State, one individual skilled in the field of architecture or engineering, and one individual who is a health care professional. (1989, c. 758, s. 1; 1999-132, s. 2.5.)

§ 58-64-85. Other licensing or regulation.

Nothing in this Article affects the authority of the Department of Health and Human Services or any successor agency otherwise provided by law to license or regulate any health service facility or domiciliary service facility. (1991, c. 720, s. 1; 1997-443, s. 11A.118(a).)

ARTICLE 65.

Hospital, Medical and Dental Service Corporations.

Part 1. In General.

Editor's Note. — Sections 58-65-1 through 58-65-165 have been designated Part 1 of Article 65 at the direction of the Revisor of Statutes in view of new G.S. 58-65-166 et seq. [Part 2] added by Session Laws 1989 (Reg. Sess., 1990), c. 1071, s. 1.

§ 58-65-1. Regulation and definitions; application of other laws; profit and foreign corporations prohibited.

(a) Any corporation organized under the general corporation laws of the State of North Carolina for the purpose of maintaining and operating a nonprofit hospital or medical or dental service plan whereby hospital care or medical or dental service may be provided in whole or in part by the corporation or by hospitals, physicians, or dentists participating in the plan, or plans, shall be governed by this Article and Article 66 of this Chapter and shall be exempt from all other provisions of the insurance laws of this State, unless otherwise provided.

The term "hospital service plan" as used in this Article includes the contracting for certain fees for, or furnishing of, hospital care, laboratory facilities, X-ray facilities, drugs, appliances, anesthesia, nursing care, operating and obstetrical equipment, accommodations or any other services authorized or permitted to be furnished by a hospital under the laws of the State of North Carolina and approved by the North Carolina Hospital Association or the American Medical Association.

The term "medical service plan" as used in this Article includes the contracting for the payment of fees toward, or furnishing of, medical, obstetrical, surgical or any other professional services authorized or permitted to be furnished by a duly licensed physician or other provider listed in G.S. 58-50-30. The term "medical services plan" also includes the contracting for the payment of fees toward, or furnishing of, professional medical services authorized or permitted to be furnished by a duly licensed provider of health services licensed under Chapter 90 of the General Statutes.

The term "dental service plan" as used in this Article includes contracting for the payment of fees toward, or furnishing of dental or any other professional services authorized or permitted to be furnished by a duly licensed dentist.

The term "hospital service corporation" as used in this Article is intended to mean any nonprofit corporation operating a hospital or medical or dental service plan, as defined in this section. Any corporation organized and subject to the provisions of this Article, the certificate of incorporation of which authorizes the operation of either a hospital or medical or dental service plan, or any or all of them, may, with the approval of the Commissioner, issue subscribers' contracts or certificates approved by the Commissioner of Insurance, for the payment of either hospital or medical or dental fees, or the furnishing of such services, or any or all of them, and may enter into contracts with hospitals for physicians or dentists, or any or all of them, for the furnishing of fees or services respectively under a hospital or medical or dental service plan, or any or all of them.

The term "preferred provider" as used in this Article with respect to contracts, organizations, policies or otherwise means a health care service provider who has agreed to accept, from a corporation organized for the purposes authorized by this Article or other applicable law, special reimbursement terms in exchange for providing services to beneficiaries of a plan administered pursuant to this Article. Except to the extent prohibited either by G.S. 58-65-140 or by rules adopted by the Commissioner not inconsistent with this Article, the contractual terms and conditions for special reimbursement shall be those which the corporation and preferred provider find to be mutually agreeable.

(b) through (c) Repealed by Session Laws 2001-297.

(d) No foreign or alien hospital or medical or dental service corporation as herein defined shall be authorized to do business in this State. (1941, c. 338, s. 1; 1943, c. 537, s. 1; 1953, c. 1124, s. 1; 1961, c. 1149; 1965, c. 396, s. 1; c. 1169, s. 1; 1967, c. 690, s. 1; 1973, c. 642; 1977, c. 601, ss. 1, 31/2; 1985, c. 735, s. 2; 1993, c. 347, s. 3; c. 375, s. 4; 464, s. 3.1; 1995, c. 223, s. 2; c. 406, s. 4; 1997-197, ss. 1, 2; 1999-186, s. 1; 1999-199, s. 2; 1999-210, ss. 5, 6; 2001-297, s. 2; 2001-487, ss. 40(h), 105(a), 105(b); 2003-212, s. 17.)

Cross References. — For the Insurance Information and Privacy Protection Act, see G.S. 58-39-1 et seq. For provisions of Chapter 58 made applicable to hospital and medical service corporations, see notes to G.S. 58-50-5, 58-51-10, 58-51-60 and 58-63-15. For provisions of Chapter 58 made applicable to medical service plan policies and hospital service plan policies issued under this chapter, see G.S. 58-51-25. As to coverage to be afforded to mentally retarded and physically handicapped children, see G.S. 58-51-25. For the Health Maintenance Organization Act of 1979, see G.S. 58-67-1 et seq. As to taxes levied on gross insurance premiums, see G.S. 105-228.5. As to authority of Commission for Health Services to regulate the sanitation of private hospitals, etc., see G.S. 130A-235. For provisions applicable to corporations governed by this Chapter which relate to the elimination of discrimination in treatment of handicapped and disabled persons, see G.S. 168-10.

Estimated Premium Tax Liability. — Session Laws 2001-489, s. 2.(e) provides that, notwithstanding the provisions of G.S 105-228.5(f), the following provisions apply to Article 65 Corporations and Health Maintenance Organizations, as defined in G.S. 105-228.3, for the 2003 taxable year in lieu of the provisions of G.S. 105-228.5(f):

Article 65 Corporations and Health Maintenance Organizations that are subject to the tax imposed by G.S. 105-228.5 and have an estimated premium tax liability for the 2003 taxable year, not including the additional local fire and lightning tax, of ten thousand dollars ($10,000) or more forbusiness done in North Carolina shall remit two estimated tax payments with each payment equal to fifty percent (50%) of the taxpayer's estimated premium tax liability for the 2003 taxable year. The first estimated payment is due on or before April 15, 2003, and the second estimated payment is due on or before June 15, 2003. The taxpayer must remit the balance by the following March 15 in the same manner provided in G.S. 105-228.5(e) for annual returns.

An underpayment of an estimated payment required by this subsection bears interest at the rate established under G.S. 105-241.1(i).

Any overpayment bears interest as provided in G.S. 105-266(b) and, together with the interest, must be credited to the taxpayer and applied against the taxes imposed upon the company under G.S. 105-228.5.

The penalties provided in Article 9 of Chapter 105 of the General Statutes apply to the estimated tax payments required by this subsection.

Editor's Note. — Articles 65 and 66 are former Chapter 57. Chapter 57 has been recodified as Articles 65 and 66 of Chapter 58 pursuant to Session Laws 1987, c. 752, s. 9, as amended by Session Laws 1987 (Reg. Sess., 1988), c. 975, s. 34.

Session Laws 1965, c. 396, s. 4, provided that nothing in the first 1965 amendment to this section, which added the exception at the end of the third paragraph (of present subsection (a)), should be construed to equate optometrists with physicians except to the extent that each must be duly licensed.

Session Laws 1967, c. 690, s. 4, provided that nothing in the 1967 amendment to this section, which added the second sentence of the third paragraph (of present subsection (a)), should be construed to equate podiatrists with physicians except to the extent that each must be duly licensed.

This section was amended by Session Laws 1993, c. 347, s. 3; c. 375, s. 4 and c. 464, s. 3.1, in the coded bill drafting format provided by G.S. 120-20.1. It has been set out in the form above at the direction of the Revisor of Statutes.

Session Laws 1995, c. 406, s. 6, had provided that the amendments to this section by Session Laws 1995, c. 406, s. 4, would expire July 1, 1999. However, Session Laws 1999-186, s. 1 deleted the July 1, 1999 expiration date.

Session Laws 2001-387, s. 154(b), provides that nothing in this act shall supersede the provisions of Article 10 or 65 of Chapter 58 of the General Statutes, and this act does not create an alternate means for an entity governed by Article 65 of Chapter 58 of the General Statutes to convert to a different business form.

Session Laws 2001-487, s. 40(h), effective December 16, 2001, substituted "licensed clinical social worker" for "certified clinical social worker" throughout the section; and in the second paragraph in subsection (c), substituted "licensed by the North Carolina Social Work Certification and Licensure Board" for "certified by the North Carolina Certification Board for Social Work." However, in subsections (a) and (c) Session Laws 2001-487, s. 40(h) failed to

take account of changes by Session Laws 2001-297, s. 2, as amended by Session Laws 2001-487, s. 105(a) and (b), effective October 1, 2001. The section has been set out in the form above at the direction of the Revisor of Statutes.

Session Laws 2003-284, s. 43.3, provides:

"Notwithstanding the provisions of G.S 105-228.5(f), the following provisions apply to Article 65 Corporations, as defined in G.S. 105-228.3, for the 2004 and 2005 taxable years in lieu of the provisions of G.S.105-228.5(f):

"Article 65 corporations that are subject to the tax imposed by G.S. 105-228.5 and have an estimated premium tax liability for the 2004 or 2005 taxable year, not including the additional local fire and lightning tax, of ten thousand dollars ($10,000) or more for business done in North Carolina shall remit two estimated tax payments with each payment equal to fifty percent (50%) of the taxpayer's estimated premium tax liability for the relevant taxable year. The first estimated payment is due on or before April 15 of the relevant year and the second estimated payment is due on or before June 15 of the relevant year. The taxpayer must remit the balance by the following March 15 in the same manner provided in G.S.105-228.5(e) for annual returns.

"An underpayment of an estimated payment required by this section bears interest at the rate established under G.S. 105-241.1(i). Any overpayment bears interest as provided in G.S. 105-266(b) and, together with the interest, must be credited to the taxpayer and applied against the taxes imposed upon the company under G.S. 105-228.5.

"The penalties provided in Article 9 of Chapter 105 of the General Statutes apply to the estimated tax payments required by this section."

Effect of Amendments. — Session Laws 2003-212, s. 17, effective October 1, 2003, in subsection (a), deleted "and Article 66 of this Chapter" once in the second, third, and fourth paragraphs, twice in the fifth paragraph, and four times in the sixth paragraph, in the fourth paragraph, deleted "2" following "for the payment," in the fifth paragraph, deleted "of Insurance" following "approval of the Commissioner," and in the last paragraph, substituted "adopted" for "promulgated," deleted "Department of Insurance" following "adopted by the," and deleted "licensed licensed"; and in former subsection (c), deleted "licensed licensed Social Work and Licensure."

Legal Periodicals. — For comment on this Chapter, see 19 N.C.L. Rev. 487 (1941).

CASE NOTES

Cited in Cato v. Hospital Care Ass'n, 220 N.C. 479, 17 S.E.2d 671 (1941).

§ 58-65-2. Other laws applicable to service corporations.

The following provisions of this Chapter are applicable to service corporations that are subject to this Article:

G.S. 58-2-125.	Authority over all insurance companies; no exemptions from license.
G.S. 58-2-155.	Investigation of charges.
G.S. 58-2-160.	Reporting and investigation of insurance and reinsurance fraud and the financial condition of licensees; immunity from liability.
G.S. 58-2-162.	Embezzlement by insurance agents, brokers, or administrators.
G.S. 58-2-185.	Record of business kept by companies and agents; Commissioner may inspect.
G.S. 58-2-190.	Commissioner may require special reports.
G.S. 58-2-195.	Commissioner may require records, reports, etc., for agencies, agents, and others.
G.S. 58-2-200.	Books and papers required to be exhibited.
G.S. 58-3-50.	Companies must do business in own name; emblems, insignias, etc.
G.S. 58-3-115.	Twisting with respect to insurance policies; penalties.
G.S. 58-50-35.	Notice of nonpayment of premium required before forfeiture.
G.S. 58-51-25.	Policy coverage to continue as to mentally retarded or physically handicapped children. (1999-244, s. 1.)

§ 58-65-5. Contract for joint assumption or underwriting of risks.

Any corporation organized or regulated by the provisions of this Article and Article 66 of this Chapter is authorized to enter into such contracts with any other firm or corporation for joint assumption or underwriting of any part or all of any risks undertaken upon such terms and conditions as are approved by the Commissioner of Insurance. (1955, c. 894, s. 1.)

§ 58-65-10. Premium or dues paid by employer, employee, principal or agent or jointly and severally.

Any premium or dues charged by a corporation regulated under the provisions of this Article and Article 66 of this Chapter may be paid by the employer, employee, principal, or agent, or jointly and severally. The term "employer" as used herein includes counties, municipal corporations, and all departments or subdivisions of the State, county, municipal corporation, and official boards including city and county boards of alcoholic control, together with all others occupying the status of employer and employee, principal and agent. (1955, c. 894, s. 2.)

§ 58-65-15. Incorporation.

Any number of persons not less than seven, desiring to form a nonprofit hospital service corporation, shall incorporate under the provisions of the general laws of the State of North Carolina governing corporations, but subject to the following provisions:

(1) The certificate of incorporation of each such corporation shall have endorsed thereon or attached thereto, the consent of the Commissioner of Insurance, if he shall find the same to be in accordance with the provisions of this Article and Article 66 of this Chapter.

(2) A statement of the services to be rendered by the corporation and the rates currently to be charged therefor which said statement shall be accompanied by two copies of each contract for services which the corporation proposes to make with its subscribers, and two copies of the type of contract which said corporation proposes to make with participating hospitals, shall have been furnished the Commissioner of Insurance; provided, however, that if the articles of incorporation of any such corporation within the meaning of this Article and Article 66 of this Chapter shall have been filed with the Secretary of State prior to March 15, 1941, the approval thereof by the Commissioner of Insurance shall be evidenced by a separate instrument in writing filed with the Secretary of State. (1941, c. 338, s. 2.)

§ 58-65-20. Members of governing boards.

(a) For the purpose of this section the words "board of directors" includes the board of directors, trustees, or other governing board.

(b) The board of directors of each hospital service corporation subject to the provisions of this Article shall include persons who are representative of its subscribers and the general public. Less than one half of the directors of any such corporation shall be persons who are licensed to practice medicine in this State or who are paid directors or employees of a corporation organized for hospital purposes. (1979, c. 538, s. 1.)

§ 58-65-25. Hospital, physician and dentist contracts.

(a) Any corporation organized under this Article may enter into contracts for the rendering of hospital service to any of its subscribers by hospitals approved by the American Medical Association and/or the North Carolina Hospital Association, and may enter into contracts for the furnishing of, or the payment in whole or in part for, medical and/or dental services rendered to any of its subscribers by duly licensed physicians and/or dentists. All obligations arising under contracts issued by such corporations to its subscribers shall be satisfied by payments made directly to the hospitals or hospitals and/or physicians and/or dentists rendering such service, or direct to the subscriber or his, her, or their legal representatives upon the receipt by the corporation from the subscriber of a statement marked paid by the hospital(s) and/or physician(s) and/or dentist(s) or both rendering such service, and all such payments heretofore made are hereby ratified. Nothing in this section shall be construed to discriminate against hospitals conducted by other schools of medical practice.

(b) All certificates, plans or contracts issued to subscribers or other persons by hospital and medical and/or dental service corporations operating under this Article shall contain in substance a provision as follows: "After two years from the date of issue of this certificate, contract or plan no misstatements, except fraudulent misstatements made by the applicant in the application for such certificate, contract or plan, shall be used to void said certificate, contract or plan, or to deny a claim for loss incurred or disability (as therein defined) commencing after the expiration of such two-year period." (1941, c. 338, s. 3; 1943, c. 537, s. 2; 1947, c. 820, s. 1; 1955, c. 850, s. 7; 1961, c. 1149; 1979, c. 755, s. 17; 1997-259, s. 16.)

Cross References. — For the Readable Insurance Policies Act, see G.S. 58-38-1 et seq.

§ 58-65-30. Dentists' services.

Any corporation organized under the provisions of this Article and Article 66 of this Chapter may, in addition to its authority to contract under G.S. 58-65-25, enter into contracts to pay duly licensed dentists for treatment of fractures and dislocations of the jaw, and cutting procedures in the oral cavity other than extractions, repairs and care of the teeth and gums. (1957, c. 987.)

§ 58-65-35. Nurses' services.

No agency, institution or physician providing a service for which payment or reimbursement is required to be made under a contract governed by this Article and Article 66 of this Chapter shall be denied such payment or reimbursement on account of the fact that the service was rendered through a registered nurse acting under authority of rules and regulations adopted by the North Carolina Medical Board and the Board of Nursing pursuant to G.S. 90-6 and 90-171.23. (1973, c. 436; 1991, c. 720, s. 37; 1993, c. 347, s. 4; 1995, c. 94, s. 4; 1997-197, s. 1.)

Editor's Note. — Session Laws 1993, c. 347, s. 5 provided that the amendment by c. 347, s. 2 applied to all plans and policies with an inception, renewal, or anniversary date on or after October 1, 1993, and expired October 1, 1998. The expiration date was deleted by Session Laws 1997-197, s. 1.

§ 58-65-36. Physician services provided by physician assistants.

No agency, institution, or physician providing a service for which payment or reimbursement is required to be made under a contract governed by this Article or Article 66 of this Chapter shall be denied the payment or reimbursement on account of the fact that the service was rendered through a physician assistant acting under authority of rules adopted by the North Carolina Medical Board pursuant to G.S. 90-18.1. (1999-210, s. 4.)

Editor's Note. — Session Laws 1999-210, s. 9, made this section effective January 1, 2000, and applicable to treatment or services rendered on or after that date.

§ 58-65-40. Supervision of Commissioner of Insurance; form of contract with subscribers; schedule of rates.

No hospital service corporation shall enter into any contract with subscribers unless and until it shall have filed with the Commissioner of Insurance a specimen copy of the contract or certificate and of all applications, riders, and endorsements for use in connection with the issuance or renewal thereof to be formally approved by him as conforming to the section of this Article entitled "Subscribers' contracts," and conforms to all rules and regulations promulgated by the Commissioner of Insurance under the provisions of this Article and Article 66 of this Chapter. The Commissioner of Insurance shall, within a reasonable time after the filing of any such form, notify the corporation filing the same either of his approval or of his disapproval of such form.

No corporation subject to the provisions of this Article and Article 66 of this Chapter shall enter into any contract with a subscriber after the enactment hereof unless and until it shall have filed with the Commissioner of Insurance a full schedule of rates to be paid by the subscribers to such contracts and shall have obtained the Commissioner's approval thereof. The Commissioner may refuse approval if he finds that such rates are excessive, inadequate, or unfairly discriminatory; or do not exhibit a reasonable relationship to the benefits provided by such contracts. At all times such rates and form of subscribers' contracts shall be subject to modification and approval of the Commissioner of Insurance under rules and regulations adopted by the Commissioner, in conformity to this Article and Article 66 of this Chapter. (1941, c. 338, s. 4; 1989, c. 485, s. 57.)

CASE NOTES

Cited in Lupton v. Blue Cross & Blue Shield of N.C., 139 N.C. App. 421, 533 S.E.2d 270, 2000 N.C. App. LEXIS 909 (2000), cert. denied, 353 N.C. 266, 546 S.E.2d 105 (2000).

§ 58-65-45. Public hearings on revision of existing schedule or establishment of new schedule; publication of notice.

Whenever any hospital service corporation licensed under this Article and Article 66 of this Chapter makes a rate filing or any proposal to revise an existing rate schedule or contract form, the effect of which is to increase or decrease the charge for its contracts, or to set up a new rate schedule, and such rate schedule is subject to the approval of the Commissioner, such hospital service corporation shall file its proposed rate change or contract form and supporting data with the commissioner, who shall review the filing in accordance with the standards in G.S. 58-65-40. Such rate revision or new rate schedule with respect to individual subscriber contracts shall be guaranteed by the insurer, as to the contract and certificate holders thereby affected, for a period of not less than 12 months; or with respect to individual subscriber contracts as an alternative to giving such guarantee, such rate revision or new rate schedule may be made applicable to all individual contracts at one time if the corporation chooses to apply for such relief with respect to such contracts no more frequently than once in any 12-month period. Such rate revision or new rate schedule shall be applicable to all contracts of the same type; provided that no rate revision or new rate schedule may become effective for any contract holder unless the corporation has given written notice of the rate revision or new rate schedule not less than 30 days prior to the effective date of such revision or new rate schedule. The contract holder thereafter must pay the revised rate or new rate schedule in order to continue the contract in force. The Commissioner may promulgate reasonable rules, after notice and hearing, to require the submission of supporting data and such information as is deemed necessary to determine whether such rate revisions meet these standards. At any time within 60 days after the date of any filing under this section or G.S. 58-65-40, the Commissioner may give written notice to the corporation of a fixed time and place for a hearing on the filing, which time shall be no less than 20 days after notice is given. In the event no notice of hearing is issued within 60 days from the date of any filing, the filing shall be deemed to be approved, subject to modification by the Commissioner as authorized by G.S. 58-65-40. In the event the Commissioner gives notice of a hearing, the corporation making the filing shall, not less than 10 days before the time of the hearing, cause to be published in a daily newspaper or newspapers published in North Carolina, and in accordance with the rules and regulations of the Commissioner of Insurance, a notice, in the form and content approved by the Commissioner, setting forth the nature and effect of such proposal and the time and place of the public hearing to be held. If the Commissioner does not issue an order within 45 days after the day on which the hearing began, the filing shall be deemed to be approved, subject to modification by the Commissioner as authorized by G.S. 58-65-40. (1953, c. 1118; 1985, c. 666, s. 60; 1989, c. 485, s. 58.)

§ 58-65-50. Application for certificate of authority or license.

No corporation subject to the provisions of this Article and Article 66 of this Chapter shall issue contracts for the rendering of hospital or medical and/or dental service to subscribers, until the Commissioner of Insurance has, by formal certificate or license, authorized it to do so. Application for such certificate of authority or license shall be made on forms to be supplied by the Commissioner of Insurance, containing such information as he shall deem necessary. Each application for such certificate of authority or license, as a part thereof shall be accompanied by duplicate copies of the following documents duly certified by at least two of the executive officers of such corporation:

   (1) Certificate of incorporation with all amendments thereto.

   (2) Bylaws with all amendments thereto.

   (3) Each contract executed or proposed to be executed by and between the corporation and any participating hospital, and/or physicians under the terms of which hospital and/or medical and/or dental service is to be furnished to subscribers to the plan.

   (4) Each form of contract, application, rider, and endorsement, issued or proposed to be issued to subscribers to the plan, or in renewal of any of contracts with subscribers to the plan, together with a table of rates charged or proposed to be charged to subscribers for each form of such contract.

   (5) Financial statement of the corporation which shall include the amounts of each contribution paid or agreed to be paid to the corporation for working capital, the name or names of each contributor and the terms or each contribution. (1941, c. 338, s. 5; 1943, c. 537, s. 3; 1961, c. 1149.)

§ 58-65-55. Issuance and continuation of license.

(a) Before issuing or continuing any such license or certificate the Commissioner may make such an examination or investigation as the Commissioner deems expedient. The Commissioner shall issue a license upon the payment of a fee of one thousand dollars ($1,000) and upon being satisfied on the following points:

   (1) The applicant is established as a bona fide nonprofit hospital service corporation as defined by this Article and Article 66 of this Chapter.

   (2) The rates charged and benefits to be provided are fair and reasonable.

   (3) The amounts provided as working capital of the corporation are repayable only out of earned income in excess of amounts paid and payable for operating expenses and hospital and medical and/or dental expenses and such reserve as the Department deems adequate, as provided hereinafter.

   (4) That the amount of money actually available for working capital be sufficient to carry all acquisition costs and operating expenses for a reasonable period of time from the date of the issuance of the certificate.

(b) The license shall continue in full force and effect, subject to payment of an annual license continuation fee of one thousand dollars ($1,000), subject to all other provisions of subsection (a) of this section and subject to any other applicable provisions of the insurance laws of this State. (1941, c. 338, s. 6; 1943, c. 537, s. 4; 1947, c. 820, s. 2; 1961, c. 1149; 1989 (Reg. Sess., 1990), c. 1069, s. 5; 1995, c. 507, s. 11A(c); 1999-435, s. 5; 2003-212, s. 26(j).)

Effect of Amendments. — Session Laws 2003-212, s. 26.(j), effective January 1, 2004, and applicable to all company licenses issued or otherwise eligible for renewal or continuation after that date, rewrote the section heading, which formerly read "Issuance of certificate"; designated the former provisions of the section as subsection (a), and added subsection (b); and in subsection (a), added "or continuing" following "Before issuing" at the beginning of the first sentence, and in the second sentence, deleted "certificate of authority or" following "shall issue a," and substituted "a fee" for "an annual fee."

§ 58-65-60. Subscribers' contracts; required and prohibited provisions.

(a) Every contract made by a corporation subject to the provisions of this Article and Article 66 of this Chapter shall be for a period not to exceed 12 months, and no contract shall be made providing for the inception of benefits at a date later than one year from the date of the contract. Any such contract may provide that it shall be automatically renewed for a similar period unless there shall have been one month's prior written notice of termination by either the subscriber or the corporation.

(b) Contracts may be issued that entitle one or more persons to benefits under those contracts. Persons entitled to benefits under those contracts, other than the certificate holder, may only be the certificate holder's spouse, lawful or legally adopted child of the certificate holder or the certificate holder's spouse, or any other person who resides in the same household with the certificate holder and is dependent upon the certificate holder.

(c) Every contract entered into by any such corporation with any subscriber thereof shall be in writing and a certificate stating the terms and conditions thereof shall be furnished to the subscriber to be kept by him. No such certificate form, other than to group subscribers of groups of 10 or more certificate holders or those issued pursuant to a master group contract covering 10 or more certificate holders shall be made, issued or delivered in this State unless it contains the following provisions, provided, however, groups between five and 10 certificate holders complying with and maintaining eligibility status under regulations approved by the Commissioner of Insurance for group enrollment may be cancelled if such participation falls below the minimum participation of five certificate holders; or if the group takes other group hospital, medical or surgical coverage:

    (1) A statement of the amount payable to the corporation by the subscriber and the times at which and manner in which such amount is to be paid; this provision may be inserted in the application rather than in the certificate. Application need not be attached to certificate.

    (2) A statement of the nature of the benefits to be furnished and the period during which they will be furnished.

    (3) A statement of the terms and conditions, if any, upon which the contract may be cancelled or otherwise terminated at the option of either party. The statement shall be in the following language:

        a. "Renewability": Any contract subject to the provisions of this subdivision is renewable at the option of the subscriber unless sufficient notice in writing of nonrenewal is mailed to the subscriber by the corporation addressed to the last address recorded with the corporation.

        b. "Sufficient notice" shall be as follows:

            1. During the first year of any such contract, or during the first year following any lapse and reinstatement, or reenrollment, a period of 30 days.

            2. During the second and subsequent years of continuous coverage, a number of full calendar months most nearly equivalent to one fourth the number of months of continuous coverage

from the first anniversary of the date of issue or reinstatement or reenrollment, whichever date is more recent, to the date of mailing of such notice.

    3. No period of required notice shall exceed two years, and no renewal hereunder shall renew any such contract for any period beyond the required period of notice except by written agreement of the subscriber and corporation.

The contract may be modified, terminated or cancelled by the corporation at any time at its option, upon:

    a. Nonpayment by the subscriber of fees or dues as required.

    b. Failure or refusal by the subscriber to comply with rate or benefit changes approved by the Commissioner under G.S. 58-65-45.

    c. Failure or refusal by the subscriber after 30 days' written notice to subscriber to transfer into hospital, medical, or dental service plan serving the area to which the subscriber has changed residence and is eligible for or to which corporation is required to transfer by interplan agreement of transfer.

    (4) A statement that the contract includes the endorsement thereon and attached papers, if any, and together with the applications contains the entire contract.

    (5) A statement that if the subscriber defaults in making any payment, under the contract, the subsequent acceptance of a payment by the corporation at its home office shall reinstate the contract, but with respect to sickness and injury, only to cover such sickness as may be first manifested more than 10 days after the date of such acceptance.

  (d) In every such contract made, issued or delivered in this State:

    (1) All printed portions shall be plainly printed;

    (2) The exceptions from the contract shall appear with the same prominence as the benefits to which they apply; and

    (3) If the contract contains any provision purporting to make any portion of the articles, constitution or bylaws of the corporation a part of the contract, such portion shall be set forth in full.

  (e) A service corporation may issue a master group contract with the approval of the Commissioner if the contract and the individual certificates issued to members of the group comply in substance to the other provisions of this Article and Article 66 of this Chapter. The contract may provide for the adjustment of the rate of the premium or benefits conferred as provided in the contract, and in accordance with an adjustment schedule filed with and approved by the Commissioner. If the contract is issued, altered or modified, the subscribers' contracts issued under that contract are altered or modified accordingly, all laws and clauses in subscribers' contracts to the contrary notwithstanding. Nothing in this Article and Article 66 of this Chapter shall be construed to prohibit or prevent the same. Forms of such contract shall at all times be furnished upon request of subscribers thereto.

  (e1) Employees shall be added to the master group coverage no later than 90 days after their first day of employment. Employment shall be considered continuous and not be considered broken except for unexcused absences from work for reasons other than illness or injury. The term "employee" is defined as a nonseasonal person who works on a full-time basis, with a normal work week of 30 or more hours and who is otherwise eligible for coverage, but does not include a person who works on a part-time, temporary, or substitute basis.

  (e2) Whenever an employer master group contract replaces another group contract, whether this contract was issued by a corporation under Articles 1 through 67 of this Chapter, the liability of the succeeding corporation for insuring persons covered under the previous group contract is (i) each person is eligible for coverage in accordance with the succeeding corporation's plan of benefits with respect to classes eligible and activity at work and nonconfinement rules must be covered by the succeeding corporation's plan of benefits; and (ii) each person not covered under the succeeding corporation's plan of benefits in accordance with (i) above must nevertheless be covered by the succeeding corporation if that person was validly covered, including benefit extension, under the prior plan on the date of discontinuance and if the person is a member of the class of persons eligible for coverage under the succeeding corporation's plan.

(f) Any hospitalization contract renewed in the name of the subscriber during the grace period shall be construed to be a continuation of the contract first issued. (1941, c. 338, s. 7; 1947, c. 820, ss. 3, 4; 1955, c. 679, ss. 1-3; 1957, c. 1085, s. 1; 1961, c. 1149; 1989, c. 775, s. 4; 1991, c. 720, ss. 38, 88; 1991 (Reg. Sess., 1992), c. 837, s. 4; 1993, c. 408, s. 4; c. 409, s. 24; 1995, c. 507, s. 23A.1(e); 1997-259, s. 17; 2001-417, s. 12.)

Cross References. — As to contracts covering newborn infants, see G.S. 58-51-30. As to the Hospital, Medical and Dental Service Corporation Readable Insurance Certificates Act, see G.S. 58-66-1 through 58-66-40.

CASE NOTES

Cited in Varnell v. Henry M. Milgrom, Inc., 78 N.C. App. 451, 337 S.E.2d 616 (1985).

§ 58-65-65. Coverage for active medical treatment in tax-supported institutions.

(a) No hospital or medical or dental service plan, contract or certificate governed by the provisions of this Article and Article 66 of this Chapter shall be delivered, issued, executed or renewed in this State, or approved for issuance or renewal in this State by the Commissioner of Insurance, after May 21, 1975, unless such plan, contract or certificate provides for the payment of benefits for charges made for medical care rendered in or by duly licensed state tax-supported institutions, including charges for medical care of cerebral palsy, other orthopedic and crippling disabilities, mental and nervous diseases and disorders, mental retardation, alcoholism and drug or chemical dependency, and respiratory illness, on a basis no less favorable than the basis which would apply had the medical care been rendered in or by any other public or private institution or provider. The term "state tax-supported institutions" shall include community mental health centers and other health clinics which are certified as Medicaid providers.

(b) No plan, contract, or certificate shall exclude payment for charges of a duly licensed state tax-supported institution because of its being a specialty facility for one particular type of illness nor because it does not have an operating room and related equipment for the performance of surgery, but it is not required that benefits be payable for domiciliary or custodial care, rehabilitation, training, schooling, or occupational therapy.

(c) The restrictions and requirements of this section shall not apply to any plan, contract, or certificate which is individually underwritten or provided for a specific individual and the members of his family as a nongroup policy, but shall apply only to those hospital service and medical service subscriber plans, contracts, or certificates delivered, issued for delivery, reissued or renewed in this State on and after July 1, 1975. (1975, c. 345, s. 2.)

§ 58-65-70. Contracts to cover any person possessing the sickle cell trait or hemoglobin C trait.

No hospital, medical, dental, or any health service governed by this Article and Article 66 of this Chapter shall refuse to issue or deliver any individual or group hospital, dental, medical, or health service contract in this State which it is currently issuing for delivery in this State, and which affords benefits or coverage for any medical treatment or service authorized or permitted to be furnished by a hospital, clinic, family health clinic, neighborhood health clinic, health maintenance organization, physician, physician's assistant, nurse practitioner or any medical service facility or personnel, on account of the fact that the person who is to be insured possesses sickle cell trait or hemoglobin C trait; nor shall any such policy issued and delivered in this State carry a higher premium rate or charge on account of the fact that the person who is to be insured possesses sickle cell trait. (1975, c. 599, s. 2.)

§ 58-65-75. Coverage for chemical dependency treatment.

(a) As used in this section, the term "chemical dependency" means the pathological use or abuse of alcohol or other drugs in a manner or to a degree that produces an impairment in personal, social, or occupational functioning and which may, but need not, include a pattern of tolerance and withdrawal.

(b) Every group insurance certificate or group subscriber contract under any hospital or medical plan governed by this Article and Article 66 of this Chapter that is issued, renewed, or amended on or after January 1, 1985, shall offer to its insureds benefits for the necessary care and treatment of chemical dependency that are not less favorable than benefits for physical illness generally. Except as provided in subsection (c) of this section, benefits for chemical dependency shall be subject to the same durational limits, dollar limits, deductibles, and coinsurance factors as are benefits for physical illness generally.

(c) Every group insurance certificate or group subscriber contract that provides benefits for chemical dependency treatment and that provides total annual benefits for all illnesses in excess of eight thousand dollars ($8,000) is subject to the following conditions:

(1) The certificate or contract shall provide, for each 12-month period, a minimum benefit of eight thousand dollars ($8,000) for the necessary care and treatment of chemical dependency.

(2) The certificate or contract shall provide a minimum benefit of sixteen thousand dollars ($16,000) for the necessary care and treatment of chemical dependency for the life of the certificate or contract.

(d) Provisions for benefits for necessary care and treatment of chemical dependency in group certificates or group contracts shall provide for benefit payments for the following providers of necessary care and treatment of chemical dependency:

(1) The following units of a general hospital licensed under Article 5 of General Statutes Chapter 131E:

a. Chemical dependency units in facilities licensed after October 1, 1984;

b. Medical units;

c. Psychiatric units; and

(2) The following facilities or programs licensed after July 1, 1984, under Article 2 of General Statutes Chapter 122C:

a. Chemical dependency units in psychiatric hospitals;

b. Chemical dependency hospitals;

c. Residential chemical dependency treatment facilities;

      d. Social setting detoxification facilities or programs;

      e. Medical detoxification facilities or programs; and

   (3) Duly licensed physicians and duly licensed psychologists and certified professionals working under the direct supervision of such physicians or psychologists in facilities described in (1) and (2) above and in day/night programs or outpatient treatment facilities licensed after July 1, 1984, under Article 2 of General Statutes Chapter 122C. After January 1, 1995, "duly licensed psychologists" shall be defined as licensed psychologists who hold permanent licensure and certification as health services provider psychologist issued by the North Carolina Psychology Board.

Provided, however, that nothing in this subsection shall prohibit any certificate or contract from requiring the most cost effective treatment setting to be utilized by the person undergoing necessary care and treatment for chemical dependency.

  (e) Coverage for chemical dependency treatment as described in this section shall not be applicable to any group certificate holder or group subscriber contract holder who rejects the coverage in writing. (1983 (Reg. Sess., 1984), c. 1110, s. 8; 1985, c. 589, s. 43(a), (b); 1989, c. 175, s. 2; 1991, c. 720, s. 64; 1993, c. 375, s. 5.)

§ 58-65-80. Meaning of terms "accident", "accidental injury", and "accidental means".

  (a) This section applies to the provisions of all subscriber contracts under this Article and Article 66 of this Chapter that are issued on or after October 1, 1989, and preferred provider arrangements under this Article and Article 66 of this Chapter that are entered into on or after October 1, 1989.

  (b) "Accident", "accidental injury", and "accidental means" shall be defined to imply "result" language and shall not include words that establish an accidental means test. (1989, c. 485, s. 11.)

§ 58-65-85. Discriminatory practices prohibited.

  No person subject to this Article and Article 66 of this Chapter shall refuse to issue or refuse to reissue to an individual any certificate, plan, or contract governed by this Article and Article 66 of this Chapter; limit the amount, extent, or kind of services available to an individual; or charge an individual a different rate for the same services, because of the race, color, or national or ethnic origin of that individual. (1989, c. 485, s. 23.)

CASE NOTES

This statute did not give rise to a private cause of action for a private hospital's refusal to render medical care to a non-Indian; it applies only to nonprofit hospitals seeking reimbursement from the North Carolina Department of Insurance and not to every private hospital. Williams v. United States, 242 F.3d 169, 2001 U.S. App. LEXIS 3126 (4th Cir. 2001).

§ 58-65-90. No discrimination against the mentally ill and chemically dependent.

  (a) Definitions. — As used in this section, the term:

   (1) "Mental illness" has the same meaning as defined in G.S. 122C-3(21); and

(2) "Chemical dependency" has the same meaning as defined in G.S. 58-65-75

with a diagnosis found in the Diagnostic and Statistical Manual of Mental Disorders DSM-3-R or the International Classification of Diseases ICD/9/CM, or a later edition of those manuals.

(b) Coverage of Physical Illness. — No service corporation governed by this Chapter shall, solely because an individual to be insured has or had a mental illness or chemical dependency:

    (1) Refuse to issue or deliver to that individual any individual or group subscriber contract in this State that affords benefits or coverage for medical treatment or service for physical illness or injury;

    (2) Have a higher premium rate or charge for physical illness or injury coverages or benefits for that individual; or

    (3) Reduce physical illness or injury coverages or benefits for that individual.

(b1) Coverage of Mental Illness. — A subscriber contract that covers both physical illness or injury and mental illness may not impose a lesser lifetime or annual dollar limitation on the mental health benefits than on the physical illness or injury benefits, subject to the following:

    (1) A lifetime limit or annual limit may be made applicable to all benefits under the subscriber contract, without distinguishing the mental health benefits.

    (2) If the subscriber contract contains lifetime limits only on selected physical illness or injury benefits, and these benefits do not represent substantially all of the physical illness and injury benefits under the subscriber contract, the service corporation may impose a lifetime limit on the mental health benefits that is based on a weighted average of the respective lifetime limits on the selected physical illness and injury benefits. The weighted average shall be calculated in accordance with rules adopted by the Commissioner.

    (3) If the subscriber contract contains annual limits only on selected physical illness and injury benefits, and these benefits do not represent substantially all of the physical illness and injury benefits under the subscriber contract, the service corporation may impose an annual limit on the mental health benefits that is based on a weighted average of the respective annual limits on the selected physical illness and injury benefits. The weighted average shall be calculated in accordance with rules adopted by the Commissioner.

    (4) Except as otherwise provided in this section, the subscriber contract may distinguish between mental illness benefits and physical injury or illness benefits with respect to other terms of the subscriber contract, including coinsurance, limits on provider visits or days of coverage, and requirements relating to medical necessity.

    (5) If the service corporation offers two or more benefit package options under a subscriber contract, each package must comply with this subsection.

    (6) This subsection does not apply to a subscriber contract if the service corporation can demonstrate to the Commissioner that compliance will increase the cost of the subscriber contract by one percent (1%) or more.

    (7) This subsection expires October 1, 2001, but the expiration does not affect services rendered before that date.

(c) Mental Illness or Chemical Dependency Coverage Not Required. — Nothing in this section requires a service corporation to offer coverage for mental illness or chemical dependency, except as provided in G.S. 58-65-75.

(d) Applicability. — Subsection (b1) of this section applies only to subscriber contracts, other than excepted benefits as defined in G.S. 58-68-25, covering more than 50 employees. The remainder of this section applies only to group contracts covering 20 or more employees. (1989, c. 369, s. 1; 1991, c. 720, s. 82; 1997-259, s. 22; 1999-132, s. 4.3.)

§ 58-65-91. Coverage for certain treatment of diabetes.

(a) Every insurance certificate or subscriber contract under any hospital service plan or medical service plan governed by this Article and Article 66 of this Chapter, and every preferred provider plan under G.S. 58-50-56 that is issued, renewed, or amended on or after October 1, 1997, shall provide coverage for medically appropriate and necessary services, including diabetes outpatient self-management training and educational services, and equipment, supplies, medications, and laboratory procedures used to treat diabetes. Diabetes outpatient self-management training and educational services shall be provided by a physician or a health care professional designated by the physician. The hospital or medical service plan shall determine who shall provide and be reimbursed for the diabetes outpatient self-management training and educational services. The same deductibles, coinsurance, and other limitations as apply to similar services covered under the policy, contract, or plan shall apply to the diabetes coverage required under this section.

(b) For the purposes of this section, "physician" is a person licensed to practice in this State under Article 1 or Article 7 of Chapter 90 of the General Statutes. (1997-225, s. 2; 1997-519, s. 3.12.)

Editor's Note. — Session Laws 1997-225, s. 4, provides: "Nothing in this act shall apply to specified accident, specified disease, hospital indemnity, or long-term care health insurance policies."

Session Laws 1997-225, s. 5, provides: "The North Carolina Commission for Health Services shall develop voluntary standards or guidelines for diabetes outpatient self-management training and educational services based on clinical practice recommendations and guidelines established by the Center for Disease Control and the American Diabetes Association. These standards or guidelines are not subject to Article 2A of Chapter 150B of the General Statutes."

§ 58-65-92. Coverage for mammograms and cervical cancer screening.

(a) Every insurance certificate or subscriber contract under any hospital service plan or medical service plan governed by this Article and Article 66 of this Chapter, and every preferred provider benefit plan under G.S. 58-50-56, that is issued, renewed, or amended on or after January 1, 1992, shall provide coverage for examinations and laboratory tests for the screening for the early detection of cervical cancer and for low-dose screening mammography. The same deductibles, coinsurance, and other limitations as apply to similar services covered under the certificate or contract shall apply to coverage for examinations and laboratory tests for the screening for the early detection of cervical cancer and low-dose screening mammography.

(a1) As used in this section, "examinations and laboratory tests for the screening for the early detection of cervical cancer" means conventional PAP smear screening, liquid-based cytology, and human papilloma virus (HPV) detection methods for women with equivocal findings on cervical cytologic analysis that are subject to the approval of and have been approved by the United States Food and Drug Administration.

(b) As used in this section, "low-dose screening mammography" means a radiologic procedure for the early detection of breast cancer provided to an asymptomatic woman using equipment dedicated specifically for mammography, including a physician's interpretation of the results of the procedure.

(c) Coverage for low-dose screening mammography shall be provided as follows:

    (1) One or more mammograms a year, as recommended by a physician, for any woman who is at risk for breast cancer. For purposes of this subdivision, a woman is at risk for breast cancer if any one or more of the following is true:

        a. The woman has a personal history of breast cancer;

        b. The woman has a personal history of biopsy-proven benign breast disease;

        c. The woman's mother, sister, or daughter has or has had breast cancer; or

        d. The woman has not given birth prior to the age of 30;

    (2) One baseline mammogram for any woman 35 through 39 years of age, inclusive;

    (3) A mammogram every other year for any woman 40 through 49 years of age, inclusive, or more frequently upon recommendation of a physician; and

    (4) A mammogram every year for any woman 50 years of age or older.

(d) Reimbursement for a mammogram authorized under this section shall be made only if the facility in which the mammogram was performed meets mammography accreditation standards established by the North Carolina Medical Care Commission.

(e) Coverage for the screening for the early detection of cervical cancer shall be in accordance with the most recently published American Cancer Society guidelines or guidelines adopted by the North Carolina Advisory Committee on Cancer Coordination and Control. Coverage shall include the examination, the laboratory fee, and the physician's interpretation of the laboratory results. Reimbursements for laboratory fees shall be made only if the laboratory meets accreditation standards adopted by the North Carolina Medical Care Commission. (1991, c. 490, s. 2; 1997-519, s. 3.6; 2003-186, s. 3.)

Editor's Note. — Session Laws 2003-186, s. 6, provides, in part, that for the purposes of this act, renewal of a health benefit plan is presumed to occur on each anniversary of the date on which coverage was first effective on the person or persons covered by the health benefit plan.

Effect of Amendments. — Session Laws 2003-186, s. 3, effective January 1, 2004, and applicable to all health benefit plans that are delivered, issued for delivery, or renewed on and after that date, in the section heading, substituted "cervical cancer screening" for "pap smears"; in the first and last sentences of subsection (a), substituted "examinations and laboratory tests for the screening for the early detection of cervical cancer" for "pap smears"; added subsection (a1); and rewrote subsections (d) and (e).

§ 58-65-93. Coverage for prostate-specific antigen (PSA) tests.

(a) Every insurance certificate or subscriber contract under any hospital service plan or medical service plan governed by this Article and Article 66 of this Chapter, and every preferred provider benefit plan under G.S. 58-50-56, that is issued, renewed, or amended on or after January 1, 1994, shall provide coverage for prostate-specific antigen (PSA) tests or equivalent tests for the presence of prostate cancer. The same deductibles, coinsurance, and other limitations as apply to similar services covered under the certificate or contract shall apply to coverage for prostate-specific antigen (PSA) tests or equivalent tests for the presence of prostate cancer.

(b) As used in this section, "prostate-specific antigen (PSA) tests or equivalent tests for the presence of prostate cancer" means serological tests for determining the presence of prostate cytoplasmic protein (PSA) and the generation of antibodies to it, as a novel marker for prostatic disease.

(c) Coverage for prostate-specific antigen (PSA) tests or equivalent tests for the presence of prostate cancer shall be provided when recommended by a physician. (1993, c. 269, s. 2; 1997-519, s. 3.7.)

§ 58-65-94. Coverage of certain prescribed drugs for cancer treatment.

(a) No insurance certificate or subscriber contract under any hospital service plan or medical service plan governed by this Article and Article 66 of this Chapter, and no preferred provider benefit plan under G.S. 58-50-56, that is issued, renewed, or amended on or after January 1, 1994, and that provides coverage for prescribed drugs approved by the federal Food and Drug Administration for the treatment of certain types of cancer shall exclude coverage of any drug on the basis that the drug has been prescribed for the treatment of a type of cancer for which the drug has not been approved by the federal Food and Drug Administration. The drug, however, must be approved by the federal Food and Drug Administration and must have been proven effective and accepted for the treatment of the specific type of cancer for which the drug has been prescribed in any one of the following established reference compendia:

    (1) The American Medical Association Drug Evaluations;
    (2) The American Hospital Formulary Service Drug Information; or
    (3) The United States Pharmacopeia Drug Information.

(b) Notwithstanding subsection (a) of this section, coverage shall not be required for any experimental or investigational drugs or any drug that the federal Food and Drug Administration has determined to be contraindicated for treatment of the specific type of cancer for which the drug has been prescribed.

(c) This section shall apply only to cancer drugs and nothing in this section shall be construed, expressly or by implication, to create, impair, alter, limit, notify, enlarge, abrogate, or prohibit reimbursement for drugs used in the treatment of any other disease or condition. (1993, c. 506, s. 4.2; 1997-519, s. 3.8.)

Editor's Note. — The number of this section was assigned by the Revisor of Statutes, the number in Session Laws 1993, c. 506, s. 4.2 having been G.S. 58-65-93.

§ 58-65-95. Investments and reserves.

(a) Corporations subject to this Article shall invest in or hold only those assets permitted by Article 7 of this Chapter for life and health insurance companies.

(b) Every such corporation shall accumulate and maintain, in addition to proper reserves for current administrative liabilities and whatever reserves are deemed to be adequate and proper by the Commissioner for unpaid hospital, medical, or dental bills, and unearned membership dues, a special contingent surplus or reserve at the following rates annually of its gross annual collections from membership dues, exclusive of receipts from cost plus plans, until the reserve equals an amount that is three times its average monthly expenditures for claims and administrative and selling expenses:

    (1) First $200,000 .... 4%
    (2) Next $200,000 .... 2%
    (3) All above $400,000 .... 1%

(c) Any such corporation may accumulate and maintain a contingent reserve in excess of the reserve required in subsection (b) of this section, not to exceed an amount equal to six times the average monthly expenditures for claims and administrative and selling expenses.

(d) If the Commissioner finds that special conditions exist warranting an increase or decrease in the reserves or schedule of reserves in subsection (b) of this section, the Commissioner may modify them accordingly. Provided, however, when special conditions exist warranting an increase in the schedule of reserves, the schedule shall not be increased by the Commissioner until a reasonable length of time has elapsed after the Commissioner gives notice of the increase. (1941, c. 338, s. 8; 1943, c. 537, s. 5; 1947, c. 820, s. 5; 1961, c. 1149; 1991, c. 720, s. 79; 1999-244, s. 6; 2003-212, s. 18.)

Cross References. — As to investments by executors, administrators and guardians, see G.S. 36A-1 through 36A-7. As to investments by banks, see G.S. 53-44, 53-45 and 53-60.

Effect of Amendments. — Session Laws 2003-212, s. 18, effective October 1, 2003, in subsection (a), substituted "Corporations" for "No corporation" at the beginning, substituted "or hold only those assets" for "any securities other than securities," and deleted "the investment of assets of" following "of this Chapter for" near the end.

CASE NOTES

"Filed Rate Doctrine" Precluded Plaintiffs' Class Action Brought Pursuant to This Section. — The trial court correctly granted insurer's motion to dismiss for failure to state a claim on the grounds that the "filed rate doctrine" precluded plaintiffs' class actions as a matter of law; because any allegation that the insurer accumulated an excessive reserve requires the recalculation of approved rates, notwithstanding plaintiffs' argument to the contrary, the plaintiffs could not prove their claim without the rates set by the Commissioner being questioned. Lupton v. Blue Cross & Blue Shield of N.C., 139 N.C. App. 421, 533 S.E.2d 270, 2000 N.C. App. LEXIS 909 (2000), cert. denied, 353 N.C. 266, 546 S.E.2d 105 (2000).

§ 58-65-96. Coverage for reconstructive breast surgery following mastectomy.

(a) Every insurance certificate or subscriber contract under any hospital service plan or medical service plan governed by this Article and Article 66 of this Chapter, and every preferred provider benefit plan under G.S. 58-50-56 that provides coverage for mastectomy shall provide coverage for reconstructive breast surgery following a mastectomy. The coverage shall include coverage for all stages and revisions of reconstructive breast surgery performed on a nondiseased breast to establish symmetry if reconstructive surgery on a diseased breast is performed, as well as coverage for prostheses and physical complications in all stages of mastectomy, including lymphademas. The same deductibles, coinsurance, and other limitations as apply to similar services covered under the policy, contract, or plan shall apply to coverage for reconstructive breast surgery. Reconstruction of the nipple/areolar complex following a mastectomy is covered without regard to the lapse of time between the mastectomy and the reconstruction, subject to the approval of the treating physician.

(b) As used in this section, the following terms have the meanings indicated:

(1) "Mastectomy" means the surgical removal of all or part of a breast as a result of breast cancer or breast disease.

(2) "Reconstructive breast surgery" means surgery performed as a result of a mastectomy to reestablish symmetry between the two breasts, and includes reconstruction of the mastectomy site, creation of a new breast mound, and creation of a new nipple/areolar complex. "Reconstructive breast surgery" also includes augmentation mammoplasty, reduction mammoplasty, and mastopexy of the nondiseased breast.

(c) A policy, contract, or plan subject to this section shall not:

    (1) Deny coverage described in subsection (a) of this section on the basis that the coverage is for cosmetic surgery;

    (2) Deny to a woman eligibility or continued eligibility to enroll or to renew coverage under the terms of the contract, policy, or plan, solely for the purpose of avoiding the requirements of this section;

    (3) Provide monetary payments or rebates to a woman to encourage her to accept less than the minimum protections available under this section;

    (4) Penalize or otherwise reduce or limit the reimbursement of an attending provider because the provider provided care to an individual participant or beneficiary in accordance with this section; or

    (5) Provide incentives, monetary or otherwise, to an attending provider to induce the provider to provide care to an individual participant or beneficiary in a manner inconsistent with this section.

(d) Written notice of the availability of the coverage provided by this section shall be delivered to every subscriber under an individual certificate, contract, or plan and to every certificate holder under a group policy, contract, or plan upon initial coverage under the certificate, contract, or plan and annually thereafter. The notice required by this subsection may be included as a part of any yearly informational packet sent to the subscriber or certificate holder. (1997-312, s. 2; 1997-519, s. 3.10; 1999-351, s. 3.2; 2001-334, s. 13.2.)

Editor's Note. — Session Laws 1997-312, s. 6, provides: "Nothing in this act shall apply to specified accident, specified disease, hospital indemnity, or long-term care health insurance policies."

Legal Periodicals. — For 1997 legislative survey, see 20 Campbell L. Rev. 469.

§ 58-65-100. Statements filed with Commissioner.

Every service corporation subject to this Article is subject to G.S. 58-2-165. (1941, c. 338, s. 9; 1999-244, s. 11.)

§ 58-65-105. Visitations and examinations.

Service corporations subject to this Article shall be examined under G.S. 58-2-131, 58-2-132, 58-2-133, and 58-2-134. (1941, c. 338, s. 10; 1995, c. 360, s. 2(l); 1999-244, s. 5.)

§ 58-65-110. Expenses.

All acquisition expenses in connection with the solicitation of subscribers to such hospital and/or medical and/or dental service plan and administration costs including salaries paid to officers of the corporations, if any, shall at all times be subject to inspection by the Commissioner of Insurance. (1941, c. 338, s. 11; 1943, c. 537, s. 6; 1961, c. 1149.)

§ 58-65-115. Licensing and regulation of agents.

Every agent of any service corporation authorized to do business in this State under this Article is subject to the licensing provisions of Article 33 of this Chapter and all other provisions in this Chapter applicable to life and health insurance agents. (1941, c. 338, s. 12; 1943, c. 537, s. 7; 1947, c. 1023, s. 1; 1961, c. 1149; 1971, c. 1080, s. 2; 1983, c. 790, s. 5; 1985 (Reg. Sess., 1986), c. 928, s. 4; 1987, c. 629, s. 2; 1999-244, s. 7.)

§ 58-65-120. Medical, dental and hospital service associations and agent to transact business through licensed agents only.

No medical and/or dental or hospital service association; nor any agent of any association shall on behalf of such association or agent, knowingly permit any person not licensed as an agent as provided by law, to solicit, negotiate for, collect or transmit a premium for a new contract of medical and/or dental or hospital service certificate or to act in any way in the negotiation for any contract or policy; provided, no license shall be required of the following:

(1) Persons designated by the association or subscriber to collect or deduct or transmit premiums or other charges for medical and/or dental care or hospital contracts, or to perform such acts as may be required for providing coverage for additional persons who are eligible under a master contract.

(2) An agency office employee acting in the confines of the agent's office, under the direction and supervision of the duly licensed agent and within the scope of such agent's license, in the acceptance of request for insurance and payment of premiums, and the performance of clerical, stenographic, and similar office duties. (1955, c. 1268; 1961, c. 1149.)

§ 58-65-125. Revocation and suspension of license; unfair trade practices.

(a) The Commissioner may revoke or suspend the license of any service corporation if:

(1) The service corporation fails or refuses to comply with any law, order, or rule applicable to the service corporation.

(2) The service corporation's financial condition is unsound.

(3) The service corporation has published or made to the Department or to the public any false statement or report.

(4) The service corporation refuses to submit to any examination authorized by law.

(5) The service corporation is found to make a practice of unduly engaging in litigation or of delaying the investigation of claims or the adjustment or payment of valid claims.

(b) Any suspension or revocation of a service corporation's license under this section may also be made applicable to the license or registration of any natural person regulated under this Chapter who is a party to any of the causes for licensing sanctions listed in subsection (a) of this section.

(c) Article 63 of this Chapter applies to service corporations and their agents and representatives. (1941, c. 338, s. 13; 1943, c. 537, s. 8; 1971, c. 1080, s. 3; 1999-244, s. 3; 1999-351, s. 8; 2003-212, s. 26(k).)

Editor's Note. — Session Laws 1999-351, s. 8 repealed subsection (c) as enacted by Session Laws 1999-224, s. 3. Thus, subsection (d) as enacted by s. 3 was redesignated as subsection (c).

Effect of Amendments. — Session Laws 2003-212, s. 26.(k), effective January 1, 2004, and applicable to all company licenses issued or otherwise eligible for renewal or continuation after that date, in the section heading, substituted "Revocation and suspension of license" for "Revocation, suspension, and refusal to renew license"; in subsection (a), substituted "revoke or suspend" for "revoke, suspend, or refuse to renew"; and in subsection (b), substituted "suspension or revocation" for "suspension, revocation, or refusal to renew."

§ 58-65-130. Amendments to certificate of incorporation.

Any corporation subject to the provisions of this Article and Article 66 of this Chapter may hereafter amend its charter in the following manner only:

(1)a. A meeting of the board of directors, trustees or other governing authority shall be called in accordance with the bylaws specifying the amendment to be voted upon at such meeting.

b. If at such meeting two thirds of the directors, trustees or other governing authority present vote in favor of the proposed amendment, then the president and secretary shall under oath make a certificate to this effect, which certificate shall set forth the call for such meeting, a statement showing service of such call upon all directors, and a certified copy of so much of the minutes of the meeting as relate to the adoption of the proposed amendment.

c. Said officers shall cause said certificate to be published once a week for two consecutive weeks in a newspaper in Raleigh and in the county where the corporation's principal office is located, or posted at the courthouse door if no newspaper be published within the county. Said printed or posted notices shall be in such form and of such size as the Commissioner may approve, and in addition to setting forth in full the certificate required in paragraph b shall state that application for amending the corporation's charter in the manner specified has been proposed by the board of directors, trustees, or other governing authority, and shall also state the time set for the meeting of certificate holders thereby called to be held at the principal office of the corporation to take action on the proposed amendment. A true copy of such notice shall be filed with the Commissioner. Such publication and filing of notice shall be completed at least 30 days prior to the date set therein for the meeting of the certificate holders and due proof thereof shall be filed with the Commissioner at least 15 days prior to the date of such meeting. If the meeting at which the proposed amendment is to be considered is a special meeting, rather than a regular annual meeting of certificate holders, such special meeting can be called only after the Commissioner has given his approval in writing, and the published notice shall show the fact of such approval. At said meeting those present in person or represented by proxy shall constitute a quorum.

d. If at such certificate holders' meeting two thirds of those present in person or by proxy shall vote in favor of any proposed amendment, the president and secretary shall make a certificate under oath setting forth such fact together with the full text of the amendment thus approved. Said certificate shall, within 30 days after such meeting, be submitted to the Commissioner for his approval as conforming to the requirement of law, and it shall be the duty of the Commissioner to act upon all proposed amendments within 10 days after filing of such certificates with him. Should the Commissioner approve the proposed amendment or amendments, he shall certify this fact, together with the full text of such amendments as are approved by him, to the Secretary of State who shall thereupon issue the charter amendment in the usual form. Should the Commissioner disapprove of any amendment, then the same shall not be allowed.

(2) All charters and charter amendments heretofore issued upon application of the board of directors, trustees or other governing authority of any corporations subject to the provisions of this Article and Article 66 of this Chapter are hereby validated.

(3) The charter of any corporation subject to the provisions of this Article and Article 66 of this Chapter may be amended to convert that corporation, so amending its charter, into a stock accident and health insurance company or stock life insurance company subject to the provisions of Articles 1 through 64 of this Chapter provided the contractual rights of the subscribers and certificate holders of the corporation are adequately protected. The proposed amendment shall be considered pursuant to G.S. 58-65-131, 58-65-132, and 58-65-133. Other provisions of this section and this Article relating to the procedure for amending the charter shall not apply. (1941, c. 338, s. 15; 1947, c. 820, s. 6; 1953, c. 1124, s. 2; 1998-3, s. 1.)

§ 58-65-131. Findings; definitions; conversion plan.

(a) Intent and Findings. — It is the intent of the General Assembly by the enactment of this section, G.S. 58-65-132, and G.S. 58-65-133 to create a procedure for a medical, hospital, or dental service corporation to convert to a stock accident and health insurance company or stock life insurance company that is subject to the applicable provisions of Articles 1 through 64 of this Chapter. Except as provided herein, it is not the intent of the General Assembly to supplant, modify, or repeal other provisions of this Article and Article 66 of this Chapter or the provisions of Chapter 55A of the General Statutes (the Nonprofit Corporation Act) that govern other transactions and the procedures relating to such transactions that apply to corporations governed by the provisions of this Article and Article 66 of this Chapter.

The General Assembly recognizes the substantial and recent changes in market and health care conditions that are affecting these corporations and the benefit of equal regulatory treatment and competitive equality for health care insurers. The General Assembly finds that a procedure for conversion is in the best interest of policyholders because it will provide greater financial stability for these corporations and a greater opportunity for the corporations to remain financially independent. The General Assembly also finds that if a medical, hospital, or dental service corporation converts to a stock accident and health insurance company or stock life insurance company, the conversion plan must provide a benefit to the people of North Carolina equal to one hundred percent (100%) of the fair market value of the corporation.

(b) Definitions. — As used in this section, G.S. 58-65-132, and G.S. 58-65-133:

(1) "Certificate holder" includes an enrollee, as defined in Article 67 of this Chapter, in a health maintenance plan provided by the corporation or a subsidiary or by the new corporation or a subsidiary.

(2) "Code" means Title 26 of the United States Code, the United States Internal Revenue Code of 1986, as amended.

(3) "Conversion" means the conversion of a hospital, medical, or dental service corporation to a stock accident and health insurance company or stock life insurance company subject to the applicable provisions of Articles 1 through 64 of this Chapter.

(4) "Corporation" means a hospital, medical, or dental service corporation governed by this Article that files or is required to file a plan of conversion with the Commissioner under subsection (d) of this section to convert from a hospital, medical, or dental service corporation to a stock accident and health insurance company or stock life insurance company.

(5) "Foundation" means a newly formed tax-exempt charitable social welfare organization formed and operating under section 501(c)(4) of the Code and Chapter 55A of the General Statutes.

(6) "New corporation" means a corporation originally governed by this Article that has had its plan of conversion approved by the Commissioner under G.S. 58-65-132 and that has converted to a stock accident and health insurance company or stock life insurance company.

(c) Compliance Required in Certain Events. — A corporation governed by this Article shall comply with the provisions of this section, G.S. 58-65-132, and G.S. 58-65-133 before it may do any of the following:

(1) Sell, lease, convey, exchange, transfer, or make other disposition, either directly or indirectly in a single transaction or related series of transactions, of ten percent (10%) of the corporation's assets, as determined by statutory accounting principles, to, or merge or consolidate or liquidate with or into, any business corporation or other business entity, except a business corporation or other business entity that is a wholly owned subsidiary of the corporation. The ten percent (10%) asset limitation in this subdivision does not apply to:

    a. The purchase, acquisition by assignment or otherwise by the corporation of individual accident and health policies or contracts insuring North Carolina residents, or with respect to accident and health group master policies or contracts, only the percentage portion of those policies or contracts covering North Carolina resident certificate holders, and that are issued by a company domiciled or licensed to do business in North Carolina, if the purchase is first approved by the Commissioner after notice to the Attorney General, no profit will inure to the benefit of any officer, director, or employee of the corporation or its subsidiaries, the purchase is transacted at arm's length and for fair value, and the purchase will further the corporation's ability to fulfill its purposes;

    b. In the case of a purchase by the corporation of all the common stock of a company domiciled or licensed to do business in North Carolina, that portion of the value of the company which is determined by the Commissioner to be attributable to individual accident and health policies or contracts insuring North Carolina residents or, in the case of accident and health group master policies or contracts, the percentage portion of those policies or contracts covering North Carolina resident certificate holders, if the purchase is first approved by the Commissioner after notice to the Attorney General, no profit will inure to the benefit of any officer, director, or employee of the corporation or its subsidiaries, the purchase is transacted at arm's length and for fair value, and the purchase will further the corporation's ability to fulfill its purposes;

    c. Granting encumbrances such as security interests or deeds of trust with respect to assets owned by the corporation or any wholly owned subsidiary to secure indebtedness for borrowed money, the proceeds of which are paid solely to the corporation or its wholly owned subsidiaries and remain subject to the provisions of this section; and

    d. Sales or other transfers in the ordinary course of business for fair value of any interest in real property or stocks, bonds, or other securities within the investment portfolio owned by the corporation or any wholly owned subsidiary, the proceeds of which are paid solely to the corporation or any wholly owned subsidiary and remain subject to the provisions of this section.

(2) Directly or indirectly issue, sell, convey, exchange, transfer, or make other disposition to any party of any equity or ownership interest in

the corporation or in any business entity that is owned by or is a subsidiary of the corporation, including stock, securities, or bonds, debentures, notes or any other debt or similar obligation that is convertible into any equity or ownership interest, stock or securities. This subdivision shall not be construed to prohibit the corporation or a wholly owned subsidiary, with the approval of the Commissioner after notice to the Attorney General, from investing in joint ventures or partnerships with unrelated third parties, if no profit will inure to the benefit of any officer, director, or employee of the corporation or its subsidiaries, the transaction is conducted at arm's length and for fair value, and the transaction furthers the corporation's ability to fulfill its purposes.

(3) Permit its aggregate annual revenues, determined in accordance with statutory accounting principles, from all for-profit activities or operations, including but not limited to those of the corporation, any wholly owned subsidiaries, and any joint ventures or partnerships, to exceed forty percent (40%) of the aggregate annual revenues, excluding investment income, of the corporation and its subsidiaries and determined in accordance with statutory accounting principles; or

(4) Permit its aggregate assets for four consecutive quarters, determined in accordance with statutory accounting principles, employed in all for-profit activities or operations, including, but not limited to, those assets owned or controlled by any for-profit wholly owned subsidiaries, to exceed forty percent (40%) of the aggregate admitted assets of the corporation and its subsidiaries for four consecutive quarters, determined in accordance with statutory accounting principles.

In determining whether the corporation must comply with the provisions of this section, G.S. 58-65-132, and G.S. 58-65-133, the Commissioner may review and consolidate actions of the corporation, its subsidiaries, and other legal entities in which the corporation directly or indirectly owns an interest, and treat the consolidated actions as requiring a conversion. An appeal of the Commissioner's order that consolidated actions require a conversion shall lie directly to the North Carolina Court of Appeals, provided that any party may petition the North Carolina Supreme Court, pursuant to G.S. 7A-31(b), to certify the case for discretionary review by the Supreme Court prior to determination by the Court of Appeals. Appeals under this subsection must be filed within 30 days of the Commissioner's order and shall be considered in the most expeditious manner practical. The corporation must file a plan of conversion within 12 months of the later of the issuance of the Commissioner's order or a final decision on appeal.

(d) Charter Amendment for Conversion. — A corporation may propose to amend its charter pursuant to this Article to convert the corporation to a stock accident and health insurance company or stock life insurance company subject to the applicable provisions of Articles 1 through 64 of this Chapter. The proposed amended charter and a plan for conversion as described in subsection (e) of this section shall be filed with the Commissioner for approval.

(e) Filing Conversion Plan; Costs of Review. — A corporation shall file a plan for conversion with the Commissioner and submit a copy to the Attorney General at least 120 days before the proposed date of conversion. The corporation or the new corporation shall reimburse the Department of Insurance and the office of the Attorney General for the actual costs of reviewing, analyzing, and processing the plan. The Commissioner and the Attorney General may contract with experts, consultants, or other professional advisors to assist in reviewing the plan. These contracts are personal professional service contracts exempt from Articles 3 and 3C of Chapter 143 of the General Statutes. Contract costs for these personal professional services shall not exceed an amount that is reasonable and appropriate for the review of the plan.

(f) Plan Requirements. — A plan of conversion submitted to the Commissioner shall state with specificity the following terms and conditions of the proposed conversion:

(1) The purposes of the conversion.

(2) The proposed articles of incorporation of the new corporation.

(3) The proposed bylaws of the new corporation.

(4) A description of any changes in the new corporation's mode of operations after conversion.

(5) A statement describing the manner in which the plan provides for the protection of all existing contractual rights of the corporation's subscribers and certificate holders to medical or hospital services or the payment of claims for reimbursement for those services. The corporation's subscribers and certificate holders shall have no right to receive any assets, surplus, capital, payment or distribution or to receive any stock or other ownership interest in the new corporation in connection with the conversion.

(6) A statement that the legal existence of the corporation does not terminate and that the new corporation is subject to all liabilities, obligations, and relations of whatever kind of the corporation and succeeds to all property, assets, rights, interests, and relations of the corporation.

(7) Documentation showing that the corporation, acting by its board of directors, trustees, or other governing authority, has approved the plan. It shall not be necessary for the subscribers or certificate holders of the corporation to vote on or approve the plan of conversion, any amendments to the corporation's articles of incorporation or bylaws, or the articles of incorporation or the bylaws of the new corporation, notwithstanding any provision to the contrary in this Article or Article 66 of this Chapter or in the articles of incorporation or bylaws of the corporation.

(8) The business plan of the new corporation, including, but not limited to, a comparative premium rate analysis of the new corporation's major plans and product offerings, that, among other things, compares actual premium rates for the three-year period before the filing of the plan for conversion and forecasted premium rates for a three-year period following the proposed conversion. This rate analysis shall address the forecasted effect, if any, of the proposed conversion on the cost to policyholders or certificate holders of the new corporation and on the new corporation's underwriting profit, investment income, and loss and claim reserves, including the effect, if any, of adverse market or risk selection upon these reserves. Information provided under this subsection is confidential pursuant to G.S. 58-19-40.

(9) Any conditions, other than approval of the plan of conversion by the Commissioner, to be fulfilled by a proposed date upon which the conversion would become effective.

(10) The proposed articles of incorporation and bylaws of the Foundation, containing the provisions required by G.S. 58-65-133(h).

(11) Any proposed agreement between the Foundation and the new corporation, including, but not limited to, any agreement relating to the voting or registration for sale of any capital stock to be issued by the new corporation to the Foundation.

(g) Public Comment. — Within 20 days of receiving a plan to convert, the Commissioner shall publish a notice in one or more newspapers of general circulation in the corporation's service area describing the name of the corporation, the nature of the plan filed under G.S. 58-65-131(d), and the date of receipt of the plan. The notice shall indicate that the Commissioner will solicit public comments and hold three public hearings on the plan. The public hearings must be completed within 60 days of the filing of the conversion plan. The written public comment period will be held open until 10 days after the last public hearing. For good cause the Commissioner may extend these deadlines once for a maximum of 30 days. The Commissioner shall provide copies of all written public comments to the Attorney General.

(h) Public Access to Records. — All applications, reports, plans, or other documents under this section, G.S. 58-65-132, and G.S. 58-65-133 are public records unless otherwise provided in this Chapter. The Commissioner shall provide the public with prompt and reasonable access to public records relating to the proposed conversion of the corporation. Access to public records covered by this section shall be made available for at least 30 days before the end of the public comment period. (1998-3, s. 2.)

OPINIONS OF ATTORNEY GENERAL

Contracts with Experts, Consultants, or Other Professional Advisors to Review Conversion Plans Are Exempt from Articles 3 and 3C of Chapter 143 of the General Statutes. — The Commissioner of Insurance has statutory authority to contract with experts, consultants, or other professional advisors to review conversion plans without adhering to the requirements set forth in Articles 3 and 3C of Chapter 143 of the General Statutes; the only statutory requirement that must be met by the Commissioner is that the costs for the personal professional service contracts must not exceed an amount that is reasonable and appropriate for the review of the plan. See opinion of Attorney General to Peter A. Kolbe, General Counsel, North Carolina Department of Insurance, 2001 N.C. AG LEXIS 28 (8/24/01).

§ 58-65-132. Review and approval of conversion plan; new corporation.

(a) Approval of Plan of Conversion. — The Commissioner shall approve the plan of conversion and issue a certificate of authority to the new corporation to transact business in this State only if the Commissioner finds all of the following:

(1) The plan of conversion meets the requirements of G.S. 58-65-131, this section, and G.S. 58-65-133.

(2) Upon conversion, the new corporation will meet the applicable standards and conditions under this Chapter, including applicable minimum capital and surplus requirements.

(3) The plan of conversion adequately protects the existing contractual rights of the corporation's subscribers and certificate holders to medical or hospital services and payment of claims for reimbursement for those services.

(4) No director, officer, or employee of the corporation will receive:

   a. Any fee, commission, compensation, or other valuable consideration for aiding, promoting, or assisting in the conversion of the corporation other than compensation paid to any director, officer, or employee of the corporation in the ordinary course of business; or

   b. Any distribution of the assets, surplus, capital, or capital stock of the new corporation as part of a conversion.

(5) The corporation has complied with all material requirements of this Chapter, and disciplinary action is not pending against the corporation.

(6) The plan of conversion is fair and equitable and not prejudicial to the contractual rights of the policyholders and certificate holders of the new corporation.

(7) The plan of conversion is in the public interest. The Commissioner shall find that the plan is in the public interest only if it provides a benefit for the people of North Carolina equal to the value of the corporation at the time of conversion, in accordance with the criteria set out in this subdivision. In determining whether the plan of conversion is in the public interest, the Commissioner may also consider other factors, including, but not limited to, those relating to the accessibility and affordability of health care. The Commissioner must determine that the plan of conversion meets all of the following criteria:

    a. Consideration, determined by the Commissioner to be equal to one hundred percent (100%) of the fair market value of the corporation, will be conveyed or issued by the corporation to the Foundation at the time the new corporation files its articles of incorporation. If the consideration to be conveyed is all of the common stock of the new corporation that is then issued and outstanding at the time of conversion, and there is no other capital stock of any type or nature then outstanding, it is conclusively presumed that the Foundation will acquire the fair market value of the corporation.

    b. At any time after the conversion, the new corporation may issue, in a public offering or a private placement, additional shares of common stock of the same class and having the same voting, dividend, and other rights as that transferred to the Foundation, subject to the applicable provisions of Chapter 55 of the General Statutes and any voting and registration agreements.

(8) The plan of conversion contains a proposed voting agreement and registration agreement between the Foundation and the proposed new corporation that meets the requirements of G.S. 58-65-133.

(9) The Attorney General has given approval pursuant to G.S. 58-65-133(h).

(b) New Corporation. — After issuance of the certificate of authority as provided in subsection (a) of this section, the new corporation shall no longer be subject to this Article and Article 66 of this Chapter but shall be subject to and comply with all applicable laws and regulations applicable to domestic insurers and Chapter 55 of the General Statutes, except that Articles 9 and 9A of Chapter 55 shall not apply to the new corporation. The new corporation shall file its articles of incorporation, as amended and certified by the Commissioner, with the North Carolina Secretary of State. The legal existence of the corporation does not terminate, and the new corporation is a continuation of the corporation. The conversion shall only be a change in identity and form of organization. Except as provided in subdivision (a)(7) of this subsection, all property, assets, rights, liabilities, obligations, interests, and relations of whatever kind of the corporation shall continue and remain in the new corporation. All actions and legal proceedings to which the corporation was a party prior to conversion shall be unaffected by the conversion.

(c) Final Decision and Order; Procedures. — The Commissioner's final decision and order regarding the plan of conversion shall include findings of fact and conclusions of law. Findings of fact shall be based upon and supported by substantial evidence, including evidence submitted with the plan by the corporation and evidence obtained at hearings held by the Commissioner. A person aggrieved by a final decision of the Commissioner approving or disapproving a conversion may petition the Superior Court of Wake County within 30 days thereafter for judicial review. An appeal from a final decision and order of the Commissioner under this section shall be conducted pursuant to G.S. 58-2-75. Chapter 150B of the General Statutes does not apply to the procedures of G.S. 58-65-131, this section, and G.S. 58-65-133. This subsection does not apply to appeal of an order of the Commissioner issued pursuant to G.S. 58-65-131(c).

(d) Attorney General's Enforcement Authority; Legal Action on Validity of Plan of Conversion. —

(1) Nothing in this Chapter limits the power of the Attorney General to seek a declaratory judgment or to take other legal action to protect or enforce the rights of the public in the corporation.

(2) Any legal action with respect to the conversion must be filed in the Superior Court of Wake County. (1998-3, s. 2.)

OPINIONS OF ATTORNEY GENERAL

Conditions Imposed by Commissioner. — The Commissioner of Insurance has the authority to enter an approval order imposing continuing conditions on a conversion, provided each condition is reasonably related to the accomplishment of one or more of the legislative goals found in the conversion law; further, conditions imposed by the Commissioner should not be structured in a manner such that the remedy for breach of the condition would be revocation of the conversion. See opinion of Attorney General to Peter A. Kolbe, General Counsel, North Carolina Department of Insurance, 2003 N.C.A.G. 2 (2/18/03).

§ 58-65-133. Creation and operation of foundation.

(a) Creation. — A Foundation shall be created to receive the fair market value of the corporation as provided in G.S. 58-65-132(a)(7) when the corporation converts.

(b) Purpose. — The charitable purpose of the Foundation shall be to promote the health of the people of North Carolina. For a period of 10 years from the effective date of the conversion, the Foundation may not, without the consent of the Attorney General, establish or operate any entity licensed pursuant to Chapter 58 of the General Statutes that would compete with the new corporation or any of its subsidiaries.

(c) Board of Directors. — The initial board of directors of the foundation shall consist of 11 members appointed by the Attorney General from a list of nominees recommended pursuant to subsection (d) of this section. The Attorney General shall stagger the terms of the initial appointees so that six members serve two-year terms and five members serve four-year terms. The board shall fill a vacancy in an initial term. Their successors shall be chosen by the board of directors of the Foundation in accordance with the bylaws of the Foundation and shall serve four-year terms. No member may serve more than two consecutive full terms nor more than 10 consecutive years. The Foundation may increase or decrease the size of the board in accordance with its bylaws, provided that the board shall have no fewer than nine directors and no more than 15 directors and that a decrease in size does not eliminate the then current term of any director.

(d) Advisory Committee. — An advisory committee shall be formed to (i) develop, subject to the approval of the Attorney General, the criteria for selection of the Foundation's initial board of directors and (ii) nominate candidates for the initial board of directors. The advisory committee shall be comprised of the following 11 members: three representatives of the business community selected by North Carolina Citizens for Business and Industry, three representatives of the public and private medical school community selected by The University of North Carolina Board of Governors, three representatives of private foundations and other nonprofit organizations selected by the North Carolina Center for Nonprofits, a representative of NCHA, Inc., and a representative of the North Carolina Medical Society. After receiving a copy of the proposed plan of conversion, the Attorney General shall immediately notify these organizations, and the advisory committee shall be constituted within 45 days thereafter.

The advisory committee's criteria shall ensure an open recruitment process for the directors. The advisory committee shall nominate 22 residents of North Carolina for the 11 positions to be filled by the Attorney General. The Attorney General shall retain an independent executive recruiting firm or firms to assist the advisory committee in its work.

(e) Foundation and New Corporation Independent. — The Foundation and its directors, officers, and employees shall be and remain independent of the new corporation and its affiliates. No director, officer, or employee of the Foundation shall serve as a director, officer, or employee of the new corporation or any of its affiliates. No director, officer, or employee of the new corporation or any of its affiliates shall serve as a director, officer, or employee of the Foundation. This subsection shall no longer apply after (i) 10 years following the effective date of the conversion or (ii) the divestment by the Foundation of at least ninety-five percent (95%) of the stock of the new corporation received pursuant to G.S. 58-65-132(a)(7)a. and subsection (a) of this section, whichever occurs later.

(f) Voting and Stock Registration Agreement. — The Foundation and the new corporation shall operate under a voting agreement and a stock registration agreement, approved by the Commissioner and the Attorney General, that provides at a minimum for the following:

(1) The Foundation will vote the common stock in the new corporation for directors of the new corporation nominated by the board of directors of the new corporation to the extent provided by the terms of the voting agreement.

(2) The voting restrictions will not apply to common stock of the new corporation sold by the Foundation.

(3) The board of directors of the new corporation will determine the timing of any initial public offering of the new corporation's common stock, either by the new corporation or by the Foundation, and the Foundation shall have demand registration rights and optional "piggy-back" or "incidental" registration rights in connection with any offerings of the new corporation's common stock by the new corporation, on the terms and conditions set forth in a stock registration agreement and agreed upon by the new corporation and the Foundation and approved by the Commissioner and the Attorney General.

(4) The voting agreement may contain additional terms, including (i) voting and ownership restrictions with regard to the common stock of the new corporation and (ii) provisions for the voting or registration for sale of any common stock to be issued to the Foundation by the new corporation.

(g) Costs. — The corporation shall pay the reasonable expenses of the advisory committee and executive search firm and the costs of any consultants, experts, or other professional advisors retained by the Attorney General incident to review under this section.

(h) Attorney General's Approval. — Before the Commissioner approves a plan of conversion pursuant to G.S. 58-65-132, the Attorney General, on behalf of the public and charitable interests in this State, must approve the determination relating to the fair market value of the corporation under G.S. 58-65-132(a)(7), the articles of incorporation and bylaws of the foundation, and all proposed agreements between the new corporation and the Foundation, including stock voting or registration agreements. The Attorney General may seek advice on these matters from consultants, investment bankers, and other professional advisors engaged by the Commissioner or Attorney General incident to review of the plan. The proposed articles of incorporation of the Foundation shall provide for all of the following:

(1) State that the Foundation is organized and operated exclusively for charitable purposes and for the promotion of social welfare.

(2) State that no part of the net earnings of the Foundation shall inure to the benefit of any private shareholder or individual.

(3) State that the Foundation shall not engage in any political campaign activity or the making of political contributions.

(4) Prohibit the Foundation from paying or incurring any amount that, if paid by an organization classified as a "private foundation" under section 509(a) of the Code, would constitute a "taxable expenditure" as defined by sections 4945(d)(1) and (2) of the Code.

(5) Prohibit the Foundation from engaging in any self-dealing for the benefit of its directors, officers, or employees.

(6) Provide for an ongoing community advisory committee to offer broad public input to the Foundation concerning its operations and activities.

(7) Provide that the Foundation, after its first three years of operation, will pay out the lesser of (i) "qualifying distributions" of "distributable amounts," as defined in section 4942 of the Code, as if the Foundation were classified as a private Foundation subject to the distribution requirements, but not the taxes imposed, under that section or (ii) substantially all of its income, less qualifying expenses. In no event shall the Foundation be required to invade its corpus to meet the distribution requirements under this subdivision.

(8) State that provisions in the articles of incorporation that are either required by this subdivision or designated by the Attorney General cannot be amended without the prior written approval of the Attorney General.

Within 120 days of the end of its fiscal year, the Foundation shall provide the Attorney General, the Commissioner, the Speaker of the House of Representatives, and the President Pro Tempore of the Senate its State and federal tax returns for the preceding fiscal year. The tax returns shall be made available for public inspection. (1998-3, s. 2; 1998-217, s. 56.)

Editor's Note. — The references in subdivisions (h)(4) and (h)(7) to "the Code" are references to Title 26 of the United States Code, the United States Internal Revenue Code of 1986, as amended, pursuant to G.S. 58-65-131(b)(2).

§ 58-65-135. Cost plus plans.

Any corporation organized under the provisions of this Article and Article 66 of this Chapter shall be authorized as agent of any other corporation, firm, group, partnership, or association, or any subsidiary or subsidiaries thereof, municipal corporation, State, federal government, or any agency thereof, to administer on behalf of such corporation, firm, group, partnership, or association, or any subsidiary or subsidiaries thereof, municipal corporation, State, federal government, or any agency thereof, any group hospitalization or medical and/or dental service plan, promulgated by such corporation, firm, group, partnership, or association, or any subsidiary or subsidiaries thereof, municipal corporation, State, federal government, or any agency thereof, on a cost plus administrative expense basis, provided said other corporation, firm, group, partnership, or association, or any subsidiary or subsidiaries thereof, municipal corporation, State, federal government, or any agency thereof shall have had an active existence for at least one year preceding the establishment of such plan, and was formed for purposes other than procuring such group hospitalization and/or medical and/or dental service coverage in a cost plus administrative expense basis, and provided only that administrative costs of such a cost plus plan administered by a corporation organized under the provisions of this Article and Article 66 of this Chapter, acting as an agent as herein provided, shall not exceed the remuneration received therefor, and provided further that the corporation organized under this Article and Article 66 of this Chapter administering such a plan shall have no liability to the subscribers or to the hospitals for the success or failure, liquidation or dissolution of such group hospitalization or medical and/or dental service plan and provided further, that nothing herein contained shall be construed to require of said corporation, firm, group, partnership, or association, or any subsidiary or subsidiaries thereof, municipal corporation, State, federal government, or any agency thereof, conformity to the provisions of this Article and Article 66 of this Chapter if such group hospitalization is administered by a corporation organized under this Article and Article 66 of this Chapter, on a cost plus expense basis. The administration of any cost plus plans as herein provided shall not be subject to regulation or supervision by the Commissioner of Insurance. (1941, c. 338, s. 16; 1943, c. 537, s. 9; 1947, c. 820, s. 7; 1961, c. 1149.)

§ 58-65-140: Repealed by Session Laws 1997-519, s. 3.16, effective January 1, 1998.

Cross References. — For present provisions regarding preferred providers, see G.S. 58-50-56.

Editor's Note. — Session Laws 1997-519, s. 3.19, as amended by Session Laws 1999-132, s. 4.8, provides: "Except as modified by G.S. 58-50-56(i), as enacted in this Part, any administrative rules that were adopted by the Commissioner under the authority of G.S. 58-65-140, 58-50-50, or 58-50-55 and that were effective before January 1, 1998, are not affected by the repeals in Section 3.16 or 3.17 of this act." Section 3.16 or 3.17 of the act provided for the repeal of G.S. 58-50-50, 58-50-55, and 58-65-140.

§ 58-65-145. Preexisting hospital service corporations.

No corporations organized under the laws of this State prior to the ratification of this Article and Article 66 of this Chapter, for the purposes herein provided, shall be required to reincorporate as provided for herein, and the provisions of this Article and Article 66 of this Chapter shall apply to said corporations only with regard to operations by said corporations with respect to subscribers' contracts, participating hospital contracts, reserves, investments, reports, visitations, expenses, taxation, amendments to charters, supervision of Commissioner of Insurance, application for certificate, issuance of certificates, licensing of agents after the date of the passage of this Article and Article 66 of this Chapter, provided, however, as soon as practical hereafter and in accordance with rules and regulations adopted by the Commissioner of Insurance said corporations shall conform to this Article and Article 66 of this Chapter as near as practical with respect to subscribers' contracts, endorsements, riders, and applications entered into prior to the ratification of this Article and Article 66 of this Chapter. (1941, c. 338, s. 17.)

§ 58-65-150. Construction of Chapter as to single employer plans; associations exempt.

Nothing in this Article and Article 66 of this Chapter shall be construed to affect or apply to hospital or medical and/or dental service plans which limit their membership to employees and the immediate members of the families of the employees of a single employer or his or its subsidiary or subsidiaries and which plans are operated by such employer of such limited group of the employees; nor shall this Article and Article 66 of this Chapter be construed to affect or apply to any nonstock, nonprofit medical service association which was, on January 1, 1943, organized solely for the purpose of, and actually engaged in, the administration of any medical service plan in this State upon contracts and participating agreements with physicians, surgeons, or medical societies, whereby such physicians or surgeons underwrite such plan by contributing their services to members of such association upon agreement with such association as to the schedule of fees to apply and the rate and method of payment by the association from the common fund paid in period-ically by the members for medical, surgical and obstetrical care; and such hospital service plans, and such medical service associations as are herein specifically described, are hereby exempt from the provisions of this Article and Article 66 of this Chapter. The Commissioner of Insurance may require from any such hospital service plan or medical service association such information as will enable him to determine whether such hospital service plan or medical service association is exempt from the provisions of this Article and Article 66 of this Chapter. (1941, c. 338, s. 18; 1943, c. 537, s. 10; 1947, c. 140; 1961, c. 1149.)

§ 58-65-155. Merger or consolidation, proceedings for.

Any two or more hospital and/or medical and/or dental service corporations organized under and/or subject to the provisions of this Article and Article 66 of this Chapter as determined by the Commissioner of Insurance may, as shall be specified in the agreement hereinafter required, be merged into one of such constituent corporations, herein designated as the surviving corporation, or may be consolidated into a new corporation to be formed by the means of such consolidation of the constituent corporations, which new corporation is herein designated as the resulting or consolidated corporation, and the directors and/or trustees, or a majority of them, of such corporations as desire to consolidate or merge, may enter into an agreement signed by them and under the corporate seals of the respective corporations, prescribing the terms and conditions of consolidation or merger, the mode of carrying the same into effect and stating such other facts as can be stated in the case of a consolidation or merger, stated in such altered form as the circumstances of the case require, and with such other details as to conversion of certificates of the subscribers as are deemed necessary and/or proper.

Said agreement shall be submitted to the certificate holders of each constit-uent corporation, at a separate meeting thereof, called for the purpose of taking the same into consideration; of the time, place and object of which meeting due notice shall be given by publication once a week for two consecutive weeks in some newspaper published in Raleigh, North Carolina, and in the counties in which the principal offices of the constituent corpora-tions are located, and if no such paper is published in the county of the principal office of such constituent corporations, then said notice shall be posted at the courthouse door of said county or counties for a period of two weeks.

Said printed or posted notices shall be in such form and of such size as the Commissioner of Insurance may approve. A true copy of said notices shall be filed with the Commissioner of Insurance.

Such publication and filing of notices shall be completed at least 15 days prior to the date set therein for the meeting, and due proof thereof shall be filed with the Commissioner of Insurance at least 10 days prior to the date of such meeting.

At this meeting those present in person or represented by proxy shall constitute a quorum and said agreement shall be considered and voted upon by ballot in person or by proxy or both taken for the adoption or rejection of the same; and if the votes of two thirds of those at said meeting voting in person or by proxy shall be for the adoption of the said agreement, then that fact shall be certified on said agreement by the president and secretary of each such corporation, under the seal thereof.

The agreement so adopted and certified shall be signed by the president or vice-president and secretary or assistant secretary of each of such corporations under the corporate seals thereof and acknowledged by the president or vice-president of each such corporation before any officer authorized by the laws of this State to take acknowledgement of deeds to be the respective act, deed, and agreement of each of said corporations.

The said agreement shall be submitted to and approved by the Commissioner of Insurance, in advance of the merger or consolidation and his approval thereof shall be indicated by his signature being affixed thereto under the seal of his office.

The Commissioner shall not approve any such plans, unless, after a hearing, he finds that it is fair, equitable to certificate holders and members, consistent with law, and will not conflict with the public interest.

The agreement so certified and acknowledged with the approval of the Commissioner of Insurance noted thereon, shall be filed in the office of the Secretary of State, and shall thenceforth be taken and deemed to be the agreement and act of consolidation or merger of said corporations; and a copy of said agreement and act of consolidation or merger duly certified by the Secretary of State under the seal of his office shall also be recorded, in the office of the register of deeds of the county of this State in which the principal office of the surviving or consolidated corporation is, or is to be established, and in the office of the registers of deeds of the counties of this State in which the respective corporations so merging or consolidating shall have their original certificates of incorporation recorded, and also in the office of the register of deeds in each county in which either or any of the corporations entering into merger or consolidation owns any real estate; and such record, or a certified copy thereof, shall be evidence of the agreement and act of consolidation or merger of said corporations, and of the observance and performance of all acts and conditions necessary to have been observed and performed precedent to such consolidation or merger. When an agreement shall have been signed, authorized, adopted, acknowledged, approved, and filed and recorded as hereinabove set forth in this section, for all purposes of the laws of this State, the separate existence of all constituent corporations, parties to said agreement, or of all such constituent corporations, except the one into which the other or others of such constituent corporations have been merged, as the case may be, shall cease and the constituent corporations shall become a new corporation, or be merged into one of such corporations, as the case may be, in accordance with the provisions of said agreement, possessing all the rights, privileges, powers and franchises as well of a public as of a private nature, of each of said constituent corporations, and all and singular, the rights, privileges, powers and franchises of each of said corporations, and all property, real, personal and mixed, and all debts due to any of said constituent corporations on whatever account, shall be vested in the corporation resulting from or surviving such consolidation or merger, and all property, rights, privileges, powers, and franchises and all and every other interest shall be thereafter as effectually the property of the resulting or surviving corporation as they were of the several and respective constituent corporations, and the title to any real estate, whether vested by deed or otherwise, under the laws of this State, vested in any such constituent corporations shall not revert or be in any way impaired by reason of such consolidation or merger; provided, however, that all rights of creditors and all liens upon the property of either of or any of said constituent corporations shall be preserved, unimpaired, limited in lien to the property affected by such lien at the time of the merger or consolidation, and all debts, liabilities, and duties of the respective constituent corporations shall thenceforth attach to said resulting or surviving corporation, and may be enforced against it to the same extent as if said debts, liabilities, and duties had been incurred or contracted by it; and further provided that notice of any said liens, debts, liabilities, and duties is given in writing to the resulting or surviving corporation within six months after the date of the filing of the agreement of merger in the office of the Secretary of State. All such liens, debts, liabilities, and duties of which notice is not given as provided herein are forever barred. The certificate of incorporation of the surviving corporation shall be deemed to be amended to the extent, if any, that the changes in its certificates of incorporation are stated in the agreement of merger. All certificates theretofore issued and outstanding by each constituent corporation in good standing upon the date of the filing of such agreement with the Secretary of State without reissuance thereof by the resulting or surviving corporation shall be the contract and agreement of the resulting or surviving corporation with each of the certificate holders thereof and subject to all terms and conditions thereof and of the agreement of merger filed in the office of the Secretary of State.

Any action or proceeding pending by or against any of the corporations consolidated or merged may be prosecuted to judgment as if such consolidation or merger had not taken place, or the corporations resulting from or surviving such consolidation or merger may be substituted in its place.

The liability of such constituent corporations to the certificate holders thereof, and the rights or remedies of the creditors thereof, or persons doing or transacting business with such corporations, shall not, in any way, be lessened or impaired by the consolidation or merger of two or more of such corporations under the provisions of this section, except as provided in this section.

When two or more corporations are consolidated or merged, the corporation resulting from or surviving such consolidation or merger shall have the power and authority to continue any contracts which any of the constituent corporations might have elected to continue. All contracts entered into between any constituent corporations and any other persons shall be and become the contract of the resulting corporations according to the terms and conditions of said contract and the agreement of consolidation or merger.

For the filing of the agreement as hereinabove provided, the Secretary of State is entitled to receive such fees only as he would have received had a new corporation been formed.

Any agreement for merger and/or consolidation as shall conform to the provisions of this section, shall be binding and valid upon all the subscribers, certificate holders and/or members of such constituent corporations, provided only that any subscriber, certificate holder and/or member who shall so indicate his disapproval thereof to the resulting, consolidated or surviving corporation within 90 days after the filing of said agreement with the Secretary of State shall be entitled to receive all unearned portions of premiums paid on his certificate from and after the date of the receipt of the application therefor by the resulting, surviving, or consolidated corporation; each subscriber, certificate holder and/or member who shall not so indicate his or her disapproval of said agreement and said merger within said period of 90 days is deemed and presumed to have approved said agreement and said merger and/or consolidation and shall have waived his or her right to question the legality of said merger and/or consolidation.

No director, officer, subscriber, certificate holder and/or member as such of any such corporation, except as is expressly provided by the plan of merger or consolidation, shall receive any fee, commission, other compensation or valuable consideration whatever, for in any manner aiding, promoting or assisting in the merger or consolidation. (1947, c. 820, s. 8; 1961, c. 1149; 1967, c. 823, s. 25.)

§ **58-65-160:** Repealed by Session Laws 1998-3, s. 3, effective May 22, 1998.

§ 58-65-165. Commissioner of Insurance determines corporations exempt from this Article and Article 66 of this Chapter.

The Commissioner of Insurance may require from any corporation writing any hospital service contracts and any corporation writing medical and/or dental service contracts or any or all of them, such information as will enable him to determine whether such corporation is subject to the provisions of this Article and Article 66 of this Chapter. (1947, c. 820, s. 9; 1961, c. 1149.)

Part 2. Indemnification.

§ 58-65-166. Policy statement and definitions.

(a) It is the public policy of this State to enable corporations organized under this Chapter to attract and maintain responsible, qualified directors, officers, employees, and agents, and, to that end, to permit corporations organized under this Chapter to allocate the risk of personal liability of directors, officers, employees, and agents through indemnification and insurance as authorized in this Part.

(b) Definitions in this Part:

    (1) "Corporation" includes any not for profit domestic hospital, medical, or dental service corporation, or successor of a corporation in a merger or other transaction in which the predecessor's existence ceased upon consummation of the transaction.

    (2) "Director" or "Trustee" means an individual who is or was a director of a corporation or an individual who, while a director of a corporation, is or was serving at the corporation's request as a director, officer, partner, trustee, employee, or agent of another foreign or domestic corporation, partnership, joint venture, trust, employee benefit plan, or other enterprise. A director is considered to be serving an employee benefit plan at the corporation's request if his duties to the corporation also impose duties on, or otherwise involve services by, him to the plan or to participants in or beneficiaries of the plan. "Director" or "Trustee" includes, unless the context requires otherwise, the estate or personal representative of a director or trustee.

    (3) "Expenses" means expenses of every kind incurred in defending a proceeding, including counsel fees.

    (4) "Liability" means the obligation to pay a judgment, settlement, penalty, fine (including an excise tax assessed with respect to an employee benefit plan), or reasonable expenses incurred with respect to a proceeding.

    (5) "Official capacity" means: (i) when used with respect to a director or trustee, the office of director or trustee in a corporation; and (ii) when used with respect to an individual other than a director or trustee, as contemplated in G.S. 58-65-172, the office in a corporation held by the officer or the employment or agency relationship undertaken by the employee or agent on behalf of the corporation. "Official capacity" does

not include service for any other foreign or domestic corporation or any partnership, joint venture, trust, employee benefit plan, or other enterprise.

(6) "Party" includes an individual who was, is, or is threatened to be made a named defendant or respondent in a proceeding.

(7) "Proceeding" means any threatened, pending, or completed action, suit, or proceeding, whether civil, criminal, administrative, or investigative and whether formal or informal.

(8) "Trustee". Whenever the term "director" or "directors" is used herein it shall include the term "trustee", or a person who is designated as a "trustee" under a corporation governed by this Article. (1989 (Reg. Sess., 1990), c. 1071, s. 1.)

§ 58-65-167. Authority to indemnify.

(a) Except as provided in subsection (d), a corporation may indemnify an individual made a party to a proceeding because he is or was a director against liability incurred in the proceeding if:

(1) He conducted himself in good faith; and

(2) He reasonably believed (i) in the case of conduct in his official capacity with the corporation, that his conduct was in its best interests; and (ii) in all other cases, that his conduct was at least not opposed to its best interests; and

(3) In the case of any criminal proceeding, he had no reasonable cause to believe his conduct was unlawful.

(b) A director's conduct with respect to an employee benefit plan for a purpose he reasonably believed to be in the interests of the participants in and beneficiaries of the plan is conduct that satisfies the requirement of subsection (a)(2)(ii).

(c) The termination of a proceeding by judgment, order, settlement, conviction, or upon a plea of no contest or its equivalent is not, of itself, determinative that the director did not meet the standard of conduct described in this section.

(d) A corporation may not indemnify a director under this section:

(1) In connection with a proceeding by or in the right of the corporation in which the director was adjudged liable to the corporation; or

(2) In connection with any other proceeding charging improper personal benefit to him, whether or not involving action in his official capacity, in which he was adjudged liable on the basis that personal benefit was improperly received by him.

(e) Indemnification permitted under this section in connection with a proceeding by or in the right of the corporation that is concluded without a final adjudication on the issue of liability is limited to reasonable expenses incurred in connection with the proceeding.

(f) The authorization, approval or favorable recommendation by the board of directors of a corporation of indemnification, as permitted by this section, shall not be deemed an act or corporate transaction in which a director has a conflict of interest, and no such indemnification shall be void or voidable on such ground. (1989 (Reg. Sess., 1990), c. 1071, s. 1.)

§ 58-65-168. Mandatory indemnification.

Unless limited by its articles of incorporation, a corporation shall indemnify a director who was wholly successful, on the merits or otherwise, in the defense of any proceeding to which he was a party because he is or was a director of the corporation against reasonable expenses incurred by him in connection with the proceeding. (1989 (Reg. Sess., 1990), c. 1071, s. 1.)

§ 58-65-169. Advance for expenses.

Expenses incurred by a director in defending a proceeding may be paid by the corporation in advance of the final disposition of such proceeding as authorized by the board of directors in the specific case or as authorized or required under any provision in the articles of incorporation or bylaws or by any applicable resolution or contract upon receipt of an undertaking by or on behalf of the director to repay such amount unless it shall ultimately be determined that he is entitled to be indemnified by the corporation against such expenses. (1989 (Reg. Sess., 1990), c. 1071, s. 1.)

§ 58-65-170. Court-ordered indemnification.

Unless a corporation's articles of incorporation provide otherwise, a director of the corporation who is a party to a proceeding may apply for indemnification to the court conducting the proceeding or to another court of competent jurisdiction. On receipt of an application, the court after giving any notice the court considers necessary may order indemnification if it determines:

(1) The director is entitled to mandatory indemnification under G.S. 58-65-168, in which case the court shall also order the corporation to pay the director's reasonable expenses incurred to obtain court-ordered indemnification; or

(2) The director is fairly and reasonably entitled to indemnification in view of all the relevant circumstances, whether or not he met the standard of conduct set forth in G.S. 58-65-167 or was adjudged liable as described in G.S. 58-65-167(d), but if he was adjudged so liable his indemnification is limited to reasonable expenses incurred. (1989 (Reg. Sess., 1990), c. 1071, s. 1.)

§ 58-65-171. Determination and authorization of indemnification.

(a) A corporation may not indemnify a director under G.S. 58-65-167 unless authorized in the specific case after a determination has been made that indemnification of the director is permissible in the circumstances because he has met the standard of conduct set forth in G.S. 58-65-167.

(b) The determination shall be made:

(1) By the board of directors by majority vote of a quorum consisting of directors not at the time parties to the proceeding;

(2) If a quorum cannot be obtained under subdivision (1), by majority vote of a committee duly designated by the board of directors (in which designation directors who are parties may participate), consisting solely of two or more directors not at the time parties to the proceeding;

(3) By special legal counsel (i) selected by the board of directors or its committee in the manner prescribed in subdivision (1) or (2); or (ii) if a quorum of the board of directors cannot be obtained under subdivision (1) and a committee cannot be designated under subdivision (2), selected by majority vote of the full board of directors (in which selection directors who are parties may participate); or

(4) By the shareholders, but shares owned by or voted under the control of directors who are at the time parties to the proceeding may not be voted on the determination.

(c) Authorization of indemnification and evaluation as to reasonableness of expenses shall be made in the same manner as the determination that indemnification is permissible, except that if the determination is made by special legal counsel, authorization of indemnification and evaluation as to reasonableness of expenses shall be made by those entitled under subsection (b)(3) to select counsel. (1989 (Reg. Sess., 1990), c. 1071, s. 1.)

§ 58-65-172. Indemnification of officers, employees, and agents.

Unless a corporation's articles of incorporation provide otherwise:
   (1) An officer of the corporation is entitled to mandatory indemnification under G.S. 58-65-168 and is entitled to apply for court-ordered indemnification under G.S. 58-65-170, in each case to the same extent as a director;
   (2) The corporation may indemnify and advance expenses under this Part to an officer, employee, or agent of the corporation to the same extent as to a director; and
   (3) A corporation may also indemnify and advance expenses to an officer, employee, or agent who is not a director to the extent, consistent with public policy, that may be provided by its articles of incorporation, bylaws, general or specific action of its board of directors, or contract. (1989 (Reg. Sess., 1990), c. 1071, s. 1; 1995, c. 193, s. 56.)

§ 58-65-173. Additional indemnification and insurance.

(a) In addition to and separate and apart from the indemnification provided for in G.S. 58-65-167, 58-65-168, 58-65-170, 58-65-171, and 58-65-172, a corporation may in its articles of incorporation or bylaws or by contract or resolution indemnify or agree to indemnify any one or more of its directors, officers, employees, or agents against liability and expenses in any proceeding (including without limitation a proceeding brought by or on behalf of the corporation itself) arising out of their status as such or their activities in any of the foregoing capacities; provided, however, that a corporation may not indemnify or agree to indemnify a person against liability or expenses he may incur on account of his activities which were at the time taken known or believed by him to be clearly in conflict with the best interests of the corporation. A corporation may likewise and to the same extent indemnify or agree to indemnify any person who, at the request of the corporation, is or was serving as a director, officer, partner, trustee, employee, or agent of another foreign or domestic corporation, partnership, joint venture, trust or other enterprise or as a trustee or administrator under an employee benefit plan. Any provision in any articles of incorporation, bylaw, contract, or resolution permitted under this section may include provisions for recovery from the corporation of reasonable costs, expenses, and attorneys' fees in connection with the enforcement of rights to indemnification granted therein and may further include provisions establishing reasonable procedures for determining and enforcing the rights granted therein.

(b) The authorization, adoption, approval, or favorable recommendation by the board of directors of a corporation of any provision in any articles of incorporation, bylaw, contract or resolution, as permitted in this section, shall not be deemed an act or corporate transaction in which a director has a conflict of interest, and no such articles of incorporation or bylaw provision or contract or resolution shall be void or voidable on such grounds. The authorization, adoption, approval, or favorable recommendation by the board of directors of a corporation of any provision in any articles of incorporation, bylaw, contract or resolution, as permitted in this section, which occurred on or prior to the effective date of this act, shall not be deemed an act or corporate transaction in which a director has a conflict of interest, and no such articles of incorporation, bylaw provision, contract or resolution shall be void or voidable on such grounds.

(c) A corporation may purchase and maintain insurance on behalf of an individual who is or was a director, officer, employee, or agent of the corporation, or who, while a director, officer, employee, or agent of the corporation, is or was serving at the request of the corporation as a director, officer, partner, trustee, employee, or agent of another foreign or domestic corporation, partnership, joint venture, trust, employee benefit plan, or other enterprise, against liability asserted against or incurred by him in that capacity or arising from his status as a director, officer, employee, or agent, whether or not the corporation would have power to indemnify him against the same liability under any provision of this Chapter. (1989 (Reg. Sess., 1990), c. 1071, s. 1; 1991, c. 172, s. 1.)

§ 58-65-174. Application of Part.

(a) If articles of incorporation limit indemnification or advance for expenses, indemnification and advance for expenses are valid only to the extent consistent with the articles.

(b) This Part does not limit a corporation's power to pay or reimburse expenses incurred by a director in connection with his appearance as a witness in a proceeding at a time when he has not been made a named defendant or respondent to the proceeding.

(c) This Part shall not affect rights or liabilities arising out of acts or omissions occurring before October 1, 1990. (1989 (Reg. Sess., 1990), c. 1071, s. 1.)

ARTICLE 66.

Hospital, Medical and Dental Service Corporation Readable Insurance Certificates Act.

§ 58-66-1. Title.

This Article is known and may be cited as the "Hospital, Medical and Dental Service Corporation Readable Insurance Certificates Act." (1979, 2nd Sess., c. 1161, s. 1.)

§ 58-66-5. Purpose.

The purpose of this Article is to provide that insurance certificates and subscriber contracts under this Article and Article 65 of this Chapter be readable by a person of average intelligence, experience, and education. All insurers are required by this Article to use certificate and contract forms and, where applicable, benefit booklets that are written in simple and commonly used language, that are logically and clearly arranged, and that are printed in a legible format. (1979, 2nd Sess., c. 1161, s. 1.)

§ 58-66-10. Scope of application.

(a) Except as provided in subsection (b) of this section, the provisions of this Article apply to the certificates and contracts of direct insurance and health care coverage that are described in G.S. 58-65-60(a) and (b).

(b) Nothing in this Article applies to:

(1) Any group contract or certificate, nor any group certificate delivered or issued for delivery outside of this State;

(2) Insurers who issue benefit booklets on group and nongroup bases explaining the certificates or contracts issued under G.S. 58-65-60. In such cases, the provisions of this Article apply only to the benefit booklets furnished to the persons insured, and not to the certificates.

(c) No other provision of the General Statutes setting language simplification standards shall apply to any certificate forms covered by this Article.

(d) Any non-English language certificate delivered or issued for delivery in this State shall be deemed to be in compliance with this Article if the insurer certifies that such certificate is translated from an English language certificate which does comply with this Article. (1979, 2nd Sess., c. 1161, s. 1.)

§ 58-66-15. Definitions.

As used in this Article, unless the context clearly indicates otherwise:

(1) "Benefit booklet" means any written explanation of insurance coverages or benefits issued by an insurer and which is supplemental to and not a part of an insurance certificate or subscriber contract.

(2) "Commissioner" means the Commissioner of Insurance.

(3) "Flesch scale analysis readability score" means a measurement of the case of readability of an insurance certificate or contract made pursuant to the procedures described in G.S. 58-66-25.

(4) "Insurance certificate or contract" or "policy" or "certificate" means an agreement as defined by G.S. 58-65-60.

(5) "Insurer" means every corporation providing contracts or certificates of coverage of insurance as described in G.S. 58-65-1. (1979, 2nd Sess., c. 1161, s. 1.)

§ 58-66-20. Format requirements.

(a) All certificates and contracts covered by G.S. 58-66-35 must be printed in a type face at least as large as 10 point modern type, one point leaded, be written in a logical and clear order and form, and contain the following items:

(1) On the cover, first, or insert page of the certificate a statement that the certificate is a legal contract between the certificate owner and the insurer, and the statement, printed in larger or other contrasting type or color, "Read your certificate carefully";

(2) An index of the major provisions of the certificate, which may include the following items:
   a. The person or persons insured by the certificate;
   b. The applicable events, occurrences, conditions, losses, or damages covered by the certificate;
   c. The limitations or conditions on the coverage of the certificate;
   d. Definitional sections of the certificate;
   e. Provisions governing the procedure for filing a claim under the certificate;
   f. Provisions governing cancellation, renewal, or amendment of the certificate by either the insurer or the subscriber;
   g. Any options under the certificate; and
   h. Provisions governing the insurer's duties and powers in the event that suit is filed against the subscriber.

(b) In determining whether or not a certificate is written in a logical and clear order and form the Commissioner must consider the following factors:

(1) The extent to which sections or provisions are set off and clearly identified by titles, headings, or margin notations;

(2) The use of a more readable format, such as narrative or outline forms;

(3) Margin size and the amount and use of space to separate sections of the policy; and

(4) Contrast and legibility of the colors of the ink and paper, and the use of contrasting titles or headings for sections. (1979, 2nd Sess., c. 1161, s. 1.)

§ 58-66-25. Flesch scale analysis readability score; procedures.

(a) A Flesch scale analysis readability score will be measured as provided in this section.

(b) For certificates containing 10,000 words or less of text, the entire certificate must be analyzed. For certificates containing more than 10,000 words, the readability of two 200-word samples per page may be analyzed in lieu of the entire certificate. The samples must be separated by at least 20 printed lines. For the purposes of this subsection a word will be counted as five printed characters or spaces between characters.

(c) The number of words and sentences in the text must be counted and the total number of words divided by the total number of sentences. The figure obtained must be multiplied by a factor of 1.015. The total number of syllables must be counted and divided by the total number of words. The figure obtained must be multiplied by a factor of 84.6. The sum of the figures computed under this subsection subtracted from 206.835 equals the Flesch scale analysis readability score for the certificate.

(d) For the purposes of subsection (c) of this section the following procedures must be used:

(1) A contraction, hyphenated word, or numbers and letters, when separated by spaces, will be counted as one word;

(2) A unit of words ending with a period, semicolon, or colon, but excluding headings, and captions will be counted as a sentence; and

(3) A syllable means a unit of spoken language consisting of one or more letters of a word as divided by an accepted dictionary. Where the dictionary shows two or more equally acceptable pronunciations of a word, the pronunciation containing fewer syllables may be used.

(e) The term "text" as used in this section includes all printed matter except the following:

(1) The name and address of the insurer; the name, number or title of the certificate; the table of contents or index; captions and subcaptions; specification pages, schedules or tables; and

(2) Any certificate language that is drafted to conform to the requirements of any law, regulation, or agency interpretation of any state or the federal government; any certificate language required by any collectively bargained agreement; any medical terminology; and any words that are defined in the certificate: Provided, however, that the insurer submits with his filing under G.S. 58-66-30 a certified document identifying the language or terminology that is entitled to be excepted by this subdivision. (1979, 2nd Sess., c. 1161, s. 1.)

§ 58-66-30. Filing requirements; duties of the Commissioner.

(a) No insurer may make, issue, amend or renew any certificate or contract after the dates specified in G.S. 58-66-35 for the applicable type of insurance unless the certificate is in compliance with the provisions of G.S. 58-66-20 and 58-66-25, and unless the certificate is filed with the Commissioner for this approval. The policy will be deemed approved 90 days after filing unless disapproved within the 90-day period. The Commissioner may not unreasonably withhold this approval. Any disapproval must be delivered to the insurer in writing and must state the grounds for disapproval. Any certificate filed with the Commissioner must be accompanied by a certified Flesch scale readability analysis and test score and by the insurer's certification that the policy is, in the insurer's judgment, readable based on the factors specified in G.S. 58-66-20 and 58-66-25.

(b) The Commissioner must disapprove any certificate covered by subsection (a) of this section if he finds that:

    (1) It is not accompanied by a certified Flesch scale analysis readability score of 50 or more;

    (2) It is not accompanied by the insurer's certification that the certificate is, in the judgment of the insurer, readable under the standards of this Article; or

    (3) It does not comply with the format requirements of G.S. 58-66-20. (1979, 2nd Sess., c. 1161, s. 1; 1995, c. 193, s. 57.)

§ 58-66-35. Application to policies; dates.

(a) The filing requirements of G.S. 58-66-30 apply to all subscribers' contracts of hospital, medical, and dental service corporations as described in G.S. 58-65-60(a) and (b) that are made, issued, amended or renewed after July 1, 1983.

(b) Repealed by Session Laws 1995, c. 193, s. 58, effective June 7, 1995. (1979, 2nd Sess., c. 1161, s. 1; 1995, c. 193, s. 58; 1995 (Reg. Sess., 1996), c. 742, s. 28.)

Editor's Note. — This section is set out in the form above at the direction of the Revisor of Statutes.

§ 58-66-40. Construction.

(a) The provisions of this Article will not operate to relieve any insurer from any provision of law regulating the contents or provisions of insurance certificates or contracts nor operate to reduce an insured's, beneficiary's or subscriber's rights or protection granted under any statute or provision of the law.

(b) The provisions of this Article shall not be construed to mandate, require, or allow alteration of the legal effect of any provision of any insurance certificate or contract.

(c) In any action brought by a subscriber or claimant arising out of a certificate approved pursuant to this Article, the subscriber or claimant may base such an action on either or both (i) the substantive language prescribed by such other statute or provision of law, or (ii) the wording of the approved certificate. (1979, 2nd Sess., c. 1161, s. 1.)

ARTICLE 67.

Health Maintenance Organization Act.

§ 58-67-1. Short title.

This Article may be cited as the Health Maintenance Organization Act of 1979. (1977, c. 580, s. 1; 1979, c. 876, s. 1.)

Cross References. — For the Insurance Information and Privacy Protection Act, see G.S. 58-39-1 et seq.

Editor's Note. — This Article is former Chapter 57A as rewritten by Session Laws 1979, c. 876, s. 1, effective July 1, 1979, and recodified as Chapter 57B, which in turn has been recodified and incorporated as Article 67 of Chapter 58 pursuant to Session Laws 1987, c. 752, s. 9, as amended by Session Laws 1987 (Reg. Sess., 1988), c. 975, s. 34.

Legal Periodicals. — For survey of 1977 law on health care regulation, see 56 N.C.L. Rev. 857 (1978).

For survey of 1979 administrative law, see 58 N.C.L. Rev. 1185 (1980).

§ 58-67-5. Definitions.

(a) "Commissioner" means the Commissioner of Insurance.

(b) "Enrollee" means an individual who is covered by an HMO.

(c) "Evidence of coverage" means any certificate, agreement, or contract issued to an enrollee setting out the coverage to which he is entitled.

(d) "Health care plan" means any arrangement whereby any person undertakes on a prepaid basis to provide, arrange for, pay for, or reimburse any part of the cost of any health care services and at least part of such arrangement consists of arranging for or the provision of health care services, as distinguished from mere indemnification against the cost of such services on a prepaid basis through insurance or otherwise.

(e) "Health care services" means any services included in the furnishing to any individual of medical or dental care, or hospitalization or incident to the furnishing of such care or hospitalization, as well as the furnishing to any person of any and all other services for the purpose of preventing, alleviating, curing, or healing human illness or injury.

(f) "Health maintenance organization" or "HMO" means any person who undertakes to provide or arrange for the delivery of health care services to enrollees on a prepaid basis except for enrollee responsibility for copayments and deductibles. For the purposes of 11 U.S.C. § 109(b) (2) and (d), an HMO is a domestic insurance company.

(g) "Person" includes associations, trusts, or corporations, but does not include professional associations, or individuals.

(h) "Provider" means any physician, hospital, or other person that is licensed or otherwise authorized in this State to furnish health care services.

(i) "Net worth" means the excess of total assets over the total liabilities and may include borrowed funds that are repayable only from the net earned income of the health maintenance organization and repayable only with the advance permission of the Commissioner. For the purposes of this subsection, "assets" means (i) tangible assets and (ii) other investments permitted under G.S. 58-67-60.

(j) "Working capital" means the excess of current assets over current liabilities; provided that the only borrowed funds that may be included in working capital must be those borrowed funds that are repayable only from net earned income and must be repayable only with the advance permission of the Commissioner.

(k) "Subscriber" means an individual whose employment or other status, except family dependency, is the basis for eligibility for enrollment in the HMO; or in the case of an individual contract, the person in whose name the contract is issued.

(l) "Participating provider" means a provider who, under an express or implied contract with the HMO or with its contractor or subcontractor, has agreed to provide health care services to enrollees with an expectation of receiving payment, directly or indirectly, from the HMO, other than copayment or deductible.

(m) "Insolvent" or "insolvency" means that the HMO has been declared insolvent and is placed under an order of liquidation by a court of competent jurisdiction.

(n) "Carrier" means an HMO, an insurer, a nonprofit hospital or medical service corporation, or other entity responsible for the payment of benefits or provision of services under a group contract.

(o) "Discontinuance" means the termination of the contract between the group contract holder and an HMO due to the insolvency of the HMO and does not mean the termination of any agreement between any individual enrollee and the HMO.

(p) "Uncovered expenditures" means the amounts owed or paid to any provider who provides health care services to an enrollee and where such amount owed or paid is (i) not made pursuant to a written contract that contains the "hold harmless" provisions defined in G.S. 58-67-115; or (ii) not guaranteed or insured by a guaranteeing organization or insurer under the terms of a written guarantee or insurance policy that has been determined to be acceptable to the Commissioner. "Uncovered expenditures" includes amounts owed or paid to providers directly from the HMO as well as payments made by a medical group, independent practice association, or any other similar organization to reimburse providers for services rendered to an enrollee. (1977, c. 580, s. 1; 1979, c. 876, s. 1; 1987, c. 631, s. 1; 1989, c. 776, ss. 2, 3, 15; 1991, c. 195, s. 4; c. 720, s. 40; 2001-417, s. 13; 2003-212, s. 19.)

Effect of Amendments. — Session Laws 2003-212, s. 19, effective October 1, 2003, deleted "provided, however, that the depreciated cost of office furniture and equipment in the principal office shall not exceed ten percent (10%) of a health maintenance organization's net worth" at the end of subsection (i).

Legal Periodicals. — For survey of 1979 administrative law, see 58 N.C.L. Rev. 1185 (1980).

§ 58-67-10. Establishment of health maintenance organizations.

(a) Notwithstanding any law of this State to the contrary, any person may apply to the Commissioner for a certificate of authority to establish and operate a health maintenance organization in compliance with this Article. No person shall establish or operate a health maintenance organization in this State, nor sell or offer to sell, or solicit offers to purchase or receive advance or periodic consideration in conjunction with a health maintenance organization without obtaining a certificate of authority under this Article. A foreign corporation may qualify under this Article, subject to its full compliance with Article 16 of this Chapter.

(b)(1) It is specifically the intention of this section to permit such persons as were providing health services on a prepaid basis on July 1, 1977, or receiving federal funds under Section 254(c) of Title 42, U.S. Code, as a community health center, to continue to operate in the manner which they have heretofore operated.

(2) Notwithstanding anything contained in this Article to the contrary, any person can provide health services on a fee for service basis to individuals who are not enrollees of the organization, and to enrollees for services not covered by the contract, provided that the volume of services in this manner shall not be such as to affect the ability of the health maintenance organization to provide on an adequate and timely basis those services to its enrolled members which it has contracted to furnish under the enrollment contract.

(3) This Article shall not apply to any employee benefit plan to the extent that the Federal Employee Retirement Income Security Act of 1974 preempts State regulation thereof.

(3a) This Article does not apply to any prepaid health service or capitation arrangement implemented or administered by the Department of

Health and Human Services or its representatives, pursuant to 42 U.S.C. § 1396n or Chapter 108A of the General Statutes, a provider sponsored organization or other organization certified, qualified, or otherwise approved by the Division of Medical Assistance of the Department of Health and Human Services pursuant to Article 17 of Chapter 131E of the General Statutes, or to any provider of health care services participating in such a prepaid health service or capitation arrangement. Article; provided, however, that to the extent this Article applies to any such person acting as a subcontractor to a Health Maintenance Organization licensed in this State, that person shall be considered a single service Health Maintenance Organization for the purpose of G.S. 58-67-20(4), G.S. 58-67-25, and G.S. 58-67-110.

(4) Except as provided in paragraphs (1), (2), (3), and (3a) of this subsection, the persons to whom these paragraphs are applicable shall be required to comply with all provisions contained in this Article.

(c) Each application for a certificate of authority shall be verified by an officer or authorized representative of the applicant, shall be in a form prescribed by the Commissioner, and shall be set forth or be accompanied by the following:

(1) A copy of the basic organizational document, if any, of the applicant such as the articles of incorporation, articles of association, partnership agreement, trust agreement, or other applicable documents, and all amendments thereto;

(2) A copy of the bylaws, rules and regulations, or similar document, if any, regulating the conduct of the internal affairs of the applicant;

(3) A list of the names, addresses, and official positions of persons who are to be responsible for the conduct of the affairs of the applicant, including all members of the board of directors, board of trustees, executive committee, or other governing board or committee, the principal officers in the case of a corporation, and the partners or members in the case of a partnership or association;

(4) A copy of any contract form made or to be made between any class of providers and the HMO and a copy of any contract form made or to be made between third party administrators, marketing consultants, or persons listed in subdivision (3) of this subsection and the HMO;

(5) A statement generally describing the health maintenance organization, its health care plan or plans, facilities, and personnel;

(6) A copy of the form of evidence of coverage to be issued to the enrollees;

(7) A copy of the form of the group contract, if any, which is to be issued to employers, unions, trustees, or other organizations;

(8) Financial statements showing the applicant's assets, liabilities, and sources of financial support. If the applicant's financial affairs are audited by independent certified public accountants, a copy of the applicant's most recent regular certified financial statement shall be deemed to satisfy this requirement unless the Commissioner directs that additional or more recent financial information is required for the proper administration of this Article;

(9) A financial feasibility plan, which includes detailed enrollment projections, the methodology for determining premium rates to be charged during the first 12 months of operations certified by an actuary or a recognized actuarial consultant, a projection of balance sheets, cash flow statements, showing any capital expenditures, purchase and sale of investments and deposits with the State, and income and expense statements anticipated from the start of operations until the organization has had net income for at least one year; and a statement as to the sources of working capital as well as any other sources of funding;

(10) A power of attorney duly executed by such applicant, if not domiciled in this State, appointing the Commissioner and his successors in office, and duly authorized deputies, as the true and lawful attorney of such applicant in and for this State upon whom all lawful process in any legal action or proceeding against the health maintenance organization on a cause of action arising in this State may be served;

(11) A statement reasonably describing the geographic area or areas to be served;

(12) A description of the procedures to be implemented to meet the protection against insolvency requirements of G.S. 58-67-110;

(13) A description of the internal grievance procedures to be utilized for the investigation and resolution of enrollee complaints and grievances; and

(14) Such other information as the Commissioner may require to make the determinations required in G.S. 58-67-20.

(d)(1) A health maintenance organization shall file a notice describing any significant modification of the operation set out in the information required by subsection (c) of this section. Such notice shall be filed with the Commissioner prior to the modification. If the Commissioner does not disapprove within 90 days after the filing, such modification shall be deemed to be approved. Changes subject to the terms of this section include expansion of service area, changes in provider contract forms and group contract forms where the distribution of risk is significantly changed, and any other changes that the Commissioner describes in properly promulgated rules. Every HMO shall report to the Commissioner for his information material changes in the provider network, the addition or deletion of Medicare risk or Medicaid risk arrangements and the addition or deletion of employer groups that exceed ten percent (10%) of the health maintenance organization's book of business or such other information as the Commissioner may require. Such information shall be filed with the Commissioner within 15 days after implementation of the reported changes. Every HMO shall file with the Commissioner all subsequent changes in the information or forms that are required by this Article to be filed with the Commissioner.

(2) The Commissioner may promulgate rules and regulations exempting from the filing requirements of subdivision (1) those items he deems unnecessary. (1977, c. 580, s. 1; 1979, c. 876, s. 1; 1983, c. 386, s. 1; 1985 (Reg. Sess., 1986), c. 1027, s. 49; 1987, c. 631, ss. 6, 7; 1989, c. 776, ss. 4-8; 1991, c. 720, ss. 41, 69; 1993, c. 529, s. 7.2; 1993 (Reg. Sess., 1994), c. 769, s. 25.48; 1997-443, s. 11A.118(a); 1998-227, s. 2.)

Cross References. — As to certificates of need for health maintenance organizations, see G.S. 131E-180.

Legal Periodicals. — For survey of 1979 administrative law, see 58 N.C.L. Rev. 1185 (1980).

§ 58-67-11. Additional HMO application information.

(a) In addition to the information filed under G.S. 58-67-10(c), each application shall include a description of the following:

(1) The program to be used to evaluate whether the applicant's provider network is sufficient, in numbers and types of providers, to assure that all health care services will be accessible without unreasonable delay.

(2) The program to be used for verifying provider credentials.

  (3) The quality management program to assure quality of care and health care services managed and provided through the health care plan.

  (4) The utilization review program for the review and control of health care services provided or paid for.

  (5) The applicant's provider network and evidence of the ability of that network to provide all health care services to the applicant's prospective enrollees.

 (b) G.S. 58-67-10(d) applies to the information specified in this section. (1997-519, s. 1.2.)

Legal Periodicals. — For 1997 legislative survey, see 20 Campbell L. Rev. 469.

§§ 58-67-12 through 58-67-14: Reserved for future codification purposes.

§ 58-67-15. Health maintenance organization of bordering states may be admitted to do business; reciprocity.

A federally qualified health maintenance organization approved and regulated under the laws of a state bordering this State may be admitted to do business in this State by satisfying the Commissioner that it is fully and legally organized under the laws of that state, and that it complies with all requirements for health maintenance organizations organized within this State; provided that the bordering state has a law or regulation substantially similar to this section. (1985, c. 666, s. 69.)

§ 58-67-20. Issuance and continuation of license.

 (a) Before issuing or continuing any such license, the Commissioner of Insurance may make such an examination or investigation as he deems expedient. The Commissioner of Insurance shall issue a license upon the payment of the application fee prescribed in G.S. 58-67-160 and upon being satisfied on the following points:

  (1) The applicant is established as a bona fide health maintenance organization as defined by this Article;

  (2) The rates charged and benefits to be provided are fair and reasonable;

  (3) The amounts provided as working capital are repayable only out of earned income in excess of amounts paid and payable for operating expenses and expenses of providing services and such reserve as the Department of Insurance deems adequate, as provided hereinafter;

  (4) That the amount of money actually available for working capital be sufficient to carry all acquisition costs and operating expenses for a reasonable period of time from the date of the issuance of the license and that the health maintenance organization is financially responsible and may reasonably be expected to meet its obligations to enrollees and prospective enrollees. Such working capital shall initially be a minimum of one million five hundred thousand dollars ($1,500,000) for any full service medical health maintenance organization. Initial working capital for a single service health maintenance organization shall be a minimum of one hundred thousand dollars ($100,000) or such higher amount as the Commissioner shall determine to be adequate.

 (b) In making the determinations required under this section, the Commissioner shall consider:

(1) The financial soundness of the health care plan's arrangements for health care services and the schedule of premiums used in connection therewith;

(2) The adequacy of working capital;

(3) Any agreement with an insurer, a hospital or medical service corporation, a government, or any other organization for insuring the payment of the cost of health care services or the provision for automatic applicability of alternative coverage in the event of discontinuance of the plan;

(4) Any agreement with providers for the provision of health care services; and

(5) Any firm commitment of federal funds to the health maintenance organization in the form of a grant, even though such funds have not been paid to the health maintenance organization, provided that the health maintenance organization certifies to the Commissioner that such funds have been committed, that such funds are to be paid to the health maintenance organization with a current fiscal year and that such funds may be used directly for operating purposes and for the benefit of enrollees of the health maintenance organization.

(c) A license shall be denied only after compliance with the requirements of G.S. 58-67-155. (1977, c. 580, s. 1; 1979, c. 876, s. 1; 1983, c. 386, s. 2; 1987, c. 631, ss. 2, 4, 8; 1987 (Reg. Sess., 1988), c. 975, s. 1; 2003-212, s. 26(n).)

Editor's Note. — Session Laws 1987 (Reg. Sess., 1988) c. 975, s. 1 amended Session Laws 1987, c. 631, s. 11, by providing that the amendment by c. 631, s. 4, which added the last two sentences of subdivision (a)(4), should apply only to health maintenance organizations licensed after the effective date of the 1987 act (July 17, 1987).

Effect of Amendments. — Session Laws 2003-212, s. 26.(n), effective January 1, 2004, and applicable to all company licenses issued or otherwise eligible for renewal or continuation after that date, rewrote the section heading, which formerly read "Issuance of certificate"; in subsection (a), substituted "Before issuing or continuing any such license" for "Before issuing any such certificate" in the first sentence, substituted "shall issue a license" for "shall issue a certificate of authority" in the second sentence, and in subdivision (a)(4), substituted "issuance of the license" for "issuance of the certificate"; and in subsection (c), substituted "A license" for "A certificate of authority."

§ 58-67-25. Deposits.

(a) The Commissioner shall require a minimum deposit of five hundred thousand dollars ($500,000) for all full service medical health maintenance organizations or such higher amount as he deems necessary for the protection of enrollees. The minimum deposit for a full service medical health maintenance organization authorized to operate on July 17, 1987, and having a deposit of less than five hundred thousand dollars ($500,000) shall be as follows:

(1) $250,000 by December 31, 1987

(2) $500,000 by December 31, 1988.

Any health maintenance organization not authorized to do business on July 17, 1987, must comply with the minimum initial deposit of five hundred thousand dollars ($500,000).

(b) The Commissioner shall require a minimum deposit of twenty-five thousand dollars ($25,000) for all single service health maintenance organizations or such higher amount as he deems necessary for the protection of enrollees.

(c) All deposits required by this section shall be administered in accordance with the provisions of G.S. 58-5-1. (1987, c. 631, s. 3.)

§ 58-67-30. Management and exclusive agreements; custodial agreements.

(a) No health maintenance organization shall enter into an exclusive agency, management, or custodial agreement unless the agreement is first filed with the Commissioner and approved under this section within 45 days after filing or such reasonable extended period as the Commissioner shall specify by notice that is given within the 45 day period.

(b) The Commissioner shall disapprove an agreement submitted under subsection (a) of this section if the Commissioner determines that the agreement:

(1) Subjects the health maintenance organization to excessive charges;

(2) Extends for an unreasonable period of time;

(3) Does not contain fair and adequate standards of performance;

(4) Enables persons under the contract to manage the health maintenance organization who are not sufficiently trustworthy, competent, experienced, and free from conflict of interest to manage the health maintenance organization with due regard for the interests of its enrollees, creditors, or the public; or

(5) Contains provisions that impair the interests of the organization's enrollees, creditors, or the public. (1987, c. 631, s. 10; 2001-223, s. 20.5.)

§ 58-67-35. Powers of health maintenance organizations.

(a) The powers of a health maintenance organization include, but are not limited to the following:

(1) The purchase, lease, construction, renovation, operation, or maintenance of hospitals, medical facilities, or both, and their ancillary equipment, and such property as may reasonably be required for its principal office or for such other purposes as may be necessary in the transaction of the business of the organization;

(2) The making of loans to a medical group under contract with it in furtherance of its program or the making of loans to a corporation or corporations under its control for the purpose of acquiring or constructing medical facilities and hospitals or in furtherance of a program providing health care services to enrollees;

(3) The furnishing of health care services through providers which are under contract with or employed by the health maintenance organization;

(4) The contracting with any person for the performance on its behalf of certain functions such as marketing, enrollment and administration;

(5) The contracting with an insurance company licensed in this State, or with a hospital or medical service corporation authorized to do business in this State, for the provision of insurance, indemnity, or reimbursement against the cost of health care services provided by the health maintenance organization;

(6) The offering and contracting for the provision or arranging of, in addition to health care services, of:

a. Additional health care services;

b. Indemnity benefits, covering out-of-area or emergency services;

c. Indemnity benefits, in addition to those relating to out-of-area and emergency services, provided through insurers or hospital or medical service corporations; and

d. Point-of-service products, for which an HMO may precertify out-of-plan covered services on the same basis as it precertifies in-plan covered services, and for which the Commissioner shall adopt rules governing:

1. The percentage of an HMO's total health care expenditures for out-of-plan covered services for all of its members that may be spent on those services, which may not exceed twenty percent (20%);

2. Product limitations, which may provide for payment differentials for services rendered by providers who are not in an HMO network, subject to G.S. 58-3-200(d).

3. Deposit and other financial requirements; and

4. Other requirements for marketing and administering those products.

(b)(1) A health maintenance organization shall file notice, with adequate supporting information, with the Commissioner prior to the exercise of any power granted in subsections (a)(1) or (2). The Commissioner shall disapprove such exercise of power if in his opinion it would substantially and adversely affect the financial soundness of the health maintenance organization and endanger its ability to meet its obligations. If the Commissioner does not disapprove within 30 days of the filing, it shall be deemed approved.

(2) The Commissioner may promulgate rules and regulations exempting from the filing requirement of subdivision (1) those activities having a de minimis effect. (1977, c. 580, s. 1; 1979, c. 876, s. 1; 1991 (Reg. Sess., 1992), c. 837, s. 8; 1997-519, s. 3.18; 2001-334, s. 8.2.)

§ **58-67-40:** Repealed by Session Laws 2003-212, s. 20, effective October 1, 2003.

§ 58-67-45. Fiduciary responsibilities.

Any director, officer or partner of a health maintenance organization who receives, collects, disburses, or invests funds in connection with the activities of such organization shall be responsible for such funds in a fiduciary relationship to the enrollees. (1977, c. 580, s. 1; 1979, c. 876, s. 1.)

§ 58-67-50. Evidence of coverage and premiums for health care services.

(a)(1) Every enrollee residing in this State is entitled to evidence of coverage under a health care plan. If the enrollee obtains coverage under a health care plan through an insurance policy or a contract issued by a hospital or medical service corporation, whether by option or otherwise, the insurer or the hospital or medical service corporation shall issue the evidence of coverage. Otherwise, the health maintenance organization shall issue the evidence of coverage.

(2) No evidence of coverage, or amendment thereto, shall be issued or delivered to any person in this State until a copy of the form of the evidence of coverage, or amendment thereto, has been filed with and approved by the Commissioner.

(3) An evidence of coverage shall contain:

a. No provisions or statements which are unjust, unfair, inequitable, misleading, deceptive, which encourage misrepresentation, or which are untrue, misleading or deceptive as defined in G.S. 58-67-65(a); and

b. A clear and complete statement, if a contract, or a reasonably complete summary, if a certificate of:

1. The health care services and insurance or other benefits, if any, to which the enrollee is entitled under the health care plan;
2. Any limitations on the services, benefits, or kind of benefits, to be provided, including any deductible or copayment feature;
3. Where and in what manner information is available as to how services may be obtained;
4. The total amount of payment for health care services and the indemnity or service benefits, if any, which the enrollee is obligated to pay with respect to individual contracts, or an indication whether the plan is contributory or noncontributory with respect to group certificates;
5. A clear and understandable description of the health maintenance organization's method of resolving enrollee complaints;
6. A description of the reasons, if any, for which an enrollee's enrollment may be terminated for cause, which reasons may include behavior that seriously impairs the health maintenance organization's ability to provide services or an inability to establish and maintain a satisfactory physician-patient relationship after reasonable efforts to do so have been made.

Any subsequent change may be evidenced in a separate document issued to the enrollee.

(4) A copy of the form of the evidence of coverage to be used in this State, and any amendment thereto, shall be subject to the filing and approval requirements of subsection (b) unless it is subject to the jurisdiction of the Commissioner under the laws governing health insurance or hospital or medical service corporations in which event the filing and approval provisions of such laws shall apply. To the extent, however, that such provisions do not apply the requirements in subsection (c) shall be applicable.

(b)(1) Premium approval. — No schedule of premiums for coverage for health care services, or any amendment to the schedule, shall be used in conjunction with any health care plan until a copy of the schedule or amendment has been filed with and approved by the Commissioner.

(2) Individual coverage. — Premiums shall be established in accordance with actuarial principles for various categories of enrollees. Premiums applicable to an enrollee shall not be individually determined based on the status of the enrollee's health. Premiums shall not be excessive, inadequate or unfairly discriminatory; and shall exhibit a reasonable relationship to the benefits provided by the evidence of coverage. The premiums or any premium revisions for nongroup enrollee coverage shall be guaranteed, as to every enrollee covered under the same category of enrollee coverage, for a period of not less than 12 months. As an alternative to giving this guarantee for nongroup enrollee coverage, the premium or premium revisions may be made applicable to all similar categories of enrollee coverage at one time if the health maintenance organization chooses to apply for the premium revision with respect to the categories of coverages no more frequently than once in any 12-month period. The premium revision shall be applicable to all categories of nongroup enrollee coverage of the same type; provided that no premium revision may become effective for any category of enrollee coverage unless the HMO has given written notice of the premium revision to the enrollee 45 days before the effective date of the revision. The enrollee must then pay the revised premium in order to continue the contract in force. The Commissioner may

adopt reasonable rules, after notice and hearing, to require the submittal of supporting data and such information as the Commissioner considers necessary to determine whether the rate revisions meet the standards in this subdivision. In adopting the rules under this subsection, the Commissioner may require identification of the types of rating methodologies used by filers and may also address standards for data in HMO rate filings for initial filings, filings by recently licensed HMOs, and rate revision filings; data requirements for service area expansion requests; policy reserves used in rating; incurred loss ratio standards; and other recognized actuarial principles of the NAIC, the American Academy of Actuaries, and the Society of Actuaries.

(3) Group coverage. — Employer group premiums shall be established in accordance with actuarial principles for various categories of enrollees, provided that premiums applicable to an enrollee shall not be individually determined based on the status of the enrollee's health. Premiums shall not be excessive, inadequate, or unfairly discriminatory, and shall exhibit a reasonable relationship to the benefits provided by the evidence of coverage. The premiums or any revisions to the premiums for employer group coverage shall be guaranteed for a period of not less than 12 months. No premium revision shall become effective for any category of group coverage unless the HMO has given written notice of the premium revision to the master group contract holder upon receipt of the group's finalized benefits or 45 days before the effective date of the revision, whichever is earlier. The master group contract holder thereafter must pay the revised premium in order to continue the contract in force. The Commissioner may adopt reasonable rules, after notice and hearing, to require the submittal of supporting data and such information as the Commissioner considers necessary to determine whether the rate revisions meet the standards in this subdivision.

(c) The Commissioner shall, within a reasonable period, approve any form if the requirements of subsection (a) of this section are met and any schedule of premiums if the requirements of subsection (b) of this section are met. It shall be unlawful to issue the form or to use the schedule of premiums until approved. If the Commissioner disapproves the filing, the Commissioner shall notify the filer. In the notice, the Commissioner shall specify the reasons for disapproval. A hearing will be granted within 30 days after a request in writing by the person filing. If the Commissioner does not approve or disapprove any form or schedule of premiums within 90 days after the filing for forms and within 45 days after the filing for premiums, they shall be deemed to be approved.

(d) The Commissioner may require the submission of whatever relevant information he deems necessary in determining whether to approve or disapprove a filing made pursuant to this section.

(e) Effective January 1, 1989, every health maintenance organization shall provide at least minimum cost and utilization information for group contracts of 100 or more subscribers on an annual basis when requested by the group. Such information shall be compiled in accordance with the Data Collection Form developed by the Standardized HMO Date Form Task Force as endorsed by the Washington Business Group on Health and the Group Health Association of America on November 19, 1986, and any subsequent amendments. In addition, beginning with data for the calendar year 1998, every HMO, for group contracts of 1,000 or more members, shall provide cost, use of service, prevention, outcomes, and other group-specific data as collected in accordance with the latest edition of the Health Plan Employer Data and Information Set

(HEDIS) guidelines, as published by the National Committee for Quality Assurance. Beginning with data for the calendar year 1998, every HMO shall file with the Commissioner and make available to all employer groups, not later than July 1 of the following calendar year, a report of health benefit plan-wide experience on its costs, use of services, and other aspects of performance, in the HEDIS format. (1977, c. 580, s. 1; 1979, c. 876, s. 1; 1987, c. 631, s. 9; 1989, c. 485, s. 59; 1991, c. 195, s. 1; c. 644, s. 13; c. 720, s. 36; 1995, c. 193, s. 59; 1997-474, s. 3; 1997-519, s. 1.3; 2001-334, ss. 8.1, 17.4; 2001-487, ss. 106(a), 106(b).)

Cross References. — For the Readable Insurance Policies Act, see G.S. 58-38-1 et seq.

§ 58-67-55. Statements filed with Commissioner.

Every HMO subject to this Article is subject to G.S. 58-2-165. (1977, c. 580, s. 1; 1979, c. 876, s. 1; 1999-244, s. 12.)

§ 58-67-60. Investments.

With the exception of investments made in accordance with G.S. 58-67-35(a)(1) and (2) and G.S. 58-67-35(b), the funds of a health maintenance organization shall be invested or maintained only in securities, other investments, or other assets permitted by the laws of this State for the investment of assets constituting the legal reserves of life insurance companies or such other securities or investments as the Commissioner may permit. (1977, c. 580, s. 1; 1979, c. 876, s. 1; 2001-223, s. 8.18.)

§ 58-67-65. Prohibited practices.

(a) No health maintenance organization, or representative thereof, may cause or knowingly permit the use of advertising which is untrue or misleading, solicitation which is untrue or misleading, or any form of evidence of coverage which is deceptive. For purposes of this Article:

(1) A statement or item of information shall be deemed to be untrue if it does not conform to fact in any respect which is or may be significant to an enrollee of, or person considering enrollment in, a health care plan.

(2) A statement or item of information shall be deemed to be misleading, whether or not it may be literally untrue, if, in the total context in which such statement is made or such item of information is communicated, such statement or item of information may be reasonably understood by a reasonable person, not possessing special knowledge regarding health care coverage, as indicating any benefit or advantage or the absence of any exclusion, limitation, or disadvantage of possible significance to an enrollee of, or person considering enrollment in a health care plan, if such benefit or advantage or absence of limitation, exclusion or disadvantage does not in fact exist.

(3) An evidence of coverage shall be deemed to be deceptive if the evidence of coverage taken as a whole, and with consideration given to typography and format, as well as language, shall be such as to cause a reasonable person, not possessing special knowledge regarding health care plans and evidences of coverage therefor, to expect benefits, services, premiums, or other advantages which the evidence of coverage does not provide or which the health care plan issuing such evidence of coverage does not regularly make available for enrollees covered under such evidence of coverage.

(b) Article 63 of this Chapter applies to health maintenance organizations and their agents and representatives.

(c) An enrollee may not be cancelled or not renewed because of any deterioration in the health of the enrollee.

(d) No health maintenance organization, unless licensed as an insurer, may use in its name, contracts, or literature any of the words "insurance", "casualty", "surety", "mutual", or any other words descriptive of the insurance, casualty, or surety business or deceptively similar to the name or description of any insurance or surety corporation doing business in this State.

(e) The HMO shall not refuse to enroll employees except when they can demonstrate they are unable to arrange adequate services.

(f) No health maintenance organization shall refuse to enroll an individual or refuse to continue enrollment of an individual in a health care plan; limit the amount, extent, or kinds of health care plans available to an individual; or charge an individual a different rate for the same health plan, because of the race, color, or national or ethnic origin of that individual. (1977, c. 580, s. 1; 1979, c. 876, s. 1; 1989, c. 485, s. 24; 1999-244, s. 14.)

Legal Periodicals. — For survey of 1979 administrative law, see 58 N.C.L. Rev. 1185 (1980).

§ 58-67-66. Collaboration with local health departments.

A health maintenance organization and a local health department shall collaborate and cooperate within available resources regarding health promotion and disease prevention efforts that are necessary to protect the public health. (1997-474, s. 4.)

§ 58-67-70. Coverage for chemical dependency treatment.

(a) As used in this section, the term "chemical dependency" means the pathological use or abuse of alcohol or other drugs in a manner or to a degree that produces an impairment in personal, social or occupational functioning and which may, but need not, include a pattern of tolerance and withdrawal.

(b) On and after January 1, 1985, every health maintenance organization that writes a health care plan on a group basis and that is subject to this Article shall offer benefits for the necessary care and treatment of chemical dependency that are not less favorable than benefits under the health care plan generally. Except as provided in subsection (c) of this section, benefits for chemical dependency shall be subject to the same durational limits, dollar limits, deductibles, and coinsurance factors as are benefits under the health care plan generally.

(c) Every group health care plan that provides benefits for chemical dependency treatment and that provides total annual benefits for all illnesses in excess of eight thousand dollars ($8,000) is subject to the following conditions:

    (1) The plan shall provide, for each 12-month period, a minimum benefit of eight thousand dollars ($8,000) for the necessary care and treatment of chemical dependency.

    (2) The plan shall provide a lifetime minimum benefit of sixteen thousand dollars ($16,000) for the necessary care and treatment of chemical dependency for each enrollee.

(d) Provisions for benefits for necessary care and treatment of chemical dependency in group health care plans shall provide for benefit payments for the following providers of necessary care and treatment of chemical dependency:

(1) The following units of a general hospital licensed under Article 5 of General Statutes Chapter 131E:
  a. Chemical dependency units in facilities licensed after October 1, 1984;
  b. Medical units;
  c. Psychiatric units; and
(2) The following facilities or programs licensed after July 1, 1984, under Article 2 of General Statutes Chapter 122C:
  a. Chemical dependency units in psychiatric hospitals;
  b. Chemical dependency hospitals;
  c. Residential chemical dependency treatment facilities;
  d. Social setting detoxification facilities or programs;
  e. Medical detoxification facilities or programs; and
(3) Duly licensed physicians and duly licensed practicing psychologists and certified professionals working under the direct supervision of such physicians or psychologists in facilities described in (1) and (2) above and in day/night programs or outpatient treatment facilities licensed after July 1, 1984, under Article 2 of General Statutes Chapter 122C.

Provided, however, that nothing in this subsection shall prohibit any plan from requiring the most cost effective treatment setting to be utilized by the person undergoing necessary care and treatment for chemical dependency.

(e) Coverage for chemical dependency treatment as described in this section shall not be applicable to any group that rejects the coverage in writing.

(f) Notwithstanding any other provision of this section or Article, any health maintenance organization subject to this Article that becomes a qualified health maintenance organization under Title XIII of the United States Public Health Service Act shall provide the benefits required under that federal Act, which shall be deemed to constitute compliance with the provisions of this section; and any health maintenance organization may provide that the benefits provided under this section must be obtained through providers affiliated with the health maintenance organization. (1983 (Reg. Sess., 1984), c. 1110, s. 9; 1985, c. 589, s. 43(a), (b); 1989, c. 175, s. 3; 1991, c. 720, s. 64.)

§ 58-67-74. Coverage for certain treatment of diabetes.

(a) Every health care plan written by a health maintenance organization and in force, issued, renewed, or amended on or after October 1, 1997, that is subject to this Article, shall provide coverage for medically appropriate and necessary services, including diabetes outpatient self-management training and educational services, and equipment, supplies, medications, and laboratory procedures used to treat diabetes. Diabetes outpatient self-management training and educational services shall be provided by a physician or a health care professional designated by the physician. The health maintenance organization shall determine who shall provide and be reimbursed for the diabetes outpatient self-management training and educational services. The same deductibles, coinsurance, and other limitations as apply to similar services covered under the policy, contract, or plan shall apply to the diabetes coverage required under this section.

(b) For the purposes of this section, "physician" is a person licensed to practice in this State under Article 1 or Article 7 of Chapter 90 of the General Statutes. (1997-225, s. 3.)

Editor's Note. — Session Laws 1997-225, s. 4, provides: "Nothing in this act shall apply to specified accident, specified disease, hospital indemnity, or long-term care health insurance policies."

§ 58-67-75. No discrimination against the mentally ill and chemically dependent.

(a) Definitions. — As used in this section, the term:
  (1) "Mental illness" has the same meaning as defined in G.S. 122C-3(21); and
  (2) "Chemical dependency" has the same meaning as defined in G.S. 58-67-70

with a diagnosis found in the Diagnostic and Statistical Manual of Mental Disorders DSM-3-R or the International Classification of Diseases ICD/9/CM, or a later edition of those manuals.

(b) Coverage of Physical Illness. — No health maintenance organization governed by this Chapter shall, solely because an individual has or had a mental illness or chemical dependency:
  (1) Refuse to enroll that individual in any health care plan covering physical illness or injury;
  (2) Have a higher premium rate or charge for physical illness or injury coverages or benefits for that individual; or
  (3) Reduce physical illness or injury coverages or benefits for that individual.

(b1) Coverage of Mental Illness. — A health care plan that covers both physical illness or injury and mental illness may not impose a lesser lifetime or annual dollar limitation on the mental health benefits than on the physical illness or injury benefits, subject to the following:
  (1) A lifetime limit or annual limit may be made applicable to all benefits under the plan, without distinguishing the mental health benefits.
  (2) If the plan contains lifetime limits only on selected physical illness and injury benefits, and these benefits do not represent substantially all of the physical illness and injury benefits under the plan, the HMO may impose a lifetime limit on the mental health benefits that is based on a weighted average of the respective lifetime limits on the selected physical illness and injury benefits. The weighted average shall be calculated in accordance with rules adopted by the Commissioner.
  (3) If the plan contains annual limits only on selected physical illness and injury benefits, and these benefits do not represent substantially all of the physical illness and injury benefits under the plan, the HMO may impose an annual limit on the mental health benefits that is based on a weighted average of the respective annual limits on the selected physical illness and injury benefits. The weighted average shall be calculated in accordance with rules adopted by the Commissioner.
  (4) Except as otherwise provided in this section, the plan may distinguish between mental illness benefits and physical injury or illness benefits with respect to other terms of the plan, including coinsurance, limits on provider visits or days of coverage, and requirements relating to medical necessity.
  (5) If the HMO offers two or more benefit package options under a plan, each package must comply with this subsection.
  (6) This subsection does not apply to a health benefit plan if the HMO can demonstrate to the Commissioner that compliance will increase the cost of the plan by one percent (1%) or more.
  (7) This subsection expires October 1, 2001, but the expiration does not affect services rendered before that date.

(c) Mental Illness or Chemical Dependency Coverage Not Required. — Nothing in this section requires an HMO to offer coverage for mental illness or chemical dependency, except as provided in G.S. 58-67-70.

(d) Applicability. — Subsection (b1) of this section applies only to group contracts, other than excepted benefits as defined in G.S. 58-68-25, covering more than 50 employees. The remainder of this section applies only to group contracts covering 20 or more employees. (1989, c. 369, s. 2; 1991, c. 720, s. 83; 1997-259, s. 23; 1999-132, s. 4.4.)

Editor's Note. — Session Laws 1989, c. 369, s. 2 made this section effective with respect to group contracts covering 20 or more employees, and health maintenance organization contracts issued, renewed, or amended on or after January 1, 1990.

§ 58-67-76. Coverage for mammograms and cervical cancer screening.

(a) Every health care plan written by a health maintenance organization and in force, issued, renewed, or amended on or after January 1, 1992, that is subject to this Article, shall provide coverage for examinations and laboratory tests for the screening for the early detection of cervical cancer and for low-dose screening mammography. The same deductibles, coinsurance, and other limitations as apply to similar services covered under the plan shall apply to coverage for examinations and laboratory tests for the screening for the early detection of cervical cancer and low-dose screening mammography.

(a1) As used in this section, "examinations and laboratory tests for the screening for the early detection of cervical cancer" means conventional PAP smear screening, liquid-based cytology, and human papilloma virus (HPV) detection methods for women with equivocal findings on cervical cytologic analysis that are subject to the approval of and have been approved by the United States Food and Drug Administration.

(b) As used in this section, "low-dose screening mammography" means a radiologic procedure for the early detection of breast cancer provided to an asymptomatic woman using equipment dedicated specifically for mammography, including a physician's interpretation of the results of the procedure.

(c) Coverage for low-dose screening mammography shall be provided as follows:

    (1) One or more mammograms a year, as recommended by a physician, for any woman who is determined to be at risk for breast cancer. For purposes of this subdivision, a woman is at risk for breast cancer if any one or more of the following is true:

        a. The woman has a personal history of breast cancer;

        b. The woman has a personal history of biopsy-proven benign breast disease;

        c. The woman's mother, sister, or daughter has or has had breast cancer; or

        d. The woman has not given birth prior to the age of 30;

    (2) One baseline mammogram for any woman 35 through 39 years of age, inclusive;

    (3) A mammogram every other year for any woman 40 through 49 years of age, inclusive, or more frequently upon recommendation of a physician; and

    (4) A mammogram every year for any woman 50 years of age or older.

(d) Reimbursement for a mammogram authorized under this section shall be made only if the facility in which the mammogram was performed meets mammography accreditation standards established by the North Carolina Medical Care Commission.

(e) Coverage for the screening for the early detection of cervical cancer shall be in accordance with the most recently published American Cancer Society guidelines or guidelines adopted by the North Carolina Advisory Committee on Cancer Coordination and Control. Coverage shall include the examination, the laboratory fee, and the physician's interpretation of the laboratory results. Reimbursements for laboratory fees shall be made only if the laboratory meets accreditation standards adopted by the North Carolina Medical Care Commission. (1991, c. 490, s. 3; 2003-186, s. 4.)

Editor's Note. — Session Laws 2003-186, s. 6, provides, in part, that for the purposes of this act, renewal of a health benefit plan is presumed to occur on each anniversary of the date on which coverage was first effective on the person or persons covered by the health benefit plan.

Effect of Amendments. — Session Laws 2003-186, s. 4, effective January 1, 2004, and applicable to all health benefit plans that are delivered, issued for delivery, or renewed on and after that date, in the section heading; in the first and last sentences of subsection (a), substituted "cervical cancer screening" for "pap smears" and substituted "examinations and laboratory tests for the screening for the early detection of cervical cancer" for "pap smears"; added subsection (a1); and rewrote subsections (d) and (e).

§ 58-67-77. Coverage for prostate-specific antigen (PSA) tests.

(a) Every health care plan written by a health maintenance organization and in force, issued, renewed, or amended on or after January 1, 1994, that is subject to this Article, shall provide coverage for prostate-specific antigen (PSA) tests or equivalent tests for the presence of prostate cancer. The same deductibles, coinsurance, and other limitations as apply to similar services covered under the plan shall apply to coverage for prostate-specific antigen (PSA) tests or equivalent tests for the presence of prostate cancer.

(b) As used in this section, "prostate-specific antigen (PSA) tests or equivalent tests for the presence of prostate cancer" means serological tests for determining the presence of prostate cytoplasmic protein (PSA) and the generation of antibodies to it, as a novel marker for prostatic disease.

(c) Coverage for prostate-specific antigen (PSA) tests or equivalent tests for the presence of prostate cancer shall be provided when recommended by a physician. (1993, c. 269, s. 3.)

§ 58-67-78. Coverage of certain prescribed drugs for cancer treatment.

(a) No health care plan written by a health maintenance organization and in force, issued, renewed, or amended on or after January 1, 1994, and that provides coverage for prescribed drugs approved by the federal Food and Drug Administration for the treatment of certain types of cancer shall exclude coverage of any drug on the basis that the drug has been prescribed for the treatment of a type of cancer for which the drug has not been approved by the federal Food and Drug Administration. The drug, however, must be approved by the federal Food and Drug Administration and must have been proven effective and accepted for the treatment of the specific type of cancer for which the drug has been prescribed in any one of the following established reference compendia:

(1) The American Medical Association Drug Evaluations;
(2) The American Hospital Formulary Service Drug Information; or
(3) The United States Pharmacopeia Drug Information.

(b) Notwithstanding subsection (a) of this section, coverage shall not be required for any experimental or investigational drugs or any drug that the federal Food and Drug Administration has determined to be contraindicated for treatment of the specific type of cancer for which the drug has been prescribed.

(c) This section shall apply only to cancer drugs and nothing in this section shall be construed, expressly or by implication, to create, impair, alter, limit, notify, enlarge, abrogate, or prohibit reimbursement for drugs used in the treatment of any other disease or condition. (1993, c. 506, s. 4.3.)

Editor's Note. — The number of this section was assigned by the Revisor of Statutes, the number in Session Laws 1993, c. 506, s. 4.3 having been G.S. 58-67-77.

§ 58-67-79. Coverage for reconstructive breast surgery following mastectomy.

(a) Every health care plan written by a health maintenance organization that is subject to this Article and that provides coverage for mastectomy shall provide coverage for reconstructive breast surgery following a mastectomy. The coverage shall include coverage for all stages and revisions of reconstructive breast surgery performed on a nondiseased breast to establish symmetry if reconstructive surgery on a diseased breast is performed, as well as coverage for prostheses and physical complications in all stages of mastectomy, including lymphademas. The same deductibles, coinsurance, and other limitations as apply to similar services covered under the policy, contract, or plan shall apply to coverage for reconstructive breast surgery. Reconstruction of the nipple/areolar complex following a mastectomy is covered without regard to the lapse of time between the mastectomy and the reconstruction, subject to the approval of the treating physician.

(b) As used in this section, the following terms have the meanings indicated:

(1) "Mastectomy" means the surgical removal of all or part of a breast as a result of breast cancer or breast disease.

(2) "Reconstructive breast surgery" means surgery performed as a result of a mastectomy to reestablish symmetry between the two breasts, and includes reconstruction of the mastectomy site, creation of a new breast mound, and creation of a new nipple/areolar complex. "Reconstructive breast surgery" also includes augmentation mammoplasty, reduction mammoplasty, and mastopexy of the nondiseased breast.

(c) A policy, contract, or plan subject to this section shall not:

(1) Deny coverage described in subsection (a) of this section on the basis that the coverage is for cosmetic surgery;

(2) Deny to a woman eligibility or continued eligibility to enroll or to renew coverage under the terms of the contract, policy, or plan, solely for the purpose of avoiding the requirements of this section;

(3) Provide monetary payments or rebates to a woman to encourage her to accept less than the minimum protections available under this section;

(4) Penalize or otherwise reduce or limit the reimbursement of an attending provider because the provider provided care to an individual participant or beneficiary in accordance with this section; or

(5) Provide incentives, monetary or otherwise, to an attending provider to induce the provider to provide care to an individual participant or beneficiary in a manner inconsistent with this section.

(d) Written notice of the availability of the coverage provided by this section shall be delivered to every subscriber under the plan upon enrollment and annually thereafter. The notice required by this subsection may be included as a part of any yearly informational packet sent to the subscriber. (1997-312, s. 3; 1999-351, s. 3.3; 2001-334, s. 13.3.)

Editor's Note. — Session Laws 1997-312, s. 6, provides: "Nothing in this act shall apply to specified accident, specified disease, hospital indemnity, or long-term care health insurance policies."

Legal Periodicals. — For 1997 legislative survey, see 20 Campbell L. Rev. 469.

§ 58-67-80. Meaning of terms "accident", "accidental injury", and "accidental means".

(a) Effective October 1, 1989, this section applies to all health maintenance organization plans under this Article.

(b) "Accident", "accidental injury", and "accidental means" shall be defined to imply "result" language and shall not include words that establish an accidental means test. (1989, c. 485, s. 12.)

§ 58-67-85. Master group contracts, filing requirement; required and prohibited provisions.

(a) A health maintenance organization may issue a master group contract with the approval of the Commissioner of Insurance provided the contract and the individual certificates issued to members of the group, shall comply in substance to the other provisions of this Article. Any such contract may provide for the adjustment of the rate of the premium or benefits conferred as provided in the contract, and in accordance with an adjustment schedule filed with and approved by the Commissioner of Insurance. If the master group contract is issued, altered or modified, the enrollees' contracts issued in pursuance thereof are altered or modified accordingly, all laws and clauses in the enrollees' contracts to the contrary notwithstanding. Nothing in this Article shall be construed to prohibit or prevent the same. Forms of such contract shall at all times be furnished upon request of enrollees thereto.

(b), (c) Repealed by Session Laws 1997-259, s. 18.

(d) Employees shall be added to the master group coverage no later than 90 days after their first day of employment. Employment shall be considered continuous and not be considered broken except for unexcused absences from work for reasons other than illness or injury. The term "employee" is defined as a nonseasonal person who works on a full-time basis, with a normal work week of 30 or more hours and who is otherwise eligible for coverage, but does not include a person who works on a part-time, temporary, or substitute basis.

(e) Whenever an employer master group contract replaces another group contract, whether the contract was issued by a corporation under Articles 1 through 67 of this Chapter, the liability of the succeeding corporation for insuring persons covered under the previous group contract is:

(1) Each person who is eligible for coverage in accordance with the succeeding corporation's plan of benefits with respect to classes eligible and activity at work and nonconfinement rules must be covered by the succeeding corporation's plan of benefits; and

(2) Each person not covered under the succeeding corporation's plan of benefits in accordance with (e)(1) must nevertheless be covered by the succeeding corporation if that person was validly covered, including benefit extension, under the prior plan on the date of discontinuance and if the person is a member of the class of persons eligible for coverage under the succeeding corporation's plan. (1989, c. 775, s. 5; 1991, c. 720, ss. 38, 88; 1991 (Reg. Sess., 1992), c. 837, s. 4; 1993, c. 408, ss. 5, 5.1; 1995, c. 507, s. 23A.1(f); 1997-259, s. 18.)

§ 58-67-88. Continuity of care.

(a) Definitions. — As used in this section:

    (1) "Ongoing special condition" means:

        a. In the case of an acute illness, a condition that is serious enough to require medical care or treatment to avoid a reasonable possibility of death or permanent harm.

        b. In the case of a chronic illness or condition, a disease or condition that is life-threatening, degenerative, or disabling, and requires medical care or treatment over a prolonged period of time.

        c. In the case of pregnancy, pregnancy from the start of the second trimester.

        d. In the case of a terminal illness, an individual has a medical prognosis that the individual's life expectancy is six months or less.

    (2) "Terminated or termination". — Includes, with respect to a contract, the expiration or nonrenewal of the contract, but does not include a termination of the contract by an HMO for failure to meet applicable quality standards or for fraud.

(b) Termination of Provider. — If a contract between an HMO benefit plan that is not a point-of-service plan and a health care provider is terminated by the provider or by the HMO, or benefits or coverage provided by the HMO are terminated because of a change in the terms of provider participation in a health benefit plan of an HMO that is not a point-of-service plan, and an individual is covered by the plan and is undergoing treatment from the provider for an ongoing special condition on the date of the termination, then, the HMO shall:

    (1) Upon termination of the contract by the HMO or upon receipt by the HMO of written notification of termination by the provider, notify the individual on a timely basis of the termination and of the right to elect continuation of coverage of treatment by the provider under this section if the individual has filed a claim with the HMO for services provided by the terminated provider or the individual is otherwise known by the HMO to be a patient of the provider.

    (2) Subject to subsection (h) of this section, permit the individual to elect to continue to be covered with respect to the treatment by the provider of the ongoing special condition during a transitional period provided under this section.

(c) Newly Covered Insured. — Each health benefit plan offered by an HMO that is not a point-of-service plan shall provide transition coverage to individuals who are undergoing treatment from a provider for an ongoing special condition and are newly covered under the health benefit plan because the individual's employer has changed health benefit plans, and the HMO shall:

    (1) Notify the individual on the date of enrollment of the right to elect continuation of coverage of treatment by the provider under this section.

    (2) Subject to subsection (h) of this section, permit the individual to elect to continue to be covered with respect to the treatment by the provider of the ongoing special condition during a transitional period provided under this section.

(d) Transitional Period: In General. — Except as otherwise provided in subsections (e), (f), and (g) of this section, the transitional period under this subsection shall extend up to 90 days, as determined by the treating health care provider, after the date of the notice to the individual described in subdivision (b)(1) of this section or the date of enrollment in a new plan described in subdivision (c)(1) of this section.

(e) Transitional Period: Scheduled Surgery, Organ Transplantation, or Inpatient Care. — If surgery, organ transplantation, or other inpatient care was scheduled for an individual before the date of the notice required under subdivision (b)(1) of this section, or the date of enrollment in a new plan described in subdivision (c)(1) of this section, or if the individual on that date was on an established waiting list or otherwise scheduled to have the surgery, transplantation, or other inpatient care, the transitional period under this subsection with respect to the surgery, transplantation, or other inpatient care shall extend beyond the period under subsection (d) of this section through the date of discharge of the individual after completion of the surgery, transplantation, or other inpatient care, and through postdischarge follow-up care related to the surgery, transplantation, or other inpatient care occurring within 90 days after the date of discharge.

(f) Transitional Period: Pregnancy. — If an insured has entered the second trimester of pregnancy on the date of the notice required under subdivision (b)(1) of this section, or the date of enrollment in a new plan described in subdivision (c)(1) of this section, and the provider was treating the pregnancy before the date of the notice, or the date of enrollment in the new plan, the transitional period with respect to the provider's treatment of the pregnancy shall extend through the provision of 60 days of postpartum care.

(g) Transitional Period: Terminal Illness. — If an insured was determined to be terminally ill at the time of a provider's termination of participation under subsection (b) of this section, or at the time of enrollment in the new plan under subdivision (c)(1) of this section, and the provider was treating the terminal illness before the date of the termination or enrollment in the new plan, the transitional period shall extend for the remainder of the individual's life with respect to care directly related to the treatment of the terminal illness or its medical manifestations.

(h) Permissible Terms and Conditions. — An HMO may condition coverage of continued treatment by a provider under subdivision (b)(2) or (c)(2) of this section upon the following terms and conditions:

(1) When care is provided pursuant to subdivision (b)(2) of this section, the provider agrees to accept reimbursement from the HMO and individual involved, with respect to cost-sharing, at the rates applicable before the start of the transitional period as payment in full. When care is provided pursuant to subdivision (c)(2) of this section, the provider agrees to accept the prevailing rate based on contracts the insurer has with the same or similar providers in the same or similar geographic area, plus the applicable copayment, as reimbursement in full from the HMO and the insured for all covered services.

(2) The provider agrees to comply with the quality assurance programs of the HMO responsible for payment under subdivision (1) of this subsection and to provide to the HMO necessary medical information related to the care provided. The quality assurance programs shall not override the professional or ethical responsibility of the provider or interfere with the provider's ability to provide information or assistance to the patient.

(3) The provider agrees otherwise to adhere to the HMO's established policies and procedures for participating providers, including procedures regarding referrals and obtaining prior authorization, providing services pursuant to a treatment plan, if any, approved by the HMO, and member hold harmless provisions.

(4) The insured or the insured's representative notifies the HMO within 45 days of the date of the notice described in subdivision (b)(1) of this section or the new enrollment described in subdivision (c)(1) of this section, that the insured elects to continue receiving treatment by the provider.

(5) The provider agrees to discontinue providing services at the end of the transition period pursuant to this section and to assist the insured in

an orderly transition to a network provider. Nothing in this section shall prohibit the insured from continuing to receive services from the provider at the insured's expense.

(i) Construction. — Nothing in this section:

(1) Requires the coverage of benefits that would not have been covered if the provider involved remained a participating provider or, in the case of a newly covered insured, requires the coverage of benefits not provided under the new policy under which the person is covered.

(2) Requires an HMO to offer a transitional period when the HMO terminates a provider's contract for reasons relating to quality of care or fraud; and refusal to offer a transitional period under these circumstances is not subject to the grievance review provisions of G.S. 58-50-62.

(3) Prohibits an HMO from extending any transitional period beyond that specified in this section.

(4) Prohibits an HMO from terminating the continuing services of a provider as described in this section when the HMO has determined that the provider's continued provision of services may result in, or is resulting in, a serious danger to the health or safety of the insured. Such terminations shall be in accordance with the contract provisions that the provider would otherwise be subject to if the provider's contract were still in effect.

(j) Disclosure of Right to Transitional Period. — Each HMO shall include a clear description of an insured's rights under this section in its evidence of coverage and summary plan description. (2001-446, s. 1.)

Editor's Note. — Session Laws 2001-446, s. 8, makes this section effective March 1, 2002, and applicable to health benefit plans that are in effect, delivered, issued for delivery, or renewed on or after that date.

Session Laws 2001-446, s. 8 provides: "Nothing in this act obligates the General Assembly to appropriate funds to implement this act."

Session Laws 2001-446, s. 7 is a severability clause.

§ 58-67-90. Licensing and regulation of agents.

Every agent of any HMO authorized to do business in this State under this Article is subject to the licensing provisions of Article 33 of this Chapter and all other provisions in this Chapter applicable to life and health insurance agents. (1977, c. 580, s. 1; 1979, c. 876, s. 1; 1985 (Reg. Sess., 1986), c. 928, s. 5; 1987, c. 629, s. 3; 1999-244, s. 8.)

§ 58-67-95. Powers of insurers and hospital and medical service corporations.

(a) An insurance company licensed in this State, or a hospital or medical service corporation authorized to do business in this State, may either directly or through a subsidiary or affiliate organize and operate a health maintenance organization under the provisions of this Article. Notwithstanding any other law which may be inconsistent herewith, any two or more such insurance companies, hospital or medical service corporations, or subsidiaries or affiliates thereof, may jointly organize and operate a health maintenance organization. The business of insurance is deemed to include the arranging of health care by a health maintenance organization owned or operated by an insurer or a subsidiary thereof.

(b) Notwithstanding any provision of the insurance and hospital or medical service corporation laws contained in Articles 1 through 66 of this Chapter, an insurer or a hospital or medical service corporation may contract with a health maintenance organization to provide insurance or similar protection against the cost of care provided through health maintenance organizations and to provide coverage in the event of the failure of the health maintenance organization to meet its obligations. The enrollees of a health maintenance organization constitute a permissible group under such laws. Among other things, under such contracts, the insurer or hospital or medical service corporation may make benefit payments to health maintenance organizations for health care services rendered by providers pursuant to the health care plan. (1977, c. 580, s. 1; 1979, c. 876, s. 1.)

§ 58-67-100. Examinations.

(a) The Commissioner may make an examination of the affairs of any health maintenance organization and the contracts, agreements or other arrangements pursuant to its health care plan as often as the Commissioner deems it necessary for the protection of the interests of the people of this State but not less frequently than once every three years. Examinations shall otherwise be conducted under G.S. 58-2-131 through G.S. 58-2-134.

(b) Repealed by Session Laws 1997-519, s. 1, effective January 1, 1998.

(c) Repealed by Session Laws 1995, c. 360, s. 2(m).

(d) Instead of conducting an examination, the Commissioner may accept the report of an examination made by the HMO regulator of another state. (1977, c. 580, s. 1; 1979, c. 876, s. 1; 1995, c. 360, s. 2(m); 1997-519, s. 1.4; 1999-132, s. 11.10.)

§ 58-67-105. Hazardous financial condition.

(a) Whenever the financial condition of any health maintenance organization indicates a condition such that the continued operation of the health maintenance organization might be hazardous to its enrollees, creditors, or the general public, then the Commissioner may order the health maintenance organization to take such action as may be reasonably necessary to rectify the existing condition, including but not limited to one or more of the following steps:

   (1) To reduce the total amount of present and potential liability for benefits by reinsurance;

   (2) To reduce the volume of new business being accepted;

   (3) To reduce the expenses by specified methods;

   (4) To suspend or limit the writing of new business for a period of time; or

   (5) To require an increase to the health maintenance organization's net worth by contribution.

(b) The Commissioner may adopt rules to set uniform standards and criteria for the early warning that the continued operation of any health maintenance organization might be hazardous to its enrollees, creditors, or the general public, and to set standards for evaluating the financial condition of any health maintenance organization, which standards shall be consistent with the purposes expressed in subsection (a) of this section. (1987, c. 631, s. 5.)

§ 58-67-110. Protection against insolvency.

(a) The Commissioner shall require deposits in accordance with the provisions of G.S. 58-67-25.

(b) Each full service health maintenance organization shall maintain a minimum net worth equal to the greater of one million dollars ($1,000,000) or the amount required pursuant to the risk-based capital provisions of Article 12 of this Chapter. Each single service health maintenance organization shall maintain a minimum net worth equal to the greater of fifty thousand dollars

($50,000) or that amount required pursuant to the risk-based capital provisions of Article 12 of this Chapter.

(c), (d) Repealed by Session Laws 2003-212, s. 21, effective October 1, 2003.

(e) Every full service medical health maintenance organization shall have and maintain at all times an adequate plan for protection against insolvency acceptable to the Commissioner. In determining the adequacy of such a plan, the Commissioner may consider:

(1) A reinsurance agreement preapproved by the Commissioner covering excess loss, stop loss, or catastrophes. The agreement must provide that the Commissioner will be notified no less than 60 days prior to cancellation or reduction of coverage.

(2) A conversion policy or policies that will be offered by an insurer to the enrollees in the event of the health maintenance organization's insolvency.

(3) Any other arrangements offering protection against insolvency that the Commissioner may require. (1987, c. 631, s. 5; 1989, c. 776, ss. 11, 12; 2003-212, s. 21.)

Effect of Amendments. — Session Laws 2003-212, s. 21, effective October 1, 2003, re- wrote subsection (b); and repealed subsections (c) and (d).

§ 58-67-115. Hold harmless agreements or special deposit.

(a) Unless the HMO maintains a special deposit in accordance with subsection (b) of this section, each contract between every HMO and a participating provider of health care services shall be in writing and shall set forth that in the event the HMO fails to pay for health care services as set forth in the contract, the subscriber or enrollee shall not be liable to the provider for any sums owed by the HMO. No other provisions of such contracts shall, under any circumstances, change the effect of such a provision. No participating provider, or agent, trustee, or assignee thereof, may maintain any action at law against a subscriber or enrollee to collect sums owed by the HMO.

(b) In the event that the participating provider contract has not been reduced to writing or that the contract fails to contain the required prohibition, the HMO shall maintain a special deposit in cash or cash equivalent as follows:

(1) Every HMO that has incurred uncovered health care expenditures in an amount that exceeds ten percent (10%) of its total expenditures for health care services for the immediately preceding six months, shall do either of the following:

a. Calculate as of the first day of every month and maintain for the remainder of the month, cash or cash equivalents acceptable to the Commissioner, as an account to cover claims for uncovered health care expenditures at least equal to one hundred twenty percent (120%) of the sum of the following:

1. All claims for uncovered health care expenditures received for reimbursement, but not yet processed; and

2. All claims for uncovered health care expenditures denied for reimbursement during the previous 60 days; and

3. All claims for uncovered health care expenditures approved for reimbursement, but not yet paid; and

4. An estimate for uncovered health care expenditures incurred, but not reported; and

5. All claims for uncovered emergency services and uncovered services rendered outside the service area.

b. Maintain adequate insurance, or a guaranty arrangement approved in writing by the Commissioner, to pay for any loss to enrollees claiming reimbursement due to the insolvency of the HMO. The Commissioner shall approve a guaranty arrangement if the guaranteeing organization has been in operation for at least 10 years and has a net worth, including organization-related land, buildings, and equipment, of at least fifty million dollars ($50,000,000); unless the Commissioner finds that the approval of such guaranty may be financially hazardous to enrollees. In order to qualify under the terms of this subsection, the guaranteeing organization shall (i) submit to the jurisdiction of this State for actions arising under the guarantee; (ii) submit certified, audited annual financial statements to the Commissioner; and (iii) appoint the Commissioner to receive service of process in this State.

(2) Whenever the reimbursements described in this subsection exceed ten percent (10%) of the HMO's total costs for health care services over the immediately preceding six months, the HMO shall file a written report with the Commissioner containing the information necessary to determine compliance with sub-subdivision (b)(1)a. of this section no later than 30 business days from the first day of the month. Upon an adequate showing by the HMO that the requirements of this section should be waived or reduced, the Commissioner may waive or reduce these requirements to such an amount as he deems sufficient to protect enrollees of the HMO consistent with the intent and purpose of this Article.

(3) Any cash or cash equivalents maintained pursuant to the terms of this section shall be maintained as a special deposit controlled by and administered by the Commissioner in accordance with the provisions of G.S. 58-5-1. (1989, c. 776, s. 13.)

§ 58-67-120. Continuation of benefits.

(a) The Commissioner shall require that each HMO have a plan for handling insolvency, which plan allows for continuation of benefits for the duration of the contract period for which premiums have been paid and continuation of benefits to enrollees who are confined in an inpatient facility until their discharge or expiration of benefits. In considering such a plan, the Commissioner may require:

(1) Insurance to cover the expenses to be paid for benefits after an insolvency;

(2) Provisions in provider contracts that obligate the provider to provide services for the duration of the period after the HMO's insolvency for which premium payment has been made and until the enrollees' discharge from inpatient facilities;

(3) Insolvency reserves such as the Commissioner may require;

(4) Letters of credit acceptable to the Commissioner;

(5) Any other arrangements to assure that benefits are continued as specified above. (1989, c. 776, s. 13.)

§ 58-67-125. Enrollment period.

(a) In the event of an insolvency of an HMO upon order of the Commissioner, all other carriers that participated in the enrollment process with the insolvent HMO at a group's last regular enrollment period shall offer such group's enrollees of the insolvent HMO a 30-day enrollment period commencing upon the date of insolvency. Each carrier shall offer such enrollees of the insolvent HMO the same coverages and rates that it had offered to the enrollees of the group at its last regular enrollment period.

(b) If no other carrier had been offered to some groups enrolled in the insolvent HMO, or if the Commissioner determines that the other health benefit plan or plans lack sufficient health care delivery resources to assure that health care services will be available and accessible to all of the group enrollees of the insolvent HMO, then the Commissioner shall allocate the insolvent HMO's group contracts for such groups among all other HMOs that operate within a portion of the insolvent HMO's service area, taking into consideration the health care delivery resources of each HMO. Each HMO to which a group or groups are so allocated shall offer such group or groups that HMO's existing coverage that is most similar to each group's coverage with the insolvent HMO at rates determined in accordance with the successor HMO's existing rating methodology.

(c) The Commissioner shall also allocate the insolvent HMO's nongroup enrollees who are unable to obtain other coverage among all HMOs that operate within a portion of the insolvent HMO's service area, taking into consideration the health care delivery resources of each such HMO. Each HMO to which nongroup enrollees are allocated shall offer such nongroup enrollees that HMO's existing coverage for individual or conversion coverage as determined by his type of coverage in the insolvent HMO at rates determined in accordance with the successor HMOs existing rating methodology. Successor HMOs that do not offer direct nongroup enrollment may aggregate all of the allocated nongroup enrollees into one group for rating and coverage purposes. (1989, c. 776, s. 13.)

§ 58-67-130. Replacement coverage.

(a) Any carrier providing replacement coverage with respect to group hospital, medical, or surgical expense or service benefits, within a period of 60 days from the date of discontinuance of a prior HMO contract or policy providing such hospital, medical or surgical expense or service benefits, shall immediately cover all enrollees who were validly covered under the previous HMO contract or policy at the date of discontinuance and who would otherwise be eligible for coverage under the succeeding carrier's contract, regardless of any provisions of the contract relating to active employment or hospital confinement or pregnancy.

(b) Except to the extent benefits for the condition would have been reduced or excluded under the prior carrier's contract or policy, no provision in a succeeding carrier's contract of replacement coverage that would operate to reduce or exclude benefits on the basis that the condition giving rise to benefits preceded the effective date of the succeeding carrier's contract shall be applied with respect to those enrollees validly covered under the prior carrier's contract or policy on the date of discontinuance. (1989, c. 776, s. 13.)

§ 58-67-135. Incurred but not reported claims.

(a) Every HMO shall, when determining liability, include an amount estimated in the aggregate to provide for any unearned premium and for the payment of all claims for health care expenditures that have been incurred, whether reported or unreported, that are unpaid and for which such HMO is or may be liable; and to provide for the expense of adjustment or settlement of such claims.

(b) Such liabilities shall be computed in accordance with rules adopted by the Commissioner upon reasonable consideration of the ascertained experience and character of the HMO. (1989, c. 776, s. 13.)

§ 58-67-140. Suspension or revocation of license.

(a) The Commissioner may suspend or revoke an HMO license if the Commissioner finds that the HMO:

    (1) Is operating significantly in contravention of its basic organizational document, or in a manner contrary to that described in and reasonably inferred from any other information submitted under G.S. 58-67-10, unless amendments to such submissions have been filed with and approved by the Commissioner.

    (2) Issues evidences of coverage or uses a schedule of premiums for health care services that do not comply with G.S. 58-67-50.

    (3) Is no longer financially responsible and may reasonably be expected to be unable to meet its obligations to enrollees or prospective enrollees.

    (4) Has itself or through any person on its behalf advertised or merchandised its services in an untrue, misrepresentative, misleading, deceptive or unfair manner.

    (5) Is operating in a manner that would be hazardous to its enrollees.

    (6) Knowingly or repeatedly fails or refuses to comply with any law or rule applicable to the HMO or with any order issued by the Commissioner after notice and opportunity for a hearing.

    (7) Has knowingly published or made to the Department or to the public any false statement or report, including any report or any data that serves as the basis for any report, required to be submitted under G.S. 58-3-191.

(b) A license shall be suspended or revoked only after compliance with G.S. 58-67-155.

(c) When an HMO license is suspended, the HMO shall not, during the suspension, enroll any additional enrollees except newborn children or other newly acquired dependents of existing enrollees, and shall not engage in any advertising or solicitation.

(d) When an HMO license is revoked, the HMO shall proceed, immediately following the effective date of the order of revocation, to wind up its affairs, and shall conduct no further business except as may be essential to the orderly conclusion of the affairs of the HMO. The HMO shall engage in no advertising or solicitation. The Commissioner may, by written order, permit such further operation of the HMO as the Commissioner may find to be in the best interest of enrollees, to the end that enrollees will be afforded the greatest practical opportunity to obtain continuing health care coverage. (1977, c. 580, s. 1; 1979, c. 876, s. 1; 1997-519, s. 1.5; 2003-212, ss. 22, 23, 26(*l*).)

Editor's Note. — Session Laws 2003-212, s. 28, provides that the amendment to the introductory paragraph of subsection (a) by s. 26(*l*) becomes effective October 1, 2003, and applicable to all company licenses issued or otherwise eligible for renewal or continuation after that date. The amendments to subdivisions (a)(3) and (a)(7) by ss. 22 and 23, respectively, become effective October 1, 2003.

Effect of Amendments. — Session Laws

2003-212, ss. 22, 23, and 26(*l*) in the introductory paragraph of subsection (a), substituted "suspend or revoke" for "suspend, revoke, or refuse to renew"; at the beginning of subdivision (a)(3), deleted "No longer maintains the financial reserve specified in G.S. 58-67-40 or"; and at the end of subdivision (a)(7), substituted "G.S. 58-3-191" for "G.S. 58-3-210." See editor's note for effective dates and applicability.

§ 58-67-145. Rehabilitation, liquidation, or conservation of health maintenance organization.

Any rehabilitation, liquidation or conservation of a health maintenance organization shall be deemed to be the rehabilitation, liquidation, or conservation of an insurance company and shall be conducted under the supervision of the Commissioner pursuant to the law governing the rehabilitation, liqui-dation, or conservation of insurance companies, except that the provisions of Articles 48 and 62 of this Chapter shall not apply to health maintenance organizations. The Commissioner may apply for an order directing him to rehabilitate, liquidate, or conserve a health maintenance organization upon one or more grounds set out in Article 30 of this Chapter or when in his opinion the continued operation of the health maintenance organization would be hazardous either to the enrollees or to the people of this State. (1977, c. 580, s. 1; 1979, c. 876, s. 1; 1989, c. 452, s. 2; c. 776, s. 14; 1998-211, s. 5.)

§ 58-67-150. Regulations.

The Commissioner may, after notice and hearing, promulgate reasonable rules and regulations as are necessary or proper to carry out the provisions of this Article. Such rules and regulations shall be subject to review in accordance with G.S. 58-67-155. (1977, c. 580, s. 1; 1979, c. 876, s. 1.)

§ 58-67-155. Administrative procedures.

(a) When the Commissioner has cause to believe that grounds for the denial of an application for a certificate of authority exist, or that grounds for the suspension or revocation of a certificate of authority exist, he shall notify the health maintenance organization in writing specifically stating the grounds for denial, suspension, or revocation and fixing a time of at least 30 days thereafter for a hearing on the matter.

(b) After such hearing, or upon the failure of the health maintenance organization to appear at such hearing, the Commissioner shall take action as is deemed advisable or written findings which shall be mailed to the health maintenance organization. The action of the Commissioner shall be subject to review by the Superior Court of Wake County. The court may, in disposing of the issue before it, modify, affirm, or reverse the order of the Commissioner in whole or in part.

(c) The provisions of Chapter 150B of the General Statutes of this State shall apply to proceedings under this section to the extent that they are not in conflict with subsections (a) and (b). (1977, c. 580, s. 1; 1979, c. 876, s. 1; 1987, c. 827, s. 1.)

§ 58-67-160. Fees.

Every health maintenance organization subject to this Article shall pay to the Commissioner a fee of two hundred fifty dollars ($250.00) for filing an application for a license and an annual license continuation fee of one thousand dollars ($1,000) for each license. The license shall continue in full force and effect, subject to timely payment of the annual license continuation fee in accordance with G.S. 58-6-7 and subject to any other applicable provisions of the insurance laws of this State. (1977, c. 580, s. 1; 1979, c. 876, s. 1; 1989 (Reg. Sess., 1990), c. 1069, s. 6; 1995, c. 507, s. 11A(c); 1999-435, s. 6; 2003-212, s. 26(m).)

Effect of Amendments. — Session Laws 2003-212, s. 26.(m), effective January 1, 2004, and applicable to all company licenses issued or otherwise eligible for renewal or continuation after that date, in the first sentence, substi-tuted "an annual license continuation fee" for "a fee," and deleted "renewal" following "for each license"; and added the last sentence.

§ 58-67-165. Penalties and enforcement.

(a) The Commissioner may, in addition to or in lieu of suspending or revoking a license under G.S. 58-67-140, proceed under G.S. 58-2-70, provided that the health maintenance organization has a reasonable time within which to remedy the defect in its operations that gave rise to the procedure under G.S. 58-2-70.

(b) Any person who violates this Article or any other provision of this Chapter that expressly applies to health maintenance organizations shall be guilty of a Class 1 misdemeanor.

(c)(1) If the Commissioner shall for any reason have cause to believe that any violation of this Article or any other provision of this Chapter that expressly applies to health maintenance organizations has occurred or is threatened, the Commissioner may give notice to the health maintenance organization and to the representatives or other persons who appear to be involved in such suspected violation to arrange a conference with the alleged violators or their authorized representatives for the purpose of attempting to ascertain the facts relating to such suspected violation, and, in the event it appears that any violation has occurred or is threatened, to arrive at an adequate and effective means of correcting or preventing such violation.

(2) Proceedings under this subsection shall not be governed by any formal procedural requirements, and may be conducted in such manner as the Commissioner may deem appropriate under the circumstances.

(d)(1) The Commissioner may issue an order directing a health maintenance organization or a representative of a health maintenance organization to cease and desist from engaging in any act or practice in violation of the provisions of this Article or any other provision of this Chapter that expressly applies to health maintenance organizations.

(2) Within 30 days after service of the cease and desist order, the respondent may request a hearing on the question of whether acts or practices have occurred that are in violation of this Article or any other provision of this Chapter that expressly applies to health maintenance organizations. The hearing shall be conducted under Article 3A of Chapter 150B of the General Statutes, and judicial review shall be available as provided by Article 4 of Chapter 150B of the General Statutes.

(e) In the case of any violation of the provisions of this Article or any other provision of this Chapter that expressly applies to health maintenance organizations, if the Commissioner elects not to issue a cease and desist order, or in the event of noncompliance with a cease and desist order issued under subsection (d) of this section, the Commissioner may institute a proceeding to obtain injunctive relief, or seeking other appropriate relief, in the Superior Court of Wake County. (1977, c. 580, s. 1; 1979, c. 876, s. 1; 1985, c. 666, s. 52; 1987, c. 827, s. 1; 1993, c. 539, s. 470; 1994, Ex. Sess., c. 24, s. 14(c); 2001-5, s. 1.)

§ 58-67-170. Statutory construction and relationship to other laws.

(a) Except as otherwise provided in this Chapter, provisions of the insurance laws and service corporation laws do not apply to any health maintenance organization licensed under this Article. This subsection does not apply to an insurer or service corporation licensed and regulated under the insurance laws or the service corporation laws of this State except with respect to its health maintenance organization activities authorized and regulated under this Article or any other provision of this Chapter that expressly applies to health maintenance organizations.

(b) Solicitation of enrollees by a health maintenance organization granted a license, or its representatives, shall not be construed to violate any provision of law relating to solicitation or advertising by health professionals.

(c) Any health maintenance organization authorized under this Article shall not be deemed to be practicing medicine or dentistry and shall be exempt from the provisions of Chapter 90 of the General Statutes relating to the practice of medicine and dentistry; provided, however, that this exemption does not apply to individual providers under contract with or employed by the health maintenance organization. (1977, c. 580, s. 1; 1979, c. 876, s. 1; 1985, c. 30; 2001-5, s. 2.)

§ 58-67-171. Other laws applicable to HMOs.

The following provisions of this Chapter are applicable to HMOs that are subject to this Article:

G.S. 58-2-125.	Authority over all insurance companies; no exemptions from license.
G.S. 58-2-155.	Investigation of charges.
G.S. 58-2-160.	Reporting and investigation of insurance and reinsurance fraud and the financial condition of licensees; immunity from liability.
G.S. 58-2-162.	Embezzlement by insurance agents, brokers, or administrators.
G.S. 58-2-185.	Record of business kept by companies and agents; Commissioner may inspect.
G.S. 58-2-190.	Commissioner may require special reports.
G.S. 58-2-195.	Commissioner may require records, reports, etc., for agencies, agents, and others.
G.S. 58-2-200.	Books and papers required to be exhibited.
G.S. 58-3-50.	Companies must do business in own name; emblems, insignias, etc.
G.S. 58-3-115.	Twisting with respect to insurance policies; penalties.
G.S. 58-50-35.	Notice of nonpayment of premium required before forfeiture.
G.S. 58-51-25.	Policy coverage to continue as to mentally retarded or physically handicapped children.
G.S. 58-51-35.	Insurers and others to afford coverage to mentally retarded and physically handicapped children.
G.S. 58-51-45.	Policies to be issued to any person possessing the sickle-cell trait or hemoglobin C trait. (1999-244, s. 2.)

Editor's Note. — Session Laws 1999-244, s. 15, made this section effective January 1, 2000.

§ 58-67-175. Filings and reports as public documents.

All applications, filings and reports required under this Article shall be treated as public documents. (1977, c. 580, s. 1; 1979, c. 876, s. 1.)

§ 58-67-180. Confidentiality of medical information.

Any data or information pertaining to the diagnosis, treatment, or health of any enrollee or applicant obtained from such person or from any provider by any health maintenance organization shall be held in confidence and shall not be disclosed to any person except to the extent that it may be necessary to carry out the purposes of this Article; or upon the express consent of the enrollee or applicant; or pursuant to statute; or pursuant to court order for the production of evidence or the discovery thereof; or in the event of claim or litigation between such person and the health maintenance organization wherein such data or information is pertinent. A health maintenance organization shall be entitled to claim any statutory privileges against such disclosure which the provider who furnished such information to the health maintenance organization is entitled to claim. (1977, c. 580, s. 1; 1979, c. 876, s. 1; 1999-272, s. 1.)

Legal Periodicals. — For legislative survey on medicine, see 22 Campbell L. Rev. 253 (2000).

§ 58-67-185. Severability.

If any section, term, or provision of this Article shall be adjudged invalid for any reason, such judgments shall not affect, impair, or invalidate any other section, term, or provision of this Article, but the remaining sections, terms, and provisions shall be and remain in full force and effect. (1977, c. 580, s. 1; 1979, c. 876, s. 1.)

ARTICLE 68.

Health Insurance Portability and Accountability.

§§ 58-68-1 through 58-68-20: Repealed by Session Laws 1997-259, s. 1(a).

Part A. Group Market Reforms.

Subpart 1. Portability, Access, and Renewability Requirements.

§ 58-68-25. Definitions; excepted benefits; employer size rule.

(a) Definitions. — In addition to other definitions throughout this Article, the following definitions and their cognates apply in this Article:

(1) "Bona fide association". — With respect to health insurance coverage offered in this State, an association that:

a. Has been actively in existence for at least five years.

b. Has been formed and maintained in good faith for purposes other than obtaining insurance.

c. Does not condition membership in the association on any health status-related factor relating to an individual (including an employee of an employer or a dependent of an employee).

d. Makes health insurance coverage offered through the association available to all members regardless of any health status-related factor relating to the members (or individuals eligible for coverage through a member).

e. Does not make health insurance coverage offered through the association available other than in connection with a member of the association.

  f. Meets the additional requirements as may be imposed under State law.
 (2) "COBRA continuation provision". — Any of the following:
  a. Section 4980B of the Internal Revenue Code of 1986, other than subdivision (f)(1) of the section insofar as it relates to pediatric vaccines.
  b. Part 6 of subtitle B of title I of the Employee Retirement Income Security Act of 1974, other than section 609 of the Act.
  c. Title XXII of the Public Health Service Act (42 U.S.C.S. § 300bb, et seq.,) as requirements for certain group health plans for certain State and local employees.
  d. Article 53 of this Chapter or the health insurance continuation law of another state.
 (3) "Employee". — The meaning given the term under section 3(6) of the Employee Retirement Income Security Act of 1974.
 (4) "Employer". — The meaning given the term under section 3(5) of the Employee Retirement Income Security Act of 1974, except that the term shall include only employers of two or more employees.
 (5) "Health insurance coverage" or "coverage" or "health insurance plan" or "plan". — Benefits consisting of medical care, provided directly through insurance or otherwise and including items and services paid for as medical care, under any accident and health insurance policy or certificate, hospital or medical service plan contract, or health maintenance organization contract, written by a health insurer.
 (6) "Health insurer". — An insurance company subject to this Chapter, a hospital or medical service corporation subject to Article 65 of this Chapter, a health maintenance organization subject to Article 67 of this Chapter, or a multiple employer welfare arrangement subject to Article 49 of this Chapter, that offers and issues health insurance coverage.
 (7) "Health status-related factor". — Any of the factors described in G.S. 58-68-35(a)(1).
 (8) "Individual health insurance coverage". — Health insurance coverage offered to individuals in the individual market, but not short-term limited duration insurance.
 (9) "Individual market". — The market for health insurance coverage offered to individuals.
 (10) "Large employer". — An employer who employed an average of at least 51 employees on business days during the preceding calendar year and who employs at least two employees on the first day of the health insurance plan year.
 (11) "Large group market". — The health insurance market under which individuals obtain health insurance coverage, directly or through any arrangement, on behalf of themselves and their dependents through a group health insurance plan maintained by a large employer.
 (12) "Medical care". — Amounts paid for:
  a. The diagnosis, cure, mitigation, treatment, or prevention of disease, or amounts paid for the purpose of affecting any structure or function of the body.
  b. Amounts paid for transportation primarily for and essential to medical care referred to in sub-subdivision a. of this subdivision.
  c. Amounts paid for insurance covering medical care referred to in sub-subdivisions a. and b. of this subdivision.
 (13) "Network plan". — Health insurance coverage of a health insurer under which the financing and delivery of medical care (including items and services paid for as medical care) are provided, in whole or

in part, through a defined set of health care providers under contract with the health insurer.

(14) "Participant". — The meaning given the term under section 3(7) of the Employee Retirement Income Security Act of 1974.

(15) "Placed for adoption". — The assumption and retention by a person of a legal obligation for total or partial support of a child in anticipation of adoption of the child. The child's placement with the person terminates upon the termination of the legal obligation.

(16) "Small employer". — The meaning given to the term in G.S. 58-50-110(22).

(17) "Small group market". — The health insurance market under which individuals obtain health insurance coverage, directly or through any arrangement, on behalf of themselves and their dependents through a group health insurance plan maintained by a small employer.

(b) Excepted Benefits. — For the purposes of this Article, "excepted benefits" means benefits under one or more or any combination of the following:

(1) Benefits not subject to requirements. —

   a. Coverage only for accident or disability income insurance or any combination of these.

   b. Coverage issued as a supplement to liability insurance.

   c. Liability insurance, including general liability insurance and automobile liability insurance.

   d. Workers' compensation or similar insurance.

   e. Automobile medical payment insurance.

   f. Credit-only insurance.

   g. Coverage for on-site medical clinics.

   h. Other similar insurance coverage, specified in federal regulations, under which benefits for medical care are secondary or incidental to other insurance benefits.

   i. Short-term limited-duration health insurance policies as defined in Part 144 of Title 45 of the Code of Federal Regulations.

(2) Benefits not subject to requirements if offered separately. —

   a. Limited scope dental or vision benefits.

   b. Benefits for long-term care, nursing care, home health care, community-based care, or any combination of these.

   c. The other similar, limited benefits as are specified in federal regulations.

(3) Benefits not subject to requirements if offered as independent, noncoordinated benefits. —

   a. Coverage only for a specified disease or illness.

   b. Hospital indemnity or other fixed indemnity insurance.

(4) Benefits not subject to requirements if offered as separate insurance policy. — Medicare supplemental health insurance (as defined under section 1882(g)(1) of the Social Security Act), coverage supplemental to the coverage provided under chapter 55 of title 10, United States Code, and similar supplemental coverage provided to coverage under a group health insurance plan.

(c) Application of certain rules in determination of employer size. — For the purposes of this Article:

(1) Application of aggregation rule for employers. — All persons treated as a single employer under subsection (b), (c), (m), or (o) of section 414 of the Internal Revenue Code of 1986 shall be treated as one employer.

(2) Employers not in existence in preceding year. — In the case of an employer that was not in existence throughout the preceding calendar year, the determination of whether the employer is a small or large employer shall be based on the average number of employees that it is

reasonably expected the employer will employ on business days in the current calendar year.
(3) Predecessors. — Any reference in this subsection to an employer shall include a reference to any predecessor of the employer. (1997-259, s. 1(c); 2002-187, s. 5.1.)

Effect of Amendments. — Session Laws 2002-187, s. 5.1, effective October 31, 2002, added subdivision (b)(1)i.

§ 58-68-30. Increased portability through limitation on preexisting condition exclusions.

(a) Limitation on Preexisting Condition Exclusion Period; Crediting for Periods of Previous Coverage. — Subject to subsection (d) of this section, a group health insurer may, with respect to a participant or beneficiary, impose a preexisting condition exclusion only if:
  (1) The exclusion relates to a condition, whether physical or mental, regardless of the cause of the condition, for which medical advice, diagnosis, care, or treatment was recommended or received within the six-month period ending on the enrollment date.
  (2) The exclusion extends for a period of not more than 12 months, or 18 months in the case of a late enrollee, after the enrollment date.
  (3) The period of any preexisting condition exclusion is reduced by the aggregate of the periods of creditable coverage, if any, applicable to the participant or beneficiary as of the enrollment date.
(b) Definitions. — For the purposes of this Part:
  (1) Enrollment date. — With respect to an individual covered under a group health insurance plan, the date of enrollment of the individual in the coverage or, if earlier, the first day of the waiting period for the enrollment.
  (2) Late enrollee. — With respect to coverage under a group health insurance plan, a participant or beneficiary who enrolls under the plan other than during:
    a. The first period in which the individual is eligible to enroll under the plan, or
    b. A special enrollment period under subsection (f) of this section.
  (3) Preexisting condition exclusion. —
    a. In general. — "Preexisting condition exclusion" means, with respect to coverage, a limitation or exclusion of benefits relating to a condition based on the fact that the condition was present before the date of enrollment for the coverage, whether or not any medical advice, diagnosis, care, or treatment was recommended or received before the date.
    b. Treatment of genetic information. — Genetic information shall not be treated as a condition described in subdivision (a)(1) of this subsection in the absence of a diagnosis of the condition related to the information.
  (4) Waiting period. — With respect to a group health insurance plan and an individual who is a potential participant or beneficiary in the plan, the period that must pass with respect to the individual before the individual is eligible to be covered for benefits under the terms of the plan.
(c) Rules Relating to Crediting Previous Coverage. —
  (1) Creditable coverage defined. — For the purposes of this Article, "creditable coverage" means, with respect to an individual, coverage of the individual under any of the following:

    a. A self-funded employer group health plan under the Employee Retirement Income Security Act of 1974.
    b. Group or individual health insurance coverage.
    c. Part A or part B of title XVIII of the Social Security Act.
    d. Title XIX of the Social Security Act, other than coverage consisting solely of benefits under section 1928.
    e. Chapter 55 of title 10, United States Code.
    f. A medical care program of the Indian Health Service or of a tribal organization.
    g. A State health benefits risk pool.
    h. A health plan offered under chapter 89 of title 5, United States Code.
    i. A public health plan (as defined in federal regulations).
    j. A health benefit plan under section 5(e) of the Peace Corps Act (22 U.S.C. § 2504(e)).
    k. The Health Insurance Program for Children established in Part 8 of Chapter 108A of the General Statutes, or any successor program.

"Creditable coverage" does not include coverage consisting solely of coverage of excepted benefits.

  (2) Not counting periods before significant breaks in coverage. —
    a. In general. — A period of creditable coverage shall not be counted, with respect to enrollment of an individual under a group health insurance plan, if, after the period and before the enrollment date, there was a 63-day period during all of which the individual was not covered under any creditable coverage.
    b. Waiting period not treated as a break in coverage. — For the purposes of sub-subdivision a. of this subdivision and subdivision (d)(4) of this subsection, any period that an individual is in a waiting period for any coverage under a group health insurance plan or is in an affiliation period shall not be taken into account in determining the continuous period under sub-subdivision a. of this subdivision.
    c. Time spent on short term limited duration health insurance not treated as a break in coverage. — For the purposes of sub-subdivision a. of this subdivision, any period that an individual is enrolled on a short term limited duration health insurance policy shall not be taken into account in determining the continuous period under sub-subdivision. a. of this subdivision so long as the period of time spent on the short term limited duration health insurance policy or policies does not exceed 12 months.

  (3) Method of crediting coverage. —
    a. Standard method. — Except as otherwise provided under sub-subdivision b. of this subdivision for the purposes of applying subdivision (a)(3) of this subsection, a group health insurer shall count a period of creditable coverage without regard to the specific benefits covered during the period.
    b. Election of alternative method. — A group health insurer may elect to apply subdivision (a)(3) of this subsection based on coverage of benefits within each of several classes or categories of benefits specified in federal regulations rather than as provided under sub-subdivision a. of this subdivision. This election shall be made on a uniform basis for all participants and beneficiaries. Under this election a group health insurer shall count a period of creditable coverage with respect to any class or category of benefits if any level of benefits is covered within the class or category.

c. Health insurer notice. — In the case of an election under sub-subdivision b. of this subdivision with respect to health insurance coverage in the small or large group market, the health insurer: (i) shall prominently state in any disclosure statements concerning the coverage, and to each employer at the time of the offer or sale of the coverage, that the health insurer has made the election, and (ii) shall include in the statements a description of the effect of the election.

(4) Establishment of period. — Periods of creditable coverage for an individual shall be established through presentation of certifications described in subsection (e) of this section or in another manner that is specified in federal regulations.

(d) Exceptions. —

(1) Exclusion not applicable to certain newborns. — Subject to subdivision (4) of this subsection, a group health insurer shall not impose any preexisting condition exclusion in the case of an individual who, as of the last day of the 30-day period beginning with the individual's date of birth, is covered under creditable coverage.

(2) Exclusion not applicable to certain adopted children. — Subject to subdivision (4) of this subsection, a group health insurer shall not impose any preexisting condition exclusion in the case of a child who is adopted or placed for adoption before attaining 18 years of age and who, as of the last day of the 30-day period beginning on the date of the adoption or placement for adoption, is covered under creditable coverage. The previous sentence does not apply to coverage before the date of the adoption or placement for adoption.

(3) Exclusion not applicable to pregnancy. — A group health insurer shall not impose any preexisting condition exclusion relating to pregnancy as a preexisting condition.

(4) Loss if break in coverage. — Subdivisions (1) and (2) of this subsection shall no longer apply to an individual after the end of the first 63-day period during all of which the individual was not covered under any creditable coverage.

(5) Condition first diagnosed under previous coverage. — A group health insurer shall not impose any preexisting condition exclusion for a condition for which medical advice, diagnosis, care, or treatment was recommended or received for the first time while the covered person held qualifying previous coverage or prior creditable coverage and the condition was covered under the qualifying previous coverage or prior creditable coverage; provided that the qualifying previous coverage or prior creditable coverage was continuous to a date not more than 63 days before the enrollment date for the new coverage.

(e) Certifications and Disclosure of Coverage. —

(1) Requirement for certification of period of creditable coverage. —

a. In general. — A group health insurer shall provide the certification described in sub-subdivision b. of this subdivision: (i) at the time an individual ceases to be covered under the plan or otherwise becomes covered under a COBRA continuation provision, (ii) in the case of an individual becoming covered under a COBRA continuation provision, at the time the individual ceases to be covered under the COBRA continuation provision, and (iii) on the request on behalf of an individual made not later than 24 months after the date of cessation of the coverage described in clause (i) or (ii) of this sub-subdivision, whichever is later.

The certification under clause (i) of this sub-subdivision may be provided, to the extent practicable, at a time consistent with notices required under any applicable COBRA continuation provision.

    b. Certification. — The certification described in this sub-subdivision is a written certification of: (i) the period of creditable coverage of the individual under the plan and any coverage under the COBRA continuation provision, and (ii) any waiting period and affiliation period, if applicable, imposed with respect to the individual for any coverage under the plan.

  (2) Disclosure of information on previous benefits. — In the case of an election described in sub-subdivision (c)(3)b. of this subsection by a group health insurer, if the health insurer enrolls an individual for coverage under the plan and the individual provides a certification of coverage of the individual under subdivision (1) of this subsection:

    a. Upon request of the health insurer, the entity that issued the certification provided by the individual shall promptly disclose to the requesting plan or health insurer information on coverage of classes and categories of health benefits available under the entity's coverage.

    b. The entity may charge the requesting plan or health insurer for the reasonable cost of disclosing the information.

(f) Special Enrollment Periods. —

  (1) Individuals losing other coverage. — A group health insurer shall permit an employee who is eligible, but not enrolled, for coverage under the terms of the plan (or a dependent of the employee if the dependent is eligible, but not enrolled, for coverage under the terms) to enroll for coverage under the terms of the plan if each of the following conditions is met:

    a. The employee or dependent was covered under an ERISA group health plan or had health insurance coverage at the time coverage was previously offered to the employee or dependent.

    b. The employee stated in writing at the time that coverage under the group health plan or health insurance coverage was the reason for declining enrollment, but only if the health insurer required the statement at the time and provided the employee with notice of the requirement and the consequences of the requirement at the time.

    c. The employee's or dependent's coverage described in sub-subdivision a.: (i) was under a COBRA continuation provision and the coverage under the provision was exhausted; (ii) was not under that provision and either the coverage was terminated because of loss of eligibility for the coverage, including legal separation, divorce, death, termination of employment, or reduction in the number of hours of employment; or (iii) employer contributions toward the coverage were terminated.

    d. Under the terms of the plan, the employee requests the enrollment not later than 30 days after the date of exhaustion of coverage described in sub-subdivision c.(i) of this subdivision or termination of coverage or employer contribution described in sub-subdivision c.(ii) of this subdivision.

  (2) For dependent beneficiaries. —

    a. In general. — If: (i) a group health insurance plan makes coverage available with respect to a dependent of an individual, (ii) the individual is a participant under the plan (or has met any waiting period applicable to becoming a participant under the plan and is eligible to be enrolled under the plan but for a failure to enroll during a previous enrollment period), and (iii) a person becomes the dependent of the individual through marriage, birth, or adoption or placement for adoption.

1125

The plan shall provide for a dependent special enrollment period described in sub-subdivision b. of this subdivision during which the person (or, if not otherwise enrolled, the individual) may be enrolled under the plan as a dependent of the individual, and in the case of the birth or adoption of a child, the spouse of the individual may be enrolled as a dependent of the individual if the spouse is otherwise eligible for coverage.

    b. Dependent special enrollment period. — A dependent special enrollment period under this sub-subdivision shall be a period of not less than 30 days and shall begin on the later of: (i) the date dependent coverage is made available, or (ii) the date of the marriage, birth, or adoption or placement for adoption described in sub-subdivision a.(iii) of this subdivision.

    c. No waiting period. — If an individual seeks to enroll a dependent during the first 30 days of the dependent's special enrollment period, the coverage of the dependent shall become effective: (i) in the case of marriage, not later than the first day of the first month beginning after the date the completed request for enrollment is received; (ii) in the case of a dependent's birth, as of the date of the birth; or (iii) in the case of a dependent's adoption or placement for adoption, the date of the adoption or placement for adoption.

(g) Use of Affiliation Period by HMO as Alternative to Preexisting Condition Exclusion. —

    (1) In general. — A health maintenance organization that does not impose any preexisting condition exclusion allowed under subsection (a) of this section with respect to any particular coverage option may impose an affiliation period for the coverage option, but only if:

        a. The period is applied uniformly without regard to any health status-related factors.

        b. The period does not exceed two months (or three months in the case of a late enrollee).

    (2) Affiliation period. —

        a. Defined. — For the purposes of this Subpart, "affiliation period" means a period that, under the terms of the health insurance coverage offered by the health maintenance organization, must expire before the health insurance coverage becomes effective. The health maintenance organization is not required to provide health care services or benefits during the period and no premium shall be charged to the participant or beneficiary for any coverage during the period.

        b. Beginning. — The period shall begin on the enrollment date.

        c. Runs concurrently with waiting periods. — An affiliation period under a plan shall run concurrently with any waiting period under the plan.

    (3) Alternative methods. — A health maintenance organization described in subdivision (1) of this subsection may use alternative methods, as approved by the Commissioner, from those described in that subdivision, to address adverse selection. (1997-259, s. 1(c); 1998-211, s. 7; 2001-334, s. 9.)

Editor's Note. — Subsection (b) was set out in the form above at the direction of the Revisor of Statutes.

§ 58-68-35. Prohibiting discrimination against individual participants and beneficiaries based on health status.

(a) In Eligibility To Enroll. —
    (1) In general. — Subject to subdivision (2) of this subsection, a group health insurer shall not establish rules for eligibility, including continued eligibility, of any individual to enroll under the terms of the health insurer's plan based on any of the following health status-related factors in relation to the individual or a dependent of the individual:
        a. Health status.
        b. Medical condition (including both physical and mental illnesses).
        c. Claims experience.
        d. Receipt of health care.
        e. Medical history.
        f. Genetic information.
        g. Evidence of insurability (including conditions arising out of acts of domestic violence).
        h. Disability.
    (2) No application to benefits or exclusions. — To the extent consistent with G.S. 58-68-30, subdivision (1) of this subsection shall not be construed:
        a. To require a group health insurance plan to provide particular benefits other than those provided under the terms of the plan, or
        b. To prevent the plan from establishing limitations or restrictions on the amount, level, extent, or nature of the benefits or coverage for similarly situated individuals enrolled in the plan.
    (3) Construction. — For the purposes of subdivision (1) of this subsection, rules for eligibility to enroll under a plan include rules defining any applicable waiting periods for the enrollment.
(b) In Premium Contributions. —
    (1) In general. — A group health insurance plan shall not require any individual (as a condition of enrollment or continued enrollment under the plan) to pay a premium or contribution that is greater than the premium or contribution for a similarly situated individual enrolled in the plan on the basis of any health status-related factor in relation to the individual or to an individual enrolled under the plan as a dependent of individual.
    (2) Construction. — Nothing in subdivision (1) of this subsection shall be construed:
        a. To restrict the amount that an employer may be charged for coverage under a group health insurance plan; or
        b. To prevent a group health insurer from establishing premium discounts or modifying otherwise applicable copayments or deductibles in return for adherence to programs of health promotion and disease prevention. (1997-259, s. 1(c).)

Subpart 2. Health Insurance Availability and Renewability.

§ 58-68-40. Guaranteed availability of coverage for employers in the small group market.

(a) Issuance of Coverage in the Small Group Market. —
    (1) In general. — Subject to subsections (c) through (f) of this section, each

health insurer that offers health insurance coverage in the small group market in this State:

    a. Must accept every small employer that applies for the coverage; and

    b. Must accept for enrollment under the coverage every eligible individual who applies for enrollment during the period in which the individual first becomes eligible to enroll under the terms of the group health insurance plan and shall not place any restriction that is inconsistent with G.S. 58-68-35 on an eligible individual being a participant or beneficiary.

  (2) Eligible individual defined. — For the purposes of this section, "eligible individual" means, with respect to a health insurer that offers health insurance coverage to a small employer in the small group market, such an individual in relation to the employer as shall be determined:

    a. In accordance with the terms of the plan,

    b. As provided by the health insurer under rules of the health insurer that are uniformly applicable in this State to small employers in the small group market, and

    c. In accordance with all applicable State laws governing the health insurer and the market.

(b) Special Rules for Network Plans. —

  (1) In general. — In the case of a health insurer that offers health insurance coverage in the small group market through a network plan, the health insurer may:

    a. Limit the employers that may apply for coverage to those with eligible individuals who live, work, or reside in the service area for the network plan; and

    b. Within the service area of the network plan, deny coverage to the employers if the health insurer has demonstrated to the Commissioner that: (i) it will not have the capacity to deliver services adequately to enrollees of any additional groups because of its obligations to existing group contract holders and enrollees, and (ii) it is applying this subdivision uniformly to all employers without regard to the claims experience of those employers and their employees (and their dependents) or any health status-related factor relating to the employees and dependents.

  (2) 180-day suspension upon denial of coverage. — A health insurer, upon denying health insurance coverage in any service area in accordance with sub-subdivision (1)b. of this subsection, shall not offer coverage in the small group market within the service area for a period of 180 days after the date the coverage is denied.

(c) Application of Financial Capacity Limits. —

  (1) In general. — A health insurer may deny health insurance coverage in the small group market if the health insurer has demonstrated to the Commissioner that:

    a. It does not have the financial reserves necessary to underwrite additional coverage; and

    b. It is applying this subdivision uniformly to all employers in the small group market in the State consistent with this Chapter and without regard to the claims experience of those employers and their employees (and their dependents) or any health status-related factor relating to the employees and dependents.

  (2) 180-day suspension upon denial of coverage. — A health insurer upon denying health insurance coverage in accordance with subdivision (1)

of this subsection shall not offer coverage in the small group market in the State for a period of 180 days after the date the coverage is denied or until the health insurer has demonstrated to the Commissioner that the health insurer has sufficient financial reserves to underwrite additional coverage, whichever is later. The Commissioner may apply this subsection on a service-area-specific basis.

(d) Exception to Requirement for Failure to Meet Certain Minimum Participation or Contribution Rules. —

    (1) In general. — Subsection (a) of this section does not preclude a health insurer from establishing employer contribution rules or group participation rules for the offering of health insurance coverage in connection with a group health insurance plan in the small group market, as allowed under this Chapter.

    (2) Rules defined. — For the purposes of subdivision (1) of this subsection:

        a. "Employer contribution rule" means a requirement relating to the minimum level or amount of employer contribution toward the premium for enrollment of participants and beneficiaries; and

        b. "Group participation rule" means a requirement relating to the minimum number of participants or beneficiaries that must be enrolled in relation to a specified percentage or number of eligible individuals or employees of an employer.

(e) Exception for Coverage. — Subsection (a) of this section does not apply to:

    (1) Health insurance coverage offered by a health insurer if the coverage is made available in the small group market only through one or more bona fide associations.

    (2) A self-employed individual as defined in G.S. 58-50-110(21a), except as otherwise provided for the basic and standard health care plans under the North Carolina Small Employer Group Health Coverage Reform Act. (1997-259, s. 1(c); 1999-132, s. 4.6.)

§ 58-68-45. Guaranteed renewability of coverage for employers in the group market.

(a) In General. — Except as provided in this section, if a health insurer offers health insurance coverage in the small or large group market, the health insurer must renew or continue in force the coverage at the option of the employer.

(b) General Exceptions. — A health insurer may nonrenew or discontinue health insurance coverage in the small or large group market based only on one or more of the following:

    (1) Nonpayment of premiums. — The policyholder has failed to pay premiums or contributions in accordance with the terms of the health insurance coverage or the health insurer has not received timely premium payments.

    (2) Fraud. — The policyholder has performed an act or practice that constitutes fraud or made an intentional misrepresentation of material fact under the terms of the coverage.

    (3) Violation of participation or contribution rules. — The policyholder has failed to comply with a material plan provision relating to employer contribution or group participation rules, as permitted under G.S. 58-68-40(d) in the case of the small group market or pursuant to this Chapter in the case of the large group market.

    (4) Termination of coverage. — The health insurer is ceasing to offer coverage in the market in accordance with subsection (c) of this section and this Chapter.

(5) Movement outside service area. — In the case of a health insurer that offers health insurance coverage in the market through a network plan, there is no longer any enrollee in connection with the network plan who lives, resides, or works in the service area of the health insurer or in the area for which the health insurer is authorized to do business and, in the case of the small group market, the health insurer would deny enrollment with respect to the network plan under G.S. 58-68-40(c)(1)a.

(6) Association membership ceases. — In the case of health insurance coverage that is made available in the small or large group market only through one or more bona fide associations, the membership of an employer in the association, on the basis of which the coverage is provided, ceases but only if the coverage is terminated under this subdivision uniformly without regard to any health status-related factor relating to any covered individual.

(c) Requirements for Uniform Termination of Coverage. —

(1) Particular type of coverage not offered. — In any case in which a health insurer decides to discontinue offering a particular type of group health insurance coverage offered in the small or large group market, coverage of the type may be discontinued by the health insurer in accordance with this Chapter in the market only if:

a. The health insurer provides notice to each policyholder provided coverage of this type in the market and to the participants and beneficiaries covered under the coverage of the discontinuation at least 90 days before the date of the discontinuation of the coverage;

b. The health insurer offers to each policyholder provided coverage of this type in the market the option to purchase all, or in the case of the large group market, any other health insurance coverage currently being offered by the health insurer to a group health insurance plan in the market; and

c. In exercising the option to discontinue coverage of this type and in offering the option of coverage under sub-subdivision b. of this subdivision, the health insurer acts uniformly without regard to the claims experience of those sponsors or any health status-related factor relating to any participants or beneficiaries covered or new participants or beneficiaries who may become eligible for the coverage.

(2) Discontinuance of all coverage. —

a. In general. — In any case in which a health insurer elects to discontinue offering all health insurance coverage in the small group market or the large group market, or both markets, in this State, health insurance coverage may be discontinued by the health insurer only in accordance with this Chapter and if: (i) the health insurer provides notice to the Commissioner and to each policyholder and to the participants and beneficiaries covered under the coverage of the discontinuation at least 180 days before the date of the discontinuation of the coverage; and (ii) all health insurance issued or delivered for issuance in this State in the market or markets are discontinued and coverage under the health insurance coverage in the market or markets is not renewed.

b. Prohibition on market reentry. — In the case of a discontinuation under sub-subdivision a. of this subdivision in a market, the health insurer shall not provide for the issuance of any health insurance coverage in that market in this State during the five-year period beginning on the date of the discontinuation of the last health insurance coverage not so renewed.

(d) Exception for Uniform Modification of Coverage. — At the time of coverage renewal, a health insurer may modify the health insurance coverage for a product offered to a group health insurance plan:

    (1) In the large group market; or

    (2) In the small group market if, for coverage that is available in the market other than only through one or more bona fide associations, the modification is consistent with this Chapter and effective on a uniform basis among group health insurance plans with that product.

(e) Application to Coverage Offered Only Through Associations. — In applying this section in the case of health insurance coverage that is made available by a health insurer in the small or large group market to employers only through one or more associations, a reference to "policyholder" is deemed, with respect to coverage provided to an employer member of the association, to include a reference to the employer. (1997-259, s. 1(c); 1997-456, s. 42.)

§ 58-68-50. Disclosure of information.

(a) Disclosure of Information by Health Insurers. — In connection with the offering of any health insurance coverage to a small employer, a health insurer:

    (1) Shall make a reasonable disclosure to the employer, as part of its solicitation and sales materials, of the availability of information described in subsection (b) of this section, and

    (2) Shall upon request of the small employer, provide the information.

(b) Information Described. —

    (1) In general. — Subject to subdivision (3) of this subsection, with respect to a health insurer offering health insurance coverage to a small employer, information described in this subsection is information concerning:

        a. The provisions of the coverage concerning the health insurer's right to change premium rates and the factors that may affect changes in premium rates;

        b. The provisions of the coverage relating to renewability of coverage;

        c. The provisions of the coverage relating to any preexisting condition exclusion; and

        d. The benefits and premiums available under all health insurance coverage for which the employer is qualified.

    (2) Form of information. — Information under this subsection shall be provided to small employers in a manner determined to be understandable by the average small employer, and shall be sufficient to reasonably inform small employers of their rights and obligations under the health insurance coverage.

    (3) Exception. — A health insurer is not required under this section to disclose any information that is proprietary and trade secret information under applicable law. (1997-259, s. 1(c).)

Subpart 3. Exclusion of Plans.

§ 58-68-55. Exclusion of certain plans.

(a) Exception for Certain Benefits. — The requirements of Subparts 1 and 2 of this Part do not apply to any group health insurance coverage in relation to its provision of excepted benefits described in G.S. 58-68-25(b)(1).

(b) Exception for Certain Benefits if Certain Conditions Met. —
   (1) Limited, excepted benefits. — The requirements of Subparts 1 and 2 of this Part do not apply to any group health insurance plan in relation to its provision of excepted benefits described in G.S. 58-68-25(b)(2) if the benefits:
     a. Are provided under a separate policy, certificate, or contract of insurance; or
     b. Are otherwise not an integral part of the plan.
   (2) Noncoordinated, excepted benefits. — The requirements of Subparts 1 and 2 of this Part do not apply to any group health insurance plan in relation to its provision of excepted benefits described in G.S. 58-68-25(b)(3) if all of the following conditions are met:
     a. The benefits are provided under a separate policy, certificate, or contract of insurance.
     b. There is no coordination between the provision of the benefits and any exclusion of benefits under any group health insurance plan maintained by the same policyholder.
     c. The benefits are paid with respect to an event without regard to whether benefits are provided with respect to that event under any group health insurance plan maintained by the same policyholder.
   (3) Supplemental, excepted benefits. — The requirements of this Part do not apply to any group health insurance plan in relation to its provision of excepted benefits described in G.S. 58-68-25(b)(4) if the benefits are provided under a separate policy, certificate, or contract of insurance. (1997-259, s. 1(c).)

Part B. Individual Market Reforms.

§ 58-68-60. Guaranteed availability of individual health insurance coverage to certain individuals with prior group coverage.

(a) Guaranteed Availability. —
   (1) In general. — Subject to the succeeding subsections of this section, each health insurer that offers health insurance coverage in the individual market in this State shall not, with respect to an eligible individual desiring to enroll in individual health insurance coverage:
     a. Decline to offer the coverage to, or deny enrollment of, the individual; or
     b. Impose any preexisting condition exclusion with respect to the coverage.
   (2) Reserved.
(b) Eligible Individual Defined. — In this Part, "eligible individual" means an individual:
   (1)(i) For whom, as of the date on which the individual seeks coverage under this section, the aggregate of the periods of creditable coverage is 18 or more months and (ii) whose most recent prior creditable coverage was under an ERISA group health plan, governmental plan, or church plan (or health insurance coverage offered in connection with any such plan);
   (2) Who is not eligible for coverage under (i) a group health plan, (ii) part A or part B of title XVIII of the Social Security Act, or (iii) a State plan under title XIX of the Act (or any successor program), and does not have other health insurance coverage;
   (3) With respect to whom the most recent coverage within the coverage period described in subdivision (1)(i) was not terminated based on a factor described in G.S. 58-68-45(b)(1) or (b)(2);

(4) If the individual had been offered the option of continuation coverage under a COBRA continuation provision or under Article 53 of this Chapter, who elected the coverage; and

(5) Who, if the individual elected the continuation coverage, has exhausted the continuation coverage under the provision or program.

(c) Alternative Coverage Permitted. —

(1) In general. — In the case of health insurance coverage offered in this State, a health insurer may elect to limit the coverage offered under subsection (a) of this section as long as it offers at least two different policy forms of health insurance coverage both of which:

    a. Are designed for, made generally available to, and actively marketed to, and enroll both eligible and other individuals by the health insurer; and

    b. Meet the requirement of subdivision (2) or (3) of this subsection, as elected by the health insurer.

For the purposes of this subsection, policy forms that have different cost-sharing arrangements or different riders shall be considered to be different policy forms.

(2) Choice of most popular policy forms. — The requirement of this subdivision is met, for health insurance coverage policy forms offered by a health insurer in the individual market, if the health insurer offers the policy forms for individual health insurance coverage with the largest, and next to largest, premium volume of all the policy forms offered by the health insurer in this State or applicable marketing or service area (as may be prescribed by rules or regulations) by the health insurer in the individual market in the period involved.

(3) Choice of two policy forms with representative coverage. —

    a. In general. — The requirement of this subdivision is met, for health insurance coverage policy forms offered by a health insurer in the individual market, if the health insurer offers a lower-level coverage policy form (as described in sub-subdivision b. of this subdivision) and a higher-level coverage policy form (as described in sub-subdivision c. of this subdivision) each of which includes benefits substantially similar to other individual health insurance coverage offered by the health insurer in this State.

    b. Lower-level of coverage described. — A policy form is described in this sub-subdivision if the actuarial value of the benefits under the coverage is at least eighty-five percent (85%) but not greater than one hundred percent (100%) of a weighted average (described in sub-subdivision d. of this subdivision).

    c. Higher-level of coverage described. — A policy form is described in this sub-subdivision if: (i) the actuarial value of the benefits under the coverage is at least fifteen percent (15%) greater than the actuarial value of the coverage described in sub-subdivision b. of this subdivision offered by the health insurer in the area involved; and (ii) the actuarial value of the benefits under the coverage is at least one hundred percent (100%) but not greater than one hundred twenty percent (120%) of a weighted average (described in sub-subdivision d. of this subdivision).

    d. Weighted average. — For the purposes of this subdivision, the weighted average described in this sub-subdivision is the average actuarial value of the benefits provided by all the health insurance coverage issued, as elected by the health insurer, either by that health insurer or by all health insurers in this State in the individual market during the previous year, not including coverage issued under this section, weighted by enrollment for the different coverage.

    (4) Election. — The health insurer elections under this subsection shall apply uniformly to all eligible individuals in this State for that health insurer. The election shall be effective for policies offered during a period of not less than two years.

    (5) Assumptions. — For the purposes of subdivision (3) of this subsection, the actuarial value of benefits provided under individual health insurance coverage shall be calculated based on a standardized population and a set of standardized utilization and cost factors.

(d) Special Rules for Network Plans. —

    (1) In general. — In the case of a health insurer that offers health insurance coverage in the individual market through a network plan, the health insurer may:

        a. Limit the individuals who may be enrolled under the coverage to those who live, reside, or work within the service area for the network plan; and

        b. Within the service area of the plan, deny the coverage to the individuals if the health insurer has demonstrated to the Commissioner that: (i) it will not have the capacity to deliver services adequately to additional individual enrollees because of its obligations to existing group contract holders and enrollees and individual enrollees, and (ii) it is applying this subdivision uniformly to individuals without regard to any health status-related factor of the individuals and without regard to whether the individuals are eligible individuals.

    (2) 180-day suspension upon denial of coverage. — A health insurer, upon denying health insurance coverage in any service area in accordance with sub-subdivision (1)b. of this subdivision, shall not offer coverage in the individual market within the service area for a period of 180 days after the coverage is denied.

(e) Application of Financial Capacity Limits. —

    (1) In general. — A health insurer may deny health insurance coverage in the individual market to an eligible individual if the health insurer has demonstrated to the Commissioner that:

        a. It does not have the financial reserves necessary to underwrite additional coverage; and

        b. It is applying this subdivision uniformly to all individuals in the individual market in this State consistent with this Chapter and without regard to any health status-related factor of the individuals and without regard to whether the individuals are eligible individuals.

    (2) 180-day suspension upon denial of coverage. — A health insurer, upon denying individual health insurance coverage in any service area in accordance with subdivision (1) of this subsection, shall not offer the coverage in the individual market within the service area for a period of 180 days after the date the coverage is denied or until the health insurer has demonstrated to the Commissioner that the health insurer has sufficient financial reserves to underwrite additional coverage, whichever is later.

(f) Market Requirements. —

    (1) In general. — Subsection (a) of this section does not require that a health insurer offering health insurance coverage only in connection with ERISA group health plans or through one or more bona fide associations, or both, offer the health insurance coverage in the individual market.

(2) Conversion policies. — A health insurer offering health insurance coverage in connection with group health plans under title XXVII of the federal Public Health Service Act shall not be deemed to be a health insurer offering individual health insurance coverage solely because the health insurer offers a conversion policy.

(g) Construction. — Nothing in this section shall be construed:

(1) To restrict the amount of the premium rates that a health insurer may charge an individual for health insurance coverage provided in the individual market under this Chapter; or

(2) To prevent a health insurer offering health insurance coverage in the individual market from establishing premium discounts or rebates or modifying otherwise applicable copayments or deductibles in return for adherence to programs of health promotion and disease prevention.

(h) Other Definitions. — As used in this section:

(1) "Church plan". — The meaning given the term under section 3(33) of the Employee Retirement Income Security Act of 1974.

(2) "Governmental plan". —

a. The meaning given the term under section 3(32) of the Employee Retirement Income Security Act of 1974 and any federal governmental plan.

b. Federal governmental plan. — A governmental plan established or maintained for its employees by the government of the United States or by any agency or instrumentality of the government.

c. Nonfederal governmental plan. — A governmental plan that is not a federal governmental plan. (1997-259, s. 1(c); 1999-132, s. 4.7.)

Editor's Note. — Subsection (a) was set out in the form above at the direction of the Revisor of Statutes.

§ 58-68-65. Guaranteed renewability of individual health insurance coverage.

(a) In General. — Except as provided in this section, a health insurer that provides individual health insurance coverage to an individual shall renew or continue in force the coverage at the option of the individual.

(b) General Exceptions. — A health insurer may nonrenew or discontinue health insurance coverage of an individual in the individual market based only on one or more of the following:

(1) Nonpayment of premiums. — The individual has failed to pay premiums or contributions in accordance with the terms of the health insurance coverage or the health insurer has not received timely premium payments.

(2) Fraud. — The individual has performed an act or practice that constitutes fraud or made an intentional misrepresentation of material fact under the terms of the coverage.

(3) Termination of plan. — The health insurer is ceasing to offer coverage in the individual market in accordance with subsection (c) of this section and this Chapter.

(4) Movement outside service area. — In the case of a health insurer that offers health insurance coverage in the market through a network plan, the individual no longer resides, lives, or works in the service area (or in an area for which the health insurer is authorized to do business) but only if the coverage is terminated under this subdivision uniformly without regard to any health status-related factor of covered individuals.

(5) Association membership ceases. — In the case of health insurance coverage that is made available in the individual market only through one or more bona fide associations, the membership of the individual in the association (on the basis of which the coverage is provided) ceases but only if the coverage is terminated under this subdivision uniformly without regard to any health status-related factor of covered individuals.

(c) Requirements for Uniform Termination of Coverage. —

(1) Particular type of coverage not offered. — In any case in which a health insurer decides to discontinue offering a particular type of health insurance coverage offered in the individual market, coverage of the type may be discontinued by the health insurer only if:

a. The health insurer provides notice, notwithstanding G.S. 58-51-20 or G.S. 58-65-60(c)(3)b., to each covered individual provided coverage of this type in the market of the discontinuation at least 90 days before the date of the discontinuation of the coverage;

b. The health insurer offers to each individual in the individual market provided coverage of this type, the option to purchase any other individual health insurance coverage currently being offered by the health insurer for individuals in the market; and

c. In exercising the option to discontinue coverage of this type and in offering the option of coverage under sub-subdivision b. of this subdivision, the health insurer acts uniformly without regard to any health status-related factor of enrolled individuals or individuals who may become eligible for the coverage.

(2) Discontinuance of all coverage. —

a. In general. — Subject to sub-subdivision c. of this subdivision, in any case in which a health insurer elects to discontinue offering all health insurance coverage in the individual market in this State, health insurance coverage may be discontinued by the health insurer only if: (i) the health insurer provides notice to the Commissioner and to each individual of the discontinuation at least 180 days before the date of the expiration of the coverage, and (ii) all health insurance coverage issued or delivered for issuance in this State in the market is discontinued and the health insurance coverage in the market is not renewed.

b. Prohibition on market reentry. — In the case of a discontinuation under sub-subdivision a. of this subdivision in the individual market, the health insurer shall not provide for the issuance of any health insurance coverage in the market and this State during the five-year period beginning on the date of the discontinuation of the last health insurance coverage not so renewed.

(d) Exception for Uniform Modification of Coverage. — At the time of coverage renewal, a health insurer may modify the health insurance coverage for a policy form offered to individuals in the individual market as long as the modification is consistent with State law and effective on a uniform basis among all individuals with that policy form.

(e) Application to Coverage Offered Only Through Associations. — In applying this section in the case of health insurance coverage that is made available by a health insurer in the individual market to individuals only through one or more associations, a reference to an "individual" is deemed to include a reference to the association of which the individual is a member. (1997-259, s. 1(c).)

§ 58-68-70. Certification of coverage.

G.S. 58-68-30(e) applies to health insurance coverage offered by a health insurer in the individual market in the same manner that it applies to health insurance coverage offered by a health insurer in the small or large group market. (1997-259, s. 1(c).)

§ 58-68-75. General exceptions.

(a) Exception for Certain Benefits. — This Part does not apply to any health insurance coverage in relation to its provision of excepted benefits described in G.S. 58-68-25(b)(1).

(b) Exception for Certain Benefits if Certain Conditions Met. — This Part does not apply to any health insurance coverage in relation to its provision of excepted benefits described in G.S. 58-68-25(b)(2), (3), or (4) if the benefits are provided under a separate policy, certificate, or contract of insurance. (1997-259, s. 1(c).)

ARTICLE 68A.

Health Care Reform Planning.

§§ 58-68A-1 through 58-68A-10: Repealed by Session Laws 1995 (Regular Session, 1996), c. 17, s. 16.

ARTICLE 69.

Motor Clubs and Associations.

§ 58-69-1: Repealed by Session Laws 1999-132, s. 12.1, effective June 4, 1999.

Editor's Note. — Article 69 is former Article 9B, G.S. 66-49.9 through 66-49.23, of Chapter 66. Article 9B of Chapter 66 has been recodified as Article 69 of Chapter 58 pursuant to Session Laws 1987, c. 752, s. 9, as amended by Session Laws 1987 (Reg. Sess., 1988), c. 975, s. 34.

§ 58-69-2. Definitions.

As used in this Article:
(1) "Branch or district office" means any physical location, other than a motor club's home office, that is used by the motor club or its representatives as a principal place of business for conducting any type of business authorized under this Article and as a place of business that is used by clients or prospective clients in meeting or dealing with the motor club or its representatives in the normal course of business authorized under this Article.
(2) "Licensee" means a motor club to which a license has been issued under this Article.
(3) "Motor club" means any person, whether or not residing, domiciled, or chartered in this State, that, in consideration of dues, assessments, or periodic payments of money, promises its members to assist them in matters relating to the ownership, operation, use, or maintenance of motor vehicles by rendering three or more of the following services:
a. Automobile theft reward service. — A reward payable to any person, law enforcement agency, or officer for information leading

to the recovery of a member's stolen vehicle and to the apprehension and conviction of the person or persons unlawfully taking the vehicle.

    b. Bail or cash appearance bond service. — The furnishing of cash or a surety bond for a member accused of a violation of the motor vehicle law, or of any law of this State by reason of an automobile accident to secure the member's release and subsequent appearance in court.

    c. Emergency road service. — Roadside adjustment of a motor vehicle so that the vehicle may be operated under its own power.

    d. Legal service. — Providing for reimbursement to a member for attorneys' fees if criminal proceedings are instituted against the member as a result of the operation of a motor vehicle.

    e. Map service. — The furnishing of road maps to members without cost.

    f. Personal travel and accident insurance service. — Making available to members a personal travel and accident insurance policy issued by a duly licensed insurance company in this State.

    g. Touring service. — The furnishing of touring information to members without cost.

    h. Towing service. — Furnishing means to move a motor vehicle from one place to another under power other than its own. (1963, c. 698; 1983, c. 542; 1985, c. 666, s. 81; 1991, c. 401, s. 1; 1999-132, s. 12.2; 2000-122, s. 7.)

Editor's Note. — Subsection (2) was originally enacted as subsection (3) and subsection (3) was originally enacted as subsection (2). They have been redesignated at the direction of the Revisor of Statutes in order to maintain alphabetical order.

The historical citation for former G.S. 58-69-1 has been incorporated in this section, as G.S. 58-69-1 was nearly identical to this section.

§ 58-69-5. License required.

No motor club, district or branch office of a motor club, or franchise motor club shall engage in business in this State unless it holds a valid license issued to it by the Commissioner as provided in this Article. The license shall at all times be prominently displayed in each office of the entity to which the license is issued. (1963, c. 698; 1991, c. 644, s. 15.)

§ 58-69-10. Applications for licenses; fees; bonds or deposits.

Licenses hereunder shall be obtained by filing written application therefor with the Commissioner in such form and manner as the Commissioner shall require. As a prerequisite to issuance of a license:

    (1) The applicant shall furnish to the Commissioner such data and information as the Commissioner may deem reasonably necessary to enable him to determine, in accordance with the provisions of G.S. 58-69-15, whether or not a license should be issued to the applicant.

    (1a) If the applicant has never been issued a motor club license it shall be required to submit an audited financial statement. If the applicant has previously been licensed the Commissioner may require that the financial statement be audited if it is reasonably necessary to determine whether or not a license should be issued to the applicant.

    (2) If the applicant is a motor club it shall be required to pay to the Commissioner a nonrefundable annual license fee of three hundred

dollars ($300.00) and to deposit or file with the Commissioner a bond, in favor of the State of North Carolina and executed by a surety company duly authorized to transact business in this State, in the amount of fifty thousand dollars ($50,000), or securities of the type hereinafter specified in the amount of fifty thousand dollars ($50,000), pledged to or made payable to the State of North Carolina and conditioned upon the full compliance by the applicant with the provisions of this Article and the regulations and orders issued by the Commissioner pursuant thereto, and upon the good faith performance by the applicant of its contracts for motor club services.

(3) If the applicant is a branch or district office of a motor club licensed under this Article it shall pay to the Commissioner a nonrefundable license fee of fifty dollars ($50.00).

(4) If the applicant is a franchise motor club it shall pay to the Commissioner a nonrefundable annual license fee of one hundred dollars ($100.00) and shall deposit or file with the Commissioner a bond, in favor of the State of North Carolina and executed by a surety company duly authorized to transact business in this State, in the amount of fifty thousand dollars ($50,000), or securities of the type hereinafter specified in the amount of fifty thousand dollars ($50,000), pledged to or made payable to the State of North Carolina and conditioned upon the full compliance by the applicant with the provisions of this Article and the regulations and orders issued by the Commissioner pursuant thereto and upon the good faith performance by the applicant of its contracts for motor club services.

(5) Any applicant depositing securities under this section shall do so in the form and manner as prescribed in Article 5 of this Chapter, and the provisions of Article 5 of this Chapter, shall be applicable to securities pledged under this Article. (1963, c. 698; 1983, c. 790, ss. 7-9; 1991, c. 425, s. 1; c. 721, s. 2.)

§ 58-69-15. Issuance or refusal of license; notice of hearing on refusal; renewal.

Within 60 days after an application for license is filed, the Commissioner shall issue a license to the applicant unless he shall find:

(1) That the applicant has not met all of the requirements of this Article, or

(2) That the applicant does not have sufficient financial responsibility to engage in business as a motor club in this State, or

(3) That the applicant has failed to make a reasonable showing that its managers, officers, directors and agents are persons of reliability and integrity. If any such finding is made, the Commissioner shall notify the applicant as soon as practicable of the reason for his refusal to issue the license, and inform the applicant of its right to a hearing on the matters as provided in G.S. 58-69-25. All licenses issued hereunder, and all renewals thereof, shall expire on June 30 following such issuance or renewal. Renewal of all licenses not previously revoked or suspended shall be automatic upon timely payment by the licensee of the annual fee. (1963, c. 698.)

§ 58-69-20. Powers of Commissioner.

The Commissioner shall have the same powers and authority for the purpose of conducting investigations and hearings under this Article as that vested in him by G.S. 58-2-50 and 58-2-70.

(1) To investigate possible violation of this Article and to report evidence thereof to the Attorney General who may recommend prosecution to the appropriate solicitor;

(2) To suspend or revoke any license issued under this Article upon a finding, after notice and opportunity for hearing, that the holder of said license has violated any of the provisions of this Article, or has failed to maintain the standards requisite to original licensing as indicated in G.S. 58-69-15 hereof;

(3) To require any licensee to cease doing business through any particular agent or representative upon a finding after notice and opportunity for hearing, that such agent or representative has intentionally made false or misleading statements concerning the motor club services offered by the motor club represented by him;

(4) To approve or disapprove the name, trademarks, emblems, and all forms which an applicant for license or licensee employs or proposes to employ in connection with its business. If such name, trademarks or emblems is distinctive and not likely to confuse or mislead the public as to the nature or identity of the motor club using or proposing to use it, then it shall be approved, otherwise, the Commissioner may disapprove its use and effectuate such disapproval by the issuance of an appropriate order; and

(5) To make any rules or regulations necessary to enforce the provisions of this Article. (1963, c. 698; 1987, c. 864, s. 3(c).)

§ 58-69-25. Hearing on denial of license.

Whenever the Commissioner denies an initial application for a license, he shall notify the applicant and advise, in writing, the applicant of the reasons for the denial or nonrenewal of the license. Within 30 days of receipt of notification the applicant may make written demand upon the Commissioner for a hearing to determine the reasonableness of the Commissioner's action. Such hearing shall be scheduled within 30 days from the date of receipt of the written demand. (1963, c. 698; 1989, c. 485, s. 32.)

§ 58-69-30. Agent for service of process.

Every motor club licensed hereunder shall appoint and maintain at all times an agent for service of process who shall be a resident of North Carolina. (1963, c. 698.)

§ 58-69-35. Violations; penalty.

Any person, firm, association or corporation who shall violate any of the provisions of this Article shall be guilty of a Class 1 misdemeanor. (1963, c. 698; 1993, c. 539, s. 471; 1994, Ex. Sess., c. 24, s. 14(c).)

§ 58-69-40. Disposition of fees.

All fees collected by the Commissioner under this Article shall be credited to the Insurance Regulatory Fund created under G.S. 58-6-25. (1963, c. 698; 1991, c. 689, s. 292; 1993 (Reg. Sess., 1994), c. 678, s. 30; 2003-221, s. 7.)

Effect of Amendments. — Session Laws 2003-221, s. 7, effective June 19, 2003, substituted "Insurance Regulatory Fund" for "Department of Insurance Fund."

§ 58-69-45. Insurance licensing provisions not affected.

Nothing in this Article shall be construed as amending, repealing, or in any way affecting any laws now in force relating to the licensing of Motor Club Membership Sales Agents or to the licensing or regulation of insurance agents and insurance companies, as provided in Articles 1 through 64 of this Chapter. (1963, c. 698; 1983, c. 802, s. 3.)

§ 58-69-50. Authority for qualified surety companies to guarantee certain arrest bond certificates.

(a) Any domestic or foreign surety company that is authorized to do business in this State may become a surety, by filing with the Department an undertaking to become a surety, in an amount not to exceed one thousand five hundred dollars ($1,500) with respect to each guaranteed arrest bond certificate issued by a motor club.

(b) The undertaking shall be in a form to be prescribed by the Department and shall state:

 (1) The name and address of the motor club or clubs with respect to which the surety company undertakes to guarantee the arrest bond certificates.

 (2) The unqualified obligation of the surety company to pay the fine or forfeiture, in an amount not to exceed one thousand five hundred dollars ($1,500) of any person who, after posting a guaranteed arrest bond certificate which the surety has undertaken to guarantee, fails to make the appearance for which the guaranteed arrest bond certificate was posted. (1985, c. 623, s. 1; 1989, c. 663, s. 1; 1999-132, s. 12.3.)

Editor's Note. — The historical citation for former G.S. 58-77-5 has been incorporated in this section, as G.S. 58-77-5 was nearly identical to this section.

§ 58-69-55. Guaranteed arrest bond certificates accepted.

(a) Any guaranteed arrest bond certificate guaranteed by a surety company under G.S. 58-69-50 shall be accepted in lieu of cash bail or other bond in an amount not to exceed one thousand five hundred dollars ($1,500) as a bail bond, when signed by the person whose signature appears on the certificate, to guarantee the appearance of that person in any court in this State at the time set by the court when the person is arrested for the violation of any motor vehicle law of this State or any motor vehicle ordinance of any municipality of this State. The guaranteed arrest bond certificate shall not apply to, and shall not be accepted in lieu of, cash bail or bond when the person has been arrested for any impaired driving offense or for any felony.

(b) A guaranteed arrest bond certificate that is posted as a bail bond in any court shall be subject to the forfeiture and enforcement provisions with respect to bail bonds in criminal cases as provided by law. (1985, c. 623, s. 1; 1989, c. 663, s. 2; 1999-132, s. 12.4.)

Editor's Note. — The historical citation for former G.S. 58-77-5 has been incorporated in this section, as G.S. 58-77-5 was nearly identical to this section.

ARTICLE 70.

Collection Agencies.

Part 1. Permit Procedures.

§ 58-70-1. Permit from Commissioner of Insurance; penalty for violation; exception.

No person, firm, corporation, or association shall conduct or operate a collection agency or do a collection agency business, as the same is hereinafter defined in this Article, until he or it shall have secured a permit therefor as provided in this Article. Any person, firm, corporation or association conducting or operating a collection agency or doing a collection agency business without the permit shall be guilty of a Class I felony. Any officer or agent of any person, firm, corporation or association, who shall personally and knowingly participate in any violation of the remaining provisions of this Part shall be guilty of a Class 1 misdemeanor. Provided, however, that nothing in this section shall be construed to require a regular employee of a duly licensed collection agency in this State to procure a collection agency permit. (1931, c. 217, s. 1; 1943, c. 170; 1959, c. 1194, s. 1; 1969, c. 906, s. 1; 1979, c. 835; 1989, c. 441, s. 1; 1993, c. 539, ss. 472, 1275; 1994, Ex. Sess., c. 24, s. 14(c).)

Editor's Note. — This Article is former Article 9, G.S. 66-41 through 66-44, as rewritten by Session Laws 1979, c. 835, and recodified as Article 9C of Chapter 66, G.S. 66-49.24 to 66-49.50, which in turn has been recodified as Article 70 of Chapter 58 pursuant to Session Laws 1987, c. 752, s. 9, as amended by Session Laws 1987 (Reg. Sess., 1988) c. 975, s. 34. Where appropriate, the historical citations to the former Articles have been added to corresponding sections in the Article as rewritten.

CASE NOTES

Contract in Violation of Article Not Enforceable. — A contract entered into and signed in this State between plaintiff, a nonresident collection agency, and defendant, a State resident, calling for the collection of the accounts of the defendant in this State, was not enforceable in this State. Divine v. Watauga Hosp., 137 F. Supp. 628 (M.D.N.C. 1956), decided under former Article 9 of Chapter 66 before its revision and recodification.

§ 58-70-5. Application to Commissioner for permit.

Any person, firm, corporation or association desiring to secure a permit as provided by G.S. 58-70-1, shall make application to the Commissioner of Insurance for each location at which such person, firm, corporation or association desires to carry on the collection agency business as hereinafter defined. Such applicant shall be entitled to a permit upon submission to the Commissioner of Insurance of the following:

(a) The name, trade name if any, street address, and telephone number of the applicant, including any home office address and telephone number, if different;

(b) If the applicant is a corporation,

    (1) A certified copy of the board of director's resolution authorizing the submission of the application;

    (2) An authenticated copy of the Articles of Incorporation and all amendments thereto;

    (3) An authenticated copy of the bylaws or other governing instruments;

(4) If the applicant is a foreign corporation, a copy of the certificate of authority to transact business in this State issued by the North Carolina Secretary of State;

(c) If the applicant is a partnership, an authenticated copy of the then current partnership agreement;

(d) If the trade name is used, certificates showing that the trade name has been filed as required by G.S. 66-68;

(e) A surety bond as required by G.S. 58-70-20;

(f) A completed statement by each stockholder owning ten percent (10%) or more of the applicant's outstanding voting stock and each partner, director, and officer actively engaged in the collection agency business, containing: the name of the collection agency, the name and address of the individual completing the form, the positions held by the individual, each conviction of any criminal offense and any criminal charges pending other than minor traffic violations of the individual, and the name and address of three people not related to the individual who can attest to the individual's reputation for honesty and fair dealings;

(g) A statement sworn to by an appropriate corporate officer, partner, or individual proprietor giving a description of the collection method to be employed in North Carolina;

(h) A statement certifying that there are no unsatisfied judgments against the applicant;

(i) A list of all telephone numbers assigned to, or to be used by the applicant in the operation of the collection agency;

(j) The appropriate permit fee as required by G.S. 58-70-35;

(k) A balance sheet as of the last day of the month prior to the date of submission of the application, certified true and correct by a corporate officer, partner, or proprietor, setting forth the current assets, fixed assets, current liabilities and positive net worth of the applicant;

(l) The address of the location at which the applicant will make those records of its collection agency business described in G.S. 58-70-25 available for inspection by the Commissioner of Insurance.

(m) A statement certifying that no officer, individual proprietor or partner of the applicant has been convicted of a felony involving moral turpitude, or any violation of any State or federal debt collection law.

(n) If the collection agency's office or records, as described in G.S. 58-70-25, are located outside of North Carolina, a statement sworn to by an appropriate corporate officer, partner, or individual proprietor consenting to and authorizing the reimbursement, to the Commissioner by the collection agency, of expenses incurred by the Commissioner in conducting routine examinations, audits, and in investigating written complaints against the collection agency or its employees. All reimbursements shall be paid to the Commissioner no more than 30 days after the date of billing.

(o) If the applicant is a foreign corporation, a statement authorizing the Commissioner to be its agent for service of process, which shall be administered pursuant to the provisions of G.S. 58-16-30. (1931, c. 217, s. 2; 1943, c. 170; 1959, c. 1194, s. 2; 1969, c. 906, s. 2; 1979, c. 835; 1989, c. 441, ss. 2, 3; 2001-269, s. 1.1.)

§ 58-70-10. Application to Commissioner for permit renewal.

Any person, firm, corporation or association desiring to renew a permit issued pursuant to G.S. 58-70-5 shall make application to the Commissioner of Insurance not less than 30 days prior to the expiration date of the then current permit. Such renewal applicant shall be entitled to a renewal permit upon submission to the Commissioner of Insurance of all the information as required by G.S. 58-70-5; provided, however, it shall be sufficient, wherever applicable, to reference the prior year's application if there has been no change as to any of the required information and it shall not be necessary to submit with a renewal application a new director's resolution. In addition, the applicant shall submit to the Commissioner a copy of a "continuation certificate" or paid receipt for renewal premiums for the collection agency bond for the year for which the renewal permit is applied. The application shall include a calculation in accordance with G.S. 58-70-20, and if the bond is increased, an endorsement by the surety. With a renewal application, the applicant shall submit a balance sheet for the last fiscal year ending prior to the application, certified true and correct by a corporate officer, partner, or proprietor, setting forth the current assets, fixed assets, current liabilities and positive net worth of the applicant. (1979, c. 835.)

§ 58-70-15. Definition of collection agency and collection agency business.

(a) "Collection agency" means a person directly or indirectly engaged in soliciting, from more than one person delinquent claims of any kind owed or due or asserted to be owed or due the solicited person and all persons directly or indirectly engaged in the asserting, enforcing or prosecuting of those claims.

(b) "Collection agency" includes:

(1) Any person that procures a listing of delinquent debtors from any creditor and that sells the listing or otherwise receives any fee or benefit from collections made on the listing; and

(2) Any person that attempts to or does transfer or sell to any person not holding the permit prescribed by this Article any system or series of letters or forms for use in the collection of delinquent accounts or claims which by direct assertion or by implication indicate that the claim or account is being asserted or collected by any person, firm, corporation, or association other than the creditor or owner of the claim or demand; and

(3) An in-house collection agency, whereby a person, firm, corporation, or association sets up a collection service for his or its own business and the agency has a name other than that of the business.

(c) "Collection agency" does not mean:

(1) Regular employees of a single creditor;

(2) Banks, trust companies, or bank-owned, controlled or related firms, corporations or associations engaged in accounting, bookkeeping or data processing services where a primary component of such services is the rendering of statements of accounts and bookkeeping services for creditors;

(3) Mortgage banking companies;

(4) Savings and loan associations;

(5) Building and loan associations;

(6) Duly licensed real estate brokers and agents when the claims or accounts being handled by the broker or agent are related to or are in connection with the broker's or agent's regular real estate business;

(7) Express, telephone and telegraph companies subject to public regulation and supervision;

(8) Attorneys-at-law handling claims and collections in their own name and not operating a collection agency under the management of a layman;

(9) Any person, firm, corporation or association handling claims, accounts or collections under an order or orders of any court;

   (10) A person, firm, corporation or association which, for valuable consideration purchases accounts, claims, or demands of another, which such accounts, claims, or demands of another are not delinquent at the time of such purchase, and then, in its own name, proceeds to assert or collect the accounts, claims or demands;

   (11) Any person attempting to collect or collecting claims, in that person's name, of a business or businesses owned wholly or substantially by that person;

   (12) Any nonprofit tax exempt corporation organized for the purpose of providing mediation or other dispute resolution services; and

   (13) The designated representatives of programs as defined by G.S. 110-129(5). (1969, c. 906, s. 3; 1973, c. 785; 1979, c. 835; 1989, c. 441, ss. 4, 5, 12; 1991, c. 387, s. 1; 1993, c. 553, s. 22; 1999-419, s. 1; 2001-269, s. 1.2.)

§ 58-70-20. Bond requirement.

  (a) As a condition precedent to the issuance of any permit under this Article, every applicant for a permit shall file with the Commissioner a bond in favor of the State of North Carolina that is executed by a surety company licensed to transact surety business in this State. The bond shall be maintained in force during the permit period, continuous in form, and remain in effect until all moneys collected have been accounted for. The bond shall expressly provide that the bond is for the benefit of any person, firm or corporation for whom the collection agency engages in the collection of accounts. The bond shall be in the amount of ten thousand dollars ($10,000) for the initial permit. The amount of the bond for any renewal permit shall be no less than ten thousand dollars ($10,000), nor more than seventy-five thousand dollars ($75,000), and shall be computed as follows: The total collections paid directly to the collection agency less commissions earned by the collection agency on those collections for the calendar year ending immediately prior to the date of application, multiplied by one-sixth.

  (b) A person required by this section to maintain a bond may, in lieu of that bond, deposit with the Commissioner the equivalent amount in cash, in certificates of deposit issued by banks organized under the laws of the State of North Carolina, or any national bank having its principal office in North Carolina, or securities, which shall be held in accordance with Article 5 of this Chapter. Securities may only be obligations of the United States or of federal agencies listed in G.S. 147-69.1(c) (2) guaranteed by the United States, obligations of the State of North Carolina, or obligations of a city or county of this State. Any proposed deposit of an obligation of a city or county of this State is subject to the prior approval of the Commissioner.

  (c) In addition to the requirements of subsections (a) and (b) of this section, as a condition precedent to the issuance of any permit under this Article, every nonresident applicant for a permit shall file with the Commissioner a bond in the amount of ten thousand dollars ($10,000) in favor of the Department that is executed by a surety company licensed to transact surety business in this State. The bond shall be maintained in force during the permit period, be continuous in form, and remain in effect until terminated by the Commissioner. The bond shall expressly provide that the bond is for the purpose of reimbursing the Department for expenses incurred in visiting and examining a nonresident collection agency in connection with a federal bankruptcy or State receivership proceeding in which the collection agency is the subject of the proceeding. (1943, c. 170; 1959, c. 1194, s. 3; 1979, c. 835; 1991, c. 212, s. 4; 2001-269, s. 1.3.)

§ 58-70-25. Record of business in State.

(a) Each person, firm, or corporation licensed as a collection agency in North Carolina shall keep a full and correct record of all business done in this State as set forth below. All such records pertaining to collection activity, concerning debtor records and client accounting records, but not general operating records, shall be open to inspection by the Commissioner of Insurance or his duly authorized deputy upon demand.

(b) Every permit holder shall maintain adequate records which shall contain the items listed below. These records must be kept separate from records of any other business and must be maintained for not less than three years after the final entry has been made:

(1) A daily collection record or cash receipt journal in which all collections are recorded and allocated as to total collections, setting forth:
   a. The amount credited to principal and to interest, if any;
   b. The amount due creditors or forwarders.
(2) The amount retained as commission or commission paid to forwardees.
(3) Payments made directly to creditors as reported to the collection agency by those creditors and commissions due the collection agency on those payments.
(4) A record of each debtor's account shall be maintained consisting of the following:
   a. The name and address of the debtor;
   b. The name of the creditor or forwarder or forwardee if the account has been forwarded;
   c. The principal amount owing and, if available, the date of the last credit or debit;
   d. The amount and date of each payment made by the debtor; and
   e. The date and time of each telephone or personal contact with the debtor.
(5) A master alphabetical record by name and address of every creditor or forwarder with whom the permit holder engages in the business of collecting accounts.
(6) A check register or carbon copies of each check issued or numerically numbered check stubs corresponding with all checks issued on the trust account for funds collected on behalf of creditors. Cancelled checks, together with voided or unused checks (adequately explained) drawn on the trust account shall be maintained in numerical order with the monthly bank statements.
(7) A record by client or client number showing the number of accounts received from the client, the date received and the principal amount of the accounts.
(8) A duplicate copy of each remittance statement furnished a creditor or forwarder, or other listing of the information contained on the statement. (1959, c. 1194, s. 3; 1979, c. 835; 1989, c. 441, s. 6.)

§ 58-70-30. Hearing granted applicant if application denied; appeal.

If, upon application, the Commissioner finds that the permit should not be issued or renewed and denies an application, he shall notify the applicant or permittee and advise, in writing, the applicant or permittee of the reasons for the denial or nonrenewal of the permit. Within 30 days of receipt of notification the applicant or permittee may make written demand upon the Commissioner for a hearing to determine the reasonableness of the Commissioner's action. Such hearing shall be scheduled within 30 days and held within 90 days from the date of receipt of the written demand. An applicant or permittee has the right to appeal any order or any unreasonable delay pursuant to Article 4 of Chapter 150B of the General Statutes. If the Commissioner shall decline an application for renewal, that applicant may continue to do business pending any appeal taken pursuant hereto. (1931, c. 217, s. 3; 1979, c. 835; 1989, c. 441, s. 7; c. 770, s. 51.)

§ 58-70-35. Application fee; issuance of permit; contents and duration.

(a) Upon the filing of the application and information required by this Article, the applicant shall pay a nonrefundable fee of five hundred dollars ($500.00), and no permit may be issued until this fee is paid. Fees collected under this subsection shall be used in paying the expenses incurred in connection with the consideration of such applications and the issuance of such permits.

(b) Each permit shall state the name of the applicant, his place of business, and the nature and kind of business in which he is engaged. The Commissioner shall assign to the permit a serial number for each year, and each permit shall be for a period of one year, beginning with July 1 and ending with June 30 of the following year.

(c) A permit is assignable or transferable only if the assignee or transferee qualifies under the provisions of this Article. Upon any change in ownership of a permittee, if a sole proprietorship or partnership, or upon a change in ownership of more than fifty percent (50%) of the shares or voting rights of a corporate permittee, a permit issued to a permittee is void unless within 30 days of the change of ownership the new owner or owners have satisfied the Commissioner that he or they qualify for a permit under this Article, and he or they maintain a bond in accordance with and in the amount required for a renewal bond under G.S. 58-70-20. (1931, c. 217, s. 4; 1979, c. 835; 1983, c. 790, s. 10; 1989, c. 441, s. 8; 1991, c. 721, s. 3.)

§ 58-70-40. Restraining orders; criminal convictions; permit revocations; other permit requirements.

(a) When it appears to the Commissioner that any person has violated, is violating, or threatens to violate any provision of this Article, he may apply to the superior court of any county in which the violation has occurred, is occurring, or may occur for a restraining order and injunction to restrain such violation, or threatened violation. If upon application the court finds that any provision of this Article has been violated, is being violated, or a violation thereof is threatened, the court shall issue an order restraining and enjoining such violations; and such relief may be granted regardless of whether criminal prosecution is instituted under any provision of this Article.

(b) The conviction by a court of competent jurisdiction of any permittee for a violation of this Article shall automatically have the effect of suspending the permit of that permittee until such time that the permit is reinstated by the Commissioner. As used in this subsection, "conviction" includes an adjudication of guilt, a plea of guilty, and a plea of nolo contendere.

(c) In addition to the other qualifications for a permit under this Article, no collection agency shall be issued or be entitled to hold a permit if the Commissioner finds as to the applicant or permittee any one or more of the following conditions:

    (1) An individual proprietor, officer, or partner of the collection agency has been convicted of a felony involving moral turpitude, or any State or federal debt collection law.

(2) There is an unsatisfied judgment which is not currently the subject of litigation against any partner, individual proprietor, or officer of the collection agency or against the collection agency.

(3) There is any materially false or misleading information in the permit application.

(4) The applicant has obtained or attempted to obtain the permit through misrepresentation or fraud.

(5) There has been an adjudication that a partner, individual proprietor, or officer of the collection agency has violated any State or federal unfair trade practice law.

(6) A partner, individual proprietor, or officer of the collection agency has violated or refused to comply with any provision of this Article or any order of the Commissioner.

(7) Another jurisdiction has suspended or revoked a collection agency or similar license or permit of the collection agency. (1931, c. 217, s. 5; 1979, c. 835; 1989, c. 441, s. 9.)

§ 58-70-45. Disposition of permit fees.

All permit fees collected under this Article shall be credited to the Insurance Regulatory Fund created under G.S. 58-6-25. (1931, c. 217, s. 8; 1943, c. 170; 1979, c. 835; 1991, c. 689, s. 293; 2003-221, s. 8.)

Effect of Amendments. — Session Laws 2003-221, s. 8, effective June 19, 2003, substituted "Insurance Regulatory Fund" for "Department of Insurance Fund."

§ 58-70-50. All collection agencies to identify themselves in correspondence.

All collection agencies licensed under this Part to do the business of a collection agency in this State, shall in all correspondence with debtors use stationery or forms which contain the permit number and the true name and address of such collection agency.

The permit to engage in the business of a collection agency shall at all times be prominently displayed in each office of the person, firm, corporation or association to whom or to which the permit is issued. (1931, c. 217, s. 9; 1969, c. 906, s. 5; 1979, c. 835.)

Part 2. Operating Procedures.

§ 58-70-55. Office hours.

If an office of a duly licensed collection agency does not maintain normally accepted business hours, the hours the office is open shall be posted so as to be prominently displayed to the public at all times. If at any time it is anticipated that the permit holder's office will be closed to the public for a period exceeding seven days, the Department of Insurance shall be notified thereof in writing. (1979, c. 835.)

§ 58-70-60. Statements to be furnished each collection creditor.

(a) Acknowledgment of Accounts. — When any account is received for collection, the permit holder shall upon request furnish the collection creditor or forwarder with a written listing or acknowledgment of the accounts received.

(b) Remittance Statements. — Each permit holder shall remit all moneys due to any collection creditor or forwarder within 30 days after the end of the collection month during which the collection was effected. The remittance shall be accompanied by a statement setting forth:

   (1) The date of remittance;

   (2) The debtor's name;

   (3) The date or month of collection and amount collected from each debtor; and

   (4) A breakdown showing money collected from each debtor and the amount due the creditor or forwarder. (1979, c. 835.)

§ 58-70-65. Remittance trust account.

(a) Each permit holder shall deposit, no later than two banking days after receipt, in a separate trust account in any bank located in North Carolina or in any other bank approved by the Commissioner, sufficient funds to pay all moneys due or owed to all collection creditors or forwarders. The funds shall remain in the trust account until remitted to the creditor or forwarder, and shall not be commingled with any other operating funds. The trust account shall be used only for the purpose of:

   (1) Remitting to collection creditors or forwarders the proceeds to which they are entitled.

   (2) Remitting to the collection agency the commission that is due the collection agency.

   (3) Reimbursing consumers for overpayments.

   (4) Making adjustments to the trust account balance for bank service charges.

(b) No refund for overpayment by a debtor in an amount of less than one dollar ($1.00) is required.

(c) Each permit holder located outside this State shall deposit in a separate trust account, designated for its North Carolina creditors, funds to pay all monies due or owing all collection creditors or forwarders located within this State. (1979, c. 835; 1989, c. 441, s. 10; c. 770, s. 52; 1991, c. 644, s. 23; 1993 (Reg. Sess., 1994), c. 678, s. 31.)

§ 58-70-70. Receipt requirement.

Whenever a payment is received in cash from a debtor, forwardee, or other person, an original receipt or an exact copy thereof shall be furnished the individual from whom payment is received. Evidence of all receipts issued shall be kept in the permit holder's office for three years. All receipts issued must:

   (1) Be prenumbered by the printer and used and filed in consecutive numerical order;

   (2) Show the name, street address and permit number of the permit holder;

   (3) Show the name of the creditor or creditors for whom collected;

   (4) Show the amount and date paid; and

   (5) Show the last name of the person accepting payment. (1979, c. 835.)

§ 58-70-75. Creditor may request return of accounts.

The written request of a creditor or forwarder for the return of any account which is not in the actual process of collection shall be complied with by the permit holder in writing within a reasonable length of time, but in any event not to exceed 60 days. All valuable papers furnished by the creditor or forwarder in connection with the account shall be returned. (1979, c. 835.)

§ 58-70-80. Return of accounts and all valuable papers upon termination of permit.

Whenever the permit of a collection agency is revoked, cancelled, or terminated for any reason, all accounts and valuable papers placed with the agency for collection shall be returned to the person placing the account for collection within five days of the termination of said permit unless, upon written application, an extension of time is granted by the Department of Insurance. All agreements between the collection agency and creditor or forwarder are automatically cancelled as of the date on which said permit is revoked, cancelled or terminated. If any of the accounts placed for collection are in the hands of others at the time of the permit termination, they shall immediately be notified by the collection agency to thereafter correspond, remit and be solely responsible to the creditor placing the accounts with the agency for collection unless the creditor has authorized a successor or other permit holder to continue to collect the accounts. In the case of dissolution of the collection agency, all accounts shall be returned within a reasonable period of time, but in any event not to exceed 60 days. Valuable papers shall include, but not be limited to, notes payable, creditor account cards and any other items placed within the collection agency by the creditor. (1979, c. 835.)

§ 58-70-85. Application of funds where there is a debtor-creditor relationship.

If a creditor has listed accounts with a permit holder for collection and also has had accounts on which he is debtor listed with the permit holder by any other creditors, collections effected in his behalf as a creditor may not be applied on accounts that he owes unless the permit holder has a written authorization on file as to how the moneys collected are to be applied. (1979, c. 835.)

Part 3. Prohibited Practices by Collection Agencies Engaged in the Collection of Debts from Consumers.

§ 58-70-90. Definitions.

As used in this Part, the following terms have the meanings specified:
- (1) "Collection agency" means a collection agency as defined in G.S. 58-70-15 which engages, directly or indirectly, in debt collection from a consumer.
- (2) "Consumer" means an individual, aggregation of individuals, corporation, company, association, or partnership that has incurred a debt or alleged debt.
- (3) "Debt" means any obligation owed or due or alleged to be owed or due from a consumer. (1961, c. 782; 1971, c. 814, ss. 1-3; 1979, c. 835.)

§ 58-70-95. Threats and coercion.

No collection agency shall collect or attempt to collect any debt alleged to be due and owing from a consumer by means of any unfair threat, coercion, or attempt to coerce. Such unfair acts include, but are not limited to, the following:
- (1) Using or threatening to use violence or any illegal means to cause harm to the person, reputation or property of any person;

(2) Falsely accusing or threatening to accuse any person of fraud or any crime, or of any conduct that would tend to cause disgrace, contempt or ridicule;

(3) Making or threatening to make false accusations to another person, including any credit reporting agency, that a consumer has not paid, or has willfully refused to pay a just debt;

(4) Threatening to sell or assign, or to refer to another for collection, the debt of the consumer with an attending representation that the result of such sale, assignment or reference would be that the consumer would lose any defense to the debt or would be subject to harsh, vindictive, or abusive collection attempts;

(5) Representing that nonpayment of an alleged debt may result in the arrest of any person;

(6) Representing that nonpayment of an alleged debt may result in the seizure, garnishment, attachment, or sale of any property or wages unless such action is in fact contemplated by the debt collector and permitted by law;

(7) Threatening to take any action not in fact taken in the usual course of business, unless it can be shown that such threatened action was actually intended to be taken in the particular case in which the threat was made;

(8) Threatening to take any action not permitted by law. (1979, c. 835.)

Legal Periodicals. — For note on intentional infliction of emotional distress, see 18 Wake Forest L. Rev. 624 (1982).

CASE NOTES

Attorney's fees are available for plaintiffs alleging violations of this section who can satisfy the requirements set forth at G.S. 75-16.1. Llera v. Security Credit Sys., 93 F. Supp. 2d 674, 2000 U.S. Dist. LEXIS 3646 (W.D.N.C. 2000).

§ 58-70-100. Harassment.

No collection agency shall use any conduct, the natural consequence of which is to oppress, harass, or abuse any person in connection with the attempt to collect any debt. Such conduct includes, but is not limited to, the following:

(1) Using profane or obscene language, or language that would ordinarily abuse the typical hearer or reader;

(2) Placing collect telephone calls or sending collect telegrams unless the caller fully identifies himself and the company he represents;

(3) Causing a telephone to ring or engaging any person in telephone conversation with such frequency as to be unreasonable or to constitute a harassment to the person under the circumstances or at times known to be times other than normal waking hours of the person;

(4) Placing telephone calls or attempting to communicate with any person, contrary to his instructions, at his place of employment, unless the collection agency does not have a telephone number where the consumer can be reached during the consumer's nonworking hours. (1979, c. 835.)

§ 58-70-105. Unreasonable publication.

No collection agency shall unreasonably publicize information regarding a consumer's debt. Such unreasonable publication includes, but is not limited to, the following:

(1) Any communication with any person other than the debtor or his attorney, except:
　　a. With the permission of the debtor or his attorney;
　　b. To persons employed by the collection agency, to a credit reporting agency, to a person or business employed to collect the debt on behalf of the creditor, or to a person who makes a legitimate request for the information;
　　c. To the spouse (or one who stands in place of the spouse) of the debtor, or to the parent or guardian of the debtor if the debtor is a minor;
　　d. For the sole purpose of locating the debtor, if no indication of indebtedness is made;
　　e. Through legal process.
(2) Using any form of communication which ordinarily would be seen or heard by any person other than the consumer that displays or conveys any information about the alleged debt other than the name, address and phone number of the collection agency except as otherwise provided in this Part.
(3) Disclosing any information relating to a consumer's debt by publishing or posting any list of consumers, except for credit reporting purposes. (1979, c. 835.)

CASE NOTES

Claim Stated. — An allegation that debt collector contacted debtor's neighbor for a purpose other than locating the debtor is sufficient to state a claim. West v. Nationwide Credit, Inc., 998 F. Supp. 642 (W.D.N.C. 1996).

§ 58-70-110. Deceptive representation.

No collection agency shall collect or attempt to collect a debt or obtain information concerning a consumer by any fraudulent, deceptive or misleading representation. Such representations include, but are not limited to, the following:
(1) Communicating with the consumer other than in the name of the person making the communication, the collection agency and the person or business on whose behalf the collection agency is acting or to whom the debt is owed;
(2) Failing to disclose in the initial written communication with the consumer and, in addition, if the initial communication with the consumer is oral, in that initial oral communication, that the debt collector is attempting to collect a debt and that any information obtained will be used for that purpose, and the failure to disclose in subsequent communications that the communication is from a debt collector; provided, however, that this subdivision does not apply to a formal pleading made in connection with legal action;
(3) Falsely representing that the collection agency has in its possession information or something of value for the consumer;
(4) Falsely representing the character, extent, or amount of a debt against a consumer or of its status in any legal proceeding; falsely representing that the collection agency is in any way connected with any agency of the federal, State or local government; or falsely representing the creditor's rights or intentions;
(5) Using or distributing or selling any written communication which simulates or is falsely represented to be a document authorized, issued, or approved by a court, an official, or any other legally

constituted or authorized authority, or which creates a false impression about its source;

(6) Falsely representing that an existing obligation of the consumer may be increased by the addition of attorney's fees, investigation fees, service fees, or any other fees or charges;

(7) Falsely representing the status or true nature of the services rendered by the collection agency or its business. (1979, c. 835; 2001-269, s. 1.4.)

CASE NOTES

Attorney's fees are available for plaintiffs alleging violations of this section who can satisfy the requirements set forth at G.S. 75-16.1.

Llera v. Security Credit Sys., 93 F. Supp. 2d 674, 2000 U.S. Dist. LEXIS 3646 (W.D.N.C. 2000).

§ 58-70-115. Unconscionable means.

No collection agency shall collect or attempt to collect any debt by use of any unconscionable means. Such means include, but are not limited to, the following:

(1) Seeking or obtaining any written statement or acknowledgment in any form containing an affirmation of any debt by a consumer who has been declared bankrupt, an acknowledgment of any debt barred by the statute of limitations, or a waiver of any legal rights of the debtor without disclosing the nature and consequences of such affirmation or waiver and the fact that the consumer is not legally obligated to make such affirmation or waiver;

(2) Collecting or attempting to collect from the consumer all or any part of the collection agency's fee or charge for services rendered, collecting or attempting to collect any interest or other charge, fee or expense incidental to the principal debt unless legally entitled to such fee or charge;

(3) Communicating with a consumer whenever the collection agency has been notified by the consumer's attorney that he represents said consumer. (1979, c. 835.)

§ 58-70-120. Unauthorized practice of law; court appearances.

Neither a collection agency nor any representative thereof who is not a duly licensed attorney shall engage in the practice of law. As used in this section, "practice of law" includes the preparation of warrants or subpoenas. A collection agency's representative is prohibited from appearing in court on behalf of a creditor except as required by court order or subpoena, and except to submit and explain claims in bankruptcy court. (1979, c. 835; 1989, c. 441, s. 11.)

§ 58-70-125. Shared office space.

The office of a collection agency shall not be shared or have a common waiting room with a practicing attorney or any type of lending institution. The office may be located in a private residence only if it is solely for business purposes, has an outside entrance and can be isolated from the remainder of the residence. (1979, c. 835.)

Part 4. Enforcement.

§ 58-70-130. Civil liability.

(a) Any collection agency which violates Part 3 of this Article with respect to any debtor shall be liable to that debtor in an amount equal to the sum of any actual damages sustained by the debtor as a result of the violation.

(b) Any collection agency which violates Part 3 of this Article with respect to any debtor shall, in addition to actual damages sustained by the debtor as a result of the violation, also be liable to the debtor only in an individual action, and its additional liability therein to that debtor shall be for a penalty in such amount as the court may allow, which shall not be less than one hundred dollars ($100.00) for each violation nor greater than two thousand dollars ($2,000) for each violation.

(c) The specific and general provisions of Part 3 of this Article shall constitute unfair or deceptive acts or practices proscribed herein or by G.S. 75-1.1 in the area of commerce regulated thereby. Notwithstanding the provisions of G.S. 75-15.2 and 75-16, civil penalties in excess of two thousand dollars ($2,000) for each violation shall not be imposed, nor shall damages be trebled for any violation under Part 3 of this Article.

(d) The remedies provided by this section shall be cumulative, and in addition to remedies otherwise available. Provided, that any punitive damages assessed against a collection agency shall be reduced by the amount of the civil penalty assessed against such agency pursuant to subsection (b).

(e) The clear proceeds of civil penalties imposed under this section in suits instituted by the Attorney General shall be remitted to the Civil Penalty and Forfeiture Fund in accordance with G.S. 115C-457.2. (1979, c. 835; 1991, c. 68, s. 2; 1998-215, s. 89(a).)

Editor's Note. — Session Laws 1998-215, s. 89, purported to add a new subsection (d). Because there is presently a subsection (d), the new subsection as enacted by Session Laws 1998-215, s. 89 has been designated as new subsection (e) at the direction of the Revisor of Statutes.

CASE NOTES

Attorney's fees are available for plaintiffs alleging violations of this section who can satisfy the requirements set forth at G.S. 75-16.1. Llera v. Security Credit Sys., 93 F. Supp. 2d 674, 2000 U.S. Dist. LEXIS 3646 (W.D.N.C. 2000).

No Proof of Actual Injury. — The jury's assessment of the minimum statutory penalty in subsection (b) of this section was insufficient to prove by a preponderance of the evidence that plaintiff suffered an actual injury; therefore, plaintiff was not entitled to recover attorney's fees under 75-16.1. Llera v. Security Credit Sys., 93 F. Supp. 2d 674, 2000 U.S. LEXIS 3646 (W.D.N.C. 2000).

Construction With Other Laws. — Debtors are protected from unfair debt collection practices under G.S. 58-70-1 et seq. and G.S. 75-1.1 et seq., and although Chapter 58, Article 70 does not set forth provisions for awarding attorney's fees, this section expressly refers to G.S. 75-1.1, which contains an attorney's fee provision at G.S. 75-16.1. Llera v. Security Credit Sys., 93 F. Supp. 2d 674, 2000 U.S. Dist. LEXIS 3646 (W.D.N.C. 2000).

Basis for Recovering Attorney's Fees. — Based on the language set forth in subsection (c), attorney's fees are available for plaintiffs alleging violations of Chapter 58, Article 70 who can satisfy the requirements set forth at G.S. 75-16.1. Llera v. Security Credit Sys., 93 F. Supp. 2d 674, 2000 U.S. Dist. LEXIS 3646 (W.D.N.C. 2000).

Evidence of "Actual Injury" Insufficient. — The assessment of a $100.00 statutory penalty but no actual damages was insufficient to prove that plaintiff suffered an "actual injury." An award of actual damages is contingent on some harm having been suffered by the plaintiff, whereas the statutory penalty is mandatory, and as such, the penalty does not necessarily provide evidence to assist a trial court in determining whether a plaintiff suffered an actual injury. Llera v. Security Credit Sys., 93 F.

Supp. 2d 674, 2000 U.S. Dist. LEXIS 3646
(W.D.N.C. 2000).

ARTICLE 71.

Bail Bondsmen and Runners.

§ 58-71-1. Definitions.

The following words when used in this Article shall have the following meanings:

(1) "Accommodation bondsman" is a person who shall not charge a fee or receive any consideration for action as surety and who endorses the bail bond after providing satisfactory evidences of ownership, value, and marketability of real or personal property to the extent necessary to reasonably satisfy the official taking bond that the real or personal property will in all respects be sufficient to assure that the full principal sum of the bond will be realized if there is a breach of the conditions of the bond. "Consideration" as used in this subdivision does not include the legal rights of a surety against a principal by reason of breach of the conditions of a bail bond nor does it include collateral furnished to and securing the surety as long as the value of the surety's rights in the collateral do not exceed the principal's liability to the surety by reason of a breach in the conditions of the bail bond.

(2) "Bail bond" shall mean an undertaking by the principal to appear in court as required upon penalty of forfeiting bail to the State in a stated amount; and may include an unsecured appearance bond, a premium-secured appearance bond, an appearance bond secured by a cash deposit of the full amount of the bond, an appearance bond secured by a mortgage pursuant to G.S. 58-74-5, and an appearance bond secured by at least one surety. A bail bond may also include a bond securing the return of a motor vehicle subject to forfeiture in accordance with G.S. 20-28.3(e).

(3) "Bail bondsman" shall mean a surety bondsman, professional bondsman or an accommodation bondsman as hereinafter defined.

(4) "Commissioner" shall mean the Commissioner of Insurance.

(4a) "First-year licensee" means any person who has been licensed as a bail bondsman or runner under this Article and who has held the license for a period of less than 12 months.

(5) "Insurer" shall mean any domestic, foreign, or alien surety company which has qualified generally to transact surety business and specifically to transact bail bond business in this State.

(6) "Obligor" shall mean a principal or a surety on a bail bond.

(7) "Principal" shall mean a defendant or witness obligated to appear in court as required upon penalty of forfeiting bail under a bail bond or a person obligated to return a motor vehicle subject to forfeiture in accordance with G.S. 20-28.3(e).

(8) "Professional bondsman" shall mean any person who is approved and licensed by the Commissioner and who pledges cash or approved securities with the Commissioner as security for bail bonds written in connection with a judicial proceeding and receives or is promised money or other things of value therefor.

(9) "Runner" shall mean a person employed by a bail bondsman for the purpose of assisting the bail bondsman in presenting the defendant in court when required, or to assist in apprehension and surrender of

defendant to the court, or keeping defendant under necessary surveillance, or to execute bonds on behalf of the licensed bondsman when the power of attorney has been duly recorded. "Runner" does not include, however, a duly licensed attorney-at-law or a law-enforcement officer assisting a bondsman.

(9a) "Supervising bail bondsman" means any person licensed by the Commissioner as a professional bondsman or surety bondsman who employs or contracts with any new licensee under this Article.

(10) "Surety" shall mean one who, with the principal, is liable for the amount of the bail bond upon forfeiture of bail.

(11) "Surety bondsman" means any person who is licensed by the Commissioner as a surety bondsman under this Article, is appointed by an insurer by power of attorney to execute or countersign bail bonds for the insurer in connection with judicial proceedings, and receives or is promised consideration for doing so. (1963, c. 1225, s. 1; 1975, c. 619, s. 1; 1995 (Reg. Sess., 1996), c. 726, s. 1; 1998-182, s. 16; 2000-180, ss. 1, 2; 2001-269, s. 2.1.)

Editor's Note. — This Article is former Chapter 85A, rewritten by Session Laws 1975, c. 619, s. 1, effective Oct. 1, 1975, and recodified as Chapter 85C, which in turn has been recodified and incorporated as Article 71 of Chapter 58 pursuant to Session Laws 1987, c. 752, s. 9, as amended by Session Laws 1987 (Reg. Sess., 1988), c. 975, s. 34.

Session Laws 1995 (Reg. Sess., 1996), c. 726, s. 21, provides that all surety bondsmen holding licenses issued under G.S. 58-33-25(e)(9) shall be issued surety bondsmen licenses under Article 71 of Chapter 58 of the General Statutes.

Legal Periodicals. — For comment on bail in North Carolina, see 5 Wake Forest Intra. L. Rev. 300 (1969).

CASE NOTES

Article 71 specifically delineates the respective responsibilities of bail bondsmen and bail bond runners, and it provides that bail bondsmen alone are liable as sureties on bonds. State v. Bridges, 89 N.C. App. 532, 366 S.E.2d 569 (1988).

Because defendants who were bail bond runners signed only their own names on bonds as sureties, they were not individually liable for bonds since defendants denoted their agency by affixing bail bondsman's license certificates to the bonds. State v. Bridges, 89 N.C. App. 532, 366 S.E.2d 569 (1988).

Cited in State v. Vikre, 86 N.C. App. 196, 356 S.E.2d 802 (1987).

§ 58-71-5. Commissioner of Insurance to administer Article; rules and regulations; employees; evidence of Commissioner's actions.

(a) The Commissioner shall have full power and authority to administer the provisions of this Article, which regulates bail bondsmen and runners and to that end to adopt and promulgate rules and regulations to enforce the purposes and provisions of this Article. Subject to the provisions of the State Personnel Act, the Commissioner may employ and discharge such employees, examiners, investigators and such other assistants as shall be deemed necessary, and he shall prescribe their duties.

(b) Any written instrument purporting to be a copy of any action, proceeding, or finding of fact by the Commissioner, or any record of the Commissioner authenticated under the head of the Commissioner by the seal of his office shall be accepted by all the courts of this State as prima facie evidence of the contents thereof. (1963, c. 1225, s. 2; 1975, c. 619, s. 1.)

§ 58-71-10. Defects not to invalidate undertakings; liability not affected by agreement or lack of qualifications.

(a) No undertaking shall be invalid because of any defect of form, omission or recital or of condition, failure to note or record the default of any principal or surety, or because of any other irregularity, if it appears from the tenor of the undertaking before what magistrate or at what court the principal was bound to appear, and that the official before whom it was entered into was legally authorized to take it and the amount of bail is stated.

(b) The liability of a person on an undertaking shall not be affected by reason of the lack of any qualifications, sufficiency or competency provided in the criminal procedure law, or by reason of any other agreement whether or not the agreement is expressed in the undertaking, or because the defendant has not joined in the undertaking. (1963, c. 1225, s. 3; 1975, c. 619, s. 1; 2001-269, s. 2.2.)

§ 58-71-15. Qualifications of sureties on bail.

Each and every surety for the release of a person on bail shall be qualified as:
   (1) An insurer and represented by a surety bondsman or bondsmen; or
   (2) A professional bondsman; or
   (3) An accommodation bondsman. (1963, c. 1225, s. 4; 1971, c. 1231, s. 1; 1975, c. 619, s. 1.)

§ 58-71-20. Surrender of defendant by surety; when premium need not be returned.

At any time before there has been a breach of the undertaking in any type of bail or fine and cash bond the surety may surrender the defendant to the sheriff of the county in which the defendant is bonded to appear or to the sheriff where the defendant was bonded; in such case the full premium shall be returned within 72 hours after the surrender. The defendant may be surrendered without the return of premium for the bond if the defendant does any of the following:
   (1) Willfully fails to pay the premium to the surety or willfully fails to make a premium payment under the agreement specified in G.S. 58-71-167.
   (2) Changes his or her address without notifying the surety before the address change.
   (3) Physically hides from the surety.
   (4) Leaves the State without the permission of the surety.
   (5) Violates any order of the court. (1963, c. 1225, s. 5; 1975, c. 619, s. 1; 1998-211, s. 30; 2001-269, s. 2.3.)

CASE NOTES

Proof of Violation Required. — Conviction of violation of this section was improper in the absence of testimony from the party who paid the premium that defendant bail bondsman had not returned it. State v. Ipock, 129 N.C. App. 530, 500 S.E.2d 449 (1998).

Punitive Damages Held Not Available in Breach of Contract Action against Bondsman. — A bail bondsman who fails to return the premium after surrendering the defendant may be liable in contract, and where arrestee's cause of action against bail bondsman consisted only of a breach of contract after the trial court decided not to submit to the jury the issues of unfair and deceptive practices and intentional infliction of emotional distress, the trial court could not submit the punitive damages issue to the jury. Shore v. Farmer, 351 N.C. 166, 522 S.E.2d 73 (1999).

§ 58-71-25. Procedure for surrender.

After there has been a breach of the undertaking in a bail bond, the surety may surrender the defendant as provided in G.S. 15A-540. (1963, c. 1225, s. 6; 1975, c. 619, s. 1; 2000-133, s. 7.)

§ 58-71-30. Arrest of defendant for purpose of surrender.

For the purpose of surrendering the defendant, the surety may arrest him before the forfeiture of the undertaking, or by his written authority endorsed on a certified copy of the undertaking, may request any judicial officer to order arrest of the defendant. (1963, c. 1225, s. 7; 1975, c. 619, s. 1.)

Legal Periodicals. — For survey of 1981 law on criminal procedure, see 60 N.C.L. Rev. 1302 (1982).

CASE NOTES

Codification of Common Law. — The bondsman's right of arrest under this section is simply a codification of the common-law rule that has been recognized in North Carolina for many years. State v. Perry, 50 N.C. App. 540, 274 S.E.2d 261, cert. denied and appeal dismissed, 302 N.C. 632, 280 S.E.2d 446 (1981).

The arrest provisions of this statute do not create a law enforcement officer in the person of the bail bondsman. State v. Mathis, 349 N.C. 503, 509 S.E.2d 155 (1998).

Miranda Warnings Not Required. — When taking a defendant who is a bail jumper into custody, a bail bondsman is not acting as a law officer or as an agent for the State, and the bondsman has no obligation to give defendant the Miranda warnings in order to render admissible incriminating statements made by defendant to the bondsman. State v. Perry, 50 N.C. App. 540, 274 S.E.2d 261, cert. denied and appeal dismissed, 302 N.C. 632, 280 S.E.2d 446 (1981).

Authority to Enter Residence Shared with Third Parties. — A surety may not enter the home of a third party where the principal does not reside without permission from the homeowner; however, a surety may break into and enter a principal's residence, even if the principal resides there with others. State v. Mathis, 349 N.C. 503, 509 S.E.2d 155 (1998).

Force to Overcome Resistance of Third Party. — Sureties or their agents may use such force as is reasonably necessary to overcome the resistance of a third party who attempts to impede their privileged capture of their principal, although they may use only such force as is reasonably necessary under the circumstances to accomplish the arrest. State v. Mathis, 349 N.C. 503, 509 S.E.2d 155 (1998).

Cited in State v. Mathis, 126 N.C. App. 688, 486 S.E.2d 475 (1997), aff'd, 349 N.C. 503, 509 S.E.2d 155 (1998).

§ 58-71-35. Forfeiture of bail.

(a) Except for bonds issued to secure the return of a motor vehicle subject to forfeiture in accordance with G.S. 20-28.3(e), the procedure for forfeiture of bail shall be that provided in Article 26 of Chapter 15A of the General Statutes and all provisions of that Article shall continue in full force and effect.

(b) At any time before execution is issued on a judgment of forfeiture against a principal or his surety, the court may direct that the judgment be remitted in whole or in part, upon such conditions as the court may impose, if it appears that justice requires the remission of part or all of the judgment. (1963, c. 1225, s. 8; 1975, c. 619, s. 1; 1998-182, s. 17.)

§ 58-71-40. Bail bondsmen and runners to be qualified and licensed; license applications generally.

(a) No person shall act in the capacity of a professional bondsman, surety bondsman, or runner or perform any of the functions, duties, or powers prescribed for professional bondsmen, surety bondsmen, or runners under this Article unless that person is qualified and licensed under this Article. No license shall be issued under this Article except to an individual natural person.

(b) The applicant shall apply for a license on forms prepared and supplied by the Commissioner. The Commissioner may propound any reasonable interrogatories to an applicant for a license under this Article about the applicant's qualifications, residence, prospective place of business, and any other matters that the Commissioner considers necessary to protect the public and ascertain the qualifications of the applicant. The Commissioner may also conduct any reasonable inquiry or investigation relative to the determination of the applicant's fitness to be licensed or to continue to be licensed.

(c) A person whose application is denied may reapply, but the Commissioner shall not consider more than one application submitted by the same person within any one-year period.

(d) When a license is issued under this section, the Commissioner shall issue a picture identification card, of design, size, and content approved by the Commissioner, to the licensee. Each licensee must carry this card at all times when working in the scope of the licensee's employment. A licensee whose license is terminated shall surrender the identification card to the Commissioner within 10 working days after the termination.

(e) This section does not prohibit the hiring of personnel by a bail bondsman to perform only normal office duties. As used in this subsection, "normal office duties" do not include acting as a bail bondsman or runner. (1963, c. 1225, s. 9; 1975, c. 619, s. 1; 1995 (Reg. Sess., 1996), c. 726, s. 2; 2001-269, s. 2.4.)

§ 58-71-41. First-year licensees; limitations.

(a) Except as provided in this section, a first-year licensee shall have the same authority as other persons licensed as bail bondsmen or runners under this Article. Except as provided in subsection (d) of this section, a first-year licensee shall operate only under the supervision of and from the official business address of a licensed supervising bail bondsman for the first 12 months of licensure. A first-year licensee may only be employed by or contract with one supervising bail bondsman.

(b) When a first-year licensee has completed 12 months of supervision, six of which shall be uninterrupted, the supervising bail bondsman shall give notice of that fact to the Commissioner in writing. If the licensee will continue to be employed by or contract with the supervising bail bondsman beyond the initial 12-month period, the supervising bail bondsman shall continue to supervise and be responsible for the licensee's acts.

(c) If the employment of or contract with a first-year licensee is terminated, the supervising bail bondsman shall notify the Commissioner in writing and shall specify the reason for the termination.

(d) If, after exercising due diligence, a first-year licensed bail bondsman is unable to become employed by or to contract with a supervising bail bondsman, the first-year licensed bail bondsman must submit to the Department a sworn affidavit stating the relevant facts and circumstances regarding the first-year licensed bail bondman's inability to become employed by or contract with a supervising bail bondsman. The Department shall review the affidavit and determine whether the first-year licensed bail bondsman will be allowed to operate as an unsupervised bail bondsman. A first-year licensed bail bondsman is prohibited from becoming a supervising bail bondsman during the first two years of licensure.

(e) Provided all other licensing requirements are met, an applicant for a bail bondsman or runner's license who has previously been licensed with the

Commissioner for a period of at least 18 consecutive months and who has been inactive or unlicensed for a period of not more than three consecutive years shall not be deemed a new licensee for purposes of this section. (2000-180, s. 3.)

§ 58-71-45. Terms of licenses.

A license issued to a bail bondsman or to a runner authorizes the licensee to act in that capacity until the license is suspended or revoked. Upon the suspension or revocation of a license, the licensee shall return the license to the Commissioner. A license of a bail bondsman and a license of a runner shall be renewed on July 1 of each year upon payment of the applicable renewal fee under G.S. 58-71-75. The Commissioner is not required to print renewal licenses. After notifying the Commissioner in writing, a professional bondsman who employs a runner may cancel the runner's license and the runner's authority to act for the professional bondsman. (1963, c. 1225, s. 10; 1975, c. 619, s. 1; 1995 (Reg. Sess., 1996), c. 726, s. 3.)

§ 58-71-50. Qualification for bail bondsmen and runners.

(a) An applicant for a license as a bail bondsman or runner shall furnish the Commissioner with a complete set of the applicant's fingerprints and a recent passport size full-face photograph of the applicant. The applicant's fingerprints shall be certified by an authorized law-enforcement officer. The fingerprints of every applicant shall be forwarded to the State Bureau of Investigation for a search of the applicant's criminal history record file, if any. If warranted, the State Bureau of Investigation shall forward a set of the fingerprints to the Federal Bureau of Investigation for a national criminal history record check. An applicant shall pay the cost of the State and any national criminal history record check of the applicant.

(b) Every applicant for a license under this Article as a bail bondsman or runner must meet all of the following qualifications:

(1) Be 18 years of age or over.
(2) Be a resident of this State.
(3) Repealed by Session Laws 1998-211, s. 23, effective November 1, 1998.
(4) Have knowledge, training, or experience of sufficient duration and extent to provide the competence necessary to fulfill the responsibilities of a licensee.
(5) Have no outstanding bail bond obligations.
(6) Have no current or prior violations of any provision of this Article or of Article 26 of Chapter 15A of the General Statutes or of any similar provision of law of any other state.
(7) Not have been in any manner disqualified under the laws of this State or any other state to engage in the bail bond business. (1963, c. 1225, s. 11; 1971, c. 1231, s. 1; 1975, c. 619, s. 1; 1987, c. 728, s. 1; 1989, c. 485, s. 39; 1991, c. 720, s. 41; 1995 (Reg. Sess., 1996), c. 726, s. 4; 1998-211, s. 23.)

Legal Periodicals. — For note on equal protection and residence requirements, see 49 N.C.L. Rev. 753 (1971).

§ 58-71-55. License fees.

A nonrefundable license fee of one hundred dollars ($100.00) shall be paid to the Commissioner with each application for license as a bail bondsman and a license fee of sixty dollars ($60.00) shall be paid to the Commissioner with each application for license as a runner. (1963, c. 1225, s. 12; 1975, c. 619, s. 1; 1983, c. 790, s. 11; 1991, c. 721, s. 4; 1995 (Reg. Sess., 1996), c. 726, s. 5.)

§ **58-71-60:** Repealed by Session Laws 1995 (Regular Session, 1996), c. 726, s. 6.

§ 58-71-65. Contents of application for runner's license; endorsement by professional bondsman.

In addition to the other requirements of this Article, an applicant for a license to be a runner must affirmatively show:

(1) That the applicant will be employed by only one professional bondsman, who will supervise the work of the applicant and be responsible for the runner's conduct in the bail bond business.

(2) That the application is endorsed by the appointing professional bondsman, who must agree in the application to supervise the runner's activities.

(3) Whether or not the applicant has ever been licensed as a bail bondsman or runner. An applicant who has been licensed as a bail bondsman must list all outstanding bail bond obligations. An applicant who has been licensed as a runner must list all prior employment as such, indicating the name of each supervising professional bondsman and the reasons for the termination of the employment. (1963, c. 1225, s. 14; 1975, c. 619, s. 1; 1987, c. 728, s. 2; 1995 (Reg. Sess., 1996), c. 726, s. 7.)

§ 58-71-70. Examination; fees.

Each applicant for a license as a professional bondsman, surety bondsman, or runner shall appear in person and take a written examination prepared by the Commissioner testing the applicant's ability and qualifications. Each applicant is eligible for examination 30 days after the date the application is received by the Commissioner. Each examination shall be held at a time and place as designated by the Commissioner. Each applicant shall be given notice of the designated time and place no sooner than 15 days before the examination. The Commissioner may contract with a person to process applications for the examination and administer and grade the examination in the same manner as for agent examinations under Article 33 of this Chapter.

The fee for each examination is twenty-five dollars ($25.00) plus an amount that offsets the cost of any contract for examination services. This examination fee is nonrefundable.

An applicant who fails an examination may take a subsequent examination, but at least one year must intervene between examinations. (1963, c. 1225, s. 15; 1975, c. 619, s. 1; 1991, c. 721, s. 5; 1995 (Reg. Sess., 1996), c. 726, s. 8.)

§ 58-71-71. Examination; educational requirements; penalties.

(a) In order to be eligible to take the examination required to be licensed as a runner or bail bondsman under G.S. 58-71-70, each person shall complete at least 12 hours of education in subjects pertinent to the duties and responsibilities of a runner or bail bondsman, including all laws and regulations related to being a runner or bail bondsman.

(b) Each year every licensee shall complete at least six hours of continuing education in subjects related to the duties and responsibilities of a runner or bail bondsman before renewal of the license. This continuing education shall not include a written or oral examination. A person who receives his first license on or after January 1 of any year does not have to comply with this subsection until the period between his first and second license renewals.

(c) Any person licensed as a runner or bail bondsman before January 1, 1994, is not subject to the prelicensing education requirement of this section, but is subject to the continuing education requirement of this section. A licensed runner or bail bondsman who is 65 years of age or older and who has been licensed as a runner or bail bondsman for 15 years or more is exempt from both the prelicensing education and continuing education requirements of this section.

(d) Educational courses offered under this section must be approved by the Commissioner before they may be offered. Before approving a course, the Commissioner must be satisfied that it will enhance the professional competence and professional responsibility of bail bondsmen and runners. No person shall offer, sponsor, or conduct any course under this section unless the Commissioner has authorized that person to do so.

(e) The license of any person who fails to comply with the continuing education requirements under this section shall lapse. The Commissioner may, for good cause shown, grant extensions of time to licensees to comply with these requirements. Any licensee who, after obtaining an extension under this subsection, offers evidence satisfactory to the Commissioner that the licensee has satisfactorily completed the required continuing professional education courses is in compliance with this section.

(f) The Commissioner may adopt rules for the effective administration of this section. (1993, c. 409, s. 22; 1993 (Reg. Sess., 1994), c. 678, s. 32; 1995 (Reg. Sess., 1996), c. 726, s. 9; 1998-211, ss. 25, 26, 28.)

§ 58-71-72. Qualifications of instructors.

(a) A person who provides, presents, or instructs a prelicensing course or continuing education course under G.S. 58-71-71 must have a certificate of authority issued by the Commissioner. The Commissioner may establish requirements for the issuance or renewal of a certificate of authority and grounds for the summary suspension or termination of a certificate of authority.

(b) The Commissioner may summarily suspend or terminate a certificate of authority to provide, present, or instruct a course if the Commissioner finds that the course is inaccurate or it received a poor evaluation from both a Department monitor and a majority of those who attended the course and responded to a Department questionnaire about the course. (1995 (Reg. Sess., 1996), c. 726, s. 10.)

§ 58-71-75. Renewal fees.

The renewal fee for a runner's license is sixty dollars ($60.00). The renewal fee for a bail bondsman's license is one hundred dollars ($100.00). A renewed license continues in effect until suspended or revoked for cause. (1963, c. 1225, s. 16; 1975, c. 619, s. 1; 1991, c. 721, s. 6; 1995 (Reg. Sess., 1996), c. 726, s. 11.)

§ 58-71-80. Grounds for denial, suspension, revocation or refusal to renew licenses.

(a) The Commissioner may deny, suspend, revoke, or refuse to renew any license under this Article for any of the following causes:

(1) For any cause sufficient to deny, suspend, or revoke the license under any other provision of this Article.

   (2) A conviction of any misdemeanor committed in the course of dealings under the license issued by the Commissioner.

   (3) Material misstatement, misrepresentation or fraud in obtaining the license.

   (4) Misappropriation, conversion or unlawful withholding of moneys belonging to insurers or others and received in the conduct of business under the license.

   (5) Fraudulent or dishonest practices in the conduct of business under the license.

   (6) Conviction of a crime involving moral turpitude.

   (7) Failure to comply with or violation of the provisions of this Article or of any order, rule or regulation of the Commissioner.

   (8) When in the judgment of the Commissioner, the licensee has in the conduct of the licensee's affairs under the license, demonstrated incompetency, financial irresponsibility, or untrustworthiness; or that the licensee is no longer in good faith carrying on the bail bond business; or that the licensee is guilty of rebating, or offering to rebate, or offering to divide the premiums received for the bond.

   (9) For failing to pay any judgment or decree rendered on any forfeited undertaking in any court of competent jurisdiction.

   (10) For charging or receiving, as premium or compensation for the making of any deposit or bail bond, any sum in excess of that permitted by this Article.

   (11) For requiring, as a condition of executing a bail bond, that the principal agree to engage the services of a specified attorney.

   (12) For cheating on an examination for a license under this Article.

   (13) For entering into any business association or agreement with any person who is at that time found by the Commissioner to be in violation of any of the bail bond laws of this State, or who has been in any manner disqualified under the bail bond laws of this State or any other state, whereby the person has any direct or indirect financial interest in the bail bond business of the licensee or applicant.

   (14) For knowingly aiding or abetting others to evade or violate the provisions of this Article.

   (15) Any cause for which issuance of the license could have been refused had it then existed and been known to the Commissioner at the time of issuance.

  (b) The Commissioner shall deny, revoke, or refuse to renew any license under this Article if the applicant or licensee is or has ever been convicted of a felony.

  (c) In the case of a first-year licensee whose employment or contract is terminated prior to the end of the 12-month supervisory period, the Commissioner may consider all information provided in writing by the supervising bail bondsman in determining whether sufficient cause exists to suspend, revoke, or refuse to renew the license or to warrant criminal prosecution of the first-year licensee. If the Commissioner determines there is not sufficient cause for adverse administrative action or criminal prosecution, the termination shall not be deemed an interruption and the period of time the licensee was employed by or contracted with the terminating supervising bail bondsman will be credited toward the licensee's completion of the required 12 months of supervision with a subsequent supervising bail bondsman. (1963, c. 1225, s. 17; 1975, c. 619, s. 1; 1989, c. 485, s. 40; 1991, c. 644, s. 17; 1993, c. 409, s. 16; 1998-211, s. 24; 2000-180, s. 4.)

Editor's Note. — Session Laws 1998-217, s. 60 repealed an amendment to subsection (b) of this section made by S.L. 1998-215, s. 90 in order to resolve a conflict with the amendment to this section made by S.L. 1998-211, s. 24.

§ 58-71-81. Notice of receivership.

Upon the filing for protection under the United States Bankruptcy Code or any state receivership law by any bail bondsman licensed under this Article or by any bail bond business in which the bondsman holds a position of management or ownership, the bondsman shall notify the Commissioner of the filing for protection within three business days after the filing. Upon the appointment of a receiver by a State or federal court for any professional bondsman licensed under this Article, or for any bail bond business in which the bondsman holds a position of management or ownership, the bondsman shall notify the Commissioner of the filing for protection within three business days after the filing. The failure to notify the Commissioner within three business days after the filing for bankruptcy protection shall, after hearing, cause the license of any person failing to make the required notification to be suspended for a period of not less than 60 days nor more than three years, in the discretion of the Commissioner. (1993, c. 409, s. 17; 1995 (Reg. Sess., 1996), c. 726, s. 12.)

§ 58-71-82. Dual license holding.

If an individual holds a professional bondsman's license or a runner's license and a surety bondsman's license simultaneously, they are considered one license for the purpose of disciplinary actions involving suspension, revocation, or nonrenewal under this Article. Separate renewal fees must be paid for each license, however. (1995 (Reg. Sess., 1996), c. 726, ss. 13, 15; 1999-132, s. 5.)

Editor's Note. — Session Laws 1995 (Reg. Sess., 1996), c. 726, s. 13, which enacted this section effective June 21, 1996, read as follows: "If licenses are issued to a bail bondsman or runner under this Article and under Article 33 of this Chapter and the license issued under Article 33 of this Chapter is suspended or revoked for cause or is not renewed, the license issued under this Article is suspended, revoked, or not renewed as of the date the order under Article 33 of this Chapter is final."

§ 58-71-85. License sanction and denial procedures.

(a) The suspension or revocation of, or refusal to renew, any license under G.S. 58-71-80 shall be in accordance with the provisions of Chapter 150B of the General Statutes.

(b) Whenever the Commissioner denies an initial application for a license or an application for a reissuance of a license, he shall notify the applicant and advise, in writing, the applicant of the reasons for the denial of the license. The application may also be denied for any reason for which a license may be suspended or revoked or not renewed under G.S. 58-71-80(a). Within 30 days after service of the notification, the applicant may make a written demand upon the Commissioner for a review to determine the reasonableness of the Commissioner's action. The review shall be completed without undue delay, and the applicant shall be notified promptly in writing as to the outcome of the review. Within 30 days after service of the notification as to the outcome, the applicant may make a written demand upon the Commissioner for a hearing under Article 3A of Chapter 150B of the General Statutes if the applicant disagrees with the outcome. (1963, c. 1225, s. 18; 1975, c. 619, s. 1; 1989, c. 485, s. 33; 1993, c. 504, s. 33; 1998-211, s. 29.)

§ **58-71-90:** Repealed by Session Laws 1999-132, s. 1.1.

§ 58-71-95. Prohibited practices.

No bail bondsman or runner shall:
  (1) Pay a fee or rebate or give or promise anything of value, directly or indirectly, to a jailer, law-enforcement officer, committing magistrate, or any other person who has power to arrest or hold in custody, or to any public official or public employee in order to secure a settlement, compromise, remission or reduction of the amount of any bail bond or the forfeiture thereof, including the payment to law-enforcement officers, directly or indirectly, for the arrest or apprehension of a principal or principals who have caused or will cause a forfeiture.
  (2) Pay a fee or rebate or give anything of value to an attorney in bail bond matters, except in defense of any action on a bond.
  (3) Pay a fee or rebate or give or promise anything of value to the principal or anyone in his behalf.
  (4) Participate in the capacity of an attorney at a trial or hearing of one on whose bond he is surety, nor suggest or advise the employment of, or name for employment any particular attorney to represent his principal.
  (5) Accept anything of value from a principal or from anyone on behalf of a principal except the premium, which shall not exceed fifteen percent (15%) of the face amount of the bond; provided that the bondsman shall be permitted to accept collateral security or other indemnity from a principal or from anyone on behalf of a principal. Such collateral security or other indemnity required by the bondsman must be reasonable in relation to the amount of the bond and shall be returned within 72 hours after final termination of liability on the bond. Any bail bondsman who knowingly and willfully fails to return any collateral security, the value of which exceeds one thousand five hundred dollars ($1,500), is guilty of a Class I felony. All collateral security, such as personal and real property, subject to be returned must be done so under the same conditions as requested and received by the bail bondsman.
  (6) Solicit business in any of the courts or on the premises of any of the courts of this State, in the office of any magistrate and in or about any place where prisoners are confined. Loitering in or about a magistrate's office or any place where prisoners are confined shall be prima facie evidence of soliciting.
  (7) Advise or assist the principal for the purpose of forfeiting bond.
  (8) Impersonate a law-enforcement officer.
  (9) Falsely represent that the bail bondsman or runner is in any way connected with an agency of the federal government or of a state or local government. (1963, c. 1225, s. 20; 1975, c. 619, s. 1; 1993, c. 409, s. 18; 1995 (Reg. Sess., 1996), c. 726, s. 16; 1998-211, s. 31; 2000-180, s. 5.)

§ 58-71-100. Receipts for collateral; trust accounts.

(a) When a bail bondsman accepts collateral he shall give a written receipt for the collateral. The receipt shall give in detail a full description of the collateral received. Collateral security shall be held and maintained in trust. When collateral security is received in the form of cash or check or other negotiable instrument, the licensee shall deposit the cash or instrument within two banking days after receipt, in an established, separate noninterest-bearing trust account in any bank located in North Carolina. The trust account funds under this section shall not be commingled with other operating funds.

(b) With the approval of the Commissioner, bail bondsmen operating out of the same business office or location may establish a shared trust account for collateral security received by them. The Commissioner may require the bondsmen desiring to establish the shared trust account to furnish the Commissioner information about their business that the Commissioner considers necessary to administer this Article effectively. (1963, c. 1225, s. 21; 1975, c. 619, s. 1; 2000-180, s. 6; 2001-269, s. 2.5.)

§ 58-71-105. Persons prohibited from becoming surety or runners.

No sheriff, deputy sheriff, other law-enforcement officer, judicial official, attorney, parole officer, probation officer, jailer, assistant jailer, employee of the General Court of Justice, nor other public employee assigned to duties relating to the administration of criminal justice, nor the spouse of any such person, may in any case become surety on a bail bond for any person. In addition, no person covered by this section may act as an agent for any bonding company or bail bondsman. No such person may have an interest, directly or indirectly, in the financial affairs of any firm or corporation whose principal business is acting as a bail bondsman. However, nothing in this section prohibits any such person from being surety upon the bond of his or her spouse, parent, brother, sister, child, or descendant. (1963, c. 1225, s. 22; 1973, c. 108, s. 39; 1975, c. 619, s. 1; 1991, c. 644, s. 18; 1995 (Reg. Sess., 1996), c. 726, s. 17.)

CASE NOTES

Cited in State v. Rogers, 68 N.C. App. 358, 315 S.E.2d 492 (1984).

§ 58-71-110. Bonds not to be signed in blank; authority to countersign only given to licensed employee.

A bail bondsman shall not sign nor countersign in blank bail bonds, nor shall he give a power of attorney to, or otherwise authorize, anyone to countersign his name to bonds unless the person so authorized is a licensed bondsman or runner directly employed by the bondsman giving such power of attorney. Copies of all such powers of attorney and revocations of such powers of attorney must be filed immediately with the Commissioner and the clerk of superior court of any county in the State where said bondsman giving the power of attorney is currently writing or is obligated on bail bonds. (1963, c. 1225, s. 23; 1975, c. 619, s. 1.)

§ 58-71-115. Insurers to annually report surety bondsmen; notices of appointments and terminations; information confidential.

Before July 1 of each year, every insurer shall furnish the Commissioner a list of all surety bondsmen appointed by the insurer to write bail bonds on the insurer's behalf. An insurer who appoints a surety bondsman in the State on or after July 1 of each year must notify the Commissioner of the appointment. All appointments are subject to the issuance of the proper license to the appointee under this Article.

An insurer terminating the appointment of a surety bondsman shall file a written notice of the termination with the Commissioner, together with a statement that the insurer has given or mailed notice to the surety bondsman and to the clerk of superior court of any county in the State in which the insurer has been obligated on bail bonds through the surety bondsman within the past three years. The notice to the Commissioner shall state the reasons, if any, for the termination. Information furnished in the notice to the Commissioner shall be privileged and shall not be used as evidence in or basis for any action against the insurer or any of its representatives. (1963, c. 1225, s. 24; 1975, c. 619, s. 1; 1995 (Reg. Sess., 1996), c. 726, s. 18.)

§ 58-71-120. Bail bondsman to give notice of discontinuance of business; cancellation of license.

Any bail bondsman who discontinues writing bail bonds during the period for which he is licensed shall notify the clerks of the superior court with whom he is registered and return his license to the Commissioner for cancellation within 30 days after such discontinuance. (1963, c. 1225, s. 25; 1975, c. 619, s. 1.)

§ 58-71-121. Death, incapacitation, or incompetence of a bail bondsman.

In the case of death, incapacitation, or incompetence of a licensed bail bondsman, the spouse or surviving spouse, next of kin, person or persons holding a power of attorney, guardian, executor, or administrator of the licensed bail bondsman may contract with another licensed bail bondsman to perform those duties to have the licensee's outstanding bail bond obligations resolved to the satisfaction of the courts. The contract must be filed with the Commissioner and every clerk of superior court where it can be determined the licensee has pending outstanding bail bond obligations. The licensed bail bondsman who has agreed to perform these duties shall not, at the time of the execution of the contract, have any administrative or criminal actions pending against him or her. (2000-180, s. 7.)

§ 58-71-125. Persons eligible as runners; bail bondsmen to annually report runners; notices of appointments and terminations; information confidential.

Every person duly licensed as a bail bondsman may appoint as runner any person who has been issued runner's license. Each bail bondsman must, on or before July 1 of each year, furnish to the Commissioner a list of all runners appointed by him. Each such bail bondsman who shall, subsequent to the filing of this list, appoint additional persons as runners shall file written notice with the Commissioner of such appointment.

A bail bondsman terminating the appointment of a runner shall file written notice thereof with the Commissioner, together with a statement that he has given or mailed notice to the runner. Such notice filed with the Commissioner shall state the reasons, if any, for such termination. Information so furnished the Commissioner shall be privileged and shall not be used as evidence in any action against the bail bondsman. (1963, c. 1225, s. 26; 1975, c. 619, s. 1.)

§ 58-71-130. Substituting bail by sureties for deposit.

If money or bonds have been deposited, bail by sureties may be substituted therefor at any time before a breach of the undertaking, and the official taking the new bail shall make an order that the money or bonds be refunded to the person depositing the same and they shall be refunded accordingly, and the original undertakings shall be canceled. (1963, c. 1225, s. 27; 1975, c. 619, s. 1.)

§ 58-71-135. Deposit for defendant admitted to bail authorizes release and cancellation of undertaking.

When the defendant has been admitted to bail, he, or another in his behalf, may deposit with an official authorized to take bail, a sum of money, or nonregistered bonds of the United States, or of the State, or of any county, city or town within the State, equal in market value to the amount of such bail, together with his personal undertaking, and an undertaking of such other person, if the money or bonds are deposited by another. Upon delivery to the official in whose custody the defendant is of a certificate of such deposit, he shall be discharged from custody in the cause.

When bail other than a deposit of money or bonds has been given, the defendant or the surety may, at any time before a breach of the undertaking, deposit the sum mentioned in the undertaking, and upon such deposit being made, accompanied by a new undertaking, the original undertaking shall be canceled. (1963, c. 1225, s. 28; 1975, c. 619, s. 1.)

§ 58-71-140. Registration of licenses and power of appointments by insurers.

(a) No professional bail bondsman shall become a surety on an undertaking unless he or she has registered his or her current license in the office of the clerk of superior court in the county in which he or she resides and a certified copy of the same with the clerk of superior court in any other county in which he or she shall write bail bonds.

(b) A surety bondsman shall register his or her current surety bondsman's license and a certified copy of his or her power of appointment with the clerk of superior court in the county in which the surety bondsman resides and with the clerk of superior court in any other county in which the surety bondsman writes bail bonds on behalf of an insurer.

(c) No runner shall become surety on an undertaking on behalf of a professional bondsman unless that runner has registered his or her current license and a certified copy of his or her power of attorney in the office of the clerk of superior court in the county in which the runner resides and with the clerk of superior court in any other county in which the runner writes bail bonds on behalf of the professional bondsman.

(d) Professional bondsmen, surety bondsmen, and runners shall file with the clerk of court having jurisdiction over the principal an affidavit on a form furnished by the Administrative Office of the Courts. The affidavit shall include, but not be limited to:

    (1) If applicable, a statement that the bondsman has not, nor has anyone for the bondsman's use, been promised or received any collateral, security, or premium for executing this appearance bond.

    (2) If promised a premium, the amount of the premium promised and the due date.

    (3) If the bondsman has received a premium, the amount of premium received.

    (4) If given collateral security, the name of the person from whom it is received and the nature and amount of the collateral security listed in detail. (1963, c. 1225, s. 31; 1975, c. 619, s. 1; 1995 (Reg. Sess., 1996), c. 726, s. 19; 2001-269, s. 2.6.)

§ 58-71-141. Appointment of bail bondsmen; affidavit required.

(a) Prior to receiving an appointment, a surety bondsman shall submit to the Commissioner an affidavit, signed under oath, by the surety bondsman and by any former insurer, stating that the surety bondsman does not owe any premium or unsatisfied judgment to any insurer and that the bondsman agrees to discharge all outstanding forfeitures and judgments on bonds previously written. The affidavit shall be in a form prescribed by the Commissioner. If the surety bondsman does not satisfy or discharge all forfeitures or judgments, the former insurer shall submit a notice, with supporting documents, to the appointing insurer, the surety bondsman, and the Commissioner, which states, under oath, that the surety bondsman has failed to satisfy, in a timely manner, the forfeitures and judgments on bonds written by the surety bondsman and that the former insurer has satisfied the forfeiture or judgment from its own funds. Upon receipt of the notification and supporting documents, the appointing insurer shall immediately cancel the surety bondsman's appointment. The surety bondsman may be reappointed only upon certification by the former insurer that all forfeitures and judgments on bonds written by the surety bondsman have been discharged. The appointing insurer or surety bondsman may, within 10 days of the receipt of notice from the former insurer, appeal to the Commissioner.

(b) The Commissioner shall adopt rules, including rules regarding the process of appeals and stays of the requirements of this section, to implement this section.

(c) As used in this section, "former insurer" means the insurer with whom the surety bondsman had a prior appointment and who is responsible for any outstanding bonds written by the surety bondsman. (2003-148, s. 1.)

Editor's Note. — Session Laws 2003-148, s. 2, made this section effective October 1, 2003, and applicable to all appointments of bondsmen on or after that date.

§ 58-71-145. Financial responsibility of professional bondsmen.

Each professional bondsman acting as surety on bail bonds in this State shall maintain a deposit of securities with and satisfactory to the Commissioner of a fair market value of at least one-eighth the amount of all bonds or undertakings written in this State on which he is absolutely or conditionally liable as of the first day of the current month. The amount of this deposit must be reconciled with the bondsman's liabilities as of the first day of the month on or before the fifteenth day of said month and the value of said deposit shall in no event be less than fifteen thousand dollars ($15,000). (1963, c. 1225, s. 29; 1975, c. 619, s. 1; 2000-180, s. 8.)

§ 58-71-150. Securities held in trust by Commissioner; authority to dispose of same.

The securities deposited by a professional bondsman with the Commissioner shall be held in trust for the sole protection and benefit of the holder of bail bonds executed by or on behalf of the undersigned bondsman in this State. A pro rata portion of the securities shall be returned to the bondsman when the Commissioner is satisfied that the deposit of securities is in excess of the amount required to be maintained with him by said bondsman and all the securities shall be returned if the Commissioner is satisfied that the bondsman has satisfied, or satisfactory arrangements have been made to satisfy, the obligations of the bondsman on all his bail bonds written in the State. The Commissioner may sell or transfer any and all of said securities or utilize the proceeds thereof for the purpose of satisfying the liabilities of the professional bondsman on bail bonds given in this State on which he is liable. (1975, c. 619, s. 1.)

§ 58-71-155. Bondsman to furnish power of attorney with securities.

With the securities deposited with the Commissioner, the professional bondsman shall at the same time deliver to the Commissioner of Insurance a power of attorney, on a form supplied by the Commissioner, executed and acknowledged by the professional bondsman authorizing the sale or transfer of said securities or any part thereof. The power of attorney shall read as follows:

POWER OF ATTORNEY

AUTHORIZING THE COMMISSIONER OF INSURANCE TO
SELL, OR TRANSFER SECURITIES DEPOSITED BY
PROFESSIONAL BONDSMEN IN
NORTH CAROLINA.

KNOW ALL MEN BY THESE PRESENTS, That _____, a professional bondsman, located in the County of _____, in the State of _____, has authorized and appointed for himself, his successors, heirs and assigns, the Commissioner of Insurance of the State of North Carolina, in the name and in behalf of said professional bondsman, his true and lawful attorney to sell or transfer any securities deposited or that may be deposited, by said professional bondsman with said Commissioner, under the laws and regulations requiring a deposit of securities to be made by professional bondsmen doing business in the State of North Carolina, insofar as the sale or transfer is deemed necessary by the Commissioner of Insurance to pay any liability arising under a bond which purports to be given by the undersigned bondsman in any county in this State and execution has been issued against said bondsman pursuant to a judgment on the bond and the same has not been satisfied. The securities so deposited are to be held in trust by the Commissioner for the sole protection and benefit of the holder of bail bonds executed by, or on behalf of, the undersigned bondsman. IN WITNESS WHEREOF, I have hereunto set my hand and affixed my seal this _____ day of _____, _____.

_____
Professional Bondsman

Before me, a Notary Public in and for the State of _____ personally appeared _____, a professional bondsman who acknowledged that he executed the foregoing power of attorney.

WITNESS my hand and Notarial Seal, this _____ day of _____, _____.

_____
Notary Public
My Commission Expires: _____

(1975, c. 619, s. 1; 1999-456, s. 59.)

§ 58-71-160. Security deposit to be maintained.

(a) Any professional bondsman, whose security deposits with the Commissioner are, for any reason, reduced in value below the requirements of this

Article, shall immediately upon receipt of a notice of deficiency from the Commissioner deposit such additional securities as are necessary to comply with the law. No professional bondsman shall sign, endorse, execute, or become surety on any additional bail bonds, or pledge or deposit any cash, check, or other security of any nature in lieu of a bail bond in any county in North Carolina until the professional bondsman has made such additional deposit of securities as required by the notice of deficiency.

(b) The Commissioner may deny the renewal of any license held by a professional bondsman under this Chapter or may deny the issuance of any license applied for by a professional bondsman under this Chapter if, at the time of the renewal application or license application, the professional bondsman has not complied with a notice of deficiency under subsection (a) of this section. The Commissioner may issue the renewal license or the new license upon compliance by the professional bondsman with the notice of deficiency. (1975, c. 619, s. 1; 2001-269, s. 2.7.)

§ 58-71-165. Monthly report required.

Each professional bail bondsman and surety bondsman shall file with the Commissioner a written report in form prescribed by the Commissioner regarding all bail bonds on which the bondsman is liable as of the first day of each month showing (i) each individual bonded, (ii) the date the bond was given, (iii) the principal sum of the bond, (iv) the State or local official to whom given, and (v) the fee charged for the bonding service in each instance. The report shall be filed on or before the fifteenth day of each month. Any person who knowingly and willfully falsifies a report required by this section is guilty of a Class I felony. (1975, c. 619, s. 1; 1989, c. 485, s. 43; 1991, c. 644, s. 20; 1993, c. 539, s. 1276; 1994, Ex. Sess., c. 24, s. 14(c); 1998-211, s. 27.)

§ 58-71-167. Portion of bond premium payments deferred.

(a) In any case where the agreement between principal and surety calls for some portion of the bond premium payments to be deferred or paid after the defendant has been released from custody, a written memorandum of agreement between the principal and surety shall be kept on file by the surety with a copy provided to the principal, upon request. The memorandum shall contain the following information:

(1) The amount of the premium payment deferred or not yet paid at the time the defendant is released from jail.

(2) The method and schedule of payment to be made by the defendant to the bondsman, which shall include the dates of payment and amount to be paid on each date.

(3) That the principal is, upon the principal's request, entitled to a copy of the memorandum.

(b) The memorandum must be signed by the defendant and the bondsman, or one of the bondsman's agents, and dated at the time the agreement is made. Any subsequent modifications of the memorandum must be in writing, signed, dated, and kept on file by the surety, with a copy provided to the principal, upon request. (1991, c. 644, s. 22.)

§ 58-71-168. Records to be maintained.

All records related to executing bail bonds, including bail bond registers, monthly reports, receipts, collateral security agreements, and memoranda of agreements, shall be kept separate from records of any other business and must be maintained for not less than three years after the final entry has been made. (1991, c. 644, s. 22.)

§ 58-71-170. Examinations.

(a) Whenever the Commissioner considers it prudent, the Commissioner shall visit and examine or cause to be visited and examined by a competent person appointed by the Commissioner for that purpose any professional bail bondsman, surety bondsman, or runner subject to this Article. For this purpose the Commissioner or person making the examination shall have free access to all records of the licensee that relate to the licensee's business and to the records kept by any of the licensee's agents.

(b) The Commissioner may conduct examinations of surety bondsmen under G.S. 58-2-195 as well as under subsection (a) of this section. (1975, c. 619, s. 1; 1991, c. 644, s. 21; 2001-269, s. 2.8.)

§ 58-71-175. Limit on principal amount of bond to be written by professional bondsman.

No professional bondsman shall become liable on any bond or multiple of bonds for any one individual that totals more than one-fourth of the value of the securities deposited with the Commissioner at that time, until final termination of liability on such bond or multiple of bonds. (1975, c. 619, s. 1; 1987, c. 728, s. 3; 1989, c. 485, s. 42.)

§ 58-71-180. Disposition of fees.

Fees collected by the Commissioner pursuant to this Article shall be credited to the Insurance Regulatory Fund created under G.S. 58-6-25. (1963, c. 1225, s. 32; 1975, c. 619, s. 1; 1991, c. 689, s. 294; 2003-221, s. 9.)

Effect of Amendments. — Session Laws 2003-221, s. 9, effective June 19, 2003, substi- tuted "Insurance Regulatory Fund" for "Depart- ment of Insurance Fund."

§ 58-71-185. Penalties for violations.

Except as otherwise provided in this Article, any person who violates any of the provisions of this Article is guilty of a Class 1 misdemeanor. (1963, c. 1225, s. 33; 1975, c. 619, s. 1; 1991, c. 644, s. 19; 1993, c. 539, s. 473; 1994, Ex. Sess., c. 24, s. 14(c); 2000-180, s. 9.)

§ 58-71-190. Duplication of regulation forbidden.

No county, city or town in this State shall license or levy a license tax on bail bondsmen nor require such bondsmen to deposit collateral security as a condition for continuing to write bail bonds. (1975, c. 619, s. 1.)

§ 58-71-195. Conflicting laws.

Section 41.1 of Chapter 105 of the General Statutes of North Carolina and all laws and clauses of laws in conflict with the provisions of the Chapter are hereby repealed. Provided, however, that in the event of any conflict between the provisions of this Chapter and those of Chapter 15A of the General Statutes of North Carolina, the provisions of Chapter 15A shall control and continue in full force and effect. (1975, c. 619, s. 2.)

Editor's Note. — Section 105-41.1, referred to in this section, was repealed by Session Laws 1975, c. 619. For present provisions as to li- cense fees for professional bondsmen and run- ners, see G.S. 58-71-55 and 58-71-75.

ARTICLE 72.

Official Bonds.

§ 58-72-1. Irregularities not to invalidate.

When any instrument is taken by or received under the sanction of the board of county commissioners, or by any person or persons acting under or in virtue of any public authority, purporting to be a bond executed to the State for the performance of any duty belonging to any office or appointment, such instrument, notwithstanding any irregularity or invalidity in the conferring of the office or making of the appointment, or any variance in the penalty or condition of the instrument from the provision prescribed by law, shall be valid and may be put in suit in the name of the State for the benefit of the person injured by a breach of the condition thereof, in the same manner as if the office had been duly conferred or the appointment duly made, and as if the penalty and condition of the instrument had conformed to the provisions of law: Provided, that no action shall be sustained thereon because of a breach of any condition thereof or any part of the condition thereof which is contrary to law. (1842, c. 61; R.C., c. 78, s. 9; 1869-70, c. 169, s. 16; Code, s. 1891; Rev., s. 279; C.S., s. 324.)

Editor's Note. — Articles 72 through 77 are former Chapter 109. Chapter 109 has been recodified as Articles 72 through 77 of Chapter 58 pursuant to Sessions Laws 1987, c. 752, s. 9, as amended by Session Laws 1987 (Reg. Sess., 1988), c. 975, s. 34.

Legal Periodicals. — For article concerning contracts and referring generally to this section, see 13 N.C.L. Rev. 65 (1935).

CASE NOTES

In General. — This section does not have the effect of introducing into an official bond provisions which are not, but ought to have been, inserted in the conditions, so as to extend the liabilities of the obligors; but the purpose is to cure certain defects and irregularities in conferring the office and accepting the instrument, and to maintain its validity as an official undertaking, as far as it goes, notwithstanding the penalty or condition may vary from those prescribed by law. State ex rel. Jordan v. Pool, 27 N.C. 105 (1844); State ex rel. Merrill v. McMinn, 29 N.C. 345 (1847); State ex rel. Murray v. Jones, 29 N.C. 359 (1847); Commissioners of Wake County v. Magnin, 86 N.C. 286 (1882). See also Midgett v. Nelson, 214 N.C. 396, 199 S.E. 393 (1938).

Retroactive Operation. — The section had a retroactive operation. State ex rel. Jordan v. Pool, 27 N.C. 105 (1844); State ex rel. Murray v. Jones, 29 N.C. 359 (1847).

Official bonds should be liberally construed and any variance in the condition of such an instrument from the provisions prescribed by the law will usually be treated as an irregularity, in view of this section, but this principle does not abrogate the freedom of contract. City of Washington v. Trust Co., 205 N.C.

382, 171 S.E. 438 (1933); Town of Scotland Neck v. Western Sur. Co., 301 N.C. 331, 271 S.E.2d 501 (1980).

Nor does this rule preclude the parties from contracting in the bond for liability for a shorter period than the official term of office of the principal. City of Washington v. Trust Co., 205 N.C. 382, 171 S.E. 438 (1933).

But where a bond is clear and unambiguous in its language, the terms of the bond cannot be extended. Town of Scotland Neck v. Western Sur. Co., 301 N.C. 331, 271 S.E.2d 501 (1980).

Validity as Common-Law or Voluntary Bonds. — A statutory bond, not duly executed, or not conditioned as required by statute, may be sustained as a common-law or voluntary bond. Chambers v. Witherspoon, 10 N.C. 42 (1824); Justices of Cumberland v. Armstrong, 14 N.C. 284 (1831); Justices of Currituck v. Dozier, 14 N.C. 287 (1831); Williams v. Ehringhaus, 14 N.C. 297 (1831); Vanhook v. Barnett, 15 N.C. 268 (1833); Davis v. Somerville, 15 N.C. 382 (1834); State ex rel. Davis v. McAlpin, 26 N.C. 140 (1843); Reid v. Humphreys, 52 N.C. 258 (1859).

County A.B.C. Board as Obligee. — The naming of county A.B.C. board as obligee in bond, rather than State, works no limitation of its character as official bond and affords no escape from its obligations as such. Jordan v. Harris, 225 N.C. 763, 36 S.E.2d 270 (1945).

Name of Constable Omitted. — Where a constable's official bond was signed by the obligors but a blank was left for the name of the constable, the omission was not cured by this section. Grier v. Hill, 51 N.C. 572 (1859).

Failure to Register Constable's Bond. — An irregularity, such as want of registration, will not, under this section, invalidate a constable's bond. Warren v. Boyd, 120 N.C. 56, 26 S.E. 700 (1897).

Failure to Name Conditions in Sheriff's Bond. — Failure to name conditions required by G.S. 162-8, relating to sheriff's bonds, will not, under this section, invalidate the bond given. State ex rel. Bd. of Comm'rs v. Sutton, 120 N.C. 298, 26 S.E. 920 (1897).

Mistake in Name of Ward in Guardian's Bond. — Where, in the order of a county court appointing a guardian, the name Margaret is by mistake inserted as that of the ward instead of Miranda, a bond taken according to the proper requisitions, with the right name recited, will, under the operation of this section, be sustained as an official bond. Shuster v. Perkins, 46 N.C. 325 (1854).

No Penalty Named in Guardian's Bond. — Where defendants signed a bond intending to make it the guardian bond of their principal, but there was no penalty named in the bond the same being filled in subsequent to the signature, it was held that this section does not apply, as it is confined to bonds wherein the amount of penalty varies from that fixed by law, being either more or less than the amount. Rollins v. Ebbs, 137 N.C. 355, 49 S.E. 341 (1904); Rollins v. Ebbs, 138 N.C. 140, 50 S.E. 577 (1905).

Who May Sue. — The chairman of a board of fence commissioners, although not named in the tax collector's bond, may bring suit on the same under this section, when the latter fails to pay the money collected for the erection of fences. Speight v. Staton, 104 N.C. 44, 10 S.E. 86 (1889).

Where a register of deeds issued a license for the marriage of a girl under 18 without the consent of her father, the father is the person injured within the meaning of this section. Joyner v. Roberts, 112 N.C. 111, 16 S.E. 917 (1893).

Cited in Barnes v. Lewis, 73 N.C. 138 (1875).

§ 58-72-5. Penalty for officer acting without bond.

Every person or officer of whom an official bond is required, who presumes to discharge any duty of his office before executing such bond in the manner prescribed by law, is liable to a forfeiture of five hundred dollars ($500.00) to the use of the State for each attempt so to exercise his office. The clear proceeds of forfeitures provided for in this section shall be remitted to the Civil Penalty and Forfeiture Fund in accordance with G.S. 115C-457.2. (R.C., c. 78, s. 8; Code, s. 1882; Rev., s. 278; C.S., s. 325; 1998-215, s. 91.)

CASE NOTES

Cited in Moffitt v. Davis, 205 N.C. 565, 172 S.E. 317 (1934); Langley v. Taylor, 245 N.C. 59, 95 S.E.2d 115 (1956).

§ 58-72-10. Condition and terms of official bonds.

Every treasurer, sheriff, coroner, register of deeds, surveyor, and every other officer of the several counties who is required by law to give a bond for the faithful performance of the duties of his office, shall give a bond for the term of the office to which such officer is chosen. (1869-70, c. 169; 1876-7, c. 275, s. 5; Code, s. 1874; 1895, c. 207, s. 4; 1899, c. 54, s. 54; Rev., s. 308; C.S., s. 326; 1985, c. 438.)

CASE NOTES

Cited in Moffitt v. Davis, 205 N.C. 565, 172 S.E. 317 (1934); State ex rel. Cain v. Corbett, 235 N.C. 33, 69 S.E.2d 20 (1952); Town of Scotland Neck v. Western Sur. Co., 301 N.C. 331, 271 S.E.2d 501 (1980).

§ 58-72-15. When county may pay premiums on bonds.

In all cases where the officers or any of them named in G.S. 58-72-10 are required to give a bond, the county commissioners of the county in which said officer or officers are elected are authorized and empowered to pay the premiums on the bonds of any and all such officer or officers. The board of commissioners of any county are further authorized and empowered to require individual or blanket bonds for any or all assistants, deputies or other persons regularly employed in the offices of any such county officer or officers, such bond or bonds to be conditioned upon faithful performance of duty, and, in the event of such requirement, to pay the premiums on such individual or blanket bonds. (1937, c. 440; 1953, c. 799.)

§ 58-72-20. Annual examination of bonds; security strengthened.

The bonds of the officers named in G.S. 58-72-10 shall be carefully examined on the first Monday in December of every year, and if it appears that the security has been impaired, or for any cause become insufficient to cover the amount of money or property or to secure the faithful performance of the duties of the office, then the bond shall be renewed or strengthened, the insufficient security increased within the limits prescribed by law, and the impaired security shall be made good; but no renewal, or strengthening, or additional security shall increase the penalty of said bond beyond the limits prescribed for the term of office. (1869-70, c. 169; 1876-7, c. 275, s. 5; Code, s. 1874; 1895, c. 207, s. 4; 1899, c. 54, s. 54; Rev., s. 308; C.S., s. 327.)

Cross References. — As to amount of bond of coroners, see G.S. 152-3. As to amount of bond of local finance officer, see G.S. 159-29. As to amount of bond of registers of deeds, see G.S. 161-4. As to amount of bond of sheriffs, see G.S. 162-8.

§ 58-72-25. Effect of failure to renew bond.

Upon the failure of any such officer to make such renewal of his bond, it is the duty of the board of commissioners, by an order to be entered of record, to declare his office vacant, and to proceed forthwith to appoint a successor, if the power of filling the vacancy in the particular case is vested in the board of commissioners; but if otherwise, the said board shall immediately inform the proper person having the power of appointment of the fact of such vacancy. (1869-70, c. 169, s. 2; Code, s. 1875; Rev., s. 309; C.S., s. 328.)

§ 58-72-30. Justification of sureties.

Every surety on an official bond required by law to be taken or renewed and approved by the board of commissioners shall take and subscribe an oath before the chairman of the board or some person authorized by law to administer an oath, that he is worth a certain sum (which shall be not less than one thousand dollars ($1,000)) over and above all his debts and liabilities and his homestead and personal property exemptions, and the sum thus sworn to shall in no case be less in the aggregate than the penalty of the bond. But nothing herein shall be construed to abridge the power of the said board of commissioners to require the personal presence of any such surety before the board when the bond is offered, or at such subsequent time as the board may fix, for examination as to his financial condition or other qualifications as surety. (1869-70, c. 169, s. 3; 1879, c. 207; Code, s. 1876; 1889, c. 7; 1891, c. 385; 1901, c. 32; Rev., s. 310; C.S., s. 329.)

Purpose and Effect of Section. — The intent of this section was to provide a statement under oath to show the solvency of the sureties and afford information to the county commissioners under like sanction that the aggregate amount of the bond equaled the penalty required, and it does not affect the doctrine of contribution as it relates to the rights of the sureties to contribution between themselves. Board of Comm'rs v. Dorsett, 151 N.C. 307, 66 S.E. 132 (1909).

Cited in State ex rel. Cole v. Patterson, 97 N.C. 360, 2 S.E. 262 (1887).

§ 58-72-35. Compelling justification before judge; effect of failure.

When oath is made before any judge of the superior court by five respectable citizens of any county within his district that after diligent inquiry made they verily believe that the bond of any officer of such county, which has been accepted by the board of commissioners, is insufficient either in the amount of the penalty or in the ability of the sureties, it is the duty of such judge to cause a notice to be served upon such officer requiring him to appear at some stated time and place and justify his bond by evidence other than that of himself or his sureties. If this evidence so produced fails to satisfy the judge that the bond is sufficient, both in amount and the ability of the sureties, he shall give time to the officer not exceeding 20 days, to give another bond, fixing the amount of the new bond, when there is a deficiency in that particular. And upon failure of the said officer to give a good bond to the satisfaction of the judge within the 20 days, the judge shall declare the office vacant, and if the appointment be with himself, he shall immediately proceed to fill the vacancy; and if not, he shall notify the persons having the appointing power that they may proceed as aforesaid. (1874-5, c. 120; Code, s. 1885; Rev., s. 316; C.S., s. 330.)

Cited in Mitchell v. Kilburn, 74 N.C. 483 (1876).

§ 58-72-40. Successor bonded; official bonds considered liabilities.

The person so appointed shall give bond before the judge, and the bond so given shall in all respects be subject to the requirements of the law in relation to official bonds; and all official bonds shall be considered debts and liabilities within the meaning of G.S. 58-72-30. (1874-5, c. 120, s. 2; Code, s. 1886; Rev., s. 317; C.S., s. 331.)

§ 58-72-45. Judge to file statement of proceedings with commissioners.

When a vacancy is declared by the judge, he shall file a written statement of all his proceedings with the clerk of the board of commissioners, to be recorded by him. (1874-5, c. 120, s. 3; Code, s. 1887; Rev., s. 318; C.S., s. 332.)

§ 58-72-50. Approval, acknowledgment and custody of bonds.

The approval of all official bonds taken or renewed by the board of commissioners shall be recorded by their clerk. Every such bond shall be acknowledged by the parties thereto or proved by a subscribing witness, before the chairman of the board of commissioners, or before the clerk of the superior court, registered in the register's office in a separate book to be kept for the registration of official bonds, and the original bond, with the approval of the commissioners endorsed thereon and certified by their chairman, shall be deposited with the clerk of the superior court, except the bond of said clerk, which shall be deposited with the register of deeds, for safekeeping. Provided that an official bond executed as surety by a surety company authorized to do business in this State need not be acknowledged upon behalf of the surety when such bond is executed under seal in the name of the surety by an agent or attorney-in-fact by authority of a power of attorney duly recorded in the office of the register of deeds of such county and such bond may be recorded by the register of deeds without an order of probate entered by the clerk of the superior court. (1869-70, c. 169, s. 4; 1879, c. 207, s. 2; Code, s. 1877; Rev., s. 311; C.S., s. 333; 1957, c. 1011.)

§ 58-72-55. Clerk records vote approving bond; penalty for neglect.

It is the duty of the clerk of the board of commissioners to record in the proceedings of the board the names of those commissioners who are present at the time of the approval of any official bond, and who vote for such approval. Every clerk neglecting to make such record, besides other punishment, shall forfeit his office. Any commissioner may cause his written dissent to be entered on the records of the board. (1790, c. 327, P.R.; 1809, c. 777, P.R.; R.C., c. 78, s. 7; 1869-70, c. 169, s. 8; Code, s. 1881; Rev., s. 314; C.S., s. 336.)

CASE NOTES

This section serves to show the light in which individual responsibility is re-garded by the legislature. See Rawls v. Deans, 11 N.C. 299 (1826).

§ 58-72-60. When commissioner liable as surety.

Every commissioner who approves an official bond, which he knows to be, or which by reasonable diligence he could have discovered to have been, insufficient in the penal sum, or in the security thereof, shall be liable as if he were a surety thereto, and may be sued accordingly by any person having a cause of action on said bond. (1869-70, c. 169, s. 6; Code, s. 1879; Rev., s. 313; C.S., s. 335.)

CASE NOTES

Section Supplements § 162-12. — This section supplements and somewhat extends the provision of G.S. 162-12, relating to the liability of sureties on a sheriff's bond. Hudson v. McArthur, 152 N.C. 445, 67 S.E. 995 (1910).

Liability of Commissioners. — Construing this section and former G.S. 153-9 together, it was held that the county commissioners may be held individually liable by a person sustain-ing loss by reason of their failure to perform their ministerial duty of requiring bond of a clerk of the superior court. Moffitt v. Davis, 205 N.C. 565, 172 S.E. 317 (1934).

As to joinder of parties and causes of action, see Ellis v. Brown, 217 N.C. 787, 9 S.E.2d 467 (1940).

Cited in State ex rel. Cole v. Patterson, 97 N.C. 360, 2 S.E. 262 (1887).

§ 58-72-65. Record of board conclusive as to facts stated.

In all actions under G.S. 58-72-60 a copy of the proceedings of the board of commissioners in the particular case, certified by their clerk under his hand and the seal of the county, is conclusive evidence of the facts in such record alleged and set forth. (1869-70, c. 169, s. 8; Code, s. 1881; Rev., s. 314; C.S., s. 336.)

§ 58-72-70. Person required to approve bond not to be surety.

No member of the board of commissioners, or any other person authorized to take official bonds, shall sign as surety on any official bond upon the sufficiency of which the board of which he is a member may have to pass. (1874-5, c. 120, s. 3; Code, s. 1887; Rev., s. 315; C.S., s. 337.)

ARTICLE 73.

Bonds in Surety Company.

§ 58-73-1. State officers may be bonded in surety company.

All persons who are required to give bond to the State of North Carolina to be received by the Governor or by any department of the State government, in lieu of personal security, may give as security for said bond and for the performance of the duties named in the said bond any indemnity or guaranty company authorized to do business in the State of North Carolina, subject to such regulations as the Governor or department may prescribe, and with power in them to demand additional security at any time. Any person presenting any indemnity or guaranty company as surety shall accompany his bond with a statement of the Insurance Commissioner as to the condition of such company as required by law. (1901, c. 754; Rev., s. 272; C.S., s. 338.)

CASE NOTES

Bond Construed Against Company. — A surety bond shall be construed most strongly against the company and most favorably to its general intent and essential purpose. Bank of Tarboro v. Fidelity & Deposit Co., 128 N.C. 366, 38 S.E. 908 (1901), discussing compliance with requirement of notice of default.

§ 58-73-5. When surety company sufficient surety on bonds and undertakings.

A bond or undertaking by the laws of North Carolina required or permitted to be given by a public official, fiduciary, or a party to an action or proceeding, conditioned for the doing or not doing of an act specified therein, shall be sufficient when it is executed or guaranteed by a corporation authorized in this State to act as guardian or trustee, or to guarantee the fidelity of persons holding places of public or private trust, or to guarantee the performance of contracts, other than insurance policies, or to give or guarantee bonds and undertakings in actions or proceedings.

The bond or undertaking of a corporation having such power shall be sufficient, although the law or regulation in accordance with which it is given requires two or more sureties, or requires the sureties to be residents or freeholders. But the clerk of the superior court may exercise his discretion as to accepting such a corporation's surety on the bonds of fiduciaries or parties to actions or proceedings. (1895, c. 270; 1899, c. 54, s. 45; 1901, c. 706; Rev., s. 273; C.S., s. 339.)

CASE NOTES

Same Liability as an Individual. — A surety corporation allowed by this section to give guardian bonds is held to the same liability on a bond given by it as an individual would be, and is responsible to the ward when the guardian's failure to properly perform his duties causes loss to the ward's estate. State ex rel. Roebuck v. National Sur. Co., 200 N.C. 196, 156 S.E. 531 (1931).

Cited in Pierce v. Pierce, 197 N.C. 348, 148 S.E. 438 (1929).

§ 58-73-10. Clerk to notify county commissioners of condition of company.

Each clerk of the superior court shall furnish the chairman of the board of county commissioners of his county with notice of each surety company licensed in this State, and of each surety company whose license has been revoked, in which any officer of the county has been bonded. (Rev., ss. 295, 4803; C.S., s. 340.)

§ 58-73-15. Release of company from liability.

A company executing such bond, obligation or undertaking, may be released from its liability or security on the same terms as are or may be by law prescribed for the release of individuals upon any such bonds, obligations or undertakings. (1899, c. 54, s. 48; Rev., s. 274; C.S., s. 341.)

CASE NOTES

Company May Be Released Only by Getting Off Bond. — Under this section a surety company can be released from its liability on a bond only by getting off the bond. Bank of Tarboro v. Fidelity & Deposit Co., 128 N.C. 366, 38 S.E. 908 (1901).

Defalcations after Expiration of Term of Office. — A surety company is not liable for defalcations committed after the expiration of the term of office to which the bond refers. Blades v. Dewey, 136 N.C. 176, 48 S.E. 627 (1904).

§ 58-73-20. Company not to plead ultra vires.

Any company which executes any bond, obligation or undertaking under the provisions of this Article is estopped, in any proceeding to enforce the liability which it assumes to incur, to deny its corporate power to execute such instrument or assume such liability. (1899, c. 54, s. 49; 1901, c. 706, s. 1, subsec. 5; Rev., s. 275; C.S., s. 342.)

§ 58-73-25. Failure to pay judgment is forfeiture.

If a surety company against which a judgment is recovered fails to discharge the same within 60 days from the time such final judgment is rendered, it shall forfeit its right to do business in this State, and the Insurance Commissioner shall cancel its license. (1901, c. 706, s. 1, subsec. 5; Rev., s. 275; C.S., s. 343.)

§ 58-73-30. On presentation of proper bond officer to be inducted.

Upon presentation to the person authorized by law to take, accept and file official bonds, of any bond duly executed in the penal sum required by law by the officer chosen to any such office, as principal, and by any surety company, as security thereto, whose insurance or guaranty is accepted as security upon the bonds of United States bonded officials (such insurance company having complied with the insurance laws of the State of North Carolina), or by any other good and sufficient security thereto, such bond shall be received and accepted as sufficient, and the principal thereon shall be inducted into office. (1899, c. 54, s. 53; 1901, c. 706, s. 1, subsec. 5; Rev., s. 276; C.S., s. 344.)

CASE NOTES

Estoppel to Deny Validity of Bond. — Although the failure of the treasurer to sign a bond was an irregularity under this section, both the treasurer and the surety recognized their liability thereon by offering a second bond in substitution, and both were estopped to deny the validity of the first bond on the ground of such irregularity. State ex rel. Bd. of Comm'rs v. Inman, 203 N.C. 542, 166 S.E. 519 (1932).

§ 58-73-35. Expense of fiduciary bond charged to fund.

A receiver, assignee, trustee, committee, guardian, executor or administrator, or other fiduciary required by law to give a bond as such, may include as part of his lawful expenses such sums paid to such companies for such suretyship to the extent of bond premiums actually paid per annum on the account of such bonds as the clerk, judge or court may allow. (1901, c. 706, s. 1, subsec. 5; Rev., s. 277; C.S., s. 345; 1939, c. 382.)

ARTICLE 74.

Mortgage in Lieu of Bond.

§ 58-74-1. Mortgage in lieu of required bond.

An administrator, executor, guardian, collector or receiver, or an officer required to give an official bond, or the agent or surety of such person or officer, may execute a mortgage on real estate, of the value of the bond required to be given by him to the State of North Carolina, conditioned to the same effect as the bond should be, were the same given, with a power of sale, which power of sale may be executed by the clerk of the superior court, with whom said mortgage shall be deposited, upon a breach of any of the conditions of said mortgage, after advertisement for 30 days. (1874-5, c. 103, s. 2; Code, s. 118; Rev., s. 265; C.S., s. 346.)

CASE NOTES

Mortgage of Intestate's Property. — A mortgage by an administrator on property of his intestate to which the administrator is heir does not comply with an order to increase the bond, as such a mortgage does not increase the penalty. Sellars v. Faulk, 118 N.C. 573, 24 S.E. 430 (1896).

Failure to Record. — The mortgage or deed in trust permitted by this section, to be given in lieu of an official bond, is, as to proper registra-tion, to be regarded as a mortgage, or deed in trust, and accordingly registered as the law required, construing the statute strictly, as requires; and its entry upon the records in the clerk's office as a bond, alone, without recording it in its proper place as a mortgage is insufficient to give notice to, or priority of lien, over a deed of a subsequent purchaser of the land. Hooper v. Tallassee Power Co., 180 N.C. 651, 105 S.E. 327 (1920).

§ 58-74-5. Mortgage in lieu of security for appearance, costs, or fine.

Any person required to give a bond or undertaking, or required to enter into a recognizance for his appearance at any court, in any criminal proceeding, or for the security of any costs or fine in any criminal action, may also execute a mortgage on real or personal property of the value of such bond or recognizance, payable to the State of North Carolina, conditioned as such bond or recognizance would be required, with power of sale, which power shall be executed by the clerk in whose court said mortgage is executed, upon a breach of any of the conditions of said mortgage.

No such mortgage on real property executed for the security for costs or fine shall allow a longer time for payment of said costs or fine than six months from the execution thereof, and no mortgage on personal property a longer time than three months, except in cases of appeal, when the time allowed shall be counted from the date of the final decision in the cause.

All legitimate expenses of sale, which shall only be made after due advertisement according to law, shall be paid out of the proceeds of the sale. (1874-5, c. 103, s. 3; Code, s. 120; 1891, c. 425, ss. 1, 2, 3; Rev., s. 266; C.S., s. 347; 1973, c. 108, s. 57.)

CASE NOTES

Applicability to Justice's Court. — This section, as it read in the Code of 1883, had no application in courts of justices of the peace. Comron v. Standland, 103 N.C. 207, 9 S.E. 317 (1889).

Foreclosure and Sale. — The clerk of the superior court may foreclose a mortgage on land given by plaintiff to secure costs of his action when the costs are awarded against him, or the clerk may report the matter to the court for a decree of sale by himself, the latter being the better practice to insure a safer title and prevent a needless sacrifice. Clark v. Fairly, 175 N.C. 342, 95 S.E. 550 (1918).

When the superior court, in term, acting through the presiding judge, has duly acquired jurisdiction to decree foreclosure, it is his duty to supervise the sale and see that the land brings a fair price; and when such sale has not been made accordingly, he may set aside the sale, and permit the plaintiff to pay the costs properly chargeable against him. Clark v. Fairly, 175 N.C. 342, 95 S.E. 550 (1918).

It is proper for the court to confirm the sale, and possibly it is necessary for him to do so. Clark v. Fairly, 175 N.C. 342, 95 S.E. 550 (1918).

A decree of confirmation of the sale of lands to pay the cost of an action under a mortgage given to secure them, under this section, may be set aside by the judge during the term of the superior court at which it was entered. Clark v. Fairly, 175 N.C. 342, 95 S.E. 550 (1918).

Cited in State ex rel. Solicitor v. Jenkins, 121 N.C. 637, 28 S.E. 413 (1897).

§ 58-74-10. Cancellation of mortgage in such proceedings.

Any mortgage given by any person in lieu of bond as administrator, executor, guardian, collector, receiver or as an officer required to give an official bond, or as agent or surety of such person or officer, or in lieu of bond or undertaking or recognizance for his appearance at any court in any criminal proceeding, or for the security of any cost or fine in a criminal action which has been registered, when such party as administrator, executor, guardian, collector, or receiver has filed his final account and when the time required by statute for the bond given by any administrator, executor, guardian, collector, or receiver to remain in force for the purpose of action thereon has expired, or when the officer required to give an official bond has fully complied with the conditions of such bond and the time within which suit is allowed by law to be brought thereon has expired, or when the person giving such mortgage in lieu of bond has made his appearance at the court to which he was bound and did not depart the court without leave, or paid the cost or fine required, may be canceled or discharged by the clerk of the superior court of the county where such action was pending or where the mortgage in lieu of bond is recorded by entry of "satisfaction" upon the margin of the record where such mortgage is recorded in the presence of the register of deeds, or his deputy, who shall subscribe his name as a witness thereto, and such cancellation shall have the effect to discharge and release all the right, title and interest of the State of North Carolina in and to the property described in such mortgage. (1905, c. 106; Rev., s. 267; C.S., s. 348; 1921, c. 29, ss. 1, 2; 1925, c. 252, s. 1.)

§ 58-74-15. Validating statute.

All acts heretofore done by the several superior court clerks, cancelling or satisfying any mortgage, or other instruments, herein mentioned and specified are hereby validated. (1925, c. 252, s. 2.)

§ 58-74-20. Clerk of court may give surety by mortgage deposited with register.

In all cases where the clerk of the superior court may be required to give surety, he may deposit a mortgage with the register of deeds, payable to the State, and conditioned, as the bond would have been required, with power of sale. The power of sale shall be executed by the register of deeds, upon a breach of any of the conditions of said mortgage; and the register of deeds shall in all cases immediately register the same, at the expense of the said clerk. (1874-5, c. 103, s. 6; Code, s. 122; Rev., s. 268; C.S., s. 349.)

§ 58-74-25. Mortgage in lieu of bond to prosecute or defend in civil case.

It is lawful for any person desiring to commence any civil action or special proceeding, or to defend the same, his agent or surety, to execute a mortgage on real estate of the value of the bond or undertaking required to be given, at the beginning of said action, or at any stage thereof, to the party to whom the bond or undertaking would be required to be made, conditioned to the same effect as such bond or undertaking, with power of sale, which power of sale may be executed upon a breach of any of the conditions of the said mortgage after advertisement for 30 days. (1874-5, c. 103, s. 1; Code, s. 117; Rev., s. 269; C.S., s. 35.)

Legal Periodicals. — For note on the North Carolina public assistance lien law and current constitutional doctrine, see 49 N.C.L. Rev. 519 (1971).

For comment on access of indigents into the civil courtroom, see 49 N.C.L. Rev. 683 (1971).

CASE NOTES

Section Strictly Observed. — This section is exceptional in its provisions, and must be strictly observed. Eshon v. Board of Comm'rs, 95 N.C. 75 (1886).

Undertaking on Appeal. — If it be granted that this section applies to an undertaking on appeal, the section was not complied with where the appellant deposited with the clerk a bond due to himself and secured by a mortgage as a substitute for the undertaking. Eshon v. Board of Comm'rs, 95 N.C. 75 (1886).

Section Does Not Require Mortgage. — This section does not authorize the court to require a party to execute a mortgage of real estate in the case therein provided for. It simply allows the party of whom an undertaking may be required in such cases to give such mortgage instead of it, and the former must be for the same amount as the latter. Wilson v. Fowler, 104 N.C. 471, 10 S.E. 566 (1889).

Not Applicable to Justice's Court. — This section had no application in courts of justices of the peace. Comron v. Standland, 103 N.C. 207, 9 S.E. 317 (1889).

Third Person Executing Mortgage for Defendant. — Where a mortgage is given by a third person for the defendant in an action, as is permitted by this section, and the mortgagor subsequently purchases a part of the mort-

gaged property, it was held, upon the plaintiff's recovering from the defendant, that the mortgagor has no such interest as will allow him to interfere with the plaintiff's rights under his judgment. Ryan v. Martin, 104 N.C. 176, 10 S.E. 169 (1889).

§ 58-74-30. Affidavit of value of property required.

In all cases where a mortgage is executed, as hereinbefore permitted, it is the duty of the clerk of the court in which it is executed to require an affidavit of the value of the property mortgaged to be made by at least one witness not interested in the matter, action or proceeding in which the mortgage is given. (1874-5, c. 103, s. 4; Code, s. 121; Rev., s. 270; C.S., s. 351; 1973, c. 108, s. 58.)

§ 58-74-35. When additional security required.

If, from any cause, the property mortgaged in lieu of a bond becomes of less value than the amount of the bond in lieu of which the mortgage is given, and it so appears upon affidavit of any person having any interest in the matter as a security for which the mortgage was given, it is the duty of the mortgagor to give additional security by a deposit of money, or the execution of a mortgage on more property, or justify as required in cases where bond or undertaking is given. (1874-5, c. 103, s. 5; Code, s. 119; Rev., s. 271; C.S., s. 352.)

ARTICLE 75.

Deposit in Lieu of Bond.

§ 58-75-1. Deposit of cash or securities in lieu of bond; conditions and requirements.

In lieu of any written undertaking or bond required by law in any matter, before any court of the State, the party required to make such undertaking or bond may make a deposit in cash or securities of the State of North Carolina or of the United States of America, of the amount required by law or, in the case of fiduciaries, of the amount of the trust, in lieu of the said undertaking or bond and such deposit shall be subject to all of the same conditions and requirements as are provided for in written undertakings or bonds, in lieu of which such deposit is made. (1923, c. 58; C.S., s. 352(a); 1947, c. 936.)

Legal Periodicals. — For comment on this section, see 1 N.C.L. Rev. 283 (1923); 25 N.C.L. Rev. 384 (1947).

CASE NOTES

Waiver of Exemptions. — When husband elected to deposit cash bond in lieu of surety bond to stay the execution of a judgment against him for spousal support and breach of separation agreement, husband waived any exemption to which he otherwise may have been entitled. Barrett v. Barrett, 122 N.C. App. 264, 468 S.E.2d 264 (1996).

Since the primary purpose of a bond is to provide a source of funds to be applied to the satisfaction of a valid judgment, as a matter of public policy, a party is not permitted to post a cash bond to stay execution of a money judgment and then avoid forfeiture of the bond after default by claiming debtor's exemptions. Barrett v. Barrett, 122 N.C. App. 264, 468 S.E.2d 264 (1996).

ARTICLE 76.

Actions on Bonds.

§ 58-76-1. Bonds in actions payable to court officer may be sued on in name of State.

Bonds and other obligations taken in the course of any proceeding at law, under the direction of the court, and payable to any clerk, commissioner, or officer of the court, for the benefit of the suitors in the cause, or others having an interest in such obligation, may be put in suit in the name of the State. (R.C., c. 13, s. 11; Code, s. 51; Rev., s. 280; C.S., s. 353.)

CASE NOTES

Cited in Lackey v. Pearson, 101 N.C. 651, 8 S.E. 121 (1888).

§ 58-76-5. Liability and right of action on official bonds.

Every person injured by the neglect, misconduct, or misbehavior in office of any clerk of the superior court, register, surveyor, sheriff, coroner, county treasurer, or other officer, may institute a suit or suits against said officer or any of them and their sureties upon their respective bonds for the due performance of their duties in office in the name of the State, without any assignment thereof; and no such bond shall become void upon the first recovery, or if judgment is given for the defendant, but may be put in suit and prosecuted from time to time until the whole penalty is recovered; and every such officer and the sureties on his official bond shall be liable to the person injured for all acts done by said officer by virtue or under color of his office. (1793, c. 384, s. 1, P.R.; 1825, c. 9, P.R.; 1833, c. 17; R.C., c. 78, s. 1; 1869-70, c. 169, s. 10; Code, s. 1883; Rev., s. 281; C.S., s. 354; 1973, c. 108, s. 59; 1997-14, s. 2.)

Cross References. — As to surety waiving his rights under G.S. 58-76-1 through 58-76-10 by appearing and answering in a summary proceeding, see G.S. 58-76-15 and the note thereto.

Legal Periodicals. — For a survey of 1996 developments in constitutional law, see 75 N.C.L. Rev. 2281 (1997).

For a survey of 1996 developments in tort law, see 75 N.C.L. Rev. 2468 (1997).

CASE NOTES

Abrogation of Common Law Immunity. — By expressly providing for a cause of action based on the negligence of public officers acting in their official capacity under this section, the General Assembly has abrogated common law immunity where a public official causes injury through "neglect, misconduct, or misbehavior" in the performance of his official duties or under color of his office. Slade v. Vernon, 110 N.C. App. 422, 429 S.E.2d 744 (1993).

Leave of Court Unnecessary. — This section gives in express terms the right to bring one or more suits upon one or more of the bonds to "every injured person," not on leave from the court, but absolutely and unconditionally so

soon as the breach occurs, except that it is to be instituted in the name of the State. Boothe v. Upchurch, 110 N.C. 62, 14 S.E. 642 (1892); Reid v. Holden, 242 N.C. 408, 88 S.E.2d 125 (1955).

Sections Construed Together. — This section and G.S. 58-76-20 relate to the same subject matter, are part of one and the same statute, and must be construed together. State ex rel. Underwood v. Watson, 223 N.C. 437, 27 S.E.2d 144 (1943).

Remedies Against Superior Court Clerks. — North Carolina statutes provide two separate and distinct remedies against clerks of the superior court — one in behalf of the injured individual for a specific fund to which he is entitled or on account of a particular wrong committed against him by the officer, as provided in this section; and one in behalf of the new clerk against his predecessor in office to recover possession of records, books, papers and money in the hands of the outgoing clerk by virtue or under color of his office, as provided for in former G.S. 2-22. State ex rel. Underwood v. Watson, 223 N.C. 437, 27 S.E.2d 144 (1943).

This section is not repugnant to the provisions of former G.S. 2-22, which required that each successive clerk shall receive from his predecessor all the records, moneys, and property of his office, but only gives an additional remedy for the benefit of individuals who have cause of complaint against an unfaithful clerk of the superior court. Peebles v. Boone, 116 N.C. 57, 21 S.E. 187 (1895). For present provisions similar to former § 2-22, see § 7A-106.

The failure of a register of deeds to properly index the registry of a mortgage renders him liable on his official bond to one injured by such neglect. State ex rel. Daniel v. Grizzard, 117 N.C. 105, 23 S.E. 93 (1895).

Person Injured. — The father of a girl under 18, to whom a marriage license has been issued without the father's consent, is the person injured within the meaning of this section. Joyner v. Roberts, 112 N.C. 111, 16 S.E. 917 (1893).

Under this section, claimants of a fund arising from a partition sale are the proper parties to sue on bond of the clerk for failure of the clerk to pay funds turned over to him by the commissioners in partition. Smith v. Patton, 131 N.C. 396, 42 S.E. 849 (1902).

An action can be maintained by the clerk of a superior court in his own name upon the official bond of the sheriff, for the recovery of costs accrued in such court and collected by the sheriff, and due and payable to said clerk and others. Jackson v. Maultsby, 78 N.C. 174 (1878).

By Virtue or Under Color of Office. — The last clause of this section is very comprehensive in its terms, scope and purpose. It, on purpose, enlarges the compass of the conditions of official bonds and their purpose, and the legislature intended by it, it seems, to prevent an evil pointed out in two or three of the cases. There were no adequate reasons why the conditions of official bonds should not extend to and embrace all the official duties of the office, and there were serious ones of justice and policy why they should. All persons interested are bound to accept the official services of such officers, as occasion may require, and they should be made secure in their rights, and have adequate remedy for wrongs done by them. Besides, all public officers should be held to a faithful discharge of their duties as such. It is singular that the clause last recited, notwithstanding a well known evil to be remedied, was not enacted until 1883. It first appears as part of the Code.

Now official bonds and the conditions of them embrace and extend to all acts done by virtue or under color of office of the officer giving the bond. Thomas v. Connelly, 104 N.C. 342, 10 S.E. 520 (1889); Kivett v. Young, 106 N.C. 567, 10 S.E. 1019 (1890).

In State ex rel. Wimmer v. Leonard, 68 F.2d 228 (4th Cir. 1934), a sheriff's bond contained a condition limiting the faithful execution of the office to specific duties such as execution of process and in view of this, and the wording of this section, the bond was held to afford no basis for a recovery by a person whom the sheriff wounded while acting in his official capacity.

This section extends the liability on the sheriff's general official bond and imposes liability for wrongful arrest and the use of excessive force in making an arrest under color of office. Price v. Honeycutt, 216 N.C. 270, 4 S.E.2d 611 (1939).

The surety on a bond of a delinquent tax collector is not liable for an arrest made by the collector in order to force the payment of a delinquent tax, since such act of the tax collector is not done under color of his office and does not come within the condition of the bond that he should "well and truly perform all the duties of his said office." Henry v. Wall, 217 N.C. 365, 8 S.E.2d 223, 127 A.L.R. 854 (1940).

The last clause of this section has been held to enlarge the conditions of the official bond to extend to all official duties of the office. State ex rel. Williams v. Adams, 288 N.C. 501, 219 S.E.2d 198 (1975).

Same — Acts Which Should Have Been Performed. — It is true that the clause seems in terms to provide only for acts done by the officer, and not for those which he should do but does not. But it would be putting a very narrow construction on the statute to say that he and his sureties are liable for what he did, but not for what he should have done and did not do, although the damage to the party was equally as great. State ex rel. Daniel v. Grizzard, 117 N.C. 105, 23 S.E. 93 (1895).

This section has been broadly construed over its long history to cover not only acts done by the officer but also acts that should have been done. State ex rel. Williams v. Adams, 288 N.C. 501, 219 S.E.2d 198 (1975).

Same — Illustrative Acts. — Where a clerk appointed the commissioner to make a partition sale, without bond, and on approving his report received and receipted the proceeds as clerk, took out his costs and entered the amount due each heir at law on his docket, and disbursed a portion of said fund to the parties entitled, this would seem to be a receipt of the fund by the clerk "by virtue of his office." The Judges v. Deans, 9 N.C. 93 (1822); McNeill v. Morrison, 63 N.C. 508 (1869); Cox v. Blair, 76 N.C. 78 (1877). But if this were otherwise the clerk received it "as clerk," and so receipted for it. This was certainly a receipt of the money "under color of his office, " and, indeed, this is admitted in the answer. The older decisions were made when these words were not in the statute. The clause embraces all cases where the officer received the money in his official capacity, but when he may not be authorized or required to receive the same. In such case the bond is responsible for the safe custody of the fund so paid in. Smith v. Patton, 131 N.C. 396, 42 S.E. 849 (1902), citing Broughton v. Haywood, 61 N.C. 380 (1867); Greenlee v. Sudderth, 65 N.C. 470 (1871); Brown v. Coble, 76 N.C. 391 (1877); Ex parte Cassidey, 95 N.C. 225 (1886); Thomas v. Connelly, 104 N.C. 342, 10 S.E. 520 (1889); Sharpe v. Connelly, 105 N.C. 87, 11 S.E. 177 (1890); Presson v. Boone, 108 N.C. 78, 12 S.E. 897 (1891).

When the clerk of the superior court is appointed receiver of a minor's estate, he takes and holds the funds by virtue of his office of clerk, and his sureties upon his official bond as such officer are liable for any failure of duty on his part in that respect. Boothe v. Upchurch, 110 N.C. 62, 14 S.E. 642 (1892).

Bonds Cumulative. — Official bonds given by an officer during any one term of office are cumulative, and the new bond does not discharge the old case. Oats v. Bryan, 14 N.C. 451 (1832); Bell's Adm'r v. Jasper, 37 N.C. 597 (1843); Poole v. Cox, 31 N.C. 69, 49 Am. Dec. 410 (1848); Moore v. Boudinot, 64 N.C. 190 (1870); Pickens v. Miller, 83 N.C. 544 (1880); Fidelity & Deposit Co. v. Fleming, 132 N.C. 332, 43 S.E. 899 (1903).

Where the surety has renewed the bond of a clerk of the court upon his election to that office a second time, acknowledged its liability and received premiums thereon, its liability is cumulative for all defalcations thereunder, whether for the second term its principal was continuing to act de facto or de jure. Lee v. Martin, 186 N.C. 127, 118 S.E. 914 (1923).

The first bonds continue to be a security for the discharge of the duties during the whole term, and the new bonds become additional security for the discharge of such of the duties as have not been performed at the time they are given. Poole v. Cox, 31 N.C. 69, 49 Am. Dec. 410 (1848). See also Oats v. Bryan, 14 N.C. 451 (1832); Bell's Adm'r v. Jasper, 37 N.C. 597 (1843).

Bond Determines Limit on Immunity. — To the extent of the bond required by this section, defendant-public officials were not immune from the claim of the plaintiff-former inmate who suffered from hemophilia and who alleged that defendants' failure to respond properly to his nose bleed ultimately caused him to be hospitalized. Summey v. Barker, 142 N.C. App. 688, 544 S.E.2d 262, 2001 N.C. App. LEXIS 180 (2001).

Action on Bond and on Case. — An action of debt on a sheriff's bond for money collected, and a nonsuit therein, is a sufficient demand to enable the plaintiff to sustain an action on the case for the same cause of action. Fagan v. Williamson, 53 N.C. 433 (1862).

Negligent Conduct of Jailer Imputed to Sheriff. — Under this section the sheriff and the surety on his official bond are liable for the wrongful death of a prisoner resulting from the negligence of the jailer in locking the prisoner, in the weakened condition, in a cell with a person whom the sheriff and the jailer knew to be violently insane, and who assaulted the prisoner during the night, inflicting the fatal injury. Dunn v. Swanson, 217 N.C. 279, 7 S.E.2d 563 (1940). For note on this case see 19 N.C.L. Rev. 101 (1941).

Action on Negligence. — This section, in so many words, provides for the prosecution of a cause of action based on negligence. State ex rel. Williams v. Adams, 288 N.C. 501, 219 S.E.2d 198 (1975).

Action for Neglect, Misconduct or Misbehavior of Sheriffs. — A cause of action was available to plaintiffs under this section for the neglect, misconduct or misbehavior of defendant sheriffs independent of plaintiffs' negligence claims against defendants. Hull v. Oldham, 104 N.C. App. 29, 407 S.E.2d 611, cert. denied, 330 N.C. 441, 412 S.E.2d 72 (1991).

A prison official is liable when he knows of, or, in the exercise of reasonable care, should anticipate danger to the prisoner, and with such knowledge or anticipation fails to take the proper precautions to safeguard his prisoners. State ex rel. Williams v. Adams, 288 N.C. 501, 219 S.E.2d 198 (1975).

Necessary Parties in Action against Deputy Sheriff. — If the defendant were acting in the capacity of deputy sheriff at the time of the alleged assault and false arrest, he and the surety on his bond, and the sheriff and the surety on his bond, would be proper and necessary parties to the action based on the cause of action for the alleged assault and false arrest. State ex rel. Cain v. Corbett, 235 N.C. 33, 69 S.E.2d 20 (1952).

Amendment of Complaint to Join Surety. — The statutory mandate that the sheriff furnish a bond works to remove the sheriff from the protective embrace of governmental immunity, but only where the surety is joined as a party to the action. The fact that the surety is not named as a party, however, is easily corrected by amendment to the complaint. Messick v. Catawba County, 110 N.C. App. 707, 431 S.E.2d 489, cert. denied, 334 N.C. 621, 435 S.E.2d 336 (1993).

Suits Against a Sheriff. — The legislature has prescribed two ways for a sheriff to be sued in his official capacity, this section and G.S.

153A-435. Smith v. Phillips, 117 N.C. App. 378, 451 S.E.2d 309 (1994).

The plaintiff failed to state a cause of action on a sheriff's official bond for the wrongful death of her husband, where she based her suit on the negligent release of a prisoner who later murdered her husband during a robbery, but she did not allege that the sheriff intentionally misbehaved in the performance of his duties, and the public duty doctrine barred any claim that the sheriff acted negligently in the performance of his duties. Stafford v. Baker, 129 N.C. App. 576, 502 S.E.2d 1 (1998), cert. denied, 348 N.C. 695, 511 S.E.2d 650 (1998).

Malicious Prosecution Claim Properly Dismissed. — Summary judgment was properly granted for the defendants, a sheriff and his officers, as to the plaintiff's malicious prosecution claim where no evidence indicated that the sheriff acted with malice when he caused the plaintiff to be arrested after repeatedly warning him to turn over some equipment which the plaintiff held pursuant to a mechanic's lien. Thomas v. Sellers, 142 N.C. App. 130, 542 S.E.2d 283, 2001 N.C. App. LEXIS 88 (2001).

Assault Claim Properly Dismissed. — Summary judgment was properly granted for the defendants, a sheriff and his officers, as to

the plaintiff's assault claim where no evidence indicated that the sheriff used excessive force when he caused the plaintiff to be arrested after repeatedly warning him to turn over some equipment which the plaintiff held pursuant to a mechanic's lien. Thomas v. Sellers, 142 N.C. App. 130, 542 S.E.2d 283, 2001 N.C. App. LEXIS 88 (2001).

Trial court erred in denying defendants' motion to dismiss all claims against them for false arrest, false imprisonment, etc., in their official capacities on the basis of governmental and sovereign immunity. Mellon v. Prosser, 126 N.C. App. 620, 486 S.E.2d 439 (1997), rev'd on other grounds, 347 N.C. 568, 494 S.E.2d 763 (1998).

Applied in Bank of Spruce Pine v. McKinney, 209 N.C. 668, 184 S.E. 506 (1936); Cole v. Cole, 633 F.2d 1083 (4th Cir. 1980).

Cited in Midgett v. Nelson, 214 N.C. 396, 199 S.E. 393 (1938); Davis v. Moore, 215 N.C. 449, 2 S.E.2d 366 (1939); Jordan v. Harris, 225 N.C. 763, 36 S.E.2d 270 (1945); State ex rel. West v. Ingle, 269 N.C. 447, 152 S.E.2d 476 (1967); Bynum v. Kidd, 570 F. Supp. 696 (W.D.N.C. 1983); Goodwin v. Furr, 25 F. Supp. 2d 713 (M.D.N.C. 1998); George v. Administrative Office of Courts, 142 N.C. App. 479, 542 S.E.2d 699, 2001 N.C. App. LEXIS 139 (2001).

§ 58-76-10. Complaint must show party in interest; election to sue officer individually.

Any person who brings suit in manner aforesaid shall state in his complaint on whose relation and in whose behalf the suit is brought, and he shall be entitled to receive to his own use the money recovered; but nothing herein contained shall prevent such person from bringing at his election an action against the officer to recover special damages for his injury. (1793, c. 384, ss. 2, 3, P.R.; R.C., c. 78, s. 2; 1869-70, c. 169, s. 11; Code, s. 1884; Rev., s. 282; C.S., s. 355.)

CASE NOTES

The relator is the real party in interest in an action brought in the name of the State on an official bond, and he will be so considered in determining the identity of the parties under a

plea of res judicata in a subsequent action. Reid v. Holden, 242 N.C. 408, 88 S.E.2d 125 (1955).

Cited in Western Carolina Power Co. v. Yount, 208 N.C. 182, 179 S.E. 804 (1935).

§ 58-76-15. Summary remedy on official bond.

When a sheriff, coroner, clerk, county or town treasurer, or other officer, collects or receives any money by virtue or under color of his office, and on demand fails to pay the same to the person entitled to require the payment thereof, the person thereby aggrieved may move for judgment in the superior court against such officer and his sureties for any sum demanded; and the court shall try the same and render judgment at the session when the motion shall be made, but 10 days' notice in writing of the motion must have been previously given. (1819, c. 1002, P.R.; R.C., c. 78, s. 5; 1869-70, c. 169, s. 14; 1876-7, c. 41, s. 2; Code, s. 1889; Rev., s. 283; C.S., s. 356; 1973, c. 108, s. 60.)

CASE NOTES

Remedy Cumulative. — It has never been understood that this cumulative and optional remedy obstructed the bringing of a regular action on the bond, when the injured party preferred to have recourse to it. Lackey v. Pearson, 101 N.C. 651, 8 S.E. 121 (1888).

Justice Had No Jurisdiction. — Since the repeal of G.S. 13 of c. 80 of Battle's Revision it was decided by repeated adjudications that a justice of the peace had no jurisdiction of an action on a constable's bond. Coggins v. Harrell, 86 N.C. 317 (1882).

To What Officers Applicable. — In Smith v. Moore, 79 N.C. 86 (1878), it was held that the power conferred by this section as it read in the Revised Code of 1856, was confined to the officers named therein, and that there was no way to hold a commissioner appointed to make a judicial sale liable for the proceeds thereof, except by an action instituted by the parties entitled to the money. Subsequent to this decision the words "or other public officer," have been inserted in the section; but applying the ejusdem generis rule it would seem that these words would not include a master in chancery and that the Smith case declares the law as it still stands. See, however, Ex parte Curtis, 82 N.C. 435 (1880), where the court states that a remedy against executrix and clerk and master should have been by summary motion under this section.

Actions by Persons Entitled to Money. — The section gives a summary remedy against public officers only to those entitled to the money, so that a new clerk cannot proceed under it against a former clerk, for not paying office money over to him as his successor. O'Leary v. Harrison, 51 N.C. 338 (1859).

There is no provision in the statute giving a preference to the party or parties who first seek such summary remedy. And, withal, before any claim, preferential or otherwise, can be established under this statute, notice must be given, the court must try the cause, and judgment must be obtained. Western Carolina Power Co. v. Yount, 208 N.C. 182, 179 S.E. 804 (1935).

It was never intended that the mere lodging of a motion under this section established a preference, or right to establish a preference, over other creditors when such other creditors had been guilty of no laches in asserting their claims. Western Carolina Power Co. v. Yount, 208 N.C. 182, 179 S.E. 804 (1935).

Minor Interested in Fund Must Be Represented by Guardian Ad Litem. — Where a judgment for personal injuries in an action prosecuted by the father as next friend for his minor son is paid only in part, it is error for the court on the father's motion under this section

to order the clerk to pay the father out of the recovery the entire amount expended by the father for necessary medical treatment of the minor, when the minor is not represented by a disinterested guardian ad litem, since the interests of the father and the minor in the fund are antagonistic. White v. Osborne, 251 N.C. 56, 110 S.E.2d 449 (1959).

Proceedings May Be Consolidated with General Creditor's Suit. — Plaintiff instituted summary proceedings under this section against the clerk of the superior court and the surety on his bond to recover for the clerk's default in failing to return to plaintiff, as ordered by the superior court, moneys deposited with the clerk. Notice and complaint in the proceeding were served on defendants. Thereafter another creditor of the clerk instituted suit in her own behalf and in behalf of all persons similarly situated, and decree was entered appointing a permanent receiver for the clerk, authorizing the receiver to bring suit on the clerk's bonds, and enjoining all creditors of the clerk from instituting any other suit or action against him or on his bonds. In the summary proceeding under this section, the surety on the clerk's bond pleaded the decree affirming receiver in bar to plaintiff's right to judgment, and the trial court dismissed the summary proceeding. It was held that the summary proceeding should have been consolidated with the suit in the nature of a general creditor's bill. Western Carolina Power Co. v. Yount, 205 N.C. 321, 171 S.E. 321 (1933).

Demand Not Necessary. — In a proceeding by the State, against a clerk of the superior court and the surety on his bond to recover sums embezzled by the clerk, the plaintiffs have the right to pursue the summary remedy under this section, upon their motion after due notice, and demand upon the clerk is not necessary. State v. Gant, 201 N.C. 211, 159 S.E. 427 (1931).

Waiver by Appearance. — Where a summary proceeding under this section has been instituted against a clerk of the superior court and the surety on his bonds to recover sums embezzled by the clerk, and the surety has entered a general appearance and filed answer, etc., the surety has waived its rights, if any it had, under G.S. 58-76-1 through 58-76-10, to object that the plaintiffs could not maintain a summary proceeding under this section. State v. Gant, 201 N.C. 211, 159 S.E. 427 (1931).

Judgment. — Under this practice, judgment was entered for the amount of the bond, the execution to be satisfied on payment of the sum collected and costs. Fell v. Porter, 69 N.C. 140 (1873). From the language of the opinion in this case it would seem that at the time of decision the operation of this section had been suspended. — Ed. note

Where A. obtained a judgment against B., clerk of the superior court, for a sum of money in his hands by virtue of his office, and B. died, and his administrator, upon demand, failed to pay the money, it was held that the court below erred in overruling a motion by the plaintiff for a judgment upon the official bond of the clerk

under the provisions of this section. Cooper v. Williams, 75 N.C. 94 (1876).

Notice. — As this section read in Battle's Revision the proceedings were "without other notice than is given by the delinquency of the officer." See Prairie v. Jenkins, 75 N.C. 545 (1876).

Applied in State v. Sawyer, 223 N.C. 102, 25 S.E.2d 443 (1943).

§ 58-76-20. Officer unlawfully detaining money liable for damages.

When money received as aforesaid is unlawfully detained by any of said officers, and the same is sued for in any mode whatever, the plaintiff is entitled to recover, besides the sum detained, damages at the rate of twelve per centum (12%) per annum from the time of detention until payment. (1819, c. 1002, s. 2, P.R.; R.C., c. 78, s. 9; 1868-9, c. 169; Code, s. 1890; Rev., s. 284; C.S., s. 357.)

CASE NOTES

This section must be considered in connection with § 58-76-15. Pasquotank County v. Hood, 209 N.C. 552, 184 S.E. 5 (1936).

And § 58-76-5. — This section and G.S. 58-76-5 relate to the same subject matter and are a part of one and the same statute. They must be construed together. State ex rel. Underwood v. Watson, 223 N.C. 437, 27 S.E.2d 144 (1943).

This Section and § 58-76-15 Are Not Applicable to Liquidation of Banks by Commissioner of Banks. — This section and G.S. 58-76-15 are inapplicable to impose liability for damages in a case where the Commissioner of Banks took over the affairs of a bank which had been theretofore constituted the financial agent of the county and which had county funds on deposit and in its possession. Pasquotank County v. Hood, 209 N.C. 552, 184 S.E. 5 (1936).

The Commissioner of Banks holding a portion of the fund, subject to the orders of the court and for the purpose of liquidation, could not be said to constitute an "unlawful detention," nor should he in his representative capacity be liable in damages as a penalty for so doing. The punishment would not fall upon a defaulting or delinquent public officer, as intended by the statute, but would penalize funds held in trust for all the creditors and stockholders whose stock assessments have helped to contribute. Pasquotank County v. Hood, 209 N.C. 552, 184 S.E. 5 (1936).

Default of Officer Must Be Shown. — In an action to recover the 12% allowed under this section, it is necessary that the plaintiff show some adequate default. Hannah v. Hyatt, 170

N.C. 634, 87 S.E. 517 (1916).

Liability of Surety. — While, as against the principal on the bond of a clerk of the superior court, interest under the statute at the rate of 12% is collectible from the time of defalcation, the amount of the penalty on his bond determines the liability of the surety thereon. State ex rel. Lee v. Martin, 188 N.C. 119, 123 S.E. 631 (1924).

Effect of Waiver of Interest from Date of Defalcation. — Where, in an action against a clerk of the superior court and his surety to recover sums embezzled by the clerk, the State waives the interest from the date of the actual defalcations, but does demand the 12% from the date of the expiration of each term of office; a judgment awarding damages at 12%, under the provisions of this section, on the sums defaulted from the expiration of each term is not error, the amount being within the penalty of the bond. State v. Gant, 201 N.C. 211, 159 S.E. 427 (1931).

Interest by Way of Damages. — Whether or not the clerk is entitled to the benefits of this section, in a suit against his predecessor, is not now decided; but, granting that he is not so entitled, the law allows interest by way of damages on money wrongfully detained. State ex rel. Underwood v. Watson, 223 N.C. 437, 27 S.E.2d 144 (1943); State ex rel. Underwood v. Watson, 224 N.C. 502, 31 S.E.2d 465 (1944).

Applied in Windley v. Lupton, 212 N.C. 167, 193 S.E. 213 (1937).

Cited in Wood v. Citizens Bank, 199 N.C. 371, 154 S.E. 623 (1930).

§ 58-76-25. Evidence against principal admissible against sureties.

In actions brought upon the official bonds of clerks of courts, sheriffs, coroners, or other public officers, and also upon the bonds of executors, administrators, collectors or guardians, when it may be necessary for the plaintiff to prove any default of the principal obligors, any receipt or acknowledgment of such obligors, or any other matter or thing which by law would be admissible and competent for or toward proving the same as against him, shall in like manner be admissible and competent as presumptive evidence only against all or any of his sureties who may be defendants with or without him in said actions. (1844, c. 38; R.C., c. 44, s. 10; 1881, c. 8; Code, s. 1345; Rev., s. 285; C.S., s. 358; 1973, c. 108, s. 61.)

CASE NOTES

Judgments as Evidence — Generally. — In action against an officer and one of the sureties on his official bond, the record of a judgment against the officer, and others of his sureties, in a previous action against them for the same demand, and on the same bond, but in which action the surety in the present action was not a party, is competent evidence to fix the amount due by the officer. Morgan v. Smith, 95 N.C. 396 (1886).

The question how far a judgment or decree is conclusive against a surety of a defendant, or against one who is liable over to a defendant, and who was not a party to the action, is involved in the greatest confusion. Between the intimate relations which exist between such a person and the defendant in the suit, on the one side, and the fundamental principle that no one ought to be bound by proceedings to which he was a stranger, on the other, the court has found it difficult to steer. Dixie Fire Ins. Co. v. American Bonding Co., 162 N.C. 384, 78 S.E. 430 (1913).

The cases are numerous in which it has been decided that a judgment rendered against a guardian is not, unaided by the statute, admissible as evidence against the surety to his bond. McKellar v. Powell, 11 N.C. 34 (1825).

The same rulings have been made in regard to the sureties to an administration bond. Chairman of Mecklenburg v. Clark, 11 N.C. 43 (1825); Vanhook v. Barnett, 15 N.C. 268 (1833); Governor ex rel. Huggins v. Montford, 23 N.C. 155 (1840); Governor ex rel. McElroy v. Carter, 25 N.C. 338 (1843). So in reference to the liability of his surety to an amercement against the sheriff.

The act of 1844 (this section), however, changed the rule of law, and rendered competent against the sureties to official bonds, and those given by executors, administrators and guardians, whatever evidence would be competent against the principals, and this was declared to be conclusive, where the evidence was a judgment against him, in Brown v. Pike, 74 N.C. 531 (1876); and in Badger v. Daniel, 79 N.C. 372 (1878).

The act of 1881 amended the previous enactment by making the evidence "presumptive only" against the sureties. Moore v. Alexander, 96 N.C. 34, 1 S.E. 536 (1887).

"It seems that our predecessors in office upon this Bench have intimated, and in one case held, that such judgments, unaided by the statute, are inadmissible in evidence against the surety. Moore v. Alexander, 96 N.C. 34, 1 S.E. 536 (1887). But an examination of the question has convinced us that the decided trend of modern authority is to the effect that such a judgment against the principal prima facie only establishes the sum or amount of the liability against the sureties, although not parties to the action, but the sureties may impeach the judgment for fraud, collusion, or mistake, as well as set up an independent defense." Dixie Fire Ins. Co. v. American Bonding Co., 162 N.C. 384, 78 S.E. 430 (1913).

While this section fixed the rule as to actions brought upon the official bonds of clerks of courts, sheriffs, coroners, or other public officers, and also upon the bonds of executors, administrators, collectors, or guardians, the precedents were in hopeless discord as to bonds not covered by the statute, until Associate Justice Brown laid down the rule in Dixie Fire Ins. Co. v. American Bonding Co., 162 N.C. 384, 78 S.E. 430 (1913). "But an examination of the question has convinced us that the decided trend of modern authority is to the effect that such a judgment against the principal prima facie only establishes the sum or amount of the liability against the sureties, although not parties to the action, but the sureties may impeach the judgment for fraud, collusion, or mistake, as well as set up an independent defense." Charleston & W.C. Ry. v. Robert G. Lassiter & Co., 208 N.C. 209, 179 S.E. 879 (1935).

Same — Evidence of Assets as Well as

Debts. — See Armistead v. Harramond, 11 N.C. 339 (1826); Brown v. Pike, 74 N.C. 531 (1876); Badger v. Daniel, 79 N.C. 386 (1878); Morgan v. Smith, 95 N.C. 396 (1886).

Same — Section Not Applicable to Tort Action. — The rule that the judgment against the principal in an official or fiduciary bond is presumptive evidence against the sureties under this section does not apply where the action is not on the bond, but in tort. Martin v. Buffaloe, 128 N.C. 305, 38 S.E. 902 (1901).

Same — Judgment Based on Admissions of Principal's Administrator, Where Interests of Administrator and Surety Conflict. — A judgment upon the admissions in the answer of the administrator bank of a deceased county treasurer is not competent in an action by the county commissioners as evidence against the surety on the official bond of the deceased when the bank has been made a party defendant and the surety at once raises the issue as to whether a part of the defalcation was moneys defaulted from the bank when the deceased was acting as its assistant cashier, the interest of the bank and the surety being in conflict, and this section not applying in such cases. Commissioners of Chowan County v.

Citizens Bank, 197 N.C. 410, 149 S.E. 380 (1929).

For case recognizing the principle adopted in Commissioners of Chowan County v. Citizens Bank, 197 N.C. 410, 149 S.E. 380 (1929), but holding the rule inapplicable under peculiar facts of case, see Charleston & W.C. Ry. v. Robert G. Lassiter & Co., 208 N.C. 209, 179 S.E. 879 (1935).

Annual account of guardian is competent evidence against him, and presumptive evidence against his sureties. Loftin v. Cobb, 126 N.C. 58, 35 S.E. 230 (1900).

Joinder of Administrator and Sureties. — Under this section the sureties on an administrator's bond are properly joined with the administrator, where it is shown that the administrator received a benefit from a falsified final account by reason of which the plaintiff's judgment against the administrators remained unpaid. State ex rel. Salisbury Morris Plan Co. v. McCanless, 193 N.C. 200, 136 S.E. 371 (1927).

Cited in Pullen v. Heron Mining Co., 71 N.C. 563 (1874); Gurganus v. McLawhorn, 212 N.C. 397, 193 S.E. 844 (1937).

§ 58-76-30. Officer liable for negligence in collecting debt.

When a claim is placed in the hands of any sheriff or coroner for collection, and he does not use due diligence in collecting the same, he shall be liable for the full amount of the claim notwithstanding the debtor may have been at all times and is then able to pay the amount thereof. (1844, c. 64; R.C., c. 78, s. 3; 1869-70, c. 169, s. 12; Code, s. 1888; Rev., s. 286; C.S., s. 359; 1973, c. 108, s. 62.)

CASE NOTES

Section Applicable to Claims, Not Executions. — This section applies only to claims placed in the hands of the sheriff or other officer for collection — such claims as are within the jurisdiction of a justice of the peace, and may be collected by judgment and process of execution granted by that magistrate. It does not apply to executions issuing from the superior or other courts of record. The reason for the distinction is clearly and certainly pointed out in McLaurin v. Buchanan, 60 N.C. 91 (1863). The statute, in effect, now is just as it was when that decision was made. Brunhild v. Potter, 107

N.C. 415, 12 S.E. 55 (1890).

What Constitutes Negligence. — The degree of diligence required is that which a prudent man would ordinarily exercise in the management of his own affairs. A constable is not bound to such strict accountability as when process is delivered to him as an officer. Morgan v. Horne, 44 N.C. 25 (1852); Lipscomb v. Cheek, 61 N.C. 332 (1867). Therefore, what constitutes negligence must depend upon the facts in each particular case; five months' delay was held negligence in State ex rel. Nixon v. Bagby, 52 N.C. 4 (1859).

ARTICLE 77.

Guaranteed Arrest Bond Certificates of Automobile Clubs and Associations in Lieu of Bond.

§§ **58-77-1, 58-77-5:** Repealed by Session Laws 1999-132, s. 12.1, effective June 4, 1999.

ARTICLE 78.

State Fire and Rescue Commission.

§ 58-78-1. State Fire and Rescue Commission created; membership.

(a) There is created the State Fire and Rescue Commission of the Department, which shall be composed of 15 voting members to be appointed as follows:

  (1) The Commissioner shall appoint 12 members, two from nominations submitted by the North Carolina State Firemen's Association, one from nominations submitted by the North Carolina Association of Fire Chiefs, one from nominations submitted by the Professional Firefighters of North Carolina Association, one from nominations submitted by the North Carolina Society of Fire Service Instructors, one from nominations submitted by the North Carolina Association of County Fire Marshals, one from nominations submitted by the North Carolina Fire Marshal's Association, two from nominations submitted by the North Carolina Association of Rescue and Emergency Medical Services, Inc., one mayor or other elected city official nominated by the President of the League of Municipalities, one county commissioner nominated by the President of the Association of County Commissioners, and one from the public at large;

  (2) The Governor shall appoint one member from the public at large; and

  (3) The General Assembly shall appoint two members from the public at large, one upon the recommendation of the Speaker of the House of Representatives pursuant to G.S. 120-121, and one upon the recommendation of the President Pro Tempore of the Senate pursuant to G.S. 120-121.

Public members may not be employed in State government and may not be directly involved in fire fighting or rescue services.

(b) Of the members initially appointed by the Commissioner, the nominees of the North Carolina State Firemen's Association and the nominees of the North Carolina Association of Fire Chiefs and the nominees of the Professional Firefighters of North Carolina Association and of the North Carolina Association of Rescue and Emergency Medical Services, Inc., shall serve three-year terms; the nominees from the North Carolina Society of Fire Service Instructors, the North Carolina Association of County Fire Marshals, and the North Carolina Fire Marshal's Association shall serve two-year terms; and the mayor or other elected city official, the county commissioner, and the member from the public at large shall serve one-year terms. The Governor's initial appointee shall serve a three-year term. The General Assembly's initial appointees shall serve two-year terms. Thereafter all terms shall be for three years.

(c) Vacancies shall be filled by the original appointer in the same manner as the original appointment was made, except that vacancies in the appointments made by the General Assembly shall be filled in accordance with G.S. 120-122.

(d) Appointed members shall serve until their successors are appointed and qualified.

(e) The following State officials, or their designees, shall serve by virtue of their offices as nonvoting members of the Commission: the Commissioner of Insurance, the Commissioner of Labor, the Attorney General, the Secretary of Crime Control and Public Safety, the Secretary of Environment and Natural Resources, and the President of the Department of Community Colleges.

(f) Members of the Commission shall receive per diem and necessary travel and subsistence allowances in accordance with the provisions of G.S. 138-5 or

G.S. 138-6, as appropriate. (1977, c. 1064, s. 1; 1981, c. 791, ss. 1, 2; 1981 (Reg. Sess., 1982), c. 1191, ss. 21, 22; 1983, c. 840, ss. 1, 2; 1985, c. 757, s. 167(b), (d); 1989, c. 727, s. 218; c. 750, s. 1; 1991, c. 720, s. 47; 1993, c. 155, s. 1; 1995, c. 490, s. 20; 1997-116, s. 1; 1997-443, s. 11A.123.)

Editor's Note. — This Article is former Part 4 of Article 11 of Chapter 143B, recodified by Session Laws 1985, c. 757, s. 167(b) as Article 2C of Chapter 58, which in turn has been recodified as Article 78 of Chapter 58 pursuant to Session Laws 1987, c. 752, s. 9, as amended by Session Laws 1987 (Reg. Sess., 1988), c. 975, s. 34.

Session Laws 1989, c. 750, s. 2 provides in part: "All rules and regulations of the State Fire Commission in effect on the effective date of Section 1 of this act [July 1, 1989] shall remain in effect as rules and regulations of the State Fire and Rescue Commission unless changed in accordance with those rules and regulations and applicable law by the State Fire and Rescue Commission."

Session Laws 1989, c. 750, s. 1 provides that the title of Article 78 of Chapter 58 now reads "State Fire and Rescue Commission."

§ 58-78-5. State Fire and Rescue Commission — Powers and duties.

(a) The Commission shall have the following powers and duties:

(1) To formally adopt a State Fire Education and Training Plan, a State Master Plan for Fire Prevention and Control, a Rescue Training Plan, and a State Master Plan for Rescue Services;

(2) To assist and participate with State and local fire prevention and control agencies in the improvement of fire prevention and control in North Carolina and to work with State and local rescue agencies to improve rescue services in the State;

(3) To increase the professional skills of fire protection and fire-fighting personnel and rescue personnel;

(4) To encourage public support for fire prevention and control and rescue services;

(5) To accept gifts, bequests, devises, grants, matching funds, and other considerations from private or governmental sources for use in promoting its work;

(6) To make grants for use in pursuing its objectives, under such conditions as are deemed to be necessary and such other powers as may be necessary to carry out the State's duties with respect to all grants to the State by the United States Fire Administration and the National Fire Academy; and all support programs brought into the State by these two entities shall be coordinated and controlled by the Commission;

(7) To make studies and recommendations for the improvement of fire prevention and control and rescue services in the State and to make studies and recommendations for the coordination and implementation of effective fire prevention and control and rescue services and for effective fire prevention and control and rescue services education;

(8) To set objectives and priorities for the improvement of fire prevention and control and rescue services throughout the State;

(9) To advise State and local interests of opportunities for securing federal assistance for fire prevention and control and rescue services and for improving fire prevention and control and rescue services administration and planning within the State of North Carolina;

(10) To assist State agencies and institutions of local government and combinations thereof in the preparation and processing of applications for financial aid and to support fire prevention and control, rescue services, and planning and administration;

(11) To encourage and assist coordination at the federal, State and local government levels in the preparation and implementation of fire prevention and control and rescue services administrative improvements and crime reduction plans;

(12) To apply for, receive, disburse and audit the use of funds received from any public and private agencies and instrumentalities for fire prevention and control and rescue services, their administration and plans therefor;

(13) To enter into monitoring and evaluating the results of contracts and agreements necessary or incidental to the discharge of its assigned responsibilities;

(14) To provide technical assistance to State and local fire prevention and control and rescue agencies in developing programs for improvement;

(14a) To serve as a central office for the collection and dissemination of information relative to fire service and rescue service activities and programs in State government. All State government agencies conducting fire service and rescue service related programs and activities shall report the status of these programs and activities to the Commission on a quarterly basis and they shall also report to the Commission any new programs or changes to existing programs as they are implemented;

(14b) To establish voluntary minimum professional qualifications for all levels of fire service and rescue service personnel;

(14c) To prepare an annual report to the Governor on its fire prevention and control activities and plans, rescue activities and plans, and to recommend legislation concerning fire prevention and control and rescue services;

(14d) To reimburse the members of the Commission's certification board, in accordance with G.S. 138-5, for travel and subsistence expenses incurred by them in their duties as certification board officers; and

(15) To take such other actions as may be deemed necessary or appropriate to carry out its assigned duties and responsibilities.

(16) To provide workers' compensation benefits under G.S. 58-87-10, to create a Volunteer Safety Workers' Compensation Board to assist it in performing this duty, and to reimburse the members of the Commission's Volunteer Safety Workers' Compensation Board in accordance with G.S. 138-5 for travel and subsistence expenses incurred by them.

(b) Each State agency involved in fire prevention and control or rescue related activities shall furnish the executive director of the Commission such information as may be required to carry out the intent of this section. (1977, c. 1064, s. 1; 1981, c. 791, ss. 3, 4; 1985, c. 757, s. 167(b); 1989, c. 750, s. 1; 1993, c. 321, s. 41; 1995, c. 507, s. 7.21A(c).)

§ 58-78-10. State Fire and Rescue Commission — Organization; rules and regulations; meetings.

(a) Organization. — The Commission shall elect from its voting members a chairman and vice-chairman to serve as provided by the rules adopted by the Commission.

(b) Rules and Regulations. — The Commission shall adopt such rules and regulations, not inconsistent with the laws of this State as may be required by the federal government for programs and grants-in-aid for fire protection, firefighting, and rescue purposes which may be made available to the State by the federal government. The Commission shall be the single State agency responsible for establishing policy, planning and carrying out the State's duties with respect to all programs of and grants to the State by the United States

Fire Administration, Federal Emergency Management Agency. In respect to such programs and grants, the Commission shall have authority to review, approve and maintain general oversight to the State plan and its implementation, including subgrants and allocations to local units of government and local fire prevention and control and rescue agencies.

All actions taken by the Commission in the performance of its duties shall be implemented and administered by the Department.

(c) Meetings. — The Commission shall meet quarterly. Seven members shall constitute a quorum. All meetings shall be open to the public. (1977, c. 1064, s. 1; 1981, c. 791, s. 5; 1983, c. 840, s. 3; 1985, c. 757, s. 167(b), (c), (e), (f); 1989, c. 750, s. 1.)

§ 58-78-15. State Fire and Rescue Commission; staff.

(a) There shall be an executive director nominated by the Commission with direct responsibilities to the Commission, who shall be appointed by the Commissioner.

(b) Personnel of the Department shall serve as staff to the Commission. The Department shall provide the clerical and professional services required by the Commission and, at the direction of the Commission, shall develop and administer the State Master Plan for Fire Prevention and Control, the State Fire Education and Training Plan, the Rescue Training Plan, the State Master Plan for Rescue Services, and any additional related programs as may be established by, or assigned to, the Commission. (1977, c. 1064, s. 1; 1985, c. 757, s. 167(b), (i); 1989, c. 750, s. 1.)

§ 58-78-20. State Fire and Rescue Commission — Fiscal affairs.

All funds for the operation of the Commission and its staff shall be appropriated to the Department. All such funds shall be held in a separate or special account on the books of the Department with a separate financial designation or code number to be assigned by the Department of Administration or its agent. Expenditures for staff salaries and operating expenses shall be made in the same manner as expenditures of any other Department funds. The Department may hire such additional personnel as may be necessary to handle the work of the Commission, within the limits of funds appropriated to it by the State and made available to it by the federal government. (1957, c. 269, s. 1; 1977, c. 1064, s. 1; 1985, c. 757, s. 167(b), (c); 1989, c. 750, s. 1.)

ARTICLE 79.

Investigation of Fires and Inspection of Premises.

§ 58-79-1. Fires investigated; reports; records.

The Attorney General, through the State Bureau of Investigation, and the chief of the fire department, or chief of police where there is no chief of the fire department, in municipalities and towns, and the county fire marshal and the sheriff of the county and the chief of the rural fire department where such fire occurs outside of a municipality, are hereby authorized to investigate the cause, origin, and circumstances of every fire occurring in such municipalities or counties in which property has been destroyed or damaged, and shall specially make investigation whether the fire was the result of carelessness or design. A preliminary investigation shall be made by the chief of fire department or chief of police, where there is no chief of fire department in municipalities, and by the county fire marshal and the sheriff of the county or the chief of the rural fire department where such fire occurs outside of a municipality, and must be begun within three days, exclusive of Sunday, of the occurrence of the fire, and the Attorney General, through the State Bureau of Investigation, shall have the right to supervise and direct the investigation when he deems it expedient or necessary.

The officer making the investigation of fires shall forthwith notify the Attorney General, and must within one week of the occurrence of the fire furnish to the Attorney General a written statement of all facts relating to the cause and origin of the fire, the kind, value and ownership of the property destroyed, and such other information as is called for by the forms provided by the Attorney General. Departments capable of submitting the required information by the utilization of computers and related equipment, by means of an approved format of standard punch cards, magnetic tapes or an approved telecommunications system, may do so in lieu of the submission of the written statement as provided for in this section. The Attorney General shall keep in his office a record of all reports submitted pursuant to this section. These reports shall at all times be open to public inspection. (1899, c. 58; 1901, c. 387; 1903, c. 719; Rev., s. 4818; C.S., s. 6074; 1943, c. 170; 1969, c. 894; 1977, c. 596, s. 1.)

Local Modification. — Guilford: 1965, c. 102; city of Kannapolis: 1987, c. 558, s. 19.

Editor's Note. — Articles 79 through 83 are former Chapter 69. Chapter 69 has been recodified as Articles 79 through 83 of Chapter 58 pursuant to Session Laws 1987, c. 752, s. 9, as amended by Session Laws 1987 (Reg. Sess., 1988), c. 975, s. 34.

§ 58-79-5. Attorney General to make examination; arrests and prosecution.

It is the duty of the Attorney General to examine, or cause examination to be made, into the cause, circumstances, and origin of all fires occurring within the State to which his attention has been called in accordance with the provisions of G.S. 58-79-1, or by interested parties, by which property is accidentally or unlawfully burned, destroyed, or damaged, whenever in his judgment the evidence is sufficient, and to specially examine and decide whether the fire was the result of carelessness or the act of an incendiary. The Attorney General shall, in person, by deputy or otherwise, fully investigate all circumstances surrounding such fire, and, when in his opinion such proceedings are necessary, take or cause to be taken the testimony on oath of all persons supposed to be cognizant of any facts or to have means of knowledge in relation to the matters as to which an examination is herein required to be made, and shall cause the same to be reduced in writing. If the Attorney General or any deputy appointed to conduct such investigations, is of the opinion that there is evidence to charge any person or persons with the crime of arson, or other willful burning, or fraud in connection with the crime of arson or other willful burning, he may arrest with warrant or cause such person or persons to be arrested, charged with such offense, and prosecuted, and shall furnish to the district attorney of the district all such evidence, together with the names of witnesses and all other information obtained by him, including a copy of all pertinent and material testimony taken in the case. (1899, c. 58, s. 2; 1901, c. 387, s. 2; 1903, c. 719; Rev., s. 4819; C.S., s. 6075; 1943, c. 170; 1955, c. 642, s. 1; 1959, c. 1183; 1973, c. 47, s. 2; 1977, c. 596, s. 2.)

§ 58-79-10. Powers of Attorney General in investigations.

The Attorney General, or his deputy appointed to conduct such examination, has the powers of a trial justice for the purpose of summoning and compelling the attendance of witnesses to testify in relation to any matter which is by provisions of this Article a subject of inquiry and investigation, and may administer oaths and affirmations to persons appearing as witnesses before them. False swearing in any such matter or proceeding is perjury and shall be punished as such. The Attorney General or his deputy has authority at all times of the day or night, in performance of the duties imposed by the provisions of this Article, to enter upon and examine any building or premises where any fire has occurred, and other buildings and premises adjoining or near the same. All investigations held by or under the direction of the Attorney General or his deputy may, in their discretion, be private, and persons other than those required to be present by the provisions of this Article may be excluded from the place where the investigation is held, and witnesses may be kept apart from each other and not allowed to communicate with each other until they have been examined. (1899, c. 58, s. 3; 1901, c. 387, s. 3; Rev., s. 4820; C.S., s. 6076; 1943, c. 170; 1977, c. 596, s. 2.)

§ 58-79-15. Failure to comply with summons or subpoena.

The failure of a person to comply with a summons or subpoena of the Attorney General or his deputy under G.S. 58-79-10 shall be brought before a court of record and punished as for contempt in the same manner as if he had failed to appear and testify before said court of record. (1955, c. 642, s. 2; 1977, c. 596, s. 2.)

§ 58-79-20. Inspection of premises; dangerous material removed.

The Commissioner of Insurance, or the chief of fire department or chief of police where there is no chief of fire department, or the city or county building inspector, electrical inspector, heating inspector, or fire prevention inspector has the right at all reasonable hours, for the purpose of examination, to enter into and upon all buildings and premises in their jurisdiction. When any of such officers find in any building or upon any premises overcrowding in violation of occupancy limits established pursuant to the North Carolina State Building Code, combustible material or inflammable conditions dangerous to the safety of such building or premises they shall order the same to be removed or remedied, and this order shall be forthwith complied with by the owner or occupant of such buildings or premises. The owner or occupant may, within twenty-four hours, appeal to the Commissioner of Insurance from the order, and the cause of the complaint shall be at once investigated by his direction, and unless by his authority the order of the officer above named is revoked it remains in force and must be forthwith complied with by the owner or occupant. The Commissioner of Insurance, fire chief, or building inspector, electrical inspector, heating inspector, or fire prevention inspector shall make an immediate investigation as to the presence of combustible material or the existence of inflammable conditions in any building or upon any premises under their jurisdiction upon complaint of any person having an interest in such building or premises or property adjacent thereto. The Commissioner may, in person or by deputy, visit any municipality or county and make such inspections alone or in company with the local officer. The Commissioner shall submit annually, as early as consistent with full and accurate preparation, and not later than the first day of June, a detailed report of his official action under this Article, and it shall be embodied in his report to the General Assembly.' (1899, c. 58, s. 4; 1901, c. 387, s. 4; 1903, c. 719; Rev., s. 4821; C.S., s. 6077; 1943, c. 170; 1969, c. 1063, s. 3; 1977, c. 596, s. 4; 1985, c. 576, s. 2.)

§ 58-79-22. Door lock exemption permit.

Any business entity licensed to sell automatic weapons as a federal firearms dealer that is in the business of selling firearms or ammunition and that operates a firing range which rents firearms and sells ammunition that desires to be exempt from the door lock requirements of Chapter 10 of Volume 1 of the North Carolina State Building Code may apply for a permit to do so with the Department in accordance with G.S. 143-143.4 and rules adopted by the Department. The Department shall charge a permit fee of five hundred dollars ($500.00) for the issuance of a permit issued pursuant to G.S. 143-143.4. (2001-324, s. 2.)

§ 58-79-25. Deputy investigators.

It shall be the duty of the Attorney General to appoint two or more persons as deputies, whose particular duty it shall be to investigate forest fires and endeavor to ascertain the persons guilty of setting such fires and cause prosecution to be instituted against those who, as a result of such investigation, are deemed guilty. (1899, c. 58, s. 6; 1901, c. 387, s. 6; 1903, c. 719, s. 2; Rev., s. 4823; 1915, c. 109, s. 2; 1919, c. 186, s. 7; C.S., s. 6078; Ex. Sess. 1924, c. 119; 1943, c. 170; 1977, c. 596, s. 2.)

CASE NOTES

Cited in O'Neal v. Wake County, 196 N.C. 184, 145 S.E. 28 (1928).

§ 58-79-30: Repealed by Session Laws 1999-456, s. 66.

§ 58-79-35. Fire prevention and Fire Prevention Day.

It is the duty of the Commissioner of Insurance, the Superintendent of Public Instruction and the State Board of Education to provide a pamphlet containing printed instructions for properly conducting fire drills in all schools and auxiliary school buildings and the principal of every public and private school shall conduct at least one fire drill every month during the regular school session in each building in his charge where children are assembled. The fire drills shall include all children and teachers and the use of various ways of egress to assimilate evacuation of said buildings under various conditions, and such other regulations as prescribed by the Commissioner of Insurance, Superintendent of Public Instruction and State Board of Education.

The Commissioner of Insurance and Superintendent of Public Instruction shall further provide for the teaching of "Fire Prevention" in the colleges and schools of the State, and to arrange for a textbook adapted to such use. The ninth day of October of every year shall be set aside and designated as "Fire Prevention Day," and the Governor shall issue a proclamation urging the people to a proper observance of the day, and the Commissioner of Insurance shall bring the day and its observance to the attention of the officials of all organized fire departments of the State, whose duty it shall be to disseminate the materials and to arrange suitable programs to be followed in its observance. (1915, c. 166, s. 5; C.S., s. 6080; 1925, c. 130; 1943, c. 170; 1947, c. 781; 1957, c. 845.)

§ 58-79-40. Insurance company to furnish information.

(a) The chief of any municipal fire or police department, county fire marshal or sheriff, or special agent of the State Bureau of Investigation may request any insurance company investigating a fire loss of real or personal property to release any information in its possession relative to that loss. The company shall release the information and cooperate with any official authorized to request such information pursuant to this section. The information shall include, but is not limited to:

 (1) Any insurance policy relevant to a fire loss under investigation and any application for such a policy;

 (2) Policy premium payment records;

 (3) History of previous claims made by the insured for fire loss;

 (4) Material relating to the investigation of the loss, including statements of any person, proof of loss, and any other relevant evidence.

(b) If an insurance company (or insurance agency) has reason to suspect that a fire loss to its insured's real or personal property was caused by incendiary means, the company shall furnish the State Bureau of Investigation with all relevant material acquired during its investigation of the fire loss, cooperate with and take such action as may be requested of it by any law-enforcement agency, and permit any person ordered by a court to inspect any of its records pertaining to the policy and the loss.

(c) In the absence of fraud or malice, no insurance company (or insurance agency), or person who furnishes information on its behalf, shall be liable for damages in a civil action or subject to criminal prosecution for any oral or written statement made or any other action that is necessary to supply information required pursuant to this section.

(d) The officials and departmental and agency personnel receiving any information furnished pursuant to this section shall hold the information in confidence until such time as its release is required pursuant to a criminal or civil proceeding.

(e) Any official referred to in subsection (a) of this section may be required to testify as to any information in his possession regarding the fire loss of real or personal property in any civil action in which any person seeks recovery under a policy against an insurance company for the fire loss. (1977, c. 520, s. 1.)

CASE NOTES

Editor's Note. — *The case below was decided under prior statutory provisions.*

Nonsuit Held Proper. — Actions to recover for personal injuries and for wrongful death resulting from a fire in defendants' building, the third floor of which was rented for sleeping quarters, were founded on former G.S. 69-8, upon allegations that defendants failed to have two exits from the sleeping quarters in case of fire. All the evidence tended to show that the building was constructed prior to 1913, and there was no evidence that the Commissioner of Insurance ever deemed practical that the building should be provided with any additional ways of egress in order that the dangers existing should be terminated. It was held that defendants' motion to nonsuit was properly allowed, since plaintiffs failed to bring themselves within the statute relied upon. Woods v. Hall, 214 N.C. 16, 197 S.E. 557 (1938).

§ 58-79-45. Fire incident reports.

(a) Whenever a fire department responds to a fire, the chief of that department shall complete or cause to be completed a fire incident report, which report shall be on a form prescribed by the Department of Insurance. When such report is made without fraud, bad faith, or actual malice, the person making the report is not subject to liability for libel or slander.

(b) The fire department shall forward a copy of the completed form to the fire marshal of the county in which the fire occurred. If there is no fire marshal in that county, the fire department shall forward a copy of the report to the county commissioners. The fire department shall retain the original of the report. The fire department and the fire marshal or county commissioners to whom reports are sent shall retain the reports for a period of five years.

(c) At the request of any person, the county fire marshal or county commissioners shall provide such person, for a reasonable copying charge, a certified copy of the report. (1989 (Reg. Sess., 1990), c. 1054, s. 7.)

ARTICLE 80.

State Volunteer Fire Department.

§ 58-80-1. Purpose of Article; meaning of "State Fire Marshal".

The purpose of this Article shall be the creation of a State Volunteer Fire Department to provide protection for property lying outside the boundaries of municipalities, and to render assistance anywhere within the State of North Carolina, in municipalities or counties, in emergencies caused by fire, floods, tornadoes, or otherwise, in the manner and subject to the conditions provided in this Article. As used in this Article and elsewhere in the General Statutes, "State Fire Marshal" means the Commissioner of Insurance of the State of North Carolina. (1939, c. 364, s. 1; 1985, c. 666, s. 66.)

§ 58-80-5. Personnel.

The personnel of the North Carolina State Volunteer Fire Department shall consist of all active members of the organized fire departments, who are members of the North Carolina State Firemen's Association, of municipalities whereof the governing bodies shall subscribe to and endorse this Article. (1939, c. 364, s. 2.)

§ 58-80-10. Organization.

The North Carolina State Fire Marshal shall be chief of the State Volunteer Fire Department; regular municipal fire chiefs shall be assistant chiefs; assistant chiefs shall be deputy chiefs; battalion chiefs, captains; lieutenants and privates shall hold the same position that they occupy in their municipal companies. When engaged in rendering assistance at the scene of any emergency, the ranking officer of the first department arriving at the scene of the emergency shall have complete charge of all operations until the arrival of a superior officer. All subordinate officers and men shall act under the direction of such ranking officer. Whenever present at the scene of an emergency, the chief shall have full and complete control and authority over operations of all members of the Department. (1939, c. 364, s. 3.)

State Government Reorganization. — The State Volunteer Fire Department was transferred to the Department of Insurance by G.S. 143A-79, enacted by Session Laws 1971, c. 864.

§ 58-80-15. Acceptance by municipalities.

Any municipality having an organized fire department and desiring to participate in the establishment of the State Volunteer Fire Department, may do so by a resolution of the governing body accepting and endorsing the provisions of this Article: Provided, that acceptance shall not be compulsory. (1939, c. 364, s. 4.)

§ 58-80-20. Withdrawal.

Any municipality which has accepted the provisions of this Article may withdraw its fire departments from membership in the State Volunteer Fire Department by resolution of the governing body thereof. Notice of such withdrawal shall be given to the State Fire Marshal and withdrawal shall not become effective until 60 days after his receipt thereof. (1939, c. 364, s. 5.)

§ 58-80-25. Dispatching firemen and apparatus from municipalities.

Municipalities endorsing this Article shall retain full and complete control and authority in sending or permitting firemen and apparatus to go beyond the limits of the municipality. The governing bodies of such municipalities shall designate and authorize a person, and at least two alternates, who shall have authority to grant or deny permission to firemen and apparatus to leave the municipality in all cases where request is made for assistance beyond its corporate limits, and the municipality shall, through the office of its municipal fire chief, furnish to the office of the State Commissioner of Insurance, and to the secretary of the North Carolina State Firemen's Association, a list of the persons so authorized by the municipality. The secretary of the State Firemen's Association shall furnish to all municipalities and counties accepting this Article a list of all such persons so designated in all municipalities within the State. (1939, c. 364, s. 6; 1943, c. 170.)

§ 58-80-30. No authority in State Volunteer Fire Department to render assistance to nonaccepting counties.

The State Volunteer Fire Department shall not have authority to render assistance in any emergency occurring within a county which has not accepted the terms and conditions of this Article by resolution of the board of county commissioners: Provided, that nothing in this Article shall be construed to prevent any municipality from voluntarily permitting its fire department to render assistance in any emergency, notwithstanding that it may arise in a county which has failed to accept this Article. (1939, c. 364, s. 7.)

§ 58-80-35. Acceptance by counties.

Any county desiring to accept the benefits of this Article may do so by resolution of the board of county commissioners. Any such county may thereupon make agreements and enter into contracts with respect to payment for services rendered by the State Volunteer Fire Department within its boundaries in the following manner:

The county may contract with any municipality which has accepted the terms of this Article, whether within or without said county, to pay to such municipality an annual fee as a consideration for the municipality providing equipment and carrying compensation insurance which will enable it to respond to calls from within the county so contracting, and to pay an additional sum per truck for each mile traveled from the station house to the scene of the emergency, and to pay an additional sum per truck per hour or fraction thereof for the use of its water or chemical pumping equipment. Said sums shall be paid to the city within 30 days after such services have been performed: Provided, that nothing in this section shall be construed to prevent the county and municipality from adopting a different schedule of fees in cases where those provided above shall be considered excessive or inadequate: Provided, that if the emergency shall occur within the limits of another city or town, such city or town and not the county wherein it lies shall be responsible for the payments and shall assume all liabilities as provided in this section. (1939, c. 364, s. 8; 1973, c. 803, s. 5.)

§ 58-80-40. Municipalities not to be left unprotected.

At no time shall the entire personnel or equipment of any municipal fire department be absent from the municipality in response to a call to another municipality, or other place lying at a distance exceeding two miles from the corporate limits, but there shall remain within the municipal limits such personnel and equipment as in the judgment of the local fire chief might provide sufficient protection during the absence of the remainder. (1939, c. 364, s. 9.)

§ 58-80-45. Rights and privileges of firemen; liability of municipality.

When responding to a call and while working at a fire or other emergency outside the limits of the municipality by which they are regularly employed or in volunteer fire service, all members of the State Volunteer Fire Department shall have the same authority, rights, privileges and immunities which are afforded them while responding to calls within their home municipality. In permitting its fire department or equipment to attend an emergency or answer a call beyond the municipal limits, whether under the terms of this Article or otherwise, a municipality shall be deemed in exercise of a governmental function, and shall hold the privileges and immunities attendant upon the exercise of such functions within its corporate limits. (1939, c. 364, s. 10.)

Cross References. — As to uniformed firemen enforcing motor vehicle laws and ordinances at fires, see G.S. 20-114.1.

CASE NOTES

Cited in Bland v. City of Wilmington, 278 N.C. 657, 180 S.E.2d 813 (1971).

§ 58-80-50. Relief in case of injury or death.

In case of injury or death of any member of the State Volunteer Fire Department arising out of and in the course of the performance of his duties, while such member is assisting at any emergency arising beyond the limits of the municipality with which he is connected, or while going to or returning from the scene of such emergency, such fireman shall be entitled to compensation under the terms of the North Carolina Workers' Compensation Act, and the municipality with which he is connected shall be liable for the compensation provided under that Act. (1939, c. 364, s. 11; 1991, c. 636, s. 3.)

§ 58-80-55. Local appropriations.

Each county and municipality is authorized to make appropriations for the purposes of this Article and to fund them by levy of property taxes pursuant to G.S. 153A-149 and 160A-209 and by the allocation of other revenues whose use is not otherwise restricted by law. Sanitary districts are authorized to make appropriations for the purposes of this Article and to fund them by annual levy of a tax on property having a situs in the district under the rules and according to the procedures prescribed in the Machinery Act (Chapter 105, Subchapter II) and by the allocation of other revenues whose use is not otherwise restricted by law. (1973, c. 803, s. 4.)

§ 58-80-60. Sums from contingent fund of State made available for administration of Article.

In order to assist in carrying out the purposes of the Article the Governor may, from time to time, make provisions for assistance to the North Carolina State Firemen's Association in a sum not to exceed two thousand five hundred dollars ($2,500), in any one year, out of the contingent fund appropriated in the General Appropriation Act. One half of the amount so provided shall, in each instance, go to the State Firemen's Relief Fund, and one half to the expenses of the said Association incurred in carrying out the provisions of this Article. (1939, c. 364, s. 12.)

ARTICLE 81.

Hotels; Safety Provisions.

§ 58-81-1: Repealed by Session Laws 1995, c. 517, s. 33.

§ 58-81-5. Careless or negligent setting of fires.

Any person who in any fashion or manner negligently or carelessly sets fire to any bedding, furniture, draperies, house or household furnishings or other equipment or appurtenances in or to any hotel or other building of like occupancy shall be guilty of a Class 1 misdemeanor. (1947, c. 1066; 1993, c. 539, s. 474; 1994, Ex. Sess., c. 24, s. 14(c).)

§ 58-81-10. Penalty for noncompliance.

Any owner, owners, proprietor or keeper of any hotel or other building of like occupancy who fails to comply with any of the foregoing provisions of this Article shall be guilty of a Class 3 misdemeanor and punished only by a fine of not less than ten dollars ($10.00) nor more than fifty dollars ($50.00). Each day of noncompliance herewith shall constitute a separate offense. (1947, c. 1066; 1993, c. 539, s. 475; 1994, Ex. Sess., c. 24, s. 14(c).)

§ 58-81-15. Construction of Article.

Nothing in this Article shall be construed to limit powers granted to and duties imposed upon the chiefs of fire departments and building inspectors by Article 11, Chapter 160 of the General Statutes of North Carolina, but the powers granted in this Article shall be in addition thereto. (1947, c. 1066.)

Editor's Note. — Article 11, Chapter 160, referred to above, was repealed by Session Laws 1971, c. 698, s. 2. For present provisions as to cities and towns, see Chapter 160A.

ARTICLE 82.

Authority and Liability of Firemen.

§ 58-82-1. Authority of firemen; penalty for willful interference with firemen.

Members and employees of county, municipal corporation, fire protection district, sanitary district or privately incorporated fire departments shall have authority to do all acts reasonably necessary to extinguish fires and protect life and property from fire. Any person, including the owner of property which is burning, who shall willfully interfere in any manner with firemen engaged in the performance of their duties shall be guilty of a Class 1 misdemeanor. (1965, c. 648; 1993, c. 539, s. 476; 1994, Ex. Sess., c. 24, s. 14(c).)

§ 58-82-5. Liability limited.

(a) For the purpose of this section, a "rural fire department" means a bona fide fire department incorporated as a nonprofit corporation which under schedules filed with or approved by the Commissioner of Insurance, is classified as not less than Class "9" in accordance with rating methods, schedules, classifications, underwriting rules, bylaws, or regulations effective or applied with respect to the establishment of rates or premiums used or charged pursuant to Article 36 or Article 40 of this Chapter and which operates fire apparatus of the value of five thousand dollars ($5,000) or more.

(b) A rural fire department or a fireman who belongs to the department shall not be liable for damages to persons or property alleged to have been sustained and alleged to have occurred by reason of an act or omission, either of the rural fire department or of the fireman at the scene of a reported fire, when that act or omission relates to the suppression of the reported fire or to the direction of traffic or enforcement of traffic laws or ordinances at the scene of or in connection with a fire, accident, or other hazard by the department or the fireman unless it is established that the damage occurred because of gross negligence, wanton conduct or intentional wrongdoing of the rural fire department or the fireman.

(c) Any member of a volunteer fire department or rescue squad who receives no compensation for his services as a fire fighter or emergency medical care provider, who renders first aid or emergency health care treatment at the scene of a fire to a person who is unconscious, ill, or injured as a result of the fire shall not be liable in civil damages for any acts or omissions relating to such services rendered, unless such acts or omissions amount to gross negligence, wanton conduct or intentional wrongdoing. (1983, c. 520, s. 1; 1985, c. 611, s. 1; 1987, c. 146, s. 2.)

CASE NOTES

This section and § 69-25.17 recognize that fire departments provide rescue and ambulance services. Geiger v. Guilford College Community Volunteer Firemen's Ass'n, 668 F. Supp. 492 (M.D.N.C. 1987).

Effect of Subsection (b). — Subsection (b) of this section does not limit a rural fire depart-

ment's liability when engaged in duties in areas other than the "suppression" of "reported fires." Geiger v. Guilford College Community Volunteer Firemen's Ass'n, 668 F. Supp. 492 (M.D.N.C. 1987).

In order for immunity to apply under this section, it is irrelevant whether the fire department's negligent act or omission occurs precisely "at the scene" of the fire as long as it relates to the "suppression of the reported fire." Spruill v. Lake Phelps Volunteer Fire Dep't, Inc., 351 N.C. 318, 523 S.E.2d 672 (2000).

Nonprofit Fire Department Entitled to Same Immunity Afforded Other Fire Departments. — Nonprofit corporation employed by a county as a fire department engaged in statutorily authorized services is entitled to receive the same immunity normally afforded to other fire departments in North Carolina. Geiger v. Guilford College Community Volunteer Firemen's Ass'n, 668 F. Supp. 492 (M.D.N.C. 1987).

Liability of a Nonprofit Fire Company in a Nonfire Related Rescue Attempt. — A nonprofit fire company employed by the county was liable for plaintiff's injuries in a nonfire related rescue attempt only to the extent of their insurance coverage since they had governmental immunity up to their insurance coverages and were engaged in duties other than the suppression of a reported fire. Geiger v. Guilford College Community Volunteer Firemen's Ass'n, 668 F. Supp. 492 (M.D.N.C. 1987).

Applied in Forrest Drive Assocs. v. Wal-Mart Stores, Inc., 72 F. Supp. 2d 576 (M.D.N.C. 1999).

ARTICLE 83.

Mutual Aid between Fire Departments.

§ 58-83-1. Authority to send firemen and apparatus beyond territorial limits; privileges and immunities.

A county, municipal corporation, fire protection district, sanitary district or incorporated fire department shall have full authority to send, or to decline to send, firemen and apparatus beyond the territorial limits which it normally serves.

When responding to a call and while working at a fire or other emergency outside the territorial limits which it normally serves, members and employees of county, municipal corporation, fire protection district, sanitary district and incorporated fire departments shall have all authority, rights, privileges and immunities including coverage under the Workers' Compensation Laws, as they have when responding to a call and while working at a fire or other emergency inside the territorial limits normally served.

A county, municipal corporation, fire protection district, sanitary district, or incorporated fire department, in attending an emergency or answering a call outside the limits of the county, municipal corporation, fire protection district, sanitary district, or other area normally served, shall have all authority, rights, privileges, and immunities that it would have in attending an emergency or answering a call inside the territorial limits normally served. (1965, c. 707; 1991, c. 636, s. 3.)

CASE NOTES

Cited in Hix v. Jenkins, 118 N.C. App. 103, 453 S.E.2d 551 (1995).

ARTICLE 84.

Fund Derived from Insurance Companies.

§ 58-84-1. Fire and lightning insurance report.

Every insurance company doing business in a fire district in this State shall report to the Secretary of Revenue by March 15 of each year a just and true account of all premiums collected and received from all fire and lightning insurance business done within the limits of each fire district during the preceding calendar year and shall pay the tax levied in G.S. 105-228.5(d)(4). The Secretary of Revenue shall provide the Commissioner the reports filed pursuant to this section and shall credit the net proceeds of the tax to the Department of Insurance for disbursement pursuant to G.S. 58-84-25. (1907, c. 831, s. 1; 1919, c. 180; C.S., s. 6063; 1929, c. 286; 1989, c. 485, s. 63; 1995 (Reg. Sess., 1996), c. 747, s. 4.)

Local Modification. — Forsyth: 1995, c. 160, s. 1; city of Hendersonville: 1993, c. 244, s. 1; city of Lenoir 1977, c. 118; 1981, c. 291; 1991 (Reg. Sess., 1992), cc. 800, 900; city of Lexington: 1981, c. 906, s. 6.1; 1983, c. 462; 1989 (Reg. Sess., 1990), c. 931; city of Reidsville: 1989 (Reg. Sess., 1990), c. 957, s. 1; city of Sanford: 1991 (Reg. Sess., 1992), c. 798, s. 10; town of Cary: 1989 (Reg. Sess., 1990), c. 924; 1991, c. 147, s. 1.

Local Supplemental Firemen's Retirement Fund. — Forsyth: 1969, c. 418; 1995, c. 160; Mount Airy: 2000-22, s. 1, 1995, c. 165, s.1; city of Asheboro: 1985, c. 186; city of Asheville: 1979, 2nd Sess., c. 1315, amending 1979, c. 208; city of Belhaven: 1981, c. 294; city of Burlington: 1969, c. 321; 1979, 2nd Sess., c. 1144; 1987, c. 612; city of Charlotte: 1947, c. 837; 1965, c. 210; city of Clinton: 1969, c. 177; 1973, c. 46; 1979, c. 264; city of Conover: 1977, c. 334; 1991, c. 260, s. 1; city of Durham: 1951, c. 576; 1973, c. 701; 1983, c. 463; 2002-114, ss. 1 and 2; 2003-325, ss. 1-3; city of Eden: 1977, c. 285; city of Fayetteville: 1979, c. 557, s. 8.3; 1987, c. 85; 1991, c. 149, s. 1, 2003-34, ss. 1, 2; city of Greensboro: 1953, c. 899; 1979, c. 289; 1983, c. 466; 1987, c. 178; 1993, c. 431, s. 1; city of Greenville: 1967, c. 570; city of Henderson: 1959, c. 810; 1969, c. 374; 1977, c. 133; 1981, c. 111; 1987, c. 173; 1991 (Reg. Sess., 1992), c. 897, s. 1; 2001-71; city of Hendersonville: 1981, c. 341; city of Hickory: 1985, c. 139; 1999-128, s. 1; city of Kings Mountain: 1979, c. 209; city of Lenoir: 1973, c. 1261; city of Lexington: 1981, c. 906, s. 6.1; 1983 c. 462; 1989 (Reg. Sess., 1990), c. 931; city of Lumberton: 1955, c. 100; 1973, c. 960; 1989, c. 357, c. 770; 1991 (Reg. Sess., 1992), c. 792; 1995 (Reg. Sess., 1996), c. 699; 2003-324, s. 1; city of Mayodan: 1985, c. 255; city of Monroe: 2000-35, s. 1; city of Mount Airy: 1995, c. 165, s. 1; 2000-22, s. 1; city of New Bern: 1969, c. 704; 1983, c. 551; city of Newton: 1969, c. 363; 1981, c. 298; 1983, c. 503; city of North Wilkesboro: 1969, c. 120; 1979, c. 366; city of Reidsville: 1979, c. 94; 1981 (Reg. Sess., 1982), c. 1235; 1989, c. 278; 1989 (Reg. Sess., 1990), c. 957, s. 1; 1977, c. 312; 1989, c. 247; city of Rocky Mount: 1969, c. 434; 1975, c. 353; 1983, c. 498; 1991, c. 497, s. 1; c. 761, s. 43; city of Sanford: 1991 (Reg. Sess., 1992), c. 798; city of Shelby: 1969, cc. 496, 552; 1985, c. 209; 1987 (Reg. Sess., 1988), c. 985; 1991 (Reg. Sess., 1992), c. 791; city of Washington: 1975, c. 418; city of Whiteville: 1971, c. 308; 1987 (Reg. Sess., 1988), c. 1018, s. 1; city of Williamston: 1985, c. 188; city of Wilmington: 1949, c. 684; 1973, c. 939; 1975, c. 247; 1983, cc. 504, 505, 906; 1987 (Reg. Sess., 1988), c. 904; city of Wilson: 1969, c. 138; 1995 (Reg. Sess., 1996), c. 678; city of Winston-Salem: 1973, c. 388; 1977, c. 15; 1979, c. 284; 1981, c. 647; 1983, c. 464; 1987, c. 508; 1989, c. 793; 1998-92; 2003-35; town of Black Mountain: 1965, c. 672; town of Canton: 1979, 2nd Sess., c. 1105; town of Edenton: 1981, cc. 286, 996; town of Elkin: 1969, c. 169; 1971, c. 391; 1987, c. 740, ss. 1 and 5; town of Farmville: 1981, c. 533; town of Lillington: 1981, c. 285; town of Mebane: 1979, c. 183; town of Mount Airy: 1967, c. 302, s. 9; 1973, c. 121; town of North Wilkesboro: 1981, c. 287; 1987, c. 176; town of Selma: 1987, c. 614; town of Smithfield: 1973, c. 941; town of Tarboro: 1973, c. 261; 1985, c. 157; 1987, c. 609; town of Valdese: 1983, c. 501; town of Wadesboro: 1967, c. 596; town of Waynesville: 1981, c. 288; town of Wilkesboro: 1985, c. 131; 1999-56, s. 1; village of Kannapolis: 1971, c. 408; 1973, c. 216; 1975, c. 423; 1983, c. 497.

Editor's Note. — Articles 84 through 88 are former Chapter 118. Chapter 118 has been recodified as Articles 84 through 88 of Chapter 58 pursuant to Session Laws 1987, c. 752, s. 9, as amended by Session Laws 1987 (Reg. Sess., 1988), c. 975, s. 34.

Session Laws 1989, c. 485, s. 63 deleted "Fire" preceding "Insurance" in the heading of Article 84.

Session Laws 1995 (Reg. Sess., 1996), c. 747, s. 16, provides: "This act does not obligate the General Assembly to appropriate funds."

§ 58-84-5. Definitions.

The following definitions apply in Articles 84 through 88 of this Chapter:
    (1) City. — A fire district.
    (2) Clerk. — The clerk of a fire district or, if there is no clerk, the person so designated by the governing body of the fire district.

   (3) Fire district. — Any political subdivision of the State that meets all of the following conditions:
     a. It has an organized fire department under the control of its governing body.
     b. Its fire department has apparatus and equipment that is in serviceable condition for fire duty and is valued at one thousand dollars ($1,000) or more.
     c. It enforces the fire laws to the satisfaction of the Commissioner.
   (4) Town. — A fire district. (1951, c. 1032, s. 1; 1995 (Reg. Sess., 1996), c. 747, s. 5.)

Editor's Note. — Session Laws 1995 (Reg. Sess., 1996), c. 747, s. 16, provides: "This act does not obligate the General Assembly to appropriate funds."

§§ 58-84-10 through 58-84-20: Repealed by Session Laws 1995 (Regular Session, 1996), c. 747, s. 6, effective January 1, 1996.

Editor's Note. — Session Laws 1995 (Reg. Sess., 1996), c. 747, s. 16, provides: "This act does not obligate the General Assembly to appropriate funds."

§ 58-84-25. Disbursement of funds by Insurance Commissioner.

The Insurance Commissioner shall deduct the sum of three percent (3%) from the tax proceeds credited to the Department pursuant to G.S. 105-228.5(d)(4) and pay the same over to the treasurer of the State Firemen's Association for general purposes. The Insurance Commissioner shall deduct the sum of two percent (2%) from the tax proceeds and retain the same in the budget of the Department of Insurance for the purpose of administering the disbursement of funds by the board of trustees in accordance with the provisions of G.S. 58-84-35. The Insurance Commissioner shall, pursuant to G.S. 58-84-50, credit the amount forfeited by nonmember fire districts to the North Carolina State Firemen's Association. The Insurance Commissioner shall pay the remaining tax proceeds to the treasurer of each fire district in proportion to the amount of business done in the fire district. These funds shall be held by the treasurer as a separate and distinct fund. The fire district shall immediately pay the funds to the treasurer of the local board of trustees upon the treasurer's election and qualification, for the use of the board of trustees of the firemen's local relief fund in each fire district, which board shall be composed of five members, residents of the fire district as hereinafter provided for, to be used by it for the purposes provided in G.S. 58-84-35. (1907, c. 831, s. 5; C.S., s. 6067; 1925, c. 41; 1985 (Reg. Sess., 1986), c. 1014, s. 168; 1989, c. 485, s. 63; 1995 (Reg. Sess., 1996), c. 747, s. 7.)

Local Modification. — City of Hickory: 1985, c. 139; 1999-128, s. 1; city of New Bern: 1983, c. 551; city of Raleigh: 1985, c. 35, s. 3; city of Shelby: 1985, c. 209; 1991 (Reg. Sess., 1992), c. 791; town of Cary: 1985, c. 159; 1991, c. 147, s. 1; town of Tarboro: 1985, c. 157; 1987, c. 609.

Editor's Note. — Session Laws 1995 (Reg. Sess., 1996), c. 747, s. 16, provides: "This act does not obligate the General Assembly to appropriate funds."

§ 58-84-30. Trustees appointed; organization.

For each county, town or city complying with and deriving benefits from the provisions of this Article, there shall be appointed a local board of trustees, known as the trustees of the firemen's relief fund, to be composed of five members, two of whom shall be elected by the members of the local fire department or departments who are qualified as beneficiaries of such fund, two of whom shall be elected by the mayor and board of aldermen or other local governing body, and one of whom shall be named by the Commissioner of Insurance. Their selection and term of office shall be as follows:

(1) The members of the fire department shall hold an election each January to elect their representatives to above board. In January 1950, the firemen shall elect one member to serve for two years and one member to serve for one year, then each year in January thereafter, they shall elect only one member and his term of office shall be for two years.

(2) The mayor and board of aldermen or other local governing body shall appoint, in January 1950, two representatives to above board, one to hold office for two years and one to hold office for one year, and each year in January thereafter they shall appoint only one representative and his term of office shall be for two years.

(3) The Commissioner of Insurance shall appoint one representative to serve as trustee and he shall serve at the pleasure of the Commissioner.

All of the above trustees shall hold office for their elected or appointed time, or until their successors are elected or appointed, and shall serve without pay for their services. They shall immediately after election and appointment organize by electing from their members a chairman and a secretary and treasurer, which two last positions may be held by the same person. The treasurer of said board of trustees shall give a good and sufficient surety bond in a sum equal to the amount of moneys in his hand, to be approved by the Commissioner of Insurance. The cost of this bond may be deducted by the Insurance Commissioner from the receipts collected pursuant to G.S. 58-84-10 before distribution is made to local relief funds. If the chief or chiefs of the local fire departments are not named on the board of trustees as above provided, then they shall serve as ex officio members without privilege of voting on matters before the board. (1907, c. 831, s. 6; C.S., s. 6068; 1925, c. 41; 1945, c. 74, s. 1; 1947, c. 720; 1949, c. 1054; 1973, c. 1365; 1985, c. 666, s. 64; 1987, c. 174, ss. 1, 5.)

Local Modification. — City of Hickory: 1985, c. 139; 1999-128, s. 1; city of Lenoir: 1977, c. 118; 1981, c. 291; 1991 (Reg. Sess., 1992), c. 800; city of Lumberton: 1989, c. 357, s. 1; 1991 (Reg. Sess., 1992), c. 792; city of Mayodan: 1985, c. 255; city of New Bern: 1983, c. 551; city of Rocky Mount: 1969, c. 434; 1983, c. 498; 1991, c. 497; city of Shelby: 1985, c. 209; 1991 (Reg. Sess., 1992), c. 791; city of Whiteville: 1987 (Reg. Sess., 1988), c. 1018, s. 1; city of Williamston: 1985, c. 188; city of Wilmington: 1983, c. 505; town of Selma: 1987, c. 614, s. 6; town of Tarboro: 1985, c. 157; 1987, c. 609; town of Valdese: 1983, c. 501; town of Wilkesboro: 1985, c. 131.

Local Supplemental Firemen's Retirement Fund. — City of Lumberton: 1995 (Reg. Sess., 1996), c. 699.

Editor's Note. — Section 58-84-10, referred to in this section, has been repealed.

§ 58-84-35. Disbursement of funds by trustees.

The board of trustees shall have entire control of the funds derived from the provisions of this Article, and shall disburse the funds only for the following purposes:

(1) To safeguard any fireman in active service from financial loss, occasioned by sickness contracted or injury received while in the performance of his duties as a fireman.

(2) To provide a reasonable support for those actually dependent upon the services of any fireman who may lose his life in the fire service of his

town, city, or State, either by accident or from disease contracted or injury received by reason of such service. The amount is to be determined according to the earning capacity of the deceased.

(2a) To provide assistance, upon approval by the Secretary of the State Firemen's Association, to a destitute member fireman who has served honorably for at least five years.

(3) Repealed by Session Laws 1985, c. 666, s. 61.

(4) To provide for the payment of any fireman's assessment in the Firemen's Fraternal Insurance Fund of the State of North Carolina if the board of trustees finds as a fact that said fireman is unable to pay the said assessment by reason of disability.

(5) To provide for benefits of supplemental retirement, workers compensation, and other insurance and pension protection for firemen otherwise qualifying for benefits from the Firemen's Relief Fund as set forth in Article 85 of this Chapter.

(6) To provide for educational benefits to firemen and their dependents who otherwise qualify for benefits from the Firemen's Relief Fund as set forth in Article 85 of this Chapter.

Notwithstanding any other provisions of law, no expenditures shall be made pursuant to subsections (5) and (6) of this section unless the State Firemen's Association has certified that such expenditures will not render the Fund actuarially unsound for the purposes of providing the benefits set forth in subsections (1), (2), and (4) of this section. If, for any reason, funds made available for subsections (5) and (6) of this section shall be insufficient to pay in full any benefits, the benefits pursuant to subsections (5) and (6) shall be reduced pro rata for as long as the amount of insufficient funds exists. No claim shall accrue with respect to any amount by which a benefit under subsections (5) and (6) shall have been reduced. (1907, c. 831, s. 6; 1919, c. 180; C.S., s. 6069; Ex. Sess. 1921, c. 55; 1923, c. 22; 1925, c. 41; 1945, c. 74, s. 2; 1985, c. 666, s. 61; 1987, c. 174, ss. 2, 3; 1997-456, s. 27.)

Local Modification. — Mecklenburg: 1949, c. 728; New Hanover: 1929, c. 328; city of Asheboro, 1985, c. 186; city of Asheville: 1959, c. 759; city of Charlotte: 1947, c. 837; 1949, c. 728; city of Conover: 1977, c. 334, s. 2; 1991, c. 260; city of Durham: 1951, c. 577; 2002-114, s. 3; city of Fayetteville: 1979, c. 557, s. 1; 1991, c. 149, s. 2; city of Gastonia: 1945, c. 183; city of Greensboro: 1953, c. 931; city of Henderson: 1959, c. 943; city of Hendersonville: 1993, c. 244, s. 2; city of Hickory: 1971, c. 65; 1981, c. 407; 1985, c. 139; 1999-128, s. 1; city of High Point: 1961, c. 523; city of Lenoir: 1977, c. 118; 1981, c. 291; 1991 (Reg. Sess., 1992), c. 800; city of Mayodan: 1985, c. 255; city of New Bern: 1983, c. 551; city of Radford: 1983, c. 496; city of Rocky Mount: 1969, c. 434; 1983, c. 498; 1991, c. 497; 1991, c. 761, s. 43; city of Shelby: 1985, c. 209; 1991 (Reg. Sess., 1992), c. 791; city of Whiteville: 1987 (Reg. Sess., 1988), c. 1018, s. 1; city of Williamston: 1985, c. 188; city of Wilmington: 1983, c. 505; town of Cary: 1985, c. 159; 1991, c. 147; 1989 (Reg. Sess., 1990), c. 924; town of Morganton: 1963, c. 689; town of Selma: 1987, c. 614, s. 2; town of Tarboro: 1985, c. 157; 1987, c. 609; town of Valdese: 1983, c. 501; town of Wilkesboro: 1985, c. 131; Windsor Firemen's Local Relief Fund: 1989 (Reg. Sess., 1990), c. 930. City of Durham: 1951, c. 577; 2002-114, s. 3.

CASE NOTES

Cited in Carroll v. North Carolina State Firemen's Ass'n, 230 N.C. 436, 53 S.E.2d 524 (1949).

§ 58-84-40. Trustees to keep account and file certified reports.

(a) Each local board of trustees shall keep a correct account of all moneys received and disbursed by them. On a form prescribed by the North Carolina State Firemen's Association, each local board shall certify by October 31 of each year the following to the Association: the balance of the local fund, proof of sufficient bonding, a full accounting of the previous year's expenditures, and a full accounting of membership qualifications. Such certification shall be made concurrently with the local unit's statement of Fire Readiness.

(b) In turn, the State Firemen's Association shall certify to the Department of Insurance by January 1 of each year on a form prescribed by the Department, the local units which have complied with the requirements of subsection (a) of this section.

(c) In the event that any board of trustees in any of the towns and cities benefited by this Article shall neglect or fail to perform their duties, or shall willfully misappropriate the funds entrusted in their care by obligating or disbursing such funds for any purpose other than those set forth in G.S. 58-84-35, then the Insurance Commissioner shall withhold any and all further payments to such board of trustees, or their successors, until the matter has been fully investigated by an official of the State Firemen's Association, and adjusted to the satisfaction of the Insurance Commissioner.

(d) In the event that any local relief fund provided for in this Article becomes impaired, then the Firemen's Relief Fund may in the discretion of its board of trustees assist the local unit administering the fund in providing for relief to injured firemen and their dependents or survivors; provided, however, that any funds so provided to such impaired units shall be repaid in full at the statutory rate of interest from future local unit receipts if the impairment resulted from violations of this Article. (1907, c. 831, s. 7; C.S., s. 6070; 1925, c. 41; 1985, c. 666, s. 63.)

§ 58-84-45: Repealed by Session Laws 2000-67, s. 26.21(a), effective July 1, 2000.

Editor's Note. — Session Laws 2000-67, s. 26.21(c), made the repeal effective July 1, 2000, and applicable retroactively to October 31, 1998.

Session Laws 2000-67, s. 1.1, provides: "This act shall be known as 'The Current Operations and Capital Improvements Appropriations Act of 2000.'"

Session Laws 2000-67, s. 28.4, contains a severability clause.

§ 58-84-46. Certification to Commissioner.

On or before October 31 of each year the clerk or finance officer of each city or county that has a local board of trustees under G.S. 58-84-30 shall file a certificate of eligibility with the Commissioner. The certificate shall contain information prescribed by administrative rule adopted by the Commissioner. If the certificate is not filed with the Commissioner on or before January 31 in the ensuing year:

(1) The city or county that failed to file the certificate shall forfeit the payment next due to be paid to its board of trustees.

(2) The Commissioner shall pay over that amount to the treasurer of the North Carolina State Firemen's Association.

(3) That amount shall constitute a part of the Firemen's Relief Fund. (2000-67, s. 26.21(b); 2001-421, s. 3.)

Editor's Note. — Session Laws 2000-67, s. 1.1, provides: "This act shall be known as 'The Current Operations and Capital Improvements Appropriations Act of 2000.'"

Session Laws 2000-67, s. 28.4, contains a severability clause.

Session Laws 2000-67, s. 26.21(c), made this section effective July 1, 2000 and applicable retroactively to October 31, 1998.

§ 58-84-50. Fire departments to be members of State Firemen's Association.

For the purpose of supervision and as a guaranty that provisions of this Article shall be honestly administered in a businesslike manner, it is provided that every department enjoying the benefits of this law shall be a member of the North Carolina State Firemen's Association and comply with its constitution and bylaws. If the fire department of any city, town or village shall fail to comply with the constitution and bylaws of said Association, said city, town or village shall forfeit its right to the next annual payment due from the funds mentioned in this Article, and the Commissioner of Insurance shall pay over said amount to the treasurer of the North Carolina State Firemen's Association and same shall constitute a part of the firemen's relief fund. (1907, c. 831, s. 9; 1919, c. 180; C.S., s. 6072; 1925, c. 41; c. 309, s. 2; 1965, c. 624.)

§ 58-84-55. No discrimination on account of race.

The local boards of trustees of the Firemen's Relief Fund shall make no discrimination based upon race in the payment of benefits. (1907, c. 831, s. 10; C.S., s. 6073; 1985, c. 666, s. 62.)

ARTICLE 85.

State Appropriation.

§ 58-85-1. Application of fund.

The money paid into the hands of the treasurer of the North Carolina State Firemen's Association shall be known and remain as the "Firemen's Relief Fund" of North Carolina, and shall be used as a fund for the relief of firemen, members of such Association, who may be injured or rendered sick by disease contracted in the actual discharge of duty as firemen, and for the relief of widows, children, and if there be no widow or children, then dependent mothers of such firemen killed or dying from disease so contracted in such discharge of duty; to be paid in such manner and in such sums to such individuals of the classes herein named and described as may be provided for and determined upon in accordance with the constitution and bylaws of said Association, and such provisions and determinations made pursuant to said constitution and bylaws shall be final and conclusive as to the persons entitled to benefits and as to the amount of benefit to be received, and no action at law shall be maintained against said Association to enforce any claim or recover any benefit under this Article or under the constitution and bylaws of said Association; but if any officer or committee of said Association omit or refuse to perform any duty imposed upon him or them, nothing herein contained shall be construed to prevent any proceedings against said officer or committee to compel him or them to perform such duty. No fireman shall be entitled to receive any benefits under this section until the firemen's relief fund of his city or town shall have been exhausted. Notwithstanding the above provisions, the Executive Board of the North Carolina State Firemen's Association is hereby authorized to grant educational scholarships to members and the children of members, to subsidize premium payments of members over 65 years of age to the Firemen's Fraternal Insurance Fund of the North Carolina State Firemen's Association, and to provide accidental death and dismemberment insurance for members of those fire departments not eligible for benefits pursuant to standards of certification adopted by the State Firemen's Association for the use of local relief funds. (1891, c. 468, s. 3; Rev., s. 4393; C.S., s. 6058; 1925, c. 41; 1981 (Reg. Sess., 1982), c. 1215; 1987, c. 174, s. 4; 1993 (Reg. Sess., 1994), c. 678, s. 33.)

CASE NOTES

A fireman may not sue the State Firemen's Association on a claim for benefits under this Chapter. Carroll v. North Carolina State Firemen's Ass'n, 230 N.C. 436, 53 S.E.2d 524 (1949).

A claim for hospital expenses incurred as a result of an injury received by a fireman in the course of his duties does not come within the benefits provided for members of the State Firemen's Association. Carroll v. North Carolina State Firemen's Ass'n, 230 N.C. 436, 53 S.E.2d 524 (1949).

§ **58-85-5:** Reserved for future codification purposes.

§ 58-85-10. Treasurer to file report and give bond.

The treasurer of the North Carolina State Firemen's Association shall make a detailed report to the State Treasurer of the yearly expenditures of the appropriation under Articles 84 through 88 of this Chapter on or before the end of the fiscal year, showing the total amount of money in his hands at the time of the filing of the report, and shall give a bond to the State of North Carolina with good and sufficient sureties to the satisfaction of the Treasurer of the State of North Carolina in a sum not less than the amount of money on hand as shown by said report. (1891, c. 468, s. 4; Rev., s. 4394; C.S., s. 6059; 1925, c. 41.)

§ 58-85-15. Who shall participate in the fund.

The line of duty entitling one to participate in the fund shall be so construed as to mean actual fire duty only, and any actual duty connected with the fire department when directed to perform the same by an officer in charge. (1891, c. 468, s. 5; Rev., s. 4395; C.S., s. 6060; 1925, c. 41.)

§ 58-85-20. Who may become members.

Any organized fire company in North Carolina, holding itself ready for duty, may, upon compliance with the requirements of said constitution and bylaws, become a member of the North Carolina State Firemen's Association, and any fireman of good moral character in North Carolina, and belonging to an organized fire company, who will comply with the requirements of the constitution and bylaws of the North Carolina State Firemen's Association, may become a member of said Association. (1891, c. 468, s. 6; Rev., s. 4396; C.S., s. 6061; 1925, c. 41.)

§ 58-85-25. Applied to members of regular fire company.

The provisions of G.S. 58-85-1, 58-85-10, 58-85-15, 58-85-20, and 58-85-25 shall apply to any fireman who is a member of a regularly organized fire company, and is a member in good standing of the North Carolina State

Firemen's Association. (1891, c. 468, s. 7; Rev., s. 4397; C.S., s. 6062; 1925, c. 41.)

§ 58-85-30. Treasurer to pay fund to Volunteer Firemen's Association.

(a) The treasurer of the North Carolina State Firemen's Association shall pay to the treasurer of the North Carolina State Volunteer Firemen's Association one sixth of the funds arising from the three percent (3%) paid the treasurer of the North Carolina State Firemen's Association by the Commissioner each year to be used by the North Carolina State Volunteer Firemen's Association for the purposes set forth in G.S. 58-84-35.

(b) Local units of the North Carolina State Volunteer Firemen's Association shall maintain records and report to the North Carolina State Firemen's Association in accordance with G.S. 58-84-40, and shall be subject to the sanctions in G.S. 58-84-40. (1925, c. 41; 1985, c. 666, s. 65; 2003-221, s. 11.)

Effect of Amendments. — Session Laws 2003-221, s. 11, effective June 19, 2003, designated the previously undesignated paragraphs as subsections (a) and (b); in subsection (a), substituted "three percent (3%)" for "five percent (5%)," substituted "the treasurer of the North Carolina State Firemen's Association" for "him," deleted "Insurance" preceding "Commissioner," and substituted "to be used by the" for "to be used by said"; and in subsection (b), substituted "in accordance with" for "in the same manner and to the same extent as provided for in," and substituted "in G.S. 58-84-40" for "as set forth therein."

ARTICLE 85A.

State Fire Protection Grant Fund.

§ 58-85A-1. Creation of Fund; allocation to local fire districts and political subdivisions of the State.

(a) There is created in the Office of State Budget and Management the State Fire Protection Grant Fund. The purpose of the Fund is to compensate local fire districts and political subdivisions of the State for providing local fire protection to State-owned buildings and their contents.

(b) The Office of State Budget and Management shall develop and implement an equitable and uniform statewide method for distributing any funds to the State's local fire districts and political subdivisions.

Upon the request of the Director of the Budget, the Department of Insurance shall provide the Office of State Budget and Management all information necessary to develop and implement the formula.

(c) It is the intent of the General Assembly to appropriate annually to the State Fire Protection Grant Fund at least three million eighty thousand dollars ($3,080,000) from the General Fund, one hundred fifty thousand dollars ($150,000) from the Highway Fund, and nine hundred seventy thousand dollars ($970,000) from University of North Carolina receipts. Funds received from the General Fund shall be allocated only for providing local fire protection for State-owned property supported by the General Fund; funds received from the Highway Fund shall be allocated only for providing local fire protection for State-owned property supported by the Highway Fund; and funds received from University of North Carolina receipts shall be allocated only for providing local fire protection for State-owned property supported by University of North Carolina receipts. (1997-443, s. 23(a); 2000-140, s. 93.1(a); 2001-424, s. 12.2(b).)

Editor's Note. — Session Laws 2001-424, s. 1.2, provides: "This act shall be known as the 'Current Operations and Capital Improvements Appropriations Act of 2001'."

Session Laws 2001-424, s. 36.5 is a severability clause.

ARTICLE 86.

North Carolina Firemen's and Rescue Squad Workers' Pension Fund.

§ 58-86-1. Fund established; administration by board of trustees; rules and regulations.

For the purpose of furthering the general welfare and police powers and obligations of the State with respect to the protection of all its citizens from the consequences of loss or damage by fire and of injury by serious accident or illness, of increasing the protection of life and property against loss or damage by fire, of improving fire fighting and life saving techniques, of increasing the potential of fire departments, rescue squads, organizations and groups, of fostering increased and more widely spread training of personnel of these organizations and groups, and of providing incentive and inducement to participate in fire prevention, fire fighting and rescue squad activities and for the establishment of new, improved or extended fire departments, rescue squads, organizations and groups to the end that ultimately all areas of the State and all of its citizens will receive the benefits of fire protection and rescue squads' activity and a resulting reduction of loss or damage to life and property by fire hazard or injury by serious accident or illness, and in recognition of the public service rendered to the State of North Carolina and its citizens by "eligible firemen and rescue squad workers," as defined by this Article, there is created in this State a fund to be known, and designated as "The North Carolina Firemen's and Rescue Squad Workers' Pension Fund" to be administered as provided in this Article.

The North Carolina Firemen's and Rescue Squad Workers' Pension Fund is established to provide pension allowances and other benefits for eligible firemen and rescue squad workers in the State who elect to become members of the fund. The board of trustees created by this Article shall have authority to administer the fund and shall make necessary rules and regulations to carry out the provisions of this Article. (1957, c. 1420, s. 1; 1959, c. 1212, s. 1; 1961, c. 980; 1981, c. 1029, s. 1.)

Cross References. — As to statutory provisions pertaining to a prior transfer of the North Carolina Firemen's and Rescue Squad Workers' Pension Fund to the Department of State Auditor, see G.S. 143A-27.1.

Editor's Note. — This Article is former Article 3 of former Chapter 118, rewritten by Session Laws 1981, c. 1029, s. 1, effective January 1, 1982, and recodified as Article 4 of former Chapter 118, which in turn has been recodified and incorporated as Article 86 of Chapter 58 pursuant to Session Laws 1987, c. 752, s. 9, as amended by Session Laws 1987 (Reg. Sess., 1988), c. 975, s. 34.

Session Laws 1981, c. 1029, s. 2, provides:

"The Fund established by Session Laws 1961 Chapter 980, G.S. 118-18 et seq., 'the Firemen's Pension Fund' is made a part of the Fund established by this act as the 'Firemen's and Rescue Squad Workers' Pension Fund'."

Session Laws 1991 (Reg. Sess., 1992), c. 833, s. 1 provides: "The statutory authority, powers, duties, and functions, records, personnel, property, unexpended balances of appropriations, allocations or other funds, including the functions of budgeting and purchasing, of the Department of State Auditor to administer the North Carolina Firemen's and Rescue Squad Workers' Pension Fund are transferred to the Department of State Treasurer."

§ 58-86-5. Creation and membership of board of trustees; compensation.

There is created a board to be known as the "Board of Trustees of the North Carolina Firemen's and Rescue Squad Workers' Pension Fund", hereinafter known as "the board".

The board shall consist of six members:

    (1) The State Treasurer, who shall act as chairman.

    (2) The State Insurance Commissioner.

    (3) Repealed by Session Laws 1993, c. 9, s. 1.

    (4) Four members to be appointed by the Governor; one a paid fireman, one a volunteer fireman, one volunteer rescue squad worker, and one representing the public at large, for terms of four years each. These members may succeed themselves.

The members presently serving on the "Board of Trustees of the Firemen's Pension Fund" shall continue to serve until the expiration of their terms. No member of the board shall receive any salary, compensation or expenses other than that provided in G.S. 138-6 for each day's attendance at duly and regularly called and held meetings of the board of trustees. (1957, c. 1420, s. 1; 1959, c. 1212, s. 1; 1973, c. 875; 1981, c. 1029, s. 1; 1991 (Reg. Sess., 1992), c. 833, s. 2; 1993, c. 9, s. 1.)

§ 58-86-10. Powers and duties of the board.

The board shall request appropriations out of the general fund for administrative expenses and to provide for the financing of this pension fund, employ necessary clerical assistance, determine all applications for pensions, provide for the payment of pensions, make all necessary rules and regulations not inconsistent with law for the government of this fund, prescribe rules and regulations of eligibility of persons to receive pensions, expend funds in accordance with the provisions of this Article, and generally exercise all other powers necessary for the administration of the fund created by this Article. (1957, c. 1420, s. 1; 1959, c. 1212, s. 1; 1981, c. 1029, s. 1.)

CASE NOTES

Board Is Agency of State. — The board of trustees of the North Carolina Firemen's Pension Fund purports to be an agency of the State, charged with the duty, among others, of administering moneys appropriated from the general fund of the State. Great Am. Ins. Co. v. Gold, 254 N.C. 168, 118 S.E.2d 792 (1961), decided under former statutory provisions.

§ 58-86-15. Director.

There is created an office to be known as Director of the North Carolina Firemen's and Rescue Squad Workers' Pension Fund. He shall be named by the board and shall serve at its pleasure. The director shall be subject to the provisions of the State Personnel Act. The director shall promptly transmit to the State Treasurer all moneys collected by him, which moneys shall be deposited by the State Treasurer into the fund. (1957, c. 1420, s. 1; 1959, c. 1212, s. 1; 1969, c. 359; 1981, c. 1029, s. 1; 1983 (Reg. Sess., 1984), c. 1116, s. 113.)

§ 58-86-20. State Treasurer to be custodian of fund; appropriations; contributions to fund; expenditures.

The State Treasurer shall be the custodian of the North Carolina Firemen's and Rescue Squad Workers' Pension Fund and shall invest its assets in accordance with the provisions of G.S. 147-69.2 and G.S. 147-69.3. The appropriations made by the General Assembly out of the general fund to provide money for administrative expenses shall be handled in the same manner as any other general fund appropriation. One-fourth of the appropriation made out of the general fund to provide for the financing of the pension fund shall be transferred quarterly to a special fund to be known as the North Carolina Firemen's and Rescue Squad Workers' Pension Fund. There shall be set up in the State Treasurer's office a special fund to be known as the North Carolina Firemen's and Rescue Squad Workers' Pension Fund, and all contributions made by the members of this pension fund shall be deposited in the special fund. All expenditures for refunds, investments or benefits shall be in the same manner as expenditures of other special funds. (1957, c. 1420, s. 1; 1959, c. 1212, s. 1; 1961, c. 980; 1971, c. 30; 1979, c. 467, s. 10; 1981, c. 1029, s. 1.)

CASE NOTES

Unconstitutionality of Former Provisions. — As to the unconstitutionality of former provisions imposing a tax on fire insurance contracts for the purpose of providing funds for the payment of pensions to retired firemen, see Great Am. Ins. Co. v. Johnson, 257 N.C. 367, 126 S.E.2d 92 (1962).

As to the invalidity for discrimination and lack of uniformity of former provisions imposing a tax on certain fire and lightning insurance policies, see American Equitable Assurance Co. v. Gold, 249 N.C. 461, 106 S.E.2d 875 (1959); In re North Carolina Fire Ins. Rating Bureau, 249 N.C. 466, 106 S.E.2d 879 (1959).

§ 58-86-25. "Eligible firemen" defined; determination and certification of volunteers meeting qualifications.

"Eligible firemen" shall mean all firemen of the State of North Carolina or any political subdivision thereof, including those performing such functions in the protection of life and property through fire fighting within a county or city governmental unit and so certified to the Commissioner of Insurance by the governing body thereof, and who belong to a bona fide fire department which, as determined by the Commissioner, is classified as not less than class "9" or class "A" and "AA" departments in accordance with rating methods, schedules, classifications, underwriting rules, bylaws or regulations effective or applied with respect to the establishment of rates or premiums used or charged pursuant to Article 36 or 40 of this Chapter or by such other reasonable methods as the Commissioner may determine, and which operates fire apparatus and equipment of the value of five thousand dollars ($5,000) or more, and said fire department holds drills and meetings not less than four hours monthly and said firemen attend at least 36 hours of all drills and meetings in each calendar year. "Eligible firemen" shall also mean an employee of a county whose sole duty is to act as fire marshal, deputy fire marshal, assistant fire marshal, or firefighter of the county, provided the board of county commissioners of that county certifies the employee's attendance at no less than 36 hours of all drills and meetings in each calendar year. "Eligible firemen" shall also mean those persons meeting the other qualifications of this section, not exceeding 25 volunteer firemen plus one additional volunteer fireman per 100 population in the area served by their respective departments. Each department shall annually determine and report the names of those firemen meeting the eligibility qualifications of this section to its respective governing body, which upon determination of the validity and accuracy of the qualification shall promptly certify the list to the North Carolina State Firemen's Association. The Firemen's Association shall provide a list of those persons meeting the eligibility requirements of this section to the State Treasurer by July 1 of each year. For the purposes of the preceding sentence, the governing body of a fire department operated: by a county is the county board of commissioners; by a city is the city council; by a sanitary district is the sanitary district board; by a corporation, whether profit or nonprofit, is the corporation's board of directors; and by any other entity is that group designated by the board. (1957, c. 1420, s. 1; 1959, c. 1212, s. 1; 1981, c. 1029, s. 1; 1983, c. 416, s. 7; 1985, c. 241; 2000-67, s. 26.22; 2001-222, s. 1; 2003-362, s. 1.)

Editor's Note. — Session Laws 2000-67, s. 1.1, provides: "This act shall be known as 'The Current Operations and Capital Improvements Appropriations Act of 2000.'"

Session Laws 2000-67, s. 28.4, contains a severability clause.

Effect of Amendments. — Session Laws 2003-362, s. 1, effective July 1, 2003, in the second sentence, inserted "deputy fire marshal, assistant fire marshal, or firefighter" and substituted "employee's" for "fire marshal's."

§ 58-86-30. "Eligible rescue squad worker" defined; determination and certification of eligibility.

"Eligible rescue squad worker" means a person who is a member of a rescue or emergency medical services squad that is eligible for membership in the North Carolina Association of Rescue and Emergency Medical Services, Inc., and who has attended a minimum of 36 hours of training and meetings in the last calendar year. Each rescue or emergency medical services squad eligible for membership in the North Carolina Association of Rescue and Emergency Medical Services, Inc., must file a roster certified by the secretary of the association of those rescue or emergency medical services squad workers meeting the requirements of this section with the State Treasurer by January 1 of each calendar year.

"Eligible rescue squad worker" does not mean "eligible fireman" as defined by G.S. 58-86-25, nor may an "eligible rescue squad worker" qualify also as an "eligible fireman" in order to receive double benefits available under this Article. (1981, c. 1029, s. 1; 1991 (Reg. Sess., 1992), c. 833, s. 3; 1995, c. 507, s. 7.21A(h).)

§ 58-86-35. Firemen's application for membership in fund; monthly payments by members; payments credited to separate accounts of members.

Those firemen who are eligible pursuant to G.S. 58-86-25 may make application for membership to the board. Each fireman upon becoming a member of the fund shall pay the director of the fund the sum of ten dollars ($10.00) per month. The monthly payments shall be credited to the separate account of the member and shall be kept by the custodian so it is available for payment on withdrawal from membership or retirement. (1957, c. 1420, s. 1; 1959, c. 1212, s. 1; 1981, c. 1029, s. 1; 1995, c. 507, s. 7.21A(d).)

§ 58-86-40. Rescue squad worker's application for membership in funds; monthly payments by members; payments credited to separate accounts of members.

Those rescue squad workers eligible pursuant to G.S. 58-86-30 may apply to the board for membership. Each eligible rescue squad worker upon becoming a member shall pay the director of the fund the sum of ten dollars ($10.00) per month. The monthly payments shall be credited to the separate account of the member and shall be kept by the custodian so it is available for payment on withdrawal from membership or retirement. (1981, c. 1029, s. 1; 1983, c. 500, s. 1; 1991 (Reg. Sess., 1992), c. 833, s. 4; 1995, c. 507, s. 7.21A(e).)

§ 58-86-45. Additional retroactive membership.

(a) Any fireman or rescue squad worker who is now eligible and is a member of a fire department or rescue squad chartered by the State of North Carolina and who has not previously elected to become a member may make application through the board of trustees for membership in the fund on or before March 31, 2001. The person shall make a lump sum payment of ten dollars ($10.00) per month retroactively to the time he first became eligible to become a member, plus interest at an annual rate of eight percent (8%), for each year of his retroactive payments. Upon making the lump sum payment, the person shall be given credit for all prior service in the same manner as if he had made application for membership at the time he first became eligible. Any member who made application for membership subsequent to the time he was first eligible and did not receive credit for prior service may receive credit for this prior service upon lump sum payment of ten dollars ($10.00) per month retroactively to the time he first became eligible, plus interest at an annual rate of eight percent (8%), for each year of his retroactive payments. Upon making this lump sum payment, the date of membership shall be the same as if he had made application for membership at the time he was first eligible. Any fireman or rescue squad worker who has applied for prior service under this subsection shall have until June 30, 2001, to pay for this prior service and, if this payment is not made by June 30, 2001, he shall not receive credit for this service, except as provided in subsection (a1) of this section.

(a1) Effective July 1, 1993, any fireman or rescue squad worker who is a current or former member of a fire department or rescue squad chartered by the State of North Carolina may purchase credit for any periods of service to any chartered fire department or rescue squad not otherwise creditable by making a lump sum payment to the Annuity Savings Fund equal to the full liability of the service credits calculated on the basis of the assumptions used for purposes of the actuarial valuation of the system's liabilities, which payment shall take into account the retirement allowance arising on account of the additional service credit commencing at the earliest age at which the member could retire on a retirement allowance, as determined by the board of trustees upon the advice of the consulting actuary, plus an administrative fee to be set by the board of trustees.

(b) An eligible fireman or rescue squad worker who is not yet 35 years old and has not previously elected to become a member may apply to the board of trustees for membership in the fund at any time. Upon becoming a member, the worker must make a lump sum payment of ten dollars ($10.00) per month retroactively to the time the worker first became eligible to become a member, plus interest at an annual rate to be set by the board for each year of retroactive payments. Upon making this lump sum payment, the worker shall be given credit for all prior service in the same manner as if the worker had applied for membership upon first becoming eligible.

A member who is not yet 35 years old, who applied for membership after first becoming eligible, and who did not receive credit for prior service may receive credit for the prior service upon making a lump sum payment of ten dollars ($10.00) for each month since the worker first became eligible, plus interest at an annual rate to be set by the board for each year of retroactive payments. Upon making this lump sum payment, the date of membership shall be the same as if the worker had applied for membership upon first becoming eligible. (1985 (Reg. Sess., 1986), c. 1014, s. 49.1(a); 1989, c. 693; 1993, c. 429, s. 1; 1995, c. 507, s. 7.21A(f); 2000-67, s. 26.17(a).)

Editor's Note. — Session Laws 1995, c. 507, which amended this section, in s. 7.21A(i) provides: "The changes made to G.S. 58-86-45 and G.S. 58-86-55 by this Part do not affect the credit received for service performed before July 1, 1995. The increase in monthly pension contributions from five dollars ($5.00) to ten dollars ($10.00) in G.S. 58-86-55 does not affect the amount of monthly contributions made prior to July 1, 1995."

Session Laws 1995, c. 507, s. 28.9, provides: "Except for statutory changes or other provisions that clearly indicate an intention to have effects beyond the 1995-97 fiscal biennium, the textual provisions of this act apply only to funds appropriated for, and activities occurring during, the 1995-97 biennium."

§ 58-86-50. Administrative fee for rejoining the fund.

Any individual who had been a member of the fund and who applies to rejoin the fund shall not be entitled to membership until he or she has paid an administrative fee of twenty-five dollars ($25.00), which fee shall be in addition to any other charges or payments required by the board of trustees to rejoin the fund based upon the fund's loss of earnings resulting from the member's withdrawal from the fund. The administrative fees collected by the fund shall be retained by the Board to defray administrative expenses, including salaries. (1987, c. 667, s. 2.)

§ 58-86-55. Monthly pensions upon retirement.

Any member who has served 20 years as an "eligible fireman" or "eligible rescue squad worker" in the State of North Carolina, as provided in G.S. 58-86-25 and G.S. 58-86-30, and who has attained the age of 55 years is entitled to be paid a monthly pension from this fund. The monthly pension shall be in the amount of one hundred fifty-eight dollars ($158.00) per month. Any retired fireman receiving a pension shall, effective July 1, 2003, receive a pension of one hundred fifty-eight dollars ($158.00) per month.

Members shall pay ten dollars ($10.00) per month as required by G.S. 58-86-35 and G.S. 58-86-40 for a period of no longer than 20 years. No "eligible rescue squad member" shall receive a pension prior to July 1, 1983. No member shall be entitled to a pension hereunder until the member's official duties as a fireman or rescue squad worker for which the member is paid compensation shall have been terminated and the member shall have retired as such according to standards or rules fixed by the board of trustees.

A member who is totally and permanently disabled while in the discharge of the member's official duties as a result of bodily injuries sustained or as a result of extreme exercise or extreme activity experienced in the course and scope of those official duties and who leaves the fire or rescue squad service because of this disability shall be entitled to be paid from the fund a monthly benefit in an amount of one hundred fifty-eight dollars ($158.00) per month beginning the first month after the member's fifty-fifth birthday. All applications for disability are subject to the approval of the board who may appoint physicians to examine and evaluate the disabled member prior to approval of the application, and annually thereafter. Any disabled member shall not be required to make the monthly payment of ten dollars ($10.00) as required by G.S. 58-86-35 and G.S. 58-86-40.

A member who is totally and permanently disabled for any cause, other than line of duty, who leaves the fire or rescue squad service because of this disability and who has at least 10 years of service with the pension fund, may be permitted to continue making a monthly contribution of ten dollars ($10.00) to the fund until the member has made contributions for a total of 240 months. The member shall upon attaining the age of 55 years be entitled to receive a pension as provided by this section. All applications for disability are subject to the approval of the board who may appoint physicians to examine and evaluate the disabled member prior to approval of the application and annually thereafter.

A member who, because his residence is annexed by a city under Part 2 or Part 3 of Article 4 of Chapter 160A of the General Statutes, or whose department is closed because of an annexation by a city under Part 2 or Part 3 of Article 4 of Chapter 160A of the General Statutes, or whose volunteer department is taken over by a city or county, and because of such annexation or takeover is unable to perform as a fireman or rescue squad worker of any status, and if the member has at least 10 years of service with the pension fund, may be permitted to continue making a monthly contribution of ten dollars ($10.00) to the fund until the member has made contributions for a total of 240 months. The member upon attaining the age of 55 years and completion of such contributions shall be entitled to receive a pension as provided by this section. Any application to make monthly contributions under this section shall be subject to a finding of eligibility by the Board of Trustees upon application of the member.

The pensions provided shall be in addition to all other pensions or benefits under any other statutes of the State of North Carolina or the United States, notwithstanding any exclusionary provisions of other pensions or retirement systems provided by law. (1957, c. 1420, s. 1; 1959, c. 1212, s. 1; 1961, c. 980; 1971, c. 336; 1977, c. 926, s. 1; 1981, c. 1029, s. 1; 1983, c. 500, s. 2; c. 636, s. 24; 1985 (Reg. Sess., 1986), c. 1014, s. 49.1(b); 1987 (Reg. Sess., 1988), c. 1099, s. 1; 1991, c. 720, s. 48; 1993 (Reg. Sess., 1994), c. 653, s. 1; 1995, c. 507, s. 7.21A(g); 1997-443, s. 33.25(a); 1998-212, s. 28.21(a); 2000-67, s. 26.18; 2002-113, s. 1; 2002-126, s. 28.7; 2003-284, s. 30.19.)

Editor's Note. — Session Laws 1983, c. 636, which inserted the next-to-last paragraph, effective with respect to all annexations where resolutions of intent are adopted on or after June 29, 1983, provides in ss. 37.1 and 38, as amended by Session Laws 1983, c. 768, s. 25:

"Sec. 37.1. The General Assembly intends by this act to repeal all acts and provisions of acts that modify the application to particular cities and towns of Parts 2 and 3 of Article 4A of Chapter 160A of the General Statutes or that exempt particular cities or towns from the application of either or both of those two Parts. Therefore, all such acts and provisions of acts, even if not specifically listed and repealed in Sections 26 through 35.4 of this act, are repealed. Neither this section nor Sections 26 through 35.4 of this act shall affect any annexation in progress on the dates of ratification of this act under any of the repealed or amended sections.

"Sec. 38. This act shall be effective with respect to all annexations where resolutions of intent are adopted on or after the date of ratification of this act, except that Sections 36 and 37 shall become effective with respect to all annexations where resolutions of intent are adopted on or after July 1, 1984, Sections 25.1 through 35.5 and Section 37.1 are effective upon ratification and Section 25 shall become effective as provided in that section. No annexation where a resolution of intent was adopted prior to the date of ratification of this act shall be affected by this act except as provided in Section 25."

The act was ratified June 29, 1983.

The references in the next-to-last paragraph of this section to Article 4 of Chapter 160A were apparently intended to refer to Article 4A of that chapter.

Session Laws 1993 (Reg. Sess., 1994), c. 653, s. 1 which amended this section was effective July 1, 1994, contingent on whether funds to implement it are appropriated in the Current Operations and Capital Improvements Appropriations Act of 1994.

Session Laws 1995, c. 507, which amended this section, in s. 7.21A(i) provides: "The changes made to G.S. 58-86-45 and G.S. 58-86-55 by this Part do not affect the credit received for service performed before July 1, 1995. The increase in monthly pension contributions from five dollars ($5.00) to ten dollars ($10.00) in G.S. 58-86-55 does not affect the amount of monthly contributions made prior to July 1, 1995."

Session Laws 1995, c. 507, s. 28.9, provides: "Except for statutory changes or other provisions that clearly indicate an intention to have effects beyond the 1995-97 fiscal biennium, the textual provisions of this act apply only to funds appropriated for, and activities occurring during, the 1995-97 biennium."

Session Laws 2002-126, s. 1.2, provides: "This act shall be known as 'The Current Operations, Capitol Improvements, and Finance Act of 2002'."

Session Laws 2002-126, s. 31.6 is a severability clause.

Session Laws 2003-284, s. 1.2, provides: "This act shall be known as the 'Current Operations and Capital Improvements Appropriations Act of 2003'."

Session Laws 2003-284, s. 49.5 is a severability clause.

Effect of Amendments. — Session Laws 2002-113, s. 1, effective September 6, 2002, and applicable to members of the Firemen's and Rescue Squad Workers' Pension Fund with at least 10 years of service on or after January 1, 2002, substituted "or whose volunteer department is taken over by a city or county, and because of such annexation or takeover is unable to perform as a fireman or rescue squad worker" for "and because of such annexation is unable to perform as a fireman" in the first sentence of the fifth paragraph.

Session Laws 2002-126, s. 28.7, effective July 1, 2002, substituted "one hundred fifty-six dollars ($156.00)" for "one hundred fifty-one dollars ($151.00)" throughout the section; and substituted "July 1, 2002" for "July 1, 2000" in the final sentence of the first paragraph.

Session Laws 2003-284, s. 30.19, effective July 1, 2003, substituted "one hundred fifty-eight dollars ($158.00)" for "one hundred fifty-six dollars ($156.00)" twice in the first paragraph, and once in the third paragraph; and substituted "effective July 1, 2003" for "effective July 1, 2002" in the third sentence of the first paragraph.

§ 58-86-60. Payments in lump sums.

The board shall direct payment in lump sums from the fund in the following cases:

(1) To any fireman or rescue squad worker upon the attaining of the age of 55 years, who, for any reason, is not qualified to receive the monthly retirement pension and who was enrolled as a member of the fund, an amount equal to the amount paid into the fund by him. This provision shall not be construed to preclude any active fireman or rescue squad worker from completing the requisite number of years of active service after attaining the age of 55 years necessary to entitle him to the pension.

(2) If any fireman or rescue squad worker dies before attaining the age at which a pension is payable to him under the provisions of this Article, there shall be paid to his widow, or if there be no widow, to the person responsible for his child or children, or if there be no widow or children, then to his heirs at law as may be determined by the board or to his estate, if it is administered and there are no heirs, an amount equal to the amount paid into the fund by the said fireman or rescue squad worker.

(3) If any fireman or rescue squad worker dies after beginning to receive the pension payable to him by this Article, and before receiving an amount equal to the amount paid into the fund by him, there shall be paid to his widow, or if there be no widow, then to the person responsible for his child or children, or if there be no widow or children, then to his heirs at law as may be determined by the board or to his estate, if it is administered and there are no heirs, an amount equal to the difference between the amount paid into the fund by the said fireman or rescue squad worker and the amount received by him as a pensioner.

(4) Any member withdrawing from the fund shall, upon proper application, be paid all moneys the individual contributed to the fund without accumulated earnings on the payments after the time they were made less an administrative fee equal to the lesser of the amount the individual contributed to the fund or twenty-five dollars ($25.00). The

administrative fees collected by the fund shall be retained by the Board to defray administrative expenses, including salaries. Notwithstanding the foregoing, if any person, firm, corporation, or other entity has made contributions on behalf of a member and that member withdraws from the fund, the person, firm, corporation, or other entity shall be entitled to a refund equal to the amount of contributions made by them after the Board has been notified of the contributor's desire to be refunded its contributions upon the member's withdrawal. Any refunds to a contributor other than a member shall also be subject to the twenty-five dollar ($25.00) administrative fee. If a refund is to be shared by a member and another party the administrative fee shall be applied to each portion on a pro rata basis. (1957, c. 1420, s. 1; 1959, c. 1212, s. 1; 1977, c. 926, s. 2; 1981, c. 1029, s. 1; 1987, c. 667, s. 1.)

§ 58-86-65. Pro rata reduction of benefits when fund insufficient to pay in full.

If, for any reason, the fund created and made available for any purpose covered by this Article shall be insufficient to pay in full any pension benefits, or other charges, then all benefits or payments shall be reduced pro rata, for as long as the deficiency in amount exists. No claim shall accrue with respect to any amount by which a pension or benefit payment shall have been reduced. (1957, c. 1420, s. 1; 1959, c. 1212, s. 1; 1981, c. 1029, s. 1.)

§ 58-86-70. Provisions subject to future legislative change.

These pensions shall be subject to future legislative change or revision, and no member of the fund, or any person, is deemed to have acquired any vested right to a pension or other payment provided by this Article. (1957, c. 1420, s. 1; 1959, c. 1212, s. 1; 1981, c. 1029, s. 1.)

§ 58-86-75. Determination of creditable service; information furnished by applicants for membership.

The board shall determine by appropriate rules and regulations the number of years' credit for service of firemen and rescue squad workers. Firemen and rescue squad workers who are now serving as such shall furnish the board with information upon applying for membership as to previous service. Notwithstanding any other provisions of this Article, the Board may grant qualified prior service credits to eligible firemen and rescue squad workers under such terms and conditions that the Board may adopt when the Board determines that an eligible fireman or rescue squad worker has been denied such service credits through no fault of his own. (1957, c. 1420, s. 1; 1959, c. 1212, s. 1; 1981, c. 1029, s. 1; 1987 (Reg. Sess., 1988), c. 1086, s. 29.)

§ 58-86-80. Length of service not affected by serving in more than one department or squad; transfer from one department or squad to another.

A fireman's or rescue squad worker's length of service shall not be affected by the fact that he may have served with more than one department or squad, and upon transfer from one department or squad to another, notice of the fact shall be given to the board. (1957, c. 1420, s. 1; 1959, c. 1212, s. 1; 1981, c. 1029, s. 1.)

§ 58-86-85. Effect of member being six months delinquent in making monthly payments.

Any member who becomes six months delinquent in making monthly payments required by G.S. 58-86-35 and G.S. 58-86-40 of this Article by the tenth of the month with respect to which the payment shall be due shall forfeit his membership in the fund. (1957, c. 1420, s. 1; 1959, c. 1212, s. 1; 1977, c. 926, s. 3; 1981, c. 1029, s. 1.)

§ 58-86-90. Exemptions of pensions from attachment; rights nonassignable.

Except for the applications of the provisions of G.S. 110-136, and in connection with a court-ordered equitable distribution under G.S. 50-20, the pensions provided are not subject to attachment, garnishments or judgments against the fireman or rescue squad worker entitled to them, nor are any rights in the fund or the pensions or benefits assignable. (1957, c. 1420, s. 1; 1959, c. 1212, s. 1; 1969, c. 486; 1981, c. 1029, s. 1; 1985, c. 402; 1989, c. 792, s. 2.1.)

§ 58-86-91. Deduction for payments to certain employees' or retirees' associations allowed.

Any member who is a member of a domiciled employees' or retirees' association that has at least 2,000 members, the majority of whom are active or retired employees of the State or public school employees, may authorize, in writing, the periodic deduction from the member's retirement benefits a designated lump sum to be paid to the employees' or retirees' association. The authorization shall remain in effect until revoked by the member. A plan of deductions pursuant to this section shall become void if the employees' or retirees' association engages in collective bargaining with the State, any political subdivision of the State, or any local school administrative unit. (2002-126, s. 6.4(f).)

Editor's Note. — Session Laws 2002-126, s. 31.7, made this section effective July 1, 2002.

Session Laws 2002-126, s. 1.2, provides: "This act shall be known as 'The Current Operations, Capitol Improvements, and Finance Act of 2002'."

Session Laws 2002-126, s. 31.6 is a severability clause.

ARTICLE 87.

Volunteer Safety Workers Assistance.

§ 58-87-1. Volunteer Fire Department Fund.

(a) There is created the Volunteer Fire Department Fund to provide matching grants to volunteer fire departments to purchase equipment and make capital improvements. The Fund shall be set up in the Department of Insurance. The State Treasurer shall invest its assets according to law, and the earnings shall remain in the Fund. The Fund shall be distributed under the direction of the Commissioner of Insurance. Beginning January 1, 1988, an eligible fire department may apply to the Commissioner of Insurance for a grant under this section. Beginning May 1, 1988, and on each May 15, thereafter, the Commissioner shall make grants to eligible fire departments subject to the following limitations:

　(1) The size of a grant may not exceed twenty thousand dollars ($20,000);

　(2) The applicant shall match the grant on a dollar-for-dollar basis;

(3) The grant may be used only for equipment purchases, payment of highway use taxes on those purchases, or capital expenditures necessary to provide fire protection services; and

(4) An applicant may receive no more than one grant per fiscal year.

In awarding grants under this section, the Commissioner shall to the extent possible select applicants from all parts of the State based upon need. Up to two percent (2%) of the Fund may be used for additional staff and resources to administer the Fund in each fiscal year.

No fire department may be declared ineligible for a grant under this section solely because it is classified as a municipal fire department.

(b) A fire department is eligible for a grant under this section if it meets all of the following conditions:

(1) It serves a response area of 6,000 or less in population.

(2) It consists entirely of volunteer members, with the exception that the unit may have paid members to fill the equivalent of three full-time paid positions.

(3) It has been certified by the Department of Insurance.

In making the population determination under subdivision (1), the Department shall use the most recent annual population estimates certified by the State Planning Officer.

(c) The Commissioner of Insurance shall submit a written report to the General Assembly within 60 days after the grants have been made. This report shall contain the amount of the grant and the name of the recipient. (1987, c. 709, s. 1; 1987 (Reg. Sess., 1988), c. 1062, ss. 6-9; 1989, c. 770, s. 30; 1995, c. 507, s. 7.21A(k); 1998-212, s. 25(a); 1999-319, s. 1.)

Editor's Note. — Session Laws 1987 (Reg. Sess., 1988), c. 1062, s. 9, effective October 1, 1988, provides that "G.S. 118-50(a) is amended by adding after the last sentence in Section 1(b) a new sentence." At the direction of the Revisor of Statutes, this new sentence is set out above as the final paragraph of subsection (a).

§ 58-87-5. Volunteer Rescue/EMS Fund.

(a) There is created in the Department of Insurance the Volunteer Rescue/EMS Fund to provide grants to volunteer rescue units providing rescue or rescue and emergency medical services to purchase equipment and make capital improvements. An eligible rescue or rescue/EMS unit may apply to the Department of Insurance for a grant under this section. The application form and criteria for grants shall be established by the Department. The Department of Health and Human Services shall provide the Department with an advisory priority listing of EMS equipment eligible for funding. The State Treasurer shall invest the Fund's assets according to law, and the earnings shall remain in the Fund. On December 15 of each year, the Department shall make grants to eligible rescue or rescue/EMS units subject to all of the following limitations:

(1) A grant to an applicant who is required to match the grant with non-State funds may not exceed fifteen thousand dollars ($15,000), and a grant to an applicant who is not required to match the grant with non-State funds may not exceed three thousand dollars ($3,000).

(2) An applicant whose liquid assets, when combined with the liquid assets of any corporate affiliate or subsidiary of the applicant, are more than one thousand dollars ($1,000) shall match the grant on a dollar-for-dollar basis with non-State funds.

(3) The grant may be used only for equipment purchases, payment of highway use taxes on those purchases, or capital expenditures.

(4) An applicant may receive no more than one grant per fiscal year.

In awarding grants under this section, the Department shall to the extent possible select applicants from all parts of the State based upon need. Up to two percent (2%) of the Fund may be used for additional staff and resources to administer the Fund in each fiscal year. In addition, notwithstanding G.S. 58-78-20, up to four percent (4%) of the Fund may be used for additional staff and resources for the North Carolina Fire and Rescue Commission.

   (b) A rescue or rescue/EMS unit is eligible for a grant under this section if it meets all of the following conditions:

     (1) Repealed by Session Laws 1989 (Regular Session, 1990), c. 1066, s. 33(a).

     (2) It consists entirely of volunteer members, with the exception that the unit may have paid members to fill the equivalent of three full-time paid positions.

     (3) It has been recognized by the Department as an organization that provides rescue or rescue and emergency medical services.

     (4) It satisfies the eligibility criteria established by the Department under subsection (a) of this section.

   (c) For the purpose of this section and Article 88 of this Chapter, "rescue" means the removal of individuals facing external, nonmedical, and nonpatient related peril to areas of relative safety. A "rescue unit" or "rescue squad" means a group of individuals who are not necessarily trained in emergency medical services, fire fighting, or law enforcement, but who expose themselves to an external, nonmedical, and nonpatient related peril to effect the removal of individuals facing the same type of peril to areas of relative safety. The unit or squad must comply with existing State statutes and with eligibility criteria established by the North Carolina Association of Rescue and Emergency Medical Services, Inc. (1987 (Reg. Sess., 1988), c. 1062, s. 2; 1989, c. 115; c. 534, s. 2; 1989 (Reg. Sess., 1990), c. 1066, s. 33(a); 1991 (Reg. Sess., 1992), c. 943, s. 2; 1995, c. 507, s. 7.21A(l); 1997-443, s. 11A.20; 1998-212, s. 25(b); 1999-319, s. 2.)

§ 58-87-10. Workers' Compensation Fund for the benefit of volunteer safety workers.

   (a) Definition. — As used in this section, the term "eligible unit" means a volunteer fire department or volunteer rescue/EMS unit that is not part of a unit of local government and is exempt from State income tax under G.S. 105-130.11.

   (b) Creation. — The Workers' Compensation Fund is created in the Department of Insurance as an expendable trust fund. Accordingly, interest and other investment income earned by the Fund accrues to it, and revenue in the Fund at the end of a fiscal year remains in the Fund and does not revert.

   (c) Use. — Revenue in the Workers' Compensation Fund shall be used to provide workers' compensation benefits to members of eligible units. Chapter 97 of the General Statutes governs the payment of benefits from the Fund. Benefits are payable for compensable injuries or deaths that occur on or after July 1, 1996.

   (d) Administration. — The State Fire and Rescue Commission, established under G.S. 58-78-1, shall administer the Workers' Compensation Fund and shall perform this duty by contracting with a third-party administrator. The contracting procedure is not subject to Article 3C of Chapter 143 of the General Statutes. The reasonable and necessary expenses incurred by the Commission in administering the Fund shall be paid out of the Fund by the State Treasurer. The Commission may adopt rules to implement this section.

   (e) Revenue Source. — Revenue is credited to the Workers' Compensation Fund from appropriations made to the Department of Insurance for this purpose. In addition, every eligible unit that elects to participate shall pay into the Fund an amount set annually by the State Fire and Rescue Commission to ensure that the Fund will be able to meet its payment obligations under this section. The amount shall be set as a per capita fixed dollar amount for each member of the roster of the eligible unit.

The payment shall be made to the State Fire and Rescue Commission on or before July 1 of each year. The Commission shall remit the payments it receives to the State Treasurer, who shall credit the payments to the Fund. (1995, c. 507, s. 7.21A(a); 1999-132, s. 1.2.)

Editor's Note. — Session Laws 1995, c. 507, which enacted this section, in s. 7.21A(b) provides: "The first per member payment that eligible fire departments and rescue/EMS units must make to the State Fire and Rescue Commission under G.S. 58-87-10 is payable on or before July 1, 1996."

Session Laws 1995, c. 507, s. 28.9, provides: "Except for statutory changes or other provisions that clearly indicate an intention to have effects beyond the 1995-97 fiscal biennium, the textual provisions of this act apply only to funds appropriated for, and activities occurring during, the 1995-97 biennium."

ARTICLE 88.

Rescue Squad Workers' Relief Fund.

§ 58-88-1. Definitions.

As used in this Article:
(1) "Association" means the North Carolina Association of Rescue and Emergency Medical Services, Inc.
(2) "Board" means the Board of Trustees of the Fund.
(3) "EMS" means emergency medical services.
(4) "Fund" means the Rescue Squad Workers' Relief Fund.
(5) "Secretary-Treasurer" means the Secretary-Treasurer of the Association. (1987, c. 584, s. 5.)

§ 58-88-5. Rescue Squad Workers' Relief Fund; trustees; disbursement of funds.

(a) The "Rescue Squad Workers' Relief Fund" is created. It consists of the revenue credited to the Fund under G.S. 20-183.7(c) and shall be used for the purposes set forth in this Article.

(b) The Executive Committee of the Association shall be the Board of Trustees of the Fund. The Board shall consist of the Commander, Vice-Commander, Secretary-Treasurer, and two past Commanders of the Association. The Commander shall be the Chairman of the Board. The Commander, Vice-Commander, and Secretary-Treasurer shall appoint the two past Commanders of the Association, who shall serve at the pleasure of the appointing officers.

(c) The Commissioner of Insurance has exclusive control of the Fund and shall disburse revenue in the Fund to the Association only for the following purposes:
(1) To safeguard any rescue or EMS worker in active service from financial loss, occasioned by sickness contracted or injury received while in the performance of his or her duties as a rescue or EMS worker.
(2) To provide a reasonable support for those persons actually dependent upon the services of any rescue or EMS worker who may lose his or her life in the service of his or her town, county, city, or the State,

either by accident or from disease contracted or injury received by reason of such service. The amount is to be determined according to the earning capacity of the deceased.

(3) To award scholarships to children of members, deceased members or retired members in good standing, for the purpose of attending a two year or four year college or university, and for the purpose of attending a two year course of study at a community college or an accredited trade or technical school, any of which is located in the State of North Carolina. Continuation of the payment of educational benefits for children of active members shall be conditioned on the continuance of active membership in the rescue or EMS service by the parent or parents.

(4) To pay death benefits to those persons who were actually dependent upon any member killed in the line of duty.

(4a) To pay additional benefits approved by the Board of Trustees of the Fund to rescue and EMS workers who are eligible pursuant to G.S. 58-88-10 and who are members of the Association.

(5) Notwithstanding any other provision of law, no expenditures shall be made pursuant to subdivisions (1), (2), (3), (4), and (4a) of this subsection unless the Board has certified that the expenditures will not render the Fund actuarially unsound for the purpose of providing the benefits set forth in subdivisions (1), (2), (3), (4), and (4a). If, for any reason, funds made available for subdivisions (1), (2), (3), (4), and (4a) are insufficient to pay in full any benefit, the benefits pursuant to subdivisions (1), (2), (3), (4), and (4a) shall be reduced pro rata for as long as the amount of insufficient funds exists. No claims shall accrue with respect to any amount by which a benefit under subdivisions (1), (2), (3), (4), and (4a) has been reduced. (1987, c. 584, s. 5; 1987 (Reg. Sess., 1988), c. 1062, s. 10; 1989 (Reg. Sess., 1990), c. 1066, s. 33(c); 1995, c. 421, s. 1.)

§ 58-88-10. Membership eligibility.

(a) Any member of a rescue squad or EMS service who is eligible for membership in the Association and who has attended a minimum of 36 hours of training and meetings in the last calendar year; and each rescue squad or EMS service whose members are eligible for membership in the Association who has filed a roster certifying to the Secretary-Treasurer who certifies to the Commissioner of Insurance by January 1 of each calendar year that all eligible members have met the requirements, shall be eligible for the Fund. Any eligible member who, in the actual discharge of his or her duties as rescue or EMS personnel, is (1) made sick by disease contracted or (2) becomes disabled, shall be entitled to the benefits from the Fund.

(b) Any organized rescue squad or EMS service in North Carolina holding itself ready for duty may, upon compliance with the requirements of the constitution and by-laws of the Association, be eligible for membership in the Fund.

(c) The line of duty entitling one to participate in the Fund shall be so construed as to mean actual rescue or EMS duty only. (1987, c. 584, s. 5.)

§ 58-88-15. Accounting; reports; audits.

The Board shall keep a correct account of all monies received and disbursed by the Board; and shall annually file a report with the Commissioner of Insurance at such time and in such form prescribed by the Commissioner of Insurance and the State Auditor. The Board shall be bonded by the sum of any money total for which it is responsible. The books, records, and operations of the Board shall be subject to the oversight of the State Auditor pursuant to Article 5A of Chapter 147 of the General Statutes. (1987, c. 584, s. 5; 1993, c. 257, s. 3.)

§ 58-88-20. Justification of claim.

The eligibility of the claimant and the justification of each claim shall be certified by the chief or chief officer of the local department before a magistrate, notary public, or other officer authorized to administer oaths, on a form furnished by the Secretary-Treasurer. This form must be accompanied by a certificate of the attending physician on a form also to be furnished by the Secretary-Treasurer. Each person receiving benefits from the Fund shall file an annual justification of claim form with the Secretary-Treasurer stating that the need for the claim still exists. (1987, c. 584, s. 5.)

§ 58-88-25. Application for benefits.

Applications for benefits from the Fund shall be made to the Secretary-Treasurer under the following conditions and procedure: Within 30 days after the contracting of a disease or the occurrence of accident for which benefits are sought, the chief or chief officer of the local department shall notify the Secretary-Treasurer in writing that the person applying for benefits is a member of the Fund and request the necessary forms from the Secretary-Treasurer's office to be submitted for the benefits. (1987, c. 584, s. 5.)

§ 58-88-30. Administration costs.

The Association shall withhold ten percent (10%) from the money received pursuant to G.S. 20-183.7(c) for the administration of the Fund. The Commissioner of Insurance shall withhold two percent (2%) from the money received pursuant to G.S. 20-183.7(c) for the administration of the Fund. (1987, c. 584, s. 5; 1989 (Reg. Sess., 1990), c. 1066, s. 33(d); 1991 (Reg. Sess., 1992), c. 943, s. 3.)

ARTICLE 89.

North Carolina Professional Employer Organization Act.

§ 58-89-1. Title.

This Article shall be known and may be cited as the "North Carolina Professional Employer Organization Act". (2002-168, s. 8.)

Editor's Note. — Session Laws 2002-168, s. 11, makes this article effective January 1, 2003, and applicable to any contracts entered into, any business conducted, and any actions taken on or after that date.

Session Laws 2002-168, s. 9, provides: "The Department of Insurance shall report to the 2005 General Assembly on the implementation, administration, and enforcement of Article 89 of Chapter 58 of the General Statutes, as enacted in Section 8 of this act. In its report, the Department shall recommend any statutory changes required to regulate professional employer organizations and enforce Article 89 of Chapter 58 of the General Statutes."

Session Laws 2002-168, s. 10, provides: "Notwithstanding G.S. 58-89-30, each professional employer organization operating within this State as of January 1, 2003, shall complete its initial registration not later than 180 days after January 1, 2003. Each professional employer organization not operating within this State as of January 1, 2003, shall complete its initial registration prior to commencement of operations within this State."

§ 58-89-5. Definitions.

In this Article:
   (1) "Applicant" means a person applying for a registration under this Article.
   (2) "Control", including the terms "controlling", "controlled by", and "under common control with", has the same meaning as in G.S. 58-19-5(2).
   (3) "Managed services" means services provided by an organization that is the sole employer of employees whom it supplies to staff and to manage a specific portion of a company's workforce or a specific facility within a company on an ongoing basis. The managed services organization has responsibility for ensuring the capabilities and skills of the employees it supplies or provides, for all employer functions, for supervisory responsibility over the employees, and for management accountability of the facility or function.
   (4) "Person" has the same meaning as in G.S. 58-1-5(9).
   (5) "Personnel placement services" means a service that offers job placement services in which the personnel placement service organization assists persons interested in finding a job with companies that are seeking employees. Companies that hire persons through a personnel placement service are the sole employers of the persons hired, and the personnel placement service does not have any responsibility as an employer.
   (6) "Professional employer organization" means a person that offers professional employer services and includes "staff leasing services companies", "employee leasing companies", "staff leasing companies", and "administrative employers" who offer or propose to offer professional employer services in this State.
   (7) "Professional employer organization group" means a combination of professional employer organizations that operates under a group registration issued under this Article.
   (8) "Professional employer services" means an arrangement by which employees of a registrant are assigned to work at a client company and in which employment responsibilities are in fact shared by the registrant and the client company, the employee's assignment is intended to be of a long-term or continuing nature, rather than temporary or seasonal in nature, and a majority of the workforce at a client company work site or a majority of the personnel of a specialized group within that workforce consists of assigned employees of the registrant. "Professional employer services" does not include services that provide temporary employees or independent contractors, personnel placement services, managed services, payroll services that do not involve employee staffing or leasing, or similar groups that do not meet the requirements of this subdivision.
   (9) "Temporary employees" means persons employed under an arrangement by which an organization hires its own employees and assigns them to a client company to support or supplement the client's workforce in a special work situation, including:
      a. An employee absence;
      b. A temporary skill shortage;
      c. A seasonal workload; or
      d. A special assignment or project. (2002-168, s. 8.)

§ 58-89-10. Rules.

(a) The Commissioner may adopt rules necessary to implement, administer, and enforce the provisions of this Article.

(b) Each registrant is subject to this Article and to the rules adopted by the Commissioner.

(c) Nothing in this Article preempts the existing statutory or rule-making authority of any other State agency or entity to regulate professional employer services in a manner consistent with the statutory authority of that State agency or entity. (2002-168, s. 8.)

§ 58-89-15. Registration required; professional employer organization groups.

(a) No person shall engage in or offer professional employer services in this State unless the person is registered with the Department of Insurance under this Article.

(b) Two or more professional employer organizations that are controlled by the same ultimate parent, entity, or persons may be registered as a professional employer organization group. A professional employer organization group may satisfy the requirements of this Article on a consolidated basis.

(c) An applicant for an initial professional employer organization registration shall file with the Commissioner the information required by subsection (d) of this section on a form prescribed by the Commissioner accompanied by the registration fee. No application is complete until the Commissioner has received all required information.

(d) The registration application shall, at a minimum, be comprised of all of the following information:

    (1) The name, organizational structure, and date of organization of the applicant, the addresses of the principal office and all offices in this State, the name of the contact person, and the taxpayer or employer identification number.

    (2) A list by jurisdiction of each name under which the applicant has operated in the preceding five years, including any alternative names, names of predecessors, and, if known, successor business entities. The list required by this subdivision shall include the parent company name and any trade name, trademark, or service mark of the applicant.

    (3) A list of all officers and controlling persons of the applicant, their biographical information, including their management background, and an affidavit from each attesting to his or her good moral character and management competence.

    (4) The location of the business records of the applicant.

    (5) Evidence that the applicant has paid all of its obligations for payroll-related taxes, workers' compensation insurance, and employee benefits. All disputed amounts shall be disclosed in the application.

    (6) Any other information the Commissioner deems necessary.

(e) An application for registration of a professional employer organization group shall contain the information required by this section for each member of the group.

(f) If the Commissioner finds that the applicant has not fully met the requirements for registration, the Commissioner shall refuse to register the applicant and shall notify the applicant in writing of the denial, stating the grounds for the denial. Within 30 days after service of the notification, the applicant may make a written demand upon the Commissioner for a review to determine the reasonableness of the Commissioner's action. The review shall be completed without undue delay, and the applicant shall be notified promptly in writing as to the outcome of the review. Within 30 days after service of the notification as to the outcome, the applicant may make a written demand upon the Commissioner for a hearing under Article 3A of Chapter 150B of the General Statutes if the applicant disagrees with the outcome. (2002-168, s. 8.)

Editor's Note. — Session Laws 2002-168, s. 10, provides: "Notwithstanding G.S. 58-89-30, each professional employer organization operating within this State as of January 1, 2003, shall complete its initial registration not later than 180 days after January 1, 2003. Each professional employer organization not operating within this State as of January 1, 2003, shall complete its initial registration prior to commencement of operations within this State."

§ 58-89-20. Fees.

(a) Each applicant for registration shall pay to the Commissioner, before the issuance of the registration, a nonrefundable application fee of two hundred fifty dollars ($250.00).

(b) Fees collected by the Commissioner under this Article shall be credited to the Department of Insurance Fund created under G.S. 58-6-25. (2002-168, s. 8.)

§ 58-89-25. Prohibited acts.

No person shall do any of the following:
(1) Engage in or offer professional employer services without being registered under this Article as a professional employer organization.
(2) Use the name or title "staff leasing company", "employee leasing company", "registered staff leasing company", "staff leasing services company", "professional employer organization", or "administrative employer" or otherwise represent that the person is registered under this Article unless the person is registered under this Article.
(3) Represent as the person's own the license of another person or represent that a person is registered if the person is not registered.
(4) Give materially false or forged evidence to the Commissioner in connection with obtaining a registration. (2002-168, s. 8.)

§ 58-89-30. Criminal penalty.

A person who violates G.S. 58-89-25 commits a Class H felony. Any officer or controlling person who willfully violates any provision of this Article may be subject to any and all criminal penalties available under State law. (2002-168, s. 8.)

Editor's Note. — Session Laws 2002-168, s. 10, provides: "Notwithstanding G.S. 58-89-30, each professional employer organization operating within this State as of January 1, 2003, shall complete its initial registration not later than 180 days after January 1, 2003. Each professional employer organization not operating within this State as of January 1, 2003, shall complete its initial registration prior to commencement of operations within this State."

TABLES OF COMPARABLE SECTIONS FOR CHAPTER 58

Present to Former

Editor's Note. — The following table shows sections of present Chapter 58 and their derivation from former Chapters 57, 57B, 58, 58A, 85C, 109, and 118, former Articles 9B and 9C of Chapter 66, and former Articles 1 to 3 and 4 to 6 of Chapter 69.

Present Section	Former Section	Present Section	Former Section	Present Section	Former Section
58-1-1	58-1	58-3-10	58-30	58-5-75	58-186
58-1-5	58-2	58-3-15	58-30.1	58-5-80	58-187
58-1-10	58-3	58-3-20	58-30.2	58-5-85	58-188
58-1-15	58-3.1	58-3-25	58-30.3	58-5-90	58-188.1
58-1-20	58-3.2	58-3-30	58-30.6	58-5-95	58-188.2
58-2-1	58-4	58-3-35	58-31	58-5-100	58-188.3
58-2-5	58-5	58-3-40	58-31.1	58-5-105	58-188.4
58-2-10	58-6	58-3-45	58-32	58-5-110	58-188.5
58-2-15	58-7.1	58-3-50	58-33	58-5-115	58-188.6
58-2-20	58-7.2	58-3-55	58-33.1	58-5-120	58-188.7
58-2-25	58-7.3	58-3-60	58-34	58-5-125	58-188.8
58-2-30	58-7.4	58-3-65	58-34.1	58-6-1	58-62
58-2-35	58-8	58-3-70	58-35	58-6-5	58-63
58-2-40	58-9	58-3-75	58-35.1	58-6-10	58-65
58-2-45	58-9.1	58-3-80	58-35.2	58-6-15	58-66
58-2-50	58-9.2	58-3-85	58-36	58-6-20	58-68
58-2-55	58-9.8	58-3-90	58-37	58-7-1	58-69
58-2-60	58-9.9	58-3-95	58-38	58-7-5	58-70
58-2-65	58-9.10	58-3-100	58-39	58-7-10	58-71
58-2-70	58-9.7	58-3-105	58-39.1	58-7-15	58-72
58-2-75	58-9.3	58-3-110	58-39.2	58-7-20	58-72.1
58-2-80	58-9.4	58-3-115	58-42.1	58-7-25	58-72.2
58-2-85	58-9.5	58-3-120	58-44.3	58-7-30	58-72.3
58-2-90	58-9.6	58-3-125	58-44.4	58-7-35	58-73
58-2-95	58-10	58-3-130	58-52	58-7-40	58-74
58-2-100	58-11	58-3-135	58-51.5	58-7-45	58-75
58-2-110	58-12	58-3-140	58-51.6	58-7-50	58-75.1
58-2-115	58-13	58-3-145	58-61.2	58-7-55	58-75.2
58-2-120	58-14	58-3-150	58-54	58-7-60	58-75.3
58-2-125	58-15	58-4-1	58-27.10	58-7-65	58-75.4
58-2-130	58-16	58-4-5	58-27.11	58-7-70	58-75.5
58-2-135	58-16.1	58-4-10	58-27.12	58-7-75	58-77
58-2-140	58-16.2	58-4-15	58-27.13	58-7-80	58-78
58-2-145	58-16.3	58-4-20	58-21.3	58-7-85	58-79
58-2-150	58-17	58-5-1	58-7.5	58-7-90	58-79.1
58-2-155	58-18	58-5-5	58-182	58-7-95	58-79.2
58-2-160	58-18.1	58-5-10	58-182.1	58-7-100	58-80
58-2-165	58-21	58-5-15	58-182.2	58-7-105	58-81
58-2-170	58-21.1	58-5-20	58-182.3	58-7-110	58-82
58-2-175	58-21.2	58-5-25	58-182.4	58-7-115	58-83
58-2-180	58-22	58-5-30	58-182.5	58-7-120	58-84
58-2-185	58-25	58-5-35	58-182.6	58-7-125	58-85
58-2-190	58-25.1	58-5-40	58-182.7	58-7-130	58-85.1
58-2-195	58-26	58-5-45	58-182.8	58-7-135	58-86
58-2-200	58-27	58-5-50	58-182.9	58-7-140	58-86.1
58-2-205	58-21.4	58-5-55	58-182.10	58-7-145	58-86.2
58-2-210	58-30.7	58-5-60	58-183	58-7-150	58-155.1
58-3-1	58-28	58-5-65	58-184	58-8-1	58-92
58-3-5	58-29	58-5-70	58-185	58-8-5	58-92.1

TABLE OF COMPARABLE SECTIONS

Present Section	Former Section	Present Section	Former Section	Present Section	Former Section
58-8-10	58-94	58-15-95	58-798	58-21-30	58-426
58-8-15	58-95	58-15-100	58-799	58-21-35	58-427
58-8-20	58-96	58-15-105	58-800	58-21-40	58-428
58-8-25	58-97	58-15-110	58-801	58-21-45	58-429
58-8-30	58-97.1	58-15-115	58-802	58-21-50	58-430
58-8-35	58-97.2	58-15-120	58-803	58-21-55	58-431
58-8-40	58-97.3	58-15-125	58-804	58-21-60	58-432
58-8-45	58-98	58-15-130	58-805	58-21-65	58-433
58-8-50	58-99	58-15-135	58-806	58-21-70	58-434
58-8-55	58-100	58-15-140	58-807	58-21-75	58-435
58-9-1	58-86.3	58-15-145	58-808	58-21-80	58-436
58-9-5	58-86.4	58-15-150	58-809	58-21-85	58-437
58-9-10	58-86.5	58-16-1	58-149	58-21-90	58-438
58-9-15	58-86.6	58-16-5	58-150	58-21-95	58-439
58-9-20	58-86.7	58-16-10	58-151	58-21-100	58-440
58-9-25	58-86.8	58-16-15	58-151.1	58-21-105	58-441
58-9-30	58-86.9	58-16-20	58-151.2	58-22-1	58-505
58-10-1	58-103	58-16-25	58-152	58-22-10	58-506
58-10-5	58-104	58-16-30	58-153	58-22-15	58-507
58-11-1	58-105	58-16-35	58-153.1	58-22-20	58-508
58-11-5	58-106	58-16-40	58-153.2	58-22-25	58-509
58-11-10	58-107	58-16-45	58-154	58-22-30	58-510
58-11-15	58-108	58-16-50	58-155	58-22-35	58-511
58-11-20	58-109	58-16-55	58-150.1	58-22-40	58-512
58-11-25	58-110	58-17-1	58-148.1	58-22-45	58-513
58-11-30	58-112	58-18-1	58-120	58-22-50	58-514
58-11-35	58-112.1	58-18-5	58-121	58-22-55	58-515
58-12-1	58-87	58-18-10	58-122	58-22-60	58-516
58-12-5	58-88	58-18-15	58-123	58-22-65	58-517
58-12-10	58-89	58-18-20	58-124	58-23-1	58-490
58-12-15	58-90	58-19-1	58-560	58-23-5	58-491
58-12-20	58-91	58-19-5	58-561	58-23-10	58-492
58-13-1	58-410	58-19-10	58-562	58-23-15	58-493
58-13-5	58-411	58-19-15	58-563	58-23-20	58-494
58-13-10	58-412	58-19-20	58-564	58-23-25	58-495
58-13-15	58-413	58-19-25	58-565	58-23-30	58-496
58-13-20	58-414	58-19-30	58-566	58-23-35	58-497
58-13-25	58-415	58-19-35	58-567	58-23-40	58-498
58-14-1	58-54.26	58-19-40	58-568	58-24-1	58-340.1
58-14-5	58-54.27	58-19-45	58-569	58-24-5	58-340.2
58-14-10	58-54.28	58-19-50	58-570	58-24-10	58-340.3
58-14-15	58-54.29	58-19-55	58-571	58-24-15	58-340.4
58-15-1	58-780	58-19-60	58-572	58-24-20	58-340.5
58-15-5	58-781	58-19-65	58-573	58-24-25	58-340.6
58-15-10	58-782	58-19-70	58-574	58-24-30	58-340.7
58-15-15	58-783	58-20-1	58-340.71	58-24-35	58-340.8
58-15-20	58-784	58-20-5	58-340.72	58-24-40	58-340.9
58-15-25	58-785	58-20-10	58-340.73	58-24-45	58-340.10
58-15-30	58-786	58-20-15	58-340.74	58-24-50	58-340.11
58-15-35	58-787	58-20-20	58-340.75	58-24-55	58-340.12
58-15-40	58-788	58-20-25	58-340.76	58-24-60	58-340.13
58-15-45	58-789	58-20-30	58-340.77	58-24-65	58-340.14
58-15-50	58-790	58-20-35	58-340.78	58-24-70	58-340.15
58-15-55	58-791	58-20-40	58-340.79	58-24-75	58-340.16
58-15-60	58-792	58-21-1	58-420	58-24-80	58-340.17
58-15-65	58-793	58-21-5	58-421	58-24-85	58-340.18
58-15-70	58-794	58-21-10	58-422	58-24-90	58-340.19
58-15-75	58-795	58-21-15	58-423	58-24-95	58-340.20
58-15-85	58-796	58-21-20	58-424	58-24-100	58-340.21
58-15-90	58-797	58-21-25	58-425	58-24-105	58-340.22

Present Section	Former Section	Present Section	Former Section	Present Section	Former Section
58-24-110	58-340.23	58-29-25	58-54.19	58-30-295	58-698
58-24-115	58-340.24	58-30-1	58-640	58-30-300	58-699
58-24-120	58-340.25	58-30-5	58-641	58-30-305	58-700
58-24-125	58-340.26	58-30-10	58-642	58-31-1	58-189
58-24-130	58-340.27	58-30-15	58-643	58-31-5	58-190
58-24-135	58-340.28	58-30-20	58-644	58-31-10	58-191
58-24-140	58-340.29	58-30-25	58-645	58-31-15	58-191.1
58-24-145	58-340.30	58-30-30	58-646	58-31-20	58-191.2
58-24-150	58-340.31	58-30-35	58-648	58-31-25	58-191.3
58-24-155	58-340.32	58-30-40	58-649	58-31-30	58-191.4
58-24-160	58-340.33	58-30-45	58-650	58-31-35	58-192
58-24-165	58-340.34	58-30-50	58-651	58-31-40	58-193
58-24-170	58-340.35	58-30-55	58-652	58-31-45	58-194
58-24-175	58-340.36	58-30-60	58-653	58-31-50	58-194.1
58-24-180	58-340.37	58-30-65	58-654	58-31-55	58-194.2
58-24-185	58-340.38	58-30-70	58-655	58-31-60	58-194.3
58-24-190	58-340.39	58-30-75	58-656	58-32-1	58-27.20
58-25-1	58-340.51	58-30-80	58-657	58-32-5	58-27.21
58-25-5	58-340.52	58-30-85	58-658	58-32-10	58-27.22
58-25-10	58-340.53	58-30-90	58-659	58-32-15	58-27.23
58-25-15	58-340.54	58-30-95	58-660	58-32-20	58-27.24
58-25-20	58-340.55	58-30-100	58-661	58-32-25	58-27.25
58-25-25	58-340.56	58-30-105	58-662	58-32-30	58-27.26
58-25-30	58-340.57	58-30-110	58-663	58-33-1	58-610
58-25-35	58-340.58	58-30-115	58-664	58-33-10	58-611
58-25-40	58-340.59	58-30-120	58-665	58-33-15	58-612
58-25-45	58-340.60	58-30-125	58-666	58-33-20	58-613
58-25-50	58-340.61	58-30-130	58-667	58-33-25	58-614
58-25-55	58-340.62	58-30-135	58-668	58-33-30	58-615
58-25-60	58-340.63	58-30-140	58-669	58-33-35	58-616
58-25-65	58-340.64	58-30-145	58-670	58-33-40	58-617
58-25-70	58-340.65	58-30-150	58-671	58-33-45	58-618
58-26-1	58-132	58-30-155	58-672	58-33-50	58-619
58-26-5	58-133	58-30-160	58-673	58-33-55	58-620
58-26-10	58-134	58-30-165	58-674	58-32-60	58-621
58-26-15	58-134.1	58-30-170	58-675	58-33-65	58-622
58-26-20	58-134.2	58-30-175	58-675.1	58-33-70	58-623
58-26-25	58-134.3	58-30-180	58-675.2	58-33-75	58-624
58-26-30	58-134.4	58-30-185	58-676	58-33-80	58-625
58-26-35	58-134.5	58-30-190	58-677	58-33-85	58-626
58-26-40	58-134.6	58-30-195	58-678	58-33-90	58-627
58-27-1	58-135	58-30-200	58-679	58-33-95	58-628
58-27-5	58-135.1	58-30-205	58-680	58-33-100	58-629
58-27-10	58-136	58-30-210	58-681	58-33-105	58-630
58-27-15	58-137	58-30-215	58-682	58-33-110	58-631
58-28-1	58-54.20	58-30-220	58-683	58-33-115	58-632
58-28-5	58-54.21	58-30-225	58-684	58-33-120	58-633
58-28-10	58-54.22	58-30-230	58-685	58-33-125	58-634
58-28-15	58-54.23	58-30-235	58-686	58-33-130	58-635
58-28-20	58-54.24	58-30-240	58-687	58-33-135	58-636
58-28-25	58-54.24A	58-30-245	58-688	58-34-1	58-575
58-28-30	58-54.24B	58-30-250	58-689	58-34-5	58-576
58-28-35	58-54.24C	58-30-255	58-690	58-34-10	58-577
58-28-40	58-54.25	58-30-260	58-691	58-34-15	58-578
58-28-45	58-164	58-30-265	58-692	58-34-20	58-579
58-29-1	58-54.14	58-30-270	58-693	58-35-1	58-55
58-29-5	58-54.15	58-30-275	58-694	58-35-5	58-56
58-29-10	58-54.16	58-30-280	58-695	58-35-10	58-56.1
58-29-15	58-54.17	58-30-285	58-696	58-35-15	58-56.2
58-29-20	58-54.18	58-30-290	58-697	58-35-20	58-56.3

TABLE OF COMPARABLE SECTIONS

Present Section	Former Section	Present Section	Former Section	Present Section	Former Section
58-35-25	58-57	58-39-15	58-383	58-41-45	58-479
58-35-30	58-57.1	58-39-20	58-384	58-41-50	58-480
58-35-35	58-57.2	58-39-25	58-385	58-41-55	58-481
58-35-40	58-57.3	58-39-30	58-386	58-42-1	58-450
58-35-45	58-58	58-39-35	58-387	58-42-5	58-451
58-35-50	58-58.1	58-39-40	58-388	58-42-10	58-452
58-35-55	58-59	58-39-45	58-389	58-42-15	58-453
58-35-60	58-59.1	58-39-50	58-390	58-42-20	58-454
58-35-65	58-59.2	58-39-55	58-391	58-42-25	58-455
58-35-70	58-59.3	58-39-60	58-392	58-42-30	58-456
58-35-75	58-59.4	58-39-65	58-393	58-42-35	58-457
58-35-80	58-59.5	58-39-70	58-395	58-42-40	58-458
58-35-85	58-60	58-39-75	58-394	58-42-45	58-459
58-35-90	58-61	58-39-80	58-396	58-42-50	58-460
58-35-95	58-61.1	58-39-85	58-397	58-42-55	58-461
58-36-1	58-124.17	58-39-90	58-398	58-43-1	58-157
58-36-5	58-124.18	58-39-95	58-399	58-43-5	58-158
58-36-10	58-124.19	58-39-100	58-400	58-43-10	58-159
58-36-15	58-124.20	58-39-105	58-401	58-43-15	58-160
58-36-20	58-124.21	58-39-110	58-402	58-43-20	58-162
58-36-25	58-124.22	58-39-115	58-403	58-43-25	58-162.1
58-36-30	58-124.23	58-39-120	58-404	58-43-30	58-172
58-36-35	58-124.24	58-40-1	58-131.34	58-43-35	58-173
58-36-40	58-124.25	58-40-5	58-131.35	58-44-1	58-174
58-36-45	58-124.27	58-40-10	58-131.35A	58-44-5	58-175
58-36-50	58-124.28	58-40-15	58-131.36	58-44-10	58-175.1
58-36-55	58-124.29	58-40-20	58-131.37	58-44-15	58-176
58-36-60	58-124.30	58-40-25	58-131.38	58-44-20	58-177
58-36-65	58-124.31	58-40-30	58-131.39	58-44-25	58-177.1
58-36-70	58-124.32	58-40-35	58-131.40	58-44-30	58-178
58-36-75	58-124.33	58-40-40	58-131.41	58-44-35	58-178.1
58-36-80	58-124.34	58-40-45	58-131.42	58-44-40	58-180
58-37-1	58-248.26	58-40-50	58-131.43	58-44-45	58-180.1
58-37-5	58-248.27	58-40-55	58-131.44	58-44-50	58-180.2
58-37-10	58-248.28	58-40-60	58-131.45	58-44-55	58-180.3
58-37-15	58-248.29	58-40-65	58-131.46	58-45-1	58-173.1
58-37-20	58-248.30	58-40-70	58-131.47	58-45-5	58-173.2
58-37-25	58-248.31	58-40-75	58-131.48	58-45-10	58-173.3
58-37-30	58-248.32	58-40-80	58-131.49	58-45-15	58-173.4
58-37-35	58-248.33	58-40-85	58-131.50	58-45-20	58-173.5
58-37-40	58-248.34	58-40-90	58-131.51	58-45-25	58-173.6
58-37-45	58-248.35	58-40-95	58-131.52	58-45-30	58-173.7
58-37-50	58-248.36	58-40-100	58-131.53	58-45-35	58-173.8
58-37-55	58-248.37	58-40-105	58-131.54	58-45-40	58-173.9
58-37-60	58-248.38	58-40-110	58-131.55	58-45-45	58-173.10
58-37-65	58-248.39	58-40-115	58-131.57	58-45-50	58-173.11
58-37-70	58-248.40	58-40-120	58-131.58	58-45-55	58-173.12
58-37-75	58-248.41	58-40-125	58-131.60	58-45-60	58-173.13
58-38-1	58-364	58-40-130	58-131.61	58-45-65	58-173.14
58-38-5	58-365	58-40-135	58-131.62	58-45-70	58-173.15
58-38-10	58-366	58-40-140	58-131.63	58-45-75	58-173.16
58-38-15	58-367	58-41-1	58-470	58-45-80	58-173.16A
58-38-20	58-368	58-41-5	58-471	58-46-1	58-173.17
58-38-25	58-369	58-41-10	58-472	58-46-5	58-173.18
58-38-30	58-370	58-41-15	58-473	58-46-10	58-173.19
58-38-35	58-371	58-41-20	58-474	58-46-15	58-173.20
58-38-40	58-372	58-41-25	58-475	58-46-20	58-173.21
58-39-1	58-380	58-41-30	58-476	58-46-25	58-173.22
58-39-5	58-381	58-41-35	58-477	58-46-30	58-173.23
58-39-10	58-382	58-41-40	58-478	58-46-35	58-173.24

TABLE OF COMPARABLE SECTIONS

Present Section	Former Section	Present Section	Former Section	Present Section	Former Section
58-46-40	58-173.26	58-51-15	58-251.1	58-55-10	58-541
58-46-45	58-173.29	58-51-20	58-251.2	58-55-15	58-542
58-46-50	58-173.30	58-51-25	58-251.3	58-55-20	58-543
58-46-55	58-173.31	58-51-30	58-251.4	58-55-25	58-544
58-47-1	58-254.19	58-51-35	58-251.5	58-55-30	58-545
58-47-5	58-254.20	58-51-40	58-251.6	58-55-35	58-546
58-47-10	58-254.21	58-51-45	58-251.7	58-56-1	58-525
58-47-15	58-254.22	58-51-50	58-251.8	58-56-10	58-526
58-47-20	58-254.23	58-51-55	58-251.9	58-56-15	58-527
58-47-25	58-254.24	58-51-60	58-252	58-56-20	58-528
58-47-30	58-254.25	58-51-65	58-254.1	58-56-25	58-529
58-47-35	58-254.26	58-51-70	58-254.2	58-56-30	58-530
58-47-40	58-254.27	58-51-75	58-254.3	58-56-35	58-531
58-47-45	58-254.28	58-51-80	58-254.4	58-56-40	58-532
58-47-50	58-254.29	58-51-85	58-254.5	58-56-45	58-533
58-48-1	58-155.41	58-51-90	58-254.6	58-56-50	58-534
58-48-5	58-155.42	58-51-95	58-254.7	58-56-55	58-535
58-48-10	58-155.43	58-51-100	58-254.8	58-56-60	58-536
58-48-15	58-155.44	58-51-105	58-254.9	58-56-65	58-537
58-48-20	58-155.45	58-51-110	58-254.4A	58-57-1	58-341
58-48-25	58-155.46	58-52-1	58-254.10	58-57-5	58-342
58-48-30	58-155.47	58-52-5	58-254.11	58-57-10	58-343
58-48-35	58-155.48	58-52-10	58-254.12	58-57-15	58-344
58-48-40	58-155.49	58-52-15	58-254.13	58-57-20	58-345
58-48-45	58-155.50	58-52-20	58-254.14	58-57-25	58-346
58-48-50	58-155.51	58-52-25	58-254.15	58-57-30	58-347
58-48-55	58-155.52	58-53-1	58-254.35	58-57-35	58-348
58-48-60	58-155.53	58-53-5	58-254.36	58-57-40	58-349
58-48-65	58-155.54	58-53-10	58-254.37	58-57-45	58-350
58-48-70	58-155.55	58-53-15	58-254.38	58-57-50	58-351
58-48-75	58-155.56	58-53-20	58-254.39	58-57-55	58-352
58-48-80	58-155.57	58-53-25	58-254.40	58-57-60	58-353
58-48-85	58-155.58	58-53-30	58-254.41	58-57-65	58-354
58-48-90	58-155.59	58-53-35	58-254.42	58-57-70	58-355
58-48-95	58-155.60	58-53-40	58-254.43	58-57-75	58-356
58-48-100	58-155.61	58-53-45	58-254.44	58-57-80	58-357
58-49-1	58-262.30	58-53-50	58-254.45	58-57-85	58-358
58-49-5	58-262.31	58-53-55	58-254.46	58-57-90	58-359
58-49-10	58-262.32	58-53-60	58-254.47	58-57-95	58-44.7
58-49-15	58-262.33	58-53-65	58-254.48	58-57-100	58-360
58-49-20	58-262.34	58-53-70	58-254.49	58-58-1	58-195
58-49-25	58-262.35	58-53-75	58-254.50	58-58-5	58-195.1
58-50-1	58-256	58-53-80	58-254.51	58-58-10	58-195.2
58-50-5	58-257	58-53-85	58-254.52	58-58-15	58-195.3
58-50-10	58-257.1	58-53-90	58-254.53	58-58-20	58-195.4
58-50-15	58-258	58-53-95	58-254.54	58-58-25	58-195.5
58-50-20	58-259.1	58-53-100	58-254.55	58-58-30	58-197
58-50-25	58-259.2	58-53-105	58-254.56	58-58-35	58-198
58-50-30	58-260	58-53-110	58-254.57	58-58-40	58-199
58-50-35	58-260.1	58-53-115	58-254.58	58-58-45	58-201
58-50-40	58-260.3	58-54-1	58-710	58-58-50	58-201.1
58-50-45	58-260.4	58-54-5	58-711	58-58-55	58-201.2
58-50-50	58-260.5	58-54-10	58-712	58-58-60	58-201.3
58-50-55	58-260.6	58-54-15	58-713	58-58-65	58-202
58-50-60	58-260.7	58-54-20	58-714	58-58-70	58-204
58-50-65	58-261	58-54-25	58-715	58-58-75	58-204.1
58-50-70	58-262	58-54-30	58-716	58-58-80	58-204.2
58-51-1	58-249	58-54-35	58-717	58-58-85	58-204.3
58-51-5	58-250	58-54-40	58-718	58-58-90	58-204.4
58-51-10	58-250.1	58-55-1	58-540	58-58-95	58-205

TABLE OF COMPARABLE SECTIONS

Present Section	Former Section	Present Section	Former Section	Present Section	Former Section
58-58-100	58-205.1	58-63-25	58-54.6	58-66-5	57-31
58-58-105	58-205.2	58-63-30	58-54.7	58-66-10	57-32
58-58-110	58-205.3	58-63-35	58-54.8	58-66-15	57-33
58-58-115	58-206	58-63-40	58-54.9	58-66-20	57-34
58-58-120	58-207	58-63-45	58-54.10	58-66-25	57-35
58-58-125	58-208	58-63-50	58-54.11	58-66-30	57-36
58-58-130	58-209	58-63-55	58-54.12	58-66-35	57-37
58-58-135	58-210	58-63-60	58-54.13	58-66-40	57-38
58-58-140	58-211	58-64-1	58-765	58-67-1	57B-1
58-58-145	58-211.1	58-64-5	58-766	58-67-5	57B-2
58-58-150	58-211.2	58-64-10	58-767	58-67-10	57B-3
58-58-155	58-211.3	58-64-15	58-768	58-67-15	57B-3.1
58-58-160	58-212	58-64-20	58-769	58-67-20	57B-4
58-58-165	58-213	58-64-25	58-770	58-67-25	57B-4.1
58-58-170	58-213.1	58-64-30	58-771	58-67-30	57B-4.2
58-59-1	58-214	58-64-35	58-772	58-67-35	57B-5
58-59-5	58-215	58-64-40	58-773	58-67-40	57B-6
58-59-10	58-216	58-64-45	58-774	58-67-45	57B-7
58-59-15	58-218	58-64-50	58-775	58-67-50	57B-8
58-59-20	58-219	58-64-55	58-776	58-67-55	57B-9
58-59-25	58-222	58-64-60	58-777	58-67-60	57B-10
58-59-30	58-223	58-64-65	58-778	58-67-65	57B-12
58-59-35	58-223.1	58-64-70	58-779	58-67-70	57B-12.1
58-60-1	58-213.6	58-64-75	58-780	58-67-75	57B-12.2
58-60-5	58-213.7	58-64-80	58-781	58-67-80	57B-2.1
58-60-10	58-213.8	58-65-1	57-1	58-67-85	57B-8.1
58-60-15	58-213.9	58-65-5	57-1.1	58-67-90	57B-13
58-60-20	58-213.10	58-65-10	57-1.2	58-67-95	57B-14
58-60-25	58-213.11	58-65-15	57-2	58-67-100	57B-15
58-60-30	58-213.12	58-65-20	57-2.1	58-67-105	57B-15.1
58-60-35	58-213.13	58-65-25	57-3	58-67-110	57B-15.2
58-61-1	58-213.18	58-65-30	57-3.1	58-67-115	57B-15.3
58-61-5	58-213.19	58-65-35	57-3.2	58-67-120	57B-15.4
58-61-10	58-213.20	58-65-40	57-4	58-67-125	57B-15.5
58-61-15	58-213.21	58-65-45	57-4.1	58-67-130	57B-15.6
58-62-1	58-155.65	58-65-50	57-5	58-67-135	57B-15.7
58-62-5	58-155.66	58-65-55	57-6	58-67-140	57B-16
58-62-10	58-155.67	58-65-60	57-7	58-67-145	57B-17
58-62-15	58-155.68	58-65-65	57-7.1	58-67-150	57B-18
58-62-20	58-155.69	58-65-70	57-7.2	58-67-155	57B-19
58-62-25	58-155.70	58-65-75	57-7.3	58-67-160	57B-20
58-62-30	58-155.71	58-65-80	57-1.3	58-67-165	57B-21
58-62-35	58-155.72	58-65-85	57-1.4	58-67-170	57B-22
58-62-40	58-155.73	58-65-90	57-7.4	58-67-175	57B-23
58-62-45	58-155.74	58-65-95	57-8	58-67-180	57B-24
58-62-50	58-155.75	58-65-100	57-9	58-67-185	57B-25
58-62-55	58-155.76	58-65-105	57-10	58-68-1	58A-1
58-62-60	58-155.77	58-65-110	57-11	58-68-5	58A-2
58-62-65	58-155.78	58-65-115	57-12	58-68-10	58A-3
58-62-70	58-155.79	58-65-120	57-12.1	58-68-15	58A-4
58-62-75	58-155.80	58-65-125	57-13	58-68-20	58A-5
58-62-80	58-155.81	58-65-130	57-15	58-69-1	66-49.9
58-62-85	58-155.82	58-65-135	57-16	58-69-5	66-49.10
58-62-90	58-155.83	58-65-140	57-16.1	58-69-10	66-49.11
58-62-95	58-155.84	58-65-145	57-17	58-69-15	66-49.12
58-63-1	58-54.1	58-65-150	57-18	58-69-20	66-49.13
58-63-5	58-54.2	58-65-155	57-19	58-69-25	66-49.14
58-63-10	58-54.3	58-65-160	57-19.1	58-69-30	66-49.15
58-63-15	58-54.4	58-65-165	57-20	58-69-35	66-49.16
58-63-20	58-54.5	58-66-1	57-30	58-69-40	66-49.17

Present Section	Former Section	Present Section	Former Section	Present Section	Former Section
58-69-45	66-49.18	58-71-160	85C-33	58-79-30	69-6
58-70-1	66-49.24	58-71-165	85C-34	58-79-35	69-7
58-70-5	66-49.25	58-71-170	85C-35	58-79-40	69-7.1
58-70-10	66-49.26	58-71-175	85C-36	58-80-1	69-14
58-70-15	66-49.27	58-71-180	85C-37	58-80-5	69-15
58-70-20	66-49.28	58-71-185	85C-38	58-80-10	69-16
58-70-25	66-49.29	58-71-190	85C-39	58-80-15	69-17
58-70-30	66-49.30	58-71-195	85C-40	58-80-20	69-18
58-70-35	66-49.31	58-72-1	109-1	58-80-25	69-19
58-70-40	66-49.32	58-72-5	109-2	58-80-30	69-20
58-70-45	66-49.33	58-72-10	109-3	58-80-35	69-21
58-70-50	66-49.34	58-72-15	109-4	58-80-40	69-22
58-70-55	66-49.35	58-72-20	109-5	58-80-45	69-23
58-70-60	66-49.36	58-72-25	109-6	58-80-50	69-24
58-70-65	66-49.37	58-72-30	109-7	58-80-55	69-24.1
58-70-70	66-49.38	58-72-35	109-8	58-80-60	69-25
58-70-75	66-49.39	58-72-40	109-9	58-81-1	69-32
58-70-80	66-49.40	58-72-45	109-10	58-81-5	69-33
58-70-85	66-49.41	58-72-50	109-11	58-81-10	69-34
58-70-90	66-49.42	58-72-55	109-12	58-81-15	69-38
58-70-95	66-49.43	58-72-60	109-13	58-82-1	69-39
58-70-100	66-49.44	58-72-65	109-14	58-82-5	69-39.1
58-70-105	66-49.45	58-72-70	109-15	58-83-1	69-40
58-70-110	66-49.46	58-73-1	109-16	58-84-1	118-1
58-70-115	66-49.47	58-73-5	109-17	58-84-5	118-1.1
58-70-120	66-49.48	58-73-10	109-18	58-84-10	118-2
58-70-125	66-49.49	58-73-15	109-19	58-84-15	118-3
58-70-130	66-49.50	58-73-20	109-20	58-84-20	118-4
58-71-1	85C-1	58-73-25	109-21	58-84-25	118-5
58-71-5	85C-2	58-73-30	109-22	58-84-30	118-6
58-71-10	85C-3	58-73-35	109-23	58-84-35	118-7
58-71-15	85C-4	58-74-1	109-24	58-84-40	118-8
58-71-20	85C-5	58-74-5	109-25	58-84-45	118-9
58-71-25	85C-6	58-74-10	109-26	58-84-50	118-10
58-71-30	85C-7	58-74-15	109-27	58-84-55	118-11
58-71-35	85C-8	58-74-20	109-28	58-85-1	118-12
58-71-40	85C-9	58-74-25	109-29	58-85-10	118-13
58-71-45	85C-10	58-74-30	109-30	58-85-15	118-14
58-71-50	85C-11	58-74-35	109-31	58-85-20	118-15
58-71-55	85C-12	58-75-1	109-32	58-85-25	118-16
58-71-60	85C-13	58-76-1	109-33	58-85-30	118-17
58-71-65	85C-14	58-76-5	109-34	58-86-1	118-33
58-71-70	85C-15	58-76-10	109-35	58-86-5	118-34
58-71-75	85C-16	58-76-15	109-36	58-86-10	118-35
58-71-80	85C-17	58-76-20	109-37	58-86-15	118-36
58-71-85	85C-18	58-76-25	109-38	58-86-20	118-37
58-71-90	85C-19	58-76-30	109-39	58-86-25	118-38
58-71-95	85C-20	58-77-1	109-40	58-86-30	118-39
58-71-100	85C-21	58-77-5	109-41	58-86-35	118-40
58-71-105	85C-22	58-78-1	58-27.30	58-86-40	118-41
58-71-110	85C-23	58-78-5	58-27.31	58-86-45	118-41.1
58-71-115	85C-24	58-78-10	58-27.32	58-86-50	118-41.2
58-71-120	85C-25	58-78-15	58-27.33	58-86-55	118-42
58-71-125	85C-26	58-78-20	58-27.34	58-86-60	118-43
58-71-130	85C-27	58-79-1	69-1	58-86-65	118-44
58-71-135	85C-28	58-79-5	69-2	58-86-70	118-45
58-71-140	85C-29	58-79-10	69-3	58-86-75	118-46
58-71-145	85C-30	58-79-15	69-3.1	58-86-80	118-47
58-71-150	85C-31	58-79-20	69-4	58-86-85	118-48
58-71-155	85C-32	58-79-25	69-5	58-86-90	118-49

TABLE OF COMPARABLE SECTIONS

Former to Present

Editor's Note. — The following table shows comparable sections for former Chapters 57, 57B, 58, 58A, 85C, 109, and 118, former Articles 9B and 9C of Chapter 66, and former Articles 1 to 3 and 4 to 6 of Chapter 69 and their disposition in present Chapter 58.

In addition, where the former section has no comparable present Chapter 58 reference due to repeal, expiration, transfer, recodification or reservation of sections, the terms Repealed, Expired, Transferred, Recodified or Reserved have been inserted.

Former Section	Present Section	Former Section	Present Section	Former Section	Present Section
57-1	58-65-1	57B-4.2	58-67-30	58-9.5	58-2-85
57-1.1	58-65-5	57B-5	58-67-35	58-9.6	58-2-90
57-1.2	58-65-10	57B-6	58-67-40	58-9.7	58-2-70
57-1.3	58-65-80	57B-7	58-67-45	58-9.8	58-2-55
57-1.4	58-65-85	57B-8	58-67-50	58-9.9	58-2-60
57-2	58-65-15	57B-8.1	58-67-85	58-9.10	58-2-65
57-2.1	58-65-20	57B-9	58-67-55	58-10	58-2-95
57-3	58-65-25	57B-10	58-67-60	58-11	58-2-100
57-3.1	58-65-30	57B-12	58-67-65	58-12	58-2-110
57-3.2	58-65-35	57B-12.1	58-67-70	58-13	58-2-115
57-4	58-65-40	57B-12.2	58-67-75	58-14	58-2-120
57-4.1	58-65-45	57B-13	58-67-90	58-15	58-2-125
57-5	58-65-50	57B-14	58-67-95	58-16	58-2-130
57-6	58-65-55	57B-15	58-67-100	58-16.1	58-2-135
57-7	58-65-60	57B-15.1	58-67-105	58-16.2	58-2-140
57-7.1	58-65-65	57B-15.2	58-67-110	58-16.3	58-2-145
57-7.2	58-65-70	57B-15.3	58-67-115	58-17	58-2-150
57-7.3	58-65-75	57B-15.4	58-67-120	58-18	58-2-155
57-7.4	58-65-90	57B-15.5	58-67-125	58-18.1	58-2-160
57-8	58-65-95	57B-15.6	58-67-130	58-19,	
57-9	58-65-100	57B-15.7	58-67-135	58-20	Repealed
57-10	58-65-105	57B-16	58-67-140	58-21	58-2-165
57-11	58-65-110	57B-17	58-67-145	58-21.1	58-2-170
57-12	58-65-115	57B-18	58-67-150	58-21.2	58-2-175
57-12.1	58-65-120	57B-19	58-67-155	58-21.3	58-4-20
57-13	58-65-125	57B-20	58-67-160	58-21.4	58-2-205
57-15	58-65-130	57B-21	58-67-165	58-22	58-2-180
57-16	58-65-135	57B-22	58-67-170	58-23,	
57-16.1	58-65-140	57B-23	58-67-175	58-24	Repealed
57-17	58-65-145	57B-24	58-67-180	58-25	58-2-185
57-18	58-65-150	57B-25	58-67-185	58-25.1	58-2-190
57-19	58-65-155	58-1	58-1-1	58-26	58-2-195
57-19.1	58-65-160	58-2	58-1-5	58-27	58-2-200
57-20	58-65-165	58-3	58-1-10	58-27.1,	
57-30	58-66-1	58-3.1	58-1-15	58-27.2	Repealed
57-31	58-66-5	58-3.2	58-1-20	58-27.3	
57-32	58-66-10	58-4	58-2-1	to 58-27.9	Reserved
57-33	58-66-15	58-5	58-2-5	58-27.10	58-4-1
57-34	58-66-20	58-6	58-2-10	58-27.11	58-4-5
57-35	58-66-25	58-7.1	58-2-15	58-27.12	58-4-10
57-36	58-66-30	58-7.2	58-2-20	58-27.13	58-4-15
57-37	58-66-35	58-7.3	58-2-25	58-27.14	
57-38	58-66-40	58-7.4	58-2-30	to 58-27.19	Reserved
57B-1	58-67-1	58-7.5	58-5-1	58-27.20	58-32-1
57B-2	58-67-5	58-8	58-2-35	58-27.21	58-32-5
57B-2.1	58-67-80	58-9	58-2-40	58-27.22	58-32-10
57B-3	58-67-10	58-9.1	58-2-45	58-27.23	58-32-15
57B-3.1	58-67-15	58-9.2	58-2-50	58-27.24	58-32-20
57B-4	58-67-20	58-9.3	58-2-75	58-27.25	58-32-25
57B-4.1	58-67-25	58-9.4	58-2-80	58-27.26	58-32-30

Former Section	Present Section	Former Section	Present Section	Former Section	Present Section
58-27.27 to 58-27.29	Reserved	58-54.9	58-63-40	58-73	58-7-35
58-27.30	58-78-1	58-54.10	58-63-45	58-74	58-7-40
58-27.31	58-78-5	58-54.11	58-63-50	58-75	58-7-45
58-27.32	58-78-10	58-54.12	58-63-55	58-75.1	58-7-50
58-27.33	58-78-15	58-54.13	58-63-60	58-75.2	58-7-55
58-27.34	58-78-20	58-54.14	58-29-1	58-75.3	58-7-60
58-28	58-3-1	58-54.15	58-29-5	58-75.4	58-7-65
58-29	58-3-5	58-54.16	58-29-10	58-75.5	58-7-70
58-30	58-3-10	58-54.17	58-29-15	58-76	Repealed
58-30.1	58-3-15	58-54.18	58-29-20	58-77	58-7-75
58-30.2	58-3-20	58-54.19	58-29-25	58-78	58-7-80
58-30.3	58-3-25	58-54.20	58-28-1	58-79	58-7-85
58-30.4, 58-30.5	Repealed	58-54.21	58-28-5	58-79.1	58-7-90
58-30.6	58-3-30	58-54.22	58-28-10	58-79.2	58-7-95
58-30.7	58-2-210	58-54.23	58-28-15	58-80	58-7-100
58-31	58-3-35	58-54.24	58-28-20	58-81	58-7-105
58-31.1	58-3-40	58-54.24A	58-28-25	58-82	58-7-110
58-31.2	Repealed	58-54.24B	58-28-30	58-83	58-7-115
58-32	58-3-45	58-54.24C	58-28-35	58-84	58-7-120
58-33	58-3-50	58-54.25	58-28-40	58-85	58-7-125
58-33.1	58-3-55	58-54.25:1	Repealed	58-85.1	58-7-130
58-34	58-3-60	58-54.26	58-14-1	58-86	58-7-135
58-34.1	58-3-65	58-54.27	58-14-5	58-86.1	58-7-140
58-35	58-3-70	58-54.28	58-14-10	58-86.2	58-7-145
58-35.1	58-3-75	58-54.29	58-14-15	58-86.3	58-9-1
58-35.2	58-3-80	58-55	58-35-1	58-86.4	58-9-5
58-36	58-3-85	58-56	58-35-5	58-86.5	58-9-10
58-37	58-3-90	58-56.1	58-35-10	58-86.6	58-9-15
58-38	58-3-95	58-56.2	58-35-15	58-86.7	58-9-20
58-39	58-3-100	58-56.3	58-35-20	58-86.8	58-9-25
58-39.1	58-3-105	58-57	58-35-25	58-86.9	58-9-30
58-39.2	58-3-110	58-57.1	58-35-30	58-87	58-12-1
58-39.3 to 58-42	Repealed	58-57.2	58-35-35	58-88	58-12-5
58-42.1	58-3-115	58-57.3	58-35-40	58-89	58-12-10
58-43 to 58-44.2	Repealed	58-58	58-35-45	58-90	58-12-15
58-44.3	58-3-120	58-58.1	58-35-50	58-91	58-12-20
58-44.4	58-3-125	58-59	58-35-55	58-92	58-8-1
58-44.4A to 58-44.6	Repealed	58-59.1	58-35-60	58-92.1	58-8-5
58-44.7	58-57-95	58-59.2	58-35-65	58-93	Transferred
58-44.8 to 58-51.4	Repealed	58-59.3	58-35-70	58-94	58-8-10
58-51.5	58-3-135	58-59.4	58-35-75	58-95	58-8-15
58-51.6	58-3-140	58-59.5	58-35-80	58-96	58-8-20
58-52	58-3-130	58-60	58-35-85	58-97	58-8-25
58-52.1 to 58-53.3	Repealed	58-61	58-35-90	58-97.1	58-8-30
58-54	58-3-150	58-61.1	58-35-95	58-97.2	58-8-35
58-54.1	58-63-1	58-61.2	58-3-145	58-97.3	58-8-40
58-54.2	58-63-5	58-62	58-6-1	58-98	58-8-45
58-54.3	58-63-10	58-63	58-6-5	58-99	58-8-50
58-54.4	58-63-15	58-64	Repealed	58-100	58-8-55
58-54.5	58-63-20	58-65	58-6-10	58-101, 58-102	Repealed
58-54.6	58-63-25	58-66	58-6-15	58-103	58-10-1
58-54.7	58-63-30	58-67	Repealed	58-104	58-10-5
58-54.8	58-63-35	58-68	58-6-20	58-105	58-11-1
		58-69	58-7-1	58-106	58-11-5
		58-70	58-7-5	58-107	58-11-10
		58-71	58-7-10	58-108	58-11-15
		58-72	58-7-15	58-109	58-11-20
		58-72.1	58-7-20	58-110	58-11-25
		58-72.2	58-7-25	58-111	Repealed
		58-72.3	58-7-30		

TABLE OF COMPARABLE SECTIONS

Former Section	Present Section	Former Section	Present Section	Former Section	Present Section
58-112	58-11-30	58-131.60	58-40-125	58-155.65	58-62-1
58-112.1	58-11-35	58-131.61	58-40-130	58-155.66	58-62-5
58-113		58-131.62	58-40-135	58-155.67	58-62-10
to 58-119	Repealed	58-131.63	58-40-140	58-155.68	58-62-15
58-120	58-18-1	58-132	58-26-1	58-155.69	58-62-20
58-121	58-18-5	58-133	58-26-5	58-155.70	58-62-25
58-122	58-18-10	58-134	58-26-10	58-155.71	58-62-30
58-123	58-18-15	58-134.1	58-26-15	58-155.72	58-62-35
58-124	58-18-20	58-134.2	58-26-20	58-155.73	58-62-40
58-124.1		58-134.3	58-26-25	58-155.74	58-62-45
to 58-124.11	Repealed	58-134.4	58-26-30	58-155.75	58-62-50
58-124.12		58-134.5	58-26-35	58-155.76	58-62-55
to 58-124.16	Reserved	58-134.6	58-26-40	58-155.77	58-62-60
58-124.17	58-36-1	58-135	58-27-1	58-155.78	58-62-65
58-124.18	58-36-5	58-135.1	58-27-5	58-155.79	58-62-70
58-124.19	58-36-10	58-136	58-27-10	58-155.80	58-62-75
58-124.20	58-36-15	58-137	58-27-15	58-155.81	58-62-80
58-124.21	58-36-20	58-138		58-155.82	58-62-85
58-124.22	58-36-25	to 58-148	Repealed	58-155.83	58-62-90
58-124.23	58-36-30	58-148.1	58-17-1	58-155.84	58-62-95
58-124.24	58-36-35	58-149	58-16-1	58-156	Repealed
58-124.25	58-36-40	58-150	58-16-5	58-157	58-43-1
58-124.26	Expired	58-150.1	58-16-55	58-158	58-43-5
58-124.27	58-36-45	58-151	58-16-10	58-159	58-43-10
58-124.28	58-36-50	58-151.1	58-16-15	58-160	58-43-15
58-124.29	58-36-55	58-151.2	58-16-20	58-161	Repealed
58-124.30	58-36-60	58-152	58-16-25	58-162	58-43-20
58-124.31	58-36-65	58-153	58-16-30	58-162.1	58-43-25
58-124.32	58-36-70	58-153.1	58-16-35	58-163	Repealed
58-124.33	58-36-75	58-153.2	58-16-40	58-164	58-28-45
58-124.34	58-36-80	58-154	58-16-45	58-165	Repealed
58-125		58-155	58-16-50	58-166,	
to 58-131.33	Repealed	58-155.1	58-7-150	58-167	Transferred
58-131.34	58-40-1	58-155.2		58-168,	
58-131.35	58-40-5	to 58-155.36	Repealed	58-169	Repealed
58-131.35A	58-40-10	58-155.37		58-170,	
58-131.36	58-40-15	to 58-155.40	Reserved	58-171	Repealed
58-131.37	58-40-20	58-155.41	58-48-1	58-172	58-43-30
58-131.38	58-40-25	58-155.42	58-48-5	58-173	58-43-35
58-131.39	58-40-30	58-155.43	58-48-10	58-173.1	58-45-1
58-131.40	58-40-35	58-155.44	58-48-15	58-173.2	58-45-5
58-131.41	58-40-40	58-155.45	58-48-20	58-173.3	58-45-10
58-131.42	58-40-45	58-155.46	58-48-25	58-173.4	58-45-15
58-131.43	58-40-50	58-155.47	58-48-30	58-173.5	58-45-20
58-131.44	58-40-55	58-155.48	58-48-35	58-173.6	58-45-25
58-131.45	58-40-60	58-155.49	58-48-40	58-173.7	58-45-30
58-131.46	58-40-65	58-155.50	58-48-45	58-173.8	58-45-35
58-131.47	58-40-70	58-155.51	58-48-50	58-173.9	58-45-40
58-131.48	58-40-75	58-155.52	58-48-55	58-173.10	58-45-45
58-131.49	58-40-80	58-155.53	58-48-60	58-173.11	58-45-50
58-131.50	58-40-85	58-155.54	58-48-65	58-173.12	58-45-55
58-131.51	58-40-90	58-155.55	58-48-70	58-173.13	58-45-60
58-131.52	58-40-95	58-155.56	58-48-75	58-173.14	58-45-65
58-131.53	58-40-100	58-155.57	58-48-80	58-173.15	58-45-70
58-131.54	58-40-105	58-155.58	58-48-85	58-173.16	58-45-75
58-131.55	58-40-110	58-155.59	58-48-90	58-173.16A	58-45-80
58-131.56	Repealed	58-155.60	58-48-95	58-173.17	58-46-1
58-131.57	58-40-115	58-155.61	58-48-100	58-173.18	58-46-5
58-131.58	58-40-120	58-155.62		58-173.19	58-46-10
58-131.59	Repealed	to 58-155.64	Reserved	58-173.20	58-46-15

Former Section	Present Section	Former Section	Present Section	Former Section	Present Section
58-173.21	58-46-20	58-191.3	58-31-25	58-213.20	58-61-10
58-173.22	58-46-25	58-191.4	58-31-30	58-213.21	58-61-15
58-173.23	58-46-30	58-192	58-31-35	58-214	58-59-1
58-173.24	58-46-35	58-193	58-31-40	58-215	58-59-5
58-173.25	Repealed	58-194	58-31-45	58-216	58-59-10
58-173.26	58-46-40	58-194.1	58-31-50	58-217	Repealed
58-173.27,		58-194.2	58-31-55	58-218	58-59-15
58-173.28	Repealed	58-194.3	58-31-60	58-219	58-59-20
58-173.29	58-46-45	58-195	58-58-1	58-220,	
58-173.30	58-46-50	58-195.1	58-58-5	58-221	Repealed
58-173.31	58-46-55	58-195.2	58-58-10	58-222	58-59-25
58-173.32,		58-195.3	58-58-15	58-223	58-59-30
58-173.33	Reserved	58-195.4	58-58-20	58-223.1	58-59-35
58-173.34		58-195.5	58-58-25	58-224	
to 58-173.51	Repealed	58-196	Transferred	to 58-241.34	Recodified
58-174	58-44-1	58-197	58-58-30	58-242	
58-175	58-44-5	58-198	58-58-35	to 58-248.10	Repealed
58-175.1	58-44-10	58-199	58-58-40	58-248.11	
58-176	58-44-15	58-200	Repealed	to 58-248.25	Reserved
58-177	58-44-20	58-201	58-58-45	58-248.26	58-37-1
58-177.1	58-44-25	58-201.1	58-58-50	58-248.27	58-37-5
58-178	58-44-30	58-201.2	58-58-55	58-248.28	58-37-10
58-178.1	58-4-35	58-201.3	58-58-60	58-248.29	58-37-15
58-179	Repealed	58-202	58-58-65	58-248.30	58-37-20
58-180	58-44-40	58-203	Repealed	58-248.31	58-37-25
58-180.1	58-44-45	58-204	58-58-70	58-248.32	58-37-30
58-180.2	58-44-50	58-204.1	58-58-75	58-248.33	58-37-35
58-180.3	58-44-55	58-204.2	58-58-80	58-248.34	58-37-40
58-181	Repealed	58-204.3	58-58-85	58-248.35	58-37-45
58-182	58-5-5	58-204.4	58-58-90	58-248.36	58-37-50
58-182.1	58-5-10	58-205	58-58-95	58-248.37	58-37-55
58-182.2	58-5-15	58-205.1	58-58-100	58-248.38	58-37-60
58-182.3	58-5-20	58-205.2	58-58-105	58-248.39	58-37-65
58-182.4	58-5-25	58-205.3	58-58-110	58-248.40	58-37-70
58-182.5	58-5-30	58-206	58-58-115	58-248.41	58-37-75
58-182.6	58-5-35	58-207	58-58-120	58-249	58-51-1
58-182.7	58-5-40	58-208	58-58-125	58-250	58-51-5
58-182.8	58-5-45	58-209	58-58-130	58-250.1	58-51-10
58-182.9	58-5-50	58-210	58-58-135	58-251	Repealed
58-182.10	58-5-55	58-211	58-58-140	58-251.1	58-51-15
58-183	58-5-60	58-211.1	58-58-145	58-251.2	58-51-20
58-184	58-5-65	58-211.2	58-58-150	58-251.3	58-51-25
58-185	58-5-70	58-211.3	58-58-155	58-251.4	58-51-30
58-186	58-5-75	58-212	58-58-160	58-251.5	58-51-35
58-187	58-5-80	58-213	58-58-165	58-251.6	58-51-40
58-188	58-5-85	58-213.1	58-58-170	58-251.7	58-51-45
58-188.1	58-5-90	58-213.2		58-251.8	58-51-50
58-188.2	58-5-95	to 58-213.5	Reserved	58-251.9	58-51-55
58-188.3	58-5-100	58-213.6	58-60-1	58-252	58-51-60
58-188.4	58-5-105	58-213.7	58-60-5	58-253,	
58-188.5	58-5-110	58-213.8	58-60-10	58-254	Repealed
58-188.6	58-5-115	58-213.9	58-60-15	58-254.1	58-51-65
58-188.7	58-5-120	58-213.10	58-60-20	58-254.2	58-51-70
58-188.8	58-5-125	58-213.11	58-60-25	58-254.3	58-51-75
58-188.9	Repealed	58-213.12	58-60-30	58-254.4	58-51-80
58-189	58-31-1	58-213.13	58-60-35	58-254.4A	58-51-110
58-190	58-31-5	58-213.14		58-254.5	58-51-85
58-191	58-31-10	to 58-213.17	Reserved	58-254.6	58-51-90
58-191.1	58-31-15	58-213.18	58-61-1	58-254.7	58-51-95
58-191.2	58-31-20	58-213.19	58-61-5	58-254.8	58-51-100

Former Section	Present Section	Former Section	Present Section	Former Section	Present Section
58-254.9	58-51-105	58-260.6	58-50-55	58-340.52	58-25-5
58-254.10	58-52-1	58-260.7	58-50-60	58-340.53	58-25-10
58-254.11	58-52-5	58-261	58-50-65	58-340.54	58-25-15
58-254.12	58-52-10	58-262	58-50-70	58-340.55	58-25-20
58-254.13	58-52-15	58-262.1		58-340.56	58-25-25
58-254.14	58-52-20	to 58-262.20	Repealed	58-340.57	58-25-30
58-254.15	58-52-25	58-262.21		58-340.58	58-25-35
58-254.16		to 58-262.29	Reserved	58-340.59	58-25-40
to 58-254.18	Reserved	58-262.30	58-49-1	58-340.60	58-25-45
58-254.19	58-47-1	58-262.31	58-49-5	58-340.61	58-25-50
58-254.20	58-47-5	58-262.32	58-49-10	58-340.62	58-25-55
58-254.21	58-47-10	58-262.33	58-49-15	58-340.63	58-25-60
58-254.22	58-47-15	58-262.34	58-49-20	58-340.64	58-25-65
58-254.23	58-47-20	58-262.35	58-49-25	58-340.65	58-25-70
58-254.24	58-47-25	58-263		58-340.66	
58-254.25	58-47-30	to 58-307	Repealed	to 58-340.70	Reserved
58-254.26	58-47-35	58-308		58-340.71	58-20-1
58-254.27	58-47-40	to 58-340	Repealed	58-340.72	58-20-5
58-254.28	58-47-45	58-340.1	58-24-1	58-340.73	58-20-10
58-254.29	58-47-50	58-340.2	58-24-5	58-340.74	58-20-15
58-254.30		58-340.3	58-24-10	58-340.75	58-20-20
to 58-254.34	Reserved	58-340.4	58-24-15	58-340.76	58-20-25
58-254.35	58-53-1	58-340.5	58-24-20	58-340.77	58-20-30
58-254.36	58-53-5	58-340.6	58-24-25	58-340.78	58-20-35
58-254.37	58-53-10	58-340.7	58-24-30	58-340.79	58-20-40
58-254.38	58-53-15	58-340.8	58-24-35	58-341	58-57-1
58-254.39	58-53-20	58-340.9	58-24-40	58-342	58-57-5
58-254.40	58-53-25	58-340.10	58-24-45	58-343	58-57-10
58-254.41	58-53-30	58-340.11	58-24-50	58-344	58-57-15
58-254.42	58-53-35	58-340.12	58-24-55	58-345	58-57-20
58-254.43	58-53-40	58-340.13	58-24-60	58-346	58-57-25
58-254.44	58-53-45	58-340.14	58-24-65	58-347	58-57-30
58-254.45	58-53-50	58-340.15	58-24-70	58-348	58-57-35
58-254.46	58-53-55	58-340.16	58-24-75	58-349	58-57-40
58-254.47	58-53-60	58-340.17	58-24-80	58-350	58-57-45
58-254.48	58-53-65	58-340.18	58-24-85	58-351	58-57-50
58-254.49	58-53-70	58-340.19	58-24-90	58-352	58-57-55
58-254.50	58-53-75	58-340.20	58-24-95	58-353	58-57-60
58-254.51	58-53-80	58-340.21	58-24-100	58-354	58-57-65
58-254.52	58-53-85	58-340.22	58-24-105	58-355	58-57-70
58-254.53	58-53-90	58-340.23	58-24-110	58-356	58-57-75
58-254.54	58-53-95	58-340.24	58-24-115	58-357	58-57-80
58-254.55	58-53-100	58-340.25	58-24-120	58-358	58-57-85
58-254.56	58-53-105	58-340.26	58-24-125	58-359	58-57-90
58-254.57	58-53-110	58-340.27	58-24-130	58-360	58-57-100
58-254.58	58-53-115	58-340.28	58-24-135	58-361	
58-255	Repealed	58-340.29	58-24-140	to 58-363	Reserved
58-256	58-50-1	58-340.30	58-24-145	58-364	58-38-1
58-257	58-50-5	58-340.31	58-24-150	58-365	58-38-5
58-257.1	58-50-10	58-340.32	58-24-155	58-366	58-38-10
58-258	58-50-15	58-340.33	58-24-160	58-367	58-38-15
58-259	Repealed	58-340.34	58-24-165	58-368	58-38-20
58-259.1	58-50-20	58-340.35	58-24-170	58-369	58-38-25
58-259.2	58-50-25	58-340.36	58-24-175	58-370	58-38-30
58-260	58-50-30	58-340.37	58-24-180	58-371	58-38-35
58-260.1	58-50-35	58-340.38	58-24-185	58-372	58-38-40
58-260.2	Repealed	58-340.39	58-24-190	58-373	
58-260.3	58-50-40	58-340.40		to 58-379	Reserved
58-260.4	58-50-45	to 58-340.50	Reserved	58-380	58-39-1
58-260.5	58-50-50	58-340.51	58-25-1	58-381	58-39-5

Former Section	Present Section	Former Section	Present Section	Former Section	Present Section
58-382	58-39-10	58-455	58-42-25	58-535	58-56-55
58-383	58-39-15	58-456	58-42-30	58-536	58-56-60
58-384	58-39-20	58-457	58-42-35	58-537	58-56-65
58-385	58-39-25	58-458	58-42-40	58-538,	
58-386	58-39-30	58-459	58-42-45	58-539	Reserved
58-387	58-39-35	58-460	58-42-50	58-540	58-55-1
58-388	58-39-40	58-461	58-42-55	58-541	58-55-10
58-389	58-39-45	58-462		58-542	58-55-15
58-390	58-39-50	to 58-469	Reserved	58-543	58-55-20
58-391	58-39-55	58-470	58-41-1	58-544	58-55-25
58-392	58-39-60	58-471	58-41-5	58-545	58-55-30
58-393	58-39-65	58-472	58-41-10	58-546	58-55-35
58-394	58-39-75	58-473	58-41-15	58-547	
58-395	58-39-70	58-474	58-41-20	to 58-559	Reserved
58-396	58-39-80	58-475	58-41-25	58-560	58-19-1
58-397	58-39-85	58-476	58-41-30	58-561	58-19-5
58-398	58-39-90	58-477	58-41-35	58-562	58-19-10
58-399	58-39-95	58-478	58-41-40	58-563	58-19-15
58-400	58-39-100	58-479	58-41-45	58-564	58-19-20
58-401	58-39-105	58-480	58-41-50	58-565	58-19-25
58-402	58-39-110	58-481	58-41-55	58-566	58-19-30
58-403	58-39-115	58-482		58-567	58-19-35
58-404	58-39-120	to 58-489	Reserved	58-568	58-19-40
58-405		58-490	58-23-1	58-569	58-19-45
to 58-409	Reserved	58-491	58-23-5	58-570	58-19-50
58-410	58-13-1	58-492	58-23-10	58-571	58-19-55
58-411	58-13-5	58-493	58-23-15	58-572	58-19-60
58-412	58-13-10	58-494	58-23-20	58-573	58-19-65
58-413	58-13-15	58-495	58-23-25	58-574	58-19-70
58-414	58-13-20	58-496	58-23-30	58-575	58-34-1
58-415	58-13-25	58-497	58-23-35	58-576	58-34-5
58-416		58-498	58-23-40	58-577	58-34-10
to 58-419	Reserved	58-499		58-578	58-34-15
58-420	58-21-1	to 58-504	Reserved	58-579	58-34-20
58-421	58-21-5	58-505	58-22-1	58-580	
58-422	58-21-10	58-506	58-22-10	to 58-609	Reserved
58-423	58-21-15	58-507	58-22-15	58-610	58-33-1
58-424	58-21-20	58-508	58-22-20	58-611	58-33-10
58-425	58-21-25	58-509	58-22-25	58-612	58-33-15
58-426	58-21-30	58-510	58-22-30	58-613	58-33-20
58-427	58-21-35	58-511	58-22-35	58-614	58-33-25
58-428	58-21-40	58-512	58-22-40	58-615	58-33-30
58-429	58-21-45	58-513	58-22-45	58-616	58-33-35
58-430	58-21-50	58-514	58-22-50	58-617	58-33-40
58-431	58-21-55	58-515	58-22-55	58-618	58-33-45
58-432	58-21-60	58-516	58-22-60	58-619	58-33-50
58-433	58-21-65	58-517	58-22-65	58-620	58-33-55
58-434	58-21-70	58-518	Repealed	58-621	58-33-60
58-435	58-21-75	58-519		58-622	58-33-65
58-436	58-21-80	to 58-524	Reserved	58-623	58-33-70
58-437	58-21-85	58-525	58-56-1	58-624	58-33-75
58-438	58-21-90	58-526	58-56-10	58-625	58-33-80
58-439	58-21-95	58-527	58-56-15	58-626	58-33-85
58-440	58-21-100	58-528	58-56-20	58-627	58-33-90
58-441	58-21-105	58-529	58-56-25	58-628	58-33-95
58-450	58-42-1	58-530	58-56-30	58-629	58-33-100
58-451	58-42-5	58-531	58-56-35	58-630	58-33-105
58-452	58-42-10	58-532	58-56-40	58-631	58-33-110
58-453	58-42-15	58-533	58-56-45	58-632	58-33-115
58-454	58-42-20	58-534	58-56-50	58-633	58-33-120

TABLE OF COMPARABLE SECTIONS

Former Section	Present Section	Former Section	Present Section	Former Section	Present Section
58-634	58-33-125	58-695	58-30-280	58-808	58-15-145
58-635	58-33-130	58-696	58-30-285	58-809	58-15-150
58-636	58-33-135	58-697	58-30-290	58A-1	58-68-1
58-640	58-30-1	58-698	58-30-295	58A-2	58-68-5
58-641	58-30-5	58-699	58-30-300	58A-3	58-68-10
58-642	58-30-10	58-700	58-30-305	58A-4	58-68-15
58-643	58-30-15	58-710	58-54-1	58A-5	58-68-20
58-644	58-30-20	58-711	58-54-5	66-49.9	58-69-1
58-645	58-30-25	58-712	58-54-10	66-49.10	58-69-5
58-646	58-30-30	58-713	58-54-15	66-49.11	58-69-10
58-647	Reserved	58-714	58-54-20	66-49.12	58-69-15
58-648	58-30-35	58-715	58-54-25	66-49.13	58-69-20
58-649	58-30-40	58-716	58-54-30	66-49.14	58-69-25
58-650	58-30-45	58-717	58-54-35	66-49.15	58-69-30
58-651	58-30-50	58-718	58-54-40	66-49.16	58-69-35
58-652	58-30-55	58-765	58-64-1	66-49.17	58-69-40
58-653	58-30-60	58-766	58-64-5	66-49.18	58-69-45
58-654	58-30-65	58-767	58-64-10	66-49.24	58-70-1
58-655	58-30-70	58-768	58-64-15	66-49.25	58-70-5
58-656	58-30-75	58-769	58-64-20	66-49.26	58-70-10
58-657	58-30-80	58-770	58-64-25	66-49.27	58-70-15
58-658	58-30-85	58-771	58-64-30	66-49.28	58-70-20
58-659	58-30-90	58-772	58-64-35	66-49.29	58-70-25
58-660	58-30-95	58-773	58-64-40	66-49.30	58-70-30
58-661	58-30-100	58-774	58-64-45	66-49.31	58-70-35
58-662	58-30-105	58-775	58-64-50	66-49.32	58-70-40
58-663	58-30-110	58-776	58-64-55	66-49.33	58-70-45
58-664	58-30-115	58-777	58-64-60	66-49.34	58-70-50
58-665	58-30-120	58-778	58-64-65	66-49.35	58-70-55
58-666	58-30-125	58-779	58-64-70	66-49.36	58-70-60
58-667	58-30-130	58-780	58-15-1	66-49.37	58-70-65
58-668	58-30-135	58-780	58-64-75	66-49.38	58-70-70
58-669	58-30-140	58-781	58-15-5	66-49.39	58-70-75
58-670	58-30-145	58-781	58-64-80	66-49.40	58-70-80
58-671	58-30-150	58-782	58-15-10	66-49.41	58-70-85
58-672	58-30-155	58-783	58-15-15	66-49.42	58-70-90
58-673	58-30-160	58-784	58-15-20	66-49.43	58-70-95
58-674	58-30-165	58-785	58-15-25	66-49.44	58-70-100
58-675	58-30-170	58-786	58-15-30	66-49.45	58-70-105
58-675.1	58-30-175	58-787	58-15-35	66-49.46	58-70-110
58-675.2	58-30-180	58-788	58-15-40	66-49.47	58-70-115
58-676	58-30-185	58-789	58-15-45	66-49.48	58-70-120
58-677	58-30-190	58-790	58-15-50	66-49.49	58-70-125
58-678	58-30-195	58-791	58-15-55	66-49.50	58-70-130
58-679	58-30-200	58-792	58-15-60	69-1	58-79-1
58-680	58-30-205	58-793	58-15-65	69-2	58-79-5
58-681	58-30-210	58-794	58-15-70	69-3	58-70-10
58-682	58-30-215	58-795	58-15-75	69-3.1	58-70-15
58-683	58-30-220	58-796	58-15-85	69-4	58-70-20
58-684	58-30-225	58-797	58-15-90	69-5	58-70-25
58-685	58-30-230	58-798	58-15-95	69-6	58-70-30
58-686	58-30-235	58-799	58-15-100	69-7	58-70-35
58-687	58-30-240	58-800	58-15-105	69-7.1	58-70-40
58-688	58-30-245	58-801	58-15-110	69-14	58-80-1
58-689	58-30-250	58-802	58-15-115	69-15	58-80-5
58-690	58-30-255	58-803	58-15-120	69-16	58-80-10
58-691	58-30-260	58-804	58-15-125	69-17	58-80-15
58-692	58-30-265	58-805	58-15-130	69-18	58-80-20
58-693	58-30-270	58-806	58-15-135	69-19	58-80-25
58-694	58-30-275	58-807	58-15-140	69-20	58-80-30

TABLE OF COMPARABLE SECTIONS

Sections of Former Chapter 58 Repealed in 1989

Editor's Note. — The following table shows sections of former Chapter 58 that were repealed during the 1989 Session.

Ch. 58 G.S. Section	1989 Ch./Sec.
58-124.1 to 58-124.11	722, s. 2
58-138 to 58-148	425, s. 2
58-155.2 to 58-155.36	452, s. 7
58-262.13 to 58-262.19	729, s. 2

Editor's Note. — Sections 58-3-125 and 58-6-10, referred to in this Section, have been repealed.

READY REFERENCE INDEX

A

ACCIDENT INSURANCE.
Aged persons.
  Joint action to insure elderly, §§58-52-1 to 58-52-25.
Credit accident and health insurance.
  Regulation, §§58-57-1 to 58-57-120.
Policies.
  Nature of policies, §§58-51-1 to 58-51-110.

ADVERTISING.
Insurance companies.
  Unauthorized insurers false advertising process act, §§58-29-1 to 58-29-25.

AGED PERSONS.
Accident insurance.
  Joint action to insure elderly, §§58-52-1 to 58-52-25.
Health insurance.
  Joint action to insure elderly, §§58-52-1 to 58-52-25.
  Medicare supplement insurance.
    Minimum standards, §§58-54-1 to 58-54-50.

B

BAIL BONDSMEN AND RUNNERS, §§58-71-1 to 58-71-195.

BOARDS AND COMMISSIONS.
North Carolina rate bureau, §§58-36-1 to 58-36-110.
Public officers and employees liability insurance commission, §§58-32-1 to 58-32-30.
State fire and rescue commission, §§58-78-1 to 58-78-20.

BONDS, SURETY.
Actions on bonds, §§58-76-1 to 58-76-30.
Deposit in lieu of bond, §58-75-1.
Insurance companies, §§58-5-1 to 58-5-124.
Mortgage in lieu of bond, §§58-74-1 to 58-74-35.
Official bonds, §§58-72-1 to 58-72-70.
Public officers and employees.
  Official bonds, §§58-72-1 to 58-72-70.
  Surety company bonds, §§58-73-1 to 58-73-35.
Surety companies, §§58-73-1 to 58-73-35.

BUSINESS CORPORATIONS.
Filings, names and registered agents, §§55D-1 to 55D-33.

C

COLLECTION AGENCIES.
Permit procedures, §§58-70-1 to 58-70-130.

CONSUMER AND CUSTOMER INFORMATION PRIVACY, §§58-31-1 to 58-39-165.

CUSTOMER INFORMATION SAFEGUARDS, §§58-39-130 to 58-39-165.

D

DEPOSITS.
Bonds, surety.
  Deposit in lieu of bond, §58-75-1.
Insurance companies, §§58-5-1 to 58-5-124.

F

FIRE INSURANCE.
Policies, §§58-44-1 to 58-44-55.
Rules and regulations.
  General regulations of business, §§58-43-1 to 58-43-40.
State property fire insurance fund, §§58-31-1 to 58-31-60.
FIRE PROTECTION AND SAFETY.
Fire departments.
  Mutual aid between fire departments, §58-83-1.
  State volunteer fire departments, §§58-80-1 to 58-80-60.
Firemen.
  Authority, §§58-82-1, 58-82-5.
  Liability, §§58-82-1, 58-82-5.
  State appropriations, §§58-85-1 to 58-85-30.
  Workers' pension fund, §§58-86-1 to 58-86-91.
Hotels, inns and other transient lodging places.
  Safety provisions, §§58-81-1 to 58-81-15.
Inspections, §§58-79-1 to 58-79-45.
Investigations, §§58-79-1 to 58-79-5.
Mutual aid between fire departments, §58-83-1.
Rescue squad workers.
  Relief fund, §§58-88-1 to 58-88-30.
  State appropriations, §§58-85-1 to 58-85-30.
  Workers' pension fund, §§58-86-1 to 58-86-91, 58-88-1 to 58-88-30.
State fire and rescue commission, §§58-78-1 to 58-78-20.
State fire protection grant fund, §58-85A-1.
State volunteer fire department, §§58-80-1 to 58-80-60.
Volunteer fire department fund, §58-87-1.
Volunteer rescue/EMS fund, §§58-87-5, 58-87-10.

FISH AND FISHERIES RESOURCES.
Insurance companies.
  Hull insurance, protection and indemnity clubs, §§58-20-1 to 58-20-40.

FUNDS.
Fire insurance.
  State property fire insurance fund, §§58-31-1 to 58-31-60.
Firemen and rescue squad workers.
  Workers' pension fund, §§58-86-1 to 58-86-91.
Rescue squad workers' relief fund, §§58-88-1 to 58-88-30.
Volunteer fire department fund, §58-87-1.
Volunteer rescue/EMS fund, §§58-87-5, 58-87-10.

G

GROUPS.
Group market reforms, §§58-68-25 to 58-68-75.

H

HEALTH INSURANCE.
Aged persons.
   Joint action to insure elderly, §§58-52-1 to 58-52-25.
   Medicare supplement insurance.
      Minimum standards, §§58-54-1 to 58-54-50.
Credit accident and health insurance.
   Regulation, §§58-57-1 to 58-57-110.
Group health insurance.
   Continuation privileges, §§58-53-1 to 58-53-40.
   Conversion privileges, §§58-53-45 to 58-53-115.
Health benefit plan external review, §§58-50-75 to 58-50-95.
Health care benefits.
   Jurisdiction over providers.
      Determination of jurisdiction, §§58-49-1 to 58-49-65.
Health care facilities.
   Continuing care facilities.
      Ombudsmen requirements, §§58-64-1 to 58-64-80.
Health maintenance organizations, §§58-67-1 to 58-67-185.
Insurance guaranty association, §§58-62-2 to 58-62-95.
Jurisdiction over providers of health care benefits, §§58-49-1 to 58-49-65.
Long-term care insurance, §§58-55-1 to 58-55-50.
Policies.
   Nature of policies, §§58-51-1 to 58-51-130.
Rules and regulations.
   General regulations, §§58-50-1 to 58-50-156.

HOME APPLIANCE VEHICLE SERVICE AGREEMENT COMPANIES,
     §§58-1-25 to 58-1-42.

HOSPITAL, MEDICAL AND DENTAL SERVICE CORPORATIONS.
Indemnification, §§58-65-166 to 58-65-174.
Readable insurance certificates act, §§58-66-1 to 58-66-40.
Rules and regulations.
   General provisions, §§58-65-1 to 58-65-165.

HOTELS, INNS AND OTHER TRANSIENT LODGING PLACES.
Fire protection and safety.
   Safety provisions, §§58-81-5 to 58-81-15.

I

INSPECTIONS.
Fire protection and safety, §§58-79-1 to 58-79-45.

INSURANCE COMPANIES.
Adjusters.
   Licensing, §§58-33-1 to 58-33-135.
Agents.
   Licensing, §§58-33-1 to 58-33-135.
   Managing general agents, §§58-34-2 to 58-34-15.
Alien insurance companies, §§58-16-1 to 58-16-55.
Assessment companies, §§58-11-1 to 58-11-35.
Asset protection act, §§58-13-1 to 58-13-25.
Bonds, surety generally, §§58-5-1 to 58-5-124.
Brokers.
   Licensing, §§58-33-1 to 58-33-135.
Deposits generally, §§58-5-1 to 58-5-124.

RULES AND REGULATIONS.
Fire insurance.
General regulations of business, §§58-43-1 to 58-43-40.
Health insurance.
General regulations, §§58-50-1 to 58-50-156.
Hospital, medical and dental service corporations.
General provisions, §§58-65-1 to 58-65-165.
Insurance department.
General regulations for insurance, §§58-3-1 to 58-3-265.
Insurance rates, §§58-40-1 to 58-40-140.
Insurance regulatory reform act, §§58-41-1 to 58-41-55.
Life insurance and viatical settlements.
General regulations of business, §§58-58-1 to 58-58-170.

S

SERVICE AGREEMENT COMPANIES, §§58-1-25 to 58-1-42.

STATE FIRE AND RESCUE COMMISSION, §§58-78-1 to 58-78-20.

STATE FIRE PROTECTION GRANT FUND, §58-85A-1.

STOCK AND STOCKHOLDERS.
Insurance companies.
Exchange of stock, §§58-9-2 to 58-9-26.
Mutual insurance companies.
Conversion of stock companies, §§58-10-1 to 58-10-10.

T

THIRD PARTY ADMINISTRATORS, §§58-56-2 to 58-56-65.

U

UNFAIR TRADE PRACTICES, §§58-63-1 to 58-63-70.

V

VIATICAL LIFE INSURANCE SETTLEMENTS.
Rules and regulations of business.
General regulations of business, §§58-58-1 to 58-58-170.

W

WORKERS' COMPENSATION INSURANCE.
Self-insurance.
Employer groups, §§58-47-60 to 58-47-205.